D0212124

Encyclopedia of
THE NOVEL

Volume 2

M – Z

Encyclopedia of
THE NOVEL

Volume 2
M – Z

Editor
PAUL SCHELLINGER

Assistant Editors
CHRISTOPHER HUDSON
MARIJKE RIJSBERMAN

FITZROY DEARBORN PUBLISHERS
CHICAGO · LONDON

Copyright © 1998
FITZROY DEARBORN PUBLISHERS

All rights reserved including the right of reproduction in whole or
in part in any form. For information write to:

FITZROY DEARBORN PUBLISHERS
919 North Michigan Avenue
Chicago, IL 60611
USA

or

FITZROY DEARBORN PUBLISHERS
310 Regent Street
London W1R 5AJ
England

British Library and Library of Congress Cataloguing in Publication Data are available.

ISBN 1-57958-015-7

First published in the USA and UK 1998

Index prepared by AEIOU Inc., Pleasantville, New York

Typeset and printed by Braun-Brumfield, Ann Arbor, Michigan

Cover design by Peter Aristedes: *The Human Condition,* by René Magritte, 1934

R
909.303
9532 2e

CONTENTS

LIST OF ENTRIES

M

Joaquim Maria Machado de Assis 1839–1908

Brazilian

Machado de Assis was a prolific novelist, short-story writer, chronicler, playwright, poet, and essayist. He left a legacy of nine novels, eight short-story collections, four volumes of poetry, 13 plays, and numerous critical essays, all of which are collected in his *Obra completa* (Complete Works). He is regarded as Brazil's most gifted and important writer of the 19th century, having significantly influenced several generations of authors in that country.

Literary critics often compare Machado to authors such as Laurence Sterne, Henry Fielding, Gustave Flaubert, James Joyce, and Marcel Proust. Machado was a voracious reader, familiar with most European writers and philosophers, to whom he made explicit reference in his texts. In the second edition of *Memórias póstumas de Brás Cubas* (1881; *Epitaph of a Small Winner*), Machado added an explanatory preface intended as a reply to puzzled critics, who could not decide if *Epitaph of a Small Winner* was a novel, a moral dissertation, or a humorous book. In his explanation, Machado defends his writing style and compares it to Laurence Sterne's and Xavier de Maistre's.

It was not until the mid-1900s that the English-speaking world acknowledged Machado as a first-rate novelist and short-story writer. Numerous English translations of his texts have appeared since then. Occasionally, contemporary writers in the United States have credited Machado with a meaningful impact on their careers as novelists. John Barth, for one, has discussed in numerous interviews how Machado's texts, particularly *Dom Casmurro* (1899; *Dom Casmurro*), inspired him to write his first novel, *The Floating Opera* (1956). Although Barth also finds similarities between Machado's and Sterne's narrative devices, he considers Machado a more passionate writer than Sterne. Susan Sontag also has acknowledged her literary debt to Machado, citing especially *Epitaph of a Small Winner.*

Machado witnessed the trends of several literary movements, including romanticism, realism, naturalism, symbolism, and impressionism, absorbing the best of them without becoming subservient to their tenets and characteristics. Although his works reflect pertinent historical and political ideals, social problems, local color, and the cultural transition that Brazilian society underwent in the 19th century, his novels transcend regionalism.

While his themes reflect the epoch in which he lived, his style distinguishes him from any other writer of that period. His use of irony, dark humor, philosophical speculation, and narrative self-consciousness has led critics to emphasize that not only did he survive the rigors of realism and naturalism in Brazil, but he also created his own aesthetic orientation.

Scholars and critics frequently overlook the gradual maturation of Machado's ideas and style, preferring to divide his works into two separate phases, pre- and post-1880. The so-called romantic or early stage includes the novels *Ressureição* (1872; Resurrection), *A mão e a luva* (1874; *The Hand and the Glove*), *Helena* (1876; *Helena*), and *Yayá Garcia* (1878; *Yayá Garcia*). The second phase, which defines him as a great writer, begins in 1881 with the publication of *Epitaph of a Small Winner* and also includes the novels *Dom Casmurro, Quincas Borba* (1891; *Philosopher or Dog?*), *Esaú e Jacó* (1904; *Esau and Jacob*), and *Memorial de Aires* (1908; *Counselor Ayres' Memorial*). Although at first glance there seems to be a separation between the two phases, a strict division of Machado's work is an oversimplification. The second phase may be considered a continuation and perfection of the first phase, presenting the maturation of his style, technique, and aesthetic principles. The Brazilian critic Afrânio Coutinho believes that Machado's literary progression is even more evident in his short stories than in his novels (see Coutinho, 1960).

In terms of experimentation with literary technique and word choice, Machado was a virtuoso whose texts parody the scientific pretensions and philosophical trends of the 19th century and question values commonly accepted as truths. Machado makes skillful use of irony and ambiguity, allowing his characters to explore their psychological world. The use of multiple perspectives, suspense, temporal dislocations, parody, and wordplay demonstrates his narrative mastery on every page.

Even though Machado belongs properly to the 19th century and his themes conform to a 19th-century reality, his experimentation with writing and the deconstructive quality of some of his novels, especially *Dom Casmurro, Epitaph of a Small Winner,* and *Philosopher or Dog?,* place him beyond the dogmas of realism and naturalism. By mastering narrative technique and probing the characters' ontological and epistemological dilemmas,

Machado anticipates narrative trends found in modern and post-modern novels.

In his last five novels, Machado often presents narrators who destabilize any concept of truth that the texts themselves attempt to formulate. He crafts a "poetics of fracture," an expression coined by Vincent Leitch in *Deconstructive Criticism* (1983), in the sense that he uses techniques of fragmentation that disrupt the linear flow of the narrative and bring forth the characters' inner conflicts. In *Dom Casmurro,* for example, the constant fluctuation between oppositions (reliability/unreliability of the narrator, truth/lie, fidelity/infidelity, appearance/reality) unravels and underscores textual contradictions and double logic.

Ambiguity and the analysis of the narrators' paradoxes and contradictions constitute the main focus of Machado's later works. His novels establish a textual dialogue with readers in the sense that the reader is invited to participate in the narrative process. At the end of each text, Machado leaves the reader with the task of reading between the lines and sorting out the multiple layers of meaning.

MARIA JOSÉ SOMERLATE BARBOSA

See also Dom Casmurro

Biography

Born in Rio de Janeiro, Brazil, 21 June 1839. Worked as a clerk and later typographer's apprentice at the National Press, 1854–58; salesman and proofreader, Paulo Brito Bookshop; published his first works in periodicals including *A Marmota Fluminense, Correio Mercantil, Diário do Rio de Janeiro,* and *A Semana Ilustrada*; clerk, then Director of accounting division, Ministry of Agriculture, Commerce and Public Works, 1873–1908; member and censor, 1862–64, Conservatório Dramático Brasileiro; granted the Order of the Rose, 1888; founding president, Academia Brasileira de Letras, 1897–1908. Died 29 September 1908.

Novels by Machado de Assis

Ressureição [Resurrection], 1872
A mão e a luva, 1874; as *The Hand and the Glove,* translated by Albert I. Bagby, Jr., 1970
Helena, 1876; as *Helena,* translated by Helen Caldwell, 1984
Yayá Garcia, 1878; as *Yayá Garcia,* translated by R.L. Scott-Buccleuch, 1976
Memórias póstumas de Brás Cubas, 1881; as *Epitaph of a Small Winner,* translated by William L. Grossman, 1952; as

Posthumous Reminiscences of Bras Cubas, translated by E. Percy Ellis, 1955
Quincas Borba, 1891; as *The Heritage of Quincas Borba,* translated by Clotilde Wilson, 1954; retitled *Philosopher or Dog?,* 1954
Dom Casmurro, 1899; as *Dom Casmurro,* translated by Helen Caldwell, 1971; also translated by R.L. Scott-Buccleuch, 1992
Esaú e Jacó, 1904; as *Esau and Jacob,* translated by Helen Caldwell, 1966
Memorial de Aires, 1908; as *Counselor Ayres' Memorial,* translated by Helen Caldwell, 1972; as *The Wager: Aires' Journal,* translated by R.L. Scott-Buccleuch, 1990

Other Writings: short stories, chronicles, plays, verse, critical essays.

Further Reading

Barbosa, Maria José Somerlate, "Sterne and Machado: Parodic and Intertextual Play in *Tristram Shandy* and *Memórias,*" *The Comparatist* 16 (May 1992)
Caldwell, Helen, *Machado de Assis: The Brazilian Master and His Novels,* Berkeley: University of California Press, 1970
Coutinho, Afrânio, *Machado de Assis na literatura brasileira,* Rio de Janeiro: Livraria Sao José, 1960; Rio de Janeiro: Academia Brasileira de Letras, 1990
Dixon, Paul B., *Retired Dreams: Dom Casmurro, Myth and Modernity,* West Lafayette, Indiana: Purdue University Press, 1989
Fitz, Earl E., *Machado de Assis,* Boston: Twayne, 1989
Gledson, John, *The Deceptive Realism of Machado de Assis: A Dissenting Interpretation of "Dom Casmurro,"* Liverpool: Cairns, 1984
Gomes, Eugênio, *Machado de Assis, influências inglesas,* Rio de Janeiro: Pallas, 1976
Grossman, William L., "The Irony of Machado de Assis," *Commonweal* 26 (1954)
Nunes, Maria Luisa, *The Craft of an Absolute Winner: Characterization and Narratology in the Novels of Machado de Assis,* Westport, Connecticut: Greenwood Press, 1983
Sena, Jorge de, "Machado de Assis and His Carioca Quintet," *Latin American Literary Review* 14 (1986)
Sontag, Susan, "Afterlives: The Case of Machado de Assis," *New Yorker* 7 (May 1990)

Hugh MacLennan 1907–90

Canadian

From the beginning of his career, Hugh MacLennan was determined, at one and the same time, to become a commercially successful writer, to employ his art in the service of pressing social themes, and, above all, to lay the firm basis for an essentially national Canadian literature. To achieve these ends, he adopted, quite openly, the principle of the sugared pill. His novels invariably contain strong and absorbing plots—including a prominent love component—specifically designed to arouse and maintain the interest of the general reader. Although they are often involved in enterprises that might be described as epic or heroic, MacLennan's characters are basically ordinary folk living in accurately represented Canadian milieux and caught up in issues concerning community and country. MacLennan was not an experimental—or even a "literary"—novelist. His preoccupation was always didactic: fiction was primarily a vehicle for the exploration of social, political, national, and religious questions. As the title of one of his essays in *The Other Side of Hugh MacLennan* (1978) indicates, for him the writer is always "The Writer *Engagé*."

His first published novel, *Barometer Rising* (1941), conveniently illustrates MacLennan's basic procedure. Set in Halifax during World War I, it is one of the first novels to be located in a specific and meticulously described Canadian city. *Barometer Rising* tells the story of Neil Macrae, who has been accused of cowardice on the battlefield and is believed to have died somewhere in France. But Neil survives, returning to Halifax incognito in order to clear his name and win the woman he loves. His return coincides with a famous disaster that took place in December 1917 when a munitions ship, involved in a collision in Halifax harbor, exploded and destroyed a large part of the city (an event to which the young MacLennan was an eyewitness). In this largest man-made explosion before Hiroshima, Neil's accuser is providentially killed, and Neil himself is able to perform acts of heroism and regain his self-esteem. Readers initially attracted to the human story are inevitably provoked to consider such questions as the nature of war and the political relation between Canada and the conflict in Europe. The explosion, presented with vivid documentary realism, is offered as a kind of Canadian rite of passage between the old world and the new.

MacLennan's subsequent novels focus on crucial aspects of Canadian experience. *Two Solitudes* (1945) examines the uneasy relations between the English- and French-speaking peoples in Quebec. Beginning with the conscription crisis during World War I and ending at the outbreak of World War II, *Two Solitudes* attempts to review all aspects of the subject, dealing also with the related clash between rural and industrial values and the conflict between religious and secular attitudes to life. A marriage at its close optimistically unites representatives of the two peoples. MacLennan returned to the subject later in *Return of the Sphinx* (1967), which is set at a time when the so-called "Quiet Revolution" and the increase of separatist sentiments in Quebec were becoming less quiet. The later novel presents a darker view of the split and boldly challenged nationalistic euphoria at the time of the Canadian centennial.

The Precipice (1948) takes up the vexed issue of Canadian/American relations, while *Each Man's Son* (1951), more social and less overtly political in intent, takes a hard look at the impact of the Calvinist religious conscience on the inhabitants of a Cape Breton mining community. Two more novels followed, *The Watch That Ends the Night* (1959) and *Voices in Time* (1980). The latter is set in a grim future after an accidentally initiated nuclear disaster has overtaken Montreal, but it reaches back to recreate the world of Nazi anti-Semitism in the 1930s and the confusion of moral values represented by the 1960s.

The Watch That Ends the Night, which enjoyed a commercial and critical success when it first appeared in 1959, is still generally regarded as MacLennan's finest novel. The plot, as so often

in MacLennan, is unlikely and melodramatic (including another character who returns after being presumed dead). But the social commentary is organically integrated with it. One of the main figures narrates the story in the first person, and MacLennan shrewdly makes him a political essayist and commentator by profession. As such, he comments naturally and acceptably on events that range from just after World War I, through the Depression, to the cold war years of the early 1950s. The struggles of ordinary human beings to survive with dignity in a dangerously threatening world are impressively evoked. The novel also contains a passionately presented religious question inspired by circumstances involving the illness and death of MacLennan's first wife. A personal urgency surfaces here that is uncommon in MacLennan's fiction. The whole is played out against a moving, detailed, and historically comprehensive portrait of Montreal in the first half of the 20th century.

Although MacLennan was hardly a technical innovator, he habitually employed an unusual combination of the realistic and the mythic. As George Woodcock was the first to point out, MacLennan (whose original training was in classical languages) offers variations on the Homeric story of Odysseus returning to his homeland. (In *Barometer Rising*, the name of Neil's beloved is Penelope.) The outcome of these Odyssean returns is often violent, as in *Each Man's Son*, where the returning husband kills his wife and her lover and almost immediately dies. Although MacLennan's stories are popular and even sensational, the use of the Homeric motif endows them with an intriguing dimension that permits symbolic and often profound psychological interpretation.

MacLennan is important in the history of Canadian fiction more for his example than for his achievement. He constructed a sturdy foundation upon which others were to build more confidently, imaginatively, and experimentally. Many subsequent Canadian novelists would have to agree with Robert Kroetsch when he remarked (in an address reprinted in Cameron, 1982): "Hugh MacLennan, more than any other writer, made it possible for me to write."

W.J. KEITH

Biography

Born 20 March 1907 in Glace Bay, Nova Scotia. Attended Halifax Academy; Dalhousie University, Halifax, B.A. 1928; Oriel College, Oxford (Rhodes scholar), B.A., M.A. 1932; Princeton University, New Jersey, Ph.D. in classical studies 1935. Classics master, Lower Canada College, Montreal 1935–45; full-time writer, 1945–51; associate professor, 1951–67, professor of English, 1967–79, and professor emeritus from 1979, McGill University, Montreal. Died 7 November 1990.

Novels by MacLennan

Barometer Rising, 1941
Two Solitudes, 1945
The Precipice, 1948
Each Man's Son, 1951
The Watch That Ends the Night, 1959
Return of the Sphinx, 1967
Voices in Time, 1980

Other Writings: essays, lectures, and other nonfiction.

Further Reading

Cameron, Elspeth, *Hugh MacLennan: A Writer's Life,* Toronto: University of Toronto Press, 1981

Cameron, Elspeth, editor, *Hugh MacLennan: 1982,* Toronto: Canadian Studies Programme, University College, 1982

Goetsch, Paul, editor, *Hugh MacLennan,* Toronto: McGraw Hill Ryerson, 1973

Keith, W.J., *Life Struggle: Hugh MacLennan's "The Watch That Ends the Night,"* Toronto: ECW Press, 1993

Leith, Linda, *Introducing Hugh MacLennan's "Two Solitudes,"* Toronto: ECW Press, 1990

MacLulich, T.D., *Hugh MacLennan,* Boston: Twayne, 1983

Woodcock, George, *Hugh MacLennan,* Toronto: Copp Clark, 1969

Woodcock, George, *Introducing Hugh MacLennan's "Barometer Rising,"* Toronto: ECW Press, 1989

Madame Bovary by Gustave Flaubert

1857

Gustave Flaubert began to write his best-known work, *Madame Bovary,* in September 1851 shortly after returning from an 18-month trip to Egypt and the Near East. (The heroine's dreams—of a honeymoon set in a bejewelled city overlooking the sea, or of the rich life awaiting her in Paris if only fate would allow her to live there—owe a great deal, no doubt, to the colorful memories accumulated during this journey.) After five years of wrestling with an increasingly uncongenial subject, Flaubert published the novel in October 1856 in the *Revue de Paris*—an unwise choice considering the *Revue de Paris'* liberal tendencies were viewed with suspicion by the imperial government. Subsequently, the author and the publisher were brought to trial in January 1857 for publishing an obscene work. The following month, thanks to a skillful defense counsel (and also, perhaps, to Flaubert's social standing as the son of an eminent doctor), they were acquitted. (Later the same year, Charles Baudelaire's *Fleurs du Mal,* on a similar charge, did not fare so well.) Published by Michel Lévy in April, the novel enjoyed an initial *succès de scandale* and excellent sales: it has remained ever after the work with which Flaubert is usually associated.

If Flaubert was, as Henry James believed, "the novelists' novelist," then *Madame Bovary* must surely be regarded as the novelists' novel. From the brief but perceptive comments by contemporaries such as Ivan Turgenev and Guy de Maupassant to the detailed analyses by 20th-century writers as diverse as Marcel Proust, Nathalie Sarraute, and Mario Vargas Llosa, Flaubert's obsessive preoccupation with the art and craft of writing has been an endless source of fascination to writers and would-be writers alike. *Madame Bovary* has also been, preeminently, a translator's novel, finding its way into all the major languages of the world. The standard bibliography by D.J. Colwell lists 14 versions in English alone, the best known of which, by Karl Marx's daughter, was revised in 1965 by Paul de Man. Above all, this apparently straightforward story of an unhappy marriage, frustrated dreams, and financial setbacks, culminating in the suicide of the heroine and death of her hapless, adoring, but ill-matched spouse, has been the work that, of all the canonical texts written in France in the 19th century, appears to have been written with future critics in mind. It has been discussed as a key example, a model, and a test case for at least three of the

major literary movements of the last 150 years, namely realism, modernism, and postmodernism.

In Flaubert's lifetime, as well as in most standard literary histories and major theoretical works such as Erich Auerbach's *Mimesis* (1946), *Madame Bovary* has been linked to the theory and practice of realism. Flaubert disliked both the term and the works associated with it: *faire rêver,* rather than *faire vrai,* was (and would remain) his chief aesthetic ambition. Nevertheless, a certain authenticity, notably in the celebrated descriptions (a true-to-lifeness not only in the detailed reality effects found on virtually every page but also, at a more general level, in the evocation of provincial life), has undoubtedly contributed to the novel's appeal to successive generations. The accounts of Emma's convent education, which alienates her from the society in which she is destined to live, and of Homais' steady progress to fame and fortune—as he says, "il faut marcher avec son siècle"—are only two among countless examples of a vein of historical realism as profound as any passages from Balzac or Tolstoi.

However, as some of Flaubert's earliest admirers were aware, the concept of realism, however defined, has never served as an entirely adequate critical tool with which to define the special qualities of *Madame Bovary.* Rather, what struck James and would remain the principal focus of several generations of critics was the quality of the writing, the carefully modulated rhythms, together with a structural integrity more reminiscent of classical tragedy than of the "loose and baggy monsters" that novels, even before Flaubert's great Russian contemporaries came on the scene, naturally tend to become. Flaubert's letters undoubtedly fostered the myth of the master-craftsman of Croisset, agonizing for hours over a single paragraph, bringing to fiction an obsessive care usually more associated with the writing of poetry. With a century and a half of hindsight, it is easy to point out both the cluster of half-truths to which this myth of *l'homme-plume*—the writer given over entirely to his art—has given rise, and, more particularly, the way in which Flaubert's stylistic difficulties were elevated into a virtue rather than a handicap, which, biographically speaking, they undoubtedly were. Nor have critics been slow to point out the contradictions in the poetics of fiction that Flaubert elaborated in his letters to Louise Colet and other friends. On some evenings, after a day spent wondering how to integrate a particular episode into the whole narrative, he would declare that a great work of art could be made out of the humblest material, since everything lies in the treatment. Elsewhere, Flaubert claimed that the key to lasting greatness may be found, rather, in the marriage of subject and style. The fact remains that it is for its formal properties—the carefully balanced sentences, the composition of individual scenes, and the overall structure—that *Madame Bovary* has received the highest praise.

This orthodox view of *Madame Bovary* as the first truly modern novel, and of Flaubert—whose belief in narrative objectivity and whose skill in treading the fine line between lyricism and irony made him the natural father figure and progenitor of high modernism—prevailed for at least half a century. However, when Nathalie Sarraute wrote in 1965 of "Flaubert *précurseur*," she was referring to affinities with her own writing and that of her *nouveaux romanciers* colleagues rather than to the experiments of Virginia Woolf or James Joyce. Since 1970, owing to the persuasive arguments of Jonathan Culler (1974) and to Jean-Paul Sartre's insistence that Flaubert's notorious difficulties with language are more revealing than the ways he found to overcome them, a more playful image of Flaubert—closer to *Bouvard et Pécuchet* (or to Julian Barnes' *Flaubert's Parrot*) than to the blend of irony and pathos that underlies *Madame Bovary*—has found widespread acceptance among academic critics. Yet Culler's claim that Flaubert's novels succeed to the extent that they prevent the reader's attempts to make sense of them may be carrying postmodern playfulness to excess. *Madame Bovary* is in no sense the "book about nothing" that Flaubert, in a quite different context, said he wanted to write. It has a subject to which readers of many different backgrounds can relate, and its formal properties, which include a beginning, middle, and end that are apparent even to the most unsophisticated reader, have stood up

to the most rigorous analysis. Above all, like Cervantes' *Don Quixote*, a book that Flaubert preferred above all others and that he re-read every year, *Madame Bovary* takes the reader into the poignant, tragicomic gap that separates life as it could be, or as it might have been (had Emma chosen a more intelligent husband or more sensitive lover), and life as it is.

GRAHAM FALCONER

See also Gustave Flaubert

Further Reading

Brombert, Victor, *The Novels of Flaubert: A Study of Themes and Techniques,* Princeton, New Jersey: Princeton University Press, 1966

Colwell, D.J., *Bibliographie des études sur G. Flaubert,* Egham: Runnymede, 1988–90

Culler, Jonathan D., *Flaubert: The Uses of Uncertainty,* Ithaca, New York: Cornell University Press, and London: Elek, 1974; revised edition, Ithaca, New York: Cornell University Press, 1985

Fairlie, Alison, *Flaubert: Madame Bovary,* London: Arnold, and Woodbury, New York: Barron's Education Series, 1962

"Flaubert," *Nineteenth Century French Studies* 12:3 (1984)

Prendergast, Christopher, "Flaubert, Quotation, Stupidity and the Cretan Liar Paradox," *French Studies* 35 (1981)

Rothfield, Lawrence, "From Semiotic to Discursive Intertextuality: The Case of *Madame Bovary,*" *Novel: A Forum on Fiction* 19 (1985)

Sartre, Jean-Paul, *L'idiot de la famille,* 3 vols., Paris: Gallimard, 1988; as *The Family Idiot: Gustave Flaubert, 1821–57,* 4 vols., Chicago: University of Chicago Press, 1981–91

Thibaudet, Albert, *Gustave Flaubert,* Paris: Plon-Nourrit, 1922; Paris: Gallimard, 1963

Magazines. *See* **Periodicals and the Serialization of Novels; Reviewers and the Popular Press**

Maghribī Novel. *See* **African Novel: Northern Africa**

The Magic Mountain by Thomas Mann

Der Zauberberg 1924

The Magic Mountain is a Bildungsroman. The novel of education, or apprenticeship novel, focuses on the hero's spiritual and emotional development toward independence and enlightenment. Many of Mann's contemporaries were puzzled that he employed this form. Although it had flourished during the 19th century, the Bildungsroman had been considered obsolete for several decades. Mann revived the form because he believed it was the best way to portray the profound spiritual changes occurring in Germany after World War I. *The Magic Mountain* is, therefore, also the story of an epoch during which an entire nation and its people are being transformed. Representing 1912 Europe in microcosm, the sick and dying inhabitants of the sanatorium Berghof frivolously refuse to face facts. With surgical precision Mann autopsies the values and attitudes that led to the catastrophe of war.

Characteristic of the novel of education is the lack of plot in the conventional sense. Hans Castorp, 23, spends seven years at Berghof. Here he meets people from whom he learns the myriad possibilities that life has to offer. That summarizes the external action. The internal action concerns Hans' self-discovery and his attainment of spiritual and emotional independence. Since Hans also functions as a representative of Germany, the implication is that the nation as a whole must embark on a similar path.

Traditionally, the hero of the Bildungsroman stands above the average and is gifted in some way. Mann deviates from the norm in that Hans is an unmotivated, average man from the middle class without any particular talent. Yet he achieves the same ideal that his more distinguished predecessors achieve. In this way, Mann shows that the road to enlightenment is open to everyone.

Another common feature of the Bildungsroman is the mentor who assists the hero. Often the member of a secret society, the mentor instructs the seeker in the principles of the group he represents. Mann again diverges from the traditional form by introducing two mentors who promote opposite ideologies. Both are equally brilliant, equally persuasive, and equally determined to gain Hans as a disciple. The first half of the novel is dominated by the Italian humanist and Mason, Ludovico Settembrini, and to a lesser extent by the Russian, Clavdia Chauchat. Settembrini represents the classical ideals of Western civilization, of the Renaissance, and of the Enlightenment. Clavdia Chauchat invokes the temptations of the East. Her mentality is basically irrational, lethargic, and submissive. (*Chauchat* in French means "hot cat.") Clavdia is replaced by Leo Naphta as the representative of Eastern mentality after Walpurgis Night (witch's Sabbath). Converted from Judaism to Catholicism and educated by the Jesuits, Naphta stands for the intellectual side of Oriental mysticism. His cast of mind is decidedly irrational. Using terror when necessary, he promotes the worship of the dark, instinctive forces. The tension and irreconcilability of East and West emerge most vividly during the scintillating, wonderfully articulate disputes between Naphta and Settembrini. The latter defends reason against the former's blind faith, monism against dualism, spirit against flesh, humanism against terrorism, the Renaissance against fanatic medievalism. According to Mann, these are the two ideologies facing Hans in particular and Germany in general.

The resolution of such conflicts is the central theme. The novel's turning point comes when Hans, torn between the two ideologies, has an epiphany in the chapter "Snow." He realizes that neither Naphta nor Settembrini has the answer. He understands that their disputes are based on the arbitrary creation of polarities. In a flash he perceives the fundamental unity beneath their standpoints. Hans speculates on the polarities of spirit and flesh, duty and inclination, reason and faith, and concludes that they exist only in the mind. A dream reveals that opposites are reconciled through enlightenment and love. This is the beginning of the new Hans.

The irrelevance of Settembrini's and Naphta's intellectual subtleties is underscored by the arrival of yet another mentor, Mynher Peeperkorn, a rich planter from the Dutch East Indies. Irrational, inarticulate, and sensual, he is devoted solely to the "simple pleasures" of food, drink, and sex. This Dionysian figure is diseased and no longer young, yet he holds center stage effortlessly through the overwhelming magnitude of his personality. He demolishes Settembrini's and Naphta's abstractions with the simple observation, "cerebrum, cerebral." Although Hans is strongly attracted to this figure, he is not influenced by him any more than he is by the others. In fact, no single ideology remains intact at the end. Peeperkorn commits suicide when his sexual powers fail. Settembrini, the advocate of enlightened humanism, is condemned to a life in the sickbed. Naphta, the spokesman for faith and obedience, blows his brains out in a maniacal rage. What remains is Hans Castorp who has learned to stay independent of ideologies and rely on himself. In the end, he is a soldier in Flanders in 1914. He is 30 years old. Ironically, "30" is editorial jargon for "end of manuscript."

Another of Mann's innovations consists of making the Bildungsroman accommodate contemporary problems in literature—in this case, the problem of time. The theme of time is one of the central concerns of modern literature. Numerous parallels to Mann's conception of timelessness are found in the works of Rainer Maria Rilke, Hermann Broch, Marcel Proust, and James Joyce. Mann's objective is to erase the reader's concept of past and future in favor of an eternal present. He achieves this in a number of ways, the most obvious of which is the repetitiveness of routine. The day at Berghof revolves around five mealtimes. The invariability of the mealtime schedule converts time into a series of unending recurrences. It also serves as a point of reference for the remainder of the novel in that the reader knows exactly what is happening at any time of day. The eternal present is further achieved by the extensive use of the leitmotiv: Hans' cigars, Settembrini's checkered trousers, and Naphta's flashing spectacles all contribute to produce the effect of a timeless present.

In other matters of style Mann displays great virtuosity. For him, language is an instrument to be played. The long and complex sentences for which he is known are rich with epithets and symbolic meaning. His superb gift of description is seen in his meticulous rendering of interiors, dress, mannerism, and character. Mann is also known for a unique stylistic device. He enjoys taking readers into his confidence and talking to them in a direct and friendly way. He frequently steps out of the story to comment on the action or to help his readers with a few remarks. Concerning this he wrote: "Discursive speech, the author's intrusion, does not need to be alien to art, it can be part of it, and itself be a means of art."

The Magic Mountain revived the German Bildungsroman. By expanding its limits and inventing new techniques, Mann breathed new life into a moribund form. Along with Hermann Hesse, Mann is directly responsible for the renaissance that the Bildungsroman has experienced this century.

JOHN D. SIMONS

See also Thomas Mann

Further Reading

Eichner, Hans, *Thomas Mann: Eine Einfuhrung in sein Werk,* Bern: Francke, 1953; 2nd edition, 1961

Faesi, Robert, *Thomas Mann,* Zurich: Atlantis, 1955

Hatfield, Henry, *From the Magic Mountain: Mann's Later Masterpieces,* Ithaca, New York: Cornell University Press, 1979

Hatfield, Henry, editor, *Thomas Mann: A Collection of Critical Essays,* Englewood Cliffs, New Jersey: Prentice-Hall, 1964

Heller, Erich, *The Ironic German: A Study of Thomas Mann,* Boston: Little Brown, and London: Secker and Warburg, 1958

Hilscher, Eberhard, *Thomas Mann: Sein Leben und sein Werk,* Berlin: Volk and Wissen, 1968

Ridley, Hugh, *The Problematic Bourgeois: Twentieth-Century Criticism and Thomas Mann's "Buddenbrooks" and "The Magic Mountain,"* Columbia, South Carolina: Camden House, 1994

Sprecher, Thomas, editor, *Das "Zauberberg"-Symposium 1994 in Davos,* Frankfurt: Klostermann, 1995

Thomas, R. Hinton, *Thomas Mann: The Mediation of Art,* Oxford: Clarendon Press, 1956

Weigand, Hermann J., *Thomas Mann's Novel: "Der Zauberberg,"* New York and London: Appleton-Century, 1933

Ziolkowski, Theodore, *Dimensions of the Modern Novel,* Princeton, New Jersey: Princeton University Press, 1969

Magic Realism

Magic realism (also called magical realism) is a style or manner of writing in which the author, through a variety of artistic techniques and strategies, seeks to combine unusual with ordinary elements of human existence in order to provide as complete a representation of reality as possible.

The term *magic realism* emerged during the interwar years in an intellectual atmosphere dominated by the political, social, and economic aftermath of both World War I and the Russian Revolution, as well as by Freud's works dealing with the unconscious and dreams. It is generally agreed that the term was first used by the German art historian Franz Roh in the title of his 1925 book, *Nach-expressionismus: Magischer Realismus: Probleme der neuesten europäischer Malerai* (Post-Expressionism: Magic Realism: Problems of the Newest European Painting). Here Roh applies *magischer Realismus* to new German painters of the period, especially those of the Munich-based *neue Sachlichkeit* (New Reality) school. Roh did not intend the term *magischer Realismus* to imply a blending of the fantastic, the absurd, and the grotesque with everyday reality, as it has come to be understood today. To Roh, magic realism was equivalent to postexpressionism, an approach to painting that sought to represent the unusual occurrences in people's lives, in contrast to the art of the contemporaneous surrealists, which embodied a more transcendent view of reality and style of representation. Surrealists hoped to understand a superior reality by augmenting their external experience, which many of them saw as shackled by human reason, laws, and mores, with the interior, unfettered force of the unconscious; hence their preoccupation with unconscious processes, especially dreams and hallucinations, and automatic writing.

Magic realists, rather than concentrating solely on the dark realms of the unconscious, sought to enrich the idea of what is real through the dimensions of magic, myth, and the unusual that occur in ordinary, everyday life. One important implication of this difference in emphasis is that the best of the surrealist writers expressed their intense interactions with the unconscious through poetry and for the most part avoided the larger, more leisurely novel form. Magic realists, by contrast, have chosen as their primary medium of expression prose fiction, both the short story and novel, where they are capable of intense flights of imagination that often seem quite surrealistic but that are contained within a logical, sequential narrative flow. Moreover, there is virtually no magic realist poetry of note. Another important distinction is that surrealists largely eschewed political engagement in their writing by comparison with magic realists, who seem to emerge from and to thrive on times of marked political foment and social turmoil.

In Spring 1927 a portion of Roh's book was published in a Spanish translation with the title "Realismo mágico" by the influential Madrid-based journal *Revista de Occidente* (Journal of the West), edited by José Ortega y Gasset. The term gained popularity in art circles in the United States during the 1940s, most notably in a 1943 show at the New York Museum of Modern Art entitled "American Realists and Magic Realists." Among those painters exhibited, Edward Hopper became the most famous. The term has retained currency in a slightly altered form with the group called the Vienna School of Fantastic Realism, associated with the painters Wilhelm Dachauer, Anton Lehmden, Peter Proksch, and others. Many of the best-known works of the contemporary American painter Andrew Wyeth are said to contain magical realist elements.

Soon the term *magic realism* was applied to written works, notably those of the Italian novelist Massimo Bontempelli and his *stracittà* (Across the City) movement of the 1920s and 1930s. In a series of novels such as *La scacchiera davanti allo specchio* (1922; The Chessboard in Front of the Mirror) and *Eva ultima* (1923; Last Eve), as well as through his work as cofounder (with Curzio Malaparte) and editor of the short-lived (1926–29) but influential Italian French-language journal *'900: Cahiers d'Italie et d'Europe* ('900: Notebooks of Italy and Europe), also known as *Il novecento* (The Twentieth Century), Bontempelli sought to "clothe the most sorrowful things with a smile and the most common things with wonder." Some literary historians cite Bontempelli as the first person to apply the term *magic realism,* known in Italian as *realismo magico,* to writing.

Shortly thereafter, in the late 1920s and early 1930s, magic realist techniques attracted three Latin American writers who, for various political and artistic reasons, were living at the time in Paris, a city whose arts were dominated by surrealism: Venezuelan Arturo Uslar Pietri, Cuban Alejo Carpentier, and Guatemalan Miguel Ángel Asturias. Uslar Pietri, a diplomat at the Venezuelan embassy in Paris and later a political exile in New York during the 1940s, may have been the first to use the term *realismo mágico* (later called *lo real maravilloso*) in Latin American literature when he applied it to two of his short stories, "La lluvia" (1936; "The Rain") and "El fuego fatuo" (1936; "Ignis Fatuus"). Later, Carpentier, whose liberal political activities precipitated his flight from Cuba to Paris, fell under the influence of his friend the French surrealist poet-novelist Robert Desnos, as well as the Irish novelist James Joyce, who was writing in Paris at the time. Carpentier elaborated on the term *magic realism* in his prologue to *El reino de este mundo* (1949; The Kingdom of This World), a novel that, like Uslar Pietri's stories, combines magic, religion, and myth from European, African, and native Latin American sources to produce its admixtures of magic realism and mundane reality. Most of Asturias' fiction stems from his profound interest in Mayan folklore and mythology. His *Leyendas de Guatemala* (1930; Legends of Guatemala), published while he was in Paris, draws its inspiration from indigenous Guatemalan sources. *Hombres de maíz* (1949; Men of Maize), initially dismissed by critics as poorly constructed, and his *Trilogía bananera* (1949–60; Banana Trilogy), together with *El alhajadito* (1961; The Bejeweled Boy) and *Mulata de tal* (1963; Mulatta), constitute his major contributions to magic realism.

Some scholars insist that the origins of magic realism are to be found farther south in Latin America, in the works of the Argentine poet, essayist, and short-story writer Jorge Luis Borges. They submit that his *Historia universal de la infamia* (1935; A Universal History of Infamy) is the first work of magic realism in Latin American literature. Borges continued to use magic realism in his best-known short stories, such as "Tlön, Uqbar, Orbis Tertius" (1941), "La biblioteca de Babel" (1941; "The Library of Babel"), "La muerta y la brújula" (1942; "Death and the Compass"), and "El Aleph" (1945; "The Aleph"). Wherever the origins of magic realism may lie, it has been a major defining feature of Latin American fiction to the present day.

Probably the most celebrated exponent of magic realism for the novel form is Colombian Gabriel García Márquez, winner of the Nobel prize for literature in 1982, whose *Cien años de soledad* (1967; One Hundred Years of Solitude) is considered the prototypical magic realist novel. Many of his subsequent works are also written in the magic realist vein. This tradition continues strongly in the writing of younger Latin American authors, such as Chilean Isabel Allende, especially her *La casa de los espíritus* (1982; The House of the Spirits), and Mexican Laura Esquivel, with her *Como agua para chocolate* (1990; Like Water for Chocolate). In the United States, magic realism is also an important aspect in contemporary southwest Chicano writing, notably in the works of Rudolfo A. Anaya and Jimmy Santiago Baca.

While a satisfactory, comprehensive definition of magic realism is impossible, critics generally agree that it is not a "movement" in the same way symbolism or surrealism were movements, but rather a mode, technique, method, or style of writing, or a tendency in writing, that is distinguished by a number of features, some of which it shares in varying degrees with other kinds of writing.

Probably the most notable characteristic of magic realism is the author's introduction of unexpected fantastic, bizarre, or absurd turns of plot or events into what is an otherwise realistic narrative flow. For example, when his sister offers him snails for lunch, the young Cosimo Piovasco di Rondò, protagonist of *Il barone rampante* (1957; The Baron in the Trees) by the Italian Italo Calvino, scampers up a tree and remains living there for the rest of his life, his mother communicating with him via military flags. Similarly, in *One Hundred Years of Solitude,* the beautiful Remedios Buendía, hanging her wash out to dry on a washday no different from any other, is bodily assumed into heaven. At age three, Oskar Matzerath, the narrator of *Die Blechtrommel* (1959; The Tin Drum) by the German Günter Grass, wills himself not to grow up and remains for many years a dwarf who possesses a voice that can shatter glass but who prefers communicating through the bang of his drum.

Critics have pointed out that many characters in magic realist novels defy gravity. Remedios Buendía's assumption into heaven, mentioned above, is one such example. In *Nights at the Circus* (1984) by Britain's Angela Carter, Sophie Fevvers, the *aerialiste extraordinaire* star of Colonel Kearney's circus, is able to perform her remarkable act because the swan wings she seems to wear as part of her costume are, in fact, extensions of her body. The two main characters in *The Satanic Verses* (1988) by Indo-British Salman Rushdie, Gibreel Farishta and Saladin Chamcha, are miraculously saved when their London-bound plane is blown up by terrorists; they float to earth singing silly Indian film songs, landing unharmed on a desolate beach. *Sexing the Cherry* (1989) by Britain's Jeanette Winterson features an entire city and its population floating above the earth. *Kniha smíchu a zapomnení* (first published in French in 1979, in Czech in 1981; The Book of Laughter and Forgetting) by Czech Milan Kundera offers two such incidents: the first, the fable entitled "Angels," in which two American girls, Gabrielle and Michelle, and their teacher, Mme. Raphael (each named after an archangel), laugh and dance heavenward in a circle; the second, in which Kundera describes a circle of young Communists dancing, levitating, and floating away, in their midst the French surrealist-turned-Marxist poet Paul Éluard, whom Kundera ironically calls "The toast of Prague" and "Prague's Darling." Gravity in magic realist novels may often be understood to refer both to the natural physical force that keeps humans attached to the earth and to the notion of seriousness, particularly in connection with the grave, sobering events transpiring in the world and in human relationships.

Fantastic elements often appear as an abrupt surprise or horrific shock, as in, for example, the famous description of eels swimming out of the dead horse head in *The Tin Drum*. Many of these fantastic or absurdist features remain unexplained, leaving the reader to guess the relationship between the seemingly unconnected event and the main narrative flow. Where realist writers might infuse coherence and logic between and among such elements, magic realists often require that readers stretch their understanding of reality and work hard at tracking what is going on in the plot, thereby creating, *inter alia*, an effect of tenuousness and uncertainty, which, for many readers, makes the magic elements all the more believable, more real. Just as the unexpected, inexplicable, and unbelievable come out of nowhere in people's daily lives, so too do such events emerge in magic realist writing.

The reader's attempts to connect these disparate, seemingly unrelated events are further complicated by the author's skillful, sometimes virtuosic, manipulations of time, which result in quick and unexpected shifts either backward or forward, requiring unusually careful attention on the reader's part. Not unique to magic realism, of course, this technique contributes as well to making magic events seem as real as mundane reality.

Like many naturalist and realist works of the 19th century, the plots of magic realist novels often cover several generations of a family or group, thereby producing not only a labyrinthine story line but also a confusing plethora of characters, some of whom have very similar or identical names. For example, *One Hundred Years of Solitude* treats three generations of the Buendía family, in which there are no fewer than three José Arcadios and four Aureliano Arcadios. Names, too, are often unusual or strange, quite in keeping with the unusual and strange events that befall the characters bearing them. Calvino's narrator in *Le cosmicomiche* (1965; *Cosmicomics*) and *Ti con zero* (1967; *T Zero*) is palindromically named Qfwfq. The novels of American Thomas Pynchon provide a veritable litany of odd, striking names: Benny Profane, Herbert Stencil, and Rachel Owlglass in *V.* (1963), Roger Mexico and Jessica Swanlake in *Gravity's Rainbow* (1973), and Prairie Wheeler and Frenesi Gates in *Vineland* (1990). Names in magic realist novels often form the basis for elaborate puns and dazzling wordplay.

Obscure or esoteric texts or knowledge often play an important part in magic realist novels. Asturias' early *Leyendas de Guatemala* is related directly to his work in Paris translating into Spanish the French rendering of two 16th-century Mayan documents, *Popul Vuh* (The Book of Counsel) and *Anales de los xahil* (*Annals of the Cakchiquels*). The old, undecipherable manuscript that the gypsy magician Melquíades brings to the Buendía house in *One Hundred Years of Solitude* is, the reader learns at the end of the novel, written in Sanskrit, the sacred language of India. Similarly, the existence of the so-called "Satanic Verses" in Islamic lore, essential to Rushdie's novel of the same name, is virtually unknown by most Muslims, except scholars, many of whom deny the authenticity or even the existence of such verses and brand as blasphemous those who even talk about them.

Literary critics and historians have discussed magic realism from a wide variety of perspectives. Some have tried, with only moderate success, to define the term precisely and to distinguish it from styles with which it shares certain qualities, especially those that fall under the headings of the fantastic, the absurd, and the grotesque. Thus, much critical inquiry has sought to establish a link between magic realism and such writers as E.T.A. Hoffman, Franz Kafka, and William Faulkner. In this context,

feminist critics see precursors to magic realism in Gothic novels written by women such as *Frankenstein* (1818) by Mary Wollstonecraft Shelley, and in modernist novels such as *Orlando* (1928) by Virginia Woolf. Other scholars are seeking to isolate magic realist elements in such disparate texts as the Arthurian cycle and Chinese ghost stories, *The Thousand and One Nights* and Italian Renaissance epics, even in Mozart and Handel operas, contemporary film, television shows, and music videos.

Reader-response analyses have attempted to identify the effects of and reactions to magic realism on the part of the reader. One view holds that magic realism offers the reader a connectedness to the past, thus a sense of security, belonging, and identity, which is well exemplified in Latin American magic realist writing. Others suggest that it provokes a sense of anxiety, estrangement, and isolation—feelings, Freudians point out, discussed by Freud in his essay "Das Unheimliche" (1919; "The 'Uncanny'"). Postmodern critics emphasize that this type of writing has flourished at times of considerable political turmoil, unrest, and stress, thus explaining its appeal to Latin American magic realists, who very often use the political and social conditions of their countries as the backdrop for their works. While Kundera's attraction may be similarly explained in relation to the complex political history of postwar Czechoslovakia, especially during the repressive Communist period, Rushdie's affinity seems to flow from the palpable atmosphere of racial tension and postcolonial aftershock found in contemporary Britain. Similarly, feminist and lesbian critics attribute the relatively recent adoption of this style by women writers to the gender and culture wars being waged in contemporary society. Such critics submit that these wars have created an atmosphere as portentous for women and minorities as those spawned earlier by dictatorships and totalitarian systems in Latin American and Central European countries.

Magic realism has attracted writers from many countries who have used its features and techniques to varying degrees. Some, such as García Márquez and Calvino, have integrated magic realism as a central artistic element of their work; others, such as Americans Maxine Hong Kingston and Nobel prize-winner Toni Morrison, have used some of its features in one or more of their major works. Some other notable novelists, not treated in this article, who employ magic realism in either of these two ways include Mikhail Bulgakov (Russian), Fausta Cialenta (Italo-Egyptian), Elsa Morante (Italian), Juan Rulfo (Mexican), John Fowles (British), John Barth (American), Umberto Eco (Italian), Fay Weldon (British), Zulfikar Ghose (Indo-British-American), Don DeLillo (American), Fabrizia Ramondino (Italian), and Emma Tennant (British).

CARLO COPPOLA

See also Historical Novel; Latin American Novel (all sections); Surrealist Novel

Further Reading

Angulo, Maria-Aliena, *Magic Realism: Social Context and Discourse,* New York: Garland, 1995

Bell-Villada, Gene H., *García Márquez: The Man and His Work,* Chapel Hill: University of North Carolina Press, 1991

Boland, Roy C., and Sally Harvey, editors, *Magical Realism and Beyond: The Contemporary Spanish and Latin American Novel,* Madrid: Vox/AHS, 1991

Brotherston, Gordon, *The Emergence of the Latin American Novel*, Cambridge and New York: Cambridge University Press, 1977

Chanady, Amaryll Beatrice, *Magical Realism and the Fantastic: Resolved Versus Unresolved Antimony*, New York: Garland, 1985

Danow, David K., *The Spirit of Carnival: Magical Realism and the Grotesque*, Lexington: University Press of Kentucky, 1995

Flores, Á., "Magical Realism in Spanish American Fiction," *Hispania* 38 (1955)

Gish, Robert, *Beyond Bounds: Cross-Cultural Essays on Anglo, American Indian, and Chicano Literature*, Albuquerque: University of New Mexico Press, 1996

King, John, editor, *On Modern Latin American Fiction*, New York: Noonday, 1989

Olken, I.T., *With Pleated Eye and Garnet Wing: Symmetries of Italo Calvino*, Ann Arbor: University of Michigan Press, 1984

Simpkins, Scott, "Magical Strategies: The Supplement of Realism," *Twentieth-Century Literature* 34 (Summer 1988)

Spindler, William, "Magic Realism: A Typology," *Forum for Modern Language Studies* 29:1 (January 1993)

Walter, Roland, *Magical Realism in Contemporary Chicano Fiction*, Frankfurt am Main: Vervuert, 1993

Zamora, Lois Parkinson, and Wendy B. Faris, editors, *Magical Realism: Theory, History, Community*, Durham, North Carolina: Duke University Press, 1995

Nagīb Maḥfūẓ 1911–

Egyptian

Nagīb Maḥfūẓ is arguably the most prominent Arab novelist to date. When he was awarded the Nobel prize for literature in 1988, many in the Arab world saw this as somewhat ironic, not least because the work for which he received the prize had been published at least three decades earlier. Maḥfūẓ had been acknowledged as the master of the Arabic novel since the 1960s, and some of his works had already acquired the status of classics. But his importance goes beyond that of an outstanding novelist and assumes a historical dimension within the context of modern Arabic literature and the novel in particular.

Maḥfūẓ wrote articles and short stories before turning to the novel. His first three novels—*ʿAbath al-aqdār* (1939; The Mockery of Fate), *Rādūbīs* (1943), and *Kifāḥ Ṭībah* (1944; Thebes' Struggle)—were historical, their subject matter and themes taken from ancient Egyptian history. They were conceived as part of a larger unfulfilled project of 30 novels meant to cover the whole history of Egypt. However, following the third novel, Maḥfūẓ shifted his interest to the present. His writings of this second period include the novels from *Al-Qāhirah al-Jadīdah* (New Cairo), published in 1946, as well as his celebrated Cairo Trilogy—*Bayn al-Qaṣrayn* (1956; *Palace Walk*), *Qaṣr al-Shawq* (1957; *Palace of Desire*), and *Al-Sukkarīyah* (1957; *Sugar Street*)—which he completed before the July Revolution of 1952. These writings made Maḥfūẓ the most celebrated Arab novelist of the period. The writings in his third period, which include *Awlād Ḥāritnā* (1967; *Children of Gebelawi*) to *Mīrāmār* (1967; *Miramar*), are more complex and controversial. The fourth period extends from 1967 to the present and includes works such as *Al-Marāyā* (1972; *Mirrors*), *Malḥamat al-ḥarāfīsh* (1977; *The Harafish*), and *Layālī alf laylah* (1981; *Arabian Nights and Days*). Some of the novels written during this period are considered by many critics to be inferior to his earlier works.

In 1970 Maḥfūẓ stated that he made a journey that started with Sir Walter Scott and ended at the gates of Nathalie Sarraute. This statement, although to a large extent true, needs many qualifications. While it is true that Maḥfūẓ's work may be divided into successive phases, some common traits appear in all of it.

Maḥfūẓ's historical novels, generally mediocre, stand as evidence of an apprenticeship through which he developed his abilities to construct a fictional world. Narrated in the third person, these stories attempt to create the illusion of merely recording events without authorial intervention.

Some of the realistic novels Maḥfūẓ wrote in his second period, such as *Al-Qāhirah al-Jadīdah*, *Zuqāq al-Midaqq* (1947; *Midaq Alley*), *Khān al-Khalīlī* (1945; Khan al-Khalili), *Bidāyah wa-Nihāyah* (1949; *The Beginning and the End*), and the Cairo Trilogy, are considered by many critics to be his best. These realistic novels include details illustrative of the practices that make up our social world, and of the storehouse of cultural stereotypes, accepted knowledge, proverbial expressions, and ethical maxims that are based upon cultural generalizations. Also during this second period, Maḥfūẓ began to explore the possibilites of representing a character's consciousness. His omniscient narrators, often through free indirect discourse, allow us to see events from different points of view (without resorting to multiple narrators as in *Miramar*). Maḥfūẓ also brought colloquial speech into modern standard Arabic prose.

Place is central in all these novels (most of them derive their titles from names of places or streets). Action and incidents usually occur in specific and well-described spaces with clear boundaries. And the temporal organization is carefully structured and reinforced by constant references to historical data, most of which would be common knowledge to Maḥfūẓ's readers. With respect to narrative time, one generally finds many ellipses, some descriptive pauses, and very little summary. The setting of a scene is encountered mostly in dialogue. Endings, on the other hand, tend to be mostly open.

Although some important changes took place during Maḥfūẓ's

third period, the fundamental principles upon which he based his strategies of fictional construction were the same. Space remained central for the works of this period (for example, the pension in *Miramar* and the houseboat in *Thartharah fawq al-Nīl* [1966; *Adrift on the Nile*]). Mahfūz was careful, too, in the temporal organization of his fiction, resorting to analepsis and memory much more than in his earlier works, usually through interior monologue. Third-person narration is mixed with interior monologues that take the place of free indirect discourse, as in *Al-Liṣṣ wa-al-kilāb* (1961; *The Thief and the Dogs*) and *Al-Summān wa-al-kharīf* (1962; *Autumn Quail*). In the case of *Miramar* Mahfūz uses a form of multiple first-person narration in which four narrators tell the story.

The most important differences between the novels of this third period and those of the second concern the relative decrease in authorial intervention and the relative democratization of the modes of narration. The question of how to represent reality becomes more complex and more problematic, but the possibility of representation is never questioned. For Mahfūz, the basic tenets of realism are still valid; what he comes to question in this period is reality itself, not its representability.

Since the 1970s, one notices the influence of many younger writers on Mahfūz's work, especially the technique of using traditional Arabic narratives as subtexts, as in *Arabian Nights and Days* and *Rihlat Ibn Fattūmah* (1983; *The Journey of Ibn Fattouma*). One noticeable technique that Mahfūz uses quite successfully is the construction of novels in chapters each one of which tells the tale of one character or one family, as in *Mirrors*, *The Harafish*, and *Hadīth al-ṣabāh wa-al-masā'* (1987; *Morning and Evening Talk*). In most of these works one notices a more dominant presence of summary rather than the meticulous detail of the previous period. The interest is now more in destinies, ideas, and human types.

Without question, Mahfūz's major accomplishment as a novelist, certainly the work for which he is best known internationally, is his Cairo Trilogy. As a set, these three texts comprise one of the most important Arabic novels written in the 20th century. However, despite its having an enormous impact on Arabic fiction that came after it, the Cairo Trilogy cannot be described as particularly innovative or revolutionary. Rather, it brings the Arabic novel to a new level of perfection within the long and venerable tradition of the realist novel.

The trilogy brings together a huge fund of social, political, economic, and anthropological materials and blends them within the fabric of the life of a middle-class Egyptian family over the course of three generations. In many ways this is a novel about history as much as it is a family saga. The history is that of 20th-century Egypt; the saga is of a family that is not only a part of that history but also emblematic of it. However, the greatness of the novel does not lie in its depiction of Egypt's history as much as in the ability of the author to write this history without in any way forcing it on the plot or turning the individual characters into representatives of the different historical currents. To the contrary, history seems to flow from the richness of the characters and from their psychological, intellectual, and social dimensions. Not reducible to history, neither can the novel be reduced to psychology, ideology, or politics. Mahfūz draws credible characters by showing the fictional individual subject to be a complex entity constituted by the interaction of multiple forces and tensions such as heredity, social environment (family, class, culture, geography),

and personal experience in relation to the social world—that is, the interaction of the personal with the public. Depicting character within such a network, rather than in a more restricted ideological scheme, counts as perhaps the Cairo Trilogy's major accomplishment and contribution to the Arabic novel.

WALID HAMARNEH

Biography

Born 11 December 1911 in Gamaliya, Cairo. Attended the University of Cairo, 1930–34, degree in philosophy 1934, postgraduate study 1935–36. Secretary, University of Cairo, 1936–38; journalist, *Ar-Risāla*, and contributor to *Al-Hilāl* and *Al-Ahrām*; civil servant, Ministry of Islamic Affairs, 1939–54; director of censorship, Department of Art; director of Foundation for Support of the Cinema for the State Cinema Organization, 1959–69; consultant for cinema affairs to the Ministry of Culture, 1969–71; retired from civil service, 1971; board member, Dār al-Maᶜāref publishing house. Awarded Nobel prize for literature, 1988.

Novels by Mahfūz

ᶜAbath al-aqdār [The Mockery of Fate], 1939
Rādūbīs, 1943
Kifāh Tībah [Thebes' Struggle], 1944
Khān al-Khalīlī [Khan al-Khalili], 1945
Al-Qāhirah al-Jadīdah [New Cairo], 1946
Zuqāq al-Midaqq, 1947; as Midaq Alley, translated by Trevor le Gassick, 1975
Al-Sarāb, 1949
Bidāyah wa-Nihāyah, 1949; as The Beginning and the End, translated by Ramses Hanna Awad, 1985
Al-Thulāthiya [The Cairo Trilogy]:
   Bayn al-Qaṣrayn, 1956; as Palace Walk, translated by W. Hutchins and Olive Kenny, 1989
   Qaṣr al-Shawq, 1957; as Palace of Desire, translated by W. Hutchins, Lorne Kenny, nd Olive Kenny, 1991
   Al-Sukkarīyah, 1957; as Sugar Street, translated by W. Hutchins and Angele Botros Semaan, 1992
Al-Liṣṣ wa-al-kilāb, 1961; as The Thief and the Dogs, translated by Trevor le Gassick and M.M. Badawi, 1984
Al-Summān wa-al-kharīf, 1962; as Autumn Quail, translated by Roger Allen, 1985
Al-Ṭarīq, 1964; as The Search, translated by Muhammed Islam, 1987
Al-Shahhadh, 1965; as The Beggar, translated by K. Walker Henry and N.K.N. al-Warraki, 1986
Thartharah fawq al-Nīl, 1966; as Adrift on the Nile, translated by Frances Liardet, 1993
Awlād Haritnā, 1967; as Children of Gebelawi, translated by Philip Stewart, 1981; as Children of the Alley, 1996
Mīrāmār, 1967; as Miramar, translated by Maged el-Komos and John Rodenbeck, 1978
Al-Marāyā, 1972; as Mirrors, translated by Roger Allen, 1977
Al-Hubb taht al-matar, 1973
Al-Karnak, 1974; in English, in Three Contemporary Egyptian Novels, 1979
Hikāyāt hāritna, 1975; as Fountain and Tomb, translated by Soad Sobhy, Essam Fattouh, and James Kenneson, 1988
Qalb al-layl [In the Heart of the Night], 1975

Ḥaḍrat al-muḥtaram, 1975; as *Respected Sir,* translated by
 Rasheed el-Enany, 1986
Malḥamat al-ḥarāfīsh, 1977; as *The Harafish,* 1994
ʿAṣr al-ḥubb [Age of Love], 1980
Afrāḥ al-Qubbah, 1981; as *Wedding Song,* translated by Olive
 Kenny, 1984
Layālī alf laylah, 1981; as *Arabian Nights and Days,* translated
 by Denys Johnson-Davies, 1995
Al-Bāqī min al-zaman sāʿah [One Hour Left], 1982
Riḥlat Ibn Faṭṭūmah, 1983; as *The Journey of Ibn Fattouma,*
 translated by Denys Johnson-Davies, 1992
Al-ʿĀʾish fī al-ḥaqīqah [Living with the Truth], 1985
Yawm maqtal al-zaʿīm, 1985; as *The Day the Leader Was
 Killed,* 1989
Ḥadīth al-ṣabāḥ wa-al-masāʾ [Morning and Evening Talk],
 1987
Thartharah ʿalā al-baḥr, 1993

Other Writings: short stories, one-act plays.

Further Reading

Allen, Roger, *The Arabic Novel: An Historical and Critical
 Introduction,* Syracuse, New York: Syracuse University Press,
 and Manchester: Manchester University Press, 1982; 2nd
 edition, Syracuse, New York: Syracuse University Press, 1995
Kilpatrick, Hilary, *The Modern Egyptian Novel: A Study in
 Social Criticism,* London: Ithaca Press, 1974
Mahmoud, Fatma Moussa, *The Arabic Novel in Egypt,
 1914–1970,* Cairo: Egyptian General Book Organization,
 1973
Sakkut, Hamdi, *The Egyptian Novel and Its Main Trends from
 1913 to 1952,* Cairo: American University in Cairo Press,
 1971
Somekh, Sasson, *The Changing Rhythm: A Study of Najib
 Mahfuz's Novels,* Leiden: Brill, 1973

Norman Mailer 1923–

United States

One of a very few novelists who has enjoyed immense fame
and critical acclaim from his first book to his most recent, Norman Mailer has nevertheless confounded the terms of his own
notoriety to become a style of writer quite different from what
both commentators and he himself expected. Although he was
eager to become a major novelist in the manner of Ernest Hemingway, writing narratives that would be fictive encapsulations
of their times, Mailer's most lasting mark on the history of the
novel will probably be his role as an innovator of what would
come to be called the nonfiction novel. Using the techniques of
fiction to investigate more deeply what most people consider
subject matter for journalism, Mailer blurred distinctions between literary artistry and fidelity to fact, even as he challenged
the novel's ability to reflect experience in a conclusive way.

As a Harvard graduate and veteran of military service in World
War II, the young Norman Mailer felt well qualified to write "the
big novel" of his generation, relating the war to both personal development and larger moral issues of the times. As such, *The
Naked and the Dead* (1948) balances microcosm and macrocosm
in a way that pits the individual (and the small group, in this case
a platoon fighting in the Pacific) against larger organizational
forces. The antecedent for this approach was obvious in the work
of John Dos Passos, whose achievement Mailer admired, and it
carries over into the domestic scene of *Barbary Shore* (1951),
which uses the circumstance of rooming house neighbors debating the radical politics of their pasts, a technique reminiscent of
Dos Passos' *Manhattan Transfer* (1925). In *The Deer Park*
(1955), the author shifted his focus to Hollywood, but once again
seemed eager to write a thematic tour de force (here of supposedly typical movieland behavior). In each case Mailer was writing
with essentially prewar notions of the novel in mind: that such fiction should totalize experience (in the manner of James T. Farrell)

while relying on the synthetic powers of all-encompassing observation (Dos Passos) to fashion a statement.

The first major shift in Norman Mailer's career came with his
fourth novel, *An American Dream* (1965). Here he took advantage of the insider's perspective won by his parallel career as a
feature essayist and commentator (*Advertisements for Myself,*
1959; *The Presidential Papers,* 1963) to blend fantasy with fact,
interweaving the fortunes of a protagonist dedicated to testing
the limits of human experience with the doings of a very real figure who in the public's imagination did much the same (John F.
Kennedy, here seen in his Senate days, but for a readership mindful of his presidency and assassination). *Why Are We in Vietnam?* (1967) unleashes this style of protagonist to an extent that
his acts eclipse even those of history. The Vietnam War, so central to American political, social, and cultural concerns during
these years that its mention in the title is unexceptional, manages
not to be cited until the novel's last sentence. But the pressure of
public events gets equal time in the work that would establish
Mailer as a pioneer of the nonfiction novel, *The Armies of the
Night: The Novel as History, History as a Novel* (1968). Here
the author not only uses the techniques of fiction (such as characterization, dialogue, and development by means of imagery
and symbolism) to dramatize a massive protest march against
the Pentagon, but studies his own reactions as a barometer of the
events themselves. Here the author faces the challenge set to his
protagonist in *An American Dream*: how to create one's self in a
world of seemingly overwhelming forces.

Throughout the 1970s, Mailer distinguished himself by treating larger than life personalities with the fictive rigor that their
cultural importance would make appropriate. Representative of
this phase are *Marilyn: A Novel Biography* (1973) and *The Executioner's Song: A True Life Novel* (1979). As Marilyn Monroe

was more than just a movie star, Gary Gilmore loomed larger in the public's estimation than simply as a convicted murderer. Her life was an iconization of sex and beauty; his execution was the first after several decades' suspension of capital punishment in the United States. Both figures riveted popular attention, and each triumphed (in this fashion) in death, something conventionally accorded only to truly great historical figures (from Jesus Christ to Napoléon Bonaparte) or to characters in novels. Mailer's quest in these works is to discover just how creatures of the imagination (as Monroe's and Gilmore's public personalities surely were) manage the same power as those who have acted deeply on the forces of history.

Sex and violence figure prominently in *Marilyn* and *The Executioner's Song*, both as indices to the exercise (if not the genesis) of power. When exploring these interests in conventional novel form, Mailer is less successful with his literary art even as he propounds the issues in almost essayistic terms. *Ancient Evenings* (1983) covers two centuries of pre-Christian history yet seems most concerned with what one reviewer called the author's "psychosomatics" and "poetics" as released from his "repressed unconscious." On the other hand, *Tough Guys Don't Dance* (1984) takes pleasure with the flat conventions of the private-eye thriller; in something of a parody of this well-worn subgeneric form, Mailer characterizes, digresses, and at times pontificates in a way that only an essential lack of respect for the medium can allow. More serious business awaits in *Harlot's Ghost* (1991) and *The Gospel According to the Son* (1997), where the author's ego is given a fair match in terms of the Central Intelligence Agency and the Christian New Testament, respectively.

Mailer's most insightful critics trace his genesis as an important writer to an essay he wrote in 1957, published as a pamphlet called *The White Negro*. A full decade before the flourishing of a countercultural revolution, the author in this piece identified the true vitality in American life as lying within the domain of the outsider, the person whose raw energy (often misconstrued as illicitly sexual and destructively violent) gives him the impetus for being an "existential hero," Mailer's code name for the type of person who can act with great determination when the future is unknown. This essay separates his early derivative novels from the groundbreaking work of the 1960s and 1970s and also explains his fascinations of the 1980s and 1990s that have led to long and (for some readers) dogmatically overbearing works.

JEROME KLINKOWITZ

Biography

Born 31 January 1923 in Long Branch, New Jersey. Attended Boys' High School, Brooklyn, New York, graduated 1939; Harvard University, Cambridge, Massachusetts (where he served as associate editor of the *Harvard Advocate*), 1939–43, S.B. (cum laude) in aeronautical engineering 1943; the Sorbonne, Paris, 1947. Served in the United States Army, 1944–46: Sergeant. Cofounded, 1955, and wrote column, 1956, for the *Village Voice*, New York; columnist ("Big Bite"), *Esquire*, New York, 1962–63, and *Commentary*, New York, 1962–63; member of the executive board, 1968–73, and president, 1984–86, PEN American Center; independent candidate for mayor of New York City, 1969.

Novels and Nonfiction Novels by Mailer

The Naked and the Dead, 1948
Barbary Shore, 1951
The Deer Park, 1955
An American Dream, 1965
Why Are We in Vietnam?, 1967
The Armies of the Night: The Novel as History, History as a Novel, 1968
Marilyn: A Novel Biography, 1973
The Executioner's Song: A True Life Novel, 1979
Ancient Evenings, 1983
Tough Guys Don't Dance, 1984
Harlot's Ghost, 1991
The Gospel According to the Son, 1997

Other Writings: short fiction, plays, screenplays, poetry, and a range of nonfictional works.

Further Reading

Adams, Laura, *Norman Mailer: A Comprehensive Bibliography,* Metuchen, New Jersey: Scarecrow Press, 1974
Bailey, Jennifer, *Norman Mailer: Quick-Change Artist,* London: Macmillan, and New York: Barnes and Noble, 1979
Manso, Peter, editor, *Mailer: His Life and Times,* New York: Simon and Schuster, and London: Viking, 1985
Mills, Hilary, *Mailer: A Biography,* New York: Empire Books, 1982
Poirier, Richard, *Norman Mailer,* New York: Viking, 1972; as *Mailer,* London: Fontana/Collins, 1972
Rollyson, Carl, *The Lives of Norman Mailer: A Biography,* New York: Paragon, 1991
Wenke, Joseph, *Mailer's America,* Hanover, New Hampshire: University Press of New England, 1987

Bernard Malamud 1914–86

United States

Bernard Malamud was an important 20th-century American fiction writer and one of the most important of post–World War II American Jewish writers. He published eight novels in his lifetime (an unfinished one, *The People* [1989], was published posthumously); some of them feature experimental techniques, while others are more traditional. All his novels are concerned with the need for the protagonist to move from a state of self-centeredness to one of selflessness; to accept moral responsibility for others; and to be able to express love, mercy, compassion, and charity. Malamud once stated, "My work, all of it, is an idea of dedication to the human. That's basic to every book. If you don't respect man, you cannot respect my work. I'm in defense of the human" (see Lasher, 1991).

His first novel, *The Natural* (1952), differs from any that followed. Baseball becomes a knightly joust at times, with the characters taking on roles from Arthurian legend. The game is played by a team called the Knights, on Knights Field. In addition, the grail legend and fertility myths are of central importance, with a Fisher King figure; a dessicated, "wasteland"-like playing field; and a concern for heroes, with hero-nurturing and hero-destroying women. There is no other American baseball novel that is so packed with mythic references, Malamud having stated that before he could write a baseball novel he found it necessary to transform the game into myth, possibly because of the game's essential lightness. Remaining as a basic stance, however, is his distinctive theme of self-development and personal growth through suffering. In this novel the hero learns too late about the importance of selflessness and does not achieve the secular salvation that marks most of Malamud's other works. American novelists generally do not place a major emphasis on these themes.

The successful fulfillment of this moral imperative may be seen in *The Assistant* (1957). Philip Roth views the suffering Malamud imposes on his characters as almost a sign of masochism. The addition of the prison motif also serves to intensify both the suffering and redemptive quality achieved. Malamud makes some use of fantasy, a device that marks his best work, and points to the limitations of a purely realistic approach to novel writing. A further important development is his use of Jewishness as a metaphor for a character's suffering and taking on of moral responsibility for others—a "Jew" being someone who is a selfless individual and not necessarily a member of the Jewish people or one who practices Judaism. This stance is reflected in Malamud's famous remark that he sees the Jew as symbolic "of the tragic experience of man existentially. I try to see the Jew as universal man. Every man is a Jew though he may not know it" (Lasher, 1991). This use of a religious/ethnic label to stand for a moral individual is peculiar to Malamud's approach to liberal humanism.

A New Life (1961) is written in a realistic vein, slightly tempered by a romantic view of nature. This "college novel" tries to come to grips with the implications of McCarthyism. It is more conventional in style than *The Fixer* (1966), which was awarded a Pulitzer Prize in literature and Malamud's second National Book Award. Malamud based *The Fixer* on the blood libel leveled at Menaham Mendel Beilis in czarist Russia, focusing on areas that were not part of the historical record—in particular, the thoughts and human development of the protagonist in his prison cell. He has said that "*The Fixer* is largely an invention. That is, I've tried to bring it as close to a folk tale as I could" (Lasher, 1991). This can be seen in its presentation of medieval beliefs concerning Jews. The themes of imprisonment (with real, not symbolic, bars), suffering, and growth in responsibility and morality are very much present, with the use of a schlemiel-like antihero figure used to carry the tale, as in previous novels. *The Assistant* and *The Fixer* mark high points in Malamud's career as a novelist, encapsulating some of his best explications of theme and suitability of form.

Pictures of Fidelman: An Exhibition (1969) is a short-story cycle in which the stories can stand on their own or serve as chapters of a novel. This form was also used in Sherwood Anderson's *Winesburg, Ohio* (1919) and William Faulkner's *The Unvanquished* (1938), both of which, as in *Fidelman*, develop common themes and characters to create unity and coherence. Viewed as a novel, which is how Malamud planned it after writing the first story, *Fidelman* is a combination Bildungsroman and *Künstlerroman*. There are also parallels with James Joyce's *A Portrait of the Artist as a Young Man* (1916) and, in its use of the picaresque and Bildungsroman, with Mark Twain's *The Adventures of Huckleberry Finn* (1884). The protagonist develops an ability to love, thus achieving a state that is of central importance in Malamud's novels.

In *The Tenants* (1971), Malamud created a novel concerned with contemporary issues, something he had not been particularly concerned with before: "Jews and blacks, the period of the troubles in New York City; the teachers strike, the rise of black activism, the mix-up of cause and effect. I thought I'd say a word" (Lasher, 1991). The novel marks a return to the use of fantasy, in which the tenement becomes a vertical island where issues of race and anti-Semitism are paramount. There is also much discussion on the nature of art and, by implication, of the novel, with Jamesian versus revolutionary views being set against each other. There are three endings, each of which reflects a different possible outcome to the racial tensions in the United States, although the novel's movement seems to point more toward tragedy than either pity or interracial marriage. Criticized by some African-Americans for taking on racial issues in part from a black perspective, the novel makes a strong case for compassion and selflessness if tragedy is to be avoided, although neither of the two main characters achieves these moral states.

Dubin's Lives (1979), although superior stylistically, resembles *A New Life* in that it is written in a traditional manner with a traditional plot structure. In Malamud's last completed novel, *God's Grace* (1982), he returns to fantasy and experimentation. Talking monkeys, a gorilla who says Kaddish, and sexual relations between the protagonist and a chimpanzee are part of this beast fable about the destruction of the human race and its relationship to God, there being continual reference to the Hebrew Bible. *God's Grace* is much more pessimistic than Malamud's earlier novels, with human beings encountering real difficulty in surviving their own moral shortcomings. This novel is firmly placed within a tradition of bestiaries—*Aesop's Fables, Gulliver's Travels,* and *Animal Farm*—and island dramas such as *Robinson Crusoe, The Tempest,* and *Lord of the Flies. Dr. Doolittle* is also relevant. Malamud uses this form to raise major theological and social issues.

A writer of deep morality, Malamud's literary legacy is one of compassion in the face of the forces of indifference (or worse) that have plagued life in the 20th century.

EDWARD A. ABRAMSON

Biography

Born 26 April 1914 in Brooklyn, New York. Attended Erasmus Hall High School, New York; City College of New York, 1932–36, B.A. 1936; Columbia University, New York, 1937–38, M.A. 1942. Teacher, New York high schools, evenings 1940–49; instructor/associate professor of English, Oregon State University, Corvallis, 1949–61; member of the Division of Languages and Literature, Bennington College, Vermont, 1961–86; visiting lecturer, Harvard University, Cambridge, Massachusetts, 1966–68; president, PEN American Center, 1979–81. Died 18 March 1986.

Novels by Malamud
The Natural, 1952
The Assistant, 1957
A New Life, 1961
The Fixer, 1966
Pictures of Fidelman: An Exhibition, 1969
The Tenants, 1971
Dubin's Lives, 1979
God's Grace, 1982
The People, 1989 (unfinished, posthumous)

Other Writings: short fiction; of particular interest for Malamud's ideas on the novel form and artistic matters is *Talking Horse: Bernard Malamud on Life and Work,* edited by Alan Cheuse and Nicholas Delbanco, 1996.

Further Reading
Abramson, Edward, *Bernard Malamud Revisited,* New York: Twayne, and Toronto: Macmillan, 1993

Alter, Iska, *The Good Man's Dilemma: Social Criticism in the Fiction of Bernard Malamud,* New York: AMS Press, 1981
Bloom, Harold, editor, *Bernard Malamud,* New York: Chelsea House, 1986
Ducharme, Robert, *Art and Idea in the Novels of Bernard Malamud: Toward "The Fixer,"* The Hague: Mouton, 1974
Field, Leslie, and Joyce Field, editors, *Bernard Malamud: A Collection of Critical Essays,* Englewood Cliffs, New Jersey: Prentice-Hall, 1975
Helterman, Jeffrey, *Understanding Bernard Malamud,* Columbia: University of South Carolina Press, 1985
Hershinow, Sheldon, *Bernard Malamud,* New York: Ungar, 1980
Lasher, Lawrence, *Conversations with Bernard Malamud,* Jackson: University Press of Mississippi, 1991
Salzberg, Joel, *Bernard Malamud: A Reference Guide,* Boston: G.K. Hall, 1985
Salzberg, Joel, editor, *Critical Essays on Bernard Malamud,* Boston: G.K. Hall, 1987

Malavoglia. *See* House by the Medlar Tree

Malaysian Novel. *See* Southeast Asian Novel: Malaysia

Malone Dies. *See* Molloy trilogy

David Malouf 1934–

Australian

It is not surprising that David Malouf has earned a reputation as what one critic has called the "lyrical epicurean" of Australian literature. Coming to prominence in the 1970s as a poet, Malouf has become widely known as one of Australia's most acclaimed novelists, a distinction supported by various international and national literary awards. His prose is characterized by a signature lyricism that blurs the boundaries between the novel form, poetry, and even music. (He is also the author of several libretti.) The broad appeal of his novels is perhaps partly owing to the fact that they all in one way or another deal with issues familiar to every culture: the question of how people map out an identifiable position in the world, particularly through language and the narratives of myth, and the ways in which people interpret their histories in order to do so.

Malouf explores these aspects of "being in" the world in his first novel, *Johnno* (1975). For its Australian audience, the novel's biographical style created an intimate portrait not only of its central characters but also of a regional setting. In telling Johnno's story, the narrator Dante tells his own story as well and invents himself as a writer; yet, perhaps more powerfully, he tells the story of a particular time and place, re-creating the local history of Brisbane, Queensland's metropolitan center, in the decades after World War II. Here Malouf explores what will become one of his later work's most characteristic features: the interweaving of private and public histories. This theme emerges in each of his subsequent novels, most strongly perhaps in *The Great World* (1990), a sweeping narrative that weaves together three generations of private histories within the broader fabric of Australia between World War I and the Vietnam War.

Early on in *Johnno*, as he traces the outline of Australia in a geography lesson, the schoolboy Dante wonders about the nature of maps and their boundaries; he has learned their names by heart, but "beyond that is a mystery. It is what begins with the darkness at our back door." The mystery, in effect, is a mystery of language. If history is the stuff from which identifying myths are made—narratives for locating one's self and one's place within time and space—then language is its most crucial vehicle, the category that expresses and determines both world and consciousness. Malouf's interest in language as both an inventive tool and a regulatory device frames the recurring material of his fiction as well as his particular quality as a writer. This interest in language has special significance in the history of colonized Australia, which was founded on a crisis between an imported language and a reticent landscape. As Malouf stated during a 1986 interview, "What we had was a highly developed language and names for everything, and a reality in front of us that did not fit." Yet as Malouf has argued elsewhere, this crisis between language and world has been, for Australia, an opportunity to "mythologise spaces and through that mythology . . . find our way into a culture." This is not to say, of course, that such a mythology fits neatly over the space of a country. The mythologies of place belonging to Aboriginal Australia, which lie like palimpsestic texts beneath and alongside those of settler Australia, form part of the tension of forces in Malouf's historical narratives. The present, Malouf has said, "is always a mess, a confusion of forces."

Malouf's internationally acclaimed novel *Remembering Babylon* (1993), in particular, pursues the crossing points between these different forces. Its protagonist, Gemmy Fairley, is a "white black man" who, taken in by an Aboriginal community as a child, seeks out his "own kind" among the white settlers of northern Queensland. As in Malouf's other novels, language is allowed a kind of primacy over the world it describes, even possessing a kind of physicality that the world itself—indeterminate until framed in language—is not given. Readers learn that Gemmy "would see [things] clearly enough, but no word was connected to them, and when his mind reached for it, the object too went thin on him." This most fundamental power of language to invent becomes the basis of the novel's exploration of the political dimension of words and of the worlds they encode. In this sense *Remembering Babylon* extends the concerns of Malouf's earlier, most poetic short novel *An Imaginary Life* (1978). A parable and a fictional autobiography, *An Imaginary Life* uses the voice of the Roman poet Ovid to articulate the capacity of world and consciousness for metamorphosis. In this process, Malouf, like Ovid in the *Metamorphoses*, recycles mythic narratives in order to explore the role of the writer as a mouthpiece for his or her cultural history. Given the "confusion of forces" that constitutes any culture's present, it is perhaps not surprising that Malouf has used the term *terrorist* to describe the writer: "A lot of what a writer has to do is to go against the grain, to go against your own nature if you are ever going to shock yourself into discovering new things."

This suggestion of balance between potentially oppositional ways of perceiving is apparent in a tension of the aesthetics that Malouf brings to his novels. In each of his works, there is a tension between what might be called a romantic conception of potential wholeness in the world and a postmodern conception of fragmentation. This tension applies not only to the novel's material but to its production. On the one hand, Malouf has suggested, his writing is an attempt to render something like Martin Heidegger's "primitive and anti-Platonic" conception of "the word and the object [as] absolutely one, as if there never was any question of mind and object being separate"; on the other hand, the writing process is like lining up a series of connected photographs: "you would get a total picture, but there would always be gaps."

The capacity of Malouf's work to express different models of interpreting the world (as well as the writing process) is lived out in the diversity of forms he brings to the novel. His use of the genre is dense with a range of narrative modes: the poetic, the autobiographical or confessional, the playfully metafictional, the historical epic, and the parable. In both the subjects and the forms he chooses for the novel, then, Malouf seems fascinated by that balance of opposites, in which the potential of one state is contained in, or shadowed by, its others.

AMANDA NETTELBECK

Biography
Born 20 March 1934 in Brisbane, Queensland. Attended Brisbane Grammar School, 1947–50; University of Queensland, Brisbane, 1951–54, B.A. (honors) in English 1954. Lecturer, University of Queensland, 1955–57; teacher, St. Anselm's College, England, 1962–68; lecturer, University of Sydney, 1968–77.

Novels by Malouf
Johnno, 1975
An Imaginary Life, 1978
Child's Play, 1982
Fly Away Peter, 1982
Harland's Half Acre, 1984
The Great World, 1990
Remembering Babylon, 1993
Conversations at Curlow Creek, 1996

Other Writings: several collections of poetry, a book of semi-autobiographical essays, a collection of short fiction, several libretti, and many essays and reviews.

Further Reading
Hansson, Karin, *Sheer Edge: Aspects of Identity in David Malouf's Writing*, Lund: Lund University Press, 1991
Indyk, Ivor, *David Malouf*, Melbourne and New York: Oxford University Press, 1993

Neilsen, Philip, *Imagined Lives: A Study of David Malouf,* St. Lucia and Portland, Oregon: University of Queensland Press, 1990

Nettelbeck, Amanda, *Reading David Malouf,* Melbourne: Sydney University Press/Oxford University Press, 1995

Nettelbeck, Amanda, editor, *Provisional Maps: Critical Essays on David Malouf,* Nedlands: Centre for Studies in Australian Literature, University of Western Australia, 1994

Tulip, James, editor, *David Malouf,* St. Lucia and Portland, Oregon: University of Queensland Press, 1990

The Man Who Loved Children by Christina Stead

1940

Of Christina Stead's 16 books—novels, novellas, and collections of short stories—*The Man Who Loved Children* has become the most highly regarded and most frequently discussed since its publication in the United States in 1940. While the novel is set on the east coast of the United States, Australian readers have been eager to claim it as an Australian novel in which Washington, D.C., and Annapolis, Maryland, stand in for parts of Sydney (Bexley and Watson's Bay) and in which Stead's experiences of family life in the 1910s have been transposed to the 1930s. Yet the novel also depends on its American references, in particular the clashing ideologies of North and South expressed in the backgrounds of husband and wife, father and mother, and the privations of the Depression and looming war. Randall Jarrell, who managed to bring the novel back into print in 1965, commented on the way its detail and particularity (clearly based on Stead's own childhood) achieve the effect of universality so that readers find themselves recognizing their own childhoods in its rendering of the horrors of family life.

In his introduction to the novel, Jarrell compares *The Man Who Loved Children* to the fiction of Fedor Dostoevskii for its combination of plausible naturalism and extreme situations. Although 19th-century naturalism is part of the novel's heritage, *The Man Who Loved Children* also demonstrates what Stead called the "drama of the person." The novel is structured around a series of dramatic scenes set entirely within the Pollit houses: the first, which takes up a third of the novel, observes 24 hours in the house in Washington in 1936; another devotes 50 pages to the day of celebration for Sam's return from Malaya; and a third (another 50 pages) covers two days of fish boiling at Annapolis, which culminate in Henny's death. Stead separates these major scenes by interludes that inform readers about life outside the home—Louie's maternal family; Henny's visit to her family home at Monocacy and her trips to town; Sam's experiences in Malaya; and Louie's life at school. In this way, Stead establishes the social and political history of each character—Louie's mother came from an abolitionist Bible-reading family at Harper's Ferry, Henny's family represents a decayed aristocracy, and Sam's foolish innocence and unwitting racism is given full expression in the adult world of Malaya. Although the settings appear as limited as the set of a stage play, the novel is full of subsidiary storytelling and textual allusion—the characters speak their own versions of existence, ordering it into stories that place them at the center of ideological universes. In fact, the novel demonstrates a remarkable self-consciousness about the nature of storytelling as exemplified by Henny's funny and scarifying pictures of a world full of sleazy and pathetic people, Sam's rhetoric of wonder at the natural world, and Louie's immersion in fairy tale, romance, and myth. Some of the characters are also writers. Sam's friend, Saul Pilgrim, writes a serial in a weekly newspaper, which he can never finish because a happy ending would be implausible and a sad ending too unpopular with his readers. Louie proffers Sam the birthday gift of a play, written in her own "Choctaw" language, in which father devours daughter, and she plans a cycle of poems (to contain a poem in every possible form and meter) for her teacher, Miss Aiden.

The novel not only draws attention to the way its characters "tell" their own stories, heavy with political and cultural meaning, but also to its own status as a structured work of art. Louie's positioning as an observer and as a writer has suggested to some readers that the novel is a version of the female artist's quest for freedom. Certainly, Louie is aligned with high-culture literary art by comparison with the populist Pollits; but Stead also suggests that literature—written stories—may be read and appropriated in myriad ways by different people to support their own worldviews. Charles Dickens' *Great Expectations* (1861) is a case in point, providing Louie with a further literary endorsement of the terrors of childhood and Grandfather Pollit with a comic turn as he plays both Wemmick and the "Aged P."

While writing the novel, Stead remarked that "there was no trouble in the subject, but the arrangement was an immense difficulty, the surplus material and surplus drama getting in the way" (Geering and Segerberg, 1994). Yet the relatively controlled structure of the finished novel may account at least partly for its success with readers. In her later novels, Stead resisted the kind of resolution established by Henny's death and Louie's determination to go for "a walk round the world." This suggests that the novel's structure may be based on the same kind of classical Greek tragedy that Louie favors for her play; like Euripides' plays, the novel explores the "middle kingdom of sexual horror" beneath the negotiations of family life, including the unspoken possibility of incestuous relationships.

With this novel and her next one, *For Love Alone* (1944), Stead seemed to purge herself of childhood and family experiences, for she was never to write in such a clearly autobiographical way again. Her novels published after 1944, although based on Stead's friends and acquaintances, explored the state of society in the United States and Europe in a much more public way. While several of her later novels, especially *Dark Places of the Heart* (1966) and *I'm Dying Laughing* (1986) have gained critical admiration, *The Man Who Loved Children* has retained its status as Stead's masterpiece.

SUSAN LEVER

See also Christina Stead

Further Reading

Geering, R.G., and A. Segerberg, editors, *Christina Stead: Selected Fiction and Nonfiction,* St. Lucia and Portland, Oregon: University of Queensland Press, 1994

Gribble, Jennifer, *Christina Stead*, Melbourne and New York: Oxford University Press, 1994

Hooton, Joy, "Mermaid and Minotaur in *The Man Who Loved Children,*" *Meridian* 8:2 (1989)

Lawson, Elizabeth, "Louie's Mother: The Feminist Inscape of *The Man Who Loved Children,*" *Meridian* 8:2 (1989)

Lever, Susan, "The Night of Which Noone Speaks: Christina Stead's Art as Struggle," *Span* 37 (1993)

McDonell, Jennifer, "Christina Stead's *The Man Who Loved Children,*" *Southerly* 44:4 (1984)

Sheridan, Susan, *Christina Stead*, New York and Brighton, Sussex: Harvester Wheatsheaf, and Bloomington: Indiana University Press, 1988

The Man Without Qualities by Robert Musil

Der Mann ohne Eigenschaften 1930–43

When Robert Musil died in Switzerland in 1942, a desperate and destitute emigrant whose books were banned in the Third Reich, his novel *The Man Without Qualities* was left unfinished. Two volumes of the book had appeared in 1931 and 1933 and a further 20 chapters were published from the corrected proofs after his death. A more complete edition published in 1952 attempted to reconstruct the whole of the torso out of early drafts, and it was only then that Musil's work was rediscovered and recognized as one of the great novels of the century, placed beside works like Thomas Mann's *Der Zauberberg* (1924; *The Magic Mountain*), Marcel Proust's *À la Recherche du temps perdu* (1913–27; translated as *Remembrance of Things Past* and also as *In Search of Lost Time*) and James Joyce's *Ulysses* (1922). A new critical edition that included even more unpublished material without constructing a particular sequence out of them was produced in 1978, and the recent English translation by Sophie Wilkins and Burton Pike is to a large extent based on that edition.

Musil's work was conceived on an ambitious scale. In a grand dialectic gesture, it was to encompass "analysis and synthesis"—nothing less than a thorough intellectual analysis of his times and a suggestion of a positive solution. Corresponding to this plan, the novel was divided into two parts, Book I starting with "a sort of introduction" and Book II finishing with "a sort of ending." It aims everywhere to represent the typical and general and seeks to integrate ideas from philosophy, psychology, and ethics into the discourse on an unprecedented scale.

Ulrich, the protagonist, is burdened with all the intellectual baggage of a modernist hero. He is not the average intelligent bourgeois, like Thomas Mann's Hans Castorp in *The Magic Mountain,* but is a highly trained mathematician, scientist, and psychologist. He engages with reality but primarily as an observer, turning his probing eye upon himself, his acquaintances, and the public sphere as a whole. With a thoroughness unprecedented in the history of the novel, Musil's hero analyzes (and decon-

structs) such concepts as the self, beauty, and love. His overriding sense of having no definite character is expressed in the formula of the title: Ulrich feels himself to be merely the convergence of impersonal qualities, gained from his membership in a class, profession, nation, and sex. Paradoxically, he sees this impersonality as a threat but embraces it as the basis of his quest for the true self in harmony with a deep morality.

In order to find the right way to live, Ulrich takes a year's holiday from life. His individual quest is submerged in a general one when he becomes honorary secretary of a patriotic committee, a kind of high-level social, humanitarian organization, which is set up to find a crowning idea for the celebration of the anniversary of the Austrian Emperor's rule. The setting is Vienna, capital of Kakania, the fictional equivalent of the Austro-Hungarian monarchy. Musil gives us no strictly historical picture, since he considered Kakania to be the prototype of a modern state, and his intention was to write a *Zeitroman* (a topical novel), developing out of the historical novel. The general setting provides Musil with a broad canvas for his investigation of the ideas, ideals, and ideologies of a time of great intellectual and political ferment. The temporal setting in the last year before World War I and the fact that celebration of the "emperor of peace" is planned for 1918 put the whole enterprise into an ironic frame and give it an added sense of urgency. The world presents itself as a chaos of unresolved contradictions that seem to lead inevitably to war.

The protagonist's general stock-taking allows Musil to introduce a number of representative figures. Musil proves to be a sparkling satirist, unmatched in 20th-century German literature, giving us delightful satiric portraits and lively scenes. Musil's wit can be humorous as well as satirical, and his strong sense of irony allows him to be serious and poetic without ever becoming pompous. His characters range from the revolutionary socialist to the aristocrat who believes that all political opposites can ultimately be reconciled in a "true" feudalism. The benevolent portrait of the general with "special cultural responsibilities" who draws up a strategic plan of the confusing array of modern ideas is counterbalanced by the biting satire of the elegant industrialist and successful writer Arnheim, based on the real-life figure of Walther Rathenau. Many of the characters are based, or partly based, on friends, acquaintances, or figures from public life. For example, the writer Franz Werfel appears in a thinly disguised portrait under the name of Feuermaul, the representative of the expressionist belief in an all-embracing brotherly love, darling of the salons and coformulator of the final, contradictory resolution of the patriotic committee. Finally, there is the pivotal figure of the sex murderer Moosbrugger, who holds a special fascination for Ulrich but takes on a different significance for all the major figures, thus providing an important thematic link.

The novel is divided into chapters, many with ironic headings. They allow the author to emphasize the principle of analogy and variation, one of the main structuring features of the novel, which is used to juxtapose and contrast the false and the genuine. According to Musil's "constructive irony," all characters reflect aspects of the protagonist's own concerns and preoccupations. Like him, they are all aware of their stagnation, and they too yearn for renewal, a state of oneness that would make their existence truly meaningful. All are, however, shown to achieve merely illusory solutions to their problems. Only Ulrich persists in his analytical and experimental attitude, treating life as a hypothesis. Even when, after all his other experiments have failed, he enters into the ultimate experiment of love in the mystical "Millennium," he does so with the critical consciousness of the scientist or Nietzschean thinker.

Love in *The Man Without Qualities* is explored from many angles. But it is in the second half of the novel, when the satire of the patriotic action recedes into the background, that the focus shifts to Musil's "ultimate love story" between the "last Romantics of love"—Ulrich and his sister Agathe. Their love is characterized as a form of self-love, love without the intrusion of anything alien, representing the possibility of total involvement. In their "utopia of the Siamese twins," each participates to such an extent in the emotions of the other that even physical unfaithfulness becomes a shared experience. Here the narrative impetus slows down, some chapters becoming essays disguised as diary entries or a kind of Platonic dialogue on love between Ulrich and his sister, Agathe, the most positive female figure Musil ever created.

The tantalizing question is, how was the novel to end? Musil himself envisaged various conclusions. Considering the date of 1913, the shadow of the war looms inevitably behind all events. Musil saw, from a new historical perspective, how everything was to lead into the great catastrophe, the destruction of European culture in the form of his, after all, nostalgically portrayed Kakania. Some critics believe that the novel should, and indeed was intended to, end with the last chapters that Musil was revising shortly before his death. The last chapter on which he was working, entitled "Breaths of a Summer Day," seemed to absorb him particularly. It might be taken as a kind of testament, containing the real message Musil had to impart to the world. Musil portrays a sublimated spiritual love, as brother and sister feel mystically united while sitting in their garden meditating on the spectacle of blossoms floating down from the trees. Doubts have been expressed as to whether the protagonist—seemingly having aged with the author during the long period of creation, although he has not reached the end of his year's holiday from life, having become much wiser, more resigned and less cynical—has reverted to the more dynamic emotions expressed in the drafts of 20 years earlier, which would have taken him and his sister on a "journey into paradise," where their union would have been physically consummated. According to the original plan, the hero would have been dismissed into the Great War to become a spy. At one time, Musil thought of replacing this with an epilogue in which Ulrich comments on his author from the point of view of 1942. What Musil might in the end have done with his material will always remain open to speculation.

Throughout the novel Musil faced the problem of how to integrate ideas into the narrative, and the question became especially urgent with the later chapters. He felt that in engaging with the "irrational" and embarking on the path of the mystics, it was even more necessary to proceed with almost scientific exactness. *The Man Without Qualities* is a unique experiment, often compared in its daring (and because of its sheer length) to the work of Joyce and Proust, but very different in its aims. Musil's ideal, which sets him apart from most novelists, was "precision in matters of the soul," in other words, in the realm of feelings and ideas. He was always conscious that he was turning the relationship between plot and ideas upside down, but he hoped that his new method would justify itself by creating a new kind of novel. Dissatisfied with story-telling but also averse to the creation of a philosophical system, he opted for a hybrid form, which Thomas Mann recognized as Musil's most important contribution to the development of the modern novel: the "elevation" (*Erhöhung*) and "intellectualization" (*Vergeistigung*) of the German novel. With the creation of this new form, Musil felt himself, with some justification, to have been more successful in pushing the boundaries of the novel than even his illustrious contemporaries Thomas Mann and Hermann Broch.

Musil's characteristic mode of writing is that of irony. He plays ironically with traditional forms, with the idea of a hero as much as the concept of reality in general. *The Man Without Qualities* is many things but never fits neatly into any of the conventional categories. It fuses the novel and essay, social portraiture and radical critique of ideology, fluctuating between abstractions and a wealth of original images, and moving from satire to utopia. The novel never presents ready-made solutions but suggests what Musil called "partial solutions"—models, patterns of "how to be a human being" ("wie man Mensch sein kann"). Although unfinished, *The Man Without Qualities* is a fascinating torso. In fact, its very incompleteness gives a postmodern feel to the romantic ruins of one of the great literary enterprises of the 20th century.

LOTHAR HUBER

See also Robert Musil

Further Reading

Bangerter, Lowell A., *Robert Musil,* New York: Continuum, 1988

Hickman, Hannah, *Robert Musil and the Culture of Vienna,* London: Croom Helm, and La Salle, Illinois: Open Court, 1984

Huber, Lothar, and John J. White, editors, *Musil in Focus: Papers from a Centenary Symposium,* London: Institute of Germanic Studies, University of London, 1982

Luft, David, *Robert Musil and the Crisis of European Culture, 1880–1942,* Berkeley: University of California Press, 1980

Payne, Philip, *Robert Musil's "The Man without Qualities": A Critical Study,* Cambridge and New York: Cambridge University Press, 1988

Peters, Frederick G., *Robert Musil, Master of the Hovering Life: A Study of the Major Fiction,* New York: Columbia University Press, 1978

Pike, Burton, *Robert Musil: An Introduction to His Work,* Ithaca, New York: Cornell University Press, 1961

Rogowski, Christian, *Distinguished Outsider: Robert Musil and His Critics,* Columbia, South Carolina: Camden House, 1994 (includes comprehensive bibliography)

The Man-Eater of Malgudi by R.K. Narayan

1961

R.K. Narayan's work was first published in Britain in the 1930s, largely thanks to the efforts of his longstanding friend and correspondent Graham Greene, who was also responsible for establishing Narayan's reputation as an Indian Chekhov, a categorization that has been applied to him repeatedly ever since. Such a label suggests that Narayan is a chronicler of the *longueurs* of provincial life. In fact, Narayan has often been regarded as a comic novelist who uses irony as a vehicle for exposing the foibles of the inhabitants of Malgudi, the fictional south Indian town (based on his own hometown of Mysore) that he has peopled for more than half a century. To classify Narayan as a comic novelist, however, only partly identifies what is distinctive in his fiction. His work also incorporates layers of Hindu myth and symbol, and it is the coexistence of these two elements—Westernized social comedy and traditional Indian fable—that establishes the highly individual flavor of his work. Narayan's fiction represents a particularly interesting response to the problems facing anglophone Indian writers. Narayan's contemporary Raja Rao clearly expressed the nature of their dilemma in the foreword to his own first novel, *Kanthapura* (1938): "One has to convey in a language that is not one's own the spirit that is one's own." In Narayan's case the interaction between language and culture is especially complex: he came from a traditional Tamil brahmin background and was educated at an English-language school, the Maharaja's College in Mysore where English and Sanskrit classics were equally familiar to him from an early age.

The Man-Eater of Malgudi belongs to the middle period of Narayan's fiction, in which he repeatedly returns to the same subject, that of a south Indian small businessman who finds his orderly life threatened by the advent of outside forces. In the novel, the protagonist Nataraj, a printer, has his daily routine disturbed by Vasu, the man-eater of the title, a bullying taxidermist newly arrived in Malgudi. From the moment he first appears in Nataraj's press, Vasu violates "its sacred traditions" by passing through a curtain that separates its inner sanctum from the outside world. This act of symbolic penetration anticipates all Vasu's subsequent behavior. When he takes over Nataraj's attic without Nataraj's explicit permission and uses it for his work

as a taxidermist, the Hindu Nataraj is horrified to find that the room has been "converted into a charnel house."

In the ensuing narrative the consequences of Vasu's invasion of Nataraj's world are, on one level, comic, as the put-upon Nataraj finds himself falling afoul of the civic authorities and incurring the displeasure of his neighbors as a result of the antisocial actions of his uninvited guest. Narayan also gently satirizes Nataraj himself. From the outset it is clear that he is capable of petty trickery: he speaks of having a staff, but his "staff" consists of a single well-wisher, Sastri, a general factotum who effectively runs the press; and he attracts would-be clients by showing them the more modern printing machine owned by his next-door neighbor.

However, underlying the comic surface of the novel are references to mythology. From the moment when Vasu first appears, he is described in terms that suggest a demonic force: "a new head appeared . . . a tanned face, large powerful eyes under thick eyebrows and a shock of unkempt hair, like a black halo." His profession flies directly in the face of Nataraj's traditional brahminical Hinduism, which maintains that all life is sacred, and this conflict is underscored by various mythological references. When Nataraj finds Vasu in the attic working on a dead eagle, he warns him that the eagle is a messenger of the god Vishnu, a sacred creature. This conflict of values appears to center on different forms of preservation, since Vishnu is said to be a protector of life, while Vasu as a taxidermist preserves his subjects in a very different sense.

As events unfold, Nataraj feels he may have to act as a Vishnu-like preserver when he suspects that Vasu is about to kill an elephant that has been chosen to play a central role in the annual spring ceremony of the local Krishna temple. However, he is never required to do this, since Vasu accidentally kills himself—in Narayan's quietistic moral universe solutions to problems are usually achieved without the intervention of the protagonist—but it is clear by this point that the novel involves an archetypal conflict (from a Hindu perspective) between Vasu, who sees himself as "a rival to nature," and Nataraj, who champions "the natural." The balance is weighted in favor of Nataraj's values. Lest the reader miss the story's mythic dimension, Sastri explains that Vasu "shows all the definitions of a *rakshasa*"and further defines Vasu as "a demoniac creature, who possessed enormous strength, strange powers, and genius, but recognized no sort of restraints of man or god." Sastri points out that *rakshasas* always contain the seeds of their own destruction; when Vasu kills himself the mythic pattern is complete.

V.S. Naipaul has written (1977) that after initially reading Narayan as a writer of social comedies, he later came to view Narayan's novels as Hindu fables dramatizing the conflict between quietism and an impulse toward social action that is usually defeated. This assessment sums up the central thematic conflict of *The Man-Eater of Malgudi,* a novel that walks a tightrope between Western and Hindu narrative modes without ever entirely allowing one mode to dominate.

JOHN THIEME

See also R.K. Narayan

Further Reading

Harrex, Syd, *The Fire and the Offering: The English-Language Novel of India, 1935–1970,* volume 2, Calcutta: Writers Workshop, 1978

Mukherjee, Meenakshi, *The Twice Born Fiction: Themes and Techniques of the Indian Novel in English,* New Delhi: Heinemann 1971; 2nd edition, 1974

Naipaul, V.S., *India: A Wounded Civilization,* London: Deutsch, and New York: Knopf, 1977

Sankaran, Chitra, *The Myth Connection: The Use of Hindu Mythology in Some Novels of Raja Rao and R.K. Narayan,* Ahmadabad: Allied, 1993

Sundaram, P.S., *R.K. Narayan,* New Delhi: Arnold-Heinemann, and New York: Humanities Press, 1973

Walsh, William, *R.K. Narayan: A Critical Appreciation,* London: Heinemann, and Chicago: University of Chicago Press, 1982

Thomas Mann 1875-1955

German

One of the most famous monographs in English on Thomas Mann is titled *The Ironic German* (see Heller, 1958). The label describes well the two determining features of Mann's fiction. At least since the romantic era, irony has been a serious matter in German literature, and since Arthur Schopenhauer and Friedrich Nietzsche German culture has entertained the idea, crucial to Mann, that illusion is existentially necessary. To this aesthetic inheritance, Mann came increasingly to add an ethical appeal to "Humanität"—a phrase conveying shades of humanity, humanitarianism, and humanism—as the barbarism of the 20th century unfolded.

The notion of ironic illusion as a component of reality—as well as the basic condition of fiction—is the leading thought in *Bekenntnisse des Hochstaplers Felix Krull* (1954; *Confessions of Felix Krull, Confidence Man*). Begun in 1910, the work was taken up again at the end of Mann's life and thus spans almost his entire oeuvre. This picaresque novel recounts the career of an attractive but penurious young man who exploits the possibilities of illusion and seduction to make his way in the world. In his hands, beautiful surfaces obscure sordid material circumstance, but they are no less real for being surfaces, no matter how deceptive. Krull tells the beguiling narrative of his confidence tricks from a prison cell, but that he has been caught does not invalidate the illusions of success. More significantly, Krull is a figure of the novelist, his tricks not essentially different from the illusions and seductions of fiction. Not Mann's most accomplished novel, *Felix Krull* nevertheless epitomizes one of the central concerns of his art.

Mann rose to fame as the author of *Buddenbrooks: Verfall einer Familie* (1901; *Buddenbrooks: The Decline of a Family*), which became the best-selling novel in Germany in the first half of the 20th century. It was the first realist novel in German to achieve international status, eventually leading to the award of the Nobel prize for literature in 1929. It combines the social realism of the great European tradition—with *Renée Mauperin* (1864) by Jules and Edmond Goncourt as a specific model—with the interest in morbid psychology of the fin de siècle. This combination is itself ironic, since the novel describes the decline of a family in incontestably splendid realist narrative and in doing so narrates the decline of the realist attitude upon which the social novel of the 19th century rested.

Mann never again referred to realism—whether as a style or a worldview—without distancing himself from its naive certainties. His second novel, *Königliche Hoheit* (1909; *Royal Highness*), expresses Mann's self-consciousness about his role as an artist. The novel points out that the figures of prince and poet are alike in that they represent the many by representing themselves. Two of Mann's shorter works deal with the same concerns. *Tonio Kröger* (1903) and *Der Tod in Venedig* (1912; *Death in Venice*) are exquisitely wrought examples of self-conscious artistry. In each, a writer-protagonist is torn between self-discipline and decadence, a dilemma created by art, which will always point both ways. As the narrator of *Death in Venice* puts it, "and does form not have two faces? Is it not at once moral and immoral?"

Yet despite this artistic self-consciousness, which remained with him always, Mann never abandoned the formal conventions of the traditional European novel, retaining a superficially unproblematic perspective on reality, as well as coherent and urbane narration, plot, setting, and characters. The broadest irony of Mann's work lies in his simultaneous and brilliant use and questioning of the novel form. His continued reliance on traditional forms helps to explain his great popularity. Mann's work was always accessible to a broad readership that did not have to come to terms with unfamiliar literary procedures. At the same time it was always evidently *about* the profound and difficult questions of the time. His art is always sustained, even at its most serious and tragic, by the trickster-artist's sense that art is an irresponsible endeavor that achieves a profundity precisely by virtue of its ludic character.

History dictated that Germany should be one of Mann's major themes. After World War I, he was obliged to think over his initial unquestioning identification with the German romantic cultural inheritance and seek, as an artist, to continue the tradition in ways compatible with modern political democracy. *Der Zauberberg* (1924; *The Magic Mountain*) parodies the German Bildungsroman in order to give an ironic portrait of prewar Europe, but the parody also attempts a renewal of the genre's humanistic tradition. Hans Castorp, the protagonist and an embodiment of "Germanness," is an engaging character with the capacity to learn and grow despite the overwhelming spiritual disorientation of the time. At once satisfying fictional creations and evidently allegorical figures, all the major characters share this quality with Hans.

While *The Magic Mountain* hoped for a democratic future in Germany, the 1930 novella *Mario und der Zauberer* (*Mario and the Magician*) is less optimistic, deftly allegorizing the ominous power of fascism in a holiday anecdote about the murder of a sinister stage hypnotist.

Mann's next two major works, *Lotte in Weimar* (1939) and *Joseph und seine Brüder* (1933–43; *Joseph and His Brothers*), are responses to the historical failure of the first German attempt at democracy and Mann's associated exile. *Lotte in Weimar* continues Mann's commitment to maintaining and renewing the German cultural legacy. The novel deals with Charlotte Kestner's visit to Weimar, residence of the already famous Johann Wolfgang von Goethe. Kestner was the real-life model for Lotte in Goethe's *Die Leiden des jungen Werthers* (1774; *The Sufferings of Young Werther*), written 24 years before the visit. Mann's novel explores the relation between art, life, and responsibility, largely through interior monologue. In the *Joseph* tetralogy, Mann falls back upon his enduring skill as a storyteller. Through the life of the biblical Joseph, the novel presents individual experience as patterned by myth. Mann uses myth in most of his works, like other more obviously modernist novelists such as James Joyce, but the Joseph novels specifically counter the Nazi abuse of mythology. Since Joseph is both interpreter of dreams and civil administrator, he thus also represents an ideal of a spiritual but practical humanity as an answer to fascist terror.

Mann's engagement with the theme of Germany culminates in *Doktor Faustus* (1947; *Doctor Faustus*). Mann had always thought of music, especially that of Richard Wagner, as a defining component of German culture, and in his version of the Faust story (once more a reference to the work of Goethe) Mann casts a composer, Adrian Leverkühn, as the representative German artist-musician who makes a pact with the devil. This is Mann's most moving and tragic work. Germany's overwhelming guilt and its suffering in World War II all but bring Mann's ludic artistry to silence. The humanist tradition speaks through the well-meaning but uncomprehending voice of the narrator, Serenus Zeitblom. Critics still argue whether or not Mann ultimately consigns Leverkühn, and Germany with him, to the devil, yet there can be no argument that the novel is itself magnificently sustained and finished, contriving to escape the disintegration that it so graphically portrays.

Mann's writing is not easy to translate, and the reader who knows his work only in translation may miss something of the lightness of touch that pervades his elaborate prose. Although in many ways a writer who belongs to a bygone era of high culture, Mann remains much loved and very widely in print as one of the very few great modern novelists who appeal as much to the ordinary reader as to the intellectual elite.

MICHAEL MINDEN

See also Buddenbrooks; Doctor Faustus; Magic Mountain

Biography

Born 6 June 1875 in Lübeck, Germany. Brother of the writer Heinrich Mann and father of the writers Erika and Klaus Mann. Attended Dr. Bussenius' school, 1882–89; Gymnasium, Lübeck, 1889–94. Served in the military, 1898–99. Employed in insurance company, Munich, 1894–95, writer thereafter; lived in Switzerland, 1933–36 (deprived of German citizenship, 1936), Princeton, New Jersey, 1938–41, Santa Monica, California, 1941–52, and Switzerland, 1952–55. Awarded Nobel prize for literature, 1929. Died 12 August 1955.

Novels by Mann

Buddenbrooks: Verfall einer Familie, 1901; as *Buddenbrooks: The Decline of a Family*, translated by H.T. Lowe-Porter, 1924; also translated by John E. Woods, 1993
Königliche Hoheit, 1909; as *Royal Highness*, translated by A. Cecil Curtis, 1916; revised translation by Constance McNab, 1979
Der Zauberberg, 1924; as *The Magic Mountain*, translated by H.T. Lowe-Porter, 1927; also translated by John E. Woods, 1995
Joseph und seine Brüder, 4 vols., 1933–43; as *Joseph and His Brothers*, 1934–44
    Die Geschichten Jakobs, 1933; as *The Tale of Jacob*, translated by H.T. Lowe-Porter, 1934
    Der junge Joseph, 1934; as *Young Joseph*, translated by H.T. Lowe-Porter, 1935
    Joseph in Ägypten, 1936; as *Joseph in Egypt*, translated by H.T. Lowe-Porter, 1938
    Joseph der Ernährer, 1943; as *Joseph the Provider*, translated by H.T. Lowe-Porter, 1944
Lotte in Weimar, 1939; as *Lotte in Weimar*, translated by H.T. Lowe-Porter, 1940; as *The Beloved Returns*, translated by Lowe-Porter, 1940
Doktor Faustus: Das Leben des deutschen Tonsetzers Adrian Leverkühn, erzählt von einem Freunde, 1947; as *Doctor Faustus: The Life of the German Composer, Adrian Leverkuehn, as Told by a Friend*, translated by H.T. Lowe-Porter, 1948; also translated by John E. Woods, 1997
Der Erwählte, 1951; as *The Holy Sinner*, translated by H.T. Lowe-Porter, 1951
Bekenntnisse des Hochstaplers Felix Krull, 1954; as *Confessions of Felix Krull, Confidence Man: The Early Years*, translated by Denver Lindley, 1955

Other Writings: novellas, short stories, essays on literary, cultural, and political subjects, speeches, radio propaganda broadcasts, as well as letters and diaries, many of which have been published, some in English translation.

Further Reading

Beddow, Michael, *Thomas Mann, Doctor Faustus,* Cambridge and New York: Cambridge University Press, 1994

Hayman, Ronald, *Thomas Mann: A Biography,* New York: Scribner, 1995; London: Bloomsbury, 1996

Heller, Erich, *The Ironic German: A Study of Thomas Mann,* London: Secker and Warburg, and Boston: Little Brown, 1958

Jonas, Klaus W., *Die Thomas-Mann-Literatur* (bibliography), Berlin: Schmidt, 1972

Koopmann, Helmut, editor, *Thomas-Mann-Handbuch,* Stuttgart: Kröner, 1990; 2nd edition, 1995

Potempa, Georg, *Thomas Mann: Eine Bibliographie,* Morsum/Sylt: Cicero Presse, 1988

Reed, T.J., *Thomas Mann: The Uses of Tradition,* Oxford: Clarendon Press, 1974; 2nd edition, Oxford: Clarendon Press, and New York: Oxford University Press, 1996

Ridley, Hugh, *Thomas Mann: Buddenbrooks,* Cambridge and New York: Cambridge University Press, 1987

Sommerhage, Claus, *Eros und Poesis: Über das Erotische im Werk Thomas Manns,* Bonn: Bouvier, 1983

Swales, Martin, *Thomas Mann: A Study,* London: Heinemann, and Totowa, New Jersey: Rowman and Littlefield, 1980

Travers, Martin, *Thomas Mann,* London: Macmillan, and New York: St. Martin's Press, 1992

Weigand, Herman J., *Thomas Mann's Novel "Der Zauberberg": A Study,* London and New York: Appleton-Century, 1933

Mann ohne Eigenschaften. *See* Man Without Qualities

Manners. *See* Novel of Manners

Manon Lescaut by Abbé Prévost

1731

In 1731, Antoine-François Prévost d'Exiles, better known as simply the Abbé Prévost (1697–1763), published the *Histoire du chevalier des Grieux et de Manon Lescaut* (*Manon Lescaut*), the seventh volume of his *Mémoires d'un homme de qualité qui s'est retiré du monde* (1728–31; *Memoirs of a Man of Quality*). Although some critics have displayed interest in Prévost's *Histoire d'une grecque moderne* (1740; *History of a Modern Greek*), Manon Lescaut survives as the primary product of an enormous output: the 1783 Serpente edition of Prévost's selected works ran to 39 volumes; his complete works included 112 volumes, including 47 translations. Readers and critics in the 18th and especially early 19th century assumed that Prévost had drawn his inspiration from his own adventures. They accepted as factual various anecdotes about him, such as that he had murdered his father and that he had died at the hand of an ignorant surgeon who performed an autopsy while the abbé was still alive.

At first, *Manon Lescaut* elicited ambivalent responses. Eighteenth-century critics such as Palissot de Monterroy and La-Harpe expressed wonder at Prévost's skill in gaining readers' sympathy for profoundly amoral characters. The blind passion that transforms Des Grieux, a young man of good family, into a cardsharp and a murderer for the sake of a feckless, pleasure-loving charmer, Manon, certainly ran counter to established 18th- and 19th-century moral tenets.

Critics and writers in the 19th century responded to its depiction of grand passion: Stendhal used *Manon Lescaut* as a source for *De l'amour* (1822; *Love*); Balzac thought of it when describing the passion of Lucien de Rubempré for the courtesan Esther in *Splendeurs et misères des courtisanes* (1844; *Splendors and Miseries of Courtesans*). Alfred de Vigny saw Des Grieux as a romantic, set apart from the common herd by his total commitment to passion. More middle-class values-oriented critics, such as Jules Michelet and Anatole de Montaiglon, criticized Manon's amorality, and Alexandre Dumas *fils* saw her as the prototype of the courtesan. Most, however, agreed on the fascination exerted by Prévost's portrayal of absolute love. The naturalness of the style and the sincerity of the emotions endowed the novel with authenticity, and readers equated Des Grieux, Prévost, and the "implied author," whose function is to articulate the work's moral values. Critics sometimes sounded guilty over the pleasure the novel gave them, and felt called upon to temper their delight with moral disapproval, often justifying Prévost's seeming amorality as, after all, being a faithful reflection of the manners and morals of a particularly libertine period, the Regency of Philippe d'Orléans. Some critics even noted that the reader sees Manon entirely through Des Grieux's eyes, but few of the early critics seemed to have been aware of the Abbé's sophisticated narrative technique.

The story of Des Grieux and Manon Lescaut concludes the memoirs of a gentleman, *un homme de qualité,* a much traveled, much tried man of the world who has loved, married, and lost a beautiful Turkish girl, Selima. The memoirs belonged to a French 18th-century genre, the memoir novel. In Prévost's *Memoirs*, the protagonist encounters only dead ends, accepts this fatality passively, and as Jean Sgard (1968) has pointed out, chooses a name, "Renoncourt"—composed of the verb *renoncer* (renounce) and the adjective *court* (short)—which reflects both his passivity and his renunciation. The stories he has related mainly happened to others. Now 70, his curiosity is piqued when he meets a young man escorting several cartsful of women who had been deported to Louisiana in punishment for their libertine ways, and wonders about the pretty deportée in chains with whom the young man is obviously in love. Renoncourt charitably gives Des Grieux some money and they part. Two years later, quite by chance, Renoncourt encounters Des Grieux in Calais and elicits from him the story of his life and of Manon's death in the "deserts" of Louisiana. The main narrator of the *Memoirs* thus steps aside, but not without remarking on the analogy between his long life and Des Grieux's story. The sympathy he feels for the young man guides the reader's response, and although the story changes its narration to the first person, it is introduced by two scenes, set two years apart, in which the narrator describes Des Grieux as a solitary "he," which contrasts with the couple around which the rest of the story is organized.

When Des Grieux relates his story, Manon has been dead only nine months. There is no distance, either temporal or moral, between the narrator and the young man who lived the passionate affair. Throughout the narration, where ostensibly Des Grieux stands aside and lets the story unfold, he, in fact, interjects comments, sometimes a word, sometimes a sentence, and occasionally a paragraph for analysis and reinforcement. These interventions blend so smoothly with the narration that it is often impossible to know whether Des Grieux the lover or Des Grieux the narrator now converted to religious sentiment is speaking. The narration, so precise in its depiction of the protagonists' emotions and of the regency's social and moral atmosphere, is vague in the extreme when it comes to Manon's appearance. The reader is told repeatedly that she is "beautiful," "charming," but never learns the color of her eyes or her hair. Des Grieux's fascination with the image of his lover robs him of his ability to describe her, and so she exists only through his memory of her.

But there she exists so strongly, however, that generations of readers have endowed Manon with a mythic quality, and she gradually displaced Des Grieux as the focus of the novel. For Prévost, the chevalier was the central character; his fall from respectability into vice and his final redemption comprised the theme. But almost immediately readers had begun shortening the title to *Histoire de Manon Lescaut,* then *Manon Lescaut,* and often simply *Manon*. Generations have seen Des Grieux as a martyr of absolute passion and Manon as an innocent, almost naive, femme fatale.

The lovers commit numerous nefarious deeds. Des Grieux cheats at cards, shares his mistress with rich lovers, acquiesces in deceiving and robbing them, and shoots the porter of the hospital where Manon is imprisoned, but his narration expresses little shame or remorse. Overall he finds excuses for his conduct in the depraved morals of his time, in the levity of youth, and especially in the overwhelming power of his passion. Imbued with the sentimental morality often found in 18th-century literature, Des Grieux feels that his wrongful deeds have not altered the innocence of his heart. Neither have Manon's misdeeds altered her fundamental goodness, so when the lovers reach Louisiana she can be redeemed and, for several months, live blissfully, although in extreme penury, with Des Grieux.

The irony of *Manon Lescaut* is that when the heroine is finally redeemed, and when European social constraints (her lowly birth, her status as a fallen woman) no longer matter, the couple seeks to be united lawfully, thus revealing to the governor's lustful nephew that Manon is single and available. Threatened with separation (the governor is most ready to give his nephew the pretty colonist he desires), the lovers flee New Orleans, and, unable to bear the harshness of the "deserts" outside the city, Manon breathes her last, a victim of her redemption.

In many respects, *Manon Lescaut* belongs to the romance tradition, its basic pattern being a typical romance device, the separation and reunion of the lovers. Shipwreck and storms play a part, and characters believed dead (such as the governor's wicked nephew) turn out to be alive. And like romances, it hinges on a love story, beginning with love at first sight and setting up love as justification for any deed, however evil. But love in *Manon Lescaut* is not the elegant passion of chivalric romances or 17th-century heroic pastorals; it is more akin to the *amour fou* of André Breton: a pathological attachment, an obsession, a madness. Moreover, *Manon Lescaut* differs from the traditional romance by the realism of its setting. The manners and morals of Paris during the Regency of Philippe d'Orléans are vividly depicted. Although Louisianians smile (when they do not laugh) at the "deserts" outside New Orleans and the sand in which Des Grieux digs a grave for his lover, the manners and morals of colonial Louisiana ring true: in the first half of the 18th century, the colony was rife with poverty, violence, corruption, and nepotism.

Prévost very much wanted to endow his story with an aura of authenticity. Not only did he use the device of a tale told to a spectator who then writes it down for the reader, but he borrowed from works composed about real people the technique of the initials and the ellipses: Monsieur de G.M., for example. This simple device endows Manon's elderly admirer, who is barely sketched, with a verisimilitude he would lack had he been given a name. Prévost's use of the pseudo-memoir enabled him, as Madsen (1978) points out, to create a situation "in which an intense subjectivity is given credence by an external objectivity."

The impact of *Manon Lescaut* can be measured by the number of imitations and adaptations it has provoked. In the 19th century Manon and the passion she inspires reappear in Dumas *fils'* *La Dame aux camélias* (1848; *Camille*), Prosper Mérimée's *Carmen* (1846; *Carmen*), and George Sand's *Leone Leoni* (1835; *Leone Leoni*), to name but a few. Besides the much performed operas by Massenet and Puccini, Manon is the eponymous heroine of plays, ballets, vaudevilles, comic operas, melodramas, and one work labeled a "cry from the heart in three acts" (*Madelon Lescaut* by P.A.A. Lambert Theboust, 1856). As recently as 1977, the historian Hurbert Jules Deschamps published *Manon l'Américaine,* which relates the Louisiana love affair between Manon's daughter and Des Grieux's younger brother. Only Dumas *fils'* *Camille* (especially in Verdi's operatic version, *La Traviata*), however, has come close to exerting the lasting fascination of *Manon Lescaut,* and Dumas' Armand is the only bereft lover to have communicated to generations of readers (or listeners) the sense of total passion and of absolute loss that pervade the narrative of Prévost's Des Grieux.

MATHÉ ALLAIN

Further Reading

Gilroy, James P., *The Romantic Manon and Des Grieux: Images of Prévost's Heroine and Hero in Nineteenth-Century French Literature,* Sherbrooke, Quebec: Naaman, 1980

Madsen, Roy Iner, Jr., "Toward an Understanding of the Abbé Prévost's *Manon Lescaut*: Structure, Mode, Genre," Ph.D. diss., UCLA, 1978

Sgard, Jean, *Prévost romancier,* Paris: Corti, 1968; 2nd edition, 1989

Smernoff, Richard A., *L'Abbé Prévost,* Boston: Twayne, 1985

Man's Fate by André Malraux

La Condition humaine 1933

Man's Fate marks a significant turn in Malraux's career as a novelist. His first widely acclaimed work, it won him the Prix Goncourt in 1933 and is generally considered his masterpiece. Although Malraux was already known in the literary world by such novels as *Les Conquérants* (1928; *The Conquerors*) and *La Voie royale* (1930; *The Royal Way*), these works had not earned him the respect and admiration that *Man's Fate* was to bring to such a young writer (he was 32 when the novel was published). These first novels, set in the Orient, were fairly well received, but the main characters were basically adventurers motivated by self-interest, and their individual quests stirred little emotional response from readers. *Man's Fate,* in contrast, exploited the interest in the Orient, told a compelling story, and engaged the audience with some of the leading political and intellectual issues of the day.

Man's Fate, along with *The Conquerors, The Royal Way,* and later on *L'Espoir* (1937; *Man's Hope*), belongs to the first stage of Malraux's evolution as a writer: during this period his fascination with death dominates. This novel reflects the concerns of the times and the worldwide political and social unrest. In the aftermath of a war (World War I), the rise of fascism, and the failure of religion to alleviate the suffering of the masses, society had become disillusioned and was looking for new ways of bringing about the changes needed. *Man's Fate* expresses the despair, alienation, and sense of emptiness that were beginning to affect the intellectual climate in France.

Until Malraux, the 20th-century French novel had focused primarily on the personal aspect of life: a character's relationship to and place in society, as in Roger Martin du Gard, or on the individual's inner world, as in André Gide and Marcel Proust. Malraux's vision is much broader; he is the first novelist to present man's relationship to an absurd universe. He, too, asks the Pascalian question: "What am I in the universe?" but unlike his Jansenist predecessor, who turned to God for answers, Malraux places his faith in man.

The story is set during the 1927 uprising in Shanghai (which ultimately failed), an appropriate stage for Malraux to play out his own sympathies for the communist ideals. He experienced the Orient as a man of action and applied his knowledge of the area to create a powerful backgound for the ideas presented in *Man's Fate.* In particular, his use of the opposing Western and Eastern world views—action (represented by the character named Kyo) versus passivity (represented by Gisors)—demonstrates the power of commitment to transcend man's fate. Katow's self-sacrifice (he gives his cyanide to two frightened young people, thus sparing them the agony of being burned alive) ends the novel on a note of hope for mankind. By contrast, Gisor's drifting off in a drug-induced fog is clearly no alternative for Malraux.

In this world of men, sentimentalism has little or no place, and the role of women remains severely limited. Valerie, Ferral's mistress, seems to have no other purpose than to be a sex object for Ferral. Hemmelrich's wife has endured a life of misery and suffering. As for May, Kyo's wife, although a capable independent doctor, she possesses few feminine traits. Malraux's women end up almost as caricatures: Valerie is a child, Hemmelrich's wife a victim, and May is really a man. They are all lacking; they are incomplete, unfinished. The depiction of women in *Man's Fate* is typical of women characters in Malraux's other novels.

Malraux breaks ground in his use of cinematic techniques (flashbacks, close-ups, shadows and lights that create a black-and-white effect), with much of the action taking place at night with artificial lights to create dramatic effects. Instead of chapters, the book is divided into seven parts and subdivided by days and by the times of the day. There is no linear plot development with clear chronological references: Malraux focuses on the torments of the individual and the spiritual quest of the characters, not on their physical appearance.

Malraux became a champion of the struggle against fascism and injustice and believed in being "engagé"—politically committed in one's writing. Likewise, Malraux's heroes in *Man's Fate* have chosen a political commitment that they believe aims at eradicating injustice. Yet the Shanghai revolution serves mainly as a pretext to demonstrate the timelessness of man's destiny. It provides a stage whereby some individuals may achieve a brief moment of glory (like Katow at the end) through a gesture that transforms their lives and ultimately gives significance to their death. In this novel, Malraux brings an awareness of the absurd as well as the idea that the meaning of existence depends upon one's acts, thus prefiguring existentialism.

MARTINE CREMERS PEARSON

Further Reading

Blend, Charles D., *André Malraux: Tragic Humanist*, Columbus: Ohio Sate University Press, 1963

Blumenthal, Gerda, *André Malraux: The Conquest of Dread*, Baltimore: Johns Hopkins University Press, 1960

Boisdeffre, Pierre de, *Metamorphose de la littérature, de Barrès à Malraux*, Paris: Alsatia, 1950

Frohock, W.M., *André Malraux and the Tragic Imagination*, Stanford, California: Stanford University Press, 1952

Horvath, Violet M., *André Malraux: The Human Adventure*, New York: New York University Press, 1969

Peyre, Henri, *The Contemporary French Novel*, New York: Oxford University Press, 1955; as *French Novelists of Today*, New York: Oxford University Press, 1967

Suares, Guy, *Malraux: Past, Present and Future: Conversations with Guy Suares*, translated by Derek Coltman, Boston: Little Brown, and London: Thames and Hudson, 1974

Manticore. *See* Deptford Trilogy

Manuscrit caché. *See* Framing and Embedding in Narrative

Alessandro Manzoni 1785–1873

Italian

An early 20th-century tribute to Alessandro Manzoni (Hachette *Almanac*, 1923) mentions his "many novels." This error is understandable: although Manzoni produced only one novel (*I promessi sposi* [first published 1827; *The Betrothed*]), it has the weight, scope, and variety possessed by most writers' collected works. Moreover, the impression that Manzoni was prolific is not so very inaccurate. What he *did* publish, in addition to *The Betrothed*, was an extraordinary range of critical disquisitions—essays on language, literature, history, and religion—as well as two tragedies, a series of poems on religious festivals (the *Inni Sacri* [1815; *The Sacred Hymns*]), and a powerful ode to Napoléon (*Il cinque maggio*). This material is just as useful to the student of the novel as might have been those phantom volumes of fiction. The concept of heroism in history offered by *Il cinque maggio* clarifies, by comparison, the very different notion of historical agency in *The Betrothed*. Manzoni's novel may be considered as an expression of his religious opinions (expressed argumentatively in *Sulla morale cattolica* [1819; *A Vindication of Catholic Morality*]). The near-obsessiveness of his linguistic interests—he once spent a series of evenings listening to most of the letter *A* read from a dictionary—helps make sense of his closely related effort to recast his great tale of the past in a national language for the future.

Among these ambitious satellite projects, his treatise on the historical novel, *Del romanzo storico* (*On the Historical Novel*), was begun in 1828 but not published until 1850, in the sixth fascicle of the author's collected works. This essay—available to English-speaking readers in Sandra Bermann's lucid translation—is one of the major theoretical statements on the power and limitations of the historical novel as a genre, and on the place of historical fiction as the inheritor of epic and tragedy. The first section of Manzoni's essay poses a double difficulty with historical novels. On the one hand, historical novelists blend fact and invention without distinguishing one from the other. Manzoni imagines the complaint of a prospective reader who has been promised "a richer, more varied, more complete history" than is to be found in conventional historical works, but who then realizes that historical fiction provides no reliable and consistent means of separating actualities from the novelist's own creations. The author makes up "falsehoods" to engage the reader's interest, but these falsehoods corrupt the process of instruction that they were intended to facilitate. Furthermore, a diametrically opposite criticism is also plausible. A second, equally just reader might well complain that the historical novel *constantly*, by implication or otherwise, suggests that some of its parts are historically based while others are mere inventions. (The most conspicuous form of such a separation is to provide footnotes signifying the truth of a particular claim—a common, often-parodied practice in 18th-century novels as well as in the works of Walter Scott.) This practice, also, is virtually impossible to avoid. Historical fiction is thus condemned doubly: initially for having too much unity and then for not having enough. It fails first on historical and second on artistic grounds.

Having posed these criticisms, Manzoni eagerly acknowledges their justice. Next he works toward successive and increasingly subtle restatements of each case, establishing by this means both that the readers whom he has mimicked have naive (and self-contradictory) expectations and that the historical novel, by its nature, is a shifting field of unities and disunities, continually readjusting the balance between invention and fact. (Along the way he skillfully dismisses the argument that history is just as fictional as fiction itself.) In conclusion, as long as the genre of historical fiction remains a narrative form working with heterogeneous materials, it can satisfy neither the historical purist nor the adherent of formal unity. "The historical novel does not have a logical purpose of its own; it counterfeits two, as I have shown." Thus, books such as Manzoni's *The Betrothed* are intrinsically unstable; the compound they presume to sustain can on no account last.

Even when running rings around his two presumed interlocutors, even when demonstrating their foolishness, Manzoni is also yielding ground to these nagging, interior voices. He is demonstrating the capabilities but also the futility of the genre in which he himself had excelled. Like some of Lev Tolstoi's essays on art, *On the Historical Novel* appears to be a retraction. Part two of the essay, however, puts a significantly different light on things. Manzoni shows in fascinating detail that if historical fiction is intrinsically unstable, so are epic and tragedy, and for similar reasons. When, at the end of the argument, he returns to the subject of historical fiction as such, the reader's perspective on the genre has been fundamentally altered. It seems now that *any* genre attempting to incorporate history and poetic invention is subject to the same contradictions as historical fiction. The death of the historical novel (predicted or perhaps just registered by Manzoni) thus repeats the fall of these more venerable and prestigious forms. If historical fiction's life span has been shorter than that of epic or historical tragedy, that is because historiography itself has flourished, diminishing the effective opportunities for original invention *within* or merely adjacent to the realm of fact. The rise of history as a discipline—an underlying cause

of historical fiction's popularity in the 19th century—is thus, concurrently, the cause of its eventual fall.

Manzoni's essay is significant on at least three levels. First, *On the Historical Novel* helps explain why its author wrote one famous novel rather than many. Second, the piece reenacts, in a more specialized and concentrated manner, a problem that had dogged novelists for centuries. In the era of Daniel Defoe, the mixing of fact and fiction had been understood as a flaw or lure of novels in general. (One frequent solution, at this stage, was to claim for first-person narratives the status of unadorned fact.) By the 19th century, this sort of mix is much more taken for granted—even in narratives, like those of William Godwin and John Galt, which echo the Defoe formula—but the arrival of the historical novel à la Scott revives the old controversies; it is as though the founding quarrels of the novel are being reenacted for a century dominated by historical thinking (and in its later decades by historical positivism). Third, the issues so subtly defined by Manzoni are apparently still alive; for instance, the controversy between Natalie Davis and Robert Finlay (on the 17th-century case of the impostor Martin Guerre) demonstrates the high passions raised in the present cultural climate by attempts to integrate historical and novelistic techniques. Manzoni's treatise still has much to teach historians, novelists, and writers who claim to work in the treacherous space between history and fictional invention.

RICHARD MAXWELL

See also Betrothed

Biography

Born in Milan, 7 March 1785. Attended the Somaschian college at Merate, 1791–96, and Lugano, 1796–98; Barnabite Collegio dei Nobili, Milan and Magenta, 1787–1801. Senator of the Kingdom, 1860; Honorary Citizen, Rome, 1872. Died 22 May 1873.

Novel by Manzoni

I promessi sposi, 3 vols., 1827; revised edition, 1840–42; as *The Betrothed Lovers*, translated by Charles Swan, 1828; also translated with *The Column of Infamy*, 1845; as *I promessi sposi*, translated by G.W. Featherstonhaugh, 1834; as *The Betrothed*, translated by Daniel J. Connor, 1924; also translated by Archibald Colquhoun, 1951; Bruce Penman, 1972

Other Writings: plays, verse, and critical works, the latter including *Del romanzo storico* (1850; *On the Historical Novel*).

Further Reading

Bermann, Sandra, "Manzoni's Essay 'On the Historical Novel': A Rhetorical Question," *Canadian Review of Comparative Literature* 10 (1983)

Colquhoun, Archibald, *Manzoni and His Times,* London: Dent, and New York: Dutton, 1954

Manzoni, Alessandro, *On the Historical Novel,* translated and with an introduction by Sandra Bermann, Lincoln: University of Nebraska Press, 1984

Negri, Renzo, *Manzoni diverso,* Milan: Marzorati, 1976

Sanctis, Francesco de, *Manzoni,* Turin: Einaudi, 1955

Viola, Pietro, "Il discorso manzoniano *Del romanzo storico,*" *Convivium* 36 (1968)

Mao Dun 1896–1981

Chinese

Mao Dun (pen name of Shen Yanbing), novelist, essayist, literary critic, social activist, and communist ideologue, is best known as the naturalist author of *Ziye* (1933; *Midnight*), a massive novel about life in Shanghai, and a rural trilogy (three short stories) entitled *Chuncan* (1932–33; "Spring Silkworms"). Mao Dun is the author of 13 novels, more than 100 short stories, and over 300 essays on Western literature and literary theory. His major works include the trilogy *Shi* (1927–28; Eclipse), *Hong* (1929; *Rainbow*), *Midnight, Fushi* (1941; Putrefaction), and *Shuangye hongsi eryuehua* (1942; Maple Leaves as Red as February Flowers). In 1921, Mao Dun became one of the founding members of the Literary Studies Society, an organization that advocated a practical program of "literature for life's sake." The organization included some of the literary giants of the period, such as Zheng Zhenduo, Zhou Zuoren, and Yu Dafu. Before he began writing novels and short stories in 1927, Mao Dun had already served a long literary apprenticeship by translating many Western works of literature into Chinese and by writing literary criticism. His works are generally well-crafted, elegant, lyrical, and reflect his interest in the works of Émile Zola and the naturalists. Mao Dun was also a Marxist. Many of his characters, often females, are in one way or another caught up in the tumultuous political and historical events of their day as they seek their own fulfillment. Mao Dun is one of the most important political and ideological writers of modern China and one of the first to explore extensively the interplay of sexuality and politics in literature.

Mao Dun's first work, *Shi*, a trilogy consisting of three slim volumes, *Huanmie* (1927; Disillusion), *Dongyao* (1928; Vacillation), and *Zhuiqiu* (1928; Pursuit), portrays a generation of young, brooding intellectuals, men and women, who are caught up in the tidal wave of revolutionary fervor without a true understanding of the nature of revolution and its aftermath. As a consequence, over a course of time spanning the May Fourth Movement (1919) to the end of Chiang Kai-shek's successful Northern Expedition (1926–28) to unite the country, which ended with the betrayal of the young communist revolutionaries, the protagonists suffer disillusionment as their fragile idealism and personal lives are shattered, and they turn from revolution to self-indulgent nihilism and ennui.

Mao Dun's next major work, *Rainbow*, tells of a young woman named Mei who escapes from her bourgeois family to join the revolutionary May Thirtieth Movement (1925) in Shanghai. Rather than succumb to the forces at home and in the school where she taught, Mei is determined "to overcome her environment, to overcome her fate." At the same time that Mei finds her identity in political action, an intricate interplay of her emergent sexuality and politics begins to unfold. Ironically, Mei finds that her newly awakened sexuality must be curtailed as she works in the underground communist organization. Geographically, Mei's liberation moves her from her home in Chengdu to the town of Luzhou, also in Sichuan, where she teaches school. Her final liberation takes place in the modern metropolis of Shanghai, where she takes part in the demonstrations of the May Thirtieth Movement and meets her revolutionary hero Liang Gangfu.

Mao Dun's next novel, his magnum opus, *Midnight,* is a Zolaesque study of the complexity of life in Shanghai, the nerve center of China's national economy, with its capitalist industrialists, striking factory workers, bourgeois youths, young communist agitators, and women in search of love and fortune. It is a long, sprawling novel of more than 500 pages, containing some 70 characters and numerous plot twists and turns. No other modern Chinese novel has been able to capture the excitement and drama of the stock market and the adventurous speculation of the foreign and nationalist capitalists as *Midnight.* Mao Dun's naturalistic depiction of the evils of city life in Shanghai, coupled with the deterministic thrust of the communist thesis on the decline of capitalism, foredoom the efforts of the shrewd silk factory owner and national capitalist Wu Sunfu in his heroic struggle against his rival, the compradore capitalist Zhao Botao. This struggle forms the main theme of the novel. Aside from this political theme, as David Der-wei Wang (1992) points out, the novel also employs a feminine/feminist theme that skillfully depicts the city of Shanghai as a voluptuous femme fatale, a city pulsating with female body parts: swaying hips, red lips, quivering breasts, and naked legs. Although this is the standard fare in Shanghai, it overwhelms the elder Mr. Wu, the protagonist's father, who has just come to Shanghai from the countryside. Shanghai is further personified in the body of the female protagonist, Xu Manli, whose bold and ribald liberated ways enable her to best the financial wizards on Shanghai's Wall Street for money and privilege. She dances a seductive "death dance" atop billiard tables for four budding Shanghai industrialists.

In 1937, after the publication of *Midnight*, Mao Dun wrote a novella entitled *Duojiao guanxi* (Polygonal Relations), which is essentially a continuation of the same theme, dealing with the many-sided relationship between landlords and workers, capitalists and peasants, bankers and industrialists. The sociopolitical circumstances are such that one group is forever exploiting and indebted to another.

Before he completed his massive novel *Midnight*, Mao Dun wrote several minor masterpieces, including his famous rural trilogy of short stories, "Spring Silkworms," "Autumn Harvest," and "Winter Ruin," which are widely regarded today as the best examples of his prose style. The rural trilogy presents touching, intimate portraits of three generations of a poor peasant family, whose fates are being determined by economic and political forces totally beyond their comprehension and control. With the passage of the seasons, the family is brought closer and closer to ruin. In *Fushi*, Mao Dun uses the first-person epistolary form to tell the story of a young woman who is a secret agent for the Nationalist Party, the Kuomintang (KMT), during the War of Resistance against Japan (1937–45). The protagonist, a young woman of 24 named Zhao Huiming, is trapped into working for the KMT as a result of her vanity and strong sense of bourgeois individualism. Her mission is to seduce a young communist revolutionary, also her lover, to force him to divulge the names of other communist party members. However, her middle-class, bourgeois sentiments conflict with the ruthlessness of her mission. In her diary she reveals her dilemma and her desperate search for her own sense of self.

Shuangye hongsi eryuehua is the tantalizing first part of a projected trilogy that was left unfinished. The story tells of the rivalry between Zhao Shouyi, a member of the powerful landed gentry, and the new-style industrial capitalist Wang Boshen, the head of a steamship company. While the Zhao and Wang families—the former representing the traditional agricultural community, the latter representing the new capitalist mercantile interests—are feuding for power, the members of the younger generation are caught in unhappy marital relationships. Zhang Xunru is listlessly married to a traditional woman, and his sister Wan-qing is unhappily married to Huang Heguang, who suffers from sexual impotence. While the marital squabbles mar the lives of these couples, an idealistic young man and widower, Qian Liangcai, carries the revolutionary banner forward to protect the farmer peasants from the incursions of Wang Boshen's steamship company. Unfortunately, the circumstances for political action are not yet ripe, and his efforts to save the farmers end in failure. In this novel, as in "Spring Silkworms," Mao Dun returns to pre–1919 China, where the internal contradictions of Chinese society among the newly emerging capitalists, the conservative landed gentry, and powerless, reform-minded intellectuals are highlighted. Because of their inability to work together, all their good intentions only result in more suffering for the peasants.

Mao Dun's other war novels include *Diyi jieduande gushi* (1937; Story of the First Stage of the War) and *Jiehou shiyi* (1942; Pieces Picked Up after the Calamity), patriotic novels about the siege of Shanghai in 1937 and the fall of Hong Kong in 1942, respectively. After 1943, Mao Dun did not produce any more major works of literature. He continued to write articles and essays after the war and became Minister of Culture after the establishment of the People's Republic of China in 1949. However, as far as his creativity as a writer is concerned, it ended essentially with the war years in 1945.

PETER LI

Biography

Born in Chekiang province, 1896. Education interrupted in 1916 because he ran out of money. Soon after became a proofreader for the Commercial Press in Shanghai, later promoted to editor and translator; in 1920 joined several other young Chinese writers in taking over editorial management of *Hsiao-shuo yüeh-pao* (Short-Story Magazine): elected editor by the group, a position he held until 1923; joined the Northern Expedition as secretary to the propaganda department of the Kuomintang (KMT) Central Executive Committee; fled to Kuling when the KMT broke with the Chinese Communist Party (CCP); helped found the League of Left-Wing Writers, 1930; founded and edited two patriotic literary journals during the Sino-Japanese War (1937–45); participated in several literary and cultural committees after the CCP came to power in 1949; Minister of Culture, 1949–1964 (dismissed from his post); later served as vice president, Chinese Writers Association, and edited a magazine of children's literature. Died 27 March 1981.

Selected Fiction by Mao Dun

Shi [Eclipse], 1927–28
  Huanmie [Disillusion], 1927
  Dongyao [Vacillation], 1928
  Zhuiqiu [Pursuit], 1928
Hong, 1929; as *Rainbow,* translated by Madeleine Zelin, 1992
San ren xing [In the Company of Three], 1931
Lu [The Road], 1932
Chuncan, 1932–33; as "Spring Silkworms," in *Spring Silkworms and Other Stories,* 1956
Ziye, 1933; as *Midnight,* 1957
Duojiao guanxi [Polygonal Relations], 1937
Diyi jieduande gushi [Story of the First Stage of the War], 1937
Fushi [Putrefaction], 1941
Shuangye hongsi eryuehua [Maple Leaves as Red as February Flowers], 1942
Jiehou shiyi [Pieces Picked Up after the Calamity], 1942

Other Writings: journalism, literary criticism and theory.

Further Reading

Chen, Yu-shih, *Realism and Allegory in the Early Fiction of Mao Tun,* Bloomington: Indiana University Press, 1986
Fu, Chih-ying, editor, *Mao Tun ping chuan* (A Critical Biography of Mao Dun), Hong Kong: Nandao, 1968
Galik, Marian, *Mao Tun and Modern Chinese Literary Criticism,* Wiesbaden: Steiner, 1969
Galik, Marian, *The Genesis of Modern Chinese Literary Criticism (1917–1930),* translated by Peter Tkac, London: Curzon Press, and Totowa, New Jersey: Rowman and Littlefield, 1980
Hsia, C.T., *A History of Modern Chinese Fiction,* New Haven, Connecticut: Yale University Press, 1961; 2nd edition, 1971
Shao Bozhou, et al., *Mao Dun de wenxue daolu* (Mao Dun's Literary Path), Wuhan: Changjiang weiyi chubanshe, 1959
Wang, David Der-wei, *Fictional Realism in Twentieth-Century China: Mao Dun, Lao She, Shen Congwen,* New York: Columbia University Press, 1992

Mar Mani. *See* Mr. Mani

Márquez, Gabriel García. *See* García Márquez, Gabriel

Marxist Criticism of the Novel

Terry Eagleton points out in *The Ideology of the Aesthetic* (1990) that the very notion of the aesthetic arose historically in conjunction with the rise of capitalism and bourgeois society. The complicity between bourgeois ideology and the whole notion of the aesthetic is particularly powerful in the case of the novel, which any number of observers have identified as a fundamentally bourgeois genre. (Ian Watt's *The Rise of the Novel* [1957] is still paradigmatic.) It should thus come as no surprise that Marxist thinkers have paid considerable attention to the realm of culture and particularly to the novel. The novel, as the literary form in which bourgeois ideology is expressed most clearly, has been a principal focus of Marxist critique from Marx and Engels on down. The tradition of the bourgeois novel also served as a central resource to Marxist thinkers such as Georgy Plekhanov when they began to develop an alternative system of aesthetics in the early 20th century. This effort received a particular boost in the early years of the Soviet Union, as Soviet writers and critics sought to develop socialist realism as a new mode of novelistic expression. The 1930s saw a burgeoning of leftist culture worldwide that involved increased production in both Marxist criticism and in leftist novels (see Murphy, 1991). As part of this phenomenon, Marxist critics such as Britain's Christopher Caudwell, Ralph Fox, and Alick West or America's Granville Hicks and V.F. Calverton examined the tradition of the bourgeois novel while seeking ways in which the novel might become an effective mode of socialist literary expression.

The dual Marxist traditions of ideological critique of the bourgeois novel and of the search for an alternative socialist novel converge in the work of the Hungarian philosopher and critic Georg Lukács. Seeking to provide guidance to revolutionary socialist writers, Lukács put forward the fundamental insight that the European bourgeoisie were at one time a revolutionary class and that bourgeois literature played a major role in the historical victory of the emergent bourgeoisie over their aristocratic predecessors. Lukács reminded his contemporaries that the European bourgeoisie, however decadent and conservative they had become by the end of the 19th century, were in their younger days the most successful revolutionary class in history, making bourgeois literature (epitomized by the realist novel) arguably the most effective revolutionary literature of all time. Lukács began his studies of literature with the early *Die Theorie des Romans* (1920; *The Theory of the Novel*), which is an essentially Hegelian account written before he became a Marxist. Lukács' later work, however, is firmly rooted in the tradition of historical materialism pioneered by Marx and Engels. In this work, Lukács consistently privileges realism as the literary mode best suited to capture the sweep of history toward socialism. In addition, he sees the realist novel as the genre best able to represent human society as a totality and thereby to counter the tendency of capitalism to fragment human experience into separate realms, thus impoverishing and unsettling the human subject.

In works such as *A történelmi regény* (1937; *The Historical Novel*), Lukács sees realism as the only literary mode capable of representing the totality of society by revealing through its narrative form the underlying movement of history. For Lukács, great 19th-century realists such as Walter Scott, Honoré de Balzac, and Lev Tolstoi thus provide potentially valuable models for 20th-century socialist writers. Indeed, Lukács believes that the greatest realist literature, embodying the forces that enable historical change, is always progressive, regardless of the political leanings of the authors themselves. Thus, in *Wider den missverstandenen Realismus* (1958; *The Meaning of Contemporary Realism*), he argues that any novel that represents history accurately is by definition a contribution to the cause of socialism, regardless of the author's actual intention. For Lukács, however, the "accurate" representation of the historical process need not imply the inclusion of exhaustive detail. Indeed, he notes in *The Historical Novel* that individual details need not even be accurate so long as the work captures the overall flow of history and the historical necessity of the situations it describes. Similarly, Lukács' insistence that the most effective literary works must strive to represent society as a totality does not imply that texts must seek, in an encyclopedic way, literally to represent all aspects of society. Rather, successful works of literature must seek to represent their characters and events in ways that show their participation in the totality of society. Crucial here, for Lukács, especially in the case of characterization, is the technique of typification, or the ability of writers such as Scott and Balzac to create vividly individualized characters who are nevertheless clearly the products of social and historical forces larger than themselves.

Rooted in the history of European civilization, Lukács' work also involves a firm sense of literary history. If the great age of realism corresponds to the rise to power of the bourgeoisie in the 18th and early 19th centuries, Lukács argues, then the bourgeois turn to conservatism after this power is achieved leads to a decline in realist literature. This decline eventually gives rise to the appearance of naturalism, which for Lukács is a degraded form of realism that focuses on description instead of narration and concentrates on local detail at the expense of the ability to represent society as a whole. In "The Ideology of Modernism" (included in *The Meaning of Contemporary Realism*), Lukács extends this historical analysis to modernism, which he sees as even more decadent and less able to represent reality accurately than naturalism. He argues that the formal fragmentation of modernist texts and the brilliance of their verbal constructions participate in the process of reification that is itself central to the fragmentation of social life under capitalism. He further condemns modernist writers like Joyce and Kafka for making technique an end in itself, without regard to the human realities that this technique might convey. For Lukács the "negation of outward reality" is a central project of modernist writing, which represents a turning away from the world and a retreat into an aesthetic realm divorced from social reality. And this disengagement is in direct complicity with the main cultural thrust of bourgeois society, which seeks to isolate art in a separate realm and thus deprive it of any potentially subversive political force. Modernist texts, for Lukács, rather than interacting with history in a positive and productive way, are sterile artifacts caught up in the inexorable drive of capitalist society to convert all it touches into mere commodities.

Many of Lukács' Marxist contemporaries, although they were influenced by his work in important ways, did not share his wholesale rejection of modernism. The disagreements led to important aesthetic debates on the left. Indeed, the "Brecht-Lukács" debate, with the Marxist dramatist Bertolt Brecht (who explored innovative modernist forms in his own writing), became one of the central aesthetic debates of 20th-century Marxism. Prominent Marxists aligned with the Brechtian position included Walter Benjamin and Theodor Adorno, both of whom were in other ways strongly influenced by Lukács.

Benjamin also made important contributions to the understanding of the novel as an expression of bourgeois ideology. In "The Storyteller" (1955), Benjamin argues that in the modern world the ability to tell meaningful stories is rapidly becoming a lost art. Always concerned with the relationship between works of art and the physical technology available to produce and distribute those works, Benjamin suggests that the demise of storytelling begins with the invention of the printing press and occurs as part of the shift from oral to print culture (and from stories to novels) that has characterized Western society for the past four centuries. Taking this argument a step further, he posits that the rise of the novel has contributed to the inability of the contemporary individual to relate to others. In contrast to the communal activity of telling (and listening to) stories, both the reading and the writing of novels are for Benjamin solitary activities that foster an individualism closely aligned with bourgeois ideology. Unlike Lukács, Benjamin thought that the new techniques developed by modernist and avant-garde artists (and new technologies such as film) offered exciting possibilities for the reversal of this cultural trend.

The American Fredric Jameson parallels Benjamin and Adorno in his belief that a critique of capitalism was an important part of the modernist project. Yet Jameson's work is informed most crucially by the influence of Lukács. In works such as *The Political Unconscious* (1981) and *Postmodernism* (1991), Jameson has elaborated an influential Marxist critical practice focused largely on the novel and based on a strong understanding of the close connection between literature and history. Jameson supplements his Marxist theoretical perspective with a sophisticated use of psychoanalytic, structuralist, poststructuralist, and other critical approaches, but he is unwavering in his insistence on the primacy of political interpretations of literature and on the fundamental superiority of Marxism to any other political approach to literature. And Jameson, while seeing great critical potential in modernism, echoes Lukács' reminder of the revolutionary role played by 19th-century realism. Meanwhile, he applies much of Lukács' critique of modernism to postmodernism, which he considers a direct reflection of the "logic" of capitalism in its late, global/consumerist phase. Jameson's most important debt to Lukács may reside in the central emphasis of both critics on history as the basic fabric of human existence. In particular, Jameson follows Lukács in placing great emphasis on the way literature (especially the novel) reflects the Marxist notion of history as class conflict. Thus, in *Signatures of the Visible* (1992), Jameson declares that history in the modern sense is an invention of the European bourgeoisie, designed to tell the story of the cultural revolution through which a particular class rose to hegemony in Europe. The story of "the transition from feudalism to capitalism," suggests Jameson, "is what is secretly (or more deeply) being told in most contemporary historiography, whatever its ostensible content." Further, Jameson argues, this view of history makes the bourgeois cultural revolution "the only true Event of history." Thus, the Lukácsian injunction "Always historicize!" with which Jameson begins *The Political Unconscious* implies not only an insistence that critics be aware of the embeddedness of literary texts in their historical contexts, but also an awareness of the way the discourses of history and literature have been used to support and legitimate bourgeois hegemony in Europe.

Given the central role of literature in the establishment and maintenance of bourgeois hegemony in Europe, it is not surprising that so many Marxist literary critics, like Terry Eagleton, have focused particularly on the realm of ideology. The most influential figure in this vein of Marxist criticism has been the Italian Marxist Antonio Gramsci, whose work is represented principally by a series of notebooks written during a ten-year imprisonment for his left-wing political activities. Gramsci focused on the way the European bourgeoisie gained and maintained their power through a complex of political and cultural practices that convinced the more numerous lower classes willingly to support bourgeois authority. Thus, bourgeois power resides principally in the ability of the bourgeoisie to obtain the spontaneous consent of the masses by having them identify with the bourgeoisie's worldview. Literature, of course, can play a central role in the development of this consent. If absolutely necessary, consensual obedience may be supplemented by more directly coercive forms of state power, that is, by institutions like the police and the army, which use physical force to impose discipline on those groups who withhold their consent. This apparatus is, Gramsci argues, largely supplemental, residing primarily in the background and coming into play only in moments of crisis when more subtle forms of control have failed.

While Gramsci himself made relatively little direct contribution to Marxist criticism of the novel, his work has proved extremely influential for a number of subsequent Marxist critics. The most important of these Gramscian Marxist critics is probably Louis Althusser, whose extensive body of work is particularly distinguished by his attempt to integrate Marxist thought with the structuralist methods of analysis that were dominant in France during the 1950s and 1960s. Especially concerned with delineating the complex relationship between art and ideology, Althusser developed the concept of "interpellation," or the "hailing of the subject"—the process through which ideology shapes the subject. According to Althusser, we do not form our attitudes so much as they form us, because the individual subject is literally created by ideology.

Echoing Gramsci, Althusser emphasizes that the process of interpellation allows the existing power structure of capitalist society to maintain its domination over the general population without resorting to violence or force. Interpellation occurs in subtle ways, through the workings of what Althusser calls "Ideological State Apparatuses" (ISAs), including official culture and specific institutions like churches and schools, although it is constantly backed up by the physical force represented by the "Repressive State Apparatus" (RSA) of the police and the military. Althusser's discussion of interpellation has much in common with the frequent arguments of Marxist critics that ideological manipulation of the individual psyche lies at the heart of the bourgeois conception of the free autonomous individual, a conception that turns out to be nothing more than a ruse to hide the fact that individuals are largely determined not by their own choices but by the needs of the economic and political systems in which they live. Indeed, Althusser directly contrasts ideology (as knowledge thoroughly conditioned by politics) with science (as direct objective knowledge). This opposition leads to a special emphasis in Althusser's work on culture and literature, which he situates somewhere between the poles of science and ideology. He argues that art plays a privileged role in ideological critique because the workings of ideology can potentially be detected in art in ways that they cannot in society at large.

Althusser was an important influence on several other critics. One of these is Pierre Macherey, whose *A Theory of Literary Production* (1978) made an important contribution to Marxist criticism of the novel from a structuralist perspective, while his later work pioneered poststructuralist Marxist criticism. Lucien Goldmann's *Towards a Sociology of the Novel* (1975), while sometimes a bit mechanical in its application of theory to the readings of actual texts, resembles Althusser's work in its structuralist approach. However, Goldmann echoes Lukács in his insistence that the realist novels of writers such as Balzac and Stendhal were ultimately artistic reflections of the capitalist market system.

The Gramscian vein of Marxist ideological critique has also been central to the tradition of British cultural materialism. A key founding figure in this tradition is Raymond Williams, whose work grows directly out of the strong British tradition of socialist class and working-class culture. However, Williams also draws extensively upon the continental Marxist tradition of thinkers like Althusser, especially later in his career. Emphasizing the role played by literature and culture in the development of society as a whole, Williams analyzes cultural artifacts as part of a project to develop a general vision of British socialism. In *The Country and the City* (1973) he presents nothing less than a Marxist revision of the entire history of British literature from the Renaissance forward. Williams' work is marked by a distinctive emphasis on the creative potential of ordinary people. He pays serious attention not only to traditional "high" culture but also to popular culture, and his work on such popular media as television has been extremely influential for cultural critics in recent years. Williams' view of culture as the embodiment of the lived experience of ordinary people and therefore as a source of organic unity has struck many contemporary Marxist critics as somewhat nostalgic and idealized. Nevertheless, his insistence on paying attention to the needs and experiences of common people as a necessary element of cultural criticism has set a positive example for many subsequent critics, particularly Eagleton, his most illustrious successor.

Eagleton's own critical practice, in works such as *Exiles and Emigrés* (1970) and *Criticism and Ideology* (1976), has focused largely on the novel, which continues to be a major emphasis of Marxist criticism, although many recent Marxists (including Lukácsians such as Jameson) have followed Williams' lead in paying serious attention to film, television, and other forms of popular culture. Sophisticated Marxist critics such as Eagleton and Jameson have in fact spearheaded a resurgence of Western Marxist criticism in the past quarter of a century, making Marxist criticism one of the most vital and innovative trends in approaches to the novel as the 20th century comes to a close. For example, Franco Moretti's *The Way of the World* (1987) continues the Lukácsian tradition with its strongly historicized treatment of the European Bildungsroman. Aijaz Ahmad's *In Theory* (1992) brings a trenchant Marxist critical practice to the study of postcolonial theory and culture, while M. Keith Booker's *Colonial Power, Colonial Texts* (1997) reads the tradition of British novels about India within a broad Lukácsian historical framework. Finally, Barbara Foley's *Radical Representations* (a 1993 study of American proletarian novels from the 1930s) makes a central contribution to the revitalization of critical interest in the long history of leftist cultural production, a history largely obscured in the West during the dark years of the Cold War.

M. KEITH BOOKER

See also Class and the Novel; Critics and Criticism (20th Century); Ideology and the Novel; Politics and the Novel; Proletarian Novel; Social Criticism; Socialist Realism

Further Reading

Ahmad, Aijaz, *In Theory: Classes, Nations, Literatures,* London and New York: Verso, 1992

Althusser, Louis, *Lenin and Philosophy and Other Essays,* translated by Ben Brewster, London: New Left Books, 1971; New York: Monthly Review Press, 1972

Benjamin, Walter, *Illuminations,* translated by Harry Zohn, edited by Hannah Arendt, New York: Harcourt Brace, 1955; London: Fontana, 1973

Booker, M. Keith, *Colonial Power, Colonial Texts: India in the Modern British Novel,* Ann Arbor: University of Michigan Press, 1997

Eagleton, Terry, *Exiles and Emigrés: Studies in Modern Literature,* New York: Schocken, and London: Chatto and Windus, 1970

Eagleton, Terry, *Criticism and Ideology: A Study in Marxist Literary Theory,* London: New Left Books, 1976

Eagleton, Terry, *The Ideology of the Aesthetic,* Oxford: Basil Blackwell, 1990

Foley, Barbara, *Radical Representations: Politics and Form in U.S. Proletarian Fiction, 1929–1941,* Durham, North Carolina: Duke University Press, 1993

Jameson, Fredric, *The Political Unconscious: Narrative as a Socially Symbolic Act,* Ithaca, New York: Cornell University Press, and London: Methuen, 1981

Jameson, Fredric, *Postmodernism; or, The Cultural Logic of Late Capitalism,* Durham, North Carolina: Duke University Press, and London: Verso, 1991

Jameson, Fredric, *Signatures of the Visible,* New York: Routledge, 1992

Lukács, Georg, *A történelmi regény*, Budapest: Hungaria, 1937; as *The Historical Novel*, London: Merlin Press, 1962; New York: Humanities Press, 1965

Lukács, Georg, *Wider den missverstandenen Realismus*, Hamburg: Claasen, 1958; as *The Meaning of Contemporary Realism*, London: Merlin Press, 1963; as *Realism in Our Time: Literature and the Class Struggle*, New York: Harper, 1964

Macherey, Pierre, *A Theory of Literary Production*, translated by Geoffrey Wall, London and Boston: Routledge, 1978

Moretti, Franco, *The Way of the World: The Bildungsroman in European Culture*, London: Verso, 1987

Murphy, James F., *The Proletarian Moment: The Controversy over Leftism in Literature*, Urbana: University of Illinois Press, 1991

Taylor, Ronald, editor, *Aesthetics and Politics*, London: New Left Books, 1977

Watt, Ian, *The Rise of the Novel: Studies in Defoe, Richardson, and Fielding*, Berkeley: University of California Press, and London: Chatto and Windus, 1957

Williams, Raymond, *The Country and the City*, New York: Oxford University Press, and London: Chatto and Windus, 1973

The Master and Margarita by Mikhail Bulgakov

Master i Margarita 1966–67

Bulgakov spent the last decade of his life working on *The Master and Margarita*, which he regarded as his masterpiece. Although essentially completed, the novel was not published during his lifetime and did not appear in print until it was published in installments in 1966 and 1967 in the journal *Moskva*. At that time, experimental fiction was again in vogue in a Soviet Union growing increasingly decadent and moribund. *The Master and Margarita* aroused great interest in the Soviet Union, and Bulgakov suddenly became, after the fact, an important predecessor of contemporary Russian writers such as Vasilii Aksenov, Andrei Siniavskii, and the Strugatskii brothers: a link between the new wave of postmodernist Soviet literature and the past tradition of Gogol' and Dostoevskii. Moreover, with its anticipations of postmodernist experimentalism, *The Master and Margarita* appealed to Western tastes and was soon widely translated and republished in the West, where its apparent satirical critique of Stalinism accorded well with the ideological requirements of the Cold War.

Dialogues between East and West (often in the form of Western scientific rationalism versus Eastern religious mysticism) are very much at the heart of *The Master and Margarita*. In the novel, a mysterious sorcerer named Woland (a figure of Satan and, presumably, the West) steps out of Goethe's *Faust* to visit modern Moscow with his entourage and wreak havoc on the populace as punishment for their philistine pettiness, greed, and vanity. Literature and writing are major subjects of the text, and much of the book's satire may be interpreted as Bulgakov's bitter commentary on his own lack of literary success in the Soviet Union. The "master" of the title is a novelist, and another major character is the poet Ivan Nikolayevich Ponyrev (who writes under the pen name Bezdomnyi, or "Homeless"). Much of *The Master and Margarita* involves representations of the work of these writers and of their difficulties with the Soviet literary establishment. Allusions to the work of previous Russian writers (like Aleksandr Pushkin and Dostoevskii) and to Western writers (like Goethe) are also prominent in the text.

The narrative that takes place in contemporary Moscow is intertwined with a second narrative strand that relates the story of Pontius Pilate and his encounter with Jeshua (Christ) in ancient Jerusalem. This second story may be variously interpreted as narrated by Satan himself, as the plot of the Master's destroyed novel, or as a story written by the failed poet Ivan Homeless. This part of the novel explores the crucial role played by cowardice in the relations between people and their rulers, as Pilate is forever tormented by the cowardice he displayed in his dealings with the tramp-philosopher Jeshua.

This highly complex narrative structure enables Bulgakov to create a dialogue between the events surrounding Woland's visit to Moscow and those surrounding the arrest and crucifixion of the Jeshua in Jerusalem. The narrative is further complicated by a combination of interacting and competing discourses from the realms of science, religion, literature, history, and politics. This dialogic mixture produces a fantastic, ambivalent satire with clear relevance to the social and political situation in the Stalinist Soviet Union of the 1930s. Bulgakov's depiction of the Soviet bureaucracy (especially the literary and medical establishments), and his delineation of the impoverished social conditions in Moscow, may be taken as severe criticisms of the Stalinist regime, just as the literary mode of the book seems to hark back to the fantastic realism of Gogol' and Dostoevskii and to radically reject the principles of socialist realism. On the other hand, much of the satire in *The Master and Margarita* appears to be aimed at lingering bourgeois elements in Soviet society, elements to which Stalin himself expressed firm opposition. Moreover, as Judith Mills has pointed out (1989), it is possible to read Bulgakov's book as a tribute to Stalin in which Woland, usually read as an anti-Stalinist figure, may potentially be interpreted as a figure of Stalin himself, working to eradicate the vestigial bourgeois elements impeding the growth of Soviet society.

The fantastic realism of *The Master and Margarita* (with its elements of ontological confusion, fantastic characters, and fantastic events based upon the ordinary pushed to its extreme) locates Bulgakov as a pioneer of the technique of magical realism. He thus becomes an important predecessor not only of many contemporary Russian writers but of numerous postmodern writers around the world, such as Günter Grass, Gabriel García Márquez, Jorge Luis Borges, Flann O'Brien, and Salman Rushdie. Indeed, Rushdie has suggested that *The Master and Margarita* provided crucial inspiration for his controversial novel, *The Satanic Verses.*

DUBRAVKA JURAGA

See also Mikhail Bulgakov

Further Reading

Barratt, Andrew, *Between Two Worlds: A Critical Introduction to "The Master and Margarita,"* Oxford: Clarendon Press, 1987

Chudakova, M., and Phyllis Powell, "*The Master and Margarita*: The Development of a Novel," *Russian Literature Triquarterly* 15 (1976)

Elbaum, Henry, "The Evolution of *The Master and Margarita*: Text, Context, Intertext," *Canadian Slavonic Papers* 37 (1995)

Gillespie, David C., *The Twentieth-Century Russian Novel: An Introduction,* Oxford and Washington, D.C.: Berg, 1996

Lakshin, Vladimir, "Mikhail Bulgakov's *The Master and Margarita,*" in *Twentieth-Century Russian Literary Criticism,* edited by Victor Erlich, New Haven, Connecticut: Yale University Press, 1975

Mills, Judith M., "Of Dreams, Devils, Irrationality and *The Master and Margarita,*" in *Russian Literature and Psychoanalysis,* edited by Daniel Rancour-Laferriere, Amsterdam and Philadelphia: Benjamins, 1989

Pittman, Riitta H., *The Writer's Divided Self in Bulgakov's "The Master and Margarita,"* London: Macmillan, and New York: St. Martin's Press, 1991

Tumanov, Vladimir, "Diabolus ex Machina: Bulgakov's Modernist Devil," *Scando-Slavica* 35 (1989)

Weeks, Laura D., "In Defense of the Homeless: On the Uses of History and the Role of Bezdomnyi in *The Master and Margarita,*" *The Russian Review* 48 (1989)

Weeks, Laura D., editor, *"The Master and Margarita": A Critical Companion,* Evanston, Illinois: Northwestern University Press, 1996

Medieval Narrative

In *The Waning of the Middle Ages* (1924), the historian Johan Huizinga says that "Of no great truth was the medieval mind more conscious than of St. Paul's phrase, 'Now we see through a glass darkly, but then face to face'"; medieval scholars, at least, strove to know the ways of God and man through the uncertain mirror of the natural world, in the hope that vision in the next world might be clearer. The desire to discern elements of reality through nature and through the representation of nature suggests three aspects of medieval literary theory that are relevant to the development of the novel. First, the writers' ability to read the message of nature wisely and to communicate that reading to an audience was beneficial to the individual reader and to society. Second, in a period when (in theory, at least) the state of the soul is of primary importance, the representation of the individual in action and in moral process within a social context becomes an instructive use of narrative. Third, therefore, through both the reading of history (*historia*) and fiction (*fabula*) a person might gain insight into his own character, into the behavior of others, and into the hidden messages of God in nature.

In his commentary on Cicero's *The Dream of Scipio,* the philosopher Macrobius defends the use not only of narrative but of fiction as a vehicle for moral instruction: "A conception of holy truths can be expressed under a seemly veil of fictions [*fabulae*], conveyed by honorable matter honorably arranged." Further, such fictions entice the youthful reader while teaching the more experienced. In *Anticlaudianus* (12th century), Alan de Lille points out that "the sweetness of the literal sense will sooth the ears of boys, the moral instruction will inspire the mind on the road to

perfection, the sharper subtlety of the allegory will whet the advanced intellect." These views reflected first a value for narrative as a vehicle for moral instruction in theology and philosophy, and led eventually to an appreciation of narrative itself as a means of revealing the hidden mysteries of fortune, character, and choice.

These principles of medieval literary theory had two sources. One source was the influence of classical rhetoric as it was taught in the medieval schools and used in the arts of persuasion and oratory. Rhetoric was dominated by a study of formal argument, tropes, and the Roman poets, especially Virgil. Narrative, in the forms of exempla, parables, and historical examples, served the purposes of the argument. The other source of theory was the monastic tradition of scriptural exegesis. Like Plato, the medieval schoolmen were suspicious of "the lies of poets," but the prevalence of narrative in scripture forced writers to analyze the forms, and the use of narrative in sermons and saints' lives led first to the retelling of scriptural stories and eventually to the instructive fictions of religious romance.

The narrative literature of the Middle Ages includes chronicle, epic, and romance. The stories, transmitted both orally and in writing, were offered in Latin and in the vernacular languages. These works may be said to precede the novel in that they developed vivid characters whose motives and actions invite interpretation rather than certainty; moral and emotional ambiguity were staples of the plots. Further, as the narrative genres developed, writers explored techniques for representing not only action but consciousness and emotional process. The early chronicles, extended accounts of towns, monasteries, or regions, were usually grounded in fact and embroidered to serve a social or political agenda. Similarly, the Icelandic sagas preserved a sense of personal and regional history and were based on the lives of real settlers. Written mostly for a courtly audience, the romances and epics combined historical event, folk material, and lively imagination to produce narratives centering on challenge or quest, moral trial, and choice. At the same time, a popular form of oral storytelling existed in the homes and marketplaces of Europe, and the conventions and values of these narratives eventually insinuated themselves into the fabric of written compositions.

Early medieval religious views of epic and romance were ambivalent. Alcuin, the eighth-century teacher and cleric of the Merovingian court, asks, "What does Ingeld have to do with Christ?" suggesting that monks should have more profitable activities than listening to the scop recast pagan Germanic and Norse legends. Nevertheless, the prevalence of narrative in scripture and subsequently in church teaching and preaching contributed to a close connection between narrative and religious thought. Certainly the early preachers were aware of the value of a good story, both as an aid to memory and as a vehicle for complex and varied interpretation. After the development of the Franciscan movement in the 13th century, with its emphasis on physical existence, the lower and middle classes, and realistic representation, religious narratives became even more concerned with representation of character and realistic psychology. Further, since Christian authors are concerned less with action than with motive ("As a man thinketh in his heart, so is he"), the representation of consciousness becomes a central element of narrative.

Early in the Middle Ages, chronicle, epic, and hagiography supplied the need for narrative, and extensions of these forms in the vernacular languages also produced romance. The romances combined elements of history, folklore, adventure, and eroticism in a form intended, at least partially, to appeal to a growing audience of women readers and patrons. And while all of these forms continued to be popular well into the 15th century, by the beginning of the 14th narratives of social commentary and psychological realism also assumed an important position in popular and secular literature. Eventually, the medieval narratives were subsumed into the adventure stories and the dramatic literature of the Renaissance. In time languages and scripts became difficult to read, and medieval literature became the property of antiquarians and philologists until the early 19th century, although elements of the stories were retained in fiction, popular drama, and children's literature. However, with the renewed interest in linguistic study in the 19th century, along with the romantic enthusiasm for medieval art and lore, the romances and epics found a new and appreciative audience. A new edition of *Le Morte D'Arthur* (1836), the novels of Sir Walter Scott, the poetry of Alfred, Lord Tennyson, and the rise of the Arts and Crafts movement all contributed to a general interest in medievalism in England. The popularity of Scott in America also ensured that the ideals of chivalry would make a significant impression on the new frontier as well as in the Old South. Thus, in the 19th century the revival of interest in medieval narrative became an influence on the development of the novel, one that continues in the present century.

In the early Middle Ages the need for public records, and indeed for national identity, fostered an interest in chronicle. The Venerable Bede's *Ecclesiastical History of the English People* (c. 731), the *Anglo-Saxon Chronicle* (597–1154), and the *Peterborough Chronicle* (the Laud manuscript of the *Anglo-Saxon Chronicle* from 1070 to 1154) reflect primarily a need for the preservation of historical information. Yet in these and other historical writings, scenes and characters may be rendered with brilliance, suggesting the beginnings of a narrative style. The scene in Bede's *History* in which the missionary Bishop Paulinus preaches to King Edwin of Northumbria and his Druid priest Colfi (Chapter 13) is justly famous, and while less well known, the descriptions in the *Peterborough Chronicle* of the Norman Conquest, and later of the civil war between Stephen and Matilda, are also dramatic, including action, character, and social comment. The anonymous author says of William I that he "had fallen into avarice, and he was completely devoted to greed," yet the account does not depend on this statement of opinion. Rather, he describes the harsh royal game laws that the king maintained in defiance not only of the common people but of the nobility and the church as well. In the passages on the civil war, the author presents a vivid picture of the disintegration of town and village caused by the warring factions; lands were destroyed, people reduced to beggars, the church ignored: "Where anyone tilled the earth, the land bore no corn, for the land was devastated by such deeds, and the people said openly that Christ and His saints were sleeping."

In the 12th century the chronicles became less about place and more about the royal houses. Wace, Walter Map, Geoffrey of Monmouth, and Laȝamon developed chronicles of the British kings, and with these accounts established not only the outline of the Arthurian narratives but also the tales of King Lear and Cymbeline, among others. Although much of the material in the British chronicles is more legendary than factual, each author maintained that his was the true story. In Laȝamon's *The Brut* he says that the Bretons "boast of and tell many lies about Arthur the king," but says of his own book that "the truth has been set down in writing, how the deeds of Arthur came to pass, from beginning to end, neither more nor less, but just as his way of life was." Nonetheless, each of these accounts offers scenes of swift action and moral choice. For example, Geoffrey of Monmouth's *History of the Kings of Britain,* in describing Uther's illicit passion for Igraine, the Duchess of Cornwall, and Merlin's complicity in her seduction, not only depicts the actions but develops the feelings and motivations of the characters as well. All of these accounts blend myth, history, and fabrication, and their descriptions become the basis of much of subsequent romance.

Another early form of narrative is found in religious instruction through saints' lives. These accounts range from straightforward accounts such as Bede's *Life of Cuthbert* to fully developed religious romances such as *The Voyage of St. Brendan*. In both kinds of saints' lives, the primary function of the narrative is to increase the devotion of the reader or hearer. Yet precisely because the pieces must reflect moral and spiritual experience, the authors must devise methods of representation that allow them to reveal the consciousness and the emotional process of the characters.

Bede's *Life of Cuthbert* reflects a scholar's commitment to accuracy and a pastor's desire for edification. The miracles are few and, according to Bede, well attested by reliable witnesses. Yet like a novelist choosing episodes that reveal character, Bede selects miracles that illustrate aspects of the saint's personality and teaching and that further serve to connect the life of the saint to the events of scripture. Healing, feeding, being fed by ravens are all miracles through which the saint enacts the gospel for his flock, and the author, by extension, for his readers. *The Voyage of St. Brendan,* on the other hand, makes little pretense to history (unlike the more straightforward *Acts of St. Brendan*). Instead, it relates the events of the Abbot Brendan's mystical journey with 14 of his brothers on the North Sea in a small coracle. The episodes of *The Voyage of St. Brendan,* many of which are frankly supernatural, are presented through action, dialogue, and description, and rather than revealing a naturalistic progress, they are made to parallel both the seasons of the liturgical year and the seasons of the individual's life. Whether realistic or magical, these and other similar hagiographical writings related events in such a way as to reveal not only individual action but also interior choice and resolution. In writing for the edification of the reader, the authors develop modes of representing motive and behavior.

A more sophisticated representation of interior experience is found in the Anglo-Saxon elegies—actually interior monologues—such as "The Seafarer" and "The Wanderer." Also a part of this tradition is the English epic *Beowulf,* one of the earliest narratives to combine mythic, historical, and fictional elements to display character, culture, and interior development. J.R.R. Tolkien, in his 1936 essay "The Monsters and the Critics," was one of the first critics to interpret *Beowulf* as a poem revealing the interior life of the hero as he reacts in youth and in old age. John Leyerle, in "The Interlace Structure of Beowulf" (1967), further suggests that the speeches, sermons, and secondary narratives, seen by 19th-century scholars as distracting digressions, are in fact a carefully plotted network of images and themes that reflect the stages of the hero's life and his relationship with his *comitatus* (action). After Beowulf has slain Grendel, his action is framed by the scop's song of Sigemund the dragonslayer and Heremod the avaricious king. These two secondary narratives suggest the range of the hero's choices, and further, they foreshadow elements of his future. Moreover, the narratives also indicate the responsibility of the hero in relation to his society. As A.C. Gibbs (1966) has pointed out, the medieval epics in general relate to actual historical and political situations, and "[their] heroes act in some way as representatives of their people, even though their conscious motivation is heroic self-assertion." However, in *Beowulf,* as in other later Germanic epics, the hero's interior landscape is presented in the light of these secondary narratives.

The word *romance* referred originally to any story written in the vernacular languages rather than in Latin. The term came to refer to a story of heroic quest, trial or challenge, erotic love, and moral choice. Supernatural events were often elements of the plot, and chivalry and courtly love were the ideal value systems. In many instances, the romance reflects the action of the knight alone in wood or wasteland, battling human opponents and supernatural beings. As Gibbs points out, the romance reflects a move from the military expedition of the *chanson de geste* to the solitary adventures of the knight. This combination of ingredients led to a personal and affective narrative form that was as concerned with feeling as with action. Northrop Frye (1985), in addressing the move from oral to written narrative, says that in the presentation of heroes alone the romance implies "a more private relationship between reader and writer" as well as "wider possibilities for the direct communication of experience."

That women are more interested than men in the discussion of feelings is a questionable truism of the late 20th century. However, it is demonstrably true that the shift in literature from *comitatus* and honor to love, quest, and sentiment corresponded to a rise in the importance of women as readers and as patrons of the arts. During the 12th century, when the Crusades produced frequent and prolonged absences of the men, women were left as administrators and guardians of the younger dependents. One such woman, Eleanor of Aquitaine (1122–1204), was the granddaughter of William IX of Aquitaine, the first troubadour whose works yet survive. She was married to two kings, first to Louis VII of France and later to Henry II of England. Her large family of children included two kings, Richard I and John I, and a daughter who was regent for her young son. Eleanor was an active proponent of the arts, especially of the development of a secular courtly poetry. Because of her worldly tastes, Bernard of Clairvaux thought her a bad influence on the French court.

Eleanor's daughter, Marie de Champagne, set up her court in Troyes, where, in addition to her skill at management, she continued her mother's artistic patronage, sponsoring both Andreas Capellanus (*The Art of Courtly Love*) and Chretien de Troyes, one of the most prolific and influential romance writers.

This period also sees one of the first women authors, Marie de France (fl. 1160–90), a French woman living in the English court. A highly educated woman, Marie is best known for her *Breton Lais,* romances derived from Celtic folk motifs and written in Anglo-Norman couplets. These stories are charming, but also psychologically astute and morally demanding. In one of her lais, *Eliduc,* the wife befriends her husband's young lover and actually arranges for their marriage, but in the end, all three of the main characters leave the courtly life to enter religious houses. The morality of this triangle is left open to the reader's judgment. While the roots of romance are clearly in the heroic literature, the women as patrons and as artists effected significant changes both in their tone and in their subject matter.

Although romances include a diverse range of sources, subjects, and techniques, they are often classified by subject matter, following the tradition established by the French romance writer Jean Bodel (12th century). Bodel refers to the "Matter of Britain," the stories of Arthur and his court, the "Matter of Rome," the classical romances, most frequently those of Alexander the Great, and the "Matter of France," the adventures of Charlemagne and his court. To these categories, modern scholars added the "Matter of England," romances about English heroes unrelated to Arthur, such as *King Horn, Sir Orfeo,* and *Havelok the Dane.* A few of the romances seem to fit none of these categories, being derived from Middle Eastern folklore, while others combine elements from several sources, for the romance reflected the fluid nature of European culture. Like the modern novel, the romance transcended regional and political boundaries and the limitations of strict categories.

The range and complexity of these categories may be seen in the summary of the largest, the Matter of Britain, including love stories of Arthur, Lancelot, and Guinevere, of Tristan and Iseult, the political and familial intrigues of Arthur's parentage and his son Mordred, the magic of Merlin, and the quest for the Holy Grail. Some of these had their early development through the chronicles and are elaborated by Chretien de Troyes and the authors of the French Vulgate cycle, and eventually in Sir Thomas Malory's *Le Morte D'Arthur* (1485). The Tristan narratives, included in Malory's account, probably derive from Celtic sources, now lost, and are depicted further in the romances of Beroul, Gottfried von Strasburg, and Wolfram von Eschenbach. The Merlin story, prominent in the later chronicles and in Malory, also forms an individual romance, *Merlin*, by Robert de Boron (13th century). The Grail quest, central to the Vulgate cycle and to Malory's account, is also found in Robert de Boron's *Joseph d'Arimathie*. And this list is far from complete.

The large number of accounts leaves ample room for diversity, even contradiction, in event, in character, and in narrative point of view. Indeed, as Charlotte Spivack and Roberta Lynne Staples (1994) point out, "Lancelot is both faithful and disloyal, Mordred both malign and vulnerable, Arthur both strong and weak." Spivack and Staples, however, see this quality as a narrative advantage both to the romances themselves and to their modern imitators: "Since the contradictory personality is an accepted fact in modern psychology, it serves as a convincing basis for the effectively complex characterizations that so many recent authors offer."

In any case, this web of narrative produces a complex vision of each individual story. In *Sir Gawain and the Green Knight* the rivalry between Morgan le Fay and Guinevere, although offered as the motive for the whole game plot, seems relatively insignificant. The romance offers only the briefest glimpses of the women's characters. Yet it is impossible to read *Sir Gawain and the Green Knight* without recalling from other romances Morgan's malice and Guinevere's disloyalty, and these memories lend weight and interest to characters about whom *Sir Gawain and the Green Knight* itself says little. In another example, the anonymous Cistercian author of *Le Conte Del Saint Graal* reveals the unsuccessful quest of Lancelot for the Holy Grail, along with his spiritual and emotional challenges. His readers might recall, however, that Lancelot, now on a religious quest, still carries the guilt of his affair with Guinevere and his disloyalty to his friend and king, Arthur. The complexity of this particular characterization is enriched by the existence of several well-known romances about the same character.

This was not, of course, a new device in the Middle Ages. In *The Odyssey,* Homer expects his hearers to know the whole story of the House of Atreus and to compare their fortunes and choices with those of Odysseus and his family. This artistic use of an extensive background narrative is occasionally a feature of modern novels as well. For example, in his trilogy *The Hamlet* (1940), *The Town* (1957), and *The Mansion* (1959), William Faulkner draws on characters who appear in other novels, and further, through the character of V.I. Ratliff, he tells the stories of a barn burning and of a herd of spotted horses, both narratives that appear from different points of view in earlier short stories. The mythos of Yoknapatawpha County may be said to form a "Matter of Mississippi" with a web of relationships, characters, and narrative points of view that enriches the individual characters and episodes of each novel.

The narrative skills of romance, epic, and chronicle culminate in Sir Thomas Malory's *Le Morte D'Arthur.* Although Malory refers to a "French Book" as a source, he clearly draws from both the French Vulgate cycle and from the English alliterative and stanzaic romances as well. Like La3amon, Malory maintains that his book is "the whole story of King Arthur and of his noble

knights," but in fact in nearly every episode he shortens his sources, making them more forceful. Moreover, Malory combines the diverse elements of the Matter of Britain with thematic unity. Certainly the book is sometimes uneven in style and coherence, yet as a whole it displays remarkable coherence in character and tone.

Nearly a century before Malory completed his romance, another form of literature was developing, at first in Florence and northern Italy and later in England. Psychological realism, narrative point of view, and the representation of consciousness produced a body of secular fiction that, although written early in the 14th century, is often classified as "Renaissance" literature.

First among these is *The Divine Comedy* of Dante Alighieri (c. 1322). This work is unusual, although not unique, as it employs a first-person narrator: "I awoke to find myself in a dark wood where the way was wholly long and gone" (Canto I). As the pilgrim moves from dark wood down through the Inferno, up Mt. Purgatory, and into Paradise, Dante not only relates realistic conversations and dramatic actions, but he also is at pains to reveal the narrator's feelings and sensations directly. Further, since Dante chooses historical characters to represent the various sins and virtues, he is able to explore their senses and experiences as well. He departs from the relative simplicity of direct allegory for a more ambiguous realism. In one famous passage (Canto V), readers often find that, despite her sin, they feel sympathy for Francesca da Rimini. She and her lover Paolo represent lust through their adultery (a sin inspired, incidentally, by their reading of a romance of Lancelot). Dante, however, through Francesca's conversation, reveals extenuating circumstances for her behavior, and her soft speech and youthful charm introduce an element of ambiguity that is not entirely dispelled by the admonitions of the Roman poet Virgil, who is the narrator's guide through *The Divine Comedy.*

Dante's most immediate successor, Giovanni Boccaccio, went even further both in subject and in technique to represent realistic character. One critic, Gregory Lucente (1981), says that with Boccaccio, "the realist mode gained full development in both stylistics and ideology." He further adds that while the life of the next world remained a major concern, "the new fascination with man himself affected every area of human endeavor," including the development of representational fiction. In both the novellas of *The Decameron* (written 1349–51) and the longer narratives of *Il Filostrato* (1340) and *Elegia di Madonna Fiammetta* (1343–45; *The Elegy of Lady Fiametta*), Boccaccio explores passions and motivations that are more often psychological than otherworldly.

Boccaccio's *Il Filostrato* is an adaptation of Benoît de Sainte-Maure's *Roman de Troie* (c. 1160). Since Benoît is principally concerned with the siege of Troy, the story of the lovers is scattered throughout the *Roman de Troie*. Through the comments of his narrator and by direct revelation of the characters' thoughts, Boccaccio centers the story on the love affair and the moral and emotional experience of his characters. He plots the progress of Troilus' passion in tormented monologues, and he also depicts Cressida's reluctance and surrender in terms that account for, if not excuse, her defection. Further, although Boccaccio appears in his conclusion to adopt the misogyny of his sources, in fact he is careful to show that Cressida's choices are gravely limited. If her actions are unfortunate, at least her motives are completely believable. In *The Elegy of Lady Fiametta,* Boccaccio not only uses a first-person narrator, but that narrator is a woman. The narrative includes very little action, but instead reveals Fiametta's feelings and reactions as she matures, marries, suffers an unrequited love, and writes her book. Several critics have seen The *Elegy of Lady Fiametta* as the progenitor of the psychological novel. As Thomas Mauch notes in an introduction to a recent edition of the novel, Fiametta represents Boccaccio's "early attempt at creating an image of a self becoming conscious of its uniqueness, ambivalence, and multiplicity." And with regard to narrative technique, the story is certainly one of the earliest protracted uses of interior monologue.

The English poet Geoffrey Chaucer traveled in Europe and read widely; thus he was much influenced first by the French poets, and even more by Boccaccio. His *Canterbury Tales* (written 1385–1400) are remarkable for their realistic portraits of the pilgrims and of the characters in their tales, for the social and religious commentary, and for the development of characters from the middle and lower classes. Of even more importance, however, to the background of the novel is his *Troilus and Criseyde* (c. 1385), for whereas the *Canterbury Tales* often employ realism in character and innovation in the use of narrators, *Troilus and Criseyde* is a sustained exploration of the lovers' emotional lives. Although Chaucer draws heavily on Boccaccio's version for scene and plot, he goes even further in developing the emotional content of the romance. In his account of Criseyde he is especially careful to show her sensations, her motives, and her alternatives, leaving moral judgments ambiguous and open to the reader's interpretation.

A third medieval account of Troilus and Cressida is Robert Henryson's *The Testament of Cressid* (c. 1460), unique in that it relates Cressida's life in the Greek camp after her unfaithfulness to Troilus. Although Cressida is jilted by Diomedes, reduced to poverty and prostitution, and afflicted with leprosy, Henryson does not offer an unambiguous condemnation of her character. Before her death she consigns her soul to the virgin goddess Diana and warns women to "Beware of men, and harken to what I say!" David Benson (1990) sees *The Testament of Cressid* as "unique in its time and . . . exceptional thereafter in refusing to make Cressida an *exemplum* of feminine wickedness." Benson goes even further to say that Henryson's poem "instead asks readers to defer judgement and to consider alternate interpretations."

By the early 16th century, because of changes in languages and in the circulation of new narratives in print, many romances were lost to the general reader. However, in the 19th century, many writers and artists revived an interest in the values and the narratives of the Middle Ages as an anodyne to the pains of modern industrialism. A new edition of Malory's *Le Morte D'Arthur* in 1836 gave new readers an opportunity to explore romance. The novels of Sir Walter Scott, with plots and characters drawn from English romances, received both popular and critical acclaim. In both his early romances such as "The Lady of Shallot" and the longer *Idylls of the King* (1859), Alfred, Lord Tennyson contributed to a public eager to enjoy the Arthurian tales. The Arts and Crafts Movement, generated by such writers as Thomas Carlyle, John Ruskin, and William Morris, offered medieval aesthetics and economics as alternatives to the corruptions of the Industrial Revolution. At the same time, Morris and the Pre-Raphaelite artists and writers made extensive use of medieval motifs and themes in poetry, fiction, and painting.

The historical fiction of Sir Walter Scott, popular in England,

was also formative in America. In southern homes, Scott's novels occupied the imaginative space afforded to John Bunyan's *The Pilgrim's Progress* (1678, 1684) in New England. According to his diaries, General Robert E. Lee enjoyed Scott's novels, and the values of southern aristocracy were directly related to their love of medieval romance. This enthusiasm translates into irony in modern fiction. In *Absalom, Absalom!* (1936), William Faulkner says that the small Compson family library included the Bible and the complete works of Sir Walter Scott, and Quentin's northern roommate Shreve refers to the southern characters as "all of those doomed Bayards and Guineveres." Thus the imaginary chivalry of the Old South was rooted in the romances of knighthood and quest and the allure of the lost cause.

The interest in medieval romance continues in the 20th century as well, as modern versions of old stories appear and as medieval motifs and images sustain novels and films of fantasy and science fiction. In *The Once and Future King* (1939), T.H. White combines elements of French and English romances with the romantic poetry of Tennyson. Rosemary Sutcliff, in *Sword at Sunset* (1963), recasts the Arthurian triangle in the light of archeological knowledge, while Marion Zimmer Bradley gives the same story a marked feminist twist in *The Mists of Avalon* (1982). In his spiritual thriller *War in Heaven* (1930), Charles Williams revives the legend of the Holy Grail, and in several of his novels the American writer Walker Percy uses the motifs of Arthurian legend to represent aspects of the preconscious experience and philosophical dismay. In fantasy and science fiction, medieval motifs have dominated such diverse works as the Dragonquest novels of Anne McCaffrey, George Lucas' *Star Wars Trilogy*, and innumerable episodes of *Star Trek*. From serious fiction to popular amusement, the themes and characters of medieval narrative continue to win readers.

The reasons for the 19th-century romantic interest in the Middle Ages and the continuing market for medieval narratives are complex and varied, but surely one must be that the medieval epics and romances offer an iconography of quest, trial, challenge, love, and choice that allows us to represent the deepest aspects of psychological experience. To paraphrase Alan de Lille in a somewhat different context, "The invention appeals to young readers, the rich characters and relationships to adults, and the layered subtlety of the structures to those readers who are willing to work for it."

JANET P. SHOLTY

See also Biblical Narrative and the Novel; Epic and Novel; Greek and Roman Narrative; Novel and Romance: Etymologies; Renaissance Narrative; Romance; Saga; Verse Narrative

Further Reading

Auerbach, Erich, *Introduction to Romance Languages and Literature: Latin, French, Spanish, Provençal, and Italian*, translated by Guy Daniels, New York: Capricorn Books, 1961

Benson, C. David, *Chaucer's Troilus and Criseyde*, London and Boston: Unwin Hyman, 1990

Fields, P.J.C., *Romance and Chronicle: A Study of Malory's Prose Style*, London: Barrie and Jenkins, and Bloomington: Indiana University Press, 1971

Frye, Northrop, Sheridan Baker, and George Perkins, *The*

Harper Handbook to Literature, New York: Harper and Row, 1985

Gibbs, A.C., editor, *Middle English Romances,* London: Arnold, and Evanston, Illinois: Northwestern University Press, 1966

Ker, W.P., *Epic and Romance: Essays on Medieval Literature,* London: Macmillan, 1897; 2nd edition, 1908

Lucente, Gregory L., *The Narrative of Realism and Myth: Verga, Lawrence, Faulkner, Pavese,* Baltimore: Johns Hopkins University Press, 1981

Mitchell, Jerome, *Scott, Chaucer, and Medieval Romance: A Study in Sir Walter Scott's Indebtedness to the Literature of the Middle Ages,* Lexington: University Press of Kentucky, 1987

Moreland, Kim, *The Medievalist Impulse in American Literature: Twain, Adams, Fitzgerald, and Hemingway,* Charlottesville: University Press of Virginia, 1996

Spivack, Charlotte, and Roberta Lynne Staples, *The Company of Camelot: Arthurian Characters in Romance and Fantasy,* Westport, Connecticut: Greenwood Press, 1994

Vinaver, Eugene, editor, *The Works of Sir Thomas Malory,* Oxford: Clarendon Press, 1947; 3rd edition, Oxford: Clarendon Press, and New York: Oxford University Press, 1990

Melmoth the Wanderer by Charles Robert Maturin

1820

Melmoth the Wanderer, arguably one of the greatest Gothic novels ever written, was, in fact, published some 20 years after the heyday of the Gothic novel proper, and effectively marks the *finis* of that form. While the Gothic novel in general quickly became the subject for mockery (witness Jane Austen's mockery of Mrs. Radcliffe in *Northanger Abbey*), *Melmoth the Wanderer* was well received from the beginning, and its influence was obvious. William Makepeace Thackeray and D.G. Rossetti praised it. Oscar Wilde was clearly thinking of it when he wrote *The Picture of Dorian Gray* (1891; indeed, Wilde took on the pseudonym of Sebastian Melmoth after his release from Brixton Prison). Edgar Allan Poe's "The Pit and the Pendulum" has often been mentioned in connection with Maturin. However, it was in France that Maturin's book had its warmest reception, being praised by successive generations of French writers and artists from the romantics to the surrealists. André Breton found Maturin "sublime"; Charles Baudelaire ranked him with Beethoven, Lord Byron, and Poe; Honoré de Balzac wrote an imitation of *Melmoth the Wanderer* under a pseudonym and then an overt sequel, *Melmoth réconcilié* (1836); Eugene Delacroix painted a picture entitled *Melmoth; ou, L'Intérieur d'un Couvent de Dominicains à Madrid* and considered illustrating the whole of *Melmoth the Wanderer.*

There are a number of things that account for this kind of reception. While other Gothic romances situate their impossible tales of the supernatural, macabre, and fantastic in the predictable setting of a haunted castle or abbey isolated among the cataracts, valleys, and precipices of some wild, romantic landscape, *Melmoth the Wanderer* appears at first to be another Anglo-Irish "Big House" novel. The main narrator, John Melmoth, is summoned from his studies at Trinity College, Dublin, to attend the deathbed of his uncle, the owner of a large and dilapidated house in Wicklow, which is occupied by the stereotypical crowd of native Irish servants eating and drinking in the kitchen below, while the uncle, a member of a Cromwellian family that had dispossessed the original inhabitants, lies neglected and despised upstairs. The description of the house, and the intense awareness of the political and historical complexities of 19th-century Ireland, locate the tale in a recognizable setting from which it then departs in a less abrupt manner than is common in other tales. The Melmoth of the title is the brother of the original Cromwellian soldier. He has entered into a compact with the Devil, who granted him an extension of life along with some supernatural powers in return for his soul. Melmoth could, however, escape his bargain if he could persuade someone else to take it upon himself. The story, spanning 160 years, moves from the prisons of the Spanish Inquisition to Bedlam (the lunatic asylum) in London, to a paradisial island in the Indian Ocean, to the house of a wealthy merchant in Seville, and finally back to the coast of Wicklow. Through discovered documents, directly personal eyewitness accounts, and reported tales, John Melmoth is told of the earlier Melmoth's wandering the world with his curse, seeking someone in the extremes of agony or fear of death who is prepared to exchange Melmoth's bargain for the sure promise of rescue from present extremity. In all his wanderings, Melmoth finds no one who will barter his soul, and the book culminates with the devil's arrival to claim his payment. The plot, then, allows limitless scope for the depiction of terror and extremes of cruelty in the most lurid and melodramatic language.

Maturin himself claimed that what he presented was realistic. He wrote against a background of intense sectarian conflict, and the violently anti-Catholic tenor of many of the passages of *Melmoth the Wanderer* reflects the tone and language of some of his, and others', sermons and the antipopery tracts that were produced in abundance at the time. In the preface to an earlier novel, *The Milesian Chief* (1812), he had written: ". . . I have chosen my own country for the scene, because I believe it the only country on earth, where, from the strange existing opposition of religion, politics, and manners, the extremes of refinement and barbarism are united, and the most wild and incredible situations of romantic story are hourly passing before modern eyes."

It is arguable that it was that "strange existing opposition of religion, politics, and manners" that was the major factor in enabling Maturin to take a comparatively worn-out form and make it capable of accomplishing something much more. It has been pointed out that the staying power of the best Gothic fiction (we might include *Frankenstein* and *Dracula* here) is owing to its ability to convey truths, attitudes, desires, and responses that are frowned upon or suppressed within the official culture—that the power of Gothic lies, to some extent, in its subversive charge that is, nevertheless, rendered less subversive by being obliquely presented or apparently fantastic. Maturin's presentation of, for example, the young lovers prepared to sacrifice all for love yet turning cannibalistically on each other when condemned to die slowly, in the dark, of starvation, while melodramatic, is, nevertheless, full of the power of *psychological* truth, as is his compelling presentation of insanity, or of the effects of starvation, poverty, or prolonged sexual repression. His subject, he said, was "the obscure recesses of the human heart."

Melmoth the Wanderer is unusual, as well, in being a profoundly religious book. Melmoth is ultimately condemned, not because of his bargain with the Devil but because he despairs of salvation. Maturin, in the conclusion to the book, does not succumb to the crudity of presenting the Devil in full view. Melmoth's damnation takes place off-stage, the details left to the terrified imagination of the reader. Neither does Maturin resort to the cozy rationalization and happy ending of Mrs. Radcliffe, for he believes in the existence of the evil he portrays. It is, ultimately, that combination of intense theological concern and profound and subtle psychological awareness that makes *Melmoth the Wanderer* rise above other examples of the Gothic novel.

ANNE CLUNE

Further Reading

Harris, Charles B., *Charles Robert Maturin: The Forgotten Imitator,* New York: Arno Press, 1980

Henderson, Peter Mills, *A Nut Between Two Blades: The Novels of Charles Robert Maturin,* New York: Arno Press, 1980

Hinck, Henry William, *Three Studies on Charles Robert Maturin,* New York: Arno Press, 1980

Idman, Niilo, *Charles Robert Maturin: His Life and Works,* London: Constable, 1923

Kramer, Dale, *Charles Robert Maturin,* New York: Twayne, 1973

Lougy, Robert E., *Charles Robert Maturin,* Lewisburg, Pennsylvania: Bucknell University Press, 1975

Monroe, Judson, *Tragedy in the Novels of the Reverend Charles Robert Maturin,* New York: Arno Press, 1972

Scholten, Willem, *Charles Robert Maturin: The Terror-Novelist,* Amsterdam: H.J. Paris, 1933; New York: Garland, 1980

Scott, Shirley, *Myths and Consciousness in the Novels of Charles Maturin,* New York: Arno Press, 1980

Melodrama

The term *melodrama* draws attention to the mixed origins of this artistic mode and to the confusing signals that it has often sent to interpreters. Simply, the term means drama with incidental music. Melodrama has never freed itself entirely from its origins on the popular stage, nor from related opprobrium. Until recently, the notion of melodrama signified, in critical and popular discourse, a coarsened and exaggerated kind of emotionalism, flamboyant language and gesture, and stylized plots in which imperiled virtue at the last moment made its escape from predatory villainy. Such a description—appropriate in outline to a good deal of Victorian fiction, not least to some of the novels of Charles Dickens—shows how melodrama has escaped generic boundaries.

This is not just a matter of the situations and idioms of stage melodrama (which was the most popular kind of theatre in the 19th century) being taken over by novelists. Narrative paintings of bourgeois life in the same period clarify the relations of melodrama with realism and show the two styles to be interdependent rather than antithetical. Those solid Victorian domestic interiors (ably analyzed by Peter Conrad in *The Victorian Treasure-house,* 1973), replete with the material objects that seem to guarantee status and prosperity, offer only the illusion of stability. They are inherently vulnerable and can swiftly be undermined by drink and gambling (as in R.B. Martineau's "The Last Day in the Old Home") and adultery (for instance in August Egg's triptych "Past and Present"). Personal indulgence and deceit can destroy the respectable appearances that sustain the edifice of middle-class family life.

Fear of dispossession is the emotional core, and hence the narrative core, of melodrama, whether this involves threats to life, property, or chastity, and whether a play, a novel, or a painting is the form in which the action is represented. Those detailed surfaces, those intricate relations of persons and properties central to realist art (or, perhaps more precisely, to its doctrinaire development into naturalism) are the stuff on which melodrama feeds, exposing their susceptibility to collapse and the hollowness of their pretensions.

The rehabilitation of melodrama was the business of creative writers long before such critics as Eric Bentley (1964), James Smith (1973), and Peter Brooks (1976) came to the task. Henrik Ibsen and Anton Chekhov are the playwrights who most profoundly explored the insubstantiality of bourgeois morality, especially as this was invested in the acquisition of property and a name. Both writers employed the devices of melodrama integrally in such plays as Ibsen's *Samfundets støtter* (1877; *The Pillars of the Community*; also rendered as *Quicksands* in a telling alternative translation) and Chekhov's *Chaika* (1896; *The Seagull*). As Bentley appositely remarked, "melodrama is the Naturalism of the dream life," or, indeed, of nightmare. He also regarded melodrama as "drama in its elemental form; it is the quintessence of drama." And Bentley conceded the emotional immaturity of the form, for whose characters "the distinction between *I want to* and *I can* is not clearly made." Speaking of its continuing power, Bentley concluded that "Melodramatic vision is paranoid: we are being persecuted, and we hold that all things, living and dead, are combining to persecute us."

Bentley's influence on theories of melodrama has been signal, notably on Peter Brooks' seminal study *The Melodramatic Imagination* (1976) which is concerned with the adaptation of elements of melodrama in the novels of Honoré de Balzac and Henry James. Brooks saw melodrama's rise and diffusion as related to the Western crisis of spiritual belief: "the vertiginous feeling of standing over the abyss created when the necessary center of things has been evacuated or dispersed." In melodrama this state of psychic and emotional extremity means that "Nothing is spared because nothing is left unsaid; the characters stand on a stage and utter the unspeakable."

Analyzing the paranoid condition ("a refusal to be left out"), psychiatrist Adam Phillips (1993) has written of a disposition to treat the outside world as "a repository for the terror inside, an elsewhere for those desires and objects that bring unpleasure." In artistic terms, as Brooks had recognized, this is to see melodrama as a fundamentally expressionistic mode. That term, borrowed from the visual arts, is another reminder of the invasive, the transgeneric demeanor of melodrama.

Melodrama's attractions for novelists may now be documented unapologetically. The villain of Mrs. Henry Wood's best-selling book *East Lynne* (1861), the aristocratic seducer and murderer Sir Francis Levison, is the classic melodramatic predator now assuming a central role in a novel. Also playing a central role is an American counterpart, the violent, drunken plantation owner and slave driver Simon Legree in Harriet Beecher Stowe's *Uncle Tom's Cabin* (1852). Both novels were dramatized, melodramatically, for the stage soon after publication.

Other figurations of the melodramatic villain in fiction are more ambiguous. Dark, brooding, of mysterious and perhaps disreputable origins (Irish or gypsy), the foundling Heathcliff is the implacable, dispossessing agent/villain of melodrama in Emily Brontë's *Wuthering Heights* (1847). At the same time (in one of those complications that perhaps more truly mark the fictional occurrences of melodrama than novels such as Wood's or Stowe's), Heathcliff may be regarded as reclaiming his rightful inheritance. And his end is peaceful. The hero of Dickens' *Oliver Twist* (1838) is more like a stock victim of melodrama, a figure of innocence traduced, robbed of his birthright, fallen among thieves, his life imperiled. Dickens' later treatments of such a victim were more complex and abstract. Willfully blind to the source of his wealth, Pip in *Great Expectations* (1861) is threatened with something more dire than poverty and the loss of his assumed social position. Magwitch's revelations mean that Pip's veritable identity is endangered, his delusive sense of self is overturned. A fragile selfhood is what he almost loses, and then painfully and partially regains.

The subduing of melodrama at the same time as its primal roles and dire threats are deployed is also a feature of the writing of celebrated 19th-century American novelists. Without doing justice to the complexity of Nathaniel Hawthorne's moral inquiry, one can see the importance of the melodramatic strain in *The Scarlet Letter* (1850), wherein Hester Prynne loses her name and her position after the birth of her illegitimate child, only to become a triumphant pariah, a sign of the hypocrisy and censoriousness of the New England community rather than of her own transgression. In Herman Melville's *Moby-Dick* (1851), the melodramatic burden is concentrated in the figure of Ahab, the hero-villain whose unbridled rhetoric, caustic and exalted, is fit for the stage. Ahab's understanding of the whale is half-aware of how he projects his own anguish upon it: "He tasks me; he heaps me; I see in him outrageous strength, with an inscrutable malice sinewing it." As Melville's narrator comments: "The White Whale swam before him as the monomaniac incarnation of all those malicious agencies which some deep men feel eating in them."

Nor did the transmutation, sophistication, and subversion of the melodramatic mode lose attraction for novelists in the 20th century. Brooks wrote of Henry James' *The Wings of the Dove* (1902) that it was "very much about how one can subtilize and complicate the terms of melodrama, their relation to individual character and their conflict, while at the same time preserving their underlying identity and nourishing drama from their substratum." The point has a wide reference. Brooks concedes that he might as well have concentrated on Dickens and Fedor Dostoevskii, on Joseph Conrad (for example "Heart of Darkness," 1902) and D.H. Lawrence, or on William Faulkner.

The number of novelists to exploit the melodramatic mode is more extensive still. Melodrama is the sovereign weather of Thomas Keneally's fiction, as for that of his compatriots Marcus Clarke (in *His Natural Life,* 1874) and Christina Stead. Clarke's hero Rufus Dawes, wrongly transported to Australia for penal servitude, has not merely suffered material loss but "knew that the name he once possessed was blotted out." The destruction of identity is the cardinal deprivation and anxiety of melodrama. Hetty Pollitt, abused wife in Christina Stead's *The Man Who Loved Children* (1940), feels that every room of her marital home is "full of living cancers of insult, leprosies of disillusion, abscesses of grudge, gangrene of nevermore, quintan fevers of divorce." This fervid speech is in the idiomatic spirit of melodrama. The location of Hetty's torments within marriage reminds us how often melodramatic fiction is concerned with family crisis.

Yet melodrama also has infused (true to its origins) some of the most popular kinds of modern fiction—notably spy thrillers. The paranoid temper of the spy novel is in the melodramatic line. Its ambiguous depiction of good in jeopardy and evil that preys upon it is congruent with the changes and complications of melodrama in the 19th-century novel. Practitioners such as Graham Greene, John Le Carre, and Len Deighton have been sensible of how melodrama's apprehension of a moral void, of the terrors of apparently motiveless persecution, can invigorate contemporary fictions. The once traditional happy ending of melodrama (in fact long withheld in the works under discussion) is a most unlikely outcome in sour tales of espionage. Their continuing popularity, however, shows the powers of renewal, mutation, and surprising enlightenment that the melodramatic mode continues to exhibit in fiction.

PETER PIERCE

See also Gothic Novel

Further Reading

Bentley, Eric, *The Life of the Drama,* New York: Atheneum, 1964; London: Methuen, 1965

Brooks, Peter, *The Melodramatic Imagination: Balzac, Henry James, Melodrama, and the Mode of Excess,* New Haven, Connecticut: Yale University Press, 1976

Conrad, Peter, *The Victorian Treasure-house,* London: Collins, 1973

Phillips, Adam, *On Kissing, Tickling and Being Bored: Psychoanalytic Essays on the Unexamined Life,* London: Faber, and Cambridge, Massachusetts: Harvard University Press, 1993

Smith, James Leslie, *Melodrama,* London: Methuen, 1973

Herman Melville 1819–91

United States

In a letter of 13 August 1852, Herman Melville offered the outline of a possible story to his newly discovered New England neighbor and fellow author Nathaniel Hawthorne. Originally told to Melville by a New Bedford lawyer, it concerned a Nantucket woman abandoned by her weak, bigamist sailor-husband. Hawthorne, Melville suggested, might care to work each "tributary" item into an imaginative whole: Agatha's patience and resignation, the rotting of the wooden post box, her cliff-side habitat and isolation, the contextual New England bleakness. In summary, he wrote, here was "a skeleton of actual reality" to be "built about with fulness & veins & beauty." Hawthorne tactfully declined the offer of the material, which contains a working credo for Melville's own fiction.

The nine full-length narratives with *Moby-Dick* (1851) as the centerpiece, the 15 or so stories written between 1853 and 1856, the novella *Israel Potter* (1855) with its lyric, haunting portrait of human isolation, and the triumph of *Billy Budd, Sailor* (written 1888–91, published 1924)—all pose a problem as to their exact kind or genre. Did Melville in fact write *novels* as such? Would not "fiction of fact" or "nonfictional novel" be more, or at least equally, apt? How best to categorize each narrative with its "isolato" storyteller (Tommo, Typee, Taji, Ishmael, Redburn, and White-Jacket)? As quest, or playfield, or anatomy? Is there not, too, most of all in *Moby-Dick, Pierre* (1852), and *The Confidence-Man* (1857), the anticipation of a later age's concern with reflexivity, self-reference, narratives told in canny and often exuberant recognition of their own telling? Little wonder that, for all his busy, firsthand factuality of Atlantic and Pacific seafaring and the modern city, Melville has increasingly been claimed as a precursor of American literary modernism and, in its wake, of the whole postmodern turn.

Certainly, Melville knew that he was not writing well-made Victorian domestic novels. His unabating curiosity and sense of the world's contradiction pressed too hard for that. Yet each "voyage thither" (to use his subtitle for *Mardi,* 1849), each of the journeys-out, labyrinths, becalmings, and entombments creates a pattern and organizing voice for the work it figures in. Perhaps his celebrated observation in "The Honor and Glory of Whaling" in *Moby-Dick*—"There are some enterprises in which a careful disorderliness is the true method"—is the most accurate description of his own work.

The balance of care and disorder can be seen in the "strife as memory" and "moods variable" of the Civil War poetry of *Battle-Pieces and Aspects of the War* (1866); in the dialectical quest for faith of his massive verse epic, *Clarel* (1876); in "Hawthorne and His Mosses" (1850), which is as much about Melville's own habits of subterfuge and ambiguity in "the great Art of Telling the Truth" as it is about Hawthorne; and in the correspondence with Hawthorne, Evert Duyckinck, and R.H. Dana ("to cook the thing up, one must throw in a little fancy," about *Moby-Dick*). Each helps to situate Melville as fiction writer with a dramatic sense of appetite tempered by craft and the shrewdest imaginative guile.

Virtually every one of his narratives ostentatiously displays a naive disorder. *Typee* (1846) speaks of offering the "unvarnished truth" of a ship desertion and Polynesian hiding-out. Yet a more equivocating orchestration of imperfect opposites could not be imagined: colonizing and exploitative Euro-America is confronted with cannibal Typee Valley, with its tattoos, sag-eyed gods, and "noble savagery." *Omoo* (1847), an island-odyssey sequel, could as easily be travelogue or diary as novel. And in *Mardi,* Melville took a practice run for *Moby-Dick,* ostensibly yet another South Seas romance but in fact a bookish, mythopoeic 16-island fantasia informed by Melville's newly acquired reading, from Dante Alighieri to Thomas Carlyle, from William Shakespeare to the English romantics.

"Cakes and ale" and "beggarly" were Melville's own dismissive phrases for *Redburn* (1849), as if the poor sales of *Mardi* and his publisher's reproofs had clipped his imaginative wings. Yet the Atlantic sea voyage of its neophyte hero again shows a far savvier compositional dexterity than he himself acknowledged. The novel carefully balances the linked narrative drama of life above and below deck aboard a merchantman; the malign, consumptive figure of Jackson; Liverpool as a City of Dreadful Night; and the powerful scenes of delirium tremens, fever, and Irish steerage. *White Jacket* (1850), seemingly lacking a clear plotline, builds the return journey of an American navy frigate from the Marquesas into a species of documentary theatre, the battleline ship replete with naval hierarchy, custom, and lore as synecdoche for a "man-of-war" world.

Moby-Dick, "woven of ships' cables & hausers," "hell-fired," and full of "sea-room," as Melville at different times described it, poses a still greater challenge. It approaches epic and mock epic in equal measure. It combines Faustian revenge drama with contemplative anatomy, "boy's own whaling adventure" with a compelling journey of mind. For all the narrative impetus of the progress of the *Pequod,* the text approaches an anti-novel. Digressions like Melville's daringly symbolist "The Whiteness of The Whale," the riddle of Queequeg as a South Seas "Indian," the use of Ishmael to mediate Melville's meditations on the world as language, enfabulation, anatomy, conundrum—such elements undermine any conventional conception of the genre. However construed, *Moby-Dick* indeed remains a pursuit of light, whale oil functioning as a tongue-in-cheek metaphor for illumination. The novel also stands at the utter center of all North American narrative.

With *Pierre,* Melville's imagination turned inland, presenting a fable of a blighted "Old New York" dynasty that starts in a mock-bucolic mode and transforms itself to an urban fiction that casts Manhattan as penitentiary, nightmare, tomb. In the portrait of Pierre Glendinning, "Fool of Truth" and angry, embittered would-be author of his own "Book of Revelation," Melville turned romance on its head and created the foundation of such later, equally self-mirroring and writerly American fictions as John Barth's *The Sot-Weed Factor* (1960) and Vladimir Nabokov's *Pale Fire* (1962).

In *The Confidence-Man,* a dark, Voltairean satire of American optimism set on the Mississippi, Melville showed that his powers had anything but diminished. Yet another kind of travel fiction, which harks back to Geoffrey Chaucer's *Canterbury Tales* (written 1385–1400), John Bunyan's *Pilgrim's Progress* (1678, 1684), and Shakespeare's *As You Like It* (1623), *The Confidence-Man* offers pointers to much of Melville's theory and practice of fiction. The most important of those reflections on fiction is the thought that fiction "should present another world, and yet one to which we feel the tie." *Billy Budd,* Melville's fable of the Fall of Man set in the Napoleonic age and told as a man-of-war drama of impressment, accusation, and hanging, also addresses the play of fable and fact, story and history.

"Truth uncompromisingly told will always have its ragged edges," Melville writes. That can serve, in part or whole, as a closing recognition of the founding principle of Melville's work.

Α. ROBERT LEE

See also Moby-Dick

Biography

Born 1 August 1819 in New York City. Attended New York Male School; Albany Academy until the age of 12. Began working at age 12 as clerk, farmhand, and schoolteacher; ship's boy on the *St. Lawrence,* bound for Liverpool, 1839–40; ordinary seaman on the whaler *Achushnet,* 1841, jumping ship in the Marquesas in 1842; departed the islands on the Sydney whaling barque *Lucy Ann,* and jumped ship in Tahiti, 1842; harpooner on whaler *Charles and Henry,* out of Nantucket, in

southern Pacific, 1842–43; clerk and bookkeeper in general store, Honolulu, 1843; returned to Boston on US Navy frigate *United States,* 1843–44; writer from 1844; lived in New York, 1847–50, and Pittsfield, Massachusetts, 1850–63; toured countries in Near East and Europe, 1856–57; traveled on lecture circuits in the United States, 1857–60; lived in Washington, D.C., 1861–62, and in New York after 1863; district inspector of customs, New York, 1866–85. Died 28 September 1891.

Novels by Melville

Narrative of Four Months' Residence among the Natives of a Valley in the Marquesas Islands; or, A Peep at Polynesian Life, 1846; as *Typee,* 1846; revised edition, 1846
Omoo: A Narrative of Adventures in the South Seas, 1847
Mardi, and a Voyage Thither, 1849
Redburn, His First Voyage, 1849
White Jacket; or, The World in a Man-of-War, 1850
The Whale, 1851; as *Moby-Dick, or, The Whale,* 1851
Pierre; or, The Ambiguities, 1852
Israel Potter, His Fifty Years of Exile, 1855
The Confidence-Man, His Masquerade, 1857
Billy Budd, Sailor, 1924

Other Writings: stories, poetry, travelogues, letters, and lectures.

Further Reading

Bowen, Merlin, *The Long Encounter: Self and Experience in the Writings of Herman Melville,* Chicago: University of Chicago Press, 1960

Brodhead, Richard H., *Hawthorne, Melville, and the Novel,* Chicago: University of Chicago Press, 1976

Bryant, John, editor, *A Companion to Melville Studies,* New York: Greenwood Press, 1986

Chase, Richard Volney, *Herman Melville: Critical Study,* New York: Macmillan, 1949

Dimock, Wai-chee, *Empire for Liberty: Melville and the Poetics of Individualism,* Princeton, New Jersey: Princeton University Press, 1991

Dryden, Edgar A., *Melville's Thematics of Form: The Great Art of Telling the Truth,* Baltimore: Johns Hopkins University Press, 1968

Lee, A. Robert, editor, *Herman Melville: Reassessments,* London: Vision Press, and Totowa, New Jersey: Barnes and Noble, 1984

Pullin, Faith, editor, *New Perspectives on Melville,* Kent, Ohio: Kent State University Press, and Edinburgh: Edinburgh University Press, 1978

Samson, John, *White Lies: Melville's Narratives of Facts,* Ithaca, New York: Cornell University Press, 1989

Seelye, John, *Melville: The Ironic Diagram,* Evanston, Illinois: Northwestern University Press, 1970

Men in the Sun by Ghassān Kanafānī

Rijāl fī al-shams 1963

The modern Arabic novel has developed in a distinctly different fashion from the modern novel in the West. While we may speak of two traditions of the modern Western novel—one experimental and avant-garde belonging to the first decades of the 20th century, the other more socially conscious succeeding it—the modern Arabic novel, emerging in the middle of the 20th century, was socially conscious from the start, and this social consciousness has always taken precedence over other literary impulses. This has nowhere been more true than in Palestine, occupied since 1948, where the modern novel has defined itself, along with other forms of literature, primarily as an expression of political resistance, while narrative experimentation and subjective expression have developed only secondarily, in the shadow of this overwhelming preoccupation.

The early 1960s was a period of deepening political tensions in the region, presaging the Six-Day War of 1967. At the same time, it was a period in which the Arabic novel began to take an experimental turn under the influence of such Western trends as existentialism and the "theatre of the absurd." Ghassān Kanafānī's work exemplifies the confluence of these tendencies. A spokesman for the Popular Front for the Liberation of Palestine, and the editor of its weekly, *Al-Hadaf,* Kanafānī fled Palestine with his family in 1948, finally settling in Damascus. Later he moved to Kuwait, and then to Beirut. He was killed in the explosion of his booby-trapped car in 1972, thought to be the work of Israeli agents. What makes Kanafānī's work remarkable, given his position as a lifelong Palestinian refugee and activist, is that, unlike most politically committed writers of the time, he refused to resort to polemicism or to impose an ideological scheme on his fiction except in a general sense. Instead, he reworked his overtly political themes to give them a more profound, universal meaning.

Men in the Sun, Kanafānī's most famous work, is a short and powerful allegorical novel. Three Palestinians, each representing different generations and stations in life, attempt the difficult journey across the desert from Iraq to Kuwait in order to escape from their past lives. They are picked up by the driver of a water truck, who agrees to take them over the border inside the closed tank. The conditions inside the tanker as it travels under the blazing desert sun are life-threatening, and the fate of the passengers depends critically on the time it will take them to cross the border. A delay at the Kuwaiti border caused by the officials' refusal to sign the driver's papers and their foul jesting causes fatal minutes to pass for the men in the oven-like tank. By the time the driver has crossed the border and can open it, his three passengers are dead. In the ignominious conclusion, he leaves the corpses at the municipal dump and, not long after departing, returns to remove their valuables.

The story of the disaster that befalls the three passengers represents the larger tragedy that has befallen the Palestinian people. In particular, the novel may be read as an exposé of the weakness of the Palestinians, depicting them as weak-willed and preferring the search for material security to the fight to regain their land. The driver, Abū Khaizurān, represents the ineffective Palestinian leadership that has ultimately betrayed its own people and led them along the road to disaster. Khaizurān is a eunuch who has lost his masculinity by being wounded in battle, and his name, which means "bamboo," symbolizes an individual who seems impressive on the outside but is weak and hollow within.

While the political message is important, the structure of the work, its narrative technique, and its degree of interiorization make it highly innovative. Kanafānī focuses on each character in turn, centering his subject in each individual's consciousness. For instance, the narrative begins with an omen of death in which the first passenger, Abū Qays, who has come the long way from Palestine to the Shatt al-Arab waterway in the southern part of Iraq (near the Kuwaiti border), is resting on the moist earth as a black bird circles high above. The stream-of-consciousness element in the narrative emphasizes the existential quality of his situation:

> He turned himself over and lay on his back, cradling his head in his hands. He started to stare at the sky. It was blazing white, and there was one black bird circling high up, alone and aimless. He did not know why, but he was suddenly filled with a bitter feeling of being a stranger, and for a moment he thought he was on the point of weeping. No, yesterday it didn't rain. We are in August now. Have you forgotten? Those miles of road speeding through a void, like black eternity? Have you forgotten it? The bird was still circling round alone like a black spot in the blaze spread out above him. We are in August. Then why this dampness in the ground? It's the Shatt. Can't you see it stretching out beside you as far as the eye can see?

It is the ending, however, that gives *Men in the Sun* its absurdist flavor. Kanafānī intends to pose the existential question of whether or not one can have control over one's destiny with respect to the issue of national will, purpose, and destiny. The conclusion is open-ended. We do not know why the passengers choose to die rather than risk discovery and imprisonment. Abū Khaizurān's questioning, however, transcends issues of individual and collective guilt, bringing the novel to a close on a subjective note of despair and questioning:

> He turned to look back to where he had left the corpses, but he could see nothing, and that glance simply set the thought ablaze so that it began to burn in his mind. All at once he could no longer keep it within his head, and he dropped his hands to his sides and stared into the darkness with his eyes wide open.
>
> The thought slipped from his mind and ran on to his tongue: "Why didn't they knock on the sides of the tank?" He turned round once, but he was afraid he would fall, so he climbed into his seat and leant his head on the wheel.
>
> "Why didn't you knock on the sides of the tank? Why didn't you say anything? Why?"

STEFAN MEYER

See also Ghassān Kanafānī

Further Reading

Audebert, C.F., "Choice and Responsibility in *Rijāl fī al-shams*," *Journal of Arabic Literature* 15 (1984)

Harlow, Barbara, "Readings of National Identity in the Palestinian Novel," in *The Arabic Novel Since 1950: Critical Essays, Interviews, and Bibliography*, edited by Issa J. Boullata and Roger Allen, Cambridge, Massachusetts: Dar Mahjar, 1992

Kilpatrick, Hilary, "Tradition and Innovation in the Fiction of Ghassān Kanafānī," *Journal of Arabic Literature* 7 (1976)

Layoun, Mary, *Travels of a Genre: The Modern Novel and Ideology*, Princeton, New Jersey: Princeton University Press, 1990

Magrath, Douglas R., "A Study of *Rijāl fī al-shams*, by Ghassān Kanafānī," *Journal of Arabic Literature* 10 (1979)

Men of Maize by Miguel Ángel Asturias

Hombres de maíz 1949

Writing in 1967, at the height of the boom of the Latin American novel, the Chilean writer Ariel Dorfman declared: "Although its origins are lost in remote regions and its socio-cultural coordinates are still debated, the contemporary Latin American novel has a quite precise date of birth. It is the year 1949, when Alejo Carpentier's *The Kingdom of This World* and Miguel Ángel Asturias' *Men of Maize* appeared. Although the latter novel is the source and backbone of all that is being written in our continent today, it has suffered a strange fate, like so many other works which open an era and close the past." The "strange fate" to which Dorfman referred was the fact that the novel was "consistently underrated by critics and neglected by readers."

Things have changed significantly in the 30 years after Dorfman's complaint. *Men of Maize* supplanted *El Señor Presidente* (1946; *The President*) as Asturias' most admired novel. It was translated into English in 1974, and it inspired critical editions in both Spanish (1981, 1992) and English (1993). Little by little, *Men of Maize* began to occupy the historical place that Dorfman had claimed for it—as precursor of the 1960s boom and as a unique and remarkable literary reflection of extraordinarily complex social, cultural, and aesthetic problems. *Men of Maize* is, indeed, a text that situates its author's own experience of life within the history of his country and his continent, implying a meditation on the meaning of Latin America within world history and, simultaneously, on the meaning of humanity's emergence from "primitive," preliterate societies on the road to the contemporary capitalist world. It is perhaps not surprising that such a conception—which might be called "Joycean"—gave rise to a literary structure whose complexity has been difficult for readers to assimilate.

In its most elementary terms, Asturias' novel sets out to resolve one of the most enduring problems confronted by Latin American novelists: namely, how to do justice to the essential "hybridity" or "heterogeneity" of the region's complex cultural identity. In the case of Guatemala, this involves exploring first of all the great Mayan civilization that dominated Central America long before the arrival of the Spaniards in the 1520s. The novel also portrays the culture of its heirs, the Indians who still live in scattered highland maize-based communities throughout the region. Finally, the European cultural traditions of the Spanish invaders and their descendants, the "Ladinos" (Mestizos) who have governed Guatemala since the early 19th century, also find a place in *Men of Maize*.

Asturias' solution is one of astonishing complexity, but also of remarkable lucidity. He shows that the struggle of the Indians against the Ladinos in the 20th century is an endlessly reenacted continuation of the war between the Spaniards and the Maya of the 16th century. These two conflictive phases are then superimposed on an even vaster canvas, itself dual, in which the experience of loss undergone by every human being from birth to maturity is used to chart humankind's inherently violent dialectical transition from the "state of nature" to the West's contemporary technological civilization. In practice, this involves a text that resembles a Maya bas-relief, in which each minute glyph is multiply connected both to the glyphs surrounding it and to the aesthetic and thematic structure of the whole. At the same time, the initial tightness of this design is gradually loosened as the dense weave of tribal culture—poetic, paradigmatic, connotative, based on economic and kinship relations that are impossible to disentangle—gradually unravels into the relentlessly linear, prosaic, and positivistic 20th-century experience, associated with metonymy and displacement, in which individualism, alienation, transience, and death form a persistent equation.

The novel is organized symbolically in three historical phases—tribal, feudal-colonial, and capitalist-neocolonial—in each of which an Indian protagonist is defeated, loses his intimate relationship both to the earth and to the feminine other, and turns to alcohol and despair. Each of these phases, based on modes of production, is aligned mythologically with the three-part Mayan structure of the universe—underworld, earth, sky (past, present, future)—which is the trajectory of Quetzalcoatl, the plumed serpent and Meso-American culture hero. His inherently Freudian trajectory, an endlessly repeated irruption from prehistory, is itself based on the sun's daily journey around the sky and beneath the earth.

The result of this conception is that the contemporary characters live in a cosmic eternity, whether they know it or not, although Asturias is also concerned to emphasize the insistent gestural spontaneity and violence that Franz Fanon identified as key aspects of third world experience and revolutionary writing. Finally, the reader may conclude that, in retrospect, it is astonishing that a novel written in 1949, with such a focus on the historical past, should also have foreseen so many central themes of Latin America's future. The most striking of these, undoubtedly, are the turn to guerrilla warfare and the shadow of ecological catastrophe: both are posited on the novel's very first page.

GERALD MARTIN

See also Miguel Ángel Asturias

Further Reading

Brotherston, Gordon, *The Emergence of the Latin American Novel,* Cambridge and New York: Cambridge University Press, 1977

Callan, Richard J., *Miguel Ángel Asturias,* New York: Twayne, 1970

Harss, Luis, and Barbara Dohmann, *Into the Mainstream: Conversations with Latin American Writers,* New York: Harper and Row, 1967

Martin, Gerald, *Journeys through the Labyrinth: Latin American Fiction in the Twentieth Century,* London and New York: Verso, 1989

Prieto, René, *Miguel Ángel Asturias's Archeology of Return,* Cambridge and New York: Cambridge University Press, 1993

George Meredith 1828–1909

English

George Meredith's career as novelist stretches over a major portion of the later Victorian period, from *The Ordeal of Richard Feverel* (1859) to his last completed novel, *The Amazing Marriage* (1895). The course of that career, and its aftermath, was and continues to be an erratic combination of success and failure, beginning with the withdrawal of *The Ordeal of Richard Feverel* from the novel list of Mudie's, the largest of the circulating libraries, owing to "the urgent remonstrances of several respectable families, who objected to it as dangerous and wicked and damnable." In spite of this unfortunate initial bout with the constraints imposed by the Victorian reading public, Meredith gradually developed an enthusiastic, if limited, following of intellectuals who admired his work. Robert Louis Stevenson, when he referred to himself as a "true-blue Meredith man," could also have been speaking for the likes of Leslie Stephen, John Morley, J. M. Barrie, and Oscar Wilde, to name a few. Meredith's popularity reached its peak in the early 1890s, and, three decades later, when Virginia Woolf looked back at this period, she ranked Meredith along with Henry James as the two most influential novelists of her parents' generation.

There is a direct connection between Meredith's rejection by "Mudie and the British Matron" and Virginia Woolf's acknowledgment of his extraordinary influence on her and her fellow practitioners of the early modern English novel. This connection consists in what Woolf herself described as the "experimental" quality of Meredith's fiction; she saw him as "a brilliant and uneasy figure" who "excites our interest as a great innovator" (*The Second Common Reader,* 1932). And this edgy, avant-garde quality is what continues to excite—and repel—interest in Meredith today, as his novels are increasingly seen as significant precursors to modernist fiction. What this quality means above all else is that Meredith seemed instinctively to question and disrupt novelistic tradition as well as Victorian popular values and taste (*pace* Mudie and the British Matron).

Meredith's novelistic experimentation, then, involved sometimes radical innovations in narrative technique and uses of genre as well as controversial contemporary themes—qualities found in abundance in such novels as *The Ordeal of Richard Feverel, One of Our Conquerors* (1891), and *The Amazing Marriage.* The innovative/protomodernist impulse in Meredith is manifested at various points in his fiction by a self-reflexive and artificial style, by a dialogic narrative interaction between playful and competing voices that suggests a corresponding distrust of such abstractions as truth and identity (in *Sandra Belloni* [1886] and *The Amazing Marriage,* for example, there is a literal struggle between two narrators, one preoccupied with storytelling, the other with analysis), by the depiction of a disintegrating subject (Richard Feverel, Purcell Barrett in *Sandra Belloni,* Richmond Roy in *The Adventures of Harry Richmond* [1871], Willoughby Patterne in *The Egoist* [1879], Victor Radnor in *One of Our Conquerors,* and Lord Fleetwood in *The Amazing Marriage* all develop into highly unstable personalities), by the use of the city as a setting for disorientation and loss, especially in *The Ordeal of Richard Feverel, The Adventures of Harry Richmond,* and *One of Our Conquerors,* and, late in Meredith's career, by a rendering of characters' thoughts that suggests the simultaneity of past, present, and future we identify with stream-of-consciousness writing, seen especially in the depiction of Victor Radnor's troubled mental associations in *One of Our Conquerors.*

In addition, we can see the questioning impulse of a modernist sensibility in Meredith's distrust of traditional generic boundaries (see separate entry on *The Ordeal of Richard Feverel* for the most famous example of Meredith's generic transgressions), in his repeated and increasingly radical questioning of proper roles for women in marriage and society (Meredith's 19th-century feminism is evident from the beginning of his career, but particularly central to his last four novels), and in his running critique of the endemic sentimental egoism he saw everywhere cloaking the presumptions of Victorian patriarchy (most famously dramatized in *The Egoist*).

Another element that is essential to appreciating Meredith's originality is his invocation of an ethic of "common sense," seen everywhere in his fiction but articulated most cogently in his famous *An Essay on Comedy* (originally titled *On the Idea of Comedy and the Uses of the Comic Spirit,* 1897). This principle of common sense provides a traditionalist basis to Meredith's experimental agenda, underlying everything from his feminism to his rejection of the limitations of genre. This recurring rationalist principle provides a coherence in Meredith's work, a consistent attitude toward the self-defeating actions of men and women, whether those actions lead to the "laughter of the mind" described in *An Essay on Comedy,* to a world of impossible romance, to tragedy, or, as is the case in *The Ordeal of Richard Feverel,* in all of these directions. For Meredith, it is betrayals of common sense—the lapses into sentimental egoism—that account for human absurdity as well as for much of human suffering. The tension that develops between Meredithian common sense and this sentimental egoism is central to all of his fiction.

There is, then, an orientation in Meredith that is both forward- and backward-looking, a radical/conservative outlook that can help one to understand Meredith's strategic role in the history of the novel. While Meredith refers to rational norms associated with classicism and the 18th century, he also invokes these traditional values as the basis for his radical critique of—and departure from—what he saw as regressive or merely trendy in Victorian art and society. The experimental and questioning instinct in Meredith is inseparable from this strong rationalist bias.

Another point is equally important in this context, however, and that is Meredith's recognition of the limitations of the rational component. From the beginning of his career Meredith insisted upon the need for harmonious balance within the triad of "blood and brain and spirit." The characterization of Sir Austin Feverel in his first novel immediately suggests Meredith's keen sense of the extreme dangers of a purely rationalist androcentric position. Instead, the term *common sense,* as he uses and dramatizes it in his fiction, suggests a Meredithian union of intellectual and emotional intelligence combined with a Goethean openness to the many-sidedness of life.

RICHARD C. STEVENSON

See also Ordeal of Richard Feverel

Biography

Born 12 February 1828 in Portsmouth, Hampshire. Attended St. Paul's Church School, Southsea, Hampshire, and another boarding school, possibly in Suffolk; Moravian School, Neuwied sur Rhine, Germany, 1843–44; articled to a solicitor in London, 1846–49. Coeditor, *Monthly Observer,* London, 1848–49; contributor, *Chambers Journal,* 1849, and *Fraser's Magazine,* 1851–52, both London; columnist, Ipswich *Chronicle,* Suffolk, 1858–68; contributor, 1860–1909, and editor, 1867–68, *Fortnightly Review,* London; reader and literary adviser, Chapman and Hall publishers, London, 1860–94, and also for Saunders and Otley publishers; contributor, *Pall Mall Gazette,* London, 1860s; special correspondent, *Morning Post,* London, during Austro-Italian war, 1866; relocated to Box Hill, Surrey, 1868; columnist ("Up

to Midnight"), *Graphic,* 1872–73; lectured on comedy at the London Institute, 1877. Died 18 May 1909.

Novels by Meredith

The Ordeal of Richard Feverel: A History of Father and Son, 1859; revised edition, 1878
Evan Harrington; or, He Would Be a Gentleman, 1861
Emilia in England, 1864; as *Sandra Belloni,* 1886
Rhoda Fleming, 1865
Vittoria, 1866
The Adventures of Harry Richmond, 1871
Beauchamp's Career, 1875
The Egoist: A Comedy in Narrative, 1879
The Tragic Comedians, 1880
Diana of the Crossways, 1885
One of Our Conquerors, 1891
Lord Ormont and His Aminta, 1894
The Amazing Marriage, 1895
Celt and Saxon, 1910

Other Writings: like Thomas Hardy, Meredith saw himself as a poet who supported himself by writing fiction; he published close to a dozen books of poetry over the period 1851–1909. His most famous poetical work, "Modern Love" (1862), is a sequence of 50 16-line poems depicting the failure of a marriage, written soon after the breakdown of Meredith's own first marriage to Mary Peacock Nicolls. In addition, he published numerous short stories and novella-length "tales." His collected letters are edited by C.L. Cline, *The Letters of George Meredith* (3 vols., 1970).

Further Reading

Beer, Gillian, *Meredith: A Change of Masks,* London: Athlone Press, 1970
Fletcher, Ian, *Meredith Now: Some Critical Essays,* London: Routledge and Kegan Paul, and New York: Barnes and Noble, 1971
Handwerk, Gary J., *Irony and Ethics in Narrative: From Schlegel to Lacan,* New Haven, Connecticut: Yale University Press, 1985
Morgan, Susan, *Sisters in Time: Imagining Gender in Nineteenth-Century British Fiction,* New York: Oxford University Press, 1989
Moses, Joseph, *The Novelist as Comedian: George Meredith and the Ironic Sensibility,* New York: Schocken, 1983
Roberts, Neil, *Meredith and the Novel,* New York: St. Martin's Press, 1997
Stevenson, Lionel, *The Ordeal of George Meredith,* New York: Scribner, 1953; London: Owen, 1954
Stone, Donald D., *Novelists in a Changing World: Meredith, James, and the Transformation of English Fiction in the 1880s,* Cambridge, Massachusetts: Harvard University Press, 1972
Williams, Ioan, editor, *Meredith: The Critical Heritage,* London: Routledge and Kegan Paul, and New York: Barnes and Noble, 1971
Wilt, Judith, *The Readable People of George Meredith,* Princeton, New Jersey: Princeton University Press, 1975

Mertvye dushi. *See* Dead Souls

Metafiction

Metafiction is a style of fictive narrative that explores the conditions of its own making. The term *metafiction* literally means "after" or "about" fiction, and practitioners of this type of writing have tended to employ metafictional techniques in order to undermine the element of illusion that characterizes the traditional realist novel. Antimimetic in nature, it discards such conventions as the reflection of reality and the willing suspension of disbelief in order to display the writer's act of fabrication as it happens. In its many varieties, metafiction may employ the author as a self-evident figure present within his or her work (as happens in Kurt Vonnegut's novel, *Slaughterhouse-Five*, 1969); highlight the physical act of typing words onto the page (as does Raymond Federman's novel *Double or Nothing*, 1971); or involve the mechanical operations of bookmaking (as does Italo Calvino in *Se una notte d'inverno un viaggiatore* [1979; *If on a winter's night a traveler*]). Especially popular during the 1960s and 1970s, "metafiction" as a term endured some critical misuse as an umbrella label for any novel or short story that was not traditionally realistic. Most properly, the term designates fiction writing that not only draws attention to the author's act of composition but makes that act the work's subject matter.

Contemporary practitioners of metafiction are fond of citing its 18th-century origins, particularly Laurence Sterne's *Tristram Shandy* (1759–67) and Denis Diderot's *Jacques le fataliste* (1796; *Jacques the Fatalist*). Because metafictional works of the 1960s and 1970s were often attacked as illegitimate forms of fiction, metafictional writers looked back to Sterne and Diderot as authors yet unencumbered by the realistic tradition. Two hundred years ago, today's metafictionalists reasoned, the novel could have developed in other ways; only long usage and enforced familiarity allowed the representational novel to become the only acceptable form for book-length fiction. Yet this argument has its limits. Even in *Tristram Shandy* the illusion is maintained that the narrator is telling a "real" story, one that is represented as having happened in the world, the same device Henry Fielding uses as a justification to counter Samuel Richardson's ploy of outfitting his own novels as bundles of letters in order to explain the narrative's reason for being. Metafiction in the hands of a contemporary master such as Ronald Sukenick or Gilbert Sorrentino forgoes even Sterne's pretense of representing an external action; in their hands, writing becomes truly metafictive, practicing no illusion whatsoever.

The first modern example of metafiction is Flann O'Brien's *At Swim-Two-Birds* (1939). Conceived as an antidote to fellow Irishman James Joyce's weighty stylistics and ponderously serious myth making, O'Brien's novel is a self-consciously comic delight in which an author writing just such a work begins by commenting on the task. Three different beginnings are submitted for the reader's choice: one involves a mythic character, the giant Finn Mac Cool; another describes a more quaint figure from Irish folklore, the Pooka MacPhellimey ("a member of the devil class"); and the third presents what would seem to be a conventionally drawn realistic character, Mr. John Furriskey. Yet no sooner do these narratives get underway than they infiltrate and corrupt one another. To make things worse, the characters of the otherwise realistic plot dislike the motivations they are given toward sin; ashamed at what their author has devised for them, they revolt, eventually lulling him to sleep so they can rewrite the action more to their liking.

Metafiction flourished in the United States during the socially disruptive decades of the 1960s and 1970s. Its challenge to traditional realism may be viewed alongside political and cultural transformations of the times. Its impulse came from an equally new quarter: not from British or continental fiction, which previously had been the strongest influences on American writing, but from South America. Signaling this shift in influence was novelist John Barth's important essay "The Literature of Exhaustion," first appearing in *The Atlantic* in August 1967 and later collected in Barth's *The Friday Book* (1984). Believing that widespread practice had exhausted the novelty of the novel and that its conventions were "used up," Barth proposed following the example of the Argentine Jorge Luis Borges and focusing on the "felt ultimacies" of such exhausted fiction as its own subject. A more metafictional angle was taken by Borges' countryman Julio Cortázar, whose novel *Rayuela* (1963; *Hopscotch*) assumes a different meaning if its 155 chapters are read in alternative orders. Climaxing this self-described "boom" in Spanish American literature were the magical realist novels of Gabriel García Márquez, a Colombian whose offhand incorporation of patently unrealistic materials made his otherwise realistic narratives read quite differently from conventional fiction.

Among the American novelists most immediately influenced by these and other South American writers were Barth himself, Robert Coover, and William H. Gass. Barth's stories collected in *Lost in the Funhouse* (1968) stem from his arguments in "The Literature of Exhaustion," which now reads as an apology for his subsequent work. In Robert Coover's *The Universal Baseball Association, Inc., J. Henry Waugh, Prop.* (1968), a metafictive situation is dramatized. Waugh, a lonely bachelor, fills his time by devising and playing a complex statistical card-table baseball game. Complete with league histories and player personalities, the action of this game takes on a viability of its own. Soon, the narrative has moved to the level of the ballplayers, who can ponder the motives of J. Henry Waugh only as humanity can construct theologies for divine purpose. The most extreme example of American metafiction is Gass' *Willie Masters' Lonesome Wife* (1971), in which writing is the subject and physical love only a metaphor for its actions. Printed on four different colors of paper and in many differing typefaces (most of which are arranged artfully on the page), Gass' novella, in its very presence, refuses to be taken for anything other than what it is: not a narrative about something else but a testimony to its own presence as a literary artifact.

"It seems a country-headed thing to say," Gass volunteers in his *Fiction and the Figures of Life* (1970), "that literature is language, that stories and the places and the people in them are merely made of words as chairs are made of smoothed sticks and sometimes of cloth or metal tubes." Yet both writer and reader can benefit from the metafictive impulse, if only to keep them anchored where they belong. "It seems incredible," Gass explains, "the ease with which we sink through books quite out of sight, pass clamorous pages into soundless dreams. That novels should be made of words, is shocking, really. It's as though you had discovered that your wife were made of rubber: the bliss of all those years, the fears . . . from sponge." Hence the attention-getting devices of *Willie Masters' Lonesome Wife* and the equally radical experiments undertaken by Gass' contemporaries, all of which are meant to reaffirm fiction's essentially metafictive nature.

A more aggressive motive for metafiction characterizes Gilbert Sorrentino's work. An accomplished poet, critic, and editor who had little patience for the thoughtlessly formulaic fiction that crowded the marketplace, Sorrentino raged against tradition in his essays and novels. "Novels are cluttered with all kinds of signals," Sorrentino notes in "The Various Isolated: William Carlos Williams' Prose," a 1972 essay collected in *Something Said* (1984)—"flashing and gesturing so that the author may direct our attention to a particular configuration of character or plot in order that his work, such as it is, may be made simpler for him, and for us." The nature of such signals is that they "assure us that we are here, oh yes, in the world that we understand; what we 'understand' are the signals." The problem with this approach, Sorrentino continues, is that "signals are gimmicks, elements of craftsmanship, or the lack of it. They allow the writer to slip out from under problems that only confrontation with his materials can solve. Novels are made of words. The difficulty in writing fiction is that the words must be composed so that they reveal the absolute reality of their prey, their subject—and at the same time, they must be real; i.e., they do not have to stand for a specific meaning."

Sorrentino's own novels are hilarious examples of how metafiction can serve such critical purpose. *Imaginative Qualities of Actual Things* (1971) has much of the roman à clef to it; as a story based on the 1960s New York art world, it is replete with insider references and slightly veiled characterizations of actual painters, poets, and critics of the time. Yet the narrative voice expresses such distaste for this world that it almost immediately becomes vindictively metafictive. When the author dislikes a character, he says so and makes gleeful comments about how he will punish this figure by subjecting him or her to astounding indignities. Passing comments are given sarcastically dismissive footnotes; themes and subthemes cross and tangle in a manner that defies any other logic than the author's own malevolent purpose. A longer example of Sorrentino's metafiction is his 200,000-word novel, *Mulligan Stew* (1979). Inspired by Flann O'Brien's *At Swim-Two-Birds,* it incorporates many of that novel's devices while taking into account a half-century of worldwide novelistic experiment subsequent to O'Brien's classic

work. Characters go on strike against their author and undertake various subversions of his text. Sorrentino also registers his complaints about the commercial publishing world, including rejection letters from a wide range of houses that were deeply dissatisfied with the manuscript.

Throughout the 1960s and 1970s, American writers reveled in the great potentiality of metafiction. Raymond Federman's *Double or Nothing* had to be published with its author's typescript photo reproduced, as typesetting would have obscured its unique typographic achievement. Each page presents a different physical structure, such as typing a page of narrative in the form of a Christmas tree. To complete the metafictive picture, Federman presents a novelist (much like himself) setting up to write a novel—renting a room to which he will confine himself with enough food and supplies to last a year. Computations necessary to effect this plan begin on page one and never end, for by the narrative's closure it becomes apparent that an initial miscalculation means the entire plan will have to be refigured.

Even more concrete metafictive devices were devised by Ronald Sukenick and Walter Abish. In his novel *Out* (1973) Sukenick numbers his chapters backward, beginning with 10 and ending with 0. For each chapter the typesetting changes, beginning with ten lines of print and then for chapter 9 dropping one line of print and adding a correlative line of space, chapter 8 offering 8 lines of print for each 2 lines of space, until as the end approaches the reader is flipping through pages at an accelerated speed. Then, with chapter 0, the print disappears, leaving nothing but blankness. This mechanical device complements the novel's action, a cross-country trip from the clutter of New York to the openness of California (ending with the vast emptiness of the Pacific Ocean). Abish's *Alphabetical Africa* (1974) uses the alphabet rather than numbers for its chapter titles. In chapter A every word begins with the letter A: "Ages ago, Alex, Allen and Alva arrived at Antibes, and Alva allowing all, allowing anyone, against Alex's admonition, against Allen's angry assertion: another African amusement, . . ." Chapter B allows words beginning with that letter to enter the mix, until by chapter Z the full alphabet is available. Thus the first-person narrator cannot appear until chapter I. It would be difficult to imagine a more emphatic reminder that fiction is made of words. Yet Abish does just this in his novel's second half, a set of chapters beginning with Z and proceeding backward. Now persons, places, and things depart from the narrative after their lettered chapter, until at the end readers are again left with only the letter A. The novel itself, together with its possibilities, expands and contracts before the viewer's eyes. A more extreme example of metafiction has not yet been written.

Metafiction's novelty enhanced its popularity, but this same novelty prompted many of its practitioners to abandon such experiments and reembrace traditions of mimetic fiction. Yet their narratives profited from their earlier rigorous interrogations, to the point that the compositional self became a much more important factor. A good example is found in the work of Kurt Vonnegut, which in the 1970s, 1980s, and 1990s took greater liberties with the writer's own obvious presence, as opposed to the subgeneric excuses (dystopian fiction, spy thrillers, apocalyptic tales) that had been used for his earlier novels of the 1950s and 1960s.

Metafiction's great success remains an American phenomenon. Although writers in England were less disposed to experiment with the form, some metafictional techniques were employed there; the most popular example is John Fowles' self-conscious storytelling. The continental novel's metafictive shadings were drawn more from language theory than from narrative art. The most successful were outright employment of details from book manufacturing by Italo Calvino, himself a publishing executive.

JEROME KLINKOWITZ

See also Framing and Embedding; Historical Writing and the Novel; Postmodernism

Further Reading

Klinkowitz, Jerome, *Literary Disruptions: The Making of a Post-Contemporary American Fiction*, Urbana: University of Illinois Press, 1975, 2nd edition, 1980

Klinkowitz, Jerome, *The Self-Apparent Word: Fiction as Language/Language as Fiction*, Carbondale: Southern Illinois University Press, 1984

Scholes, Robert, *Fabulation and Metafiction*, Urbana: University of Illinois Press, 1979

Spencer, Sharon, *Space, Time and Structure in the Modern Novel*, New York: New York University Press, 1971

Sukenick, Ronald, *In Form: Digressions on the Act of Fiction*, Carbondale: Southern Illinois University Press, 1985

Thiher, Allen, *Words in Reflection: Modern Language Theory and Postmodern Fiction*, Chicago: University of Chicago Press, 1984

Waugh, Patricia, *Metafiction*, London and New York: Methuen, 1984

Mexican Novel. *See* Latin American Novel: Mexico

Middlemarch by George Eliot

1872

In a review of *Middlemarch*, Edith Simcox remarked, "To say that *Middlemarch* is George Eliot's greatest work is to say that it has scarcely a superior and very few equals in the whole wide range of English fiction." This opinion reflected the contemporary consensus, and although Eliot's reputation declined in the early modernist period, by midcentury *Middlemarch* had again achieved a firm standing as one of the greatest of all English novels, and it can reasonably be ranked among the masterpieces of world fiction.

Middlemarch is Eliot's seventh substantial piece of fiction, her sixth novel, and her penultimate novel. In retrospect, all her previous works seem like preliminary studies or sketches for portions of this one grand novel. While absorbing her previous experiments in genre, characterization, and theme, *Middlemarch* adds entirely new elements, and it fuses all the elements into a satisfying artistic whole. The one novel that follows *Middlemarch, Daniel Deronda* (1876), is equal in intellectual sophistication, but it has a smaller scope of action and less variety of portrayal, and it has commonly and correctly been felt to fall into two parts, a psychological study in the mode of severe ironic realism and a symbolic drama, strained and fantastic, in the mode of utopian idealism. For most readers, *Middlemarch* remains the richest and most complete realization of Eliot's genius.

There are three main stories or sets of dramatic relations: Dorothea Brooke and her two husbands, Edward Casaubon and Will Ladislaw; Tertius Lydgate and Rosamond Vincy; and Fred Vincy and Mary Garth. The banker Bulstrode is involved in Lydgate's downfall, but late in the narrative he also emerges as a center of dramatic interest. For many readers the central character of the novel is Dorothea Brooke, a spiritually ardent and emotionally passionate young woman. Dorothea seeks to break free from the constraints of the conventional roles accorded to women and to achieve some higher order of existence. In this effort she is the culminating figure in a sequence that includes—from Eliot's other works—the methodist preacher Dinah Morris in *Adam Bede* (1859), the autobiographical Maggie Tulliver in *The Mill on the Floss* (1860), and the Renaissance Florentine Romola in the novel of that title (1863). In her moral and social idealism, Dorothea also assimilates Eliot's depiction of the eponymous Felix Holt (1866), and in her energetic exercise of imaginative sympathy she prefigures Daniel Deronda.

Fred Vincy is the culminating figure in a series of weak but well-intentioned young men that includes Arthur Donnithorne in *Adam Bede* and Godfrey Cass in *Silas Marner* (1861). Adam Bede, a young carpenter, is modeled on Eliot's own father, and a similar character, in middle age, appears as Mary Garth's father,

Caleb. Will Ladislaw's sympathy with Dorothea's desire for a wider life affiliates him with Philip Wakem in *The Mill on the Floss,* and his cultivated aesthetic temperament affiliates him with Stephen Guest in the same novel. Mrs. Poyser, the sharp-tongued, strong-minded matron from *Adam Bede,* prefigures Mary Garth's mother. The relationship between Fred Vincy and Mary Garth turns on the sacrosanct character of fidelity, and it thus resumes a central theme from *The Mill on the Floss.* The reverend Farebrother, closely involved with both Lydgate and the Garths, is Eliot's finest depiction in a gallery of worldly clergymen, scant on doctrine but of sterling character, that includes Mr. Gilfil in *Scenes of Clerical Life* (1858) and Mr. Irwine in *Adam Bede.*

Two of the main characters in *Middlemarch,* Lydgate and Mary Garth, have no antecedents in Eliot's work. These two characters personify crucial aspects of Eliot's own narrative persona, and their inclusion no doubt helps account for the exceptional range and power of Eliot's commentary in this novel. Lydgate is a young doctor with ardent scientific aspirations, and Mary is a young woman who is plain and socially obscure but who has impressive powers of humorous observation and vigorous moral judgment. Through Lydgate, Eliot depicts an intellectual passion for diagnostic understanding. "He wanted to pierce the obscurity of those invisible thoroughfares which prepare human misery and joy." Eliot, too, seeks to pierce this obscurity, and Lydgate is one of the chief objects of her incisive analysis. Mary holds the perspective of the satirist, taking life as a comedy and observing that "people were so ridiculous with their illusions, carrying their fool's caps unawares." Through Dorothea, Lydgate, and Mary, Eliot fashions an internal dramatic correlative for the tonal interplay among chief elements of her own persona: her spiritual fervor, the cerebral intensity of her dispassionate scientific analysis, and the angry contempt of her satiric revelations.

The formal order of the novel integrates two polar principles: one of social and psychological realism and the other of thematic and symbolic structure. At the level of social and psychological realism, the plan of the novel is suggested in the subtitle, *A Study of Provincial Life.* The setting is given precise geographical and historical specification: a Midlands industrial and commercial town in the years just before the first reform bill and the coming of the railroads. The multitude of characters provides a representative cross section of this social world. At the level of symbolic and thematic signification, the main characters exemplify both elemental qualities of temperament and sexual identity and also cultural forces specific to their time. Dorothea's marriage with Ladislaw symbolically represents traditional Christian spiritualism in the process of being absorbed and transformed both by romantic aestheticism and by Victorian social idealism. Lydgate's scientific objectivity is correlated with his arrogance and his insensitivity, and in the larger movement of the plot, his specifically masculine ethos is subordinated to Dorothea's female ethos of communitarian sympathy. At a period of political upheaval and tumultuous industrial development,

Fred Vincy ineffectually clings to an older tradition of genteel idleness, but he ultimately submits to the bourgeois work ethic exemplified by the Garths.

In the geniality of its humor, the moral resonance of its satire, and the rich array of its tonal palette, *Middlemarch* has qualities peculiarly English. Eliot is the legitimate heir to Henry Fielding and Jane Austen, and a peer of Charles Dickens and William Makepeace Thackeray. Although capable of an ironic social realism as tough-minded as that of Honoré de Balzac or Gustave Flaubert, she also has qualities of kindly humor and moral refinement that are alien to them. Eliot shares with Lev Tolstoi the power of panoramic social display and sustained psychological analysis, and she influences the efforts of Marcel Proust to evoke the development of an inner sense of personal identity. By making the psychological development of her characters the chief moving principle in the construction of her narrative, Eliot serves as the single most important model for Henry James. Through her assimilation of the subjects of fiction to the meditative power of the modern intellect, she is the progenitor to Thomas Hardy, Joseph Conrad, and D.H. Lawrence. Among the surprisingly few novelists who concern themselves with depicting the dramatic quality of intellectual experience, perhaps only Thomas Mann is Eliot's equal.

JOSEPH CARROLL

See also George Eliot

Further Reading

Adam, Ian, editor, *This Particular Web: Essays on "Middlemarch,"* Toronto: University of Toronto Press, 1975

Allen, Walter, *George Eliot,* New York: Macmillan, 1964; London: Weidenfeld and Nicolson, 1965

Bloom, Harold, editor, *George Eliot's "Middlemarch,"* New York: Chelsea House, 1987

Carroll, David, editor, *George Eliot: The Critical Heritage,* New York: Barnes and Noble, and London: Routledge and Kegan Paul, 1971

Cecil, David, *Early Victorian Novelists: Essays in Revaluation,* London: Constable, 1934; Indianapolis: Bobbs-Merrill, 1935

Haight, Gordon Sherman, *George Eliot: A Biography,* New York: Oxford University Press, and London: Clarendon Press, 1968

James, Henry, *Literary Criticism: Essays on Literature, American Writers, English Writers,* edited by Leon Edel and Mark Wilson, New York: Literary Classics of the United States, 1984

Leavis, F.R., *The Great Tradition: George Eliot, Henry James, Joseph Conrad,* London: Chatto and Windus, and New York: New York University Press, 1948

Levine, George Lewis, and Patricia O'Hara, *An Annotated Critical Bibliography of George Eliot,* Brighton, Sussex: Harvester Press, 1984; New York: St. Martin's Press, 1988

Stephen, Leslie, *George Eliot,* London and New York: Macmillan, 1902

Midnight's Children by Salman Rushdie

1981

Salman Rushdie was only 34 years old in 1981 when the publication of his second novel, *Midnight's Children,* turned him into an overnight celebrity of international stature. It won him the Booker Prize, Britain's top award for fiction. *Midnight's Children* was acclaimed by critics as a literary event of international importance and drew favorable comparisons to such classics as Laurence Sterne's *Tristram Shandy* (1759–67), Gabriel García Márquez's *Cien años de soledad* (1967; *One Hundred Years of Solitude*), and Günter Grass' *Die Blechtrommel* (1959; *The Tin Drum*). The success of *Midnight's Children,* a work that expresses the experience of postcolonial Indians, spawned a whole genre of postcolonial fiction, helping to bring to the attention of Western readers the fiction of Indian writers such as Anita Desai, Amit Chaudhuri, and Vikram Chandra.

Midnight's Children is narrated in the first person by Saleem Sinai, who was born on 15 August 1947, along with 1,000 other infants, during the first hour after India acquired independence from Britain. Prematurely aged at 31, Saleem reflects on a lifetime during which, he claims, "I had been mysteriously handcuffed to history, my destinies indissolubly chained to those of my country." The novel attempts to recoup the major events in the history of the Indian subcontinent through the protagonist's fallible memory of his experiences during the first three decades of independence and through his family's history during the three decades before that. Rushdie has said that the novel is intended to read as a comic epic. Saleem's unreliable narration reflects his own outsider's recollection of India, which includes the separation of Pakistan from India, the rebellion leading to the establishment of Bangladesh, and Indira Gandhi's declared emergency in 1975. "To understand me, you'll have to swallow a world," Saleem insists. Saleem gets dates (such as the date of Indira Gandhi's assassination) wrong, attributes victories to the wrong generals, mixes up the Mahabharata with the Ramayana, and commits numerous other historical errors. These mistakes underline the author's insistence on the superiority of imaginative over factual truths to produce what Rushdie has called "intensified images of reality." Saleem's vision of India turns sour by the last of the three books into which the novel is divided, where his nightmarish participation in the Bangladesh war parallels the epic's obligatory visit to the underworld. The subsequent emergency represents the dark underside of the hopes born with India's independence.

By contrast, the first two books offer a comic, personalized account of Saleem's interaction with his country's chaotic progress. Saleem's narrative teems with others' stories, many of which remain incomplete, suggesting the inexhaustible superabundance of Indian life. Saleem is the child of a poor Indian woman and a departing Englishman. His mixed parentage enables him to embody Rushdie's own duality, born Indian but educated and living in Britain. As Rushdie says of Indian writers living abroad, they "are capable of writing from a kind of double perspective." Rushdie's success in rendering this experience of being both an insider and an outsider in both countries accounts for the novel's wide appeal. Even Saleem's huge nose is an intertextual reference both to the elephant-headed Hindu god Ganeesh and to such Western models as Tristram Shandy and Cyrano de Bergerac. The

book implies that in the same way, modern India is the outcome of miscegenation. The novel parallels British atrocities such as the Amritsar massacre with Indira Gandhi's program of forcible sterilization. Saleem is further faced with his double, or shadow, in the form of Shiva (also the name of the Hindu god of destruction), who mocks Saleem's search for a purpose to the birth of the 1001 children of midnight: "there is only me-against-the-world," he insists. A common theme in all of Rushdie's works concerns individuals divided, as he is, from themselves.

Saleem's narration is addressed to Padma, an ignorant and superstitious woman whose "what-happened-nextism" highlights Saleem's nonlinear narrative. This is not just Saleem's story but the story of his writing it. Rushdie's use of an unreliable narrator, magic realism, and fabulation (a witch dematerializes him at one point) unite to create a story of displacement, alienation, and life seen by the dispossessed. In adopting this strategy, Rushdie invented a voice uniquely suited to the postcolonial experience. *Midnight's Children* uses a combination of Western and Indian forms of the English language. The linguistic struggle that ensues reflects the ideological struggles between colonizer and colonized that still linger. This is apparent in the various receptions that his book has received in the West and in the East. Where Western readers have seen it primarily as a fantasy, Indians have talked about it in historical and political terms. Western critics tend to praise it for its formal complexities, intertextuality, and metafictional innovations, or to criticize it for its loose episodic structure and didacticism. Indian critics prefer to dwell on the novel's political dimensions, for example its exposure of the corruption and exploitation of those in power, rather than its portrayal of "representative" individual characters and events. As Rushdie says, "description is itself a political act." The truth of this proposition has subsequently been confirmed by the violent reception of *The Satanic Verses* (1988). It is Rushdie's ability to force the language of the West to communicate the experiences of the non-Western world while appealing to both worlds that has turned him into a major influence and international figure within the field of postcolonial literature.

BRIAN FINNEY

See also Salman Rushdie

Further Reading

Brennan, Timothy, *Salman Rushdie and the Third World: Myths of the Nation,* New York: St. Martin's Press, and London: Macmillan, 1989

Cundy, Catherine, *Salman Rushdie,* Manchester: Manchester University Press, and New York: St. Martin's Press, 1996

Dhawan, R.K., and G.R. Taneja, editors, *The Novels of Salman Rushdie,* New Delhi: Indian Society for Commonwealth Studies, 1992

Harrison, James, *Salman Rushdie,* New York: Twayne, 1992

Parameswaran, Uma, *The Perforated Sheet: Essays on Salman Rushdie's Art,* New Delhi: Affiliated East-West Press, 1988

Rushdie, Salman, *Imaginary Homelands: Essays and Criticism, 1981–1991,* London and New York: Granta Books, 1991

Migrations by Miloš Crnjanski

Seobe, 1929, and Druga kniga Seoba, 1962

The first volume of Miloš Crnjanski's novel *Seobe* (*Migrations*) appeared in 1929. The second, *Druga kniga Seoba* (The Second Book of Migrations), was written soon after the first but was not published until 1962, because of the author's self-imposed exile after World War II and the official proscription of his works until his return in 1965. The two publication dates frame a turbulent period in his career, which took him from a lofty position as leading Serbian poet and as diplomat in the royal Yugoslav government to a difficult life as an emigrant in London during and after the war. The war years are depicted in his later novel *Roman o Londonu* (1971; Novel about London).

Migrations follows the fate of the Serbs in the Austro-Hungarian province of Voyvodina in the 18th century, decades after they emigrated to the area north of Belgrade, to escape the wrath of the Turks after the War of Succession. Even though the Voyvodina Serbs were granted a special status and many privileges by the Austrian rulers in exchange for their military services, *Migrations* portrays them as never feeling quite at home. They are allowed to use their own language, practice the Orthodox religion freely, and possess land. Yet they yearn to live with other Serbs—an impossibility because the Serbian lands are still under Turkish rule. Deprived of that option, they dream of emigrating to another Slavic and Orthodox country, Russia, where they hope to feel more at home. In the second volume, they finally realize their dream, although not perfect happiness.

The protagonist, Vuk Isakovič, a colonel in the Austrian army, admonishes his people to resist being drowned in a foreign sea. While serving the Austrian army bravely and more or less faithfully on long campaigns that take him and his soldiers all the way to Mainz, Isakovič never loses sight of his people in the fertile homeland. Isakovič dreams of going to Russia, where the Serbs would enjoy greater freedom and a sense of belonging among their racial brethren. The second book of *Migrations* brings the story to a successful conclusion. After many years, Isakovič's son, Pavle, arrives in Russia with a number of his people and begins a new life. But slowly and inexorably the small Serbian colony is eroded and assimilated, until only the Serbian names of a few little towns and villages are left.

Crnjanski uses this broad canvas to present the plight of a national minority serving a foreign power and attaining independence only through migrating in search of a better life. But the author does not stop there. Ending the book with the statement that "There is no death, there are only migrations," he seems to say that the whole of mankind is constantly migrating, in search of its true identity. Such philosophical undertones give Crnjanski's novels a deeper and universal meaning.

The novels are based on historical facts and derive an air of authenticity from Crnjanski's careful use of archaisms. But he uses history only as a decor for his tale about a small nation that is always in an inferior position. To underscore this unfortunate fact, the author presents the protagonist in a constant state of melancholy and in need of basic care: "he looked like a straw-stuffed monster. . . . His skin was flaccid, his gray yellowish hair

bristly, his mustachio unkempt and twitching." His relations with other characters are hardly such as to dispel his misery. His beautiful wife Dafina, for instance, left behind to pine for her husband, seeks solace in an affair with his own brother. This subplot lends the novel a tragic thrust, as she dies from a frightful disease, which she thinks of as God's punishment for her sins. She leaves behind a sickly child, symbolizing perhaps the predicament of the entire nation.

Combining the qualities of a linguist, historian, ethnographer, and psychologist, Crnjanski created a masterful, at times stunning, novelistic achievement that is almost impossible to imitate. Like Boris Pasternak, Crnjanski is primarily a poet and not a novelist. Nevertheless, this epic is one of the most significant novels in contemporary Yugoslav literature. It is indeed "the novel of a nation," as Zoran Gluščević calls it in *Perom u raboš* (1966). It adroitly encompasses, in the words of Ken Kalfus in *The New York Times Book Review* (1994), the four "sorrowful themes" of Serbian history: defeat, suppression, exile, and encirclement. It is also one of the first lyrical novels in Serbian literature, which broadened the horizons of the predominantly realistic Serbian novel.

VASA D. MIHAILOVICH

Further Reading

Banković, Jelena S., *Metamorfoze pada u delu Miloša Crnjanskog,* Belgrade: Mašić, 1996

Džadžić, Petar, *Prostori sreće u delu Miloša Crnjanskog,* Belgrade: Nolit, 1976

Leovac, Slavko, *Romansijer Miloš Crnjanski,* Sarajevo: Svjetlost, 1981

Milošević, Nikola, *Roman Miloša Crnjanskog: Problem univerzalnog iskaza,* Belgrade: Srpska književna zadruga, 1970

Norris, David, *The Novels of Miloš Crnjanski: An Approach Through Time,* Nottingham: Astra Press, 1990

Norris, David, editor, *Miloš Crnjanski and Modern Serbian Literature,* Nottingham: Astra Press, 1988

Palavestra, Predrag, and Svetlana Stipčević, editors, *Književno delo Miloša Crnjanskog: Sbornik radova,* Belgrade: Institut za književnost i umetnost, 1972

Petrov, Aleksandar, *Poezija Crnjanskog i srpsko pesništvo,* Belgrade: Vuk Karadzić, 1971

Visković, Velimir, "*Seobe*: Njihovo mjesto u stvaralaštvu Miloša Crnjanskog," *Književna istorija* 5 (1973)

Vladiv, Slobodanka, "Miloš Crnjanski's Novels *Migrations* I, II, III: The Quest for a National and Historical Identity," *Australian Slavonic and East European Studies* 4:1–2 (1990)

Vladiv, Slobodanka, "Miloš Crnjanski's Novel *Migrations* (1929) and Modernism," *Melbourne Slavonic Studies* 19 (1985); *Relations* 1 (1994)

Vujičić, Stojan, "Miloš Crnjanski and His External Wanderings," *Acta Litteraria Academiae Scientiarium Hungaricae* 28:1–2 (1986)

The Mill on the Floss by George Eliot

1860

From its first publication in 1860, much has been made of autobiographical elements in *The Mill on the Floss*. These elements include the sibling relationship between Tom and Maggie Tulliver, the drawing of characters based on people from Eliot's pre-London life, and the evocation of the landscape and small town environment Eliot had herself lived in. It must be said at once, however, that Eliot's decision to transmute the normally comic Bildungsroman into tragedy, whether from her own psychological conflicts or from her avowed purpose of treating the genre of the novel as a vehicle for "experiments in life," and thus to give it a status reflected in Virginia Woolf's assertion that Eliot was the first novelist to write for adults, radically separates Maggie Tulliver's tragically unfulfilled potential from what Eliot herself had been able to achieve as a Victorian intellectual.

Before *The Mill on the Floss*, the Bildungsroman had proved a successful genre for male and female novelists. Dickens' *David Copperfield* (1850), Charlotte Brontë's *Jane Eyre* (1847), and Elizabeth Gaskell's *North and South* (1855) used the form both to trace the development of an individual through the school of experience and to treat issues of social and economic importance. In all of the earlier novels, however, despite the seriousness with which they engaged contemporary issues, the essential plot structure remained that of romantic domestic comedy. They reached closure through various forms of wish fulfillment that compromised their realism. David Copperfield's marriage to Agnes Wingfield and the unexpected fortunes that allow Jane Eyre and Margaret Hale to marry the men they love are cases in point.

In rejecting the romance plot of these versions of the Bildungsroman in favor of a tragic ending, Eliot aimed at a greater realism. At the same time, however, she turned to literary and scientific sources as well. She mined Greek tragedy, which she read as the complex interplay between character and fate. Wordsworth served as an exemplar, not merely for his focus on nature and country life, but also for the way he located tragedy in the everyday world. Darwin yielded the concept of natural selection, which shapes the portrayal of Maggie, who has inherited characteristics that are useless to her as a woman in her particular culture but which would have been of advantage to her brother Tom. To these sources Eliot adds empirical observations derived from her own experience. Her precise recording of provincial life, particularly in her descriptions of the way behavior is determined and controlled by powerful social and family conventions, amounts to a sociology of the provincial petty bourgeoisie.

Eliot clearly conceived *The Mill on the Floss* as a tragedy from the first: Maggie's eventual death by drowning is foreshadowed in the opening chapters. Only the disproportionate space she gives to the detailed treatment of Maggie's childhood in relation to the more condensed presentation of Maggie as an adult may obscure the overall conception. In spite of such foreshadowing, however, some readers of the novel continue to regard the flood at its end as a *deus ex machina* brought in to impose closure and related in no obvious way to the impasse in the lives of the principal characters. Moreover, the flood seems to contradict an essential premise of the novel, which adheres to a gradualist theory both of individual development and of changes and modifications in social structures—a theory of processive change that Eliot shares with Darwin. The ending, then, replaces that gradualism with a catastrophic mechanism of change.

Perhaps a more important contradiction in the novel results from a disparity between the commentary of the omniscient narrator and the representation of events, characters, and relationships within the novel—a disparity between telling and showing. One important instance of this contradiction is the narrator's evocation of an almost edenic pastoralism, in which Tom and Maggie's childhood relationship is described as "the days when they clasped their little hands in love and roamed the daisied fields together." This idealized Wordsworthian image of childhood innocence is nowhere reflected in Eliot's acutely realized and psychologically probing depiction of the conflicted relationship between Maggie and Tom, a depiction sensitive to the age and gender differences between the children. A measure of the importance of this difficult relationship is that Eliot generalizes and thematizes it later in the novel as the problematic situation of a gifted woman in a male-dominated culture, which denies her any degree of self-fulfillment.

Eliot's strong focus on Maggie throughout the novel almost inevitably invites feminist readings of *The Mill on the Floss* as a female Bildungsroman. The usual premise behind feminist critiques is that, given the restrictive forces that repress or deny autonomous female identity and individuality in a patriarchal culture, a Maggie Tulliver will either be forced into one of the culturally acceptable roles for women, such as wifehood, or, in resisting these roles, she will be silenced—as the adage goes, marriage or death.

Eliot is more subtle than this. The novel is a double Bildungsroman, following, although not in so detailed a way, Tom Tulliver's development as well as Maggie's. Just as Maggie's personality and intelligence make it impossible for her to assume the conventional roles for a woman in provincial society, so Tom's innate characteristics do not permit him successfully to assume the expected male roles in the same society. In the world of the novel, both Maggie and Tom are anomalous, in quite different ways. In Eliot's version of the tragic concept of character as fate, fate is the historical condition of culture and circumstance that overwhelms both Maggie and Tom. It should be pointed out that it is not specifically the flood, with its primordial and mythical associations, that overwhelms them, but a piece of modern technology, in the form of a large wooden structure in the harbor, unmoored by the flood, that finally sinks their boat. In Darwinian terms, neither of them is fit for the world in which they live. Maggie represents a type that her world is not yet ready to accept, while Tom, almost as a throwback, is thrust into a world for which he is not equipped.

This tragic vision of the fate of the individual trapped and crippled by historical circumstance will be developed to its fullest in Eliot's masterpiece, *Middlemarch*. Its final statement in the 19th century, after Eliot's death, will be the late novels of Thomas Hardy.

JAMES L. HILL

See also George Eliot

Further Reading

Auerbach, Nina, "A Power of Hunger: Demonism and Maggie Tulliver," in *Romantic Imprisonment: Women and Other Glorified Outcasts*, New York: Columbia University Press, 1985

Beer, Gillian, *George Eliot,* Brighton, Sussex: Harvester, and Bloomington: Indiana University Press, 1986

David, Deirdre, *Intellectual Women and Victorian Patriarchy: Harriet Martineau, Elizabeth Barrett Browning, George Eliot,* Ithaca, New York: Cornell University Press, and London: Macmillan, 1987

Ebbatson, Roger, *George Eliot, "The Mill on the Floss,"* London and New York: Penguin, 1985

Ermarth, Elizabeth, "Maggie Tulliver's Long Suicide," *Studies in English Literature* 14:4 (Autumn 1974)

Haight, Gordon, *George Eliot: A Biography*, New York: Oxford University Press, and London: Clarendon Press, 1968

Homans, Margaret, *Bearing the Word: Language and Female Experience in Nineteenth-Century Women's Writing,* Chicago: University of Chicago Press, 1986

Mimesis

Representation and Referentiality in the Novel

Henry James, in "The Art of Fiction," remarked that "the only reason for the existence of a novel is that it does attempt to represent life." The question of how the novel seeks to represent "life" or "reality" in language is one of the most complex issues in literary theory. The question touches on the fields of philosophy (particularly the philosophy of language), linguistics, poetics, and narratology, insofar as a novel's narrative technique may be seen as an expression of its worldview. Historically, different types of referentiality underlie different conceptions of mimesis, which in turn correspond, although not along strictly chronological lines, to phases in the development of the novel.

Different aspects of linguistic representation need to be considered here. Representation can be heteroreferential (referring to an extralinguistic or extratextual reality) or autoreferential (referring to language itself). The type of sign used in linguistic representation is usually symbolic (having an arbitrary relation to its referent, or object of representation, via the signified, the mental concept it generates) as opposed to iconic (resembling the referent). Finally, the referent can be either reality or a fictional world. Normal linguistic representation may thus be described as symbolic heteroreferentiality, via the signified, to "reality."

In poetics, this referential use of language finds an equivalent in the classical concept of mimesis, which has exerted an enormous influence on Western thought about the arts in general. Translated broadly as "imitation," mimesis refers to the relation between experiential reality and its imitative representation in the arts. For Plato and Aristotle, mimesis was the essence of artistic representation. Far from the postmodernist view that works of art create their own reality, Plato saw art as purely imitative and emphasized the inferiority of the imitation to the original, dismissing the poets from his ideal state for this reason. Aristotle, with his very different understanding of the material world, regarded the referentiality of art in a positive light. Rather than detract from the essence of things (which for Plato lay in a world of ideas beyond the material world), art, Aristotle argued, has the power to clarify the essential, which remains obscure in the phenomenal world.

During the Renaissance, the concept of mimesis resurfaced with the rediscovery of classical poetics. Frequently, the mimetic function of art was expressed in the image of the mirror, the best-known example probably being Hamlet's statement that art should "hold, as 'twere, the mirror up to nature." The traditional conception of mimesis regarded external reality primarily as a medium partially revealing some "higher reality," which it was the function of the work of art to reveal more clearly. The neoclassical understanding of mimesis rejected the exact imitation of reality in all its bewildering detail in favor of the delineation of generally valid truths, the higher reality intimated in the phenomenal world. Reflections of this aesthetic are still to be found in the 18th-century novel.

According to two widely influential accounts of the genesis of the novel, Ian Watt's *The Rise of the Novel* (1957) and Erich Auerbach's *Mimesis: Dargestellte Wirklichkeit in der abendländischen Literatur* (1946; *Mimesis: The Representation of Reality in Western Literature*), the rise of the novel is intimately related to the genre's pursuit of mimesis. Watt operates on the premise that "the novel is a full and authentic report of human experience," including "details which are presented through a more largely referential use of language than is common in other literary forms." The primary function of language in the novel is thus not aesthetic but referential, providing the reader with the information relevant to his or her appreciation of the individuality of the characters and the specificity of temporal and topographical locations. According to Watt, the novel's reference to reality is grounded in its representation of individual experience, which replaces traditional subjects as the main concern of fiction. The works of Defoe, Richardson, and Fielding, upon which Watt draws as his prime examples, are related to, if not directly influenced by, the empiricist philosophy of Locke and Hume with its emphasis on individual experience. They reflect the rise of a mercantile middle class and its ethos of individual initiative. Therefore, Watt claims, the novel appears as the congenial literary medium of a culture that emphasizes the new (cf. the very term "novel"), as individual experience is always singular and thus "new."

The novel's attempt to represent the diversity of human experience is manifest in its accurate descriptions of geographical, topographical, and historical setting, as well as of social milieu (Watt cites Defoe's *Robinson Crusoe* [1719] as an important early narrative with a sustained focus on topographical detail and the quotidian activities of the hero). It features highly individualized characters who are true to life and act within specific circumstances, instead of types acting within archetypal situations. Moreover, the attention paid to chronology in 18th-century novels indicates the growing recognition of time as an important dimension in the physical world and as a shaping force in individual and collective human history. In this respect, the novel's functionalizing of the past through its emphasis on "past experience as the cause of present action" appears as a significant innovation, with teleological, realistic plots replacing the fantastic or mythological plots of romance along with the latter's reliance upon "disguises and coincidences," as Watt describes them.

Like Watt, Erich Auerbach is concerned with locating the comparatively new genre of the novel in European cultural and literary history. Auerbach studies "the interpretation of reality through literary representation or 'imitation'," discussing examples from Homer to the modern novel, along with much drama and nonfiction. Assuming the essential unity of European culture, Auerbach's *Mimesis* identifies the stages of cultural history with a variety of literary styles. His method relies on the close parallel analysis of content and language. Of the two basic varieties of style Auerbach identifies, one, he argues, was to become decisive for the emergence of the novel as a literary form. Descriptive, balanced, and cohesive, this plain style is characterized by directness and lack of ambiguity. It is restricted to the presentation of historical phenomena and to an assessment of the human condition. The rigid separation of stylistic levels in classical antiquity between the high and low styles (*sermo sublimis* and *sermo humilis*), which prescribed the low, comic mode for the description of everyday life, gradually dissolved in the course of European literary history to allow for a combination of the realistic and the serious. Realistic works of literature, in Auerbach's sense, locate the tragic, the problematic, the serious, and the sublime within everyday life—whereas in antiquity such material would have been the exclusive domain of the heroic mode and the high style.

According to Auerbach, it was Stendhal who first rendered a modern worldview in the sense that his work evinces not only a consciousness of continuous historical change but also an uncompromising pursuit of mimesis. Stendhal's programmatic sentence in *Le Rouge et le noir* (1830; *The Red and the Black*) that a novel is a mirror moving along a road ("... un roman est un miroir qui se promène sur une grande route") postulates an understanding of mimesis that transforms the old metaphor of the mirror, identifying fiction with the mirror. George Eliot also uses the mirror image in *Adam Bede* (1859):

> my strongest effort is ... to give a faithful account of men and things as they have mirrored themselves in my mind. The mirror is doubtless defective; the outlines will sometimes be disturbed, the reflection faint or confused; but I feel as much bound to tell you as precisely as I can what that reflection is, as if I were in the witness-box narrating my experience on oath.

One can perceive behind these statements a heightened self-con-

fidence on the part of the novelist. Instead of the previous presentation of novels as authentic "histories" (with the implicit acknowledgment of fiction's comparatively low prestige), we find a conviction that the novel is a medium as well suited to the scientific exploration of reality as any other. Such claims of scientific validity, made explicitly by Honoré de Balzac, for instance, are based on verisimilitude or *vraisemblance,* the notion of realist fiction's "fidelity" to the external world. Privileged by its capacity to render circumstantial detail, the novel can achieve an impression of truth, a semblance of reality. In the words of Flaubert, the novel is reality transposed into writing, "le réel écrit."

It must be emphasized that realism is not coextensive with mimesis. While all realistic novels are mimetic, not all mimetic novels are realistic, since mimesis encompasses not only the realist aesthetic. Similarly, mimesis presupposes an ontological difference between "original" reality and the mimetic artifact, from which it follows that a work of art will at best offer only an illusion of reality. Thus, there is considerable overlap between the concept of mimesis and that of aesthetic illusion, which involves the tacit acknowledgment of the fictionality of the work by author and reader, as well as the reader's "willing suspension of disbelief." Aesthetic illusion is a feature of many novels that are not mimetic. The utopian novel, for instance, endeavors to create an illusion of the truth of the world it presents but certainly lacks any direct reference to an empirical reality.

In the 20th century, mimesis lost its hold on theories of art in general and on the novel in particular and was supplanted by *poiesis*. In contrast to the mimetic concept of language and art, the poietic concept plays down the importance of reference to an external reality and emphasizes instead the capacity of the work of art to create its own reality. In poietic views, reality itself is predominantly understood not as something that exists independently of our sense perception but as a mental construct. Hans Blumenberg, for instance, has described "reality" as the result of a process of realization (see Blumenberg, 1979). The poietic view is as old as the mimetic and may be traced back in the English tradition to Sir Philip Sidney's *An Apology for Poetry* (1595). Goethe, in his *Maximen und Reflexionen* (*Maxims and Reflections*), emphasized that "we know of no world except in relation to man, and we want no art except that which is an image of this relation." The novel, according to Goethe, is a "subjective epic, in which the author takes the freedom to present the world in his own manner." Central to the aesthetics of romanticism, the poietic model of literature has had considerable currency since then, but has only recently ousted mimetic views of the novel.

The poietic model has profound implications for an understanding of the relation between the novel and reality: the question, it appears, can no longer be how the novel represents reality as something external or other (reality *in* the novel), but how the novel builds up its own reality (reality *of* the novel). Referentiality, according to this view, is to be understood in the sense of a symbolic heteroreferentiality via the signified—but now to a fictional world, rather than to "reality."

The fragmentation of a unified worldview in literary modernism also plays down the significance of external reality as an object of mimesis. Focusing on the perceiving subject, modernist novels move away from symbolic heteroreferential relationships between the literary artifact and (outer) reality. They come closer to an iconic use of language, as speech, whether uttered or not, becomes the object of representation. In Erich Auerbach's words, modern fiction, as exemplified by such seminal texts as Virginia Woolf's *To the Lighthouse* (1927), "dissolves reality into multiple and multivalent reflections of consciousness." Testifying to a change in human experience, the realism of the modern novel lies in its presentation of conjectures instead of convictions, of individual consciousness instead of facts, of doubts and possibilities instead of assurance and knowledge.

The novel's increasing preoccupation with the inner states of its characters, with the subconscious and irrational, not only parallels the development of modern psychology but reflects the conviction that reality is constructed in the mind. Indeed, we have come to regard modernist novels that focus on inner life as more truthful and "realistic" than realist novels with their focus on an external world. Even in the poietic model, then, mimesis still plays an important role, albeit in a reconceived, metaphorically extended formulation.

As the object of mimesis has shifted from the external world to the inner world of consciousness, critics have begun to redefine the concept so as to efface the central idea of imitation. George Whalley, for instance, describes mimesis not as static imitation but as "the continuous dynamic relation between a work of art and whatever stands over against it in the actual moral universe, or could conceivably stand over against it" (see Whalley, 1985). Some critics even go so far as to say that mimesis involves an imaginative transformation of reality, a mimetic text being "like a set of instructions for constructing a fictional world" (see Ron, 1981). This understanding of mimesis is highly problematic, as the original meaning of the term ("imitation of reality") appears to have been obliterated. The tendency in contemporary aesthetics to extend the concept of mimesis makes it increasingly difficult to establish criteria for what is mimetic in literature and what is not.

Other critics have attempted to limit the applicability of the term to speech representation. Plato already refers to mimesis as direct representation of speech (when the poet impersonates a character) as opposed to diegesis (when the poet speaks *in propria persona*). As an illustration of this kind of mimesis, Plato cites an example from the *Iliad*, Chryses' plea to Agamemnon to release his daughter. Like Plato, Aristotle recognizes the significance of speech representation in Homer, yet unlike Plato he does not place mimesis in opposition to diegesis. Rather, he divides mimesis into two modes: the direct (dramatic) and the diegetic. In the 20th century, Gérard Genette has expounded on these differences between Plato and Aristotle to show that the concept of mimesis as "imitation of reality" can be applied to narrative only in a restricted sense, as narrative either falls short of imitation (in narrative discourse) or transcends it (in dialogue):

> In contrast to dramatic representation, no narrative can "show" or "imitate" the story it tells. All it can do is tell it in a manner which is detailed, precise, "alive" and in that way give more or less the illusion of mimesis—which is the only narrative mimesis, for this single and sufficient reason: that narration, oral or written, is a fact of language, and language signifies without imitating.

It is only when "the object signified (narrated) be itself language" that the mimetic principle applies, as "mimesis in words can only be mimesis of words." Mimesis is thus to be used, according to Genette, in the Platonic sense as an equivalent for dialogue (see Genette, 1980).

Different ways of representing speech will create various "degrees of mimetic illusion" (see Rimmon-Kenan, 1983). This insight underlies the dichotomy between "showing" and "telling" as proposed by Percy Lubbock, following Henry James, and the postulate that the novelist should aspire to the objectivity of drama by suppressing the voice of the narrator and letting the characters reveal themselves in dialogue. Opposing this simple model, Wayne C. Booth has suggested that the novel is in fact a rhetorical genre capable of accommodating a variety of communicative situations (see Booth, 1983). What distinguishes the novel from drama, however, is its internal frame of communication including the fictional narrator and addressee. F.K. Stanzel has demonstrated that "showing" (or "figural narration," as he calls it) can at best achieve an illusion of immediacy, as mediation by a narrator "is the generic characteristic which distinguishes narration from other forms of literary art."

The work of Mikhail Bakhtin once again extends the analysis of speech representation, proposing that the novel represents the social sphere through the representation of speech. Treating language as a social phenomenon and as a constituent of social reality, Bakhtin argues that the novel encompasses a multiplicity of social perspectives through "heteroglossia"—the internal stratification of language into dialects, sociolects, and ideolects, as well as myriad instances of individual usage. Although every novel is polyphonic in the sense of capturing the full social complexity of a culture at a given moment, Bakhtin finds the fullest realization of the polyphonic potential in the work of Dostoevskii: a "plurality of independent and unmerged voices and consciousnesses, a genuine polyphony of fully valid voices is in fact the chief characteristic of Dostoevsky's novels."

Raymond Williams in *The English Novel from Dickens to Lawrence* (1970) similarly characterizes the novel as a medium uniquely able, through the subtlety of its narrative techniques, to represent the intricacies of social development through language. However, Williams argues that "the most deeply known human community is language itself." The view that human images of reality are linguistically generated reaches back to C.S. Peirce's *Theory of Cognition* (1868) and has found its most uncompromising formulation in our century in the theories of Sapir and Benjamin Whorf. This view opens up almost unlimited perspectives to the novel: if language is the shaping force in our perception of the phenomenal environment, then no aspect of this environment will be unavailable to literary representation. Fiction and reality are thus to be understood as complementary rather than as opposed concepts.

Structuralism and poststructuralism emphasize the nonreferentiality and autonomy of literary discourse. As many critics have felt, there is indeed something paradoxical about postulating the novel's proximity to reality while at the same time acknowledging its status as fiction. Against the traditional view of the novel as a realistic representation of human experience, structuralism has argued that all narratives are first and foremost engendered by narrative conventions. Jonathan Culler in his *Structuralist Poetics* (1975) has identified categories of verisimilitude or "naturalization" that are employed to endow a text with an appearance of referentiality. Along the same lines, David Lodge has suggested that realism should be defined as "the representation of experience in a manner which approximates closely to descriptions of similar experience in non-literary [i.e. referential] texts of the same culture" (*The Modes of Modern Writing*, 1977). This involves a decisive modification of the problem of mimesis: "Literary mimesis does not aim at truth ... it aims at conveying an impression that it is a *semblance* of true discourse" (see Ron, 1981). Thomas Pavel has criticized structuralist "mythocentrism," that is, its overemphasis on plot and narrative structure: "By overemphasizing the logic of plot, mythocentrism helped to create the impression that problems of reference, mimesis, and more generally of relations between literary texts and reality were merely aftereffects of a referential illusion, spontaneously projected by narrative syntax" (see Pavel, 1986).

Among deconstructionists, representation has become increasingly problematic, even simply impossible, as language has come to be conceived as decentered and incapable of conveying meaning. J. Hillis Miller in *Fiction and Repetition* (1982), for instance, is concerned with demonstrating the invalidity of referential techniques of interpretation. Thus, in the sentence "The novel is a representation of human reality in words," the emphasis should be placed on the last element, as "all the turnings of language away from straightforward representation" in a literary work will "inhibit ... the coherent or noncontradictory working of the other two dimensions of fiction" addressed in the sentence, "representation" and "reality." The disregard of the novel's fictionality all too easily results from an over-emphasis on human experience, in the same way that a purely phenomenological criticism arises from too close a focus on representation.

Poststructuralist and deconstructionist positions have deeply influenced the postmodernist novel, causing novelists to question traditional concepts of representation by underlining the self-referentiality of all literature. Authors like John Barth, William Gass, Donald Barthelme, Richard Brautigan, and Robert Coover in the United States, as well as Jorge Luis Borges and Julio Cortázar in Latin America, use experimental techniques to replace any sense of heteroreferentiality with autoreferentiality. Their novels constantly refer back upon themselves through a variety of metafictional devices. One view, however, holds that the postmodernists' apparent abandonment of mimesis in fact carries the mimetic principle to an extreme: "what postmodernist fiction imitates, the object of its mimesis, is the pluralistic and anarchistic ontological landscape of advanced industrial cultures" (see McHale, 1987). This statement may well be seen as symptomatic of the ferment in the debate about mimesis in the novel.

MARTIN LÖSCHNIGG

See also Critics and Criticism (all sections); Description; Dialogism; Diegesis and Diegetic Levels of Narration; Discourse Representation; Genre Criticism; Historical Writing and the Novel; Narratology; Narrator; Postmodernism; Psychological Novel; Realism; Structuralism, Semiotics, and the Novel

Further Reading

Auerbach, Erich, *Mimesis: Dargestellte Wirklichkeit in der abendländischen Literatur*, Bern: Francke, 1946; as *Mimesis: The Representation of Reality in Western Literature*, Princeton, New Jersey: Princeton University Press, 1953

Bakhtin, M.M., *The Dialogic Imagination: Four Essays*, translated by Caryl Emerson and Michael Holquist, edited by Holquist, Austin: University of Texas Press, 1981

Bakhtin, M.M., *Problemy tvorchestva Dostoevskogo*, Leningrad: Priboi, 1929; 2nd edition, revised, as *Problemy poetiki Dostoevskogo*, Moscow: Sov. Pisatel, 1963; as *Problems of Dostoevsky's Poetics*, Ann Arbor, Michigan: Ardis, 1973; new edition and translation, Minneapolis: University of Minnesota Press, and Manchester: Manchester University Press, 1984

Blumenberg, Hans, "The Concept of Reality and the Possibility of the Novel," in *New Perspectives in German Literary Criticism*, edited by Richard Amacher and Victor Lange, Princeton, New Jersey: Princeton University Press, 1979

Booth, Wayne C., *The Rhetoric of Fiction*, Chicago: University of Chicago Press, 1961; 2nd edition, Chicago: University of Chicago Press, and London: Penguin, 1983

Bruck, Jan, "From Aristotelean Mimesis to 'Bourgeois' Realism," *Poetics* 11:3 (1982)

Culler, Jonathan, *Structuralist Poetics: Structuralism, Linguistics, and the Study of Literature*, London: Routledge and Kegan Paul, and Ithaca, New York: Cornell University Press, 1975

Fludernik, Monika, *The Fictions of Language and the Languages of Fiction: The Linguistic Representation of Speech and Consciousness*, London and New York: Routledge, 1993

Genette, Gérard, "Boundaries of Narrative," translated by Anne Levonas, *New Literary History* 8:1 (1976)

Genette, Gérard, *Discours du récit*, in *Figures III*, Paris: Seuil, 1972; as *Narrative Discourse*, Ithaca, New York: Cornell University Press, 1980

Harding, O.B., *Aristotle's Poetics: A Translation and Commentary for Students of Literature*, Englewood Cliffs, New Jersey: Prentice-Hall, 1968

Kohl, Stephan, *Realismus: Theorie und Geschichte*, Munich: Fink, 1977

Lamarque, Peter, and Stein Haugom Olsen, *Truth, Fiction, and Literature: A Philosophical Perspective*, Oxford: Clarendon Press, and New York: Oxford University Press, 1994

Lodge, David, *The Modes of Modern Writing: Metaphor, Metonymy, and the Typology of Modern Literature*, London: Arnold, and Ithaca, New York: Cornell University Press, 1977

McHale, Brian, *Postmodernist Fiction*, London and New York: Methuen, 1987

Melberg, Arne, *Theories of Mimesis*, Cambridge and New York: Cambridge University Press, 1995

Miller, J. Hillis, *Fiction and Repetition: Seven English Novels*, Cambridge, Massachusetts: Harvard University Press, and Oxford: Blackwell, 1982

Pavel, Thomas G., *Fictional Worlds*, Cambridge, Massachusetts: Harvard University Press, 1986

Plato, *The Republic*, translated by Allan David Bloom, New York: Basic Books, 1968

Ricoeur, Paul, *Temps et récit*, Paris: Seuil, 1983–85; as *Time and Narrative*, 3 vols., Chicago: University of Chicago Press, 1984–88 (see especially volumes 1 and 2)

Rimmon-Kenan, Shlomith, *Narrative Fiction: Contemporary Poetics*, London and New York: Methuen, 1983

Ron, Moshe, "Free Indirect Discourse, Mimetic Language Games and the Subject of Fiction," *Poetics Today* 2:2 (1981)

Stanzel, Franz Karl, *Theorie des Erzählens*, Göttingen:

Vandenhoeck and Ruprecht, 1979; as *A Theory of Narrative,* Cambridge and New York: Cambridge University Press, 1984

Watt, Ian, *The Rise of the Novel: Studies in Defoe, Richardson and Fielding,* Berkeley: University of California Press, and London: Chatto and Windus, 1957

Whalley, George, *Studies in Literature and the Humanities:*

Innocence of Intent, London: Macmillan, and Kingston, Ontario: McGill-Queen's University Press, 1985

Williams, Raymond, *The English Novel from Dickens to Lawrence,* London: Chatto and Windus, and New York: Oxford University Press, 1970

Les Misérables by Victor-Marie Hugo

1862

When Victor Hugo published *Les Misérables* from exile in 1862, he was already the most famous French poet, playwright, and novelist of his time—and a figure of considerable literary and political controversy. The author of three earlier historical novels, including the widely celebrated *Notre-Dame de Paris* (1831; *The Hunchback of Notre-Dame*), he had begun drafting in 1845 a tale of moral degradation and spiritual redemption in post-Revolutionary France. Originally entitled *Jean Tréjean,* then *Les Misères,* the text was well on its way to completion when the Revolution of 1848 swept Hugo into a full-time career as a constitutional and legislative representative to the Second Republic. His move from the Right to the Left during the next three years, his experience after the 1851 coup d'état as an outcast from Napoléon III's Second Empire, and the maturation of his epic, lyric, satiric, and visionary genius in the poetic works of the 1850s all affected the expansion and conclusion of *Les Misérables* during 1861–62.

Appearing simultaneously in Paris, Rio de Janeiro, and a host of European cities from Lisbon to St. Petersburg, the long-awaited novel was an instant success with readers of every race, class, and nationality. As one of the world's best-selling classics to this day, it has ensured Hugo's literary immortality, notwithstanding the virulent critical attacks that marked most of the first 100 years of its history. Indeed, the novel's immense popularity is closely linked to the negative reactions of political and literary conservatives alike. If the people embraced it, as such contemporary exponents of stylized fiction as Gustave Flaubert, Théophile Gautier, and Charles-Augustin Sainte-Beuve indicated, it could not be very good literature. (Thirty years earlier the aesthetic iconoclasm of Hugo's novels and plays had similarly outraged and threatened the reigning neoclassicists, who had also accused the young romantic of "bad taste.") Other critics contended that the outlaw characters and sprawling design of *Les Misérables* were merely derivative of *Notre-Dame de Paris,* Honoré de Balzac's *La Comédie humaine (The Human Comedy),* or Eugène Sue's *Les Mystères de Paris* (1843; *The Mysteries of Paris*). The novel's mass appeal likewise provoked reactionary defenders of the Second Empire and French Catholicism during the 1860s, of the Third Republic at the turn of the century, and of fascism during the 1930s and 1940s.

By the same token, the moral, social, and visionary aspects of *Les Misérables* were warmly received by Émile Zola, who transposed entire passages in *Le Ventre de Paris* (1873; *The Belly of Paris*) and *Germinal* (1885); by Fedor Dostoevskii, in his conception of both *Prestuplenie i nakazanie* (1867; *Crime and Punishment*) and *Idiot* (1869; *The Idiot*); by Lev Tolstoi, as the inspiration for *Voina i mir* (1863–69; *War and Peace*); by the republican opponents of Napoléon III's empire; by the communist bloc countries during the 20th century; and by people in revolution and upheaval everywhere. Finally, the dramatic and lyrical qualities of the text have made it a favorite of children's literature and of operatic, theatrical, cinematic, and televised adaptations the world over.

Whether admired or reviled, Hugo's epic tale of individual and collective progress occupies a unique position in the history of the novel. As the variety of critical responses suggests, it combines virtually all literary genres—drama, lyricism, myth, epic, comedy, tragedy, satire, romance, confession, and prophecy—into an enormous, heterogeneous ensemble that has no real models or imitators. Drawing on a wealth of shared myths and images, Hugo reshapes the story of Satan's fall from grace into the struggles of the ex-convict Jean Valjean for social and spiritual redemption. His unrecognized moral superiority is emblematic of the untapped potential of all of society's rejects, beginning with the poor and uneducated men, women, and children who populate the text. At the same time, the fugitive's exemplary displays of moral daring, physical prowess, and self-sacrifice are intimately intertwined with the glory and martyrdom not only of Jesus Christ but also of the French revolutionaries of 1789, Napoléon Bonaparte, the young insurgents who died on the 1832 barricades, and the exiled writer himself atop his rock in the Channel Islands. Although historical references in the novel end in 1848, such cross-generational correspondences enable the reader to perceive the satirical thrusts aimed at the Second Empire, as well as Hugo's vision of the resurrected republic in the not-too-distant future.

On first approach, then, the interplay in *Les Misérables* of numerous generic modes and rhetorical registers, running from legend to historical digression, from romantic idealism to realist observation, and from the grotesque to the sublime, results in a random, discontinuous, even chaotic appearance. But through recurring themes, motifs, and patterns at every textual level, Hugo consolidates his work into a well-orchestrated, coherent whole. While his dramatic genius structures a memorable plot full of suspense, ambushes, confrontations, chases, moral dilemmas, and recognition scenes, his *poetic* mastery of the French language generates the system of analogies that permeates the novel. In the end, Hugo demonstrates that the sublime is not the antithesis of the grotesque but its other, luminous, transcendent side. The multiple structural, metaphorical, and symbolic resonances of the text, which inflect its characters, story line, digressions, and thematics, enable Hugo to transcend the conventions of prose fiction and to explore the formal limits of the genre.

A stunning verbal tour de force, *Les Misérables* may be compared to the equally ambitious projects represented by Marcel Proust's *À la recherche du temps perdu* (1913–27; translated as *Remembrance of Things Past* and also as *In Search of Lost Time*) and James Joyce's *Ulysses* (1922). More frequently, however, critics class it with major epic poems such as Virgil's *Aeneid* (19 B.C.) or Dante's *Divine Comedy* (1321), parallels that Hugo himself readily fostered. Given the absence in 1862 of any French national epic of such scope and stature, the novelist's aspirations for his work seem clear. *Les Misérables'* unrivaled international fortune shows that Hugo's faith in his work was not misplaced. Today, readers and critics alike consider *Les Misérables* to be the abiding literary anthem of the French republic.

KATHRYN M. GROSSMAN

See also Victor Hugo

Further Reading

Brochu, André, *Hugo, Amour, Crime, Révolution*: *Essai sur "Les Misérables,"* Montreal: Presses de l'Université de Montréal, 1974

Brombert, Victor, *Victor Hugo and the Visionary Novel*, Cambridge, Massachusetts: Harvard University Press, 1984

Grant, Richard B., *The Perilous Quest: Image, Myth, and Prophecy in the Narratives of Victor Hugo*, Durham, North Carolina: Duke University Press, 1968

Grossman, Kathryn M., *Figuring Transcendence in "Les Misérables": Hugo's Romantic Sublime*, Carbondale: Southern Illinois University Press, 1994

Grossman, Kathryn M., *"Les Misérables": Conversion, Revolution, Redemption*, New York: Twayne, and London: Prentice-Hall International, 1996

Laforgue, Pierre, *Gavroche: Etudes sur "Les Misérables,"* Paris: SEDES, 1994

Rosa, Guy, editor, *Victor Hugo: "Les Misérables,"* Paris: Klincksieck, 1995

Ubersfeld, Anne, and Guy Rosa, editors, *Lire "Les Misérables,"* Paris: Corti, 1985

Mishima Yukio 1925–70

Japanese

Mishima Yukio's spectacular suicide by seppuku (the traditional samurai method of slitting open the belly) in 1970 has tended to cast a pall over critical evaluations of his work, especially in his native Japan. Alarmed and even embarrassed by his right-wing politics, Mishima's contemporaries often dismissed his writing as a poisonous blend of fascistic romanticism and fanatical, emperor-centered supernationalism. To be sure, Mishima's works are characterized by colorful imagery, a yearning for past glories, and larger-than-life characters, all of which may be summed up under the "romantic" label. Furthermore, the writings of his final decade do contain a striking number of paeans to the Japanese imperial house. Overall, however, Mishima's oeuvre contains more hard-edged realism than most of his detractors would admit. Even his most lushly romantic work is usually balanced by a tough-minded awareness of the constraints of the real world. Mishima's work shows both the allure and the impossibility of the romantic ideal, and this may be one reason that, confounding the critics, his writing remains internationally popular decades after his death.

Critics in Japan also lambasted Mishima's writing style. Compared to the confessional approach of the mainstream *shishōsetsu* (I-novel), which tended toward meandering autobiographical revelations, Mishima's work possesses what Japanese critics have called an artificial quality. Although there are occasional autobiographical elements, Mishima's fiction touches on an enormous variety of subjects, ranging from Adolf Hitler in his 1968 play *Waga tomo Hitler* (My Friend Hitler) to a pair of star-crossed lovers in the first novel of his final tetralogy *Haru no yuki* (1969; *Spring Snow*). Mishima's novels are also strongly plotted and action-packed, a far cry from the subtle and lyrical meditations of such older writers as Kawabata Yasunari or Shiga Naoya. As opposed to the confessional style that often privileges sincerity over art, Mishima's work glories in its fictive qualities, in its function of opening a window into richer and more romantic possibilities than the *shishōsetsu* could ever encompass.

Mishima's first major work, *Kamen no kokuhaku* (1949; *Confessions of a Mask*), is clearly autobiographical, but, unlike the *shishōsetsu*, it is also remorselessly analytical. A stark exploration of a young man's inner life, especially his development as a homosexual in the stratified and repressive society of 1930s and 1940s Japan, the novel coolly examines its agonized young subject's attempt to create a mask of normality to protect himself from the outside world. No knowledge of Mishima's own life is necessary to appreciate the cold beauty and tight artistic control with which the young man's sado-masochistic fantasies, fumbling attempts at love, and paroxysms of suicidal despair are described. *Confessions of a Mask* remains one of the truly great Bildungsromane of the 20th century.

Confessions of a Mask was Mishima's only truly autobiographical work, but he continued to explore the major themes of that novel, especially the tension between art and reality, throughout the rest of his fictional oeuvre. Perhaps he examined this theme most fully in his 1956 masterpiece *Kinkakuji* (*The Temple of the Golden Pavilion*), which uses an actual historical incident, the burning of a centuries-old temple in 1953 by a crazed acolyte, to produce a rigorous but fascinating meditation on beauty, violence, and, as in *Confessions of a Mask,* the intense power of the mind's inner visions.

Like the hero of *Confessions of a Mask,* the protagonist Mizoguchi is also an outsider, an ugly stuttering loner who becomes, through Mishima's prose, a mouthpiece for the writer's theoretical preoccupations with the nature of action and the romantic ideal. Unlike the protagonist of *Confessions of a Mask,* however, Mizoguchi turns his inner obsessions (in this case the impossible beauty of the golden temple) into real-world action, burning down the temple so he can retain its true beauty forever in his soul. Mishima also develops this theme of protecting one's ideal, even to the point of destroying it, in the 1963 novella *Gogo no eikō* (*The Sailor Who Fell from Grace with the Sea*).

The early 1960s also saw Mishima beginning to wed his personal political ideology, his preoccupations with beauty and death, and his idiosyncratic view of his country's history into his most important and controversial works. "Yukoku" ("Patriotism"), one of his best-known stories both in the West and in Japan, is a particularly good example of Mishima's bending of history to create his own artistic vision. As with *The Temple of the Golden Pavilion,* Mishima uses an actual historical incident, in this case an attempted coup by young officers in February 1936, to weave another meditation on the preservation of the romantic ideal through violence. In the case of "Patriotism," however, Mishima creates two larger-than-life characters, the stalwart Lieutenant Takeyama and his beautiful and docile wife Reiko, whose spectacular traditional suicides embody their creator's distinctive blend of ideology and art. The story itself consists of two almost equal parts. The couple's decision to die and their final lovemaking, described in vivid detail, make up the first half of the story, and their suicides, also vividly described, make up the second half.

"Patriotism" is Mishima's clearest expression of the equivalence of Eros and Thanatos. But perhaps even more interestingly, it is also Mishima's clearest attempt to rewrite history, to impose a colorful romantic vision on the events of the 1930s that ultimately crushed certain Japanese traditions, perhaps forever. The lieutenant and his wife die proclaiming "Long live the Imperial Forces," but by the time Mishima wrote this, he knew that the Imperial Forces and the world that produced them were long gone. And even in this story's most dizzyingly romantic moments, Mishima builds in ironies, especially ones suggesting the lieutenant's inherent narcissism, which tend to undermine a solidly romantic message.

The twin themes of a longing for romance and the need to undercut the romantic ideal achieve their fullest expression in Mishima's final tetralogy, *Hōjō no umi* (*The Sea of Fertility*). In these four volumes, *Spring Snow, Homba* (1969; *Runaway Horses*), *Akatsuki no tera* (1970; *The Temple of Dawn*), and *Tennin gosui* (1971; *The Decay of the Angel*), Mishima relates the history of modern Japan from the early 20th century to 1972. This is a story of a decline from aristocratic and martial nobility to decay and pathos. It begins in the aristocratic world of the turn of the century with *Spring Snow* and carries on to a soldierly flowering in the 1930s terrorism/heroism of *Runaway Horses,* but declines into corruption and decadence in the two novels set in the postwar era. *Spring Snow*'s aristocratic young hero is supposedly reincarnated in each of the novels, to tantalize readers with the potential for realization of the romantic ideal even in the fallen postwar world. However, the final scene of the aptly titled *The Decay of the Angel* removes even that possibility, as we learn that the incarnations are false. The novel's aging protagonist stumbles out into a world in which reality's relentless truth blinds him like the midsummer sun.

Throughout his works, Mishima played with and even seemed to endorse the possibility that art and the romantic ideal could offer an alternative to the dreariness of real life and the overpowering events of actual history. His last work explores this belief again, only to suggest that, in the end, artifice will not suffice against the crushing finality of reality. Yet Mishima's books are still read precisely because they consistently present those alternatives, offering the reader a colorful world made more appealing by its very ephemerality.

SUSAN J. NAPIER

Biography

Born Hiraoka Kimitake in Tokyo, 14 January 1925. Attended Peers School and College, graduated 1944; Tokyo University, degree in jurisprudence 1947. Civil servant, Finance Ministry, 1948; then freelance writer; also worked as film director, designer, stage producer, and actor. Died (suicide) 25 November 1970.

Fiction by Mishima

Hanazakari no mori [The Forest in Full Bloom], 1944
Misaki nite no monogatari [Tales at a Promontory], 1947
Yoru no shitaku [Preparations for the Night], 1948
Tozoku [Thieves], 1948
Shishi [Lion], 1948
Kamen no kokuhaku, 1949; as *Confessions of a Mask,* translated by Meredith Weatherby, 1958
Hoseki baibai [Precious-Stone Broker], 1949
Magun no tsuka [Passing of a Host of Devils], 1949
Ai no kawaki, 1950; as *Thirst for Love,* translated by Alfred H. Marks, 1970
Kaibutsu [Monster], 1950
Janpaku no yoru [Snow-White Nights], 1950
Ao no jidai [The Blue Period], 1950
Kinjiki; Higyo, 2 vols., 1951–53; as *Forbidden Colours,* translated by Alfred H. Marks, 1968
Natsuko no boken [Natsuko's Adventures], 1951
Manatsu no shi, 1953; as *Death in Midsummer,* translated in *Death in Midsummer and Other Stories,* 1966
Nipponsei [Made in Japan], 1953
Shiosai, 1954; as *The Sound of Waves,* translated by Meredith Weatherby, 1957
Shizumeru taki [The Sunken Waterfall], 1955
Kinkakuji, 1956; as *The Temple of the Golden Pavilion,* translated by Ivan Morris, 1959
Kofuku go shuppan, 1956
Bitoku no yorimeki [The Tottering Virtue], 1957
Hashizukushi [A List of Bridges], 1958
Kyoko no ie [Kyoko's House], 1959

Utage no ato, 1960; as *After the Banquet,* translated by Donald Keene, 1963
Suta [Movie Star], 1961
Nagasugita haru [Too Long a String], 1961
Utsukushi hoshi [Beautiful Star], 1962
Gogo no eikō, 1963; as *The Sailor Who Fell from Grace with the Sea,* translated by John Nathan, 1966
Ken [The Sword], 1963
Nikutai no gakko [The School of Flesh], 1964
Kinu to meisatsu [Silk and Insight], 1964
Han-teijo daigaku [College of Unchasteness], 1966
Eirei no koe [Voices of the Spirits of the War Dead], 1966
Death in Midsummer and Other Stories, various translators, 1966
Fukuzatsuma kare [A Complicated Man], 1966
Yakaifuku [Evening Dress], 1967
Taiyo to tetsu, 1968; as *Sun and Steel,* translated by John Bester, 1971
Hōjō no umi, as *The Sea of Fertility,* 1985
  Haru no yuki, 1969; as *Spring Snow,* translated by Michael Gallagher, 1972
  Homba, 1969; as *Runaway Horses,* translated by Michael Gallagher, 1973
  Akatsuki no tera, 1970; as *The Temple of Dawn,* translated by E. Dale Saunders and Cecilia Segawa Seigle, 1973

Tennin gosui, 1971; as *The Decay of the Angel,* translated by Edward Seidensticker, 1974
Kemono no tawamure [The Play of Beasts], 1971
Acts of Worship: Seven Stories, translated by John Bester, 1989

Other Writings: short stories, plays, literary criticism, travelogues, political articles.

Further Reading

Napier, Susan Jolliffe, *Escape from the Wasteland: Romanticism and Realism in the Fiction of Mishima Yukio and Ōe Kenzaburō,* Cambridge, Massachusetts: Harvard University Press, 1991
Nathan, John, *Mishima: A Biography,* Boston: Little Brown, 1974; London: Hamilton, 1975
Scott-Stokes, Henry, *The Life and Death of Yukio Mishima,* New York: Farrar, Straus and Giroux, 1974; London: Owen, 1975; revised edition, New York: Noonday Press, 1995
Starrs, Roy, *Deadly Dialectics: Sex, Violence and Nihilism in the World of Yukio Mishima,* Sandgate, Folkestone, Kent: Japan Library, and Honolulu: University Press of Hawaii, 1994
Yourcenar, Marguerite, *Mishima: A Vision of the Void,* London: Ellis, and New York: Farrar, Straus and Giroux, 1986

Mission to Kala by Mongo Beti

Mission terminée 1957

Mongo Beti has played an important role in the development of the Cameroonian novel. Together with Ferdinand Oyono, he made the novel into an instrument of protest against French colonial rule. *Le Pauvre Christ de Bomba* (1956; *The Poor Christ of Bomba*) and *Le Roi miraculé* (1958; *King Lazarus*), for instance, strongly criticize French colonial policy in West Africa and attack the Catholic Church as a tool of colonial power. To express his political themes, Beti created sophisticated narrative forms by building on Cameroon's already highly developed autobiographical and folktale traditions. He has also acknowledged the influence of Richard Wright and Chester Himes on his work. Although Beti is interested in African narrative forms, he has consistently written in French—a practice he has frequently been called upon to defend. His later work, vehement attacks on the independent Cameroonian government of Ahidjo, was written in exile and dramatizes Cameroonian history.

Mission to Kala, which originally appeared in the United States as *Mission Accomplished,* is Beti's third novel and belongs to the early phase of his career. The story is the first-person narrative of Jean-Marie Medza, a young man educated in a French school in the city, who goes to a village in the bush to retrieve the adulterous wife of a relative. Apart from references to forced labor and the colonial practice of corrupting local chiefs, there is

little direct mention of the European presence in Cameroon. However, Jean-Marie sees his mission as a parallel to the quest to bring back Helen of Troy. Some critics read the novel primarily as an attack on a young man's exaggerated enthusiasm for the foreign and imported. Others see it as a critique of the colonized mentality that produces such enthusiasm.

The novel contrasts young Cameroonians educated in French schools in the city and villagers with limited knowledge of European culture. The encounter between the educated youth and his village relatives produces a comic situation in which the villagers frequently prove to be more intelligent than he is. However, *Mission to Kala* suggests that the mentality of both city and village Cameroonians has been affected by colonization and recognizes that the residents of the village of Kala never lived in a golden age of pastoral simplicity and natural virtue. For instance, they are greedy. When Jean-Marie's uncle speaks of the importance of family ties in the traditional village, his unstated purpose is to justify appropriating half of the sheep the villagers have given to their educated relative from the city. Moreover, the novel points out that Jean-Marie is at least as influenced by his tyrannical father as by his French-language schooling. *Mission to Kala* places the blame for the disorder and corruption of Cameroonian society on both French colonization and human nature in general.

Mission to Kala uses Jean-Marie's forced parallel with the *Iliad* as an occasion to parody the heroic epic. In the prologue, presumably addressed to a former schoolmate, a much older Jean-Marie attempts to give an inflated historical dimension to his experience, which, in its insignificance, compares to the famous bathetic conclusion of Gustave Flaubert's *L'Éducation sentimentale* (1869; *Sentimental Education*). Chapters begin with plot summaries reminiscent of the 18th-century picaresque novel. As a tale of an innocent confronting the corruption of society, *Mission to Kala* can also be compared to Voltaire's *Candide* (1759). Ironically, Beti's narrator is more innocent than Candide, unable to accept the offers of village girls and embarrassed to lose his virginity. Beyond the humor of such echoes of European literature lies a subtle criticism of Jean-Marie, who can only see his life in European terms. However, the European society he has attempted to imitate cannot be a model, nor can he adopt the easygoing hedonism and lack of ambition of the young men of Kala. His initiation into adulthood is clearly a failure.

On the surface, *Mission to Kala* is a lighthearted satiric comedy of manners, but its humor frequently deepens into irony. Critics agree that Beti's playfulness masks an underlying pessimism. The ironic tone of *Mission to Kala* and Beti's other novels has been a significant influence on the work of younger francophone African novelists such as Boris Birago Diop.

ADELE KING

Further Reading

Bjornson, Richard, *The African Quest for Freedom and Identity: Cameroonian Writing and the National Experience,* Bloomington: Indiana University Press, 1991

Blair, Dorothy, *African Literature in French: A History of Creative Writing in French from West and Equatorial Africa,* Cambridge and New York: Cambridge University Press, 1976

Drame, Kandioura, *The Novel as Transformation Myth: A Study of the Novels of Mongo Beti and Ngugi wa Thiong'o,* Syracuse, New York: Maxwell School of Citizenship and Public Affairs, Syracuse University, 1990

Fame Ndongo, Jacques, *L'Esthétique Romanesque de Mongo Beti,* Paris: Présence Africaine, 1985

Melone, Thomas, *Mongo Beti, L'homme et le destin,* Paris: Présence Africaine, 1971

Mouralis, Bernard, *Comprendre l'oeuvre de Mongo Beti,* Paris: Classiques Africains, 1981

Présence Francophone (1993), special issue on Mongo Beti

Mo Yan 1956–

Chinese

Few writers in the post-Mao era (1976–) have caused as much controversy or reached as wide an audience in China and in the West as the northern (Shandong) novelist Mo Yan (pen name of Guan Moye). A member of the so-called root-seeking generation of disillusioned young Chinese who grew up during the Cultural Revolution (1966–1976), Mo Yan, who is also the author of dozens of short stories and novellas, has reinvigorated and recast the art of historical fiction in China, merging historiography and myth in a series of novels that have been labeled breakthroughs by his supporters and blasphemies by his detractors. Indeed, they are both.

In 1985, five linked Mo Yan novellas subsequently were published together as a novel entitled *Hong gaoliang jiazu* (*Red Sorghum: A Novel of China*), resulting in the most significant literary event of its time. Often compared to Gabriel García Márquez's *Cien años de soledad* (1967; *One Hundred Years of Solitude*) as a work of magic realism and historical imagination, *Red Sorghum* both baffled and exhilarated its readers with a blend of myth and history (personal and national) that spans the entire Chinese Republican era (1911–49) and the post-liberation era into the Cultural Revolution. Using a first-person omniscient narrator who convincingly relates events he could not have witnessed and investing his characters with supernatural qualities, Mo Yan quickly established himself as the most innovative novelist of his generation. The narrative power of *Red Sorghum* is accomplished not only by its startling evocation of the bloody history of one quasi-autobiographical family across three generations, but also by its uncommonly sensuous prose, creating a text filled with scenes of graphic violence, pulsating eroticism, and an idiosyncratic manipulation of colors and odors, plus a series of bizarre mutations of nature.

The tone of *Red Sorghum* carries over into Mo Yan's second, and most ideological, novel, *Tiantang suantai zhi ge* (1988; *The Garlic Ballads*), which constitutes an angry denunciation of the government's inhumane policies toward the peasantry. Based upon an actual 1986 incident in which local garlic farmers rose up in revolt against local bureaucrats who denied them their livelihood, the novel centers on two families who are exploited in turn by real people and supernatural forces. The struggle of marginalized peasants to survive replaces the heroics of the *Red Sorghum* family in this "subversive" novel, which was banned briefly in the wake of the 1989 Tiananmen Square massacre for fear that it would increase resentment among the populace.

The following year *Shisan bu* (Thirteen Steps) was published, Mo Yan's densest and most obscure novel to date. A political allegory based upon the 13 symbolic steps of a mythological bird, *Shisan bu* is a virtuoso, if not totally successful, attempt to create a modernist text in an age when only realist works were favored by the literary bureaucracy or appreciated by domestic readers (interestingly, only the French have shown an interest in translating this novel).

An experimentalist by nature, Mo Yan followed up the publication of *Shisan bu* with his most artistically ambitious work, *Jiu guo* (1992; Wine Country), a long metafictional novel of such startling originality and creative energy that its eminent publication in translation will likely elevate its author into the top ranks of international novelists. *Jiu guo* is a sardonic tale of cannibalism, gourmandism, intrigue, murder, adultery, and drunkenness. The novel is interrupted by a series of fictional correspondences between the narrator (a novelist named Mo Yan) and a fawning yet contentious hack writer from the mining town of Wine Country who sends his stories to "Mo Yan" for publication. The stories dutifully appear in the text, each one more bizarre than its predecessor, and each shortening the distance between the narrator and the narrated text, as the epistolary insertions and story line bleed into and intersect one another. Unity is achieved at the end of the novel, as the fictional correspondent appears to have descended into madness, and the story's protagonist, a government functionary sent to investigate rumors of children raised for the jaded palates of local dignitaries, dies in a cesspool. The symbolic nature of these events—mirroring a society mired in chaos—is impossible to overlook.

Mo Yan's most recent and longest work, *Fengru feitun* (1996; Full Breasts and Ample Hips), is, in many ways, reminiscent of *Red Sorghum*: the historical sweep, the vitality, and the gripping interfamily intrigues and struggles capture the reader's imagination. But *Fengru feitun*, which spans the same historical period, is bawdier, livelier, and more controversial than its predecessor. Winner of China's most prestigious literary prize, the novel and its author have been vilified by the conservative literary establishment for an inappropriately earthy tone and a "cavalier" approach toward sex and violence. More importantly, the novel has been attacked for a historical view of 20th-century China that privileges the role of the "losers" in the decades-long political struggle with the Chinese Communist Party. Interweaving fictionalized history and real events, *Fengru feitun* tells the stories of several daughters from a single family to reveal a mixed and highly provocative legacy.

Mo Yan is not a "careful" writer, either in his use of language, much of which is a response to the "Maoist dialogue" that has monopolized literary productions for decades, or in his revisionist view of official communist history. Like Milan Kundera, Mo Yan is convinced of the metaphorical power of depicting sexual acts; that aspect of his art is further enhanced by incidents of brutality—characterized as gratuitous by his detractors—that permeate his fictional world. Highly cinematic tales and colorful prose are the hallmarks of a body of work by an author who has barely entered middle age, yet continues to amaze his reading public with remarkably inventive novels of 20th-century China.

HOWARD GOLDBLATT

Biography
Born in rural Gaomi County, Shandong province, 5 March 1956. Graduate of Lu Xun Literature Academy. During the Cultural Revolution (1966–76) worked as a peasant, then as a common laborer; joined the People's Liberation Army, 1976, serving first as a political instructor, then was assigned to the Cultural Affairs Department as a professional writer; first short story appeared in 1981. Currently lives in Beijing.

Novels by Mo Yan
Hong gaoliang jiazu, 1985; as *Red Sorghum: A Novel of China*, translated by Howard Goldblatt, 1993
Tiantang suantai zhi ge, 1988; as *The Garlic Ballads*, translated by Howard Goldblatt, 1995
Shisan bu [Thirteen Steps], 1990
Jiu guo [Wine Country], 1992
Fengru feitun [Full Breasts and Ample Hips], 1996

Other Writings: short stories and novellas.

Further Reading
Duke, Michael S., "Worse than a Tiger," *The World & I* (November 1995)
Goldblatt, Howard, "Of Heroes and Bastards," *The World & I* (August 1992)
Inge, M. Thomas, "Mo Yan and William Faulkner: Influences and Confluences," *The Faulkner Journal* 6:1 (Fall 1990)
Laifong Leung, editor, "Mo Yan: Creator of the Red Sorghum Series," in *Morning Sun: Interviews with Chinese Writers of the Lost Generation*, Armonk, New York, and London: M.E. Sharpe, 1995
Lu Tonglin, "*Red Sorghum*: Limits of Transgression," in *Misogyny, Cultural Nihilism, & Oppositional Politics*, Stanford, California: Stanford University Press, 1995

Moby-Dick by Herman Melville

1851

Any account of the place *Moby-Dick* occupies in the history of the novel must address itself to the vexed question of whether Herman Melville's masterpiece is, indeed, a novel. A fictional narrative that begins with an etymology, in 13 languages, "supplied by a late consumptive usher to a grammar school," and a list of extracts "supplied by a sub-sub-librarian" (each of them little more than provocations toward an understanding of whales and whaling, and each admitting the impossibility of ever completing the task), and that contains soliloquies and dramatic staging, must, as so many commentators have noted, be something more than a novel. The opening chapter, however, reads rather like a novel by Charles Dickens in its atmospheric evocations of character and place; and the subsequent adventures that take Ishmael to Nantucket, his comic-erotic encounter with Queequeg, and his signing on for a three-year journey on the *Pequod* belong to the conventions of 19th-century comic realism, not merely those of Dickens but also those of Nikolai Gogol' and Honoré de Balzac. But *Moby-Dick* quickly dispels our sense of familiar territory, for the entrance of Ahab and other seamen on *The Pequod* brings not only a dramatic change of mood but also a suspension of techniques and conventions associated with fictional realism. Indeed, so great is the shift that the reader is confronted by a plurality of linguistic discourses, including those appropriate to the scientific essay, to the Bible, to philosophical speculation, to history and historiography, and, above all, to the conventions of the stage, especially the Shakespearean stage.

What are we to make of all this? By the standards of fictional realism established in the 19th-century novel and, particularly, by Henry James in his prefaces, Melville cannot tell a story and is confused by some of the most basic matters of fictional technique. Ishmael, his first-person narrator, seems to possess a preternatural ability to hear the thoughts of others and has an extraordinary amount of information about the past lives of characters he has barely met. We quickly conclude that Ishmael is really Melville embellishing his experiences on a whaler with elements of quasi-Shakespearean rhetoric and dramatic staging while simultaneously displaying his prodigious knowledge of whales and the whaling industry. But the reader seems unperturbed by these "mistakes" and reads on. This is partly due to the power of Melville's prose and the depth of his intelligence, but it is explained more persuasively by our unstated awareness that prose fiction is not constrained by rules or conventions and that, to a large extent, each major work of fiction erects a structure and a form that best serves its intentions.

Paradoxically, however, *Moby-Dick* does have much in common with some of the great works of 19th-century realism: for example, in Balzac's *Illusions perdues* (1837–43; *Lost Illusions*) there are long stretches of fairly inert technical narrative describing the workings of the French printing industry that as expository prose have much in common with the cetological chapters of *Moby-Dick*; and Tolstoi in *Voina i mir* (1863–69; *War and Peace*) is not at all averse to intercalary chapters devoted to his analysis of the nature of war, history, and causality. But it would be a mistake to think of Melville's novel in its total effect as being like these other works, for it possesses strengths and, indeed, weaknesses that bespeak its uniqueness as a work of fiction.

Not surprisingly, critics have struggled to find a terminology for *Moby-Dick,* a work largely ignored by contemporaries but rediscovered by 20th-century readers for whom it is considered one of the great achievements of the North American imagination. D.H. Lawrence in his influential *Studies in Classic American Literature* (1923) recognized the epic qualities in what he describes as "one of the strangest and most wonderful books in the world," and E.M. Forster in *Aspects of the Novel* (1927) speaks of Melville, alongside Fedor Dostoevskii, Lawrence, and Emily Brontë, as a writer of "prophetic fiction," arguing that it is the quality of "song" in *Moby-Dick* that lends it its distinctiveness. Some 20 years later, Charles Olson in *Call Me Ishmael* (1947) sees the novel in both dramatic and musical terms, noting both its immense indebtedness to Shakespearean tragedy and its effects of contrasting cadence (the differing "voices" of Ishmael

and Ahab) and counterpoint. More recent critics, for example Edward H. Rosenberry and John P. McWilliams, have also pointed to its epic and mock-epic qualities, so much so that we might be tempted to conclude that to call *Moby-Dick* an epic, or an epic-romance, is sufficient for taxonomic purposes. The novel does, indeed, contain much that is epic in character—catalogues, interludes, information, elements of the oral folktale, epic simile, its registers of the heroic and the sublime, and what Melville himself called its "mighty theme"—but it steadfastly resists such a final classification because the terms of classical epic were no longer available to the 19th-century writer (particularly an American one), in part because the very history of the novel, combined with a writer's awareness of the resourcefulness of the genre, made any appeal to the epic mode fraught with difficulties and constraints.

Melville's own understanding of the nature of his work is articulated on many occasions in *Moby-Dick,* and it is this self-referentiality that has tempted some critics to construe it as a peculiarly modernist work, one insistently aware of its own ontology and of the necessary limitations on what can be achieved in prose fiction. What Melville says, through Ishmael, about writing frequently points to romantic and organic theories of composition: works of art grow like plants or trees; they take their shapes from their material, not from some preexistent idea of form that is immutable and unchanging; they are often left incomplete, merely gestures toward something that can never be realized; although they seek to express, they often end up expressing inexpressibility.

In such "theorizing" about art we can see the adumbrations of writers like James Joyce, Jorges Luis Borges, Vladimir Nabokov, and Thomas Pynchon. But to see only these adumbrations would do a disservice to our sense that *Moby-Dick* is, in many ways, a very 19th-century book, one engaging with the possibilities of what is, especially for the American writer, a new medium and, at the same time, engaging with 19th-century intellectual and moral preoccupations. If we put aside our knowledge that *Moby-Dick* is the story of a whaler captain's hunt for a monstrous white whale, we find that its meditative and reflective moments are very much concerned with the claims of religious faith in a world increasingly dominated by the claims of science, issues that were as real to Melville as they were to contemporaries such as George Eliot and Alfred Tennyson. For all his sense that he had written a "wicked book," Melville remains in the novel uncertain about faith and the workings of God's intelligence, and he is as sceptical at times about the conclusions of naturalistic science as he is about those of Christian orthodoxy. (Melville was not to resolve these matters until his last great work, *Billy Budd, Sailor,* a story left unfinished at his death in 1891.) *Moby-Dick,* in other words, is a complex book that frequently warns us against the dangers of complexity, a book that equivocates while simultaneously mocking those who equivocate.

In many ways *Moby-Dick* was a failure, derided and misunderstood by those who read and reviewed it, and resurrected long past the date when Melville could gain any pecuniary reward for what he had achieved. Although he continued to write prose fiction in the years immediately following *Moby-Dick*'s publication, his efforts were confused and faltering. *Pierre; or, The Ambiguities* (1852) has moments of brilliance but is more often artificial and unreadable; *Israel Potter* (1855) courts popularity by presenting a story of drama and high adventure, but the historical materials—the novel is set during the Revolutionary War—are accorded none of the urgency and immediacy Melville was able to give to his whaling experiences; and *The Confidence-Man, His Masquerade* (1857) allows the enigmatic and the ambiguous so central a role that many readers set the book aside, perplexed and bewildered. It is, arguably, in his anonymously authored stories, notably "Bartleby" and "Benito Cereno" (published in the volume *The Piazza Tales* in 1856), that Melville's real achievement in fiction after the publication of *Moby-Dick* is to be found. After *The Confidence-Man* no more of Melville's fiction was published during his lifetime. His later years were taken up entirely by verse, until sometime in the late 1880s when he began the story of the innocent English foretopman, Billy Budd. Forty years separate this last unfinished work and Melville's masterpiece, 40 years that saw the suicide of a son, the Civil War, and Melville's decline as an author of international repute (secured largely by his first two works, *Typee* [1846] and *Omoo* [1847]) to almost total public neglect. But *Moby-Dick* and *Billy Budd, Sailor* have much in common: each is a work searching for an appropriate form, each is a work at whose moral center lies a profound enactment of the problems of duty and responsibility in a world of uncertainties, and each is a work of a uniquely American kind in the history of the novel, caught between the world of romantic narrative fiction and that of a more complex, symbolic protomodernism.

HENRY CLARIDGE

See also Herman Melville

Further Reading

Berthoff, Warner, *The Example of Melville,* Princeton, New Jersey: Princeton University Press, 1962

Brodhead, Richard H., *Hawthorne, Melville, and the Novel,* Chicago: University of Chicago Press, 1976

Brodhead, Richard H., editor, *New Essays on "Moby-Dick,"* Cambridge and New York: Cambridge University Press, 1986

Brodtkorb, Paul, Jr., *Ishmael's White World: A Phenomenological Reading of "Moby-Dick,"* New Haven, Connecticut: Yale University Press, 1965

Duban, James, *Melville's Major Fiction: Politics, Theology, and Imagination,* DeKalb: Northern Illinois University Press, 1983

Forster, E.M., *Aspects of the Novel,* London: Arnold, and New York: Harcourt Brace, 1927

Guetti, James, *The Limits of Metaphor: A Study of Melville, Conrad, and Faulkner,* Ithaca, New York: Cornell University Press, 1967

Lawrence, D.H., *Studies in Classic American Literature,* New York: Seltzer, 1923; London: Heinemann, 1924

Matthiessen, F.O., *American Renaissance: Art and Expression in the Age of Emerson and Whitman,* London and New York: Oxford University Press, 1941

McWilliams, John P., Jr., *The American Epic: Transforming a Genre, 1770–1860,* Cambridge and New York: Cambridge University Press, 1989

Olson, Charles, *Call Me Ishmael,* New York: Reynal and Hitchcock, 1947

Percival, Milton Oswin, *A Reading of "Moby-Dick,"* Chicago: University of Chicago Press, 1950

Rogin, Michael Paul, *Subversive Genealogy: The Politics and Art of Herman Melville,* New York: Knopf, 1983

Rosenberry, Edward H., *Melville,* London and Boston: Routledge and Kegan Paul, 1979

Sedgwick, William Ellery, *Herman Melville: The Tragedy of Mind,* Cambridge, Massachusetts: Harvard University Press, 1944

Vincent, Howard Paton, *The Trying-Out of "Moby-Dick,"* Boston: Houghton Mifflin, 1949

Modernism

The Modern Novel

The Period of Modernism

All literary schools and movements are somewhat incoherent and divided in their aims and purposes, but the group of revolutionary approaches to writing loosely referred to as modernism is more various than most. In literature, these aesthetic initiatives start with the movement *el modernismo* in Latin America in the early 1890s—which despite the name was not yet fullfledged modernism—and may be said to reach a climax (or a dead end) with the publication of James Joyce's *Finnegans Wake* in 1939. But modernism took a surprising variety of forms in different countries, and even within the same national literature. It has been described as less a style of writing than as a search for style. Critics disagree even as to the period of modernism, but many date it from around the turn of the century, regarding the innovations of writers of the 1890s as preparatory. Some feel the key years for modernism are those immediately preceding the outbreak of World War I in 1914; these critics stress the experiments in narrative form of Joseph Conrad in *Lord Jim* (1900) and Henry James in *The Ambassadors* (1903), or the various portraits of modern alienation in books like Thomas Mann's *Tonio Kröger* (1903), E.M. Forster's *Howards End* (1910), or the early stories of Katherine Mansfield. Certainly the prewar years in modernist poetry are crucial, with the early work of Ezra Pound and T.S. Eliot.

Immediately following the war, Joyce's *A Portrait of the Artist as a Young Man* (1916) uniquely combined a number of modernist themes with striking formal experiments. Its sensitive, suffering modern protagonist was rivaled only by that in Eliot's influential volume of poetry *Prufrock and Other Observations*

(1917). But the preeminent decade of modernist masterpieces is the 1920s, which featured D.H. Lawrence's *Women in Love* (1920), Joyce's *Ulysses* (1922), Italo Svevo's *La coscienza di Zeno* (1923; *Confessions of Zeno*), Mann's *Der Zauberberg* (1924; *The Magic Mountain*), F. Scott Fitzgerald's *The Great Gatsby* (1925), Franz Kafka's *Der Prozess* (1925; *The Trial*), Willa Cather's *The Professor's House* (1925), Gertrude Stein's *The Making of Americans* (1925), André Gide's *Les Faux-monnayeurs* (1926; *The Counterfeiters*), Virginia Woolf's *To the Lighthouse* (1927), Alfred Döblin's *Berlin Alexanderplatz* (1929), and William Faulkner's *The Sound and the Fury* (1929), as well as most of the volumes in Marcel Proust's *À la recherche du temps perdu* (1913–27; *Remembrance of Things Past*; translated recently as *In Search of Lost Time*). The 1920s also witnessed the Harlem Renaissance, and some critics feel that works like Jean Toomer's multigenre *Cane* (1923) should be approached as modernist novels; others argue that the Harlem Renaissance marked a separate achievement that in fact pointed beyond (white) modernism.

Most critics agree, however, that by the 1930s a counterreaction had set in; novels appearing in the 1930s were markedly less experimental (especially in Anglophone countries) and in many ways returned to the conventions of 19th-century realism, against which modernism had rebelled. On the other hand, outstanding novels directly in the modernist tradition have continued to appear up to the present day, such as Lawrence Durrell's *Alexandria Quartet* (1957–60) and many of the works of Vladimir Nabokov. While most critics now see modernism yielding to a separate literary movement called postmodernism sometime after World War II, there is little agreement as to the exact distinction between the two movements—or, indeed, whether postmodernism is not simply an exaggeration of certain modernist tendencies. In any case, the vast majority of novels published today, just as in 1890 or in 1925, are neither modernist nor postmodernist but written within the classical realist tradition developed during the 19th century.

Modernism and Modernity

Modernism, in both its Anglo-American and European forms, was first a response to the experience of modernity and often assumed the form of a reaction against it. The modern condition was most deeply marked by a century's worth of increasing industrialization, with its vertiginous effects, including urbanization and the social displacements resulting from the shift from an agricultural to an industrial economy. At least to people who had felt themselves at home in an earlier time, the experience of the 20th century seemed fragmentary and violent, without the consolation of the old truths offered by religion and social consensus. Charles Darwin had displaced mankind from its central location and replaced Providence with a world of brute struggle and random changes, while Karl Marx had challenged not only the right of the bourgeoisie to power but also its social and moral assumptions, which he reduced to mere ideology.

While science, technology, and a belief in social engineering were in the ascendant in the new century, and the creed of progress served as the semi-official doctrine of most of the Western world, the great majority of modernist artists and thinkers seemed driven by an impulse to protest against that creed along with most other bourgeois beliefs. Some, like the futurists associated with the Italian artist Filippo Marinetti or (to a degree) the vorticists associated with Wyndham Lewis and Pound, embraced the new world of speed, violence, and immensely powerful machines, and called for a new aesthetic to celebrate it. This was one of the trends to which the philosopher José Ortega y Gasset pointed in his 1925 essay entitled "The Dehumanization of Art." On the other hand, modernist writers as different as Lawrence, Forster, Eliot, and the southern American writers associated with the "Fugitive" group all harkened back to a premodern agrarian world of lost unity. Indeed, for many modernists it was art itself that offered the only chance of restoring lost unity to a fragmented world.

Rebellion and Fragmentation

For conservative critics, however, modernist art of all kinds seemed only to exacerbate the fragmentation. Writing in 1930, G.K. Chesterton saw modernism as a "jagged sensibility"—"music cut up into notes, pictures cut up into cubes, prose cut up into impressions and episodes, and poetry often cut up into isolated images." In music, modernism was closely associated with the abandonment of the diatonic scale and the exploration of atonality, while in the graphic arts cubism was the most memorable of the many modern schools and movements, most of them embodying a move toward increasing abstraction. Pablo Picasso's "Les Demoiselles d'Avignon" (1907) is often called the first truly 20th-century painting. The "International Style" of modernist architecture was noted for its emphasis on form as function and its abandonment of architecture's historical inheritance and its traditional use of ornament (these were replaced by pure expanses of concrete, glass, and steel). Perhaps all that truly unites these disparate "modernist" arts is the insistence on novelty, a fresh start, an art that defines itself against its own immediate past—an art that adopted Pound's slogan, "Make It New." Indeed, in some splinter groups, such as the dadaists and surrealists, the insistence on novelty and revolution became so extreme as to constitute an attack upon the concept of art itself. Still, there are many examples of modernist artists in different fields who claimed to learn from one another despite the differences in their forms—Gertrude Stein and Pablo Picasso, for example, or Pound and the sculptor Henri Gaudier-Brzeska. In the 1910s and 1920s a galaxy of modernist artists collaborated in the world of dance and theatre in Paris, while another remarkable synergy of graphic artists, writers, and musicians comprised the Harlem Renaissance.

Modernist writers quite self-consciously saw themselves as engaged in a rebellion against the characteristic forms, themes, and attitudes of the 19th century. In poetry this often was manifested as a revolt against what Pound called "the tyranny of the iamb"—that is, regular meter—and against regular rhyme as well. For novelists, a revolt against 19th-century fiction might lead in various directions. In her essay "Modern Fiction" (1919) Virginia Woolf complains of the superficial realism of novelists such as Arnold Bennett, H.G. Wells, and John Galsworthy, whom she terms "materialists" because their entire interest seems to be in plot and in external descriptions of items like clothing. "If a writer were a free man and not a slave" to literary conventions, she writes, there would be "no plot, no comedy, no tragedy, no love interest, or catastrophe in the accepted style, and perhaps not a single button sewn on as the Bond Street tailors would have it." Woolf points to James Joyce as a "spiritual" innovator, for his interest in the movements of the mind itself, the way he traces the impressions of the "atoms as they fall upon the mind"—no matter how odd, difficult, or uncommercial the result may be. One of the casualties of this revolution was character as it had been conceived in the 19th century. For all its complexity, the major 19th-century novelists conceived character as attributes that could be specified and rationally analyzed. In contrast, character in modernist works became far more mysterious, fluid, and intangible. Robert Musil's unfinished novel sequence *Der Mann ohne Eigenschaften* (1930–43; *The Man Without Qualities*) may be said to trace the effects of a disintegrating society on selfhood.

The Move Inward

Woolf's discussion of the modern novel applies most directly to the group of concerns and techniques of "literary impressionists," among whom one usually counts not only Woolf and Joyce but also Conrad, Ford Madox Ford, James, and some of Stephen Crane. But it also points more broadly to the modernist novel's concern with subjectivity, especially the subjectivity of a mind that is in some way set against social norms. For one branch of the modernist novel this results in an increasing interiority in fiction, a shift of novelistic focus from external action and description to the question of perception, the complexity of temperament, and the movements of the mind itself. This shift is evident in the extended stream-of-consciousness passages in Woolf's *Mrs. Dalloway* (1925), Joyce's *Ulysses,* and Dorothy Richardson's multivolume *Pilgrimage* (1915–67); moreover, Henry James in his later works and Thomas Mann often employ a narrator who expands generously upon a character's consciousness. The Norwegian writer Knut Hamsun, early in the century, explicitly devotes himself to exploring "the life of the mind" (in this sense Fedor Dostoevskii is an important precursor of modernism). But not all modernist novels express their interest in subjectivity this way: Wyndham Lewis in his novel *Tarr* (1918) expresses a fascination with the varieties of personality almost entirely through stylized descriptions of the external world. This secondary tendency of modernism is sometimes associated with *expressionism,* and evolves from another modernist tendency—more evident in painting—to restrict representation to flat, external surfaces.

Along with the dominant focus on interiority often came an interest in the quality of experienced time—what the philosopher Henri Bergson called *la durée*—as opposed to external, measurable "clock-time." Joyce, Woolf, and Döblin all published long novels that take place in a single day, each of them exploring the movements of consciousness back and forth from past to present. Perhaps the masterpiece of "time-consciousness" is Proust's *In Search of Lost Time,* in which the protagonist Marcel finds that the taste of a particular cake, the *madeleine,* almost magically brings back forgotten memories. Marcel's moment of sudden memory recall upon tasting the *madeleine* is related to a repeated motif in modernist art, which is best known under the title Joyce gave it, the *epiphany*: a single momentary flash of almost magical perception that is closely related to creation. Woolf speaks of "moments of being," and the idea probably descends from William Wordsworth's "spots of time," but in the 20th century the concept carries the inevitable suggestion that there is no fixed, stable point of reference from which the truth of things can be determined, independent of any individual observer. Both Joyce's *Ulysses* and Faulkner's *The Sound and the Fury* exploit

the effect of using very different organizing consciousnesses in different sections of the novel, and *Ulysses* also features unusual, unnaturalistic narrators—an insanely pedantic questioner in one section, a narrator borrowed from popular romance fiction in another. The overall effect is to suggest that no viewpoint is uniquely privileged—including that of the traditional godlike omniscient narrator frequently employed in 19th-century fiction.

Extremity and the Irrational

But the epiphany implied more. Because it is a moment of rather mysterious emotional and spiritual insight, not one in which a rational conclusion is drawn, this aesthetically privileged instant constituted a rejection of discursive reason and positivistic thought. Much modernist art turns instead to an exploration of irrationality and to various sources of prerational thought: to dream, myth, and the unconscious, and to what were then figured as "primitive" cultures. Sigmund Freud was the most influential of several researchers in the 1890s who began an investigation of the unconscious contents of the human mind, and his model of a divided mind and self permanently altered Western conceptions of selfhood. Where the novelistic romances of Sir Walter Scott and Victor Hugo had featured adventure and dramatic tableau and the realist novels of Honoré de Balzac, George Eliot, William Thackeray, and Charles Dickens had examined the workings of social justice, the rise and fall of characters in society, and the permutations of the "marriage plot," the 20th-century novel's inward turn led to explorations of the antisocial impulses of exceptional protagonists. In Conrad's "Heart of Darkness" (1902), Kurtz, who indulges in unspeakable horrors as a chieftain and god in Africa, is one such figure; but the more representative character is the "good man" Marlow, who is baffled by his own loyalty to Kurtz, frightened by his response to the native drums, and horrified by the colonial exploitation that brings into question so much of European civilization. All of Europe went into the making of Kurtz, Marlow observes, and the revelation that this apostle of enlightenment can be so easily transformed into a gluttonous tyrant constitutes a typically modernist indictment of bourgeois rationalism with all its romantic aspirations.

Modernist novels often explore extremities. Conrad's novels, set on shipboard and in exotic islands and countries, explore the strains on men under pressure who are far from home in less sophisticated milieus, as do many of Ernest Hemingway's stories and novels. The settings of Mann's *The Magic Mountain* (a sanatorium) and Ford Madox Ford's *The Good Soldier* (a spa) both serve to isolate the characters and intensify the relations among them. Both Stephen Crane in *The Red Badge of Courage* (1895) and Hemingway are interested in the reactions of men under the extreme pressure of war. Lafcadio, the protagonist of Gide's *Les Caves du Vatican* (1914; *The Vatican Cellars*), embraces the irrational by committing an apparently motiveless murder as a liberating *"acte gratuit"*—a theme anticipated in Dostoevskii's *Prestuplenie i nakazanie* (1867; *Crime and Punishment*) and echoed later by Albert Camus' *L'Étranger* (1942; *The Stranger*).

D.H. Lawrence is well known for his celebration of irrational, instinctive drives and what he terms "blood knowledge" as opposed to abstract mental activity. Several of his novels are set in more "primitive" countries (Australia and Mexico, for instance) where he believes people are more in touch with the body and the "dark sources" of wisdom and less corrupted by a European society that crushes individuality in its unhealthy emphasis on mechanism and abstraction. Like some other modernists, Lawrence's thought shows the influence of Nietzsche's demolition of positivistic science, his attacks on Christianity as a "herd religion," and his celebration of the exceptional man who is beyond the reach of ordinary morality. Characters as Lawrence conceived them are no longer stable, self-enclosed egos but are impelled by larger, mysterious forces of which they are usually ignorant. Lawrence carefully traces the swells of emotion that shape and transform his characters, but his vision was ultimately mythic, subordinating individual character to superhuman forces of creation and destruction.

As plot and the movement toward rational and moral conclusions on the part of a novel's protagonist become less important, alternative ways of structuring the novel, especially those based on myth and symbol, become correspondingly more important. In a well-known essay Eliot praised Joyce's practice of using the myth of Odysseus to structure a novel about a young Dublin writer and an advertisement canvasser. This "mythic method," he suggested, was a way to order the anarchy and futility of contemporary life. Other writers, especially poets, seemed to develop their own myths. Some, like Lawrence, alluded frequently to a wide variety of myths from different cultures, while a late-modernist writer like Malcolm Lowry in *Under the Volcano* (1947) deployed a complex series of references to Mexican religious belief. But writers who had no particular interest in myth in any classical sense still relied upon mysterious symbols at key points in their novels (the huge eyeglasses brooding over an urban wasteland in Fitzgerald's *The Great Gatsby,* for instance) to suggest a larger pattern of meaning. While symbolism as a doctrine originated among 19th-century French poets and has been of primary importance to modern poetry, it has also profoundly, although unsystematically, influenced the novel.

Sexuality and Alienation

As early as 1900, in *Die Traumdeutung* (*The Interpretation of Dreams*), Freud had argued that through dreams, free-association, or creative work the unconscious mind expresses itself through symbols and that the primary content of that expression is sexual. Meanwhile, late-19th-century "sexologists" such as Krafft-Ebing and Havelock Ellis were exploring the enormous variety of sexual expression, including those farthest from what 19th-century society considered normal. The 20th-century novel probably made its largest impression on the reading public by the degree to which it brought the discussion of sexuality into the open. Books by Lawrence and Joyce were banned for their sexual frankness, while many of the works of Colette from 1900 on won notoriety because of their scandalous nature. Women especially seemed sensitive to the depravations of sexuality and sexual politics; the fiction of Jean Rhys, Katherine Mansfield, Djuna Barnes, and Anaïs Nin all carried a disturbing suggestion of bohemian depravity for bourgeois readers. Sexual ambivalence characterizes important modernist characters, such as Eliot's Tiresias in *The Waste Land* (1922) or Bloom, the "new womanly man," in *Ulysses.* Meanwhile, a very large proportion of modernist writers, especially in England, considered themselves either homosexual or bisexual—the "Bloomsbury Group" was especially well known for this—almost as if "normal" sexual orientation were one of the Victorian verities that the 20th

century would demolish. Although few made this an explicit theme of their work, the author's experience of marginalization by the surrounding society certainly is reflected in the novels of many homosexual and bisexual modernist writers.

In fact, the alienation of the artist is a dominant theme in modernist works, whether that alienation be sexual, aesthetic, or broadly ideological. The critic Lionel Trilling memorably characterized modernism as "a culture of opposition." Kafka's protagonist who awakens to find himself transformed into a giant cockroach is the most famous emblem of modern alienation, but the modernist period is also filled with examples of the *künstlerroman,* in which the artist, by virtue of his being an artist in an age of Philistines, finds himself an emotional (or literal) exile. The protagonist of Ralph Ellison's late-modernist masterpiece *Invisible Man* (1952) is clearly marginalized because of his race, but his final retreat into some hidden cellar mirrors the plight of alienated protagonists starting with Dostoevskii's *Zapiski iz podpol'ia* (1864; *Notes from Underground*). Modernists themselves, however, tended to flee abroad. Indeed, a surprising number of modernist novelists were either permanently displaced (including Joyce, Stein, Rhys, and Mann) or temporarily self-exiled (including the host of American artists living in Paris in the 1920s). Some, like Lawrence and Rilke, spent an enormous amount of time traveling. This condition no doubt gave modernism its status as preeminently an *international* movement, so that a writer as difficult as Joyce might find himself actually better known and far more appreciated in Paris than in Dublin or London, even as literary London found itself dominated by the American-born Pound and Eliot.

Form and Style

Feeling themselves less valued by a society they saw as materialistic and hypocritical, and increasingly inclined to turn elsewhere even for entertainment, modernist novelists exercised increasing control over the one thing wholly in their power: the form of their work. Style and structure, the formal concerns of a novelist, became prominent concerns of fiction writers who, in the wake of Gustave Flaubert and Henry James, came to see themselves as artists more than entertainers. There is some irony in the fact that some of the most carefully and elaborately structured modernist works, such as Joyce's *Portrait of the Artist as a Young Man* and *Ulysses,* were at first seen by hostile reviewers as chaotic and formless—no doubt because their form was not conventional. By abandoning convention and turning inward, modernist authors exacerbated the already strained relationship between themselves and their audience. As a result, their readership dwindled.

In some modernist novels there is a sense of the author at play, exhausting formal possibilities simply for the sake of doing so; as such, the work's ultimate subject appears to be its own construction rather than some idea regarding the world to which it putatively refers. Extreme personal styles of writing proliferated during the modernist period. Gertrude Stein's highly repetitious, run-on strings of simple but rather vague words, which most readers found unreadable, nonetheless influenced Hemingway, who helped type one of Stein's novels. Indeed, even Hemingway's more accessible minimalist style was far more original and mannered than it now appears (if Hemingway's prose style now seems conventional this is because it has been so heavily imitated). Faulkner's huge, ornate, winding sentences are equally famous. Joyce is known less for any given style than for the exploration of a multitude of styles, although in the language of *Finnegans Wake*—an English substratum with a host of (mainly European) languages punningly interlayered—he reaches some sort of limit of stylistic innovation. It was with reference to *Finnegans Wake* that Samuel Beckett claimed that Joyce was not writing *about* something but rather *writing something.* The work becomes its own world, and writing becomes increasingly self-referential. In Gide's *The Counterfeiters,* a major character is the novelist Edouard, who is writing a novel entitled *The Counterfeiters* and who keeps a journal about the writing of that novel whose entries obviously apply to the book in which he appears. Edouard's favorite model for fiction is Bach's "Art of the Fugue," and both he and Gide are interested in what a British imitator of Gide, Aldous Huxley, termed "the musicalization of fiction."

In fact, it is easy to overstate the formalism of the modernist novel. Following Flaubert, modernist artists were very much inclined to speak in terms of formal control, and the critical movement most closely associated with modernism—the "New Criticism" that dominated American literature departments in mid-century—reflected this emphasis. But in retrospect it is surprising how much daily chaos modernist novels included—in some respects, far more than did the "loose, baggy monsters" of 19th-century fiction. *Ulysses,* for all its complex formal patterning, contains a huge amount of random "street furniture" and is seeded with loose narrative ends, withheld climaxes, and major and minor mysteries—all the chaos of both life and literature. John Dos Passos' trilogy *U.S.A.* (1930–36) mingles narratives focusing on a large variety of fictive characters with the biographies of actual historical persons, and sets such narratives next to the impressionist descriptions of the "Camera Eye" sections and the newspaper montages of the "Newsreel" sections.

Another aspect of modernist formalism is what the New Criticism saw as the apolitical nature of modernist works. But (again, in retrospect) this seems debatable. Dos Passos wrote political protest throughout his career. Woolf was an avowed feminist, like Rebecca West and Katherine Mansfield, and indeed several of the most important modernist journals were also feminist organs. Joyce was a socialist, and whatever else it may be about, *Ulysses* certainly raises the issue of anti-Semitism. Both Pound and Eliot had strong social agendas. Pound was imprisoned for treason because of his vocal support of fascism, while Mann was nearly as famous for denouncing Hitler. Perhaps it is more accurate to say that modernist writers seldom made overt and unambiguous statements about politics in their own novels. With politics, as with most issues, their artistic means were indirect.

Modernism and National Literatures

Many critics have focused their discussion of modernism in the novel on the English, Anglo-Irish, and North American literary traditions, since there more than elsewhere modernism was a self-conscious movement among writers of fiction—and recognized as such by literary historians. In part this may be owing to the lack of a native tradition of avant-garde writing in English-speaking countries; literary movements like naturalism gained less foothold and were far less coherent in England than in France, for example. French writers and literary critics later in the 20th century were less inclined to speak in terms of modernism and more inclined to speak in terms of self-promoting avant-garde movements such as surrealism or dada, which barely registered on the British or American literary scenes. Even within the Anglo-American critical establishment consensus was slow to form. It could hardly even be said that modernism was generally regarded as the most important literary movement of the century until the 1960s, when critics began discussing whether the movement had ended and been superseded. Another difficulty in discussing the modernist novel internationally arises from the fact that most European countries have been much quicker to recognize a native modernist movement in the genre of poetry than in fiction. Finally, local historical circumstances have had enormous and varied effects on the shape and timing of international movements. In Russia, an early, energetic modernist flowering after 1900 was cut short by the revolution and driven underground by Stalinism. Although the Scandinavian dramatists Henrik Ibsen and August Strindberg, writing in the late 19th century, were crucial to the modernist writers who followed them, the Scandinavian countries produced few important novelists one might call modernist. In Iceland and Finland a movement called modernism did not flourish until the 1940s and 1950s, and in Denmark not until the 1950s and 1960s—and in each case the movement featured poets.

Even within Anglo-American modernism, there is a distinction between American modernism and the variety practiced in Great Britain, although this is probably more true for novelists than for poets, where Pound and Eliot were mediators between the two countries. But it is difficult to locate precisely where the difference lay. The critic Hugh Kenner entitled his book on American modernism *A Homemade World,* implying that there was a provisory, informal, and perhaps a domestic flavor to the American movement. Some writers, such as William Carlos Williams, in fact conflated the project of modernism with the development of a rebellious, distinctively American voice that would owe little to literary tradition. To an extent, this emphasis on Americanness ran counter to the internationalist trend of the British and European branches. Some themes of American novels, such as the protest against sexual repression in Sherwood Anderson or the attack on small-minded capitalism in Theodore Dreiser and Sinclair Lewis, differ substantially from the themes of European novels. Even in the most European of American modernists, Gertrude Stein, there is the sense of a radical individual project that stands or falls with the individual author. The American novelist with the greatest influence on European and Latin American writers, William Faulkner, was valued less for the Joycean play with time and narration of *The Sound and the Fury* than for his continuing poetic evocation of dark regional themes, to the verge of obsession; this quality was picked up both by French writers of the *nouveau roman* such as Claude Simon and by the great Latin American novelists who rose to prominence in the 1960s and 1970s, such as Gabriel García Márquez. The intonation given to modernism by writers of the Harlem Renaissance—or by later African-American novelists such as Richard Wright—was unique to the situation of the United States.

In Latin America the movement called *modernismo,* led by the Nicaraguan poet Rubén Darío in the 1890s, took a cosmopolitan approach and incorporated elements of art-for-art's sake. While it produced some evocative, impressionistic poetry, and even exerted influence back in Spain, it had little effect on the Latin American novel, and in any case has only tenuous connections to modernism. Up until the 1960s the Latin American figure with the greatest international impact on fiction was the Argentine Jorge Luis Borges, whose writings from the 1940s through the 1970s offer brilliant and complex explorations of metafictional themes; whether he should be approached as a late modernist figure or an early postmodernist is another question. Meanwhile, two Spanish literary figures younger than Borges, neither of them primarily novelists, are important to the early development of modernism. Miguel de Unamuno, a major figure of the "generation of '98," in his essays, poems, and novels is a paradoxical and often suffering exponent of the interior life as against the false objectivity of historians or sociologists, and reflects the influence of Henri Bergson and Søren Kierkegaard. A generation younger than Unamuno, Ortega y Gasset was influential throughout Europe as both an apologist for early modernist art and its ironic critic. Another member of the generation of '98 was the Basque Pío Baroja, a prolific novelist who attained modernist effects by putatively abandoning form and style in favor of the messiness of "real life." A Nietzschean element is evident in his widely-praised *El arbol de la ciencia* (1911; *The Tree of Knowledge*). Another remarkable figure is the rather theatrical Ramón del Valle-Inclán, Baroja's countryman and contemporary. In his best novel, *Tirano Banderas* (1926; *The Tyrant Banderas*), he developed the modernist style he termed *esperpento,* which suggests the distorting mirrors found at carnivals.

But if we are to step back and look at Latin America as a whole, it is possible to distinguish between, on the one hand, a varied group of early modernist novelists, including Borges, Mario de Andrade, Miguel Ángel Asturias, Alejo Carpentier, Juan Rulfo, and João Guimarães Rosa, and on the other the famous "boom" generation of novelists who came to prominence beginning in the 1960s, including Carlos Fuentes, Julio Cortázar, Mario Vargas Llosa, and Gabriel García Márquez. The so-called magic realist novels of these authors have been seen as the climax and consummation of Latin American modernism, but they also have been claimed for postmodernism.

The style of several European and Latin American novelists, such as Valle-Inclán, could easily be termed "expressionist," and indeed European literary critics—as opposed to Anglo-American ones—frequently use this term to refer to the aspect of modernism that stresses distortion, forceful representation of the emotions, and an antinaturalistic approach to art that frequently leads to satire and the grotesque. Expressionism flourished especially in Germany, where the term has been applied to early 20th-century work in painting, theatre, and the cinema. Much of Alfred Döblin's work has been called expressionist. Other German writers dealt with the irrational in more restrained ways. *Die Schlafwandler* (1931–32; *The Sleepwalkers*) and the densely poetic novel *Der Tod des Vergil* (1945; *The Death of Virgil*) shows the depth of Hermann Broch's fascination with philosophy and the richness of his formal innovations. Broch's work shows the influence of Joyce, who praised him and helped him to escape Germany after his arrest by the Nazis. Like Wyndham Lewis and Robert Musil—but unlike most Anglo-American modernists—Broch deploys satire and pastiche as a form of critique. A similarly philosophical novelist was Hermann Hesse, who became a Swiss citizen in midlife, and whose novels became a rage on American campuses during the 1960s and 1970s. From *Demian* (1919) through the utopian *Das Glasperlenspiel*

(1943; *The Glass Bead Game*), Hesse plays upon the material of Jungian psychoanalysis and Eastern mysticism, producing effects that might be termed magic realist. Like Thomas Mann, Hesse received the Nobel prize. Like many of the major figures in the German novel of the 20th century, such as Mann, Broch, Musil, and Döblin, Hesse wrote books that are explicitly concerned with philosophical issues to a far greater extent than are the major novels in the Anglo-American tradition. This relative emphasis on exposition of abstract ideas contrasts with the Anglo-American emphasis on formal experimentation, considered a hallmark of modernism; but in fact both are significant departures from the dominant 19th-century modes of narrative romance and the novel of manners.

French literary historians, like their German counterparts, tend not to see the 20th-century novel in terms of modernism, although Proust and Gide are two fundamental figures in most histories of that movement. Many modern French writers fit only uneasily into a modernist mold. Colette, for instance, shows a "modern" attitude toward sexuality but comes too close to nostalgia and sentimentality for the taste of most modernists. The entirely bizarre Raymond Roussel, whose best-known work is *Impressions d'Afrique* (1910; *Impressions of Africa*), was championed first by the surrealists and then by the *nouveau romanciers* of the 1960s; he employed a formal linguistic method of invention that led to highly un-novelistic novels. Far more conventional novelists are Roger Martin du Gard and François Mauriac, both of whom—like a large proportion of 20th-century French writers, from Joris-Karl Huysmans to Georges Bernanos—wrestle with Catholicism in their novels. Another significant writer without parallel in the Anglo-American tradition is Louis-Ferdinand Céline, a brilliant, unbalanced anti-Semite whose hallucinatory *Voyage au bout de la nuit* (1932; *Journey to the End of the Night*) might well be termed expressionist.

An avant-garde movement often seen as ushering in modernism, but whose effects were limited in Britain and America, was futurism, which was founded by the Italian Filippo Marinetti but had its greatest impact in Russia. The Italian novelist Massimo Bontempelli was briefly a futurist; his novel *La scacchiera davanti allo specchio* (1922; The Chessboard in Front of the Mirror) is a modernist fantasy, although not particularly futurist. Apart from Italo Svevo, Italy has produced surprisingly few important modernist novelists; among its best-known 20th-century writers, Ignazio Silone and Alberto Moravia both are realists. Cesare Pavese is also a realist, although his work shows the influence of Gertrude Stein and William Faulkner, whom Pavese translated. The Russian variety of futurism, which abjured Marinetti's celebration of war, had an important impact on modernist poets such as Vladimir Mayakovsky, Velimir Khlebnikov, and Andrei Voznesenskii, but on few novelists. Russia gave the world arguably the most distinguished group of realist novelists of any country during the 19th century, including Tolstoi, Turgenev, and Gor'kii, but its contribution to novelistic modernism is far less recognized in the West. Anton Chekhov is a tremendously important forerunner, especially in leading writers to abandon the well-made plot. His influence on other European writers, both directly and through admirers such as Katherine Mansfield, is considerable.

Perhaps the major Russian modernist novelist from early in the century is the former symbolist poet Andrei Belyi, whose

Peterburg (1916; *Petersburg*) shows a delight in wordplay and elaborate literary allusion that is reminiscent of Joyce. Aleksei Remizov's *Epopeya* (1927) gave a portrait of the revolution as seen through dreams, while Boris Pil'niak's *Golyi god* (1922; *The Naked Year*), a stylistic experiment, was an attempt to represent the upheavals of the civil war. Evgenii Zamiatin's novel of the future *My* (*We*), written in 1920 and first published in a garbled translation in 1925, is a remarkable work that influenced George Orwell, and is modernist in a wholly different key from the works of Joyce, Woolf, and Faulkner.

Zamiatin ended his life in exile, as did several potentially modernist writers, while others disappeared during the Stalinist purges. Vladimir Nabokov, arguably the dominant Russian modernist novelist for much of the century, lived abroad after the age of 20, published in the Russian language between 1926 and 1940, and in English from then on. From other Slavic countries, for reasons in part political, in part cultural, relatively few modernist novelists are known in the West; perhaps the best known are the Poles Witold Gombrowicz, whose *Ferdydurke* (1937), a playful exploration of gross appetites, was circulated in the 1960s in the United States, and Stanisław Witkiewicz, who preached the doctrine of "pure form" but explored his characters' sexual fantasies in his own odd verbal style. Among other Eastern European novelists, the Hungarian Dezső Kosztolányi produced several remarkable works, including *Nero, a véres költő* (1922; *The Bloody Poet: A Novel About Nero*), a visionary historical novel about the emperor Nero that Mann called "astonishing." From the perspective of literary theory, perhaps the major Eastern European contribution to international modernism has been the critical work of the Russian formalists, notably Roman Jakobson, Boris Eikhenbaum, and Viktor Shklovskii. Their work, which began to be regarded as important in the West around the early 1960s, paralleled the New Critical emphasis on the autonomy of art and on the verbal aspect of literature—interests shared by most modernist writers. Ironically, in the 1970s the Russian formalists were most frequently invoked by Western critics who wished to hail the movement now called postmodernism.

Modernism and Postmodernism

Starting around the late 1950s, a number of critics began to suggest that the modernist movement had more or less exhausted itself and that another movement had begun to succeed it; by the 1970s this position had many supporters, and the broad term *postmodernism* was most frequently invoked to designate the new movement. The entire issue was complicated by several factors, however. First was the fact that what some critics saw as a new departure in literature and especially in the novel was seen by other critics as simply an exaggeration of certain modernist tendencies. Second was the fact that over a 30-year period critics were concerned to point to and validate a contemporary and experimental kind of writing, and that of course changed from the early novels of Norman Mailer through the "metafictions" of John Barth and Vladimir Nabokov to the politically-charged, magical-realist novels of Toni Morrison (American examples come most immediately to mind because the preponderance of discussion of postmodernism was American). Finally, there was some confusion between the continental critical approaches that came to replace the New Criticism (and that themselves validated contemporary experimental writing) on the one hand and on the other the new type of novels being written. Indeed, the new critical approach (poststructuralism) tended to minimize any difference between "critical" and "creative" writing, so that the later writing of the highly creative critic Roland Barthes (for example) was called both "poststructuralist" and "postmodern." The fact that some practitioners of the French *nouveau roman,* such as Alain Robbe-Grillet and Michel Butor, wrote both criticism and novels only added to the confusion in terminology—as did the fact that "postmodern" novels began to look less and less like novels and came to include writing in a variety of genres, fictive or not.

There have been two dominant conceptions of the postmodern novel, and critics sometimes strain to account for both. One paradigm features the novel of formal play that announces its own arbitrary fictionality and freely appropriates from its own past through citation. Perhaps the ancestor of this strain is the Irish writer Flann O'Brien's *At Swim-Two-Birds* (1939), which features a novelist who believes fiction should be a "self-evident sham," and which involves the adventures of figures from Irish myth and folklore, lower-middle-class Dubliners, Irish cowboys, and various demons. In one of the novel's numerous subplots, characters plan to assassinate their own author. Other writers often claimed for this "metafictional" genre are Italo Calvino, especially in *Se una notte d'inverno un viaggiatore* (1979; *If on a winter's night a traveler*), William Burroughs, John Fowles, Thomas Pynchon, Kathy Acker, and Georges Perec. Another dominant strain maintains a kind of fictional illusion, usually through something approximating magic realism, and foregrounds the experience of socially marginalized characters. This includes, in addition to the famous Latin American writers of the "boom," Europeans such as Günter Grass and Milan Kundera as well as a host of contemporary American novelists, many of whom, like Morrison or Louise Erdrich, construct alternate novelistic realities that participate in the imaginative or mythic life of their respective ethnic groups. This strain of postmodernism is often conceived as politically activist, and in fact populist, in contrast to modernism, which supposedly held itself aloof from the ordinary reader and from political action. A number of critics, in fact, now call the first (formal and intellectual) strain late-modernist and reserve the term *postmodernist* for the second strain, which is more popular and more historically oriented.

Attempts to distinguish modernism from postmodernism have been hampered over the past 20 years by the relatively rapid changes in academic fashion and by the desire to impose a coherence (whether political or formal) on a remarkably various literature. Historical approaches that posit postmodernism as following World War II or the cultural upheavals of the 1960s (for instance) suffer because so many works that predate these watersheds (such as Laurence Sterne's *Tristram Shandy* [1759–67]) are arguably postmodern in form. Clearly, postmodernism's experiments in novelistic form link it closely to modernism, but where should we draw the line between the two? Further, several important figures, such as the later Joyce, Beckett, Kafka, and Borges, are often claimed for both postmodernism and modernism. John Barth has argued that some writers during their career work alternately in realistic, modernist, and postmodernist modes. If we accept that premise, then this exercise in literary periodizing becomes even more problematic. We may well live in a postmodern age, although the implications of that are far from clear; but we are still in modernism's shadow.

R. Brandon Kershner

See also City and the Novel; Critics and Criticism (20th Century); Myth and the Novel; Nouveau Roman; Postmodernism; Science and the Novel; *and see entries on countries, writers, and novels discussed in this essay*

Further Reading

Berman, Marshall, *All That Is Solid Melts into Air: The Experience of Modernity,* New York: Simon and Schuster, 1982; London, Verso, 1983

Berman, Russell A., *The Rise of the Modern German Novel: Crisis and Charisma,* Cambridge, Massachusetts: Harvard University Press, 1986

Bradbury, Malcolm, and James MacFarlane, editors, *Modernism: 1890–1930,* London and New York: Penguin, 1976

Bree, Germaine, and Margaret Guiton, *An Age of Fiction: The French Novel from Gide to Camus,* New Brunswick, New Jersey: Rutgers University Press, 1957; London: Chatto and Windus, 1958; as *The French Novel from Gide to Camus,* New York: Harcourt Brace, 1962

Brown, Edward James, *Russian Literature Since the Revolution,* New York: Collier, 1963; revised and enlarged edition, Cambridge, Massachusetts: Harvard University Press, 1982

Butler, Christopher, *Early Modernism: Literature, Music and Painting in Europe, 1900–1916,* Oxford: Clarendon Press, 1994

Ellmann, Richard, and Charles Feidelson, Jr., editors, *The Modern Tradition: Backgrounds of Modern Literature,* New York: Oxford University Press, 1965

Eysteinsson, Astradur, *The Concept of Modernism,* Ithaca, New York: Cornell University Press, 1990

Felski, Rita, *The Gender of Modernity,* Cambridge, Massachusetts: Harvard University Press, 1995

Green, Martin, *The English Novel in the Twentieth Century,* London: Routledge and Kegan Paul, 1984

Huyssen, Andreas, *After the Great Divide: Modernism, Mass Culture, Postmodernism,* Bloomington: Indiana University Press, 1986

Kenner, Hugh, *The Pound Era,* Berkeley: University of California Press, 1971; London: Faber, 1972

Kershner, R.B., *The Twentieth-Century Novel: An Introduction,* London: Macmillan, and Boston: Bedford, 1997

Lee, Brian, *American Fiction, 1865–1940,* London and New York: Longman, 1987

Levitt, Morton, *Modernist Survivors: The Contemporary Novel in England, the United States, France, and Latin America,* Columbus: Ohio State University Press, 1987

Martin, Gerald, *Journeys through the Labyrinth: Latin American Fiction in the Twentieth Century,* London and New York: Verso, 1989

Nicholls, Peter, *Modernisms: A Literary Guide,* London: Macmillan, and Berkeley: University of California Press, 1995

Seymour-Smith, Martin, *New Guide to Modern World Literature,* New York: Bedrick, 1985

Stevenson, Randall, *Modernist Fiction: An Introduction,* London and New York: Harvester Wheatsheaf, 1992

Trotter, David, *The English Novel in History, 1895–1920,* London and New York: Routledge, 1993

Wagner-Martin, Linda, *The Modern American Novel, 1914–1945: A Critical History,* Boston: Twayne, 1990

Williams, Raymond, *The Politics of Modernism: Against the New Conformists,* edited by Tony Pinkney, London and New York: Verso, 1989

Moll Flanders by Daniel Defoe

1722

Most readers are familiar with Daniel Defoe as a writer of travel and adventure novels, picaresque narratives of derring-do in the face of seemingly impossible physical obstacles and odds, like those encountered by the castaway hero of *Robinson Crusoe* (1719), Defoe's first novel. And because of the concrete particularity, referential language, and contemporaneous settings of his stories, literary critics have long assigned Defoe a special place in the history of the novel, if not quite as the father of the mature form of the novel then certainly as the originator of the techniques famously defined by Ian Watt (1957) as "formal realism."

Moll Flanders was the first of Defoe's novels to bring this new realism to bear on an urban setting. Moll's adventures are overtly social (a fact underscored by her eventual transformation into a gentlewoman), and suggest the need to redefine one's initial understanding of adventure in Defoe's canon. Indeed, all Defoe's novels dramatize the confrontation of a solitary individual with the social and material world, usually in the form of a fictional life. Crusoe alone on his island is the obvious example, but the solitude is often metaphoric: H.F. confronting the plague in *A Journal of the Plague Year* (1722) and Moll Flanders suffering sexual ruin are also examples. In the context of such solitude, Defoe's use of first-person narration emphasizes the role of psychic alienation, while autobiographical techniques allow him to dramatize the internal struggle of his narrators to evaluate both their world and their own conduct.

The power of *Moll Flanders* as the dramatization of a plebian woman's life was evident soon after it was published. To many early readers, the novel was a morally dubious expression of plebian criminality, and they worried about its appeal to members of the servant and laboring classes (a popular rhyme read as follows: "Down in the Kitchen, honest Dick and Doll / Are studying Colonel Jack and Flanders Moll"). Given the popularity of inexpensive ballad and chapbook versions of *Moll Flanders,* these fears were hardly groundless. Although still concerned with the social implications of Defoe's novels, 19th-century evaluations acknowledged the art of his narrative realism, what William Hazlitt called Defoe's "fac-similes" of low-life character. Only in the 20th century has interest in Defoe's documentary realism been joined by appreciation of his perspectival realism. It is *Moll Flanders*' latter brand of realism—its anticipation of stream-of-consciousness narration, for example—that intrigued modern novelists such as Virginia Woolf and E.M. Forster.

Defoe approached the representation of social perspective well aware, from his experience as a political journalist during the early decades of the 18th century, of the popularity of the "secret history" of fashionable life practiced by writers such as Delarivier Manley in *The New Atalantis* (1709). These party-political works adapted the language, style, and narrative patterns of romance for the coded revelation of court intrigues. Defoe reversed this precedent in his own novels, however, by adapting biographical genres such as travel writing and the political memoir to the expression of a fictional life and by employing documentary techniques from the literature of common, rather than fashionable, life. This is especially clear in *Moll Flanders,* where the influence of trial reports and criminal biography is striking; indeed, the fictional Moll Flanders may have been modeled in part on Moll King, a then-contemporary thief and whore.

Situated in a plebian milieu, Moll's criminal practices are linked to the social isolation of a clever malcontent rather than the sinning nature of humankind. Yet even as the events of Moll's life reflect the worldly orientation of the picaresque, Defoe draws the psychological intensity and narrative coherence of his novel from the confessional form of the spiritual autobiography, in which first-person narration is tied to the exposure of a shameful and unflattering past. A good example is Moll's account of her robbery of a valuable necklace from a little girl. The combination of these contrary narrative modes results, perhaps unpredictably, in a coherent synthesis. Alone in a world bent on her physical and moral destruction, Moll proves herself a survivor; yet unlike the typical *pícaro,* Moll's struggle to interpret her own conduct remains as central as her pursuit of material success.

Defoe's choice of a female protagonist in *Moll Flanders* reflects his interest, well before *Roxana* (1724), in the female experience of psychic alienation. According to Margaret Anne Doody (1974), women writers of the early 18th century sought to assert the importance of woman as an "agent of feeling," especially in relation to the experience of love. It is thus interesting to find that, like Amena in Eliza Haywood's *Love in Excess* (3 vols., 1719–20), for example, Moll suffers romantic disillusionment when she is ruined at the hands of a cynical male seducer. By staging the topos of sexual ruin early in Moll's life, Defoe makes the social crisis of his novel a fundamentally female one. He goes on, however, to modify the context of female sexual crisis: the female protagonist is not a member of the social elite but an illegitimate child of low birth, and her earliest erotic experiences are linked to the exchange of money. Defoe thus plebianizes the protagonist of amatory fiction, a sign of which is Moll's criminalization: rather than entering a continental nunnery to bury her shame, Moll eventually becomes a whore and a thief.

This plebianization underscores the moral-narrative problem of Defoe's novels that subsequent writers attempted to resolve. Clearly attracted to Defoe's perspectival realism was Samuel Richardson, whose use of the epistolary form in *Pamela* (1740) was an attempt to advance fictional self-narration technically. *Pamela* also presents a plebian female heroine, although unlike Moll Pamela is meant as an exemplary figure, and Richardson replaces Defoe's narrative relativism with the typification of middle-class values. Suspicious of all self-narration, Henry Fielding rejected both Defoe's and Richardson's approaches to the dramatization of a life by creating an ironic, third-person, omniscient narrator to control and objectivize the moral framework of his novels.

The essence of Defoe's technique is impersonation. *Moll Flanders* is a book-length dramatic monologue, and both the power and the moral heterogeneity of the novel spring from its dramatic enactment of a voice and perspective. Defoe was, of course, well known for his abilities in written mimicry (in works such as *The Shortest Way with the Dissenters,* 1702), and he carried this power over to his historical fiction (*Memoirs of a Cavalier,* 1720). The concept of impersonation also clarifies the presentation of personal self-fashioning in the world of *Moll Flanders*: Moll engages in literal impersonations, such as when she disguises herself as a man during her thieving days; she is an artist of personalities—or at least of personae—much like her author (even her name is an alias); and she employs the same art when she disguises her inner sentiments (for example, during her negotiations with her Lancashire husband). On the evidence of the editor's preface, which frames the ethical challenge of *Moll Flanders* in terms of the analogy of the stage, Defoe was well aware of the dramatic provenance of his technique. Far from taking the individual for granted as an object of representation or ludic representation, however, *Moll Flanders* is an extended inquiry into the nature of individualization itself through introspection, retrospection, and impersonation.

Moll is born plebian, but she lives to become a gentlewoman through the spoils of a successful colonial plantation. Although Defoe's own views on the criminalization of plebian life in the 18th century may not be apparent in Moll's narration, social conflict and mobility are clearly dramatized. Viewed in these terms, *Moll Flanders* does more than document 18th-century life or the experiences of a loose-living victim of necessity; it also embodies a collision of social perspectives that neither the conduct-based moralizing of Richardson nor the Augustan elitism of Fielding can resolve. Only in the novels of another keen-eyed dramatist of social conflict, Jane Austen, will Defoe's response to precursors such as Haywood and Manley be reappropriated by the tradition of women's writing and the novel.

FRASER EASTON

See also Daniel Defoe

Further Reading

Backscheider, Paula R., *Daniel Defoe: Ambition and Innovation,* Lexington: University Press of Kentucky, 1986
Bender, John, *Imagining the Penitentiary: Fiction and the*

Architecture of Mind in Eighteenth-Century England,
Chicago: University of Chicago Press, 1987

Blewett, David, Defoe's Art of Fiction, Toronto and Buffalo,
New York: University of Toronto Press, 1979

Doody, Margaret Anne, A Natural Passion: A Study of the
Novels of Samuel Richardson, Oxford: Clarendon Press,
1974

Faller, Lincoln B., Crime and Defoe: A New Kind of Writing,
Cambridge and New York: Cambridge University Press, 1993

Gallagher, Catherine, Nobody's Story: The Vanishing Acts of
Women Writers in the Marketplace, 1670–1820, Berkeley:
University of California Press, and Oxford: Clarendon Press,
1994

Kay, Carol, Political Constructions: Defoe, Richardson, and
Sterne in Relation to Hobbes, Hume, and Burke, Ithaca, New
York: Cornell University Press, 1988

Mitchell, Juliet, introduction to Moll Flanders, London:
Penguin, 1978

Novak, Maximillian E., Realism, Myth, and History in Defoe's
Fiction, Lincoln: University of Nebraska Press, 1983

Starr, George A., Defoe and Spiritual Autobiography, Princeton,
New Jersey: Princeton University Press, 1965

Watt, Ian, The Rise of the Novel: Studies in Defoe, Richardson,
and Fielding, Berkeley: University of California Press, and
London: Chatto and Windus, 1957

Molloy, Malone Dies, The Unnamable by Samuel Beckett

Molloy, Malone meurt, L'Innommable 1951–53

By the end of World War II Samuel Beckett, aged 39, had published only one volume of linked short stories, *More Pricks Than Kicks* (1934), one novel, *Murphy* (1938), and had written a second novel, *Watt,* that did not find a publisher until 1953. On a visit to Ireland in April 1946 Beckett found himself late at night at the end of a pier in Dublin harbor during a storm. He experienced a vision in which he realized that "the dark" he had "struggled to keep under" should constitute the true material of his work. He determined to embark on an internal excavation of the darkness that lay within him, and this led Beckett to develop the art of the monologue, what he called "the battle of the soliloquy."

Beckett next entered into the most prolific phase of his writing career. Anxious to curb the natural excesses of what he referred to as his Gothic Irish, he decided to start writing in French, the language of his adopted country, claiming that in French "it is easier to write without style." In a spurt of creativity Beckett wrote four *nouvelles*, or stories; two plays (including *En attendant Godot* [*Waiting for Godot*]); and four novels between 1946 and 1949. Because he drew on the first of these four novels, *Mercier et Camier* (*Mercier and Camier*) to write *Waiting for Godot,* he withheld the novel from publication until 1970. The remaining three novels rapidly evolved one from the other between 1947 and 1949. *Molloy* was published in French in 1951, *Malone meurt* (*Malone Dies*) in 1951, and *L'Innommable* (*The Unnamable*) in 1953.

The trilogy has long been recognized as the summit of Beckett's work in fiction. Although many of the novels' early reviewers made flattering comparisons between Beckett's work and that of James Joyce, Beckett was moving in quite the opposite direction from Joyce. Where Joyce's later fiction exploits and celebrates the polysemantic nature of language, Beckett used language to defeat its endless proliferation of meanings. His aim was to produce "a literature of the un-word." Convinced that we inhabit a world without meaning, he sought to take meaning out of the world of language. But he knew that his desire to turn words into the equivalent of abstract splashes of paint was destined to be thwarted by the signifying function of words. Failure was unavoidable. Thus, Beckett made a virtue of necessity. "To be an artist is to fail," he wrote, "as no other dare fail." The trilogy celebrates this art of failure by showing each successive narrating voice attempting in vain to tell his story in a definitive form that will enable the "I" to relapse into silence. Each successive "voice-exister" in the three novels shows a more extreme level of physical deterioration as Beckett pursues his own narrative tail or tale. Molloy starts off on a bicycle, regresses to crutches, then to crawling, and finally to stasis in bed. Malone starts off in bed and expects to die imminently. The voice in *The Unnamable* belongs to a postmortem limbless trunk and head and then to a rudimentary creature with minimal human attributes. But the narrating voice continues to tell stories that attempt to track down the elusive self.

Beckett referred to the self as "the narrator narrated." The narrator can never overcome the obvious fact that as soon as it speaks of "I" it has divided itself between the speaking and the spoken subject. The speaking subject is forever exiled from the real self. All the speaker can do is tell stories about the spoken self, who grammatically remains distinct from the speaking self. This is the quandary with which the narrator of *The Unnamable* begins: "Unquestioning. I, say I. Unbelieving." So, according to Beckett, the artist bent on self-immersion can never penetrate into the darkness of the true self because that darkness recedes as the light of the investigating writer tries to penetrate it. Where modernists made art out of the angst they experienced, Beckett shows himself to be postmodernist in his determination to make art out of the absence of all meaning. The famous conclusion to *Molloy* illustrates just how well he does this. The narrating voice is finishing his written account of his failed attempt to track down an earlier avatar of himself: "Then I went back into the house and wrote, It is midnight. The rain is beating on the windows. It was not midnight. It was not raining." With perfect symmetry Beckett balances the assertion (made in the continuous present) of written fiction with the negation (in the past tense) of spoken actuality. Yet that actuality has immediately become itself a part of a new fiction. The conclusion refuses closure by offering an endless vista of receding mirror-like images that, like the signifying chain of language itself, forever postpones a final signified.

The trilogy explores and exploits this paradox at the heart of human consciousness. The speaking voice seeks to reach itself, a self that resides in the nonverbal realm of silence. As *The Unnamable* puts it, "Where I am there is no one but me, who am not." Grammatically correct, yet awkward, that sentence illustrates the way Beckett employs language against itself. Adding to the metafictional tendency that began to display itself in modernist fiction, Beckett employs metalinguistics in an effort to force language to reveal its duplicitous nature. As *The Unnamable* says, "I'm in words, made of words, others' words." Beckett in effect anticipates the poststructuralist view of the subject as a verbal construct divided from itself and constituted by intertextuality. *The Unnamable* is the provisional end of the line of a whole series of fictional antecedents in what he calls "a ponderous chronicle of moribunds," the narrative personae that began with Belacqua, the protagonist of *More Pricks Than Kicks,* and continued through all of Beckett's novels. Particularly in *The Unnamable,* Beckett mounts a frontal assault on the language that simultaneously he is forced to use to define himself. Syntax defeats him: "I'll begin again." He plays fast and loose with pronouns: "To get me to be he." Or rather words play fast and loose with *The Unnamable,* as the last words of the trilogy beautifully demonstrate: "I must go on, I can't go on, I'll go on."

The circularity of Beckett's three novels (they begin where they end) is quite different from the circular structure of Joyce's *Finnegans Wake* (1939). Joyce's use of form turns the language system into a closed structure wherein he plays inventively with its components. Beckett's form illustrates the futility of a life wherein birth itself is a kind of death and where narration displays its inability to leave its point of departure. Caught in what *The Unnamable* calls the "wordy-gurdy" of human consciousness, the narrating voice does not try to add to the resources of language as in Joyce's work. Instead, the voice tries to reach the reality of the silence by using linguistic counterpoint, paradox, and verbal balance. Beckett's attack on the deceptive nature of language, combined with his rigorous deflation of the pretenses of human endeavor—especially its claims to philosophical insight—make him a precursor of postmodernism as defined by Jean-François Lyotard. Since World War II and the horrors of the Holocaust, Lyotard has argued, the grand narratives of the Enlightenment have lost their credibility. The postmodern work of art is heterogeneous, unstable, and forced to construct its own

rules as it proceeds. Beckett's trilogy, a work in process and about being in process, exhibits these qualities brilliantly.

Beckett's fictional world is so distinctively his own that it is hard to discern his direct influence on subsequent writers. Like Joyce, he seems to have written himself into a cul-de-sac. As he remarked upon completing *The Unnamable,* "there's complete disintegration. . . . There's no way to go on." Although he did go on to write one more full-length novel, his fictional works after that consisted of short, condensed fictions that constructed variations around the themes adumbrated in the trilogy. One could argue that in the trilogy he not only invented a subgenre of fiction but also went on to exhaust it as soon as he had created it. Yet the fictional world Beckett conjured is not only unique. It also has become a paradigm of the postwar Western world. "Beckettian" has been used to describe the laughable pretensions of humankind to dignity or even to meaningfulness. Nowhere, not even in his plays, is Beckett's negative yet humorous vision of Western civilization's contemporary plight more satisfactorily expressed than in the great trilogy he wrote at the height of his powers.

BRIAN FINNEY

See also Samuel Beckett

Further Reading

Abbott, H. Porter, *The Fiction of Samuel Beckett: Form and Effect,* Berkeley: University of California Press, 1973

Dearlove, J.E., *Accommodating the Chaos: Samuel Beckett's Nonrelational Art,* Durham, North Carolina: Duke University Press, 1982

Fletcher, John, *The Novels of Samuel Beckett,* London: Chatto and Windus, and New York: Barnes and Noble, 1964; 2nd edition, 1970

Kenner, Hugh, *A Reader's Guide to Samuel Beckett,* London: Thames and Hudson, and New York: Farrar, Straus and Giroux, 1973

Knowlson, James, *Damned to Fame: The Life of Samuel Beckett,* London: Bloomsbury, and New York: Simon and Schuster, 1996

Levy, Eric, *Beckett and the Voice of Species: A Study of the Prose Fiction,* Totowa, New Jersey: Barnes and Noble, and Dublin: Gill and Macmillan, 1980

Murphy, Peter J., *Reconstructing Beckett: Language for Being in Samuel Beckett's Fiction,* Toronto: University of Toronto Press, 1990

Rabinovitz, Rubin, *Innovation in Samuel Beckett's Fiction,* Urbana: University of Illinois Press, 1992

Toyama, Jean Yamasaki, *Beckett's Game: Self and Language in the Trilogy,* New York: Peter Lang, 1991

The Moonstone by Wilkie Collins

1868

Although 19th-century English fiction is replete with mystery and crime, as in the novels of Collins' older contemporary and friend Charles Dickens, critics often credit Wilkie Collins with the invention of the English detective novel. What sets *The Moonstone* apart from later detective fiction, however, is not the intricacy of its plot, brilliantly constructed as it is, but its sheer length. Of course, length was a staple requirement of the Victorian publishing marketplace, whether in novels published serially like *The Moonstone* or issued in the standard three-volume format. Constructing novels of such length also allowed Victorian writers ample room for the development of complex characters, as well as for the leisurely fleshing out of those characters' worlds, but these strategies told against tightness of plot—so much so that plot, per se, is of relatively minor importance in much of the period's fiction.

Collins thus faced a challenge: how to raise plot to a level of primary importance while participating in a novelistic tradition that appeared to militate against such a strategy. He solved the problem by returning to a structural device he had used in his earlier best-seller, *The Woman in White* (1860): multivocal narrative that imitates the presentation of testimony from a number of witnesses in a court case. In this narrative form, each witness is called upon to give evidence strictly limited to his or her direct involvement in events connected with the theft of the moonstone. The device harks back to such epistolary novels as Samuel Richardson's *Clarissa* (1747–48), Tobias Smollett's *Humphrey Clinker* (1771), and Mary Shelley's *Frankenstein* (1818). As producers of evidentiary narratives, however, Collins' witnesses do not engage in the exploration of the private world of the self that provides the main interest in Richardson and Shelley. This method allows Collins freedom to develop his characters through ventriloquism—particularized idiom, highly individualized responses to events and to other characters, and self-justifications—in what is perhaps more nearly a dramatic rather than a novelistic method of character presentation.

There is another sense, also connected with plot, in which the detective novel is at odds with the general tendencies of the Victorian novel. The essential questions for the detective novel are, of course, "Who did it?" and its corollaries "How?" and "Why?" Thus the direction of the plot is backward, from effect to cause, from the crime to the criminal. And while the detective novel, like many Victorian novels, is multiplotted, these plots again proceed in reverse order: the plot of detection precedes the plot of the crime. By contrast, novels such as William Makepeace Thackeray's *Vanity Fair* (1848) develop plots in parallel, alternating sequence. The typical Victorian novel, rather than moving backward, moves its plot(s) forward, and is involved with growth and development, the unfolding of effects or consequences from cause, and, in its more determinedly realistic examples (*Vanity Fair*; George Eliot's *Middlemarch*, 1872; Anthony Trollope's *The Way We Live Now*, 1875), gives us a sense of the rapidly increasing complexity of the modern world and its effects on the lives of its characters. The detective novel, on the other hand, begins with an overdetermined situation in which everyone and everything are potentially involved in the crime, and then, through the deductive efforts of the detective, reduces everything to its normal valence except for the essential clues that point to the criminal.

Although the vital clue in *The Moonstone* is found quite early (a smudge in the fresh paint on the door of the room where the stone was kept on the night of its disappearance), Collins manages to suspend the discovery of the person who caused the smudge for at least 200 pages. He also takes the opportunity to develop a frustrated but eventually successful romance plot and to introduce a number of eccentric or marginalized characters of the sort in which he delights. Thus we meet Miss Clack, an evangelical relative of the robbed aristocratic Verinder family and one of Collins' best comic characters. We also encounter Rosanna Spearman, a former London thief taken in as a servant by the Verinders who falls hopelessly in love with the gentlemanly hero of the novel (himself far above her in station) and is driven to despair and suicide. Ezra Jennings, a physician's assistant who is haunted by a murky past and cursed by a repellent physical appearance, fascinates because he also shares Collins' own eventual fate: he is addicted to massive doses of opium as an anodyne for an unspecified disease that finally kills him.

These characters, along with others, such as Gabriel Betteredge, the elderly butler for the Verinder household, recall Dickens' eccentric creations, but their prominence in *The Moonstone* makes the novel an atypical example of the detective novel. Furthermore, these creations implicitly set the novel at odds with the ideological stance many critics have argued the typical detective novel assumes. In *Signs Taken for Wonders* (1988), Franco Moretti has argued that the detective novel is conservative, protective of a bourgeois status quo that appears contaminated by a criminal act, but which is vindicated as innocent by the detective who, by identifying the criminal (usually from a social level either above or below the middle class), exposes him as the alien "Other." *The Moonstone*, however, does not allow such consoling reductionism. The history of the fabulous moonstone itself also makes this point clear. Originally set in the forehead of a figure of a Hindu god, the stone was stolen by the invading Moghuls, who were Muslim, and stolen in turn by an English aristocrat serving in the British Army, who brought it back to England. As a consequence, the diamond, an object of religious veneration, becomes a marketplace commodity in a demi-monde world of dealers in valuable objects of questionable provenance, where its value, because of a flaw at its center, stands to be increased if it can be smuggled to Amsterdam and recut as a number of smaller stones. This process, however, would cause the jewel to lose its identity as a sacred stone. Whether Collins intended the stone's story to symbolize the growing materialism of 19th-century England or the rapaciousness of British imperialism, which itself destroyed the indigenous histories of other cultures as it sought to create new markets, the novel offers itself to these as well as other subversive readings, particularly in Collins' willingness to give voices to the underclasses (Rosanna Spearman, Gabriel Betteredge) and to the marginalized (Ezra Jennings, Miss Clack).

Finally, in contradiction to Moretti's formula for the standard detective novel, in which the criminal comes from a class above or below the bourgeoisie, the thief who steals the diamond from the Verinder estate is Godfrey Abelwhite, a cousin of the family and a suitor for the hand of the Verinder heiress. By making the criminal a member of the same class as the victim, Collins challenges the ideological fiction of a middle class bound together in commitment to a common moral code. Since Collins' readers were themselves middle class, they found themselves confronted with the possibility that crime could come from their own group, and could not be dismissed as the antisocial act of an alien in their midst. As the first of its kind, *The Moonstone* reaches levels of complexity that few of its successors can match—both in terms of the brilliance of its plot construction and the subtlety of its social vision.

JAMES L. HILL

Further Reading

Brooks, Peter, *Reading for the Plot: Design and Intention in Narrative,* New York: Knopf, and Oxford: Clarendon Press, 1984

Clarke, William M., *The Secret Life of Wilkie Collins,* London: Allison and Busby, 1988; Chicago: Dee, 1991

Heller, Tamar, *Dead Secrets: Wilkie Collins and the Female Gothic,* New Haven, Connecticut: Yale University Press, 1992

Lonoff de Cuevas, Sue, *Wilkie Collins and His Victorian Readers: A Study in the Rhetoric of Authorship,* New York: AMS Press, 1982

Miller, D.A., *The Novel and the Police,* Berkeley: University of California Press, 1988

Moretti, Franco, *Signs Taken for Wonders: Essays in the Sociology of Literary Forms,* London: Verso, 1983; revised edition, London and New York: Verso, 1988

O'Neill, Philip, *Wilkie Collins: Women, Property and Propriety,* London: Macmillan, and Totowa, New Jersey: Barnes and Noble, 1988

Peters, Catherine, *The King of Inventors: A Life of Wilkie Collins,* London: Secker and Warburg, 1991; Princeton, New Jersey: Princeton University Press, 1993

Rance, Nicholas, *Wilkie Collins and Other Sensation Novelists: Walking the Moral Hospital,* London: Macmillan, and Rutherford, New Jersey: Fairleigh Dickinson University Press, 1991

Taylor, Jenny Bourne, *In the Secret Theatre of Home: Wilkie Collins, Sensation Narrative, and Nineteenth-Century Psychology,* London and New York: Routledge, 1988

George Moore 1852–1933

Irish

An important early English-language exponent of French prose styles, George Moore plays a pivotal role in the transformation of the Victorian novel, with all its bourgeois certitude, into modernist fiction with its uncertainties and reservations. Richard Allen Cave has gone so far as to suggest that to read George Moore's novels in chronological sequence "is to watch in miniature the transformation of the novel itself as a genre from its typically nineteenth-century to its typically twentieth-century mould" (see Cave, 1978).

Moore is the earliest writer in English to experiment with the stream-of-consciousness technique, later refined in the work of writers such as James Joyce and Virginia Woolf. His interest in Wagnerian opera found support in the work of French writer Édouard Dujardin, who attempted to capture in prose the uninterrupted musical pattern of Wagner's operas. Moore took Dujardin's ideas further, pursuing a rhythmic and uninterrupted flow of prose to indicate the flow of thought.

Moore was an experimentalist, and most critics agree that there is no such thing as a "typical" George Moore novel. He was also prolific. At the time of his death—just short of his 81st birthday—he had published 21 volumes of prose fiction (both novels and short stories), 9 plays, 11 volumes of essays, criticism, and autobiographical sketches, 2 volumes of poetry, and a number of translations.

Despite spending a significant part of his working life in England, Moore was much less influenced by English writers than he was by continental styles and values, in particular those of Émile Zola, Gustave Flaubert, Ivan Turgenev, Charles Baudelaire, Édouard Dujardin, as well as the painters Edgar Degas and Édouard Manet. The experiences of his early, bohemian lifestyle in France as an aspiring painter influenced Moore throughout his life. He never lost his love of art, and much of his writing not only focuses on artists but illustrates literary techniques derived directly from the visual arts.

Although Moore's fiction is most often classified as naturalistic, his extensive experimentalism makes his work difficult to classify with any accuracy. His first novel, the three-volume *A Modern Lover* (1883), written when he was 31 years old, was the first of many to center on artists and the art world. His second novel, *A Mummer's Wife* (1884), is often described as the first naturalistic novel in English and was acknowledged by Arnold Bennett to have inspired his own novels about the Five Towns. However, the novel, bearing evidence of the influence of Zola and Flaubert, marked the beginning and end of Moore's strictly naturalistic period, since he began to look to a more diverse range of sources and became more intent on honing his own stylistic skills.

A Drama in Muslin (1886) explicitly confronts Moore's own Irish (Ascendancy) background. The events of the novel take place in an atmosphere of class warfare, involving rent strikes, absentee landlords, and abject poverty. Moore juxtaposes the privileged foolishness of the upper-class women of the novel against the gloom of peasant life. However, like many contemporaneous Anglo-Irish writers, his sympathetic portrayal of peasant exploitation is always qualified by a sense of sadness for the decline of his own class.

Moore continued the theme of Irish life in his *Confessions of a Young Man* (1888), an autobiographical novel regarded by many critics as an early "portrait of the artist as a young man." It is in this novel that Moore makes clear his complex and often dichotomous artistic views. The central narrator, Edward Dayne, gives two quite distinct views of the Impressionists, Zola, and Shakespeare, stating that "Art is not nature. Art is nature digested. Art is sublime excrement."

It was not until the publication and success of *Esther Waters* (1894), one of many Moore novels to have a central female character, that Moore's literary reputation was established. Acknowledged as a "tale that marks a period in our literature" by a group of prominent artists, writers, and critics on the occasion of Moore's 80th birthday, *Esther Waters* is considered by many to represent a particular stage in the development of the English novel through, on the one hand, its use of naturalism in both style and material and, on the other hand, its adoption of a cyclical narrative and an optimistic ending, thus challenging any existing understanding of that generic classification. Initially the novel was critically acclaimed for its "beauty of moral effort" and the author's "respect for common life." However, even for some who liked the novel, such as Katherine Mansfield and H.G. Wells, Moore remained too detached from his tale, omitting any sense of warmth or humor. Similarly, contemporary critics such as Ian Gregor and Brian Nicholas see the novel as melodramatic and simplistic in its theme of the good girl victimized by the wicked society. It seems possible, however, that Moore has attracted such criticism through his attempt to challenge the two main strands of writing dealing with the working classes during the 19th century—the sentimental and the comical—by creating a story that sets the brutal aspects of the protagonist's reaction toward her surrounding material conditions against her inner strength, beauty, and compassion.

Moore's stated intention in *Esther Waters* was to break away from the strictures of naturalism in relation to linear structure and the conventions of determinism. In contrast to the conventions of the naturalistic novel, then, inherited social status and environment are not the overwhelming factors in deciding Esther's fate. Moore found naturalism limiting because it took such small account of the inner lives of characters and, particularly in Zola's work, reduced human instinct to the level of animal urges. In *Esther Waters,* Moore challenges such determinism by allowing the inner, individual determination to survive over everything else.

Between 1899 and 1911, Moore returned to live and work in Ireland as part of the Irish Literary Renaissance. Among his most successful writing from this period was a collection of short stories, *The Untilled Field* (1903), which was inspired by Turgenev's *Tales of a Sportsman* and which is considered the precursor to James Joyce's *Dubliners.* However, his most enduring writing from the Irish period is an autobiographical trilogy, initially published as *Ave* (1911), *Salve* (1912), and *Vale* (1914). The books were ultimately amalgamated under the title of *Hail and Farewell* (1914). While these accounts offer an interesting and lively view of social and political life in Dublin, they ultimately register Moore's disillusionment with Ireland and the Irish Literary Theatre. His differences with W.B. Yeats are evident in the trilogy, where Yeats is caricatured. Unable to resolve his differences with the Gaelic movement and the leaders of the Literary Revival, Moore left Ireland in 1911.

In his later work, Moore revealed a greater interest in oral narration and, as a result, much of his writing was directed toward the stage. As his last novels indicate, Moore was more interested in style than in story. He endlessly revised new and existing work, testing for rhythm by tapping out a beat as he read. This procedure testifies to his lifelong interest in achieving a rhythmic and uninterrupted flow of prose, which he first spoke of in *Confessions of a Young Man.*

REBECCA PELAN

Biography

Born 24 February 1852 at Moore Hall, Ballyglass, County Mayo; moved with his family to London, 1869. Attended Oscott College, Birmingham, 1861–67; took art classes in the evenings at South Kensington Museum, and studied with an army tutor, 1870; studied painting in London, 1870–73, and at Académie Julian and Ecole des Beaux Arts, Paris, 1873–74. Lived in Paris, 1873–79, and in London and Ireland from 1879; contributed to the *Spectator* and the *Examiner*; art critic, the *Speaker*, 1891–95; cofounder, with Lady Gregory, Edward Martyn, and William Butler Yeats, Irish Literary Theatre (later the Irish National Theatre Society at the Abbey Theatre, Dublin), 1899; lived in Dublin, 1901–11, and in London from 1911; High Sheriff of Mayo, 1905. Died 21 January 1933.

Novels by Moore

A Modern Lover, 1883; as *Lewis Seymour and Some Women,* 1917
A Mummer's Wife, 1884; as *An Actor's Wife,* 1889
A Drama in Muslin, 1886; revised edition, as *Muslin,* 1915
Confessions of a Young Man, 1888
Spring Days: A Realistic Novel—A Prelude to Don Juan, 1888; as *Shifting Love,* 1891
Mike Fletcher, 1889
Vain Fortune, 1891
Esther Waters, 1894
Evelyn Innes, 1898
Sister Teresa, 1901
The Lake, 1905
The Brook Kerith: A Syrian Story, 1916
Héloïse and Abélard, 1921; as *Fragments,* 1921
Ulick and Soracha, 1926
Aphrodite in Aulis, 1930

Other Writings: stories, plays, poetry, essays, criticism, autobiography.

Further Reading

Cave, Richard Allen, *A Study of the Novels of George Moore,* Gerards Cross: Smythe, and New York: Barnes and Noble, 1978
Dunleavy, Janet Egleson, *George Moore: The Artist's Vision, the Storyteller's Art,* Lewisburg, Pennsylvania: Bucknell University Press, 1973

Farrow, Anthony, *George Moore*, Boston: Twayne, and London: Prior, 1978

Gilcher, Edwin, *A Bibliography of George Moore*, DeKalb, Illinois: Northern Illinois University Press, 1970

Hone, Joseph M., *The Life of George Moore*, New York: Macmillan, and London: Gollancz, 1936

Hughes, Douglas A., editor, *The Man of Wax: Critical Essays on George Moore*, New York: New York University Press, 1971

Owens, Graham, editor, *George Moore's Mind and Art*, Edinburgh: Oliver and Boyd, 1968; New York: Barnes and Noble, 1970

Alberto Moravia 1907–90

Italian

Although generally regarded by critics as an existentialist writer of the same school as Albert Camus and Jean-Paul Sartre, Alberto Moravia is, as Joan Ross and Donald Freed point out in *The Existentialism of Alberto Moravia* (1972), "first and foremost . . . a storyteller, and human behavior is at the core of his fictional world."

Moravia was a sickly child—he suffered from tuberculosis of the bones from the age of nine until his late teens. As he was frequently too ill to attend school, his family, anxious that his studies should not suffer, provided him with the works of such authors as Arthur Rimbaud, Fedor Dostoevskii, Alessandro Manzoni, Marcel Proust, Franz Kafka, Sigmund Freud, Molière, Shakespeare, and James Joyce. His first novel, *Gli indifferenti* (1929; *The Time of Indifference*), was the product both of this somewhat unusual education and of the political climate of the age. Although Moravia himself frequently maintained that he conceived of *The Time of Indifference* as an exercise in fusing the techniques of the novel with those of the theatre, and that he had no political point to prove, public opinion failed to appreciate his intention, and the novel received a far from positive response upon its publication.

Many of the themes that dominate Moravia's later works were already discernible in this first novel: the dangers inherent in a consumerist, bourgeois society; a sense of alienation, along with an inability to comprehend society; the struggle of an intellectual protagonist who must choose between conformity and integrity; voyeur/exhibitionist relationships whose impetus stems not from sexual fantasy but from the desire of the narrating voyeur for self-revelation; and, despite an essentially tragic view of the human condition, an underlying conviction that people can ultimately overcome even the most destructive forms of adversity and suffering.

Starting in 1930, Moravia worked as foreign correspondent for the newspapers *La Stampa* and *La Gazzetta del Popolo*, during which time he published several collections of short stories and novels, among them the crudely moralistic *Le ambizioni sbagliate* (1935; *The Wheel of Fortune*) and the political caricature *La mascherata* (1941; *The Fancy Dress Party*). He returned in 1936 to Italy and, as Oreste del Buono quotes him in *Moravia* (1962), "ad un'atmosfera avvelenata dalla menzogna, dalla pau-

ra e dal conformismo" (to an atmosphere poisoned by lies, by fear and by conformism).

Following the fall of Mussolini in 1943, Moravia, who had published vehemently antifascist articles in *Il Popolo di Roma*, suffered considerable persecution at the hands of the remnant fascist regime and was obliged to flee Rome and take refuge with the peasant community in Fondi. This experience was the foundation for *La ciociara* (1957; *Two Women*), which highlights the devastation and inhumanity of fascism. Its influence may also be seen in several other works, including *La romana* (1947; *The Woman of Rome*), which is set during the late 1930s and depicts the optimistic fascist and imperialistic expansionism of the age, juxtaposed with the nascent stirrings of antifascist activity.

A self-confessed Marxist—Moravia remarked to Alain Elkann in *Vita di Moravia* (1990) that "per la prima volta in vita mia mi trovai più o meno completamente d'accordo con un movimento politico" (for the first time in my life I found myself more or less completely in agreement with a political movement)—Moravia's political ideology became a major theme in his writings.

La vita interiore (1978) is somewhat sensationally translated into English as *Time of Desecration*, thus maintaining the "Time of" style so popular with Moravia's translators but doing away with the Marxist alienation implicit in the original idea of "the life inside." It is a more modernist work, composed in the form of an interview between the ostensible narrator *io* (I) and the interviewee, Desideria, in which the author produces an oblique reflection of the events of 1968, the subsequent period of protest, and the rise of the "Movimento." The tone is static, impersonal, and externalized. Any interaction between those characters of whom Desideria speaks but whom readers never actually "meet" is narrated so subjectively that readers remain alienated from any form of objective reality. The only true interaction discernible in the novel takes place between Desideria and her interlocutor, the authoritative, privileged *io*.

This stylization of character had often been commented on, both before and after the publication of *Time of Desecration*, by Moravia's critics. Giancarlo Pandini in *Invito alla lettura di Alberto Moravia* (1973) remarks that "[i personaggi moraviani] patiscono il rapporto dificile con la realtà; tutti sono in conflitto con la verità di una vita che invano si sforzano di vivere autenticamente" ([Moravia's characters] suffer from a difficult relationship with reality; they cannot come to terms with the truth that they are trying in vain to live life in an authentic manner). Thomas Bergin in his article "The Moravian Muse" (1953) notes that "his characters speak fluently enough . . . but their speech is always a little literary in flavor; they talk indeed very much like characters in a book." Only Rocco Capozzi in his preface to *Homage to Alberto Moravia* (1993) is able to see beyond this artificiality when he observes that, "though at times the writing is tedious, a little contrived, or a little too polished, it is always very much alive."

Moravia's criticism of his society is at once shocking and brutal: rape, sodomy, and murder occur frequently and often graphically in his works. His representation of what is essentially the distasteful, seamy side of life can be located in his reaction to the violence of life as he understands it. On an allegorical level, then, the rape of Rosetta in *Two Women* symbolizes the rape of the proletariat by capitalism, the failed sodomizing of Desideria in *Time of Desecration* indicates the failure of bourgeois society to quash the revolutionary youth, and the murder of Quinto in the same novel represents the corruption running through all levels of society.

Moravia's courage in addressing subjects that many other authors would consider taboo has ensured that all his novels have been received either with praise or with opprobrium, but never with indifference. He remains one of Italy's most important and influential novelists.

SALLY-ANN POULSON

Biography

Born Alberto Pincherle in Rome, 28 November 1907. Educated privately. Contracted tuberculosis at the age of nine and spent considerable time in sanatoriums from 1916 to 1925. Foreign correspondent, *La Stampa*, Milan, and *La Gazzetta del Popolo*, Turin, in the 1930s; traveled extensively, staying for long periods in France, Britain, the United States, Mexico, Greece, and China; lived in Anacapri (on Capri), 1941–43; persecuted by the fascist regime for publishing antifascist articles, and so fled Rome in 1943 and went into hiding in Fondi, near Cassino, until the Allied Liberation; film critic, *La Nuova Europa*, 1944–46; coeditor, with Alberto Carocci, *Nuovi Argomenti*, Milan, from 1953; film critic, *L'Espresso*, Milan, from 1955; State Department lecturer in the United States, 1955; traveled throughout the world, 1958–70; coeditor with Leonardo Sciascia and Enzo Siciliano, *Nuovi Argomenti*, 1982. Died 26 September 1990.

Novels by Moravia

Gli indifferenti, 1929; as *The Indifferent Ones*, translated by Aida Mastrangelo, 1932; as *The Time of Indifference*, translated by Angus Davidson, 1953

Le ambizioni sbagliate, 1935; as *The Wheel of Fortune*, translated by Arthur Livingstone, 1937; as *Mistaken Ambitions*, translated by Livingstone, 1955

La mascherata, 1941; as *The Fancy Dress Party*, translated by Angus Davidson, 1947

Agostino, 1945; as *Agostino*, translated by Beryl de Zoete, 1947

La romana, 1947; as *The Woman of Rome*, translated by Lydia Holland, 1949

La disubbidienza, 1948; as *Disobedience*, translated by Angus Davidson, 1950; as *Luca*, translated by Davidson, in *Five Novels*, 1955

Il conformista, 1951; as *The Conformist*, translated by Angus Davidson, 1951

Il disprezzo, 1954; as *A Ghost at Noon*, translated by Angus Davidson, 1955

La ciociara, 1957; as *Two Women*, translated by Angus Davidson, 1958

La noia, 1960; as *The Empty Canvas*, translated by Angus Davidson, 1961

L'attenzione, 1965; as *The Lie*, translated by Angus Davidson, 1966

Io e lui, 1971; as *Two: A Phallic Novel*, translated by Angus Davidson, 1972; as *The Two of Us*, translated by Davidson, 1972

La vita interiore, 1978; as *Time of Desecration*, translated by Angus Davidson, 1980

L'uomo che guarda, 1985; as *The Voyeur: A Novel*, translated by Tim Parks, 1986

Il viaggio a Roma, 1988; as *Journey to Rome*, translated by Tim Parks, 1990

La donna leopardo, 1990

Other Writings: short stories, plays and screenplays, travel writings, film criticism, essays.

Further Reading

Bergin, Thomas, "The Moravian Muse," *Virginia Quarterly Review* (Spring 1953)

Capozzi, Rocco, and Mario B. Mignone, editors, *Homage to Alberto Moravia*, Stony Brook, New York: Forum Italicum, 1993

Dego, Giuliano, *Moravia*, Edinburgh and London: Oliver and Boyd, 1966; New York: Barnes and Noble, 1967

del Buono, Oreste, *Moravia*, Milan: Feltrinelli, 1962

Elkann, Alain, and Alberto Moravia, *Vita di Moravia*, Milan: Bompiani, 1990

Pandini, Giancarlo, *Invito alla lettura di Alberto Moravia*, Milan: Mursia, 1973; 3rd edition, 1977

Ross, Joan, and Donald Freed, *The Existentialism of Alberto Moravia*, Carbondale: Southern Illinois University Press, 1972

Wood, Sharon, *Woman as Object: Language and Gender in the Work of Alberto Moravia*, London: Pluto Press, and Savage, Maryland: Barnes and Noble, 1990

Toni Morrison 1931–

United States

Toni Morrison is acknowledged as the foremost writer of the contemporary black women's renaissance, which includes the writers Alice Walker, Gloria Naylor, Maya Angelou, and others such as Toni Cade Bambara and Gayle Jones, whom Morrison herself promoted from her position as senior editor at Random House. The award of the Nobel prize for literature in 1993 crowned a career that already glittered with major literary prizes and honors: the National Book Award, the National Book Critics Circle Award, the American Academy and Institute of Arts and Letters Award, the Pulitzer Prize, and the appointment to the National Council on the Arts. Such accolades attest to Morrison's significance and the importance of her contribution to American literature generally and to African-American literature specifically. However, the exact nature of her novelistic innovations resists easy categorization. Her work blends realism, history, myth, folktale, the fantastic and the grotesque; she draws upon a rich artistic heritage that is at once black, American, and European; and her fiction is contemporary, yet it stands apart from the postmodern mainstream. Her achievement has been to open African-American literary expression to a world of possibilities.

Morrison's first novel, *The Bluest Eye* (1970), demonstrates her commitment to inventing a novelistic form that meets the needs of the specific story. This story of the Breedlove family brims with their loathing of their own poverty, powerlessness, ugliness, and blackness. The family is unlovable and unloving. Pecola prays for the blue eyes she believes will make her beautiful and loved and transform her world. Morrison uses a complex narrative point of view, moving between the perspective offered by the child-narrator Claudia, various first-person narrators, and an anonymous third-person omniscient narrator. In this way, Morrison creates a vivid picture of the black community of Lorain, Ohio, and the past and present experiences of the main characters, as well as a bitingly critical and ironic perspective, as the adult Claudia re-creates her youthful innocence and lack of understanding. The narrative contains no suspense—all is given at the beginning: Pecola's rape by her father, the death of her baby, her madness. The novel asks not "what?" but "how?" and takes the form of recollection in order to encourage analysis on the part of the reader.

The Bluest Eye forms a foundation, stylistic and thematic, for Morrison's subsequent work. The language is heavily textured and highly imagistic; it invites participation in the production of meaning, because it is open to interpretation rather than being transparent to the reader. This is indicated in the opening pages, where sentences taken from a "Dick and Jane" primer are gradually flattened into gibberish, garbling the middle-class family ideal the words represent. It is upon the capacity of the racial values of white America to poison and destroy the lives of African-Americans that the novel concentrates. Pecola's final victimization by Soaphead Church imprisons her in his 19th-century colonial attitudes; he uses her insane desire for blue eyes to take revenge upon her blackness. His is an act of moral and spiritual violence that destroys Pecola's mind just as Cholly's physical violence destroys her body. Throughout the novel, Morrison sustains a distinction between the view of the narrator, Claudia, and the adults of the black community. Only the children Claudia and Frieda have hope for Pecola's child and for the future. Claudia clearly sees Pecola's fate and recognizes that the consequences of her fate must be borne by the other characters: "It's too late. At least on the edge of my town, among the garbage and the sunflowers of my town, it's much, much too late."

The power of white culture to corrupt entire communities that cannot meet its cultural demands because of their race is a theme that occupies Morrison's fiction. The inverted values of wealth and beauty cause Pecola to be rejected by the corrupted black community and transformed into a pariah, a focus for all their fears of unworthiness. Even Pecola, the "innocent" victim, accepts that only beauty merits love and that, because she is black, she is ugly and therefore unworthy of love. Cultural artifacts like Shirley Temple dolls, Mary Jane candy, and Hollywood movie actresses transform female sexuality into commodities that are sold to black women, who consume these images in a doomed attempt to make themselves into reflections of the cultural ideal. Sula, the eponymous heroine of Morrison's second novel (1974), is similarly cast as a pariah. The novel charts the friendship between Sula and Nel to explore issues of responsibility and fear, the possibilities of love in a corrupted world, and the identity and reclamation of self within the context of a black community in which values have been turned upside down as a consequence of internalized racism. In this novel, evil may be good and good may be evil. Destruction, murder, and self-mutilation may be necessary expressions of love. In *Sula* there are no easy equations, and moral decisions are always difficult.

In Morrison's fiction the motif of double-consciousness or seeing double represents the ways in which race permeates every aspect of experience—white and black—and complicates every action. Characters see themselves reflected variously in white and black eyes. Thus, in *The Bluest Eye* the blue eyes Pecola desires symbolize her desire for physical beauty and for approval within a racist culture. Throughout the book, the self-image reflected in the eyes of others symbolizes the way in which people experience themselves in society. People often seek confirmation of their self-worth in the eyes of those they encounter every day. In the eyes of the storekeeper, Mr. Yacobowski, Pecola finds the "absence of human recognition . . . she had seen it lurking in the eyes of all white people. So. The distaste must be for her, her blackness. . . ." The connection between self and world that is symbolized by vision is then symbolically severed when Pecola seeks to exchange her brown eyes for blue. She surrenders irrevocably any hope for an authentic relationship with the world. In her final madness, she stares into mirrors and talks schizophrenically to an imaginary friend who is but a reflection of part of herself. In *Tar Baby* (1981), Morrison takes this theme further. Jardine is an African-American woman who has been adopted by a white millionaire and educated in Europe as an art historian. While visiting her family's Caribbean mansion, Jardine encounters Son, a violent criminal on the run, and in his eyes she reads all that she has surrendered, all that she has paid as the price for her metaphorical blue eyes. The life she lives comes into focus in a racial perspective as a consequence of this harrowing encounter.

Morrison takes a more optimistic approach to racial self-definition in *Song of Solomon* (1977). "Milkman" Dead resists the pressure imposed by his family to emulate white standards. Instead, he seeks the meaning of the legacy left to him by his aunt Pilate, the woman with no navel who knows folk magic. Milkman leaves his Northern town for the Southern rural community where his family has its roots. Hagar, the woman who loves him, represents the danger of racial conformity he leaves behind, as she dies in the futile attempt to transform herself into an image of white beauty. Through the discovery of community, of a rich history and a personal place in it, and through the ritual repetition of mythic events, Milkman discovers transcendence through self-acceptance and self-knowledge.

In her novels *Beloved* (1987) and *Jazz* (1992), Morrison examines the impact of slavery and Reconstruction upon African-American life. In a more openly political style of writing, Morrison offers two novels in a planned trilogy that will reconstruct postbellum history from an African-American perspective. These novels represent a culmination of Morrison's treatment of black America as conditioned by white racial ideology. *Beloved* tells the story of an escaped slave, Sethe, who attempts to kill her children rather than see them returned to slavery. Her murdered baby eventually returns in corporeal form to exact retribution, causing Sethe to relive agonizing memories of the past before she can exorcise them. *Jazz* moves forward in time, from Reconstruction to the period of mass migration from the South in the early 20th century. Like *Beloved,* this novel asks how freed slaves are to deal with the complexities of a freedom over which they have no control. With no successful models to follow, crisis is the inevitable consequence, as individuals attempt to become agents in their own lives.

Morrison's work displays an increasing interest in the reconstruction of American history, literary and otherwise, to incorporate a previously unacknowledged racial perspective. Her 1988 essay, "Unspeakable Things Unspoken," sets out the views Morrison has since explored further in the critical work *Playing in the Dark* (1992) and in her contribution to *Race-ing Justice, En-gendering Power* (1992).

DEBORAH L. MADSEN

See also Beloved

Biography

Born in Lorain, Ohio, 18 February 1931. Attended Howard University, Washington, D.C., B.A. 1953; Cornell University, Ithaca, New York, M.A. 1955. Instructor in English, Texas Southern University, Houston, 1955–57, and Howard University, 1957–64; senior editor, Random House, publishers, New York, 1965–84; Associate Professor, State University of New York, Purchase, 1971–72; Visiting Lecturer, Yale University, New Haven, Connecticut, 1976–77, Rutgers University, New Brunswick, New Jersey, 1983–84, and Bard College, Annandale-on-Hudson, New York, 1986–88; Schweitzer Professor of the Humanities, State University of New York, Albany, 1984–89; Regents' Lecturer, University of California, Berkeley, 1987; Santagata Lecturer, Bowdoin College, Brunswick, Maine, 1987. Since 1989 Goheen Professor of the Humanities, Princeton University, New Jersey. Awarded Nobel prize for literature, 1993.

Novels by Morrison

The Bluest Eye, 1970
Sula, 1974
Song of Solomon, 1977
Tar Baby, 1981
Beloved, 1987
Jazz, 1992
Paradise, 1998

Other Writings: essays, including *Playing in the Dark: Whiteness and the Literary Imagination* (1992).

Further Reading

Bloom, Harold, editor, *Toni Morrison,* New York: Chelsea House, 1990
Callaloo 13:3 (Summer 1990), special issue on Toni Morrison
Carmean, Karen, *Toni Morrison's World of Fiction,* Troy, New York: Whitston, 1993
Harris, Trudier, *Fiction and Folklore: The Novels of Toni Morrison,* Knoxville: University of Tennessee Press, 1991
Heinze, Denise, *The Dilemma of "Double-Consciousness": Toni Morrison's Novels,* Athens: University of Georgia Press, 1993
Mbalia, Doreatha D., *Toni Morrison's Developing Class Consciousness,* Selinsgrove, Pennsylvania: Susquehanna University Press, and London: Associated University Presses, 1991
Otten, Terry, *The Crime of Innocence in the Novels of Toni Morrison,* Columbia: University of Missouri Press, 1989
Rigney, Barbara Hill, *The Voices of Toni Morrison,* Columbus: Ohio State University Press, 1991

Mr. Mani by A.B. Yehoshua

Mar Mani 1990

Mr. Mani, A.B. Yehoshua's most innovative novel and an Israeli best-seller, is an historical novel and a family saga that subverts the literary genres and narrative techniques that it employs and relies upon. In a postmodernistic spirit of play with conventional genres, Yehoshua reconstitutes traditional presentations of history, particularly Jewish history and ethnicity, offering a Sephardic and Mediterranean-oriented account riddled with ambiguity. In a certain sense, this novel holds a distorted mirror to Jewish history by presenting it *backward* through a series of partially unreliable and uninformed sources, who focus upon a family that never gathers and is perpetually tottering on the verge of extinction.

The nine generations of the Mani family, whose life stories constitute the core of this novel, are Sephardic Jews who, for different reasons, wander through a Mediterranean world during the course of some 200 years. In a series of five intensely dynamic conversations, the Manis' vicissitudes are narrated, mostly by strangers—three Ashkenazic Jews, one Nazi soldier, and only one family member—to audiences who in most cases do not know the Manis.

As eccentric and disturbed as some of the Manis are, the characters who describe them are almost equally so. Each has a private motive for telling his or her account to a parent, officer, teacher, or other authoritative figure who judges both the storyteller and the respective Mani family member. The storytellers manipulate their audience's attention while admitting that their information is subjective and somewhat flawed. In fact, the Manis themselves know relatively little about their ancestors because contacts between generations are often severed during the course of tragic relocations. Moreover, the sometimes awful Mani history can be uttered only by an outsider, or by a family member to a listener who is unable to repeat the compromising information. Each storytelling performance is thus exposed as an imaginative reconstruction bursting with gaps and ambiguities.

The most striking feature of Yehoshua's novel is that it shows only one side of each conversation, inviting the reader to fill in the absent interlocutor's lines. The attitudes, and even the very words, of the interlocutor can easily be reconstructed from the arguments, apologies, and requests of the speaker. As Wendy Zierler (1993) points out, *Mr. Mani* thus approximates Roland Barthes' ideal modern text: a "writerly" text in which the reader becomes actively involved in the process of producing and interpreting literature.

The second striking feature of this novel is its nonchronological arrangement. The opening conversation, which takes place between a young Israeli woman and her mother in a contemporary kibbutz, is set in 1982 during the Peace for the Galilee war. The last conversation, between Avraham Mani and an old rabbi who dies during the course of Mr. Mani's horrific revelations, is set in 1848 Athens. Three intermediate conversations, set around critical moments in Jewish history such as the Holocaust, the British Mandate of Palestine, and the First Zionist Congress, occur respectively in 1944 Crete, 1918 Jerusalem, and 1899 Poland. A testimony to Yehoshua's extraordinary linguistic and stylistic virtuosity is his ability to mimic traits from the supposed language and period-style of each conversation, be it Hebrew, German, English, Yiddish, or Judeo-Spanish.

Historical milestones coinciding with salient developments in the characters' lives provide more than just a backdrop to their tumultuous and convoluted existences. In fact, the historical events propel the action: the British presence in Palestine triggers Yosef Mani's political and histrionic ambitions; meeting a Jerusalemite at the Zionist Congress in Switzerland provides the Shapiros with an opportunity to venture into the Holy Land. Such historical junctures expose obsessive tendencies lying dormant in the characters, whose fantasies and anxieties lead them to commit treason, adultery, incest, and even infanticide.

The past is made present through *Mr. Mani*'s nonchronological structure and its series of conversations set at the time of the narrated events. Yet the personal and supposedly authoritative witnessing of places and events—the "I was there so I should know" assumption—is as riddled with gaps as conventional historiographies that attempt to approach the past from a present outlook. Globally, *Mr. Mani* is the product of a conventional historiographical gesture, but internally it is built from a series of subjective accounts that expose the limitations of any totalizing and teleological master narrative. In the classical historical novel, an objective and authoritative truth is always assumed, while in the postmodern novel, and specifically in *Mr. Mani*, the subjectivity of storytelling and interpretation is systematically exposed.

This novel also challenges traditional Jewish historiographies by pitting Sephardic, Jerusalemite, and Mediterranean perspectives against dominant Ashkenazic, intellectual, and Central European-oriented accounts of the Jewish people and their wanderings. *Mr. Mani*'s ethnic dimension is a dual one, however, for the novel's Sephardic core is processed through the psyches of Ashkenazic and even non-Jewish storytellers whose curiosity about the Manis and their Sephardic ways highlights ethnic differences.

Despite the terrible events that befall the Manis, the novel's overall spirit is comic and playful. Yehoshua delights in twisting a wide range of literary rules and readerly-writerly conventions, engaging the reader in an entertaining decoding of the novel's multiperspectival layers of information. While *Mr. Mani* belongs to the family-saga genre, according to Gershon Shaked (1991) it is equally an *anti*saga and an *anti*family novel, since, in an antichronological sequence, strangers tell the story of a family they barely know, a family that never consolidates as a functional entity.

Yehoshua steps beyond the precedent of William Faulkner's chronologically-disjointed and narratologically-fragmented sagas, as well as Joseph Conrad's and James Joyce's instances of one-sided dialogue, to offer a playful threefold reconfiguration of narrative dialogue, historical writing, and family saga. Coupled with a deliberate denial of certainty and closure, this successful experimentation with the novel's form marks new and wider boundaries now available to contemporary writers.

YAEL HALEVI-WISE

See also A.B. Yehoshua

Further Reading

Ben-Dov, Nitza, editor, *Be-kivun ha-negdi: Kovetz Mehkarim al "Mar Mani" Le-A.B. Yehoshua* (In the Opposite Direction: Articles on *Mr. Mani*), Tel Aviv: Hakibbutz Hameuhad, 1995

Meiron, Dan, "Behind Every Thought Hides Another Thought: Meditations on *Mr. Mani*," *Siman Kriyah* 21 (December 1990)
Shaked, Gershon, "A Puzzle Greater Than Its Solutions," *Modern Hebrew Literature* (Spring/Summer 1991)
Zierler, Wendy, "*Mr. Mani* by A.B. Yehoshua," *Ariel* 91 (1993)

Mrs. Dalloway by Virginia Woolf

1925

Mrs. Dalloway is the novel that established Virginia Woolf as a successful modernist writer. In the course of writing it she discovered her true voice as well as a method suited to her expression. Her fourth novel, *Mrs. Dalloway* ushered in the succession of major novels that were to follow, most notably *To the Lighthouse* (1927) and *The Waves* (1931). *Mrs. Dalloway* was published concurrently with *The Common Reader*, a collection of essays exploring Woolf's ideas about the nature of fiction. Significantly, it contained her modernist manifesto "Modern Fiction," in which she gives an account of the psychological novel, the novel that is inward looking. This was a new kind of fiction dedicated to the search for reality or "life itself" situated within the individual consciousness, and it required new forms and structures. Through this new idea Virginia Woolf was rejecting the tradition of realism and, more specifically, the traditional forms of fiction as they were used by many Edwardian novelists. When *Mrs. Dalloway* was almost completed, Woolf published her essay "Mr. Bennett and Mrs. Brown" (1924), in which she made her celebrated pronouncement that human nature changed in 1910, the year of the Post-Impressionist Exhibition at the Grafton Galleries in London. This event, which was organized by Roger Fry, profoundly influenced Woolf's thinking about the art of fiction. With respect to the visual arts, Fry believed that instead of photographic representation there should be expressive images and "a closely-knit unity of texture" that would convey reality through "a necessitated form." Virginia Woolf's theorizing about fiction in the early 1920s was closely linked to Fry's theory of painting and reflects what she was attempting to do in *Mrs. Dalloway.*

Mrs. Dalloway captures the mood of a city slowly recovering from the trauma of World War I through Woolf's inward exploration of a small group of characters as she connects their various responses to life and death, social conditions, illness, changing social mores, oppression, and so on. But the surface of the novel is itself trivial. A society hostess goes out to buy flowers for a party she is to give that evening. She meets people, reflects on her past, is visited by a former suitor in the middle of the morning, and by her husband in the middle of the afternoon. She mends a dress and orders ices for the party. The reality explored below that banal surface, however, is immense. Woolf reaches in her fiction from the outer to the inner, searching for the implications of the insignificant and the trivial, and the depth of human experience that she explores is communicated through a richly textured prose that has the resonant power of poetry.

Virginia Woolf sometimes has been criticized for being more concerned with form than content. Although she did work out the design of *Mrs. Dalloway* very carefully, the substance of the novel actually dictated its final form. As she put it figuratively in the Introduction to the Modern Library Edition (1928), "The idea started as the oyster starts or the snail to secrete a house for itself." The novel began as the short story "Mrs. Dalloway in Bond Street" but changed direction when Woolf discovered her "tunneling process" that enabled her to "dig out" the "caves" of a character's consciousness.

The two important thematic strands of *Mrs. Dalloway* are its critique of the social system and its study of madness. These were conceived at an early stage of composition, as Woolf recorded in her diary (14 October 1922, 19 June 1923). Through the technique of stream of consciousness, she fuses the two thematic strands, chiefly by following the associative connection between Septimus Warren Smith and the Dalloways. The Dalloways represent the ruling classes, while Septimus is at the lower end of the social scale; a scapegoat figure, he is one of the tragedies of the war (a war the ruling classes prolonged unnecessarily). At a deep level Septimus and Clarissa Dalloway are linked through the imagistic patterning of their interior monologues, which move from the ebb and flow of the ordinary and outer life to the strange world of the unconscious, where a larger reality is reached. Clarissa and Septimus never meet, yet he is her double, embodying the irrational side of her nature. Virginia Woolf's original intention had been that Clarissa should die at the end of the party. She then invented Septimus as her double who would die instead. Virginia Woolf successfully fuses the surface world of the London streets—the shops, the parks, the social scene—with the alienated individual psyche of her characters as they try to make sense of, and come to terms with, their own personal situations, the wider human condition, and the bleak nature of the modern world.

Mrs. Dalloway is arguably Virginia Woolf's most modernist text and has been compared with James Joyce's *Ulysses* (1922). These two novels have many technical features in common. Both are set in a metropolis and have a one-day time scale, for instance, and Joyce's epiphanic moments correspond to Woolf's "moments of being." Moreover, their respective narratives are built up through connecting and reflecting interior monologues that exploit the poetic possibilities of language. *Mrs. Dalloway* places Virginia Woolf at the center of the postwar explosion of modernist experimentation.

STELLA MCNICHOL

See also Virginia Woolf

Further Reading

Abel, Elizabeth, *Virginia Woolf and the Fictions of Psychoanalysis,* Chicago: University of Chicago Press, 1989

Bennett, Joan, *Virginia Woolf: Her Art as a Novelist,* Cambridge: Cambridge University Press, and New York: Harcourt Brace, 1945

Guiguet, Jean, *Virginia Woolf et son oeuvre,* Paris: Didier, 1962; as *Virginia Woolf and Her Works,* London: Hogarth Press, and New York: Harcourt Brace, 1965

Johnstone, J.K., *The Bloomsbury Group,* London: Secker and Warburg, and New York: Noonday Press, 1954

Kelley, Alice van Buren, *The Novels of Virginia Woolf: Fact and Vision,* Chicago: University of Chicago Press, 1973

Laurence, Patricia Ondek, *The Reading of Silence: Virginia Woolf in the English Tradition,* Stanford, California: Stanford University Press, 1991

McNichol, Stella, *Virginia Woolf and the Poetry of Fiction,* London and New York: Routledge, 1990

Naremore, James, *The World Without a Self: Virginia Woolf and the Novel,* New Haven, Connecticut: Yale University Press, 1973

Richter, Harvena, *Virginia Woolf: The Inward Voyage,* Princeton, New Jersey, Princeton University Press, 1970

Mudun al-milḥ. *See* Cities of Salt

Muerte de Artemio Cruz. *See* Death of Artemio Cruz

ʿAbd al-Raḥmān Munīf 1933–

Saudi Arabian

ʿAbd al-Raḥmān Munīf started out in life as an economist with a specialization in oil markets. Subsequently, he became a political activist, protesting human rights abuses, particularly the suppression of the freedom of speech. When he was imprisoned (and later exiled) for his political activities, he turned to fiction. Munīf devoted himself full time to writing novels in 1981.

Munīf's novels and critical writings have played an important role in revitalizing the Arab novel. Repudiating the slavish imitation of Western models, he has called for an authentic Arab novel written specifically for an Arab audience. Rather than please Western readers, he has argued, the novelist should respond to the needs of the Arab people and to the realities of the Arab world. Munīf has also pointed to the need for critical norms in the evaluation of literature that are similarly responsive to Arab society and culture.

Munīf's work is dominated by the conviction that the Arab novel fulfills an important historical function, given that the history of the region has largely been written by Westerners, while Arab historians have tended to write from the perspective of the social elite. As a result, official history falsifies Arab experience, particularly that of ordinary people, Munīf argues. He makes the point not only in his critical writings but also in his novels. The early novel *Al-ashjār wa-ightiyāl Marzūq* (1973; The Trees and the Assassination of Marzūq), for instance, takes as its subject the resistance to the imposition of false histories and the fight for freedom of expression.

According to Munīf, the novel offers the opportunity for an alternative, more truthful, historiography, and he has described his work as an "archive" for future generations. Through his novels, he intends to write "the history of those who have no history, the history of the poor and the oppressed, as well as those who dream of a better world." At the same time, he warns against the stagnation that results from hiding behind heritage and history to avoid the fact that the world, including the Arab world, is changing rapidly.

Munīf's most important work, the five-volume *Mudun al-milḥ* (1984–89; Cities of Salt), which earned him an international reputation, puts these beliefs into practice. The quintet of novels gives a gripping portrait of traditional Bedouin society, and the detailed narrative conveys the slow pace of time in the desert. The highly allusive style effectively creates a compelling ambience of mystery. However, Munīf's political and historical interests counteract the familiar romanticizing tendencies inherent in the focus on traditional desert life. Starting with the gradual establishment of the Kingdom of Saudi Arabia in the first decades of the 20th century, Cities of Salt also tells the story of British interventions in Arab politics and chronicles the transformation of traditional desert society following the discovery of oil.

Munīf's masterpiece is also remarkable for its handling of Arabic dialects. The narrative is written entirely in classical Arabic, but every character speaks in the colloquial Arabic (Gulf Arabian, Syrian, and so on) of the tribe to which he or she belongs. Munīf uses a variety of techniques, including the use of proverbs, to help make the meaning clear in the case of the less familiar dialects. A virtuoso accomplishment, this fidelity to the realities of the Arabic language contributes significantly to Munīf's goal of authenticity.

Despite Munīf's historical focus, his work is not romanticized history. The fictional narrative takes precedence over the linearity of historical events, which distances his work from purely historical narrative. In the novel entitled *Cities of Salt* in English, for instance, the story leaps backward and forward in time and the ending is revealed at the beginning. Munīf's concern with psychology—particularly evident in early works such as *Qiṣṣat ḥubb mājūsiyyah* (1974; Magician Love Story) and *Sharq al-Mutawasiṭ* (1975; East of the Mediterranean), which consist almost entirely of interior monologue—also shifts his novels away from straight history.

Given that he turned to fiction when he was a political prisoner, it is not surprising that Munīf's novels have an overtly political function. He believes that revealing the degree of a society's degradation will—once the initial shock has passed—provoke the reader to ask, "Do we have to put up with this, or should we revolt?" Much of his fiction targets the British, particularly *Al-ashjār wa-ightiyāl Marzūq*, *Sibāq al-masāfāt al-ṭawīlah* (1979; Long-Distance Race), *Taqāsīm al-layl wa-al-nahār* (1989; Variations on Night and Day), and *Bādiyat al-ẓulumāt* (1989; The Desert of Darkness). But he has been equally blunt with Arab regimes, which he also accuses of falsifications of history and of restricting the freedom of expression.

Another enduring aspect of Munīf's fiction is his celebration of place. Whether he describes deserts, cities, or prisons, his prose vividly evokes physical places and endows them with symbolic significance. Cities, central to the feeling of exile, both re-

pel and attract, an example being the tragic case of Ilyās in *Al-ashjār wa-ightiyāl Marzūq*. Munīf himself has returned to his native city, Amman, in the imagination, in *Sīrat Madīnah* (memoir, 1994; Story of a City). But in the Arab context, the absence of a specific identifiable geographic location takes on a special significance, since, as Munīf comments, "the similarity of situation in the Arab countries . . . changes every generalization into a specification."

AIDA A. BAMIA

See also Cities of Salt

Biography

Born in Amman, Jordan, in 1933. Educated in Egypt. Worked as an oil economist in Baghdad, and for OPEC; later exiled; since mid-1980s has lived in Damascus.

Fiction by Munīf

Al-ashjār wa-ightiyāl Marzūq [The Trees and the Assassination of Marzūq], 1973
Qiṣṣat ḥubb mājūsiyyah [Magician Love Story], 1974
Sharq al-Mutawasiṭ [East of the Mediterranean], 1975
Al-nihāyāt, 1978; as *Endings*, translated by Roger Allen, 1988
Sibāq al-masāfāt al-ṭawīlah [Long-Distance Race], 1979
ʿĀlam bi-lā kharāʾ iṭ [World without Maps], with Jabrā Ibrāhīm Jabrā, 1982
Mudun al-milḥ [Cities of Salt]
   Al-tīh, 1984; as *Cities of Salt*, translated by Peter Theroux, 1987
   Al-ukhdūd, 1985; as *The Trench*, translated by Peter Theroux, 1991
   Taqāsīm al-layl wa-al-nahār, 1989; as *Variations on Night and Day*, translated by Peter Theroux, 1993
   Al-munbatt [The Uprooted], 1989
   Bādiyat al-ẓulumāt [The Desert of Darkness], 1989
Hina tarakna al-jisr [When We Left the Bridge], n.d.
Al-ān hunā [Here and Now], 1991
Urwat al-Zaman al-bahi [Bond of Radiant Time], 1997

Other Writings: critical writings, including *Al-dīmuqrāṭiyyah awalan, al-dimuqrāṭiyyah dāʾiman* (1992; Democracy First, Democracy Always).

Further Reading

Allen, Roger, *The Arabic Novel: An Historical and Critical Introduction*, Syracuse, New York: Syracuse University Press, and Manchester: Manchester University Press, 1982; 2nd edition, Syracuse, New York: Syracuse University Press, 1995
Allen, Roger, "The Mature Arabic Novel Outside Egypt," in *Modern Arabic Literature*, edited by Muhammad Mustafa Badawi, Cambridge and New York: Cambridge University Press, 1992
Munīf, ʿAbd al-Raḥmān, *Al-Kātib wa-al-manfā* (The Writer and Exile), 2nd edition, Beirut: Al-Muʾassassa al-ʿArabiyya Lit-Ṭība ʿa Wan-Nashr, 1994
Tomiche, Nadia, *La Littérature arabe contemporaine*, Paris: Maisonneuve et Larose, 1993

Alice Munro 1931–

Canadian

Alice Munro is best known as a short-story writer: since 1977 she has been a regular contributor to the *New Yorker*. Along with fellow Canadian Mavis Gallant, Munro has pioneered the genre of the novel-length short-story sequence. Besides several traditional collections, Munro has published three short-story sequences, *Lives of Girls and Women* (1971), *Who Do You Think You Are?* (1978; published in the United States as *The Beggar Maid: Stories of Flo and Rose,* 1979), and, most recently, *Open Secrets* (1994). These sequences, which focus on a single developing character, participate in a searching investigation of what novelistic forms like the retrospective first-person narration, the Bildungsroman, or the historical novel can and cannot encompass. Munro's linked short stories fracture the singular plotline that in a novel might tie things together. In its place are freestanding yet overlapping stories that may seem only a few steps removed from "the scraps of papers and torn envelopes . . . records of the weather, bits of information about the garden, things he had been moved to write down" that one character finds in her father's work shed after his death. The short-story sequence probes the pretensions of narrative forms that discover an explanatory design or an historical continuity in experience. Experience in Munro's fiction is both mundane and unfathomable. Without warning or explanation, ordinary inhabitants of small-town Ontario go missing or fall in love, or the relationship between actions and rewards and punishments simply goes out of kilter. In such contexts, the efforts of narrators to provide explanations or locate origins or ends seem simultaneously overweening, pointless, and redemptive.

The gossip of Munro's characters, especially the women, most explicitly registers the gap between the certitudes of the historical record and the muddle of everyday life. Gossip challenges the literary conventions that determine what can be legitimately narrated and remembered, eroding distinctions between the public and the private, the significant and the trivial. Gossip challenges linear time, keeping alive alternative, dead and buried identities, especially the shadowy pasts of certain pillars of the community. Challenging the hegemony of literary conventions, Munro's reliance on gossip also revalues what has traditionally been deemed female discourse. Although they may seem to go round and round, small-town stories form an infra-historical lore, commemorating the lives of girls and women and others who would otherwise be forgotten. Because it is notoriously hard to say how a rumor starts, gossip presents a problem of origins, of legitimate and illegitimate historical knowledge, which Munro links to questions about genealogy and gender. Her work connects a resistance to linear narrative with a resistance to patrilineal arrangements for the transmission and inheritance of tradition. While Munro reminds us of the patrilineal schemes that make literary traditions into father-son affairs, she regularly arranges her fictions so that a woman character, whether a would-be writer, a librarian, or a bookseller, becomes the heir to literary legacies. In "Heirs of the Living Body" (the second story in *Lives of Girls and Women,* Del Jordan is chosen, by default, to complete her Uncle Craig's manuscript history of Wawanash County, even though her great-aunts generally draw the firmest of lines between men's and women's work. In *Who Do You Think You Are?* Rose learns to mimic the evocatively named Milton Homer, the mentally deranged man who himself mimics the town fathers, marching in every Orangeman's parade and making speeches at every christening. Rose's mimicry, combined with Milton Homer's own, suggests models of literary succession less "classic" than those Homer's aunt inculcates at the local high school.

This is not to overlook the fact that Munro, herself a descendant via her father of the 19th-century Scottish novelist James Hogg, has a particularly rich relationship to the genealogies of the novel and of Canadian literature. Her attempt to embed an elliptical Bildungsroman within the history of a particular place recalls at once the modernist historical novel—William Faulkner's *Go Down Moses* (1942), for instance, or Virginia Woolf's *The Years* (1937)—and the impressionist local color writing of the fin de siècle—Charles Chesnutt's *The Conjure Woman* (1899), Sarah Orne Jewett's *The Country of the Pointed Firs* (1896), or Katherine Mansfield's New Zealand stories. Munro's most recent short-story sequence, *Open Secrets,* makes visible another literary inheritance: refusing chronological order altogether, the book is held together by its returns to the locale of Carstairs, Ontario, and to the fortunes of the Doud family, as well as by its focus on letter-writing, which keeps alive otherwise dispersed communities and alliances. *Open Secrets* makes more apparent than earlier work that Munro's annalistic sensibility—her interest in the small town as the unit of social and historical analysis and her attention to the history of Scottish settlement in Canada—owes much to 19th-century Scottish regionalist fiction. The meditations of James Hogg, John Galt, Walter Scott, and Margaret Oliphant on the nature of historical experience, their experiments with narrative temporality, and their case studies of the micro-operations of modernization in specific small towns all form a distinct presence in *Open Secrets.*

This Scottish fiction also exercised a formative influence on the 19th-century literature of English-speaking Canada. There, as elsewhere in the British empire, the first fictions usually took the form not of novels but rather of epistolary, descriptive, or satirical "sketches." Munro's "A Wilderness Station" (the fourth story in *Open Secrets*) explicitly revisits the 19th-century sketches of Susanna Moodie and Catharine Parr Traill (pioneering settlers and chroniclers of the Ontario bush). It also incorporates materials from Munro's own family history. In helping to invent the linked short-story sequence as a specifically Canadian literary genre, Munro thus works to revitalize or at least to reconsider the most important indigenous fictions and fictional forms of colonial Canada. Appropriately, she now serves on the editorial board of McClelland and Stewart's canon-forming "New Canadian Library" series.

KATIE TRUMPENER AND DEIDRE LYNCH

Biography

Born 10 July 1931 in Wingham, Ontario. Attended Wingham public schools; University of Western Ontario, London,

1949–51. Lived in Vancouver, 1951–63, Victoria, British Columbia, 1963–71, London, Ontario, 1972–75, and Clinton, Ontario, from 1976; artist-in-residence, University of Western Ontario, 1974–75, and University of British Columbia, Vancouver, 1980.

Fiction by Munro

Dance of the Happy Shades, 1968
Lives of Girls and Women, 1971
Something I've Been Meaning to Tell You: Thirteen Stories,
    1974
Who Do You Think You Are? 1978; as *The Beggar Maid: Stories of Flo and Rose,* 1979
The Moons of Jupiter, 1982
The Progress of Love, 1986
Friend of My Youth, 1990
Open Secrets, 1994
Selected Stories, 1996

Further Reading

Blodgett, E.D., *Alice Munro,* Boston: Twayne, 1988
Godard, Barbara, "'Heirs of the Living Body': Alice Munro and the Question of the Female Aesthetic," in *The Art of Alice Munro: Saying the Unsayable,* edited by Judith Miller, Waterloo, Ontario: Waterloo University Press, 1984
Heble, Ajay, *The Tumble of Reason: Alice Munro's Discourse of Absence,* Toronto and Buffalo, New York: University of Toronto Press, 1994
MacKendrick, Louis K., editor, *Probable Fictions: Alice Munro's Narrative Acts,* Downsview, Ontario: ECW Press, 1983
Rasporich, Beverly J., *Dance of the Sexes: Art and Gender in the Fiction of Alice Munro,* Edmonton: University of Alberta Press, 1990
Redekop, Magdalene, *Mothers and Other Clowns: The Stories of Alice Munro,* London and New York: Routledge, 1992

Iris Murdoch 1919–

English

Between 1953 and 1995 Dame Iris Murdoch published 26 novels and many essays about the theory and practice of fiction. She also established a serious reputation as a philosopher with a particular interest in the relation between ethics and metaphysics as it bears on the difficult human search for what Plato, her philosophic mentor, called the Good. Although a certain moral philosophy suffuses her novels, her fiction does not stage debates about ideas but paints portraits of obsessed persons in situations that are finely detailed and rich in ironies. The principal characters interest us by virtue of their stories, which often trace a tragicomic pilgrimage from illusion and vanity toward a clearer recognition of the truth, hence of what promotes life. Sometimes, however, she leads a character beyond this goal toward becoming "good for nothing," toward an "unselfing" that symbolizes in her work contact with divinity. Plato's myth of the cave is the image governing the former of these stories; the myth of Apollo flaying Marsyas is associated with the latter.

Because of Murdoch's skill from the start in creating both an inner life for her characters and placing them in a worldly comedy of manners, the early novels were often linked to the influence of George Eliot and Henry James. As her concern shifted toward darker obsessions and more strenuous struggles with egotism, critics came to associate her novels also with those of Fedor Dostoevskii and D.H. Lawrence. Yet they are finally like no one else's. They combine exciting storytelling with elaborate, symbolic patterning; immediate sensuous charm with a highly literate intelligence; a grounding in the credible and realistic with an inclination toward the fantastic and even supernatural. The maelstrom of sexual emotion is Murdoch's principal subject, but the contemporary reader who makes a connection with Freud also will want to remember Plato. Although Freud helped Murdoch modernize Plato by psychologizing the themes of eros-as-fundamental-energy and the falseness of appearances, her more mature fiction moves from a psychology (of determinism and choice) to a cosmology (of necessity and chance).

Murdoch's first novel, *Under the Net* (1954), launched her reputation. Its central relationship between a kind of artist and a kind of saint established a thematic focus that Murdoch sustained for many years. In the subsequent early novels, these types may represent alternative paths to the Good, as do Dora and Michael in *The Bell* (1958), often considered the best of the early novels. (The portrait of Michael, incidentally, is the first of half a dozen that demonstrate exceptional sensitivity to homosexual feeling.) In others, the artist is associated with a problematic moral magic, a power to exert a charismatic influence (as in *A Severed Head,* 1961, the most widely read of the early novels), while a figure of good (like Ann in *An Unofficial Rose,* 1962) is associated with an absence of self, an obedience to something beyond self.

The novels of the early 1960s are said to belong to Murdoch's "Gothic phase" and are generally less valued, but they make a serious effort to complicate, even if they do not coordinate very well, her developing notions of good and evil. Then in *The Nice and the Good* (1968), and especially in *A Fairly Honourable Defeat* (1970), this coordination is successfully achieved. These two novels are often said to mark the beginning of a new phase of her career.

Yet the novels of the 1970s and 1980s ambitiously break the new mold. They are considerably longer, abandon chapter divisions for space breaks, use more frequent emphasis, and are both more freewheeling in the style and more audacious in the use of imperfectly trustworthy narrators. One may guess that Murdoch had become dissatisfied with the simple moral opposition of art and magic to power, realizing that the writer herself was inevitably an artist-magician. In the most impressive of these, *The Black Prince* (her 1973 masterpiece) and *The Sea, The Sea* (which won the Booker Prize for 1978), the central consciousness is an unreliable narrator. Bradley Pearson in *The Black Prince* is introduced to us after his death by an "editor," who at the conclusion offers the most authoritative of four versions of the novel's events. The core is his narration of an exciting story of murder and blackmail permeated by his intense celebration of love and art as questionable but redeeming powers, leading him on a Platonic quest for the Good that must, however, remain out of reach. In another novel of this period that best rounds out the struggle, *The Good Apprentice* (1985), the power of magic and art, once problematic, has become benign.

But Murdoch's ever restless imagination created in the late novels (most evidently in *The Message to the Planet*, 1989, and *The Green Knight*, 1993) a central figure who is both magical and saintly and who, moreover, seems to belong to a different world from that of the circle of realistically conceived characters. At considerable risk to the integrity of the novel as an aesthetic structure, Murdoch goes beyond her stories of moral questers who are fairly honorably defeated and seeks to create a religious model that the age requires, someone who can lead us, living in an age that can no longer believe in a personal God, to a new conception of virtue.

In all her art and thought, Murdoch has struggled to reconcile fascination with a strong pattern or organizing myth to a scrupulous respect for the precious separateness of individualities, to unite "form" with "contingency," "necessity" with "chance," both imagined as aspects of the Good. The perfect can never be achieved, but the resulting tension generates a great deal of intellectual and novelistic energy, and is the mark of an ambitiousness often on the verge of overreaching itself.

It is difficult to predict the future of Murdoch's reputation, even though the recent diagnosis of Alzheimer's disease probably means that her career is effectively concluded. Her books have enjoyed a wide readership, but they are not much discussed among trend-setting critics and theorists, perhaps because the somewhat formulaic procedures of her elaborate plots seem to suggest a traditional rather than groundbreaking literary sensibility. Certainly she has earned a place as one of the leading British persons of letters of her generation, and her influential literary partnership with her husband, the distinguished critic John Bayley, is almost legendary. But any more precise assessment must await the next turn in the history of taste. In addition to the titles mentioned in this article, new readers may also wish to look up her two most important works of nonfiction, *The Sovereignty of Good* (1970) and *Metaphysics as a Guide to Morals* (1992).

DAVID J. GORDON

Biography

Born 15 July 1919 in Dublin. Attended the Froebel Education Institute, London; Badminton School, Bristol; B.A., Somerville College, Oxford, 1942; Newnham College, Cambridge, 1947–48. Assistant principal in the Treasury, London, 1942–44; administrative officer with the United Nations Relief and Rehabilitation Administration (UNRRA) in London, Belgium, and Austria, 1944–46; fellow, St. Anne's College, Oxford, and lecturer in philosophy, Oxford University, 1948–63; lecturer, Royal College of Art, London, 1963–67.

Novels by Murdoch

Under the Net, 1954
The Flight from the Enchanter, 1956
The Sandcastle, 1957
The Bell, 1958
A Severed Head, 1961
An Unofficial Rose, 1962
The Unicorn, 1963
The Italian Girl, 1964
The Red and the Green, 1965
The Time of the Angels, 1966
The Nice and the Good, 1968
Bruno's Dream, 1969
A Fairly Honourable Defeat, 1970
An Accidental Man, 1971
The Black Prince, 1973
The Sacred and Profane Love Machine, 1974
A Word Child, 1975
Henry and Cato, 1976
The Sea, The Sea, 1978
Nuns and Soldiers, 1980
The Philosopher's Pupil, 1983
The Good Apprentice, 1985
The Book and the Brotherhood, 1987
The Message to the Planet, 1989
The Green Knight, 1993
Jackson's Dilemma, 1995

Other Writings: essays on philosophy and on the theory and practice of fiction, plays, poetry.

Further Reading

Antonaccio, Maria, and William Schweiker, editors, *Iris Murdoch and the Search for Human Goodness*, Chicago: University of Chicago Press, 1996

Bloom, Harold, editor, *Iris Murdoch*, New York: Chelsea House, 1986

Byatt, A.S., *Degrees of Freedom: The Novels of Iris Murdoch*, London: Chatto and Windus, and New York: Barnes and Noble, 1965

Conradi, Peter J., *Iris Murdoch: The Saint and the Artist*, New York: St. Martin's Press, and London: Macmillan, 1986; 2nd edition, London: Macmillan, 1989

Dipple, Elizabeth, *Iris Murdoch: Work for the Spirit*, Chicago: University of Chicago Press, and London: Methuen, 1982

Gordon, David J., *Iris Murdoch's Fables of Unselfing*, Columbia: University of Missouri Press, 1995

Murphy by Samuel Beckett

1938

Samuel Beckett's *Murphy* is a rollicking philosophical *jeu d'esprit* in the tradition that runs from Cervantes and Rabelais, through Swift and Fielding, to *Ulysses*. Yet the book has never received the close attention it warrants. For all its brevity, it has an intricacy and complexity that justify its being placed among the giants of novelistic invention. The few longer studies of *Murphy* are distressingly poor, and while other accounts of Beckett's fiction are valuable for their treatment of certain aspects of the book, not one has yet brought these together, nor paid proper attention to the particulars—demented and otherwise—that for Beckett constitute the only possible straws of understanding, philosophical and fictional. The essential nature of the book, a gigantic joke made up of an infinitude of tiny ones, has been acknowledged. But the tiny jokes themselves have received too little attention. Every paragraph, most sentences, and many individual phrases or words constitute "phrase-bombs," to use Beckett's term—verbal and philosophical land mines laid through the text. If these have not all exploded, it is simply because most critics and readers have walked too lightly.

In *Murphy*, one of the greatest writers of the 20th century first found his authentic voice and gave expression to themes and images that would haunt his prose and drama for decades to come. *Murphy* is also that rarity, a genuine novel of ideas that parodies the form and content of conventional fiction to promote new ways of looking at the relationship of literature to philosophy. Perhaps it is not surprising, then, that Beckett had difficulty finding a publisher, the book making the rounds of some 40 houses before being accepted by George Reavey. Then—nothing. Despite enthusiasm from Kate O'Brien in *The Spectator* and qualified approval from Dylan Thomas and Iris Murdoch, the novel sold poorly and remained frozen until the 1950s, when the success of *En attendant Godot* (1952; *Waiting for Godot*) created a mild climate of interest in Beckett's earlier works and led to their reissue. Even now, *Murphy* is much undervalued.

When Beckett in 1935 embarked upon *Murphy*, he was the arrogant young author of an essay on Joyce, a monograph on Proust, a slim volume of difficult verse, a first novel, *Dream of Fair to Middling Women* (published posthumously in 1992), emphatically rejected, and a set of short stories, *More Pricks Than Kicks* (1934), that, surprisingly, had been accepted for publication. None of them had made his fame or fortune. *Murphy* drew on Beckett's experiences in Dublin and London and on a program of self-education that ranged widely into the classics and philosophy from the Presocratics to Kant and beyond. A decade of intense reading and study of music and the visual arts went into the making of *Murphy* and into its comic subversion of thought.

The structural principle of the novel is Cartesian dualism and its expression the *reductio* of rationalism. Murphy's attempts to retreat into the little world of the mind are foiled by his "deplorable susceptibility" to the contingencies of a contingent world. Even apart from the dislocations of narrative expectation (notably, the notorious chapter 6), the compositional technique is curious: the text subdivides into irregular units of sense, each structured around a philosophical or literary witticism or conundrum, but linked by a narrative plot and subplot in which, as an expression of pre-established harmony, all things limp to an appointed end in the Big World of the physical fiasco, where the Cartesian God and cosmic machinery are replaced by the very astrology Descartes despised. The key question, however, concerns the viability of Murphy's retreat into the mind where (according to the philosopher Geulincx and the Occasionalists, to say nothing of Schopenhauer) he may be free. In an ironic denouement that only Beckett could have contrived, Murphy is unable to become a microcosmopolitan because he recognizes, tragically, that he is sane.

Every premise of the novel is equally absurd: a Pythagorean Academy in Cork operates under the rational guidance of Neary, whose very reasoning is unbuttoned by the thought of Miss Counihan or whatever figure currently obtrudes on his awareness. Neary is a comic creation of Falstaffian proportions, his every utterance an implosion of literary or philosophical absurdity, the only impediment to delight being the reader's ignorance of the specifics of Beckett's wit. The book's erudition, presumably, is why it has had few followers, despite its remarkable innovations of content and form. Even for Beckett, it marked the end of a line; he would never write like this again, moving henceforth toward simplification of expression. Beckett could be dismissive of his early work, yet on the rare occasions that he would venture an opinion of it, he might refer to *Murphy* and cite as points of departure for the further study of his writing the axiom of Democritus, "Nothing is more real than nothing," and the central ethical principle of Arnold Geulincx, "Ubi nihil vales, ibi nihil velis" (where you are worth nothing, there you should want nothing). Both are central to *Murphy*, yet between them lies the realm of consciousness that Beckett would spend the rest of his life exploring.

CHRIS ACKERLEY

See also Samuel Beckett

Further Reading

Barale, Michèle Aina, and Rubin Rabinovitz, *A KWIC Concordance to Samuel Beckett's "Murphy,"* New York and London: Garland, 1990

Farrow, Anthony, *Early Beckett: Art and Illusion in "More Pricks Than Kicks" and "Murphy,"* Troy, New York: Whitson, 1991

Harrison, Robert, *Samuel Beckett's Murphy: A Critical Excursion,* Athens: University of Georgia Press, 1968

Henning, Sylvie Debevic, *Beckett's Critical Complicity: Carnival, Contestation, and Tradition,* Lexington: University Press of Kentucky, 1988

Hesla, David, *The Shape of Chaos: An Interpretation of the Art of Samuel Beckett,* Minneapolis: University of Minnesota Press, 1971

Kennedy, Sighle, *Murphy's Bed: A Study of Real Sources and*

Sur-Real Associations in Samuel Beckett's First Novel,
Lewisburg, Pennsylvania: Bucknell University Press, 1971

Kenner, Hugh, *Samuel Beckett: A Critical Study,* New York:
Grove Press, 1961; London: Calder, 1962; new edition,
Berkeley: University of California Press, 1968

Knowlson, James, *Damned to Fame: The Life of Samuel
Beckett,* London: Bloomsbury, and New York: Simon and
Schuster, 1996

Rabinovitz, Rubin, *The Development of Samuel Beckett's
Fiction,* Urbana: University of Illinois Press, 1984

Robert Musil 1880–1942

Austrian

Robert Musil's true stature as a representative figure of literary modernism is probably not yet as widely appreciated outside the German-speaking world as it deserves to be. The intellectual rigor of his writing and the complexity of what he attempts, coupled with the fact that his major work, *Der Mann ohne Eigenschaften* (1930–43; *The Man Without Qualities*), remained an incomplete fragment of some 1,600 pages at his death, have meant that the reading public has been slow to accord Musil's work the recognition given to that of James Joyce, Marcel Proust, or Franz Kafka, with which in one way or another it has been compared. During the course of his writing career, however, Musil made remarkable contributions to the development of narrative techniques for exploring both the life of the mind and the intellectual dilemmas of Western culture in the 20th century.

Musil trained as an engineer between 1898 and 1903, did original work in experimental psychology, and wrote his doctoral dissertation on the Viennese philosopher Ernst Mach, who had achieved notoriety in the 1880s with his radical insistence that the reality we know is constituted only in our sensations. These interests, combined with his early reading of Nietzsche and Freud, are reflected in the assiduous techniques for evoking the experiences of thinking and feeling that characterize Musil's early literary writings. His first novel, *Die Verwirrungen des Zöglings Törless* (1906; *Young Törless*), tells a tale of adolescent self-discovery set in a remote military academy in the Eastern marches of the Hapsburg Empire. But while the outward plot of the work evokes a case of manifest brutality and victimization, the real focus of the narrative is on the central character's bewildering experiences of his own responses to what he witnesses. Törless finds disturbing chains of association entering his consciousness that link his emotional responses in the presence of the local prostitute, for example, to the memory of his mother; and faced with the task of explaining to his schoolteachers what he had experienced of the sadistic persecution of a fellow pupil, he emphasizes the sense in which his own rational understanding had seemed to operate separately from the life within himself that was prompting his own thoughts. Musil further pursued the refinement of his techniques for conveying the fine texture of mental activity in two extraordinarily dense texts published under the title *Vereinigungen* (Unions) in 1911, which use extensive physiological analogies for the expression of minutely observed psychic processes.

Finely observed evocations of heightened emotional awareness are to be found in Musil's later writing as well, where they are related to an investigation—still inspired by Nietzschean self-scrutiny—into the moral and psychological insights yielded by quasi-mystical experience. But acute psychological observation is only part of the reason that *The Man Without Qualities* is regarded as a landmark in the development of modernist narrative. By setting the work in the 12-month period preceding the outbreak of World War I, Musil is able not only to exploit the irony of hindsight but also to evoke the ambiguous implications of long-term tendencies in modern intellectual culture. The central figure through whom this 20th-century world is observed, and whom we know only by his forename Ulrich, has passed through varieties of professional training that mirror the author's—as engineer, soldier, and mathematician; but Ulrich has detached himself from the career goals of conventional society because he has come to experience that characteristic dilemma of modernity (as Max Weber describes it), namely that the possibility of understanding many specific things is accompanied by the loss of any overall sense of purpose. Ulrich's "holiday from life," which he dedicates largely to investigating how to achieve some dependable orientation for living in a modern, secularized world, is one of the comic devices with which Musil structures his narrative; the other is a public campaign to celebrate the 70th anniversary of Emperor Franz Joseph's ascending the Austrian throne. In and around that campaign, we experience the strivings and yearnings of the members of a social elite who are afflicted, like Ulrich, by the absence of any unifying meaning in their lives, but who lack his rigor in the analysis of their own emotive responses to that predicament. Through their various precipitate attempts to find unifying principles, Musil satirizes the volatile intellectual culture of Central Europe in his day.

A delicate ironic tension is at work in *The Man Without Qualities,* not only in the portrayal of individual characters but also in the compositional technique of the work. Musil deploys the traditional techniques of novel writing in flexible ways that allow the narrative to slip in and out of the perspective of a particular character, or indeed in and out of the various perspectives in which an issue might present itself to that character's mind. Ulrich is made to notice on a number of occasions how his own ideas take on a different complexion when they reappear in the thought sequences of others. In particular scenes Musil plays off one perspective against another, having an Austrian general conduct a survey of the world of ideas, for example, and having a Prussian industrialist speculate about the coming cultural changes of the 1920s. The opening chapter plays, famously, with the traditional conventions for setting the time and place of the action, only to dismiss such specifics as irrelevant to the issues with which the work is chiefly concerned. Other early chapters emphasize the senses in which human personality has become a function of diverse impersonal factors, and suggest that the individual human being has ceased to be a plausible measure of significance in the world of the 20th century, a world of "qualities without the man." Musil's approach to narration is "essayistic" in a sense that is made explicit within the novel, namely that the most appropriate means of evaluating a world recognized as consisting of a potentially infinite system of connections is in the manner of an essay, by examining the object from a variety of sides without claiming to be able to grasp it in its entirety. The very notion of narrative continuum is disrupted by the constant deferral of any decisive action, and by the predominantly discursive nature of the text. The inherent indeterminacy of such writing has led some to question whether *The Man Without Qualities* qualifies as a novel at all; but the real delight of the work arises precisely from the dynamic relationship between its aspiration to become a finished work and the essayistic exploration of the implications of particular situations.

Musil, then, is one of the true pioneers of techniques that take the novel into new dimensions of psychological and moral investigation in the 20th century. The radical nature of his experimentation means that—like that of Joyce, Proust, or Kafka—it does not lend itself readily to further development. But by exploring extreme possibilities he, like them, contributes significantly to that self-consciousness about the processes of narrative writing that is inseparable from the way the novel has subsequently been conceived.

DAVID MIDGLEY

See also Man Without Qualities

Biography
Born 6 November 1880 in Klagenfurt, Austria. Attended a school in Steyr; military school in Eisenstadt, 1892–94, and in Mährisch-Weisskirchen, 1895–97; engineering student at Technische Hochschule, Brno, 1898–1901; philosophy student, University of Berlin, 1903–05, Ph.D. 1908. Military service, 1901–02; served in Austrian army, 1914–16 (hospitalized 1916); editor of army newspaper, 1916–18; bronze cross. Engineer in Stuttgart, 1902–03; in Berlin until 1911; archivist, 1911–13; editor, *Die Neue Rundschau,* Berlin, 1914; in press section of Office of Foreign Affairs, Vienna, 1919–20, and consultant to Defense Ministry, 1920–23; freelance writer in Berlin, 1931–33, in Vienna, 1933–38, and in Switzerland, 1938–42. Died 15 April 1942.

Novels by Musil
Die Verwirrungen des Zöglings Törless, 1906; as *Young Törless,* translated by Eithne Wilkins and Ernst Kaiser, 1955
Der Mann ohne Eigenschaften, completed by Martha Musil, 3 vols., 1930–43; edited by Adolf Frisé, 1952; as *The Man Without Qualities,* translated by Eithne Wilkins and Ernst Kaiser, 3 vols., 1953–60; translated by Sophie Wilkins and Burton Pike, 2 vols., 1995

Other Writings: stories, plays, and critical writings (including those gathered in *Selected Writings* [edited by Burton Pike, 1986] and *Precision and Soul: Essays and Addresses* [edited and translated by Pike and David S. Luft, 1990]).

Further Reading
Brokoph-Mauch, Gudrun, editor, *Robert Musil: Essayismus und Ironie,* Tübingen: Francke, 1992
Cohn, Dorrit, *Transparent Minds: Narrative Modes for Presenting Consciousness in Fiction,* Princeton, New Jersey: Princeton University Press, 1978
Corino, Karl, *Robert Musil: Leben und Werk in Bildern und Texten,* Reinbek: Rowohlt, 1988
Harrison, Thomas, *Essayism: Conrad, Musil and Pirandello,* Baltimore: Johns Hopkins University Press, 1992
Hickman, Hannah, *Robert Musil and the Culture of Vienna,* London: Croom Helm, and La Salle, Illinois: Open Court, 1984
Large, Duncan, "Experimenting with Experience: Robert Musil, *Der Mann ohne Eigenschaften,*" in *The German Novel in the Twentieth Century: Beyond Realism,* edited by David Midgley, Edinburgh: Edinburgh University Press, and New York: St. Martin's Press, 1993
Luft, D.S., *Robert Musil and the Crisis of European Culture 1880–1942,* Berkeley: University of California Press, 1980
Payne, Philip, *Robert Musil's "The Man Without Qualities": A Critical Study,* Cambridge and New York: Cambridge University Press, 1988
Rogowski, Christian, *Distinguished Outsider: Robert Musil and His Critics,* Columbia, South Carolina: Camden House, 1994
Webber, Andrew, "Reality as Pretext: Robert Musil, *Die Verwirrungen des Zöglings Törless,*" in *The German Novel in the Twentieth Century: Beyond Realism,* edited by David Midgley, Edinburgh: Edinburgh University Press, and New York: St. Martin's Press, 1993

My. *See* We

The Mysteries of Paris by Eugène Sue

Les Mystères de Paris 1843

The Mysteries of Paris was the most widely read and discussed work by the "king of the popular novel," Eugène Sue. Marx and Engels saw fit to write their most sustained engagement with literature on it; Victor Hugo, George Sand, and Alexandre Dumas praised it; Charles Dickens and G.W.M. Reynolds among others were influenced by it. Théophile Gautier went so far as to say that the sick delayed dying in order to read the next installment. Other less hyperbolic anecdotes relate how, inspired by the work, soup kitchens for the unemployed were opened and an agricultural colony was founded for the young. What these anecdotes reveal is that the influence of the novel was felt not only in the international literary marketplace, but also in politics. With *The Mysteries of Paris* the serial novel rose to new heights in persuading the reader to buy installment after installment, and its politics played a decisive role in this. Dealing mainly with the poorest sections of Parisian society, the novel offered different kinds of pleasure to different readers: for the poor it seemed to hold up a mirror to their lives; it gave novelists a political raison d'être for their work; for the bourgeoisie it offered a justification for reform and charity (and thus political power) together with the transgressive pleasures of visiting low-life haunts while remaining safely within their armchairs. The tension between utopian socialist politics and a savvy manipulation of the market lies at the heart of the novel.

The Mysteries of Paris was not Sue's first work. Born into the wealthy upper middle class of Paris, Marie-Joseph (Eugène was a pseudonym) seemed destined for a medical career like his father. He rebelled, however, leaving school with no qualifications, and in 1823 joined the navy as a lowly auxiliary surgeon, traveling the world. In 1830, after his father's death, Sue returned to Paris where he carved a reputation for himself as an extravagant aesthete and dandy. He explicitly modeled his lifestyle upon Beau Brummel and Lord Byron, and the influence of the latter is clear in his literary output. Sue now turned to literature with novels inspired by his experiences at sea, most notably *Atar-Gull* (1831) and *La Salamandre* (1832; *The Salamander*). With their fashionable cynicism and sensational exoticism, these novels won him fame among the cultivated elite. Sue later gained a wider audience through writing feuilletons to pay off the debts he had incurred after running through his inheritance. *Mathilde: Mémoires d'une jeune femme* (1841; *Mathilde; or, Memoirs of a Young Woman*) was the first of these, although he had published fragments of other works in newspapers before this. *Mathilde* was very successful, but it was *The Mysteries of Paris* shortly afterward that firmly established Sue as the most widely read author of his day. Shortly before beginning work on *The Mysteries of Paris*, Sue had been converted to socialism, yet he left the more liberal *La Presse*, in which his previous works had appeared, to publish *The Mysteries of Paris* in *Le Journal des débats*, a pro-government newspaper that promoted the interests of financiers, since it offered him 26,500 francs for the novel. As a result of the novel's serialization, *Le Journal* increased its circulation to around 25,000, a huge number for the time. Since *The Mysteries of Paris* seems to have drawn in left-leaning readers who would otherwise never have purchased the paper, the novel may be regarded as an attempted seduction of such readers into the ideology promoted by the rest of the paper.

The Mysteries of Paris was subsequently published in volume format and quickly translated into many languages; in 1844 alone at least ten translations appeared, including Italian, German, Dutch, and English. On the strength of this novel, Sue was given the hitherto unheard of sum of 100,000 francs for his next novel, *Le Juif errant* (1844; *The Wandering Jew*), by yet another paper, *Le Constitutionnel*, whose sales figures now increased by over 1,000 percent. But Sue was now rivaled by Dumas, who had learned from Sue's techniques, and later works such as *Martin l'enfant trouvé* (1846; *Martin the Foundling*) and *Les Sept péchés capitaux* (1848–51; *The Seven Deadly Sins*) were markedly less successful. Elected on a socialist ticket to the National Assembly in 1850 (where his political idleness was heavily criticized), Sue went into exile after the royalist coup of 1851, continuing to work on his vast novelistic history of France *Les Mystères du peuple* (1850; *The Mysteries of the People*) until his death in semi-obscurity. Yet as late as 1862 the influential *Revue des deux mondes* preferred *The Mysteries of Paris* to Victor Hugo's recently published *Les Misérables* (which had in fact been inspired by the earlier work).

The Mysteries of Paris marks a turning point in literary history not only for its sales figures. Remarkably, some 1,100 letters to Sue regarding it survive today, and by means of his readers' comments Sue was able to offer them a version of the world that they already knew but had never before seen in print. The truthful analysis of society that was so much trumpeted was rather his readers' own construction of reality. In this sense the novel was tailored to its purchasers through an early example of market research. Another innovation of the novel still has powerful resonance today, for Sue created a new kind of alienated and solitary protagonist in Rodolphe, an offshoot of the Byronic hero and a prefiguration of Batman or Superman (Dumas' slightly later Monte Cristo is another of the same type). Rodolphe is the Prince of Gerolstein, but for most of the novel he explores the Parisian underworld disguised as a painter of fans, secretly punishing the wicked and rewarding the good with the aid of his immense physical strength, intelligence, and limitless wealth. Rather than solve social problems through collective action (as in socialism), the novel offers an individual aristocratic saviour. Finally, instead of locating the sensational and exotic in distant lands as in his earlier novels, Sue shows the "barbarian" to be just as characteristic of the national capital, thus both paving the way for the crime novel of later years and playing on the contemporary vogue for travel literature. Whereas Balzac had already used convicts and lowly shopkeepers in his novels, Sue went even further down the social scale to show appalling wretchedness, degradation, and violence, described in a language that juxtaposes the shockingly concrete, the mystically abstract, and the colorful jargon of criminals.

ANDREW L. KING

See also Roman-Feuilleton

Further Reading

Bory, Jean Louis, *Eugène Sue*, Paris: Hachette, 1962

Eco, Umberto, *The Role of the Reader: Explorations in the Semiotics of Texts*, Bloomington: Indiana University Press, 1979; London: Hutchinson, 1981

Europe: Revue littéraire mensuelle 644 (November-December 1982)

Grubitzsch, Helga, editor, *Materialien zur Kritik des Feuilletons-Romans: "Die Geheimnisse von Paris" von Eugène Sue*, Wiesbaden: Athenaion, 1977

Luce, Louise Fiber, "The Masked Avenger: Historical Analogue in Eugène Sue's *Les Mystères de Paris*," *French Forum* 1 (1976)

Marx, Karl, and Friedrich Engels, *The Holy Family*, in *Collected Works*, volume 4, London: Lawrence and Wishart, and New York: International Publishers, 1975

Olivier-Martin, Yves, *Histoire du roman populaire en France*, Paris: Albin-Michel, 1980

Queffélec, Lise, *Le Roman-feuilleton français au XIXe siècle*, Paris: Presses Universitaires de France, 1989

Svane, Brynja, *Le Monde d'Eugène Sue*, 2 vols., Copenhagen: Forlag, 1986

The Mysteries of Udolpho by Ann Radcliffe

1794

Since the publication of Horace Walpole's *The Castle of Otranto* (1764), Gothic fiction had been gaining gradual prominence in the tastes of Britain's 18th-century readership. In the 1790s, however, with the contributions of Ann Radcliffe, Gothic fiction became a dominant literary mode. *The Mysteries of Udolpho* followed the success of Radcliffe's third novel, *The Romance of the Forest* (1791). In addition to being the novelist's most popular and enduring work, *Udolpho* was perhaps the most significant Gothic novel of the romantic period, spawning numerous imitations. Jane Austen immortalized the novel in her satire of Gothic writing, *Northanger Abbey* (1817), and her unqualified praise of Radcliffe contrasts remarkably with Austen's general disparagement of other Gothic novelists. Writing about Radcliffe, Sir Walter Scott emphasized her undeniable appeal: "[*Udolpho's*] very name was fascinating, and the public, who rushed upon it with all the eagerness of curiosity, rose from it with unsated appetite" (see Scott, 1824; edited by Williams, 1968). By the 1790s Radcliffe had become so popular that she was the best-selling author of the decade and received the unprecedented sum of £500 for the publication of *Udolpho*, which by 1799 had gone into its fourth edition. Reviewers, however, generally frowned upon Radcliffe's inclusion of supernatural events within the fundamentally realistic form of the novel; more particularly, many felt cheated by Radcliffe's last-minute "explanations" of these supernatural occurrences.

Central to Radcliffe's fiction is the notion of the "sublime," which the Gothicists developed from Edmund Burke's theories of the 1750s. The characteristic sublime emotion is "astonishment," and the most astonishing—hence sublime—feelings are those elicited by visions of death, the most terrible of all images. The superlative imagery of the sublime is that of the natural landscape, which simultaneously reminds the viewer of human insignificance, while confronting one with the vast, dangerous spectacle of the world beyond. Gothicists such as Radcliffe moved beyond this merely specular aspect of the sublime and refocused it through the tropes of excess and repetition. Thus, the heroine of *Udolpho*, Emily St. Aubert, repeatedly confronts tableaux of extreme suffering and death, whether from the past, the present, or a threatened future. Still, it is the very landscape itself that comes to symbolize Emily's increasing journey into danger. This progression is measured in the differing descriptions of the mountain ranges she encounters: from the calm Pyrenees of her homeland to the sublimely awful Alps, which represent a midpoint between idyll and Gothic romance, culminating in the terror of the Apennines, the location of the castle of Udolpho.

Robert Hume (1968) subdivides the Gothic into two types, "terror-Gothic" and "horror-Gothic." Hume comments that "terror opens the mind to the apprehension of the sublime, while (according to Mrs. Radcliffe) the repugnance involved in horror closes it." For Radcliffe, the terrifying, *imaginative* reaction to the sublime allows access to the sublime; horror, a more *instinctive* reaction, denies such a connection, focusing on the immediacy of the spectacle. Terror depends on suspense and imagined fears (hence deferment) for its effect, and Emily's half-glimpsed, disconcerting encounters with the "supernatural" are typical examples. Although Radcliffe's Gothicism was popular during the 1790s, by the turn of the century there was a distinct shift toward the horror-Gothic novel, beginning with Matthew Lewis' *The Monk* (1796)—with its affirmation, rather than denial, of the supernatural—and culminating with Mary Shelley's *Frankenstein* (1818) and Charles Maturin's *Melmoth the Wanderer* (1820).

As an 18th-century writer, Radcliffe's focus on landscape serves to display and test the delicacy of Emily's taste. Daniel Cottom (1985) notes that in Radcliffe's novels aesthetic judgment correlates with moral, social, and religious beliefs: Emily's father states that "virtue is little more than active taste." One's sensitivity to the landscape itself becomes a paradigm for every aspect of human character, and this usage is later developed by both Austen and Scott in their novels. This ideal, however, conflicts with another 18th-century legacy: that of the newer form of sensibility, which identifies the novel as a primarily *affective* form. That is, rather than being led to draw moral analogies from the events and images of the novel, the reader is encouraged to empathize with the heroine and view the novel's world through her eyes. Although some accommodation between these two divergent forms is achieved, particularly in the St. Auberts' household, where taste and sentiment are in harmony, the existence of such a dynamic places Radcliffe significantly within an age of both political and cultural transition.

The affective form of *Udolpho* has encouraged modern interpreters to associate it with the political turmoil of the 1790s. The Gothic form had been perceived by various critics as subversive and radical; it dethroned the rationalism and quotidian comfort of the bourgeois world with primitive and mysterious forces. It also had been viewed as conservative, in its valorization of typical middle-class values of sympathy, prudence, and the importance of family ties, as exemplified by the St. Auberts. In her development of the affective model, Radcliffe inherited much of the apparatus of her sentimental predecessors; however, she was less than accepting of its implications. *Udolpho,* more than any other of Radcliffe's novels, challenges and interrogates the standards of sensibility that many other "Radcliffean" novelists—notably Regina Maria Roche—simply accepted. Sentimental and Gothic fiction share common methods of characterization, form, and narration that anticipate a single aim—the correspondence between the sufferings of the protagonists and the reader's sympathetic response. However, *Udolpho* begins to question how empowering such emotionalism is. Emily is the victim of the villainous Montoni, incarcerated at his whim, and duped into signing over her estates to him. Ultimately, neither she nor the sentimental hero, Valancourt, is responsible for her liberation, and Montoni himself dies off-stage in battle. Emily finds that sensibility as an epistemological frame can be destructive and deluding: "the influence of superstition now gained on the weakness of her long-harassed mind." In sentimental literature, the reader is solicited to admire the virtuous feelings of the protagonists; in Gothic fiction, one is held in suspense with the characters themselves, whose very (sentimental) feelings are interrogated. Increasingly there is an effort to shock, disturb, and otherwise rouse—rather than reassure—the reader's emotional response.

In addition to questioning the antecedent literary conventions of her age, Radcliffe was a notable innovator, and these innovations are most successful in *Udolpho.* Much of her language is lyrical, and poetry forms an integral mechanism of the narrative. Unlike her neoclassical predecessors, Radcliffe quotes British—rather than classical—poets at the openings of her chapters. In employing such methods, Radcliffe demonstrates an awareness of her essentially female audience, who would have been generally unacquainted with the writers of antiquity. Furthermore, her inclusion of poetry intratextually, primarily in the compositions of Emily, again demonstrates how Radcliffean Gothic is to be understood as an affective form, the poetry itself being integral to one's understanding of Emily's psychological frame. The most notable instance occurs during Emily's imprisonment, when she composes several poems, especially that of the "Sea-Nymph," in which she dreams of being free, untamed, and at the whim of no man.

More significant than Radcliffe's use of poetry, however, is her introduction of suspense as a primary device in the novel. This is perhaps her most important contribution to the development of

the novel, and it combines with *Udolpho*'s affective form to develop an empathic relationship between Emily and the reader. Because the reader is as ignorant of the situation as Emily, the reader tends to feel what she does and experiences a concern for her safety. Radcliffe was the first author to employ suspense in this centralized manner, and suspense is the supreme paradigm of the novel. From Radcliffe's time onward, the use of suspense as an affective form became an integral part of the novelistic mechanism, its most obvious proponents being the Brontës, Charles Dickens, and the sensation novelists, especially Wilkie Collins, whose *Woman in White* (1860) displays evident Radcliffean tendencies. Scott, too, owed much to Radcliffe's Gothic, and elements of Radcliffean suspense and terror abound in his novels, especially in tales such as *Waverley* (1814) and *Guy Mannering* (1815).

Critics have often dismissed Radcliffe as another "genre novelist," and while acknowledging her innovations they have denied her importance to the development of the novel form in general. *Udolpho* loomed so large in 18th-century literature that it was not only imitated but was written *against*—Lewis composed *The Monk* in contradiction to *Udolpho*'s central premises. Radcliffe, in turn, responded with *The Italian* (1797). *The Mysteries of Udolpho* not only displays the signs of an age in transition, with its sometimes contradictory juxtapositions of taste and sensibility, morality and affective form, but it also foreshadows numerous changes in the novel itself. Radcliffe's charismatic villains evolve into the fallen antiheroes of horror-Gothic in the early decades of the 1800s, then into the Heathcliffs and Rochesters of the Victorian era. Similarly, the suspense mechanisms employed by Radcliffe—unexplained family secrets, mysterious dream sequences, the vaguely supernatural—are traditions that continued in the work of "respected" novelists such as Scott and Dickens, as well as in the more sensational works of Mary Elizabeth Braddon and Wilkie Collins. Victorian critics' marginalization of Radcliffe has led to her exclusion from the canon of English literature; however, critical reappraisal since the 1960s has encouraged an understanding of her literary contribution. Novelists who have followed Radcliffe have testified to her significance in the development of their own works, whether in what they have said or in the way they have written. As Scott noted, "Mrs Radcliffe has a title to be considered as the first poetess of Romantic fiction, that is, if actual rhythm shall not be deemed essential to poetry."

A.A. MANDAL

See also Gothic Novel

Further Reading

Botting, Fred, *The Gothic,* London and New York: Routledge, 1996

Cottom, Daniel, *The Civilized Imagination: A Study of Ann Radcliffe, Jane Austen, and Sir Walter Scott,* Cambridge and New York: Cambridge University Press, 1985

Hume, Robert D., "Gothic versus Romantic: A Revaluation of the Gothic Novel," *PMLA* 84 (1968)

Kiely, Robert, *The Romantic Novel in England,* Cambridge, Massachusetts: Harvard University Press, 1972

Miles, Robert, *Ann Radcliffe: The Great Enchantress,* Manchester and New York: Manchester University Press, 1995

Morris, David B., "Gothic Sublimity," *New Literary History* 16 (1985)

Poovey, Mary, "Ideology in *The Mysteries of Udolpho*," *Criticism* 21 (1979)

Schroeder, Natalie, "*The Mysteries of Udolpho* and *Clermont*: The Radcliffean Encroachment on the Art of Regina Maria Roche," *Studies in the Novel* 12 (1980)

Scott, Sir Walter, "Ann Radcliffe," *Ballantyne's Novelist's Library*, 1 September 1824; reprinted in *Sir Walter Scott on Novelists and Fiction*, edited by Ioan Williams, London: Routledge and Kegan Paul, and New York: Barnes and Noble, 1968

Smith, Nelson C., "Sense, Sensibility, and Ann Radcliffe," *Studies in English Literature* 13 (1973)

Mystery Novel. *See* Crime, Detective, and Mystery Novel

Myth and the Novel

Myth has entered into many arrangements with the *longue dureé* of the novel, from Alexandrian fiction to George Eliot's *Middlemarch* (1872) and James Joyce's *Ulysses* (1922), to the novels of Salman Rushdie, and to Wilton Barnhardt's *Gospel* (1993). Myth has often been the subject, an archetypal form, or an allegorical or prefigurative engine of a novel. The ratio of these competing functions has been determined in the past by myth's inexorable secondary relation to religion in the West: myth is what others believe. It is not until the modern period, broadly construed, when comparative religion and irreligion in the 19th century begin to threaten Christianity itself, that myth in Western literature assumes a positive alternative status to religion in content and in form, as an alternative recognizably not definitive, authoritative, totalitarian.

Alongside the great comparative studies in the 19th century—of elements, religions, languages, and social and skeletal structures—the novel plays its own role. The great 19th-century novelists are profoundly comparative in their study of human behavior, in effect if not always in intention. In consequence, their work (as René Girard has argued in *Mensonge romantique et vérité romanesque* [1961; *Deceit, Desire, and the Novel*]) also needs to be read as a vast comparative research project, whose results could be coordinated with those of other discourses.

George Eliot (herself the translator of D.F. Strauss' *Das Leben Jesu* [*The Life of Jesus Critically Examined*, 3 vols., 1846]—one of the century's "biographies" that proposes a secular Christ) signals the new dispensation in fiction by her characterization in *Middlemarch* of Edward Casaubon, whose lifework is to discover the secret key to all mythology. *Middlemarch* foretells that the propagation of theories of myth, as well as theories of human behavior (even debunked theories), can themselves provide the form or the content of the novel and suggests that novels can aspire to their own theoretical potential and their own status as myths.

To do more than reiterate the ubiquity of myth and theorize myth's resurgence in modern literature, particularly the novel, is not easy. Northrop Frye has offered the most ambitious hypothesis for literature's relation to mythology in this century, although his work is now perhaps itself (de)classed as yet another mythology. Frye proposed two versions of the relation of literature to myth over his long career. In *Anatomy of Criticism* (1957), a book that made an important early contribution to the human sciences and theory in American humanities, Frye synthesized a formally methodological or protostructural theory of literature's "displacement" of myth. Beginning in *The Secular Scripture* (1976), he developed a racier hypothesis of social myth "hijacking" literature.

Frye's early concept of "mode" measures the degree of displacement of literature from myth by asking the question: how far does a character in a literary work stand from being a god? For Frye, all narratives contain typically recurring features, and modern narratives represent the most extreme displaced versions of the stories myth tells in radical form. Frye also argues that the modern is at the end of a historical process of progressive displacement. Myths tell stories of the unlimited power and desires of the gods, and they often suggest that their teller is divine, also. By contrast, modern narratives are written by and about those who can connect nothing with nothing.

Frye's first answer to the ubiquity of myth in modern literature is itself a formal one: so many modern novels refer to myth because the modern is itself the place where the totality of narrative structure becomes part of the subject of literature. But Frye's own remarkable schema of this hypothesis, with four archetypal narratives as stages of a single romance cycle, the monomyth of dying and resurrecting hero or god, suggests that modern ironic narratives, which seemingly invoke myth only to disparage their own comparative powerlessness, in fact prepare the ground for a "return" to myth.

For instance, Leopold Bloom, one of the "heroes" of James Joyce's *Ulysses,* falls far short of the stature of the "archetypal" hero figure of Odysseus. But if Bloom were no Odysseus at all, comparison could not take place. If there is more than a little of Odysseus in Bloom, and of Bloom in Odysseus, they belong to a common archetype, whose lineaments are more visible in myth. This relativization of the divine and the ordinary anticipates postmodern metanarratives, which relish any and all myth. It is worth remembering, however, that John Barth, an early proponent of postmodern writing, had listed the prescription of mythotherapy in *The End of the Road* (1958) as contraindicated.

The problem of going back to (any) myth as the articulation of the desirable finally forced Frye to set aside "displacement," which, for example, might require one to identify the goals of human desire with Zeus' amorous practices. *The Secular Scripture* thus reverses the priority of archetype and individual work. The structure we find in a novel no longer represents the goals of human desire; rather, the structure represents the *hijacking* of the spirit of romance, the integrity and equality of all living things, by the successive histories which hurt us, the seemingly inexorable form of exploitative events and desires for which Zeus and Bacchus can stand well enough as archetypes. Frye's title indicates he could give no more time to modern writing before turning to sacred scripture as his final project.

What then is to be done with the modern "collocation" (T.S. Eliot's term for the mythic method of *Ulysses* as applied in the notes to *The Waste Land* [1922]) of Odysseus and Bloom, myth and modern experience in the novel? Eliot critiqued humanism's "snack at the bar" relativization of religions and cultures, yet he granted an ethical value to Joyce's "mythic method" of pairing Dubliners and Achaeans, which, Eliot argued, made the immense panorama of futility of contemporary history a possible representational ground for modern art.

René Girard, like Frye, will perhaps never return to an extended meditation on the secular scripture of modern narrative. Girard's *Deceit, Desire, and the Novel* decodes the presumed autonomy and isolation of the desires and the very being of modern fictional heroes and antiheroes as a mask for their mimetic secondariness to others. Like all human behavior, Girard argues, desire is mimetic.

Girard's discovery of the mimetic hypothesis latent in novels led him to revise Freud's model for human desire and to redress Freud's preference for myths, including Freudian ones, in favor of Sophocles. For Girard, myth rationalizes the covertly violent origin and structure of all human societies by telling the stories of ritual victimization from the point of view of their benficiaries. In myth, Oedipus' guilt pollutes the community. At specific historical moments, however, literature of a certain theoretical power desymbolizes myth to reveal the victimization it masks, which in turn allows the community to deflect its own violence away from itself. Sophocles' play *Oedipus Rex,* unlike the myth that stands behind it, considers, at least for a while, that Oedipus is no guiltier than anyone else for the ills that have befallen Thebes.

The long devolution (adapting Raymond Williams' phrase for the modern) that distances literature from myth up to the modern period is not a falling away from instinctual grace, as Frye's concept of displacement might suggest. In *La violence et le sacré* (1972; *Violence and the Sacred*), Girard reads "that strange culture or nonculture we call modern" as the beneficiary of a long historical process of de-differentiation of myths, languages, and

structures. This process, in turn, makes our great comparative studies possible. According to Girard, we can theorize the world's great kinship systems because our own system has degraded to the absolute minimum required. We speak all the languages of kinship because we hardly have one of our own. In the modern period, ancient and modern myths, as well as our hypotheses for them, can coexist.

Girard's mimetic hypothesis allows us to theorize the historical development (or dedevelopment) of literature that Frye termed the secular scripture, as well as the attempts to hijack this revelation. Bloom and Marlow coexist with Odysseus and Aeneas because they decline heroism for a reluctance to do violence, or to glorify violence by making oneself its perfect victim.

The great challenge of the modern return to myth is to avoid re-glorifying violence by the twin hazards of fetishizing domination (as in Nietzsche) or victimization as the sign of a new divinity. To use the Christian myth to divinize suffering from persecution as the primary indication of virtue, of superiority to those who persecute the victim, leads finally to the paralysis Joyce considers the maimed and venal soul of Ireland.

We can perhaps indicate the alternative to these twin hazards by considering a great couplet of modern narratives that form a particular link on the chain of the long devolution but which themselves have assumed the status of myth: Joseph Conrad's "Heart of Darkness" (1902) and Chinua Achebe's *Things Fall Apart* (1958).

"Heart of Darkness" bears the pattern of the descent to the underworld, one of the most well-attested archetypes in any version of the relation between myth and the novel. In Marlow's two successive versions of narrative to answer the "gigantic tale" told by his cohorts on the deck of the *Nellie* (they continue the long historical process of nobilizing as knight errantry all English sailors who bring light to the dark places of the earth), he moves from a relativization of all cultural myths (England, too, as Marlow points out near the beginning of the novella, was once a place of darkness lit by Roman imperialism), to a second, unfinished narrative, which his auditor/narrator himself can only continue, but not complete.

If "Heart of Darkness" (as the narrator's provisional title for Marlow's second narrative, or Conrad's provisional title for the narrator's tale) began perhaps as Marlow's defense of power that promotes efficiency at the (regrettable) expense of its victims, it also has suffered a parallel misreading by critics of the glorification of victimization: Africa has a white soul proved by the black soul of its "white" victimizers. But "Heart of Darkness" does not bear out such a reading. Kurtz's "unsound methods" of divinizing violence are shown to be persuasive in every culture, winning "Intendeds" and followers on both sides of the racial divide.

Ultimately, when we retell the narrative again in our criticism, our theories should not stop where the title stops, which suggests that there is some geographical core of barbarity to which one brings light, and from which one brings back some treasure (or, conversely, plague). As our narrator advises, we should find Marlow's meaning outside, not inside, the tale. The narrator's image of Marlow's new kind of story is an image of a new kind of theory not yet named. Read collaboratively, within the archive of postcolonialism, Conrad's fictions may now be seen to stand on the borderline of reflecting and/or revealing (devolving) racism.

While Chinua Achebe has rejected Conrad as the "projector" and "representer" of racist myth, Achebe is no essentialist of *négritude,* changing out Western for African myths. After all, W.B. Yeats' odd combination of myth and theory of myth give Achebe just the title he needs for his first novel, as well as the notion that things can fall apart or desymbolize into clarity ("but now I know/That twenty centuries of stony sleep/Were vexed to nightmare by a rocking cradle," Yeats wrote in "The Second Coming"). In fact, Achebe's work shows *two* myth systems "falling apart" and narrates his story with a comparatist viewpoint and comparatist terminology. The great scandal to the usual oppositional and essentializing postcolonial theory is that the Christian missionaries hijack the long (de-)development of the Umuofian culture, so that they can no longer pursue their own suspicion that their gods do not require blood victims and child sacrifices.

Achebe's interpretation of the rituals and prohibitions by which the Umuofian clan avoids violence follows the standard anthropological literature. More profoundly, *Things Fall Apart* corroborates the analysis of the primitive social order delineated by Girard in *Violence and the Sacred* and suggests the interrelation of all human societies at whatever stage of dedevelopment—an interrelation only partially understood by postcolonial theory. Achebe "translates" the local device "among these people" for blaming and expunging one who pollutes the entire community with the modern secular and comparatist term "ostracism." The social history of this word, which begins in the action of Greek soldiers shaking pellets or shards mixed with others in a helmet to blame Chance alone for whoever "draws" the off-colored one indicating a deadly assignment, and finally comes to name the common, modern recognition of a transcultural strategy of all saving themselves in their alliance against one, thus measures the long devolution from myth and the sacred to modern theories of myth and modern novels.

WILLIAM A. JOHNSEN

See also Epic and Novel; Genre Criticism; Greek and Roman Narrative; Modernism; Romance

Further Reading

Bell, Michael, *Literature, Modernism, and Myth: Belief and Responsibility in the Twentieth Century,* Cambridge and New York: Cambridge University Press, 1997

Eliot, T.S., "Ulysses, Order, and Myth," *The Dial* 75 (1923)

Falck, Colin, *Myth, Truth, and Literature: Towards a True Post-Modernism,* Cambridge and New York: Cambridge University Press, 1989; 2nd edition, 1994

Frye, Northrop, *Anatomy of Criticism: Four Essays,* Princeton, New Jersey: Princeton University Press, 1957

Frye, Northrop, *The Secular Scripture: A Study of the Structure of Romance,* Cambridge, Massachusetts: Harvard University Press, 1976

Girard, René, *Mensonge romantique et vérité romanesque,* Paris: Grasset, 1961; as *Deceit, Desire, and the Novel: Self and Other in Literary Structure,* Baltimore: Johns Hopkins University Press, 1965

Girard, René, *La violence et le sacré,* Paris: Grasset, 1972; as *Violence and the Sacred,* Baltimore: Johns Hopkins University Press, 1977

Gould, Eric, *Mythical Intentions in Modern Literature,* Princeton, New Jersey: Princeton University Press, 1981

Lucente, Gregory L., *The Narrative of Realism and Myth,* Baltimore: Johns Hopkins University Press, 1981

Righter, William, *Myth and Literature,* London and Boston: Routledge and Kegan Paul, 1975

Segal, Robert A., editor, *Literary Criticism and Myth,* New York: Garland, 1996

White, John J., *Mythology in the Modern Novel: A Study of Prefigurative Techniques,* Princeton, New Jersey: Princeton University Press, 1971

N

Na Drini ćuprija. *See* Bridge on the Drina

Vladimir Nabokov 1899–1977

United States

Nabokov concludes chapter six of his autobiographical memoir *Speak, Memory* with the following paragraph.

> I confess I do not believe in time. I like to fold my magic carpet, after use, in such a way as to superimpose one part of the pattern upon another. Let visitors trip. And the highest enjoyment of timelessness—in a landscape selected at random—is when I stand among rare butterflies and their food plants. This is ecstasy, and behind the ecstasy is something else, which is hard to explain. It is like a momentary vacuum into which rushes all that I love. A sense of oneness with sun and stone. A thrill of gratitude to whom it may concern—to the contrapuntal genius of human fate or to tender ghosts humoring a lucky mortal.

This paragraph, like the book it belongs to, sounds several strong thematic elements characteristic of all of Nabokov's heartening work: a joyous independence of time as conceived in the empiricist era, the emphasis on reiterative patterns that can trip unaccustomed readers, the tender interval and its accompanying rush of love, the tribute to contrapuntal human genius, and, most of all, the ever-present, ever-surprising demonstration of the generosity and elegance possible to those who inhabit the English language.

There is also in this passage, as in the work, a defiance of the historical, materialist approach to biography. Who can tell the real story of someone else's life? Who can tell the story of his own life? One gets lost on such roads. Especially for Nabokov, whose life had among its themes some dramatic historical events, this problem of biography has been acute. The more interesting the life, the more it has become a lens for reading the art, but espe-

cially with Nabokov this is the wrong way around: the balance should lie the other way, with the art being a lens for reading the life, as happens in *Speak, Memory*. Evanescent, immortal "ecstasy" found in moments of high, bright life: that is the byword of Nabokov's art, whether it deals with "rare butterflies and their food plants" or with the play and power of language.

Fortunately for those interested in Nabokov's life Brian Boyd has published two definitive volumes: *Vladimir Nabokov: The Russian Years* (1990) and *Vladimir Nabokov: The American Years* (1991). These impressive and balanced books describe the childhood and youth in St. Petersburg and in the country at Vyra; the potential career as a major, even preeminent Russian poet, a career that was, along with so much else in Russia, first derailed by the Bolshevik Revolution and then effectively terminated by the Nazi *Anschluss* into France; the new life in the United States (and later, after the success of *Lolita,* in Switzerland), where he wrote the novels in English that resulted in an unprecedented renewal of the language, and where he began an ambitious project as a lepidopterist (completed by others decades after his death), in which he identified and classified a new genus of blue butterfly (informally known as Mr. Nabokov's Blues), 25 species of which have since been named after characters in his novels.

There would be no point in summarizing the plots of Nabokov's novels because, as he says, you only get on with the business of art "once plot is let out the door." At best, plot is an excuse for digression, a theme for anthematic elaboration, a correctable misuse of time. The "action" in his books has to do with language: with the play of sound and sequence, with the powers of English, with the formulations and scrambled formulations that produce double and triple versions of what seemed single, with the hilarious dismissal of fixed positions (known especially by various Freudonyms), and with the perpetual refusal of explanatory history that consigns the potentially ecstatic consciousness to "the disaster of receding time." Reading his novels has been a trial for those committed to such things, but a joyous opportunity for those who take him on his own terms, the terms that favor Eros in the large sense, in which the unexpected produces a surprise, a recognition of alterity crucial to life. This life-affirming power is what his novels provide; and this must be what the US novelist John Barth meant when, summing it up, he said that "Nabokov sustains us."

Nabokov's novels come in two groups: first, the Russian novels that he later translated himself or in collaboration with others into English; and, second, his English novels, which he spent a significant part of his last years translating or overseeing the translating into Russian. Nabokov's work is thus double-complete: existing as a complete body of original texts in two different languages, the (chronologically) first half originally in Russian, and the (chronologically) second half originally in English. As a translator himself, most notably of Pushkin, Nabokov was far too wise to leave his fate as a writer in the hands of others. His published work is immense, and includes beside the novels many stories, translations, essays, and letters, all of which are listed in Brian Boyd's biography.

Finding "development" in a writer so complex as Nabokov would beggar the achievement, but a few preferential points might be made. Nabokov began his literary career as a poet and, if the Germans had not arranged for Lenin's sealed train to pass unobstructed to Moscow, Nabokov might have been remembered primarily as one of the great poets of his Russian language. As it was, and publishing under the pseudonym of "Sirin," Nabokov was a preeminent poet of an emigré circle, first in Berlin (1922–37) and then in Paris (1937–40). In Berlin he began publishing novels in Russian in the mid-1920s, and his last Russian novel, *Dar* (*The Gift*) was finally published partially in 1937 and in its complete form in 1952. *The Gift* thematizes many of the issues about language, time, and writing that later appear fully orchestrated in his most sublime English novels, especially *Lolita* (1955), *Ada; or, Ardor: A Family Chronicle* (1969), and *Transparent Things* (1972). Although fluent in several languages from childhood, Nabokov chose to make his transition as a writer, for a fateful, mysterious collection of reasons, from Russian poet to English novelist, and in so doing reinflected dormant powers in the English language.

Nabokov's last two novels, *Ada* and *Transparent Things*, offer readers very rich and complete expressions of the way the magician folds his magic carpet, so that pattern becomes superimposed upon pattern, and ordinary expectations of plot dissolve into different kinds of attention and produce new focus on the multiplied, poetic power of language. *Ada* plays with time, inverting the relation between chapter length and the length of chronological time that passes, and constructing what Nabokov calls "anthemion" patterns, or interlaced, flower-like arrangements in which readers experience new ways to make connections, as well as some vital lessons on how not to do it. The same parallel comparison occurs in *Transparent Things*, between the sad recessions of "history" on the one hand, and on the other the life-affirming powers that Nabokovian language and sequence engender.

ELIZABETH DEEDS ERMARTH

See also Gift; Lolita

Biography

Born in St. Petersburg, Russia, 22 April 1899. Attended Tenishev school, St. Petersburg; fluent English and French speaker. Wrote under the pseudonym Vladimir Sirin until 1940. Family emigrated in 1919; studied Romance and Slavonic Languages at Cambridge University, England; moved to Berlin: worked as translator and writer, 1922–37; father assassinated by monarchist extremists, 1922; moved to Paris, 1937: worked as translator, language teacher, and tennis instructor; as Europe fell to the Nazis, sailed to the United States, 1940; thereafter wrote in English and translated important works of Russian literature; taught at Wellesley College; also held a Harvard Research Fellowship in lepidoptera; Professor of Russian Literature, Cornell University, Ithaca, New York, 1948–59; retired after the success of *Lolita*; moved to Montreux, Switzerland, 1960, where he continued to write and set about finalizing his literary affairs. Died 2 July 1977.

Novels by Nabokov

Mashen'ka, 1926; translated by the author and Michael Glenny as *Mary*, 1970
Korol', Dama, Valet, 1928; translated by the author and Dmitri Nabokov as *King, Queen, Knave*, 1968
Zashchita Luzhina, 1930; translated by the author and Michael Scammell as *The Defense*, 1964
Kamera Obskura, 1932; translated by W. Roy as *Camera Obscura*, 1936; revised and translated by the author as *Laughter in the Dark*, 1938
Podvig', 1933; translated by the author and Dmitri Nabokov as *Glory*, 1971
Otchayanie, 1936; translated by the author as *Despair*, 1937
Soglyadataj, 1938; translated by the author and Dmitri Nabokov as *The Eye*, 1965
Priglashenie na Kazn', 1938; translated by the author and Dmitri Nabokov as *Invitation to a Beheading*, 1959
The Real Life of Sebastian Knight, 1941
Bend Sinister, 1947
Dar, 1952; translated by the author and Michael Scammell as *The Gift*, 1963
Lolita, 1955; translated by the author into Russian, 1967
Pale Fire, 1962
Ada; or, Ardor: A Family Chronicle, 1969
Transparent Things, 1972
Look at the Harlequins!, 1974

Other Writings: stories, plays, poetry, memoirs, letters, and literary criticism.

Further Reading

Appel, Alfred, and Charles Newman, editors, *Nabokov: Criticism, Reminiscences, Translations, and Tributes*, Evanston, Illinois: Northwestern University Press, 1970; London: Weidenfeld and Nicolson, 1971
Boyd, Brian, *Vladimir Nabokov: The Russian Years*, London: Chatto and Windus, and Princeton, New Jersey: Princeton University Press, 1990
Boyd, Brian, *Vladimir Nabokov: The American Years*, London: Chatto and Windus, and Princeton, New Jersey: Princeton University Press, 1991

Dembo, L.S., editor, *Nabokov: The Man and His Work,* Madison: University of Wisconsin Press, 1967

Ermarth, Elizabeth, "Vladimir Nabokov's *Ada; or, Ardor: A Family Chronicle,*" in her *Sequel to History,* Princeton, New Jersey: Princeton University Press, 1992

Parker, Stephen Jan, "Professor Nabokov: A Review Essay," *Vladimir Nabokov Research Newsletter* 8 (Spring 1982)

Pifer, Ellen, *Nabokov and the Novel,* Cambridge, Massachusetts: Harvard University Press, 1980

Quennell, Peter, editor, *Vladimir Nabokov, His Life, His Work, His World: A Tribute,* London: Weidenfeld and Nicolson, 1979; New York: Morrow, 1980

Roth, Phyllis, editor, *Critical Essays on Vladimir Nabokov,* Boston: G.K. Hall, 1984

Rowe, William, *Nabokov's Spectral Dimension,* Ann Arbor, Michigan: Ardis, 1981

V.S. Naipaul 1932–

Trinidadian

V.S. Naipaul's first published novel, *The Mystic Masseur* (1957), established themes that reappear in his later works—the displacement of individuals in colonial and postcolonial contexts and the struggle of the writer to create a sense of order from chaotic social history. *The Mystic Masseur* also represents an equally remarkable diversity in the range of Naipaul's fictional technique. While today Naipaul is widely regarded as a British novelist, his work embodies a postcolonial quest to find an appropriate tradition in which to write and is more satisfactorily explained in relation to his Indo-Caribbean origins. Naipaul draws broadly on English literature without ever engaging in the counter-discursive stance toward the English canon that characterizes the work of such Caribbean writers as Jean Rhys (who writes back to Jane Eyre in *Wide Sargasso Sea*), Derek Walcott (who playfully subverts the Robinson Crusoe-Man Friday relationship in his play *Pantomime*), and George Lamming (who contests the colonial paradigms constructed in Shakespeare's *The Tempest* in his novel *Water with Berries* and in his nonfiction study *The Pleasures of Exile*).

Naipaul's response to the English tradition has never been so hostile or direct. Consequently, certain critics contend that Naipaul writes within that tradition in an unquestioning way. For example, the Guyanese novelist Wilson Harris asserts that Naipaul is an exponent of "the novel of persuasion," a genre that he relates to the traditions of 19th-century realism. Yet from the beginning of his career, Naipaul's fiction demonstrates a deeply ambivalent response to his European precursors—of whom Charles Dickens and Joseph Conrad are the most obvious. In fact, Naipaul's later works challenge the conventions of the novel form in a number of ways—most notably by blurring the boundaries between fiction and autobiography.

In "Jasmine" (an essay included in *The Overcrowded Barracoon,* 1972), Naipaul explains the ambiguous response he had to English literature as a young aspiring writer: "The language was ours to use as we pleased. The literature that came with it was therefore of peculiar authority; but this literature was like an alien mythology. . . ." He goes on to discuss how he attempted to adapt the books he read to his own environment. His early novels include traces of a similar adaptation process at work. Novels such as *The Mystic Masseur, The Suffrage of Elvira* (1958), and *A House for Mr. Biswas* (1961)—his early masterpiece—draw on the Charles Dickens-H.G. Wells tradition of the English novel, employing broad caricatures and comic portraiture of an externally observed social world. George Lamming (in *The Pleasures of Exile*) attacks Naipaul's early fiction, saying "His works can't move beyond a castrated satire." Lamming implies that Naipaul's fiction lacks the positive moral function that often offsets the vituperative side of satire. Naipaul answers this charge by saying that he is an ironist employing a large comic vision, based on acceptance rather than the "anger" of satire.

Naipaul's early fiction and sensibilities can be related to his political predicament of colonial disempowerment. His first two novels part company with the Dickensian tradition in their lack of any sense of indignation at the corruption they chronicle, while the tragicomic *A House for Mr. Biswas,* which bears striking similarities to Wells' *The History of Mr. Polly* (1910), offers its protagonist none of the solace of the happy ending that Wells affords his hero. In short, Naipaul's early fiction represents a fragmented colonial world and employs a fictional form that is its correlative, as it subtly undermines the sense of comic providence that underlies its European equivalents.

In the 1960s Naipaul turned to another fictional precursor, Joseph Conrad, who has been the most important influence on Naipaul's later work. He speaks of Conrad as a writer who "had been everywhere before me. Not as a man with a cause, but a man offering, as in *Nostromo,* a vision of the world's half-made societies" ("Conrad's Darkness" in *The Return of Eva Perón,* 1980). From *The Mimic Men* (1967) onward, Naipaul's fiction is written in Conradian modes. *The Mimic Men* employs a fragmentary and chronologically disordered narrative mode—reminiscent of *Lord Jim* (1900) and *Nostromo* (1904)—and a first-person narrator who, like Conrad's Marlow, sets up various ambiguities and creative tensions in the telling of the tale. Such destabilization of the authority of the narrative voice is part of

Naipaul's distinctive contribution to the postcolonial novel (and in this sense Conrad, a writer sometimes criticized for his supposed colonial attitudes, may be seen to have anticipated Naipaul as a postcolonial precursor). After *The Mimic Men*, Naipaul went on to shadow "Heart of Darkness" in *In a Free State* (1971) and *A Bend in the River* (1979)—fiction that reflects the psychological turbulence of displaced characters caught up in the aftermath of colonialism. His narrative forms, ostensibly realistic, subtly undermine the sense of security afforded by European realism.

Since the publication of his travelogue *The Middle Passage* (1962), Naipaul has alternated between fiction and nonfiction writing. Among his numerous nonfiction works are three books about India, a study of Islam (*Among the Believers*, 1981), and an account of a journey through the American South (*A Turn in the South*, 1989). Increasingly, his later work has eroded the borderline between fact and fiction. His 1987 "novel" *The Enigma of Arrival* (1987) is autobiographical, describing the life of a Caribbean-born writer who settles in Wiltshire—just as Naipaul himself did. Generic categories are also blurred in the central tale, which gives the novel its title (taken from a painting by the surrealist artist Giorgio De Chirico). This novel resembles the fiction of a postmodern writer like Jorge Luis Borges; it has less in common with classic realism or conventional autobiography. Naipaul asserts that the novel form is dead, and his 1994 book *A Way in the World*, which follows *The Enigma of Arrival* in blending fact and fiction, refuses status as a novel, preferring to call itself "a sequence." It intersperses a range of public and personal histories to illustrate a complex investigation of origins, which suggests that pasts are layered and cannot be described through a unitary narrative method. Naipaul's compulsive storytelling complicates the issue of how to narrate the past. Despite the view that he is no innovator, Naipaul's approach has much in common with the French philosopher Michel Foucault's archaeological approach to the discursive inscription of the past, which has influenced several postcolonial critics of European historiography.

JOHN THIEME

See also Bend in the River

Biography

Born 17 August 1932 in Trinidad; brother of the writer Shiva Naipaul. Attended Tranquility Boys School; Queen's Royal College, Port of Spain, Trinidad, 1943–49; University College, Oxford, 1950–54, B.A. (honors) in English 1953. Editor, "Caribbean Voices," BBC, London, 1954–56; fiction reviewer, *New Statesman*, London, 1957–61. Knighted, 1990.

Novels by Naipaul

The Mystic Masseur, 1957
The Suffrage of Elvira, 1958
A House for Mr. Biswas, 1961
Mr. Stone and the Knights Companion, 1963
The Mimic Men, 1967
Guerrillas, 1975
A Bend in the River, 1979
The Enigma of Arrival, 1987

Other Writings: short stories, a novella (*In a Free State*, 1971), travel writing, and other nonfiction.

Further Reading

Boxill, Anthony, *V.S. Naipaul's Fiction: In Quest of The Enemy*, Fredericton, New Brunswick: York Press, 1983
Cudjoe, Selwyn R., *V.S. Naipaul: A Materialist Reading*, Amherst: University of Massachusetts Press, 1988
Hamner, Robert, *V.S. Naipaul*, New York: Twayne, 1973
Hamner, Robert, editor, *Critical Perspectives on V.S. Naipaul*, Washington, D.C.: Three Continents Press, 1977; London: Heinemann, 1979
Hughes, Peter, *V.S. Naipaul*, London and New York: Routledge, 1988
Kelly, Richard, *V.S. Naipaul*, New York: Continuum, 1989
Modern Fiction Studies 30:3 (1984), special issue on Naipaul
Nixon, Rob, *London Calling: V.S. Naipaul, Postcolonial Mandarin*, New York: Oxford University Press, 1992
Thieme, John, *The Web of Tradition: Uses of Allusion in V.S. Naipaul's Fiction*, London: Dangaroo Press, 1987
White, Landeg, *V.S. Naipaul: A Critical Introduction*, London: Macmillan, and New York: Barnes and Noble, 1975

Naked Lunch by William Burroughs

1959

William Burroughs' *Naked Lunch* is infamous because of the various ways it stretched literary boundaries, in terms both of content and form. Following in the footsteps of writers such as Arthur Rimbaud, Andre Gidé, and Louis-Ferdinand Céline, Burroughs in *Naked Lunch* focused on the deviant subcultures thriving beneath the surface of modern society. By describing the experiences of drug addicts and homosexuals in graphic detail, he alienated many readers and became a cult hero to others.

Naked Lunch was first published in Paris in 1959 by the Olympia Press, which was known at the time primarily for its line of pornographic literature. Olympia's publisher, Maurice Girodias, had been trying to branch out by publishing controversial literary works (just four years prior to publishing *Naked Lunch* Girodias had also released Vladimir Nabokov's *Lolita*). After Grove Press obtained the US publishing rights for *Naked Lunch* from Girodias, it soon found itself embroiled in a highly publicized obscenity lawsuit. The courts ultimately ruled that *Naked Lunch* was not obscene, and the trial helped expand the legal boundaries of acceptable literary expression.

The obscenity charge directed against *Naked Lunch* stemmed most obviously from its vivid depictions of sadomasochistic homosexual encounters. All of these scenes, however, are exaggeratedly perverse and violent and are more likely to arouse disgust in the reader than a state of erotic arousal. As many critics have noted, Burroughs deliberately set out to offend his readers in order to demonstrate how sexual relations can be used as perverse expressions of power, and how power itself eventually exerts an addictive control over those engaged in sexual activities.

Obscenity charges were also leveled against *Naked Lunch* for its portrayal of drug use and addiction. Burroughs' personal experience as a heroin addict in the 1940s and 1950s led him to use the metaphor of addiction to describe the mechanisms by which governments maintain control over their citizens, and the manner in which these mechanisms of control reduce modern life to an animalistic nightmare. By focusing on the experiences of junkies and sexual deviants, then, Burroughs was not only suggesting that these subcultures are the natural products of an inherently diseased society, but also that even so-called "normal" social relations are predicated upon similarly malignant expressions of power.

Burroughs' experiments with literary form in *Naked Lunch* helped him expose and destroy these more subtly pervasive techniques of social control. Burroughs felt that language itself exerts a tyranny over modern thought that can only be undone by breaking up the apparently "logical" connections between words and sentences. As a result, the language of *Naked Lunch* is more akin to surrealist or symbolist poetry than the realist prose typically associated with novelistic discourse. This freewheeling attitude toward linguistic decorum most clearly demonstrates Burroughs' literary relation to such Beat writers as Allen Ginsberg and Jack Kerouac. Both Ginsberg and Kerouac were instrumental in assembling the manuscript of *Naked Lunch* and getting it published, and Ginsberg ultimately campaigned to have Burroughs accepted to the American Academy and Institute of Arts and Letters in 1983. While Burroughs' literary sensibility is much darker and more pessimistic than the Beats', both Burroughs and Kerouac opened up the poetic possibilities of the novel to a greater extent than ever before in American fiction.

Burroughs' most obvious attempt to open up the poetic possibilities of novelistic discourse is displayed in the structure—or what many critics would call the nonstructure—of *Naked Lunch*. Rather than being arranged in a linear, chronological fashion, *Naked Lunch* unfolds in an apparently haphazard manner, its poetically charged vignettes linked thematically rather than causally. As a result, some readers have found the book to be unduly repetitive and feel that the lack of a progressive storyline creates a monotonous, impenetrable narrative. But by allowing *Naked Lunch* to unfold in such a fashion, Burroughs accomplishes two things. First, he realistically depicts the timeless quality of what he terms "junk experience," a state of being in which there are only repeated cycles of abject need and physical gratification. Secondly, he forces the reader's imagination to

break free of the logical structures that typically condition his or her responses to reality. By willfully disrupting the reader's narrative expectations, he imposes upon the reader the arbitrary nature of all representations of human experience.

Ironically, however, the reader's only choice is to submit to Burroughs' own arbitrary arrangement of human experience. As Burroughs writes toward the end of the book, "*Naked Lunch* demands Silence from The Reader. Otherwise he is taking his own pulse." Thus, even Burroughs' relation to the readers of *Naked Lunch* reproduces the dominant power structures he exposes throughout the book. Burroughs is very much aware of this irony, and his bleak pessimism regarding the possibility of transcending the systems of addiction and control that (he argues) permeate modern society is perhaps the most disturbing aspect of *Naked Lunch*.

While many reviewers found little to praise in the novel, others pointed to its literary merits. Mary McCarthy defended the novel as a form of Swiftian satire, but finally concluded that "what saves *Naked Lunch* is not a literary ancestor but humour. Burroughs' humour is peculiarly American, at once broad and sly. It is the humour of a comedian, a Vaudeville performer playing in 'One,' in front of the asbestos curtain of some Keith Circuit or Pantages house long since converted to movies" (See McCarthy, 1963). Norman Mailer, during the course of the *Naked Lunch* obscenity trial, said of Burroughs, "The man has extraordinary style. . . . I think he catches the beauty, at the same time the viciousness and the meanness and the excitement, you see, of ordinary talk, the talk of criminals, of soldiers, athletes, junkies." Burroughs' satirical outlook resembles Joseph Heller's in *Catch-22* (1961) and Thomas Pynchon's in *Gravity's Rainbow* (1973). Burroughs' outlaw sensibility has also become a major reference point in popular culture, most notably helping to shape the punk ethos of the late 1970s and early 1980s. While many readers will continue to find the willful perversity of much of *Naked Lunch*'s imagery repulsive, and be daunted by the interpretive difficulties posed by its poetic character, just as many will find inspiration in its subversive sensibility, uncompromising integrity, and daring experiments with literary form.

ANDRES VIRKUS

Further Reading

Bockris, Victor, editor, *With William Burroughs: A Report from the Bunker,* New York: Seaver, 1981; London: Vermilion, 1982; revised edition, New York: St. Martin's Press, 1996.

Goodman, Michael, *Contemporary Literary Censorship: The Case History of Burroughs' "Naked Lunch,"* Metuchen, New Jersey: Scarecrow, 1981

McCarthy, Mary, "Burroughs' *Naked Lunch*," *Encounter* 20 (April 1963)

McLuhan, Marshall, "Notes on Burroughs," *Nation* 199 (28 December 1964)

Morgan, Ted, *Literary Outlaw: The Life and Times of William Burroughs,* New York: Holt, 1988; London: Pimlico, 1991

Mottram, Eric, *William Burroughs: The Algebra of Need,* Buffalo, New York: Intrepid Press, 1971; London: Boyars, 1977

Skerl, Jennie, *William S. Burroughs,* Boston: Twayne, 1985

Tytell, John, *Naked Angels: The Lives and Literature of the Beat Generation,* New York: McGraw-Hill, 1976

R.K. Narayan 1906–

Indian

R.K. Narayan's prolific literary career, which now spans seven decades, includes novels, short stories, and works of nonfiction. Since his entry onto the international literary stage in 1935, his books alone comprise 15 novels, 10 collections of stories, and 11 works of nonfiction, including volumes of autobiography and collections of essays. He is without doubt one of India's best-known writers and has received considerable recognition for his work both in and out of India. Narayan's work is characterized by a preference for premodernist fictional techniques, and by the strong vein of comedy and irony that runs through the whole body of his writing. But the most remarkable aspect of his oeuvre is undoubtedly his creation of an India in microcosm in the imaginary town of Malgudi—which bears a striking resemblance to Narayan's hometown, the South Indian city of Mysore. Malgudi was introduced to the world in his first novel, *Swami and Friends* (1935), and has been developed through a succession of novels and stories spanning more than 60 years. His work has long been compared with that of various European writers, notably Anton Chekhov and Jane Austen, and, more recently, with a range of postcolonial writers including Chinua Achebe, Anita Desai, Ruth Prawer Jhabvala, George Lamming, Salman Rushdie, Kurt Vonnegut, and Patrick White.

Narayan's early novels are heavily autobiographical. *Swami and Friends* draws on his experiences as a schoolboy, his second novel, *The Bachelor of Arts* (1937), on his experiences as a college student, and his fourth novel, *The English Teacher* (1945), on his short-lived teaching career, as well as his marriage and the early death of his wife. Together these works form a loose trilogy and indeed were published as such in the United States under the title *Grateful to Life and Death* (1953). His third novel, *The Dark Room* (1938), with its bleak portrait of the ill-treatment of a traditional Hindu wife, stands somewhat apart from the rest of Narayan's predominantly comic oeuvre.

Narayan's next five novels, from *Mr. Sampath* (1949) to *The Man-Eater of Malgudi* (1961), map the boundaries of his fictional world and populate that world with many of its most enduring and endearing characters. *Waiting for the Mahatma* (1955), which is of considerable historical interest for its portrait of Gandhi, suffers for stepping outside the usual pattern of the Malgudi novels. *The Guide* (1958), however, which also strays from that pattern, is regarded widely as his most outstanding novel. By the time he wrote *The Man-Eater of Malgudi*, Narayan had developed a formula for his fiction, a formula which captures both the strengths and limitations of his work. *The Vendor of Sweets* (1967) demonstrates this pattern clearly. Narayan typically focuses his powers of observation on a single protagonist, in this case the shopkeeper Jagan as he goes about his daily business. Once Narayan firmly establishes the daily routine of the central character, he then disrupts the routine by a series of crises that are more often than not caused by the arrival of an outsider of some kind—here the return of Jagan's son Mali from America. Similarly, in *The Man-Eater of Malgudi* Nataraj's life is disrupted when he meets the mad taxidermist Vasu; the problems in *Talkative Man* (1986) stem from the arrival of Dr. Rann on the train from Delhi; and in *The World of Nagaraj* (1990) Nagaraj's routine is disturbed by the arrival of his nephew Tim. In *Talkative Man, The World of Nagaraj,* and *The Vendor of Sweets,* the interruption is complicated further by the presence of a wife.

This deceptively simple pattern, which Narayan invariably exploits to great comic and ironic effect, masks a series of penetrating explorations of Indian life. *The Man-Eater of Malgudi,* rooted in Indian mythology, is at once the story of an arrogant person receiving his come-uppance and a vivid portrait of madness. Beneath its comic surface, *The Vendor of Sweets* offers a complex reading of the oppositions between East and West, between the traditional and the modern, and between generations. Jagan's lifelong commitment to the teachings of Mahatma Gandhi also provides the opportunity for a subtle reexamination of Gandhism that can usefully be compared to Narayan's earlier treatment of Gandhi's teaching in *Waiting for the Mahatma. The Painter of Signs* (1976), ostensibly the story of Raman's love for Daisy (and something of a companion piece to *Waiting for the Mahatma*), takes on India's population problem and the controversial subject of birth control. *A Tiger for Malgudi* (1983), another unusual novel in Narayan's oeuvre, is narrated by the talking tiger Raja. There is a clear shift here toward fantasy, but behind the fantastic elements lies Narayan's serious examination of reincarnation.

The more recent and very short novel *Grandmother's Tale* (1992) is the only one of Narayan's 15 novels not to be set in the environs of Malgudi, although some of Narayan's short stories, notably "A Horse and Two Goats," are also set outside the imaginary town.

RALPH J. CRANE

See also Man-Eater of Malgudi

Biography
Born 10 October 1906 in Madras. Attended Collegiate High School, Mysore; Maharaja's College, Mysore, graduated 1930. Teacher, and later journalist, early 1930s; owner, Indian Thought Publications, Mysore.

Novels by Narayan
Swami and Friends: A Novel of Malgudi, 1935
The Bachelor of Arts, 1937
The Dark Room, 1938
The English Teacher, 1945; published together with *Swami and Friends* and *The Bachelor of Arts* as *Grateful to Life and Death,* 1953
Mr. Sampath, 1949; as *The Printer of Malgudi,* 1957
The Financial Expert, 1952
Waiting for the Mahatma, 1955
The Guide, 1958
The Man-Eater of Malgudi, 1961
The Vendor of Sweets, 1967; as *The Sweet-Vendor,* 1967
The Painter of Signs, 1976
A Tiger for Malgudi, 1983
Talkative Man, 1986
The World of Nagaraj, 1990
Grandmother's Tale, 1992

Other Writings: short stories, essays, travel writing, sketches, autobiography, and shortened modern prose versions of *The Ramayana* (1972) and *The Mahabharata* (1978).

Further Reading
Beatina, Mary, *Narayan: A Study in Transcendence*, New York: Peter Lang, 1993
Crane, Ralph J., "'Oft of One Wide Expanse Have I Been Told': An Evaluation of the Criticism of R.K. Narayan's Works," *Littcrit* 22:1 (1996)
Harrex, S.C., "Celebrating Malgudi's Golden Jubilee," *CRNLE Reviews Journal* (Adelaide) 1–2 (1988)

Holmstrom, Lakshmi, *The Novels of R.K. Narayan*, Calcutta: Writers Workshop, 1973
McLeod, A.L., editor, *R.K. Narayan: Critical Perspectives*, New Delhi: Sterling, 1994
Naik, M.K., *The Ironic Vision: A Study of the Fiction of R.K. Narayan*, New Delhi: Sterling, 1983
Vanden Driesen, Cynthia, *The Novels of R.K. Narayan*, Nedlands: Centre for South and South East Asian Studies, University of Western Australia, 1986
Walsh, William, *R.K. Narayan: A Critical Appreciation*, London: Heinemann, and Chicago: University of Chicago Press, 1982

Narratee. *See* Narratology; Narrator

Narrative Poetry. *See* Verse Narrative

Narrative Theory

Where narratology describes a particular way of analyzing texts in order to arrive at interpretation or categorization, narrative theory considers more philosophical questions about the nature of narrative by viewing it from a variety of linguistic, social, and political perspectives. While not every narrative theory is narratology, narratology implies a narrative theory or a way of defining and contextualizing the term *narrative* itself. Narrative theory studies much more than just the novel or even prose fiction, seeking instead to understand all forms of narrative, including historical, scientific, and philosophical writing. For instance, Donna Haraway's highly influential book about the rhetoric of science, *Simians, Cyborgs, and Women* (1991), argues that certain "allowable stories" exist within all fields of study and that these kinds of stories determine how authority is granted and ultimately what conclusions research will reach. Nontextual narrative has also been included in the scope of narrative theory, as in Anthony Paul Kerby's argument in *Narrative and the Self* (1991) that individuals constantly tell stories about themselves as a way to understand everyday experience, or as in Peter McCormick's *Fictions, Philosophies, and the Problems of Poetics* (1988), which claims that we judge future events by pro-

jecting ourselves into hypothetical narratives with ourselves as "virtual persons."

What qualifies these types of discourse as narrative? In *Narrative as Communication* (1989), Didier Coste defines narrative as discourse describing things that change over time and "elicits thinking about the passage of time." We might add that narrative (and narrative theory) is concerned with the nature of identity. Narrative theory is closely related to models of time and meaning, and, more than most subfields of literary theory like feminism, marxism, or theories of metaphor, the different "schools" of narrative theory carry on relatively independently of each other. We can fairly distinguish five broad approaches to narrative that have had a "turn" in the theoretical spotlight over the last 30 years.

Syntactic Narrative Theories

Narrative theory is usually traced to Russian formalism. A group of linguists and literary historians, this school sought to take a scientific approach to the "laws" of art and to move away from more subjective theories of aesthetic response. Their best known claim was that art functioned essentially to defamiliarize linguistic expression. Although the methods by which a poem might accomplish such defamiliarization are fairly obvious—rhyme and rhythm, the striking use of metaphor, and so on—the means by which a narrative accomplishes this task are less obvious. Out of this difficulty was born a distinction that became fundamental to the study of narrative: the difference between *fabula* and *syuzhet,* or story and plot. A story is simply the events ordered chronologically; the plot is the careful arrangement and presentation of these events for the sake of some moral or artistic purpose. Viktor Shklovskii concludes his famous essay on Laurence Sterne's *Tristram Shandy* by remarking, "The forms of art are explainable by the laws of art; they are not justified by their realism. Slowing the action of a novel is not accomplished by introducing rivals, for example, but by simply *transposing* parts. In so doing the artist makes us aware of the aesthetic laws which underlie both the transposition and the slowing down of the action." Although Shklovskii uses the distinction between story and plot to explain narrative aesthetics, other formalist critics were able to use the terms and general scientific approach to describe the structural building blocks of narrative more generally. Vladimir Propp's *Morfologiia skazki* (1928; *Morphology of the Folktale*) uses the distinction to study the constituent elements of the Russian folktale, discovering that the diversity of the actual characters in the tales reduces to 31 basic plot functions associated with stock chracters, such as the villain, the provider, the helper, the hero, the dispatcher, and so on. By using the distinction between narrative surface and depth, Propp showed that the Russian folktale obeys a structural rule, offering the first clear example of what we may call the syntactic approach to narrative, based on the assumption that some fundamental law controls the way that individual narratives are constructed. But the urge to make sense of events by seeing them as the product of some more basic and logical system precedes Russian formalism. For instance, Marx and Engels' claim in the *Communist Manifesto* (1848) that economic history could be understood in terms of the inevitable movement from feudalism to capitalism to communism essentially anticipates syntactic narrative theory, examining the messy details of history and reducing them to a logical structure that underlies and causes them.

The syntactic approach to narrative represented by Russian formalism underwent a profound change when Roman Jakobson introduced it to the French intellectual community, which had already adopted Ferdinand de Saussure's semiological theory of language. Saussure had distinguished the "diachronic" process of how languages change over time from the "synchronic" order of a whole language at a given moment, and he had distinguished individual utterances (*parole*) from a given linguistic system (*langue*). The explanatory power of Saussure's theory and the elegance and economy of Propp's morphology suggested that other forms of communication might have the equivalent of *langue*—a fundamental narrative system from which individual narratives are generated. The most obvious and extreme example of the resulting structuralist narrative theory is Tzvetan Todorov's *Grammaire du Décaméron* (1969; Grammar of *The Decameron*). Todorov's study of Giovanni Boccaccio's 100 tales applies the grammatical categories of the sentence to narrative, claiming that it is made up of basic propositions that are formed like a sentence: with a noun (a character) and either a verb (action) or an adjective (attribute). Todorov's study exemplifies the

characteristic tendency of syntactic approaches to see the surface of the text *merely* as the manifestation of some syntactic depth.

Yet precisely the reductiveness of semiotic analysis may also work to open up a text to multiple interpretations. This possibility is most clear in Roland Barthes' work. Where Barthes' early essay "Introduction à l'analyse structurale des récits" (1966; "An Introduction to the Structural Analysis of Narratives") looks very much like Todorov's and Propp's discussion of the basic building blocks of narrative, later work like *S/Z* (1970; *S/Z*) identifies fundamental syntactic elements in order to complicate rather than simplify a narrative. In *S/Z*, Barthes distinguishes between five basic codes and looks for their appearance throughout Balzac's "Sarrasine": the *hermeneutic* code raises a question for the narrative, the *semantic* code describes the connotations of individual elements in the work, the *symbolic* code refers to thematic oppositions in the narrative, the *proairetic* code describes the actions that characters follow to logical ends, and the *gnomic* code refers to generally accepted cultural "wisdom." Barthes claims that his analysis reveals a kind of "musical score" in the novella because each of the codes moves into the foreground at different moments. According to Barthes, this kind of structural analysis is possible because Balzac's novella is "readerly" (as opposed to "writerly"), that is, it allows room for the reader to participate in its construction. In contrasting readerly to writerly texts, Barthes argues against traditional literary criticism, which takes the book as a complete thing to be approached passively and without interpretive intervention.

Semantic Narrative Theories

Syntactic narrative theories suffer from two main problems. First, they tend to be profoundly reductive. Todorov's analysis of Boccaccio is the most obvious example of this reduction, but the same charge can be made against Russian formalism, which reduces all literature to the pursuit of "defamiliarization." Second, syntactic theories ignore the imaginative experience of the narrative text for the sake of an unseen structure that "causes" the surface of the text and that may be inaccessible to an untrained reader. Both problems have led theorists to complain that the syntactic approach to narrative is the result of critical arrogance and the mistaken belief that narrative is a generative system. Thomas Pavel notes in *Fictional Worlds* (1986) that "it is difficult to believe that all myths, stories, or texts can be reduced to single elementary semantic structures. . . . Semiotic objects are complex constructions, overloaded with meaning; to postulate so rudimentary a sense involves a considerable loss of information." Semantic narrative theory tries to avoid the reductiveness of syntactic approaches.

The French critic A.-J. Greimas functions as an interesting transitional figure between syntactic and semantic narrative theories. Greimas believes that Saussurean linguistics is limited because it does not consider its underlying semantic oppositions, the tensions that make words meaningful within a culture. For instance, a Saussurean would claim that the decision to use the word "tree" in an English sentence is determined by the availability of related words—the fact that English has a word for "bush" and "forest" but no word to distinguish deciduous from evergreen trees. Greimas, conversely, studies the fundamental oppositions organizing individual words, distinguishing, in *Sémantique structurale* (1966; *Structural Semantics*), for example, spatial words like "high," "long," and "wide" from those like "vast" and "dense." The former terms reflect a concern for "dimensionality," whereas the latter do not. Greimas applies this search for underlying semantic structures to Propp's work on character "functions." In Propp's analysis Greimas sees a narrative syntax that has not been sufficiently reduced to its fundamental meaningful oppositions. Examining Propp's 31 functions, he finds three pairs of opposed "actants": subject versus object, sender versus receiver, and helper versus opponent. In this respect, then, Greimas' analysis is reductive in the extreme. On the other hand, Greimas leaves the relation between surface and depth somewhat ambiguous. If we assume that the deep structure generates the surface manifestations, then Greimas is ultimately offering a reductive syntactic theory of narrative. However, if we assume that the structures we find in the narrative are produced by our actions as readers—and this is Fredric Jameson's reading of Greimas in his foreword to the English translation of *On Meaning* (1987) and in Jameson's own *The Prison-House of Language* (1972)—then these structures are the result of our attempts to make the work meaningful, part of a semantic approach.

The field of fictional semantics shares with Jameson's reading of Greimas a concern for how narrative is made meaningful, but it often begins at sentence-level reference. At its simplest, fictional semantics asks what it is we refer to when we speak about fictional characters and objects. Although fictional semantics raises very broad questions about reference that have little application to the task of literary interpretation, semantics does address an important issue: the construction of a textual "world" in which we place events and characters to make them meaningful. Fictional semanticists will point out that our experience of a text is often less of the actual events and characters and more of the whole "style" of the text's world. For a semanticist, a narrative is a network of "modalized" events—that is, events with various degrees of likelihood and actuality. In *Possible Worlds, Artificial Intelligence, and Narrative Theory* (1991), Marie-Laure Ryan distinguishes events with various kinds of existence on the basis of three systems: the deontic (concerning permissibility or prohibition), the axiological (concerning goodness or badness), and the epistemic (concerning knowledge and belief). The text, then, is made up of wished-for, expected, prohibited, allowed events, and so on. The tissue of actual and nonactual events that Ryan describes can also be applied to the way a narrative constructs characters and objects. Thomas Pavel notes that our "everyday" world is comprised of many kinds of entities that arise from our belief systems and that often survive after explicit belief in those systems begins to erode. Other critics have noted that this same approach to the layering of real, possible, and impossible objects and events within narrative applies to the types of space contained within a work: some spaces are actually occupied by characters, others are viewed by them, others are potential sites for visits, and still others are merely imagined.

Semantic approaches to narrative share with syntactic ones the assumption that the surface level of the text depends on a more logical structure that underlies it. It departs from syntactical theories in implying that these structures are constructed by our own interpretive acts more than by the causality of the narrative form itself. A good example of this interpretive approach to narrative semantics is Lubomír Doležel's "Intensional and Extensional Narrative Worlds" (1979). Doležel distinguishes between two general categories of "worlds" within a narrative: those composed of entities (extensional) and those that sort these entities according to some principle of value (intensional). Doležel notes that there are primary extensional worlds, which are simply the sum of all the objects and characters within a given narrative, and secondary extensional worlds, which are more abstract "types" that we can recognize in many individual texts. For instance, one of the ways that we interpret a work is by recognizing that a given character is part of a larger tradition. Thus, Anna Karenina, to use one of Doležel's examples, shares with other tragic 19th-century female characters like Emma Bovary certain qualities that allow us to grasp the thematic point of this work more clearly. Interpreting a work means recognizing the elements of the primary extensional world, seeing cross-textual parallels in the secondary extensional world, and understanding what the work has to say about this general type by considering the values implied within the intensional world. As this example makes clear, the secondary extensional world that helps to illuminate the work is the product of our own interpretive background, rather than some internal structure that causes the narrative to be produced in a certain way.

Phenomenological Narrative Theories

The syntactic and the semantic approaches to narrative theory both assume that we can distinguish between the surface level of the text and some logical or formal deep structure. In this sense, both approaches to narrative arise from a fundamental linguistic model and assume that narrative should be treated as a communicative activity that obeys certain rules, whether these rules are thought to control a particular narrative's generation or its interpretation. We should now turn to a largely independent strain of narrative theory that arises out of phenomenology and that takes the temporality of narrative less as a discursive feature (an element of a text) and more as a part of lived experience in general. Edmund Husserl's phenomenological theory claims that our experience of the world always involves "retensions" and "protensions" in that our perception of the present is conditioned by how we place it in the context of the past and how we anticipate the future to proceed from this point. One of the best illustrations of the phenomenological approach to time is the experience of music. When listening to a piece of music, we do not hear individual notes; rather, we are aware of the tempo, changes in tone, repetitions and variations of themes, and the likely continuation of specific musical phrases and patterns.

Critics have applied the idea that our everyday experience has a temporal and therefore narrative quality in many contexts. Michel de Certeau, for example, speaks about the experience of urban space as a kind of narrative in *L'Invention du quotidien* (1980; *The Practice of Everyday Life*). De Certeau argues that moving between spaces within a city demands that we follow various trajectories and that we experience locations in terms of their history. With reference to text, the claim that our basic experience of the world involves creating narratives has led theorists to reconsider the question of how our own acts of textual interpretation struggle with historical distance. That question has a long tradition in hermeneutics, the philosophy originally concerned with biblical interpretation, but which has become generalized to include any attempt to understand the original meaning of a given text. Paul Ricoeur's three-volume study, *Temps et récit* (1983–85; *Time and Narrative*) provides a sweeping synthesis of theories of temporality applied to narrative. Our temporal experience, Ricoeur argues, involves constructing and negotiating three ways in which our place in the temporal world is "plotted" and made meaningful: the time of individual actions, the time of the total "plot," and the time in which these two are reconciled and the narrative is brought to bear on our personal actions. As Ricoeur concludes about this third form of time, "what is interpreted in a text is the proposing of a world that I might inhabit and into which I might project my ownmost powers." Each of these forms of time imply a type of "mimesis" that represents them, and Ricoeur claims that different literary, scientific, and historical works shape human time by negotiating these kinds of mimesis in different ways.

Many critics have applied these very sweeping philosophical issues about human experience to literary interpretation in a more narrow sense. Wolfgang Iser, the best known critic working in this field, claims that we should approach an individual text as a kind of script for producing a response. According to him, underlying patterns that we discover when we interpret a story are meaningless if we fail to take into account the temporal process through which a reader comes to recognize those patterns. As Iser remarks at the outset of *Der Akt des Lesens* (1976; *The Act of Reading*), "As meaning arises out of the process of actualization, the interpreter should perhaps pay more attention to the process than to the product. His object should therefore be, not to explain a work, but to reveal the conditions that bring about its various possible effects." Iser's work has given rise to a major strain of contemporary literary theory called "reader response" criticism, which studies how readers are led to respond to a given work. Ricoeur's claim about the fundamentally temporal nature of human experience is transformed in this approach to the reader's temporal experience of narrative. Iser argues that, although experience is personal, readers share the rough outlines of their experience because they accept the role that a text defines for them—they are willing to become the "implied reader" the text asks them to be. This leap is essential for being able to interpret a given narrative using the tools of our temporal movement through it. Once we agree that a text defines an implied reader, then a critic can identify this reader, analyze how the text encourages her to adopt that role, and explain the purpose behind this manipulation.

Rhetorical Theories of Narrative

Rhetorical theories focus on the rhetorical repertoire of narrative elements, such as voice, perspective, temporal organization, and so on, that are at the author's disposal. The seeds of the rhetorical approach lie in Wayne Booth's highly influential *The Rhetoric of Fiction* (1961). Booth assumes that narratives always imply a judgment and thus always tell us how to interpret a given scene. Booth's theory is fundamentally temporal in the same way as Iser's, although it lacks the theoretical justification that Iser draws from phenomenology. But by emphasizing the *effect* that a text has on a reader, Booth treats literary experience from a rhetorical perspective that has largely dominated the study of narrative in the American academy in the last two decades.

The rhetorical approach to narrative begins from the common-sensical definition of a writer's basic choices. Seymour Chatman's widely taught overview of narratology, *Story and Discourse* (1978), enumerates the elements of narratives that in-

dividual authors use to achieve their purposes. As Chatman notes, "Language is an extremely versatile tool, and clever authors can deploy a wide range of verbal underlinings and concealments, promotions and deceptions." Although early (syntactic) French theories of narrative like Todorov's *Qu'est-ce que le structuralisme?*, volume 2: *Poétique* (1968; *Introduction to Poetics*) often drew directly or indirectly on Booth's work and described the *langue* of narrative in terms of authorial choices, this rhetorical approach to narrative is at odds with the syntactic model in that it does away with the "deep level" posited by syntactic theories. Narrative for Booth and Chatman is fundamentally unmysterious. The advantages of this rhetorical approach to narrative are obvious and significant: by considering the conclusions toward which a writer hopes to draw a reader, critics are able to speak about the political implications of various texts. James Phelan's discussion of a Hemingway novel in his *Reading People, Reading Plots* (1989), for instance, examines the ways in which readers are able to "resist" the role of the "implied reader" that a text might hope to provide: "To [become the implied reader], we are asked . . . to assent to a definition of the fine life in which the female is endlessly self-effacing, tirelessly available, and continually sacrificing." Phelan's discussion shows the problems with reading works that have an implied reader one is unwilling to accept, and yet he also manages to distinguish these individual points of conflict from larger thematic purposes in the work that readers might still find meaningful.

This rhetorical understanding of narrative has had an effect on debates about the nature of contemporary knowledge in general. In *La Condition postmoderne* (1979; *The Postmodern Condition*), Jean-François Lyotard argues that contemporary knowledge claims are changing. In the past, individuals appealed to broad "metanarratives" that allowed them to make factual statements. In the narrative of the "hero of liberty," for example, "All peoples have a right to science. If the social subject is not already the subject of scientific knowledge, it is because that has been forbidden by priests and tyrants. The right to science must be reconquered." Postmodern knowledge, conversely, is characterized by less stable "language games," each with a tentative authority in which "the rules defining a game and the 'moves' playable within it *must* be local, in other words, agreed on by its present players and subject to eventual cancellation." Lyotard's claims about the nature of contemporary knowledge have been challenged by a number of critics—mostly because many forms of social critique demand that individuals *do* construct large interpretive "stories." Nancy Fraser and Linda Nicholson argue in their influential article "Social Criticism without Philosophy" (1988) that "it would be apparent that many of the genres rejected by postmodernists [i.e., metanarratives] are necessary for social criticism. For a phenomenon as pervasive and multifaceted as male dominance simply cannot be adequately grasped with the meager critical resources to which they would limit us." The debate surrounding the role of large narratives in defining and justifying criticism is a particularly broad and abstract context for understanding the rhetorical deployment of narrative. Rather than only thinking about narrative as a series of discursive positions that the reader is encouraged to adopt, Lyotard's association of narrative and the way that we establish our right to make knowledge claims suggests a much broader sense in which culturally accepted "stories" circulate and serve social and political purposes.

Theories of Narrative Instability

For all its common-sensical appeal, rhetorical narrative theories make several problematic assumptions: that writers are more or less fully self-conscious, that readers pick up on all rhetorical clues, and that reading is a more or less unified march toward the conclusion that the author wishes the reader to draw. Although many rhetorical theories of narrative try to account for the ways in which response may be unpredictable, speaking about an author's rhetorical strategies implies a stability of intention and response. At the opposite end of the spectrum lie narrative theories that focus on sources of instability—on the *lack* of identity between two moments within a text.

Probably the most significant example of this open-ended understanding of narrative, at least for readers of the novel, is Mikhail Bakhtin's theory of narrative dialogue. In *The Dialogic Imagination*—a work written during the 1930s but not published until 1981—Bakhtin argues that dialogic speech contains "traces" of expected responses. Bakhtin calls the mixture of real and anticipated voices in any element of novelistic speech "heteroglossia":

> the prose writer witnesses as well the unfolding of social heteroglossia *surrounding* the object, the Tower-of-Babel mixing of languages that goes on around any object; the dialectics of the object are interwoven with the social dialogue surrounding it. For the prose writer, the object is a focal point for heteroglot voices among which his own voice must also sound.

According to Bakhtin, novelistic discourse at its best is not the "monologic" construction of an author but "polyphonic" play of many character voices that function relatively independently within the novel. Bakhtin's distinction between monologic and polyphonic writing has had a strong influence on narrative theorists, who see in it an approach to the novel based not on totalizing structures—some rhetorical "point" that an author is trying to make or some underlying "structure" that causes the work to be written—but instead on an unstable but ultimately democratic pluralism.

Where Bakhtin believes that narrative voices *exceed* any one unifying perspective, other critics have posited a lack in the text that undermines the meaning the text projects. Paul de Man's theory in *Allegories of Reading* (1979) uses narrative as a way of speaking about how a text wanders or fails to remain consistent in its definition of terms. Speaking of Rousseau's *Pygmalion*, de Man describes how the slippage of meaning within the text creates a kind of narrative "progression." De Man explains, "The various steps in this progression do not simply cancel each other out; they are 'aufgehoben,' surpassed but maintained . . . which does not mean that they are allowed to reach their teleological closure." De Man's use of the narrative figure of allegory is a good example of how narrative can embody the slippage of meaning in a text. Other theories strive for a balance between Bakhtin's notion of narrative excess and de Man's idea of narrative lack. Homi Bhabha's "DissemiNation: Time, Narrative, and the Margins of the Modern Nation" (in *Nation and Narration*, 1990) describes the creation of the cultural entity of the nation using terms reminiscent of Lyotard's claims about the functioning of narratives in a culture. Bhabha hopes to describe "the complex strategies of cultural identification and discursive address that function in the name of 'the people' or 'the nation' and make them the immanent subjects and objects of a range of social and literary narratives." Rather than arguing that narratives are imposed on a nation as untouchable wholes, Bhabha sees the very conditions out of which narratives are produced to make them unstable. According to Bhabha, "the people are neither the beginner or the end of the national narrative; they represent the cutting edge between the totalizing powers of the social and the forces that signify the more specific address to contentious, unequal interests and identities within the population." Because the nation is always the site of conflict and struggle for definitions, the narratives that circulate within a culture can never be stable or simple. They are simultaneously incomplete and the product of excess and multiplicity.

In an important sense, narrative theory participates in the philosophical inquiry into the discursive representation of the passing of time, an inquiry that underlies both the history of the novel and the more practical interpreting and categorizing goals of narratology. Critics have increasingly come to see narrative as itself something with which writers struggle (especially in the analysis of narrative instabilities and in some of the more sophisticated rhetorical and phenomenological criticism) rather than merely as a mechanical, quasi-linguistic system for the transmission of ideas. In a sense, we can observe a fusion of form and content in narrative theory of the last decade, where stories are increasingly taken to be "about" the problems of constructing a narrative. If temporality is a fact with which human society must come to terms, the novel will be one of the richest cultural expressions of this struggle. As a result, the novel today is most often studied as a reflection of fundamental philosophical, even metaphysical problems contained within narrative itself.

DANIEL PUNDAY

See also Critics and Criticism (20th Century); Dialogism; Discourse Representation; Feminist Criticism of Narrative; Formalism; Historical Writing and the Novel; Narratology; Narrator; Plot; Point of View; Postmodernism; Structuralism, Semiotics, and the Novel; Time in the Novel

Further Reading

Bakhtin, M.M., *The Dialogic Imagination: Four Essays*, translated by Caryl Emerson and Michael Holquist, edited by Holquist, Austin: University of Texas Press, 1981

Barthes, Roland, "Introduction à l'analyse structurale des récits," *Communications* 8 (1966); as "An Introduction to the Structural Analysis of Narrative," *New Literary History* 6 (1975)

Barthes, Roland, *S/Z*, Paris: Editions du Seuil, 1970, as *S/Z*, London: Cape, and New York: Hill and Wang, 1975

Bhabha, Homi K., editor, *Nation and Narration*, London and New York: Routledge, 1990

Booth, Wayne C., *The Rhetoric of Fiction*, Chicago: University of Chicago Press, 1961; 2nd edition, with afterword "The Rhetoric in Fiction and Fiction as Rhetoric: Twenty-One Years Later," Chicago: University of Chicago Press, and London: Penguin, 1983

Brooks, Peter, *Reading for the Plot: Design and Intention in Narrative*, Oxford: Clarendon Press, and New York: Knopf, 1984

Chatman, Seymour, *Story and Discourse: Narrative Structure in Fiction and Film*, Ithaca, New York: Cornell University Press, 1978

Coste, Didier, *Narrative as Communication*, Minneapolis: University of Minnesota Press, 1989

Haraway, Donna, *Simians, Cyborgs, and Women: The Reinvention of Nature*, New York: Routledge, and London: Free Association, 1991

Iser, Wolfgang, *Der Akt des Lesens: Theorie ästhetischer Wirkung*, Munich: Fink, 1976; as *The Act of Reading: A Theory of Aesthetic Response*, Baltimore: Johns Hopkins University Press, 1978

Lemon, Lee T., and Marion J. Reis, editors, *Russian Formalist Criticism: Four Essays*, Lincoln: University of Nebraska Press, 1965

Martin, Wallace, *Recent Theories of Narrative*, Ithaca, New York: Cornell University Press, 1986

McHale, Brian, and Ruth Ronen, editors, "Narratology Revisited I," special edition of *Poetics Today* 11:1 (1990)

McHale, Brian, and Ruth Ronen, editors, "Narratology Revisited II," special edition of *Poetics Today* 11:4 (1990)

Miller, J. Hillis, "Narrative," in *Critical Terms for Literary Study*, edited by Frank Lentricchia and Thomas McLaughlin, Chicago: University of Chicago Press, 1990; 2nd edition, 1995

Nicholson, Linda J., editor, *Feminism/Postmodernism*, New York: Routledge, 1990

Pavel, Thomas G., *Fictional Worlds*, Cambridge, Massachusetts: Harvard University Press, 1986

Phelan, James, *Reading People, Reading Plots: Character, Progression, and the Interpretation of Narrative*, Chicago: University of Chicago Press, 1989

Rabinowitz, Peter J., *Before Reading: Narrative Conventions and the Politics of Interpretation*, Ithaca, New York: Cornell University Press, 1987

Ricoeur, Paul, *Temps et récit*, Paris: Seuil, 1983–85; as *Time and Narrative*, 3 vols., Chicago: University of Chicago Press, 1984–88

Ryan, Marie-Laure, *Possible Worlds, Artificial Intelligence, and Narrative Theory*, Bloomington: Indiana University Press, 1991

Scholes, Robert, and Robert Kellogg, *The Nature of Narrative*, Oxford and New York: Oxford University Press, 1966

Todorov, Tzvetan, *Quést-ce que le Structuralisme?*, volume 2: *Poétique*, Paris: Seuil, 1968; as *Introduction to Poetics*, Brighton, Sussex: Harvester Press, and Minneapolis: University of Minnesota Press, 1981

White, Hayden, *Tropics of Discourse: Essays in Cultural Criticism*, Baltimore: Johns Hopkins University Press, 1978

Narratology

Narratology is a branch of narrative theory. The term was first used by the structuralist French critic Tzvetan Todorov in his *Grammaire du Décaméron* (1969; The Grammar of *The Decameron*) to refer to a structuralist description of narrative parameters that constitute narrative discourse and are in systematic interaction with each other. Not necessarily structuralist, narratology is centrally concerned with the establishment, rearrangement, and mediation of plot and typically provides a systematic account of functionally related elements such as plot levels, narrative mediation, person, perspective, and temporal arrangement, frequently in the shape of a typology of narrative forms.

Although Todorov was the first to use the term, narratology can in fact be traced back to Käte Friedemann's seminal study *Die Rolle des Erzählers in der Epik* (1910; The Role of the Narrator in Epic). Work by Percy Lubbock and Norman Friedman on narrative perspective as well as the early work of Käte Hamburger and Eberhart Lämmert laid the groundwork for the classic texts that have played a central role in the development of the discipline: F.K. Stanzel's *Die typischen Erzählsituationen im Roman* (1955; *Narrative Situations in the Novel*), Wayne C. Booth's *A Rhetoric of Fiction* (1961), and above all Gérard Genette's *Discours du récit* (in *Figures III*, 1972; *Narrative Discourse*).

Classical Genettean narratology concentrates on the surface structure of narrative and on the mediation of the story within the narrative discourse. Thus, characters are said to function as nouns, their characteristics as adjectives, and their actions as verbs. Genette also uses mood, voice, and tense but applies them to surface features of the narrative. Building on Genette's work, critics have developed a number of different, but roughly compatible, accounts of the basic narrative constituents, narrative levels, and major discourse features of narration. Recent developments have been in the direction of a greater refinement of individual categories. For instance, Mieke Bal's *De theorie van vertellen en verhalen* (1978; *Narratology: An Introduction to the Theory of Narrative*) and Seymour Chatman's *Coming to Terms* (1990) introduce refinements to Genette's theory of focalization, that is, the handling of perspective. Susan Lanser's *The Narrative Act* (1981) proposes a complex web of subcategories, and Shlomith Rimmon-Kenan's *Narrative Fiction* (1983) extends the range of narratorial functions.

The analysis of deep structure elements and minimal constitutive features represents another tributary to narratology. It originated with Vladimir Propp's seminal work *Morfologiia skazki* (1928; *Morphology of the Folktale*), and comprises the narrative poetics of Claude Bremond and Tzvetan Todorov, Roland

Barthes' work on narrative codes in *S/Z* (1970; *S/Z*) and "Introduction to the Structural Analysis of Narrative," as well as the work of Philippe Hamon, Uri Margolin, Gerald Prince, Thomas Pavel, and Marie-Laure Ryan. Unlike classic narratology, which has largely neglected the issue of character even while it lionized the equally anthropomorphic narrator, deep-structural narratology puts a premium on character functions. In its heyday, this branch of narratology produced a number of proposals for grammars of narrative, a project that coincided with linguistic attempts at defining cognitive story schemata. Thus, A.-J. Greimas proposed a narrative grammar that is "to consist in a limited number of principles of structural organization of narrative units, leading to the production of narrative objects." Meanwhile, however, narrative grammar has been discredited in the wake of the paradigm shift in linguistics away from Chomskyan syntax to pragmatics.

Traditionally, narratology has focused on written narrative, especially fiction, and has tended to exclude performance texts and the media. Since the 1970s, however, the concept of narrative has been applied more broadly and narratology has begun to focus on narrative discourse couched in a variety of media, including cartoons, film, drama, and ballet. At the same time, linguistic analysis of conversational story-telling by William Labov and Mary Louise Pratt has provided crucial insights into key features of narrative as an anthropological universal.

In recent years, narratology has developed in directions that supersede narrowly typological formulas, including psychoanalytic studies of narrative, possible world theory, and linguistic narratology. In psychoanalytic studies, as in Peter Brooks' *Reading for the Plot* (1984), plot becomes the focal point for the reader's suspense-driven desire for narrative closure that motivates the reading process. In Ross Chambers' formulation in *Story and Situation* (1984), the story "seduces" the reader by means of its persuasive authority and undermines the narrator's interpretive authority. In possible world theory, developed by Marie-Laure Ryan (1991) and Ruth Ronen (1994), the analysis of the way narratives establish virtual realities replaces the traditional narratological analysis of plot mediation. Linguistic narratology, in Monika Fludernik's *Towards a "Natural" Narratology* (1996), focuses on linguistic surface structure phenomena, such as tense, deictic signals, discourse markers, and the like, in a historical framework, attempting a more precise description of the development of narrative forms through the centuries. Fludernik's work illustrates narratology's increasing interest in the diachronic perspective of literary history, focusing on such issues as the origins of the novel and the development of the historical novel.

The Structure of the Typologies

Classical typologies of narrative have proposed a double- or triple-tiered base structure of narrative levels that provides a frame for other narrative phenomena. In the case of Gérard Genette, this is the division into *histoire* (story), *récit* (discourse), and *narration*. Narration refers to the process or act of narration, the transaction between the narrator and the narratee. The narrative discourse (*récit*) is the actual text produced by the act of narration, and it conveys, or "signifies," the story of the narrative. Genette's categories of tense (*temps*) and mood (*mode*) describe the relationship between the levels of discourse and story as instantiated in the surface structure of the text. Seymour

Chatman's model in *Story and Discourse* (1978), by contrast, extrapolates voice phenomena from the textual level, adhering to a bipartite schema.

F.K. Stanzel's typology is the most complex of all since it superimposes a triad of person, mode, and perspective on the basic binary opposition between the story and its mediation through the narrative instance. The text, although it is the material entity from which story and narration are extrapolated, does not occupy a theoretical position in Stanzel's schema.

In *Towards a "Natural" Narratology*, Fludernik proposes a four-level model of mediation through cognitively anchored modes of consciousness. Fludernik also shifts the central emphasis from the story or plot to the notion of experientiality—a concept that includes story but does not reduce narrative to action sequences.

Definitions of Narrative

There have been three approaches to the definition of narrative: in opposition to drama (F.K. Stanzel); in opposition to other text types (Chatman and Fludernik); and in reference to the presence of one constitutive feature (story in Genette, Bal, Prince; the story/discourse complex in Chatman; experientiality in Fludernik).

On the basis of the opposition between narrative and drama, Stanzel posits mediacy as the constitutive feature of narrative. Since a great number of younger narratologists base their definitions on the presence of a story, to accommodate the media of film, theatre, ballet, and so on, narrative now needs to be contrasted to other text types. Chatman contrasts narrative to argument and description; Jon Adams (1996) to exposition and description; and Fludernik to argument, conversation, metalanguage, and instruction.

The most traditional definition of narrative refers to the story or plot, in particular to a minimal narrative base unit consisting of at least two events in temporal sequence. Such a definition needs to be supplemented by qualitative factors, to account for the aesthetic properties and signification of narrative. Eventfulness in and of itself does not imply a superior quality of narrativity: narrative transforms mere events into plot, adding motivation and causation to the basic event sequence. Narratology must account both for these elements embedded in the plot and for the techniques by which story is transformed into plot.

A more general definition of narrative is based on the commonalities between historical writing and narrative fiction. Hayden White and Paul Ricoeur correlate narrativity with constructedness or emplotting. They define narrative on the basis of its fictionality, counterpointing the equivalences and differences between "real" (i.e., historical) and fictional (i.e., literary) narratives. By contrast, linguistic discourse analysis in the wake of William Labov's work suggests that narratives of personal experience are amenable to a very literary analysis, arguing for a continuity between literary and nonliterary types of narration.

The Narrator

Most traditional narrative theories assume that every narrative has a narrator even if that narrator is not personalized, that is, even if the narrator figure does not display attributes of existence beyond the mere speaker function as indicated by the use of the first-person pronoun, address formulae directed at the narratee, or instances of colloquial speech. Such a conception of the narrator presupposes a communicative model of narration, in which somebody tells a story to the narratee. This communication pattern has been articulated in narrative theory on several levels: communication between the real author and the real reader; between the implied author and the implied reader, especially in unreliable narration; and between the narrator and the narratee in the frame of the narrative text. Inside the narrative, characters also communicate with one another.

Against this communicative model of narrative, some narratologists have pointed out that the narrative is no mere message shunted from the author to the reader and that texts with a merely covert narrator function cannot be interpreted as the equivalence of an utterance or speech act in conversation. The most radical stand in this line of argument was taken by Ann Banfield in her book *Unspeakable Sentences* (1982). In Banfield's model, narrative and communication are mutually exclusive categories, her title alluding to the thesis that third-person narrative clauses are "unspeakable."

The narrator may either be a part of the narrative world as a character or stand outside the story world. In the first case, the narrative is homodiegetic in Genette's term or homocommunicative in Fludernik's. In the second case, the narrative is classified as heterodiegetic or heterocommunicative. Concerning the issue of narrative levels, Genette distinguishes between the diegetic level of the story, the extradiegetic level of the narration about the story world, and the intradiegetic (or metadiegetic) level of the story within the story. The classic omniscient narrator is an extradiegetic heterodiegetic narrator in Genette's model.

Focalization

One of the most extensively debated aspects of narrative is that of focalization or point of view. Although these metaphors are visual, referring to "who sees" in a narrative, the term has been extended to cover perspective in general, including spatial, ideological, linguistic, and epistemological points of view. Chatman questions the adequacy of this visual conception since the narrator, from his position outside the narrative world, cannot see but merely describe through the "filter" of a character's psyche or through external focalization on the character—a factor Chatman links to knowledge or access to characters' consciousness rather than point of view. Fludernik, on the other hand, sees little heuristic value in the concept of focalization and conceives of various points of view as mental schemata that are elicited by the linguistic make-up of the text, particularly by the narrative's deictic structure.

Focalization, even though it continues to be controversial, is important to narrative because it attempts to account for access to characters' interiority and the prevailing perspectivity of the novel of consciousness, in which the narrative is filtered through the eyes and mind of a protagonist. Whereas the first issue is one of the management of knowledge or information, the other relates to narrative presentation from the inside rather than from the outside. Internal perspective restricts the field of vision, limiting access to information. Focalization is also crucial to first-person (homodiegetic) narrative since the narrator, as a character, has similarly limited access to information. Another manipulation of point of view that has played an important role in literary narrative is the first-person narrator who filters the narrative through the eyes of his or her former self as opposed to his or her present, more knowledgeable perspective on the past. In homodiegetic narrative, the distinction between access to

knowledge and filtering collapses. More radically still, the now very popular genre of the first-person present-tense narrative problematizes the narrator's mastery over his or her experience, challenging traditional formulations of the point-of-view question. The same is true of much second-person narrative.

Narrative Situation

Much of the discussion about focalization fails to distinguish between small-scale and large-scale contexts. In most narratives, focalization changes frequently, with the presentation moving from a brief description of a character's intimate thoughts to an external summary of the goings-on, perhaps alternated with snatches of the character's perception of the scenery (in internal focalization). Although such alternation on the sentence-by-sentence level of narratives is admitted to exist by most narratologists, models of focalization (with the exception of Bal) stress overall macrotextual perspectives of entire narratives. Stanzel calls these larger perspectives narrative situations, which he defines as complexes of prototypical alignments between the categories of person, perspective, and mode. Stanzel's three narrative situations operate as abstract prototypes, which, Fludernik argues, are open to modifications as the narrative progresses.

Whereas the Genettean typology proposes a combinatory of all categories (homo/heterodiegetic; extra/intradiegetic; internal/external/zero focalization), Stanzel's narrative situations maintain the regular co-occurrence of certain features associated with historically observable generic types. This is most obviously the case for Stanzel's authorial narrative situation, in which external perspective, teller mode, and heterodiegesis combine into one prototypical schema. Henry Fielding's *Tom Jones* (1749) is the prototypical authorial narrative, displaying—in Genettean terminology—an extradiegetic-heterodiegetic narrator persona and employing zero focalization, or narratorial omniscience in the sense of access to the characters' thoughts and full access to the fictional world. Stanzel's second narrative situation, the figural narrative situation (in German, "personale Erzählsituation"), is the recurrent prototype of an internally focalized narrative, or, as Stanzel calls it, a narrative in the reflector mode. Figural texts can employ third, second, and first person narrative diegesis. Stanzel's third narrative situation, first-person narrative, refers to the prototypical scenario of quasi-autobiography in which a homodiegetic, autodiegetic narrator evaluates and comments on his or her life story. This schema, again, is a historically recognizable type of narrative that combines a prominent teller figure with an alternation between external and internal perspective involving the distancing of the now wiser, morally superior, and sedate first-person narrator, the narrating self, from his or her earlier naive, wicked, or adventurous incarnation, the experiencing self.

Stanzel arranges these three narrative situations on a typological circle that allows for intermediary forms, such as peripheral first-person narrative in which the "I" functions as a witness to another's story. Thomas Mann's *Doktor Faustus* (1947; *Doctor Faustus*), for example, is situated in the transitional area between first-person and authorial narrative. Novels like Thomas Hardy's *Tess of the D'Urbervilles* (1891), on the other hand, belong to the recurring intermediary form of the authorial-figural continuum, in which the narrative continually shifts between the authorial and figural mode.

Character and Setting

Traditional narratology subsumes characters and setting under the title of plot: characters are the necessary agents (or actants) effecting the succession of events. Likewise, since events need to be located in space and time, the where and when of narrative have always been implicit in the standard definitions of plot. For this reason, the analysis of description in narrative and the investigation of character have attracted little interest in classical narratology. Description used to be treated as a pause in the much more important sequence of events constituting plot, while characters seemed to function as propellors of the plot. Narratology therefore counterintuitively backgrounded what in the traditional analysis of novels was quite crucial: the delineation of character and the realistic evocation of a fictional setting.

In conversational narrative, as we know from Labov's work, the establishment of the setting in the orientation section of the story is an important constituent of the narrative structure, as is character in narratives of personal experience. At the same time, experimental writing has undermined traditional plotting in various ways, so that the plot definition of narrative is no longer adequate in capturing the properties of narrative art. When plot is displaced as the central defining feature of narrative, then the setting and temporal anchoring of narrative and the constitution of character move back into focus. Under this aspect, the presentation of a (pseudo-) human subject within a specific environment becomes very important, particularly when narrative is contrasted with poetic discourse. "All roses are fragrant" does not evoke a narrative scenario, but "The rose was red and emitted an alluring fragrance" does. The second sentence contains a primitive narrative scenario with a specific rose and a specific time, and somebody is registering the rose's color and smell. It is possible, for example, that the person who perceives the rose will materialize to pluck the rose and thereby effect the change of state formerly taken to be a base requirement of narrative discourse.

Temporal Structure and Chronology

Narratology has devoted much attention to time, in such large-scale analyses as Paul Ricoeur's magisterial *Temps et récit* (1983–85; *Time and Narrative*) and in Genette's seminal study, with its exhaustive account of possible temporal relations between the story and the discourse and between narrated time and narrating time, a distinction first proposed by Günther Müller in 1968.

Ricoeur concentrates on the philosophical issues of temporality, such as the elusive quality of the present, and presents a very thorough comparison between fictional and historical narratives. The temporality of narrative, according to Ricoeur, can be located in the dynamic tension between chronological sequence, plot progression, and the teleological factor that reconfigures the story in relation to its closure. More recently, Philip Sturgess and Jon Adams have insisted on plot dynamics. Like Ricoeur's, their work explicitly considers the reader's active cognitive involvement in the establishment of plot, and they critique merely chronological definitions of story.

Gérard Genette, on the other hand, like Seymour Chatman, bases his analysis of temporal relations in narrative on a fundamental dichotomy between the story, the chronological sequence of events underlying the discourse, and the textualization of that story in the discourse. Whereas narrated time is uniform, narrat-

ing time can speed up (one chapter summarizing the events of several years in the hero's life, for instance), slow down (an entire novel being devoted to several moments of consciousness, as in William Golding's *Pincher Martin* [1956], in which the protagonist's entire imaginative life passes before his mind's eye in the brief moments before his death by drowning), or it can come to a standstill or pause (allegedly so in descriptions where no "action" occurs). Ellipsis refers to the complete elision of an event from the narration: in Agatha Christie's *The Murder of Roger Ackroyd* (1926), for instance, the first-person narrator strategically "fails" to tell us that he committed the murder. Gerald Prince's concept of the disnarrated (1988), on the other hand, serves to designate events that never happened but are related in the narrative discourse. Narrating time, which is measured in terms of the time it takes to read the text or in terms of the number of printed pages, is therefore set in relation to a supposedly pre-given sequence of events, the story. In actual fact, as Genette is certainly aware, the story is a construct that the reader pieces together on the basis of the "deviations" in the discourse.

Besides the noted changes in tempo, Genette also subdivides the narrative restructurations on the temporal plane into changes in frequency (e.g., telling one event twice, or several events only once) and in chronological reshufflings.

Order is of course the category that has been most carefully analyzed in criticism since rearrangements of chronological order are so very prominent in the modernist novel. Genette's terminology for different types of anachrony comprises flashbacks (analepsis), anticipatory passages (prolepsis), and indeterminate items whose position on the temporal scale cannot be specified in relation to other events (achrony). Genette's most original contribution lies in the study of chronological frequency: some events may be told again and again in one novel (like the episode of the killing of the centipede in Alain Robbe-Grillet's *La Jalousie* [1957; *Jealousy*]). In other texts, as in Marcel Proust's *À la recherche du temps perdu* (1913–27; translated as *Remembrance of Things Past* and also as *In Search of Lost Time*), one scene of a dinner at the Guermantes may serve as a consideration of many such dinners, a technique that Genette labels iterative.

These distinctions and subcategories under the headings of order, duration, and frequency presuppose that a story, a chronology, can indeed be made out from the text. In experimental fiction this option often disappears, and in a text like Robert Coover's "The Babysitter" (1969) temporal reshufflings or iterative renderings of events prevent the construction of a consistent storyline. Achrony, in Genette's terminology, prevails.

Mimesis/Diegesis

The distinction between mimesis and diegesis was originally a distinction between types of speech representation (indirect versus direct speech). The dichotomy has now come to signify the opposition between the narrative and dramatic genres, or—in Stanzel's typology—between openly mediated and apparently unmediated parts of narrative discourse. As a consequence, dialogue in the narrative text is traditionally taken to be pure mimesis, but some types of action report have also been seen as mimetic.

In a more general sense, narrative as a whole is frequently taken to be mimetic in the sense of representing a (fictional) reality. This kind of representationality comes close to the evocation of an illusion of reality since literary texts are, after all, linguistic constructs. The nonrepresentational nature of narrative has been foregrounded in recent literature on experimental fiction. The anti-novel and several forms of anti-illusionistic fiction have deliberately inverted and subverted traditional narrative technique. In the wake of such narrative experiments, the consistency of plot dissolves to create hierarchically indeterminate levels of the story (heterarchy)—the functional analogues of Möbius strips, Chinese boxes, or metaleptic constructions (transgressions of narrative level as when characters appear in search of their author). Plot is also reduced to nearly complete uneventfulness or proliferates to staggering proportions. Characters, setting, voice or focalization, and temporal structure have undergone similar experimentation. Experimental texts further undermine mimetic presuppositions by utilizing pronominal or temporal choices that are odd or deviant, such as "we" narrative and future-tense narration, or they rearrange the narrative text in typographic shapes that are reminiscent of concrete poetry, as Raymond Federman does in his novel *Double or Nothing* (1971). Moreover, experimental texts undermine mimesis by means of self-reflexive textual strategies and metafictional techniques, foregrounding the constructedness of the narrative text.

On a very pragmatic level, narratology provides a toolkit for historical analysis, for the precise description of individual texts, and for the examination of generic modes. It also suggests to us how narrative levels overlap and interact, complicating all-too-simplistic definitions of genres or narrative modes.

Much research still remains to be done in the realm of the history of the novel, since traditional narratology has tended to neglect diachronic issues. Thus, we do not have any studies that attempt to trace the origins of unreliable narration or analyze the properties of verse narrative, and we also lack a comprehensive history of focalization before the 18th century, to name just three lacunae in the field. Narratology need not be as formalistic as its reputation would suggest, and in recent years it has accommodated more thematic concerns, including the ideology of the narrator function, the significance of gender in narrative, and the repurposing of narrative technique in marginalized ethnic and postcolonial texts. However, some of these thematic questions are posed in narrative theories that do not see themselves as narratological.

MONIKA FLUDERNIK

See also Character; Description; Diegesis and Diegetic Levels of Narration; Discourse Representation; Framing and Embedding; Historical Writing and the Novel; Implied Author; Mimesis; Narrative Theory; Narrator; Person in Narrative; Plot; Point of View; Space; Structuralism, Semiotics, and the Novel; Tense in Narrative; Time in the Novel; Unreliable Narrator

Further Reading

Adams, Jon K., *Narrative Explanation: A Pragmatic Theory of Discourse,* Frankfurt: Lang, 1996
Bal, Mieke, *De theorie van vertellen en verhalen,* Mulderberg: Coutinho, 1978; as *Narratology: An Introduction to the Theory of Narrative,* Toronto and Buffalo, New York: University of Toronto Press, 1985
Banfield, Ann, *Unspeakable Sentences: Narration and Representation in the Language of Fiction,* Boston: Routledge and Kegan Paul, 1982
Barthes, Roland, "Introduction à l'analyse structurale des récits," *Communications* 8 (1966); as "An Introduction to the Structural Analysis of Narrative," *New Literary History* 6 (1975)
Barthes, Roland, *S/Z,* Paris: Seuil, 1970; as *S/Z,* London: Cape, and New York: Hill and Wang, 1975
Booth, Wayne C., *The Rhetoric of Fiction,* Chicago: University of Chicago Press, 1961; 2nd edition, Chicago: University of Chicago Press, and London: Penguin, 1983
Branigan, Edward, *Narrative Comprehension and Film,* London and New York: Routledge, 1992
Bremond, Claude, *Logique du récit,* Paris: Seuil, 1973
Brooks, Peter, *Reading for the Plot: Design and Intention in Narrative,* Oxford: Clarendon Press, and New York: Knopf, 1984
Carrard, Philippe, *Poetics of the New History: French Historical Discourse from Braudel to Chartier,* Baltimore: Johns Hopkins University Press, 1992
Chambers, Ross, *Story and Situation: Narrative Seduction and the Power of Fiction,* Minneapolis: University of Minnesota Press, and Manchester: Manchester University Press, 1984
Chatman, Seymour, *Story and Discourse: Narrative Structure in Fiction and Film,* Ithaca, New York: Cornell University Press, 1978
Chatman, Seymour, *Coming to Terms: The Rhetoric of Narrative in Fiction and Film,* Ithaca, New York: Cornell University Press, 1990
Cohan, Steven, and Linda M. Shires, *Telling Stories: A Theoretical Analysis of Narrative Fiction,* New York: Routledge, 1988
Cohn, Dorrit, "Fictional versus Historical Lives: Borderlines and Borderline Cases," *The Journal of Narrative Technique* 19:1 (1989)
Dijk, Teun A. van, and Walter Kintsch, *Strategies of Discourse Comprehension,* New York: Academic Press, 1983
Fludernik, Monika, *The Fictions of Language and the Languages of Fiction: The Linguistic Representation of Speech and Consciousness,* London and New York: Routledge, 1993
Fludernik, Monika, "Second-Person Narrative as a Test Case for Narratology: The Limits of Realism," *Style* 28:3 (1994)
Fludernik, Monika, *Towards a "Natural" Narratology,* London and New York: Routledge, 1996
Friedemann, Käte, *Die Rolle des Erzählers in der Epik,* Leipzig: Haessel, 1910; reprinted, Darmstadt: Wissenschaftliche Buchgesellschaft, 1965
Friedman, Norman, "Point of View in Fiction: The Development of a Critical Concept," *PMLA* 70 (1955)
Genette, Gérard, *Discours du récit,* in *Figures III,* Paris: Seuil, 1972; as *Narrative Discourse,* Ithaca, New York: Cornell University Press, 1980
Genot, Gérard, *Elements of Narrativics: Grammar in Narrative, Narrative in Grammar,* Hamburg: Buske, 1979
Greimas, A.-J., "Narrative Grammar: Units and Levels," *Modern Language Notes* 86 (1971)
Greimas, A.-J., *Sémantique structurale: Recherche de méthode,* Paris: Larousse, 1966; as *Structural Semantics: An Attempt at a Method,* Lincoln: University of Nebraska Press, 1983
Hamburger, Käte, *Die Logik der Dichtung,* Stuttgart: Klett,

1957; as *The Logic of Literature,* Bloomington: Indiana University Press, 1973; 2nd revised edition, 1993

Hamon, Philippe, "Pour un statut sémiologique du personnage," *Littérature* 6 (May 1972)

Jahn, Manfred, "Windows of Focalization: Deconstructing and Reconstructing a Narratological Concept," *Style* 30:2 (1996)

Labov, William, *Language in the Inner City: Studies in the Black English Vernacular,* Philadelphia: University of Pennsylvania Press, 1972; Oxford: Blackwell, 1977

Lämmert, Eberhard, *Bauformen des Erzählens,* Stuttgart: Metzler, 1955

Lanser, Susan Sniader, *The Narrative Act: Point of View in Prose Fiction,* Princeton, New Jersey: Princeton University Press, 1981

Lanser, Susan Sniader, *Fictions of Authority: Women Writers and Narrative Voice,* Ithaca, New York: Cornell University Press, 1992

Lubbock, Percy, *The Craft of Fiction,* London: Cape, and New York: Scribner, 1921

Müller, Günther, *Morphologische Poetik: Gesammelte Aufsätze,* Tübingen: Niemeyer, 1968

Nünning, Ansgar, *Von historischer Fiktion zu historiographischer Metafiktion: Theorie, Typologie, und Poetik des historischen Romans,* 2 vols., Trier: Wissenschaftlicher, 1995

Pavel, Thomas G., *La syntaxe narrative des tragédies de Corneille,* Paris: Klincksieck, 1976

Pavel, Thomas G., *The Poetics of Plot: The Case of English Renaissance Drama,* Minneapolis: University of Minnesota Press, and Manchester: Manchester University Press, 1985

Pratt, Mary Louise, *Toward a Speech Act Theory of Literary Discourse,* Bloomington: Indiana University Press, 1977

Prince, Gerald, *A Grammar of Stories: An Introduction,* The Hague: Mouton, 1973

Prince, Gerald, *Narratology: The Form and Functioning of Narrative,* Berlin and New York: Mouton, 1982

Prince, Gerald, "The Narratee Revisited," *Style* 19:3 (1985)

Prince, Gerald, *A Dictionary of Narratology,* Lincoln: University of Nebraska Press, 1987; Aldershot: Scolar, 1988

Prince, Gerald, "The Disnarrated," *Style* 22:1 (1988)

Prince, Gerald, *Narrative As Theme: Studies in French Fiction,* Lincoln: University of Nebraska Press, 1992

Propp, Vladimir, *Morfologiia skazki,* Leningrad: Academia, 1928; as *Morphology of the Folktale,* Bloomington: Research Center, Indiana University, 1958; 2nd edition, Austin: University of Texas Press, 1968

Quasthoff, Uta M., *Erzählen in Gesprächen: Linguistische Untersuchungen zu Strukturen und Funktionen am Beispiel einer Kommunikationsform des Alltags,* Tübingen: Narr, 1980

Ricoeur, Paul, *Temps et récit,* Paris: Editions du Seuil, 1983–85; as *Time and Narrative,* 3 vols., Chicago: University of Chicago Press, 1984–88

Rigney, Ann, *The Rhetoric of Historical Representation: Three Narrative Histories of the French Revolution,* Cambridge and New York: Cambridge University Press, 1990

Rimmon-Kenan, Shlomith, *Narrative Fiction: Contemporary Poetics,* London and New York: Methuen, 1983

Ronen, Ruth, *Possible Worlds in Literary Theory,* Cambridge and New York: Cambridge University Press, 1994

Ryan, Marie-Laure, "On the Window Structure of Narrative Discourse," *Semiotica* 64:1–2 (1987)

Ryan, Marie-Laure, *Possible Worlds, Artificial Intelligence, and Narrative Theory,* Bloomington: Indiana University Press, 1991

Stanzel, Franz Karl, *Die typischen Erzählsituationen im Roman,* Vienna: Braumüller, 1955; as *Narrative Situations in the Novel,* Bloomington: Indiana University Press, 1971

Stanzel, Franz Karl, *Theorie des Erzählens,* Göttingen: Vandenhoeck and Ruprecht, 1979; as *A Theory of Narrative,* Cambridge and New York: Cambridge University Press, 1984

Sturgess, Philip J.M., *Narrativity: Theory and Practice,* Oxford: Clarendon Press, and New York: Oxford University Press, 1992

Tannen, Deborah, *Talking Voices: Repetition, Dialogue, and Imagery in Conversational Discourse,* Cambridge and New York: Cambridge University Press, 1989

Todorov, Tzvetan, *Grammaire du Décaméron,* The Hague: Mouton, 1969

Uspenskii, Boris A., *Poetika Kompozitsii: Struktura Khudozh. teksta i tipologiia Kompozits. formy,* Moscow: Isskustvo, 1970; as *A Poetics of Composition: The Structure of the Artistic Text and Typology of a Compositional Form,* Berkeley: University of California Press, 1973

White, Hayden, "The Value of Narrativity in the Representation of Reality," in *On Narrative,* edited by W.J.T. Mitchell, Chicago: University of Chicago Press, 1981

Wolf, Werner, *Ästhetische Illusion und Illusionsdurchbrechung in der Erzählkunst: Theorie und Geschichte mit Schwerpunkt auf englischem illusionsstörenden Erzählen,* Tübingen: Niemeyer, 1993

The Narrator

Fictional narratives have two dimensions: 1) the *story,* that is, the chain of actions and events performed or experienced by characters in a setting, and 2) the *discourse,* the means by which the story is told or otherwise transmitted. In rough terms, the story is the "what," and the discourse is the "how." Although story (sometimes called the "narrated") and discourse (the "narrating" or "narration") are useful terms devised by narratologists to explain the structure of the novel, each novel, of course, actually comes to a reader as a string of words. That string—the published text—is an actualization or instance of the narrative structure. The reader reads the words and interprets them as events, characters, settings, and the like.

The main agent of the discourse is the *narrator*. Some narratologists believe that every narrative has a narrator; others believe that narratives are "non-narrated" if the reader cannot discern an audible voice. In the simplest kind of narrative, the oral personal anecdote, the narrator is the speaker; he or she tells what happened, usually after the fact, to another person, the listener. On the analogy of "narrator," this audience has been named (by Gerald Prince) the *narratee.*

A narrative is one of several types of text—others are descriptions, arguments, expositions, lists, and so on. Unlike the other text types, narrative necessarily communicates a chain of events or happenings. Recall the main events of Charles Dickens' *Great Expectations* (1861). Upon the invitation of an anonymous benefactor, Pip, a poor country boy, leaves his humble home for London to become a gentleman. He believes that his benefactor is the lady of the manor, Miss Havisham, but later learns that it was really Magwitch, a convict whom he had helped escape and who has made a fortune abroad. When Magwitch returns to England, sacrificing everything for a chance to see "his boy," Pip learns the truth and is ashamed of the snobbishness he has developed toward the poorer classes, including Magwitch and his brother-in-law, Joe. Pip goes to the Orient to seek his fortune, returns to his village, makes amends, and finally goes off to a glorious future with Estella, Miss Havisham's ward.

Time-sequence is essential to the text type we call narrative: every story rests on a chronology of events. That chronology may be called *story-time*. But there is another kind of narrative time, namely the time (whether stated by the narrator or reconstructed by the reader) that it takes the narrator to tell the story; this kind of time may be called *discourse-time*. In story-time, events can only occur in one sequence, following the natural order of life. Jack has to climb the hill before he can fall down it; he has to fall down before his crown is broken. In the nursery rhyme "Jack and Jill," the discourse-time follows the same order as the story-time. But the discourse-time could have been arranged in a different way: "Jack lay on the ground moaning. He had just broken his crown after falling down the hill." Here the last event is told first, and the earlier events are told later. This discourse arrangement is usually called *flashback* (or *analepsis*). It appears as early as Homer's *Iliad.*

Narrative, then, unlike the other text types, has a double time arrangement. Compare the double time-scheme of narrative with the single time of a different kind of text, argument. An argument turns not on events but on propositions and proofs. Of course, a story may be used by an arguer to support the argument. In that case, however, the story is not told for its own sake, but as evidence. A defendant's attorney may tell a story of how his client was bowling when the murder occurred, so a chronology is invoked. Yet the larger structure of the lawyer's argument does not depend on time-sequence, but on the support furnished by the reasons to the assertion in question (in this case, "He is not guilty"). Of course, the argument is a text that unfolds in time, the time it takes to read or hear it. But that is external text-time: it is not intrinsic to the structure of the argument.

The story the defense attorney tells about his client's bowling at the time of the murder is an instance of a narrative subserving an argument. The reverse also happens: in Henry Fielding's *Tom Jones* (1749), the narrator often interrupts the story by advancing a moral argument. The text type of description even more typically subserves narratives, for instance, in setting the scene. (Narratives may subserve descriptions, also, as when a travel book recounts the history of a castle as part of its description of the building.)

Just as we distinguish between story-time and discourse-time, we may distinguish between *story-space* and *discourse-space*. Story-space is the setting, the place(s) where the story events occur. Story-space in *Great Expectations* includes Joe's forge, where Pip lives as a boy, Miss Havisham's manor, and London. Discourse-space, on the other hand, is the place occupied by the narrator when he tells the story. In *Great Expectations*, the discourse-space occupied by the narrator is indeterminate; but in some novels it is clearly located. In Joseph Conrad's "Heart of Darkness" (1902) the discourse-space is the yacht *Nelly,* lying becalmed in the London estuary, whereas the space of Marlow's story extends from Belgium to Africa, up the Congo River. The discourse-space of Emily Brontë's *Wuthering Heights* (1847) is Thrushcross Grange, the house Lockwood has rented from Heathcliff; it is there that Lockwood, the initial narrator, becomes narratee to Mrs. Dean's story of Heathcliff's tempestuous love for Catherine. The story-space of Mrs. Dean's tale, of course, is the estate of Wuthering Heights.

In the personal oral anecdote, the narrator is also the author. If I tell you about something that happened to me yesterday, I am both the author of the story and its narrator or transmitter. If I tell you a joke that I heard, I am only the narrator; the person who originally made the joke up is the author. The situation in novels and short stories is still more complex. When an author decides to write a novel, she chooses not only the story elements—events, characters, and settings—but also the discourse elements, including the best kind of narrator. Mark Twain decided to have Huckleberry Finn narrate the novel *The Adventures of Huckleberry Finn* (1884) because he wanted a naive spokesman, the better to ironize life on the Mississippi River. Jane Austen decided on an anonymous narrator to narrate *Pride and Prejudice* (1813), the better to convey the conflict between Elizabeth's prejudice and Darcy's pride. It is important not to confuse the real author with the narrator, even if the narrator refers to herself as "your author" or the like. The author is or was a real historical person; the narrator, on the other hand, is a personage in the novel, no less fictional than any character, who comes to life each time the novel is read.

Some narrators are also characters in the story; some only tell the story and do not participate in it. The first kind may be called *character-narrators*; the second *external narrators*. Pip, in addition to being the narrator of *Great Expectations*, is also its hero or protagonist. The character-narrator can tell what happened in the story even up to the present moment, the "now" of the discourse. He was a character "back then," during story-time, and is now a narrator in present discourse-time. A more technical term for the character-narrator is *homodiegetic narrator*. ("Diegetic" refers to story-telling, and "homo-" means "the same.") Thus, the narrator-Pip is the same person as the protagonist-Pip. However, it is important to recognize that "Pip" refers to two different narrative agents, even though Pip is a single person. Sometimes the character-narrator is not the protagonist but a lesser character who tells what happened to the protagonist. For example, in F. Scott Fitzgerald's novel *The Great Gatsby*

(1925), Gatsby is the protagonist, but the narrator is his neighbor, Nick Carraway. The narrator of Fedor Dostoevskii's *The Devils* (1872) is an even more minor character, an unnamed and undistinguished inhabitant of a provincial Russian town. A character-narrator who is only an observer is called a *witness narrator.*

Character-narrators often are referred to as "first-person-" or "I-narrators," but those terms can be misleading since an external narrator, one who does not inhabit the story-world but only the discourse-world, could just as well refer to herself as "I." A more technical term for the external narrator is *heterodiegetic narrator.* Classic examples are the narrators of Henry James' *The Ambassadors* (1903) and his short story "The Beast in the Jungle" (1903). The narrator of the former, for example, says on the first page "The principle I have just mentioned . . ." and the latter alludes to himself in sentences beginning "Our point is . . ." or "What we are especially concerned with . . .". But neither narrator is a character in the story. In a few cases the first-person plural "we" is used to refer to the external narrator, either in the royal sense (the monarch is so grand a figure as to encompass a plurality, not an individuality, speaking as she does for the entire kingdom) or, contrarily, as a mark of modesty, to avoid the suggestion of egotism. But some narrators *are* plural in the ordinary sense: in William Faulkner's short story "A Rose for Emily" (1931), the "we" represents a village community who witness the bizarre aftermath of Miss Emily's jilting by her fiancé. The collective "we"-narrator is rare, even in modern fiction, and often ambiguous. It can refer to such different entities as an actual community of speakers speaking as one (like the chorus in a Greek tragedy), to one speaker presuming to speak for others (who may or may not be willing to let her be spokesperson), to a speaker who includes the addressee in the group (that is, makes the narratee, by definition a "you," into a member of his party), and so on.

The expression "third-person narrator" is even more confusing than "first-person narrator," since the third person in question is generally not a speaker or an addressee but some other person. Grammatically, the first person is the one who speaks, the second person is the one spoken to, and the third person the one spoken about. That means that the latter is by definition a non-participant in the immediate communication of the discourse, although her consciousness may "filter" the story-world. To call the narrator a third person is to confuse story and discourse. (An exception is the narrative in which, for some extranarratorial reason, the first-person speaker refers to himself by his own name, as does Julius Caesar in *The Gallic Wars*.) However, one may reasonably speak of third-person narratives, remembering that the focus is now on the character, not on the narrator.

Is there such a thing as a second-person or "you"-narrator? Again we can speak of "second-person narratives," but in this unusual form the "you" again seems always to refer to a character (or to the character aspect of a character-narrator). In second-person narration, the narrator may be referring to him-/herself in past (or future) time, but also may be the narratee, or a third person who, for some reason, is spoken to as well as about. Some examples are Rex Stout's *How Like a God* (1929), Michel Butor's *La Modification* (1957; *Change of Heart*), a short story by Mary McCarthy called "The Genial Host," in *The Company She Keeps* (1942); Jay McInerney's *Bright Lights, Big City* (1984), and Lorrie Moore's *Self-Help*

(1985). How are we to understand this rather unnatural way of telling a story? In some cases we seem to be dealing with an external narrator telling the events to some "you" who actually has experienced them but is either unwilling or unable to articulate the story (as a psychiatrist might tell an amnesiac patient his own story to help him recover his memory, or a prosecuting attorney might tell the accused his version of a crime in the hopes that the accused will break down and admit that it is true). In other cases, the narrator may be speaking to himself about himself, as if from the outside. Or the passage may be in interior monologue, the narrator simply recording what the character who refers to himself as "you" is thinking. In some cases, as in parables, the "you" may be generic, indicating that what is happening to the character may easily happen to anyone. Or "you" may simply be a vivifying form of "I" (as in some detective novels). Whatever the case, the "you" form seems intended to make the reader identify closely with the addressed character.

Despite the fact that they inhabit only the discourse, some external narrators emerge as full-blown personages in their own right, expressing opinions, attitudes, and prejudices, even describing their own personality, appearance, and so on. Others are simply voices, giving us few clues, either explicit or implicit, about themselves. The former are sometimes called *overt*, the latter *covert.*

Narratees are even more likely to be blanks, simply ears, listeners living in the discourse-world, or "dear readers," who make no response to the narrator's tale. But sometimes they are fleshed out, as when the text is "nested" and the discourse becomes itself a little narrative. The outer or containing narrative may be called the *frame*, and the inner, contained narrative the *framed.* For instance, in Conrad's "Heart of Darkness," the framing narrative recounts a conversation among four men on a yacht. An unnamed member of the party narrates the story of the men's conversation; mentioning no narratee, he is presumably telling the story of the conversation to "us readers." At a certain point, another member of the party, Marlow, embarks on the framed story, about his trip to Africa and meeting with Kurtz. Marlow is the narrator of the inner, framed story, and his narratees are the other three men, including the anonymous narrator of the outer, framing story. (A similar structure informs *Wuthering Heights*.)

We can also distinguish among narrators according to the kind and amount of information they provide. At one end of the scale is the narrator who has the power to tell the narratee explicitly, and at any moment he likes, everything one needs to know to understand the story. Traditionally, such a narrator has been called the omniscient narrator, but we might do better to call her the *unlimited* narrator. "Omniscient"—"all-knowing" (from Latin "omni-" "all" and "sciens" "knowing")—is not felicitous because the narrator's function is not to know something, but simply to tell the story. To do that she must already know the story. It makes even less sense to say that the author is omniscient, since in a fiction the author is the one who has invented everything. Ordinarily, the only one for whom knowing is an issue is the reader, who learns everything in the course of reading the novel.

There are, however, some exceptions, that is, narrators who do not know the whole story from the outset. For example, a correspondent in an epistolary novel, like Samuel Richardson's *Pamela* (1740), or the diarist of a diary novel, like Jean-Paul

Sartre's *La Nausée* (1938; *Nausea*), do not know in mid-novel how things will ultimately turn out for them. It could be argued, however, that these are not the main narrators of their novels, that the narrator, rather, is the one who compiled and/or edited the letters or diary. Such a narrator is like the passive narrator of a story told completely through the quoted dialogue of one or more of the characters (for example, Dorothy Parker's short story "Lady with a Lamp").

Another narrator who may not know the whole story, or who knows it only inaccurately, is called an *unreliable narrator*. An unreliably narrated story is one whose "true version," we infer, differs strikingly from what the narrator actually tells us. We piece together the "real" story because we find reasons in the narrator's character, age, intelligence, the way he expresses himself, or whatever, for doubting that he understands the import of the events, or that he is being truthful about them. In the former case, when the narrator does not undersand, we may speak of *naive* unreliability, which we find in *Huckleberry Finn* and Ford Madox Ford's *The Good Soldier* (1915), for instance. When the narrator is all too knowing, we may speak of *lying* unreliability (as, for instance, in Jason Compson's section of William Faulkner's *The Sound and the Fury* [1929]).

The *unlimited* narrator can, at any moment of his choosing, provide a great deal of information directly to the narratee; he can summarize events and situations, interpret, judge, and comment upon what characters do, think, and feel (or what they don't do, think, or feel), introduce metaphoric language, philosophize about the real world (as opposed to the fictional world of the story), make comments about the narrating process itself, and so on. The narrator of *Tom Jones* offers copious explanations of his narrative procedures, explaining, for example, why he has withheld the information that Mr. Square as well as Tom Jones was Molly's lover (he saw no reason for doing so, since Mr. Square hadn't announced it either). Such a narrator is sometimes called *self-conscious*. The (implied) author puts no limits on what the unlimited narrator can say.

On the other hand, the narrator may be *limited*. Usually the limitation takes the form of restricting what can be told at any given story-moment to what one character experiences. A classic example is Henry James' *What Maisie Knew* (1897): the adult external narrator narrates the erotic carryings-on of a small girl's estranged parents, but only insofar as she perceives and understands—or fails to understand—them. Another example is Gustave Flaubert's *Madame Bovary* (1857), most of which is screened through Emma Bovary's flawed consciousness. As for character-narrators, like Marlow in "Heart of Darkness," most are limited, but some may enter the minds of other characters without explaining how they could do so (the minor character-narrator of *The Devils* recounts the secret thoughts of the protagonist, which neither he nor anyone else possibly could have known).

The limited narrator tends not to give overt clues about his own personality, but we can often catch hints of it. The stories in James Joyce's *Dubliners* (1914), often cited as classic examples of limited narration, imply some attitudes of the narrator. For example, in "A Painful Case," a sentence summarizing the protagonist's general attitude toward life—"Mr Duffy abhorred anything which betokened physical or mental disorder"—is followed by "A mediaeval doctor would have called him saturnine. His face, which carried the entire tale of his years, was of the

brown tint of Dublin streets." Here the narrator stands back from the character's consciousness and gives an independent view of the character's appearance, as well as hints of his own attitude toward Dublin and its inhabitants (not to speak of his knowledge of medical history).

There are extreme cases of limitation in which the narrator has the power to present only the contents of a character's mind. This is the effect called *interior monologue* or *stream of consciousness*. The most celebrated example is the last section of Joyce's *Ulysses* (1922), which presents nothing but the rambling thoughts of the heroine, Molly Bloom. It is important to understand that the character whose flow of thoughts is recorded is not the narrator. She is not telling anybody a story but simply living her life in the story. The narrator here is a kind of mind-reading recorder faithfully reproducing her every thought. He is even more restricted than the narrators of *Dubliners*.

Finally, there is a kind of narrator who may not enter *any* character's mind. This sort of objective narrator functions somewhat like a camera—hence such colorful synonyms as *camera-eye* or *fly-on-the-wall narrator*. Objective narratives are sometimes said to be "shown" rather than "told," but the terminology is only metaphoric: you can literally "show" a story only in a visual medium like a movie or comic strip. The objective narrator, common in hard-boiled detective novels that insist on hard evidence, usually recounts only what could be seen by someone standing in the vicinity of the events narrated. A classic example is Ernest Hemingway's "The Killers." The objective narrator "follows" the protagonist, Nick Adams, but tells us practically nothing of what he is thinking, leaving us to guess Nick's state of mind as the events transpire before him. Not that the objective narrator need be the equivalent of a photographic device. He—or better "it"—may "overhear," like an audiotape recorder or stenographer who does nothing more than transcribe the dialogue of the characters. Another Hemingway story, "Hills Like White Elephants" (1927), consists almost entirely of the speeches, wrapped in quotation marks, of the two characters. Or the objective narrator may present only written documents, like letters. This kind of narrator functions like a fax machine or manuscript copyist.

These categories—*unlimited*, *limited*, and *objective*—only roughly explain the characteristics of narrators of novels and short stories. Often it is difficult to place individual narrators. Some seem to belong in more than one category or blur the norms of a given category. Some novels switch repeatedly among different kinds of narrators (James Joyce's *Ulysses* is a preeminent example). Some tales are narrated multiply by narrators whose versions conflict, leaving what "really" happened open to question. Robert Browning's narrative poem *The Ring and the Book* (1868–69) and the Japanese short story and film *Rashomon* are good examples of this technique. Instead of forcing narrators into one or another of the categories listed above, we may do better to characterize them in terms of the individual powers assigned them. Take, for example, Marcel Proust's *À la recherche du temps perdu* (1913–27; *In Search of Lost Time*; also translated as *Remembrance of Things Past*). Although narrated by the character-narrator Marcel, and in many ways limited to what Marcel-as-character could know, Marcel-as-narrator also has the power to delve into the intimate thoughts of other characters. The narrator of John Barth's "Lost in the Funhouse" (1968) has access only to the consciousness of the protagonist Ambrose but at the same time feels free to comment and generalize, not only about events and characters in the story, but also about the art and mechanics of writing fiction.

Whatever the powers of the narrator, he or she inevitably presents the story from a certain point of view or perspective. This point of view, which we can call the narrator's *slant,* may be stated quite explicitly by the narrator. In the first chapter of *Tom Jones,* the narrator argues that authors should provide plenty of information—in introductions, chapter headings, and the like—about what the reader may expect to find in the text. His slant takes the ostensible form of honest business dealings: like a good restauranteur, he offers the reader a menu by which to decide whether to partake of the text. The narrator of Joyce's "A Painful Case," comparing Duffy's saturnine face with the "brown tint" of Dublin's streets, conveys a rather negative slant on life in Ireland. In the opening sentence of *Pride and Prejudice,* the narrator reveals her slant about a social class whose sole occupation is to marry off its daughters to affluent men: "It is a truth universally acknowledged, that a single man in possession of good fortune must be in want of a wife." In "Heart of Darkness," Marlow's slant is against the brutal treatment of indigenous peoples by entrepreneurs, although not necessarily against colonialism as an institution.

Unlike the external narrator, the character-narrator has two perspectives—her present, narrator's slant toward the story and her earlier, character's perspective. We may call the character's point of view "filter." The character-narrator can report the filtered attitude that she had back when she was a character (what I did made sense at the time) but then modify it with her current slant (but I see now that it was quite stupid). The narrator's slant may reveal psychological, moral, political, ideological, and economic attitudes—indeed, any mental predisposition whatsoever.

Slant entails the notion of distance. A narrator may be said to be more or less distant from the characters, the action, the setting, or all three. This distance may be literally spatial, as in "Heart of Darkness," in which the narrator recounts events that happened thousands of miles away. Sometimes, distance is used to refer to a broad perspective. *Tom Jones* begins as if high above England: "In the western half of this kingdom . . .". Critics speak of the *bird's-eye* or *God's-eye view,* as opposed to the *microscopic view.* It is common to use terms like "long shot" and "close-up," but we must remember that these apply only metaphorically to verbal fiction.

Another kind of distance is temporal; that is, the time of the telling of the story may begin only moments after the last story-event occurred, as in Richardson's *Pamela,* or long after, as in Sir Walter Scott's historical novels or John Fowles' *The French Lieutenant's Woman* (1969), whose narrator lives in the 1960s but narrates events that took place 100 years before.

Most novels are told by the narrator after the fact, that is, retrospectively. But a few novels suggest that the discourse and the story are simultaneous. There are even a few novels cast in the future tense, which give the effect of prophecy, or in the conditional mood, that is, envisaging what might have happened.

In English, the standard verb form for retrospective accounts is the ordinary past or preterite tense. Conrad's *The Secret Agent* (1907) begins, "Mr. Verloc, going out in the morning, left his shop nominally in charge of his brother-in-law." Sometimes, however, the retrospective discourse is couched in the present tense, whether progressive (the verb "to be" followed by the present participle—"John is singing") or simple ("John sings").

The present tense is used in ordinary conversational narrative to impart a kind of vivid immediacy to the tale: the person next to you in a bar says "So I'm standing there and he comes up to me and makes this remark . . .". Some novels do the same: Ann Beattie's *Chilly Scenes of Winter* (1976) begins, "It is raining, and Sam's hair streams down his face." Quite often in fiction, when the narrator tells the story in the simple present tense, we understand that the account is retrospective, that the present tense refers to past activity. This is a use of the "historical present" tense to vivify the action.

Even when the narrator tells the story in the preterite, the story may be vivified by the use of present time adverbs (technically called *deictics*) to convey the sense of immediacy felt by a character. In Edgar Allan Poe's "The Tell-Tale Heart" (1843), for example, the narrator refers to his feelings upon being interrogated by the police: "No doubt I *now* grew very pale" (rather than "No doubt I *then* grew very pale").

Finally, there is a kind of distance that we may call personal, referring to the degree of sympathy or empathy that the narrator exhibits toward the character, whether emotionally, morally, sociologically, or philosophically. The narrators of Virginia Woolf's *Mrs. Dalloway* (1925) and Katherine Mansfield's "The Garden Party" (1922), for instance, are mostly in harmony with the protagonists. But the narrator may be very distant, speaking of the protagonist with detachment or even distaste, as is the case in Conrad's *The Secret Agent.* Even a character-narrator may be very distant from and unsympathetic toward her former self. Sympathy toward the protagonist has been termed *consonance*; indifference or antipathy has been termed *dissonance* (see Cohn, 1978).

The properties of narrators described above are not rules but norms, that is, conventional characteristics of narrators as manifested throughout the history of the novel. But art is dynamic, and authors press the limits of these norms, seeking ever new ways to tell stories. This is particularly true of 20th-century novelists, both modernist and postmodernist. To many an author, a narratorial norm is like a red cape to a bull, not something to be revered but something to be subverted or transformed into new realms of expression.

SEYMOUR CHATMAN

See also Beginnings and Endings; Character; Description; Diegesis and Diegetic Levels of Narration; Discourse Representation; Framing and Embedding; Historical Writing and the Novel; Implied Author; Mimesis; Narratology; Person in Narrative; Plot; Point of View; Realism; Stream of Consciousness and Interior Monologue; Tense in Narrative; Unreliable Narrator

Further Reading

Bal, Mieke, *De theorie van vertellen en verhalen,* Mulderberg: Coutinho, 1978; as *Narratology: An Introduction to the Theory of Narrative,* Toronto and Buffalo, New York: University of Toronto Press, 1985

Booth, Wayne C., *The Rhetoric of Fiction,* Chicago: University of Chicago Press, 1961; 2nd edition, Chicago: University of Chicago Press, and London: Penguin, 1983

Chatman, Seymour, *Story and Discourse: Narrative Structure in*

Fiction and Film, Ithaca, New York: Cornell University Press, 1978

Chatman, Seymour, *Coming to Terms: The Rhetoric of Narrative in Fiction and Film,* Ithaca, New York: Cornell University Press, 1990

Cohn, Dorrit, *Transparent Minds: Narrative Modes for Presenting Consciousness in Fiction,* Princeton, New Jersey: Princeton University Press, 1978

Fludernik, Monika, editor, *Style* 28:3 (Fall 1994), special issue on second-person narrative

Genette, Gérard, *Discours du récit,* in *Figures III,* Paris: Seuil, 1972; as *Narrative Discourse,* Ithaca, New York: Cornell University Press, 1980

Genette, Gérard, *Nouveau discours du récit,* Paris: Seuil, 1983; as *Narrative Discourse Revisited,* Ithaca, New York: Cornell University Press, 1988

Margolin, Uri, "Telling Our Story: On 'We' Literary Narratives," *Language and Literature* 5 (1996)

Prince, Gerald, *Narratology: The Form and Functioning of Narrative,* Berlin and New York: Mouton, 1982

Prince, Gerald, *A Dictionary of Narratology,* Lincoln: University of Nebraska Press, 1987; Aldershot: Scolar, 1988

Rimmon-Kenan, Shlomith, *Narrative Fiction: Contemporary Poetics,* London and New York: Methuen, 1983

National Tale

The national tale was a short-lived but extremely influential novelistic genre that flourished during the first three decades of the 19th century. Developed primarily by women novelists who resided in Ireland or Scotland rather than in London, the genre was intended not only to introduce English readers to the particular history, culture, beauty, and political problems of the British "peripheries," but also to model a new mode of viewing and interpreting unfamiliar cultures. Written under the direct influence of a new cultural nationalism, and influenced as well by new modes of ethnographic writing, national tales were particularly interested in the relationship between gender and national identification, drawing clear parallels between the domestic world and the national community. Most early national tales share the same basic plot: a young hero or heroine, raised in England or on the continent, travels to Ireland or Scotland expecting to find barbarism. Instead, the protagonist falls in love with his or her new surroundings and with the aristocratic native guide who has helped him or her to understand the region's beauty and cultural interest. The novel ends with the marriage of the lovers—and thus also with the allegorical union of Britain and its constituent "national characters."

Although strongly influenced by Maria Edgeworth's *Castle Rackrent* (1800) and *Ennui* (written 1803–05), the genre really took shape in 1806 when Sydney Owenson (later Lady Morgan) published her *Wild Irish Girl,* a phenomenally popular novel that influenced Madame de Staël's *Corinne, ou l'Italie* (1807; *Corrine; or, Italy*) and spawned a lasting fad not only for harp playing (the favored activity of Owenson's glamorous Irish princess-heroine, Glorvina) but for the national tale itself. Although Owenson wrote several national tales set in Greece (*Woman; or, Ida of Athens,* 1809), India (*The Missionary: An Indian Tale,* 1811), and Belgium (*The Princess; or, The Beguine,* 1835), it was her Irish national tales—*Wild Irish Girl, O'Donnel: A National Tale* (1814), *Florence Macarthy: An Irish Tale* (1818, a novel complete with long internal meditations on the nature and role of the national tale), and *The O'Briens and the O'Flahertys: A National Tale* (1827)—that most inspired her contemporaries. The genre became a particularly important vehicle for Irish nov-

elists, influencing Charles Maturin's *Wild Irish Boy* (1808), *The Milesian Chief* (1812), and *Women; or, Pour et Contre* (1818); Edgeworth's *The Absentee* (1812) and *Ormond* (1817); Regina Maria Roche's *The Tradition of the Castle* (1824); John Banim's *The Anglo-Irish of the Nineteenth Century* (1828); and Alicia LeFanu's *Tales of a Tourist* (1823). But Scottish authors developed corresponding Scottish national tales, ranging from Walter Scott's *Waverley* (1814) and Christian Johnstone's *The Saxon and the Gaël* (1814) and *Clan-Albin: A National Tale* (1815) to Susan Ferrier's *Marriage* (1818), *The Inheritance* (1824), and *Destiny* (1831). Meanwhile, Elizabeth Appleton's *Edgar: A National Tale* (1816) attempted—albeit with limited success—to develop a national tale for England itself. As many of these titles suggest, publishers commonly employed the generic designation "national tale" as a marketing device. Interestingly, the national tale serves as an early example of the marketing of a genre by a particular press: many of the national tales were published by a single London publisher, Henry Colburn, who probably deserves considerable credit for the genre's enormous success and wide range of influence.

The obvious political catalyst for the genre was the 1798 United Irishmen's rebellion and the subsequent 1800 Union of Ireland with Britain. Many of the Irish national tales address these events directly and at length, attempting to explain the specific tensions that led to the rebellion; Owenson's *O'Donnel* and *The O'Briens and the O'Flahertys,* Theodore Melville's *The Irish Chieftain and His Family* (1809), and Maturin's *The Milesian Chief,* for instance, focus on the dispossession of Irish aristocrats as one long-term source of political unrest. Other novelists, however, worked to lay to rest the specters of revolution and radicalism, calling instead for mutual understanding and reconciliation between different nationalities, to be achieved through intermarriage and a new sensitivity to cultural differences.

The national tale had a profound, if paradoxical, influence on Scott's early Waverley novels, and thus on the modern development of the historical novel; together these parallel and closely interrelated genres laid much of the conceptual ground for the 19th-century realist novel. If the national tale celebrates the richness of a national culture as accreted, over centuries, in a particular place, the historical novel describes the way historical forces disrupt and destroy this national culture. In turn, the national tale itself is influenced by Scott's historical novels: Johnstone's *Clan Albin* thus describes the dispersal of the Highland clans and the attempt to reassemble a new national community in the wake of that diaspora, while Owenson's *The O'Briens* suggests the repetitiveness and irredeemable suffering of the Irish under centuries of English imperialism. A genre designed to attract the attention and sympathy of English readers for the cultural traditions of Ireland or Scotland thus becomes one that can express anti-English sentiment—and that addresses itself more and more clearly to Scottish or Irish readers. If national tales often see themselves pedagogically, as modeling a new kind of touristic attitude and thus inaugurating a new epoch of cultural understanding, they also can function—as in Edgeworth's *Ennui* or Owenson's *O'Donnel*—as satires on new modes of individual and mass tourism, or as satiric commentaries on the lasting inability of English travelers to transcend their own parochialism. In Ferrier's *Marriage,* for instance, when the English character continually fails to comprehend the Scottish Highlands on its own terms, the national union ultimately gives way to national divorce.

Absorbed into other forms of militant, idyllic, and nostalgic national fiction over the course of the 1820s, the national tale gradually lost clear definition and currency as a novelistic genre within Britain itself. Overseas, however, it continued to have a profound influence on the early literature of the British Empire throughout the 19th century, particularly on the fictional sketches, travel reports, and ethnographic and historical novels written in and about Canada, Australia, and British India. Despite its lasting influence on the historical novel, realist novel, colonial fiction, and local-color writing, the genre of the national tale was all but forgotten until very recently. During the 1980s, however, a new attention to early female novelists and feminist reprint programs that republished key novels by Owenson and Edgeworth catalyzed renewed scholarly discussions about the romantic novel in general and the national tale in particular.

KATIE TRUMPENER

See also English Novel (1800–40); Historical Novel; Regional Novel; Romantic Novel

Further Reading

Eagleton, Terry, *Heathcliff and the Great Hunger: Studies in Irish Culture,* London and New York: Verso, 1995

Ferris, Ina, *The Achievement of Literary Authority: Gender, History, and the Waverley Novels,* Ithaca, New York: Cornell University Press, 1991

Garside, Peter, "Popular Fiction and National Tale: Hidden Origins of Scott's *Waverley,*" *Nineteenth-Century Literature* 46:1 (June 1991)

Kelly, Gary, *English Fiction of the Romantic Period, 1789–1830,* London and New York: Longman, 1989

Lloyd, David, *Anomalous States: Irish Writing and the Post-colonial movement,* Durham, North Carolina: Duke University Press, 1993

Trumpener, Katie, *Bardic Nationalism: The Romantic Novel and the British Empire,* Princeton, New Jersey: Princeton University Press, 1997

Watson, Nicola, *Revolution and the Form of the British Novel, 1790–1825: Intercepted Letters, Interrupted Seductions,* Oxford: Clarendon Press, and New York: Oxford University Press, 1994

Native Son by Richard Wright

1940

In the 1994 film biography *Richard Wright—Black Boy,* historian John Henrik Clarke claimed that with the publication of *Native Son* Wright "came like a giant out of the mountain with a sledgehammer." Although this description may seem somewhat hyperbolic, it actually captures quite well the initial response to the publication of *Native Son.* In fact, in some bookstores stock was sold out within hours; the novel sold 215,000 copies in the first three weeks, a new record for Harper's, its publisher. Wright immediately became a prominent figure in American literature of the 1940s and the first African American to earn his living from writing.

Initial reviews of the novel were enthusiastic, comparing Wright to John Steinbeck, Theodore Dreiser, Fedor Dostoevskii, and Charles Dickens. The novel was also a Book-of-the-Month Club selection, Wright being the first black author to profit from the club's wide circulation. Well-known African-American intellectuals, such as literary critic Alain Locke and NAACP president James Ivy, praised the novel, although African-American reviewers and readers alike were dismayed over the characterization of the black protagonist, Bigger Thomas. Many people feared that the depiction of Bigger Thomas as a violent young black man would only reinforce societal stereotypes, while others felt that this characterization was necessary in order to shock at least some white readers into a recognition of America's racial problems, which is certainly what Wright intended to do. Despite the novel's representation of social and racial values within a specifically communist context, communist party reviewers waited almost a month before commenting on or reviewing *Native Son,* which in itself signaled the party's ambivalent feelings about the novel. But Mike Gold, columnist for the *Daily Worker,* praised the novel and defended it against attacks from other party members. Detractors such as Benjamin Davis Jr. and James

W. Ford noted the novel's "nationalist racial spirit" and were perhaps troubled by the fact that the novel primarily takes an African-American point of view rather than an exploited worker's perspective. In a letter to Mike Gold, Wright responded to the criticisms and took the party to task for its encouragement of "types of writing that can be used for agitprop purposes" and its "tendency to sneer at more imaginative attempts. . . ." Also upsetting to party members was the fact that Bigger Thomas was not amenable to any political movement. Wright characterized him as so alienated and isolated from the rest of society that the party's efforts to erase racial lines had become futile, as demonstrated in the character of Jan Erlone, a communist party member who attempts to befriend Bigger.

The conflicts between Wright and the communist party over *Native Son* are representative of their ongoing disagreements about the role of the artist and of literature in the party. But despite this, Wright's depiction of the party in the novel is fairly positive, and the last third of the book is largely a speech given by Boris Max, a party attorney, in Bigger's defense at his trial. Wright clearly uses Max to convey his own Marxist assessment of the racial situation in the United States, arguing that the problem stems from the hierarchical and exploitative nature of a capitalist society. The speech is also based on Clarence Darrow's defense of Leopold and Loeb, a case to which Wright often alludes in *Native Son*.

Native Son is one of the best examples of social protest fiction, and Wright is one of its most well-known proponents. In order to use the novel as a protest against racism, Wright drew from his experiences working with the South Side Youth Club in Chicago, as well as actual newspaper accounts of an incident involving Robert Nixon and Earl Hicks that happened while Wright was working on *Native Son*. Also evident is his study of sociology at the Chicago School of Urban Sociology and with his friend the sociologist Horace R. Cayton. This study, combined with Wright's Marxist analysis of American society and his indictment of racism, created a novel unlike any American novel published previously. Although structure and characterization in *Native Son* are fairly conventional, influenced mainly by American realism (as in Dreiser's *An American Tragedy*, 1925) and Russian existentialism (as in Dostoevskii's *Crime and Punishment*, 1867), Wright also incorporates symbols involving color, temperature, and objects. One of the most vivid uses of these symbols is the opening scene of the book in which Bigger is forced to kill a large black rat in his family's wretched kitchenette on Chicago's poverty-stricken South Side. This scene also demonstrates what Michel Fabre calls one of the novel's "most striking if not original devices: the use of a symbolic detail or episode to announce a crisis or future event" (see Fabre, 1993). But perhaps the most important feature of the novel is Wright's

representation of Bigger's point of view, as a result of which the black characters come to life and the white characters are reduced to stereotypes. This shift marks a distinct change from literature published previously that portrayed only stereotypical black characters. Although novels such as Harriet Beecher Stowe's *Uncle Tom's Cabin* (1852) attempted to treat blacks sympathetically, the black characters in these novels appear as though drawn from a white point of view, as though they do not truly understand black culture, thought, and feeling. Wright reverses this tradition and is able to show the gaps between the two races through Bigger's total alienation from the white world around him.

The widespread fear of communism incited by the Cold War and McCarthyism led to the diminished popularity of *Native Son* during the 1950s. But even though many African-American writers differed with Wright politically and artistically, his influence was, and is, felt widely and is evident in the works of writers such as Ralph Ellison, James Baldwin, and Chester Himes. Writer and activist Amiri Baraka (LeRoi Jones) seems to speak for many writers when he says in *Richard Wright—Black Boy* that "it was Wright who was one of the people who made me conscious of the need to struggle." Since the 1960s, Wright's work has seen something of a revival, and works such as *Native Son* and his autobiography *Black Boy* have been placed firmly in the canon of American literature.

ANGELA K. ALBRIGHT

Further Reading

Butler, Robert J., editor, *The Critical Response to Richard Wright*, Westport, Connecticut: Greenwood Press, 1995

Fabre, Michel, *The Unfinished Quest of Richard Wright*, New York: Morrow, 1973; 2nd edition, Urbana: University of Illinois Press, 1993

Gates, Henry Louis, and Anthony Appiah, editors, *Richard Wright: Critical Perspectives Past and Present*, New York: Amistad, 1993

Hakutani, Yoshinobu, *Richard Wright and Racial Discourse*, Columbia: University of Missouri Press, 1996

Kinnamon, Keneth, *The Emergence of Richard Wright*, Urbana: University of Illinois Press, 1972

Kinnamon, Keneth, editor, *New Essays on "Native Son,"* Cambridge and New York: Cambridge University Press, 1990

Kinnamon, Keneth, editor, *Critical Essays on Richard Wright's "Native Son,"* New York: Twayne, and London: Prentice-Hall International, 1997

Macksey, Richard, and Frank E. Moorer, editors, *Richard Wright: A Collection of Critical Essays*, Englewood Cliffs, New Jersey: Prentice-Hall, 1984

Natsume Sōseki 1867–1916

Japanese

The decision of the Treasury of Japan to grace the 1,000 yen note with an idealized portrait of Natsume Sōseki exemplifies the unintended irony only a bureaucracy can produce. The Japanese government has chosen for the symbol of its economy an artist who wrote cautionary tales about the emptiness of material society, and has made a cultural hero of a man who relentlessly exposed the dislocations and loss of meaning that were the price of Japan's modernity.

Natsume Sōseki's career as a writer spanned a single productive decade, beginning in 1905 with the serialization of *Wagahai wa neko de aru* (*I Am a Cat*). A series of vignettes narrated by a cat, the work presents a satirical view of bourgeois society in the late Meiji period (1868–1912). The cat belongs to a Mr. Kushami (Mr. Sneeze), a lazy, dyspeptic academic who is a self-mocking portrait of Sōseki. The early installments of the novel became very popular and brought the author considerable fame. *I Am a Cat* reflects the general Meiji project of modernizing literary practice by abandoning the ornate language of the Edo period (1600–1868) in favor of a standardized style based on the speech patterns of the Tokyo dialect. Even so, the structure of the novel resembles the anecdotal fiction of Edo more than the Western realistic novels that were the ideal for many late Meiji writers.

Sōseki continued experimenting with a vernacular style in his second novel, *Botchan* (1906; *Botchan*), a broad satire of a sincere young man who, although not very bright, ends up teaching high school in Japan's provinces. Sōseki draws on his own experiences for much of the humor, and his protagonist, an orphan dispossessed of his family's former status as samurai, typifies the rootless young man who figures prominently in Sōseki's later fiction.

In *Kusamakura* (1906; *The Three-Cornered World*), Sōseki departs from the form he used in his first two novels. Sōseki referred to it as a novel in the manner of a haiku, and certain passages resemble the *haibun,* or poetic journals, of the great Edo poets Bashō and Buson. The narrator is a Tokyo painter who comes to a village in the mountains to work and is attracted to a mysterious young woman, Onami, whose apparent lack of passion inspires his lyrical evocations of place and his musings on the nature of art.

In *Nowaki* (1907; Autumn Wind), Sōseki begins moving toward the psychological realism that would eventually distinguish his mature style. The story depicts the relationships between Takayanagi, a poor young man who is dying of tuberculosis; Shirai, a poor teacher; and the wealthy Nakano. Class tensions and the poor's hatred of the rich give the story a melodramatic quality, but Sōseki achieves an edgy depth in his characterization of Takayanagi, who realizes that Shirai's hatred is borne by political principle, while his own is borne by envy. Takayanagi's growing self-awareness forces him to acknowledge his spiritual emptiness and leads him to sacrifice his ambitions and his health for the sake of Shirai.

Sōseki next published *Gubijinsō* (1908; Red Poppy), a throwback to the didactic novels of late Edo in its plotting, characterization, and heavily sinicized language. He felt ambivalent about completely abandoning the values of pre-Meiji literature in favor of Western modes of representation, and that ambivalence is apparent in his peculiar misogynist obsession with the character Fujio, a Neo-Confucian version of the femme fatale. This obsession is apparent in Sōseki's journals, where he insists that he must kill off this woman. By writing *Gubijinsō*, Sōseki reluctantly purged himself of traditional literary values and practices in pursuit of his own narrative mode.

Kōfu (1908; *The Miner*) departed radically from *Gubijinsō,* leaving many critics of the time befuddled. The story of a troubled young man who runs away from home and finds work in a mine, this work also explores the art of the novel by parodying narrative conventions, including the conventions of the poetic journal. The protagonist's descent into the hellish world of the mine is ultimately redemptive, but the tale of redemption is so overtly framed by the narrative's concerns with the nature of literary art that it struck some contemporary readers as avant garde.

Sanshirō (1908; *Sanshirō*), *Sorekara* (1910; *And Then*), and *Mon* (1911; *The Gate*) form a trilogy in which Sōseki settles into a distinctive style that enables him to give full expression to the theme of the loneliness of the individual in modern Japan. Because these works employ a tightly controlled psychological realism, their novelty is often overlooked. However, during these years Sōseki achieved an original and unsettling narrative synthesis, part commentary on and part product of the profound cultural tensions of his times.

The novels of Sōseki's final years—*Higan Sugi made* (1912; *To the Spring Equinox and Beyond*), *Kōjin* (1914; *The Wayfarer*), *Kokoro* (1914; *Kokoro*), *Michikusa* (1915; *Grass on the Wayside*), and *Meian* (1917; *Light and Darkness*)—for the most part elaborate on the style he achieved in his middle period. The most notable feature of these novels is their increasingly dark and pessimistic tone. *Kokoro* is now generally acknowledged as Sōseki's masterwork. Some critics read *Kokoro* as part of a trio of books that begins with *To the Spring Equinox and Beyond* and *The Wayfarer,* while others group the work with *Grass on the Wayside* and *Light and Darkness* to form a trilogy that is the culmination of his life's work. While certain thematic concerns (especially the problem of the individual's isolation in modern society) link all of these late works, *Kokoro* particularly resembles *To the Spring Equinox and Beyond* in that it follows two narrative strains: the first half, comprising parts 1 and 2, deals with the efforts of the narrator, a young man referred to as "I" throughout, to uncover the past—and thus the true character—of his mentor, who is referred to simply by the honorific title of *Sensei,* teacher or master; the second half is a long confessional suicide note written by *Sensei* that helps explain the circumstances of his life—the betrayals he has suffered at the hands of relatives and also his own betrayal of his friend, who is referred to simply as "K." Although *Sensei* presents his story as a way of instructing his young student, Sōseki creates disturbing parallels between the path *Sensei* has followed and the path the young "I" seems doomed to follow.

The title of the work, which Edwin McClellan has noted may be translated as "spirit" or "the heart of things," suggests an identification by the author of the individual's spirit with the spirit of the age, an interpretation supported by the fact that Sōseki began work on the novel in response to the suicide of General Nogi after the death of the Meiji Emperor in 1912. Nogi's death, the implications of which are discussed in the narrative, was a ritual form of suicide called *junshi* (following one's lord in death) that recalled all of the older values of a feudal era. The death of the Emperor was by itself enough to suggest the passing of an age, but Nogi's death, and that of his wife, was a sensational event that riveted the nation's attention, calling forth the basic questions concerning traditional values and national identity that the Japanese had confronted during an age of unprecedented social and cultural transformation. Sōseki was not the only Japanese writer profoundly affected by this event, but, given his intellectual and emotional inclinations, he was especially sensitive to the implications of Nogi's action. In *Kokoro*, the isolation of the modern individual is linked closely to an apocalyptic view of the present that sees the act of revealing one's inner self—exemplified by both Nogi's death and *Sensei*'s narrative—as alienating and destructive.

The problem of moral confusion and the pessimism that became increasingly prominent elements in his writing may be the result of his failing health, but Sōseki's propensity for narrative experimentation probably stemmed from his attempts to fully explore the darker implications of modernity. As he searched for a distinctive voice, Sōseki created a compelling and terrible vision of the costs of asserting the autonomy of the self and of looking into the chasm of spiritual emptiness opened up by the cultural discontinuity of Meiji Japan.

DENNIS C. WASHBURN

Biography

Born Natsume Kinnosuke in Tokyo, 9 February 1867; given up for adoption at age 2 but returned to his birth parents at age 9. Attended schools in Tokyo; Tokyo Imperial University, 1890–93. Teacher, Tokyo Normal College, 1894–95, and Middle School, Matsuyama, 1895–1900; studied in England, 1900–02; Professor of English, Tokyo Imperial University, 1903–07; staff member, *Tetsugaku Zasshi*, 1892; associated with *Asahi* from 1907. Died 9 December 1916.

Novels by Natsume Sōseki

Wagahai wa neko de aru, 1905; as *I Am a Cat*, translated by K. Ando, 1906; revised by K. Natsume, 2 vols., 1906–09; also translated by Katsue Shibata and Motonari Kai, 1971 (volume 1), and A. Ito and G. Wilson, 1980 (volume 2)

Botchan, 1906; as *Botchan (Master Darling)*, translated by Yasotaro Morri, 1918; as *Botchan*, translated by Umeji Sasaki, 1927; also translated by Alan Turney, 1972

Kusamakura, 1906; as *Kusamakura*, translated by Umeji Sasaki, 1927; as *Inhuman Tour*, translated by Kazutomo Takahashi, 1927; as *The Three-Cornered World*, translated by Alan Turney, 1965

Nowaki [Autumn Wind], 1907

Gubijinsō [Red Poppy], 1908

Kōfu, 1908; as *The Miner*, translated and with an afterword by Jay Rubin, 1988

Sanshirō, 1908; as *Sanshirō*, translated and with a critical essay by Jay Rubin, 1977

Sorekara, 1910; as *And Then*, translated and with an afterword and selected bibliography by Norma Moore Field, 1978

Mon, 1911; as *The Gate*, translated by Francis Mathy, 1982

Higan Sugi made, 1912; as *To the Spring Equinox and Beyond*, translated by Kingo Ochiai and Sanford Goldstein, 1985

Kōjin, 1914; as *The Wayfarer*, translated and with an introduction by Beongcheon Yu, 1967; as *The Wanderer*, translated by Yu, 1967

Kokoro, 1914; as *Kokoro*, translated by Ineko Sato, 1941; also translated by Iñeko Kondon, 1956, and Edwin McClellan, 1957

Michikusa, 1915; as *Grass on the Wayside*, translated and with an introduction by Edwin McClellan, 1969

Meian, 1917; as *Light and Darkness*, translated and with a critical essay by V.H. Viglielmo, 1971

Other Writings: stories, literary criticism and theory.

Further Reading

Doi, Takeo, *The Psychological World of Natsume Sōseki*, Cambridge, Massachusetts: Harvard University Press, 1976

Fujii, James, *Complicit Fictions: The Subject in the Modern Japanese Prose Narrative*, Berkeley: University of California Press, 1993

McClellan, Edwin, *Two Japanese Novelists: Sōseki and Tōson*, Chicago: University of Chicago Press, 1969; London: University of Chicago Press, 1970

Pollack, David, "Framing the Self: The Philosophical Dimensions of Human Nature in *Kokoro*," *Monumenta Nipponica* 43:4 (Winter 1988)

Rubin, Jay, "Sōseki on Individualism: 'Watakushi no Kojinshugi'," *Monumenta Nipponica* 34:1 (Spring 1979)

Washburn, Dennis, *The Dilemma of the Modern in Japanese Fiction*, New Haven, Connecticut: Yale University Press, 1995

Naturalism

The influence of naturalism was pervasive in the arts in the latter half of the 19th century, as much in drama and the visual arts as in the novel, and any account of its place in the history of the novel must necessarily be judged as only one part of a larger history. It is equally important to note the place that the term *naturalism* has in the history of philosophy and the history of ideas, for its philosophical implications, while not coterminous with its literary ones, are an important aid to our understanding of what naturalism is and what its practitioners sought to achieve. In philosophical usage *naturalism* is frequently invoked alongside *materialism* to explain the phenomena of nature within the terms (and the languages) of the physical sciences and with no appeal to metaphysical or supernaturalist explanations. Naturalism concludes that everything that exists is spatial and temporal and is itself either a physical system or is inseparable from one, so much so that the naturalistic philosopher holds that there can be no knowledge of the world other than that which we ordinarily call *scientific*. Such a philosophical system of course takes much of its intellectual and explanatory force from the great advances made by the natural sciences in the 19th century, notably in physics, but advances in other areas, especially in evolutionary theory and psychology, reinforced the claims of naturalism and materialism. It would be wrong to overstate the proximity that exists between naturalist ideas in philosophy and those in the arts, but it is important to point to their most salient areas of common ground: an emphasis on science and scientific method, a distrust of the metaphysical and the supernatural, and a belief that the external world can be investigated without recourse to a doctrine of ultimate causes.

Naturalism, moreover, must be understood in relation to realism. Again, ideas about realism in philosophy have a significant relationship to ideas about realism in the arts. The relationship between philosophical realism and artistic realism cannot be explored fully here, but it is sufficient to say that philosophical realism seeks to attribute to objects and things a reality independent of the process by which they are known and, at the same time, to accord to humankind its proper place in the world of finite things, insisting on the unexceptional character of man's position among other living beings. Not only does naturalism in the arts follow realism in historical chronology, it is also dependent on realism for its existence. Thus, while we might say that realistic works are not naturalistic, the reverse is not true: all naturalist works must be realistic—it is a necessary condition of all naturalistic works that they involve the techniques and methods of realism. This is because the assumptions about life and objects explained above are common to both, as is the assumption that it is possible for the artist to present a neutral, disinterested, and objective report on the world of quotidian reality. Thus, our interest is not so much with the common ground that exists between the realist and the naturalist as with where their dissimilarities lie, with what, in effect, naturalism *adds* to realism. The following discussion about naturalism and realism is concerned more or less exclusively with their fictional manifestations.

We can say of naturalism that it was a movement in a way that realism was not. Many of those who saw themselves as adherents to naturalism identified with its tenets as if they were comparable with the policy statements of a political manifesto; many moved in the literary salons and circles associated with the naturalist cause; and, above all, those who saw themselves as naturalists read and criticized one another's work. The word *naturalism* had been widely used in France in the criticism of the fine arts in the 1850s and 1860s, but the importation of the term into the world of fiction is largely attributed to the leading French proponent of naturalism, Émile Zola, although one should be wary of suggesting with any certainty that he was the first important writer to employ the term in a literary context. Like the realists, Zola challenged the widely held assumption that it was the function of art to represent the ideal and, like Gustave Flaubert, the Goncourt brothers (Edmond and Remy), and the critics Champfleury (the pseudonym of Jules Fleury-Husson) and Edmond Duranty, he es-

poused the virtues of scientific observation and objectivity in the novelist's presentation of everyday reality. For both realist and naturalist, the hero was the painter Gustave Courbet, for it was Courbet, above all, who had resisted the idealizing entreaties of the French art salons and who, in defending his unsentimental treatment of the peasantry and the proletariat, had called realism forward as his defense. But while realism and naturalism are, in part, defined by their subject matter (in particular, the depiction of contemporary middle- and lower-class life), the character that Zola was to give to naturalism was such that it limited whatever prescriptiveness realism possessed, binding it, especially, to a strongly biological and evolutionary understanding of man's place in the universe. The strongly scientific character of naturalism made it, as Lillian R. Furst and Peter N. Skrine (1971) have remarked, at once "more concrete and at the same time more limited than Realism"; it also made it more vulnerable to intellectual (and, indeed, moral) attack than realism, and, of course, it made it more vulnerable to the very advances of science itself.

We can best understand the scientific character of naturalism if we look at two important works by Zola, his 1868 preface to the second edition of *Thérèse Raquin* (1867; *Thérèse Raquin*) and *Le Roman expérimental* (1880; *The Experimental Novel*). In the preface, written to defend himself against the charge that *Thérèse Raquin* was pornographic and obscene, Zola writes of his intention to study temperaments and not characters:

> I have chosen people completely dominated by their nerves and blood, without free will, drawn into each action of their lives by the inexorable laws of their physical nature. Thérèse and Laurent [the eponymous heroine and her lover] are human animals, nothing more. I have endeavoured to follow these animals through the devious working of their passions, the compulsion of their instincts, and the mental unbalance resulting from a nervous crisis. The sexual adventures of my hero and heroine are the satisfaction of a need, the murder they commit a consequence of their adultery, a consequence they accept just as wolves accept the slaughter of a sheep. And finally, what I have had to call their remorse really amounts to a simple organic disorder, a revolt of the nervous system when strained to breaking-point. There is a complete absence of soul, I freely admit, since that is how I meant it to be.

While there are legitimate questions we might raise about Zola's ingenuousness in his account of the novel's composition, the preface is a striking illustration of how in his hands (and subsequently in the hands of others) the assumptions of realism had been sharpened by naturalist theory. The language invokes scientific and deterministic models of character and action: human behavior is a matter of "nerves" and "blood"; free will is an illusion; people are drawn to one another by "inexorable laws" of "physical nature" or what he alternatively calls "the compulsion of their instincts"; and anything that might seem to be the expression of a sentiment or an emotion is to be explained away as "a simple organic disorder." The discoveries of biology and physics are clearly at work here, but so too is the language of the chemist, for Zola reduces the creative role of the novelist to that of an observer who clinically and dispassionately records the reactions of two chemical agents as they are mixed together in the test tube of life. The novel is the laboratory.

In *The Experimental Novel*, Zola attempts a more concerted conception of the novel drawing on the theoretical exactitude of the natural sciences. While he is indebted to the positivism of the philosopher Auguste Comte and the scientific literary history of Hippolyte Taine (particularly his *Histoire de la littérature anglaise* [1863; *History of English Literature*]), Zola draws above all on a model provided for him by Claude Bernard's *Introduction à l'étude de la médecine expérimentale* (1865; *Introduction to the Study of Experimental Medicine*) and Bernard's later *Leçons sur les phénomènes de la vie communs aux animaux et aux végétaux* (1878–79; *Lessons on the Phenomena of Life Common to Animals and Plants*). Zola imports into his theory of the novel Bernard's emphasis on the acquisition of empirical data and the importance of the experimental method. The novelist, Zola concludes, is both observer and experimenter: "The observer in him presents data as he has observed them, determines the point of departure, establishes the solid ground on which his characters will stand and his phenomena take place. Then the experimenter appears and institutes the experiment, that is, sets the characters of a particular story in motion, in order to show that the series of events will be those demanded by the determinism of the phenomena under study." This insistence on the scientific and empirical nature of the novelist's task and the deterministic conception of human character is worked out by Zola in *Les Rougon-Macquart,* the collective title given to the 20 novels from *La Fortune des Rougon* (1871; *The Fortune of the Rougons*) to *Le Docteur Pascal* (1893; *Doctor Pascal*) and afforded a subtitle that itself urges on us Zola's claim to have written a scientific document: *Histoire naturelle et sociale d'une famille sous le Second Empire.*

The degree to which naturalism became identified with Zola and his writings is such that many literary historians think that few movements in the arts have been so dominated by one individual. Indeed, by the late 1880s Zola's dominance was such that some, notably Alphonse Daudet and Edmond de Goncourt, both of them prominent members of the movement, came to the conclusion that Zola was exploiting naturalism for his own ends. Zola built up around him a small group of like-minded writers, amongst them Paul Alexis, Léon Hennique, J-K. Huysmans, and Guy de Maupassant. They were collectively known as *Le Groupe de Médan,* drawing their name from the house near Paris where Zola lived, although they met more frequently in Paris itself than in Médan. Maupassant was, without question, the most accomplished of Zola's disciples, and in works such as *Boule de Suif* (1880)—written, one might say programmatically, for *Les Soirées de Médan,* a collection of tales with a common theme, the Franco-Prussian War, that would advertize the naturalist manifesto—and *Bel-Ami* (1885; *Bel-Ami*) Maupassant's indebtedness to Zola is pronounced, although it was Flaubert whom Maupassant revered above all.

As naturalist techniques and interests moved beyond France to other parts of continental Europe, Great Britain, and the United States, it expanded into other forms of writing as well. In Germany naturalism was found as much in drama as in prose, and dramatists such as Gerhardt Hauptmann and Arno Holz were instrumental in bringing naturalism to the attention of the German public, if only to find that some of their works were excoriated as much as they were acclaimed. Hauptmann's first play, *Vor Sonnenaufgang* (1889; *Before Sunrise*), established his naturalistic style. A later play, *Die Weber* (1892; *The Weavers*),

thought to be his finest, is written entirely in dialect, and its subject, the plight of poverty-stricken Silesian weavers, is both national and thus to an extent patriotic and socially conscious; naturalism in Germany was driven both by the recent unification of the nation in the wake of the Franco-Prussian War and the "discovery" (partly a consequence of the influence of Henrik Ibsen) that art can be an instrument of social reform.

In the German novel the naturalistic tradition that derives from Zola is found in minor writers such as Conrad Alberti and Max Kretzer, but there are markedly naturalistic elements in the early writings of Thomas Mann, particularly *Buddenbrooks* (1901; *Buddenbrooks*), which, while not strictly speaking evidence of a Zolaesque inheritance, are suffused with much of the intellectual and pseudoscientific character of Zola's model. Mann is free of Zola's tendency to relentlessly construe the naturalist subject as primarily a matter of the lives of the working classes or the *lumpen-proletariat,* and his study of degeneration and decay (both individual and social) is played out among the genteel, propertied classes of an ancient Hanseatic city; the catastrophe that befalls the Buddenbrooks (it is chiefly the female characters who survive at the end) is not a matter of the "tragic flaw" or the unreality of romantic genius but is a process that is natural in its inevitability, a process that is analyzed by Mann with due attention to its scientific, and deterministic, causes. Naturalist elements surface also in the late 19th-century Italian novel in the style known as *verismo,* of which the chief exponent is Giovanni Verga, whose *I Malavoglia* (1881; *The House by the Medlar Tree*), *Novelle Rusticane* (1882; *Short Sicilian Novels*), and *Mastro-don Gesualdo* (1889; *Master Don Gesualdo*) are informed both by careful attention to the detailing of peasant life and by a quasi-naturalistic objectivity and dispassionateness.

In the English and American novel naturalism occupies a somewhat contradictory position: in the English novel, if one excepts Thomas Hardy, it is in a distinctly minor key, while in the American novel naturalism emerges as a major movement. English literature, it might be argued, has been particularly resistant to theorizing about literary forms, and the English novel has traditionally been characterized by its concreteness and particularity. Zola's reputation in Great Britain, moreover, was more a matter of indignation than admiration: the Vigilance Association's denunciation of any literature that depicted the seamier or more degrading aspects of human life led to a House of Commons motion opposing the importation of "immoral" literature, and Henry Vizetelly, the English publisher of Zola, was tried and imprisoned for making *La Terre* (1887; *The Earth*) available to the English reader, despite the fact that his was a heavily expurgated translation. Thus the climate of the age was not conducive to the growth of a recognizably English strain of Zolaesque naturalism, but those very aspects of 19th-century culture that contributed so much to the intellectual current of which naturalism was one part were, of course, as apparent in Great Britain as they were in continental Europe, and many writers were unable to escape the effects of the challenges to faith and to the received wisdom of a traditional society that scientific determinism brought in its wake.

The current of English naturalism runs strongest in Hardy, George Moore, and George Gissing. Moore and Gissing, much more so than Hardy, write of the "lower depths"; in their treatment of this they sometimes walk a tightrope between imaginative art and dramatized sociology. Hardy avoids the excesses of the sociological and frequently breaks through naturalistic verisimilitude to find a symbolic, even quasi-mythical, register, but the deterministic strains that give much force to naturalist fiction are palpably present in his work, even if in a novel such as *Tess of the D'Urbervilles* (1891) they can seem somewhat mechanistically reductive. In Moore's *A Mummer's Wife* (1884) the central character, Kate Ede, slides into alcoholism and near prostitution, and in his greatest novel, *Esther Waters* (1894), the eponymous heroine is a "general domestic" whose life is treated with a sober unsentimentality. This method owes much to Zola, of whom Moore remembered in *Confessions of a Young Man* (1888) that reading an article by him ("Naturalisme, la vérité, la science") was like receiving a "violent blow on the head": "I read that one should write with as little imagination as possible, that plot in a novel was illiterate and puerile, and that the art of M. Scribe was an art of strings and wires, etc." (Moore was subsequently to visit Zola at Médan and to befriend Paul Alexis.) Later Moore concluded that Zola's theories were only the "simple crude statements of a man of a powerful mind, but singularly narrow vision," though on Zola's death in 1902 he declared "That man was the beginning of me."

In Gissing naturalistic elements exist, somewhat uneasily, alongside idealistic ones in novels such as *Demos* (1886) and *New Grub Street* (1891). The critical response of English writers to naturalism reflects the misgivings of many readers; sometimes these misgivings assume a moralistic tone, naturalism being criticized for the lapses in taste to which it can frequently give rise. But in the articles and reviews of Edmund Gosse and Henry James they take on a more measured aesthetic and philosophical character. In his essay "The Limits of Realism in Fiction" (*Forum* 9 [June 1890]), Gosse challenges the first-order principles that underlie it:

> The first principle of the school was the exact reproduction of life. But life is wide and it is elusive. All that the finest observer can do is to make a portrait of one corner of it. By the confession of the master spirit himself, this portrait is not to be a photograph. It must be inspired by imagination, but sutained and confined by the experience of reality. It does not appear at first sight as though it should be difficult to attain this, but in point of fact it is found almost impossible to approach this species of perfection.

For James the appeal in Zola, and naturalism more generally, to the models of science is, in itself, deeply questionable and, ultimately, inconsequential:

> But the formula really sees us no further. It offers a definition which is no definition. 'Science' is soon said—the whole thing depends on the ground so covered. Science accepts surely *all* our consciousnes of life; even, rather, the latter closes materially round it—so that, becoming thus a force within us, not a force outside, it exists, it illuminates only as we apply it. We do emphatically apply it in art. But Zola would apparently hold that it much more applies us" ("Émile Zola," *Atlantic Monthly* [1903]).

If James' view of Zola's naturalism is admiring, yet finally distanced and unsympathetic, that of his American contemporaries

is markedly less critical. Although *The Earth* was attacked in the United States for its gross sexuality, *La Débâcle* (1892; *The Debacle*) was widely admired. Frank Norris spoke for many writers (and, indeed, readers) when he adverted to Zola's achievement as the most advanced of "the present stage of literary development." Norris, however, constructed naturalism as part of a dialectic in which, as Donald Pizer (1966) argues, "realism and romanticism were opposing forces, and naturalism was transcending synthesis." Norris elsewhere referred to Zola as a "romanticist," a terminological confusion that is probably to be understood as distinguishing the kind of realism to be found in Zola from the uncritically optimistic realism associated with William Dean Howells. Norris says little about the philosophical determinism and scientific "experimentation" that lends such intellectual force to Zola's theorizing; he sees naturalism, essentially, as a matter of truthfulness to contemporary reality conjoined with sensationalism and the treatment of the "lower depths." There can be no doubt, however, that ideas played a major part in the development of an indigenous naturalist movement in America, in part because American society has been generally more receptive to scientific breakthroughs (the differing responses of the United States and Great Britain to the publication in 1859 of Charles Darwin's *The Origin of Species* is an illustrative case in point), but also because the social and economic conditions that faced the United States in the years following the end of the Civil War called for a fiction of greater moral urgency about social matters than had hitherto been demanded as well as a commitment to the use of art as an instrument of social reform. Norris' *The Octopus* (1901), with its powerful depiction of the struggle between California ranchers and the railroad that controls the transportation of their grain, and his later *The Pit* (1903), set largely in the world of the Chicago grain exchange (the novels were the first two in a projected "Epic of the Wheat"), are naturalistic both in their emphasis on the economic forces that shape the lives of their characters and in their implicit appeal to their readers to turn from fiction to life and correct the excesses of laissez-faire capitalism Norris depicts.

Similarly reformist in spirit, Upton Sinclair's *The Jungle* (1906), with its grim depiction of the life of Lithuanian immigrant workers in the Chicago stockyards at the turn of the the century, led to a federal investigation both of working conditions in the stockyards and of the meat-packing process. In the novels of Stephen Crane, Theodore Dreiser, and Jack London, the reformist objectives play a less obvious role, but in Crane's *Maggie: A Girl of the Streets* (1893) and London's *Martin Eden* (1909) a spirit of reforming zeal is at work, although neither work caused any public indignation of the kind that attended *The Jungle*. For Dreiser and London, especially, naturalism was very much bound up with the supposed explanatory power of mechanistic determinism and social Darwinism. Dreiser's characters live in a Darwinian universe in which, as in *The Financier* (1912), strong eat weak, or predators consume prey, although evolutionary biology is often uneasily situated alongside a rather crude theory of chemical agency (perhaps *pace* Zola), as in his first novel, *Sister Carrie* (1900). London similarly insists on a social Darwinian view of man and his place in nature (London writes in the semi-autobiographical *Martin Eden* of undergoing a kind of intellectual conversion after reading Herbert Spencer, the English philosopher and social scientist whose application of the doctrines of evolution to ethics and the study of human society did much to promote American social Darwinism). For London, naturalism was more a matter of intellectual and scientific authority than it was of literary indebtedness: "I am a hopeless naturalist," he wrote in a letter of June 1914 to Ralph Kaspar, "I see the soul as nothing else than the sum of the activities of the organism plus personal habits, memories, experiences of the organism." In works such as *The Call of the Wild* (1903), *White Fang* (1906), and *Before Adam* (1907), London elaborated his primitivist, often violent, thesis and enjoyed a commercial success denied to almost all his naturalist contemporaries.

Naturalism persisted longer in the American novel than it did in any other national literature. Its traces are found in the fiction of Ernest Hemingway, William Faulkner (notably in his study of familial degeneration in *The Sound and the Fury* [1929]), James T. Farrell, John Steinbeck, Nelson Algren, and the early novels of Saul Bellow (particularly *Dangling Man* [1944] and *The Victim* [1947]). Arguably its most important manifestation in recent years is found in Hubert Selby's grim, "street-level" depiction of Brooklyn life, *Last Exit to Brooklyn* (1964). But in most other countries the "naturalist movement," if it can be so designated, was more or less dead by about 1910, having enjoyed an active life of little more than 40 years. The reasons for this are various, though among them lies the simple fact that artistic revolutions of a formulaic character are by definition ephemeral and quickly exhausted. Naturalism is, above all, a creation of Victorian science and, being a child of science and the scientific outlook, it was therefore acutely vulnerable to those advances in science (particularly in the areas of evolutionary biology, anthropology, and genetics) that would undermine its very intellectual foundations. It asserted, moreover, an account of the relationship between art and science that is philosophically untenable, for it sought to disclaim the importance of the creative imagination and to turn the writing of novels into an act of photographic recording that no self-respecting novelist would find either possible or believable. D.H. Lawrence remarked of Verga that in *Master Don Gesualdo* he is a realist "in the grim Flaubertian sense of the word," but he found this a realism that "has no more to do with reality than romanticism has," since "Realism is just one of the arbitrary views man takes of man" ("Introduction" to *Mastro-Don Gesualdo*, 1928). The same might be said of naturalism, perhaps more so. The criticism of Henry James and others points to the besetting limitations of any fiction grounded in a "theory," especially one so intractably reductivist in its view of the role of the author. Indeed, it is James himself, along with Joseph Conrad, James Joyce, Marcel Proust, and others, who marks the end of naturalism's brief reign while simultaneously enacting the very fiction, essentially modernist in method, that announces its demise.

HENRY CLARIDGE

See also Critics and Criticism (19th Century); English Novel (1880–1920); French Novel (1850–1914); Proletarian Novel; Realism; Rougon-Macquart; Science and the Novel; United States Novel (1850–1900 *and* 1900–1945)

Further Reading

Ahnebrink, Lars, *The Beginnings of Naturalism in American Fiction*, Cambridge, Massachusetts: Harvard University Press, 1950

Becker, George J., editor, *Documents of Modern Literary Realism*, Princeton, New Jersey: Princeton University Press, 1963

Bell, Michael Davitt, *The Problem of American Realism: Studies in the Cultural History of a Literary Idea*, Chicago: University of Chicago Press, 1993

Block, Haskell M., *Naturalistic Triptych: The Fictive and the Real in Zola, Mann, and Dreiser*, New York: Random House, 1970

Brunetière, Ferdinand, *Le Roman naturaliste*, Paris: Levy, 1883

Furst, Lilian R., and Peter N. Skrine, *Naturalism*, London: Methuen, 1971

Grant, Damian, *Realism*, London: Methuen, 1970

Henkin, Leo J., *Darwinism in the English Novel, 1860–1910*, New York: Russell, 1963

Levin, Harry, *The Gates of Horn: A Study of Five French Realists*, New York: Oxford University Press, 1963

Martino, Pierre, *Le Naturalisme Français*, Paris: Colin, 1923

Persons, Stow, editor, *Evolutionary Thought in America*, New Haven, Connecticut: Yale University Press, 1950

Pizer, Donald, *Realism and Naturalism in Nineteenth-Century American Literature*, Carbondale: Southern Illinois University Press, 1966; revised edition, 1984

Salvan, Albert J., *Zola aux Etats-Unis*, Providence, Rhode Island: Brown University Press, 1943

Starkie, Enid, *From Gautier to Eliot: The Influence of France on English Literature, 1851–1939*, London: Hutchinson, 1960

Stromberg, Roland N., editor, *Realism, Naturalism and Symbolism: Modes of Thought and Expression in Europe, 1848–1914*, London: Macmillan, and New York: Harper and Row, 1968

Walcutt, Charles C., *American Literary Naturalism: A Divided Stream*, Minneapolis: University of Minnesota Press, 1956

Zola, Émile, *Le Roman expérimental*, Paris: Charpentier, 1880; as *The Experimental Novel*, New York: Cassell, 1893

Zola, Émile, *Les Romanciers naturalistes*, Paris: Charpentier, 1881

Nature Novel. *See* Environmental Novel

Nausea by Jean-Paul Sartre

La Nausée 1938

When *Nausea* appeared, Jean-Paul Sartre was at an early point in his career as a philosopher and literary critic: he had written none of the dramas that would bring him fame, and he had not yet assumed his later roles of militant political journalist, spokesman, and activist. Whereas from the late 1940s on, his name would be recognized by hundreds of thousands and then millions, in the mid-1930s he was known only to a few, as a teacher and author of short critical pieces and sketchy, although provocative, philosophical essays. This novel, his first, was an initial step in carrying out his youthful resolution to become great through literature. It is now viewed by critics (except hostile ones, still numerous—for he succeeded in his aim of being offensive) as highly original, his best fiction, excepting perhaps the stories collected in *Le Mur* (1939; *The Wall*).

Despite obvious ties between *Nausea* and Sartre's early philosophical positions, the novel is not merely a parable or methodological illustration of the phenomenological existentialism set out in his major treatise, *L'Etre et le néant* (1943; *Being and Nothingness*). It may be viewed, however, as an introduction to the more rigorous treatise. The replacement of the original title, *Melancholia* (a reference to Albrecht Dürer's engraving), by the definitive one may be seen now as a brilliant move: the physiological phenomenon that presides over the novel indicates Sartre's understanding of the mind-body relationship and suggests his horror at the world.

Nausea is a modern work in an antique frame, that of the "found manuscript" in diary form; this 18th-century device suits the contents, since the main character, Roquentin, is supposedly working on a biography of a figure from that period. Excepting explanatory publisher's notes, Roquentin's voice is heard throughout, as he records his few activities, carries out self-analysis, and makes various philosophical discoveries. He is a quintessential antihero, whose antecedents go back to such figures as Gustave Flaubert's Frédéric Moreau in *L'Éducation sentimentale* (1869; *Sentimental Education*), André Gide's narrator in *Paludes* (1895; *Marshlands*), Marcel Proust's narrator in *À la recherche du temps perdu* (1913–27; translated as *Remembrance of Things Past* and also as *In Search of Lost Time*), and Louis-Ferdinand Céline's Bardamu in *Voyage au bout de la nuit* (1932; *Journey to the End of the Night*). (It is known that Sartre read all four writers.) Like these works, *Nausea* is a dissecting of various social, aesthetic, and philosophical errors. Very little happens; Roquentin's adventures are mostly mental, consisting primarily of an increasing awareness of the raw existence of things (a stone, a beer glass) and of his own consciousness, separate, yet clinging to them, unable to wrench itself away and empty itself, spinning out indefinitely its saliva-like thought. These discoveries lead to paralysis of mind, passivity, and nausea. Yet Roquentin is not uninteresting, and the novel is highly inventive, even comic. He wants to follow what may be seen as a philosophical method; but as the world impinges on his perception, his style becomes highly subjective, often poetic (although sometimes coarse, even obscene). His sensitivity to his surroundings is extraordinary; things undergo metamorphosis under his gaze; his paranoia leads to absurd mad dashes through the streets, in a parody of adventure fiction. Sartre's acquaintance with surrealism served him well in Roquentin's stream-of-consciousness musings.

Like Gide's and Proust's narrators, Roquentin struggles with the problem of expressing phenomena in words; unlike Proust's, he ultimately gives up (as biographer and, apparently, as diarist), discovering that language simply does not convey meaning. Better put, there is no meaning. In a passage recalling epiphanies in other novels, he discovers that objects, such as trees in the public garden, exist independently of him, beyond words, beyond ideas and concepts (which do not exist), beyond any human grasp; the mind, sticky as glue and without any being of its own, is invaded by raw, undifferentiated impressions. All are superficial; none is grounded or justified. This discovery is profoundly disgusting. Moreover, human projects are similarly empty, void, and unjustified: Roquentin has no belief in social progress, no understanding of deep personal relationships. (It is ironic that Sartre, who became the philosopher of political commitment, insisting that human beings must use their complete philosophical freedom for politically meaningful purposes, sets forth in *Nausea* only the negative side of human availability.) Art alone, especially music, may offset, as an antireal, the world's powerful denial of human emptiness and desire. (Sartre would later denounce this one remaining value.) In an act of honesty, Roquentin abandons his few activities and ties (including a dead love affair to which he has clung and a vague acquaintance with another loner, whose solitude is both pathetic and hilarious) and acknowledges that existence consists in meaningless, pointless physical functioning. Only fiction—like music, a type of ideal—might justify his existence. That his papers were "found" leaves open the question of what becomes of him; talk about writing a novel is only in the conditional tense, and there is no sign of its existence, unless, in Proustian fashion, it is *Nausea* itself.

Illustrating one mode of philosophical fiction, *Nausea* eschews treating individual psychology and group behavior to examine the very foundations of human existence. Whereas Balzac attempted to embrace in fiction the whole of French society, *Nausea* is embracing in a different way, offering a comprehensive (if not unchallenged) view of human existence by means of a philosophical adventure starting from tabula rasa, carried out by a central consciousness whose contacts with the world and reflection on itself lead to denunciation of bogus humanistic values and recognition of things as they are. Grounded in the concrete, fiction suits Sartre's purposes well, allowing him to show, not merely explain, how he understands existence; he excels in conveying the very feel of things and of embodiment. A radical novel in the strictest sense, since it goes to the root of existence, *Nausea* foreshadows Sartre's postwar radicalism, according to which there can be no salvation in a meaningless world except by a drastic redesigning of human beliefs, structures, and relationships through political revolution.

CATHARINE SAVAGE BROSMAN

Further Reading

Aronson, Ronald, and Adrian van den Hoven, editors, *Sartre Alive*, Detroit, Michigan: Wayne State University Press, 1991

Brosman, Catharine Savage, *Jean-Paul Sartre*, Boston: Twayne, 1983

Champigny, Robert, *Stages on Sartre's Way*, Bloomington: Indiana University Press, 1959

Falk, Eugene, *Types of Thematic Structure: The Nature and Function of Motifs in Gide, Camus, and Sartre*, Chicago: University of Chicago Press, 1967

Frohock, Wilbur M., *Style and Temper: Studies in French Fiction, 1925–1960*, Cambridge, Massachusetts: Harvard University Press, and Oxford: Blackwell, 1967

Kellman, Steven G., *The Self-Begetting Novel*, New York: Columbia University Press, and London: Macmillan, 1980

Kermode, Frank, *The Sense of an Ending: Studies in the Theory of Fiction*, New York: Oxford University Press, 1967; London: Oxford University Press, 1968

Leak, Andrew N., *The Perverted Consciousness: Sexuality and Sartre*, London: Macmillan, and New York: St. Martin's Press, 1989

Nuttall, A.D., *A Common Sky: Philosophy and the Literary Imagination*, Berkeley: University of California Press, and London: Chatto and Windus, 1974

Thody, Philip, *Jean-Paul Sartre*, New York: St. Martin's, and London: Macmillan, 1992

Wardman, Harold W., *Jean-Paul Sartre: The Evolution of His Thought and Art*, Lewiston, New York: Edwin Mellen Press, 1992

Nedjma by Kateb Yacine

1956

In 1956, at the height of the Algerian war of independence (1954–62), Editions du Seuil in Paris published a novel by a young Algerian writer, Kateb Yacine. The novel, entitled *Nedjma*, was an immediate and stunning success. Not only was it authored by a colonized person from a country that had reaped the benefits and suffered the humiliations of the French policies of "assimilation" and the "civilizing mission" applied to governance of her colonies; it was also a novel that seemed to come out of nowhere, so to speak, for the literature in French by native Algerians that had begun to burgeon around 1950 consisted mostly of what are termed "ethnographic novels," in which the writers tend to describe in straightforward terms local habits and personal lives in narratives destined primarily for consumption in Europe.

Nedjma, characterized by a powerful vision, a fragmented style, and an authoritative manipulation of French, was a product of Kateb's own intellectual development and his obsession with the figure of Nedjma, a cousin whom he loved but could not properly court, about whom he had been writing since 1948 when a poem seminal to his overall work, "Nedjma ou le poème ou le couteau," appeared in *Mercure de France*. But the novel *Nedjma* also seemed to share some common ground with the writing of the fledgling *nouveau roman* (New Novel) emerging in Paris. Indeed, in *Le nouveau roman* (1973; The New Novel),

Jean Ricardou—apologist and self-proclaimed guru of the *nouveaux romanciers*—includes Kateb's *Nedjma* in an extensive list of contemporary works in which he says one can find *traces de nouveauté* (traces of newness) in comparison to the academic novel.

To be sure, the fractured lens through which objects and especially time are distorted in Kateb's work provide us with a facile link to the Parisian school. Yet *Nedjma* is more properly understood as a reflection of the fertile imagination of the young Algerian and as an indication of his ability to translate into discourse and narrative structure the violence surrounding him during the pre-Revolution years (he claimed to have discovered his two great loves, poetry and revolution, when, still a schoolboy, he was imprisoned after the demonstrations turned to rioting and massacres in Eastern Algeria on 8 May 1945) and during the early years of the Algerian war.

Kateb did, it is true, draw inspiration from a literary ancestor who was also admired by Robbe-Grillet and other *nouveaux romanciers*: William Faulkner. At first loath to acknowledge an influence many readers sensed in his work, Kateb admitted in lectures and interviews later in his life that Faulkner was the most important influence on his style of writing. The deep-lying passion and eroticism, the violence and such turpitudes as incest, and the decadence and pervasive sense of doom and isolation that we find in Faulkner's special Mississippi world parallel Kateb's portrayal—in *Nedjma* and other works such as *Le Polygone étoilé* (1966; The Stellated Polygon) that resulted from his salvaging of extensive cuts that the editors at Editions du Seuil requested he make in the excessively long manuscript of *Nedjma* first submitted to the publisher—of the decadent remnants of the ancestral Keblouti clan.

The novel came as a surprise to the metropolitan critics who did not expect such a powerful and sophisticated work to come from the pen of a writer in the colonized Arab-Berber population. The text was sufficiently alien to European readers that the editors provided a preface that has, in itself, remained a subject of controversy owing to its generalities concerning the alleged dynamics of Arab thought:

> The narrative techniques Kateb Yacine uses are occasionally disconcerting to the Western reader. The latter, as a last resort, will take refuge in the subtleties of comparative literature to exorcise the mystery: apropos of *Nedjma*, some readers will undoubtedly cite Faulkner. It seems to us that the explanation of this novel's singularities are to be found elsewhere. The narrative's rhythm and construction, if they indisputably owe something to certain Western experiments in fiction, result in chief from a purely Arab notion of *man in time*. Western thought moves in *linear* duration, whereas Arab thought develops in a *circular* duration, each turn a *return,* mingling future and past in the eternity of the moment.

If there is a small element of truth in this assumption of relative mentalities, it is yet a fact that Maghribī readers and critics find it typically "Orientalist" and possibly designed to diminish the fundamental originality of the work.

At a colloquium held in Philadelphia in March 1988, in response to a question about the structure of *Nedjma*, Kateb explained the discontinuity of the work by drawing a line on the blackboard from left to right, saying that he had a certain narrative itinerary to follow from point A to point Z. He embarked on this path only to find that there were things he wanted to plumb, from ancient Berber history to recent political events, so that he would descend along vertical lines to these substrata and return to the A–Z story line, only to descend again and again to one or another of the substrata to add further elements.

The structure of *Nedjma*—which Kateb acknowledges is suggestive of a timepiece owing to the novel's numbering of sections that sometimes contain 12 subchapters and other times 24 subchapters numbered twice from I to XII—has been the cause of heated debate and critical casuistry in numerous books and articles by scholars such as Arnaud (1982), Gontard (1985), and Bonn (1990).

The plot of *Nedjma* is difficult to follow, owing to the quilt-like structure of its episodes. Indeed, scholars have even ex-

changed barbs over the chronological sequence as they see it unfolding behind the various vignettes. The editors who suggested differences between Western and Arab thought durations came to the conclusion—not incompatible with Kateb's own description of an A–Z trajectory interrupted by descents going back to different levels of history—that "we cannot follow *Nedjma*'s plot development, but rather its involution: the passage from one level of consciousness to another is effected by a kind of intellectual slide down spirals of indefinite length." They decided that the wary reader may require the "guarantee" of a summary and so provided one with the warning that "in truth it summarizes nothing, merely piling up blocks which, as such, will never make a house."

The story of *Nedjma*, set as it is against the backdrop of the revolution, has also been interpreted as a metaphorical paradigm defining the complex obscurities and interactions of Algeria's colonial past and its quest for self-determination and the recovery of an identity sabotaged by the colonial presence: *nedjma* means "star" and is, like the crescent, an emblem of national identity.

Nedjma has, since its publication, been acclaimed by many as the "Great North African Novel," and the work exerted a strong influence on a generation of writers in Africa and elsewhere in the Third World. Today younger readers in an Algeria in turmoil and faced with other imminent problems are sometimes unable to share the excitement or sense the provocative political pertinence that *Nedjma* stimulated in readers in the immediate post–World War II intellectual climate. Nevertheless, *Nedjma* was the first Maghribī novel to be instantly recognized as a classic in the pantheon of world literature, a stature it maintains to this day.

ERIC SELLIN

Further Reading

Aresu, Bernard, introduction to *Nedjma*, by Kateb Yacine, Charlottesville: University Press of Virginia, 1991

Aresu, Bernard, *Counterhegemonic Discourse from the Maghreb: The Poetics of Kateb's Fiction,* Tübingen: Günter Narr, 1993

Arnaud, Jacqueline, *Recherches sur la littérature maghrébine de langue française: Le cas de Kateb Yacine,* volume 2, Lille: Université Lille III, 1982

Aurbakken, Kristine, *L'étoile d'araignée: Une lecture de "Nedjma" de Kateb Yacine,* Paris: Publisud, 1986

Bonn, Charles, *Kateb Yacine: "Nedjma,"* Paris: Presses Universitaires de France, 1990

Bonn, Charles, editor, *Bibliographie Kateb Yacine,* Paris and Montreal: L'Harmattan, 1997

Gontard, Marc, *"Nedjma" de Kateb Yacine: Essai sur la structure formelle du roman,* Paris: L'Harmattan, 1985

Raybaud, Antoine, "Poème(s) éclaté(s) de Kateb Yacine," *Revue de l'Occident Musulman et Méditerranéen* 22 (1976)

Netherlandish Novel

At the end of the 16th century, the political entity of the Low Countries disintegrated into two parts. The seven northern provinces constituted an independent state, the protestant Republic of the United Netherlands. The Catholic southern provinces, or Flanders, which then consisted of what is now Belgium as well as part of the northern province of France, rapidly decayed into a distant territory of Spain, later ruled by Austria. The political reorganization of the Dutch Republic was paralleled by the so-called "Golden Age," a period of intense cultural activity, to which immigrants from the south contributed greatly. As a consequence of the talent drain to the north, cultural life in the south suffered serious setbacks for several centuries. This divergence in the Dutch-speaking provinces persisted until the end of the 19th century.

Holland had a strong tradition of vernacular prose fiction, rooted in late 15th-century chapbooks, which by the end of the 18th century gave rise to a large variety of popular genres. These included picaresque tales, adventure stories, stories of women disguised as men, erotic tales, imaginary travel narratives (often used as a vehicle of social criticism), and crime stories. The more realistic vein was introduced by Justus van Effen, a great admirer of Jonathan Swift, who founded *De Hollandsche Spectator* in 1731, a journal modeled after *The Spectator* of Joseph Addison and Richard Steele. The journal contained commentary on subjects of topical interest and included short fiction, both modes playing an important formative role in the development of realistic prose narrative.

The Dutch epistolary novel of manners emerged in the 1750s, but the real success of the genre is due to the publication, in 1782, of *De Historie van Mejuffrouw Sara Burgerhart* (The History of Miss Sara Burgerhart), written by two women, Elizabeth Wolff and Aagje Deken. Although the epistolary genre was modeled on Samuel Richardson's *Pamela* (1740) and *Clarissa* (1747–48), the authors wrote an original and very lively novel, in which they introduced a network of 24 correspondents around the main character. These correspondents comment in various styles not only on Sara's letters, but also on many different subjects of daily and more general interest. The novel recounts the life story of Sara Burgerhart, a young and intelligent orphan who is educated by her aunt. Sara escapes from the "narrow" milieu in which she grows up and turns to a life of adventures. In the course of the novel, she falls into the hands of a rascal, but in the end she is respectably married to a man named Edeling (the name, which means "nobleman," is indicative of his noble character). The novel faithfully depicts everyday life, but this realist impulse is overshadowed by the novel's bourgeois morality—Sara's ultimate purpose in life is an honorable middle-class domesticity, symbolized by the name Burgerhart, or "bourgeois heart," where bourgeois is a term of praise. *Sara Burgerhart* thus illustrates with exceptional clarity the middle-class origin of the modern Dutch novel.

Quite remarkably, the sentimental epistolary novel *Julia* (1783) by Rhijnvis Feith proved equally successful at the time. One could hardly imagine a contrast more sharp than the one between those two novels. While the reader knows everything about the circumstances of Sara's life, Julia's remains wholly undefinable. She lives entirely in her feelings for her friend Eduard.

Julia is a masterpiece of the literature of sentiment, characterized by a style that avoids naming emotions so as to intimate their transcendent boundlessness and fluidity. Punctuation marks such as hyphens, ellipsis points, and exclamation points are pressed into service to evoke the unnamable. The irrationality of this sentimentalism met with the derision of contemporary critics but was avidly received by a broad reading public.

In contrast with the realistic concerns of *Sara Burgerhart*, *Julia* foreshadows the motifs and themes of romantic literature. Julia and Eduard preferably meet in cemeteries on gloomy tombstones, and Julia eventually dies as a result of being parted from her (spiritual) lover. Nevertheless, both *Julia* and *Sara Burgerhart* have the same didactic purpose. Both novels bring home the message of "virtue rewarded" and were intended to edify the young and to urge middle-class 18th-century morality on their readers. The educational aims of these novels are typical of the genre in this early phase of its development. By the end of the 18th century, a new middle class was reading popular scientific works and informative periodicals. But the novel, gaining in popularity and discussed in ever-growing reading circles, still carried the brand of frivolity, which, it was feared, would undermine the morals of the young women who formed the novel's most enthusiastic audience. For the wide reading public the new genre was then still associated with the fear that the morality of the Age of Reason should be undermined. The often heavy-handed moralizing compensates for the suspicion in which the genre was held.

The realism and the plea for domestic virtue were to form the mainstream of the novel in the Netherlands. Initially, however, the influence of sentimentalism proved stronger. Feith's *Julia* was imitated by Elisabeth Post in *Het Land* (1788; The Land), a very successful novel that, improbably, glamorizes country life. But Post's novel leaves some space for reason. In addition, *Reinhart; of, Natuur en godsdienst* (1793; Reinhart; or, Nature and Religion), set in Latin America and dealing with colonialism and slavery, shows Post's interests in material reality. The most "modern" and independent, nonconformist writer of the age, however, was Belle van Zuylen, better known in the French-speaking world as Isabel de Charrière. She was of Dutch origin, but, having married a Swiss, she lived in Switzerland most of her adult life. She published widely but wrote exclusively in French. Her best and best known work is *Caliste; ou, Suite des lettres écrites de Lausanne* (1787; Caliste, or Sequel to the Letters Written from Lausanne).

During the French domination of the Low Countries, from the 1790s until 1813, the economy suffered both in the north and in the south. French rule manifested itself by a repression of national cultural life and the imposition of strict censorship. The climate was not favorable to literature. Nevertheless, the very same situation contributed to the success of the first historical novel in the Netherlands, Adriaan Loosjes' *Het leven van Maurits Lijnslager* (1808; The Life of Maurits Lijnslager), in which the author evokes the brilliant period of the "Golden Age." Unlike the later historical novel inspired by Scott, *Maurits Lijnslager* did not aim to portray an age and its culture. Rather, it harked back to more prosperous times in order to "divert" the mind from the "calamities" to which the nation had fallen victim.

In the Netherlands, as elsewhere in Europe, the historical novel became enormously popular as a result of the widely imitated work of Walter Scott. Jacob van Lennep, Scott's first follower in the Netherlands, focused on 14th-century medieval history in his popular novel *De roos van Dekama* (1836; The Rose of Dekama). The influence of Scott is clear in Van Lennep's copious descriptions of market and war scenes and in the touches of obviously scrupulously investigated local color. Van Lennep's most outstanding novel is *Ferdinand Huyck* (1840), which might be called a novel of adventure as well as a historical novel. Van Lennep is above all a storyteller who succeeds in captivating his readers with intricate plots and rousing adventures.

The historical novel presented itself in different guises. With *Hermingard van de Eikenterpen* (1832; Hermingard of the Oak-Hills), Arnout Drost wrote a historical novel of ideas that deals with a meticulously documented past in pagan Roman times but is equally concerned with propagating an evangelical Christianity. (Drost was a representative of the so-called *Réveil* movement, a protestant romantic religious movement that stressed personal devotion and brotherly love.) The most important historical novel of the period, however, was written by a woman, A.L.G. (Geertrui) Bosboom Toussaint. Her *Het huis Lauernesse* (The House of Lauernesse), published in 1840, was set in the period of the Reformation, in the first years of the reign of Charles V, when the Inquisition was claiming its first victims in the Low Countries. Besides being novels of ideas, the historical works of Bosboom Toussaint may also be characterized as psychological novels. Her major work was the trilogy *Leycester,* set in the late 16th century, when the Earl of Leicester was sent to the Netherlands as governor by Queen Elizabeth. In one of her last novels, *Majoor Frans* (Major Frans), published in 1874, Toussaint chose a modern setting and pictured the development of the main character, a passionate young girl, in a more modern, dynamic manner.

In the south, meanwhile, vernacular literature survived to a large extent, mainly because of the continuing influence of the Chambers of Rhetoric that had taken over the organization of literary life in the early 16th century. During the short reunion of the Low Countries, from 1815 to 1830, in the Kingdom of the Netherlands, Flemish intellectuals enjoyed a brief period of near-autonomy. However, soon after the formation of the Nation of Belgium (constituted by a Dutch-speaking part in the north and a French-speaking part in the south), Flemish culture was again rigidly gallicized. Yet from this new nation emerged a writer, Hendrik Conscience, who was fully representative of the international romantic movement and its genre *par excellence,* the historical novel. Conscience's father was of French descent, and the author was a dedicated Francophile and admirer of the French novelist Victor Hugo. But Conscience wrote in Dutch (his mother was Flemish). A spokesman for the nascent Flemish nationalism, he also became "the man who taught his people to read." He wrote 100 novels and attained a tremendous popularity that lasted until well after World War II. By then, the ideals of the Catholic Flemish movement he stood for had become obsolete, and his works were demoted to children's literature.

Conscience's debut, *In 't Wonderjaer* (1837; The Year of Miracles), was the first historical novel to be written in Belgium. Set in the 16th century, it glorifies the liberation struggle of the Sea Beggars (a loosely organized seaborne guerrilla movement) against the Spanish rulers in 1566. Conscience's best known novel is *De leeuw van Vlaenderen* (The Lion of Flanders), pub-

lished in 1838 and describing the victory of a small group of Flemish warriors over a well-organized French army in the Battle of the Golden Spurs in 1302. Locating Flemish identity in this glorious past, the novel is virtually a manifesto for the Flemish movement. While its heroes have no psychological depth and both plot and style are quite deficient, yet the novel has a vision and conveys a depth of conviction that soon turned it into a national epos. After publishing *Jacob van Artevelde* (1849), technically his best novel, set in the Middle Ages and again glorifying the martial exploits of a popular Flemish hero, Conscience turned to different genres, such as the novel of manners and regional work that glorifies the idylls of country life.

The most successful prose work of the 19th century in the Netherlands was not a historical novel but a *roman à clef: Max Havelaar,* published in 1860 by Multatuli, pseudonym (meaning "I suffered greatly") of Eduard Douwes Dekker, who had tried to make a career in the colonial administration of the former Dutch Indies. The political impact of the book was enormous, and it is still discussed today. *Max Havelaar* is a bitter complaint against the colonial policy of the Netherlands in Indonesia, which encouraged local rulers to squeeze the native population and disavowed all responsibility for the resulting misery while taking the lion's share of the wealth. Dekker had been dismissed and wrote *Max Havelaar* to rehabilitate himself: the eponymous hero, an idealistic young man who tries to change the system, is Dekker's romanticized self-portrait. The immediate and lasting success of the novel is now attributed to its literary qualities more than to its message. From a purely literary point of view, the events at Lebak that lead to Havelaar's resignation are narrated in a manner that was at first thought to be very incoherent but in fact has a strikingly modern feel. Dekker makes use of three narrators and even more layers of narration. At the end, the implied author Multatuli breaks through the frame of narration, dismisses his narrators as his own despicable creatures, and explicitly addresses himself to the reader in order to plead his cause. *Max Havelaar* caused an uproar that has never been matched since by any novel written in Dutch. The book was widely read and translated (twice into English). Douwes Dekker, who was never rehabilitated as a colonial administrator, enjoyed his celebrity as an author and continued to write. The most complete expression of his rebellious and romantic personality is to be found in his seven-volume *Ideën* (1862–77; Ideas), a miscellaneous work in which he vents his opinions in essays, stories, dramatized scenes, and even a novel of childhood, *Woutertje Pieterse.*

With the exception of *Max Havelaar,* mainstream fiction during the second half of the 19th century in the Netherlands is in a realistic vein, plainly narrated. This realism has a *Biedermeier* touch, however, as it seems to have brought about a compromise with the dominant idealistic poetics of the time, which demanded an embellishing representation of reality. The first half of the century had produced a painstaking fidelity to everyday reality, as in the *Betuwsche novellen* (1856; Novellas from the Betuwe) by J.J. Cremer and the humoristic *Camera obscura* (1839) by Nicolaas Beets and *Studententypen* (1839–41; Student Types) by Johan Kneppelhout. Their manner of "copying everyday life" was criticized by the leading critic of the time, J. Potgieter, for its lack of "higher ideals." Although some accommodations were made in the second half of the century, the focus on small-scale domestic life set the standard for the Dutch realist tradition until today. In the south, a similar form of realism prevailed in the work of Anton Bergmann, who published *Ernest Staes, Advocaat* (Ernest Staes, Lawyer) in 1874, and in the novellas of Rosalie and Virginie Loveling. However, Virginie Loveling later published provocative political novels in which she criticized the intolerance of the young Catholic clergy in the Flemish countryside. Thus she established a tradition of social criticism that was to remain characteristic of Flemish prose in general and is evident in the work of 19th-century novelists such as Eugeen Zetternam, P.F. van Kerckhoven and in the 20th century in the novels of Cyriel Buysse, Gerard Walschap, Louis Paul Boon, Walter van den Broeck, and Monika van Paemel.

In *Een Vlaamsche jongen* (A Flemish Boy), published in 1879 by Wazenaar (pseudonym of Amand de Vos), both the "harsh" realism and the omission of the traditional happy ending anticipate the breakthrough of naturalism. However, naturalism was first introduced in the Netherlands by Marcellus Emants and Frans Netscher, a direct follower of Émile Zola. Dutch and Flemish naturalism, with its focus on biological determinism, is intimately related to fin-de-siècle decadence that expresses itself as a fascination with perversion, morbidity, family secrets, mental illness, and an obsessive interest in sensual experience. A new type of hero emerged—the hypersensuous, nervous, and oversensitive protagonist whose life story consisted of a gradual and absolute disillusionment and ended in suicide. The main representatives of the genre were Lodewijk van Deyssel's *Een liefde* (1887; A Love), Marcellus Emants' *Juffrouw Lina* (1888; Miss Lina), Louis Couperus' *Eline Vere* (1889) and a few years later Frederik van Eeden's *Van de koele meren des doods* (1900; *The Deeps of Deliverance*).

The prose works of Herman Heijermans, who was above all a playwright, introduced a significant variant of realism, which allowed for a strong social commitment. His *Kamertjeszonde* (1899; Chamber Sin) evoked severe protest because of its "overt" discussion of sexuality and its criticism of contemporary conjugal ethics. His social realism links him with Belgian naturalism as practised by Cyriel Buysse, Stijn Streuvels, Gustaaf Vermeersch, and Reimond Stijns. As was the case with other naturalist novels, Buysse's *Het recht van de sterkste* (1893; The Law of the Strongest), which opens with the description of a rape, proved to be very offensive to the reading public, which by then consisted for the most part of middle-class ladies who gathered in reading circles.

For the greatest novelists who emerged in the 1890s, decadence soon won out over naturalism. A typical case is that of Louis Couperus, whose novels are still widely read today. *De stille kracht* (1900; The Silent Force), set in Indonesia where Couperus had lived, describes the complete disintegration of the main character as a result of his incapacity to deal with magic oriental forces. His subsequent novels dissect small sections of Dutch society, especially the close-knit circles of repatriated colonial families in The Hague, whose lives are still completely dominated by their Indonesian experience, as in *Van oude mensen, de dingen die voorbijgaan* (1906; *Old People and the Things That Pass*). Couperus later considered these "psychological, bourgeois novels" irrelevant and took to writing historical novels, all situated in Greek and Roman antiquity. To him, antiquity was synonymous with freedom and *joie de vivre,* a world in which he could express his own androgynous personality. Clearly *De berg van licht* (1905–06; The Mountain of Light) stands in the romantic-decadent tradition of Charles Baudelaire,

Remy De Gourmont, Théophile Gautier, Oscar Wilde, Alfred Bruce Douglas, and Algernon Charles Swinburne. The novel depicts the life and decay of the child-emperor Heliogabalus, the incarnation of a supreme androgynous being whose superhuman love cannot possibly be realized on earth.

Between 1890 and 1920 a more or less coherent artistic movement grew out of a reaction against naturalism. Only in German historiography is the term *neoromanticism* officially accepted as the name of this international movement. The Dutch reaction against impressionism and naturalism was clearly marked by such neoromantic tendencies. Neoromantic novels were located in unreal, vaguely indicated historical and exotic settings and took as their central theme the longing to escape from a fixed petty bourgeois existence. Several novelists explored new, distant, and preferably mysterious worlds and reinforced the mystery of their settings in a vague and suggestive style related to symbolism. Some of the early works of Couperus can be associated with this movement, as can the short stories of the Flemish symbolist poet Karel van de Woestijne, including *Janus met het dubbele voorhoofd* (1918; Janus Bifrons) and *De bestendige aanwezigheid* (1928; The Permanent Presence). The early prose works of Arthur van Schendel also belong to the neoromantic vein. His *Een zwerver verliefd* (1904; A Wanderer in Love) and its sequel *Een zwerver verdwaald* (1907; A Wanderer Lost) introduce the main character Tamalone, a lonely wanderer who is driven by a vague, undefinable desire and remains entirely indifferent to the people surrounding him. Van Schendel's early prose was widely appreciated for the simplicity and the natural suggestiveness of its style. A more short-lived success was that of *Quia absurdum* (1906) by Nico van Suchtelen. The novel's central theme is the longing for an unattainable dream, and the main character collapses under the weight of the discrepancies between his ideals and his experience of an absurd reality.

In 1930 Arthur van Schendel published *Het Fregatschip Johanna Maria* (The Frigate Johanna Maria), which marked a return to classic realism. It was to be followed by a number of novels with a contemporary Dutch setting and a cast of middle-class characters: *Een Hollands drama* (1935; A Dutch Tragedy) and *De grauwe vogels* (1937; The Grey Birds). A similar turn to realism had already taken place earlier in the work of the Flemish naturalists Cyriel Buysse and Stijn Streuvels, although Buysse's realist novels were not recognized as such for decades. To Buysse's classics of psychological realism belong *'t Bolleken* (1905; The Little Ball), which tells the life story of a *bon vivant* with great relativizing humor, and *Tantes* (1926; The Aunts), which brings into conflict two generations of nieces who have withdrawn from life. Streuvels' work, by contrast, was immediately successful. Concerned with the Flemish rural population living in constant struggle with nature, his work evinces a broad, even cosmic, vision influenced by his reading of German, Scandinavian, and Russian novelists and later also of English and French ones. Streuvels' undisputed masterpiece is *De vlaschaard* (1907; The Flax Field), in which the human struggle for survival in nature is shaped by the conflict between a father and his son. In *De teleurgang van de Waterhoek* (1927; The Fall of Water's Edge), Streuvels records the disintegration of a closed rural Flemish community by the spread of industrialization.

Dutch realism was qualified by remnants of naturalism. Fate was still the dominant theme in the works of J. Van Oudshoorn, but a new, milder realism came to the fore in a number of novels depicting bourgeois family life by Herman Robbers, Ina Boudier-Bakker, Nescio (pseudonym of J.H.F. Grönloh), and the Fleming Willem Elsschot. The latter two wrote prose that was too "modern" and exceptional to be widely appreciated by contemporary readers, however. Nescio's oeuvre is collected in *Dichtertje. De uitvreter. Titaantjes* (1918; The Little Poet. Eating Out. Tiny Titans), in which he portrays some unforgettable idealistic revolutionaries who are unable to adapt themselves to society. Nescio's unaffected, ironic style shows similarities with the work of Elsschot, whose debut in 1913 with *Villa des Roses* went virtually unnoticed. In *Lijmen* (1924; *Soft Soap*) and *Het been* (1938; *The Leg*), both autobiographical novels of business life, Elsschot presents two opposing "universal" characters: Laarmans, a benevolent but rather soft and helpless man, who confronts the cynical, business man Boorman, who does not shun fraud.

Elsschot's style is distantly related to the "Nieuwe Zakelijkheid" ("Neue Sachlichkeit" or New Objectivity), which was dominant in the period between the world wars. Several Dutch novelists were affected by this new style, which presented itself as a significant variant of high modernism. The most important, if not fully representative, of the genre was Ferdinand Bordewijk, who wrote an early dystopian novel in *Blokken* (1930; Blocks), a metaphor for a dictatorial state. The strength of Bordewijk's characterization lies in his grotesque foregrounding of minute details and his tendency to endow human behavior with animal traits. His best known work is *Karakter* (1938; *Character*), which tells the story of a merciless father who tries to subdue his natural son, supposedly in order to strengthen his character.

The Dutch novel of the interbellum period was clearly influenced by the French analytical novel. Its variants were the psychological novel and the novel of ideas, all of them focusing on the individual, his inner conflicts, and his conflicts with society. Eddy du Perron, coeditor of the famous periodical *Forum* and a novelist himself, was the most authoritative critic of the time, together with his friend Menno ter Braak. Du Perron was a great admirer of André Malraux, who dedicated *La Condition humaine* (1933; *Man's Fate*) to him. The title of this novel came to function as a manifesto for its generation. Protagonists often turned out to be antiheroes, meditating on their fate and obsessed by their defeats. Above all, however, the interbellum generation judged its authors according to the strength of their temperament or personality. In Flemish literature, the analytical novel was represented by Maurice Roelants and Gerard Walschap, known for his problematization of Catholic faith. (Herman Teirlinck, however, much closer to the turn-of-the-century spirit, was then writing his classic "vitalistic" and psychological novels.) The most prolific writer coming to the fore in the Netherlands in the 1930s was Simon Vestdijk. His oeuvre is usually divided into autobiographical novels, historical novels, novels of fantasy, and psychological novels, but no classification will ever come to terms with the variety of his work. Vestdijk's approach to his characters can easily be traced in all of them: he is concerned with finding out who and what they are and what their place or role is in the society they live in. In *De koperen tuin* (1950; *The Garden Where the Brass Band Played*), a contemporary Bildungsroman, as well as in *Het vijfde zegel* (1937; The Fifth Seal), a novel about the painter El Greco, Vestdijk tries to penetrate the inner reality of his characters. In addition, his historical novels provide an elaborate picture of the age they are set in, including food, drinking, and dressing habits. Above all, Vestdijk became famous for a series of

eight autobiographical novels, *Anton Wachter,* named after the central character. His lasting success is confirmed by his influence on later generations, including the most prominent contemporary writer of historical novels, Hella Haasse.

The postwar novel is dominated by the traumatic experiences of violence, chaos, and disillusion, and it is directly or indirectly linked with existentialist philosophy. The theme of war and the common feeling that life is absurd are central and omnipresent. Moreover, the process of dealing with the traumatic results of the war has not yet come to an end. Writers such as Harry Mulisch and Hugo Claus, Hellema (pseudonym of Alexander Bernard van Praag), and G.L. Durlacher, but also representatives of the younger generation, such as Leon de Winter, Marcel Möring, and Arnon Grünberg, are still trying to come to terms with the past. In the immediate postwar period the direct representation of the invasion and occupation was at the center of attention, as in Simon Vestdijk's *Pastorale 1943* (1948) and Alfred Kossmann's *De nederlaag* (1950; The Defeat), but gradually the historical events became the setting, the background against which more general problems were dealt with. The generation that came to the fore in the late 1940s presents a very pessimistic worldview, depicting mankind in decline and without any prospects. One exception in this atmosphere of general nausea is the magic realism developed by the Fleming Johan Daisne in *De trap van steen en wolken* (1942; The Staircase of Stone and Clouds) and in *De man die zijn haar kort liet knippen* (1947; The Man Who Had His Hair Cut Short), both of which offer an escape from a reality devoid of illusion. After Daisne, this interweaving of myth and reality was further to achieve success in the early works of Hubert Lampo.

The postwar worldview was presented in its most provocative gloominess by G.K. van het Reve. In his debut, *De avonden* (1947; The Evenings), younger readers discovered a self-portrait in the discontented, rudderless main character, Frits van Egters, whereas the older generation was shocked by the young man's ultimate lack of intellectual ambition. The ten chapters describe ten evenings in his life, in which he listlessly and indifferently watches others, only showing some critical interest in symptoms of decay and decomposition. Willem Frederik Hermans struck the nihilistic key in a different way. From his debut onwards he criticized any form of ideology, including religion, as collective insanity. From his early masterpieces, *De tranen der acacia's* (1949; The Tears of the Acacias) and *De donkere kamer van Damokles* (1958; *The Dark Room of Damocles*), he dealt with the unknowability of man, the central theme of his work. In addition, he criticized the general belief that the Dutch had effectively resisted the German oppressor. Hermans shows the ambiguities of the human situation by a subtle manipulation of narrative point of view. Hermans' "nihilistic universe" finds a close equivalent in the fictional world of the Fleming Louis Paul Boon, who pursued a unique combination of technical innovation and political and social commitment. In *Mijn kleine oorlog* (1947; My Little War) he cast his shocking war experiences in the form of fragmented reportage and documentary, "to kick the people into gaining a conscience." The fragmentation suggests the chaos of contemporary society, and Boon used the technique on a larger scale in the diptych *De Kapellekensbaan* (1953; *Chapel Road*) and *Zomer te Ter-Muren* (1956; Summer at Ter-Muren).

Hugo Claus and Ivo Michiels brought about further technical innovations. Claus made his debut with *De Metsiers* (1950;

Duck Hunt), inspired by Faulkner's *As I Lay Dying* (1930). Claus' ambitious war novel, *De verwondering* (1962; Wonderment) received a late sequel in *Het verdriet van België* (1983; *The Sorrow of Belgium*), a postmodern masterpiece that can be read on different levels and traces the narrow-mindedness of the average Belgian, exemplified by the (autobiographical) portrait of the young protagonist and his family.

Harry Mulisch began his career in a lighthearted manner, expressing himself in bizarre phantasies. But he, too, soon turned to the war problem and the recurrent question of guilt and retaliation. *Het stenen bruidsbed* (1959; *The Stone Bridal Bed*) tells the story of an American bomber crew member during the war who returns several years later to Dresden, which he helped to destroy. Coping with traumatic war experiences was also the central theme in *De aanslag* (1982; *The Assault*). Mulisch's major accomplishment is *De ontdekking van de hemel* (1992; *The Discovery of Heaven*), which has a plot that turns on the notion that the proof of divine presence on earth has to be returned to heaven. The construction allows for a hard-edged critique of the bankruptcy of the "central values" of our era.

Contemporary writers who appeared on the literary scene in the late 1970s and the 1980s were above all marked by the style introduced in the periodical *Revisor,* in which reality and its representations are questioned in many different ways in true postmodern fashion. Meanwhile, realism persists at the same time that autobiographical writing appears to become paramount.

ANNE MARIE MUSSCHOOT

See also Belgian Novel

Further Reading

Anbeek, Ton, *Na de oorlog: De Nederlandse roman, 1945–1960,* Amsterdam: Arbeiderspers, 1986

Anbeek, Ton, *Geschiedenis van de Nederlandse literatuur tussen 1885 en 1985,* Amsterdam: Arbeiderspers, 1990; 3rd edition, 1991

Bousset, Hugo, and Theo Hermans, editors, "New Flemish Fiction," *The Review of Contemporary Fiction* 14:2 (Summer 1994)

Drop, W., *Verbeelding en historie: Verschijningsvormen van de Nederlandse historische roman, in de negentiende eeuw,* Assen: Van Gorcum, 1958; 2nd edition, Utrecht: HES, 1972

Goedegebuure, Jaap, *Nederlandse literatuur 1960–1988,* Amsterdam: Arbeiderspers, 1989

Goedegebuure, Jaap, and Anne Marie Musschoot, *Contemporary Fiction of the Low Countries,* Rekkem: Stichting Ons Erfdeel, 1991; 2nd revised edition, 1995

Kemp, Bernard, *Van "In 't wonderjaer" tot "De verwondering": Een poëtica van de Vlaamse roman,* Antwerp: Nederlandsche Boekhandel, 1969; 2nd edition, 1974

Meijer, Reinder P., *Literature of the Low Countries: A Short History of Dutch Literature in the Netherlands and Belgium,* Assen: Van Gorcum, and New York: Twayne, 1971; new edition, Cheltenham: Stanley Thornes, and Boston: Nijhoff, 1978

Rutten, Mathieu, and Jean Weisgerber, editors, *Van "Arm Vlaanderen" tot "De voorstad groeit": De opbloei van de Vlaamse literatuur van Teirlinck-Stijns tot L.P. Boon (1888–1946),* Antwerp: Standaard, 1988

Schenkeveld-Van der Dussen, Maria A., and Ton Anbeek, editors, *Nederlandse literatuur: Een geschiedenis,* Groningen: Nijhoff, 1993

Stouten, J., *Verlichting in de letteren,* Leiden: Nijhoff, 1984

Weisgerber, Jean, *Formes et domaines du roman flamand, 1927–1960,* Brussels: La Renaissance du Livre, 1963; as *Aspecten van de Vlaamse roman, 1927–1960,* Amsterdam: Polak and Van Gennep, 1964

New Criticism. *See* Critics and Criticism: 20th Century

New Humor Novel

The phenomenon that came to be known as New Humor first surfaced in the late 1880s, when English writers like Barry Pain, William Pett Ridge, W.W. Jacobs, Jerome K. Jerome, and Israel Zangwill began to publish short stories and sketches in popular periodicals. Prior to these productions, English humor had tended to have an aristocratic slant, requiring a certain minimum of literary knowledge and education to be appreciated. The New Humorists were the first generation of writers who benefited from W.E. Forster's Education Act of 1870, which spawned a multitude of new readers. While not as sophisticated as earlier Britons, these consumers created a book and magazine buying market that provided unprecedented earning capacity in the field of literature. Employing lower-class subject matter, heavy use of accurate dialect, and working-class heroes and heroines, these authors made large sums in a profession that had previously withheld its monetary rewards from all but a privileged few.

Although primarily known as short-story writers, all of these authors successfully composed novels in the same comic vein. W.W. Jacobs, whose nautical tales appeared in the *Strand Magazine* for more than 30 years, published several novels, most issued serially. *The Skipper's Wooing* (1897), *Dialstone Lane* (1904), and *Salthaven* (1908) are all longer fictional works with the New Humor stamp. These books deal with sailors ashore and provide their readers with a light comic fare that skirts the popular realism then in fashion, a bequest from French naturalists like Émile Zola. The New Humorists, while essentially realistic in tone, bypassed the sordid portrayal of slum conditions that the naturalists and their English and American disciples embraced. Lower-class denizens of the comic novels of the Jacobs-Pain coterie might be poor, but they are never debased.

Barry Pain's detective novel *The Memoirs of Constantine Dix* (1905) features a lay pastor who is also a consummate burglar. This protagonist's concern for the spiritual welfare of humanity reaches even farther—into concern for its pecuniary interests as well. The sardonic Dix is amusing in his ability to extract confessions from hardened miscreants, later employing the information toward his own light-fingered ends. Other novels in the New Humorist vein include William Pett Ridge's *Mord Em'ly* (1901), Jerome K. Jerome's *Three Men in a Boat* (1889), and Israel Zangwill's *The King of Schnorrers* (1894). Ridge's book concerns the adventures of a young slum urchin (Maud Emily) who goes to reform school for stealing pastry as a lark. Her manipulations of the warders in the institution are resourceful and often hilarious, showing a good-hearted child who is a victim of her environment but who turns out well in the end. Jerome's popular tale of the anything but relaxing vacation of three lower middle-class clerks and their dog is still read today; his books created such demand in Europe that they frequently were employed as foreign language readers. Zangwill's novel of a Jewish rapscallion in poverty-stricken East London gives valuable insights into the living conditions of Jews in turn-of-the-century England. The New Humorists tended to paint a positive picture of lower middle-class life with which a horde of readers could identify. The characters of these works possessed no super-human traits; their very foibles contributed to their immense popularity.

There is nothing didactic in the productions of this group of writers whose main view was the entertainment of the reader; many times the heroes of these fictions are amiable scoundrels with questionable morals. The weary clerk or laborer found nothing intellectually taxing in these books; rather, the light, restful fare buoyed the spirits without tiring the mind. These comic authors helped to democratize the profession of letters in turn-of-the-century Britain, although they were snobbishly excluded from the ranks of the established literati. They were remarkably successful writers who inspired many imitators, showing that the profession of authorship was open to all who had talent, regardless of class. British novelists who were influenced by the New Humorists include P.G. Wodehouse, Oliver Onions, and Anthony Hope.

JOHN D. CLOY

See also Comedy and Humor in the Novel

Further Reading

Adcock, Arthur St. John, *The Glory That Was Grub Street: Impressions of Contemporary Authors*, London: Low, Marston, and New York: Stokes, 1928

Cloy, John D., "Barry Pain," in *Dictionary of Literary Biography*, volume 135, edited by Annegret S. Ogden, Detroit, Michigan: Gale, 1994

Cloy, John D., *Pensive Jester: The Literary Career of W.W. Jacobs*, Lanham, Maryland: University Press of America, 1996

Jerome, Jerome K., *My Life and Times*, London: Hodder and Stoughton, 1926

Pound, Reginald, *Mirror of the Century: The Strand Magazine 1891–1950*, South Brunswick, New Jersey: Barnes, 1966

Ridge, William Pett, *A Story Teller: Forty Years in London*, London: Hodder and Stoughton, 1923

Trail, H.D., "The Future of Humour," *The New Review* 10 (1894)

New Journalism and the Nonfiction Novel

The New Journalism involves using the conventions of fiction—including focused characterization, development by dialogue, structuring by imagery, and deepening of thematic statement by use of metaphor and symbol—as a way of presenting a factual subject. In the hands of its more radical practitioners, such as Tom Wolfe and Hunter S. Thompson, the methodology placed the reporter at the center of the experience he was reporting. Its major contribution to literary history is the nonfiction novel, an extended treatment drawing on the traditional novel's power of broad effect and satisfactory closure.

Both the New Journalism and the nonfiction novel are products of the 1960s in the United States. Both can be traced to the broader palettes and more personal allowances for style granted to writers by *Esquire* and *New York* magazine during this period. From the *New York Times*, the *New York Herald Tribune*, and *The Atlantic*, established feature journalists such as Gay Talese, Tom Wolfe, and Dan Wakefield were recruited by rival editors Harold Hayes and Clay Felker to shake up the pages of their magazines with articles that were controversial in both subject matter and treatment. Controversy of treatment meant involving the writer with his or her subject, both as a literary artist (who would shape the material according to the dictates of creative imagination as well as the traditional reporter's code of factuality) and as a necessary part of the coverage itself (an analogue to the modern scientific principle that the presence of an experimenter influences the experiment's results). The style itself was much looser than customary reportage and was allowed to develop as if by chance. To take one important early instance of this looser style, Tom Wolfe, when he had missed his deadline for a piece on customized cars and their attendant subculture in southern California, was asked to send in a radical summation of his rough notes, from which another writer would draft an essay. *Esquire*'s editors, who found these notes to be compelling, published them without any further work, thus giving birth to Wolfe's exuberant, unfettered style.

The nonfiction novel is a more serious affair. Most noteworthy were Truman Capote's *In Cold Blood* (1966), about sensational multiple murders in Kansas, and Norman Mailer's *Armies of the Night* (1968), about a massive march on the Pentagon protesting the war in Vietnam. Mailer's subtitle, "The Novel as History, History as a Novel," indicates the motivation behind both works. Just as the novel mimics the cavalcade of rationally organized events that become known as history, so too is history understood as a narrative shaped by humans. To what extent, both Mailer and Capote ask, does the penchant for story-making influence not just our record of events but the events themselves?

Many New Journalists felt that their trade had become necessary because of a failure on the part of novelists themselves to address current reality. Tom Wolfe voiced this complaint in the introduction to his anthology, edited with E.W. Johnson, *The New Journalism* (1973). His principal objection was to the new style of fiction, particularly metafiction, that avoided mimetic representation of the world in favor of drawing attention to the makings of fiction itself. Such practice neglected the social realities of contemporary life, Wolfe believed. Who would become the Dickens of late 20th-century London, the Balzac of today's Paris, the Henry James of Wolfe's own New York? The answer was Tom Wolfe himself, doing so not by writing conventional fiction (although he eventually did much later, in *The Bonfire of the Vanities*, 1987) but by importing the novelistic elements of character development, dialogue, setting, and symbol into feature journalism.

Wolfe's subsequent collections give a colorful picture of the era. *The Kandy-Kolored Tangerine-Flake Streamline Baby* (1965) collects early form-setting essays on the great varieties of 1960s American culture; *The Electric Kool-Aid Acid Test* (1968) rides the bus with novelist Ken Kesey and his roving band of pranksters, spreading messages of artistic freedom and imaginative liberation by means of drugs such as LSD and mescaline. For New York City itself, Wolfe was able to portray (and criticize) its intellectual life in *Radical Chic and Mau-Mauing the Flak Catchers* (1970) and challenge its hegemony as the world's art center in *The Painted Word* (1975). The climax of his New Journalism, taking the form less of collected essays than of the sustained nonfiction novel, was his story of the astronauts' personal role in America's space program, *The Right Stuff* (1979). Made into a major Hollywood motion picture, this work fulfilled Wolfe's ambitions of contributing to the culture's deeper realization of itself by means of literary art.

The New Journalism's lasting contribution to American letters is evident in the way it eventually blended into the mainstream of fiction itself. Many of its practitioners began writing successfully in both genres; Joan Didion and Dan Wakefield, for example, are now as famous for their novels as for their New Journalism, with little real difference between their styles in the two forms. With the work of Hunter S. Thompson and James S. Kunen, New Journalism comes full circle and begins to emulate the metafictive exploits of writers such as Kurt Vonnegut and Ronald Sukenick, emphasizing the act of writing as much as the subject portrayed. *Fear and Loathing in Las Vegas* (1971) begins as Thompson's ostensible coverage of a motorcycle race and a drug law-enforcement convention but soon deteriorates into vividly characterizational reportage of his inability to see the race and his own illicit adventures with drugs. Kunen's *The Strawberry Statement* (1969) is much like Kurt Vonnegut's novel published that same year, *Slaughterhouse-Five*; Kunen finds his subject, the student revolution at Columbia University, just as unreportable as Vonnegut finds the firebombing of Dresden. Each writer winds up depicting his own inability to make sense of these events. These methods square with transformations of American culture during the 1960s and afterward, especially in their privileging of the personal imagination and their rigorous interrogation of previously unquestioned assumptions.

JEROME KLINKOWITZ

See also Journalism and the Novel; United States Novel (1945–)

Further Reading

Hellmann, John, *Fables of Fact: The New Journalism as New Fiction*, Urbana: University of Illinois Press, 1981

Hollowell, John, *Fact and Fiction: The New Journalism and the Nonfiction Novel*, Chapel Hill: University of North Carolina Press, 1977

Johnson, Michael L., *The New Journalism: The Underground Press, the Artists of Nonfiction, and Changes in the Established Media*, Lawrence: University Press of Kansas, 1971

Lounsberry, Barbara, *The Art of Fact: Contemporary Artists of Nonfiction*, New York: Greenwood Press, 1990

Polsgrove, Carol, *It Wasn't Pretty, Folks, But Didn't We Have Fun? Esquire in the Sixties*, New York: Norton, 1995

Weber, Ronald, *The Literature of Fact*, Athens: Ohio University Press, 1980

Weber, Ronald, editor, *The Reporter as Artist: A Look at the New Journalism Controversy*, New York: Hastings House, 1974

Wolfe, Tom, and E.W. Johnson, editors, *The New Journalism*, New York: Harper Row, 1973; London: Pan Books, 1975

New Novel. *See* Nouveau Roman

New Zealand Novel

The story of the novel in New Zealand is inevitably bound up with the story of the emergence of a distinctive national culture from a dependent colonial context and, more recently, with its increasing closeness to international culture. The story starts with the importation and adaptation of British and US fictional models before moving to the exploitation and then exploration of indigenous themes. The maturation of New Zealand fiction was matched by the emergence of an indigenous reading public and a publication infrastructure to serve it. The story may be traced through four distinct but overlapping periods: the pioneer period (1840–89), the late colonial period (1890–1934), the provincial period (1935–64), and the postprovincial period (1965 to the present).

The late 18th- and early 19th-century exploratory expeditions to New Zealand gave rise to several works of prose fiction, but the first published novel to be written in New Zealand seems to have been Henry Butler Stoney's *Taranaki, A Tale of the War*, published in 1861, more than 20 years after the beginning of organized European settlement. It is typical of the novels of the pioneer period in several ways: it was written in the midst of a busy colonial life by an amateur writer (the only exceptions to this amateurism were British writers such as Samuel Butler or Benjamin Farjeon, who resided for brief periods in New Zealand and then returned to England); it incorporated the three major fictional modes of the time—naive documentary realism, didacticism, and melodrama; it was intended as a justification of the colonial endeavor; and it was a very bad novel. It was atypical only in that it was published in New Zealand for a New Zealand audience, while most novels of the period were published in London for an English audience, to inform them about life in the colonies. (Serialized novels, appearing in newspapers and obviously aimed at a local audience, never achieved publication as books.)

Documentary realism was the most obvious mode to present New Zealand materials to a primarily English audience. Some of the early novels were thinly fictionalized autobiographies presenting the author's experiences in New Zealand in a loose, picaresque sequence, as in William Mortimer Baines' *The Narrative of Edward Crewe; or, Life in New Zealand* (1874), with its artless accounts of fishing, pig hunting, milling and dam building, gum digging, and goldmining in the New Zealand of 1850. Often such adventures were given a kind of containing shape by a melodramatic plot, usually a romance. Alexander Bathgate defined the formula for this kind of book when he described his *Waitaruna: A Story of New Zealand Life* (1881) as a series of "true pictures of life in the southern portion of the colony of New Zealand . . . strung together, as it were, by a story." A different kind of work of documentary realism was the ethno-graphic description of Maori life in fictional form, such as John White's *Te Rou; or, The Maori at Home* (1874).

A few novels of the period were written in a didactic mode. They often contained elements of autobiography or romance but subordinated these to the didactic intent. Ellen R. Ellis' *Everything Is Possible to Will* (1882) uses autobiographical fiction to present opinions about marriage, feminism, and the moral fiber needed for successful colonization. Prime Minister Julius Vogel's strange *Anno Domini 2000; or, Woman's Destiny* (1889) uses a more romantic plot to present Vogel's ideas about sexual equality, the British Empire, and a welfare state based on economic expansion and increased consumption. Vogel's didactic novel, like Ellis', ends with an essay. The most interesting of the didactic fictions is Samuel Butler's *Erewhon* (1872), which moves from a realistic picture of life in the Canterbury high country as he had experienced it to a presentation of an imagined society "over the range" on the West Coast of the South Island as a vehicle for a satire of English society.

The dominant form of the period was the melodramatic romance, with the indigenous materials simply plugged into the imported structures of Victorian popular fiction. One popular variety was the Maori romance, fitting Maori elements to the conventions popularized by Sir Walter Scott and James Fenimore Cooper, as in the Australian Rolf Boldrewood's *"War to the Knife"; or, Tangata Maori* (1899), which dealt with the Land Wars of the 1860s. A similar exploitation of New Zealand materials was evident in the South Island goldfield romances such as Vincent Pyke's lively *Wild Will Enderby* (1873). Rather more complex in plot structure was a group of sensation novels written in imitation of Wilkie Collins and using New Zealand materials within the formulae that Collins established. Oliver Growden's *Matthew Redmayne: A New Zealand Romance* (1892; serialized in 1889–90 as *The Mark of Cain*) was the most elaborate of these.

Whatever the modes, these early novels were mostly justifications of the colonizing endeavor as well as the Victorian work ethic and the doctrine of imperial expansion that lay behind it. They praise the pioneer purpose of building a "better Britain of the South Seas" and present the Land Wars as necessary for achieving that purpose. Attitudes varied from those who saw the Maori as noble savages sadly but necessarily sacrificed to progress, as did Boldrewood, to those who, like John Featon in his didactic *The Last of the Wakatos: A Sensational Tale of the Province of Auckland* (1873), wanted a war of extermination to eliminate all obstacles to pioneer material progress. However, several of the most interesting novels of the period step outside both the conventional fictional modes and these accepted attitudes. Sygurd Wisniowski, in *Tikera or Children of the Queen of*

Oceania (published in Polish in 1877 but not translated into English until 1972) rejects the conventions of melodrama and romance in favor of a kind of picaresque realism through which he presents a thoughtfully critical view of New Zealand settler society, both in its material aspirations and in its race relations. Similarly, George Chamier's *Philosopher Dick: Adventures and Contemplations of a New Zealand Shepherd* (1891) and its sequel, *A South Sea Siren: A Novel Descriptive of New Zealand Life in the Early Days* (1895), present an intelligently sceptical view of Canterbury society in the 1860s. Loose, capacious picaresque novels in the 18th-century mold, they are held together by the development of the hero from naive idealism to a tempered realism.

The late colonial period, despite some abortive attempts to found national literary journals, saw no real development of an indigenous reading public or publishing infrastructure. Most New Zealand novels were still published in England and aimed primarily at an English audience. There was no development of a coherent indigenous literary tradition. Nevertheless, in isolation from one another, four significant novelists (three of them New Zealand-born) developed between 1890 and 1930, each producing at least four novels: Edith Searle Grossmann, William Satchell (the only immigrant among them), Jane Mander, and Jean Devanny. All of them worked within and to some extent transformed the main modes and attitudes of the period, although none of them received much recognition.

Grossmann, an outspoken radical feminist, worked primarily in the didactic mode. Her *In Revolt* (1893) and its sequel, *The Knight of the Holy Ghost* (1907), express through heightened symbolic moral melodrama an exalted vision of the period's faith in social progress. She presents the struggle for female equality as part of "our efforts to emancipate the race from the past and make ways for its evolution in the future" (as she put it in the preface to the 1907 novel). Her last novel, *The Heart of the Bush* (1910), attempts to present an ideal relationship between man and woman but is able to do so only by slipping into an escapist pastoral idyll. None of the many other didactic novels of the turn of the century were as powerful as Grossmann's at their best, but all shared with them some form of faith in social evolution, whether focusing on temperance or women's rights or trade unionism or projecting the accomplishments of the liberal government onto a utopian future.

That faith in social evolution also underlies most of the melodramatic romances of the period. Satchell in *The Land of the Lost* (1902), *The Toll of the Bush* (1905), and *The Greenstone Door* (1914) expresses that optimism most fully in works that in some ways transcend the melodramatic romance but still depend on its plot contrivances. Buoyed by religious faith in spiritual evolution (which found most explicit expression in the symbolic romance of 1907, *The Elixir of Life*), Satchell saw the pioneer effort and the Land Wars as painful but necessary steps toward achieving the better society of the future. A similar, if more limited, vision of social progress underlay many of the period's melodramatic romances set in frontier society, including John Bell's *In the Shadow of the Bush* (1899), and was present in the melodramas of marriage by "Alien" (Louisa Baker), published between 1894 and 1910, and those of frontier and empire by "G.B. Lancaster" (Edith Lyttleton), published between 1904 and 1943. Both Baker and Lyttleton achieved popular success in England and the United States.

Devanny in her first seven novels (her last nine were written and set in Australia) set out, like the heroine of her *Lenore Divine* (1926), to write books "instinct with the germs of progress, vital to achieve, a real fighting force for the good of the race." Her vision of social progress, a strange amalgam of feminism, Marx and Engels, social Darwinism, and Nietzsche, was the most radical of these late colonial novelists, and her method was the crudest. She seemed to be struggling to find something like D.H. Lawrence's method of presenting intense feeling, but she fell back into rhetorical melodrama.

Mander, Devanny's older contemporary, had a similar but less radical faith in evolutionary progress, "the flow of the great human current that carries all men, great and small, towards some goal of understanding and goodwill which they see as in a glass darkly," as she described it in her first novel, *The Story of a New Zealand River* (1920). That tendency, she thought, was toward a more enlightened society, no longer hindered by puritan repression, with greater social and sexual equality and more opportunity for individual fulfillment. Mander's mode for presenting this, a typically English blend of realism with modified romance, was more conservative than Devanny's and was also more successful, especially in *Allen Adair* (1925), the best novel of the period.

A similar blend is found in some of the other significant novels of the period, such as Arthur Adams' *Tussock Land: A Romance of New Zealand and the Commonwealth* (1904), which incorporates elements of realism and begins to move beyond reliance on the contrivances of melodramatic romance. Alan Mulgan's *Spur of Morning* (1934) successfully blends romance and realism and reprises most of the important themes of the age, viewing the hardships of frontier life, the destruction of the bush, the disruption of Maori culture, and the relative lack of a European high culture as necessary costs of the early stages of the struggle for social progress. Mulgan's two heroes, one a New Zealand nationalist, the other an anglophile, represent the divided national culture of the age, looking fondly back to England (Mulgan published in 1927 a popular book about a visit to England called *Home: A New Zealander's Adventure*) but also beginning to develop a sense of nationalism (Mulgan's autobiography, published in 1958, was entitled *The Making of a New Zealander*).

The revolution that New Zealand writing underwent in the provincial period, beginning in the 1930s, can be dramatically shown by placing Alan Mulgan's novel next to *Man Alone*, a novel by his son John, which appeared only five years later. The differences in attitude and method are profound. That literary revolution is usually seen as beginning with the publication of the first issue of the periodical *Phoenix* at the University of Auckland in 1932. For poetry that view holds, but the novel lagged behind both poetry and the short story, so that the new structure of feeling did not find expression until late in the 1930s with John Mulgan's novel and the novels of Robin Hyde. That changed structure of feeling emerges from an interchange between Alan Mulgan and Robert Chapman in the literary periodical *Landfall* in 1953. Chapman, in his classic essay "Fiction and the Social Pattern: Some Implications of Recent N.Z. Writing," saw the fiction writers of the previous 20 years as practicing a critical, even clinical, realism to expose "what lies beneath the crust of the everyday" and to offer "a clinical report . . . on the state of the patient," a report that indicated that the patient was suffering from an overdose of irrelevant imported Victorian puritanism and needed a dose of healthy new-world humanism. Alan Mulgan protested, stating that "the main business of the novelist" was not this "deliberate sociological probing and exposure" but rather the entertaining and uplifting of the reader by showing "what is *right*" with society. John Mulgan's novel, published in England in 1939 but finally reprinted in New Zealand in 1949, engages in Chapman's brand of critical "probing." It provides a model both for the critical analysis of society (with its sharply observed portrait of New Zealand between the wars as a constricted puritan and capitalist society) and for the method of that analysis (a Hemingwayesque vernacular realism focusing on the figure of the marginalized man alone whose interactions with his society show its deficiencies). As early as 1934, in his essay "Some Aspects of New Zealand Art and Letters" in the periodical *Art in New Zealand,* the poet A.R.D. Fairburn had said that *Huckleberry Finn* was "from the point of view of the New Zealand writer . . . the most important novel ever written," and his point was validated within several years when Frank Sargeson revolutionized the New Zealand short story by drawing on Sherwood Anderson as an exponent of the Twain tradition. Mulgan's use of Ernest Hemingway as a model for his novel was a further development in the same direction, as was David Ballantyne's choice of James T. Farrell for his model in his first novel, *The Cunninghams* (1948), a critical exposure of the cultural poverty of New Zealand provincial life. Ian Cross' independent discovery of Anderson as a model for his first novel, *The God Boy* (1957), resulted in a classic account of the difficulties of growing up puritan (in this case an Irish Catholic variety of puritanism).

At the same time that this US-inspired mode of critical realism was employed to present a critical view of New Zealand society, other novelists were developing a modernist mode for a similar vision, taking Virginia Woolf, Katherine Mansfield, James Joyce, and William Faulkner as their models. Robin Hyde drew on Woolf and Mansfield for a more internalized, impressionistic method. She presents isolated men and women as victims in New Zealand society between the wars in *Nor the Years Condemn* and focuses on the pains of growing up puritan in the autobiographical *The Godwits Fly* (both 1938). Sargeson turned to the Joyce of *A Portrait of the Artist as a Young Man* for his semi-autobiographical *I Saw in My Dream* (1949), while Janet Frame used a method closer to Faulkner's *The Sound and the Fury* for her semi-autobiographical *Owls Do Cry* (1957)—both intense accounts of the trauma of growing up in a society that was "homogeneous, dull, conformist, philistine, puritanical, bourgeois, materialist, Anglo-Saxon, and hostile," to quote from Peter Simpson's analysis of the provincial novelist's sensibility (see Peter Simpson, *Ronald Hugh Morrieson,* 1982). Other novelists stayed closer to traditional English models while presenting somewhat less critical views of New Zealand society, as did the expatriates Dan Davin in his *Roads from Home* (1949) and James Courage in his *The Young Have Secrets* (1954), further accounts of growing up in New Zealand.

By 1960, the provincial novel had an established set of themes and methods. It had declared a kind of postcolonial independence from the English novel (as part of the cultural nationalist agenda of the period's literature) and had something of an indigenous readership and the beginning of a cultural infrastructure. Nevertheless, the situation presented difficulties for the novelist. From its inception in 1939, the weekly *New Zealand Listener* reviewed

New Zealand fiction, and the literary quarterly *Landfall,* founded in 1947, published not only reviews but also occasional critical articles, while both journals published short stories. However, there was not such a clear path for the publication of novels. The Caxton Press of Denis Glover, the main publisher of the significant poetry and short fiction of the period, published few novels. The few established conservative New Zealand publishers accepted novels occasionally, depending on their editors, but there was no regular outlet. Thus Ballantyne's and Cross' first novels were published in the United States and all of Hyde's were published in England, as were Sargeson's. While there was some critical celebration that an unprecedented number of promising novelistic debuts were made in the years 1957 to 1959, including not only Cross and Frame but also Sylvia Ashton-Warner, Ruth France, M.K. Joseph, Marilyn Duckworth, Errol Brathwaite, and Gordon Slatter, only Frame, Brathwaite, and Slatter were published in New Zealand.

At the end of the period, the provincial novel widened its focus to include Maori experience in Noel Hilliard's *Maori Girl* (1960), to take on a fuller social range together with its historical origins in Cross' *After Anzac Day* (1961), and to present a whole community in cross-section in Bill Pearson's *Coal Flat* (1963), but Cross and Hilliard could not find a New Zealand publisher, and Pearson's book was published in New Zealand only after considerable difficulty. It was recognized on publication as the major novel of the period, answering Sargeson's call for a book that would "seek out the threads of our lives, and show us where they all lead to." However, it had taken Pearson about ten years of on-and-off part-time writing to finish the novel and another three years to get it published. It remained his only novel.

Difficulties of the sort that Pearson faced have eased in the years since 1963. Since then full-time novelists have arisen, such as Maurice Shadbolt and Maurice Gee, although most must supplement their income from novels with journalism or children's books or writing for television. About two-thirds of all New Zealand novels ever published have appeared since 1965, mostly published in New Zealand by local firms (including active university presses) or by the local branches of multinationals. This unprecedented flow of fiction has gained a new audience, so that when Keri Hulme's *The Bone People* won the Booker Prize in 1984 the writer received something like the acclaim of a national sporting hero. Alan Duff's *Once Were Warriors* (1990) became part of the national debate on race relations (intensified when the novel was made into a successful film). The conscious national culture that the provincial writers had desired, the "invention of New Zealand" that poet Allen Curnow had called for in his dialogue with Ngaio Marsh in 1945 (in *Yearbook of the Arts*), has taken shape, and the novel has played a vital part in the process. The cultural ties to England have become as loose as the economic ones after England's entry into the common market. Ironically, cultural independence from Britain was realized at the same time that New Zealand drew closer to international culture and a multinational free-trade economic system. To date, despite the invasive power of US popular culture, evident especially in New Zealand television, the presence of such forces has not overwhelmed the growth of a vigorous national culture.

The postprovincial novel, then, has developed in a situation of cultural expansion and rapid social and economic change. Such changes have come in two waves, 1984 marking a convenient

line of demarcation. In the 1960s and 1970s, increasing afflu-
ence (and threats to it in the form of Britain's move toward Europe and of the oil shocks) brought increased urbanization and
suburbanization, the sexual revolution, the feminist revolution,
Maori urban migration and the growth of Maori cultural and
political consciousness, the emergence of a more distinctive
youth subculture, and changes in family patterns. The second
wave of change, which engulfed the country with the election of
the Lange Labour government in 1984, has seen a continuation
of the earlier changes, qualified by the rise of the new capitalism
and the end of the Cold War and its alliances and oppositions.
Recent developments include an increased economic and social
individualism, increased economic stratification and the re-
trenchment of the welfare state, increased economic internation-
alization, and radically changed patterns of immigration
bringing more cultural pluralism. These and related phenomena
have given novelists very different material from the more narrow, monocultural society of the previous period, material for
which the conventions and explanatory patterns worked out in
the provincial novel are no longer entirely suitable.

Social change has resulted in an increasing diversity of theme
and mode in the novel. Through the late 1960s and the 1970s,
the critical realism and the humanistic values of the provincial
novelists remained dominant, but they were much modified to
take in social change. They moved beyond a simple opposition
to a puritan monoculture, widening their vision to include those
who had been excluded or marginalized by the provincial novel, especially women and Maori. The emergence of a younger
generation of writers not raised under puritanism in the 1980s
and 1990s has brought an even greater diversification of subject, attitude, and mode, expressed in an increasing quantity of
novels.

Some postprovincial novels, such as Gee's *In My Father's Den*
(1972), sharply contrast a period from the provincial past with
the present, to show the extent of social change. Others, such as
Gee's Plumb family trilogy (*Plumb,* 1978; *Meg,* 1981; *Sole Survivor,* 1983) or Maurice Shadbolt's *Strangers and Journeys*
(1972), trace a long curve of social change. More frequently,
novelists directly confront contemporary society, some in large
social cross-sections, as in Barbara Anderson's *Girls High*
(1990), others in smaller domestic groups, as in Duckworth's
Disorderly Conduct (1981), or in a focus on isolated characters,
as in Shonagh Koea's *The Grandiflora Tree* (1989). Fiona Kidman's *True Stars* (1990) and other novels of society focus on political and social issues, but the great majority center on personal
relations. These differ from the novels of the provincial period in
their greater emphasis on individual rather than social responsibility, in their more psychological or therapeutic approach to
their characters, and in their greater willingness to deal explicitly with sexuality. The period is marked by increasingly frank
treatment of various forms of sexuality, whether it be heterosexual passion, as in Sheridan Keith's *Zoology* (1995), male homosexual love, as in Witi Ihimaera's *Nights in the Gardens of Spain*
(1995), lesbian love, as in Renee's *Daisy & Lily* (1993), or even
pedophilia, as in Mike Johnson's *Lear* (1986).

A different kind of widening of novelistic range has come
about since the 1970s with the advent of Maori novelists writing
about Maori life from the inside. Ihimaera in *Whanau* (1974)
and Patricia Grace in *Potiki* (1986) deal with the rural Maori
community in the postprovincial time of sharp social change.

Grace especially focuses on cultural conflict over land. Duff in
Once Were Warriors and its sequel, *What Becomes of the Broken Hearted?* (1996), focuses on the plight of dispossessed urban
Maori. Hulme in *The Bone People* tries to point to new social
patterns, bringing Maori and Pakeha together in new configurations that transcend past failures and break out of the confinement of the nuclear family.

Ihimaera in *The Matriarch* (1986) and Grace in *Cousins*
(1992) deal with the historical aspects of the change in the
Maori situation, Ihimaera going back to the Land Wars from the
present and Grace going back to the 1940s. Such historical interest has been a feature of many novels of the period, and there
have been historical novels on many segments of the past from
many perspectives. The historical sections of Ian Wedde's
Symmes Hole (1986) and Graham Billing's *The Chambered
Nautilus* (1993) deal with the pre-1840 whaling days, while
C.K. Stead's *The Singing Whakapapa* (1994) treats the early missionaries. The central section of *The Matriarch* treats the Land
Wars from the Maori side, while Shadbolt's historical trilogy
(*Season of the Jew,* 1986; *Monday's Warriors,* 1990; *The House
of Strife,* 1993) looks at the same events primarily from the
Pakeha side. Kidman's *The Book of Secrets* (1987) gives a femi-
nist interpretation of a 19th-century religious settlement, and
Rachel McAlpine's *Farewell Speech* (1990) presents a revisionist
view of the struggle for female suffrage. Stevan Eldred-Grigg's
Oracles and Miracles (1987) gives a working-class view of the
Depression, Elizabeth Knox's *Glamour and the Sea* (1996) is a
re-creation of the home front in World War II, and Stead's *All
Visitors Ashore* (1984) presents a postmodern treatment of the
1951 Waterfront confrontation. The whole range of New
Zealand history has been open to the postprovincial novelists,
not for costume drama but for varied reinterpretations and revisionist readings. A range of futuristic fiction includes the feminist fantasies of McAlpine as well as postapocalyptic dystopias
such as the future section of Frame's *Intensive Care* (1970) and
the post-AIDS world of Johnson's *Lear.*

This great diversity of subject and attitude has been matched
by a diversity in mode and method. Critical realism has not been
superseded but rather has continued to develop beyond that of
the provincial novelists. However, it has become less dominant,
as other modes have developed alongside it. Gee, the most significant novelist of the period, through a career encompassing 12
novels, has consistently expanded the possibilities of realism. Using the model of Joyce Cary's trilogies, he developed in the
Plumb trilogy a use of a retrospective first-person point of view
moving back and forth through several chronological levels,
with three different narrators dealing with overlapping material
from different perspectives in the three novels. In novels since
then, including *Prowlers* (1987) and *Going West* (1992), he has
further elaborated the method. He uses a shifting omniscience
within a more restricted time frame with a larger social cross-
section in such novels as *The Burning Boy* (1990), *Crime Story*
(1994), and *Loving Ways* (1996). Shadbolt among others has
also continued to develop the realist mode while incorporating
some postmodern elements. The continued vitality of realism is
evident in the work of the two most significant novelists to
emerge in the 1990s, Barbara Anderson and the younger
Damien Wilkins, whose *The Miserables* (1993) and *Little Masters* (1996) show an already accomplished mastery of a range of
realistic techniques.

Frame's novels of the 1960s and 1970s follow *Owls Do Cry* in their basically modernist mode, although her most recent fiction has moved toward postmodernism. Of her modernist novels, *Intensive Care* shows the greatest virtuosity, with its shifting interior viewpoints, some in limited third-person, some in stream of consciousness, some in first-person narration, linked by a rich and enigmatic pattern of recurring symbol and motif. Maori novelists have been particularly innovative in their use of modernist and impressionist techniques. Hulme in *The Bone People* adventurously combines first- and third-person external and internal viewpoints, using interior monologue, recurring symbols, and mythic patterns. Grace in *Potiki* uses a similar range of techniques but for a simpler oral, storytelling effect. Ihimaera experiments with intercut levels of chronology in *Tangi* (1973); in his highly complex *The Matriarch* he combines this method with shifting first- and third-person points of view, recurring motifs and symbols, and a web of allusions to Italian opera.

More recently, New Zealand novelists have supplemented realist and modernist modes of writing with postmodern ones. Elements of magic realism appear in Fiona Farrell's *The Skinny Louie Book* (1992) and Christine Johnston's *Blessed Art Thou Among Women* (1991). An expressionist mode of presenting "Kiwi Gothic" pictures of small-town and rural New Zealand life first used by Ronald Hugh Morrieson in his novels of the early 1960s (including *The Scarecrow*, 1963) reappears in the nostalgic fictions of Noel Virtue (*In the Country of Salvation*, 1990), in the mannered novels of Terence Hodgson in the 1990s, and, most prominently, in Mike Johnson's *Dumb Show* (1996). A "factional" mix of fact and fiction appears in such works as Michael Jackson's autobiographical *Pieces of Music* (1994) and Lloyd Jones' fictionalized travel book *Biografi* (1993). Intertextual interplay is taken beyond allusion and parody in Eldred-Grigg's *The Siren Celia* (1989), which incorporates parts of Chamier's *A South Sea Siren* and rewrites that novel to express contemporary attitudes toward gender and class. Most striking has been the range of metafictional devices developed by contemporary New Zealand novelists. Frame, who had from early in her career destabilized her narratives by revealing "fictions" within the fictions, as in *Scented Gardens for the Blind* (1963) and *Daughter Buffalo* (1972), plays more elaborate postmodern metafictional games in *Living in the Maniototo* (1979) and *The Carpathians* (1988). Stead plays wittier, less destabilizing games in *All Visitors Ashore* and *The Death of the Body* (1986). The two most thoroughly postmodern New Zealand novels to date, Gregory O'Brien's *Diesel Mystic* (1988) and Anne Kennedy's *Musica Ficta* (1993), show the complexity of the contemporary situation in that the former uses the devices of international postmodernism to transform a recognizably New Zealand regional world while the latter employs similar devices to create a world with no overt sign of relationship to New Zealand.

LAWRENCE JONES

See also Bone People; Janet Frame; Postcolonial Narrative and Criticism of the Novel; Maurice Shadbolt

Further Reading
Alley, Elizabeth, and Mark Williams, editors, *In the Same Room: Conversations with New Zealand Writers,* Auckland: Auckland University Press, 1992
Chapman, Robert, "Fiction and the Social Pattern: Some Implications of Recent N.Z. Writing," *Landfall* 7 (1953)
Evans, Patrick, *The Penguin History of New Zealand Literature,* Auckland and New York: Penguin, 1990
Hankin, Cherry, editor, *Critical Essays on the New Zealand Novel,* Auckland: Heinemann Educational, 1977
Holcroft, M.H., *Islands of Innocence: The Childhood Theme in New Zealand Fiction,* Wellington: Reed, 1964
Ireland, Kevin, *The New Zealand Collection: A Celebration of the New Zealand Novel,* Auckland: Random House, 1989
Jones, Joseph Jay, and Johanna Jones, *New Zealand Fiction,* Boston: Twayne, 1983
Jones, Lawrence, *Barbed Wire and Mirrors: Essays on New Zealand Prose,* Dunedin: University of Otago Press, 1987; 2nd edition, 1990
McCormick, Eric Hall, *New Zealand Literature: A Survey,* London: Oxford University Press, 1959
New, William H., *Among Worlds: An Introduction to Modern Commonwealth and South African Fiction,* Erin, Ontario: Porcepic Press, 1975
O'Brien, Gregory, *Moments of Invention: Portraits of 21 New Zealand Writers,* Auckland: Heinemann Reed, 1988
Rhodes, H. Winston, *New Zealand Fiction since 1945,* Dunedin: McIndoe, 1968
Rhodes, H. Winston, *New Zealand Novels: A Thematic Approach,* Wellington: Price Milburn, 1969
Roberts, Heather, *Where Did She Come From? New Zealand Women Novelists 1862–1987,* Wellington: Allen and Unwin/Port Nicholson Press, 1989
Sargeson, Frank, *Conversation in a Train and Other Critical Writing,* edited by Kevin Cunningham, Auckland: Auckland University Press, and Oxford: Oxford University Press, 1983
Smith, Elizabeth Maisie, *A History of New Zealand Fiction from 1862 to the Present Time with Some Account of Its Relation to the National Life and Character,* Wellington: Reed, 1939
Stevens, Joan, *The New Zealand Novel, 1860–1960,* Wellington: Reed, 1961; 2nd revised edition as *The New Zealand Novel, 1860–1965,* 1966
Sturm, Terry, editor, *The Oxford History of New Zealand Literature in English,* Auckland and New York: Oxford University Press, 1991
Williams, Mark, *Leaving the Highway: Six Contemporary New Zealand Novelists,* Auckland: Auckland University Press, 1990

Ngugi wa Thiong'o 1938–

Kenyan

Ngugi wa Thiong'o dominates what may be considered the transitional period of the African novel (1964–78), and his works function as an important link between the pioneers of African writing, most notably Chinua Achebe, and the younger generation of postcolonial African writers such as Ben Okri. As a novelist and a literary critic, Ngugi has been one of the most perceptive students of the politics of writing in colonial and postcolonial Africa, and his thoughts on the nature of the novel as a genre committed to social justice have influenced two generations of writers in Africa and its diaspora. Although he has produced work in other genres, Ngugi has privileged the novel as the form most attuned to the culture and politics of societies undergoing the process of radical change. If, as he noted in 1973, a culture embodies "a community's structure of values" and is ultimately "an ideological expression of the totality of [communal] activities," then the novel functions as the vehicle of such values and activities at different historical phases. Ngugi's novels are marked by this desire to represent communities undergoing change and to map out the crisis of modernity that emerges in this process.

Since he started to write on the cusp of colonialism and decolonization, Ngugi's early novels comprise both retrospective examinations of a violent imperial past and a sceptical prognosis of the culture of the independent African nation. His later works were produced within the harsh cultural and political conditions imposed on writers and artists by the postcolonial state and were thus preoccupied with the question of power within the symbolic economy of what has come to be known as arrested decolonization. In both phases, however, Ngugi also was searching for a new language to represent the postcolony and its insurgent narratives. Considered chronologically, then, Ngugi's novels map the difficult politics of one African state (Kenya) as it moves from the culture of colonialism, through the euphoria of independence, and into the harsh realities of what Frantz Fanon once called "the pitfalls of national consciousness." One of the most salient aspects of Ngugi's narrative practice, then, is a self-conscious engagement with the central issues that have determined African writing since independence: cultural nationalism, the romance of the nation, and the politics of knowledge.

While such concerns have drawn attention to the sociological significance of Ngugi's novels, they are perhaps more important in the way they have demanded a certain aesthetic response. In *Weep Not, Child* (1964), Ngugi used the Bildungsroman form to probe how the life of a boy growing up under colonial terror was caught between individual desires and communal demands. Hence, there was a close relationship between the *bildung* structure of this novel and its primary theme—education and social change—as the novelist used a romantic relationship to mediate conflicting historical and social forces. The most prominent theme in Ngugi's early work—the conflict between the individual and the community—was revisited in his second novel, *The River Between* (1965), which was cast as a retrospective look on the emergence of Gikuyu cultural nationalism in the 1920s but is most memorable for its representation of the divided consciousness of a colonial subject trying to reconcile the dream of national restoration and the most fundamental form of erotic desire.

A Grain of Wheat (1967) represents an important transition in Ngugi's career: it marked his break with cultural nationalism and his embracing of Fanonist Marxism; it also marked his first attempt to grapple with the possibilities and difficulties of modernist aesthetic ideologies. Ngugi was attracted to the modernist form like his mentor, Joseph Conrad, because it provided him with a forum for representing the culture of rupture (the transition from colonialism to postcoloniality so vividly dramatized in the novel). He recognized, at the same time, that the instability of form inherent in the modernist aesthetic could provide him with techniques for expressing the dashed expectations of nationalism. In *A Grain of Wheat,* then, the story of one man's mistaken heroism and capacity for betrayal came to be read as an allegory for the culture of postcolonialism.

When he wrote *Petals of Blood* (1977) after a hiatus of almost ten years, Ngugi had consolidated his reputation as one of the most radical African writers. He was now quite clear about the kinds of questions he wanted his novels to address—the political economy of the postcolonial state in all its manifestations. While other African writers were turning away from the realism of the first generation of African writers in order to delegitimize nationalism, Ngugi sought to delegitimize nationalist narratives by using more realist forms. This attachment to realism drew mixed responses from readers: African critics admired it for its epic representation of the history and culture of the continent as well as its keen sense of contemporary political events, but some European and American critics found its subject alienating and its form old-fashioned.

In 1978 Ngugi was arrested and imprisoned for a year (without trial) for his involvement with a communal theatre in his home village. He has narrated the circumstances surrounding his arrest and imprisonment in *Detained: A Writer's Prison Diary* (1981), in his prison memoirs, and in *Caitaani Mutharaba-ini* (1980; *Devil on the Cross*), the novel he wrote in prison. Following his imprisonment, Ngugi abandoned using English as the primary language of his work in favor of Gikuyu, his native tongue, a linguistic shift that provoked many debates about the nature of the African novel. Ngugi saw his break with English as nothing less than the radical rupture that would give the African novel its own genealogy and grammar. Focusing on the needs of his immediate audience, he wrote a story drawing on their quotidian world and also on literary traditions they knew well, especially oral and biblical narratives. Against this background *Matigari* (1987; *Matigari*) came to be read as one of Ngugi's most important works, not only because it marks a crucial space of transition—both in linguistic and aesthetic terms—but also because it takes up questions he had bypassed in earlier works: questions about the influence of African oral literatures on written forms and the problem of cultural translation. Building his narrative on a famous Gikuyu folktale, Ngugi succeeded in turning old sources into new instruments for representing the postcolony.

If Ngugi is now one of the most influential voices in the continuing debate on the nature of the novel in the Third World, it is because his works have provided readers with powerful stories about what it means to be an African subject in a hostile world, and what it means to be a writer under colonial and postcolonial conditions. With regard to matters of language and ideology, it may be said that as early as the 1960s Ngugi had preempted the issues that have come to dominate the study of literature and culture at the end of the 20th century—issues such as nation and narration, power and performance, language and identity, and empire and postcoloniality.

SIMON GIKANDI

See also Grain of Wheat

Biography

Formerly wrote as James T. Ngugi. Born 5 January 1938 in Kamiriithu, near Limuru, Kiambu District. Attended Kamaandūra School, Limuru; Karing'a School, Maanguū; Alliance High School, Kikuyu; University College, Kampala, Uganda (editor, *Penpoint*), 1959–63, B.A. 1963; Leeds University, Yorkshire, 1964–67, B.A. 1964. Columnist ("As I See It"), early 1960s, and reporter, 1964, *Nairobi Daily Nation*; editor, *Zuka*, Nairobi, 1965–70; Lecturer in English, University College, Nairobi, 1967–69; Fellow in Creative Writing, Makerere University, Kampala, 1969–70; Visiting Lecturer, Northwestern University, Evanston, Illinois, 1970–71; Senior Lecturer, Associate Professor, and Chairman of the Department of Literature, University of Nairobi, 1972–77; imprisoned under Public Security Act, 1978; left Kenya, 1982.

Novels by Ngugi

Weep Not, Child, 1964
The River Between, 1965
A Grain of Wheat, 1967
Petals of Blood, 1977
Caitaani Mutharaba-ini, 1980; as *Devil on the Cross*, 1982
Matigari, 1987; as *Matigari*, translated by Wangui wa Goro, 1989

Other Writings: short stories, plays, memoirs, a diary (*Detained: A Writer's Prison Diary*, 1981), literature for children, and essays on a variety of cultural, political, and literary topics, including *Decolonising the Mind* (his "goodbye" to English, 1986) and *Penpoints, Gunpoints and Dreams: Towards a Critical Theory of the Arts and the State in Africa* (1998).

Further Reading

Cantalupo, Charles, editor, *The World of Ngugi wa Thiong'o*, Kirksville: Northeast Missouri State University, 1993
Cantalupo, Charles, editor, *Ngugi wa Thiong'o: Text and Contexts,* Trenton, New Jersey: Africa World Press, 1995
Cook, David, and Michael Okenimpke, *Ngugi wa Thiong'o: An Exploration of His Writings,* London: Heinemann, 1983
Gikandi, Simon, *Ngugi wa Thiong'o: The Ideology of Form,* Cambridge: Cambridge University Press, 1998
Killam, G.D., *An Introduction to the Writings of Ngugi wa Thiong'o,* London and Exeter, New Hampshire: Heinemann Educational, 1980
Robson, Clifford B., *Ngugi wa Thiong'o,* London: Macmillan, and New York: St. Martin's Press, 1979
Sicherman, Carol, *Ngugi wa Thiong'o: The Making of a Rebel,* London and New York: Hans Zell, 1990

Nineteen-Nineteen. *See* U.S.A. Trilogy

Nonfiction Novel. *See* New Journalism and the Nonfiction Novel

---

Norwegian Novel. *See* Scandinavian Novel

Nostromo by Joseph Conrad

1904

Although now acknowledged as Conrad's supreme imaginative achievement and one of the greatest novels in English, *Nostromo* was at first very badly received. The poor critical reception of the novel was a major and lasting disappointment to Conrad. The form of the work caused reviewers most dismay; they saw the detailed evocations of scene and frequent disruptions of chronology and narratorial perspective as evidence of the author's inability to control or sustain the narrative. Early reviewers almost universally judged that *Nostromo* was over-long and that the discontinuous style of narration made it, as one critic unsympathetically remarked, "difficult to say when or where we are" (*British Weekly,* 10 November 1904, reprinted in Sherry, 1973). Nevertheless, Arnold Bennet thought it "the finest novel of [its] generation," and Edward Garnett praised its disregard for the conventions of realism that dominated the bulk of popular fiction (Sherry, 1973).

In the preface he added to *Nostromo* in 1917, Conrad focused on the content of the novel, making no reference to the formal attributes that had prompted the hostile reviews. In fact, by describing himself in the preface as a kind of travel writer who was the temporary "guest" and "friend" of the imaginary country and characters he created in Sulaco, Conrad emphasized the realistic nature of the novel, locating *Nostromo* in a literary tradition whose conventions and rules the early reviewers considered the novel to flout. Perhaps this was Conrad's tacit denial of the formal objections raised by those initial criticisms.

In *Nostromo,* the form of narration is notoriously complicated, interspersing a broadly omniscient, all-knowing, all-seeing mode with the personal reflections and perspectives of various characters in the story. By abandoning in this novel the singular focus provided by the character of Marlow, who was the narrator of previous works such as *Lord Jim* (1900) and "Heart of Darkness" (1902), Conrad dispenses with any fixed point of reference or personality in the unfolding of the narrative. He opts instead for a diffuse, impressionistic style that incorporates a variety of perspectives and attitudes deriving from various characters and chronological vantage points in the novel itself. For example, in chapter 7 of Part II, the narrative momentarily adopts the epistolary mode, describing people and events from the perspective of a letter written by the character Decoud. The summary provided by the letter, which momentarily restores order and sequence to the impressions and events of earlier chapters, is nevertheless tainted by the "sane materialism" that is the ultimate downfall of Decoud, undercutting the letter's apparently rational, orienting function.

The time scheme of the novel is equally complex, moving between past, present, and future, often without indication either of a change in the narratorial perspective or the sequence of events (in the first chapter of Part III the point of view changes at least ten times in five pages). These disruptions of chronology and dislocations of narratorial voice could be seen to reflect a view of history as inconsecutive and repetitive, in which events occur without reason, purpose, or hope of progress. This effect of the narration certainly parallels the bleak moral and political outlook of the novel, which portrays the corruption of the apparently "incorruptible" Nostromo (our man), adopted son of the European and American commercial interests in the town of Sulaco—a coastal port in the imaginary South American republic of Costaguana.

Apart from Nostromo, the dominating presence in Sulaco is the silver mine owned by Charles Gould. Given the abandonment of the stylistic techniques associated with literary realism, which emphasize the "organic" unity and linear development of the plot, *Nostromo* instead portrays the silver of the mine as the principal organizing symbol around which the action turns. To quote Nostromo's phrase, the silver is the "deadly disease" that invades the whole life of the novel, as if binding events together in the absence of a conventional formal unity. It is an ambivalent symbol both of moral corruption and regeneration, destroying the marriage of the Goulds, but reviving the crushed spirit of Dr. Monygham and "reforming" the bandit Hernandez, who becomes a respected general and protector of Sulaco. In Conrad's political universe the silver represents the dominating "material interests" of imperialism, providing an ironic illusion of political cohesion and progress where the form of the novel reflects a dissolution of such order.

Nostromo stages a confrontation between the "sophisticated" ideals of national progress and the primitive desire for wealth and power, symbolized by the dominating pursuit of the silver. As critics have noted, Gould's plan for the "salvation" of the mine, and the ultimately corrupting effect of its treasure, suggests the biblical account of the fall of humankind. Yet the style of narration, suggesting the moral and material vacuity of existence and the failure of moral or political progress, refutes the spiritual hope that might be implied by these religious overtones. In this respect, the revolutionary form of *Nostromo* reflects the perpetual revolution and corruption at the heart of Costaguanan politics and may be read as a paradigm of the greed and constant social upheaval that intrudes upon the peace of the republic.

The corruption of the honorable Nostromo refutes the moral salvation of Lord Jim, the hero of Conrad's previous novel whose peaceful government and honorable death in Patusan atones for the act of cowardice that haunts his life. In the sordid and labyrinthine connections between commerce and politics in Costaguana, there are also echoes of the ivory trading and political corruptions of "Heart of Darkness." Each of these earlier works explored the failure of "noble" moral and imperial intentions, realizing in the stark disjunctions of their form the anxieties and tensions of the colonial enterprise. In the shadowy and mysterious figure of Marlow, who relates these earlier stories, Conrad poses questions about the reliability of the narrator; in the multiple narrators and perspectives of *Nostromo,* he pushes these questions to their utmost limits. As the hostility of the early reviews indicate, *Nostromo* was, and remains, an adventurous and innovative work, whose formal developments and outlook influenced a range of modernist writings in the early 20th century, of which T.S. Eliot's *The Waste Land* (1922) is perhaps the most celebrated example.

ANDREW HAGIIOANNU

See also Joseph Conrad

Further Reading

Guerard, Albert J., *Conrad the Novelist,* Cambridge, Massachussetts: Harvard University Press, 1958

Gurko, Leo, *Joseph Conrad: Giant in Exile,* New York and London: Collier Books, 1962

Karl, Frederick, editor, *Joseph Conrad: A Collection of Criticism,* New York: McGraw-Hill, 1975

Knapp Hay, Eloise, *The Political Novels of Joseph Conrad,* Chicago: University of Chicago Press, 1963

Mudrick, Marvin, editor, *Conrad: A Collection of Critical Essays,* Englewood Cliffs, New Jersey: Prentice-Hall, 1966

Parry, Benita, *Conrad and Imperialism: Ideological Boundaries and Visionary Frontiers,* London: Macmillan, 1983

Sherry, Norman, *Conrad's Western World,* Cambridge: Cambridge University Press, 1971

Sherry, Norman, editor, *Conrad: The Critical Heritage,* London and Boston: Routledge and Kegan Paul, 1973

The Notebooks of Malte Laurids Brigge by Rainer Maria Rilke

Die Aufzeichnungen des Malte Laurids Brigge 1910

Rainer Maria Rilke's work is mostly known as that of a supreme 20th-century lyrical poet, articulating the self-alienation of the modern subject. His prose writings are usually understood as aesthetic reflections accompanying the poetic work or as preparatory exercises toward his mature poetic work (*Die Sonette an Orpheus* [1923; *Sonnets to Orpheus*], *Duineser Elegien* [1923; *Duino Elegies*]). Rilke's novel, *The Notebooks of Malte Laurids Brigge,* published in 1910, is thus often read in a poetic context stressing self-reflection and poetic transcendence. As such, the novel is said to belong to the genre of the *Künstlerroman* (the artistic novel), which in the fashion of a romantic teleology records the growth and natural unfolding of an artist's mind. More astute critics have engaged in a comparison with the poetic reflections of Rilke's contemporary Hugo von Hofmannsthal ("Ein Brief" [1905; "The Chandos Letter"]) in order to stress the considerable degree of alienation and pathological self-reflexivity that undermines the developmental scheme of the artistic novel. However, until recently few critics have been willing to go further and grant *The Notebooks of Malte Laurids Brigge* the exceptional status that it occupies within Rilke's body of work.

Rilke's diary novel, drawing from the author's own biography and his extended stays in Paris, records the impressions and recollections of a young Danish aristocrat, Malte Laurids Brigge, during his stay in the metropolitan center of Europe. Malte Laurids Brigge, while attempting to gain in his notes a poetic understanding of his own predicament, must do so without the traditional shelters of identity such as tradition, genealogy, and social status. As a 28-year-old son whose parents are dead, he is exposed both to impoverishment and exile and has to some extent become as marooned as the many *Fortgeworfene* (social castaways) he encounters during his daily walks through the streets of Paris. Nevertheless, Malte's cultural training allows him to absorb his crisis intellectually so as not to succumb to the forces of urban modernity and displacement entirely. Rilke's novel retains in this respect the enlightenment notion of the autonomous male bourgeois subject capable of self-mediation and self-determination. However, it is the venture beyond this autonomy that generates the most provocative and uncanny aspects of this novel, placing it into a productive tension between tradition and modernity.

It is thus urban modernity and displacement that challenges the childhood memories of Malte and forces him to recall traumatic experiences that shatter the illusion of a harmonious and unimpaired upbringing. At the same time, the vitality of a premodern life of the village in which death has not yet become an expedient affair is recalled by Malte as he visits the Parisian hospitals for the dying poor, where death has become anonymous and institutionalized. This tension between modern depersonalization and a traditional confidence in self-determination challenges the diary keeper to find a new and distinct voice in his poetic reflections. The notebooks open up the lyrical voice of the poet-protagonist to modernity and its mass-mediated experiences both in their terrifying (Georg Simmel's "bombardment of the senses") and redemptive sense of disclosing new ways of seeing (Walter Benjamin's "flaneur" and Siegfried Kracauer's "cult of distraction"). This "school of vision," as Malte calls the immersion into modern mass experience, anticipates James Joyce's Leopold Bloom, who, while wandering through the streets of Dublin, absorbs the city's complex web of tactile, aural, and visual sensory stimuli. Rilke's Malte appears likewise under the sway of Joyce's "ineluctable modality of the visible" and on the threshold to a new way of conceiving himself, questioning the bourgeois precepts that had kept him at a safe distance from this new urban and mass environment.

Malte's identification with mass anonymity and the ensuing suspension of identity allow him to reconstruct a critical family genealogy marked by rupture, narcissistic wounding, and hallucinatory dissolution of the body's presence and physical boundaries. Repeated images of failed self-recognition and fragmentation not only call into doubt the body's and the subject's assumed co-originality but also place them into a relation of dissymmetry. Thus, the independence and material contingency of the physical becomes at once the site of terror (loss of self-control and return of repressed knowledge of mortality) and the site of visionary embodiment for Malte, the achieved dying and immersion in human mortality and depersonalization as represented by the experience of the city. Malte's staging of a crisis of identity, indebted to Friedrich Nietzsche and Søren Kierkegaard, represents in part an early example of existentialist prose in which mortality becomes the reflective limit situation for the authentic affirmation of the human condition (Martin Heidegger's "Being-towards-death," Jean-Paul Sartre's "l'être pour soi").

Structurally, the notebooks emphasize the deflection from self-identity in their episodic and discontinuous form, shifting between past and present and laying bare Malte's partial and incomplete reflections. The novel's temporality with its co-simultaneity of past, present, and future in an extended present prefigures the stream-of-consciousness novel (James Joyce, Virginia Woolf) and its spontaneous reflective phenomenology built on the random and contiguous order of sense impressions. While Rilke's novel clearly breaks with 19th-century novelistic traditions such as the Bildungsroman and the realist novel in its modernist insistence on the dramatic present of consciousness (echoing Hugo von Hofmannsthal and Arthur Schnitzler), it has not entirely abandoned its concerns of reflective self-clarification and a critical analysis of social structures. Rather, "consciousness" in Rilke's novel becomes the immediate site of tension between a bourgeois desire for sustained interiority and the recognition of disruptive social conditions (mass poverty, oppression of women) preventing this type of harmonized closure. The enlightenment subject presented by Rilke has thus become critical of itself and its infatuation with the mythology of enlightenment that results in an instrumentalization of reality. In this respect, Rilke's novel clearly departs from high-modernist attempts, mostly given in poetry (Stefan George, Gottfried Benn), to contain the lyrical voice hermetically in a world of pure form and vision. In fact, Rilke's own poetry may benefit from a reassessment against this earlier novel, which shows the poet more comfortably at home among modernists such as Walter Benjamin or Siegfried Kracauer, who similarly stressed the emergence of the modern subject in mass culture.

MATTHIAS KONZETT

Further Reading

Blanchot, Maurice, "Rilke and Death's Demand," in *The Space of Literature,* by Blanchot, Lincoln: University of Nebraska Press, 1982

Cervi, Andrea, "The Composition of Reality: Rainer Maria Rilke's *Die Aufzeichnungen des Malte Laurids Brigge,*" in *The German Novel in the Twentieth Century: Beyond Realism,* edited by David Midgley, Edinburgh: Edinburgh University Press, and New York: St. Martin's Press, 1993

Donahue, Neil H., "Fear and Fascination in the Big City: Rilke's Use of Simmel in *The Notebooks of Malte Laurids Brigge,*" *Studies in Twentieth Century Literature* 16:2 (1992)

Huyssen, Andreas, "Paris/Childhood: The Fragmented Body in Rilke's *Notebooks of Malte Laurids Brigge,*" in *Modernity and the Text: Revisions of German Modernism,* edited by Andreas Huyssen and David Bathrick, New York: Columbia University Press, 1989

Kleinbard, David, *The Beginning of Terror: A Psychological Study of Rainer Maria Rilke's Life and Work,* New York: New York University Press, 1993

Kruse, Bernhard Arnold, *Auf dem extremen Pol der Subjektivität: Zu Rilkes "Aufzeichnungen des Malte Laurids Brigge,"* Wiesbaden: Deutscher Universitäts Verlag, 1994

MacLeod, Jack, "Writing as Paradox in Rilke's *Notebooks of Malte Laurids Brigge,*" *Modern Fiction Studies* 38:2 (Summer 1992)

Sokel, Walter H., "Zwischen Existenz und Weltinnenraum: Zum Prozess der Ent-Ichung in *Malte Laurids Brigge,*" in *Rilke Heute: Beziehungen und Wirkungen,* edited by Ingeborg H. Solbrig and Joachim W. Storck, Frankfurt am Main: Suhrkamp, 1975

Sokel, Walter H., "Rainer Maria Rilke's *The Notebooks of Malte Laurids Brigge,*" in *Reflection and Action: Essays on the Bildungsroman,* edited by James Hardin, Columbia: University of South Carolina Press, 1991

Nouveau Roman

The cluster of authors who for a brief time after World War II came to be known as practitioners of the *nouveau roman,* or New Novel, pulled together as cobelligerants against the increasingly politicized role ascribed to the creative writer by such giants as Jean-Paul Sartre and Albert Camus. The alliance was driven by a common interest in preserving the autonomy of the artistic impulse more than by any particular guidelines or compositional recipes, although the *nouveaux romanciers* were prolix in their theorizing and in their discussion of the epistemological and ontological implications of the text. The authors associated with the group vary according to the degree of their conformity to an overall notion of what the novel should be and do, as well as to the length of time they aligned themselves with the group. Early works by some authors, such as Alain Robbe-Grillet and Michel Butor, signaled the origins of the New Novel, while other authors, such as Nathalie Sarraute, Marguerite Duras, and the poet Francis Ponge, whose works and/or theories predated or developed independently of the movement, were adopted by the group.

It was apparent in the 1950s that something new was occurring on the literary scene, but typically the name *nouveau roman* was not immediately consecrated. The publisher most frequently associated with the New Novel is Editions de Minuit, a house directed by Jérôme Lindon that had been a combat or resistance press during the war (in 1941 Minuit published Vercors' *Le silence de la mer,* the best known resistance novel). Critics, in an effort to define the new movement, labeled it *l'Ecole de Minuit* (the Midnight School) or *l'Ecole du Regard* (the School of the Gaze). Even Robbe-Grillet did not necessarily like the term *New*

Novel. In an early essay dated 1955, "A quoi servent les théories" ("The Use of Theory"), which later was used to open his *Pour un nouveau roman* (1963; *For a New Novel: Essays on Fiction*), Robbe-Grillet writes:

> If in many of the pages that follow, I readily employ the term *New Novel*, it is not to designate a school, nor even a specific and constituted group of writers working in the same direction; the expression is merely a convenient label applicable to all those seeking new forms for the novel, form capable of expressing (or of creating) new relations between man and the world, to all those who have determined to invent the novel, in other words, to invent man.

The name New Novel emerged as the principal label, but we should retain Robbe-Grillet's reservations regarding the amorphous nature of the group; for some writers, such as Marguerite Duras, aligned themselves with the group only soon to withdraw, and even the idiom and interests of major New Novelists such as Robbe-Grillet and Michel Butor were to evolve into a different style later in their careers.

The core of writers associated with the New Novel movement are Alain Robbe-Grillet, Michel Butor, Nathalie Sarraute, Marguerite Duras, Robert Pinget, Claude Mauriac, Jean Ricardou, and 1985 Nobel prize winner Claude Simon. Dozens of other writers have written works that in some way betray, according to Jean Ricardou, "par rapport au roman académique, des traces de nouveauté" ("traces of newness in relation to the academic novel"); and in *Le nouveau roman* (1973), Ricardou lists more than 50 such authors, including those already listed above as well as such different authors as Samuel Beckett, Jean Cayrol, Hélène Cixous, J.M.G. Le Clézio, Jean Pierre Faye, Raymond Jean, Claude Ollier, Georges Perec, Jorge Semprun, Philippe Sollers, Monique Wittig, and Kateb Yacine. As for ancestors, Robbe-Grillet asserts in *For a New Novel* that literature is alive and that the novel has always been "new":

> How could its style have remained motionless, fixed, when everything around it was in evolution—even revolution—during the last hundred and fifty years? Flaubert wrote the new novel of 1860, Proust the new novel of 1910. The writer must proudly consent to bear his own date, knowing that there are no masterpieces in eternity, but only works in history; and that they survive only to the degree that they have left the past behind them and heralded the future.

Here Robbe-Grillet articulates the concept of a Marxist dynamic of social, political, and artistic phenomena in which the underpinnings of society that prevail will necessarily shape the superstructure of society, whether gradually or—as Thomas Kuhn, in his book on scientific revolutions, would have it—in abrupt upheavals, toppling the old ideas, making way for the new ones that will one day suffer the same fate.

It is no accident that Robbe-Grillet speaks of the place of the novel in history, nor that Ricardou could list so many writers as "new"; the New Novel was a product of the post-World War II era, and the same forces that were at play in the New Novel also influenced most other writers. The era also lionized writers whose styles were really the product of an earlier modernism (Samuel Beckett), or who had independently found "things" to be objects of desire (Francis Ponge), or who had always considered literature's mission to seize and define things and moments, or "tropisms" (Nathalie Sarraute), in what we might characterize as *états d'âme* (states of soul, being, or mind) or *tranches d'âme* (slices of soul, being, or mind—in contrast to "slice of life" writing).

The political climate before, during, and after World War II led to a polarization of the intellectuals whose exacerbated ideological differences led to the break-up of some movements in the 1920s and 1930s. The surrealists split between André Breton, who endorsed the French Communist Party, and purists who felt that to accept the dialectics of Marxism was to negate the absolute individual freedom basic to surrealist philosophy. The cataclysm of the war and the real threat of annihilation of the entire human race, represented by the atomic bomb, led to a period of anxiety that would last until another generation deemed activism preferable to pessimism and defeatism. These years of anxiety coincided roughly with the period of the New Novel, which would be supplanted by the so-called *nouveau nouveau roman* and the activities of the Tel Quel group.

A by-product of the sense of doom of the late 1940s, the 1950s, and the early 1960s was a natural reassessment of the world of objects around us: stones, plants, the sun, manmade objects, all as a reaction to the pessimism and instability of the postwar world. For instance, a poem by G.-E. Clancier is made up entirely of names of objects and tools found on a farm, and it should come as no surprise that intellectuals and writers of the time could identify with the prose poems of Francis Ponge that did, indeed, take "a stand on behalf of things" (c.f., *Le part-pris des choses,* 1942). The war's destruction had placed man and objects at odds, and it became clear that humanistic truth systems had failed to avert the monumental horror man had visited upon man. After 1945, it also became clear that man had to give greater consideration to the elements of the environment, those mute witnesses that would alone survive the ultimate cataclysm should it occur, to become, in a sense, man's custodians.

It is somewhat ironic that the phenomenological philosophy of Sartre and his cohorts—derived from such *maîtres à penser* as Fedor Dostoevskii, Karl Jaspers, Søren Kierkegaard, Edmund Husserl, and others—placed special emphasis on objects in the world, be they manmade or natural; the very things that preoccupied the New Novelists. Their quarrel, which fed on itself for a decade or more, seems largely based on Sartre's advocacy of a utilitarian art and his endorsement of the pragmatics of the Soviet Zhdanov, for whom art had no role save to further the revolutionary ideals and social engineering of Communism. The New Novelists, if Robbe-Grillet's views are taken as doctrine, could not accept that art should serve politics or ideology, maintaining rather that art should be sufficient unto itself, nothing less, nothing more, a latter-day Art for Art's Sake. In addition, the humanizing touch is suspect, and objects should not be expropriated by man but rather left as parts of their own paradigm. Thus, even though a New Novelist such as Robbe-Grillet could appreciate the fact that Sartre and Camus valorized objects, he did not appreciate their version of phenomenology that tends to impart to things—even on the level of semantics—the various preoccupations and qualities of humans. Although the New Novel demonstrates parallels with the cinema of the *nouvelle vague* (New

Wave), the Theatre of the Absurd, and concrete poetry of the same general period, it rejects the desperate nihilism of existential absurdity that is exemplified by Camus, in "Le Mythe de Sisyphe" (1942; "The Myth of Sisyphus"), as the dialogue of man interrogating the heavens and the silence of the reply (nor should one forget that the term Theatre of the Absurd is a misnomer).

Robbe-Grillet (1963) criticizes Sartre and especially Camus for not letting objects in the world *be*, insisting rather on embuing them with man's own emotions:

> Freedom of observation should be possible, and yet it is not. At every moment, a continuous fringe of culture (psychology, ethics, metaphysics, etc.) is added to things, giving them a less alien aspect. Sometimes the camouflage is complete: a gesture vanishes from our mind, supplanted by the emotions which supposedly produced it, and we remember a landscape as *austere* or *calm* without being able to evoke a single outline.

Even on the semantic level, Sartre and Camus endow the object with human attributes, Camus by inference through the use of anthropomorphic verbs, adjectives, and metaphors. As Ben F. Stoltzfus (1964) writes,

> Robbe-Grillet [in his essay "Nature, Humanisme, Tragédie" published in the *Nouvelle Nouvelle Revue Française* in October 1958 and reprinted in *For a New Novel*] goes on to say that Meursault, protagonist of [Camus'] *The Stranger,* engages in a kind of bitter and fascinated connivance with the world, whose "absurdity" leads to disappointment, withdrawal, and finally revolt. It is the specific manner in which Meursault humanizes the world about him which Robbe-Grillet seems to object to; that in spite of Meursault's apparent indifference to and alienation from his environment, Camus has used metaphors in such a way as to negate this alienation.

Stoltzfus then cites Robbe-Grillet's list of examples of Camus' verbal humanization of objects, including references to a countryside "gorged with sunlight," an evening "like a melancholy truce," a pot-holed pavement exposing the "shining flesh" of the tar, and the "blood colored" earth.

The metaphor is highly suspect to the New Novelist, since it tends to mediate a merger between the world of objects and the human psyche. In "Nature, Humanisme, Tragédie," Robbe-Grillet writes that the metaphor is "never an innocent figure of speech," since when one speaks of the "heart" of the forest, of a "majestic" mountain, or of a "pitiless" sun one tends to lend characteristics to the objects themselves: the mountain's height takes on moral value, the sun's rays seem to result from the sun's will rather than from the reaction of the person to the neutral fact of the universe, and so forth.

There is no stylistic ornamentation in Robbe-Grillet's *La Jalousie* (1957; *Jealousy*). The technical descriptions are so devoid of signified substance that, despite their utter precision, they fail to yield a concrete image of what is described; for instance, the word "house" is stripped of any physicalness by virtue of the cold painstaking dimensions, directions, and coordinates provided by the narrator/protagonist; and this blankness exists to such a degree that the editors of the Grove Press edition

of *Jealousy* in English translation deemed it necessary to precede the novel with a floor plan of the house and the layout of the grounds surrounding it, complete with a legend identifying various locations and objects mentioned in the narrative, all interpreted from the novel's own mathematical precisions. The editors did not realize that they were, by thus interpreting in readily understandable terms the objects evoked in the novel, actually humanizing and normalizing the narrative and thwarting the creative and ideological position of the author.

The world is, for Robbe-Grillet and other novelists in the group, simply other than us and not dependent on us: "The world is neither significant nor absurd. It *is*, quite simply." The writers against whom the New Novelists reacted were, as far as the latter are concerned, deficient in alienation, bridging the gap, as we have seen, by humanizing the objects from which they are supposedly isolated. As John Calder has written, "Robbe-Grillet's basic philosophical message is that there is no objective reality, that reality is what we choose to make it, and the will of man is more important and offers more hope and happiness to mankind than any attempt to deduce doubtful truths from nature with our discredited scientific and critical investigative methods" (see Fletcher and Calder, 1986). Thus the main apologist for the New Novel rejects the romantic or transcendental notion of Nature as the great Teacher (as, for example, in Chateaubriand, Rousseau, or Emerson); indeed, he debunks the validity of empiricism for anything but the very act, for to suggest that the empirical eye might have a therapeutic effect on man or any utilitarian value is inappropriate.

If Robbe-Grillet remains—despite Claude Simon later being awarded the Nobel prize for literature (1985)—the premier New Novelist and theoretician of the movement, others have contributed to the theory as well. A less well-known novelist, Jean Ricardou, became the self-proclaimed leader of the movement, although his ideas are perhaps more readily identifiable with the Tel Quel group than those of the New Novelists. Ricardou's *Pour une théorie du nouveau roman* (1971; *For a Theory of the New Novel*), published not by Editions de Minuit but by Editions du Seuil in their "Tel Quel" series, offers guidelines for creating New Novels and underlines the fact that the New Novelists were prompt to explain and defend their writing and their stand on behalf of writing. As Gerald Prince (1989) writes, "[the New Novel] stressed the realities of representation instead of the representation of realities; or, as Jean Ricardou once argued, it focused on the adventures of writing rather than on the writing of adventures."

Nathalie Sarraute had already developed her unique style before World War II, but found herself embraced by the New Novelists. Her *Tropismes* (1939; *Tropisms*) consists of a series of vignettes in which the line between fiction and poetry blurs and which seize on moments of reality or awareness. It is easy to see in this work and in lengthier novels such as *Le Planétarium* (1959: *The Planetarium*), in which many pages are devoted to the question of re-upholstering a chair, why Sarraute would be a welcome collaborator in the movement of the New Novel, but it is equally obvious that she had an agenda of her own that was distinct from theirs. Her essays collected in *L'Ère du soupçon* (1956; *The Age of Suspicion*), similar to Robbe-Grillet's introspections in *For a New Novel,* analyze what she as an author tries to achieve in her work and discuss past authors who have influenced her creative vision.

From a theoretical viewpoint, the New Novelists appear to have distanced themselves from the humanization of objects by metaphor as well as to have valued the microscopic analysis of critical moments in space and time, removing, as it were, personal interpretation. And yet, one might well ask if a writer can ever have total "liberty of observation" and is not, perforce, bound to convey obsessions that he or she personally harbors. Much has been written about the relative roles of narrator and author in the works of Butor, Sarraute, Duras, and Robbe-Grillet. Some contend that even if the narrator is an independent entity, his or her very implementation must result from the author's will to project his or her viewpoint. For instance, Robbe-Grillet was originally an agronomist, or agricultural engineer, which may explain to some extent his narrators' eye for mathematical alignments.

What, then, are the traits that we find in the actual works of the New Novelists? As the theory would suggest, they are usually intent upon describing with camera-like precision the world around them (and us) without letting the objects become rhetorically tainted by traces of moralistic or humanizing imagery. The patently experimental nature of their works takes varying forms, from Robbe-Grillet's blend of cold observation and ambiguous or contradictory assertions to Michel Butor's unusual use of verb tense to create the implication that what has occurred may only be a conditional idea, as in *La Modification* (1957; *A Change of Heart*).

The New Novel was, indeed, new. Much of its worth resided in its shock value, its function as "antinovel" rejecting the complacencies of traditional fiction. This iconoclasm necessarily entailed frustration on the part of readers who are usually product-oriented and expect a logical closure in response to their efforts.

Upon first reading *Jealousy*, when it appeared in English translation published by Grove Press, I was on the point of returning my copy to the bookstore, believing it to be defectively bound, for whole passages were repeated verbatim. Then I verified the pagination and realized—and was fascinated by—the author's compositional strategy; and the anecdote illustrates the degree to which the style of this literature was, indeed, "new" compared to that of the preceding generation of writers like André Malraux, Sartre, and Camus. The style continues to have the capacity to perplex and annoy readers more comfortable with a facilitating style that doesn't impose itself between the text and the reader's imagination. Whenever I teach Robbe-Grillet's *Jealousy* and *La Maison de rendez-vous* (1965; *La Maison de rendez-vous*) and Butor's *A Change of Heart*, many students feel cheated or betrayed by:

1. *Jealousy*'s tedious measurement of objects and interminable descriptions of mundane gestures such as those of a person eating, as well as by its frequent contradictions, which they could not tolerate, such as when the narrator describes with logically incompatible phrases the plot of a book that is being read and discussed by A . . . and Franck:

The main character of the book is a customs official. This character is not an official but a high-ranking employee of an old commercial company. This company's business is going badly, rapidly turning shady. This company's business is going extremely well. The chief character—one

learns—is dishonest. He is honest, he is trying to re-establish a situation compromised by his predecessor, who died in an automobile accident. But he had no predecessor, for the company was only recently formed; and it was not an accident. Besides, it happens to be a ship (a big white ship) and not a car at all.

2. The inconsistent spelling of the name of the main character in *La Maison de Rendez-vous* (Johnson/Johnston/Johnstone) which caused students to express resentment at the fact that a famous author couldn't even properly proofread his book, and they felt the need to know what the "real" spelling of his name was); and

3. The fact that they plodded through *A Change of Heart* to see what would "happen" only to find that at the end of the novel the narrator—who for the entire text has been describing in detail how a tryst will hopefully develop—decides not to pursue the affair and, instead, returns home.

These examples, covering the past 35 years, bear witness to the fact that the New Novel was not only "new" in the 1950s and 1960s, but also show that its shock effect endures, for today's average reader, like the one of the immediate post–World War II era, continues to have difficulty realizing that descriptions, names, and actions in fiction can very well derive their essence not from life but from their own textual existence and its momentum.

ERIC SELLIN

See also French Novel (1945–); Postmodernism; Alain Robbe-Grillet

Further Reading

Britton, Celia, *The Nouveau Roman: Fiction, Theory, and Politics,* New York: St. Martin's Press, 1992

Fletcher, John, and John Calder, editors, *The Nouveau Roman Reader*, introduction by John Calder, London: Calder, and New York: Riverrun Press, 1986

Heath, Stephen, *The Nouveau Roman: A Study in the Practice of Writing,* London: Elek, and Philadelphia: Temple University Press, 1972

Oppenheim, Lois, editor, *Three Decades of the New Novel,* Urbana: University of Illinois Press, 1986

Prince, Gerald, "The Nouveau Roman," in *A New History of French Literature*, edited by Denis Hollier, Cambridge, Massachusetts: Harvard University Press, 1989

Ricardou, Jean, *Pour une théorie du nouveau roman,* Paris: Editions du Seuil, 1971

Ricardou, Jean, *Nouveau Roman: Hier, aujourd'hui,* Paris: Union générale d'éditions, 1972

Ricardou, Jean, *Le nouveau roman,* Paris: Editions du Seuil, 1973

Robbe-Grillet, Alain, *Pour un nouveau roman,* Paris: Editions de Minuit, 1963; as *For a New Novel: Essays on Fiction,* New York: Grove Press, 1965

Stoltzfus, Ben F., *Alain Robbe-Grillet and the New French Novel,* Carbondale: Southern Illinois University Press, 1964

Sturrock, John, *The French New Novel: Claude Simon, Michel Butor, Alain Robbe-Grillet,* London and New York: Oxford University Press, 1969

Nouvelle historique. *See* Historical Novel

Novel and Romance: Etymologies

Samuel Johnson, writing his *Dictionary of the English Language* (1755) during the first flowering of the English novel, entered the following definition: "novel: a small tale, generally of love." To modern sensibilities, Johnson's novel resembles more closely the novella in dimension and the romance in substance. He was of course thinking of the novel's proximate etymology from the Italian *novelle,* much like Dryden, who spoke disparagingly of "the trifling novels which Ariosto inserted in his poems." Since then, the word *novel* has come to embrace different generic criteria of subject, meter, length, and unity of action designating in the main a long piece of fiction in prose. Likewise, the term *romance,* or *roman,* once interchangeable with *novel* in English, retains the meaning of *novel* in Germany, France, Russia, and most of Europe, while in the anglophone world it has been demoted to frivolity. Although the etymologies of *novel/novella, romance/roman* are discrete, the history of their evolution and the connotative prejudices and linguistic snobberies that underlie their application to the same narrative form is shared. *Novel* connotes a newness in form, a deviation into more colloquial prose from epic and lyric meters; *romance* suggests a newness in idiom, a rejection of the Latin of antiquity for the common speech of Europe.

Romance/Roman

In the Middle Ages and early Renaissance, the history of the word *romance* was itself the subject of romance. As Daniel Huet attests in *De l'Origine des Romans* (1670; *A Treatise of Romances and Their Original*), one bumpkin etymology maintained that *romance* was an eponym deriving from the city of Reims, where the famous Turpin, hero of the battle of Roncesvalles and *La Chanson de Roland* (*The Song of Roland*), had been archbishop. The reality is somewhat less romantic.

A corruption of the Latin adverb *romanice, romance* was the word used by vulgar Latin speakers in the further marches of the Roman Empire to describe the "manner of speaking in Rome," or *romanica loqui.* After the fall of the empire in the fifth century, the noun *romans* referred to the dialects formed by the mixture of vulgar Latin first with the Celtic and later the Germanic languages of Europe. As a linguistic term, *romans* served to distinguish European vernaculars from the low Latin of the Church and of diplomacy.

Romans remained an oral language until the Carolingian era, when it was first used in texts: *La Chanson de Sainte Eulalie* (The Song of St. Eulalia), a 9th-century French sermon, and the *Oaths of Strasbourg* (c. 842), a treaty between two Carolingian kings written partly in French. The leap from language to literary form occurred most likely via sermons that increasingly needed to be translated from Church Latin for congregations who could no

longer understand the service. *Romance* thus derives narrowly from the verbs *enromancier* and *romancar,* meaning "to translate into the vernacular," the product of which was a *romanz, romant,* or *romanzo.* In Spain from the 15th century onward, *romanza* designated exclusively a song or ballad such as the French *lai* and distinct from the long, chivalric tale called a *historia,* or *corónica.* France seems to have been the origin of the latter. According to the 16th-century Italian scholar Giraldi, the chivalric romance passed from France to Spain and thence to Italy. At the same time, the Italian poet Tasso was arguing for a rapprochement of the *romanzo* with Aristotelian epic conventions, giving the form a new literary weight. From the late 17th century on, this new heroic romance, fortified by the *gravitas* of epic, took on the modern European sense of *roman* equivalent to *novel* in English.

Novel/Novella

Ancient Rome was a society that often valued tradition over novelty. In Latin ethical vocabulary, the words *novus, novitas,* and its relatives regularly bear pejorative connotations. Consequently, when Cicero wanted to revile modern poets such as Catullus who had revived the Greek Alexandrian style, he called them *neoteroi* or *poetae novi.* The Ciceronian stigma on novelty was to plague letters until Dante, poet of the *dolce stil nuovo* and author of the linguistic tract *De vulgari eloquentia* (c. 1305; *Literature in the Vernacular*), restored virtue to literary newness, playing unwitting midwife to the term *novel.* The word *novel* is a foreshortening of the vulgar Latin *novella,* the neuter plural of *novellus,* meaning "news" but leaning more toward "rumors." By connotation, "novel/novella" is a form whose subjects and characters are drawn largely from the middle and lower classes. As "news" or "rumor," it suggests a story told on the corner, an indecorous tidbit narrated orally in a familiar style yet pretending at a journalistic immediacy that belies the fiction it is.

Novel first appeared as a literary term in 14th-century Italy in Guardati's *Novellino* (1367), a collection of stories and anecdotes overshadowed a few years later by Boccaccio's *Decameron* (1371). In his preface Boccaccio searches for a genre to fit his compilation of tales, proposing tentatively "parables," "fables," or "novels" (*novelle*). Widely translated and imitated throughout Europe, the *Decameron* inscribed the word *novella* indelibly in the terminology of genre. As a short story of the common classes, however, *novella* was at an evolutionary crossroads. Transmitted north to France, it became the *nouvelle,* retaining its narrow focus on a single episode but growing in length and regaining courtly pretensions. German authors of the 18th and early 19th centuries authoritatively formulated the rules for the modern novella, whose subject Goethe characterized in a manner reminiscent of its Latin roots in rumor: "What else is a *Novelle* about but an event which is unheard of but has taken place?" Transmitted west to Spain, *novelle* became *novelas*, allying itself with the *exemplum* or exemplary tale. *Novelas* was still a recent term when Cervantes wrote the *Novelas Ejemplares* (1613), a work that both lengthened the Italian form and imbued it with added moral seriousness. Shakespeare and other English playwrights frequently mined *novelle* for dramatic plots, and as the term gained popularity, its Italian pronunciation was Englished to *novél*. With influence from the longer French nouvelle and Cervantes' more substantial *novelas*, the long modern novel of middle-class affairs finally found definition in the early 19th century. The last word belongs to Sir Walter Scott, who commented on Jane Austen's *Emma* in *The Quarterly Review* (1815), arguing that it belonged "to a class of fictions which has arisen almost in our own times, and which draws the characters and incidents introduced more immediately from the current of ordinary life."

GREGORY HEYWORTH

See also Critics and Criticism (18th Century); Genre Criticism; Novella; Prose Novelistic Forms; Renaissance Narrative; Romance; Romantic Novel

Further Reading

Anderson, James, and Bernard Rochet, *Historical Romance Morphology,* Ann Arbor: University of Michigan Press, 1978

Auerbach, Erich, *Introduction to Romance Languages and Literature: Latin, French, Spanish, Provencal, Italian,* New York: Capricorn, 1961

Dryden, John, "Preface to the Fables," in *Essays of John Dryden,* volume 2, edited by W.P. Ker, Oxford: Clarendon Press, 1900; New York: Macmillan 1903

Huet, Daniel, "De L'Origine des Romans" (1670), in *Œuvres Complètes de Madame de La Fayette,* edited by Auger, Paris: Lepetit, 1820

Kern, Edith, "The Romance of Novel/Novella," in *The Disciplines of Criticism: Essays in Literary Theory, Interpretation, and History,* edited by Peter Demetz, Thomas Greene, Lowry Nelson, and Rene Welleck, New Haven, Connecticut: Yale University Press, 1968

Krauss, Werner, "Novela-Novelle-Roman," *Zeitschrift für romanische Philologie* 60 (1940)

McKeon, Michael, *The Origins of the English Novel, 1600–1740,* Baltimore: Johns Hopkins University Press, 1987; London: Radius, 1988

Paulin, Roger, *The Brief Compass: The Nineteenth Century German Novelle,* New York and Oxford: Clarendon Press, 1985

Reeve, Clara, *The Progress of Romance,* Colchester: Keymer, 1785; New York: Facsimile Text Society, 1930

Novel Cycles. *See* Romans Fleuves

Novel of Ideas

The novel as a genre is inherently well suited to the exploration of ideas, and all novels to a greater or lesser extent engage in dialogues with various political and philosophical notions. However, some novels, which might be termed novels of ideas (closely related to the French term *roman à thèse*), rely more centrally on the exploration of ideas than others. In these novels, the exploration of ideas becomes paramount, while normally important aspects of the novel such as plot and characterization are secondary. In some ways the novel of ideas has its roots in texts such as the dialogues of Plato and may be related to the tradition of Menippean satire as elaborated not only in the ancient Greek texts of Lucian but also in more modern works such as François Rabelais' *Gargantua and Pantagruel* (1532–34), Robert Burton's *The Anatomy of Melancholy* (1621), Jonathan Swift's *Gulliver's Travels* (1726), Herman Melville's *Moby-Dick* (1851), James Joyce's *Ulysses* (1922), and Thomas Pynchon's *Gravity's Rainbow* (1973). However, the novel of ideas experienced a particular flowering in the 19th century. The realist novel became the dominant Western genre during this century because it was the form best suited to the expression of ideas that informed the worldview of the newly dominant European bourgeoisie. Yet the very dominance of the novel as a genre of bourgeois expression often tended to make it the genre of choice for writers who, for whatever reason, wished to express ideas in opposition to bourgeoisie ideology.

To an extent, the great French realist novels of the 19th century should all be considered novels of ideas, despite their typical emphasis on plot. The works of writers such as Honoré de Balzac, Stendhal, Gustave Flaubert, and Émile Zola may be read as dramatizations of the struggle for hegemony among various ideas that periodically erupted in the postrevolutionary society of France throughout the 19th century. In England, on the other hand, bourgeois hegemony was so stable and well established by the 19th century that most mainstream English novels of the period tend to operate in a mode that obscures the ideological status of bourgeois thought and presents bourgeois ideas instead as "nature" or "common sense." Thus, most 19th-century English novels that present themselves overtly as novels of ideas are to some extent antibourgeois in nature. Even the works of writers such as Charles Dickens, Benjamin Disraeli, and Elizabeth Gaskell, while certainly not revolutionary in their advocacy of political change, are critical of certain aspects of the existing social order. And genuinely revolutionary English novels do appear in this period, ranging from the chartist novels of Ernest Jones and Thomas Merton Wheeler, to the utopian fantasies of William Morris, to the beginnings of a genuine working-class novelistic tradition (informed by the work of writers such as William Edwards Tirebuck, Allen Clarke, and Margaret Harkness) by the end of the century. Meanwhile, the production of socialist novels worldwide was spurred in the late 19th century by the work of Karl Marx and Friedrich Engels and by events such as the founding of the Second International in 1889.

Nowhere, however, did the 19th-century novel of ideas flourish more prominently than in Russia, a country that was struggling at the time to define its very cultural identity, both in relation and in opposition to the West. An early example of this phenomenon is Aleksandr Radishchev, who, influenced by the ideas of the Western Enlightenment, passionately argues in his influential novel *Puteshestvie iz Peterburga v Moskvu* (1790; *A Journey from St. Petersburg to Moscow*) against the ills of czarist Russia. Most importantly, Radishchev attacks the institution of serfdom and advocates the establishment of a more just and humane Russian society. Following Radishchev's humanistic model, Aleksandr Herzen also focuses his literary activities on a critique of Russian society. His novel *Kto vinovat?* (1847; *Who Is To Blame?*) addresses the problem of the so-called Russian "superfluous man," the symbol for a class of educated and bright young men unable to find a suitable place in society. Herzen points out that these men, instead of applying themselves to the betterment of society, are at best useless and at worst a destructive force. In *Who Is To Blame?* Herzen also examines the position of women in 19th-century Russian society, criticizing that society for preventing women from becoming strong and independent individuals by forcing them into passive roles.

During the 19th century, novels became a common territory in which Russian authors examined various issues and ideas. For example, the meditations on the nature of history that punctuate the narrative of Lev Tolstoi's *Voina i mir* (1863–69; *War and Peace*) should be read within the context of a larger uncertainty about the role of Russia in European history. Many of the great Russian novels of the 19th century were written specifically as contributions to important national debates, the most important of which took place between the Westernizers and the Slavophiles. The former (following a path first advocated in Russia by Peter the Great) believed the best way for Russia to achieve a more just and prosperous society was to emulate the process of capitalist modernization that had transformed Western European society in the prior two centuries. The Slavophiles, on the other hand, believed capitalist modernization was spiritually impoverishing and that Russia's best course lay in the pursuit of indigenous values based on the Russian Orthodox religion and the traditional (Eastern) cultures of Russia's people. Novels such as Nikolai Gogol's *Mertvye dushi* (1842; *Dead Souls*) are, among other things, diatribes against the Western Enlightenment emphasis on rationality, celebrating instead the advantages of Russian spirituality.

On the other hand, many of the various revolutionary groups that sprang up in 19th-century Russia espoused a strong belief in Western science as a potential cure for the ills of czarist Russia. Bazarov, the protagonist of Ivan Turgenev's *Ottsy i deti* (1862; *Fathers and Sons*), is an early literary figuration of the new scientific man in Russia. Turgenev apparently considered his treatment of the rationalist Bazarov sympathetic, but many of the radicals of the day reacted violently against Turgenev's book, viewing Bazarov as crudely depicted in his scientific beliefs, in mockery of their own. Nikolai Chernyshevskii's *Chto delat'?* (1863; *What Is To Be Done?*) was written at least partially as a response to what many thought of as Turgenev's satire by openly embracing the kind of scientism demonstrated by Bazarov. Chernyshevskii's book is a powerful plea for science and rationality as important guiding principles in life. *What Is To Be Done?* also pays substantial attention to the need for the emancipation of women and for workers to take positive but peaceful collective action to oppose their exploitation by capitalism. It quickly became an important inspiration for many materialist radicals of the time and for decades to come, up to and including the Bolsheviks of the 1917 revolution. Meanwhile, the success of Chernyshevskii's book brought an immediate response from Fedor Dostoevskii in the form of *Zapiski iz podpol'ia* (1864; *Notes from Underground*), whose protagonist bitterly rails against the coldly impoverishing materialism of Chernyshevskii's rationalist vision. In fact, the novels of Dostoevskii play a special role in the Russian 19th-century novel of ideas. Even though they are explicitly written as denunciations of Western influences on Russian culture, Mikhail Bakhtin has argued in his important study *Problemy poetiki Dostoevskogo* (originally published 1929; *Problems of Dostoevsky's Poetics*) that all of Dostoevskii's novels may be read as balanced dramatizations of conflicts among various ideas, very much in the tradition of Menippean satire.

The tradition of intellectual debate established in the Russian 19th-century novel carried forward into the 20th century as well. For example, the dystopian warnings of Evgenii Zamiatin's *My* (1924; *We*) owe a great deal to the critique of rationality contained in the 19th-century novels of Dostoevskii and others. Similarly, dissident novels that explicitly criticized the postrevolutionary Soviet regime, many of which gained considerable attention in the West, often grew out of either the Slavophile tradition (as in the works of Aleksandr Solzhenitsyn) or the Menippean tradition (as in the works of Iuz Aleshkovskii or Aleksandr Zinov'ev). But the impressive array of pro-Soviet novels that were produced during the Soviet years (often written in the mode of socialist realism, including novels by Maksim Gor'kii, Mikhail Sholokhov, and Aleksei Tolstoi) stands as probably the most important single phenomenon in the 20th-century novel of ideas, while drawing directly upon the works of 19th-century predecessors such as Tolstoi and Chernyshevskii.

DUBRAVKA JURAGA

See also Conte Philosophique; Ideology and the Novel; Russian Novel; Social Criticism; Socialist Realism

Further Reading

Acton, Edward, *Alexander Herzen and the Role of the Intellectual Revolutionary*, Cambridge and New York: Cambridge University Press, 1979

Andrew, Joe, *Writers and Society During the Rise of Russian Realism,* London and New York: Macmillan, 1980

Bakhtin, M.M., *Problemy tvorchestva Dostoevskogo,* Leningrad: Priboi, 1929; 2nd edition, revised, as *Problemy poetiki Dostoevskogo,* Moscow: Sov. Pisatel, 1963; as *Problems of Dostoevsky's Poetics,* Ann Arbor, Michigan: Ardis, 1973; new edition and translation, Minneapolis: University of Minnesota Press, and Manchester: Manchester University Press, 1984

Berlin, Isaiah, *Russian Thinkers,* London: Hogarth Press, 1977; New York: Viking, 1978

Hingley, Ronald, *Russian Writers and Society, 1825–1904,* London: Weidenfeld and Nicolson, and New York: McGraw-Hill, 1967; 2nd revised edition as *Russian Writers and Society in the Nineteenth Century,* London: Weidenfeld and Nicolson, 1977

Lodge, David, *The Art of Fiction: Illustrated from Classic and Modern Texts,* London: Penguin, 1992; New York: Viking, 1993

Rzhevsky, Nicholas, *Russian Literature and Ideology: Herzen, Dostoevsky, Leontiev, Tolstoy, Fadeyev,* Urbana: University of Illinois Press, 1983

Suleiman, Susan Rubin, *Authoritarian Fictions: The Ideological Novel as a Literary Genre,* New York: Columbia University Press, 1983

Walicki, Andrzej, *Rosyjska filozofia i mysl spoleczna od oswiecenia do marksizmu,* Warsaw: Wiedza Powszechna, 1973; as *A History of Russian Thought from the Enlightenment to Marxism,* Stanford, California: Stanford University Press, 1979; Oxford: Clarendon Press, 1980

Zelinskii, Kornelii, *Soviet Literature: Problems and People,* Moscow: Progress, 1970

Novel of Manners

Considering how often one novel or another is designated a "novel of manners," it is astonishing how little critical energy has been devoted to discerning what precisely the "novel of manners" is, from which tradition or traditions this subgenre derives, and what novels of manners do. Scholars working within the Anglo-American tradition(s) are quick to claim the works of Jane Austen, Henry James, and Edith Wharton as quintessential novels of manners and, depending on what they consider the salient qualities of these novels, will then expand their lists to include such authors as Samuel Richardson, Anthony Trollope, George Eliot, Frances Burney, Maria Edgeworth, Virginia Woolf, Barbara Pym, Dorothy Sayers, Margaret Drabble, F. Scott Fitzgerald, even Nathaniel Hawthorne as novelists of manners. This—admittedly partial—list suggests that there is little consensus, even within Anglo-American culture, about what a novel of manners is. And when we admit the productions of other language cultures into consideration, reading Madame de Lafayette (*La Princesse de Clèves* [1678; *The Princess of Cleves*]), Choderlos de Laclos (*Les Liaisons dangereuses* [1782; *Dangerous Acquaintances*]), Honoré de Balzac (*Le père goriot* [1835; *Le Père Goriot*]), Marcel Proust (*À la recherche du temps perdu* [1913–27; translated as *Remembrance of Things Past* and also as *In Search of Lost Time*]), Theodor Fontane (*Frau Jenny Treibel* [1892; *Jenny Treibel*]), Thomas Mann (*Buddenbrooks* [1901; *Buddenbrooks*]), Johann Wolfgang von Goethe (*Die Wahlverwandtschaften* [1809; *The Elective Affinities*]), Lev Tolstoi (*Anna Karenina* [1875–77])—just to mention the French, German, and Russian writers known to a general Anglo-American readership—as novelists of manners, the task of defining the novel of manners becomes all the more difficult.

It is equally difficult to adduce any one history or tradition of the novel of manners, since a particular culture's literary appropriation of conventions of manners depends so much on the class structure of that culture and the relation between codes of behavior and social organization. Hence, for example, the Continental novel is indebted to Renaissance and ancien régime courtly protocol, whereas the English tradition of manners—at least as this tradition achieves articulation in the novel—is more readily traced to social and literary forms associated with the rise of the bourgeoisie in the 18th century.

The *Oxford English Dictionary* defines manners as "the way something is done or takes place" in a certain society; more specifically, they are the "customary mode of acting or behavior, whether of an individual or of a community, habitual practice, usage, custom, fashion . . . external behavior in social intercourse, estimated as good or bad according to its degree of politeness or of conformity to the accepted standard of propriety." In the spirit of this definition, James Tuttleton (1972) describes the novel of manners as one in which "the manners, social customs, folkways, conventions, traditions, and mores of a given social group play a dominant role in the lives of fictional characters, exert control over their thought and behavior, and constitute a determinant upon the actions in which they are engaged, and in which these manners and customs are detailed realistically—with, in fact, a premium upon the exactness of their representation."

In addition to representing the context in which the action of the novel takes place, manners also constitute the system of representation of the novel of manners. That is to say that manners are not simply the conventions, mores, customs, and traditions in terms of which the characters in a novel articulate their desires and emplot their fulfillment; manners also are the novelistic conventions in which these desires and their emplotment achieve representation.

Through manners, the novel's closed society articulates its boundaries, and the novel itself articulates the terms of its closure. Manners organize a closed society in such a way that what it considers improper—that is, both unseemly and not proper (belonging) to it—is simultaneously proscribed and granted indirect articulation. In his brilliant eponymous essay on the French writer La Bruyère (1964), Roland Barthes distinguishes between the "inland" and the "outland" delineated by the manners of a closed society: the laws governing what one does and does not do both constitute the boundaries of a society and allow those members who agree to behave according to these laws a certain latitude in which to play with them. For instance, in a society in which afternoon and morning visits signal entirely different registers of intimacy, the appearance in the morning of a relative stranger with a plausible excuse (i.e., "an intimate mutual friend asked me to deliver a message") can—but need not—precipitate a socially yet-unsanctioned new intimacy that will either continue to operate under cover of other similarly engineered ruses or seek public legitimation. The way in which the novel's plot deals with this "infraction" (immediate censure, continued dalliance, legitimation, scandal) determines its closural strategies. Since the novel of manners' repertoire of plots is determined by the rules governing social behavior, it is possible to assert that its narrative economy is governed by the same laws that regulate the actions of its characters.

The reason that manners allow for play at the same time as they designate the boundaries of that play is that they encode what they apparently proscribe; they represent a mode of indirection whose functioning depends on their ability to maintain in a state of dynamic repression much of their own constitutive energy. Hence, as James R. Kincaid argues in an article entitled "Anthony Trollope and the Unmannerly Novel" (in Bowers and Brothers, 1990):

> Manners—and the novel of manners—do not just happen but are tied to forms of cultural power and control; further . . . actual novels of manners tend to allow a pretty fierce criticism of the system upholding any given set of manners. No novels . . . are more relentlessly political and ideological than these presumably domestic and personal works. They resist the dissociation of the personal from the political and see forms of power everywhere. . . . The novel of manners is most interestingly seen as an attack on the novel of manners.

As Kincaid suggests, the subgenre that is so often associated with conservatism—because of its circumscription of a closed, elitist society and its acute preoccupation with affairs that are of apparently no interest outside of this society—has explosive political potential, albeit potential that is often not exploited and even more often not noticed. The way, for example, that the novels of Jane Austen have been appropriated by all kinds of readers, from the far right to the far left, suggests that in her deployment of manners Austen mobilizes more energies than are containable in one single political economy, even though the economy of manners of her novels seems to accommodate these energies quite neatly.

Yet the energies that novels of manners encode within the gestural economy of "good" society need not be figured as political energies. Long before critics started paying serious attention to the political subtexts of novels of manners, manners—in Austen and elsewhere—were seen to give expression to psychological depths. As Gloria Sybil Gross claims in "Jane Austen and Psy-

chological Realism: 'What Does a Woman Want'" (in Bowers and Brothers, 1990), "a word, a gesture, a look, a tone of voice, these significant small details of social intercourse are the clues to the deepest sources of feeling. . . . Austen exposed profound unconscious dynamics and their powerful influence upon conscious life." More dramatically than Austen, perhaps, Balzac and James use manners to both mask and give expression to profound psychological dramas—what Peter Brooks (1976) calls "melodrama"—whose sheer force would do violence to the representational economy were manners themselves not capable of containing excess at the same time as they allow it to negotiate some of its claims. In Balzac's *Le Père Goriot,* the Vicomtesse de Beauséant gives a ball on the evening that she quits society forever because she has been forsaken by her lover; the brilliant social performance that belies her humiliation and masks her intention to leave the world not only gives powerful expression to her abjection but comments on the drama of Goriot, an old man dying in poverty several blocks away, ruined and abandoned by the daughters who attend the ball and mourn the departure of the Vicomtesse more than they do the impending demise of their father. In this episode, exquisite manners both divert attention from and give expression to a many-layered drama of ambition and betrayal. The famous card-playing scene in Henry James' *The Golden Bowl* (1904) articulates the entire drama of betrayal and retribution being acted out through manners within the arrangement of four people at a card table being watched by a fifth:

> The facts of the situation were upright to [Maggie Verver] round the green cloth and the silver flambeaux; the fact of her father's wife's lover [Maggie's husband] facing his mistress; the fact of her father sitting, all unsounded and unblinking, between them; the fact of Charlotte keeping it up, keeping up everything, across the table; the fact of Fanny Assingham, wonderful creature, placed opposite to the three and knowing more about each, probably . . . than either of them know of either. Erect above all for her was the sharp-edged fact of the relation of the whole group, individually and collectively, to herself. . . .

Because manners here are working to keep a nexus of deception and knowledge from exploding into destruction and pain, Maggie can look at this scene and imagine it "like a stage awaiting a drama, it was a scene she might people, by the press of her string, either with serenities and dignities and decencies, or with terrors and shames and ruins . . .". The ability to "work" manners such that they preserve appearances even as the "terrors and shames and ruins" are being silently acknowledged and distributed enables both Maggie and James to bring the plot to a close without violating the superficial formality figured in the first citation.

It should be clear from the examples just discussed that the quality of affect represented as being encoded into manners depends upon the role manners play within a novel's historical context. Certainly, a Balzacian or Jamesian melodrama of manners would be anathema to the ideology of propriety governing the novels of Jane Austen. In Balzac and James, it is clearly anachronistic to use manners to organize a discourse about the social world as a whole; the pressure that is brought to bear on manners by what is so palpably "beneath and behind" them (to use James' phrase) allows for the representation through them of both a sociopolitical and a personal unconscious as well as a dramatization of the inadequacy of manners to the task of truly representing "le monde comme il est" ("the world as it is," *Le Père Goriot*).

In the case of Austen, the world circumscribed by manners is more plausibly identical with the world whose parameters the novel's discourse recognizes. Although recent scholarship has convincingly challenged the notion of Austen as a conservative miniaturist of manners entirely disengaged from the historical events and political debates of her day, it is true that historical and political discourse are present in her novels in much the same manner as they are present to the characters in these novels. As Edward Said (1993) points out, *Mansfield Park* (1814) does bring up the issue of British imperialism, but it does so only insofar as Sir Thomas Bertram's concern about his plantations in Antigua compels him to leave Mansfield at a crucial moment in the development of the novel's domestic crisis. Although a responsible reading of the novel demands attention to this highly significant detail, its importance to the characters has more to do with the protracted absence of the head of the family than with the economic and political implications of the sugar trade in the early 19th century—and our interpretation of this detail must consider it in relation to the crises it precipitates: Maria Bertram's engagement to Mr. Rushworth, the introductions of the worldly Crawfords, the theatricals. In Austen's novels, manners domesticate the larger world's infractions upon the domestic sphere: the presence of a militia encampment in *Pride and Prejudice* (1813) and of naval officers learning to cope with peacetime in *Persuasion* (1818) certainly gestures toward a world outside the domestic and a class outside the gentry, but their interest to the characters in the novels is resolutely domestic and romantic; in a world in which there seem always to be more marriageable young women than there are bachelors willing to marry them, the military represents a resource seemingly divorced from its national or imperial mission.

But if in Austen's novels manners domesticate the world's infractions upon the private sphere, they do not solve the conflicts raised by these infractions. The conflicts that Austen's novels represent directly are personal—and social only to the extent that the personal comes into conflict with those social concerns that achieve articulation within the family. Yet the way in which the sociopolitical becomes visible at the margins of the world of manners lends force to the impression generated by the novels' domestic plots that, even though manners continue to manage the gender politics of Austen's few families, they do not manage them satisfactorily: there is no way to prevent Mr. Collins from taking Elizabeth's refusal to marry him as a polite deferral of her acceptance of his proposal. Indeed, at the same time as manners envision no resolution other than marriage for a woman's plot, they seem only barely capable of protecting women from making, or being forced into, the wrong marriage. Moreover, the inabilities of the economy of manners of *Mansfield Park*, for instance, to accommodate some trivial home theatricals, Mary Crawford's worldliness, and her brother's rakishness suggest that the manners that govern the world of Mansfield are inadequate to the tasks that are being set for them. If, ideally, manners mask and negotiate the claims they claim not to recognize, in Austen, the force of nonrecognition that manners must exert makes them incapable of entirely masking or adequately negotiating these claims.

As early as the beginning of the 19th century, then, those novels that have been most often canonized as novels of manners seem to be using manners to gesture toward their own insufficiency both in the organization of society and of literary texts. Perhaps this is why it is so difficult to claim any particular history of this subgenre. Within the Continental tradition, it is possible to derive a genealogy for the novel of manners such as that described by Peter Brooks (1969) that derives from Renaissance literature about courtly behavior, includes the romances of Madeleine de Scudéry, the maxims of La Bruyère and La Rochefoucauld, the libertine novels of Crébillon *fils*, Denon, and others, and what might be termed the first novel of manners in the form we know it today, Lafayette's *La Princesse de Clèves.* Yet the English novel of manners derives less from courtly models than it does from those attempts to legislate conduct associated with the rise of the bourgeoisie and of the distinctions in gender roles that develop with bourgeois forms of domesticity. Hence, perhaps, the explicit centrality of questions of erotics and power in the Continental novel of manners, questions that can be addressed in the English tradition only through indirection, or, as in the case of Frances Burney's *Evelina* (1778), through the introduction of foreigners. And when Henry James appropriates the tradition at a relatively late point in its protracted obsolescence, he orchestrates precisely the conflicts that occur when manners, as construed in the Anglo-American tradition, encounter manners in their Continental application (see especially *The American*, 1876). If the novel of manners has its origin in texts working toward or even celebrating the homogeneity of a closed society that could designate its closure through its manners, its function in the 20th century seems to have been the foregrounding and exploration of the differences to which forms of social closure are such a tempting response.

In 1950, Lionel Trilling called upon the novel of manners to do the work of moral discernment ("to penetrate to the truth which, as the novel assumes, lies hidden beneath all the false appearances") in a world that is poor in institutions that "raise questions in our minds not only about conditions but about ourselves, that lead us to refine our motives and ask what might lie behind our good impulses." Nearly 40 years later, Kazuo Ishiguro's postmodern, postcolonial novel of manners *The Remains of the Day* (1989) demonstrates as eloquently as Laclos' *Les Liaisons dangereuses* that manners, and the novels that exploit them, are subject to the same mystifications and seductions that they claim to expose, and that, as Goethe put it in *The Elective Affinities*, "Through what is called behavior or good manners we are supposed to achieve what is otherwise achievable only through violence, or perhaps not even through violence."

SUSAN WINNETT

See also English Novel (18th Century); Epistolary Novel; French Novel (18th Century)

Further Reading

Armstrong, Nancy, and Leonard Tennenhouse, editors, *The Ideology of Conduct: Essays in Literature and the History of Sexuality,* New York: Methuen, 1987
Auerbach, Erich, "La Cour et la Ville," translated by Ralph Manheim, in *Scenes from the Drama of European Literature,* New York: Meridian, 1959
Barthes, Roland, "La Bruyère," in *Critical Essays,* translated by

Richard Howard, Evanston, Illinois: Northwestern University Press, 1972; volume originally published as *Essais critiques*, 1964

Bentley, Nancy, *The Ethnography of Manners: Hawthorne, James, Wharton*, Cambridge and New York: Cambridge University Press, 1995

Bowers, Bege K., and Barbara Brothers, editors, *Reading and Writing Women's Lives: A Study of the Novel of Manners*, Ann Arbor, Michigan: UMI Research Press, 1990

Brooks, Peter, *The Novel of Worldliness: Crébillon, Marivaux, Laclos, Stendhal*, Princeton, New Jersey: Princeton University Press, 1969

Brooks, Peter, *The Melodramatic Imagination: Balzac, Henry James, Melodrama, and the Mode of Excess*, New Haven, Connecticut: Yale University Press, 1976

Johnson, Claudia L., *Jane Austen: Women, Politics, and the Novel*, Chicago: University of Chicago Press, 1988

Price, Martin, "Manners, Morals, and Jane Austen," *Nineteenth-Century Fiction* 30 (December 1975)

Said, Edward, *Culture and Imperialism*, New York: Knopf, and London: Chatto and Windus, 1993

Trilling, Lionel, "Manners, Morals, and the Novel," in *The Liberal Imagination: Essays on Literature and Society*, New York: Viking, 1950; London: Secker and Warburg, 1951

Tuttleton, James W., *The Novel of Manners in America*, Chapel Hill: University of North Carolina Press, 1972

Winnett, Susan, *Terrible Sociability: The Text of Manners in Laclos, Goethe, and James*, Stanford, California: Stanford University Press, 1993

Novella

The novella, a short to medium-length narrative in prose, differs from the novel principally through its greater concision and its traditional exploitation of a central event. It is realistic, often tightly plotted, with a relative lack of dialogue. The novella's demand for economy commonly means that setting, characters, mood, and inner meaning may all be subordinate to what actually happens, while the central event (or situation) may be recounted in such a way that it seems more important than the figures themselves. The central event may sometimes be seen to overshadow the characters, with their psychology expressed by means of that event rather than by gradual description and revelation—another distinguishing mark between this genre and the novel itself.

Throughout its history the novella has continued to provoke new definitions, and in Germany writers often have been as much aware of the views of the critics as of literary tradition itself. The model established in the 19th century remains the accepted norm, however, and writers have experimented far less with this genre than they have with the novel. It is remarkable how consistently writers of novellas employ a framework narrative (that is, the technique of a "double narrator"), how prominent the actual process of narration has tended to be, how regularly the central event has come closer to the mysterious, or unfathomable, rather than the simply "unusual," and how often there has been an element of paradox.

Novellas obviously lie between novels and short stories. Although the key distinction among the three is generally regarded as one of length, little may actually divide extreme examples of each form. Most novellas fall between 15,000 and 50,000 words, but these are obviously limits within which one could place a long short story or a short novel. A more useful distinction may be in what each genre seeks to cover. Novellas typically involve a smaller range of characters than novels (focusing on a small group or, more likely, an individual), snatches of an existence rather than a full survey, and a swift and indirect revelation of character rather than full and detailed development.

Despite its economy, the novella contains a certain complexity that distinguishes it from the short story. In the latter, the story itself is supreme; there tends to be a minimum of character, plot, and idea; and the force of the work normally derives from the twist of its conclusion. The clearer brevity of the short story may lead it toward the amusing or even the flippant. The novella, by contrast, is never trivial. Its implications are often profound, and often something problematic occurs at its center. Although it, too, may have a twist in its ending, readers may have anticipated the twist, which serves as an integral part of the novella's effect.

The novella (Italian for "piece of news") was a precursor of the novel. It originated in Renaissance Italy with Boccaccio's *Decameron* (written 1349–51), a collection of contemporary tales told by a group of different narrators. The *Decameron* marked the first appearance of stories recognizable as being akin to the modern novella, with compact, intricate narratives and an economy of detail. The collection ranges in length, however, from what we might nowadays term anecdote to long short story. The "story within the story" technique of the *Decameron* remained popular, as writers first sought to encourage identification between narrator and reader and then exploited the obvious, or concealed, prejudices of the framework narrator in order to introduce ambiguity. The first type of novella flourished in Italy with numerous imitators of Boccaccio and came to Spain a little later, most prominently with Miguel de Cervantes. There were recognizable novellas in 17th- and 18th-century France and England (written by Voltaire, Jonathan Swift, and others), and from the late 18th century, under the influence of Western Europe, especially Germany, there were examples in Russia (authored by Ivan Turgenev, Lev Tolstoi, Anton Chekhov). Partly for social and even technical reasons relating to publishing possibilities, novellas did not emerge in Germany until the very end of the 18th century, but it was in this country that the genre quickly acquired its most important foothold and where it has remained triumphant to the present day. Indeed, almost every great German (and Austrian) writer has attempted the form. Literary analyses of the genre, too, tend to have largely been drawn from Germany and German scholars; examples from other national literatures are usually discussed with reference to the German-language tradition.

The first German commentator was Christoph Martin Wieland, who distinguished the novella from the novel by length and simplicity of conception. Johann Wolfgang von Goethe, the true originator of the form in Germany, provided what is perhaps the first piece of theoretical writing on the novella in German. In part of the framework to his *Conversations of German Refugees* (1794–95), he advocates simplicity and concentration, suggesting that the novella should have a concentrated unity of form and mood—like a poem—and that emphasis should be placed on form, speed, concentration, and economy. Furthermore, the novella is to be a social form, presupposing a known narrator and a known audience. Friedrich Schlegel developed Goethe's ideas by emphasizing that the genre was a subjective one, but that the subjectivity was indirect, hidden; it was a sophisticated, social genre, basically detached and ironical. The hidden subjective element led to allegory, or symbol. Friedrich's brother, August Wilhelm, emphasized the importance of realism and introduced the notion of "turning points," a key concept for Ludwig Tieck, who claimed that there is a single point at which the novella takes a decisive narrative turn, an idea that carried considerable weight with later theoreticians. Tieck, a romantic, also emphasized such aspects as the "wonderful," preferring not to distinguish between fairy tale and novella but embracing a hybrid of the two. Also important for Tieck was the idea that something should remain mysterious, something for which readers needed to search and on which they needed to reflect.

The classic German example of the genre was provided during the early 19th century by Goethe, who decided to give a new story the title *Novelle*, "for what is a novella other than an event of which no one has heard, but which has actually taken place?" In the story, a duke goes on a hunting expedition, leaving his wife in the charge of an uncle and a young officer, Honorio. While the three are riding in the mountains, a fire breaks out at a fair in a neighboring town. A tiger and a lion escape and the tiger, who pursues the duchess, is killed by Honorio. The gypsy owners of the menagerie plead for the life of the lion, which is led back into its cage by a gypsy boy, who plays on his flute and sings variations on a simple verse about the goodness of God and the powers of gentleness. In this piece are all the features mentioned by the theorists up to this point: a simple, concentrated action; a well-defined social context; a hidden subjective meaning (the taming of the passions of Honorio, who is in love with the duchess); a symbol (the wild animals, killed or tamed); the "wonderful" (the gypsies with their strange powers of magic and incantation); a decisive turning point (the outbreak of the fire); and, finally, as B.A. Rowley (1977) has put it in his interpretation of Goethe's obiter dictum, "the ambiguous interplay of the realistic with the extraordinary," that is, the sense of uncertainty experienced by the reader in distinguishing between the real and the supernatural.

Later 19th-century theoreticians restated earlier views more crisply or suggestively but added little that was new. The German writer Paul Johann Ludwig von Heyse put forth the "falcon theory," the view that each novella should be distinguishable from others through a specific image, such as the falcon in Boccaccio's story of that title. Popular though the theory became, it was essentially covered by earlier views on symbolism. And the writers of this age—Gottfried Keller, Adalbert Stifter, Theodor Storm, Conrad Meyer—were probably less concerned with contemporary views than with what was by now a well-established heritage. Nevertheless, some writers wrote almost as if to illustrate the theory, while, as with all genres, critics redefined the concept in order to admit new texts that seemed to resist earlier definitions.

Other parts of Europe showed markedly less interest in the novella as such. Although Marguerite de Navarre's *L'Heptaméron* (1558–59; *The Heptameron*) provided French authors with a model similar to that of Boccaccio, the preference in France proved to be rather for the novel, or for the *nouvelle* (short story) rather than the *conte* (originally the concept employed for the novella). The demand created by newspaper and magazine publishers for fiction with a strong narrative and of a particular length (digestible at a single sitting) aided the rise of short fiction. The French, however, remained largely indifferent to questions of classification, and eventually the concepts *nouvelle* and *conte* became interchangeable. Even an obvious novella like Benjamin Constant's *Adolphe* (1816) was originally referred to as a *roman*. There was equally little concern for the classification of later examples like Prosper Mérimée's *Carmen* (1846) and Gérard de Nerval's "Sylvie" (1854). Yet neither of these authors was fully at home in the genre, with even Mérimée just as likely to compose long short stories as novellas. Guy de Maupassant, often regarded as the greatest master of short prose in French, likewise favored the short story. In Italy the novella reached something of a plateau after the initial impetus from Boccaccio and his imitators, but novellas continued to be written. Prime modern examples are Alberto Moravia's *L'amore coniugale* (1949; *Conjugal Love*) and Ignazio Silone's *La volpe e le camelie* (1960; *The Fox and the Camellias*).

Questions of classification rarely troubled English or American writers either, and although one can identify a fair number of works that may be assigned to the genre, the authors probably were not modeling themselves on a tradition: they simply happened to be writing at the length and in the form that suited their subject matter. D.H. Lawrence's stories of a man between two women (*The Fox*, 1923) and of a dangerous stallion (*St. Mawr*, 1925) contain material that breaches the bounds of the short story but that is insufficient for a short novel. The same is clearly true of Ernest Hemingway's *The Old Man and the Sea* (1952), which deals with a three-day struggle to land a massive fish. Other famous American examples include Stephen Crane's *The Red Badge of Courage* (1895), William Faulkner's *The Bear* (1942), and J.D. Salinger's pair *Franny and Zooey* (1961).

Henry James, a master of the short form, revealed a keen interest in classification, although his comments were largely retrospective about his own work rather than prescriptive for literature in general. Well read in European literature and a critic as well as a writer, James was anxious to devote himself both to what was "short" and what was "perfect." He produced a very large number of shorter works that he referred to as anecdotes, tales, short stories, and especially *nouvelles*, the latter inspired by French writing rather than by German, which he rejected as "slow reading for its very suggestiveness and intellectual resources." Despite this rejection, certain of his long short stories have been claimed as examples of the novella—*Daisy Miller* (1878) and *The Turn of the Screw* (1898), in particular.

These pieces, however, do contain more dialogue than is traditionally common in the genre, and, in terms of length, the latter reaches the absolute limit for the novella.

Joseph Conrad is perhaps the greatest English exponent of the novella, with "Heart of Darkness" (1902) and "The Secret Sharer" (1912) regarded as exemplary. The former recounts the story of a disturbing journey upstream into the heart of the Congo to bring back a highly successful ivory trader who has succumbed to savage practices in order to achieve his goal. One may identify in this text several features of the German novella: the turning point, the unexpected event, and the interplay of the real and the mysterious. "Heart of Darkness" makes little use of dialogue and develops a single-stranded and tightly structured plot. In addition, Conrad employs a set of framing and ironic techniques that create a sense of uncertainty about what the narrator, Marlow, really sees and thinks—uncertainty that develops into a challenge to the reader. The contradictions and ambiguities of the tale oblige the reader to create his or her own construction of events and of meaning. The story itself provides playfully ambiguous nautical and nature imagery to encourage yet also frustrate the reader's deduction with such concepts as snags, fogs, and mist. As Marlow puts it at one point, "the essentials of this affair lay deep below the surface, beyond my reach." Marlow's inability to recognize the distinctions between the often repeated and ambiguous motifs of light and dark (knowledge/ignorance, civilization/savagery) reveal his disorientation in a complex world where traditional values have been perverted. For the reader, too, the full meaning of the "heart of darkness" remains elusive, and the brevity of the piece heightens such mystery. In this respect, too, then, Conrad's novella follows the German tradition.

Another uncertainty may intrigue the reader of "Heart of Darkness": like so many novellas, this one seems to shift in its nature. It is clearly far from the simple "yarn" with which the principal narrator decides to entertain his listeners, just as the "story" that so many narrators of German novellas suggest they are about to tell is far from being slight. Plot may be the initial spring, but at different points the reader may wonder whether the principal aim or ideological purpose might not be rather, in turn, a character study of an abnormal individual, a psychoanalytic study, a sociological investigation into colonialism, or psychological and philosophical reflections on the world and on human nature.

These same considerations hold true for Thomas Mann, writing shortly after Conrad and generally regarded as the last great master of novella form. *Der Tod in Venedig* (1912; *Death in Venice*), his best-known achievement, reveals a subtle approach to the "unusual event," which, superficially, could be seen as commonplace—the death of a famous writer from the plague. Yet one of the aims of the novella is rather to suggest that the death of Gustav von Aschenbach is most unusual; the plague may be regarded as an external factor only. The novella gives us a succession of scenes that are important for our understanding of the central figure, and each brief encounter contains a symbolic message for Aschenbach, whose life of self-discipline is seen to crumble as the wild "Dionysian" features of his nature come into conflict with the restraining, preserving "Apollonian" features. By using such concepts recently popularized by Friedrich Nietzsche, and by hinting at the numerous levels on which Aschenbach operates (the physical, genetic, sensual, and moral, as well as the philosophical, psychological, sociological, and historical), Mann shows the complexity of the writer's demise. The technique of compression for which the novella is famous is here exploited in the style itself: as partial parody of the dense prose in which Aschenbach himself would have composed, the narrator condenses information and ideas into lengthy and complex sentences with extensive use of irony. Like Mann's earlier famous novella *Tonio Kröger* (1903), the plot seeks to illuminate timeless human attributes and dilemmas.

The tradition in Germany is so rich and so well established that practically every major German-language writer of prose has recognized the novella form as a natural challenge. Traditions elsewhere have tended to lead writers to avoid the form in favor of the short novel or the long short story. Genre criticism has followed a comparable path, with an extensive and meticulous approach to the concept by scholars with a grounding in German literature and a looser one elsewhere. It is, therefore, often possible to find the concept applied in a rather broad sense, with length alone taken as the key factor. In the narrower, German sense, however, technique and scope clearly provide equally important considerations.

PETER HUTCHINSON

See also German Novel; Prose Novelistic Forms; Renaissance Narrative

Further Reading

Good, Graham, "Notes on the Novella," *Novel: A Forum on Fiction* 10 (1976–77)

Lee, A. Robert, *The Modern American Novella*, London: Vision Press, and New York: St. Martin's Press, 1989

Paine, J.H.E., *Theory and Criticism of the Novella*, Bonn: Bouvier, 1979

Paulin, Roger, *The Brief Compass: The Nineteenth-Century German Novelle*, Oxford and New York: Clarendon Press, 1985

Rowley, B.A., "To Define True Novellen . . . : A Taxonomic Enquiry," *Publications of the English Goethe Society* 47 (1977)

Swales, Martin, *The German Novelle*, Princeton, New Jersey: Princeton University Press, 1977

Weing, Siegfried, *The German Novella: Two Centuries of Criticism*, Columbia, South Carolina: Camden House, 1994

Yarbro-Bejarano, Yvonne, *The Tradition of the Novela in Spain, from Pedro Mexía (1540) to Lope de Vega's Novelas a Marcia Leonardo (1621, 1624)*, New York: Garland, 1991

Zelinsky, Bodo, editor, *Die Russische Novelle*, Düsseldorf: Bagel, 1982

Nuit sacrée. *See* **Sand Child and Sacred Night**

Flora Nwapa 1931–93

Nigerian

Flora Nwapa played a revolutionary role in African literature in the second half of the 20th century. She has left a phenomenal legacy. In 1966, she broke down the male monopoly over African writing with the publication of her first novel, *Efuru.* By that singular act, Nigeria had produced not just its own first female novelist but also black Africa's first internationally published female novelist in the English language. *Efuru* was a historic landmark.

Before *Efuru,* nationally and internationally known African writers were all men, but their subject matter was quite often women. Their depictions of women were utterly sexist. Women were portrayed essentially as household help, never on equal terms with their husbands, and their primary function was to procreate, beginning preferably with male children. They were molded to fit the roles of silent participants in their social environment. If they exhibited any exuberance, it was in the abuse of their bodies. The dominant image was that of a pleasure-seeking, prurient creature with little or no inner qualities. In the rural setting her relevance was depicted in her subservience to men; in an urban environment, her significance shifted to her appearance and ability to gratify male desire. Nwapa offered a new perspective of African womanhood.

Nwapa launched her career in fiction writing with a tacit commitment to wage war on the stereotypical image of women in African fiction. In an interview with Marie Umeh (1995), Nwapa expressed her disappointment at the way men had portrayed female characters but declared that her efforts to present a positive image of womanhood do not make her a feminist:

> I don't think that I am a radical feminist. I don't even accept that I'm a feminist. I accept that I'm an ordinary woman who is writing about what she knows. I try to project the image of women positively. I attempt to correct our menfolks . . . when they write little or less about women, when their female characters are prostitutes and ne'er-do-wells. I started writing to tell them that this is not so. When I do write about women in Nigeria, in Africa, I try to paint a positive picture about women because there are many women who are very, very positive in their thinking, who are very, very independent, and very, very industrious.

Nwapa also pioneered the projection of the female perspective in the African novel. In doing this, she not only forcibly changed a tradition, she also began a trend that was followed with remarkable success by other African women writers such as Buchi Emecheta, Ama Atta Aidoo, Ifeoma Okoye, Zynab Alkali, and a host of others across the African continent.

Efuru takes its title from the name of the heroine, a choice that proudly proclaimed Nwapa's position. No novel had done such an honor to womanhood before. Efuru has a mind of her own. She distinguishes herself by her industrious nature, administrative acumen, and economic prudence—an attack on the myth of female irrelevance to national development. Where male writers had cast the childless or barren woman as unfulfilled in marriage, Nwapa's heroine, whose only child died in infancy, is full of energy, plans, and aspirations and leads a satisfactory, rewarding life. This portrayal would have been controversial enough by itself, but Nwapa fans the fire by depicting Efuru's husband as an insignificant character: "Efuru was her name. She was a remarkable woman. It was not only that she came from a distinguished family. She was distinguished herself. Her husband was not known and people wondered why she married him."

Dominated by men, the Nigerian literary establishment reacted negatively to *Efuru.* However, Nwapa was not discouraged by adverse reviews and her subsequent work also endows female characters with versatile talent, a strong voice and identity, a vivid imagination, a potent intellect, articulate wit, and enduring wisdom in human affairs. *Efuru* was followed by *Idu* (1970), a novel that raises similar issues and subtly challenged traditional marriage and a married woman's role. *Idu* examines the opposing needs of self and society and the tensions between female competence on the one hand and patriarchal authority and male ego on the other.

Nwapa became increasingly prolific with her rising recognition nationally and internationally. *Never Again* (1975), based on the Nigerian civil war, was released about the same time that male Nigerian writers were also publishing fiction about the war. But unlike her male counterparts, Nwapa focused on the role of women in the war effort and in combat, while underscoring the futility of war in resolving human conflicts. In 1981, Nwapa published the epochal *One Is Enough,* hailed by critics as one of her strongest expressions of feminism. It addresses the issue of single mothers, who in many African societies are stigmatized and held in derision and contempt. Nwapa's heroine in *One Is Enough,* Amaka, refuses to marry the father of her twin sons and decides to raise them by herself because she can afford to. Amaka's decision is in line with Nwapa's conviction that "every woman, married or single, must have economic independence . . . a woman who holds her husband as a father, dies an orphan." In 1986, Nwapa, still concerned with the issue of independence, contended that "there are different ways of living one's life fully and fruitfully—marriage is not the only way." In that year, she published *Women Are Different,* in which the protagonists are married women and professionals in their own right. Through them, Nwapa provides a window onto alternative feminine roles even in the midst of male malevolence. Nwapa's sixth and last novel, *The Lake Goddess* (1995), was published posthumously and focuses on the legendary lake goddess Mammy Water, the eternal spring and mythical inspirer of Nwapa's fiction and creativity, the fairy godmother whose abode is the bottom of Oguta Lake, near Nwapa's birthplace.

Nwapa was equally prolific outside the novel form. She wrote two collections of short stories (*This Is Lagos and Other Stories,* 1971, and *Wives at War and Other Stories,* 1980), a book of prose poems (*Cassava Song; and, Rice Song,* 1986), and seven children's books. Some of her children's fiction consists of simplified versions of well-known myths and legends, and others recreate folktales. Still others are simple stories told for the purpose of educating and entertaining young minds, as well as providing role models for children in their formative stages of life.

Nwapa concealed her talents as a playwright until the very end of her life, but she saw her three published plays, *The First Lady* (1993), *Two Women in Conversation* (1993), and *The Sycophants* (1993), performed shortly before her death. These plays came as the crowning glory of her career as a committed writer deeply concerned with the plight of womanhood in Africa and beyond. Of the three, *Two Women in Conversation* is the most volatile and expressive. In it, Nwapa articulates her feminist ideology in the clearest of terms. The play is a scathing and incisive attack on marriage, portrayed as a social institution created and manipulated by men for the subjugation of women, with the tacit acquiescence of law and religion under patriarchal authority. The play explores the ugly secrets of marriage and exposes ideas and prejudices in such a way as to raise doubts about the necessity of continuing the institution in its present form. The final message in the play is an appeal for a better understanding of the female predicament, especially of the dehumanization of women by religious bigotry and antiquated cultural norms. Nwapa thus becomes the voice of disenfranchised women everywhere.

Nwapa, the doyenne of African women's writing, was also an accomplished woman in other spheres. She was the first black African woman to establish a publishing company—Tana Press, Africa's first womanist press—to facilitate the publication and distribution of her own works as well as those of other African female writers. She was awarded by her town (Oguta) the highest chieftaincy title—*Ogbuefi,* a title usually reserved for men of achievement but given also to women who accomplish great feats in their lifetime. In 1982 the Nigerian government bestowed on her one of the country's highest honors, the OON (Order of the Niger).

Flora Nwapa's greatest honor resides in the hearts and minds of African female writers, to whom she has bequeathed an invaluable legacy. Through a variety of literary works, she sought to restore dignity to womanhood and paved the way for pragmatic feminism (womanism) in Africa.

ERNEST N. EMENYONU

Biography

Born 13 January 1931 in Oguta, in the present Imo State of Nigeria; her mother was a wealthy trader and her father a palm produce agent of the United Africa Company, a well-known British trading company in the colonial era. Attended Archdeacon Crowther Memorial Girls' School, Elelenwa; C.M.S. Girls School, 1949–50, and Queen's College, 1951, both in Lagos; University of Ibadan, B.A. in English, History, and Geography; University of Edinburgh, Scotland, Diploma in Education 1958. Worked variously as education officer, teacher, university administrator, and civil servant, the latter culminating in her appointment to the cabinet of the first post–Nigerian civil war government of Eastern Nigeria, first serving as Commissioner for Health and Social Welfare (1970) and later as Commissioner for Lands, Survey, and Urban Development (1971–75). Died 16 October 1993.

Novels by Nwapa

Efuru, 1966
Idu, 1970
Never Again, 1975
One Is Enough, 1981
Women Are Different, 1986
The Lake Goddess, 1995

Other Writings: short stories, poetry, plays, children's books.

Further Reading

Umeh, Marie, and Ogunyemi Chikwenye Okonjo, editors, *Research in African Literatures* 26:2 (Summer 1995), special issue on Flora Nwapa
Umeh, Marie, editor, *Emerging Perspectives on Flora Nwapa,* Trenton, New Jersey: Africa World Press, 1997

O

Oblomov by Ivan Goncharov

1859

The radical contemporary critic Nikolai Dobroliubov set the agenda for future Russian criticism of *Oblomov* by arguing that it "reflects Russian life" and shows "the living contemporary Russian type": a member of the gentry who has become alienated and corrupted by serfdom. He assigned the eponymous hero to a line of such "superfluous men" (the phrase is Turgenev's) as Pushkin's Onegin, Lermontov's Pechorin, and Turgenev's Rudin.

Modern criticism, in the West and more recently in Russia, has been more sympathetic to Ilia Oblomov and less inclined to read the novel solely as social commentary. Its reputation has not diminished. Now, however, we tend to view it as a highly idiosyncratic work. Russian novelists such as Gogol', Dostoevskii, Tolstoi, and Leskov wrote works that challenge our preconceptions of what a novel should be, and Goncharov's *Oblomov* is similarly unconventional. It combines high comedy, lyricism, symbolism, and the stylizations of romance in a narrative structure that hovers on the periphery of the realist tradition.

The peculiarities of *Oblomov* may owe in part to the duration of its writing. Begun in 1847, it was completed only in 1858. In Russia the 1840s marked the birth of realism or, as it was then called, "the natural school." However, romanticism had not entirely ebbed, and the influence of Gogol's grotesque universe was still powerful. Part one of *Oblomov* reflects the "physiological sketches" of the natural school in its static depiction of a typical day in the life of its hero. The monumentally inert Oblomov and his nagging servant Zakhar (as well as an assortment of visitors) are comically fanciful in the Gogolian manner. Master and man, isolated from the normal world of activity, perform a verbal dance whereby despair is turned into burlesque. They anticipate the modernist impulse to play out existential dramas in a timeless world (Samuel Beckett, for one, has been called "an Irish Oblomov").

The famous chapter nine of part one, entitled "Oblomov's Dream," is in turn a portrait of typical days on Oblomov's ancestral estate, Oblomovka. It is a prose poem of unusual beauty, owing something to the lyric side of Gogol', if more subdued. This mythic evocation of a homely Russian land of Cockaigne stands at the center of the novel, exerting a seductive fascination, although nuanced by irony. "Oblomov's Dream," like his earlier daydreaming, pulls him away from caricature and adds psychological causality to the story of his life. His dreams tell of his desires but also reveal the trauma of his childhood. From the static comedy of part one, the novel gradually evolves into that characteristic novelistic form—the biography of a soul. The paradisiacal landscape of Oblomovka is the object of Oblomov's desire; his unwillingness to settle for less is the cause of his doom.

Goncharov struggled with his novel for roughly ten years until a great burst of creative activity in the summer of 1857 allowed him to write most of the remainder in a month's time. The romance of parts two and three reflects the changed literary interests of the late 1850s. Russia had known the novel as a poem in verse (Pushkin's *Eugene Onegin*, 1831), the novel as a prose poem (Gogol's *Dead Souls*, 1842), the novel as a string of stories (Lermontov's *Hero of Our Time*, 1840), the novel as disguised autobiography (Aksakov's *Family Chronicle*, 1856, and Tolstoi's *Childhood*, 1852). In the late 1850s and early 1860s Turgenev brought into Russia the novel of contemporary social life that had long dominated the scene in France and England. *Rudin* (1856), *Home of the Gentry* (1859), *On the Eve* (1860), *Fathers and Sons* (1862; also translated as *Fathers and Children*) represent the "form and pressure" of the period in dramatic structures (Turgenev began as a playwright).

This new dramatic interest gave Goncharov a way to overcome the stasis of the sketch of daily life or the dream-like reminiscence. In parts two and three Oblomov gets out of bed and enters the common world of activity. He has a purpose—to win the love of the radiant Olga—and a rival, his childhood friend and alter ego, the practical half-German Stolz. Stolz is wooden, Olga is idealized, the tones of romance color Oblomov's entrance into society—the central portion of the novel has been criticized extensively for these characteristics. But in stumbling against the demands of love, Oblomov's story acquires a pathos that it would otherwise lack, and at the same time takes on a more conventionally novelistic realism: Oblomov has shucked off his comic motley and become like the rest of us, a man struggling to find his place in the world.

Part four, the most powerful piece of writing in Goncharov's oeuvre, traces Oblomov's decline into vegetative existence and death. Largely eventless, it is yet too rich in psychological insight and poetic imaginings to be identified with the sketch-like burlesque of the opening. The novel moves in a circle. But where Oblomov's earlier dreamings were a refuge from the demands of life, his recovery of Oblomovka at the elbow of the loving Agafia Matveevna is a kind of achievement. A failure in the world of action, Oblomov has yet found love and a measure of self-knowledge. The ending asserts the power of the imagination to coalesce beginnings and ends into a meaningful pattern. Oblomov's dreaming mind has returned to the past not only for escape but to discover who he is—for what it was that "had laid a heavy hand upon him in the beginning of his journey and had thrown him away from his true human purpose." Oblomov has learned to accept himself, limited as he is, and the reconciliations of the ending keeps the novel, for all its pain, in the mode of comedy.

The theme of alienation, central to *Oblomov,* is also central to much modern fiction, as is the assertion of the power of memory to restore the self; Proust's writings echo through the best pages of *Oblomov* (although Proust, of course, came after Goncharov). The mixtures of lyricism and absurdist farce, idealizations and parody, dream and reality are also modern (and romantic), although the detailed explorations of psychological and social causality place the novel in the mid–19th century. *Oblomov* is a quirky masterpiece, rarely, if ever, imitated.

MILTON EHRE

Further Reading

Dobrolyubov, N.A., "What Is Oblomivitis," in *Belinsky, Chernyshevsky, and Dobrolyubov: Selected Criticism,* edited by Ralph E. Matlaw, New York: Dutton, 1962

Ehre, Milton, *Oblomov and His Creator: The Life and Art of Ivan Goncharov,* Princeton, New Jersey: Princeton University Press, 1973

Krasnoshchekova, E., *Oblomov I.A. Goncharova,* Moscow: Khudozhestvennaia literatura, 1970

Macauley, Robie, "The Superfluous Man," *Partisan Review* 19:2 (1952)

Mirsky, D.S., *A History of Russian Literature,* edited by Francis J. Whitfield, New York: Knopf, and London: Routledge and Kegan Paul, 1949

Peace, Richard, *Oblomov: A Critical Examination of Goncharov's Novel,* Birmingham: Department of Russian Language and Literature, University of Birmingham, 1991

Poggioli, Renato, *The Phoenix and the Spider,* Cambridge, Massachusetts: Harvard University Press, 1957

Pritchett, V.S., *The Living Novel and Later Appreciations,* revised edition, New York: Random House, 1964

Prutskov, N.I., *Masterstvo Goncharova-romanista,* Leningrad: Izd-vo Akademii nauk SSSR, 1962

Stilman, Leon, "Oblomovka Revisited," *The American Slavic and East European Review* 7 (1948)

Thiergen, Peter, editor, *Ivan A. Goncarov: Leben, Werk und Wirkung,* Cologne: Böhlau, 1994 (collection of essays, some in English)

Flann O'Brien 1911–66

Irish

If Samuel Beckett could arrive into the world on Good Friday, it seems fitting that Flann O'Brien should exit on April Fools' Day. In his 55 years, he jested and imbibed his way from the poverty of a large Catholic family through University College Dublin and the Irish civil service, eventually becoming a celebrated figure in the Irish literary landscape. Born Brian Nolan, he rounded the name to O'Nolan or Ó Nualláin, alias Brother Barnabas, Myles na gCopaleen (Myles of the Little Horses, from Bouccicault's *The Collen Bawn*), and Flann O'Brien (the Brian O'Lynn or O Fhloinn of popular ballad). Best known outside Ireland for two fine comic novels, *At Swim-Two-Birds* (1939) and *The Third Policeman* (1967), he was for some 20 years a columnist for the *Irish Times,* his witty sallies injested [*sic*] with the morning rashers. His reputation faded, and the stout and whiskey failed to restoke the wit, but he is pictured in these final years in an unforgettable photograph, standing in his bowler beside a road sign that reads: "Dublin Diversion." In a final bilingual tribute he would have appreciated, the plaque marking his birthplace has the Gaelic for "writer" (*scriobhnóir*) misspelled.

Described as the most stolen book of its time, *At Swim-Two-Birds* for one glorious week replaced *Gone with the Wind* as Dublin's top seller. Reading for Longmans, Graham Greene had described it as (a) a book about a man called Trellis who is (b) writing a book about certain characters who (c) are turning the tables on him. Calling this a wild, fantastic notion, Greene commented that by no other method could the realistic, the legendary, and the novelette be worked together. O'Brien, however, mocks the postmodernism that claims him as forerunner. In fact, he wished to write a "modern" novel, whatever that might be, with Sterne and Rabelais as ancestors and Joyce and Beckett as peers. Indeed, *At Swim-Two-Birds* may be described as A Portrait of the Artist Who Stayed at Home and did not reject his family, country, or religion. While it was much talked about, the novel was criticized for its undergraduate wit and the many private allusions it is studded with. Only recently has the novel come to be seen as an artful form of magniloquent frenzy. Its blending of the ordinary, the bizarre, the mythological, and the self-conscious is now thought to have redefined the comic—in the words of the Good Fairy, to have evolved a Fifth Excellence from Four Futilities.

Perhaps the greater novel is *The Third Policeman.* The book was rejected by Longmans, which seriously damaged O'Brien's confidence. Equally zany and extravagant ("Is it about a bicycle?"), *The Third Policeman's* wit is more disciplined and its form more complex. The "third man" theme is handled with a great deal of philosophical and structural sophistication. The Chinese-box effects and games with infinity intimate a delight in Dunne's experiments with time and seriality. Huysmans' *À rebours* is the parallel universe most avidly explored. From atomic theory to omnium, wooden-legged men to that form of forms, Policeman Fox, the novel is a dazzling delight. Its writing marks new departures for O'Brien, notably in the "second dimension" after the narrator, unbeknownst to himself, has been killed by a bomb. In this posthumous narrative, the landscape of middle Ireland on a fine spring day is made to sing even as its legoland unreality disturbs. Uniquely for O'Brien, *The Third Policeman* has a stern Catholic streak, particularly in the "third dimension" after the narrator, unbeknownst to himself, has been hanged, and he returns to the scene of his crime to face for all eternity the recurrent consequences of what he has done. The US edition was entitled *Hell Goes Round and Round,* which captures the themes of circularity and guilt. However, it fails to convey the moral terror implicit in the ability forever to avert but never altogether avoid punishment for a crime.

These two experimental novels are O'Brien's lasting contributions to the genre. His other works are fascinating but of less consequence. The finest is *An Béal Bocht* (1941), translated as *The Poor Mouth* (1973). This parody of Tomás O'Crohan's *The Islandman* (1934) is a comic masterpiece. A Beckett-like vision of bleakness, *The Poor Mouth* is a celebration of what it satirizes. Less exuberant are *The Hard Life: An Exegesis of Squalor* (1961) and *The Dalkey Archive* (1964). Despite his insistence that the most crackpot invention must be subject to its own stern logic, neither novel dazzles. The "exegesis of squalor" in *The Hard Life* rests uneasily with the satire of Catholicism, and the jokes (Father Kurt Fahrt, S.J.) are furtive and fleeting. *The Dalkey Archive* is largely a recycling of *The Third Policeman* but lacks its rigor. Its strengths are various, but the obsession with Joyce becomes tedious, and the protagonist, de Selby, is less ingenious. Yet there is one brilliant passage, an underwater interview with St. Augustine, which exemplifies O'Brien at his best. Nor should one ignore the posthumously published selections from the "Cruiskeen Lawn" (little overflowing jug), the gatherings of his newspaper columns, which for all their passing parochialism and repetition can be quite heady. The best of these involve the lunatic conversations of Keats and Chapman, the local wisdom of The Brother and the Plain People of Ireland, the Catalogue of Clichés, and the bus that always arrives before the point can be made. O'Brien will be remembered for his two innovative novels, but the other writings testify to the rich store of comic invention from which these arose.

CHRIS ACKERLEY

See also At Swim-Two-Birds

Biography
Born 5 October 1911 in Strabane, County Tyrone, Northern Ireland. Attended the Christian Brothers School, Synge Street, Dublin; Blackrock College, Dublin; University College, Dublin (where he served as editor of *Blather* magazine), 1929–32, B.A. 1932, M.A. 1935; traveling scholarship to Germany, 1933–34. Employed in local government branch of Irish civil service, Dublin, 1935–53; columnist, as Myles na gCopaleen ("Cruiskeen Lawn"), *Irish Times,* Dublin, 1940–66. Died 1 April 1966.

Novels by O'Brien
At Swim-Two-Birds, 1939
An Béal Bocht: nó, An Milleánach, 1941; as *The Poor Mouth: A Bad Story about the Hard Life,* translated by Patrick C. Power, 1973
The Hard Life: An Exegesis of Squalor, 1961
The Dalkey Archive, 1964
The Third Policeman, 1967

Other Writings: stories, plays, an *Irish Times* newspaper column entitled "Cruiskeen Lawn."

Further Reading
Asbee, Sue, *Flann O'Brien,* Boston: Twayne, 1991
Booker, M. Keith, *Flann O'Brien, Bakhtin, and Menippean Satire,* Syracuse, New York: Syracuse University Press, 1995
Clissmann, Anne, *Flann O'Brien: A Critical Introduction to His Writing: The Story-teller's Book-web,* New York: Barnes and Noble, and Dublin: Gill and Macmillan, 1975
Clissmann, Anne, and David Powell, editors, *The Journal of Irish Literature* 3:1 (January 1974), special Flann O'Brien issue
Costello, Peter, and Peter Van der Kamp, *Flann O'Brien: An Illustrated Biography,* London: Bloomsbury, 1987
Cronin, Anthony, *No Laughing Matter: The Life and Times of Flann O'Brien,* London and Toronto: Grafton, 1989
Hopper, Keith, *Flann O'Brien: A Portrait of the Artist as a Young Post-Modernist,* Cork: Cork University Press, 1995
O'Keeffe, Timothy, editor, *Myles: Portraits of Brian O'Nolan,* London: Martin Brian and O'Keeffe, 1973
Shea, Thomas F., *Flann O'Brien's Exorbitant Novels,* Lewisburg, Pennsylvania: Bucknell University Press, and London: Associated University Presses, 1992

The Obscene Bird of Night by José Donoso

El obsceno pájaro de la noche 1970

Originally published in Barcelona by Editorial Seix Barral, a major player in bringing outstanding young Spanish-language writers before the international reading public, *The Obscene Bird of Night* has been hailed as the last great novel of the Latin American "boom." These novels, most of which appeared in the 1960s, brought to a close the era of realistic, linear, and unambiguous narrative that had dominated Hispanic writing since the novel's heyday in the 19th century. Relying on avant-garde techniques that challenged the basic assumptions of the traditional narrative, José Donoso and his contemporaries (Gabriel García Márquez, Julio Cortázar, Mario Vargas Llosa, and Carlos Fuentes) ushered in a bold new approach to fiction writing. Donoso's first three novels, *Coronación* (1957; *Coronation*), *Este domingo* (1966; *This Sunday*), and *El lugar sin límites* (1966; *Hell Hath No Limits*), brought him recognition within his country and some acclaim abroad, but it was *The Obscene Bird of Night,* his fourth novel, that established him as a writer of the first order and a leading exponent of the Latin American "new narrative."

In this novel, Donoso eschews the straightforward delineation of plot and character that had served him so well in his earlier works, producing instead a technically complex novel fraught with such obstacles to comprehension as temporal disjunctions, chaotic shifts in narrative perspective, interior monologues, and indeterminacy of plot, all seemingly designed for the purpose of bewildering the reader. Fragmenting into a multiplicity of voices, the narrator vacillates between first and third person and at times resorts to second person. The constant altering and distorting of events and the presentation of conflicting versions of crucial elements of the principal storyline place additional burdens on readers searching for verisimilitude.

The novel owes its title to a quotation from Henry James, Sr., who wrote that life proceeds from an "essential dearth" and that our inheritance as human beings is the forest of nightmare, populated by the wolf and the "obscene bird of night." Appearing as an epigraph, this statement prefigures the chaotic surreal world that eventually engulfs all of the novel's principal characters.

In *The Obscene Bird of Night*, the question of identity occupies center stage. Characters overlap and fuse with one. The narrator, the deaf servant Mudito, works in the Casa de Ejercicios Espirituales de la Encarnación, a home for old women and orphans. Often, he narrates as Humberto Peñaloza, a frustrated writer in search of his identity, who once served as secretary to the illustrious Don Jerónimo Azcoitía, a descendant of the Casa's founder. Living at the Casa de la Encarnación, he undergoes a series of incarnations and assumes multiple identities; he is at various times one of the old women, a dog, a baby, a giant with a papier-mâché head, and the mythical *imbunche,* a hideous figure who has had all its orifices sewn up (the fate of children who have been stolen by witches). In short, the reader must decide which identity is real.

Other primary characters similarly merge and separate at random. Inés, Don Jerónimo's wife, devotes herself to lobbying in Rome for the beatification of her double and namesake, the legendary daughter of the founder. Inés' identity also becomes confused with that of Iris, an orphan living at the Casa. Jerónimo is obsessed with producing an heir, and when his son, Boy, is born with hideous deformities, Jerónimo has him placed in La Rinconada, a country estate he populates with dwarfs, giants, and other human monstrosities that pervert the natural order by making the abnormal seem the norm. Mudito-Humberto alternately loses his identity to Jerónimo and Boy, thus providing further illustration of the divided self. Reworking a centuries-old legend that concerns a wealthy landowner's daughter and witchcraft, the narrator transfers attributes of the legendary characters (the witch and the yellow dog) onto the modern-day ones (Inés and her old servant, Peta Ponce). Even the two houses, the Casa in the city and La Rinconada in the country, seem like two manifestations of a single locale, since both are labyrinths where monsters roam.

Irony pervades the novel, and nothing is what it seems to be. The Casa, for example, once a religious retreat and now purportedly a refuge for old women and orphans, has become a haven for witches who have conjured the diabolical *imbunche*. At the novel's apocalyptic conclusion, the Casa is about to be closed in preparation for demolition, and the old women-witches, awaiting the miraculous birth of a child to the "virgin" Iris, expect to be carried away to heaven in beautiful hearses. Instead, they are about to be transported in buses across town to a new home. In the final analysis, they are the novel's survivors. As in legends, which survive through oral tradition in multiple versions, much of the novel is reported as pure hearsay ("dicen que . . ."). Readers must, therefore, eventually confront the question of the nature of reality and determine which events really happen and which are only dreams or the product of a character's imagination, and what meaning to assign them.

The fact that the Azcoitía family, like the Casa it founded, is in danger of dying out, serves as a lucid commentary on the decay and demise of the aristocracy and the collapse of archaic social and political institutions. In the case of Mudito-Humberto, his schizophrenia and psychic disintegration mirror his physical deterioration. On a metaphysical level, his spiritual decline proclaims the absurdity and hopelessness of existence, which leads to ultimate annihilation.

The Obscene Bird of Night is a phantasmagoric, neobaroque text, dominated by the ugly and the grotesque, that conjures up visions of the paintings of Hieronymus Bosch. It destroys literary conventions and offers something radically new in Latin American literature. If reality is in essence chaotic, then the orderly presentation of characters, setting, and events typical of the conventional novel seems inappropriate for the "new novel," where fragmentation, distortion, and ambiguity reign supreme. If Mudito-Humberto is, as one suspects, insane, the chaotic form his narrative takes is what one would expect of a madman.

MELVIN S. ARRINGTON, JR.

Further Reading

Bacarisse, Pamela, "*El obsceno pájaro de la noche*: A Willed Process of Evasion," in *Contemporary Latin American*

Fiction, edited by Salvador Bacarisse, Edinburgh: Scottish Academic Press, 1980

Castillo-Feliú, Guillermo I., editor, *The Creative Process in the Works of José Donoso,* Rock Hill, South Carolina: Winthrop College, 1982

Caviglia, John, "Tradition and Monstrosity in *El obsceno pájaro de la noche,*" PMLA 93 (1978)

Finnegan, Pamela May, *The Tension of Paradox: José Donoso's "The Obscene Bird of Night" as Spiritual Exercises,* Athens: Ohio University Center for International Studies, 1992

González Mandri, Flora, *José Donoso's House of Fiction: A Dramatic Construction of Time and Place,* Detroit, Michigan: Wayne State University Press, 1995

Magnarelli, Sharon, *Understanding José Donoso,* Columbia: University of South Carolina Press, 1993

McMurray, George R., *José Donoso,* Boston: Twayne, 1979

Rodríguez Monegal, Emir, "José Donoso: La novela como happening," *Revista Iberoamericana* 37 (1971)

Swanson, Philip, "José Donoso: *El obsceno pájaro de la noche,*" in *Landmarks in Modern Latin American Fiction,* edited by Swanson, London and New York: Routledge, 1990

Wood, Michael, "José Donoso: Where the Wolf Howls," in *On Modern Latin American Fiction,* edited by John King, New York: Noonday Press, and London: Faber, 1987

Obsceno pájaro de la noche. *See* Obscene Bird of Night

Odin den' Ivana Denisovicha. *See* One Day in the Life of Ivan Denisovich

---

Ōe Kenzaburō 1935–

Japanese

When Ōe Kenzaburō won the Nobel prize for literature in 1994, the Nobel Committee cited his mythic imagination, in particular his extraordinary ability to create complex universal worlds out of intensely personal and regional characters and incidents. Ōe himself puts it another way: in an interview with Rob Wilson in *boundary,* he explains, "You know, I feel that literature is something you do when you're trying to make an experience into something that, even though it's not really happening in real time, is still palpably, suddenly, in the here and now" (*boundary* 20:2 [1993]).

Throughout his career, Ōe has consistently taken a variety of experiences, ranging from the personal, through the intellectual, to the transcendent, and translated them into a "here and now" that engages, disturbs, and sometimes confounds his readers. This is clear from his first major work, "Shiiku" ("Prize Stock and the Catch"), a story that garnered the young Ōe the prestigious Akutagawa prize in 1958 for its unique portrait of wartime Japan. The story of a black US fighter pilot captured by villagers during World War II, the work uses the pilot's slowly developing and ultimately tragic relationship with the village children to weave an intense antiwar parable concerning the sacrifice of the innocent. But "Prize Stock and the Catch" is by no means a simple allegory. Far from sentimentalizing the black soldier or the children, the narrative privileges the children's spontaneous violence and sexuality, in contrast to the controlled brutality of the village elders, especially the young narrator's father.

In his early novels, Ōe continued to explore the cathartic nature of antisocial violence as well as frequently perverse sexuality, sometimes in the semi-autobiographical pastoral spaces first emblematized in "Prize Stock and the Catch," such as in his 1958 novella *Memushiri kouchi* (*Nip the Buds, Shoot the Kids*). His other favorite site, however, was the urban wasteland of big city Japan. In novels such as *Seiteki ningen* (1963; J), *Sevuntiin* (1961; *Seventeen*), and *Warera no jidai* (1959; Our Era), he depicts antisocial protagonists such as perverts or terrorists, pitting them against an indifferent but ultimately all-powerful establishment that inevitably crushes them. Frequently his fiction connects this establishment with the Japanese imperial house, a holdover from traditional Japan that Ōe excoriates.

One of Ōe's most brilliant works of this type is *Seventeen*, his bleak but strangely poignant portrayal of right-wing activism. *Seventeen* chronicles the rise and demise of a pathetic adolescent who becomes involved in right-wing terrorism, largely for the sense of belonging this association provides him. The youth assassinates a socialist politician and then kills himself in the emperor's name. Based on an actual historical incident, *Seventeen* shocked and horrified contemporary Japanese, not only because of its brutally realistic portrait of the often tawdry motivations behind political activism but for its insistent equation of the emperor with sexuality. In the novella's most controversial scene, for example, the youth is taken to a brothel by his new right-wing friends; while a prostitute masturbates him he sees a vision of the emperor and climaxes. Perhaps even more disturbing, in the novella's final scene the youth masturbates one last time before hanging himself, while calling on the emperor to take care of his "Beloved Seventeen."

The dynamic between the political and the sexual is a central aspect of Ōe's work, but in 1964 he added another vital element: the strange, touching, and fascinating relationship between a father and his brain-damaged child. Two works published that year begin a still ongoing exploration of Ōe's own relationship with his severely brain-damaged son, Hikari. In both works Ōe uses his personal experience to create two distinctive visions of the "palpable here and now" that he is searching to convey.

The first, *Kojinteki na taiken* (*A Personal Matter*), is essentially a contemporary Bildungsroman in which a young man attempts to escape the responsibility of having fathered a brain-damaged child. Bird, the novel's protagonist, attempts a variety of increasingly desperate strategies of self-abasement, including deciding to murder the child, but at the very last moment submits to the demands of fatherhood and maturity. The second work, a novella entitled *Sora no kaibutsu Aguii* (*Agwhee the Sky Monster*), is a metafictional examination of the same situation; in this case the story begins after the young father, a composer, has allowed his child to die at the hands of unscrupulous doctors and has apparently gone mad with guilt. The composer is visited by a ghost baby called Aghwee whom only he can see, while the tale is narrated by a young student who has been hired to watch over him. In a sly variation on Henry James' *The Turn of the Screw* (1898), however, both narrator and reader are ultimately led to the point where they almost believe in Agwhee too. The novella ends with the narrator becoming aware of creatures (myths, fiction, etc.) populating his own personal sky.

Ōe's increasing concern with metafictional modes, including a fascination with language itself, comes to the fore in his extraordinary 1972 novella *Waga namida o nuguitamū hi* (*The Day He Himself Shall Wipe My Tears Away*), a work that combines many of his major preoccupations, such as the emperor, cathartic violence, and a somewhat autobiographical father-son relationship, with an intense and challenging meditation on the nature of language as a tool for perceiving reality. The novel's narrator is a 38-year-old man who, believing he is dying, secludes himself in a hospital room and returns obsessively to a memory of what he calls his "happy days," when he was ten years old and plotted with his dying father to save the emperor during the final days of World War II. Two other figures, the man's mother and his wife, continually question his memory of the events, however, leaving the reader to question the reliability of language and memory as well. True to Ōe's belief in writing fiction with a message, *The Day He Himself Shall Wipe My Tears Away* also has a strongly ideological subtext: with its problematic narrator's implicitly insane valuation of rewriting history and memory for the sake of terrorism, the novella is actually a sustained attack on Ōe's fellow novelist Mishima Yukio, whose attempt at a right-wing coup and subsequent suicide by seppuku in 1970 epitomized to Ōe the dangers of fanatical beliefs. The novel weaves together a variety of factors—Ōe's own personal and ambivalent memories of World War II, his contempt for Mishima and his politics, and his fascination with language—to create a memorable new "here and now."

Ōe transforms his memories into a new "here and now" throughout his later writings as well. His landmark 1979 novel *Dōjidai gemu* (*The Game of Contemporaneity*) creates a hidden village, reminiscent of his own birthplace in rural Shikoku but mythologized into a small universe whose mythic connotations coexist with the personal. His 1993 trilogy *Moegaru midori no ki* (*The Burning Green Tree*) also returns to a pastoral setting in an exploration of themes of faith and salvation, heavily interwoven with complex allusions to William Blake, Dante, and William Butler Yeats.

At the height of his career, Ōe remains a complex and demanding writer, willing to experiment both with language and the concept of fiction itself. At the same time, however, he remains true to his fascination with creating a palpable "here and now." Ōe's writings are challenging, whether in Japanese or English, but they are among the most vivid and powerful fiction being produced today.

SUSAN J. NAPIER

Biography

Born 31 January 1935 in Ōse village, Shikoku island, Japan. Attended Tokyo University, 1954–59, B.A. in French literature 1959. Traveled to China as member of Japan-China Literary Delegation, 1960; traveled to Western and Eastern Europe, 1961, the United States, 1965, 1968, Australia, 1968, and Southeast Asia, 1970; visiting professor, Colegio de México, Mexico City, 1976. Awarded Nobel prize for literature, 1994.

Novels and Novellas by Ōe

Memushiri kouchi, 1958; as *Nip the Buds, Shoot the Kids*, translated by Paul Mackintosh and Maki Sugiyama, 1995
Warera no jidai [Our Era], 1959
Seinen no omei [The Young Man's Stigma], 1959
Kodoku na seinen no kyūka, 1960
Okurete kita seinen [The Youth Who Arrived Late], in *Shinchō*, September 1960–February 1962; in book form, 1962
Sevuntiin, in *Bungakukai*, January 1961; as *Seventeen*, translated by Masao Miyoshi, 1996
Seiji shōnen shisu [The Death of a Political Boy], in *Bungakukai*, February 1961
Sakebigoe [Outcries], in *Gunzō*, November 1962; in book form, 1963
Seiteki ningen, 1963; as *J*, translated by Masao Miyoshi, 1996
Nichijō seikatsu no bōken [Adventures of Everyday Life], 1963

Kojinteki na taiken, 1964; as *A Personal Matter,* translated by John Nathan, 1968

Sora no kaibutsu Aguii, 1964; as *Aghwee the Sky Monster,* translated by John Nathan, in *Teach Us to Outgrow Our Madness: Four Short Novels,* 1977

Man'en gannen no futtobōru [Football in the First Year of the Man'en Era], 1967; as *The Silent Cry,* translated by John Bester, 1974

Warera no kyoki o iki nobiru michi o oshieyo, 1969; augmented edition, 1975; as *Teach Us to Outgrow Our Madness,* translated by John Nathan, in *Teach Us to Outgrow Our Madness: Four Short Novels,* 1977

Waga namida o nuguitamū hi, 1972; as *The Day He Himself Shall Wipe My Tears Away,* translated by John Nathan, in *Teach Us to Outgrow Our Madness: Four Short Novels,* 1977

Kōzui wa waga tamashii ni oyobi [The Flood Has Reached My Soul], 2 vols., 1973

Pinchiranna chōsho, 1976; as *The Pinch Runner Memorandum,* translated by Michiko N. and Michael K. Wilson, 1994

Teach Us to Outgrow Our Madness: Four Short Novels (includes *Teach Us to Outgrow Our Madness; The Day He Himself Shall Wipe My Tears Away; Prize Stock; Aghwee the Sky Monster*), translated by John Nathan, 1977

Dōjidai gemu [The Game of Contemporaneity], 1979

"Ame no ki" o kiku onnatachi [Women Listening to "Rain Tree"], 1982

Atarashi hito yo mezameyo [Rouse Up O Young Men of the New Age!], 1983

Natsukashii toshi e no tegami [Letters to the Lost Years], 1986

Jinsei no Shinseki, 1989; as *An Echo of Heaven,* translated by Margaret Mitsutani, 1996

Chiryō no tō [The Treatment Tower], 1990

Moegaru midori no ki [The Burning Green Tree], 1993

Other Writings: short stories and essays (including *Hiroshima nōto* [1965; *Hiroshima Notes*]).

Further Reading

Napier, Susan Jolliffe, *Escape from the Wasteland: Romanticism and Realism in the Fiction of Mishima Yukio and Ōe Kenzaburō,* Cambridge, Massachusetts: Harvard University Press, 1991

Wilson, Michiko, *The Marginal World of Ōe Kenzaburō: A Study in Themes and Techniques,* Armonk, New York: M.E. Sharpe, 1986

On the Road by Jack Kerouac

1957

On the Road was not Jack Kerouac's first published novel—he made his debut as a novelist with *The Town and the City* in 1950—but he dismissed his first book as being written before he had found his own voice. Modeled after the fiction of Thomas Wolfe, *The Town and the City* was written, according to Kerouac, after "what they told me at Columbia University, Fiction. But . . . the novel's dead. Then I broke loose from all that and wrote picaresque narratives. That's what my books are."

In April 1951, after three weeks of inspired typing on a 120-foot roll of long sheets of drawing paper held together with scotch tape (so he wouldn't have to break off at the bottom of a page to put new sheets of paper into his typewriter), Kerouac created the novel published nearly seven years later as *On the Road.* At the age of 29, he had written his first successful autobiographical picaresque narrative. Six months later he discovered his experimental prose style, which he called "spontaneous prose" or "sketching." He immediately began to revise *On the Road,* creating another book covering the same period in his life entitled *Visions of Cody.* This narrative was so unconventional that it did not find a publisher in its complete form until 1973, more than three years after Kerouac's death.

The models for *On the Road* were the autobiographical books *Junkie* (1953) by William Burroughs and *Go* (1952) by John Clellon Holmes, both of which Kerouac read in manuscript shortly before he set to work on the marathon typing of his own novel. Between 1948 and 1950, he had made several attempts to begin *On the Road,* but he abandoned them because they failed

to tap what he called "the reverent mad feelings" he had about his experiences.

Kerouac found his own voice as a writer only after composing a series of long letters in December 1950–January 1951 to Neal Cassady, the friend who became the central character (Dean Moriarty) in the novel. Kerouac's letters were a response to an initial letter from Cassady describing his sexual exploits in Denver as a young man with two teenage girlfriends, Joan Anderson and Cherry Mary. Kerouac was so impressed by Cassady's letter that he told his friend:

> I thought it ranked among the best things ever written in America. . . . I say truly, no Dreiser, no Wolfe has come too close to it; Melville was never truer. I know that I don't dream. It can't possibly be sparse & halting, like Hemingway, because it hides nothing; the material is painfully necessary . . . the material of Scott Fitz was so sweetly unnecessary. It is the exact stuff upon which American Lit is still to be founded. You must and will go on at all costs including comfort & health & kicks; but keep it kickwriting at all costs too, that is, write only what kicks you and keeps you overtime awake from sheer mad joy.

The series of letters Kerouac wrote Cassady were a conscious attempt to "proceed into the actual truth" of his life for his close friend, and they became the foundation for all of Kerouac's subsequent books, beginning with the successful completion of *On the Road.* In the letters Kerouac experimented with flashbacks and interjections within the chronology of his narrative, developing the voice he would use in *On the Road.* He told Cassady that he felt as if he were talking to his friend on the front seat of a car "driving across the old U.S.A. in the night with no mysterious readers, no literary demands, nothing but us telling."

Previously, Kerouac had encouraged Cassady, Burroughs, and Holmes to write the story of their own lives, and he had even started his second wife Joan on a project to describe her life "in utter detail from beginning to end." Joan had asked him, "What did you and Neal really do?" on the cross-country trips Jack and Neal had taken together before their marriage. Kerouac decided to write his "road book" as if telling her the story of his adventures with Cassady, choosing first-person narration like Burrough's laconic autobiography but imitating Cassady's confessional style to dramatize the emotional effect his road experiences had had on him. Kerouac might have been critical of the romantic fiction of "Scott Fitz," but he had made a study of *The Great Gatsby* (1925) for a literature course at the New School and had learned the value of using a sympathetic narrator (himself as the character he called "Sal Paradise") to tell the story of an American hero (Neal Cassady as Dean Moriarty) who flees his past to embrace what he imagines as the freedom of his future. Kerouac's fictional portrait of Neal Cassady as a "great amorous soul" is the central achievement of *On the Road,* but the persona Kerouac created for himself as the innocent "Sal Paradise" who "shambled after" Dean is an equally skillful creation. Sal is a morally consistent presence in the book, a solid backdrop for the reader's encounter with the dazzlingly unpredictable whirlwind called Dean Moriarty.

Most reviewers of the novel read it as a description of what Kenneth Rexroth in *The San Francisco Chronicle* (1 September 1957) called "the delinquent younger generation." Others, like the more sympathetic critic William Hogan in the same issue of the newspaper, understood that the novel was "on more than one level, the account of postwar youth trying madly to get somewhere, someplace, somehow." Hogan read *On the Road* as a jazz novel, realizing that Kerouac "is of a generation that has willingly acknowledged jazz as its voice, that identifies itself with jazz." Early in the book Kerouac refers to "that sound in the night which bop has come to represent for all of us," and Hogan recognized that, "faced with a society which he considers has rejected him" (because he doesn't share its materialistic values), Kerouac "has come to identify himself in a great degree with jazz music because this is also the position of the jazz artist." Even the hostile review in *Newsweek* magazine (9 September 1957), which described Dean Moriarty as "a frantic, animal-like delinquent . . . a kind of T-shirted Ahab of the automobile," praised Kerouac's "fast-tempoed, bop-beat prose."

The sound of bop and the example of jazz musicians such as Charlie Parker, Lester Young, and Thelonious Monk were important influences on Kerouac as he developed his style in books after *On the Road.* Kerouac's "sketching" or "spontaneous prose," an unedited and unrevised spontaneity, impressed his fellow Beats Allen Ginsberg and William Burroughs. Kerouac compared himself to a jazz musician improvising on a musical theme: "sketching language is undisturbed flow from the mind of personal secret idea-words, blowing (as per jazz musician) on a subject of image." There was to be no revision: "Never afterthink to improve or defray impressions . . . tap from yourself the

song of yourself, *blow!—now!—your way* is your only way—good—bad—always honest."

In 1952, after completing *On the Road* and *Visions of Cody,* Kerouac went on to create the series of autobiographical novels he conceived of as his life's work, "The Legend of Duluoz," or "The Legend of Kerouac" (Duluoz was another of Kerouac's pseudonyms for himself). *On the Road* appears midway in this sequence after novels about his childhood and adolescence: *Visions of Gerard* (1963), *Doctor Sax* (1959), *Maggie Cassidy* (1959), and *Vanity of Duluoz* (1968). In the chronology of books about Kerouac's life, *On the Road* is followed by *The Subterraneans* (1958), *Tristessa* (1960), *The Dharma Bums* (1958), *Desolation Angels* (1965), *Big Sur* (1962), and *Satori in Paris* (1966), in which he describes his last trip abroad three years before his death from alcoholism in 1969.

As Allen Ginsberg wrote the poet Charles Olson on 18 February 1957, Kerouac's "material is not historical saga but personal." All of Kerouac's novels were based on autobiographical material, because—as Ginsberg went on—"The only way I know to stay solid is to keep my individual firsthand feelings . . . or goofy imaginations of Poe in attic, still strictly personal, actually each poem a confession, for Jack each novel a confession or vision—of someone he loves usually."

Kerouac's "vision" of his friend Neal Cassady in *On the Road* has become an archetypal vision of the outsider for generations of young readers in the United States. Kerouac's description of his cross-country adventures on America's highways with "Dean Moriarty" is as compelling a visionary description of his experience as another outsider's visionary account of his sojourn at Walden Pond 100 years earlier. Both Thoreau's *Walden* (1854) and Kerouac's *On the Road* are classic works of literature that have succeeded in capturing the imagination of generations of readers who want to dream the beautiful dream of self-reliance as the essential quality of the American experience.

ANN CHARTERS

Further Reading

Charters, Ann, *A Bibliography of Works by Jack Kerouac,* New York: Phoenix Book Shop, 1967; revised edition, 1975

Charters, Ann, *Kerouac: A Biography,* San Francisco: Straight Arrow Books, 1973; London: Deutsch, 1974

Charters, Ann, editor, *The Beats: Literary Bohemians in Postwar America,* 2 vols., Detroit, Michigan: Gale Research, 1983

Charters, Ann, editor, *The Portable Jack Kerouac,* New York: Viking Press, 1995

Charters, Ann,, editor, *The Selected Letters of Jack Kerouac, 1940–1956,* New York: Viking Press, 1995

Gifford, Barry, and Lee Lawrence, *Jack's Book: An Oral Biography of Jack Kerouac,* New York: St. Martin's Press, 1978

Holmes, John Clellon, *Representative Men: The Biographical Essays,* Fayetteville: University of Arkansas Press, 1988

Hunt, Tim, *Kerouac's Crooked Road: Development of a Fiction,* Hamden, Connecticut: Archon, 1981

Nicosia, Gerald, *Memory Babe: A Critical Biography of Jack Kerouac,* New York: Grove Press, 1983; Harmondsworth: Viking, 1985

Tytell, John, *Naked Angels: The Lives and Literature of the Beat Generation,* New York: McGraw-Hill, 1976

One Day in the Life of Ivan Denisovich by Aleksandr Solzhenitsyn

Odin den' Ivana Denisovicha 1962

One Day in the Life of Ivan Denisovich was a major Soviet literary event of the post-Stalinist period known as "the thaw." At the 22nd Congress of the Soviet Communist Party in 1961, Nikita Khrushchev continued the de-Stalinization campaign that he had started at the 20th Party Congress in 1956. Aleksandr Solzhenitsyn judged the moment propitious for an attempt to publish a literary account of the Soviet labor camp or Gulag experience. Having overcome numerous hurdles, his novella was finally printed in the monthly *Novyi mir* in November 1962, with Khrushchev's personal permission.

Ivan Denisovich is primarily a vehicle for a fictionalized testimony about the world of the Soviet labor camps. Aiming at the broadly representative, the novella gives a systematic account of a typical day in a camp, from reveille to lights out. The cast of characters is a cross section of Soviet society. And the charges that serve as the reason for the characters' imprisonment run the gamut of those commonly brought against Soviet citizens after World War II. The story is occasionally interrupted by blocks of information about camp procedures and the typical behavior of inmates and guards. Many of these blocks take the form of lists of possibilities: what might be done by prisoners in a particular set of circumstances, what might be done by the guards in response, what might be expected should circumstances change.

Solzhenitsyn integrates the documentary function of *Ivan Denisovich* into an overarching narrative framework. By and large, camp events are presented through the experiences of Ivan Denisovich Shukhov, a canny, cagey, observant, and somewhat unscrupulous peasant. Ivan holds the reader's attention as his character slowly takes shape and draws the reader into the story. He is engaged in unceasing efforts to alleviate his lot—sometimes at the expense of others, sometimes also on their behalf. Although Ivan can predict the possible outcomes of his efforts, he usually has no way of telling whether he will be successful in improving his situation. The resulting suspense helps to carry the reader through the documentary sections that are interspersed among the events of Ivan's day.

Solzhenitsyn places the information blocks at strategic points in the story. The jobs that are typically done before morning roll-call, for instance, are listed immediately after Ivan wakes up. All the possible outcomes of a frisking are described when Ivan undergoes that "ritual." The information blocks tend to fall in places where the pace of events slows down, for instance, when Ivan has his temperature taken in the infirmary and is waiting for the thermometer to show the result. Almost apologetically, Solzhenitsyn creates the illusion that these segments are only filling the dull stretches in the story-time—since the reader would otherwise just be waiting around, she might as well use the time to find out more about the Gulag.

Ivan Denisovich has been attacked for giving an uncharacteristically mild account of life in the Soviet labor camps. One reason that the camp conditions tend to be understated in the novella is that, of all the outcomes of Ivan's maneuvering, the luckiest usually ensues. But more than that, according to camp veterans such as the writer Varlam Shalamov, the camp depicted in the story is much more humane than the average camp. Although he creates the impression that *Ivan Denisovich* describes a representative camp, Solzhenitsyn chose the particulars of the story so as to tone down the typically harsh conditions and to avoid the worst atrocities. Ivan's camp is in the relatively warm Kazakhstan, and the work to which the prisoners are assigned is construction rather than mining or timbering, which were associated with far more grueling conditions. The only indication that *Ivan Denisovich* does not represent typical conditions in the Gulag comes in Ivan's reminiscences of a different camp, where he nearly died of privation.

Solzhenitsyn indirectly reflects, in the narrative itself, on his choice not to represent the full extent of the atrocities and suffering in the Gulag. Ivan overhears an argument between two intellectuals concerning the distortion of history in Eisenstein's movies, and this discussion lays out the artist's dilemma as a choice between, on the one hand, understating the miseries and abuses so as to be able to publish and, on the other hand, representing history accurately and being silenced by the censor. Obviously, Solzhenitsyn chose the former and had the satisfaction of seeing the labor camps become a subject of literary exploration in the wake of *Ivan Denisovich*'s publication.

But *Ivan Denisovich* is more than an exploration of the logistics of survival in the camps. The novella raises other "forbidden" issues in a veiled manner and invites a critique not only of the Soviet penal system but of Stalinist political repression and Soviet communism in general. The letters of Ivan's wife and the dialogue of the guards suggest that the majority of Soviet citizens are only serving a lighter sentence, without the benefit of barbed wire, of the same bondage and oppression that Ivan and his fellow prisoners are condemned to inside the camps. In this respect, *Ivan Denisovich* also made a significant contribution to the literary phenomenon of veiled political criticism that has flowered in the Soviet Union and other totalitarian regimes.

Shortly after the publication of *Ivan Denisovich*, manuscripts of Gulag narratives started flooding editorial offices. It soon became apparent, however, that Khrushchev's "thaw" was only a brief stage in Soviet history. Only a few tendentiously selected camp narratives were published in the years after Solzhenitsyn's novella came out. But many of the manuscripts turned down by official journals surfaced in the literary Samizdat (underground publication). These, together with other works by Solzhenitsyn, formed an important element in the cultural background of the end of Soviet communist rule.

LEONA TOKER AND MARIJKE RIJSBERMAN

See also Aleksandr Solzhenitsyn

Further Reading

Hosking, Geoffrey, *Beyond Socialist Realism: Soviet Fiction since "Ivan Denisovich,"* London: Granada, and New York: Holmes and Meier, 1980

Lukács, Georg, *Solschenizyn,* Neuwied: Luchterhand, 1970; as *Solzhenitsyn,* London: Merlin, 1970; Cambridge, Massachusetts: MIT Press, 1971

Luplow, Richard, "Narrative Style and Structure in *One Day in* the Life of Ivan Denisovich," *Russian Literature Triquarterly* 3 (1971)

Medvedev, Zhores A., *Ten Years after "Ivan Denisovich,"* translated by Hilary Sternberg, New York: Knopf, and London: Macmillan, 1973

Ruttner, Ekhard, "The Names in Solzhenitsyn's Short Novel *One Day in the Life of Ivan Denisovich*," *Names: Journal of the American Name Society* 23 (1975)

Scammell, Michael, *Solzhenitsyn: A Biography*, New York: Norton, 1984; London: Hutchinson, 1985

Solzhenitsyn, Aleksandr, *The Oak and the Calf* (memoirs), translated by Harry Willetts, London: Collins, and New York: Harper and Row, 1980

Toker, Leona, "Some Features of the Narrative Method in Solzhenitsyn's *One Day in the Life of Ivan Denisovich*," in *In Honour of Professor Victor Levin: Russian Philology and History*, edited by W. Moskovich, J. Frankel, I. Serman, and S. Shvarzband, Jerusalem: Praedicta, 1992

One Hundred Years of Solitude by Gabriel García Márquez

Cien años de soledad 1967

Gabriel García Márquez's first three novels went unnoticed by scholars and critics, despite the aesthetic merit of the books. With the publication of *One Hundred Years of Solitude*, however, the response of critics and readers alike was uniformly enthusiastic. Never before had a Latin American novel received such instantaneous and widespread acclaim. The novel's unprecedented commercial success, as well as its exploration of Latin American history and its humor, have made it one of the most remarkable literary phenomena of the century.

In the years following its publication in Spanish, *One Hundred Years of Solitude* was translated into English and numerous other languages. During this period (the late 1960s and early 1970s), the international recognition of the "boom" of the Latin American novel was at its zenith, and *One Hundred Years of Solitude* was one of the main reasons for the renown of this literature. It popularized the type of literature often identified as magic realism.

Latin American literature associated with magic realism had been widely published since the 1940s. The Cuban writer Alejo Carpentier had articulated a concept similar to magic realism in 1949, proposing that Latin American literature was an expression of "lo real maravilloso" (marvelous reality). In the 1950s and 1960s, several prominent critics of Latin American literature, including Angel Flores, attempted to describe or define magic realism. Most of these descriptions and definitions emphasize how Latin American literature in the magic realist vein uses a realist base as a point of departure and then moves into a fantastic realm while maintaining the realist tone. Gabriel García Márquez considers himself fundamentally a realist who writes about Colombian and Latin American reality exactly as he has observed it. Much of his writing, and particularly *One Hundred Years of Solitude*, has roots in the oral storytelling tradition of the northern Caribbean coast of Colombia, a tradition with several characteristics similar to magic realism, including hyperbole.

García Márquez claims that he learned everything he needed to know as a novelist by the time he was eight. He learned the oral tradition from his grandmother during his childhood in Aracataca, Colombia, for his parents left him to be reared by his grandparents. He began writing stories in his adolescence in Bogotá in the 1940s and published fiction set in the fictional town of Macondo in the 1950s and 1960s, fiction written under the obvious influence of William Faulkner. *One Hundred Years of Solitude* was the culmination, for García Márquez, of a cycle of novels centering on Macondo. At the same time, it was his first novel to incorporate the oral tradition.

One Hundred Years of Solitude abounds in social and political themes. The novel relates much of the social and political life in Colombia and Latin America from the three centuries of the colonial period to the 20th century. During the 19th century, liberals and conservatives in Colombia engaged in several civil wars, and these battles, as fantastic as they seem in the novel, were real. At the end of the 19th century, the United Fruit Company was established in Colombia, and this historical fact places the arrival of Mr. Herbert in the novel within the context of the historical arrival of North Americans. In 1928 the banana workers struck against the United Fruit Company, a catastrophic event that is central to the novel and involved the massacre of hundreds, possibly thousands, of workers.

It is possible to view the endless series of repetitions in *One Hundred Years of Solitude* as a metaphor for a capitalist society without social or economic vitality. Read in this manner, the colonel's endless battles are quite similar to his repetitive creation of little gold fish: both activities present a paradigm of action for the sake of action (or production for the sake of production) with no worthwhile return. Interestingly enough, Macondo never really functions as a bona fide participant in the political or economic processes of the nation. It is always marginal.

One Hundred Years of Solitude is a unique social document in that it captures a wide gamut of Colombia's social, political, and economic realities. For Colombia, this novel is anomalous in its portrayal and critique of the social and political consequences of the export economy that was in existence for only a short period in a small region in Colombia. It is a paradigm that applies, however, for much of Latin America. At the same time, García Márquez portrays the central conflict between Colombia's traditional political and economic sectors in the civil wars between liberals and conservatives. His method for fictionalizing this conflict is to use the most vividly remembered legendary figure of this period, a general named Rafael Uribe Uribe, as the model for the character Colonel Aureliano Buendía.

Technically speaking, *One Hundred Years of Solitude* has a third-person omniscient narrator. This narrator does occasionally reveal what the characters think. The predominant mode, however, is external: the reader observes the characters as they act and speak. The narrator is detached from what he narrates, offering an apparently neutral presentation of the fictional world. Nevertheless, certain variations in this format belie total neutrality. On the one hand, the narrator often functions as if he were a character in the novel. At times he demonstrates an innocence or amazement with the world that is similar to that of the characters. The narrator thinks like them, demonstrating on occasion the same prejudices and at other times the same oral-culture point of view.

One Hundred Years of Solitude contains a variety of languages to create numerous resonances. Resonances of biblical language, for example, help make it possible to read the novel as a total history of mankind since creation. The narrator incorporates languages that have the resonance of distinct historical periods, each of which also contributes to the book's universal overtones. The narrator, for example, uses a language associated with the Middle Ages when he describes José Arcadio Buendía's attack on Prudencio Aguilar as a "duel of honor." He uses an equally antiquated, and humorous, language to describe Rebeca's reaction to the physical masculinity of José Arcadio.

The central role of memory is underscored by the insomnia epidemic of the third chapter, which threatens the loss of all the layers of identity and history that saturate the consciousness of Macondo. The epidemic reduces culture to the recognition of only the most basic objects, by the labels they have been provided with.

Rarely does a novel attract such a vast response from scholars and critics of Latin American literature. Numerous critics have been interested in explaining how the beginning and end of this novel function. For John Brushwood (1975), the opening line is one of the most remarkable in all of Latin American fiction. Seymour Menton (1978) has observed how the first sentence immediately involves the reader in three aspects of time: the future, an assumed present, and the past. Time thus becomes a problematic matter for the reader from the very first line and continues to elude definition. Critics point out that the matter of "discovering ice" also stands out in this first sentence. It suggests a primitiveness and innocence that surprise the reader yet characterize much of Macondo in the first two chapters. The town, in effect, is a type of biblical paradise where innocence reigns. In addition, the naming of things in the novel's beginning suggests that the act of creation will be important in the novel, as indeed it is.

These and other critics have pointed out that the last three pages reveal several important secrets and change the reader's experience of the novel considerably. For most of the novel, the reader is allowed to forget the book's status as fiction. It is above all a story of a family and a town, as opposed to a self-referential reflection on fiction. Near the end, however, the novel becomes a more playful metafiction, including characters from the fiction of other writers, to mention only one example.

One Hundred Years of Solitude has had considerable influence on fiction in Latin America, the United States, and beyond. In the Spanish-speaking world, this novel opened the door to fiction that emphasizes the magical qualities of life in Latin America, portrayed in a humorous tone. The one writer whose work is most in this vein since the publication of *One Hundred Years of Solitude* is the Chilean novelist Isabel Allende. Several North American writers, too, have mentioned how the wild imagination and invention in this novel gave them a sense of vitality and reaffirmed the possibilities of writing fiction. Throughout the world, writers, too, have used García Márquez's model to tell humorous stories portraying the peculiarities of everyday life in their own towns. Given its status as one of Latin America's most widely read and studied novels of the century, *One Hundred Years of Solitude* appears to be destined to survive several more decades—if not centuries—of analysis, discussion, and enjoyment.

RAYMOND LESLIE WILLIAMS

See also Gabriel García Márquez

Further Reading

Brushwood, John Stubbs, *The Spanish American Novel: A Twentieth-Century Survey,* Austin: University of Texas Press, 1975

Fau, Margaret Eustella, *Gabriel García Márquez: An Annotated Bibliography, 1947–1979,* Westport, Connecticut: Greenwood Press, 1980

Harss, Luis, and Barbara Dohmann, *Into the Mainstream: Conversations with Latin American Writers,* New York: Harper and Row, 1967

Levine, Suzanne Jill, *El espejo hablado,* Caracas: Monte Avila, 1975

Ludmer, Josefina, *"Cien años de soledad": Una interpretación,* Buenos Aires: Tiempo Contemporáneo, 1972; 2nd edition, 1974

McMurray, George, *Gabriel García Márquez,* New York: Ungar, 1977

McMurray, George, editor, *Critical Essays on Gabriel García Márquez,* Boston: G.K. Hall, 1987

Menton, Seymour, *La novela colombiana: Planetas y satélites,* Bogotá: Plaza y Janés, 1978

Oberhelman, Harley D., *The Presence of Faulkner in the Writings of García Márquez,* Lubbock: Texas Tech Press, 1980

Williams, Raymond Leslie, *The Colombian Novel: 1844–1987,* Austin: University of Texas Press, 1991

The Ordeal of Richard Feverel by George Meredith

1859

When Virginia Woolf assessed the remarkable impact of George Meredith on her generation, she stressed his role as a breaker of novelistic conventions. Writing during the centenary of his birth (1928), she took his remarkable first novel, *The Ordeal of Richard Feverel,* as primary evidence that Meredith was writing against tradition: "He has been, it is plain, at great pains to destroy the conventional form of the novel. He makes no attempt to preserve the sober reality of Trollope and Jane Austen; he has destroyed all the usual staircases by which we have learnt to climb" ("The Novels of George Meredith," in *The Second Common Reader*).

What particularly interests Woolf here is Meredith's technique in *The Ordeal of Richard Feverel*—the jettisoning of many of the traditional narrative strategies that had become the staples of 19th-century realism, with its stylistic immersion in quotidian detail and implied simulacrum of the "actual" world. This sacrifice of "the usual staircases," what Woolf also calls the "defiance of the ordinary" in *The Ordeal of Richard Feverel*, contributes to much of what is both fascinating and, at times, maddening about the experimentation in this novel and in Meredith's later work: if fiction had remained what it was to Austen and Trollope, fiction would by this time be dead. Thus Meredith deserves gratitude and excites interest as a great innovator. Many of the doubts about him and much of the inability to frame any definite opinion of his work comes from the fact that it *is* experimental and thus contains elements that do not fuse harmoniously. The reader must not expect the perfect quietude of a traditional style nor the triumphs of a patient and pedestrian psychology.

The experimental and questioning impulse in Meredith's first novel found expression through a variety of means, both thematic and technical. Its thematic center is found in its scathing critique of Victorian patriarchy and gender relations; its technical innovation is evident where Meredith develops these themes by playing with language and genre to test and extend traditional novelistic boundaries, at the same time creating tensions, awkwardnesses, and apparent contradictions that his efforts at revision in the 1878 edition failed to resolve.

The reader is confronted with a good illustration of how this innovative process operates at the opening of *The Ordeal of Richard Feverel*. Meredith begins with an arch narrative style distinctly reminiscent of the satirical language he used in the two highly stylized burlesques with which he had begun his fiction-writing career, *The Shaving of Shagpat: An Arabian Entertainment* (1855) and *Farina: A Legend of Cologne* (1857). While the tone of *Richard Feverel's* opening chapters is considerably more urbane and sententious than that of the two earlier works, the predominant note is still broadly satiric: the inhabitants of Raynham Abbey—like the oddities who inhabit Meredith's father-in-law's *Nightmare Abbey* (1818)—are presented in a blend of parodistic styles that would seem to prepare for anything but tragedy, but that is in fact the direction the novel eventually takes, resulting for many readers in a sense of incongruity— what Woolf identified as lack of harmonious fusion.

On the other hand, the pointed satiric references to Sir Austin Feverel's "Pilgrim's Scrip" that begin on the opening page provide a continually telling ironic commentary on the action. Almost the first of the aphorisms quoted—"Life is a tedious process of learning we are Fools"—makes fun of Sir Austin not only because he is a fool, but because he never learns he is one. At the novel's end we see him still trapped in the aphoristic monologue with which he begins. What Meredith produces in his portrait of Sir Austin is quite literally a psychological critique and parody of the patriarchal claim to objectivity: the father, posturing as "Scientific Humanist," is intent not on dispassionate, methodical, or humane thinking but rather on an elaborate scheme of retribution that he himself cannot fully recognize. Abandoned by his wife after the birth of their son, he has proceeded to sublimate his extreme sense of damaged self-esteem into a "scientific System," ostensibly to protect Richard from the dangers of a similar ordeal. That this elaborate project should run its course by helping to produce similar patriarchal arrogance and consequent disaster in the life of the son gains an increasing sense of inevitability as the novel proceeds.

What Meredith does in *The Ordeal of Richard Feverel,* then, is to take an initially comic situation—based upon the male egoism and self-ignorance that are thematic hallmarks of all his fiction—and develop by degrees what he saw as its tragic implications. This crossing of generic boundaries has produced outcries from critics since the novel first appeared and probably contributed to its being dropped by Mudie's circulating library. In fact, the critical history of the novel has often been marked by the determination of its readers to recast and conventionalize Meredith's experimentation by attempting to view the work consistently through a comic lens. Joseph Warren Beach solved the difficulty of the more somber elements in the novel by dividing it into two parts: the tragedy of Richard and Lucy and the comedy of Sir Austin and his System. Beach then proceeded, logically enough, to devote his discussion to the latter. (See Beach, 1911.) Many critics have subsequently returned to Beach's basic premise—*The Ordeal of Richard Feverel* is or ought to be essentially comic—and have treated the novel as comedy *manqué*. But this monogeneric approach misses an essential element of Meredith's genius, in this and subsequent novels: his purposeful playfulness in the face of the constraints of traditional form, his instinctive habit of presenting a range of sometimes competing narrative voices in his fiction.

One of the most interesting recent developments in Meredith criticism has been the recognition of this dialogic quality of his work (see Roberts, 1997; Stone, 1988), that is, the impulse to "become more free and flexible" that Mikhail Bakhtin associates with the role of the dialogic imagination in the novel as a genre (*The Dialogic Imagination,* 1981). Donald Stone, arguing that Meredith is the most Bakhtinian of 19th-century English novelists, puts the point this way: "Other genres respond to the rules laid down for stabilized forms, but the novel flaunts its instability; it thrives on the rejection of rules" (Stone, 1988), and this observation applies especially well to *The Ordeal of Richard Feverel*.

Meredith, then, is becoming increasingly appreciated as a rule breaker, as one who questioned and deconstructed conventions such as those of genre and "the perfect quietude of a traditional style." The countervailing narrative voices in *The Ordeal of Richard Feverel* are a manifestation of a dialogic impulse that propels the narrative away from any kind of generic unity to a dizzying mixture of satire, comedy, romance, and, finally, tragedy. Or, one could simply say that Meredith seems sometimes to delight in disrupting our conventional notions of how a plot or a narrative voice should be constructed. Bakhtin, when he describes the process in fiction he calls the "novelization of other genres," provides what may serve as a useful description of this aspect of *The Ordeal of Richard Feverel*: language becomes "dialogized, permeated with laughter, irony, humor, elements of self-parody and finally—this is the most important thing—the novel inserts an indeterminacy, a certain semantic openendedness, a living contact with unfinished, still-evolving contemporary reality" (*The Dialogic Imagination*). In *The Ordeal of Richard Feverel*, we find this "certain semantic openendedness" with a vengeance, a quality that helps to explain the importance of this work in the development of the modern English novel.

RICHARD C. STEVENSON

See also George Meredith

Further Reading

Beach, Joseph Warren, *The Comic Spirit in George Meredith,* New York: Longmans, Green, 1911

Beer, Gillian, *Meredith: A Change of Masks,* London: Athlone Press, 1970

Buckley, Jerome Hamilton, *Season of Youth: The Bildungsroman from Dickens to Golding,* Cambridge, Massachusetts: Harvard University Press, 1974

Foster, David E., "Rhetorical Strategy in Richard Feverel," *Nineteenth-Century Fiction* 26 (1971)

Korg, Jacob, "Expressive Styles in *The Ordeal of Richard Feverel,*" *Nineteenth-Century Fiction* 27 (1972)

Moses, Joseph, *The Novelist as Comedian: George Meredith and the Ironic Sensibility,* New York: Schocken, 1983

Roberts, Neil, *Meredith and the Novel,* New York: St. Martin's Press, 1997

Spanberg, Sven-Johan, *"The Ordeal of Richard Feverel" and the Traditions of Realism,* Uppsala: Acta Universitatis Upsaliensis, 1974

Stevenson, Richard C., "The Spirit of Critical Intelligence in Richard Feverel," in *The Worlds of Victorian Fiction,* edited by Jerome Hamilton Buckley, Cambridge, Massachusetts: Harvard University Press, 1975

Stone, Donald D., "Meredith and Bakhtin: Polyphony and Bildung," *Studies in English Literature* 28 (Autumn 1988)

Wilt, Judith, *The Readable People of George Meredith,* Princeton, New Jersey: Princeton University Press, 1975

Oroonoko by Aphra Behn

1688

Aphra Behn turned to fiction writing only after a varied career as wife, spy, poet, and playwright. The choices she made throughout her life, both in her behavior and in her fictional self-expression, often ran counter to the expectations for women of her time. To many of her contemporaries she was a scandal, an enemy of femininity and chastity; to many of the scholars who now study her she was a protofeminist, an early abolitionist, and a literary innovator. Behn's *Oroonoko* clearly shows both the complexity of her position as a woman writer and the complexity of the narrative strategies she used to negotiate her position.

The story recounts a presumably real encounter with the African slave Oroonoko, which occurred during a visit to Surinam in 1663. So as to leave no doubt about the veracity of her narrative, Behn opens with a truth claim: she is not writing about a "feign'd *Hero,*" nor is she going to "adorn" the "Truth" for the reader's entertainment. Her story is a "History"; it will describe only those things that she has personally witnessed or that were told to her by Oroonoko himself. To reinforce her status as documentarian, Behn then provides copious and minute details about her West Indian surroundings. She also makes so many historical and biographical references that the narrative has often been viewed both as straightforward biography fleshing out Behn's otherwise scantily recorded life and as an accurate account of West Indian colonial culture.

There is much in the narrative that relates it to the actual political conflicts of the late 17th century. From one perspective, Behn addresses the political controversies of the day, using her hero as a shadowy representation of James II. It is the monarchist Tories in the narrative (Behn, Trefry) who respect and admire Oroonoko, while the cruel, greedy Whigs want only to destroy him. From another perspective, the narrative touches on the difficult issue of colonialism. Oroonoko has been interpreted as an antiracist, abolitionist narrative through Oroonoko's impassioned speech decrying slavery as well as Behn's vivid depictions of the cruel treatment suffered by the slaves.

The narrative also raises the issue of the political and literary disenfranchisement of women. In her claim to truth, Behn stakes out ground for herself as a woman writer, for a woman writing professionally was viewed with the greatest suspicion. To write at all was to assert her private, feminine self in a masculine, public world. Yet Behn claims the authority of the observer: her descriptions of Surinam, the natives, and Oroonoko have a proprietary tone. Also, despite her concluding demur that Oroonoko deserves a "more sublime Wit than mine to write his

Praise," Behn lays claim to narrative authority; she is the teller of her tale as well as the tales of others.

In an equally powerful way, however, Behn locates her narrative within the world of romance that her realism and politics attempt to deny. *Oroonoko* is a romance of the very sort that Behn claims she is not writing. The narrative is divided into two sections—Oroonoko's and Imoinda's adventures in love and war in Africa and their enslavement in Surinam—and each section is colored by romance as much as realism. In Africa, Oroonoko is a king endowed with natural virtues and natural authority. As star-crossed lovers, Oroonoko and Imoinda are idealized figures of Western heroic romance, whose love for each other transcends time, place, and race. In Surinam, Behn's hero is the "noble savage" who is socially and morally superior to the white men around him. Surinam is represented as an Edenic world whose native Indians possess a natural beauty, an innocent curiosity, and an innate sense of justice. The white colonists, in contrast, are depicted for the most part as corrupt, drunken louts—England's political and social rejects.

In *Oroonoko,* these two worlds—the realistic world of colonialism and the idealistic world of romance—exist in a contestatory relationship. For instance, the narrative's possible antislavery message is complicated by Oroonoko's own acceptance of slavery as a viable institution: it is permissible as long as the right people are dominated. The injustice of his own enslavement derives not from the essential injustice of the institution but from his royal origins. Paradoxically, Oroonoko is beautiful and noble because he is unlike the rest of his race; with his fine Roman profile and preternaturally black skin, his vast wisdom and superhuman strength, he transcends race to claim the kind of majesty that resides in supreme artistic creations. Thus, Behn's descriptions of Oroonoko complicate her claims to fact. Was he an actual man whose goodness and intelligence are simply amplified to create a character sufficiently heroic? Or is he an entirely fictional paragon, derived from romance and devised to attract attention and to make a particular point?

In the end, Behn resolves the tension between these two narratives—one forceful in its bloody realism and rebellious politics, the other insistent on maintaining an idealized status quo of transcendent nobility—through the strategies of romance. Having boldly raised private history into public heroism, Behn finally transmutes the public, political problem of slavery into a private, doomed love story. In her depictions of "glorious" Oroonoko and the "brave, the beautiful, and the constant" Imoinda, Behn represents a hero and heroine who seem simultaneously authentic and artificial, both true and too good to be true.

Behn's attitude toward and treatment of her material places her within the 17th- and 18th-century epistemological dialogue over the substantiality and authenticity of narrative literature. Numerous early writers of the novel—Behn, Daniel Defoe, Jonathan Swift, Henry Fielding, and Samuel Richardson—attempted to separate their own "real" narratives from the fantasy romances that were the main staple of fiction at the time. Thus *Oroonoko* falls into the uncertain domain between empirical fact and acknowledged fiction. It is a hybrid of a number of narrative forms: romance, travelogue, reportage, and polemic. Later writers were to resolve more successfully the conflicting demands of realism and idealism. However, even though it is a narrative technically flawed and thematically unstable, *Oroonoko* opened for the novel a space within which the discourses of realism and romance, feminism and Tory politics, and abolitionism and colonialism could contest one another in a fascinating and instructive fashion.

JUDITH BURDAN

See also Aphra Behn

Further Reading

Ballaster, Ros, "New Historicism: Aphra Behn's *Oroonoko*: The Body, the Text, and the Feminist Critic," in *New Feminist Discourses: Critical Essays on Theories and Texts,* edited by Isobel Armstrong, New York and London: Routledge, 1992

Brown, Laura, "The Romance of the Empire: *Oroonoko* and the Trade in Slaves," in *The New Eighteenth Century,* edited by Felicity Nussbaum and Laura Brown, New York: Methuen, 1987

Davis, Lennard J., *Factual Fictions: The Origins of the English Novel,* New York: Columbia University Press, 1983

Gardiner, Judith Kegan, "The First English Novel: Aphra Behn, the Canon, and Women's Tastes," *Tulsa Studies* 8:2 (1989)

Macheski, Cecilia, and Mary Anne Schofield, editors, *Fetter'd or Free? British Women Novelists, 1670–1815,* Athens: Ohio University Press, 1986

McKeon, Michael, *The Origins of the English Novel, 1600–1740,* Baltimore: Johns Hopkins University Press, 1987; London: Radius, 1988

Rogers, Katharine M., "Fact and Fiction in Aphra Behn's *Oroonoko,*" *Studies in the Novel* 20 (1988)

Spencer, Jane, *The Rise of the Woman Novelist: From Aphra Behn to Jane Austen,* Oxford and New York: Blackwell, 1986

Spengemann, William C., "The Earliest American Novel: Aphra Behn's *Oroonoko,*" *Nineteenth-Century Fiction* 38 (1984)

Todd, Janet, editor, *Aphra Behn Studies,* Cambridge and New York: Cambridge University Press, 1996

Ottsy i deti. *See* Fathers and Sons

Outlaws of the Marsh. *See* Six Classic Chinese Novels

Outsider. *See* Stranger

Owls Do Cry by Janet Frame

1957

When Janet Frame began to write *Owls Do Cry* in the summer of 1954–55, she had published only one book, *The Lagoon and Other Stories* (1952) and had spent seven of the years since 1945 in mental hospitals. Since her discharge from the hospital, she had been seeking, as she later said, "a place to live and write, with enough money to support myself." Her attempts at writing in her hometown of Oamaru and in Dunedin had been unsuccessful, but in Auckland she established herself in a shed in the garden of the writer Frank Sargeson and was able to dedicate herself to the writing of her first novel, which she completed in the late winter of 1955.

The novel was published in New Zealand in 1957, which proved propitious, for 1957–58 was soon being claimed as an annus mirabilis for the New Zealand novel. Within that year Sylvia Ashton-Warner, Ian Cross, M.K. Joseph, and Ruth France also published significant first novels. There had been few notable New Zealand novels since World War II, but a breakthrough seemed to be occurring. Previously, Sargeson's short stories and John Mulgan's novel, *Man Alone*, in the late 1930s had established critical realism as the primary mode of New Zealand fiction in the provincial period and the conflict between the isolated individual and society as the primary theme. Frame's vision continued in that tradition but deepened it. At the same time she chose a very different mode of expression that could be classified as modernist or impressionist. New Zealand fiction had had one of the makers of that mode in Katherine Mansfield, but the only writer who had incorporated modernist methods into the novel before Frame was Robin Hyde, the most productive, but not the most influential, of New Zealand novelists of the 1930s.

Frame's dualism between the sensitive individual and the uncaring world was directly in the tradition of New Zealand fiction, but more extreme, with a metaphysical dimension. The world where "owls do cry" (the title comes from the song in Shakespeare's *Tempest*) is one in which, in the words of Daphne, the protagonist, "time and death pinned human in the pocket of my land not rest from taking underground the green all-willowed and white rose and bean flower and morning-mist picnic of song in pepper-pot breast of thrush." For the sensitive individual, the only escape in such a world is the imagination—the only true treasure in Frame's world—which is immediately available to children but something that the society of Waimaru strives to destroy by the process of socialization. When an individual refuses to give up childlike imagination, as in Daphne's case, society's means of socialization is the mental hospital, with its electric-shock treatment and its ultimate weapon—the leucotomy—which is used against Daphne to cut out the offending imagination.

To express a more extreme version of the provincial writers' dualism, Frame uses the devices of the modernist novel rather than those of the dominant realist tradition. *Owls Do Cry*'s point of view is not the limited third-person perspective of Mulgan but a constantly shifting series of inside views, including Daphne's lyrical interior monologues from the mental hospital and the ironic first-person narrative of her sister Chicks' diary. The style is not the consistent and basically utilitarian prose of the realist novel but is poetic, imagist, allusive, and constantly changing. Frame's characterization does not rely primarily on speech and action supplemented by summaries of thought but on a relatively direct presentation of the inner life by free indirect thought and interior monologue. The plot does not recount a long, chronologically ordered causal chain of events but supplies the reader with a series of intensely realized inner experiences, often out of chronological order. The structure, too, is not purely temporal and linear but also "spatial," with recurring motifs and symbols reflecting back and forth upon each other. No New Zealand novelist before Frame had so exploited the devices associated with James Joyce, Virginia Woolf, and William Faulkner. Hyde had used some, especially in *The Godwits Fly* (1938), *Owls Do Cry*'s most significant New Zealand predecessor, but not to the extent that Frame does.

New Zealand reviewers sensed that the novel was a significant work, although some were puzzled by its seeming fragmentariness and quick transitions. E.H. McCormick in his magisterial *New Zealand Literature: A Survey* (1959) spoke of the "explosive publication" of the novel and justified Frame's methods because they enabled her "to evoke objects and people with an immediacy that imparts to them almost palpable existence." Publication followed in the United States in 1960 and in England in 1961, and reviewers who were more familiar with modernist conventions were quick to note the resemblances to Woolf and other modernists. The novel received favorable reviews in most of the important journals on both sides of the Atlantic, which helped launch Frame's international career.

Owls Do Cry, then, marked the beginning of Frame's career as a novelist, both within New Zealand and internationally. It was followed by *Faces in the Water* (1961), Frame's "documentary" novel about mental hospital experiences, and *The Edge of the Alphabet* (1962), the sequel to *Owls Do Cry.* With *Scented Gardens for the Blind* (1963), Frame moved into a more complex mode and never returned to the methods of her first novel. Such works as *Intensive Care* (1970) and *Living in the Maniototo* (1979) surpass *Owls Do Cry* in complexity and sophistication, but nothing Frame has written since surpasses in vividness and power this dark song of innocence.

LAWRENCE JONES

See also Janet Frame

Further Reading

Dalziel, Margaret, *Janet Frame,* Wellington: Oxford University Press, 1980

Delbaere, Jeanne, editor, *Ring of Fire: Essays on Janet Frame,* Sydney: Dangaroo Press, 1992

Evans, Patrick, *Janet Frame,* Boston: Twayne, 1977

Hankin, Cherry, editor, *Critical Essays on the New Zealand Novel,* Auckland: Heinemann Educational, 1977

Jones, Lawrence, *Barbed Wire and Mirrors: Essays on New Zealand Prose,* Dunedin: University of Otago Press, 1987; 2nd edition, 1990

Journal of New Zealand Literature 11 (1993), special issue on Janet Frame

Lawn, Jenny, "The Many Voices of *Owls Do Cry,*" *Journal of New Zealand Literature* 8 (1990)

Mercer, Gina, *Janet Frame: Subversive Fictions,* Dunedin: University of Otago Press, 1994

Amos Oz 1939–

Israeli

Ever since the publication of his first collection of short stories, *Artsot hatan* (1965; *Where the Jackals Howl*), Amos Oz has been regarded as one of the leading writers in Israel. The first collection of stories as well as his first novel, *Makom acher* (1966; *Elsewhere, Perhaps*), placed him within the 1960s "New Wave" in Israel, a movement that attempted to break away from cultural and literary traditions and begin the process of revision of social and aesthetic norms. Oz's works are widely read and translated and have drawn critical responses both praising and critical, but never indifferent.

In both *Where the Jackals Howl* and *Elsewhere, Perhaps,* Oz's depiction of the kibbutz, which represents a condensed social context and mirrors intensely the most important issues in Israeli society, questions fundamental assumptions of the Israeli ethos, such as the assumed unity between individuals and the collective and the realization of the founders' Zionist vision. Social critique, like most other elements of the narrative, becomes the means to an existential and metaphysical investigation into archetypal oppositions: suppressed emotions and drives versus social conventions; individuality and the collective; nature versus civilization; the rational and the irrational. Basic thematic and structural principles found in the early works are also present in the later works. This pattern is particularly evident in the novel *Menuchah nechonah* (1982; *A Perfect Peace*), which studies and develops the conflicts and the characters of *Elsewhere, Perhaps,* and in the relation between the novella *Har ha'etsah hara'ah* (1976; *The Hill of Evil Counsel*) and *Panter ba'martef* (1995;

Panther in the Basement). In other cases the relationship between novels is more subtle; in *Al tagidi lailah* (1994; *Don't Call It Night*), one of the protagonists, Noa, is analogous to Hanna Gonen, the protagonist and narrator of *Micha'el sheli* (1968; *My Michael*). The repeated basic structures underscore similarities and dissimilarities between the various works.

Characters, plots, and landscapes intensify the extreme polarization of fundamental oppositions. Landscapes project either the characters' moods and passions or the narrator's metaphysical viewpoint—for example, the desert threatening the cities of Jerusalem or Tel-Kedar, the jackals lurking, or the nomads infiltrating the settled kibbutz. The characters are either antiheroes or heroes stripped of their public mask. They are for the most part people who live at the margins of society, suppressing their passions. Unlike postmodern antiheroes, who when pushed into the forefront might challenge the establishment, Oz's characters belong to the establishment and, most of the time, are unable to shift dominant trends. Their lives reach a climactic, sometimes destructive, relief when they clash, inevitably, with the rational social conventions. In this respect, Oz's works are romantic, and their dramatic, richly figurative language intensifies this tendency, although the characters lack the extraordinary qualities usually associated with romantic heroes.

Later works seem more subtle and provide deeper psychological and political insight, although the basic metaphysical dichotomy is repeated in all of Oz's works. The narrators of his late works tend to prefer subjective points of view. In *The Hill of*

Evil Counsel, the narrator reconstructs his childhood through the child's view. This perspective also organizes both *Soumchi* (1978; *Soumchi*), a novel written for younger readers, and *Panther in the Basement,* which at first was intended for younger readers. These novels may be seen as Bildungsromane, stories about the coming of age in which the narrator recalls and reflects upon traumatic or significant events that shaped his life. *The Hill of Evil Counsel, Soumchi,* and *Panther in the Basement* all take place in Jerusalem toward the end of the British Mandate over Palestine. In each a sensitive and alienated child grows up through a realization of loss (of the mother, of innocence) and the polarization of his world (emotions and rationality, loyalty to national causes and loyalty to personal relationships). Subjectivity of the discourse is intensified in *Kufsah shechorah* (1987; *Black Box*), which is structured around the exchange of letters between Ilana and her ex-husband seven years after their bitter divorce.

While most of Oz's works take place in Israel, whether in a kibbutz or a town, the novella *Ahavah me'ucheret* (1971; *Unto Death*) removes the plot from the present time into the medieval world, telling the story of Count Galliume, who sets out on a crusade to Jerusalem in 1096. The novella breaks away from the genre of the historical novel and becomes a journey into the soul, as the Count and his fellow crusaders set out to free their souls of sin and evil. On their way they sadistically murder the Jews they encounter, whom they see as the source of evil. They abuse their victims for fear of their own evil, and their attempt to cleanse their souls through violence brings about their demise. The crusaders' failure becomes a metaphor through which issues of oppression, victimization, sin, and redemption are discussed as fundamental oppositions relevant to our time. In this respect, *Unto Death* is linked to other of Oz's works that may be interpreted as metapolitical, such as *A Perfect Peace* and *The Hill of Evil Counsel.* By removing the discourse into the past, whether as far back as the Middle Ages or the 1940s in Israel, Oz intensifies the implications of his stories by pointing to the archetypal forces underlying Israeli society.

TSILA RATNER

Biography

Born 4 May 1939 in Jerusalem. Attended Hebrew University, Jerusalem, B.A. in Hebrew literature and philosophy 1963. Served in Israeli army, 1957–60; fought as reserve soldier in tank corps in Sinai, 1967, and in the Golan Heights, 1973. Teacher of literature and philosophy, Hulda High School, Kibuts Hulda, and Regional High School, Givat Brenner, 1963–86; also has taught at colleges and universities in Israel, the United States, and Britain.

Novels and Novellas by Oz

(All translations by Nicholas De Lange)
Makom acher, 1966; as *Elsewhere, Perhaps,* 1973
Micha'el sheli, 1968; as *My Michael,* 1972
Ahavah me'ucheret, 1971; as *Unto Death,* 1975
Laga'at bamayim, laga'at baruach, 1973; as *Touch the Water, Touch the Wind,* 1974
Anashim acherim [Different People], 1974
Har ha'etsah hara'ah, 1976; as *The Hill of Evil Counsel,* 1978
Menuchah nechonah, 1982; as *A Perfect Peace,* 1985
Kufsah shechorah, 1987; as *Black Box,* 1988
Lada'at ishah, 1989; as *To Know a Woman,* 1991
Hamatsav hashelishiy, 1991; as *Fima,* 1993
Al tagidi lailah, 1994; as *Don't Call It Night,* 1995
Panter ba'martef, 1995; as *Panther in the Basement,* 1997

Other Writings: short stories, a children's novel (*Soumchi* [1978; *Soumchi*]), a book on poetics (*Shetikat ha'shamayim* [1993; *The Silence of Heaven*]), and other nonfiction.

Further Reading

Gertz, Nurith, *Amos Oz, Monografyah,* Tel Aviv: Sifriyat poalim, 1980
Miron, Dan, *Pinkas Patuah: Sihot al ha'siporet be-738,* Tel Aviv: Sifriyat poalim, 1979
Shaked, Gershon, *Gal hadash ba'siporet ha'ivrit,* Tel Aviv: Sifriyat poalim, 1970; 2nd edition, 1974
Shaked, Gershon, *The Shadows Within: Essays on Modern Jewish Writers,* Philadelphia: Jewish Publication Society, 1987

P

Pai Hsien-yung 1937–

Taiwanese

As a leading figure among the modernist writers in Taiwan, Pai Hsien-yung (also romanized as Bai Xianyong) is best known for his skillful employment of the Chinese language, for his artistic portrayal of human psychology, and for his depiction of marginalization, displacement, and exile. Pai was instrumental in introducing Western modernism to Taiwan through a literary journal, *Hsien-tai wen-hsueh* (Modern Literature), that he cofounded with a group of young writers while he was still in college. With the publication of his first novel, *Niezi* (1983; *Crystal Boys*), Pai was also the first writer in modern Chinese literary history to portray the unspeakable and insufferable dark side of gay life in Taiwan, which he did through experiments in modernist techniques such as stream of consciousness, free association, and interior monologue. Some of his stories and *Crystal Boys* have been adapted into motion pictures.

Pai Hsien-yung was born in mainland China in 1937 and emigrated to Hong Kong and then Taiwan with his father, a famous general with the Nationalist government, along with thousands of other mainlanders who left their families behind after the communist takeover. Pai's fondness for exploring the themes of exile and displacement originated partially from his background, which had given him ample opportunity to observe the lives of émigrés in Taiwan and later in the United States (where he moved in 1963). The experience of separation, displacement, and the longing for one's homeland and glorious past are the subjects of his 1971 collection of 14 short stories, *Taibei ren* (*Tales of Taipei Characters*). The title of this collection is ironic, for these characters never consider Taipei their home, nor can they return to their homeland in China. Be they former generals or lowly servants, these characters are either middle-aged or older, and a sense of irretrievable youth runs deeply through the stories. Pai also dealt with political and historical issues, such as the retreat of the Nationalist government, a dangerous topic at the time of writing. Personal experience is thus intertwined with national history, past and present forming a striking contrast. But these stories do not concern themselves only with a specific time or place; their significance lies in the universal themes of the gap between past and present, the conflict between nation and individual, the agony of displacement and rootlessness, and the eternal human struggle between body and soul.

Pai has written other short stories, some of which are grouped as "Niuyue ke" (New Yorkers) and deal with Chinese expatriates living in the United States. But he is best known for his novel *Crystal Boys*, about the underworld of gay life in Taipei and the quest for emotional and sexual fulfillment. The novel is divided into four sections: "Banishment," "In Our Kingdom," "The Cozy Nest," and "Young Birds on the Wing." "Banishment," a one-page section, introduces the narrator, Ah-Qing, who is expelled from high school after a sexual act with the school's janitor and subsequently is chased out of the house by his father. The second section follows Ah-Qing into the gay world of Taipei's New Park, where he becomes a male hooker and mingles with gay boys of similarly anguished backgrounds. "The Cozy Nest" shifts the setting to a tavern newly opened by Chief Yang, patriarch of the gay world in New Park. The tavern is closed down because of its "unsavory" and "illicit" nature of operation. The last short section tells of the incorporation of some of the novel's characters into society.

Crystal Boys has been compared to John Rechy's pioneering novel *City of Night* (1963), but the homosexual theme is only one aspect of the novel. *Crystal Boys'* depiction of conflict between father and son reveals the oppressive authority of Chinese patriarchy and its tormenting effects on Chinese sons. The title "Niezi" refers to a sinful son and implies retribution to a man for begetting a homosexual son, a blasphemy against Confucian morality. The banishment and reconciliation between father and son thus plays a conspicuous role in the novel. A former general becomes the benefactor of the gay community after his gay son commits suicide, while a paternal relationship takes shape between Chief Yang and the "crystal boys" he takes under his wing.

A less obvious concern of the novel but one that is common to Pai's early works—the image of the nation—also runs through *Crystal Boys*. Indeed, the long section of the novel entitled "In Our Kingdom" is replete with references to the framework of a nation. This illegitimate kingdom is the ideological opposite of the orthodox nation of the outside world, from which the crystal boys are forever banished, and is a direct challenge to the homogeneous and homophobic country of their fathers. Through this juxtaposition of personal and national realms, local and universal themes, Pai Hsien-yung, who has been called the preeminent stylist of his generation, has created a novel that addresses universal pathos within the Chinese milieu.

SYLVIA LI-CHUN LIN

Biography
Born 11 July 1937 in Guilin, Guangxi province, the son of Pai Chong-hsi, a well-known general with the Nationalist government. Before emigrating with the government to Taiwan in 1952, Pai lived in Chongqing, Shanghai, Nanjing, and Hong Kong. Cofounded *Hsien-tai wen-hsueh* (Modern Literature) with his classmates in the Department of Foreign Languages at Taiwan University, 1960; joined the International Writers' Workshop at the University of Iowa, 1963; taught Chinese literature at the University of California at Santa Barbara, 1965–94.

Selected Fiction by Pai Hsien-yung
Taibei ren, 1971; as *Wandering in the Garden, Waking from a Dream: Tales of Taipei Characters*, translated by Pai Hsien-yung and Patia Yasin, 1982
Niezi, 1983; as *Crystal Boys*, translated by Howard Goldblatt, 1990

Other Writings: short stories.

Further Reading
Chang, Sung-sheng Yvonne, *Modernism and the Nativist Resistance: Contemporary Chinese Fiction from Taiwan*, Durham, North Carolina: Duke University Press, 1993
Lau, Joseph S.M., "'Crowded Hours' Revisited: The Evocation of the Past in *Taipei Jen*," *Journal of Asian Studies* 35:1 (1975)
Ou-yang, Tze, "The Fictional World of Pai Hsien-yung," in *Chinese Fiction from Taiwan: Critical Perspectives*, edited by Jeannette L. Faurot, Bloomington: Indiana University Press, 1980

The Palm-Wine Drinkard by Amos Tutuola

1952

Amos Tutuola's first novel, *The Palm-Wine Drinkard and His Dead Palm-Wine Tapster in the Deads' Town*, was the first West African europhone novel to receive wide critical acclaim in Europe and North America. *The Palm-Wine Drinkard* tells the story of the eponymous drinkard's journey to the world of the dead to retrieve his tapster, who died while tapping wine. It is a quest story woven from traditional adventure tales, in language that betrays the writer's limited competence in English. Tutuola's primary model was D.O. Fagunwa's Yoruba-language *Ògbójú Ode Nínú Igbo Irúnmalè* (1938), later translated into English by Wole Soyinka as *The Forest of a Thousand Daemons: A Hunter's Saga*.

Upon its publication, *The Palm-Wine Drinkard* provoked a major controversy between Western critics who proclaimed it a remarkable achievement and African critics who found it embarrassing. The controversy was directly related to African europhone literature's emergence in the mid–20th century as an extension of Africa's decolonization struggle. Africans were primarily dissatisfied with the Western penchant for primitivist imagery and a patronizing tone and suggested that the novel reinforced Western racial prejudices. Dylan Thomas' enthusiastic description of Tutuola's language as "young English by a West African" was considered racially condescending. Even more clearly objectionable was Selden Rodman's comment that Tutuola was "not a revolutionary of the word, not a mathematician, not a surrealist [but] a true primitive," who remained outside "European rational and Christian traditions."

The Palm-Wine Drinkard marks a crucial phase in the development of the African novel from oral narratives to the written tradition, reflecting a society in which oral cultures were incorporating, reshaping, and being reshaped by material realities and technologies rooted in the culture of writing. In Tutuola's fictional world, a "half-bodied baby" speaks "with a lower voice like a telephone," while a "Spirit of Prey" has eyes "which brought out a flood-light like mercury." However, Tutuola is not consciously striving after a synthesis of the two worlds, and conventions of oral aesthetics found in plot, language, and characterization are there primarily by default rather than by design. The language is replete with redundancy structures that characterize oral rhetoric, such as repetitions and reformulations, alongside certain print conventions, as in "when we reached there with these three fellows, my wife and myself etc., stopped . . . N.B. We did not want to follow them . . .".

Tutuola's meticulous attention to minute details of temporal and spatial setting, material items, measurements, lists, and characters' appearances easily attains that "circumstantial realism" that Ian Watt, in *The Rise of the Novel* (1957), identifies as characterizing the emerging middle-class novel in 18th-century Britain. Tutuola's "measures" simply follow the British imperial system with the pound sterling and its units and the mile and its subdivisions, while the 12-hour clock measures daily time. The drinkard and his wife met highway robbers "after [they] had travelled about eighty miles away" from one town. Going to "Unreturnable-Heaven's Town," they traveled "from two o'clock till seven o'clock in the evening." It is instructive to compare such passages with Chinua Achebe's *Things Fall Apart* (1958): "During the planting season, Okonkwo and his family worked daily on his farm from cock-crow until the chickens went to roost."

Despite the absence of any nationalistic literary or cultural theory, Tutuola addresses some issues that Achebe and his followers eventually consciously worked into themes of cultural nationalism. Interestingly, Tutuola—unlike better educated African writers who generally follow Western usage—avoids the generic representation of humankind with masculine grammatical forms. Many African languages provide gender-neutral nouns and pronouns, and Tutuola attempts to reproduce their effect by consistently specifying the two sexes, as in "everybody would be returning to his or her destination or to where he or she came from," or "If any earthly person mistakenly entered their town, they would catch him or her and begin to cut . . . his or her body into pieces." Tutuola's struggle with pronouns shows that sexist grammar is not universal and anticipates Western writing in its attempts to grapple with the problem.

Early expectations that Tutuola might set off a trend were quickly disappointed. Gabriel Okara's *The Voice* in 1964, at the height of the controversy over the choice of language in African literature, briefly rekindled those expectations because of its experimental infiltration of English with the syntax and idioms of the Ijaw language. The fact is that Tutuola's style is not one an aspiring writer would benefit from emulating. Its most striking feature, the substandard language, is a handicap that Tutuola has struggled to overcome. Some of his subsequent writing, notably *The Village Witch Doctor and Other Stories* (1990), suggests that his efforts have met with some success.

Tutuola's work was reevaluated by major African scholars in the late 1960s. Bernth Lindfors' *Critical Perspectives on Amos Tutuola* (1975) includes "reappraisals" of his work, especially *The Palm-Wine Drinkard,* by Eldred Jones, Taban lo Liyong, E.N. Obiechina, and Omolara Ogundipe-Leslie, among others. The major turning point, however, came with Chinua Achebe's "Work and Play in Tutuola's *The Palm-Wine Drinkard*" (1988). Achebe characterized Tutuola as "the most moralistic of all Nigerian writers, being fully as single-minded . . . as the chapbook authors of the Onitsha Market" but superior to them in possessing "a richer imagination and a more soundly based moralism." With this, Tutuola has been firmly situated within the moral universe of African literature, in which art is a mode of participating in the society's struggles.

CHIDI OKONKWO

See also Amos Tutuola

Further Reading

Achebe, Chinua, "Work and Play in Tutuola's *The Palm-Wine Drinkard,*" in *Hopes and Impediments: Selected Essays,* London: Heinemann, 1988; New York: Doubleday, 1989

Collins, Harold R., *Amos Tutuola,* New York: Twayne, 1969

Ibitokun, B.M., "Amos Tutuola," in *Perspectives on Nigerian Literature: 1700 to the Present,* volume 2, edited by Yemi Ogunbiyi, Lagos: Guardian, 1988

Lindfors, Bernth, "Amos Tutuola: Literary Syncretism and the Yoruba Folk Tradition," in *European-Language Writing in Sub-Saharan Africa,* edited by Albert S. Gérard, Budapest: Akadémiai Kiadó, 1986

Lindfors, Bernth, editor, *Critical Perspectives on Amos Tutuola,* Washington, D.C.: Three Continents Press, 1975; London: Heinemann, 1980

Ogundipe-Leslie, Omolara, "*The Palm-Wine Drinkard*: A Reassessment of Amos Tutuola," *Journal of Commonwealth Literature* 9 (July 1970)

Snead, James, "European Pedigrees/African Contagions: Nationality, Narrative, and Communality in Tutuola, Achebe, and Reed," in *Nation and Narration,* edited by Homi Bhabha, London and New York: Routledge, 1990

Zabus, Chantal, *The African Palimpsest: Indigenization of Language in the West African Europhone Novel,* Amsterdam and Atlanta, Georgia: Rodopi, 1991

Paperback

In *American Authors and the Literary Marketplace since 1900* (1988), James L. West points to "two of the most important innovations in book distribution during this century"—book clubs and paperbacks. While some believe paperback books have broadened the gap between serious and popular literature, others argue that paperbacks actually have blurred that distinction.

There is some disagreement among historians concerning the appearance of the first paperback book, but it is generally agreed that the paperback as we know it today originally appeared on newsstands and in bookstores in June 1939. The founder of the Pocket Books company, which issued the first ten paperbacks in the United States, was Robert Fair de Graff, and he apparently got the idea from Allen Lane, England's Penguin Books publisher, who had lifted the concept from a German line of books called Albatross, which was begun to compete with another German paperback firm, Tauchnitz Editions.

Entrepreneurial ideas were not the only ones subject to imitation during the paperback revolution. As John Unsworth points out in *The Columbia History of the American Novel* (1991), early paperbacks were mostly recycled versions of "texts originally produced by trade publishing houses through conventional means." Indeed, the first ten titles de Graff issued in paperback had been hardcover best-sellers, including *Lost Horizon* (1933) by James Hilton, *The Murder of Roger Ackroyd* (1926) by Agatha Christie, Emily Brontë's *Wuthering Heights* (1847), and Thornton Wilder's *The Bridge of San Luis Rey* (1927). The list seemed designed to cater to general literary taste. De Graff believed that different readers comprised the audience for the paperback and hardcover versions of the same book, that those who purchased paperbacks simply did not have access to or money for the hardcover editions. In other words, he believed paperback readers represented a lower economic sphere than did hardcover readers but that they were readers, nonetheless.

The way to the paperback revolution was paved by the marriage of the books themselves to the magazine distribution system. Potential readers of paperbacks often were those perusing the magazine racks or newsstands, people whose eyes fell on the paperbacks now shelved nearby. Realizing this, paperback publishers began churning out books to appeal to readers who, previously, had not been considered readers at all. As a result of this knowledge, numerous subcategories of the mystery, the romance, the Western, and the science-fiction novel began to appear.

The original mission of paperback publishers seems to have been to make serious literature, to which only those with money and proximity to retail bookstores had access, available to the general population. Once the idea took off and its profitability became apparent, that mission changed. Paperback publishers began issuing more formulaic works of fiction, sure-bet sellers, that would attract the less highbrow members of society. In addition, emphasis on flashy covers underscored the presumed new role of paperbacks.

After the postwar boom in mass-market paperbacks, some in the hardcover industry worried about the future of literature. In her book *The American Dream and the Popular Novel* (1985), Elizabeth Long reports that Viking founder Harold Guizberg said at the 1954 American Scholar Forum on "The Future of Books in America," "My worry is that you may repeat in the book field what has happened in other fields—in entertainment and communication—you may make it increasingly difficult to do anything that is not geared to large low common denominators." It is true that during the 1940s and 1950s, novels that pandered to what many would deem the more base human instincts, novels with much graphic violence and sexual content and with naked bodies on the covers, proliferated to the point that the publishing industry was the subject of a congressional investigation in 1952. But the paperback publishing industry continued to evolve, and one step in that evolution was engendered by the New American Library and may have been the answer Guizberg was looking for. Bucking the constraints of the 25-cent paperback model, the New American Library issued a 35-cent paperback, Richard Wright's *Native Son* (1940). This was a move toward publishing higher quality literature and targeting a more limited audience with paperbacks. Ironically, however, this development—publishing and successfully selling higher quality paperback books for more money—led publishers to realize that they could raise their newsstand prices. This ultimately resulted in paperback publishing houses purchasing manuscripts for millions of dollars and the subsequent hype of those

properties through advertising campaigns, book tours, and movie deals.

As the dominance of mass-oriented paperback publishing has tied some sectors of the publishing industry to other mass media, novels that translate easier to those other formats (e.g., television) have become the most profitable and therefore the most published. The historical profile of the novel's audience is middle class and female. In 18th- and 19th-century America, because women were excluded from the realms of formal education and business, they made up the majority of novel readers. Today's paperback product—the mass-market realist narrative—continues that tradition as it is marketed mainly to women through the use of what John Unsworth calls "essentialist stereotypes of the proclivities and desires of that gendered market."

Statistics point to a more positive result of the paperback revolution. Elizabeth Long reports in *The American Dream and the Popular Novel* that for every 1,000 Americans, the number of new book titles doubled between 1955 and 1977, a fact that reflects the rising literacy rates of those years. Also, it can no longer be argued that paperbacks in general reach a different audience than do hardcovers. Quality softcover books, including novels and works in other genres, have been available for decades.

JENNIFER WHEELOCK

See also Dime Novels and Penny Dreadfuls

Further Reading

Bonn, Thomas L., *Under Cover: An Illustrated History of American Mass-Market Paperbacks,* New York and London: Penguin, 1982

Crider, Allen Billy, editor, *Mass Market Publishing in America,* Boston: G.K. Hall, 1982

Davis, Kenneth C., *Two-Bit Culture: The Paperbacking of America,* Boston: Houghton Mifflin, 1984

Gedin, Per, *Literature in the Marketplace,* London: Faber, and Woodstock, New York: Overlook Press, 1977; originally published as *Litteraturen i verkligheten*

Hackett, Alice Payne, and James Henry Burke, *80 Years of Best Sellers, 1895–1975,* New York: Bowker, 1977

Kadushin, Charles, Lewis A. Coser, and Walter W. Powell, *Books: The Culture and Commerce of Publishing,* New York: Basic Books, 1982

Kostelanetz, Richard, *The End of Intelligent Writing: Literary Politics in America,* New York: Sheed and Ward, 1974

Tebbel, John William, *A History of Book Publishing in the United States,* volume 2: *The Expansion of an Industry: 1865–1919,* New York: Bowker, 1975

Whiteside, Thomas, *The Blockbuster Complex: Conglomerates, Show Business, and Book Publishing,* Middletown, Connecticut: Wesleyan University Press, 1981

Parody and Pastiche

Parody and pastiche are not absolutely distinct, and in the climate of critical thought about fiction since World War II they have tended steadily to converge. Parody is the intentional reproduction, usually for critical, humorous, or satirical purposes, of an original whose features are exaggerated, distorted, inverted, or in some way recognizably changed. Parody is thus repetition-with-a-difference, as its etymology suggests (from the Greek "counter song," where the ambiguity of the Greek prefix "para" yields two meanings: "beside" or "against"). Pastiche is a form of allusion—a quotation from, or a reference to, the style of one or more originals, without necessarily comic, satirical, mocking, or even critical implications. The term comes from painting, not music, and originally signifies a mélange of styles in a single work. It is related to the Renaissance *cento,* or literary patchwork, the impulse to the macaronic. Pastiche can be straightforward homage or self-conscious compliment. It is often traditionally a technical exercise by a young artist: Proust's first book, for example, *Les Plaisirs et les jours* (1896; *Pleasures and Regrets,* the title an ironic allusion to Hesiod's *Works and Days*), is a literary pastiche in the strict sense of a tissue of stylistic quotations from a wide variety of literary sources.

As a simple example of the traditional distinction in usage, consider the following extract from Garrick's Prologue to Goldsmith's *She Stoops To Conquer* (1773):

> *Enter Mr. Woodward, dressed in black, and holding a Handkerchief to his Eyes*
>
> Excuse me, sirs, I pray—I can't yet speak—
> I'm crying now—and have been all the week!
> 'Tis not alone this mourning suit, good masters;
> I've that within—for which there are no plasters!

This is a parody of Hamlet's famous speech to his mother. A pastiche, on the other hand, would simply be "written in the style of," instead of dissociating itself from the style of Shakespeare by comic markers of metrical distortion and bathos in the text. When we come to the phrase "I've that within . . . ," the audience is invited mentally to complete Shakespeare's original line, "I have that within *which passeth show*" (emphasis added), and thus to mark the difference, while the Prologue distorts it on two levels: at the level of content, it proposes absurd medical remedies for a mysterious condition of mind that, as T.S. Eliot put it, is without "objective correlative"; and at the level of form, it transposes heroic blank verse into burlesque couplets.

That there is a relative difference between pastiche and parody is thus evident. Parody tends to use as its original the text, and pastiche the style. The relation between Milton and his 18th-century imitators (Thompson, Collins, or Gray) involves pastiche, their genial but general stylistic reminiscences of Milton being designed to lend weight and authority to their poetry. On the other hand, Alexander Pope, in the obscene and twistedly precise echoes of the *Dunciad* (1728), often produces comic parody of Milton's actual lines as well as epic style. Characteristically, parody introduces a marked drop in tone.

The difference, however, is only relative. Pastiche suppresses the differences between original and reproduction whereas parody exaggerates them. Pastiche tends to operate exclusively at the level of style, rather than text or content. But both of these activities can occur at the micro or the macro end of literary production: one can have parody or pastiche at the level of the phrase, the sentence, the paragraph, the chapter, or complete structural repetition. Both activities imply an intention, whether one attributes it to the text or the author. I will begin by taking *parody* as the more inclusive term and will then go on to discuss *pastiche* as a subset, with significant differences in modern critical vocabulary and thought.

Parody is a special form of imitation that has always had a critical aspect. It exists simultaneously at the level of a literary practice and as a part of the critical metalanguage: the cultivation of difference often acts both as comic performance and as a critical interpretation of a text. In this it differs crucially from a term like caricature, for example, which implies a distorting mirror held up directly to life. William Hogarth in *Gin Lane* or *The Rake's Progress* (1735) distorts the lineaments of real, historically existing 18th-century prostitutes or surgeons. His "original" is a historical society, whereas the original of a parody is always a prior representation. Compared with caricature, parody exists on two levels. It always has one eye on the representation and one on the content.

This double level is significant in the change of prestige and range of the term in postwar thought about the novel. Traditionally parody has often been thought parasitic and local. Modern criticism has come to see it differently. Parody is not just a local operation. As Joseph A. Dane puts it:

> Parody has moved to a central position in literary history. It is a literary system reflecting on itself, at war with itself. Rather than being a marginal literary genre—one of the curiosities and oddities of literature—parody becomes an exemplary genre, in which the dynamics of the literary system are expressed.

The shift in importance, as Dane suggests, involves the question of how we see the literary system in which the novel takes its place, how we understand the history of the literary genres and the novel genre in particular (see Dane, 1988). This phrase itself, the "literary system," reveals, archaeologically, the presence in contemporary critical discourse of the formalist and structuralist heritage and the universal discursive category of intertextuality, in which both parody and pastiche are prominent. Poststructuralism's stress on *écriture,* writing that overflows infinitely into other writing, enhances this formalist endorsement of the "intertext" as central to all literary meaning.

The early 20th-century Russian formalists began the process of bringing parody in from the margins of literary history by characterizing it as a "revolutionary" force; they thought of it as essential to the "refunctioning" process of literature's ability to transform itself (see Hutcheon, 1985). Sterne's *Tristram Shandy* (1759–67), with its continuous anarchic parodies of Locke and its arch pastiche of Cervantes, becomes, for Viktor Shklovsky, the archetypal novel that lays bare its own processes of construction (see Lemon and Reis, 1965). Parody thus becomes central, not marginal, because it is the sign of literary self-consciousness and reflexive textuality, and therefore of the novel's dynamic ability to break the chains of habitualized perception.

Thought about parody has been most spectacularly influenced by the contribution of Mikhail Bakhtin, a Russian critic whose work has changed our picture of the history of the novel and the place of parody within "the literary system." Bakhtin's argument is as follows: conventional literary history is based on the isolation from classical times of the "straightforward genres"—epic, tragedy, and lyric. Parody is the fourth genre, which paves the way for the novel. Before Bakhtin's views became widely disseminated, critics like Ian Watt were anxious to prove that the beginnings of the English novel were part of a reaction to the 18th-century Enlightenment, and that the novel, as a new, "straightforward" genre, evolved out of that reaction. Bakhtin shows us that the novel is much older than we had thought and began as parody.

Bakhtin argues that the ancient, discredited "low" forms, like Greek Menippean satire or the mixed narratives of writers like Petronius, which parody the "high" genres of lyric, epic, and tragedy, paved the way for the "impiety of the novel form." The first genre manifestation of the novel is in the Greek romances that parody the epic. This struggle of the classical cultures between "straightforward" genres and the parodic Bakhtin terms a clash between monoglossia and polyglossia or heteroglossia. This polyglot or heteroglot world is paradoxically a kind of whole without genre:

> Consequently this extra-generic or intergeneric world is internally unified and even appears as its own kind of totality. Each separate element in it—parodic dialogue, scenes from everyday life, bucolic humor, etc.—is presented as if it were a fragment of some kind of unified whole. I imagine this whole to be something like an immense novel, multi-generic, multi-styled, mercilessly critical, soberly mocking, reflecting in all its fullness the heteroglossia and multiple voices to a given culture, people and epoch. In this huge novel—in this mirror of constantly evolving heteroglossia—any direct word and especially that of the dominant discourse is reflected as something more or less bounded, typical and characteristic of a particular era, aging, dying, ripe for change and renewal. And in actual fact, out of this huge complex of parodically reflected words and voices the ground was being prepared in ancient times for the rise of the novel, a genre formed of many styles and many images ("From the Prehistory of Novelistic Discourse").

This view challenges the notion that classical culture is the seamless dominance of a literary ideal, that genres are "pure," and that the novel is an essentially modern form dominated by realism as had been claimed by critics like Lukács and Raymond Williams. Culture in Bakhtin's view becomes a struggle of representations, and parody works to liberate language from the homogenizing power of myth. The home of parodic, travestying language is the novel, a genre that incorporates dialogue into its very texture.

The implications for parody are interesting here. Bakhtin is changing our view of language and culture along with our notions of literary genre. Traditionally, parody is parasitic upon a literary original (although not exclusively so if it is, as I have said, critical). But Bakhtin's view institutes another relationship between original and reproduction that affects the way we see parody: everything serious in classical culture, he argues, had a comic double. Parody becomes thus an "intentional dialogic hybrid" that "doubles" language, since the original is no longer in the originating position; instead, it becomes a quotation, existing alongside its mocking double.

This doubling effect is an important feature of the usefulness of parody to contemporary writers. Parody does not create a new point of origin but rather allows a space between original and imitation, which is one of its most attractive features to novelists now writing in a period when the language itself has expanded to include the cultures of the developing world and when the old certainties of literary history and the canon have been broken up by a vast influx of new writing. Since the structuralism of the late 1950s and early 1960s, there has been a pervasive attack on myths of origin and homogenizing narratives of the dominant culture. This cultural hostility to the dominance of such narratives informs the parodic strategies of a writer like Salman Rushdie, for example. His intercultural style is specifically aimed at celebrating migration and cultural impurity and travestying the theological certainty and the cultural hegemony of certain classes and groups in the postcolonial situation of both Britain and the Indian subcontinent.

In fact, since modernism, which was intensely conscious of stylistic experiment, parody has become a vital destabilizing presence in the novel. James Joyce's *Ulysses* (1922) famously parodies, in its "Oxen of the Sun" episode, the development of the English language from the early medieval period to the Black American argot that was contemporary in 1922. Joyce's parody attacks myths of cultural purity and is now seen as part of an anticolonial satire. However, even in this case, identifiable original texts are present behind the paragraphs of "Oxen of the Sun," which, comically, are made "representative" of certain stages in the development of the language. Here we touch on the un-Bakhtinian paradox that parody may sometimes have the opposite effect of its apparent intention: it may authorize, and therefore recuperate, the transgressive nature of an original.

Nabokov's *Lolita* (1955) underwent a similar process. Initially a subversive and even offensive work, it has become, over the last 40 years, an iconic text, a narrative model for novelists as diverse as John Banville, Joyce Carol Oates, Martin Amis, and Erica Jong. But are their novels parodies? This is a nice point: they use *Lolita* as a model but do not introduce parody's specific textual reference and characteristic tonal bathos. Yet we would often loosely call them parodies. This kind of rewriting would suggest that pastiche can spring from the head of parody, like Athena from the head of Zeus. Parody, as I have argued above, includes pastiche because it already has a double focus: referring to a text, it necessarily refers to a style. Parody is thus already an imitation and a difference. Marcel Proust parodied his precursors of the 19th century—Honoré de Balzac, Gustave Flaubert, and Jules and Edmond de Goncourt, for example—but he also calls this activity pastiche. On the other hand, Proust's own style, like Joyce's, is very distinctive despite its continuous traffic with imitation. So in these examples the two may be said to coexist. Pastiche is parody, viewed as the suppression of difference.

A tendency to tongue-in-cheek imitation has increased dramatically among postwar novelists, resulting in a general repudiation of any neo-romantic aesthetic of "originality." This repudiation is often said to be one of the features of postmodernism in the novel, but it can be traced back in part to the modernists. Humbert Humbert's attempts (in *Lolita*) to possess and yet not possess Dolly Schiller are themselves a parody of Marcel's quest for Albertine in Proust's *À la Recherche du temps perdu* (1913–27; translated as *Remembrance of Things Past* and also as *In Search of Lost Time*). And Marcel is, in his turn, a parodic version of the Platonic lover. The idealist tradition thus enters Nabokov's text through the parodic chain.

Both parody and pastiche play an important role in contemporary fiction's use of replication, allusion, citation, and facsimile. Recursive structures are now taken for granted in many fields of science and technology, and in popular culture. Generative models have become a universal part of thought. The Freudian analysis of desire is a rich meditation on repetition and difference in the narrative life of the psyche. The theory of transference has given a strong leaning toward repetition and facsimile in psychoanalytic discourse about human relationships and in the post-Freudian narrative analysis of fiction. In criticism, there have been several influential adaptations of the Oedipal model to describe rewriting in literary history, which are based on the idea of the appropriation (and exorcism) of an original by repetition and difference.

This recent cult of the simulacrum in novelistic style led Fredric Jameson to draw together parody and pastiche, for if parody becomes a dominant mode itself, then its critical power inevitably disappears. Jameson argues that postmodernism has appropriated parody as a new universal style and calls it pastiche: "Pastiche is blank parody, parody that has lost its sense of humor: pastiche is to parody what that curious thing, the modern practice of a kind of blank irony, is to what Wayne Booth calls the stable and comic ironies of, say, the 18th century" (see Jameson, 1985). This is a historical argument: parody proper has given way to blank parody or pastiche. Jameson links this effect to the death of the subject and the supersession of private language by consumer fetishism, a supermarket of styles, in which all we have is stylistic diversity and heterogeneity. This is a world in which parody (which would imply, says Jameson, the existence of a private language with identifiably idiosyncratic features) is impossible. All contemporary stylistic effort is subject to the "white noise" of pastiche.

Compare this view, however, with the following defenses of parody by the contemporary American novelist Joyce Carol Oates (1972):

> Parody is an act of aggression. Twentieth-century literature is never far from parody, sensing itself anticipated, overdone, exhausted. But its power lies in the authenticity of its anger, its parodistic instinct, the kind of art in which Mann's Adrian Leverkuhn and Dostoievsky's Ivan Karamazov excel: "the playing of forms out of which life has disappeared."

Oates separates parody from pastiche here by relating it to tragic anger and comes up with a much more positive view of parody as a form of energy. And yet, in her allusion to the way modern literature feels itself anticipated, the convergence of parody and pastiche is also visible, via the implication of an inevitable "belatedness" in modern and contemporary style. And it is significant that Oates herself, in her scores of novels, is a notoriously accomplished, chameleonic *pasticheur* as well as a parodist.

VICTOR SAGE

See also Comedy and Humor in the Novel; Dialogism; Genre Criticism; Satirical Novel

Further Reading

Almansi, G., "L'Affaire Mystérieuse de l'Abominable 'tongue-in-cheek'," *Poétique* 36 (1978)

Amossy, Ruth, and Elisheva Rosen, "La Dame aux catleyas: Fonction du pastiche et de la parodie dans *À la recherche du temps perdu*," *Littérature* 14 (1974)

Bakhtin, M.M., *The Dialogic Imagination: Four Essays,* translated by Caryl Emerson and Michael Holquist, edited by Holquist, Austin: University of Texas Press, 1981

Bauerle, Ruth, "A Sober Drunken Speech: Stephen's Parodies in 'The Oxen of the Sun'," *James Joyce Quarterly* 5 (1967)

Blackmur, R.P., "Parody and Critique: Mann's *Doctor Faustus*," in his *Eleven Essays in the European Novel,* New York: Harcourt Brace, 1964

Cobley, Evelyn, "Sameness and Difference in Literary Repetition," *Recherches Sémiotiques/Semiotic Inquiry* 4 (1984)

Dane, Joseph A., *Parody: Critical Concepts Versus Literary Practices, Aristophanes to Sterne,* Norman: University of Oklahoma Press, 1988

Freeman, Rosemary, "Parody as a Literary Form," *Essays in Criticism* 13 (1963)

Heller, Eric, "Parody Tragic and Comic: Mann's *Doktor Faustus* and *The Holy Sinner*," *Sewanee Review* 66 (1958)

Hutcheon, Linda, *A Theory of Parody: The Teachings of Twentieth-Century Art Forms,* New York: Methuen, 1985

Jameson, Fredric, "Postmodernism and Consumer Society," in *Postmodern Culture,* edited by Hal Foster, London: Pluto Press, 1985

Josipovici, Gabriel, "Lolita: Parody and the Pursuit of Beauty," *Critical Quarterly* 6 (1964)

Lemon, Lee T., and Marion Reis, editors, *Russian Formalist Criticism: Four Essays,* Lincoln: University of Nebraska Press, 1965

Oates, Joyce Carol, *The Edge of Impossibility: Tragic Forms in Literature,* New York: Vanguard Press, 1972; London: Gollancz, 1976

Poirier, Richard, "The Politics of Self-Parody," *Partisan Review* 35 (1968)

Riffaterre, Michael, "The Poetic Function of Intertextual Humour," *Romanic Review* 65 (1974)

Partigiano Johnny. *See* Johnny the Partisan

Pasos perdidos. *See* Lost Steps

A Passage to India by E.M. Forster

1924

Forster's *A Passage to India* was ten difficult years in the making, from 1913, following his first visit to the Indian Subcontinent, until 1923, after his second. The interim had seen such horrors as World War I in Europe and the Amritsar massacre of 1919. In India, the noncooperation movement against the British grew under the leadership of the National Congress and Moslem League in uneasy alliance. Forster's sympathies were clearly with the Indians ("How could one possibly be unfair to the English?" he would later retort). In *A Passage to India,* in the character of Fielding, he explores a liberal humanism that affirms the moral good of friendship even as it remains disconcertingly aware of the realities of India threatening such an affirmation. The novel's title derives from Walt Whitman, but the American poet's celebration of the opening of the Suez Canal as bringing together East and West is qualified by Kipling's assertion that "ne'er the twain shall meet." The colorful panorama Forster describes, his uncanny predictions, complex ambiguities, and the tonal complexities of an impossible dream ensure that what is essentially a conventional novel has remained problematic and provocative to this day.

Although close to the Bloomsbury group and appreciative of Virginia Woolf's "wonderful new method" of rendering consciousness, Forster was a dubious modernist, appalled by Joyce's *Ulysses* and choosing instead to work with traditional realism, albeit tinged by irony and not without contemporary awareness. *Aspects of the Novel* (1927) effectively defines his achievement: the novel, he affirms, must tell a story, and at the heart of *A Passage to India* is a fine story, a drama of passions, tensions, and conflict. This is shaped by Forster's conceptions of character, perspective, plot, fantasy, prophecy, pattern, and rhyme, in accordance with an aesthetic of wholeness, with subtleties of rhythm and time regulating movement and occasionally culminating in the "great chords" that Forster found in Tolstoi.

A Passage to India may be placed in a realist tradition and shows affinities to George Eliot and other Victorians—and, indeed, to Forster's earlier novels. Yet the dictum of "only connect" formulated in *Howards End* (1910) is here subdued, not only by the immensities of an India not easily assimilated to English fictional form but by Forster's own uncertainties. The structural divisions of "Mosque," "Cave," and "Temple" place the friendship of Aziz and Fielding, Muslim and Englishman, in the realm of mysticism, which can be apprehended but not rationalized. Forster was perturbed by the relationship of "muddle" and "mystery," and although he handles the problem poetically, through unforgettable images of the caves and the wasp that links the Hindu mystic Godbole to Mrs. Moore, a sense of uneasiness prevails in the novel, as the impossibilities of reconciliation are experienced. This is not dramatic failure but enigma, cosmic ironies combining with the more localized comic ones.

Much of the novel's appeal lies in its drama and spectacle, qualities that made David Lean's film version of *A Passage to India* attractive despite its simplistic vision. There is descriptive authenticity—not just documentary accuracy but a genuine sympathy. Old-fashioned as the concept may be, the novel becomes "alive" in its evocation of an imagined world: the reader cannot forget the awfulness of the large ladies, Mrs. Turton and Mrs. Callendar, the inanities of the "bridge party," or Aziz's difficulties with the collar-stud. This quality of precise ironic observation is shared with Paul Scott, in *The Raj Quartet* (1976), and Kipling at his best; but, as a number of Indian critics have affirmed, Forster is unique among Europeans in his handling of the dissolution of British India, capturing the moments of the transformation into the new nation(s) with a disturbingly accurate vision, notably in the final paragraph where the prophetic voice has rung disconcertingly true. For this reason, novels such as Salman Rushdie's *Midnight's Children* (1981) and Ruth Prawer Jhabvala's *Heat and Dust* (1975), celebrating the new India, pay tribute to Forster's evocation of the old.

The novel is not without its critics. Forster's liberal humanism has been condemned as inappropriate to the realities of the subcontinent, for sublimating the brutal realities of the conflict between Independence and the Raj to tame Bloomsburian pieties, and for implying that if people could be nice to one another all this nastiness might be avoided. The book has been criticized for not having a major Hindu protagonist; for suggesting that if India is a state of mind then that mind is Forster's; and, in the postcolonial context, for failing to examine the material and imperial roots of colonialism and capitalism. Forster might have replied that the novel was simply telling its story, but politically aware criticism has led to significant revaluations of such a position. Scholars studying Western Orientalism, for instance, have shown that, for all Forster's professed detachment, phrases such as "Like most Orientals" indicate a fundamental inability to relinquish the Eurocentric perspective. A number of gender-based and post-Freudian studies have stressed the homoerotic nature of Fielding's attraction to Aziz, or the ambiguities of Forster's depiction of Miss Quested. They affirm that Forster's appropriation of the Orient for display and exploration intersects with his own repressed desires. Followers of Bakhtin have celebrated the carnivalesque in *A Passage to India* as well as the colloquy between Western and Indian modes of thought and language. Paradigmaticists of the discourse of disconnection have translated Forster's muddles into their own aporias. When it first appeared, *A Passage to India* was acclaimed by such critics as Leavis and Trilling, who saw in literature the only salvation from the dark forces assailing civilization. Current perspectives may soon seem equally dated, but the novel continues to engage with contemporary discourse without losing its power to enchant.

CHRIS ACKERLEY

See also E.M. Forster

Further Reading

Beauman, Nicola, *Morgan: A Biography of E.M. Forster*, London: Hodder and Stoughton, 1993; New York: St. Martin's Press, 1994

Beer, John, editor, *"A Passage to India": Essays in Interpretation*, London: Macmillan, and Totowa, New Jersey: Barnes and Noble, 1986

Bradbury, Malcolm, editor, *"A Passage to India": A Casebook*, London: Macmillan, 1970

Crews, Frederick, *E.M. Forster: The Perils of Humanism*, Princeton, New Jersey: Princeton University Press, 1962

Das, G.K., *E.M. Forster's India*, London: Macmillan, and Totowa, New Jersey: Rowman and Littlefield, 1977

Davies, Tony, and Nigel Wood, editors, *A Passage to India*, Buckingham and Philadelphia: Open University Press, 1994

Furbank, P.N., *E.M. Forster: A Life*, 2 vols., London: Secker and Warburg, and New York: Harcourt, 1977

Gardner, Philip, editor, *E.M. Forster: The Critical Heritage*, London and Boston: Routledge and Kegan Paul, 1973

Herz, Judith Scherer, *A Passage to India: Nation and Narration*, New York: Twayne, and Toronto: Macmillan, 1993

Lago, Mary, *E.M. Forster: A Literary Life*, London: Macmillan, and New York: St. Martin's Press, 1995

Stape, J.H., editor, *E.M. Forster: Interviews and Recollections*, New York: St. Martin's Press, 1993

Stone, Wilfrid H., *The Cave and the Mountain: A Study of E.M. Forster*, Stanford, California: Stanford University Press, 1966

Pastiche. *See* Parody and Pastiche

Pastoralism in the Novel

A pastor is a shepherd, one who makes his living by grazing flocks of sheep, often in rugged mountain territory, and selling their fleeces to merchants who convert them into woolen goods. But the economic basis of the pastoral life is obscured in most traditional pastoral literature. Shakespeare's Corin in *As You Like It* is exceptional in his awareness of the problems of money and churlish masters, and even he rests his defense of "this shepherd's life" on the placid contentment that it makes possible: "I earn that I eat, get that I wear, owe no man hate, envy no man's happiness, glad of other men's good, content with my harm; and the greatest of my pride is to see my ewes graze and my lambs suck." More characteristically, the shepherds of pastoral are otherworldly lovers basking by Mediterranean shores and piping to their equally conventionalized mistresses songs of love that invite them, as Marlowe's "passionate shepherd" does, to

> "Come live with me, and be my love,
> And we will all the pleasures prove,
> That Valleys, groves, hills and fields,
> Woods, or steepie mountaines yields. . . .

This is the landscape that the Italian Sannazaro dubbed Arcadia, which the English Sir Philip Sidney used as the setting for his complexly plotted proto-novel of the same name. The tradition is most notably represented in Spain by Jorge de Montemayor's *Diana* (1559) and Miguel de Cervantes' *Galatea* (1585), and in

France by Honoré d'Urfé's *Astreé* (1607–27). The narrative form of pastoral, the pastoral romance, from which these Renaissance writers drew their inspiration, was a late Greek form, exemplified by the three most quoted and imitated models, the 2nd-century *Daphnis and Chloe* by Longus, the 3rd-century *Ethiopian Story* by Heliodorus, and *Leucipppe and Clitophon* by Achilles Tatius. Greek romance is full of spectacular disasters and harrowing misfortunes, which, however, lead to a miraculously happy ending wherein equally spectacular episodes of good fortune are involved. Its true offspring is the tragicomedy manifested in Battista Guarini's *Il Pastor Fido* (1590), in which the tragicomic form is both theorized and exemplified, and the plays of Beaumont and Fletcher—works in which the idealized landscape of pastoral forms the setting for events that are built up to excruciating dilemmas and resolved by histrionic reversals.

Yet it is untrue to say that pastoral is merely a form of escapism that idealizes country pleasures. It is invariably predicated on a contrast, implicit or explicit, with the unpleasant conditions that obtain in the real world. Marlowe's invitation to the shepherdess is countered, in Sir Walter Raleigh's reply, with a grim recognition of time, which "drives the flocks from field to fold." Countless examples of pastoral are directed at the corruption and vices of the world as it actually is: the commonest of themes is the opposition of country life to that of the court or city; of the peaceful, creative pursuits of the shepherd to the destructive scheming of the politician and the selfish greed of the merchant. Needless to say, although love is the frequent burden, broken hearts abound.

Arcadia as the mythical land of pastoral is likewise a critique of the real world. It is the fictional projection of longings for lost innocence. The impetus that gives rise to it—and historically it is the product of mature Greek civilization, unlike the epic celebrating war, which is the product of more primitive times—is disillusionment with, and critique of, a decadent society. Its ideological analogue, from which the notion of pastoral becomes virtually inseparable, is the classical concept of the Golden Age, which, in its turn, is conflated by a Christian society (which often represents the shepherd as a "pastor" in the religious sense, as a man of God caring for the souls of his human flock) with the prelapsarian condition of Eden before the Fall. The description of the Golden Age on which most subsequent variations are based is that given by Ovid in Book I of the *Metamorphoses*: men keep faith and live righteous lives without the imposition of laws; they are content with their homeland and fell no trees for ships in which to cross the seas; war is unknown; the earth gives abundantly all things necessary for life, and there is no need to wound its surface with the hoe or the ploughshare; the distinction between "mine" and "thine" is unknown, and a benevolent communism prevails. To subsequent Christian writers this innocent nature—contrasting with the fallen nature bequeathed to their universal offspring by the original sin of Adam and Eve, as Ovid's Iron Age contrasted with his Golden Age—was a condition of divinely ordained unity matching God's perfect creature with a perfect creation, at once pure and fertile, free and yet obedient, loving and yet unashamed. To Milton it was, in addition, a condition of sexual harmony. To his Italian predecessor, Torquato Tasso, it was the very heart of the pastoral ideal, as expressed in the great Golden Age chorus of his pastoral play *Aminta* (1573), for its freedom from the latter-day tyranny of honor. For Cervantes, incorporating both the Ovidian and Christian topoi in Don Quixote's absurdly inappro-

priate, yet nonetheless imaginatively appealing, vision of the Golden Age, it was a time of instinctive chivalry when "out of sheer courtesy, the sturdy cork-trees shed their light and broad bark, with which men first covered their houses." A favorite Renaissance addition to the commonplace of the Golden Age was an emphasis on unadorned nature, which completely outshines the decadent contrivances of art.

If nostalgia is the hallmark of all these idealizations, it is worth noting how pastoralism dominated the Renaissance response to the discovery of America. Peter Martyr, for example, rapturizes on Hispaniola as an Ovidian Eden come true: "the Ilande enjoyeth perpetuall springe tyme, and is fortunate with contynuall soomer and harvest. The trees floryshe there all the hole yeare: And the medowes contynue always greene: All thyngs are exceadynge fortunate, and growe to great perfection" (*Les Huit decades*, translated into English by Richard Eden, 1555). The indigenous peoples are worthy inhabitants of this newfound paradise, living without the corrupt luxuries of Europe, "So that if we shall not be ashamed to confesse the truthe, they seeme to lyve in that goulden worlde of the which owlde wryters speake so much." From this to Rousseau's noble savage is no great step; nor to the paradisal forest and exalted blood-brotherhood of Chingachgook and Natty Bumppo in what D.H. Lawrence dubs the "romance" and "myth-meaning" aspects of Fenimore Cooper's Leatherstocking novels (*The Pioneers*, 1823; *The Last of the Mohicans*, 1826; *The Prairie*, 1827; *The Pathfinder*, 1840; and *The Deerslayer*, 1841); nor yet again to the pond-worship of Thoreau's *Walden* (1854), which, as Marcus Cunliffe suggests, belongs to a time when some Americans "thought it possible to find the godhead in the nearby woods," and "to be like Adam before the Fall." Both in style and content Mark Twain is a long way from such a prelapsarian vision, but in *Tom Sawyer* (1876) and *Huckleberry Finn* (1884) the juxtaposition of natural energies with the ambiguous benefits of adult civilization is still recognizably within a New World pastoralism.

If the novel as such is regarded as the literary form most closely associated with the rise of the middle classes in the 18th century, the pastoral novel may be regarded as in the main the product of the Industrial Revolution. There are notable exceptions. Samuel Johnson's *Rasselas* (1759) begins by situating its hero in an innocent pastoral haven, but its exploration of the wider world is conducted on a plan of disillusionment, which is perhaps only to be expected from an author who notoriously denounced the pastoral as "easy, vulgar and therefore disgusting." Defoe's *Robinson Crusoe* (1719)—although arguably the precursor of desert island pastorals such as R.M. Ballantyne's *The Coral Island* (1857) and the more Johnsonian counterpastoral of William Golding's *Lord of the Flies* (1954)—is a fictional projection of dissenting pragmatism rather than idealization in the traditionally pastoral mold. Golding has other predecessors in the poets of the late 18th and early 19th century who looked back to a kind of pastoral golden age enjoyed in the consciousness of childhood, exemplified in Blake's *Songs of Innocence* (1789) and the "fair seedtime" of the soul, which is the guiding autobiographical principle of William Wordsworth's *The Prelude* (1850).

Early 19th-century pastoralism is part of a complex reaction against the "civilizing" rationalism and commercial expansionism that culminated in industrialization and urbanization, which were accompanied by pollution, poverty, overcrowding, and squalor. The idealization of childhood combined with nostalgia for a lost paradise of natural surroundings to create an opposition between country and city that gave new meaning to the well-worn traditional pastoral opposition between country and court. Whereas the traditional pastoral was a highly conventionalized form largely ignoring the actual conditions in which shepherds and shepherdesses lived their lives, the new fictional form that emerged in the 19th century, although subject still to idealization, celebrated a psychological innocence and freedom to be found in characters and circumstances that were realistically drawn.

Dickens is not perhaps a pastoral novelist, but pastoral elements are of considerable importance in works such as *Pickwick Papers* (1837) and *Great Expectations* (1861). Pickwick belongs to the city rather than the country, but his adventures in the countryside exemplify his benevolence, which borders on the naive. His enforced re-immersion in the city because of legal difficulties involving supposed breach of promise echoes the traditional opposition between pastoralism's unsuspecting innocence and the Iron-Age duplicity of court and city. On the same lines, but more deeply disturbing in its exploration of urban corruption, *Great Expectations* balances the boyhood world of Pip and the innocence of Joe Gargery (constituting an idyllic, yet realistic, pastoral of life on the marshes) against the withered and withering frustration of Miss Havisham, the disillusioned cunning of the law embodied in Jaggers, and the criminal world to which Magwitch belongs. But cutting across these broad antitheses of traditional pastoral are complexities and contradictions, such as Pip's false idealization of Estella (a deluded pastoral) and his self-deception as to the nature and identity of his "benefactor" (ultimately giving a different dimension to Magwitch), which compel the reader to a new adjustment of the relationship between innocence and experience.

George Eliot's early novels reveal a more direct derivation from pastoral and pastoral romance, but they also make a typically 19th-century accommodation to realism. *Adam Bede* (1859) offers in its titular hero an idealized version of a simultaneously noble and natural character, situated, however, in a grim rural setting. Its triangular love story (Adam in love with Hetty, Hetty infatuated with the seemingly glamorous Arthur, and Arthur captivated by his sentimental image of the innocent country maid) represents several of the features of traditional pastoral in a truly fallen world of class distinction, social prejudice, and uncompromising legality. *The Mill on the Floss* (1860) likewise takes the childhood vision of the romantics and couples it with a glamorous view of the sibling love between Maggie and Tom. The story transmutes the idyll of Longus' *Daphnis and Chloe,* while rooting it in a contemporary, 19th-century world that is observed with sociological accuracy and that has harsh consequences for Maggie's dreaming aspirations. For George Eliot the romantics' version of the pastoral ideal has a powerful attraction, but it is countered by an equally powerful sense of the historical conditioning of men and women by the ties of family and society and their moral and religious beliefs. It has often been remarked that *The Mill on the Floss* reads like a latter-day *Winter's Tale,* but even here the precision with which the village community of Raveloe is presented distinguishes it from the hazy aura surrounding traditional Arcadia and creates a background against which the fairy-tale plot stands out in ambiguous relief.

Two novelists who take up this kind of juxtaposition from George Eliot and move it on into the later 19th and early 20th centuries are Thomas Hardy and D.H. Lawrence. Hardy's *Under the Greenwood Tree* (1872) acknowledges its pastoral debt in its Shakespearean title and has it counterpart in Lawrence's first novel, *The White Peacock* (1911). Both have stylistic elements that belong to the self-consciously literary manner sanctioned by the pastoral tradition, a manner also continued by such writers as Kenneth Grahame and Laurie Lee. But both are also fully aware of the fragile and literary nature of the form they imitate, creating a delicate counterpoint between the conventional and the real. This counterpoint is evident in the ending, slightly coy, slightly sardonic, of *Under the Greenwood Tree,* in which Fancy agrees with Dick to "have no secrets from each other," or rather, "None from to-day," to the ironical accompaniment of the nightingale's singing, again echoing *As You Like It*: "Tippiwit! Swe-e-et! ki-ki-ki! Come hither, come hither, come hither!"

Hardy includes another literary allusion in the title of his second pastoral novel, *Far from the Madding Crowd* (1874), where again tradition is played off against modern realism. The allusion is ironic, for Hardy's rustics are not permitted "[a]long the cool sequestered vale of life" to keep "the noiseless tenor of their way." The false glamour of the outside world intrudes, like the pirate incursions in *Daphnis and Chloe,* exploiting Fanny's innocence and all but destroying Bathsheba's peace of mind. This development is a portent of what is to come in the subsequent Wessex novels, where the old order faces the new and tragically succumbs. *The Woodlanders* (1887), given the most deeply secluded, rural setting of all Hardy's pastoral novels, is, yet, paradoxically, the most modern in its Darwinian anti-pastoralism. And *Tess of the d'Urbervilles* (1891), rich as it is in echoes of the classical Golden Age and the Christian Eden, is Hardy's most tragic and most indignant lament for a rural society subverted by Victorian "progress." His last novel, *Jude the Obscure* (1895), marks his shift to a scathing modernity that is more urban than rural and suggests profound disillusionment with the pastoral.

The opposition between modern industrialism and pastoral tradition is key to much of Lawrence's work. His theme, as stated in the essay "Nottingham and the Mining Country" (1929), is that "the tragedy of England . . . is the tragedy of ugliness. The country is so lovely: the man-made England is so vile." But this is not just a scenic preference. For Lawrence, the country-city opposition maps onto the opposition between "mental consciousness" and "intuitive and instinctive consciousness." *Sons and Lovers* (1913), *The Rainbow* (1915), *Women in Love* (1920), and, after a long interval, *Lady Chatterley's Lover* (1928) all chart the devastating impact of mental consciousness and its accompanying technological sterility on the Nottinghamshire "country of his heart." The novels and tales between, including *Kangaroo* (1923), *St. Mawr* (1925), *The Woman Who Rode Away* (1928), and *The Plumed Serpent* (1926), are latter-day variations on the search for a lost paradise, which Lawrence, despite his repeated and increasingly bitter disappointments, persisted in believing was still to be recovered in the Australian bush, or among Native Americans, or in his neo-utopian community of Rananim. In a characteristically pastoral dualism, the ideal and the real meet head-on in his work. Passionate wishful thinking is juxtaposed with a critical diagnostic of 20th-century civilization. But it must be conceded that Lawrence often emphasizes a primitive energy that is difficult to distinguish from savagery and violence, especially in parts of *Women in Love* and in his writings set in Mexico and New Mexico, and virtually stands the original pastoral idyll on its head.

More recent 20th-century fiction belongs primarily to an urban, suburban, and technological world that seems to exclude this partial dualism, except, perhaps, in an ironically distancing fashion. But there are nonetheless signs of its survival. The role accorded the Australian outback in the novels of Patrick White and the Canadian wilderness in those of Margaret Atwood builds on the "pastoral" element in 19th-century American literature of the frontier and of the wilderness. With Atwood, pastoralism becomes allied with feminism in a way that gives the critical function of pastoral—its persistent opposition between a lost, or buried, ideal and the corrupt, contemporary reality—a new meaning and relevance. The vogue for magic realism also contributes to this renewal. Pastoralism has always clung to an imaginative, fantastic dimension that challenges the accepted assumptions of a fallen, everyday world. It continues to offer itself to writers who are urged not only to question the norms of their intellectual and social worlds, but also to explore alternatives, however elusively utopian they may seem to be.

R.P. DRAPER

See also Astrée; Diana; French Novel (16th and 17th Centuries); Greek and Roman Narrative; Regional Novel; Renaissance Narrative; Spanish Novel; Utopian and Dystopian Novel

Further Reading

Alcorn, John, *The Nature Novel from Hardy to Lawrence,* New York: Columbia University Press, and London: Macmillan, 1977

Alpers, Paul J., *What Is Pastoral?* Chicago: University of Chicago Press, 1996

Bakker, Jon, *Pastoral in Antebellum Southern Romance,* Baton Rouge: Louisiana State University Press, 1989

Bromberg, Rachel, *Three Pastoral Novels* [Montemayor's *Diana,* Ribeiro's *Menine e Moa,* and Sannazaro's *Arcadia*], Brooklyn, New York: Postar Press, 1970

Damiani, Bruno M., and Barbara Louise Mujica, *Et in Arcadia Ego: Essays on Death in the Pastoral Novel,* Lanham, Maryland: University Press of America, 1990

Draper, R.P., editor, *George Eliot: "The Mill on the Floss" and "Silas Marner": A Casebook,* London: Macmillan, 1977

Draper, R.P., editor, *Hardy, Three Pastoral Novels,* London: Macmillan, 1987

Empson, William, *Some Versions of Pastoral,* London: Chatto and Windus, 1935; as *English Pastoral Poetry,* Freeport, New York: Books for Libraries Press, 1938

Ettin, Andrew V., *Literature and the Pastoral,* New Haven, Connecticut: Yale University Press, 1984

Gerhardt, Mia Irene, *La Pastorale: Essai d'analyse littéraire,* Assen: Van Gorcum, 1950

Harrison, Elizabeth Jane, *Female Pastoral: Women Writers Re-Visioning the American South,* Knoxville: University of Tennessee Press, 1991

Hunter, Shelagh, *Victorian Idyllic Fiction: Pastoral Strategies,* Atlantic Highlands, New Jersey: Humanities Press, and London: Macmillan, 1984

Jehenson, Myriam Yvonne, *The Golden World of the Pastoral: A Comparative Study of Sidney's "New Arcadia" and d'Urfé's "L'Astrée,"* Ravenna: Longo, 1981

Keith, W.J., *Regions of the Imagination: The Development of British Rural Fiction,* Toronto and Buffalo, New York: University of Toronto Press, 1988

Lawrence, D.H., "Fenimore Cooper's Leatherstocking Novels," in *Studies in Classic American Literature,* New York: T. Seltzer, 1923; London: Heinemann, 1924

Lawrence, D.H., "Nottingham and the Mining Countryside," in *Phoenix: The Posthumous Papers of D.H. Lawrence,* London: Heinemann, and New York: Viking, 1936

Levin, Harry, *The Myth of the Golden Age in the Renaissance,* Bloomington: Indiana University Press, 1969; London: Faber, 1970

Lincoln, Eleanor Terry, editor, *Pastoral and Romance: Modern Essays in Criticism,* Englewood Cliffs, New Jersey: Prentice-Hall, 1969

Marinelli, Peter V., *Pastoral,* London: Methuen, 1971

Sole-Leris, Amadeo, *The Spanish Pastoral Novel,* Boston: Twayne, 1980

Squires, Michael, *The Pastoral Novel,* Charlottesville: University Press of Virginia, 1974

Sussex, R.T., *Home and the Homeland Novel: Studies in French Regional Literature,* Townsville, Queensland: Department of Modern Languages, James Cook University of North Queensland, 1979

Westling, Louise Hutchings, *The Green Breast of the New World: Landscape, Gender, and American Fiction,* Athens: University of Georgia Press, 1995

Williams, Raymond, *The Country and the City,* London: Chatto and Windus, and New York: Oxford University Press, 1973

Pedro Páramo by Juan Rulfo

1955

Published in 1955, Juan Rulfo's only novel, *Pedro Páramo,* is one of the most innovative works of all Mexican fiction. Its highly experimental use of time, space, and narrative voices makes this work a key point of reference for understanding the evolution of the contemporary Latin American novel and the international recognition it has received since the 1960s. Writers such as Gabriel García Márquez have repeatedly acknowledged their artistic debt to Rulfo.

Much of Rulfo's originality as a writer resides in the innovative structure and narrative strategies set forth in *Pedro Páramo.* His prose successfully combines realistic, tragic, and dramatic elements with a poetic narrative voice that is the novel's most praised artistic feature.

Rulfo was born in a small town in the state of Jalisco in 1918. While his place of birth is never directly mentioned in his books, Rulfo's fictional universe centers on the lives of peasants in rural Mexico. Rulfo previously portrayed such a setting masterfully in his only collection of short stories, *El llano en llamas (The Burning Plain)*, published in 1953. Rulfo's prose breaks from the conventions of realistic regional writers of Mexico who had identified characters and scenes belonging to a specific local reality (Gregorio López y Fuentes, Martín Luis Guzmán). These traditional modes of representation were used by many of Rulfo's predecessors to denounce the historical neglect of the peasant population and the nation's failure to incorporate this group into mainstream society, particularly in the aftermath of the Mexican Revolution. Without sacrificing social commitment, Rulfo moves away from documentary-type approaches to Mexico's indigenous question and develops new ways of expressing the perspective of peasant characters. For example, he does not depend on educated narrators to explain the lives of uneducated, rustic individuals; instead, he chooses to focus on the inner selves of these abandoned antiheroes, whose immediate concerns are mostly related to basic survival (rain for their crops, the loss of a cow). Hence, Rulfo's characters speak a basic, common language that in its colloquial nature redefines the representation of peasant psychology. The down-to-earth orality of Rulfo's characters at first appears to be the product of an uncalculated artlessness, characterized by few words and short sentences. But, in fact, their speech is the product of a perfectly crafted lyrical stylization that is absent from the Latin American novel prior to Rulfo. This artistic perfection in the use of language allows for the treatment of themes such as death and violence to transcend local or regional references, and the lives of many of Rulfo's characters ultimately become mythical symbols of a deprived human existence.

Pedro Páramo tells the story of Juan Preciado's arrival in the town of Comala. Preciado journeys to Comala in order to keep a promise he made to his mother, Dolores Preciado, on her deathbed—to find his unknown father, Pedro Páramo, and avenge Páramo's abandonment of Juan and his mother. But Juan is only one of many children abandoned by his father, Comala's despotic *cacique,* or political boss, who uses his wealth and vast landownings to control the town. Significantly, Pedro Páramo's name means "barren plain." Once a green and flourishing town, Comala has been a wasteland ever since Pedro Páramo decided

to punish the town for organizing a fiesta after the death of Susana San Juan, his only true love. Upon arrival in Comala, Juan Preciado finds an abandoned ghost town. Comala's people are dead but they have maintained a capacity to reminisce about their unfinished lives from their graves. Because the narration is made up of fragmented sequences, the revelation that the characters are speaking from the cemetery only becomes clear midway through the story. The conversations among the dead add a new dimension to the novel's initial realism by confronting the reader with the mysterious humanity of these lost souls. Rulfo creates a narrative tone that combines the real with the fantastic in a nonchronological sequencing. In this way, Comala becomes a purgatory of anguish, pain, and guilt.

Pedro Páramo's life unfolds from three different points of view—one belonging to Juan Preciado, another to an omniscient narrator, and a third to the inhabitants of Comala. This multiplicity gives the novel a rich psychological dimension. Consequently, the events in Comala move easily from objective reality to the subjective and phantasmagoric, and a final revelation challenges the reader's sense of logic once again: Juan Preciado, like the others, is also speaking from the dead. Such a fragmented sense of reality, with many juxtapositions in time and space, repeatedly challenges the reader to organize the novel's information to reach a full understanding of the town's destruction. In the process, the reader discovers that Juan Preciado survived only two days after his arrival in Comala, and that the many comments about his life were addressed to a woman buried alongside him. Eventually, the reader realizes that Pedro Páramo was murdered by another of his abandoned offspring, a muleteer who at the outset of the novel served as Juan Preciado's guide to Comala. Juan Preciado's descending journey into Comala is, in short, an inexorable encounter with death, a never-ending curse of guilt and dispossession, to which all of Comala's dwellers are condemned.

Rulfo's complex use of space, time, and language was at first little understood in Mexico, but his artistic contributions to the contemporary Latin American novel are today undisputed. While *Pedro Páramo* historically has close ties with the novel of the Mexican Revolution and explores a new aesthetic representation of the indigenous novel in Latin America, Rulfo early on crafted a new type of speech that depicts universal human solitude and the material spareness of life in rural Latin America. The anguished expressions of his characters are marked by a sense of timelessness and universality, imbuing them with classical or mythical identities. The people of Juan Rulfo's fictional world are so permanently tainted by a sense of abandonment and guilt that not even death can bring them peace.

CÉSAR FERREIRA

Further Reading

Brotherston, Gordon, "Province of Lost Souls: Juan Rulfo," in *The Emergence of the Latin American Novel,* by Brotherston, Cambridge and New York: Cambridge University Press, 1977

Brushwood, John S., *Mexico in Its Novel: A Nation's Search for Identity,* Austin: University of Texas Press, 1966

Crow, John A., "*Pedro Páramo*: A Twentieth Century 'Dance of Death'," in *Homage to Irving A. Leonard: Essays on Hispanic Art, History, and Literature*, edited by Raquel Chang-Rodríguez and Donald A. Yates, East Lansing: Latin American Studies Center, Michigan State University, 1977

Fuentes, Carlos, "Mugido muerte y misterio: El mito de Rulfo," *Revista Iberoamericana* 43 (1981)

Harss, Luis, and Barbara Dohmann, "Juan Rulfo, or the Souls of the Departed," in *Into the Mainstream: Conversations with Latin-American Writers*, New York: Harper and Row, 1967

Leal, Luis, *Juan Rulfo*, Boston: Twayne, 1983

Leal, Luis, "Juan Rulfo," in *Modern Latin-American Fiction Writers*, first series, edited by William Luis, Detroit: Gale Research, 1992

Peavler, Terry J., "Textual Problems in *Pedro Páramo*," *Revista de Estudios Hispánicos* 19 (1985)

Rodríguez-Alcalá, Hugo, *El arte de Juan Rulfo*, Mexico City: Instituto Nacional de Bellas Artes, 1965

Sommers, Joseph, *After the Storm: Landmarks of the Modern Mexican Novel*, Albuquerque: University of New Mexico Press, 1968

Penny Dreadful. *See* Dime Novels and Penny Dreadfuls

People of the City by Cyprian Ekwensi

1954

People of the City originated in a series of stories that Cyprian Ekwensi wrote and broadcast on radio over several years to entertain demobilized West African veterans of Britain's World War II campaigns in Southeast Asia. The inspiration to rework these stories came during a 13-day sea voyage to Britain in 1951, when he "found a pattern of city life" in them (see Nichols, 1981). Through the activities of the central character, the journalist and band leader Amusa Sango, the novel offers a panoramic view of Nigerian society in the final phase of British colonial rule, particularly the moral confusion resulting from colonialism's destruction of indigenous normative institutions.

Although generally favorable, early criticism of *People of the City* emphasized its urban setting and themes rather than its literary features. This fact is significant, for it highlights a major difference between Ekwensi's early writing and the first wave of African europhone literature in the mid–20th century. Ideologically motivated, this literature was designed to contest European colonialist hegemony and its sustaining myths of race. Conversely, Ekwensi's main artistic motivation resulted in novels that offer snapshots of life without probing its undercurrents. In his opinion, "The Nigerian loves a good story [and] spectacle. . . . We like to hear scandalous things about people. . . . We want to see how we can acquire the wealth to build twenty-story buildings. And we also like to see those who have twenty-story buildings being impeached for getting their wealth in a corrupt way. So it's all part of the ebullience of life [and] the joy of living in the Africa of today" (see Nichols, 1981). Given such a combination of journalistic sensationalism and ideological ambivalence, the novel treats colonialism mainly as a minor detail in support of larger incidents. Ekwensi makes moral statements about such issues as poverty, crime, moral and material corruption, and the 1949 massacre of dozens of striking coal miners by British colonial police without offering a coherent critique of history, social institutions, or human limitations. His journalistic pretensions notwithstanding, Amusa Sango is brought face to face with the wretchedly poor and recoils in horror, not out of pity but from fear of contamination. With the exception of background characters, Ekwensi virtually associates poverty with criminality.

People of the City also differs from other first-generation African novels by the absence of conscious exploitation of indigenous aesthetic codes, either for creating literary effects or as part of an artistic-ideological program of cultural affirmation. Yet Ekwensi actually began his writing career by retelling indigenous oral tales, as in *Ikolo the Wrestler and Other Ibo Tales* (1947), and subscribed to the nationalistic view of African literature. This inconsistency results primarily from the fact that the dominant literary influences and worldview that shaped Ekwensi's narrative art were not African but European and oriental, including the English literature that made part of the syllabus of colonial schools, as well as Westerns, detective thrillers, oriental tales like the *Arabian Nights*, "European-hero-in-Africa" tales like those of H. Rider Haggard, adventure tales like Robert Louis Stevenson's, and Indian films.

Such influences account for other aberrations in Ekwensi's cultural values. For instance, he derides traditional married life, as in the portrayal of Lajide's polygamous marriage, but romantic love intrigues based on foreign models are treated sympathetically. In one romantic subplot, Sango's friend Bayo and his Lebanese or Syrian lover are murdered by her brother who opposes their cross-racial relationship. Bayo would not be out of place in Elizabethan drama and was perhaps inspired by the ubiquitous *Lambs Tales from Shakespeare*. Descriptions such as the following are not uncommon: "Bayo's condition was pitiful to see. Dull were his shoes, wrinkled his tie; and the hair of this erstwhile dapper youngster was for once uncombed." Sango preys on a succession of African women before opportunistically marrying Beatrice the Second, who hails from an aristocratic Dahomeyan family with hinted Portuguese-Brazilian connections. Ekwensi even retains the color and name symbolism of "European-hero-in-Africa" tales. The young woman whom Amusa seduces and abandons within 24 hours bears a Nigerian name, Aina, and is portrayed as "the dark temptress who was such a threat to his happiness," while her mother is a witch and "the blackmailing woman of the tempting daughter." The fiancée abandoned by Amusa has a foreign name, perhaps Helena or Eleanor, localized to Elina. Conversely, the three women who arouse noble emotions of love bear foreign names: the two Beatrices and Suad.

Oral aesthetics exert a significant influence on this novel's vaguely didactic conception, glimpsed, for example, in the tone and phrasing of the epigraphs to the two parts. The epigraph to Part One reads, "How the city attracts all types and how the unwary must suffer from ignorance of its ways," while the epigraph to Part Two reads, "When all doors are Closed." Yet Ekwensi's didacticism is only on the surface, in a manner reminiscent of Daniel Defoe, with whom he has frequently been compared. For the resolution Ekwensi manipulates the plot to secure a happy ending for the unreformed protagonist by the simple expedient of giving him the rich, adoring, and faintly Europeanized Beatrice the Second for a bride.

People of the City set the pattern for Ekwensi's fiction up to the Nigeria-Biafra war (1967–70). Its affinities are not with the mainstream African europhone novel of the 1950s and 1960s but with the chapbook tradition known as Onitsha Market Literature:

People of the City thrives in the commercial town of Onitsha, along with Amos Tutuola's mythopoeic *The Palm-Wine Drinkard* (1952). The romantic intrigues, the manipulation of plot to achieve desired resolutions, and use of Eurocentric color and name symbolism in characterization are common features of the Onitsha tradition. Interestingly, one of the earliest and most successful Onitsha novelettes, *When Love Whispers* (1947), was also written by Ekwensi. *People of the City* is the best achievement of that tradition.

CHIDI OKONKWO

See also Cyprian Ekwensi

Further Reading

Emenyonu, Ernest, *Cyprian Ekwensi,* London: Evans, 1974
Emenyonu, Ernest, editor, *The Essential Ekwensi: A Literary Celebration of Cyprian Ekwensi's Sixty-fifth Birthday,* Ibadan, Nigeria: Heinemann, 1987
Inyama, N.F., "Language and Characterisation in Cyprian Ekwensi's *People of the City* and *Jagua Nana,*" *African Literature Today* 17 (1991)
Mackay, Mercedes, "People of the City," *Venture* 6:10 (Autumn 1965)
Nichols, Lee, interviewer and editor, *Conversations with African Writers,* Washington, D.C.: Voice of America, 1981
Okonkwo, J.I., "Ekwensi and the 'Something New and Unstable'," in *Literature and Modern West African Culture,* edited by D.I. Nwoga, Benin City, Nigeria: Ethiope, 1978
Povey, John, "Cyprian Ekwensi: The Novelist and the Pressure of the City," in *The Critical Evaluation of African Literature,* edited by Edgar Wright, London: Heinemann, 1973; Washington, D.C.: INSCAPE, 1976
Zabus, Chantal, *The African Palimpsest: Indigenization of Language in the West African Europhone Novel,* Amsterdam and Atlanta, Georgia: Rodopi, 1991

Le Père Goriot by Honoré de Balzac

1835

With the publication of *Le Père Goriot,* Balzac established himself as the leading French romantic novelist. To be sure, Balzac's voice in the novel is consistently impassioned, even melodramatic, and is qualitatively different from the objective tone that characterizes later French realism. Nevertheless, *Le Père Goriot* has a close affinity to literary realism by virtue of the novel's wealth of historical and sociological detail. For all the subjectivity and idealism of the narrator's commentary, *Le Père Goriot* is a study of *milieu,* or social environment, which is clearly understood, for the first time in the history of the French novel, as one of the basic determinants of character. Balzac later explained that his writing was inspired by science, notably the

work of Georges Cuvier and Geoffroy Saint-Hilaire. (In fact, *Le Père Goriot* is dedicated to the latter.) As these naturalists studied plant and animal species, so Balzac set out to study social species in his *La Comédie humaine* (The Human Comedy), conceiving his entire oeuvre as a single, unified portrait of 19th-century French society. (*See separate entry,* Human Comedy.)

Le Père Goriot marks a crucial step in Balzac's conceptualization of *La Comédie humaine,* not only in the novel's emphasizing environmental influences on character but also because it contains characters who will reappear in later novels and thus give coherence to Balzac's entire novelistic output. Stories partially known in earlier works are fleshed out in later ones.

Secondary characters acquire more depth, and, indeed, some minor figures become major characters later on. Of the main characters in *Le Père Goriot*, the title character dies, but Rastignac's rakish rise in French society may be tracked in subsequent novels; the arch-criminal Vautrin returns for a wild adventure in *Splendeurs et misères des courtisanes* (1845; *A Harlot High and Low*); Bianchon, the medical student, becomes *the* doctor of *La Comédie humaine*; and Mme de Beauséant, who leaves Paris after her betrayal by a faithless lover, will undergo the same painful experience in the provinces in later novels. Subsequently, when republication gave him the opportunity, Balzac retouched his reappearing characters to shape them into more cohesive personages, sometimes changing their names to do so. With such characters, Balzac's novels no longer formed a discontinuous series but became building blocks in a larger design, a design Balzac intended as a portrait of all of French society.

Le Père Goriot is set in a sleepy quarter of Paris, where a series of characters lives in genteel poverty in the seedy Vauquer pension. In a long descriptive passage of the type for which Balzac is famous, they are presented as being in perfect harmony with their environment. Chief among them are Goriot, a retired merchant who has sacrificed his once considerable fortune for the dowry of his egotistical daughters, who have made brilliant marriages but now shun their father; Eugène de Rastignac, a young provincial law student of meager fortune but noble lineage; and the mysterious Vautrin, who turns out to be an escaped convict. The novel is constructed so that "old man" Goriot's demise coincides with the completion of Rastignac's education in the selfish ways of a corrupt society. Thus Balzac develops one of the classic patterns of 19th-century fiction: the novel of apprenticeship or education, in this case, of the *arriviste*.

Family connections allow Rastignac to be received into the stronghold of aristocratic Paris ruled by his influential cousin, Mme de Beauséant (loosely translated, "Mme Sitting-Pretty"). She explains Goriot's situation and cynically urges Rastignac to make use of female patronage to make his way in the world. Delphine de Nucingen, one of Goriot's daughters, she points out, would "lap up all the mud of Paris" in order to receive an invitation to Mme de Beauséant's ball—wealthy she may be, but still she is married to a bourgeois financier, and a Jew to boot. Back at the pension, Vautrin, who has divined Rastignac's ambitious character, makes him a cruder proposal. He could marry a fellow pensioner who will become rich once her brother, her wealthy father's sole heir, is killed in a duel that Vautrin will arrange in exchange for a share in the fortune. As justification, Vautrin remarks, "Il n'y a pas de principes, il n'y a que des événements" ("There are no principles, only events"). Rastignac reflects that this philosophy is morally not very different from his cousin's.

Eventually the plot explodes into the multiple events of the famous "long day," during which the pension's denizens all decamp. Vautrin is unmasked and arrested by the police, and Goriot (now a figure echoing Shakespeare's King Lear), devastated by his daughters ingratitude, dies comforted only by Rastignac and Bianchon. Rastignac must pay out of his own pocket for the funeral to which the families send their emblazoned, empty carriages. In the dramatic, concluding scene set on the heights of the Père Lachaise cemetery, Rastignac crosses his "Parisian Rubicon": gazing at the city below where evening lights are just beginning to twinkle, he issues a challenge to the Paris he now resolves to conquer by whatever means: "A nous deux, maintenant!" ("Now it's between the two of us!"). At novel's end, Rastignac is prepared to "adapt" himself to his chosen milieu.

Le Père Goriot is a novel of deep social pessimism. Indeed, Henry James wrote that the true protagonist of *La Comédie humaine* was the 20 franc piece. The corruption of society and the violence of human passion are the novel's grand themes. Mud is one of its dominant metaphors. Its notorious "open ending" shocked many readers, who hoped and expected that Rastignac would renounce the wickedness of Paris and return virtuously to the provinces. Later novels indeed bear out the suggestion that Rastignac is finally ready to stoop to anything, showing him to be a perfect scoundrel, massively enriched through shady business dealings and married to Augusta de Nucingen, the daughter of a former mistress.

Balzac's emphasis on the shaping influence of *milieu* on his characters found many followers among later French novelists. His most obvious descendant is Émile Zola, who, in his unified, serial portrait of French society, *Les Rougon-Macquart* (1871–93; *The Rougon-Macquart*), demonstrated an affinity not only with Balzac's interest in social determinism but also with his penchant for the encyclopedic.

STIRLING HAIG

See also Human Comedy

Further Reading

Auerbach, Erich, *Mimesis: Dargestellte Wirklichkeit in der abendländischen Literatur,* Bern: Francke, 1946; as *Mimesis: The Representation of Reality in Western Literature,* Princeton, New Jersey: Princeton University Press, 1953

Barbéris, Pierre, *"Le Père Goriot" de Balzac: Écriture, structures, significations,* Paris: Larousse, 1972

Bardèche, Maurice, *Balzac romancier,* Paris: Plon, 1940; reprint, Geneva: Slatkine Reprints, 1967

Bellos, David, *Honoré de Balzac: "Old Goriot,"* Cambridge and New York: Cambridge University Press, 1987

Brooks, Peter, *The Melodramatic Imagination: Balzac, Henry James, and the Mode of Excess,* New Haven, Connecticut: Yale University Press, 1976

Levin, Harry, *The Gates of Horn: A Study of Five French Realists,* New York and London: Oxford University Press, 1963

Longaud, Félix, *Dictionnaire de Balzac,* Paris: Larousse, 1969

Picon, Gaëtan, *Balzac par lui-même,* Paris: Editions du Seuil, 1956

Pugh, Anthony R., *Balzac's Recurring Characters,* Toronto: University of Toronto Press, 1974; London: Duckworth, 1975

Georges Perec 1936–82

French

Georges Perec was an experimentalist, a writer intrigued by the possibilities of literary form. Although he is best known for his novels, he also wrote plays, poetry, essays, film scripts, opera librettos, and many other texts that elude traditional generic categories. In a 1978 interview, Perec spoke of his goals: "My ambition as a writer would be to traverse all of contemporary literature, without ever feeling that I am retracing my own steps or returning to beaten ground, and to write everything that someone today can possibly write." Elsewhere, he suggested that four major concerns animated his work: an interest in the apparently trivial details of ordinary life, a tendency toward confession and autobiography, an impulse toward formal innovation, and a desire to tell engaging, absorbing stories.

His first novel, *Les Choses: Une histoire des années soixante* (1965; *Things: A Story of the Sixties*), is an account of a young couple grappling with the materialism of contemporary consumer society. Well received both critically and commercially, it was awarded the prestigious Prix Renaudot. Hailing it as a "sociological novel," critics suggested that *Things* offered a fresh direction for a literature exhausted by the esotericism of the *nouveau roman. Quel petit vélo à guidon chromé au fond de la cour?* (1966; *Which Moped with Chrome-plated Handlebars at the Back Yard?*) is undoubtedly Perec's least-known novel. In mock-heroic style, Perec tests the possibilities of satire as he describes the efforts of a young French conscript to avoid military service in Algeria. *Un Homme qui dort* (1967; *A Man Asleep*) is an experiment in narrative voice. Told in the second-person singular in an eerily confessional, reflexive tone, it is the tale of a young man's struggles with depression.

In 1967 Perec joined the Ouvroir de Littérature Potentielle (Oulipo), a group founded by Raymond Queneau and François Le Lionnais and devoted to the principle of formal innovation. *La Disparition* (1969; *A Void*) arises directly out of this association: it is an astonishing 312-page novel written without the letter *e,* the most frequently used letter in French. Cast as a detective novel whose central enigma is the "disappearance" of the letter *e* from the alphabet, it also tells a broader and more somber story about absence, loss, and disaster. Perec followed this with a shorter novel called *Les Revenentes* (1972: *The Exeter Text: Jewels, Secrets, Sex*) in which *e* is the only vowel used. Curious formal relations pertain between those two texts since, given their compositional constraints, not one word is common to both.

In *W ou le souvenir d'enfance* (1975; *W, or, the Memory of Childhood*), autobiographical and fictional narratives compete, alternating chapter by chapter. In this novel, Perec confronts the memories of his early years and the catastrophe of his parents' deaths, trying to save his personal story from collective history, that is, from the vast narrative of the Holocaust that threatens to subsume his own history. The autobiographical narrative and the fictional narrative gradually converge in the text, each leading toward a concentrationary universe dominated by oppression and death. Perec vexes those two narratives one against the other with great canniness in order to deal with the problem of the unspeakable: in many cases, one narrative says what the other cannot.

La Vie mode d'emploi (1978; *Life, a User's Manual*) is a massive novel of 700 pages telling a vertiginous multiplicity of closely interrelated stories. Received warmly upon its publication, it was awarded the Prix Médicis. *Life, a User's Manual* is considered by many to be Perec's major literary statement, defining a key moment in the history of the modern European novel. (*See separate entry,* Life, a User's Manual.)

Un Cabinet d'amateur (1979; *A Gallery Portrait*) is the tale of a painter and his most elaborate canvas, a painting that depicts, in ever more precise and minute detail, a collection of other paintings. Here Perec plays on the notion of specularity, a central term of postmodernist art and literature, exploring the aesthetic artifact as mirror of itself and its conventions. Through analogy, Perec reflects upon literature, for the painting is offered as the mirror of the book—of this book, clearly, but of Perec's other books as well, and of the literary tradition out of which they spring, and which they question so radically.

«53 Jours» (1989; *53 Days*), Perec's last novel, was left unfinished at his death. Edited by his friends and fellow Oulipians Harry Mathews and Jacques Roubaud, this posthumous publication includes the 11 chapters Perec had finished, as well as the detailed notes he had kept for the 17 remaining chapters. *53 Days* seems to be many things: a travel book, a tale of adventure, a detective story.

From 1965 until his death, Perec produced what many regard as the richest body of work in French literature during the second half of the 20th century. Over that 15-year period he changed the direction of the French novel, injecting new life and vigor into a literary form that many critics viewed as moribund. By the mid-1960s the *nouveau roman* had become stagnant, increasingly remote from the general reader; its practitioners had in effect written themselves into a corner. Perec set himself the task of making the French novel "legible" again, and each of his texts furnishes a generous space for the reader. Integrating principles of contemporary structuralist theory into his writing, he advanced the notion that form must *signify* within any narrative economy, that narrative structure must be both motivated and motivating. Although clearly avant-gardist in inspiration, his novels exerted—and continue to exert—broad popular appeal. More than anything else perhaps, Georges Perec's oeuvre may be seen as a sustained meditation on writing itself, a deliberate, painstaking interrogation of the limits and possibilities of literature.

WARREN MOTTE

See also Life, a User's Manual

Biography

Born 7 March 1936 in Paris, into a family of Polish Jews who had emigrated to France in the 1920s; father died in World War II, mother and other members of family arrested, deported, and murdered in the Nazi concentration camps. Attended a Catholic boarding school in the South of France during the war and returned to Paris with his adoptive aunt in 1945; studied sociology at the Sorbonne, 1954–56. Began writing reviews and essays for the *Nouvelle Revue Française* and *Les Lettres*

Nouvelles, 1955; military service, 1958–59; lived in Tunis and Sfax, 1960–62, then worked as an archivist at the Centre National de la Recherche Scientifique in Paris, 1962–79. Died (of cancer) 3 March 1982.

Novels by Perec

Les Choses: Une histoire des années soixante, 1965; as *Things: A Story of the Sixties*, translated by David Bellos, published with *A Man Asleep*, 1990

Quel petit vélo à guidon chromé au fond de la cour?, 1966; as *Which Moped with Chrome-plated Handlebars at the Back Yard?*, translated by Ian Monk, published in *Three by Perec*, 1996

Un Homme qui dort, 1967; as *A Man Asleep*, translated by Andrew Leak, published with *Things: A Story of the Sixties*, 1990

La Disparition, 1969; as *A Void*, translated by Gilbert Adair, 1994

Les Revenentes, 1972; as *The Exeter Text: Jewels, Secrets, Sex*, translated by Ian Monk, published in *Three by Perec*, 1996

W ou le souvenir d'enfance, 1975; as *W, or, the Memory of Childhood*, translated by David Bellos, 1988

La Vie mode d'emploi: Romans, 1978; as *Life, a User's Manual: Fictions*, translated by David Bellos, 1987

Un Cabinet d'amateur: Histoire d'un tableau, 1979; as *A Gallery Portrait*, translated by Ian Monk, published in *Three by Perec*, 1996

«53 Jours», edited by Harry Mathews and Jacques Roubaud, 1989; as *53 Days*, translated by David Bellos, 1992

Other Writings: plays, radio plays, essays, journals, poetry; a treatise on the Japanese game of Go, 1969; wrote crossword puzzles for the weekly news magazine *Le Point*, a selection of which were published as *Les mots croisés*, 1979; a book about Ellis Island, 1980; other works resisting generic categorization.

Further Reading

Bellos, David, *Georges Perec: A Life in Words*, London: Harvill, and Boston: Godine, 1993

Burgelin, Claude, *Georges Perec*, Paris: Editions du Seuil, 1988

Lejeune, Philippe, *La Mémoire et l'oblique: Georges Perec autobiographe*, Paris: POL, 1991

Magné, Bernard, *Perecollages 1981–1988*, Toulouse: Presses Universitaires du Mirail-Toulouse, 1989

Magné, Bernard, *Tentative d'inventaire pas trop approximatif des écrits de Georges Perec* (bibliography), Toulouse: Presses Universitaires du Mirail-Toulouse, 1993

Motte, Warren, *The Poetics of Experiment: A Study of the Work of Georges Perec*, Lexington, Kentucky: French Forum Monographs, 1984

Schwartz, Paul, *Georges Perec: Traces of His Passage*, Birmingham, Alabama: Summa Publications, 1988

Benito Pérez Galdós 1843–1920

Spanish

Benito Pérez Galdós is the most important Spanish representative of the European realist tradition since Cervantes. His output consists of 31 novels about contemporary society, 46 historical novels based on the course of events in Spain between 1808 and 1875, and 21 plays, 5 of them based on his novels. Although some of his plays, notably *Electra* (1901), were acclaimed for their courage in tackling the issue of religious intolerance, Galdós had little sense of theatrical dynamics, and his works for the stage are verbose and slow moving. Some of his later novels, such as *Realidad* (1889; *Reality*) and *El abuelo* (1897; The Grandfather), are experimental, to the extent that they are written in pseudo-theatrical dialogue form, and others, such as *El caballero encantado* (1909; The Enchanted Squire), have fantastic and allegorical elements. Galdós' reputation, however, rests primarily on the novels in which he analyzes the character and mores of contemporary society.

Galdós' understanding of his role as a novelist was shaped principally by two forces. When he arrived in mainland Spain from his native Canaries in 1862, the country was governed by the clerical-dominated regime of Isabella II, and Galdós soon earned a reputation as an outspoken opponent of reaction. In 1865 he embarked on a journalistic career characterized by his unswerving defense of liberal values and an implacable opposition to clericalism, political and religious fanaticism, and corruption in both public and private life.

The second major factor that shaped Galdós' literary development was the lamentable state of prose fiction at the time of his arrival in Spain. The taste of the reading public was dominated by decadent romantic literature such as the melodramatic historical novels of Ortega y Frías or Fernández y González. In one of his newspaper articles in 1866, Galdós wittily satirized the genre: "We want to see the most atrocious disasters described with an unflinching hand. If there is a hospital scene, better still; if a redeeming consumption, capital; if a gallows, splendid! Reality at all costs!" His own literary credo, set out in an important essay of 1870, "Observaciones sobre la novela contemporánea en España" (Observations on the Contemporary Novel in Spain), upholds the values of verisimilitude, sobriety, detachment, and impartiality.

Some of the assumptions underlying this approach were undoubtedly culled from writers such as Honoré de Balzac and Charles Dickens, both of whom Galdós had read extensively by the mid-1860s. In light of this, and given the stage to which the novel had developed in Europe by 1870, it is remarkable that the "Observaciones" say nothing about non-Spanish models. Galdós chooses instead to present himself as heir to an indigenous realist tradition represented principally by Miguel de Cervantes and Diego Velázquez. In so doing, he reveals two attitudes that he shared with his more conservative contemporaries: a deep-seated cultural nationalism and a fastidiousness toward what he considered the excessively explicit treatment of sordid and ugly realities by contemporary French writers.

Galdós' novelistic practice did not always fulfill the theoretical postulates contained in the "Observaciones," for his liberal views led him at times to adopt a polemical posture. *Doña Perfecta* (1876; *Doña Perfecta*) was written while a civil war was raging in northern Spain, and it portrays the forces of clericalism in a way that borders on caricature. Galdós' characteristic voice, however, is tolerant and humorous, projecting an inclusive vision of human behavior and avoiding facile judgments while still retaining moral authority. This voice emerges in the less politically stressful circumstances of the 1880s, when the institutionalization of a two-party system seemed to hold out the prospect of stability. The first really mature work in this new mode is *El amigo Manso* (1882; *Our Friend Manso*), in which Galdós, depicting with gentle irony the efforts of the philosopher-narrator to mold the personality of the woman he loves, not only presents a subtle portrayal of human feelings but also pokes fun at his own efforts, only a few years before, to carry on a liberal crusade in the pages of his novels.

Our Friend Manso indicates clearly the direction in which Galdós' major preoccupations were to develop, for side by side with the detailed portrayal of the behavior of individuals in society there is a deep concern with how they represent their actions to themselves and others, reflected in the ironic light that Galdós casts over the reliability of Manso's narrative. Galdós' early hostility to the popular novel is thereby brought into a relationship with his moral concerns, for moral corruption consists not merely in social posturing, materialism, and sexual license, but includes the characters' efforts to construct, with the help of preexisting literary stereotypes, accounts of their behavior that flatter their self-esteem and encourage self-deception. Thus, for example, *Tormento* (1884; *Torment*) is deliberately written as an ironic counterpoint to a conventional romantic rags-to-riches story dreamed up by the hack writer José Ido del Sagrario. Ido also appears in Galdós' longest and most accomplished work, *Fortunata y Jacinta* (1886–87; *Fortunata and Jacinta*), but he is not the only one engaged in presenting a partial vision of events, for the unnamed narrator of that novel purveys a complacent and uncritical view of the corrupt, middle-class society to which he belongs. Here, as in other novels, such as *Lo prohibido* (1884–85; *Forbidden Fruit*), the stark reality of greed, dishonesty, and exploitation of women is allowed to emerge despite the failure of the narrator to question the values of the society he is indulgently chronicling.

This constant preoccupation with the problematical nature of narration confers on Galdós' best work a modernity that has been unjustly ignored by some later writers and critics who have dismissed his novels for allegedly being concerned with everyday trivialities. His potential influence on the European novel as a whole has not been realized, partly because he has not been particularly well served by translators, and partly because, by the end of his long life, new and more experimental currents of writing, represented by, for example, James Joyce, had made his work seem old-fashioned.

EAMONN RODGERS

See also Fortunata and Jacinta

Biography

Born 10 May 1843 in Las Palmas, Grand Canary Island. Attended an English School, Las Palmas; Colegio de San Agustín, 1856–62; law student at the University of Madrid, 1862–65. Staff member, *La Nación,* from 1865, and associated with *La Revista de España,* from 1870; forsook journalism for writing and travel, 1873; Liberal deputy for Puerto Rico, 1886–90; Republican deputy for Madrid, from 1907. Blind after about 1912. Died 4 January 1920.

Fiction by Pérez Galdós

La Fontana de Oro, 1870; as *The Golden Fountain Cafe,* translated by Walter Rubin, 1989

La sombra, 1871; as *The Shadow,* translated by Karen O. Austin, 1980

El audaz: Historia de un radical de antaño, 1871

Doña Perfecta, 1876; as *Lady Perfecta,* 1883; also translated by Mary Wharton, 1894; as *Doña Perfecta,* 1883; also translated by Mary J. Serrano, 1895, and Harriet de Onís, 1960

Gloria, 1877; as *Gloria,* translated by Nathan Wetherell, 1879; also translated by Clara Bell, 1882

Marianela, 1878; as *Marianela,* translated by Clara Bell, 1883; also translated by Helen W. Lester, 1892, and Mary Wharton, 1893

La familia de León Roch, 1878; as *The Family of Leon Roch,* translated by Clara Bell, 1886; as *Leon Roch,* translated by Bell, 1888

La desheredada, 1881; as *The Disinherited Lady,* translated by Guy E. Smith, 1957; as *The Disinherited,* translated by Lester Clark, 1976

El amigo Manso, 1882; as *Our Friend Manso,* translated by Robert Russell, 1987

El doctor Centeno, 1883

Tormento, 1884; as *Torment,* translated by J.M. Cohen, 1952

La de Bringas, 1884; as *The Spendthrifts,* translated by Gamel Woolsey, 1951

Lo prohibido, 1884–85

Fortunata y Jacinta, 1886–87; as *Fortunata and Jacinta,* translated by Lester Clark, 1973; also translated by Agnes Moncy Gullón, 1986

Miau, 1888; as *Miau,* translated by J.M. Cohen, 1963

La incógnita, 1889; as *The Unknown,* translated by Karen O. Austin, 1991

Realidad, 1889; as *Reality,* translated by Karen O. Austin, 1992

Torquemada en la hoguera, Torquemada en la cruz, Torquemada en el purgatorio, Torquemada y San Pedro, 4 vols., 1889–95; as *Torquemada,* translated by Frances M. López-Morillas, 1986; *Torquemada en la hoguera* as *Torquemada in the Fire,* translated by Nicholas G. Round, 1985

Ángel Guerra, 1890–91; as *Ángel Guerra,* translated by Karen
  O. Austin, 1990
Tristana, 1892; as *Tristana,* translated by R. Selden Rose, 1961
La loca de la casa, 1892; as *La loca de la casa,* translated by
  Frances Exum, 1963
Nazarín, 1895; as *Nazarin,* translated by Jo Labanyi, 1993
Halma, 1895
Misericordia, 1897; as *Compassion,* translated by Toby Talbot,
  1962; also translated by Joan MacLean, 1966
El abuelo, 1897
Casandra, 1905
El caballero encantado, 1909
La razón de la sinrazón, 1915

Fiction: *Episodios Nacionales* series

Trafalgar, 1873; as *Trafalgar,* translated by Clara Bell, 1884
La Corte de Carlos IV, 1873; as *The Court of Charles IV,*
  translated by Clara Bell, 1888
El 19 de marzo y el 2 de mayo, 1873
Bailén, 1873
Napoleón en Chamartín, 1874
Zaragoza, 1874; as *Saragossa,* translated by Minna Caroline
  Smith, 1899
Gerona, 1874; as *Gerona,* translated by G.J. Racz, 1993
Cádiz, 1874
Juan Martín, el Empecinado, 1874
La batalla de los Arapiles, 1875; as *The Battle of Salamanca,*
  translated by Rollo Ogden, 1895
El equipaje del Rey José, 1875
Memorias de un cortesano de 1815, 1875
La segunda casaca, 1876
El Grande Oriente, 1876
El 7 de julio, 1876
Los Cien Mil Hijos de San Luis, 1877
El terror de 1824, 1877
Un voluntario realista, 1878
Los apostólicos, 1879
Un faccioso más y algunos frailes menos, 1879
Zumalacárregui, 1898
Mendizábal, 1898
De Oñate a La Granja, 1898
Luchana, 1899
La campaña del Maestrazgo, 1899
La estafeta romántica, 1899
Vergara, 1899
Montes de Oca, 1900

Los Ayacuchos, 1900
Bodas reales, 1900
Las tormentas del 48, 1902
Narváez, 1902
Los duendes de la camarilla, 1903
La revolución de julio, 1904
O'Donnell, 1904
Aita Tettauen, 1905
Carlos VI en La Rápita, 1905
La vuelta al mundo en la Numancia, 1906
Prim, 1906
La de los tristes destinos, 1907
España sin Rey, 1908
España trágica, 1909
Amadeo I, 1910
La primera República, 1911
De Cartago a Sagunto, 1911
Cánovas, 1912

Other Writings: plays, journalism, and essays.

Further Reading

Aldaraca, Bridget, *El ángel del hogar: Galdós and the Ideology
  of Domesticity in Spain,* Chapel Hill: University of North
  Carolina Press, 1992
Bly, Peter, *Galdós's Novel of the Historical Imagination: A
  Study of the Contemporary Novels,* Liverpool: Cairns, 1983
Dendle, Brian J., *Galdós y la novela histórica,* Ottawa:
  Dovehouse, 1992
Gilman, Stephen, *Galdós and the Art of the European Novel,
  1867–1887,* Princeton, New Jersey: Princeton University
  Press, 1981
Jagoe, Catherine, *Ambiguous Angels: Gender in the Novels of
  Galdós,* Berkeley: University of California Press, 1994
Labanyi, Jo, editor, *Galdós,* London and New York: Longman,
  1993
Ribbans, Geoffrey, *History and Fiction in Galdós's Narratives,*
  Oxford: Clarendon Press, and New York: Oxford University
  Press, 1993
Rodgers, Eamonn, *From Enlightenment to Realism: The Novels
  of Galdós 1870–1887,* Dublin: [E. Rodgers], 1987
Smith, Alan, *Los cuentos inverosímiles de Galdós en el
  contexto de su obra,* Barcelona: Anthropos, 1992
Urey, Diane F., *Galdós and the Irony of Language,* Cambridge
  and New York: Cambridge University Press, 1981
Urey, Diane F., *The Novel Histories of Galdós,* Princeton, New
  Jersey: Princeton University Press, 1989

Periodicals and the Serialization of Novels

Serial publication of novels in magazines in England had an uncertain origin in the 18th century. It came into its own as an important means of publishing new novels in the Victorian period and then declined to the fringes of popular culture in the 20th century. At its peak between 1860 and 1890, it was the initial means of publication for many of the most important novels of the period, and its unique demands had a profound effect on the novels themselves.

Originally, the serial publication of novels was the response of newspaper proprietors to new tax laws after 1712. They sometimes used serialized versions of already printed novels, such as Daniel Defoe's *Robinson Crusoe*, as fillers. A different kind of serialized fiction—brief, moralized epistolary tales spread over several issues—appeared in essay-centered periodicals such as Joseph Addison and Richard Steele's *Tatler* and *Spectator* (1709–14), Samuel Johnson's *Rambler* and John Hawkesworth's *Adventurer* in the 1740s, and Henry Mackenzie's *Mirror* (1779–80). There was no attempt to adapt any of this fiction to serial form, as the editors simply cut the stories into installments to fit available space. The general magazines of the time such as the *Gentleman's Magazine* very occasionally ran original serialized fiction, such as the anonymous *A Story Strange as True*, which ran in seven parts in that magazine in 1737 and 1738. However, most of the fiction in magazines was made up of short pieces or abridgments or excerpts from previously published novels. The major novelists of the time such as Samuel Richardson and Henry Fielding did not publish serials in magazines (although *Clarissa, Sir Charles Grandison,* and Laurence Sterne's *Tristram Shandy* appeared serially in the sense that they came out over a period of time in multiple volumes). The one exception and the first important English novel to be originally published as a magazine serial was Tobias Smollett's *The Life and Adventures of Sir Lancelot Greaves*, which appeared in the *British Magazine* in 1760 and 1761 in 25 installments, with illustrations. The novel was written expressly for serialization, each installment being comprised of a single chapter that was complete in itself. The completed novel was published in two volumes in 1762.

Smollett's serialized novel anticipates those of the Victorian period, but it seems to have made little impact at the time. Charlotte Lennox attempted a similar novel, *The Story of Harriot and Sophia,* in her *Lady's Museum* in 1760 and 1761, and it ran for 11 numbers. However, in the years that followed there were few other imitators and no serialized novels by significant writers. Various periodicals of the late 18th and early 19th centuries such as the *London Magazine* and the *Lady's Magazine* ran irregular fictional serials, but these were mostly amateur efforts by readers, often in imitation of Sterne or Richardson. Other more sensational periodicals such as *Marvellous Magazine and Compendium of Prodigies* (1802–04) ran Gothic serials formed by cribbing and abridging all the sensational events from novels such as Ann Radcliffe's *The Mysteries of Udolpho* or M.G. Lewis' *The Monk* and changing the names of the characters. The only novels of literary quality that were serialized at the time were those in the weekly *Novelist's Magazine* (1780–89) and similar publications, but these were all previously published novels that were out of copyright, including all those of Richardson, Fielding, Smollett, and Sterne, as well as European novels.

The first journal since Smollett's *British Magazine* to print serious fiction written expressly for serialization was *Blackwood's Edinburgh Monthly Magazine,* founded in 1817. Its first important serialized novel was John Galt's *The Ayrshire Legatees* in 1820 and 1821, which, according to the editor, "increased our sale prodigiously," and drew so much correspondence from readers that a separate section was set up to print the letters and Galt's answers. However, Galt's succeeding novels, published as books by Blackwood, were not serialized in the magazine, and throughout its first 20 years *Blackwood's* published serialized fiction only sporadically. Often the installments appeared at irregular intervals. The 18 installments of Samuel Warren's *Passages from the Diary of a Late Physician,* for instance, were published from 1830 to 1837.

The first magazine to specialize in high quality serialized novels published regularly was Frederick Marryat's *Metropolitan Magazine* in the 1830s, featuring his very popular navy fiction (much of *Blackwood's* fiction had been military), with four of his novels running between 1832 and 1837. Similarly, the *Dublin University Magazine* contained a serial from its first issue in 1833 and came to feature especially the picaresque military novels of Charles Lever, who served as the magazine's editor from 1842 to 1845. At the same time, *Fraser's Magazine* was moving more tentatively into serial fiction, mostly through the efforts of William Makepeace Thackeray, whose various satires and parodies were serialized from 1837, *The Luck of Barry Lyndon* of 1844 being the first that was unequivocally a complete novel. As the first editor of *Bentley's Miscellany*, Charles Dickens published Samuel Lover's irregularly serialized *Handy Andy* in the first issue, while his own *Oliver Twist* led off the second and ran until 1839, with Harrison Ainsworth's *Jack Sheppard* beginning before *Oliver Twist* ended. One of the magazine's rivals, the *New Monthly,* had been published since 1814 and had begun serializing novels by 1834, but it emphasized serialization much more after the initial success of *Oliver Twist,* running concurrent serials by Theodore Hook and Marryat in 1837. Through the 1840s it featured serials by Marryat, Mrs. Trollope, and Robert Surtees.

Oliver Twist was a great success, but Dickens already had had an even greater success with a different method of serialization with *The Posthumous Papers of the Pickwick Club.* The new publishing firm Chapman and Hall had approached him in 1836 to provide the texts for a series of sporting engravings by Robert Seymour, to be sold in monthly numbers for one shilling. The firm was modeling its project on the illustrated sporting and society sketches of Pierce Egan (which had appeared in part-issue in the 1820s) and Surtees and John Poole (which had been appearing as series in the *New Sporting Magazine* and the *New Monthly*), and perhaps on the recent reprinting in paper-covered part-issues of popular novels and stories by Edward Bulwer-Lytton, Marryat, and William Carleton. For *The Pickwick Papers,* the text was originally to be subordinate to the plates, but when Seymour committed suicide after the second number, Dickens took over as the dominant partner and Hablot K. Browne (Phiz) became his illustrator. Their partnership was to last several years. The series started slowly, with only 400 copies of the first number and 500 of the second, but it took off after Sam Weller came in with the fourth number. By the 15th number 40,000 copies were being printed and sold (as well as great quantities of the reprinted back numbers). A publishing phenomenon was born.

While *Oliver Twist* was still appearing in *Bentley's,* Dickens began a third novel, *The Life and Adventures of Nicholas Nickleby,* in 20 one-shilling numbers. Sales for *Nicholas Nickleby* reached 50,000 per part. Thus Dickens took part at the beginning of both of the major Victorian modes of serial publication, the magazine serial and the separate part-issue series. He attempted to combine the two methods with his next novel, *The Old Curiosity Shop,* as it appeared in his new weekly magazine, *Master Humphrey's Clock.* This novel began in the 12th issue and soon the "magazine" consisted primarily or even exclusively of the novel (1840–41), as was the case with Dickens' following novel, *Barnaby Rudge* (1841). At that point Dickens quit the "magazine" and returned to issuing his full-length novels in 20 numbered parts with *The Life and Adventures of Martin Chuzzlewit* (1843–44) and *Dealings with the Firm of Dombey and Son* (1846–48).

The part-issue method received another boost with Thackeray's first great success, *Vanity Fair: Pen and Pencil Sketches of English Society,* which appeared in 20 separate numbers (with illustrations by the author) in 1847 and 1848. His *History of Pendennis* (1848–50) ran almost in tandem with Dickens' *The Personal History and Experience of David Copperfield the Younger* (1849–50), both being published by Bradbury and Evans. Dickens continued to employ this method with *Bleak House* (1852–53), *Little Dorrit* (1855–57), and *Our Mutual Friend* (1864–65). Thackeray published *The Newcomes* (1853–55) and *The Virginians* (1857–59) in separate part-issue. By the 1860s this method of publication was used less frequently, but Anthony Trollope still used it for five of his novels between 1861 and 1875 (two of those being in 32 weekly parts) and issued *The Prime Minister* in 8 monthly numbers of 120 pages each in 1875 and 1876. With that last novel, Trollope probably followed the example of George Eliot, who had used an ingenious variation on part-issue publication with *Middlemarch* in 1871 and 1872, publishing it in eight separate books at bi-monthly (and later monthly) intervals. Eliot went on to use the same method with her last novel, *Daniel Deronda,* in 1876. William Black's *Sunrise* in 1880 was probably the last novel to appear in part-issue.

The decline of part-issue publication was caused by revolutionary changes in the magazine world. First, in the 1850s, came Dickens' two-penny weekly periodicals, *Household Words* (1850–59) and *All the Year Round* (1859–70), which were designed to provide a middle-class alternative to the popular one-penny papers such as *Reynolds' Miscellany* and *Lloyd's Penny Weekly Miscellany,* which had been presenting serialized popular fiction to the masses since the 1830s. *Household Words* featured short fiction more than novels, but it did include Elizabeth Gaskell's episodic *Cranford* (1851–53) and her *North and South* (1854–55) and *My Lady Ludlow* (1858), Dickens' *Hard Times* (1854), and Wilkie Collins' *A Rogue's Life* (1856) and *The Dead Secret* (1857). In *All the Year Round,* Dickens shifted the emphasis to serialized novels, probably in recognition of developments in other magazines. Throughout his editorship there was always at least one serial running. To get the new periodical off to a flying start, Dickens published his own *A Tale of Two Cities*

(1859). He followed it with Collins' *The Woman in White* (1859–60), one of the great popular successes of the age. He had hoped to follow that with a new novel by George Eliot, but when she refused he turned to Lever, whose *A Day's Ride: A Life's Romance* was a relative failure. When circulation dropped, Dickens came back with his own *Great Expectations* (1860–61), which he had originally hoped to publish separately in part-issue. Other novelists he published in the 1860s included Collins (his *Moonstone* in 1868 was notable), Charles Reade, and Gaskell. In North America, *Harper's Weekly* started up in 1850. It always ran a serialized novel and even used some of the same novels (including some by Dickens, Collins, and Gaskell), although it had more political content and was, famously, illustrated. It had the largest circulation of any "quality" periodical of the times. From 1867 it was complemented by the weekly *Harper's Bazar,* aimed at the women's market, which also ran serials.

Even more important for serialized fiction than the rise of the weeklies was the appearance of the new mass-circulation monthlies at one shilling per issue. The older monthlies such as *Bentley's* and *Fraser's* had been priced at two shillings, sixpence, but lower printing costs, a larger audience, and the willingness of book publishers to subsidize their house magazines as advertising for their books brought prices down. The two central monthlies were *Macmillan's Magazine,* founded 1859, and Smith, Elder's *Cornhill,* founded 1860 and first edited by Thackeray. These were complemented by a large group of imitators including *Belgravia* (1866, edited by the sensation novelist M.E. Braddon), *Temple Bar* (1860), *The Argosy* (1865, edited by the sentimental novelist Mrs. Henry Wood), *St. James* (1861), *Tinsley's,* and *St. Pauls* (1867, edited by Trollope). In America a little earlier, *Harper's Monthly* (1850) and the *Atlantic Monthly* (1857) appeared, with *Lippincott's* entering on the scene in 1868 and *Scribner's Monthly* in 1870 (becoming the *Century Illustrated Monthly* in 1881). These magazines usually offered their readers an illustrated monthly serial similar in quantity and quality to separately published part-numbers plus a rich diet of nonfiction and poetry by the leading writers of the age. To the writer, they could offer huge fees, such as the unprecedented £10,000 that Smith, Elder offered George Eliot for a new novel to be serialized in *Cornhill.* (The novel was *Romola,* which appeared in 1862 and disappointed readers who wanted another *Adam Bede*). Until the 1890s the monthlies dominated serial publication.

For novelists who had already begun publication in other modes, the monthlies provided new outlets. Anthony Trollope had already published nine novels between 1847 and 1859, none very popular or remunerative. Invited to offer the first full-length serial for *Cornhill* (to complement Thackeray's own briefer *Lovel the Widower*), Trollope obliged with *Framley Parsonage* (1860–61), which was a great popular success. He followed it up with three other serials in the magazine over the next six years, the most notable being *The Small House at Allington* (1862–64). Although at about the same time Trollope also began utilizing part-issue publication, magazine serialization became his main mode of initial publication, and over the following 20 years he supplied the initial serial novel for the *Fortnightly Review* (*The Belton Estate,* 1865–66), appeared there twice more, started off his own *St. Pauls* with *Phineas Finn* (1867–68), appeared in *Blackwood's* three times, and *Good Words,* the *Graphic,* and *All the Year Round* twice each, and once each in *Macmillan's, Temple Bar,* and the *Whitehall Review.*

In the 1860s and 1870s, then, there were numerous possibilities for serial publication in the monthly magazines. The older journals had continued to run serials. *Blackwood's* had especially featured Bulwer-Lytton and Margaret Oliphant, she becoming almost the "house novelist" and achieving special success with her "Chronicles of Carlingford" beginning with *Salem Chapel* in 1862–63, while George Eliot had begun there with *Scenes of Clerical Life* (1857). *Fraser's* had run Charles Kingsley's *Yeast* in 1848 and his *Hypatia* in 1852–53, but the magazine achieved its most popular success with G.J. Whyte-Melville's numerous novels. Meanwhile, Ainsworth published ten serials in *Bentley's* between 1855 and 1868. Lever and Joseph Sheridan Le Fanu dominated the *Dublin University Magazine.* Mrs. Henry Wood's *East Lynne* (1860–61) was the one great success in the otherwise undistinguished *New Monthly.* The newer monthlies in these years established themselves in a hierarchy with *Cornhill* at the top, featuring fiction by Thackeray, Trollope, Collins, Harriet Beecher Stowe, Eliot, and Thomas Hardy, among others. *Cornhill* was followed by *Macmillan's,* which opened with Thomas Hughes' *Tom Brown at Oxford* (1859–61) and enjoyed its greatest success with Kingsley's *The Water Babies* (1862–63). *St. Pauls* achieved quality only with Trollope and with Nathaniel Hawthorne's *Septimus: A Romance of Immortality* in 1872. The lower end of the scale, specializing in sensation novels and sentimental fiction, was served by *Tinsley's, Belgravia, Temple Bar,* and *Argosy. Temple Bar,* for example, occasionally rose to the heights of Trollope, and ran three serials by Collins, but mostly featured the likes of M.E. Braddon or Rhoda Broughton.

The division between "quality" monthlies and "popular" monthlies points to the increasing division between reading publics. No novelist in the future would have the breadth of Dickens' readership. A further sign of this division was the formation of Tillotson and Sons' Newspaper and Fiction Bureau in 1873, which supplied syndicated serials and short fiction to provincial weekly newspapers. Although they recruited such novelists as Collins, Reade, and later Thomas Hardy and H.G. Wells, they were looking for immediately appealing and uncontroversial fiction for a less literate audience than that of the great monthlies. By the end of the century, newspaper serials were a form well below the serious novel. Thus even as popular a novelist as Collins found in the 1880s, when he tried to place serials with provincial papers, that his novels were often found too difficult and "high class" for their readers. Always the literary businessman, Arnold Bennett made a clear distinction between the serious novels that he wrote for book publication and the potboilers he wrote as serials. He sold *For Love and Life,* an example of the latter, to Tillotson's in 1898 (it appeared in book form, much revised, in 1907 as *The Ghost: A Fantasia on Modern Themes*).

With the increased possibilities of magazine serialization in a diversifying market, the new novelists fit themselves into the system. The experience of Hardy shows something of the opportunities and difficulties. After publishing two unserialized novels, he was asked to provide a serial for *Tinsley's,* and supplied *A Pair of Blue Eyes* (1872–73). Meanwhile, his second novel, *Under the Greenwood Tree* (1872), had caught the eye of Leslie Stephen, editor of *Cornhill,* and he was invited to submit a plan for

a serial. His proposal for *Far from the Madding Crowd* was accepted and the novel was serialized in 1874 to critical acclaim. That success earned him the chance of another serial in *Cornhill,* but he was so anxious to show that he was not imitating George Eliot, as some of the reviewers had charged, that he tried a quite different kind of novel in *The Hand of Ethelberta* (1875–76) and failed. In consequence, both *Cornhill* and *Blackwood's* turned down his proposal for his next serial, *The Return of the Native.* That novel appeared in *Belgravia* "of all places," as Hardy said, in 1878. This fall to a lower level, however, was partly offset by simultaneous American serial publication in *Harper's New Monthly.* He attempted to interest *Cornhill, Macmillan's,* and *Blackwood's* in his next effort, *The Trumpet-Major,* but failed, and that novel ended up being published in a Scottish religious monthly, *Good Words* (1880). However, in that same year he received an invitation from Harper Brothers to write the initial serial for their new European edition of *Harper's New Monthly Magazine* and offered them *A Laodicean.* After finishing the first three installments, Hardy was struck with a very serious illness but bravely continued to supply copy on time for the rest of the serial (1880–81). Although it was not a critical success, Hardy nevertheless received an invitation for a new serial from the *Atlantic Monthly,* and *Two on a Tower* duly appeared there in 1882. Thomas Bailey Aldrich, the editor, was not happy with the more controversial aspects of the book, nor were the critics, and Hardy's next serial publications—*The Romantic Adventures of a Milkmaid* (1883) and *The Mayor of Casterbridge* (1886)—were published in the less prestigious illustrated weekly, the *Graphic* (but also in *Harper's Weekly* in America). He made it back to the prestigious monthlies when he placed *The Woodlanders* in *Macmillan's* in 1887, but there was again some trouble with the editor over that novel's sexual frankness, an issue that became even more problematic for Hardy with his next novel, *Tess of the d'Urbervilles.* Hardy orginally placed it with Tillotson to fulfill a contract for a serial, but they rejected it when they saw how controversial it would be, as did the editors of *Murray's* and *Macmillan's,* to whom Hardy next sent the manuscript. He had to recast and dismember the novel to make it suitable for serial publication in the *Graphic* and *Harper's Bazar* in 1891. He then responded to Tillotson's request for "something light" with *The Pursuit of the Well-Beloved,* and they arranged for the publication of it in another popular weekly, the *Illustrated London News,* and also *Harper's Bazar* in 1892 (it was thoroughly recast for publication as *The Well-Beloved* in 1897). Finally, when Harper and Brothers asked for a novel "in every respect suitable for a family magazine," he supplied *The Simpletons* (which became in the second number *Hearts Insurgent*) and once again had to cut and bowdlerize for serial publication, this time in *Harper's Monthly* (1894–95). Restored to its original form, it appeared in 1896 as *Jude the Obscure,* his last novel.

Other writers responded to serialization in other ways. George Meredith ran *Evan Harrington* in *Once A Week* (the successor to *Household Words*) in 1859 and *The Adventures of Harry Richmond* in *Cornhill* in 1870 and 1871. With his reputation as a "difficult" novelist, he appeared mostly in the *Fortnightly Review,* edited by his friend John Morley, which did not feature much fiction and catered to what it considered an enlightened liberal minority. In contrast, Henry James had no trouble at all placing his early novels in the best monthlies, getting *Watch and Ward* in the *Atlantic Monthly* in 1871 and following it there with *Roderick Hudson* in 1875 and *The American* in 1875 and 1876. He so succeeded on both sides of the Atlantic that *Washington Square* appeared simultaneously in *Cornhill* and *Harper's Monthly* (1880), while *The Portrait of a Lady* came out in *Macmillan's* and the *Atlantic Monthly* (1880–81). However, by the time of his more difficult later works all had changed: *The Awkward Age* appeared in *Harper's Weekly* (1898–99), but of the last four novels only *The Ambassadors* was serialized—in the *North American Review,* where it was the first novel that sober journal had published. James' friend William Dean Howells began publishing his work around the same time and found it relatively easy to place serials throughout his long career. He printed all his early novels in the *Atlantic Monthly* while he was editor (1871–81). His major novels of the 1880s, including *The Rise of Silas Lapham* (1885), appeared in the *Century,* while his fiction of the 1890s, including *A Hazard of New Fortunes* (1890), appeared in *Harper's Monthly,* of which he had become an editor. By the time Howells completed his last novels, the main Harper and Brothers journals no longer printed serials, but they placed *The Son of Royal Langbrith* in the *North American Review* in 1904 following *The Ambassadors.* His last novel, *The Leatherwood God,* was serialized in the *Century* in 1916.

Joseph Conrad's career coincided with a decline in the serialization of serious fiction. Conrad was anxious to have his novels published in magazines and did place *The Nigger of the Narcissus* (1897) in the *New Review* and "Heart of Darkness" (1899) and *Lord Jim* (1899–1900) in *Blackwood's.* But after that he had difficulties placing a novel in any large magazine. Harper and Brothers, after an initial interest, backed away from *Nostromo,* which eventually appeared in *T.P.'s Weekly* (1904). *Under Western Eyes* (1911) and *The Shadow-Line* (1916–17) appeared in his friend Ford Madox Ford's *English Review; The Secret Agent* (1907) appeared in *Ridgeway's,* which Conrad referred to as a "rag"; and *Chance* (1913) appeared in the *New York Herald.*

As the "serious" and "popular" reading publics pulled further apart, serialization in newspapers and magazines was becoming the mode of publication primarily for popular fiction. The survivors among the more serious, middlebrow magazines increasingly printed only short stories for their fiction component. Quite a few serious novels still appeared as serials in the 1890s but mostly in publications other than the famous monthlies. Under W.E. Henley's brief editorship, the *New Review* published not only *The Nigger of the Narcissus* but also H.G. Wells' *The Time Machine* (1895), James' *What Maisie Knew* (1897), and Arthur Morrison's *A Child of the Jago* (1895). *McClure's Magazine* in America, primarily a political journal, published novels by Kipling and Mrs. Humphry Ward among others, *Scribner's Magazine* published Robert Louis Stevenson's *The Master of Ballantrae* (1888–89) and *The Wrecker* (1891–92), *Cosmopolis* published Stevenson's *Weir of Hermiston* (1896), and *Lippincott's* published Oscar Wilde's *The Picture of Dorian Gray* (1890). But by 1900 the great days of serialization for serious novels were ending. Those novelists who did manage to continue magazine serialization of their work tended to straddle the popular/serious distinction. Jack London, for instance, placed his novels in a variety of periodicals: *The Call of the Wild* in the *Saturday Evening Post* (1903), *The Sea-Wolf* in the *Century* (1904), *White Fang* in *Outing* (1906), *Martin Eden* in the *Pacific*

Monthly (1908–09). Edith Wharton placed all of her early fiction in *Scribner's* and was a best-seller for that publishing house. Beginning with *The Age of Innocence* (1920), she placed her later novels in the slicker, more popular *Pictorial Review* and *Delineator.* Sinclair Lewis placed his lesser novels in such popular magazines as the *Woman's Home Companion, Collier's, Redbook,* the *Saturday Evening Post,* and *Cosmopolitan.*

Serialization of the more difficult serious novelists took place, if at all, in little magazines. With Ezra Pound's help, James Joyce's *A Portrait of the Artist as a Young Man* appeared in the little magazine the *Egoist* in 1914 and 1915. Similarly, parts of Joyce's *Ulysses* appeared in the *Egoist* in 1919 and, with censorship difficulties, in the *Little Review* from 1919 to 1920. Likewise, parts of his *Finnegans Wake* appeared in Ford's *Transatlantic Review* in 1924 as "Work in Progress." That same periodical in its one illustrious year also serialized Gertrude Stein's *The Making of Americans* and Ford's *Some Do Not.* Since 1930 little serious longer fiction has been serialized. There has been the occasional one-off effort, such as *Esquire's* serialization of Norman Mailer's *An American Dream* (1964), the *Atlantic Monthly's* serialization of Saul Bellow's *Mr. Sammler's Planet* (1969), and *Rolling Stone's* serialization of Tom Wolfe's *The Bonfire of the Vanities* (1987), but serialization has largely ceased to be the method of publication for anything but popular fiction.

At its peak during the Victorian period the method had a significant impact on novelists and their novels. Serialization affected writers' working methods. Most novelists began publication of a serial before they had finished writing it, and many cut or expanded their work in order to fit it into the requisite parts. Thackeray would make final cuts and additions up to a week before publication of each part, contracting or expanding his material to make it exactly 32 pages. Trollope, on the other hand, liked to complete his novels before serialization began, although he conceived of them as serials and mapped out what he thought would be the appropriate divisions into parts as he wrote. The dangers of starting serial publication before the manuscript was finished led to writers missing deadlines because of illness (Thackeray with *Pendennis* in 1849) or a death in the family (Dickens with *The Pickwick Papers* and *Oliver Twist* in 1837). At the time of their deaths, Dickens, Thackeray, and Gaskell all left serials unfinished during publication.

Serialization also affected the structure of novels. As Trollope observed, the need to catch readers' interest at the very beginning ruled out the leisurely expository opening such as Sir Walter Scott had used. The need to fill 20 numbers and yet maintain action and narrative interest in each number led to the interweaving of multiple plots and the use of a wide-ranging omniscient point of view, as in Dickens' *Our Mutual Friend* and Eliot's *Middlemarch.* The interweaving of plots made possible parallels and contrasts such as Eliot used so well in individual books of *Middlemarch,* and the kind of orchestration of emotional effects within a number that Dickens mastered. The shorter installments in the weeklies made for greater compression, as may be seen in *Hard Times* and *The Woman in White.* For both kinds of serials the writer needed to keep a forward momentum, often by creating suspense. Hardy in *A Pair of Blue Eyes* even went so far as to have a literal cliff-hanger, leaving Henry Knight clinging to a cliff face at the end of one number and then describing his rescue at the beginning of the next.

The serialization of novels also altered the relationship between novelists and their readers and editors. For readers, living with a novel for a year or more and trying to anticipate what would happen next could mean quite an intimate involvement with the text and its implied (and sometimes its actual) author. Dickens received many letters asking him not to let Little Nell die in *The Old Curiosity Shop*, and one of Hardy's readers wrote while *Far from the Madding Crowd* was running that "It is perhaps a taste of Purgatory to wait for the drop of cold water" of the next installment to find out what happens to Sergeant Troy and Bathsheba Everdene at one of the novel's climaxes. George Eliot commented that she was "enormously gratified" that serial publication allowed *Middlemarch* to "develop . . . on the minds of worthy readers by keeping the characters longer before them," although in general she did not like the pressures of serialization and refused offers to have *Adam Bede* and *The Mill on the Floss* serialized. For writers, this prolonged contact with the reader could develop almost into a personal relationship, as is evident in the addresses to the reader at the end of serials by Dickens and Thackeray. Fluctuations in sales figures, especially under the part-issue system, gave novelists feedback as to what succeeded and what did not, as did the comments in weekly journals such as the *Athenaeum,* which reviewed the parts or installments as they appeared. The reviewers of the part-issues of *Middlemarch*, for example, probably spoke for many readers in hoping for an eventual marriage between Dorothea Brooke and Dr. Lydgate (both reviewers and readers were disappointed when it did not happen).

Magazine serialization also put novelists in prolonged contact with editors, who could have significant effects, for good or ill, on the novel. For example, Leslie Stephen initially communicated to Hardy that although he did not "want a murder in every number" of *Far from the Madding Crowd,* he did want a "distinct and well arranged plot" that would "catch the attention of readers." Hardy, concerned to "be considered a good hand at a serial" and thus "willing, and indeed anxious, to give up any points which may be desirable in a story when read as a whole, for the sake of others which shall please those who read it in numbers," supplied such a plot to order, including a death in childbirth and a murder, and arranged the serial breaks for maximum suspense, even arranging the turning point of the novel—Bathsheba Everdene's marriage to Sergeant Troy—to take place off-stage and to be retrospectively narrated by her later as a means of keeping up suspense between installments. That death in childbirth, however, raised a different problem for Stephen, for he was concerned about the seduction and pregnancy of Fanny Robin, and asked that the first "be treated in a gingerly fashion" and that the second, and the resulting birth, be left as implicit as possible for the sake of a family audience. Thus was anticipated the kind of trouble that was to accompany the publishing of *Tess of the d'Urbervillles* and *Jude the Obscure.* Hardy was an extreme case, so bothered by the editorial censorship of his late novels that he said in 1890 that the price the novelist "has to pay for the privilege of writing in the English language" is "the complete extinction, in the mind of every mature and penetrating reader, of sympathetic belief in his personages" because of the restrictions put upon him. Many other novelists felt and resented similar editorial pressure. George Eliot was so upset at William Blackwood's criticism of the "coarser" elements in "Janet's Repentance" in *Scenes of Clerical Life* that she decided

to end the series at that point. James resisted Howells' editorial pressure to supply a happy ending for *The American,* while Dickens yielded to the advice of his colleague Bulwer-Lytton to provide a happy ending for *Great Expectations.* Dickens himself as editor pressured Gaskell to speed up the narrative pace of *North and South.*

The serialized novel at the height of its popularity, then, offered readers sustained and inexpensive access to the best fiction of the day. Serialization gave writers more opportunities for publication, a larger readership, and greater remuneration, but it also placed pressures and limits on them. The Victorian novel, with its ingenious multiple plots, often melodramatic action, usually happy endings, sometimes garrulous omniscient narrators, social inclusiveness, and sexual reticence, is intimately related to the serial mode of publication for which many of its greatest texts were written.

LAWRENCE JONES

See also Illustrations and Engravings; Roman-Feuilleton

Further Reading

Butt, John Everett, and Kathleen Mary Tillotson, *Dickens at Work,* London: Methuen, 1957; Fair Lawn, New Jersey: Essential Books, 1958

Chase, Mary Ellen, *Thomas Hardy from Serial to Novel,* Minneapolis: University of Minnesota Press, 1927

Coolidge, Archibald Cary, *Charles Dickens as Serial Novelist,* Ames: Iowa State University Press, 1967

Feltes, N.N., *Modes of Production of Victorian Novels,* Chicago: University of Chicago Press, 1986

Hamer, Mary, *Writing by Numbers: Trollope's Serial Fiction,* Cambridge and New York: Cambridge University Press, 1987

Harden, Edgar F., *The Emergence of Thackeray's Serial Fiction,* Athens: Univeristy of Georgia Press, and London: Prior, 1979

Hardy, Thomas, "Candour in English Fiction," in *Thomas Hardy's Personal Writings: Prefaces, Literary Opinions, Reminiscences,* edited by Harold Orel, New York: Macmillan, 1966; London and Melbourne: Macmillan, 1967

Hopkins, Annette B., "Dickens and Mrs Gaskell," *Huntington Library Quarterly* 9 (1946)

Hughes, Linda K., and Michael Lund, *The Victorian Serial,* Charlottesville: University Press of Virginia, 1991

Jones, Lawrence, "'A Good Hand at a Serial': Thomas Hardy and the Serialization of *Far from the Madding Crowd,*" *Studies in the Novel* 10 (1978)

Martin, Carol A., *George Eliot's Serial Fiction,* Columbus: Ohio State University Press, 1994

Mayo, Robert D., *The English Novel in the Magazines, 1740–1815,* Evanston, Illinois: Northwestern University Press, 1962

Patten, Robert L., *Charles Dickens and His Publishers,* Oxford: Clarendon Press, and New York: Oxford University Press, 1978

Pollard, Graham, "Serial Fiction," in *New Paths in Book Collecting,* edited by John Carter, London: Constable, and New York: Scribner, 1934

Shillingsburg, Peter L., *Pegasus in Harness: Victorian Publishing and W.M. Thackeray,* Charlottesville: University Press of Virginia, 1992

Sutherland, John, *Thackeray at Work,* London: Athlone Press, 1974

Sutherland, John, *Victorian Novelists and Publishers,* Chicago: University of Chicago Press, and London: Athlone Press, 1976

Sutherland, John, "Chips off the Block: Dickens's Serialising Imitators," in *Dickens and Other Victorians: Essays in Honour of Phillip Collins,* edited by Joanne Shattock, London: Macmillan, 1988

Tillotson, Kathleen Mary, *Novels of the Eighteen-Forties,* Oxford: Clarendon Press, 1954

Vann, J. Don, *Victorian Novels in Serial,* New York: Modern Langauge Association of America, 1985

Persian Novel. *See* Iranian Novel

Person in Narrative

In the nontechnical sense, "person" is often used as synonymous with "a character in a story world." In the technical sense, it designates the communicative position of the main character(s) of the narrated story with respect to the voice or individual who narrates it and who is always an "I." Following the theorist Monika Fludernik, we can say that the category of person depends directly on the construction of the dramatis personae and on the relation between story world and narrative communication. In other words, "person" refers to the relation between teller and told, the speaker and those spoken of, narrator and acting/experiencing individuals. Together with time (tense) and space, person forms one of the three major coordinates for locating the narrated relative to the act of narration.

There are first-, second-, and third-person singular narratives (I, you, s/he), "we" and "they" novels, and some experimental novels in the impersonal "one" mode. (It is not clear if any plural "you" novels exist). By far most novels, however, are written in the first- or second-person singular modes. Novels are primarily, but not exclusively, in one of the three persons. Almost all first-person novels include some "he" or "she" segments, and numerous third-person novels include the "I" as a minor or peripheral character. Third-person novels are heterodiegetic, that is, they tell "someone else's" story. The narrator may remain an anonymous voice, and the narratee, to whom the story is addressed, may remain unspecified. In first- and second-person novels, on the other hand, the teller and addressee positions respectively are of necessity textually marked, so that signs of narration and of the narrated are present. In second-person novels (you did such and such) the narrated individuals are simultaneously spoken of and to. First-person novels (I did such and such) are autodiegetic, telling the narrator's own story. The addressee may remain unspecified or may be a specific individual, including the speaker him- or herself.

In third-person novels, the narrator often has direct access to the minds of characters and can roam freely in time and space. If the voice remains anonymous, it is equated with the voice of truth as regards both information and judgments supplied. Third-person, past tense (preterite), omniscient narration by an anonymous voice has often been considered the prototype of fictional narration. In first-person novels, the "I" as narrator is always personalized to some degree. The only narrated individual (character) to whose mind such a narrator has direct access may be him- or herself, while other characters are seen from the outside. The teller of a first-person narrative can always be doubted as to the reliability or completeness of the information or judgments provided.

Second-person novels have become prominent in the last generation, and many of them are written in the present tense, synchronizing action with narration and address functions. Second-person narration is rather unnatural: why tell someone her own life story, of which she is presumably aware anyway? and how can a personalized narrator have access to the mind of another person? Depending on the specific text, several motivations may be offered. The narrator may wish to remind his addressee or make him aware of things he has forgotten, repressed, or been unaware of. Or there may really be a situation of self-address, the speaker being the alter ego of "you," the voice of conscience or self-consciousness, reviewing and judging the character's actions and experiences. The "you" form, especially when employing appeals, admonitions, or orders, may also be conducive to the actual reader assuming the role of the textual "you," so that she becomes the major actor in the unfolding game of make-believe. This is especially true when many of the "you" character's activities are concerned with reading.

"We" novels are rare and occupy an unstable position between first-person narratives and second- and third-person ones. The narrator is always a single individual making assertions about the identity, actions, and concerns of the "we" group to which he belongs. But he is not its spokesman, and therefore speaks about it, but not on its behalf. "We" narratives focus on the group's collective actions, its sense of solidarity, and self-image as a collective subject. But claims about the group's mental states may not apply to all its members and may combine uneasily the narrator's own immediate knowledge with inferences about other members. It is also difficult to sustain a narrative, even of external actions, entirely on the collective level, without describing individual members' distinct activities. At least one French novel, Monique Wittig's *L'Opoponax* (1964; *The Opoponax*), and the Swiss-German E.Y. Meyer's *In Trubschachen* are written throughout in the "on" and "man" pronouns respectively, roughly corresponding to the English "one," and, like it, initially unspecified for gender, number, and person (first, second, or third). These two texts end up referring to female and male singular characters respectively, complete with their mental life, but this pronominal usage has both a strong depersonalizing or distancing effect as well as a clear implication of general or generic validity, a "whoever" slot that allows for reader identification. One could even argue that the impersonal form of narration is the most elementary or basic position, a matrix from which all other forms are derived through different optional specifications.

In some first-person novels, the narrator refers to his narrated self, alternately or in different sections, as "he" or "she" or "you," in addition to the standard "I" reference. This usage is grammatically a "transferred or displaced person deixis," in which the textual speaker refers to himself by means of a personal pronoun that is inappropriate to the current speech situation. Such transfers, in which the speakers adopt the point of view of a specific or generalized other toward themselves, may be mimetically motivated to convey how others saw, thought, and talked about them at some point. Another motivation could be that the narrator speaks to and of himself as of another, implying an estrangement from some past phases of one's life as if they belonged to someone else, an inability to appropriate them as part of the narrator's current sense of self.

URI MARGOLIN

See also Character; Diegesis and Diegetic Levels of Narration; Discourse Representation; Narrator; Point of View; Tense in Narrative

Further Reading

Brooke-Rose, Christine, *A Rhetoric of the Unreal: Studies in Narrative and Structure, Especially of the Fantastic*, Cambridge and New York: Cambridge University Press, 1981

Duchan, Judith, Gail Bruder, and Lynne Hewitt, editors, *Deixis in Narrative: A Cognitive Science Perspective*, Hillsdale, New Jersey: Erlbaum, 1995

Fludernik, Monika, "Second-Person Narrative: A Bibliography," *Style* 28:4 (1994)

Fludernik, Monika, *Towards a "Natural" Narratology*, London and New York: Routledge, 1996 (see chapter 6)

Fludernik, Monika, editor, "Second-Person Narrative," *Style* 28:3 (1994)

Genette, Gérard, *Nouveau discours du récit*, Paris: Editions du Seuil, 1983; as *Narrative Discourse Revisited*, Ithaca, New York: Cornell University Press, 1988

Hamburger, Käte, *Die Logik der Dichtung*, Stuttgart: Klett, 1957; as *The Logic of Literature*, Bloomington: Indiana University Press, 1973; 2nd revised edition, 1993

Margolin, Uri, "Telling Our Story: On 'We' Literary Narratives," *Language and Literature* 5 (1996)

Romberg, Bertil, *Studies in the Narrative Technique of the First-Person Novel*, Stockholm: Almqvist and Wiksell, 1962

Stanzel, Franz Karl, *Die typischen Erzählsituationen im Roman*, Vienna: Braumüller, 1955; as *Narrative Situations in the Novel*, Bloomington: Indiana University Press, 1971

Stanzel, Franz Karl, *Theorie des Erzählens*, Göttingen: Vandenhoeck and Ruprecht, 1979; as *A Theory of Narrative*, Cambridge and New York: Cambridge University Press, 1984

Tamir, Nomi, "Personal Narration and Its Linguistic Foundation," *PTL* 1 (1976)

Persuasion by Jane Austen

1818

Jane Austen began *Persuasion* in 1815, although it was not published until 1818, when it appeared in a posthumous volume alongside a much earlier novel, *Northanger Abbey*. Originally entitled "The Elliots," *Persuasion* is the only one of Austen's completed novels to have been written after the Napoleonic Wars, or certainly after their end was in sight. This fact explains why the novel is different from Austen's earlier work, which remains within the idioms governing 18th-century fiction, particularly those deriving from epistolary narrative.

Persuasion provides a starting point for a discussion of the English 19th-century novel in a number of respects. Austen's use of

free indirect discourse highlights the consciousness of a single character and deemphasizes the objective perspective of an ironic omniscient narrator. This shift in emphasis marks an important departure from Austen's earlier fiction, in which the landed social world provides a sense of security, grounds the narrative voice, and provides a means of plot resolution. The tension between these perspectives gives *Persuasion* an atmosphere both of anxiety and freedom—a heightened emotional quality and a relativistic awareness of, and toleration for, what Anne Elliot, the novel's central character, calls the matters of discourse belonging to "other commonwealths." Peppered with realistic historical details, especially those concerning life in the Royal Navy, and permeated by the moral exhaustion and emotional isolation Anne experiences, *Persuasion* is generally seen as Austen's break from Augustan literary conventions and an anticipation of the more inwardly turned, emotionally unsettled, and socially realistic Victorian novel. In *Persuasion,* the individuation of character, the specificity of personal experience, and the representation of psychological interiority take on a new urgency. These elements are present in earlier novels but are not always loaded with the same social and structural significance. For that reason, many critics have followed F.R. Leavis in placing *Persuasion* at the beginning of the "great tradition" of technically complex and socially reflexive realist fiction.

The anxiety attendant on intellectual dislocation, the moral failure of authority, and the ethical fragmentation of traditional social structures are seen as the novel's peculiarly modern characteristics. *Persuasion*'s representation of time—for example, the pressing presence of the past—works in Wordsworthian fashion to strengthen the construction of Anne's interiority, but it operates on a structural plane as well. *Persuasion* begins with Sir Walter Elliot's poring over his favorite book, the Baronetage, where the marriages, births, and deaths of the aristocracy are recorded. The only time Austen represents the act of reading so self-consciously, the scene demonstrates that the Baronetage, as an institution and as a book, has fallen silent. There is, in this most literal sense, a failure of narration, emphasized by the aborted romance encapsulated in these first few pages: Anne might have married the young and ambitious hero, but that story too was repressed by a surrogate mother who persuaded Anne against connecting herself to a young naval officer whose capitalistic, self-made spirit had not yet received the professional rewards and communal approval that usher him back to Anne's neighborhood at the beginning of this afterword-like novel. The past and its failed narratives—the generational narrative of the Baronetage and the romantic narrative of Anne's memory—convey a sense of cultural crisis on the one hand, but on the other allow prior submerged narratives of the past to find new forms of representation.

What is most remarkable about *Persuasion* when compared to Austen's other fiction and to the 18th-century novelistic tradition of Fielding and Richardson is that it concludes with a homeless heroine. Anne Elliot, like so many of Austen's other heroines, has little income and no family to receive her chosen mate properly. Unlike her predecessors, however, she has no home awaiting her post-nuptial arrival. In Austen's earlier fiction, property and the small community it encircles provide the individual heroine with an appropriate expression of herself, which in turn implies a faith that the self can be fulfilled in the socialized terms of a traditional landed community. Politically, this paradigm allows the moral values of the gentry to rejuvenate a morally exhausted aristocracy without abandoning the traditional social structure. Structurally, the plot reproduces a fairy tale as a comedic fable in which a deserving subject errs, learns, and is rewarded by finding her personal desires socially and morally sanctioned after all.

By replacing the landed estate with the community of sailors to which the hero, Wentworth, belongs, *Persuasion* marks a radical departure from the earlier paradigm. The novel has to work harder to maintain the comedic structure, to make the self-society "fit" credible, which contributes to making it such an important transitional novel. Of particular importance in this respect is the scene in which Anne visits Lyme and admires the warm companionship of Wentworth's brother officers; the cozy and ingeniously equipped boarding house they inhabit; and the free and easy manner in which naval wives converse with their husbands and friends, intelligently, reasonably, and confidently. The seascape home in Lyme impresses by virtue of its ingenious contrivances and affectionate company rather than generational continuity and historical order, and an entirely new vocabulary emerges as central in English narrative. In this sense, the courtship plot is deflected from a social hierarchy organized around landed property and toward one centered on ingenuity. The repudiation of land as property in favor of some intellectual equivalent is established early on when Anne, however admiring of her sister's family, the happy Musgroves at Uppercross, is saved from envying them by not wanting to surrender "her own more elegant and cultivated mind." For Anne Elliot, there really are no rejuvenating possibilities associated with the traditionally landed and conventionally moneyed classes. Their moral bankruptcy is profound. Indeed, the failure of the subplot concerning the fate of the Elliot estate—which forces Anne to relinquish the possibility of keeping her rank, her home, and even her name—is often viewed as inept and cursory, but it exemplifies the process of reinvention at work. By the end of the novel, "mind" has surfaced as the only desirable property and ingenuity as an ascendant value. Politically, this shift implies a radically new view of the aristocracy and conveys a more tolerant attitude toward the "modern" values associated with an increasingly influential professional class. Formally, the shift in cultural values from land to mind resonates in the expansion of the novelistic space devoted to the representation of individual interiority.

The difficulties of representing interiority emerge through an exploration of *Persuasion*'s two endings: the original chapter in which a chance encounter and an accidental verbal slip force Wentworth and Anne to confess their love, and the two replacement chapters in which Wentworth eavesdrops on Anne and Harville's discussion of the cultural construction of sexual difference. Here Harville argues that the constant leave-takings and homecoming that characterize a man's extradomestic work life should make his love more constant. Anne, knowing that Wentworth is listening, argues that the immobility of a woman's anchored life makes her love not only more constant but more unhappy—constant even when constancy no longer applies. Constancy and persuadability, the twin focus of the novel, place it in the context of 1790s feminist writing, conservative fiction, and conduct literature. The plot of romantic commitment among the young, particularly young women, and the generational strife that it could engender is thought to have emerged at this time because it pitted revolutionary and romantic ideas of autonomy and Godwinian individualism against the generational continuity and traditional authority of parents. When Wentworth enters the novel in search of a woman who is both sweet and firm, he broaches the question central to novels popular during the period: should a woman obey the authority of tradition or that of her own mind? Austen makes it clear in *Persuasion* that the question is important not only because it concerns the cultural condition of women but because it concerns the nature of authority and obedience generally. Although Austen is unrelenting in demonstrating the failure of traditional authority by stripping the novel's parents and aristocrats of all redeeming qualities, she refuses to sanction rebellion. Anne never says that she had been wrong to obey Lady Russell. Obedience continues to have value even when authority has forfeited its right to it. The characteristic way in which Austen conjures dichotomies and resolves their implied contradictions takes *Persuasion* beyond the Johnsonian tidiness of its predecessors and opens a portal to Victorian fiction.

MONICA F. COHEN

See also Jane Austen

Further Reading

Auerbach, Nina, *Romantic Imprisonment: Women and Other Glorified Outcasts,* New York: Columbia University Press, 1986

Brown, Julia Prewitt, *Jane Austen's Novels: Social Change and Literary Form,* Cambridge, Massachusetts: Harvard University Press, 1979

Butler, Marilyn, *Jane Austen and the War of Ideas,* Oxford: Clarendon Press, 1975; New York: Oxford University Press, 1987

Johnson, Claudia L., *Jane Austen: Women, Politics, and the Novel,* Chicago: University of Chicago Press, 1988

Kelly, Gary, *Women, Writing, and Revolution, 1790–1827,* Oxford: Clarendon Press, and New York: Oxford University Press, 1993

Poovey, Mary, *The Proper Lady and the Woman Writer: Ideology as Style in the Works of Mary Wollstonecraft, Mary Shelley, and Jane Austen,* Chicago: University of Chicago Press, 1984

Roberts, Warren E., *Jane Austen and the French Revolution,* London: Macmillan, and New York: St. Martin's Press, 1979

Tanner, Tony, *Jane Austen,* London: Macmillan, and Cambridge, Massachusetts: Harvard University Press, 1986

Peruvian Novel. *See* Latin American Novel: Peru

Petersburg by Andrei Belyi

Peterburg 1916/1922

At the beginning of the 20th century, Russian literature enjoyed a renewal led by poets and dramatists. Groups with names like "Symbolists," "Futurists," and "Acmeists" developed new techniques and proposed new principles of art with astonishing rapidity. While these artists hardly agreed on a single method or goal for literary creation, they generally concurred in demanding a rethinking of the nature of art, perception, and tradition. Andrei Belyi's *Petersburg* was the first novel to register this cry successfully.

Born in 1880, Boris Bugaev began publishing poetry under the pseudonym "Andrei Belyi" ("Andrew White") in 1902. Around the same time he carried out a series of innovations he called four "symphonies" in prose. Although he did not repeat this radical experiment, Belyi nonetheless remained syncretic all his life and strove to make his prose poetic, philosophical, musical, and picturesque. In 1909 he wrote his first novel, *Serebrianyi golub'* (*The Silver Dove*), which was published in 1910. It was to be the first installment of a trilogy entitled "Vostok ili zapad" (East or West?). The second metamorphosed into *Petersburg,* which remains by common consent the pinnacle of Belyi's artistic career. He continued to produce poetry, several more novels, and mountains of critical and theoretical writings.

The textual history of *Petersburg* is itself a long and crooked tale. In 1911, P.B. Struve rejected the novel for publication in the journal *Russian Thought*. K.F. Nekrasov of Yaroslavl then published a few chapters, and Belyi continued to work on the novel while traveling in Russia and Europe. The rights were transferred to the almanac *Sirin,* which published the first full edition, in three parts, in 1913 and 1914, and then in book form in 1916. Dissatisfied almost immediately, Belyi began a series of revisions (mostly subtractions), leaving the text shorter by a full one-third. The final result was published in Berlin by *Epokha* in 1922 when Belyi was living in that city; an earlier version served as the basis for a German translation in 1919. A Soviet edition followed in 1928, faithful to the 1922 version save the excision of much religious and mystical imagery and a few other miscellaneous changes. The 1916 (1913–14) and 1922 versions are considered canonical, with dispute simmering as to which is superior or otherwise preferable.

Set in 1905, when revolution spread throughout Russia and threatened to demolish the social order, the novel revolves around a reactionary senator and his son, who has agreed to carry out a political assassination, the target being his own father. Subplots and themes abound; indeed, the novel is virtually an encyclopedia of the history of Russian literature. The conception of the city of St. Petersburg as grandiose, artificial, and unhealthy comes from Aleksandr Pushkin's long poem *Mednyi vsadnik* (1841; *The Bronze Horseman*) and from much of the work of Nikolai Gogol' and Fedor Dostoevskii. Intergenerational conflict had been a staple of Russian fiction at least since Ivan Turgenev's *Ottsy i deti* (1862; *Fathers and Sons*); revolutionary terror since Dostoevskii's *Besy* (1872; *Devils*); and the vacillating, indecisive "superfluous man" since Aleksandr Griboedov's play *Gore ot uma* (1825; *Woe from Wit*), Pushkin's novel in verse *Evgenii Onegin* (1831; *Eugene Onegin*), and Mikhail Lermontov's novel *Geroi nashego vremeni* (1840; *A Hero of Our Time*). With these and other themes, as well as borrowed motifs and quoted passages, the novel emphasizes its debt to tradition.

Yet *Petersburg* is also emphatically of its own time. In its themes of mysticism, masks, apocalyptic rebirth, and Russia's unique position between East and West; in its hazy, gloomy, fantastical images of the city; and in its preoccupation with the thought of Friedrich Nietzsche, Nikolai Fedorov, and Vladimir Solov'ev, the novel rehearses elements that pervade the writings of Belyi and his fellow symbolists (Aleksandr Blok, Viacheslav Ivanov, Valerii Briusov, Konstantin Bal'mont, and others). And *Petersburg* alludes, at times transparently, to important political figures and issues of the early 20th century. Moreover, with its urban setting, its delight in synesthesia, and its encoded cultural history, the novel shares many of the themes of European modernism.

However, *Petersburg*'s historical significance—and to many minds its greatest achievement—lies not in its themes but in its form. Fragmentary, repetitive, quizzical, and downright contrary, the novel's style epitomizes what Belyi wants to say about St. Petersburg, about revolution, and about history and his position in it. Although the novel is self-consciously philosophical, its verbal behavior tends to devalue (even to sabotage) logic in favor of the heightened experience of images, of sounds, of emotions, of things. Belyi's most important stylistic debt is to Nikolai Gogol', a debt he later acknowledged in a book-length study devoted to the 19th-century writer. Gogol' perfected the techniques of personification and depersonification, metonymy and isolation, and

narrative earnestness and buffoonery that saturate *Petersburg*. Belyi recombines these elements and others into a composite style that communicates both Gogolian ridicule and deep sympathy, both the farce and the tragedy of human endeavors.

This new prose style, which came to be called "ornamentalism," dominated the Soviet prose of the early 1920s, in particular that of Isaak Babel', Boris Pil'niak, and Evgenii Zamiatin. The influence waned during the subsequent period of socialist realism, with the demand for clarity of exposition and the rejection of stylistic "decadence." The question of Belyi's—and more generally the "modernists'"—persisting influence has occasioned debates and hypotheses, but beyond serious question are the immediate historical impact and the enduring merits of *Petersburg*, the novelistic apotheosis of early 20th-century Russian literature.

Timothy Colin Langen

Further Reading

Alexandrov, Vladimir, *Andrei Bely: The Major Symbolist Fiction*, Cambridge, Massachusetts: Harvard University Press, 1985

Dolgopolov, L., *Andrey Bely i ego roman ÇPeterburgÈ*, Leningrad: Sovietskii Pisatel', 1988

Elsworth, J.D., *Andrey Bely: A Critical Study of the Novels*, Cambridge and New York: Cambridge University Press, 1983

Janecek, Gerald, editor, *Andrey Bely: A Critical Review*, Lexington: University Press of Kentucky, 1978

Malmstad, John E., editor, *Andrey Bely: Spirit of Symbolism*, Ithaca, New York: Cornell University Press, 1987

Mann, Robert, *Andrei Bely's "Petersburg" and the Cult of Dionysus*, Lawrence, Kansas: Coronado Press, 1986

Mochulskii, Konstantin, *Andrei Bely: His Life and Works*, Ann Arbor, Michigan: Ardis, 1977

Steinberg, Ada, *Word and Music in the Novels of Andrey Bely*, Cambridge and New York: Cambridge University Press, 1982

Woronzoff, Alexander, *Andrej Belyj's "Petersburg," James Joyce's "Ulysses," and the Symbolist Movement*, Bern: Lang, 1982

Philippines. *See* Southeast Asian Novel: Philippines

Philosophical Novel. *See* Conte Philosophique; Novel of Ideas

---

Picaresque

The picaresque has very precise cultural and historical roots, but it has mutated into a number of different literary forms during the past 400 years. In its original mode as a Spanish narrative of roguery, the picaresque follows the adventures of the *pícaro,* whose inclinations toward wayward living and moral proclivity position him in opposition to qualities of virtue and decency. A study of the genesis of the picaresque provides a way of understanding the transition between 16th-century pastoral romances and the development of the European novel in the 18th century. Written within and set against the backdrop of a society in transition from fixed feudal relationships to a more flexible social structure in which the middle classes began to have significant economic and moral influence, the picaresque foreshadows the novel, charting the rise of bourgeois individualism in its exploration of the tensions between oppressive societies and disaffected individuals. Since emerging as a distinct form of Spanish antipastoral narrative in the late 16th century, the picaresque has undergone a series of cultural, geographical, and historical displacements, from a dominant form of 18th-century narrative in England to a series of modernist reactions to the 19th-century European realist novel and, later, to forms of postmodern narrative that contribute to the structure and tone of much American postfrontier writing and postcolonial stories of cultural dislocation in the 20th century.

Most picaresque narratives form a series of loosely connected episodes or phases in the life of the *pícaro,* who usually relates his adventures retrospectively in the first person or whose encounters are recounted by a secondary figure who happens upon records of the *pícaro*'s life. Picaresques are often rambling and digressive as the *pícaro* relates his nomadic wandering through various communities, reveling in his own versatility and ingenuity in his attempts to deal with difficult and exacting encounters. There is some critical disagreement as to the essential qualities of the *pícaro*: generally he is thought to be either a delinquent figure who, although transgressing social and moral values, is essentially nonviolent, or he is seen as a character whose roguish tendencies are redeemed by a good heart and human compassion. There are enough versions of picaresque to defend either view of the *pícaro* as rebel or ultimate conformist, but most critics agree he is a prototype of the literary antihero, providing the author with a vehicle for ridiculing or exposing dominant social beliefs. In most cases, the picaresque forms a loose comic narrative, making use of caricature, burlesque, and satire in order to attack dogma, hypocrisy, and high seriousness. The satirical strain of the picaresque is especially evident in the often digressive and meandering nature of its narrative, a characteristic that reflects the meaning of the Latin term *satira*: a mixture, or hodge-podge. Indeed, although generic similarities can be discerned in all its historical manifestations, the picaresque is far from a pure narrative form or one that adheres to a strict literary agenda. The mutability of the picaresque has much to do with its intrinsic hybridity as a result of a variety of different cultural and social pressures.

The picaresque narrative emerged in Spain for various and complex reasons. Some critics claim it reflected a country in economic and moral decline, which bred the kind of delinquency epitomized by the character of the *pícaro,* whereas Alexander Parker (1967) claims that Spain was in no worse economic state than other countries. For example, the social conditions of Elizabethan England were reflected in Thomas Nashe's episodic romance narrative *The Unfortunate Traveller* (1594), although there is evidence to support the argument that Nashe was influenced by early Spanish picaresques. For Parker, the Spanish picaresque picks up on the spirit of the Counter-Reformation in its religious and moral reaction to the exceptional and virtuous hero of the chivalric romance, a dominant literary form in Europe, and especially Italy, in the 16th century. The picaresque was deemed to be more truthful than the idealistic romance for two main reasons: first, the picaresque does not offer a mythical or allegorical pattern that would provide ultimate meaning to the chance encounters and random events of the *pícaro*'s life, and second, unlike the ennobled figure of the romance, the *pícaro* is depicted as being more sinner than saint; his contempt for the world often leads to his being outcast from society into a misanthropic state of cynicism. As such, the picaresque blends elements of romance with moral commentary and a realistic treatment of social issues and values.

An anonymous Spanish work published in 1554 entitled *La vida de Lazarillo de Tormes* is commonly thought to be the most important precursor to the picaresque tradition. On the surface the narrative relates the passage of a boy Lázaro from inauspicious family beginnings to a skillful and wily negotiator of social values, ending his life as the successful town crier of Toledo. However, the story really serves to comment critically on the prevalent codes of selfishness and hypocrisy that Lázaro has to learn and appropriate in order to succeed in the world. Although *Lazarillo de Tormes* reflects various aspects of the picaresque, it was not until the publication of *Primera parte de la vida del pícaro Guzmán de Alfarache* (1600) and *Segunda parte de la vida del pícaro Guzman de Alfarache* (1604) by the Spanish writer Mateo Alemán that the picaresque came to fruition as an identifiable mode of writing. *Guzmán de Alfarache* is framed as an autobiographical sketch in which the eponymous protagonist from Seville reveals his own complex psychology in his moralizing reflections on and adventures through and beyond lower-class life in Spain. The narrative is similar to *Lazarillo de Tormes* in the respect that Guzmán becomes skilled in the arts of deception and exploitation in order to advance his own material interests, but Alemán's narrative also deals with more obvious aspects of criminality and social transgression. In a convoluted tale in which the protagonist is given a number of chances to reform, Guzmán is eventually exposed as a sham saint and sentenced to spend life as a galley slave, at which point he undergoes a conversion experience. Again, the real point of the narrative is to provide an entertaining but nevertheless satirical commentary on prevailing social values. Although the picaresque often deals with religious hypocrisy, it is usually a very secular mode of writing in which the protagonist is forever complicit in the way of the world, a world from which he is unable to escape into an idealized realm of virtue.

Some critics consider Miguel de Cervantes' *Don Quixote,* published in two parts in 1605 and 1615 and often referred to as the first European novel, to be a picaresque narrative. However, although *Don Quixote* conforms to an episodic and digressive pattern, it is firmly rooted in the mode of pastoral romance against which the Spanish picaresque reacted. The eponymous hero is deluded by excessive reading of chivalric tales and undergoes a series of bizarre and disconnected adventures, but unlike the *pícaro* he maintains his dignity and innocence throughout the narrative. However, *Don Quixote* does share with the picaresque a critique of chivalric idealism and a number of implicit attacks on materialism, the Catholic Church, and Spanish politics. Better examples of picaresque tales are to be found in Cervantes' collection *Novelas Ejemplares* (1613; *Exemplary Novels*), a series of 12 short narratives varying in content, two of which—"Rinconete y Cortadillo" and "El coloquio de los perros"—typify the picaresque. Despite the uncertain position *Don Quixote* occupies in the development of the Spanish picaresque, its numerous translations were partly responsible for influencing the growth of the genre in Western Europe in the 17th and 18th centuries, particularly in the work of the French writers Charles Sorel (*Histoire Comique de Francion,* 1623) and Alain René Lesage (*Histoire de Gil Blas de Santillane,* 1715). *Lazarillo de Tormes* and *Guzmán de Alfarache* were also translated widely in the 17th century in England, France, and Germany, but were usually loosely adapted to fit in with particular cultural trends and tastes.

The most famous British exponents of the picaresque novel are Daniel Defoe, Henry Fielding, and Tobias Smollett, who, between them, covered much of the same ground as the Spanish writers fused with contemporary issues pertaining to the rise of the middle-class consciousness in 18th-century England and Scotland. Defoe's early novel *Robinson Crusoe* (1719) weaves an episodic adventure narrative on the Puritan model of John Bunyan's *The Pilgrim's Progress* (1678, 1684). However, whereas Bunyan's exemplary tale is purely allegorical, Defoe's story is discursive and opens the way for a number of subsequent narratives that are more obviously written in the picaresque mode. For example, Defoe's novel *Moll Flanders* (1722) follows the adventures of his eponymous protagonist (although this is an assumed name), whose wayward life as opportunist, thief, and prostitute provides a means of commenting on the growth of self-interest in 18th-century English society. The story of Moll Flanders begins in London's Newgate prison and follows the twists and turns of a life that fluctuates between the promise of material success and the harshness of failure. Like *Robinson Crusoe,* Defoe's picaresque narrative explores issues of sinfulness and providence in order to explore prevailing metaphysical assumptions and the social realities of the period. Although the erosion of Moll's moral character corresponds to the Christian idea of sin, some critics argue that the reader is encouraged to respond favorably to her duplicity, vitality, and exuberance as she revels in her depraved state. Similarly, despite Defoe's prefatorial comment that the tale should have "vertuous and religious uses," its pseudo-autobiographical nature blurs the boundaries between Moll's self-image and the moral values by which she is judged. Consequently, it is possible to read the ending of *Moll Flanders,* when she is sent once more to Newgate, either as a genuine or an ironic moment of repentance as she and her criminal husband "resolve to spend the Remainder of our Years in sincere Penitence, for the wicked Lives we have lived."

Although Fielding's *Jonathan Wild* (1743) and *The History of Tom Jones* (1749) both display picaresque elements in their episodic plots and the morally dubious activities of their respective protagonists, Smollett's first two novels—*The Adventures of Roderick Random* (1748) and *The Adventures of Peregrine Pickle* (1751)—provide better examples of the British picaresque. Like the Spanish writers, Smollett sets up his satirical antiromances in opposition to the romance tradition, which he claims "owes its origin to ignorance, vanity and superstition." *Roderick Random* was self-consciously modeled on *Gil Blas,* but whereas Lesage's protagonist was a rogue who Smollett claims excites the reader's "mirth," his hero represents "modest merit" in the hope of evoking "compassion" in the reader. Accordingly, as with his later writing such as *The Adventures of Ferdinand Count Fathom* (1953) and *The Life and Adventures of Sir Launcelot Greaves* (1762), Smollett creates relatively innocent characters who remain untarnished by the evils of the world and yet still manage to succeed in it. Roderick Random is a Scottish orphan, blessed nevertheless with the "advantages of birth and education," who eventually discovers his nobility when he finds his long lost father in South America and finally returns to the British Isles to reclaim the family estate. Similarly, although Peregrine Pickle is more of a rogue than his fictional predecessor, after wasting a fortune and imprisonment he inherits again and, like Roderick Random, ends the tale prosperous and happily married.

While picaresque conventions appear in the 19th century, notably in Dickens' *Pickwick Papers* (1837), the next significant emergence of the picaresque in European literature occurs as a minor strain in modernist literature. The widespread reaction against the 19th-century realist novel stimulated some modernist writers to adopt experimental modes of composition that deliberately flouted the upward and prospective form of the bourgeois narrative, the early signs of which are evident in the 18th-century novel. The growth of the modern technological world created the material conditions for the erosion of traditional European art forms; some writers adopted impressionistic, fragmented, and chaotic modes of description while others chose to adopt the picaresque for their own ends. One of the most interesting cultural manifestations of the modernist picaresque arose in Germanic writing. The Czech writer Franz Kafka in *Amerika* (1927; *America*), the Austrian Robert Musil in *Der Mann ohne Eigenschaften* (1930–43; *The Man Without Qualities*), and the German Thomas Mann in *Bekenntnisse des Hochstaplers Felix Krull* (1953; *Confessions of Felix Krull, Confidence Man*) all subvert the idealistic tradition of self-cultivation and personal development of the German Bildungsroman, the chief example of which was Johann Wolfgang von Goethe's *Wilhelm Meister's Lehrjahre* (1795–1821; *Wilhelm Meister's Apprenticeship*). Like 18th-century English novelists, these modernist writers loosely adapted the picaresque to their own literary ends: all the narratives are episodic and discursive, and the characters range from an innocent abroad (Kafka's Karl Rossmann), a morally suspect antihero (Musil's Ulrich), and a master of deception (Mann's Felix Krull). It is significant in the light of more recent trends in picaresque writing that each of these writers appropriates the picaresque to deal with issues of cultural displacement: Kafka and Musil worked on the borders of the German tradition, and Mann spent 20 years in Switzerland and America as a German exile.

Other examples of modernist modification of the picaresque can be discerned in the meandering narrative structure of James Joyce's *Ulysses* (1922), Samuel Beckett's novels *Watt* (1953) and

Molloy (1951), which deal with the devastated landscapes in the aftermath of war, and Albert Camus' existentialist work *L'Étranger* (1942; *The Stranger*). A purer example of the modernist picaresque is the Spanish novelist Camilo José Cela's ironic novel *La familia de Pascual Duarte* (1942; *The Family of Pascual Duarte*). This novel deals obliquely with the cataclysm of the Spanish Civil War, as the eponymous antihero relates his violent tale while awaiting execution for murder. Like Camus and Beckett, Cela deals with the nihilism stimulated by a chaotic and absurd world in which faith in divinity and humanity has entirely eroded.

There is also a strong tradition of the picaresque in American literature, which stems out of 19th-century frontier narratives. The frontier represented the westward line of advancement of American civilization in the 18th and 19th centuries and is a flexible topological term that describes various regions at particular historical junctures. American frontier narratives place special emphasis on the particular qualities of the landscape and the trials of the protagonist in forging an existence in the face of difficult and exacting circumstances. James Fenimore Cooper's quintet of novels The Leatherstocking Tales (1823–41) provide the most sustained treatment of the conflict between the natural and civilized worlds. However, unlike the European *picaro*, the central character of the tales, Natty Bumppo, epitomizes the moral codes of native Americans and the virtues of nature as opposed to the exploitation of white settlers. Mark Twain's *The Adventures of Tom Sawyer* (1876) and *The Adventures of Huckleberry Finn* (1884) offer better examples of the devious and mischievous antihero common to European picaresques, but the descriptions of the landscape, racial unrest, and the variety of lifestyles that the protagonists encounter on their adventures all serve to make the American picaresque different in essence from the European model.

Although the American historian Frederick Jackson Turner's essay "The Significance of the Frontier in American History" (1893) marked the closing of the frontier in 1890 and thus the completion of westward expansion, as Philip Melling (1985) argues, the depictions of the rootless *picaro* survived the passing of the frontier into the 20th century. For example, the character of Tom Joad in John Steinbeck's novel *The Grapes of Wrath* (1939), dealing with the Great Depression in the 1930s, embodies what Melling describes as a complex mixture of "attractive criminality, destitution and rebellious poeticism." Other manifestations of the post-frontier picaresque in American literature are evident in 1950s Beat writing, the most famous example of which is *On the Road* (1957) by the Canadian-born writer Jack Kerouac; novels dealing with the consequences of the Civil War for Southern writers, such as Flannery O'Connor's *Wise Blood* (1952); and Jewish-American narratives that explore conflicting cultural expectations, moral hardships, and the possibilities of personal renewal, important examples of which are Nathanael West's *A Cool Million* (1934), Saul Bellow's *The Adventures of Augie March* (1953), and Bernard Malamud's *The Assistant* (1957).

The postmodern picaresque moves even farther away from its Spanish roots and is often assimilated into a pastiche of other literary forms. The two American writers who have been most influential in reinventing the picaresque in postmodern guise are John Barth, who, in *The Sot-Weed Factor* (1960), adopts a variety of 18th-century literary conventions in order to reassess the

history of American colonization, and Thomas Pynchon, whose epic novel *Gravity's Rainbow* (1973) explores the aftermath of war and the conspiratorial myths prevalent in American society. The European novel of displacement emerged from the ashes of World War II in, for example, Günter Grass' groundbreaking novel *Die Blechtrommel* (1959; *The Tin Drum*) and Heinrich Böll's *Ansichten eines Clowns* (1963; *The Clown*), and later became an identifiable element in novels of magic realism, such as the Italian writer Umberto Eco's discursive novel *L'isola del giorno prima* (1994; *The Island of the Day Before*). Other exponents of the postmodern picaresque have explored postcolonial issues of racial identity and hybridity by writing stories in which the protagonist cannot or will not wholly assimilate into the culture in which he finds himself. Although the chief elements of the traditional picaresque cannot always be identified, novels such as Salman Rushdie's *Midnight's Children* (1980) and Bharati Mukherjee's *Jasmine* (1989) both depict the vitality, daring, and shrewdness of the *picaro* within episodic narrative forms.

MARTIN HALLIWELL

See also Miguel de Cervantes; Comedy and Humor in the Novel; English Novel (18th Century); Lazarillo de Tormes; Prose Novelistic Forms; Romance; Spanish Novel

Further Reading

Alter, Robert, *Rogue's Progress: Studies in the Picaresque Novel,* Cambridge, Massachusetts: Harvard University Press, 1964

Bjornson, Richard, *The Picaresque Hero in European Fiction,* Madison: University of Wisconsin Press, 1977

Brennan, Timothy, *Salman Rushdie and the Third World: Myths of the Nation,* London: Macmillan, and New York: St. Martin's Press, 1989

Galloway, David D., *The Absurd Hero in American Fiction: Updike, Styron, Bellow, Salinger,* 2nd revised edition, Austin: University of Texas Press, 1981

Harris, Charles, *Passionate Virtuosity: The Fiction of John Barth,* Urbana: University of Illinois Press, 1983

Melling, Philip H., "Samples of Horizon: Picaresque Patterns in the Thirties," in *Nothing Else to Fear: New Perspectives on America in the Thirties,* edited by Stephen W. Baskerville and Ralph Willett, Manchester and Dover, New Hampshire: Manchester University Press, 1985

Miller, Stuart, *The Picaresque Novel,* Cleveland, Ohio: Press of Case Western Reserve University, 1967

Monteser, Frederick, *The Picaresque Element in Western Literature,* University: University of Alabama Press, 1975

Parker, Alexander Augustine, *Literature and the Delinquent: The Picaresque Novel in Spain and Europe,* Edinburgh: Edinburgh University Press, 1967

Rousseau, G.S., and Paul-Gabriel Bouce, editors, *Tobias Smollett: Bicentennial Essays Presented to Lewis M. Knapp,* New York: Oxford University Press, 1971

Sieber, Harry, *The Picaresque,* London: Methuen, 1977

Smith, Stan, *A Sadly Contracted Hero: The Comic Self in Post-War American Fiction,* British Association for American Studies, 1981

The Pickwick Papers by Charles Dickens

1837

The Posthumous Papers of the Pickwick Club, to give this work its full title, not only launched the career of the greatest Victorian novelist but also set a fashion for serialized fiction that persisted until the end of the century. The novel originated almost by accident: in late 1835 a well-known illustrator named Robert Seymour planned a series of sketches for monthly publication, to be based on the well-tried formula of the adventures of a London sporting club. In February 1836, Dickens, just 24 and relatively unknown, was invited to write the text to accompany these illustrations. With amazing self-confidence, he proposed that the roles of artist and writer be reversed and the pictures subordinated to the text. Seymour's suicide in April, followed by the appointment of an artist, H.K. Browne, even younger than Dickens, further strengthened Dickens' control over the project. He wrote very rapidly, and the first of 19 monthly installments appeared in April 1836. The serial continued until November 1837, in which month the work also appeared in volume form. Since Victoria had become queen in June of that year, *The Pickwick Papers* may claim to be the first great Victorian novel and for generations remained in some respects the most celebrated.

Dickens used the serial mode of publication, with some variations, to the end of his career, and it was also widely adopted by other Victorian novelists, including William Makepeace Thackeray, Anthony Trollope, George Eliot, and Thomas Hardy. Serialization exerted a profound influence on form and technique, creating problems and opportunities for the writer—as well as providing experiences for the reader—that were different in many important ways from those offered by fiction appearing only in volumes. Dickens' own writing, particularly his conception of plot and character, was radically affected by the serial form. And since writing and publication proceeded hand in hand, he was acutely aware of the response of readers and critics and was prepared to modify his original intentions as a work progressed. More broadly, the history of 19th-century English fiction would have been very different if serialization had not become such a popular practice. Among other results, the cheapness of serial publications made fiction available to a far wider audience than had read the novels of Jane Austen a generation earlier. In turn, Dickens, like many of his successors, consciously wrote for a socially diverse readership.

Although *Pickwick* is primarily a comic masterpiece, Dickens, ever mindful of the importance of providing variety, blended other elements with the comedy. A series of interpolated tales, in which the dominant atmosphere is one of pathos, melodrama, and Gothic darkness, alternate with the comic scenes. The narrative also contains satirical depictions of contemporary institutions and characters—for example, in the account of the Eatanswill election campaign with its bribery, drunkenness, and windy political rhetoric. In this and other passages, Dickens made good use of his experiences as a young reporter who had traveled widely to cover similar events. The famous trial scene, later adapted by Dickens as one of his most successful public readings, drew material from his time as a shorthand-reporter in the London law-courts.

Although written at the beginning of the railway age, *Pickwick* portrays the world of coach travel of Dickens' childhood—the world of Fielding's *Tom Jones* (1749) and other 18th-century prototypes. As a child, Dickens had devoured the novels of Fielding and Smollett, and his own first novel owes much to the 18th-century English picaresque tradition, itself heavily indebted to such Continental models as Cervantes' *Don Quixote* (1605-15) and Lesage's *Gil Blas* (1715-35). Just as Don Quixote and other picaresque heroes had been accompanied on their travels by faithful retainers, Mr. Pickwick is looked after on his ramblings by Sam Weller, the street-wise Cockney who is one of Dickens' greatest comic creations.

The realistic, sometimes brutal world of Fielding and Smollett is, however, modified by another 18th-century influence, the sentimental tradition of Sterne and Goldsmith. Their focus on tender emotion and moral nicety provides an antecedent for the benevolent and innocent Mr. Pickwick, whose excesses we may be invited to laugh at, but whose goodness we nevertheless cannot help but respect. A central concern in the novel, in fact, is the collision between the sentimental and picaresque traditions, between the hero's idealized view of the world and its harsh realities.

Although the novel did not create an immediate sensation, the introduction of Sam Weller provoked a strong public response, and monthly sales rose rapidly from a few hundred for the early numbers to nearly 40,000 by the end of the run. With his first novel, Dickens had become famous, not only in England but throughout the English-speaking world. The novel spawned imitations, parodies, stage adaptations, and other literary and dramatic attempts to capitalize on the book's success, as well as an industry offering Pickwick hats, canes, and china figures, Sam Weller joke books, and other commodities. Its popularity did not wane, and during the next 100 years approximately 100 further editions appeared in England and even more in the United States. It has even been claimed that no other book in the history of English literature has aroused such enthusiasm on an international scale.

The original illustrations, reproduced in most modern editions, serve as a reminder of the curious origins of *Pickwick*. Browne, who adopted the pseudonym "Phiz," went on to illustrate many of Dickens' subsequent novels under the author's close supervision. His renderings of character and scene have had an important influence on readers' visualization of the Dickensian world and have an intimate relationship with the written text.

NORMAN PAGE

See also Charles Dickens

Further Reading

Andrews, Malcolm, *Dickens and the Grown-up Child,* London: Macmillan, and Iowa City: University of Iowa Press, 1994

Auden, W.H., "Dingley Dell and the Fleet," in *The Dyer's Hand and Other Essays,* New York: Random House, 1962; London: Faber, 1963

Butt, John, and Kathleen Tillotson, *Dickens at Work,* London: Methuen, 1957

Daldry, Graham, *Charles Dickens and the Form of the Novel,* Totowa, New Jersey: Barnes and Noble, 1986; London: Croom Helm, 1987

Marcus, Steven, *Dickens: From Pickwick to Dombey,* London: Chatto and Windus, and New York: Simon and Schuster, 1965

Morgan, Nicholas H., *Secret Journeys: Theory and Practice in Reading Dickens,* London: Associated University Presses, and

Rutherford, New Jersey: Farleigh Dickinson University Press, 1992

Page, Norman, *A Dickens Companion,* London: Macmillan, 1984; New York: Schocken, 1987

Patten, R.L., "The Art of *Pickwick*'s Interpolated Tales," *English Literary History* 34 (1967)

Smith, Grahame, *Charles Dickens: A Literary Life,* London: Macmillan, and New York: St. Martin's Press, 1996

The Pilgrim's Progress by John Bunyan

Part I, 1678; Part II, 1684

John Bunyan seemed to his contemporaries an unlikely candidate for literary genius. Part-time tinker and Puritan preacher, he was proud of his lack of formal education—it left him more open to the inspired truth of God as revealed through His scriptures. And Bunyan most certainly had a thorough knowledge of the Bible and Puritan theology.

Part I of *The Pilgrim's Progress,* probably composed while Bunyan was imprisoned for his radical preaching, was his first essay into literary narrative. His previous works were mainly sermons, religious treatises, and homilies. Clearly, Bunyan's intentions in *Pilgrim's Progress* are didactic as well: he means to reveal the way to salvation. But his approach is less straightforward than the plain style of his nonfiction works. In *Pilgrim's Progress,* Bunyan chooses allegory, and his attitude to this narrative strategy is defensive. In his prefatory verses to Part I, Bunyan justifies the imaginative style of his work by saying first that the allegory came to him involuntarily and second that allegory is used often by scripture to make a theological point. He argues that his "dark and cloudy words they do but hold/ The Truth, as Cabinets inclose the Gold." His fiction is not a divergence from or a decoration of the truth for amusement's sake. His "little Book," he asserts, contains "Nothing but sound and honest Gospel-strains."

The structure and style of the narrative follow the conventions of spiritual autobiography, such as Bunyan's own *Grace Abounding to the Chief of Sinners* (1666): it is the personal account of an individual's conversion and spiritual maturation, presented as a journey from an unregenerate condition to the safety of salvation and the ongoing struggle of sanctification. Indeed, Christian's story of his conversion experience and his subsequent journey, which he tells over and over again, becomes emblematic for those who follow after him. Christian's travels also reflect those of earlier allegorical journeys such as Langland's *Piers Plowman* and Edmund Spenser's *The Faerie Queene,* and they anticipate the more complexly figurative travels of Robinson Crusoe and Gulliver.

Bunyan's narrative stands between a fading religious allegorical tradition and a developing secular novelistic one. Thus, *Pilgrim's Progress* represents a negotiation between two narrative strategies. On the one hand, it is a spare, allegorical journey. The story opens with a dream and a dreamer, and the reader is thrust into an otherworldly place of vision and interpretation. The dreamer sees a man who also faces the task of interpretation: he reads a book whose contents instruct him of his condemned state. Evangelist gives Christian another "parchment roll" and instructs him to "fly from the wrath to come." The narrative thus begins in fear, and this sense of urgency does not diminish in the course of Christian's life. In Part I, time is compressed as Christian hurries along through a world whose landscape and inhabitants are clearly emblematic. He struggles through the Slough of Despond, battles Satan's minion in the Valley of Humiliation, receives instruction in the House of the Interpreter, faces trial in Vanity Fair, languishes in Doubting-Castle, and finally crosses fearfully over the River into the Celestial City. Along the way, he is tested by Obstinate, Worldly-wise, Talkative, Atheist, and Ignorance, and encouraged by Faithful and Hopeful.

On the other hand, Christian, although allegorical, is not one dimensional. He is both an Everyman and an individual. He grows both as a spiritual warrior and as a character in the course of the narrative. Christian's development is not smoothly linear—he succumbs to the same sorts of doubts both early and late in the narrative—but he does grow and learn, moving from pupil to teacher. He is a wiser, if still flawed, character in the end. Bunyan's narrative thus anticipates the teleological structure of the novel in the spiritual journey that he describes. Moreover, Bunyan's gradual development of Christian stands at the beginning of the novelistic tradition of psychological character representation through the internal reasoning of meditation and reflection and the external reasoning of conversation and instruction.

If Part I shows a novelistic interest in the development of individual character, then Part II reveals a novelistic interest in social relationships. In this part, the narrative incorporates more of the everyday details characteristic of novelistic realism. In Part II, which recounts the journey of Christiana and her children, the frame of the dream loses its certainty—at times the fictional world is a dream landscape and at other times it is an actual place. Furthermore, the emphasis is less on the allegorical significance of the places and people that the pilgrims encounter and more on the responses that they have to their adventures. These pilgrims become more fully realized as ordinary characters: Christiana and her companions are much aware of the commonplace material concerns of food, clothing, and shelter. In this half of the narrative there is also more conversation and less sermonizing, more socializing in welcoming houses and less isolated traveling on the road. Time slows down, and the narrative concerns itself with social interaction and social institutions. Thus, Bunyan combines the realistic portrayal of character, incident, and colloquial conversation with his allegorical framework to produce a work that touches both the eternal world of spiritual welfare and the immediate world of day-to-day concerns.

Pilgrim's Progress was an immediate best-seller: it went through 13 editions in ten years. But this popularity was largely among Bunyan's peers—working-class people who shared his religious values. Augustan writers such as Alexander Pope, Joseph Addison, William Congreve, and John Gay ridiculed Bunyan as a vulgar hack. By the end of the 18th century, however, the literary merit of Bunyan's work underwent a revaluation. Romantics such as Samuel Taylor Coleridge, Robert Southey, John Keats, Sir Walter Scott, and Charles Lamb established *Pilgrim's Progress* as an English classic, both for its spiritual and its aesthetic merit. His originality and plainspoken style became assets rather than liabilities. Bunyan's allegory became a mainstay for Victorian novelists on both sides of the Atlantic, including George Eliot, Charlotte Brontë, William Makepeace Thackeray, Charles Dickens, Nathaniel Hawthorne, and Louisa May Alcott. In the work of these authors, spiritual pilgrimage is transmuted into Bildungsroman—the social, psychological, and moral testing of the protagonist through a series of trials that results in maturity. Thus has Bunyan's "little Book" about individual testing and individual triumph become woven into the form and the substance of the novel genre.

JUDITH BURDAN

Further Reading

Baird, Charles W., *John Bunyan: A Study in Narrative Technique,* Port Washington, New York: Kennikat Press, 1977

Batson, E. Beatrice, *John Bunyan: Allegory and Imagination,* London: Croom Helm, and Totowa, New Jersey: Barnes and Noble, 1984

Fish, Stanley, *Self-Consuming Artifacts: The Experience of Seventeenth Century Literature,* Berkeley: University of California Press, 1972

Hill, Christopher, *A Tinker and a Poor Man: John Bunyan and His Church, 1628–1688,* New York: Knopf, 1989

Iser, Wolfgang, *The Implied Reader: Patterns of Communication in Prose Fiction from Bunyan to Beckett,* Baltimore: Johns Hopkins University Press, 1974

Kaufmann, U. Milo, *"The Pilgrim's Progress" and Traditions in Puritan Meditation,* New Haven, Connecticut: Yale University Press, 1966

Keeble, N.H., editor, *John Bunyan: Conventicle and Parnassus: Tercentenary Essays,* Oxford: Clarendon Press, and New York: Oxford University Press, 1988

Newey, Vincent, editor, *"The Pilgrim's Progress": Critical and Historical Views,* Totowa, New Jersey: Barnes and Noble, and Liverpool: Liverpool University Press, 1980

Sharrock, Roger, editor, *Bunyan: "The Pilgrim's Progress": A Casebook,* London: Macmillan, 1976

Swaim, Kathleen M., *Pilgrim's Progress, Puritan Progress: Discourses and Contexts,* Urbana: University of Illinois Press, 1993

Pinocchio. *See* Adventures of Pinocchio

Andrei Platonov 1899–1951

Russian

At first glance it seems paradoxical to discuss Andrei Platonov in the context of the novel. Although Platonov was a prolific writer of short stories, who at various times tried his hand at journalism, poetry, plays, film scenarios, and critical essays, he left only two complete novels. Of these, *Chevengur* (written 1926–29) was never published in its entirety in Russian until late in the Soviet era, even though it had been scheduled for printing in 1929 and parts of it were published as stories. *Schastlivaia Moskva* (completed around 1937; Happy Moscow) was left as an unfinished manuscript. Nonetheless, Platonov's writings embody one of the major dissenting responses to the socialist-realist novel that became the centerpiece of the Stalinist literary aesthetic. The two novels also engage, in ways complicated by the Soviet experience, a secondary but important line within the broader tradition of the Russian novel: the utopian narrative, which in Russia has often taken novelistic form without being confined to it.

It is this utopian line, rather than the mainstream "critical realism" of writers like Fedor Dostoevskii, Ivan Turgenev, and Lev Tolstoi, that is most relevant to *Chevengur*. Platonov once said that this novel was meant to be a tale of "how history begins and when it will end." It recounts the travels of two heroes, Dvanov and Kopenkin, as they wander through the Russian steppes at the height of the civil war, eventually finding their way to a remote town called Chevengur whose inhabitants believe they have managed to establish a communist utopia overnight. The utopia turns out to have pursued its radically egalitarian ideal in a bizarrely literal manner: the bourgeoisie has been forcibly exiled, destitute vagabonds have been herded into the town from the surrounding steppes to serve as the proletariat, and labor has been suspended in the belief that the sun will raise enough grain to feed everyone. The houses are moved around town once a week in the belief that communism is "eternal motion." Eventually, however, autumn arrives, and a marauding band of cossacks invades the town.

A brief summary of *Chevengur*'s plot, however, lends it more coherence than the reader encounters on its pages. The novel actually consists of loosely conjoined episodes suggestive of the picaresque novel with interwoven elements of the epic (or mock-epic) and the Bildungsroman. Its ideas draw significantly on the eccentric utopian philosophy of the 19th-century thinker Nikolai Fedorov and such successors of his as Aleksandr Bogdanov (author of a science-fiction utopian work entitled *Krasnaia zvezda* [1922; *Red Star*]). Its ideology hovers between a parody of revolutionary fervor and a lament at its passing. In summation, *Chevengur* may be thought of as a complex meditation on utopian thought in the early Soviet context.

While not technically a novel, Platonov's long story *Kotlovan* (*The Foundation Pit*), completed in 1930 but published in a full, corrected version only in 1987, presents, in inverted form, the key elements of what soon after was labeled the "socialist-realist" novel. Specifically, it parodies the kind of narrative central to that genre, in which politically enlightened heroes struggle against daunting obstacles in order to launch a new factory or organize a collective farm. The story amounted to a satire on the aims of the first "five-year plan" of rapid industrialization that was central to Stalinist economic policy. *The Foundation Pit*'s characters, every bit as eccentric as those in *Chevengur*, labor at an increasingly frenetic pace to excavate the foundation pit for a "proletarian home," which is to provide permanent shelter for Moscow's working class. As the projected size of the edifice increases, so does the pit, until in the end all that has been created is a giant hole. Parallel to this plot line runs another that portrays the efforts to create a model collective farm. This plot is marked by surreal episodes during which horses voluntarily collectivize themselves and a semi-mythical bear (who works as a blacksmith) metes out capital punishment to kulaks (wealthy peasant farmers). The tale's focal point is a dour character named Voshchev, a literal outsider who has been fired from a factory job and now wanders the outskirts of town. Like *Chevengur*, *The Foundation Pit* is poised between utopia and dystopia: it remains unclear whether Platonov's heretical refraction of the production novel arose out of disaffection with Soviet utopianism in general or, more narrowly, with the authoritarian and bureaucratic means by which it was being pursued under Stalin. But the tale's import is not limited to the political. Throughout, its characters are obsessed with one of

Platonov's abiding themes: the troubled nature of existence within a physical body, in a physical world (an idea that led him to a complex dialogue with Soviet "materialist" Marxism). What is most striking, however, is the verbal style of *The Foundation Pit*: an odd, deformed rendition of Soviet political clichés as they might have been processed by a semi-literate folk-consciousness, which in fact constitutes one of the signal achievements of modern Russian prose.

From the 1930s onward, hostility toward his works from the Soviet literary establishment forced Platonov to attempt a more conventional literary manner—something he never really accomplished. *Schastlivaia Moskva*, on which he worked in the mid-1930s, appears to have arisen out of such aims, but, despite a toned-down verbal style and visible efforts to camouflage itself as a socialist-realist novel, it remains a very odd candidate for the genre. Instead of a coherent "production" plot, it offers a meandering series of encounters between its allegorical heroine (Moskva Chestnova—roughly, "Moscow the Honest") and a motley group of mostly alienated characters, who, while anxiously following the development of socialism, are in fact more preoccupied with existential questions about the nature of the body, the soul, and physical death. Tantalizingly, it may have been intended as part of an even longer work to be entitled *Puteshestvie iz Leningrada v Moskvu* (A Journey from Leningrad to Moscow), but of that work only a few mentions survive.

THOMAS SEIFRID

Biography

Born 1 September 1899 in Iamskaia sloboda, a suburb of the Russian town of Voronezh. His father was a railway mechanic and inventor and his mother the daughter of a watchmaker. Received early education at a parochial school and later enrolled in a polytechnical school associated with the railway. An early sympathizer with the Bolshevik Revolution, Platonov became a visible figure in the local Proletarian Culture movement from 1918–21; worked as a land reclamation engineer in the Voronezh and Tambov regions, 1922–25; moved to Moscow to establish himself as a writer, 1926; after some initial success his works increasingly came under suspicion, and between 1931 and 1934 he was not allowed to publish; worked for the journals *Literaturnyi kritik* and *Literaturnoe obozrenie*, 1937–40; served in the Soviet Army as a war correspondent for the newspaper *Krasnaia zvezda* and managed to publish several stories during World War II; in 1943 his son, who had been arrested in 1938 as an alleged saboteur, was released from the camps infected with tuberculosis; Platonov contracted the disease himself and eventually died from it on 5 January 1951.

Novels by Platonov

Kotlovan, 1969; also in *Novyi mir*, 1987; as *The Foundation Pit*, translated by Thomas P. Whitney, 1973, reprinted in *Collected Works*, 1978; also translated by Mirra Ginsburg, 1975, and by Robert Chandler and Geoffrey Smith, 1996
Chevengur, 1972 (incomplete); also in *Druzhba narodov*, 1988; separate edition, 1989; as *Chevengur*, translated by Anthony Olcott, 1978
Schastlivaia Moskva [Happy Moscow], 1991

Other Writings: short stories, poetry, journalism, and critical essays.

Further Reading

Bethea, David M., *The Shape of Apocalypse in Modern Russian Fiction*, Princeton, New Jersey: Princeton University Press, 1989

Brodsky, Joseph, "Catastrophes in the Air," in *Less Than One: Selected Essays*, New York: Farrar, Straus and Giroux, and London: Viking, 1986

Clark, Katerina, *The Soviet Novel: History as Ritual*, Chicago: University of Chicago Press, 1981; 2nd edition, 1985

Geller, Mikhail, *Andrei Platonov v poiskakh schast'ia*, Paris: YMCA Press, 1982

Langerak, Thomas, *Andrei Platonov: Materialy dlia biografii, 1899–1929 gg.*, Amsterdam: Pegasus, 1995

Seifrid, Thomas, *Andrei Platonov: Uncertainties of Spirit*, Cambridge and New York: Cambridge University Press, 1992

Plot

Until recently, novel theory and criticism has given plot little respect. Indeed, plot summary is still widely considered to be the lowest form of critical discourse, and teachers of the novel always want their students to do more than just read for plot. Yet in the last decade or so, plot has received increasing attention and respect from theorists of the novel, and although it cannot claim the pride of place once given to it by Aristotle, who called it the "soul of tragedy" and elevated it above character and thought in his hierarchy of elements, plot no longer needs to apologize for its own existence. The story of plot in novel theory can be told in three chapters: (1) its treatment from the early part of the 20th century up to the 1980s, with particular focus on E.M. Forster, the Russian formalists and French structuralists, the New Critics, especially Cleanth Brooks and Robert Penn Warren, and the Chicago neo-Aristotelians; (2) the new attention to plot generated during the 1980s and early 1990s in works by Peter Brooks (1984), James Phelan (1989), and Susan Stanford Friedman (1993); (3) the recent move, accompanying theory's general turn to politics and culture, to link plots to ideology and politics.

Chapter One

Unlike the situation in Aristotle's Athens, plot in the 20th-century Western world has been most commonly defined in relation to story, with the latter being the chronological sequence of events recounted in a narrative and plot being that sequence plus something else. For E.M. Forster (1927), who said with a sigh that "yes, oh dear, yes, the novel tells a story," the difference between story and plot is causality. "The king died and then the queen died" is a story, whereas "The king died and then the queen died of grief" is a plot. For the Russian formalists, the difference between story and plot is the difference between the chronological sequence of events, which they labeled the *fabula,* and the actual rendering of those events in the narrative, which they labeled the *syuzhet.* The structuralists observe a similar distinction between *histoire,* the events abstracted from any narration in any medium, and *récit,* the events in combination with the discourse. Brooks and Warren (1979) distinguish between "sequence of action," by which they mean the chronological sequence of events, and plot, by which they mean "the structure of the action *as presented* in a piece of fiction." In other words, they operate with their own version of the *fabula/syuzhet* distinction, although they do not use those terms.

Although none of these conceptions of plot as story-plus-X automatically entails a lack of respect, such treatment has accompanied each. Forster does admire careful plotting, but he sees plot and character as competing for dominance in the novel, and he prefers character to plot, because character, in his view, connects the novel to life, while plot connects it to artifice. The Russian formalists, and especially the French structuralists, tend to focus less on *syuzhet* and *récit* than on the mechanisms of narrative discourse that transform story into plot. Thus, their work has offered valuable insights into the *how* of the novel but has not been as productive for the reader's thinking about the *what.* The most useful structuralist contribution is Roland Barthes' (1966) distinction between "kernels," events that are central to a narrative's sequence, and "satellites," events that revolve around those kernels. In Jane Austen's *Pride and Prejudice* (1813), for example, Elizabeth's reading of Darcy's letter explaining his behavior toward Wickham and Jane is a kernel, while Darcy's delivering the letter by his own hand is a satellite. If Elizabeth did not read the letter, Austen would seriously alter her plot, but if the letter were delivered by a servant rather than by Darcy himself, the plot would not be significantly changed.

The New Critics see plot not as an end in itself but as the means toward some larger thematic end; for them, plot is important because it participates in the novel's communication of some truth about or attitude toward life.

The neo-Aristotelians buck the critical tide because they, like Aristotle, give plot pride of place in a hierarchy of literary elements. They look back to the Stagirite less for a definition of plot than for a method of discussing it. Aristotle's (translated 1984) view of plot follows from his definition of tragedy: an imitation of an action that is serious, complete, and of a certain magnitude designed first to arouse the emotions of pity and fear and second to expurgate those emotions through what he called catharsis. For Aristotle, to imitate an action is to construct a plot, and to construct a plot is to produce a trajectory of emotions in one's audience. Consequently, one can reason back from the effects of a work to its causes in the construction, especially in the construction of the plot. R.S. Crane (1952), Sheldon Sacks (1964), and other neo-Aristotelian critics employed this method in order to correct what they saw as the New Critics' misplaced emphasis on language and theme and to develop a theory of novelistic form that would be adequate to the range of plots that had been developed throughout the history of literature.

Before moving to chapter two in our story of plot, one may consider how these different conceptions would lead to different analyses of Austen's *Pride and Prejudice*. Forster would say that Austen is telling the story of how Elizabeth Bennet comes to marry Fitzwilliam Darcy, but the plot proper is found in the sequence of causation that moves them from their initial dislike to their final union. Chief among these causes are Darcy's close observations of Elizabeth, first at Netherfield Park, where she nurses her sister Jane, and second at Rosings, where she visits her friend Charlotte Collins, while he visits his aunt Lady Catherine de Bourgh. These observations lead to Darcy's first proposal, which Elizabeth flatly refuses because of her conviction that he has ruined Wickham and interfered with Jane's chances of marrying Bingley. Elizabeth's refusal, in turn, produces Darcy's letter of explanation of his role in these matters, an explanation that goes a long way toward revising Elizabeth's views and feelings toward Darcy. An additional cause of Elizabeth's change of feeling is her visit with her aunt and uncle Gardiner to Darcy's estate, Pemberley, where both the careful cultivation of the grounds and the testimony of Darcy's housekeeper give her a fuller view of his exemplary character. Austen then introduces an event that initially seems to be a cause of their permanent separation but actually turns out to be a cause of their coming together: the elopement of Elizabeth's sister, Lydia, with Wickham. Although Elizabeth is sure that Lydia's rash act will damage the Bennet family name so much that the proud Darcy will not want anything else to do with her, Darcy, in large part because of his feelings for Elizabeth, intercedes in the crisis and arranges the marriage between Lydia and Wickham. When Elizabeth finds out, she expresses her gratitude to Darcy, which in turn leads him to venture his second proposal, and this time Elizabeth happily accepts. For all this masterful plotting on Austen's part, Forster would be more interested in her characters, particularly the wonderfully flat Mrs. Bennet, Mr. Collins, and Lydia, as well as the delightfully round Elizabeth. Indeed, Forster would likely anticipate the complaints of some feminist critics who view Elizabeth as sacrificing too much liveliness and independence in her marriage to Darcy. For Forster, this curtailment of Elizabeth's liveliness would be an example of plot dominating character.

The Russian formalists and the French structuralists would note that, for the most part, the plot of *Pride and Prejudice* follows the chronological sequence of the events, with notable exceptions occurring when Darcy's letter recounts the earlier history of his relations with Wickham and when Mrs. Gardiner recounts for Elizabeth Mr. Darcy's significant role in the marriage of Lydia and Wickham. These critics would also emphasize the way that the narrative discourse fluctuates primarily between the perspective of the omniscient narrator and that of Elizabeth, with occasional departures to the perspectives of various letter writers, chiefly Darcy, Mr. Collins, Jane, and Mrs. Gardiner. This way of converting *fabula* into *syuzhet*, *histoire* into *récit*, makes Elizabeth rather than Darcy the central figure, and it allows Austen to emphasize not only her change of feeling and of character but also the situation of being a single woman of small fortune in Regency England.

The New Critics would be willing to accept these previous descriptions, but they would want to thematize the plot much more. Taking one cue from the title, they would say that the structure of the action shows the necessity and desirability of getting past both pride and prejudice as the reader responds to others. Taking another cue from the focus of the discourse on Elizabeth, they would also emphasize the way that the structure of the action exposes the importance of economic and social status in the Regency marriage market.

The neo-Aristotelians would emphasize the way in which the plot is designed to make the audience feel something like Elizabeth's own sense of satisfaction in the marriage. They would note that Austen structures the action to give the audience the comic assurances that, despite the initial complications of the plot, Elizabeth will end up in a happy situation, and they would analyze the discourse to show how Austen carefully modulates the audience's sympathy and Elizabeth's judgment so that the reader observes but does not condemn her initial misjudgments and applauds the self-analysis she undertakes after reading Darcy's letter. In the neo-Aristotelian's analysis, too, Lydia's elopement is a crucial event, not only because of its causal importance but also because of its emotional consequences. At this point in the comic plot, the reader—but not the character—knows that Elizabeth will marry Darcy; thus, the reader, witnessing Elizabeth's belief that she has now lost Darcy, takes greater satisfaction in the eventual engagement. The reader knows that Elizabeth has faced the full consequences of her initial pride.

Chapter Two

In 1984 Peter Brooks made an important intervention in theoretical accounts of plot by arguing that the problem with structuralist accounts is that they encourage a spatial rather than temporal understanding of narrative: looking at how story is transformed into discourse means viewing plots as static wholes rather than as phenomena that are experienced in time. Furthermore, he wanted to link the temporality of plot to the temporality of life, so he analyzed reading for the plot in terms of Freud's *Beyond the Pleasure Principle* and developed a model that describes narrative as a desire for the ending. Thus, he sees the beginning of plot as the introduction of desire, the middle as deferral and delay, largely through repetition, until the end of the plot brings about discharge or satisfaction of that desire. Thus, in *Pride and Prejudice*, the plot begins by introducing a desire for the marriage of Elizabeth and Darcy, the long middle defers the marriage through the complications of the plot and repetitions with the difference of their various meetings and misunderstandings, and, finally, the ending satisfies the desire with their engagement. Brooks' model has been appropriately criticized by feminist theorists such as Susan Winnett (1990) for its assumption that the trajectory of male sexual response is the underlying pattern of all plots.

Phelan's work on progression (1989) offers a different critique of Brooks, even as it tries to link plot with the arousal, development, and resolution of a reader's interests. Rather than saying that plot is story-plus-X, Phelan proposes progression as a concept that incorporates plot: progression is the synthesis of the temporal unfolding of the narrative with the developing attitudes the audience is asked to take to that unfolding. Progressions can be generated either by instabilities (unstable relations among characters) or by tensions (discrepancies in knowledge, beliefs, values, or opinions between narrators and their audiences). Beginnings, therefore, introduce instabilities, tensions, or both; middles complicate the instabilities and tensions; and endings seek to resolve these complications. Phelan suggests further that there are three main kinds of readerly interest: mimetic, the way in which the fiction gives an illusion of life; thematic, the way in which the fiction is concerned with generalizations from its action and the representativeness of its characters; and synthetic, the way in which the fiction is an artificial construct. Progressions of different novels will establish different relations between these kinds of interests; furthermore, attending to them helps one see that reading novels involves emotions, intellect, psyche, and ethics. Phelan also develops the following differences between his concept of reading for the progression and Brooks' concept of reading for the plot. First, endings are not, as Brooks would have it, determinative of beginnings and middles; instead, beginnings, middles, and ends are mutually determinative, and are themselves subordinated to some larger design for the whole. Second, as a consequence, middles are more important than Brooks' model acknowledges; they are not just devices of delay and repetition but places for the development of various dimensions of plot and various levels—affective, cognitive, and ethical—of readerly response. Third, reading for progression will get the reader closer to the experiential quality of reading narrative because it attends not just to developing themes, as Brooks' practical criticism tends to do, but also to developing judgments, expectations, desires, and emotions. Finally, rather than looking for the deep structure of narrative plots in psychoanalysis or any other discipline cognate to literature, readers should continue to analyze the variety and complexity of individual novelistic progressions.

Susan Friedman's (1993) concept of spatialization goes beyond the aforementioned arguments by suggesting that narrative has not only a horizontal movement through time but also a vertical dimension that brings back a spatial view of plot. The vertical dimension links the horizontal surface to literary, historical, and psychic intertexts. Literary intertexts include both generic patterns and specific prior narratives; historical intertexts involve the broader social order, including cultural narratives; and psychic intertexts involve the patterns of repression and return within the text itself as well as those involved in the author's relation to the material.

Thus, in *Pride and Prejudice* Phelan would emphasize the interaction of Elizabeth's progression toward Darcy with Austen's thematizing of her situation as a single woman of little fortune so that the reader's pleasure in the mimetic story is deepened and deeply contextualized by the novel's thematizing. Collins' proposals, first to Elizabeth, who refuses him, and then to Charlotte Lucas, who accepts him, are more than just deferrals or anticipations of Darcy's later proposals to Elizabeth. Instead they represent an alternate fate for Elizabeth, the awareness of which strengthens our desire and satisfaction in her marriage to Darcy, even as it emphasizes that Elizabeth's good fortune is just that. Friedman would emphasize the way in which *Pride and Prejudice* interacts with previous marriage plots and makes Elizabeth both partly responsible for Darcy's reform and partly the fortunate beneficiary of his generosity of spirit. Friedman would also emphasize the novel's commentary on the marriage market and the constrictions and restrictions it places on female experience and choice, and she would look for implied relations between Austen's own experiences as a single woman and the horizontal unfolding of Elizabeth's fate.

Chapter Three

Susan Friedman's work participates in the ideological turn of recent criticism, but the most notable feature of that turn of plot theories is the effort to link plot patterns with political beliefs. Rachel Blau DuPlessis succinctly articulates the assumption behind this effort: "ideology is coiled in narrative structure." History, both social and literary, has privileged certain plots and in so doing has linked them with certain cultural values. *Pride and Prejudice,* for example, is one version of the marriage plot, a plot given great prominence in Anglo-American social and literary history, a plot that privileges heterosexuality, marriage, and the patriarchal order that sets up the rules of the marriage market and defines women's proper place in the domestic sphere. Experimentation with plot by women writers, gay and lesbian novelists, and novelists of color needs to be understood, according to this argument, as both formal innovation and political statement: breaking the sequence, as Virginia Woolf (1929) put it, is a way both to protest against the usual plot patterns and to find forms for experiences and values that those patterns have not attended to.

Jeanette Winterson's *Written on the Body* (1992), for example, can be profitably read as breaking the sequence of the marriage plot: it traces not the coming together of a single couple but rather the character-narrator's multiple experiences of love and loss; where the marriage plot confines sex to the couple's untold life after the novel ends, Winterson's protagonist has multiple sexual partners. Winterson moves in the direction of the marriage plot by representing the character-narrator's temporary union with Louise, but she then turns away from that plot to focus on the loss of Louise and the character-narrator's effort to come to terms with that loss. Furthermore, while the marriage plot reinforces heterosexuality, Winterson challenges that taken-for-granted position first by showing that the character-narrator has sexual partners of both sexes, and, second, by refusing to identify the character-narrator's own sex. Meanwhile, as the title suggests, *Written on the Body* is also an allegory of reading, one that analogizes the relationship between the central lovers to that between author/narrator and implied reader/actual reader. In this way, the formal choice not to identify the character-narrator's own sex has the political consequence of queering the experience of reading, of exposing the way desire in reading, like desire in general, cannot be readily confined to the clearly demarcated categories of gender and sexuality.

Even as critics and theorists have become more attuned to the link between form and politics, this Winterson-like awareness—that simple one-to-one correspondences between plot X and political belief Y are inadequate—has spread. Novelists continue to revise established ways of moving from beginning to end and continue to reinvigorate old plots and to find new ones. Lovers of the novel hope it will be ever thus.

JAMES PHELAN

See also Beginnings and Endings; Character; Description; Framing and Embedding; Narratology; Space; Structuralism, Semiotics, and the Novel; Time in the Novel

Further Reading

Aristotle, *Poetics,* in *The Rhetoric and the Poetics of Aristotle,* New York: Modern Library, 1984

Barthes, Roland, "Introduction à l'analyse structurale des

récits," *Communications* 8 (1966); as "An Introduction to the Structural Analysis of Narrative," *New Literary History* 6 (1975)

Blau DuPlessis, Rachel, *Writing Beyond the Ending: Narrative Strategies of Twentieth-Century Women Writers,* Bloomington: Indiana University Press, 1985

Brooks, Cleanth, and Robert Penn Warren, *Understanding Fiction,* New York: Crofts, 1943; 3rd edition, Englewood Cliffs, New Jersey: Prentice-Hall, 1979

Brooks, Peter, *Reading for the Plot,* New York: Knopf, and Oxford: Clarendon Press, 1984

Chatman, Seymour, *Story and Discourse: Narrative Structure in Fiction and Film,* Ithaca, New York: Cornell University Press, 1978

Crane, Ronald S., "The Concept of Plot and the Plot of *Tom Jones,*" in *Critics and Criticism: Ancient and Modern,* edited by Crane, Chicago: University of Chicago Press, 1952

Forster, E.M., *Aspects of the Novel,* London: Edward Arnold, and New York: Harcourt Brace, 1927

Friedman, Susan Stanford, "Spatialization: A Strategy for Reading Narrative," *Narrative* 1 (1993)

Homans, Margaret, "Feminist Fictions and Feminist Theories of Narrative," *Narrative* 2 (1994)

Phelan, James, *Reading People, Reading Plots: Character, Progression, and the Interpretation of Narrative,* Chicago: University of Chicago Press, 1989

Rimmon-Kenan, Shlomith, *Narrative Fiction: Contemporary Poetics,* London and New York: Methuen, 1983

Sacks, Sheldon, *Fiction and the Shape of Belief,* Berkeley: University of California Press, 1964

Winnett, Susan, "Coming Unstrung: Women, Men, Narrative, and Principles of Pleasure," *PMLA* 105 (1990)

Woolf, Virginia, *A Room of One's Own,* London: Hogarth Press, and New York: Fountain Press, 1929

Plum in the Golden Vase. *See* Six Classic Chinese Novels

Point of View

The narrative term *point of view* derives from its ordinary non-literary usage, which designates one's literal visual orientation or perspective: "From John's point of view, standing as he was on top of the mountain, the castle seemed tiny, but from my point of view at the base of the building, it was enormous." Sight is not the only sense to which the term can apply: "From Mary's point of view, the music was dreadful," "From the famished man's point of view, the smell was delicious," "The experience was too touchy-feely from Ron's point of view."

The phrase is also used metaphorically. The object(s) viewed may be quite vague or intangible: "from the point of view of a child, many things in the adult world are mysterious" (*Webster's Third New International Dictionary*). One can have a point of view about a person long dead ("From the student's point of view, Shakespeare was an enigma") or a state of affairs or abstraction ("Totalitarianism, from everyone's point of view, is evil"). In such cases, point of view refers not to literal vision, but to thinking, believing, opining. Clearly there are conceptual, emotional, ideological, and other kinds of point of view.

Further, the term applies not only to the way something is mentally considered, but to the person considering it—*Webster's* defines this sense as "a particular manner of considering or evaluating something." When we say "John has a conservative point of view," we refer to an aspect of John's personality, his disposition to perceive and conceive things conservatively. This sense of point of view may extend to "a particular reasoned mental attitude toward or opinion about something" (*Webster's*). When we ask someone "Please state your point of view," we are asking her to articulate her reasoning.

Although a point of view usually suggests a human perceiver or conceiver, it may also apply to individuals who cannot mentally entertain any object or idea but somehow have a stake in it. For example, "The judge tried to look at the question from the fetus' point of view." The fetus neither perceives nor thinks, but presumably has an interest in the judicial process. Even insensate objects or high-level abstractions may be said to have a point of view: "From the *point of view* of climate and soils [this procedure] is best suited to agriculture" (an example in *Webster's*). This sense of the phrase entails the welfare, well-being, or general interests of the subject.

As novels and short stories involve persons who perceive and conceive things in the fictional world, it was natural that the term *point of view* should be applied to them by literary critics and theorists. In fact, consideration of point of view has become a staple of 20th-century discussions of fiction. But its narratological usage is more complicated than its conversational usage because of the dual nature of narrative texts. Every narrative consists of something told, the *story,* and the means or mechanism by which the story gets told, the *discourse.* In consequence, there are two kinds of persons or agents in narratives: characters, that is, participants in the actions and happenings of the story, and narrators, that is, those who tell or otherwise communicate the story. Characters are agents in the story; narrators are the agents of the discourse recounting the story. Some narrators, speaking "now" in discourse-time, were characters "back then" in story-time. These are *character-narrators* or *homodiegetic narrators.* Both narrators and characters have points of view. The reference of the term is sometimes unclear, so the underlying components of narratorial versus characterial points of view need to be understood.

Several names besides point of view have been proposed, and, as might be expected, these different names lead the discussion in different directions. Henry James was one of the first to discuss the topic seriously. In his extensive deliberations on narrative theory (especially in the prefaces to his novels in the collected New York edition [1907–17]), James wrote of his efforts to endow one (or a few) central characters with a consistent point of view and to tell the story through that point of view. He used various words to describe the point-of-view character, including "reflector" or "reflecting center," "mirror," "vessel" (of consciousness), and "register." James felt that a novel should turn on the "drama of consciousness," the events in the plot being less important than the record of a character's engagement in or "take" on those events. The play of the character's thinking was what counted. Each of James' terms (and many others proposed by later narratologists, like "vision," "post of observation," "inner view," "focus," and "focalization") suggests its own nuance. "Reflector" or "mirror," for instance, favors the character's physical visual powers but makes the character seem a passive replicator of them. "Vessel" gives good insight into the character as bearer of consciousness but does not invoke the communicative implication that the narrator tells the tale, as it were, *through* the character, as the character experienced it.

Not only the character's experience, but the narrator's discourse, like any other communication, entails a point of view—an attitude, a disposition that pervades the telling of the tale, sometimes overtly, sometimes by implication. Thus, literary critics assign the term point of view also to the narrator, generally without making any theoretical distinction between the character's and the narrator's points of view.

But clearly some novels express a conflict between how a character perceives plot events and how the narrator does. In a classic discussion in *The Rhetoric of Fiction* (1961), Wayne Booth showed how Jane Austen's *Emma* (1815) turns on that conflict. The heroine, whose point of view is conveyed in the narrative, is charming but misguided, and the narrator's point of view helps us see Emma's faults (and also to hope that she will ultimately see the light). However, applying the term *point of view* to both the character and the narrator may give rise to confusion. A particularly troubling confusion is involved in the belief that telling the story through a character's point of view makes that character into the narrator, even though the character is referred to in the third person. Booth, for instance, wrote: "The most important unacknowledged narrators in modern fiction are the third-person "centers of consciousness" through whom authors have filtered their narratives. . . . [T]hey fill pre-

cisely the function of avowed narrators—though they *can* add intensities of their own." With respect to *Emma,* Booth argued, "The solution to the problem of maintaining [the reader's] sympathy despite almost crippling faults was primarily to use the heroine herself as a kind of narrator, though in third person, reporting on her own experience." "Reporting on" seems an odd way to express what happens in the novel since it implies that Emma was consciously telling her story. But Emma is not telling her story; rather she is *living* it. It seems unwise to confuse the third person—the person spoken about—with a genuine narrator.

The French narratologist Gérard Genette has argued the need to recognize the profound difference between the narrator's act of telling, expressing the story in words, and the physical and mental orientation of the story through a character who experiences the events from a particular position inside the story-world. We must recognize, argues Genette, the difference between who speaks and who sees. These terms are, of course, synecdoches: "speaks" stands for "communicates a story in any way," so that even a movie camera may be said to act as a narrator, while "sees" stands for "experiences in the story-world," whether through the physical senses or through mental conceptualization.

Most narratologists agree with Genette that it is the narrator who speaks or reports and the character who sees or experiences the story-world. But there is some difference of opinion about how to distinguish these functions terminologically. Genette introduced the word *focalization* (but later reverted to an older term, French *foyer,* or focus) to communicate the "seeing" function, reserving "narrating" or "narration" for the "speaking" function. Mieke Bal, to whom events "are always presented from within a certain 'vision'," argued that both characters and narrators focalize: ". . . the focalizor, the point from which the elements are viewed . . . can lie with a character . . . or outside" (see Bal, 1980). This is her way of accounting, for example, for the expository beginnings of some novels, wherein the narrator may orient or delimit a certain space and time as the story-world even before the first character appears. Where the narrator alone orients the setting, Genette and Bal speak of *external focalization.* *Internal focalization,* on the other hand, is the orientation performed as through some character's consciousness. The object of focalization Bal calls the *focalized* ("focalisé"). In a sentence like "John saw Mary smile," the narrator speaks the sentence, John is the focalizer, and Mary is the focalized.

But if no terminological distinction is drawn between the narrator's orienting the scene and the character's doing so, if the narrator can "see" as well as "speak," the confusion that Genette warned against is potentially reintroduced. The two kinds of orientation must be distinguished. Both narrator and character can orient the scene spatially and temporally, but this power need not be referred to by the same term. Should they be lumped together as points of view or focalizations? The answer can be yes only with respect to non-perceptual orientations. Conceptually, the narrator, like the character, can obviously express or imply a certain attitude (even if it is one of neutrality) toward what happens in the story. He or she may also exhibit a certain interest in how and which aspects of the story get told; for example, some narrations contain confessions or excuses for the narrator's past behavior, as in Vladimir Nabokov's *Lolita* (1955) or Charles Dickens' *Great Expectations* (1861). People have reasons for telling stories, and, especially where the narrator is a character-narrator, those reasons may be more important than the story itself. For instance, in Manuel Puig's *Kiss of the Spider Woman* (1976), the homosexual Molina recounts the trite plots of Hollywood and Nazi movie thrillers to his cellmate Valentin partly to while away the time, but also in the hopes of seducing him. (An excellent explanation of the pragmatic function of story-telling—or *why* a story is told—is given by Ross Chambers, 1984.)

The application of point of view or focalization to the perceptions of the narrator, however, is more problematic. Obviously, the narrator can orient the story in time and space independently of any character's perceptions. But there is an important difference between orienting the reader to a setting, through the choice of certain words, and literally perceiving the scene. It doesn't really make sense to say that the narrator perceives the events, characters, and setting in the act of telling the story. A character-narrator may perceive them in his mind's eye, as a memory or an imagination, but not literally, the way a character perceives them. Only characters inhabit the world of the story. Only *they* see, hear, and otherwise experience the events, the other characters, and the setting. The narrator does not experience the events, but rather reports them, and in reporting, orients (or in Bal's term, focalizes) the scene in such a way that the reader can grasp it.

To ensure the clarity of this distinction, some narratologists prefer to speak of two kinds of point of view, according to whether it belongs to the narrator or to a character. It has been proposed, for example, that we call the narrator's point of view *slant* and the character's point of view *filter*. When the narrator tells a story through a character's point of view, we can say that the story is *filtered* and that the character in question is a *filter-character*. These different terms help us remember that the narrator does not inhabit the world of the story but rather the world of the discourse. The narrator's discourse may (or may not) use the filter of one or more characters, and it may (or may not) state or imply an independent conceptual and/or interest slant. But the narrator has no direct perceptual access to the story-world; his or her post is outside, in the discourse. Since only characters have direct perceptions within the story-world, the narrator must use them as filters to establish an effect of direct witnessing. The narrator does not have a perceptual view into the story-world (although he does have one inside the discourse-world; for example, the character-narrator Whitey in Ring Lardner's "Haircut" [1929] can obviously see the hair of the man whom he is barbering as he tells the story of the death of Jim Kendall). It should be noted, too, that the narrator's slant is a conscious part of his or her method of presenting the story to the reader. The character's filter, on the other hand, is not directed at the reader—normally, the character is not even aware of the reader's existence. Rather, it is simply a product of the character's living her life in the story. She does not consciously orient us, but we can infer an orientation in space and time from what she does, says, and thinks.

The filter-slant distinction may seem to break down in first-person (homodiegetic) narratives. Doesn't Pip both speak about the events and characters of *Great Expectations* and also see them? Yes, but at different times: as a character he saw them back in story-time; as a narrator he recalls them "now," in discourse-time. A character-narrator, although a single person, is two different narrative agents. As reminiscing narrator of the story, he lives in the present moment of the discourse; as experiencing character he lived back then during the story. Thus, each first-person narrator necessarily has two points of view. His present point of view, or narrator's slant, states or implies his current attitudes, what he feels at the moment of telling the story. But usually he also tells the story through himself-as-filter-character, that is, he reports, as a memory, his earlier impressions about the events, other characters, and setting back when they occurred in the story-world. The character-narrator's slant and filter may or may not coincide: Pip-as-narrator views some things quite differently in discourse time from the way he viewed them back when he was a frightened boy on the moor in the grip of an escaped convict, or later in London, when he became something of a snob, awaiting his great inheritance. In the first chapter of Conrad's "Heart of Darkness" (1902), Marlow tells us a good deal about his present slant—for instance, when he reminds his listeners that England "also has been one of the dark places of the earth." In later chapters, however, much of what he says about the Congo jungle and the mysterious Kurtz is filtered through the experience of the younger Marlow-as-character.

Many narrative ironies turn on the distinction between slant and filter. Consider the following sentence: "Unfortunately, despite every insult, John listened with admiration to the conversation of company assembled at dinner, feeling that he was being treated very well indeed." From John's perceptual point of view (as reported by the narrator), the conversation sounds admirable, and, from his conceptual point of view, he is being treated very well indeed. But the narrator's "Unfortunately, despite every insult" explicitly slants the narrative to show that John's admiration of the company is misguided, that John's interest point of view, although he doesn't know it, are at odds with his perceptual and conceptual points of view. "Unfortunately" must be the narrator's word and hence presents his slant.

A good literary example of this kind of irony opens Joseph Conrad's *The Secret Agent* (1907). Mr. Verloc, the protagonist, an anti-hero double agent for both the British and the Russians in pre-World War I London, is on his way to a secret meeting with his employer at the Russian Embassy:

> He surveyed through the park railings the evidence of the town's opulence and luxury with an approving eye. All these people had to be protected. Protection is the first necessity of opulence and luxury . . . the whole social order favourable to their hygienic idleness had to be protected against the shallow enviousness of unhygienic labour. It had to—and Mr. Verloc would have rubbed his hands with satisfaction had he not been constitutionally averse from every superfluous exertion. His idleness was not hygienic, but it suited him very well.

The narrator tells the story through Mr. Verloc's perceptual filter and through Verloc's conceptualization of his mission—to protect the British upper class' "hygienic idleness" against the unhygienic working class. But the last two sentences convey the narrator's slant: he considers Verloc himself lazy, unhygienic, and shabby compared to the people he claims to be protecting. This slant persists through the rest of the novel, attaching as well to the anarchists with whom Verloc associates.

Consider the means by which the character's filter and the narrator's slant are conveyed in the above passage. Perceived objects are not ordinarily expressed in words that the character would articulate in his own mind. We do not assume that the first sentence is equivalent to "Verloc said to himself 'Look at that evidence of the town's opulence and luxury'." The perception is Verloc's, but the words are the narrator's ("approving" is the narrator's general characterization of Verloc's attitude toward what he sees). But when we conceptualize, words do seem to be going through our minds. (That we think in words is no mere convention but a common experience in the real world: out in the streets we can hear unfortunate souls shouting their inner reveries aloud.) In novels, the words passing through the character's mind may be directly quoted, just as if they were speech. Conrad could have written "'All these people have to be protected,' Verloc thought." Notice that to achieve the greatest degree of immediacy, such direct quotation of a character's thought uses the present tense (*have* to be protected). Or that the character's thought might have been indirectly quoted: "Mr. Verloc thought that all those people had to be protected." Indirect quotation introduces a slight degree of distance, but not as much as would have been the case if the narrator had used his own words. The indirect quotation could be further abbreviated by the deletion of the tag "He thought"—that is, by deleting the attribution of the thought to Verloc. Such a truncated indirect quotation is called *free indirect thought* (and its spoken equivalent *free indirect speech*). That is the form Conrad actually chose to represent Verloc's thinking: "All these people had to be protected."

Thought quotation, whether direct or indirect, purports to reproduce the words that pass through a character's mind. Whatever the scientific truth about human cognition, the narrative convention is that characters conceptualize in language. Perception, as we have seen, does not entail words—when you see smoke, you don't say to yourself "I'm seeing smoke." But in novels and short stories, perceptions too must be conveyed through words, so the words depicting them can only be the narrator's. Any representation of a character's perception, and of those cognitions not couched in the character's own language, have been conveniently labeled *psychonarration* (see Dorrit Cohn, 1978). That is the form used in the later sentences from *The Secret Agent* quoted above. From what the narrator hints about Verloc's personality and level of culture (confirmed throughout by the character's directly quoted dialogue), we can infer that although Verloc felt that "the whole social order favourable to the hygienic idleness of the upper classes had to be protected against the shallow enviousness of unhygienic labour," such an uncouth man probably could not have expressed that feeling in such elegant words. The words are clearly those of the literate and ironic narrator.

Our ability to distinguish between psychonarration and indirect free thought rests upon our ability to distinguish speech styles. External narrators are usually well-spoken, whereas a character's command of the language necessarily depends upon his or her dialect, age, education, class, intelligence, and the like—information that readers acquire in various ways in a novel, but most explicitly through direct quotations of the character's speech. The greater the gap between the narrator's linguistic capabilities and the character's (however we divine or infer it), the easier it is to distinguish the character's indirect free thought from the narrator's psychonarration. Consider, for example, an early passage in Joyce's *A Portrait of the Artist as a Young Man* (1916). The whole novel is filtered through the consciousness of

Stephen Dedalus. In the second section, he is five or six years old, a pupil at Clongowes Woods school. His weak eyes and frail body prevent him from succeeding in sports, but he is forced to try. Some of his feelings are expressed through psychonarration: for instance, "The evening air was pale and chilly and after every charge and thud of the footballers the greasy leather orb flew like a heavy bird through the grey light." Though very young, Stephen already shows much sensitivity: the title of the novel tells us that he will become an artist. So we can believe that at some level he may see a resemblance between the football and a bird sailing through gray light. But it is doubtful that those exact words, let alone "the greasy leather orb," literally passed through the mind of a five-year-old. They come from the narrator's vocabulary, in psychonarration. However, we do pass into Stephen's indirect free thought in the course of the following passage: "He felt his body small and weak amid the throng of players and his eyes were weak and watery. Rody Kickham was not like that: he would be the captain of the third line all the fellows said. Rody Kickham was a decent fellow but Nasty Roche was a stink." "Throng" is still the narrator's word, but "stink" is clearly Stephen's.

When the character's linguistic abilities approach those of the narrator, however, it is sometimes difficult to recognize whose point of view prevails. It may be the character's, through indirect free thought or psychonarration, or the narrator's, or indeterminately both. This ambiguity often gives rise to an interesting effect of sympathetic harmony of point of view between character and external narrator. The effect occurs in many modernist novels, including, prominently, Virginia Woolf's *Mrs. Dalloway*.

SEYMOUR CHATMAN

See also Diegesis and Diegetic Levels of Narration; Discourse Representation; Film and the Novel; Implied Author; Narrative Theory; Narratology; Narrator; Person in Narrative; Tense in Narrative; Unreliable Narrator

Further Reading

Bal, Mieke, *De theorie van vertellen en verhalen*, Mulderberg: Coutinho, 1980; as *Narratology: An Introduction to the Theory of Narrative*, Toronto and Buffalo, New York: University of Toronto Press, 1985

Booth, Wayne C., *The Rhetoric of Fiction*, Chicago: University of Chicago Press, 1961; 2nd edition, Chicago: University of Chicago Press, and London: Penguin, 1983

Chambers, Ross, *Story and Situation: Narrative Seduction and the Power of Fiction*, Minneapolis: University of Minnesota Press, and Manchester: Manchester University Press, 1984

Chatman, Seymour, *Story and Discourse: Narrative Structure in Fiction and Film*, Ithaca, New York: Cornell University Press, 1978

Chatman, Seymour, *Coming to Terms: The Rhetoric of Narrative in Fiction and Film*, Ithaca, New York: Cornell University Press, 1990

Cohn, Dorrit, *Transparent Minds: Narrative Modes for Presenting Consciousness in Fiction*, Princeton, New Jersey: Princeton University Press, 1978

Genette, Gérard, *Discours du récit*, in *Figures III*, Paris: Seuil, 1972; as *Narrative Discourse*, Ithaca, New York: Cornell University Press, 1980

Genette, Gérard, *Nouveau discours du récit,* Paris: Seuil, 1983;
as *Narrative Discourse Revisited,* Ithaca, New York: Cornell
University Press, 1988

Lanser, Susan Sniader, *The Narrative Act: Point of View in
Prose Fiction,* Princeton, New Jersey: Princeton University
Press, 1981

Miller, James E., Jr., *Theory of Fiction: Henry James,* Lincoln:
University of Nebraska Press, 1972

Rimmon-Kenan, Shlomith, *Narrative Fiction: Contemporary
Poetics,* London and New York: Methuen, 1983

Toolan, Michael, *Narrative: A Critical Linguistic Introduction,*
London and New York: Routledge, 1988

Polish Novel

The first Polish novels started appearing at about the same time the genre matured in Western Europe, i.e., in the second half of the 18th century. And although the Polish word for novel, *powieść,* had been used even earlier, in medieval writings, it meant no more than a prose work, mostly a free translation from Latin, which until the Renaissance period in the 16th century dominated Polish letters.

As a milestone in that modern development there stood a novel *Mikołaja Doświadczyńskiego przypadki* (1776; The Adventures of Mr. Nicholas Wisdom), published under the pen name X.B.W., an abbreviation for Xiążę Biskup Warmiński (Prince Bishop of Warmia), the official title of Ignacy Krasicki, one of the most illustrious representatives of the Polish Enlightenment. Its author had distinguished himself with numerous poems, fables, satires, mock-heroic poems, etc., making him a favorite with the reading public. This time, however, he combined several genres into one, and wrote an educational novel, slightly cynical, slightly humorous, resembling Voltaire's *Candide,* which was published earlier, in 1759. The protagonist of Krasicki's novel, a young gentleman, experiences all sorts of adventures at home, abroad, and in a fantastic utopian neverland, thus gathering practical education in many fields, with the intention of bringing the improvements to his own country. Narrated in a witty, often satirical manner, the story obviously fostered the Age of Reason philosophy and served a pedagogical rather than artistic purpose. The same is true of Krasicki's next novel, *Pan Podstoli* (1778–1803; Mr. Pantler), which turns into a socio-moral treatise, realistically presenting the problems facing Poland at the end of the century.

The problems were many and most serious. The partitioning of Poland between the three neighboring powers, Russia, Prussia, and Austria, took place between 1772 and 1795, effectively erasing Poland from the map of Europe for the next 123 years, a period crucial in the history of the European novel. That circumstance alone affected the Polish novel's further development and character. Partitioning inspired the writing of romantic poetry and poetic novels (notably by Poland's most prominent poets, Adam Mickiewicz and Juliusz Słowacki), among other literary forms, but did not contribute to a free, creative presentation of social and political problems typical of the modern novel of the early 19th century. The romantic spirit suited patriotic poetry, nostalgic in character and spiritual in yearning, but did not help in keeping up with the rapid change in European literature at that time. Compounding the problem was the fact that, in the lands occupied by the three foreign powers, the possibility of free expression was quite limited. Indeed, some romantic Polish poets, including Mickiewicz, left the country after an anti-Russian uprising in 1830 failed, thus removing themselves from the thick of the problems facing Polish society at home.

It was then up to those writers who remained in Poland to create a modern, contemporary novel adequate to express political questions—as much as this was permissible—as well as social questions, and, at the same time, to match the literary developments in the West, which for centuries had served as a model for Polish literature, as part of the Western heritage in the national ethos. They followed the Western example quite closely, with all its trends and fashions. While women writers, numerous at that time, embraced sentimentalism and wrote countless tearful romances for the new reading public created by the educational policies of the late 18th century, there happened to be in Poland an almost equal number of writers impressed by the Gothic novel. An interesting example is *The Manuscript Found in Saragossa* (1805) by Jan Potocki, an international adventurer and Polish writer who wrote in French, published in Russia, and eventually became quite popular in Western Europe as a hero of that genre, with all its horrors, adventures, mystery, and romance. That particular novel was rediscovered only in the late 1960s, and enjoyed for a while a cult following in the United States.

Polish writers at the beginning of the 19th century embraced early realism in all its forms, including, curiously enough, the historical novel. That latter phenomenon could be ascribed to the captive nation's political situation, in which the glories of the past served as a reminder that "Poland has not been lost yet," in the words of a 1797 mazurka that later became the national anthem in 1918. Thus the enormous popularity of Sir Walter Scott's novels, discovered by the romantic poets and translated into Polish as early as the 1820s, strongly impacted the creation of the original Polish historical novel in later decades. However, in the first half of the 19th century, next to romantic poetry, the Polish novel emerged as a popular genre dealing mostly with contemporary issues—at least those that could be voiced with permission from the occupying authorities. Among those "safe" subjects were the situations of the peasantry, thus far neglected in literature, of the petty gentry, and of the Jewish minority in the Eastern provinces of Poland. In short,

Polish writers developed new forms for presenting new problems, beginning with journalistic sketches, collections of vignettes, novellas, and eventually full-fledged novels.

Among the large number of new novelists entering the field in the mid–19th century, a special place was occupied by Józef Ignacy Kraszewski, who authored nearly 700 volumes, most of them social and historical novels. As Czesław Miłosz phrased it in his *The History of Polish Literature* (1969), Kraszewski's achievement "must be reckoned among the highest outputs ever on a world scale." As large, socially oriented panoramas of country and urban life, full of human compassion for misery and misfortune, and yet optimistic in their final message, Kraszewski's novels somewhat resemble those of Charles Dickens (interestingly, Dickens' novels were promptly translated and widely read in Poland). That type of fiction turned out to be generally accepted by Polish readers, many of whom considered it an educational experience, even substituting it for the formal education that was gradually being curtailed by the occupying authorities. Among Kraszewski's most ambitious and successful projects was a series of novels chronicling the history of Poland, from its early beginnings in the 10th century to the end of Rzeczpospolita (from Latin *Res Publica*, the Republic), as the Kingdom of Poland was officially called, and even to the 1863 national uprising against the Russians.

For his literary and civic endeavors Kraszewski was greatly admired by his contemporaries and considered by some to be a patriotic role model. When a baby boy was born to a young poet, Apollo Korzeniowski, the happy father asked Kraszewski for a birthday blessing, and the novelist gladly obliged his neighbor. The boy was christened Józef Teodor Konrad, and later on, after many heartbreaking experiences and adventures, he was to become England's foremost novelist, Joseph Conrad. Hence his French biographer, G. Jean-Aubry, rightly remarked, "It looked as if literature had presided over the first moments of his destiny."

Kraszewski's contemporary Teodor Tomasz Jeż (real name Zygmunt Miłkowski) sought his topics in the Balkans, writing a series of novels on the Turkish yoke over South Slavs. Clearly, that type of fiction had strong bearings on the Polish readers who could compare their own political situation with the glories of the past and the struggles to regain national freedom.

The Polish writer with the greatest popular appeal, however, was Henryk Sienkiewicz, Nobel prize winner in 1905. Sienkiewicz's historical novels of the 1880s have topped the national best-seller lists ever since. He wrote, as he put it at the end of his historical trilogy, "to uplift human hearts," and perhaps nobody understood that message better than a modern master of US literature, William Faulkner, who wrote in 1953, recalling his youthful readings of Sienkiewicz's historical novel, "This book was written at the expense of considerable effort, to uplift men's hearts, and I thought: *What a nice thing to have thought to say. But no more than that. I didn't even think, Maybe some day I will write a book too and what a shame I didn't think of that first so I could put it on the front page of mine* . . . until suddenly one day he saw that old half-forgotten Pole had had the answer all that time. To uplift man's heart; the same for all of us. . . . Some of us don't know that this is what we are writing for. . . . But we all write for this one purpose."

The trilogy consists of three novels, *Ogniem i mieczem* (1884; *With Fire and Sword*), *Potop* (1886; *The Deluge*), and *Pan*

Wołodyjowski (1887–88; *Pan Michael* or *Fire in the Steppe*), dealing with a series of wars Poland conducted in its defense against the Cossacks, the Swedes, and the Turks, respectively, over the course of the 17th century. It is, on the surface, an almost classical type of adventure novel, made highly popular by Alexandre Dumas *père* in the 1840s, and, for its Polish readers living in a country partitioned off and deprived of basic freedoms, it had an uplifting effect, indeed. Sienkiewicz's trilogy told of the nation's past glories and defeats in such a manner that people could identify with the fictitious heroes, emulate their efforts, and once more believe in the resurrection of their homeland. As an interesting example one can recall that, during World War II, with the country once more divided between Nazi Germany and Soviet Russia, an impressive number of freedom fighters assumed their pseudonyms from the protagonists of Sienkiewicz's novels. His granddaughter Maria recollected how a guerilla detachment rode in on horseback to their family estate, Oblęgorek, many of the young men having pseudonyms taken from the trilogy. What could be a more lasting testimony to the author's fame than his fictitious heroes coming alive half a century later?

Although Sienkiewicz repeated his national success with yet another historical novel, *Krzyżacy* (1900; *The Teutonic Knights*), international recognition and fame came earlier, with the publication of his masterpiece *Quo vadis?* (1896; *Quo Vadis?*), a novel about the persecution of early Christians in Rome during the reign of Emperor Nero. Vivid with colorful characters, fast action, and impressive images of the ancient world, *Quo Vadis?* deftly introduces a striking contrast between the superficial Roman splendor and the true values represented by Christianity, while the novel's intrigue is sustained by a romance between a Roman officer and a Christian girl.

While Sienkiewicz dominated the field of Polish novel writing with these and many other works at the turn of the century, occasionally he shared the literary limelight with his contemporary Bolesław Prus (real name Aleksander Głowacki). Starting as a journalist and short-story writer, Prus emerged as a major novelist with the publication of his most popular work, *Lalka* (1890; *The Doll*), perhaps the first truly modern novel of that period. Set in Warsaw in the late 1870s, it introduces a rich gallery of characters as a background for the main conflict, the uphill struggle of a young businessman, Stanisław Wokulski, whose ambition is to be accepted by an artistocratic girl as a symbol of his social climb in a society rapidly changing its priorities (modern readers may be reminded of F. Scott Fitzgerald's *The Great Gatsby*, 1925). Prus' next novel, *Emancypantki* (1893; The Emancipated Women), deals with an equally modern problem, the need for better education for girls. No less important were the issues in his major historical novel *Faraon* (1897; *The Pharaoh*); with the colorful scenery of ancient Egypt serving as a background for the main problem, the novel focuses on the power struggle between the young pharaoh Ramses and the priests who actually ruled the country. On a philosophical level, Prus focuses on the conflict between enthusiasm and reason, but presents it in a character contrast, in an action novel based on historical research.

One more writer from this period should be mentioned: Eliza Orzeszkowa. Living in the provincial town of Grodno, remote from the centers of cultural life, she managed not only to follow modern trends but also introduced some bold and new problems into her writings, such as the role of women in contemporary society, the plight of young girls from the lower social strata, the question of the Jewish population in their self-imposed ghettos, etc., always telling her stories in a low-key, simple, and yet convincing style of narration. In *Nad Niemnem* (1888; On the Niemen River), the populist-minded Orzeszkowa addressed some vital national issues (such as hidden references to the 1863 uprising) under the surface of a family saga set in the northeastern provinces of Poland.

Sienkiewicz, Prus, and Orzeszkowa, more than any other authors of that epoch, represented the philosophy of positivism, which called for a new approach to all social and national problems, the repudiation of romantic ideas, and a new, sober, and realistic way of thinking and doing. Since that philosophy coincided with the international rise of realism as a method of writing, the Polish novel of the second half of the 19th century on the one hand faithfully reflected the changes occurring in that country and elsewhere, and on the other hand reached new artistic heights, signifying the maturity of the genre. Scores of authors, novelists, short-story writers, essayists, and playwrights testified to those changes with a large number of works, but it seems that the example of the three above-mentioned novelists illustrates it better than anything else.

With the artistic merits of the 19th-century Polish novel second to none, one wonders why it has never achieved a duly deserved international reputation. The reasons seem to be twofold. First, Polish novels have not been translated widely enough into languages generally known in European and US critical circles. While Sienkiewicz happened to be lucky enough to be translated into English and French, and W.S. Reymont (his fellow Nobel recipient) into German, making their novels available to, among others, the Nobel prize committee, their contemporaries did not enjoy the same opportunity. Prus' *The Doll* had to wait 72 years for its English translation, and Reymont's *Chłopi* (1902–09; *The Peasants*) as well as Żeromski's *Popioły* (1904; *The Ashes*), both of which were published once in English translation in the mid-1920s, have never been reprinted in the United States, while a modern version of Sienkiewicz's trilogy did not appear on the US book-market until 100 years after its first translation into English. The second reason for the Polish novel's failure to gain a stronger international reputation is perhaps more complicated. As a German critic, Marcel Reich-Ranicki, put it in discussing Polish novels, "It is not the problem of fights for freedom and independence at all. Nobody in the world cares for that, because not only the Poles, but also the Hungarians and Italians fought for it. But nobody wants to read about it. This is—more or less, *praeter propter*—national literature. Perhaps an excellent national literature, but international it is not. People are not interested in such topics."

At the turn of the century, Poland, like most European countries, succumbed to the new trends and fashions fostered in France and Germany, the two national cultures with the greatest influence on Polish intellectual life. While the French brand of naturalism, characterized by violence, cruelty, and unbridled passions, did not find many followers in Poland, traces of its influence can be found in the early writings of Władysław Stanisław Reymont, who became famous after the publication of his folkloristic novel *The Peasants,* a work that eventually won him the Nobel prize in 1924. Polish letters instead seemed to be falling under the spell of modernism, often referred to

in that country as symbolism, neoromanticism, or the Young Poland movement. The first to incorporate modernist elements into his novels was Stanisław Przybyszewski, a writer who had achieved a fairly large following first in Germany, where he published a number of works, and then, after returning to Poland in 1898, a notoriety for his preoccupation with "the naked soul" (as he called the libido), liberated sex, Satanic cults, and so on. But with an ever-growing interest in poetry and drama at the turn of the century, that type of fiction faded away rather quickly, replaced by novels dealing either with folklore (Reymont) or recent national history, particularly the ill-fated 1863 uprising.

That topic seemed to be an obsession with Stefan Żeromski, who focused on it in a number of his early short stories and several novels that won him public recognition. His most successful novel, *The Ashes,* deals with the Napoleonic wars and the question of Poland's very existence emerging at that time. Often compared to Tolstoi's *Voina i mir* (1863–69; *War and Peace*), Żeromski's novel is perhaps less ambitious in philosophical scope but more modern in novelistic technique, introducing a number of protagonists, international scenery, shifting points of view, and a variety of narrative forms. His last novel, *Przedwiośnie* (1925; Before the Spring), published after Poland regained her independence in 1918, discusses the more contemporary issues of neighboring Soviet Russia and its potential revolutionary influence. It offers no solution and ends on an ambiguous note of suspense as to the future of the newly reborn republic.

The period between the wars (1918–39) was dominated by psychological and social fiction written in many cases by women authors emerging in the mid-1920s. While Maria Dąbrowska distinguished herself with a broad, social panorama of the early years of the 20th century with her novel *Noce i dnie* (1932–34; Nights and Days), a significant number of her contemporaries addressed social ills in modern Poland, focusing on such issues as unemployment, poverty, injustice, and the plight of ethnic minorities and women. Two men who made their mark on that period, Andrzej Strug (real name Stefan Gałecki) and Juliusz Kaden-Bandrowski, emphasized in their respective novels antiwar sentiments and pleas for world peace (Strug) and the life of the working class, coal miners in particular (Bandrowski). The interwar period brought about a revival of the best traditions in the Polish novel and, at the same time, allowed for formal experimentation and the introduction of new types of novels that reflected the changes in literature and society following World War I.

Among the best-known representatives of that new type of fiction there emerged Stanisław Ignacy Witkiewicz (also known as Witkacy) and Witold Gombrowicz. The former, a painter, playwright, and amateur philosopher, wrote two grotesque, loosely composed novels, *Pożegnanie jesieni* (1927; Farewell to Autumn) and *Nienasycenie* (1930; *Insatiability*), set in some unidentified future, the time of universal revolutions, when Western civilization would be annihilated by communism and "the yellow peril," the Chinese. With its psychological defenses down, eliminated by a mysterious pill that breaks the will to resist, the West would succumb to a new (we could call it Orwellian today) social order under totalitarian control. Witkacy's dark vision was largely misunderstood during his lifetime, and only after World War II has it been recognized as almost prophetic. Gombrowicz, on the other hand, was more preoccupied with the problems of individuals in modern society, and his first novel, *Ferdydurke* (1937; *Ferdydurke*), was received by critics as a challenge to the existing societal norms. Gombrowicz happened to be in South America at the outbreak of World War II, and, in spite of a number of problems created by his reluctant emigration, he went on writing novels and theatrical plays, eventually emerging as one of the leading modern writers of the postwar period. Interestingly, his novel *Trans-Atlantyk* (1953; *Trans-Atlantyk*) satirically repeats some of the experiences of the protagonist of Krasicki's 18th-century novel and imitates that novel's baroque style.

Germany's attack on Poland on 1 September 1939 marked the beginning of World War II and the end of an era in Poland's literary history. Polish writers who stayed home were not permitted to publish for the next five years in the German-occupied part of the country, while those living under Soviet occupation, which was undertaken two weeks after the German onslaught, were either deported to the Soviet labor camps and prisons or "persuaded" by force to accept the standards of "socialist realism," i.e., to follow the ideological and political dictate of the communist party. Only in view of such a reality could one appreciate Witkacy's foresight and understand why he committed suicide upon hearing of the Soviet invasion. If it were not for a small group of writers who managed to escape abroad, mostly to France, Great Britain, and the United States, Polish literature would have come to a complete standstill. Thus a new emigré literature was born with the self-imposed task of salvaging whatever was left, and bearing testimony to all that was taking place. Initially the emigré writers produced occasional poetry and short stories—neither the circumstances nor settings encouraged the production of more elaborate forms like the novel—and yet, as early as 1941, there appeared a semi-fictitious report on the combat experience of Polish troops participating in an Allied Expeditionary Force defending Norway against the German invasion in 1940, *Droga wiodła przez Narvik* (The Narvik Way) by Ksawery Pruszyński, a roving reporter, soldier, and journalist. The same author, writing as a critic, coined the label "literature of the fighting Poland," a literature that grew to become the free voice of the captive nation for the next half-century, defying both German control and Soviet indoctrination in the years and decades to come. It took other emigré writers a few years to follow suit, and eventually to reestablish that genre as a counterpart to novels that began to appear in 1945 in Poland, a country forced to become a member of the Soviet bloc in the aftermath of political decisions undertaken at the end of World War II.

The postwar period may be divided into several stages of the Sovietization of the Polish novel. The initial years, 1945–48, were marked by a fairly liberal policy by the authorities who took over control of the publishing market, a market strictly monitored by the communist party. Naturally, Polish novelists focused their attention on the two basic problems of the recent past: the politics of the interwar period and the national war experience. While the first topic resulted in a few novels that criticized the government for not being sufficiently prepared to defend the country against the German and Soviet invasions, the war novels generally praised rank-and-file soldiers, pointing the accusing finger at the higher military ranks, who were allegedly responsible for the lost campaign. Another event angering Polish writers was the tragedy of the 1944 Warsaw Uprising, which re-

sulted in the almost total destruction of the Polish capital. One of the first novels to discuss the uprising, *W rozwalonym domu* (In a Ruined House) by Jan Dobraczyński, appeared in 1946 and opened a never-ending flow of similar novels. The fact that it had been written by a Catholic writer, a man ideologically opposed to the new regime, alleviated the suspicion that the issue had been manipulated and used by the communist propaganda machine, which wanted to put the blame for the national tragedy on the Polish government-in-exile in London.

During those first years after World War II, it was possible for the Catholic writer Jerzy Andrzejewski to write and publish his novel *Popioł i diament* (1948; *Ashes and Diamonds*), a possibly objective presentation of the armed conflict between the patriotic young soldiers of the Polish underground Home Army and the communist regime entering Poland with the Soviet troops. Highly dramatic, realistic in detail, and topical as far as the political situation was concerned, *Ashes and Diamonds* eventually was translated into more than 20 languages and made into a successful movie by Andrzej Wajda.

This period did not last long. Early in 1949 the Union of Polish Writers adopted the Soviet model of socialist realism, and for the next six years Polish novels attempted to depict "positive heroes," the alleged achievements of the communist economic system, social conflicts in the "class struggle," and so on. The black-and-white scheme of that dogma—good guys (communists) versus bad guys (capitalists and their followers)—never hitched well with the sophisticated Polish novelists of the previous decades, hence the production of generally substandard works, in spite of the fact that quite a few writers with well-established credentials contributed to the promulgation of that type of literature. As an example one may cite the case of Wojciech Żukrowski, who had achieved a good literary reputation with his collections of short stories published just after the war, and who undertook to write a major novel on the September 1939 campaign in Poland. In 1952, at the height of the socialist realism period, he published the novel *Dni klęski* (The Days of Disaster), which realistically and objectively follows the footsteps of a young Polish protagonist until the day of 17 September 1939, when he welcomes the invading Soviet soldiers as "the liberators" of his country. Igor Newerly's (real name Igor Abramow) industrial novel *Pamiątka z Celulozy* (1952; *A Night of Remembrance*) focuses on the social development and advancement of a young worker in the newly established socialist system.

Polish writers had to register with the Union of Polish Writers and follow its political and even technical dictate. Most authors, either out of fear of persecution or the simple necessity of survival, followed the Union's dictate to the letter, with devastating artistic results. Only a few, mostly Catholic novelists, tried to escape into the field of the historical novel or, like Stanisław Lem, ventured into the unexplored field of science fiction. Lem achieved considerable international success, particularly in the following decades, with novels such as *Solaris* (1961), a philosophical work of existential dimensions. His books have been translated into 34 languages, placing him atop the international list of science-fiction authors.

A special mention should be given to a handful of Jewish writers who survived the Holocaust and were determined to give an artistic testimony to the national tragedy. Among that small group, Adolf Rudnicki left a few collections of prose works, including the novella *Złote okna* (1953; *The Golden Windows,* in *The Dead and Living Sea and Other Stories*), a moving account of the Warsaw Ghetto Uprising in 1943. His writings were free of communist propaganda, an exceptional case during the period of Stalinist pressure on Polish literature between 1949 and 1955. He left Poland after 1968 and settled as an emigré in Paris.

The first breakthrough came as early as 1954, when socialist realist dogma was challenged in its homeland, the Soviet Union. Polish writers soon followed suit with the publication of Maria Dąbrowska's novella *Na wsi wesele* (1955; *The Village Wedding*), which signaled the end of an artificial, politically motivated presentation of contemporary life. And readers generally received it as such. Much broader appeal with the reading public was achieved by Leopold Tyrmand's crime thriller *Zły* (1955; *The Man with White Eyes*), which openly disclosed for the first time that, under the surface of the officially promoted image of peaceful life in contemporary Warsaw, there existed and thrived a mafia-type underworld of violence, crime, and social dissatisfaction immune to the inefficient police force. Tyrmand's novel became an instant international hit, particularly in countries of the Soviet bloc, and was translated into more than 20 major European languages. After leaving Poland for the United States in 1966, Tyrmand wrote and published a number of novels, including *Życie towarzyskie i uczuciowe* (1967; Social and Emotional Life) and his Warsaw notebook *Dziennik 1954* (The 1954 Diary), both critically focusing on the corrupted moral and social standards of that city's intellectual elite.

Many novelists, who hitherto promoted socialist realism as the only method acceptable in creative writing, quickly rejected it and came forward with novels and novellas critical of the political pressure that had motivated them. Kazimierz Brandys' novel *Matka Królów* (1957; *Sons and Comrades*) disclosed the internal struggle in the upper echelons of the ruling communist party, while a number of his short stories advocated revisions of the communist ideology. "The Thaw"—as the period between 1955 and 1960 was generally referred to after the Soviet example—brought about a number of distinguished novels by older as well as newer writers. For example, Tadeusz Konwicki, who had achieved a dubious distinction as the author of the communism-affirming novel *Władza* (1954; Power), now wrote a number of novels, such as *Sennik współczesny* (1963; *The Dreambook for Our Time*) and *Kompleks polski* (1977; *The Polish Complex*), that won well-deserved international acclaim as examples of modern fiction, free of political ideology, artistically mature, and deep with symbolic, existential meaning.

Suddenly, Polish novels were fashionable in- and outside the country, heralding dramatic changes taking place in the Soviet bloc. The Polish novel's progress was recognized with an ever-growing number of translations and international awards.

Domestic political factors, however, hampered its further development in the 1960s and 1970s, resulting in a period called "a little stabilization," with no major results in the field of fiction. Once more, it was the proper time for emigré Polish writers to pick up the baton and promote what was missing at home—freedom of expression. Czesław Miłosz, an emigré poet since 1951, and Witold Gombrowicz, both writing for the Institut Littéraire, a Polish publisher in Paris, came to the fore with a number of novels that brought them fame and recognition. Miłosz won the Nobel prize for literature in 1980; although that highest literary honor was granted mostly for his achievements in poetry, two

novels, *Zdobycie władzy* (1955; *The Seizure of Power*) and *Dolina Issy* (1955; *The Issa Valley*), contributed to his success perhaps no less than his famous essay on the literary situation in postwar Poland, *Zniewolony umysł* (1953; *The Captive Mind*).

Two other emigré writers deserve recognition: Józef Mackiewicz, a rabid anti-communist who promoted his campaign against the Soviets in a number of novels, including *Nie trzeba głośno mówić* (1969; One Is Not Supposed to Speak Out Loud), and Włodzimierz Odojewski, who left Poland in order to publish, free of censorship, his major novel *Zasypie wszystko, zawieje . . .* (1973; And the Snow Will Cover Everything). Both authors devoted the bulk of their novelistic writings to the subject of *Kresy*, the Eastern regions of Poland taken over by the Soviets in 1939.

The following years witnessed a revival of biographical novels on personalities whose fate had been passed over in silence in Poland proper. One example is *Generał* (1980; The General) by Jerzy R. Krzyżanowski, which tells the story of Leopold Okulicki (1898–1946), the last commandant-in-chief of the Polish Home Army, who was kidnapped by the Soviets, put on trial, and sentenced to ten years in prison, where he eventually died. That novel had to wait another ten years for its new edition in Warsaw, free of the communist censorship.

For the record one should also remember two Polish writers who emigrated to the United States in the 1950s and not only decided to write and publish in English only but also made their respective contributions to contemporary US fiction. W.S. Kuniczak won the Book-of-the-Month Club selection for his first novel, *The Thousand Hour Day* (1966), and, following it up with *The March* (1979) and *Valedictory* (1983), created a modern trilogy on the Polish troops fighting in World War II. Jerzy Kosinski became a best-selling author of a series of contemporary novels that "illuminate the quest for identity, which is constantly threatened by the encroachments of modern society," in the words of US critic Samuel C. Coale.

The central distribution of books in Poland from the 1950s through the 1970s contributed to at least two interesting phenomena: on the one hand, it made books easily available and inexpensive, thus widening the circle of readers considerably; on the other hand, it promoted only those books printed by state-owned or state-controlled publishers, for whom ideological and political considerations were more important than artistic merits. As a result, most novels published during this period promoted the communist system and established its ideology, particularly among young readers. That method, however, backfired as soon as political controls were weakened by social protests and economic unrest. When communist authorities arrested a number of striking workers in 1976, a group of students and young intellectuals came to their defense and soon started a publication network, first underground, on a limited scale, then quickly growing to a significant number of publications known as "the second circuit," functioning under and beyond the officially approved and censored net of publication and distribution. The dissidents managed to publish a regular literary quarterly, *Zapis* (1979–82), and three of its 21 issues contained complete novels. Many major Polish novelists decided to have their respective works printed in *Zapis* or by emigré publishers in order to avoid censorship and political control. Jerzy Andrzejewski, Kazimierz Brandys, Tadeusz Konwicki, Włodzimierz Odojewski—to list only a few authors mentioned earlier—either started writing for the underground and emigré publishers or decided to leave the country, hence breaking the totalitarian monopoly of the communist party on literature. One of the most prominent novelists belonging to that group is Marek Nowakowski, whose work gradually evolved from novels depicting the lowest strata of Warsaw society to ambitious, critical presentations of that city's intellectuals and their political involvement.

Interestingly, the major political upheavals of 1980—the workers' strikes in Gdańsk and the Solidarity movement—have not been adequately reflected in fiction, except for the short, topical novel *Moc truchleje* (1981; *Give Us This Day*) by Janusz Głowacki. Nonetheless, the repercussions of that political change were loud and clear. A gradual relaxation of censorship, partial privatization of the publishing industry, and easier contacts with the West and the Polish emigré community all helped to promote contemporary fiction and to free it from the constraints imposed on it by the communist regime.

In 1989 the collapse of the system brought about a complete freedom of expression in Poland, with all of the problems that occur after a major political change. The book market has since been flooded with US fiction and romances, often of a cheap, sensational nature; private publishers, deprived of state subsidies, struggle to survive; authors are denied adequate royalties for their work; light entertainment seems to be more popular than serious novels; the reading public cannot afford high-priced books—in short, all the pitfalls of employing a capitalist system in a country that is used to state financial support manifest themselves with often devastating results. And yet, in spite of all these problems, there appear on the market interesting and valuable novels as signs of the cultural revival taking place alongside the political one.

Foremost among the changes has been the return of emigré books (and sometimes the authors themselves) to the reading public. Gustaw Herling-Grudziński had been deported by the Soviets in 1940 and consequently banned from publication in Poland. After the war he published in the West his devastating autobiographical novel *Inny świat* (1951; *A World Apart*), disclosing the evils of the Soviet labor camp system; he is now one of the most popular writers in Poland. Czesław Miłosz has made his partial residence in Cracow, which is also the home of the poetess Wisława Szymborska, 1996 Nobel prize winner, and Polish satirist Sławomir Mrożek, now returned after several years spent in Mexico. Włodzimierz Odojewski regularly contributes to Polish periodicals, and Witold Gombrowicz is regarded by many critics as the most important Polish writer of the century. The domestic novelists, both older and newer, are coming forward with new publications, openly discussing issues and problems hitherto forbidden by the censors, particularly the period of Soviet deportations and Stalinist persecutions in Poland after the war. Personal recollections and memoirs have become the novelistic stuff, with a heavy emphasis on politics, the horrors of forced exile, difficulties of returning to normal life in the postwar years, and so on. There is, in a way, a similarity between that type of novel and that which dealt with the German occupation, written in the late 1940s.

In the constant flow of such topical novels there appears once in a while a work of lasting value. Such is the case of Wiesław Myśliwski, who had written a number of peasant novels, returning to the well-established tradition of Reymont, before publishing *Kamień na kamieniu* (1984; A Stone upon a Stone), on which a contemporary critic, Andrzej Mencwel, commented, "The traditional peasant culture, which in its substance and structure steps down to its grave before our very eyes, happens to be the oldest Polish culture, the culture of the great majority of this nation. Perhaps it's three quarters, perhaps nine tenths . . . Myśliwski . . . meticulously, wisely, with inspiration and patience, with energy and piety, built for its remnants an impressive, everything else surpassing, carefully polished gravestone." Twelve years later, after all the changes occuring in Poland and in its literary life, he followed it up with *Widnokrąg* (1996; The Horizon), a novel about coming of age in a provincial Polish town during and immediately after World War II. Many critics regard it as one of the finest modern novels of its kind.

The majority of writers have remained preoccupied with more contemporary issues and problems. The events of 13 December 1981, when the communist regime imposed martial law to suppress the growing freedom movement, became a topic of several novels, including *Dezerter* (1992; The Deserter) by Tadeusz Siejak, who combined the psychological profiles of numerous characters from various walks of life with an ironic presentation of the political realities of that period. In *Dezerter,* as well as in some of his previous novels, such as *Pustynia* (1987; The Desert), Siejak demonstrates an almost uncanny ability to render in fiction the forms of speech used by ill-educated, petty officials of the communist party, making his prose a penetrating linguistic and cultural document of the 1980s in Poland.

Many other novelists focus their attention on the problems of a society undergoing a rapid, and often dramatic, transition from totalitarian rule to a free-market economy, with all of the complicated issues that accompany such changes. The Polish novel insists on remaining true to its basic mission, to be—as Stendhal put it—a mirror walking along the road.

JERZY R. KRZYŻANOWSKI

See also Witold Gombrowicz; Bolesław Prus; Władysław Stanisław Reymont; Henryk Sienkiewicz

Further Reading

Coleman, Marion Moore, editor, *Polish Literature in English Translation: A Bibliography,* Cheshire, Connecticut: Cherry Hill, 1963

Danilewicz Zielińska, Maria, *Szkice o literaturze emigracyjnej,* Paris: Instytut Literacki, 1978

Eile, Stanislaw, *Modernist Trends in Twentieth-Century Polish Fiction,* London: School of Slavonic and East European Studies, 1996

Gillon, Adam, and Ludwik Krzyzanowski, editors, *Introduction to Modern Polish Literature,* New York: Twayne, and London: Rapp and Whiting, 1964

Głowiński, Michał, *Gry powieściowe,* Warsaw: PWN, 1973

Kridl, Manfred, *A Survey of Polish Literature and Culture,* The Hague: Mouton, and New York: Columbia University Press, 1956

Krzyżanowski, Julian, *A History of Polish Literature,* Warsaw: PWN–Polish Scientific Publishers, 1978

Kuncewiczowa, Maria, editor, *The Modern Polish Mind: An Anthology,* Boston: Little Brown, and London: Secker and Warburg, 1962

Miłosz, Czesław, *The History of Polish Literature,* New York:

Macmillan, 1969; 2nd edition, Berkeley: University of
California Press, 1983

Terlecki, Tymon, editor, *Literatura polska na obczyznie
1940–1960*, 2 vols., London: Swiderski, 1964–65

Wieniewska, Celina, editor, *Polish Writing Today*, Baltimore
and London: Penguin, 1967

Wyka, Kazimierz, *Pogranicze powieści*, Warsaw: Kot, 1948;
2nd edition, Warsaw: Czytelnik, 1974

Zawodziński, Karol Wiktor, *Stulecie trójcy powieściopisarzy:
Studia nad społecznem i artystycznem znaczeniem dzieła
Orzeszkowej, Prusa, Sienkiewicza*, Łódź, 1948

Politics and the Novel

The relation of politics to the genre of the novel is a modern question and a contentious one. In the sense that all literature and all writers are products of specific historical and cultural conditions, it is often argued that all novels are political. The apparent lack of a specific political viewpoint or of specific political material, or claims by the author of political neutrality, are seen in this context as a political stance. At the other end of the spectrum, many artists and critics have regarded any direct connection between aesthetic productions and the real world as an illusion, the result of literary and linguistic trickery. These extremes form the parameters of a debate that generally focuses on four major areas of discussion: the nature of political content and its relation to aesthetic form; the use of the novel as an agent of social change; the role of public reception in determining a novel's impact as political; and, finally, the possible tension between the politics of the writer and the politics of the writing.

When we talk about politics and the novel, it is generally assumed that we are talking about content, about the body of realistic material that provides the context, the thrust, and the rationale of the fictional narrative. Novels that are judged to be political in this sense may not necessarily describe or even refer to specific political processes and/or events, but are critical representations of social structures, social mores, and social relations. They are perceived as political partly because of the writer's viewpoint but also because of the writer's power to influence and/or change the viewpoint of the reader. More specifically, the political novel is one whose intention is demonstrably to act as an agent of social change.

Most critics would accept that definition as a starting point. However, even such apparently straightforward ideas present difficulties. Many critics claim that the relation between a writer's political viewpoint and the political statement his or her novel makes is an unstable and problematic one. The conjunction of an individual's viewpoint, a specific historical context, and a particular stage in the evolution of literary form may obscure or transform the writer's intention, giving the reader uncertainty of focus and suggesting a variety of responses. These critics would also argue that content is not easily separated from form and that the relation of politics to the novel is mediated not only through the writer and the reader but also through the literary forms available to him or her at the time. Others would claim that a novel is not a political pamphlet but a literary construct that cannot intervene in social processes the way a pamphlet may. Attempts to make it do so, such critics maintain, contradict the function of art.

However, despite these arguments, in practice many novelists continue to use their novels as social critiques and as agents of change, and the novel has continued to make powerful interventions in social and political issues. What is certain is that the novel form has always shown itself to be peculiarly suited to the investigation of social relations, emerging again and again in times of historical change and public and political crisis as the literary form of protest.

The novel's rapid rise to popularity in 18th-century England is commonly explained in political terms as closely linked to the rise of the bourgeoisie. Indeed, the novel has been called a bourgeois literary form because of its early focus on the world of the rising middle classes and its materialist perspective on the daily world of social intercourse, in contrast to the heroic themes of classical poetry and drama. However, early novels such as Jonathan Swift's *Gulliver's Travels* (1726)—a savagely specific political allegory attacking the ruling classes—and Henry Fielding's *The Adventure of Joseph Andrews* (1742)—a razor-sharp satire on the hypocrisy of social institutions—located the novel from the beginning in an emerging tradition of social and political commentary. However, despite the political implications of such novels, typical literary treatment in the 18th century pointed toward a moral rather than driving at political resolution.

The forces of industrialization and the rapidly worsening conditions in England's cities in the mid–19th century began to draw the novel form into closer alliance with the politics of change. Writers such as Elizabeth Gaskell, Charles Dickens, and Charles Kingsley used their novels to intervene in social processes and to contribute to social reform by framing their narratives with detailed and realistic descriptions of social conditions. Elizabeth Gaskell's *Mary Barton* (1848) exposed the plight of the industrialized classes in Manchester and diagnosed the social malaise at the heart of class relations. Child labor, debt, poverty, and the Poor Law were issues Dickens addressed in novels such as *Oliver Twist* (1838), *Little Dorrit* (1857), and *Our Mutual Friend* (1865), while Charles Kingsley advocated the benefits of education for the working classes in *Alton Locke* (1850) and joined in the attack on child labor in *The Water-Babies* (1863).

These "condition of England" novels mark an important development in the political function of the novel. Although Gaskell, Dickens, and Kingsley all claimed to write from a

Christian perspective for humanitarian reform and avoided political pleading, the implications of their fictions are not reformist, but revolutionary. Many contemporary readers and critics responded to them in this spirit. These novels also mark the beginning of a long tradition of British social protest novels that continued into the 20th century and includes the novels of William Makepeace Thackeray, Thomas Hardy, and George Moore. The success of these novels had the effect of transforming literary realism into a radical literary mode. In France, realism developed in the late 19th century into naturalism, which emphasized authenticity and accuracy of detail in the representation of middle- and working-class life. Émile Zola's *Les Rougon-Macquart* series, which includes *Germinal* (1885) and *La Terre* (1887; *The Earth*), exposed the misery and poverty of contemporary French society and the violence of human instincts and had considerable influence on British realist writers.

The late 19th century registered a further change in the relation between politics and the novel. Waning religious authority, the increase in literacy, and the rise of Marxist socialism and labor politics after 1880 gave the novel greater public influence and an increasingly specific political edge. This was not an entirely new phenomenon. In the 1840s in England, for instance, the Chartists—a working-class movement struggling for political freedom—had demonstrated an intimate relation between literature and politics. They had transformed popular literary forms, harnessing narrative to a specific ideological viewpoint. However, the turn of the century saw such writing becoming more frequent and more international as socialist ideas spread across the world. In the United States, works such as Jack London's *The People of the Abyss* (1903) and *The Iron Heel* (1908), socialist analyses of the injustices of capitalism, and Upton Sinclair's attack on working conditions in the Chicago stockyards, *The Jungle* (1906), began to appear. In England, there was a wave of socialist novels such as Margaret Harkness' *Out of Work* (1888), George Bernard Shaw's *An Unsocial Socialist* (1887), and Robert Tressell's *The Ragged Trousered Philanthropists* (1914). While realism continued to be the hallmark of such novels, this period also saw increasing diversity of form as writers struggled to express their social visions. Utopias and dystopias flourished, including H.G. Wells' *The Time Machine* (1895) and William Morris' *News from Nowhere* (1890) in England and Edward Bellamy's *Looking Backward: 2000–1887* (1888) in the United States.

In the early part of the 20th century, the emergence of modernist literary techniques and the identification of modernism with the articulation of modern sensibilities (although not necessarily of modern conditions) drove an abiding wedge between those writers who saw the world of public values and collective experience as their material and those, like Virginia Woolf, James Joyce, and William Faulkner, for whom the interior world of private value and experience was paramount. The dominance of modernism in Western Europe and the United States temporarily marginalized the interest and relevance of the political as material and/or motivation for the novel.

It was not until the 1930s that politics and the novel again became a subject for public debate. This decade proved a period of dramatic upheaval and political instability throughout Europe and the United States as the Depression shook economic security and the rise of fascism in Germany and communism in Soviet Russia threatened world peace. In 1934, socialist realism was adopted as the official artistic doctrine by the Congress of Soviet Writers, a decision approved by Stalin. The doctrine of socialist realism required that the creative artist serve the proletariat, and it denounced all forms of literary experimentation as degenerate. Socialist realism is associated with a long period of literary oppression and censorship in the Soviet Union. It is interesting to note that this official use of literature as a weapon of political propaganda was of strictly limited success. On the other hand, many novels about the Russian Revolution, such as *Doktor Zhivago* (1957; *Doctor Zhivago*) by Boris Pasternak, and about Stalin's proscriptive regime, including *Odin den' Ivana Denisovicha* (1962; *One Day in the Life of Ivan Denisovich*) and *Rakovyi korpus* (1968; *Cancer Ward*) by Aleksandr Solzhenitsyn, which were written to question and challenge the official party line and were banned at the time, have retained their power to influence generations of readers.

The consequence of political and literary oppression generally has been a politicization of novelists, who are encouraged to reconsider their artistic role. This was particularly true of American novelists, who had no native tradition of political writing. The *Partisan Review* was founded in 1934—initially in a spirit of support for communism—for the express reason of engaging writers in the historical and political process. The editors rapidly moved away from such a restrictive orthodoxy and established the *Partisan Review* as an influential force in making literature almost synonymous with politics by providing a platform for critical debate and new writing. The new left-wing tendency, whether accepting or critical of Stalinism, was pervasive. The new generation of writers—John Steinbeck, Erskine Caldwell, James T. Farrell, and Richard Wright—stirred their readers with powerful and moving accounts of a range of social issues, including the life of workers in the American West in Steinbeck's *The Grapes of Wrath* (1939), and in the South in Caldwell's *Tobacco Road* (1932), urban disintegration in Farrell's *Young Lonigan* (1932, the first novel of a trilogy), and the plight of black Americans in Wright's *Native Son* (1940). Ernest Hemingway and F. Scott Fitzgerald, already established writers, changed direction to express the new social and historical concerns. *For Whom the Bell Tolls* (1940), for instance, draws on Hemingway's experience of the Spanish Civil War in 1936.

Marxism has had a formative influence on literary theory and on our understanding of what defines a political novel since its emergence in England in the early 1880s. In their letters and essays of this period, Marx and Engels recognize the political influence of the realist novel and declare the importance of the representation of typical characters and situations. Neither of them advocated a closed ideological perspective and both praised the work of Dickens, Gaskell, the Brontës, Thackeray, and particularly the French novelist Honoré de Balzac, for their authentic and honest portrayals of the ills of their societies.

This acceptance of the difference between the politics of a writer and the political import of his or her writing has stimulated much critical debate. Leon Trotsky in *Literatura i revoliutsiia* (1923; *Literature and Revolution*) supports and extends this notion as does Georg Lukács, the Marxist critic, in *Essays über Realismus* (1948; *Studies in European Realism*) and *Wider den missverstandenen Realismus* (1958; *The Meaning of Contemporary Realism*). Lukács' self-appointed task—to rid communism of the legacy of Stalinism and to rediscover the creative core of the teachings of Marx, Engels, and Lenin—was a difficult one.

He emphasized the instability of intentionality, claiming that realism was the basis of fiction and that any writer who concerned himself honestly with history and society, whatever his personal convictions, would contribute toward a socialist future.

The struggle to understand the relation of politics to the novel spilled over into the 1940s, when the debate moved on from narrow ideological concerns to the question of how political commitment and artistic autonomy can be reconciled. Two men were largely responsible for articulating the thoughts of a generation that could no longer believe in the validity of a single political truth. The first was Jean-Paul Sartre, the French philosopher, novelist, and playwright whose association with the communist party was always mediated through his search for artistic freedom. Sartre developed the idea of "littérature engagée" in his seminal work "Qu'est-ce que la littérature" (in *Situations II,* 1948; *What Is Literature?*), a refutation of the familiar criticism that politics is the death of art. In this series of essays, Sartre dismisses the idea of transcendence and universality in literature and argues that people cannot escape their historical identity and their responsibility to the age they live in. At the heart of Sartre's argument is the conviction that art has the power to liberate consciousness and to act as a kind of secondary form of action. Therefore, the writer can and should work to dispel inertia, dogma, and false emotion. Sartre's own novels, such as the *Roads to Freedom* series (1945–49), do not have an overt political agenda. Rather, they concentrate on the individual and offer the possibility of changing society by exploring ways in which people—as individuals—can assert or deny their personal freedom.

The second influential contributor to the politics and literature debate in this period is the Englishman George Orwell. In the essays "Why Write?" and "Politics and the English Language" (1948), Orwell argues forcefully that writers have an obligation to commit their creativity to the task of fighting social injustice, oppression, and the power of totalitarian regimes. His two last novels, exemplifying these principles, are biting political satires aimed at the threat posed to the modern world by the twin dangers of fascism and Stalinist communism. *Animal Farm* (1945) is an allegory that exposes the contradictions and cruelties of the Russian Revolution. Orwell's last novel, *Nineteen Eighty-Four* (1949), uses a realistic representation of postwar Britain cityscapes as the fictional location for a totalitarian future in a powerful narrative about the extinction of individual freedom of thought, emotion, and creativity.

Much of the literary controversy and literary history around the issue of the relation of politics to the novel is closely identified with the development of left-wing thought and the history of Western societies in crisis. It is also true that, today, to talk about the relation of writers to politics is to become aware of a whole spectrum of belief and of diverse movements which cut across national borders and historical periods. The genre of the novel still retains its political function for writers who wish to reach a wide public and, from the 1950s to the present day, has become the means by which writers construct and explore new social and political identities and help to articulate distinctive voices for African-American, African, and Caribbean communities, for women, for gays and lesbians, and for other formerly "silent" communities.

This new potential for the novel form has been stimulated by those writers and critics who have challenged the literary canon, the processes of literary criticism, and the academy, analyzing

them as political projects in themselves. Feminists have been particularly successful in arguing that the marginalization of women's writing has been the direct result of male-dominated literary, economic, and political structures. The recovery, publication, or republication of "lost" women's writing from medieval times to the present, then, has political implications, whether the writing itself has a political orientation or not.

The continuing political power of the novel is illustrated by the experience of Ngugi wa Thiong'o, a Kenyan novelist whose early work—*The River Between* (1965) and *Grain of Wheat* (1967)—was written in English. His decision to write in his own language, Gikuyu, when he became an established writer was sufficiently threatening to his government that he was imprisoned. It seems that the novel is still in alliance with those writers whose mission is to inform, to criticize, and to change the society they live in and that those who hold political power are fully aware of the danger a novel may and can pose to the status quo.

LYNNE HAPGOOD

See also Canon; Class and the Novel; Critics and Criticism (20th Century); Ideology and the Novel; Marxist Criticism of the Novel; Naturalism; Proletarian Novel; Social Criticism; Socialist Realism

Further Reading

Craig, David, editor, *Marxists on Literature: An Anthology,* London and Baltimore: Penguin, 1975

Jameson, Fredric, *The Political Unconscious: Narrative as a Socially Symbolic Act,* Ithaca, New York: Cornell University Press, and London: Methuen, 1981

Klaus, H. Gustav, *The Socialist Novel in Britain: Towards the Recovery of a Tradition,* Brighton: Harvester, and New York: St. Martin's Press, 1982

Kostelanetz, Richard, *Politics in the African-American Novel: James Weldon Johnson, W.E.B. Du Bois, Richard Wright, and Ralph Ellison,* New York: Greenwood Press, 1991

Kurzweil, Edith, and William Phillips, *Writers and Politics: A "Partisan Review" Reader,* Boston: Routledge and Kegan Paul, 1983

Lauter, Paul, "Race and Gender in the Shaping of the American Literary Canon," *Feminist Studies* 9:3 (Fall 1983)

Lukács, Georg, *Wider den missverstandenen Realismus,* Hamburg: Claasen, 1958; as *The Meaning of Contemporary Realism,* London: Merlin Press, 1963; as *Realism in Our Time: Literature and the Class Struggle,* New York: Harper, 1964

Miller, Jane Eldridge, *Rebel Women: Feminism, Modernism and the Edwardian Novel,* London: Virago, 1994; Chicago: University of Chicago Press, 1997

Orwell, George, *Collected Essays, Journalism and Letters,* vols. 1–4, edited by Sonia Orwell and Ian Angus, London: Penguin, 1970

Said, Edward W., "Representing the Colonized: Anthropology's Interlocutors," *Critical Inquiry* 15:2 (Winter 1989)

Sartre, Jean-Paul, "Qu'est-ce que la Littérature?," in *Situations II,* Paris: Gallimard, 1948; as *What Is Literature?,* New York: Philosophical Library, 1949; London: Methuen, 1950

Showalter, Elaine, *A Literature of Their Own: British Women Novelists from Brontë to Lessing,* Princeton, New Jersey:

Princeton University Press, 1977, and London: Virago, 1978; revised edition, London: Virago, 1982

Trotsky, Leon, *Literatura i revoliutsiia,* Moscow: Krasnaia nov', 1923; as *Literature and Revolution,* London: Allen and Unwin, and New York: International Publishers, 1925

Williams, Raymond, *The English Novel from Dickens to Lawrence,* London: Chatto and Windus, and New York: Oxford University Press, 1970

Williams, Raymond, *Marxism and Literature,* Oxford: Oxford University Press, 1977

Polyphonic Narrative. *See* Dialogism

Pornographic Novel

The pornographic novel in English may be traced to the European style of writing known as "whore dialogues" or "whore letters," and its development runs parallel to that of the English novel as a literary genre. The Greek word *porne* means sexual purveyor, which, in the context of early pornographic writing, came to be interpreted literally as "the writing of whores." These early novels include Pietro Aretino's *Ragionamenti,* which consists of two parts of three dialogues each, the last of which was published in English in 1658 as *The Crafty Whore.* Similarly, Pallavicino's *La retorica delle puttane* appeared in an English version titled *The Whore's Rhetoric* in 1683. Limited literacy meant that these tales of supposed firsthand experiences were written largely for middle-class readers who wanted a glimpse of the underworld of crime and prostitution. Most early examples of the genre are bawdy anticlerical satires and celebrations of human sexuality rather than writing for sexual stimulation.

The early Italian exponents were followed by French writers who refined the genre. *The School of Venus* (c. 1688), thought to be written by either Michel Millot and/or Jean l'Ange, replaced the conventional central figure of a prostitute with two female members of the middle class. English translations of Nicolas Chorier's *Satyra sotadica,* published as *The School of Women* (1682), and *A Dialogue Between a Married Lady and a Maid* (1688), extended the genre further to include aspects of lesbianism and flagellation. This last novel also largely omitted any of the comic or satiric elements earlier associated with the genre and was published with explicit engravings.

Peter Wagner has pointed out that, in the course of the development of the whore dialogue into the pornographic novel, there is evidence of an increasing exactness in the description of sexual details. Wagner also notes the change of setting from brothel to private home and, eventually, to monastery, where both moral and sexual taboos are violated in a claustrophobic atmosphere that serves the general pornographic purpose (see Wagner, 1988). *Venus in the Cloister; or, The Nun in Her Smock* (1728), by Abbé Du Prat (a pseudonym for Abbé Barrin) and published by Edmund Curll (who is said to be the father of pornographic publishing), is generally considered to be the prototype of such anti-monastic, pornographic novels, which also exhibit an interest in sexual deviation. The novel, translated from the French, describes the amorous activities of clerics, nuns, and friars and also includes explicit pornographic illustrations.

Sado-masochism, homosexuality, incest, and flagellation appear in even the earliest examples of erotic texts. The two most notable writers of perverted sexual practices were Donatien-Alphonse-Francois, Marquis de Sade (French) and Leopold von Sacher-Masoch (Austrian), from whose names have derived the terms sadism and masochism, respectively. De Sade's principal works (described by Havelock Ellis as a sort of 18th-century encyclopedia of sexual perversions) are *Justine* (2 vols., 1791), *Les 120 Journées de Sodome* (written approximately 1785; *The 120 Days of Sodom*), *Aline et Valcour* (4 vols., 1785; *Aline and Valcour*), *La Philosophie dans le boudoir* (2 vols., 1795; *The Philosopher in the Boudoir*), *La Nouvelle Justine; ou, Les Malheurs de la vertu, suivie de L'Histoire de Juliette, sa soeur* (10 vols., 1797; *Juliette*), and *Les Crimes de l'amour* (4 vols., 1800; *The Crimes of Love*). Sacher-Masoch's best known work is *Venus in Furs.*

The first strictly English pornographic novel is usually said to be John Cleland's *Memoirs of a Woman of Pleasure,* alternatively known as *Memoirs of the Life of Fanny Hill* and, ultimately, *Fanny Hill* (1749). Production and trade in pornographic books and prints in England steadily increased from the time of the appearance of *Fanny Hill,* reaching a peak in the later Victorian period. Donald Thomas has suggested that it was, ironically, an atmosphere of increased censorship in England just before 1800 that caused the pornographic novel to flourish. Victorian moral piety and the novel as a literary genre, popular with a newly emerged, literate middle class, reached their peaks at the same time. The introduction of obscenity laws and government censorship inevitably made the production of pornography into a flourishing black market activity.

While there are cases of prosecution for publishing pornographic books or pictures as obscene libel prior to 1824 (when such publishing became a misdemeanor by parliamentary statute), most of the early cases were undertaken on the basis of impiety against religious or political bodies rather than on grounds of indecency. It was not until 1857, in fact, with the passing of the Obscene Publications Act (commonly known as Lord Campbell's Act) that magistrates throughout England had the power to order the destruction of any material considered to be obscene, thus introducing an element of strict government censorship. It is significant that the word "pornographer" is first recorded in the *Oxford English Dictionary* in 1850 and is defined as "one who writes of prostitutes or obscene matters; a portrayer of obscene subjects," clearly linking our modern understanding of the term to the Victorian period.

Three of the most famous obscenity trials of the 20th century were those against D.H. Lawrence's *Lady Chatterley's Lover* (1928), Radclyffe Hall's *The Well of Loneliness* (1928), and James Joyce's *Ulysses,* first published in Paris in 1922 and America in 1933, although it did not appear in England until 1936. Despite attempts to define the term, however, an understanding of what constitutes pornography depends on the value of any given society from one historical period to another.

One of the ongoing debates concerning pornographic literature, a debate that has intensified since the second wave of feminism in the late 1960s, has been whether there is any place for pornographic novels—as one part of a larger body of pornographic material—in the lives of women. Even the most cursory glance at pornographic novels in historical context reveals that, despite the etymology of the word, very little of it has been produced either by or for women. One of the most well known exceptions to this is Pauline Réage's *Histoire d'O* (1954; *The Story of O*). In general, the debate over the place of such novels cen-

ters, on the one hand, on the notion that pornography of any kind debases women and, on the other, the idea that women have the same need for sexual pleasure as men. One of the changes brought about by the debate has been the shift in terminology within feminist discourse from "pornographic novel" to "erotic" or "romance" fiction.

REBECCA PELAN

See also Censorship; Fanny Hill; Justine; Libertine Novel

Further Reading

Brownmiller, Susan, *Against Our Will: Men, Women and Rape*, New York: Simon and Schuster, and London: Secker and Warburg, 1975

Dworkin, Andrea, *Pornography: Men Possessing Women*, New York: Putnam, and London: Women's Press, 1981

Foxon, David, *Libertine Literature in England 1660–1745*, London: Shenval Press, 1964; New Hyde, New York: University Books, 1965

Hoffmann, Frank, *Analytical Survey of Anglo-American Traditional Erotica*, Bowling Green, Ohio: Bowling Green University Popular Press, 1973

Hughes, Douglas H., editor, *Perspectives on Pornography,* New York: St. Martin's Press, 1970

Hyde, H. Montgomery, *A History of Pornography*, London: Heinemann, 1964; New York: Farrar, Straus and Giroux, 1965

Wagner, Peter, *Eros Revived: Erotica of the Enlightenment in England and America,* London: Secker and Warburg, 1988

Portnoy's Complaint by Philip Roth

1969

Portnoy's Complaint was Philip Roth's fourth book and his third novel. At the age of 26, he had been awarded the National Book Award for fiction for his novella *Goodbye, Columbus* (1959). As a result of that piece, and the stories collected with it, he was pilloried by the Jewish community in the United States as a self-hating Jew and, possibly, an anti-Semite. Roth wrote articles and gave speeches defending himself, pointing out that he was pleased to be a Jew. That accident of birth had given him a morally demanding experience, a complicated history, and a particular lens through which to view the world. In part to placate his critics, he then wrote two uncontroversial novels; however, the criticism continued unabated, and this aided his decision to write *Portnoy's Complaint,* which would really give people something to complain about. Also, Roth saw this novel as a break with the more conventional approach that he had taken in *Letting Go* (1962) and *When She Was Good* (1967), both rather

gloomy works that he said made him feel a need to loosen up, to use his comic gifts. Both novels were set in the Midwest and neither stressed Jewish issues. Indeed, *When She Was Good* contained no Jewish characters at all. In part because of continual criticism, which had begun with *Goodbye, Columbus* and continued with *Portnoy's Complaint* (as though the two conventional, serious novels in between had not been written), Roth felt forced to focus upon Jewish issues to an extent he had not intended. Indeed, he felt that his critics gave him a subject that proved to be of immense value: Jews and Jewish perspectives became an important part of his writing.

Portnoy's Complaint was viewed as scandalous because of its protagonist's use of obscene language and the blatant sex scenes and allusions to masturbation it contained. Many readers, Jewish and non-Jewish, found it not only offensive but pornographic. These complaints, far from destroying the novel's reception, seemed to aid in its huge popularity and helped to keep it on the best-seller list for months. Paperback and movie rights were fought over. Whether the book added to Roth's reputation as a writer is another matter. Brendan Gill, the reviewer for *The New Yorker*, called it "one of the dirtiest books ever published," and *Time*'s reviewer thought Roth's characters mere stereotypes. Even Alfred Kazin, who found the novel funny and praised Roth's ability at mimicry, castigated him for being able to depict Jews only as hysterics and for reducing their experience to psychology. The novel marked a turning point in Roth's career, as afterward he was sometimes viewed as "the author of *Portnoy's Complaint*," almost as though he had written nothing else. In particular, he has suffered from overidentification with his characters, a situation that led him to comment that, according to his critics, he must be the only fiction writer in history who never made anything up.

Alex Portnoy is 33 years old and was born in 1933—the year that Judge John M. Woolsey gave his decision to allow the publication of James Joyce's *Ulysses*. That decision included the statement that "although it contains . . . many words usually considered dirty, I have not found anything that I consider to be dirt for dirt's sake." It is probable that Roth is alluding to this decision, as it made the publication of *Portnoy's Complaint* possible. He has said that "Obscenity is not only a kind of language that is used in *Portnoy's Complaint*, it is very nearly the issue itself. . . . [T]his is a man speaking out of an overwhelming obsession: he is obscene because he wants to be saved" (Roth, 1975).

The novel uses a first-person narrator through whom everything is seen and interpreted. As with many of Edgar Allan Poe's narrators, Portnoy is suspect. There is no objectivity in what he presents and no opportunity to receive another interpretation of events. At times Portnoy drifts into caricature to depict his views. Particular criticism has been leveled at his presentation of the Jewish mother, which many critics have seen as false and as not giving due credit to the courageous role played by the mother in Jewish history. Indeed, the Jewish family and its values are held up to ridicule, as much or more than in any other Jewish-American novel. Roth uses an oral, conversational style, the stress being upon the spoken language. Portnoy's approach to experience is often ironic and has the effect of a stand-up comedian's patter. The inspiration behind Portnoy has been variously attributed to Lenny Bruce's nightclub act and to other stand-up comedians, such as Shelley Berman and Mort Sahl.

Portnoy's Complaint may be appropriately viewed as an attempt to place within US literature a novel that combines ribald, urban, and sometimes adolescent humor (reminiscent of Holden Caulfield's in *The Catcher in the Rye*); a parody of psychoanalysis and psychiatrists; and a peek into an ethnic family as seen through the eyes of one of its guilt-ridden members. In Alex Portnoy readers see the disastrous results of one man's attempts to sever his moral conscience from his desires. He is a crippled hero—an antihero—the hero of the post–World War II world.

EDWARD A. ABRAMSON

Further Reading

Baumgarten, Murray, and Barbara Gottfried, *Understanding Philip Roth*, Columbia: University of South Carolina Press, 1990

Halio, Jay, *Philip Roth Revisited*, New York: Twayne, and Toronto: Macmillan, 1992

Lee, Hermione, *Philip Roth*, London and New York: Methuen, 1982

McDaniel, John, *The Fiction of Philip Roth*, Haddonfield, New Jersey: Haddonfield House, 1974

Milbauer, Asher, and Donald Watson, *Reading Philip Roth*, London: Macmillan, 1988

Peterson, Judith Hillman, and Guinevera A. Nance, *Philip Roth*, New York: Ungar, 1981

Pinsker, Sanford, editor, *Critical Essays on Philip Roth*, Boston: G.K. Hall, 1982

Roth, Philip, "On *Portnoy's Complaint*," in *Reading Myself and Others*, London: Cape, 1975; new expanded edition, New York: Penguin, 1985

A Portrait of the Artist as a Young Man by James Joyce

1916

Although James Joyce's largely autobiographical *A Portrait of the Artist as a Young Man* has certainly benefited from the huge reputation and controversy aroused by his later *Ulysses* (1922), it was in fact quickly recognized as a work of great originality, even genius. Most reviewers were struck by the quality of the writing, although several were put off by what H.G. Wells called Joyce's "cloacal obsession": even the reference on the novel's first page to Stephen wetting the bed was seen as a breach of decorum. The book's "advanced" subject matter—its indirect treatment of the protagonist Stephen Dedalus' masturbation and sexual encounters with prostitutes, as well as his conflict with the Roman Catholic Church—was hailed by some reviewers, deplored by others. Many readers were struck by the lifelike quality of the "naturalistic" passages, and Joyce's dialogue earned praise from different critics, such as A. Clutton-Brock's comment that "no living writer is better at conversation." Some, however, found it impossible to follow the concerns of so spiritual and so aesthetically serious a young man, and many found Stephen a dangerously unhealthy model for youth. Considering the huge amount of critical energy that has since gone into explicating the book's formal structure, it is amusing that a majority of early reviewers saw the book as annoyingly formless.

A Portrait of the Artist as a Young Man in fact has a minimal plot, but a wealth of events. The novel treats the development of a sensitive middle-class Irish Catholic boy from infancy through his graduation from University College, Dublin, and imminent departure from Ireland, dedicated to "silence, exile and cunning." But then apparently so did *Stephen Hero,* the draft version of *A Portrait of the Artist as a Young Man* that Joyce abandoned and mostly destroyed. A comparison of the two shows the radical compression and streamlining of *Portrait,* as well as its relative freedom from authorial commentary. The story is told in five chapters, each broken into three to five subsections, separated by a row of asterisks. Unlike *Stephen Hero,* in *Portrait* Joyce makes no attempt at a continuous narrative, instead allowing vivid scenes and descriptive passages to stand in for entire phases of Stephen's development, with little transition between the passages. Symbolism and indirect suggestion carry much of the weight traditionally carried by plot. For instance, in a crucial episode in which Stephen is asked whether he feels a vocation for the priesthood, Joyce avoids the obviously dramatic scene in which the boy articulates his repugnance for the joyless, sterile life of the Jesuits. Instead, the priest who makes the offer is shown with his back to the light, the bones of his skull deeply shadowed, as he dangles and makes a loop with the cord of a blind—making a visual image that effectively conveys Stephen's feelings. Similarly, Stephen's choosing life and art is captured in his sight of a young woman knee-deep in the ocean who reminds him, in a heavily lyrical passage, of a bird. Such scenes have been termed *epiphanies,* following a suggestion of Stephen himself, and the word has been applied to crucial moments in other works of fiction as well.

The book's writing is as distinctive as its structure. The opening sentence reads, "Once upon a time and a very good time it was there was a moocow coming down along the road and this moocow . . . met a nicens little boy named baby tuckoo." The syntax and vocabulary of the remainder of the chapter similarly suggests a child's consciousness, or even stories written for children, although, like the remainder of the book, it is written in third-person free indirect discourse, allowing the narrator to move smoothly into and out of Stephen's consciousness. Sometimes the narration is displaced by outside voices, as in the third chapter, which is taken over by an extended, terrifying sermon on hell delivered by one of the boy's teachers. By the fifth chapter, the style has become elaborate, even precious at times. Dense lyrical passages alternate with passages of brutal descriptive realism or highly colloquial conversation. The book's final section is in the form of entries from Stephen's diary—fragmentary, gnomic, written in a variety of styles, addressing a potpourri of subjects on the young man's mind as he prepares to leave. Rather than traditional novelistic closure, this technique suggested to some early reviewers a disturbing chaos, or what we would now term openness, in the book's ending.

A Portrait of the Artist as a Young Man belongs to a familiar genre for British readers. As a novel displaying the education of a sensitive youth, it follows George Meredith's *The Ordeal of Richard Feverel* (1859) and Samuel Butler's *The Way of All Flesh* (1903), as well as a host of less famous turn-of-the century novels in French and English specifically dealing with the religious crisis of a youth. What made *A Portrait of the Artist as a Young Man* different from these and gave it, in the eyes of some critics, a claim to being the first fully modernist novel in English, was its remarkable interiority. In a well-known essay, Virginia Woolf compared *Portrait* and several installments of *Ulysses* that had appeared in a journal to more conventional fiction by John Galsworthy, Arnold Bennett, and H.G. Wells, and concluded that Joyce was the more "spiritual" writer. By this she meant that unlike his "materialist" elders, Joyce was less concerned with representing the outward circumstances of his characters than with an attempt to "trace the pattern, however disconnected and incoherent in appearance, which each sight or incident scores upon the consciousness."

In this respect, modern subject and modernist form are, of course, inseparable. Perhaps because the novelistic tradition in many European countries had always paid more attention to the vagaries of consciousness than had the British tradition, Joyce's novel fit somewhat better into an international modernist context than it did into the British tradition (with which Joyce's relationship, as a citizen of a colonized country, was in any case problematic). By the 1950s it seemed natural to group *A Portrait of the Artist as a Young Man* with works by Marcel Proust, Thomas Mann, and André Gide, rather than with earlier British novels exploring the aesthetic and romantic sensitivies of a young man, such as Thomas Hardy's *Jude the Obscure* (1895). Joyce's unprecedented combination of naturalism with highly charged lyrical and symbolic passages, his deployment of impressionist technique in conveying details of Stephen's experience, as well as the extended passages of intense interiority verging on stream-of-consciousness narration, pointed in a variety of directions that were explored by later modernist narratives.

R. BRANDON KERSHNER

See also James Joyce

Further Reading

Harkness, Marguerite, *"A Portrait of the Artist as a Young Man": Voices of the Text,* Boston: Twayne, 1990

Joyce, James, *A Portrait of the Artist as a Young Man: Text, Criticism, and Notes,* edited by Chester G. Anderson, New York: Viking Press, 1964

Joyce, James, *A Portrait of the Artist as a Young Man: Complete, Authoritative Text with Biographical and Historical Contexts, Critical History, and Essays from Five Contemporary Critical Perspectives,* edited by R.B. Kershner, Boston and New York: Bedford Books of St. Martin's Press, 1993

Kiberd, Declan, *Inventing Ireland: The Literature of the Modern Nation,* London: Cape, 1995; Cambridge, Massachusetts: Harvard University Press, 1996

Parrinder, Patrick, *James Joyce,* Cambridge and New York: Cambridge University Press, 1984

Scholes, Robert, and Richard M. Kain, editors, *The Workshop of Daedalus: James Joyce and the Raw Materials for "A Portrait of the Artist as a Young Man,"* Evanston, Illinois: Northwestern University Press, 1965

Seed, David, *James Joyce's "A Portrait of the Artist as a Young Man,"* New York: St. Martin's Press, and Hemel Hempstead: Harvester Wheatsheaf, 1992

The Portrait of a Lady by Henry James

1881

Henry James, according to F.R. Leavis (1948), belongs to the great tradition of English novelists, or novelists writing in English, keeping company with Jane Austen, George Eliot, and Joseph Conrad. James' admiration for George Eliot is well documented, as are the parallels between the character of Gwendolen Harleth in Eliot's novel *Daniel Deronda* (1876) and James' portrayal of Isabel Archer in *The Portrait of a Lady*. Moreover, James published *Daniel Deronda: A Conversation* in 1876, and in the character of Constantius says, "Gwendolen is a masterpiece. She is known, felt and presented psychologically altogether in the grand manner." This could well have been written later of Isabel Archer. Leavis goes so far as to say that James could not have written *The Portrait of a Lady* if he had not read George Eliot's novel.

What Leavis admired in James was his moral strenuousness, his engagement with life, and the seriousness of his commitment to his art, all of which he has in common with Nathaniel Hawthorne, whose biography James had published two years before *The Portrait of a Lady*. In the biography, James has written his own apologia, or at least his justification for his preoccupation with Europe and Europeans. He called the America that Hawthorne wrote about "a thin society" and explained that in order to create a more interesting and complex fictional world it would be necessary for him to turn to a more complex society, an older and richer culture where he could partake of "the banquet of initiation." Like Hawthorne, however, his ultimate inspiration and the deepest territory he would quarry was to be found "among the shadows and substructions, the dark-based pillars and supports of our moral nature." The influence of both Eliot and Hawthorne can be seen to lie behind *The Portrait of a Lady*, but James had grown away from both. James' achievement in this novel is that while writing a recognizably traditional, chronological novel, he had pushed the form further. He has done this chiefly in the depth of the psychological study of the moral situation, and in this he points the way to D.H. Lawrence and Virginia Woolf.

The Portrait of a Lady is the culmination of James' early phase. His major themes and preoccupations with the "international theme," with its clash and interplay of, at its simplest, American innocence and European corruption, new money and old traditions, commerce and aesthetics, and the moral implications of all transactions, had been explored in such early works as *Roderick Hudson* (1875), *The American* (1877), *The Europeans* (1878), and *Daisy Miller* (1878). All come together with greater subtlety and sophistication in *The Portrait of a Lady*. Ultimately it was not so much the dialetic of the old and the new that concerned James as the fine connections between layers of meaning and the free play of meaning generated between the dualities he had set up as he explored the moral consciousness of his central character, the subject of his "portrait."

What also contributes to the richness and depth of *The Portrait of a Lady* is James' exploitation of his theory of point of view, whereby he maintains a consistent viewpoint in telling his story or recounting events. The viewpoint he has chosen is Isabel Archer's consciousness, and he has made it the central structuring locale of the novel. All events and actions contribute to its development and are colored and illuminated in turn by it, and as James wrote in his preface to *Roderick Hudson*, the drama of the novel is "the very drama of that [central] consciousness." Although there is a surface linearity to James' narrative, the real plot—all events, characters, and developments—is generated centrally from Isabel Archer's thoughts and emotions, her reflections, her choices and decisions.

The Portrait of a Lady is the story of a young American woman "affronting" her destiny. It is a novel about choice and destiny, and about the nature of human freedom exercized and controlled between both. Isabel Archer is given a fortune so that she can be free and independent. Ironically her fortune turns out to be the vehicle of her entrapment. The man she chooses for a husband is a fortune hunter; hence the generous and independent young American woman finds herself constricted within a loveless marriage. The high point of the novel is the moral choice she makes not to leave him when she could, but to remain with him for the sake of his step-daughter Pansy, the child he had by his mistress before his marriage to Isabel Archer.

The complex and interesting world that James has created in his *The Portrait of a Lady* is the world of Europe that he himself left America to find. The art world of Florence, the ancient, tragic world of Rome, and the elegant "country house" world of English society, all belong to the idealized world of European culture of which he was enamored and that enabled him to create his greatest fictions. That vivid and varied world is presented with such spaciousness and solidity in the novel that the reader is not at first aware of the taut structure underpinning the whole that enables every part of it to fall into place. That is the achievement of the Jamesian "point of view." In his preface to the novel James refers to *The Portrait of a Lady* as the most proportioned of his fictions. The proportion is built up, he explains, from the center, and the center must have its "satellites, especially the male," but their interest must be one that is "contributive only to the greater one." This concern with the aesthetics of structure, together with his psychological study of a central consciousness, anticipates modernist preoccupations of the 1920s.

STELLA McNICHOL

See also Henry James

Further Reading

Fussell, Edwin, *The Catholic Side of Henry James*, Cambridge and New York: Cambridge University Press, 1993

Gale, Robert L., "Henry James and Italy," *Nineteenth Century Fiction* 14 (September 1959)

Kenney, Blair Gates, "The Two Isabels: A Study in Distortion," *Victorian Newsletter* 25 (Spring 1964)

Leavis, F.R., *The Great Tradition: George Eliot, Henry James, Joseph Conrad*, London: Chatto and Windus, and New York: New York University Press, 1948

Mackenzie, Manfred, "Ironic Melodrama in *The Portrait of a Lady*," *Modern Fiction Studies* 12 (Spring 1966)

Matthiessen, F.O., and Kenneth B. Murdock, editors, *The Notebooks of Henry James,* New York and Oxford: Oxford University Press, 1961

Smith, Virginia Llewellyn, *Henry James and the Real Thing: A Modern Reader's Guide,* London: Macmillan, and New York: St. Martin's Press, 1994

Tanner, Tony, *Henry James,* London: Macmillan, 1968

Tintner, Adeline, *Henry James and the Lust of the Eyes: Thirteen Artists in His Work,* Baton Rouge: Louisiana State University Press, 1993

Walton, Priscilla, *The Disruption of the Feminine in Henry James,* Toronto and Buffalo, New York: University of Toronto Press, 1992

Possessed. *See* Devils

Postcolonial Narrative and Criticism of the Novel

The term *postcolonial novel* may be understood to cover two broad categories of writing: imperial outpost novels, produced by Europeans, including the European diaspora in countries like Australia, Argentina, Canada, New Zealand, and the United States; and decolonization novels, produced by writers from the ex-colonial states as well as indigenous and ethnic minorities in the settler-dominated countries. The prevailing definition of the postcolonial novel follows from the work of Australian critics Bill Ashcroft, Gareth Griffiths, and Helen Tiffin, who describe postcolonial literature as "emerging in their present form out of the experience of colonization and asserting themselves by foregrounding the tension with the imperial power, and by emphasizing their differences from the assumptions of the imperial centre" (see Ashcroft, Griffiths, and Tiffin, 1989).

The postcolonial mode of critique itself has its foundations in Third-World critical practice since the 1950s, which rejects Eurocentric aesthetic judgments and insists on the validity of indigenous codes of aesthetic representation. European academic critics appropriated postcolonial criticism into Western postmodernist cultural theory in the late 1980s, some would say as a strategic response to the imperatives of the post-Soviet "New World Order." For academics of the European diaspora, this approach facilitates their construction of new identities out of their ambiguous positions as heirs to the fruits of colonial conquest. Hence, Ashcroft, Griffiths, and Tiffin have argued of the United States that "[despite] its current position of power, and the neo-colonizing role it has played . . . its relationship with the metropolitan centre as it evolved over the last two centuries has been paradigmatic of post-colonial literatures everywhere." The new approach further postulates parallels "between the power relationship of the colonizer to the colonized and that of men to women, the upper classes to the lower, or men to the landscape" (see Goodwin, 1993). Bill Pearson has extensively demonstrated, however, that Australian and New Zealand Europeans treated the indigenous peoples as other Europeans did, with the Australian Henry Lawson employing the adjective "Maori" as "an

epithet of contempt" and portraying Maoris as dirty, stinking, and lazy animals (see Pearson, 1974). Naturally, in postcolonial novels from these territories, it is almost invariably these settlers rather than imperial Europe who are portrayed as colonizers and oppressors.

The Imperial Outpost Narrative

The first major imperial outpost novel is probably Daniel Defoe's *Robinson Crusoe* (1719). By the 19th century, the form was popular in Europe and all European settler territories. It ranged from the Western, which emerged in North America to celebrate the military conquest of the Indian territory west of the Mississippi River, to the Anglo-Indian novel. Plot, character, and conflict follow a pattern: a European hero's adventures among non-European people—who are often depicted as subhuman—is transformed through Manichean symbolism into a conflict pitting European light, rationality, and order against the invaded people's darkness, instinct, and chaos. The significance of events is based on shared assumptions between writer and reader. Early examples include James Fenimore Cooper's *The Pioneers* (1823), *The Last of the Mohicans* (1826), and *The Prairie* (1827).

The imperial outpost novel was such an undemanding form that an Ohio dentist, Zane Grey, was able to write at least 50 of them (including the popular *The Spirit of the Border*, 1906, and *Riders of the Purple Sage*, 1912), while a woman, B.M. Bower, so successfully portrayed frontier adventures that her readers took her for a real cowboy. When Polish writer Joseph Conrad, his health and finances ruined by his Congo expedition, was asked for a story by *Blackwood's* magazine to celebrate its 1,000th issue, he wrote "Heart of Darkness" (1902), a fictional enactment of European myths of Africa, for which he has been denounced by Chinua Achebe as "a thoroughgoing racist" (see Achebe, 1988).

Even writers of liberal persuasion have not hesitated to exploit racial stereotypes. In *A Passage to India* (1924), E.M. Forster's characters are defined primarily according to European stereotypes of East and West, and in *Three Continents* (1987) by the German-born Polish writer Ruth Prawer Jhabvala, "good comes to be represented by scions of a once-noble white family, whereas evil is perennially associated with the characters belonging to the races of the ancient, mysterious East" (see Afzal-Khan, 1993). Although married to an Indian, Ruth Prawer Jhabvala has insisted that "the central fact of all my work . . . is that I am a European living permanently in India."

The imperial outpost novel flourished right into the mid-20th century, and still survives in various forms, although it is steadily losing place to audio-visual entertainment media like film, television, and, since the 1980s, computer games.

Decolonization Narratives

Resistance to colonialism found a literary expression from the moment some of the colonized people acquired the ability to write and the political consciousness to put this ability to use. The 18th-century campaigns to abolish slavery and the slave trade encouraged a crop of "slave narratives" that recounted in graphic detail the horrors of slavery. In India, political impetus was unintentionally supplied by the contemptuous dismissal (in 1835) of India's literary heritage by Thomas Babington Macaulay, an advisor on Indian affairs to the British government. But it was the worldwide upsurge of anticolonialist nationalism in the 20th century, aided by the two world wars, that led to the full emergence of the European-language decolonization novel. The phenomenon has been described as a "Prospero-Caliban syndrome" since O. Mannoni's *Psychologie de la colonisation* (1950; *Prospero and Caliban: The Psychology of Colonization*). The postcolonial novel has assumed the role of a metafiction contesting racial myths used to rationalize imperialism. The Indian Mulk Raj Anand's assertion that "all art is propaganda" has recently been reformulated by the Maori novelist Witi Ihimiaera: "Just as all literature is politics, so too I am not only a writer but a political person." The Nigerian novelist Chinua Achebe spoke for most when he declared that his aim was "to help my society regain its belief in itself and put away the complex of years of denigration and self-denigration."

Decolonization novels also reflect the uniqueness of local cultures and histories, and the whole tradition is really best understood as a mosaic of discrete regional traditions that share certain common threads. The first wave of novels in each culture was much concerned with the creation of countermyths of the self and revisions of colonialist historiography. They explored themes of cultural conflict in terms of the historical process by which indigenous civilizations were overthrown by European colonialist forces, as in Chinua Achebe's *Things Fall Apart* (1958) and *Arrow of God* (1964), or the struggle for sovereignty from colonial oppression as in Raja Rao's *Kanthapura* (1938), V.S. Reid's *New Day* (1949), Ngugi wa Thiong'o's novels, from *The River Between* (1965) to *A Grain of Wheat* (1967), and Witi Ihimiaera's *The Matriarch* (1986). In *A Brighter Sun* (1952), Samuel Selvon explores questions of identity, individual adaptability, and multiracial living in a colonial society undergoing wartime transformation.

Where decolonization struggle involved actual warfare, decolonization novels, including Ngugi's, Reid's, and Ihimiaera's, portray the guerrilla fighters as heroes and the colonial forces as terrorists. For Maori novelists, the threat of Maori dissolution in the European settler-dominated culture and the challenges of multiracial accommodation are recurrent themes, as in Witi Ihimaera's *Tangi* (1973) and *Whanau* (1974) and Patricia Grace's *Mutuwhenua: The Moon Sleeps* (1978), while in *The Bone People* (1983) Keri Hulme's heroine Kerewin Holmes effectively challenges the prevailing error of equating modernity with the West. However, given that India's traditions of writing are older than those of many European cultures, major Indian novelists of the period—Mulk Raj Anand, Raja Rao, and R.K. Narayan—also showed early concern with social problems in the manner that would later be identified as critical realism. The Marxist-oriented Anand raised issues of poverty and social injustice, caste contradictions, problems of the working class, and women's status in novels like *Untouchable* (1935), *The Coolie* (1936), and *The Big Heart* (1945). Raja Rao showed early concern with language and consciousness, an issue that would engage Chinua Achebe later. Rao's foreword to *Kanthapura* comments on the difficulty of conveying "in a language that is not one's own the spirit that is one's own," and conveying "the various shades and omissions of a certain thought-movement that looks maltreated in an alien language." Problems of language and metaphysical issues of life and death lie at the heart of Rao's *The Serpent and the Rope* (1960), *The Cat and Shakespeare* (1965), and *Comrade Kirillov* (1976). Rushdie's comic epics *Midnight's Children* (1981) and *The Satanic Verses* (1988) explore the postcolonial predicament of India from a cosmopolitan stance that debunks both colonialist and self-massaging indigenous myths. Rushdie has asserted that "central to the purposes of *The Satanic Verses* is the process of reclaiming language from one's opponents." Yet his postmodernist love of endless verbal play, mystifying complications of plot, and general obliqueness of expression subvert his "purposes" so effectively that the Revolutionary Islamic government of Iran sentenced him to death in 1989 for supposedly blaspheming Islam.

Novelists' concerns and techniques have also varied over the years in response to historical developments. The wave of euphoria that accompanied the attainment of ceremonial independence in the years following the end of World War II quickly collided with the reality that "independence" had changed very little. With few exceptions, the new elite who came to power generally lacked political vision. Endemic social instability and poverty resulted from a complex mesh of economic and technological weakness; a resurgence of ethnic rivalries that had been suppressed by colonial governments or suspended in the face of a common enemy; and sustained aggression by European imperial powers, the United States, and the Soviet Union. Orlando Patterson powerfully projects this vicious cycle in *The Children of Sisyphus* (1964), while George Lamming's prophetic *In the Castle of My Skin* (1953) foreshadows the alliance of the indigenous elite with the former colonizers in a new era of self-betrayals and violations. Such increased critical realism inevitably led to a search for viable nationhood and the emergence of tendentious writing. The Ghanaian Ayi Kwei Armah advocated a return to primal racial values in such novels as *Two Thousand Seasons* (1973) and *The Healers* (1978). The Indian Mulk Raj Anand and the Kenyan Ngugi wa Thiong'o produced novels influenced by Marxist ideology. R.K. Narayan's *The Painter of Signs* (1976) explores a broad spectrum of intertwined social issues: love and marriage, gender conflicts, family planning, and problems of adapting established customs to radical new values.

Ngugi's *Devil on the Cross* (1982) explores problems of poverty, class, and exploitation of the working class under neocolonialist socio-economic systems, although close examination reveals that Ngugi's socialist blueprints are actually drawn from traditional African social systems. In New Zealand, Maori disillusionment arose from discrepancies between successive governments' proclaimed goals of creating racial justice in a multicultural society and the bitter reality of programs that continued Maori marginalization. These are prominent issues in Patricia Grace's *Potiki* (1986) and, to a lesser degree, *Cousins* (1992). In Samoan-New Zealander Albert Wendt's novels, pakeha racism against Maoris and other ethnic minorities becomes a major theme for the first time. As Wendt has explained in an interview,

> The New Zealand section [of *Ola*] is a look at colonialism in New Zealand. It was intended to disturb. . . . [It has] upset some Pakeha New Zealanders . . . : *Ola* is performing the function of fishing racism even out of some literary critics . . . . My commitment to the Maori struggle is even deeper . . . . Especially when I see the emergence of a "new" racism in this country, a racism articulated not only by politicians and business leaders, but former academics and so-called pundits and journalists.

Disillusionment apart, the second wave of the postcolonial novel's development was also marked by the greater contribution of women, beginning in the 1960s and 1970s. In the West Indies, this means greater participation of West Indian women, as expatriate European women's writing is much older. Contributing to this emergence were improved educational opportunities for women, transformations in gender roles, and sponsorship of women's writing by Western feminist interests. Naturally, many of these novels give sharper focus to women's problems in male-dominated colonial or neocolonial society—obsessive themes in the novels of the Nigerian Buchi Emecheta but subordinated to decolonization politics in a novel like *A Small Place* (1988) by the Antiguan Jamaica Kincaid. For the Indian novelist Anita Desai, feminist and existential themes are interwoven in *Voices in the City* (1965) and *Fire on the Mountain* (1977).

While much of the response to the European imperial outpost novel has taken the form of challenge and refutation, there has also been extensive borrowing or adaptation of literary motifs and archetypes. Poets like W.B. Yeats, T.S. Eliot, and Walt Whitman have been particularly influential, and poems like "The Second Coming," "Journey of the Magi," and "This Compost" are exploited to shape movements of plot and theme in novels projecting contrasting social visions and ideologies. While many claims of Western influence are no more than instances of similarity in underlying narrative or thematic motifs, increasing globalization of culture has also led to greater openness of Third-World novelists to Western cultural and literary currents. Emphasis on intertextuality by current literary scholarship has uncovered intricate webs of cross-references, allusions, and echoes in the work of most decolonization novelists.

On the whole, development of the postcolonial novel has suffered from theory and criticism that reflect the theorists' priorities and anxieties more than the realities of the narrative traditions. With postcolonial discourse developing in more theoretical kinds of writing, the postcolonial novel is studied and appreciated less today in the late 1990s than at mid-century. Without a vigorous, self-directed critical culture to nourish it, the postcolonial novel is displaying signs of an identity crisis.

CHIDI OKONKWO

See also Adventure Novel; *and entries on countries and writers discussed in this essay*

Further Reading

Achebe, Chinua, "An Image of Africa: Racism in Conrad's *Heart of Darkness*," in *Hopes and Impediments: Selected Essays,* London: Heinemann, 1988; New York: Doubleday, 1989

Afzal-Khan, Fawzia, *Cultural Imperialism and the Indo-English Novel: Genre and Ideology in R.K. Narayan, Anita Desai, Kamala Markandaya, and Salman Rushdie,* University Park: Pennsylvania State University Press, 1993

Anim-Addo, Joan, editor, *Framing the Word: Gender and Genre in Caribbean Women's Writing,* London: Whiting and Birch, and Concord, Massachusetts: Paul, 1996

Ashcroft, Bill, Gareth Griffiths, and Helen Tiffin, *The Empire Writes Back: Theory and Practice in Post-Colonial Literatures,* London and New York: Routledge, 1989

Barfoot, C.C., and Theo D'haen, editors, *Shades of Empire in Colonial and Post-Colonial Literatures,* Amsterdam and Atlanta, Georgia: Rodopi, 1993

Barker, Francis, Peter Hulme, and Margaret Iversen, editors, *Colonial Discourse, Postcolonial Theory,* Manchester: Manchester University Press, and New York: St. Martin's Press, 1994

Boehmer, Elleke, *Colonial and Postcolonial Literature: Migrant Metaphors,* Oxford and New York: Oxford University Press, 1995

Frank, Katherine, "Women Without Men: The Feminist Novel in Africa," *African Literature Today* 15 (1987)

Goodwin, Ken, "Studying Commonwealth Literature," *College Literature* (double issue on teaching postcolonial and commonwealth literatures) 19:3 (October 1992) and 20:1 (February 1993)

JanMohamed, Abdul R., *Manichean Aesthetics: The Politics of Literature in Colonial Africa,* Amherst: University of Massachusetts Press, 1983

King, Bruce, editor, *The Commonwealth Novel since 1960,* London: Macmillan, 1991

Moses, Michael Valdez, *The Novel and the Globalization of Culture,* New York: Oxford University Press, 1995

Parker, Michael, and Roger Starkey, editors, *Postcolonial Literatures: Achebe, Ngugi, Desai, Walcott,* London: Macmillan, 1995

Pearson, Bill, "Attitudes to the Maori in Some Pakeha Fiction," in *Fretful Sleepers and Other Essays,* London: Heinemann, 1974

Postmodernism and the Novel

To discover which narratives might be postmodern novels we must first sort out the various and conflicting definitions of the term *postmodernism*. Depending on the interpretive code that governs its use, this term can mean almost anything. A Marxist, for example, defines postmodernism negatively, in such a way as to suit the agendas of Marxism. The cultural critic defines postmodernism historically, as a set of discursive conditions requiring readjustment of traditional values. The conventional moralist treats it as an unfair assault on All We Hold Dear. Such differences in usage testify to the resilience of the term that has become a kind of system-marker; what it marks is not the identity of postmodernism but the values and limitations of the various interpretive codes.

Whatever else it is, postmodern narrative is a feat of language: an effort to resurrect powers of language that have become constrained by mechanisms of production, especially the production of "meaning." Language, postmodern writing reminds us—and all the systems of meaning and value that operate like language—has many other functions than the production of "meanings," which are the portable property produced by narratives of a bygone cultural moment. Because usage of the term *postmodernism* vacillates in this way, between the excessively narrow and the meaninglessly broad, this entry will frame a definition of postmodernity in broadly historical terms.

Across a wide range of activity since World War II, European culture has sustained a multivalent challenge to some of its founding assumptions. From academic disciplines to practical science, from physics to philosophy, from politics to art, the description of the world has changed in ways that upset some basic assumptions of modernity about identity and structure, about the nature of space and time, and about transcendence and particularity. And these developments are not local events; they have been long-prepared and reflect tectonic shifts in founding cultural arrangements.

As a historical term, *postmodernism* indicates something that comes after modernity. Consequently its definition varies with the term *modern*. Sometimes *modern* indicates movements in the arts around the turn of the 20th century known as modernism, and in that case *postmodernism* refers to a fairly local phenomenon of the mid– to late–20th century. Alternatively, *modern* indicates the period that follows the medieval—that is, Renaissance culture and its sequels—in which case *postmodern* refers to a broadly distributed cultural phenomenon.

The present account accepts the broad usage of the term *modern* and conceives *post*modernism as whatever it is that follows and transforms that particular Renaissance (or Reformation, or even Enlightenment) modernity. Some of the more ahistorical contributions of recent French philosophy (Derrida, Lyotard, Irigaray) trace their postmodern critique of Western metaphysics back to the Greeks, but while these efforts are important they blur practical issues because they occupy a period so vast that they scarcely allow for historical change at all. Postmodernity is a historical term and a historical event, and the practical and political issues it raises took their particular definition from postmedieval modernity.

Two key assumptions in particular characterize postmodernism. The first is the assumption that all human systems operate like language, that is, as systems of differential (rather than referential) function: systems that are finite and that powerfully construct and maintain whatever we know of meaning and value. The second and related assumption is that no common denominators exist to guarantee either the One-ness of the world or the possibility of neutral or objective thought: in short, no "Nature" or "Truth" or "God" or "The Future" or any of the explanatory narratives based upon those fictions exist to rescue any value from finitude and any individual from choice.

The first of these assumptions—that language, not more traditional notions of structure, is the model for all human systems of meaning and value—expands the notion of language to include a variety of symbolic systems, whether they involve politics, fashion, gender relations, wrestling, or money. Language can act as such a model because language is conceived as a system of differential function, not as a collection of referential pointers. This view of language was stated influentially by Ferdinand de Saussure at the beginning of the 20th century in a series of lectures at Geneva on linguistics (c. 1906–11, published from notes by his students as *Cours de linguistique générale* [1916; *Course in General Linguistics*]). The linguistic sign, as Saussure defined it, does not refer to objects in the world (each of which has different names in different languages), but instead it specifies a particular linguistic system. To read or understand a linguistic sequence, even the simplest, is to recognize difference, and at a level of complication of which we are blissfully unaware; it is to perform an incalculably complex and continuous act of differentiation, more and more balanced and rich the more that linguistic sequence inclines toward poetry or other complex usage. (Technically, Saussure's word points not to an object but to an idea, and that idea is itself linguistic; there is nothing prior to language.)

So, for example, the word *tree* has no natural relation to any object, and we understand it only because we understand what it is not (not *free*, not *trow*, not verb)—in other words, we understand the entire system called "English" in which this term functions and which it specifies. Even a simple word like *tree* has no exact equivalent either in other languages or in the world. It is not translatable; it is only readable according to a set of tacit rules (called "grammar") that enables us to differentiate between a nonsense sequence of words (for instance "Sleep ideas green furiously colorless") and an "English" sentence, however nonsensical (for instance "Colorless green ideas sleep furiously"). One cannot translate Baudelaire exactly into English, nor English nouns into Chinese, because each language is a system of functions, not a collection of pointers. Each system differs from all other languages except in *being* such a system. A "native" speaker is someone who understands that complex code-system; by extension, we "speak" or "write" in various nonverbal code systems simultaneously and continuously as we go through ordinary life.

These rather dry terms in fact are describing language's capacity for poetry: its capacity as a living language to provide its speakers with particular alphabets and lexicons of possibility, and to modify, even radically, the usages with which we constitute our worlds. It is here we begin to see a main agenda of narrative that could be called postmodern: the narrative that emphasizes those alphabets of possibility and that requires of us new acts of attention. And we begin to see why the term *narrative* may be preferred over *novel* as more inclusive in its implication of those narratives that act like but are not primarily verbal constructs.

The postmodern moment, as Derrida puts it in his essay "La Structure, le signe et le jeu" ("Structure, Sign and Play"), is the moment "when language invaded the universal problematic": that is, when it has become broadly evident that everything operates by such codes, that everything behaves like language including the silent gesture, the plan of a city, the unspoken agenda, the fashion statement. The postmodern writer engages us not in the objectifying practices that belong to plot-and-character reruns of the same old stories, but instead in the recognition of the complexity and richness of our most unnoticed daily practices where coded systems function in multiples; they interest us in an expertise we have already but have depreciated in the interest of producing portable property ("meaning"). "There is no message," as Julio Cortázar says in *Hopscotch*, "only messengers."

Probably it is worth distinguishing postmodernism from deconstruction, with which it is sometimes confused. As an interpretive method, deconstruction seeks like postmodernism what is *not* present; but unlike postmodernism, which finds in that negative definition a liberation and an opportunity, the keynote of deconstruction too often rivets attention on loss—on points of crisis and breakdown in a system or coded rationalization—and in so doing gets lost in circularities and negative, even paranoid, questioning. It is almost as though deconstruction operates a kind of permanent nostalgia for lost objectivity. Postmodernism poses slightly different questions: what is the system of meaning and value? What are its limits and its capabilities? How does one negotiate between one and another?

The linguistic turn just described amounts to a major shift in the foundations of knowledge because it challenges the bases of consensus and representation that Renaissance culture inscribed in science, in politics, and in art. That knowledge-system or "episteme" is founded in the humanistic belief that the world is One. This belief, codified in centuries of realist art, representational politics, and empirical science, is tantamount to the assertion that a common denominator can be found for all systems of belief and value: that the world is a unified field, explicable by a single explanatory system that belongs to nobody in particular, but to everybody in general.

However, as this belief informed increasingly secular and materialistic practices it became less secure in its claims to universal applicability. After the Renaissance, the "totalizing" claim to universal applicability was increasingly transferred from divinity to infinity, that is, from God to the infinite neutralities of humanist time and space: especially the infinity of space and time as they were radically reconstructed by Renaissance art and science. These developments established the neutral media of modernity in which so much has been possible. Postmodernism is the condition of coping without these absolute common denominators, especially without the neutral and homogeneous media of time and space that are the quintessential, field-unifying media of modernity.

By the 19th century the relativism not just of individual achievement but of systems was generally understood, but implicitly the belief in Truth remained. Darwin's theory of natural selection was not merely one among a number of unreconcilable

theories but one that more closely approximated Truth than prior ones. Implicitly, "totalization" or complete realization of a system's potential remains possible, even though it may not be visible from any single historical moment.

In postmodernism, on the other hand, relativism tips over into relativity, and "totalization" is positively to be avoided as a form of system-death. A system—for example the Latin language—once it has been universally achieved, fulfilled, or expressed, dies out literally and morally; it can be useful in limited ways but it lacks living tolerance and capacity for change.

Postmodern narrative positively avoids the kind of explanatory fullness that would "totalize" its instruments; full descriptions of motive and causality of the kind that formulate "character" and "event" are to be avoided because they tend toward objectification; a margin of multiplicity always remains, and usually a wide margin. This is not to be confused with vagueness, for postmodern narrative language is preternaturally precise. But as Alain Robbe-Grillet (1963) said of Kafka, "nothing is more fantastic than precision." It is the lack of mediating conditions, conditions that unify the world in a common horizon and system of explanation, that postmodern narrative lacks. In this it tips over into relativity.

The work of Robbe-Grillet, for example, thrives on the complete reduction of history and totality in favor of what he called the "obscure enterprise of form." His narrative strategies appear both in novels such as *La Jalousie* (1957; *Jealousy*) and in films such as *L'Année dernière à Marienbad* (1961; Last Year at Marienbad). The nature of the sequence is similar in both: the written description or the camera trace various elliptical trajectories in which repetitions and variations are compounded and multiplied until they produce a kind of absorption and even emotional investment of a sort customarily associated with traditionally meaningful plots, and which yet have no plot or "meaning" in any customary sense of the term. Of course, one has to be capable of letting plot "out the door," but to the well-intentioned reader the effect is almost always one of delight and pleasure in the pattern-making and, perhaps, in the priority the narratives give to such activity. As in Cortázar or Nabokov, Robbe-Grillet's witty film and novel tease the conventional reader with vestiges of the old plot-and-character convention, only to undermine them completely.

Readers are either alarmed or inspired by the implication in postmodern narrative that all systems are self-contained, that therefore all beliefs and values are systemic, that none involves "Truth," and that Truth is impossible and undesirable. This implication goes beyond the recuperable relativism of the 19th century to unrecuperable difference in the 20th. In modernity, relative systems still cohabit more or less uneasily in a common world; in postmodernity, finite systems (Marxism or "English") *construct* the world, which means the world is *not* One but many. Words like *truth, nature, reality*, and even *human* imply, falsely, that an autonomous world of meaning and values exists that *transcends* all finite and mutually exclusive human systems and somehow guarantees them. Postmodernism denies that absolute basis. The questions always remain: What truth? Which nature? Whose reality?

When Truth and Reality disappear so does the objectivity that supported them through the humanist era: an objectivity that itself proves to be a finite system that operates like language, a differential system of function that the "objects" and the referential language of modernity exist to sustain. In postmodern narrative, those "objects" and their psychic counterpart, "subjects," cease to have interest; instead, language can have new functions because it is sprung from the need to refer to "objects" and "subjects" or to support objectifying enterprises such as empiricism or the Napoleonic Code. So, for example, Cortázar's *Rayuela* (1963; *Hopscotch*) offers different sequences for its chapters. The conventional sequence, which produces plot, event, and character, concludes midway through the novel. The recommended "hopscotch" sequence elides event and character for the sake of a protracted, delightful improvisation that continues well past "the end."

Postmodern narrative is a feat of language that plays with the elements of systems and refuses responsibility for consistency within this or that totalized explanation. What one wants to avoid at all costs is something without play, without slack, without the living capacity for movement; one wants play in the line, play in the structure, in the sense of flexibility and variability even to the point of reorganizing the structure. So, for example, Italo Calvino's *Se una notte d'inverno un viaggiatore* (1979; *If on a winter's night a traveler*) consists of a series of first chapters in a never-ending opening gambit. This process, rather than anything that could be summarized in terms of character or plot motivation, constitutes Calvino's novel. We have only beginnings, no endings; by implication the reader who wants an explanatory narrative must construct it herself.

The postmodern attenuation of history and individualism means that narrative seeks other sources of energy and satisfaction than the development of plot and character. Postmodern narrative focuses on the multiplicity of code-systems—of languages in the widest sense—and thus problematizes the ideas of "individuality" and of "history" that were so important to humanism.

The "individual"—and the related idea of "self"—was constructed by and for Enlightenment knowledge and social projects. In postmodern narrative this "founding subject" of history, as Michel Foucault called it, disappears, and instead the possible individuality suggested by terms like *identity* or *self* or *consciousness* remains opaque, problematic, mobile. Marguerite Duras' narrative voice in *L'Amant* (1984; *The Lover*) is problematic as it vacillates between "she" and "I" as if unwilling to settle for one or the other. Duras' I/She is neither the stable entity belonging to a Cartesian *cogito* nor a helpless function of systems, but part of a rhythmic element in the novel that has little or nothing to do with psychological definitions and much to do with the power of language and the strength of a writer. Readers of postmodern narratives must accept that the romantic "individual" is no more; that whatever is "individual" about a life does not at all arise from a cultivated "natural" essence—a romantic soul trailing clouds of glory—but instead from the activity and the work a subject does: from its particular specification of the discursive complex that it inhabits.

Different writers problematize identity in different ways, depending on their commitment to history. Duras abandons the romantic self with positive delight; in her text, past and present belong to the same oscillation, the same rhythmic element that effaces individual identity, effacing the coherence of history in favor of a different relation to the past. Heinrich Böll, on the other hand, anatomizes with more nostalgia the corrosive effects on identity of a society motivated by multinational corporations

and the tabloid press in *Die verlorene Ehre der Katharina Blum* (1974; *The Lost Honor of Katharina Blum*). In this novel the multiplied systems of power and value only bleed into each other by violence, a violence that makes individual integrity viable only in prison. But while Böll's thematic undertones are nostalgic for a European tradition reaching back in narrative from Camus' *L'Étranger* (1942; *The Stranger*) to Stendhal's *Le Rouge et le noir* (1830; *The Red and the Black*), his narrative strategies disrupt the thematic agendas at every turn and belong to the complex interplay of systems characteristic of postmodern narrative. His narrative voice longs for but conspicuously fails to achieve a history; that is, the power to bring all stories into a single story.

The absence of historical conventions in postmodern narrative is perhaps its most noticeable feature. History is a kind of perspective system that potentially aligns all viewpoints in space and time into a single, common-denominator medium—into the same putatively "neutral" time that objectifies a common world subject to common rules. This idea of history is crucial to most 19th-century narrative, especially under the influence of Sir Walter Scott, whose work was celebrated throughout Europe and North America because it provided a new narrative medium for a new social order of things. It is a narrative suitable to democratic social agendas because it assumes, and thus inscribes, a universal connectedness between past and present.

Historical narrative, however, is a totalizing system of the subtlest kind because its totalizing mechanism is not a dogma but a medium. By constructing a temporal medium that is neutral, historical conventions make possible universally applicable systems of human, social, and even scientific explanation. Postmodernist narrative puts history in the interesting position of considering its own historicity. Time does not pass in Duras or Böll or Nabokov, and characters who try to discover underlying causalities or to understand the past come to grief. Vladimir Nabokov's novels always submit "history" to the characteristically postmodern play of systems. Once plot is "let out the door," as he says in his last important book, *Ada; or, Ardor: A Family Chronicle* (1969), the writer and reader can get on with the main business of postmodern narrative, which is to experience the powers of language unconstrained by teleological necessities. Especially in *Ada*, in *Lolita* (1955), and in *Transparent Things* (1972), Nabokov abandons "the disaster of receding time" in favor of the process by which the so-called "individual" subjectivity, inhabiting its complex systemic structures (its language), develops its unique and unrepeatable "poetry."

Postmodern narrative, then, belongs to a cultural reformation that implicates the entire range of cultural practices, and includes academic fields from anthropology to philosophy, from physics to art. Many of the best examples of postmodern writing, especially those from the Latin American "boom," have become best-sellers in English-speaking countries and have gained international recognition. And, with a few notable exceptions, the most original postmodern writing has been done in Latin languages (French, Spanish, Italian) and not in English. This is a politically interesting fact. The postmodern critique of culture and knowledge is least understood and most resisted in Anglo-American cultures because they are so thoroughly invested in empiricism and in the representational politics and capitalist economies that seem to accompany empiricism.

The philosophical critiques of modernity and of rationalism

have in many cases been anticipated by the creative work of artists and scientists who have gone well beyond philosophers in locating the practical implications of postmodernism. Artists such as René Magritte and various surrealists, filmmakers such as Luis Buñel, Alain Resnais, and the Coen brothers, post-Einsteinian scientists interested in quanta and chaos, feminists interested in new acts of personal and political attention, and architects who play with traditional conventions—all these have explored more fully than most theoretical writers the practical and material implications of postmodernism.

Postmodern writers make possible for readers something that even filmmakers cannot achieve: a new habitation in language, a new sense of the autonomous powers of words, of writing, of speech. In fact, one of the most immediate material conditions of life is precisely language. What is more material than the kinesis and sonority of language, or than the torque and tension created by the not-said? Postmodern writers are thoroughly invested in exploring the play of meaning and value that differential systems of all kinds make available.

What postmodern writers do, then, is to make visible both the powers of verbal language that have been suppressed by rationalist agendas as well as the degree to which all systems in their plurality operate like language. Earlier narrative strategies work to mediate plurality by resorting to history, where difference can always be reconciled by the temporal common denominator essential to the dramas of emergent form. By comparison, postmodern writers attempt what the surrealists attempted: to make the limits of systems appear by pluralizing them and by providing no common denominators but language itself. Postmodern novels supply pieces of systems, alphabets of possibility, and the problem of linkage; but they leave the actual linkages precariously up to readers. To paraphrase Jean-François Lyotard's definition of politics in *Le Différend* (1983; *The Differend*), the postmodern narrative condition consists of differences in need of linkage. That condition is something that we already experience daily, and practically everywhere except in the traditional (historical) novel. Postmodern novels simply call attention to and validate that practical experience and its knowledge.

To classify postmodern novels or novelists leads to lists of qualifiers and finalists and obscures the point, which is to validate experiment and adventure. It is not difficult to round up the usual suspects and texts: the *nouveaux romanciers* in France (including Duras, Robbe-Grillet, Raymond Queneau, Robert Pinget); a few German, Italian, and East European writers (such as Böll, Calvino, and Milan Kundera), following the lead of Kafka; in English, writers such as John Hawkes, Gerald Murnane, Vladimir Nabokov, Thomas Pynchon; and of course the writers of the Latin American boom (Isabel Allende, Jorge Luis Borges, Julio Cortázar, José Donoso, Gabriel García Márquez, Octavio Paz, and many others). In ascertaining what is or is not a postmodern narrative, anything qualifies that is consistent with the large agendas of postmodernity described earlier. How or whether a particular writer or text conforms to those agendas depends on the uncertain enterprise of reading as an enterprise of renewal.

"To speak of knowledge is futile," Virginia Woolf says in *The Waves* (1931), and postmodern novelists agree with her; "all is experiment and adventure." At the level of the sentence and in the entire text, the postmodern novel experiments with the possibilities opened up by the erasure of an objectified world. The postmodern writer above all experiments with sequence, varying the syntactical development of traditional plot with various paratactic developments running parallel to and even sometimes in contradiction with any main plot line.

Postmodern narratives always proceed with tremendous zest and buoyancy, not anxiously regretting the passing of Truth and Reality but, on the contrary, rejoicing in the limitations of all systems and in the recovery of buried potentialities in ordinary languages, sequences, and discourses. Postmodern artists call full attention to the medium; that is the message, that is the "meaning." So-called "content" is a religious relic. While it is unprofitable to classify postmodern novels, one negative rule might apply: if the novel is not playful, enjoyable, pleasurable, erotic in the largest sense of life-affirmation, then it probably is not a postmodern novel.

Postmodernist writing offers both new freedoms and new constraints. The freedoms lie in the emphasis on the constructed nature of all knowledge and projects; this means that, because they have been invented, knowledge and projects can be changed. That there is morally or socially speaking no "nature" of things is a liberation, not a loss. The countervailing constraint is the enforced recognition of how many of our supposedly "personal" beliefs and values are not unique to us but things we are born into, that we inherit with the whole complex of interpretations and grammars that govern what we can say and who can speak. Modernity gave us World Historical models and goals. Postmodernity offers us more local, more collective, less heroic opportunities. Postmodernism gets rid of "character" and "point of view," but it by no means extinguishes individuality; it simply denaturalizes it and insists on its discursive function.

ELIZABETH DEEDS ERMARTH

See also Historical Writing and the Novel; Metafiction; Nouveau Roman; Realism; Time in the Novel

Further Reading

Derrida, Jacques, "La Structure, le signe et le jeu dans le discours des sciences humains," in *L'Écriture et la différence*, Paris: Editions du Seuil, 1967; as "Structure, Sign and Play in the Discourse of the Human Sciences," in *Writing and Difference*, Chicago: University of Chicago Press, 1978

Donoso, José, *Historia personal del "boom,"* Barcelona: Anagrama, 1972; as The *"Boom" in Spanish American Literature: A Personal History*, New York: Columbia University Press in association with the Center for Inter-American Relations, 1977

Ermarth, Elizabeth Deeds, *Realism and Consensus in the English Novel*, Princeton, New Jersey: Princeton University Press, 1983; new edition, with subtitle *The Construction of Time in Narrative*, Edinburgh: Edinburgh University Press, 1998

Ermarth, Elizabeth Deeds, *Sequel to History: Postmodernism and the Crisis of Representational Time*, Princeton, New Jersey: Princeton University Press, 1992

Foucault, Michel, *L'Archéologie du Savoir*, Paris: Gallimard, 1969; as *The Archaeology of Knowledge*, New York: Pantheon, and London: Tavistock, 1972

Harvey, David, *The Condition of Postmodernity: An Enquiry into the Origins of Cultural Change*, Oxford and Cambridge, Massachusetts: Blackwell, 1989

Hutcheon, Linda, *The Politics of Postmodernism,* London and New York: Routledge, 1989

Lyotard, Jean-François, *La Condition postmoderne: Rapport sur le savoir,* Paris: Editions de Minuit, 1979; as *The Postmodern Condition: A Report on Knowledge,* Minneapolis: University of Minnesota Press, and Manchester: Manchester University Press, 1984

Lyotard, Jean-François, *Le Différend,* Paris: Editions de Minuit, 1983; as *The Differend: Phrases in Dispute,* Minneapolis:

University of Minnesota Press, and Manchester: Manchester University Press, 1988

Robbe-Grillet, Alain, "La Nature, l'humanisme, et la tragédie," in *Pour un nouveau roman,* Paris: Editions de Minuit, 1963; as "Nature, Humanism and Tragedy," in *For a New Novel: Essays on Fiction,* New York: Grove Press, 1965

Tyler, Stephen, *The Unspeakable: Discourse, Dialogue, and Rhetoric in the Postmodern World,* Madison: University of Wisconsin Press, 1987

Pramoedya Ananta Toer 1925–

Indonesian

Since he first won recognition as a writer in 1950, Pramoedya Ananta Toer has exercised a shaping influence on Indonesian literature. Unified not so much by genre as by a unique style of storytelling, Pramoedya's work includes novels, novellas, short stories, political pamphlets, biographies, and historical studies. His significance as a novelist of international acclaim was established with the Buru tetralogy, the set of four historical novels about the emergence of anticolonial Indonesian nationalism: *Bumi Manusia* (1980; *This Earth of Mankind*), *Anak Semua Bangsa* (1980; *Child of All Nations*), *Jejak Langkah* (1985; *Footsteps*), and *Rumah Kaca* (1988; *House of Glass*). Discussing these novels in 1992, Pramoedya wrote, "I began deliberately with the theme of Indonesia's National Awakening—which, while limited regionally and nationally, nonetheless remains part of the world and of humanity. Step by step I am writing to the roots of its history."

Pramoedya's abiding theme is Indonesian nationalism. Throughout the 1950s, most of his stories, tales, and novels return to the period of revolutionary struggle for independence (1945–50). His first two novels, *Perburuan* (*The Fugitive*) and *Keluarga Gerilya* (Guerrilla Family), both smuggled out of a Dutch prison and published in 1950, tell stories of resistance to Japanese occupation (in *The Fugitive*) and against the Dutch and Allied forces (in *Keluarga Gerilya*). Strongly autobiographical, they recount the spirit of youthful nationalism simultaneously as the memory of solidarity and of betrayal and as liberation and trauma. Like many of Pramoedya's early stories, they give literary form to the experiences of a generation (the so-called Generation of '45) that came of age with the declaration of the Indonesian Republic.

Synthesizing a wide variety of literary traditions, Pramoedya's narrative form is premised on a clear break with Javanese literary conventions. From the work of Chairil Anwar and Idrus (pioneers of the literature of Indonesian revolution) and various American and European writers (John Steinbeck, William Saroyan, and the Flemish writer Lode Zielens), Pramoedya developed techniques of realistic narrative, ironic distance, and satire to form his own distinctive styles of storytelling. His work also draws on the Javanese storytelling patterns of *wayang* shadow puppetry and *babad* historical chronicles, although in ways

that have led critics to write of Pramoedya's "guerrilla war" against his Javanese heritage (see Anderson, 1990; Foulcher, 1993a).

Language is essential for the innovations of novel writing Pramoedya has forged from many different traditions. All his works are written in Bahasa Indonesia, a language developed from the old lingua franca Malay of interisland communication throughout the Malay Archipelago. Adopted by the nationalist movement in 1928 for the needs of an emerging new nation, Bahasa Indonesia is the linguistic workshop from which Pramoedya refashions literary and cultural form. The role of Malay in Indonesia's "national awakening" is one of the many threads running through the Buru tetralogy. It is thematized in the dilemma faced by the main character, Minke, who must decide which language to choose as writer, journalist, and political activist. It also provides an important literary model in the form of Minke's surprise discovery of the short novel "Tjerita Njai Dasima" (1900; The Story of Nyai Dasima) by G. Francis—"a truly European-style novel. But in Malay."

With the Buru tetralogy, there is a significant shift in the scope of Pramoedya's storytelling, as personal memory modulates into historical record. Set in the turn-of-the-century Dutch-controlled East Indies, these novels trace the path of Minke, a Dutch-educated Javanese aristocrat, as he becomes increasingly involved in mass movements of resistance to Dutch colonial rule. *This Earth of Mankind,* which unfolds in many respects as a European Bildungsroman, also draws explicitly on the Malay *nyai* (concubine-slave-mistress) narrative form. Minke's Dutch education is set in counterpoint to what he learns at the Buitenzorg agricultural company—from Sanikem, the native "concubine," and her Eurasian daughter Annelies, who together run the estate in the name of their Dutch master who has gone insane. It is Sanikem who introduces Minke to *Nyai Dasima,* and it is her own narrative of enslavement and then struggle as a *nyai* that provides a primary model both for Minke's writing and for storytelling throughout the tetralogy. As with all of the novels, the story of Minke's awakening is in many respects less important than the set of stories that accumulate around him—and which he then, in turn, transcribes.

All four novels are based on the encyclopedic historical research into the "roots" of anticolonial nationalism that Pramoedya conducted in the late 1950s and early 1960s. His wide-ranging research included study of pre-Indonesian literature, the life and works of the Dutch-educated Javanese feminist Kartini (1879–1904), and the journalism and activism of Tirto Adi Suryo (1880–1918), the model for Minke. The Buru tetralogy, however, and the scope of all Pramoedya's writing since 1965, has been decisively shaped by the disappearance of almost all this historical work following Pramoedya's arrest in 1965 and by the events that precipitated the military takeover and massacres inaugurating Indonesia's "New Order." This lost work is the basis for Pramoedya's novelistic feat of memory, first told orally to his fellow political prisoners in exile on Buru Island.

The lasting impact of Pramoedya's Buru exile is registered in the motif of deafness that runs through *Nyanyi Sunyi Seorang Bisu* (1995; Song of a Deafmute). A compelling two-volume work of documentation, autobiography, and personal, familial, and historical record, *Nyanyi Sunyi Seorang Bisu* records the conditions within which Pramoedya conceived the historical novel-writing that has so far produced, besides the Buru quartet, the long historical novel of 16th-century Indonesia, *Arus Balik* (1995; The Turning of the Tide). Novels yet to be published include *Arok and Dedes,* about historical changes in early Javanese Hindu society, and *Mangir,* about the situation after Majapahit fell and the formation of Mataram. The prison memoirs dwell, too, on the ossification of the ideals of the Indonesian nationalism in "New Order" Indonesia. In its art of storytelling, *Nyanyi Sunyi Seorang Bisu* reiterates all those problems of memory and forgetting, autobiography and history, and revolutionary nationalism and world history to which Pramoedya's novel writing gives shape.

CHRIS GOGWILT

Biography

Born in Blora, Java, in 1925. Imprisoned under the Dutch, 1947–49; in 1958 became member of Lekra, the Institute of People's Culture, an organization championing the nationalist ideals of the 1945 revolution; editor, *Lentera* (Lantern), 1962–65, the weekly section on cultural issues in the left-wing *Bintang Timur* (Eastern Star); also lecturer of Indonesian language and literature, University of Res Publica, and teacher, "Dr. Abdul Rivai" Academy of Journalism; founder, "Multatuli" Literature Academy, Jakarta; arrested in October 1965 during the events that led to the establishment of "New Order" Indonesia under Suharto, at which time his works were banned and his unpublished works, personal archives, and research materials were taken from him and either destroyed or lost; imprisoned, 1965–79, and exiled to Buru island prison camp, 1969–79.

Novels by Pramoedya

Perburuan, 1950; as *The Fugitive,* translated by Willem Samuels, 1990
Keluarga Gerilya [Guerrilla Family], 1950

Bukan Pasarmalam, 1951; as "No Night Market," translated by Harry Aveling, published in *A Heap of Ashes,* 1975
Ditepi Kali Bekasi [On the Banks of the Bekasi River], 1951
Mereka Yang Dilumpuhkan [The Paralyzed Ones], 1951
Gulat di Djakarta [Struggles in Jakarta], 1953
Korupsi [Corruption], 1954
Midah—Simanis Bergigi Emas [Midah—the Sweetheart with the Gold Tooth], 1955
Sekali Peristawa di Bengen Selatan [It Happened in Southern Banten], 1958
Buru tetralogy:
    Bumi Manusia, 1980; as *This Earth of Mankind,* translated by Max Lane, 1990
    Anak Semua Bangsa, 1980; as *Child of All Nations,* translated by Max Lane, 1990
    Jejak Langkah, 1985; as *Footsteps,* translated by Max Lane, 1990
    Rumah Kaca, 1988; as *House of Glass,* translated by Max Lane, 1990
Gadis Pantai, 1987; as *The Girl from the Coast,* translated by Harry Aveling, 1991
Arus Balik [The Turning of the Tide], 1995

Other Writings: collections of stories (including *Subuh: Tjerita-Tjerita Pendek Revolusi* [1950; Subuh: Short Stories of Revolution] and *Tjerita dari Djakarta* [1957; Stories from Jakarta]), biographical and historical works (including *Sang Pemula dan karya-karya non-fiksi (jurnalistik)-fiksi (cerpen/novel) R.M. Tirto Adhi Soerjo* [1985; The Originator: Life and Work of Tirto Adi Suryo]), and memoirs (*Nyanyi Sunyi Seorang Bisu* [1995; Song of a Deafmute]).

Further Reading

Anderson, Benedict, *Language and Power: Exploring Political Cultures in Indonesia,* Ithaca, New York: Cornell University Press, 1990
Foulcher, Keith, "Post-Modernism or the Question of History: Some Trends in Indonesian Fiction since 1965," in *Culture and Society in New Order Indonesia,* edited by Virginia Matheson Hooker, Kuala Lumpur and New York: Oxford University Press, 1993a
Foulcher, Keith, "The Early Fiction of Pramoedya Ananta Toer, 1946–1949," in *Text/Politics in Island Southeast Asia: Essays in Interpretation,* edited by D.M. Roskies, Athens: Ohio University Center for International Studies, 1993b
Hering, Bob, editor, *Pramoedya Ananta Toer 70 Tahun: Essays to Honour Pramoedya Ananta Toer's 70th Year,* Stein, Netherlands: Yayasan Kabar Seberang, 1995
Mrázek, Rudolf, "Only the Deaf Hear Well," *Indonesia* 61 (April 1996)
Teeuw, A., *Pramoedya Ananta Toer: De verbeelding van Indonesië,* Berchem: De Geus, 1993

Preface. *See* Framing and Embedding in Narrative

Prestuplenie i nakazanie. *See* Crime and Punishment

Pride and Prejudice by Jane Austen

1813

As a stylist, Jane Austen is perhaps best known through two phrases from her letters. In the first, Austen assures a nephew that she is not responsible for his missing manuscript. Austen asks, "What should I do with your strong, manly, vigorous sketches, full of variety and glow? How could I possibly join them on to the little bit (two inches wide) of ivory on which I work with so fine a brush, as produces little effect after much labour?" To a niece, she writes that "3 or 4 Families in a Country Village is the very thing to work on." These two statements, generally interpreted as Austen's self-deprecating confession that she was a literary miniaturist, have long been used to trivialize, sometimes to venerate, but always to demarcate her talents as a novelist.

While her works have been condemned as predictable romances or superficial comedies of manners, Austen is best understood as a writer of realistic novels. She was conversant with and influenced by the psychological dramas of Samuel Richardson and the social comedies of Henry Fielding, Frances Burney, and Maria Edgeworth. Above all, plausibility of character and action is the guiding principle of Austen's fiction. Seeking to paint a true portrait of human nature and social behavior as she perceived it through the lens of her own experience and judgment, Austen uses her deceptively small world to offer both trenchant social commentary and intricate psychological portraits.

Ostensibly, *Pride and Prejudice* is a courtship novel, but, as its title indicates, it is actually a novel of education. Its main character is taught how to perceive her world accurately and ethically, and how to act responsibly in that world without forfeiting individual expression and satisfaction at the same time. To enact these lessons, Austen deploys two narrative points of view. The first is an omniscient narrator who stands outside the action, reporting and judging it with a delicious sense of irony. The second is that of Elizabeth Bennet, who positions herself early in the novel as a disinterested observer and a shrewd judge of character. Her voice echoes that of the omniscient narrator in its wit and intelligence; however, unlike the omniscient narrator who already knows all the "right" answers, Elizabeth must learn them during the course of the novel. Austen integrates these two

perspectives in a masterful portrait of human character in both its public and private dimensions.

One technique that Austen uses to reveal character is the opaque narrative of dramatization. In scenes dominated by action and conversation, Austen puts her characters through their paces in a variety of circumstances. The novel's minor characters are largely two-dimensional. They are motivated principally by a single characteristic, whether it is Jane Bennet's naive kindness, Mr. Bingley's good-natured pliancy, Mrs. Bennet's myopic desire to marry off her daughters, or Mr. Collins' obsequious groveling. The characters act predictably again and again, providing little doubt about how to judge them. Elizabeth also participates in this dramatic narrative; she joins in the conversations, the balls, and the visits right along with her fellow characters. Readers experience her as a full participant in her town's social whirl as she dances, converses, and flirts.

More significantly, Austen permits her readers to learn about Elizabeth through her judgments about those around her and about herself. It is through Elizabeth's more complex perspective that Austen gives voice to the individual, a voice that balances out that of the community. Early in the novel, the reader is presented with Elizabeth's judgments through her conversations, as she mulls things over with her sister Jane, her friend Charlotte, and her aunt Mrs. Gardiner. Her perspective, so different from those of the lesser intellects around her, initially seems accurate. But Elizabeth is not so much an exception to her society as an exemplar of the willful, self-interested individuals that it produces. Like her mother, she is proud of her feelings; like her father, she is proud of her cleverness. As a result, she fulfills neither the role of observer nor that of judge with complete success. The novel's double-narrative perspective reflects and reinforces Elizabeth's growing difficulties. Her moments of reflection are increasingly internalized as she becomes isolated and is forced to rely only on her now dubious ability to judge. At the same time, however, she must continue to participate in a social world that is no longer so easy to maneuver.

At the beginning of the novel Elizabeth believes that her individual perspective allows her a comprehensive view of her world and an intimate view of individual human nature. This perspective leads her to blindly defend her elder sister's passivity and her father's sarcasm. It leads her willfully to dislike Darcy and to believe Wickham. During the course of the novel, however, she learns to read the characters of those around her, so that, in the end, she does approach the comprehensive understanding of Austen's wise omniscient narrator. She learns to negotiate the demands of proper social behavior and individual desire. Elizabeth cannot really change her culture, or even her family, but she can change herself, her perceptions, and her values. The two narrative perspectives—external and internal—allow for a combination of dramatization and reflection that enables readers to watch Elizabeth as she matures in her judgments. In the transparent narrative—Elizabeth's thoughts—the reader watches her learn to separate appearance from reality; in the opaque narrative—Elizabeth's actions—the reader watches her learn to separate manners from mannerisms.

Pride and Prejudice continues to be Austen's most popular novel, and Elizabeth Bennet her most popular heroine. But while Austen's novels have always had a faithful following and have never gone out of print, they were never as popular as those of her contemporary, Sir Walter Scott, and had little impact on influential 19th-century novelists such as Charlotte Brontë and Charles Dickens. Austen's novel of manners did, however, provide a model for writers as diverse as George Eliot, Henry James, and Virginia Woolf. Each of these novelists, in his or her own way, attempts to offer an expansive view of humanity through the very small aperture of individual characters operating within their own limited social circles and their own limited perceptions. For them, as for Austen, the whole world could be distilled into, but not limited by, a deceptively small point in time and space.

JUDITH BURDAN

See also Jane Austen

Further Reading
Brown, Julia Prewitt, *Jane Austen's Novels: Social Change and Literary Form,* Cambridge, Massachusetts: Harvard University Press, 1979
Halperin, John, editor, *Jane Austen: Bicentenary Essays,* Cambridge and New York: Cambridge University Press, 1975
Kaplan, Deborah, *Jane Austen Among Women,* Baltimore: Johns Hopkins University Press, 1992
Looser, Devoney, editor, *Jane Austen and Discourses of Feminism,* London: Macmillan, and New York: St. Martin's Press, 1995
MacMaster, Juliet, *Jane Austen the Novelist: Essays Past and Present,* London: Macmillan, and New York: St. Martin's Press, 1996
Monaghan, David, editor, *Jane Austen in a Social Context,* London: Macmillan, and Totowa, New Jersey: Barnes and Noble, 1981
Mooneyham, Laura G., *Romance, Language, and Education in Jane Austen's Novels,* London: Macmillan, and New York: St. Martin's Press, 1988
Poovey, Mary, *The Proper Lady and the Woman Writer: Ideology as Style in the Works of Mary Wollstonecraft, Mary Shelley, and Jane Austen,* Chicago: University of Chicago Press, 1984
Thompson, James, *Between Self and World: The Novels of Jane Austen,* University Park: Pennsylvania State University Press, 1988
Thompson, James, "Jane Austen," in *Columbia History of the British Novel,* edited by John Richetti, New York: Columbia University Press, 1994

La Princesse de Clèves by Madame de Lafayette

1678

La Princesse de Clèves is considered the first psychological novel and stands out as one of the most successful attempts to meld history and fiction. As a result, it has been extremely influential in the subsequent evolution of the novel in France.

A highly cultured aristocrat with access to the court of Louis XIV, Madame de Lafayette chose to revert to an earlier period in situating the tragic story of a young woman's renunciation of illicit love. The action takes place during the undistinguished reigns of Henri II (reigned 1547–59), husband of Catherine de' Medici, and Francis II (reigned 1559–60), husband of Mary Stuart. Because Madame de Lafayette's primary concern was psychological rather than historical, she made free use of historical characters and events in order to lend credibility and verisimilitude to her fiction. The initial focus on the glamorous life at the court of the pleasure-loving and amorous Henri II, depicted in

the opening pages of the novel, soon switches to the eponymous heroine.

Mademoiselle de Chartres, the future Princesse de Clèves, has been brought up away from the pleasures and temptations of the court by a lovingly protective mother who warns her only child against the fatal dangers that lurk behind men's seductive ways and words. Soon after the young woman's arrival in the capital, the exceedingly worthy Prince de Clèves falls in love with her and succeeds in winning her hand in marriage, realizing, however, that his love is not reciprocated. When the princess meets the strikingly handsome and accomplished Duc de Nemours, she experiences real passion, and it overwhelms her with dread and panic. During their public encounters at court events and their rare private moments, she attempts desperately to hide her true feelings behind a facade of dignified decorum and distant hauteur. Whenever possible, she flees from his presence. Determined to remain virtuous and reproachless, the princess continues to flee from Nemours for fear of yielding to him.

Forced to the extraordinarily painful dilemma of choosing between a respected elderly husband and an impetuous young lover, the princess decides on a course of action that will have unexpected and disastrous results. Remembering the stern admonitions of her deceased mother—that a wife should always turn to her husband for help and guidance—the princess undertakes the morally courageous but naive act of confessing her powerful attraction to Nemours to her husband, all the while proudly insisting that she is blameless and strenuously resisting his jealous entreaties to reveal the identity of the man who has conquered her heart. Instead of finding in the prince the moral and emotional support the princess so desperately needs to resist Nemours' advances and her own feelings, she finds she must deal with her spouse's tormented distrust and anxiety. That the prince failed to appreciate his wife's extraordinary sincerity is hardly difficult to understand. Her great pride and lack of worldliness led the princess to make the fatal psychological error of taking her husband into her confidence, an unheard-of act, especially considering the cynical mores of Old Regime courtly society. (In fact, contemporary critics found the princess' honesty too improbable to believe.)

The princess' wholly negative attitude toward sexual passion is doubtless better understood in light of the way in which 17th-century society viewed the "passions." On the whole, the moral ideal is what the language of the time called *repos* (self-possession and inner tranquillity), a term the Princesse de Clèves frequently invokes in her travails. Such moralists and thinkers as Descartes, Pascal, La Rochefoucauld, and La Bruyère, as well as such dramatists as Corneille and Racine, depict in the direst images and most eloquent language the dreadful effect the passions, and especially sexual passion, have on the human soul. Seen in this cultural and literary context, the Princess de Clèves' tragic attempts to resist her attraction to the Duc de Nemours become more understandable. She fears, above all, losing her self-mastery and her peace of mind. In these terms, amorous passion is like a disease of the soul. The transgression of the marriage contract is, of course, also a central theme in the novel. Adultery is no small matter in a society in which a woman is totally dependent on the authority of a father or a husband. A wife's unfaithfulness, when uncovered, is a scandal and a disgrace. How could the princess then entrust her honor and reputation to a man notorious for his amorous conquests? In a society such as hers, men are the enemy and are to be feared and distrusted. There is safety only in respectability and marital loyalty.

It does not take an overly attentive reader to detect a wealth of emotional overtones and stylistic nuances in the formal, elevated prose of *La Princesse de Clèves*. Madame de Lafayette's finely wrought sentences are as well balanced and imposing as classical architecture, with its fondness for symmetrical arrangements and effects of grandeur. A deliberate lack of concreteness and specificity in the descriptions and a tendency to use repetition for expressive effect characterize the classical style. There are two voices in the novel: the voice of a third-person narrator, who sets the dignified tone, and the voices of the characters, who frequently engage in dialogue that remains elevated and stately, even in the most dramatic circumstances. The scene of the princess' confession to her husband is a good example. Yet such decorum does not preclude strong sexual and erotic overtones. Powerful human emotions can be expressed just as effectively in the restrained, classical language of Madame de Lafayette as in the hyperbolic, overheated prose of the romantics. It is no coincidence, therefore, that *La Princesse de Clèves* had such a profound influence on successive generations of French novelists. Jean-Jacques Rousseau, Stendhal, and Albert Camus, among many others, have acknowledged their admiration for Madame de Lafayette's masterpiece.

GITA MAY

Further Reading

Coulet, Henri, *Le Roman jusqu'à la Révolution*, Paris: Armand Colin, 1967

DeJean, Joan E., *Tender Geographies: Women and the Origins of the Novel in France*, New York: Columbia University Press, 1991

Duchêne, Roger, *Madame de Lafayette: La Romancière aux cent bras*, Paris: Fayard, 1988

Force, Pierre, "Doute métaphysique et vérité romanesque dans *La Princesse de Clèves* et *Zaïde*," *Romantic Review* 83 (1992)

Harth, Erica, *Ideology and Culture in Seventeenth-Century France*, Ithaca, New York: Cornell University Press, 1983

Henry, Patrick, editor, *An Inimitable Example: The Case for "The Princesse de Clèves,"* Washington, D.C.: Catholic University of America Press, 1993

Laugaa, Maurice, editor, *Lectures de Madame de Lafayette*, Paris: Colin, 1971

Kamuf, Peggy, *Fictions of Feminine Desire: Disclosures of Heloise*, Lincoln: University of Nebraska Press, 1982

Kaps, Helen Karen, *Moral Perspective in "La Princesse de Clèves,"* Eugene: University of Oregon Books, 1968

Redhead, Ruth Willard, *Themes and Images in Fictional Works of Madame de La Fayette*, New York: Lang, 1990

Showalter, English, *The Evolution of the French Novel, 1641–1782*, Princeton, New Jersey: Princeton University Press, 1972

Stanton, Domna, "The Ideal of 'repos' in 17th-Century French Literature," *L'Esprit Créateur* 15 (1975)

The Private Memoirs and Confessions of a Justified Sinner by James Hogg

1824

Published anonymously in one volume in June 1824, James Hogg's *The Private Memoirs and Confessions of a Justified Sinner* received little attention for almost 100 years. Nervous (he would later claim) of having written "a story replete with horrors," Hogg attempted to pass it off as a Glasgow production, and complained when his identity was leaked by *Blackwood's Edinburgh Magazine*. After his death, the novel was reissued in a corrupt, bowdlerized text, retitled *Confessions of a Fanatic* (1837); the original did not become current again until the 20th century. Robert Louis Stevenson, Andrew Lang, and George Saintsbury noticed it in the 1890s, and in the 1920s it was taken up by André Gide and Julien Green. Gide's advocacy, in particular, repositioned *Confessions* as a modernist classic *avant la lettre*; more recent criticism has made it a postmodernist one. At least four editions are currently in print. Critics have come to admire the novel for its analysis of radical evil, its portrayal of psychopathic dissociation, its evocation of moral collapse in a condition of epistemological undecidability, and its unrelenting satire of the cultural assumptions and literary conventions of the Scottish romance revival.

The Private Memoirs and Confessions of a Justified Sinner marked the end of Hogg's attempt to establish himself as a "Scotch novelist" in the wake of Sir Walter Scott in the early 1820s. Abandoning the attempt as a critical and commercial failure, Hogg returned to short fiction and poetry. *The Private Memoirs and Confessions of a Justified Sinner* reflects on that failure as an index of a larger cultural predicament, and it undertakes a powerful critique of the form of national historical romance instituted by Scott. Hogg's text, like everything it contains, is divided into two parts: the "Private Memoirs and Confessions of a Sinner, written by himself," and "The Editor's Narrative," which frames it. In an epilogue, the reader learns how the editor has exhumed the manuscript of the "Confessions" along with the corpse of an 18th-century suicide: Hogg makes the antiquarian retrieval of an ancestral national culture amount to grave robbery. The editor pieces the "Confessions" together with fragments of documentary evidence and oral tradition but fails to produce a coherent, unified story, leaving us with his own confession of bafflement.

"The Editor's Narrative" opens with a repudiation of the ideological themes of union established with Scott's *Waverley* (1814). Scandalous divisions within the family characterize the Laird of Dalcastle's marriage and the parentage and upbringing of his children; these divisions are both causes and effects of historic divisions in the religious and political institutions of public life in Scotland at the end of the 17th century. The brothers, or (in a systematic ambiguity) stepbrothers, George Colwan and Robert Wringhim, grow up apart as merry Episcopalian Tory and dour Presbyterian Whig. They are thrown together in Edinburgh during the political debates preceding the Treaty of Union between Scotland and England—a historical event never named in this novel about the impossibility, or futility, of "union" as a state of psychic and collective life. Impelled by a perverse antagonism, Robert haunts his brother, who is killed in a duel under mysterious circumstances. The resourceful investigations of two women,

George's stepmother and the prostitute Bell Calvert, discover the further haunting of a shadowy stranger, who appears to be Robert's friend but betrays him to them as his brother's murderer.

The narrative then passes to Robert in the "Confessions" proper. Robert relates his upbringing by a fanatical Calvinist stepfather who teaches him that he is "justified," one of God's elect. A glamorous stranger comes to demand Robert's allegiance and convinces him that all actions are permissible to the man predestined for salvation. The narrative structure prevents the reader from deciding whether the stranger, called Gil-Martin, is actually the devil or Robert's hallucinatory projection. Gil-Martin, who has the power to assume people's likenesses and to read their thoughts, sets Robert on a course of debauchery and murder. Robert's psychic splitting proceeds from a radical dislocation at his origins and culminates in his wretched flight across country at the end of the narrative. Rejected by his biological father, he is brought up in a false community based on the individualist yet authoritarian interpretation of the written word. Hogg represents the opposite condition to this in the oral-traditional culture of the Scottish countryside, the novel's authentic site of community (shown in the interpolated dialect tale of the preaching at Auchtermuchty, in which a peasant's native sagacity detects the devil). But Hogg also represents that community as historically bounded, and inaccessible to the outcast Robert, who ineffectually seeks refuge in it on his way to a lonely end.

That traditional community, we discover in a last, startling turn, is equally unavailable to the author of *The Private Memoirs and Confessions of a Justified Sinner*. In his closing account of the book's origins, the editor reprints the description of the suicide's grave, with its uncannily preserved contents, from a letter to *Blackwood's Magazine* written in August 1823 by none other than James Hogg, the well-known shepherd-poet. The editor and some of his friends (associated with Scott's circle) seek out Hogg for further information, but he unexpectedly lives up to his folk persona of "the Ettrick Shepherd" and refuses to assist them in the unwholesome business of ransacking old graves. This James Hogg, loyal to the community that, as a shepherd, he still serves, cannot be the same person as the shadowy, nameless, thoroughly alienated author of *The Private Memoirs and Confessions of a Justified Sinner*. Hogg's masterpiece achieves its lucid and disturbing formal perfection upon the representation of an incoherence that includes the identity of the author.

IAN DUNCAN

Further Reading

Duncan, Ian, "The Upright Corpse: James Hogg, National Literature, and the Uncanny," *Studies in Hogg and His World* 5 (1994)

Gifford, Douglas, *James Hogg*, Edinburgh: Ramsay Head Press, 1976

Groves, David, *James Hogg: The Growth of a Writer*, Edinburgh: Scottish Academic Press, 1988

Kelly, Gary, *English Fiction of the Romantic Period, 1789–1830*, London and New York: Longman, 1989

Mack, Douglas S., "'The Rage of Fanaticism in Former Days': James Hogg's *Confessions of a Justified Sinner* and the Controversy over *Old Mortality*," in *Nineteenth-Century Scottish Fiction: Critical Essays*, edited by Ian Campbell, Manchester: Carcanet New Press, and New York: Barnes and Noble, 1979

Manning, Susan, *The Puritan-Provincial Vision: Scottish and American Literature in the Nineteenth Century*, Cambridge and New York: Cambridge University Press, 1990

Miller, Karl, *Cockburn's Millennium*, London: Duckworth, 1975; Cambridge, Massachusetts: Harvard University Press, 1976

Petrie, David, "The Sinner versus the Scholar: Two Exemplary Modes of Mis-taking Signs in Relation to Hogg's *Justified Sinner*," *Studies in Hogg and His World* 3 (1992)

Redekop, Magdalene, "Buried Alive with Hogg's *Justified Sinner*," *English Literary History* 52:1 (1985)

Sedgwick, Eve Kosofsky, *Between Men: English Literature and Male Homosocial Desire*, New York: Columbia University Press, 1985

Watson, Nicola, *Revolution and the Form of the British Novel: Intercepted Letters, Interrupted Seductions*, Oxford: Clarendon Press, and New York: Oxford University Press, 1994

Proletarian Novel

Socialist Realism in the United States and Great Britain

If the novel is the most important literary genre through which the European bourgeoisie has explored its own class identity and expressed its collective vision of the world, it is also the case that the novel has been one of the most important literary vehicles for the expression of antibourgeois positions. Indeed, proletarian novels (which one might roughly define as those that represent the position of workers as the class antagonists of the ruling bourgeoisie) have a long and rich history in both Britain and the United States. In Britain, novels that might be considered proletarian (or at least antibourgeois) in their orientation go back as far as William Godwin's *Caleb Williams* (1794), although Godwin's essentially anarchist position lacks any real proletarian class consciousness. Even though the rudiments of a critique of capitalism may be found in the works of bourgeois Victorian novelists such as Elizabeth Gaskell or Charles Dickens, such writers remained highly antagonistic to the idea of working-class political action. The 19th-century US novel contains similar gestures toward a literature of the working class. Rebecca Harding Davis' *Life in the Iron Mills* (written 1861, published 1972) is a notable example, and even Hermann Melville's venerable *Moby-Dick* (1851), with its cast of mostly working-class characters, might be considered the first US proletarian novel.

Nevertheless, the 19th-century roots of leftist culture are far deeper and stronger in Britain than in the United States. As E.P. Thompson points out in his monumental work *The Making of the English Working Class* (1963), English working-class culture developed in vibrant and dynamic ways during the 19th century. Workers sought, within the confusion of the sweeping social transformations associated with the Industrial Revolution, to establish a viable cultural identity for themselves as individuals and as a class. Nevertheless, working-class culture remained an essentially marginal phenomenon, promulgated through informal channels and generally set in stark opposition to an official English culture that tended to represent workers in negative and stereotypical ways. Indeed, the more workers sought to seize control of their lives, the more they became the objects of fear and loathing in the official English press—and in English literature. The Chartist movement of 1837 to 1853 marks a particular watershed in the history of this phenomenon. As the most significant attempt of English workers in the 19th century to gain political and cultural power, the Chartist movement spurred the expansion of working-class culture into realms hitherto dominated by the middle and upper classes. This expansion included the production of working-class novels by writers such as Ernest Jones and Thomas Merton Wheeler. Not surprisingly, the movement triggered a reaction in middle-class literature as well, providing some of the inspiration for Dickens and Gaskell and even leading a decidedly right-wing writer like Benjamin Disraeli to warn in novels like *Sybil* (1845) that economic inequality was making England into two nations that might eventually end up at war with each other. In Disraeli's case, the concern was less for the plight of English workers than for the possibility that these workers, given their supposed brutish tendencies toward savagery and mob violence, might wreak havoc on the upper classes. Nevertheless, "condition of England" novels by writers like Disraeli and Gaskell helped to establish precedents for the literary treatment of issues that would be crucial to the literature of the left in future decades.

The middle part of the 19th century, especially after the end of the Chartist movement in 1853, saw a relative dearth in the production of working-class literature in Britain. Still, works such as John W. Overton's *Harry Hartley; or, Social Science for the Workers* (1859) and W. Lynn Linton's *The True History of Joshua Davidson* (1872) continued to agitate for greater justice and equality in Britain. Working-class literature then underwent a resurgence late in the 19th century as depressed economic conditions worsened the plight of the working class and brought new urgency to the treatment of issues of social and economic equality. Specific events, including the London Dock Workers strike of 1889 and the founding of the Second International in that same year, marked a renewed concern with the problems of capitalism but also renewed hope of the potential of socialism to solve those problems. Meanwhile, literature played an important role in developments that led to a number of political and social reforms designed to alleviate the plight of the poor—a plight so extreme that many felt it might lead to revolution. Novels such as George Gissing's *The Nether World* (1889) and Arthur Morrison's *A Child of the Jago* (1896) attempted to make a middle-class audience aware of the miserable living conditions of the underclasses, especially in London. More importantly, writers such as William Edwards Tirebuck, Allen Clarke, and Margaret Harkness (publishing as John Law) produced novels designed to express a genuinely working-class perspective on contemporary social and political issues. Moreover, many of these writers were influenced by socialism, as were William Morris, H.G. Wells, and George Bernard Shaw. The last years of the 19th century also saw an increase in the production of historical novels from a working-class perspective by writers such as William Hale White (*The Revolution in Tanner's Lane,* 1887), James Haslam (*The Handloom Weaver's Daughter,* 1904), and E.L. Voynich (*The Gadfly,* 1897).

Thus, by the end of the 19th century, there was already an impressive body of working-class novels in Britain, ranging from naturalistic descriptions of working-class poverty, to rousing calls for working-class political action, to utopian visions of a better socialist future, to historical novels intended to help delineate a usable past for working-class action in the present. Nevertheless, the impetus for leftist literature seemed to wane in the first decade of the 20th century, in part because of several democratizing reforms. World War I contributed to a further decline in British left literary production in the second decade of the 20th century. Proletarian novels did continue to be produced, however, including *The Sorcery Shop* (1907) by the socialist propagandist Robert Blatchford. Moreover, 1914 saw the publication (albeit in expurgated form) of Robert Tressell's *The Ragged Trousered Philanthropists,* probably the most vivid literary evocation of working-class experience to that date and a book that would become the single most influential text in British proletarian literature in the 20th century. Tressell's book, informed by a solid socialist political perspective, is made all the more effective by the fact that Tressell himself (an Irish-born house painter whose real name was Robert Noonan) had experienced proletarian life first hand. Indeed, his book has been called the first realistic novel of British working-class life actually written by a member of that class.

The 1920s then saw another surge in the production of proletarian literature in Britain, spurred by British social and economic problems in the wake of World War I and inspired partly by the success of the Russian Revolution and the project to build socialism in the Soviet Union. James Welsh's *The Underworld* (1920), H.R. Barbor's *Against the Red Sky* (1922), Ethel Carnie Holdsworth's *This Slavery* (1925), Henry Green's *Living* (1929), Ellen Wilkinson's *Clash* (1929), and others once again turned literary attention to class-related social and economic issues. With the coming of the Great Depression of the 1930s (and with the threat of fascism looming over British society—both internally and externally—during most of that decade), British proletarian literature underwent a veritable explosion of productivity. This

decade saw the publication of hundreds of proletarian novels, again often influenced by trends in the Soviet Union and by the work of Soviet writers such as Maksim Gor'kii and Mikhail Sholokhov. It should be emphasized, however, that Soviet socialist realism (which sought to contribute to the building of socialism in a society officially committed to that project) faced problems very different from those faced by Western proletarian fiction, the principal mission of which was to contribute to the growth of proletarian class consciousness in capitalist societies.

The proletarian works of the 1930s were produced in a wide variety of modes and from a significant range of political perspectives. Some of them, such as Lewis Grassic Gibbon's trilogy, *A Scots Quair* (1932–34), employed sophisticated modernist literary strategies that helped them to become accepted as classics of British literature. Olaf Stapledon's socialist utopian fantasies (*Last and First Men,* 1930; *Star Maker,* 1937) eventually gained recognition as classics of science fiction. Middle-class writers such as Alec Brown (*Daughters of Albion,* 1935), Rex Warner (*The Wild Goose Chase,* 1937), and Edward Upward (*Journey to the Border,* 1938) produced works, sometimes in experimental avant-garde forms, that attempted to convey the need for radical social and political change in Britain. Walter Greenwood (*Love on the Dole,* 1933), Walter Brierley (*Means Test Man,* 1935), and others wrote best-selling novels using realist and naturalist strategies to convey working-class experience to a primarily middle-class audience. Meanwhile, writers such as Harold Heslop (*Last Cage Down,* 1935) and Lewis Jones (*Cwmardy,* 1937; *We Live,* 1939) began to make genuine progress toward the development of a legitimately proletarian literature that breaks free of the limitations of the bourgeois aesthetic tradition. Finally, Christopher Caudwell, Alick West, Ralph Fox, and other critics made important contributions in the 1930s to the development of British literary criticism from a genuinely Marxist perspective. Fox also wrote proletarian novels, while Caudwell (writing as Christopher St. John Sprigg) joined Cecil Day Lewis (writing as Nicholas Blake) and numerous others in writing detective novels sympathetic to the proletarian cause.

The development of US proletarian fiction lagged somewhat behind that of its British counterpart, largely because industrialization (and thus the creation of a genuine proletariat) occurred later in the United States than in Britain. Nevertheless, important works were produced in the early 20th century that began to represent the point of view of the US industrial working class. One might single out, for example, Jack London's *The Iron Heel* (1908) or Ernest Poole's *The Harbor* (1915) as early novels that sought to introduce US workers to socialist principles and to the need for collective working-class action to oppose the inequities of the emergent capitalist system. Meanwhile, US naturalist writers Frank Norris (*McTeague,* 1899; *The Octopus,* 1901), Theodore Dreiser (*Sister Carrie,* 1900; *An American Tragedy,* 1925), and Upton Sinclair (*The Jungle,* 1906) had begun to produce compelling novels that documented the sometimes appalling human consequences of capitalism, although not necessarily from a specifically proletarian perspective. Radical labor unions, particularly the Industrial Workers of the World (IWW), also participated in the development of US proletarian culture in the first decades of the 20th century.

The 1930s saw an explosion in the production of US proletarian novels, paralleling developments in Britain and for many of the same reasons. Indeed, one could argue that this movement contained the most important energies in US culture of the 1930s, influencing in important ways even mainstream writers such as F. Scott Fitzgerald and Ernest Hemingway, whose *For Whom the Bell Tolls* (1940) remains the most important US literary treatment of the Spanish Civil War. Indeed, some works that came to be regarded as classics of US literature were produced very much in sympathy with the proletarian movement of the 1930s. In this regard, one might single out John Dos Passos' *U.S.A.* trilogy (1930–36) and John Steinbeck's *The Grapes of Wrath* (1939). It is also true, however, that the canonization of Dos Passos' trilogy was aided by its growing scepticism toward the realization of the utopian goals of socialism in a US context, while the continuing critical acceptance of *The Grapes of Wrath* occurred at the expense of a consistent effacement of its radical political message.

Many of the most important US proletarian novels of the 1930s dealt directly with the experience of work and the phenomenon of labor activism. Strikes became a central theme of proletarian fiction during this period, and fictionalized documentaries of real events became common. The crucial Gastonia Mill strike of 1929 formed the basis for an entire family of works of proletarian fiction, including Mary Heaton Vorse's *Strike!* (1930), Sherwood Anderson's *Beyond Desire* (1932), Fielding Burke's *Call Home the Heart* (1932), Grace Lumpkin's *To Make My Bread* (1932), Myra Page's *Gathering Storm* (1932), and William Rollins' *The Shadow Before* (1934). Much of this kind of fiction was produced by workers themselves. Encouraged by radical journals such as *New Masses* and aided by Communist Party workshops and organizations like the John Reed Clubs, numerous workers turned their hand to writing in this decade. An important work produced as part of this phenomenon was *Jews Without Money* (1930), an autobiographical novel by *New Masses* editor Mike Gold that was produced partially in an attempt to provide a model for other proletarian writers. Indeed, many proletarian writers, attempting to find a literary mode for the expression of working-class experience, wrote in an autobiographical vein, including Jack Conroy (*The Disinherited*, 1933), Isidor Schneider (*From the Kingdom of Necessity*, 1935), and Agnes Smedley (*Daughter of Earth*, 1929).

While class remained the central social category in their work, proletarian writers also led the way toward more cogent treatment of issues involving gender, race, and ethnicity in US literature in the 1930s. Women writers were particularly prominent among the proletarian novelists of this decade. In addition to Smedley, Vorse, Burke (the pen name of Olive Tilford Dargan), Lumpkin, and Page, this movement also included such figures as Tess Slesinger (*The Unpossessed*, 1934), Josephine Herbst (*Rope of Gold*, 1939), Tillie Olsen (*Yonnondio*, written in the 1930s but not published in book form until 1974), and Meridel Le Sueur (*The Girl*, written in the 1930s and early 1940s, published in book form in 1978). Meanwhile, writers such as Gold and Henry Roth (*Call It Sleep*, 1934) focused on the experiences of Jewish immigrants in the United States, while James T. Farrell (*Studs Lonigan* trilogy, 1932–35) and Pietro Di Donato (*Christ in Concrete*, 1939) did the same for Irish and Italian immigrants, respectively. Participants in the Harlem Renaissance, including Langston Hughes (*The Ways of White Folks*, 1934) and Claude McKay (*Banjo*, 1929; *Banana Bottom*, 1933), called attention to racial inequalities in the United States in works that were closely aligned with the proletarian movement. And some of the most important US proletarian writers of the 1930s were African Americans writing about racial issues within the framework of class, including Richard Wright (*Native Son*, 1940) and William Attaway (*Blood on the Forge*, 1941).

World War II interrupted this tremendously rich cultural production in both Britain and the United States. The subsequent climate of the Cold War made it impossible for that production to regain its former momentum. It should be noted, however, that the decline in production owed partly to the fact that many reforms supported by proletarian writers of the 1930s were actually implemented in the years after World War II. Nevertheless, social problems and class inequality remained, and proletarian writers continued to respond to those phenomena. In Britain, Jack Common wrote effective autobiographical novels of working-class experience, including *Kiddar's Luck* (1951) and *The Ampersand* (1955). Jack Lindsay, whose career began in the 1930s, remained a tremendously prolific writer of leftist texts throughout the 1950s, specializing in historical novels. Doris Lessing, responding especially to issues related to gender and colonialism, produced *Martha Quest* (1952) and *The Golden Notebook* (1962), novels that broke genuinely new ground in the literature of the left. Likewise, John Berger brought the British novel of the left fully into the realm of postmodernism with *G.* (1972). In the meantime, writers like David Caute kept alive the leftist tradition of historical novels, while Barry Hines, Alan Sillitoe, David Storey, the Marxist critic and theorist Raymond Williams, and others continued to produce novels centering on working-class life within the new context of post-1960s Britain.

In the United States, the McCarthyite repression brought particularly difficult times for proletarian writers in the late 1940s and early 1950s. Many of the prominent writers of the 1930s were silenced altogether. Others, like Dos Passos, continued to work but drifted to the right in their political orientation. Nevertheless, writers such as Howard Fast (*Freedom Road*, 1944; *Spartacus*, 1951) continued to produce novels sympathetic to the proletarian cause in the 1940s and 1950s, while others turned to the more indirect modes of political expression offered by popular genres, including science fiction (as in the satires of Frederik Pohl and Cyril Kornbluth) and detective and crime fiction (as in the case of Chester Himes, William Gardner Smith, and Ed Lacy). Not surprisingly, the 1960s saw a resurgence in anti-authoritarian political fiction, although little of it was specifically proletarian in its orientation. Nevertheless, writers such as E.L. Doctorow (*The Book of Daniel*, 1971; *Ragtime*, 1975) have brought proletarian sympathies to the realm of postmodernism, while John Nichols (*The Milagro Beanfield War*, 1974), Denise Giardina (*Storming Heaven*, 1987), and others have continued to produce novels of proletarian experience in recent decades.

The 1980s and 1990s have witnessed a resurgence in attention to proletarian fiction as critics on both sides of the Atlantic have sought to recover and reassess this rich literary tradition that had been all but forgotten during the Cold War. Gustav Klaus, Jeremy Hawthorn, David Bell, and Pamela Fox have worked to bring renewed attention to the long tradition of British socialist and working-class literature. Raymond Williams, Terry Eagleton, and Perry Anderson have drawn upon the heritage of British cultural materialism to make important new contributions to the development of Marxist theory. In the United States, Fredric Jameson has made similar contributions to Marxist theory, while critics such as Barbara Foley, Alan Wald, Constance Coiner, Michael Denning, and James Bloom have brought much-needed sympathetic critical attention to the long-disparaged tradition of US proletarian culture.

M. KEITH BOOKER

See also Class and the Novel; English Novel (1920–50); Ideology and the Novel; Marxist Criticism of the Novel; Naturalism; Politics and the Novel; Social Criticism; Socialist Realism; United States Novel (1900–45)

Further Reading

Aaron, Daniel, *Writers on the Left: Episodes in American Literary Communism,* New York: Harcourt, 1961

Bell, David, *Ardent Propaganda: Miners' Novels and Class Conflict, 1929–1939,* Umea, Sweden: University of Umea, 1995

Bloom, James D., *Left Letters: The Culture Wars of Mike Gold and Joseph Freeman,* New York: Columbia University Press, 1992

Coiner, Constance, *Better Red: The Writing and Resistance of Tillie Olsen and Meridel Le Sueur,* New York: Oxford University Press, 1995

Denning, Michael, *Mechanic Accents: Dime Novels and Working-Class Culture in America,* London and New York: Verso, 1987

Denning, Michael, *The Cultural Front: The Laboring of American Culture in the Twentieth Century,* London and New York: Routledge, 1997

Foley, Barbara, *Radical Representations: Politics and Form in U.S. Proletarian Fiction, 1929–1941,* Durham, North Carolina: Duke University Press, 1993

Fox, Pamela, *Class Fictions: Shame and Resistance in the British Working-Class Novel, 1890–1945,* Durham, North Carolina: Duke University Press, 1994

Hawthorn, Jeremy, editor, *The British Working-Class Novel in the Twentieth Century,* London: Arnold, 1984

Klaus, H. Gustav, editor, *The Socialist Novel in Britain: Towards the Recovery of a Tradition,* Brighton, Sussex: Harvester, and New York: St. Martin's Press, 1982

Klaus, H. Gustav, editor, *The Rise of Socialist Fiction, 1880–1914,* Brighton, Sussex: Harvester, and New York: St. Martin's Press, 1987

Murphy, James F., *The Proletarian Moment: The Controversy over Leftism in Literature,* Urbana: University of Illinois Press, 1991

Rideout, Walter B., *The Radical Novel in the United States, 1900–1954: Some Interrelations of Literature and Society,* Cambridge, Massachusetts: Harvard University Press, 1956

Smith, David, *Socialist Propaganda in the Twentieth-Century British Novel,* London: Macmillan, 1978; Totowa, New Jersey: Rowman and Littlefield, 1979

Thompson, E.P., *The Making of the English Working Class,* revised edition, London: Penguin, 1980

Vicinus, Martha, *The Industrial Muse: A Study of Nineteenth-Century British Working-Class Literature,* London: Croom Helm, 1974; New York: Barnes and Noble, 1975

Wald, Alan, *Writing from the Left: New Essays on Radical Culture and Politics,* London and New York: Verso, 1994

Prologue. *See* Framing and Embedding in Narrative

Promessi sposi. *See* Betrothed

Prose Novelistic Forms

Although various critics, from Northrop Frye (1976) to Margaret Doody (1996), have stressed the continuity between the modern novel and such ancient narrative traditions as the myths and romances of classical Greece, most commentators regard the early 18th century as the period that witnessed the birth of what scholars recognize as the novel. Ian Watt (1957) credited Daniel Defoe, Samuel Richardson, and Henry Fielding with having founded the genre, a canonical interpretation that was lent authority by the self-consciousness with which Richardson and Fielding had discussed their artistic innovations in prefaces, essays, and authorial asides. The realism of their narratives, combined with their formal mastery, has often seemed unprecedented in the history of English prose fiction and has been taken as sufficient explanation of the popular and critical success they enjoyed with their contemporaries and with posterity. (Defoe, being less rigorously moralistic than Richardson and less decorous in aesthetic terms than Fielding, suffered relative neglect until the 20th century.) Their influence on contemporary and subsequent writers is plainly visible; Richardson is, if not the first, then the most prominent in a long tradition of sentimental novelists, while Fielding's imitators from the 1750s onward were legion.

It may be tempting to take at face value the respective claims of Richardson and Fielding to have instituted a "new species of writing," but the marked differences of content and technique that exist between the two authors' works should warn readers against the assumption that the novel was their invention, pure and simple. From its very beginnings the novel has been a highly pluralistic form, able to accommodate widely different artistic practices and moral perspectives. Ethics and aesthetics are closely linked in narrative fiction, as Michael McKeon's magisterial study (1987) of the relationship between truth and truthfulness in the early novel seeks to explain. Not surprisingly, therefore, "the novel" has drawn on a very broad spectrum of "pre-novelistic" prose forms from the 16th, 17th, and early 18th centuries, although the relative (and indeed absolute) importance of these individual narrative traditions for the novel continues to provoke disagreement. Given the diversity of themes, forms, and narrative techniques to be found in the novel, it would be impossible, as well as undesirable, to determine which of its ancestors clamors loudest for recognition. Indeed, the genealogical model implied by studying a genre in terms of its progenitors or precursors is a contentious one, and of limited value in explaining how and why one narrative mode apparently came to displace or assimilate a number of others.

Nonetheless, commentators from the 18th century onward have noted that certain distinctive features of the novel—among others, its contemporary settings, "ordinary" characters, circumstantiality, and emphasis on the psychological inner life of an individual or individuals—were foreshadowed by various earlier narrative traditions dating from at least as far back as the 16th century. One of the earliest of these narrative traditions is the courtly prose romance as exemplified by the works of John Lyly and Sir Philip Sidney (although Lyly had his precursors, too, in the ancient Greek and Roman romances and the Italian *novelles* collected and translated into English as *The Palace of Pleasure* by William Painter between 1566 and 1575).

Lyly is most often remembered for the highly mannered, elaborate style of his *Euphues: The Anatomy of Wit* (1578), a slenderly plotted romance that was intended primarily as a handbook for courtly lovers. Lyly's decision to cast this narrative in prose, and his thematic emphasis on matters of the heart, may have distantly influenced the novel's development. More directly influential, however, was Sir Philip Sidney's *Arcadia* (1590), one of the most widely read works of 17th-century English prose fiction.

Like *Euphues*, the *Arcadia* was intended for a sophisticated, courtly readership; originally written for the author's sister, Mary Sidney, it was subsequently circulated in manuscript. It had a pastoral setting, reflecting the revival of neoclassicism in the period, and it depicted the trials and eventual triumphs in love of various courtiers disguised as shepherds. The *Arcadia's* popularity with 17th-century women readers has been attributed to its preoccupation with love and the exalted nature of its char-

acters, but Sidney's essay *The Defence of Poesy* (1595) argued strenuously for poetry's superior powers over history-writing to inculcate virtue in its readers, and those who have regarded the *Arcadia* as romantic escapism have been challenged by those who insist on its serious moral and political implications.

Eighteenth-century commentators regarded the romance and novel as antithetical, on the grounds that the latter was more true to life than the former, but modern literary historians anxious to trace the origins of the novel frequently have pointed to the courtly romance as an earlier narrative form that apparently anticipated, if not directly influenced, 18th-century novelists in its preference for complicated plots (especially true of the *Arcadia*), its focus on love, and its determination to unite entertainment and instruction.

The relationship between the novel and the 17th-century French romance is perhaps easier to establish since the two traditions are historically closer, and a number of romances in English deliberately set out to imitate the French heroic style (e.g., Roger Boyle's *Parthenissa* [1651–69]). Nonetheless, the connection is far from self-evident. Although some French romances, notably Honoré D'Urfé's *L'Astrée* (1607–27), used pastoral settings as Sidney had done, most preferred to situate their heroic stories of love and war in a remote and idealized past. Gauthier de Costes de la Calprenède's *Cassandre* (1644–50), for example, told the story of the wife of Alexander the Great, while his *Cléopatre* (1647–56) dealt with the daughter of Antony and Cleopatra and *Pharamond* (1661–70) with the exploits of the various royal lovers of the Cambrian princess, Rosamonde. The works of Madeleine de Scudéry, *Artamène, ou le Grand Cyrus* (1649–53) and *Clélie* (1654–61), were similar to La Calprenède's in emphasizing the abjection of the knight and the extraordinary beauty and virtue of his mistress. The moral and emotional power that romances typically gave their heroines over their lovers often has been seen by modern critics (e.g. Terry Lovell, 1987; Rosalind Ballaster, 1992) as accounting for their extraordinary popularity well into the 18th century with women readers. At a time when middle-class women enjoyed little autonomy, many clearly were entranced by a fictional world in which men were held in thrall by their imperious and exacting mistresses (as is strongly implied in Charlotte Lennox's comic novel *The Female Quixote* [1752]).

Although the French heroic romance was quite unlike the novel in deliberately eschewing contemporaneity, its influence is apparent in terms of narrative technique. In particular, the long digressions that characterize these romances have their counterparts in the interpolated tales with which Fielding, Tobias Smollett, and other 18th-century novelists punctuate their main plots. The loose structure associated with the novel from the 18th century to the present may thus be seen to have its origins in an earlier prose fictional form. The French heroic romance also helped to establish the letter as a versatile tool for the novelist; the letters that relay the complex love affairs in the works of La Calprenède and Scudéry anticipate Aphra Behn's *Love Letters Between a Nobleman and His Sister* (3 vols., 1683–87) and the work of Richardson and his successors in the epistolary tradition. Richardson's famous prolixity, too, is attributable to the heroic romance, which was notoriously long as well as digressive (typically extending to between 10 and 12 volumes).

Although the novel would share both English and French romances' preoccupations with characters' emotional lives, the greater psychological realism of the novel has been attributed in large part to a single work, Madame de Lafayette's *La Princesse de Clèves* (1678), in which the analysis of character became less idealizing and more acute. In addition, the newer form rejected the aristocratic, courtly settings of the romance in favor of stories of middle- and lower-class life. Even in the late 16th century, however, a short-lived but very popular English subgenre of prose fiction had chosen to focus on the lives of ordinary people, rendering them more realistically than any author would do until Defoe. The best-known 16th-century popular romances included Robert Greene's coney-catching pamphlets, *A Notable Discovery of Cosenage* (1591) and *The Black Book's Messenger* (1592), and Thomas Nashe's vivid and lively tale in the picaresque tradition, *The Unfortunate Traveller; or, The Life of Jacke Wilton* (1594), which describes the varied fortunes of a one-time page at the court of Henry VIII.

Yet it is Thomas Deloney who is most often cited as having created the popular romance. Deloney published four narratives that, like Nashe's *The Unfortunate Traveller,* used historical settings but which reflected the anti-aristocratic, middle-class values of late 16th-century Protestantism. In his best-known prose works, *Jack of Newbery, The Gentle Craft,* and *Thomas of Reading* (all published between 1597 and 1600), Deloney celebrated the virtues of apprentices and craftsmen whose sobriety and industry were justly rewarded with material and social success. At the same time he attacked the corruption he identified with the court, particularly (or ostensibly) the pre-Reformation court of Henry VIII.

One of Deloney's most significant fictional achievements was to incorporate realistic dialogue into his narratives, but critics have always acknowledged the hiatus between the popular prose romances of the late 16th century and the works of Restoration and early 18th-century authors such as Richard Head, Francis Kirkman, and Defoe. The gap between elite and popular culture widened so dramatically during the course of the 17th century that Deloney and his contemporaries fell from view, and no direct evidence exists of their having influenced works such as Head and Kirkman's *The English Rogue* (1665), let alone Defoe's criminal biographies, *Colonel Jack* (1722) and *Moll Flanders* (1722). Incidentally, the same is true of the fairy tale, which might be supposed to belong among the precursors of the novel but which enjoyed so little respect in the 17th century (being associated exclusively with juvenile, female, and lower-class readers) that it played little if any part in the development of the genre. Since most fairy tales were orally transmitted (e.g. "Jack the Giant-Killer") or written in verse (e.g. the medieval romances *Bevis of Hampton* and *Guy of Warwick*), they cannot be said to have served the same cultural functions that the novel would later serve. Where the novel would address a silent, solitary reader, the fairy tale belonged to a preliterate world of collective storytelling. Most fairy tales were lost until their self-conscious revival by antiquarian scholars in the mid–18th century.

By contrast, the many travel narratives of the 16th and 17th centuries were believed, until recently, to have had a significant influence on the novel. Fictional voyages such as Defoe's *Captain Singleton* (1720) appear to have been closely modeled on nonfictional works such as Woodes Rogers' popular *A Cruizing Voyage Round the World* (1712). The fantastic travelers' tales exemplified by those of the apocryphal Sir John Mandeville (1356–57) seem to have established a precedent for the many wonderful and unlikely travel fictions of the 18th century, including Jonathan Swift's *Gulliver's Travels* (1726) and Robert Paltock's *The Life and Adventures of Peter Wilkins* (1750).

Yet the debt to travel narratives now appears less certain and perhaps merely an illusion created by the novel's perennial reliance on the metaphor of life-as-journey and the loosely constructed plot that tends to result from it. Moreover, the novel's roots in the picaresque tradition—the influences of Alain-René Lesage and Paul Scarron were acknowledged by many 18th-century novelists—was bound to produce an emphasis on adventure and exploration independent of the travel narrative's similar preoccupations. Recent critics such as J. Paul Hunter (1990) suggest that travel literature did not exert a one-way influence on the novel but that the two traditions shared certain concerns—with cultural difference, with the recording of data, and with the evocation of marvels—all of which reflected the cultural shift toward empiricism attributable to the Protestant Reformation.

The question of influence may be virtually impossible to resolve, however, given the tendency of many supposedly "scientific" travel writers to exaggerate and even fabricate material and, conversely, the pressure novelists felt to assert the authenticity of their narratives. As numerous commentators point out, the categories of fact and fiction were unstable in the early 18th century, so that individual texts may well straddle the boundaries between them. While the relationship between novel and travel narrative may not have been characterized by straightforward influence, the relationship was undoubtedly intimate, as Henry Fielding's *Journal of a Voyage to Lisbon* (1755), Tobias Smollett's *Travels Through France and Italy* (2 vols., 1766), and Laurence Sterne's *A Sentimental Journey* (1768) testify. All three are narrated as idiosyncratically and personally as any novel, but in Fielding's and Smollett's cases the journeys were real and the narratives firmly based on firsthand experience.

The metaphor of life-as-journey that underpins so many novels more likely derives from the spiritual biographies and autobiographies of the puritan tradition than from the literature of travel. The most famous such biography is, of course, John Bunyan's *Pilgrim's Progress* (1678, 1684), an allegorical account of its protagonist's journey to grace. Commentators have noted certain superficial similarities with Defoe's *Robinson Crusoe* (1719); however, although Bunyan's hero, Christian, is sharply individualized, the narrative lacks the circumstantial realism that characterizes Defoe's novel. More significant for the novel than the use of allegory was the spiritual biography's concern with the workings of providence in human affairs and with the evidence of providential intervention in the life of an individual. Most portrayed that life as conforming to a familiar pattern from sin to repentance to salvation, and studies of *Joseph Andrews* by Martin Battestin (1959) and *Robinson Crusoe* by G.A. Starr (1965) suggest how easily the novel was able to appropriate and modify this pattern.

Spiritual biographies grew out of the saint's life as exemplified by John Foxe's work of Protestant hagiography, the *Book of Martyrs,* which was first published in English in 1563. Secular biographies were also made popular by Sir Thomas North's 1579 translation of Plutarch's *The Lives of the Noble Grecians and Romanes,* a work that was very widely read in the 16th and 17th centuries. Izaak Walton, Lucy Hutchinson, Margaret Cavendish, John Aubrey, and Anthony à Wood all wrote lives of their contemporaries, while Clarendon's *History of the Rebellion* (1702–04) contains many biographical essays on individuals prominent in the civil wars. The success of the "life" reflected an increased interest in history-writing in general, but it was undoubtedly reinforced by the Reformation emphases on the importance of the individual soul and on the value of (self-)examination.

The spiritual biography tended to be cast retrospectively, in the light of the protagonist's eventual salvation, and in this sense it anticipated the novel, which is usually written in the past tense. In terms of content, spiritual biographies were strongly didactic, as were many 18th-century novels, and most (e.g. Bunyan's *Life and Death of Mr. Badman* [1680]) were as anxious as the average novel to proclaim their truthfulness. Lastly, they resembled the novel in their concern for detail, which was prompted by the desire to document the spiritual journey of the individual subject as fully and authentically as possible. As McKeon (1987) has suggested, this interest in the particular circumstances of the individual coexists in the spiritual biography with an emphasis on the overarching pattern from sin to grace to which all Christian lives may be seen to conform. The novel, too, dependent on an unresolved tension between its protagonist as both a unique and a representative figure, aims to blend the circumstantial with the familiar. A fundamental difference exists, therefore, between the Everyman of medieval morality drama and the protagonists of 17th-century spiritual biographies and 18th-century novels respectively, even where these are only thinly characterized by the standards of 19th- and 20th-century fiction.

Like travel narratives, spiritual biographies seem rather to share a common worldview with the novel—a preoccupation with observing, recording, and interpreting the experience of an individual or individuals—than to have offered the novelist themes or techniques for imitation. This relationship to the novel is even more true of the diary, another narrative mode that antedates the novel but which should not necessarily be regarded as one of its progenitors. Journals and diaries first began to appear in print during the 16th century, but the best-known date from the 17th century: those of Anne Clifford, Thomas Browne (in the published form of his autobiography, *Religio Medici* [1642]), John Evelyn, Samuel Pepys, and Celia Fiennes, for example.

The motivations of diarists varied greatly. Pepys, for instance, appears to have been prompted by an urge to record the turbulent times in which he lived, while Clifford uses her diaries to record the history of her family. Some diarists were intensely private—Pepys wrote in a modified shorthand cipher—while others clearly had a wider audience in mind: Evelyn's diary was written some time after the events he described and underwent authorial revision. Yet the practice of keeping a diary, for whatever purpose, became increasingly commonplace in the 18th century. Moreover, like the spiritual biography, the diary shared a fundamental assumption with the novel: that the life of an individual constitutes a narrative. Richardson's *Pamela* (1740) is written as a series of extended letters that gradually turn into a journal; Defoe's *A Journal of the Plague Year* (1722) is an even clearer illustration of the shared aims of the diarist and novelist for narrative completeness, continuity, and immediacy. However, attempts to read *Robinson Crusoe* as a thinly disguised memoir of its author seem contrived.

Diaries were necessarily unstructured and spontaneous, even when subsequently edited; in this respect they may appear to be responsible for the cheerful disregard for formal coherence of which many 18th-century novelists are accused. Yet the criteria for judging the "coherence" of any literary work are largely subjective, and in one regard—the approach to character—the 18th-century novel tends to be very tightly structured. Most often when new characters are introduced their previous histories are given in exhaustive detail. This practice involves suspending the main plot and hence risking the impression of disorganization, but it also allows the novelist to provide a potted biographical sketch with something of the succinctness and satirical edge of the "character," a prose form that the novel otherwise appears to have rendered obsolete.

The "character," a kind of biographical essay (or character sketch), first appeared in the wake of Casaubon's translation of Theophrastus, the ancient Greek, in 1592. Theophrastus' essays on various kinds of personality were imitated by, among others, Joseph Hall, Sir Thomas Overbury, and John Earle. The aim was to provide a satirical portrait of a contemporary type—a roaring boy, for instance—and the genre became very popular at the Stuart court, where Cecily Bulstrode and Lady Frances Southwell both wrote characters satirizing the vanity and artifice of the female courtier.

By the 18th century the short character sketch had given way to the more extended treatment of social types in periodicals such as *The Spectator,* in which Addison and Steele introduce readers to Sir Roger de Coverley, a stereotypical Tory squire, and Sir Andrew Freeport, an equally stereotypical Whig merchant. From there it appears to have been a short step to the more complex satires of character in novels such as Fielding's *Joseph Andrews* (1742), which featured the hilariously unworldly parson, Abraham Adams; or to Oliver Goldsmith's *The Vicar of Wakefield* (1766), whose protagonist was similarly vulnerable to abuse; and, rather later, to Frances Burney's wickedly sharp-eyed *Evelina* (1778), which exposed examples of hypocrisy and greed from across the social spectrum.

Given that the novel had much greater scope for sustained satire, it is not surprising that the character did not survive beyond the early 18th century. By contrast, the novel does not appear to have sounded the death knell of another narrative tradition, the criminal life, which, however, it assimilated just as effectively as it had done the character. Criminal lives continued to flourish within and outside the novel, perhaps partly because so many readers of the genre could not afford to buy book-length fiction. Criminal lives, otherwise known as rogue and whore biographies, were at the height of their popularity by the 1720s, along with a diverse literature of crime, which included the accounts of the Newgate "Ordinaries" (i.e., chaplains) and the Sessions papers of the Old Bailey. John Reynolds' collection of stories recording the divine punishments meted out to violent criminals, *The Triumph of God's Revenge against the Crying and Execrable Sin of Wilful and Premeditated Murder,* had first appeared in 1621, and a century later it had been joined by numerous sensational works, most of which adopted a formula by which an individual's crimes were described, followed by an account of his or her repentance, confession, and (usually) execution. This pattern contains echoes of the spiritual biography, but most criminal biographies contrived to be both salacious and comic as well as serious and cautionary; indeed, for one modern critic, John Richetti (1969), their chief appeal lay in the escapism they offered their readers.

Like the novel, the criminal biography was concerned with "low" characters and subjects, as compared to the aristocratic milieus associated with most romances. Like the majority of novels, criminal biographies tended to be written in the first person, since they sought the credibility of personal testimonies. The novel did not render the criminal biography extinct, but the distinction between the two genres was blurred by authors such as Mary Carleton, who published numerous accounts of her exploits, some heavily fictionalized, others apparently not, and Defoe, whose *Colonel Jack* and *Moll Flanders* made strenuous efforts to seem authentic. Meanwhile, Fielding's slightly later *The Life of Mr. Jonathan Wild the Great* (1743) used a real-life gangster as the vehicle for a two-pronged satire of public life (which likened politics to the London underworld), while a number of well-known subsequent novels by Fielding, Smollett, and others focused on themes of crime and punishment. For John Bender (1987) the explanation lies in the parallel between the novel's understanding of character as something susceptible to education and change and the analogous assumption that the individual can be reformed, an assumption that underlay the 18th-century penal system. It is certainly true that prisons and penitentiaries are recurrent motifs in early novels.

Criminal lives form one of the most significant byproducts of the mid- to late 17th-century explosion in popular print. The civil wars had encouraged an exponential growth in reportage, and the newsbooks of the mid-century facilitated the development of a less ephemeral journalistic form, the periodical, in the 1690s. The most successful periodical was John Dunton's *Athenian Mercury,* which, along with a number of comparable publications, helped to create an urban readership of "coffee-house politicians" whose avid interest in current affairs arguably reflects the same cultural changes that allowed the novel to gain its eventual dominance over other narrative forms. Although the groups who would read novels in the second half of the 18th century were not necessarily those who had read periodicals 50 years earlier, critics such as Lennard J. Davis (1983) have suggested that novels and printed news satisfy the same basic desires for novelty and narrative continuity, while Hunter (1990) speculates that the sense of intimacy with the reader fostered by the narrator of, say, *Tom Jones,* is akin to the public consciousness newly created by the periodicals, pamphlets, and broadsheets of the late 17th century.

The theory that the novel came to fulfill—and further stimulate—the desire for observing and interpreting the experiences of an individual previously satisfied by other narrative traditions, such as news or the spiritual biography, is an attractive one. Yet it does not entirely explain how or why the novel became hegemonic during the course of the 18th century. The 18th-century novel retains many similarities to the romance it supposedly replaced and has been shown to combine its impulse toward realism with a host of antirealist traits, from classical allusions to implausible plots, stylized characters, and formal self-reflexiveness. Since the 1960s, successive critics have argued that the novel did not appear overnight, as if from nowhere, with the publication of Defoe's *Robinson Crusoe* in 1719 or of Behn's *Oroonoko* in 1688—or, indeed, any single work—but that the novel was preceded by a wide range of "pre-novelistic" prose forms, many of which it eventually supplanted. Yet even this revisionist interpretation is limited by its reliance on a biological metaphor to explain generic change. The novel may well have competed with, adapted to, or evolved in parallel with other narrative traditions, but why it did so and why it eventually triumphed over so many of its predecessors is still little understood. While it is certainly important to recognize the novel's antecedents, the suggestive similarities between the novel and forms such as the romance, the spiritual biography, the criminal life, and other narrative traditions should not be taken to imply causal links between the novel and its so-called precursors; after all, the connections between them are circumstantial and ultimately impossible to prove.

KATHERINE A. ARMSTRONG

See also Critics and Criticism (18th Century); English Novel (18th Century); Epistolary Novel; French Novel (16th and 17th Centuries); Genre Criticism; Greek and Roman Narrative; Journalism and the Novel; Medieval Narrative; Novel and Romance: Etymologies; Novella; Parody and Pastiche; Pastoralism in the Novel; Picaresque; Realism; Renaissance Narrative; Romance; Sentimental Novel

Further Reading

Adams, Percy G., *Travelers and Travel Liars, 1660–1800,* Berkeley: University of California Press, and London: Cambridge University Press, 1962

Ballaster, Rosalind, *Seductive Forms: Women's Amatory Fiction 1684–1740,* Oxford: Clarendon Press, and New York: Oxford University Press, 1992

Bartolomeo, Joseph F., *A New Species of Criticism: Eighteenth-Century Discourse on the Novel,* Newark: University of Delaware Press, and London: Associated University Presses, 1994

Battestin, Martin C., *The Moral Basis of Fielding's Art: A Study of "Joseph Andrews,"* Middletown, Connecticut: Wesleyan University Press, 1959

Bender, John, *Imagining the Penitentiary: Fiction and the Architecture of Mind in Eighteenth-Century England,* Chicago: University of Chicago Press, 1987

Davis, Lennard J., *Factual Fictions: The Origins of the English Novel,* New York: Columbia University Press, 1983

Doody, Margaret, *The True Story of the Novel,* New Brunswick, New Jersey: Rutgers University Press, 1996

Frye, Northrop, *The Secular Scripture: A Study of the Structure of Romance,* Cambridge, Massachusetts: Harvard University Press, 1976

Hunter, J. Paul, *Before Novels: The Cultural Contexts of Eighteenth-Century English Fiction,* New York: Norton, 1990

Lovell, Terry, *Consuming Fiction,* London and New York: Verso, 1987

McKeon, Michael, *The Origins of the English Novel 1600–1740,* Baltimore: Johns Hopkins University Press, 1987; London: Raduis, 1988

Richetti, John, *Popular Fiction Before Richardson: Narrative Patterns 1700–1739,* Oxford: Clarendon Press, 1969

Salzman, Paul, *English Prose Fiction, 1558–1700: A Critical History,* Oxford: Clarendon Press, and New York: Oxford University Press, 1985

Starr, G.A., *Defoe and Spiritual Autobiography,* Princeton, New Jersey: Princeton University Press, 1965

Watt, Ian, *The Rise of the Novel: Studies in Defoe, Richardson and Fielding,* Berkeley: University of California Press, and London: Chatto and Windus, 1957

Protagonist. *See* Character

Marcel Proust 1871–1922

French

Marcel Proust is best known as the novelist who exalted the infinite richness of the interior life of the mind. The beauty and intricacy of his prose, eliciting ecstasy in some readers and exasperation in others, represents above all an exhaustive exploration of the particular over and against the universal. The first published collection of Proust's essays, sketches, and poems, *Les Plaisirs et les jours* (*Pleasures and Regrets*), appeared in 1896. His initial literary endeavors also include the novel *Jean Santeuil*, written during the period 1895–99 and which, despite its considerable length, remained an unfinished work and did not appear in print until 1952. Proust wrote a number of essays and reviews that were published in 1954 under the title *Contre Saint-Beuve* (*Against Saint Beuve and Other Essays*). *Pastiches et mélanges* (1919) is an assemblage of parodies and sketches. Additionally, Proust translated two works by John Ruskin, *The Bible of Amiens* (1904; translated as *La Bible d'Amiens*) and *Sesame and Lilies* (1906; translated as *Sésame et les lys*). A prolific writer, he also was an avid letter writer, and multiple volumes of his correspondence reveal an inexhaustible mind at work.

However, Proust is most revered for his classic work, *À la recherche du temps perdu*, published in multiple volumes between 1913 and 1927 and translated first as *Remembrance of Things Past* and later as *In Search of Lost Time* (5 vols., 1992). It is considered by many to be the pinnacle of a fictional style that engages in painstaking self-analysis. Indeed, many consider Proust and this masterpiece to be synonymous. There is a striking difference between his earlier works and his grand oeuvre with regard to stylistic complexity. It is precisely the exquisite detail in Proust's renderings of societal life, the slow maturation of the narrator, the sometimes astonishing intensity of everyday aesthetic experiences, and the ultimate ambiguity of each individual's perception of the world that lends this sprawling novel its prominent status within 20th-century fiction. The overall structure of *In Search of Lost Time* is not readily apparent to the first-time reader; indeed, it is only in the final volume that a subtly executed organization reveals itself. For Proust, the discovery of unity in and through the process of creating and experiencing merits the label of art. Thus, what he calls a "retroactive unity" is contrasted with an artificial, false unity that is superimposed upon experience. Proust believed the proper role of the novelist is one of discovery; hence the narrator Marcel is initially ignorant—only slowly, in the role of apprentice, does he begin to grasp the essence of his experience. The fundamental disequilibrium of the self in time and the individual process of relating to that disequilibrium are central to *In Search of Lost Time*.

A harsh critic of realism, Proust considered such fiction to be dangerous when it substitutes its own truth for stimulating the reader to think and create his or her own reality. In *The Guermantes Way,* for instance, Mme de Guermantes pronounces the grand master of fictional realism, Gustave Flaubert, "bourgeois through and through" and his personal correspondence, described by the Comtesse d'Arpajon, as more intriguing and valuable than his novels.

The art of the novel for Proust was inextricably bound with the communication (or as he termed it, the "translation") of "our passionate dialogue with ourselves." If the writer is presumptuous enough to impose an overriding truth that effectively blankets the essence of individual sensory and emotional experience, then that writer has committed a grave error. In short, Proust asked the following question of realist writers: "How could the literature of description possibly have any value, when it is only beneath the surface of the little things that such a literature describes that reality has its hidden existence (grandeur, for example, in the distant sound of Saint-Hilaire, the past in the taste of a madeleine, and so on) and when the things in themselves are without significance until it has been extracted from them?" It is the process of extraction that fascinated Proust and constituted the *raison d'être* of his novels.

The question of unity is perhaps one of the most complex in any consideration of Proust's contribution to the novel form, and it also accounts for the continued scholarly interest in his work. The close of the 20th century, with its insistence on fragmentation and denunciation of firm foundations upon which to construct permanent truths, lends a certain urgency to the questions of unity raised by Proust in *In Search of Lost Time*. At work in the oeuvre is an insoluble tension between the veracity of sensory, emotional experience on the one hand and the illumination of such experience by the intellect on the other. Metaphor, above all, provides unity for Proust. The real truth of life is found in the distilled essence common to two or more qualities, as captured within a metaphor. It is through metaphor and the surprise of involuntary memory that the individual achieves a timeless state of being. The taste of the madeleine, the steeples of Martinville, or the uneven paving stones—because they are experienced identically in the past and in the present—produce moments that are "outside of time." This surge of sensory experience in involuntary memory frees the individual from time. In turn, the decipherment of such moments constitutes the proper methodology of the writer.

Grief is one emotion in particular whose depths Proust plumbs in order to demonstrate the enormous complexity of the interior life of the individual. In the final volume, *Le Temps retrouvé* (1927; *Time Regained*), he uses the metaphor of a storm to describe this complexity: "only during a storm, when our thoughts are agitated by perpetually changing movements do they elevate to a level at which we can see the whole law-governed immensity which normally, when the calm weather of happiness leaves it smooth, lies beneath our line of vision." Of all the emotions, grief is most closely linked to the interrelated elements of existence that shape our perceptions of self and others: habit, time, and forgetting.

For Proust, the importance of sharpening our vision to the essence of existence is what lends the novel its distinctive value; narrative art permits the retroactive clarification of the chaos of impressions. Although he ultimately placed a higher value on these sensory and emotional impressions, Proust recognized the necessity of the intellect's power to bring together into a coherent whole such disparate elements. The precious quality and rarity of these impressions call for the more solid structure of the art form. For Proust, the writer's true vocation is the individual act of creation rather than the mere art of observation. Equally important is that the reader of fiction become a more sophisticated reader of his or her own self: the true worth of fiction is the reader's self-recognition in the author's words.

ROBYN BROTHERS

See also In Search of Lost Time

Biography
Born 10 July 1871 in Auteuil, Paris, France. Attended Lycée Fontanes (renamed Lycée Condorcet, 1883), Paris, 1882–89; the Sorbonne, Paris, 1891–93, bachelor of law 1893. Military service at Orleans, 1889–90; cofounded the review *Le Banquet* with Fernand Gregh, 1892; occasional contributor to newspapers and journals, but gradually withdrew from society. Died 18 November 1922.

Novels by Proust
À la recherche du temps perdu, 1913–27; as *Remembrance of Things Past*, translated by C.K. Scott Moncrieff, 1922–31; revised translation by C.K. Scott Moncrieff and Terence Kilmartin, 3 vols., 1981; as *In Search of Lost Time*, revised translation by D.J. Enright, 5 vols., 1992
Jean Santeuil, 3 vols., 1952; as *Jean Santeuil*, translated by Gerard Hopkins, 1955

Other Writings: letters, poems, prose on art and literature.

Further Reading
Bersani, Leo, *Marcel Proust: The Fictions of Life and of Art*, New York: Oxford University Press, 1965; London: Oxford University Press, 1969
Brée, Germaine, *The World of Marcel Proust*, London: Chatto and Windus, and Boston: Houghton Mifflin, 1966
Compagnon, Antoine, *Proust entre deux siècles*, Paris: Seuil, 1989; as *Proust: Between Two Centuries*, New York: Columbia University Press, 1992
Deleuze, Gilles, *Proust et les signes*, Paris: Presses Universitaires de France, 1964; as *Proust and Signs*, London: Lane, and New York: Braziller, 1972
Descombes, Vincent, *Proust: Philosophie du roman*, Paris: Minuit, 1987; as *Proust: Philosophy of the Novel*, Stanford, California: Stanford University Press, 1992
Kristeva, Julia, *Le Temps sensible: Proust et l'expérience littéraire*, Paris: Gallimard, 1994; as *Time and Sense: Proust and the Experience of Literature*, New York: Columbia University Press, 1996
Tadié, Jean-Yves, *Proust et le roman: Essai sur les formes et techniques du roman dans "À la recherche du temps perdu,"* Paris: Gallimard, 1971

Prozess. *See* Trial

Bolesław Prus 1847–1912

Polish

Bolesław Prus contributed more to the development of Polish fiction than is usually recognized. Regarded as a classic of 19th-century fiction, he is not adequately appreciated as a reformer of narrative art who played a similar role in Poland that Flaubert played in France. Prus had an early career as a humorist, contributing light-hearted sketches to comic magazines, which attached to him the label of popular entertainer. Living at a time of strenuous effort to modernize Polish social and economic structures, Prus was dedicated deeply to reform and delivered his message in his many newspaper articles known as the "Weekly Chronicles." His journalism, a palpable presence throughout his fiction, gave him a reputation for social didacticism. These judgments, in themselves not inaccurate, have obscured his accomplishments as a frequently sceptical thinker, with mature and well-argued views on social and political problems as well as the function of art. His fiction was certainly affected by his ideological commitments, but his most accomplished novels, *Lalka* (1890; *The Doll*) and *Faraon* (1897; *Pharaoh*), ask fundamental questions that go far beyond the issues of the day.

Prus' attachment to realism was based on the ideas of the French critic Hippolyte Taine, who saw the arts as a vehicle of intellectual enlightenment, drawing attention to things unnoticed by the general public and thus shedding "light on the surrounding darkness." Prus believed that its insights into human psychology made literature a counterpart to science: "Such characters as Hamlet, Macbeth, Falstaff, Don Quixote are findings in psychology at least as important as the laws of planetary motion in astronomy. Shakespeare is worth as much as Kepler." A typical supporter of the middle way, Prus rejected both the idealism and fantasy of romanticism and what he saw as the vulgarity of naturalism. Respectful of Fedor Dostoevskii, he was interested in unexpected human reactions, and in his best novels he created a plurality of narrative perspectives, placing the perspective of the narrator alongside rather than above that of his characters. Prus also exploited humor to create serious and comic views of things simultaneously. His work was often close, therefore, to the novels of Charles Dickens and William Makepeace Thackeray, from which he sometimes borrowed characters. Such borrowed characters are matched by his own creations, which display a penetrating insight into the human mind that equals the most remarkable achievements of contemporary psychological fiction. Although he was a positivist devoted to "provable" facts and to a concrete use of language, he was also greatly interested in parapsychology and the subconscious impulses that precede rational thinking.

Initially, Prus was most successful with his short stories, and his first novel, *Kłopoty babuni* (1874; Granny's Troubles), was a failure. Even this unsuccessful early novel shows an ability to combine humor with seriousness, factual descriptions with emotionalism or comic exaggeration sometimes bordering on the absurd, and realism with a romantic fascination with mystery. The short novel or rather novella *Anielka* (1880) again demonstrates those qualities. Its use of free association in the interior monologue of a delirious little girl was unusual in Poland at the time of publication. The first important novel, *Placówka* (1885; *The Outpost*), is best known for its nationalist content, portraying the resistance of Polish peasants to German settlers seeking to buy their land. Following the practice of the naturalists, Prus chose a social conflict, represented by groups rather than individuals, for his subject and described events in simple chronological order.

The next novel, *The Doll*, is certainly the best achievement of Polish 19th-century fiction and constitutes a watershed in the development toward modernist forms. The novel reworks the old motif of illusion and disillusionment, borrowed from *Don Quixote*, but gives it the character of an open-ended cycle. The protagonist swings between an idealized vision of his beloved woman inspired by romantic poetry and the sober disclosures of her actual ordinariness. Disillusionment invariably follows the scenes of emotional "madness" and impels the protagonist to consider another alternative: scientific research, useful for humanity. The complexities of the protagonist's inner life are counterbalanced by the surrounding world of superficial characters "borrowed" from traditional novels and here representing the suffocating power of mediocrity.

Emancypantki (1893; The Emancipated Women) is the longest of Prus' novels and actually consists of four independent parts, united by the presence of the same character, Miss Brzeska (who is, however, not the protagonist throughout). Dominated by dialogues, the novel contains a variety of literary techniques, which predominate in different parts: dramatic plot, episodic story line with comic and satirical scenes, and lengthy philosophical disputes. Moving back and forth between Prus' condemnation of women's emancipation and a defense of the existence of God and the immortal soul, the novel lacks unity both in its content and structure. But while the angelic image of the heroine is unconvincing, Prus provides once again an impressive gallery of caricatures even more distressing in their selfishness and narrow-mindedness than in *The Doll*.

Pharaoh is set in the ancient Egypt of the legendary Ramses XIII and formally belongs to the genre of the historical novel, which, despite its great popularity in Poland, was generally of little interest to Prus. The past, however, serves here only as an example of more general concerns about state mechanisms, the nature of historical progress, and the role of exceptional individuals in its development. The allegorical tendencies account for some of the novel's anachronisms, particularly the modernizing representation of Egyptian society, its scientific achievements and political structure. The general pattern of the Bildungsroman, following the education of a compassionate prince, is coupled with the dramatic struggle between the protagonist and his powerful opponents, the priests. The realistic representation of everyday life and the painstaking descriptions of ancient temples coincide with a vivid interest in the mysterious and unknown that contributes to the novel's suspense. Although the main argument follows the then popular utilitarian principles of organic working conditions and mutual cooperation between all social groups, the novel leaves open the question of personal commitment versus historical determinism and the moral aspect of social progress in relation to individual happiness.

The last novel, *Dzieci* (1908; Children), about the revolution of 1905, is barely more than a journalistic and rather naive account of social upheavals in the Russian-ruled Polish lands. In his best works, nonetheless, Prus had achieved results comparable to the best European novels of the time. His hesitant approach to form, his unusual blend of the old and the new, reflects the scepticism of the author and his unrelenting search for the most suitable medium of expression.

STANISLAW EILE

Biography

Born Aleksander Głowacki, near Hrubieszów, Poland, 20 August 1847. Educated in Lublin, 1856, and in Siedlce and Kielce, from 1861; after uprising completed school in Lublin, 1866; studied mathematics and physics at Szkola Głowna in Warsaw, two years. Participated in uprising, 1863; injured in battle between Siedlce and Lublin; imprisoned in Lublin but later released because of his young age. Wrote weekly chronicles in *Kurier Warszawski*, from 1874; editor of daily newspaper, *Nowiny*, 1882–83, and *Kurier Warszawski* and *Kurier Codzienny*, from 1886; literary journalist, 1884–87; traveled to Germany, Switzerland, and France in 1895. Died 19 May 1912.

Novels by Prus

Kłopoty babuni [Granny's Troubles], 1874

Anielka, 1880

Placówka, 1885; as *The Outpost*, translated by Else Benecke, 1921; as *Ten Morgs of Land*, translated by Christina Rockover Eatus, 1957

Lalka, 1890; as *The Doll*, translated by David Welsh, 1972

Emancypantki [The Emancipated Women], 1893

Faraon, 1897; as *The Pharaoh and the Priest: An Historical Novel of Ancient Egypt*, translated by Jeremiah Curtin, 1910; as *Pharaoh*, translated by Christopher Kasparek, 1991

Dzieci [Children], 1908

Other Writings: short stories, journalism, literary criticism, comic sketches.

Further Reading

Eile, Stanislaw, *Modernist Trends in Twentieth-Century Polish Fiction*, London: School of Slavonic and East European Studies, 1996

Łoch, Eugenia, and Stanisław Fita, editors, *Bolesław Prus: Twórczość i recepcja*, Lublin: Lubelskie Towarzystwo Naukowe, 1993

Markiewicz, Henryk, *Prus i Żeromski: Rozprawy i szkice literackie*, Warsaw: Panstwowy Instytut Wydawniczy, 1954; 2nd amended edition, 1964

Melkowski, Stefan, *Poglądy estetyczne i działalność krytycznoliteracka Bolesława Prusa*, Warsaw: Panstwowy Instytut Wydawniczy, 1963

Piesácikowski, Edward, editor, *Prus: Z dziejów recepcji twórczości*, Warsaw: Panstwowe Wydawn Naukowe, 1988

Pietrkiewicz, Jerzy, "Justified Failure in the Novels of B. Prus," *Slavonic and East European Review* 92 (1960)

Przybyła, Zbigniew, *"Lalka" Bolesława Prusa: Semantyka, kompozycja, konteksty*, Rzeszów: Wydawnictwo Wyzszej Szkoly Pedagogicznej, 1995

Szweykowski, Zygmunt, *Twórczość Bolesława Prusa*, Poznan: Wielkopolska Ksiegarnia Wydawnicza, 1947; 2nd edition, Warsaw: Panstwowy Instytut Wydawniczy, 1972

Welsh, David, "Realism in Prus' Novel *Lalka* (*The Doll*)," *Polish Review* 4 (1963)

Psychoanalytic Models of Narrative and Criticism of the Novel

From its inception, psychoanalytic theory has been informed by readings of literature, including novels. This close relationship quickly grew into a distinctive approach to literature that took its techniques from psychoanalysis. Early psychoanalytic criticism was characterized by a strong focus on the psychology of the author. The critic interpreted—according to the terminology of the time—the latent content hidden in the manifest content of the text, in much the same way that an analyst draws meaning from dream material. Later criticism shifted attention to characters, to the nature of narrative, and to the relationships among the text, the reader, the critic, the earlier literary tradition, and so on.

In the earliest period, in what is now called the id psychology phase of the development of psychoanalysis, research and thinking were directed in the main to processes associated with the unconscious, seething, biologically driven id, which are dominated by the pleasure principle. Freud frequently turned to art, myth, and literature, especially drama, to elucidate, and perhaps even to validate, features of his theories, such as psychic determinism (the idea that all mental events—dreams, fantasies, parapraxes, jokes, neurotic symptoms—have a meaning beyond the obvious), the importance of the unconscious and its role in the treatment of acceptable and unacceptable desires, and the centrality of early childhood experiences, notably childhood sexuality, in shaping the adult personality. The Oedipus complex, a cornerstone of psychoanalytic theory, is probably the best known example of a theory that was formulated in conjunction with a literary interpretation. Freud could treat literature as evidence for his theories because he posited that all art is essentially a compromise formation between the unconscious impulses of the artist to express a wish (usually infantile) and an uncon-

scious, or perhaps even conscious, attempt to defend against, or deny, that wish. The characterization of literature as an expression of psychic processes also laid the foundation of psychoanalytic criticism.

Freud applied his psychoanalytic model to novels in only two essays. "Der Wahn und die Träume in W. Jensens 'Gradiva'" (1907; "Delusion and Dreams in W. Jensen's 'Gradiva'") analyzes the delirium and dream sequences in *Gradiva: Ein pompejanisches Phantasiestück* (1903; *Gradiva: A Pompeiian Fantasy*) by Wilhelm Jensen, and unearths a metaphor of burial and excavation that Freud maps onto the psychoanalytic concepts of repression and analysis. "Dostojewski und die Vatertötung" (1928; "Dostoyevsky and Parricide") investigates Oedipal themes in *Brat'ia Karamozovy* (1880; *The Brothers Karamazov*) by Fedor Dostoevskii. In that essay, Freud argues that Dostoevskii's novel reflects various features of his personality—masochism, sadism, repressed homosexuality, criminal tendencies, and a passion for gambling, among others.

Various early students of Freud also used literature as the basis for their investigations. The best known work from this early period is probably *Hamlet and Oedipus* (original essay 1910; book-length version 1949) by the British analyst Ernest Jones. Jones' analysis of Shakespeare's play centers on his contention that Hamlet hesitated to kill Claudius because he realizes that his uncle has actually carried out his own Oedipal desire to kill his father. Another important early work, Marie Bonaparte's *Edgar Poe, étude psychanalytique* (1933; *The Life and Works of Edgar Allan Poe: A Psycho-Analytic Interpretation*) symbolically decodes the poetry and fiction of Edgar Allan Poe as multifaceted expressions of grief, tinged with necrophilia, over his mother's death when he was two. In *Der Doppelgänger: Eine psychoanalytische Studie* (1914; *The Double: A Psychoanalytic Study*), Otto Rank analyzes a number of novels, notably Dostoevskii's *Dvoinik* (1846; *The Double*) and *The Brothers Karamazov, The Strange Case of Dr. Jekyll and Mr. Hyde* (1886) by Robert Louis Stevenson, and *The Portrait of Dorian Gray* (1891) by Oscar Wilde. Rank utilizes Freud's notions of projection and narcissism to conclude that the self and the double in these works are, in spite of surface differences, one and the same in their origin, that the rival is a reflection of self-love, and that both the self and the rival are projections of the author.

The classical Freudian model served as the basis for numerous analyses of the novel by a generation of literary critics from the 1940s to the 1960s. In *Freudianism and the Literary Mind* (1945), Frederick J. Hoffman discusses in detail Freud's views about dreams, sex, religion, and money as reflected in the works of various modernist novelists. This tradition continued in Henry A. Murray's well-known essay "In Nomine Diaboli" (1951). The title translates as "In the Name of the Devil," a satanic imitation of a portion of the Roman Catholic baptismal ceremony that is used as a secret code in *Moby-Dick* (1951). Murray offers a tripartite reading of *Moby-Dick* based on Freud's model of the psyche: Ahab, a figure of Lucifer, is analogous to the id, uncontrollable and isolated; the God-fearing Starbuck, attempting to serve as mediator between external reality and Ahab's monomaniacal drive to kill the whale, represents the ego; and the white whale, usually treated as a symbol for some kind of special or preternatural knowledge, is here viewed as a symbol of rigid and repressive New England Puritanism, a projection of Melville's superego, which, suggests Murray, seeks to control and direct the ego to act within socially acceptable limits.

The early work of Frederick Crews, notably his *The Sins of the Fathers: Hawthorne's Psychological Themes* (1966), is classically Freudian, investigating Oedipal themes in Hawthorne's various novels and stories. These are often underscored by sexualized descriptions of the landscape, night, darkness, and images of flora. Crews concludes that Hawthorne never resolved the Oedipal tensions within himself. However, about ten years later, Crews had become disaffected by psychoanalytic criticism and repudiated it in such works as *Out of My System: Psychoanalysis, Ideology, and Critical Method* (1975).

Breaking with Freud in 1914, Carl Jung explored myth to develop his theory of personality, which he based on the notion of potent, genetically transmitted dispositions, or archetypes, which have evolved in the collective unconscious of the human species. Jung's essay "Ulysses" (1934; "Ulysses: A Monologue"), an analysis of James Joyce's *Ulysses* (1922), suggests that the novel's radical use of language possesses qualities akin to schizophrenia, from which its author may have suffered. More significantly, Jung's theories served as the foundation for the first important offshoot of classical Freudian psychoanalytic model of criticism: archetypal theory and criticism. Borrowing certain aspects of Jung's work on archetypes, Northrop Frye's seminal *Anatomy of Criticism: Four Essays* (1957) attempts an exhaustive classification of literature and offers salient discussions of various 19th- and 20th-century novelists. Frye argues, for example, that the sodden tavern keeper Humphrey Chimpden Earwicker in Joyce's *Finnegans Wake* (1939) is, through various transmutations, changes, and adjustments, a contemporary manifestation of the "Divine King," whose archetype is found in

such diverse writings as the Bible, the Egyptian Book of the Dead, and the Icelandic prose Edda. Much of the critical work of Leslie A. Fiedler on the novel is similarly archetypal in nature. His controversial essay "Come Back to the Raft Ag'in, Huck Honey!" (1948) is an exposition of the archetype of the young boy with an infantile, homoerotic crush on a man of color in a variety of American novels, including classics such as *The Adventures of Huckleberry Finn* (1884) by Mark Twain, Melville's *Moby-Dick,* the Leatherstocking tales of James Fenimore Cooper, and *Two Years Before the Mast* (1840) by Richard Henry Dana, Jr. Fiedler also identifies various permutations of this archetype in mid-20th-century fiction, including Gore Vidal's *The City and the Pillar* (1948), Truman Capote's *Other Voices, Other Rooms* (1948), and Carson McCullers' *The Member of the Wedding* (1946).

The 1930s produced a new phase in psychoanalysis with the development of ego psychology, with its emphasis on pre-Oedipal development and object relations in the work of such scholars as Melanie Klein and Donald W. Winnicott. Rather than concentrate on the development of the Oedipus complex and its resolution, as Freud and his earlier followers had done, these revisionists studied the earliest relationships between the newborn and objects, including its caretakers, especially the mother, and even more particularly, the mother's breast, as the basis for the formation of certain kinds of mental representations and models of interaction that are played out in later life with other people.

The influence of the ego psychologists is found in the writings of the second wave of psychoanalytic criticism. One of the earliest and most innovative of second-wave critics was Simon O. Lesser, whose *Fiction and the Unconscious* (1957) broke new ground by suggesting that the very act of reading a text elicits a "struggle between impulse and inhibition" in the reader. Broadly defining "fiction" as any literary form that possesses narrative or tells a story, Lesser differentiates between three unconscious processes when a reader responds to a text: passive, unconscious understanding; unconscious identification with characters; and, importantly, unconscious analogizing, referring to the reader's identification of the story contained in the narrative with his or her own story. Each of these then makes a different appeal to the id, the ego, and the superego.

Norman N. Holland is the author of several key texts in this type of literary criticism. In *The Dynamics of Literary Response* (1968), Holland posits the notion of "identity themes," particular kinds of psychological inclinations or predispositions that a reader brings to the act of reading. These identity themes determine in good part the kind of reactions or responses a reader has to the text. Reading, responding to, and interpreting a text, Holland argues, is a highly personal, idiosyncratic act that escapes the limits of any objective or correct interpretation. Reading is a "transactive" activity between the reader and the text, a kind of negotiation between the ego as it seeks to satisfy its desire for pleasure in the text and the limitations that the text possesses. Both Lesser and Holland are also associated with reader-response theory and criticism.

Yet another reconceptualizing of Freud is found in the work of Erik H. Erikson. Modifying Freudian principles, especially those relating to childhood sexuality and trauma, Erikson theorized that, throughout the life span, people pass through a series of psychosocial, as opposed to psychosexual, crises, each marked by a set of oppositions (e.g., basic trust versus basic mistrust).

How people negotiate these crises is essential to the formation of their personality and accounts for major actions in their later life. While Erikson's work did not directly affect literary theory or criticism, it did give rise to the development of psychobiography, the study of historical and literary figures that stresses key incidents in that person's psychosocial development—frequently adolescence—that motivate important actions and activities later in life. In *Young Man Luther* (1958), Erikson suggests that the reformer's later challenges to authority could be traced to a number of factors, including "anal defiance" and a late adolescent identity crisis. Similarly, *Gandhi's Truth: On the Origins of Militant Nonviolence* (1969) explains Gandhi's politics in terms of the teenaged Gandhi's failure to keep watch at his dying father's bedside, making love to his young wife instead. Distinguished psychobiographies of novelists include the magisterial five-volume *Henry James* (1953–72) by Leon Edel; *Swift and Carroll: A Psychoanalytic Study of Two Lives* (1955) by Phyllis Greenacre, who also contributed significantly to the scientific theoretical literature on object relations, the psychology of women, and on creativity; *Joseph Conrad: A Psychoanalytic Biography* (1967) by Bernard C. Meyer; and *Mark Twain and His World* (1974) by Justin Kaplan. Building on Bonaparte's study of Poe and using the Eriksonian psychobiographical approach, Daniel Hoffman wrote *Poe Poe Poe Poe Poe Poe Poe* (1972).

The French psychoanalyst Jacques Lacan, who began publishing in the early 1950s, radically reread and reinterpreted Freud, effecting a major change in psychoanalysis itself and in literary criticism based on psychoanalytic models. Lacan was influenced by the theories of the Swiss structural linguist Ferdinand de Saussure, who characterized language as a self-contained, self-referential system operating on principles of contrast and difference and existing separately and independently of reality. Additionally, Saussure posited that language consists of signs, which, in turn, are made up of two aspects, the signifier (roughly, the word) and the signified (roughly, the meaning of that word), neither of which is linked to the other or to reality in any natural or absolute way. Instead, this flexible, fluid linkage exists through convention and by participation of the sign with countless other signs in the entire system of language. Reworking Freud through the prism of Saussurean linguistics and writing in a pointedly difficult, sometimes abstruse, style, Lacan theorized a model of the psyche made up of three separate but interactive orders, or registers: the Imaginary Order, which is similar to Freud's pleasure principle; the Symbolic Order, roughly equivalent to Freud's reality principle; and the Real Order, which is concerned with fleeting, powerful, primal human experiences, for example joy and terror as experienced in connection with sex and death.

At birth, the infant participates in the Imaginary Order, a preverbal state of blissful fusion with the mother. Here, boundaries between the infant and mother are flexible and fluid; there is no differentiation between the self (the infant) and the other (the mother). Some time between six and 18 months, the infant enters into what Lacan calls the "mirror stage," when the infant, possibly, but not necessarily, seeing itself in a mirror for the first time, starts to differentiate itself as a subject in language separate from other objects, especially the mother. Unlike ego psychologists, who see mirroring as the first step in the formation of a healthy ego, Lacan believes this stage to be one of alienation from and splitting of one's sense of self. The infant begins to de-

fine itself in terms of its differences from others, of what it is not or what it lacks, of its separateness from significant things, or key objects, termed *objet a* by Lacan. Now operating in the Symbolic Order, the infant begins to develop language as it tries to achieve subjective wholeness through a reunion with the lost key objects. This Symbolic Order is the domain of the father, where the Oedipal drama is carried out. If the Oedipal drama is successfully negotiated, the child is able to take the subject position in a relational system of self and other, male and female, parent and child, and so on, as a genuine subject. Lacan describes entry into this order as a type of symbolic castration for both sexes, an initiation into the rules of language and the subject's role in society. The father as signifier in language enjoys the privilege of naming and defining roles. Such naming, according to Lacan, is as flexible and unstable as the match between Saussure's signifier and signified. In addition, the child takes on gender identity as well, which, for Lacan, is also a construct of language based on contrast, difference, and loss. At this juncture, the child starts to accept his or her limitations as a speaking, gendered subject. Boys accept paternal dominance and give up their sexual desire for the mother, which springs from the desire to return to the Imaginary Order. Girls negotiate the Symbolic Order in a more complex fashion, for they must accept masculine hegemony. Although suppressed in this order, Lacan argues that girls seem to retain the ability to access the Imaginary Order more easily than boys. The essence of the human condition for Lacan is absence and loss and the desire of the subject to regain *objet a* and to return to the Imaginary Order. But this desire is repressed, and the act of repression gives rise to the unconscious, another construct of language, that "is structured like a language." Literature is important in Lacan's theories because of its potential to aid in the recovery of the Imaginary Order and, in the works of a few exceptional authors, for allowing the attuned reader to participate briefly and fleetingly in the Real Order. Lacan devoted one of his famous seminars to Poe's "The Purloined Letter" (1845), where, he claims, the narrative is shaped neither by the characters of the story nor the contents of the stolen letter, but rather by the position of the letter in its relationship to the characters in the two parts of the story. The story does not offer a governing narrative position; instead, the letter functions as a signifier because it produces subject positions for the various characters in the narrative. Lacan also taught seminars on the works of James Joyce in which he suggested that Joyce's works, perhaps more than any other 20th-century novelist's, provide the reader with access to the Real Order.

Lacan called into question the authoritative role of the analyst in the analyst-analysand dyad. By extension, he challenged that same role enjoyed by the critic vis-à-vis the text. The extent of his influence in literature, not to mention psychoanalysis, is shown by the degree to which his terminology—especially "the subject," "the decentered subject," "position," and "symbolic order"—has become a staple in the vocabulary of current literary criticism, critical theory, and cultural studies.

Lacan's theories have provoked a strong reaction, positive and negative, in psychoanalytic and literary circles. His views on gender, especially the notion that it is a construct of language, have elicited fierce agreement and disagreement from feminist literary theorists and critics. The work of the radical French feminists Luce Irigaray, Hélène Cixous, and Julia Kristeva is particularly notable. These theorist-critics share a number of traits:

each comes out of a markedly leftist philosophical and political tradition; each has extensive training in linguistics; each uses the deconstructionist techniques espoused by Jacques Derrida and Lacanian principles as points of departure for her own theorizing. Two of the three are non-French born and have lived through political and economic domination by another country (Kristeva in Bulgaria; Cixous Algeria); two (Irigaray and Kristeva) are practicing psychoanalysts; and two (Kristeva and Cixous) are creative writers. While there are also some similarities in various aspects of their theories, each is unique and distinctive in her particular thinking.

The work of Irigaray is perhaps the most influential and provocative. Her ground-breaking *Speculum de l'autre femme* (1974; *Speculum of the Other Woman*), for example, led to her exclusion from French psychoanalytic and academic circles. Here she posits that Western systems of thought and discourse, laid out along exclusively masculine parameters as they are, have failed to represent validly or to treat seriously the feminine and its desires. In both *Speculum* and her other major work, *Ce Sexe qui n'en est pas un* (1977; *This Sex Which Is Not One*), she deconstructs Freud's concept of femininity, which, by giving primacy to the phallus, relegates the feminine to a lack, or absence, to merely a desire for what it cannot possess. Hence, hierarchical relationships emerge in which the masculine is considered superior, solid, active, fixed, associated with the self (father), etc., and the feminine is treated as inferior, malleable, inactive, fluid, associated with the other (mother), etc. Ultimately Irigaray seeks to erase hierarchical relations, not only between the sexes, but in society generally, even in the analytic situation between the analyst and the analysand, as Lacan also suggested. Instead, she wishes to offer nonhierarchical articulation in all instances.

Cixous is, in addition to being a highly prolific literary critic and theoretician, a poet, novelist, and dramatist. She is perhaps best known for her development of the concept of *écriture féminine*, a type of discourse that finds its origins in the pre-Oedipal drives of the body, or, more specifically, it is writing from/by the female body, a revolutionary kind of writing, she asserts, that will demolish the oppressive structures and strictures of conventional (i.e., male) language and thought dominating the Western philosophical and literary tradition. *Écriture féminine* gains its power by being subversive and multiple in character, much like female sexuality, wherein the sex organs are multiple and afford the woman multiple orgasms. It is in opposition to the directness and singularity characteristic of male writing, and, by extension, of male sexuality, wherein the phallus, a single organ, allows the man a single orgasm. Delight, pleasure, sexual enjoyment, and orgasm are all subsumed under the key term *jouissance*. Cixous' most important theoretical works are found among her many essays, notably "Le Rire de la Méduse" (1975; "The Laugh of Medusa") and "La Venue à l'écriture" (1977; "Coming to Writing"), while one of her best-known creative works is the play *Portrait de Dora* (1976; *Portrait of Dora*), a trenchant dramatization of incidents in the life of Freud's Dora.

Kristeva made her initial impact on French intellectual life in the late 1960s through her incisive explications of the theoretical work of Mikhail Bakhtin and the Russian Formalists. Then, through a highly nuanced reading of Saussurian linguistics, which were combined with Marxist principles, she developed her important theory about the development of subjectivity in language. Working with Lacan's concept of the Symbolic Order, she devised her notion of the Semiotic, which accounts for the presence and circulation of presignifying drives in the body of the pre-Oedipal child. Reluctant to identify herself as a feminist, Kristeva has even suggested doubt about the necessity or relevancy of the gender category "woman."

Throughout the 20th century, then, psychoanalysis has provided the Western intellectual tradition with one of its most powerful, influential methodological tools. It has had a profound effect in nearly every field of intellectual endeavor, but its effect in the fields of literature and literary criticism have proven especially felicitous. Throughout the century psychoanalysis has changed in significant ways and transformed itself repeatedly in both the clinical setting and in the academy. At the present time, many of its detractors, like their predecessors at various junctures throughout the 20th century, insist that psychoanalysis has run its course and has been superseded by other newer, more demonstrably scientific methodologies. However, to paraphrase Mark Twain, rumors of the demise of psychoanalysis in its various avatars have been exaggerated.

CARLO COPPOLA

See also Feminist Criticism of Narrative; Psychological Novel

Further Reading

Berman, Jeffrey, *Narcissism and the Novel,* New York: New York University Press, 1990

Davis, Robert Con, editor, *Lacan and Narration: The Psychoanalytic Difference in Narrative Theory,* Baltimore: Johns Hopkins University Press, 1983

Ellmann, Maud, editor, *Psychoanalytic Literary Criticism,* London and New York: Longman, 1994

Felman, Shoshana, editor, *Literature and Psychoanalysis: The Question of Reading, Otherwise,* Baltimore: Johns Hopkins University Press, 1982

Holland, Norman N., *Holland's Guide to Psychoanalytic Psychology and Literature-and-Psychology,* New York: Oxford University Press, 1990

Kaplan, Morton, and Robert Kloss, *The Unspoken Motive: A Guide to Psychoanalytic Literary Criticism,* New York: Free Press, 1973

Knapp, Bettina L., *A Jungian Approach to Literature,* Carbondale: Southern Illinois University Press, 1984

Kurzweil, Edith, and William Phillips, editors, *Literature and Psychoanalysis,* New York: Columbia University Press, 1983

Lesser, Simon O., *Fiction and the Unconscious,* Boston: Beacon Press, 1957; London: Owen, 1960

Paris, Bernard J., *A Psychological Approach to Fiction: Studies in Thackeray, Stendhal, George Eliot, Dostoevsky, and Conrad,* Bloomington: Indiana University Press, 1974

Schapiro, Barbara A., and Lynne Layton, editors, *Narcissism and the Text: Studies in Literature and the Psychology of Self,* New York: New York University Press, 1986.

Skura, Meredith A., *The Literary Use of the Psychoanalytic Process,* New Haven, Connecticut: Yale University Press, 1981

Wright, Elizabeth, *Psychoanalytic Criticism: Theory in Practice,* London and New York: Methuen, 1984

Psychological Novel and Roman d'analyse

The terms *psychological novel* and *roman d'analyse* denote a fiction in which the internal moods, thought processes, and behavioral traits of character are more important than the external action of plot and incident. This definition, however, is descriptive rather than generic. Both labels are able to include a vast range of literature, including fiction that predates or even ignores psychological theory. Indeed, the tag *psychological novel/roman d'analyse* can be applied to almost any novel that pays a heightened attention to the nature of identity and the subtle workings of personality. The French term (literally *analytical novel*) is generally applied to fiction subsequent to the writings of Gustave Flaubert, especially his novel *Madame Bovary* (1857) with its style of interior monologue. Yet there are many exceptions to this time scale, not least because all literature contains some degree of what we might term *psychological content*.

Arguably the psychological novel begins with Madame de Lafayette's *La Princesse de Clèves* (1678; *The Princess of Clèves*), a work driven by an intense character analysis of Madame de Chartes, yet also an ambiguity as to the motivational center of human behavior. This emphasis on the inner workings of personality became especially focused in the epistolary novels of the 18th century. Samuel Richardson's *Pamela* (1740) gave an unusually privileged access to character with a narrative form that unfolds Pamela's inner action as it happens. Richardson's characterization often seeks to problematize identity by having ethical and spiritual ideals clash with the unpredictable tendencies of personality. The blending of psychological realism and literary form was much more dramatically pursued by Laurence Sterne, whose *Tristram Shandy* (1759–67) displayed markedly modern tendencies through a psychological exploration of time. This unconventional narrative, with its digressionary structure, indicated that consciousness does not work in linear and chronological sequence, but in an unpredictable network of association and connection.

The 19th century saw a heightening of interest in the hidden centers of mind and personality, particularly those nebulous regions of character that could drag the individual toward the base action or the compulsive predilection. For example, Stendhal expressed his belief that the passions were the seat of all humankind's higher instincts through novels such as *Le Rouge et le noir* (1830; *The Red and the Black*) and *La Chartreuse de Parme* (1839; *The Charterhouse of Parma*). Interest in the obscure but influential regions of mind naturally led to a novelistic exploration of the domain of sleep, dreams, and hallucinations. Although this journey could often have more to do with metaphysics than mind, many such novels do fit into the psychological category because of their premise that through the dream or the vision a genuine identity could be revealed. Novels of the dream included Victor Hugo's *Les Travailleurs de la mer* (1866; *The Toilers of the Sea*) and *L'Homme qui rit* (1869; *The Laughing Man*) and Charles Nodier's *Smarra* (1821) and *La Fée aux miettes* (1832; The Crumb Fairy).

The concern with the unveiling of unconscious mental realities was a prevalent interest in romantic fiction. From the romantic obsession with the conflict between reason and the dark, irrational self was born the literary theme of the double or doppelgänger. (It should be pointed out that the double was not theorized as a specifically literary device until the late 1940s.) A theme originating in the German romantics, the double was an opposite self, perceivable to the senses, that haunted the protagonist and often resulted in the disintegration of the character's self-possession. Influenced by psychologists such as Mesmer and Schubert, a wide variety of novels were written that bewitchingly represent the dark alter ego as a psychological opposite of our rational self. Examples include William Godwin's *Caleb Williams* (1794), James Hogg's *The Private Memoirs and Confessions of a Justified Sinner* (1824), Adelbert von Chamisso's *Peter Schlemihls wundersame Geschichte* (1814; *Peter Schlemihl*), and Mary Shelley's *Frankenstein* (1818). Although the theme of the double declined in popularity somewhat after the romantic period, mainly because of the questioning of romantic psychology, it was maintained into the later years of the 19th century by the likes of Edgar Allan Poe, Fedor Dostoevskii, Guy de Maupassant, Robert Louis Stevenson, and W.H. Mallock. With the increase in scientific rationalism, however, came a double that was less a metaphysical extension than a scientifically observable phenomenon, as is famously the case in Stevenson's *The Strange Case of Dr. Jekyll and Mr. Hyde* (1886) and Mallock's *An Immortal Soul* (1908). Despite the fact that the idea of the subconscious was in its infancy, the fictional theme of the double or doppelgänger gave 19th-century fiction a haunting psychological dimension that suggested many hidden layers to human character.

The approach of the 20th century initiated a new realism into the psychological novel, a realism that had its most influential precedent in the detailed psychological veracity of Flaubert's *Madame Bovary*. Dostoevskii's *Prestuplenie i nakazanie* (1867; *Crime and Punishment*), *Idiot* (1869; *The Idiot*), and *Brat'ia Karamazovy* (1880; *The Brothers Karamazov*) all involved a focus on the clash between idealistic hopes for life and the psychological reality of living, a clash illustrated through the characters' intense inner dialogues. In the same period Thomas Hardy reflected upon human complexity by creating protagonists whose tortured perceptions and pained understandings expressed themselves in the tension between high sentiments and more base instincts. The context of this clash included not only concerns about the preservation of social order, but also developments in psychological theory that dissolved the boundaries between spirit/body and subject/object. More importantly, an increasing interest in theories of the unconscious resulted in more novelists examining themes of human limitations and repressed identities. Henry James, in *The Portrait of a Lady* (1881), *The Ambassadors* (1903), and *The Golden Bowl* (1904), depicted individuals whose aspirations are fettered by psychological restrictions of which they are frequently unaware. In some of James' later stories, "The Jolly Corner" (1908) often being seen as the most psychologically significant, James expanded the theme of the double. In "The Jolly Corner" the character Spencer Brydon is being haunted by the ghost of his other, darker self, a ghost that seems to act as a visualization of repressed, unconscious being. Joseph Conrad pursued a similar representation of the self and its other in "Heart of Darkness" (1902), where Marlow's journey toward the haunting presence of Kurtz becomes more an encounter with the enigmatic and cruel realities of self.

Apart from its American, English, and Russian exponents, many innovative psychological novels were being produced in continental Europe during the fin de siècle and early years of the 20th century. One of the most influential was France's Paul Bourget, who, reacting against the deterministic psychology of Hippolyte Taine, wrote moralistic novels that combined psychological theory with a Catholic spirituality. In *Le Disciple* (1889; *The Disciple*), *Cruelle énigme* (1885; Love's Cruel Enigma), and *André Cornélius* (1887), Bourget focused on the dilemmas of morality, with characters often illustrating the psychological efforts of working through problems of conscience. One of the most significant psychological novelists of the early 20th century was Thomas Mann. Mann's predominant influence was Sigmund Freud, and he created his novels around many different aspects of contemporary psychology. In *Der Zauberberg* (1924; *The Magic Mountain*) and *Der Tod in Venedig* (1912; *Death in Venice*) Mann concentrated on the divisions between the theoretical and the practical aspects of life. However, perhaps his most interesting contribution to the psychological novel was *Mario und der Zauberer: Ein tragisches Reiseerlebnis* (1930; *Mario and the Magician*). In this novel Mann depicts a hypnotist controlling his audience and manipulating their personalities, thus conveying the principle that human beings hold multiple identities and are often controlled by forces far beyond their will. Questions regarding the composition of human identity are also addressed in Marcel Proust's *À la recherche du temps perdu* (1913–27; *Remembrance of Things Past*; also translated as *In Search of Lost Time*), one of the pinnacles of the 20th-century psychological novel. The vast, first-person narrative of this work describes the development of the protagonist, Marcel, in a broken, digressionary form that goes toward demonstrating Proust's theories on the relation between memory and identity. Proust saw identity as lying in those moments of "involuntary memory" whereby the individual has an unmediated and spontaneous remembrance of a past event. In *In Search of Lost Time* Proust depicts the working of this process throughout the development of an individual life and attempts to show the way in which a person can momentarily step outside of the shifting and changing structures of subjectivity.

From the 1920s onward the rapidly expanding currency of Freudian psychoanalysis and other schools of psychology in the contemporary artistic world meant that more and more writers were producing novels that reflected theories such as the unconscious, the Oedipus complex, and the primacy of sexual motivation. D.H. Lawrence, although rejecting Freud's theories because of what he saw as an emphasis on determinism, expressed his abiding interest in matters psychological through novels such as *The Rainbow* (1915) and *Lady Chatterley's Lover* (1928). Lawrence's antisocial literary themes were a product of both his belief in an innate capacity for self-determination and an acceptance that sexuality lay at the seat of the human psyche.

Sexuality also formed a significant element in the novels of James Joyce, Dorothy Richardson, and Virginia Woolf, yet the literary form that they developed attempted a faithfulness to psychological processes that far exceeded Lawrence's work. Dorothy Richardson's epic *Pilgrimage* (1915–67), charting the day-to-day life of Miriam Henderson, used a flowing style to show that identity and subjectivity are continually reframed by temporality and the present, a style that May Sinclair labeled "stream of consciousness," using terminology from William James' *Principles of Psychology* (1890). It is in James Joyce that stream of consciousness as a form of psychological representation reached its fullest expression. Joyce's *Ulysses* (1922), which deals with 24 hours in the lives of three Dubliners, is a massive novel that strives to represent the flux of experience, although this point should not be pushed too far, as Joyce's masterpiece is tightly structured around mythical models and national stereotypes. We must perhaps look to *Finnegans Wake* (1939), where Joyce conveys the mental activity of a sleeping man, H.C. Earwicker, to see a more extensive attempt at presenting the fluidity of consciousness. The mishmash of words and the incredible intensity of allusion in *Finnegans Wake* suggest a mutable and unpredictable order of consciousness that defies reduction to logical principles of meaning. Yet, once again, the cleverness of Joyce's work prohibits us from making the claim that Joyce offers an unmediated picture of mental randomness, although Joyce was certainly influenced by Freudian theory. What he does contribute to the growth of the psychological novel is a more faithful portrait of human mental processes than is given by the character who delineates thought in logical patterns of language and imagery.

William Faulkner and Virginia Woolf stand as two other great modernist practitioners of the psychological novel. Faulkner used a type of stream of consciousness in *The Sound and the Fury* (1929) to scrutinize the conflicts that can exist in the individual and his society, while Woolf in such novels as *The Waves* (1931) presents a collection of characters whose identities are relational to those around them rather than being independent entities. Woolf in particular shows how the self is often conditioned by social models that are already in place. This situation creates a difficulty in the psychological act of self-definition, and it was this manner of problem that was often treated in the French *nouveau roman*. The *nouveau roman*, beginning in France in the 1950s and including such authors as Alain Robbe-Grillet, Claude Ollier, and Robert Pinget, expressed, among other things, an intense concern with the connection between reality and perception. In *La Jalousie* (1957; *Jealousy*) and *Dans le Labyrinthe* (1959; *In the Labyrinth*), Robbe-Grillet shows how perceptions of the external world are dramatically altered by internal moods, while Michel Butor in novels like *L'Emploi du temps* (1956; *Passing Time*) demonstrates the impossibility of defining oneself through the events of one's past. Many novels from the *nouveau roman* fit the profile of the psychological novel, and even later existentialist writers, such as Jean-Paul Sartre, voice psychological arguments or principles. Sartre's novels *La Nausée* (1938; *Nausea*) and *Les Chemins de la liberté* (1945–49; *Roads to Freedom*) reject Freudian ideas of the unconscious and fragmented self to posit an individual living in a radical freedom with the ability to define his or her own existence. For Sartre, therefore, the tolerance of opposed ideas within consciousness amounts to an act of "bad faith" and remains a matter of personal choice. Indeed, choice is a defining term in Sartre's fiction, with his characters often facing acts of decision as the climax to the narrative. As a psychological novelist Sartre should be distinguished from many of his French contemporaries because of his existentialist impetus. Sartre himself voiced a greater allegiance to the literary traditions established by American novelists such as Ernest Hemingway and Norman Mailer, who invented characters that define themselves through personal effort and independent action. Such characters must be juxtaposed against those of novelists such as Arthur Koestler, George Orwell, and Albert Camus, who reflected on the way that the freedom to choose could be an unobtainable ideal when psychological processes are often steered and controlled by social forces.

Many novels written since the 1960s must be considered within the framework of the psychological novel, mainly because the language of psychoanalysis is now thoroughly ingrained into social and artistic vocabularies. Even postmodern works like William Gaddis' *The Recognitions* (1955), Thomas Pynchon's *Gravity's Rainbow* (1973), and Margaret Atwood's *Life Before Man* (1979) are all indebted to psychological language and themes, if only in presenting the absolute complexity of character and the difficulty of self-analysis. Moreover, postmodern fiction has perhaps expanded the boundaries of the psychological novel by illustrating how the forces of media and technology are able to occupy the individual's sense of reality and her modes of perception. Recent feminist writers have also contributed to the psychological novel by exploring through fiction the potential of Freud's Oedipus theory and the psychological implications of the female body. Atwood's *The Edible Woman* (1969) and Fay Weldon's *The Life and Loves of a She-Devil* (1983), for example, show how for a woman psychological imprisonment can result from the way that society views certain types of bodily form. The psychological novel has also been maintained in the continuing traditions of crime and detective fiction, with the intensive analysis of a particular criminal mind being juxtaposed with the psychological tangles of the investigator.

Since all novels are open to psychological analysis, one must be careful in distinguishing the critical traditions that have grown around "psychological fiction." The psychoanalysis of the text, author, and reader has tended to grab center stage over the treatment of the psychological novel as a distinct genre, although the 20th century in particular has seen many important critical voices attracted to psychological fiction. Henry James wrote upon the work of Ivan Turgenev, George Eliot, Flaubert, and Nathaniel Hawthorne, approving of their display of psychological realism, while in the early to middle part of the 20th century Marie Bonaparte and Phyllis Greenacre offered studies on Poe, Jonathan Swift, and Conrad through the mediation of Freud's ideas of the unconscious. Bonaparte's *Edgar Poe, étude psychanalytique* (1933; *The Life and Works of Edgar Allan Poe: A Psycho-Analytic Interpretation*) notably analyzed Poe's fiction through his life experience, and Edmund Wilson's psychological studies in *The Triple Thinkers* (1938) also accepted the premise that the author's life was significant in considering the theme of a text.

Since the 1950s, more critics have begun to treat psychoanalysis as a defining tool of literary criticism. Leon Edel's *The Psychological Novel: 1900–50* (1955) saw in psychological writing "the most characteristic aspect of twentieth-century fiction." Also around this time reader-response theory started to take hold, with Norman Holland's *The Dynamics of Literary Response* (1968) being a good example of theory that considered the reader as important as the author in the psychological mechanisms of fiction. This approach to psychological texts has continued into recent years through such critics as Shoshana Felman. Felman's article on Henry James, "Turning the Screw of Interpretation" (in Felman, 1977), has argued that as the meaning of the text is never consolidated the reader is as much an analysand as an analyzer. Apart from such general approaches, much criticism of the psychological novel has fixed upon particular texts and authors rather than give itself to all-embracing considerations of genre. Frederick Crews' *The Sins of the Fathers: Hawthorne's Psychological Themes* (1966) considered what Crews saw as Hawthorne's "buried impulses," while D.H. Lawrence looked for ideas of predominant sensuality in Poe and Hawthorne in his *Studies in Classic American Literature* (1923). A good recent example of this style of analysis would be Anita Sokolsky's interpretation of Austen's *Persuasion* (in "The Melancholy Persuasion," 1994) through Freudian theories of melancholy. As psychoanalysis became more interfused with linguistics in the 1970s through the influence of Jacques Lacan, the critique of psychological fiction shifted to issues of communication and linguistic identity, with Lacan's "Seminar on The Purloined Letter" (1972) being perhaps the landmark of this complex branch of criticism. Although the influence of this critical perspective has tended toward pure theory rather than literary study, it has emphasized the fact that all fiction, not just the psychological novel, is situated within complex psychological issues that extend well beyond artistic confines.

CHRISTOPHER McNAB

See also Mimesis; Modernism; Psychoanalytic Models of Narrative and Criticism of the Novel; Stream of Consciousness and Interior Monologue

Further Reading

Edel, Leon, *The Psychological Novel, 1900–1950*, London: Rupert Hart-Davis, and Philadelphia: Lippincott, 1955

Ellman, Maud, editor, *Psychoanalytic Literary Criticism*, London and New York: Longman, 1994

Felman, Shoshana, editor, *Literature and Psychoanalysis: The Question of Reading, Otherwise*, New Haven, Connecticut: Yale French Studies, 1977

Holland, Norman N., *Holland's Guide to Psychoanalytic Psychology and Literature-and-Psychology*, New York: Oxford University Press, 1990

May, Keith, *Out of the Maelstrom: Psychology and the Novel in the Twentieth Century*, London: Elek, and New York: St. Martin's Press, 1977

Tymms, Ralph, *Doubles in Literary Psychology*, Cambridge: Bowes, 1949

Williams, Linda, *Critical Desire: Psychoanalysis and the Literary Subject*, London: Arnold, and New York: St. Martin's Press, 1995

Wilson, Edmund, *The Triple Thinkers: Ten Essays on Literature*, London: Oxford University Press, and New York: Harcourt Brace, 1938; revised edition as *The Triple Thinkers: Twelve Essays on Literary Subjects*, New York: Oxford University Press, 1948; London: Lehmann, 1952

Wright, Elizabeth, *Psychoanalytic Criticism: Theory in Practice*, London and New York: Methuen, 1984

Puerto Rican Novel. *See* Latin American Novel: Hispanic Caribbean; Latino-American Novel

---

Manuel Puig 1932–90

Argentine

Mixed critical reactions have greeted Manuel Puig's novels in Argentina: early novels such as *La traición de Rita Hayworth* (1968; *Betrayed by Rita Hayworth*) and *Boquitas pintadas* (1969; *Heartbreak Tango: A Serial*) were considered simplistic and sentimental because of intertextual Tango lyrics and their emphasis on pop culture. The general popularity they achieved caused critics to view them as shallow and lacking literary merit. Conversely, later books that did not emphasize mass culture were criticized because they were difficult for average readers and perhaps too elitist.

Scholars generally divide the novels of Manuel Puig into three cycles, the first being the cycle of General Vallejos (a reference to the town where the novels take place) comprising *Betrayed by Rita Hayworth* and *Heartbreak Tango*. The second, or Buenos Aires cycle, includes *The Buenos Aires Affair* (1973; *The Buenos Aires Affair*) and *El beso de la mujer araña* (1976; *Kiss of the Spider Woman*). The third, or American novels cycle, encompasses *Pubis angelical* (1979; *Pubis angelical*), set in Mexico; *Maldición eterna a quien lea estas páginas* (1980; *Eternal Curse on the Reader of These Pages*), set in the United States; and *Sangre de amor correspondido* (1982; *Blood of Requited Love*), which takes place in Brazil. Puig's last novel, *Cae la noche tropical* (1988; *Tropical Night Falling*), also takes place largely in Brazil.

Puig's first two novels, *Betrayed* and *Heartbreak Tango*, portray small-town Argentina of the 1940s and 1950s and masterfully parody the serial novel. These works consciously incorporate popular culture and Hollywood kitsch, defying conventional boundaries between genres and the traditional separation of canonical and paraliterary forms. In *Betrayed*, the characters are revealed largely through dialogue and interior monologue, although narrative perspectives include a letter and a school notebook, all of which trace the story of a young boy from infancy to age 15 as he grows up with his provincial parents and later moves on to a boarding school in Buenos Aires. The title alludes to betrayals enacted by Rita Hayworth's character in the movie *Blood and Sand* and those of several characters in the novel. *Heartbreak Tango* approximates the serial novel still more, as it presents underdeveloped characters and a structure that emphasizes narration over presentation and character development. The novel portrays members of the Argentine middle class of the 1930s and 1940s whose quest for identity falters when they adopt values supplied by the mass media. The novel's several "episodes" feature as epigraph the words from tangos and other popular songs. Lacking a narrator per se, the novel is told via numerous one-sided telephone conversations, newspaper articles, letters, interior monologues, photograph albums,

police reports, a palm reader's statements, obituaries, and so on. The protagonist, Juan Carlos, dies prematurely of tuberculosis, a romantic death that parodies the sentimentality of serials.

The Buenos Aires Affair has virtually no dialogue since the characters are much too caught up in their own dreams. Puig experiments in this novel with another genre deemed paraliterary, the detective story. Its structure is duplicated here with a whodunit and two opposing points of view: the narrator, who obfuscates with false clues and *cul de sacs,* and the reader, who seeks the truth. Eventually, the crime is solved and the guilty are punished. Characterization suffers in this mystery thriller, as it depends on the stereotypical criminal, victim, and investigator. Within such a simple form, however, underlying ethical and moral values emerge. The victim, Gladys—a stereotypically submissive female—is masochistic by virtue of her patriarchal upbringing. The criminal, Leo—the typical sadist macho—provides the female with what she wishes. (Gladys is an artist, Leo an influential art critic.) Puig achieves a tour de force by choosing unlikely professions for his two characters, then setting up contrasting but complementary psychological needs that correspond to the victim/victimizer dichotomy.

Kiss of the Spider Woman takes place almost entirely inside a Buenos Aires prison cell. Two characters, one homosexual, spend their time seeking respite through discussions of Hollywood movies. (A successful Hollywood production was based on this novel.) Likewise, *Pubis angelical* features two characters confined to a small space, in this case a hospital room. Ana and Pozzi's dialogue creates and re-creates their lives, their fantasies, and the Argentine sociopolitical process. Ana's diary depicts her fears and most intimate desires plus many of her oneiric self-projections. These two novels resemble each other in the way they present the dialogue of two characters confined to a small and restricted space; additionally, they both contain certain aspects of the psychodrama, as the characters' dreams, fantasies, and recollections merge and acquire allegorical implications.

Eternal Curse on the Reader of These Pages is presented almost entirely through dialogue, although it does include various documents such as police reports and letters near its conclusion. The story concerns an elderly invalid, eventually revealed to have escaped Argentina, who suffers from amnesia as a reaction both to the mistreatment he received there as well as to the murder of his family at the hands of Argentine authorities.

Blood of Requited Love is narrated by several voices in first and third person who re-create past events, some fantasy and some real. The novel develops as a conversation that centers on the supposed deflowering of Ana at age 15, an occurrence that might not have actually happened.

Tropical Night Falling, Puig's last novel, presents a dialogue between two female octogenarians who recall the past, their children, and all that might have been. Structure and technique in this last novel recall previous works: the limitating of characters to two, an almost claustrophobic restriction of space, a narrative driven by dialogue, and the reconstruction of memories and dreams. Supplementing the women's conversation are letters, newspaper reports, advertisements, and other pseudo-intertexts.

Manuel Puig, one of Latin America's most important writers of the second half of the 20th century, employs an elaborate, conscious craftsmanship that brings into sharp focus his favorite theme and motif: the representation and frequent subversion of modern mass-culture values. His novels incorporate a multi-voiced discourse that depends heavily upon intertexts from popular culture: the cinema, serial romances, popular songs, and the periodical press. This emphasis upon the ephemera of the moment—songs, movies, historical trivia—limits Puig's claim to universality, but his exceptional artistry will maintain his name in the canon for years to come. His ability to fuse best-seller writing with academic writing will ensure that his works continue to be read by the general public as well as more serious students of literature.

GENARO J. PÉREZ

Biography

Born in General Villegas, Province of Buenos Aires, Argentina, 28 December 1932. Moved to Buenos Aires, 1946. Attended US boarding school in the capital from 1946; studied architecture in 1950, then philosophy, from 1951, at the University of Buenos Aires; received scholarship to study film directing, with Vittorio De Sica, and screenwriting with Cesare Zavattini at the Centro Sperimentale di Cinematografia, Rome, 1956. Traveled throughout Europe, 1956–63, and worked at a variety of jobs, including: translator and teacher of English and Spanish, London and Rome, 1956–57, dishwasher and language tutor, London and Stockholm, 1958–59, assistant film director and translator of subtitles, Rome, Paris, and Buenos Aires, 1957–61; clerk for Air France, New York, 1963–67; returned to Buenos Aires, 1967; visiting lecturer, Columbia University,

New York; lived in Brazil, 1973–75, New York, 1976–80, and based in New York and Rio de Janeiro, 1980–89; settled in Cuernavaca, Mexico, 1989. Died 22 July 1990.

Novels by Puig

La traición de Rita Hayworth, 1968; as *Betrayed by Rita Hayworth*, translated by Suzanne Jill Levine, 1971
Boquitas pintadas, 1969; as *Heartbreak Tango: A Serial*, translated by Suzanne Jill Levine, 1973
The Buenos Aires Affair, 1973; as *The Buenos Aires Affair*, translated by Suzanne Jill Levine, 1976
El beso de la mujer araña, 1976; as *Kiss of the Spider Woman*, translated by Thomas Colchie, 1979
Pubis angelical, 1979; as *Pubis angelical*, translated by Elena Brunet, 1986
Maldición eterna a quien lea estas páginas, 1980; as *Eternal Curse on the Reader of These Pages*, translated by Puig, 1982
Sangre de amor correspondido, 1982; as *Blood of Requited Love*, translated by Jan L. Grayson, 1984
Cae la noche tropical, 1988; as *Tropical Night Falling*, translated by Suzanne Jill Levine, 1991

Other Writings: plays and essays.

Further Reading

Bacarisse, Pamela, *The Necessary Dream: A Study of the Novels of Manuel Puig*, Cardiff: University of Wales Press, and Totowa, New Jersey: Barnes and Noble, 1988
Bacarisse, Pamela, *Impossible Choices: The Implications of the Cultural References in the Novels of Manuel Puig*, Calgary, Alberta: University of Calgary Press, and Cardiff: University of Wales Press, 1992
Kerr, Lucille, *Suspended Fictions: Reading Novels by Manuel Puig*, Urbana: University of Illinois Press, 1987
Lavers, Norman, *Pop Culture into Art: The Novels of Manuel Puig*, Columbia: University of Missouri Press, 1988
Merrim, Stephanie, "For a New (Psychological) Novel in the Works of Manuel Puig," *Novel: A Forum on Fiction* 17:2 (1984)

Pulp Fiction. *See* American Western Novel; Crime, Detective, and Mystery Novel; Dime Novels and Penny Dreadfuls; Science Fiction Novel

---

Aleksandr Pushkin 1799–1837

Russian

Aleksandr Pushkin's national standing as Russia's greatest poet equates with that of William Shakespeare in England and Dante in Italy. With his extensive and multifarious body of work, he almost single-handedly created a classical literary heritage for the nation as well as a new literary language, the first successful blending of vernacular, archaic, and modern (Frenchified) Russian.

Pushkin's contribution to the novel is based on two very different works, *Evgenii Onegin* (1833; *Eugene Onegin*) and *Kapitanskaia dochka* (1836; *The Captain's Daughter*), the latter being of lesser significance. *Eugene Onegin,* probably the best loved of all Russian literary works, is a highly distinctive work that stands at the head of modern Russian literature. As foremost in a grand series of 19th-century realist novels for which no allowances had to be made in terms of everyday realism, *Eugene Onegin* was the first one in which the underlying story is surpassed in interest and significance by the characters, their behavior, psychology, and moral responsibility. The great Russian novelists who followed, including Mikhail Lermontov, Nikolai Gogol', Ivan Turgenev, Fedor Dostoevskii, and Lev Tolstoi, would not have been able to write as they did without Pushkin as forebear.

Eugene Onegin is one of the shortest novels in world literature, consisting of eight chapters and only about 21,000 words. The first secret of its success and memorability—many Russian speakers know large sections of it by heart—is that it contains some of the best Russian poetry ever written. Moreover, the poet packs into a single stanza of fewer than 60 words as much information, oblique and implied, as an orthodox prose novelist would deliver in a large paragraph. Succinctness is the hallmark of this writer's general style in both poetry and prose; nowhere is that quality better exemplified than in *Eugene Onegin.*

Although this work deliberately imitates the amusingly discursive manner of Laurence Sterne's *Tristram Shandy* (1759–67), it took as its true starting point not a novel but Lord Byron's long narrative poem *Don Juan* (1819–24). Nevertheless, from the outset it proclaimed itself a novel ("the devil of a difference") and because of its disciplined structures, seriousness of purpose, solid characterization, and natural incorporation of dialogue in verse, it is universally acknowledged as belonging to that genre.

The poetic strength of *Eugene Onegin* is grounded on a happy decision of Pushkin's to reject the constraints of Byron's *ottava rima* form in favor of a new, purpose-built stanza. This 14-line structure reads much like a sonnet, even though the lines are shortened from the traditional pentameter to Pushkin's favorite tetrameter. The protean rhyme scheme, AbAbCCddEffEgg (capital letters denoting two-syllable rhymes), allows each stanza to adopt its own shape, tending sometimes toward the Shakespearean (three quatrains plus couplet) and sometimes toward the Italian (octave plus sestet). The experience of reading *Eugene Onegin* is a curious one, like enjoying a selection of the best English sonnets that happen successively to present characters and tell a story.

Much of the pleasure of this novel derives from the amiable chatter of the narrator on a wide range of subjects (carefully controlled and modulated so as to avoid the garrulity of *Don Juan*), although the plot is rather slender. Tatiana Larina, a passionate country girl, falls in love with a new neighbor, Eugene Onegin, who refuses her advances. He leaves the district following a duel in which he has shot to death a young acquaintance, Vladimir Lensky. After two or three years spent traveling, he returns to St. Petersburg, where he meets Tatiana again, this time in her new role as a well-married society hostess. Now it is his turn to fall in love, but Tatiana makes a pointed declaration of marital fidelity. These apparently straightforward occurrences are more complicated than they seem. Subtle questions of motivation and moral responsibility arise at every corner. Was the younger Tatiana truly in love, or did she see Onegin as a saturnine deliverer akin to the heroes of the many romances she had read? Onegin's shallowness of character, established at the outset in an extended portrait of the man-about-town, becomes clear to her in chapter seven when she visits his castle and looks at his possessions. Could it be that her high moral tone at the end is less than it seems, since she has little difficulty rejecting him? What is Onegin's motivation in destroying young Lensky under circumstances that could have been controlled and directed otherwise? Critics are still arguing about these and many other issues arising from a novel of striking irony and ambiguity. Without appearing to do so because of its apparent flippancy, *Eugene Onegin* goes beyond storytelling and invites consideration in a way that later Russians would develop on a massive scale of serious human issues: moral values, truth and falsehood, the pursuit of happiness, the wonder of life, and the mystery of death.

Pushkin's finest work of prose is undoubtedly his story "Pikovaia dama" (1834; "The Queen of Spades"), a psychologically fascinating tale of the supernatural. A small collection of short narratives, *Povesti pokoinogo I.P. Belkina* (1830; *The Tales of Belkin*), appears lightweight by comparison, and the offerings under this title are best regarded as parodies. *The Captain's Daughter,* the result of a period of historical research by the author, was a more serious enterprise, but it achieved only limited success. Both the characters and the events are thinly substantiated, Pushkin's economy of style having been pressed into service of the wrong cause. Sometimes mistaken for a historical novel, this work may be described as a novella. Its broad range of characterization (from the Empress Catherine to the servants and peasants) may have had some influence on Tolstoi, as evidenced in his technique. The overall significance of Pushkin's achievement in prose is less momentous than that of *Eugene Onegin,* a novel that must count as one of the most unusual works to have earned definition by that generic title.

A.D.P. Briggs

See also Eugene Onegin

Biography

Born 26 May 1799 in Moscow. Educated at home, and at Imperial lycée in Tsarskoe Selo, near St. Petersburg, 1811–17. Civil servant, St. Petersburg, 1817–20; exiled in southern

Russia and Pskov province for his unpublished political poetry, 1820–26, after which he returned to St. Petersburg; fought with the Russian army against the Turks in Transcaucasia, 1829; editor, *Sovremennik* [The Contemporary], 1836–37. Died (in a duel) 29 January 1837.

Novels by Pushkin

Evgenii Onegin, 1833; translated as *Eugene Onegin,* 1881; also translated by Oliver Elton, 1937, revised by A.D.P. Briggs, 1992; Vladimir Nabokov, 1964, revised editions, 1976, 1981; Charles Johnston, 1977; Walter Arndt, 1963, revised edition, 1981; S.D.P. Clough (bilingual edition), 1988; James E. Falen, 1995

Kapitanskaia dochka, 1836; as *The Captain's Daughter,* translated by Rosemary Edmonds in *The Queen of Spades and Other Stories,* 1962; also translated by Alan Myers in *The Queen of Spades and Other Stories,* 1997

Other Writings: poetry, stories and tales, plays, critical prose, and letters.

Further Reading

Bayley, John, *Pushkin: A Comparative Commentary,* Cambridge: Cambridge University Press, 1971

Briggs, A.D.P., *Alexander Pushkin, Eugene Onegin,* Cambridge and New York: Cambridge University Press, 1992

Clayton, J. Douglas, *Ice and Flame: Aleksandr Pushkin's "Eugene Onegin,"* Toronto and Buffalo, New York: University of Toronto Press, 1985

Dalton-Brown, S., *Pushkin's "Evgenii Onegin,"* London: Bristol Classical Press, 1997

Hoisington, Sona Stephan, editor *Russian Views of Pushkin's "Eugene Onegin,"* Bloomington: Indiana University Press, 1988

Thomas Pynchon 1937–

United States

Students of the novel consider Thomas Pynchon a primary developer and practitioner of the postmodern novel. Pynchon has attained his stature while shunning literary celebrity, and the paucity of details about his life has both frustrated readers wanting to connect the books to the man and intrigued readers who use the absence of biographical details as an invitation to a free play of textual meaning. From his early short stories to his five novels, Pynchon has been a quintessential examiner of the postmodern condition. His fiction represents the stakes of living in a world characterized by decreasing certainty, by a proliferation of both literary and conspiratorial plots, and by absurd and often futile attempts by individuals to understand and act upon a world that appears to exceed the grasp of any single individual. Nevertheless, as Kathryn Hume observes in *Pynchon's Mythography* (1987), Pynchon's "heroes" engage in small acts of kindness that redefine heroism in the nonlinear cosmos of his fiction.

In *V.* (1963), Pynchon begins his postmodern critique of epistemological ways of knowing, such as historical reconstructions. Split into two narratives that ultimately converge, *V.* focuses (1) on a 1956 pseudo-beat group of characters called "the Whole Sick Crew," particularly Benny Profane, a self-confessed schlemiel; and (2) on the historical reconstructions of the lady V. by Herbert Stencil, who defines his life as a quest to understand the malevolent forces operating under the surface of the 20th century and somehow connected to V. Alternating between comedy and pathos, *V.* introduces readers to Pynchon's examination of not only the failure of history to provide clear access to the truth but the failure of individuals to attain traditional heroism. Although Profane may sometimes be roused to make an effort to help another character, even his "noble" actions are essentially

meaningless, leaving him at the novel's close in an existential flight into darkness. Stencil doesn't fare much better, endlessly approaching yet avoiding any final truth about V. Despite looking backward stylistically to high modernism, *V.* begins to map Pynchon's postmodern worldview.

As in *V., The Crying of Lot 49* (1966) also presents a quest/detective plot focusing on Oedipa Maas, who, in the process of executing a former lover's will, appears to stumble onto a centuries-old secret postal service called Tristero. Even as her inquiries accumulate "facts" of Tristero's existence, Oedipa becomes less sure if what she is finding is real, a hoax, or the product of her own paranoia. Oedipa's uncertainty transfers to the reader, who receives no help from the narrator in determining which possibility is true. In Pynchon's writing, paranoia is both a theme and an analog to the whole process of the novel and its reading. Eschewing techniques of science fiction, Pynchon's postmodern poetics stage narrative constructions of possible worlds that expose the entropic breakdown of everyday life. Characters such as Oedipa are given glimpses of other alternatives that, paradoxically, are too fantastic to believe.

Publication of *Gravity's Rainbow* (1973) solidified Pynchon's place as his generation's preeminent novelist. This sprawling novel, with its 400 characters, multiple plot lines, and encyclopedic frame of reference, challenged readers to find new methods for processing its complex narrative. Taking place between December 1944 and autumn 1945, *Gravity's Rainbow* focuses on a rich context of characters and issues surrounding the V-2 rocket terrorizing London. The scope of the novel, however, extends far beyond the last days of World War II to include questions of how the war set the stage for the politics of the Cold War and the politics of rocketry for both space and military applications. Significantly, *Gravity's Rainbow* marked, as Brian McHale (1992) argues, the complete shift from the epistemological dominant of modernism to the ontological dominant of postmodernism. Readers emerge from the fictional "Zone" of the text with questions about how the "real" world is conceptualized. Pynchon structures his novel to capitalize on scientific theories of indeterminacy and incompleteness, presenting a superb example of a self-deconstructing text. Nevertheless, some readers have interpreted the novel's textual uncertainty as neither nihilistic nor apocalyptic but as a site of possibility if only the signs could be read correctly.

Seventeen years elapsed between *Gravity's Rainbow* and *Vineland* (1990). Although *Vineland* is less complex than *Gravity's Rainbow*, it is Pynchon's most straightforwardly political novel, critiquing the failure of 1960s radicals to prevent the injustices of Ronald Reagan's America of the 1980s. Pynchon's typical themes of paranoia and conspiracy abound in this novel, but he adds an inquiry into how television (the "Tube") and computers have come to dominate everyday existence. At the same time, the novel explores the ethics of loyalty and responsibility within the postmodern landscape of California. Frenesi Gates, her former husband Zoyd Wheeler, and their daughter Prairie form the focus of a genealogical narrative, and their low-key reunion at the novel's conclusion marks a mellower turn to Pynchon's fictional vision.

Long rumored to be in the writing, *Mason & Dixon* (1997) marked a return to the standards Pynchon set with *Gravity's Rainbow*. This richly dense novel, told in an 18th-century diction and narrative style interlaced with postmodern stylistic turns, tells the story of the association between British surveyors Charles Mason and Jeremiah Dixon, who gave their names to the famous line separating north and south in America. In this "historical" novel Pynchon continues his inquiry into the ongoing construction of America, especially its moral and ethical dimensions. Always on the side of the Preterite rather than the Elect, Pynchon uses the metaphor of the "line" to argue that the historical destiny of America was fixed by forces operating behind the scenes. As in his other novels, the characters only sense the larger implications of their actions or the deeper context in which they are enmeshed. Pynchon's postmodern reimagining of America's origin is one more chapter in his ongoing project of exposing the forces behind the scenes that, for their own interests, create the fictions by which everyday life is constructed.

BERNARD DUYFHUIZEN

See also Gravity's Rainbow

Biography

Born 8 May 1937 in Glen Cove, Long Island, New York. Attended Oyster Bay High School, Glen Cove; Cornell University, Ithaca, New York, B.A. 1959. Served in the US Naval Reserve, 1955–57. Technical writer, Boeing Aircraft, Seattle, 1960–63.

Novels by Pynchon

V., 1963
The Crying of Lot 49, 1966
Gravity's Rainbow, 1973
Vineland, 1990
Mason & Dixon, 1997

Other Writings: short stories (collected in *Slow Learner,* 1984), essays, book reviews, and liner notes.

Further Reading

Berressem, Hanjo, *Pynchon's Poetics: Interfacing Theory and the Text,* Urbana: University of Illinois Press, 1993

Duyfhuizen, Bernard, "Taking Stock: 26 Years Since V. (Over 26 Books on Pynchon!)," *Novel* 23 (Fall 1989)

Grant, J. Kerry, *A Companion to "The Crying of Lot 49,"* Athens: University of Georgia Press, 1994

Hite, Molly, *Ideas of Order in the Novels of Thomas Pynchon,* Columbus: Ohio State University Press, 1983

Hume, Kathryn, *Pynchon's Mythography: An Approach to "Gravity's Rainbow,"* Carbondale: Southern Illinois University Press, 1987

Levine, George, and David Leverenz, editors, *Mindful Pleasures: Essays on Thomas Pynchon,* Boston: Little Brown, 1976

McHale, Brian, *Constructing Postmodernism,* London and New York: Routledge, 1992

McHoul, Alec, and David Wills, *Writing Pynchon: Strategies in Fictional Analysis,* London: Macmillan, and Urbana: University of Illinois Press, 1990

Mead, Clifford, *Thomas Pynchon: A Bibliography of Primary and Secondary Materials,* Elmwood Park, Illinois: Dalkey Archive Press, 1989

O'Donnell, Patrick, editor, *New Essays on "The Crying of Lot 49,"* Cambridge and New York: Cambridge University Press, 1991

Pynchon Notes (bibliography), 1979–

Schaub, Thomas H., *Pynchon: The Voice of Ambiguity,* Urbana: University of Illinois Press, 1981

Slade, Joseph W., *Thomas Pynchon,* New York: Warner Paperback Library, 1974; revised edition, New York: Peter Lang, 1990

Tanner, Tony, *Thomas Pynchon,* New York and London: Methuen, 1982

Weisenburger, Steven, *A "Gravity's Rainbow" Companion: Sources and Contexts for Pynchon's Novel,* Athens: University of Georgia Press, 1988

Q

Quer pasticciaccio brutto de via Merulana. *See* That Awful Mess on Via Merulana

---

Quiet Flows the Don by Mikhail Sholokhov

Tikhii Don 1928–40

Set in the years 1912–22, this four-volume novel offers a panoramic view of the Don Cossacks' life in times of peace, war, and revolution. Like *The Iliad, Quiet Flows the Don* deals with momentous historical events and has a heroic central character endowed with dignity and formidable martial skills. Both works abound in fierce military engagements, presenting gore and suffering in a calm epic manner. Furthermore, both works vividly depict the grief of those whose sons or husbands perished in combat. However, similarities between *Quiet Flows the Don* and *The Iliad* stem not from Sholokhov's borrowing from Homer, but from a subject matter furnished by analogous historical situations and from an authorial predilection for the portrayal of battles.

A closer link exists between *Quiet Flows the Don* and Lev Tolstoi's *Voina i mir* (1863–69; *War and Peace*). Both works blend elements of family and historical novels with the heroic war focus. Some artistic features of Sholokhov's epic—chronological arrangement of the narrative, attention to detail, certain methods of characterization and psychological probing, and contrasts of peaceful landscapes with scenes of murderous human fighting—bespeak Tolstoi's influence. These similarities are, however, outweighed by differences in the novels' endings and style. While *War and Peace* immortalizes the triumph of the Russian people and the nobility, *Quiet Flows the Don* shows the destruction of the centuries-old existence of the Cossacks as a unique segment of Russia's population. This outcome gives the closing part of Sholokhov's novel a somber air absent from the conclusion of *War and Peace*. In his lavish use of dialectic, tropes, and colorful description, Sholokhov sharply departs from Tolstoi. There are more than 2,000 similes in *Quiet Flows the Don,* three times as many as in *War and Peace*. In terms of style, Sholokhov's epic

has more in common with Soviet ornamental prose of the 1920s than with the Russian realistic novel of the 19th century.

Two kinds of Russian ornamental prose flourished in the 1920s. One was represented by writers like Isaak Babel' and Iurii Olesha, who strove to create striking figures of speech while maintaining a traditional authorial voice that featured the vocabulary of standard Russian and clear, correct diction. Other writers, notably Fedor Gladkov and Artem Veselyi, not only filled their fiction with tropes but also introduced the vernacular and experimented with the syntax of spoken dialogue. Sholokhov was closer to this group. He used syntactical inversions and rivaled Gladkov in the copious employment of similes expressed by means of the instrumental case. What distinguishes Sholokhov from all practitioners of ornamental prose of the 1920s, as well as from later Soviet writers, was his choice of genre, the epic novel.

Quiet Flows the Don is an unusual work of Soviet literature because Sholokhov presents the struggle of the Whites against the Reds and does so with remarkable impartiality. The novel's protagonist Grigorii Melekhov vacillates between the two warring sides, but his determination to defend his native Cossack land against the Bolshevik invaders brings him into the ranks of the Whites for nearly the entire duration of the civil war. Grigorii's political and war experiences, however, are overshadowed by the story of his tragic love. The novel's romantic element exemplifies the author's idea that nearly every true love ends with separation or loss.

Quiet Flows the Don is rich in tense situations resulting from personal or sociopolitical conflicts. This realism of sharp confrontations imparts a dramatic quality to the novel. Sholokhov portrays the Cossacks as full-blooded individuals and faithfully reproduces their racy speech. The many-sidedness of Sholokhov's talent is manifested in his masterly handling of epic, lyrical, and comic elements. The plot unfolds smoothly, except in volume two, which suffers from fragmented narrative, an overabundance of marginal characters, and an overuse of documentary materials.

With the possible exception of Boris Pasternak's *Doktor Zhivago* (1957; *Doctor Zhivago*), no Soviet novel attaches such significance to nature as does *Quiet Flows the Don*. Sholokhov views human beings as part of nature, since their lives revolve around love and procreation. Human feelings and actions are often related to processes occurring in nature, which is described with keen attention to details of shape, color, sound, and smell. Yet, as this novel demonstrates, the complexities of human spiritual and emotional life are unknown to nature, while humans also surpass nature in cruelty and destructiveness. For Sholokhov, who was an atheist, the sun is the source of life. The black sun that Grigorii sees after burying his beloved not only symbolizes his grief but also presages his loss of the will to live, since the generator of life has burned out for him.

Nature description often takes a strategic place in the structure of Sholokhov's epic. Nature constitutes the novel's title and figures prominently in the Cossack songs forming the epigraphs to its first and second halves. Four parts as well as one-fourth of the novel's chapters begin or end with representations of nature. In all these positions the natural imagery plays an important role, illustrating the action, foreshadowing future events, or conveying the author's philosophy.

While *Quiet Flows the Don* had a great success with the general reading public, the reactions of literary critics varied. Some reviewers praised the novel's epic sweep; others, particularly orthodox Communists, criticized it for its idealization of reactionary Cossacks, admiration of the Whites, and neglect of the class struggle.

Assertions that Sholokhov could not have written *Quiet Flows the Don* or at least not parts of it, considering his young age and pro-Soviet orientation, have been made since 1928 but are not supported by proof. Indeed, the evidence of his authorship is growing, especially now that rough drafts and manuscripts of the novel's first two volumes have been found.

Early English-language publications of Sholokhov's epic entitled *And Quiet Flows the Don* (1934), *The Don Flows Home to the Sea* (1940), and *The Silent Don* (1941) were spoiled by inadequate translation and extensive editorial abridgments. The best English translation appeared under the title of *Quiet Flows the Don* in 1996 in Great Britain and the United States. Thanks to the almost complete restoration of material removed by Soviet censorship, this edition offers the fullest text of the novel in any language, including Russian.

HERMAN ERMOLAEV

Further Reading

Bearne, C.G., *Sholokhov,* Edinburgh: Oliver and Boyd, 1969

Ermolaev, Herman, *Mikhail Sholokhov and His Art,* Princeton, New Jersey: Princeton University Press, 1982

Kjetsaa, Geir, *The Authorship of "The Quiet Don,"* Oslo: Solum Forlag, and Atlantic Highlands, New Jersey: Humanities Press, 1984

Kolodnyi, Lev Efimovich, *Kto napisal "Tikhii Don": Khronika odnogo poiska,* Moscow: Golos, 1995

Medvedev, Roy Aleksandrovich, *Problems in the Literary Biography of Mikhail Sholokhov,* Cambridge and New York: Cambridge University Press, 1977

Murphy, A.B., V.P. Butt, and Herman Ermolaev, *Sholokhov's "Tikhii Don": A Commentary in 2 Volumes,* Birmingham: Department of Russian Language and Literature, University of Birmingham, 1997

Sivovolov, G.Ia., *"Tikhii Don": Rasskazy o prototipakh,* Rostov-on-Don: Rostovskoe knizhnoe izdatel'stvo, 1991

Stewart, David Hugh, *Mikhail Sholokhov: A Critical Introduction,* Ann Arbor: University of Michigan Press, 1967

R

François Rabelais 1484?–1553

French

Rabelais is generally credited with transforming French into a modern literary language. His comic narratives known collectively as *Gargantua and Pantagruel* are arguably the most innovative works of narrative prose written in French, and they are among the very few to have attained an undisputed place in literary canons outside of France. Their ebullience, linguistic inventiveness, encyclopedic inclusiveness, and characteristic blend of broad popular humor and exquisite humanist irony are among the features that exercised a decisive influence on a long line of writers extending from Thomas Nashe and Cervantes through Voltaire and Laurence Sterne to James Joyce, André Gide, and Céline. Less influential was the massive erudition that makes Rabelais' work a virtual summa of Renaissance learning.

Although commonly referred to as *romans,* Rabelais' books are in fact nothing of the kind. They contain no trace of the multiple plots, marvelous adventures, or romantic intrigues of earlier romances, nor any premonition of the psychological depth, social realism, or polyphonic density of the novel to come. They appear in fact to defy classification by genre, incorporating as they do elements that derive from a variety of unrelated genres: long narrative genres like the chronicle; short narrative forms such as the *fabliau,* the *conte,* and the humanist *facetia;* dramatic genres like the farce and *sotie;* philosophical genres like the dialogue and the commentary; even such lyric genres as the *rondeau* and the epigram. This generic eclecticism has led many to think of Rabelais' books in modal rather than generic terms, as comedies, satires, burlesques, or "Menippean satires"—the latter term referring to the episodic and apparently open-ended character of Rabelais' narratives and the highly corrosive, often fantastical nature of his satire. All such characterizations are valid to varying degrees, and the palpable influence of late Greek writers like Lucian and Plutarch and of near-contemporary ironists like Erasmus and Thomas More seems to authorize the view that Rabelais' books are generically indeterminate by design.

But Rabelais himself conceived of his books as epics and deliberately inscribed them in the heroic tradition extending from Homer and Virgil through the late prose redactions of medieval *chansons de geste* (e.g. *Fierabras* and *Perceforest*) to Renaissance burlesques such as Pulci's *Morgante Maggiore* (1483), Folengo's *Baldus* (1521), and the anonymous *Chroniques de Gargantua* (1532?). He alludes explicitly to all these antecedents and even states in the prologue to *Pantagruel* (1532) that his book is a direct sequel to the last mentioned in this long line of heroic narratives. Indeed, the heterogeneous elements of all four books are clearly subordinated to an overall epic design, which Rabelais comically subverts and adapts to his own satirical ends.

This design is most obvious in the first two books, which in their broad outlines narrate the birth, education, and unique epic exploits of a single giant hero—"giant hero" being itself an absolute contradiction in terms according to immutable epic convention. In *Pantagruel* the eponymous hero is prepared by an encyclopedic humanist education for an ultimate epic confrontation with the ungodly forces of ignorance and violence represented by the outlaw king Anarche and his cannibalistic general, Loup Garou (Werewolf). His providential victory at the end occasions a definitive return to the Golden Age. This simple epic plot culminates, significantly, with a burlesque of Virgil's *Aeneid* in which Epistemon ("the Learned") descends into Hades where he observes all the great heroes of epic and history—including Achilles, Ulysses, Aeneas, Perceforest, and Morgante—performing menial tasks, while the poor and the meek of the world are exalted. This systematic inversion of hierarchies suggests that *Pantagruel* is in essence a burlesque *anti*-epic, which adopts the structures and topoi of traditional epic in order to turn the ethos of heroism on its head.

Gargantua (1534) retells essentially the same story in a more natural, "novelistic" mode. The chapters on Gargantua's early years constitute the first realistic representation of childhood in French literature; scenes of a drinking bout and a peasant quarrel are perfectly plausible representations of life in the country; and Gargantua's epic war against the tyrant Picrochole offers a realistic glimpse at 16th-century techniques of warfare and ideals of diplomacy, as well as topographical details so precise that a modern visitor to the Chinonais can still identify the site of each skirmish. The familiarity of such touches of realism today tends to obscure their original function in a work generically marked as an epic. Like the burlesque inversion of epic in *Pantagruel,* the popular domestication of epic in *Gargantua* serves to demystify the heroic ethos from within.

Rabelais' last two books work within and against heroic convention in even more original ways, by deliberately subverting epic teleology. The *Tiers Livre* (1546), especially, is an unprecedented experiment in unheroic, nonteleological narrative. This belated sequel to *Pantagruel* relates the purely domestic failures of the hero's erstwhile epic companion, Panurge, in a decidedly post-epic world situated in Touraine. No longer constrained by a predetermined epic role, Panurge is free to forge his own destiny but lacks the will to do so. Resolved to marry but unwilling to accept the inevitable risks of marriage, he sets out on an interminable quest for a guarantee that he will never be cuckolded by his future wife. The hero, meanwhile, directs this ill-conceived quest in such a way as to prevent the kind of assurance his companion is seeking so as to force him to act on his own will without illusion or constraint. He fails in his purpose, and the book ends inconclusively as the two set sail for the "Temple de la Dive Bouteille," a pure fabrication invented by Panurge as an excuse to continue his heedless quest indefinitely and thus avoid free agency forever.

The *Quart Livre* (1552) returns to a more conventional epic structure by narrating the Pantagruelians' sea voyage to Cathay in search of the "Dive Bouteille." The book is modeled on the *Odyssey,* the *Argonautica,* Lucian's *True Story,* and the *Queste del Sainct Graal,* as well as on such contemporary voyages to the New World as that of Jacques Cartier, but ends once again inconclusively, far from its ostensible, nonexistent telos. The voyage has become an end in itself, while the description of strange, often phantasmagorical islands functions as a fictional pretext for political and religious satire. A posthumous, unauthorized *Cinquiesme Livre* (1564), consisting largely of rejected and superseded drafts of the two preceding books, completes the voyage with the final "mot" of the Dive Bouteille. Although this spurious sequel destroys the internal logic of both the *Tiers Livre* and the *Quart Livre,* it was assumed to be the authentic conclusion of "*Gargantua and Pantagruel*" by generations of readers from the late 16th to the early 20th century.

Certain technical innovations in Rabelais' books—their vigorous narrative, efficacious dialogue, unprecedented realism, and vividly drawn characters (including Panurge, Frère Jean, Janotus de Bragmardo, and Judge Bridoye)—undoubtedly contributed indirectly to the evolution of a genre that Rabelais and his readers could not possibly have foreseen. The most innovative book of the series, the *Tiers Livre,* even looks astonishingly like a proto-novel, portraying as it does the desires and hesitations of a free agent in a post-epic world of contingency. But this was far too radical and unrepeatable an experiment to have any direct influence on narrative fiction before the 20th century.

EDWIN M. DUVAL

Biography
Born in 1484(?). Possibly studied law, 1500–10, in Bourges, Angers, or Poitiers; became a member of the Franciscan convent at Fontenay-le-Comte (Poitou) in 1520s; studied medicine, possibly in Paris, then in Montpellier, bachelor of medicine 1530; doctor of medicine, 1537. Lectured on Hippocrates and Galen, Montpellier, 1531; practiced in southern France; physician at Hôtel-Dieu, Lyons, 1532; visited Italy as physician to his friend and patron Bishop (later Cardinal) Jean Du Bellay, 1534, and later visited with Guillaume Du Bellay, governor of Piedmont; Canon at Benedictine Abbey of Saint Maur-les-Fossés, 1536; obtained the livings of Meudon, near Paris, and Jambet, near Le Mans, 1550, but does not appear to have discharged the duties of either personally. Died 9 April(?) 1553.

Fiction by Rabelais
Pantagruel, 1532
Gargantua, 1534
Tiers Livre de Pantagruel, 1546
Quart Livre de Pantagruel, 1552
Gargantua and Pantagruel, translated by Thomas Urquhart, 1653, continuation by P.A. Motteux, 1694; also translated by J.M. Cohen, 1955, and Burton Raffel, 1990

Further Reading
Bowen, Barbara C., *The Age of Bluff: Paradox and Ambiguity in Rabelais and Montaigne,* Urbana: University of Illinois Press, 1972

Coleman, Dorothy Gabe, *Rabelais: A Critical Study in Prose Fiction,* Cambridge: Cambridge University Press, 1971

Duval, Edwin M., *The Design of Rabelais's "Pantagruel,"* New Haven, Connecticut: Yale University Press, 1991

Duval, Edwin M., *The Design of Rabelais's "Tiers Livre de Pantagruel,"* Geneva: Droz, 1997

Duval, Edwin M., *The Design of Rabelais's "Quart Livre de Pantagruel,"* Geneva: Droz, 1998

Gray, Floyd, "Structure and Meaning in the Prologue to the *Tiers Livre,*" *L'Esprit Créateur* 3:2 (1963)

Kaiser, Walter, *Praisers of Folly: Erasmus, Rabelais, Shakespeare,* Cambridge, Massachusetts: Harvard University Press, 1963

La Charité, Raymond C., "Du *Pantagruel* au *Quart Livre*: Projet narratif et lecteur," *French Forum* 20:2 (1995)

Nykrog, Per, "Thélème, Panurge et la Dive Bouteille," *Revue d'Histoire Littéraire de la France* 65:3 (1965)

Quint, David, "Rabelais: From Babel to Apocalypse," chapter 6 in *Origin and Originality in Renaissance Literature: Versions of the Source,* New Haven, Connecticut: Yale University Press, 1983

Schwartz, Jerome, *Irony and Ideology in Rabelais: Structures of Subversion,* Cambridge and New York: Cambridge University Press, 1990

Screech, Michael A., *Rabelais,* London: Duckworth, and Ithaca, New York: Cornell University Press, 1979

Weinberg, Florence M., *The Wine and the Will: Rabelais's Bacchic Christianity,* Detroit, Michigan: Wayne State University Press, 1972

The Radetzky March by Joseph Roth

Radetzkymarsch 1932

The Radetzky March has long been recognized as Joseph Roth's masterpiece, and it is still his best-known and best-loved book. Publication in 1932, however, meant that it did not initially find a German readership, since Roth, as a Jewish author, was banned in 1933. Although 25,000 copies of a German first edition were eventually sold, Roth was not able to benefit. The novel was rediscovered by mass audiences when Michael Kehlmann's two-part TV version was produced in 1965.

The novel has been widely translated. Indeed, it has the unusual distinction—for a 20th-century novel in German—of existing in three different English versions. It has not, however, entered the European canon, and, despite its continuing popularity and its status as a school text in Germany, *The Radetzky March* barely features in all but the most recent accounts of the development of the German novel. The principal reasons for this omission lie in the novel's relatively conservative form and in the difficulty commentators have encountered in classifying it. Where German writers of the early 20th century tended increasingly to challenge notions of character and plot and the given apparatus of the 19th-century novel, incorporating essayistic and discursive elements that ultimately swamped narrative lines, Roth remained a storyteller, whose plotting and skillful deployment of characters are nowhere better illustrated than in *The Radetzky March*.

The Radetzky March chronicles the rise and fall of the male line of the Trotta family, but it is not a dynastic novel as such. In a review published in *Literturnaja Gazeta* (15 August 1939), Georg Lukács asserted that *The Radetzky March* was a historical novel, since its main characters were middle-ranking officers and officials placed in situations that lifted them out of the prosaic and gave their psychological reactions artistic significance. Uncertainties over Lukács' definition of the historical novel have continued to inform the debate on *The Radetzky March*, but it is clear that significant aspects of the novel relate to major historical themes. The figure of the Emperor Franz Joseph, for example, appears in the story, and the action spans a precise historical period, from the Battle of Solferino in 1859 to the emperor's death in 1916. Roth is, however, less concerned with the workings of history and more with the impact of that history on the individuals caught up in events beyond their grasp or control. Fruitful comparison might be made with Thomas Mann's *Buddenbrooks* (1901; *Buddenbrooks*), an intellectual novel in the form of a family saga, or perhaps with the novellas of Austrian writers such as Ferdinand von Saar (1833–1906) or Marie von Ebner-Eschenbach (1830–1916).

The Radetzky March deals with three generations. The story opens with a young infantry lieutenant, Joseph Trotta, who saves his emperor's life on the battlefield at Solferino and is ennobled for his deed. When the account of his actions is transformed into a propagandistic school text, he complains and resigns his commission, forbidding his only son to take up a military career. That son, Franz von Trotta, becomes a *bezirkshauptmann* (district governor) in a small Moravian town. Most of the novel, however, is devoted to the third generation, that of the grandson Carl Joseph von Trotta, who becomes a cavalry officer but lacks the conviction and courage of his grandfather and shows little aptitude for military life. Carl Joseph's career develops against a backdrop of mess life in far-flung garrison towns at the margins of the Hapsburg Empire, where officers squander their time in gambling, drink, and visits to the local brothel. Carl Joseph's best and only friend, a Jewish regimental doctor, is killed in a duel and he seeks transfer to a less prestigious infantry regiment. Here he takes to drink and runs up gambling debts. An incident where a party of soldiers commanded by Carl Joseph shoots at striking workers causes a scandal, and the emperor intervenes at the request of Franz von Trotta to save the young lieutenant's career. Disillusioned, Carl Joseph resigns but is recalled at the outbreak of World War I. He dies attempting to fetch water for his men, a moment whose ambiguity (is he brave or merely foolhardy?) is typical of its author. The novel ends with the parallel deaths of Franz von Trotta and Emperor Franz Joseph.

In the context of Austro-German literature of the interwar years, *The Radetzky March* has frequently been read as an ambivalent commentary on the "Hapsburg Myth." In Claudio Magris' account of this myth, memories of the vanished dual monarchy are woven into the fabric of a longstanding Austrian tradition that sought shelter from uncomfortable realities in a nostalgic past (see Magris, 1966). *The Radetzky March* articulates a powerful critique of mythmaking in Joseph Trotta's rejection of the authorities' version of his heroism and in the "commonplace end" of Carl Joseph, "not suitable for textbooks in the elementary schools and high schools of Imperial and Royal Austria."

Philip Manger (1985) indicates three components of the Hapsburg myth that are pertinent to a discussion of Roth's novel: supranationality, bureaucratism, and hedonism. The Trottas, as Austro-Germans of Slovene descent, embody the supranational ideal of the Hapsburg state, that all its peoples were equal in the sight of the emperor. Yet the harsh reality of Austro-German hegemony is plain to see in District Governor Franz von Trotta's contempt for Czech nationalists. *Bureaucratism* refers to the three pillars of the Hapsburg state: church, army, and civil service. Avoiding the role of the Catholic hierarchy, Roth presents Franz Joseph as supreme civil servant, Franz von Trotta as one of thousands of mutton-chop-whiskered reflections of the all-powerful emperor who sought to uphold an order threatened by modernizing social and economic forces. The army has degenerated from the heroic days of grandfather Joseph Trotta. Its final phase is embodied in the dissolute and unheroic Carl Joseph. The leitmotif of Strauss' jaunty Radetzky March accompanies Carl Joseph through his career, like the dark gaze of his grandfather's portrait, a constant ironic reminder of vanished glories. Strauss' march also symbolizes the hedonism of late Hapsburg Austria, a quality always linked to anti-Prussian feeling. Roth explores similar themes in his later novel *Die Kapuzinergruft* (1938; *The Emperor's Tomb*) and in the shorter novel *Die Büste des Kaisers* (first published in French in 1934; *The Bust of the Emperor*).

A further significant context for any discussion of the novel is the spate of novels on military themes that began in the late 1920s in Germany with Ludwig Renn's *Krieg* (1929; *War*) and Erich Maria Remarque's *Im Westen nichts Neues* (1929; *All Quiet on the Western Front*). Similar Austrian examples are Robert Mimra's *Batterie 4* (1930; Battery No. 4) and Fritz Weber's *Das Ende einer Armee* (1936; The End of an Army). While most of these novels focus on World War I, in Austria a number of popular writers took up the military theme in a more nostalgic vein. Good examples may be found in Rudolf von Eichthal's short-story collection *Miczike* (1931) or Ferdinand Fauland's *Die schwarz-gelbe Passion* (1930; The Black and Yellow Passion) and later in Alexander Lernet-Holenia's *Die Standarte* (1934; *The Standard*), among others. Such writers drew on a pre-1914 tradition of soldiering writing exemplified by the novels of Carl von Torresani in the 1880s and 1890s, a context to which Roth's literary text explicitly refers at various points when examining the "false consciousness" of its major protagonist.

IAN FOSTER

See also Joseph Roth

Further Reading

Böning, Hansjürgen, *Joseph Roths "Radetzkymarsch,"* Munich: Fink, 1968

Bronsen, David, *Joseph Roth, Eine Biographie*, Cologne: Kiepenheuer and Witsch, 1974

Chambers, Helen, editor, *Co-Existent Contradictions: Joseph Roth in Retrospect,* Riverside, California: Ariadne Press, 1991

Gordimer, Nadine, "The Empire of Joseph Roth," *New York Review of Books* 38 (1991)

Kaszyński, Stefan H., "Die Mythisierung der Wirklichkeit im Erzählwerk von Joseph Roth," *Literatur und Kritik* 243–244 (1990)

Magris, Claudio, *Der habsburgische Mythos in der österreichischen Literatur,* Salzburg: Müller, 1966; 2nd edition, 1988

Manger, Philip, "The Radetzky March: Joseph Roth and the Habsburg Myth," in *The Viennese Enlightenment*, edited by Mark Francis, London: Croom Helm, and New York: St. Martin's Press, 1985

Müller, Klaus-Detlef, "Joseph Roth: *Radetzkymarsch*, Ein historischer Roman," in *Interpretationen, Romane des 20. Jahrhunderts,* volume 1, Stuttgart: Reclam, 1993

Stillmark, Alexander, editor, *Joseph Roth—Der Sieg über die Zeit*, Stuttgart: Heinz, 1996

Wörsching, Martha, "Die rückwärts gewandte Utopie: Sozialpsychologische Anmerkungen zu Joseph Roths *Radetzkymarsch*," in *Joseph Roth*, edited by Heinz Ludwig Arnold, Munich: Boorberg, 1974

The Radiance of the King by Camara Laye

Le Regard du roi 1954

The Radiance of the King is the second novel published by Camara Laye, a young Guinean who at the time was living and working in Paris. (His name is properly Laye Camara. Camara is the family name; Laye is a shortened version of Abdoulaye. Some scholars now refer to Laye Camara, but all of his works—three novels and a retelling of a traditional African griot's tale—were published under the name Camara Laye.) His first novel, the autobiographical *L'Enfant noir* (*The African Child*), published a year before *The Radiance of the King,* received critical acclaim and was the first African novel to win the Prix Charles Veillon. *The Radiance of the King* is considerably different from his first novel, both in subject matter and in style. It tells the story of a white man who comes to Africa for no discernible purpose and loses his money gambling. He hopes to find some kind of job with the king of the country, but is bartered by a disreputable beggar to an African chieftain.

The Radiance of the King is the first novel published by a writer from francophonic Africa to tell its story from the perspective of a white European. It is also one of the earliest African novels to go beyond autobiography or criticism of colonial policy, to treat a universal theme. The novel combines considerable humor, some of it rather earthy, with a religious message, particularly in the final chapters when the protagonist, Clarence, feeling ashamed of his life in the village (where he was employed without his knowledge as a stud for the chief's harem), is accepted, in spite of his sense of unworthiness, into the bosom of the king, a young black man with divine qualities.

The novel is written in standard metropolitan French, with almost no African expressions or usage. It is set in an unnamed African country, with few identifying characteristics. (Many of the early novels of West Africa do not identify a country, perhaps an indication of loyalties either to an ethnic group or to Africa as a whole.) The young black king is described in almost mystical terms from the perspective of the European, who is the focal point of the narration.

The Radiance of the King shows influences of both European and African narrative forms. The European influence is apparent in the opening scenes, which show Clarence awaiting the arrival of the king and then being arraigned for having supposedly stolen a jacket. The surrealism of these scenes owes debts to Franz Kafka's *Der Prozess* (1925; *The Trial*) and *Das Schloss* (1926; *The Castle*), particularly in its representation of an incomprehensible system of justice. Conversations among a group of young men early in the novel suggest an underlying homosexuality, a theme seldom present in West African literature in the 1940s and 1950s. However, Clarence's trip south through a dense forest in the company of the beggar who will trade him to the village chief shows similarities to traditional African tales of initiation. There are also several dream narratives, which some critics have compared to those in traditional African tales.

The novel inverts the hackneyed scenario of Africans arriving in Europe, showing Clarence completely out of his depth in a world that is unproblematic to the local population. Clarence cannot pay his bills. His possessions are confiscated by a hotel keeper. He is treated as a figure of fun by the dominant culture, and he finds it difficult to adjust to a new way of life. Laye also takes his revenge on the European stereotype of the hyperpotent African male by making Clarence a stud for the chieftain's harem who sires many mulatto babies. (Like Africans of earlier centuries, he is sold into slavery.) *The Radiance of the King* is also a plea for interracial understanding, as Clarence gradually loses his feeling of superiority as a white man and the villagers accept him as similar to themselves.

Beyond the cultural themes, however, the novel is a story of the search for God, for forgiveness and salvation, inspired in part by Sufi mysticism. In later commentary, Camara Laye suggests that his protagonist becomes African in sensibility and that the novel evokes a feeling of religious hope that stands in contrast to the Kafkaesque despair of the opening scenes.

Initial critical reactions to *The Radiance of the King* were highly favorable in France. Camara Laye was sharply criticized, however, by Mongo Beti, a Cameroonian novelist, critic, and spokesman for African independence. According to Beti, Camara Laye's work was too far removed from the political reality of life in a West African colony (see Beti, 1955). L.S. Senghor, the leading francophone poet of *négritude*, criticized the novel for suggesting that Clarence is right to feel ashamed of his sexual ap-

petites. According to Senghor, such a moral judgment is an imposition of European values on African culture.

The Radiance of the King has not served as a source of inspiration to many later African writers. Its religious theme was parodied in Yambo Ouologuem's *Le Devoir de Violence* (1968; *Bound to Violence*), a satiric portrayal of African spiritual values.

Because of its great stylistic difference from *L'Enfant noir,* and more importantly because of the lesser literary quality of Camara Laye's third novel, *Dramouss* (*The Dream of Africa*), published in 1966, *The Radiance of the King* has attracted critical speculation about its authenticity. Lilyan Kesteloot, who knew Camara Laye when he was in exile in Senegal after his political problems with the Guinean dictator Sekou Touré, claimed in print, after Camara Laye's death in 1980, that Laye admitted the novel was written by a European. The paternity of the novel remains in dispute.

ADELE KING

Further Reading

Beti, Mongo, "Afrique noire, littérature rose," *Présence Africaine* (1955)

King, Adele, *The Writings of Camara Laye,* London: Heinemann, 1980; Exeter, New Hampshire: Heinemann, 1981

Obumselu, Ben, "The French and Moslem Backgrounds of *The Radiance of the King,*" *Research in African Literatures* (1980)

Senghor, L.S., "Laye Camara et Lamine Niang, ou l'art doit être incarné," in *Liberté I,* Paris: Editions du Seuil, 1964

Shelton, Austin J., "Cultural Reversal as a Motif of Protest by Laye and Dadié," *L'Esprit créateur* (1970)

Soyinka, Wole, *Myth, Literature and the African World,* Cambridge and New York: Cambridge University Press, 1976

Rayuela. *See* Hopscotch

Realism

The problems in conducting meaningful discussion about realism are considerable. First we have to get rid of the notion that realism has something to do with the presence of circumstantial detail. As Franz Kafka's or Jorge Luis Borges' detailed but entirely unrealistic stories demonstrate, detail in itself indicates nothing. Circumstantial evidence—"background" information—can exist only in the presence of rules whereby anything can be measured or judged as mutually positioned with respect to anything else—that is, in the presence of the rules of realism.

Literature never is "information" unless it is not art at all. Whatever the detail or the apparent informational horizon, art only becomes realism when it observes a particular grammar, a system of rules.

Before outlining those rules, it is worth considering the degree to which "realism" has been confused with good art in general; "it is very realistic" often means "it is very good art." If the best art is always realistic, then we must claim Kafka or Borges as realists, and to do so is not only to lose perception of the crucial difference that Kafka and Borges have made to narrative and to realism, it is also to confuse our understanding of what realism is and what it is not.

This confusion has been pervasive across the arts, in painting and film as well as narrative. Even in university courses, the term "realism" often has been used in the 20th century as an evaluative rather than a descriptive term. In the not-too-distant past, for example, university courses were quite likely to inform students, either directly or (perhaps more often) by implication, that "realism" is the norm of all high art, one that can be found fledgling in Roman frescoes or in Chaucerian narrative but that flourished fully during and since the Renaissance (or some other historical marker) and that flourishes still wherever true art is to be found. According to this approach, then, two interchangeable and self-confirming assumptions are codified: that all high art is realist and that realism is the most fully achieved form of art.

This false and doubtless now surpassed usage of the term *realism* belongs to the history of art but also to the history of philosophy in which the term *realism* still indicates a kind of Reality Quotient, an indication that presumes the existence of a timeless Reality or stable truth that informs and accounts for appearances and that even presumes a distinction exists between "reality" and "appearances." Such constructions of "realism" may be traced back through the empiricist tradition of the 17th century, but also as far back in Western philosophy as the Scholastic Realists of the Middle Ages and to Plato.

Given this long and mixed history of the term, it comes as no surprise to find *realism* inconsistently applied in literary interpretation. In relation to the novel particularly, the term has referred to at least two very different kinds of narrative. On the one hand, it has been used to describe the normative, delightfully pristine, atmosphereless, hierarchical, morally static universes of 18th-century novels by Daniel Defoe, Samuel Richardson, Henry Fielding, Laurence Sterne, and (in their tradition) Jane Austen (and see Dale Spender's modification of this canon, *Mothers of the Novel*, 1986). On the other hand, the term *realism* has been used to describe the historical novels of the 19th century, which, beginning with the seminal and international influence of Sir Walter Scott, present narrative worlds full of atmosphere, distance, common-denominator enterprises, and emergent values.

Using the term *realism* to describe two very different kinds of narrative has blurred a crucial distinction between the realist novel, which flourished after 1800 and very largely after 1850, and prior narrative traditions from which it differs radically. Applying the term *realism* in narrative to both sides of that watershed elides the difference; after all, how radical could the oft-remarked 19th-century shift to realism in narrative be if it is only what all art since the Romans has been striving to become? Moreover, recognizing the distinctness of realism as a culturally determinate phenomenon rather than a universal norm for art allows us to understand, historically and comparatively, the cultural context in which realism has had its function.

This confusion of realism with a universal norm extends to the collateral term, *representation*. The same universalizing applies to *representation*, but that confusion is the more damaging because *representation* has political as well as aesthetic connotations that align it with a particular humanist discourse and a particular empiricist methodology. A "re-presentation" is a "realistic" presentation of objects or relationships according to certain rules, whether those rules have to do with writing or politics

or art or even scientific description. Unfortunately, both *realism* and *representation* have become interchangeable terms for a standard that is typical of a particular discursive order of things, one that has been mistaken for a universal.

One good example of this conflation of a particular discourse with universal reason may be found in an often cited text on the cultural history of art, Erich Auerbach's widely disseminated book *Mimesis: Dargestellte Wirklichkeit in der abendländischen Literatur* (*Mimesis: The Representation of Reality in Western Literature*). The book is full of splendid textual analyses and sheer intelligence, but it has an often-missed political agenda that reduces its reliability as history. Written in Istanbul between 1942 and 1945 by a refugee from German Nazism and published in 1946, *Mimesis* is an apologia for a humanist tradition that Auerbach conceived as a single property of Western culture since classical times but believed was threatened by a catastrophic war. Despite its apparent interest in historical periods, this important and influential book accomplishes precisely a reduction of historical difference. Auerbach's argument locates humanist values in the classical world and traces their probable demise in Virginia Woolf, thus unifying very disparate cultural traditions in the service of a single set of unifying values that he presumed to be universal. Auerbach's tone, as well as his distinctions, caught on and were perpetuated. Auerbach, not without reason, associates realism with those favored humanist values; thus he links realism with strength in art, whether that is found in Homer or Boccaccio, and lack of realism with weakness in art, something he finds in Virginia Woolf.

The single most influential book on realism in the English novel has been Ian Watt's *The Rise of the Novel* (1957), which treats Defoe, Richardson, and Fielding particularly as the early originators and exemplars of realism in the novel. Watt's social and cultural criticism situates the new interest in details of domestic life within an argument that a rising middle class produced readers whose interests substantially redirected novel writers toward a new subject matter and through it to new forms. Watt's use of Lockean terminology for perception and knowledge and his descriptions of changing social conditions, especially new ideas of privacy and of the relation between private and public life, have interested generations of readers, although various revisionist readings have now challenged his view of history and his gender bias in constructing it (see Ermarth, 1983; Spender, 1997).

Taking a different tack from Auerbach and Watt, Robert Alter's *Partial Magic* (1975) reverses the usual privilege given to specifically 19th-century realism and prepares for revisionist thinking about the whole matter of realism in the novel tradition. Alter argues that 19th-century realism represents an exception in the history of the novel that otherwise has favored precisely the kind of "magic" found in novels from the whimsical hero of Cervantes through the fragmentary works of Laurence Sterne to the magic realism of the 20th century.

Looked at through a different lens, however, the narrative realism of the 19th-century novel appears to have less in common with the 18th-century novel than it has with 16th-century painting or 17th-century mathematics. That different lens belongs to the kind of interdisciplinary or multidisciplinary method that refuses to treat art as information and that as a method has more of humanist value to it than the narrowly conceived "literary" histories of the kind Auerbach wrote and used to such effect. The multidisciplinary method treats art as a particular kind of practice that has expression in other cultural forms as well, including political, religious, psychological, or scientific ones.

Since the mid–20th century, for example, this kind of interdisciplinary method has taught us to recognize narrative in various cultural forms as well as in novels; this method also sees in narrative forms like "realism" certain principles, rules, and assumptions that apply more broadly. Literary narratives have special prominence among cultural artifacts, however, because they are the most highly achieved of cultural narratives, and thus the most accessible to interpretive use.

Considered in this light, "realism" is only one form of narrative among the many that exist, and not the preeminent narrative form that Auerbach and others considered it. Realism, however, also exists as a preeminently accessible form among cultural narratives and a site for discovering fundamental cultural principles and changes. Realism or representation thus belong, not to a constrained "literary" field, but to a cultural field in which its values of neutrality, mobility, and emergent form find expression in cultural practices at large. In discussing realism, therefore, we are undertaking to single out discursive principles or rules or codes from a broad range of cultural practice, and not merely considering local differences in ways of looking at literature. Where intelligent and well-prepared interpreters differ about what constitutes realism, the difference usually stems from 20th-century differences of opinion, not actual differences on the ground between the art forms of the past.

Realism, then, regardless of whether the medium is pictorial, narrative, or political, involves the production of certain values, particularly the values of neutrality and objectivity. As a cultural practice, this production may be found distributed throughout Europe from Italy to Scotland and throughout the period from the early 15th to the late 19th centuries. Its major cultural productions appear across the range of practice: in Quattrocento realist painting (Filippo Brunelleschi, Piero della Francesca, Raphael, Michelangelo, and the rest of the Renaissance painters and architects who together with their heirs still constitute the pantheon of Western art); in representational political institutions (parliamentary structure, libertarian revolutions in the United States, 1776, and in France, 1789); in empirical science (Galileo, the Royal Academy, John Locke, Linneaus, Sir Isaac Newton, and the technologies that flowed from them); and in historical narrative—which could be called the master narrative of humanist culture—from John Foxe's *Book of Martyrs* (16th century) to Walter Scott's novels to much of the humanities curriculum of European universities. Philosophy, cosmology, physics, technology, politics, art, and education: a common system of value and organization prevails across the culture of representation in Europe.

That discursive system and those values are particularly accessible to observation and analysis in the work of the great realist painters and novelists, who, in different terms and different eras, present the peculiarly public values inherent in the culture of representation. For purposes of clarity and simplification, two will be considered here, realist painting and realist narrative, which flourished, respectively, at the early and late ends of this European cultural development.

The key to these forms of realism is the presence of a grammar of perspective. It appeared first in spatial terms and much later (following considerable cultural upheaval, especially in post-Reformation politics) in temporal terms. This grammar of perspective has its roots in the Renaissance; its most memorable visual record can be found in the perspective painting of the Quattrocento. There, in spatial terms, Italian painters and architects like Masaccio and Brunelleschi began to re-present the aspects of the world from a single, arbitrary, and implicitly changeable position and thereby to construct a world with one single vanishing point: in other words, a world with common coordinates that apply universally regardless of position. This effort in painting not only depicted a world of common coordinates but was itself a testimonial to the rationalization of human faculties (what William J. Ivins Jr. calls "the rationalization of sight" in painting).

In 1424—a full decade prior to Alberti's codification of their implied rules—several painters provided the lead. Masolino and Masaccio painted frescoes in Northern Italian chapels according to a technique that, for the first time, made possible the exact duplication of spectator awareness. Until this time, in Ivins' words, no image "could be exactly duplicated" because there was no "grammatical scheme for securing either logical relations within the system of pictorial symbols" or correspondence with the appearance of objects in space. This lack of a "grammar" of perspective accounts for "much of the failure of classical and medieval science" (Ivins, 1938). It is precisely this grammar of perspective that painters and architects developed in Europe during the early Renaissance; this effort, in turn, had fateful consequences for centuries of social, political, and scientific organization. Long before Descartes, this realist grammar, the hidden control of which was a single spectator, asserted the primacy of the individual subject whose faculties are rationalized by the very pictorial image it supposedly "sees." This representation asserted that time and space are media shared in common by all positions and vantage points—an argument that had endlessly creative possibilities not only for pictorial representation but for politics and science.

Many years were to pass before the vast implications of this assertion of perspective were fully recognized, and only several centuries later were its mechanical implications understood. The work of Raphael and the early career of Michelangelo clarified its pictorial implications, but the period between 1424 and 1524 had seen only the beginning of the influence of these new pictorial representations in cartography and exploration, in religion, and in mathematical and scientific application. Many of the greatest painters of the Italian Renaissance already had flourished by the time Columbus set sail for the Indies and opened a new geopolitical era. The Quattrocento also was well past by the time its new grammar of perspective found expression in the neutral time and space of empirical science and Newtonian laws. The full mathematical implications of these representations did not appear until 1630 in France, and the political and social implications—the political development of the idea of representation, for example, and its translation into conventions of representational time—still were taking shape in the 18th and 19th centuries (see Ermarth, 1983). The construction of the historical subject and its power of consensus, those ultimate achievements of this representational convention, was an achievement that took hundreds of years to reach its apogee in the 19th century.

During the late 18th and early 19th centuries, writers of narrative began to experiment with the problem of producing a single coordinated system by which the many moments of narrative perception could be organized, as pictorial realism had been, according to a single system of coordinates rather than according to some typological sequence already established by tradition. The instrument of this production was a kind of narrative that provided a vantage point that remained outside and in the future of the action: a vantage point provided by the past tense that confers upon every moment a double identity, which is both newly emerging and, at the same time, already past and located in a larger pattern of significance. This narrative system, in which the powers of the past tense are fully exploited for the first time, is called History. History is single-point perspective in time, and the writers who accept and explore that convention appear mainly in the 19th century, when European culture was considering the intimately related problem of producing democratic society.

Realist narrative depends upon the successful construction of a narrating constant (often misleadingly personalized as "the narrator") that provides the bridge, the mediation, the connection across silence and limitation that most characters cannot supply. This narrative voice has a double life: it always exists in the future of every action reinscribed as such by each past tense declaration and serves as an implicit or explicit commentator on events, their causes, and their outcomes. Simultaneously, this voice is always present, always realized in every narrated moment, including those "dramatic" speeches that it quotes. The narrative system literally is collected in the sense that it includes potentially every vantage point (including readers) in a commanding structure of awareness. This commanding structure of awareness maintains the common denominators, the agreements of realism. It differs entirely from the equipoise of satire, which multiplies viewpoint in order to split the false from the true, rather than to coordinate and rationalize.

Realism, or the grammar of single-point perspective, first and foremost produces the value of neutrality. A perspective system produces neutrality when it achieves a unified system in which all possible moments (viewpoints) are made to agree in the formal sense that they do not contradict. As with the "realist" space of painting, the historian, which is to say the realist in time, establishes the neutral medium by maintaining a formal agreement (consensus) among all possible viewpoints: an "agreement" in the sense that there is no contradiction to threaten the establishment of a common temporal medium.

But this supposedly infinite neutrality actually depends upon the serial collection of conscious moments to constitute it. This neutral narrative time materializes only as a collected phenomenon. Each conscious moment produces an "individual" vantage, which exists as a discrete element "in" the narrative medium and, at the same time, forms a constituent part of the system to which it belongs. The individual vantage creates the system it belongs to. Thus, "the individual" acts primarily as the necessary condition or (from another viewpoint) the necessary alibi from which common-denominator time develops; it is what the philosopher Michel Foucault calls the "founding subject" of history.

Most important, historical conventions embody collected memory. Organized from an indistinct "future" situated beyond the end of the sequence, the mnemonic reflex by definition coordinates the variety of temporal moments into a common time. This mnemonic reflex is not personal; it collects the multitude of various personal expectations, memories, fears, and plans into a single, collectedly "remembered," social sequence. The memory thus belongs to everybody (that is, to nobody in particular; see Ermarth, 1983), despite the occasional devolution of the narrative voice into the personal mode (both in first- and third-person narratives). The historical mode is thus not the property of personal memory but rather a collective, and, literally, a collected result. That result is time in the realist mode: a time that is neutral because, putatively and unlike prior conventions, it appears all-inclusive and infinite; it makes no distinction between human and divine time as medieval writers do, or between time-frames as postmodern writers do. It is this neutrality, and not mere chronology or linearity, that characterizes the grammar of single-point perspective in time.

Realism thus achieves a formal consensus by producing a common-denominator world. In realist painting, the perspective grid produces for the first time a space that is neutral and homogeneous: the medium of a common world, one undivided by architectural, hierarchical, or other considerations; one that is neutral and unproblematic; one that makes possible mutually informative measurement across gaps of separation that once had been absolute and irreducible. In narrative, or history, realism accomplishes the same thing by producing a time that is neutral and homogeneous. The term is not riven by divine agency or other fatality but exists as a neutral, unproblematic medium "in" which all events and moments, public and private, are mutually informative. We always know in history that what seems unrelated can, and often does, turn out to be linked; it is the business of realist (historical) narrative to establish and maintain that possibility. Realistic art, whether in narrative or in painting, chiefly represents not objects but a medium: space itself and time itself, and specifically the neutral space and time "in" which we think that so much is possible. The "objects" of realist painting and narrative act as the carriers of this perspective system, and although they are often delicious objects, they are no more than that. The representational conventions associated with realism aim primarily to found the media of neutrality, the time and space "in" which emergent forms develop, identities are recognized or altered, and mutually relevant "human" laws obtain.

These conventions also emphasize mobility. "In" space and time, things develop distributively, that is, in ways that retain and do not forget initial states and conditions. In fact, the only way to exist in neutral media and in a limited horizon is to keep moving, to keep learning, to keep discovering, measuring, and linking what has remained undiscovered, unmeasured, or unconnected. What is the link between symptom and cause? What is the link between the orphan boy and the fine lady in town? These are the questions that occupy realist artists in the culture of representation, and, whatever the answers, the feat consists in having asked these questions, and in having produced the conditions in which such questions can be asked.

It will be seen from this discussion that "realism" is only partially achieved in 18th-century narrative for want of the mediating device that neutralizes the medium and provides the democratic impulse. Eighteenth-century writers were not inferior realists, they simply had other motivations than those of the high realists of the 19th century.

One might well ask why there has been so much developmental interest in realist narrative. The medium positively insists on the linkage between now and then, here and there, us and them. Such interest cannot properly be accounted for with terms like *plot* and *character*, which are borrowed from other, older arts, chiefly drama, and which leave out the crucial element of realism: that mediating perspective system which the narrative's particular details exist primarily to support. That system, and all it promises in the way of increase, growth, and capitalization, constitutes the primary representation or realism in narrative.

The emphasis in all forms of realism upon serial development—on the evolution of identity as distributed through a series of cases—also has a radical potential that the 19th century only began to explore. Does identity emerge through time with several dimensions? If so—that is, if individual identity is simultaneously gendered, political, and economic—then what is its status as an entity? And on the level of collective action, is there such a thing as society or "human" whole? If so, is that social entity universal, common to all humanity? If not, do single determinants like nationality, language, ethnicity, or gender constitute communities? Because a series, especially a historical series, can take unexpected turns, the identity that depends upon such a series endures a certain tenuousness at the same time that it enjoys a certain opportunity. The ambiguity of identity and causality might seem to threaten the neutralities of realism. But so long as no one of these contradictions is great enough to rupture common time, the grammar of realist perspective remains secure.

Although realism remains the preferred form of popular fiction in the late 20th century, its most original and creative period was the 19th century. A few examples from this high period will demonstrate how narrative realism works. Walter Scott was the first and most influential of realist (historian) novelists, but his heirs are more fun to read, especially among those Anthony Trollope and George Eliot. These two writers intrigue not only because their narrative language is witty but also because they engage most explicitly with two key cultural projects—political representation and scientific advance—that we associate with the history of realism.

Trollope presents the best such example because his narrative mediations take place not only within novels but between them as well: main characters in one novel become background figures in the next, and they reemerge in yet another novel with new interest. Particularly, his six so-called "Palliser" novels deal with the political and social conditions in which democratic politics can exist. These conditions, in the narrative medium, have to do with the continually floating, shifting narrative perspective that aligns by mediating an immense variety of potentially conflicting views.

This basic mediating gesture of narrative realism is apparent continuously in Trollope's work; his treatment of the ambitious Crosbie in *The Small House at Allington* (1864) serves as one such example. Crosbie has jilted the heroine at Allington, Miss Lily Dale (even her name carries the edge of ironic commentary), for comfortless proximity to a title. The novel partly turns on the social losses and on the failure of proper connection that this choice entails. The issue of hierarchical and inherited social privilege is especially central to a narrative formally committed to common-denominator values, and Trollope certainly makes an example of Crosbie. The character's obsequious focus on class hierarchy and precedent, and, for that matter, the aristocracy's supine reliance on class hierarchy and precedent, effectually defeats aspiration and achievement and mystifies all enterprise.

These messages, however, are not carried to readers in so many words, but indirectly through the comparative acts of

readerly attention constantly required by the single-point perspective system of history. Readers are immersed in the narrative problematic of realism, one that engages them in a continually doubled, even multiplied perspective. This doubled perspective is always present as Trollope's narrative voice not only plays alongside but exists in the future of every action. This pervasive effect in realism is so familiar that it has become subliminal, so to raise it into view some particular instances are necessary. The point of the examples that follow is to bring into focus the degree to which the constructive rules of realist (historical) narrative operate constantly in the language.

We begin with these descriptions of Crosbie succumbing to the "air" of Courcy Castle:

> The air of Courcy was too much for him. In arguing the matter with himself he regarded himself as one infected with a leprosy from which there could be no recovery, and who should, therefore, make his whole life suitable to the circumstances of that leprosy (*The Small House at Allington*, chapter 18).

One could imagine another conclusion to that sentence, in which Crosbie resolves to flee from contamination; the fact that this idea does not occur to Crosbie pretty well pegs him, right down to the phony heroics of his self-image. As the narrative voice continues, several levels of commentary are in play simultaneously, one commenting on another, all of them placed in perspective by a yet-wider horizon. Note the tense, productive gap between the character's private thoughts and the wider horizon maintained by narrative hindsight:

> It was of no use for him to tell himself that the Small House at Allington was better than Courcy Castle. Satan knew that heaven was better than hell; but he found himself to be fitter for the latter place. Crosbie ridiculed Lady Dumbello, even there among her friends, with all the cutting words that his wit could find; but, nevertheless, the privilege of staying in the same house with her was dear to him. It was the line of life into which he had fallen, and he confessed inwardly that the struggle to extricate himself would be too much for him. All that had troubled him while he was yet at Allington, but it overwhelmed him almost with dismay beneath the hangings of Courcy Castle (chapter 18).

The levels of perspective here are delightfully complex, involving Crosbie's helpless desire to be near a title, his own self-criticism concerning that desire, and the narrative voice's ironies, which in turn add other levels of implicit commentary through the cosmic heroics from Milton ("Satan knew that heaven was better than hell"), the worship of someone called "Dumbello," the image of a social group depreciating and fawning on its hostess, and the final ironic, even satiric imputation at the expense of those overawed by drapery. The alternative points of view at every step mediate the character's own double awareness with a yet-wider range of relevancies.

The fun of hunting down Crosbie depends on such complex discriminations that each moment sustains. These discriminations, however, also reduce to nothing any possibility of simplistic interpretation: it is after all readers belonging to a class-ridden society to whom Trollope directs this writing. And the plot has further ironies in store when we eventually discover that Crosbie, having thrown in with titles and thrown over superior companions, gets promoted on the basis of merit in the end, so that, unbeknownst to him, all his fawning for promotion has been pointless: "he had really been promoted because he knew more about his work than any of the other men, and Lady De-Courcy's influential relation at the India Board had not yet even had time to write a note upon the subject." For good measure, and not content with irony only at Crosbie's and Courcy Castle's expense, Trollope also implicates an entire office staff in the same obsequiousness when he notes how Crosbie's promotion is accompanied by an air of sudden "deference" from his office colleagues.

Despite his treatment of Crosbie, Trollope is not a leveler; he has more complex views on social class than just those in view in this case (in the same novel, Lord de Guest helps the commoner, Johnny Eames, with both money and also advice on how to change his social position; the subsequent results make Eames, also a suitor of Lily Dale, an instructive counterpart to Crosbie). All these additional considerations must be taken into account before Crosbie's behavior can be fully judged, but by this time in the narrative judgment itself seems almost anticlimactic. By the time Crosbie eventually recognizes his losses, we are into a subsequent "Barchester" novel. The point of the local narrative treatment lies in the expanding revelation of mutual relevance between apparently discrete or separate events, details, and choices.

Like other great realists, Trollope thematizes the issues presented formally in realism. The Palliser novels are particularly concerned with the echoes between personal problems of agreement and political ones. Tension between two different ways of life plays out "in" the common-denominator time that implicitly favors one over the other: the pull of the world toward democracy on the one hand, and, on the other, the pull of tradition and heritage toward qualitative distinction. These tensions drive the sequence in the great Palliser novels: *Phineas Finn* (1869), *Phineas Redux* (1874), *The Prime Minister* (1876), and *The Duke's Children* (1880). The latter begins with the assertion that "it is impossible" to set aside the aristocracy's codes in England, and, in the end, the impossible has been accomplished.

Through complex sequences of shifting vantage, Trollope reveals the personal dimensions of Plantagenet Palliser, the aristocrat central to the Palliser novels. These sequences, however, also sustain an increasingly democratic vision, not only thematically but also formally through the common perspective system. The following passage, for example, demonstrates both at work; it is typical of the process of shifting perspective in time by which narrative realism objectifies the world.

> The peer who sat next to him in the House of Lords, whose grandmother had been a washerwoman and whose father an innkeeper, was to him every whit as good a peer as himself. And he would as soon sit in counsel with Mr. Monk, whose father had risen from a mechanic to be a merchant, as with any nobleman who could count ancestors against himself. But there was an inner feeling in his bosom as to his own family, his own name, his own children, and his own personal self, which was kept altogether apart from his grand political theories. It was a subject on which he never spoke; but the feeling had come to him as a part of his birthright. . . . That one and the same man

should have been in one part of himself so unlike the other part,—that he should have one set of opinions so contrary to another set,—poor Isabel Boncassen did not understand (*The Duke's Children*, chapter 49).

The key shift in the passage comes with a "But . . ." where the duke's two minds become evident. The US heiress whom the Duke's son wants to marry finds this "inconsistency" tellingly difficult to understand; it is the kind of split that favors hierarchy, and Isabel Boncassen's understanding is formed by thoroughly democractic assumptions. The constant undertow of irony and the risibility and pleasure of realist narration both come from this exploitation of the doubled, systematized perspective that realism provides. Each event in realistic narration consists simultaneously of present and past—constituted both as something immediate and also as something over and done and already seen from the vantage of a future hindsight.

The final example of this gradually building perspective system concerns yet another issue of debate that touches on the deep structures of social definition and commitment in realism, and one that still, in some parts of the world, galvanizes public discussion on radio and television in the late 20th century: foxhunting. A brief passage from *The Duke's Children* approaches the issue as follows:

> Everything had been made to give way to deer and grouse. The thing had been managed so well that the tourist nuisance had been considerably abated. There was hardly a potato patch left in the district, nor a head of cattle to be seen. There were no inhabitants remaining, or so few that they could be absorbed in game-preserving or cognate duties. . . . Reginald Dobbes was a man of about forty. . . . Sport was the business of his life. . . . But it never occurred to him that his whole life was one of self-indulgence (chapter 38).

In the course of this passage, various potential observers—tourists, farmers, rural inhabitants, and the huntsman—all congregate in the margin to constitute the problem as a common, shared one; they bring testimony to the presence of common denominators that mediate what seems separate and unrelated. The passage's effect has everything to do with inscribing a public power—the collective, literally collected power to shift preferences and opinions in the interest of widening public enlightenment; it has relatively little to do with the author's private opinions. Trollope was an avid foxhunter who eventually renounced it on principle, but the powers of his text cannot meaningfully be traced to his personal views. The attempt to do so trivializes the narrative achievement of a common, objective world and suggests that that world is constituted by somebody in particular, instead of by everybody.

The constant zig-zag of narrative attention in realism is what surprises and retains the interest of readers; this process sometimes even implicates readers as well in issues raised by the text. But this sequential shift from one moment to another always takes place within a horizon where difference is mediatable. And the mediation, in the best writers, usually provides amusement: "It will come to pass with some of us soon that we must deny ourselves the pleasure of having young friends, because their marriage presents are so costly" (*The Duke's Children*, chapter

89). In all the other great 19th-century realists such as Stendhal, George Eliot, Balzac, Tolstoi, Elizabeth Gaskell, George Gissing, and Henry James, and continuing into the 20th century especially with James Joyce, variants of this cumulative perspective system may be found. Each novelist textualizes in different ways the values maintained and problems posed by the cultural grammar of perspective. A different texture of time exists in each. And none of them produces "perfect" realism—the goal, it would seem, of a great many second-rank novelists in the 20th century. The great novelists of the realist tradition simply maintain the realist problematic.

In the 18th-century English novel, by contrast, writers ordered matters differently. English narratives by the canonical writers achieve an initial but ultimately incomplete experiment with realist narrative strategies and values. Writing after a century of religious and political wars, 18th-century novelists treat the common-denominator values of neutrality, mediation, mobility, and serial development with some scepticism; in their books, the providential universe also remains a powerful discursive convention. Daniel Defoe's and Samuel Richardson's characters, for example (Robinson Crusoe and Moll Flanders, Pamela and Clarissa), lack the depth and realist interest of Trollope's people, but that is because they operate in a providential universe and are not "characters" in Trollope's sense at all. Such a providential context, where all human "measures" (to use Crusoe's word) necessarily come to nothing, does not provide an entirely salubrious environment for the development and infinite neutralities of realist narrative. In fact, 18th-century English novels often joke at the expense of realist values such as neutrality, mobility, the economics of development (capitalization), and the politics of neutrality. These novels were written for a sophisticated readership, but not one prepared for the values associated with realism.

Because 18th-century writers do not fully or even primarily exploit the grammar of single-point perspective, the narrative form of their books remains episodic and unmediated. This is true both in the case of novels that are written as journals or personal memoirs and in the case of the period's most favored narrative form, the epistolary novel. Both journals and letters favor what Richardson called "writing to the moment," and they often obscure any far-reaching potentialities for the sake of home truths on the local scale. Such writing entirely undermines the suspension of judgment and the patient watching of outcomes that belong to later, more fully realist novels. The same may be said of most other 18th-century novelists, including Fielding and Sterne, whose treatment of temporality and perspective limit attention to short, sometimes very short, vignettes that may be delightful in themselves but that are organized not according to developmental agendas but by already well-established conventions of narrative such as the pilgrim's (or rake's) progress or the voyage of discovery.

These episodic 18th-century novels concentrate upon moments in which all can be won or lost at a stroke. Particular episodes do not take place in an emerging structure of significance as indicated by the grammar of perspective in realism but instead in moments that verge on the heroic—a kind of epic of inner life. Compared to realism, the episodes recorded in a journal or a collection of letters belong to sequences that often involve chance as much as choice and that devote themselves to rhetorical purposes rather than to the historical purposes associated with realism.

Such sequences precisely do not invite interest in character or plot development or in hidden explanations that link what seemed unconnected. Such interests, in fact, are precisely the ones assigned to the worst characters, such as Richardson's evil Lovelace in *Clarissa* (1747–48) or Fielding's conniving London aristocrats in *Tom Jones* (1749). The neutral homogeneous temporal medium and the common-denominator world "in" which all events happen are products of the realist perspective system; such a temporal schema does not materialize in these 18th-century works. Instead, sequences in 18th-century novels entail a competition between the concerns of worldly time and those of a higher, providential, unfallen nature outside time. This theme reiterates everywhere in 18th-century narrative, and it is at odds with the full development of a single-point perspective system, and thus always partially at odds with realism, often substantially so.

To a narrative project that directs attention to essential and eternal affairs, temporal and spatial coordinates ultimately are irrelevant. *Robinson Crusoe* (1719) offers an especially useful example of how the standard pre-realist text operates because it has been claimed misleadingly as a standard of "realism" by those who conceive of realism as little more than the judicious selection of detail. Even by such a measure, however, Defoe's novel does not achieve realism. In Defoe's usage, detail tends to evanesce and to become porous and spiritualized in ways entirely inconsistent with realism. Of the many detailed descriptions of some action undertaken by Crusoe (to salvage material from his shipwreck or to build up fortifications or supplies on his island), most stand as a kind of moral warning about the folly of such action. Crusoe's fortifications are never needed, and although he has increased his supplies significantly, he remains solitary and unable to consume all that he produces. Defoe follows most of these episodes with a moral observation against covetousness, bad planning, fear, or expectation. He does not use detail to support the perspective system but, on the contrary, to confound it.

What is more, the novel is full of jokes for a highly literate urban audience about economic theories that are essentially capitalist, about conflicts between religious belief and actual behavior, about racism, and about politics. A more evocative example of cultural misapprehension would be difficult to find than the 20th-century treatment of this complex, politically satirical novel as an adventure book for children (although as a critique of a world-on-the-make the novel may carry salutary lessons to children). As a political functionary in his time who served several different sides of political debate, and as an editor and journalist and essayist attempting to survive without protectionist legislation in a turbulent political era, Defoe wrote under circumstances of risk, sometimes extreme personal risk, and routinely took very different positions across a range of political or religious commitment. That adopting of positions was in fact a crucial part of his early education (see Ermarth, 1983). *Robinson Crusoe* is a witty book about politics and morality, not a children's adventure or a handbook of survival strategies for shipwrecked seapersons.

The charm of such 18th-century novels lies precisely in their differences from subsequent realist redefinitions of personal identity, social life, and narrative sequence. To approach them with historical values in tow invites major difficulties in accounting for their quite unhistorical appeal. The mnemonic overview that maintains the formal consensus of realism in 19th-century narrative simply does not have much play in the 18th century, where neutrality was not yet a broadly disseminated cultural value. When Crusoe and Pamela set down their experiences, they write in the spirit of religious self-examination rather than to create a historical record to be secured and re-read. When knowledge comes from experience, memory (as realism constructs it) can have value. But in the providential universes of 18th-century narrative, knowledge often comes prior to experience, or in spite of it. Characters are not invited to travel as a way of extending or developing themselves, but more as a way to see in the universality of moral problems the advantages of staying home. Confinement, not travel, is more the prevailing figure for this form of psychic life when that life is measured by norms of constancy and changelessness.

It is worth noting in conclusion that the term *realism* has been appropriated by writers who, by the standard defined in this essay, are not realist writers. Alain Robbe-Grillet, for example, one of the most original novelists of the 20th century, writes books in which time does not pass or even seem to exist at all except as reading time, and in which character does not develop or even exist. Nevertheless, he can claim that because "reality" has changed, his novels are more "realistic" for a late 20th-century audience than, say, novels by Trollope or Tolstoi would be. And he has a point. In any case, the term *realism* should be carefully and clearly defined for local use so that it does not merely confuse any argument. Historically, "realism" belongs to a broad cultural agenda—manifested across a wide range of practices based on a grammar of perspective—whose epoch may have come to a close.

ELIZABETH DEEDS ERMARTH

See also Class and the Novel; Critics and Criticism (all sections); Description; English Novel (1840–80); French Novel (1800–50; 1850–1914); Genre Criticism; Historical Novel; Historical Writing and the Novel; Journalism and the Novel; Mimesis; Naturalism; Postmodernism; Prose Novelistic Forms; Romance; Space; Time in the Novel

Further Reading

Alberti, Leon Battista, *Della pittura*, Florence: Sansoni, 1950; as *On Painting*, New Haven, Connecticut: Yale University Press, and London: Routledge and Kegan Paul, 1956; revised edition, New Haven, Connecticut: Yale University Press, 1966

Alter, Robert, *Partial Magic: The Novel as a Self-Conscious Genre*, Berkeley: University of California Press, 1975

Armstrong, Nancy, *Desire and Domestic Fiction: A Political History of the Novel*, New York: Oxford University Press, 1987

Auerbach, Erich, *Dargestellte Wirklichkeit in der abendländlischen Literatur*, Bern: Francke, 1946; as *Mimesis: The Representation of Reality in Western Literature*, Princeton, New Jersey: Princeton University Press, 1953

Ermarth, Elizabeth Deeds, *Realism and Consensus in the English Novel*, Princeton, New Jersey: Princeton University Press, 1983; new edition, with subtitle *The Construction of Time in Narrative*, Edinburgh: Edinburgh University Press, 1998

Ermarth, Elizabeth Deeds, "The Crisis of Realism in Postmodern Time," in *Realism and Representation: Essays on the Problem of Realism in Relation to Science, Literature, and Culture*, edited by George Levine, Madison: University of Wisconsin Press, 1993

Ermarth, Elizabeth Deeds, *The English Novel in History, 1840–1895*, London and New York: Routledge, 1997

Ivins, William, Jr., *On the Rationalization of Sight; with an Examination of Three Renaissance Texts on Perspective*, New York: Metropolitan Museum of Art, 1938; reprinted, New York: Da Capo, 1973

Ivins, William, Jr., *Art and Geometry: A Study in Space Intuitions*, New York: Dover, 1946; reprinted 1964

Levine, George, *The Realistic Imagination: English Fiction from Frankenstein to Lady Chatterley*, Chicago: University of Chicago Press, 1981

Levine, George, editor, *Realism and Representation: Essays on the Problem of Realism in Relation to Science, Literature, and Culture*, Madison: University of Wisconsin Press, 1993

Lukács, Georg, *Wider den missverstandenen Realismus*, Hamburg: Claasen, 1958; as *The Meaning of Contemporary Realism*, London: Merlin Press, 1963; as *Realism in Our Time: Literature and the Class Struggle*, New York: Harper, 1964

MacCabe, Colin, "Realism and the Cinema: Notes on Some Brechtian Theses," in *Theoretical Essays: Film, Linguistics, Literature*, Manchester: Manchester University Press, 1985

Nochlin, Linda, editor, *Realism and Tradition in Art, 1848–1900: Sources and Documents*, Englewood Cliffs, New Jersey: Prentice-Hall, 1966

Panofsky, Erwin, *Early Netherlandish Painting: Its Origins and Character*, 2 vols., Cambridge, Massachusetts: Harvard University Press, 1953

Panofsky, Erwin, *Renaissance and Renascences in Western Art*, 2 vols., Stockholm: Almqvist and Wiksell, 1960; New York: Harper and Row, 1969; London: Paladin, 1970

Robbe-Grillet, Alain, *Pour un nouveau roman*, Paris: Editions de Minuit, 1963; as *For a New Novel: Essays on Fiction*, New York: Grove Press, 1965

Spender, Dale, "Women and Literary History," in *The Feminist Reader: Essays in Gender and the Politics of Literary Criticism*, edited by Catherine Belsey and Jane Moore, London: Macmillan, and New York: Blackwell, 1989; 2nd edition, 1997

Stern, J.P., *On Realism*, London and Boston: Routledge and Kegan Paul, 1973

Vargish, Thomas, *The Providential Aesthetic in Victorian Fiction*, Charlottesville: University Press of Virginia, 1985

Watt, Ian, *The Rise of the Novel: Studies in Defoe, Richardson, and Fielding*, Berkeley: University of California Press, and London: Chatto and Windus, 1957

Williams, Ioan, *The Realist Novel in England: A Study in Development*, London: Macmillan, 1974; Pittsburgh, Pennsylvania: University of Pittsburgh Press, 1975

The Red and the Black by Stendhal

Le Rouge et le noir 1830

As every reader of Stendhal soon recognizes, the world of his novels is organized around a set of oppositions: France and Italy, the 19th century and the Renaissance, passion and vanity, the red and the black. On the first level of his text, the "black" vanity of 19th-century France is rejected by the narrator who, like his heroes, longs for a past in which true, "red" passion was possible, which, in *The Red and the Black,* is the time of the Napoleonic wars—especially the Italian campaign.

A nostalgia for a past idealized as a period of naturalness, spontaneity, and immediacy of desire, and the rejection of the present which is marked, in opposition to that past, by a fall into mediation, imitation, and lack of authenticity—these two features may be considered the hallmarks of romanticism. In his influential study of the novel, *Mensonge romantique et vérité romanesque* (1961; *Deceit, Desire, and the Novel*), René Girard considers the belief in a natural, spontaneous, and unmediated desire to be the "romantic lie" (*mensonge romantique*), which the novel as a genre demystifies, thus constituting its own truth (*vérité romanesque*). According to this reading Stendhal's novel is divided not between passion and vanity but between a romantic nostalgia for the past and its novelistic demystification.

Vanity and mediated desire are presented in the novel as characteristic of the 19th century. Early in the novel M. de Rênal hires Julien as a tutor for his children. His decision is based not on Julien's intrinsic qualities but on Rênal's fear that M. Valenod, his rival in the city, may also be interested in hiring Julien. It is the mediation of Valenod that turns Julien from a carpenter's son who happens to know Latin into a tutor worth 400 francs a year. M. de Rênal is opposed to his wife, who is described as a natural person (she is repeatedly compared to the countryside where she resides), completely lacking not only in vanity but also in self-consciousness.

Julien himself is also different from M. de Rênal and his double/rival, M. Valenod, both of whom he despises. Unlike them, he longs for the Napoleonic past, which he sees as a period of freedom (the revolutionary army) when people acted spontaneously, out of enthusiasm for a cause, and were rewarded for their accomplishments, for what they themselves were. In his alienation from the present and his longing for a heroic past, Julien is similar to Mathilde. She too despises the men of the present (her brother and his noble friends) and longs for the time of her ancestor, Boniface de la Mole, who is characterized by his passion, courage, and daring.

But of course neither Julien nor Mathilde can belong to the past they idealize. Moreover, by imitating this past they show themselves as belonging to the age they despise, since that age is characterized precisely by the loss of spontaneity and its replacement by mediation and imitation. In other words, Julien's and Mathilde's imitation of the past—the sign of their not belonging in the present—shows them also to be cut off from the past they admire and long for. The narrator's irony exposes each character's blindness to his true predicament.

But the ironization of the hero's self-conception as different from and superior to his surroundings does not mean that Julien is like everybody else, only that his difference has to be under-

stood differently. Julien is repeatedly (and somewhat tautologically) described as exceptional by virtue of his ability to do the unexpected (*l'imprévu*). At the same time, however, Julien is also a simple memory machine: he can memorize everything and anything, from the New Testament to the classified ads in the *Constitutionel,* and hence can be (rather startlingly) a pious student of theology, an excellent humanist, a passionate lover, a faithful political agent. His unpredictability is not a sign of authenticity or spontaneity (his being "red") but rather of his complete emptiness, of his ability to be everything or anything. At the same time, his memorizing and reciting from memory are not signs of hypocrisy or "black" Tartuffery. Though it is true that his rise in the world to a large extent has to do with his memorizing texts (more or less explicitly described as meaningless to him or even as contradicting his deep convictions) and reproducing them in front of others, this memorization is somewhat haphazard, and the recitation meets with mixed results: Julien does not determine this operation or its effects but is rather determined by it. His memorizing (as well as his reciting from memory) is an almost automatic action; he does not choose to memorize certain texts with the goal of using them in particular circumstances for his advancement. Indeed, he does not have a clear idea whether what he memorizes is useful or in what circumstances it may be useful. What he memorizes becomes useful—and thus acquires meaning—on a future occasion that is unknown at the moment of memorizing.

Thus both red passion and black hypocrisy are shown to be illusory, predicated as they are on the myth of an autonomous, "instrumental," subject. The mediation that Stendhal represents through the figure of Julien does not have to do with a volitional imitation (by a self of another) but rather with the power texts (or, more generally, language) hold over our lives. This power does not come from the truth or knowledge we gain from texts, their ability to "educate" us, but rather from their social circulation, of which we are the more or less unconscious agents (texts are appropriated and repeated without being believed in, without even being fully understood; it is their circulation that endows them with meaning). The exemplary self Stendhal represents is a subject without "self," without interiority, made entirely of surfaces (hence "beautiful," or, to use the language of *The Charterhouse of Parma,* "adorable"); it is an empty subject that lends itself to the circulation of various discourses whose incalculable effects make him appear unpredictable, mysterious, unconventional—superior.

Written around the same time as Honoré de Balzac's *Le père goriot* (1835; *Le Père Goriot*) and *Illusions perdues* (1837–43; *Lost Illusions*), *The Red and the Black* seems, at first, to be best understood as belonging to the tradition of the Bildungsroman. Like a Bildungsroman, it features a young hero who is about to enter the social world and whose story of "socialization" the novel recounts. Julien's shooting of Mme de Rênal and his speech in court may be then interpreted as a rejection of his social education: reuniting with Mme de Rênal in prison, Julien would be seen as choosing the innocence of childhood over the mature knowledge that had enabled him to become a husband, a father, and a member of the upper class. But reading the novel in this way requires attributing to Julien a knowledge that he never really gains. Julien, in fact, comes closer to the hero of an older genre—the picaresque—who travels along the road and has a number of adventures along the way, but whose journey does not represent a progress since it has no specific goal and therefore no closure. The peculiarity of *The Red and the Black* may thus reside in its generic ambiguity: like its hero, it does not fully belong in either the 19th century (whose "symbolic form" is the Bildungsroman) or in an earlier, and supposedly simpler, past.

MICHAL PELED GINSBURG

See also Stendhal

Further Reading

Auerbach, Erich, *Mimesis: Dargestellte Wirklichkeit in der abendländischen Literatur,* Bern: Francke, 1946; as *Mimesis: The Representation of Reality in Western Literature,* Princeton, New Jersey: Princeton University Press, 1953

Brodsky Lacour, Claudia, *The Imposition of Form: Studies in Narrative Representation and Knowledge,* Princeton, New Jersey: Princeton University Press, 1987

Brombert, Victor, *Stendhal et la voie oblique: L'auteur devant son monde romanesque,* New Haven, Connecticut: Yale University Press, and Paris: Presses Universitaires de France, 1954

Brooks, Peter, *Reading for the Plot: Design and Intention in Narrative,* New York: Knopf, and Oxford: Clarendon Press, 1984

Girard, René, *Mensonge romantique et vérité romanesque,* Paris: Grasset, 1961; as *Deceit, Desire, and the Novel,* Baltimore: Johns Hopkins University Press, 1965

Hemmings, F.W.J., *Stendhal: A Study of His Novels,* Oxford: Clarendon Press, 1964

Miller, D.A., *Narrative and Its Discontents: Problems of Closure in the Traditional Novel,* Princeton, New Jersey: Princeton University Press, 1981

Moretti, Franco, *The Way of the World: The Bildungsroman in European Culture,* London: Verso, 1987

Regard du roi. *See* Radiance of the King

La Regenta by Clarín [Leopoldo Alas]

1884

If there is an author who has definitively stated his ideas about the literature of his time and his own conception of the ideal novel, it is Leopoldo Alas, who is better known by his pseudonym, Clarín. A highly respected, as well as feared, literary critic during most of his writing career, Clarín left a wealth of testimonies and opinions on the literary currents and production of his time. He also left no doubt about his intentions when writing his masterpiece, *La Regenta*. In one of his letters to Benito Pérez Galdós, whom he admired more than any other writer in the world, he candidly pointed out that "I write first of all because I want to, then to see if I can please a handful of people, especially Galdós and Pereda, and most particularly Galdós" (*Cartas a Galdós* [1964; Letters to Galdós]).

La Regenta shows similarities with previous novels and in fact may in some ways have been inspired by such works as Gustave Flaubert's *Madame Bovary* (1857), Émile Zola's *La Conquête de Plassans* (1874; *The Conquest of Plassans*), and Eça de Queiros' *O primo Basilio* (1878; *Cousin Bazilio*). But that does not mean that Clarín took those novels as models for his own. The only model he consciously sought to emulate was that of Pérez

Galdós, especially after the latter's turn toward the Spanish version of naturalism with *La desheredada* (1881; *The Disinherited Lady*). The critique Clarín wrote about this novel was as much an attempt to define Spanish naturalism as a more intense form of realism as was Emilia Pardo Bazán's *La cuestión palpitante* (1883; The Burning Question). It was no coincidence that Clarín wrote a prologue to this series of articles about realism and naturalism, since both he and Pardo Bazán were of the opinion that inspiration for a novel must come primarily from reality, considered from a physical and psychological perspective. In his prologue, he points out the difference between his interpretation of naturalism and Zola's. Unlike the French author, Clarín does not consider naturalism to be an unflinching description of all things, including the ugly or repulsive, nor does he think of it as the scientific exploration of biological and social causation.

It is in the balance between realism and naturalism, conceived in Spanish terms, that *La Regenta* is far superior to any other Spanish novel of the 19th century, perhaps with the exception of Pérez Galdós' masterpiece *Fortunata y Jacinta* (1886–87; *Fortunata and Jacinta*). Its depiction of the stifling atmosphere of a typical 19th-century provincial town and its detailed description of an amazing variety of characters is pervaded by a deep sense of religion, philosophy, and irony. Pérez Galdós himself wrote in his prologue to the second edition of *La Regenta* that the novel was a beautiful example of naturalism restored to its original meaning, "to adjust fiction to the reality of nature and the soul, representing things and persons, characters and places as God made them." In his praise of the novel's broad spectrum of characters, representation of reality, and the humor with which all this is presented, he states that "I have read very few works whose profound interest, realistic characters and vivid language have made me forget so much as this one the limits of dimensions, and I finished reading it with the sadness of not having another volume of it to read with the same kind of events and the reappearance or reincarnation of the same characters."

The focus of the novel is on Ana Ozores, a woman who stands out for her sincerity. Unlike the deeply cynical or thoughtlessly amoral people around her, Ana wishes to be good and true. But her inclinations toward an ecstatic mysticism, considered unseemly, are strongly discouraged. When it is discovered that she writes poetry, she is punished for fear that she might turn into a blue-stocking. Denied a meaningful education, Ana cannot focus her energies on intellectual pursuits either. Without a meaningful occupation, Ana is left vulnerable to her longing for romantic and sexual fulfillment and eventually succumbs to temptation.

The language is vivid because the deftly portrayed characters speak for themselves, in dialogue or through free indirect discourse. The story is open-ended, leaving the reader in the middle of an ongoing situation with infinite possibilities for its continuation. These two characteristics make *La Regenta* into one of the remarkable achievements of 19th-century realism.

La Regenta was generally well received by Clarín's contemporaries, earning high praise particularly from Pérez Galdós. However, the novel was criticized on account of its frank portrayal of an adulterous relationship. A few critics accused Clarín of plagiarizing *Madame Bovary*. The appreciation of *La Regenta* and Clarín among today's writers and critics is manifest in the many editions of the novel available and the great number of homages, critical studies, and conferences dedicated to the author and his work. According to Mario Vargas Llosa, "*La Regenta* is the best 19th-century novel of Spain."

ALMA AMELL

See also Clarín

Further Reading

Brent, Albert, *Leopoldo Alas and "La Regenta": A Study in Nineteenth-Century Spanish Prose Fiction,* Columbia: Curators of the University of Missouri, 1951
Durand, Frank, "Characterization in *La Regenta*: Point of View and Theme," *Bulletin of Hispanic Studies* 41 (1964)
Rutherford, John, *Leopoldo Alas: "La Regenta,"* London: Grant and Cutler, 1974
Sieburth, Stephanie A., *Reading "La Regenta,"* Amsterdam and Philadelphia: Benjamins, 1990
Sobejano, Gonzalo, prologue to *La Regenta*, by Leopoldo Alas, Madrid: Castalia, 1984
Valis, Noël Maureen, *The Decadent Vision in Leopoldo Alas: A Study of "La Regenta" and "Su único hijo,"* Baton Rouge: Louisiana State University Press, 1981

Regional Novel

Generic Traits and the Development of the Regional Novel in Britain

This first section on the regional novel attempts a loose definition of the subgenre as a whole, summarizes the subject matter and corresponding dominant formal elements associated with regionalism in fiction, and traces the origins and sources of the regional novel with brief reference to its development in Britain. The entry following this one will consider regionalism in the US novel.

The regional novel represents a particular social and cultural world, usually in relation to a particular topography. Setting, therefore, becomes especially important in regional fiction, as do closely related formal elements such as description, characterization, and dialogue. A particular regional setting does not in itself necessarily mark a novel as "regional," however; this setting should be emphatically distinctive, manifestly central to the novel's purpose, and determinative of its formal construction, rather than just informative or an aspect of its formal realism.

Conventionally, the region as represented in regional novels and other genres (e.g., drama, narrative poetry) refers to a more or less extended geographical area having a complex yet distinctive topographical character with associated social, economic, cultural, and political life and institutions, which are shown or implied to have grown out of the landscape and its economy. Conventionally, too, the region is predominantly rural and agrarian, rather than urban and industrial, and consequently many regional novels have been discussed as "pastoral" novels, in a long tradition of representations of more or less idealized rural life. Nevertheless, a city or town may also be represented as a region, and urban novels are sometimes considered a particular type of the regional novel.

Many regional novels represent social life at some distance from a national or imperial center. Accordingly, many regional novels are also referred to as novels of provincial life, although usually the region is explicitly or implicitly presented as part of a larger natural and social world, especially the nation, nation-state, or empire. In this aspect, regional novels often emphasize community as interrelated social, cultural, and economic relationships at the local level. The community of a regional novel often has a particular relationship to the wider nation and empire, often some kind of conflict, resolved or superseded through the plot: the community may have lessons in social relations and cohesion for the wider nation and empire; or the community may be represented, implicitly or explicitly, as a microcosm of the wider nation and empire.

Authors of regional novels frequently address contemporary social, economic, and political issues, often as a means of suggesting a tension between "progress" and nostalgia for a supposedly simpler and more authentic way of life. Accordingly, many regional novels are also historical novels that confront, directly or indirectly, issues of difference between a region's past and present. To resolve such differences, regional novels often represent regional character and life, for all its distinctiveness, as essentially, typically, or even archetypically human and social. These tendencies of the regional novel reveal its origins in particular ideas, concerns, and forms of writing in Western Europe of the late 18th and early 19th century.

Works of narrative fiction in prose and verse have had more or less identifiable geographical and topographical settings ever since ancient times, but the distinctively regional novel was founded on two major ideas of Enlightenment materialist philosophy: first, that each society and culture is shaped by the character of its natural environment, including its distinctive economy; second, that each individual's character is shaped, for better or worse, by his or her natural and social environment. Motivating these interests in the regional novel and related kinds of literature was a movement that historians call modernization. This was the supplanting of an older economic and social order, based on customary relations of mutual responsibility within a hierarchical society, by a new order, based on capitalism and a wage economy. A broad and complex array of social, economic, cultural, and political changes accompanied, facilitated, or followed the process of modernization, which proceeded unevenly in various parts of Europe and its empires or former empires. The regional novel drew on several forms of writing that promoted modernization, including a type of travel writing, topographical surveys of economic, social, and cultural resources, local and regional scientific research and antiquarian studies, and linguistic studies and the formation of standard written "national" languages (which turned other forms of a language into dialects).

New ideas and anxieties about national identity, unity, history, culture, and destiny directly affected the formation of the regional novel. These ideas and anxieties developed during the revolutions of the late 18th and early 19th century in America, France, and elsewhere. During this period, civil wars broke out, centuries-old regimes were overthrown, and new ideas of nationhood were advanced based on "the people" rather than a royal dynasty. Examples of these incidents include the revolt against the revolutionary government by people of the Vendée in western France, the Irish uprising of 1798 against British rule, the various revolts against foreign rule or local puppet governments in Spain and Italy during the Napoleonic period and after, and the various revolts in South and Central America against the Spanish imperial government that eventually led to the establishment of new independent states. After the fall of Napoléon (1815) and the restoration of monarchic regimes and imperial control in many places, the chronic instability of such regimes,

as well as the new social tensions that resulted from such economic and social change, kept anxieties about national solidarity alive well into the 20th century. The ideology of a national identity based on a combination of language, culture, or religion produced aspirations for independence in many regions—aspirations the regional novel could stimulate and sustain. Over the past two centuries the regional novel has continued to serve such aspirations and purposes in many parts of the world.

In Britain, the regional novel developed to address the differences and conflicts among regions of England that have existed at least since Anglo-Saxon times. For example, differences have persisted between England proper and Wales ever since the latter became a principality of the English crown during the Middle Ages. The English and Scottish crowns were united in 1603, and England and Scotland were united constitutionally in 1707 to create Great Britain, yet differences and tensions have persisted in that relationship, too, occasionally erupting into armed conflict and open rebellion by Scots. Ireland has been a kingdom of the English monarchy since the Middle Ages, though its acute linguistic, cultural, religious, political, and economic differences with England have caused chronic violence and occasional widespread armed conflict, as when the Catholic Irish supported the monarchy against parliament in the English Civil War, and in the Catholic Stuart dynasty's opposition to the Protestant House of Orange during the 17th century. The parliaments of Great Britain and Ireland were united in 1800 to create the United Kingdom of Great Britain and Ireland, partly in response to the bloody Irish Rebellion in 1798.

The regional novel in Britain and elsewhere emerged during the period of the French Revolution and the Napoleonic wars. The debate on the French Revolution, with its interest in revolutionary claims to a universal social identity, set against the supposed uniqueness of national social cultures and their accompanying political orders and constitutions, gave new significance to Enlightenment ideas about the relationship between social cultures and their natural environments, and to resulting differences in what was then called "national character" but which would nowadays be called ethnic differences. There had long been tales supposedly representing or illustrating, sympathetically or otherwise, various ethnic traits, or what would now be considered stereotypes, but this kind of tale was recontextualized and its elements appropriated to more complex and extended descriptions of region in various novels written during the Napoleonic period, which was characterized by global conflict of states and empires, so-called "citizen-armies" (at least on the French side) apparently motivated by patriotic nationalism, and campaigns of French imperialism conducted in the name of universal liberty.

In some places, such as Italy, French conquest created a sense of national identity linked to reform and a rejection of monarchic rule, especially by foreign monarchic states. In Germany and Spain, resistance to Napoleonic imperialism formed around a largely invented national identity to unite disparate social and regional interests in a common cause. After the fall of Napoléon, these identities came under repeated stress, for various reasons, especially uneven economic development in different regions and countries, commercial and territorial competition between empires, and clashes of religion, ethnic and racial identity, and class. Although the circumstances behind the regional novel's first appearance have changed, issues of national difference and unity remain important to many writers today whose fiction might be described as regional.

In keeping, then, with the tensions manifested in the regional novel between imperial center and distant margins, the first regions to be represented in regional and regional-historical fiction in Britain were on the margins of the United Kingdom, namely Ireland and Scotland, where modernization was incomplete, unevenly distributed, and lagging behind much of England. The first clearly regional novel in Britain, Maria Edgeworth's *Castle Rackrent* (1800), was written by the daughter of a member of the dominant Anglo-Irish landowning class. Published just after the Irish rebellion of 1798 (an uprising that was inspired partly by the French Revolution and assisted futilely by a French invasion), Edgeworth's novel openly promoted the union of Britain and Ireland as a way of removing the economic, political, and cultural differences that seemed to have led to the rebellion. Although Edgeworth wrote other novels set in the cosmopolitan and supposedly "central" world of upper- and middle-class southern English society, she also produced further "Irish tales" (e.g., *The Absentee*, 1812). The success of these works with the reading public, and the way they addressed anxieties about the capacity of modernization to create a common national interest, let alone a common identity, inspired other writers who developed the form in various ways over the next couple of decades.

It is significant, however, that Edgeworth's narrative method changed (with one exception) in the "Irish Tales" published after *Castle Rackrent*. *Castle Rackrent* is based formally on the earlier and long-established short fiction form known as the conte, which foregrounds the story's narrator. Accordingly, Edgeworth's story is narrated by an Irish domestic servant, in a watered-down written version of Irish speech, and illustrates the ideological and cultural dependence of the Irish folk on a decadent upper class, both classes appearing as obstacles to the modernization of the Irish economy and society. To ensure readers got her message, Edgeworth went beyond the conte to frame her story within a complex and authoritative, yet partly ironic, "editorial" apparatus. The reading public seemed charmed rather than alarmed by the Irish "voice" and its attitudes, however, and henceforth Edgeworth used what would become the more common narrative method of regional and historical novels: third-person omniscient narration, in the then recently established standardized written English, containing dialogue in written versions of vernacular and dialect speech. Thus the regional, as a form of language, was clearly distinguished from, and subordinated to, the "standard," "normal," and presumably "national" dialect that was in fact cultural property of the educated, and mainly professional, urban (indeed metropolitan), middle-class reading public. The regional-historical novel, as devised by Edgeworth and developed by Walter Scott, and a host of other writers around the world, represents in its linguistic structure an implied cultural and social hierarchy and diversity-in-unity.

Scottish writers were among the first to follow Edgeworth's lead. An early imitator was Elizabeth Hamilton in her *The Cottagers of Glenburnie* (1808), a book about a retired Scottish female servant who single-handedly modernizes the village of Glenburnie. This heavily didactic tale became the literary fad of its season and charmed readers as a piece of quaint, rustic realism rather than serve as a blueprint for modernization at the local level and, by extension, of the region and nation as a whole. Walter Scott, considered the first major historical novelist, made arguably his most original contribution to the form of the novel in his treatment of Scotland as a geographical, cultural, economic, and political unit, roughly divided into the Highland and Lowland regions. Scott acknowledged Edgeworth's "Irish Tales" as his model. Other Scottish writers, such as John Galt and James Hogg, quickly responded to Edgeworth's, Hamilton's, and Scott's representations.

Later in the 19th century, the Scottish regional novel was taken up by the so-called Kailyard School, a group of writers who depicted rural Scottish life. Very broadly, the historical plot underlying these regional and historical novels, as it had been for Edgeworth, involved the benefits and costs of modernization. The intended readership for some of these novels was English—certainly for Edgeworth and for Scott—although Hamilton, Galt, and Hogg seem to address a Scottish readership. The Kailyard School was partly Scots nationalist in motivation; thus the first regional novels of the romantic era were largely addressed from a regional margin to a "national" and imperial center. In other novelists, the address became more regional.

Novelists were slower to subject England itself to fictional regionalization. Jane Austen's novels, published in the 1810s, are often taken to represent a southern England of the so-called "home counties" (shires around London) and immediately beyond. This does not seem to have been her main intention, however, and her reputation for such regionalism developed after her death—partly inspired by Mary Mitford's *Our Village* (1824–32), which claims Austen as an antecedent.

Through the 19th and into the 20th century, other writers represented other regions of England in novels of provincial life. George Eliot wrote about the towns and countryside of the Midlands of England where she herself grew up—"Middlemarch," according to the title of her best known work. She also strongly developed the Victorian novel's device of interwoven, parallel stories rendering a complex representation of regional life. The Brontë sisters represented rural and partly industrialized life in their native Yorkshire, focusing more intensely on personal and familial relationships and conflicts. Anthony Trollope is now known principally for his representation of provincial life in the fictitious region of "Barsetshire"—roughly Wiltshire and Somersetshire. R.D. Blackmore and Sabine Baring-Gould wrote several popular regional-historical novels of the West Country, or southwest counties of England. Thomas Hardy represented rural life in fictitious Wessex, roughly corresponding to the historic Anglo-Saxon kingdom of Wessex, present-day Dorset, Devonshire, and Wiltshire. Hardy in his regional novels invoked the late Victorian sense of a regional prehistory, and an almost mythic folk memory and culture, to give his tales the grandeur of classical tragedy. In novels such as *The Rainbow* (1915), D.H. Lawrence continued this practice.

The 20th century has witnessed a proliferation of regional novels of a more popular, often best-selling, variety. Examples include Winnifred Holtby's depiction of Yorkshire, Mary Webb's of Shropshire, Mary Butts' and the Powys brothers' (John Cowper, Theodore, and Llewellyn) treatment of Dorset, Sheila Kaye-Smith's of Sussex, and Richard Llewellyn and Alexander Cordell's depiction of Wales. Arnold Bennett and Francis Brett-Young have depicted Midlands life, Hugh Walpole the Lake District, and Catherine Cookson—perhaps the best-selling regional novelist of the 20th century—the South Tyneside region.

The major theme of English (as distinct from Irish and

Scottish) regional novels has been the authenticity and "realism" of provincial and regional life set against the corrupt and corrupting centers of urban life especially, and increasingly in industrial towns. However, because the urban novel can also be considered a form of regional novel, there is another important strain of the regional novel to be traced, perhaps beginning from Pierce Egan's best-selling picaresque novel *Life in London* (1821). In this novel, Egan divides London into at least two regions: the fashionable West End and the unfashionable yet lively, energetic "City" and East End, characterized by its working-class underworld of urban "folk." This regionally divided London was also represented in the popular Silver Fork Novels (novels of fashionable society) and Newgate Novels (named after a major London prison) of the later 1820s and 1830s. These regional characterizations, in turn, were taken up by Charles Dickens, who created a popular image of "Dickensian" London that, like Austen's supposed rural England, still has selling power in the tourist and heritage industries, and evidenced further by the continued film and television adaptations of Dickens' and Austen's novels. Sir Walter Besant also wrote a series of socially crusading novels depicting the harshness of working-class life in the East End of London. In the 20th century, the novel of the "provincial" town or city, especially in economic decline, eventually overlapped with what is called the industrial novel, as in Alan Sillitoe's work, or Henry Green's *Living* (1929).

A parallel outline of the regional novel could likely be written for any country whose crisis of national identity was or is addressed by the novel. In the 19th-century French novel, the provinces are often set against Paris in terms that mark a passage from rural authenticity to urban corruption—a geographical move that mirrors the character's movement from innocence to experience. The regional novel of Britain exemplifies many of the possible developments of this subgenre, and the form as it developed in Britain did have an important influence on its development elsewhere. Despite common conditions of origin and development, the regional novel, by its nature, must always be considered in relation to the peculiarities of its individual instances.

Gary Kelly

See also City and the Novel; English Novel (1800–40); National Tale; Pastoralism in the Novel

Further Reading

Anderson, Benedict, *Imagined Communities: Reflections on the Origin and Spread of Nationalism,* London: Verso, 1983; 2nd edition, London and New York: Verso, 1991

Collins, Laura Roberts, *English Country Life in the Barsetshire Novels of Angela Thirkell,* Westport, Connecticut: Greenwood Press, 1994

Edwards, Peter David, *Idyllic Realism from Mary Russell Mitford to Hardy,* New York: St. Martin's Press, and London: Macmillan, 1988

Hunter, Shelagh, *Victorian Idyllic Fiction: Pastoral Strategies,* Atlantic Highlands, New Jersey: Humanities Press, and London: Macmillan, 1984

Keith, W.J., *Regions of the Imagination: The Development of British Rural Fiction,* Toronto and Buffalo, New York: University of Toronto Press, 1988

Newman, Gerald, *The Rise of English Nationalism: A Cultural History, 1740–1830,* New York: St. Martin's Press, and London: Weidenfeld and Nicolson, 1987; revised edition, New York: St. Martin's Press, 1997

Squires, Michael, *The Pastoral Novel: Studies in George Eliot, Thomas Hardy, and D.H. Lawrence,* Charlottesville: University Press of Virginia, 1974

Williams, Raymond, *The Country and the City,* New York: Oxford University Press, and London: Chatto and Windus, 1973

Regional Novel

Regionalism in the US Novel

What critics today refer to as the American regional novel was not, as is often the case, the product of a conscious literary movement or the philosophical or aesthetic aspirations of a particular group of authors. Regional fiction first appeared shortly before the start of the US Civil War and reached its height of popularity between 1875 and 1910, although contemporary regional authors continue to publish. Critics and readers alike often have difficulty distinguishing between regionalism, realism, and local color, and with good reason. Like most labels, these three are often applied arbitrarily, and in many cases their use can obscure as much information as it reveals. The question of what constitutes regional, as opposed to universal, literature is as old as Western culture, dating at least to Horace's decision in the first century B.C. to write not about Greece, as was the fashion of the time, but about his native Rome. The question is as open to debate in the works of contemporary writers such as Maxine Hong Kingston's *The Woman Warrior* (1976) or Dorothy Allison's *Bastard Out of Carolina* (1992) as it was in Horace's time.

Regionalism emerged from a number of economic, social, and literary trends, as well as from the diverse geographic and ethnic composition of the United States. Prior to the Civil War, and in some locales for many years thereafter, most Americans viewed themselves as citizens of their respective states and regions first, and as citizens of the United States second. How dearly citizens held these regional differences is reflected in the bloodiness and bitterness of the Civil War and its aftermath. In addition to these ideological differences, regional identity was heightened by slow and difficult transportation and communication systems. Before the completion of the transcontinental railroad in the 1870s, a trip from New York to London was both quicker and safer than either a land or sea journey from New York to San Francisco. Economic and publishing interests were equally regional in scope. Because large corporations and the national distribution of books and magazines did not become common until late in the 19th century, strong regional cultures were fostered at the expense of a national one. After the Civil War, many social and literary critics saw the need for a more unified American culture and literature. At the same time, the necessary tools to begin to unify such a large and diverse nation came into being: most importantly the railroad, the telegraph, and the steam press. The first two made rapid and efficient transportation and communication possible for the first time, while the latter allowed for the production of large quantities of inexpensive printed materials. Ironically, this push for nationalization in large part fostered the growth and popularity of regional literature, because appreciation for regional differences grew as the differences themselves began to be engulfed by an emerging, homogeneous national culture.

William Dean Howells, perhaps the most influential editor and literary critic of the last half of the 19th century, edited the *Atlantic Monthly* in Boston from the 1860s to the 1870s. His move in the 1880s to New York and *Harper's Monthly* signaled the shift of the seat of the literary establishment from Boston to New York. Howells' criticism, commentaries, and reviews in these two journals set the tone for American literature for the 35 years at the end of the 19th century. In both his criticism and in his own novels, such as *The Rise of Silas Lapham* (1885), Howells advocated literary realism, a movement out of which regionalism in the US developed. Howells' vision of realism called for authors to focus their works on familiar locales and characters—to be true to the surface realities of American life. It focused on authentic American speech rather than a more literary language, and it often shifted the narrative point of view from an omniscient narrator to the first-person voice of an individual character. Realist fiction is also characterized by its nonjudgmental narrative position toward issues of ethics and morality. Rather than the author or the narrator passing judgment on characters' actions, the characters and readers of realist fiction are left to assess such issues for themselves. This narrative stance caused many works, such as Kate Chopin's *The Awakening* (1899), to receive scathingly hostile critical reviews. Howells provided an important forum for works of realism and for some of the more established regionalists, such as Mark Twain, as well. A more important outlet for emerging regional fiction, especially works with a populist political slant, was the journal *Arena,* founded in 1889 by William Orange Flower. The *Arena* published works by writers such as Hamlin Garland, author of *Main-Traveled Roads* (1891), along with reviews of many other regionalist authors.

Regional fiction in the US may be defined on one level as anything focused outside of Boston or New York and the interests of the literary establishment based there. More than one critic has observed that William Faulkner, author of many novels set in the American South, ceased to be a regional writer the day he was awarded the Nobel prize for literature. More recently, a New York publisher dismissed Norman Maclean's *A River Runs Through It* (1976) with the comment that "this story has too many trees in it." Regionalism has, in fact, been largely the domain of those marginalized by mainstream culture and its institutions: women, people of color, recent immigrants, and residents of rural areas. Regional fiction is not only closely focused on its geographic setting, but that setting is invariably rural, and often a rural area in decline or undergoing unwelcome modernization. This attachment to a specific, rural place and culture is one of the defining characteristics of regionalism, and place and culture inevitably play a major role in these works.

A second, related characteristic of regionalism is its careful attention to regional and cultural differences in the presentation of dialogue and narrative voice. The earliest example of this realistic presentation of regional dialect is seen in Mark Twain's record of the speech patterns of a ten-year-old African-American. Published in 1874, "Sociable Jimmy" presents a regional dialect that is remarkably similar to the speech patterns given to the protagonist of his novel *The Adventures of Huckleberry Finn* (1884). Kate Chopin's fiction is also characterized by the accurate and detailed portrayal of speech patterns and social customs, specifically those of the Creole and Acadian characters who populate her tales of New Orleans and the Cane River country of Louisiana. The New England Yankees of Sarah Orne Jewett's *The Country of the Pointed Firs* (1896) are every bit as terse as their real life counterparts—reserved to the point that they cannot even articulate their experiences. Jewett presents characters who are not able to communicate effectively in words; their actions must literally speak for them, reflecting a New England cultural ideal. Alice Walker's *The Color Purple* (1982) may be written in the style of an 18th-century epistolary novel, but her characters speak the language of rural African-Americans of the early 20th century.

This emphasis on place, culture, and dialect is especially characteristic of local color, which is perhaps best viewed as a subgenre of regionalism. If regionalism is characterized by its marginalization from the power structure of mainstream culture, then local color is best distinguished by its optimistic point of view. At the same time that Howells and much of the US literary establishment were calling for a more realistic portrayal of life in literature, Howells also argued that US literature should present "the large cheerful average of health and success and happy life." Local color fiction is characterized by its unwavering focus on humor and the bright side of life, often at the expense of harsher social realities. For example, Joel Chandler Harris is most noted for his collection *Uncle Remus: His Songs and His Sayings* (1880), a well-known collection of African-American folk tales. While this collection provided a great service in preserving African-American vernacular speech and folklore, it has been justly criticized for presenting a false image of happy, contented slaves and gentle, understanding masters. Yet to his credit, Harris' *Free Joe and Other Georgian Sketches* (1887) presents a sympathetic and far more accurate portrayal of the plight of even "free" African-Americans prior to the Civil War. Harris seems to have been well aware of the harsh realities facing African-Americans in the rural South, but he was evidently blinded by his love of the language and culture of his characters. His optimistic tales may also have been to some extent driven by the market for literature that existed in the late 19th-century United States.

By the late 19th century, largely owing to the influence of Howells as a publisher and critic, a booming market had evolved for local color fiction of the most optimistic and least controversial sort. Works such as George Washington Cable's *The Cavalier* (1901) are today criticized for being excessively genteel. At the time, these works were considered more on the order of light entertainment, especially suitable for women, as opposed to the "serious" literature written by the likes of Henry James, or Howells himself. This perception on the part of publishers and critics allowed women authors an unprecedented opportunity to publish their work. This opportunity arose despite a lingering prejudice that had been articulated decades earlier in Nathaniel Hawthorne's railings against "those damned scribbling women," whom he viewed as inferior competitors. Yet these same "scribbling women" were more successful commercially than Hawthorne and many of the other literati. Grace King's work presents what is perhaps the best example of the sort of local color fiction that was especially popular at the end of the 19th century. King's *Monsieur Motte,* published in 1888, is the story of an African-American slave's devotion to her young white mistress, explicitly intended to promote the Southern view of so-called "good darkies" and white patrician noblesse oblige. King began the novel in response to Cable's treatment of the repression of African-Americans in New Orleans, which had been sympathetic to their plight. King's works portray a romanticized, antebellum South that never existed in the first place, transplanted into the post-Reconstruction era. She was unabashedly patrician in both her life and her novels. Despite providing interesting glimpses of Southern society and dialect, King's work presents a narrow and unrealistic, almost naive, view of her world. Yet such a view was very much in demand by both publishers and the reading public at the turn of the century.

Perhaps the greatest contribution of writers such as Cable and King is that their vision of local color opened the doors of publishers for writers who were more challenging stylistically. Kate Chopin was considered by her contemporaries to be a local colorist, and her work is still compared with that of Cable and King. Yet Chopin herself despised both the label and the comparison. While some of her short fiction might rightly be termed local color, Chopin's best work lacks both the optimism and the romanticism that characterize the subgenre. Chopin's novel *The Awakening,* along with portions of her short fiction, deals openly and nonjudgmentally with controversial themes such as female sexuality, adultery, women's place in society, and suicide. As she began to deal more openly with such themes, the critical response to her work became markedly more hostile. Chopin did not even attempt to publish one of her finest and most critically acclaimed stories, "The Storm," because she was aware that its frank and explicit (for its time) treatment of sexual passion would never be accepted by a contemporary audience. Yet Chopin was not the only author for whom the demand for local color opened the door to far more serious topics than the genteel editors of the day might have imagined. Mary E. Wilkins Freeman's *Pembroke,* published in 1894, presents a vivid account of a patriarch's default on the assumed domestic contract of the time. He nearly allows his family to starve as the women work away at domestic chores. Freeman frames this more universal social critique in the people, places, and language of rural New England. Like Chopin, she offers the reader an opportunity to focus on either her serious themes, or on the quaint setting and characters of her stories.

Arguably, the South has made the largest contribution to regional literature in the US, in part because of the strong regional identity that still exists in the American South. This sense of regional identity is a troubled one, however, as its roots lie in a legacy of slavery and oppression. Writers from both the North and the South have tended to romanticize the antebellum period, offering characters such as Margaret Mitchell's Scarlett O'Hara and Rhett Butler who live on as the prototypical, misunderstood, and on some level lovable Southerners. The inherently evil source of these characterizations, and the culture that produced them, is slavery, but this fact is often discounted in favor of more palatable versions of historical fact. Contemporary Southern literature draws heavily on the stereotypical "redneck" figure, who swills beer, drives a pickup truck, has a long-suffering, often abused wife, and has many children by an equal number of women. Although most regions of the United States have their stock characters, such as the lumberjack of the Pacific Northwest and Alaska, and the working class of Cannery Row portrayed in John Steinbeck's fiction, the prototypes of the South are the most well known and enduring. Often, contemporary Southern regionalism is told from the point of view of the "trash," the descendants of the "crackers" of antebellum Southern society, although even in these stories, which often feature incest, violence, alcoholism, and abuse, the roles of the characters are often romanticized, despite their realistic portrayal. Dorothy Allison's *Bastard Out of Carolina* exemplifies these stock characters, and although Allison's protagonist ultimately gets the best of her abusers, she is patently Southern, and does not show any inclination to change or be embarrassed by her Southernness. The underlying message is that the Southerner's lot in life may be bad, but life as a "damned Yankee" would surely be worse. Perhaps the attraction of regional fiction, in part, is the voyeuristic vision that it offers of someone who is worse off than the reader.

As the nation and the national literature and culture of America became more homogenized during the 20th century, regional fiction grew in popularity for many of the same reasons that it became popular in the first place. As a national identity became more firmly entrenched, these regional figures became more attractive to readers because they offered a believable but nonthreatening means of escape from a sense of sameness inherent in modern society.

DAVID J. CAUDLE AND SUZANNE D. GREEN

Further Reading

Campbell, Donna M., *Resisting Regionalism: Gender and Naturalism in American Fiction, 1885–1915,* Athens: Ohio University Press, 1997

Elliott, Emory, editor, *The Columbia Literary History of the United States,* New York: Columbia University Press, 1988

Elliott, Emory, editor, *The Columbia History of the American Novel,* New York: Columbia University Press, 1991

Holman, David Marion, *A Certain Slant of Light: Regionalism and the Form of Southern and Midwestern Fiction,* Baton Rouge: Louisiana State University Press, 1995

Jones, Anne Goodwyn, *Tomorrow Is Another Day: The*

Woman Writer in the South, 1859–1936, Baton Rouge: Louisiana State University Press, 1981

Jordan, David, *New World Regionalism: Literature in the Americas,* Toronto and Buffalo, New York: University of Toronto Press, 1994

Rubin, Louis D., Jr., editor, *The History of Southern Literature,* Baton Rouge: Louisiana State University Press, 1985

Stephens, Robert O., *The Family Saga in the South: Generations and Destinies,* Baton Rouge: Louisiana State University Press, 1995

Remembrance of Things Past. *See* In Search of Lost Time

Renaissance Narrative

The question of the relationship of the modern novel to earlier narrative forms, still controversial, is central to our understanding of the genre. Ian Watt, in *The Rise of the Novel* (1957), argued that the proliferation of prose narratives in late 17th- and early 18th-century England was a direct result of the development of capitalism and that these literary forms signaled a complete break with earlier models of imaginative writing. The spread of capitalism led to the concomitant development of the individual as the conceptual center of social reality, all knowledge being mediated through an understanding of the self, as Descartes argued in his famous "cogito ergo sum." Also crucial, according to Watt, were the spread of literacy and the growth of a reading public, more democratic forms of political expression, and, most importantly, the demands of a political economy that required continual innovation. In Watt's account, the first real novel was *Robinson Crusoe* (1719), tellingly written in England, the first major capitalist nation in Europe.

Watt's claims have been challenged, most successfully and sympathetically by Michael McKeon in *The Origins of the English Novel, 1600–1740* (1987). McKeon challenges Watt's assumption that the rise of the middle class as a reading public for the novel took place in the 18th century and argues that Watt has posited too great a distinction between proto-forms of the novel and the novel proper. They share a number of formal features, which makes it improbable that only the novel proper expresses the experience of the individual. Moreover, the novel cannot simply be equated with realism, as Watt does: many prenovelistic forms can claim to be realistic in a number of ways, depicting the brutal facts of ordinary life, centering on the consciousness of one individual, and deliberately eschewing the fairytale elements of courtly fictions. Neither did romantic forms of writing die out after the early 18th century, and the history of the realistic novel is entwined with that of the prose romance.

Nevertheless, McKeon does not dismiss Watt's insights out of hand. He merely suggests that to present the rise of the novel as an absolute break in literary history is to push the evidence too hard. Instead, he argues, the novel became an important and separately conceived genre when the complexity of early modern social experience required new forms. The novel emerged only at the end of a long period of "novelistic usage," when varieties of experience had outlived existing media of expression. Hence, no hard and fast distinction can be made between the novel and the proto-novel form, even though the quantity, status, and importance of individual examples signal a qualitative transformation. To give one example, it could be argued that the Arthurian romances of the French Vulgate cycle (early 12th century) exhibit as realistic a notion of character as many 18th-century novels, especially in the representation of the love triangle between Arthur, Guinevere, and Lancelot. However, to conclude from this example that the novel has always existed and that literary forms have never altered would clearly be an absurdity in the face of overwhelming counterexamples. Such a case, however, is made in Margaret Anne Doody's *The True Story of the Novel* (1996), which dates the rise of the novel back to ancient Greece and Rome. Doody's argument has not found favor with many scholars, but her work is stimulating and a timely reminder that there is no straightforward break between premodern and modern literary forms.

Another important argument is contained in Julia Kristeva's *Le Texte du roman* (1970; The Text of the Novel), based on a study of the late medieval French writer Antoine de la Sale (c. 1385–c. 1460). Kristeva argues that the novel became possible as a literary form because of a transformation of the nature of the linguistic sign. According to Kristeva, in the Middle Ages the sign was perceived as a transcendental entity beyond human comprehension and criticism, but as the medieval period gave way to modernity, the sign came to be regarded as an "open-ended material structure" able to change in significance. This gave rise to the novel as a more democratic literary form, in which stable meanings could be disputed and appropriated by writers and readers. Kristeva's work owes much to the theories of Mikhail Bakhtin, who argues that the novel form developed as the official culture of the medieval period crumbled and more carnivalesque and disruptive modes of writing became possible, concentrating on representing the hitherto disguised "lower bodily stratum." Neither Kristeva nor Bakhtin sees a sudden *rise* of the novel, but they do discern a distinct break between epochs brought about by a transformation in practices of reading and writing.

This rather complex understanding of literary history has two corollaries. First, it is not only impossible but undesirable to suggest that realistic and romantic modes of prose fictional narrative written in the European Renaissance should be separated as two distinct generic forms, only one of which led to the rise of the novel. I shall include a discussion of both forms in this survey. Second, it is not reasonable to single out English literature as particularly significant in terms of its proto-novelistic forms; accordingly, I shall include a discussion of fictional prose narratives in Spain, France, Italy, and Germany.

The most significant writer of prose fiction in Renaissance Italy was Giovanni Boccaccio, an unusual literary figure on two counts: he chose to write in the Italian vernacular rather than Latin, and he wrote as much in prose as he did in verse. Boccaccio's first surviving experiment in prose fiction is the romance *Filocolo* (c. 1336), which narrates the story of the love affair between Florio and Biancofiore and includes a digression comprising a number of stories told by the main characters in Naples. Two stories from the digression reappear in Boccaccio's major work, the *Decameron* (written 1349–51), a collection of 100 stories set against the background of an outbreak of the plague that afflicted Florence in 1348. The narrators, having escaped from the disease-ridden city, decide to beguile their time by telling each other stories. These vary in content, style, moral, and allegorical significance, ranging from the story of patient—and morally exemplary—Griselda, who endures her husband's tyrannical tests and remains faithful to him despite the odds, to a number of fabliaux, bawdy tales of husbands or wives indulging in extramarital affairs and escaping the consequences through their cunning ingenuity. Boccaccio's influence on later writers was immense, not least for the range of literary styles and forms contained in his work.

Also important was the genre of pastoral romance, which had been inherited from classical Greece. The most important pastoral romance was probably Jacopo Sannazaro's *Arcadia* (1502), which had a major influence throughout Europe and helped to establish the popularity of Arcadia as a literary location. *Arcadia* tells the story of Sincero, a Neapolitan shepherd who leaves Naples for the remote Greek province of Arcadia to recover from unrequited love. There he is revitalized by the happy shepherds and their simple lifestyle and is able to return to Naples, where he finds that his love has died. Sannazaro's work led to much more complicated treatments of the pastoral in prose romance, which often used rural locations as a means of making political criticisms of the existing order of society. Alternatively, the idyllic setting serves to convey the idea that mankind will never free itself of fundamental problems.

Story collections were a significant feature of Italian literary output in the Renaissance. The most influential of these in the 15th century was Masuccio Salernitano's *Novellino* (c. 1460), which contains five distinct parts and deals with themes from the moral misconduct of the clergy to examples of magnanimity.

Novellino is also remarkable for containing the first extant version of the story of Romeo and Juliet. In the following century, the stories of Giovanambattista Giraldi Cinthio, who was also an important literary critic, were collected in his *Hecatomitthi* (1565), which follows the example of Boccaccio in setting the framing story in the aftermath of a major disaster, the sacking of Rome in 1527. Cinthio suggests that his stories have a therapeutic function and are based on eye-witness accounts. Throughout the *Hecatomitthi,* Cinthio stresses the horror of the destruction of Rome and the impiety of the invaders who desecrate the church, giving his stories a sternly moralistic style. Cinthio's stories had a particular impact in England, as did the novellas of Matteo Bandello. Bandello's stories, like Cinthio's, were written in the aftermath of tragic destruction, in his case the invasion of Milan in 1525. Bandello's works possess a simple and often understated style, and are designed to represent "real events as random occurrences, more amenable to opinion than to principled analysis" (see Kirkpatrick, 1995). Bandello's realism illustrates the difficulty of separating the novel from the proto-novel form. Italian prose fiction is also important for a number of utopian works, notably Tommaso Campanella's *La città del sole* (written in 1602; *The City of the Sun*).

The 17th century produced little in the way of startling innovation in prose fiction, although there were more collections of stories and novellas, notably Giambattista Basile's *Lo Cunti de li cunti* (1634; *The Story of Stories*), which has claims to be the first collection of folktales in Europe. Once again, the 50 stories are held together by a framing fiction, perhaps illustrating the influence of Scheherazade's dire situation in *The Arabian Nights*. In Basile's collection, a prince and his wife, a former Moorish slave who has achieved her status under false pretenses, hear ten stories by women on five successive afternoons until the rightful princess appears as the last storyteller and claims her rightful due. The stories told include Beauty and the Beast, Cinderella, Puss in Boots, and other well-known tales.

In France, probably the most significant prose written before the 18th century was François Rabelais' work, which is usually referred to as *Gargantua and Pantagruel* and was written over the course of two decades from 1532 onward. Rabelais' work is the subject of *Tvorchestvo Fransua Rable i Narodnaja Kul'tura Srednevekovija i Renessansa* (1965; *Rabelais and His World*), an influential study by Mikhail Bakhtin that argues that Rabelais occupies a pivotal position in the development of the modern novel. Rabelais brings together a host of subjects and styles and mixes such a variety of modes and literary forms—utopian, realistic, satirical, fantastic, tragic, comic—that it is difficult to classify his writing or to describe the purpose of the ongoing project. *Gargantua and Pantragruel* tells the story of a dynasty of giants whose gross behavior and habits combine with shrewd wit and native intelligence to mock the pretensions of medieval authorities, particularly the church. Rabelais promotes the beliefs and practices of humanism, with its insistence on simplifying and purifying the complex intellectual heritage of the Middle Ages. Notable sections attack the power of monks over the population at large, defend free will, mocking papal authority and superstition, and parody chivalric romances, as does Cervantes in *Don Quixote* (1605–15). The work is also important for its linguistic innovations and use of rhetoric, often providing great lists of synonyms as a means of exposing pedantry and hair-splitting distinctions.

The vogue for collections of stories with a framing narrative also asserted itself in France, where Boccaccio was widely imitated. Important collections include *Les nouvelles récréations et joyeux devis* (1558) by Bonaventure Des Périers and an unfinished collection by Marguerite de Valois. Des Périers also wrote political and religious allegory. Pierre de Bourdeilles de Brântomes is significant for his posthumously published *Mémoires* (1663–66), which recount his adventurous life in a style that has been described as naturalistic.

In the 17th century, numerous novels were published, a further challenge to the view that England was preeminent in this literary form because of the advanced state of its capitalistic development. Honoré d'Urfé's *L'Astrée* (1607–27) is the most important French pastoral novel and is heavily indebted to Spanish and Italian sources. *L'Astrée* tells the story of the shepherd Celadon who loves the shepherdess Astrée. After a misunderstanding, Celadon is banished and, in despair, tries to drown himself but is rescued by nymphs. One of these falls in love with him, but he rejects her advances and eventually succeeds in marrying Astrée. The intricate plot has numerous interwoven subplots. The success of *L'Astrée* resulted in widespread imitations and a strengthening of the pastoral strain in the novel's history.

Another developing subgenre was the novel of adventure, with notable examples written by Gauthier de Costes de la Calprenède. His two most celebrated novels are *Cassandre* (1644–50), a historical work set in the time of Alexander the Great, and *Cléopatre* (1647–56), which describes the passion of Juba, Prince of Mauritania, for the Egyptian queen. Madeleine de Scudéry, together with her brother Georges, also wrote a series of historical novels with subjects taken from Turkish, Roman, and Persian history. Their most influential work was *Artamène, ou le Grand Cyrus* (1649–53), which tells the story of Artamène's love for Mandane, daughter of the king of the Medes. The novel can also be read as a roman à clef, the characters representing Scudéry's immediate circle of friends. Antoine Furetière, in his *Roman bourgeois* (1666), produced a more realistic text that parodies the extravagances and polite manners of such novels as Scudéry's by concentrating on the lives of a number of less privileged lawyers.

Cyrano de Bergerac's two posthumously published accounts of fantastic voyages, *Voyage dans la lune* (1657) and *L'Histoire des états et empires du soleil* (1662), published together as *L'Autre Monde; ou, Les États et empires de la lune* (*Other Worlds: The Comical History of the States and The Empires of the Moon and the Sun*), belong to the Rabelaisian tradition of satire and generic mixing. Expressing a scepticism based on faith in the powers of reason, realism, satire, and science fiction, these works are difficult to classify. They prefigure not only the novelistic experiments of the following century and beyond, but also the rationalism of the Enlightenment. Another more realistic novel was Paul Scarron's *Le Roman comique* (1651–57; *The Comic Romance*), which tells the story of a group of itinerant actors. Scarron creates a series of strongly drawn individuals who are, as often as not, grotesque and ridiculous. Charles Perrault's collection of stories derived from folktales, *Contes* (1697; *Fairy Tales*) parallels similar Italian collections.

Probably the most widely read novel written in 17th-century France was Madame de Lafayette's *La Princesse de Clèves* (1678; *The Princess of Cleves*). Madame de Lafayette was already well known as a society figure who associated with important intellectuals. She had published two novels that consider the vicissitudes of love, *La Princesse de Montpensier* (1662; *The Princess of Montpensier*) and *Zaïde* (1670). Her brief masterpiece tells the story of the Princess of Clèves, who is married to a man whom she respects but does not love. She falls in love with the gallant Duke of Nemours, who reciprocates her passion, but she decides to confess all to her husband and ask for his protection. The prince admires her resolve and virtue, but dies of a broken heart. The princess refuses to marry the duke and enters a convent. Owing much to the work of Brântomes—but without his flamboyant style—*La Princesse de Clèves* is important as a psychological study that had a profound influence on the subsequent development of the European novel.

Early Spanish Renaissance literature exercised a strong influence on the development of the novel through the picaresque. This highly episodic form follows the diverse adventures of a *pícaro* who is usually characterized as a dishonest delinquent. Serving as a vehicle for often mordant social satire, the picaresque developed the unreliable first-person narrator-protagonist which has played such an important role in the modern novel. The most influential early picaresque tale was the anonymous *Lazarillo de Tormes* (1554), which tells the story of Lazaro's youthful misadventures in the service of a series of rascally masters. The realism of the novel is matched by its brutal and unsettling comedy. Its incidental structure, loosely describing the most important moments in Lazarillo's "education," was often imitated when novels were published in serial form.

Side by side with these realistic narratives—and in competition with them—Renaissance Spain produced several idealistic and romantic narrative forms. The most popular were the chivalric romances so famously satirized in Miguel de Cervantes' *Don Quixote*—and so successfully that modern readers usually believe them, unfairly, to be worthless. One of the most frequently reprinted of these was the Arthurian romance *Amadís de Gaula*, which went through 30 different editions in the 16th century. It tells the story of the son of King Perión of Gaul, who is born in secret to Elisena after an illicit affair. The child is set adrift in an ark containing a letter giving his name as Amadís and is eventually found by a Scottish knight, Ganadales, who brings him up. Amadís falls in love with Oriana, daughter of the King of Great Britain, and the story follows their trials and tribulations until they are eventually married, despite the hostility of Oriana's father, Lisuarte. The book was so widely read that a number of different sequels were written, including *Las sergas de Esplandián* (1510). Other important romances are *Palerin de Oliva* (1511); Pedro Hernandez de Villumbales' *El caballero del sol* (1552); and *Caballeria cristiana* (1570). Altogether some 60 romances were published in more than 300 editions in the 16th century, making the form the most popular kind of fiction in Spain. Although *Amadís* is principally significant for its sophisticated interlacing of plot elements, other chivalric romances are notable for their psychological analysis.

As in France and Italy, pastoral romance was also widely read in Spain, much of it heavily influenced by Sannazaro's *Arcadia*. Jorge de Montemayor's *La Diana* (1559) went through 20 editions in the 16th century, while Gil Polo's *La Diana enamorada* (1564), Cervantes' *La Galatea* (1585), and Lope de Vega's *Arcadia* (1598) provided variations on the same theme. Many of these works deal with the complexities of the problem of love, particularly its power as an all-encompassing and irrational force that humans are ill-equipped to resist.

The most influential Spanish narrative of the Renaissance was undoubtedly Cervantes' *Don Quixote,* which tells the story of an amiable, aged eccentric who, having read too many chivalric romances, becomes convinced that he is a knight errant and so sets out on a variety of ludicrous quests in order to set the world to rights. Don Quixote is accompanied by his squire, Sancho Panza, a much more earthy creature, and one of the novel's major attractions for readers has been the fluctuating relationship between the two men. Interestingly, *Don Quixote* not only trounces the unrealistic chivalric romance but incorporates its forms into the fabric of its own narrative, and the book also contains elements of the pastoral romance in its interpolated tales. This generic mixing underscores the open boundaries between types of narratives in the 16th and 17th centuries. Cervantes' *Novelas ejemplares* (1613; *Exemplary Novels*), a collection of 12 tales dealing with the relationship between good and evil and between love and sex, similarly contains realistic and romantic tales. The collection exercised a massive influence on subsequent Spanish writers, spawning numerous imitations throughout the 17th century. Probably the most significant novelist after Cervantes in 17th-century Spain was Baltasar Gracián, a stern moralist whose allegorical works deal with questions of self-knowledge, prudence, and the use of reason. A large number of satirists, including Francisco de Quevedo y Villegas and Cristóbal Suárez de Figueroa, vividly portrayed contemporary Spanish society and its foibles.

Germany experienced similar developments to those occurring in France at the start of the 15th century, the prose romance replacing the medieval verse epic as the main vehicle for narrating stories. Notable examples are Elisabeth von Nassau-Saarbrücken's *Loher und Maller* (c. 1437) and *Huge Scheppel* (c. 1437). But narrative approximating the modern novel did not emerge until the second half of the 17th century, when the influence of French and Spanish models ushered in a literary transformation. Probably the most significant novel of the century was Hans Jacob Christoffels von Grimmelshausen's *Der Abenteurliche Simplicissimus Teutsch und Continuatio* (1668; *Simplicius Simplicissimus*), set during the Thirty Years' War (1618–48) and heavily indebted to the picaresque novel. The protagonist is of noble birth but brought up by peasants as a shepherd until he encounters a band of brutal soldiers who burn down the village where he lives. A series of far-flung adventures finally concludes when Simplicissimus settles down among his books to reflect on the vicissitudes of the world. Also of importance are the satirical novels of Christian Reuter and Christian Wiese, whose works chastised mankind for the folly of war and saw education as the only possible salvation. The heroic adventure novels of Philipp von Zesen, Eberhard Werner Happel, Anton Ulrich, and Heinrich Anshelm von Ziegler und Kliphausen may be compared with similar work in France and Spain.

Although the development of the European novel was by no means dependent on the literary history of England, it is probably not misleading to suggest that more forms of prose fiction developed in England, or, rather, the English-speaking British Isles. Sir Thomas Malory's prose epic, *Le Morte D'Arthur* (written c. 1469–71 and first printed by William Caxton in 1485) consists of a series of interrelated tales woven together into a polyphonic narrative that balances the different accounts and switches from one episode to another. In so doing, Malory arguably produced a literary model of causation that is far more sophisticated than that employed by many later novelists. Also significant was Thomas More's *Utopia* (1516), which became the foundation for a new genre of fiction.

Many English writers were influenced by Italian collections of short stories, sometimes via French translations. William Painter produced the highly influential *Palace of Pleasure* in 1566, a series of some 60 tales translated from Boccaccio and Bandello. The collection mirrors the mixture of styles and subjects of the Italian models but lacks the sophisticated framing devices. Similar collections were produced by George Whetstone, who culled the stories in his *Heptameron* (1582) from Italian courtesy literature; and Barnabe Rich, whose *Farewell to Militarie Profession* (1581) provided the sources for a number of Shakespeare's plays. These collections contain stories of cynical realism that deal with the problems of sexual jealousy (often involving revenge for perceived slights or the deception of decrepit husbands by sexually voracious young women) side by side with romances in which the devotion of lovers overcomes all odds.

Longer novellas written in the middle of the 16th century were mostly concerned with love in a courtly setting. George Gascoigne's *The Adventures of Master F.J.* (1573) tells the story of F.J.'s wooing of the lady Elinor through a series of letters. John Lyly's *Euphues: The Anatomy of Wit* (1578) and *Euphues and His England* (1580) were hugely popular works and particularly important for their stylistic influence on subsequent fiction during the following 50 years. Lyly's style, characterized by a profusion of finely balanced antitheses, became the courtly style *par excellence* and the epitome of wit that other writers either had to imitate or react against to find their own distinctive voice. The first of the two romances tells the story of Euphues, a talented but arrogant young Athenian gentleman, who becomes a severe moralist after the failure of his love affair with the scheming Lucilla, which nearly destroys his friendship with Philautus. In the sequel, the two friends travel to the English court and are favorably impressed with the virtues of the English.

Other prose romances were written by Thomas Lodge and Robert Greene, who also wrote important journalistic works describing the low life of London. The most significant Elizabethan prose romance was undoubtedly Sir Philip Sidney's lengthy *Arcadia,* which appeared in two separate versions. The first, *The Old Arcadia* (c. 1580), circulated widely in manuscript but was not published until the 20th century. It is carefully constructed in five parts linked together by a series of poems and tells two interrelated stories. The main plot concerns the fears of Duke Basilus, who retires to an Arcadia marred by an excessively harsh moral law. The revised version, *The New Arcadia,* left unfinished at Sidney's death, was posthumously published in 1590 and is a much longer work, adding a new subplot, interlacing the various stories more carefully, and confronting moral questions with far greater earnestness.

More realistic fiction was written by Thomas Nashe, most importantly in his *The Unfortunate Traveller* (1594), another novel that owes much to the picaresque tradition, recounting the often dangerous and bloody adventures in France and Italy of Jack Wilton, a young English page. Nashe describes executions, rapes, murders, and tortures in vivid detail, and there is a famous account of the slaughter of the Anabaptists at Munster. Thomas Deloney, a silk-weaver, wrote a number of works that may be contrasted to the courtly style of Lyly, Greene, and Sidney, as they deal with the lives of artisans rather than courtiers. *Jack of Newbery* (c. 1597) concerns the adventures of a number of weavers. *Thomas of Reading* (c. 1602) focuses on clothiers, and *The Gentle Craft* (c. 1597) on shoemakers.

In the 17th century, many of these forms developed and proliferated as new generic subcategories also appeared. Sidney's *Arcadia* was much imitated by a number of writers. For instance, *Urania* (1621), by Sidney's niece, Lady Mary Wroth, transformed the epic style of her uncle's work back into a chivalric romance and, in doing so, commented on current political events, an increasing trend in Arcadian works, as well as pointing out the vulnerable position of women in the game of love. A number of picaresque novels were also written, notably Richard Head's *The English Rogue* (1665), which sold extremely well. Also significant was the genre of satirical and allegorical romance, which included John Barclay's *Argenis* (1621), a work of political criticism, and that of heroic romance, such as Roger Boyle's *Parthenissa* (1651–69).

The two writers from the second half of the century most important for the subsequent development of the novel are probably John Bunyan and Aphra Behn. Bunyan's religious allegories, written in a prose that eschews the elaborations of the courtly style, were owned by a large number of English households in the following two centuries. Bunyan's most celebrated work is *The Pilgrim's Progress* (1678, 1684), an extended fable or allegory of the model Christian, who has to leave his wife and family behind and undertake a journey to escape the City of Destruction. *The Pilgrim's Progress* had a major influence on the development of the English novel, opening possibilities of a broader audience for fictional prose and establishing the plain style as an appropriate standard for the English novel. Aphra Behn's prolific output enabled her to sustain an income as the first professional English woman writer, and her example created the possibility of a writing career for nonaristocratic women. (Virginia Woolf commented that "All women together ought to let flowers fall upon the tomb of Aphra Behn . . . for it was she who earned them the right to speak their minds.") Her most significant prose romance was *Oronooko; or, The Royal Slave* (1688), which told the story of an African prince sold into slavery in Surinam, where he is reunited with his beloved, Imoinda. After Oronooko leads the other slaves to escape, the lovers are hunted. Oronooko kills Imoinda with her consent to prevent her capture and is then executed with barbarous cruelty. *Oronooko*, until relatively recently excluded from accounts of the "rise of the novel," had an especially important influence on the development of women's fiction in the following century.

ANDREW HADFIELD

See also Astrée; Aphra Behn; Miguel de Cervantes; Diana; French Novel (16th and 17th Centuries); Genre Criticism; Lazarillo de Tormes; Novella; Pastoralism in the Novel; Picaresque; Pilgrim's Progress; Princesse de Clèves; Prose Novelistic Forms; François Rabelais; Romance; Simplicicius Simplicissimus; Spanish Novel; Verse Narrative

Further Reading

Bakhtin, M.M., *Tvorchestvo Fransua Rable i Narodnaja Kul'tura Srednevekovija i Renessansa,* Moscow: Khudozh, 1965; as *Rabelais and His World,* Cambridge, Massachusetts: MIT Press, 1968

Bakhtin, M.M., *The Dialogic Imagination: Four Essays,* translated by Caryl Emerson and Michael Holquist, edited by Holquist, Austin: University of Texas Press, 1981

Clements, Robert, and Joseph Gibaldi, *Anatomy of the Novella: The European Tale Collection from Boccaccio and Chaucer to Cervantes,* New York: New York University Press, 1977

Day, Geoffrey, *From Fiction to the Novel,* London and New York: Routledge and Kegan Paul, 1987

Doody, Margaret Anne, *The True Story of the Novel,* New Brunswick, New Jersey: Rutgers University Press, 1996; London: HarperCollins, 1997

Hunter, J. Paul, *Before Novels: The Cultural Contexts of Eighteenth-Century English Fiction,* New York: Norton, 1990

Hutson, Lorna, "Fortunate Travellers: Reading for the Plot in Sixteenth-Century England," *Representations* 41 (1993)

Jones, R.O., *A Literary History of Spain: The Golden Age, Prose and Poetry, The Sixteenth and Seventeenth Centuries,* London: Ernest Benn, and New York: Barnes and Noble, 1971

Kirkpatrick, Robin, *English and Italian Literature from Dante to Shakespeare: A Study of Source, Analogue, and Divergence,* London and New York: Longman, 1995

Kristeva, Julia, *Le Texte du roman: Approche sémiologique d'une structure discursive transformationnelle,* The Hague: Mouton, 1970

Lucas, Caroline, *Writing for Women: The Example of Woman as Reader in Elizabethan Romance,* Milton Keynes and Philadelphia: Open University Press, 1989

McKeon, Michael, *The Origins of the English Novel, 1600–1740,* Baltimore: Johns Hopkins University Press, 1987; London: Raduis, 1988

Relihan, Constance C., *Fashioning Authority: The Development of Elizabethan Novelistic Discourse,* Kent, Ohio: Kent State University Press, 1994

Rodax, Yvonne, *The Real and the Ideal in the Novella of Italy, France, and England: Four Centuries of Change in the Boccaccian Tale,* Chapel Hill: University of North Carolina Press, 1968

Salzman, Paul, *English Prose Fiction, 1558–1700: A Critical History,* Oxford: Clarendon Press, and New York: Oxford University Press, 1985

Schlauch, Margaret, *Antecedents of the English Novel: 1400–1600 (from Chaucer to Deloney),* London: Oxford University Press, 1963

Watt, Ian, *The Rise of the Novel: Studies in Defoe, Richardson, and Fielding,* Berkeley: University of California Press, and London: Chatto and Windus, 1957

René by François-René de Chateaubriand

1802

René established Chateaubriand's literary reputation as the "father of romanticism" and transformed French literature. References and allusions to the structure, themes, and language of *René* abound in French poetry and prose late into the 19th century, at least through the time of Gustave Flaubert.

Only a few dozen pages long, *René* presents the framed narrative of a young French aristocrat who flees to North America in the early 18th century. From the moment of its publication, this plot was understood to be a barely disguised description of Chateaubriand's youth and his travels in America at the end of the century.

The impoverished younger son of a Breton aristocrat, Chateaubriand left the chaos of revolutionary France for North America in 1791, having received some governmental monies for the purpose of seeking out the elusive Northwest Passage. He was also, he claims, in search of "true colors" for an epic poem, *Les Natchez,* which would presumably have portrayed the disastrous effects of European colonization on the "noble savage." For four months Chateaubriand traveled in America, from Baltimore and Philadelphia, up the Hudson, to Niagara, and down the Ohio River. He briefly returned to France and then spent almost a decade in exile in England. There, he published his first book, *Essai historique, politique, et moral sur les révolutions* (1797; *An Historical, Political, and Moral Essay on Revolutions, Ancient and Modern*), in which he showed himself to be a follower of the 18th-century *philosophes* and a supporter of the French Republic. In the conclusion, he wrote speculatively about the "Religion that will replace Christianity."

However, on his return to France, Chateaubriand rapidly completed a work of Christian apologetics, *Le Génie du christianisme* (1802; *The Genius of Christianity*). It appeared opportunely in 1802, at the very time of Napoléon's reestablishment of Christianity in France. *The Genius of Christianity,* which included *René,* was intended to show that Christianity is the most "beautiful" of religions and the most favorable to the arts. Like *Atala* (1801), *The Genius of Christianity*'s other interpolated story, *René* was presented as the illustration of a particular advantage of Christianity. In introducing *René,* Chateaubriand wrote of a kind of melancholy that he considered characteristic of modern times, in which "the imagination is rich, abundant, and full of wonders, existence poor, dry, and disenchanted." Christianity, although its beliefs foster such melancholy, provides refuges, such as convents, for the suffering.

This argument is grafted onto René's story, which he himself tells to Indian sachem Chactas and Père Souël, a French missionary, as they sit overlooking the Natchez village and rising French colony. René tells of his unhappy youth and adolescence; his restless travels throughout Europe, pursued by an instinctive desire for an unknown good ("un bien inconnu, dont l'instinct me poursuit"); and his abandonment by his only friend, his sister Amélie, who fell in love with him and took refuge in a convent. René's story is egocentric and complacent, and at the end of it he is sternly reproved by Père Souël, who tells him that, instead of "giv[ing] himself up to useless reveries," he should "use his strength in the service of his fellows."

René had announced at the beginning of the story that he would not tell "the adventures of his life, since he had not experienced any, but the secret sentiments of his soul." The tale is structured by motifs and themes such as falling leaves, bells, autumn winds, solitude, desire, and an aimless yearning ("le vague des passions"). Its prevailing tone is lyric. It embraces the common romantic notion that emotional anguish indicates moral superiority: "A great soul must contain more sorrows than a little one," Chactas says to comfort him.

Père Souël's unexpected rebuke is so out of keeping with the preceding pathos (the French romantic critic Sainte-Beuve called it a "moralité plaquée"—a stuck-on moral) that many readers suspect it resulted from an attempt to force a Christian lesson onto a previously existing narrative. *René* was originally conceived by Chateaubriand in the unchristian context of the never completed *Les Natchez.* In that poem, the primitive American sanctuary, about to be spoiled by European civilization and religion, would have served as an appropriate (if temporary) refuge for a disenchanted European. No religious moral was needed to round out the romantic tale.

Critics and readers embraced the romantic narrative despite Chateaubriand's disavowal. Sainte-Beuve saw that unsatisfied, narcissistic René was a startlingly new kind of novel hero and that a "multitude of Renés" recognized themselves in him. Although René stands in a long line of French autobiographical characters, including Michel de Montaigne and Jean-Jacques Rousseau, René is among the first of the romantic protagonists (with the almost contemporary Oberman [1804] of Etienne de Senancour) who lays claim to our attention not because he is a public figure but simply because he is *himself* and unhappy. The story was persuasive enough that in his later autobiography, *Les Mémoires d'outre-tombe* (1849–50; *Memoirs*), published long after he was an important political figure, Chateaubriand had to struggle constantly to distinguish what he then considered his true self from his readers' (and perhaps his own) belief that, in some basic way, he was René.

Although *René* is primarily a sentimental tale, metonymically it represents the plight of the uprooted French aristocracy during the Revolution. Chateaubriand situated his story in the troubled period after the death of Louis XIV in 1715, but his readers understood clearly that the tale was contemporary. Like René's many descendents, this early romantic hero evolves in the context of a society in upheaval.

Chateaubriand's several earlier published poems and prose pieces reveal a naturally gifted writer; *Atala* and *René* further display a fully developed and original prose style, marked by rhythmical sentences, colorful descriptive vocabulary, and sensuous verbal molding of emotional states. *René*'s portrayal of unfocused adolescent yearning and the sense of purposelessness felt by the aristocrat in a society undergoing rapid change are of unparalleled accuracy and force. From its not completely coordinated triple origin, this tale, manifesting the selfish desire to flee (*Les Natchez*), a conservative religious morality (*The Genius of Christianity*), and an autobiographical search for self-understanding, produces a tension, almost an anxiety, that makes *René* strikingly modern.

CHARLES PORTER

Further Reading

Barbéris, Pierre, *René de Chateaubriand, un nouveau roman,* Paris: Larousse, 1973

Chateaubriand, François-René de, *Œuvres romanesques et voyages,* 2 vols., edited by Maurice Regard, Paris: Gallimard, 1969 (volume 1 includes the text of *René,* with excellent commentary and notes)

Chateaubriand, François-René de, *Les Natchez, Atala, René,* edited by Jean-Claude Berchet, Paris: Librairie Générale Française, 1989 (includes excellent commentary and notes)

Painter, George D., *Chateaubriand: A Biography,* London: Chatto and Windus, 1977; New York: Knopf, 1978

Porter, Charles A., *Chateaubriand: Composition, Imagination, and Poetry,* Saratoga, California: ANMA Libri, 1978

Sainte-Beuve, Charles-Augustin, *Chateaubriand et son groupe littéraire sous l'empire,* new edition, Paris: Garnier frères, 1948; originally published 1849

Representation. *See* Mimesis

Reviewers, the Popular Press, and Their Impact on the Novel

For a book to receive any sort of review at all, it seems, is something of a miracle. The Women in Publishing group in England reports that more than 50,000 books are published in Great Britain yearly, yet the *Times Literary Supplement* has the space to review only about 3,000, or approximately 6 percent (see Women in Publishing, 1987). Books reviewed in the *TLS* are likely to be sufficiently high-profile to be covered multiply in other, less prestigious organs, further limiting the total number of titles covered.

Even if as many as 2,000 additional titles are reviewed in media from specialty journals to small-town newspapers, a new book has only a one in ten chance of receiving even a single review, and no more than a 50–50 chance of being reviewed positively. Novelists whose books are reviewed negatively are likely to wish their work had been ignored; at least they must ask themselves, "Who reviews these books anyway?" We might ask two related questions: 1) do reviews affect the writing and publishing of novels? 2) if so, in what ways? There is, as it turns out, a symbiotic relationship between the novel and the critical review, both of which came into being at approximately the same time and matured at roughly the same pace. A look at the historical record shows that indeed reviews do have an impact on writing and publishing, although that impact is probably less strong than many think. Conversely, if reviewers affect novelists to some degree, so may it be claimed that novelists improve reviewing standards by broadening reviewers' horizons.

First, the matter of who writes reviews. Although there are loosely-organized societies for reviewers such as the National Book Critics Circle in the United States, there are no associations to enforce standards comparable to the American Medical Association and the American Bar Association and certainly no procedures established for the certification or even the training of reviewers. Indeed, the first reviewers scarcely reviewed at all: J.M.S. Tompkins reveals that the typical 18th-century English reviewer preferred lengthy quotation of the novel in hand to critical commentary, often quoting as many as a dozen pages and further lightening his work load by taking them from the book's first chapters only (see Tompkins, 1932). Bad novels were dismissed briefly and witheringly; good ones were praised at slightly greater length for such dubious qualities as decency, plausibility, and freedom from affectation.

But if early reviewing practices were so slipshod and even lazy, surely part of the reason for this lack of professionalism may be traced to the equivocal state of the novel itself. After all, if measured by present-day standards, the first novels often seem unworthy of the name. Looking back at 17th-century France, when the first full-length books of prose fiction began to appear with some frequency in that country, Martin Turnell notes that

> the writers were not without talent but their works, as we can see from the practice of Honoré d'Urfé and Madeleine de Scudéry, often consisted of lengthy collections of adventure and love stories which today are found unreadable and a serious burden for literary historians. The plot was used to introduce and link them together, but there were no compelling relations between them or with the main plot, which meant that the novel was usually lacking in a unified experience (see Turnell, 1978).

No wonder reviewers found themselves stymied in the face of such an ungainly form.

The task of early reviewers was further complicated by the early novel's disreputable aura. Each new medium is viewed suspiciously in contrast to the old, and, just as new forms of pop music or electronic media are seen today as threats to established values, so the novel was seen as inferior to the poem. As late as 1828, a writer for the English *Athenaeum* maintained that a reader whose intellectual faculties are at their peak will pick up a poem, although when fatigued we are more likely to "court embicility [sic] and inanition in the pages of a novel." An anonymous colleague writing in the *Methodist Magazine* suggested rhetorically that readers "ask the man, who with smiling but vacant countenance, rises from reading *Tom Jones, Don Quixote,* etc., if his judgment is better informed; if his mind is more expanded; his stock of ideas increased; or if he is better prepared for performing the duties of his station?"

The implied answer, of course, is no. Yet even if this smiling, vacant reader finds himself unable to adequately perform his duties as merchant or barrister or clergyman because of the novel's pernicious influence on his intellect and sense of purpose, his continued interest in and support of the novel as literary commodity has now become absolutely essential. For two events occurring in the last half of the 18th century combined to change forever the nature of publishing: the birth of the novel, which would rapidly become the popular form it remains today; and the death of the patronage system, which meant that writers would have to be supported in their industry by thousands of individual purchasers of their books instead of a single wealthy nobleman. And these two developments led to a third: the installation of the reviewer at midpoint between the writer and the book-buying public.

Frank Donoghue (1996) sees in the career of Laurence Sterne the emblematic story of the first modern novelist. At the beginning of his career, Sterne, like other authors of his day, believed that reliance on a wealthy and noble patron was the only road to publication. He struck out on his own, however, when he decided to promote the sales of *Tristram Shandy* (1759–67) with the help of David Garrick, actor, theatre manager, and, perhaps most important, influential member of fashionable London society. Wildly successful, *Tristram Shandy* spawned an immense amount of "Sterneiana"—imitations of and pamphlets about the novel. When these fell off in number, Sterne found his work treated in two of the most influential of the new journals devoted to reviewing, the *Monthly Review* in 1749 and the *Critical Review* in 1755.

Far from praising Sterne's work, however, as had the amateurish yet enthusiastic imitators and pamphleteers, writers for the two literary reviews urged Sterne to abandon the learned satire of *Tristram Shandy* and take on instead the familiar world of feeling. The result is the very different *A Sentimental Journey* (1768), based on Sterne's own travels in France and Italy. Within less than a decade, then, Sterne not only went from dependence to self-promotion to reliance on reviews but also changed his way of writing in order to accommodate critical opinion.

If Sterne's relations with the critical reviews were not entirely happy, at least reviewers took his work seriously. Women novelists of the day found their work regarded uniformly as second-rate; male reviewers condescended to female novelists, although they spared them the withering scorn that they unleashed on inferior male novelists. Women writers resorted to various strategies to win critical approval, seeking endorsements from male

literary sponsors, for example, or addressing exclusively female audiences in the hopes of avoiding the charge of meddling in serious (i.e., masculine) affairs.

Frances Burney, however, took the matter directly in hand by dedicating her first novel, *Evelina* (1778), to the "Authors of the *Monthly* and *Critical Review,*" reminding the critics of the principles they themselves had defined in their own pages (integrity, candor, and so on) and arguing that *Evelina* satisfied every one of their criteria. The immediate effect of this bold stroke was slight, since *Evelina* received polite but perfunctory notices in both reviews. But both reviews praised extensively her next novel, *Cecilia* (1782). Thus Burney's initiative and its effect make her, as Donoghue says, the first author to acknowledge openly and seriously that critical reviews "occupy a legitimate place of power in the field of literature." (Not that the reviewers took women as a whole any more seriously; a century later, a reviewer said of George Eliot's work, "There is a good deal of coarseness, which it is unpleasant to think of as the work of a woman." Yet when Eliot was believed to be a man by reviewers, she was thought to be "a gentleman of high church tendencies.")

For the fact is that, in general, if most reviewers throughout history have proven to be more open to novelty and variety in fiction than most readers, they have also shown themselves to be more conservative than most literary (as opposed to mass-market) novelists. Henry Nash Smith (1978) points out that, in the United States, Nathaniel Hawthorne, Herman Melville, and Henry James all started out successfully but suffered drastic declines in sales in mid-career; William Dean Howells could not break from the hackneyed convention of the genteel love story, even though his own tastes were shaped by the achievements of the groundbreaking English, French, and Russian novelists of his day; and Mark Twain was treated as little more than a comedian by reviewers who failed to notice the thematic depth of his work.

Part of the problem, of course, was that these authors opposed what Herbert F. Smith (1980) calls "the Protestant ethic of the American heartland of the mid-nineteenth century . . . based upon the triumvirate of values that support it still: success, reform, and piety." For example, in his novels Hawthorne explored ancestral guilt, a topic of little interest to the reader whose self-concept was based on the fundamental American premise of rebirth and renewal in a New World. Not surprisingly, the reviewer for a magazine called *To-Day* found *The Scarlet Letter* (1850) "gloomy from beginning to end," and other reviewers found both "pollution" and "mentally diseased" ideas in *The Scarlet Letter* and *The Blithedale Romance* (1852).

And after delighting audiences with early novels based on his real-life travels in the South Pacific and then baffling them with the more demanding *Mardi* (1849) and *Moby-Dick* (1851), the always unpredictable Herman Melville tried to resolve the conflict between audience demand and artistic desire with *Pierre* (1852), one of the most bizarre works in US or any literature. As Henry Nash Smith writes, the plan was "to produce a novel that on the surface would conform to the conventions of mass fiction as these were represented in weekly 'story papers,' yet would embody an undercurrent of subversive implication repudiating the basic articles of the dominant value system." Melville hoped he could accomplish two goals at once: win back his readership with, on the surface, the kind of sentimental pulp fiction that was devoured unthinkingly by the masses, yet gain the admiration of the few elite readers capable of responding to true genius by including a second, subtler layer of thought that could be detected only by the cognoscenti.

The result is that *Pierre* is a bizarre hybrid, something vaguely reminiscent of the romances Charles Brockden Brown had written half a century before, long before Hawthorne had perfected the American form of that genre in *The Scarlet Letter*, yet freighted, especially in the final chapters, with personal grousings. An aristocratic country youth in the beginning, Pierre is revealed as a writer and misunderstood genius (much like his creator) halfway through; by the end he is a killer, a prisoner, and, finally, a suicide.

Some happy ending! Reviewers were not pleased—even Melville's friend Evert Duyckinck, writing in the *Literary World*, condemned Pierre's inconsistencies and overreachings, observing that "the combined power of New England transcendentalism and Spanish Jesuitical casuistry could not have more completely befogged nature and truth, than this confounded Pierre has done." Others were more direct: following the publication of *Pierre*, one New York newspaper ran the headline "HERMAN MELVILLE CRAZY." Whereas conservative reviewers had persuaded Laurence Sterne to be less experimental in his writing and more conciliatory to a mass audience, the literary press was as violent to Melville's outlook as he to theirs; in effect, devastating notices killed the public's desire for his writings altogether.

It should be noted, however, that reviewers' opinions are not always so influential and that the reviewing system is only part of a vast industry whose output is shaped by a variety of factors, some of which lie beyond anyone's control. For example, there is nothing more relentless (and less predictable) than literary fashion: as H.R. Klieneberger points out, after the German translation of *Robinson Crusoe* was published in 1720, some 20 imitations of it appeared in German over the next ten years and several more during the following decade; in effect, this story of self-reliance and Christian piety had created its own self-renewing publicity machine (see Klieneberger, 1981).

In the same way, a work adored by professional readers is doomed to a respectful neglect if lay readers do not embrace it. Christoph Martin Wieland's *Die Geschichte des Agathon* (1766–67; *The History of Agathon*), although it initiated the tradition of the Bildungsroman or educational novel, "was to share the fate of many outstanding contributions to German fiction," says Klieneberger: "it was acclaimed by creative writers and critics, but not widely read." A later Bildungsroman, Goethe's *Wilhelm Meisters Lehrjahre* (1795–1821; *Wilhelm Meister's Apprenticeship*), is probably the first example of the genre that comes to the minds of most readers, but probably less because of expert opinion than the fact that it, too, was, like *Robinson Crusoe*, widely read and imitated not only in its country of origin but internationally.

So reviewers do not affect sales of novels perhaps as much as they would like to. Obviously, best-sellers like Judith Krantz and Danielle Steele sell very well at present, even though they are reviewed very rarely and, even then, usually negatively. On the other hand, reviewers are able to shape the production of serious novelists, as the examples of Sterne and Melville show. And, of course, serious novelists who do not discourage easily are able to change reviewers' minds as well; as we have seen, Frances Burney's dedication of her first book to reviewers may have influenced their overwhelming acceptance of her second. And Henry Nash Smith points out that, whereas James' *The Portrait of a Lady* (1881) was accused of being overly analytical by reviewers and *The Bostonians* (1886) and *The Princess Casamassima* (1886) were called "heartless," a change of tone began to appear in reviews of *The Spoils of Poynton* (1897) and *What Maisie Knew* (1897) as critics began to write more positively of the subtlety and refinement of James' method.

The historical record suggests that, to the extent that they are influential at all, reviewers are somewhat supportive of the public's fairly conservative taste in reading, although, as a group, they are more willing to accept new developments in writing; thus reviewers help general readers to change their literary attitudes, although probably not as quickly as the novelists themselves would like. The Women in Publishing group asked literary editors what sorts of books they selected for reviewing; such answers as "fairly widely available, reasonably cheap, not too academic" suggest that the books most likely to be reviewed will be serious yet accessible, books that fall into the mid-range somewhere between potboilers and scholarship.

In a recent survey of some 20 regional US newspapers, Robert Johnson found that reviewers are considerably more professional now than they were in the 18th century (see Johnson, 1993). "Writing styles . . . seemed carefully weighed," with "little, if any, bombast, let alone fluff. Comfortably colloquial, but formal, diction and sentence patterns dominated," even if "highly educated diction appeared to be on holiday." Overall, Johnson found popular reviewing in the US to be serious, if not stuffy, a matter of "avowed book people talking to other book people . . . not the odd tourist who got lost while paging through on the way to NBA scores."

No doubt many novelists have felt and continue to feel that reviewers are not sufficiently respectful of their best efforts. However, an astute writer will offer change gradually rather than ask the reading public to alter its habits overnight. In this sense, a tolerant if sceptical reviewer may serve a function somewhat like that of a sea anchor, keeping the boat from lurching forward so quickly that the passengers fall off.

DAVID KIRBY

See also Critics and Criticism (all sections); Journalism and the Novel

Further Reading

Baym, Nina, *Novels, Readers, and Reviewers: Responses to Fiction in Antebellum America,* Ithaca, New York: Cornell University Press, 1984

Donoghue, Frank, *The Fame Machine: Book Reviewing and Eighteenth-Century Literary Careers,* Stanford, California: Stanford University Press, 1996

Johnson, Robert, "Pop Criticism Provides Non-Academic Readers a Unique Service," *St. Louis Journalism Review* 22 (1993)

Klieneberger, H.R., *The Novel in England and Germany: A Comparative Study,* London: Wolff, 1981

Mott, Frank L., *A History of American Magazines,* 5 vols., Cambridge, Massachusetts: Belknap Press of Harvard University Press, 1930–68

Smith, Henry Nash, *Democracy and the Novel: Popular Resistance to Classic American Writers,* New York: Oxford University Press, 1978; Oxford: Oxford University Press, 1981

Smith, Herbert F., *The Popular American Novel, 1865–1920*, Boston: Twayne, 1980

Taylor, John Tinnon, *Early Opposition to the English Novel: The Popular Reaction from 1760 to 1830*, New York: King's Crown Press, 1943

Tompkins, J.M.S., *The Popular Novel in England, 1770–1800*, London: Methuen, 1932; Lincoln: University of Nebraska Press, 1961

Turnell, Martin, *The Rise of the French Novel*, New York: New Directions, 1978; London: Hamish Hamilton, 1979

Women in Publishing, *Reviewing the Reviews: A Woman's Place on the Book Page*, London: Journeyman, 1987

Władysław Stanisław Reymont 1867–1925

Polish

Few Nobel prize winners in literature are so little known internationally as Władysław Stanisław Reymont. Having won the prize in 1924, he died a year later and did not have a chance to become better known outside of his native Poland. And yet he deserved not only that highest literary distinction but also the fame that escaped him. A shortage of translations into internationally known languages and a lack of promotional devices besides his untimely death—all those factors contributed to the fact that his name is barely known outside Poland, and even in his native land critics have challenged Reymont's place as the most outstanding Polish novelist of the early 20th century. Nevertheless, he is undoubtedly one of the giants of the modern novel.

The beginnings of his literary career in the mid-1890s were as modest as his cultural background. Born into a lower-middle-class rural family, he was sent to Poland's capital, Warsaw, to learn a trade rather than to pursue his interest in intellectual matters. However, as a young tailor's apprentice, he started frequenting city theatres and developed a lasting love for the stage. Consequently, he joined a traveling theatrical company as an actor, but a lack of talent forced him to return to more practical jobs, including that of railroad inspector in the remote Polish countryside. But in spite of his lack of formal education, his literary interests persisted and prompted him to try his hand at journalism and short stories. His early work served to introduce him to a closed circle of Polish intellectuals and writers. His journalistic report on the pilgrimage to Jasna Góra, a holy shrine in Częstochowa, appeared in 1894 and won him an instant literary reputation. His apprentice fiction drew heavily on his own experience and was rendered in the naturalistic style of the period.

His first two novels, *Komediantka* (1896; *The Comedienne*) and *Fermenty* (1897; The Ferments), dwelled upon his theatrical experience, but for an ambitious young writer they were only the first step in a literary career. Having worked near Łódź, a fast-growing center of manufacturing industry, he had been able to observe the impact of the Industrial Revolution on rural areas, and he decided to use it as the main theme in his next novel, *Ziemia obiecana* (1899; *The Promised Land*), which must rank with the best novels dealing with industrialization in world literature. It is, above all, a realistic image of the creation of a modern industrial center at the turn of the century. But realism mingles with symbolism, which enriches the novel with powerful images of factories as modern monsters, the city sucking in human resources from the land like a huge dragon. Similarities to the metaphors used by US industrial novelists, such as Frank Norris and Upton Sinclair, are striking, but there are no lines of influence in either direction. Reymont anticipated the modern concern with the environment and ensuing social problems:

> For that "promised land," for that octopus, the villages have been deserted, the forests have disappeared, the land has been despoiled of its treasures, the rivers dried out. For that land people were born. And it sucked everything in, crushed it in its powerful jaws, and chewed people and objects, the sky and the earth, in return giving useless millions to a handful of people, and hunger and hardship to the whole throng.

The vitality of *The Promised Land* was underscored when the well-known Polish director Andrzej Wajda made the book into a motion picture in 1975.

Reymont began to emerge as a leading Polish novelist at the turn of the century, as Henryk Sienkiewicz and Bołeslaw Prus were winding up their literary careers. He was determined to establish himself firmly with yet another major work, this one entirely devoted to the Polish peasant tradition he knew so well from his own experience. He started working on his tetralogy *Chłopi* (1902–09; *The Peasants*) while temporarily living in France and completed it after the short but stormy 1905 Revolution in Warsaw. With each of the four novels titled after a season of the year, the tetralogy begins with *Autumn,* following the agricultural cycle of life and death in nature, here transposed into the history of a peasant family, the Borynas, in central Poland. This close link between nature and human beings enlarges the scope of the novel and makes it into an epic panorama of life—full of love, suffering, birth and death, sorrow and joy. To give the novel a truly epic dimension, Reymont employed techniques characteristic of classical epic: two parallel plots, nature and society as main poles in the protagonists' actions, a multitude of events making up a panoramic picture, lengthy descriptions, and an abundance of stylistic devices such as metaphors, similes, periphrases, rhythmic cadences in prose, and so on.

Focusing on the Boryna household—symbolically placed in the center of the village Lipce—Reymont skillfully mirrors in it all vital elements of peasant lore, which are treated as central to the understanding of society. The plot turns on a conflict derived from classical Greek tragedy, a love triangle, with Antek, Boryna's son, becoming the lover of his young stepmother, Jagna. To complicate the plot even more, Reymont introduced a fourth party, Antek's wife, who cannot reconcile herself with the situation and fights back to claim her rights to her husband and the property. The drama is eventually resolved by the old man's death and Antek's decision to abandon the seductive woman since "'everything must go its own way. One has to plow in order to sow, one has to sow in order to harvest, and what is disturbing has to be weeded out, like a bad weed,' a strict prehuman voice was talking inside him as if it were the voice of the land and the village." That close relationship between man and nature makes *The Peasants* a work of a truly universal dimension, an existential drama of the human condition. A Polish television series and a movie based on the novel were made in 1975, on the 50th anniversary of the novelist's death.

Besides an impressive number of short stories and novellas written in the same period and in the years to follow, Reymont wrote a historical trilogy, *Rok 1794* (1913–18; The Year 1794). The work was meant to equal the famous trilogy of Henryk Sienkiewicz, a truly national classic. Reymont focused on the last years of the Polish Republic before its partition among Russia, Prussia, and Austria, introducing a vast panorama of events and characters. However, he was not able to match his predecessor's success. Clearly, the historical novel was not his genre, and the work's publication during World War I did not contribute to its popularity, Poland being involved in a dramatic struggle for its independence that left it anything but willing to turn back to the causes of national disasters which had occurred more than 100 years ago. Equally unsuccessful was his attempt to explore American culture for an intended sequel to *The Peasants,* and his two trips to the United States, in 1919 and 1920, resulted only in a few minor short stories. It seemed that Reymont's fame was in decline, overshadowed by the talent of his famous contemporary Stefan Żeromski (1864–1925), generally considered by critics to be a natural candidate for the Nobel prize in the postwar period. However, for a number of reasons, including politics, moral issues, and personal preferences, the 1924 Nobel prize went to Reymont, on the basis of *The Peasants* in particular. Apparently, it came too late. Having learned the news, he wrote in a letter to a friend, "That is terrible! Nobel Prize, money, world-wide fame, and a man who cannot undress without getting very tired. This is a real irony of life, sneering and satanic indeed."

He did not live long enough to enjoy the honor, and his works in translation hardly outlived him either. The US edition of *The Peasants* (1924–25) has never been reprinted, nor has the 1927 translation of *The Promised Land* been made available in print either. If an American reader wants to get acquainted with either of these two major novels, he or she can find them only as movies on video tapes with English subtitles, a poor substitute for the novelist's rich and impressive style. *The Peasants* has fared much better in translations other than English: between 1957 and 1984 alone, according to the available bibliographical data, it was published in 13 European countries and Cuba, while translations of his other works appeared either in separate editions or in anthologies in many countries, including China and Peru. In Poland, the centennial of Reymont's birth resulted in official celebrations and many publications, including new editions of his works and a number of critical studies. But his contribution to the genre of the novel still remains to be discovered in the English-speaking world.

JERZY R. KRZYŻANOWSKI

Biography

Born in Kobiele Wielkie in 1867. Received no formal education, despite his interest in intellectual matters; worked at many jobs before establishing his literary career, including tailor's apprentice and railroad inspector; also joined a traveling theatrical company for a time. Awarded Nobel prize for literature, 1924. Died in 1925.

Novels by Reymont

Komediantka, 1896; as *The Comedienne,* translated by Edmund Obecny, 1920
Fermenty [The Ferments], 1897
Ziemia obiecana, 1899; as *The Promised Land,* translated by Michael Dziewicki, 1927
Chłopi, 1902–09; as *The Peasants,* translated by Michael Dziewicki, 1924–25
Marzyciel, 1908
Wampir, 1911
Rok 1794 [The Year 1794], 1913–18

Other Writings: short stories, novellas, and sketches.

Further Reading

Dyboski, Roman, "Zeromski and Reymont," *The Slavonic Review* 4 (1926)
Kocowna, Barbara, *Reymont: Opowieśc biograficzna,* Warsaw: LSW, 1971; 2nd edition, 1973
Kocowna, Barbara, editor, *Reymont: Z dziejów recepcji twórczości,* Warsaw: PWN, 1975
Krzyżanowski, Jerzy R., *Wladyslaw Stanislaw Reymont,* New York: Twayne, 1972
Krzyżanowski, Julian, *Władysław Stanisław Reymont: Twórca i dzieło,* Lwow: Zakładu Narodowego im. Ossoliskich, 1937
Polakowska, Anna, *Reymont, Władysław Stanisław,* in *Bibliografia Literatury Polskiej: Nowy Korbut,* 15, Warsaw: PIW, 1977
Prace polonistyczne 24 (1968)
Rzeuska, Maria, "*Chłopi* Reymonta," Warsaw: TNW, 1950
Stender-Petersen, Adolf, "Reymont, Winner of the Nobel Prize," *The Living Age* (1925)
Wyka, Kazimierz, "Próba nowego odczytania *Chłopów,*" *Pamiętnik Literacki* 59 (1968)
Zielinski, Tadeusz, "The Peasant in Polish Literature," *The Slavonic Review* 2 (1923–24)

The Rice Sprout Song by Eileen Chang

Yang ko 1955

Eileen Chang (Zhang Ailing) is a Chinese writer with an educated and upper-class background who emigrated to the United States as a young adult. She is the author of several novels, including *The Rice Sprout Song, Jidi zhi lian* (1954; *Naked Earth*), and *The Rouge of the North* (1967). She is also the author of the acclaimed novella *Jin suo ji* (1943; The Golden Cangue), which draws heavily upon her experience of her father's opium habit and the familial destruction it caused. This novella was later expanded into her novel *The Rouge of the North*.

Chang's critical reputation rests largely upon her masterful novel *The Rice Sprout Song*, which, like *The Naked Earth*, was originally written in Chinese but was later translated into English by Chang herself. Significantly, both novels were commissioned by the United States Information Agency for barely-concealed propaganda purposes. The initial inspiration for *The Rice Sprout Song* was an article written by a communist party cadre who had been involved in quelling a peasant attack on a granary store during a period of particular hardship. The party member questioned in his article how the communist party could have veered so far from its original ideals that it was now aligned against the people it sought to help. The cadre subsequently published a retraction of his articles, and it is these two viewpoints expressed by the party member that Chang explores in her novel. *The Rice Sprout Song* is more successful than *The Naked Earth* in transcending the narrow contractual brief within which Chang was forced to work, as she herself has admitted. *The Rice Sprout Song* offers a subtle but sophisticated critique of the values spawned by communist China through the dual lenses of both the peasant hardship created by the revolution and subsequent government, and the party itself.

The novel opens with a peasant village wedding and then proceeds to follow the lives of party members such as Ku, the party intellectual prone to petty deceptions. The contact between Ku and peasant hardship poignantly illustrates the distance between the ideals and the realities of communist China. The narrative also charts the activities of a higher-ranking party member, Comrade Wong, whose demands upon the peasants culminate in a riot that he is forced to viciously suppress. These characters provide the means for Chang to demonstrate the impossible demands and conditions of survival in communist China, as well as the fracture of both the party's ideas and ideals, as Wong finally notes: "We have failed." The rice sprout song, or *yang ko*, is the dance of the revolution that ultimately provides a powerful and ironic symbol in Chang's novel.

Chang's critical reputation predominantly rests upon *Jin suo ji* and *The Rice Sprout Song*. Although critics have described Chang as "the only novelist of real competence who has deserted Red China and written of life in that country from this side of the Bamboo curtain" (Preston Schoyer, "The Smell of a Hidden World," *Saturday Review* 21 May 1955), her work may be compared with Nien Cheng's autobiographical *Vida e morte em Xagai* (1986; *Life and Death in Shanghai*), another account of the Cultural Revolution and its aftermath. Chang's work has also been compared with that of other Chinese women writers who have made the United States their home, including Han Suyin, Helena Kuo, Hazel Lin, and Yuan-tsung Chen (see Ling, 1990). As the renowned Chinese literary expert C.T. Hsia (1971) has noted, *The Rice Sprout Song*'s position at the forefront of Chinese writing in English extends beyond its linguistic boundaries, so that it may be considered "among the classics of Chinese fiction." The novel's importance may be attributed to the critical and ruthlessly unsentimental account that it offers of life in communist China, in which respect it may be placed alongside Maria Yen's *The Umbrella Garden: A Picture of Student Life in Red China* (1954) and Yuan-tsung Chen's *The Dragon's Village* (1980). However, *The Rice Sprout Song*'s reputation is equally explained by Chang's literary skill. As Amy Ling has noted, Chang's sparse but effective descriptions and striking images also contribute much to the success of this novel.

HELENA GRICE

See also Eileen Chang

Further Reading

Chang, Sung-sheng Yvonne, "Yuan Qiongqiong and the Rage for Eileen Chang among Taiwan's Feminine Writers," *Modern Chinese Literature* 4 (1988)

Hsia, C.T., *A History of Modern Chinese Fiction, 1917–1957*, New Haven, Connecticut: Yale University Press, 1961; 2nd edition, 1971

Kingsbury, Karen Sawyer, "Reading Eileen Chang's Early Fiction: Art and a Female Sense of Self," *Dissertations Abstract International* 56 (1995)

Ling, Amy, *Between Worlds: Women Writers of Chinese Ancestry*, New York and Oxford: Pergamon, 1990

Sheuh Ching-i, *Chang Ai-ling de Shao Shou Yi Shu* (The Art of Zhang Ailing's Fiction), Taipei: Kuo Yai Ying Shu Gwan, 1973

Samuel Richardson 1689–1761

English

Since the 18th century, discussions of Samuel Richardson's contribution to novel writing have centered on a debate about whether his works should be considered realist or sentimental—a debate that is virtually synonymous with the history of the English novel itself. In his *Eloge de Richardson,* Denis Diderot highly commended Richardson's work—and compared it to that of Moses, Homer, Euripides, Sophocles, Sir Isaac Newton, and John Milton. *Clarissa* (7 vols., 1747–48), he argued, resembled the *Iliad* or Newton's *Principia Mathematica* (1687) because Richardson had managed to evoke a world that both resembled and helped to explain our own. But not all readers followed Diderot in his enthusiasm for Richardson's social or psychological realism. Richardson's reputation steadily declined in the latter part of the 18th century as critics turned against the sentimentality that was increasingly seen as his main contribution to the novel as a genre. Indeed, just a year after his death, a contributor to the *New and General Biographical Dictionary* (1762) insisted that Richardson "describe[s] human nature, rather as he wished her to be, than as she really is" and that "whoever shall form their judgment of the human kind from [him], and affix to it all those effeminate and fantastic ideas of *sentiment, delicacy,* and *refinement,* which his descriptions are too apt to suggest, will find themselves little qualified for commerce with the world."

By all indications, Richardson was, himself, well qualified for commerce with the world. Born in rural Derbyshire in 1689 into a family of "middling note" (his father was a joiner, or woodworker), he spent his formative years in the shops, docks, warehouses, and waste-filled streets of London. Poverty forced him to leave school at an early age and enter an apprenticeship as a printer. In 1715 he became a freeman of the Stationers' Company and a Citizen of the City. Richardson's work as a printer belies his reputation for "delicacy" and his presumed commitment to the private sphere. He twice narrowly escaped prison and pillory, once for printing the duke of Wharton's *True Briton* (1722)—a Jacobite critique of the Walpole government and the Hanoverian succession—and again for his involvement with the Tory periodical *Mist's Weekly Journal* in 1728. In his professional capacity, he was familiar with works of cultural and political history, both national and international. He revised and edited the second edition of Daniel Defoe's *Tour Thro' the Whole Island of Great Britain* (3 vols., 1724–27), and printed Sir Thomas Roe's *The Negotiations of Sir Thomas Roe, in His Embassy to the Ottoman Porte 1621 to 1628* (1740), Sir Henry Morgan's *History of Algiers* (1728), and William Maitland's *The History of London* (1739). Richardson's facility with legal and parliamentary practices, evident in his novels, may be traced to his role in compiling *A Compleat Collection of State-Tryals* in 1730, and to his role as printer to the House of Commons, a position he occupied from 1733 until his death. (By 1742, when he was contracted to print the Commons journals, he had a virtual monopoly over parliamentary printing, and in 1760 he became joint partner with Catherine Lintot in the office of Law Printer to His Majesty.)

Moreover, the first identifiable work written by Richardson, *Apprentice's Vade Mecum; or, Young Man's Pocket-Companion* (1733), is precisely about negotiating "commerce with the world." In his preface, he says that the work is "principally designed for Youth of tender years . . . just stepping out into Life, and who, like tender Plants . . . require the gentlest Management." Likewise, his *Letters Written to and for Particular Friends* (1741) were written in response to a request that he compose a "little Volume of Letters" offering practical advice on general social behavior to "Country Readers." And *A Seasonable Examination of the Pleas and Pretensions of the Proprietors of, and Subscribers to, Play-Houses, Erected in Defiance of the Royal License* (1735) not only represents Richardson's entry into a long-standing national debate over the social costs and benefits of the stage, but is a response to a highly topical issue—the attempt to set up a theatre in Goodman's Fields in defiance of the "Royal Licence."

The turn to novel writing, as biographers have pointed out, came only after Richardson's printing business was well established and he himself was financially secure. In 1738 he was able to lease a country home, and there he began his epistolary novel *Pamela; or, Virtue Rewarded* (1740). That work—the story of a maidservant whose exemplary virtue and integrity win her the heart and hand of her master, and thus a dramatic rise in the status hierarchy—made Richardson famous. It was the first modern "best-seller." Indeed, the popularity of *Pamela* approached contemporary marketing phenomena—everyone read it, and scenes from the novel decorated fans, teapots, and theatre boxes.

The novel also initiated the debate pitting sentimentalism against realism: some readers were impressed by the credibility of the heroine (enhanced by details of dress, diction, foot-stomping, and Pamela's rigorous introspection). Others—most notably Henry Fielding—found her supremely unrealistic and considered her successes at moral conversion and economic uplift unpersuasive (as well as unhelpful as a model for emulation). This debate has characterized discussions of the English novel ever since. Is the novel, at its inception, a realistic genre describing the emergence of the bourgeoisie in England—with Pamela herself an icon of that class representing its characteristic commitment to self-scrutiny (derived from Puritan autobiography), moral integrity, contractual negotiation, and affective marriage? Or is the novel fundamentally a sentimental—and thus unrealistic if not nostalgic—genre based on a didactic tradition that primarily constructs typological models of things as they should be (rather than as they are)?

As if in response to this problem, Richardson's second novel, *Clarissa,* rewrites *Pamela* in the tragic mode. Here, attempts to negotiate successful domestic and matrimonial relationships fail, and the paragon's moral exemplarity and vigilance are mainly ineffectual. Clarissa does not convert the rake who pursues her and cannot prevent the attack on her virtue. She is a model not for her success, but for her failure. British readers were devastated by Richardson's denial of poetic justice in this cautionary tale. As the novel was circulated in manuscript form and published in volume installments, readers launched furious letter-writing campaigns hoping to persuade him to spare his heroine her igno-minious fate. This time the charge was not that the scenario lacked credibility, but that it was all too real. Anglican divines worried over the "warmth" of the scenes between Lovelace and Clarissa; others feared that Richardson had made his villain so charismatic—so impressive to men, so desirable to women—that the novel would produce a generation of copycat rakes who would erode the virtue of English womanhood (and manhood). Continental translators were so concerned about *Clarissa*'s vulgar realism that they expurgated offending passages: in Johannes Sinstra's Dutch translation of *Clarissa* the heroine is not raped; the Abbé Prevost's French translation excises the "low, the vivid, and prolix" in Richardson's text (the scenes with Mrs. Sinclair and her brood of foul-mouthed whores, for example) in order to produce a "decorous" and elegant narrative.

Yet in England, families read *Clarissa*—a novel that in the unabridged Penguin edition currently weighs in at 1,499 pages and is officially the longest novel in English—aloud at table. When Richardson published a revised and expanded edition of the text in 1751, Samuel Johnson rejoiced that the author had "got above all fears of prolixity." Richardson himself argued in the postscript to the novel that this prolixity was a necessary consequence of his fidelity to the real: "there was frequently a necessity," he explained, "to be very circumstantial and minute, in order to preserve and maintain that air of probability, which is necessary to be maintained in a story designed to represent real life." Thus in contradistinction to some of his detractors he insisted upon a convergence between the pedagogical and senti-mental aspects of the text and its circumstantial realism. "The letters and conversations, where the story makes the slowest progress," he asserted, "are presumed to be *characteristic*. They give occasions likewise to suggest many interesting *personalities*, in which a good deal of the instruction essential to a work of this nature is conveyed."

In his next, and final, novel, *The History of Sir Charles Gran-dison* (7 vols., 1753–54), Richardson returned to the sentimental mode, to the successful paragon whose reward for exemplary virtue is once again economic and domestic stability. The epon-ymous hero was designed as an anti-Lovelace—a *male* paragon who has Lovelace's good looks and charm, but who directs his energies toward socially beneficial ends. The work received more ambivalent reviews than his previous two novels, and for some readers *Sir Charles Grandison* came to exemplify the weakness-es and excesses of sentimental fiction—the unbearable senten-tiousness of its heroes and heroines, the ubiquitous tears, and the moralizing diatribes. Robert Burns complained of Richardson that his "Dramatis personae are beings of some other world; & however they may captivate the unexperienced, romantic fancy of a boy or a girl, they will ever, in proportion as we have made human nature our study, disgust our riper minds." In fact, *Gran-dison* did influence "ripe" and "romantic" minds: its admirers included Mme de Staël, Sir Walter Scott, William Hazlitt and François-René de Chateaubriand (all of whom expressed prefer-ences for either Clementina or Harriet, Grandison's warring in-amorata), Stendhal (who wept over the novel), and Aleksandr Pushkin (whose characters in *Evgenii Onegin* [1833] know it al-most by heart). In England, *Grandison* set the stage for the high sentimentalism of Henry MacKenzie's *Man of Feeling* (1771), for the domesticity and provincialism of Jane Austen's and An-thony Trollope's novels, for George Eliot's Bildungsroman

Daniel Deronda (1876), and George Meredith's *The Egoist* (1879; Meredith's novel includes an *anti*-Grandison hero—a character who in the late 18th and 19th centuries is as familiar as the anti-Lovelace of an earlier generation).

To a considerable extent, the complaint about Richardson's sentimentality (one reiterated well into the 20th century by critics who consider him responsible for countless volumes of bad writ-ing) was motivated by a hostility to the encroaching numbers of "scribbling" women he had influenced and often actively sup-ported. *Pamela* and *Clarissa* were revolutionary—especially for women writers—not only because these novels managed to evoke a world, but because of the particular contours of the world they evoked—a world of homes and gardens, dressing tables and writ-ing closets. In these novels—in contrast to picaresque fiction or heroic romance—the action is mainly confined to domestic spaces, and thus they legitimized as the very stuff of fiction a mi-lieu that women could recognize and reproduce. Richardson en-thusiastically assumed the role of midwife to such reproductions. He frequently acted as an agent for women writers and as an in-termediary between them and their printers. He aided Charlotte Lennox with the publication of *The Female Quixote; or, The Ad-ventures of Arabella* (1752), which he eventually printed, and helped Frances Sheridan through the writing of the *Memoirs of Miss Sidney Bidulph* (3 vols., 1761). He encouraged Sarah Field-ing, printing works by her and her friend Jane Collier, and at the end of his life he assisted Anne Meades with revisions of the man-uscript of her novel *Sir William Harrington* (1771).

But Richardson's greatest influence was formal, and for that reason it is possible to consider writers as distinct as Susanna Rawson and James Joyce as heirs to Richardson's legacy. What he (or rather, Clarissa) called "writing to the moment"—the breathless transmission of an individual's thoughts and emo-tions: subjectivity made visible—gave narrative an increased psy-chological complexity that has become virtually synonymous with the novel itself. So while few but academics now read his weighty and "minute" texts, and the centuries have not, as Diderot demanded, made "haste to run and bring with [them] the honors which are due to Richardson," it is yet possible to say with Diderot that Richardson "brings [us] back to the important concerns of life" and to the foundations of the novel.

SANDRA MACPHERSON

See also Clarissa; Epistolary Novel

Biography

Born July 1689 in Mackworth, Derbyshire. May have attended Merchant Taylors' School, London, 1701–02. Apprenticed to the stationer John Wilde, London, 1706–13: admitted freeman of the Stationers' Company, 1715 (liveryman, 1722); worked for several years as a compositor and corrector in a London printing office; proprietor of his own printing firm in Salisbury Court, Fleet Street, 1721–61 (printed works by Defoe, Aaron Hill, James Thomson, and David Mallet, among others); printer for the House of Commons from 1733, printing their journals from 1742; bought North End house in Fulham, 1738; built new printing offices in Salisbury Court, 1755; Master of the Stationers' Company, 1754–55. Died 4 July 1761.

Novels by Richardson

Pamela; or, Virtue Rewarded. In a Series of Familiar Letters from a Beautiful Young Damsel, to Her Parents. Now First

Publish'd in Order to Cultivate the Principles of Virtue and Religion in the Minds of the Youth of Both Sexes, 2 volumes, 1740

Clarissa: or, The History of a Young Lady: Comprehending the Most Important Concerns of Private Life. And Particularly Shewing, the Distresses That May Attend the Misconduct Both of Parents and Children, in Relation to Marriage, 7 volumes, 1747–48

The History of Sir Charles Grandison. In a Series of Letters. Publish'd from the Originals, by the Editor of Pamela and Clarissa, 7 volumes, 1753–54

Other Writings: correspondence, political pamphlets, an instructional manual for letter writing (*Letters Written to and for Particular Friends,* 1741), and a guide for young men entering the world of commerce (*Apprentice's Vade Mecum,* 1733).

Further Reading

Braudy, Leo, "Penetration and Impenetrability in *Clarissa,*" in *New Approaches to Eighteenth-Century Literature: Selected Papers from the English Institute,* edited by Phillip Harth, New York: Columbia University Press, 1974

Castle, Terry, *Clarissa's Ciphers: Meaning and Disruption in Richardson's Clarissa,* Ithaca, New York: Cornell University Press, 1982

Doody, Margaret Anne, *A Natural Passion: A Study of the Novels of Samuel Richardson,* Oxford: Clarendon Press, 1974

Duncan Eaves, T.C., and Ben D. Kimpel, *Samuel Richardson: A Biography,* Oxford: Clarendon Press, 1971

Eagleton, Terry, *The Rape of Clarissa: Writing, Sexuality and Class Struggle in Samuel Richardson,* Oxford: Blackwell, and Minneapolis: University of Minnesota Press, 1982

Ferguson, Frances, "Rape and the Rise of the Novel," *Representations* 20 (1987)

Goldberg, Rita, *Sex and Enlightenment: Women in Richardson and Diderot,* Cambridge and New York: Cambridge University Press, 1984

Kinkead-Weekes, Mark, *Samuel Richardson: Dramatic Novelist,* Ithaca, New York: Cornell University Press, and London: Methuen, 1973

McKillop, Alan Dugald, *Samuel Richardson: Printer and Novelist,* Chapel Hill: University of North Carolina Press, 1936

Sale, William Merrit, Jr., *Samuel Richardson: A Bibliographical Record of His Literary Career with Historical Notes,* New Haven, Connecticut: Yale University Press, 1936

Smith, Sarah W.R., *Samuel Richardson: A Reference Guide,* Boston: Hall, 1984

Warner, William Beatty, *Reading Clarissa: The Struggles of Interpretation,* New Haven, Connecticut: Yale University Press, 1979

Watt, Ian, *The Rise of the Novel: Studies in Defoe, Richardson and Fielding,* Berkeley: University of California Press, and London: Chatto and Windus, 1957

Zomchick, John, *Family and the Law in Eighteenth-Century Fiction: The Public Conscience in the Private Sphere,* Cambridge and New York: Cambridge University Press, 1993

Mordecai Richler 1931–

Canadian

As a well-known novelist and prominent critic of cultural and political nationalism, Mordecai Richler is perhaps Canada's foremost contemporary writer and certainly one of its most controversial. For more than 40 years, his ten novels and nearly 500 journalistic pieces have earned him both rabid denunciations and enthusiastic praise. His detractors argue that he dislikes Jews, *les Québécois,* and Canadians, and ridicules them without restraint, while his admirers champion his works as superb entertainments that, although seasoned with black humor and satiric bite, are ultimately concerned with affirming moral responsibility.

This diverse critical reaction mirrors Richler's own dual response to the principal subjects of his fiction. He was, in his youth, torn between the rigid values and severe morality of his Jewish immigrant grandparents and the more flexible values and tolerant attitudes of his own time. His break with orthodoxy would later have a significant impact on the style and substance of his novels: blending satire and nostalgia, his novels often il-lustrate the difficulty of balancing personal and cultural identity while formulating a viable moral code. Richler's ambivalent protagonists—often expatriate Jews—are fervent in their rejection of the Montreal-Jewish ghetto but are compelled, finally, to acknowledge their sentimental connection to it. For instance, Noah Adler, in *Son of a Smaller Hero* (1955), condemns the insularity of the community he has left behind but admits that "that cage, with all its faults, had justice and safety and a kind of felicity." Like Jake Hersh in *St. Urbain's Horseman* (1971) and Joshua Shapiro in *Joshua Then and Now* (1980), Noah learns that he must accept his origins if he is to grow beyond them. Before leaving for Europe, he tells his grandfather, "I am going and I'm not going. I can no more leave you, my mother, or my father's memory, than I can renounce myself. But I can refuse to take part in this. . . ." Such ambiguous conclusions grow out of the harrowing emotional journeys the protagonists undertake; in fact, some suffer, or narrowly avert, nervous breakdowns before their ordeals are over.

Since Richler's novels are often peopled with Canadians who ultimately learn that self-knowledge comes from going home again, his novels, alongside those of fellow Canadians such as Margaret Atwood, Robertson Davies, and Margaret Laurence, are sometimes described as fictional representations of the infamous national identity crisis. However, Richler concentrates primarily on individuals struggling with fundamentally human problems. He has often argued in interviews that novel writing is a "moral office." If Richler is a moralist, he never plays the pontiff: his narrative voice is not didactic but instead falters between sympathy and censure; he does not draw characters with impeccable morals against whom rogues may easily be measured; and he does not plot his novels toward poetic justice for clearly defined heroes and villains. True to postmodern literature's proclivity for positing irony in all levels of existence, Richler's narrative voice satirically impugns vice and folly while simultaneously conceding that it is hard to avoid. He is, finally, less concerned with producing moral judgments than with exploring the arduous process of moral deliberation.

Richler carefully crafts his novels to reflect his own conflicting moral responses to the modern world and, perhaps more importantly, to recreate similar responses in his readers. Textual strategies such as frames, part divisions, set pieces, mirroring, repetition, and circular narration draw attention not only to the choices available to the characters in their quests for success, acceptance, and self-knowledge but to the sources of their failures. Readers are prompted to judge Richler's characters and yet are shown how difficult it is to do so fairly. In *The Apprenticeship of Duddy Kravitz* (1959), for instance, the image of the dangling telephone spinning over two of Duddy's victims—Mrs. Macpherson at the beginning of the novel and Virgil at the end—is a framing device that induces readers to judge Duddy's interim moral development. While they may condemn his evolution from a thoughtless prankster to a heartless swindler, they must also recognize the extenuating circumstances of his upbringing and wonder what they might have done in his place. Richler thereby provokes moral responses from his readers while demonstrating that predefined, simplistic categories fail to encompass the vast range of complex human behavior.

The angst that underpins these serious thematic concerns is apparent throughout Richler's career. Beginning with *The Apprenticeship of Duddy Kravitz*, he expresses it comically. The late-germinating influence of writers such as Terry Southern, Mason Hoffenberg, Nathanael West, and Evelyn Waugh can be seen in the flashes of black humor and forceful satire that punctuate this novel and that dominate Richler's next two, *The Incomparable Atuk* (1963) and *Cocksure* (1968). The use of film script excerpts in several of Richler's novels points to another key influence on his artistic development: soon after he began writing screenplays in the late 1950s, he experimented with incorporating the techniques of that literary medium into his novels. The resulting effects are now characteristic features of Richler's fiction: a fast narrative pace, a complex time line, jump cuts between scenes and eras, the combination of brisk dialogue and startling visual images, and the inclusion of entertaining set pieces.

St. Urbain's Horseman, and the three novels that follow it, represent a successful reconciliation of the various themes and styles of Richler's earlier work, fusing serious topics with comic entertainment in complexly structured and highly cinematic

works. They also reveal Richler's growing tendency to adapt fact for fictional purpose in the creation of characters who are involved in, or preoccupied with, real historical events. For instance, Jake is haunted by passages of testimony from the Nuremberg Trials. Similarly, in *Barney's Version* (1997), Richler complicates the issue of narrative reliability by including footnotes written by Barney's son that profess to correct the factual errors and outright lies that pepper his forgetful and self-interested father's manuscript.

Richler's novels do not simply tell stories; they create textual experiences through which readers are urged to explore the complexity of the modern spirit and the difficulty of personal morality, and thereby learn something of themselves. His focus on the Jewish community has prompted critical comparisons with Jewish American writers such as Budd Schulberg, Saul Bellow, Jerome Weidman, Karl Miller, and Philip Roth. However, Richler is not absorbed by racial and ethnic issues. As his narratives reveal, the constant search for moral values and tenable myths that might offer meaning in a post-Holocaust world is not a Jewish dilemma but a human one.

ANGELA ROBBESON

See also Apprenticeship of Duddy Kravitz

Biography

Born 27 January 1931 in Montreal. Attended the Montreal Hebrew Academy; Baron Byng High School, Montreal, 1944–49; Sir George Williams University, Montreal, 1949–51. Lived in Europe, 1951, 1954–72; worked for the Canadian Broadcasting Corporation, 1952–53; writer-in-residence, Sir George Williams University, 1968–69; Visiting Professor, Carleton University, Ottawa, 1972–74; judge, Book-of-the-Month Club, 1972–88; columnist ("Books and Things"), *Gentlemen's Quarterly/GQ*, New York.

Novels by Richler

The Acrobats, 1954
Son of a Smaller Hero, 1955
A Choice of Enemies, 1957
The Apprenticeship of Duddy Kravitz, 1959
The Incomparable Atuk, 1963; as *Stick Your Neck Out,* 1963
Cocksure, 1968
St. Urbain's Horseman, 1971
Joshua Then and Now, 1980
Solomon Gursky Was Here, 1989
Barney's Version, 1997

Other Writings: short stories, screenplays, children's literature, essays, and journalism.

Further Reading

Darling, Michael, "Mordecai Richler: An Annotated Bibliography," in *The Annotated Bibliography of Canada's Major Authors,* edited by Robert Lecker and Jack David, Downsview, Ontario: ECW Press, 1979
Darling, Michael, editor, *Perspectives on Mordecai Richler,* Toronto: ECW Press, 1986
Davidson, Arnold, *Mordecai Richler,* New York: Ungar, 1983
Gibson, Graeme, "Mordecai Richler," in *Eleven Canadian*

Novelists Interviewed by Graeme Gibson, Toronto: Anansi, 1973

Lucking, David, "'Between Things': Public Mythology and Personal Identity in the Fiction of Mordecai Richler," *Dalhousie Review* 65:2 (1985)

McSweeney, Kerry, "Mordecai Richler," in *Canadian Writers and Their Works,* fiction series, edited by Robert Lecker et al., Downsview, Ontario: ECW Press, 1983

Metcalf, John, "Black Humour: An Interview with Mordecai Richler," *Journal of Canadian Fiction* 3 (Winter 1974)

Ramraj, Victor, *Mordecai Richler,* Boston: Twayne, 1983

Sheps, G. David, editor, *Mordecai Richler,* Toronto and New York: Ryerson Press, 1971

Woodcock, George, *Mordecai Richler,* Toronto: McClelland and Stewart, 1970

Rickshaw Boy. *See* Camel Xiangzi

Riḥlat Ghāndī al-ṣaghīr. *See* Journey of Little Gandhi

Rijāl fī al-shams. *See* Men in the Sun

Alain Robbe-Grillet 1922–

French

In the early 1950s, Alain Robbe-Grillet burst on the French literary scene with a series of articles on the theory of the novel published in the widely distributed news magazine *L'Express.* Some hailed this obscure 30-year-old agricultural engineer as a bringer of gospel, while others have thought him a carrier of the plague, responsible for the subsequent death of the French novel. He quickly rounded up other writers under the banner of the *nouveau roman* (the new novel), including Claude Simon, Nathalie Sarraute, Michel Butor, Robert Pinget, Claude Ollier, and Marguerite Duras. The group claimed kinship with Franz Kafka, Marcel Proust, James Joyce, Raymond Roussel, and William Faulkner and were eager to see their works read and recognized by a wider public.

The theoretical premises of the *nouveau roman* converge on a total break with the Balzacian construction of realism, the belief in the power of language to render the specific density and complexity of the real. The *nouveau roman* undermines the realist illusion by using description to new purposes. Robbe-Grillet sought to show that description is the stuff of temporality and creativity and that it diverges sharply from the immediacy of sensual perception. In Robbe-Grillet's theory and practice both, description—exhaustive, obsessive description of sometimes the simplest objects—*is* the story, the story of a problematic, inescapably subjective apprehension of impossibly complex relationships and histories.

Robbe-Grillet attacked Jean-Paul Sartre and Albert Camus

for using metaphors to maintain "a dubious relationship" with the world. He argued that metaphors are to be avoided, as they anthropomorphize objects, referring them to an "outside," that is, to metaphysics. That the world does not answer Man's anguished cries is not an absurd tragedy, according to Robbe-Grillet, but simply a recognition that the old humanistic belief in transcendence had been a mistake. Yet Robbe-Grillet's novels are resolutely phenomenological, putting into practice what Sartre had extracted from Edmund Husserl's theory of human consciousness. They describe objects but refuse to interiorize them. The characters' consciousness is constantly "outside of itself," projecting itself on the different phenomena of the world while denying them any anthropomorphic qualities.

Despite its focus on objective reality, Robbe-Grillet insisted, the *nouveau roman* is entirely subjective—its world is always perceived through the eyes of a character, not an omniscient narrator. In *Le Voyeur* (1955; *The Voyeur*), this narrative perspective is expressed in the title. In *La Jalousie* (1957; *Jealousy*), the narrating "absence-presence" is a jealous husband. Instead of analyzing, in Proustian fashion, the effects of his wife's suspected betrayal on his heart and mind, the narrator spies on his wife and her alleged lover through the openings of a Venetian blind (*jalousie* in French) and meticulously describes the "cut-up" reality filtered through this device.

Robbe-Grillet's creative production and thought took a different turn in the mid-1960s, starting with *La Maison de rendez-vous* (1965; *The House of Assignation*), where there is not just one narrating voice as in *The Voyeur*, but different points of view that intersect, contradict each other, and create a playful surface completely immune to psychological or metaphysical interpretation. Concurrently, in Robbe-Grillet's production, the erotic obsessions become more obvious and aggressive. The novel plays with society's unconscious stereotypes without judgment or condemnation. We seem to be in a post-Christian world devoid of guilt and dedicated to the pursuit of pleasure in this "nouveau nouveau roman," a term coined in 1972.

In 1984, Robbe-Grillet published *Le Miroir qui revient* (*Ghosts in the Mirror*), the first volume of an autobiographical trilogy, *Romanesques*. He states, "I have never spoken about anything but myself. As it was from the inside, no one really noticed. Thank God." As he points out, he is using three terms that he had helped to discredit: "myself," "inside," and "spoken about." But, according to Robbe-Grillet, the iconoclasm of the *nouveau roman* has itself become dogma. The focus on himself in *Romanesques* is not a return to traditional psychologizing, but a defiant assertion of the joy of writing, anathema to a Christian society, where creativity must be equated with sweat and suffering. Thus Robbe-Grillet practices, alongside Marguerite Duras and Nathalie Sarraute, what he calls "nouvelle autobiographie." In his latest works, Robbe-Grillet acknowledges Claude Simon's dictum that "Everything is autobiographical, even the imaginary." Indeed, read retrospectively, Robbe-Grillet reveals the fictionalization of the self by language in even his earliest work.

MICHELE PRAEGER

See also Jealousy; Nouveau Roman

Biography

Born 18 August 1922 in Brest, France. Attended Lycée de Brest; Lycées Buffon and St. Louis, Paris; National Institute of Agronomy, Paris, diploma 1944. Sent to work in German tank factory during World War II; engineer, National Statistical Institute, Paris, 1945–49, and Institute of Colonial Fruits and Crops, Morocco, French Guinea, and Martinique, 1949–51; full-time writer thereafter; literary consultant, Editions de Minuit, Paris, since 1955.

Novels by Robbe-Grillet

Les Gommes, 1953; as *The Erasers*, translated by Richard Howard, 1964

Le Voyeur, 1955; as *The Voyeur*, translated by Richard Howard, 1958

La Jalousie, 1957; as *Jealousy*, translated by Richard Howard, 1959

Dans le labyrinthe, 1959; as *In the Labyrinth*, translated by Richard Howard, 1960; also translated by Christine Brooke-Rose, 1967

L'Année dernière à Marienbad, 1961; as *Last Year at Marienbad*, translated by Richard Howard, 1962

Instantanés, 1962; as *Snapshots*, translated by Barbara Wright, with *For a New Novel*, 1965; also translated by Bruce Morrissette, 1968

L'Immortelle, 1963; as *The Immortal One*, translated by A.M. Sheridan Smith, 1971

La Maison de rendez-vous, 1965; as *La Maison de Rendez-vous*, translated by Richard Howard, 1966; as *The House of Assignation*, translated by Howard, 1970

Glissements progressifs du plaisir, 1974

La Belle Captive, with René Magritte, 1975; as *La Belle Captive*, translated by Ben Stoltzfus, 1995

Topologie d'une cité fantôme, 1976; as *Topology of a Phantom City*, translated by J.A. Underwood, 1977

Un Régicide, 1978

Souvenirs du triangle d'or, 1978; as *Recollections of the Golden Triangle*, translated by J.A. Underwood, 1984

Djinn, 1981; as *Djinn*, translated by Yvonne Lenard and Walter Wells, 1982

Other Writings: autobiography, including *Le Miroir qui revient* (1984; *Ghosts in the Mirror*); film scripts, including *L'Année dernière à Marienbad* (1961), based on his novel; and critical essays, including *Pour un nouveau roman* (1963; *For a New Novel*).

Further Reading

Allemand, Roger-Michel, *Duplications et duplicité dans les "Romanesques" d'Alain Robbe-Grillet*, Paris: Lettres Modernes, 1991

Barthes, Roland, "The Last Word on Robbe-Grillet?" and "There Is No Robbe-Grillet School," both in *Critical Essays*, translated by Richard Howard, Evanston, Illinois: Northwestern University Press, 1972

Jost, François, editor, *Robbe-Grillet*, Nyons: Obliques (a special number [16–17] of *Obliques* containing a bibliography by Michel Rybalka and a filmography), 1978

Morrissette, Bruce, *Les Romans de Robbe-Grillet*, Paris:

Editions de Minuit, 1963; as *The Novels of Robbe-Grillet,* Ithaca, New York: Cornell University Press, 1975

Ramsay, Raylene L., *Robbe-Grillet and Modernity: Science, Sexuality, and Subversion,* Gainesville: University Press of Florida, 1992

Ricardou, Jean, editor, *Robbe-Grillet: Analyse, théorie,* Paris: Union générale d'éditions, 1976

Ricardou, Jean, *Pour une théorie du nouveau roman,* Paris: Editions du Seuil, 1971

Robbe-Grillet, Alain, *Pour un nouveau roman,* Paris: Editions de Minuit, 1963; as *For a New Novel: Essays on Fiction,* New York: Grove Press, 1965

Stoltzfus, Ben, *Alain Robbe-Grillet and the New French Novel,* Carbondale: Southern Illinois University Press, 1964

Vareille, Jean-Claude, *Alain Robbe-Grillet, l'étrange,* Paris: A.-G. Nizet, 1981

Robinson Crusoe by Daniel Defoe

1719

Early and mid-20th-century critics tended to identify *Robinson Crusoe* unproblematically as the first English novel. An increased awareness of Defoe's many precursors has led recent commentators to be more circumspect, although it is still generally accepted that Defoe instituted a new kind of fictional realism that had profound consequences for the novel form. His immediate influence, however, is difficult to assess, since many of Defoe's contemporaries read *Robinson Crusoe* as a work of nonfiction; furthermore, although *Robinson Crusoe* spawned numerous imitations, it had little direct impact on later well-known 18th-century novels such as those of Richardson and Fielding. Not until the end of the century was *Robinson Crusoe* widely recognized as a work of fiction, by which time it had given rise to a whole new European subgenre, the Robinsonade. If Defoe did not exactly invent the myth of the desert island castaway (*Robinson Crusoe* is based on the life of Alexander Selkirk, whose story had been published some years earlier), his version was undoubtedly responsible for the myth's enduring fascination for novelists across the world. Early reworkings of the myth include Johann David Wyss' *The Swiss Family Robinson* (1812–13) and R.M. Ballantyne's *The Coral Island* (1857); more recently, William Golding, J.M. Coetzee, and others have transposed the Crusoe myth to modern settings.

All of Defoe's major works of prose fiction appeared toward the end of his life when he already had enjoyed a long career as a poet, journalist, and pamphleteer. *Robinson Crusoe*—Defoe's first major work of prose fiction—represented a departure from his earlier writing in terms of the protagonist's individuality and the sheer imaginative power with which his remarkable experiences were described. Employing a first-person narrator whose account included apparently genuine journal entries, and who related his spiritual life with as much earnest detail as he did his efforts to make a loaf of bread or fortify his shelter, Defoe created an authenticity and sense of immediacy unparalleled in his earlier writing. The text's popularity with its first readers is witnessed by Defoe's rapid publication of two sequels, *The Farther Adventures of Robinson Crusoe* (1719) and *Serious Reflections*

During the Life and Surprising Adventures of Robinson Crusoe (1720), although pirate versions were swift to appear, as was a life of Defoe by Charles Gildon, *The Life and Strange Surprizing Adventures of Mr. D. . . De F. . . of London, Hosier* (1719), which drew satirical parallels between Defoe and his famous creation. But if enemies such as Gildon, Pope, and Swift objected on class and sectarian grounds to Defoe's success (he was a tradesman and a Dissenter), the plainness and accessibility of his style were precisely what endeared him to generations of "ordinary" readers. As Charles Lamb observed more than a century later, *Robinson Crusoe* was "written in a phraseology peculiarly adapted to the lower conditions of readers. Hence, it is an especial favourite with sea-faring men, poor boys, servant-maids, &c." (letter to Walter Wilson, 22 December 1822).

Numerous editions of *Robinson Crusoe* were published before 1800, and as a consequence of the 18th-century enthusiasm for travel literature the novel was frequently anthologized, although it was not until the 19th century that it achieved canonical status as a result of its inclusion in collections of classic English novels by Anna Laetitia Barbauld and Sir Walter Scott. In a century that placed great store by deeds of empire and adventure, *Robinson Crusoe* became a children's classic, not least because of its pious tone, although a number of critics, including Samuel Taylor Coleridge, applauded Defoe for his exceptional and unprecedented realism, and for the sophisticated irony detectable in the conflict between Crusoe's moral self-righteousness and his ruthless pursuit of material gain.

The precise nature of the realism that seems to distinguish Defoe from his predecessors continues to preoccupy critics. For Ian Watt (1957) the circumstantial details that characterize Crusoe's account, coupled with the stolidly middle-class background of his protagonist, reflect the emphasis of early modern capitalism on economics as the root of individual identity, an emphasis that Protestantism may be seen to share rather than preclude. Although some critics have preferred to stress the romantic, antirealist aspects of the text, most acknowledge that Defoe's evocation of Crusoe's life on his island is based on a sustained attention to concrete detail unmatched in previous works of prose fiction.

Other 20th-century critics have looked beyond *Robinson Crusoe*'s celebrated realism and socioeconomic contexts to its spiritual and moral dimensions. George Starr (1965) and J. Paul Hunter (1966) examine Defoe's indebtedness to the Puritan autobiography, noting his focus on the inner, religious life of his protagonist and the journey he undergoes from sin to despair to revelation and repentance. Defoe's Protestantism has rather different implications for Manuel Schonhorn (1991), who reads *Robinson Crusoe* as a coded defense of William III as the Protestant champion who will save Britain from Popery and Stuart absolutism.

The diversity of interpretations to which *Robinson Crusoe* has given rise in recent times supports the novel's identification by Ian Watt (1996) as one of the founding myths of "modern individualism." While it would be wrong to regard *Robinson Crusoe,* or indeed any single text, as the first English novel (it borrows from many earlier narrative traditions and combines realism with substantial elements of fable and romance), it is difficult to think of a work that has had greater symbolic significance for the genre, or a greater international impact. Defoe both anticipated and helped to establish the characteristic themes of the novel form, for like so many of its successors *Robinson Crusoe* is a deeply ambivalent text, concerned with both solitude and society, spirituality and materialism, domesticity and travel, prudence and adventure.

KATHERINE A. ARMSTRONG

See also Daniel Defoe

Further Reading

Armstrong, Katherine A., *Defoe: Writer as Agent,* Victoria, British Columbia: University of Victoria, 1996

Bell, Ian A., *Defoe's Fiction,* London: Croom Helm, and Totowa, New Jersey: Barnes and Noble, 1985

Blewett, David, *Defoe's Art of Fiction—"Robinson Crusoe," "Moll Flanders," "Colonel Jack" and "Roxana,"* Toronto and Buffalo, New York: University of Toronto Press, 1979

Hunter, J. Paul, *The Reluctant Pilgrim: Defoe's Emblematic Method and Quest for Form in "Robinson Crusoe,"* Baltimore: Johns Hopkins University Press, 1966

Novak, Maximillian E., *Economics and the Fiction of Daniel Defoe,* Berkeley: University of California Press, 1962

Novak, Maximillian E., *Defoe and the Nature of Man,* London: Oxford University Press, 1963

Richetti, John J., *Defoe's Narratives: Situations and Structures,* Oxford: Clarendon Press, 1975

Rogers, Pat, *Robinson Crusoe,* London and Boston: Allen and Unwin, 1979

Schonhorn, Manuel, *Defoe's Politics: Parliament, Power, Kingship, and "Robinson Crusoe,"* Cambridge and New York: Cambridge University Press, 1991

Seidel, Michael, *"Robinson Crusoe": Island Myths and the Novel,* Boston: Twayne, 1991

Spaas, Lieve, and Brian Stimpson, editors, *Robinson Crusoe: Myths and Metamorphoses,* London: Macmillan, and New York: St. Martin's Press, 1996

Starr, George, *Defoe and Spiritual Autobiography,* Princeton, New Jersey: Princeton University Press, 1965

Watt, Ian, *The Rise of the Novel: Studies in Defoe, Richardson and Fielding,* Berkeley: University of California Press, and London: Chatto and Windus, 1957

Watt, Ian, *Myths of Modern Individualism: Faust, Don Quixote, Don Juan, Robinson Crusoe,* Cambridge and New York: Cambridge University Press, 1996

Woolf, Virginia, "Defoe," in *The Common Reader,* London: Hogarth Press, and New York: Harcourt Brace, 1925

Roman à clef

A roman à clef is a subgenre of the novel that presents actual people in the guise of fictional characters. When readers identify the historical individuals and events that form the basis of a roman à clef, they unlock the novel's hidden (or not so hidden) meaning. The French phrase roman à clef, in fact, alludes to this detective process. Literally translated, the phrase means "novel with a key"; the equivalent term in German is *schlüsselroman.* Many authors have in fact published keys that identified the characters in their novels; in the case of Benjamin Disraeli's scandalous success *Coningsby* (1844), numerous *other* writers even produced such keys.

The roman à clef originated in mid- to late 17th-century France. One of the most prominent literary figures in Parisian salon society during this period was Madeleine de Scudéry, who wrote several voluminous romans à clef, including *Clélie* (1654–61; *Clelia*). In their guise as historical epics, Scudéry's novels explore contemporary social mores and celebrate or satirize contemporary figures within the related worlds of the Bourbon court and Parisian salon society. In other words, the historical frameworks allowed for depictions of some court and salon intrigues that remained unrepresented in the court histories produced by some of her contemporaries.

By publishing her works under her brother's name during her lifetime, Scudéry also avoided the contemporary charge that literary efforts were beneath ladies of her social rank. Throughout its history, in fact, the roman à clef as a genre has often thrived upon supplying gossip or wicked caricatures of individuals to readers, while providing sufficient social and legal cover (or anonymity) to its practitioners. Because authors and publishers can claim that the romans à clef they produce are fictional rather than slanderous, for example, they are difficult targets for lawsuits. This sort of unlimited fictional license has attracted many authors to the genre, and some authors have manipulated this license for political aims. *Coningsby* ridicules Disraeli's political enemies, while playing up the political importance of the author's hitherto marginal "Young England" faction. Joe Klein's recent "anonymous" account of the 1992 US Democratic presidential campaign in *Primary Colors* (1996) also illustrates the roman à clef's ability to generate political intrigue. Other authors have deployed this novelistic form to reinvent their personal lives or public personae. Ernest Hemingway's *The Sun Also Rises* (1926) is a very thinly veiled account of events in the lives of American expatriots in Europe in the 1920s. In a novel that chronicles the relationship between two brothers during World War I, Heinrich Mann's *Der Kopf* (1925; The Chief) suggests the author's deteriorating rapport with his own brother, author Thomas Mann.

Because a relatively small number of these novels have been written, the roman à clef has remained a somewhat obscure novelistic subgenre, and despite its distinct historical origins, the genre does not have a well-defined history. As the numerous articles that consider whether specific novels may be classified as romans à clef attest, the problems inherent in distinguishing this genre from other novelistic forms add to the problems inherent in charting an accurate history of the roman à clef. For instance, if authors (in part) invent their fictions by writing what they know, then all literary works implicitly have autobiographical, biographical, and fictional elements. How, therefore, can critics differentiate a roman à clef from a novel with autobiographical emphases? For some readers, F. Scott Fitzgerald's *Tender Is the Night* (1934) might look like a roman à clef that covertly depicts episodes and characters from the author's social life in 1920s Antibes; for other readers, the novel might resemble a meditation on marriage and madness with certain autobiographical elements.

Because they fictionalize the lives of the famous and the infamous, and thus provide enticing stories and gossip for their readers, many romans à clef are immensely popular immediately after publication. The vicissitudes of fame and the often topical nature of these works, however, age many of them quickly. For instance, Thomas Love Peacock's *Nightmare Abbey* (1818) tweaks romantic poets Coleridge, Byron, and Shelley, but these poets' lives and poetry are less accessible to audiences today. More obviously, Aldous Huxley's *Point Counter Point* (1928) targets many figures, but some of these individuals, such as critic Middleton Murry and political extremist Oswald Mosely, have already been consigned to the historical margins. Nonetheless, making categorical claims that contend that the impact of all romans à clef greatly diminishes over time would unfairly dismiss a number of very interesting novels. Some other famous romans à clef include W. Somerset Maugham's *Cakes and Ale* (1930), Nathaniel Hawthorne's *The Blithedale Romance* (1852), Simone de Beauvoir's *Les Mandarins* (1954; *The Mandarins*), and Truman Capote's *Answered Prayers* (1986).

WILLIAM WEAVER

Further Reading

Applegate, Debby, "Roman à Clef," *American Literary Renaissance* 7 (1995)

Brady, Patrick, *"L'oeuvre" de Émile Zola: Roman sur les arts, Manifeste, Autobiographie, Roman à clef,* Geneva: Librairie Droz, 1967

DeVore, Lynn, "The Backgrounds of *Nightwood*: Robin, Felix, and Nora," *Journal of Modern Literature* 10 (1983)

Godenne, René, *Les Romans de Mademoiselle de Scudéry,* Geneva: Librairie Droz, 1983

Hallet, Richard, "Beneath a Closed Visor: Dimitry Panin and the Two Faces of Sologdin in Solzhenitsyn's *The First Circle,*" *Modern Language Review* 78 (1983)

McFate, Patricia, "The Interpreters: AE's Symposium and the Roman à Clef," *Eire-Ireland: A Journal of Irish Studies* 11 (1976)

Moran, Margaret, "Bertrand Russell as Scogan in Aldous Huxley's *Crome Yellow,*" *Mosaic: A Journal for the Interdisciplinary Study of Literature* 17 (1984)

Railton, Stephen, *Authorship and Audience: Literary Performance in the American Renaissance,* Princeton, New Jersey: Princeton University Press, 1991

Swallow, Noreen J., "Portraits: A Feminist Appraisal of Mme. de Stael's *Delphine,*" *Atlantis: A Women's Studies Journal* 7 (1981)

Roman à thèse. *See* Ideology and the Novel

Roman d'analyse. *See* Psychological Novel

Roman-Feuilleton

Novels that are read in installments are known as *romans-feuilletons*. The word *feuilleton* (leaf) originally referred to the lower, detachable section of a French daily newspaper. As news communication was unreliable, alternative material was published below the feuilleton line. At first the fill-in material consisted of indexes, literary and dramatic criticism, and short tales. Gradually, however, episodic fiction took over the space, and for about 15 years in the mid–19th century the feuilleton dominated French literature and literature worldwide. *Roman-feuilleton* became a generic, and usually derogatory, term for light literature.

In 1836, on the same July day, two innovative daily newspapers were launched: Émile de Girardin's *La Presse* (1836–) and Armand Dutacq's *Le Siècle* (1836–1917). Mechanized printing and paper making and improved transportation created a print medium that was accessible and affordable: these two publications were available for 40 francs a year instead of the usual 80-franc subscription rate. The new audience for this early form of mass media did not only want to be enlightened or informed—some readers wanted to be entertained. *Le Siècle,* noting that its translation of the Spanish *Lazarillo de Tormes* (1554) was well received, next published what is generally considered to be the first *roman-feuilleton*, Honoré de Balzac's *La Vieille Fille* (1837; The Old Maid) in 12 installments. The public responded to the new daily offering of fiction by purchasing the paper in unprecedented numbers. *La Presse* and *Le Siècle* achieved circulations of roughly 10,000 and 11,000 respectively, whereas previously publications anticipated circulations of around 1200. Alexandre Dumas' stories increased *Le Siècle*'s circulation from 14,066 in 1838 to 33,366 in 1840. The immense success of *Le Siècle* and *La Presse* alerted other periodicals to the need for light, imaginative literature that could be run in successive issues and would establish readers' loyalty and sustain circulation figures. Within a year, the populist infection spread to other publications. Even the conservative *Le National* published a serial novel, albeit a parody. Eugène Sue's *Les Mystères de Paris* (1842–43; The Mysteries of Paris), doubled the circulation of the *Journal des débats* and his *Le Juif errant* (1844–45; The Wandering Jew) increased the flagging circulation of *Le Constitutionnel* from 5,944 to 24,771 in the course of its publication. However, the *roman-feuilleton* was not immediately embraced as a serious literary form; it engaged critical and literary circles in a long and heated debate.

In general, the novel had divided the French literary community. For example, the *Quarterly Review* printed statistics that purported to demonstrate a positive correlation between crime and fiction. Conservative newspapers such as *La Revue des deux mondes, Le Journal des débats,* and *La Revue de Paris* displayed little enthusiasm about the novel as an art form. They were particularly unimpressed by a popular, sensational daily story with few pretenses to high literary style. Literary critics were severe: Charles Augustin Sainte-Beuve decried the invasion of democratic literature and coined the deprecating term "industrial" for this new literature, while Alfred Nettement wrote that *The Wandering Jew* reflected the literary and social disorder of France. Fellow novelists were no less critical: Gustave Flaubert wrote that Eugène Sue's *Arthur* made him want to vomit; Théophile Gautier is reported to have said that Paul de Kock had the advantage of being exactly like his readers; and Émile Zola said the feuilletons had created a new public of those who were incapable of reading anything else. On the other hand, proprietors and authors met a public need, to which even the most conservative journals succumbed, and many "literary" authors eventually published their work in feuilleton format. The issue became so hotly debated that comments by Armand Carrel of *Le National* about Émile de Girardin's *La Presse* resulted in a duel and Carrel's death.

The dramatic increase in newspaper sales created an economic cycle with immense repercussions for the literary scene. Periodical publications needed to maintain a large and loyal readership to attract more advertisers, whose money commissioned popular authors, whose stories maintained circulation figures. Newspaper proprietors courted authors and paid them extraordinary commissions. Writers who had previously sold novel rights for a pittance found that the tide had turned and that their names were now lucrative commodities. Indeed, Dumas told his agent that the time would come when no publisher would bring out a novel that had not appeared in a newspaper. For the first time, writing could be considered an occupation and one which brought fame and money.

While a laborer earned about 2 francs per day, the average *feuilletonist* earned between 75 centimes and 1 franc per line. Dumas received 1.5 francs per line for 100,000 lines per year from *Le Siècle*. Balzac received a franc per line from the elite *Débats*. George Sand moved from *Revue de Paris* to *Revue des Deux Mondes* when she was not satisfied with her remuneration. *Le Constitutionnel* paid Sue 100,000 francs for *The Wandering Jew,* while circulation increases realized a profit of about 600,000 francs. Later Sue signed a 14-year contract for 100,000 francs per year with *Le Constitutionnel*. Luckily for readers and newspaper proprietors, the authors' fiscal skills did not match their writing skills and few reached financial independence, forcing them to keep churning out story after story. Proprietors launched publicity campaigns boasting of the huge, often fictitious, amounts paid to secure new feuilletons. For example, Gustave Flaubert's publisher advertised a 30,000 franc fee for *Salammbo,* but Flaubert received only 10,000 francs. In consequence, the once disreputable field of novel writing attracted many aspiring authors. Many received enormous amounts of money and went on to collect literary and state honors.

The definitive *roman-feuilleton* is Sue's *The Mysteries of Paris,* the best-selling book of the century. Cashing in on Sue's success, Paul Féval wrote *Les Mystères de Londres* (1844; The Mysteries of Modern London), preceding G.W.M. Reynolds' *Mysteries of London* (1846–50) by two years. Féval abandoned his career as a lawyer and joined *Le Siècle*'s coterie, where he enjoyed considerable popularity. His novel of Breton legends *Le Loup Blanc* (1843; The White Wolf) forged a long-lasting reputation. Not only did he dominate the writing of the second empire, he was also the president of several literary associations. His other writings include *Le Bossu* (1857) and *La Ville vampire* (1875). Féval's closest rival, Pierre-Alexis Ponson du Terrail, penned the Rocambole series, which endowed the French language with the adjective *rocambolesque,* meaning far-fetched, a testament to his style. Emile Gaboriau, Paul Féval's secretary, wrote what some consider the first modern detective story, *L'Affaire Lerouge* (1863; *The Widow Lerouge*). Paul de Kock's novels were energetic, often lurid stories filled with wry observations of French life. Karl Marx praised de Kock's realistic depictions, while the public seemed entranced by his coarse humor and bawdy scenes. De Kock's name became synonymous with risqué literature, as in James Joyce's *Ulysses* (1922), where a character sends de Kock's *The Three Girls with the Three Pairs of Stays* to a woman in the hope it will inflame her desires. Another fecund *feuilletonist* of this period was Frédéric Soulié, who wrote for the *Journal des débats* from 1837 to 1845. His best known novel was *Les Mémoires du diable* (1837–38; The Devil's Memoirs).

Perhaps the best known *feuilletonist* was Alexandre Dumas. His greatest novels, written during the height of the feuilleton phase, were penned in collaboration with Auguste Maquet: *Les Trois Mousquetaires* (1844; *The Three Musketeers*), *Vingt ans après* (1845; *After Twenty Years*), and *Le Vicomte de Bragelonne* (1848–50; *The Man in the Iron Mask*) all appeared in *Le Siècle*, while *Le Comte de Monte-Cristo* (1844–45; *The Count of Monte-Cristo*) appeared in *Le Journal des débats*. Dumas' preoccupation with the past no doubt stemmed from Maquet's historical training. Dumas' case, involving the virtually complete erasure of Maquet as collaborator, demonstrates the gaps that exist in the history of the feuilleton. How much was contributed by Dumas' stable of secretaries and assistants is also unclear.

While the central feuilleton figures—Sue, Soulié, Féval, and Dumas/Maquet—filled one niche, other feuilleton writers such as Honoré de Balzac, George Sand, Alphonse de Lamartine, François-René Chateaubriand, Gustave Flaubert, and Émile Zola filled another. Their stories appeared in the more conservative literary journals, including *Revue de Paris, Revue des deux mondes,* and *Journal des débats.* The stories in these journals tend to be better crafted. For example, Flaubert's *Madame Bovary* (1856–57; in the *Revue de Paris*) made only one concession to the feuilleton style in its melodramatic ending.

Feuilleton writing developed distinctive traits, some imposed by the exigencies of daily writing, others by the need to entertain less sophisticated readers and hold their attention across episode breaks. The popular feuilleton writers did not have the luxury, as Flaubert did, of polishing their prose. At the same time, the lack of revision, some have argued, tended to make the writing more immediate and energetic. Penny-a-line payment encouraged a richly circumlocutory style and dialogue, and the latter's "stagy" character often was motivated by authors' desire to see their works adapted for the theatre (many *feuilletonists* realized considerable profits dramatizing their own stories). Event-heavy narratives sustained the reader's interest throughout the many months of the story's run, while a rich cast of characters allowed an author to stretch a tale well past its credible life. The feuilletons also created an array of stereotypes, such as the villainous épicier (grocer), who became a stock French caricature. Perhaps the most characteristic trait was the cliff-hanging episode ending, which evolved from the theatre's end-of-act dramatic scenes.

The feuilleton was influenced by melodrama and by the enormously successful 18th-century episodic and picaresque tales of Georges and Madeleine de Scudéry and Alain-René Lesage. The penchant for the sensational, and particularly sensational crime, is thought to have stemmed from the crime periodical *Gazette des tribunaux,* a publication that is said to have inspired many

authors. The lines between journalism and imaginative writing often blur in the feuilleton, as in Sue's careful mapping of the underbelly of Paris, its urban squalor and criminal classes.

If the feuilletons failed as great literature, they succeeded as entertainment and as social history. Few literary forms are more influenced by the tastes of readers and by their cultural context than daily writing. Readers exercised their influence indirectly through their newspaper buying, but also through direct communication with authors in the course of serial publication. The many letters Sue received while writing *The Mysteries of Paris,* for instance, influenced him to adopt a more didactic moral stance. New technologies, "scientific" theories, and political commentary all found their way into the daily installment. The historical adventures of Dumas/Maquet reflect the rise in French nationalism caused by the political unrest of the time. The second empire felt threatened enough by feuilleton writing to impose taxes on periodicals that contained literature and to ban works such as Sue's *Mystères du peuple* and Flaubert's *Madame Bovary* (the latter more as a punishment of the journal that had opposed the regime than of Flaubert's writing).

Exactly who read feuilletons is impossible to know. There is a myth that copies were passed from mistress to maid, but it seems that the average readers were lower-middle-class. The *roman-feuilleton* appeared at a time when literacy was growing as a result of the 1833 education reforms, jumping from 45 percent in 1829 to 64 percent in 1847. This increase created an audience eager for reading material—and one for whom books were too expensive. Even pirated Belgian editions cost approximately 3.5 francs, nearly two days' wages for working-class people. The daily press offered a cheap alternative for those who wanted original fiction, although at 40 francs per year subscriptions were still most likely affordable for middle-class readers. However, ingenious schemes were worked out to make the papers available to poorer people, who could rent copies at 10 centimes for half an hour from *Cabinets de lecture* (public reading rooms). Most information about reading practices is anecdotal: Gautier commented that the feuilletons were read aloud by erudite janitors to their willing audiences, by apprentices reading aloud to their fellows while they worked, by maids who burned meals because they were absorbed in the latest story. Today, the feuilleton form is still considered populist.

The feuilleton proves that publishing borders are much more permeable than geographical ones. Sue, Soulié, and Dumas appeared in the popular periodicals in the United Kingdom, the United States, and Australia, no doubt pirated by agents who were employed to send copy of the latest popular serials, illustrations and all, to other newspapers. The host of imitations of Sue's *Mystères—Mysteries of San Francisco, Mysteries of Fitchburg, Massachusetts,* and *Mysteries of Melbourne—* demonstrates that the idea had worldwide appeal even if the subject matter was regional. Eventually, other countries tired of pirating French *feuilletonists.* In London, *Reynolds' Miscellany* (1847–69), the *London Journal* (1845–90), the *Family Herald* (1844–90), and *Cassells* (1853–83) established their own coterie of penny-a-line writers, J.F. Smith, G.W.M. Reynolds, and M.E. Braddon. In the United States, periodicals such as *Ballou's Dollar Monthly,* the *Philadelphia Saturday Courier,* and the *New York Ledger* all developed a core of feuilleton writers such as E.D.E.N. Southworth, Leon and Harriet Lewis, and Sylvanus Cobb, Jr. Other European countries, many divided by wars, political unrest, and regionalism, took longer to adopt their own *romans-feuilletons*. In Germany, *Gartenlaube* (1853–1918), an illustrated weekly journal, increased its 1853 circulation of 5,000 to 225,000 in 1876 largely as a result of publishing the fiction of women writers such as E. Marlitt, E. Heimburg, and E. Werner. Their gentle stories of honest burghers and village life espoused middle-class values and provided women readers with good Christian domestic models. In Italy, the *romanzi d'appendice,* such as Emilio de Marchi's *Demetrio Pianelli* (1890) and the stories of Francesco Mastriani, provided readers with thrilling adventures of humble people. Spain's *la literatura por entregas* were printed in fascicles as supplements for newspapers and magazines. The prolific Manuel Fernandez y Gonzalez imitated Sue and Hugo in his 200-plus novels, as did Wenceslao Ayguals de Izco. Ramón de Mesonero Romanos was the proprietor of Spain's first illustrated weekly newspaper, *Semanario pentoresco español,* in which he published *Panorama matritense* (1835–38), creating the influential costumbristo regionalism. The Russian Nikolai Karamzin printed "Bednaia Liza" (Poor Liza) in his short-lived *Moscow Journal* (1791–92). Later Russian "thick journals" printed installment fiction, including Fedor Dostoevskii's *Bednye liudi* (1846; *Poor Folk*) and *Dvoinik* (1846; *The Double*) in the *Petersburgski sbornik* (St. Petersburg Miscellany), and *Prestuplenie i nakazanie* (1866; *Crime and Punishment*) and *Brat'ia Karamazovy* (1879–80; *The Brothers Karamazov*) in *Russky Vestnik* (*Russian Herald*).

Alhough the *roman-feuilleton* may be considered an idiosyncratic 19th-century literary form, it still survives in various forms today. After peaking in France in the 1840s, it declined when the second empire began to levy a stamp tax on newspapers containing fiction. The form resurfaced in the 20th century, with Maurice LeBlanc's Arsène Lupin series in *Le Journal* (1907–39) and the Fantomas series created by Marcel Allain and Pierre Souvestre. With technological advances, the serialized form continues to draw an audience through radio plays, television soap operas, and now the internet's interactive novels.

Toni Johnson-Woods

See also Alexandre Dumas; Mysteries of Paris; Periodicals and the Serialization of Novels

Further Reading

France, Peter, editor, *The New Oxford Companion to Literature in French,* Oxford: Clarendon Press, and New York: Oxford University Press, 1995

Green, Frederick C., *French Novelists: From the Revolution to Proust,* New York: Appleton, and London: Dent, 1931; republished, New York: Ungar, 1964

Hemmings, F.W.J., editor, *The Age of Realism,* London and Baltimore: Penguin, 1974

Hollier, Denis, editor, *A New History of French Literature,* Cambridge, Massachusetts: Harvard University Press, 1989

Kunitz, Stanley, and Vineta Colby, editors, *European Authors, 1000–1900: A Biographical Dictionary of European Literature,* New York: Wilson, 1967

Levi, Anthony, *Guide to French Literature: 1789 to the Present,* Chicago and London: St. James Press, 1992

Queffèlec, Lise, *Le roman-feuilleton français au XIXe siècle,* Paris: Presses Universitaires de France, 1989

Roman-Fleuve

Series and Novel Cycles

Although the roman-fleuve appeared before World War I, the term being coined by Romain Rolland to describe his novel cycle *Jean-Christophe* (1904–12), it is a genre that belongs essentially to the interwar years and the immediate post–World War II period and that is dominated by French novelists, in particular Roger Martin du Gard, Georges Duhamel, Jules Romains, and Henri Troyat, in spite of the success of non-French examples, such as John Galsworthy's *The Forsyte Saga* (1906–21) or Anthony Powell's *A Dance to the Music of Time* (1951–75).

A roman-fleuve is an extended series of novels (the term translates literally as "novel-river"), each of which may be free-standing and read separately, but which form part of a coherent and continuous narrative. As such, the genre derives from the early publication of novels in feuilleton form starting in 1836, a practice that dominated the novel in the 19th century and that continued in newspaper and magazine serialization well into the 20th century. Rolland's *Jean-Christophe* was serialized in Péguy's *Cahiers de la Quinzaine,* and episodes of Martin du Gard's *Les Thibaults* (1922–40; *The Thibaults*) appeared in the most important literary review of the interwar years, *La Nouvelle Revue Française.* The roman-fleuve draws upon the tradition of recurrent characters peopling a large number of individual novels, as in Honoré de Balzac's *La Comédie humaine* (1842–48; *The Human Comedy*), which also provides an overarching structure, together with a system of subcategories, into which the individual novels themselves are fitted. The culmination of this process in France in the 19th century is found in Émile Zola's *Les Rougon-Macquart* (1871–93), a unified collection of 20 novels, with recurrent characters, a coherent genealogy, and a quasi-scientific sociological mission. It is by comparing Zola's collection of 20 novels with the romans-fleuves, which followed it in the next century, however, that the crucial difference between the two enterprises becomes apparent: Zola's novels may have recurrent characters, and there may be allusions, both backward and forward, to common plot elements, but they do not constitute a single narrative, progressing in chronological order through the contributory volumes.

In the same way, although romans-fleuves share common features with other forms of fictional output, including the quasi-sociological ambitions of Balzac and Zola, they remain distinct from them. An autonomous fictional world, with recurrent characters and a constant location, for example, in William Faulkner's Yoknapatawpha County, is not sufficient to guarantee a roman-fleuve. Nor is sheer length by itself: even multivolume modernist works such as Marcel Proust's *À la recherche du temps perdu* (1913–27; translated as *Remembrance of Things Past* and also as *In Search of Lost Time*), John Dos Passos' *U.S.A.* trilogy (1930–36), or, indeed, post–World War II works such as Lawrence Durrell's *The Alexandria Quartet* (1957–60) are no more romans-fleuves than James Joyce's *Ulysses* (1922) or Thomas Mann's *Der Zauberberg* (1924; *The Magic Mountain*), although the frontiers are more blurred in the cases of works such as Olivia Manning's *The Balkan Trilogy* (1960–65) or Evelyn Waugh's *The Sword of Honour* (1952–62). The important distinction is that the roman-fleuve, unlike the multivolume modernist text, puts its length at the service of the development of plot and theme, and, in so doing, it asserts its highly traditional fictional nature.

The real origins of the roman-fleuve lie in the German Bildungsroman and its European imitators, in which the novelist recounts and explores the extended moral and social development of an individual over a long period. Rolland's *Jean-Christophe,* which portrays the long gestation of a spectacular musical vocation in the eponymous hero against the broader cultural and political background of the relations between France and Germany in the first interwar period, between 1870 and 1914, is clearly acknowledging the importance of Johann Wolfgang von Goethe's *Wilhelm Meisters Lehrjahre* (1795–1821; *Wilhelm Meister's Apprenticeship*). At the same time, like the Bildungsroman itself, the roman-fleuve is a novel form rooted in the family, even, and especially, if the character's "education" takes the form of a temporary departure from and rebellion against the family institution, thus reaffirming the genre's inherent conservatism, both thematically and formally. Some of the best known examples of the roman-fleuve, Galsworthy's *The Forsyte Saga,* Martin du Gard's *The Thibaults,* Georges Duhamel's *La Chronique des Pasquier* (1933–45; *The Pasquier Chronicles*), or Henri Troyat's *Les Eygletière* (1965–67), all take their titles from the family dynasty whose fortunes they record. In relation to the family, however, the roman-fleuve is invariably ambiguous, charting the sometimes spectacular decline of the bourgeois family while retaining a nostalgic admiration for its dynastic strength. As such, the genre is a powerful affirmation of bourgeois social and moral values, set against external or chronological forces against which it is sometimes powerless. Indeed, a novel cycle such as Duhamel's *Vie et aventures de Salavin* (1920–32; *Life and Adventures of Salavin*), describing the increasing alienation of the isolated hero, constitutes an implicit recognition of the positive values of the family and society from which the hero is separated. It is for this reason that, while the narrative perspective of such novel cycles is invariably liberal humanist, and, as such, often condemns the authoritarianism and restricted vision of the dynastic bourgeoisie, it is essentially hostile to change, whether coming from inside a society in the form of revolutionary action or from outside in the form of war.

It is no coincidence that war is the dominant explicit or implicit theme of the roman-fleuve. *Jean-Christophe* is not merely an exploration of the growth of an unusual artistic talent but an anguished reflection on the differences between the German and French national characters that had already led to the catastrophic defeat of 1870 and were pushing the two nations to a renewed conflict in 1914. Nor is it surprising that the great period of the novel cycle was the interwar years in Europe, when the need to understand the origins and the impact of World War I was rendered even more urgent by the imminence of a second world conflict. In this respect, Martin du Gard's *The Thibaults* is exemplary: begun in the 1920s as the account of a bourgeois family during the Belle Epoque, it changed direction in the 1930s in order to alert the reader to the danger of a further war by devoting its final volumes to an intricate description of the impersonal and fatalistic interplay of diplomatic alliances that made World War I inevitable, in *Été 1914* (1936; *Summer 1914*), followed by a description of the conflict itself, in which the two Thibault brothers, Jacques, the anarchist rebel, and Antoine, the liberal doctor, are both killed. Similarly, although Jules Romains' massive 27-volume novel cycle *Les Hommes de bonne volonté* (1932–47; *Men of Good Will*) has an ambitious, quasi-sociological concern with the operation of the principle of Unanimism and provides some extraordinary set-piece evocations of Paris in all its simultaneous diversity, its two most dramatic and best-known volumes are *Prélude à Verdun* (1938; *Prelude to Verdun*) and *Verdun* (1939), which take the novel's heroes to the greatest French battle of World War I. This preoccupation with warfare continues in novel cycles that appeared after World War II. The second volume of Troyat's *Les Semailles et les moissons* (1953–58; *The Seed and the Fruit*) follows his hero Pierre to the World War I trenches, while Olivia Manning's *The Balkan Trilogy* observes the life of British expatriates before and during the German invasion of the Balkans in 1941.

If war is so important to the roman-fleuve, it is because it is the most extreme threat to the humanism which, for the most part, is the genre's moral perspective. In the case of Martin du Gard's *The Thibaults,* that humanism is all but extinguished by despair and the conflict being described, yet the final volume, *Epilogue* (1940), comprising the cool scientific notes made by the liberal scientist Antoine Thibault on the process of his own inexorable death from gas poisoning, constitutes an affirmation of the values of reason and objectivity in the face of the irrational and the inhumane. Similarly, Troyat's complementary novel cycles, *Tant que la Terre durera* (1947–50; *While the Earth Endures*) and *The Seed and the Fruit,* which follow the combined fortunes of a Russian bourgeois family under the revolution and in exile in France and those of a French petit-bourgeois family who survive both the transition from the rural peasantry to the Parisian petite-bourgeoisie and the trauma of World War I, celebrate, as their titles suggest, the resilience and continuity of common humanity and ordinary people in the face of war and social change. Repeatedly in his novel cycles, Troyat's characters ask despairingly "Qu'allons-nous devenir?" ("What is to become of us?"), emphasizing the awesome vulnerability of the individual in the face of history, whereas the novels themselves demonstrate a modest faith in human survival. Indeed, the "river" that supplies the formula for Rolland's original roman-fleuve, *Jean-Christophe,* the Rhine, appears both as the barrier between two cultures, France and Germany, that results in cataclysmic conflict, and as a powerful symbol of the continuity of human endeavor.

If the roman-fleuve is essentially conservative thematically, highly distrustful of any departure from liberal bourgeois democracy, it is hardly surprising that it should formally constitute a most dramatic example of the continued health of the realist tradition in 20th-century fiction. It is no coincidence that one of the most successful practitioners of the genre, Roger Martin du Gard, should specifically prefer the technique and world-view of Lev Tolstoi to the more fashionable example of Fedor Dostoevskii, who proved much more fruitful to the European avant-garde. In contrast to the Dostoevskiian tradition, the roman-fleuve exploits the length available to it in order to develop the illusion that it is exploring "real" people in a "real" world. In this respect, the use of the term *chronicle* in the title of Duhamel's most famous novel, or of *saga* in Galsworthy's, points both to a particular relationship with history and to a concept of fiction ostensibly rooted in the unproblematic narration of events. As such, one may trace a lineage to the work of Balzac and Zola, in which the bourgeois reader's thirst for knowledge about psychology and society is satisfied, along with the desire to see a mirror image of a familiar world. It is no coincidence that Romains' *Men of Good Will* should spring from a grandiose pseudo-scientific theory of the psychology and sociology of the group, in Unanimism, or that novel cycles should be so unusually peopled with scientists who, when they are also liberal doctors, satisfy both the moral and intellectual aspirations of the reader. In other words, the novel cycle is concerned ostensibly with a recognizable external world that it is both elucidating and defending; where it distances itself from modernist fiction, even novels that adopt a comparable length, is in its refusal ever to endanger the illusion of reality, to draw attention to its own fictional identity, and to adopt explicitly a frame of reference that is aesthetic rather than thematic. Even a cycle such as Powell's *A Dance to the Music of Time,* which appears to engage with aesthetic issues, is in fact more interested in describing, often as a roman à clef, the political and artistic life of London over a long period. Thus it is no coincidence that Louis Aragon's first flirtation with the roman-fleuve should adopt the overarching title *Le Monde réal* (1934–44; The Real World), and that, in spite of considerable technical virtuosity, it should mark something of a regression in relation to the earlier surrealist texts, looking forward to the socialist realism of the cycle *Les Communistes* (1949–51). Similarly, Jean-Paul Sartre's unfinished attempt to chart the intellectual and political history of France from the interwar years to the Occupation in *Les Chemins de la liberté* (1945–49; *Roads to Freedom*), in spite of the homage to Dos Passos in the middle volume, *Le Sursis* (1945; *The Reprieve*), marks the adoption of a traditional novel form after the irony and self-reflectiveness of *La Nausée* (1938; *Nausea*).

It is not difficult to account for the success of such a genre, although it is less easy to explain national variations. In general, novel cycles built upon the tradition of serialization in the 19th century, exploiting serialization's thematic and realist properties as well as its commercial potential in terms of popular publishing. There is some evidence to suggest, however, that in countries that developed mass paperback publishing in the interwar years, such as the United States and Britain, popular reading taste was satisfied by loyalty to author rather than by commitment to a continuing cycle and by recurrent characters, especially heroes,

rather than by an extended narrative. In France, the situation was significantly different: not only, through Balzac and Zola, was there a 19th-century tradition of serious fiction using extended collections of novels to introduce recurrent characters and explore important sociological, psychological, and political subjects, but also the publishing market was more primitive and more restrictive than in Britain or the United States, at least during the first half of the 20th century. As Theodore Zeldin recalls in *France, 1848–1945* (1973), until the period following World War II, the French reading public was relatively small and essentially restricted to the middle classes. Cheap mass paperback publishing did not become available until the postwar era, and avant-garde texts had low sales. The lucrative core of French publishing, therefore, lay in its middle-class and middle-brow readership: it was they who had the financial resources, the intellectual and aesthetic interest, and the political concerns to enable them to respond to the regular appearance of individual novels in any one cycle, with echoes of the 19th-century masters. In this respect, aesthetic concerns became intertwined with the commercial: not only did the roman-fleuve, with its middle-class characters threatened by the encroachment of history but nevertheless capable of survival, constitute an acceptable mirror for its readership, it also appealed to that readership's bibliophile collector's instinct. In other words, in France during the interwar years, the roman-fleuve was able to exploit a particular moment in middle-class taste that was not infinitely renewable into the postwar period. This is not to say, however, that the formula was a guaranteed success: sales of *The Thibaults* were notoriously sluggish until the final volumes regarding World War I, when the certainty of a renewed conflict between France and Germany gave the narrative heightened immediacy.

Nevertheless, in spite of the high intrinsic quality of novel cycles like *The Thibaults* or Rolland's *Jean-Christophe,* the genre as a whole is never far removed from the realm of popular fiction: Galsworthy's *Forsyte Saga,* itself the basis for a highly successful television series in the 1960s, looks forward to an unambiguously popular collection such as Mazo de la Roche's *Whiteoaks* cycle, while in France in the 1940s, the continued success of the roman-fleuve owed much to publishers' needs to satisfy popular demand for French equivalents of American historical romances, such as Margaret Mitchell's *Gone with the Wind* (1936) and Kathleen Winsor's *Forever Amber* (1944). Indeed, Troyat figured as one of France's best-selling authors in the 1950s, along with Françoise Sagan and Georges Simenon. Since the 1960s, the genre appears to have definitively gone into decline, supplanted in its popular aspects both by television drama and by "blockbuster" paperback publishing, and challenged in its serious ambitions both by the sociological change in the composition of its readership and by prevailing formal concerns in the fictional genre itself.

NICHOLAS HEWITT

Further Reading

Boak, Denis, *Roger Martin du Gard,* Oxford: Clarendon Press, 1963

Boisdeffre, Pierre de, *Une Histoire vivante de la littérature d'aujourd'hui, 1939–1961,* Paris: Perrin, 1962

Chaigne, Louis, *Les Lettres contemporaines,* Paris: Del Duca, 1964

Cuisenier, André, *L'Art de Jules Romains*, Paris: Flammarion, 1948

Escarpit, Robert, *Le Littéraire et le social: Éléments pour une sociologie de la littérature,* Paris: Flammarion, 1970

Ganne, Gilbert, *Messieurs les best-sellers*, Paris: Perrin, 1966

Hewitt, Nicholas, *Henri Troyat,* Boston: Twayne, 1984

Marill, Rene, *Le Roman d'aujourd'hui, 1960–1970*, Paris: Albin Michel, 1970

Nathan, Jacques, *Histoire de la littérature contemporaine,* Paris: Nathan, 1954

Starr, William Thomas, *One Against All: A Biography of Romain Rolland,* The Hague: Mouton, 1971

Roman Narrative. *See* Greek and Roman Narrative

Romance

Defining literary genres is a task more like lexicography than taxonomy: a description of historically variable vernacular usage, rather than the scientific formulation of a synchronic order. The distinction between *novel* and *romance* is peculiar to English. Other European languages, and languages of cultures in which the novel has represented a Westernizing development, tend to designate extended works of prose fiction by a single name derived from the French *roman: il romanzo* (Italian), *der Roman* (German), *Roman* (Russian), *roman* (Turkish), etc. (*Nouvelle* and its analogues signify a shorter form, as in the English *novella*.) Accordingly, this essay will concentrate on the anglophone fortunes of romance as a category posed in differential relation to (and within) the novel.

In English, *romance* has carried a wide range of meanings, including the following: a chivalric poem of the later Middle Ages; a Renaissance court fiction in prose or verse; any work of fiction; four of the late plays of Shakespeare; the 19th-century tradition of American novels; contemporary, highly conventionalized mass-market novels read by women; a love affair or story; a fanciful, erotic, or sentimental enhancement of any situation or event; a supergenre containing all fictional forms and figures corresponding with the human imagination. The principal meaning of romance in the lexicon of modern criticism—a departure from the normative conventions of narrative realism—records a disjunction in British cultural history. Following the political revolutions of the 17th century, romance came to signify those cultural elements from which the new hegemony—Whig, Protestant, middle class, masculine—progressively strove to differentiate itself. From the mid–18th century, romance thus denoted a variable (and unstable) antithetical category: the discredited stories of the "other," beginning with the *ancien régime* and its continental avatars, but soon including women, adolescents, aliens, the colonized, and the common people. Attempts to stabilize romance with a positive definition as a genre or (more loosely) "mode" have led to much critical confusion, usually by the fixation on some contingent formal or thematic feature: improbable or marvelous events; a preference for action over character; a "poetic" or "atmospheric" emphasis; a plot defined by a wandering, quest, homecoming, or discovery of lost or secret origins; an ethos determined by desire, wish-fulfillment, or escapism; a feminine predominance; conservatism; individualism; and so on. Conversely, the function of romance as the sign of imaginative forms and energies excluded from the official culture of modernity has made it a creative resource for poets and novelists, as advertised in a series of titles: *The Romance of the Forest* (Ann Radcliffe), *Ivanhoe: A Romance* (Sir Walter Scott), *The Blithedale Romance* (Nathaniel Hawthorne), *The Moonstone: A Romance* (Wilkie Collins), *A Romance of Two Worlds* (Marie Corelli), *Green Mansions: A Romance of the Tropical Forest* (W.H. Hudson), *Romance: A Novel* (Joseph Conrad and Ford Madox Ford), *A Glastonbury Romance* (J.C. Powys), and *Possession: A Romance* (A.S. Byatt).

Romance, as its etymology tells us, originally referred to the Latin-derived vernacular languages of Europe after the fall of the Roman Empire, and subsequently to heroic metrical narratives composed and circulated in those languages, especially in France. By the advent of printing (which encouraged the diffusion of long prose forms) *romance* meant any extended fiction in the vernacular, in prose or verse, that might occupy a book: medieval chivalric poems and their more recent revisions and imitations (*Amadis de Gaul, Orlando Furioso*); reedited ancient Greek novels (the *Æthiopica, Daphnis and Chloe*); and modern court or côterie fictions drawing on both of those along with other sources (*Arcadia, Artamènes*). The categorical abstraction of *romance* to mean "a fiction antithetical to historical reality" was rehearsed within some of these Renaissance romances through an internal movement of self-critique and ironical apologia, notably in works by Ariosto and Miguel de Cervantes. Cervantes' *Don Quixote* (1605–15), especially, prepared the modern way of the novel as a romance form attached to the

Aristotelian canons of probability that increasingly came to define the epistemological regime of truth. The two parts of *Don Quixote* make sophisticated dialectical play with the categories of truth, fiction, and illusion, rather than crudely debunking fiction as such, to produce a modern romance that licenses itself through the recognition of its own fictiveness.

As mentioned earlier, the continental development of the novel through these and other narratives was not marked by the terminological discontinuity that has troubled the historiography of fiction in English. In 17th-century England a generic distinction emerged, and began to stabilize, between romance and history, in company with the new discourses of empiricism (see McKeon, 1987). *Romance* became the stigma of a writing adrift from religious truth and scientific fact alike; in the age of an expanding reading public and the proliferation of religious and political dissent, the term acquired a disciplinary, censorious charge. To be culturally acceptable, fiction would have to assume another title. The "rise of the novel" in England between 1660 and 1750 has become the field of productive debate in recent literary scholarship. According to the traditional account (Watt, 1957), the novel established itself as the emergent form of modern culture by developing a new mimetic technology of "formal realism" committed to the ideology of Protestant individualism, an innovation that entailed a clean break with the past and with the obsolete conventions of romance. It seems clear that this account (perpetuating the ideological commitment it describes) has exaggerated the discontinuities between the novel and its premodern traditions and affiliations, as well as the novel's own investment in the rhetoric of fiction—in deviations from a strictly mimetic imperative.

An 18th-century English rhetoric of "antiromance," taking its cue from *Don Quixote*, burlesqued in particular the so-called *romans héroïques* or *romans à longue haleine* produced by the salons of the *précieuses*, the côteries of women writers and readers attached to the court of Louis XIV. Ostensibly aimed at a French, Catholic, Royalist culture of fiction addicted to extravagance and idolatry, the satire by mid-century involved the domestic ascendancy of the new form, the novel itself, associated with an expansion of the reading public to include the lower classes and, especially, women—who, like the *précieuses*, also happened to be the authors of many of these books. Henry Fielding repudiated the title of romance in order to claim a suitably masculine generic dignity for his own fictional practice ("comic epic poem in prose," "heroic, historical, prosaic poem") in *Joseph Andrews* (1742) and *Tom Jones* (1749). Charlotte Lennox's *The Female Quixote* (1752) invokes the French salon romances as vessels of a feminine countertradition of desire and heroism in a patriarchal culture: in a last-minute conversion, the heroine must submit to correction by the official sentences of reason, morality, and historical truth. If the female Quixote's most celebrated avatar is the heroine of Jane Austen's *Northanger Abbey* (1817), the figure, and the association of women with romance, has recurred throughout the history of the novel (see Langbauer, 1990).

These and other works rehearsed a convention that would recur in apologies for fiction for the next century and a half. The novel claimed the legitimacy of a formal realism bound to the representation of truth and morality by rejecting a disreputable prior fiction called romance. Romance thus meant two things: a failure of representation (a deficiency of realism, a straying from truth and morality) that reduces it to nothing but fiction; and the representation of other, illegitimate cultural energies.

Antiromance sought to conflate these two categories, so that the heroic values of a feudal monarchy, or representations of female autonomy and pleasure, are cast as illusions with no basis in experience or reason. But the seeds of a reversal, and a revaluation of romance, are already sown: the recognition of other cultural styles and values as such (rather than as defections from a norm) would license fiction as a means of evoking alternative structures of reality, forms of desire and fantasy that turn against the received story of the way things are. This turn is already latent in the shift of romance to denominate different sites of cultural otherness, from the absolutist court, to female literacy, to a host of ideological regimes of the other, such as popular communities and primitive societies. The positive revaluation of romance gets under way with the miscellaneous cultural movement of the second half of the 18th century called the "romance revival," devoted to the antiquarian reconstruction and poetic imitation of premodern, native, and nonclassical literary forms. Driven by broadly nationalist as well as commercial motives, romance revival comprised modern editions and dissertations upon elite and popular older literature (Edmund Spenser, William Shakespeare, English and Scottish ballads), and ancestral and exotic inventions, from James Macpherson's Ossian epics to a vogue for Oriental tales. The movement expanded via 19th-century colonialism to accommodate an anthropological interest in the collection and synthesis of all cultural forms, including the preliterary forms of myth and subliterary forms of manners and customs, into a timeless universal order—a department of what one critic has called "the imperial archive" (see Richards, 1993).

By the end of the century, the premodern and nonclassical forms of cultural expression, along with the consolidation of the novel as an ascendant literary genre, framed the appearance of novels confident enough to claim "romance" as a title of distinction. These were the so-called Gothic romances, a category covering miscellaneous ideological claims and formal experiments rather than a unified tradition. More militantly than *romance*, the term *Gothic* would signify a cultural identity set in problematical opposition to a classical-based modernity. It might bear barbarous, outrageous energies of sex and power, as in Matthew Lewis' *The Monk, a Romance* (1796), or native, ancestral virtues of liberty and endurance, as in the novels of Anne Radcliffe, the genre's most prestigious author. In *A Sicilian Romance* (1790) and its successors, Radcliffe revised the female Quixote scenario to refashion female subjectivity as the narrative center of truth and value, rewarding rather than correcting its (to be sure, entirely proper) desire. Radcliffe fortified her heroine's sensibility with an intensified rhetoric of scenic description and the authority of a national poetic tradition, consisting of the Shakespeare-based romance-revival canon established by modern poets such as Thomas Gray, Thomas Warton, and William Collins.

The strategy of investing modern romance with the authority of a national tradition was amplified, with formidable scholarship and literary sophistication, by Sir Walter Scott, who more than anyone else established the primary modern senses of romance as both a subjective state of the imagination and as the literary form of a premodern culture. Beginning with *Waverley* (1814), Scott's novels turn critically upon their own history and genealogy, invoking a range of materials and techniques that constitute a vital body of artistic resources rather than a lapsed past. Scott's novels thus activate a categorical mixture of thematic and formal sources: national, regional, and imperial; ancient and modern; courtly, urban, and rural; native and exotic. The earlier novels address the social and cultural constitution of modern Scotland; Scott began to subtitle his novels "A Romance" with *Ivanhoe* (1819), signaling the move away from this proximate history to remoter, exotic settings accessible only through literary sources. As the cultural history of the novel includes the traditional opposition between romance and history, so the progress of the hero and the evolution of the nation toward modernity together rehearse a complex, dialectical movement. Figures of romance, designating the hero's adolescent illusions as well as premodern cultural habits, fall under the inexorable pressure of "real history," but romance also returns as the medium in which the subject is able to inhabit modernity, released from the conflicts of historical development. In a complex (Cervantean) irony, romance signifies the faculty of aesthetic self-consciousness through which modern readers imagine their relation to past and present conditions. Scott's romance thus performs a co-option and containment of historic cultural differences, and their oppositional energies, in a dynamic imperial regime; at the same time, the final turn to romance advertises the fictive, provisional status of the narrative resolution, and of the dispensation of modernity, inviting a critical interrogation—an extension of the imaginative play—that a seamless insistence on "the real" would have excluded.

Romanticism, the title retrospectively given to the era, describes the resort of many poets (even more than novelists) to the nationalist and/or adversary cultural energies signified by romance, moving the term toward its modern sense of a human desire in critical tension with modern life. The examples of Lord Byron and John Keats as well as Scott indicate the range of politics with which the term could be charged, although the critical or transcendental principle tended to claim the form of lyric, and the internalization of narrative tropes (Bloom, 1971). Novelists who assumed the title of romance often did so in response to Scott's example, especially if they were Scottish novelists. James Hogg's *The Three Perils of Man; or, War, Women and Witchcraft: A Border Romance* (1822) activates the demonic figures of Border folklore in subversive opposition to Enlightenment canons of historical realism.

The 1830s saw a regothicization of historical romance in the wake of Scott by younger writers such as W. Harrison Ainsworth and G.P.R. James. Henceforth, historical fiction would largely be confined to the status of "mere romance" as the Victorian social novel, from the 1840s onward, took up Scott's dialectical combination of romance and realism. The most prestigious of the Victorian novelists tended to follow the example of Scott's Scottish novels in avoiding the taxonomic trap of the novel-romance distinction. Dickens' novels, for example, deploy the narrative techniques of romance adapted from Scott, such as plots hinging on lost or secret origins, the providential intervention of demonic or guardian figures, etc., to represent an uncanny enhancement and visionary transformation of modern social reality. With his ideological objections to historicism, which he associated with Toryism, Dickens abandons premodern culture as the referential basis for romance, preferring instead the transcendental yearnings of an alienated individual imagination. Dickens' sources are urban popular culture, spiritual allegory

(divested of a theological framework), and the nursery rhymes and tales of childhood (accommodating the figure of an unfallen fancy, the most potent of all). The authentic avatars of romance—children or childlike young women—bear a special grace, a salvational aura (*Dombey and Son*, 1848; *Little Dorrit*, 1857).

Victorian women writers, in the wake of Scott's strong historicizing and masculinizing of romance, were especially conscious of the stigma that remained attached to the term, reinforced by the designation of domesticity as their proper cultural sphere. Now that the novel was established as a canonical genre practiced by male professional authors, romance was even more likely to be the label of an inferior literature in which the feminine and the popular were conflated, especially with the industrialization of a genuine mass market for fiction in the second half of the 19th century. This did not mean that women did not continue to use romance tropes and signifiers to challenge the ideological freight of realism. If Emily Brontë's *Wuthering Heights* (1847) offers a "wild" deconstruction of the Scott regional-historical romance after the post-Gothic manner of Hogg, Charlotte Brontë's *Shirley* (1849) claims the title of the real ("unromantic as Monday morning") in order to contest it from within, most strikingly in a series of allegorical didactic interpolations. George Eliot moved from the assertion of an amplified and rigorous realism (*Adam Bede*, 1859) to a synthesis of romance devices in order to represent the dynamic, transformative energies of "culture" as such. *Daniel Deronda* (1876), perhaps the century's most ambitious extension and revision of the Scott model, explodes the 19th-century narrative of national identity by counterpointing an "English" plot of courtship and marriage (corresponding to a feminine domestic realism) with a "Hebraic" romance of revealed origins and world-historical destiny.

Otherwise, the term romance remained the unstable signifier of narrative modes divergent from domestic realism, even if it often meant nothing much more precise than "popular work of fiction." As the century progressed, romance became linked to the proliferation of genres that represented sites or forces more radically alien to a modern social order: primitive, pagan, mystic, demonic, or otherwise exotic. The pioneer of the development was Edward Bulwer-Lytton, who wrote (besides historical romances) a range of experimental fictions exploring alternative genres, including post-Gothic occult fantasy (*Zanoni*, 1842) and prototypical science fiction (*The Coming Race*, 1871). The neo-Gothic "sensation novel" of the 1860s (and its offspring, detective fiction) subverted domestic realism from within its *mise-en-scène*; the movement's most original practitioner, Wilkie Collins, gave the subtitle "A Romance" to *The Moonstone* (1868) in recognition of the triumph of an alien cultural power, as Hindu secret agents reclaim a looted diamond in defiance of English policework. As the literary market diversified in the 1880s and 1890s, so did nonrealist or antirealist genres, as well as author specialization: occult fantasy (Marie Corelli), ghost and horror fiction (Margaret Oliphant, Bram Stoker), imperial adventure (H. Rider Haggard), utopian romance (William Morris), "scientific romance" (H.G. Wells), and many more. In the eyes of many writers and reviewers, romance stood for a thoroughly commodified state of fiction and a literary production absolutely controlled by the market, strictly distinguished from the didactic realism of a George Gissing or the serious artistry of a Henry James. Few were the authors allowed to be masters of romance rather than its drudges. If Robert Louis Stevenson was admired as a connoisseur-practitioner who made consummate aesthetic play with romance conventions (*Prince Otto*, 1885), Joseph Conrad offered the riskier case of an author investing a popular genre with advanced philosophical content and formal experimentation. (If Stevenson's *Kidnapped* [1886] miniaturizes the Scott novel to adolescent scale, Conrad's *Lord Jim* [1900] updates it as the vessel of an inquiry into the epistemology of character and action.) The appearance of the modern category of the bestseller at the end of the century sealed this stratification of the literary market, with romance consigned—when not the project of select masters—overwhelmingly to "scribbling females."

North American developments were somewhat different, although again the woman writer was cast as the producer of frivolous if not deleterious rubbish. In the middle decades of the 20th century, American academic criticism set up a masculine dynasty of 19th-century novelists (James Fenimore Cooper and Edgar Allen Poe through Hawthorne and Herman Melville) who boldly departed from English norms in their exploration of nonrealist modes of romance, allegory, and fable. Indeed, an influential account defined the American tradition as one of romance rather than the novel (Chase, 1957). The central figure, Hawthorne, theorized his own work as "romance" (*The House of the Seven Gables,* 1851; *The Marble Faun,* 1860) and dissociated it from an inferior industry of sentimental domestic fiction by women writers. The gender hierarchy, in other words, reversed the English genre hierarchy, so that romance became the badge of a masculine aesthetic exceptionalism (played out, in works by Cooper, Melville, et al., in antidomestic homosocial adventures). Since the 1970s, Americanist scholars have been debating and revising this literary history. For the purposes of the present essay, it remains to be noted that the mid-century election of romance to the dignity of a national form derived from interesting developments in modernist cultural theory.

The fate of romance in early 20th-century Britain faithfully traced the literary demography of modernism: on the one hand, a decisive fall into the abyss of a feminized mass culture, where romance carried on a degraded material existence as best-selling fiction by and for women; on the other, an idealized exaltation to the sphere of modernist theory, where romance came to articulate the essential structures of a collective (racial or universal) imagination, yielding the potent figures of myth and archetype. It was at once the principle of that literature empirically most embedded in modernity and, in an ultimate fulfillment of the logic of romance revival, of an archaic or natural narrative transcending it. The dichotomy is memorably posed in the "Nausicaa" episode of James Joyce's *Ulysses* (1922): the mythic narrative schema taken from the *Odyssey* ironically frames a stylistic pastiche of the trashy romances that constitute Gertie MacDowell's subjectivity—which, like every other subjectivity in the book, has no access to the mythic schema (an irony that cuts both ways). The empirical declension of romance issued in its contemporary vernacular association with a popular brand-name commodity, defined more by wholesale manufacture and marketing (Harlequin, Mills, and Boon) than by the work of an author. Recent scholarship has defended this romance subculture against the traditional charge of female Quixotism, arguing that reading constitutes a domain of discrimination and reflection

here just as much as anywhere else (Radford, 1986; Radway, 1984).

The theoretical aggrandizement of romance was prepared by Victorian intellectuals. According to John Ruskin, the premodern symbolic systems of Gothic architecture and Greek mythology represented the free expression of objective forms of nature by individual artisans in an organic society; imitation of their example could heal the ontological trauma of modernity, reconnecting the national sensibility with a defaced natural order. Ruskin's account of Greek myth in *The Queen of the Air* (1869) anticipates later accounts of narrative forms grounded in sacred, primordial intuitions and processes. With its interest in primitive culture and prehistoric "survivals," Victorian anthropology claimed a global, transhistorical field of reference, fortified by a rhetoric of scientific authority. In the most ambitious example, *The Golden Bough* (1890), Sir James Frazer's encyclopedic synthesis of mythologies is arranged in a master narrative rooted in the seasonal cycles of death and regeneration. At about the same time, Freudian psychoanalysis scripted the structural dynamics of the psyche as a set of fundamental plots of desire and prohibition. Freud provided for a scientific justification of romance, conventionally associated with fantasy states, as an authentic chart of inner psychic reality. It was Carl Jung who decisively (not to say reductively) combined psychoanalysis with Frazerian cultural anthropology to explicate the narrative themes of a "collective unconscious," locking individual, historical identities into a taxonomy of essential, mythic agencies or "archetypes." Jungianism, with its hermeneutic of universal binary oppositions, flourished in the West, especially in the United States, during the Cold War, with consequences for the discourse of romance.

These developments marked a completion of the modern revaluation of romance as a category of narrative alienated from (yet investing) modernity. Now romance represented a domain *more real* than realism's socially and historically contingent, transient phenomenology; it emerged no longer merely from a national or psychic past, through the discourses of history and culture, but from an atemporal domain of origins, structurally essential and thus eternally recurring, through the discourses of myth and race. Jessie L. Weston (*From Ritual to Romance,* 1920) injected Frazer's scheme into historical literature with an argument that the medieval Grail romances expressed ancient vegetation rituals. Weston's thesis was taken up by T.S. Eliot (who coined the self-descriptive phrase "mythical method" in a 1923 review of *Ulysses*); his poem *The Waste Land* (1922) invokes the shadow of a grand primordial narrative of the Aryan race, bound to natural rhythms and forces, which might contain the fractured utterances of modernity. John Cowper Powys' *A Glastonbury Romance* (1932) recapitulates both works of Weston and Eliot to rehearse, on the grandest scale, the forms and ambitions of the 19th-century novel in its dialectical relation to "romance," the mystic double that inhabits and exceeds it. In many ways Powys stands at the end of the novel-romance tradition his work summarizes. The crisis of realism proclaimed by modernism brought the end of its prestige as a representation adequate to the world; realism declined to the status of just another romance, the outdated historical expression of a bourgeois hegemonic confidence. The role of romance as its antithetical double was accordingly attenuated. The nonrealist or magic realist modes of postmodern fiction draw on an enlarged cultural horizon, including non-European traditions, so that it is not especially illuminating to speak of, for example, Maxine Hong Kingston, Salman Rushdie, or Jeanette Winterson as authors of "romance," except perhaps from the perspective of an imperial Jungianism. Those writers who might plausibly be seen as still working the vein affiliate their work to specific traditions: Iris Murdoch (Powys' most interesting successor) invokes British and continental literary and philosophical genealogies of "romance and realism" (*The Sea, The Sea,* 1978; *The Green Knight,* 1993); Fay Weldon mobilizes ancient vernacular conventions through the styles of contemporary popular fiction (*The Hearts and Lives of Men,* 1987). Otherwise, recent Anglo-American fiction has preferred the more reliably oppositional connotations of "Gothic."

The modernist high-cultural account of romance persisted in postwar literary criticism, which generated a remarkable canon of romance-revival mythographies by poets and scholars such as G. Wilson Knight, Robert Graves, Northrop Frye, and Harold Bloom. Frye, the most influential of these, composed the apotheosis of romance as a "secular scripture," the total form of all plots and figures, thus the register of the human imagination (1976). More recently, the rhetoric of identity politics has encouraged a recovery of archetypalist criticism from the poststructuralist critique of essentialism; Margaret Doody's *True Story of the Novel* (1996) is an outstanding recent attempt to recast the history of fiction through a romance typology, now grounded on a female nature (a gentler version of Robert Graves' 1948 *White Goddess*). Interestingly, Doody repeats the ancient gesture of claiming the legitimate title "novel" by repudiating that of "romance," suggesting that an old story is far from over.

IAN DUNCAN

See also Adventure Novel and Imperial Romance; Critics and Criticism (18th and 19th centuries); Genre Criticism; Gothic Novel; Greek and Roman Narrative; Historical Novel; Historical Writing and the Novel; Medieval Narrative; Mimesis; Myth and Novel; Novel and Romance: Etymologies; Prose Novelistic Forms; Realism; Renaissance Narrative; Romantic Novel

Further Reading

Beer, Gillian, *The Romance,* London: Methuen, 1970; New York: Methuen, 1982

Bloom, Harold, "The Internalization of Quest Romance," in *The Ringers in the Tower,* Chicago: University of Chicago Press, 1971

Chase, Richard, *The American Novel and Its Tradition,* Garden City, New York: Doubleday, 1957; London: Bell, 1958

Doody, Margaret Anne, *The True Story of the Novel,* New Brunswick, New Jersey: Rutgers University Press, 1996; London: HarperCollins, 1997

Duncan, Ian, *Modern Romance and Transformations of the Novel: The Gothic, Scott, Dickens,* Cambridge and New York: Cambridge University Press, 1992

Frye, Northrop, *The Secular Scripture: A Study of the Structure of Romance,* Cambridge, Massachusetts: Harvard University Press, 1976

Jameson, Fredric, "Magical Narratives," in *The Political Unconscious: Narrative as a Socially Symbolic Act,* Ithaca, New York: Cornell University Press, and London: Methuen, 1981

Langbauer, Laurie, *Women and Romance: The Consolations of Gender in the English Novel,* Ithaca, New York: Cornell University Press, 1990

McKeon, Michael, *The Origins of the English Novel, 1600–1740,* Baltimore: Johns Hopkins University Press, 1987; London: Raduis, 1988

Radford, Jean, editor, *The Progress of Romance: The Politics of Popular Fiction,* London and New York: Routledge and Kegan Paul, 1986

Radway, Janice, *Reading the Romance: Women, Patriarchy and Popular Literature,* Chapel Hill: University of North Carolina Press, 1984; London: Verso, 1987

Richards, Thomas, *The Imperial Archive: Knowledge and the Fantasy of Empire,* London and New York: Verso, 1993

Watt, Ian, *The Rise of the Novel: Studies in Defoe, Richardson and Fielding,* Berkeley: University of California Press, and London: Chatto and Windus, 1957

Williams, Ioan, *Novel and Romance 1700–1800: A Documentary Record,* London: Routledge and Kegan Paul, and New York: Barnes and Noble, 1970

Romance of the Three Kingdoms. *See* Six Classic Chinese Novels

Romanian Novel

The emergence of the novelistic form in Romania should be discussed in terms not only of foreign influences but also of the culture's internal evolution, as "one of the manifestations that the transition from a traditional to a modern mentality took in Romania" (Cosma, 1985). The novel emerges when the traditional horizon of expectations, which encouraged a collective transmission of mythic models, is converted into what philosopher Constantin Noica has called a "horizon of questioning" (*Sentimentul românesc al fiinţei*), which promotes individual experience and mental mobility. In Romania the traditional narrative ethos, based on the idea of the cyclic nature of phenomena, was replaced by a forward-looking, transformative mentality in the second half of the 18th century, when the Romanian principalities of Transylvania, Wallachia, and Moldavia assimilated the ideas of the Enlightenment. The beginning and the end of the 19th century were separated by two distinct worldviews: one medieval and village-centered, the other bourgeois and city-centered. Against this evolving background, the Romanian novel emerged as a synthesis of local storytelling traditions and foreign influences. The success of the novel depended upon the creation of a credible narrative form, an adequate public, and a modern form of authorship. All three processes came together in the middle of the 19th century, which is generally regarded as the starting point of the indigenous Romanian novel.

The weakest component in the genesis of the Romanian novel was the reading public. Due to the high rate of illiteracy and the late development of the middle class, the Romanian novel for a while did not have an adequate audience. As Ioan Slavici confessed in 1874, the existence of a limited readership discouraged Romanian novelists from producing too much; but since they had fewer novels to write, these pioneers could spend more time on quality, producing persuasive works meant to educate a reluctant public. Thus, even though important, the reading public was not the ultimate determining factor in the genesis of the novel. Writers could break and modify the horizon of expectations, producing works that were not called forth by the existing cultural conditions. As historian Nicolae Iorga argued at the beginning of the 20th century, "The history of our literature speaks about books that have not been read. This is its main difference from the history of Western literatures which deal with books that have been read, preserved, rediscovered, loved, admired and converted by those impacted by them into a living sociopolitical reality" (see Iorga's *Oameni care au fost*, 1967). As in the case of modern historiography, drama, or poetry, Romanian fiction developed heroically in the absence of an adequate reading public or favorable political conditions. The first Romanian writers (Heliade, Kogălniceanu, Bolintineanu, and Alecsandri) had to create several new literary traditions, a literary language, and even a receptive culture. Eclectic rather than specialized, these founding figures had little time for aesthetic-generic distinctions. Authors in the modern sense of the word emerged only in the latter half of the 19th century: poet Mihai Eminescu, playwright Ion Luca Caragiale, and novelists Ioan Slavici and Duiliu Zamfirescu. By contrast to the earlier imitators of Western romances, Slavici and Zamfirescu wrote the first aesthetically conscious "novels," building on but also disentangling the genre from older forms of storytelling, such as oral tales, religious narratives, historical annals, epics, travelogues, or "physiologies."

Described as *romanţuri*—a term that in Romanian designates an uncertain cross between traditional romance and the modern novel—the first works of fiction, which imitated French models, fell into three subcategories: M. Kogălniceanu's fragmentary *Tainele inimii* (1850; The Heart's Mysteries) and Dimitrie Bolintineanu's *Manoil* (1855) and *Elena* (1862) are sentimental romances; G. Baronzi's *Misterele Bucureştilor* (The Mysteries of Bucharest) and C. Boerescu's *Aldo şi Aminta sau banditii* (Aldo and Aminta or the Bandits) are adventure romances; and I. Ghica's unfinished *Istoria lui Alecu* (1848; The History of Alecu), Pantazi Ghica's *Un boem român* (1860; A Romanian Bohemian), and Radu Ionescu's *Don Juanii din Bucureşti* (1862; The Don Juans of Bucharest) are social romances with elements of moral satire. Subtitled "a national novel," Bolintineanu's *Manoil* makes an effort to recast a foreign model in terms of the local history. Beyond its sentimental plot, which describes the erotic tribulations of a romantic idealist turned social playboy, and the epistolary structure inspired by Johann Wolfgang von Goethe's *Die Leiden des jungen Werthers* (1774; *The Sufferings of Young Werther*), one finds informative descriptions of everyday life in Moldavian villages and satirical portrayals of the fashionable circles in Bucharest. Bolintineanu's popular second novel, *Elena*, introduces another romantic hero, Alexandru, but its main focus is on the refined and introspective Elena, who suggests that women have an important role to play in the spiritual emancipation of Romania.

The second phase in the evolution of Romanian fiction (1863–65) produced the first genuine social novel, *Ciocoi vechi şi noi* (1863; Upstarts Old and New). Written by Nicolae Filimon, this work, labeled *romanţ* in the subtitle and a *nuvelă* (novella) in the dedication, marked a significant departure from the weaker imitative romances of the previous phase. The author's declared intention in the prologue was to move from Stendhal's study of isolated *arrivistes* to the physiology of an entire class of upstarts that included both the Greek bureaucrats brought to govern Wallachia at the end of the previous century (their representative in the novel is Andronache Tuzluc) and the rapacious local profiteers, "leaders of Bucharest upstartism and villainy," represented by Dinu Păturică. Filimon's physiology was supposed to end with the newer, Westernized type of *ciocoi* emerging midway through the 19th century, but the writer never completed the projected second part. As Eugen Lovinescu wrote in 1913, "The future of our novel emerged from the furrow of Filimon's Upstarts." If this furrow seemed typologically naive, opposing the villainous *ciocoi* to idealized traditional types such as the enlightened landowner C., Tuzluc's bailiff Gheorghe, or the native Prince Ghica who replaces foreign rule in Romania, it provided readers with an entertaining plot driven by memorable villains such as Păturică and Kera Duduca, with excellent social and psychological forays into an epoch (1814–30) that marked the transition of Romanian society from feudalism to capitalism.

The period that followed was dominated by historical romances written by I.C. Drăgescu, N.D. Popescu, Th.M. Stoenescu, Al. Pelimon, and G. Baronzi that passed easily into sensational fiction, especially when their main characters were *haiduci* (outlaws) rendered lucrative by P. Macri and Ilie Ighel. There were also a few observant social romances, such as Iosif Vulcan's *Ranele naţiunii* (1876; The Wounds of a Nation), which was dedicated to the plight of Transylvanian Romanians, Nicolae D. Xenopol's *Brazi şi putregai* (1880; Pine Trees and Rot), which focused on social inequities in rural Moldavia, and Grigore H. Grandea's *Vlăsia sau Ciocoii noi* (1887; Vlăsia or the New Upstarts), which updated Filimon's novel by comparing mid-19th-century Romanian society to the wild Vlăsia woods. However, with the exception of Constantin Mille's *Dinu Milian* (1887), which advocated aesthetic and ideological principles borrowed from Émile Zola's naturalism, these works had a rudimentary aesthetic consciousness.

Two transition figures who contributed to the aesthetic professionalization of the novel were Mihai Eminescu, Romania's preeminent poet, and Ioan Creangă, the greatest 19th-century Romanian storyteller. Eminescu's unfinished novel *Geniu pustiu* (Barren Genius), written between 1866 and 1868 but published only posthumously, followed *The Sufferings of Young Werther*'s example in structuring the narrative around an introspective artistic character with strong feelings, disquieting experiences, and heroic passions that include participation in the 1848 national democratic revolution in Transylvania. The novella *Sărmanul Dionis* (1873; Poor Dionis) introduced a new narrative tradition in Romanian fiction, romantic-fantastic, violating time and space relationships and pursuing new configurations "within a framework of the extraordinary" (Ciopraga, 1973). Eminescu's synthesis of Romanian fantastic folklore with classic myths and Oriental initiatory doctrines paved the way for every important mythopoetic writer of the 20th century, from Sadoveanu and Voiculescu to Mircea Eliade and A.E. Baconsky.

Ion Creangă has been praised as the embodiment of the pure faculty of narration, a Romanian Homer who in his autobiographical *Amintiri din copilărie* (1881–89; Memories of My Boyhood) created the "image of universal childhood" (George Călinescu, 1941). Beyond the good-humored recapitulation of the author's childhood exploits, *Memories of My Boyhood* treats the reader to events with unexpected dramatic implications for the life of a patriarchal Moldavian village. Nică, the autobiographical protagonist, is a comic-tragic character who confronts not only petty cultural divisions in his native village but also an all-present *vreme* (time/destiny/season/weather), which gives him a painful historical consciousness. His journeys away from his native northern Moldavian village anticipate the more significant drama of his final uprooting. The book's acute sense of time splits the narrating self from the experiencing self, and the two further from author Creangă, introducing a novelistic complication between the space of memory, that of history, and the mythic space of childhood.

Like Creangă, Ioan Slavici took his primary inspiration from oral storytelling rather than from contemporary European fiction, but he was well acquainted with the work of Honoré de Balzac, Émile Zola, and Alphonse Daudet. Both his association with the literary-philosophic society Junimea (Youth) and his studies in Vienna aroused Slavici's interest in questions of aesthetics and novelistic form. His essays reveal not only the novelist's need to articulate characters, arrange situations, and give sentiments a direction but also his obligation to provide questions for the reader to solve. Rejecting sentimentality, Slavici insisted that situations and characters be true to the situation of a certain place. Even more interestingly, Slavici asked (much like Joseph Conrad) that every word contribute to a consistent narrative atmosphere. These working ideas emerged out of Slavici's slow career as a novelist, which took him through two botched novels and about 80 successful short stories before he wrote his masterpiece, *Mara*. Serialized in 1894 without reference to its genre, with the subtitle "roman" (novel) added in 1904 when it was republished in book form, *Mara* consolidated the Romanian novel, introducing the first well-rounded, strong-willed characters torn between an implacable destiny and what Slavici called a "predominant passion" that enabled characters to challenge their "bastardly condition."

Examples of embattled, "problematic heroes"—as Georg Lukács would later call them—can be found in the work of other writers of the period, particularly in Alexandru Vlahuţă's *Dan* (1894), which portrays the first Romanian *inadaptabil*, or intellectual misfit in conflict with bourgeois society. Unlike Vlahuţă's intellectual dreamers, however, Slavici's characters begin as average people, so that their later efforts to transcend their dull condition appear even more impressive. Ghiţă, the protagonist of Slavici's novella *Moara cu noroc* (1881; The Mill of Luck and Plenty), starts as a relatively happy cobbler and husband, but his newfound capitalistic ambitions push him into a dangerous partnership with outlaw Lică Sămădăul that defies basic laws of society and nature. Mara also begins as a humble, impoverished widow and mother of two, but turns into a resourceful businesswoman who escapes her condition and class. On a higher, ethical level, Slavici's novel tries to find answers to old ethnic prejudices, portraying the passionate love of Mara's daughter, Persida, for a German ethnic, Ignaz Huber. With his cross-cultural sensitivity acquired during a childhood spent in a multi-ethnic Transylvanian town, Slavici ends the stormy affair with an interethnic marriage, but does not gloss over the inherent contradictions in 19th-century family life. Slavici's importance as the creator of realistic rural fiction and of the first bourgeois epic was recognized only gradually, after the author had been contested by his rival Duiliu Zamfirescu and his rural fiction had entered an eclipse in the first decades of the 20th century, as modernism established itself in fiction in direct opposition to rural traditionalism. Today Slavici is recognized not only for his rural realism but also for the modernity of his narrative constructions and of his incursions into deep psychology.

Unlike Slavici, who had developed his artistic consciousness instinctively, Duiliu Zamfirescu arrived at an understanding of the possibilities of the novel through a study of already existing models, such as Gustave Flaubert's, Zola's, Filimon's, or Slavici's. By contrast to the naturalistic position, focused on the external determinants of life, Zamfirescu emphasized character psychology and intellectual analysis. After a false start with two youthful novels, Zamfirescu developed the first narrative cycle in Romanian literature, comprised of *Viaţa la ţară* (serialized 1894–95; republished in volume 1898 [*Sasha*]), *Tănase Scatiu* (1895–96; 1907), *În război* (1897–98; 1902 [In Time of War]), *Îndreptări* (1901–1902; 1908 [Restitutions]), and *Anna, sau Ceea ce nu se poate* (1906–10; 1911 [Anna, or What Cannot Be Done]). Focused on the Comăneşti family, this cycle excelled in its presentation of characters with contradictory psychologies, split between reality and ideality. Matei Damian, the protagonist of *Viaţa la ţară,* returns to his home village with dreams to reform it, but he never translates them into action. His marriage to

Saşa Comăneşteanu is motivated by deep intellectual affinities: both characters live absorbed in their rich inner lives, relating to each other from the remoteness of an illusion. Like his characters, Zamfirescu wavered between the space of ideality and that of social reality, opposing the idealized landed aristocracy to the rising class of leaseholders memorably embodied in a Filimon-type character, the venal and boorish Tănase Scatiu. As *Îndreptări* suggested, a partial recovery of the rural aristocracy could take place through the marriage of the last Comăneşti with a spirited middle-class woman from the recently reintegrated province of Transylvania, but on the whole Zamfirescu's Comăneşti cycle reads like an elegy for the Romanian *boyar* class.

The last decades of the 19th century also consolidated the aesthetic understanding of the genre. Previous discussions had been primarily concerned with the morality of the novel or with its place among the other genres. The term *romanţ* (romance), introduced in the preface to a 1799 translation and defined by I. Eliade Rădulescu as "an invented history or the narration of a real event adorned with imagined events" (1839), competed for quite a while with that of *roman* (novel), defined by D. Gusti in 1852 as an instructive narrative whose purpose was to improve social mores through the castigation of vices and uncontrolled passions. The term *nuvelă* (novella) was also used in alternation with *roman,* suggesting that the latter was still considered to be too close to the term *romanţ* associated with imitative products. After 1860, Romanian writers felt an increasing need to move beyond their foreign models, stretching them to accommodate Romanian realities. The articulation of the first Romanian theories of the novel thus went hand in hand with the plea for an original Romanian realism. Thus Pantazi Ghica argued in *Un boem român* (1860) that fiction needed to reflect a recognizable, autobiographical, or more generally human experience; and Radu Ionescu, after conceding apropos of his own *Don Juanii din Bucureşti* (1862) that the Romanian novelist could emulate the spacious genius of Balzac, set before Romanian writers the task of representing single facets of Romanian society in novels of manners modeled after William Makepeace Thackeray and Charles Dickens. In time these partial representations could constitute a veritable social comedy of a Romanian society. This idea was reconceptualized later in terms of a specific national typology both by the influential critic of the 19th century, Titu Maiorescu, who in "Literatura română şi străinătatea" (1882; Romanian Literature and the Foreign Influence) argued for an original novel focused on representative national characters, such as peasants and the lower classes, and by the naturalist C. Mille, who in 1887 defended his right to represent in an unadorned way the "blurred, contradictory features of everyday people."

At the beginning of the 20th century, Romanian literature went through a brief period of stagnation. "The great achievements of romanticism and realism in poetry, prose, and drama—as illustrated by Mihai Eminescu, Ion Creangă, Ion L. Caragiale, and Ioan Slavici—lay behind, and the great critical-intellectual mentors, the aestheticist Titu Maiorescu and the Marxist Constantin Dobrogeanu-Gherea, were long past their prime" (Nemoianu, 1981). In fiction, two emerging writers, Ion Agârbiceanu and Gala Galaction, followed the model of the rural novel established during the 19th century, keeping their prose simple and traditionalistic and blending social awareness with

sentimental Christian humanism. Their work fit into the ethnographic and moralist literature promoted by the magazine *Sămănătorul* (1901–10; The Sower). The chief advocate of rural traditionalism was critic and historian Nicolae Iorga. Two other critics and theorists associated with the populist trend, Garabet Ibrăileanu and Constantin Stere, wrote novels themselves, but their works illustrated two new types established after World War I: the psychological novel and the political satire.

The two most important novelists of the first half of the 20th century, Mihail Sadoveanu and Liviu Rebreanu, began to publish before World War I but brought out their major work after 1920. Author of more than 100 volumes, Sadoveanu alternated between ample historical novels that defined the fundamental moral and psychological features of the Romanian people and shorter mythic-poetic narratives that explored the relationship between man and nature, body and soul, and guilt and punishment. The first category, organized in ample cycles inspired by traditional legends and historical chronicles, spanned Romanian history from its ancient roots (*Creanga de aur* [1933; The Golden Bough]), through the medieval period of chivalrous, anti-Turkish struggle (*Şoimii* [1904; The Hawks], *Neamul Şoimăreştilor* [1915; The Şoimaru Clan], *Zodia cancerului* [1929; Under the Sign of the Crab], *Nunta Domniţei Ruxandra* [1932; Princess Ruxandra's Wedding], *Viaţa lui Ştefan cel Mare* [1934; The Life of Stephen the Great], *Fraţii Jderi* [1935–42; The Jderi Brothers], *Nicoară Potcoavă* [1952; Nicoară Horseshoe]), to modern history (*Strada Lăpuşneanu* [1917; The Lăpuşneanu Street], *Venea o moară pe Siret* [1925; A Mill Was Floating Down the Siret]). The second category of works consisted of clusters of interrelated stories (*Hanul Ancuţei* [1928; Ancuţa's Inn], *Ţara dincolo de negură* [1926; The Land Beyond the Mists]) or of more structured mythic-realistic narratives such as *Creanga de aur, Divanul persian* (1940; The Persian Divan) and *Baltagul* (1930; The Hatchet), which restated the theme of crime and punishment through its memorable character Vitoria Lipan, the novel's sturdy, illiterate heroine who avenges the death of her husband killed by fellow shepherds. Chiding historians for their excess of factuality, Sadoveanu reminded them that "Reality is not constituted only of stone buildings and pieces of paper: the light in the souls of generations is preserved in myth." However, Sadoveanu's own work alternated between enchanted mythopoetic vistas and well-documented, unadorned descriptions of everyday life in Moldavian villages and provincial towns.

If Sadoveanu illustrated the possibilities of lyrical-mythic fiction, remaining primarily a great storyteller, Rebreanu represented the culmination of classic realism. No other Romanian writer has had more memorable characters or a finer, geometric sense of novelistic construction. Rebreanu's work covers a variety of subjects and social environments, from the elementary rituals of peasant life in *Ion* (1920; *Ion*) to the complex conflicts of city life: political in *Gorila* (1938; Gorilla), social-psychological in *Răscoala* (1932; The Uprising); subject matter ranges from Horea's 18th-century uprising against the Hungarian domination of Transylvania (*Crăişorul* [1929; Prince of the Mountains]) to the tragedy of Romanian ethnics in Transylvania forced to defend the Austro-Hungarian Empire against their Romanian brethren during World War I (*Pădurea spînzuraţilor* [1922; The Forest of the Hanged]). Continuing the rural tradition inaugurated by Slavici, Rebreanu raised it to a classic art in *Ion,* described by its author as a "spheroidal object which ends just as it began." The quasi-Aeschylian tragedy caused by the character Ion's unappeased desire for more farming land shakes a Transylvanian village community, leaving several characters dead; but in the end the turmoils of life are erased by indifferent time, which restores the village to its original image "as if nothing had changed in it." *The Uprising,* devoted to the dramatic events of 1907, also has a symmetrical structure alternating between a well-documented description of the life of deprivation led by peasants in the Argeş county and the narcissistic life of landowners, leaseholders, and politicians in Bucharest and their properties.

Believing that "the foundation of all writing is expression as a means not as an aim in itself," Rebreanu avoided "beautiful writing," keeping his style unadorned and his narrative presentation direct and impersonal. His complex social frescoes revolve around strong-willed but contradictory characters such as Ion Glanetaşu, who represented for critic Eugen Lovinescu (1928) "the expression of an instinct for the domination of the land." Intricate ideological conflicts are negotiated at the level of human interrelations, as in *Pădurea spînzuraţilor,* which opposes to both imperialist internationalism and the idea of national-ethnic duty a humanistic emphasis on man's duty to his fellow man. While Rebreanu's major novels had a remarkably complex narrative structure, his later works were held together through sensational plot motifs, such as that of bestial sexuality and metempsychosis in *Adam şi Eva* (1936; Adam and Eve), or class miscegenation and mental pathology in *Ciuleandra* (1927).

Rebreanu's exploration of an elementary universe was later continued by Pavel Dan, whose *Urcan Bătrînul* (published posthumously in 1987; Old Urcan) introduced fantastic elements in realistic rural settings, as did two Romanian writers with distinguished careers abroad, Panait Istrati and Peter Neagoe. Living most of his adult life in France, Istrati wrote in French about an elemental world of peasants, outlaws, small entrepreneurs, and existential bums on the Danube plains. His novels, some of which he himself translated into Romanian, won him the reputation of the "new Gor'kii of the Balkans." *Kyra Kiralina* (1924; Kirah Kiralinah) showed not only a knack for vibrant, unconventional characters but also cinematic skill in handling the temporal and spatial shifts of narration. The motley origins and status of his Romanian, Turkish, Greek, and Gypsy characters suggested a utopian multicultural space along the Danube, whose fluid boundaries and uninhibited behaviors contrasted with the increasing divisions in Europe. The later novels, gathered under the common title of the "Stories of Adrian Zografi" (*Oncle Anghel* [1924; Uncle Anghel], *Les Haidoucs* [1925; The Bandits], *La Maison Türinger* [1933; The Türinger House], *Le bureau de placement* [1933; Office for the Unemployed], *Mediteranée* [1934]), and his independent masterpieces *Codin* (1925) and *Les Chardons du Baragan* (1928; The Thistles of the Baragan) added other memorable characters to his Danubian gallery of liminal existential heroes. The English fiction of Peter Neagoe, written after his emigration to the United States, recalls typical peasant experiences in his native Transylvania. *Easter Sun* (1934) echoes Rebreanu's *Ion,* portraying simultaneously exceptional passions and everyday life in a rural environment; *There Is My Heart* (1936) takes a typical peasant character to New York, exploring the problems of cultural acclimatization. Two later works, *No Time for Tears* (1958), which focuses on Jewish emigration, and the posthumous *The Saint of Montparnasse* (1965), devoted to the rural Romanian

childhood and the Parisian adulthood of sculptor Constantin Brâncuşi, continue to explore the dramatic dichotomies of exile.

Rebreanu's preoccupation with the psychology and politics of city life was continued by Ion Călugăru, who described Jewish life in provincial Moldavian towns, and George M. Zamfirescu, who in *Maidanul cu dragoste* (1936; The Lovers' Gutter) represents the outlandish life of shantytowns around Bucharest. But the most important urban novelist of the first half of the 20th century was Cezar Petrescu, who in *Întunecare* (1927; Gathering Clouds), *Calea Victoriei* (1930; Victory Road), and *Apostol* (1933) explored the radical shifts in the culture of big cities during and after World War I. Radu Comsa, the hero of *Întunecare,* inaugurated a concern with Romania's own lost generation of disillusioned war heroes. Petrescu also modernized novelistic techniques, resorting to simultaneous presentation, cinematic splicing, and blending of document and fiction. Like Petrescu, Ionel Teodoreanu focused on the breakup of the prewar patriarchal Romanian society. Both novelists displayed a mixture of sentimental nostalgia and satire in reflecting the degradation of the rural environment and the political intrigues of the new urban class. Critic George Călinescu also focused his novel *Enigma Otiliei* (1938; Otilia's Enigma) on the decadent upper middle class, but his human comedy takes a more Balzacian approach, pitting the pretentiously opulent Giurgiuveanus against bewildered young idealists such as Felix Sima, cynical upstarts such as Stănică Raţiu, and a rare vestige of the landed aristocracy such as Leonida Pascalopol.

The momentous changes brought about by the end of World War I, from the increase in territory and population to major modernizing reforms in all areas, created conditions for the emergence of Romanian modernism, promoted primarily by critic and novelist Eugen Lovinescu. His imposing syntheses, *Istoria civilizaţiei române moderne* (1924–25; History of Modern Romanian Civilization) and *Istoria literaturii române contemporane* (1926–29; History of Contemporary Romanian Literature), encouraged synchronization with the urban-liberal cultures of the West, and "all sincere efforts of exploration and innovation" in literature. Lovinescu's own cycle of psychological novels— *Bizu* (1932), *Firu'n patru* (1933; Splitting Hairs), *Diana* (1936), *Mili* (1937), and *Acord final* (1939; Final Chord)—recalls themes of 19th-century fiction but breaks spectacularly with the expected conventions of form, mixing confession, psychological analysis, and conceptual discussion.

Lovinescu's theoretical aspirations for the novel were more persuasively carried out by Camil Petrescu, Hortensia Papadat-Bengescu, Anton Holban, Gib I. Mihăescu, Ury Benador, and Marcel Blecher. Intimately acquainted with European analytic fiction and the theories of Bergson, Freud, and Husserl that had influenced it, Camil Petrescu proposed in his 1935 essay "Noua structură şi Marcel Proust" (The New Structure and Marcel Proust) to substitute a flexible phenomenology of events for the old positivistic causality, and authenticity of experience for the classical rules of fiction. In his desire to represent life *dans toute vérité,* Camil Petrescu chose personal forms of narration (diary, letters, confession) that emphasized process writing without "composition or style." His novels, however, did not lack discipline: Ladima's drama in *Patul lui Procust* (1933; Procustes' Bed) is put together by Fred Vasilescu with the rigor of a historian-detective from Ladima's diaries and articles, the recollections of his friends and lover Emilia, and the prosecutor's conclusions concerning the causes of Ladima's suicide. *Ultima noapte de dragoste, întîia noapte de război* (1930; Last Night of Love, First Night of War) also shifts from a self-absorbed first volume focused on Ştefan Gheorghidiu's jealous feelings toward his wife to the more objectified, multivoiced journal of the war in the second volume.

Herself an admirer of Marcel Proust, Hortensia Papadat-Bengescu wrote seven novels focused on the Halippa family—descendants of former leaseholders turned big-time capitalists—that replaced external narration with minute inner analysis. *Concert din muzică de Bach* (1927; A Concert of Music by Bach) presents characters not through a stable narrator but through other characters' impressions of them. Many of these inner reflectors are unusually perceptive, seeing everything through a magnifying glass. Mini in *Fecioarele despletite* (1926; Disheveled Virgins) can see even the "density of her thoughts," and tries to do the same with other characters, revealing their intimate structure the way "the whole anatomy of steel fibers and veins was revealed when you raised the lid of a piano." Papadat-Bengescu was also interested in exploring liminal states of the subconscious, enhanced by some malady, handicap, or social-moral decadence, such as the social disenchantment of the landowner Baldovin in *Rădăcini* (published posthumously in 1974; Roots), or the narcissistic self-absorption of Coca-Aimée, Doctor Walter, and Prince Maxenţiu in *Concert din muzică de Bach*. Papadat-Bengescu's preoccupation with morbid moods was shared by the younger Gib I. Mihăescu, who described himself as a "diver into the subconscious." His novels *Rusoaica* (1933; The Russian Woman) and *Donna Alba* (1935) offer an original mix of sensationalism and analytic insight, modern psychology and romance. Ury Benador took the analysis of obsessive states even further, crossing in *Subiect banal* (1935; Banal Subject) the border between normality and pathology, describing a self-destructive male character caught between his human desire to fail in his demonstration that all women are adulterous and his "scientific" desire to succeed.

The exploration of liminal subconscious states had other purposes besides that of suggesting a psychopathology. For example, the blurring of the boundary between reality and fantasy in Marcel Blecher's *Întîmplări în irealitatea imediată* (1930; Occurrences in the Immediate Unreality) create not only psychological disturbances, but also useful ontological expansions of the world as we know it. In Anton Holban's fiction, introspection combines with moral reflection. His static narratives *O moarte care nu dovedeşte nimic* (1931; A Death That Proves Nothing), *Ioana* (1934), and *Jocurile Daniei* (1935; Dania's Games) record the disruptions that the imponderables of love, sickness, and death create in the certitudes of the male protagonists. The rational male perspective was put to test also in critic G. Ibrăileanu's *Adela* (1959), subtitled "A Fragment of Emil Codrescu's Diary." In his monologic confession, Codrescu worries over Adela's sentiments for him, trying to reduce feminine ambiguities to male certitudes. More weighty political concerns are reflected in playwright Mihail Sebastian's novel *De două mii de ani* (For Two Thousand Years), in which an autobiographical Jewish hero tries to safeguard his human and intellectual identity against the background of the anti-Semitic manifestations of 1923.

The evolution of the Romanian novel from Sadoveanu through Rebreanu to Camil Petrescu and Papadat-Bengescu had followed one primary direction, moving from lyrical subjectivity to objectified analysis, and from authorial intrusion to imperson-

ality. This dominant trajectory, however, was interrupted by writers who returned fiction to lyricism, myth, and a nostalgic-picaresque Balkanic decor. In addition to George M. Zamfirescu and Panait Istrati, Mateiu Caragiale deserves mention; in *Craii de curtea veche* (1929; Old Court Libertines) he offers a sumptuous recreation of the fin-de-siècle atmosphere of Bucharest's suburbs ruled over by Paşadia and Pantazi, two "old court philanderers" who mix oriental hedonism with Western cultural ambitions. By contrast to these "Danubian Don Quixotes," Gore Pirgu is a perverse lower-class upstart. Descended directly from Filimon, this character suggests Caragiale's antipathy for the rising suburban class, recruited from the "brawlers and throat cutters" of the slums.

The mythic-fantastic element also reemerged in the fiction of Vasile Voiculescu and Mircea Eliade. Voiculescu's posthumously published *Zahei Orbul* (1968; Blind Zahei) traces the symbolic experiences of the title character in an apocalyptic fin-de-siècle world that includes a Gothic "court of thieves" and a salt mine for forced labor. A similar mixture of myth and Gothic tension can be found in Eliade's early novels, which describe the agitated life of young intellectuals before World War II (*Isabel şi apele diavolului* [1930; Isabel and the Devil's Waters], *Întoarcerea din rai* [1934; Return from Eden]). Eliade also wrote novels of analysis, whose in-depth psychological focus he considered a good substitute for a magic consciousness on the wane. *Şantier* (1935; Building Site), subtitled an "indirect novel" and written entirely as an intellectual journal, records the narrator's struggle between his passion for science and his attraction to adventure. *Maitreyi* (1933) relocates the struggle for self-definition in the Orient, focusing on Eliade's spiritual adventure in India and his effort to reconcile the conflict of cultures through "an integrative consciousness" of love and myth.

In 1941, at the end of one of the most productive periods in the history of the Romanian novel, Pompiliu Constantinescu could finally state that Romanian fiction had come of age. Multiformed and thematically varied, the Romanian novel was truly the "resonating chamber of all the individual and collective struggles of our society." But criticism also noticed signs of devitalization in fiction, as newer writers mimicked rather superficially the previously successful techniques of analytic fiction. The signs of exhaustion were aggravated during the next period (1948–60), when the Soviet-occupied Romania underwent a process of Stalinization that radically disrupted its culture and civil society. At a time when, as André Stil proudly announced, every Eastern European writer had "a little Stalin in him, watch[ing] from inside, smiling and serious, giving confidence," few novelists managed to publish thematically and formally viable work. The doyen of Romanian fiction, Sadoveanu, produced a dubious novel, *Mitrea Cocor* (1949), about an opportunist who turns the Soviet occupation to his advantage, and *Nicoară Potcoavă* (1952; Nicoară Horseshoe), a rewriting of *Şoimii* that makes Nicoară into a philosophic man of arms who announces the rise of a "new world." Camil Petrescu's monumental historical fresco, *Un om între oameni* (1954–57; A Man Amongst Men), based on the events leading to the 1848 revolution in Wallachia and the part played in it by the militant historian Nicolae Bălcescu, was painstakingly documented but predictable in its ideological conclusions. The works that succeeded were primarily devoted to pre–World War II events handled in traditional forms, such as the chronicle novel with memorialistic insertions. Most popular at the time was Zaharia Stancu, who wrote rhapsodic, structurally digressive novels such as *Desculţ* (1948; *Barefoot*), *Dulăii* (1952; *Hounds*), the five-volume *Rădăcinile sînt amare* (1958–59, Bitter Are the Roots), and the trilogy *Vîntul şi ploaia* (1969; The Wind and the Rain). Focused on the life of peasants and small tradesmen in the southern plains during the first half-century, these novels are loosely structured by the subjective perspective of a youthful, partly autobiographical protagonist called Darie. *Jocul cu moartea* (1962; *A Gamble with Death*), *Pădurea nebună* (1963; The Crazy Forest), and *Şatra* (1968; *The Gypsy Tribe*) moved beyond Stancu's favorite autobiographical themes—the first exploring Bucharest under German occupation, the second provincial life, and the third the fate of a displaced community of gypsies after the war—but continued to rely on the loose structuring techniques of oral storytelling.

Călinescu's *Bietul Ioanide* (1953; Wretched Ioanide) and *Scrinul negru* (1960; The Black Chest of Drawers) exemplify a more rigorous form of documentary novel, focused on the microsocial shifts produced by the historical and political events of the mid-century. *Bietul Ioanide* filters the momentous events of the 1930s and 1940s through the sceptical consciousness of its title character, a disenchanted architect and "ageless faun." *Scrinul negru* describes the dissolution of the former landed aristocracy and professional class during the 1950s, mixing classic narrative with documents, letters, and even snatches of Călinescu's own magazine columns. The example of Călinescu's baroque narratives of a decaying class was followed by Petru Dumitriu in the trilogy *Cronica de familie* (1957; *Family Jewels*), completed after the writer's self-imposed exile to France with historical frescoes such as *L'homme aux yeux gris* (1968; The Man with Grey Eyes). To compensate for the political compromises made in Romania with *Pasărea furtunii* (1952; Bird of Storm), which tries to justify the existence of a Romanian communist gulag, Dumitriu also published *Incognito* (1962), which denounces the depersonalizing system of the communist dictatorship, and a number of reflections on his spiritual crisis, such as *Au Dieu inconnu* (1979; *To the Unknown God*) and *Zéro, ou le point de depart* (1982; Zero, or the Point of Departure). Updating thematic strands inaugurated by Rebreanu, Titus Popovici published two successful novels during the 1950s: *Străinul* (1955; *The Stranger*), portraying a provincial milieu experienced by an adolescent hero during the traumatic years of World War II, and *Setea* (1958; *The Thirst*), which focuses on ancestral peasant mentalities about to be disrupted by the communist socialization.

The writer who contributed most to the rehabilitation of Romanian literature during the 1950s was Marin Preda. His early masterpiece, *Moromeţii* (volume 1, 1955; volume 2, 1967; *The Morometes*), portrays a traditional rural society enjoying its last days of freedom before the communist takeover. Preda's subsequent novels, from *Risipitorii* (1962; The Squanderers), *Intrusul* (1968; The Intruder), and *Marele singuratic* (1972; The Great Loner) to the three-volume *Cel mai iubit dintre pămînteni* (1980; The Most Beloved Man on Earth), spearheaded the revival of the novel, contributing to the emergence of two new types of fiction: the new analytic novel and the novel of political debate. Preda's last published work openly interrogates the communist ideology through Victor Petrini, an aspiring philosophy professor fired during the Stalinistic purges and imprisoned several times for political reasons.

A more contradictory transition figure from the dogmas of socialist realism was Eugen Barbu. His work alternated between propagandist novels, such as *Şoseua nordului* (1959; The Northern Highway), which pits communist heroes against fascist villains, and *Facerea lumii* (1964; Genesis), which represents the forced collectivization of agriculture, and authentic fiction. In the latter category mention deserves to be made of the poetic-grotesque evocation of the Bucharest underworld in *Groapa* (1957; The Pit), which builds on the interwar prose of the slum (Rebreanu, Mateiu Caragiale, George M. Zamfirescu); as well as a richly documented chronicle of 18th-century Wallachia, *Principele* (1969; The Prince), which opposes an idealized local scholar and moralist, Ion Valahul, to the corrupt Greek princes that rule the country for the Turks. Barbu's vision of an 18th-century Wallachia fallen prey to foreign ideologies could easily be read as a somewhat xenophobic allegory of Romania's postwar history.

During the 1960s, novelists became acutely aware of the prohibitive boundaries placed by the communist power around social truth and of their need to challenge them, first by rediscovering the transformative power of symbolic imagination, then by expanding their focus from documentary reconstruction to cultural analysis. Both trends had political as well as aesthetic consequences: by insinuating an element of subjective fantasy in their fiction, writers such as A.E. Baconsky, Fănuş Neagu, Ştefan Bănulescu, Sorin Titel, and Sütö András violated the prescriptions of socialist realism. Their rich, metaphoric vision made the social reporting of the 1950s appear trite and escapist. Likewise, the political novels of Laurentiu Fulga, Constantin Ţoiu, Alexandru Ivasiuc, Nicolae Breban, Dumitru Radu Popescu, Paul Goma, George Bălăiţă, Norman Manea, Bujor Nedelcovici, Augustin Buzura, and Romulus Guga call into question official representations of recent history (especially the Stalinistic 1950s), gaining new insights not only into objective history but also into its subjective refractions in the life of individuals. Both trends showed concern with narrative approach, borrowing polyphonic techniques from Fedor Dostoevskii, Albert Camus, Jean-Paul Sartre, or the masters of South American magic realism. They also had strong ties with Romanian fiction of the 1930s and 1940s. Fănuş Neagu's mythic-realistic description in *Îngerul a strigat* (1968; The Angel Has Cried) of a rural community disrupted by World War II recalls the poetic realism of Sadoveanu and Istrati, and A.E. Baconsky's apocalyptic vision of postwar Romania in *Echinoxul nebunilor* (1967; Equinox of the Fools) draws on both Eminescu's fantastic prose and on the Gothic tradition of Poe and Hoffmann. The political novel, on the other hand, inherited features of the "end of a world" fiction as illustrated by Cezar Petrescu, Mateiu Caragiale, or George Călinescu, as well as introspective-essayistic strategies of the interwar analytic novel.

The apocalyptic dynamics of history play an important role in Bujor Nedelcovici's *Ultimii* (1970; The Last Ones), Laurenţiu Fulga's *Moartea lui Orfeu* (1970; Orpheus' Death), Romulus Guga's *Nebunul si floarea* (1970; The Madman and the Flower), and D.R. Popescu's *Vînătoarea regală* (1973; The Royal Hunt). In particular, Popescu's polyphonic, multiplotted novel invites comparison with William Faulkner and Gabriel García Márquez, but also with Mircea Eliade's political-philosophic novel *Pe strada Mântuleasa* (1970; The Old Man and the Bureaucrats). Begun in the 1950s in Paris and completed later in Chicago, this novel has a redeeming narrative-metaphysical theme: its protagonist, an old man named Zaharia Fărîmă (Zaharia "Crumb"), mesmerizes his communist interrogators with fabulous, labyrinthine stories of the past. Eliade's "*Arabian Nights* in a Stalinistic World" did not merely ensure the storyteller's survival, it also created important disturbances in the power machinery of communist Romania. Eliade's search for a mythopoetic form of narrative that would redeem history was further echoed in novels published in Romania during the 1970s. George Bălăiță's *Lumea în două zile* (1975; A World in Two Days) mixes fantastic-metaphysical insertions among realistic narratives on political themes, creating a narrative hybrid on all levels. A similar conjunction of politics and metaphysics can be found in Ştefan Bănulescu's *Cartea de la Metopolis* (1977; The Book of Metopolis), an epic-mythic reconstruction of a Danubian world through the first half of the 20th century that opposes an imaginative tailor-writer, Polydor, to half-demented social reformers like Bazacopol who make the future of Metopolis miserable. Few Romanian readers missed the hint to the fate of historical Bucharest demolished by Ceauşescu in the late 1970s, as well as to the collective dream of salvation from the contemporary kitsch through an improvised hero figure. That Romanian dream, naive as it may have seemed, is also expressed in Breban's *Drumul la zid* (1984; Journey to the Wall), which portrays the spiritual conversion of a humble functionary into a hero endowed with charismatic powers and a mysterious message.

The introspective methods of Camil Petrescu, updated with Sartre and Camus, were carried to their ultimate consequences by Alexandru Ivasiuc. His *Vestibul* (1967; Antechamber) and *Interval* (1968) employ confession and analysis to explore the subterranean changes in the life of middle-aged men; *Cunoşterea de noapte* (1969; Night Knowledge) uses a personal crisis (the imminent death of the protagonist's wife) to trigger a process of historical and political reexamination that turns a "professionist of total understanding" into an alienated sceptic. Ivasiuc's later work, such as *Păsările* (1970; The Birds) and *Apa* (1975; The Water), addresses the moral failures of the communist revolution through problematizing analysis and a more direct narration, while *Racul* (1976; The Crawfish) illustrates the dangers of totalitarian power against a Conradian background (an invented Latin American republic). In Nicolae Breban's fiction, psychological and ethical speculation have been used to support a comprehensive analysis of Romanian society in *Francisca* (1965), *În absenţa stăpînilor* (1966; In the Absence of the Masters), *Animale bolnave* (1868; Sick Animals), and *Îngerul de ghips* (1973; The Plaster Angel), but also the more ambiguous, erotic-experimental theme of *Don Juan* (1981). Norman Manea has also oscillated between straightforward political novels such as *Captivii* (1970; The Captives) and *Anii de ucenicie ai lui August Prostul* (1976; The Apprentice Years of August the Dull-Witted) and poetic-experimental novels such as *Atrium* (1974), which reconstructs the wandering psychological and social perspective of an adolescent. His last novel published in Romania, *Plicul negru* (1986; *The Black Envelope*), combines approaches, recording both the somber details of daily life in Ceauşescu's Romania and their allegorical implications.

A more unwavering analytic focus can be found in Augustin Buzura's fiction. Beginning with *Absenţii* (1970; Absentees) and *Feţele tăcerii* (1974; Faces of Silence), Buzura's novels record with clinical lucidity the minutest aspects of the Romanian psy-

chological and social experience. Even though later novels like *Vocile nopţii* (1980; The Voices of Night) envision history as a formidable labyrinth through which individual characters move defeated in search of an elusive truth, Buzura's ambition throughout his pre-1989 career was to transcribe, in a kind of uncensored total recall, the atmosphere of (post-)Stalinistic Romania. Buzura's single-minded concentration on the truth of history was matched only by Paul Goma's political novel-essays, which could only appear abroad. *Ostinato,* first published in Germany and then retitled *La cellule des libérables* (1971; The Cell of the Liberatable) in France, *Elles étaient quatre . . .* (1974; They Were Four), *Gherla* (1976), *Dans le cercle* (1977; Within the Circle), *Garde inverse* (1977; Reversed Guard), *Le tremblement des hommes* (1979; The Trembling of Men), *Les Chiens de mort* (1981; The Dogs of Death), *Bonifacia* (1986), and *Le Calidor* (1987) expose in brutally honest detail reminiscent of Aleksandr Solzhenitsyn the treatment of political prisoners such as Goma himself in the Romanian communist gulag.

Of the younger writers, mention deserves to be given to Petru Popescu, who focused the fiction published in Romania on the disgruntled generation of the 1970s. Continuing the tradition of the confessional urban prose illustrated by Cezar Petrescu, Popescu's *Dulce ca mierea e glonţul patriei* (1971; Sweet as Honey Are Mother Land's Bullets) reconstructs in quick-paced cinematic sequences the author's autobiographical experiences in the army and the bureaucratic culture of Bucharest. The conflict between generations with their different ideological positions, one dogmatic-conservative, the other cynical-defiant, also is pursued in *Să creşti într-un an cît alţii într-o zi* (1973; To Grow as Much in a Year as Others in a Day). Since his defection to the United States, Popescu has published a number of highly successful novels that combine techniques of the thriller with historical and psychological analysis (*The Last Wave,* 1978; *Obsessive Love,* 1982) or revalorize narrative formulas, such as the vampire narrative (*In Hot Blood,* 1986) and the fiction of geographic/ecological exploration (*Amazon Beaming,* 1991).

The role of criticism throughout the 1960s and 1970s was to vigorously promote these new works. Each review became implicitly a rereading of cultural contexts and a polemical engagement with the dogmatic tenets of socialist realism. A more theoretical type of analysis, interested in reconceptualizing the function and strategies of the novel, emerged only during the late 1970s, when the terminology of structuralist narratology, semiotics, and phenomenological criticism was finally accepted in Romania. Both newly published academic critics such as Marian Papahagi, Al. Călinescu, Livius Ciocârlie, Mihai Zamfir, Monica Spiridon, and Cornel Mihai Ionescu, and well-established practical critics such as Nicolae Manolescu, Eugen Simion, and Lucian Raicu became interested in matters of narrative poetics and typology. The political fiction of the previous two decades came under new critical scrutiny, particularly from the point of view of its lacking narrative poetics. Participants in a 1983 debate on "Today's Romanian Fiction" agreed that the political novel of the so-called obsessive decade had exhausted its "thematic possibilities; aesthetically it has been exhausted from the start." To a young innovator such as Gheorghe Crăciun, these political narratives seemed huge rhetorical "mincers," haphazardly processing reality. After 20 years of undisputed domination in Romania, the political novel had been reduced to a manneristic recycling of themes and motifs that Preda himself had parodied in *Cel mai iubit dintre pămînteni* (1980). The erosion of the appeal and credibility of the political novel made the emergence of alternative modes of fiction (self-reflexive, psychological, feminist) finally possible.

The first innovative, self-reflexive trend to emerge during the late 1960s was the short-lived oneiric group (Dumitru Ţepeneag, Virgil Tănase, and Sorin Titel), which explored states of psychological and social liminality with surrealistic imagery reminiscent of Franz Kafka and the *nouveau roman* (New Novel). Because of the subversive implications of experimental works such as Sorin Titel's *Noaptea inocenţilor* (1970; The Night of Innocents) and *Lunga călătorie a prizonierului* (1971; The Prisoner's Long Journey), the oneiric trend was vehemently denounced by Ceauşescu in 1971. Titel's later fiction from *Ţară îndepărtată* (1974; Remote Country) to *Pasărea şi umbra* (1977; Bird and Shadow), *Clipa cea repede* (1979; The Fleeting Moment), and *Mamă, Iată-ţi fiul* (1983; Mother, This Is Your Son) problematized the very notion of reality. A similar self-reflexive mixture of analytic narrative and mythic fantasy was also present in Mircea Ciobanu's influential *Martorii* (1968; The Witnesses), and in Matei Călinescu's prize-winning novel published before his transplantation to the United States, *Viaţa şi opiniile lui Zacharias Lichter* (1969; The Life and Opinions of Zacharias Lichter).

The "Tîrgovişte school" of self-reflexive fiction, belatedly discovered during the 1970s, is the first manifestation of Romanian postmodernism. Drawing on both the Romanian avant-gardist traditions (Urmuz, Tzara, and Eugen Ionescu) and on the Latin American experiment, writers such as Mircea Horia Simionescu, Radu Petrescu, Costache Olăreanu, and Al. George produced deconstructive-ironic texts that questioned conventional modes of representation. The most spectacular example was offered by Simionescu's *Ingeniosul bine temperat* (1969–84; The Well-Tempered Ingenious). This narrative cycle composed of a pseudo-"onomastic dictionary," a general bibliography of themes and myths, a "breviary" of the century's real or imagined catastrophes, and an autobiographical "toxicology" subverted almost every procedure in the realistic repertory. Its comic inventory of types and clichés depicts a real-fictive world, "sick with inertia and stereotypy." The influence of the Tîrgovişte school was felt even by political novelists such as Constantin Ţoiu, who in *Galeria cu viţă sălbatică* (1976; A Gallery of Wild Vine) shifted attention from the investigation of the wrongs suffered by a typical victim of the 1950s to a discussion of the limits of narrative representation itself.

The inventive, self-reflexive strategies of the Tîrgovişte school and of other metafictional novelists such as Sorin Titel, Mircea Ciobanu, or Constantin Ţoiu were transposed in a stronger political key by the "new wave" fiction of the 1980s. Emerging at the height of Ceauşescu's "totalitarian absurd," this last wave of innovative fictionists (Mircea Nedelciu, Gabriela Adameşteanu, Ioan Groşan, Gheorghe Crăciun, Constantin Stan, and Adina Kenereş) exposed the paternalistic-ethnocentric mentalities of Ceauşescu's Romania. Much of this fiction written by novelists in their 20s and 30s was candidly autobiographical, a narrative shorthand of sorts that wished to convey an atmosphere of unadulterated truth. But their ironic recitation of surface realities had more in common with the American surfictionists than with any neorealistic trend. The reality recovered by their narratives is an ironic anthology of cultural clichés and prepackaged discourses. To exemplify, the two soldier friends in Mircea

Nedelciu's *Zmeura de cîmpie* (1984; Field Raspberry), one with historical ambitions, the other fancying a career as a film director, seek a notion of representation closer to history's "soul of facts," only to discover that reality cannot be extricated from public fictions that masquerade as truths. *Nopţi de trecere* (1984; Night Passages), by Constantin Stan, presents its young protagonist with the difficult task of making some sense of a socially and narratively disarticulated world in which even the hero's paternity is in question. The protagonist is helped in his endeavor by his lover and amateur reporter, Cristina, and a magic typewriter that records the story of his experience between the lines. As these experimental works suggested, the novelist's response to the loss of cultural grounding was appropriately dialogic, involving a continuous disarticulation/rearticulation of individual narratives around more imaginative plots.

An important theme in the new fiction is also the struggle to assert previously silenced voices such as those of female and male adolescents in Adina Kenereş' *Îngereasa cu pălărie verde* (1983; The Female Angel with Green Hat) or of a more mature woman in Gabriela Adameşteanu's *Dimineaţa pierdută* (1984; Wasted Morning). In order to find their voice, Kenereş' characters must break not only expected social conventions but also linguistic codes. Adameşteanu also makes the assertion of repressed, feminine themes directly dependent on a successful recuperation of individual speech, shifting from an objectified style of narration to a first-person voice; but she subsequently moves beyond the level of self-expression to a dialogic "you" that includes the reader in the process of narrative reconstruction.

Inspired by this new antirealistic, self-reflexive trend in fiction, the criticism of the 1980s revisited the issue of narrative representation, seeking alternatives to the mimetic tradition that had dominated the Romanian novel since its inception. A revisionistic-experimental concept of representation was articulated in the postmodern criticism of the 1980s (Radu G. Ţeposu, Ioan Buduca, Ion Bogdan Lefter, and Cristian Moraru); this concept challenged what another critic, Ov. S. Crohmălniceanu, had called "artistic illiteracy, the reduction of art to faithful copies after nature." A few years earlier, Nicolae Manolescu had posited a similar narrative category specific to Eastern European fiction in his typological study suggestively entitled *Arca lui Noe: Eseu despre romanul românesc* (1980–82; Noah's Ark: An Essay on the Romanian Novel). Improving upon A. Thibaudet's classification of fiction into a masculine, epic branch (the doric style) and a feminine, analytic branch (the ionic style), Manolescu added a third category, the corinthian novel of "tragic irony that unfolds in the forms of the grotesque, burlesque, or the parodic." By contrast to the doric novel, which was "a myth-maker, like the rising middle class," and to the "ionic novel [which] is the fruit of a pensive and lucid age that sets inner revelations above the pleasures of action," the corinthian novel erodes even further the author's faith in realistic mastery, resorting instead to satirical-parodic modes of narration.

The full ideological import of the self-problematized, oppositional discourse of postmodern fiction has been recognized only more recently in the freer, post-Ceauşescu political climate. The two most important gains brought by the so-called post-communist phase are the diversification of narrative production, with unpredictable hybrid works that call into question the pre-1989 fictional categories, and the reintegration of expatriated Romanian theorists (Matei Călinescu, Thomas Pavel, Sorin Alexandrescu, Mihai Spariosu, Marcel Cornis-Pope, and Christian Moraru) in the critical discourse about the novel produced today in Romania.

MARCEL CORNIS-POPE

Further Reading

Călin, V., "Postwar Developments of the Prewar Tradition in Romanian Prose," in *Fiction and Drama in Eastern and Southeastern Europe: Evolution and Experiment in the Postwar Period,* edited by Henrik Birbaum and Thomas Eekman, Columbus, Ohio: Slavica Publishers, 1980

Călinescu, George, *Istoria literaturii române de la origini pînă în prezent,* Bucharest: Fundaţia regală pentru literatură şi artă, 1941; translated by Leon Leviţchi in abridged form as *History of Romanian Literature,* Milan: Nagard-UNESCO, 1988

Călinescu, Matei, "Romanian Literature: Dealing with the Totalitarian Legacy," *World Literature Today* (Spring 1991)

Ciopraga, Constantin, *Personalitatea literaturii române: O incercare de sinteza,* Iaşi: Junimea, 1973; as *The Personality of Romanian Literature: A Synthesis,* translated by Ştefan Avădanei, Iaşi: Junimea, 1981

Cornis-Pope, Marcel, "Narration Across the Totalistic Gap: On Recent Romanian Fiction," *Symposium* 43:1 (Spring 1987)

Cornis-Pope, Marcel, *The Unfinished Battles: Romanian Postmodernism Before and After 1989,* Iaşi: Polirom, 1996

Cosma, Anton, *Geneza romanului românesc,* Bucharest: Eminescu, 1985

Impey, Michael, "Historical Figures in the Romanian Political Novel," *Southeastern Europe* 7:1 (1980)

Lăzărescu, Gheorghe, *Romanul de analiză psihologică în literatura română interbelica,* Bucharest: Minerva, 1983

Lovinescu, Eugen, *Istoria literaturii române contemporane,* volume 4, *Evoluţia poeziei epice,* Bucharest: Ancora, 1928

Manolescu, Nicolae, *Arca lui Noe,* 3 vols., Bucharest: Minerva, 1980–83

Munteanu, Romul, *La Civilisation des livres: Littérature roumaine, littérature européene,* Bucharest: Univers, 1986

Nemoianu, Virgil, "Romanian Literature," in *Encyclopedia of World Literature in the 20th Century* (Leonard S. Klein, general editor), volume 4, New York: Ungar, 1981

Odangiu, Marian, *Romanul politic,* Timişoara: Facla, 1984

Pârvu, Sorin, *The Art of the Romanian Novel,* Iaşi: Romanian Cultural Foundation, 1995

Perry, Thomas Amherst, "The Romanian Search for Realism," *Yearbook of Romanian Studies* 4 (1979)

Ţeposu, Radu G., *Viaţa şi opiniile personajelor,* Bucharest: Cartea Românească, 1983

Ţeposu, Radu G., *Istoria tragică şi grotescă a întunecatului deceniu literar nouă,* Bucharest: Eminescu, 1993

Vargolici, Teodor, *Aspecte ale romanului românesc din secolul al XIX-lea,* Bucharest: Eminescu, 1985

Vlad, Ion, "Contemporary Romanian Fiction as History and Aesthetic Experience," in *Romanian Essayists of Today,* translated by Anda Teodorescu and Andrei Bantaş, Bucharest: Univers, 1979

Romantic Novel

Defining the romantic novel presents difficulties similar to those of defining romanticism itself. Romanticism is usually viewed as a predominantly cultural movement in late 18th- and early 19th-century Western Europe. Yet the term *romantic* was not applied to the movement until late in that period. Furthermore, historians have defined romanticism in diverse and sometimes contradictory ways and have given it varying temporal dimensions in different national cultures. For example, many literary historians find romanticism developing in Britain during the late 18th and early 19th centuries; after 1800 in France, Germany, and Poland; perhaps later in Italy, Spain, Hungary, and Russia; and later still in Europe's various colonies and former colonies, especially in the New World. In addition, cultural historians often assign different degrees of importance to different arts in various national romantic movements—giving, for example, the prominent role to music in Germany; to painting in France; and to literature in Britain, Italy, Hungary, Poland, and Russia. Similarly, literary historians often give different genres the leading role in various national romantic literary movements, with poetry prominent in Britain and Central and South America; fiction and poetry in France, Germany, and Russia; the

drama in Spain and Portugal; and fictional and nonfictional prose in the new United States of America. Moreover, romanticism, however defined, was not the only important movement in its time. There were also movements such as political economy, utilitarianism, religious revivals of various kinds, and regionalism and nationalism. These movements also had cultural expressions, sometimes implicated in romanticism. In some parts of Europe, such as Poland and Hungary, which had ceased to exist as separate nation-states, the novel, along with other literary forms, became an important means of promoting and sustaining national consciousness during the romantic period, and after. Finally, romanticism is often seen as an ideology or culture without temporal limits, manifested in various times, places, and societies, down to the present.

Using the term *novel* in relation to the romantic period also presents difficulties. The common definition of *novel* today—an extended work of prose fiction—would have covered a broad range of literary and subliterary forms bearing different names during the romantic period, in different European languages. The English term *novel* cannot easily be equated with a single term in other languages. *Roman* (French, German, and Russian) and *romanzo* (Italian) were all used to designate novels during the romantic period, as now, but most English speakers would have distinguished the English cognate of these terms, *romance*, from *novel*. Spanish speakers used the term *novela*, which resembles *novella*, a modern but not early 19th-century English usage for prose fiction that falls between the short story and the novel in length. During the romantic period, *novel* could designate most kinds of extended prose fiction in English, but the term also continued to designate a kind of late 17th- and early 18th-century shorter prose fiction, usually dealing with courtly amorous intrigue. In English, *modern novel* was the romantic period's usual designation for extended prose fiction "realistically" representing contemporary or near contemporary life; *romance* designated novels with exotic and extravagant characters and settings, often using the improbable or supernatural. *Romance* also had and continues to have particular historical applications, including a form of later 20th-century cheap popular fiction that imitates *romance* of the romantic period. In Britain and Europe many works that would now be considered novels, or at least novellas, were called tales in English and equivalent terms in other languages. Such works were considered distinct from full-scale novels in being not just shorter in length but also simpler, more direct, less sophisticated in language and form, and closer to common life, including the life of the "folk."

Thus it is difficult to describe the romantic novel as a unified form with a clear or established place in literature, the arts, culture, and society. Nevertheless, what could be considered a historically specific romantic form of the novel developed in Europe, especially Western Europe, roughly during the late 18th and early 19th centuries. It embodies certain major themes of the historic romantic movement, including the nature and development of individual subjectivity; the local and domestic sphere of common life; the relationship among nature and individual, social, and national character; certain social conflicts; and the national history, identity, and (imperial) destiny. It employs and develops a certain repertory of forms and techniques, including romance plots, socially representative characters, first-person narration or third-person narration centered on a particular character, a great deal of description, an interest in authenticating its representations as facts, an emphasis on the realism of common life with an interest in the liminal and even supernatural, an interest in incorporating various non-novelistic discourses, and the incorporation of dialect and sociolect within a framework of the new or emergent standard written form of the national language.

In these respects the romantic novel, like that of any period, served the diverse and often conflicting interests of its readers. As the most widely read form of print in its time, apart from newspapers and magazines, and as the most widely consumed literary form, approached only by drama, the novel was both highly commercialized and highly responsive to the interests of its readers. Like newspapers and magazines and drama, novels disseminated information of interest to their readers, including new social and cultural practices, from conversation to courtship, from dress to education, from manners to emotion. At a time when the disciplines now known as psychology, sociology, cultural studies, and so on were only beginning to be contructed as distinctive practices and institutions, novels circulated new information and ideas about these domains to their readership. Novels also disseminated a wide range of information about the arts, learning, society, culture, topography, politics, economies, and similar topics, rivaled in this respect only by travel books. Accordingly, the novel was used to serve a variety of social, religious, cultural, political, and intellectual movements, coteries, and parties. The romantic novel was not only diverse in itself but comprised a field of conflict between various factions within its different national and regional reading publics.

Most obviously, the romantic novel, like romantic poetry and the late 18th-century literature of sensibility, developed new techniques for describing and representing individual subjectivity. To render the representation of afflicted subjectivity more immediate and rhetorically effective, many romantic novels use first-person narration of various kinds, including the epistolary form—although the epistolary novel was less prominent than it had been in the 18th century—and especially autobiographical and confessional narration. The representation of subjectivity as rich, authentic, and complex was of central interest to the predominantly middle-class reading public. This readership was deeply committed to a discourse of merit, of inner acquired worth as distinct from and often opposed to "merely" social categories of identity based on birth, rank, inherited wealth, and ascribed status. The conflict between the authentic individual and an inauthentic social and political order, the struggle between merit and an unequal and unjust social structure, is often represented in autobiographical novels of victimization, harassment, and persecution. Subjectivity, politicized in this way, was a prominent theme in a wide variety of romantic novels, including late 18th-century novels of sensibility, overtly political novels of the 1790s, Gothic romances from the 1780s to the 1820s, and a wide range of education and adventure novels, or bildungsroman.

Romantic lyric poetry aimed especially at representing subjectivity, and the expressivity and lyricism of such poetic discourse were carried over into the romantic novel in such works as Bernardin de St. Pierre's *Paul et Virginie* (1787), Nikolai Karamzin's *Bednaia Liza* (1792; *Poor Liza*), François-René de Chateaubriand's *Atala* (1801) and *René* (1802), Étienne de Senancour's *Obermann* (1804), Germaine de Staël's *Corinne* (3 vols.,1807), Adalbert von Chamisso's *Peter Schlemihls wundersame Geschichte* (1814), and Benjamin Constant's *Adolphe* (1816). The bildungsroman represents the construction of individual subjectivity as an idealized middle-class self, morally disciplined, intellectually informed, and ethically astute as a result of formation in the domestic sphere and adventures of various kinds in the wider social world. Accordingly, the bildungsroman as such was a central form in the romantic period, from Thomas Day's *Sandford and Merton* (1783–89) through Johann Wolfgang von Goethe's *Wilhelm Meisters Lehrjahre* (1795–96) and *Wilhem Meisters Wanderjahre* (1821) to Stendhal's *Le Rouge et le noir* (1830; *The Red and the Black*). Romantic narrative poems, ranging from Lord Byron's *Don Juan* (1819–24) to Aleksandr Pushkin's *Evgenii Onegin* (1833), influenced and were influenced by such novels. Furthermore, elements of the bildungsroman are found in other romantic novels of several kinds, from political novels to historical novels.

Gothic romances also specialized in representation of subjectivity, following the model established in England by Ann Radcliffe in the early 1790s. The Gothic was given a more erotic and sensationalist turn in Freidrich von Schiller's *Der Geisterseher*

(1789; *The Ghost-Seer*), M.G. Lewis' *The Monk* (1796), and Charlotte Dacre's *Zofloya; or, The Moor* (1806). The Gothic extravaganza, or fantastic, became especially associated with German writers such as E.T.A. Hoffmann. Mary Shelley's *Frankenstein* (1818) and C.R. Maturin's *Melmoth the Wanderer* (1820) present critiques of romantic individualism, referring obliquely to the French Revolution and Napoleonic era. The dependence of the Gothic on increasing sensationalism produced diminishing returns, however; elements of the Gothic were appropriated into other forms, and from the 1830s the Gothic romance and the various forms of adventure novel were taken up by producers of cheap fiction for the new lower-class and lower middle-class mass reading public.

Another variety of romantic novel was related to the Gothic and the picaresque tradition of the adventure novel, often with overtly satirical purpose. This kind of novel represents the relationship of the individual to society as problematic, or even inescapably conflicted. According to the 18th-century materialist philosophy of sensibility, the individual is constructed by natural, material, social, and cultural circumstances. Thus a divided and conflicted social world could also manifest itself in divided and conflicted subjectivity, as represented in sentimental novels such as Henry Mackenzie's *The Man of Feeling* (1771), Karamzin's picaresque *Pisma russkago puteshestvennika* (1790; *Letters of a Russian Traveller*), overtly political novels such as William Godwin's *Caleb Williams* (1794), and comic picaresque novels such as Robert Bage's *Man as He Is* (1792) and *Hermsprong* (1796) and Charles Pigault-Lebrun's *Mon oncle Thomas* (1799).

Also related to the Gothic and the picaresque was the so-called robber novel, often set in exotic lands in the past and featuring social outcasts and exiles in the romanticized Robin Hood tradition. These novels glamorize the outcast or self-defined social exile and rebel, as in the bandit novels of the German writer Heinrich Zschokke and the Newgate novels (after an infamous London prison) of Edward Bulwer-Lytton and Charles Dickens. The damaging effects of a faulty or decadent society on individual subjectivity are represented in romantic novels from Dr. John Moore's *Zeluco* (1789), a study of moral degeneration resulting from power over others, to Mikhail Lermontov's *Geroi nashego vremoni* (1840; *A Hero of Our Time*), a sardonic representation of the man of merit excluded from effective action in the public and political sphere. Often such novels represent not only a divided but a doubled self—in German, doppelgänger—as in Shelley's *Frankenstein* and James Hogg's *Private Memoirs and Confessions of a Justified Sinner* (1824).

In the culture of the middle-class reading public, the authentic individual subject was ideally created, nurtured, and educated in a broad sense within the domestic sphere and by the "domestic affections" (which included friendship as well as familial relations). The authentic individual was also repaired and healed in the domestic sphere after encounters with the hostile outside social world. The achievement of an idealized, almost paradisal and utopian domesticity is the objective of the plot in many novels of the late 18th-century culture of sensibility. The domestic ideology was emphasized even more in the romantic period, after the prolonged cataclysm of the French Revolution, the Napoleonic wars, and the continued struggle for reform in many parts of the Old and New Worlds. Domestic novels depict not so much an idealized domesticity, however, as the intrusion of the

outside social and political world into the domestic sphere, destroying the domestic affections and dividing families or driving them into some kind of flight or exile. The romantic novel usually idealizes the domestic sphere in the face of upper-class courtly decadence, or the destructive conflicts of the public sphere, as in the novels of Félicité de Genlis in France, Frances Burney in England, Maria Edgeworth in Ireland, and Sophie von La Roche in Germany. In some romantic novels, domesticity is openly problematized, as in Elizabeth Inchbald's *A Simple Story* (1791) or Goethe's *Die Wahlverwandtschaften* (1809; *Elective Affinities*). A different, still conflicted, but more comic and positive domesticity is represented in Jane Austen's novels of the 1810s.

The domestic sphere as the "home" of the individual is extended outward in several ways by the romantic novel. The large body of romantic poetry of local and daily experience has its equivalent in the romantic novel's detailed representation of the local as the appropriate field for individual action and for the formation of social relationships beyond the domestic sphere. This emphasis on the local implies rejection of the metropolitan and cosmopolitan as physical, social, and cultural spaces dominated by the fashionable upper class on one hand and the undisciplined and dangerous lower classes on the other. In this respect, the novels of Jane Austen are not antiromantic but typical of a strong line in the romantic novel. Often this emphasis on the local is generalized, with the regional or national character represented as arising from the local. The region or nation is often represented as an agglomeration of locales, different yet unified by common traits that are inherently local and even domestic. Novels and (especially) tales of regional identity, often incorporating folkloric elements, by writers such as Maria Edgeworth in Ireland, I.A. Krylov in Russia, Honoré de Balzac in France, András Dugonics in Hungary, and Alessandro Manzoni in Italy, represent the nation in this way, as a series of domestic spheres in particular localities, neighborhoods, and regions.

Romanticism in several arts emphasized the material conditions of the formation of individual subjectivity, local communities, and the wider nation. In the novel, as in poetry and travel writing of the romantic period, this theme takes the form of lengthy description of nature and topography, usually rendered through the subjective experience of the protagonist or narrator. Physical nature not only forms the individual, but also guides the individual through moral and ethical dilemmas in everyday life. This is especially so in the Gothic novels of the period. Nature is also shown to influence the social structures and culture and the economic system that form the individual, especially at the local and regional level. Landscape is often contrasted with townscape in this respect. The development of these themes requires a good deal of description—a feature that the Romantic novel shared with travel writing at this time, with similar significance. Handling of description is an important formal innovation of the romantic novel, from the Gothic romances of Ann Radcliffe to the social-historical novels of Scott, Manzoni, Balzac, and others.

Novelists everywhere, along with writers in several subgenres, however, used the description novel to represent continuity and change in terms specific to emergent regional and national identities. In fact, these predominantly middle-class writers were also interested in tradition and change as problems of what historians call modernization, or the transformation from feudal and medieval customary society, culture, and economy to capitalist national and international economic development. At the same time, the "traditionary" culture, soon to be called "folklore," that was to be displaced by modernization was carefully incorporated in regional novels, national tales, and historical novels. Such representations were central to Maria Edgeworth's Irish tales, John Galt's novels of western lowland Scotland, numerous German tales by writers such as Heinrich von Kleist, I.A. Krylov's *Basni* (1809; *Fables*), sketches by the Scottish-Canadian writers Thomas McCulloch and T.C. Haliburton, and the American Washington Irving's tales and novels. Significantly, the first novel of national identity in Spain's former colonies, *El Periquillo Sarniento* (1816), was written by a liberal patriotic journalist, the Mexican José de Lizardi.

In romantic culture, the theme of space, as communal, regional, and national space, was strongly related to the theme of time, especially social and historical time, and was also a source of formal innovation, especially in the novel. As a largely postrevolutionary movement, Romanticism was concerned with continuities of all kinds. The French Revolution and sympathetic movements in many countries and regions of Europe, as well as Europe's colonies near and far, had revealed that continuities and traditions hitherto taken for granted were fragile, perhaps even illusory. In addition, the romantic period saw accelerating change in many fields, especially organized around modernization. Romantic preoccupation with regional or national history, identity, and destiny required representation of historic continuity and change and the reproduction of the national character over time.

The historical novel addresses this preoccupation. It merges historiography and fiction in order to show the operation of history, and especially large historical movements of change, of disruption and restabilization, at the level of individual, domestic, and local life—conventionally, the special domains of novelistic representation. Historical fact is used to authorize the fictionalized representations of individual and local experience of the historical process, often with scholarly apparatus of footnotes, prefaces, and glossaries. This has been perhaps the most influential form of the novel over the past two centuries, produced in successive regions and nations on all continents to represent or invent emergent national consciousness and to serve various regional and national independence movements, predominantly led by professional middle-class people—precisely those who have been the dominant element of the reading public.

The historical novel was pioneered by women writers such as Maria Edgeworth in *Castle Rackrent* (1800) and Jane Porter in *The Scottish Chiefs* (1810). Sir Walter Scott gave the historical novel its most popular form, beginning with *Waverley* (1814) and the succession of his Waverley novels down to the 1830s. Scott's example was taken up by novelists all over Europe and its colonies and former colonies. In Italy there was Manzoni's *I promessi sposi* (3 vols., 1827; *The Betrothed*), often imitated by others during the long struggle for Italian national independence and unification. In France, Balzac's series of historical, regional, and domestic novels, known collectively as the *La Comédie humaine,* was initiated, significantly, by *Le Dernier Chouan* (1829; *The Chouans*), a novel about regional resistance to the French Revolution. The leading French romantic poet and dramatist Victor Hugo followed Scott in representing the medieval roots of modern society in his novel *Notre-Dame de Paris* (1831). In Germany, historiography and philosophy of history were powerful instruments in the formation of a romantic nationalism opposed both to revolutionary and Napoleonic imperialism and to German aristocratic cosmopolitanism. In the United States, the historical novels of James Fenimore Cooper were designed to invent a national character for the new nation, but were also very popular in Britain. A number of writers used fictionalized history in the novel, as well as poetry, drama, and folklore studies, independently of Scott's influence. Nevertheless, the example of the Waverley novels reinforced German literary historicism in fiction by such writers as "Novalis" (Friedrich von Hardenberg), Friedrich de la Motte Fouqué, Ludwig von Arnim, Wilhelm Hauff, and "Willibald Alexis" (Wilhelm Häring). In Russia, Aleksandr Pushkin represented the period of the Empress Catherine II in his novel *Kapitanskaia dochka* (1836; *The Captain's Daughter*). The major Russian historical novels, such as those of Lev Tolstoi, did not appear until some decades later, however. In Hungary, Baron Miklós Jósika adapted the pattern of the Waverley novels to sustaining Hungarian identity at a time when the upper aristocracy still followed German cultural leadership. Poland disappeared as a nation-state in 1796, not to reappear as such until 1918, and romanticism quickly became a mainstay of national consciousness, especially in the hands of writers in exile. Julian Ursin knew English literature very well and adapted Scott's model of the historical novel to Polish in *Jan z Teczyna* (1825). In Spain, where modernization and change were deeply implicated in the prolonged political crisis from Napoléon's takeover through the post-Napoleonic liberal revolts, the historical national novel was also taken up by several poets and dramatists impressed by Scott's example. These included Mariano José de Larra, Angel Saavedra, Duke of Rivas, and Jose de Espronceda. In Portugal, too, fictionalized national history was first practiced in narrative verse and drama, but Alexandre Herculano's novel *O Monástico* (1844–48) followed the example of the Waverley novels, and many Portuguese novelists followed Herculano's lead.

Finally, the novel was used to embody romantic culture's concern with continuities, distinctions, and conflicts of discourse and language, including genre, and literature itself. Romantic social and historical novels include varieties of the national language in representations of dialect within a narrative framework in the standard form of the language. Many romantic novels include discourses of other kinds, including antiquarian scholarship, historiography, poetry, dialogue set out in playscript form, and so on. There were also experiments with form, such as narratives set within narratives, linked narratives, the inclusion of obviously autobiographical matter, obvious reference to real-life characters, as in the roman à clef, and the inclusion of different and incompatible narrative accounts within the same text.

Such diversity, tensions, complexities, and ambiguities may represent the central romantic anxiety about the coherence and stability of human and social meaning, an anxiety unleashed by revolutionary violence, transgression, and disruption and by Napoleonic imperialism and struggles for national identity and independence. More positively, the romantic novel's testing of the boundaries and limits of discourse, genre, and language may be seen as what the 20th-century Russian theorist M.M. Bakhtin calls dialogism. As applied to the novel, this means the inclusion of many "voices," or styles, genres, and discourses, within a single text, thereby relativizing them, depriving any one dialect, style, genre, and so on of special literary or cultural authority. Such dialogizing would be a democratizing move, contributing to the founding of the modern liberal state. According to Bakhtin this move is characteristic of the novel; perhaps it is characteristic of the romantic novel in particular.

GARY KELLY

See also Adventure Novel and Imperial Romance; Bildungsroman; Critics and Criticism (19th Century); English Novel (1800–40); French Novel (1800–50); Genre Criticism; German Novel; Gothic Novel; Historical Novel; National Tale; Novel and Romance: Etymologies; Romance; Scottish Novel; Sentimental Novel

Further Reading

Adams, Percy G., *Travel Literature and the Evolution of the Novel*, Lexington: University Press of Kentucky, 1983

Allen, James Smith, *Popular French Romanticism: Authors, Readers, and Books in the Nineteenth Century*, Syracuse, New York: Syracuse University Press, 1981

Anderson, Benedict, *Imagined Communities: Reflections on the Origin and Spread of Nationalism*, London: Verso, 1983; revised edition, London and New York: Verso, 1991

Bakhtin, M.M., *The Dialogic Imagination: Four Essays*, translated by Caryl Emerson and Michael Holquist, edited by Holquist, Austin: University of Texas Press, 1981

Christiansen, Rupert, *Romantic Affinities: Portraits from an Age 1780–1830*, New York: Putnam, 1988

Furst, Lilian R., *Romanticism in Perspective: A Comparative Study of Aspects of the Romantic Movements in England, France and Germany*, London: Macmillan, and New York: St. Martin's Press, 1969; 2nd edition, London: Macmillan, 1979

Hollingsworth, Joseph Keith, *The Newgate Novel, 1830–1847*, Detroit, Michigan: Wayne State University Press, 1963

Jones, Howard Mumford, *Revolution and Romanticism*, Cambridge, Massachusetts: Harvard University Press, and London: Oxford University Press, 1974

Kelly, Gary, *English Fiction of the Romantic Period, 1789–1830*, London and New York: Longman, 1989

Lukács, Georg, *A történelmi regény*, Budapest: Hungaria, 1937; as *The Historical Novel*, London: Merlin Press, 1962; New York: Humanities Press, 1965

Stahl, Ernest Ludwig, and William Edward Yuill, *German Literature of the Eighteenth and Nineteenth Centuries*, London: Cresset Press, and New York: Barnes and Noble, 1970

Ward, Albert, *Book Production, Fiction, and the German Reading Public, 1740–1800*, Oxford: Clarendon Press, 1974

Wilson, James D., *The Romantic Heroic Ideal*, Baton Rouge: Louisiana State University Press, 1982

Joseph Roth 1894–1939

Austrian

When Joseph Roth's first novel was being serialized in a Viennese newspaper in 1923, life uncannily began to imitate art. *Das Spinnennetz* (*The Spider's Web*) tells of a young man's rise to power and influence aided by the antidemocratic and anti-Semitic prejudices he shares with others, of the way his ruthlessness is fueled by his own cowardice and fear of retribution, and of how the climate of mutual manipulation in the early 1920s makes life in its entirety come to resemble a "web" of machination and double-dealing suspended above a void. Publication was halted by the news of Hitler's Munich putsch. This episode in Roth's early writing career illustrates both his flair for identifying the decisive factors at work in Central European society in the aftermath of World War I, which Roth had developed by working as a journalist, and also his talent for finding the expressive imagery with which to evoke a world suddenly bereft of any sense of fundamental value and legitimizing authority.

In his novels of the 1920s, Roth depicts the effects of postwar disruption with a close attention to the detail of personal circumstances, but also in ways that confer a wider symbolic significance on such detail. The hotel he describes in *Hotel Savoy* (1924), with its seven stories stratified according to the wealth and status of the clientele, is like an emblematic chunk of Western civilization set down in a Polish provincial town. It provides temporary accommodation for a variety of figures who are searching in the postwar world for vestiges of a past life, or for intimations of a future one, and who are destined to be disappointed in both respects. *Die Flucht ohne Ende* (1927; *Flight Without End*) traces the experiences of an Austrian soldier who confronts the fragility of personal identity as he makes his way back from captivity in Siberia, and whose sense of dislocation becomes all the more intense when he reaches the West and finds himself alienated from what now seem to be the mechanical laws of bourgeois society and paralyzed by the sense of his own superfluity. It was this work that led Roth's name to be associated with the vogue for documentary writing in the 1920s, because he claimed in the preface to be reporting the authentic experience of a personal friend rather than creating a fiction. By 1930 Roth was firmly distancing himself from any such naive reliance on factual veracity as a criterion for the value of literary writing, but what continued to characterize his narrative style was the combination of a sharp focus on immediate experiences and perceptions with a chilling sense of the hollowness that lay behind them.

Radetzkymarsch (1932; *The Radetzky March*), the work for which Joseph Roth is most commonly remembered, contains many descriptive and reflective passages that capture the flavor and the ambience of a more measured life in the prewar Hapsburg Empire, with its peculiar combination of precarious multiethnic equilibrium, bureaucratic correctness, and hedonistic sensuality. But it also depicts that society as burdened with the consciousness of its own impending demise. The first chapter shows a political myth being created out of the spirit of self-delusion: at the battle of Solferino in 1859 a young lieutenant saves the life of the still younger emperor by pulling him to the ground just in time to avoid an enemy bullet, and the incident is subsequently stylized into an act of extravagant military bravery. Through his account of the descendants of this "hero of Solferino," Roth shows a world in which, from one generation to another, all sense of purpose drains away from the preservation of inherited practices until the last member of the family finds a meaningless death in the opening skirmishes of World War I. A Spenglerian vision of European culture in decline is an inescapable feature of Roth's novels, but it is accompanied by a passionate commitment to the assiduous recording of the personal and cultural experiences of loss.

Roth's ambivalence toward Western civilization led him increasingly to draw on the heritage of Eastern European, and particularly Jewish, storytelling that was familiar to him from his Galician Jewish background. In *Hiob* (1930; *Job*) he self-consciously presents the afflictions visited upon an Eastern European Jewish family in legendary rather than realist terms, offering a story of sufferings endured—and eventually dispelled as if by a miracle—as a model of truth-to-self on the level of simple piety. In *Tarabas* (1934; *Tarabas*) he develops a story he found in a Ukrainian newspaper into a self-consciously religious account of the ambivalences of the human condition, presenting the title figure as a ruthless military commander who also develops the potential for becoming a pentitent and a holy fool of the kind familiar from Russian literature. Roth's *Die hundert Tage* (1936; *The Ballad of the Hundred Days*) shows us a Napoléon who renounces the aspiration to power after learning to recognize his own human frailty, while *Das falsche Gewicht* (1937; *Weights and Measures*) tells of a weights-and-measures inspector in the borderlands of the Tsarist Empire who experiences both intense emotional disappointments and the emptiness of a life dedicated wholeheartedly to duty ("out of a fear of fear," as the text makes explicit), and who ends up imagining that he will be prosecuted for "false weights" in heaven, as he has prosecuted others on earth. *Die Kapuzinergruft* (1938; *The Emperor's Tomb*), which is a sequel to *The Radetzky March*, shows Roth responding to the National Socialist takeover in Austria with an expression of true nostalgia for the Hapsburg dynasty. *Die Legende vom heiligen Trinker* (1939; *The Legend of the Holy Drinker*) conveys a self-ironic impression of Roth's own condition in his last years, presenting the inveterate alcoholic as a disheveled but pure emblem of a kind of honor that can ultimately find refuge only in God's mercy.

There is arguably a tendency in Roth's later works to present life in the form of prefashioned fictional structures, but his talent for the sharp realist representation of detail remained undiminished. The model he has offered to subsequent generations of writers is that of sharply observed sensory experience as the medium for conveying an intense sense of cultural and existential crisis.

DAVID MIDGLEY

See also Radetzky March

Biography

Born in Brody, Galicia, Austria (now in the Ukraine), 2 September 1894. Attended Baron-Hirsch-Schule, Brody, 1901–05; Imperial-Royal Crown Prince Rudolph Gymnasium, 1905–13; University of Lemberg, Vienna, 1913; studied German literature, University of Vienna, 1914–16. Served in the Austrian army, 1916–18; claimed to have spent months in Russian captivity as a prisoner of war; journalist, Vienna, 1919–23; staff member, Berlin, 1923–25, and cultural correspondent, Paris, 1925, Soviet Union, 1926, Albania, 1927, and Poland, 1928, for the *Frankfurter Zeitung*; moved to Paris to escape the Nazi regime, 1933, where he lived the remainder of his life; traveled to Poland, 1933 and 1937, on PEN lecture tour; suffered from poor health for most of his life. Died 27 May 1939.

Novels by Roth

Hotel Savoy, 1924; translated by John Hoare, in *Hotel Savoy; Fallmerayer the Stationmaster; The Bust of the Emperor*, 1986

Die Rebellion, 1924

April: Die Geschichte einer Liebe, 1925

Der blinde Spiegel, 1925

Die Flucht ohne Ende, 1927; as *Flight Without End*, translated by Ida Zeitlin, 1930; also translated by David Le Vay and Beatrice Musgrave, 1977

Zipper und sein Vater, 1928; as *Zipper and His Father*, translated by John Hoare, with *The Spider's Web*, 1988

Rechts und Links, 1929; as *Right and Left*, translated by Michael Hofmann, 1991

Hiob: Roman eines einfachen Mannes, 1930; as *Job: The Story of a Simple Man*, translated by Dorothy Thompson, 1931

Radetzkymarsch, 1932; as *The Radetzky March*, translated by Geoffrey Dunlop, 1933; also translated by Eva Tucker, 1974, and by Joachim Neugroschel, 1995

Tarabas: Ein Gast auf dieser Erde, 1934; as *Tarabas: A Guest on Earth*, 1934; also translated by Winifred Katzin, 1987

Le Buste de l'Empereur (in French), 1934; as *Die Büste des Kaisers*, 1964; as *The Bust of the Emperor*, translated by John Hoare, in *Hotel Savoy; Fallmerayer the Stationmaster; The Bust of the Emperor*, 1986

Der Antichrist, 1934; as *Antichrist*, translated by Moray Firth, 1935

Die hundert Tage, 1936; as *The Ballad of the Hundred Days*, translated by Moray Firth, 1936; as *The Story of the Hundred Days*, 1936

Beichte eines Mörders, erzählt in einer Nacht, 1936; as *Confession of a Murderer, Told in One Night*, translated by Desmond L. Vesey, 1938

Das falsche Gewicht, 1937; as *Weights and Measures*, translated by David Le Vay, 1982

Die Kapuzinergruft, 1938; as *The Emperor's Tomb*, translated by John Hoare, 1984

Die Geschichte von der 1002. Nacht, 1939; as *The Tale of the 1002nd Night*, translated by Michael Hoffmann, 1998

Die Legende vom heiligen Trinker, 1939; as *The Legend of the Holy Drinker*, translated by Michael Hofmann, 1989

Der Leviathan, 1940

Romane, Erzählungen, Aufsätze, 1964
Der stumme Prophet, 1966; as *The Silent Prophet,* translated by David Le Vay, 1979
Das Spinnennetz (first serialized in 1923), 1967; as *The Spider's Web,* translated by John Hoare, with *Zipper and His Father,* 1988
Die Erzählungen, 1973

Other Writings: essays.

Further Reading

Bronsen, David, *Joseph Roth: Eine Biographie,* Cologne: Kiepenheuer and Witsch, 1974
Bronsen, David, editor, *Joseph Roth und die Tradition: Aufsatz- und Materialiensammlung,* Darmstadt: Agora, 1975
Chambers, Helen, editor, *Co-Existent Contradictions: Joseph Roth in Retrospect,* Riverside, California: Ariadne Press, 1991

Henze, Viktor, *Jüdischer Kulturpessimismus und das Bild des alte Osterreich im Werk Stefan Zweigs und Joseph Roths,* Heidelberg: Winter, 1988
Magris, Claudio, *Lontano da dove. Joseph Roth e la tradizione ebraico-orientale,* Turin: Giulio Einaudi, 1971; as *Weit von wo. Verlorene Welt des Ostjudentums,* Vienna: Europa, 1974
Müller-Funk, Wolfgang, *Joseph Roth,* Munich: Beck, 1989
Nürnberger, Helmuth, *Joseph Roth in Selbstzeugnissen und Bilddokumenten,* Reinbek: Rowohlt, 1981; 8th edition, 1995
Siegel, Rainer-Joachim, *Joseph Roth, Bibliographie,* Morsum, Sylt: Cicero, 1995
Steinmann, Esther, *Von der Würde des Unscheinbaren: Sinnerfahrung bei Joseph Roth,* Tübingen: Niemeyer, 1984
Trommler, Frank, *Roman und Wirklichkeit: Eine Ortsbestimmung am Beispiel von Musil, Broch, Roth, Doderer und Gütersloh,* Stuttgart: Kohlhammer, 1966

Rouge et le noir. *See* Red and the Black

Les Rougon-Macquart by Émile Zola

1871–93

In the years just preceding the Franco-Prussian war of 1870, Émile Zola conceived his famous *Rougon-Macquart* cycle. Born in 1840, Zola had pursued a respectable career as a journalist and novelist during the 1860s, churning out a series of popular works that, if they prefigured the important themes of the great series, did not match their literary quality. He was sufficiently well known to have his portrait painted by Édouard Manet and shown at the Salon of 1868.

Émile Zola was a man of determination, if not of great self-confidence. In the late 1860s he immersed himself in the vast project of reading and research that was to form the basis of his proposed cycle. Like most novelists of his generation, he labored under the crushing presence of Honoré de Balzac. Between 1829 and 1851, Balzac had constructed an elaborate social saga of about 100 novels, *La Comédie humaine,* many of them tied together by means of reappearing characters. Balzac's large-scale introduction of the material world into fiction represented a formidable challenge to every subsequent novelist. Zola was particularly sensitive to Balzac's achievement for he, too, had "universalist" ambitions. He saw that he could not simply replicate Balzac's pattern for his own times. Between 1850 and 1870, society—and literature—had changed radically. Preparing his own great cycle, he jotted down a list of what he called "the dif-

ferences between Balzac and myself." The differences, he thought, were explained by the changing times.

Twelve years old when the Second Empire (1852–70) was established and 30 when it fell, Zola grew up just when the Industrial Revolution reached France. By the time he reached maturity around 1855, technology and the sciences—especially biology, chemistry, and physics—were firmly established on a modern footing. The life sciences especially enjoyed enormous prestige and seemed on the way to resolving the major problems of human existence. These were the concerns that interested him when he began to research the *Rougon-Macquart* cycle. He was fascinated by scientific methodology and determined to apply it to literature. Perhaps the most influential source he found was Prosper Lucas' book *Natural Heredity,* from which he took the somewhat dubious scientific theories of human genetics that inform his novels.

Zola was not much concerned with the objective accuracy of biological science—he was not, after all, a trained scientist himself. Rather he was concerned with the usefulness of science for literature. In later years, Zola claimed that literature could be as "experimental" as science and that he had created an "experimental novel." To a great extent, this was sheer public relations, and Zola eventually admitted as much. What he really intended was to endow literature with the same prestige as science by giving it similar methodologies. This approach to literature eventually came to be known as naturalism, which has sometimes been described as the realism of the laboratory. But it is obvious that experiment in literature did not mean anything like experiment in the sciences. A novelist does not determine the nature of his characters the way a chemist in his laboratory determines the nature of his reagents. In his heart of hearts, Zola understood this.

Of all the biological notions floating about, heredity proved to be ideal for literary adaptation. It had two great advantages. On the one hand, it could be viewed as the modern version of the classical notion of Fate, thus connecting to a long tradition in the European novel. On the other hand, it raised the question of "nature versus nurture" and that, in its turn, immediately gave his novels an important political dimension.

Whereas Balzac had explored the influence of social environment (milieu) on individual destiny, Zola focused on the fortunes of a single family a generation at a time to illustrate the workings of heredity. Before he had written a word of the *Rougon-Macquart* cycle he was drawing up genealogical trees and making brief notes on the novels' contents. His family would spring from an ancestor known as Aunt Dide who had both legitimate (Rougon) and illegitimate (Macquart) offspring. This arrangement allowed Zola to apply the notions of heredity he had picked up from Lucas. While the Rougon branch comprised small shopkeepers and petty bourgeois, the Macquart branch was a family of poachers and smugglers. Through combinations of talent, luck, scheming, and skullduggery, some members of this somewhat unsavory family would rise to the highest levels of French society. Others would fall by the wayside, victims of both society and heredity. Zola included characters in all sorts of occupations: manual workers, coal miners, railroad workers, priests, businessmen, artists, politicians, diplomats, and even prostitutes. In 1869 this was embodied in a project for a series of ten novels, which he submitted to the publisher Lacroix. Of course, many changes and additions occurred as he worked, and the final cycle contained 20 rather than ten works. But the essential elements were all in the so-called Lacroix Project.

As his historical frame, he chose the Second Empire, that is, the period of his adolescence and young manhood. The choice was fraught with significance. Zola had completed the first novel of the cycle, *La Fortune des Rougon* (*The Fortune of the Rougons*), when its serial publication in 1869 was interrupted by the outbreak of the Franco-Prussian war. He was launched on the second novel of the series when the French army suffered defeat at the battle of Sedan and Paris was threatened with siege. Zola was forced to flee Paris for the south of France, leaving his papers and manuscripts behind. The war, however, was relatively brief, and Zola returned in 1871 to find his material intact. The Second Empire was now gone, replaced by the Third Republic. Zola greeted this political event with peculiar relief, for now—in contrast to Balzac, whose historical view was open-ended—Zola knew precisely how the social dimension of his cycle would work out. Such constraints gave Zola a secure conceptual framework within which he could chart the fortunes of his family and experiment with some quite radical departures in the form and substance of the novel.

His first problem was how to turn the biological theory of heredity into the literary notion of Fate, or Destiny. To do this, Zola chose the theme of alcoholism—a serious public health problem in 19th-century France. At the time, even less was known about alcoholism than now. But it was clear that alcoholism and its consequences could pass from generation to generation. Like a scientist working with a test group and a control group, Zola made the Macquarts alcoholics while keeping the Rougons sober. The *Rougon-Macquart* novels study the permutations of the theme in successive generations of this double-branched family.

But Zola was clearly not about to write 20 novels on alcoholism. The only work to deal directly with the problem is *L'Assommoir* (1877; translated as *The Dram Shop*, *The Gin Palace*, and *Drink*), but elsewhere the theme lurks in the background, shadowing the characters and their actions. Ranging widely over French society of the Second Empire, the novels deal with the social and political problems implied by the naturalist method of research. Zola was no friend of the Second Empire, which had been a conservative, even oppressive, regime. The arts had been largely stifled, especially literature, with its potential for causing "trouble." Zola naturally found himself in the political opposition, and this is reflected in almost all his works, even though he wrote them after the downfall of the regime. *The Gin Palace* is concerned with the sufferings of the down-trodden Parisian working class. *Germinal* (1885) is a story about the miserable, exploited coal miners in the north of France. *Son Excellence Eugène Rougon* (1876; *His Excellency Eugene Rougon*) deals with corruption in politics and high society. *Au bonheur des dames* (1883; *The Ladies' Paradise*) describes the devastation wrought on small Parisian businesses by the first department stores. *L'Oeuvre* (1886; *The Masterpiece*) deals with the dangerous links between artistic creativity and mental instability. *Nana* (1880), perhaps his most direct attack on the Second Empire, deals with the prostitution—both literal and moral—that corroded the entire society of the Second Empire, where everything, or so it seemed, was for sale.

Obviously, the debased, corrupt, money-grubbing society of the Second Empire was not the consequence of heredity, and, as Zola explored these themes, the question of alcoholism very often receded far into the background. Indeed, it occasionally disappeared altogether. The Macquarts may have had alcoholism in their genes, but Second Empire society favored and facilitated their venality. Zola saw this with utmost clarity. He also saw that a "sober" heredity did not exempt the Rougons from their own forms of corruption. The high sense of morality that later led him to defend Colonel Dreyfus in the famous article "J'accuse" is already clear in the *Rougon-Macquart* novels. Like all great artists, Zola outran his own initial intentions.

The idea of portraying various levels of society was not in itself new. It had been the basis of the picaresque novel two centuries earlier. But the 19th-century novel was a middle-class form, aimed at a middle-class reading public. Obviously, then, its topics and protagonists had been largely middle class. Even Balzac had introduced only a relative handful of peasants and urban workers into his vast panorama. This was perhaps because prior to the mid-century the working class had little consciousness of being a distinct group within the different European societies. In France, industrial workers were often lumped together with out-and-out criminals under the term *classes dangereuses*.

Zola swept all these limitations away. He explored every imaginable social stratum, described his characters' worlds in their own language, and allowed them to speak as they actually did in the streets, the shops, the mines, and the factories. In a culture that worshiped the purity of its literary language, the dialogue in some of Zola's novels was considered positively scandalous. For his part, Zola contended that he was simply an observer—a scientific one at that—and that he tried to be as accurate in presenting a laundress as in presenting a banker.

So much for naturalism as a thematic approach. There was another and far more significant dimension to Zola's scientific assumptions. However questionable its theoretical application to literature, the sciences suggested to Zola a unique working methodology, which is the essence of naturalism and has influenced writers ever since. Zola was a researcher in the modern sense of the word. Each novel was preceded by an intense period of research that resulted in a set of thick dossiers. These dossiers (now preserved at the Bibliothèque nationale in Paris) all follow the same, or nearly the same, pattern. There is an *ébauche,* or preliminary plan, followed by a more or less extensive series of notes on whatever the particular topic of the novel was to be. These were usually followed by a second, more elaborate *ébauche.* Then would come a Plan, which was a series of paragraphs outlining the action of each chapter. Along with it usually came a file of Personnages, or characters, containing thumb-nail biographies of each protagonist. Finally there was usually a second Plan, in which the paragraphs of the first might be expanded to several pages each. At this point, Zola was ready to begin the actual redaction of the novel. The final text rarely deviated from the outline of the last plan in any significant way. Despite appearances, the process was far from mechanical. Zola moved back and forth from one set of files to another. Research generated thick sheaves of notes, which would bring on dramatic changes in his plans. Such changes would then spark further research. But in the main, he tended to be methodical and precise where Balzac was headlong, disorganized, and often surprised by what turned up in his writing.

The research itself was particularly modern in nature. It involved not only the consultation of books and interviews with experts but the exploration of reality itself. Preparing *La Bête humaine* (1890; *The Beast in Man*), a novel about the railroads, he rode in the cab of a locomotive from Paris to Mantes and took extensive notes on his experience. Researching *Germinal,* he pretended to be an engineer visiting coal mines in the north of France. Exploring the emergence of large modern department stores, he spent many hours wandering through them and examining their administrative workings. If anything defines naturalism, it is this immediate connection with real life.

This method gave Zola's novels a sense of reality not found elsewhere. Indeed, his novels were so pertinent that they were often treated as if they were sociological tracts. On this score, they often raised readers' hackles. For example, workers' groups read *The Gin Palace* as a right-wing tract assaulting the proletariat for its supposed tendency to drink. *Germinal,* on the other hand, was attacked by right-wing political groups as a call to revolution. Zola always maintained that he was merely writing down what he saw. Despite this claim, it was not lost on anyone that his basic sympathies lay with the poor and the disinherited.

Despite the naturalistic bias, one should not underestimate the sheer power of Zola's imagination. *The Beast in Man* may be replete with technical details about the French railways, but its real power lies in the treatment of the locomotive "La Lison,"

which under his pen becomes a breathing, panting monster, rushing through dark tunnels and cavernous stations, flashing its malevolent eye, spitting fire and smoke. *The Gin Palace* conjures up the alcohol still like an evil god-beast, crouching in the corner of a neighborhood bar, dripping out the liquid that will destroy so many lives. *Germinal* gives us the mine as a ravenous animal that swallows the miners, torments and injures them, then vomits out their mangled bodies. To such an extent do these fevered images fill his pages that many of his contemporaries "accused" him of being the last of the romantics. He did not object. In fact, his own last years were devoted to two new cycles (neither of the quality of the *Rougon-Macquart* cycle), in which romantic elements almost swamped the naturalism that had become associated with his name.

From 1870 to 1893, Zola worked ceaselessly at the *Rougon-Macquart* cycle and eventually published 20 novels as part of it. The most famous are undoubtedly *The Gin Palace* and *Germinal*; others among the more popular titles are *Le Ventre de Paris* (1873; *The Belly of Paris*), *Nana, La Terre* (1887; *The Earth*), and *La Débâcle* (1892; *The Debacle*).

What, then, is Zola's legacy? Was he a naturalist? A romantic? In a sense, these questions mean little because the categories are so difficult to define. In any case he was too large a figure to be contained in any one category. Zola's legacy to world literature lies elsewhere. He demonstrated that precise documentation could underpin a sympathetic portrayal of the dispossessed and that accurate portrayals did not prevent the soaring of the imagination. And he showed that personal integrity helped rather than hindered literary achievement.

Worldwide, novelists followed his lead. Beyond the frontiers of France, realism and the more extreme naturalism owed more to Zola's methods and attitudes than to his particular themes, which were, after all, specific to France. From the United States and the realist school around Theodore Dreiser to Turgenev and his generation in Russia; from August Strindberg in Scandinavia to Emilia Pardo-Bazan and Clarín in Spain and the *verismo* movement in Italy, the influence of Zola was felt everywhere.

But just as Zola outstripped his initial project, so he outlived the literary movement he had helped to create. After his death in 1902, naturalism itself fell out of favor among novelists and playwrights, buried under a swarm of literary movements that eventually gave birth to Dada and surrealism—two attitudes that could hardly be more distant from his own work. On the other hand, his popular readership never abandoned him. Critical interest revived in the 1950s, and he is now recognized as a prose writer of unmatched power—a romantic realist who has left us perhaps a half dozen masterpieces that justify his place among the greatest novelists of all times.

MARTIN KANES

See also Naturalism

Further Reading

Baguley, David, editor, *Critical Essays on Emile Zola*, Boston: G.K. Hall, 1986
Berg, William J., and Laurey K. Martin, *Emile Zola Revisited*, New York: Twayne, 1992
Bernard, Marc, *Zola*, Paris: Editions du Seuil, 1988
Buuren, Maarten van, *"Les Rougon-Macquart" d'Emile Zola: De la métaphore au mythe*, Paris: Corti, 1986

Chessid, Ilona, *Thresholds of Desire: Authority and Transgression in the Rougon-Macquart,* New York: Peter Lang, 1993

Cogny, Pierre, "Realism and Naturalism: Roots of the Twentieth Century," in *L'Hénaurme Siècle: A Miscellany of Essays on Nineteenth-Century Literature,* edited by Will McLendon, Heidelberg: Carl Winter, 1984

Hemmings, F.W.J., *Emile Zola,* Oxford: Clarendon Press, 1953; 2nd edition, 1966

Lethbridge, Robert, editor, *Zola and the Craft of Fiction,* Leicester: Leicester University Press, 1990

Nelson, Brian, editor, *Naturalism in the European Novel: New Critical Perspectives,* New York: Berg, 1992

Nelson, Roy Jay, *Causality and Narrative in French Fiction from Zola to Robbe-Grillet,* Columbus: Ohio State University Press, 1990

Petrey, Sandy, *Realism and Revolution: Balzac, Stendhal, Zola, and the Performances of History,* Ithaca, New York: Cornell University Press, 1988

Schom, Alan, *Emile Zola: A Bourgeois Rebel,* London: MacDonald, 1987; as *Emile Zola: A Biography,* New York: Holt, 1988

Gabrielle Roy 1909–83

Canadian

Gabrielle Roy has the distinction of having made two very different contributions to Quebec literature: first as the author of what is widely considered to be the first true urban novel of Quebec literature, *Bonheur d'occasion* (1945; *The Tin Flute*), a masterpiece of social realism, and second as one of the finest practitioners of a more personal, intimate type of writing whose major subject is childhood memories and their transformation over time.

Roy's literary career began in the late 1930s and early 1940s, when she contributed short stories and sketches to a number of general interest publications and wrote well-researched and vibrantly humane articles on various Canadian regions and on religious and ethnic groups, some of which were later collected in *Fragiles lumières de la terre* (1978; *The Fragile Lights of Earth*). This work as a freelance journalist developed her powers of observation, her interest in the social problems of the day, her sympathy for the poor and downtrodden, including women and minorities, and her ability to describe the physical world around her. *The Tin Flute,* her first novel, appeared to immediate critical acclaim in Canada, the United States, and abroad. Ironically, Roy was soon to fall victim to her early success: the public and critics expected her to continue in the realist vein of *The Tin Flute.* Her second novel, *Le Petit Poule d'eau* (1950; *Where Nests the Water Hen*), could not have been more different. In it, she abandoned social realism for a series of three linked short stories about a family living on a remote island in rural Manitoba. Critical reaction to this idyllic, dreamlike work was severe. In subsequent years Roy alternated between the social realist mode and the semi-autobiographical novels that ultimately dominated her output.

Over the years, as she notes in her autobiography, Roy lost interest in describing the concrete details of the world around her, as she did to such effect in *The Tin Flute,* and became more concerned with exploring her own inner life. In *Rue Deschambault* (1955; *Street of Riches*) and *La Route d'Altamont* (1966; *The Road Past Altamont*), she portrays herself as a child and a young woman, her parents, some of her many siblings, and the small street where she grew up in St. Boniface, Manitoba, a French-speaking suburb of Winnipeg. Many episodes, however, were transformed or invented, and the narrator is called Christine rather than Gabrielle, underscoring the fictional status of these works. Often humorous, even playful, these works offer extremely profound meditations on complex philosophical questions such as the nature of time and memory, the reasons for human existence, and the birth of the artistic vocation. *Ces enfants de ma vie* (1977; *Children of My Heart*) returns once again to Roy's youth, describing her early years as a schoolteacher and the love she felt for her pupils, many of whom, like Roy herself, had artistic ability. The status of all these works is somewhat ambiguous in that, although labeled as novels, they are in fact linked short stories narrated by a central adult character many years after the fact. This juxtaposition of brief texts with a unifying focus is a hallmark of Roy's writing. At the end of her life, Roy abandoned autobiographical fiction for true autobiography. *La Détresse et l'enchantement* (1984; *Enchantment and Sorrow*), published posthumously in 1984, is considered by many critics to be her finest work and one of the best autobiographies ever published in Quebec.

While some commentators have criticized Roy for turning away from the social criticism of her early novels, abandoning, in their view, serious issues in favor of innocuous ruminations on her own childhood, it appears that Roy, despite a concern for social progress and justice that never left her, saw writing for writing's sake, not writing for a cause, as her true mission. She was reluctant to actively espouse any political cause, including the defense of minority French-language status in her native Manitoba, where, as her autobiography later revealed, French-Canadians were humiliated and deprived of their basic rights. Increasingly, however, it has become clear that Roy raised major issues for Quebec society, often before other writers had done so. *Alexandre Chenevert, caissier* (1954; *The Cashier*), one of the first novels to portray the French-Canadian white-collar worker, deals with subjects that were not widely discussed in the Quebec novel until much later, including the Americanization of French-Canadian society, the clash of languages and cultures in Montreal, and the impact of the mass media on human feelings and thought processes. Another key theme of Roy's writing, little discussed in Quebec literature until the 1980s, is ethnic diversity. Immigrants are among the major characters of *Where Nests the Water Hen* and are generally portrayed in a positive light. In *La Rivière sans repos* (1970; *Windflower*) and the three "Eskimo Stories" published with it in the French-language edition, Roy deals sensitively with the meeting of white and Inuit cultures, probing the strengths and the flaws of both; a number of short stories, including some included in *Un jardin au bout du monde* (1975; *Garden in the Wind*), feature Chinese or Eastern European immigrants to Canada and their struggles to belong. According to Ben-Zion Shek (1976), Gabrielle Roy was the first Quebec author to move beyond suspicion and fear of foreigners to see them as human beings and as equals. Her writing expresses a longing for universal fraternity and world peace, to be achieved through better understanding among individuals.

Questions related to natural and human ecology are also emphasized in Roy's work, particularly in *The Cashier* and in *Cet été qui chantait* (1972; *Enchanted Summer*), a series of brief meditations on nature, the seasons, and animals in the Charlevoix area of Quebec, where the author spent her summers writing in a tiny house overlooking the St. Lawrence River. Roy was a lifelong proponent of feminism, and even her earliest writing, although not overtly political, engages with a number of key debates that were to dominate feminist circles in the 1970s and 1980s, including mother-daughter relationships, gender relations and social power, and women and art. Although social concerns are nearly always present in her writing, Roy is most remarkable for her limpid, deceptively simple prose style and for the love and compassion she felt for her characters. As a feminist, a humanist, and an original thinker and writer, Roy played a key role in shaping Quebec fiction. A number of important contemporary writers, including Jacques Poulin, Michel Tremblay, Jovette Marchessault, and Francine Noël, have paid tribute to her influence.

LORI SAINT-MARTIN

See also Tin Flute

Biography

Born 22 March 1909 in St. Boniface, Manitoba. Attended St. Joseph Academy, St. Boniface; Teachers Training School, Winnipeg, Manitoba. Taught at a village school, 1928–29, and in St. Boniface, 1929–37; associated with newspapers and magazines in Quebec and France, especially *Le Jour*, 1939–40, and *Bulletin des Agriculteurs*, 1940–45. Died 13 July 1983.

Novels by Roy

Bonheur d'occasion, 1945; as *The Tin Flute*, translated by Hannah Josephson, 1947; also translated by Alan Brown, 1980
La Petite Poule d'eau, 1950; as *Where Nests the Water Hen*, translated by Harry Lorin Binse, 1951
Alexandre Chenevert, caissier, 1954; as *The Cashier*, translated by Harry Lorin Binse, 1955

Rue Deschambault, 1955; as *Street of Riches*, translated by Harry Lorin Binse, 1957
La Montagne secrète, 1961; as *The Hidden Mountain*, translated by Harry Lorin Binse, 1962
La Route d'Altamont, 1966; as *The Road Past Altamont*, translated by Joyce Marshall, 1966
La Rivière sans repos, 1970; as *Windflower*, translated by Joyce Marshall, 1970
Cet été qui chantait, 1972; as *Enchanted Summer*, translated by Joyce Marshall, 1976
Un jardin au bout du monde, 1975; as *Garden in the Wind*, translated by Alan Brown, 1977
Ces enfants de ma vie, 1977; as *Children of My Heart*, translated by Alan Brown, 1979
Courte-Queue, 1979; as *Cliptail*, translated by Alan Brown, 1980
La Pékinoise et L'Espagnole, 1987; as *The Tortoise-Shell and the Pekinese*, translated by Patricia Claxton, 1989

Other Writings: short stories, journalism, and autobiography.

Further Reading

Babby, Ellen Reisman, *The Play of Language and Spectacle: A Structural Reading of Selected Texts by Gabrielle Roy*, Toronto: ECW Press, 1985
Gilbert Lewis, Paula, *The Literary Vision of Gabrielle Roy: An Analysis of Her Works*, Birmingham, Alabama: Summa, 1984
Harvey, Carol J., *Le cycle manitobain de Gabrielle Roy*, St. Boniface, Manitoba: Editions des Plaines, 1993
Ricard, François, *Gabrielle Roy, une vie*, Montreal: Boréal, 1996 (a biography of Gabrielle Roy including a chronology of her works)
Romney, Claude, and Estelle Dansereau, editors, *Portes de communications: Études discursives et stylistiques de l'oeuvre de Gabrielle Roy*, Quebec: Presses de l'Université Laval, 1995
Saint-Martin, Lori, *Lectures contemporaines de Gabrielle Roy: Bibliographie analytique des écrits critiques, 1978–1997*, Montreal: Boréal, 1998
Shek, Ben-Zion, *Social Realism in the French-Canadian Novel*, Montreal: Harvest House, 1976
Smart, Patricia, "Quand les voix de la résistance deviennent politiques: *Bonheur d'occasion* ou le réalisme au féminin," in *Écrire dans la maison du père: L'émergence du féminin dans la tradition littéraire du Québec*, Montreal: Éditions Québec/Amérique, 1988; English version in *Writing in the Father's House: The Emergence of the Feminine in the Quebec Literary Tradition*, Toronto: University of Toronto Press, 1991
Socken, Paul, "Gabrielle Roy: An Annotated Bibliography," in *The Annotated Bibliography of Canada's Major Authors*, edited by R. Lecker and J. David, Toronto and Boston: ECW Press, 1979
Socken, Paul, *Myth and Morality in "Alexandre Chenevert" by Gabrielle Roy*, Frankfurt am Main and New York: Peter Lang, 1987
Whitfield, Agnès, "Gabrielle Roy's *Children of My Heart* or Portrait of the Artist as a Young Woman," in *Redefining Autobiography in Twentieth-Century Women's Fiction*, edited by Janice Morgan and Colette T. Hall, New York: Garland, 1991

Rulin waishi. *See* Six Classic Chinese Novels

Salman Rushdie 1947–

English

Salman Rushdie writes postcolonial picaresque novels that explore themes of loss and metamorphosis triggered by absurd, often incomprehensible, political and religious events in a world that is rapidly, even alarmingly, becoming heterogeneous and, for some, a terrifyingly disenchanting place. One of the world's most famous and most controversial late 20th-century novelists, Rushdie is perhaps best known for his *The Satanic Verses* (1988), which, ironically, most of his critics and detractors have not read.

The title of his first novel, *Grimus* (1975), is an anagram of the name "Simurg," the immense, all-wise, fabled bird of pre-Islamic Persian mythology. Although a mélange of fantasy, myth, and science fiction, *Grimus* germinally sets forth several concerns that Rushdie addresses more comprehensively in his later novels: the intersection of Eastern and Western characters, themes, features, and language; the bicultural conflict of protagonists who are peripheral, marginal people in a mainstream culture; religious and cultural rootlessness; and the ability of people to change in the face of overwhelming odds.

In his second novel, *Midnight's Children* (1981), Rushdie hit his stride as a novelist. Winner of numerous literary prizes, including Britain's highly prestigious Booker Prize, this novel was hailed as a major literary achievement and brought Rushdie international attention and critical praise as a virtuosic, brilliant prose stylist. Exploiting the magic-realist and fantastic modes more convincingly than in *Grimus, Midnight's Children* is an allegory of India's history during the first three-quarters of the 20th century told from the point of view of Saleem Sinai, one of 1,001 magic children born between midnight and 1:00 A.M. on 15 August 1947, when India received its independence from Britain. The prematurely aged, impotent Sinai, dying in a pickle factory near Bombay, tells his tragic story with such comic élan and mythic exuberance that the reader can only react with amusement and laughter. On the quarter-century anniversary of the Booker Prize in 1993, *Midnight's Children* was named the "Booker of Bookers," the best among all Booker winners.

Rooted in a more realistic narrative mode than his earlier works, *Shame* (1983), which was short-listed for the Booker Prize, is an unsettling meditation on several themes: shame and shamelessness, the uses and abuses of power, and the relationship between shame and violence. Centered on a well-to-do, seemingly pious Pakistani family, the novel depicts that group's struggle to come to terms with the ruthless politics and increasing religious obscurantism that define everyday life in Pakistan. *Shame*'s themes of parricide and the type of inhuman cruelty associated with the establishment of Pakistan are woven into a family history that serves as a metaphor for the country at large, ravaged by shameless acts that previously would have remained hidden but that now no one even bothers to conceal.

Many critics believe that Rushdie's fourth novel, *The Satanic Verses* (1988), is his masterpiece. After its publication, some Muslim clerics alleged that the book blasphemes Islam, the Prophet Muhammed, and the Koran; thus, it was immediately banned in India, proscribed in other Muslim countries, and publicly burned by British Muslims. On 14 February 1989, Iranian leader Ayatollah Khomeini issued a *fatwā,* or religious decree, calling for Rushdie's death for this alleged blasphemy. A reward of $5 million was placed on his head, and the author was forced into hiding. As of this writing, he continues to live in hiding but emerges periodically to appear at both public and private events.

The Satanic Verses, also short-listed for the Booker Prize, is concerned with South Asian immigrants in Britain, people marginalized by Thatcherian economic policies and politically sanctioned racial prejudice. With flights of magic realism, elaborate imagery, and dazzling puns and wordplay in five languages, the novel depicts the interaction between WASP Britons and that country's people of color, most of whom, like Rushdie, come from the empire's former colonies, the ever increasing "others" from the Third World whom the British had in earlier times suppressed, exploited, and humiliated but who now are demanding the right to define themselves and to control their destinies.

Rushdie wrote *Haroun and the Sea of Stories* (1990) in response to his son Zafar's claim that his father wrote books for adults only. Narrated as a fairy tale, this work addresses, not surprisingly, censorship and the curbing of artistic freedom. Rushdie weaves an intriguing story of betrayal, tyranny, and finally redemption told from the point of view of a child in this work suffused with Saturday morning cartoon-type characters, an affable robot, genies, talking fish, dark villains, and even an Arabian princess in need of saving. An engaging bedtime tale for children on its literal level, this work also possesses a metaphorical intent that is equally powerful and cautionary for adults.

The Moor's Last Sigh (1995), which can seen as an update of *Midnight's Children,* continues to focus on contemporary India, the foibles of modern Indians, and that country's former colonizers—this time the Portuguese—with trenchant satire, dazzling wordplay in several languages, and complex, magic-realist storytelling, features that have become identified with Rushdie's style. The story of public life in the India of the 1970s and 1980s is reflected in the declining fortunes of the extremely wealthy and powerful, highly eccentric, and morally compromised Gama-Zogoiby family, whose roots are both Portuguese and Jewish. This novel is one of the first in English to address the matter of amoral, right-wing Hindu terrorist activities directed at Indian

Muslims and lower castes. The Gama-Zogoiby family, like India itself, is, in Rushdie's view, on the rocks, self-destructing as it lunges toward the millennium.

Through his novels Rushdie has introduced, and even popularized, one of the most important voices of the postcolonial, end-of-millennium period, that of the "other." It is not without irony, an irony that Rushdie relishes, that one of the foremost writers of contemporary English fiction is an "other" from India, once Britain's most precious colony. Rushdie depicts with what one critic calls "funambulistic" vigor the world's quick-paced, postcolonial multicultural transformation. Some critics ask whether Rushdie's powers of observation and his ability to write will be adversely affected by his forced hiding. To date, he seems to continue to grow artistically, hampered but undaunted.

CARLO COPPOLA

See also Midnight's Children

Biography

Born 19 June 1947 in Bombay. Attended Cathedral School, Bombay; Rugby School, Warwickshire, 1961–65; King's College, Cambridge, 1965–68, M.A. (honors) in history 1968. Worked in television in Pakistan and as actor in London, 1968–69; freelance advertising copywriter, London, 1970–81; council member, Institute of Contemporary Arts, London, from 1985; forced into hiding in February 1989 after being sentenced to death for *The Satanic Verses* in a religious decree (*fatwā*) by Ayatollah Khomeini.

Novels by Rushdie

Grimus, 1975
Midnight's Children, 1981
Shame, 1983
The Satanic Verses, 1988
The Moor's Last Sigh, 1995

Other Writings: stories, television screenplays, children's fiction, a travelogue, and essays.

Further Reading

Afzal-Khan, Fawzia, *Cultural Imperialism and the Indo-English Novel: Genre and Ideology in R.K. Narayan, Anita Desai, Kamala Markandaya, and Salman Rushdie,* University Park: Pennsylvania State University Press, 1993

Appignanesi, Lisa, and Sara Maitland, editors, *The Rushdie File* (bibliography), London: ICA, Fourth Estate, 1989; Syracuse, New York: Syracuse University Press, 1990

Brennan, Timothy, *Salman Rushdie and the Third World: Myths of the Nation,* London: Macmillan, and New York: St. Martin's Press, 1989

Cundy, Catherine, *Salman Rushdie,* Manchester: Manchester University Press, and New York: St. Martin's Press, 1996

Fletcher, M.D., editor, *Reading Rushdie: Perspectives on the Fiction of Salman Rushdie,* Amsterdam and Atlanta, Georgia: Rodopi, 1994

Gorra, Michael Edward, *After Empire: Scott, Naipaul, Rushdie,* Chicago and London: University of Chicago Press, 1997

Harrison, James, *Salman Rushdie,* New York: Twayne, and Toronto: Macmillan, 1992

Kuortti, Joel, *The Salman Rushdie Bibliography: A Bibliography of Salman Rushdie's Work and Rushdie Criticism,* Frankfurt am Main and New York: Lang, 1997

Parameswaran, Uma, *The Perforated Sheet: Essays on Salman Rushdie's Art,* New Delhi: Affiliated East-West Press, 1988

Petersson, Margareta, *Unending Metamorphoses: Myth, Satire and Religion in Salman Rushdie's Novels,* Lund, Sweden: Lund University Press, 1996

Pipes, Daniel, *The Rushdie Affair: The Novel, the Ayatollah, and the West,* New York: Carol, 1990

Rao, Madhusudhana, *Salman Rushdie's Fiction: A Study,* New Delhi: Sterling, 1992

Taneja, G.R., et al., editors, *The Novels of Salman Rushdie,* New Delhi: Indian Society for Commonwealth Studies, 1992

Weatherby, William, *Salman Rushdie: Sentenced to Death,* New York: Carroll and Graf, 1990

Russian Formalists. *See* Formalism

Russian Novel

1750–1830

For 18th-century Russian writers the means of achieving cultural parity with the West lay in the renovation of their national literature. They worked to create a native canon written in the vernacular rather than in Slavonic and to stock it with the full complement of genres. The birth of Russian literary criticism produced clear theoretical prescriptions that corroborated the work of the various competing poetic schools. By the 1750s writers of pastoral verse, odes, and elegies could orient themselves with equal success on native and alien models. Although the period from 1730 to the 1770s saw a successful assimilation by Russian writers of verse-forms and poetic themes from Western sources, a parallel development of the novel in Russia based on Western models was slow to come.

The status of the novel in 18th-century Russia offers therefore a more problematic case study in Russia's self-conscious treatment of its literary belatedness. Before 1763 Russia produced no original novels and few translations; during the period 1763–75, Russian presses produced 123 novels in translation, which enjoyed substantial press-runs, yet only 12 original Russian novels were published. Despite the increase in popular demand for fiction that rose significantly after the Free Press law of 1783 dissolved the government monopoly on printing, there was little financial reward for novelists in a system where copyright had not been established, where royalty payments from the new private presses were precarious, and where the writer had yet to achieve professional status. While readers bought up grammars, histories, and law books (these were reprinted by the thousands), the market for literary texts was confined to the urban elite that expanded substantially only after the 1820s.

That no tradition of novel writing was firmly established or sanctioned by the literary establishment may be attributed in part to economic circumstances. Yet this failure is surprising and difficult to explain when viewed in the context of a literary environment that was otherwise rapidly accommodating European models while satisfying the demands of the Russian readership by translating works of English and French fiction. Polyphonic and polymorphous, the novel as a genre was problematic for Russian writers who gravitated to narrative forms that were found to be most compatible with native models. Hence, considerable continuity may be observed between the morality tale and adventure tale—already familiar narrative modes from oral and folkloric literature—and their elaboration into the Russian variant of the utopian, philosophical, and even political novel. The increasing realism of the English novel was admired by Russian readers who enjoyed the works of Daniel Defoe and Henry Fielding in translation, but there was no corresponding attempt to match these achievements in Russia. Often singled out for its strains of realism, even Mikhail Chulkov's *Prigozhaia povarikha* (1770; *The Comely Cook*), which as a picaresque has enjoyed greater popularity among readers than the larger corpus of neoclassical novels, has now been shown by a number of revisionist critics to be a work based more on stylization and parody than realism. Although it is more self-consciously literary, like other adventure and travel novels, including Chulkov's own *Peresmeshnik* (1789; The Mocker),

The Comely Cook employs the conventions of the romance and fabliau; it incorporates themes and expressions of urban folklore within the devices and frame structures of an older form without allowing more than token space to the close representation of the world for characters of any psychological depth.

Several other reasons underlie the tenuous position of the novel in literary production of the period. The 18th century in Russian literature mirrors the systemic and epistemological shift from an ecclesiastical to a secular culture that had been set in motion during the reign of Peter the Great. While the chronicle, sermon, historical narrative, and tale remained viable types of prose (an author could publish these under his own name, subject to the approval of the Church), the tradition of narrative fiction that flourished before and immediately after the Petrine period was of an oral and popular provenance that had been perpetuated anonymously in written form. Even well into the late 17th century the official creation of literary texts had chiefly been the preserve of figures based either at the court, in chanceries, or in monasteries and other institutions of the church; the production of texts therefore was geared either to utilitarian purposes, such as ceremonial occasions when panegyric poetry was performed, or a doctrinal function, such as a theological commentary.

There was, then, scarcely precedent in 1730 for the translation by Vasilii Trediakovskii of Paul Tallemant's *Voyage de l'isle d'amour* (*Ezda v ostrov liubvi*). A minor work of *preciosité*, written in a mixture of prose and verse, the French work served as a vehicle for Trediakovskii's linguistic experimentation in forging a literary language based on the vernacular. From a sociological standpoint it also represented a pathbreaking attempt to introduce into Russian culture the values of sensibility enshrined in the salon. Often misdescribed as the first Russian novel when it might more plausibly be called a throwback to the romance, *Ezda v ostrov liubvi* was, however, one of the first fictions composed in Russia with a view toward entertaining a secular if very small elite audience. With no sponsorship from the Academy of Sciences, which funded the dissemination of technical works, lexicons, and translations of exemplary literature, it is hardly surprising that Trediakovskii failed to set a trend.

Cultural bias continued to dampen interest and demand. Enthusiasm for the tenets of neoclassical doctrine led to bad press for novels in literary journals. Aleksandr Sumarokov and Mikhail Lomonosov, two of the most influential authors of the period, approved the low rank that the theory of styles and the hierarchy of genres accorded the novel, excepting classics of didactic fiction such as Fénelon's *Télémaque* (1699), first translated into Russian in 1734, and Barclay's *Argenis*. It is a measure of the status of the novel that both of these works were, later on, adapted by Trediakovskii into verse and not prose. Didactic fiction could be tolerated because it used invention, which was widely equated with lying, for the greater good of moral teaching. In his poetic treatises written in imitation of Boileau, Sumarokov had laid down rules governing poetic style, but as the author of popular songs and elegant elegies he had no time for "novels that weigh a ton, but do not have a pound worth of essence." In his *Remarks on the Novel* (1759), he condoned only those novels that served a moral purpose, otherwise villifying novels because "they teach readers an affected and deformed outlook on life and lead them away from what is natural." Similarly, Lomonosov, whose seminal writings on rhetoric, poetics, and grammar established definitive features of literary decorum, weighed in against the novel. The absence of critical benchmarks for prose at a time when debate concerning poetic style was prominent is clearly symptomatic of the inferior status of prose fiction.

Scarcely any boundaries can be drawn between the adventure novel and the didactic novel of this period. Both draw heavily on the conduct books, rule books, primers, and instructions that enjoyed official sanction and publication. It is inconceivable that the novelists producing these fictions included moralistic passages simply as a ruse to satisfy the censor, since these fictions entirely subordinate pyschological characterization and even entertainment value to their larger ethical purpose, which was typically expressed in monologues. No amount of outlandish plotting could curb the public taste for tales of the privileged who get their come-uppance. Ivan Novikov's *Pokhozhdenie Ivana gostinago syna, i drugiia skazski* (1785–86; Adventures of Ivan, the Merchant's Son, and Other Stories and Tales), charts the descent of a respectable youth into the world of a thieving Muscovite underclass by way of warning parents of the material temptations of urban life and the dangers of luxury. After an elaborate series of adventures, containing multiple embedded narratives by a fleeting cast of characters, the merchant's son has a dream that reveals the path of Truth and to the Temple of Virtue. The 17th-century *Povest'o Gore-Zlochastii* (*Tale of Woe-Misfortune*), whose protagonist seeks piety in the monastery and is everywhere thwarted by the devil, evidently influenced this work, which is one of very few novels of the period to be set in Russia. Similar lessons on the inconstancy of fortune and the precariousness of social mobility inform the anonymous *Unfortunate Nikanov; or, The Adventure of the Life of a Russian Nobleman* (1775, 1787–89), in which a Russian army officer recounts in seven evenings the tale of his own ruin.

The prevalence of allegorical novels reflects the heavy preference for didactic literature at this time. Concern about the nature of the benevolent ruler had been made topical by Catherine the Great in her own writings and official decrees. Satirical journals provided the liveliest and safest forum whereby writers under the protection of a pen name could open discussion on politically sensitive topics, but such interest also informed novels that could afford an elaborate screen of generality and exoticism as camouflage for a political viewpoint. Early Russian novels imitated neoclassical works like *Télémaque* and the abbé Barthélemy's *Le Voyage du jeune Anacharsis en Grèce* (1788) by featuring quests across the city states of ancient Greece in search of the good king. As a literary subject the formation of the ideal monarch inspired Fedor Emin's *Prikliucheniia Femistokla* (1763; The Adventures of Themistocles), where the expulsion of Themistocles provides a lightly veiled allegory for Catherine the Great's deposition of her husband Peter III and assumption of the throne. Mikhail Kheraskov's *Numa, ili protsvetaiushchii Rim* (1768; Numa; or, Flourishing Rome), the least forgotten of his three neoclassical novels, translated into fictional dialogue the obsession with the art of good government. Here too the language of statecraft is borrowed from Catherine's own manifestos, breathing faltering life into an ancient monarch who is idealized as the prototype. Implicitly, these and other works en-

dorsed or succumbed to the image of the Enlightenment ruler that Catherine had fashioned for herself. Yet at the same time, at least in the case of Kheraskov's *Polidor, syn kadma i Garmonii* (1794; Polydorus, Son of Cadmus and Harmony), these books, while affirming the status quo, also suggest a neo-Stoic message typical of the neoclassical novel, that virtue is to be sought through reason and mystical contemplation in the private cultivation of a quiet life in rustic retreat.

A taste for Fielding and Samuel Richardson that persisted into the late 1820s (if we accept as evidence the reading list that Aleksandr Pushkin gives Tatiana in *Evgenii Onegin* [*Eugene Onegin*]) spawned moralistic novels in the sentimentalist tradition. Translations of Richardson's *Pamela* (1787), *Sir Charles Grandison* (1793–94), and *Clarissa* (1791–92) gave impetus to imitation that fostered an indigenous culture of sensibility and appealed to a largely female readership. Impossible plots, hackneyed characterizations, and routine rhetoric mark imitations that nonetheless also managed for the first time to address social questions in a specifically Russian context. A few years before Nikolai Karamzin raised the question in his famous story "Bednaia Liza" (1792; "Poor Liza"), P.Iu. L'vov's *The Russian Pamela* (1789) addressed the issue of unequal marriage between members of different social classes. Dubbed a caricature of Jean-Jacques Rousseau's *Julie; or, La Nouvelle Héloïse*, Fedor Emin's *Pis'ma Ernesta i Doravry* (1766; The Letters of Ernest and Dovrara) was for all its tendentiousness the most successful of the sentimental novels. Although Emin's attempt at psychological nuance is hampered by his inability to differentiate between the discourse of the two characters (they are made to sound identical), this first epistolary novel in Russia captured the emotional upheavals of Ernest and Dovrara who, like Julie and St. Preux, remain separated by class and by sexual (if not emotional) fidelity to their respective spouses. Eventually Russian literary sentimentalism, directed by Karamzin and his supporters, supplanted the sentimental novel with short prose tales and lyric verse where the static and intimate communion between the self and nature could be represented on a more appropriate scale.

In the ever-popular adventure novel, Russian fiction widened its geographic range to embrace Europe, often bypassing the home landscape. Informing Russian readers about European life and customs (past and present) fell within the compass of fiction rather than the travelogue, which scarcely existed until the publication of Karamzin's epistolary account of his travels in 1792. It is open to conjecture whether the purpose of these foreign fictitious itineraries was to inculcate an image to which the Russian readership was meant to aspire; more likely, the writers of these fictions latched onto a surefire formula that proved viable and marketable in a tradition where the conventions of folklore supervened. In one of the best-selling fictions, *Povest' o prikliuchenii anglinskogo milorda Georga i o brandenburgskoi markgrafine Friderike Luize* (1782; The Story of the Adventure of the English Milord George and Frederica Louise, Margravine of Brandenburg), M. Komarov further integrated the frame-story and secondary plots in his recounting of the amorous adventures of George, who moves across Europe in search of pleasure. However, Komarov's survey of European reality is little more than an overlay on the knightly tale that serves as the basic replicating structure of the novel; there is typically no attempt to Russianize the sources. Most successful of the frame-story novels was Emin's *Nepostoiannaia fortuna, ili Pokhozhde-*

nie Miramonda (1763; Inconstant Fortune; or, Miramond's Peregrinations). From robbery to shipwreck, from military service in Egypt to marriage and baptism in Turkey—improbably meant to remind the reader of Emin's own strange biography—the episodic plot also proves a vehicle for a historical, geographic, and ethnographic commentary. To be sure, some works did more than maximize entertainment value by splicing together disparate features of the adventure tale and the travelogue. In *The Sad Love of the Marquis of Toledo* (1763), Emin attempted to reform his archaic habits by adapting a more realistic manner; he also encouraged readers to consider philosophical questions about the relation between man and nature, but again without reference to a Russian setting.

Although conspicuous anachronisms militate against a realistic reading, Chulkov's *The Comely Cook* qualifies as a landmark in Russian literature for its use of first-person narrative in a historically recognizable Russian context. Russia's answer to Moll Flanders (from Daniel Defoe's novel of that name), the heroine Martona is a *pícara* who uses her native wit and cunning to withstand misfortune. Gifted with a proverbial wisdom and a verbal inventiveness, two attributes that serve to animate her characterization (the novel is often referred to as an early example of the technique of *skaz*), Martona is the first heroine in Russian literature to offer the reader a vicarious view of urban life; her numerous observations, including comments on custom, money, serfdom, and jail, provide a context in which the heroine's philosophy of life develops as part of the novel's lived experience (as opposed to being imposed by the author through interpolated speech). But Chulkov's vivid creation of the subculture that Martona negotiates uses the novel form less as a medium of realism than as a celebration of the power of fiction to parody and send up cultural institutions and conventions. In subverting a range of cultural fixtures, from the salon (depicted as a bordello) to the neoclassical novel (where characters with none of Martona's palpable experience moralize pompously), *The Comely Cook* creates an unstable world that perfectly illustrates the author's stated belief in the inconstancy of fortune, which is revealed in the story of a character (Martona) who cuts her moral cloth to suit those mutable circumstances and values. Through her speech, erotic daring, and lawless behavior, Martona sets in opposition the morally contradictory worlds of the subculture and official literature while at the same time refusing to judge in favor of one side or the other.

Such moral relativism informs the philosophical project of Aleksandr Radishchev's *Puteshestvie iz Peterburga v Moskvu* (1790; A Journey from St. Petersburg to Moscow). Suppressed upon publication by Catherine II, it immediately became a classic of Russian dissident literature for its radical views on serfdom and its application of Enlightenment theories to the political economy of the Russian state. Yet as a work of literature *A Journey from St. Petersburg to Moscow* is far more than a *roman à these*. If predecessors like Chulkov drew on the Russian literary resources of the folkloric and carnival genres, Radishchev mined Western literary sources, from the ancient historians to Rousseau, to produce a work that has more in common with European fiction than Russian models. Radishchev employs the single frame-story of the traveler in a series of vignettes on the evils of serfdom, history, prostitution, censorship, court-life, excess, and luxury. For the first time a Russian fiction deployed the resources of the novel to create a polyphony of dis-

courses in which the authoritative speech of the narrator and the fictional speech of characters are independent; to the extent that the discourse of characters reflects their own psychology rather than an authorial message, they fulfill the expectation that the literary theorist Mikhail Bakhtin laid down for the novel as a genre in which characters come to life precisely through speech that exists apart from the narrator's control and sometimes in conflict with the narrator's views. The goal of Radishchev's novel is to educate and test the sensibility of the reader by using stories to reveal the ambiguities and moral complexity of social problems, rather than simply to indoctrinate the reader. The extent to which Radishchev imbues his novel with the spirit of relativism visibly affects the structure of the narrative, which, in the manner of fictions like Laurence Sterne's *Tristram Shandy*, openly calls into question its own status through metaliterary devices, thereby forcing the reader to consider the nature of the novel itself. Such a sophisticated use of literature to make literature would not recur in the Russian novel until Pushkin's *Kapitanskaia dochka* (1836; The Captain's Daughter), the early fiction of Gogol', and Mikhail Lermontov's *Geroi nashego vremeni* (1840; A Hero of Our Time). In the intervening period from Radishchev to Pushkin, the novel found few practioners among writers of sentimentalism and pre-romanticism, who favored instead poetic genres or shorter tales either suffused with emotion or packed with exotic action. In fact, the most accomplished extended narrative work of the period, and the most widely read (selling more than 3,000 copies), was Karamzin's *Istoriia gosudarstva rossiiskogo* (1818–29; History of the Russian State). The historical novels of the Napoleonic wars, despite their popular success, fell far short of artistic distinction. These works looked backward to the didactic style of 18th-century fiction rather than to the advances in writing national fiction that had been made chiefly by Sir Walter Scott, the example from which Pushkin would make his departure point.

ANDREW KAHN

Further Reading

Brown, William Edward, *A History of 18th Century Russian Literature*, Ann Arbor, Michigan: Ardis, 1980

Budgen, David, "Fedor Emin and the Beginnings of the Russian Novel," in *Russian Literature in the Age of Catherine the Great: A Collection of Essays*, edited by Anthony Cross, Oxford: Meeuws, 1976

Garrard, John, *Mixail Culkov: An Introduction to His Prose and Verse*, The Hague: Mouton, 1970

Gasparetti, David, "The Carnivalesque Spirit of the Eighteenth-Century Russian Novel," *The Russian Review* 52 (April 1993)

Kahn, Andrew, "Self and Sensibility in Radishchev's *Puteshsestvie iz Peterburga v Moskvu*: Dialogism and the Moral Spectator," *Oxford Slavonic Papers* (New Series) 30 (1998)

Levin, Iu. D., *Istoriia russkoi perevodnoi khudozhestvennoi literatury*, St. Petersburg: Dmitrii Bulanin, 1996

Marker, Gary, *Publishing, Printing and the Origins of Intellectual Life in Russia, 1700–1800*, Princeton, New Jersey: Princeton University Press, 1985

Rogger, Hans, *National Consciousness in Eighteenth-Century Russia*, Cambridge, Massachusetts: Harvard University Press, 1960

Russian Novel

1830–1855

The aged countess in Aleksandr Pushkin's short story "Pikovaia dama" (1834; "The Queen of Spades") asks a pointed question: "Are there such things as Russian novels?" In one sense, of course, the answer must be positive. There already was a budding novelistic tradition in the 18th century, with such writers as Mikhail Chulkov, Fedor Emin, and Nikolai Karamzin, which was carried on into the 19th century by such novelists as Vasilii Narezhnyi, Antonii Pogorel'skii, and Aleksandr Marlinskii. But the "Russianness" of such writing might be questioned. This early fiction was patently based on foreign models, as the very title of Narezhnyi's best-known novel *Rossiiskii Zhil'blaz* (1814; *Russian Gil Blas*) makes plain. In addition, it often had a strong Ukrainian flavor, as in Pogorel'skii's *Monastyrka* (1833; *The Convent Girl*) and the writings of Narezhnyi as well. Yet the countess' scepticism might also be a question about genre. Karamzin's "Bednaia Liza" (1792; "Poor Liza") was in effect a long short story (*povest'*), and many Russian writers seemed more comfortable with this shorter form than the full-blown novel. The word for novel in Russian—*roman*—also means "love affair," and Pushkin's countess (given her distaste for the tendency toward violence in the contemporary French novel) may well have considered love the true subject matter of the genre.

D.S. Mirsky (1949) regards the threshold of this period, 1829, as the year in which the Russian novel ceased "vegetating rather half-heartedly." In that year, Faddei Bulgarin published *Ivan Vyzhigin,* a moralistically reactionary novel about Russian life, and Mikhail Zagoskin brought out *Iurii Miloslavskii, ili Russkie v 1612 godu* (*The Young Muscovite, or the Poles in Russia*) and laid the foundations of the Russian historical novel in the vein of Sir Walter Scott. Despite these developments, the countess' questions about "Russianness" and genre haunt the development of the Russian novel throughout this period.

These doubts affect Pushkin himself and his masterpiece *Evgenii Onegin* (first published in full in 1833; *Eugene Onegin*). This work laid the foundation for the classical Russian novel, yet it is not a work in prose but rather a verse narrative written in a strict stanza form (adapted from the sonnet). Moreover, it is in effect unfinished. While the superficial influence may well be Byron's *Don Juan,* the impact of foreign literature on the novel is more profound. Vissarion Belinskii, who had begun his career as a critic by saying "we have no literature," saw in *Eugene Onegin* an "encyclopedia of Russian life." Nevertheless, the work could more fittingly be called an "encyclopedia of European literature," for, as Vladimir Nabokov has demonstrated in great detail, the whole of Pushkin's novel is permeated by literary allusion. Yet the matter goes even deeper: character motivation takes us back to the origins of the European novel itself—to *Don Quixote* and Cervantes' perception of the way life is molded by fiction. The behavior of all Pushkin's protagonists is conditioned by what they read, and it is the irreconcilability of different fictional worlds that leads to misunderstanding and tragedy.

The heroine, Tatiana, is brought up on sentimental novels and perceives Onegin as a Richardsonian hero. True to the conventions of the epistolary novel, she declares herself to him in a letter, but he, an aloof Byronic figure, spurns her love. It is only later, having seen the marks he has made in his own books, that Tatiana realizes exactly who he is. By then, the fatal clash between Onegin's cynical Byronism and the idealistic, German romanticism of his friend, Lenskii, has already occurred in an inevitable confrontation of fictional worlds that leads to a duel and to Lenskii's death. At the end of the novel, the amorous positions are reversed. It is Tatiana, a married woman, who now rejects Onegin. We may agree with Dostoevskii that her reply is one of high moral virtue, and still note the parallel with Richardson's Pamela. As for Onegin, the now "forbidden" liaison, which in its earlier purity he had rejected, still retains its Byronic attractions.

The self-conscious literariness of the novel is reinforced by the teasing presence of the author. He enters the novel as a friend of Onegin's and later seems as much concerned with his own literary autobiography as with the life of his hero. At other times, he teases his readers about the banality of their expectations in matters of rhyme and provides an introduction to the novel only at the end of the penultimate chapter.

If *Eugene Onegin* is an "encyclopedia of Russian life," it is so only as a literary paradigm of those Western influences that had penetrated the national imagination since the reforms of Peter I. The central figure, for all his foreign trappings, indeed because of them, was seen as a typically Russian figure—the rootless nobleman at odds with his own society, the so-called "superfluous man." The novel captivated its readers not with any down-home Russian qualities but with its urbanity: the elegance of its form, the epigrammatic wit of its aperçus, the polish of its verse.

There are clear signs that by the end of his brief life Pushkin was turning toward prose fiction. Influenced by Sir Walter Scott, he wrote a brief historical novel, *Kapitanskaia dochka* (1836; *The Captain's Daughter*), and he was working on an adventure novel when he was killed in a duel in 1837. But his move in the direction of prose fiction was continued by Mikhail Lermontov, who published *Geroi nashego vremeni* (*A Hero of Our Time*) in 1840. Lermontov appears consciously to be taking the portrait of the "superfluous man" a stage further. Much as Pushkin had named his hero after the River Onega, so Lermontov chooses another northern river, the Pechora, to "baptize" his hero, Pechorin, using the course of a river as an image of life itself. In fact the lives of both heroes are dogged by futility, and it is perhaps no coincidence that the Onega and the Pechora both find their outlet in the wastes of the Arctic Ocean.

Lermontov's work also poses a problem of genre, for if *Eugene Onegin* is a novel in verse, *A Hero of Our Time* is a novel made up of short stories. It is clear that the author conceived the work as a collection of short stories until he arrived at the plan of weaving them into a novel. This compositional heterogeneity allows Lermontov great subtlety in the portrayal of his hero, whom we see from many sides: through the eyes of others, through ironic self-exposure in the section "Taman," and finally through the self-questioning and revelations of his own journal. As in *Eugene Onegin,* the romantic themes of love and friendship reveal the ruthless attitude of the hero in his personal relations. However, where in *Eugene Onegin* Pushkin questions the motives and the nature of his hero, in *A Hero of Our Time* Pechorin interrogates himself on the enigma of his own character. When compared with the earlier novel, *A Hero of Our Time* marks a radical inward shift both in terms of psychological portrayal and narrative procedures. The friend killed by Onegin is his very opposite both in character and fictional values, but Grushnitskii, Pechorin's victim, is his alter ego—a parody of the hero himself. In his preface to the novel, Lermontov stresses authorial irony and mocks his readers' naiveté (much as Pushkin had teased his readers). Lermontov's playing with his readers' expectations is particularly noticeable in his arrangement of the original stories. Their chronological dislocation serves the ironically evolving psychological portrayal of the "hero." The sophistication of these procedures looks ahead to similar formal experiments in the 20th century.

A Hero of Our Time is a poet's novel, written in a clear but pungent prose. It is set in the Caucasus, and Lermontov's poetic eye enriches his prose with lyrical descriptions of natural scenery. Symbol and metaphor inform the novel's structure. In its analysis of the wayward human spirit, it laid the foundation of the Russian psychological novel, later brought to new heights by such novelists as Dostoevskii and Tolstoi.

The procedures of that other great figure of the 1830s and 1840s, Nikolai Gogol', are entirely different. His stories ostensibly shun all psychological analysis, yet the bizarre details and logical dislocations of the text manage to suggest a disturbing psychological dimension. At the same time, his magnum opus, *Mertvye dushi* (1842; *Dead Souls*), shows that typically Russian equivocation with regard to genre. It is, of course, a novel, yet Gogol' insisted (perhaps with Pushkin in mind) that the work was a prose poem—an epic (*poema*). Other features also appear to look back to Pushkin's novel. There is a similar playing with literary convention, for instance. The hero's biography is not given at the outset but relegated to the final chapter of part I, and it is only then that the reader learns the reasons for Chichikov's enigmatic behavior. As with Pushkin, an autobiographical element enters the work, and the condescending attitude toward the reader, latent in Pushkin's teasing and more obvious in Lermontov's ironic preface, now seems to have developed into open hostility. Thus the author denies responsibility for such negative heroes as Chichikov: their appearance in his work is the reader's fault. The influence of Laurence Sterne is evident, particularly in the final chapter of part I, where fictional time is treated as real time. It may also be seen in the nonsensical inserted tale of Captain Kopeikin.

Gogol' originally conceived his *poema* as a picaresque: a rogue hero travels Russia to buy up documents giving him ownership of dead peasants. Since a landowner's tax liability was based on the number of "souls" (serfs) he owned and since records were revised infrequently, tax had to be paid on dead or run-away peasants. Chichikov exploits this anomaly by buying "dead souls" at a give-away price, to form what appears on paper to be a wealthy estate capable of being mortgaged for real money. Yet as the work progressed, Gogol' began to see his theme in more positive terms. He wanted to make the novel into an apotheosis of Russian values in the planned parts II and III. However, he was dissatisfied with his attempts to achieve this goal and burned two separate versions of part II, so that part II as it now exists is merely a conflation of what survived. In this

respect, the unfinished nature of the novel recalls, yet again, Pushkin's *Eugene Onegin*.

Part I develops as a series of portraits of typical landowners who are depicted in a wealth of grotesque detail. Gogol's mastery presents each one as bizarrely unique, yet somehow typical. The master stroke is Chichikov himself, who, in a truly Gogolian paradox, is a nonperson with a palpable presence, a "dead soul" of a different order. *Dead Souls* is a great comic novel, yet it raises serious issues and, whatever Gogol's intentions, was widely seen as an exposé of the evils of serf-owning. Its emphasis on the banal, the provincial, and the seedy marks it off from the more aristocratic worlds of Pushkin and Lermontov, as does its reduction of amorous matters to the comic and the peripheral. Strangely, this work with its unrealistic detail bordering on the fantastic laid the foundation of the Russian realist novel.

In 1846 Dostoevskii launched his literary career with a short novel that brought him overnight fame, *Bednye liudi* (*Poor Folk*). Once again genre is an issue, for Dostoevskii sought his form in the 18th-century epistolary novel. The title, singling out the lower orders of society, suggest the world of Gogol', but the self-revelation which the epistolary form allows the characters is closer to the psychological methods of Lermontov. A Pushkinian dimension may also be detected in the prominence of what the characters are reading. Two works assume an emblematic role: Pushkin's short story "Stantsionnyi smotritel'" (1831; "The Stationmaster") and Gogol's "Shinel'" (1842; "The Overcoat"). "The Overcoat" arouses the strongest emotions in the male protagonist, Makar Devushkin, who is offended by Gogol's comically naturalistic portrayal of a poor clerk and his attachment to his greatcoat. In effect, *Poor Folk* is a polemical rewriting of this story, with Dostoevskii seeking to humanize the theme of an improbable love. The name of Gogol's hero is Bashmachkin, which, as Gogol' points out, is derived form the word for shoe (*bashmak*), but the name of Dostoevskii's hero, Devushkin (*devushka* means "young girl"), hints at the way Dostoevskii has transmogrified the love object from an inanimate article of clothing into a living person. Dostoevskii not only humanizes the Gogolian theme, he "psychologizes" it. Gogol' refuses to enter the thought processes of his character, but the novel of letters allows Dostoevskii to present the psychological world of his protagonists from the inside. Nevertheless, the Gogolian world of objects finally reasserts itself, when Makar, having lost his love to another man, is sent to buy clothing for her trousseau. The novel ends with a pathetic outburst in which he contrasts the values of human life to mere frippery.

Dostoevskii's next short novel, *Dvoinik* (1846; *The Double*), was a further attempt to add psychological depth to themes already suggested in Gogol's short stories "Nos" (1836; "The Nose") and "Zapiski sumasshedshego" (1835; "Diary of a Madman"). Its hero, Goliadkin, is a clerk, a typically Gogolian figure. With great psychological insight, Dostoevskii explores his sense of inferiority and the delusion that he is being persecuted by a more successful double. This greater focus on psychology and the interest in doubles looks forward to the mature Dostoevskii. However, his contemporaries were not ready for his work, and the novel was not received well. Later he would give it the subtitle "A Petersburg Poem" (*poema*), not only indicating his debt to Gogol' but also raising the perennial question of genre.

An important new development took place in the Russian novel with the publication of Aleksandr Herzen's *Kto vinovat?* (*Who Is to Blame?*) in 1847. It is one of the first Russian "problem novels," addressing social and moral issues. Bel'tov, a nobleman brought up on Western values and unfit for Russian life, is a "superfluous man," but Krutsiferskii, a man of humbler origins, who is an anomaly in his native land for being highly educated despite his social status, is the more interesting figure. He is a déclassé intellectual (*raznochinets*) and forerunner of a hero who would assume greater prominence in the post-reform literature of the 1860s. Herzen's heroine, Liubon'ka, in rejecting Bel'tov in favor of Krutsiferskii, exemplifies the moral rectitude of Pushkin's Tatiana, and it has become a critical commonplace to point out the moral strength of the Russian heroine when confronted with the failings of the superfluous man.

This theme is again present in another novel of 1847, Aleksandr Druzhinin's *Polin'ka Saks* (*Polinka Saks*), a work with a sentimental strain inspired by the writings of George Sand. Its partly narrative, partly epistolary style again shows a customary generic ambiguity. The sympathetic portrayal of its eponymous heroine reinforces a dominant feature of the Russian novel in general—the positive portrayal of women. Indeed, Druzhinin suggests that society itself is to blame for any shortcomings in its womankind, since it treats them either as children or as angels. Karolina Pavlova's *Dvoinaia zhizn'* (1848; *A Double Life*), which also adopts the theme of the treatment of women, is a novel written both in poetry and in prose, again raising the issue of genre.

The final years of the period, from 1848 to 1855, became known as "the gloomy seven years." Europe had seen widespread revolution in 1848, and Nicholas I reacted by taking draconian measures at home. The development of the Russian novel suffered a serious setback during this period. Censorship was redoubled, seriously inhibiting literary production. Dostoevskii was arrested and sentenced to penal servitude in Siberia. Ivan Turgenev was arrested and briefly exiled to his own estate. Gogol' committed suicide in 1852. Herzen had left Russia for good in 1847.

Nevertheless, one forward-looking literary event took place in 1849 with the publication of "Son Oblomova" ("Oblomov's Dream") by Ivan Goncharov. "Oblomov's Dream" was published as a separate and independent sketch, and it took another ten years for Goncharov's masterpiece, *Oblomov,* to appear. "The Dream of Oblomov" in many ways evokes the atmosphere of the last years of the reign of Nicholas I. On one level, it appears to poeticize an obsolescent feudalism and a society in stagnation, with its proscribed areas (the ravine) where unknown terrors lurk. Goncharov presents his "dream" with a gentle irony that in effect questions the very values he appears to endorse. This sketch of a doomed way of life is in every sense the kernel of the later novel.

The years from 1830 to 1855, then, saw a tremendous rise in the production and quality of the Russian novel. Although generic ambiguities continued to haunt many of the novel published during this time, a foundation was laid for the realistic novel in Gogol's work, for the psychological novel in *A Hero of Our Time* and Dostoevskii's early fiction, for the "problem novel" in Herzen's *Who Is to Blame?* All of these beginnings came to fruition in the decades following the death of Nicholas I in 1855.

RICHARD PEACE

See also Fedor Dostoevskii; Nikolai Gogol'; Hero of Our Time; Oblomov; Aleksandr Pushkin

Further Reading

Barratt, Andrew, and A.D.P. Briggs, *A Wicked Irony: The Rhetoric of Lermontov's "A Hero of Our Time,"* Bristol: Bristol Classical Press, 1989

Bowman, Herbert, *Vissarion Belinski, 1811–1848: A Study in the Origins of Social Criticism in Russia,* Cambridge, Massachusetts: Harvard University Press, 1954

Briggs, A.D.P., *Alexander Pushkin: A Critical Study,* London: Croom Helm, and Totowa, New Jersey: Barnes and Noble, 1983

Debreczeny, Paul, *The Other Pushkin: A Study of Alexander Pushkin's Prose Fiction,* Stanford, California: Stanford University Press, 1983

Ehre, Milton, *Oblomov and His Creator: The Life and Art of Ivan Goncharov,* Princeton, New Jersey: Princeton University Press, 1974

Fanger, Donald, *Dostoevsky and Romantic Realism: A Study of Dostoevsky in Relation to Balzac, Dickens, and Gogol,* Cambridge, Massachusetts: Harvard University Press, 1965

Gippius, Vasilii, *Gogol,* Leningrad: Mysl, 1924; as *Gogol,* Ann Arbor, Michigan: Ardis, 1981

Mersereau, John, *Mikhail Lermontov,* Carbondale: Southern Illinois University Press, 1962

Mirsky, D.S., *A History of Russian Literature,* New York: Knopf, and London: Routledge and Kegan Paul, 1949

Moser, Charles A., editor, *The Cambridge History of Russian Literature,* Cambridge and New York: Cambridge University Press, 1989; revised edition, 1992

Peace, Richard, *The Enigma of Gogol: An Examination of the Writings of N.V. Gogol and Their Place in the Russian Literary Tradition,* Cambridge and New York: Cambridge University Press, 1981

Peace, Richard, *"Oblomov": A Critical Examination of Goncharov's Novel,* Birmingham: Department of Russian Language and Literature, University of Birmingham, 1991

Terras, Victor, *The Young Dostoevsky (1846–49): A Critical Study,* The Hague: Mouton, 1969

Todd, William Mills, *Fiction and Society in the Age of Pushkin: Ideology, Institutions, and Narrative,* Cambridge, Massachusetts: Harvard University Press, 1986

Russian Novel

1855–1900

The emergence of the novel as the dominant genre in Russian literature during the last half of the 19th century may be explained partly by certain sociopolitical and socioeconomic factors. The major historical event was the defeat of imperial Russia in the Crimean War of 1854–55. National humiliation led to national rethinking and a recognition of the need to modernize the state along European lines.

The reforms involved measures of near-revolutionary proportions. The abolition of serfdom, for instance, promulgated in 1861, required the introduction of limited forms of self-government at the local level to replace the former authority of the serf-owning nobility. As a consequence the liberated peasantry gradually began a large-scale migration to the cities, into industries and commerce.

Other forces were unleashed in the process. Among these was a younger intelligentsia, a meritocracy known as the "new men," who belonged neither to the nobility nor to the peasantry. Following the teachings of Nikolai Chernyshevskii (1828–83) and his young protégé Nikolai Dobroliubov (1836–61) in materialism, atheism, anti-aestheticism, and, above all, total commitment to the laws of the natural sciences, they were branded "nihilists" for their social and political radicalism.

The reforms created social tensions that were thrown into sharper relief by the nihilist intelligentsia. The Russian novel of the 1860s took its inspiration from this situation and provided the only real public forum for the discussion of political ideas. The earliest example of a novel focusing on sociopolitical issues and chronicling the growth of the intelligentsia was Ivan Turgenev's first novel, *Rudin* (1856; *Rudin*). Diagnosing the inability of the older generation of the intelligentsia to act upon their ideals, the novel revealed the hero's inadequacies while emphasizing the heroine's strengths. It was basically an elaborate portrait somewhat like *Tysiacha dush* (1858; *One Thousand Souls*) by Aleksei Pisemskii, which traced, in loose chronicle style, the rise and fall of an ambitious bureaucrat corrupted by greed. Rudin's formlessness compares badly with the elegiac elegance of Turgenev's second novel, *Dvorianskoe gnezdo* (1859; *Home of the Gentry*), a love story poignantly illustrating the seemingly irreconcilable difference between the indigenous (Slavophile) and European (Westernizing) choices facing Russia.

Yet Turgenev's novel could not match Ivan Goncharov's *Oblomov* (1859; *Oblomov*) in scope. The appearance of this masterpiece elicited from Dobroliubov a brilliant review interpreting the hero, the serf-owner who sinks into inertia as a result of the privileges of serfdom, as the ultimate "superfluous man," morally as servile as the serf upon whom he depended. The implication of such a tendentious approach was that the "new men" were the only people capable of changing Russian society. Goncharov's portrait had, in fact, more universal appeal and greater complexity than Dobroliubov allowed, just as his novel as a whole, in its scale and its detailed verisimilitude, established new norms for the genre in Russian literature.

The gradual evolution of the Russian novel from concentration on portraiture into a form capable of embracing cross-sections of society occurred most conspicuously in the work of Turgenev and heralded a purposefulness in the genre that produced a marked formal enlargement. *Nakanune* (1860; *On the Eve*), Turgenev's third novel, attempted to provide an insight into the younger generation's aspirations through the character of its heroine, but the result was a disjointed work, impressive as much for its pessimism as for its multiple locales. Yet it clearly attempted to grapple objectively with the quixotic, altruistic aims of the younger intelligentsia.

Real success greeted Turgenev's efforts with his fourth novel, *Ottsy i deti* (1862; *Fathers and Sons*). Recognized as his masterpiece, this novel, set in 1859, uses a series of rural locales to portray different aspects of the hero, Bazarov, emphasizing both his nihilism and his tragic end. (Bazarov, having failed in love, needlessly dies in the service of the people.) As a scientist and a potential Jacobin, Promethean in his challenge to divine supremacy, Bazarov represents a real threat to the status quo. The novel also stresses the continuity of family life and society, the need for understanding between the generations, the promise "of eternal reconciliation and of life everlasting" as the final words declare.

Turgenev's legacy to the Russian novel was a new objectivity, a disengaged liberalism in the treatment of relevant sociopolitical issues. However, polemics and partisanship assumed dominance in the 1860s. The influence of Chernyshevskii undoubtedly played a part in this increased political engagement. His novel *Chto delat'?* (1863; *What Is To Be Done?*) stressed the purposefulness of fiction in a deliberately polemical sense. Intended as "a textbook on life," a blueprint for educating a generation of "new men" in the precepts of rational egoism, it showed how the heroine could emancipate herself and dream of a socialist future and how the revolutionary hero could begin to implement that future through a course of self-improvement. Hostility toward the novel's radicalism stimulated a series of "anti-nihilist" novels, the greatest examples of which are those by Fedor Dostoevskii.

Dostoevskii's model was initially Dickens. *Unizhennye i oskorblennye* (1861; *The Insulted and the Injured*), his first (unsuccessful) attempt at a large-scale novel, had a Dickensian plot dominated by two portraits of quite unusual intensity, but his first great novel was *Prestuplenie i nakazanie* (1867; *Crime and Punishment*). The novel contains such a rich diversity of characters that "polyphony" (Bakhtin's term) or multivocality seem specifically designed to describe Dostoevskii's achievement here. It is doubtful, however, whether the common assumption that the narrator's voice has no greater authority than that of the characters can withstand close scrutiny. Although originally conceived as a first-person confession, the final product is closer to a detective fiction incorporating elements of the morality play and Greek tragedy. Within a dramatically condensed time-scheme, *Crime and Punishment* explores the motives of the student dropout Raskolnikov who commits murder to rid society of an evil and to prove his own nihilist freedom of will. The love of the prostitute Sonia ultimately redeems him (although this is open to question), but his soul is equally under threat from the sinister Svidrigailov, whose own parody of nihilism finally leads to suicide as the ultimate self-willed act.

The national reassessment that followed the Crimean War also involved a reassertion of Russian religious uniqueness. Dostoevskii's second novel, *Idiot* (1869; *The Idiot*), written largely in Dresden during his second exile, advanced the notion of a Russian Christ who would save a corrupt Europe. Yet the central image of the childlike Prince Myshkin preaching that beauty will save the world does not withstand the murderous forces of nihilism and venal capitalism that surround him. He is finally reduced to his former idiocy. Magnificent in its boldness of conception and in its opening and concluding scenes, the novel is too overburdened with subplots and polemics to be wholly satisfactory. Turgenev's contribution to the same question in *Dym* (1867; *Smoke*), his fifth, only partially successful novel, set in Baden-Baden, portrays Russia as essentially consumed by dark forces that can only be countered by pro-Western influences.

No novel did more to confront the issue of Russian nationalism in this period than Lev Tolstoi's masterpiece, *Voina i mir* (1863–69; *War and Peace*). A historical novel describing the Napoleonic invasion of Russia in 1812, it was not exactly topical. But it addressed all the issues of the day in its celebration of both the patriotic unity of Russia and the selflessness of the nobility, both the determinism of the historical process and a countervailing search for faith, God, and social justice. As a family chronicle, it describes the experiences of two exemplary noble families, the Rostovs and the Bolkonskiis, and the heroines central to each, Natasha and Mar'ia. As a historical fiction describing the battles of Austerlitz (1805) and Borodino (1812) and the later French retreat from Moscow, *War and Peace* vitally enhances history by representing it as a truth seen mostly through the eyes of the two central heroes, Andrei Bolkonskii and Pierre Bezukhov. The heroes' search for faith is part of the larger issue of the meaning of history as Tolstoi attempted to define it. It also informs the notion that there is an "active virtue" in life that can change society for the better.

The majestic scale of *War and Peace* gave new stature to the Russian novel. Dostoevskii became consumed by the desire to match it and conceived "The Life of a Great Sinner" for the purpose. Lesser writers, equally antinihilist and nationalist—Goncharov, for instance, in *Obryv* (1870; *The Precipice*), Pisemskii in *Vzbalamuchennoe more* (1863; Troubled Seas), Nikolai Leskov in *Nekuda* (1864; No Way Out) and *Na nozhakh* (1871; At Daggers Drawn)—offered their often shapeless and contrived novels as grist to the same mill, as did Vasilii Sleptsov in *Trudnoe vremia* (1865; Hard Times) and Innokentii Omulevskii in *Shag za shagom* (1870; Step by Step) with their pronihilist works. But none plumbed the depths of the problem as fully as Dostoevskii did in his third great novel, *Besy* (1872; *Devils* or *The Possessed*).

His darkest, most politically oriented work, ostensibly told by a busy-body narrator, *Devils* aimed to diagnose the ills facing Russia by showing how Western ideology had entered the intelligentsia (on the pattern of the man possessed by devils in the gospel of St. Luke) and infected the hero Stavrogin as well as his "disciples," his ideological progeny. Possessed respectively by the idea of a God-fearing people but unable to believe in God (as in the case of Shatov), or by the notion of suicide as a self-willed crucifixion that will liberate humanity from the fear of death (as in the case of Kirillov), both "disciples" ultimately fall victim to the machinations of an unscrupulous political fixer (based on the historical Nechaev) who aims to turn Stavrogin into a revolu-

tionary leader. In fact, he turns out to be an empty, impotent husk. Unmasked in his "confession" (in an unpublished chapter) as a pervert whose "great sin" is the rape of a young girl, he eventually hangs himself like his wretched victim. Despite such *grand guignol* horrors, the novel contains a succession of splendidly realized satirical scenes laced with black humor and brilliant characterizations, none more wicked than the satire of Turgenev in the figure of the writer Karmazinov.

The enlargement of the Russian novel's scale that occurred during the 1860s continued into the 1870s. That decade, however, saw a marked change of tone. If the reforms of the preceding period had led to a rethinking of national issues, the 1870s, known as "the epoch of great deeds" (*epokha velikikh del*), saw a younger intelligentsia actively pursuing a populist ideal in the belief that only the peasantry were capable of overthrowing the autocracy. Meanwhile, official Russia embarked on a vague Panslavism in the hope of uniting the Slav peoples. Both ideals ended in bloodshed—Panslavism in the Russo-Turkish War (1877–78) and populism in terrorism and the bloody assassination of Alexander II in 1881.

Against this background of unrest and conflict, the Russian novel, mainly through the work of Tolstoi and Dostoevskii, became the conscience of the nation and virtually its second government. Only two other writers contributed novels of any value to this process. Turgenev's last novel, *Nov'* (1877; *Virgin Soil*), attempted to regain the favor of the younger intelligentsia by depicting the activities of the populists although without professing any real support for their cause. Mikhail Saltykov-Shchedrin in *Gospoda Golovlevy* (1880; *The Golovlevs*) focused on the place of women and the sanctity of marriage and the family in a rapidly changing society. Saltykov's blackly satirical portrayal of a former serf-owning family dominated by a grasping matriarch and consumed by greed, hypocrisy, and alcoholism dealt a significant blow to the pieties of traditionalism. The most memorably awful portrait was that of the deceitful Iudushka, the final inheritor of the matriarchal wealth.

Generally regarded as Dostoevskii's least successful major novel, *Podrostok* (1875; *An Accidental Family*, also translated as *A Raw Youth* and *The Adolescent*) analyzes the causes of family breakdown through the bitter experience of the young illegitimate narrator who is in search of his biological and spiritual father. He dreams of becoming as rich as a Rothschild, while his father Versilov, a representative of the Westernized intelligentsia, dreams of a Golden Age at the beginning of European civilization. Dostoevskii suggests that, in their evasion of reality, both ideals betoken a refusal to deal with the here and now.

Tolstoi's *Anna Karenina* (1875–77) examines the issue of a family breakdown far more deeply. The famous epigraph "Vengeance is mine and I will repay" suggests authorial bias as much as the opening sentence "All happy families are alike, each unhappy family is unhappy in its own way," but the moral intent of the novel, however skewed to Tolstoi's purposes, does not seriously distract from the grandeur and tragedy of the central portrait of Anna herself. Her vitality and her allure arguably redeem her in the end, despite the way her infatuation with Vronskii brings on a tragedy compounded by her lack of faith, her social disgrace, and the fatalism of her suicide. The positive example offered by Konstantin Levin mirrors Tolstoi's own experience in marriage and his discovery of faith. *Anna Karenina* presents marriage as the basic social contract and argues for the superiority of rural to urban values and the need for a spiritual dimension in life. Throughout *Anna Karenina,* Tolstoi exhibits his psychological insight, his sense of the sheer physicality of the world, and a characteristic kinetic energy in moving his novel forward scene by scene.

Another high point of the period followed a few years later, with Dostoevskii's last, if incomplete, novel *Brat'ia Karamazovy* (1880; *The Brothers Karamazov*). A novel about deep family enmities, it evolved from Dostoevskii's attendance at the trial of the terrorist Vera Zasulich in 1878. Culminating in the trial of Dmitrii Karamazov for parricide—a miscarriage of justice—the novel may be seen as an in-depth analysis of the three days prior to the parricide and of the true reasons for the crime. Justice is the novel's central theme—both within a family setting and at the level of society at large, through the intervention of church and state. Although ostensibly about money and murder, the novel explores the choices facing Russia, between Ivan Karamazov's atheist and implicitly socialist attack on Christ's gospel in the name of moral freedom (in the famous chapter "The Grand Inquisitor") and his brother Alesha's discovery of mutual responsibility for sin based on the teaching of his spiritual mentor, Father Zosima. Raising the level of debate about the human dilemma far beyond national concerns and boundaries, the novel does not resolve the central choice.

Always topical and in a realistic mode, the great novels of this period by Turgenev, Goncharov, Dostoevskii, and Tolstoi have never been out of print and are still read throughout the world for the profundity of their psychological insight, their ideas, their candor in dealing with human pathology, and their power as works of art. In each case, these novels originally appeared in serialized form in major journals and had a close association with the demands of journalistic publication. Although always subject to censorship, the major novels of these writers, according to the available evidence, suffered an even harsher regime of drafting and remodeling at their creators' hands. They may be regarded as integral parts of the European tradition of the novel in a broad sense, but they have features that relate them to classical norms, including the Homeric epic, Attic drama, and Menippean satire. Apart from their relationship to their time and a tendency, also typical of Russian criticism, to blur the distinction between fiction and reality, the Russian novels of this period relied on historical events rather than fantasy, on psychology rather than plot. They were distinguished by what Dostoevskii described as "a penetration of reality" and what Viktor Shklovski (1928), writing about Tolstoi, described as *ostranenie* ("defamiliarization"). They acquired in the process the right to edify as well as typify, to be vehicles for heroes and heroines as positive role models, endowing the Russian novel with a unique moral and sociopolitical authority.

Between 1881 and the end of the century the situation changed. The most important work in the genre to appear was Tolstoi's last novel, *Voskresenie* (1899; *Resurrection*), which resurrects his early hero Prince Nekhliudov. Despite several successful scenes, the novel is little more than a political tract. Regionalism and a concern with the merchant class were marked features of novels by Dmitrii Mamin-Sibiriak (including *Privalovskie milliony* [1883; *Privalov's Millions*]) and Pavel Mel'nikov-Pecherskii (*V lesakh* [1875; *In the Woods*] and *Na gorakh* [1881; *In the Hills*]).

A.I. Ertel had a major success with epic novels on the rise of capitalism (*Gardeniny* [1889; The Gardenins]) and change in the countryside (*Smena* [1891; Change]). Throughout these two decades P.D. Boborykin produced novels of varying value on issues of topical relevance. The first sign of a revival in the genre came on the eve of the next century with Maksim Gor'kii's *Foma Gordeev* (1899). Fresh and vivid, it sounded the first note of protest for two decades.

RICHARD FREEBORN

See also Fedor Dostoevskii; Novel of Ideas; Oblomov; Lev Tolstoi; Ivan Turgenev; What Is To Be Done?

Further Reading

Bakhtin, M.M., *Problemy tvorchestva Dostoevskogo,* Leningrad: Priboi, 1929; 2nd edition, revised, as *Problemy poetiki Dostoevskogo,* Moscow: Sov. Pisatel, 1963; as *Problems of Dostoevsky's Poetics,* Ann Arbor, Michigan: Ardis, 1973; new edition and translation, Minneapolis: University of Minnesota Press, and Manchester: Manchester University Press, 1984

Bonamour, Jean, *Le Roman russe,* Paris: Presses Universitaires de France, 1978

Bushmin, Aleksei Sergeevich, et al., editors, *Istoriia russkogo romana,* 2 vols., Moscow and Leningrad: Izd-vo Akademii Nauk SSSR, 1962–64

Freeborn, Richard, *The Rise of the Russian Novel: Studies in the Russian Novel from "Eugene Onegin" to "War and Peace,"* Cambridge: Cambridge University Press, 1973

Freeborn, Richard, *The Russian Revolutionary Novel: Turgenev to Pasternak,* Cambridge and New York: Cambridge University Press, 1982

Garrard, John, editor, *The Russian Novel from Pushkin to Pasternak,* New Haven, Connecticut: Yale University Press, 1983

Gifford, Henry, *The Novel in Russia: From Pushkin to Pasternak,* London: Hutchinson University Library, 1964; New York: Harper and Row, 1965

Golovin, K., *Russkii roman i russkoe obshchestvo,* St. Petersburg: Porokhovshchikov, 1897

Ivanov, V.I., *Borozdy i mezhi: Opyty esteticheskie i kriticheskie,* Moscow: Musaget, 1916

Moser, Charles, editor, *The Cambridge History of Russian Literature,* Cambridge and New York: Cambridge University Press, 1989; revised edition, 1992 (see especially chapters 6 and 7)

Moser, Charles, *Antinihilism in the Russian Novel of the 1860s,* The Hague: Mouton, 1964

Reeve, F.D., *The Russian Novel,* New York: McGraw-Hill, 1966; London: Muller, 1967

Shklovskii, Viktor, *Material i stil' v romane L'va Tolstogo' "Voina i mir,"* Moscow: Federatsiia, 1928

Steiner, George, *Tolstoy or Dostoevsky: An Essay in the Old Criticism,* New York: Knopf, 1959; 2nd edition, New Haven, Connecticut: Yale University Press, 1996

Vogue, Eugene-Melchior, *Le Roman russe,* Paris: Plon-Nourrit, 1886; as *The Russian Novelists,* Boston: Lothrop, 1887

Russian Novel

1900–1945

The turn of the century found the Russian novel in crisis, no major novelist having succeeded the 19th-century giants, Ivan Turgenev, Fedor Dostoevskii, and Lev Tolstoi. Instead, various groupings argued over the direction the novel was to take in a highly politicized debate. The Socialist Left propagated its revolutionary ideology, writing "around" czarist censorship. The liberal position, highlighted in a collection of essays entitled *Landmarks* (1909), was that the radical intelligentsia had reached an impasse and that it was time to pursue limited social goals by nonviolent means.

Writers of a socialist and liberal persuasion tended to publish with the *Znanie* (Knowledge, 1898–1913) publishing association, whose "Low-Priced Library" series featured mainly works of the "critical realism" type. Maksim Gor'kii, ideologically and personally close to Lenin and the Bolsheviks, joined the *Znanie* group in 1900. His novels *Foma Gordeev* (1899), *Zhizn' Matveia Kozhemiakina* (1911; *The Life of Matvei Kozhemyakin*), *Delo Artamonovykh* (1925; *The Artamonov Business*), and *Zhizn' Klima Samgina* (The Life of Klim Samgin, 1925–36; translated in 4 vols. as *The Bystander, The Magnet, Other Fires,* and *The Spectre*) follow an identical pattern: an older generation of bourgeois entrepreneurs clashes with an emergent generation of revolutionaries, pitting fathers against sons. Gor'kii's *Mat'* (1906; *Mother*) became the archetype of the Soviet socialist-realist novel. Nilovna, the heroine, is a revolutionary worker's mother who, at novel's start, is a cowed, religious housewife, but develops into a fearless fighter for the revolution.

Among the liberal members of the *Znanie* group were Ivan Bunin and Aleksandr Kuprin, both primarily short-story writers. Bunin's short novel *Derevnia* (1910; *The Village*) is composed of brief episodes of life in the Russian provinces at the time of the Revolution of 1905. *Sukhodol* (1912; Dry Valley) tells the story of the decline of the family that owns the Sukhodol estate. Bunin is an impressionist who makes use of significant detail to generate a gamut of emotions, mostly melancholy. Kuprin, a former army officer, in his short novel *Poedinok* (1905; *The Duel*), describes the life of army officers as wretched, brutish, and tedious. Other writers of a liberal persuasion who reacted to topical issues found as many readers and were discussed as heatedly as Tolstoi or Chekhov. Such were Aleksandr Amfiteatrov (1862–1928). Their work is provocative but lacks depth.

The symbolist movement, influenced by Nietzsche, Theosophy, and the philosophy of Vladimir Solov'ev (1853–1900), generated much of what was new about the Russian novel of the 1900s. Its decadent branch showed a tendency for fin-de-siècle pessimism and a penchant for the perverse and macabre. The symbolists proper pursued religious and metaphysical ideals.

Fedor Sologub, a decadent, in *Melkii bes* (1908; *Petty Demon*) tells the story of a dull-witted and brutish schoolteacher's descent into delusions, irrational fears, and eventually murderous paranoia against a background of the banality and tedium of life in a provincial city; the novel also offers occasional glimpses of erotic enchantment in episodes featuring young people.

Andrei Belyi's fiction is defined by the notion that symbolic representation—verbal, musical, or visual—is an avenue to true reality. Techniques of musical and pictorial composition appear in Belyi's prose along with intricate language games. His masterpiece, *Peterburg* (1916; *Petersburg*), is a medley of fast and furious action (the plot revolves around a bomb), topical issues (a workers' uprising, "the yellow peril"), the topography and literary mythology of Petersburg, and a series of confused dreams.

Dmitrii Merezhkovskii authored a trilogy of historical novels: *Smert' bogov: Iulian Otstupnik* (1896; *The Death of the Gods*), *Voskresshie bogi: Leonardo da Vinchi* (1902; *The Romance of Leonardo da Vinci*), and *Antikhrist: Petr i Aleksei* (1905; *Peter and Alexis*). It reflects the idea that a Nietzschean Hellenism and Christianity were two halves of an as yet unrealized higher truth. Mikhail Kuzmin, poet, playwright, and essayist, was close to the symbolists, although he leaned toward "beautiful clarity" with respect to style and was opposed to their mysticism. His personal concern was with homoerotic experience, which is the subject of his short novel *Kryl'ia* (1907; *Wings*).

The prose of Aleksei Remizov (1877–1957) is distinguished by a persistent foregrounding of the word-as-such and a stylized diction adapted to the theme at hand. His novels *Prud* (1908; The Pond) and *Chasy* (1908; *The Clock*), composed of short lyric vignettes, are difficult although fascinating reading because of constant changes in the tone of the narrative voice, colloquial syntax, frequent use of poetic tropes, and the confusion of dream, fiction, and reality.

The Revolution of 1917 had an immediate effect on Russian literature. Many major writers emigrated and new groupings emerged, all ostensibly loyal to the Soviet regime. The most radical writers gathered around the journals *October* (1924–) and *On Guard* (1923–25; as *On Literary Guard*, 1926–32). They called themselves the All-Union or the Russian Association of Proletarian Writers (VAPP and RAPP, respectively) and advocated close cooperation with the Communist Party. From their ranks came Dmitrii Furmanov, Iurii Libedinskii, Aleksandr Fadeev, Mikhail Sholokhov, and Aleksandr Serafimovich.

Pereval (Watershed), a group of less radical writers, gathered around the journal *Red Virgin Soil* (1921–42), edited by Aleksandr Voronskii, a Bolshevik. Pereval welcomed fellow travelers and subscribed to the principle according to which, in Voronskii's words, "consciously or unconsciously, a scholar or artist fills orders which he has received from his [social] class." Among the signers of Pereval manifestoes were Ivan Kataev, Andrei Platonov, and Anna Karavaeva.

A group that published the journal *LEF* (Left Front, 1923–28) consisted of futurists, formalists, and constructivists, most of whom were non-party members but nurtured the hope that the Soviet government would welcome progressive, modernist art. The formalists, headed by Viktor Shklovskii, Iurii Tynianov, and Boris Tomashevskii, are known primarily for their critical and theoretical writings. They found the significance of the novel primarily in formal aspects, analyzing it as an aggregate of themes, motifs, and devices. The constructivists, including Boris Arvatov and Kornelii Zelinskii, sought simple formulas and models to clarify the complexity of modern life. The third grouping, the futurists, expressed an unreserved enthusiasm for scientific and technological advances, including such 20th-century phenomena as cars and planes, communications technology, and highly mechanized manufacturing and construction techniques.

LEF advocated a frankly utilitarian art, addressed to the masses in readily visualized and entertaining form. The group wished to replace fiction with "factographic" genres, such as biography, documentary, and reportage. Viktor Shklovskii wrote several novels that combine all three and Iurii Tynianov wrote some historical novels that were, in effect, scholarly biographies.

The Serapion Brothers (1921–29), an informal group of writers, took their name from E.T.A. Hoffmann's work of that title to signal their creative freedom, camaraderie, and creative spirit. Among the "Serapions" were Vsevolod Ivanov, Konstantin Fedin, and Veniamin Kaverin. Several other groups were in existence during the New Economic Policy period (1921–28), during which writers were allowed a relatively free choice of styles and topics. The Revolution and civil war were leading topics. Some writers dealt with them in a manner of "revolutionary romanticism." *Nedelia* (1922; *A Week*) by Iurii Libedinskii, for instance, describes the heroic and tragic struggle of a rural Communist Party cell against a murderous peasant uprising. *Zheleznyi potok* (1924; *The Iron Flood*) by Aleksandr Serafimovich relates how a heroic communist leader converts a ragged band of proletarians into a disciplined fighting force. Dmitrii Furmanov used factographic reportage for his novel *Chapaev* (1923; *Chapaev*), celebrating the exploits of a Red Army general of legendary fame. Vsevolod Ivanov's trilogy *Partizany* (1921; Partisans), *Bronepoezd 14–69* (1922; *Armored Train 14–69*), and *Tsvetnye vetra* (1922; Colored Winds) deals with the civil war in Siberia. Its basic device is that of a series of rapidly changing still images, supported by ample factographic material.

Goroda i gody (1924; *Cities and Years*) by Konstantin Fedin gives an account of the Revolution from an intellectual's viewpoint. Close to the 19th-century novel in many ways, it uses several formal devices that indicate its 20th-century provenance. Time sequences are inverted to signal that time is out of joint. Tone and tempo of the narrative are modulated for suspense and estrangement. *Golyi god* (1922; *The Naked Year*) by Boris Pil'niak was even more modernist. Its style, derived from Belyi and Remizov, became the model for postrevolutionary ornamentalist prose.

Other writers chose the conventional epic manner of Tolstoi. Aleksandr Fadeev's novel *Razgrom* (1927; *The Rout*) deals with the civil war in the Far East in a restrained and objective manner. The rout is that of a Red guerilla detachment by White Cossacks. *Tikhii Don* (1928–40; *Quiet Flows the Don*) by Nobel prize winner Mikhail Sholokhov is one of a number of works modeled after *War and Peace*. It covers life in a community of Don Cossacks from 1912 to 1922 against a panoramic background of historical events. Aleksei Tolstoi likewise sought to emulate his namesake in a novel trilogy, *Khozhdenie po mukam* (1920–42; *Road to Calvary*), which covers the same period as Sholokhov's novel but from the viewpoint of the progressive intelligentsia. *Belaia gvardiia* (1927–29; *The White Guard*) by Mikhail Bulgakov sees the Revolution through the eyes of a divided middle-class famiily.

The least conventional novel dealing with the Revolution was fashioned by Andrei Platonov. His novel *Chevengur* (partially published in 1929, fully in 1972, in the West) tells of an imaginary city where the ideals of the Communist Revolution are fa-

bled to have been realized within a short span of time. The quest of the simple people headed for Chevengur ends in heartbreak and tragedy. A dystopian novel, *My* (1924; *We*) by Evgenii Zamiatin, like Platonov a communist activist, appeared in English translation long before a Russian text was published, also in the West. *We* predicts a technological dystopia that will deprive man of his freedom and stifle emotion and artistic creativity. Other Soviet writers, Aleksei Tolstoi for one, were more optimistic in their utopian fiction.

The other main theme of the 1920s was the transformation of Russian society after the Revolution. *Tsement* (1925; *Cement*) by Fedor Gladkov is the inspirational story of a worker-activist who succeeds in resuming production at a cement plant. *Cement* became the prototype of the Soviet "production novel," in which the plot is defined in terms of the production of goods or services, while the human factor plays an ancillary role. The coming of the Soviet order to the Russian countryside was also a popular subject, treated in such novels as *Lesozavod* (1928; The Sawmill) by Anna Karavaeva and *Bruski* (1928–37; *Bruski: A Story of Peasant Life in Soviet Russia*) by Fedor Panferov. Ivan Kataev was bold enough to describe successful small dairy farms on the very eve of collectivization in *Moloko* (1930; Milk).

Writers of the 1920s also dealt with real problems of Soviet society. The hero of Leonid Leonov's novel *Vor* (1927; *A Thief*) is a communist hero of the civil war who has turned to crime. *Skandalist, ili Vechera na Vasil'evskom ostrove* (1928; The Troublemaker, or Evenings on Vasilevskii Island) and *Khudozhnik neizvesten* (1931; *The Unknown Artist*) by Veniamin Kaverin exposed the cultural isolation, even lag, of Russia in the 1920s. These novels are set in literary and academic circles and contain portraits of some of the writers and literary theorists of the period. In a similar vein, *Kozlinaia pesn'* (1928; The Satyr Song) by Konstantin Vaginov draws a phantasmagoric picture of Leningrad as a cultural necropolis.

Zavist' (1928; *Envy*) by Iurii Olesha is a modernist tour de force. A well-organized discourse, it has no plot in the conventional sense. The whole novel is a web of ambiguities. An apparent celebration of the new order, it is also a devastating satire. It features Freudian symbolism, cinematic techniques in visual effects and treatment of time, and constant estrangement through unconventional diction, far-fetched metaphors, and bizarre imagery.

With the launching of Stalin's first Five-Year Plan (1928–32), the relative freedom of the New Economic Policy period came to an end. Many writers perished in the purges of the 1930s. A decree of the Central Committee of the Communist Party, dated 23 April 1932, dissolved all existing literary organizations and replaced them by a single Union of Soviet Writers. At their first congress in 1934, the doctrine of socialist realism was adopted as "the basic method of Soviet literature and literary criticism, which requires of the artist a truthful, historically concrete representation of reality in its revolutionary development."

Most writers tried to jump on the bandwagon of the Five-Year Plan and collectivization. Some made study trips to industrial plants, construction sites, or collective farms. Marietta Shaginian, for instance, went to work at a newly constructed hydroelectric plant and produced the novel *Gidrotsentral'* (1931; Hydrocentral). *Vremia, vpered!* (1932; *Time, Forward!*) by Valentin Kataev describes a single action-packed day on the construction site of the Magnitogorsk metallurgical plant. Leonid

Leonov's novels *Sot'* (1930; *The Sot*), *Skutarevskii* (1932; *Skutarevsky*), and *Doroga na okean* (1935; *Road to the Ocean*) were devoted to the construction of a paper mill, the workings of a research institute, and a railway depot, respectively. *Podniataia tselina* (1932–60; *Virgin Soil Upturned*) by Mikhail Sholokhov was the most significant novel dealing with the collectivization of agriculture. *Kak zakalialas' stal'* (1932–34; *How the Steel Was Tempered*) by Nikolai Ostrovskii joined Gor'kii's *Mother* and Gladkov's *Cement* as a communist classic. It tells the story of a working-class youth who becomes a leader in the Komsomol (Young Communists). High-minded and pure, he lives entirely for the cause, combatting defeatism, selfishness, and lax morality wherever he encounters them, even when he is stricken by a debilitating illness.

The anticipation of an impending war in the 1930s led to an emphasis on Russian patriotism and military traditions. The historical novel made a strong comeback. Aleksei Tolstoi's *Petr Pervyi* (1929–45; *Peter the First*) followed the myth of Peter the Great as a progressive ruler who made Russia strong, while also having a heart for the people. (It is known that Stalin identified with the great czar.) Viacheslav Shishkov wrote several historical novels, among them *Emel'ian Pugachev* (1941–47; *Emelian Pugachev*), about the leader of an 18th-century peasant uprising, the best of several similar efforts. Sergei Sergeev-Tsenskii told of the heroic defense of Sevastopol in the Crimean War in *Sevastopol'skaia strada* (1937–39; *The Ordeal of Sevastopol*).

Mark Aldanov emerged as a major historical novelist in emigration. Among his many novels, a cycle linking Russia and the West in the age of Napoléon is the most remarkable: *Deviatoe termidora* (1923; *The Ninth Thermidor*), *Chortov most* (1925; *The Devil's Bridge*), and *Zagovar* (1927; *The Conspiracy*). Russian emigré literature produced far fewer novels than Soviet literature, mainly because publishing long fiction was difficult for financial reasons. Ivan Bunin produced a single novel, *Zhizn' Arsen'eva* (1930–39; *The Life of Arsen'ev*), a fictionalized autobiography.

The only novelist of real stature to emerge in emigration was Vladimir Nabokov. None of his nine short novels in Russian is set in Russia. Their ingenious and suspenseful plots are often focused on a fateful obsession. The more remarkable of Nabokov's Russian novels are *Zashchita Luzhina* (Luzhin's Defense, 1930; *The Defense*), based on a parallel between the hero's fate and a chess game (Luzhin is a chess master); *Dar* (published in part 1937–38, in its entirety 1952; *The Gift*), the story of a young writer's growth; and *Priglashenie na kazn'* (1938; *Invitation to a Beheading*), an allegory whose hero is awaiting execution for what appears to be the crime of being "different." Nabokov's most innovative work was not written in Russian, however, and cannot be counted as part of the history of the Russian novel. As a consequence, it may be said that in the first half of the 20th century, even while an enormous range of interesting fiction was written, the Russian novel disappeared from the stage of world literature.

VICTOR TERRAS

See also Mikhail Bulgakov; Maksim Gor'kii; Formalism; Vladimir Nabokov; Novel of Ideas; Petersburg; Andrei Platonov; Socialist Realism; Quiet Flows the Don; We

Further Reading

Brown, Edward J., *Russian Literature Since the Revolution*, New York: Collier, 1963; revised and enlarged edition, Cambridge, Massachusetts: Harvard University Press, 1982

Clark, Katerina, *The Soviet Novel: History as Ritual*, Chicago: University of Chicago Press, 1981; 2nd edition, 1985

Connolly, Julian W., *Nabokov's Early Fiction: Patterns of Self and Others*, Cambridge and New York: Cambridge University Press, 1992

Elbaum, Henry, "Industrialism vs. Primitivism in the Soviet Russian Literature of the Twenties and Thirties," *Sociocriticism* 2:1 (October 1986)

Erlich, Victor, *Modernism and Revolution: Russian Literature in Transition*, Cambridge, Massachusetts: Harvard University Press, 1994

Karlinsky, Simon, and Alfred Appel, editors, *The Bitter Air of Exile: Russian Writers in the West, 1922–72*, Berkeley: University of California Press, 1977

Maguire, Robert A., *Red Virgin Soil: Soviet Literature in the 1920s*, Princeton, New Jersey: Princeton University Press, 1968

Mirsky, D.S., *Contemporary Russian Literature, 1881–1925*, New York: Knopf, and London: Routledge, 1926

Poltoratzky, Nikolai P., "Russian Literature, Scholarship and Publishing in the United States," in *Ethnic Literatures Since 1776: The Many Voices of America*, edited by Wolodymyr T. Zyla and Wendell M. Aycock, Lubbock: Interdepartmental Committee on Comparative Literature, Texas Tech University, 1978

Striedter, Jurij, "Three Postrevolutionary Russian Utopian Novels," in *The Russian Novel from Pushkin to Pasternak*, edited by John Garrard, New Haven, Connecticut: Yale University Press, 1983

Struve, Gleb, *Russian Literature Under Lenin and Stalin, 1917–1953*, Norman: University of Oklahoma Press, 1971; London: Routledge and Kegan Paul, 1972

Terras, Victor, editor, *Handbook of Russian Literature*, New Haven, Connecticut: Yale University Press, 1985

Russian Novel

1945–

Between 1945 and the end of the century, the Russian novel underwent greater changes than in any period of comparable length in its history, going from socialist realism to conceptualism via the "Thaw," *samizdat* and *tamizdat,* fantasy, allegory, satire, anti-utopias, the picaresque and grotesque, socialist realism in reverse, new realism, quasi-pornography, and the Russian version of postmodernism. In the first postwar years, the Russian novel continued to be bound by the socialist-realist dogma of the 1930s. World War II temporarily brought a greater freedom to writers, but as early as 1946 ideological pressures again were placed on literature. Few novels of any real worth were produced during Stalin's last years, although the state continued to support conformist writers with immense print-runs and prizes. Officially approved works included numerous dull and unrealistic production novels, such as *Daleko ot Moskvy* (1948; *Far from Moscow*), a particular favorite of Stalin's, by Vasilii Azhaev and the notorious *Kavaler zolotoi zvezdy* (1947–48; *The Cavalier of the Golden Star*) by Semen Babaevskii, a work that for many symbolized the "pastrycook fabrications" of Stalinist fiction. There were also many epics about the Revolution and civil war as well as the recent war, in which victory had merely strengthened the iron grip of the authorities: *Molodaia gvardiia* (1946; *The Young Guard*) by leading literary functionary Aleksandr Fadeev is one of the best known.

War novels improved radically after the death of Stalin, but one early example of the genre stands out, namely *V okopakh Stalingrada* (1946; *In the Trenches of Stalingrad*) by Viktor Nekrasov, a work that gave its name to a new concept in Soviet war writing, *okopnaia pravda* (the truth of the trenches). The novel achieved exceptional success (by 1974 Nekrasov's novel had appeared in 120 editions and 30 languages) for its harsh realism at a time when even the reality of war was prone to varnishing. Another remarkable novel about the battle of Stalingrad was the panoramic *Zhizn' i sud'ba* (1965; *Life and Fate*), which was only published, abroad, in 1985. The author of this novel, Vasilii Grossman, destroys the myth of Soviet wartime unity and arrives at the grim conclusion that from a Jewish viewpoint there was little to choose between communism and fascism.

Although Fadeev, Azhaev, and Babaevskii were merely literary functionaries, many better writers also retained the habits of socialist realism after the death of Stalin. The content of literature, however, expanded rapidly as novels became once again, as they had been in the 19th century, a forum for debate and the discussion of new ideas. One such novel, epitomizing the new atmosphere of the Thaw and creating a sensation at the time despite its modest literary qualities, was *Ne khlebom edinym* (1957; *Not by Bread Alone*) by Vladimir Dudintsev. Khrushchev promptly denounced the author as a "calumniator" for his picture of the suppression of a talented young engineer by the corrupt scientific establishment, which at the end of the novel remains unchanged. Another key work of the immediate post-Stalin period was *Russkii les* (1953; *The Russian Forest*), a huge and dense final novel by Leonid Leonov, who in the 1920s had shown great literary imagination and vitality. *The Russian Forest* is in a sense pure socialist realism but without the moral simplification and ideological orthodoxy characteristic of this doctrine, showing that long Soviet novels on scientific or industrial themes did not have to be riddled with primitive falsification.

Quite different from the works of Dudintsev and Leonov was Boris Pasternak's *Doktor Zhivago* (published in Milan, 1957; *Doctor Zhivago*). The most important novel of the decade, it won its author the Nobel prize and broke new ground in many ways. Philosophically reminiscent of Lev Tolstoi, Pasternak's novel is imbued with evidence of the poet's perception and craft. Written in a highly lyrical style and with a rich pattern of imagery, it has an appendix with 25 poems. A historical novel that minimizes historical events, focusing instead on fate and the human condition, *Doctor Zhivago* continues to be the object of critical controversy.

An important development of the 1960s that lasted into the 1970s, much encouraged by the Soviet authorities, was so-called "village prose," an investigative, sympathetic, and even nostalgic literary reexamination of life outside the city. The principal writers of village prose were Vasilii Belov and Valentin Rasputin, although neither cared to be so labeled. Characteristic of the trend (some would say genre) was a wealth of ethnographic detail, a heavy use of dialect, sympathy for the peasants' hard lot, and a tendency to idealize country folk, particularly old women and children. One of the most discussed novels in all Soviet literature of the 1960s was Belov's *Privychnoe delo* (1966; *That's How It Is*), whose feckless but spiritually innocent hero Ivan Afrikanovich was to some critics a symbol of peasant virtues, to others an insult to Soviet Russian dignity. Belov's strength lies in characterization and style rather than form, as is also evident in his three-volume novel about events leading to the catastrophic collectivization of agriculture in a North Russian village in the late 1920s, *Kanuny* (1976; *Eves*), continued in *God velikogo pereloma* (1989; The Year of the Great Transformation). The later parts of this sprawling epic become increasingly chauvinistic and anti-Semitic, reflecting the overtly right-wing stance Belov adopted toward the end of the Soviet era, which lost him many admirers. The Siberian Rasputin also adopted an extreme political position in the late 1980s. The author of many well-plotted novels about village communities, he focuses on moral problems in all his works, with a particular emphasis on ecology in his magnum opus, *Proshchanie s Materoi* (1976; *Farewell to Matyora*), describing resistance to the flooding of an island community for the sake of a hydroelectric project. In his *Den'gi dlia Marii* (1968; *Money for Maria*) and *Poslednii srok* (1970; *Borrowed Time*), various moral questions relating to village and town life are highlighted, while *Zhivi i pomni* (1975; *Live and Remember*) presents a subtle story of loyalty and betrayal when a deserter from the army secretly returns to his village and saintly wife. A later novel, *Pozhar* (1985; *The Fire*), expresses despair at the cynicism of contemporary village people. Despite Rasputin's use of dialect, his novels were popular on account of their absorbing plots, sound construction, and a sense of genuine tension not often found in the work of other village writers.

Urban prose also developed in the 1960s (most socialist realism had avoided the political hazards of writing about Moscow and

Leningrad), and a number of novelists made lasting contributions in this area. Of the older generation, Iurii Trifonov particularly developed in the 1970s, writing a series of slow-moving, reflective, realistic novels about the convoluted moral problems of the Muscovite privileged classes. Some, like *Obmen* (1969; *The Exchange*), *Predvaritel'nye itogi* (1970; *Taking Stock*), and *Dolgoe proshchanie* (1971; *The Long Goodbye*), treated contemporary life, while Trifonov looked back to the repressions of 1937 and 1949 in *Dom na naberezhnoi* (1976; *The House on the Embankment*) and *Starik* (1978; *The Old Man*). *The House on the Embankment,* which caused the greatest controversy, also offers the best example of Trifonov's many-layered, sometimes almost Byzantine, narrative technique.

Quite different from Trifonov is Andrei Bitov, another cerebral urban writer who is drawn to serpentine syntax to convey subtleties of mood and emotion. Bitov mostly uses shorter forms, but the novel *Pushkinskii dom* (1978; *Pushkin House*) is a work of great historical and cultural depth that uses a variety of modernist devices to celebrate the riches of classical Russian literature in a witty and seemingly light-hearted vein, with a plot centered on the official vandalism of Russia's most famous literary museum. Complete with an alternative ending and many episodes in different genres, some of them repeated, as well as several subplots, this 400-page book is a kaleidoscopic compendium of Russian culture as it existed in the 1960s. An imperfect but entertaining work, it recalls Vladimir Nabokov's more sophisticated *Dar* (published in part 1937–38, in its entirety 1952; *The Gift*) in its close engagement with Russian literature. In the bleak context of Brezhnev's reign, it marked a refreshing new development, even though it could not be published at that time.

In many ways the most brilliantly imaginative novel of the 1960s was the endlessly inventive epic of alcoholism *Moskva-Petushki* (1969; *Moscow Circles* or *Moscow to the End of the Line*) by Venedikt Erofeev. This short picaresque tale of a possibly imaginary journey down a godforsaken suburban railway line is the most damning and hilarious of all indictments of Soviet culture, as well as a vivid although impressionistic portrayal of the minutiae of chronically heavy drinking. Erofeev and his masterpiece are unique in the history of the Russian novel.

As a young man in the 1960s, Bitov had belonged to an important literary grouping of writers known as Youth Prose who, taking advantage of the new liberal atmosphere of the Thaw, challenged the stilted language and attitudes of their elders and, particularly, of Stalinist literature. The principal among them were Vasilii Aksenov, Vladimir Voinovich, and Georgii Vladimov. At first they preferred short forms, perhaps reacting against the gigantism of the conventional Soviet novel. Vladimov's *Bol'shaia ruda* (1961; *The Great Ore*) and his *Tri minuty molchaniia* (1969; *Three Minutes' Silence*), however, bear a superficial resemblance to Soviet production novels, with changed moral values and more realism. Vladimov's masterpiece, however, was *Vernyi Ruslan* (1963–65; *Faithful Ruslan*), a magnificent allegory of the Stalinist period centered on the experience of a prison camp dog. Released when his camp is closed, the dog is unable to adjust to a world of freedom where total loyalty to authority is not enough for survival. Classical Russian literature had occasionally turned to animals for an original viewpoint, but in the 20th century Vladimov's work, which circulated for many years in *samizdat* and was for a time rumored to be written by Solzhenitsyn, is an outstanding example of imaginative writing that greatly expanded the bounds of the Russian novel.

Although modern Russian literature is far from humorless, there have been few truly comic novels. One of the best is Voinovich's *Zhizn' i neobychainye prikliucheniia soldata Ivan Chonkina* (*The Life and Extraordinary Adventures of Private Ivan Chonkin*), which, written in 1963, also circulated in *samizdat* before being published illegally abroad in 1969. The novel reverses the basic idea of Jaroslav Hašek's *The Good Soldier Švejk*: where the cunning Švejk defeats his enemies by feigning simplicity, simple Chonkin overcomes his by genuine naiveté. Since his emigration, Voinovich has written a sequel entitled *Pretendent na prestol* (1979; *Pretender to the Throne*). The promised third part seems unlikely to appear. Also noteworthy as an inventive comic novel is *Moskva 2042* (1987; *Moscow 2042*), a witty satire on the Soviet Union in the guise of a futuristic anti-utopia.

Elements of satirical fantasy are also to be found in one of the two novels that Aksenov wrote in the Soviet Union and published immediately on his arrival in the West: *Ostrov Krym* (1981; *The Island of Crimea*) is a free-rolling satirical novel built around the idea that Crimea is an island that has somehow escaped Soviet power in analogy to Taiwan's relationship to China. Always a writer of powerful imagination, Aksenov created a very Westernized blockbuster in this compendious and imaginative novel. His masterpiece, however, was *Ozhog* (1980; *The Burn*), on which he worked for six years, publishing it almost simultaneously with *The Island of Crimea*. A modernist work of high textual density and complexity, it abounds in spatial, temporal, stylistic, linguistic, and narrative shifts. The novel paints a phantasmagoric collective picture of the young Muscovite intelligentsia of the 1960s through a polypersona of five brothers and their women, but it also contains a moving quasi-realistic picture of Aksenov's own childhood in the prison city of Magadan.

The Third Wave of emigration from the Soviet Union soon split into two major camps on both political and literary grounds: those who favored a basically realistic type of writing and a robustly pro-Western position on the one hand, and, on the other, writers who sought to pursue the kind of fantastic writing that had been proscribed in the Soviet Union. The former, and larger, group looked up to Solzhenitsyn as an unofficial leader, although Solzhenitsyn had virtually abandoned fiction by 1974 when he arrived in the West, turning instead to writing an alternative history of the Russian Revolution. One of the major realistic novelists of the emigration was the prolific Vladimir Maksimov. Among the best of his work was his first novel, *Sem' dnei tvoreniia* (1971; *The Seven Days of Creation*), unpublishable in the Soviet Union. It gives a very negative account of Soviet society from a Christian viewpoint. The autobiographical *Proshchanie iz niotkuda* (1974; *Farewell from Nowhere*) is also noteworthy. Another basically realistic novelist who was, nevertheless, anathema to Maksimov and Solzhenitsyn was Eduard Limonov. His scandalous Bildungsroman *Eto ia, Edichka!* (1979; *It's Me, Eddie!*) broke the linguistic and sexual taboos of Russian literature and the political taboos of the emigration, flaunting homosexual escapades and despising America for not recognizing his genius. As a quasi-pornographic novelist, Limonov has had several lesser followers among émigré writers and, in the 1990s, in Russia itself. Far more interesting as a taboo-breaker was Iuz Aleshkovskii, who, writing in America, has used obscenity with virtuosic creativity in various novels depicting the evil and ridiculous aspects of the Soviet regime. His best-known novel is *Kenguru* (1981; *Kangaroo*), a modern picaresque in which an old thief at his trial proudly relates a series of escapades in the late Stalin years.

Maksimov's opposite in Paris was undoubtedly the critic and writer Andrei Siniavskii, who, under the pen name of Abram Terts, wrote phantasmagorical criticism as well as fiction. One of the best of his early novels is *Liubimov* (1963; *The Makepeace Experiment*), essentially a historical chronicle but rich in imagery and displaying a dazzling range of narrative devices and tricks, as well as elaborate play with the academic apparatus of footnotes. In 1984 Siniavskii wrote the fascinating novel *Spokoinoi nochi* (*Goodnight!*), which recalls the years of his political exile, pays rich tribute to his wife and father, and tries to clear his name of persistent rumors of KGB involvement. A protean writer and critic, he was one of the most intellectually lively of the late 20th-century Russian novelists. Another major figure was Sasha Sokolov, author of three very different novels. In the first, *Shkola dlia durakov* (1976; *A School for Fools*), the narrator is a schizophrenic youth whose stream of consciousness often turns into dialogue with his alter ego and other characters, both alive and dead. A highly lyrical piece, it won Nabokov's praise. *Mezhdu sobakoi i volkom* (1980; Between the Dog and the Wolf) is a grim surrealist picture of Soviet provincial life in a text comprising both prose and verse of a linguistic complexity that has so far defied translators. Sokolov's third nove, *Palisandriia* (1985; *Astrophobia*), unlike its predecessors, has a plot of sorts, which mainly consists of comic and scabrous episodes satirizing émigré historiography. Rarely have three so different novels been produced by the same author in such a brief time span.

With the collapse of communism, émigré novelists could once again visit Russia and find an appreciative new audience for their work, while metropolitan writers were freed from political censorship. However, many complained of the new, no less rigorous, pressure of commerce. Several new writers came to prominence in the late 1980s and early 1990s. Viktor Pelevin, one of the most promising of the younger generation, achieved success with his novel *Omon ra* (1992; *Omon ra*), a fantastic tale in a realistic setting, parodying the Soviet space program in a reversal of socialist realism; his *Zhizn' nasekomykh* (1993; *The Life of Insects*) intertwines the fantastical with the factual, presenting serious discussions in an absurd form. Of the older generation, Vladimir Makanin attracted attention in the post-Soviet period particularly with his allegorical, rather Dostoevskian, novel *Laz* (1991; *Escape Hatch*), which shows a flourishing life below ground while misery reigns on the surface; the anti-utopian allegory is plain, but the atmosphere is anti-intellectualist. The author appears to be attacking his own kind. Dostoevskii takes the foreground in Viacheslav P'etsukh's short novel *Novaia moskovskaia filosofiia* (1989; New Moscow Philosophy), which, in describing four days in the life of the inhabitants of a communal flat, produces a parody of Dostoevskii's *Crime and Punishment.*

Evgenii Popov, who enjoyed considerable underground popularity for his wild and whimsical humor in Soviet times, has since written the complex novel *Dusha patriota ili razlichnye poslaniia Ferfichkinu* (1989; *The Soul of a Patriot, or Various Epistles to Ferfichkin*). Like Bitov's *Pushkin House,* it relies on free association and requires an extensive knowledge of Russian history

and culture. It has been aptly compared to Laurence Sterne's *Tristram Shandy.* Mark Kharitonov won the first Russian Booker prize with an ambitious postmodern novel, *Linii sud'by, ili Sunduchok Milashevicha* (1992; *Lines of Fate, or Milashevich's Little Trunk*). *Lines of Fate* is marked by intense cross-referentiality and literary self-consciousness: the opening dozen pages raise questions of plagiarism, intertextuality, coincidence, reader reception, the reader as author, modes of image creation, and much else. The conceptualist erotic novel *Okolo ekolo* (1992; Around and About) by Valeriia Narbikova, which relies heavily on free association, also deserves mention. Floating from "straight" narrative to the dream world and back again via the most liberated of word associations and stream of consciousness, this is among the most iconoclastic of all post-Soviet novels

The continuing vigorous development and variety of the contemporary Russian novel undoubtedly bode well for its future.

ARNOLD MCMILLIN

See also Doctor Zhivago; Vladimir Nabokov; Aleksandr Solzhenitsyn

Further Reading

Brown, Deming, *Soviet Russian Literature Since Stalin,* Cambridge and New York: Cambridge University Press, 1978

Brown, Deming, *The Last Years of Soviet Russian Literature: Prose Fiction, 1975–1991,* Cambridge and New York: Cambridge University Press, 1993

Clark, Katerina, *The Soviet Novel: History as Ritual,* Chicago: University of Chicago Press, 1981; 2nd edition, 1985

Clowes, Edith W., *Russian Experimental Fiction: Resisting Ideology After Utopia,* Princeton, New Jersey: Princeton University Press, 1993

Hosking, Geoffrey, *Beyond Socialist Realism,* London and New York: Granada, 1980

Lowe, David, *Russian Writing Since 1953: A Critical Survey,* New York: Ungar, 1987

Parthé, Kathleen F., *Russian Village Prose: The Radiant Past,* Princeton, New Jersey: Princeton University Press, 1992

Porter, Robert, *Four Contemporary Russian Writers,* Oxford: Berg, and New York: St. Martin's Press, 1989

Porter, Robert, *Russia's Alternative Prose,* Oxford and Providence, Rhode Island: Berg, 1994

Shneidman, N.N., *Soviet Literature in the 1970s: Artistic Diversity and Ideological Conformity,* Toronto and Buffalo, New York: University of Toronto Press, 1979

Shneidman, N.N., *Soviet Literature in the 1980s: Decade of Transition,* Toronto and London: University of Toronto Press, 1989

Shneidman, N.N., *Russian Literature, 1988–1994: The End of an Era,* Toronto and Buffalo, New York: University of Toronto Press, 1995

Struve, Gleb, *Russian Literature Under Lenin and Stalin, 1917–1953,* Norman: University of Oklahoma Press, 1971; London: Routledge and Kegan Paul, 1972

Svirskii, Grigorii, *A History of Post-War Soviet Writing: The Literature of Moral Opposition,* Ann Arbor, Michigan: Ardis, 1981

Vail, Petr, and Aleksandr Genis, *Sovremennaia russkaia proza,* Ann Arbor, Michigan: Hermitage, 1982

S

Sacred Night. *See* **Sand Child and Sacred Night**

Nawāl al-Saʿdāwī 1931–

Egyptian

Nawāl al-Saʿdāwī, Egyptian doctor, feminist and political activist, novelist and essayist, born in Kafr Tahla in the Egyptian delta, represents most forcefully today the synthesis of feminist and literary issues challenging Eastern and Western ideologies alike. Indeed, if one were to assess al-Saʿdāwī's writings, one would have to take into account its dissident nature. This position allows the author to transgress literary conventions and imposed codes of femininity in order to forge new horizons in both spheres. On the one hand, her fiction defies rigid classification of genre. On the other hand, it is precisely this nonconformist approach toward fiction and feminist theory that has earned her a place on the "black list" of the Egyptian government under Gamal Abdel Nasser's regime (1962), incarceration under Sādāt's regime (1981), and a place on the Islamist death list (1993), all of which are punitive measures designed to silence her uncompromising views.

Nawāl al-Saʿdāwī's literary career spans more than 30 years. She first achieved public recognition in the Egyptian press for her medical research papers and sociological studies, in which she discussed women's sexuality and presented women's sexual neuroses as the consequence of patriarchy and class divisions. She demonstrates how cultural and political exclusion of women is historically linked to slavery and property ownership practices. When she began publishing short stories, plays, and novels, she embedded them in her nonfiction work, a quasi-scientific amalgam of sciences ranging from anthropology to history, philosophy, religion, and psychology. This "comprehensive" approach to "sources of knowledge" foregrounds her case against established epistemological paradigms, which, she argues, are all components of patriarchal ideology aimed at sustaining male supremacy and female submissiveness.

In what may be considered an early phase (1961–76), al-Saʿdāwī published five novels, three of which develop the theme of "creativity" versus "science" and their relationship to the well-being of women. In this phase she developed her own form of the autobiographical novel. In *Mudhakkirāt ṭabībah* (1958; *Memoirs of a Woman Doctor*), *Imra'atāni fī mra'ah* (1968; *Two Women in One*), and *Emra'ah ʿinda nuqṭat al-ṣifr* (1975; *Woman at Point Zero*), al-Saʿdāwī demonstrates that the sexual, the social, the political, and the economic are interrelated. She convincingly argues against the false hypothesis that gender equality is associated with the "sexual," the "feminine," and therefore the marginal. Demystifying women's issues allows her to deconstruct their paradigms, to redefine and reconstruct them in light of her new findings. These novels also focus on the "gaze," an issue inherent to gender debate in the Arabo-Islamic tradition. The author seeks to redefine this debate using medical science as a forum. In this first period of her writing, the author favors middle-class and lower-class women protagonists. The former may find their way to independence through a career, but the latter can only achieve liberation through self-destruction.

The second phase (1977–86) may be called the transitional stage. Turning on al-Saʿdāwī's incarceration and her role in the founding of the International Association (1982–91; The Arab Women Solidarity Association), this period marks a turning point in the author's personal life and literary career and includes two poignant novels: *Ughniyyat al-aṭfāl al-dā'iriyyah* (1977; *The Circling Song*) and *Mudhakkirāti fī sijn al-nisā'* (1983; *Memoirs from the Women's Prison*). In the first novel, gender-related issues supersede class issues in the focus on the plight of lower-class male and female victims of patriarchy, imprisoned in the rituals of false honor and revenge. *The Circling*

Song marks the beginning of the postmodernist stage in al-Saʿdāwī's fiction, in which temporal discontinuities serve to highlight the circular pattern of abuse and revenge. A transition from a woman protagonist to a child-protagonist indicates the growing reach of al-Saʿdāwī's analysis of gender oppression.

Memoirs from the Women's Prison is a poignant testimony of the author's incarceration. The experience and its "documentation" signal the beginning of a new phase in her political activism, as it took on a wider scope. Interestingly, the narrative structure again raises the question of the biographical. The work is considered a novel by literary critics, since fictional and nonfictional elements are combined. However, some collections list the work under "nonfiction" or "other." This may stem from confusion over the Arabic title, which uses the possessive form of the word, *Mudhakkirāti* (my memoirs) as opposed to *Mudhakkirāt* (memoirs). The same issue arises with respect to her *Riḥlātī ḥawl al-ʿālam* (1986; *My Travels Around the World*), listed under "other" in collections, while critics identify fictional aspects of the text.

Since 1987 al-Saʿdāwī has published three novels that clearly manifest an even greater leap toward the metafictional postmodernist novel. Character identity and plot lose their referential function in a multivocal narrative of repeated events in *Suqūṭ al-Imām* (1987; *The Fall of the Imam*), *Jannāt wa-Iblīs* (1992; *The Innocence of the Devil*), and *Al-Ḥubb fī zamān al-nafṭ* (1993; *Love in the Time of Oil*). Their "gender-oriented intertextual games," to use a phrase by Fedwa Malti-Douglas, merge holy scriptures and other classical Arabic texts into fictions in a polemic strategy that seeks to redefine, recontextualize, and reconstruct their meaning. Even though these intertextual games with sacred texts are highly risky, given the Islamists' rise in Egypt, they have also been used by other Egyptian authors such as Jamāl al-Ghīṭānī, Muḥammad Mustajāb, and Nagīb Maḥfūẓ. But among Egyptian women writers, al-Saʿdāwī is the only one to have broken with social and literary conventions to expand the horizons of the contemporary Egyptian Arabic novel while drawing international attention to her cause.

As for al-Saʿdāwī's impact on the development of the Egyptian novel, certain factors need to be considered. First, she writes only in Arabic and is read widely by Arab audiences. Therefore, her impact on national as well as pan-Arab readership is considerable. The numerous editions of her works in Arabic and in translation increase her influence at home and abroad. Second, her work is a powerful example to women writers who seek to challenge the classical Arabic language that marginalizes them. Women's marginalization is due to the "sacred" status of Arabic, the language of divine revelation, as well as to the predominance of male writers. Third and equally important is the visibility of the author within Eastern and Western literary and academic scholarship, as well as the notoriety she received when the Egyptian government disbanded her women's association in 1991. Nawāl al-Saʿdāwī has encouraged debates seeking to redefine the structural and aesthetic parameters of the novel. But most significantly, she will be best remembered for her humanist vision and her search for the most persuasive articulation of the dissenting word of the oppressed.

THÉRÈSE MICHEL-MANSOUR

See also Woman at Point Zero

Biography

Born 27 October 1931 in Kafr Tahla. Attended the University of Cairo, M.D. 1955; Columbia University, New York, M.P.H. 1966; Ain Shams University, 1973–75. Physician, University of Cairo, 1955–56, and Rural Health Center, Tahla, 1956–58; director of health education, Ministry of Health, Cairo, 1958–72 (dismissed on publication of her study on women's sexuality); writer, High Institute of Literature and Science, Cairo, 1973–78; director of African Training and Research Center for Women, United Nations Economic Commission for Africa, Addis Ababa, 1978–80; adviser for women's programs, UN Economic Commission for West Asia, Beirut, 1978–80; arrested under Egyptian "Law for the Protection of Values from Shame" and imprisoned for two months, 1981; editor-in-chief, *Health* magazine, 1968–72 (dismissed); cofounder, African Women's Association for Research and Development, 1977; her books have been banned in Egypt and some other Arab countries.

Novels by al-Saʿdāwī

Mudhakkirāt ṭabībah, 1958; as *Memoirs of a Woman Doctor,* translated by Catherine Cobham, 1989
Al-Ghāʾib, 1965; as *Searching*, translated by Shirley Eber, 1991
Imraʾatāni fī mraʾah, 1968; as *Two Women in One*, translated by Osman Nusairi and Jana Gough, 1985
Emraʾah ʿinda nuqṭat al-ṣifr, 1975; as *Woman at Point Zero*, translated by Sherif Hetata, 1983
Mawt al-rajul al-waḥīd ʿalā al-arḍ, 1976; as *God Dies by the Nile,* translated by Sherif Hetata, 1985
Ughniyyat al-aṭfāl al-dāʾiriyyah, 1977; as *The Circling Song,* translated by Marilyn Booth, 1989
Mudhakkirātī fī sijn al-nisāʾ, 1983; as *Memoirs from the Women's Prison*, translated by Marilyn Booth, 1986
Suqūṭ al-Imām, 1987; as *The Fall of the Imam*, translated by Sherif Hetata, 1988
Jannāt wa-Iblīs, 1992; as *The Innocence of the Devil*, translated by Sherif Hetata, 1994
Al-Ḥubb fī zamān al-nafṭ [Love in the Time of Oil], 1993

Other Writings: short stories, plays, essays, and sociological studies.

Further Reading

Al-Ali, Nadje Sadig, *Gender Writing/Writing Gender: The Representation of Women in a Selection of Modern Egyptian Literature,* Cairo: American University in Cairo Press, 1994
Badran, Margot, and Miriam Cooke, "Nawal el Saadawi," in *Opening the Gates: A Century of Arab Feminist Writing,* edited by Margot Badran and Miriam Cooke, Bloomington: Indiana University Press, and London: Virago, 1990
Cooke, Miriam, "Arab Women Writers," in *The Cambridge History of Arabic Literature: Modern Arabic Literature,* edited by Muhammad Mustafa Badawi, Cambridge and New York: Cambridge University Press, 1992
Djébar, Assia, preface to *Ferdaous, un voix en enfer,* by Nawāl al-Saʿdāwī, translated by Assia Trabelsi and Assia Djébar, Paris: Des Femmes, 1981
Hetata, Sherif, and Peter Hitchcock, "Living the Struggle: Nawal el Saadawi Talks about Writing and Resistance," *Transition: An International Review* 61 (1993)

Malti-Douglas, Fedwa, *Woman's Body, Woman's Word: Gender and Discourse in Arabo-Islamic Writing,* Princeton, New Jersey: Princeton University Press, 1991

Malti-Douglas, Fedwa, *Men, Women and God(s): Nawal El Saadawi and Arab Feminist Poetics,* Berkeley: University of California Press, 1995

Sacdāwī, Nawāl al-, "Mon expérience de création," translated by L. Barbulesco, *Quantara: Cultures en Mouvement* 10 (1994)

Saiti, Ramzi, "Paradise, Heaven and Other Oppressive Spaces: A Critical Examination of the Life and Works of Nawal el-Saadawi," *Journal of Arabic Literature* 25:2 (1994)

Ṭarābīshī, Georges, *Woman against Her Sex,* London and Atlantic Highlands, New Jersey: Saqi, 1988; originally published as *Unthā Ḍod al-Unūthah,* 1984

Zeidan, Joseph T., *Arab Women Novelists: The Formative Years and Beyond,* Albany: State University of New York Press, 1995

Saga

The Icelandic sagas are long prose narratives that were transmitted orally for about 100 years before they were written anonymously during the 13th century. The genre covers a wide range of material distinguished primarily by subject matter, but the sagas that have received the most scholarly attention and inspired the most literary imitators are the family sagas (*islendinga sogur*), which include about 30 narratives varying in length in modern editions from about 20 pages (*Thorstein Staffstruck*) to more than 400 (*Njals saga*). The family sagas deal with historical events that occurred in Iceland and Norway during the period of settlement, from about 870 to 1050, yet they are not simply chronicles of a district; indeed, the complexity of their characterization has led some critics to conclude that the sagas were written as historical fiction with the attendant alterations and elaborations appropriate to the novel.

In *The Medieval Saga,* Carol J. Clover (1982) suggests a division in the family sagas between those that are primarily biographical (*Egils saga, Grettis saga, Gislis saga*) and those concerned with families (*Laxdaela saga, Njals saga*). However, all of the family sagas deal with the dramatic tension between individuals and the communities in which they live. In *Grettis saga,* Grettir, the hero, grows from a difficult child into an even more difficult adult, but all his exploits involve conflicts with or in support of his family or acquaintances, and the pathos of his outlawry and eventual death lies at least partly in his isolation. *Laxdaela saga,* on the other hand, relates several generations of family relationships, yet here also the action derives from the tension between the individual, the family, and neighbors. In the sagas no character is introduced without a complete genealogy. The family ties, both immediate and extended, place each individual solidly within a web of relationships that shapes his or her character and defines the parameters of choice and action.

Character and relationship are the primary concerns in the family sagas, and, unlike romances, the sagas employ few elements of the supernatural. Although episodes sometimes feature a ghost or monster, the supernatural being is a part of the pattern of human action. In *Grettis saga,* for example, when Thorhall's farm is haunted by the ghost of Glam, the ghost is merely continuing the violence Glam practiced in life. When Grettir wrestles Glam to the ground and cuts off his head, he avenges Glam's injuries to Thorhall and the farm is no longer haunted. Other Icelandic literature demonstrates a lively interest in supernatural events, but the family sagas, even when telling of ghosts or monsters, are entirely occupied with matters of human character.

Saga plots typically follow the pattern of feud and resolution. Theodore Anderson (1978) lists the six phases of the feud as quarrel, conflict, killing, revenge, counter-revenge, and resolution, although in the longer sagas the elements of revenge and counter-revenge may go on for many episodes and span a period of years. The violence is pervasive, but here also the emphasis is on the characters, their choices, and the consequences. The reader who comes to the sagas from the medieval romances will find the sagas peculiarly modern, with characters who are intelligent, obstinate, overbearing, weak in judgment, loving, violent, and often afflicted with bad luck. As Clover notes, the characters are represented so vividly that "one is tempted to ascribe them primarily to life and only secondarily to art. . . . The saga authors may be regarded as the foremost portrait artists in medieval literature."

In their use of frontier events, the sagas are very similar to novels of the American West written after the Civil War. After Frederick Jackson Turner declared the closing of the frontier, American writers looked back with nostalgia upon what they regarded as a heroic past. The Icelandic authors, writing a century after their own frontier period, also admired the strength and vitality of their ancestors. Further, American writers admired gunfighters and trailblazers, the Daniel Boones and Wyatt Earps who had performed heroic feats but whose individualism made them uncomfortable residents in a settled community. Similarly, the Icelanders looked with admiration on their outlaws, such as Grettir and Gisli, who dealt handily with monsters, berserks, or thieves, but whose touchy sense of honor often led to violence and made them uncomfortable companions.

The Icelandic sagas were not widely known until late in the 19th century and may have had no direct influence on the development of the novel. Echoes of saga plot and character resonate in the western novels of Willa Cather and even in the generational conflicts of William Faulkner; these are, however, coincidental. However, a revival of interest in the historical and literary past inspired several Scandinavian writers to imitate the devices of the saga in historical fiction. Of these, Sigrid Undset's *Kristin Lavransdatter* trilogy (1920–22), including *Kransen (The Gar-*

land), *Husfrue* (*The Mistress of Husaby*), and *Korset* (*The Cross*), is best known. In these novels, for which she was awarded the Nobel prize in 1928, Undset demonstrates the genealogical and dynastic themes of the saga. Among American novels, O.E. Rolvaag's *Giants in the Earth: A Saga of the Prairie* (1927) and its sequels make use of multigenerational motivation, character, and experience, focusing on the Norwegian immigrants who settled the midwest. Both Undset and Rolvaag revive the frontier experience, and their careful development of character reflects their regard for the sagas.

The tension between individual, family, and community extending over several generations, and actions motivated by genealogy and balanced by choice: these are the contributions of the saga to prose narrative, apparent directly in historical novels and indirectly in accounts of family and of frontier experience.

JANET P. SHOLTY

See also Scandinavian Novel

Further Reading

Anderson, Theodore, "The Icelandic Sagas," in *Heroic Epic and Saga: An Introduction to the World's Great Folk Epics,* edited by Felix J. Oinas, Bloomington: Indiana University Press, 1978

Clover, Carol J., *The Medieval Saga,* Ithaca, New York: Cornell University Press, 1982

Hallberg, Peter, *The Icelandic Saga,* Lincoln: University of Nebraska Press, 1962

Johnston, George, translator, *The Saga of Gisli,* Toronto: University of Toronto Press, and London: Dent, 1963

Palsson, Herman, and Denton Fox, translators, *Grettir's Saga,* Toronto: University of Toronto Press, 1974

The Sand Child and The Sacred Night by Tahar Ben Jelloun

L'Enfant du sable, 1983, and La Nuit sacrée, 1987

Despite having authored a steady flow of distinguished texts since the early 1970s, the Moroccan French-language writer Tahar Ben Jelloun labored in relative obscurity until he was awarded the prestigious Prix Goncourt for his seventh novel, *The Sacred Night,* and his work finally drew the international acclaim it clearly deserves—although some Maghribī (North African) critics have blamed Ben Jelloun for allegedly pandering to European readers and for committing thereby the same sins as the French colonial exoticists did with their "postcard" mentality.

It is a fact that Ben Jelloun's oneiric and lyrical prose style, later lauded by many, was present to varying degrees in his works from the outset, from the early prose poems collected in *Les Amandiers sont morts de leurs blessures* (1976; The Almond Trees Have Died from Their Wounds) and his eclectic first novel, *Harrouda* (1973), to the brilliant narrative technique displayed in two of his finest novels to date—*La Prière de l'absent* (1981; The Prayer for the Absent One) and *L'Écrivain public* (1983; The Public Scribe). Ben Jelloun always had a small but ardent set of fans; however, true fame came only with the publication and favorable reception of *The Sand Child* and *The Sacred Night* and the subsequent recognition stimulated by the Prix Goncourt.

Ben Jelloun's work—particularly the two novels discussed here—has been the subject of numerous conference papers and articles, and he has been adopted and lionized as an exponent of various critical discourses, from feminist to postmodernist, from postcolonial to cultural and bicultural studies.

It is, for several reasons, appropriate to consider *The Sand Child* and *The Sacred Night* as a unit; indeed, based exclusively on analysis of their intertwined plots, the two works appear to have been conceived as one opus, in addition to which both were made available in 1987 in one bound volume. It is, in fact, necessary to read both novels to appreciate either fully; and some of the enigmas of *The Sand Child* were not clarified until the sequel appeared—although Ben Jelloun's works do indeed thrive on ambiguity and enigma and readers must be willing to expect no logical closure in his works.

Any attempt to convey a clear-cut linear plot would be futile, for Ben Jelloun develops his narratives using multiple points of view (expressed in oral *contes,* letters, diaries, verbalized arcana, mystical manifestoes, and the like) and by exploring several registers of the imagination, from what might be called description of cognitive reality (recognizable streets or towns; physical objects meant to be taken literally at face value, not as symbols), to "loaded" iconic evocations of objects such as trees, wells, mirrors, and so on, to automatic writing of the sort practiced by the surrealists (to whom Ben Jelloun is admittedly indebted) and the insertion of dreams that blur with the other registers to the point that we feel justified in deeming all the points of view as essentially oneiric.

Some readers are frustrated by the lack of closure in Ben Jelloun's episodes, as when, for example, in the final paragraph of *The Sand Child,* the reader is impishly told that the narrator of the moment has progressively forgotten the characters in the manuscript he is reciting and has seen its pages turn blank under the full moon. He adds that he, too, has forgotten everything and concludes with a curious and mystifying invitation: "If any of you really wants to know how this story ended, he will have to ask the moon when it is full. I now lay down before you the book, the inkwell, and the pens." This inconclusive ending to *The Sand Child* provides an excellent transition to the "real" story recounted in the sequel. In the "Preamble" of *The Sacred Night*, we are told by the protagonist/narrator of her arduous identity quest, and we realize that this sequel will be the "definitive" notebook, fully aware that "definitive" is at best a multivalent notion in any work by Ben Jelloun:

> Don't forget, I was a child whose identity was clouded, unsteady, a girl disguised as a male by a willful father who felt demeaned and humiliated because he had no son. I became the son he dreamed of. Some of you know the rest; others have heard bits and pieces of it. Those of you who ventured to tell the story of that child of sand and wind ran into trouble. Some suffered amnesia, others nearly lost their souls. You've heard stories, but they were not really mine. . . . I knew that when I disappeared, I would leave behind fuel for the most extravagant tales. But my life is not a tale, and I am determined to establish the facts, to yield the secret hidden under a black stone in a house with high walls at the end of an alleyway sealed by seven gates.

The principal thrust of the two stories—developing as it does on several levels in which reality and imagination are in constant symbiosis and evolve in a cyclical rather than linear fashion—involves a girl whose father, ashamed at having already sired only seven girls and no son, raises her as a boy, Ahmed. The father resorts to the complicity of an old servant and to a subterfuge—cutting his finger held between the infant's legs—to stage the circumcision and grooms Ahmed to be the head of the household as his heir. Appearances are maintained when Ahmed marries an invalid who suspects the truth but does not object to the charade. Ahmed begins to be tormented and attracted by the yearnings of his true identity and finally disappears with the father's fortune that he, as sole male heir, has inherited; and of course Ahmed's uncle had anticipated inheriting his brother's fortune were the latter to have no son.

Ahmed joins a circus and is given a sideshow act to perform in which he plays an androgynous person who emerges as Zahra. Ahmed/Zahra's sexuality becomes more and more a path to self-discovery, even when the experience is painful. Various people step forward to offer alternate versions of what happened to Ahmed after he absconded. Some of these versions are patently self-serving on the part of the narrator of the moment, while others permit Ben Jelloun to indulge in lucid intertextuality, as when he presents the reader with a blind storyteller obviously based on the Argentine author Jorge Luis Borges. In the end, the above-mentioned conclusion leaves the reader's curiosity unappeased.

The second novel relates the supposedly true story of the fate of Ahmed/Zahra, a story that the reader is told is not a tale but a revelation of the facts; but the reader soon understands that he or she is merely being entertained with yet another tale, albeit a more sustained one than those constituting *The Sand Child*. In *The Sacred Night*, Zahra is a willing victim to rape at the hands of a stalker she never sees, and when she is taken under the wing of a woman who guards the door of the *hammam* (public bath), Zahra embarks on a journey of redemption, rediscovery, and ultimate deliverance. She goes to live with L'Assise (The Seated Woman) and her blind brother, known as Le Consul (The Consul). There, in a series of sexual adventures and metaphysical

discussions with the Consul (the latter activity leading to intellectual growth), Zahra recovers her female identity. The uncle, who has learned of Zahra's real gender and has discovered her whereabouts, arrives and accuses her of having illegally obtained his brother's property through imposture. Zahra kills the uncle with a pistol found in one of the Consul's drawers. She goes to prison, where she tries to remain close to the Consul by pretending to be blind. After release from prison she enters a nebulous realm, or Pantheon of sorts, where she is reunited with the late Seated Woman and the Consul, and appears to be, herself, apotheosized as a saint.

Even without such clues as the Borges reference, one readily associates Ben Jelloun's novels with the Latin American trend of magic realism, although there is a difference between his work and most of those in that tradition. If the works of Gabriel García Márquez, Borges, and others are surreal and loaded with a myriad of interpolated small dramas, they seem to be truth that is stranger than fiction and thus preponderantly realistic; Ben Jelloun relies more heavily on mysticism and the ethereal and thus depends more on magic, or, as some naysayers would have it, sleight of hand.

The story line is, of course, interesting, but Ben Jelloun's fundamental value resides in his ability to tell an entertaining story, or many stories, in beautiful poetic prose, a stylistic trait characteristic of many Maghribī novels. Intertextual references to the seminal work *The Thousand and One Nights* are contained in most of Ben Jelloun's novels; and, indeed, *The Sand Child* and *The Sacred Night* are heavily involuted frame stories permitting their author both caprice and variety. As in the frame narratives, many of the passages in the two novels could just as easily have been situated elsewhere, in another order. The structure and plotline are less important than the texture and the unit of the tale or chapter that often is an element unto itself.

Much of the intellectual charm of Ben Jelloun's work is derived from his biculturalism and bilingualism. Asked by a journalist whether he preferred the Arabic or the French language, Ben Jelloun quipped that Arabic was his wife, French his mistress, and that he had been unfaithful to both. In fact, Ben Jelloun's work draws on both Moroccan and French culture. Sometimes he seems deliberately to tease his non-Maghribī readers, as when he writes that the Seated Woman is called that because of her *fessier impressionnant* (impressive rump), suggesting a comical image of a woman so stout that she seems to be seated even when she stands; but the epithet is, in fact, no more than the literal translation of the Arabic *gellasa* (seated woman), which is the Moroccan term for the superintendent seated at the entrance to the *hammam* on women's day.

As for the oneiric style of his works, Ben Jelloun has, through his character in *L'Homme rompu* (1994; *Corruption*), described the process well:

> For the time being, I dream the world since I cannot transform it. To dream is to assemble incongruous things and beings, and from that point of departure, to weave a trite or extraordinary story. I am simply following Schopenhauer's idea that "life and dreams are pages in a single book; to read the pages in order is life; to read them out of order is to dream."
>
> For a long time I tried to follow the order of things, Now . . . I place greater trust in disorder and the dream.

Ben Jelloun's predilection for disorder and the vagaries of the dream is particularly at play in *The Sand Child* and *The Sacred Night,* in which the very concept of "true" chronology and "true" events is repeatedly undermined by the capricious intervention of interpretations various individuals would "write" on the blank pages of a mystical manuscript, these interventions themselves being the setting for texts and dreams within texts.

The Sand Child and *The Sacred Night* remain gratifying yet tantalizing reading, and—despite the fact that some readers consider *La Prière de l'absent* his masterpiece and despite Ben Jelloun's having published several fine novels since *The Sacred Night*—this diptych or dyadic narrative represents the culmination of Ben Jelloun's opus to date.

ERIC SELLIN

Further Reading

Bourkhis, Ridha, *Tahar Ben Jelloun: La poussière d'or et la face masquée: Approche linguistique,* Paris: L'Harmattan, 1995

M'Henni, Mansour, editor, *Tahar Ben Jelloun: Stratégies d'écriture,* Paris: L'Harmattan, 1993

Natij, Salah, "Dialogue interculturel et complaisance esthétique dans l'oeuvre de Tahar Ben Jelloun," *Itinéraires et Contactes de Cultures* 14 (1991)

Novèn, Bengt, *Les Mots et le corps: Etude des procès d'écriture dans l'oeuvre de Tahar Ben Jelloun,* Uppsala: Acta Universitatis Upsaliensis, 1996

Sellin, Eric, "Signes migrateurs: Approche transculturelle d'une lecture de la littérature maghrébine d'écriture française," *Itinéraires et Contactes de Cultures* 14 (1991)

George Sand 1804–76

French

From the enthusiasm generated by *Indiana* (1832) in the early days of France's July Monarchy through the successes and polemics of a professional career that spanned more than 50 years, George Sand played a pivotal, if long underestimated, role in the evolution of the novel. Initially famous for "family romances" that explored the tangled webs of role identification, desire, and power, Sand rapidly expanded her repertoire to include philosophical or metaphysical novels, the utopian-socialist novels of the late 1830s and 1840s, her celebrated pastoral novels, autobiographical texts, and the so-called Second Empire novels. While this widely accepted and roughly chronological categorization accurately defines the major trends within the rich Sandian corpus, it ignores a coherence that the French Senate itself recognized, albeit negatively, in its 1867 opposition to the presence of Sand's works in public libraries. Indeed, the only real error of the legislative body lay in underestimating the extent to which the pastoral novels, generally considered exempt from blame, refined rather than refuted Sand's earlier evaluations of the aesthetic and ideological principles dominating postrevolutionary society. Complex representations of the political, economic, affective, and symbolic structures in French society that prohibit personal and collective fulfillment, George Sand's novels also offer models for a material and conceptual revolution.

Free from the nostalgia for Old Regime institutions that haunted romantics such as Chateaubriand and Balzac, Sand nonetheless shared the desire of her peers to interpret the weight of history in a society under construction. Her early works most poignantly demonstrate the failures of recent political history and canonical fictions to accommodate change. In *Indiana,* for example, where the main male characters incarnate Republican, Napoleonic, and Restoration values, survival is only possible outside of society and after a symbolic death. A commoner's attempt in *Jacques* (1834) to defy the combined fatality of desire, literary tradition, and aristocratic, feminine wrong-doing results

in isolation and apparent death, as does the quest of the travestied female protagonist in her play *Gabriel* (1840), who dies at the hand of a government hit man after failing to convince her cousin and lover to reject the violent politics of their princely grandfather. Reciprocity and communication are Sand's laws of the future, which explains the importance of education in all her novels (see Mozet, 1997). Her own personal "literary dialogism" with Balzac is an example of the fruitful exchanges that mark her fictional quests for spiritual and interpersonal knowledge. Continual creation and collective responsibility replace dogma and patriarchal privilege. Mixtures of letters, journal entries, and pure dialogue in many of her novels, including *Lélia* (1833), *Isidora* (1846), and *Marianne* (1876), privilege shared voice over monolithic discursive authority. Although more conservative in their sexual and political implications, later novels such as *Le Dernier Amour* (1867; Last Love), *Césarine Dietrich* (1871), and *Nanon* (1872) nevertheless extend earlier experiments and explorations of the interpersonal and collective dynamics of power, desire, and violence (see Frappier-Mazur, 1996).

Many late 19th- and 20th-century critics have dismissed all Sandian texts, or at the very least utopian novels like *Le Meunier d'Angibault* (1845; The Miller of Angibault) and *Le Péché de Monsieur Antoine* (1846; The Sin of M. Antoine), as so many heavy-handed *romans à thèse,* collections of naive, idealized characters articulating dangerously misleading lies (see Schor, 1993). However, Sand's novels recognize the material constraints and, more significantly perhaps, the intense violence of desire that stand in the way of a social order without violence. Moreover, the idealization in which Sand engages is anything but naive. On the contrary, even as she builds a theory of mimesis in prefaces, essays, and novels such as *Les Maîtres mosaïstes* (1838; The Master Mosaic Workers) and earned great praise for her descriptions of landscape and her psychological portraits, she emphasizes the transforming power of the visionary, of a literature that provides positive new models for human relations (see Naginski, 1991, and Rossum-Guyon, 1996).

Sand's reliance on the emblematic value of sexual union corresponds to traditional novelistic practice, but the persistence with which she reworks this trope for all social contracts takes on added pertinence in light of her own authorial position. As a woman writing, publishing, and living under a man's name, George Sand never ceased affirming her place within and distance from a culture increasingly committed to defining itself through the supposed truths expressed in and by sexually differentiated "realist" bodies. Whether it be in private letters of her youth or in later novels such as *Monsieur Sylvestre* (1865), the androgynous figures of the traveler and the hermit embody a desire to displace sexual identity from its position as a privileged marker of personal identity (see Naginski, 1991). When the subversive use of realist referentiality in *Indiana* gave way to its simultaneous appropriation and rejection in *Lélia,* readers rightfully recognized her text as a sweeping attack on sexually defined rules for social intercourse and aesthetic creation (see Schor, 1993).

Sand's subsequent novels acknowledge and contest the power of gendered destinies promoted in canonical fictions. A misguided but loving female protagonist in *Horace* (1842), for example, demonstrates her superiority to the model she found in *Manon Lescaut* (1731) by Abbé Prévost by escaping the demise traditionally reserved for sexually active women. The male student privileged in so many 19th-century novels reveals himself in *Horace* to be dangerous in his very weakness. In similar fashion, the musically gifted heroine of *Consuelo* (1843) defies the tragic destiny depicted in Madame de Staël's *Corinne* (1807), which makes the novel into France's major portrayal of female artistic genius and initiation. Moreover, it prepared the way, by association, for Sand's mid-life autobiography, *Histoire de ma vie* (1854–55; *Story of My Life*). This chronicle of a journey from youth, under the name of Aurore Dupin, to authorship and maturity as George Sand displaces conventional distinctions separating male from female, fact from fiction, and public from private life.

Widespread critical attention accompanied the publication of most of Sand's novels, which exerted great influence on other writers. Fedor Dostoevskii and Lev Tolstoi found in her utopian novels inspiring representations of a new society; Gustave Flaubert saw in her later novels not only the traps of romantic delusion but inspiring representations of simple if limited goodness. Sand's representations of the maternal inspired the narrator of Marcel Proust's *À la recherche du temps perdu* (1913–27; *Remembrance of Things Past*, also translated as *In Search of Lost Time*), while her autobiographical resurrection and idealization of both the maternal and paternal are recalled in the attention that Marguerite Yourcenar gives her own maternal and paternal lineage. Through her artistic and personal example, George Sand also enriched the pool of future women writers, for whom she figured as an icon. Juliette Adams, George Eliot, Louise Aston, and Rosalía de Castro are just a few of the women who were indeed "infected," as Balzac wrote disparagingly in the *Muse du Département*, with a malady called "Sandism," that is, with a confidence that impelled them to brave social conventions and act with more or less lucidity upon their talents and desires. Nonetheless, for several decades the vicissitudes of George Sand's liaisons with Alfred de Musset, Chopin, and other well-known men occupied critics more than the scope and breadth of her literary influence.

The temporary effacement from which romantic writers suffered at the end of the 19th century lasted much longer for George Sand, precisely because of her sex and the provocative nature of her writing. But changing literary fashion, the rise of feminist criticism, and a greater interest in the mechanics of cultural exclusion have fostered an appreciation for the artistic originality and subversive content of her writing. George Sand's novels persistently destabilize the purported normalcy of centralized authority, whether it be individual political power, the primacy of Paris, patriarchal privilege, or realist mimesis, leaving in its place models for a new and as yet unrecognized community of beings.

ANNE E. McCALL

See also Indiana

Biography

Born Amantine Aurore Lucile Dupin in Paris, 1 July 1804. Received education at Nohant, her grandmother's estate, and at Couvent des Anglaises, Paris, 1817–20. Married the baron Dudevant in 1822 (judicially separated 1836), to whom she bore one son and one daughter; had liaisons with Jules Sandeau, Alfred de Musset, 1833–34, Chopin, 1838–47, Alexandre Manceau, 1849–65, and others; inherited Nohant, 1821; left, with her husband's acquiescence, to live in Paris, 1831; journalist, *Le Figaro*, 1831; adopted pseudonym George (briefly Georges) Sand, 1832; contributor, *Revue des Deux Mondes,* 1832–41; coeditor, *Revue Indépendante*, 1841; contributor, *La République,* 1848; settled at Nohant, 1848; lived in Palaiseau, near Versailles, 1864–67. Died 8 June 1876.

Fiction by Sand

Rose et Blanche, with Jules Sandeau (jointly as J. Sand), 1831
Indiana, 1832; as *Indiana*, translated anonymously, 1850
Valentine, 1832; as *Valentine,* translated by George Burnham Ives, in *The Masterpieces of George Sand,* 1900–02
Lélia, 1833; revised edition, 1839; as *Lélia,* translated by Maria Espinosa, 1978
Le Secrétaire intime (includes *Métella; La Marquise; Lavinia*), 1834; *Lavinia* as *Lady Blake's Love-Letters,* translated by Page McCarty, 1884; as *Lavinia,* translated by George Burnham Ives, in *The Masterpieces of George Sand,* 1900–02
Jacques, 1834; as *Jacques,* translated by Anna Blackwell, 1847
Leone Leoni, 1835; as *Leone Leoni,* translated by George Burnham Ives, in *The Masterpieces of George Sand,* 1900–02
André, 1835; as *André,* translated by Eliza A. Ashurst, in *The Works of George Sand,* 1847
Simon, 1836; as *Simon,* translated by Matilda M. Hays, in *The Works of George Sand,* 1847
Mauprat, 1837; as *Mauprat,* translated by Matilda M. Hays, in *The Works of George Sand,* 1847; also translated by V. Vaughan, 1870; H.E. Miller, 1891; Stanley Young, 1902
Les Maîtres mosaïstes, 1838; as *The Mosaic Workers,* translated by Eliza A. Ashurst, 1844; as *The Mosaic Workers,* translated by Ashurst, in *The Works of George Sand,* 1847; as *The Master Mosaic Workers,* translated by C.C. Johnstone, 1895

L'Uscoque, 1838; as *The Uscoque*, translated by J. Bauer, 1850

La Dernière Aldini, 1839; as *The Last Aldini*, translated by
  Matilda M. Hays, in *The Works of George Sand*, 1847; as
  The Last of the Aldinis, translated by George Burnham Ives,
  in *The Masterpieces of George Sand*, 1900–02

Spiridion, 1839; as *Spiridion*, translated anonymously, 1842

Pauline, 1840

Le Compagnon du tour de France, 1841; as *The Companion of
  the Tour of France*, translated by Matilda M. Hays, in *The
  Works of George Sand*, 1847; as *The Journeyman Joiner*,
  translated by Francis G. Shaw, 1849

Horace, 1842

Consuelo, 1843; as *Consuelo*, translated by Francis G. Shaw,
  1846; also translated by Fayette Robinson, 1851; Frank H.
  Potter, 1889

La Comtesse de Rudolstadt, 1844; as *The Countess of
  Rudolstadt*, translated by Francis G. Shaw, 1847; also
  translated by Fayette Robinson, 1870; Frank H. Potter, 1891

Jeanne, 1844

Lettres à Marcie, 1844; as *Letters to Marcie*, translated by
  Betsy Wing, 1988

Le Meunier d'Angibault, 1845; as *The Miller of Angibault*,
  translated by Edmund R. Larkin, in *The Works of George
  Sand*, 1847; also translated by M.E. Dewey, 1871

Teverino, 1845; as *Teverino*, translated anonymously, 1855; as
  Jealousy; or, Teverino, translated by O.S. Leland, 1870

Le Péché de Monsieur Antoine, 1846; as *The Sin of M.
  Antoine*, translated by George Burnham Ives, in *The
  Masterpieces of George Sand*, 1900–02

Isidora, 1846

La Mare au diable, 1846; as *The Devil's Pool*, translated by
  Francis G. Shaw, 1847; Frank H. Potter, 1890; Jane M. and
  Ellery Sedgwick, 1895; Hamish Miles, 1929; Antonia
  Cowan, 1966; as *The Haunted Marsh*, translated
  anonymously, 1848; as *The Enchanted Lake*, translated by
  Shaw, 1850; as *Germaine's Marriage*, translated 1892; as *The
  Haunted Pool*, translated by Potter, 1890

Lucrezia Floriani, 1846; as *Lucrezia Floriani*, translated by
  Julius Eker, 1985

The Works of George Sand, edited by Matilda M. Hays and
  translated by Hays, Eliza A. Ashurst, and Edmund R. Larkin,
  6 vols., 1847

Le Piccinino, 1847; as *The Piccinino*, translated by George
  Burnham Ives, in *The Masterpieces of George Sand*, 1900–02

François le Champi, 1848; as *Francis the Waif*, translated by
  Gustave Masson, 1889; also translated by Jane M. Sedgwick,
  1894; as *The Country Waif*, translated by Eirene Collis, 1930

La Petite Fadette, 1849; as *Little Fadette*, translated by Joseph
  Mazzini, 1850; also translated by Hamish Miles, 1928, and
  Eva Figes, 1967; as *Fadette*, translated anonymously, 1851;
  also translated by Jane M. Sedgwick, 1893; J.M. Lancaster,
  1896; as *Fanchon the Cricket*, translated anonymously, 1863;
  as *Petite Fadette*, translated by F.A. Binas, 1892

Le Château des déserts, 1851; as *The Castle in the Wilderness*,
  translated 1856

Mont-Revêche, 1853

La Filleule, 1853

Les Maîtres sonneurs, 1853; as *The Bagpipers*, translated by
  K.P. Wormeley, 1890

Adriani, 1854

Le Diable aux champs, 1856

Évenor et Leucippe, 1856; as *Les Amours de l'âge d'or*, in
  Oeuvres, 1871

La Daniella, 1857

Les Dames vertes, 1857; as *The Naiad: A Ghost Story*,
  translated by K. Berry di Zéréga, 1892

Les Beaux Messieurs de Bois-Doré, 1857; as *The Gallant Lords
  of Bois-Doré*, translated by Steven Clovis, 1890

L'Homme de neige, 1858; as *The Snow Man*, translated by V.
  Vaughan, 1871

Narcisse, 1859

Elle et lui, 1859; as *He and She*, translated by George Burnham
  Ives, in *The Masterpieces of George Sand*, 1900–02, this
  translation also published as *She and He*, 1902

Flavie, 1859

Jean de la Roche, 1860

Constance Verrier, 1860

La Ville noire, 1860

Le Marquis de Villemer, 1860–61; as *The Marquis of Villemer*,
  translated by R. Keeler, 1871

Valvèdre, 1861

La Famille de Germandre, 1861; as *The Germandre Family*,
  translated by George Burnham Ives, in *The Masterpieces of
  George Sand*, 1900–02

Tamaris, 1862

Antonia, 1863; as *Antonia*, translated by V. Vaughan, 1870

Mademoiselle la Quintinie, 1863

Laura, voyage dans le cristal, 1864; as *Journey Within the
  Crystal*, translated by Pauline Pearson-Stamps, 1992

La Confession d'une jeune fille, 1864

Monsieur Sylvestre, 1865; as *M. Sylvestre*, translated by Francis
  G. Shaw, 1870

Le Dernier Amour, 1867

Cadio, 1868

Mademoiselle Merquem, 1868; as *Mademoiselle Merquem*,
  translated anonymously, 1868

Pierre qui roule; Le Beau Laurence, 1870; as *A Rolling Stone;
  Handsome Laurence*, translated by Carroll Owen, 1871

Malgrétout, 1870

Césarine Dietrich, 1871; as *Césarine Dietrich*, translated by E.
  Stanwood, 1871

Francia, 1872

Nanon, 1872; as *Nanon*, translated by Elizabeth Wormeley
  Latimer, 1890

Ma soeur Jeanne, 1874; as *My Sister Jeannie*, translated by S.R.
  Crocker, 1874

Flamarande; Les Deux Frères, 1875

La Tour de Percemont; Marianne, 1876; first part as *The Tower
  of Percemont*, translated anonymously, 1877; second part
  translated as *Marianne*, 1880; also translated by Siân Miles
  (includes letters), 1987

Other Writings: plays, autobiography, journals, letters, stories
for children, and essays.

Further Reading

Crecelius, Kathryn J., *Family Romances: George Sand's Early
  Novels*, Bloomington: Indiana University Press, 1987

Frappier-Mazur, Lucienne, "Ecriture et violence chez Honoré de
  Balzac et George Sand," in *George Sand et l'écriture du*

roman, edited by Jeanne Goldin, Montreal: Université de Montréal, 1996

Godwin-Jones, Robert, *Romantic Vision: The Novels of George Sand,* Birmingham, Alabama: Summa, 1995

Goldin, Jeanne, *George Sand et l'écriture du roman,* Montreal: Université de Montréal, 1996

Hecquet, Michèle, *Poétique de la parabole: Les romans socialistes de George Sand, 1840–1845,* Paris: Klincksieck, 1992

McCall Saint-Saëns, Anne, *De l'être en lettres: L'Autobiographie épistolaire de George Sand,* Amsterdam and Atlanta, Georgia: Rodopi, 1996

Mozet, Nicole, *George Sand: Ecrivain de romans,* Saint-Cyr-sur-Loirc: Pirot, 1997

Naginski, Isabelle Hoog, *George Sand: Writing for Her Life,* New Brunswick, New Jersey: Rutgers University Press, 1991

Petrey, Sandy, "George and Georgina Sand: Realist Gender in *Indiana,*" in *Textuality and Sexuality: Reading Theories and Practices,* edited by Judith Still and Michael Worton, Manchester: Manchester University Press, and New York: St. Martin's Press, 1993

Powell, David, *George Sand,* Boston: Twayne, 1990

Rossum-Guyon, Françoise, "Sand, Balzac et le roman," in *George Sand et l'écriture du roman,* edited by Jeanne Goldin, Montreal: Université de Montréal, 1996

Schor, Naomi, *George Sand and Idealism,* New York: Columbia University Press, 1993

Szabo, Anna, *Le Personnage sandien: Constantes et variations,* Debrecen: Kossuth Lajos Tudomanyegyctem, 1991

Sanguo zhi yanyi. *See* Six Classic Chinese Novels

Satirical Novel

The first satirical novels were written in the 18th century, but, like the novel proper with its roots in narrative verse and folk tales, they have antecedents in earlier works, for example Geoffrey Chaucer's *Canterbury Tales* (written 1385–1400), the prose fiction of François Rabelais' *Gargantua and Pantagruel* (1532–34) and Miguel de Cervantes' *Don Quixote* (1605–15). Rabelais' work was first translated into English in 1653, and his influence is most apparent in the satirical novels of Jonathan Swift, Laurence Sterne, Thomas Love Peacock, Samuel Butler, and James Joyce. Alain-René Lesage's *Gil Blas* (1715–35), translated by Tobias Smollett in 1749, also influenced the English satirical novel in its infancy. Swift's *A Tale of a Tub* (1704) and *Gulliver's Travels* (1726), as well as Daniel Defoe's *Moll Flanders* (1722)—while their status as novels is debatable—may be seen to have influenced its development considerably.

The satirical novel also inherited some of the features of the formal verse satires of the classic Roman satirists, Horace, Persius, and Juvenal. Joseph Hall (1574–1656) introduced Juvenalian satire to England and wrote a somewhat bawdy satire in Latin while studying at Cambridge. The word *satire,* dating from the 16th century, derives from the Latin *satura* (medley) and originally referred to a poetic form developed by the Romans.

Satire in verse or prose generally offers an attack on historically specific targets by way of irony, parody, and ridicule. It is difficult to arrive at a satisfactory definition of satire, however, as the term suggests not only a type of literature but also a mode and spirit that may find expression in numerous genres. Critics have very often treated satire as a low genre while insisting on its moral stance, conservative nature, and reformist intentions, when in fact much satire, while indicting the behavior of its victims, is amoral, radical in viewpoint, and anarchic. Satire, rooted in its contemporary context, powerfully comments on the history of its own period, another feature of the genre overlooked by critics.

While not all satirical novels are comic, the satirical novel frequently includes a strong comic element. Rather than restoring harmony or resolving tension as "pure" comedy does, the comedy found in the satirical novel is usually purposeful and carries the author's criticisms. The satirical novel exposes folly and vice, using a mixture of rhetorical strategies and literary devices. It has frequently adopted the beast fable, anecdotes, homilies, the utopia, and various fantastic and invented experiences. Nearly every satirical novel features a display of invective, mockery, distortion, exaggeration, sarcasm, wit, and denunciation in order to arouse contempt in the reader for its satiric targets.

Satirical novelists very often attack specific individuals. For example, Swift and Henry Fielding satirize Robert Walpole, and Aldous Huxley denounced Middleton Murry and D.H. Lawrence as well as a number of writers of his own circle, following the convention set by Juvenal of identifying satiric victims. But satirical novels may focus their attack on particular social groups or ideologies. For example, Evelyn Waugh mocks the English aristocracy in many of his novels, George Orwell denounces communism in *Animal Farm* (1945), and the Australian novelist Christina Stead satirizes both the American left and right in her novel about postwar politics in the United States, *I'm Dying Laughing* (1986).

Many satirical novels rely heavily on dialogue as well as utilize the comic monologue. Grotesque imagery is a feature of the satirical novel in all periods. In fact, many satirists revel in whatever is ugliest and most excessive in their satiric targets. For example, Swift's Gulliver is revolted by the deformities of the Brobdingnagian women and by the disgusting behavior of the Yahoos. Dickens' characters are frequently depicted as grotesques, and, in the contemporary context, the Australian satirist David Foster reveals a recurring fascination with castration that is as disturbing as the cannibalistic feasts described by Rabelais. However, the significance of the grotesque is as varied as the satirical novels themselves and is not always simply a method of conveying the demonic or morally dissipated nature of the satiric victims portrayed.

Perhaps the earliest satirical novel is Henry Fielding's *An Apology for the Life of Mrs. Shamela Andrews,* published in 1741, a parody of Samuel Richardson's popular work *Pamela; or, Virtue Rewarded* (1740). Fielding acknowledged his debt to Lucian, Swift, and Cervantes in his comic prose epics. Tobias Smollett's *Roderick Random* (1748) developed the picaresque, and Laurence Sterne's *Tristram Shandy* (1759–67) continued Fielding's impulse to parody the developing conventions of the new novel form. Sterne's witty and frequently salacious prose presents an early example of the stream-of-conciousness technique, linking his satire with modernists of the 20th century such as James Joyce. Voltaire's pessimistic and savage philosophical tale *Candide,* also published in 1759, offered an intricate satire of ideas, a fable, and an argument on the limitations of rationalism in the face of evil.

In the 19th century, the novel was used extensively for social satire. Early in the century Thomas Love Peacock published three satirical novels, *Headlong Hall* (1816), *Melincourt* (1817), and *Nightmare Abbey* (1818), in which the author casts a cold eye on the political culture of his day, drawing on the classical "anatomy" or miscellaneous prose satire and the Socratic dialogue. Peacock caricatures some of his contemporaries: William Wordsworth, Samuel Taylor Coleridge, Robert Southey, Lord Byron, and Percy Bysshe Shelley. William Thackeray's *Vanity Fair* (1848) satirizes the increasingly materialistic society of his times, and Anthony Trollope's Barsetshire series of six novels (1855–67) achieved extraordinary popularity featuring a remarkable realism in the satirical depiction of social life in rural England at mid-century. Charles Dickens' novels are among the most popular satirical novels ever written. Dickens' fiction ranged from the comic and sometimes sentimental early works (serialized from 1837) to the darker and more serious novels of social criticism of his later period, of which *Our Mutual Friend* (1865) is a good example. His interest in social reform is paramount, and his satiric effect is achieved through the development of character and the drama of incident, rather than through denunciation or rhetoric (see Manning, 1971).

Flaubert's posthumously published and unfinished satirical work *Bouvard et Pécuchet* (1881; *Bouvard and Pécuchet*) anticipates Joyce and other modernists in its portrayal of the minds of two men utterly cluttered with the detritus of 19th-century popular and pseudo-science. On the other side of the Atlantic, Mark Twain combined the picaresque adventure story with scathing social criticism in *The Adventures of Tom Sawyer* (1876) and *The Adventures of Huckleberry Finn* (1884).

The satirical novel of the 20th century takes many forms. In the early part of the century, it ranged from the richly allusive blend of parody, naturalism, and fantasy in Joyce's *Ulysses* (1922) to the much more narrowly focused attacks on the Bloomsbury group in Roy Campell's *The Georgiad: A Satirical Fantasy in Verse* (1931) and the social satire of Anthony Powell, Evelyn Waugh, George Orwell, and Aldous Huxley. Later in the century, the potent satirical comedy of Kingsley Amis dominated the genre in Great Britain.

In the United States, the novels of Nathaniel West and Sinclair Lewis marked the end of the satirical novel in its modernist phase. However, the American postmodernist novel is frequently satirical, particularly the fiction of Vladimir Nabokov, William Gaddis, Thomas Pynchon, and William Burroughs. Pynchon's use of fantasy and fable and his sweeping surveys of contemporary life link his novels with the controversial allegorical works of the Indian-born Salman Rushdie. Both authors write encyclopedic satire in which the texts present the full range of knowledge and beliefs of a national culture (see Weisenburger, 1995). Rushdie's novels offer cross-cultural analysis and preserve the strong comic elements of traditional satire. Whereas the works of Nabokov and Burroughs seems dissociated from the political, Rushdie's fiction is highly attuned to *realpolitik.* Although more often subsumed under the label of magic realism, the novels of Gabriel García Márquez and the stories of Jorge Luis Borges are heavily satirical, and their magic realist elements recall the extravagant distortions of the fabular in the earliest satirical novels.

Since the 18th century, the satirical novel has flourished in English, with significant examples of the form in French, German, and Russian. Yet critics have consistently regarded satire as a separate and unequal genre, one that simply cannot live up to the complexities demanded by the novel form. However, the history of the satirical novel demonstrates that satire manifests itself in many genres as a mode or spirit and that satire is a feature of many of the great novels published in the last three centuries.

ANNE PENDER

See also Comedy and Humor in the Novel; Conte Philosophique; Greek and Roman Narrative; Parody and Pastiche

Further Reading

Connery, Brian A., and Kirk Combe, editors, *Theorizing Satire: Essays in Literary Criticism,* London: Macmillan, and New York: St. Martin's Press, 1995

Feinberg, Leonard, *Introduction to Satire,* Ames: Iowa State University Press, 1967

Griffin, Dustin, *Satire: A Critical Reintroduction,* Lexington: University Press of Kentucky, 1994

Hodgart, Matthew, *Satire,* London: Weidenfeld and Nicolson, and New York: McGraw-Hill, 1969

Manning, Sylvia Bank, *Dickens as Satirist,* New Haven, Connecticut: Yale University Press, 1971

Palmeri, Frank, *Satire in Narrative: Petronius, Swift, Gibbon, Melville, and Pynchon,* Austin: University of Texas Press, 1990

Weisenburger, Steven, *Fables of Subversion: Satire and the American Novel, 1930–1980,* Athens: University of Georgia Press, 1995

Scandinavian Novel

Denmark

Losing much of its political importance in Europe in the early 19th century, Denmark experienced an upsurge in national awareness and a flowering of the arts, resulting in what is sometimes referred to as the Danish Golden Age. The Danish novel first arose in this context of vigorous artistic activity. Associated primarily with the middle and upper classes, the novel of the Golden Age is narrowly focused on Copenhagen society and displays a far greater interest in psychological analysis than in social realism or political engagement.

Denmark's close cultural connections with Germany ensured the dominant influence of such romantic writers as Johann Wolfgang von Goethe, Joseph von Eichendorff, and E.T.A Hoffmann, which explains why the early Danish novel had little or no concern for realism. The popularity of Walter Scott's historical novels did little to counter that general tendency. However, in conjunction with the rise of Danish nationalism, the vogue for Scott's work did produce a spate of historical novels.

Johannes Carsten Hauch, a dramatist and poet, wrote several ambitious historical novels that generally fall far short of their aspirations. The best known is *Vilhelm Zabern* (1834), a novel about the 16th-century Danish King Christian II. Evincing an eclectic imagination, his other novels take as their subjects the French Revolution, the invention of the steamboat, and the development of capitalism. Bernhard Severin Ingemann was a more accomplished novelist and won a lasting popularity as "the Danish Walter Scott." His first work was a highly derivative novel in verse, *Varners poetiske Vandringer* (1813; Varner's Poetic Wanderings), based on Goethe's *Die Leiden des jungen Werthers* (1774; The Sufferings of Young Werther) and Ludwig Tieck's *Franz Sternbalds Wanderungen* (1798; Franz Sternbald's Travels). His four novels about the Middle Ages—*Valdemar Seir* (1826; *Waldemar, surnamed Seir or the Victorious*), *Erik Menveds Barndom* (1828; *The Childhood of Erik Menved*), *Kung Erik og de Fredløse* (1826; *King Erik and the Outlaws*), and *Prins Otto af Danmark* (1835; Prince Otto of Denmark)—became common reading property in all cultured Danish homes. The strength of these novels lies in their detailed settings, their weakness in the characters' rather simple psychology. A third voice in the historical novel belonged to Carl Bernhard, pseudonym of Andreas Nicolai de Saint Aubain, whose short and polished novels were modeled on Prosper Mérimée's *Chronique du Regne de Charles IX* (1829; Chronicle of the Reign of Charles IX). Bernhard's *Krøniker fra Christians IIs Tid* (1847; Chronicles from the Age of Christian II) and *Krøniker fra Erik af Pommerns' Tid* (1850; Chronicles from the Age of Erik of Pomerania) won great popularity for their crystalline style and sense of drama.

Ingemann's *Varner* was not the only verse novel published in Denmark. Christian Winther's very popular historical novel *Hjortens Flugt* (1855; The Flight of the Stag) is written in the strophic form of the German *Nibelungenlied*. Fredrik Paludan-Müller also wrote in verse, employing the strophic form of Byron's *Don Juan* in his *Adam Homo* (1841, 1848) to brilliant effect.

The strong romantic and idealistic inclinations of these writers also characterize the work of Poul Martin Møller, Steen Steensen Blicher, and Carl Bagger, but tempered by more realistic elements. Møller is remembered for the unfinished novel *En dansk Students Eventyr* (1845; A Danish Student's Adventures). The absence of a clear plot in the four completed chapters is made up for by the careful characterization of persons and locales. Reminiscent of Eichendorff's *Aus dem Leben eines Taugenichts* (1826; From the Life of a Ne'er-Do-Well), *En dansk Students Eventyr* is often classified as protorealist for its focus on everyday life. Blicher espoused an idiosyncratic regionalism, depicting life in distant and wild Jutland in the crushingly pessimistic stories of *Traekfuglene* (1838; The Birds of Passage), which stand out for their use of the Jutland dialect. Carl Bagger's reputation also rests on a single work, *Min Broders Levned* (1835; My Brother's Life), in which the "good" brother, the pastor Johannes, tells the story of his frivolous sibling Arthur. The two characters appear to express different aspects of Bagger's own tormented and unstable self.

As early as the 1830s, a different, more realistic, sensibility had announced itself in Danish fiction. This so-called poetic realism displayed a stronger realist bent, a concern for social issues, and a greater interest in formal considerations. For instance, the novels of Hans Christian Andersen—now forgotten outside Denmark but once very popular in Germany and England—are divided between quasi-autobiographical explorations and attacks on social injustice. The protagonists of *Improvisatoren* (1835; The Improvisatore), *O.T.* (1836; O.T.), and *Kun en Spillemand* (1837; Only a Fiddler) reflect Andersen's own hopes and self-doubts. *De to Baronesser* (1848; The Two Baronesses) is a tightly constructed book about social injustice and the nobility of the spirit, while *At være eller ikke være* (1857; To Be or Not To Be?) expresses Andersen's philo-Semitism and his quite unorthodox Christianity. *Lykke Peer* (1870; Lucky Peer) returns to Andersen's dreams of artistic success.

Thomasine Gyllembourg was Denmark's first woman writer. Her *Familien Polonius* (1827; The Polonius Family) and *En Hverdags-Historie* (1828; An Everyday Story) deal with problems of love and marriage, looking forward to the social discussions of the 1880s. *To Tidsaldre* (1845; Two Ages) is a more ambitious work contrasting the revolutionary spirit of the 1790s with the bourgeois concerns of the 1830s. Gyllembourg was much admired in her time for her wit and the complex structures of her novels and today enjoys a renaissance as a pioneer woman writer.

Looking to such models as Honoré de Balzac and Eugène Sue, Meir Aron Goldschmidt began his creative career with *En Jøde* (1845; A Jew), which dissects various aspects of anti-Semitism and earned him the enmity of Copenhagen's Jewish community. His subsequent work, *Hjemløs* (1853–57; Homeless), *Arvingen* (1863; The Heir), and *Ravnen* (1867; The Raven), tackled the subject more obliquely. *Ravnen* has been praised for its depiction of the last years of the reign of Christian VIII (1839–48), the Slesvig Wars (1848–50), and the end of Danish absolutism.

The capstone of the psychological literature of the Golden Age is Hans Egede Schack's *Phantasterne* (1857; The Phantasists), which analyzes the empty formalism of Danish government and the lazy dreaminess that is widely thought to be a trait of the Danish national character. One of *Phantasterne*'s dreamers ends his days in a madhouse, while the other manages to retain his sanity only by overcompensating in the direction of an equally extreme objectivity. The novel is remarkable for its destruction of romantic attitudes toward life, its political commentaries, and for its depiction of sexual fantasies.

The Golden Age came to an end with Denmark's ignominious defeat in an armed confrontation with Prussia and Austria over the duchies of Slesvig and Holstein in 1864. Losing territory, Denmark suffered an immense sense of loss that also made itself felt in literature. Several established writers tried to confront the tragedy, but the most popular postwar author, Vilhelm Bergsøe, owed his success to his evasion of the issue. His *Fra Piazza del Popolo* (1867; From the Piazza del Popolo) is a compendium of seven long novellas told by members of the Danish artists' colony in Rome as they wait for the release of a colleague kidnapped by brigands. The characters, some of whom move from story to story, come from a large range of social levels and national backgrounds—British lords and ladies, Byronic Danish students, Italian *putane* and thieves. *Fra Piazza del Popolo*, retrospective and romanticizing, is a last product of the Golden Age, whose literature, however fascinating in its refinement, is socially narrow. In fact, Bergsøe's *Fra den gamle Fabrik* (1869; From the Old Factory), a fictionalized account of his own childhood, features one of the first appearances of factory life in the Danish novel, albeit from the perspective of the director's son.

Denmark emerged from the trauma of the 1860s with a strong economy, experiencing a rapid industrialization that transformed the small and cozy capital into a modern metropolis. In literature, the critic Georg Brandes led the so-called modern breakthrough, a shift away from the inward-looking and hyperaesthetic writing of the Golden Age. In amazingly short order, Brandes succeeded in changing the tone of Scandinavian letters from cultural idealism to a realism that no longer ignored social problems and biological factors. In *Hovedstrømninger i det 19de Aarhundredes Litteratur* (1872–90; *Main Currents in 19th Century Literature*), Brandes shows himself fully cognizant of the work of Gustave Flaubert and Émile Zola in France and George Eliot and George Meredith in England, as well as the writings of Charles Darwin, John Stuart Mill, Hippolyte Taine, Auguste Comte, and Ernest Renan. Brandes also did much to spread the reputation of the new Norwegian dramatists, Henrik Ibsen and Bjørnstjerne Bjørnson, both in Scandinavia and abroad.

Jens Peter Jacobsen was Brandes' closest Danish follower. The naturalist *Fru Marie Grubbe* (1876; *Marie Grubbe: A Lady of the Seventeenth Century*) recounts a sensational case of downward mobility, telling the story of a noblewoman who ends up as the contented wife of a drunken ferryman and sometime convict. Jacobsen's psychological penetration, his close, quasi-scientific observation, and his evocation of atmosphere make for a radically new approach to the historical novel. Jacobsen's other novel, *Niels Lyhne* (1880), with a Golden Age setting, paints a portrait of the passive dreamer. In effect a miniature Bildungsroman, *Niels Lyhne* recalls the major debates of the 1870s on such subjects as realism in art, women's erotic choices, and atheism. Although Jacobsen is Denmark's strongest naturalist writer, Brandes was uncomfortable with his delicate sensualism and lyricism.

Jacobsen's nearest rival was Holger Drachman, who was primarily a poet and devoted much energy to self-dramatization. Drachman's novel *En Overkomplet* (1876; A Supernumerary) looked back to Bagger's *Min Broders Levned,* depicting the half-brothers Erik and Adolf. The gifted but undisciplined Erik, the self-styled supernumerary, is inspired by Ivan Turgenev's superfluous man from *Dnevnik lishnego cheloveka* (1850; *The Diary of a Superfluous Man*), a novel much read in Denmark. Like *En Overkomplet,* Drachman's *Forskrevet* (1890; Signed Away) has a pair of contrasting heroes, the Bohemian would-be artist Ulf and the hard-working and productive painter Henrik. Both fall in love with the same woman, a warm-hearted nightclub singer, who in the end opts for Henrik—just as well, since it turns out that she is Ulf's sister. The title may be a thrust at Brandes, whose insistence on strict realism, Drachman thought, could lead to a signing away of artistic creativity to the theory of an imposing but noncreative mind. The sometimes silly extravagances of *Forskrevet*'s plot do not detract from the novel's main strength—an impression of the growing Copenhagen of the 1880s.

Diametrically opposed protagonists likewise turn up in *Nutidsbilleder* (1878; Modern Images) by the journalist Vilhelm Topsøe, who contrasts the hard-working farmer and politician Harald Holst with the dreamer Flemming. Yet Topsøe gives the story a different twist by letting Holst grow corrupt as a member of the Danish diet, while Flemming casts off his ineffectual self and becomes a principled and disciplined man. Topsøe's earlier novel, *Jason med det gyldne Skind* (1875; Jason with the Golden Fleece), had also portrayed the ultimate failures of a practical man—an engineer and physician who commits suicide when his mistress betrays him. Topsøe's concern with marriage and sexual morality was shared by many of his contemporaries. Erik Skram's *Gertrud Colbjørnsen* (1879) argued for the necessity of adultery after a woman is pushed by family pressures into an unhappy marriage. This novel, recently rediscovered, ends with Gertrud's divorce and her marriage to the painter Fabricius, a constant "tin soldier" in Andersen's mold. Women writers also took up the subject of marital unhappiness, including Skram's wife, the Norwegian Amalie Skram, whose personal experience in a previous marriage lent force to fictional descriptions of conjugal misery. Olivia Levison provided another harrowing picture of an unhappily married woman's deprived life in *Konsulinden* (1887; The Consul's Wife). Adele (Adda) Marie Ravnkilde depicted a romantic and misled young woman in *Tantaluskvaler* (1884; The Torments of Tantalus).

Henrik Pontoppidan's masterful work grows out of the modern breakthrough, showing a connection particularly in its persistent attention to social, economic, and political factors. He described his chef d'œuvre as "a trilogy in which a connected picture of modern Denmark [is presented] by means of portrayals of human beings and human minds and human fates, in which social, religious, and political conflicts are included." The trilogy consists of *Det forjættede Land* (1891–95; *The Promised Land*), describing the aspirations, temptations, and ultimate destruction of the pastor Emanuel Hansted; *Lykke-Peer* (1898; *Lucky Peer*), the saga of the plans and, at last, the defeat of the engineer, surveyor, and highway inspector Per Sidenius; and *De Dødes Rige* (1912–16; The Kingdom of the Dead), about a high-minded Jutland estate owner who wishes to aid the workers on his properties but sees them turn against him. All three of Pontoppidan's protagonists have the best of intentions, but their idealism is their destruction. Seeking happiness in a series of sexual relationships, they either find happiness too late or not at all. Pontoppidan was awarded a shared Nobel prize in 1917 with Karl Gjellerup, a writer justly forgotten. However, Pontoppidan has never won a large international reputation, not even in Germany. The heavy quality of his prose and the pessimism that dominates his novels may be responsible for the fact that he is less well known than he should be.

The contrast between Pontoppidan and Herman Bang could not be greater. Bang's books, all brief, contain a strong element of sheer entertainment in their wonderfully vivid dialogue and their evocative impressionism. As a very young man, Bang created a sensation with his novel of family degeneration and shattered theatrical ambitions, *Haabløse Slægter* (1880; Hopeless Generations), later revised to remove portions charged with indecency. A classic of decadent literature, the novel anticipates Joris-Karl Huysmans' *À rebours* (1884; *Against Nature*). In subsequent novels, Bang focused on seduced and deserted young women, giving rise to speculations that he described his own unfortunate romantic experiences. *Det hvide Hus* (1898; The White House) and *Det graa Hus* (1901; The Gray House), taking place respectively in a country parsonage and the grand Copenhagen mansion of an aging physician (a portrait of Bang's paternal grandfather), are tributes to his mother. *Det graa Hus* centers on Bang's conviction that sexual passion is the primary root of human suffering. A comic jeu d'esprit, *Sommerglæder* (1902; Summer Pleasures), the compressed account of a single day in a Danish country inn, is the last work in which Bang is at the top of his form.

The aim of the modern breakthrough—the exposure of society's numerous hypocrisies and deformities—was still pursued by authors around the turn of the century, as in Karl Larsen's sweet-tempered *I det gamle Voldkvarteret* (1899; In the Old Wall Section), an elegy for an older Copenhagen, and the double novel *Hvis ser du Skæven* (1902; If You Spy the Mote) and *En modern Hverdagshistorie* (1906; A Modern Everyday Story). In stark contrast, the bitterly funny novels about provincial life of the gifted Gustav Wied, *Livsens Ondskab* (1899; Life's Malice) and *Knagsted* (1902), are examples of the malicious humor of which Danes are so proud. Seen from a more serious side, Wied's books gave the coup de grâce to the high-minded reforming zeal of the modern breakthrough. Sniping at small-town hypocrisy is also central to the novels of Knud Hjortø, who, in *To Verdener* (1905; Two Worlds), returned to psychological analysis and the perennial type of the Danish dreamer. Jakob Knudsen's *Sind* (1903; Disposition) and Harald Kidde's *Helten* (1912; The Hero), both with remote settings, also focus on the psychology of their characters. *Sind,* about the main character's discovery that he is as tyrannical as his loathed father, is set in Jutland. In *Helten,* the pure fool Clemens Bek (who has grown up, undefiled, in a Copenhagen whorehouse) becomes an elementary school teacher on the little Baltic island of Anholt and tries to bring some of its inhabitants to a Christian way of life.

The passing of the modern breakthrough also made room for a revival of the historical novel. *Æbelø* (1895; Apple Island), the medievalizing and highly poetic prose narrative of Sophus Michaelis, is a tale of much-tried love on an island of preternatural beauty. But Michaelis' fragile talent was put completely in the shade by the vigor of Johannes V. Jensen. After some floundering, Jensen's actual career began with *Danskere* (1896; Danes) and *Einar Elkjær* (1898), both of which are about contemporary dreams and dreamers. But Jensen turned to a pair of historical dreamers in *Kongens Fald* (1900–01; *The Fall of the King*), which recounts the intersecting lives of a Jutland peasant's son, failed student, and mercenary soldier, Mikkel Thøgersen, and the hard-handed but indecisive Christian II: both are brutal, wildly ambitious, given to fantasies, and unable to realize their own potential. Jensen uses poetic prose far more brilliantly and inventively than Michaelis, telling the story in three "seasonal" sections, "The Death of Spring," "The Great Summer," and "Winter." Jensen's incomparable knowledge of the history and folkways of the late 15th and early 16th centuries, employed more in allusion than in direct narration, and his insight into the superstitious minds of the two men made *The Fall of the King* into what the literary historian Sven H. Rossel calls "the finest historical novel in Danish literature."

Jensen never again equaled this early accomplishment. An admirer of the United States, he wrote two rather original novels set in the New World before returning to the historical genre in *Den lange Rejse* (1908–21; *The Long Journey*), which he regarded as his masterpiece. It begins in the forests of the Tertiary Age, moves to the Ice Age, and trudges forward through the aeons to the Vikings and Christopher Columbus. The epic contains elements of proto-Nazism, celebrating the emergence of the supremely energetic Nordic people. However, the suppression of human bestiality and the triumph of love mitigate Jensen's politics. He continued to write during the German occupation but carefully maintained his distance from the occupiers, believing that the Nazis had destroyed "everything that is called race and evolution"—that they had given racism a bad name. Jensen was awarded the Nobel prize in 1944, partly on the strength of *The Long Journey*.

The Danish novel took a very different turn with the work of Martin Andersen-Nexø. Nexø, a communist with a working-class background, spoke for landless agricultural workers and the industrial proletariat, which had been signally absent from Danish literature. Nexø established himself with the series *Pelle Erobreren* (1906–10; *Pelle the Conquerer*). The first volume describes the boyhood of a working-class child cursed with a feckless father. Later Pelle rises above the humiliations of his childhood to become a successful labor organizer. Another series, *Ditte Menneskebarn* (1917–21; *Ditte, Girl Alive, Daughter of Man, Towards the Storm*), tells the heart-rending story of poor Ditte, born out of wedlock, who goes to Copenhagen to support her own illegitimate child and is crushed by the forces of capitalism.

Hans Kirk, another communist, wrote the collective novel *Fiskerne* (1928; The Fishermen), a narrative of far greater subtlety and brevity than Nexø's stories. In *Fiskerne*, a community of fishermen moves from its original home, ravaged by the North Sea, to a safer haven. There, pious Christians, they directly outdo the lazy local inhabitants by their self-discipline and industry, but they pay a high price for their success in selfish personal conflicts.

Jacob Paludan was the political opposite of Nexø and Kirk and used his work to express his reactionary aestheticism, particularly in *De vestlige Veje* (1922; The Western Roads) and *Søgelys* (1923; Search Light), which pillories technological developments for the aesthetic and ecological damage they cause.

His best work is *Jørgen Stein* (1932–33), a novel chronicling the decline and fall of the cultivated bourgeoisie.

The 1920s saw a great deal of social experimentation, answered by limited technical experimentation in the novel. Tom Kristensen's *Hærværk* (1930; *Havoc*) is the most incisive portrait of the age, about the parasitical newspaper critic Ole Jastrau, who slowly goes to pieces despite his hopes of finding an intellectual, political, or religious handhold. The novel was one of the first to use interior monologue and stream of consciousness. Less experimental, Knud Sønderby's work also captures the Jazz Age, particularly his debut novel, *Midt i en Jazztid* (1931; In the Midst of a Jazz Age). Børge Madsen's strange little *Jeg er salig* (1933; I Am Blest) is technically more adventurous, using a first-person narrative interrupted by feigned conversations, mini-novels, poems, musical compositions, aphorisms, and so on. The narrator, like so many Danish characters before him, ends as a patient in an insane asylum.

The 1920s and 1930s also saw the arrival of several novelists who explored sexuality. Jens August Schade, for instance, depicted the complete surrender to impulses in the plotless *Den himmelske Elsker paa Jorden* (1931; The Heavenly Lover on Earth) and in *Mennesker mødes og sød Musik opstaar i Hjertet* (1944; People Meet, and Sweet Music Arises in the Heart). Charges of pornography were brought against the latter for its plot: a man and a woman meet on a train, are attracted to one another, and immediately retire to one of the Danish State Railroad's spacious lavatories. Jørgen Nielsen found more complexity in sexuality, as in his debut novel, *Offerbaal* (1929; Sacrificial Fire), in which a peasant girl is doubly seduced by men willing to take advantage of her passive nature and by born-again Christianity. Some of Nielsen's characters acquire considerable self-insight, as in *De Hovmodige* (1930; The Prideful Ones), in which Kathy finally realizes that she keeps choosing the wrong suitors because they shore up her self-esteem. Jutland farm life provides the background of *En Kvinde ved Baalet* (1933; A Woman by the Bonfire), a popular success with a melodramatic story about the tortured passion of the devoted Daniel for the promiscuous Lisa.

Other writers dominating the 1930s included Nis Petersen, who established an international reputation with a playfully comical novel about Rome in the age of Marcus Aurelius, *Sandalmagernes Gade* (1931; *The Street of the Sandalmakers*) and the topical *Spildt Mælk* (1934; *Spilt Milk*), about the Irish civil war of the 1920s. The gifted Mogens Klitgaard wrote about disreputable characters, including an alcoholic debt-collector in *Der sidder en Mand i en Sporvogn* (1937; A Man Is Sitting in a Streetcar) and a petty crook in *Gud mildner Luften for de klippede Faar* (1938; God Tempers the Wind for Shorn Sheep). After April 1940, Klitgaard used the historical novel to make oblique comments on the German occupation, publishing *De røde Fjer* (1940; The Red Feathers), *Ballade paa Nytorv* (1940; Row at Nytorv), and *Den guddomelige Hverdag* (1942; The Divine Everyday Life). Klitgaard had an interest in contemporary narrative technique and used a collage of newspaper reports and narrative snapshots similar to Alfred Döblin's *Berlin Alexanderplatz* (1929) and John Dos Passos' *U.S.A* (1930–36). Another author of the 1930s was Hans Scherfig, who wrote biting social satire. His mystery novel *Den forsvundne Fuldmægtig* (1938; *The Missing Bureaucrat*) exposes the soul-killing monotony of bureaucratic life. Scherfig's next target was the Danish lyceum

system and its ability to deform the spirits of its pupils, in *Det forsømte Foraar* (1940; *Stolen Spring*). *Idealister* (1945; Idealists) and *Frydenholm* (1962) portray Denmark in the 1930s and during the occupation, respectively.

The postwar period was dominated by younger novelists, many writing about the occupation. Willy-August Linnemann published *Natten for Freden* (1945; The Night before the Peace), dedicated to the Danes who openly opposed the Germans. Linnemann's work largely stood in the service of his antinationalism, which, however admirable, did not benefit his fiction. Hans Christian Branner began with *Legetøj* (1936; Toys), an account of the workings of a toy factory that has been read as a criticism or warning of the dangers of Nazism. Branner then returned to psychological analysis in several novels before achieving a genuine breakthrough with two novels about the occupation, *Rytteren* (1949; *The Riding Master*) and *Ingen kender Natten* (1955; *No One Knows the Night*).

The occupation also left a mark on Martin A. Hansen, whose *Jonatans Rejse* (1941; Jonathan's Journey) is a picaresque novel that asks how one can oppose evil without becoming to some extent evil oneself. Hansen's two postwar novels—*Lykkelige Kristoffer* (1945; *Lucky Kristoffer*) and *Løgneren* (1950; *The Liar*)—are considered masterpieces of 20th-century Danish literature. *Lucky Kristoffer* takes place in the 16th century, telling the story of a young idealist through the reminiscences of one of his companions. The crux of the novel lies in the difficulties of forming a moral judgment about the complex characters. Loyalty and greed are hopelessly mixed in Martin, for example, and in the tears of the turncoat Gabel "duplicity and sincerity are so fervently united." *The Liar* is a novel written for radio. Its protagonist is a middle-aged schoolmaster on an isolated island who has written a manuscript about his moral and intellectual failings. Vig is a manipulator, a constant falsifier of fact and emotional relationships, but at last he finds peace in renunciation.

The 1950s and 1960s brought more novels about World War II. Ole Sarvig's *Stenrosen* (1955; Stone Roses) pictures survival in Berlin before and after May 1945. Tage Skou-Hansen's *Dagstjernen* (1960; The Day Star) describes the fates of an informer and the man designated to kill him. Peter Seeberg's remarkable little *Bipersonerne* (1956; The Extras) focuses on a group of foreign workers assigned to a film studio in Berlin during the last days of the war. In *Hyrder* (1970; Shepherds), Seeberg called for a greater sense of mutual responsibility in the relatively untroubled Danish welfare state, an argument that has marked Seeberg's subsequent production. A similar thread also runs through the later work of Sarvig and Skou-Hansen.

Sven Holm's *Termush—Atlanterhavskysten* (1967; *Termush*) describes an atomic disaster, while short novels such as *Langt borte taler byen med min stemme* (1976; Far Away the City Speaks with My Voice) focus on lives coming apart in Copenhagen, his favorite setting. Disorientation, if not disintegration, shapes Sven Åge Madsen's *Besøget* (1963; The Visit), in which a man dwells in a mysterious hotel, directed by some distant authority, and *Lystbilleder* (1964; Pictures of Lust), in which a rape is seen from several points of view. Madsen called this second work an *uroman,* or non-novel. Irresponsibility, fey humor, and pervasive melancholy characterize Frank Jæger's mock Wertheriad *Den unge Jægers Lidelser* (1953; The Sufferings of Young Jæger), *Danskere: Tre fortællinger af Fædrelandets historie* (1966; Danes: Three Tales from the History of the Fatherland),

and *Døden i Skoven* (1970; Death in the Forest). The 1960s also saw the rediscovery of the work of Albert Dam, who had written *Mellem de to søer* (1906; Between the Two Lakes) and *Saa kom det ny brødkorn* (1934; Thus There Came New Bread-Grain) decades earlier.

The dominant voice of the 1970s and 1980s belonged to Klaus Rifbjerg, who first made a name for himself as a lyric poet. Rifbjerg's œuvre displays a constant curiosity about humanity that has had a strong appeal for the Danish reading public. His novels are always located in recent or contemporary Denmark (or Europe), even the fantastic *De hellige aber* (1981; *Witness to the Future*), in which two boys in the occupied Denmark of 1941 crawl through a cave and come up 40 years later, finding the city in an uproar at the prospect of nuclear war. *Den kroniske oskyld* (1958; The Chronic Innocent) is a novel about the entanglements of puberty in the vein of Schack's *Phantasterne*. No one in Rifbjerg's novels is quite sound. The sybaritic middle-aged mathematics professor in *Operaelskeren* (1966; The Opera Lover), deeply devoted to his wife, becomes involved with a Norwegian diva, a situation ending for the amateur Don Juan in his total emotional dissolution. In *Et bortvendt ansigt* (1977; A Face Turned Away), the conventional middle-aged Henrik, also happily married, is nonetheless a kind of Tristan yearning for an Isolde, whom he finds, disastrously, in a student revolutionary. A female protagonist in Rifbjerg's gallery of tormented personalities is *Anna (jeg) Anna* (1969; Anna [I] Anna). Rifbjerg's vaunted ability to create extraordinary but quite believable female characters has recently found a rival in Peter Høeg, whose *Frøken Smillas fornemmelse for sne* (1992; *Smilla's Sense of Snow*) has become an international best-seller. Høeg's work is similar to Rifbjerg's in many respects, but he lacks Rifbjerg's highly professional sense of brevity, coherence, and form.

Thorkild Hansen's documentary novels on painful episodes from Danish history challenge traditional genre distinctions in that they could easily be taken for scholarly monographs. *Det lykkelige Arabien* (1962; *Arabia Felix*), on an ill-fated scientific expedition of the 1760s, *Jens Munk* (1965; *The Way to Hudson Bay*), on a catastrophic voyage to the Canadian sub-arctic during the reign of Christian IV, and a trilogy on the Danish slave trade, *Slavernes kyst* (1967; The Slave Coast), *Slavernes Skibe* (1968; The Slave Ships), and *Slavernes Øer* (1970; The Slave Islands), have all been well received. Hansen's investigation of the trial of the aged Knut Hamsun, *Processen mod Hamsun* (1978; The Case Against Hamsun), won him no friends in Norway. Henrik Stangerup's historical fiction, *Vejen til Lagoa Santa* (1981; The Road to Lagoa Santa) on the Danish naturalist Peter Vilhelm Lund and *Det er svært at dø i Dieppe* (1985; It Is Hard to Die in Dieppe) on the fate of the Danish critic P.L. Møller, is in much the same vein as Hansen's work.

In Denmark as in the rest of the North, woman's literature underwent a radical expansion after about 1970. But even before then, several women writers had made a mark, including Tove Ditlevsen. Ditlevsen first attracted attention in 1941, when she wrote a novel about child molestation, *Man gjorde et barn fortræd* (Someone Harmed a Child). She cast a wholly unsentimental light on the slums of Copenhagen she came from in *Barndomens gade* (1943; Childhood's Street). The much more free-wheeling Elsa Gress wrote largely about her own life in novels and memoirs and offered a model to Suzanne Brøgger, whose autobiographical *Fri os fra kærligheden* (1973; Deliver Us from

Love) and *Crème Fraiche* (1978; Sour Cream) defy genre norms and are highly critical of Danish society. Dea Trier Mørch's work has hewed to a much more traditional line, with paeans to motherhood in *Aftenstjernen* (1982; *Evening Star*) and *Vinterbørn* (1976; *Winter's Child*). Kirsten Thorup has written "factual novels" about the development of a young girl on the island of Fyn in the 1950s, *Lille Jonna* (1977; Little Jonna) and *Den lange sommer* (1979; The Long Summer). In *Baby* (1976), she explored female sexual degradation in a brittle society devoid of genuine love. Following the persistent urge of Scandinavian authors to write in series, she expanded and continued her Jonna books in *Himmel og Helvede* (1982; Heaven and Hell) and *Den yderste grænse* (1987; The Outermost Boundary).

Finland and Finnish-Language Literature

Finland had a very rich oral tradition, with the Kalevala epic and the folk songs of the Kanteletar, but Finnish became a written language only with the Bible translations of the Reformation and did not receive official status until 1863, by order of the liberal czar Alexander. Every educated Finnish speaker also spoke Swedish and could read Danish and Dano-Norwegian, making for strong connections between the different literatures, reinforced by the fact that many Finnish novels were immediately translated into Swedish and so became available to Finland's Swedish speakers and the rest of Scandinavia.

Soon after the official recognition of Finnish, Aleksis Kivi (pseudonym of Alexis Stenvall) wrote a novel of world rank, *Seitsemän veljestä* (1870; *Seven Brothers*), a story of seven youths who flee to the wilderness to evade the Lutheran Church's requirement that they learn to read and write before confirmation. At first attacked because of its boisterous depiction of willful ignorance and sloth, its mixture of comical, mythological, pedagogical, and tragic elements was slowly but surely appreciated, and it became a national novel, enjoyed and interpreted at many levels.

During the remarkable expansion of Finnish literature in the 1880s and 1890s, the impact of realism, primarily in the depiction of social problems, was quickly evident. The playwright Minna Canth assailed sexual inequality in the novel *Hanna* (1886), while *Köyhää kansaa* (1886; Poor Folk) demanded responsible care for the mentally ill. Teuvo Pakkala was a pioneer of the collective novel long before Denmark's Hans Kirk exploited the genre in *Fiskerne*. Pakkala's best collective novel is *Vaaralla* (1891; On the Hill), focusing on social class rather than individuals. Pakkala also experimented with narrative strategy, as in *Pieni elämäntarina* (1902; A Little Story of a Life), which tells its story not consecutively but in flashes. His work is particularly strong in psychological analysis.

Juhani Aho (born Johannes Brofeldt) is better known for his short stories, but his novels are also important in the Finnish canon. *Rautatie* (1884; The Railroad) reflects the impact of the railroads on a small community. *Papin tytär* (1885; The Parson's Daughter) and *Papin rouva* (1893; The Parson's Wife) consider the aspirations and ultimate disappointments of the intellectually gifted and emotionally thwarted Elli. Aho's later work departs from his realist beginnings: his neoromantic historical novel *Panu* (1897), set in 17th-century Karelia, presents its eponymous hero, a shaman, as the last champion of paganism. *Juha* (1911), again set in Karelia, is a novel about adultery and suicide that casts the border province as a hotbed of passion.

Other writers carried this neoromanticism forward into the 20th century. Volter Kilpi's early short novels in poetic prose, *Bathseba* (1900), *Parsifal* (1902), and *Antinous* (1903), took up in turn three great themes of the European fin de siècle: overwhelming passion, artistic vocation and purity, and the contemplation of beauty. Echoes of Walter Pater and Oscar Wilde can easily be heard. Johannes Linnankoski (pseudonym of Vihtori Peltonen) was responsible for a pleasantly vulgar contribution in somewhat the same vein, with *Laulu tulipunaisesta kukasta* (1905; *The Song of the Blood-Red Flower*), a great success at home and abroad, thanks to its operetta-like plot and its improbably virile hero.

A disciple of Lev Tolstoi and an ardent nationalist, Arvid Järnefelt wrote novels marked—and sometimes weighed down—by his patriotism. *Isänmaa* (1893; The Fatherland) offers a particularly clear example of Järnefelt's politics. One of his characters, with the author's evident approval, demands that all Swedish-speakers leave Finland. Although his novels were widely read, he found complete critical favor only with *Greeta ja hänen Herransa* (1925; Greeta and Her Lord), in which an elderly Swedish-speaking woman, whose son has married a Finn, tries to come to terms with the son's suicide, both in her relationship to the widow and to her Christian faith. Järnefelt's fictionalized account of his gifted but difficult parents, *Vanhempieniromaani* (1928–30; My Parent's Novel), depicts the new Finnish intelligentsia of the 1880s and 1890s.

By the turn of the century, Swedish hegemony in Finland's economic, governmental, and cultural life was rapidly waning. Czarist rule showed little respect for Finnish autonomy. The landless people of the countryside were growing restive, and the new urban proletariat was drawn toward a radical socialism. In response to a program of Russification, a persistent demand for independence arose, particularly among younger intellectuals. Internal unrest erupted repeatedly during the first decade of the new century, and news of the Russian Revolution of October 1917 was followed by a wave of political killings, mostly carried out by members of the revolutionary Red Guard, opposed by a conservative "defense corps." On 6 December 1917, Lenin granted Finland independence; on 30 January 1918, a short and brutal civil war broke out between the Whites and the Reds, who were sometimes joined by officerless Russian army units left behind in Finland. Carl Gustaf Mannerheim, who had served in the imperial Russian army, commanded a White officer corps made up in good part of Finlanders who had volunteered in the German army. The Whites triumphed, with the aid of a German expeditionary force, and terrible acts of reprisal ensued. After the end of World War II, Finland officially became a republic.

During these tumultuous years, the novel often served as an indicator of moods in the country. The imperious Maila Talvio had started out with a cogent demand for much needed reform of the tenant farm system in *Pimeänpirtin hävitys* (1901; The Destruction of the Dark Cottage). Her subsequent work, once much read, contrasted the purity of the Finnish countryside with the rottenness of the capital, which still had a significant Swedish presence. Her *Niniven lapset* (1915; Children of Nineveh) indicates by its very title what her argument was: Finns were corrupted by high living and Swedish associations. She moved ever farther to the right with *Kurjet* (1919; The Cranes), about the civil war, and the historical trilogy *Itämeren tytär* (1926–30; The Daughter of the Baltic), in which she presents the city as throwing off its Swedish beginnings in order to fulfill a Finnish destiny.

Aino Kallas (born Aino Krohn) was the first Finnish-language author to attract substantial attention in the anglophone world. Married to an Estonian, Kallas wrote about Estonia. Her early novel *Ants Raudjalg* (1907) expresses her shock at the double oppression of Estonian peasants by the German aristocracy and the Russian bureaucracy. Reverting to neoromanticism, she came fully into her own with her short, tragic "ballad novels," written in an archaizing language, about 16th- and 17th-century Estonia, including *Barbara von Tisenhusen* (1923), in which a blue-blooded girl is tried and drowned by her family for falling in love with a clerk. In *Reigin pappi* (1926; The Pastor of Reigi), the wife of the pastor on the island of Hiiumaa falls in love with her husband's curate. They run away and are apprehended and executed. (The story is told by the cuckolded husband.) *Sudenmorsian* (1928; The Wolf's Bride) is the tale of a forester's wife who can assume a wolf's shape and is killed by her husband's silver bullet.

Such neoromantic work stands in strong contrast to the social criticism of Ilmari Kianto, whose *Punainen viiva* (1909; The Red Line) is an indictment of the grinding poverty of the Finnish backwoods and the empty promises of democracy. The red line is the mark of illiterate voters, and it is the bloody mark left when the central character is killed by a bear. *Punainen viiva* also has strong elements of humor and continues the tradition established by Kivi. In his *Ryysyrannan Jooseppi* (1924; Joseph of Ryysyranta), Kianto likewise treats his lazy protagonist, a bootlegger and the father of many children, with affectionate contempt. Joel Lehtonen—whose first novel, *Paholaisen viulu* (1904; The Devil's Violin), was in the neoromantic mode—also deconstructed the time-honored literary picture of the backwoods hero in *Putkinotko* (1919–20). The novel is a condemnation of the pastoral dreams of the bourgeoisie and the inability of the peasantry to understand or even to imagine an improvement in their lot.

Other authors who began writing in the troubled years before the civil war similarly portrayed feckless and irresponsible country and village folk. Maria Jotuni began with cynical short stories about love in *Rakkautta* (1907; Love) and then wrote a collective novel, *Arkielämää* (1909; Everyday Life), in which the central character persuades the inhabitants of a remote village to confess their secret sorrows and pleasures. The radical journalist Maiju Lassila, pseudonym of Algoth Tietäväinen-Untola, published his *Tulitikkuja lainaamassa* (1910; Borrowing Matches), in which a naïve but goodhearted farmer sets out to borrow matches and, with a crony, manages in short order to get himself thrown into jail.

During the civil war, the variously idealized or smiled-at inhabitants of the Finnish countryside suddenly became monsters in White eyes, capable of terrible atrocities. Frans Eemil Sillanpää exposed the political motivation of this demonization in *Hurskas kurjuus* (1919; Meek Heritage). Ground down by years of poverty, the protagonist is swept along by the Red Guards, captured, and executed by the Whites after a court-martial of which he understands almost nothing. Sillanpää's sympathy with harmless little people, often victimized, was also the inspiration of *Nuorena nukkunut* (1931; The Maid Silja), a story of an innocent girl who blissfully dies young, and *Ihmiset suviyössä* (1934; People in the Summer Night), which portrays people who are good because they have not been abused. Sillanpää was awarded the Nobel prize for literature in 1939.

The 1920s and 1930s brought more variety to the Finnish novel. In 1928, Mika Waltari published *Suuri illusioni* (The Great Illusion), about Helsinki's well-educated and well-to-do middle-class Finnish youth. Waltari proved to be startlingly prolific, and his short psychological novels, including *Ei koskaan huomispäivää!* (1942; *Never a Tomorrow*) and *Fine van Brooklyn* (1943), received much critical acclaim. But he won an international reputation with his historical epics, compared in their day to Thomas Mann's Joseph novels. *Sinuhe egyptilainen* (1945; *Sinuhe the Egyptian*) became a Hollywood film. Waltari then quickly wrote *Mikael Karvajalka* (1948; *Michael the Finn*), *Mikael Hakim* (1949; *The Sultan's Renegade*), and *Johannes Angelos* (1952; *The Dark Angel*). With *Turms, kuolematon* (1955; *The Etruscan*) he repeated the feat of *Sinuhe the Egyptian,* hanging an amazingly detailed reconstruction of an ancient civilization on a somewhat flimsy plot.

Pentti Haanpää's *Kenttä ja kasarmi* (1928; Exercise Field and Barracks), an unsparing attack on the brutal training methods of the Finnish army, so upset patriotic reviewers that for the next seven years no publisher would touch his work. During this enforced silence, he wrote *Noitaympyrä* (1956; The Magic Circle), considered to be his best work, which takes up the theme of a retreat into the wilderness from an unbearable and hypocritical "civilized" world. *Vääpeli Sadon tapaus* (1956; The Case of Sergeant Sato) deals with the sadism of petty authority. Pessimism and grim humor also mark *Jauhot* (1949; Grain), which is based on a historical event, when peasants seized a government granary during the great famine of 1867–68.

At about the same time, Volter Kilpi embarked on a second career as a novelist, leaving his neoromantic beginnings far behind and associating himself with the tradition of sly humor and tragic undercurrents begun by Kivi. In 1933, he published the giant *Alastalon salissa* (In the Hall of Alastalo), in which he tried to capture, almost minute by minute, the doings of the shipowners, captains, fishermen, and farmers who had been his forebears in extreme southwestern Finland. The slow tempo of the work, which relies on minutely recalled conversation and slow-motion action, has limited its popularity, but admirers regard him as a neglected colleague of James Joyce, Marcel Proust, Hermann Broch, and Robert Musil.

For Finland, World War II began with the "Winter War" of 1939–40, which put an end to the class hatred and the language squabble left over from the civil war. Even Haanpää could bring himself to adopt a patriotic stand in *Korpisota* (1940; Wilderness War), one of the many works of fiction to emerge from what was rightly seen as a justified and heroic conflict. Yet the "Continuation War" (1940–44), in which the Finnish army invaded Soviet Karelia with the grandiose goal of creating a "Great Finland" on the model of Hitler's "Grossdeutschland," was viewed with a vast scepticism, as expressed by Haanpää's *Yhdeksän miehen saappaat* (1945; Nine Men's Boots), in which the same pair of boots passes from one trooper to another. The "Lapland War" took place in the winter and spring of 1944–45, when an army made up of young draftees was sent to the north of Finland to drive German forces into Arctic Norway. Parts of Karelia were permanently incorporated into the Soviet state, Finnish reparations to the Soviets caused economic hardships, and war crimes trials contributed to a mood of great anxiety.

Positive developments included the emergence of a more egalitarian society, a rapprochement to the rest of Scandinavia, and a more questioning attitude toward long-accepted norms, allowing a more open mentality and a more experimental literature.

The most striking novel to come out of the war was *Tuntematon sotilas* (1954; *Unknown Soldier*) by Väinö Linna. Using the conversations and experiences of a small group of enlisted men, Linna demonstrates the grimy valor of the Finnish soldier without glorifying the war itself. Linna's other great accomplishment was the trilogy *Täällä Pohjantähden alla* (1959–62; Here Beneath the North Star), which comments on the difficult moments in Finnish history by following three generations of a poor farm family.

Lauri Viita made a contribution to social realism with *Moreeni* (1950; The Moraine), set in working-class Pispala, a run-down but fiercely independent community. *Moreeni* parallels Linna's trilogy in that the time span is roughly the same, but it focuses on the industrial, not the agricultural, proletariat. Viita also displays a stronger sense of irony. In somewhat the same spirit, Eeva Joenpelto took a small town in Uusimaa in southern Finland as her bailiwick in a series of novels beginning with *Neito kulkee vetten päällä* (1955; *The Maiden Walks upon the Water*). Her work, particularly *Elämän rouva, rouva Glad* (1982; *The Bride of Life*), portrays strong women and is popular among moderate feminists.

The psychological novel was developed by Jorma Korpela, who depicted a disappointed idealist in *Martinmaa, mies henkilö* (1948; Martinmaa, A Male Being) and an icy individualist who undergoes a shattering mental crisis in *Tohtori Finckelmann* (1952; Doctor Finckelmann). The psychological novels of Marja-Liisa Vartio—*Se sitten kevät* (1957; This Then Is Spring), *Mies kuin mies, tyttö kuin tyttö* (1958; Man as Man, Girl as Girl), *Kaikki naiset näkevät unia* (1960; All Women See Dreams), and *Tunteet* (1962; Feelings)—mostly focus on love and are distinguished by their spare and objective style. In *Hänen olivat linnut* (1967; Hers Were the Birds), the satiric undertones of her work develop into wry comedy.

Marko Tapio, pseudonym of Marko Vihtori Tapper, explored the emotional torments of a war veteran in a long interior monologue in *Aapo Heiskanen viikatetanssi* (1956; Aapo Heiskanen's Scythe Dance). Tapio also completed two parts of a planned tetralogy exploring Finnish national psychology and tellingly named *Arktinen hysteria* (Arctic Hysteria): *Vuoden 1939 ensiluma* (1967; The First Snow of 1939) and *Sana todella rakastatko minua* (1968; Tell Me That You Really Love Me).

Paavo Rintala drew on a radical application of Christian tenets in *Kuolleiden evankellumi* (1954; The Gospel of the Dead) and *Rikas ja köyhä* (1955; Rich and Poor). Disturbed by the perversion of moral values during the war, Rintala portrays adolescents led astray by the hectic atmosphere of the times in *Pojat* (1958; The Boys). He dealt with Finland's troubled history during the last Russian years and the first days of the republic in *Mummoni ja Mannerheim* (1980; My Grandmother and Mannerheim) by following the parallel lives of an obscure and humble countrywoman and Carl Gustaf Mannerheim, the vainglorious scion of the Finland-Swedish upper class. His war novel *Sissiluutnantti* (1963; *The Long Distance Patrol*) created a scandal because it included an episode in which an officer develops a sexual relationship with a member of the Finnish women's auxiliary corps, whose "purity" was still a source of national pride.

Veijo Meri also drew on material from the wars but presented it with a sardonic humor. *Manillaköysi* (1957; The Manilla Rope), *Irraliset* (1959; The Rootless Ones), *Vuoden 1918 tapahtumat* (1960; Events of the Year 1918), and *Sujut* (1961; Equal) are highly episodic and revolve around distinctly unheroic characters. Meri also made fun of the absurdities of military life in *Yhden yön tarinat* (1967; Tales of a Single Night) and *Everstin autokuljettaja* (1966; The Colonel's Driver).

Meri's short novels display a resemblance to the *nouveau roman,* which is also the case with the minimalist novels of Antti Hyry, who described his childhood in *Kotona* (1960; At Home), *Isä ja poika* (1971; Father and Son), and *Silta liikkuu* (1975; The Bridge Moves). Similarities to the *nouveau roman* notwithstanding, Hyry's stance also seems disconcertingly like that of the Austrian Adalbert Stifter, another master of noncommittal prose. Paavo Haavikko also espoused an apparent objectivity, writing about a fact-and-object-obsessed salesman who refuses to become involved in *Yksityisiä asoita* (1960; Private Matters), dissecting events leading to a double suicide in *Toinen taiva ja maa* (1961; Another Heaven and Earth), and dispassionately describing the life of a tramp in *Vuodet* (1962; The Years).

The radicalism of the 1960s (even then very muted) was gradually replaced by a belief in the efficacy of political ideologies in the 1970s and by the individualism of the prosperous 1980s. Then, in the 1990s, the collapse of the Soviet Union caused an economic recession. In the novel, these shifts of atmosphere were reflected in the exploration of previously tabooed subjects. A drunken mock-sermon with remarks about Christ's sex life delivered by a character in Hannu Salama's *Juhannustanssit* (1964; The Midsummer Dance) incurred a charge of "intentional blasphemy of God." Found guilty, Salama was sentenced to three months in jail but pardoned by President Kekkonen. Since then, authors have been free to write about whatever they want. Salama himself gave a fictionalized history of a communist group in the working-class community of Pispala in *Siinä näkijä missä tekijä* (1972; Where the Doer Is, There's the Witness). The novel features Harri Salminen, a character who stands in for the author and makes an appearance in almost all of Salama's novels. In *Finlandia* (1976–), Salminen, periodically insane, moves through a similarly psychotic Finnish society.

Alpo Ruuth, who made a debut with *Kämppä* (1969; The Den), set in a working-class neighborhood of Helsinki, is another politically engaged novelist, concerned with such problems as the migration of workers to Sweden (*Kotimaa* [1974; Homeland]) and strife within the People's Democratic Party (*Nousukausi* [1967; Boomtime]). *Korpraali Julin* (1975; Corporal Julin) is similar to Jaroslav Hašek's *The Good Soldier Švejk,* portraying a character who flouts authority in a comparable way.

Kerttu-Kaarina Suosalmi long stood out among women writers because of her obvious unwillingness to espouse a feminist program, sparing neither gender in *Jeesuksen pieni soturi* (1976; The Little Warrior of Jesus), in which a slow-witted junk dealer is caught between a tough business woman and his nervous wife. *Onnen metsämies* (1982; The Huntsman of Happiness) focuses on an egomaniacal male author. *Ihana on Altyn-Köl* (1988; Lovely Is Altyn-Köl) illuminates the emotional and intellectual confusions of the postwar period. Anu Kaipainen, looking farther into the past, comments on the present in *Arkkienkeli Oulussa* (1967; The Archangel in Oulu), about the Russo-Swedish War of 1808–09 and the peace movement of the 1960s. In *Magdaleena ja maailman lapset* (1969; Magdalena and the Children of the World), she uses a dual perspective that encompasses biblical and contemporary matters. Kaipainen may be seen as a magic realist writer, because she incorporates the miraculous in such novels as *Kellomorsian* (1977; The Bell Bride) and *Poimisin heliät hiekat* (1979; I'd Collect the Shining Grains of Sand). Eeva Kilpi achieved international fame with *Tamara* (1972), depicting the quasi-erotic relationship between an impotent paraplegic and a sexually active woman. Kilpi is more interested in solving larger social problems in *Elämä edestakaisin* (1964; Life Round Trip) and *Häätanhu* (1973; The Wedding Dance).

Timo K. Mukka acquired literary-historical importance as the harbinger of a new regionalism. His *Maa on syntinen laulu* (1964; Earth Is a Sinful Song) is a historical account of the struggle between born-again Christianity and the fleshly temptations besetting the people of the far north. *Laulu Sipijan lapsista* (1966; The Song of the Children of Sipija) is also set in the far north. Kalle Päätalo's Koillismaa series, including *Koillismaa* (1960; Our Daily Bread) and *Myrsky Koillismaassa* (1963; Storm over the Land), set against a background of wilderness farming, exemplifies a similar regionalism. Heikki Turunen's *Joensuun Elli* (1974; Elli of Joensuu) and *Kivenpyörittäjän kylä* (1976; Stoneroller's Village) romanticize North Karelia in a similar way. His series about a small farmer and his family ends, inevitably, with a move to the city and complete corruption in *Maan veri* (1987; Blood of the Land). Antti Tuuri depicted his native Ostrobothnia—long notorious for the legendary hot tempers and unreasonableness of its inhabitants—in *Pohjanmaa* (1982; Ostrobothnia), a generational novel bordering on the burlesque in its depictions of a family's peculiarities and festivities. His subsequent work has a more open perspective. *Amerikan raitti* (1986; The Open Road of America) is about migrants from Ostrobothnia in the new world. *Uusi Jerusalem* (1988; The New Jerusalem) is set in the mines of western Canada and the beach towns of Florida. *Maan avaruus* (1989; Breadth of the Earth) searches for a utopian community that turns out not to be so utopian after all.

An altogether different and little observed side of Finland emerges from the work of Daniel Katz, a member of Finland's minute Jewish community. His *Kun isoisä Suomeen hiihti* (1969; When Grandfather Skied to Finland) stands in the Yiddish tradition of the episodic-comic novel. Jewish themes also dominate in *Orvar Kleinin kuolema* (1976; The Death of Orvar Klein) and *Saksalainen sikakoira* (1993; German Schweinehund). The likableness and ambivalence of Katz's heroes inevitably calls to mind characters in Saul Bellow and Bernard Malamud.

Finnish Literature in Swedish

The great strength of Finnish-language literature lies in the novel, while Swedish-language (or "Finland-Swedish") literature has been preeminent in the lyric. However, during the national awakening of the first half of the 19th century, almost all literature was composed in Swedish. The first Finland-Swedish novelist was Zachris Topelius, who primarily wrote historical fiction, such as *Hertiginnan af Finland* (1850; The Duchess of Finland), marred by psychologically simplistic characterization. Fredrika Runeberg also wrote historical novels, including the carefully constructed *Fru Catharina Boije och hennes döttrar* (1859; Mistress Catharina Boije and Her Daughters), about the

Russian occupation of Finland from 1712 to 1721, and the clumsier *Sigrid Liljeholm* (1862), about the civil wars at the end of the 16th century.

The first novel to recognize the Finland-Swedish community as a minority was Karl August Tavaststjerna's *Barndomsvänner* (1892; Childhood Friends), about a singer who ends up as the inglorious inspector of an isolated railroad station. Tavaststjerna's *Hårda tider* (1891; Hard Times) contrasts the self-sacrifice of some members of the Finland-Swedish upper class with the unthinking selfishness of others. *Lille Karl* (1897; Little Karl) recounts the author's own childhood as the son of an estate owner and retired general.

In Gustav Alm, pseudonym of Richard Malmberg, the language struggles of the early 20th century found a bitterly sardonic observer, who condemned both Finnish zealotry and Finland-Swedish narrowness and materialism in his *Höstdagar* (1907; Autumn Days). Alm turned his unblinking gaze on the Swedish-speaking small town in *Herr Agaton Vidbäck och hans vänner* (1915; Mr. Agaton Vidbäck and His Friends). A more fully realized talent belonged to Mikael Lybeck, whose short novels *Den starkare* (1900; The Stronger), *Tomas Indal* (1911), and *Breven till Cecilia* (1920; The Letters to Cecilia) read almost like the late dramas of Henrik Ibsen in their compression and ambivalence. The poet Arvid Mörne described the disillusionment of a sometime activist and socialist in his autobiographical novel *Ett liv* (1925; A Life). In later life, he came to think of his language group as proud remnants of history, standing with their backs to the sea.

Modernism, generally reckoned to be Finland-Swedish literature's greatest age with respect to poetry, also produced some interesting experiments with the novel, including Henry Parland's *Idealrealisation* (1929; Sale of Ideals), about a youthfully cynical visit to the jazz age, and Diktonius' *Janne Kubik* (1932). The latter is a series of cameos, accompanied by authorial commentaries, of a member of the Red Guard, a rumrunner during Finland's prohibition, a fascist sympathizer, a prematurely aged dockworker, and other disreputable characters. Diktonius, who was completely bilingual, claimed that *Janne Kubik* was conceived in Finnish and published the "original," *Janne Kuutio,* in 1946.

Hagar Olsson, the premier modernist literary critic, made her mark as a novelist as well. Her one unflawed triumph is the Dickensian and autobiographical *Chitambo* (1932), named after the village in Africa where David Livingstone died. Her fairy-tale novel, *Träsnidaren och döden* (1940; The Woodcarver and Death), tells the story of a woodcarver who, drawn to mysterious Karelia, learns to understand the nature of existence when he witnesses the death of the unintentionally abused child of an irresponsible horse-trader. Eva Wichman's *Mania* (1937) and *Ohörbart vattenfall* (1944; Inaudible Waterfall) and Margit Niininen's *Tora Markman och hennes syster* (1936; Tora Markman and Her Sister) are notable for their portraits of female characters.

Jarl Hemmer made a powerful statement about the civil war in his *En man och hans samvete* (1931; A Fool of Faith), in which a defrocked pastor, a volunteer chaplain who witnesses the White atrocities committed at the concentration camp on Suomenlinna in Helsinki harbor, takes the place of a married prisoner about to be executed. Sigrid Backman's *Ålandsjungfrun* (1919; The Åland Maid) is a legend about the last days of the civil war involving a seamstress, a kind of Undine figure who drowns herself when her lover is executed by a White court-martial. Three of Backman's novels are set in Punavuoret, a bilingual working-class district in Helsinki. *Familjen Brinks öden* (1922; The Fates of the Brink Family) describes the tragedies and injustices of the war; *Bostadslaget Sjuan i Lergränden* (Condominium Company Number Seven in Mud Alley) chronicles the comic errors of a housing cooperative; and *De fåvitska trollen* (1932; The Foolish Trolls) is a novel in praise of free spirits like the heroine, a stand-in for the author.

A general disengagement from reality marked Finland-Swedish novels of the 1930s and 1940s. Narratives from these years have the air of ignoring their own Helsinki background. Many are set in a dream-like Karelia, including Olof Enckell's *Ett klosteräventyr* (1930; A Cloister Adventure) and Göran Stenius' *Det okända helgonets kloster* (1934; The Cloister of the Unknown Saint), or in the Russian Orthodox refugee enclaves of Estonia, as portrayed by the convert Tito Colliander in *Korståget* (1937; The Procession with the Cross). A comparable exoticism can be found in the classic novels of childhood by Oscar Parland, who had already painted a lightly concealed family portrait of great sophistication and subtlety in *Förvandlingar* (1945; Transformations), which is influenced by Thomas Mann, Marcel Proust, and the Russian novelist Juriy Olyeshya. Taking place during World War I and the Russian Revolution on a tumbledown Karelian estate, Parland's *Den förtrollade vägen* (1953, 1974; The Enchanted Way) is an account of a loving if bizarre extended family and almost mythical natural surroundings. Intimations of violent death appear in *Tjurens år* (1962; The Year of the Bull).

Christer Kihlman caused a change of mood by accusing the Finland-Swedish novel of bloodlessness, total estrangement from the rest of Finland's population, and empty devotion to tradition. His *Se upp Salige!* (1960; Watch Out, Ye Blest!) gives a merciless commentary on the willful irrelevance of the Finland-Swedish community. The novel is set in "Lexå," from the Latin *lex,* or law, a name coined to emphasize the exaggerated Finland-Swedish respect for the Swedish legal code. The novel provoked a towering dislike among conservative Finland-Swedes, who spoke of birds that dirty their own nest. *Den blå modern* (1963; The Blue Mother) is a sequel examining a Finland-Swedish industrial family. *Madeleine* (1965), using some of the same characters, is an attack on the bourgeoisie in the wake of the murder of John F. Kennedy. *Dyre prins* (1978; Sweet Prince) and *Gerdt Bladhs undergång* (1987; The Downfall of Gerdt Bladh) are the first volumes of a multivolume family novel about another Finland-Swedish family. Despite his early call for a novel reflecting the whole of Finland's society, then, Kihlman's novels confine themselves to the narrow upper-class Finland-Swedish community.

Jörn Donner began with a familiar sort of autobiographical novel, *Jag, Erik Anders* (1955; I, Erik Anders), and *Bordet* (1957; The Table). Much later, he wrote a serial family novel beginning with *Nu måste du* (1974; Now You Must). Because of the skill with which he moves through the minefields of patrician intrigue, industry, and finance, Donner has been called a Finland-Swedish Balzac, but his characters do not always come to life.

Henrik Tikkanen made a career of parading the real or fancied eccentricities of the Finland-Swedish upper-middle class. His early novels *Hjältarna är döda* (1961; The Heroes Are Dead) and *Ödlorna* (1965; The Lizards) are about his experiences as a young volunteer in the Continuation War. He then launched an autobiographical series, beginning with *Brändövägen 8. Brändö. Tel.35* (1975; A Winter's Day), in which he recounts all the embarrassing details of his family's life. His *30-åriga kriget* (1977; The Thirty Years' War) is based on his own *Unohdettu sotilas* (1974; The Forgotten Soldier), an earlier Finnish-language text, and on newspaper stories of a Japanese soldier left behind on Guam in 1945, unaware that the war had ended. *Efter hjältedöden* (1979; After the Hero's Death) is a sequel.

Märta Tikkanen embarked on her literary career in *Nu imorron* (1970; Now Tomorrow) and *Ingenmansland* (1972; No Man's Land), narratives about a troubled couple, easily recognizable in hindsight as the Tikkanens themselves. She branched out into more objective discussions of male dominance and brutality such as *Män kan inte våldtas* (1975; Manrape), in which a woman, offended by a man's improper advances, takes revenge by raping him. Her subsequent work has been mostly in verse.

Other novelists of considerable talent have pursued a less sensational kind of narrative. Hans Fors' *Livets bryggor: En berättelse om Österbotten* (1980; Life's Bridges: A Tale about Ostrobothnia) and *Under höga träd* (1990; Beneath Lofty Trees) have their roots in his home province. Anders Cleve's dithyrambic novels, influenced by Thomas Wolfe, are hymns of love to his native Helsinki. Johann Bargum's tightly made, laconic novels often specialize in family mysteries.

The Finland-Swedish novel displays a greater diversity since 1960. Kjell Westö has taken up a much younger generation's identity problems. Pirkko Lindberg's *Byte* (1991; Prey) registers a sharp awareness of the possibilities of linguistic play. Fredrik Lång's *Porträttet av Direktör Rask* (1988; The Portrait of Director Rask) tells of the rise and fall of the founder of a timber-export firm, determined to erase the stigma of his father's rumored communism. In Lars Sund's *Colorado Avenue* (1990), a young woman migrates to America before World War I, marries a fellow Ostrobothnian who is later killed in a labor dispute at Telluride, and goes back to Finland as a veritable "Dollar Hanna." Sund is a virtuoso narrator, full of feints and dodges, appealing to an altogether different audience than did the venerated Anni Blomquist, whose tales of skerry life in Åland were made into a long-running television series. Ulla-Lena Lundberg created a special kind of family novel out of the great Åland sailing tradition in *Leo* (1989), *Stora världen* (1991; The Great World), and *Allt man kan önska sig* (1995; Everything One Could Wish For). These fictions answer Kihlman's call for a more open Finland-Swedish novel.

The Faroe Islands

The Faroe Islands possess a rich popular heritage of ballads and folktales, but the novel developed only in the 20th century. A first novel in Faroese, *Bábelstornid* (1909; The Tower of Babel), by Regin i Líd, pseudonym of Rasmus Rasmussen, was issued in newspaper installments. It dealt with the contrasts between the Faroese and Danish temperaments, with the tensions between an extremely conservative peasant mentality and currents for reform, and with the islands' desire for independence from Denmark.

The literary critic Jørgen-Frantz Jacobsen left an almost finished novel, *Barbara* (1939), at his death. A singular work about sexual compulsion and sexual destruction, *Barbara* became a classic in Denmark, fitting well into the tradition of short erotic novels by such authors as Jens Peter Jacobsen and Jørgen Nielsen. His cousin, William Heinesen, gave the book a final polishing. Heinesen emerged as a novelist in his own right with *Blæsende Gry* (1934, 1961; Stormy Daybreak) and *Noatun* (1938; Niels Peter), both collective novels in the fashion of Hans Kirk's *Fiskerne* (1938). *Den sorte Gryde* (1949; The Black Cauldron) is a satirical picture of the moral decay fostered in Tórshavn by the prosperity of World War II, a rot embodied in the profiteer Oppermann. *De fortabte Spillemænd* (1950; The Lost Musicians) is again set in Tórshavn, but now at the beginning of the century. With its musical structure in four movements and its core group of amateur musicians, all portrayed with whimsical affection by the creator, it is the most immediately appealing of Heinesen's works. *Moder Syvstjerne* (1952; The Kingdom of Heaven), containing several characters from *The Lost Musicians*, recounts the various spiritual and emotional experiences of a small boy. *Det gode Håb* (1946; The Lively Hope) is set in Tórshavn in 1669 and 1670 when the islands were held in personal fief by King Fredrik III's privy councillor and his son. This most disciplined of Heinesen's works is an epistolary novel in which the Danish pastor Peder Børresen describes the evils he attempts to oppose.

The third important novelist from the Faroes, Hedín Brú, pseudonym of Hans Jacob Jacobsen, was the first novelist of artistic importance to write in the mother tongue. His semi-autobiographical novels about village life—*Lognbrá* (1939; Mirage) and *Fastatøkur* (1935; Firm Grip)—take a sensitive farmboy out to sea, into the world of love, and back to the family homestead. *Leikum fagurt* (1948; Fair Play) is a satirical account of Faroese political life and the struggle for self-determination. Brú's *Fedgar á ferd* (1940; The Old Man and His Sons) presents traditional Faroese ways as no longer tenable in the 20th century.

Iceland

The first Icelandic novels were written by Jón Thorodssen, whose *Piltur og stúlka* (1850; Bachelor and Girl) seems to have been inspired by the comical characters in the novels of Walter Scott and Charles Dickens. *Madur og kona* (1876; Man and Wife) has the same cheerful mood and happy ending as its predecessor. Both novels, in their good spirits and peasant coloring, are equivalents of Norwegian poetic realism. A more disturbing and original work was the burlesque *Sagan af Heljarslódarorrustu* (1861; The Saga of the Battle on Hell Field), Benedikt Sveinbjarnarson Gröndal's retelling of the Battle of Solferino. This satirical narrative uses the language of the Icelandic chivalric sagas (*riddara sögur*) but with a strong admixture of the slang spoken by Icelandic students in Copenhagen.

In the next decades, Icelandic novelists tried to apply the social realism advocated by Georg Brandes. Einar Hjörleifsson Kvaran wrote a pair of novels, *Ofurefli* (1908; Overwhelming Odds) and *Gull* (1911; Gold), that concerned themselves with the capital's growing bourgeoisie and its materialism. Jón Stefánsson, who published under the pseudonym Thorgils Gjallandi, wrote about the difficulties of life in extreme isolation in *Upp vid fossa* (1902; Up by the Rapids). Jón Trausti, pseudonym of Gudmundar Magnússon, wrote about farm life in *Halla* (1906) and *Heidarbylid* (1911; The Heath Farm), turning to political themes in *Leysing* (1907; Spring Floods), *Borgir* (1909; Castles), and *Bessi gamli* (1918). Finally, he tried historical subjects in *Sögur frá Skaftáreldi* (1912–13; Stories from the Skafta Eruption) and *Góðir stofnar* (1914–15; Good Stock).

Gunnar Gunnarsson was determined to break out of the geographical and linguistic isolation of his native country, leaving Iceland at 18 and creating the largest part of his work in Danish to reach a larger public. He began with a family tetralogy under the collective name *Af Borgslægtens Historie* (1913–14; From the History of the Family at Borg). *Salige er de enfoldige* (1920; Seven Days' Darkness) is a disaster novel about the eruption of Mount Hekla and the Spanish flu epidemic in 1918. After a five-volume autobiographical suite, Gunnarsson entered a historical phase, choosing sensational or stirring episodes from Icelandic history, as in the tightly constructed *Svartfugl* (1929; The Black Cliffs), on a double murder that took place in 1802 amid the "pestilential atmosphere" of an inaccessible farm, and *Jón Arason* (1930), the dramatic story of the last Catholic bishop of Iceland, executed with his two sons in 1550.

Kristmann Gudmundsson wrote novels dealing—in Norwegian—with erotic passion, earning him a reputation as a northern D.H. Lawrence, particularly for *Livets morgen* (1929; Morning of Life). Gudmundur (Jónsson) Kamban's European reputation was based on his Danish-language dramas and the historical novel *Skálholt* (1930–35; partially translated as The Virgin of Skalholt), based on a notorious 17th-century family conflict. *Jeg ser et stort skønt land* (1936; I See a Great Fair Land), portraying masterful Nordic men, brings out his racial politics.

Gudmundar Gíslason Hagalín's work is distinguished by his use of the speech of the Western Fjords in *Vestan úr fjördum* (1924; From the West out of the Fjords), a celebration of the independent patriarch who battles nature. The novel may have been influenced by Knut Hamsun's Nobel prize-winning *Markens grøde* (1917; The Growth of the Soil). Unlike Hamsun's, Hagalín's old-fashioned hero succumbs to the forces of the modern world. The clash between the old and the new and an admiration for obstinacy recurs in almost all of Hagalín's novels, most memorably in the portrait of a stubborn old woman in *Kristrún í Hamravík* (1933; Kristrún at Hamravík).

Thórbergur Thórdarson's whimsical eccentricity finds expression in the unusual *Bréf til Láru* (1924; Letter to Laura), a giant letter in 36 sections to a young woman in northern Iceland. The letter serves as a framework for yarns, essays, fragments of autobiography, and reflections on superstition, spiritism, socialism, and communism. In the semi-autobiographical *Íslenzkur adall* (1938; partially translated as In Search of My Beloved), Thórdarson turned his gift for comedy on himself, as he did in the autobiographical *Ofvitinn* (1940–41; The All Too Wise One).

Halldór Kiljan Laxness made a breakthrough as a novelist with *Vefarinn mikli frá Kasmír* (1927; The Great Weaver from Kashmir), a veiled autobiographical work about a gifted and sensitive youth. Laxness then spent some time in the United States, an experience that seems to have driven him back to his Icelandic roots, because his next novels—*Thú vínviður hreini* (1931; Thou Pure Vine) and *Fuglinn í fjörunni* (1932; The Bird on the Beach), later issued together as *Salka Valka*—portray a small Icelandic fishing community struggling to retain its identity despite the encroachments of commercial interests. Laxness' internationally most popular work, *Sjálfstætt folk* (1934–35; Independent People) is a de-romanticization of the Icelandic small

farmer. The four-volume *Heimsljós* (1937–40; World Light) is a remarkable extended character portrayal based on the life of the minor poet, Magnús Hjaltason. The historical trilogy *Íslandsklukkan* (1943–46; Iceland's Bell) is set around 1700, when Iceland's impotence under Danish rule and German mercantile power was at its worst. Its unadorned style is said to have been influenced by Ernest Hemingway's *A Farewell to Arms* (1929), which Laxness had translated in 1941. *Gerpla* (1952; The Happy Warriors), written in mock-saga style, reaches back to the 11th century, using *Fóstbrœdra saga* (The Foster Brothers Saga) as the basis for reflections on World War II and the Cold War. Laxness was awarded the Nobel prize in 1955.

No subsequent Icelandic novelist has been able to escape from Laxness' giant shadow. Agnar Thórdarson's *Ef sverd thitt er stutt* (1955; The Sword) is a recasting of the Hamlet story, in which the narrator, sensing that something is rotten in the state of Iceland, attempts to placate his late father's spirit by a futile act of violence. Thórdarson's *Hjartad í borði* (1968; A Medal of Distinction) penetrates further still into the moral decay of Iceland's urban society. Jakobina Sigurdardóttir charges that all authenticity has been lost in Icelandic life in the long monologue *Snaran* (1968; The Snare) and in *Lifandi vatnið* (1974; Living Water). Gudbergur Bergsson's *Tómas Jónsson metsölubok* (1966; Tómas Jónsson Best-Seller) and Thor Vilhjálmsson's *Madurinn er alltaf einn* (1950; The Man Is Always Alone) and *Fljótt, fljótt sagdi fuglinn* (1968; Quick, Quick Said the Bird) offer a similar picture of emptiness, falseness, and self-delusion. Other novels portray a longing for home and traditional ways no longer within reach, such as Indridi G. Thorsteinsson's *79 af stödinni* (1955; 79 from the Station) and *Land og synir* (1963; Land and Sons). Svava Jakobsdóttir's *Leigjandinn* (1969; The Lodger) is an allegory of the American military presence. Her *Gunnladar saga* (1987; The Saga of Gunnlöd) seeks to legitimate feminine creativity in traditional myth.

In the 1970s, Thorgeir Thorgeirsson wrote a documentary novel on the last execution in Iceland (1830), following it with the more unusual *Einleikur á glansmynd* (1976; Solo on a Shining Image), which Thorgeirsson described as "a surrealistic documentary novel," told in a series of dialogues and repeating motifs. The traditional historical novel was represented by Njördar P. Njardvík, whose *Daudamenn* (1982; Dead Men) is a Lutheran pastor's account of his own successful efforts to have a father and son burned at the stake for witchcraft. Einar Kárason's *Thar sem djöflaeyjan ris* (1983; Where the Devil's Island Rises) and *Gulleyjan* (1985; Gold Island), burlesque narratives about Camp Thule, an abandoned American installation squatted by a group of social outcasts, give a very different picture of modern Iceland.

Norway

The first Norwegian novel is Camilla Collett's *Amtmandens Døtre* (1854–55; The District Governor's Daughters), a fictionalized account of Collett's unrequited love for the poet Johan Sebastian Welhaven. The novel offers a detailed portrait of life among the privileged official and clerical classes of Norway, forming the basis for the development of the realist novel.

After this auspicious start, the Norwegian novel entered a golden age. The idealizing peasant stories of Bjørnstjerne Bjørnson—*Synnøve Solbakken* (1857; Trust and Trial), *Arne* (1858), *En glad gut* (1860; A Happy Boy), *Fiskerjenten* (1868; The

Fisher Girl)—established a distinctly Norwegian regionalism. Bjørnson's novels in the realistic style are less successful because of weak characterization.

Jonas Lie was one of the principal representatives of the realist novel of the later 19th century. *Den Fremsynte eller Billeder fra Nordland* (1870; *The Visionary or Pictures from Northland,* also translated as *The Seer*), *Tremasteren "Fremtiden"* (1872; *The Barque "Future"*), and *Lodsen og hans hustru* (1874; *The Pilot and His Wife*) deal with maritime life in the far north. *Livsslaven* (1883; *One of Life's Slaves*), more disillusioned, was influenced by Émile Zola. *Familjen paa Gilje* (1885; *The Family at Gilje*) and *Kommandørens døtre* (1886; *The Commodore's Daughters*) portray the constraints on women and other problems of Norway's increasingly irrelevant upper class. Lie stands out for his impressionistic style, picking out only significant details of setting, atmosphere, and speech.

Alexander Kielland was drawn to the formal polish and social engagement of French literature. His masterpiece, *Garman og Worse* (1880), telling of the decline of a family and a firm, served as a model for Thomas Mann's *Buddenbrooks* (1901). Kielland combined stylistic elegance with a pronounced reformatory zeal: *Skipper Worse* (1882) is an indictment of religious fanaticism; the harrowing *Else* (1881; *Elsie, A Christmas Story*) attacks the sexual exploitation of women; *Arbeidsfolk* (1881; *Workers*) is critical of the cynical tyranny of Kristiania officialdom; and *Gift* (1882; *Poison*) and *Fortuna* (1884; translated with *Gift* as *Professor Lovdahl*) expose the shortcomings of classical education. However, Kielland's contempt for the ill-bred and unrefined, surfacing in his last novel, *Jacob* (1891), reaffirms the traditional class structure.

Amalie Skram, married to the Danish novelist Erik Skram, settled in Copenhagen and became a leading champion of women's rights. *Constance Ring* (1885), exposing the constraints of marriage on women, is a fascinating psychological study. *Lucie* (1888), *Fru Inès* (1891), and *Forraadt* (1892; *Betrayed*) are also concerned with the problems of marriage. Skram told the generational story of a fisher-family's rise and fall in the tetralogy *Hellemyrsfolket* (1887–98; *The People of Hellemy*), but returned to the short form in two autobiographical novels about her own mental illness, *Professor Hieronymus* (1895) and *Paa St. Jørgen* (1895; translated together as *Under Observation*). Skram boldly broached sexual topics at which Lie and Kielland only hinted, but her novels are weighed down by her clumsy style.

Arne Garborg reinvigorated regionalism, writing in a self-constructed *landsmål,* or country language, subsequently called *nynorsk,* or New Norwegian. *Landsmål* was closer to the speech patterns of country folk than normative Dano-Norwegian, which was later transformed into *riksmål.* Garborg employed *landsmål* for his naturalist *Bondestudentar* (1883; *Peasant Students*), *Mannfolk* (1886; *Men*), and *Hjaa ho mor* (1890; *At Mother's*). However, *Trætte Mænd* (1891; *Tired Men*), the diary of a decadent government clerk, was couched in a brilliant Dano-Norwegian and became Norway's prime contribution to the continental literature of the fin de siècle. *Fred* (1892; *Peace*), again in *landsmål,* portrays the religion-ridden home of Garborg's boyhood and his difficult relationship with his father, which remained a theme in his last novels.

Another significant novelist of the late 19th century was Tryggve Andersen, whose *I cancelliraadens dage* (1897; *In the Days of the Councillor*) is a historical novel made up of connected stories. His *Mot Kvæld* (1900; *Toward Evening*) describes the end of the world as beheld in a Norwegian coastal town. Another great stylist, Hans Kinck brought out two novels about a sensitive man caught between Norway's ever more fragile official class and the world of vigorous peasants, *Sus* (1896; *Soughing*) and *Hugormen* (1898; *The Adder*), which were eventually combined under the title *Herman Ek* (1928).

Knut Hamsun called for a break with the realism and naturalism that had dominated Scandinavian literature for the latter part of the 19th century in an essay entitled "From the Unconscious Life of the Soul." His *Sult* (1890; *Hunger*) and *Mysterier* (1892; *Mysteries*) exemplified a new emphasis on psychological analysis, particularly of the irrational forces underlying human behavior. His novels of the 1890s are also notable for their lyrical descriptions of nature and their powerful depictions of love. In subsequent decades, Hamsun's work gravitated to a more traditional realism, including such works as *Børn av tiden* (1913; *Children of the Age*), *Markens grøde* (1917; *The Growth of the Soil*), and *Landstrykere* (1927; *Wayfarers*). *The Growth of the Soil,* in particular, exemplifies a strong nationalist tendency, idealizing a traditional Protestant Norwegian family and its dedication to hard work and obedience. Hamsun received the Nobel prize in 1920, but his achievement was tarnished by his collaboration with the Nazis during World War II, which also throws a suspicious light on the idealism of *The Growth of the Soil.*

Sigrid Undset also set a new direction with her first three novels—*Fru Marta Oulie* (1907; *Mrs. Marta Oulie*), *Jenny* (1911), and *Splinten av troldspeilet* (1917; *Images in a Mirror*)—which focus on the contradictions between new opportunities for women and their traditional duties. But Undset's greatest importance for Norwegian literature lies in her historical trilogy *Kristin Lavransdatter* (1920–22), set in the Middle Ages and chiming in with the growing patriotism of the age. Although the role of women was one of Undset's principal concerns, her masterful depiction of the medieval culture of Norway earned her the Nobel prize in 1928. Undset's subsequent work showed a growing preoccupation with religious questions.

Norwegian nationalism found a counterpoint in Nini Roll Anker's elegies for the old Norway in such novels as *Huset i Søgaten* (1922; *The House on Lake Street*), *I Amtmandsgaarden* (1925; *On the District Governor's Estate*), and *Under Skraataket* (1927; *Beneath the Slanting Roof*), and in Christian Elster's significantly titled *Av skyggernes slægt* (1919; *From the Realm of Shadows*). However, the nationalist novelists who championed peasant culture were generally more successful. Peter Egge trotted out the sturdy people of the hinterland of Trondheim in his *Inne i fjordene* (1920; *Within the Fjords*) and other novels. Gabriel Scott's historical novel *Jernbyrden* (1915; *The Burden of Iron*), set in the south of Norway, pits good peasants against evil officials. Inge Krokann's *I Dovre-sne* (1929; *In Dovre Snow*) considers the troubled 15th century, when Norway was on the eve of Danish rule. The novel is written in *nynorsk,* which Krokann apparently did not see as incompatible with his hope for the preservation of an older, more authentic Norway.

Johan Bojer grappled with the question of the power of falsehood in public life, as in *Et folketog* (1896; *A Procession of the People*) and *Troens magt* (1903; *The Power of a Lie*). The idealistic *Den store hunger* (1916; *The Great Hunger*) sees human and national selfishness as the root of all evil. But Bojer's subsequent work also revolves around the notion that Norwegians possess unusual virtue and strength, whether they live on the Lofoten Islands or in the American Midwest, as in *Den siste Viking* (1921; *The Last of the Vikings*). Ole E. Rølvaag, writing in Minnesota, similarly glorifies Norwegian immigrants in the Midwest in *I de dage* and *Riket grundlægges* (1924–25; translated together as *Giants in the Earth*) and other novels. The nationalist fervor of Bojer and Rølvaag does not make up for the technical weaknesses of their work.

Olav Duun's *Juvikfolke* (1918–23; *The People of Juvik*), a more skillful epic, is written in a highly idiosyncratic *nynorsk*, little resembling the supple *riksmål* of Hamsun and Undset. Kristofer Uppdal, another *nynorsk* epicist, took up the cause of industrial workers in his ten-volume *Dansen genom skyggeheimen* (1911–24; The Dance Through the Realm of Shadows). The best of Johan Falkberget's historical novels, *Den fjerde nattevakt* (1923; *The Fourth Night Watch*), gives a portrait of a community of miners in the early 19th century.

Novelists who struck out in different directions included Johannes Thrap-Meyer, who celebrated the beauty of Oslo in *Anakreons død* (1928; Anacreon's Death), and Cora Sandel (pseudonym of Fabricius), whose Alberte trilogy—*Alberte og Jakob* (1926; *Alberte and Jacob*), *Alberte og friheten* (1931; *Alberte and Freedom*), and *Bare Alberte* (1939; *Alberte Alone*)—presaged many other accounts of women unwilling to take on traditional roles. Sandel's painful and laconically expressed vision had its most bitter expression in *Kranes Konditeri* (1945; *Crane's Café*), which ends with the defeat of the heroine. Tarjei Vesaas, one of the greatest *nynorsk* stylists, initially seemed destined to become a typical peasant writer with such novels as *Det store spelet* (1934; *The Great Cycle*). But he later wrote a series of symbolic and allegorical narratives, including *Kimen* (1940; *The Seed*), which obliquely addresses the dangers of mass hysteria, *Huset i mørkret* (1945; *The House in the Dark*), about occupied Norway, and *Is-slottet* (1963; *The Ice Castle*), an allegory of love. Vesaas' symbolic apparatus can be heavy-handed, but admirers argue that his stripped-down narrations have a hypnotic effect.

Sigurd Hoel, on the other hand, was a vigorous advocate of *riksmål* and published two satirical novels about Norway's linguistic battles, *Sesam Sesam* (1938; Open Sesame) and *Sprogkampen i Norge: En kriminalfortelling* (1951; The Language Struggle in Norway: A Detective Story). Long interested in psychoanalysis, Hoel applied its theories in *Syndere i sommersol* (1927; *Sinners in the Summer Sun*), *En dag i oktober* (1931; *One Day in October*), and *Fjorten dager før frostnettene* (1934; Two Weeks before the Frost Nights). His *Trollringen* (1958; *The Troll Circle*), which has a strong political component, makes extensive use of folklore and symbols.

More spiritual approaches to the psychological novel were explored by Ronald Fangen, a Christian humanist, in *Allerede nu* (1937; Even Now), and by Sigurd Christiansen in *Vort eget liv* (1918; Our Own Life), *Ved Golgota* (1920; At Golgotha), and two trilogies, a family saga and a fictional autobiography. Aksel Sandemose, the most self-revelatory of the explorers of the psyche, wrote his first six works in Danish, then translated the most striking of them, *Klabautermanden* (1927; The Klabauterman), a tale of strange beliefs at sea, into Norwegian in 1932. His work is a disturbing mixture of the tormented Strindberg and the self-aggrandizing Jack London. *En sjöman går iland* (1931;

A Sailor Goes on Land) begins a long series about Sandemose's alter ego. He continued to plumb the depths of erotic and other behavior in *Det svundne er en drøm* (1944; The Past Is a Dream), written in Swedish, and *Tjærhandleren* (1945; The Tar Dealer). Sandemose's *Varulven* (1958; *The Werewolf*) is about the destructive force of the libido and the trauma of adolescence.

World War II and the experience of occupation and collaboration, as well as the aftermath of recrimination and trials, provided material for authors who came into their own during the postwar years. The journalist Sigurd Evensmo scored overnight with his *Englandsfarere* (1945; Boat for England), about the Alesund Gang, a band of Norwegians who, trying to escape to Britain, were apprehended and executed. Johan Borgen, who was imprisoned in the domestic concentration camp of Grini, wrote a trilogy about a character who eventually serves as a border guard for the Nazis and as a guide for Jewish refugees escaping to Sweden. As the war ends, he is hunted down as a collaborator by a mob and drowned. The protagonist of Kåre Holt's *Det store veiskillet* (1949; The Great Crossroads) is split into three different identities, a black marketeer, an informer for the Nazis, and a leader of the home front—a clever way to present the choices Norwegians made in the occupation years. Holt also wrote a long fictional history of organized labor, beginning with *Det stolte nederlag* (1956; The Proud Defeat) and a historical trilogy with the collective title *Kongen* (1965–69; Kings), in which a pretender to the Norwegian throne, in his lust for power, plunges Norway into civil war. Holt also wrote three documentary novels, following the example of Thorkild Hansen in Denmark and Per Olof Enquist in Sweden, that demystify national heroes, including *Kappløpet* (1974: *The Race: A Novel of Polar Exploration*), about the polar explorer Roald Amundsen.

Alfred Hauge's historical novels, less realistically detailed and more spiritual, include *Mysterium* (1967; Mystery) and a trilogy about Norwegian migration to the United States consisting of *Hundevakt* (1961; Dog Watch), *Landkjenning* (1964; Landfall), and *Ankerfeste* (1965; Anchorage), translated together as *Cleng Peerson*. Hauge's later novels, including *Perlemorstrand* (1974; Mother-of-Pearl Shore), conjure up a present-day Norway beset by avarice and anxiety.

Terje Stigen tried theme after theme and setting after setting in novels about the Norwegian past, about World War II, about industrialization, and about imaginary authoritarian states. But his most convincing performances have come in the short novel of psychological tension, including the early *Vindstille underveis* (1956; *An Interrupted Passage*) and *Besettelse* (1970; Obsession), in which a middle-aged teacher falls in love with one of his charges.

Nevertheless, a feeling of estrangement dominates many postwar novels, including Torborg Nedreaas' *Av måneskin gror det ingenting* (1947; *Nothing Grows from Moonshine*), Finn Carling's documentary accounts of groups feared or ignored by society (the blind, homosexuals, the terminally ill), and Carling's novel about nuclear disaster *Museumstekster* (1982; Museum Texts). Brutality became the specialty of Jens Bjørneboe in his trilogy comprised of *Frihetens øjeblikk* (1966; *Moment of Freedom*), *Kruttårnet* (1969; The Powder Tower), and *Stillheten* (1972; The Silence).

Agnar Mykle provoked one of the last obscenity trials because of the unabashed sexual descriptions in his novels about the super-potent Ask Burlefot, *Lasso kring fru Luna* (1954; *Lasso*

Round the Moon) and *Sangen om den røde rubin* (1956; *The Song of the Red Ruby*). Mykle's sensationalism has long since been outdone by Knut Faldbakken, who peers into corners of erotic experience such as incest and necrophilia in *Maude danser* (1971; *The Sleeping Prince*) and other novels.

The second half of the 20th century has also seen many novels with a strong political motivation, possibly inspired by Nedreaas' *De varme hender* (1952; The Warm Hands), in which the writer polemicized against the North Atlantic Treaty Organization. Dag Solstad's Marxism resulted in *Arild Arnes 1970* (1941), in which the protagonist learns to be an "organized communist" in conduct and language. Solstad also wrote three documentary novels on the immediate pre-occupation and occupation years: *Svik: Førkrigsår* (1977; Betrayal: Pre-War Years), *Krig, 1940* (1978; War, 1940), and *Brød og vapen* (1980; Bread and Weapons), about Oslo's working people under the pressure of occupation.

Although the Norwegian novel has never strayed far from realism, a resurgence of traditional realist narrative is notable in new regional narratives. Edvard Hoem, writing in *nynorsk*, showed how honest people have become disoriented and aimless in *Kjærleikens ferjereiser* (1974; *The Ferry Crossing*), in which the mind-deadening movement back and forth across a fjord, from dismal town to dying factory, stands for uneasiness and decay. Kjartan Fløgstad described the changes wrought in a community and family by the shift away from fishing, farming, and—a favored Norwegian calling—the merchant marine to an industrial society, as in *Rasmus* (1974). Jan Kjaerstad's *Speil: Leseserie fra det 20, århundre* (1982; Mirror: A Series of Readings from the Twentieth Century) also avoids the broken narrative line and constant retrospections of postmodernism as it mulls the century's violence and penchant for war. However, Kjaerstad's *Homo falsus eller: Det perfekte mord* (1984; Homo Falsus or The Perfect Murder) does experiment with narrative technique. Herbjørg Wassmo also uses a straightforward realism in her series about Tora, the child of a German soldier and a Norwegian mother, shunned by her self-righteous north Norwegian community and sexually abused by her stepfather, beginning with *Huset med den blinde glassveranda* (1981; *The House with the Blind Glass Windows*).

Sweden

The first Swedish novel, Urban Hiärne's *Stratonice*, written between 1665 and 1668, circulated in manuscript among the members of his Uppsala circle. A roman à clef modeled on Honoré d'Urfé's *L'Astrée* (1607-27), the novel features characters based on the late Karl X Gustaf, his son Karl XI, Hiärne himself, and members of his family and is set in thinly disguised cities of the Swedish empire. *Stratonice* had no progeny, remaining the sole novel of the Swedish baroque. Another early novel, *Adalrik och Giöthildas äfventyr* (1742-44; The Adventures of Adalrik and Giöthilden), by Jacob Mörk and Anders Törngren, inspired by the medieval Icelandic sagas, also remained an isolated effort.

The true beginning of the Swedish novel comes with Frederik Cederborgh's *Uno von Thrazenbergh* (1809-10), the adventures of a naive and much traveled nobleman, and *Ottar Trallings Levnads-Målning* (1810-18), a considerably more concentrated account with strong autobiographical elements. Both narratives are critical of class privilege. Clas Livijn's *Spader Dame* (1824; The Queen of Spades), a "tale in letters, found at Danviken" (an

insane asylum outside Stockholm) and another criticism of class prejudice, showed a debt to the German romantics. Its multiple plots and its hero's mental dissolution as a result of a romantic attachment both derive from the tales of E.T.A. Hoffman.

Other early novels, including the work of Carl Jonas Love Almqvist, mixed romantic traits with proto-realism and social criticism. Almqvist's *Det går an* (1839; Sara Videbeck, also translated as *Why Not?*) has remained the most widely read of his many narratives because of its topicality, its attractive heroine, and its descriptions of the central Swedish landscape. His *Amorina* (1822, 1839) is a Gothic story of incest and murder that describes the formation of a criminal personality. Almqvist's masterpiece, *Drottningens juvelsmycke* (1834; The Queen's Diadem) recounts the assassination of Gustaf III at the Stockholm Opera in 1792. Concentric circles of political and erotic intrigue center on the androgynous Azouras Lazuli Tintomara, both a clarinetist in the opera orchestra and a danseuse.

Fredrika Bremer's "family novels"—*Grannarne* (1827; The Neighbors), *Hemmet* (1839; The Home or Life in Sweden), *Hertha, eller en själs historie* (1856; Hertha)—praised virtue at the same time that they advocated nonrevolutionary social change, including greater freedom for women. Bremer has been called "the mother of the Swedish novel," because her work, despite its sentimentality, carved out a convincing realism in its description of the prosperous middle class.

Sophie von Knorring initially wrote about the (generally unhappy) upper nobility in *Cousinerna* (1834; The Cousins). She subsequently startled her readership with *Torparen och hans omgifing* (1843; The Peasant and His Landlord), noteworthy as the first Swedish novel about peasant life, replete with drink, seduction, and murder. The incredibly prolific Emilie Flygare-Carlén developed a colorful regionalism filled with believable dialogue and fast action. Her best known novel is one of the earliest, *Rosen på Tistelön* (1842; *The Rose of Tistelön: A Tale of the Swedish Coast*), which set the tone for later regional novels with a focus on sinister deeds and insanity on a remote island.

Viktor Rydberg wrote horror stories as a young man and made a name for himself with the historical adventure novel *Fribytaren på Östersjön* (1857; The Freebooter of the Baltic), which rose above the genre with its attack on contemporary religious fanaticism. But Rydberg is best known for *Singoalla* (1856), which leaves realism in the dust with its interest in parapsychological phenomena—the protagonist becomes a split personality as a consequence of being haunted by a disowned child. For many years *Singoalla* was standard reading in Swedish schools, its antique style and heartrending plot provoking much admiration. *Den sista atenaren* (1859; The Last Athenian) is a historical novel set in the age of Julian the Apostate and follows Charles Kingsley's *Hypatia* (1853) in its condemnation of ignorant fanaticism. *Vapensmeden* (1891; The Armorer), set during the Swedish reformation, again combines polemics with careful historical reconstruction.

August Strindberg's *Röda rummet* (1879; The Red Room), a satire about the professional and emotional training of a journalist in a Sweden just getting used to a certain liberalization of its political life, has been called Sweden's first modern novel. Offering a remarkable picture of contemporary Stockholm, the novel has a highly episodic structure and intertwined plots. *Hemsöborna* (1887; The Natives of Hemsö), more traditional and more widely read, is a broad comedy with tragic undertones. His historical novel *Tschandala* (1889, 1897), revolving around a 17th-century *Übermensch,* focuses on sexual obsession and debasement. *I havsbandet* (1890; *By the Open Sea*) is an interesting formal experiment, combining elements from Joris-Karl Huymans' *À rebours* (1884; *Against Nature*), geological and ichthyological treatises, Friedrich Nietzsche, and the peasant murder story as practiced by Flygare-Carlén.

Gustaf af Geijerstam, an exceptionally derivative author, is chiefly notable for a naturalist novel, *Erik Grane* (1887). His *Medusas hufvud* (1895; Medusa's Head) incorporates neoromantic elements. The depiction of extreme psychological and emotional states, pursued by Strindberg and Geijerstam, was also a central concern in Ola Hansson's *Sensitiva amorosa* (1884), a short novel made up of stories on the "secret processes [by which] we are ruled."

The novels of Strindberg, Geijerstam, and Hansson tend to have a strong regional flavor, a tendency brought out more clearly by Victoria Benedictsson, who wrote under the nom-de-plume Ernst Ahlgren. Benedictsson used Scania as the background for her stories in *Från Skåne* (1884; From Scania). Her autobiographical novel *Pengar* (1885; Money) is based on the events of her unhappy marriage and a plea for women's social and intellectual emancipation. August Bondeson's *Skollärare John Chronschougs memoarer* (1897–1904; Schoolteacher John Chronschoug's Memoirs) is an embodiment of a more comic regionalism. Written in an intentional and exaggerated imitation of academic rhetoric, it describes the struggles of the culturally ambitious Chronschoug with peasants, pupils, and the fair sex.

The 1890s saw an upsurge in neoromantic historical fiction in response to a growing nationalism. Verner von Heidenstam called for a rejection of the treatment of social problems—or "shoemaker's realism"—and a return to imagination, a sense of beauty, and wit. His *Hans Alienus* (1892), partly written in verse, is best described as a phantasmagoria and exploits the exoticism of its Near-Eastern setting to the fullest. *Karolinerna* (1897–98; *The Charles Men*) is a series of stories connected by the figure of "the warrior king," Karl XII, seen together with his devoted men at several stages of his career, particularly during the disastrous invasion of the Ukraine that ended at Poltava in 1709. The cycle's true heroes are the patient and loyal Swedish soldiers, willing to make any sacrifice. Heidenstam, who now may have seen himself as the voice of the nation, continued with *Heliga Birgittas pilgrimsfärd* (1901; Saint Birgitta's Pilgrimage), another devoted but not uncritical portrait of a Swedish idol. His *Folkungaträdet* (1905–07; *The Tree of the Folkungs*) describes the foundation of the kingdom of Sweden. Heidenstam won the Nobel prize in 1916.

Heidenstam's great neoromantic rival was Selma Lagerlöf, winner of the Nobel prize in 1909 and the first woman elected to the Swedish Academy, in 1914. Growing up, Lagerlöf had been an avid listener to stories about the glorious past of the great estates in the Värmland region, a world of cavaliers, sleighing parties, and superstitions that she recreated in her novels. The floridly romantic *Gösta Berlings saga* (1891; *The Story of Gösta Berling*) is predicated on a double vision. In accordance with the plan of the evil Sintram, in league with the devil, an estate is run to wrack and ruin by the 12 wild "cavaliers of Ekeby," among them the drunken sometimes pastor and ladies' man Berling. Yet the cavaliers, and certainly Gösta, bring a sense of adventure (the equivalent of Heidenstam's beauty) to the place they plun-

der. The novel's charm lies in the ambiguity of Lagerlöf's attitude, both moralizing and loving, toward her creations, and in her unique storytelling style, melodramatic and even sensational but nonetheless altogether convincing. *Gösta Berling* was followed by a novelistic geography and history lesson, *Nils Holgerssons underbara resa genom Sverige* (1906–07; *The Wonderful Adventures of Nils*)—a children's classic with a double vision of life in the air (on the back of a giant goose) and on the ground. *Antikrists mirakler* (1897; The Miracles of Anti-Christ) also belongs to the spirit of the neoromantic 1890s, but shows an awareness of such social ills as child labor. Such realist elements were eventually drowned out by Lagerlöf's interests in Christianity and extreme emotional states.

Hjalmar Söderberg rejected regionalism in favor of pessimistic, often cynical, psychological studies of middle-class life in Stockholm, including *Förvillelser* (1895; Aberrations) and *Martin Bircks ungdom* (1901; *Martin Birck's Youth*). The latter novel shows a Danish influence, featuring a dreamer in the Danish mold, sensitive, unable to act, aware that his talents are second rate—the quiet prisoner of a sadly stunted life. The protagonist of *Doktor Glas* (1905; *Doctor Glas*) is another incarnation of the type. The novel's dream sequences constitute an important advance in the Swedish psychological novel. The importance of Stockholm as a literary background was even greater in Sigfrid Siwertz's *En flanör* (1914; A Stroller), in which well-to-do young men wander aimlessly through well-tended streets and cafés.

Siwertz built a more substantial reputation with *Selambs* (1920; *Downstream*), about a family driven by avarice, egotism, lust, or, in one instance, unfulfilled Nietzscheanism, giving expression to a general dissatisfaction with contemporary middle-class values that pervaded Swedish literature in the wake of World War I. Sven Lidman's *Huset med de gamla fröknarna* (1918; House with the Old Ladies) is a defense of old-fashioned values voiced by three admirably snobbish ladies and a pendant to Lidman's five-volume series about the Silfverstååhls (1910–13), an ambitious picture of the inevitable decline of old and honorable traditions, which is marred by flashes of anti-Semitism. Elin Wägner wrote about the corruption of a good woman by her marriage into a wealthy but notoriously dishonest peasant family in *Åsa-Hanna* (1918). Gustaf Hellström, with *Snörmakare Lekholm får en idé* (1927; *Lace-Maker Lekholm Has an Idea*), is another critic of Swedish social striving and the narrowness of the Swedish small town. Birger Sjöberg's *Kvartetten som sprängdes* (1924; The Quartet That Went to Pieces) and Ludvig Nordström's *Tomas Lack och hans familj* (1912, 1930; Tomas Lack and His Family) belong to the same group. In many respects the authors of the 1910s and 1920s hark back to the 1880s in their wish to indicate the folly of the middle class.

The most important of the authors who seemed to regret the passing of the old-fashioned provincial town and its ingrown society, even as they applauded its demise, is the regionalist Hjalmar Bergman. Most of his work centers on "Wadköping" (a fictional re-creation of Örebro and the Bergslagen mining region just to the north). Novels such as *Loewenhistorier* (1913; Loewen Stories), *Mor i Sutre* (1917; Mother of Sutre), and *Farmor och vår Herre* (1921; *Thy Rod and Thy Staff*) are inspired by Lagerlöf's romantic melodrama. Interestingly, Bergman was one of the few Swedish novelists to embrace the technical experimentation of modernism in his family novel *En döds memoarer*

(1918; A Dead Man's Memoirs), which plays with factual and subjective time. His next novel, the satirical *Markurells i Wadköping* (1919; *God's Orchid*), abandons technical innovation, and *Herr von Hancken* (1920; *Mr. von Hancken*) is an imitation of the literary style of the early 19th century. Bergman delivered a dark commentary on his own dedication to entertaining the reader in his final work, *Clownen Jack* (1930; *Jack the Clown*), in which the main character, a projection of the author, insists that a clown's art springs from terror: the clown must frighten himself so that "children and fools would have the chance to laugh at their fear."

Voices of a new kind began to appear in the Swedish novel around 1930, with writers from a proletarian background who represented a distinctly working-class point of view in both autobiographical and historical novels. Vilhelm Moberg's work deals with the impoverished, tradition-bound Småland peasant society from which he came, particularly in the autobiographical trilogy *Sänkt sedebetyg* (1935; *Memory of Youth*), *Sömnlös* (1937; *Sleepless Nights*), and *Giv oss jorden!* (1939; *The Earth Is Ours*). In *Soldat med brutet gevär* (1944; partially translated as *When I Was a Child*), Moberg idealizes himself as a fighter for the common man, for pacifism, and for the Social Democratic Party. Moberg's greatest accomplishment was a tetralogy about emigration to the United States, consisting of *Utvandrarna* (1949; *The Emigrants*), *Invandrarna* (1952; *Unto a Good Land*), *Nybyggarna* (1956; *The Settlers*), and *Sista brevet till Sverige* (1959; *Last Letter Home*).

Jan Fridegård's historical novels, *Trägudars land* (1940; *The Land of Wooden Gods*), *Gryningsfolket* (1944; *People of the Dawn*), and *Offerök* (1949; *Sacrificial Smoke*), feature a thrall as a fighter for social justice in a pre-Sweden of human sacrifice and wooden idols. A later series on the fates of ordinary soldiers in the wars of imperial Sweden, from *Svensk soldat* (1959; *Swedish Soldier*) to *Hemkomsten* (1963; *Homecoming*), clings to a central democratic message—the constant disregard of the Swedish crown for its cannon-fodder.

Among the working-class novelists, Ivar Lo-Johansson had the least concern with history and the greatest commitment to the correction of present miseries. His *God natt, jord* (1933; *Breaking Free*), a collective novel on the wretched existence of day laborers, is thought to have helped to prompt extensive reform measures by the government. Lo-Johansson also wrote an autobiographical series, starting with *Analfabeten* (1951; *The Illiterate*), through *Gårdfarihandlaren* (1942; *Peddling My Wares*), to *Författaren* (1957; *The Author*). Josef Kjellgren is associated with the urban working-class man in Swedish literature, and his *Människor kring en bro* (1935; *People Around a Bridge*) is a classic example of the collective novel.

Moa Martinson (née Helga Swartz), the only woman writer among the worker-novelists, rose from the miserable existence of day-laborers on the great central Swedish estates. Her *Kvinnor och äppelträd* (1933; *Women and Appletrees*) and *Sallys söner* (1934; *Sally's Sons*) describe the hard lives of defiant women. The attempts of women to free themselves also form the subject of an autobiographical trilogy by Martinson, beginning with *Mor gifter sig* (1936; *Mother Gets Married*). Martinson served as a role model for women writers in Swedish Finland as late as the 1970s, and feminist criticism has recently refurbished her reputation.

Eyvind Johnson began as a worker-novelist with *Stad i mörk-* er (1927; *Town in Darkness*) and *Avsked till Hamlet* (1930; *Farewell to Hamlet*), the latter novel being the first in a series of five books about Mårten Torpare, a character with a background like Johnson's own, who learns to reject his ambivalence toward his simple past. During stays in Berlin (1921–23) and Paris (1925–30), Johnson read the work of John Dos Passos, Alfred Döblin, Marcel Proust, André Gide, and James Joyce, as well as Henri Bergson and Sigmund Freud. His own novels show the influence of his reading. *Minnas* (1928; *Remembering*), for instance, is a study of repressed memory that uses interior monologue. In *Regn i gryningen* (1933; *Rain in the Dawn*), Johnson embraced a form of primitivism, briefly becoming a follower of D.H. Lawrence. *Strändernas svall* (1946; *Return to Ithaca*) uses myth—the story of Ulysses' return from Calypso's island to Ithaca—to comment on Allied excesses during World War II. A similar dual perspective dominates *Drömmar om rosor och eld* (1949; *Dreams of Roses and Fire*), which looks at political trials and executions through the witchcraft trial of the 17th-century French priest Urbain Grainier. *Molnen över Metapontion* (1957; *Clouds over Metapontion*) combines Xenophon's *Anabasis* with the fate of a Swedish survivor of a German concentration camp. Johnson's political idealism and his undoubted technical virtuosity were rewarded by a Nobel prize in 1974, shared with Harry Martinson, who is best known for his travel books, his poetry, and his vision of the end of the world in the space epic *Aniara*, 1956.

In startling contrast to the worker-novels of the 1930s, Agnes von Krusenstjerna's chronicles of Sweden's moribund nobility carry such deceptive titles as *Tony växer upp* (1922; Tony Grows Up) and *Fröknarna von Pahlen* (1930–35; The Misses von Pahlen). The novels grow ever darker, describing the nervous breakdown and institutionalization of Tony and delving into the sometimes lurid sexual lives of the nobility. Krusenstjerna's admirers compare her with Proust and D.H. Lawrence, although a comparison with Radclyffe Hall, the author of the once popular lesbian novel *The Well of Loneliness* (1928), may be more to the point.

Sweden also produced two comic novelists at mid-century. Fritiof Nilsson Piraten, best known for his Bombi Bitt novels (*Bombi Bitt och jag* [1932; *Bombi Bitt: The Story of a Swedish Huckleberry Finn*] and *Bombi Bitt och Nick Carter* [1946; Bombi Bitt and Nick Carter]), both inspired by American sources. Frans G. Bengtsson is chiefly notable for his great Viking burlesque, *Röde Orm* (1941–45; *The Long Ships*), which parodies romantic Viking pageants, in poetry and prose.

Writers responded in various ways to the rise of the Nazis and to World War II. Sweden's neutrality was morally tainted by the fact that the country supplied iron ore to Germany and that German troop trains traveling from Norway to Finland were given free passage. Pär Lagerkvist, who received the Nobel prize in 1951, was a particularly outspoken critic of totalitarianism, publishing a series of novels that raise a protest against political oppression and inquire into the nature of evil, beginning with *Bödeln* (1933; *The Hangman*). *Dvärgen* (1944; *The Dwarf*), an allegorical novel about the struggle between good and evil, is often cited for its stylistic achievements. His later novels—*Sibyllan* (1956; *The Sibyl*) and *Ahasverus död* (1960; *The Death of Ahasuerus*)—were chiefly concerned with religious themes. Karin Boye's futuristic *Kallocain* is another allegorical novel about the totalitarian threat, but it registers a great deal of ambivalence.

The scientist Leo Kall invents a truth serum, "kallocain," which brings out a person's innermost thoughts. Besides its obvious negative uses, Kall realizes after some hesitation, the drug can be employed for good in that it breaks down the defenses that prevent human contact.

Sivar Arnér grappled with the moral questions raised by World War II in *Plånbok borttappad* (1943; Lost Wallet), a study of the motivation and costs of resistance to oppression. Arnér's historical novel *Knekt och klerk* (1945; Soldier and Clerk) and his *Fyra som var bröder* (1955; Four Who Were Brothers) argue for pacifism, justifying Sweden's neutrality. The very young Stig Dagerman captured the pervasive anxiety of the war years in Sweden in *Ormen* (1945; *The Snake*), which set the tone for the rest of his dark oeuvre, including *De domdas ö* (1946; Isle of the Condemned), a fantasy on the fear of death, *Bränt barn* (1948; *Burnt Child*), a family novel in which a father and son are caught in a torturous Oedipal relationship, and *Bröllopsbesvär* (1949; Wedding Difficulties), which describes the drunken, sometimes grossly comical, and finally tragic events of a peasant wedding.

The work of Lars Ahlin mingles the grotesque with the spiritual, as in *Min död är min* (1945; My Death Is Mine), in which a traveling salesman is given away by his wife to a laundress, who needs a husband to legitimize her children. They have a mystical sexual experience and, in due time, fall in love. The climax of the novel is set in a morgue, where the salesman and a friend overcome their fear by drinking alcohol intended for the bathing of corpses. Constantly mixing sexual involvements and mystical experiences, Ahlin's novels are marked by complex narrative situations using such techniques as interior monologue, as in *Bark och löv* (1961; Bark and Leaf).

Lars Gyllensten's work resembles Ahlin's in its often grotesque characters, but Gyllensten substitutes a pervasive questioning for Ahlin's mysticism. *Senilia* (1956) has a 30-year-old protagonist who tries to protect himself against shocks by pretending to be an old man. Proceeding dialectically, Gyllensten then wrote a reply to his own book in *Juvenilia* (1965). In *Sokrates död* (1960; The Death of Socrates), the philosopher (who does not actually appear in the novel) seeks shelter in his teaching of scepticism and then in the imminence of his death. His daughter Aspasia believes that he is incapable of feeling normal human love, and his wife Xanthippe is convinced that his desire to die is an expression of his will to power. In *Kains memoarer* (1961; *The Testament of Cain*), a quasi-Christian sect, having decided that God, if He exists, must be evil, because of the wretchedness of the world, venerates Cain and others who have revolted against God. *Palatset i parken* (1970; The Palace in the Park) brands compassion as a selfish or ineffectual emotion. Gyllensten's scepticism resolved itself in *Det himmelska gästabudet* (1991; The Heavenly Banquet), essentially an affirmation of the greatness of the creation. Gyllensten's mental experiments find a counterpart of sorts in the mini-novels of Willy Kyrklund, such as *Mästaren Ma* (1952; Ma the Master), while Sven Fagerberg takes flight in the abstractions of Eastern philosophy, particularly Zen, in such novels as *Höknatt* (1957; Hawk Night) and *Svärdfäktarna* (1963; The Fencers).

Besides these more unusual novels, the 1950s and 1960s witnessed a flourishing of traditional realism, sometimes expressing a strong sense of social engagement. Per-Anders Fogelström published several semi-historical and autobiographical series set in Stockholm. Pår Rådström's Greg Bengtsson series (*Tiden väntar inte* [1952; Time Doesn't Wait], *Greg Bengtsson och kärleken* [1953; Greg Bengtsson and Love], and *Ärans portar* [1954; The Gates of Honor]) are interesting today for their remarkable stylistic variety and their ebullient humor. Another series with an international cast of characters, consisting of *Paris—en kärleksroman* (1955; Paris—A Novel of Love) and *Ballong till månen* (1958; Balloon to the Moon), is remembered for Rådström's oblique criticism of a burgeoning celebrity cult.

Sara Lidman represents a new development in the Swedish novel with several early novels expressing a profound political engagement. *Tjärdalen* (1953; The Tar Valley), a story of collective guilt, is the first of a series of novels set in remote Norrland, followed by *Hjortronlandet* (1955; The Cloudberry Land), *Regnspiran* (1958; The Rain Bird), and *Bära mistel* (1960; Carrying Mistletoe). All save the first concentrate on the oppressed, providing portraits of sensitive women caught in or tainted by their unforgiving surroundings. Two of her novels have African settings. *Jag och min son* (1961; I and My Son) tells the story of a Swede living in Johannesburg who sympathizes with the plight of the blacks but feels compelled to betray his friends in order to provide for his physically fragile son. *Med fem diamanter* (1964; With Five Diamonds) is set in Kenya and has an entirely black cast. In the 1970s, Lidman wrote a series of novels that focus on the building of a railroad to Norrland in the last years of the 19th century and the inevitable upheaval it caused in that primitive world, from *Din tjänare hör* (1977; Your Servant Hears) to *Jernkronan* (1985; The Crown of Iron). The series is notable for its close observation of dialectical and social differences.

Birgitta Trotzig, less political than Lidman, wrote several historical novels that also evince a strong concern with human suffering. Her novels are usually set in Scania, in the far south of the country. *De utsatta* (1957; The Exposed Ones) takes place during the Danish-Swedish wars of the 17th century, while *En berättelse från kusten* (1961; A Tale from the Coast) is set at the end of the 15th century. Later novels center on the relationship between a father and a daughter in *Sveket* (1966; The Betrayal); between father and son in *Sjukdomen* (1972; The Illness); and between mother, daughter, and grandson in *Dykungens dotter* (1985; The Bog King's Daughter). The bog king, inspired by a tale by Hans Christian Andersen, is a sailor who long ago seduced the grandmother, thus starting a chain of unhappiness and degradation. The legendary quality of Trotzig's novels presages Torgny Lindgren's *Ormens väg på hälleberget* (1982; Way of a Serpent), a tale about sexual exploitation and revenge told in a dialectically colored and old-fashioned Swedish.

The "new provincialism" prevalent in the Swedish novel in the second half of the 20th century (see Lidman's and Lindgren's Norrland, Trotzig's Scania, even Fogelström's Stockholm) took a different turn in the small but extremely provocative oeuvre of Per Olof Sundman. Sundman's work, describing action without commentary or emotional exploration, bears a resemblance to the French *nouveau roman*. The main source of Sundman's laconic art is the Icelandic saga, a debt particularly clear in *Berättelsen om Såm* (1977; The Story about Såm), a modern retelling of *Hrafnkels saga Freysgoda* (The Saga of Hrafnkel, Priest of Frey). Sundman's Swedish landscape of preference was Jämtland, the mountainous region stretching along the Norwegian border in Sweden's northwest, as in *Jägarna* (1957; The Hunters) and *Två dagar, två nätter* (1965; *Two Days, Two*

Nights). Sundman also played an important role in the development of the documentary novel with his *Expeditionen* (1962; *The Expedition*), modeled on Henry Morton Stanley's safaris in the Congo, and *Ingeniör Andrés luftfärd* (1968; *The Flight of the Eagle*), closely based on the documentation surviving from a disastrous attempt to cross the North Pole by balloon by three Swedish aeronauts in 1897. Another documentary novelist is Per Olof Enquist, who wrote *Magnetisörens femte vinter* (1964; *The Magnetist's Fifth Winter*), based loosely on the life of the German hypnotist Franz Anton Mesmer, *Hess* (1966), about Rudolf Hess, and *Legionärerna* (1968; *The Legionaries*), which dealt with a group of Baltic refugees, mostly Latvians, who had served in the Wehrmacht against their will and fled to Sweden when the German eastern front collapsed. Buckling under Soviet pressure, the Swedish government eventually turned them over to the Soviet authorities. Still another documentarist is Per Gunnar Evander, whose early works again have the nature of factual reports. However, Evander's characters turn out to share a great propensity for lying (as in *Uppkomlingen—en personundersokning* [1969; *The Upstart—A Personal Investigation*]), which seriously compromises the documentary status of the novels they appear in.

Sven Delblanc's oeuvre is marked by great variety. *Eremitkräftan* (1962; *The Hermit Crab*) is an allegory revealing a debt to Franz Kafka; *Prästkappan* (1963; *The Cassock*) is a picaresque tale set in 18th-century Germany; *Homunculus* (1965) is a fantasy; and *Åsnebrygga* (1969; *Ass' Bridge*) is the fictionalized account of a guest professorship at the University of California at Berkeley. The "Hedeby" tetralogy (*Åminne* [1970; River Memory], *Stenfågel* [1973; Stone Bird], *Winteride* [1974; Winter Lair], and *Stadsporten* [1975; The Town Gate]) and the Samuel tetralogy (*Samuels bok* [1981; Samuel's Book], *Samuels döttrar* [1983; Samuel's Daughters], *Kanaans land* [1984; Canaan's Land], and *Maria ensam* [1985; Maria Alone]) appealed to the nostalgia of a Swedish public comfortably settled in the modern cities of the welfare state. Delblanc's creative urge also found an outlet in short historical novels, including *Kastrater* (1975; *The Castrati*), which featured in its cast of characters the great soprano castrato Luigi Marchesi, the besotted sometime "Bonnie Prince Charlie," and Gustaf III of Sweden, staying incognito in Rome, and *Speranza* (1980), which showed the transformation of an idealist into an oppressor onboard a slave ship.

Kerstin Ekman began with a set of eight detective novels, culminating in the open-ended mystery *Pukehornet* (1967; *The Devil's Horn*). Her next work was a semi-documentary novel, *Menedarna* (1976; *The Perjurers*), focused on the Swedish-American agitator Joe Hill. Her major social-historical tetralogy (*Häxringarna* [1972; The Witches' Rings], *Springkällan* [1976; The Spring], *Änglahuset* [1979; The Angel's House], and *En stad av ljus* [1983; A Town of Light]) shows the transformation of a Swedish railroading community during a century of radical change, from 1870 on. The epic has a feminist point of view. With *Rövarna i Skuleskogen* (1988; The Robbers in Skule Forest), Ekman undertook a historical-mythological experiment, creating as a protagonist a troll who has watched human behavior for some 500 years. *Hunden* (1986; *The Dog*) also offers a commentary on human behavior from a nonhuman perspective. A detective novel, *Händelser vid vatten* (1993; *Blackwater*) reverts to Ekman's beginnings.

Taken together, Lidman, Delblanc, and Ekman offer a vast panorama of Sweden in transition. Göran Tunström's canvas is more modestly scaled, but his plainly autobiographical stories are presented with great narratological virtuosity, as in his three Sunne novels, *De heliga geograferna* (1973; The Holy Geographers), *Guddöttrarna* (1975; The Goddaughters), and *Prästungen* (1976; The Pastor's Boy). A strong Christian interest becomes apparent in *Ökenbrevet* (1978; The Letter from the Wilderness), Jesus' account of his life before he enters upon his public mission. *Juloratoriet* (1983; The Christmas Oratorio) displays a magic realism (in the appearance of Selma Lagerlöf and the Swedish explorer Sven Hedin) not often found in the Swedish novel. The same blend of imaginative flights with great good humor puts a special stamp on *Tjuven* (1986; The Thief).

The historical novel enjoyed a come-back in Sweden in the 1970s. Lars Widding, Lars Ardelius, Hans Granlid, and Gunnar E. Sandgren explored the riches of Sweden's prehistory and history, from the fancied connection with the Ostrogothic empire in Italy to the great Baltic empire of the 17th century, its abrupt destruction, and the country's subsequent role as a theatre of grand illusions, as in the Gustavian age.

P.C. (Per Christian) Jersild has made a specialty of satirizing the perils and absurdities of the welfare state and its possible transmogrifications in the future, as in *Till varmare länder* (1961; To Warmer Lands), in which a housewife's visions of warmer climes turn out to be hell; *Ledig lördag* (1963; Free Saturday), in which the participants in a company party are trapped in a subway train; and *Prince Valiant och Konsum* (1966; Prince Valiant and the Co-Op), about a girl's dreams of a comic-book hero in the monotony of a Swedish grocery store. In *Grisjakten* (1968; The Pig Hunt), a skewering of Swedish bureaucracy and brainless obedience, a respectable government official is given the assignment of killing all the pigs in Sweden, starting with the island of Gotland. At several points in his career, Jersild has extrapolated from the icy efficiency of modern health care to visions of the future, as in *Djurdoktorn* (1973; Animal Doctor) and *En levande själ* (1980; A Living Soul). Like other Scandinavian authors, Jersild envisioned a post-nuclear-disaster world in *Efter floden* (1982; After the Flood). In *Holgerssons* (1991), he made fun of an icon of Swedish's children's literature, confronting a dignified and distinctly uncomfortable Selma Lagerlöf with Nils Holgersson from *The Wonderful Adventures of Nils*.

GEORGE C. SCHOOLFIELD

See also Knut Hamsun; Pär Lagerkvist; Sigrid Undset

Further Reading

Björck, Staffan, *Romanens formvärld: Studier i prosaberättarens teknik,* Stockholm: Natur och Kultur, 1953

Brøndsted, Mogens, editor, *Nordens Litteratur,* 2 vols., Copenhagen: Gyldendal, 1972

Brønner, Hedin, *Three Faroese Novelists,* New York: Twayne, 1973

Budd, John, *Eight Scandinavian Novelists: Criticism and Reviews in English,* Westport, Connecticut: Greenwood Press, 1981

Einarsson, Stefán, *A History of Icelandic Literature,* New York: Johns Hopkins Press for the American-Scandinavian Foundation, 1957

Friese, Wilhelm, *Nordische Literaturen im 20. Jahrhundert,* Stuttgart: Kröner, 1971

Gustafson, Alrik, *Six Scandinavian Novelists,* New York: Princeton University Press for the American-Scandinavian Foundation, 1940

Holmberg, Olle, *Lovtal över svenska romaner,* Stockholm: Bonnier, 1957

Höskuldsson, Sveinn Skorri, editor, *Ideas and Ideologies in Scandinavian Literature since the First World War,* Proceedings of the 10th Study Conference of the International Association for Scandinavian Studies, held in Reykjavík, 22–27 July 1974, Reykjavík: Institute of Literary Research, University of Iceland, 1975

Karkama, Pertti, *Sosiaalinen konfliktiromaani: Rakennetutkimus suomalaisen yhteiskunnallisen realismen pohjalta,* Helsinki: Tammi, 1971

Kristensen, Sven Møller, *Impressionismen i dansk prosa 1870–1900,* Copenhagen: Gyldendal, 1955

Kristensen, Sven Møller, *Den store generation,* Copenhagen: Gyldendal, 1974

Mawby [Garton], Janet, "The Norwegian Novel Today," *Scandinavia* 14 (1975)

Mazzarella, Merete, *Det trå rummet: En finlandssvensk romantradition,* Helsinki: Söderström, 1989

Mjöberg, Jöran, *De sökte sanningen: En studie i fem romaner (1879–1886),* Stockholm: Raben and Sjögren, 1977

Naess, Harald S., editor, *A History of Norwegian Literatures,* volume 2, *A History of Scandinavian Literatures,* Lincoln: University of Nebraska Press, 1993

Nettum, Rolf Nyboe, editor, *I diktningens brennpunkt: Studier i norsk romankunst, 1945–1980,* Oslo: Aschehoug, 1982

Paul, Fritz, editor, *Grundzüge der neueren skandinavischen Literaturen,* Darmstadt: Wissenschaftliche Buchgesellschaft, 1982

Polkunen, Mirjam, editor, *Romaani ja tulkinta,* Helsinki: Otava, 1973

Rossel, Sven H., editor, *A History of Danish Literatures,* volume 1, *A History of Scandinavian Literatures,* Lincoln: University of Nebraska Press, 1992

Schoolfield, George C., "The Postwar Novel of Swedish Finland," *Scandinavian Studies* 34 (1962)

Schoolfield, George C., editor, *A History of Finland's Literature,* volume 4 of *A History of Scandinavian Literatures,* Lincoln: University of Nebraska Press, 1988

Scottie, Irene, editor, *Aspects of Modern Swedish Literature,* Norwich: Norvik Press, 1988

Warme, Lars G., editor, *A History of Swedish Literature,* volume 3, *A History of Scandinavian Literatures,* Lincoln: University of Nebraska Press, 1996

Weinstock, John M., and Robert Rovinsky, editors, *The Hero in Scandinavian Literature,* Austin: University of Texas Press, 1975

Zuck, Virpi, editor, *Dictionary of Scandinavian Literature,* New York: Greenwood Press, and London: St. James Press, 1990

Scarlet and Black. *See* Red and the Black

The Scarlet Letter by Nathaniel Hawthorne

1850

Few American works of fiction have proved more enduring, or influential, than *The Scarlet Letter.* Written in 19th-century New England and set in 17th-century Puritan Massachusetts, the novel's explorations of sexual power relations and of self and society could not seem more wholly, or even more startlingly, modern. It has functioned as a mainstay of the American Renaissance and of American writing in general.

The main action of Hawthorne's story, the illicit love affair of Hester Prynne with the Reverend Arthur Dimmesdale and the birth of their child Pearl, takes place before the book opens. What follows is a kind of animated narrative tableau, a meticulously scripted sequence of exchanges of accusation and guilt, hope and remorse, revenge and resignation, that turns upon the silent presence of Hester's husband, the Old World physician-savant Roger Chillingworth.

Hawthorne knew that he had written something very different from the traditional realist novel. Calling his work a "romance," he identified as antecedents the narratives of Edmund Spenser, Walter Scott, Washington Irving, and Charles Brockden Brown, embodying a storytelling tradition of emblems, figuration, biblical and Bunyanesque typology, and transforming moments. The result is a highly visual, even pictorial fiction. Hawthorne presents the lives of Hester, Arthur, Roger, and Pearl against the backdrop of a Puritan settlement revolving around church, scaffold, cemetery, and fear of forest and witchery, as a drama of seeing and being seen. Henry James—whose novels testify to Hawthorne's influence—calls this emphasis on spectacle "the ordeal of consciousness." Describing *The Scarlet Letter* as "beautiful, admirable [and] extraordinary," James added that Hawthorne's manner is prone to "an abuse of the fanciful element," "a certain superficial symbolism."

Hawthorne may be thought to have anticipated these doubts. In the prefatory "The Custom House," mistakenly left out in some editions, he carefully prepares the reader for the narrative that follows. Presenting itself as a historically accurate account of the novel's genesis, "The Custom House" is in fact an important fiction in its own right. Within the conventional conceit of the fortuitous discovery of Hester's story through the find of the "capital letter A" with its intricate needlework and golden embroidery, Hawthorne's text adroitly brings together autobiography, genealogy, and history, as well as genre theory and musings on the nature of fiction and its relationship to reality in a twilight atmosphere that adumbrates Hawthorne's world of romance— "a neutral territory, somewhere between the real world and fairy-land, where the Actual and the Imaginary may meet, and each imbue itself with the nature of the other."

The following 24 chapters—geometric, stylized, complementary—are focused on the three pivotal scaffold scenes at the beginning, middle, and end. The principal characters are inextricably entwined and defined by their relationships to each other: Hester as she moves from lover to protectress-mother and finally to nurse and wisewoman; Arthur as the haunted, duplicitous minister and guilt-laden bearer of his own psychosomatic scarlet letter; Roger as the "unpardonable sinner"—cold, prying, a medical technologist of head over heart; and Pearl, whose waywardness embodies the spirit of art under a sexually obsessive yet fearful puritanism. Setting an example for Henry James' Isabel Archer and Daisy Miller, Pearl will in due course abandon New England for Europe.

Each scene-setting ("The Prison Door," "The Market-Place," and so on) belongs to a symbolic geography of gates, pathways, thresholds, and borders. The central opposition contrasts the unregulated wild rose-bush, associated with Hester, with the "black flower" of the township's prison—an oppositional mapping of Nature and Society. Hester's transgressive, mock-sacral "What we did had a consecration of its own," spoken to Arthur in the forest, challenges the established authority of family, magistracy, and ministers. Hawthorne probes all forms of social ascendancy, inquiring into the foundation and moral authority of temporal power and the rules embraced by the community and balancing these against the call of life and feeling.

Hester Prynne has been seen as a pioneer feminist in the line from Anne Hutchinson to Margaret Fuller, an incarnation of the "witch" as sexually autonomous woman, an early American martyr to patriarchy, a classic nurturer and so part of the "feminization" of American culture, and, indeed, a teasing blend of each. An American equivalent of Anna Karenina or Emma Bo-

vary, she has held the attention of readers and critics since her appearance.

Hawthorne's legacy has been so potent that critics sometimes refer to the "School of Hawthorne," inspired by his psychological querying, his apparent withdrawal of his own authority ("the Inmost Me" as he teasingly calls it in "The Custom House"), his rich obliquities of style and metaphor, and his transforming use of the historical donnée to open up perennial issues and concerns. All of these are most powerfully embodied in *The Scarlet Letter*.

The influence of *The Scarlet Letter* is apparent in Henry James' *The Portrait of a Lady* (1881) and *The Bostonians* (1886); in Kate Chopin's *The Awakening* (1899), with its conflict between feminine autonomy and male writ; in William Faulkner's *As I Lay Dying* (1930), which replays the "betrayal" of Hester with Dimmesdale in the form of Addie Bundren's affair with the preacher Whitfield; and in John Updike's *Roger's Version* (1986), which gives the "gender politics" of *The Scarlet Letter* a contemporary Bostonian twist. Each bears witness to Hawthorne's turns of intelligence and craft and his continuing hold on American fiction.

A. ROBERT LEE

See also Nathaniel Hawthorne

Further Reading

Baym, Nina, *The Shape of Hawthorne's Career*, Ithaca, New York: Cornell University Press, 1976

Bercovitch, Sacvan, *The Office of "The Scarlet Letter,"* Baltimore: Johns Hopkins University Press, 1991

Brodhead, Richard, *Hawthorne, Melville, and the Novel*, Chicago: University of Chicago Press, 1976

Brodhead, Richard, *The School of Hawthorne*, New York: Oxford University Press, 1986

Dryden, Edgar, *Nathaniel Hawthorne: The Poetics of Enchantment*, Ithaca, New York: Cornell University Press, 1977

Dunne, Michael, *Hawthorne's Narrative Strategies*, Jackson: University Press of Mississippi, 1995

Hutner, Gordon, *Secrets and Sympathy: Forms of Disclosure in Hawthorne's Novels*, Athens: University of Georgia Press, 1988

Lee, A. Robert, editor, *Nathaniel Hawthorne: New Critical Essays*, London: Vision Press, and Totowa, New Jersey: Barnes and Noble, 1982

Millington, Richard H., *Practicing Romance: Narrative Form and Cultural Engagement in Hawthorne's Fiction*, Princeton, New Jersey: Princeton University Press, 1992

Sewall, Richard B., *The Vision of Tragedy*, New Haven, Connecticut: Yale University Press, 1959; new, enlarged edition, 1980

Swann, Charles, *Nathaniel Hawthorne: Tradition and Revolution*, Cambridge and New York: Cambridge University Press, 1991

Scholars. *See* **Six Classic Chinese Novels**

Science and the Novel

The original meaning of the word "science" was "knowledge acquired by study," and it was not until the 19th century that its meaning became restricted to the systematic study of the natural universe. At that time, science began to make its mark in the world, and the consequences of scientific developments frequently affected humanity as a whole. Every invention, every new theory, every new explanation of life or the universe made its effects felt in many ways. The beginning of the 19th century also witnessed the proliferation of new sciences and subsciences. These became part of the general culture of the age, which included a belief in an ultimately uniform and regular reality that left no room for randomness. Nature's laws ruled and humbled humans, as Darwin's theory of evolution showed, but they were thought to apply universally. While 19th-century science had troubling implications, it also held out the hope that humanity would ultimately be able to explain, predict, even conquer, the natural universe.

The literature of the 19th century—most noticeably its dominant form, the novel—responded to particular scientific discoveries, but perhaps of greatest importance is the way it reflects the shifts in worldview that scientific developments provoked. In the most general terms, this appears in the 19th-century novel's fascination with origins, growth, and transformation, and with progress, the struggle for existence, and extinction. It is also evident in the desire on the part of many 19th-century novelists to reconcile the implications of scientific developments and the need for religious reassurance. As science pushed back or undermined religion, literature jumped in the breach, addressing the need for adjustment in religious orientation. The need for this adjustment became more evident after the mid-century mark, with the gradual shift in philosophical perspective, from belief in a world order under divine control to the (frequently ambivalent) affirmation of human control over the natural order.

Ambivalence and Adjustment

One of European fiction's first evaluations of science, *Frankenstein; or, The Modern Prometheus* (1818), was openly critical, identifying scientific experimentation with an overstepping of natural boundaries, and Frankenstein's monster has become synonymous with science gone rampant. Reflecting widespread fear of technological innovation, Mary Shelley's novel is a complex critique of science and its assertion of the right to pursue knowledge by any means. Shelley based her novel about the scientist who creates a monster he cannot control on an understanding of the most recent scientific developments of her day. Although the scientific background of the novel, with its Gothic trappings, may seem fantastic nowadays, Shelley took care to make it consistent with current scientific theories, including ideas about electricity that were still somewhat magical. She used this knowledge to analyze and criticize the more dangerous implications of the scientific method and its practical results. More importantly, Shelley contrasted what she considered "good" science (the classification and description of the natural world, which had been the primary focus of the sciences throughout the 18th century) to "bad" science (the manipulation of natural forces to serve man's interests, which is more typical of scientific endeavor in the 19th century).

Recent feminist criticism argues, in addition, that Shelley condemns science and the scientific method for its grounding in a gendered understanding of nature as female, which justifies its violation. Shelley compares the evil science of Victor Frankenstein and his attempts to create a living creature from dead organic matter through the use of chemistry and electricity with the natural process of procreation—which, of course, involves women, as Frankenstein's approach does not. The novel suggests, then, that Frankenstein's pursuit of science is inspired at least in part by a fear of female sexuality and the desire to evade female power. Such a suggestion finds some support in the work of recent historians of science, who have shown that many 19th-century scientific projects were little more than attempts at sexism.

The genre of the novel has not been unreservedly hostile to science, and even *Frankenstein* expresses a fascination with the tremendous possibilities science opens up. More than a simple moral parable against scientific hubris, Shelley's novel voices a deep ambivalence about science, which appears in many other 19th-century novels. The irrepressible optimism of the age, now usually thought of as naive, counterbalanced doubts that scientific advances in fact benefited human society. While Charles Dickens satirizes scientific "progress" as it expressed itself in the miseries of industrialization in the novel *Hard Times* (1854), he also celebrates the scientific spirit in *Little Dorrit* (1857). The work of the Spanish novelist Benito Pérez Galdós expresses a less qualified optimism about scientific achievement. Respect for science, rather than fear of it, permeates his massive novel *Fortunata y Jacinta* (1886–87; *Fortunata and Jacinta*). This novel derives some of its cheerfulness from the fact that it has managed to integrate evolutionary theory with its religious convictions. Shifting the emphasis from the past to the future, it discerns in the evolution of species a plan that glorifies spiritual attainment. It is easy to go a step further and suppose that God is directly at work in the evolutionary process.

Naturalism

Pérez Galdós illustrates one of the adjustments to science taking place in the general culture and literature of the 19th century. A very different literary response to scientific developments is to be found in naturalism, a movement marked by pessimism. To understand its development, one needs to consider the broad philosophical shifts occurring in the 18th and 19th centuries.

The Deism of Descartes and Newton had shaped the 18th century's optimistic, orderly worldview, which neatly separated God and nature. Human beings and all other species were thought of as separate creations that had specially assigned places in a grand scheme; each was systematically classifiable and each conformed to an established pattern. A divine being, although in control of creation, stood apart from it. As a result, science and religion (or materialism and spiritualism) were not in conflict. It was possible to believe in determinism and free will at the same time. This worldview was dominant in Europe, especially in England, and persisted well into the 19th century, finding expression in several novels by Charles Dickens and in the work of the Spanish writer José María de Pereda, to mention just two examples. But then Western thought shifted from a dualistic view of the world to a unitary concept of being. Newtonian and Cartesian dualism was slowly abandoned in favor of a philosophical monism that discarded religion as a valid consideration in the attempt to reach an understanding of nature. This monism ushered in the age of the naturalistic novel, colored in large measure by advances in the biological sciences.

Naturalism asserted itself in Europe late in the 19th century and was characterized by a strong leaning toward science, conceived in opposition to religion. The life sciences, particularly evolutionary theory, had a shaping influence on naturalism, which abandoned belief in the separate creation and fixity of species. Rather, species were seen as completely overshadowing and determining the individual. All things and people were thought to obey an irrational force, or will. Among novelists, the Frenchman Émile Zola is most closely associated with naturalism. In his essay *Le Roman expérimental* (1880; *The Experimental Novel*), Zola argued that the modern novel should be experimental in the scientific sense of the word and follow scientific method. Given the dominant role accorded to science, some would say that Zola proposed that novelists write sociological or physiological treatises rather than literary works. His own novel *Germinal* (1885), although it goes beyond such a narrow framework, is indeed a socioeconomic study of the wretchedness and injustice suffered by the working class. It also analyzes the way human beings relate to the forces of nature and focuses on the question of the individual, as opposed to the human species as a collective entity. Zola's conception of heredity led him to view man as primarily a member of the species, entirely determined by external influences. At the time, heredity was conceived without the benefit of genetics to explain the mechanism by which traits are passed from one generation to the next. It was thought that all kinds of traits were heritable, including characteristics acquired during the lifetime of an individual organism, which do not in fact "enter" the genetic code. This faulty understanding of heritability contributed to an extreme determinism in naturalistic fiction, virtually excluding the possibility of individual freedom. Both plotting and characterization bear the stamp of this determinism in the work of Zola and other naturalist writers, and characters are often conceived primarily as the expression of the natural forces of heredity, environment, and sex.

In Italy, naturalism was known as "verismo," its paradigmatic examples being *La Lupa* (1912; *The She-Wolf*) and *I Malavoglia*

(1881; *The House by the Medlar Tree*) by Giovanni Verga. In England, George Eliot's novel *Middlemarch* (1872) is sometimes considered a forerunner of naturalism, with its frequent allusions to the exact sciences and its tendency toward determinism in characterization. Thomas Hardy's *Tess of the d'Urbervilles* (1891) also shares Darwin's view of a biologically active universe, although Hardy's novel is deliberately anthropocentric. The Anglo-Irish novelist George Moore is commonly considered the most important representative of naturalism in English fiction, particularly in his novel *Esther Waters* (1894). In Spain, Zola's influence is best seen in the novelists Emilia Pardo Bazán and Leopoldo Alas (who wrote under the name Clarín) in the 1880s and Vicente Blasco Ibáñez in the next decade. Pardo Bazán did not in fact approve of Zola's proposal to use the novel as an instrument of science and, as an orthodox Catholic, opposed the philosophical implications of his view of life. Nevertheless, she was attracted to the French writer's concepts and adopted naturalism for what she claimed to be purely formal purposes. Her most naturalistic novels are *Los pazos de Ulloa* (1886; *The House of Ulloa*) and its sequel, *La madre naturaleza* (1887; Mother Nature). A unifying theme is the representation of nature as a powerful force that takes its toll on human beings, who are, in turn, portrayed as opposing forces rather than as individuals. Blasco Ibáñez's best known naturalistic novel is perhaps *Cañas y barro* (1902; *Reeds and Mud*), whereas Leopoldo Alas' masterpiece is *La Regenta* (1884; *La Regenta*), a novel often compared to Gustave Flaubert's *Madame Bovary* (1857) because both novels focus on the weight of the material world and the failure of love as a means of liberation. Such novels give an indication of the bleak pessimism that marks most naturalistic fiction. Naturalism may have embraced scientific theory, but it found little hope or promise of social improvement in its own scientific worldview.

Science Fiction

A more hopeful response to science is to be found in the work of Jules Verne, who is often seen as the father of science fiction and whose name is synonymous with enthusiasm for scientific progress. Exhibiting an interest primarily in technology, Verne's writings popularized scientific advances of the 19th century and fueled speculation about the future possibilities of science: travel around the world in 80 days, flight, deep-sea exploration, travel to the moon, and so on. Seeing their world changed out of all recognition by the steam-engine, the mechanized factory, the use of gas and electricity, Verne and other 19th-century enthusiasts of science became fascinated by machines and gadgets, and they saw in technology a promise of universal health and happiness. Verne's novels that express this infatuation with science and technology most clearly are *Voyage au centre de la terre* (1864; *A Journey to the Center of the Earth*), *De la terre à la lune* (1865; *From the Earth to the Moon*), and *Vingt mille lieues sous les mers* (1870; *20,000 Leagues under the Sea*). He treated the novel primarily as a vehicle of information, a form not far removed from scientific journalism. This conception of the novel survives in modified form in contemporary science-fiction writing.

Verne's enthusiasm for technological innovation is by no means an invariable characteristic of science fiction. In fact, another formative influence on the genre was the work of H.G. Wells, whose novels moulded the frightening dystopias of 20th-century science fiction. Wells used Darwin's theory of evolution extensively in his writings, bringing together sociology and biology. His novel *The Time Machine* (1895), for example, describes a journey through the various stages of human evolution. But Wells did not consider science to be, on the whole, a positive force, as becomes clear in *The Island of Dr. Moreau* (1896), which tells the story of a visionary but misguided scientist who attempts to turn beasts into men. Although science started as a liberation from religious dogma, this novel suggests, it has become an uncontrollable power, incapable of governing itself. Wells' later novels continue this pessimistic attitude about the use of science and set the tone for most science-fiction works of the 20th century. Dystopian novels like Aldous Huxley's *Brave New World* (1932) and George Orwell's *Nineteen Eighty-Four* (1949) are cases in point, presenting a totalitarian future made possible by technology.

The 20th Century

The 20th century starts with two major scientific upheavals that had far-reaching effects on Western culture and on the novel: Albert Einstein's theory of relativity and Sigmund Freud's psychoanalytic theories. The universe, ever since Einstein, has been conceived as unstable, variable, a product of chance, all its points of reference equally valid. Time and space are conceived as continuous entities. Modern physics encourages the imagination to construct new concepts of reality that violate common-sense expectations. With the undermining of time and space as absolutes in themselves, it is no longer appropriate to think of objects as inhabiting concrete, localized space. Time, space, and the objects that exist within them are merged, and we are forced to depend heavily upon abstract mental constructions in our search for new meanings.

Physics has had an enormous impact on literature in the 20th century, primarily in relation to the concept of individual freedom. Whereas 19th-century science led to an understanding of the ways that heredity and environment constrain individual freedom, the new science has given us a more open universe, in which humans may feel more free. However, the vastness of available choices and the perceived randomness of events intrudes on any feeling of liberation.

While physics caused a transformation in the prevailing image of the universe, Freud changed the vision humans had of themselves by bringing sexuality, the unconscious, and irrationality to the foreground. Old models of human behavior and motivation, intimately related to traditional Judeo-Christian morality with its focus on sin, started to disintegrate.

The loss of faith in reason and religion, the suggestion that caprice is a major factor in nature, and Freud's theories concerning dreams and sexuality have all left their mark on the imaginations of 20th-century writers. The association of absurdity with the concept of divinity is evident in French existentialism. Jean-Paul Sartre suggests in his novel *La Nausée* (1938; *Nausea*) that a recognition of the fundamental conditions of human existence is liable to induce an insuperable alienation and repugnance to life. Many novels published in Spain after the Civil War (1936–39) replace God with a capricious will that governs the universe, and this also produces a pervasive sense of alienation. For example, Ramón J. Sender's *El lugar del hombre* (1939; The Place of Man) focuses on the question of freedom in a nonrational universe. *El túnel* (1948; *The Tunnel*) by the Argentine physicist-turned-novelist Ernesto Sábato is a perfect example of

the 20th-century novel of alienation, as is Albert Camus' *L'É-tranger* (1942; *The Stranger*).

Another response to modern scientific theory has been a progressively deepening doubt of the effectiveness, even attainability, of objectivity. The primary expression of this doubt in literature is to be found in modernist techniques that discarded omniscient narrators and their claims of being privy to the truth. In modernist fiction, truth became relative and began to multiply with the focus on subjective experience and the use of interior monologue. The most prominent examples include the novels of Virginia Woolf (especially *Jacob's Room*, 1922; *Mrs. Dalloway*, 1925; *To the Lighthouse*, 1927; *The Waves*, 1931), James Joyce (*Ulysses*, 1922), William Faulkner (*As I Lay Dying*, 1930; *Absalom, Absalom!*, 1936), and André Gide (*Les Faux-monnayeurs*, 1926; *The Counterfeiters*).

Postmodernist fiction has continued this trend by progressively undermining the certainties of form demonstrated by the realistic novel. Jorge Luis Borges' stories freely mix the realistic and fantastic. John Fowles' *The French Lieutenant's Woman* (1969) provides a set of mutually exclusive endings, which takes away the univocality and the false security of closure. *Rayuela* (1963; *Hopscotch*) by the Argentine Julio Cortázar, invites the reader to create the story by reading the chapters in whatever order seems appropriate. William Gaddis' *The Recognitions* (1955), focusing on a painter who forges the "lost works" of early Flemish masters, gradually undermines the distinctions between the genuine and the fake, between authenticity and imposture, between reality and illusion. Other novelists who reflect on the implications of ideas from the new physics in their novels include John Barth with *Giles Goat-Boy* (1966) and "Lost in the Funhouse" (1968), John Updike with *Couples* (1968) and *Rabbit Redux* (1971) and Kurt Vonnegut, with *Slaughterhouse-Five* (1969) and *Breakfast of Champions* (1973).

The Information Age

Other novelists have focused specifically on information technology. John Dos Passos' trilogy *U.S.A.* (1930–36), considered the first fiction of the information age, shows how the mass media rewrite American culture every day. In these three novels, the writer is compared to the scientist in that both produce knowledge and interpretations of reality that are ultimately commodified by the mass media.

In recent decades, the novel has also embraced cybernetics, the formal study of systems in machines and animals, which has been at the core of the computer revolution during the postwar era. Terms we now use to express ourselves in our daily lives such as *positive and negative feedback, entropy, information, noise,* and *sender-receiver* all have their origins in or have been inflected by cybernetics. Cybernetics suggests that everything in the knowable universe can be modeled in a logico-mathematical system of quantifiable information. The idea is controversial, since it implies that the richness of the human spirit, human spontaneity, and human inspiration are just the product of mechanical processes that can be imitated and even surpassed by cybernetic mechanisms. Nevertheless, both the sciences and the arts often describe human behaviors in mechanical terms and share the fundamental idea that humans are machines.

Contemporary literature has confronted the central question of cybernetics both as a subject matter and by dramatizing the problem. Computers and robots, cyborgs and androids have proliferated especially in science-fiction works, but the question has also been tackled in other genres. Although cybernetic fiction has been written in different countries (Italo Calvino's *Ti con zero* [1967; *T Zero*] is perhaps the best known novel focusing on cybernetics), American authors, most of them male, have probed the issues raised by cybernetics most searchingly. Most famously, Thomas Pynchon's novels *V.* (1963), *The Crying of Lot 49* (1966), and *Gravity's Rainbow* (1973) have all shown a direct engagement with the science of cybernetics. Other examples include Kurt Vonnegut's *Player Piano* (1952); William Burroughs' fiction of the 1950s and 1960s, such as *The Soft Machine* (1961) and *The Ticket That Exploded* (1962); John Barth's *Giles Goat-Boy* and *Letters* (1979); Joseph McElroy's *Lookout Cartridge* (1974) and *Plus* (1977); Marianne Hauser's *The Talking Room* (1976); and Don DeLillo's *White Noise* (1985). Most recently, the subject has produced a movement in science fiction called "cyberpunk," which is usually traced to William Gibson's novel *Neuromancer* (1984), still the classic cyberpunk text.

For the 20th-century novelist, science may be feared or embraced, but it cannot be ignored. The characters in contemporary novels cannot be presented simply as the product of heredity and environment anymore, for the individual psyche is perceived as far more problematic, its responses less dependent on specific stimuli, its actions far more random. The 19th-century novel reflects an effort to shift from a dualistic to a unitary worldview spurred on primarily by the theory of biological evolution. The 20th century has inherited that same problem and acquires in addition the burden of having to accommodate itself to the implications of relativity, psychoanalysis, and, most recently, cybernetics.

YOLANDA MOLINA GAVILÁN AND MARIJKE RIJSBERMAN

See also Critics and Criticism (19th Century); Naturalism; Science Fiction Novel

Further Reading

Bronowski, Jacob, *Science and Human Values,* New York: Messner, 1956; London: Hutchinson, 1961; revised edition, New York: Harper, 1965

Butterfield, Herbert, *The Origins of Modern Science, 1300–1800,* London: Bell, 1949; New York: Macmillan, 1951; new edition, London: Bell, and New York: Macmillan, 1957

Chapple, J.A.V., *Science and Literature in the Nineteenth Century,* London: Macmillan, 1986

Cosslett, Tess, *The "Scientific Movement" and Victorian Literature,* Brighton, Sussex: Harvester, and New York: St. Martin's Press, 1982

Eastman, Max, *The Literary Mind: Its Place in an Age of Science,* New York and London: Scribner, 1931

Haynes, Roslynn D., *From Faust to Strangelove: Representations of the Scientist in Western Literature,* Baltimore: Johns Hopkins University Press, 1994

Henkin, Leo J., *Darwinism in the English Novel, 1860–1910: The Impact of Evolution on Victorian Fiction,* New York: Russell, 1963

Levine, George, *Darwin and the Novelists: Patterns of Science in Victorian Fiction,* Cambridge, Massachusetts: Harvard University Press, 1988

Levine, George, editor, *One Culture: Essays in Science and Literature,* Madison: University of Wisconsin Press, 1987

Limon, John, *The Place of Fiction in the Time of Science,* Cambridge and New York: Cambridge University Press, 1990

Losee, John, *A Historical Introduction to the Philosophy of Science,* London and New York: Oxford University Press, 1972; 3rd edition, 1993

Nadeau, Robert, *Readings from the New Book on Nature: Physics and Metaphysics in the Modern Novel,* Amherst: University of Massachusetts Press, 1981

Russett, Cynthia Eagle, *Sexual Science: The Victorian Construction of Womanhood,* Cambridge, Massachusetts: Harvard University Press, 1989

Scholnick, Robert J., editor, *American Literature and Science,* University Press of Kentucky, 1992

Warrick, Patricia S., *The Cybernetic Imagination in Science Fiction,* Cambridge, Massachusetts: MIT Press, 1980

Whitehead, Alfred North, *Science and the Modern World,* New York: Macmillan, 1925; Cambridge: Cambridge University Press, 1926

Science-Fiction Novel

Science fiction is a variety of fantastic literature, a descendant of myth, and a close cousin of the fairy tale, the detective story, and the Western. Science fiction is that variety of fantastic literature that presents its fantastic elements as plausible against a background of science. The science-fiction novel is the central literary expression of science fiction and as such participates in the whole realm of science fiction at large, a realm that extends well beyond written works of art.

Science fiction is arguably the most characteristic and influential cultural mode of our times, imagining the splendid and fear-some meanings of science and technology. Uniquely modern myths invariably have a connection to science, like that of Frankenstein's monster, from Mary Shelley's *Frankenstein* (1818), a terrifying tale of science escaping from the scientist's control. We long feared "Big Brother," the implacable and ubiquitous face of the totalitarian, industrialized state from George Orwell's *Nineteen Eighty-Four* (1949). For a decade the United States played with the deployment of a space-based antimissile system, a science-fiction weapon if ever there was one—universally known simply as Star Wars, in a reference to the title of a

1977 science-fiction movie that was structured as a fairy tale with a princess in distress and a talking animal sidekick. From "Industrial Rock" music to industrial design to computer games to World's Fairs to the world's most popular tourist destination, EPCOT (Experimental Prototype Community Of Tomorrow), we live in a world in which both science and science fiction are pervasive. Small wonder that the majority of the all-time highest grossing films have been fantasy and, more specifically, science fiction or that science-fiction novels so often top best-seller lists.

The term *science fiction,* first used in 1851 in a work advocating the poetic presentation of science in literary form, achieved currency only in 1929. In that year Hugo Gernsback, a pioneering editor of pulp magazines, promised to supply "science fiction" as the content of *Amazing Stories,* a magazine he had launched in April 1926. But this first publication self-consciously embracing science fiction recognized some of its own antecedents, defining its field retrospectively as including works by H.G. Wells, Jules Verne, and Edgar Allan Poe. Indeed, science fiction as we know it today has many sources, some literary, others extraliterary, as well as many outlets, some literary, others extraliterary. The evolution of the science-fiction novel is long and complex. We will consider, in order, the continuing tributaries of the science-fiction mainstream, the central contributions of Verne and Wells, and science fiction's place in American culture and modern culture.

Tributaries of the Science-Fiction Mainstream

In a broad sense, science fiction takes its origin in myths about the search for knowledge. In a narrower sense, there are five tributaries of the science-fiction mainstream worthy of special attention: the tradition of utopian fiction, the literature of fantastic voyages, the so-called *contes philosophiques* (philosophical tales), Gothicism, and "tales of ratiocination."

Utopian fiction, like science fiction, is a term that came very late to a tradition that long antedated it. Thomas More called his Latin political travelogue *Utopia* (1516), after an imaginary country in which all share labor according to their abilities and receive material goods according to their needs. The English neologism *utopia* is More's Greek pun. *Eu-topos,* which means "good place," is homophonous (at least in the English pronunciation) with *ou-topos,* which means no-place. This may mean that no current place is a good place or that no possible place is a good place. The majority have read More's text in the first way. More's *Utopia* is an island nation with money. Within its regulated realm, any citizen may move freely, using guest houses in any other sector, but must contribute some labor in compensation to his local hosts. The tale is narrated to a character named Thomas More by another character, Raphael Hythloday, a sailor, who claims to have visited this ideal island. The double narrative distancing here, as well as the geographical and ideological distancing, is typical both of utopian fiction and of the wider category of science fiction in providing a vantage point from which to criticize, or at least scrutinize, the world of the writer and his or her readers. Although More is undoubtedly criticizing the corruption and greed of English life, some critics speculate that he subtly criticizes the Utopians, too. For example, they consider themselves pacifists but employ mercenaries to conquer the islands next to theirs to create a protective buffer. In this respect, More's *Utopia* is characteristic of the genre, in which utopia and dystopia commonly are the two sides of the same coin. At bottom, all utopias are ambiguous. They are usually written to serve not so much as social blueprints as teaching devices.

The first significant utopian narrative is Plato's *Republic* (c. 380 B.C.), a dialogue in which Plato's character Socrates lays out the conditions of the ideal state. Famous among these is the banishment of poets—not, as popularly recalled, all poets, but only the imaginative ones who can arouse potentially disruptive ideas in people's heads. "Austere" poets are welcome in the training of the ideal citizens who live, as did many ancient Athenians, by the labor of slaves. To Plato, it seems clear, this republic was an ideal. To modern readers, reacting against its slave-based economy, it is closer to a dystopia. If we view political science as a science, providing the background against which a utopia's fantastic elements can be seen as plausible, then utopian fiction, as Darko Suvin (1979) has argued persuasively, is rightly understood as the oldest variety of science fiction.

All utopian fiction, no matter what its themes, must address the matter of economics, for without adequate material goods people are unhappy and may be driven to conflict. In terms of economics, utopian novels have moved through four broad phases. Ancient utopias, like those of Plato and Plutarch ("The Life of Lycurgus," c. 70 A.D.), based their economies on slave labor. Beginning in the Renaissance and influenced by Christian communitarianism, utopias like More's based their economic success on the efficient regulation of labor and the abolition of competition. Notable in that vein were *Civitas Solis* (1602; *The City of the Sun*), by Tommaso Campanella, the first utopian novel to reject slavery and to value work per se, and *Christianopolis* (1619), by Johann Valentin Andreae, a work based on John Calvin's theocratic Geneva that extolls the segregation of citizens by their occupations.

With the machine age came utopian economies based on machine labor, such as Edward Bellamy's *Looking Backward: 2000–1887* (1888), arguably the most influential utopian novel ever written. This 21st-century social tour is narrated by a reawakened 19th-century Bostonian in the form of reflections and history lessons for his new contemporaries. It tells of a world of equality in which all may eat at communal kitchens, pneumatic tubes deliver goods to homes from neighborhood warehouses, and a government-regulated market of jobs (the less desirable the job, the shorter the hours required) distributes labor equitably. A conscripted "Industrial Army" provides labor for those jobs so undesirable (for example, coal mining) that they cannot be filled. Bellamy's vision of "state capitalism" led to the formation of more than 400 Bellamy Clubs, which nearly succeeded in electing a candidate to the US presidency, but others saw this vision as what we would today call fascism. William Morris wrote *News from Nowhere* (1890), about a 25th-century dream world likened to a romanticized 14th century, as a reply to Bellamy. In Morris' world, the British Parliament buildings are used to store manure (More had used gold for chamber pots), and each person works purely for the love of the job and the pleasure of service in this anarchic paradise. In the world created by Morris, great floating barges convey coal across the landscape without need of human drudgery.

Samuel Butler's *Erewhon* (1872), an anagram for *nowhere,* ushered in the fourth phase of utopianism, that in which mechanization is seen as a threat to, rather than a source of, human happiness. In the two chapters known together as "The Book of the Machines," Butler argued, only 13 years after the publication of Charles Darwin's *The Origin of Species* (1859), that machines might have an autonomous evolution of their own and eventually enslave or obviate humanity. Right now, he wrote, street cars require humans to ring and respond to the signal bells by which cars warn each other of their approach to blind street corners. Someday, those signals would be made and heeded by other machines, and eventually machines would make, and even improve, themselves. For that reason, the Erewhonians had banned the development of machinery beyond the level of the early 19th century.

In the 20th century, dystopias, reacting against the dehumanization of industrialization, have been far more numerous than utopias. Evgenii Zamiatin's *My* (1920; *We*), a fierce satire of the Soviet state, is set in an implacable future in which "L=f(D), love is a function of death." Moreover, "every Number [citizen] can use any other Number as a sexual product," according to the "Lex Sexualis." All work according to a "Table of Hours" in a relentless Taylorism, named for the American Frederic Winslow Taylor, the founder of scientific industrial management and time-motion studies. The narrator, D-503, the chief builder of *The Integral*, a space ship, tells us that his instrument will be used to "impose a mathematically faultless happiness" on all people in the domain of the "United State." D-503 finds himself struggling ever more fiercely against this state as he becomes more aroused by I-330, a revolutionary woman. But eventually the state develops a medical procedure to remove the imagination from all its numbers, and D-503 watches emotionlessly as I-330 is publicly executed in the name of social order for, as the novel's last line says, "Reason must prevail."

Zamiatin's novel is the precursor of Aldous Huxley's *Brave New World* (1932), Orwell's *Nineteen Eighty-Four*, and a host of other grim novels, such as Anthony Burgess' *A Clockwork Orange* (1962), now all recognized as solidly at the center of modern science fiction. Nonetheless, utopian work has continued in the fourth phase. For example, B.F. Skinner wrote *Walden Two* (1948), in which people, trained like his famous experimental pigeons by "operant conditioning," are raised to be perfect contributors to a communist paradise. Skinner echoed Karl Marx, who believed that the process of maturing in a state in which each gave in accordance with his abilities and received in accordance with his needs would necessarily create "the new communist man." In such a vision, humans are similar to machines in being susceptible to conditioning by social forces. To Marx and Skinner, such conditioning presaged utopia; to Zamiatin and others, it led to dystopia. To all, utopian fiction, which certainly since the beginning of the 19th century has largely meant science fiction, has been a prime literary arena for social speculation and protest, particularly against the ravages of the modern industrial state.

The second important antecedent, fantastic voyages, also takes its beginning in the ancient world. Some scholars call Lucian of Samosata's satiric dialogue *Icaro-Menippus* (c. 170 A.D.) the first work of science fiction because the title character gains new perspectives on human folly by flying to the moon (which affords him a literally distant physical viewpoint) and to the summit of Olympus. His conversation with Jupiter results in a metaphorically distant philosophical perspective. From Lucian's day to ours, fantastic voyages have made possible the aesthetic distancing that supports social critique, whether those voyages

are made by the writer's compatriots to distant realms of space or time or by denizens of those realms to the space and time of the writer. Space travel and time travel, the archetypal tropes of science fiction, serve crucial ideological goals. As Olaf Stapledon wrote in the preface to his best-selling novel, *Last and First Men* (1930), "To romance of the far future, then, is to attempt to see the human race in its cosmic setting, and to mould our hearts to entertain new values. . . . Yet our aim is not merely to create aesthetically admirable fiction . . . nor mere fiction, but myth . . . true myth."

The category of the *conte philosophique* cuts across fantastic voyages and utopian works. Lucian's *Icaro-Menippus* is a good candidate for inclusion under *conte philosophique*, as is the utopian fantastic voyage in the fourth book of Jonathan Swift's *Gulliver's Travels* (1726), which portrays the peaceful realm of the intelligent, horse-like Houyhnhnms who do not understand war, lying, or sexual passion. Certainly More's *Utopia* qualifies as a philosophical tale in its exposition of the role of money and law in social relations. Francis Bacon, often held to have first codified what many call "the scientific method" in his *Novum Organum* (1620; *The New Tool*), wrote *The New Atlantis* (1626), a work that is at once utopian fiction, fantastic voyage, and philosophical tale. Bacon's ideal state, the name of which recalls a mythical lost realm praised by Plato, is ruled by a hereditary line of scientist-kings who order all behavior for the common good, a situation Swift satirized memorably in the third book of *Gulliver's Travels* with its description of the flying city of Laputa (Spanish for "the whore"). The citizens of Laputa are so lost in their thoughts that they employ "flappers" to whack them on the head to rouse them to conversation with other citizens or to prevent their walking off the edge of the city to their deaths. Rather than surviving on well-regulated labor, as one would expect in a utopian work, Laputa survives by tribute exacted from those living on the land below under threat of having the Laputans either move their city over the groundlings' farms, thus blocking their sunlight, or, in extreme cases, floating down and crushing them. Swift was clearly satirizing not merely Bacon's vision of utopia but 18th-century aristocracy and its relations to the working masses. As such, his satire shares aims with other philosophical tales that are not thought of as fantastic voyages at all, such as Voltaire's *Candide* (1759) and Samuel Johnson's *Rasselas* (1759), both of which take naive title characters from their sheltered childhood realms and expose them to hardship and corruption. The philosophical tale certainly includes works such as *Histoire comique des etats empires du soleil* (1655; *The States of the Moon and the Sun*), satiric travel tales written by the historical Cyrano de Bergerac. Voltaire wrote *Micromégas* (1752), a satire of our world from the viewpoint of giant visitors from space, and other tales that certainly qualify as both *contes philosophiques* and science fiction. Indeed, those who prefer the term "speculative fiction" (such as Robert A. Heinlein) would see the whole genre of science-fiction literature as a subset of the *conte philosophique*. Other critics, however, such as Brian Aldiss, trace science fiction to the Gothic.

Gothicism is a general artistic term that first arose in the 18th century for narratives that are strongly colored by the atmosphere that Gothic architecture evoked to English Protestants—a romantic, decadent, crumbling vestige of a benighted, sexually charged, Catholic, superstitious, medieval past. Still enormously popular in many forms, including the so-called "bodice rippers" mass marketed to appeal to repressed sexual desire, Gothicism has had many fine practitioners, including Percy Bysshe Shelley (*St. Irvyne, or The Rosicrucian,* 1811), Edgar Allan Poe ("The Fall of the House of Usher," 1839), and Nathaniel Hawthorne (*The House of the Seven Gables,* 1851). As Gothic novels grew in popularity and thus familiarity, writers, in addition to concocting new horrors, sought ways to combat their readers' aesthetic fatigue. While some took the tack of satirizing the form, as did Jane Austen in *Northanger Abbey* (1817), others, like Ann Radcliffe in *The Mysteries of Udolpho* (1794), created Gothic *expliqué,* or "explained Gothic," in which the surprises of the apparently supernatural were superseded by a final revelation that all these supposedly impossible events in fact had quite natural, albeit amazing, explanations. Out of this arose what most critics consider the first true science-fiction novel.

In 1818, Mary Shelley published *Frankenstein; or, The Modern Prometheus,* a thoroughly Gothic novel set in desolate garrets, windswept islands, and icebound ships, and featuring a tortured Faustian seeker of power, a direct but alienated descendant of William Shakespeare's Prospero (*The Tempest,* 1611), who consciously strives to fulfill the ancient myth of undoing death and unconsciously seeks to reproduce himself without the help of a woman. Structurally, *Frankenstein* made one crucial advance over Gothic *expliqué*: it moved the explanation from the end of the novel to the beginning. The 1818 preface begins by asserting that "[t]he event on which this fiction is founded, has been supposed, by Dr. [Erasmus] Darwin, and some of the physiological writers of Germany, as not of impossible occurrence." The never-named monster is clearly Frankenstein's double, just as Mephistopheles is Faust's, and takes his lineage from Adam shaped of clay and the Jewish legend of the Golem, the clay man given supernatural life to protect the community. But in Shelley's case, seeking knowledge alienates the seeker from the moral compass of his community, and the product of that seeking, the monster (probably from the Latin *monere,* "to warn"), destroys the community. One of the very first science-fiction novels, then, demonstrates the fearful consequences both of love of knowledge and of knowledge itself.

Tales of ratiocination was the term Poe gave to a group of his own narratives. Like *Frankenstein,* these tales exploit the atmosphere and interests of the Gothic, but they foreground something that is only implicit in *Frankenstein* and is typically absent in traditional Gothic—an aesthetic engagement through the love of intellectual exploration. Works that Poe put into this category we would now put into two, science fiction (for example, "The Facts in the Case of M. Valdemar," 1845) and the detective novel (for example, "The Purloined Letter," 1845). In "Valdemar," the title character is experimentally hypnotized at the point of death and thereby kept in an unbreathing limbo state for months. When the trance is finally broken, his body liquefies at once into "detestable putridity." There are some things man was not meant to know. In "The Purloined Letter," only the detective who is able to match his mind to the criminal's realizes that the stolen letter is right in plain view, hidden as it were among many other letters casually left on a desktop. By exercising his mind, as the hypnotist had exercised his, the letter is recovered and the detective's political will is served. Both works engage our intelligence in addition to our emotions, but the former ratifies our fears of new science while the latter ratifies what W.H. Auden called "the fantasy that hidden guilt will be revealed." By adding an explicit recognition that the intellect has a special place in certain narratives, Poe helped create modern science fiction.

Verne and Wells

Jules Verne, a Frenchman, is considered one of the cofounders of modern science fiction. He was the first person ever to support himself completely as a science-fiction writer, producing a lengthy series of extraordinary voyages typified by *Vingt mille lieues sous les mers* (1870; *20,000 Leagues under the Sea*). Almost every one of Verne's voyages is a so-called Robinsonade (after Daniel Defoe's *Robinson Crusoe,* 1719), in which European protagonists encounter the truly alien and respond by creating a familiar interior space and projecting old ideas and meanings on newly encountered lands and peoples. In *20,000 Leagues under the Sea,* we have a submarine tricked out as a club for Victorian gentlemen, complete with library, natural history museum, and wine cellar. The action is a tour of wonders but also includes a concrete reference to contemporary world affairs in the encounter among the Greek islands between the captain of the submarine, the stateless Nemo ("no one"), and an unidentified swimmer, who is, apparently, a Greek freedom fighter and who receives a sack of gold from Nemo to aid in the fight against tyranny, the fight in which Byron himself participated. In *Les Cinq Cents Millions de la Bégum* (1879; *The Begum's Millions*), not a Robinsonade, Verne contrasts two competing ideal cities, each built according to their founders' utopian designs, in the Olympic Mountains of the American Northwest. One city is Frankville, a French vision of satisfied middle-class life, and the other is Stahlstadt, a German vision of centrally directed industrial growth. In Verne's novel, Frankville wins. In these two works, and throughout Verne's career, we see many of the continuing realities of the science-fiction novel: an engagement with the intellectually new, the politically important, and the mythically moving, all often melded in works that rely on easy stereotyping for both satiric and didactic purposes and charged with a fascination with science and technology.

H.G. Wells, an Englishman, is considered the other founder of modern science fiction. Although today he is best remembered for his early, elegantly monitory science-fiction novels, throughout his prolific career as journalist, essayist, and writer of both fiction and nonfiction, Wells considered himself to be primarily a teacher. In his famous public dispute with novelist Henry James, Wells, rejecting James' interest in individual psychological states, argued that the duty of the novel was to explore the social forces that shape us. Wells followed his own advice, whether writing in a utopian vein or not. *The Time Machine* (1895), which introduced the radical notion of controllable time travel as a literary trope, dramatized the consequences of the split between the managerial and working classes of Wells' time in the conflict between our evolved descendants, the effete Eloi and the savage Morlocks. Both *The Island of Dr. Moreau* (1896) and *The War of the Worlds* (1898) stand as fierce indictments of British colonialism. And *The Invisible Man* (1897) suggests, as Mary Shelley had done, that knowledge without community is inevitably self-destructive.

Wells, who trained under T.H. Huxley, Charles Darwin's great disciple and popularizer, was the first science-fiction writer to understand science well. The theory of evolution taught him to search for patterns everywhere, including the patterns of social forces. Revolving around the "not impossible" workings of evolution, Wells' works still stand as inspirations to the genre. He is, in this sense, the father of what is called "hard science fiction," those works that rely on the so-called hard sciences, in which the imagined societies of tomorrow make sense in terms of what we know today.

American Culture and Science Fiction

Ever since Shakespeare set *The Tempest* in "the Bermoothes" (the newly discovered Bermuda), America and science fiction have had intertwined histories. America, as the setting for dreams of perfection, rejuvenation, and the taming of nature, was a natural locale for science fiction, and the literary forms that arose in the United States marked the course of science fiction worldwide. We see this clearly in the evolution of so-called pulp culture. Pulp, the cheap, brittle, wood-based paper used for printing dime novels, which were first published in 1860, gave its name to a whole family of demotic genres, from "true romances" to "true detectives" to "tales of horror." Inexpensive to produce and intended to be disposable, pulp novels and short-story magazines, unlike the works of Shelley and Wells, had no ambitions as literature but did offer the sort of sensationalism that first led to national news publication, via the newly invented telegraph, in Civil War reportage. The earliest pulp novels were Westerns, tales of the American frontier, works shaped by the social conditions of American westward expansion. As John Cawelti (1976) demonstrates, these pulp novels followed a formula acording to which an in-group (the townsfolk, the ranchers, the wagon train) is in conflict with an out-group (the ranchers, the outlaws, the Indians). The in-group has the values of the East (law and settled social relations), closely associated with the presence of women, while the out-group has the values of the frontier (individualism and nomadism) and rugged survival skills. Into this conflict, set in a vast landscape, rides the Lone Hero, someone who has the values of the in-group but the skills of the out-group. He typically settles the conflict in favor of the in-group but then necessarily becomes the most dangerous figure on the scene and so must either hang up his guns, as does the hero of Owen Wister's *The Virginian: A Horseman of the Plains* (1902), or ride out of town, as does the hero of Jack Schaefer's *Shane* (1953). This formula, already clear in Edward Sylvester Ellis' 1868 pulp novel *The Huge Hunter; or, The Steam Man of the Prairies,* marked what we would today call science fiction. From the pulps onward, adolescent inventors save the world against marauding threats or mad scientists seek to dominate the world. In both cases, the landscape is vast, the division between the forces of the good in-group and the bad out-group is clear, and the principal character is the most dangerous person. At the end of *Frankenstein*, the title character dies and his monstrous double wanders off alone into the uncharted Arctic ice. Shelley had already predicted the pattern that would typify most popular science fiction.

Edgar Rice Burroughs is a central figure in pulp science fiction. Earlier in the year in which he published his first Tarzan book (1912), Burroughs published *A Princess of Mars*, his first Mars book. As the book opens, the hero, John Carter, formerly a captain in the Army of the Confederate States of America, is being chased, along with a riding companion, across the barren Arizona landscape by howling Indians. The companion is killed by an arrow, but Carter escapes deep into a cave where he is overcome by a green miasma and awakens in another desert, this one

red. He is magically on Mars, a Western-type setting in which, because he has the strength of a man born on a planet with gravity three times that of Mars, he is able to become the successful hero he never could be on earth (in view of the fact that he found himself on the losing side of the Civil War). In the course of 11 novels, Carter settles Martian conflicts, marries a Martian princess by whom he has a child, and manages to bring peace to a world of "red Martians" and "green Martians."

Burroughs' Mars novels may in many senses be seen as costumed Westerns. They offer a power fantasy (conquest and inclusion) that is particularly appealing to the young and marginalized. We understand the lone hero's powers—good or bad—as reflecting some scientific truth (e.g., evolution and environment determines our strengths). The exposition of the novel depends on the deployment of stereotypes (in this case racial). And the outcome, as with all true fairy tales, indulges the protagonist's illusion of centrality (by marrying a princess, Carter becomes a legitimately dominant figure on Mars), an illusion that Sigmund Freud had identified as infantile. Such works readily lend themselves to series publication, for readers return to them not so much to be challenged as to be aroused and then reassured, each work reliably showing the triumph of the "viewpoint character," who often used the evocative initials J.C. In all, Burroughs published three more series of science-fiction novels for a total of 25 books, besides the Tarzan series, itself consisting of 24 novels, in which the lone hero has the skills of the outgroup (the apes), the values of the in-group (he is a lost scion of the English peerage), and settles conflicts usually in a rugged, unsettled landscape. Indeed, given Burroughs' use in the Tarzan books of speculations in linguistics, archaeology, and so on, one can say that these novels, too, are science fiction, where the science that generates plausibility is anthropology.

American pulp science fiction takes a happier view of science than Shelley, Wells, and Zamiatin. It embraces the progressive optimism of Verne, whose extraordinary voyages set the model for series publication, but typically without Verne's satiric bite. These pulps aimed to give the public what they wanted. Into this field came a Luxembourgian immigrant, Hugo Gernsback, who founded the first science-fiction magazine and gave the genre its name. Gernsback argued that the role of science fiction was to create scientists by making science appealing. He began the letters columns that still mark science-fiction magazines, creating the first popular genre with a tight and continuing conversation among writers, editors, and readers. Pulp science fiction not only aimed to give the public (most typically teenage boys) what they wanted; it knew what they wanted and gave it to them again and again. This habit of formulaic production, of course, led to the disparagement of science fiction by high-brow critics and ghettoized the genre.

From 1926, when Gernsback launched *Amazing Stories*, to 1954, science-fiction magazines thrived. By the end of that period, 38 science-fiction monthlies were being published in the United States. Writers were paid by the word and then, for the stories that proved most popular, produced "fix-ups," series stories lightly reworked into novels, which could be separately published in hardback. Many fans call the period from 1938 to 1946 the Golden Age of Science Fiction. It was shaped by John W. Campbell, Jr., the influential editor of *Astounding*, who demanded much better characterization than had previously ruled the pulps, and science that, like Burroughs' gravity-granted strength and unlike Burroughs' green miasma, worked. The stories of this period, produced by such American notables as Isaac Asimov (born in Russia), Robert Heinlein, and A.E. van Vogt (born in Canada), and such non-American notables as Arthur C. Clarke (born in England), refined an ideology that dominated science fiction. They valorized progress, tolerance, and democracy in the form of a natural meritocracy. They saw science and technology as providing the tools to solve all problems, even while recognizing their misuse as a grave danger. These were power fantasies set in a world in which one bright young man could save the universe.

Science fiction participated in the American cultural hegemony that arose after World War II, so that the growing global appetite for science fiction in a world brought to "peace" by the atom bomb and kept by that same technology on the brink of destruction was fed largely by English-language, typically American, productions. But those American productions changed significantly in each of the next two decades.

In the early 1950s, the American News Company, the only national periodical distributor, was bought by a Wall Street conglomerate and slowly sold for the value of its downtown warehouses, properties originally acquired during and after the Civil War for selling the pulps. By 1960, the American News Company was dismantled, and no other channel of distribution replaced it. Thus, while large circulation magazines, like *Time* and *Newsweek,* could work profitably through a series of regional distribution companies, small circulation magazines failed. The 38 science-fiction magazines were reduced to four. No longer could writers support themselves with short stories. But in the early 1950s, Ian Ballantine and others began to develop the paperback original as a means of novel publication. These works did not have the prestige of hardbacks, but, being undated, they did not have to be pulled off the newsstands to make way for their successors. Distribution became possible again, but only if science-fiction writers concentrated on the longer form. They did, of course, but retained the practice of writing works in series. From this arose the modern system of science-fiction publication.

In content, these globally marketed novels began to change in the 1960s, reflecting the political rethinking of Americans. "Soft" science fiction began to make its mark. While the first novel ever to win both the Hugo Award (named after Gernsback, the highest honor given by science-fiction fandom) and the Nebula Award (the highest honor given by the professional writers' association) was Frank Herbert's *Dune* (a 1965 fix-up that led to a whole series of works in a desert world), the second was *The Left Hand of Darkness* (1969), by Ursula K. Le Guin, a self-contained novel that valorized Taoist thought (under other names). Also in the 1960s, science fiction participated in the questioning idealism that marked the wider culture, leading to experimentation with form, in the work of writers such as Philip K. Dick. At this point, science fiction, in a sense, began to outgrow its largely stereotypical Americanness and to develop new roles in modern world culture.

Science Fiction in Modern Culture

Because American-dominated science fiction depended in large part on invention within the limits of formulae and stereotypes, it was aesthetically conservative, at least as interested in feeding the consumer as in challenging the thinker. Retrospectively, we can now recognize that many challenging works, such as *Lord of the Flies* (1954) and *The Inheritors* (1955) by English Nobel laureate William Golding, are also science fiction, but given the high-brow denigration of the genre, the label was not used in publishing, reviewing, or distributing Golding's work. But in the 1960s two related developments affected the scope of science fiction: the so-called New Wave writers adopted the stylistic experimentation of non–science-fiction writers, and the progressive industrialization of modern life, particularly the creation of a "global village" by way of communication technology, impelled non–science-fiction writers to embrace the tropes of science fiction.

In the 1960s, E.J. Carnell and Michael Moorcock, successive editors of the English magazine *New Worlds,* called aggressively for science-fiction writers to attempt the artistic explorations long characteristic of non–science-fiction writers, the stream-of-consciousness of James Joyce, for example, or the fragmented forms of John Dos Passos. They gave writers such as Brian Aldiss (*Barefoot in the Head,* 1969), J.G. Ballard (*The Atrocity Exhibition,* 1969), and John Brunner (*Stand on Zanzibar,* 1968) an outlet. Back across the Atlantic, atypical American science-fiction writers, such as Philip K. Dick, Samuel R. Delany, and Harlan Ellison, had independently been experimenting aesthetically.

In 1984, William Gibson's *Neuromancer* appeared, with this famous first line: "The sky above the port was the color of television, tuned to a dead channel." Gibson's style was an outgrowth of New Wave influenced by his observation in darkened video arcades of the transfixed faces of customers intent on the lights flashing before them. *Neuromancer* created a new subgenre called cyberpunk, which, in Gibson's case, is characterized by the radical conflation of vehicles and tenors in metaphors; by the presumption that society is controlled by an insidious, loose oligarchy of secret corporate and government interests; by the promulgation of the notion that this oligarchy functions through control of technology, especially information technology; and by the depiction of the lone hero as struggling but finally powerless in the world of cyberspace (a term Gibson coined). But cyberpunk, of course, is also the artistic mode of the film *Blade Runner* (1982, directed by Ridley Scott based on the Dick novel *Do Androids Dream of Electric Sheep?* [1968]) and of MTV, which appears to some as an emblem of a generation living through the lights flashing before them.

In the move from American genre fiction to New Wave to cyberpunk, the geographic center of science fiction also moved, reflecting cultural and economic realities. In Wells' day, the Martians in *The War of the Worlds* landed outside London. In the movie *The Day the Earth Stood Still* (1951), by Robert Wise, the cinematic aliens landed in Washington, D.C. In *Blade Runner,* the post-industrial future was Los Angeles. And in *Neuromancer,* we find our protagonist, a Native American, struggling to survive on the fringes of Tokyo. This westward movement has helped to globalize the domain of science fiction.

In the years preceding the demise of the Soviet Union in 1989, the single most popular writer in eastern Europe was Stanislaw Lem, the brilliant Polish science-fiction writer who, like Arkady and Boris Strugatsky, his only rivals in popularity in the Soviet Union, could criticize the state by hiding his critique in a genre literature set in the United States and aimed at the (very sophisticated) masses. In this he followed Zamiatin, of course, but also Jonathan Swift and Cyrano de Bergerac. Modern writers of all ostensible persuasions employ science-fiction tropes because, as so many advertisements for new technologies assert, "It's not just science fiction anymore." In Japan, Abe Kōbō (*Daiyon kan-pyoki* [1959; *Inter Ice Age 4*]), a great science-fiction writer, is regarded simply as one of his nation's greatest writers. Margaret Atwood, one of Canada's premier psychological novelists, achieved her greatest popular success with a dystopian science-fiction novel, *The Handmaid's Tale* (1985). Richard Powers, a MacArthur Fellow, has published such excellent philosophical science fiction (although not so called) as *Galatea 2.2* (1995).

Before the 1920s, the science-fiction novel did not have a recognized separate identity, although once noticed, that identity leaped into the foreground. Since the 1980s, the label has once more come to designate genre productions, while the concerns of science fiction have become so widespread that they are now part of all arts everywhere in modern industrialized culture. What began in myth, fairy tale, and fear has been transformed into the content of our lives. In that sense, "the science-fiction novel" is a historical label, while science fiction itself, the content of such novels, is a cultural dominant of our lives.

ERIC S. RABKIN

See also Dime Novels and Penny Dreadfuls; Science and the Novel; Utopian and Dystopian Novel

Further Reading

Aldiss, Brian, *Billion Year Spree*, London: Weidenfeld and Nicolson, 1973; as *Trillion Year Spree: The History of Science Fiction*, New York: Atheneum, 1986

Alkon, Paul K., *Origins of Futuristic Fiction*, Athens: University of Georgia Press, 1987

Amis, Kingsley *New Maps of Hell: The History of Science Fiction*, New York: Harcourt Brace, 1960; London: Gollancz, 1961

Bailey, James Osler, *Pilgrims Through Space and Time: Trends and Patterns in Scientific and Utopian Fiction*, New York: Argus Books, 1947

Bainbridge, William Sims, *Dimensions of Science Fiction*, Cambridge, Massachusetts: Harvard University Press, 1986

Barr, Marleen, *Feminist Fabulation: Space/Postmodern Fiction*, Iowa City: University of Iowa Press, 1992

Berneri, Marie Louise, *Journey Through Utopia*, London: Routledge, and Boston: Beacon Press, 1950

Carter, Paul Allen, *The Creation of Tomorrow: Fifty Years of Magazine Science Fiction*, New York: Columbia University Press, 1977

Cawelti, John G., *Adventure, Mystery, and Romance: Formula Stories as Art and Popular Culture*, Chicago: University of Chicago Press, 1976

Clarke, I.F., *Voices Prophesying War: Future Wars, 1763–3749*, New York and London: Oxford University Press, 1992

Clute, John, and Peter Nicholls, editors, *The Encyclopedia of Science Fiction*, New York: St. Martin's Press, and London: Orbit, 1993

Frye, Northrop, *The Secular Scripture: A Study of the Structure of Romance*, Cambridge, Massachusetts: Harvard University Press, 1976

Hayles, N. Katherine, *The Cosmic Web: Scientific Field Models and Literary Strategies in the Twentieth Century*, Ithaca, New York: Cornell University Press, 1984

Hume, Kathryn, *Fantasy and Mimesis: Responses to Reality in Western Literature*, New York: Methuen, 1984

Huntington, John, *The Logic of Fantasy: H.G. Wells and Science Fiction*, New York: Columbia University Press, 1982

Jackson, Rosemary, *Fantasy, the Literature of Subversion*, New York and London: Methuen, 1981

Landon, Brooks, *The Aesthetics of Ambivalence: Rethinking Science Fiction Film in the Age of Electronic (Re)Production*, Westport, Connecticut: Greenwood Press, 1992

Manuel, Frank Edward, and Fritzie Prigohzy Manuel, *Utopian Thought in the Western World*, Cambridge, Massachusetts: Belknap Press of Harvard University Press, and Oxford: Blackwell, 1979

Meyers, Walter Earl, *Aliens and Linguists: Language Study and Science Fiction*, Athens: University of Georgia Press, 1980

Panshin, Alexei, *The World Beyond the Hill: Science Fiction and the Quest for Transcendence*, Los Angeles: Tarcher, 1989

Rabkin, Eric S., *The Fantastic in Literature*, Princeton, New Jersey: Princeton University Press, 1976

Rose, Mark, *Alien Encounters: Anatomy of Science Fiction*, Cambridge, Massachusetts: Harvard University Press, 1981

Scholes, Robert E., *Fabulation and Metafiction*, Urbana: University of Illinois Press, 1979

Scholes, Robert E., and Eric S. Rabkin, *Science Fiction, History, Science, Vision*, New York and London: Oxford University Press, 1977

Suvin, Darko, *Metamorphoses of Science Fiction: On the Poetics and History of a Literary Genre*, New Haven, Connecticut: Yale University Press, 1979

Sir Walter Scott 1771–1832

Scottish

The most important novelist of the early 19th century and one of the key figures in the history of the form, Sir Walter Scott established the novel as a canonical literary genre fitted for the representation of national life. Scott's historical romance decisively enlarged the technical repertoire of prose fiction, raised its cultural status, bound it to a modern publishing industry and an international reading public, and precipitated the monumental figure of the author.

According to early reviewers, *Waverley* (1814) elevated the novel to the professionalized sphere of literary authority defined by the new critical quarterlies, rescuing it from a decadent, feminine culture of "romance" (see Ferris, 1991). Scott's turn to an Enlightenment historicism invigorated fiction with an empirical, materialist narrative of the progress of society so that individual lives, with their literary burden of pathos and comedy, could dramatize collective processes of social transformation (see Lukács, 1962; McMaster, 1981). At the same time, the new historical novel relied on prior traditions of fiction by (predominantly) women writers, as well as literary resources contained in the category of romance. The plot of *Waverley*—a young Englishman gets involved in the 1745 Jacobite rising before settling down to a safe Scottish marriage—adapts the allegory of political union worked out in the Anglo-Irish national tale to an imperial absorption of the Celtic fringe in the modern British state (see Trumpener, 1997). Scott's representation of "archaic" cultural forms sedimented within the nation's historical geography draws on the repertoire of the 18th-century antiquarian and poetic movement of romance revival, activating a content—regional native culture—that tended to remain episodic in the national tale (see Duncan, 1992). This repertoire, including both "naive romance" forms of native popular culture (ballads, folklore) and "sentimental romance" forms of an earlier national literature (Edmund Spenser, William Shakespeare), gives Scott's fiction not only a superior density of social mimesis in its depiction of customs and mentalities of traditional cultures, but also a richer register of poetic forms and techniques informing his own narrative practice. Some of these forms and techniques were specified in the dominant sentimental or literary romance of the preceding generation, the Gothic novel (see Robertson, 1994). Gothic fiction provided the model for a subjective narrative of psychological crisis and sexual politics, which Scott used to focus the objective narrative of historical transformation. Beginning with *Waverley*, Scott transferred the strong representation of a central sensibility from the traditional figure of the Gothic heroine to a male protagonist, the celebrated "passive hero" borne along by large historical forces (see Welsh, 1992).

Scott's adaptation of these precursor forms accomplished a significant thematic, rhetorical, and aesthetic expansion of the novel, creating a more flexible and capacious narrative vehicle. The characteristics of this expansion were, on the one hand, a thicker, referentially saturated historical and social mimesis, and, on the other, an increased complexity and resourcefulness of literary technique, marked by a rhetorical insistence on the non-mimetic conventions of romance. Scott effectively invented the modern form of the novel that articulates together, in a homologous relationship, private and public destinies, individual and cultural developments, inward psychological states, and a broad canvas of "society." With their innovative heteroglossia of dialects, styles, discourses, and genres, Scott's novels founded the 19th-century project of representing society as a complex, dynamic totality, a national and imperial range of generations, regions, classes, and ethnic groups; at the same time, the Waverley novels establish that amplified realism as a condition of "romance," of the modes of interpretation, thought-experiment, and fantasy encoded in particular cultural forms.

Waverley was followed by *Guy Mannering* (1815) and *The Antiquary* (1816); far from repeating a formula, Scott wrote three different kinds of novels, covering the making of modern Scotland from 1745 to the French revolutionary wars and the era of the author's youth. *Waverley* sets the classic pattern of the historical novel, with a fictional character as the focus of an epic historical crisis, while the historical context of *Guy Mannering*—the expansion of the British Empire after the Seven Years' War—frames a romance plot allegorizing the long-durational shifts of modernization. *The Antiquary* is a kind of meta–*Waverley* novel: an intricate, allusive meditation on Scott's materials and techniques and their conservative cultural politics. The ensuing series of *Tales of My Landlord* constitute a more ambitious set of historical novels of national life, three of which (*Old Mortality*, 1816; *The Heart of Mid-Lothian*, 1818; *The Bride of Lammermoor*, 1819) have generally been praised as Scott's finest. Turning from his persona as "The Author of Waverley," Scott adopted a more elaborate apparatus of editorial masks in an ongoing "anonymity game" (see Millgate, 1984). If *Old Mortality*, a tale of the Covenanting wars, offers the most concentrated version of the *Waverley* type of historical novel, *The Heart of Mid-Lothian* would prove most fertile for Scott's successors, instituting the polyphonic, mixed-genre form of the Victorian novel with its vision of a complex society symbolically organized around the prison, its focus on scandalous maternity, and its peasant-class heroine.

Scott pioneered the role of the prolific, best-selling novelist commanding an international reading public; *Rob Roy* (1817) sold out its huge edition of 10,000 copies in two weeks. *Ivanhoe* (1819), even more popular, marked a turning point. Scott forsook the modernization of Scotland for a new setting, the medieval greenwood, and a more overt commitment to romance, in a brilliant fantasia on the origins and constitution of an imperial English culture. The romances that followed ranged across early modern Europe, from the Scottish Reformation (*The Monastery* and *The Abbot*, 1820), through the Elizabethan court (*Kenilworth*, 1821: a glittering exercise in Tudor Gothic), to the waning of the Middle Ages in France and Burgundy (*Quentin Durward*, 1823, and *Anne of Geierstein*, 1829). In two novels published in 1824 Scott returned to modern Scotland: *St. Ronan's Well* was an unsuccessful attempt at a satirical melodrama of contemporary manners, while *Redgauntlet*, one of his best works, sustains a complex reflection upon the "Scotch novels" of his earlier career. With the *Tales of the Crusaders* (1825) Scott exaggerated the fantastic medievalism of *Ivanhoe* toward burlesque.

The financial crash of 1825–26 destroyed the Author of *Waverley*'s anonymity, as well as his fortune, and exposed him to the general public as Sir Walter Scott. The event helped bring the modern figure of the author into focus, as an identity at once heroically aloof from the commercial conditions of literary production and fatally bound by them. One of the major projects of Scott's last years involved the full-scale reassembly and marketing of his literary identity in a collected edition of the novels, the so-called Magnum Opus (1829–33), with revisions, notes, and introductions by the author. Just as Scott's first editions had done much to fix the material form of the novel in Britain for the remainder of the century—the three-volume, post-octavo set priced at a guinea and a half—so the "Magnum Opus" edition established a new cultural formation: the novelist as author, presiding over and informing his oeuvre, in an organic unity of life and works. Scott had prepared such a formation by editing a canon of British novels with biographical and critical prefaces (*Ballantyne's Novelist's Library*, 1821–24), and it was sealed with a monumental biography, *Memoirs of the Life of Sir Walter Scott, Bart.* (1837–38), by his son-in-law John Gibson Lockhart.

Scott's authority and influence remained preeminent for a generation after his death. His historical romances redefined both history and the novel as the major narrative genres of modernity and supplied a model for the developing literatures of Europe and the colonial periphery. As well as learning their technique from Scott, the Victorian novelists were haunted by his example, a career of superhuman industrial production issuing in glory and ruin. By the late 19th century, subsequent developments in fiction had appeared to supersede the Waverley novels. Modernist taste relegated Scott to the category of the subliterary or juvenile, and after 1945 even the novels' popularity suffered obsolescence, with many of them falling out of print. The last couple of decades have brought a significant revival of critical and scholarly interest, and a new collected edition is in progress.

IAN DUNCAN

See also Historical Novel; Ivanhoe; Realism; Romance; Scottish Novel; Waverly

Biography

Born 15 August 1771 in Edinburgh; as a child lived for a time in the Border country. Attended the High School, Edinburgh; University of Edinburgh; studied law: admitted to the Faculty of Advocates, 1792. Sheriff-deputy of Selkirkshire, 1799–1832; became partner to James Ballantyne in the latter's printing company, 1804 (the company went bankrupt in 1826, and it took Scott nearly the rest of his life to discharge the joint debt of £126,000); clerk of the Court of Session, 1806–30; helped found the *Quarterly Review*, 1809; built and resided at Abbotsford from 1812; founding president, Bannatyne Club, 1823; created a baronet, 1820. Died 21 September 1832.

Novels by Scott

Waverley; or, 'Tis Sixty Years Since, 1814
Guy Mannering; or, The Astrologer, 1815
The Antiquary, 1816
Tales of My Landlord, First Series: The Black Dwarf, Old Mortality, 1816
Rob Roy, 1817
Tales of My Landlord, Second Series: The Heart of Mid-Lothian, 1818
Tales of My Landlord, Third Series: The Bride of Lammermoor, A Legend of Montrose, 1819
Ivanhoe; A Romance, 1819
The Monastery, 1820
The Abbot; or, The Heir of Avenel, 1820
Kenilworth; A Romance, 1821
The Pirate, 1821
The Fortunes of Nigel, 1822
Peveril of the Peak, 1823
Quentin Durward, 1823
St. Ronan's Well, 1824

Redgauntlet; A Tale of the Eighteenth Century, 1824
Tales of the Crusaders: The Betrothed, The Talisman, 1825
Woodstock; or, The Cavalier, 1826
Chronicles of the Canongate: The Highland Widow, The Two Drovers, The Surgeon's Daughter, 1827
Chronicles of the Canongate, Second Series: Saint Valentine's Day; or, The Fair Maid of Perth, 1828
Anne of Geierstein; or, The Maiden of the Mist, 1829
Tales of My Landlord, Fourth Series: Count Robert of Paris, Castle Dangerous, 1832

Other Writings: stories and tales, poetry, plays, prefaces, a history of Scotland, biography, letters, a journal, and other miscellaneous prose works.

Further Reading

Duncan, Ian, *Modern Romance and Transformations of the Novel: The Gothic, Scott, Dickens,* Cambridge and New York: Cambridge University Press, 1992

Ferris, Ina, *The Achievement of Literary Authority: Gender, History and the Waverley Novels,* Ithaca, New York: Cornell University Press, 1991

Grierson, H.J.C., editor, *The Letters of Sir Walter Scott,* 12 vols., London: Constable, 1932–37

Hayden, John O., editor, *Sir Walter Scott: The Critical Heritage,* New York: Barnes and Noble, and London: Routledge and Kegan Paul, 1970

Lukács, Georg, *A történelmi regény,* Budapest: Hungaria, 1937; as *The Historical Novel,* London: Merlin, 1962; New York: Humanities Press, 1965

McMaster, Graham, *Scott and Society,* Cambridge and New York: Cambridge University Press, 1981

Millgate, Jane, *Walter Scott: The Making of the Novelist,* Edinburgh: Edinburgh University Press, and Toronto and Buffalo, New York: University of Toronto Press, 1984

Robertson, Fiona, *Legitimate Histories: Scott, Gothic, and the Authorities of Fiction,* Oxford: Clarendon Press, and New York: Oxford University Press, 1994

Sutherland, John, *The Life of Walter Scott: A Critical Biography,* Oxford and Cambridge, Massachusetts: Blackwell, 1995

Trumpener, Katie, *Bardic Nationalism: The Romantic Novel and the British Empire,* Princeton, New Jersey: Princeton University Press, 1997

Welsh, Alexander, *The Hero of the Waverley Novels,* New Haven, Connecticut: Yale University Press, 1963; expanded edition, Princeton, New Jersey: Princeton University Press, 1992

Williams, Ioan, editor, *Sir Walter Scott on Novelists and Fiction,* New York: Barnes and Noble, and London: Routledge and Kegan Paul, 1968

Wilt, Judith, *Secret Leaves: The Novels of Walter Scott,* Chicago: University of Chicago Press, 1985

Scottish Novel

The first vernacular Scottish prose romance appears to have been Sir George Mackenzie's *Aretina* (1660), a politically coded pastoral romance that looks backward both in its reliance on Renaissance courtly forms and in its Royalist politics. A recognizably modern form of the novel appears in Scotland only after the final failure of Stuart dynastic ambitions in 1746, and well after the political absorption of Scotland into Great Britain at the Treaty of Union of Parliaments in 1707. This loss of national sovereignty poses problems for delineating a Scottish tradition of the novel, as opposed to surveying, within a broadly British literary history, novelists who happen to be Scots.

The case of Margaret Oliphant, writing in the second half of the 19th century, illustrates some of the problems involved with identifying a specifically Scottish form of the novel. Born and raised in Scotland, Oliphant spent most of her life in London; she began her career by writing Scottish domestic regional tales and historical romances (including *Passages in the Life of Margaret Maitland,* 1849, and *Katie Stewart,* 1853), but she achieved her greatest success with the "Chronicles of Carlingford" (1863–76), tales of English provincial life on the model of Anthony Trollope's Barsetshire series. Although she would occasionally return to Scottish themes (as in *Kirsteen,* 1890), Oliphant effectively established herself as a prominent Victorian author whose works were addressed to a general British reading public and situated in a 19th-century tradition defined more by English women novelists (Jane Austen, Elizabeth Gaskell, George Eliot) than by Sir Walter Scott. Gender, in other words, reinforced an economic determination of the author's cultural identity as primarily Anglo-British rather than Scots. (Oliphant's Scots publisher, Blackwood and Sons, had been based in London since the 1840s.) Or consider Muriel Spark, arguably the best known contemporary Scots-born novelist. While her Edinburgh novel *The Prime of Miss Jean Brodie* (1961) brilliantly reprises the Scottish psychosocial anatomy of power and manners instituted early in the 19th century by John Galt and James Hogg, her other fiction assumes English, even European and US styles, topics, and points of cultural reference (such as Roman Catholicism), attuned to an international reading public.

For much of its history Scottish fiction has been inextricably mixed with, if not absorbed into, English and British constructions of literary tradition. This is due not so much to a failure of will (or genius, or virtue) on the part of Scottish writers as to specific material conditions and to the limited significance that could be claimed for "Scotland" as a figure of national identity, not only in Scotland itself but in the larger cultural fields—Anglo-British, European, imperial, and postcolonial—to which modern Scotland has irreducibly belonged. Twice in its postnational history Scotland has acquired that representatively national status, but with quite different meanings: the consolidation of a Great British imperial national identity in the early 19th century, and (borrowing the phrase used by Tom Nairn, 1981) the break-up of that national identity at the end of the 20th. On each occasion, an historical crisis of national representation *within Britain as a whole* created the opportunity for Scottish novelists to convene an effectively national movement or tradition.

Scottish institutions of literary production and reception—the local presence not simply of authors but of publishers, editors, and reviewers—made possible the appearance of the "Scotch novel" (so called) as a distinct, indeed dominant, genre in early 19th-century Britain. The conditions for this appearance were laid in the Scottish Enlightenment of the second half of the 18th century, with its metropolitanization of native institutions and discourses, and the formation (through the Scottish academies) of an empirical, historicist, and sociological understanding of modernity. While Scottish philosophy would be theoretically fertile for the rise of the novel, its material base was formed by the expansion of gentry and middle-class prosperity through capitalist "improvement," widespread popular literacy in Lowland Scotland, and the predominance of key institutions—the church, law, and education, including the universities—that had survived the Union, to become the bearers of national identity as (in the absence of political sovereignty) a *culture,* a distinctive body of rites, laws, and customs codifying national life. These institutions supported a powerful professional-class intelligentsia, separated from the exigencies of court or parliament and (progressively throughout the period) from the dogmatic wing of the Presbyterian Church of Scotland (the Kirk). Nevertheless, the Kirk remained vigorous enough to make the novel itself, along with the drama, a suspect literary form until the end of the 18th century. Furthermore, despite a lively printing industry dispersed throughout the Lowland burghs (but increasingly centered in Edinburgh, especially after the anti-Jacobin crackdown of the 1790s), there was as yet no large-scale publishing industry in Scotland. Allan Ramsay, the poet, had opened the first British circulating library in Edinburgh in 1725, but it was not until 1771 that William Creech turned his printing shop into a salon for the Enlightenment literati and began to produce books and periodicals by Scottish authors—although not yet novels, which remained a foreign commodity, imported from England and France.

Novelists of Scots origin included Charlotte Lennox (*The Female Quixote,* 1752) and John Moore (*Zeluco,* 1789), but their works, published in England, scarcely differentiate themselves from an English cultural norm. The two most important 18th-century figures for the development of a Scottish novel were Tobias Smollett and Henry Mackenzie, whose most characteristic novels—Smollett's last, Mackenzie's first—both appeared in 1771. Of the two Smollett has been the more consequential. Following a typical career trajectory, Smollett went south to London, the grand center of patronage, the theatres, and Grub Street. His first novel, *The Adventures of Roderick Random* (1748), a violent and salacious picaresque, takes the antihero from Scotland through London to the imperial peripheries. With this expanded geography, Smollett militantly charted a "British" rather than English domain of fictional reference, an achievement that the conventional comparisons of Smollett with Fielding have tended to obscure. Smollett thus plays an important part in that largely Scottish enterprise, the literary invention of "Great Britain" (see Crawford, 1992).

Mackenzie, meanwhile, retained his Edinburgh legal career but traveled in London, a visit to which (he claimed) gave him his impetus to write his first, wildly popular novel, *The Man of Feeling* (1771). Its programmatic excesses of "sensibility" align

The Man of Feeling with English and French models, an affiliation sustained (with some didactic hardening) in Mackenzie's later novels, *The Man of the World* (1773) and *Julia de Roubigné* (1777). As F.R. Hart observes (1978), these novels influenced a didactic, disciplinary offshoot of the novel of sentiment through the early 19th century in Scotland, including the works of Mary Brunton and John Gibson Lockhart. Mackenzie lived to become the grand old man of the Edinburgh post-Enlightenment, dying only one year before Scott. His influence consists less in his fiction than in his contribution, through his editorship of the periodicals *The Mirror* (1779–80) and *The Lounger* (1785–87), to the refinement of literary discourse according to English models; Scott eulogized him in the postscript to *Waverley* as "our Scottish Addison."

Smollett's last novel, *The Expedition of Humphry Clinker* (1771), proved to be the seminal work for a modern tradition of Scottish fiction that makes the postnational status of Scotland its self-identifying theme. The decisive text in the tradition, Scott's *Waverley* (1814), followed a spate of Anglo-Irish "National Tales" (see Trumpener, 1997); these in turn drew their national scheme from *Humphry Clinker,* which narrates, in a polyphony of dialects and sociolects, a family's journey from "British" origins (Wales) through the fashionable and commercial core (Bath, London) up to the author's native Scotland, and back. Scotland, the ancient nation fallen out of a political into an aesthetic mode of being, activates a healing deployment of romance conventions against the metropolitan register of satiric realism, so reaffirming the new national entity of the British imperial Union. In the next generation the wars with revolutionary and Napoleonic France gave a new urgency to the ideological consolidation of the British nation, a project that became yet more critical in the postwar years of economic recession, industrial restructuring, and class struggle.

Early national tales by Scottish women authors used a regional setting to frame domestic narratives of liberal-reformist social improvement (examples include Elizabeth Hamilton, *The Cottagers of Glenburnie*, 1808; Christina Johnstone, *Clan-Albin*, 1815) and the disciplinary regulation of sensibility (such as Mary Brunton's *Self-Control,* 1811, and *Discipline,* 1814). These novels tended to be formally as well as politically more conservative than their Irish models. Brunton's novels, fulfilling the dour promise of their titles with considerable technical panache, reprise an anti-Jacobin tradition of moral correction. Scott himself drew on the full cultural repertoire of Enlightenment sociological history and romance revival to amplify elements in the national tale, as well as in early historical romances set in Scotland (Ann Radcliffe's *Castles of Athlin and Dunblayne,* 1789; Jane Porter's sensational biographical romance of William Wallace, *The Scottish Chiefs,* 1810). Scott's Waverley novels, as they came to be called, exhibit an expanded range and density of both "realism" and "romance" that would be extremely influential not only in Scotland but throughout Britain, Europe, and the 19th-century colonial peripheries.

The wartime economic boom, with the closing of the continent, stimulated a revival of letters in Edinburgh following the freeze of the anti-Jacobin reaction. The founding of the *Edinburgh Review* in 1802 marked the pioneering ascendancy of Archibald Constable (1774–1827), who effectively transformed the 18th-century bookseller into the 19th-century entrepreneurial publisher, not least by becoming the principal publisher of the Waverley novels. Like his rival William Blackwood, Constable amassed his capital selling fine libraries and antiquarian books during the war, before expanding into book production. This allowed Constable to provide unprecedented financial incentives to his editors and authors while allowing them something like professional independence, and to invest heavily in promotion and distribution, especially in the London market.

With its powerful publishers and periodicals, drawing on the cultural capital of the city's institutions and professional literati, Edinburgh became a center of literary production to rival London during and after the war. Scott himself, with his close ties to the Scots Tory administrative junta as well as to the old guard Moderate or Old Whig intelligentsia, was the city's most powerful cultural broker, a source of social and political as well as literary influence. A lively local industry of "Scotch novel-writing" flourished around the success of the Waverley novels. Blackwood became the leading specialist in the genre, serializing some of these tales in his scandalously successful *Blackwood's Edinburgh Magazine* (1817–), which pioneered the role of the monthly miscellany as a major vehicle for prose fiction in 19th-century Britain. Scott, inevitably, was a patron of *Blackwood's Magazine,* and many of the firm's prominent novelists (Hogg, Lockhart, Wilson, Ferrier) were his protégés.

Sir Walter Scott's most important contribution to the fortunes of the Scottish novel is in his great Scottish historical novels of 1814–19, from *Waverley* through the third series of *Tales of My Landlord,* with the important supplement of *Redgauntlet* (1824), Scott's retrospective, critical summation of the genre he had established. Apart from sustaining, by their continuous success, the commercial conditions for Scottish regional and historical fiction as a major genre, the Waverley novels explore an influential solution to the predicament of modern Scottish identity in a postnational province, administratively attached to the state apparatus of a global commercial and military empire. First, Scott's generic resort to "history" recovered the novel from a disparaged feminine cultural zone of "romance" and united it with the public domain of a professional, masculine literary discourse staked out by the Enlightenment human sciences and the *Edinburgh Review* (see Ferris, 1991). Second, the novels themselves typically reconstitute national identity as cultural, mediated through aesthetic forms, rather than as political. Scott obtains these aesthetic forms through the "romance revival" of ancestral and popular native literatures; it is the posthistorical character of the romance that now signifies its contemporaneity (see Duncan, 1992). The nation is recovered and cherished in a knowledge of historical loss that provides the very opening of consciousness onto modernity—elegiac, to be sure, but comic or ironic rather than tragic.

Fellow Scotch novelists would imitate Scott's inventions of national history and culture (and a supply of historical topics, character types, romance tropes, etc., that would sustain fiction for a century or more); but for the most gifted of them, imitation meant contest and critique as well as emulation. In response to Scott's controversial novel of the Covenanting wars, *Old Mortality* (1816), which had offended the evangelical Presbyterians, James Hogg worked up one of his Border tales, *The Brownie of Bodsbeck* (1818), to vindicate the popular culture of the rural Borderers; and a few years later John Galt ventriloquized the Covenanter version of Scottish history in *Ringan Gilhaize* (1823). Both novels reject Scott's authoritarian-centrist, synthetic, and objective mode of historical narration for something radically different—in Hogg's case an imitation of the local vivacity and indeterminacy of oral tale-telling, in Galt's a cumulatively obsessive monologue spanning three generations. Both Hogg and Galt were premier Blackwood's authors; the magazine, with its volatile mixture of experimental forms and genres, intemperate Tory politics, bourgeois populism, nationalism, imperialism, and religious zealotry, represented the cutting edge of fiction through the 1830s.

John Gibson Lockhart and John Wilson, both of whom held editorial roles at the magazine, produced their best work at the edges of the novel form: Lockhart's satiric national-cultural anatomy, *Peter's Letters to His Kinsfolk* (1819), and the collaborative serial symposium *Noctes Ambrosianae* (1822–35), mainly by Wilson (as "Christopher North"). Wilson otherwise distinguished himself by reviving Mackenzian sentimentalism for a proto-Victorian style of morbid, lachrymose pietism (*Lights and Shadows of Scottish Life,* 1822), Lockhart by turning from the novel to biography (notably of his father-in-law, Scott). Susan Ferrier, another Scott protégée, leavens the Brunton tradition of domestic antisentimentalism with a satiric attention to social surfaces and the distinction of manners between Scotland and the metropolitan South (*Marriage,* 1818; *The Inheritance,* 1824; *Destiny; or, The Chief's Daughter,* 1831). And, in addition to specializing in Gothic and sensation tales, Blackwood's accommodated a characteristic Scottish vein of imperial fiction, looking back to Smollett, in the serials of Michael Scott (*Tom Cringle's Log,* 1829–31; *The Cruise of the Midge,* 1834–35).

The most original of the Blackwood authors, those who most strongly established a critical alternative to Scott's Waverley novels, were Hogg and Galt. Although they shared certain aims and techniques—notably, the promotion of vernacular Scots to the narrative foreground, in contrast to Scott's enclosure of Scots speech within an English narration—they produced strikingly different kinds of fiction. James Hogg was patronized in his lifetime as "the Ettrick Shepherd," a genuine primitive, the author of dialect songs and ballads. His remarkable experiments in prose fiction were neglected until the 20th century, when the startling success of one of them, *The Private Memoirs and Confessions of a Justified Sinner* (1824), has tended to overshadow the rest. Hogg's wild and subversive narratives offended polite taste by disrupting the conventions within which "folk" material was expected to be packaged, and by laying presumptuous claim to metropolitan styles and genres. Throughout the early 1820s, at the height of the vogue for the form, Hogg made a concerted attempt to set himself up as a Scottish novelist in the wake of his chief patron, Scott. The result was three extended works of fiction culminating in the *Confessions of a Justified Sinner,* none of which enjoyed any critical or commercial success, but each of which represents a radical, original reinvention of the dominant genres of Scottish fiction. *The Three Perils of Man: War, Women and Witchcraft* (1821), a prose romance of the medieval Borders, rebuts Scott's brilliant antiquarian inventions (*Ivanhoe, The Monastery*) with a fiercely comical mode of magic realism. *The Three Perils of Woman: Love, Leasing and Jealousy* (1823), a series of interlinked narrative "circles," turns back to the domestic national tale and traces its declension into the historical romance of *Waverley:* but Hogg performs a vertiginous deconstruction of this development, and of the cultural politics of a narrative synthesis of national life.

The literary career of John Galt spanned a mobile and fragmented life, traversing the "national" geography of the age and its varied commercial enterprises, from Greenock to London to Canada (where Galt founded the town of Guelph). Galt's "tales of the West," his most original works (published by Blackwood, 1820–23), explore an innovative domestic historical realism, while later novels reflect on his colonial experience (*Lawrie Todd; or, The Settlers in the Wood,* 1830; *Bogle Corbet; or, The Emigrants,* 1831) and satirize London political life (*The Member* and *The Radical,* both 1832). Galt intended his Scottish fiction of the early 1820s "to exhibit a kind of local theoretical history." *Annals of the Parish* (1821) and *The Provost* (1822), in particular, eschew the plot-intensive romance forms of Scott for a *trompe-l'oeil* satiric chronicle or annalistic record of the micropolitics of everyday life, while in *The Entail* (1823), his most ambitious work, Galt takes on (via the type of multigenerational family chronicle characteristic of a later period of the European novel) the scope of national romance. Galt's 19th-century influence descended, however, through a softened version of the depiction of local manners, performed by Galt himself in *Sir Andrew Wylie* (1822), and imitated, for example, by fellow Blackwoodian David Moir (*Mansie Wauch, Tailor of Dalkeith,* 1824) and Andrew Picken (*The Dominie's Legacy,* 1830). This mode of sentimental comic regionalism, a loosely knit anecdotal series devoted to the foibles of parish life and quaint or "pawky" characters, would effectively constitute the native tradition of a self-consciously Scottish fiction for the rest of the century.

Indeed, a strong school of Scottish fiction did not outlast the generation of Scott, Hogg, and Galt, as Edinburgh ceased to be a major national center of literary production after the 1830s. Nationalist critics once ascribed this cultural collapse to an organic fatality or decadence—the consequences of the Union, or of the corrupt aesthetic of Scott (see Muir, 1936; Craig, 1961). It is clear, however, that a combination of political, economic, and social forces undermined the regional institutions that sustained a metropolitan literary culture and a distinct tradition of Scottish fiction. The 1825–26 business crash that ruined Scott and Constable depressed the publishing trade throughout Great Britain, and when it recovered it was more centralized, decisively London-based (although Edinburgh would remain important for printing well into the 20th century). The modernization of transport and financial technologies brought Edinburgh too close to London for it to retain the gravitational integrity of a rival center. The 1832 Reform Act modernized Scottish institutions, bringing them into line with English models, but also eroding their local autonomy. London emerged as the definitive world-city, the undisputed center of literary as of other markets; ambitious Scots, and Scottish cultural capital, fled south. The case of Thomas Carlyle is exemplary. In the 1820s Carlyle began his literary career at *The Edinburgh Review* and flirted with novel writing, translating Goethe's *Wilhelm Meister* novels and starting one of his own; but with *Sartor Resartus* (1833–34), an antinovelistic experiment very much in the Blackwoodian manner, Carlyle scrambled the boundaries of both fiction and narrative, and darkly announced his own move from Scotland to the imperial center.

The net result of these changes was that no Victorian Scottish realism arose comparable to what was achieved in the English novel during the mid–19th century. Fiction in vernacular Scots flourished, to be sure, in the popular press rather than in the middle-class circulating library (see Donaldson, 1986). The most successful work of this provenance, William Alexander's *Johnny Gibb of Gushetnuik* (1869–71), appeared in book form after serialization in the *Aberdeen Free Press*; here the parish comedy (tied to a specific historical event, the 1843 schism in the Church of Scotland) inclines toward the sardonic rather than mawkish. George MacDonald, another Aberdonian, divided his literary labor between allegorical or juvenile fantasies (*Phantastes*, 1858; *At the Back of the North Wind*, 1871) and melodramatic rural Scottish tales (*David Elginbrod*, 1863; *Alec Forbes of Howglen*, 1865). The latter type yielded a full-blown movement at the end of the century, the so-called Kailyard ("cabbage-patch") school, assiduously promoted by the editor of the evangelical *British Weekly*, William R. Nicoll. Its principal authors, J.M. Barrie (*Auld Licht Idylls*, 1888), S.R. Crockett (*The Lilac Sunbonnet*, 1894), and John Watson (who wrote as "Ian Maclaren"; *Beside the Bonnie Brier Bush*, 1894), cultivated a parish idyll steeped in piety, nostalgia, and morbid sentimentality. (The "Celtic twilight" romances of William Sharp ["Fiona Macleod"] and William Black formed a Highland counterpart.) The Kailyard provoked the counterblast of George Douglas Brown's *The House with the Green Shutters* (1901), a bitter exposure of the moral squalor of small-town life that is as programmatic, in its way, as the model it sought to demolish.

The most accomplished realist novels by a Victorian Scottish writer, Margaret Oliphant's, make it clear that "provincial life" would have to be English in order to represent the life of the nation. The best of these (such as *Miss Marjoribanks*, 1866) rank among the best novels written in English during the 19th century. Oliphant produced the finest of her Scottish novels near the end of her career, as though in a critical return upon the Scottish tradition: *Kirsteen* (1890) is a feminist revision of Scott's *The Heart of Mid-Lothian* (1818). Forced by circumstances to be prolific even by mid-Victorian standards, Oliphant wrote across a wide range of genres, otherwise distinguishing herself in the supernatural tale (*A Beleaguered City*, 1880).

The other major Scottish fiction writer of the late 19th century, Robert Louis Stevenson, followed a more drastic path of exile—across North America and the Pacific to Samoa—and a career marked by the rejection of English cultural norms. Stevenson refused, in particular, to produce the conventional three-volume novel, the market dominance of which was secured with Scott's success and sustained by the all-powerful circulating libraries until the year of Stevenson's death, 1894. Stevenson established himself as a fiction writer in the magazine genres of tale (ludic fabulations such as *New Arabian Nights*, 1882, and *The Dynamiter*, 1885) and serial (the brilliant juvenile romances *Treasure Island*, 1883, and *Kidnapped*, 1886). In the 1890s Stevenson addressed his consummate technique to the far reaches of the European world-system in the South Pacific, with the mixed-genre experimental romance *The Wrecker* (1892) and the novella *The Ebb-Tide* (1894), an ironic colonial adventure that anticipates (and in some respects exceeds) Joseph Conrad. The other development of Stevenson's last years was a serious, reflexive return to the Scottish tradition established at the beginning of the century. *The Master of Ballantrae* (1889), the Stevenson work that most resembles a novel, begins as a Scott historical romance about Jacobitism and swerves into post-Gothic irony in the manner of Hogg, while *Weir of Hermiston* (1896), left incomplete at the author's death, stages (through its father-son

conflict) a complex reckoning with modern Scottish literary culture, above all with the formidable literary father, Scott.

Stevenson's huge critical and popular success released a flood of historical, imperial, and adventure romances, some of them distinguished. If the vivid historical romances of S.R. Crockett (*The Raiders*, 1894) and Neil Munro (*John Splendid*, 1898) have faded into the archive, Violet Jacob's grim, antiromantic *Flemington* (1911) has been revived to recent acclaim in Scotland, and the adventure novels of John Buchan have never been out of print. Buchan wrote expertly across a wide range of genres, favoring histories, historical novels (including two of the best modern exercises in the genre, *Witch Wood*, 1927, and *The Blanket of the Dark*, 1931), and thrillers, the modern form of which he did much to establish (with such novels as *The Thirty-Nine Steps*, 1915). Buchan's thrillers are best described as counterespionage quest romances; the best of them, such as *Greenmantle* (1916), achieve a radiant narrative lightness.

Buchan was a Tory, Unionist, and Imperialist intellectual of some stature, and he set his romances polemically against what he perceived to be the cultural politics of European high modernism (see especially *The Three Hostages*, 1924). Scotland's own modern movement, the so-called Scottish Renaissance, marched with a leftist political nationalism (the formation of the Scottish National Party, 1926–34) and was largely Glasgow-based; industrial Glasgow, hit hard by the post–World War I depression, became a viable alternative to genteel Edinburgh as a national cultural capital, an eminence it still holds in many respects. This Renaissance largely was guided by poets (above all Christopher Murray Grieve, "Hugh MacDiarmid"), although by the 1930s the movement would number several novelists among its fellow travelers, notably James Leslie Mitchell ("Lewis Grassic Gibbon") and Neil Gunn.

Scottish fiction of the modern period awaits a comprehensive critical reappraisal. Gibbon appears likely to stay the course as its most substantial figure (his trilogy *A Scots Quair* recently was reprinted in a scholarly edition), while Gunn has been a canonical figure in Scotland at least since the 1940s. *A Scots Quair* (1932–34) is an original and powerful achievement, although, like most trilogies or tetralogies, it falls off in its latter stages. Otherwise, the Scottish novels of the modern period are less impressive than their contemporaneous English, Irish, and North American counterparts; in range and quality they are exceeded both by the work of the Scott generation and by contemporary practitioners. Among the poets and critics who were the major figures of the Scottish Renaissance, MacDiarmid (like Carlyle, whom he in some respects resembles) held the novel in programmatic disdain, while Sydney Goodsir Smith produced the movement's bona fide modernist experiment, the sub-Joycean *Carotid Cornucopius* (1947). (The most striking "experimental" novel of the age turned out to be something quite different, David Lindsay's science-fiction allegory on national ideological themes, *A Voyage to Arcturus*, 1920.)

The nationalism of the Scottish Renaissance issued in one distinctively modernist preoccupation among mid-century Scottish novelists, namely with archetypalist and symbolist techniques of mythopoetic revival. This concern was informed by the Scottish conjectural anthropology of Andrew Lang and (especially) Sir James Frazer, sometimes reinforced with a Jungian allegorical framework. The reverie of a prehistoric, Pictish or pre-Pictish, Scottish Golden Age pervades Gibbon's *Scots Quair* and takes over Gunn's *Sun Circle* (1933); this essential, archetypal Scotland persists in a critical relationship to a modernity imagined in apocalyptic terms (whether utopian or infernal). The heroine of Gibbon's trilogy, Chris Guthrie, traverses an historical cycle from rural crofting community to provincial burgh to industrial city to become, equivocally, the nation as eternal feminine, mystically attuned to "the land." (*A Scots Quair* is also remarkable for its keen social consciousness, wit, and narrative style, a lyrical amplification of the Scots-inflected English of John Galt.) In *The Bull Calves* (1947) Naomi Mitchison underwrites a familiar national genre and theme (historical novel, Jacobite rising) with Jungian archetypalism; elsewhere she elaborates "universal" mythic themes in romances set in a more or less fantastic archaic world (*The Corn King and the Spring Queen*, 1931). Neil Gunn's most admired novels, set in Highland crofting and fishing communities (*The Silver Darlings*, 1941), depict the realization of primordial human identities (i.e., male sexuality: see Whyte, 1995) in relation to the elemental presence of, once more, the land and sea. An unsympathetic view might describe all this archetypalism as a late, muscular reinvigoration of the Kailyard with modern themes of mythicism, violence, and sexual yearning. The most distinguished contemporary author in the vein is the Orkney poet and novelist George Mackay Brown (*Greenvoe*, 1972; *Magnus*, 1973).

The most versatile novelist of the mid-century, Eric Linklater, produced his best work in a mode of cosmopolitan ironic picaresque (*Juan in America*, 1931; *Private Angelo*, 1946), alongside modern reinventions of Norse sagas. Scottish traditions of historical romance (as practiced by Nigel Tranter and Dorothy Dunnett) as well as Kailyard idyllicism (carried on by A.J. Cronin and Compton Mackenzie) have continued to flourish in the 20th century as mass-market genres. A feminine domestic realism, owing much to the Victorian women novelists, issued through Jane and Mary Findlater (*Crossriggs*, 1908), the Glaswegian bourgeois comedy of Anna Buchan ("O. Douglas"), and anatomies of provincial life by Willa Muir (*Imagined Corners*, 1931) and Jane Duncan ("Janet Sandison"), with a distinctively modern variant in the autobiographical protest fiction of Catherine Carswell (*Open the Door!*, 1920; *The Camomile*, 1922). The line of masculine social realism, with which Gibbon's trilogy intersects in *Grey Granite* (1934), goes back to the anti-Kailyard of Brown's *The House with the Green Shutters* and John MacDougall Hay's *Gillespie* (1914; a kind of demonic elaboration of Galt's *The Provost*). Notwithstanding the Highland novels of Thomas MacDonald ("Fionn MacColla"), this type of novel's setting tends to be urban, industrial, and proletarian—typically focused on working-class Glasgow, as in James Barke's *Land of the Leal* (1939) or Edward Gaitens' *Dance of the Apprentices* (1948). The tradition continues to prosper and diversify in the work of William McIlvanney (*Remedy Is None*, 1966; *Docherty*, 1975), James Kelman (*A Disaffection*, 1989; *How Late It Was, How Late*, 1994), and Jeff Torrington (*Swing Hammer Swing!*, 1992).

Both Kelman and Alasdair Gray, the most influential figures among the present generation of Scottish novelists, are products of Glasgow and its strong 20th-century tradition of a socially engaged, politically and aesthetically progressive art. Gray's *Lanark*, which in 1981 initiated the current flowering of Scottish fiction, might indeed be viewed as the authentic if long-belated masterpiece of the Scottish Renaissance, with its marriage of an engaged social and autobiographical realism to "experimental" modes of allegorical fantasy and metafiction. Just as the socio-economic and ideological reinvention of Great Britain after the Napoleonic wars allowed Scott and his contemporaries to make the Scottish novel a major cultural form, so the 1980s and 1990s brought something like the reverse process, the implosion of the imperial nation—a crisis that has been no less fruitful for fiction. Political alienation from England within a federalizing Europe has brought the possibility of devolution—and the vision of at least a virtual sovereignty within whatever postnational epoch lies ahead—closer to realization. "Scotland" is a figure invested with new imaginary possibilities, and novelists have responded accordingly. More immediately, the onset of Thatcherism and decline of the old Labour party (which had always had a strong Scottish industrial base) radicalized Scottish cultural production; small publishers such as Canongate and Polygon (both in Edinburgh) played a key role in the 1980s and 1990s, launching many promising careers.

Kelman, Gray, and their younger contemporaries make up the most gifted generation of Scottish novelists since the post-Enlightenment group that grew up around Scott. At first glance, Kelman and Gray themselves might seem to personify different tendencies within Scottish fiction: Kelman a sardonic realism cast in vernacular Scots (the narrative resources of which he has done much to renew), Gray a highly wrought formalism and a virtuosic literary English (*Poor Things*, 1992; *A History Maker*, 1994). But Kelman's fictions tend just as much to lyricism and fantasy, while Gray's encompass the devices of a politically engaged realism. Among the younger generation, Janice Galloway, Duncan McLean, and Irvine Welsh all extend the possibilities of vernacular narration, but in very different directions, while Iain Banks, A.L. Kennedy, and Candia McWilliam exhibit a consummate English style—although the cool, litotic Kennedy has little in common with the aureate McWilliam, save strength and wit.

Among these contemporary Scottish novelists, form, genre, and topic vary as widely as stylistic practice, as evidenced, for example, by Banks' brilliant performances of mass-market genres (the thriller in *Complicity*, 1993; science fiction in a series of novels by "Iain M. Banks"), the scabrous, delirious urban nomadologies of Welsh (*Trainspotting*, 1993), Galloway's feminist critical naturalism (*Foreign Parts*, 1994), Kennedy's startling suture of fantastic conceit onto low-key domestic realism (*So I Am Glad*, 1995). If Scottish novels of the late 20th century share a distinctive preoccupation, it would appear to be with sexual politics: male as well as female writers are engaged with a feminism the more energized and various for its breaching the culture so late, while the lavish representation of violence, especially sexual violence, is in large part a masculine preoccupation (Banks, *Complicity*; Welsh, *Marabou Stork Nightmares*, 1995; McLean, *Bunker Man*, 1996).

IAN DUNCAN

See also English Novel (19th-century sections); Historical Novel; National Tale; Private Memoirs and Confessions of a Justified Sinner; Romance; Romantic Novel; Sir Walter Scott; Robert Louis Stevenson

Further Reading

Burgess, Moira, *The Glasgow Novel: A Survey and Bibliography,* 2nd edition, Glasgow: Scottish Library Association, 1986

Campbell, Ian, editor, *Nineteenth-Century Scottish Fiction,* Manchester: Carcanet New Press, and New York: Barnes and Noble, 1979

Craig, Cairns, editor, *The History of Scottish Literature,* 4 vols., Aberdeen: Aberdeen University Press, 1988 (see volumes 2, 3, and 4)

Craig, David, *Scottish Literature and the Scottish People 1680–1830,* London: Chatto and Windus, 1961

Crawford, Robert, *Devolving English Literature,* Oxford: Clarendon Press, and New York: Oxford University Press, 1992

Crawford, Robert, *Literature in Twentieth-Century Scotland: A Select Bibliography,* London: British Council, 1995

Donaldson, William, *Popular Literature in Victorian Scotland: Language, Fiction and the Press,* Aberdeen: Aberdeen University Press, 1986

Drescher, Horst W., and Joachim Schwend, editors, *Studies in Scottish Fiction: Nineteenth Century,* Frankfurt am Main and New York: Peter Lang, 1985

Drescher, Horst W., and Joachim Schwend, editors, *Studies in Scottish Fiction: Twentieth Century,* Frankfurt am Main and New York: Peter Lang, 1990

Duncan, Ian, *Modern Romance and Transformations of the Novel: The Gothic, Scott, Dickens,* Cambridge and New York: Cambridge University Press, 1992

Ferris, Ina, *The Achievement of Literary Authority: Gender, Genre and the Waverley Novels,* Ithaca, New York: Cornell University Press, 1991

Fielding, Penny, *Writing and Orality: Nationality, Culture and Nineteenth-Century Scottish Fiction,* Oxford and New York: Clarendon Press, 1996

Hart, Francis Russell, *The Scottish Novel: A Critical Survey,* London: John Murray, 1978; subtitled *From Smollett to Spark,* Cambridge, Massachusetts: Harvard University Press, 1978

Letley, Emma, *From Galt to Douglas Brown: Nineteenth-Century Fiction and Scots Language,* Edinburgh: Scottish Academic Press, 1988

MacQueen, John, *The Enlightenment and Scottish Literature,* volume 2: *The Rise of the Historical Novel,* Edinburgh: Scottish Academic Press, 1982

Manning, Susan, *The Puritan-Provincial Vision: Scottish and American Literature in the Nineteenth Century,* Cambridge and New York: Cambridge University Press, 1990

Muir, Edwin, *Scott and Scotland: The Predicament of the Scottish Writer,* London: Routledge, 1936

Nairn, Tom, *The Break-Up of Britain: Crisis and Neonationalism,* 2nd edition, London: New Left Books/Verso, 1981

Royle, Trevor, *The Macmillan Companion to Scottish Literature,* London: Macmillan, 1983

Stevenson, Randall, and Gavin Wallace, editors, *The Scottish Novel Since the Seventies: New Visions, Old Dreams,* Edinburgh: Edinburgh University Press, 1993

Trumpener, Katie, *Bardic Nationalism: The Romantic Novel and the British Empire,* Princeton, New Jersey: Princeton University Press, 1997

Whyte, Christopher, editor, *Gendering the Nation: Studies in Modern Scottish Literature,* Edinburgh: Edinburgh University Press, 1995

Ousmane Sembène 1923–

Senegalese

The Senegalese novelist Ousmane Sembène is the most important practitioner of the 20th-century francophone-African novel and one of the leading figures in modern African culture as a whole. His work, in its sincere socialist political commitment and intense engagement with African history, has provided inspiration for a whole generation of African novelists. Sembène's novels have established important structural and stylistic models as well. For example, his best known novels are written largely in a mode reminiscent of European realism, and he is rightly considered one of the founders of the African realist tradition. Yet these realist novels establish and maintain a voice that is distinctively African. They are, from the beginning, influenced in important ways by African oral storytelling traditions. Sembène's novels are thus exemplary of the kinds of intercultural dialogues that have given the modern African novel much of its distinctive richness.

Sembène's experience as a dockworker in Marseilles provided

him with the material for his first novel, *Le Docker noir* (1956; *Black Docker*), in which the protagonist, Diaw Falla, is a young Senegalese man who works on the docks in Marseilles while struggling to become a writer. Suffering injustice both because he is black and because he is poor, Diaw winds up in prison for life, having killed a white woman who tried to take credit for a prize-winning book that he himself wrote. Meanwhile, his half-French, half-African fiancée, Catherine, is forced to turn to prostitution to support herself and their young son. The book ends with Diaw's passionate pleas that poverty be ended before society collapses from sickness.

The theme of injustice on the basis of class, race, and gender central to *Black Docker* remains at the heart of Sembène's subsequent work as well. In *O Pays mon beau peuple!* (1957; *O My Country, My Good People!*), Sembène moves his setting from France to a small fishing village in Senegal, and broadens the scope of his critique of racism by juxtaposing white prejudice against blacks to black prejudice against a white European woman who marries an African man. In 1960 Sembène published *Les Bouts de bois de Dieu* (*God's Bits of Wood*), regarded by many as his masterpiece and as one of the most important works of African literature. A historical novel, it dramatizes the 1947 strike (in which Sembène himself participated) against the Dakar-Niger railway in French colonial Africa. It pays particular attention to the crucial role African women played in support of the striking men, thus anticipating the emphasis on women both as objects of oppression and sources of resistance that would characterize the rest of Sembène's oeuvre. The anticolonial orientation of the book is strong, and Sembène presents in graphic terms the brutal attempts of the rulers of colonial French West Africa to put down the strike. Still, while the strikers are black Africans and their ultimate bosses are white Europeans, Sembène makes clear his socialist orientation by presenting the strike in terms of class struggle rather than racial oppositions. Meanwhile, the main emphasis of the book is a positive depiction of the heroic efforts of the Senegalese workers to resist French (and thereby capitalist) domination. The strike is to a large extent successful, and in the end most of the workers' demands are met.

The 1963 novel *L'Harmattan* employs the image of the hot, dry winds that blow through West Africa from December to March to suggest the spirit of independence that was blowing across colonial Africa in the late 1950s. However, in a mode somewhat reminiscent of Frantz Fanon, the book suggests that independence alone cannot bring genuine freedom, which for Sembène can only be achieved through socialism. During the early years of his career, Sembène also wrote and published a number of short stories with similar socially engaged themes. Many of these were published in the volume *Voltaïque* (1962; *Tribal Scars, and Other Stories*), while two brief novels, *Véhi-Ciosane* and *Le Mandat* were published in 1964 (these were published together in English translation as *The Money Order* and *White Genesis*). These novellas explore the breakdown in Senegalese society under the impact of colonialism but are careful to suggest that the alternative to the bourgeoisification of Africa is not a return to the traditional past but a forward movement to a socialist future.

By 1973 Sembène had turned his attention from colonialism to neocolonialism with the short novel *Xala* (*Xala*). Employing a mode of comic satire somewhat in the vein of predecessors like Mongo Beti, Sembène explores the ongoing neocolonial exploitation of Senegal through a depiction of El Hadji Abdou Kader Beye, a member of the rich, decadent indigenous bourgeoisie who continues to do the bidding of his French masters in order to maintain his wealth and status in postcolonial Senegal. However, vestigial remnants of precolonial social practices (such as polygamy) are satirized as well. The book is structured around parallels between El Hadji's business activities as a member of the postcolonial bourgeoisie and his sexual activities as the patriarch of his family and husband of three wives. Sembène again makes clear his belief that liberation in Africa must be achieved through socialism rather than through a return to precolonial tradition.

Sembène's latest full-length novel, *Le Dernier de l'empire* (1981; *The Last of the Empire*), satirizes the complex political scheming of various groups in postcolonial Senegal and exposes the mutual folly of French-controlled neocolonialists and

staunch Senegalese nationalists. Also published in the 1980s were the novellas *Niiwam* and *Taaw* (1987; published together in English translation as *Niiwam and Taaw*).

In addition to being one of the most respected figures in African literature, Sembène is one of the founding figures of the African cinema. In 1966 he directed the feature-length film *La Noire de . . .* (The Black Girl from . . .), the first ever produced by an African filmmaker. This film, in French, won a prize at the 1967 Cannes Film Festival, and Sembène's career as a successful filmmaker was launched. With the 1968 *Mandabi* (The Money Order), based on his own novella, Sembène turned to making films in the Wolof language, thus increasing his Senegalese audience. Indeed, many of Sembène's films in Wolof (the language most widely spoken in Senegal) have been based on his novels in French (the language in which Sengalese are most widely literate). The films thus effectively provide translations of the novels, as well as a distinctive solution to the controversies that have surrounded the continuing production of postcolonial African novels in the languages of former colonial rulers. Sembène has continued to gain international recognition as a filmmaker, and his films have been immensely popular in Africa, although the socialist political commentary that informs films such as *Xala* (1973) and *Ceddo* (1977) has sometimes gotten him into trouble with the Senegalese authorities, who have banned or censored several of his productions.

M. KEITH BOOKER

Biography

Born 1 January 1923 in the Zinguinchor-Casamance region of Senegal in colonial French West Africa. After receiving only a limited education, he was drafted into the French army in 1939; following France's official surrender to Germany early in World War II, Sembène joined the Free French forces in 1942 and landed with them in France in 1944 as they swept to victory against France's Nazi occupiers; returned to Senegal after the war, where he participated in the Dakar-Niger railway strike of 1947; later returned to France, joining a community of African dock workers in the port city of Marseille, where he taught himself to read and write in French and began his career as a novelist before moving back to Senegal; developed an interest in the cinema about 1960 and began to devote a large part of his energy to the making of films; traveled to Moscow in the early 1960s, where he studied at the Moscow Film School; founding editor, *Kaddu* newspaper, 1972; at this writing he continues to live and work in Senegal.

Novels by Sembène

Le Docker noir, 1956; as *Black Docker*, translated by Ros Schwartz, 1987

O Pays mon beau peuple! [O My Country, My Good People!], 1957

Les Bouts de bois de Dieu, 1960; as *God's Bits of Wood*, translated by Francis Price, 1962

L'Harmattan, 1963

Véhi-Ciosane and *Le Mandat*, 1964; published together as *The Money Order* and *White Genesis*, translated by Clive Wake, 1972

Xala, 1973; as *Xala*, translated by Clive Wake, 1976

Le Dernier de l'empire, 1981; as *The Last of the Empire*, translated by Adrian Adams, 1983

Niiwam; Taaw, 1987; as *Niiwam and Taaw,* translated by Catherine Glenn-Lauga, 1991

Other Writings: short stories and screenplays.

Further Reading

Bayo, Ogunjimi, "Ritual Archetypes—Ousmane Sembène's Aesthetic Medium in *Xala,*" *Ufahamu* 14:3 (1985)

Bestman, Martin T., *Sembène Ousmane et l'esthétique du roman négro-africain,* Sherbrooke, Quebec: Editions Naaman, 1981

Cham, Mbye Baboucar, "Ousmane Sembène and the Aesthetics of African Oral Traditions," *Africana* 13:1–4 (1982)

Gadjigo, Samba, Ralph Faulingham, Thomas Cassirer, and Reinhard Sander, *Ousmane Sembène: Dialogues with Critics and Writers,* Amherst: University of Massachusetts Press, 1993

Mulvey, Laura, "*Xala,* Ousmane Sembène 1976: The Carapace that Failed," in *Colonial Discourse and Post-Colonial Theory: A Reader,* edited by Patrick Williams and Laura Chrisman, New York and London: Harvester Wheatsheaf, 1993

Pfaff, Françoise, *The Cinema of Ousmane Sembène, a Pioneer of African Film,* Westport, Connecticut: Greenwood Press, 1984

Tsabedze, Clara, *African Independence from Francophone and Anglophone Voices: A Comparative Study of the Post-Independence Novels by Ngugi and Sembène,* New York: Lang, 1994

Semiotics. *See* Critics and Criticism: 20th Century; Narrative Theory; Narratology; Structuralism, Semiotics, and the Novel

---

Sensation Novel. *See* Gothic Novel; Horror Novel; Melodrama; Romance

---

Sensibility. *See* Sentimental Novel

A Sentimental Education by Gustave Flaubert

L'Éducation sentimentale 1869

Perhaps no other 19th-century French author has been more radically reinterpreted in the last few decades than has been Gustave Flaubert. Whereas for critics in the first half of the 20th century he represented the epitome of realist writing, more recent critics have seen in Flaubert's novels the precursor of the *nouveau roman.* Although this critical reversal has been very productive (for one thing, it made people read works—such as *Bouvard et Pécuchet* [1881]—previously dismissed as complete failures), it should not obscure the main point about Flaubert: that he neither wholly adhered to nor wholly dismissed the form of the novel as he inherited it. As *A Sentimental Education* in particular demonstrates, Flaubert's relation to the traditional novel is critical: he seeks to undermine its conventions from within.

By its very title *A Sentimental Education* marks itself as belonging to one of the most important subgenres of the 19th century—the Bildungsroman. The novel of education tells the process by which the young protagonist moves from a state of childhood innocence to that of mature knowledge (of the world, of society, of himself). Especially in the French tradition, this journey of education is often represented as a passage from the provinces—the realm of innocence and spontaneity, moral integrity, and stable social relations whose model is the family—to the capital, a complex social world characterized by corruption and hypocrisy but also by knowledge. Education, then, is defined negatively—as the loss of certain ideas (or ideals) redefined, from the perspective of the capital, as illusions. Often the story of the protagonist is contrasted with that of a childhood friend who remains in the provinces—that is, remains throughout the novel what the protagonist was at its beginning; this "double" serves as a yardstick by which we measure the "progress" of the protagonist.

Flaubert's novel seemingly adheres to this model: Frédéric Moreau leaves his childhood home in Nogent for Paris, there to acquire the knowledge that will enable him to succeed in the social world, and he leaves behind him his childhood friend, Deslauriers. But Flaubert constantly blurs the distinction between Paris and the provinces, between the hero who leaves and the friend who stays, thus ultimately undermining the very possibility that education (or its negative variant, disillusionment) may take place. The novel, symptomatically, begins with a return: coming back to Nogent-sur-Seine from a visit to Le Havre, Frédéric, on the first page of the novel, leaves Paris—sees it disappearing from the deck of a boat—before he ever sets foot in it. In Nogent he joins Deslauriers who is also back from Paris, having spent two years there. Two months later Frédéric leaves for Paris but comes back soon after, owing to lack of funds. Only at the beginning of Part II, after he has inherited from his uncle, does Frédéric make his "real" entry into the capital—an entry that by then inevitably occurs under the sign of repetition and loss. What the first hundred pages of the novel accomplish, then, is the dismantling of the symbolic structure of oppositions through which the process of education is conventionally articulated.

As a *sentimental* education, the novel is also a love story. But what kind of love story? On the one hand, it is the story of one love for an unattainable, hence privileged, object of desire—Mme Arnoux; on the other hand, it is the story of many objects of desire—Mme Arnoux, Rosanette, Mme Dambreuse, Louise Roque. Frédéric is both Werther—the lover who sustains his desire by never consummating it—and Don Juan—the hero whose endless search for new objects of desire demonstrates the inability of any particular object ever to fulfill his desire. But the coexistence of these two models in the same story compromises both: Frédéric neither sticks to his one ideal/impossible love nor does he substitute new objects of desire for old ones, discarded when possessed. His love story takes place in a middle zone between consummation and non-consummation since the object possessed is never the object desired at that particular moment. Hence Frédéric ends his life with none of his desires fulfilled in spite of the fact that in the course of the novel each one of the women he initially desired but could not possess ends up offering herself to him.

The extreme detail with which historical events are described invites us to read *A Sentimental Education* as a historical novel.

But here again we encounter a paradox: in a novel so couched in historical context, history plays no role. In depicting the revolution of February 1848, the insurrection of June 1848, and the coup d'état of December 1851, the novel shows individuals to have no influence over history. Historical events take place independently of particular individuals, who are mere spectators (this is clearest in the case of Frédéric) or, at best, mere actors—as is Dussardier—but never playwrights. If Frédéric's passivity and detachment may be seen as the sign of certain individuals' inability or lack of desire to shape history, Dussardier's staged suicide during the coup d'état is the sign of the futility of even attempting such action. In getting himself killed, Dussardier makes manifest his realization that he—and the people he symbolizes—failed in shaping history.

But there is more: Frédéric's life, unfolding through some of the greatest tribulations in French history, is at no point influenced by these historical events (which, moreover, show a tendency to repeat failures of the past rather than inaugurate a change in the future). The most striking example of this "irrelevance" of history is the episode in which Frédéric waits several hours for Mme Arnoux, who fails to arrive. Outside, in the streets, the February revolution is gradually taking shape. It occurs to Frédéric that Mme Arnoux's failure to arrive may be caused by the riots. This would have been an example of historical events impinging on the lives of individuals. If this were the case, Frédéric's life story would have been the tragic story of individual happiness thwarted by the impersonal forces of history. But Mme Arnoux is in fact prevented from meeting Frédéric because of her son's sickness, a chance event that has nothing to do with history. Frédéric and Mme Arnoux are neither agents nor victims of history; the revolution raging in the streets remains external to their lives. The impossibility—or futility—of change joins the impossibility or futility of education and of erotic fulfillment.

In registering all these impossibilities, *A Sentimental Education* brings to an end an important chapter in the history of the French novel: the chapter we usually associate with the name of Balzac and where individualized characters engage in a plot that moves forward, toward resolution, through a sequence of decisive events. The failure—or futility—of action writ large in *A Sentimental Education* will turn the French novel away from the social world—the privileged arena of the "realists"—and toward the world of feelings, thoughts, and art. The successor of Frédéric Moreau is not only Huysmans' Des Esseintes; it is also Proust's Marcel.

MICHAL PELED GINSBURG

See also Gustave Flaubert

Further Reading

Brombert, Victor, *The Novels of Flaubert: A Study of Themes and Techniques,* Princeton, New Jersey: Princeton University Press, 1966

Brooks, Peter, *Reading for the Plot: Design and Intention in Narrative,* New York: Knopf, and Oxford: Clarendon Press, 1984

Culler, Jonathan, *Flaubert: The Uses of Uncertainty,* Ithaca, New York: Cornell University Press, and London: Elek, 1974; revised edition, Ithaca, New York: Cornell University Press, 1985

Ginsburg, Michal Peled, *Flaubert Writing: A Study in Narrative*

Strategies, Stanford, California: Stanford University Press, 1986

Moretti, Franco, *The Way of the World: The Bildungsroman in European Culture,* London: Verso, 1987

Sartre, Jean-Paul, *L'idiot de la famille,* 3 vols., Paris: Gallimard, 1988; as *The Family Idiot: Gustave Flaubert, 1821–57,* 4 vols., Chicago: University of Chicago Press, 1981–91

Terdiman, Richard, *The Dialectics of Isolation: Self and Society in the French Novel from the Realists to Proust,* New Haven, Connecticut: Yale University Press, 1976

Thorlby, Anthony, *Gustave Flaubert and the Art of Realism,* London: Bowes, 1956; New Haven, Connecticut: Yale University Press, 1957

Sentimental Novel

The sentimental impulse recurs in literature: in all literary ages there are pathetic and moving scenes involving domestic relationships and distressed virtue. In the 18th century, however, sentiment and pathos for a while became the central motif of creative writing, especially in Britain and to a lesser extent in France and Germany. The cult of sensibility, occurring roughly from the 1740s to the 1770s, was a cultural movement devoted to tear-demanding exhibitions of pathos and unqualified virtue; in fiction it was notably expressed in the novels of Laurence Sterne, Henry Mackenzie, Jean-Jacques Rousseau, and Johann Wolfgang von Goethe, but it was also the dominant mode of a host of lesser-known men and women who responded to the increasing middle-class demand for sentimental fiction.

The rise of sentimental fiction has been associated with a growing hegemony of bourgeois cultural values, a decline in England of aristocratic court culture with the coming of the Hanoverians, the separation of public and private spheres, the valorization of the domestic and familial, and an increase in leisure, as well as with the movement in literary production from patronage to the market. It was also related to the entry of women into literary culture as readers and producers of fiction at a time when they were, on the whole, declining in economic importance. Sentimental fiction stressed the provincial and placed the country over the city; where 17th-century literature had been overwhelmingly metropolitan, suggesting that wit stopped at the suburbs, sentimental literature valued country locations and saw the city as the locus of vice, corruption, and greed. The typical sentimental novel takes its country hero or heroine to the capital, where he or she is distressed and abused, the denouement being a return to seclusion in the country and to rural values.

Sentimental fiction was supported by a moral philosophy that insisted on the value of the virtuous sensation as the root of goodness and benevolence. Beyond the explanations of Christian doctrine, this philosophy, associated with the Anglican Latitudinarians, held to a notion of innate virtue and stressed charity as the supreme quality and the proper manifestation of Christian faith. The most influential philosopher of this sort in England was probably the Earl of Shaftesbury, whose *Characteristics* (1711) preached a kind of secular humanism; for Shaftesbury, nature was an expression of God, while natural laws declared divine beneficence. The mind was in harmony with nature, and knowledge came through the senses, so one should be open to the world. An inborn conscience was a source of moral distinction that made the uncorrupted soul yearn naturally for benevolence and friendliness and swerve from the egotism and selfishness posited as the springs of human nature by such earlier philosophers as Thomas Hobbes and Bernard de Mandeville. Shaftesbury's thought was developed and modified by later moral philosophers, especially the Scots, Francis Hutcheson, David Hume, and Adam Smith, who continued his association of morals and aesthetics and his emphasis on good actions being their own reward. All rejected the ethics of rationalism, insisting that morality was *felt,* and all found community natural, part of a human desire for fellowship. In France, Rousseau, in his *Lettre à d'Alembert sur les spectacles* (1758; *A Letter to M. d'Alembert*) and again in *Julie; ou, La Nouvelle Héloïse* (1761; *Julie; or, The New Eloise*), advocated emotional rituals to bind a community while preserving its basic hierarchy. A microcosm of social community in much of fiction was the representation of women bonding in friendship, especially united in defense against some male assertion of power.

Sensibility suggested a capacity for very refined emotion and a quickness to compassion. As innate sensitivity or susceptibility, *sensibility* is defined in 1797 by the third edition of the *Encyclopædia Britannica* as a "nice and delicate perception of pleasure or pain, beauty or deformity" that, as far as it is natural, "seems to depend upon the organization of the nervous system." Frequently it appears physically based on a quality of nerves turning easily into illness, and it is described in contemporary medical treatises in terms of movements within the body. Its rise is inevitably linked with changes in the representation of the body, a transformation from the old humoral system to one that separated the sexes. This made the female body in particular the site of subtle emotions, since it was especially susceptible to influence; hence, women's propensity to blushing, crying, and fainting. In *L'Homme Machine* (1748), La Mettrie saw the mind and body as different forms of the same substance, and he linked sexuality and sensibility. The linkage was not accepted in women, however, in whom approved sensibility invariably implied chastity; only when sensibility was denigrated was it connected with sexuality in women.

Criticism influenced by sentimental ideas stressed the affective nature of literature, as Edmund Burke does in his *A Philosophical Enquiry into the Origin of our Ideas of the Sublime and*

Beautiful (1757). The work of art does not necessarily contain an intellectual meaning but rather it provokes the reader's participation in a mood. In Lord Kames' *Elements of Criticism* (1762), for example, the reader's experience becomes a rhapsody or reverie in which the consciousness of self entirely disappears. In Germany, Gotthold Lessing's *Hamburgische Dramaturgie* (1767–69; *The Hamburg Dramaturgy*) described the tragic effect as educative; it refines the audience's capacities to feel. Works of art reach out into life and change pity into virtue.

At its most basic and extreme, sentimental literature sought to arouse pathos through conventional situations, stock domestic characters, and rhetorical devices that demanded of the reader an emotional and often physical response. It was based on an assumption of the aesthetic quality of virtue displayed in a hostile world through a powerful distress that was somehow inevitable and religiously validated. In early sentimental novels, virtue in distress tended to be the central theme; in later works it was often the effect of misery on the observed that took center stage. The distress was rarely deserved, and the distressed tended to be natural victims whose suffering sprang from the predicament of being a defenseless young woman, an aging father, a helpless child, or even a melancholic and benevolent youth in a harsh world. The novels that displayed sensibility might sometimes be self-mocking, but they were rarely ironic. They provoked tears and distress in the reader in a way no other literature aimed to do. Perhaps more than any other writing, the acceptance of sentimental fiction relied on fashion, and it could become thoroughly outmoded when the modes of sentiment changed. So Mackenzie's *The Man of Feeling*, published in 1771 in the middle of the high period of the cult of sensibility when the public was emotionally prepared for his sentimental scenes, was ignored or mocked only a few decades later.

The literature of sensibility included all genres—the novel, essay, poetry, and drama—but the cult of sensibility was largely defined by fiction. In the mid–18th century this fiction taught readers how to behave and express themselves and how to respond properly to life's experiences. Later on it was more concerned with making its readers weep in various and prescribed degrees. In both eras it delivered the great archetypal victims: chaste, suffering women rewarded with marriage or elevated into almost martyr significance with a noble death, the scene of which was rendered redemptive for onlookers. In the later years it also delivered the benevolent and sensitive man whose feelings were too exquisite for the vulgarity, selfishness, and economic predatoriness of a wicked world. The assumption was that life and literature were linked not through mimesis and any demand for verisimilitude but rather through the belief that the experience of reading must intimately affect other aspects of living. Sentimental literature taught emotions, showing its readers how to produce an equivalent response to the one presented in the text. It moralized rather than analyzed, and insisted that the feelings it described were common; hence the emphasis on the domestic and familial, often delivered in an emotional tableau that arrested the action of the plot. Children, motherhood, and affectionate marriage were emphasized, and the small, loving family unit and kindly parenting were stressed, suggesting a change in family structure from the large kinship group of former times to the more modern nuclear family.

The bulk of sentimental novels were conventional, using such prescribed terms as *virtue* and *transport*. Some words shifted meaning to accommodate the new mood. The word *weakness*, which Samuel Johnson's *A Dictionary of the English Language* (1755) had defined as "want of judgment and foolishness of mind," came closer to suggesting a pardonable excess of a quality in which the sentimentalist might have proper pride, such as tenderness or pity. Most of the vocabulary was overcharged and hyperbolic, with adjectives running to extremes, from sweet and delicate to cruel and base. Words, tending to come in pairs and triplets and in prepackaged phrases, were not left to carry the meaning alone: they were augmented by heightening typographical and punctuation devices such as italics, exclamation marks, dashes, and gaps, indicating an emotion beyond speech. Because emotion was the concern, the work of sensibility tended to meander rather than move toward an inevitable destination. This was taken to the extreme by Sterne in *Tristram Shandy* (1759–67) and *A Sentimental Journey Through France and Italy* (1768); in the former, characters digress and muse so often that there is no chance of overtaking the historic moment and finishing the book, while in the latter, after many gaps and unfinished tales, the whole breaks off with the hand grasp of the narrator who has never reached Italy. The novels of Sterne, Samuel Richardson, Mackenzie, and a host of women writers of the late 18th century declare themselves fragmented: gaps are included in the works through the conceit of missing sheets or torn letters. Writing is intended to be to the moment, catching the minute fluctuations of sensation and emotion.

For purposes of the history of sentimental fiction it is useful to distinguish the novel of *sentiment* from the novel of *sensibility*, although the distinction is by no means clean. Moral sentiments, or reflections on human conduct, abound in the work of Samuel Richardson, the principal exponent of the early sentimental novel, with *Pamela* (1740–41), *Clarissa* (1747–48), and *Sir Charles Grandison* (1753–54). Often these sentiments are thoughts influenced by emotion, combining head and heart, and they are there for the edification of the reader, who should learn from the exemplary characters. Novels of sentiment, such as Sarah Fielding's *David Simple* (1744–53), praise a generous heart, often delay the narrative to philosophize about benevolence and virtue, and provide displays of emotional rituals. Both Richardson and Sarah Fielding wrote overtly to instruct, and they considered that morality was at the core of their endeavor. With some readers the effect was as intended, and Denis Diderot affirmed that Richardson's fiction had softened his heart and compelled him to choose oppressed virtue over triumphant vice. The novel of sentiment was not all exemplary and cautionary in effect, however, and Richardson's achievement was to have made the sentimental construction of woman a dominant motif of the novel throughout the century, as well as—against his stated intention—to have suggested how fiction could be used to investigate areas of sexual fantasy and domination quite out of keeping with the moral message. Female virtue is displayed best in distress in the midst of an extreme context of hostility and aggression that falls easily into a display of sadomasochism, as the Marquis de Sade made clear in *Justine* (1791) and *Juliette* (1797).

The novel of *sensibility* came in with the use of the latter term, which was little employed before the mid-century, although Joseph Addison had earlier used it to suggest delicate emotion and physical susceptibility. It honored the capacity for refined feeling, and it stopped the story to display this feeling and elicit the reader's response. Many of the novels, such as Mackenzie's *The Man of Feeling* and Sterne's *A Sentimental Journey,* have no plots beyond journeys. The episodes yield emotion as the compassionate, sensitive Shaftesburian soul travels through a callous and materialistic world, finding himself amazed but largely unchanged by his experiences. In Sterne's work, sensibility exists with some bawdiness and humor, but it was a formula no one else was able to follow. More common is the Mackenzie delineation, similar to that of Goethe in *Die Leiden des jungen Werthers* (1774; *The Sorrows of Young Werther*), of a man of feelings too refined for a wicked world, whose emotions are less a pattern for life than an object of the reader's admiration.

In the works of Mackenzie and Goethe, the hero is a victim of his refinement and of a corrupt society; he thus comes close to the position of the woman so mythologized by Richardson. In extreme moments of tenderness or pathos, the heroes often declare themselves like a woman or suffused with womanly emotions. In such remarks there is an implication that women excel in sensibility and that with women there is, as Richardson had amply shown, a ready-made plot of virtue in distress—that of sexual suffering. In fact, few later women writers followed Richardson into this dark territory. They were more concerned, during the high sentimental period, with portraying the woman of feeling as a domestic creature, an affectionate wife, a dutiful daughter, or a benevolent mother. Motherhood in particular was elevated in sentimental novels after the middle of the century, and the heroines of Rousseau, Henry Fielding in *Amelia* (1751), Charlotte Smith in *Desmond* (1792), and a hundred others took some of the sentimental power from their position as mothers. In other works, women achieved immense influence simply through their extraordinary sensibility, coupled with their extraordinary beauty. In the novels of the 1770s and 1780s, scene after scene provided the female reading public with a display of male venerations before this potent icon. Female innocence and passivity are pitted against aggressive male libertinage or parental power, and the woman, usually a well-born orphan, invariably wins; in the Gothic novel of the form usually written by women, which can be seen as a branch of the sentimental novel, the feeling heroines usually achieve both man and their own property.

The sentimental novel declined as an elite form toward the end of the 18th century, although it endures in today's popular forms of romance and melodrama. In the 1790s, popular and elitist taste began to move farther apart. Sentimental fiction, especially that written by women, came to seem an effeminizing force and a pandering to unintellectual and vulgar tastes; William Beckford noted its fantasy of aristocratic marriage for the passive sensitive girl and dismissed it as an escape from plebeian vulgarity. Classically educated men regarded the novel as undermining literary standards and diffusing authority from London and the universities. However, perhaps the most famous attack on sentimental fiction came from a woman, Jane Austen, herself steeped in sentimental novels. She saw them as dangerously promoting self-indulgence and supporting unanalyzed feeling over

proper reason and common sense. In the sincere, the overvaluation of sensibility attacked common sense and proper social behavior, as it does in Marianne Dashwood in *Sense and Sensibility* (1811), while in the insincere, sensibility became a mere mask over selfishness, a point made in the character of the vulgar Lucy Steele. The change in taste can be well seen in Mary Wollstonecraft, whose first novel, *Mary: A Fiction* (1788), praised her melancholy heroine's sensibility, while *A Vindication of the Rights of Women* (1792) made a sustained attack on both sensibility and the sentimental novel that promoted it.

JANET TODD

See also Critics and Criticism (18th Century); English Novel (18th Century); French Novel (18th Century); Gothic Novel; Melodrama; Novel of Manners; Sex, Gender, and the Novel

Further Reading

Barker-Benfield, G.J., *The Culture of Sensibility: Sex and Society in Eighteenth-Century Britain,* Chicago: University of Chicago Press, 1992

Birkhead, Edith, "Sentiment and Sensibility in the Eighteenth-Century Novel," *Essays and Studies* 11 (1925)

Braudy, Leo, "The Form of the Sentimental Novel," *Novel* 7 (1973–74)

Bredvold, Louis I., *The Natural History of Sensibility,* Detroit, Michigan: Wayne State University Press, 1962

Brissenden, R.F., *Virtue in Distress: Studies in the Novel of Sentiment from Richardson to Sade,* London: Macmillan, and New York: Barnes and Noble, 1974

Cox, Stephen D., *"The Stranger Within Thee": Concepts of the Self in Late-Eighteenth-Century Literature,* Pittsburgh, Pennsylvania: University of Pittsburgh Press, 1980

Crane, R.S., "Suggestions toward a Genealogy of the 'Man of Feeling,'" in *The Idea of Humanities, and Other Essays Critical and Historical,* Chicago: University of Chicago Press, 1967

Dussinger, John A., *Discourse of the Mind in Eighteenth-Century Fiction,* The Hague: Mouton, 1974

Friedman, Arthur, "Aspects of Sentimentalism in Eighteenth-Century Literature," in *The Augustan Milieu: Essays Presented to Louis A. Landa,* edited by Henry Knight Miller, Eric Rothstein, and G.S. Rousseau, Oxford: Clarendon Press, 1970

Frye, Northrop, "Toward Defining an Age of Sensibility," *English Literary History* 23 (1956)

Hagstrum, Jean H., *Sex and Sensibility: Ideal and Erotic Love from Milton to Mozart,* Chicago: University of Chicago Press, 1980

Starr, G.A., "Only a Boy: Notes on Sentimental Novels," *Genre* (1977)

Todd, Janet, *Sensibility: An Introduction,* London: Methuen, 1986

Serialization. *See* Periodicals and the Serialization of Novels; Roman-Feuilleton; Roman-Fleuve

---

Setting. *See* Description; Space

Sex, Gender, and the Novel

Throughout its history the novel has repeatedly acted as a site for the conflicts and consolidations of gender identities and sexual propriety. While there are long-standing traditions of erotic and gender-conscious fiction, such as Greek romance and the Don Juan narratives, prior to the 20th century the novel has generally mediated its sexual content with other themes, particularly reflection upon female sexual morality. In the early 18th century, a pejorative association was frequently assumed between the novel form and the female gender, an association that connected fictionality and femininity with the irrational, lazy, and romantic.

Although the 17th and 18th centuries saw a growth in the number of women writing professionally, the novel in particular, with its revelatory character and its scandalous potential, was often deemed an especially disreputable or licentious form of writing for women outside of the polite pamphlet or the ordered poem. *The Countesse of Montgomeries Urania* (1621) by Lady Mary Wroth, incited such vitriol on account of its romantic frankness and contemporary allusions that it had to be withdrawn from sale. However, before the rise of sentimental fiction in the mid–18th century, women writers such as Delarivier Manley and Aphra Behn did write with a sexual honesty on topics such as lesbianism and infidelity that distinguished them from the more "modest" female writings.

The deliberate engagement with sexual rather than romantic love marked a shift away from the conventions of the influential French romance, a form especially popularized through the novels of La Calprenède and Madame de Scudéry's *Clélie* (1654–61; *Clelia*). With its telos in the moral state of love, French romance retained a certain heroic influence that Jane Barker appreciated through works such as *A Patch-Work Screen* (1723) and *Exilius; or, The Banish'd Roman* (1715). The anxiety, however, that Barker's novels exhibit about the acceptability of being a woman writer seems justified by the experience of Delarivier Manley. Manley's *Secret Memoirs and Manners of Several Persons of Quality of Both Sexes from the New Atalantis* (1709), a novel in the style of the *chronique scandaleuse*, contained eroticisms and allusions that eventually led to her arrest. The literary world of the 18th century was one in which women writers, who often dominated novelistic output, could attract criticism because of the disapproval of female authorship. Thus in Germany in the 1770s, although women's education had become more widespread, female literary powers were still considered either aberrant or inappropriate. Sophie La Roche's novel *Geschichte des Fräuleins von Sternheim* (1771; The Story of Fräulein von Sternheim) caused a scandal purely because La Roche was a wife and a mother of five and should have been attending to more domestic matters than literary composition.

Considering these pressures, it is hardly surprising that the 18th century saw a widespread shift to a more didactic type of gender characterization and sexual lesson. Mary Davys' *The Reform'd Coquet* (1724) and Eliza Haywood's *The History of Miss Betsy Thoughtless* (1751) were novels that sought to reestablish the protectionist role of the good man in contradistinction to more predatory male characters. The heroines of such novels were based on a gendered ideology that classed the coquettish female as somehow predisposed toward error through flirtatious ignorance, and whose inevitable mistakes would educate her in the need for masculine support. This picture of fallible innocence must be balanced by the general 18th-century interest in the fallen woman, especially within the context of prostitution. Against a social increase in prostitution came novels that either celebrated its sexual liberty, as in the case of John Cleland's *Fanny Hill* (1748–49), which originally appeared anonymously as *Memoirs of a Woman of Pleasure*, or practiced a salacious condemnation, such as in the anonymous *The London Bawd* (1711) and *The Present State of Whorecraft* (1749). This type of novel, which detailed all manner of sexual act from sodomy to coprophagia, straddled pornography and social comment, although it became less acceptable with the increased sympathy toward the fallen woman as the century progressed.

The advent of the novels of sentimentality and sensibility consolidated a tradition of female passivity in such novels as Pierre Marivaux's *La Vie de Marianne* (1731–41; *The Life of Marianne*) and Goethe's *Die Leiden des jungen Werthers* (1774; *The Sufferings of Young Werther*). The sentimental novel in Europe found itself situated in times of immense change as the expansion in trade, leisure, consumerism, and women's education combined with the decline in literary patronage to produce an explosion of professional female writers operating in a more open, perhaps more accepting, literary market. Sentimental fiction fashioned the ideal woman as emotional, domestic, pure—although texts such as Elizabeth Griffith's *The History of Lady Barton* (1771) and Harriet Lee's *The Errors of Innocence* (1786) also depicted the psychological problems of the upright woman trapped in a loveless marriage. Marriage, however, was typically represented as an ideal state that could tame the rakish man in domestic equilibrium, such as in Frances Brooke's *The History of Lady Julia Mandeville* (1763) and Susannah Gunning's *Coombe Wood* (1783). The model housewife, promoted from the Netherlands in such works as *Sara Burgerhart* (1782) by Elizabeth Bekker Wolff and Agatha Deken and the Puritan writings of North America, was indeed well established before the advent of the overtly masculine Victorian age.

A gendered dominant of 18th-century fiction was the theme of "virtue in distress," with literal beauty operating as physical indicator of this virtue. Samuel Richardson's *Pamela* (1740) and *Clarissa* (1747–48) elevated the status of chastity and the resistance to seduction, although the virtue of characters such as the raped Clarissa Harlowe is always threatened by the physical vulnerability of their gender. Richardson not only created "feminized" male characters as an alternative to the more predatory man (sentimental male characters often displayed female characteristics, although the equation was never made in reverse), but also influenced the novels of many women writers, including Frances Sheridan's *Memoirs of Miss Sidney Bidulph* (1761) and Sarah Fielding's *The Adventures of David Simple* (1744–53), *The Governess* (1749), and *The History of the Countess of Dellwyn* (1759). The male heroes of these novels made heightened, "feminine" sensibility into a universal attribute that crossed gender divides, although as the century progressed there was an increasing tendency to ironize the weakness of the sentimental personality and, indirectly, femininity.

The gendered paradox of the sentimental novel seems to issue from the contemporary proprieties regarding female authorship. Francis Brooke's *The Excursion* (1777), which depicts the downfall of heroine Maria Villiers directly because of her pursuit of a literary career, exemplifies the tensions for women whose writing eulogized domesticity while simultaneously attesting to their nonincorporation in that ideal. Indeed, many female writers wrote out of financial necessity, annually producing large amounts of work for a reward that often amounted to little more than a subsistence wage.

The late 18th century saw radical changes in the nature of society and the gendered concerns of literature. Within the context of the political radicalism of Mary Wollstonecraft, Thomas Paine, and William Godwin, and the French and American revolutions, the vogue for sentimentality and sensibility began to decline. Part of the reason for this was a growing concern over the moral dangers of reading fiction. Sentimentalism had always been accompanied by the suspicion that reading romantic and emotive novels could predispose women toward a sexual fall. Emily Atkins, the heroine of Henry Mackenzie's *The Man of Feeling* (1771), notes that her reading of novels makes her vulnerable to male sexual threat, while anonymous works such as *The Evils of Adultery and Prostitution* even drew a connection between the reading of novels and the increase in soliciting. Yet there were also writings that offered new reflections upon the fallen woman and female sexual liberty. Mary Hays' *The Victim of Prejudice* (1799), Elizabeth Inchbald's *Nature and Art* (1796),

and Mary Wollstonecraft's *The Wrongs of Women; or, Maria* (1798) are among many late 18th-century novels that questioned the literary confines of female sensibility and male sexual double standards. In this last novel, Wollstonecraft went as far as defiantly assaulting male definitions of adultery and asserting the presence of a female sexuality. Such writings, however, must be contextualized within a definite growth of a masculine work ethic and the hardening belief in the power of the husband over the wife. In North American fiction writing of the 1790s, the common theme of seduction and sexual predation repeated the message that the romanticism of fiction could result in moral downfall. William Hill Brown's *The Power of Sympathy; or, The Triumph of Nature* (1789), Susanna Rowson's *Charlotte Temple* (1791), and Hannah Foster's *The Coquette* (1797) all suggested that sexual vulnerability was allied with the preoccupation with novel reading. Consequently, the late 18th century saw a move toward an emphasis on thematic verisimilitude rather than aesthetic indulgence. Moreover, as prose writing began to be claimed as a male form by Samuel Johnson among others, female writers found themselves increasingly criticized as debasers of prose fiction, criticism that tended to push female writing more toward the more ethical and reformatory.

The picture of relations between gender and literature in the 19th century is, like any other period, a complex one, although the influence of Victorian values from the middle part of the century led to a considerable solidification in the roles expected of fictional gender identities. Comment on the gender politics of the romantic period found a formidable voice in the person of Jane Austen. *Northanger Abbey* (1818) goes beyond questions of sexual and marital propriety by reflecting upon the issue of women's exclusion from historical narratives. Austen's drive behind such observations was not the desire for the rigid separation of the sexes but for a rational equality that accepted female intellectual capacities. It is not surprising, therefore, that Austen repeated the questioning of fanciful or excessively imaginative writing, with *Northanger Abbey* attacking Gothic fiction and *Sense and Sensibility* (1811) posing a general critique of the "cult of feeling." The explicit defense of female novel writing in chapter five of *Northanger Abbey* shows Austen as one who saw in fiction a chance for women to rise up as an "injured body" and establish their equality through demonstrations of wit and inventiveness. Naturally enough, Austen admired the writings of Wollstonecraft and set herself against the popular French writings of such as Germaine de Staël. Although de Staël wrote about the fetters that restricted talented women and also addressed the need of sexual liberation in novels like *Delphine* (1802) and *Corinne* (1807), Austen disliked the aesthetic elitism inherent in her work. Thus *Mansfield Park* (1814) mocks the aesthetic sensibility through the character of Fanny Price, although Fanny also represents a much more rounded female character than was previously seen in most fiction.

As we move into the Victorian period distinctions must be made between developments in Britain and the United States and some of the distinct forms originating in continental Europe and Russia in the 1830s. In postrevolutionary France the literary traditions of romance and seduction combined to establish a genre that considered the origins, societal context, and effects of female adultery. Fear of female emancipation and the desire to protect bourgeois property relations led several novelists to explore didactically the fall of woman from marital grace. The novel of female adultery, as Bill Overton (1996) has pointed out in his critical work of that name, explored the directly sexual nature of infidelity instead of playing on the theme of ignorance common to many British narratives of seduction.

Influenced by libertine novels such as Laclos' *Les Liaisons dangereuses* (1782; *Dangerous Acquaintances*) and the Marquis de Sade's *Justine* (1791), Honoré de Balzac's collection *La Comédie humaine* (1842–48; *The Human Comedy*) frequently probed adultery as a theme through which French social conditions could be explored in works such as *La femme de trente ans* (1834–42; *A Woman of Thirty*) and *Muse du département* (1843; *The Muse of the Department*). Balzac's context was a postrevolutionary France that was generally caught within two traditions regarding gender identity. There were those novelists like Théophile Gautier (in *Mademoiselle de Maupin*, 1835) who perceived gender distinctions in a state of breakdown, or those like Charles Augustine Sainte-Beuve whose work sought to confirm rigid gender categorizations. However, this simple distinction belies the complex attitudes to adultery that existed within Continental fiction. George Sand in *Indiana* (1832) and *Valentine* (1832), for example, considered adultery more as a by-product of the excessive power of the husband and of generally unjust sexual relations. This idea went on to hold currency in some Russian writing with Nikolai Chernyshevskii's idealistic novel *Chto delat'* (1863; *What Is To Be Done?*) directly expanding Sand's work into a consideration of interpersonal relationships outside of propertied values. Chernyshevskii's focus on female adultery was paralleled by Lev Tolstoi in *Anna Karenina* (1875–77) and *Kreitserova Sonata* (1891; *The Kreutzer Sonata*), although Tolstoi was equally critical of male adultery and desire in novels such as *D'iavol* (1911; *The Devil*) and *Voskresenie* (1899; *Resurrection*). Again in France, Champfleury's *Les Bourgeois de Molinchart* (1855; *The Bourgeois of Molinchart*) lent an exculpatory feel to female adultery by not only playing down the consequences of infidelity but also by showing the husband of the protagonist as being a selfish and boring individual. While other novels, such as Flaubert's *Madame Bovary* (1857), considered adultery through ideas of female sexual magnetism, some European writers shifted the focus of female infidelity to the context of male abuse. The Danish novelist J.P. Jacobson, writing under Denmark's more liberated divorce laws, shows in *Marie Grubbe* (1876) the need for female resistance against male exploitation. The heroine not only goes through two divorces but also physically attacks her rapist first husband and his mistresses. Iberian writers at this time, such as Eça de Queiros, Benito Pérez Gáldos, and Leopoldo Alas, likewise gave attention to male sexuality and social power as vehicles of exploitation. De Queiros *O primo Basílio* (1878; *Cousin Bazilio*) explored the callous activities of the seducer rather than the seduced, while the novels of Alas looked at the Church as an environment particularly adapted to sexual corruption.

Whatever the individual emphasis of the 19th-century novel of adultery, its basic motivation was an intense concern with the interrelationship of sexual morality, gender roles, and social stability. In a time when traditional social identities were being continually challenged or subverted, sexuality could act as an indicator of social transformation in terms of propertied relations and moral values. The instability of gender identity, although certainly sensed, was managed more rigidly in the United States and Britain. In 19th-century North America, women writers began to express gender identity through the standards of a popular fiction with an overtly religious content. Owing to the influence of Christian populism, women were able to form an extensive and potent community of producers and consumers of literature; indeed between 1820 and 1870 women's novels dominated the literary market, much to the chagrin of their male counterparts, who predictably accused them of lowering artistic standards. The early to middle part of the century was dominated by novels of domesticity such as Susan Warner's *The Wide, Wide World* (1850), Elizabeth Oakes Smith's *Bertha and Lily* (1854), and Harriet Beecher Stowe's *Uncle Tom's Cabin* (1852). The pious heroines of these novels displayed an otherworldly virtue that set them apart from the worlds of business, commerce, and mercantile masculinity that surrounded them. Yet the gendering of these novels was closely allied to the massive expansion of bourgeois consumerism in 19th-century America. The moralistic and worthy heroine is often visibly distinguished by fine clothes and goods, as is the case in Stowe's *The Pearl of Orr's Island* (1862), *My Wife and I* (1871), and *We and Our Neighbours* (1875). Consumer goods in 19th-century novels were not only capable of defining social place but also of assigning a separate sphere of gender reality allied to a specifically bourgeois ideology.

The gendered ideality of the domestic novel did not find universal acceptance. In France, alongside the standard romance, women started to write erotic fiction while novels such as André Léo's *Un mariage scandaleux* (1862; *A Scandalous Marriage*) and Daniel Stern's *Valentia* (1883) started to comment on the injustices that existed within the state of marriage. Reflections on the social conditions that supported female exploitation became common as more women entered the workforce out of economic necessity. Bruno Sperani's *Nell'ingranaggio* (1885; *Caught in the Wheel*), Krupa Satthianadhan's *Kamala* (1894), and Charlotte Brontë's *Jane Eyre* (1847) are examples of, respectively, Italian, Indian, and English works that expressed a distinct consciousness of the social restrictions and sexual exploitations to which women were subject by virtue of contemporary economics and vocational opportunities. Nineteenth-century America also contained many determined feminist champions like Margaret Fuller and Kate Chopin. Yet, generally speaking, the definition in the West of a stoical, creative masculinity and an enduring, ethical "muscular Christianity" ensured the dichotomy of female passivity and male activity in fictional characters, if not in direct action then at least in spiritual principle. Writers such as Herman Melville saw the increasing force of femininity in American society and literary audiences as a genuine threat to the definition of masculinity. Against the backdrop of a reading public who were mainly middle-class women, Melville wrote *Pierre* (1852), a novel that attempts to address the complexities of sexuality and society and refuse the easy absorption of masculinity into religiosity and sentimentalism. Victorian Britain was also responding in various ways to what it saw as the feminine threat. The stentorian campaigns for women's suffrage and the 1861 census, which showed more women than ever engaged in hardworking subsistence employment, disrupted the superficial construct of the "angel in the house." Thus writers such as Charles Dickens created a whole company of aggressive and unattractive female characters as a way of personifying the threat of the dominant female. Inspired by his disapproving witness of feminism in the United States, Dickens went on to sculpt characters such as Sairy Gamp

1212 SEX, GENDER, AND THE NOVEL

in *Martin Chuzzlewit* (1844) and Miss Havisham in *Great Expectations* (1861). These were vindictive figures who for Dickens illustrated the de-gendering that took place in the presence of the assertive woman. As a corrective measure, Dickens portrayed what he saw as the correct female credentials of passivity, quiet industry and deference through the likes of, among others, Amy Dorrit in *Little Dorrit* (1857).

Despite being conscious of the excesses of masculinity, exemplified in the Gradgrindian utilitarianism of *Hard Times* (1854), Dickens was among several Victorian writers who sensed that masculine qualities were somehow eroded or stolen from their rightful owners by the strong-minded woman. Thackeray in *The Newcomes* (1854–55) shows how the aged Colonel Newcome is steadily emasculated by his young wife, the forthright Sophia Newcome, who for Thackeray represented a base mercantile personality that saps Colonel Newcome's older, more noble values. Donald Hall in *Fixing Patriarchy* (1996) has pointed to the paradox that for the Victorian male writer, such as Thackeray and Thomas Hughes in *Tom Brown's Schooldays* (1857), female identity designated both strength and weakness, as femininity contained the enfeeblement that man must fear and from which he had to escape. There were novels written by men, such as Charles Kingsley's *Alton Locke* (1850) and, more strongly, Wilkie Collins' *The Woman in White* (1860), that expressed approval for the confident and industrious woman. Moreover, as the 19th century draws to a close we find writers like Thomas Hardy portraying the exigencies of being a female in an exploitational world of subsistence labor and sexual risk. In *Tess of the d'Urbervilles* (1891) Hardy does not shy away from the sexual desirability of Tess, but he does show that sexual relations take place within social codes that privilege male possession of land and title. Much late 19th-century fiction is characterized by an acute tension between the image of the domestic and quiescent woman and the reality of female working conditions. As we move into the 20th century we encounter a revolution both in the understanding of gendered identity and the way in which sex and sexuality are treated in the novel.

The novelistic expression of sexuality and gender in the 20th century is distinguished by a steady liberation of gender boundaries and attitudes to sexual being. Throughout the Edwardian and modernist periods we find the growth of novels that begin to detach sex from its reproductive and social functions and consider it in the light of its own pleasurability. *The Blue Lagoon* (1908), H. de Vere Stacpoole's representation of a teenage couple's sexual explorations, shows sexuality in the framework of spontaneous desire rather than reproductive intention. However, by emphasizing the innocence of the couple and their edenic tropical surroundings, Stacpoole preserves a certain sexual modesty. Others were more explicit. H.G. Wells in *Ann Veronica* (1909) drew a vigorous critical response by depicting a woman being sexually aroused by a man and making appropriate advances toward him of her own accord. Indeed it was around this time that the *femme fatale* started to become an established fictional motif, especially in the work of Wyndham Lewis, Ford Madox Ford, and Alduous Huxley. These authors admitted that women could both possess and express a sexual motivation, although their latent anxiety about this phenomenon may well have been informed by the increasing potency of the women's suffragette movement.

The early part of the 20th century saw more novelists denoting the body itself as the primary vehicle of sexual relations, with close description of physical details linking sexuality, appearance, and desire at a fundamental level. Sexuality started to be equated with individuality and, famously in the case of D.H. Lawrence, resistance to the lifeless processes of early 20th-century industrialization. Lawrence's direct descriptions of sexual congress issued from an almost mystical sense of the potential of sexual union and placed the pleasure principle of sex directly above that of its reproductive function, arguing from such realities as the female orgasm. Famous works such as *Lady Chatterley's Lover* (1928, withheld from publication in Britain until 1959, after the notorious court battle over obscenity laws) and *The Rainbow* (1915) not only revolutionized the graphic standards of sexual representation and language, but also introduced characters who occasionally pursued nonheterosexual behavior.

The prodigious controversies that raged over Lawrence's work served to place sexuality in a central position within fiction. In the same period women writers such as Virginia Woolf and Dorothy Richardson were making fictional journeys into sexual behavior in the context of oppressive male sexual conventions. Woolf's *Three Guineas* (1938) and *Between the Acts* (1941) draw parallels between the rise of fascism and the male control of women through economic, social, and psychological coercion. The commitment that Woolf and others showed toward feminism led them into the attempt to develop a new "feminine" style more suited to exploring the subject/object dichotomies of female social identity. Woolf's *The Waves* (1931), Richardson's 13-volume *Pilgrimage* (1915–67), and May Sinclair's *Mary Olivier* (1919) are examples of modernist fiction that sought through the free indirect style a release from the confrontational models of masculine writing and a unity between gender identity and novelistic form.

The modernist movement, set against the historical upheavals of war and successful campaigns for women's suffrage, laid the groundwork for the almost complete liberty of sexual expression in the Western novel, particularly from the 1960s when issues such as women's identity and contraception irrevocably changed gender consciousness. The fiction of the latter half of the 20th century has seen a vast exploration of all aspects of sexual persuasion and gender identity, from heterosexual and homosexual sex to perversions and sex crimes. (It must be recognized that this revolution has had a qualified or nonexistent presence in the many countries that maintain the prohibitions of rigorous censorship laws.) The 1950s and 1960s saw the publication of many novels previously banned for their explicit sexual content: Vladimir Nabokov's *Lolita* (1958), William Burroughs' *The Naked Lunch* (1962), Lawrence's *Lady Chatterley's Lover* (1959), and Henry Miller's *The Tropic of Cancer* (1961). In the 1970s the forceful resurgence of the feminist movement produced many radical women novelists, such as Marilyn French, Marge Piercy, Kate Millet, Rita Mae Brown, and Fay Weldon, who vigorously assaulted the double standards of male sexuality and asserted female resistance and sexual freedom.

The revolution in women's sexual expression and gendered defiance does indeed appear to be worldwide in the 20th century, often assisted by political turmoil and national transformation. The reflections this revolution has spawned are diverse. In the Netherlands, Andreas Burnier's *Een tevreden lach* (1965; A Satisfied Laugh) openly discusses transsexuality and lesbianism, while in Germany novels such as Elisabeth Plessen's *Mitteilung an den Adel* (1976; Message to a Noble) and Karin Struck's *Die Mutter* (1975; The Mother) examine issues of mother/daughter father/daughter relationships in the context of psychoanalytic theories of gender. The Soviet Union, although allowing under communism a certain degree of openmindedness regarding sex and gender, was increasingly liberalized with the advent of Perestroika, the result being novels such as Iuliia Voznesenskaia's *Zhenskii dekameron* (1987; *The Women's Decameron*). African women writers such as Muthoni Likimani have discussed the problematic issues of gender identity within the context of tribal loyalties, and in the West novelists such as Alice Walker, Amy Tan, and Toni Morrison have widened the specificity of gender debates by considering sexuality and male/female relations within different racial settings. In Japan, Masuda Mizuko and Yamada Eimi have written novels that look to the possibility of human interaction between the sexes that does not base itself on any sexual precondition or expectation. Many countries, especially in the Arab Middle East and Southeast Asia, still operate within stringent codes of censorship in regard to sexual writing and the accompanying politics of that writing. The literature of the Arab Middle East generally prioritizes powerful male protagonists with female characters usually assuming the role of emblems of nationhood. However, the theme of national liberation or the struggle for independence has enabled some writers to vocalize female individuality, such as in *The Open Door* (1960) by Latifada al-Zayyat, which aligns the development of a young girl with the course of Egyptian independence.

Of course, any appraisal of the 20th-century novel's representations of sexuality and gender would be incomplete without acknowledging the extensive contribution made by gay and lesbian fiction. Oscar Wilde's *The Picture of Dorian Gray* (1891), which contained the attraction between two male characters, famously contributed to his imprisonment for homosexuality, and exemplified the oppression of homosexuality in literature for the next 60 years. Texts that did engage with homosexual characters tended toward a predictable tragedy, as is the case in Alfred J. Cohen's *A Marriage Below Zero* (1899), whose gay protagonist is compelled to suicide by society's fetters and Cohen's own literary restrictions. Historically, more tolerance was to be found in France, where a tradition of homosexual writers such as Paul Verlaine, Arthur Rimbaud, Marcel Proust, and André Gide operated under a greater social freedom and where many foreign writers, including William Burroughs, could publish their work. With the gay liberation movements of the 1960s and the subsequent establishing of gay publishers in the United States, there has been an explosion of diverse gay literature. James Barr's *Quatrefoil* (1950), which showed a gay relationship between two naval officers, was perhaps the first successful gay novel. Since then the community of gay novelists has grown internationally, among them writers such as Christopher Bram, James Purdy, Allan Hollinghurst, José Lezama Lima, Reinaldo Arenas, Pier Paolo Pasolini, and Yukio Mishima. Undoubtedly the biggest influence on recent gay writing has been the AIDS pandemic, with Hervé Guibert and Paul Monette being among many gay writers who have dealt with the trauma, loss, and persecution suffered by the gay community since the initial effects of the disease in the early 1980s.

The postwar period has also seen the development of lesbian fiction as a distinct genre, stemming particularly from the interest in lesbian writing in the 1950s. Lesbian subtexts were present in the fiction of Virginia Woolf, but it took the liberalism of the 1960s to establish the openness necessary for lesbian fictional expression. Since then a vivid pageant of lesbian writers including Mary Renault, Sara Teasdale, Margaret Cruickshank, Jewelle Gomez, and Bonnie Zimmerman have produced novels of intense lesbian physical and emotional expression and highlighted heterosexual society's frequently reactionary attitudes.

The 20th century has perhaps seen the greatest development in the open representation of sexuality than in all the previous centuries, at least in what is considered to be literary fiction. The direction of future understandings of sexuality and gender is impossible to predict, especially in a world that is becoming increasing unshockable and where sex has become a merchandising standard.

Christopher McNab

See also Feminist Criticism of Narrative; Libertine Novel; Modernism; Pornographic Novel; Sentimental Novel

Further Reading

Charney, Maurice, *Sexual Fiction,* London and New York: Methuen, 1981

Cranny-Francis, Anne, *Feminist Fictions: Feminist Uses of Generic Fiction,* Cambridge: Polity Press, and New York: St. Martin's Press, 1990

Davies, Carole Boyce, *Black Women, Writing, and Identity: Migrations of the Subject,* London and New York: Routledge, 1994

Douglas, Ann, *The Feminization of American Culture,* New York: Knopf, 1977

Grier, Barbara, *The Lesbian in Literature,* San Francisco: Daughters of Bilitis, 1967; 3rd edition, Tallahassee, Florida: Naiad Press, 1981

Hall, Donald E., *Fixing Patriarchy: Feminism and Mid-Victorian Male Novelists,* London: Macmillan, and New York: New York University Press, 1996

Ingham, Patricia, *The Language of Gender and Class: Transformation in the Victorian Novel,* London and New York: Routledge, 1996

Markman, Ellis, *The Politics of Sensibility: Race, Gender, and Commerce in the Sentimental Novel,* Cambridge and New York: Cambridge University Press, 1996

Overton, Bill, *The Novel of Female Adultery: Love and Gender in Continental European Fiction, 1830–1900,* London: Macmillan, and New York: St. Martin's Press, 1996

Peterson, Carla L., *The Determined Reader: Gender and Culture in the Novel from Napoleon to Victoria,* New Brunswick, New Jersey: Rutgers University Press, 1986

Showalter, Elaine, *Sexual Anarchy: Gender and Culture at the Fin de Siècle,* New York: Viking Press, and London: Bloomsbury 1991

Spencer, Jane, *The Rise of the Woman Novelist: From Aphra Behn to Jane Austen,* Oxford and New York: Blackwell, 1986

Summers, Claude J., *Gay Fictions: Wilde to Stonewall: Studies in a Male Homosexual Literary Tradition,* New York: Continuum, 1990

Maurice Shadbolt 1932–

New Zealander

Maurice Shadbolt is one of New Zealand's most popular and prolific writers. To date he has published ten novels, five collections of short fiction, a play, a volume of autobiography, and various works of nonfiction. However, it is as a historical novelist that Shadbolt has established his reputation.

His first two books, *The New Zealanders* (1959) and *Summer Fires and Winter Country* (1963), are both collections of short stories in which Shadbolt chronicles New Zealand's social history during the first half of the 20th century, focusing particularly on the lives of young New Zealanders of his own generation. In these collections, Shadbolt introduces themes that have remained important throughout his work. The impressive opening story of *Summer Fires and Winter Country*, "Ben's Land," sees Shadbolt making use of material that would later be reworked in his first novel, *Among the Cinders* (1965), expanded in *The Lovelock Version* (1980), and revisited again in his autobiographical work, *One of Ben's: A New Zealand Medley* (1993).

Among the Cinders explores New Zealand's history from the early days of European settlement to the 1950s through the relationship between the adolescent Nick Flinders and his grandfather Hubert. Here Shadbolt found a pattern for treating past and present that he would reuse and develop in later works. His next two novels, *This Summer's Dolphin* (1969) and *An Ear of the Dragon* (1971), have been referred to as distractions from the task of completing *Strangers and Journeys* (1972). *This Summer's Dolphin* is a short novel that focuses on a number of isolated characters whose separate stories are linked only by their tenuous connection to Opo, a dolphin. Although Shadbolt's blatant reconstruction of the life of Renato Amato in *An Ear of the Dragon* attracted a great deal of criticism, his use of historical flashbacks—both in the story of Pietro Fratta (Amato) and of Frank Firth (possibly a persona of the author)—is particularly skillful. *Strangers and Journeys* is a long, ambitious, and only partially successful novel that took Shadbolt ten years to complete. It draws together many of the themes and characters of his earlier novels and stories, in what is essentially a contrast between the lives of two representative fathers and sons. The earlier sections of the novel, which deal with the lives of the fathers as they battle against the environment and the harsh economic times, are generally recognized as the strongest.

In many respects, *Strangers and Journeys* marked the end of a phase in Shadbolt's writing during which he had largely focused on contemporary New Zealand and explored the position of the artist in New Zealand society. His next two novels, *A Touch of Clay* (1974) and *Danger Zone* (1975), two parts of a projected but unfinished trilogy, constitute something of a digression in Shadbolt's development as a historical novelist. *A Touch of Clay* focuses on the relationship between Paul Pike, an ex-lawyer turned potter, and Irene, a drug-dependent young woman from a nearby commune. Of particular interest in this novel is the introduction of the past in the form of Pike's grandfather's 19th-century diaries, which may have inspired Shadbolt to turn his attention more fully to the 19th century, first in *The Lovelock Version* and later in his New Zealand Wars trilogy. *Danger Zone* focuses on New Zealand's opposition to nuclear testing in the

South Pacific and is based loosely on Shadbolt's voyage to Mururoa on board the protest vessel *Tamure* in 1972.

In 1980 Shadbolt published his first historical novel, *The Lovelock Version,* his most exuberant and, in the view of many critics, his most accomplished novel to date. This novel marked a definite shift to an engagement with 19th-century history, which has turned out to be the most fertile ground Shadbolt has ploughed thus far in his fiction. The past is foregrounded in the stories of the three pioneering Lovelock brothers and their families, which, along with the many digressions those stories engender, present the full sweep of 19th-century Pakeha history in New Zealand. First and foremost a magnificent storyteller, Shadbolt skillfully employs the techniques of magic realism and metafiction to present a tragicomic, spirited version of New Zealand history. Shadbolt reworked the Gallipoli strand in *The Lovelock Version* into his only published play, *Once on Chunuk Bair* (1982), and later into a work of nonfiction, *Voices of Gallipoli* (1988).

Shadbolt's triptych of revisionist historical novels, *Season of the Jew* (1986), *Monday's Warriors* (1990), and *The House of Strife* (1993), commonly referred to as his New Zealand Wars trilogy, forms what is perhaps the most important work of historical fiction yet produced by any New Zealand writer. *Season of the Jew* tells the story of Te Kooti's Poverty Bay campaigns of the 1860s. *Monday's Warriors,* also set in the 1860s, moves to Taranaki and is concerned with Titokawaru's war and the story of the rebel American Kimball Bent. Here Shadbolt reaps the reward of ground already prepared in *The Lovelock Version,* where Titokawaru, Kimball Bent, and Von Tempsky all make an appearance. The final volume of the trilogy, *The House of Strife,* moves still further back in time to the early skirmishes of the New Zealand Wars and the 1845–46 rebellion of Hone Heke. Common to each novel is a central Pakeha figure—George Fairweather, Kimball Bent, and the Ferdinand Wildblood/Henry Youngman doppelgänger respectively—whose sympathies are more with the Maori than with the colonizers, and who provides Shadbolt with an apparently objective perspective from which to narrate the events of his stories. Together the three volumes of the trilogy offer a revised version of the New Zealand Wars. More importantly, they remind us that history is above all else *story,* and that there are many versions of it, including the Shadbolt version.

RALPH J. CRANE

Biography
Born 4 June 1932 in Auckland. Attended Te Kuiti High School; Avondale College; University of Auckland. Journalist for various New Zealand publications, 1952–54; documentary scriptwriter and director, New Zealand National Film Unit, 1954–57; began writing full-time in 1957; lived in London and Spain, 1957–60, then returned to New Zealand.

Novels by Shadbolt
Among the Cinders, 1965
This Summer's Dolphin, 1969

Other Writings: short stories, a play, an autobiographical work (*One of Ben's: A New Zealand Medley,* 1993), and other non-fiction.

Further Reading

Crane, Ralph J., editor, *Ending the Silences: Critical Essays on the Works of Maurice Shadbolt,* Auckland: Hodder Moa Beckett, 1995

Ḥanān al-Shaykh 1945–

Lebanese

Ḥanān al-Shaykh, one of the leading contemporary women writers in the Arab world, has written novels that have been translated into English, French, Dutch, German, Danish, Italian, Korean, Spanish, and Polish. Originally from southern Lebanon, al-Shaykh was born and raised in Beirut, Lebanon, where she received her high school education. By the age of 16, she had already published essays on themes such as freedom, boredom, and infidelity. Al-Shaykh left Lebanon for Cairo to pursue her college education. While in Cairo, she wrote her first novel *Intiḥār rajul mayyit* (Suicide of a Dead Man) at the age of 19; it was later published in Beirut in 1970. The novel tells the story of a journalist—in his forties, married, with a teen-aged son—who falls in love with an 18-year-old woman. Al-Shaykh's concern in this novel is to show the double-standard of a married man who imposes certain rules and regulations on his wife while permitting himself more libertine conduct. Al-Shaykh adopted a male's perspective and voice because she wanted to differentiate herself from other female writers; she was afraid of being labeled a woman writer with "one story to tell." She admits, however, that in so doing she was untrue to herself: "I was camouflaging events by creating and being concerned with description and a beautiful style and sentences which sometimes didn't fit the novel."

Back in Beirut, while working as a journalist for a leading newspaper as well as in television, she published a series of articles on famous women entitled "The Portrayal of Women" that explored the circumstances that shaped them. Al-Shaykh's second work, *Faras al-shayṭān* (1975; The Praying Mantis), is a defiant novel that critically exposes the suffocating societal values and traditions of the Arab world. This novel, which has a female narrator, also includes biographical elements related to al-Shaykh's extremely religious father, aspects of her own love story, as well as her subsequent marriage. Al-Shaykh considers this novel to be artistically weak because its two sections are thematically unconnected. Some critics consider the importance of this novel to lie in its faithful depiction and frank discussion of subjects rarely treated in the Arab world.

No publisher in Lebanon accepted al-Shaykh's third novel, *Ḥikāyat Zahrah* (1980; The Story of Zahra), so she published it at her own expense with the children's publishing house Dār al-fatā al-ʿarabī. This novel, which brought her immediate fame and recognition, was banned in most Arab countries because of its frank treatment of the repressed sexuality and general predicament of women in the Arab world. *The Story of Zahra* is significant not only for its social commentary, or in its historical moment, the Lebanese Civil War, but also in its narrative structure. This novel, and those subsequent to it, are evidence of al-Shaykh's maturity in mastering techniques such as voice and internal monologue.

Al-Shaykh's fourth novel, *Misk al-ghazāl* (1988; Women of Sand and Myrrh) was chosen as one of the 50 Best Books of 1992 by *Publishers Weekly,* and it won the 1993 Elle Literary Prize for the Bourgone, France. Set in an unnamed Persian Gulf state, *Women of Sand and Myrrh* tells the stories of four women caught in a patriarchal order. Although the stories initially appear to be independant from one another, they are nevertheless connected through the women's oppression and their struggle with their immediate surroundings. Al-Shaykh sensitively captures the dilemmas and experiences of these defiant women as they attempt to transform their societal values and traditions.

Barīd Bayrūt (1992; Beirut Blues) can be considered both a sequel to *The Story of Zahra* and as an independent work. *Beirut Blues* investigates the nature of memory by testing its ability to order and explain life. The novel is comprised of ten letters "written" by Asmahān, the narrator, and addressed either to specific persons, both living and dead, or places. A novel of correspondance can call attention to stories told in opposition to a more dominant, public narrative; in this novel it becomes a form of resistance to the atrocities and destruction of war, as well as a resistance to annihilation by the inscription of the self in history. The structure of the novel, allowing stories to emerge from within other stories, connects and relates various themes—rural versus urban life, disdain for exile, religion as an imposed fact of birth, fundamentalism, and nationalism—to the concept of nationhood. Again al-Shaykh is at her best in the creation of a distinctive voice. In an interview, al-Shaykh once noted that narrative voice "should be correct to my ear. This is what counts. If I don't hear it as I want to, I might change all of it, and this is what happened with *Beirut Blues*. I changed the narrative voice. It became [ten] letters."

Although al-Shaykh is best known for her novels, she also has published two collections of short stories, *Wardat al-Ṣaḥrāʾ* (1982; The Desert Rose), and *Aknus al-shams ʿan al-suṭūḥ* (1994; I Sweep the Sun off Rooftops). She wrote two plays, *Dark Afternoon Tea* and *Paper Husband*, which were staged in London in 1995 and 1997. Currently she is working on a novel exploring emigré and intercultural relationships in London.

SABAH GHANDOUR

See also Story of Zahra

Biography
Born 12 November 1945 in Beirut. Attended Alamiliah traditional Muslim girls' primary school, Beirut; Ahliyyah School, Beirut; American College for Girls, Cairo, 1963–66. Journalist, *Al-Ḥasnaʾ* women's magazine, 1966–68, and *Al-Nahār* literary supplement, 1968–75; left Lebanon in 1976 because of civil war; lived in Saudi Arabia until 1982, when she moved to London.

Novels by al-Shaykh
Intiḥār rajul mayyit [Suicide of a Dead Man], 1970
Faras al-shayṭān [The Praying Mantis], 1975

Ḥikāyat Zahrah, 1980; as *The Story of Zahra*, 1986
Misk al-ghazāl, 1988; as *Women of Sand and Myrrh*, 1989
Barīd Bayrūt, 1992; as *Beirut Blues*, 1995

Other Writings: journalism, short stories, and plays.

Further Reading

Accad, Evelyne, *Sexuality and War: Literary Masks of the Middle East,* New York: New York University Press, 1990
Allen, Roger, *The Arabic Novel: An Historical and Critical Introduction,* Syracuse, New York: Syracuse University Press, and Manchester: Manchester University Press, 1982; 2nd edition, Syracuse, New York: Syracuse University Press, 1995
Cooke, Miriam, *War's Other Voices: Women Writers on the Lebanese Civil War,* Cambridge and New York: Cambridge University Press, 1988
Ghandour, Sabah, "Ḥikāyat Zahrah: al-riwāyah al-muḍādah . . . al-tārīkh al-muḍād," *Fuṣūl* (Autumn 1993)
Sunderman, Paula, "An Interview with Hanan al-Shaykh," *Michigan Quarterly Review* (1992)
Sunderman, Paula, "Hanan al-Shaykh: An Annotated Bibliography of Primary and Secondary Sources," *Meisei Review* 12 (1997)

Shen Congwen 1902–88

Chinese

Shen Congwen was among the most resourceful founders of China's New Literature of the 1920s, a brilliant prose stylist who demonstrated that modern creativity in Western genres and a new literary Mandarin could be as subtle and allusive as the canon in classical Chinese. A humble autodidact whose personal understanding of rural as well as modern life outflanked that of many Marxist writers, Shen by the 1930s epitomized professional independence and devotion to artistic and cultural experimentalism over political revolution, as he did again during the post-Mao thaw, even though he had ceased writing in 1949.

Besides his versatility in styles—from folkloric to modernist—and his celebration of the courage and dignity of the common Chinese, Shen is known for having broadened Mandarin's expressive power and created a visually appealing lyric rural fiction. The pastoral *Bian cheng* (1934; *The Frontier City,* or *The Border Town*), perhaps the most perfectly conceived and enduring novella of pre-Communist China, seemed retrospectively to 1980s critics a reproof and antidote to the overblown socialist peasant "epics" mandated by Shen's fellow Hunanese Mao Zedong. Yet particularly in the novel, Shen was also a major chronicler of urban Chinese manners.

The modern Chinese novel emerged in the 1920s, and Shen's

first contributions are typical. Composing serially for periodicals, he stretched and linked together shorter forms, always his forte, into diary, epistolary, and free-form novels of social criticism and romance. *Bu si riji* (1928; A Pre-Posthumous Diary) and *Yi ge tiancai de tongxin* (1930; Correspondence from a Born Talent) are gloomy autobiographical evocations of social oppression, genteel urban poverty, and the sexually frustrating titillation of modern life. More humorous are *Huang jun riji* (1928; The Diary of Master Huang) and *Dai guan riji* (1929; An Inane Official Diary), which are satires of stupidity and ennui in Republican bureaucratic circles. *Dushi yi furen* (1932; A Lady of the City) and *Shenshi de taitai* (1933; The Gentry Wife) skewer bourgeois hypocrisy and vanity as they affected women. *Chang xia* (1928; Long Summer), *Jiu meng* (1930; Past Dreams), and *Ahei xiao shi* (1933; The Story of Ahei) are romantic comedies of manners, the last about teenage sexuality among the nonliterate Miao (Hmong) aborigines in Shen's native West Hunan.

Shen's closest approximation to the European novel of social manners is *Yi ge nü juyuan de shenghuo* (1931; The Life of an Actress), featuring third-person narrative, a unified plot, and revelation of psychology through dialogue. The heroine—attractive, headstrong, politically progressive, and personally liberated, not unlike Shen's friend Ding Ling, the writer—goes through suitors like roles. Shen dissects modern personality role confusion and political grandstanding as by-products and surrogates of the drama while lampooning the Chinese dramatic profession.

Contemporary Chinese cultural critics found his writing inadequately "ideologized," but today Shen's early novels seem original, diverting, and in the revolutionary mainstream with their new vocabulary, "foreignized" syntax, and confessional realism. These works were also popular, until they were "politically superseded" in the 1930s. Shen later tried to suppress his erotic works, although probably they had encouraged Ding Ling to express her sexuality in her pioneering works of Chinese feminism.

Alisi Zhongguo youji (1928; Alice's Adventures in China) is Shen's most often cited early novel despite structural weaknesses that Shen himself lamented. After parodying Lewis Carroll, Western travel guides, Jonathan Swift, and the Chinese literary revolution (as depicted in a writers' congress of birds twittering at each other in modern verse), Shen takes Alice to see Miao poverty. To C.T. Hsia (1971), this novel and Lao She's parody *Mao chengji* (1932; Cat Country) typify an "obsession with China" among Shen's nationalistic generation of writers.

Shen's mature work is famous for its local color, regionalism, and portraits of the Miao as a people unspoiled by Confucianism and urbanism, as in *Shenwu zhi ai* (1929; The Shaman's Love), a modern myth woven around Miao festivals, love serenading, and religion. The title story of *Yuexia xiaojing* (1933; Under Moonlight), a tribal legend about the superiority of human romantic devotion over local taboos against marrying one's first lover, introduces a collection of Indian Buddhist Jatakas, all rewritten in an economical modern prose and linked after the fashion of Boccaccio.

The pastoral *The Border Town* sublimates and refines such exotic ethnic and regional lore in an understated paean to the simple beauty of rural southern landscapes and unmaterialistic folkways. The heroine, a dark pubescent beauty of ambiguous ethnicity named Cuicui (Green Jade), as "wild" as her surrounding state of nature, awakens to her sexuality in a subconscious ecstasy triggered by erotic songs. The devices used in the novel include Freudian symbolism and Cuicui's tension-laden emergence from an Electra dependency on her grandfather, an old ferryman. Li Jianwu, speaking for nonleft 1930s critics, called the novella Shen's masterpiece, "a poem, like the love songs that move the heroine."

Four unfinished later novels about West Hunan differ remarkably in tone and style. The idyll *Fengzi* (1933–37; Phoenix) meditates on the lives of Shen's friends in light of West Hunanese mores. *Xiaozhai* (1937; A River Town), also unfinished owing to the war, begins a naturalistic saga of a river town's descent into poverty, violence, and moral degradation. *Chang he* (1943; Long River), the first volume of an intended regional epic of "permanence amid change" and still Shen's longest novel, is regarded by Hsia and Sima Changfeng as his greatest work and the "most inclusive of the many facets of his talent" (Hsia, 1971), "a tone poem like *Border Town* but with the rumblings of history" (Sima). Bittersweet suggestions of tragedy punctuate intimations that "love, friendship, work, and ritual will survive tyranny and rapacity" (Hsia). Still another regional saga, retrospectively titled *Xue qing* (1945–47; Clearing after the Snow), contains more forebodings of social violence. Its characterizations, plot,

and ornate language suggest a still self-renewing creativity that was terminated in 1949 by the Communist Revolution.

Episodic, unfinished, and politically incorrect or not, Shen's "little Greek temple" worshiping "humanity," as he called his classic works, ultimately superseded Mao's drafty exposition halls worshiping the proletariat. Chinese writers rediscovered the beauty and hidden psychological conflicts of rural China when they rediscovered Shen Congwen; the lush but psychologically wrenching 1980s novels and films that resulted helped lead Chinese culture back onto the world stage.

JEFFREY C. KINKLEY

Biography

Born 28 December 1902 in Feng-huang, Hunan province. Began writing fiction in 1922 when he arrived in Peking (Beijing); taught Chinese literature at several Chinese universities during the Sino-Japanese War (1937–45) to support himself; prolific writer until 1949, when his writings came under the attack of the new Communist regime. Died 10 May 1988 in Beijing.

Novels by Shen Congwen

Alisi Zhongguo youji [Alice's Adventures in China], 2 vols., 1928
Huang jun riji [The Diary of Master Huang], 1928
Chang xia [Long Summer], 1928
Bu si riji [A Pre-Posthumous Diary], 1928
Dai guan riji [An Inane Official Diary], 1929
Shenwu zhi ai [The Shaman's Love], 1929
Yi ge tiancai de tongxin [Correspondence from a Born Talent], 1930
Jiu meng [Past Dreams], 1930
Yi ge nü juyuan de shenghuo [The Life of an Actress], 1931
Dushi yi furen [A Lady of the City], 1932
Ahei xiao shi [The Story of Ahei], 1933
Fengzi [Phoenix], 1933, continued in 1937 (unfinished)
Yi ge muqin [A Mother], 1933
Yuexia xiaojing [Under Moonlight], 1933
Nuofu [The Coward], 1933
Shenshi de taitai [The Gentry Wife], 1933
Bian cheng, 1934; as *The Frontier City*, translated by Ching Ti and Robert Payne, published in *The Chinese Earth*, 1947; as *The Border Town*, translated by Gladys Yang, 1981
Xiaozhai [A River Town], 1937 (unfinished)
Chang he [Long River], 1943 (unfinished)
Xue qing [Clearing after the Snow], 1945–47 (unfinished); extant chapters assembled in *Shen Congwen wen ji*, 1983

Other Writings: short stories, plays, poetry in modern and classical Chinese, letters, essays, literary criticism and history, biographies, autobiography, reminiscences, and travelogues; noted also for his calligraphy and, after the Communist Revolution, art history research on Chinese dress, textiles, painting, handicrafts, and various aspects of Chinese material culture.

Further Reading

Hsia, C.T., *A History of Modern Chinese Fiction*, New Haven, Connecticut: Yale University Press, 1961; 2nd edition, 1971
Kinkley, Jeffrey C., *The Odyssey of Shen Congwen* (contains

bibliography), Stanford, California: Stanford University Press, 1987

Nieh, Hua-ling, *Shen Ts'ung-wen,* New York: Twayne, 1972

Peng Hsiao-yen, *Antithesis Overcome: Shen Congwen's Avant-Gardism and Primitivism,* Taipei: Institute of Chinese Literature and Philosophy, Academia Sinica, 1994

Shen Congwen, *The Chinese Earth,* New York: Columbia University Press, 1982

Wang, David Der-wei, *Fictional Realism in Twentieth-Century China: Mao Dun, Lao She, Shen Congwen,* New York: Columbia University Press, 1992

Shitou ji. *See* Six Classic Chinese Novels

Short Story. *See* Novella

Shuihu zhuan. *See* Six Classic Chinese Novels

Henryk Sienkiewicz 1846–1916

Polish

Henryk Sienkiewicz was a best-selling author who achieved a popularity unknown by any other Polish novelist. The Nobel prize for literature (1905) and the fact that his most liked novels were made into films carried his reputation into the second half of the 20th century. However, more demanding readers have frequently objected to his shallow populism and novelistic stereotypes. Bolesław Prus, his contemporary, denounced the nationalist distortion of historical facts and the stock quality of Sienkiewicz's characters. The best known pioneer of modernist Polish fiction, Witold Gombrowicz, called him "the first-rate secondary writer" but nevertheless recognized the compelling magic of his narrative skill. New translations of Sienkiewicz's fiction published in the United States seem to prove an international interest in his novels of historical adventure even in our times. The dilemmas facing anyone attempting a critical assessment of his output are identified by Czesław Miłosz in *The History of Polish Literature* (2nd edition, 1983): "To appraise him objectively is quite a task, for he combined a rare narrative gift with

shortcomings that are serious enough to disqualify him from the title of a truly great writer."

Sienkiewicz first trained his narrative skills in short stories, novellas, and travel reports. His great popular success came with the publication of a trilogy about the tempestuous years of Polish history in the middle of the 17th century: *Ogniem i mieczem* (1884; *With Fire and Sword*), *Potop* (1886; *The Deluge*), and *Pan Wołodyjowski* (3 vols., 1887–88; *Pan Michael*). In this cycle, where relentless fighting eclipses all other events, Sienkiewicz followed the example of Alexandre Dumas *père,* complementing the colorful narrative with patriotic morale boosting. Similar to Dumas' *The Three Musketeers,* the trilogy focuses on a chain of exciting adventures of invented characters, which not only overshadows history but comes to affect its course. Narrative techniques borrowed from Homer and the *chanson de geste* (epic poems about the exploits of Charlemagne) are subordinated to the popular appeal of fairy tales, legends, romances of adventure, and even American stories about the heroic West, visited by the author a few years before (1876–78). The central love story in these and Sienkiewicz's other historical novels rings the changes on the pattern of a dragon kidnapping the king's daughter. Similarly, the trilogy contains the usual complement of invincible heroes and their extraordinary exploits, the theme of everlasting friendship, spectacular duels, heroic death, and a miraculous weapon. The uncomplicated stock characters of Sienkiewicz's novels have pleased the general public because of vivid portrayals often accompanied by humor. Criticized severely for the gross distortions and simplifications of historical facts and for its lack of genuine originality in plotting and characterization, the trilogy nevertheless offers compelling reading to those who do not request much more than good storytelling.

The trilogy was followed by two contemporary novels, *Bez dogmatu* (1889; *Without Dogma*) and *Rodzina Połanieckich* (1895; *Children of the Soil*). The author made it clear in a letter that the former was intended as an explicit warning against intellectual overrefinement and scepticism, which might undermine the purity of traditional certitudes. The novel follows the form of a diary written by a decadent and inconsolable lover, somewhat resembling Goethe's Werther. Sienkiewicz combines the directness of the protagonist's confessions with his own unequivocal message by exploiting the doubleness of the main character-narrator. Sienkiewicz presents the experiencing mind, whose inner drama is sometimes portrayed with a profundity rarely present in contemporary Polish novels, and the narrating diarist, who not only reports his experience but assesses his own follies with amazing distance and criticism. While Sienkiewicz's moral code hardly appealed to more liberal contemporaries, the psychological perspicacity of the novel still finds admirers. Apart from some realistic episodes and vivid background characters, *Children of the Soil* was a failure, providing an easy target for unfriendly critics ever since.

Quo vadis? (1896; *Quo Vadis?*), translated into many languages, including Persian and Japanese, and filmed in Hollywood several times, is probably Sienkiewicz's internationally most popular novel. Set in the Rome of Nero, it portrays the decadence of the pagan world and the advent of persecuted Christianity. As usual in Sienkiewicz's historical fiction, a sentimental love story comes to the foreground, this time featuring the ups and downs of a Roman patrician and a Christian girl, whose "barbarian" status is offset by her royal descent. The drama of action and suspense overshadows historical events and Sienkiewicz's moral message. Similarly, the magnificence of the emperor's court and the splendor of Roman feasts and mass entertainment eclipse the colorless life of the Christians. While Nero plays the role of sinister tyrant, refined Petronius, Tacitus' *arbiter elegantiae*, is a far more appealing character than the Apostles Peter and Paul, who do nothing but say the right things. Even the martyrs are upstaged by the athletes, as sensuality and the appealing descriptions of pagan life, contrary to the author's ostensible message, tower above noble ideas and admirable sentiments.

Sienkiewicz's last important novel, *Krzyżacy* (4 vols., 1900; *The Teutonic Knights*), attempted to rise above the author's main stereotypes. Set in medieval Poland at the time of its conflict with the Teutonic Order, the novel is devoted much more than the trilogy to nonmilitary activities, such as social events, hunting, and tournaments. Although the main characters possess great physical fitness, they certainly are more ordinary than in earlier works. Above all, the heroes of *The Teutonic Knights* do not play a major role in the course of history, which, to the contrary, determines the condition of their lives and remains distinct from Sienkiewicz's invented story lines. Even the traditional plot of the heroine's abduction and recovery has been reworked, as the young lady eventually dies, making room for another woman to marry the protagonist.

Among four later novels only one was successful. In *W pustyni i w puszczy* (1911; *In Desert and Wilderness*) Sienkiewicz does for a children's audience what he had always done well: spin a yarn of thrilling events, now located in the deserts and savannahs of Africa in the year of Mahdi's rebellion and the capture of Khartoum. Adventure, courage and a sense of honor, well-established narrative techniques, and traditional values distinguish the work of this outstanding storyteller once again. In spite of criticism by more sophisticated readers, Sienkiewicz represents the popular novel at its best.

STANISLAW EILE

Biography

Born 5 May 1846 in Wola Okrzejska, Poland. Attended Warsaw Gymnasium, 1858–65; Polish University, Warsaw, 1866–71. Journalist and freelance writer; co-owner and editor of the biweekly *Niwa*, 1874; coeditor of the newspaper *Słowo* [The Word], 1882–87; founding member, Mianowski Foundation, 1882; cofounder and president, Literary Foundation, 1899, and Swiss Relief Committee for the War Victims in Poland, 1915; given an estate by the Polish government at Oblęgorek, near Kielce, 1900. Awarded Nobel prize for literature, 1905. Died 15 November 1916.

Novels by Sienkiewicz

Ogniem i mieczem, 1884; as *With Fire and Sword,* translated by Jeremiah Curtin, 1890; also translated by Samuel A. Binion, 1898; W.S. Kuniczak, 1991

Potop, 1886; as *The Deluge,* translated by Jeremiah Curtin, 1891; also translated by W.S. Kuniczak, 1991

Pan Wołodyjowski, 3 vols., 1887–88; as *Pan Michael,* translated by Jeremiah Curtin, 1893; also translated by Samuel A. Binion, 1898; as *Fire in the Steppe,* translated by W.S. Kuniczak, 1992

Bez dogmatu, 1889; as *Without Dogma,* translated by Iza Young, 1893

Rodzina Połanieckich, 1895; as *Children of the Soil,* translated by Jeremiah Curtin, 1895; as *The Irony of Life,* translated by Nathan M. Babad, 1900

Quo vadis?, 1896; as *Quo Vadis?,* translated by Jeremiah Curtin, 1896; also translated by Samuel A. Binion and S. Malevsky, 1897; William E. Smith, 1898; C.J. Hogarth, 1914; Stanley F. Conrad, 1992; W.S. Kuniczak, 1997

Krzyżacy, 4 vols., 1900; as *The Knights of the Cross,* translated by S.C. de Soissons, 1897; also translated by Samuel A. Binion, 1899; Jeremiah Curtin, 1900; B. Dahl, 1900; translated as *Danusia*, 1900; as *The Teutonic Knights,* translated by Alicja Tyszkiewicz, 1943, revised by Miroslav Lipinski, 1993

Na polu chwały, 1906; as *On the Field of Glory,* translated by Jeremiah Curtin, 1906; as *The Field of Glory,* translated by Henry Britoff, 1906

Wiry, 1910; as *Whirlpools,* translated by Max A. Drezmal, 1910

W pustyni i w puszczy, 1911; as *In Desert and Wilderness,* translated by Max A. Drezmal, 1912; as *Through the Desert,* translated by Mary Webb Artois, 1912

Legiony [The Legions], 1913–14

Other Writings: short stories, plays, literary criticism, journalism.

Further Reading

Bujnicki, Tadeusz, *Sienkiewicza "Powieści z lat dawnych": Studia,* Krakow: Universitas, 1996

Gardner, Monica, *The Patriot Novelist of Poland Henryk Sienkiewicz,* London: Dent, and New York: Dutton, 1926

Giergielewicz, Mieczyslaw, *Henryk Sienkiewicz,* New York: Twayne, 1968

Jodełka-Burzecki, Tomasz, editor, *Trylogia Henryka Sienkiewicza; Studia, szkice, polemiki,* Warsaw: Panstwowy Instytut Wydawniczy, 1962

Kosko, Marja, *Un "best-seller" 1900: "Quo vadis?"* Paris: Jose Corti, 1960

Krzyżanowski, Jerzy R., editor, *The Trilogy Companion: A Reader's Guide to the Trilogy of Henryk Sienkiewicz,* New York: Copernicus Society of America, 1991

Krzyżanowski, Julian, *Twórczość Henryka Sienkiewicza,* Warsaw: Panstwowy Instytut Wydawniczy, 1970; 3rd edition, 1976

Lednicki, Waclaw, *Henryk Sienkiewicz: A Retrospective Synthesis,* The Hague: Mouton, 1960

Silence by Endō Shūsaku

Chinmoku 1966

It is difficult to assess whether the critical interest accorded the novel *Silence* when it emerged on the literary scene was greater in theological or literary circles. For the Japanese Catholic community, a minority grouping to which Endō was affiliated in light of his baptism, albeit reluctantly, as a teenager in the 1930s, the decision to select the act of apostasy as the ostensible focal point of his novel aroused considerable controversy. Indeed, to several prominent Catholic critics, the portrayal of Rodrigues, a 17th-century missionary who enters Japan in defiance of the anti-Christian edicts of the time and who, following his inevitable capture, offers public renunciation of God and all that his life to date has stood for, represented an act of heresy. Equally vociferous, however, were the majority of literary critics who insisted on locating Endō within a Western literary tradition of "Catholic authors."

To be sure, it would be hard to exaggerate Endō's literary debt to European letters—most noticeably to Claude Mauriac, Georges Bernanos, Julien Green, and the other French Catholic authors who had long represented the primary focus of his studies. Endō himself had made much, in both his fictional and nonfictional publications, of his desire to root his literature in his experience, as one of the first Japanese students to study abroad in the postwar period, and to come to terms with the apparently irreconcilable gap, both spiritual and cultural, between the East and West.

In all this, the position of *Silence* within the Japanese prose narrative tradition was largely ignored. The reassessment when it came, however, was highly revealing, and it is in this light, as a novel with readily identifiable debts to various indigenous literary developments, that the contribution of *Silence* as exemplar of the Japanese novel is best considered. Two particular trends within the 20th-century Japanese prose narrative tradition merit special attention in this regard. The first was the generation of fin-de-siècle authors who had sought to address the question of "selfhood" in their literature. Developing the focus on "the inner life" of Kitamura Tōkoku, and inspired in no small measure by their schooling in the English romantic poets and Christianity, the contribution of authors such as Shimazaki Tōson, Natsume Sōseki, and Kunikida Doppo in the formulation of Endō's approach to literary subjectivity cannot be overlooked. Of equal significance to the creation of the novel *Silence* was the legacy of the *shishōsetsu* tradition of confessional literature crucial to the literary direction adopted not just by Endō but by fellow members of the *daisan no shinjin* coterie of postwar writers. Comparisons with the predominantly mundane experiences of daily life depicted, with minimum rhetorical flourish, in the prewar *shishōsetsu* may appear unwarranted. And yet, in serving to convince Endō of the suitability of his spiritual journey as material for his fiction and of the novel as an ideal forum for such considerations, the influence of the *shishōsetsu* may be seen as no less than that of the French Catholic novelists with whom Endō's name is more readily associated.

Such indigenous roots merit considerable emphasis. Equally significant, yet equally often overlooked, is the extent to which *Silence* represents, not a radical new departure within the author's oeuvre, but a logical progression from the earlier novels, which, although less overt in their identification with the author's personal struggle to reconcile his adopted faith with his cultural heritage, may nevertheless be seen as containing allusion to the various narrative threads taken up in *Silence.* The literary portrayals of Christ, not as an awe-inspiring figure but as a pitiful being suffering alongside his creations in the persons of Gaston in *Obakasan* (1959; *Wonderful Fool*) and Mitsu in *Watashi ga suteta onna* (1964; *The Girl I Left Behind*), and the early attempts at fusing qualities initially established as irreconcilable (e.g. East and West, strong and weak) as portrayed in the pair of novellas *Shiroi hito* (1955; White Man) and *Kiiroi hito* (1955; Yellow Man) and in *Umi to dokuyaku* (1957; *The Sea and Poison*), in retrospect demonstrate that the ground was well developed in advance of *Silence*.

For all the tendency to divorce *Silence* from the mainstream of literary criticism, however, the majority of critics were united in their acclaim of the extended depiction of the psychological drama in which Endō's protagonist becomes embroiled. And yet implicit in such criticism was the suggestion that "the *fumie* scene" toward the end of the novel, in which Rodrigues ultimately accedes to the shogunate demands to place his foot on the image of Christ attached to a crucifix (the *fumie* that was traditionally employed by shogunate officials as a means of rounding up those who clung to the outlawed faith), represents the climax of the novel. In practice, however, the drama does not finish at this point; instead, Endō's narrator is at pains to stress in a brief concluding chapter that, for all his outward capitulation, inwardly Rodrigues is now possessed of a faith more real and profound than that which had inspired him to risk all in embarking on his mission to Japan in the first place. The section is all-important: it is only at this point that the full extent of Rodrigues' journey of self-discovery becomes apparent. The subsequent narrative focuses on a protagonist who, in agreeing to hear the confession of Kichijirō, the very man who had betrayed him, Judas-like, to the authorities, appears confident in the knowledge that "even if he was betraying his fellow priests, he was not betraying his Lord. He loved him now in a different way from before."

It is with this dramatic image—and with the protagonist's ultimate recognition that "Our Lord was not silent. Even if he had been silent, my life until this day would have spoken of him"—that the novel actually ends. In thus challenging the traditional distinction between apostasy and martyrdom, Endō succeeds, paradoxically, in merging these two opposites into alternative expressions of the same concept—that of human love. At the same time, in placing the emphasis firmly on the inner growth occasioned in his protagonist as a result of his gradual renunciation of his earlier pride and heroism, Endō here succeeds not only in plumbing ever deeper into human psychology but also in hinting at the possibility of reconciling seeming incompatibilities that would remain the hallmark of his subsequent literature.

MARK WILLIAMS

See also Endō Shūsaku

Further Reading

Gessel, Van C., "Voices in the Wilderness: Japanese Christian Authors," *Monumenta Nipponica* 37 (1982)

Gessel, Van C., "Salvation of the Weak: Endō," in *The Sting of Life: Four Contemporary Japanese Novelists,* New York: Columbia University Press, 1989

Johnston, William, "Translator's Preface" to *Silence,* by Endō Shūsaku, London: Penguin, 1988

Kaufman, Gordon, "Towards the Reconception of Christ and Salvation," in *Theology for a Nuclear Age,* Manchester: Manchester University Press, and Philadelphia: Westminster Press, 1985

Mathy, Francis, "Shūsaku Endō: Japanese Catholic Novelist," *Thought* (Winter 1967)

Quinn, Philip L., "Tragic Dilemmas, Suffering Love, and Christian Life," *Journal of Religious Ethics* 17 (Spring 1989)

Claude Simon 1913-

French

Claude Simon published his first novel, *Le Tricheur,* in 1945. Forty years and more than a dozen books later, he won the Nobel prize for literature. (He was the first French laureate after Jean-Paul Sartre, who, unlike Simon, refused the prize.) Today Simon's oeuvre includes an early volume of memoirs (*La Corde raide,* 1947), 15 novels, two experimental texts that include reproductions of visual works of art, 2 albums of photographs, as well as a travel tale that satirizes the former USSR (*L'Invitation,* 1987). He has given numerous interviews and written articles on the aesthetics of the novel. Many of his ideas about writing and the craft of fiction-making are found in his acceptance speech for the Nobel prize (*Discours de Stockholm,* 1987). Translated into many languages, his works are better known outside of France than in his native country, as he is reputed to be a difficult writer. In fact, Simon is perhaps best appreciated as a "primitive," i.e., an artist who refuses to follow the conventions of academic art, which in this case means the conventions of the traditional novel, whether of the psychological or the realist mode. The freshness of his vision, at once unchanging and renewed over many years of writing, is witness to his fascination for all things visual, especially painting and photography. Although much academic criticism has been devoted to Simon's works, his novels are among the most anti-intellectual of current French fiction. At the same time, his works subvert many of the values honored by the French people, both in terms of historical context (the myth of France's glorious history at the time of the Revolution or of World War II) and at the level of style (the famous love of clarity and simplicity). For Simon, "clear" prose does little more than disguise what none of us can really express adequately or even perceive with any accuracy.

Although influenced by William Faulkner, Fedor Dostoevskii, and Marcel Proust, Claude Simon is a writer with a unique style. His works have also been associated with the French *nouveau roman* (New Novel), but this alignment was something of a journalistic accident and is in fact erroneous. For Simon, unlike some of the practitioners of the *nouveau roman*, metaphor, autobiography, history, and storytelling are all important, although he does experiment with various narrative techniques and stylistic practices in his fiction that can sustain comparison with the *nouveaux romanciers*.

Perhaps the most representative of Simon's novels is *L'Herbe* (1958; *The Grass*), a protofeminist tale about an old woman (Marie) who is dying. Nothing actually happens in this novel, for Marie never dies, and Louise, the wife of Marie's nephew Georges, never leaves her husband as she planned. Filled with long descriptions of houses and gardens, as well as the civilian exodus of June 1940 in the face of the German invasion of France, this novel is an attack on the traditional writing of history (and the novel for that matter). For Simon, history—one is tempted here to say "herstory"—is not the stuff of textbooks and monuments, but rather the everyday occurrences in the life of an unmarried woman who lived with her sister, taught elementary school, ran a farm, and refurbished the family's ancestral home before selling it to help her nephew make his way in the world after the war. In the context of Simon's oeuvre, Marie represents the hidden, unwritten side of history, which is the very kind that is now examined in cultural studies devoted to the "nobodies" (women in particular) of history: as Simon puts it, "not tragedy, screams, the accidental, the spectacular, but what constitutes, so to speak, the very warp of existence."

The sequel to *The Grass, La Route des Flandres* (1960; *The Flanders Road*), tells the story of Georges' wartime experiences as he grapples with the personal histories of various people associated with him and his family, including a cousin, Captain de Reixach, who apparently allowed himself to be killed during the 1940 invasion, and the same officer's wife, the beautiful Corinne, with whom Georges becomes sexually involved after the war. But neither the storytelling that went on in the German prison camp nor the passionate love-making with Corinne allows Georges to reconstitute the truth of the past. It is a futile quest, leading him to conclude that there is no way to know what really happened. But this failure does not qualify the novel as a failure; rather, it contains some of the most luxuriant, sensuous, and erotic pages of French prose in the 20th century. Using a collage technique, Simon juxtaposes scenes of Georges lying in a field guarded by German soldiers and their dogs with scenes of postwar sex with Corinne. This type of writing is allegorized within the novel according to the technique of *mise-en-abyme* in a description of an 18th-century engraving of a hybrid creature, half woman, half horse. For Simon, transitions are all-important; as each piece of the puzzle is added to the others, the work begins to resemble a fine work of marquetry.

Much of Simon's fiction is autobiographical in origin (he himself says he is incapable of inventing anything); the three best examples of this tendency are *Histoire* (1967; *Histoire*), *Les Géorgiques* (1981; *The Georgics*), and *L'Acacia* (1989; *The Acacia*), all of which tell the stories of Simon's father and mother, as well as their ancestors. In *Histoire* the long engagement of his mother is described as she waits for her future husband to return from the Far East, where he is serving in the French colonial army. These family tales are interspersed with fragments of 20th-century history. For example, in *The Georgics* Simon rewrites the adventures of George Orwell during the Spanish Civil War (1936–39) as recounted in the famous English writer's *Homage to Catalonia* (1938). Here 20th-century history is juxtaposed with events from the 18th century as Simon explores the life and times of two of his ancestors, one of whom was a soldier and later an officer, while the other was executed for betraying the cause of the French Revolution. In *The Acacia* the third-person character most closely resembling Simon watches helplessly as a train of deportees leaves a railway station in pre–World War II Berlin. In all these novels Simon employs a rich and often difficult form of intertextuality, incorporating references to his own novels and to other texts; that quality, along with Simon's intense preoccupation with language—with the many connotations, flavors, sounds, and rhythms of words—mark his work as among the most challenging and rewarding of 20th-century French novels.

RALPH SARKONAK

Biography

Born 10 October 1913 in Tananarive, Madagascar. Attended Collège Stanislas, Paris; Lycée Saint-Louis (for naval career: dismissed); studied at Cambridge and Oxford universities for a brief time; studied painting with André Lhote. Served in the French Cavalry, 1934–35 and 1939–40; in the latter tour he was captured, but escaped; joined resistance movement in Perpignan. Awarded Nobel prize for literature, 1985.

Novels by Simon

Le Tricheur [The Cheater], 1945
Gulliver, 1952
Le Sacre du printemps [The Rite of Spring], 1954
Le Vent: Tentative de restitution d'un rétable baroque, 1957; as *The Wind: Attempted Restoration of a Baroque Masterpiece*, translated by Richard Howard, 1959
L'Herbe, 1958; as *The Grass*, translated by Richard Howard, 1960
La Route des Flandres, 1960; as *The Flanders Road*, translated by Richard Howard, 1961
Le Palace, 1962; as *The Palace*, translated by Richard Howard, 1963
Histoire, 1967; as *Histoire*, translated by Richard Howard, 1968
La Bataille de Pharsale, 1969; as *The Battle of Pharsalus*, translated by Richard Howard, 1971
Les Corps conducteurs, 1971; as *Conducting Bodies*, translated by Helen R. Lane, 1974
Triptyque, 1973; as *Triptych*, translated by Helen R. Lane, 1976
Leçon de choses, 1975; as *The World About Us*, translated by Daniel Weissbort, 1983
Les Géorgiques, 1981; as *The Georgics*, translated by Beryl and John Fletcher, 1989
L'Acacia, 1989; as *The Acacia*, 1991

Other Writings: a play and miscellaneous prose, including a travel satire of the former Soviet Union, *L'Invitation* (1987; *The Invitation*).

Further Reading

Birn, Randi, and Karen Gould, editors, *Orion Blinded: Essays on Claude Simon*, Lewisburg, Pennsylvania: Bucknell

University Press, and London: Associated University Presses, 1981

Brewer, Mária Minich, *Claude Simon: Narrativities Without Narrative,* Lincoln: University of Nebraska Press, 1995

Britton, Celia, *Claude Simon: Writing the Visible,* Cambridge and New York: Cambridge University Press, 1987

Britton, Celia, editor, *Claude Simon,* London and New York: Longman, 1993

Dällenbach, Lucien, *Claude Simon,* Paris: Seuil, 1988

Duncan, Alastair, editor, *Claude Simon: New Directions,* Edinburgh: Scottish Academic Press, 1985

Duncan, Alastair, *Claude Simon: Adventures in Words,* Manchester and New York: Manchester University Press, 1994

Longuet, Patrick, *Lire Claude Simon: La polyphonie du monde,* Paris: Minuit, 1995

Loubère, J.A.E., *The Novels of Claude Simon,* Ithaca, New York: Cornell University Press, 1975

Newmann, Guy, editor, *Claude Simon,* Villeneuve d'Ascq: University of Lille 3, 1990

Sarkonak, Ralph, *Claude Simon: Les carrefours du texte,* Toronto: Paratexte, 1986

Sarkonak, Ralph, *Understanding Claude Simon,* Columbia: University of South Carolina Press, 1990

Sarkonak, Ralph, *Les Trajets de l'écriture: Claude Simon,* Toronto: Paratexte, 1994

Sarkonak, Ralph, editor, *À la recherche du référent . . . ,* Paris: Lettres Modernes Minard, 1994

Séguier, Marcel, editor, *Claude Simon,* Rodez: Subervie, 1972

Starobinski, Jean, *Sur Claude Simon,* Paris: Minuit, 1987

Sykes, Stuart, *Les Romans de Claude Simon,* Paris: Minuit, 1979

Simplicicius Simplicissimus by Hans Jakob Christoffel von Grimmelshausen

Der abenteurliche Simplicissimus Teutsch und Continuatio 1668

The title page of *Simplicicius Simplicissimus* opens with a fictional text that tells of a most simplistic yet adventurous protagonist of German background. Not only that, the title continues, but the story describes the life of a vagrant, from birth through adventurous experiences to the ultimate rejection of the world. Each component of the extended title links the novel to German and to wider European traditions of the literary form.

The central character, Simplicissimus, is involved in numerous adventures. Of indeterminate familial origin, he grows up in the woods in central Germany, is educated there by a hermit, and goes out into a world defined by the Thirty Years War (1618–48). For five books and many years he traverses the territories of the German empire, across the northern tier of Westphalia, to the Black Forest in the southwest. He is battered by real-life horrors and charmed by otherworldly experiences; he outwits rivals and is himself duped; he gains and loses friends; he makes love and is put upon sexually; he rises and falls through military ranks. His life is proof positive that nothing is as constant as inconstancy. At last, in book six, Simplicissimus, the survivor, abandons it all. He undertakes a halfhearted pilgrimage through southern Europe and ends up as an involuntary castaway on an island off Africa, a Robinson Crusoe-like fate some 50 years before Daniel Defoe's novel. There he writes his biography on palm fronds, the novel's manuscript, in order to atone for his moral shortcomings.

On one level, then, *Simplicicius Simplicissimus* poses as an autobiographical confession written by an old man looking back. The story is, however, anything but wistful and is not a novel of education (Bildungsroman). True, the reader is dragged through the shock of battle and the degradations of an outlaw predator, through the extremes of inhuman experience, events that might seem to trace a process of maturation. Yet he never seems to learn; the eremitic life of contrition on the island occurs more by happenstance than as a conceptual endpoint.

The narrative seems so realistic that scholars have used its text as a source for biographical details on Grimmelshausen (1622–76). But this is a tricky proposition, since some of the most graphic descriptions were lifted verbatim from novels by other writers. As faithfully as the confessional story line seems to represent the wartime realities of the 17th century, the representation of reality is ever beholden to the demands of entertaining literary satire in the service of the actual author's morality.

Simplicissimus is no pious pilgrim progressing in accordance with any plan, divine or not. He is, instead, every inch a picaresque vagrant, subject to the vagaries of fortune, sharing the characteristics of craftiness and undetermined familial origin with other picaresque heroes. Little wonder, for Grimmelshausen had absorbed the imagination of Spanish (Mateo Alemán, Miguel de Cervantes) and French (Charles Sorel) epic traditions, texts available to him in published translations. He also relied on German sources (the folktale of Till Eulenspiegel and the works of Hans Sachs) as well as the instructive tales published by his Nuremberg contemporary Georg Philipp Harsdörfer. The Bible and various encyclopedic collections also served Grimmelshausen, who also was familiar with classical epics in translation, especially the *Odyssey*. Grimmelshausen's novel is, however, no mere compilation of sources but rather a richly textured narrative sustained by a resonant language, a vibrant imagination, and, above all, a fascinating central character.

Simplicicius Simplicissimus was quite unlike the contemporary courtly novels written to legitimate the political values of late 17th-century German absolutism. If anything, Simplicissimus was an irreverent anti-courtier, a fact that accounts for the novel's early popularity. Grimmelshausen rode the wave of success, publishing *Courasche* (1670; *Mother Courage*) and *Springinsfeld* (1670; *The Singular Life Story of Heedless Hopalong*), shorter novels detailing the adventures of Simplicissimus' sidekicks. Known, but essentially unappreciated throughout the subsequent century, it was not until the uncovering of Grimmelshausen's identity in the first half of the 19th century that the scholarly and popular reception of the novel commenced. The likes of Thomas Mann and Alfred Döblin drew inspiration from Grimmelshausen's creativity. Bertolt Brecht dramatized *Mutter Courage und ihre Kinder* (produced 1941; *Mother Courage and Her Children*) and more recently the novelist Günther Grass has expressed his indebtedness to Grimmelshausen. *Die Blechtrommel* (1959; *The Tin Drum*) details the exploits of a childlike protagonist caught in three decades of crisis, a latter-day Thirty Years War (1914–45), and Simplicissimus appears as a spirited presence in Grass' story *Das Treffen in Telgte* (1979; *The Meeting at Telgte*).

The recent positive reception of Grimmelshausen mirrors an unabated academic appreciation of the novel, much of which has been published in the journal *Simpliciana* (ongoing from 1979). Translations into English have increased the novel's accessibility and enhanced its reputation. Since the tercentenary of Grimmelshausen's death, scholars have considered the work's putative astrological structure, that is, whether the narrative traces identifiable planetary phases. The debate has ended in a draw, but not without catalyzing an ongoing reexamination of all aspects of the novel. Useful results have been achieved, for example, by interpreting the author's intentions as expressed by cryptic frontispieces—moralizing images dependent on early modern iconographic traditions. The viewpoints of feminist scholarship have better explained the author's timebound antipathies, particularly with regard to *Courasche,* and a fresh evaluation of the era's philosophy and theology have embedded *Simplicicius Simplicissimus* in the rich context of the premodern European imagination.

RICHARD E. SCHADE

Further Reading

Meid, Werner Volker, *Grimmelshausen: Epoche, Work, Wirkung,* Munich: Beck, 1984

Negus, Kenneth, *Grimmelshausen,* New York: Twayne, 1974

Schade, Richard E., "Text and Images: Representation in Grimmelshausen's *Continuatio,*" *The German Quarterly* 64 (1991)

Schade, Richard E., "Simplicissimus in Paris: The Allegory of the Beautiful Lutenist," *Monatshefte* 88 (1996)

Simpliciana: Schriften der Grimmelshausen Gesellschaft (1979–)

Isaac Bashevis Singer 1904–91

United States

The novels of Isaac Bashevis Singer, the renowned 20th-century Yiddish writer, are an achievement of rare distinction. Written in Yiddish, but read throughout the world largely in translation, Singer's novels are noted for their unconventional portrayals of Jewish life past and present. His works explore the darker side of the human psyche, especially as it manifests itself in the erotic and the mystical. Whether focusing on medieval Poland or on New York City during the years following World War II, Singer conjures up in his novels a Yiddish-speaking world that no longer exists, breathing life into the past in a way that is unlike that of any other Yiddish writer.

Singer's first novel, *Der sotn in Goray* (1935; *Satan in Goray*), helped establish his reputation as a master stylist. Written in a linguistic and rhetorical style imitative of a medieval Yiddish book of chronicles, the novel is narrated as if it were a rediscovered text of premodern Jewish piety. This also allowed Singer to initiate a technique that was to become one of his trademarks—the literary use of the supernatural—which serves as an imaginative means of capturing the way in which premodern people defined their inner reality prior to the advent of psychology. Singer loosely bases *Satan in Goray* on historical fact, modeling his story on the events surrounding the 17th-century false messiah Shabbatai Zvi. Exploring the phenomenon of charismatic leadership and the exploitation of the masses, Singer paints a compelling portrait of individual Jews who gradually become caught in the grip of messianic fever after their town is devastated by brutal pogroms. The consequent moral breakdown and the excesses that follow are graphically depicted to show the extreme forms that human depravity can take when cut loose from the strictures of religious law.

Historically and thematically linked to *Satan in Goray* is the novel *The Slave* (1962). Similar to the earlier novel, *The Slave* concentrates on 17th-century Polish Jewry in the aftermath of pogroms. *The Slave,* however, is essentially a love story about two individuals—a Jewish man and a gentile woman—whose love is threatened by the extreme disparity between their two backgrounds. Singer wrote a third novel entitled *The King of Fields* (1988) that continues this theme of Jewish-gentile love in an even earlier era of Jewish life in Poland. Sexual passion is a key element in these novels and is something Singer regularly integrated into many of his works, earning him both notoriety and scorn from the Yiddish-reading public. Indeed, Singer was often charged with being a sensationalist who misrepresented the true nature of Jewish life in Eastern Europe. His works, however, should surely not be read as history but as imaginative re-creations that strive not so much for factual truth as for psychological and spiritual authenticity.

Singer in fact wrote a number of highly unconventional

"love" novels in which erotic attraction follows a specific pattern. In works such as *The Magician of Lublin* (1960), *Enemies: A Love Story* (1972), *Shosha* (1978), and *The Certificate* (1992), Singer creates male protagonists who fall in love with three (and occasionally four) different women: the political radical, the cultured intellectual, the warm-hearted naïf, and sometimes also the wealthy matron. Unable to choose between these women, the protagonist involves himself with all of them simultaneously, leading to a crisis of conscience and an attempt at self-analysis. Some critics view these female character types as Singer's symbolic way of mapping out the social, political, and spiritual choices available to the modern Jew. Interpreted as such, these works depict much more than the exploits of a Yiddish-speaking Don Juan, for each novel is a drama of ideas expressed through the dynamics of character and plot.

Singer is not, however, a writer who is ideologically motivated. He never identified with any specific system of belief and remained decidedly aloof from most of the prevailing attitudes of his lifetime. This scepticism tends to set Singer apart from most of his contemporary Yiddish writers, who were decidedly secular and left-leaning. His independence from ideology allowed Singer the freedom to explore a wide spectrum of options through the diverse characters he created. This is particularly evident in Singer's "family novels," such as *Di Familie Mushkat* (1950; *The Family Moskat*), *The Manor* (1967), and *The Estate* (1969), in which atheists and pietists, communists and capitalists are all constructed as characters worthy of being heard. Setting also plays a crucial role in these novels; Singer's characters are often formed as much by contemporary historical events as they are by their own innate tendencies.

A central stylistic feature of Singer's novels is his frequent use of the monologue as a means by which his main characters convey their story in the first person. The novel that perhaps employs this technique most compellingly is *The Penitent* (1983), in which the protagonist relates his personal story of how he came to embrace ultra-orthodox Judaism after becoming increasingly disillusioned with modern life. This confessional approach to narrative is one that Singer used to maximum effect, enabling him to closely imitate the art of simple storytelling, which he believed to be the basic and primary form of literature.

The facts of Singer's own biography and the times he witnessed form the basis for a series of novels he wrote in the style of the memoir. These quasi-autobiographical novels, such as *In My Father's Court* (1966) and *Love and Exile* (1984), focus mostly on Singer's Hasidic upbringing in Poland and his subsequent rebellion against it. Presented as a kind of ongoing personal chronicle, these works round out Singer's oeuvre, giving flesh and blood to this seemingly inexplicable writer who has been able to wondrously re-create, as if by magic, the lost world of Yiddish-speaking Jewry, in a fictional form that may not be historically accurate but is nevertheless brimming with a relentless passion for life.

Sharon Green

Biography

Born Icek-Hersz Zynger 14 July 1904 in Leoncin, Poland; emigrated to the United States (gained citizenship 1935). Attended the Tachkemoni Rabbinical Seminary, Warsaw, 1921–22. Proofreader and translator, *Literarishe Bleter*, Warsaw, 1923–33; associate editor, *Globus*, Warsaw, 1933–35; journalist, *Vorwärts* (*Jewish Daily Forward*) Yiddish newspaper, New York, from 1935. Awarded Nobel prize for literature, 1978. Died 24 July 1991.

Novels by Singer

Der sotn in Goray, 1935; as *Satan in Goray*, translated by Jacob Sloan, 1955

Der zindiker meshiekh: Historisher roman [The Sinning Messiah: A Historical Novel], serialized in the *Forverts*, 1935–36

Der feter fun Amerike: Roman [The Uncle from America: A Novel], serialized in the *Forverts*, 1949–51

Di Familie Mushkat, 1950; as *The Family Moskat*, translated by A.H. Gross, 1950

A Shif keyn Amerike [A Ship to America], serialized in the *Forverts*, 1958

The Magician of Lublin, translated by Elaine Gottlieb and Joseph Singer, 1960

The Slave, translated by Isaac Bashevis Singer and Cecil Hemley, 1962

In My Father's Court, translated by Channah Kleinerman-Goldstein and others, 1966

The Manor, translated by Joseph Singer and Elaine Gottlieb, 1967

The Estate, translated by Joseph Singer, Elaine Gottlieb, and Elizabeth Shub, 1969

Enemies: A Love Story, translated by Alizah Shevrin and Elizabeth Shub, 1972

Shosha, translated by Joseph Singer and Isaac Bashevis Singer, 1978

Meshuge, 1981–83; as *Meshugah*, translated by Isaac Bashevis Singer and Nili Wachtel, 1994

The Penitent, translated by Joseph Singer, 1983

Love and Exile: The Early Years: A Memoir, 1984:
    A Little Boy in Search of God: Mysticism in a Personal Light, illustrated by Ira Moskowitz, 1976
    A Young Man in Search of Love, translated by Joseph Singer, 1978
    Lost in America, translated by Joseph Singer, 1981

The King of Fields, translated by Isaac Bashevis Singer, 1988

Scum, translated by Rosaline Dukalsky Schwartz, 1991

The Certificate, translated by Leonard Wolf, 1992

Shadows on the Hudson, 1998

Other Writings: short stories, children's novels and stories, autobiography, plays, literary criticism, essays.

Further Reading

Alexander, Edward, *Isaac Bashevis Singer*, Boston: Twayne, 1980

Allentuck, Marcia, *The Achievement of Isaac Bashevis Singer*, Carbondale: Southern Illinois University Press, 1969

Farrell, Grace, editor, *Critical Essays on Isaac Bashevis Singer*, New York: G.K. Hall, 1996

Friedman, Lawrence S., *Understanding Isaac Bashevis Singer*, Columbia: University of South Carolina Press, 1988

Hadda, Janet, *Isaac Bashevis Singer: A Life*, New York: Oxford University Press, 1997

Malin, Irving, editor, *Critical Views of Isaac Bashevis Singer*, New York: New York University Press, 1969

Miller, David Neal, *Fear of Fiction: Narrative Strategies in the Works of Isaac Bashevis Singer*, Albany: State University of New York Press, 1985

Miller, David Neal, editor, *Recovering the Canon: Essays on Isaac Bashevis Singer*, Leiden: Brill, 1986

Roskies, David, "The Demon as Storyteller: Isaac Bashevis Singer," in *A Bridge of Longing: The Lost Art of Yiddish Storytelling*, Cambridge, Massachusetts: Harvard University Press, 1995

Six Classic Chinese Novels

The six classic novels of China are canonic for good reason: they represent important landmark achievements in the history of Chinese fiction. Each of the novels is original and innovative in its own way and provides its own vision of Chinese culture. Long favored by educated Chinese, these novels have exerted a strong influence on Chinese society. The four novels from the 16th century, *Sanguo zhi yanyi* (*Romance of the Three Kingdoms*, or simply *The Three Kingdoms*), *Shuihu zhuan* (long known in English as *Water Margin* but better represented in the translation *Outlaws of the Marsh*), *Xiyou ji* (*The Journey to the West*), and *Jin Ping Mei* (*The Golden Lotus*; again, the more recent translation as *The Plum in the Golden Vase* is to be preferred), represent the culmination of long-evolving Chinese oral and written narrative traditions. Filled with vitality, these 16th-century novels established several new subgenres and set trends that other novelists would follow. The two novels from the 18th century, *Rulin waishi* (*The Scholars*) and *Honglou meng* (*The Dream of the Red Chamber*), which is also known under the title *Shitou ji* (with the preferred modern translation as *The Story of the Stone*), further transform and refine the subgenres. *The Story of the Stone*, in particular, epitomizes the finest achievement in the Chinese art of narrative.

All six novels have significant sociocultural, political, philosophical, religious, and aesthetic dimensions. While reflecting to a certain extent various social realities of the past, the novels also convey their authors' feelings about the times in which they lived, their frustrations as well as their desires, their moral agenda, and their outlook on life. These novels often draw upon—and sometimes reevaluate and critique—the teachings of Confucianism, Taoism, and Buddhism. Simultaneously entertaining and educating their readers, they employ comedy and satire while also providing insight into human nature. To a certain degree the six novels share the following formal characteristics: they are extremely lengthy and include many characters and events, resulting in relatively episodic structures; they contain diverse themes and styles and employ various levels of language ranging from classical to colloquial; they have an omniscient narrator using the storyteller's formulaic phraseology and modes of presentation and commentary; and the 16th-century works use poetry (either composed by the novelist or quoted from earlier literary sources) and set pieces (often in parallel prose) to describe characters, scenery, and battles as well as to comment on characters and their actions. Some of these features are adaptations of the oral storytelling tradition.

The Three Kingdoms (the Chinese title translates literally as "Elaboration of the *Chronicle of the Three Kingdoms*"), from the early 16th century, is actually not a romance at all. Often categorized as a historical novel, it is, rather, a popularized and partially fictionalized history. Underscoring the intimate connection between history and fiction in the Chinese tradition, as well as the creative tension such a connection may bring about, this novel at times approaches epic grandeur. The author is compelled to negotiate between adherence to historical facts and his desire to imprint these facts with his own moral philosophy and vision. While the novel serves aesthetic and expressive functions, it is also pedagogical, educating the common reader in the proper interpretation of history. This is achieved by the use of plainer diction and the inclusion of more dramatized situations than those found in standard historical texts. Thus, the novel establishes a new genre in world fiction that could be called "exposition of history."

Although traditionally attributed to Luo Guanzhong (c. 1330–1400), the novel's authorship is unclear. It is one of the earliest Chinese novels, evolving over time from the Tang (618–907) oral tales about the history of the Three Kingdom Period to the earliest extant text bearing a preface dated 1522, and finally to the revised and most widely read version by Mao Zonggang in the late 17th century. The author relies primarily on historiography, drawing considerably from Chen Shou's third-century *Sanguo zhi* (Chronicle of the Three Kingdoms) and Pei Songzhi's fifth-century commentary. The author's use of semiclassical language indicates his familiarity with and admiration for the historical texts. The author was influenced to some extent by oral traditions and drama as well as the *Sanguo zhi pinghua* (Prose Narrative of the Chronicle of the Three Kingdoms), dating from the 14th century. While the author incorporates folk traditions, he remains faithful to history and does not falsify or exaggerate as is common in those traditions. At the same time, he employs much fictional imagination in elaborating and re-creating historical scenes and figures.

The Three Kingdoms depicts heroes and events from the tumultuous period of A.D. 169–280, during the collapse of the Han dynasty and the establishment of a new dynasty. It was a period of opportunities for ambitious heroes contending for the throne and for those who attached themselves to those heroes in the hope of future success and fame. Out of the crowd of princes, ministers, generals, and heroes vying for power, three major contenders emerged—Cao Cao, Liu Bei, and Sun Quan. They attracted talented and courageous followers and founded the three kingdoms of Wei, Shu, and Wu, respectively. After many heroic battles, the stouthearted first generation gradually died off, giving way to the weaker second generation. Eventually, the grandson of one of Cao Cao's generals was able to reunify the empire.

Celebrated for its narration of battles and ingenious military strategies as well as for its intricate plot, the novel is also noted for its character portrayals. Since the author's sympathy lies with the kingdom of Shu founded by Liu Bei, a descendant of the Han royal family, he portrays Liu's rival Cao Cao as a cunning usurper and Liu Bei as the legitimate leader. Episodes about Liu Bei demonstrate his leadership abilities, emphasizing the traditional themes of recognition, loyalty, and righteousness. For example, Liu Bei recognizes the talents of, and becomes sworn brothers with, Guan Yu and Zhang Fei. Liu Bei secures the service of the extraordinary strategist Zhuge Liang by demonstrating much sincerity, humility, and patience. And because Liu Bei is loyal to his sworn brothers and treats his followers with kindness, they render him faithful and dedicated service.

The author is a master of characterization. He gives even a negative figure such as Cao Cao some admirable qualities, and positive characters have their weaknesses and limitations. The great general Guan Yu, for example, is vainglorious and overly self-confident, while Liu Bei, eager to avenge his sworn brother's death, willfully leads an expedition against Wu that results in his own ruin. In addition to such tragic flaws of character, the author demonstrates the inability of human will to overcome the designs of fate. Despite his foreknowledge of the eventual downfall of Shu, Zhuge Liang, the excellent strategist-cum-minister, perseveres in faithfully serving first Liu Bei and then Liu's foolish son. The author thus creates a character who perfectly embodies Confucian virtues and exhibits a tragic grandeur.

Like *The Three Kingdoms, Outlaws of the Marsh* is based on historical events during the last reign of the Northern Song (1119–25). According to the brief record contained in *The History of the Song Dynasty,* Song Jiang and his band of 36 outlaws initially triumphed over government troops but later opted for honorable surrender and even successfully fought against other rebels on the side of the government. *Outlaws of the Marsh* fictionalizes these historical events to a far greater extent than that found in *The Three Kingdoms.* The novel depicts 108 outlaw-heroes of mythical origins, showing them to be incarnations of demon spirits, and elaborates on the recruitment and assemblage of the heroes as well as on the pronouncement of their grand ideals. *Outlaws of the Marsh* sharpens the contrast between these righteous outlaw-heroes and the corrupt ministers who keep the kind but inept emperor ignorant of the sufferings of the common people. Other departures from the historical record include the embellishment of the heroes' early battles against government troops; a heightening of the tension between Song Jiang and those of his followers who are reluctant to surrender to the government; an increase in the number of expeditions against other rebels once the heroes join with government forces; and the dramatization of the final dissolution of the band.

But *Outlaws of the Marsh* is more than just a fictionalized history. Much of the novel—especially the more fascinating episodes of the first 70 chapters—celebrates the stalwarts' almost superhuman martial skills, courage, and strength, focusing in particular on their avoidance of sexual indulgence as evidence of their self-discipline. While praising loyalty to one's leader (and to the emperor), the novel emphasizes the chivalric ideals of sworn brotherhood and righteousness. Much violence is committed in the name of justified vengeance. In this sense, *Outlaws*

of the Marsh may be considered the first "heroic" novel in China, initiating a subgenre that later became very popular, with works such as *Shuihu houzhuan* (1664; The Water Margin: A Sequel) and *Sanxia wuyi* (1879; Three Knights and Five Heroes).

Outlaws of the Marsh went through a complex process of evolution and a complicated textual history. It is definitely a work of collective authorship, but it may not necessarily have been written by Shi Nai'an (1296–1370) and Luo Guanzhong, to whom authorship is traditionally attributed. In addition to *The History of the Song Dynasty,* the novel was influenced by *Xuanhe yishi* (probably dating from the 13th century; Neglected Events of the "Proclaiming Harmony" Reign Period), as well as by stories, legends, and plays about the heroes' band written during the Yuan dynasty. While the earliest extant text dates from the early 16th century, the novel has appeared not only in the full 120-chapter version but also in versions of 100, 110, 115, and 124 chapters. In 1641, the famous fiction commentator Jin Shengtan produced a 70-chapter version by retaining only the first 71 chapters and renaming chapter 1 as the prologue. Although this 70-chapter version became popular in the Qing, it is incomplete and reductive, ending with the execution of all the heroes soon after their assemblage.

In addition to its fame for dramatic action, *Outlaws of the Marsh* creates more than a dozen memorable characters. It focuses on the outstanding heroes' marginalization within society as well as their sworn brotherhood and subsequent deeds and exploits. As in the case of *The Three Kingdoms,* the complexity of any individual character may be fully appreciated only when he is viewed in the context of other characters. For example, C.T. Hsia notes the contrasting yet complementary relationship between Song Jiang, the leader of the band, and Li Kui, his sworn brother: the more civilized Song Jiang favors the band's honorable surrender to the government, while the impulsive Li Kui—perhaps representing Song's "suppressed desire" to become emperor—opposes surrender (see Hsia, 1968).

Outlaws of the Marsh has been greatly praised for its skillful use of the vernacular language. Moreover, it is the first Chinese novel consciously to employ extensive dream episodes as a literary and aesthetic device. The dreams contribute psychological depth to the characterizations and provide essential coherence to this seemingly loosely organized novel. Moreover, as part of the novel's supernatural framework, the dreams create dramatic irony and introduce a Buddhist perspective in which all phenomena appear to be illusory.

The Journey to the West, commonly known in the West as *The Monkey* through Arthur Waley's abridged 1943 translation, is attributed to the Ming writer Wu Cheng'en (c. 1500–82). The earliest extant edition dates from 1592, although controversies still surround the textual history of the novel. Humorous and fantastic, this 100-chapter novel is the first extended religious and satiric allegory as well as the first comic novel in China. It also spawned a number of other accounts of imaginary journeys that include contests between gods and demons. One example is the collection *Siyou ji* (The Four Journeys) in the Ming with *Dongyou ji* (The Journey to the East) and *Nanyou ji* (The Journey to the South).

Although based on the historical pilgrimage to India undertaken by the famous seventh-century Tang monk Xuanzang for the purpose of bringing back Buddhist texts, the novel is full of original invention and fantasy. *The Journey to the West* transforms the historical saintly personage Xuanzang into the fearful monk Tripitaka. Believing his flesh can confer longevity, many monsters yearn to consume Tripitaka, and he constantly fears for his own safety. The novel, focusing on Monkey as the true protagonist, describes his birth and acquisition of magical power, his frustrations leading to rebellion in Heaven, and his ultimate subjugation by Buddha. Monkey, together with the Pig, the Sand Monk, and the dragon-horse—all possessing supernatural skills—become Tripitaka's animal disciples and travel escorts. The bulk of the novel concerns the 81 ordeals they undergo during their pilgrimage. After fulfilling their mission of obtaining sacred texts, they return to China and become canonized.

Although the author incorporated many earlier legends, oral and written tales, and plays into his writing, he composed most of the verses and poetic set pieces himself to suit specific contexts in the novel. His use of vernacular language is expressive, and his narrative voice refreshing and vivacious.

The author humanizes, to various degrees, the deities, Tripitaka's animal disciples, and the monsters and demons encountered along the way, thereby infusing social reality into a seemingly fantastic tale. He succeeds in depicting strong individual characters such as the intelligent, loyal Monkey and the gluttonous, indolent Pig, as well as the dynamic and changing relationships among these characters. Corresponding to the five elements of Water, Fire, Wood, Metal, and Earth, the five principal characters contrast with as well as complement one another.

Like *Outlaws of the Marsh*, *The Journey to the West* bestows mythic origins on its heroes. Having committed misdeeds in a previous existence, they must perform good deeds in their present incarnations in order to redeem themselves. Viewed within a religious framework, the ostensible purpose of the pilgrimage—obtaining scriptures—indicates a desire for Buddhist salvation. Nevertheless, the novel does not refrain from ridiculing Buddhist and Taoist deities and ideologies. Its frequent satire of Confucian bureaucracy and institutions also marks it as a carnivalesque novel in the sense developed in the 20th century by the Russian theorist Mikhail Bakhtin.

The Journey to the West is entertaining as fantasy, yet it also evinces deep insight into human realities. However, it was not until *The Plum in the Golden Vase* that the first Chinese novel of manners clearly located in the human realm made its appearance. Written in the late 16th century by an author who used the pseudonym of "The Scoffing Scholar," the 100-chapter *The Plum in the Golden Vase* was probably first published in 1617. Unlike *The Three Kingdoms* and *Outlaws of the Marsh*, which set forth numerous grand battles and heroic deeds, *The Plum in the Golden Vase* describes quotidian life in a rich merchant's household in an urban setting. Focusing on the depraved Ximen Qing and his six wives, the novel has a tighter, more cohesive plot than any of its three predecessors.

The composition of *The Plum in the Golden Vase* is rather unusual. Set between 1112 and 1127, the novel overlaps with the historical period of *Outlaws of the Marsh* but departs somewhat in its plot design. The author took an episode from *Outlaws of the Marsh*, in which the tiger-slaying hero Wu Song avenges his older brother Wu Da by killing Wu Da's adulterous and murderous wife Pan Jinlian (golden lotus). In *The Plum in the Golden Vase*, Wu Song goes into exile (chapter 10) after Jinlian kills her husband. Jinlian then lives with her paramour, and it is not until much later that Wu Song has a chance to kill her (chapter 87). In addition to the Wu Song episode, the author incorporates a great variety of other sources in his work. As identified by Patrick Hanan, these sources include histories of the Song dynasty, one erotic story in literary Chinese, vernacular stories, *chantefable* literature, plays, and popular songs (see Hanan, 1963).

Its appropriation of existing material notwithstanding, the novel is original, well structured, and artistically appealing. The author relates numerous episodes with obvious relish, such as Jinlian's marriage into Ximen Qing's household; their amorous pleasure; Ximen's many sexual exploits; Jinlian's frustration and adulterous escapades; her fights with the other wives, especially her jealousy of Li Ping'er, Ximen's favorite; her hand in the deaths of Ping'er's son and Ping'er herself; Ximen's death from an overdose of aphrodisiac; Jinlian's gruesome murder by Wu Song; and, finally, the dissolution of Ximen's household, which results in his heir becoming a Buddhist monk.

The author's attention to detail, skillful narration, and lively dialogues result in a vivid—if not necessarily completely faithful—representation of late Ming life. Moreover, the author uses poetic pieces and song lyrics to communicate the inner views and emotions of the characters and to provide a different or contrasting perspective to that conveyed by the narrative. For example, the largely negative portrayal of Jinlian in the narrative is mitigated by the sympathetic lyrics of her songs in which she expresses her frustration. Various levels of diction and style contribute to the creation of complex human experiences.

The author's borrowing from other sources might have been one reason for the difficulty in ascribing a consistent meaning to the novel. When it first appeared, it was read as a roman à clef. Later, some read it as pornography, while others regarded it as an exposition of Buddhist enlightenment. Still others argued for its demonstration of orthodox Confucian principles. Scholars continue (albeit to little avail) to seek a uniform interpretation under which all elements of the novel can be subsumed. Like *Outlaws of the Marsh* and *The Journey to the West*, *The Plum in the Golden Vase* should be read as a mixture of many layers of meaning. It contains something of all the above interpretations, but none should be seen as absolute and all-encompassing. Indeed, the novel not only has realistic, erotic, moral, and religious dimensions: it satirizes social ills and human foibles and may also be seen as a political allegory in which Ximen stands for the emperor and his six wives represent the six ministers.

The Scholars (c. 1750; literally "Unofficial History of the Literati World") has not provoked the same controversy over authorship as the four masterworks of the 16th century. This 55-chapter novel, written by Wu Jingzi, who hailed from an established official family in Anhui province, is one of the first semi-autobiographical novels in China. Although well educated, Wu was not interested in taking the civil service examination to become an official. Deliberately avoiding contact with official bureaucrats, he instead befriended socially marginal figures such as poets, painters, and actors. After squandering his inheritance, he led an impoverished life as a recluse in Nanjing. In his novel, he expressed his frustration and cynicism about the literati world, endowing the novel's protagonist Du Shaoqing with many of his own qualities and weaving in his own observations and personal experiences.

The Scholars has long been described by Lu Xun (1881–1936) and other scholars as China's first satirical novel. It is in fact not the first, since it was preceded by earlier examples such as Dong

Yue's *Xiyou bu* (1641; Supplement to Journey to the West) and the 100-chapter *Xingshi yinyuan zhuan* (c. 1661; Marriage Destinies to Awaken the World). However, *The Scholars* is the most consistent and focused satire, as well as the most subtle in tone. While criticizing many aspects of society, the novel targets phony scholars as well as the examination and official recruitment systems. It also directly influenced many late Qing satiric novels of social criticism such as *Guanchang xianxing ji* (1903; Exposure of the Official World) and *Ershinian mudu zhi guai xianzhuang* (1909; Strange Happenings Eyewitnessed in the Last Twenty Years).

Tailored to Wu Jingzi's satiric intent, *The Scholars* compares and contrasts Confucian ideals with sordid reality. Employing a framing device in the first and last chapters, the author presents the Confucian eremitic ideal in characters dedicated to moral self-cultivation who stand beyond the temptations of society. Chapters 2 to 30 ridicule opportunistic scholars who try to pass examinations and become officials. In caricaturing these scholars who frantically pursue status, wealth, and fame, the author reveals the underlying corruption of the examination and recruitment systems. Chapters 31 to 37 form the climax of the idealistic core, describing the gathering of genuine scholars to perform a grand sacrifice at the Confucian temple in Nanjing. Chapters 37 to 54 are episodic and contain stories satirizing other characters who are intent on the profit motive. In particular, the hypocrisy and pretensions of those who abuse the existing social system—often in the name of defending Confucian morality—are exposed.

The Scholars is exceptional in its narrative art. Adopting a fairly objective mode of presentation, the narrator relates facts while refraining from commentary or interruption, thereby allowing the reader to form an independent judgment of characters and events. In his ability to provide multiple perspectives on characters, Wu Jingzi is influenced by historiography and classical tales. But instead of using formulaic set pieces or verses, Wu Jingzi chooses to describe characters, objects, and scenes in vernacular prose. Wu's prose is clean and fluid, and many of his descriptive passages have been praised for their vividness.

Considered the most refined and profound novel in China, *Story of the Stone* (c. 1760) is the great favorite among Chinese intellectuals. So much has been written that scholarship on this novel, termed *Hongxue*, or *Redology*, has become a field in and of itself. Like *The Scholars*, *Story of the Stone* incorporates a good deal of autobiographical material concerning the author, Cao Xueqin (Cao Zhan). Born into a wealthy official family in Nanjing, Cao witnessed the decline of his family's fortune and spent the last part of his life in poverty in the suburbs of Beijing. During the time he was writing it, the novel circulated in manuscript form among his friends. However, he completed only 80 chapters before his death. In 1792, a complete 120-chapter edition appeared. Its prefaces were written by Cheng Weiyuan (c. 1742–c. 1818) and Gao E (c. 1740–c. 1815). Gao E has now been identified as the most likely author of the last 40 chapters.

Like *The Plum in the Golden Vase*, *Story of the Stone* presents diverse themes and interweaves many layers of meaning. It has been read as a roman à clef, a political allegory with hidden criticism of the Manchus, a triangle love story, an illustration of the Buddhist philosophy of detachment, a novel of social criticism, and a novel of manners. Although both epic and lyrical, it should primarily be regarded as a novel of manners with philosophical and religious overtones. Influenced by *The Plum in the*

Golden Vase, the novel revolves around the domestic world and the conflict between desire and duty, detailing the initial glory and later decline of a wealthy family. It includes many complex female characters and is far more refined and subtle in its representation than *The Plum in the Golden Vase*. In shifting its focus from sexual desire to romantic love, *Story of the Stone* is able to explore a broader range of human emotions as well.

The structure of the novel is characterized by a back-and-forth movement between various interweaving themes: sociopolitical versus philosophical, Confucian versus Taoist and Buddhist, natural versus supernatural and mythical, dream versus reality, and literal versus metaphorical. The protagonist, Jia Baoyu (precious jade), is born into an aristocratic household with a piece of jade in his mouth. He falls in love with his female cousin Lin Daiyu (black jade), a beautiful, talented, but also sickly and hypersensitive girl. Baoyu and Daiyu share a mythical affinity: in a former existence, Baoyu was a magical stone who watered and gave life to a fairy flower; the fairy flower was later incarnated as Daiyu to pay back her "debt of tears."

Despite otherworldly affinities, Baoyu and Daiyu are doomed to suffer in this world and their love to end in tragedy. Having lost his jade as well as his wits, Baoyu is fooled by his family into marrying Xue Baochai (precious hairpin), another cousin who is an intelligent and sensible girl, beautiful in her own way. Daiyu dies meanwhile of consumption and bitter disappointment (chapters 97–98). Baoyu comes to his senses and realizes his mistake, becoming disillusioned and resolving to detach himself from this world. But before leaving home to become a monk, he first fulfills his Confucian duty. He passes his examination, thereby bringing his family honor, and also leaves his family with an heir. From a Buddhist perspective, the ending is by no means tragic. Having suffered much in the world of craving and desire, Baoyu is eventually enlightened and obtains personal salvation. Moreover, according to Buddhist belief, by becoming a monk he guarantees salvation for nine generations.

The Prospect Garden is the major locus for events in chapters 23 to 80 and also an important metaphor throughout the novel. Originally built for the visit of Baoyu's eldest sister, the imperial concubine, the garden is inhabited by Baoyu together with the beautiful and talented young girls who are his sisters and female cousins. The garden is situated within, and yet partially secluded from, the two adjoining Jia family mansions inhabited mainly by prodigal members of the clan. As such, it represents an idyllic and untainted contrast to the corrupt world outside, reminiscent of the divine Land of Illusion Baoyu once visited in his dreams. It is also an allegory of human existence and its attendant processes of birth, change, and death. And so the garden must inevitably be disturbed, scattering its residents.

The motifs of dream and mirror are skillfully used to underscore the novel's philosophical themes, and the ambiguous dualities of truth and falsehood, reality and illusion, are shown to be contrasting yet also complementary. The novel explores character psychology with more subtlety and depth than any of its predecessors. Moreover, its language is superb: elegant and poetic, very expressive, but also colloquial and humorous, depending on the context. The author's dexterous use of such devices as pun, riddle, and rebus further creates pluralistic meanings in the text. While providing a wealth of information on Chinese culture and aesthetics, the novel is in itself an invaluable work of art.

In conclusion, each of the six novels yields a complexity of meaning through the use of diverse themes, levels of meaning, and intertextual allusions that can be fully appreciated only through repeated reading. These novels provide fertile ground for studying the emotions, ideas, and culture of the Chinese people, but they are more than a national record, as their cognitive insights into human nature are universal. The six classic novels have been fortunate to receive much scholarly attention. Hu Shi (1891–1962) has contributed admirable studies, and C.T. Hsia has written the best introduction in English and helped to build the fame of "the Big Six." Many other scholars have focused study on one or more of the six novels. All of them have been translated into English, most of them in full. However, it still remains for these novels to be better known and appreciated by Western readers.

It should be emphasized that these novels do not exist in isolation. They are related to many other fine novels that are still considered "marginal" in current scholarship. The 17th-century satire *Marriage as Retribution, Awakening the World* and Li Haiguan's 18th-century novel *Qilu deng* (The Warning Light at the Crossroads) are two examples of the understudied "minor" works. The six classic novels can thus offer an advantageous starting point for the reading and evaluation of noncanonical works.

Yenna Wu

See also Chinese Novel (Beginnings to the 20th Century)

Six Classic Chinese Novels

Sanguo zhi yanyi, published early 16th century; as *Romance of the Three Kingdoms*, translated by C.H. Brewitt-Taylor, 2 vols., 1925; as *The Three Kingdoms: A Historical Novel*, translated by Moss Roberts, 1991

Shuihu zhuan, published c. 1550; as *All Men Are Brothers*, translated by Pearl S. Buck, 2 vols., 1933; as *Water Margin*, translated by J.H. Jackson, 2 vols., 1937; as *Outlaws of the Marsh*, translated by Sidney Shapiro, 2 vols., 1981; as *The Broken Seals: Part One of The Marshes of Mount Liang*, translated by John Dent-Young and Alex Dent-Young, 1994

Xiyou ji, published c. 1580; as *Monkey, Folk Novel of China*, translated by Arthur Waley, 1942 (abridged); as *The Monkey King*, translated by George Theiner, 1965; as *The Journey to the West*, translated by Anthony C. Yu, 4 vols., 1977–83

Jin Ping Mei, published c. 1617; as *The Golden Lotus*, translated by Clement Egerton, 4 vols., 1939; as *Chin P'ing Mei: The Adventurous History of Hsi Men and His Six Wives*, translated by Bernard Maill, 1939 (translated from Franz Kuhn's German translation of 1930); as *The Plum in the Golden Vase; or, Chin P'ing Mei, Volume One: The Gathering*, translated by David Tod Roy, 1993 (5 vols. projected)

Rulin waishi, published c. 1750; as *The Scholars*, translated by Yang Hsien-yi and Gladys Yang, 1957, revised edition 1987

Honglou meng, published c. 1760; as *The Dream of the Red Chamber*, translated by Chi-chen Wang, 1929 (abridged); as *A Dream of Red Mansions*, translated by Yang Hsien-yi and Gladys Yang, 3 vols., 1978–86; Chinese text is also known as *Shitou ji*, in English as *The Story of the Stone*, translated by David Hawkes and John Minford, 5 vols., 1973–86

Further Reading

Carlitz, Katherine, *The Rhetoric of Chin P'ing Mei*, Bloomington: Indiana University Press, 1986

Chang Ching-erh, "The Monkey-Hero in the *Hsi-yu chi* Cycle," *Chinese Studies* 1:1 (June 1983) and 1:2 (December 1983)

Dudbridge, Glen, *The Hsi-yu chi: A Study of Antecedents to the Sixteenth-Century Chinese Novel*, Cambridge: Cambridge University Press, 1970

Hanan, Patrick, "The Text of the *Chin P'ing Mei*," *Asia Major* 9:1 (1962)

Hanan, Patrick, "Sources of the *Chin P'ing Mei*," *Asia Major* 10:2 (1963)

Hegel, Robert E., *The Novel in Seventeenth-Century China*, New York: Columbia University Press, 1981

Hegel, Robert E., and Richard C. Hessney, editors, *Expressions of Self in Chinese Literature*, New York: Columbia University Press, 1985

Hsia, C.T., *The Classic Chinese Novel: A Critical Introduction*, New York: Columbia University Press, 1968

Huang, Martin W., *Literati and Self-Re/Presentation: Autobiographical Sensibility in the Eighteenth-Century Chinese Novel*, Stanford, California: Stanford University Press, 1995

Kao, Karl S.Y., "An Archetypal Approach to *Hsi-yu chi*," *Tamkang Review* 5:2 (October 1974)

Li, Wai-yee, *Enchantment and Disenchantment: Love and Illusion in Chinese Literature*, Princeton, New Jersey: Princeton University Press, 1993

Liu Ts'un-yan, *Buddhist and Taoist Influences on Chinese Novels*, Wiesbaden: Harrassowitz, 1962

Lu Xun, *Zhongguo xiaoshuo shilüe*, Beijing, 1924; as *A Brief History of Chinese Fiction*, Beijing: Foreign Languages Press, 1959; 3rd edition, 1976

Ma, Y.W., "The Chinese Historical Novel: An Outline of Themes and Contexts," *Journal of Asian Studies* 34:2 (February 1975)

McMahon, Keith, *Misers, Shrews, and Polygamists: Sexuality and Male-Female Relations in Eighteenth-Century Chinese Fiction*, Durham, North Carolina: Duke University Press, 1995

Nienhauser, William H., editor, *Indiana Companion to Traditional Chinese Literature*, Bloomington: Indiana University Press, 1986

Plaks, Andrew H., *Archetype and Allegory in the "Dream of the Red Chamber,"* Princeton, New Jersey: Princeton University Press, 1976

Plaks, Andrew H., editor, *Chinese Narrative: Critical and Theoretical Essays*, Princeton, New Jersey: Princeton University Press, 1977

Rolston, David L., editor, *How To Read the Chinese Novel*, Princeton, New Jersey: Princeton University Press, 1990

Rolston, David L., *Traditional Chinese Fiction and Fiction Commentary: Reading and Writing Between the Lines*, Stanford, California: Stanford University Press, and Cambridge: Cambridge University Press, 1997

Ropp, Paul S., *Dissent in Early Modern China: "Ju-lin wai-shih"* [*Rulin waishi*] *and Ch'ing Social Criticism*, Ann Arbor: University of Michigan Press, 1981

Rushton, Peter H., *The Jin Ping Mei and the Non-Linear*

Dimensions of the Traditional Chinese Novel, Lewiston, New York: Edwin Mellen Press, 1994

Wang, Jing, *The Story of Stone: Intertextuality, Ancient Chinese Stone Lore, and the Stone Symbolism of "Dream of the Red Chamber," "Water Margin," and "The Journey to the West,"* Durham, North Carolina: Duke University Press, 1992

Widmer, Ellen, *The Margins of Utopia: Shui-hu hou-chuan and the Literature of Ming Loyalism,* Cambridge, Massachusetts: Council on East Asian Studies, Harvard University, 1987

Wong, Timothy C., *Wu Ching-tzu,* Boston: Twayne, 1978

Wu, Shih-ch'ang, *On the Red Chamber Dream: A Critical Study of Two Annotated Manuscripts of the XVIIIth Century,* Oxford: Clarendon Press, 1961

Wu, Yenna, *The Chinese Virago: A Literary Theme,* Cambridge, Massachusetts: Council on East Asian Studies, Harvard University, 1995

Wu, Yenna, "Outlaws' Dreams of Power and Position in *Shuihu zhuan,*" *Chinese Literature: Essays, Articles, Reviews* 18 (1996)

Yang, Winston L.Y., Peter Li, and Nathan K. Mao, editors, *Classical Chinese Fiction: A Guide to Its Study and Appreciation: Essays and Bibliographies,* Boston: G.K. Hall, and London: Prior, 1978

Yu, Anthony C., "Heroic Verse and Heroic Mission: Dimensions of the Epic in the *Hsi-yu chi,*" *Journal of Asian Studies* 31:4 (August 1972)

Yu, Anthony C., "Two Literary Examples of Religious Pilgrimage: The *Commedia* and the *Journey to the West,*" *History of Religions* 22:3 (February 1983)

Yu, Anthony C., *Rereading the Stone: Desire and the Making of Fiction in "Dream of the Red Chamber,"* Princeton, New Jersey: Princeton University Press, 1997

Small House at Allington. *See* Barsetshire Novels

Snow Country by Kawabata Yasunari

Yukiguni 1937/48

In 1937 Kawabata Yasunari published under the title *Yukiguni* (*Snow Country*) a collection of related short stories that had appeared previously in magazines. The book was well received and earned the author a prominent literary prize, which encouraged him to devote less time to writing reviews of new fiction and more to his own creative efforts. But this version of *Snow Country* was not the piece for which Kawabata was awarded the Nobel prize for literature in 1968. The final version of *Snow Country* was not published until 1948, after a number of additions to the 1937 version and much revision.

Structurally, *Snow Country* and many of Kawabata's other longer works have been compared to the traditional Japanese linked-verse poetry, or *renga*. The ancient form involves one or more poets who compose a sequence of verses, with each new verse playing off the one immediately preceding. *Renga* shows little architectural regard for the overall structure of the poem; instead it focuses on the linear development of each succeeding link. The sequence of scenes in *Snow Country* does suggest just such a train of traditionally linked associations. It also exhibits the occasionally puzzling or even jarring juxtaposition of images of the modernism that Kawabata promoted early in his career as a theorist for the New Perception school. This work also has been likened to stream-of-consciousness techniques with which

Kawabata was familiar from translations of Marcel Proust and James Joyce.

In the case of *Snow Country,* Kawabata had had no intention of writing a novel when he began it and had no vision of what the full work would encompass. The publishing history of *Snow Country* is one of the most complex in Japanese literature, although not particularly unusual for Kawabata. His first story, about a Tokyo dilettante (Shimamura) and the geisha (Komako) he visits in a snowy northern province, "Yugeshiki no kagami" (Mirror of an Evening Scene), was published in the literary magazine *Bungei Shunju* in January 1935. Unable to include all he wished to write about these characters before the magazine's copy deadline, Kawabata continued the story in a second piece, "Shiroi asa no kagami" ("Mirror of a White Morning"), which he published in a different magazine whose deadline for the January issue was some days later. Kawabata claimed that the feeling for the story stayed with him and induced him to write more and more about the characters—Shimamura, Komako, and the young woman Yoko. Each time he wrote about these characters it was as if he were recalling forgotten scenes. Toward the end of 1935, the third and fourth installments of the "Snow Country" sequence were published in yet a different magazine; the fifth appeared in still another magazine in 1936. Kawabata went on to write a sixth and a seventh "Snow Country" story, and these were published in 1936 and 1937 in two magazines in which earlier pieces had appeared. The completed 1937 book proved popular with readers and was adapted for the stage. However, Kawabata published two more "Snow Country" chapters in magazines in 1939 and 1940. He revised the whole work for the 1948 edition—on which translations into English and other languages are based. Even after the definitive version of *Snow Country* was published, Kawabata considered adding another chapter to the novel in order to clarify the vague relationship between Komako and Yoko, but ultimately he decided to abandon the project.

The opening of the novel is one of the most famous in Japanese literature. For years, college applicants in Japan have been required to memorize the first lines in preparation for entrance examinations. "After the long border tunnel, the snow country appeared. The depths of the night turned white." The setting remains far removed from the mundane obligations of home and the city. Its other-worldly quality is apparent from the moment the train enters the snow country: the windows become imperfect mirrors that afford Shimamura glimpses of points of light in the dark. The passing landscape outside merges with scenes inside the car and evokes tenuous memories of Shimamura's previous encounter with Komako. Mirrors figure prominently in Kawabata's literature, and those in *Snow Country* serve to link the characters without actually bringing them into direct contact with one another. Kawabata's style—his tendency toward ellipsis and fascination with oblique encounters—seems particularly suited to his recurrent theme of yearning for love and avoidance of direct involvement.

Kawabata stated that *Snow Country* was "the kind of work that could be cut off at any point." Indeed, one of the last works Kawabata wrote before his death in 1972 was a distillation of his most famous novel into the form of one of Kawabata's noted "palm-of-the-hand stories," entitled "Gleanings from Snow Country." This miniature version ends with the same scene with which Kawabata ended the story "Mirror of a White Morning" in 1934: as she prepares to leave his room, Shimamura sees Komako's face in a mirror as if it is floating, surrounded by the white of the snowy mountains.

In *Snow Country*, Kawabata was writing as he did for most of his career—against the prevailing or popular form. The dominant form of the time was the confessional I-novel, a descendent of the Japanese version of naturalism. Proponents of the I-novel

eschewed the artifice that Kawabata's work entailed. And some critics, reluctant to read the novel as anything other than confessional, insisted that the author himself must be the model for Shimamura, to which Kawabata offered his famous remark that if he was any character in the novel, he existed in the person of the geisha Komako. The influence of *Snow Country* can be measured by the extent to which it has been translated and has served to introduce many non-Japanese readers to Japanese literature. *Snow Country* and other works by Kawabata have often been read as representative of modern Japanese fiction, establishing somewhat skewed expectations of the modern Japanese novel. Kawabata's stories about the anxiety of love repeat motifs found in early Japanese literature. The ellipsis and suggestiveness common to much of modern Japanese fiction find their most extreme manifestations in Kawabata's work.

J. MARTIN HOLMAN

See also Kawabata Yasunari

Further Reading

Araki, James T., "Kawabata and His Snow Country," *Centennial Review* 8 (1969)

Gessel, Van C., *Three Modern Novelists: Soseki, Tanizaki, Kawabata,* Tokyo and New York: Kodansha International, 1993

Liman, Anthony V., "Kawabata's Lyrical Mode in *Snow Country,*" *Monumenta Nipponica* 26 (1971)

Miyoshi, Masao, *Accomplices of Silence: The Modern Japanese Novel,* Berkeley: University of California Press, 1974

Petersen, Gwenn Boardman, *The Moon in the Water: Understanding Tanizaki, Kawabata, and Mishima,* Honolulu: University Press of Hawaii, 1979

Swann, Thomas E., and Katsuhiko Takeda, *Essays on Japanese Literature,* Tokyo: Waseda-Daigaku-Shuppanbu, 1973

Tsuruta, Kinya, and Thomas E. Swann, *Approaches to the Modern Japanese Novel,* Tokyo: Sophia University, 1976

Ueda, Makoto, *Modern Japanese Writers and the Nature of Literature,* Stanford, California: Stanford University Press, 1976

Yamanouchi, Hisaaki, *The Search for Authenticity in Modern Japanese Literature,* Cambridge and New York: Cambridge University Press, 1978

Social Criticism

The Novel of Social Criticism in the Victorian Era

While in a general sense most novels either implicitly or explicitly critique society, the Victorian period in England saw the publication of a group of novels consciously devoted to exposing social ills, particularly those thought to have arisen as a result of industrialization and urbanization. These novels were first identified and discussed as a group by French critic Louis Cazamian (1903), in which novels by Charles Dickens, Benjamin Disraeli, Elizabeth Gaskell, and Charles Kingsley were included in his groundbreaking study, as well as those by several other writers, such as Harriet Martineau, Charlotte Brontë, Frances Trollope, and Charlotte Elizabeth Tonna. While Cazamian confined his study to England and ended it with the year 1850, most of these writers, as well as many others from England and other nations as well, continued to write novels of social criticism during the next decade and well beyond.

Like the novels Cazamian identified as "social novels with a purpose," a few novels published earlier in the 19th century also focused on working-class characters and could be called precursors or early examples of social problem novels. Some of the most notable of these would be the radical philosopher William Godwin's *Caleb Williams* (1794) and Maria Edgeworth's portrayals of Irish peasants and landlords in *Castle Rackrent* (1800) and *The Absentee* (1812). Edward Bulwer-Lytton's *Paul Clifford* (1830) is sometimes called a novel with a purpose; its use of lowlife characters and language made it the first of a group of novels called "Newgate novels" for their association with criminals and social deviance. Harriet Martineau's *Illustrations of Political Economy* (1832–34), an immensely successful series of tales meant to demonstrate individual principles of political economy in fictional form, are often credited as the first social problem narratives.

The social problem novel or novel with a purpose that began to appear in the late 1830s and early 1840s combined the techniques of literary realism with a clearly marked didacticism; in other words, these novels claimed to be representations of actual social conditions in order to teach their primarily middle-class readers about specific social problems and to influence them to take action toward solving these problems. The earliest of these novels looked not only to earlier socially conscious narratives, such as those of Godwin or Martineau, but also took as models slave narratives and antislavery literature from the late 18th and early 19th centuries, using "white slavery" as a metaphor to describe the English working classes. Frances Trollope, for instance, began her series of novels about social problems in 1836 with a savage antislavery novel, *Jonathan Jefferson Whitlaw*. The most famous antislavery novel of the 19th century, of course, was American Harriet Beecher Stowe's *Uncle Tom's Cabin* (1852), whose subtitle, *Life Among the Lowly*, ties it to British novels about working-class life. Stowe's novel, in fact, could be called the most influential of all social-problem novels, dealing, as it does, with America's most pressing social problem in the 19th century and using many of the same techniques as the British "novels with a purpose."

Most 19th-century novels of social criticism focused at least in part on poor or working-class characters victimized by brutal social forces beyond their control or by greedy and vicious employers who refused to see them as human beings. Such novels typically gave many details of working-class life, particularly the unsanitary state of urban slums and the grueling and dangerous working conditions in the factories, often contrasting them with the idle and luxurious lives of factory owners, government leaders, or other authority figures. Despite their poverty and lack of education or religious training, however, the working-class protagonists of these novels usually exemplified middle-class values such as cleanliness, respect, gratitude, thrift, hard work, and domestic affection so that readers would identify and sympathize with them and their plight. Most also included at least one altruistic observer or reformer from the middle classes, and some social problem novels, especially those written after the 1840s, also featured capitalists or landowners who, although portrayed

sympathetically, are misguided and must change their opinions after learning the truth about the condition of the workers. Some social problem novels ended by rescuing the poverty-stricken protagonists into middle- or even upper-class prosperity and security, while others had these characters' lives end tragically. However, few were able to dramatize actual widespread societal solutions to the problems they so graphically represented, because most of the middle-class authors of social problem novels were ambivalent about, if not downright mistrustful of, unions, strikes, and other forms of collective action; neither could they imagine the kind of widespread social change that later socialists would advocate. Thus their imagined solutions to social problems tended toward either a return to a paternalistic model of social responsibility or vague plans for improving class relations through individual understanding and brotherly love, both supported by protective legislation for factory workers and other laborers.

The Victorian novel of social criticism was closely akin to several other important forms of discourse that addressed social problems related to the rise of industrialization, urbanization, and other widespread changes in English social, political, and economic relations. Journalists, government inspectors and commissioners, statisticians, political economists, social theorists, and philosophers all addressed the living and working conditions of the poor and prescribed solutions to social ills. Journalist Henry Mayhew's *London Labour and the London Poor* (1862), for instance, devoted four volumes to a painstaking catalog of conditions among dozens of different types of laborers, while parliamentary "blue books" proliferated on almost every social problem imaginable. Blue books, in fact, frequently were used by novelists as sources for the conditions described in their novels, while novels, in turn, especially those by Charles Dickens, were sometimes quoted in parliamentary debates as evidence of social conditions. Victorian novels of social criticism, therefore, were intimately tied to these other forms of discourse about social problems and often were received with equal authority by their readers. Because such novels were written by and addressed to members of the middle and upper classes, they should not be confused with "proletarian novels," which were usually written by members of the working classes rather than about or to them.

Early Victorian novels of social criticism dealt primarily with factory conditions or with the effects of the New Poor Law (which, enacted in 1834, revolutionized the way the needs of the poor were handled by the government) and with virtually redefining the very idea of poverty. Early factory novels included Frances Trollope's *The Life and Adventures of Michael Armstrong, Factory Boy* (1840) and Charlotte Elizabeth's *Helen Fleetwood* (1841). These two novels had a powerful influence on the reading public because of their graphic depictions of the insides of factories and slums, places most readers had never seen personally. Both also portrayed idealized child factory workers, contrasted with selfish, callused factory owners, in an effort to promote a specific legislative movement—the "Ten-Hours Bill." Dickens' *Oliver Twist* (1838) and Frances Trollope's *Jessie Phillips, A Tale of the Present Day* (1843) both attacked the New Poor Law, portraying the plight of deserving children thrust into the horrific workhouse by its provisions.

Also published during the period known as "the hungry forties" was Benjamin Disraeli's *Sybil; or, The Two Nations* (1845), one of a subgroup of social problem novels often called "condition-of-England" novels. The "two nations" of the title are the rich and poor; the novel portrays conditions in depressed agricultural districts, industrial slums, and mining towns, including the "truck system," which forced workers to buy provisions at inflated prices at "company stores." In the end, the working-class heroine Sybil turns out to be an aristocrat, and her union with Charles Egremont, the younger son of an earl, is meant to symbolize the union of the two nations in an idealized neofeudalism advocated by Disraeli and the "Young England" movement as a solution to the problems of industrialism. Disraeli, who later became prime minister, also wrote two other condition-of-England novels, entitled *Coningsby; or, The New Generation* (1844) and *Tancred; or, The New Crusade* (1847).

Elizabeth Gaskell's *Mary Barton: A Tale of Manchester Life* (1848) was probably even more widely read and influential than Disraeli's novels. Set almost entirely among factory workers in the slums of Manchester, Gaskell's novel managed to depict its working-class characters both sympathetically and realistically, relying less on idealized stereotypes and simplistic oppositions between owners and workers than had many previous social problem novels. *Mary Barton* introduced several pressing social issues, including Chartism, unionism, cholera epidemics, prostitution, and opium abuse. Charlotte Brontë, whose earlier novel *Jane Eyre* (1847) had portrayed the problems faced by gentlewomen without fortunes, also took on the issue of factory workers in *Shirley* (1849). *Shirley* differed from *Mary Barton* and most previous factory novels by focusing on young, single, middle-class women rather than working-class characters as protagonists and by being set in the period of the Luddite riots of 1811–12 rather than in the present or very recent past. The social problems discussed in the novel include both relations between factory owners and workers and the challenges faced by unmarried, portionless, middle-class women, who are portrayed as being in sympathy with the workers. In 1850 the Christian Socialist clergyman Charles Kingsley published *Alton Locke, Tailor and Poet*, another social problem or condition-of-England novel. The title character, a self-educated sweatshop tailor, becomes a poet and activist and is influenced by both sympathetic and unsympathetic middle-class characters representing the views of figures such as Thomas Carlyle and John Henry Newman.

Two novels published in the mid-1850s, Dickens' *Hard Times* (1854) and Gaskell's *North and South* (1855), are also usually considered part of the group of novels described as "factory novels" or "industrial novels." Written by mature writers during a more prosperous time than the depressed 1840s, these two novels are somewhat more complex and broad ranging than many of the earlier instances of the genre, focusing less on specific historical events or legislative issues and more on the general issue of how to conduct relations between the classes. Both novels were first published concurrently in Dickens' journal *Household Words,* with the authors in correspondence with each other; however, the two are quite different in style and emphasis.

Dickens' novel is a savage satire of industrial relations, utilitarian philosophy, current educational theories, unjust divorce laws, and the popular ideal of the "self-made man." Against several exaggerated figures representing these various targets, Dickens sets his model of an ideal domestic woman, a girl named Sissy Jupe, and a circus troop that represents the imaginative and intuitive faculties. His representative working-class characters

are betrayed by both fellow workers (Dickens' criticism of union activism) and their employers, and their lives end tragically. *North and South,* on the other hand, although set in the same place (Manchester) and time period, is a more realistic and psychological novel that attempts to reconcile oppositions between representatives of the old gentry and the new capitalists, as well as between factory owners and workers. The agent of mediation is a young middle-class woman whose new insights into the theories of political economy and the working and living conditions of the laborers are taught to readers at the same time they are shared with opposing characters. Singlehandedly stopping a riot and saving the life of the factory owner, whom she later marries, Margaret Hale is an example of what Constance D. Harsh has called a "subversive heroine" (1994).

The novels discussed here as factory novels, condition-of-England novels, or social problem novels are, of course, only a few major examples of what was a very popular and widely imitated genre in the England of the 1840s and 1850s. Many other novels, with titles such as *William Langshawe, the Cotton Lord* (Elizabeth Stone, 1842), *The White Slave: A Romance for the Nineteenth Century* (James Malcolm Rymer, 1844), *Fanny, the Little Milliner; or, The Rich and the Poor* (Charles Rowcroft, 1846), *Colton Green: A Tale of the Black Country* (William Gresley, 1848), *Masters and Workmen; A Tale Illustrative of the Social and Moral Condition of the People* (Richard Frederick Chichester, Earl of Belfast, 1851), *The White Slaves of England* (John Cobden, 1853), *It Is Never Too Late to Mend* (Charles Reade, 1853), *Progress and Prejudice* (Catherine Gore, 1854), and *The Strike* (Anonymous, 1858), took up the same themes and through the medium of fiction attempted to identify and resolve the social problems their authors saw facing the nation.

Besides the novels that focused specifically on the social problems related to factories and the working and living conditions of the poorer classes, many other Victorian novels explored different kinds of social issues. William Makepeace Thackeray's *Vanity Fair* (1848), for instance, considered class relations between the rising middle class and the old gentry through the medium of a poor but unscrupulous governess, thus also tangentially treating the problem of impoverished gentlewomen (otherwise known as the "redundant woman problem"), an issue also addressed in several of Charlotte Brontë's novels.

The most well known British novelist of social criticism of all varieties was, of course, Charles Dickens. In addition to the already mentioned instances that focus on the poor law and factory conditions, almost all of Dickens' output of fiction dealt with social criticism of one variety or another. *Bleak House* (1853), for instance, took on the English legal system and its victims, as well as the plight of the unemployed urban poor and factory workers. *Little Dorrit* (1857) addressed the evils of the debtors' prison, while *Great Expectations* (1861) depicts a prison ship and a felon transported to Australia. In addition to the major social issues his novels confront, almost all of Dickens' works, including the Christmas stories, address a number of other social questions or practices, ranging from the plight of street sweepers and prostitutes to loveless marriages and the endless bureaucracy of the patent office. Most of Dickens' famous "grotesques," or humorously exaggerated characters, are meant as criticism of various social types, while many of his important symbols, such as the railway in *Dombey and Son* (1848) or the fog in *Bleak House,* are introduced as vehicles of social critique.

After the 1850s, many English novels still dealt with various individual social problems or mounted a critique of society as a whole. Many of the novels of Anthony Trollope, for instance, treat the problems of the clergy or of politicians, while a number of new women writers took on various aspects of the "woman question," ranging from divorce and custody laws to the problem of middle-class women with nothing to do. The novels of George Eliot, especially *Adam Bede* (1859) and *Middlemarch* (1872), examine societal relations in more general terms, portraying characters from many segments of society and scrutinizing their social aspirations and ambitions. Eliot also authored a late example of a factory novel with her 1866 *Felix Holt, the Radical*, as did Charles Reade with *Put Yourself in His Place* (1870), a novel about trade unions, and George Gissing with *Demos* (1886), which portrays socialist ideals in a naturalistic style. Some of the novels of Thomas Hardy also may be classed as social problem novels. *Tess of the d'Urbervilles* (1891), for instance, focuses on some of the effects of agricultural capitalism in a manner not unlike some of the earlier factory novels. These later novels, however, while often representing working-class characters or treating specific social problems, tend to have less coherence as a group than the earlier social problem novels. Authors from the latter third of the century also tend to be less optimistic than the earlier novelists about resolving the social issues they raise.

A number of prominent 19th-century writers of other nations, notably the United States, France, and Russia, also produced novels of overt social criticism. Harriet Beecher Stowe, of course, leads the list of those who wrote antislavery novels, while the novels of other American writers such as Lydia Maria Child and Rebecca Harding Davis feature mill girls, child prostitutes, abusive husbands, working women, and even circus performers, much like their English contemporaries. Later in the century, American naturalists such as Theodore Dreiser would also represent life among the working classes. In France, famous novelists such as Honoré de Balzac, George Sand, Victor Hugo, Eugène Sue, and Gustave Flaubert also wrote realist novels of social criticism, as did later naturalists such as Émile Zola. Russian novelists Fedor Dostoevskii and Lev Tolstoi also wrote works of social realism during the 19th century. Throughout the 20th century, of course, novelists from many nations and regions and of a variety of political persuasions followed the tradition of the Victorian novel of social criticism by using their novels as vehicles of social criticism and even political activism.

DORICE WILLIAMS ELLIOTT

See also City and the Novel; Class and the Novel; English Novel (19th-century sections); Ideology and the Novel; Marxist Criticism of the Novel; Politics and the Novel; Proletarian Novel; Socialist Realism

Further Reading

Bodenheimer, Rosemarie, *The Politics of Story in Victorian Social Fiction*, Ithaca, New York: Cornell University Press, 1988

Born, Daniel, *The Birth of Liberal Guilt in the English Novel: Charles Dickens to H.G. Wells*, Chapel Hill: University of North Carolina Press, 1995

Brantlinger, Patrick, *The Spirit of Reform: British Literature and Politics, 1832–1867*, Cambridge, Massachusetts: Harvard University Press, 1977

Cazamian, Louis François, *Le Roman social en Angleterre, 1830–1850: Dickens, Disraeli, Mrs. Gaskell, Kingsley*, Paris: Société nouvelle de libraire et d'édition, 1903; as *The Social Novel in England 1830–1850: Dickens, Disraeli, Mrs. Gaskell, Kingsley*, London and Boston: Routledge and Kegan Paul, 1973

Colby, Robert Alan, *Fiction with a Purpose: Major and Minor Nineteenth-Century Novels*, Bloomington: Indiana University Press, 1967

Colmer, John, *Coleridge to "Catch-22": Images of Society*, London: Macmillan, and New York: St. Martin's Press, 1978

Flint, Kate, editor, *The Victorian Novelist: Social Problems and Social Change*, London and New York: Croom Helm, 1987

Gallagher, Catherine, *The Industrial Reformation of English Fiction: Social Discourse and Narrative Form, 1832–1867*, Chicago: University of Chicago Press, 1985

Guy, Josephine M., *The Victorian Social-Problem Novel: The Market, the Individual, and Communal Life*, New York: St. Martin's Press, and London: Macmillan, 1996

Harsh, Constance D., *Subversive Heroines: Feminist Resolutions of Social Crisis in the Condition-of-England Novel*, Ann Arbor: University of Michigan Press, 1994

Kestner, Joseph A., *Protest and Reform: The British Social Narrative by Women, 1827–1857*, Madison: University of Wisconsin Press, and London: Methuen, 1985

Kettle, Arnold, "The Early Victorian Social-Problem Novel," in *From Dickens to Hardy*, edited by Boris Ford, volume 6 of *The Pelican Guide to English Literature*, Baltimore: Penguin, 1958

Kovačević, Ivanka, editor, *Fact into Fiction: English Literature and the Industrial Scene, 1750–1850*, Leicester: Leicester University Press, 1975

Krueger, Christine L., *The Reader's Repentance: Women Preachers, Women Writers, and Nineteenth-Century Social Discourse*, Chicago: University of Chicago Press, 1992

Lucas, John, *The Literature of Change: Studies in the Nineteenth-Century Provincial Novel*, Hassocks: Harvester Press, and New York: Barnes and Noble, 1977; 2nd edition, Brighton: Harvester, and Totowa, New Jersey: Barnes and Noble, 1980

Smith, Sheila Mary, *The Other Nation: The Poor in English Novels of the 1840s and 1850s*, Oxford: Clarendon Press, and New York: Oxford University Press, 1980

Sutherland, John, *The Stanford Companion to Victorian Fiction*, Stanford, California: Stanford University Press, 1989

Vicinus, Martha, *The Industrial Muse: A Study of Nineteenth Century British Working-Class Literature*, London: Croom Helm, 1974; New York: Barnes and Noble, 1975

Webb, Igor, *From Custom to Capital: The English Novel and the Industrial Revolution*, Ithaca, New York: Cornell University Press, 1981

Socialist Realism

The Socialist-Realist Novel in the Soviet Union

In the wake of the October Revolution of 1917 and the subsequent civil war, writers in the newly formed Soviet Union set out to create a literature that would reflect the phenomenal events of the era and contribute to the construction of a genuinely new cultural identity for the emergent Soviet society. Not surprisingly, this unprecedented project ushered in a rich period of literary experimentation as writers sought a literary mode appropriate to the profound historical transformation underway in the society around them. Many writers of the period sought to adapt the modernist and avant-garde art then emergent in the West to the Soviet situation, while others attempted to update the 19th-century realism of writers such as Lev Tolstoi to the new Soviet world. Other Soviet writers, however, sought entirely new literary modes, leading to debates that eventually culminated in the first Soviet Writers' Congress of 1934, when socialist realism was officially endorsed as the most effective means through which writers could contribute to the Soviet project. The congress began with the Leninist idea (an idea that itself builds on the work of earlier theorists such as Nikolai Chernyshevskii, Vissarion Belinskii, and Georgii Plekhanov) that art ought to concern itself directly with the lives of real people. The basic premise of socialist realism, as endorsed at the congress, was to describe truthfully Soviet society in its historical development toward socialism. Karl Radek (1935), in one of the central addresses of the congress, noted that socialist realism

> means giving a picture not only of the decay of capitalism and the withering away of its culture, but also of the birth of that class, of that force, which is capable of creating a new society and a new culture. Realism . . . means reflecting reality as it is, in all its complexity, in all its contrariety, and not only capitalist reality, but also that other, new reality—the reality of socialism.

As the novelist Aleksandr Fadeev would later put it, socialist realism is "first of all a true depiction of reality in the process of development, in its basic tendencies and its living wealth" (see *Za tridtsat' let* [1957; Over Thirty Years]). "Socialist realism," as endorsed at the congress, essentially represented the declaration of a truce in the Soviet culture wars of the 1920s. The congress abandoned the attempt to agree on a single best style or form, leaving that choice up to the individual writer as long as that writer's work reflected the sense of historical transformation that characterized the Soviet society of the time. As a result of this openness (and of the dedication of the Soviet regime to promoting literature as a means of contributing to the growth of socialism), a large number and wide variety of novels were subsequently produced under the banner of socialist realism.

Of course, many works from before 1934 (or even before 1917) meet the broad requirements of socialist realism as well, and critics often identify Maksim Gor'kii's novel *Mat'* (1906; Mother) as the first work of socialist realism. Moreover, Gor'kii himself (a major figure at the 1934 congress) typically is considered the father of socialist realism. *Mother* is rooted in the events of the abortive 1905 revolution in Russia. A novel about the hardships of working-class and peasant life in prerevolutionary Russia, it clearly suggests that the only solution to these hardships lies in the revolutionary class struggle toward the eventual establishment of a communist society. The book thus set the tone for the numerous socialist-realist novels that followed it. Gor'kii's other works, such as the play *Na dne* (1902; The Lower Depths), the novel *Delo Artamonovykh* (1925; The Artamonov Business), the unfinished tetralogy *Zhizn' Klima Samgina* (1925–36; translated in 4 vols. as *The Bystander, The Magnet, Other Fires,* and *The Spectre*), and others also encourage readers not only to see reality in its sordid colors but also to challenge that reality and actively engage in a search for a better society based on human labor and reason.

Not surprisingly, many early postrevolutionary works of socialist realism focused on the cataclysmic civil war of 1917–20 as a major step toward the historical development of socialism in the Soviet Union. One of the most popular works of the 1920s was Dmitry Furmanov's semidocumentary and semibiographical novel, *Chapaev* (1923; Chapaev). Establishing a model that later became very popular, *Chapaev* was based on the life of a real person, a legendary leader under whom Furmanov himself had served in the Red Army during the civil war. Furmanov gives a lively and positive portrayal of his protagonist, as a devoted builder of the new society and a dedicated warrior against the enemies of the young Soviet state. The novel, in its realism, marked a departure from the then common romanticized depictions of Bolsheviks and Communists as flawless "men in leather jackets." *Chapaev* was later made into a film that was immensely popular with the Soviet audience.

Fadeev's *Razgrom* (1927; The Rout), another influential book about the civil war, narrates the almost complete destruction of a Bolshevik company in the Far East by the White Cossacks and the Japanese. Fadeev portrays Soviet partisans and their supporters, the peasants, in a realistic manner, showing both their strengths and weaknesses but also showing the suffering and ordeals they undergo. Fadeev emphasizes the dedication of these people to their cause, their firm belief in a better Soviet future, and their willingness to bear any sacrifices for its realization.

In *Zheleznyi potok* (1924; The Iron Flood), Aleksandr Serafimovich depicts a massive exodus of poor peasants from Kuban who are fleeing rebellious Cossack forces set out to destroy the Soviet power and its supporters. Narrated in an epic manner, the novel attempts to convey the enormity of sacrifices and suffering of the people and their dedication to socialism. Konstantin Fedin's *Goroda i gody* (1924; Cities and Years) relates events from Fedin's life in Germany and Russia during World War I and the Russian civil war. Isaak Babel's story collection *Konarmiia* (1926; Red Cavalry) depicts the events and people Babel encountered while serving with Semen Budenny's Red Cavalry during the war with Poland in 1920. Other noted works about the civil war include Vsevolod Ivanov's novels *Partizany* (1921; Partisans) and *Bronepoezd 14–69* (1922; Armored Train 14–69) and Aleksandr Malyshkin's *Padenie Daira* (1923; The Fall of Dahir).

Such works became immensely popular with a new Soviet audience that saw its own recent experience reflected in them. This direct engagement with reality continued to distinguish socialist-realist fiction as it moved beyond the early emphasis on the civil war to a depiction of life in the Soviet Union following the Red victory in that war. Many authors based leading works on their own lives or those of their acquaintances. For example, Nikolai Ostrovskii's *Kak zakalialas' stal'* (1932–34; *How the Steel Was Tempered*), a Bildungsroman, relates the growth of its protagonist, Pavel Korchagin, who is clearly based on Ostrovskii himself. Korchagin's strength and enthusiasm proved to be a constant inspiration to the Soviet audience and its writers.

Many novels of the 1920s and 1930s dealt with the difficult process of the Sovietization of the vast Russian countryside, including Lidiia Seifullina's *Virineia* (1924), Leonid Leonov's *Barsuki* (1924; *The Badgers*), Anna Karavaeva's *Lesozavod* (1928; *The Sawmill*), and Fedor Panferov's *Bruski* (1928–37; *Bruski: A Story of Peasant Life in Soviet Russia*). One of the most important of these novels, Mikhail Sholokhov's *Podniataia tselina* (1932–60; *Virgin Soil Upturned*), portrays the impact of agricultural collectivization on the Soviet peasant population. Like many socialist-realist works, *Virgin Soil Upturned* is a highly topical novel that reflects events occurring even as it was being written. Sholokhov actually interrupted the writing of his other great novel, *Tikhii Don* (1928–40; *Quiet Flows the Don*), in order to write *Virgin Soil Upturned* while the events he describes were still fresh in his mind and in the memory of Soviet society.

Numerous other novels, including Valentin Kataev's *Rastratchiki* (1927; *The Embezzlers*), Boris Gorbatov's *Iacheika* (1928; *The Cell*), Iurii Krymov's *Tanker "Derbent"* (1938; *The Tanker "Derbent"*), and Anton Makarenko's *Pedagogicheskaia poema* (1933–35; *The Road to Life*) and *Kniga dlia roditelei* (1937; *A Book for Parents*) explore various aspects of socialist reality in the new Soviet state. Most of these novels were written in a popular style that featured protagonists with whom Soviet readers could identify from their own experience. Likewise, Konstantin Fedin portrays a variety of Soviet people in his novels *Pokhishchenie Evropy* (1935; *The Rape of Europe*) and *Sanatorii Arktur* (1940; *Sanatorium Arktur*). Marietta Shaginian's *Mess-Mend* (1924; *Mess-Mend*) takes the form of a detective novel but shifts the code of this genre to feature proletarian heroes who are struggling against capitalist villains trying to thwart Soviet accomplishments.

Many socialist-realist novels represent modifications of Western genres. On the other hand, the shift away from the depiction of private experience led to the development of several entirely new types of novels. For example, Fedor Gladkov's novel *Tsement* (1925; *Cement*) is an early example of the Soviet production novel, a type of socialist-realist novel that focuses on the intensive project of modernization and industrialization that was central to the first decades of Soviet rule. Gladkov situates his novel amid attempts to rebuild the Soviet economy in the immediate aftermath of the civil war. In *Cement* a Red Army veteran returns to his hometown after serving in the civil war, but there he must continue his fight for socialism, which now focuses on bringing new life to his shattered community by resuming production in a neglected cement factory. Gladkov's other production novel, *Energiia* (1939; *Energy*), describes the construction of Dneprostroy. Other leading production novels include Leonid Leonov's *Sot'* (1930; *The Sot*), *Skutarevskii* (1932; *Skutarevsky*), and *Doroga na okean* (1935; *Road to the Ocean*); Shaginian's *Gidrotsentral'* (1931; *Hydrocentral*); Valentin Kataev's *Vremia,*

vpered! (1932; *Time, Forward!*); and Il'ia Erenburg's *Den' vtoroi* (1934; *The Second Day*) and *Ne perevodia dykhaniia* (1935; *Without Pausing for a Breath*).

Given socialist realism's emphasis on engagement with historical reality, it is not surprising that many of its leading works were historical novels. Gor'kii again sets the stage for this phenomenon, beginning with *The Artamonov Business*, a sweeping family saga relating the lives of several generations of the Artamonovs as they participate in the movement from semifeudal czarist society to the emergent capitalism of early 20th-century Russia to the socialist development of the postrevolutionary years. Gor'kii's massive *Zhizn' Klima Samgina* is the centerpiece of his postrevolutionary writing. *Zhizn' Klima Samgina* demonstrates the historical necessity of the Russian Revolution by detailing, in epic proportions, the temporary replacement of the feudal system in Russia by a movement toward a new bourgeois order that was already decadent before it even began, followed by the collapse of this order and the beginnings of socialism. Gor'kii makes his revolutionary point inescapable when he has his eponymous protagonist symbolically drop dead at the moment of Lenin's triumphant arrival in St. Petersburg on his way to power, thus announcing the death of the bourgeois alternative and the birth of the socialist one.

In 1928 Mikhail Sholokhov published the first parts of his acclaimed historical novel, *Quiet Flows the Don*. This epic work describes in documentary detail the impact of the events of the first part of the 20th century on the Don Cossack peasant/warrior community. In this encyclopedic novel, Sholokhov portrays the effects of World War I on traditional Cossack life and customs and the class conflicts that ripped apart the traditional community during the revolution and civil war. Sholokhov then focuses in great detail on the Cossack revolt against the Bolsheviks in 1918–20, when the Cossacks sided with the Whites in an attempt to oust the Bolsheviks from Cossack land. Kornelii Zelinskii describes *Quiet Flows the Don* as one of the two "peaks of Soviet fiction." The other he identifies as Aleksei Tolstoi's historical novel *Petr Pervyi* (1929–45; *Peter the First*), which vividly evokes the texture of Russian life in the dark and barbarous time of its protagonist, capturing very well the complexity and contradictions of this crucial turning point in Russian history.

Peter the First presents characters from all layers of Russian society, which is depicted as an intricately interrelated totality, very much in the way described by Georg Lukács in *A történelmi regény* (1937; *The Historical Novel*), as a crucial project of the greatest historical novels. Indeed, Russia as a whole seems to be the true protagonist of Tolstoi's text, although Peter himself is certainly the book's central character in the traditional sense. And, although Tolstoi carefully avoids depicting Peter's attempted revolution as a sort of allegorical anticipation of the Soviet project, he does characterize Peter as a predecessor to the Bolsheviks and a modernizer who helped take a primitive Russia one step closer to the day when the Soviet Union might become a historical possibility. Peter, although presented in anything but a simplistic way, is thus portrayed in an essentially positive light, as is his modernizing project. Tolstoi also wrote another important trilogy of historical novels, *Khozhdenie po mukam* (1920–42; *Road to Calvary*).

Ol'ga Forsh, a particularly prolific socialist-realist historical novelist, wrote *Goriachii tsekh* (1926; *Hot Shop*), a novel about the revolution of 1905; *Sumasshedshii korabl'* (1931; *Crazy Ship*), set in the 1920s; *Voron* (1933; The Raven), set in the 1910s; and *Perventsy svobody* (1950–53; *Pioneers of Freedom*), a novel about the Decembrists. Forsh's trilogy, *Iakobinskii zakvas* (1932; Jacobin Ferment), *Kazanskaia pomeshchitsa* (1934; A Landed Lady of Kazan), and *Pagubnaia kniga* (1939; A Fateful Book) is an important historical work about the life and times of 18th-century liberal Aleksandr Radishchev. Other prominent postrevolutionary Soviet historical novels include Fadeev's *Poslednii iz Udege* (1941; The Last of the Udege) and Fedin's *Pervye radosti* (1946; *Early Joys*), *Neobyknovennoe leto* (1948; *No Ordinary Summer*), and *Koster* (1961–67; *The Conflagration*). Vasilii Grossman's *Stepan Kol'chugin* (1937–40; *Kol'chugin's Youth*) depicts the life of a protagonist who lives from the late czarist period to the 1930s. Leonid Leonov's innovative historical novel *Russkii les* (1953; *The Russian Forest*) narrates events that began during the prerevolutionary period and extended to the early 1950s. Anatolii Ivanov's *Vechnii zov* (1971; *The Eternal Call*) describes the events in Siberia from the early 20th century to the aftermath of World War II.

During the 1940s, 1950s, and later, the Great Patriotic War of 1939–45, known in the West as World War II, preoccupied Soviet socialist-realist writers. The heroic struggle of the Soviet people and the immense devastation and suffering they experienced during this war left an indelible impression on Soviet society and its writers. Konstantin Simonov depicts the defense of Stalingrad in his *Dni i nochi* (1944; *Days and Nights*); his *Zhivye i mertvye* (1959; *The Living and the Dead*) and *Soldatami ne rozhdaiutsia* (1963; Soldiers Are Made, Not Born) are also about the Great Patriotic War. The siege of Stalingrad is the theme of Viktor Nekrasov's *V okopakh Stalingrada* (1946; *In the Trenches of Stalingrad*). Aleksandr Fadeev's *Molodaia gvardiia* (1946; *The Young Guard*), Boris Polevoi's *Povest' o nastoiashchem cheloveke* (1946; *A Story about a Real Man*), Vera Panova's *Sputniki* (1946; *The Train*), Leonid Leonov's *Vziatie Velikoshumska* (1944; The Battle for Velikoshumsk), Emmanuil Kazakevich's *Vesna na Odere* (1949; Spring on the Oder), and Galina Nikolaeva's *Zhatva* (1950; *Harvest*).

The decade after the Great Patriotic War featured novels that depicted the reconstruction of the ravaged country. Important socialist-realist novels published during this decade included Vasilii Azhaev's *Daleko ot Moskvy* (1948; *Far from Moscow*) and Vsevolod Kochetov's *Zhurbiny* (1952; *The Zhurbins*). Meanwhile, socialist-realist literature in the postwar years was enriched by new contributions from national literatures other than Russian, including the work of Mukhtar Auezov, a Kazakh, and Chingiz Aitmatov, a Kirghiz. However, socialist realism declined after the war as authors continued the uncritical pro-Soviet stance that, understandably, characterized the literature of the war years and drifted away from the critical engagement with reality that was typical of socialist-realist fiction during the 1920s and 1930s. After the death of Stalin in 1953, Soviet literature sought new directions, especially after Khrushchev's denunciation of Stalin in 1956. The mid-1950s thus initiated a period known as the "thaw" (following Erenburg's 1954 novel of that title), in which Soviet writers began to investigate new forms

that deviated substantially from the socialist-realist tradition. Science fiction (including the surrealist science fiction of the brothers Arkadii and Boris Strugatskii) became a particularly important movement in Soviet literature, while authors such as Erenburg and Vasilii Aksenov began to move toward Western modernism and even postmodernism. Important works of socialist realism continued to be produced by authors such as Vsevolod Ivanov and Konstantin Simonov. Soviet-realist fiction, however, came to be dominated by the so-called village prose movement, which was a reaction against socialist realism. It is, in fact, symptomatic that the most important writer to emerge from the village prose movement (and the most internationally prominent Soviet realist writer of the post-Stalinist years) was the decidedly antisocialist Aleksandr Solzhenitsyn.

DUBRAVKA JURAGA

See also Class and the Novel; Ideology and the Novel; Marxist Criticism; Politics and the Novel; Proletarian Novel; Social Criticism

Further Reading

Barabash, Yuri, *Aesthetics and Poetics,* Moscow: Progress, 1977

Clark, Katerina, *The Soviet Novel: History as Ritual,* Chicago: University of Chicago Press, 1981; 2nd edition, 1985

Freeman, Joseph, Joshua Kunitz, and Louis Lozowick, *Voices of October: Art and Literature in Soviet Russia,* New York: Vanguard, 1930

Lahusen, Thomas, and Eugeny Dobrenko, editors, *Socialist Realism Without Shores,* special issue of *South Atlantic Quarterly* 94:3 (Summer 1995)

Lenin, Vladimir Ilich, *O literature: iskusstve,* Moscow: Gos. izd-vo polit. lit-ry, 1957; as *On Literature and Art,* Moscow: Progress, 1975

Lukács, Georg, *A történelmi regény,* Budapest: Hungaria, 1937; as *The Historical Novel,* London: Merlin Press, 1962; New York: Humanities Press, 1965

Lukács, Georg, *Wider den missverstandenen Realismus,* Hamburg: Clausen, 1958; as *The Meaning of Contemporary Realism,* London: Merlin Press, 1963; as *Realism in Our Time: Literature and the Class Structure,* New York: Harper, 1964

Markov, D.F., *Socialist Literatures: Problems of Development,* Moscow: Raduga, 1984

Ovcharenko, A.I., *Socialist Realism and the Modern Literary Process,* Moscow: Progress, 1978

Parkhomenko, Mikhail, and Aleksandr Miasnikov, editors, *Socialist Realism in Literature and Art,* Moscow: Progress, 1971

Radek, Karl, "Contemporary World Literature and the Tasks of Proletarian Art," in *Problems of Soviet Literature: Reports and Speeches at the First Soviet Writers' Congress,* Westport, Connecticut: Greenwood Press, 1979; originally published in Russian in 1935

Zelinskii, Kornelii, *Soviet Literature: Problems and People,* Moscow: Progress, 1970

Aleksandr Solzhenitsyn 1918–

Russian

In the 1960s and 1970s Aleksandr Solzhenitsyn produced a number of major novels based on his own experience of Soviet prison and hospital life before turning to what he had come to regard as his primary mission, namely the semificionalized rewriting of Russian history of the revolutionary period in the multivolumed *Krasnoe koleso* (1983–91; The Red Wheel). Solzhenitsyn first dreamed of writing novels about the revolution as early as 1937. By the 1970s he had become the most famous of all Soviet dissidents, and his works were greatly feared by the Soviet regime, which did all it could to minimize their effect. In the United States he became an almost reclusive émigré, pronouncing on many aspects of the West and Russia, but he returned to Russia after the collapse of communism in the hope of leading a national revival. His novels, which were all written in the Soviet Union but were for the most part published abroad by *tamizdat,* are more remarkable for their content than their literary finesse, although Solzhenitsyn, who clearly belongs to the 19th-century novelistic tradition, made many controversial innovations in the use of language and, particularly, lexicon. Together with his nonfiction *Arkhipelag GULag: 1918–1956* (1973–76; The Gulag Archipelago) his novels stand as a memorable and lasting record of the abuse of Soviet power.

Odin den' Ivana Denisovicha (1962; One Day in the Life of Ivan Denisovich) marked the beginning of Soviet prison-camp literature and is remarkable for the skillful use of third-person direct speech and for the creation of a microcosm of Soviet life as seen through the eyes of a simple Everyman. Another outstanding early story, "Matrenin dvor" (1963; "Matryona's House"), highlights Solzhenitsyn's dominant concern with moral values.

Only two of his fictional works may be called novels without equivocation. *Rakovyi korpus* (1968; Cancer Ward) was submitted for publication in the leading Soviet literary journal *Novyi mir* (New World), and its rejection and subsequent publishing abroad led to its author's disgrace and eventual expatriation. Sharply political points are made, but the book's main concerns are moral, as the characters confront questions of life and death, truth and falsehood—emphasized by the discussion of Lev Tolstoi's "What Do Men Live For?" in the ward.

As in *One Day in the Life of Ivan Denisovich,* Solzhenitsyn presents in *Cancer Ward* a cross-section of society that seems to be a microcosm of Soviet life during the time of transition after Stalin's death. Kostoglotov, the central character, is no Everyman but a semi-authorial figure, and the patients reassess their lives less on account of the new political situation than as a result of their life-threatening condition. In contrast to Tolstoi's *Smert' Ivana Il'icha* (1886; The Death of Ivan Ilyich), however, Solzhenitsyn does not punish his characters: Rusanov, the unrepentant party boss, emerges from the ward alive.

Solzhenitsyn's particular form of realism owes something to both Tolstoi and Fedor Dostoevskii: from the former he draws the moral inspiration and strength of vision; from the latter a desire to create what Mikhail Bakhtin called polyphonic novels, but—for all the individual voices and viewpoints of the characters in *Cancer Ward*—Solzhenitsyn's own beliefs remain present. The strength of the novel's physical realism may be seen in the detailed way the author depicts sensations of love, right down to the precise area of the body where it is first felt, in many ways echoing the way the location of cancer is described. The realities of the X-ray treatment are shown no less graphically. Solzhenitsyn shared the aversion Thomas Mann showed to chemical and mechanical treatment in *Der Zauberberg* (1924; *The Magic Mountain*), believing the only true therapy for all ills to be in the psyche and spirit. A further aspect of the book's realism is the relative openness about sexuality.

This novel also demonstrates clearly Solzhenitsyn's linguistic innovations by which he sought to release the Russian language from the grayness of Sovietization, rediscovering many old and neglected roots. Solzhenitsyn once said, "My main character is all of Russia," and it is clear that, although Europe was manifestly sick with wars and death camps, for Solzhenitsyn it was Russia's tragedy that mattered most. The cancer of Stalinism is symbolized by the tragedy of those in the hospital, both as a group and as individuals: an informer has cancer of the tongue and a promiscuous girl suffers from breast cancer. *Cancer Ward* is rich in human interest as well as symbolism, and its lasting popularity speaks of universal qualities.

Polyphony in Solzhenitsyn's understanding of the concept ("each character becomes the central one while he is in the field of action") is best seen in his *V kruge pervom* (1968, restored full edition 1978; The First Circle). Set during the late 1940s and early 1950s, the novel provides a panoramic view of the circle of Russian society that is caught up in the system of prisons and camps. A whole range of characters with individual views and concerns create an entire moral cosmos that is based on the duality of freedom and imprisonment, seen in a spiritual as well as a physical light. Like other novels by Solzhenitsyn, it has a closed setting, in this case a special prison for intellectuals engaged in secret work for the state. Naturally, the background is Dante's first circle, in which God put the sages of antiquity whom He cannot admit to paradise but does not like to consign to hell. *The First Circle* is, indeed, a highly intellectual work in which characters debate endlessly the first principles of morality as well as the abstract and the particular aspects of Soviet and world politics. Many of the main protagonists seem to have been based on living models, a factor that added greatly to the controversy the book spawned when it was published.

All Solzhenitsyn's novels are devoted to understanding and explaining the power of the lie that pervaded the Stalin years, but their lasting qualities rest in their engagement with universal moral values rather than purely local concerns, however tragic and important. Although Solzhenitsyn has now adopted a quite different role, he will continue to be regarded as one of the great realistic novelists of the 20th century.

ARNOLD McMILLIN

See also One Day in the Life of Ivan Denisovich

Biography

Born in Kislovodsk, Russia, 11 December 1918. Attended school at Rostov-on-Don; studied mathematics and physics at

Rostov University, 1936–41; correspondence course in literature, Moscow Institute of Philosophy, Literature, and History, 1939–41. Served in the Soviet army, 1941–45; captain of artillery, twice decorated; arrested at the East Prussian front for having written a letter containing disparaging remarks about Stalin, 1945, and given an eight-year sentence for anti-Soviet agitation; served in camps and prisons near Moscow, and camp in Ekibastuz, Kazakhstan, 1945–53; exiled to South Kazakhstan village of Kok-Terek, 1953–56; worked as mathematics and physics teacher, and wrote in secret; gravely ill with cancer, but successfully treated in Tashkent, 1954–55; released from exile, 1956; "rehabilitated" and settled in Riazan as teacher, 1957; unable to publish from 1966; charged with treason and expelled from Soviet Union, 1974; lived in Zurich, 1974–76, then Cavendish, Vermont, 1976–94; reinstated to Union of Soviet Writers, 1989; Soviet citizenship restored, 1990; treason charges formally dropped, 1991; returned to Russia, 1994. Awarded Nobel prize for literature, 1970.

Novels by Solzhenitsyn

Odin den' Ivana Denisovicha, 1962; as *One Day in the Life of Ivan Denisovich,* translated by Ralph Parker, 1963; also translated by Max Hayward and Ronald Hingley, 1963; Bela Von Block, 1963; Gillon R. Aitken, 1971, revised edition, 1978; Harry T. Willetts, 1990

Rakovyi korpus, 1968; as *Cancer Ward,* translated by Nicholas Bethell and David Burg, 2 vols., 1968–69; as *The Cancer Ward,* translated by Rebecca Frank, 1968

V kruge pervom, 1968; restored complete edition, 1978; as *The First Circle,* translated by Thomas P. Whitney, 1968; also translated by Michael Guybon, 1969; Max Hayward, Manya Harari, and Michael Glenny, 1988

Other Writings: stories, prose miniatures, plays, film scripts, verse, memoirs, documentary writing, speeches, quasi-history, political tracts, books and articles on religion and on the future of Russia.

Further Reading

Burg, David, and George Feifer, *Solzhenitsyn,* London: Hodder and Stoughton, and New York: Stein and Day, 1972

Curtis, James M., *Alexander Solzhenitsyn's Traditional Imagination,* Athens: University of Georgia Press, 1984

Dunlop, John B., Richard Hough, and Alex Klimoff, editors, *Alexander Solzhenitsyn: Critical Essays and Documentary Materials,* New York: Collier Macmillan, 1973; revised edition, 1975

Dunlop, John B., Richard S. Hough, and Michael Nicholson, editors, *Solzhenitsyn in Exile: Critical Essays and Documentary Materials,* Stanford, California: Hoover Institution Press, 1985

Feuer, Kathryn B., editor, *Alexander Solzhenitsyn: A Collection of Critical Essays,* Englewood Cliffs, New Jersey: Prentice-Hall, 1976

Fiene, Donald M., *Alexander Solzhenitsyn: An International Bibliography of Writings by and about Him,* Ann Arbor, Michigan: Ardis, 1973

Kodjak, Andrej, *Alexander Solzhenitsyn,* Boston: Twayne, 1978

Krasnov, Vladislav, *Solzhenitsyn and Dostoevsky: A Study in the Polyphonic Novel,* Athens: University of Georgia Press, 1980

Lukács, Georg, *Solschenizyn,* Neuwied: Luchterhand, 1970; as *Solzhenitsyn,* London: Merlin Press, 1970; Cambridge, Massachusetts: MIT Press, 1971

Rothberg, Abraham, *Alexander Solzhenitsyn: The Major Novels,* Ithaca, New York: Cornell University Press, 1971

Scammell, Michael, *Solzhenitsyn: A Biography,* New York: Norton, 1984; London: Hutchinson, 1985

Sons and Lovers by D.H. Lawrence

1913

Sons and Lovers, Lawrence's third novel, marks the turning point in his writing career. It shows him definitively turning away from the external formal conventions of the Edwardian novel and groping his way to a modernist understanding of the genre. Between 1910 and 1913, Lawrence transformed what started out as a melodramatically told imaginary family saga into a powerful fictionalized rendition of his own growth to manhood in a Midlands working-class family split by differences of gender and class. In the course of those three years, the interventions of his boyhood sweetheart, Jessie Chambers, and his new wife, Frieda, induced Lawrence to excavate his own inner feelings and to shape the novel to reflect them. That looser shape met with the disapproval of Edward Garnett, the publisher's lit-erary adviser, who pruned about a tenth of the finished manuscript without further consultation. The published novel of 1913, which was further bowdlerized by the publisher because of its sexually explicit material, remained the standard text even after Mark Schorer published *Sons and Lovers: A Facsimile of the Manuscript* in 1977. In 1992 Cambridge University Press finally published *Sons and Lovers* in its original manuscript form. But Garnett was not the only reader to take offense. The manifestly autobiographical basis of the book bedeviled its reception from the start. Although the reviews were generally favorable, a number of them blamed Lawrence for his acquiescence in the protagonist's selfish treatment of the women in his life.

Lawrence chose to work within the genre of the Bildungsroman because it offered him a looser, more internalized form than that associated with the traditional novel of his time. The Bildungsroman concerns itself with the growth and development from childhood to manhood of its often autobiographically based protagonist. It made its first appearance in 1795–96 with the publication of Goethe's *Wilhelm Meisters Lehrjahre* (*Wilhelm Meister's Apprenticeship*). By 1913 Lawrence had at his disposal a form that had been used and modified by Dickens, Flaubert, Thomas Mann, and Samuel Butler, among others. *Sons and Lovers* actually belongs to a subgenre known as the *Künstlerroman*, that is, a novel concerned with the growth to maturity of the artist. Another famous instance of the *Künstlerroman* is Joyce's *A Portrait of the Artist as a Young Man,* which Ezra Pound started publishing serially in 1914. Lawrence used the major conventions of the genre to give fictional objectivity to his subjective material. His change of title from "Paul Morel" (the protagonist) to *Sons and Lovers* is indicative of his larger ambition to write "a great tragedy," "the tragedy of thousands of young men in England." Lawrence welcomed the freedom to depart from the remembered facts of his own life that the Bildungsroman offered, although his choice of this mixed genre did expose him to inevitable charges of not perceiving the failings of his protagonist.

Sons and Lovers constitutes a significant moment in the arrival of literary modernism. While insisting that his novel had form, Lawrence was equally insistent that "we need an apparent formlessness, definite form is mechanical." Lawrence was not interested in the premodernist conception of form as a reflection of social or moral patterns of conduct. He was searching for a new way of rendering the workings of the human psyche, the development of which "is slow like growth." The novel alternates between brief scenes of actions and behavior typifying a phase in the development of the protagonist and longer, highly particularized scenes heavily reliant on dialogue to dramatize that phase. Lawrence described his technique as "accumulating objects in the powerful light of emotion and making a scene of them." Although the novel is largely chronological, this mode of organization transforms temporal succession into causal connection—the connections forming a composite of the young artist's internal psychological growth into manhood.

Lawrence's modernist approach to the narrative is responsible for an ambivalence that runs through every aspect of the novel. Thus the depiction of an oedipal conflict within Paul, who is torn between his powerful mother and his childhood sweetheart, is complicated by the fact that Lawrence was still undergoing a similar conflict while writing the book. The text itself shows the workings of unconscious desire and refuses to conform to the textbook case history of the Oedipus complex (which Lawrence offered Garnett in an attempt to justify its radically different concept of form). In addition, Lawrence's concern with the workings of the unconscious is matched by a competing desire to show how all his characters are shaped by the disruptive effects of industrialization at the turn of the century. If Paul's motivation turns on unconscious fantasies of murdering his father, the narrator goes beyond that frame of reference to show how all the major characters are alienated from one another and themselves by the pernicious class war that capitalism fostered for its own purposes. Lawrence's earlier references to his "collier novel" emphasize the fact that this conception of his characters as exemplary of the predicament his generation faced at that stage of British industrial capitalism was as important a factor as the psychological. The novel's political allegiance is illustrated by the fact that Paul does not rise out of the working class to join the middle class; rather, he leaves class-ridden English society to become an alienated and *déclassé* artist.

In more recent times, *Sons and Lovers* has become a pivotal text in the ongoing debate about the representation of women in fiction written by men. First Simone de Beauvoir, then Kate Millett argued that all the women in the book are defined by men (whether Paul or the narrator) and are used by them. Later feminist critics have pointed to Lawrence's support for the suffragette movement, while noting that he felt the real revolution that needed to take place was a sexual and spiritual revolution in individual women. While Lawrence was tainted by certain male prejudices common among his contemporaries, he championed women's as much as men's right to sexual freedom in the face of the Victorian mores that still characterized his time.

BRIAN FINNEY

See also D.H. Lawrence

Further Reading

Farr, Judith, editor, *Twentieth-Century Interpretations of "Sons and Lovers": A Collection of Critical Essays,* Englewood Cliffs, New Jersey: Prentice-Hall, 1970

Finney, Brian, *D.H. Lawrence: "Sons and Lovers,"* London and New York: Penguin, 1990

Harvey, Geoffrey, *Sons and Lovers,* London: Macmillan, and Atlantic Highlands, New Jersey: Humanities Press International, 1987

Moynahan, Julian, editor, *"Sons and Lovers": Text, Background, and Criticism,* New York: Penguin, 1977

Salgado, Gamini, editor, *D.H. Lawrence's "Sons and Lovers,"* London: Arnold, 1966

Tedlock, E.W., editor, *D.H. Lawrence and "Sons and Lovers": Sources and Criticism,* New York: New York University Press, 1965; London: University of London Press, 1966

Worthen, John, *D.H. Lawrence: The Early Years, 1885–1912,* Cambridge and New York: Cambridge University Press, 1991

Sorrows of Young Werther. *See* Sufferings of Young Werther

The Sound and the Fury by William Faulkner

1929

The Sound and the Fury, Faulkner's fourth novel, received little critical attention when it appeared. Faulkner came to public notice with his notorious potboiler *Sanctuary* (1931), but it was not until Malcolm Cowley's *The Portable Faulkner* (1946) presented Faulkner as a historian of the South that his work began to be taken seriously. Subsequently, countless volumes of critical analysis have been dedicated to his fiction, and *The Sound and the Fury,* arguably his greatest novel, has become his most discussed book.

Faulkner's unique achievement is that in his best work he is both a regional novelist—a chronicler of the Deep South—and also an important figure of international modernism. As a regional novel *The Sound and the Fury* is about the decline of a southern family, the Compsons, and is set in Faulkner's imagined county of Yoknapatawpha, Mississippi, based on the area around Oxford, Mississippi, in Lafayette County where he grew up. He began his social and historical exploration of that world with *Sartoris* (1929), the novel that preceded *The Sound and the Fury,* and went on to chronicle the lives of his southern families through his accounts of provincial Mississippi life in later novels so that cumulatively his works acquire an epic and at times mythic status. The distinctive feature of *The Sound and the Fury* and the following novel, *As I Lay Dying* (1930), is that they are internalized accounts of the disintegrating world of the South conveyed through the psychological experience of a few characters. With *The Sound and the Fury* Faulkner shifted from realism to the symbolic and the mythic, from the social and historical mode to the psychological, and from traditional narrative structures to an extreme form of experimentation, producing complex and difficult avant-garde literary texts. The decline of the southern family in *The Sound and the Fury* becomes, through Faulkner's resonant use of symbol, and particularly through his exploration of the theme of time and elaborate experimental use of time structurally, an account of 20th-century unease and sense of disintegration, an exploration of the modern consciousness.

The Sound and the Fury has a four-part structure, the narrative being not linear but repetitive. The "story" is told four times over, the events and significance of the story becoming clearer with each account. The first account is Benjy's, and it is a tale "told by an idiot." It proceeds as an uninterrupted interior monologue in which the 33-year-old child recalls incidents from the past associatively by something said or done in the present, as when, for instance, in the novel's opening, Benjy, hearing a golfer call for his caddie, thinks of his sister Caddy and begins to moan. Benjy's chronological time is obliterated, and past and present merge in his mind. His life is lived essentially in emotional responses to either kindness or the lack of it. The relationship between Caddy and her retarded brother is most movingly conveyed throughout this section of the novel; Benjy finds security in her presence, Caddy understands instinctively what his needs are and knows how to satisfy them.

In contrast to Benjy's intuitive consciousness is the highly developed intellectual consciousness of his brother, Quentin, which is explored in the novel's second section. Like Benjy, however, Quentin, too, is trapped in his past. His story is one of ontological despair conveyed by a highly charged poetic language in which he argues and rationalizes his journey toward suicide. Beginning with the opening image of his grandfather's watch as "a mausoleum of all hope and desire," the theme of time is abstractly explored through images of aridity and emptiness as they occur in his tormented mind. Quentin, the most gifted of the Compson children, and given every opportunity to make something of his life (his father sold land in order to send him to Harvard), can find no reason to go on living.

The third section belongs to the third brother, Jason, who is cold, cynical, and cruel. Of the three his story is stylistically the most straightforward and easiest to follow. Unlike his brothers he lacks all fine sensibilities, and in his egoism and materialism he is perfectly attuned to the spirit of his age. In him are found the final signs of the disintegration of the Compson family. The fourth section of the novel is a third-person narrative given over to the negro servant, Dilsey, the only character to find meaning and fulfillment in life. She has dedicated her life to caring for the Compson family and finds consolation in her religion.

Caddy, who was the origin and inspiration of the novel, is given no section of her own; she is presented entirely through the interior monologues of her brothers. At a Class Conference at the University of Virginia (15 February 1957) Faulkner was asked why he chose not to give Caddy her own section of the novel. His oblique reply was that the explanation of the whole book lay in that question. The book was about Caddy, and he had chosen the right tools "to draw a picture" of her. This was also one of several occasions on which he gave an account of the genesis of the novel. It began with the image of the little girl's muddy drawers seen when she climbed a tree to look into the parlor window on the day of her grandmother's funeral. Her story is complete, and the story of the novel is complete in its opening section. The next two sections were added to elucidate the first. Finally, Faulkner added the fourth to contextualize the whole.

In an interview with Cynthia Grenier (1955) Faulkner revealed that *The Sound and the Fury* was the novel he felt tenderest toward. "I couldn't leave it alone," he said. Indeed, he did not. He wrote an Introduction—it exists in two versions—in

1933, and an Appendix entitled "Compson: 1699–1945" in 1945, and added a map inscribed "Jefferson, Yoknapatawpha Co., Mississippi. Area, 2,400 Square Miles — Population, Whites, 6,298; Negroes, 9,313 . . ." For all of these embellishments, however, it was his experimental, often obscure, way of presenting the Compson world that brought him recognition as a major modernist writer.

STELLA McNICHOL

See also William Faulkner

Further Reading
Adams, Richard P., *Faulkner: Myth and Motion,* Princeton, New Jersey: Princeton University Press, 1968; 2nd edition, 1973
Backman, Melvin, *Faulkner: The Major Years: A Critical Study,* Bloomington: Indiana University Press, 1966

Barbour, James, and Tom Quirk, editors, *Writing the American Classics,* Chapel Hill: University of North Carolina Press, 1990 (contains essay on *The Sound and the Fury*)
Brown, Calvin, *A Glossary of Faulkner's South,* New Haven, Connecticut: Yale University Press, 1976
Litz, Walton, "William Faulkner's Moral Vision," *Southwest Review* 37 (1952)
Polk, Noel, editor, *New Essays on "The Sound and the Fury,"* Cambridge and New York: Cambridge University Press, 1993
Snead, James A., *Figures of Division: William Faulkner's Major Novels,* New York: Methuen, 1986
Swiggart, Peter, *The Art of Faulkner's Novels,* Austin: University of Texas Press, 1962
Vickery, Olga W., *The Novels of William Faulkner: A Critical Interpretation,* Baton Rouge: Louisiana State University Press, 1959

South African Novel. *See* African Novel: South Africa

Southeast Asian Novel

Indonesia

The development of the novel in the Dutch East Indies, later to become Indonesia, has its origins in the polyglot social world of the great port cities of the north coast of Java around the turn of the 20th century. It was here that a cosmopolitan, multi-ethnic, racially mixed society, oriented toward commerce and trade, first underwent the changes introduced by print capitalism and the modern state to produce the beginnings of mass literacy and the habit of private reading essential to the emergence of the novel form. Newspapers began to appear in Java in the mid–19th century and by the early 20th century were available in most of the major urban centers in the Indies. Apart from local and international news items, advertisements, and public notices, these newspapers encouraged the exchange of views on issues of topical interest in a style of writing that had no precedent in the indigenous traditions of the Indonesian Archipelago. The writing was secular and described actual events with a claim to accuracy of representation and reportage. Importantly, the main newspaper language was urban Malay, the language of interethnic communication and exchange in the entrepot cities of north Java.

Increasingly after 1900, a regular feature of some of these newspapers was the publication of stories and serialized stories in urban Malay. This was fiction based on actual events, or events claimed by their authors to be drawn from "real life." Through the story feature, established newspapers came to nurture a new concept of the "writer," usurping the role of court or village audience as the storyteller's patron and supporting the development of a new type of fictional expression whose goal was verisimilitude along with the moral education and entertainment of the reader (see Wahab Ali, 1991). Private printing houses soon joined in this type of publication, indicating that readership was sufficiently widespread to constitute a source of potential commercial gain.

These precursors of the modern Indonesian novel reflected in themselves the polyglot, multi-ethnic nature of the urban societies from which they emerged. They were written by Eurasians of mixed Dutch or other European and indigenous parentage, by Chinese from families long established in the archipelago who had intermarried with local people and adopted elements of their language and culture, as well as by representatives of the new indigenous elite, sons of local aristocrats who had been educated in the Dutch primary and secondary school system. One of the earliest of these stories was "Tjerita Njai Dasima" (The Story of Nyai Dasima), written by G. Francis, a Eurasian of apparently English descent, published in Batavia (later Jakarta) by a Chinese printing house in 1896. It tells, in about 7,000 words, the well-known and tragic tale of a young indigenous woman who lives peacefully and contentedly as the concubine (*nyai*) of a resident Englishman. She is lured away, through the practice of magic spells and appeals to her Muslim identity, by an unscrupulous local landowner who covets her wealth and finally has her murdered after making her his second wife. This story, said to be based on actual events of the early 19th century, was followed by the publication of other *nyai* stories, indicating the attraction that stories of cultural marginalization and the appropriation of women's sexuality across racial lines exercised on the imagination of readers in contemporary colonial society.

The first work of truly novelistic proportions to be written in urban Malay by a representative of late colonial society in the Indies is *Hikayat Siti Mariah* (The Tale of Siti Mariah), written by another Eurasian who went by the name of Hadji Mukti. Originally published in 284 installments in the newspaper *Medan Prijaji* between November 1910 and January 1912, it first appeared in book form only in 1987, as part of the efforts of the prominent modern novelist Pramoedya Ananta Toer to recover and make known the work of his earliest predecessors. Until Pramoedya's own research of the early 1960s, this picaresque novel of romance and melodrama set on the sugar estates of 19th-century colonial Java remained lost, buried by the efforts of the colonial government after World War I to control the reading matter available to the new class of educated Indonesians. Educational reforms, coming in the wake of the so-called "Ethical Policy" of the early years of the 20th century, had by 1920 begun to produce significant numbers of newly literate young men and women, some of whom were beginning to question the politics and morality of colonial authority. Some of the new works in novel form were acquiring a distinctly nationalistic, anti-capitalist and anti-imperialist edge. Indeed, at least two writers of serialized stories who were prominent around 1920, Semaun and Mas Marco Kartodikromo, were also leading figures in the newly established Communist Association of the Indies, soon to become the Indonesian Communist Party (PKI). Novelistic stories published by commercial printers, meanwhile, had begun to take on a racy character that was offensive to the colonial authorities in other ways. All in all, conditions were ripe for the assertion of the colonial control.

In 1908, a commission had been formed to advise the colonial government on the provision of reading matter for "natives and native schools." The commission published a report in 1917 that became the basis for the foundation of Balai Pustaka (The Hall of Good Reading), the institution that came to dominate the development of the Indonesian novel for the remainder of the colonial period. (It became a major printing house for the Indonesian government following the transition to independence in 1949.) Balai Pustaka was a printer and publisher with an elaborate editorial structure spread over sections devoted to all the major indigenous languages of the archipelago. In addition, it managed an extensive system of libraries and agencies, including itinerant distributors, by which its publications were disseminated among the indigenous population of the colony. It published books and magazines with a popular educational character, as well as works of fiction, both selections from the indigenous literary traditions of the archipelago and translations and adaptations of European works (these were mainly popular classics such as *The Three Musketeers, Treasure Island, The Count of Monte-Cristo,* and *Tom Sawyer*). Balai Pustaka encouraged original writing, within the bounds of a "neutral" stand toward matters of religion, race, and politics. Original submissions were also subjected to highly moralistic standards and had to conform to language standardization policies.

Novels published in the Malay section of Balai Pustaka were far overshadowed in number and popularity by publications in Javanese and Sundanese, the major indigenous languages of Java. However, these Malay novels later came to be seen as the first genuinely "Indonesian" novels because they were the work of writers of purely "indigenous" blood, unlike the earlier writers of mixed race. In addition, they were recognizable as "novels" according to the European and American models, and they were written in a form of Malay that was beginning to be called Bahasa Indonesia, "the Language of Indonesia," the envisioned national language of an independent Indonesian state. One of the earliest and most popular of the Balai Pustaka novels in Malay was *Sitti Nurbaya* by Marah Rusli, appearing in 1922. It was a melodramatic tale of the tribulations of a young West Sumatran couple who are separated by the force of indigenous custom, which disallowed the free choice of marriage partner. *Sitti Nurbaya* set the tone for a whole series of Balai Pustaka novels dealing in sentimental style with the struggle of young people against the *adat*, or customary law of traditional societies. Another early Malay novel of lasting interest is *Salah Asuhan* (1928; Wrong Upbringing) by Abdul Muis. Questions about the extent of editorial intervention in the original manuscript remain unanswered, but what survives is the first extended exploration in Indonesian literature of the psychological ravages of Western education in the colonial context. The novel chronicles the tragic consequences of the denial of the culture of one's birth in pursuit of identification with the colonizer's world.

Outside of Balai Pustaka, the popular novel in paperback format and the serialized newspaper story, both in Malay and in Javanese, continued to grow in popularity. Literacy in Roman script had grown only to a miniscule 6.4 percent by 1930, but, in a total population of over 60 million, the actual number of potential readers was significant. As Western-style education continued to expand, the reading public continued to grow. Writers with nationalist convictions and those who rejected the moralistic and educational demands of the Balai Pustaka editors, meanwhile, had little room to maneuver. It was only at the very end of the colonial period that two important novels rejected by Balai Pustaka found their way into print. The first of these was *Belenggu* (Shackles) by Armijn Pane, published in 1940 as a special three-in-one edition of the nationalist cultural periodical *Pujangga Baru* (The New Writer). Rejected by Balai Pustaka on moral grounds, it was the first Indonesian novel to probe the cultural and psychological condition of the new Western-educated Indonesian elite, and it was fully engaged in the cultural politics of its time. It told the story of a crisis in the marriage of a young doctor and his independent-minded wife and his ultimately futile attempt to seek an alternative relationship with a woman who appears to fulfill his ideal of "a real woman." Pane described the story as one of "psychic disequilibrium," an exploration of the issues of cultural identity that confronted his generation.

In the same year, one of the most important novels by an Indonesian woman first saw publication, Surwarsih Djojopuspito's

Buiten Het Gareel (Out of Harness), an autobiographical novel first written in the author's native Sundanese, rejected by Balai Pustaka, rewritten in Dutch, and published in the Netherlands in the year of its occupation by Nazi Germany, the event that would ultimately usher in the collapse of the Dutch empire in the East and the birth of the Indonesian Republic. It describes from an explicitly female point of view the writer's experiences as an activist and a teacher in the anticolonial nationalist school system during the 1930s. Although its status as an Indonesian novel has always been contested because it was written in the colonial language, it has no equal among other novels by Indonesian authors of its time. The circumstances of its publication meant that it was little known and little read in Indonesia until its translation by Djojopuspito herself not long before her death in 1977, but it symbolically marks the end of the colonial period and the transition to an independent Indonesia.

The occupation of the Dutch East Indies by Japan in March 1942 ushered in a period of almost eight years of warfare, instability, and upheaval that finally came to an end with the final recognition of Indonesian sovereignty by the Dutch in November 1949. These upheavals swept aside all the apparent certainties and predictability of the colonial order and inevitably left their mark on the character of the Indonesian novel. A new literary and cultural movement, describing itself as the voice of the Indonesian revolution, looked confidently to the international stage as a source of influence and identification. Escaping the paternalistic constraints of Balai Pustaka, writers took on certain aspects of European modernism in the search for new literary forms and accents. Conditions, however, were hardly conducive to either the production or consumption of novels, and it was not until after the transfer of sovereignty that a small number of novels written during the revolution found their way into print. The first of these was Achdiat Karta Mihardja's *Atheis* (1949; An Atheist), the story of a failed attempt to make the transition from the pious certainties of village Islam to the exciting yet profoundly disturbing world of the urban-based artist and intellectual. This novel was followed by the publication of the early work of Pramoedya Ananta Toer, much of it written in Dutch prisons between 1947 and 1949, including the novels *Di Tepi Kali Bekasi* (1951; On the Banks of the Bekasi River), *Keluarga Gerilya* (1950; A Guerilla Family), and *Perburuan* (1950; The Fugitive).

Another novelist of the new, revolutionary generation was Mochtar Lubis, whose *Tidak Ada Esok* (1950; There Is No Tomorrow) and *Jalan Tak Ada Ujung* (1952; A Road with No End) illustrated, like the novels of Pramoedya, the characteristic tendency of the period to seek out the underlying moral and ethical questions that accompanied active involvement in the struggle for independence. Drawing for the first time on such models as John Steinbeck, Ernest Hemingway, and William Saroyan, novelists of this period developed a fast-moving and uncluttered narrative style and a free-flowing use of language that imitated contemporary spoken and journalistic Indonesian, in contrast to the heavily edited, scholastically correct Malay of the prewar Balai Pustaka novels. They were read, and much discussed and debated, by the intellectual elite of the new nation, and with the establishment of a mass-based Indonesian-language school system, a potential mass readership crossing the ethnic and linguistic divisions of the archipelago began to emerge. Certain novels, like *Keluarga Gerilya,* found their way onto national curricula,

but the actual production of novels was soon eclipsed by the growth of the poem and the short story as the characteristic forms of Indonesian literature in the early post-independence period.

The new, Indonesian-educated generation of writers and readers did not read foreign languages, as their Dutch-educated predecessors had done, and thus took less account of both foreign literary models and the grand, universalist moral and ethical questions that had come to motivate the Indonesian novel. Most of the novels written after independence were short, lyrical evocations of life lived beyond the reach of the city and its problems, such as Toha Mohtar's evocative story of reintegration and healing, *Pulang* (1958; Going Home).

The social and political conditions of the 1950s worked against the development of the novel as an extended critical engagement with ethical and moral questions, such as had motivated the writers of the revolutionary period. Mochtar Lubis completed his realist narrative of corruption, social chaos, and moral decay, *Senja di Jakarta* (1963; *Twilight in Djakarta*), while under house arrest in 1957, but it was many years before the novel found its way into print. It was first published in English, and its appearance served to confirm the West's worst fears about political and economic decline and the rise of communist influence in Indonesia during the last years of Sukarno's rule. It was not published in Indonesia until 1970, five years after Sukarno's fall. Pramoedya, meanwhile, published a novel about moral and political decline, *Korupsi* (Corruption) in 1954, but soon thereafter he moved increasingly away from creative literature in a search for a new basis for cultural development. By the early 1960s, Pramoedya joined the call for a socialist-realist literature, in contrast to the so-called "universal humanism" of the revolutionary period. Returning to the earliest traditions of the novel in Indonesia, he finally published *Gadis Pantai* (*The Girl from the Coast*) in serialized form in the newspaper *Bintang Timur* over a three-month period in 1962.

Although the period before 1965 saw an increasing polarization of writers along political and cultural lines, the Indonesian novel by and large adhered to the format of a realist narrative giving the writer's critical perspective on an aspect of social or political life. Writers focused overwhelmingly on situations of conflict, of suffering and psychological turmoil. Narrative endings sometimes posited the resolution of conflict and looked hopefully toward the future, but even within such a vision characters often faced death and defeat. Humor was almost totally absent and engagement with the rich traditions of the indigenous cultures and literatures of the archipelago was rare, swept aside in the urgent pursuit of the "modern."

All this was to change, however, in the diversity that came to characterize the Indonesian novel after 1965. The year 1965 itself saw the fall of the radical nationalist Sukarno government and the purge of communist influence in an unprecedented wave of killings and imprisonments that accompanied the rise to power of the military-backed "New Order" government of Indonesia's second president, Suharto. Among the priorities of the new government was economic reform and social development, and by the 1970s the moribund Indonesian publishing industry began to experience an unprecedented boom, backed by government subsidies and the rapid rise of an economically stable urban middle class. The popular romance and crime fiction of earlier times, including increasingly large numbers of foreign translations, soon became a huge industry, its products dominating the burgeoning number of new bookshops and publishing outlets across the major urban centers. "Serious" publishers were not left behind, however. As new writers—increasingly college educated, literate in English, and in touch with world trends—came to join their older, established counterparts, the Indonesian novel entered a new and productive phase of development.

Initially, as though in reaction to the trauma of the 1965 upheavals, the Indonesian novel seemed to turn away completely from its characteristic realist form. The first "New Order" novels were the absurdist, antirealist novels of Iwan Simatupang, actually written at the beginning of the 1960s but for reasons both political and economic not published until the late 1960s and early 1970s. For a time, Simatupang's *Merahnya Merah* (1968; The Red of the Red), *Ziarah* (1969; The Pilgrim), and *Kering* (1972; Drought) were seen as setting a new direction for the development of the Indonesian novel. They were followed by the 1970s novels of Putu Wijaya, *Telegram* (1973) and *Stasiun* (1977), some of the first works by an extraordinarily prolific writer of novels, stories, and dramas who continues to attract a wide audience of particularly young readers with his lively stories of the unexpected, the fantastic, and the absurd. Often overturning conventional wisdom and morality, unfailingly humorous in the blackest of situations, the more recent stories and novels of Putu Wijaya often incorporate irreverent reworkings of classical motifs and stories drawn from indigenous theatrical and literary traditions.

Humor and classical allusion were turned to different effect in the satirical novels of Yudhistira A.N.M. Massardi, *Arjuna Mencari Cinta* (1977, 1980; Arjuna in Search of Love) and *Arjuna Wiwaha* (1984; Arjuna's Wedding). These novels, also popular with young readers, transpose the noble heroes of the traditional shadow play (*wayang*) onto the world of the indulged teenagers of the new Jakarta super-rich, effectively subverting the authority of classical Javanese culture and the status of the military-bureaucratic elite in the same novelistic gesture of youthful rebellion.

At the same time that Yudhistira engaged in satire as a means of social commentary, other writers were returning to the Indonesian novel's traditional concern with realist narrative and social criticism. Ahmad Tohari's novel *Ronggeng Dukuh Paruk* (1982; The Dancer from Paruk Village), the first part of a trilogy that explores life in a Javanese village as it struggles to deal with the intrusion of the outside world, does not shy away from the events of 1965 and 1966. Other writers turned to modern Indonesian history. Y.B. Mangunwijaya's *Burung-Burung Manyar* (1981; The Weaverbirds), for instance, became a widely translated reconsideration of moral questions at the time of the revolution. Lesser known but of equal importance is Ajip Rosidi's *Anak Tanahair* (1985; Child of the Homeland), which re-created in fictional form the cultural political struggles of the 1950s and 1960s. Most widely known, and most widely read, was the great prison tetralogy of Pramoedya Ananta Toer, the series of four novels based on the nationalist awakening of the early years of the 20th century that began to appear in print with the publication of *Bumi Manusia* (This Earth of Mankind) in 1980, following the author's release from 14 years of political imprisonment in 1979. In 1995 Pramoedya published *Arus Balik* (The Turning of the Tide), which deals with the fall of the last Hindu Javanese kingdom and the coming of Islam to Java in the early 16th cen-

tury. His work remains uncompromisingly realist and modernist in its orientation.

Indonesian history as a field for postmodernist experimentation in the novel comes to the fore in Mangunwijaya's *Durga Umayi* (1991; The Goddess Durga Umayi), a whirlwind romp through postcolonial Indonesian history that explores the author's own fascination with the limitations of binary oppositions. Durga and Umayi are the malevolent and benevolent forms, respectively, of the consort of Shiva in the Hindu Javanese pantheon. In Mangunwijaya's novel they embody the demonic and the charitable faces of the female character who traverses the course of recent Indonesian history.

Although the world of the Indonesian novel in the 1990s presents a picture of diversity and growth, to what extent the reading of novels has taken root among Indonesia's population of nearly 200 million remains unclear. The habit of private reading remains a largely foreign import in Indonesian cultural life, and novels generally have small print runs and a short life on the shelves of Indonesian bookshops. Even in schools and universities, many of the "classic" novels of the modern tradition are better known through short summaries than through reading of the originals. Indeed, some observers believe that the globalized technology that now dominates Indonesian public culture will cause a transition from the "primary orality" of traditional societies to the "secondary orality" of the visual media of global culture without the immersion in the "literacy" phase that allowed the novel to flourish in the cultures of the West. As a form of creative expression, the Indonesian novel is undoubtedly alive. Whether it will be able to sustain itself in the face of this shift between "primary" and "secondary" oralities, however, remains to be seen.

KEITH FOULCHER

See also Pramoedya Ananta Toer

Further Reading

Foulcher, Keith, "Post-Modernism or the Question of History: Some Trends in Indonesian Fiction since 1965," in *Culture and Society in New Order Indonesia,* edited by Virginia Matheson Hooker, Kuala Lumpur and New York: Oxford University Press, 1993

Foulcher, Keith, "The Early Fiction of Pramoedya Ananta Toer, 1946–49," in *Text/Politics in Island Southeast Asia: Essays in Interpretation,* edited by D.M. Roskies, Athens: Ohio University Center for International Studies, 1993

Hellwig, Tineke, *In the Shadow of Change: Women in Indonesian Literature,* Berkeley: Centers for South and Southeast Asian Studies, University of California, 1994

Johns, Anthony H., *Cultural Options and the Role of Tradition: A Collection of Essays on Modern Indonesian and Malaysian Literature,* Canberra: Australian National University Press, 1979

Kartini, Raden Adjeng, *Letters of a Javanese Princess,* edited and with an introduction by Hildred Geertz, translated by Agnes Louise Symmers, New York: Norton, 1964

Kartini, Raden Adjeng, *Letters from Kartini: An Indonesian Feminist, 1900–1904,* translated by Joost Cote, Clayton, Victoria: Monash Asia Institute, Monash University, 1992

Quinn, George, *The Novel in Javanese: Aspects of Its Social and Literary Character,* Leiden: KITLV Press, 1992

Roskies, D.M., editor, *Text/Politics in Island Southeast Asia: Essays in Interpretation,* Athens: Ohio University Center for International Studies, 1993

Salmon, Claudine, *Literature in Malay by the Chinese of Indonesia: A Provisional Annotated Bibliography,* Paris: Editions de la Maison des sciences de l'homme, 1981

Teeuw, A., *Modern Indonesian Literature,* 2 vols., 2nd edition, The Hague: Martinus Nijhoff, 1979

Wahab Ali, A., *The Emergence of the Novel in Modern Indonesian and Malaysian Literature: A Comparative Study,* Kuala Lumpur: Dewan Bahasa dan Pustaka, 1991

Southeast Asian Novel

Malaysia

The novel—as a genre recognizably similar to the form in Western literature—has had a long and complex gestation in Malaysia. Since Malay is the national language of this nation state, which achieved independence from Britain in 1957, this survey will consider literary works written only in that language. The history of the novel in English in Malaysia belongs almost exclusively to authors from Chinese or Indian backgrounds, who chose English as their medium to reach a non-Malay, international audience. Their choice of language indicates a decision not to identify fully with Malaysia as constructed by the Malays. While their writing is inspired by their connections with Malaysia, their themes are those of a personal anguish stemming from fragmented identity and social alienation, as expressed in such works as K.S. Maniam's *The Return* (1981), Lee Kok Liang's *Flowers in the Sky* (1981), and Catherine Lim's *The Serpent's Tooth* (1982).

The Malay Peninsula, heartland of the Malay race, is mountainous and watered by a number of impressive rivers. From prehistoric times, the estuaries and harbors of these waterways offered landing places to the vessels that engaged in local and international trade in the region. From the 15th century, local Malay sultanates were centered along the coast to claim taxes from passing traders. The texts sponsored by these courts describe kingdoms organized around total loyalty to traditional leaders, an increasing division between elite and nonelite Malays, and a concern with identifying what was particular about "the Malays" (in contrast to other races and cultures, especially the Javanese) and preserving for posterity Malay customs and traditions. Two epic works that epitomize these characteristics are *Sejarah Melayu* (*The Malay Annals*) and *Hikayat Hang Tuah* (The Story of Hang Tuah), both of which describe the splendor of the entrepot city of Melaka (Malacca) before its conquest by the Portuguese in 1511. They were probably compiled by several hands through the 17th century and live on in contemporary Malaysia as set school texts. Stylistically, they are a skillful blend of reportage, high adventure, "folk" tales, and witty vignettes serving to flesh out a genealogical skeleton of Malay sultans. They are essentially didactic texts to educate Malays in history, morals, and manners.

Neither the Portuguese nor the Dutch who replaced them as masters of Melaka left a lasting influence on the intellectual world of the Malays. The major outside influences on Malay culture came from Arab and Indian scholars and traders who brought Islamic religion and learning. As Malays converted to Islam, the demand arose for greater knowledge of the Quran and its exegetic texts, and with these came also tales of the great Muslim heroes who had battled the infidels to spread the faith. Such tales were enjoyed through oral renditions by professional tellers who often performed together with the tellers of traditional tales (*hikayat*), whose stories were a mix of local and Indian-derived (Hindu) repertoires. Evidence from the 19th century shows that Malay narrative traditions encompassed verse and prose, oral and written forms, and themes that were an eclectic blend of indigenous, Indian, Middle-Eastern and Muslim sources. The patterned repetition of stock epithets and a rich store of conventions for the description of beauty, bravery, correct behavior, and so on in the written literature from the last century indicates its close relationship with oral composition (see Sweeney, 1987).

During the 19th century, urged on by Stamford Raffles' belief that the British should balance Dutch power in the region, increasing numbers of British colonial officials and private traders worked in Malaya, particularly in the cosmopolitan ports of Penang and Singapore. Indian, Arab, and Javanese entrepreneurs whose business activities included lithographic and later printing enterprises were attracted to these enclaves of British free trade (see Proudfoot, 1993). Europeans and locals met on a new footing of equality as they transacted their business. As a result of his observations of European knowledge and behavior in this context, Abdullah bin Abdul Kadir, a clerk and Malay language teacher of Arab-Indian ancestry, compiled his autobiography, *Hikayat Abdullah* (*The Hikayat Abdullah*) in 1849. Abdullah is recognized by 20th-century Malays as the founder of their modern literature because in both style and content he emphasized realism (in contrast to the fantasy of traditional literature). He praised the printing press for being more accurate than scribal copying in the production of texts, and he railed at Malays for blindly following rulers who oppressed them. Abdullah wrote that Malays would be left behind in the age of "progress" if they did not value their language, improve their education, and work harder (see Milner, 1994).

Education in the Malay world had traditionally taken place on a small scale, following the master-pupil model and focused on the explication of specialist texts. European missionaries and then British colonial officials established schools for Malay secular education from the mid–19th century, but these were directed particularly at the children of the Malay elite and focused on education in English. In the early years of the 20th century, the British set up schools for ordinary Malays, using Malay as the medium of instruction to provide a very basic education. Some of the graduates from these schools went on to Malay Teachers' College, reading voraciously in Malay and sometimes in English about the "modern" world and the economic and technological changes it offered. From Malay newspapers, magazines, and journals from the Dutch East Indies, from Malay versions of English classics, and from their teachers, they formed a picture of what Malay society could be and contrasted it with what they actually saw. The extracts from *The Malay Annals* and from other Malay traditional texts, presented as evidence of a formerly great Malay culture, inspired them to combat foreign influence in their own country. Malay newspaper editorials urged the Malays not to allow the foreign immigrants to dominate the economy completely. The concern of Abdullah, that the Malays would be left behind, was constantly repeated by each new generation of educated Malays.

Muslim education developed alongside secular education, as it still does in Malaysia. Within that system, a variety of attitudes developed about the way Islam should be expressed in a changing world. The traditionalists (known as *Kaum Tua,* the "old" group) believed in the literal interpretation of the Quran and resisted innovation, which they considered a threat to the purity of the religion. Another group, known as the "modernists" (*Kaum Muda*), believed that God gave mankind intelligence to be used to further His glorious religion and that the power of reason should be used to keep Muslim civilization flowering as it had in its early history. These modern-minded Muslims believed that they should learn from the West and use that knowledge to better understand the Quran and to adapt it to the contemporary world. Debate between these two groups in the 1920s and 1930s was heated.

One of the most radical of the modernists was Sayyid Shaykh al-Hadi, of Arab background but born in Malaya, who had studied in Cairo, worked as a lawyer in the religious courts, founded his own schools and journals, and was a prolific writer. In 1925 and 1926, he printed on his own press in Penang two volumes of his *Hikayat Faridah Hanom* (The Story of Faridah Hanom), which Malays acknowledge as their first novel. Sayyid Shaykh opens his work with a note to his readers explaining that he has written a story (*hikayat*) in a new form, to entertain, to guide, and to give lessons for the benefit of his readers and their native land. The intrusive narratorial voice continues through the work, guiding the reader through the story line and commenting on the behavior of the characters. The story is set in Cairo in 1894 and concerns a young, aristocratic Egyptian woman, Faridah Hanom, who has had a Muslim education and has read widely in French literature. She falls in love with a Western-educated Egyptian aristocrat but is forced to marry her cousin. She avoids the consummation of this marriage and is finally granted a ruling by the Mufti of Egypt declaring her marriage invalid because it was entered into without her consent. She is thus able to marry the man she loves and persuades him that his Western education is not as appropriate for their life as a ratio-

nal interpretation of Islam. The story concludes with a description of the women who have graduated from schools she has founded, who go into the world to work for women's rights and women's education. The final sentence is a condemnation of Muslims who blindly follow outdated traditions and neglect the true message of Islam.

Hikayat Faridah Hanom is a radical work seeking to persuade its readers that what has been achieved in Egypt can also be achieved in Malaya. Its heroine is an example of how modernist Islam can be lived. Her modernism is linked also to her native land as she explains in a long didactic passage how working to improve one's own condition also advances the homeland. In his story, Sayyid Shaykh blends reality with fiction, interweaving references to "real" people, dates, events, and places with his constructed story. His formal inspiration may have been an early Arabic novel (itself influenced by French models), but the system of moral values and social action Faridah elaborates is based on the teachings of Egyptian Muslim modernists. The choice of the love story as a form had immediate results, and the first edition of *Hikayat Faridah Hanom* sold out within a year, to be followed by numerous reprintings.

Hikayat Faridah Hanom was followed by many similarly constructed stories of young lovers who advocate modern education, industry, thrift, and initiative. In these works, which still refer to themselves as "new stories," individuals work for change in their lives and, as in Faridah's case, enjoin others to work for the greater good of race, religion, and homeland. In *Melor Kuala Lumpur* (1930; The Jasmine of Kuala Lumpur) by Harun Aminurrashid, the main characters sublimate their romantic love by dedicating themselves instead to their homeland as each works to improve the condition of the Malays. Through these works runs a strong thread of ethno-nationalism, overtly expressed through devotion to race, religion (Islam), and homeland, but more subtly encoded in their choice of Malay as their medium and their use of the Arabic script (closely linked with Islam) for its presentation.

Through the late 1920s and until the Japanese occupation in 1942, small, privately owned presses printed runs of 1,000 or so of these "new stories", which became recognizable as a group. They developed conventions of constructed realism, emphasized their contemporaneity, presented modern-minded themes through young characters, and expressed anxiety about the condition of the Malay race. Their characters showed that it was possible to acquire knowledge for oneself from books and to use this knowledge for personal advancement. In the stories, characters are not dependent on the Malay elite for their welfare but can use their energies and skills to achieve goals they have set for themselves. The strategies the narrators outline for readers provide a means of control and advancement in a time of social transition, and the voices of the dramatized narrators that speak through these stories offer encouragement and support to those for whom change may be threatening.

In physical appearance, these published editions of stories also announced their type. They were small, inexpensive, of poor quality paper and with soft covers, and often crudely printed, but all in Arabic script and in the Malay language. It is evident that their authors were writing for ordinary Malays, offering them programs for empowerment and advancement in a new world. They were critical of the English-educated Malay elite, as Abdullah had been in the mid–19th century.

By the late 1930s some Malays had formed anticolonial organizations and were condemning the British administration of Malaya. The English-educated Ishak Haji Muhammad left a promising administrative career to become a Malay-language journalist. He also wrote a wicked parody of the colonial system in a mini-novel entitled *Putera Gunung Tahan* (1938; *The Prince of Mount Tahan*). In this and a following work, *Anak Mat Lela Gila* (1941; *The Son of Mad Mat Lela*), he challenged readers by questioning basic assumptions and urged Malays to return to their indigenous values and way of life, to become self-sufficient, and to develop without recourse to Western knowledge. Ishak and fellow activists such as Ahmad Boestamam were continually in and out of detention, both under the British and after independence.

The self-reliance theme was further developed by Abdullah Sidek, who in mini-novels such as *Mari Kita Berjuang* (1941; Let Us Strive) brought together the themes of self-support, Malay cooperatives, and the bounty of the homeland, themes taken up again in the 1960s. The Malay experience of the Japanese occupation is described in *Nyawa di Hujung Pedang* (1946; Life at the Point of a Sword) by Ahmad Murad bin Nasruddin. There is a sense of shared suffering by all the inhabitants of Malaya, a new sense of self-confidence in the face of oppression, and an explicit awareness of human life as bestowed by God, but also a preoccupation with individual agency and a conviction that it is worthy of literary representation. The question of divine will versus human agency is explored in *Bilek 69* (1949; Room 69) by Ahmad Lutfi, where the death of a young woman resulting from a failed abortion allows the author to question not divine will but human understanding and the application of God's laws.

The post–World War II period was one of social dislocation and political activity in Malaya as Malays organized political parties and positioned themselves to negotiate independence. There was no violent revolution as in Indonesia, but a restlessness and tension is written into narratives that express disillusionment with old ways. *Mata Intan* (1951; Sparkling Eyes) by Wijaya Mala describes the transformation of a character who leaves his village to work in Singapore as a writer, believing that through his writing he can change the destiny of his people and serve his homeland. The heroine believes that "novels are the mirror of society," thus capturing the concept of engaged art that has become the guiding principle of Malay writing.

In 1950 a group of writers formed the "Generation of Writers of the '50s" and actively promoted the slogan "Art for Society." The concept was not uncontested, and Hamzah argued for a creativity unfettered by social engagement. His experimental novel *Rumah Kosong* (1954; The Empty House) is a rare example in Malay fiction of extended symbolism and the exploration of emotions. *Hari Mana Bulan Mana* (1960; Which Day, Which Month), the first novel by a female author, Salmi Manja, also explores a character's interior world through a first-person narrator, but it has been criticized in Malaysia for being self-indulgent. The "Generation of the '50s," led by Keris Mas, successfully lobbied the government of newly independent Malaya to establish a Language and Literature Agency, Dewan Bahasa. This body initiated a novel competition in 1957, which has been repeated at regular intervals. The competition marked the official recognition of the novel as a genre in Malay writing, and since then the term *nobel* has been used to describe extended prose fiction.

The novel that was awarded a runner's-up prize in the first competition is now regarded as Malaya's first significant modern novel. *Salina* (1961; *Salina*) by A. Samad Said is set in the squalor of a Singapore shanty town whose inhabitants are "the victims of time and circumstance." The author uses detailed descriptions of milieu and relationships between characters to produce a new depth of realism, and his style has influenced many Malay writers. Noteworthy among them is Shahnon Ahmad, arguably Malaysia's most famous novelist. His *Ranjau Sepanjang Jalan* (1966; No Harvest But a Thorn) details the cycle of wet-rice growing and the world of a struggling peasant family with heart-rending realism. The magnitude and frequency of the trials they face provoke the reader to ask why God allows such suffering. Shahnon is a prolific novelist whose works probe violence, oppression, and the nature of leadership.

The 1960s and 1970s saw rapid economic development in Malaysia that was not matched by social development. Social tensions erupted in the tragic anti-Chinese race riots of 1969 and simmered within Malay society as the poorer (usually rural) Malays did not share in the wealth that began to flow to educated, urban-employed Malays, who were being developed by the government as a new, indigenous middle class. These tensions were reflected in Malay novels of the time, particularly the novels of women writers Adibah Amin (*Seroja Masih di Kolam* [1968; The Lotus Is Still in the Pond]) and Khadijah Hashim (*Merpati Putih Terbang Lagi* [1972; The White Dove Flies Again]). The concern for economic development at the expense of spiritual growth was also a theme in novels of this period. Anwar Ridhwan's *Hari-Hari Terakhir Seorang Seniman* (1979; The Last Days of an Artist) is a complex account of the last year in the life of an old man whose profession as a teller of traditional tales is coming to an end with modern technology. The novel employs a rich layering of symbolism to represent the spiritual growth of the old man, as he recalls his past and prepares for death. The loss of identity that accompanies the alienation from a traditional past is also the theme of Fatimah Busu's novel *Kepulangan* (1980; Homecoming), a grandmother's stream-of-consciousness reminiscence of her life.

Malay novels of the 1980s experimented with a variety of literary techniques and applied international trends to the Malay context. A. Samad Said used magic realism in his *Daerah Zeni* (1985; The Region of Zeni) and *Hujan Pagi* (1986; *The Morning Post*), while Anwar Ridhwan used psychoanalytical techniques in *Arus* (1985; Current). All three novels received warm critical responses. Meanwhile, reflecting another aspect of international influence, the late 1970s witnessed a debate concerning the role of Islam in literature. Through the 1980s and 1990s, supported by state and federal government prizes, a series of "Islamic novels" has appeared. Many of these novels have been described as overly imbued with missionary fervor, but Shahnon Ahmad's series of Islamic novels, *Al-Syiqaq* (1985; Firm Guidance), *Tok Guru* (1988; The Religious Teacher), and *Ummi dan Abang Syeikhul* (1992; Ummi and Syeikhul), presents a more complex interweaving of worldly and religious interests, particularly with regard to human sexuality (see Aveling, 1996).

Mainstream Malay novels of the 1990s continue the theme of ethno-nationalism evident in the "new stories" of the 1920s and 1930s. The Malaysian government's promotion of the "New Malay" as the ideal that all Malays should strive to match is a figure abreast of modern technology, proactive, internationally competitive, and with advanced entrepreneurial skills. The

"New Malay" is at home in the international world of business and must therefore speak English. Although Malay is the national language, in the push for recognition in the global world of technological innovation Malay and many aspects of Malay identity are regarded as inappropriate. While on the one hand the government continues to sponsor Malay novel competitions, on the other hand it urges Malays to compete in the English-speaking international arena.

The short story and poetry remain the preferred genres of most Malay writers. Fewer than 10 publishers print novels in Malaysia, and, as elsewhere, the visual and popular print media attract most of the Malay audience. As long as it continues to be supported by official sponsors such as the government, the novel in Malay will continue to be written; but its reception by ordinary Malays may become limited to its function as a set school text unless the official rhetoric that upholds Malay as the national language also promotes Malay as the accepted language of business and elite intercourse.

VIRGINIA MATHESON HOOKER

Further Reading

A. Wahab Ali, *The Emergence of the Novel in Modern Indonesian and Malaysian Literature: A Comparative Study,* Kuala Lumpur: Dewan Bahasa dan Pustaka, 1991

Ahmad Kamal Abdullah, *History of Modern Malay Literature,* volume 2, Kuala Lumpur: Dewan Bahasa dan Pustaka, 1992

Aveling, Harry, "Islam, Power, and Gender: The Pious Man in the Works of Shahnon Ahmad," Ph.D. diss., National University of Singapore, 1996

Banks, David J., *From Class to Culture: Social Conscience in Malay Novels since Independence,* New Haven, Connecticut: Yale University Southeast Asia Studies, 1987

Banks, David J., "Resurgent Islam and Malay Rural Culture: Malay Novelists and the Invention of Culture," *American Ethnologist* 17:3 (August 1990)

Maimunah Mohd. Tahir, Ungku, *Modern Malay Literary Culture: A Historical Perspective,* Singapore: Institute of Southeast Asian Studies, 1987

Matheson Hooker, Virginia, "Persuading the Reader: Modernisation in Malay Novels of the 1920s–30s and the 1960s," in *Telaah Sastera Melayu,* edited by Ainon Abu Bakar, Kuala Lumpur: Dewan Bahasa dan Pustaka, 1993

Milner, Anthony, *The Invention of Politics in Colonial Malaya: Contesting Nationalism and the Expansion of the Public Sphere,* Cambridge and New York: Cambridge University Press, 1994

Mohd. Yusof Hasan, *Novels of the Troubled Years: A Study of Shahnon Ahmad's Novels, 1965–1978,* Kuala Lumpur: Dewan Bahasa dan Pustaka, 1989

Proudfoot, I., *Early Malay Printed Books,* Kuala Lumpur: Academy of Malay Studies and the Library, University of Malaya, 1993

Sweeney, Amin, *A Full Hearing: Orality and Literacy in the Malay World,* Berkeley: University of California Press, 1987

Southeast Asian Novel

Philippines

The Philippine novel is written in many languages—Filipino, Pampango, Tagalog, Ilocano, Cebuano, Hiligaynon, Pangasinan, Spanish, English. This multilingual environment creates tremendous difficulties for the scholar who pursues an integrated understanding of the development of the Philippine novel. Translations and, in their absence, summaries written by other scholars must often stand in for original texts. Only tentative observations can be made in this unusual research context.

Although the first Philippine novel—Pedro Paterno's *Ninay: Costumbres filipinas* (Ninay: Filipino Customs)—was published only in 1885, the novel in the Philippines may be said to have its origins in the extended verse narratives or epics (in more than 100 languages) of small communities on the archipelago as early as 1500 B.C. The most famous of these epics, for example, *Darangen* of the Maranaos in the southern Philippines, written probably around the tenth century, already contains structural characteristics, thematic concerns, character types, and ideological elements found in 20th-century novels.

Many scholars of Philippine literature, however, trace the roots of the novel to the more recent 16th-century metrical romance, variously called *awit* or *korido* (Tagalog), *corido* (Cebuano, Hili-gaynon, Bicol), *kuriru* (Pampango), *biag* or *panagbiag* (Ilocano), and *impanbilay* (Pangasinan), modeled after European popular tales introduced into the country by Spanish Catholic priests. Extended prose narratives during the Spanish colonial period (1521–1898) include the *manual de urbanidad* (conduct book), the *ejemplo* (exempla), and the *tratado* (polemic narrative). These were not novels in the modern sense of the word, but they continued the structural and thematic traditions of the epic that eventually evolved into elements of the modern novel.

In particular, most scholars identify four traditions or modes in Philippine narratives—the romantic, the didactic, the realist, and the radical—that have persisted through four centuries of narrative development.

Ninay follows the epics and the metrical romances in its use of antitheses (savage/civilized, country/city, tradition/progress, poor/rich, younger/older) and its plot devices (mistaken identity, coincidences, unfamiliar settings, magic or divine intervention). Usually considered a prime example of the romantic mode in Philippine fiction, *Ninay* set the tone for hundreds of novels in the 20th century, most notable of which are the best-seller *Lidia* (1907), written in Pampango by Juan Crisostomo Soto; Amando

Osorio's *Daylinda, ang Walang Palad* (1913; Daylinda, the Unfortunate), written in Cebuano; Magdalena Jalandoni's *Ang Bantay sang Patyo* (1925; The Graveyard Caretaker), written in Hiligaynon; Leon Pichay's *Apay a Pinatayda ni Naw Simon?* (1935; Why Was Simon Killed?), written in Ilocano; Macario Pineda's *Ang Ginto sa Makiling* (1947; The Gold in Makiling), written in Tagalog; Ramon Muzones' *Margosatubig: Maragtas ni Salagunting* (1946; Margosatubig: History of Salagunting), written in Hiligaynon; and Maria P. Magsano's *Samban ag Nabenegan* (c. 1935; Unretracted Vow), written in Pangasinan.

The romantic mode is the mainstream tradition in the Philippine novel, appealing to a deep-seated belief among Filipinos in the benevolence of the natural and supernatural worlds. In the epics, for example, the hero usually dies after a particularly difficult battle or undertaking but is magically brought back to life by friends, either natural (such as animals) or supernatural. In the romantic mode, plots reserve a positive ending for characters who are in tune with nature and spirits. In terms of the traditional antitheses, the savage, the rural, the traditional, the poor, and the young are privileged.

Many novels, however, focus not on the romantic elements but on moralistic preaching. These are usually considered to be in the didactic mode started by Spanish conduct books, which were written primarily to justify Catholic Christianity and Spanish imperialism. Valeriano Hernandez Peña's *Ang Kasaysayan ng Magkaibigang si Nena at si Neneng* (The Story of the Friends Nena and Neneng), written in Tagalog in 1903, is the most important example of the didactic mode. The main appeal of the book for many readers is its love story, full of betrayals and passion, but much of the book is devoted to a justification of traditional manners. Other novels in this mode are Angel Magahum's *Benjamin* (1907), written in Hiligaynon; Mariano Gaerlan's *Biag ti Maysa a Lakay, wenno Nakaam-ames a Bales* (1909; Life of an Old Man or Frightful Revenge), written in Ilocano; and Flaviano Boquecosa's *Ang Palad ni Pepe* (1937; Pepe's Fate), written in Cebuano.

Heavily influenced by 19th-century European realism and naturalism and later by early 20th-century American realistic fiction, Philippine realist novels strive to re-create actual political, economic, and social conditions, particularly in a postcolonial context. Many of them written by Filipinos who have lived outside the country for some period in their lives, this type of novel most closely approximates European or American fiction, even in the occasional use of expressionist techniques. In fact, most novels of this type are written in foreign languages. Examples of realist novels are Sulpicio Osorio's *Mga Bungsod nga Guipangguba* (1929; Destroyed Fish Corals), written in Cebuano; Antonio Abad's *La Oveja de Nathan* (1928; Nathan's Sheep), written in Spanish; Nick Joaquin's *The Woman Who Had Two Navels* (1961); Bienvenido N. Santos' *The Volcano* (1965); Carlos Bulosan's *America Is in the Heart* (1946); F. Sionil Jose's *Mass* (1979); Linda Ty-Casper's *The Peninsulars* (1964); Lina Espina Moore's *Ang Balay nga Baraha* (1973; House of Cards), written in Cebuano; and Jessica Hagedorn's *Dogeaters* (1990).

In the radical tradition, Philippine novels generally follow a Marxist line of cultural analysis, particularly in its Maoist guise, advocating armed revolution to dislodge capitalist and feudal interests. Like antagonism between social classes, the radical tradition antedates Western Marxism, but authorial sympathies and solutions may be said to foreshadow or follow that sort of mod-

ern analysis. Most commonly cited as belonging to this mode are Lope K. Santos' *Banaag at Sikat* (1905; Glimmer and Light), written in Tagalog; Amado V. Hernandez's *Mga Ibong Mandaragit* (1960; Birds of Prey), written in Tagalog; Lualhati Bautista's *Dekada '70* (1976; Decade of the '70s), written in Filipino; Mano de Verdades Posadas' *Hulagpos* (1980; Breaking Free), written in Filipino; Jun Cruz Reyes' *Tutubi, Tutubi, 'Wag Kang Magpahuli sa Mamang Salbahe* (1987; Dragonfly, Dragonfly, Don't Let the Bad Man Catch You), written in Filipino; and Humberto Carlos' *Sebyo* (1990), written in Filipino.

The four traditions do not divide so neatly in the hands of major novelists. The writer considered internationally as the best Philippine novelist, Jose Rizal, for example, clearly had didactic aims in his realist novels *Noli Me Tangere* (1887; *Touch Me Not*), written in Spanish, *El Filibusterismo* (1891; *Subversion*), written in Spanish, and *Makamisa* (Following Mass), written in both Tagalog and Spanish and unfinished at the time of his execution by Spanish authorities. But the main plot of the first two novels involves a romantic love story, that of a Spanish-educated rich young man and the long-suffering illegitimate daughter of a Spanish priest. The main reason the novels became tremendously influential (they helped to provoke the Philippine Revolution of 1896) was their realistic depiction of the corrupt Catholic clergy who had deprived Filipinos of freedom, land, and personal dignity through torture, theft, and sexual harassment. Considered the most important novels in the realist mode, Rizal's novels nevertheless also display the characteristics identified with the didactic and romantic modes.

More recent readings of Rizal, moreover, point to elements in his work that are in the radical tradition. Rizal's protagonist in *Touch Me Not*, for example, is an upper-class intellectual who believes in educational reform rather than armed revolution, but readers easily identify with some of his ostensibly minor characters who lead armed guerrilla groups against the Spanish colonial government. In *Subversion*, the disillusioned protagonist of the earlier novel returns as a terrorist, although his plot to assassinate all the key Spanish government and church officials with one bomb is frustrated by a young man afraid that a particular young lady would be killed together with the colonial villains. This typical plot twist, found mostly in romantic novels, serves as the climactic device in what is supposedly a realist novel, but which is tinged with radicalism and filled with didactic sections meant to provoke readers to change their behavior. (Curiously, Rizal apparently never read Marx, although the Filipino writer spent a number of years living in Germany and England at a time when Marxist ideas were very fashionable.)

Intellectual currents such as Catholic Christianity, European Marxism, Chinese Maoism, and naturalism clearly introduced elements of verisimilitude and ideology into the Philippine narrative tradition. What is more interesting, however, is the way the Philippine novel, particularly in the hands of Rizal, has shaped Philippine intellectual and political life. Rizal's two novels were published in Europe and had to be smuggled into the Philippines to evade Spanish government censorship, but they were read eagerly by both intellectuals and peasants, who joined to organize the successful revolution against Spain. The novels of Rizal are required reading for all high school and college students in the Philippines, a sign of their continuing relevance to nationalist education. After the Filipinos established a republic in 1898, the United States waged war against the Philippines and won, claiming it as a colony. It was in novels again, particularly in those of Hernandez (proclaimed eventually a "National Artist"), that patriotic sentiments were kept alive. Like Rizal's work, Hernandez's novels are often read in high school.

The novel is less influential today than during the Spanish and American colonial periods. When Philippine independence was finally recognized by the United States in 1946, novelists became more receptive to foreign trends and started to lose the edge that centuries of writing epics had given earlier writers. Thus, today, it is becoming more and more common to see novels written in imitation of North American or Latin American models, a sad paradox considering that what is heralded as modern magic realism was present in the early Philippine epics as a given.

Although the Chinese who invented printing came to the country and brought with them copies of their classical books as early as 982 (the date the Philippines were first mentioned in Chinese archives), print technology really arrived in the Philippines from Europe, or, more accurately, Mexico, from where the colony was ruled. The first books printed in the Philippines were, not surprisingly, books on Christianity, but soon even such books contained poetry by Filipinos. It was only a matter of time before the forerunners of the modern novel saw print. By the time of *Ninay,* it was already commonplace to see vernacular translations of European novels such as *Don Quixote* being sold in marketplaces. There was, in other words, a sizable audience for extended fiction.

Most vernacular novels today, however, are not written primarily for the book market. Because of low royalties offered by commercial or academic publishers, most novelists prefer to publish their novels in weekly installments in commercial magazines. The result of this preference is not only more income for the writers but a novelistic structure that reflects serial publication—chapters of roughly equal length that usually end in some suspenseful action. The need to provide action in every chapter—today even more pronounced owing to the influence of Mexican *telenovelas,* which are fantastically popular throughout the islands—forces novelists to focus on plot complications rather than on complex character portrayal. Seen in the context of the Philippine narrative tradition, today's novels may be said to continue the tendency in early epics to stereotype characters,

albeit with the qualification that most modern heroes lose their grand battles and their lives.

Rizal's first novel, for example, ends with the protagonist being shot at by Spanish soldiers. The reader is not told whether the protagonist is actually killed, but an unidentified person is buried at novel's end. The second novel starts with the revelation that it was the revolutionary who was killed in the first novel and not the protagonist—who has returned to wreak havoc on the Spanish colonial government and on the Catholic Church. However, he does not survive the second novel, which ends with the protagonist's death. Since Rizal started a third novel and since he was one of the first Filipino scholars to realize that the country had had a long but unappreciated history before colonization, he may be presumed to have thought of a way to resurrect his protagonist in accordance with the epic tradition. Unfortunately, he never finished his third novel.

Other novelists have tried to finish Rizal's fiction for him. Hernandez's Birds of Prey, for example, starts with his protagonist finding a treasure chest that was thrown into the sea at the end of *Subversion.* Santos' socialist *Banaag at Sikat* (another high school text in the Philippines) follows the polemical structure of *Subversion.* All the novels of F. Sionil Jose, who has the distinction of being the most translated living Filipino writer, clearly follow Rizal's lead in narrative technique, although the working-class Jose aims his anger also at the upper class, to which Rizal himself belonged.

ISAGANI R. CRUZ

Further Reading

Galdon, Joseph A., S.J., editor, *Essays on the Philippine Novel in English,* Quezon City: Ateneo de Manila University Press, 1979

Mojares, Resil B., *Origins and Rise of the Filipino Novel: A Generic Study of the Novel until 1940,* Quezon City: University of the Philippines Press, 1983

Reyes, Soledad S., *Nobelang Tagalog, 1905–1975* (The Tagalog Novel, 1905–1975), Quezon City: Ateneo de Manila University Press, 1982

Tiongson, Nicanor G., editor, *CCP Encyclopedia of Philippine Art,* 10 vols., Manila: Cultural Center of the Philippines, 1994 (volume 9 is on Philippine literature)

Southern Balkan Novel

The southern Balkans—Greece, Macedonia, Bulgaria, and Albania—are characterized by a strange mixture of unity and diversity. Greek, Bulgarian, and Albanian are all Indo-European languages, but they are as distinct as English, French, and Polish. In addition, they are all written in different alphabets. (However, Macedonian is very close to Bulgarian, closer than Spanish is to Italian.) Nevertheless, linguists have been able to trace a large

number of loan words and a degree of syntactical similarity between the different languages. Other unifying factors are their shared political history and the presence of substantial ethnic minorities in each country, while their different religious and educational policies reinforce the diversity.

Until the fall of Constantinople in 1453, most of the Balkans for most of its history had been ruled by the Byzantine empire, although there was a strong independent Bulgarian state incorporating Macedonia in the 8th to 10th centuries and again in the 13th. Albania was never really independent except briefly under the great hero Scanderbeg in the late 15th century. By this time most of the Balkans was under Ottoman rule and remained so until the 19th century, when the rise of nationalism brought about the creation of small independent states. Southern Greece became independent in 1832, northern Bulgaria in 1878. The Balkan wars of 1912 and 1913 liberated the rest of the Ottoman territories apart from a small area near Istanbul. Albania became independent, but the area we now know as Macedonia passed to Serbia. Greece, which gained extensive territory near Salonika, claimed that the term *Macedonia* is more properly used for this territory, while Bulgaria, the loser in the Balkan wars, claimed to have been deprived of Macedonia. After World War I, there were further minor adjustments of territory; Bulgaria was again the loser, and Macedonia together with Serbia became part of the new kingdom of Yugoslavia, under a Serbian dynasty. Invaded by the Axis powers in World War II, the Balkans suffered the consequences of occupation, resistance, and civil strife. The communists emerged as the strongest power after the war, except in Greece. Macedonia was given more autonomy in a federal Yugoslavia, and Macedonian was finally recognized as a literary language. The collapse of communism in the 1990s led to the break up of Yugoslavia, precarious independence for Macedonia, and troubled times for Albania and Bulgaria. This summary of the complicated history of the Balkans is necessary for an understanding of the history of the novel, which reflects these complications.

The Ottoman authorities, generally and perhaps unfairly represented in fiction as cruel and tyrannical, were certainly uninterested in promoting education and culture. Greek, with its glorious literary tradition and its strong standing as the language of the church, enjoyed a head start over its rivals in schools and in commercial activities. Macedonian had no status until after World War II, and Albanian did not achieve even an alphabet until 1908. Bulgarian prospered greatly when the Turks allowed the establishment of a separate Bulgarian church in 1870, but the unhappy result was that the supporters of this church fought with the supporters of the Greek church over a great swath of the southern Balkans.

Albanian today is spoken by about 3 million people inside the country and a slightly smaller number in other parts of the Balkans, primarily in the Serbian-ruled province of Kosovo, where the Albanians form the majority of the population, and in Macedonia, where they form a substantial minority. A primitive form of Albanian is still spoken in southern Italy and central Greece. At the time of the formation of the Albanian state, the number of Albanian speakers was much smaller owing to a high mortality rate, and the number of those able to read and write Albanian was even smaller owing to a high rate of illiteracy. Indeed, the creation of the Albanian language was something of a miracle, considering that at the beginning of this century there was no Albanian state, no Albanian schools, and no Albanian alphabet. Albanians were divided between three religions and two different dialects, Gheg (or Geg) being spoken in the north and Tosk in the south.

Even today there are still small Albanian-speaking minorities in Greece, Greek-speaking minorities in Albania, and Macedonian-speaking minorities in Greece. There are large Turkish groups in all countries apart from Albania, and Macedonia has a large Albanian community. Vlachs, speaking a language akin to Romanian, live in all four countries. The fortunes of war and postwar population exchanges have greatly reduced these minorities. Northern Greece is now largely Greek speaking, whereas in 1920 less than half of the population spoke Greek. Among the intelligentsia who wrote and read novels, we often find a fierce patriotism blending oddly with a cosmopolitan knowledge of the languages and cultures of other countries. Thus Bulgarian and Albanian authors often show a surprising knowledge of Greek. There is also an odd oscillation between a wish to concentrate on particular local problems and a wish to take in worldwide movements, springing largely from the sophisticated West.

The 19th-century novel in the West was produced to satisfy a leisured educated class with supposedly shared values, including a wish to solve the social problems caused by such factors as the growth of industrialization. Such a flat generalization is impossible for Balkan countries, where the educated population was much smaller, values were less likely to be shared, and problems went far beyond those associated with industrialization. Initially, writers found it easier to publish poetry and short stories rather than novels because of publication difficulties and a lack of a receptive audience. Historical, political, and national themes have always been popular in Balkan literature because they bring out shared values and because many poets have found themselves cast as politicians.

Albania

Among leading Albanian politicians and writers, we can note some interesting careers. Naim Frashëri wrote in Turkish, Greek, and Persian and was director of the board of censorship for the Ottoman government. Yet he is considered one of Albania's greatest poets. Even more impressively, Fan Noli was born on the Bulgarian/Turkish border, was educated at a Greek school, acted in Greek theatrical companies, taught in a school in Egypt, emigrated to America, and then at the age of 26 was ordained as the first deacon of a breakaway Albanian orthodox church. Noli became the head of the Albanian community, visited Albania for the first time in 1913, and in 1919 became Bishop of the Albanian Church in America. After a spell as Albanian delegate to the United Nations and foreign minister, Noli became the first (and some might say the last) democratically elected prime minister of Albania. The rest of his career was a slight anticlimax. He left Albania at the end of 1924, giving way to Ahmet Zogu, later King Zog, and withdrawing from politics. However, he wrote prolifically as a dramatist, poet, historian, and translator. Perhaps sadly, he never tried his hand at the novel.

The title of Albania's first novelist should probably go to Sami Frashëri, the youngest of a remarkable family of three brothers, the eldest of whom, Abdul, was both a member of the Turkish parliament and a leading light of the League of Prizren, a movement for Albanian autonomy. Sami Frashëri published in 1872 what could be counted both as the first Albanian novel and as the first Turkish novel, *Taaşşuk-u Tal'at ve Fitnat* (The Love of Tal'at and Fitnat), a sentimental tale in Turkish that involved some social commentary on the position of women. Frashëri worked as a Turkish lexicographer and pioneered a new Albanian alphabet, which left him little time for fiction. Pashko Vasa was another activist in the Albanian cause who was simultaneously a loyal servant to the Ottoman empire. His *Bardha de Témal* (1890) was written in French, but at least it has an Albanian background, being set in Shkodër in the year 1842. It has an interesting political theme and contains some insight into life in north Albania. Another claimant to the title of first Albanian novelist is Francesco Antonio Santori from southern Italy, who wrote *Sofia Kammate,* a novel in Italian with a shorter version in Albanian, but both versions remained unpublished until the 20th century. Dom Ndoc Nikaj (1864–1951) has been called the father of the Albanian novel, but, during a long, interesting, and ultimately tragic life as priest, publisher, and political prisoner, Nikaj published journalism, short stories, and didactic works, but not really anything that amounted to a novel. The Albanian age of national awakening and educational enlightenment, known as the Rilindja, produced some fine literature but virtually no long fiction.

Novels written after independence were not of high literary quality. Zef Harapi produced historical novels in a lively but discursive style. His first novel, *Pushka e tratharit* (1914; The Traitor's Gun), has a surprisingly romantic thrust in view of the fact that the author was a priest. Foqion Postoli, like Fan Noli an emigré to America, wrote two sentimental novels, *Per mprojten e atdheut* (1921; In Defense of the Homeland) and *Lulja e kujtimit* (1924; The Flower of Remembrance), both full of gushing patriotism. Medhi Frashëri was a member of the famous Frashëri family and a writer and politician who fell out of favor because of his opposition to communism. His short novel *Nevruzi* (1923) is full of Balkan history but devoid of narrative skill. Llambi Dardha's *Kthimii Skenderbeut në Krujë* (1929; Scanderbeg's Return to Krujë) and *Deshmöret e lirisë* (1933; The Martyrs of Freedom) combine historical fiction and nationalist bias. Haki Stërmilli and Sterjo Spasse bridge the gap between interbellum Albania under King Zog and communist Albania after World War II. Both were born on the Macedonian-Albanian border, Spasse in a Macedonian-speaking village. Both ended their lives as favored sons of the communist regime, although Stërmilli had tutored King Zog's sister. Spasse ended his life writing dreary novels of socialist realism, but before and during the war he had produced the critical *Nga jeta në jetë—Pse?* (1936; From Life to Life—Why?) and *Afërdita* (1944). Stërmilli's *Sikur t'isha djalë* (1936; If I Were a Boy) is also critical of conventional morality, dealing with the revolt of a young girl against an arranged marriage to an elderly merchant. Stërmilli's second novel, begun in 1938 but not published until 1967, *Kalesori Skenderbeut* (Scanderbeg's Horsemen), deals with a familiar historical theme.

The communist victory at the end of World War II introduced a period of stifling restraint on intellectual curiosity and a strong emphasis on Albanian patriotism, which grew increasingly isolationist as Albania broke with the Western powers, with Yugoslavia, with the Soviet Union, and finally with all other countries, including China. To its credit, the regime of Enver Hoxha did much to improve standards of literacy, and the reading public became much larger. There was thus an ideal market for novels of gritty social realism, praising heroic Albanian workers striving for a better world against the foreign, capitalist forces of darkness. Novelists like Shevqet Musaraj and Fatmir Gjata wrote accounts of the struggle for national liberation, painting characters and events in a black-and-white fashion, although the total effect is grimly grey. The work of Musaraj and Gjata has

been translated into English, as has that of Dritëro Agolli, whose novels *Komisari Memo* (1970; The Bronze Bust) and *Njeriu me top* (1975; The Man with the Gun) deal with the German occupation. Agolli was for many years head of the Albanian Union of Writers, although his work was occasionally felt to be out of touch with the party line, and he did write one novel, not translated into English, *Shkelqimi dhe rënja e shokut Zylo* (1973; The Rise and Fall of Comrade Zylo), which can be interpreted as a satire hostile to the regime. Writers hostile to Hoxha suffered persecution, and some fled into exile. Martin Camaj was one of them, a scholar and poet working for Albanian literature outside Albania. His novels *Rrathë* (1978; Circles) and *Karpa* (1987; Karpa) have a psychological depth totally lacking in the realistic novels of his contemporaries who remained in Albania.

The one Albanian novelist to gain world fame is Ismail Kadare, many of whose works have been translated into English, although there have been difficulties with translations made indirectly through a French version. Kadare's attitude to the Hoxha regime is ambiguous. His mysterious tales, usually set in the past, are critical of stifling tyranny. The somber picture of Albania in many of his novels is in marked contrast to the travel-brochure prose of his contemporaries. His first novel, *Gjenerali i ushtrisë së vdekur* (1963; The General of the Dead Army), begins in pouring rain, while *Dimri i madh* (1977; The Great Winter), describing the break with the Soviet Union, starts with snow. *Ura me tri harque* (1978; The Three Arched Bridge) and *Kush e Solli Doruntinën* (1979; Doruntine) expand two grim Balkan folktales into novels, while the famous *Prilli i thyer* (1978; Broken April) considers the savage Albanian blood feud tradition. *Nëpunësi i pallatit te ëndrrave* (1981; The Palace of Dreams), set in the days of the Ottoman Empire, evokes in a savagely humorous fashion a Kafkaesque world of totalitarian bureaucracy. Kadare dealt with the rupture with China in a novel entitled *Koncert në fund të dimrit* (1988; Concert at the End of Winter), a sequel to *The Great Winter*. On the surface, Kadare seems to attack the abuses that the communists were trying to eradicate, but clearly his works have a deeper symbolic meaning and deal with universal themes. They also paint a more truthful picture of Albania past and present than do the works of his contemporaries, with whom Kadare remains on uneasy terms.

Hoxha died in 1985, and his successor, Ramiz Alia, was a less powerful figure. By the end of 1990, the communist regime had collapsed, but Kadare had already left Albania for Paris together with his wife, also a writer of distinction. His writing in exile has been disappointingly personal and bitter. A novel written in French, *La Pyramide* (1992; The Pyramid) is clearly an attack on Hoxha's fondness for elaborate statues, the pyramid form also reflecting any dictator's love of hierarchy and absolute power. But the title proved sinisterly prophetic in another way. In 1992 democratic elections brought into power President Sali Berisha. Albania was suddenly opened up to the West, and there should have been a flowering of culture. The old state publishing company was dismantled, and 70 private publishing houses were founded. The work of dissidents was published, while some writers who had taken the party line recanted their communist allegiances. But there was a shortage of money, and after 50 years of oppression writers found it hard to start from scratch. The new regime encouraged the pursuit of wealth, and the writing of fiction did not lead in that direction. Fairly soon, intellectuals found themselves at odds with the new regime, which they accused of reverting to the dictatorial practices of Hoxha. In 1997, the regime collapsed in anarchy after a series of scandals involving pyramid schemes. The current situation leaves little room for optimism about the novel in Albania.

Bulgaria

Bulgaria's history is not altogether dissimilar from Albania's, and the history of the novel in that country has followed a roughly similar pattern. Bulgarian national consciousness did not really develop until the 19th century, although there had been powerful Bulgarian empires in the Middle Ages. Turkish influence in civil matters and Greek influence in educational affairs were always strong. In 1762 Father Paisi Khilandarski wrote a history of Bulgaria in Bulgarian, and this largely fictional account may be taken as the starting point for any survey of the Bulgarian novel. It is of course in no sense a novel, but it did establish that Bulgarian was a written language. As it turned out, the Bulgarian novel was always to have a strong historical component and nationalist bias. The first Bulgarian dictionary prepared by Petar Beron appeared in 1824, and the first collection of Bulgarian folk songs was assembled by Vasil Aprilov in 1841. Beron and Aprilov were wealthy Bulgarians who lived abroad. Inside Bulgaria, churchmen like Neofit Rilski and Neofit Bozveli worked hard for Bulgarian education. The first Bulgarian newspaper appeared in 1842. The writers Georgi Rakovski, who died in 1867, and Khristo Botev, who died in 1869, both fought for Bulgarian independence and wrote poetry with a strongly nationalist bias. Lyuben Karavelov, who died in 1869, was strongly influenced by Russian writers like Gogol' and wrote short stories along the same lines. However, it was not until 1878, when most of Bulgaria gained independence from Turkey, that the first Bulgarian novel was published. Up to that moment, there had been neither the market nor the distribution system for a long work of fiction. Even after independence, poetry and short stories remained more popular forms of literary expression.

Ivan Vazov dominated Bulgarian literature during his lifetime, and his work has remained in favor ever since, although his conservatism was not very popular with the communist regime. He produced poetry, plays, and novels in vast quantities, and might have written more if he had not been called upon to play a prominent part in public life, editing newspapers and even serving as minister of education. All his work is strongly realist and is steeped in a simple and robust patriotism. His most famous novel, *Pod igoto* (1889; *Under the Yoke*) describes Bulgaria at the time of the national uprising against the Turks in 1876. It ends tragically with the deaths of the revolutionary Boycho Ognyanov and his fiancée, the idealist schoolteacher Rada Gospojina. *Nova Z-zemya* (1896; The New Land) deals rather less dramatically with the problems arising from the incorporation of the southern province of Eastern Rumilia into Bulgaria. In *Kazalarskata tzaritsa* (1903; The Empress Kazalar), Vazov attacks materialism and contemporary intellectual fashions: he opposed both radicalism and symbolism.

Most of Vazov's contemporaries wrote short stories rather than novels. The exception is Aleko Konstantinov, whose *Baj Ganju* (1894; Uncle Ganya) describes, in a series of satirical sketches, a villainous character who has been interpreted as an embodiment of all that was wrong in the Bulgarian character. Bulgaria fared badly in World War I and in the Balkan War that preceded it, being on the losing side on both occasions. After the war, there was a brief period when the agrarian leader Alexander Stambolyski was in power, but he was assassinated in 1923, and a right-wing government then ruled until World War II, when again the Bulgarians joined the losing side. Conditions were not favorable for the writing of literature. Novelists flirted with symbolism and with communist ideas. Bulgaria's contemporary and recent misfortunes inspired novelists to retreat to the remote past. Dimitar Shishmanov wrote three novels attacking corruption and bureaucracy—"*High Life*" (1920; High Life), *Deputat Stoyanov* (1920; Deputy Stoyanov), and *Buntovnik* (1921; The Rebel)—before the assassination of Stambolyski, but his final work, *Blyanova kray Akropola* (1937; Shadows on the Acropolis), is a whimsical contrast between the ancient and modern world. Dobri Nemirov (1882–1945), Stilyan Chilingirov (1889–1969), and Fani Popova Moutafova (1902–1977) all wrote historical novels. Konstantin Konstantinov wrote a novel, *Kruv* (1933; Blood), about provincial society just after the war.

Some of these writers fell afoul of the communists who took over with the invading Russian army in 1944. By contrast, Lyudmil Stoyanov, who had flirted with symbolism and had written a novel praising Stambolyski, became president of the Union of Writers. Communist themes appear in his novels *Holera* (1935; Cholera) and *Zhenski doushi* (1929; Women's Souls). Stoyan Zagorchinov wrote a story, "Den posleden-den gospoden" (1931–34; The Lost Day), about life before the Turkish invasion; the story is also a merciless attack on the upper classes. Dimitur Talev wrote four novels about Macedonia, and Dimitur Dimov wrote about the Spanish Civil War. These two novelists were much favored by the communists, who did not wish to see Bulgaria's problems exposed. Emilyan Stanev set some of his novels in medieval Bulgaria, as did Vera Moutafchieva. Stefan Dichev wrote novels about the national liberation movement, *Za svobodata* (For Freedom) and *Putyat kum Sofia* (The Road to Sofia). Anton Donchev discussed forced conversions to Islam in *Vreme razdelno* (Time of Parting). In spite of a large Islamic population, the official party line encouraged a strongly nationalist Bulgarian approach, as these novels indicate. There was also a tendency to follow Russian novels, with Maksim Gor'kii's influence predominating.

Some tried to break away from rigid orthodoxy. Emil Manov published a novel, *The Unauthentic Case*, in which the hero, a good, sincere communist, takes to drink and goes mad. Pavel Vezhinov escaped to the realm of science fiction, while Nikola Haitov and Ivailo Petrov escaped to the countryside. Dimitur Koroudzhiev expressed genuinely democratic views in *Domut na Alma* (The House of Alma) and *Deset godini po-kusno* (Ten Years After). Viktor Paskov's satirical novel *Balada za Georg Henig* (1988; A Ballad for George Henig) has been well translated into English.

The great Soviet thaw was not very comfortable for Bulgaria. The country was ruled alternately by old style communists, renamed socialists, and democrats, and sometimes there was an uneasy balance of power, with the Turkish minority holding the scales. It was not an easy time for publishing novels. But Blaga Dimitrova rises above the general mirk of Bulgaria's literary world, above the corruptions of communism and capitalism. The author of nine novels as well as numerous collections of poetry, Dimitrova was occasionally banned in communist times and served as vice president of Bulgaria in noncommunist times.

Her protests against the Vietnam War lift the Bulgarian novel from its parochial interest, but her work is nevertheless firmly Bulgarian.

Macedonia

The history of Macedonia is like the history of the Balkans—tragically complicated. Its literature encompasses and sometimes even transcends these tragic complications. A beautiful but rugged landscape, high mountains and surprising lakes, great heat in summer and stark cold in winter, a friendly people with a monstrous past, a name universally known and hotly disputed—these are but a few of the contradictions in Macedonian history and literature.

Because the language spoken by most of the inhabitants of Macedonia was not recognized until 1945, it is difficult to speak of Macedonian literature until that date. Of course people spoke and sang in Macedonian under the Turks, the Serbs, and the Bulgarians, and they continued to do so when Macedonia became part of Yugoslavia. But there was little opportunity or incentive to write in Macedonian. Not surprisingly, folklore and oral poetry form an important part of the Macedonian literary heritage, while the novel took a long time to develop. The first Macedonian to attempt a novel was Kocho Ratsin (1908–41), who published some poems in Macedonian but wrote mainly in Serbo-Croatian. Only a few fragments of his novel *Opium Poppy* survive.

Tito's wise recognition of Macedonia as separate from and yet integral to the new Yugoslavia untapped the literary genius of the Macedonians. There were of course many problems to overcome, foremost among them the lack of a standard language. However, the philologist, patriot, poet, and academic Blaze Koneski did his best to create one. His fellow poet Slavko Janevski published the first complete Macedonian novel, *Selo zad sedumte jaseni* (The Village behind the Seven Ash Trees), in 1952. The novel blends an account of partisan activity during the war with reminiscences of earlier days amid subtle insights into human psychology.

By this time Yugoslavia had broken with Stalin and was thus more open to Western literature. But Macedonia was a backward part of Yugoslavia and faced enormous economic problems. The writing of novels in Macedonian was not high on the agenda of the Yugoslav state, which through tourism, education, roads, and folklore tried to drag Macedonia from the 17th to the 20th century. Modernization was a cruel process, and perhaps Macedonian novels reflect this cruelty. An added cruelty lay in wait. In order to escape the murderous Yugoslav civil war, Macedonia declared independence in 1991. Western countries were slow to recognize the fledgling state and Greece objected to the name. Through no fault of its own, Macedonia now faces isolation, poverty, and problems with the minority Albanians. The situation does not invite novelistic production.

Nevertheless, there are several novelists of note in Macedonia, although poetry has attracted more writers and perhaps, given limited publishing opportunities, even more readers. Dimitar Solev wrote movingly about his unhappiness in the war. Zivko Cingo's primary interest in Macedonian life is to escape from it into the world of the imagination in his bitter novels *Srebreni snegori* (1967; Silver Snows) and *Golemata voda* (1971; The Great Water). In spite of its unpromising present and uncertain future, Macedonia has a rich past, and its gifted writers, given more opportunities, will probably draw on this past in future novels.

Greece

The huge shadow of ancient Greek literature and history falls less heavily on the novel than on other modern Greek genres. There are fictional romances in ancient and medieval Greek, but these are usually thought to have had little influence on the modern novel. The rise of the novel in Western Europe coincided with the collapse of the epic, and it has been reasonably argued that this coincidence was partly due to a growth in literacy among people who did not have the benefit of a classical education. In Greece, some of the classics remained in folk memory, and others were well known in educated circles, although fossilized by antiquarian prejudice and distorted by ecclesiastical pressure. But on the whole, ancient Greek remained a closed book to the average modern Greek until the 19th century, when interest in and imitation of the classics revived under Western influence. As a result, modern Greek drama is full of classical allusions. But the novel followed a path of its own, even though many novelists were also poets and dramatists and were caught up in the general enthusiasm for ancient Greece.

Thus, the great Greek patriot Adamantios Korais claimed in 1804 that the novel was an ancient Greek invention. Korais wrote four fictional letters as a preface to the *Iliad* between 1811 and 1820, and this epistolary quartet has been put forward as the first modern Greek novel. However, the honor more usually goes to *Ho Leandros* (Leander), written by the poet Panayotis Soutsos and published at Nauplia in 1832, the date of Greek independence. *Ho Leandros* is a romantic epistolary novel with obvious debts to Goethe and Foscolo, but it also tried to incorporate an ancient Greek influence. Alexander Soutsos, Panayotis' brother, published *Ho exoristos tou 1831* (The Exile of 1831) in 1833. Before 1850, similar works of fiction appeared, often with a strong historical and patriotic theme. These novels are now not easy to obtain or understand, owing to their artificial rhetorical style and their use of archaic language.

The only two novels of any literary merit in the first period of Greek independence from 1832 to 1881 are *Thanos Vlekasas* (1855) by Pavlos Kalligas and *Hē Papissa Iōanna* (1866; Pope Joan) by Emmanuel Roidis. Both Kalligas and Roidis had been educated in the West, each attacked social ills, and each wrote only one novel. The tragic fate of Kalligas' eponymous hero has an appealing pathos, but the novel's elaborate allegories stood in the way of a popular success. Roidis, cultivating a highly allusive style and playing elaborate games with the reader, is a difficult and rhetorical writer. Interestingly, his work anticipates many 20th-century trends in fiction. He tells the story of a ninth-century pope who was in fact a woman, but *Hē Papissa Iōanna* is fairly obviously an attack on the contemporary Greek church, which was quick to condemn the novel (and ensure its lasting fame). *Hē Papissa Iōanna* is also an attack on the romantic historical novel, showing that the past was no better than the present.

In 1881, Greece advanced its frontiers to include Thessaly and the Ionian islands, which had a more continuous literary history because of their freedom from Ottoman rule. After this expansion, Greek politicians became obsessed with further expansion to include other Greek communities that remained under the Turkish yoke on the northern and eastern shores of the Aegean. Rather quaintly known as the Great Idea, this policy was temporarily successful after some initial setbacks and a long struggle in Macedonia. Greece eventually gained northern Greece and, if only for a short time, large areas in western Turkey. But in 1922, trying to expand their acquisitions in Anatolia, the Greeks suffered a disastrous defeat: they lost territory and gained a large number of refugees from the lands they were forced to sacrifice. Even when successful, the country had experienced social and economic strains as a result of war and the absorption of new territory and people. Novels of the period, as elsewhere in the Balkans, reflect a febrile patriotism, as well as the tensions it produced.

During the last two decades of the 19th century, Greece produced a number of novels dealing with small contemporary communities, usually in a rural setting. Such novels and many more short stories asserted an essential Greekness while displaying the influence of foreign writers like Zola. The influence of Thomas Hardy is apparent in the work of Andreas Karkavitsas (1860–1922), whose novels seem to tell simple stories of country life but in fact describe the collapse of peasant society in the face of 20th-century progress. By the end of the century, many rural Greeks had moved to Athens, and novelists abandoned their obsession with folkloric realism. They still continued to write about small communities, but these were part of the urban environment of Athens. Thus Gregorios Xenopoulos (1807–1951) and Iannis Kondylakis (1861–1920) wrote their first novels about life in the capital, although later works are set in their native islands of Crete and Zakynthos. Acknowledging the influence of Balzac and Dickens, Xenopoulos wrote prodigiously and carelessly. His very popularity and his evident wish to entertain without voicing serious social criticism have not helped his reputation.

Konstandinos Hatzopoulos, a poet in the symbolist tradition, wrote two novels, *Ho purgos tou akropotamou* (1909; The Manor by the Riverside) and *Phtinopōro* (1917; Autumn), that break free from the realism that dominated the Greek novel. The work of Konstandinos Theotokis, a friend of Hatzopoulos and a socialist, displays a resemblance to Dostoevskii's novels. *Hoi slavoi sta desma tous* (1922; Slaves in Their Chains), while recording with melancholy exactness the decline of idealism at the hands of the rapacious middle class, is principally significant for the elegance of its style and formal construction and its sophisticated use of leitmotivs. In contrast, the politician Ion Dragoumis wrote simple, realistic patriotic novels, describing the Greek struggle in Macedonia, for instance, in *Martyrōn kai herōōn haima* (1907; Blood of Martyrs and Heroes).

In between the wars, Greece made a surprisingly successful recovery from the Asia Minor disaster and the international slump, but collapsed into dictatorial rule before the German invasion in 1941. The disaster in Asia Minor inspired a number of works. Four novelists lived in Mytilene, a few miles from the Turkish coast, and three of them were refugees from the Turks. Stratis Doukas wrote *Historia enos aichmalotou* (1929; Prisoner's Story) about a refugee from Anatolia who had escaped by pretending to be a Turk, while Stratis Myrivilis described the Macedonian campaign in *Hē zōē en taphō* (1924; Life in the Tomb). Ilias Venezis tells us of the fate of the Anatolian Greeks in *To noumero 31328* (1924; Number 31328). All three novels blur the boundaries between fact and fiction and were expanded during their authors' long lives. Venezis and Myrivilis produced second novels showing the cruel consequences of the aftermath of war. Fotis Kondoglou in *Pedro Kazas* (1923) tells an escapist tale of adventure set outside Greece.

Another group of novelists explored urban life and the difficulties that ensued as a result of the Asia Minor disaster. Yorgos Theotokas wanted to break away from the provincialism and photographic realism of earlier writers and published a broadside entitled *Eleſthero pneuma* (Free Spirit) in 1929. His own novel *Argo* was planned on an ambitious scale, the first volume of what was to be a vast trilogy appearing in 1933, but a much shorter second volume completed the work in 1936. *Argo* shows the weight of history and myth with which Greek fiction has to contend. There are references to contemporary historical characters like Venizilos and Mussolini as well as glances back to Byzantine history and classical legend. The novel is full of religious symbolism and shows the influence of European fiction as well. In spite of the breathless speed of its second volume, *Argo* achieves a kind of detachment while preserving its essential Greekness. These latter features are lacking in the work of M. Karagatsis, whose tragic characters, all foreigners, are driven to their doom by a sexual passion too powerful for them to control.

Karagatsis and Theotokas were able to bring Greek fiction into line with the European mainstream, as represented by such authors as Gustave Flaubert and Fedor Dostoevskii. Another group of writers based on Thessaloniki were more interested in the work of James Joyce and other modernists, and they tried to break away from realism altogether. Yannis Skarimbas (1893–1984) anticipates Samuel Beckett, and Nikos Pentzikis (1909–92) shows the influence of Franz Kafka.

Literary experimentation came to a fairly abrupt end with the imposition of the Metaxas dictatorship in 1936, which was followed by three years of Axis occupation. None of the writers previously mentioned were particularly sympathetic to communism or subject to censorship and repression, but a number of the novelists who had seemed experimental in the 1920s and early 1930s now returned to more traditional themes, often reverting to the experiences of their early years and sometimes delving back into the remoter past. Myrivilis and Venezis wrote about rural villages before 1922, Theotokas about Constantinople at the turn of the century. In his second novel, *Ho pethamenos kai hē anastasē* (The Dead Man and the Resurrection), finished in 1938 and published in 1944, Pentzikis described the history of Thessaloniki. Kosmas Politis, who had previously written novels about smart Athenian society, deftly blended memories of his native Smyrna with parallels from the *Iliad* in *Eroica* (1937; Eroica). Both novels contain innovative touches, although, as is the case with Melpi Axioti's *Dyskoles nychtes* (1938; Difficult Nights), they perhaps try to do too much in linking modernist trends with the weight of oral tradition.

The same accusation can be leveled against Nikos Kazantzakis, whose second novel, *Vios kai politeia tou Alexe Zorba* (Zorba the Greek), brought him immense fame, as it was made into a successful film. As a result, all his novels were translated into English and reached a worldwide audience. *Zorba the Greek* was written in 1941 and 1943 during the Axis occupation, but it was not published until 1946. Kazantzakis' fame and the fact that he lived for most of his career outside Greece have led some of his countrymen to despise him, but in fact his work is very typical of the Greek novel of the period.

Zorba is a rough Cretan peasant whose earthy philosophy is contrasted with the timid nature of his employer, the narrator of the story. The dialogue between these two characters is reminiscent of the dialogues of Plato, and there are obvious if surprising resemblances between the novel and Plato's *Republic*. Kazantzakis also includes religious commentary and many details of Greek traditional life, elements largely lost in the film version.

Kazantzakis' subsequent novels, such as *Ho Christos xanastaurōnetai* (1954; *Christ Recrucified*), *Ho kapetan Michalēs* (1953; *Freedom and Death*), *Ho phtochoules tou Theou* (1956; *God's Pauper*), and *Ho teleutaios peirasmos* (1955; *The Last Temptation*), were all written after Kazantzakis had left Greece, where thought and culture were dominated by the savage civil war following the German defeat. Opinion was polarized between the losing communist side and the successful right wing. Kazantzakis wrote a novel entitled *Hoi aderphades* (1963; *The Fratricides*), which deals with the civil war, but it was published posthumously. In *Christ Recrucified* he wrote about Anatolia on the eve of the Turkish disaster, and in *Freedom and Death* about Crete in the Turkish period. His last two novels retreat from the historical present but are not really escapist, as all Kazantzakis' novels preach a message of reconciliation.

Some found the subject of the civil war too painful to handle. Two women novelists, writing at its very beginning, chose to retreat to the 1930s, although both *Ta psathina kapela* (1946; Straw Hats) by Margarita Lymberaki and *Contretemps* (1947) by Mimiki Kranaki are full of ominous portents, and the latter novel does touch upon the German invasion and the People's Army. *Ho allos Alexandros* (1950; The Other Alexander), a curious allegorical novel, also makes explicit reference to the civil war. Angelos Terzakis and M. Karagatsis wrote long novels, *Dichōs Theo* (1951; Without a God) and *Ho Kitrinos Phakellos* (1956; The Yellow File), respectively, that end on the brink of World War II but contain implied criticisms of communism. *Ho Kitrinos Phakellos* is an elaborate construction about the life of a novelist who thinks he can view the world with scientific objectivity and even reform it accordingly but ignores human nature. Yannis Beratis, who also wrote experimental novels, produced realistic accounts of the Albanian campaign and the struggle of the right-wing guerillas in Epirus in *To platy potami* (1946; The Broad River) and *Hodoiporiko tou 43* (1946; Itinerary of 1943). Yorgos Theotokas wrote *Hiera hodos* (1950; Sacred Way) and *Astheneis kai hodoiporoi* (1964; Invalids and Travelers) about the war against the Germans and the civil war in the same, almost documentary, style.

Experimental novels came to the fore in the more prosperous 1960s. Tatiana Gritsi-Milliex in *Idou hippos chlōros* (1963; Behold a Pale Horse) and Stratis Tzirkas in *Akybernetes politeies* (1960–65; Drifting Cities) wrote accounts of recent events from a left-wing viewpoint with a certain amount of experimentation. The best-selling novel of the 1960s was *Matōmena chomata* (1962; Farewell, Anatolia) by Dido Sotirou, which deals with the Anatolian disaster and blames it on international capitalism. Other noteworthy novels include *To phragma* (1967; The Dam) by Spyros Plaskovitis, a surprising last novel by Theotokas, *Hoi kampanes* (1960; The Bells), and Pentzikis' masterpiece, *To mythistorēma tēs Kurias Ersēs* (1966; The Novel of Mrs. Ersi), a good combination of traditional Greek motifs and Western postmodernism.

From 1967 to 1974 Greece was ruled by a military junta, which was overthrown in 1974. Since that time, the country has been governed by the conservative New Democracy Party, associated with Konstantinos Karamanlis, and the socialist PASOK party, associated with Andreas Papandreou. Both governments were an improvement over the junta but both were accused of corruption, and the polarization of Greek politics continued. Writers tended to approach contemporary Greek life with a certain amount of cynicism. Greece joined the European Community in 1981, and the country joined the mainstream of European culture, although in a peculiarly Greek way.

Lymberaki's *To Mystērio* (1976; The Rite), Margarita Karapanou's *Hē Kassandra kai ho lukos* (1977; *Cassandra and the Wolf*), Alexander Kotzias' *Antipoiēsis archēs* (1979; Usurped Authority), and Maro Douka's *He archaia skouria* (1979; Fools' Gold) reflect conditions under the Colonels, and *To kibotio* (1974; The Box) by Aris Alexandrou is an allegorical tale of the civil war made more bitter by recent experiences. All of these works deal with Greek history, but not as objective truth; the narrator's search for the exact truth in *To kibotio* is shown to be as empty as the box in which he supposedly carries the papers that record his mission. *He archaia skouria* admits that the heroine's reminiscences of the 1967 coup may be inaccurate and points out the inadequacy of language to describe reality.

Three novels of the 1980s, *Historia* (1982; *History of a Vendetta*) by Yoryis Yatromanalakis, *To hevdomo roucho* (1983; *The Seventh Garment*) by Evyenia Fakinou, and *Ho vios tou Ismail Ferik Pasha* (1989; *The Life of Ismail Ferik Pasha*) by Rea Galanaki, deal with the recent Greek past, recall the ancient Greek past, and try to come to terms with modern Western influences. Like other writers, notably Kazantzakis, they may be accused of taking on too much, of trying to do many things at once, but they achieve a fair amount of success. These novels also show similarities to more famous novels from other countries. *History of a Vendetta*, dealing with a blood feud in a Cretan village, and *The Seventh Garment*, the story of three generations of women amid the disasters of Greek history, are reminiscent of the cyclical chronicles of Gabriel García Márquez. Galanaki's novel, recounting the life of an Ottoman commander who was born a Cretan Christian, has been compared with the work of Jorge Luis Borges. This novel encapsulates many of the ambiguities of Greek history but is perhaps the first to recognize that Greece had an Ottoman as well as a Hellenic past.

The Greek novel has a rich past and a promising future. There have been times when its complex history has threatened to overwhelm it, and it is difficult to sum up its history except in a desperate rash of proper names, whereas other Balkan nationalities are less richly endowed and have suffered more from Turkish oppression. Nevertheless, the Greek novel is not all that different from novels in other southern Balkan countries. A poetic emphasis on the eternal and the transcendent, in keeping with the influence of Orthodox Christianity, lifts the reader away from the harsh world of reality. A bitter environment of hot summers and cold winters, rural poverty and urban squalor, is not ignored, but the past is used to bring the present into perspective. Heroism going back as far as Homer and humor going back as far as Herodotus make Balkan novels worth studying.

TOM WINNIFRITH

See also Nikos Kazantzakis; Turkish Novel

Further Reading

Beaton, Roderick, *An Introduction to Modern Greek Literature,* Oxford: Clarendon Press, and New York: Oxford University Press, 1994

Bien, Peter, *Nikos Kazantzakis: Novelist,* Bristol: Bristol Classical Press, 1989

Clogg, Richard, *A Concise History of Greece,* Cambridge and New York: Cambridge University Press, 1992

Crampton, Richard J., *A Short History of Modern Bulgaria,* Cambridge and New York: Cambridge University Press, 1987

Elsie, Robert, *History of Albanian Literature,* New York: Columbia University Press, 1995

Jelavich, Barbara, *History of the Balkans,* Cambridge and New York: Cambridge University Press, 1983

MacDermott, Mercia, *A History of Bulgaria, 1393–1885,* London: Allen and Unwin, and New York: Praeger, 1962

Manning, Clarence Augustus, and Roman Smal-Stocki, *The History of Modern Bulgarian Literature,* New York: Bookman, 1960

Moser, Charles A., *A History of Bulgarian Literature, 1865–1944,* The Hague: Mouton, 1972

Naughton, J.D., editor, *Traveller's Literary Companion to Eastern and Central Europe,* Brighton: In Print, 1995

Polites, Linos, *A History of Modern Greek Literature,* Oxford: Clarendon Press, 1973

Vickers, Miranda, *The Albanians: A Modern History,* London and New York: Tauris, 1995

West, Rebecca, *Black Lamb and Grey Falcon: A Journey through Yugoslavia,* London: Macmillan, and New York: Viking, 1941

Winnifrith, Tom, *Shattered Eagles, Balkan Fragments,* London: Duckworth, 1995

Space

Spatial Metaphors and Narrative, the Novel's Representation of Space, and the Space of the Book

Theoretical discussions of space in relation to the novel or to narrative in general often begin by opposing space and time, an opposition that inevitably leads to claims for the greater relevance of one or the other coordinate. For example, Joseph Frank's frequently cited concept of "spatial form" in literature assesses texts in terms of their oscillation between the "two poles" of space and time and defines modernist writers as "intend[ing] the reader to apprehend their work spatially, in a moment of time, rather than as a sequence" (see Frank, 1963). For Frank and his followers, "spatial form" is "the technique by which novelists subvert the chronological sequence inherent in narrative," thus drawing attention to the way that "units of narrative" are "juxtaposed in space, not unrolling in time" (see Smitten and Daghistany, 1981). In this definition, space has no positive characteristics but becomes manifest only as, and after, the negation of time. Not surprisingly, then, the notion of spatial form does little to specify what space means. It also overlooks how modernist techniques undermine space along with time, and conflates two very different spaces, the space of the narrative (where chronology gets subverted) and the space of the printed book (where textual units are juxtaposed).

By contrast, the more or less exclusive focus on space in this entry is not a claim for its autonomy or primacy. A more fruitful approach is expressed in Mikhail Bakhtin's concept of the chronotope, a portmanteau word that expresses "the intrinsic connectedness of temporal and spatial relationships . . . in literature" (see Bakhtin, 1981). Certain texts—for example, Dante's *Commedia* (written 1307–21; *The Divine Comedy*) or Georges Perec's *La Vie mode d'emploi* (1978; *Life, a User's Manual*)—do try to suppress time by presenting, in cross-section, simultaneous events that the narrator claims to grasp in a single moment. However, even those texts take time to be read and include narratives that refer both back and forward in time.

An article on space owes its readers a map of what follows. Our trajectory will follow that of the novel's historical development toward increasingly particular and concrete notions of space. The first section discusses spatial metaphors in narrative and novel theory, focusing on how theorists use figures of space to make abstract notions concrete. The second section addresses the representation of space in the novel, particularly in relation to realism. The final section deals with the novel as a book, as a physical object in space whose materiality authors and readers can either efface or highlight.

Spatial Metaphors and Narrative

So ingrained and naturalized are certain spatial terms as metaphors for narrative processes that their status as metaphors has become invisible. When we speak of a text's point of view, its linear or circular structure, its narrative gaps, parallels, and digressions, its background, foreground, and frames, or even the narrator's relative distance from or proximity to narrative events, we seem to be describing attributes of the text. In fact, we are inventing spatial relations that do not actually exist in it. When we speak of a gap in the text, for example, we do not refer to a literal hole in the page, nor even, in many cases, to an expanse of blank space between words or lines. Rather, we use gap as a metaphor, to express the difference between the degree of change in narrative space and time (from Russia to Rome) relative to the degree of change in the printed text (from one sentence to another).

Narrative theory uses spatial metaphors to make abstract structures more conceptually concrete, but their metaphorical nature is obscured by the greater proximity between textual relations and spatial relations than is usual for the terms of a metaphor. Both spatial relations and textual relations are relatively abstract; spatial metaphors make textual relations more concrete only because geometry and technologies of vision have familiarized us with visual symbols of abstract spatial concepts. But in less familiar uses, the metaphor becomes unmistakable. For example, Joseph Kestner argues that the "spatiality" of the novel is heightened in depictions of "egoism, loneliness, and monomania" because those qualities represent isolated "points" in the "plane" of society (see Kestner, 1978). His terms do not seem at all descriptive, because neither conventionally nor logically do we easily translate feelings into shapes. Jurii Lotman describes this revalorization as a common literary process by which "the spatial order of the world . . . becomes an organizing element around which its non-spatial features are also constructed," so that, for example, high and low signify good and bad and near and far signify self and other (see Lotman, 1977).

The metaphoricity of spatial terms in narrative theory should serve as a caution against taking them literally, but not as sign of their falsehood or sterility. Writers and critics often make productive use of metaphors of space and architecture (understood as the organization of space) to represent mimesis and narration. Philippe Hamon has noted that architecture and literature frequently involve each other as metalanguages, and accounts for this mutual usefulness in terms of analogies between them: each has an outside and inside, each works to classify and organize, each gives form to space and time (see Hamon, 1992). At the same time, each makes up for an apparent lack in the other: architectural metaphors for writing lend to it a materiality that it strives for but is often perceived as lacking, particularly relative to speech. Metaphors of writing in architectural theory and actual inscriptions on buildings can anchor the often elusive significance of architectural objects, endowing them with legible meanings.

In her study of *Literary Architecture,* Ellen Eve Frank terms the process of formulating an architectural metalanguage for literature "ut architectura poesis," in which "writers respect and imitate in their literary style principles of architectural construction or structure" (see Frank, 1979). She shows that Walter Pater, Gerard Manley Hopkins, Henry James, and Marcel Proust all used spatial metaphors to concretize consciousness and memory, the acts of perceiving and recording, and the literary artifact itself. James described consciousness in terms of mass and extension, as large and deep. Proust called *À la recherche du temps perdu* (1913–27; translated as *Remembrance of Things Past* and also as *In Search of Lost Time*) a cathedral. Honoré de Balzac presented himself as both architect and archeologist, and *La Comédie humaine* (1842–48; *The Human Comedy*) as a gallery of rooms and a monument. Émile Zola equated representing the world with looking out a window.

Critics often cast narration itself—the process of recounting a sequence of events—in terms of the spatio-temporal complex of the journey. Indeed, many argue that journeys feature so frequently as themes in novels because they mimic the acts of narration (moving from one event to the next) and of reading (moving from the space surrounding the reader's body to the space represented by the text). That convergence of acts of narration with the actions narrated may also be associated with the novel's consistent attention to the representation of space.

The Novel's Representation of Space

Bakhtin argues that the history of the novel is the history of the chronotope, that is, the history of the novel's representation of time and space. While all novels develop chronotopes, different subgenres have different chronotopes, which function as generic markers. The chronotope gives substance to historically variable ways of experiencing and perceiving space and time, and changes in chronotope also indicate changing relationships between the literary work and historical reality, particularly with respect to such factors as subjectivity, social relations, and knowledge production.

Representations of space are related to the way novels designate place. Lennard Davis explains that place in novels (and other literary works) can be actual, fictitious, or renamed. For example, Paris in Honoré de Balzac's novels is actual because we presume that the city Balzac calls Paris refers to the real city called Paris. George Eliot's Middlemarch is fictitious because we deduce that she invented it and that, while it may stand generally for a type of place at a particular time, it does not correspond to a specific, existing locale. Elizabeth Gaskell's Milton or F. Scott Fitzgerald's West and East Egg are renamed places that we translate, if we have the requisite knowledge, into the real places to which their descriptions correspond (see Davis, 1987). In a different typology, Earl Miner describes three types of fictional place: common, proper, and improper. Common place refers to an unnamed, unidentified location. Proper place, corresponding to Davis' actual place, is named and taken to exist. Improper place is taken not to exist and is often a metaphorical place such as the underworld or heaven (see Miner, 1990).

Most of Miner's examples come from early modern literature (Dante, Shakespeare, Spenser), while all of Davis' come from 19th- and 20th-century literature. The trajectory from Miner's schema to Davis' is the trajectory of the novel, moving from relatively abstract and undifferentiated space in the early Greek novel to increasingly particularized space in the realistic novels of the 18th and 19th centuries, followed by self-conscious reactions against or intensifications of particularization in 20th-century modernism.

Bakhtin begins "Forms of Time and Chronotope in the Novel" with a discussion of the Greek romances written between the second and sixth centuries A.D. In the contingent world of adventure romances, he argues, small increments of time can have enormous significance in relation to space: one minute sooner or later in the right or wrong place can bring fortune or misfortune to the hero or heroine. Because chance meetings and encounters are crucial in the romance, the road predominates as a site of contact. The characters' actions oscillate between extreme movement across space—pursuit, abduction—and the stasis of captivity. Although space is important to the romance, Bakhtin notes that for "adventure time to work, one must have an *abstract* expanse of space," since the protagonists would be less subject to the workings of chance if they were able to map and classify space. In addition to anatomizing the space of romance, Bakhtin demonstrates that time in the romance is reversible, while spaces are generally interchangeable. Neither definite nor familiar, space in the romance is not typical of any region or historical moment. Moreover, small units of space are not put into relation with larger ones.

Bakhtin identifies an increase in "realism" in two Roman adventure novels of everyday life, Petronius' *Satyricon* and Apuleius' *The Golden Ass*. Those works represent time as irreversible and linked to the development of characters who are discrete, particular, and evolving. Similarly, space is both more concrete and more integrally fused to character. Bakhtin also remarks on the "exclusively personal and private" nature of the everyday life that Roman novels depict. "This life takes place between four walls and for only two pairs of eyes," that is, in a closed space. The protagonist, however, violates that privacy by witnessing secret events, recounting them to characters in the narrative, and conveying them to readers outside the narrative. The realist protagonist becomes an observer, spy, and eavesdropper, and a contradiction develops between "the public nature of the literary form and the private nature of its content."

Literary historians tend to downplay the early modern period's significance for the novel's representation of space and to emphasize the innovations of the 18th-century novel. The present entry will proceed accordingly—not as a sign of agreement with the judgment just summarized, but to remark on the need for further research on the early modern novel. The most influential discussion of the 18th-century novel's representation of space remains Ian Watt's *The Rise of the Novel* (1957). Watt defines the novel in opposition to the romance, as opposed to Bakhtin, who sees the romance as a type of novel. He discusses the particularization of characters, time, and space in the context of 18th-century philosophy, particularly the immediate and individual apprehension of reality espoused by Descartes and Locke. The novel's plot, in Watt's argument, "had to be acted out by particular people in particular circumstances, rather than, as had been common in the past, by general human types against a background primarily determined by the appropriate literary convention."

In *Resisting Novels,* Lennard Davis expands on Watt's notion of the particularization of space. According to Davis, the novel not only describes space in detail but also saturates space with a protagonist's purpose and intention. While Watt accounts for the rise of formal realism in terms of philosophical developments and changes in the reading public, Davis provides what he calls an ideological account that links novelistic descriptions of space to debates about property ownership, to the rhetorical conventions of travel narratives, and to imperial acts of staking territorial claims. Davis' reading of Daniel Defoe's *Robinson Crusoe* (1719) thus equates Crusoe's description of territory with his appropriation of it, a point developed by other recent studies of imperialist discourse. At the same time, however, the *failure* to specify and describe the space of the colonies also became a novelistic strategy for differentiating between England and "other" spaces, as Edward Said has shown in his reading of Jane Austen's *Mansfield Park* (1814) and as Gayatri Spivak has shown in her readings of Charlotte Brontë's *Jane Eyre* (1847) and Jean Rhys' *Wide Sargasso Sea* (1966).

Critical texts such as Erich Auerbach's *Mimesis* (1953) have trained us to view the 19th-century novel as the apotheosis of detailed representations of everyday spaces. Certainly, novels by Balzac, Zola, Charles Dickens, and Elizabeth Gaskell feature extended descriptions of city streets, the exteriors and interiors of houses, the furniture of rooms, and the clothing of inhabitants.

This view, however, obscures the considerable variety in 19th-century novelistic treatments of space. For example, the sentimental and idealist fiction that dominated early 19th-century French literature deliberately represents space in vague terms. A variety of avowed realists, including Anthony Trollope, George Eliot, and Henry James, often eschewed exhaustive narratorial inventories of place and space.

The dominance of realistic representations of space and place in 19th-century literature should be recast, then, not as an attribute of every novel of the period, but rather as a cultural consensus about how to perceive and describe space. Indeed, 19th-century realists could choose not to describe space in detail or to forgo a bird's-eye view of a setting precisely because the increased scope of discourses like statistical studies, illustrated newspapers, and cartography made it easy for most readers to supply those details and views unprompted. Readers did not need to be told that a city was divided into neighborhoods, streets, and buildings to map urban space into those units. Even in the absence of explicit detail, they might imagine the particular stones of a house, the definite smells pervading a street, and the exact fabric in which a style of chair would be upholstered. Readers ascribe incremental construction, sensual immediacy, material specificity, and commodified aesthetic qualities to literary worlds independently of what any individual literary text describes. Thus, although critics have often attributed the verisimilitude of realism to the ways that its descriptions attempt to replicate a real, substantial world, it would be more accurate to say that realist novels seem real because their narrators invoke culturally current frameworks for perceiving space and time.

As a result of the particularity accorded to space in the 19th-century novel, specific types of places became crucial to types of plot. The country, the city, and the suburbs; the provinces and the capital; picturesque ruins and cottages; Gothic castles; slums; sewers; the salon; the family mansion; the apartment building: all became significant spatial categories for the 19th-century novel. The particularity accorded to space also enabled writers to turn places into symbols for increasingly individualized characters and to represent space as the external expression of internal emotions, wishes, and temperaments. Space became subjectivity. Dickens frequently personified buildings and streets. In *Jane Eyre,* the red room and the attic articulate the heroine's fears, anger, and desires; the elaborate rooms in Joris-Karl Huysmans' *À rebours* (1884; *Against Nature*) or Oscar Wilde's *The Picture of Dorian Gray* (1891) enact the refined, decadent, aesthetic sensibilities of the characters who design them.

The realistic cataloguing of space continues to characterize many 20th-century novels, but in its modernist and postmodernist incarnations, the 20th-century novel has also registered new modes of perceiving and construing space by conducting literary experiments in simultaneity, juxtaposition, panorama, collage, and the blurring of space and time. Those experiments in the narrative representation of space also often play with the physical space of the book.

The Space of the Book

Reading trains us to ignore many aspects of the space of the book. We learn not to stop at the end of a line of prose, not to read across facing pages, not to assign significance to the blank spaces that demarcate text on the page. At the same time, other aspects of the book's spatial and material existence do have salience for us. We assign meaning to the clusters of type we call paragraphs and chapters. We recognize that quotation marks and dashes set dialogue apart from narration. We know that typographical shifts to boldface or italics draw our attention to words and sentences. We understand that borders around words and changes in typeface simulate the presence of another text, such as a business card, a letter, or a newspaper article, within the one we read. And the running titles at the top of every page common in 19th-century serial novels provide a kind of narrative gloss.

Occasionally, authors deliberately accentuate the material status of the book, and in so doing, they construct the book as a space with a particular form. Romantic writers in France and England, for example, constructed the space of the book in terms of a contrast between its inside (the text) and outside (the cover). In order to draw attention to the increasing commercialization of literature, they contrasted elaborate covers, whose engraved, florid letters and illustrations resembled advertisements, to the simple typefaces of the actual texts. Drawing on the book's superior capacities for cross-referencing relative to scrolls or magnetic tapes, Julio Cortázar's *Rayuela* (1963; *Hopscotch*) reshapes both narrative and the book in the image of its eponymous game, encouraging the reader to read the chapters in any order, and highlighting the physical ease with which the reader of a book can skip from page to page.

Finally, one of the best recent examples of a work that encourages the reader to explore the book's actual arrangement of space also significantly revises 19th-century representations of space. Georges Perec's *Life, a User's Manual* provides an exhaustive description of a Parisian apartment building, a major topos in 19th-century French realist fiction. While the classic realist novel tended to subsume description within narration, Perec's novel subordinates narration to description. Each chapter takes as its topic a room in the apartment building and begins with an inventory of objects and decor; human characters enter the scene only as part of the room's tableau, and narratives become digressions from descriptions. A series of tables and indices (lists of stories told, a timeline, a map of the building) highlight the reader's ability to read the text in alternative orders. Perec thus aligns the reader's mobility within the space of the book with the narrator's mobility through the space he represents, undermining the illusion, so particularly created by realism, of the novel's spatial dimensions.

SHARON MARCUS

See also City and the Novel; Description; Framing and Embedding; Mimesis; Narratology; Plot; Realism; Time in the Novel

Further Reading

Auerbach, Erich, *Mimesis: Dargestellte Wirklichkeit in der abendländischen Literatur,* Bern: Francke, 1946; as *Mimesis: The Representation of Reality in Western Literature,* Princeton, New Jersey: Princeton University Press, 1953

Bachelard, Gaston, *La Poétique de l'espace,* Paris: Presses Universitaires de France, 1957; as *The Poetics of Space,* New York: Orion Press, 1964

Bakhtin, M.M., "Forms of Time and of the Chronotope in the Novel," in *The Dialogic Imagination: Four Essays,* translated by Caryl Emerson and Michael Holquist, edited by Holquist, Austin: University of Texas Press, 1981

Butor, Michel, "The Space of the Novel" and "The Book as Object," in *Inventory: Essays,* New York: Simon and Schuster, 1968; London: Cape, 1970

Cohen, Margaret, *Why Were There No French Women Realists?* Princeton, New Jersey: Princeton University Press, 1998

Davis, Lennard J., *Resisting Novels: Ideology and Fiction,* London and New York: Methuen, 1987

Frank, Ellen Eve, *Literary Architecture: Essays Toward a Tradition,* Berkeley: University of California Press, 1979

Frank, Joseph, "Spatial Form in Modern Literature," in *The Widening Gyre: Crisis and Mastery in Modern Literature,* New Brunswick, New Jersey: Rutgers University Press, 1963

Hamon, Philippe, *Expositions: Littérature et architecture au XIX siècle,* Paris: Corti, 1989; as *Expositions: Literature and Architecture in Nineteenth-Century France,* Berkeley: University of California Press, 1992

Kestner, Joseph, *The Spatiality of the Novel,* Detroit, Michigan: Wayne State University Press, 1978

Laufer, Roger, "L'espace graphique du livre au XIXe siècle," *Romantisme* 43 (1984)

Lotman, Jurij, *Struktura Khudozhestvennogo teksta,* Moscow: Iskusstvo, 1970; as *The Structure of the Artistic Text,* Ann Arbor: Department of Slavic Languages and Literature, University of Michigan, 1977

Marcus, Sharon, *Apartment Stories: The City and the Home in Nineteenth-Century Paris and London,* Berkeley: University of California Press, 1998

Miner, Earl, "Common, Proper, and Improper Place," in *Proceedings of the XIIth Congress of the International Comparative Literature Association,* volume 3, Munich: Iudicium Verlag, 1990

Poulet, Georges, *L'Espace Proustien,* Paris: Gallimard, 1963; as *Proustian Space,* Baltimore: Johns Hopkins University Press, 1977

Pratt, Mary Louise, *Imperial Eyes: Travel Writing and Transculturation,* London and New York: Routledge, 1992

Said, Edward, *Culture and Imperialism,* New York: Knopf, and London: Chatto and Windus, 1993

Smitten, Jeffrey, and Ann Daghistany, editors, *Spatial Form in Narrative,* Ithaca, New York: Cornell University Press, 1981

Spivak, Gayatri Chakravorty, "Three Women's Texts and a Critique of Imperialism," *Critical Inquiry* 12:1 (Autumn 1985)

Watt, Ian, *The Rise of the Novel: Studies in Defoe, Richardson, and Fielding,* Berkeley: University of California Press, and London: Chatto and Windus, 1957

Spanish Novel

The origins of the Spanish novel may be traced back to a variety of medieval narrative forms. The rollicking verse chronicles of the 12th and 13th centuries, including the *Libro de Aleixandre* (1178–1250; Book of Alexander) and the *Libro de Apolonio* (1223; Book of Apollonius), drew on history, legend, and Latin epic to patch together narratives that feature improbable coincidences, fortuitous encounters, shipwrecks, kidnappings, disguises and mistaken identities, misdiagnosed deaths, and wondrous resuscitations. The structure of the typical verse chronicle plot, ending inevitably in the reward of virtue and the punishment of vice, may be recognized in the work of later writers from Lope de Vega and Miguel de Cervantes in the 16th century to Pérez de Ayala in the 20th.

The Spanish Middle Ages also saw the development of many shorter narrative forms in verse, including the Castilian translation of an Arabic collection of apologues, *Calila e Digna* (c. 1261), derived from the Hindu *Panchatantra,* and the *Libro de los engaños y los asayamientos de las mujeres* (c. 1253; Book of Deceits and Women's Wiles). Achieving enormous popularity, the *Libro de los engaños* consists of 23 tales inserted into a frame narrative. The first Spanish prose narrative, the *Libro de Patronio o el Conde Lucanor* (1330–35) by Juan Manuel, also adopts a framing device to justify the fables and didactic tales it brings together.

The verse *Libro de buen amor* (1389; The Book of the Archpriest of Hita), by Juan Ruiz, Archpriest of Hita, is the fictional autobiography of a repudiated lover and has a wealth of interpolated tales, exempla, fables, and allegories, as well as satiric, lyric, and religious passages. Interpolated tales remained characteristic of Spanish narrative for a long time, as witness the interpolated tales in Cervantes' *Don Quixote.* However, Ruiz' narrative is of interest in the history of the novel principally for the development of the protagonist's character.

Hagiography, pseudobiographical works, dynastic chronicles, and novels of chivalry, which resembled and influenced one another, form another set of novelistic antecedents. Laying a claim to historical fidelity, each of these forms incorporated myth, folklore, and legend. The most immediate forerunners of the modern novel are the chivalric novels, particularly those of the Amadís and Palmerín cycles, which enjoyed a continuing popularity from the 14th through the 16th centuries. Their flagrant disregard for verisimilitude is balanced by careful plot construction and exceptional characterization, particularly in the 16th-century Palmerín novels. Since the bourgeoisie emerged in Spain in the 16th century, critics consider it logical that the novel comes of age at that time, which also saw the beginnings of a national publishing industry.

Many critics go further back and situate the beginnings of the modern European novel in the 15th-century Catalan courtly romances, which in turn derive from the poetry of the Provençal troubadours. Such romances as *Blanquerna, L'espill, Tirant lo Blanc,* and *Curial y Guelfa* show the earliest beginnings of realism: incredible elements are rare, the main characters are not all of noble birth, and historical episodes are anchored in the experience of the characters. Although the Catalan romances exerted a decided influence on the history of the Spanish novel, Catalan literature itself died a premature death with the proclamation of Castilian as the official language in 1492.

Another significant influence on the Spanish novel is Alfonso Martínez de Toledo's *Arcipreste de Talavera: Reprobación del amor mundano* (1438; Little Sermons on Sin), known popularly as *Corbacho* for its reminiscences of Boccaccio. The book rebukes "insane love," listing both the physical and spiritual ills of lust and the evidence of the evil nature of women. Its realistic dialogue and frequent use of colloquialism made it an important example in the development of the novel and theatre. *La Celestina* by Fernando de Rojas in particular shows its influence.

Spanish sentimental romances of the late 15th century show strong affinities to the modern novel. Structurally sophisticated, they replace soliloquies with abundant realistic dialogue and are characterized by penetrating psychological analysis. Diego de San Pedro's *Tractado de amores de Arnalte y Lucinda* (1491; Treatise of the Loves of Arnalte and Lucinda), a sentimental exaltation of women in epistolary form, and his *Cárcel del Amor* (1492; Prison of Love) incorporate chivalric elements as well as poetry from the medieval songbooks and motifs from Italianate narratives. A lyric, intimate tone and developing erotic psychology are combined with Platonic ideals and mysticism. The "Cruel Lady" of courtly poetry becomes pious or merciful in sentimental novels, while fantastic episodes are replaced by the hero's efforts to become the perfect lover, loyal to the death. The sentimental romances distinguish themselves from the modern novel in their exotic settings, stylized geography, and idealized, stereotyped characters. While the early sentimental romances are characterized by a highly artificial style, Diego de San Pedro adopted Renaissance rhetorical norms, moving away from stylistic ornamentation.

Critics have been puzzled by *La Celestina*'s relationship to the sentimental romances. Attributed to Fernando de Rojas, *La Celestina* is a pseudo-theatrical work consisting almost exclusively of dialogue arranged into 21 acts (in its best known version). The aged bawd Celestina arranges a love affair between two young members of the nobility, who, following their brief indulgence, meet with a violent death. Critical opinion is divided as to whether *La Celestina* belongs to the tradition of sentimental romances or parodies them. Although it may be difficult to gauge whether Rojas is serious, his work undeniably represents a major advance toward realism in its serious treatment of the humbler characters.

The Spanish Golden Age, generally dated from 1545 to 1681, saw a tremendous flowering of the arts. Narrative art underwent rapid development and made a significant contribution to the European novel, with the publication of *Lazarillo de Tormes* (1554) and the novels of Cervantes, Francisco de Quevedo, Lope de Vega, and Baltasar Gracián. Some of the impetus for these achievements came from the 16th-century vogue for the Italian *novella,* as exemplified particularly by Boccaccio. The collections that appeared in mid-century and later were highly derivative of the Italian examples, but by the beginning of the 17th century original work began to appear. Chief among these is Cervantes' *Novelas ejemplares* (1613; Exemplary Novels), which contains several realistic tales that are still highly readable and entertaining today. Spain's first woman novelist, María de Zayas, also worked in this shorter genre and is remembered primarily for her *Novelas amorosas y ejemplares* (1637; *The Enchantment of Love: Amorous and Exemplary Novels*) and *Desengaños amorosos* (1647; *Love's Disillusionments*). Both employ the structure of Boccaccio's *Decameron* (written 1349–51): a group of men and women tell each other stories on the themes of love and disillusionment. Zayas' two collections feature the same storytellers, which allows for some character development. The most important character, Lisis, proffers a feminist defense of education for women.

Pastoral romances displaced chivalric romances as Spain's most popular fictional form in the mid-16th century. The most important of these are Cervantes' *La Galatea* (1585; *La Galatea*), Lope de Vega's *La Arcadia* (1598; *Arcadia*), and Jorge de Montemayor's *La Diana* (1559). However, their pervasive artificiality places them at the opposite end of the spectrum from the novel.

In fact, many critics view the picaresque as a reaction against the idealizing romances, chivalric, sentimental, or pastoral. The beautiful, young, noble, valiant, honorable, and virtuous hero of the romances is parodically inverted into the ugly, cowardly, cynical rogue (*pícaro*) of humble or infamous origin, who mocks love, virtue, and social convention. Picaresque settings are typically realistically portrayed environments, peopled with bawds and beggars, criminals, and indigent students. The picaresque is sometimes called the epic of hunger, and the *pícaro*, living by his wits, is ruled by his stomach instead of such luxuries as honor, love, or the chivalric code. Generally, the *pícaro* comes to a bad end and repents his amorality, but that does not invalidate the social criticism that forms a hallmark of the genre.

Not only its unflinching realism makes the picaresque important to the development of the Spanish (and indeed the European) novel, but also its use of first-person narrative. The anonymous *Lazarillo de Tormes* deploys the first-person narrative to maximum ironic effect, although critics disagree whether the irony is used by or against Lazarillo. The *Lazarillo*, after a gap of several decades, was followed by Mateo Alemán's *Guzmán de Alfarache* (1599; *The Rogue; or, The Life of Guzmán de Alfarache*) and *La vida del buscón llamado don Pablos* (1626; translated as *The Scavenger* and *The Swindler*) by Francisco de Quevedo. A satirist of enormous intellect, Quevedo had a keen eye for absurdity and corruption. His superb verbal inventiveness and wit are vehicles of a relentlessly pessimistic and grotesque worldview. Like other picaresque novels, however, Quevedo's *The Scavenger* is highly episodic, consisting of disparate scenes completely lacking psychological analysis or character development.

A variant of the picaresque features feminine protagonists who, instead of serving many masters, had many lovers, deceiving, swindling, and robbing them all. Francisco Delicado anonymously published the most erotic and lascivious of these, *Retrato de la lozana andaluza* (1528; *Portrait of Lozana: The Lusty Andalusian Woman*), employing a dialogue format and presenting a cast of 125 depraved characters. Documenting moral and social corruption in Renaissance Italy, Delicado glorifies obscenity, sensuality, and lasciviousness. *Portrait of Lozana* presents the only female protagonist until *La pícara Justina* (1605; *The Life of Justina, the Country Jilt*), which has been attributed to Francisco Lopez de Ubeda. The picaresque also

makes itself felt in Cervantes' *Don Quixote* (1605–15), which has several picaresque episodes, and in the *Exemplary Novels*. In the 17th century, however, the genre becomes a mere vehicle for social satire, as in *Vida del Escudero Marcos de Obregón* (1618; *The History of the Life of the Squire Marcos de Obregón*) by Vicente Espinel, and *El diablo cojuelo* (1641; *The Limping Devil*) by Luis Vélez de Guevara. Such satiric novels retained their popularity into the 18th century in Spain, reappearing intermittently thereafter, including a revival during the early Franco regime in the 20th century.

Don Quixote, often touted as the "first modern novel" and a remarkable achievement in many ways, is significant to the history of the novel primarily for its characterization. In earlier fiction, one knightly protagonist resembled another, and the *pícaros*, although more individualized, do not exhibit any kind of fundamental moral or psychological change. *Don Quixote*'s major characters, however, undergo continuing change throughout their adventures, resembling each other more and more: Sancho waxes "quixotic," idealistic, and impractical, while the hero becomes more realistic, finally renouncing his existence as a wandering knight. Cervantes' masterpiece, a compendium of earlier narrative forms, contains several interpolated novellas in the pastoral, picaresque, sentimental, and Italianate forms. No simple parody, *Don Quixote* also contains a chivalric novella. Prototypical metafictional elements include the author's self-criticism, the characters' extensive, self-conscious role-playing, their manipulation of other characters, and the characters' awareness of their fictionality. The modern novel has been pervasively influenced by this paradigmatic text to an unparalleled extent: numerous great characters have been created imitating Cervantes' knight-errant, and the basic premise of a protagonist who rejects reality in favor of a fictional world has been reworked by authors throughout succeeding centuries.

In *Don Quixote*, one character concludes that epics can be written in prose as well as in verse, and some critics consider Cervantes' Christian allegory *Los trabajos de Persiles y Sigismunda* (1617; *The Trials of Persiles and Sigismunda*) his prose epic. Its acknowledged model is the Renaissance translation of Heliodorus' *An Ethiopian Story*. *Persiles* incorporates Byzantine conventions—disguise, extended journeys and pilgrimages, prolonged separations, marvelous and perilous adventures, interpolated anecdotes and tales, physical and spiritual trials, and a final reunion following the revelation of true identities. *Persiles* enjoyed great popularity in the 17th century, with translations into all major European languages. Although neglected after the 18th century, some contemporary critics proclaim it Cervantes' supreme achievement.

Cervantes inspired no immediate followers or imitators. Lope de Vega, roughly a contemporary, adopted different fictional models. For instance, *La Dorotea* (1632)—probably Lope's best fictional creation—exudes disillusionment, ending with the triumph of materialism and corruption. Like *La Celestina*, it combines real with fictional characters and an exalted vision of love with picaresque elements.

The most significant 17th-century novel following Cervantes' death is the three-part allegorical novel entitled *El Criticón* (1651, 1653, 1657; *The Critick*) by Baltasar Gracián. His prose is the culmination of the baroque literary style termed *conceptismo*, a complex, intentionally difficult fashion analogous to British euphuism or French *préciosité*. Gracián emphasizes subtlety, complexity, and novelty of metaphor, employing Latinate allusions, lexicon, and syntax, conceits, wordplay, paradox, antithesis, parallelisms, and comparisons. The primary contemporary theorist of baroque aesthetics, Gracián defines the poetics of *conceptismo*. *The Critick*'s protagonists, Critilo and Andrenio, a father and his son, undertake a pilgrimage from the isle of St. Helena across 17th-century Spain and Europe to Rome in search of Felisenda, their wife and mother, traversing both real and allegorical places. This voyage is a "journey of life" from youth to old age and a simultaneous quest for the afterlife and earthly happiness. It combines Byzantine and picaresque elements, although the primary genre model is the epic. The title, inspired by John Barclay's *Satyricon* (1603), suggests a penetrating critique of baroque society, evoking the individual's precarious situation. The elder protagonist, Critilo, personifies critical judgment, reason, and experience, while Andrenio personifies instinct, man in the "natural" state. Their metaphorical quest, somewhat in the manner of John Bunyan's *Pilgrim's Progress* (1678, 1684), pits them against challenges that raise philosophical questions and provoke moral reflection. The novel's three parts correspond to the stages of life: Springtime of Childhood, Autumn of Maturity, Winter of Old Age.

Spanish literature's relative decline after the Golden Age affected all genres. Most literary historians mention only two 18th-century novels, one of which is now deemed a memoir, the *Vida* (1752; Life) of Diego de Torres Villarroel, author of poetry, prose, dramas, essays, and almanacs and prognostications. Although it was once classified as a picaresque novel, the *Vida* differs markedly from that genre in the character of the narrator. No social outcast, but a successful member of the bourgeoisie, he lives quietly as a somewhat unconventional university professor. The initial misclassification was motivated by the fact that Spanish autobiographies were relatively uncommon. Not until two centuries later did critics understand the nature of Torres Villarroel's work, realizing that it marks the appearance of the bourgeoisie as a social conscience, anticipating the epoch of realism.

The only 18th-century novel of any consequence, then, is José Francisco de Isla's *Historia del famoso predicador Fray Gerundio de Campazas, alias Zotes* (1758; *The History of the Famous Preacher, Friar Gerund de Campazas, Otherwise Gerund Zotes*), a parody of the florid pulpit oratory of the day. It was banned by the Inquisition. Blending picaresque and Cervantean models, Isla satirizes histrionics, ridiculing inaccurate biblical quotation, ignorance of sources, and the use of overly erudite, artificial, flowery rhetoric that values brilliance of discourse above spiritual content. He advocates clarity, simplicity, and order. *Friar Gerund*'s realistic descriptions of regional customs and rustic life, its portrait of the village of Campazas (based on direct observation), and its use of dialectical speech prefigure the 19th-century regional novel.

Lesser writers of the 18th century include José Cadalso y Vásquez, a well-educated noble, and Pedro Montengón. Neoclassical influences, the Enlightenment, and antecedents of romanticism converge in Cadalso. *Cartas marruecas* (completed 1774, published 1793; Moroccan Letters), his best-known work, comprises 90 fictional letters that, like the epistolary works of Montesquieu and Oliver Goldsmith, satirize national customs and the country's lagging industrialization, an archaic educational system, and stagnant social welfare. Cadalso's *Noches lúgubres* (completed 1774, published 1798; Lugubrious Nights), once considered autobiographical, reflects a tragic emotional turbulence anticipating romanticism. Structured in three "nights," the work employs a dialogue format. Tediato, despairing over lost love, seeks help from the gravedigger Lorenzo in disinterring his lover's body. Vaguely allegorical figures appear, including a Jailer, a Justice, and a Child. Romantic elements include the setting (the cemetery), tone, characters, and themes, Tediato's cosmic grief, and dramatic atmospheric conditions.

Pedro Montengón wrote five novels, two being philosophical or pedagogical in the mold of Jean-Jacques Rousseau's *Émile* (1762; Emile); two others, *El Atenor* (1788) and *El Rodrigo* (1793), are prose epics, while the fifth, *Mirtilo* (1795), is a pastoral novel in prose and verse. Montengón's best known novel is *Eusebio* (1786–88), a sentimental, moralizing, didactic work that anticipates romanticism. Montengón's pedagogical doctrines resemble Rousseau's, advocating progressive education in a natural environment, and he exchanges traditional religious dogma for Stoic philosophy and the ethics of Seneca. Montengón also wrote about feminine education in *Eudoxia, hija de Belisario* (1793; Eudoxia, Daughter of Belisario), which emphasizes domestic occupations and the teaching of an Enlightenment moral philosophy.

The most prestigious prose of the period was not fiction but journalism, erudition, or descriptions of customs. Critic José I. Montesinos affirms that "after the middle of the 17th century, there is scarcely a Spanish novel worthy of the name." Nevertheless, novels appeared in considerable quantity and were avidly read by growing numbers of readers. Juan Ignacio Ferreras, in *Los orígenes de la novela decimonónica* (1973; Origins of the 19th-century Novel), indicates that during the 19th century some 200 novels appeared in Spain and nearly 600 translations were marketed. Probably the greatest influence on Spain's romantic novel was the work of Sir Walter Scott, widely translated from 1825 onward. Once romanticism took hold in Spain, women writers began to appear and women readers multiplied. Novels were serialized in newspapers and distributed to homes as weekly pamphlets by subscription. Hacks prospered, the most prolific being Manuel Fernández y González, followed by Ayguals de Izco, Julio Nombela, and Enrique Pérez Estrich. Improvisation, frequent changes of direction, unpolished prose, and the practice of ending each episode with a cliffhanger are common characteristics of these serialized fictions. The Gothic subgenre exalted irrationality, death, mystery, and dark forces, featuring macabre or gory scenes. Agustín Pérez Zaragoza's *Galería fúnebre de historias trágicas, espectros y sombras ensangrentadas* (1831; Funereal Gallery of Tragic Tales, Spectres, and Bloody Ghosts), in 12 volumes containing 21 tales, is typical. The abundant historical and social novels were mostly mediocre. Spanish romanticism's "historical" fictions—set in imaginary, mythic, vaguely medieval worlds, populated by valiant knights and peerless ladies, governed by chivalric codes and uncontrolled passions—blended exalted religiosity with a heroic ambiance. The "history" represented was not the result of historical study but a patchwork of myth, legend, sentimentalism, and fantasy set against a historical background. Prolonged intrigues—complicated by witches, magicians, astrologers, and seers, by conspiracies, disguises, disappearances, and presumed deaths—almost invariably are revealed as mere mistakes. "Social" novels (motivated by socialist aspirations) combined aspects of the *roman à thèse* and sentimental novel, using contemporary settings.

The most significant achievement of romanticism is its development of *costumbrismo,* a minor genre dating from the late 17th century that consists of sketches of customs, manners, and types that celebrate particular locales and are usually laced with dialectical expressions and colloquialisms. Although *costumbrismo* sentimentally exaltated the picturesque, it nevertheless constitutes an advance in the direction of realism. Associated with political conservatism, *costumbrismo* idealized tradition, denounced progress, and promoted a backward-looking agenda. Cecilia Bohl de Faber, who wrote under the pseudonym of Fernán Caballero and dubbed her works "novels of customs," represents conservative *costumbrismo*. The prologue to her best known novel, *La Gaviota* (1849; *The Sea Gull*), advocates careful observation of scenery, settings, and customs as novelistic raw material, even though earlier she had written typical romantic fiction full of sentimentality and melodramatic elements. Bohl produced several volumes of *costumbrista* sketches in addition to some dozen overtly moralizing novels, including a *roman à thèse, Clemencia* (1852), which advocates the use of reason against savage, destructive passion and raw sexuality. Another prolific novelist, María del Pilar Sinüés, who is ignored by most literary historians, published some 100 extremely popular books of women's fiction and moralizing conduct works, advocating the cult of bourgeois domesticity and virtuous Christian motherhood, contributing to the discourse on Spanish womanhood and articulating the contradictions women writers faced.

Pedro Antonio de Alarcón began as a political revolutionary. He was a unionist organizer and the founder of a Republican newspaper. His early work expresses a very strong anticlericalism, as in *El final de Norma* (1855; *Norma's End*). Following his conversion, however, he became conservative, evolving an intense Catholicism, as in *El escándalo* (1875; *The Scandal*), *El niño de la bola* (1880; *The Infant with the Globe*), and *La pródiga* (1881; *The Prodigal Daughter*). Alarcón's fame rests primarily upon *El sombrero de tres picos* (1874; *The Three-Cornered Hat*), a tale of a foiled seduction that inspired operas, several dramas, and a ballet. Based upon a traditional tale featuring a stereotypical jealous older husband and flirtatious young wife, *The Three-Cornered Hat* is a work of Andalusian *costumbrismo,* full of humor and realistic local color.

Costumbrismo characterizes many regionalist novels, including the work of José María de Pereda, an ultraconservative rural aristocrat from the mountains of Santander, the setting of his best known novels. A paternalistic, rightist politician, he began as a journalist, publishing two well-received volumes of *costumbrista* sketches, *Escenas montañesas* (1864; Mountain Scenes) and *Tipos y paisajes* (1871; Types and Landscapes). His life and work reflect contemporary conflicts between liberals and conservatives, and the settings of his novels alternate between the traditionalist, Catholic northern countryside of his youth and the relatively progressive cities, which are portrayed as irreligious, degenerate places that undermine faith and tradition. Pereda's heavy-handed moralizing weakens such novels as *El buey suelto* (1878; The Bachelor), an ideological tract on the benefits of marriage. Slightly better is his political satire *Don Gonzalo González de la Gonzalera* (1879). *De tal palo, tal astilla* (1880; A Chip off the Old Block) is a melodramatic *roman à thèse* peopled with good Catholic traditionalists and wicked liberals. Its situations are contrived, and its characterization is wooden. By contrast, *El sabor de la tierruca* (1882; The Feel of the Good

Earth), a paean to Pereda's native soil, contains magnificent descriptions exalting his region's specificity and uniqueness. *Pedro Sánchez* (1883), a Bildungsroman narrated in the first person, compellingly portrays a provincial youth corrupted by politics, money, and sex in Madrid, while *Sotileza* (1885), set in the port of Santander, successfully combines individual and collective characters, plots, and setting, demonstrating Pereda's command of popular language. *Sotileza,* considered by many critics his masterpiece, also exemplifies Pereda's best efforts at characterization. His other fictional high point, *Peñas arriba* (1895; Up the Peaks), revives the *beatus ille* motif, idealizing simple, idyllic rural life and patriarchal hierarchy. Pereda's realism, unlike the critical variant pioneered by Gustave Flaubert, depends primarily upon the depiction of popular types, creative use of popular language, and intensely detailed descriptions.

Juan Valera, a Cordoban aristocrat, career diplomat, lifelong "Don Juan," and the most cosmopolitan of Spain's 19th-century novelists, came late to fiction, publishing his first five novels between 1874 and 1879 and three more between 1895 and 1899. An ironic, sceptical observer of human behavior, Valera excels in character delineation and psychological analysis. The author's unabashed delight in physical comforts, elegance, and gastronomy hints at the fundamental role of pleasure in his essentially hedonistic life and works. Politically liberal and socially conservative, Valera presents a surprising range of nontraditional, unstereotypical characters, defending the values of modernity while attempting to preserve the status quo. Officially Catholic but often voicing reservations concerning official dogma, Valera incurred the wrath of fanatics by portraying struggles between physical and spiritual love that resulted in spiritual crises, as in his two best known novels, *Pepita Jiménez* (1875; *Pepita Jiménez*) and *Doña Luz* (1879; *Doña Luz*). Both novels titillated readers with the portrayal of the sinful attraction between a beautiful woman and a priest and suggested that mysticism is the sublimation of erotic impulses. An avowed foe of naturalism, Valera professed a classicism that recommends the elimination of disagreeable aspects of reality. He depicted settings marked by *costumbrismo* with typical Andalusian foods, popular gatherings, and dress.

Spanish terminology for fiction fluctuated until the late 19th century. Novels were termed *leyenda* (legend) or *historia* (history) in the romantic era, while one eight-volume work was subtitled *cuento* (tale or short story). Not until the triumph of the realistic novel did *novela* definitively come to designate the novel in its modern connotation (and modern Spanish does not distinguish between the novel and the novella). The key date for Spain's realistic novel is 1868, when the liberal and bourgeois September Revolution initiated the short-lived First Republic. In fact, many Spanish literary histories use the label "Generation of 1868" for the realist novelists—Pereda, Valera, Jacinto Octavio Picón, Armando Palacio Valdés, and above all, Benito Pérez Galdós. Motivated by the bloodless coup and resulting social change, Spanish realists focus on bourgeois problems, defend bourgeois values, and observe the world from a bourgeois perspective—even while criticizing that class and its ideals. Unlike Pereda and Valera, Galdós and other realists concentrated on urban life, symbolized by Madrid. In their work, the city becomes a place of positive connotations, while the country is equaled with obscurantism and stagnation. Their protagonists are predominantly middle-class figures who oppose the parasitic aristocracy and combat the bureaucracy. Most Spanish realists avoid proletarian conflicts. Privileging economic issues, omniscient narrators proffer complex explanations of cause and effect, reading the hearts and minds of their middle-class characters.

Benito Pérez Galdós, often compared to Charles Dickens and Honoré de Balzac, is Spain's realist par excellence. He produced 31 novels and 46 "National Episodes," novelized re-creations of recent historical events, blending fiction and eyewitness sources. Galdós adapted several of his novels for the stage, writing others in dialogue form. The six novels of his first period (1871–76) treat ideological conflicts, religious disagreement and fanaticism, hypocrisy and intolerance. They include some of his best known titles: *Doña Perfecta* (1876; *Doña Perfecta*), *Gloria* (1877; *Gloria*), *Marianela* (1878; *Marianela*), and *La familia de León Roch* (1878; *Leon Roch*). In 1881 Galdós published *La desheredada* (*The Disinherited Lady*), the first of 24 volumes of "contemporary novels" that analyze the national propensity for self-delusion.

Zola's ideas reached Spain early in the 1880s, and Galdós went through a naturalist phase, which was followed by his best fiction: the two-volume masterpiece *Fortunata y Jacinta* (1886–87; *Fortunata and Jacinta*), *Miau* (1888; *Miau*), *Nazarín* (1895), and *Misericordia* (1897; *Compassion*). Together with lesser Spanish realists, Galdós exhibited a marked preference for third-person narration. Characteristic realist novels more or less faithfully reflect surrounding reality, using objective elements in extensive, dispassionate descriptions. Closed spaces that reveal details about their inhabitants are common, especially in urban novels. Main characters are psychologically "rounded," not flat types as in earlier fiction, but secondary figures tend to caricature.

The late 19th century was marked by a resurgence of Catalan literature. Father of the modern novel in Catalan is Narcís Oller (1846–1930), a realist in the tradition of Galdós, Balzac, and Dickens, whose works chronicle the effects of the Industrial Revolution and the decline of the aristocracy. Oller admired Zola, who wrote a prologue for the French translation of *La papallona* (1882; *The Butterfly*), calling Oller a literary brother. Nevertheless, only one short novel, *L'escanyapobres* (1882; *The Miser*), follows Zola's deterministic principles. Oller stands out for his depictions of the world of high finance, tracing the rise and fall of capitalist Gil Foix in *La febre d'or* (1890–92; *Gold Fever*), and the daily life of the Catalan bourgeoisie in *Pilar Prim* (1906).

Spain's best known, most controversial woman novelist of the 19th century, Emilia Pardo Bazán is credited with introducing naturalism to the Spanish reading public in her series of critical articles, *La cuestión palpitante* (1882–83; The Burning Question). She had a major impact on the Spanish literary world and provoked a bitter polemic with Valera, who considered her an apologist for naturalism. However, Pardo Bazán's prologue to *Un viaje de novios* (1881; *A Wedding Trip*) rejects naturalism's pessimism and crude subject matter. Later, she advocated a compromise between naturalist and idealist aesthetics. *La tribuna* (1883; The Woman Orator) is based on her observation of tobacco factory workers in La Coruña. It deals compassionately with the plight of the proletariat and may be considered naturalistic. Pardo Bazán's best known novel, *Los pazos de Ulloa* (1886; *The Son of the Bondswoman*), which traces the decadence of an aristocratic rural Galician dynasty, is marked by nat-

uralistic themes and contains scenes that were deemed too crude and violent "for a woman" at the time. Its sequel, *La madre naturaleza* (1887; Mother Nature) presents the incestuous love between a brother and sister unaware they are siblings, set against a lush, sensual countryside, arousing animal and sexual instincts. *Insolación* (1889; *Midsummer Madness*) likewise depicts the power of natural instincts to overcome social and moral taboos. On the other hand, *Una cristiana* (1890; *Secret of the Yew Tree; or, A Christian Woman*) and *La prueba* (1891; The Test) present moral, social, and religious duty as more powerful than natural inclinations. Pardo Bazán also examined domestic problems and women's position in Spanish society, as in *Doña Milagros* (1894) and *Memorias de un solterón* (1896; Memories of a Bachelor).

Caterina Albert, a Catalan novelist, poet and playwright who wrote under the pseudonym of Victor Catalá and resembles Oller, was a more committed naturalist. She conveys a dark, pessimistic vision of rural life in essentially naturalistic fiction and drama, peopled by primitive, brutal, alienated characters. *Solitud* (1908; *Solitude*), her best known novel, combines naturalistic descriptions and determinism with legendary and mythic elements in a narrative that is both beautiful and unsettling.

Also categorized as a naturalist, Leopoldo Alas, better known as "Clarín," was an Asturian critic, law professor, satirist, and educator whose novel *La Regenta* (1884; *La Regenta*) ranks as Spain's most significant novel of the 19th century. Actually, Clarín is closer to Flaubert than Zola, using the moral decline and fall of a tormented, neurotic, provincial socialite to present the pervasiveness of evil and degeneration in Spanish Restoration society. A profound exploration of the individual psyche, *La Regenta* anticipates Freudian views of hysteria, achieving a depth and complexity not found in typical naturalistic novels. Clarín distanced himself still further from the realist-naturalist mold in *Su único hijo* (1890; *His Only Son*) to concentrate on subjective realities and dreams.

Vicente Blasco Ibáñez became the most read and translated European novelist of the first half of the 20th century. Yet his work is slighted by Spanish literary historians. While his early work was reasonably well received, his leftist activism, numerous incarcerations, and international popularity alienated Spain's establishment, as did his radical views in *La catedral* (1903; *The Shadow of the Cathedral*), *El intruso* (1904; *The Intruder*), *La bodega* (1905; *The Fruit of the Vine*), *Los muertos mandan* (1908; *The Dead Command*), and *La horda* (1905; *The Mob*). These novels develop such themes as the poverty of migratory workers, the activities of anarchist organizers, unequal treatment of the poor, and conflicts created by religious traditions. Two novels that greatly increased Blasco's fame center on World War I: *Los cuatro jinetes del Apocalipsis* (1916; *The Four Horsemen of the Apocalypse*) and *Mare Nostrum* (1916; *Our Sea*), which denounces German submarine warfare in the Mediterranean. Blasco's vivid, colorful, and imaginative narratives develop from an initial adherence to naturalism to an increased emphasis on the inner self.

Pío Baroja was a disciple of Galdós and Blasco Ibáñez. Much admired by Hemingway, he was the most prolific and successful novelist of his generation, producing 67 novels, mostly neo-naturalistic. He defined the genre as *un saco en donde cabe todo* (a sack that holds everything). Unconcerned with method or theory, he wrote in direct, uncomplicated fashion, terming it the "style of a man in house-slippers." A sceptic who viewed life as unrelenting misery, he possessed sufficient storytelling talent to make his works popular and entertaining despite his pessimism. Baroja catalogs humanity's flaws and society's indifference in loosely organized works allegedly written "without a plan." The struggle for life (title of one of his best known trilogies) is his most constant theme. Fast-paced action revolves around protagonists who fall into two major categories, intellectual misfits and "men of action" (adventurers, wanderers, or voyagers). Baroja's best known novel representing contemporary, urban, intellectual life is *El árbol de la ciencia* (1911; *The Tree of Knowledge*), while the most popular of his Basque adventure novels is *Zalacaín el aventurero* (1909; Zalacaín the Adventurer). Baroja also wrote more than 20 pseudo-historical novels that document the exploits of a distant relative, enigmatic 19th-century adventurer Aviraneta during several decades of war and conspiracy.

Modernism was first introduced by the heterogeneous intellectuals of the "Generation of 1898," whose commitment to regeneration following the Spanish-American War included major aesthetic change. Along with other European modernists, many reacted against realism and naturalism and experimented with novelistic form. Miguel de Unamuno, an essayist, poet, and dramatist, is credited with introducing the "existential novel" to Spain. His tongue-in-check use of the invented term "nivola" is symbolic of his rejection of realism with its bourgeois allegiance to and faith in objectivity. His work is characterized instead by shadowy or stylized settings and passionate characters defined primarily by their anguished obsessions. Unamuno revived the "exemplary" novella, alluding to Cervantean precedent with his *Tres novelas ejemplares y un prólogo* (1920; *Three Exemplary Novels*), which present an unadorned vision of intimate human drama and depend primarily upon dialogue, monologue, and what he termed *monodiálogo*, which uses silent interlocutors to avoid the artificiality of soliloquy. Scorning the concept of genres, Unamuno repeatedly proclaimed that all novels are autobiography (or theatre, or poetry). His fiction is indeed highly autobiographical, in the sense that many characters, described as *ex-futuros yos* (aborted potential selves), are alter egos of the author. In both short and full-length novels such as *Abel Sánchez* (1917; *Abel Sanchez*) and *La tía Tula* (1921; Aunt Gertrude), Unamuno typically placed his tormented characters in what Karl Jaspers termed "boundary situations," extreme or critical moments in their lives. His most studied novel is *Niebla* (1914; *Mist*), which focuses on the questionable existence of the main character. The characterless, disoriented protagonist, Augusto—an existential non-entity—achieves self-discovery through the anguish of rejection and humiliation. Self-referential, meta-novelistic conversations between Augusto and his friend Victor highlight the author's emphasis on conversation and action, lack of plot and description. Augusto contemplates suicide and visits Unamuno, who reveals to him his fictional status, leading the character to struggle with his creator for control over his destiny. The outcome is left to the reader to imagine. Unamuno's insertion of himself into the text as ontological equal of his fictional entities had profound reverberations in 20th-century Spanish fiction. Typically brief, intense, intellectualized, and ultimately enigmatic, yet often ludic as well, his fiction also anticipates significant aspects of postmodernism.

José Martínez Ruiz, writing under the name Azorín, wrote 16 novels that were disparaged by traditional critics but are seen now to anticipate surrealism and the anti-novel. The early trilogy comprising *La voluntad* (1902; Will), *Antonio Azorín* (1903), and *Las confesiones de un pequeño filósofo* (1904; Confessions of a Little Philosopher) features the autobiographical protagonist Antonio Azorín (whose name the author adopted thenceforth as his own) and presents the intellectual development of a resigned, melancholy, reflective misfit. Azorín later wrote two novels based on the Don Juan legend, *Don Juan* (1922; *Don Juan*) and *Doña Inés* (1925). Both novels consist of a fragmented series of vignettes with little action that leave much unsaid. Azorín's favorite themes, the slow passage of time, the difficulties of writing, and interior duplication producing a sense of déjà vu dominate the novels. Recent critics see them as anticipating Marcel Proust in the slow-paced reconstruction of memories. The experimental novels *Félix Vargas* (1928), *Superrealismo* (1929; Surrealism), and *Pueblo* (1930; People) lack plots and abound in minute description. They employ free association and dwell on characters' psychological states. Between 1942 and 1944, Azorín published another half-dozen novels distinctly metafictional and self-reflective, treating themes of the writer and creative process.

Ramón del Valle-Inclán, a picturesque, eccentric bohemian, began as a decadent and modernist, went through a realist phase, and eventually evolved a personal brand of expressionism, which he termed *esperpento* (grotesque caricature). *Tirano Banderas* (1926; *The Tyrant: A Novel of Warm Lands*) typifies the *esperpento* aesthetic, which mediates a commentary on reality through its expressionist deformations. Its cabalistic structure is based on the numbers three and seven. Chronological disorder begins with the prologue, whose events paradoxically occur after the novel itself but before the climax (in the epilogue). *The Tyrant* is set in Tierra Caliente, a collage of Latin American republics, and depicts revolution against a composite of archetypal dictators while satirizing all levels of society—especially the Spaniards. Valle's final novelistic project, an ambitious series of three trilogies entitled *El ruedo ibérico* (The Iberian Ring), was truncated at his death with the completion only of *La corte de los milagros* (1927; Court of Miracles) and *Viva mi dueño* (1928; Long Live My Lord). Including characters and subject matter from earlier works, the final novels—satirizing the reign of Isabel II—resemble *The Tyrant* in technique and ideological content. Valle, often shocking and little appreciated by Spanish readers and critics of his day, has risen steadily in esteem during the last three decades, ranking today as a novelist, poet, and dramatist of the highest order.

Other avant-garde novelists of the early 20th century include Ramón Pérez de Ayala, who tried to bring the novel closer to poetry, Gabriel Miró, who took decadent concerns to new extremes, and Benjamín Jarnés. Jarnés fictionalized the ideas of the philosopher Ortega y Gasset, with varying aesthetic success.

Concha Espina, the best known woman writer of the period, published 17 novels, mostly interesting and well-written narratives best classified as sentimental realism. Her most characteristic works feature female protagonists, as in *La niña de Luzmela* (1909; The Girl from Luzmela), *La esfinge maragata* (1913; *Mariflor*), and *Altar mayor* (1926; High Altar). Preferred by many critics, *El metal de los muertos* (1920; The Metal of the Dead) is an exposé of the unhealthy and dangerous living and working conditions of copper miners. The novel is atypical for Espina, an essentially conservative writer who became more reactionary with the years.

Also writing in the period between the wars were several incipient "social novelists" whose politico-economic emphases usually sacrificed aesthetic to ideological concerns. The most important are Joaquín Arderius, Antonio Espina, and José Díaz Fernández. Dubbed the "New Romantics," their return to critical realism—a reaction against "dehumanized" art—was interrupted by the Spanish Civil War, which left many of them dead, imprisoned, or in exile.

Rosa Chacel, the most significant woman author of the vanguard generation, produced novels, short stories, essays, and poetry. Her works, preoccupied with formal perfection and philosophical issues, befit a disciple of Ortega y Gasset. Chacel's contacts with European modernism, especially the works of James Joyce and Marcel Proust, profoundly affected her aesthetics and her novelistic production. Cosmopolitanism and aestheticism came naturally to Chacel, who lived for decades as an expatriate (Italy, 1921–27; Rio de Janeiro and Buenos Aires, 1940–77). Her first novel, *Estación, ida y vuelta* (1930; Station, Round Trip), directly influenced by Joyce's *Portrait of the Artist as a Young Man* (1916), exhibits an internalized focus and minimal action, proto-existential elements, and experiments with the autonomy of characters, developing Unamuno's treatment of the theme. The later novel *La sinrazón* (1960; Unreason) is also a variation on the *Künstlerroman,* depicting the maturation of disoriented, petulant, aspiring intellectuals. The novel also contains Freudian elements and explores hidden psychological depths. Chacel's *Teresa* (1941), a novelized biography of Teresa Mancha, tragic lover of the romantic poet José de Espronceda, blends implicit feminist and existential concerns. *Memorias de Leticia Valle* (1945; *Memoirs of Leticia Valle*) narrates in diary format the coming-of-age of a precocious adolescent. The apocryphal autobiography recreates the girl's psychological seduction and incipient sexual relationship with a married professor. Other themes are artistic apprenticeship, adolescent moral ambiguity, and possible child molestation—a daring topic for the day. *Barrio de Maravillas* (1976; *The Maravillas District*), the first installment of a novelized trilogy on Chacel's generation, follows the development of two adolescent girls in Madrid, depicting 1914-era music, painting, sculpture, cinema, and new literature. Spanish critics recognized this portrayal of female adolescence by awarding it the Critics' Prize. *Acrópolis* (1984; Acropolis), the trilogy's second part, follows the same girls as they encounter modernist art and begin their own artistic careers. The third part, *Ciencias naturales* (1988; Natural Sciences) demands much of readers, given its intellectual density, interior monologues, and Chacel's challenging lexicon. The trilogy's title, *The Platonic School,* alludes to its philosophical concerns and its inspiration in the Platonic dialogues.

Francisco Ayala, novelist, essayist, critic, diplomat, political scientist, and sociologist before his exile, published his first novel at 18: *Tragicomedia de un hombre sin espíritu* (1925; Tragicomedy of a Man without a Spirit) introduces the literary allusions and metaliterary devices of his mature fiction. Ayala's distilled intellectualism and philosophically dense fiction exhibits major tenets of existentialism, as well as Ortega's perspectivism. His exile works, following a 14-year hiatus, seem radically different—deceptively mimetic, deeply ironic, sceptical, and humorous. Ayala's exceptonal stylistic skill foreshadows his belated recognition as one of the Spanish language's foremost living prose writers, but that reputation rests on his straightforward postwar historical narratives. Mastering the difficult art of simplicity and clarity, Ayala achieves astounding narrative economy in masterful works apparently bereft of literary artifice but marked by rare moral and philosophical intensity. The 17th-century world re-created in his brilliant demythologizing novelette, *El Hechizado* (1944; The Bewitched), and the ten "exemplary tales" of *Los usurpadores* (1949; *Usurpers*) with their medieval and Renaissance settings contain no identifiable distortions of accepted historical accounts, yet they subversively undermine the Franco regime's idealization of Spain's past glory. One unifying theme—usurpation of power—underlies these seemingly innocuous re-creations of familiar historical figures, illustrating how power corrupts those who hold it. Ayala (who insists that all of his fictions are novels, regardless of length) holds that all control exercised by one man over another is a form of usurpation. *La cabeza del cordero* (1949; *The Lamb's Head*) comprises four novelettes united by the common background of Spain's civil war, illustrating the human shortcomings and errors that shape history, while *Historia de macacos* (1955; Monkey Story) presents six depictions of the human tendency to abuse, ridicule, humiliate, and debase others. Ethical concern with moral and physical outrage unifies the sardonic tales of *El as de Bastos* (1963; Ace of Clubs) and reappears in his masterful interconnected novels *Muertes de perro* (1958; *Death as a Way of Life*) and *El fondo del vaso* (1962; The Bottom of the Glass), which portray tyranny, demagoguery, and existential alienation in an imaginary Latin American dictatorship. Satiric, sometimes sarcastic, deceptively simple in their re-creation of journalistic style and mass mentality, Ayala's novels examine difficult questions of the rights of the individual in a mass society, probing the myriad ways contemporary man falls short of existential authenticity.

The New Romantics' most controversial, talented, and prolific member was Ramón J. Sender, novelist, journalist, and later professor of Spanish during his exile in the US. He was also one of the few of the group who continued to write after the civil war. Sender wrote more than 40 novels, which typically blend objective realism and autobiographical and testimonial fiction with elements of the *roman à thèse*. A colorful, passionate, adventurous revolutionary, Sender focused on recent Spanish history in most of his novels. Sender's extensive fiction, alternately allegorical, fantastic, and humorous, contains numerous infelicities along with some inspired moments. In his masterpiece, *Mosén Millán* (1953), revised as *Réquiem por un campesino español* (1960; *Requiem for a Spanish Peasant*), the guilt-ridden priest Mosén Millán recalls the life and death of the Christ-like former altar boy turned socialist organizer, whom he betrayed to Falangist executioners. Although Sender occasionally experimented with narrative perspective, most of his novels follow the realism of Galdós or the naturalism of Baroja.

The first significant new novelist to arise in Spain under Franco was Camilo José Cela, whose *La familia de Pascual Duarte* (1942; *The Family of Pascual Duarte*) is the prison confession of a condemned serial killer who may have died for a political murder he did not commit. The pseudo-autobiographical narrative, filled with horrendous scenes of neo-naturalistic violence, misery, illness, filth, depravity, and death, initiated a new movement called *tremendismo.* Cela produced generally neo-realistic works but he experimented with structure, perspective, and technique in his subsequent novels. *La colmena* (1951; *The Hive*), his masterpiece, is a complex orchestration of hundreds of characters, lacking plot and protagonist, that depicts the moral bankruptcy and misery of Franco's Madrid. Always unorthodox, Cela's novels are often extremely difficult to read. His later work is commonly classified as postmodernist, particularly *San Camilo, 1936* (1969; *San Camilo, 1936*) and *Oficio de tinieblas, 5* (1973; Office of Darkness), written principally in the second person. The first offers an interminable monologue-chronicle of events in Madrid the week before the civil war began. An "antinovel," *Oficio* comprises nearly 1,200 "monads" or fragments lacking plot, protagonist, characterization, temporality or sustained action, identifiable place or epoch. The fragments are unified only by the reiteration of themes of boredom, sexuality, absurdity, eroticism, death, bestiality, war, violence, fear, betrayal, defeat, pain, and excrement. They are punctuated by unexpected lyric intervals.

Tremendismo, vaguely connected to existentialism in rejecting abstractions to portray absurdity, loneliness, despair, and anguish, flourished during the 1940s and inspired various imitators, none especially distinguished. A psychological variant of *tremendismo* occurs in Carmen Laforet's *Nada* (1945; *Andrea*), narrated by a Canary Islands girl attending university in postwar Barcelona and living with eccentric, mentally disturbed relatives: a sadistic uncle occupied in some clandestine business, a masochistic maiden aunt, another uncle who is a frustrated artist and abuses his wife and child, and a senile grandmother. Abundant emotional and psychological abnormalities, plus the dirty, overcrowded, run-down house, hunger, despair, and violence mark this novel and *La isla y los demonios* (1952; The Island and Its Demons).

Tremendismo gave way to the less violent social realism of the 1950s and early 1960s. Most social realist novelists were politically motivated, portraying poverty, social inequities and injustice, and economic stagnation—indirect denunciations of the Franco regime's conservatism. Some adopted *objetivismo* (modeled on French objectivism and the *nouveau roman*) with its impassive stance, rejection of psychological development, and abandonment of authorial omniscience. The social novel, objectivism, and *tremendismo* are all neo-realist modes. Frequently, two or three modes appear in a single writer. Both objectivists and "social" novelists or neo-realists were influenced by the cinema, imitating the "impartiality" of the camera eye and collage and montage techniques. Rejecting linear plot and character analysis, objectivists chose collective protagonists, either in large groups or one by one in serial mini-episodes. Some critics include Cela's *The Hive* with objectivist novels, while others consider it neo-realist. Typically, no single character acquires primacy; instead, the confrontation of social classes and dissimilar types creates a sociological dialectic. These works associate superficial values, egotism, boredom, and alienation with the parasitic privileged bourgeoisie, while attributing more positive traits to the poor. Objectivists depict a continual present, without remembrances except those communicated orally, presenting only surface reality. Juan García Hortelano's *Tormenta de verano* (1962; *Summer Storm*), Juan Goytisolo's *La isla* (1961; *The Island of Women*), Luis Goytisolo's *Las mismas palabras* (1962; The Same Words), and Jorge [Cela] Trulock's *Inventario base* (1969; Basic Inventory) represent the movement. Rafael Sánchez Ferlosio produced Spanish objectivism's masterpiece, *El Jarama* (1955; *Jarama River*), with Ignacio Aldecoa's *Gran Sol* (1957; Great Sole) a close second. Both relate the monotonous same-

ness of quotidian existence among generic working-class characters, deprived of opportunity, devoid of ambition, ideas, and *joie de vivre*.

One critic identifies "problem orientation" as the distinguishing characteristic of social novelists, i.e., their commitment to the critical depiction of problematic contemporary reality, implicitly denouncing injustice and hoping to effect reform. Continuing the tradition of Blasco Ibáñez and the prewar New Romantics including Sender, these writers allude to Marxism and theories of Jean-Paul Sartre, Georg Lukács, Bertolt Brecht, Emma Goldmann, and Friedrich Engels. The social novel's situational exposés produced certain thematic constants: rural or urban regional experiences, work-related problems, and class or group conflicts. Typically, protagonists are lower class, usually peasant farmers or members of the urban proletariat, living in misery, ignorance, and backwardness. Examples include José Manuel Caballero Bonald's *Dos días de setiembre* (1962; Two Days in September), portraying Andalusian viniculture; Alfonso Grosso's *La zanja* (1961; The Ditch), depicting a cross-section of a small Andalusian town; and Luisa Isabel Alvarez de Toledo's *La huelga* (1967; *The Strike*), about class confrontation in southern Spain.

The legacy of Galdós and Baroja appears intermittently, although social novelists vehemently reject 19th-century techniques. Unjust, exploitative, or indifferent political bosses, employers, or rich landowners usually play the villain, as in *El cacique* (1963; The Boss) by Luis Romero. Big business is the villain in Jesús López Pacheco's *Central eléctrica* (1958; Powerhouse), in which the construction of a hydroelectric station eventually victimizes those it should have helped. Dolores Medio's *Funcionario público* (1956; Public Servant) denounced the substandard wages paid to postal and telegraph employees and actually resulted in a wage increase for minor government employees. Intolerable urban conditions also appear in Juan Antonio de Zunzunegui's *Esta oscura desbandada* (1951; This Dark Disbandment), Armando López Salinas' *Año tras año* (1962; Year after Year), García Hortelano's *Nuevas amistades* (1959; New Friendships), Angel María de Lera's *Los olvidados* (1957; The Forgotten Ones), and Francisco Umbral's *Travesía de Madrid* (1966; Across Madrid). Juan Goytisolo paints horrifying conditions in Barcelona's slums in *La resaca* (1958; The Undertow), *El circo* (1957; The Circus), and other works. Tourism also became a frequent theme among social novelists, given the regime's headlong rush to develop the tourist industry, ignoring ecology, conservation, or local social impact. Major shortcomings of the social novel include its exaggeration of social dichotomies and a naive identification of good with poverty, evil with wealth.

Miguel Delibes is one of Spain's most significant 20th-century realists. In *El camino* (1950; *The Path*), *Diario de un cazador* (1953; Diary of a Hunter), *Diario de un emigrante* (1958; An Emigrant's Diary), *La hoja roja* (1959; The Red Leaf), *Las ratas* (1962; *Smoke on the Ground*), *Las guerras de nuestros antepasados* (1975; *The Wars of Our Ancestors*), and *El disputado voto del señor Cayo* (1978; The Disputed Vote of Mr. Cayo), Delibes portrays the forgotten inhabitants of dwindling villages in rural Castile, often with satire and humor but also with passionate concern. Concern for the rural poor likewise underlies *Los santos inocentes* (1981; The Blessed Innocents) and *El tesoro* (1985; The Treasure). Delibes' preoccupation with the bitter divisions preceding and following the civil war permeates several novels, including the masterful *Cinco horas con Mario* (1966; *Five Hours with Mario*), in which marital conflict symbolizes Spain's social and ideological strife as conveyed by the widow's unintentionally ironic internal monologue. *El príncipe destronado* (1973; Dethroned Prince) employs the peculiarly limited, distorted consciousness of a three-year-old who witnesses the skirmishes between his warring parents. In Spain's most significant novel on the civil war, *377a, madera de héroe* (1987; 377A, The Stuff of Which Heroes Are Made), Delibes meditates upon the relativity of heroism and treason.

Major postwar women novelists include Elena Quiroga, Ana María Matute, and Carmen Martín Gaite. Quiroga, socially conservative but committed to literary experimentation, becomes more progressive and critical in later novels. Quiroga deliberately varies form and structure, trying to make each novel different, and employs uncommon perspectives. *La sangre* (1952; Blood) adopts the viewpoint of a chestnut tree to chronicle three generations of decadent rural gentry. *Algo pasa en la calle* (1954; Something's Happening in the Street), one of her best works, employs multiple perspectives to reconstruct the dead protagonist's enigmatic personality. The protagonist of *La enferma* (1955; The Sick Woman) is mute and immobilized; other characters dispute the facts and motivations of her past life and present state. Quiroga's best novels are *Tristura* (1960; Sadness), winner of the Critics' Prize, and *Escribo tu nombre* (1965; I Write Your Name), two parts of a longer cycle unified by a common protagonist, seen at a different stage of life in each installment.

Ana María Matute figures among the most significant postwar writers on the civil war. She applies the story of Cain and Abel to the warring factions in *Los Abel* (1948; The Abel Family), the masterful short novel *Fiesta al noroeste* (1952; *Celebration in the Northwest*), and *Los hijos muertos* (1958; The Dead Children), winner of the Critics' Prize. Like *En esta tierra* (1955; In This Land), *Los hijos muertos* examines conflicting forces in the war, analyzing the loss of ideals, youth, and hope. Matute's trilogy *Los mercaderes* (The Moneychangers) divides humanity into two groups, moneychangers, for whom everything has its price, and heros, capable of sacrificing everything for an ideal. The three novels share thematic relationships, especially the social inequities and injustices underlying the civil conflict. *La torre vigía* (1971; The Watchtower) is a disconcerting allegory in which knightly quest themes and chivalric honor are juxtaposed with sordid poverty, fanatic superstitions, sexual depravity, and hypocrisy. *Olvidado Rey Gudú* (1996; Forgotten King Gudú), a quarter-century in gestation, continues these concerns.

Carmen Martín Gaite gained prominence with *Entre visillos* (1957; *Behind the Curtains*), about the entrapment or imprisonment of women in their houses. The critics' favorite, *El cuarto de atrás* (1978; *The Back Room*), a postmodern hybrid, blends mystery novel, memoirs, and meditations on the creative process. *Nubosidad variable* (1992; *Variable Cloud*) and *La reina de las nieves* (1994; The Snow Queen) reveal Martín Gaite as a voice for women's concerns, interested in gender equity and feminine creative potential.

Differences notwithstanding, prevailing novelistic modes during the first 25 years under Franco were representational. Content prevailed over form, and most works had a testimonial thrust. Covert political resistance, motivating much postwar writing, muted the importance of aesthetic considerations, but during the final decade of dictatorship and most emphatically in the post-Franco period, aestheticism, experimentalism, form and language per se, and interest in theory replace "message" and extraliterary goals. Neo-baroque, neo-vanguardist, and postmodern experimentation forge aesthetic links between the prewar and post-Franco periods. Luis Martín Santos' *Tiempo de silencio* (1962; *Time of Silence*) reintroduced personal, subjective tone, complex and esoteric lexicon, polished language, multiple perspectives, and experimental style and form. This brilliant first novel by a practicing psychiatrist reasserted in Spain the literary viability of psychological interpretation, character development, and intellectualism, breaking with the pretense of depersonalized authorial objectivity and rejecting notions that literature must try to change society. Typographically recalling avant-garde formats, the novel features arbitrary and unconventional punctuation, syntax, and subdivisions, with baroque contortions of language, foreign words, neologisms, and technical jargon employed to expose the backwardness of Spain's scientific establishment. Martín Santos died in an automobile accident in 1964.

Juan Benet, commonly referred to as the father of Spain's "new novel," adopted European and American models, scorning neo-realism's "tavern" mentality and slice-of-life approach, rejecting the facile, the simplistic, and the transparent. Following William Faulkner, Benet created a fictional microcosm which he named "Region," site of the pivotal *Volverás a Región* (1967; *Return to Region*) and most of his subsequent fiction. A miniature, parallel world resembling Spain, Region acquired mythic traits and often escaped the physical laws of quotidian reality. Benet's narratives, deliberately obscure and contradictory, follow his conviction that mystery constitutes the writer's greatest attraction. Often deemed arrogant and elitist, Benet cultivated ambiguity, enigma, polysemy, hermeticism, multivalence, and indeterminacy, reintroducing the sensibility of modernity that had disappeared from Spanish letters with the passing of Ramón del Valle-Inclán. Benet reaffirms the modernist concept of the centrality of language as both agent and substance, but he does not subscribe to postmodernism. His major works include *Una meditación* (1970; *A Meditation*), *Un viaje de invierno* (1972; A Winter's Trip), *La otra casa de Mazón* (1973; Mazon's Other House), *En el estado* (1977; In the State), and *En la penumbra* (1982; In the Shadows).

Gonzalo Torrente Ballester, with a sensibility formed in the modernist period, is one of Spain's most distinguished novelists, a master of erudite humor and meta-literary satire. His *Don Juan* (1963) places the immortal seducer in 20th-century Paris where, rejected by heaven and hell, he can no longer indulge his sexual desire: 400 years have so perfected his sexual technique that his paramours die of ecstacy, precipitating legal complications. *La sagafuga de J.B.* (1972; The SagaFlight of J.B.) is a more major work, which exhibits a radical intensification of concern for narrative theory, shifting and fragmented temporal planes, parody, and linguistic play. A ludic exercise in pure invention, mythic, satiric, and wholly postmodern, *La sagafuga* has much in common with *Fragmentos de apocalipsis* (1977; Fragments of Apocalypse) and *La isla de los jacintos cortados* (1980; The Isle of Cut Hyacinths), the latter novel's premise being that Napoléon never existed. Torrente's subsequent works equate fiction and history.

Camilo José Cela also evolved a postmodern aesthetic, with *Mazurca para dos muertos* (1983; *Mazurka for Two Dead Men*), which presents a mythic reflection of the civil war in Galicia; *Cristo versus Arizona* (1988; Christ Against Arizona), which adopts a lyric, fragmentary technique; *El asesinato del perdedor* (1994; *The Murder of the Loser*); and *La cruz de San Andrés* (1994; St. Andrew's Cross), complex exercises in rewriting or unwriting that always return to motifs of sexual perversion and violent death.

In his "new novel" trilogy, *Señas de identidad* (1966; *Marks of Identity*), *Reivindicación del Conde don Julián* (1970; *Count Julian*), and *Juan sin tierra* (1975; *Juan the Landless*), Juan Goytisolo experiments with language and shifting narrative viewpoint, utilizes a self-aware narrator, and borrows extensively from other texts. He moves progressively closer to oral poetry held together by patterns, repetitive themes, motifs, and epigraphs, away from complex plots, characterization, conventional story, and structure. Arabic culture becomes a dominant element, pervading *Makbara* (1980) and several later works. With *Paisajes después de la batalla* (1982; *Landscapes after the Battle*), Goytisolo's social critiques become universal, with new humor and subversiveness, while characters become increasingly unstable, shifting identities and form.

Luis Goytisolo likewise abandons simple neo-realism and the social novel for more experimental structures in *Ojos, círculos, buhos* (1970; Eyes, Circles, Owls) and *Devoraciones* (1976; Devourings). His tetralogy, *Antagonía*, begun with *Recuento* (1973; Recounting), turns the focus to language and style, consciously attempting to develop formalist and structuralist poetics. The cycle includes *Los verdes de mayo hasta el mar* (1976; The Green of May unto the Sea), *La cólera de Aquiles* (1979; Achilles' Rage), and *Teoría del conocimiento* (1981; Theory of Knowledge). Mythic concepts, emblematic and allegorical characters, and the transformation of the narrative into an epically erotic, Neptunian universe are shared characteristics. A consummate practitioner of the art of metafiction, Luis Goytisolo explores the nature and limits of the self-conscious novel, questioning the power of language and the creative process. *Estela del fuego que se aleja* (1984; Wake of Fire Fading Away), an intricate labyrinth of mirrors and multiple levels of meaning, blends fiction with theoretical commentary. Other important writers who began writing "social" novels but have adopted more aesthetic orientations include Juan García Hortelano, José María Caballero Bonald, and Juan Marsé.

Following Franco's death in 1975, Spanish literature underwent an orgy of indulgence in the previously prohibited: a wave of porno-political frenzy accompanied an exploding interest in novels, autobiographies, and memoirs of exile, war (from the unaccustomed anti-Franco perspective), and clandestine opposition during the dictatorship. *Franquismo* itself became a thematic nucleus, with primarily unfavorable portrayals of the dictatorship, its ideology, history, and minions. The same era saw rapid expansion of publishing in minority "vernaculars," not only the historically significant languages, primarily Catalan and Galician, but Basque—whose literature was largely oral until the 20th century—and dialects such as Leonese, Bable (Asturian), Andalan (Aragonese), and Andalusian. Many regional languages became official, alongside Castilian, in their respective regions with the passage of the local autonomy laws, fragmenting the linguistic, literary, and cultural scene. Many younger writers are publishing in the regional vernaculars.

Women writers have proliferated as well in the last two decades, with especially significant names including Josefina Aldecoa, Esther Tusquets, Ana María Moix, Lourdes Ortiz, Marina Mayoral, Cristina Fernández Cubas, and Soledad Puértolas. Some novelists omitted by literary histories have acquired new prominence, including banker-diplomat José Luis Sampedro and José Jiménez Lozano, the latter cultivating themes drawn from the esoteric background of various religions. The recently recognized "Generation of 1968" includes writers born in the 1940s: Juan J. Armas Marcelo, Juan José Millás, Luis Mateo Díez, José María Merino, Juan Pedro Aparicio, plus several women mentioned above. Other successful younger novelists in Castilian are Alvaro Pombo, Ramón Hernández, Mariano Antolín Rato, Enrique Murillo, Félix de Azua, Germán Sánchez Espeso, Raúl Guerra Garrido, José Leyva, Pedro Zarraluki, Javier Tomeo, José María Vaz de Soto, Enrique Vila-Matas, Vicente Molina Foix, Javier Marías, Paloma Díaz-Mas, and Ignacio Martínez de Pisón.

No fictional mode clearly predominates over others, and traces from the various movements and tendencies of the Spanish novel from the beginning of the 20th century and before may be found among current practitioners. Although some critics perceive a "crisis" because no mode or movement is in the ascendency, the impressive variety, vigor, and quality suggest that the Spanish novel ends the 20th century alive and well.

JANET PÉREZ

See also Camilo José Cela; Celestina; Miguel de Cervantes; Clarín; Diana; Juan Goytisolo; Lazarillo de Tormes; Pastoralism in the Novel; Benito Pérez Galdós; Picaresque; Miguel de Unamuno

Further Reading

Bjornson, Richard, *The Picaresque Hero in European Fiction*, Madison: University of Wisconsin Press, 1977

Boehne, Patricia, *The Renaissance Catalan Novel*, Boston: Twayne, 1989

Cox, Merritt, *Eighteenth-Century Spanish Literature*, Boston: Twayne, 1979

Eisenberg, Daniel, *Castilian Romances of Chivalry in the Sixteenth Century: A Bibliography*, London: Grant and Cutler, 1979

Eisenberg, Daniel, *Romances of Chivalry in the Spanish Golden Age*, Newark, Delaware: Juan de la Cuesta, 1982

Eoff, Sherman Hinkle, *The Modern Spanish Novel*, New York: New York University Press, 1961; London: Owen, 1962

Jones, Margaret E.W., *The Contemporary Spanish Novel, 1939–1975*, Boston: Twayne, 1985

Landeira, Ricardo, *The Modern Spanish Novel, 1898–1939*, Boston: Twayne, 1985

Medina, Jeremy T., *Spanish Realism: The Theory and Practice of a Concept in the Nineteenth Century*, Potomac, Maryland: Porrúa, 1979

Nora, Eugenio G[arcía] de, *La novela española contemporánea, 1898–1927*, Madrid: Gredos, 1958; 2nd edition, 1963

Parker, Alexander Augustine, *Literature and the Delinquent: The Picaresque Novel in Spain and Europe, 1599–1753*, Edinburgh: Edinburgh University Press, 1967

Patchell, Mary Frances Corinne, *The Palmerín Romances in*

Elizabethan Prose Fiction, New York: Columbia University Press, 1947

Pérez, Janet, *Women Writers of Contemporary Spain,* Boston: Twayne, 1988

Rico, Francisco, *La novela picaresca y el punto de vista,* Barcelona: Seix Barral, 1970; as *The Picaresque Novel and Point of View,* Cambridge and New York: Cambridge University Press, 1984

Roca-Pons, Josep, *Introduction to Catalan Literature,* Bloomington: Department of Spanish and Portuguese, Indiana University, 1977

Solé-Lerís, Amadeo, *The Spanish Pastoral Novel,* Boston: Twayne, 1980

Thomas, Henry, *Spanish and Portuguese Romances of Chivalry,* Cambridge: Cambridge University Press, 1920; reprinted, New York: Kraus, 1969

Christina Stead 1902–83

Australian

In 1942 Christina Stead wrote in Kunitz and Haycraft's *Twentieth Century Authors* that "The essence of style in literature, for me, is experiment, invention, 'creative error' . . . and change: and of its content, the presentation of 'man alive'. . . ." Thus, she linked the two elements of her own achievement as a novelist—the impulse to experiment at the risk of failure and the dedication to realism in the observation of the lives around her. Most of Stead's novels have been deemed failures at some time, accused by critics of formlessness, excess, and lack of control. Yet her stated belief in the importance of "creative errors" alerts the reader to her interest in the process of writing: art as the record of a living struggle rather than as a completed and closed work.

Stead's approach to the novel was undoubtedly founded on her reading of the great 19th-century European naturalists and British realists, including Guy de Maupassant, Charles Dickens, Fedor Dostoevskii, and Honoré de Balzac. She called herself a naturalist in the scientific sense, claiming only to observe and record reality rather than criticize it. Yet Stead also admired James Joyce and, although she always preferred external drama to interior monologue, her use of myth and symbol within realist modes aligns her work with modernism. At the same time, her associations with the communist party especially through her husband, William Blake, ensured that she was fully aware of socialist-realist theory, with its class analysis and concern for depicting the "typical." While her novels could never be identified with the formulaic socialist realism that dominated communist writing in the 1930s and 1940s, her characters are always situated within specific historical moments and endure particular economic constraints. Consequently, her first novel, *Seven Poor Men of Sydney* (1934), details the material and emotional hardship of the 1920s while at the same time plumbing the psychological despair of its individual characters. Stead allies an experimental modernism with carefully detailed social observation, spanning the two dominant modes of the mid-century novel—modernism and social realism.

Terry Sturm (1974) has argued that Stead's *drama of the person* (Stead's term) represents a new mode of realism that can be credited with finding a way out of the division between the public and the private that restricted both "bourgeois" and "socialist" realism. None of her novels has conventional plot structures, and all of them depend on the close observation of individual characters. In her "Uses of the Many-Charactered Novel," reprinted in Geering and Segerberg (1994), Stead explains that a novel of multiple characters is an attempt "to fix" the plurality of the modern world. While her characters often emerge as grotesque and excessive rather than "typical," they are always allowed room to express the logic of their particular worldview as they talk their way through the novels. Stead's technique of characterization through speech coincides with her interest in cinema—*House of All Nations* (1938) is structured into 104 scenes rather than chapters—and her brief period working in Hollywood left its mark on her style. Through their talking, Stead demonstrates that the seemingly extraordinary individuals at the center of her novels belong irremovably to a public world that provides the rationale for their being. Jonathan Crow, of *For Love Alone* (1944), for example, offers eugenic and latent fascist theory among his revolutionary ideas; Sam Pollit, of *The Man Who Loved Children* (1940), calls on scientific attitudes and the Uncle Sam ideology of middle America in constructing himself; Nellie Cotter, of *Dark Places of the Heart* (1966; published in Great Britain as *Cotters' England*), uses Marxist theory, including socialist realism, to dominate her relatives and friends.

Several critics have argued that Stead's contribution to the novel lies in her commitment to narrative—not in the sense of providing unified plot structures but in acknowledging the multiple possibilities for storytelling. For her the world was an "ocean of story," infinite beyond the novelist's powers to record. Her first book, *The Salzburg Tales* (1934), mimicked the structure of Geoffrey Chaucer's *Canterbury Tales* as its characters—a group of visitors to Salzburg—stepped forward as storytellers, each adopting a different narrative mode for his or her tale. In this way, Stead placed fairy tale and myth beside contemporary realist stories. *The Man Who Loved Children* and *For Love Alone* depict 20th-century lives informed by fairy tale and myth. As her career progressed, Stead's authorial voice increasingly withdrew in favor of her characters' versions of reality. *The Man Who Loved Children,* for example, pits Henny's narrative of "rotten luck" against Sam's patriarchal delusions while allowing the children to observe the adult world as "tragic faery." In *Letty Fox: Her Luck* (1946), the title character recounts her own picaresque sexual journey through wartime New York, and Nellie Cotter dominates *Dark Places of the Heart* by her conviction that she knows "reality." *Letty Fox: Her Luck* is the only novel that employs first-person narration throughout; the other novels prefer third-person narrators who at times become so tactful that readers have been confused about their meaning. *Miss Herbert (The Suburban Wife)* (1976), for example, observes Miss Herbert's career in close detail without offering judgment on the corruption and vapidity of her existence. The reader must deduce these from both the abundance of sordid detail and Miss Herbert's incomprehensible lack of historical awareness.

At the center of Stead's interest in experiment and change lies her interest in history. Her papers indicate that she researched the background for each novel assiduously. Her characters move through a corrupt 20th-century world—specifically the world of the 1930s and 1940s. It is a world in which the possibility of reform or revolution has been destroyed, leaving idealists to act out an often unself-conscious hypocrisy. Stead's interest in "man alive" leads her to stunningly original subject matter; her account of the black market in New York during World War II in *A Little Tea, a Little Chat* (1948), for example, has no historical parallel; and her final, posthumously published novel, *I'm Dying Laughing* (1986), provides an incisive account of communists in Hollywood during the 1940s and also focuses on the lifestyles of Americans in France at the war's end. Stead's ability to see the most intimate aspects of a life as part of an ideological position with public implications may be her most noteworthy achievement. In this last novel, for example, Emily Wilkes Howard's unrestrained eating expresses the capacity for US capitalism (disguised as idealism) to feed off the rest of the world.

While *The Man Who Loved Children* remains her best-known work, and while Australian readers favor *Seven Poor Men of Sydney* and *For Love Alone* for their local settings, *I'm Dying Laughing* may prove to be Stead's most ambitious achievement. Creative errors lie here aplenty—the manuscript was pieced together by R.G. Geering after Stead's death—yet they cannot detract from the satiric power of this sharp, bitter, funny examination of the relationship between Europe and the United States during and after the war. Everything about this novel is excessive—its generous accumulation of detail, its vitality, and its central figure, the gargantuan Emily.

In retrospect and in the light of the notes she left, Stead's novels after 1944 may be seen as forming a satirical history of failed radicalism, with *The People with the Dogs* (1952) providing a lighthearted and affectionate counter to *I'm Dying Laughing*. While feminist or socialist readers may prefer the earlier novels for their clear commitment to the oppressed, the later satires together mount a strong if bitter critique of Western civilization.

SUSAN LEVER AND ANNE PENDER

See also Man Who Loved Children

Biography

Born 17 July 1902 in Rockdale, Sydney, New South Wales. Attended Sydney University Teachers' College, graduated 1922. Demonstrator, Sydney University Teachers' College, in Sydney schools, 1922–24; secretary in Sydney from 1925 until she moved to Europe in 1928; office clerk in London, 1928–29, and in Paris, 1930–35; lived in the United States, 1937–47; senior writer, Metro-Goldwyn-Mayer, Hollywood, 1943; instructor, New York University, 1943–44; traveled, 1948–52; lived in England, mainly in Surbiton, Surrey, 1953–73, and in Australia, 1974–83; fellow in creative arts, Australian National University, Canberra, 1969. Died 31 March 1983.

Novels and Novellas by Stead

Seven Poor Men of Sydney, 1934
The Beauties and the Furies, 1936
House of All Nations, 1938
The Man Who Loved Children, 1940
For Love Alone, 1944
Letty Fox: Her Luck, 1946
A Little Tea, a Little Chat, 1948
The People with the Dogs, 1952
Dark Places of the Heart, 1966; as *Cotters' England,* 1967
The Puzzleheaded Girl: Four Novellas, 1967
The Little Hotel, 1973
Miss Herbert (The Suburban Wife), 1976
The Palace with Several Sides: A Sort of Love Story, 1986 (posthumous)
I'm Dying Laughing, 1986 (posthumous)

Other Writings: reviews, edited anthologies; *Ocean of Story,* edited by R.G. Geering, a collection of Stead's short stories, was published in 1985, after her death. A two-volume collection of her letters was published as *A Web of Friendship: Selected Letters (1928–1973)* and *Talking into the Typewriter: Selected Letters (1973–1983)* in 1992, edited by Geering.

Further Reading

Brydon, Diana, *Christina Stead,* London: Macmillan, and Totowa, New Jersey: Barnes and Noble, 1987
Carter, Angela, *Expletives Deleted: Selected Writings,* London: Chatto and Windus, 1992
Geering, R.G., and A. Segerberg, editors, *Christina Stead, Selected Fiction and Nonfiction,* St. Lucia and Portland, Oregon: University of Queensland Press, 1994
Gribble, Jennifer, *Christina Stead,* Melbourne and New York: Oxford University Press, 1994
Rowley, Hazel, *Christina Stead: A Biography,* Port Melbourne: Heinemann Australia, 1993; New York: Holt, 1994; London: Secker and Warburg, 1995
Sheridan, Susan, *Christina Stead,* Brighton, Sussex, and New York: Harvester, 1988
Sturm, Terry, "Christina Stead's New Realism," in *Cunning Exiles: Studies of Modern Prose Writers,* edited by Don Anderson and Stephen Thomas Knight, Sydney: Angus and Robertson, 1974
Wilding, Michael, "Christina Stead's *The Puzzleheaded Girl*: The Political Context," in *Words and Wordsmiths: A Volume for H.L. Rogers,* edited by Geraldine Barnes, Sydney: Department of English, University of Sydney, 1989
Williams, Chris, *Christina Stead: A Life of Letters,* Melbourne: McPhee Gribble, and London: Virago, 1989

Gertrude Stein 1874–1946

United States

Of Gertrude Stein's immense literary output only the epic *The Making of Americans*, which she began in 1903 and published in 1925, can be classified as a novel in the traditional sense. Stein was a modernist writer who experimented continually with both form and style in order to question the parameters of conventional genres of writing. Her early sequence *Three Lives* (1909) is formally divided into three distinct tales—"The Good Anna," "Melanctha," and "The Gentle Lena"—on the model of Gustave Flaubert's *Trois Contes* (1877; *Three Tales*). However, the three stories form a loose narrative sequence that pushes the triadic structure closer toward the novel in a manner similar to two other influential US modernist collections: Sherwood Anderson's *Winesburg, Ohio* (1919) and Ernest Hemingway's *In Our Time* (1925). *Three Lives* may be read as a late naturalist book (developing the work of US writers Theodore Dreiser and Upton Sinclair), but the shifting and equivocal narrative voice creates an ironic tone that serves to highlight the method of narration over the subject matter of the stories. *Three Lives* has been interpreted as one of the earliest high modernist texts; Stein's interest in the unstable nature of language is connected with her attempts to apply to fiction the theories of consciousness expounded by the US psychologist and philosopher William James during her time at Harvard University.

Stein, as well as other expatriate US writers, lived in Paris during the years prior to World War I. After the publication of *Three Lives* her work developed in a more experimental direction. She was interested in replicating in her writing the painterly techniques of French Postimpressionists (especially Paul Cézanne) and, later, the cubism of Pablo Picasso. The radical sequence *Tender Buttons* (1914), like *Three Lives,* is divided into three parts—"Objects," "Food," and "Rooms"—in which Stein developed a mode of writing that challenged not only the nature of narrative but the possibility of representing the world accurately through the medium of language. *Tender Buttons* is really a collection of fragments (perhaps heavily coded messages to her lover and companion Alice B. Toklas) that are structured by the juxtaposition of images and the repetition and modulation of words, phrases, and sentences. The series of discrete formal components combine to create a phenomenological flow of idiosyncratic impressions in which the subject of perception (as traditionally represented in literature) is expunged from view. Consequently, the text conveys the impression of a perpetually moving and unstable perceptual moment that is neither contained nor ordered by an identifiable subject. This mutable narrative perspective is further complicated in *Tender Buttons* because the reader's attention is rarely directed closely toward the domestic objects that the section titles purport to introduce. Instead, Stein devises a technique labeled in 1917 by the Russian formalist critic Viktor Shklovskii as "defamiliarization," in which she questions the usually unconscious correlation between words and things. For example, the paratactic sentence structure and the instability of visual impressions are both evident in the following fragment entitled "A Blue Coat": "A blue coat is guided guided away, guided and guided away, that is the particular color that is used for that length and not any width not even more than a shadow."

In *The Making of Americans* Stein went on to develop the themes of consciousness, perception, and time within the framework of a much longer narrative sequence. On one level *The Making of Americans* describes the history of two American families, the Dehnings and the Herslands, whose histories are traced back to their middle-class roots in Europe. As such, the book represents an epic US history that explores aspects of American exceptionalism and the tensions between European and US culture; the narrator states early on in the novel: "The old people in a new world, the new people made out of the old, that is the story that I mean to tell, for that is what really is and what I really know." However, on a more profound level, the novel is about the process of its own composition and formation: as the title suggests, it is constructed around a series of techniques that highlight the changes experienced by different generations of the two families. To demonstrate the difficulties as well as the possibilities of telling this epic story, which incorporates the whole history of the United States as much as the history of two families, Stein fills the novel with digressions, narrative discontinuities, and idiosyncratic syntax. Furthermore, in her notebooks on *The Making of Americans* Stein quotes the 16th-century English dramatist John Lyly—"In faith Euphues thou hast told me a long tale, the beginning I have forgotten, the middle I understand not and the endeth hangeth not together"— to emphasize the potentially endless nature of such a story.

In an important essay entitled "Composition as Explanation," published in London a year after *The Making of Americans,* Stein introduced the term *continuous present* to describe the kind of fiction she had attempted to develop after *Three Lives.* She describes the writing of *The Making of Americans* as "a groping for using everything and there was a groping for a continuous present and there was an inevitable beginning of beginning again and again and again." As well as indicating the necessarily voluminous length of such a project (*The Making of Americans* runs to more than 1,000 pages to take its place alongside the modernist epics written by Marcel Proust, James Joyce, John Dos Passos, Thomas Mann, Robert Musil, and Hermann Broch), Stein stresses the composition and process of writing over and above the finished aesthetic product.

Stein's later works are less experimental in nature than her earlier writings, which is perhaps indicative of the ultimately frustrated work *The Making of Americans* was to become. Nevertheless, Stein continued to explore alternative narrative perspectives: she adopts the voice of her lover in order to comment on her own life in *The Autobiography of Alice B. Toklas* (1933), and she oscillates between the reported speech of young US soldiers abroad and her own stylized prose in the late sequence *Brewsie and Willie* (1946).

MARTIN HALLIWELL

See also Three Lives

Biography

Born 3 February 1874 in Allegheny, Pennsylvania; spent childhood in Vienna, Paris, and Oakland, California. Attended schools in Oakland and San Francisco; Radcliffe College, Cambridge, Massachusetts, 1893–97: studied philosophy under William James, B.A. (Harvard University), 1897; studied medicine at Johns Hopkins Medical School, Baltimore, 1897–1901. Lived in Paris from 1903, with Alice B. Toklas from 1908; moved in a circle of artists and writers including Picasso, Matisse, Braque, Hemingway, and Fitzgerald; lived in Mallorca, 1914–16; worked with American Fund for French Wounded, 1917–18; founded Plain Edition, Paris, 1930–33; lectured in the United States, 1934–35. Died 27 July 1946.

Novels by Stein

Three Lives, 1909
Tender Buttons, 1914
The Making of Americans, 1925
The Autobiography of Alice B. Toklas, 1933
Brewsie and Willie, 1946

Other Writings: stories, plays, verse and prose poetry, children's literature, letters, critical writings, and an assortment of other experimental works.

Further Reading

Berry, Ellen E., *Curved Thought and Textual Wandering: Gertrude Stein's Postmodernism,* Ann Arbor: University of Michigan Press, 1992

Copeland, Carolyn Faunce, *Language and Time in Gertrude Stein,* Iowa City: University of Iowa Press, 1975

DeKoven, Marianne, *A Different Language: Gertrude Stein's Experimental Writing,* Madison: University of Wisconsin Press, 1983

Dubnick, Randa, *The Structure of Obscurity: Gertrude Stein, Language and Cubism,* Urbana: University of Illinois Press, 1984

Neuman, Shirley, and Ira B. Nadel, *Gertrude Stein and the Making of Literature,* London: Macmillan, 1987; Boston: Northeastern University Press, 1988

Quartermain, Peter, *Disjunctive Poetics: From Gertrude Stein and Louis Zukovsky to Susan Howe,* Cambridge and New York: Cambridge University Press, 1992

Ruddick, Lisa, *Reading Gertrude Stein: Body, Text, Gnosis,* Ithaca, New York: Cornell University Press, 1990

Stein, Gertrude, "Composition as Explanation," reprinted in *A Stein Reader,* edited by Ulla E. Dydo, Evanston, Illinois: Northwestern University Press, 1993; essay originally appeared in 1926

Steiner, Wendy, *Exact Resemblance to Exact Resemblance: The Literary Portraiture of Gertrude Stein,* New Haven, Connecticut: Yale University Press, 1978

Walker, Jayne L., *The Making of a Modernist: Gertrude Stein from "Three Lives" to "Tender Buttons,"* Amherst: University of Massachusetts Press, 1984

Weinstein, Norman, *Gertrude Stein and the Literature of Modern Consciousness,* New York: Ungar, 1970

Stendhal [Marie-Henri Beyle] 1783–1842

French

Marie-Henri Beyle, better known under his pen name, Stendhal, had not intended to become a novelist and had hoped instead to make his mark in the literary world as a dramatist. While he never completed a play, his prenovelistic career included the publication of books about music and Italian painting, an analytical treatise on love, travel literature, pamphlets on the romantic movement, and magazine articles on contemporary French culture. Only in 1827, when he was 44 years old, did Stendhal finally publish a novel, *Armance,* and even that work was in part a literary hoax intended to make fun of another novelist. *Armance* was followed by *Le Rouge et le noir* (1830; *The Red and the Black*), *Lucien Leuwen* (written 1834–35, published 1894; *Lucien Leuwen*), *La Chartreuse de Parme* (1839; *The Charterhouse of Parma*), and *Lamiel* (written 1839–42, published 1889; *Lamiel*).

Stendhal's novels are continuous with the 18th-century concept of the genre in their retention of an overt role for the narrator. Freely intervening in the text, occasionally addressing the reader directly, and sometimes adopting an ironic stance toward his own characters, the narrator maintains a presence intended to heighten the reader's consciousness of the text's fictionality. In *The Red and the Black* especially, Stendhal enjoys highlighting the arbitrariness of fiction, even exhibiting a ludic concept of textuality in his use of epigraphs, most of which are falsely attributed or fictitious, becoming markers of textual play and invitations to the reader to recognize the author's playfulness. This ludic propensity is also present in his affection for inserting brief narrative sequences informing the reader of what would have happened had the hero, Julien, acted differently. We sense Stendhal's pleasure in telling the story of two heroes, one the actual hero and the other a potential hero who would be smarter and more astute.

While extending the 18th-century understanding of the novel as a self-conscious genre, Stendhal made major contributions in the development of the realistic novel. This is already evident in *Armance* in which the characters live in a historically defined world. Indeed, the plot is dependent on the outcome of a historical act of parliament in 1825. In *The Red and the Black,* Stendhal broadly expanded this dimension so that the complexities of the political and social conditions are woven into the fabric of the narrative more tightly than in any previous novel. Julien Sorel's entanglement with his society led the scholar Erich Auerbach to see in this novel the first expression of "a modern consciousness of reality" (see Auerbach, 1946).

Yet Stendhal's contribution to the realist orientation of the novel differs considerably from that of his contemporary Honoré de Balzac. Refusing a microrealism centered on descriptive detail, Stendhal is primarily interested in describing the forces—religious, political, and economic—at play in society. This approach serves him particularly well in representing the political realities of Europe after the Congress of Vienna, whether those realities be the subtle and petty politics of reactionary regimes in *The Charterhouse of Parma* or the deadening weight of government corruption under Louis-Philippe, which *Lucien Leuwen* so brilliantly unveils. Stendhal is astute in representing political institutions, but he is most interested in the reverberations of politics on individuals. He is therefore more prone than Balzac to filter the representation of reality through the individual consciousness of the hero. The most famous example of this technique is the representation of the battle of Waterloo through the eyes of Fabrice del Dongo, the protagonist of *The Charterhouse of Parma*—a technique that much impressed Lev Tolstoi, who acknowledged his own debt to it.

It is within such social, political, and historical contexts and under the watchful eye of a sophisticated narrator that Stendhal presents heroes and heroines as self-conscious young people coping with the transition to adulthood in post-Napoleonic Europe. From his first novel, Stendhal relies heavily on the interior monologue as a way of making the reader aware of the inner thoughts of his protagonists, all of whom suffer problems of identity. The protagonists deal with their identity problems in different ways: Octave, the hero of *Armance*, who harbors a secret so shameful that he cannot reveal it, tries to live according to a model of duty and Cornelian honor; Julien Sorel, whose ambitions are fueled by a heightened sense of class consciousness, attempts to conform his life to his reading of Napoléon's, intending to achieve greatness through the force of his will. Unlike Octave, Julien finally succeeds in seeing through his own mythology and understanding its falseness. Lucien Leuwen, the hero of the novel of the same name, assumes various identities in an anguished search for self-definition. Only toward the end of the novel does Lucien realize that he can be himself only if he cuts his ties with his wealthy father whose paternal generosity and control undermine his self-confidence. Fabrice del Dongo, another character in search of himself, is the first Stendhalian hero to rid himself of the obsession with an ideal model and to forgive himself for being a man. One character who does not share the propensity for self-questioning that characterizes Stendhal's male heroes is Lamiel, the protagonist of his last, unfinished, and most audacious novel. A young woman of incredible energy, Lamiel reverses gender roles in courtship without experiencing any of the internal debates about love that plague Stendhal's male heroes. Stendhal's projected ending for this novel, namely Lamiel's self-immolation in the conflagration of the Palace of Justice is both a paean to passion and an indictment of the corruption of power. In the end, all Stendhal's heroes finally recognize that only love has the power to destroy their fear of the judgment of others. As the stories of Julien and Fabrice attest, passionate love can transform even a prison into a place of happiness. This representation of love as the noblest of human emotions situates Stendhal's novels within the European romantic movement.

EMILE J. TALBOT

See also Red and the Black

Biography

Born 23 January 1783 in Grenoble, France. Schooled by tutors at home, and attended École Centrale, Grenoble, 1796–99. Influence procured him an army commission, 1800: 2nd lieutenant of dragoons; resigned commission, 1802; lived in Paris, 1802–06; civil servant: provisional deputy, deputy, and intendant to Commissariat of Wars at Brunswick, Vienna, and Hungary, 1806–09; commissioner for Council of State and Inspector of Crown Furnishings and Buildings, Paris, 1810; courier to Napoléon's armies in Germany, Russia, and Austria, 1812–13; administrator in Silesia and Dauphiné; quit civil service, 1814; lived in Milan, 1814–21, and in Paris, working as a freelance journalist for French and English papers, 1821–30; French Consul, Trieste, 1830–31, and Civitavecchia, from 1831; lived in Paris on extended leave, 1836–39, and on sick leave from 1841. Died 23 March 1842.

Novels by Stendhal

Armance; ou, Quelques Scènes d'un Salon de Paris en 1827, 1827; as *Armance*, translated by C.K. Scott Moncrieff, 1928
Le Rouge et le noir, 1830; as *Red and Black*, translated by E.P. Robins, 1898; as *The Red and the Black*, translated by Horace B. Samuel, 1913; as *Scarlet and Black*, translated by C.K. Scott Moncrieff, 1927
La Chartreuse de Parme, 1839; as *La Chartreuse de Parme*, translated by E.P. Robins, 1895; as *The Chartreuse of Parma*, translated by Lady Mary Loyd, 1901; as *The Charterhouse of Parma*, translated by C.K. Scott Moncrieff, 1925; Margaret R.B. Shaw, 1958; Margaret Mauldon, 1997
Lamiel, 1889; as *Lamiel*, translated by Jacques Le Clerq, 1929; also translated by T.W. Earp, 1951
Lucien Leuwen, 1894; as *Lucien Leuwen: The Green Huntsman* [and] *The Telegraph*, translated by Louise Varèse, 2 vols., 1950; also translated by H.L.R. Edwards, 2 vols., 1951

Other Writings: books on Italian art, biographies of composers, a treatise on love, autobiography, memoirs, travel books, essays.

Further Reading

Alter, Robert, *A Lion for Love: A Critical Biography of Stendhal*, Cambridge, Massachusetts: Harvard University Press, 1979
Auerbach, Erich, *Mimesis: Dargestellte Wirklichkeit in der abendländischen Literatur*, Bern: Francke, 1946; as *Mimesis: The Representation of Reality in Western Literature*, Princeton, New Jersey: Princeton University Press, 1953
Boll-Johansen, Hans, *Stendhal et le roman: Essai sur la structure du roman stendhalien*, Aran: Editions du Grand-Chêne, and Copenhagen: Akademisk Forlag, 1979
Brombert, Victor, *Stendhal: Fiction and the Themes of Freedom*, New York: Random House, 1968

Day, James T., *Stendhal's Paper Mirror: Patterns of Self-Consciousness in His Novels,* New York: Peter Lang, 1987

Jefferson, Ann, *Reading Realism in Stendhal,* Cambridge and New York: Cambridge University Press, 1988

Pearson, Roger, *Stendhal's Violin: A Novelist and His Reader,* Oxford: Clarendon Press, and New York: Oxford University Press, 1988

Talbot, Emile J., *Stendhal Revisited,* New York: Twayne, and Toronto: Macmillan, 1993

Steppenwolf by Hermann Hesse

Der Steppenwolf 1927

Hermann Hesse's novel *Steppenwolf* is a text of midlife in several ways: it lies midway in its author's publishing career, which spanned roughly the first half of the 20th century; also, the novel's protagonist is a man facing the anguished uncertainties both of middle age and of a social world—the Germany of the 1920s—in transition. Despite the more obvious charm and serenity of some of Hesse's other narrative works, his reputation as a modernist writer is largely founded on *Steppenwolf,* which has received the most critical acclaim.

Hesse's literary roots lie in German romanticism. Romanticism's antirationalist spirituality and its critique of bourgeois culture inform much of Hesse's writing, which is intensified by knowledge of Far Eastern religious thought as well as by Nietzschean philosophy—especially the defiant Nietzsche of *Also sprach Zarathustra* (1892; *Thus Spoke Zarathustra*). In addition, Hesse's thinking was enriched by a deep interest in psychoanalysis, derived from his systematic study of the discipline and his personal experiences of analysis, which included sessions with Carl Jung. Evidence of Hesse's interest in psychoanalysis is apparent in several earlier works. The novel *Demian* (1919; *Demian*) incorporated Jungian motifs but attempted rather awkwardly to integrate them into a relatively conventional first-person narrative frame. Hesse had in the essay *Sprache* (1917; Language) written of the way art might learn to move easily between the conscious and unconscious. In his autobiographical *Kurgast* (Spa Guest) of 1925 he yearned for a "double melody" in language that would unite the physical and the spiritual simultaneously.

With *Steppenwolf* Hesse finally found an adequate vehicle to embody the complexity of his thinking on personality, to which the painful experience of two failed marriages and of being reviled as a pacifist after World War I undoubtedly contributed. The title *Steppenwolf* is rich with resonances. There are echoes of Nietzsche's predatory beast outside the "herd," of Freud's Wolf Man case with its split between decency and unbridled instinct, and of "steps" in the sense of dance. Hesse had himself only learned to dance at approximately the age of 50, and his letters of the time play directly on the word association of "steppes" and "steps"—the idea of dance as a wild and ecstatic release from overrational bourgeois constraint. Thus, the title signals the text's concern with antibourgeois attitudes, with the life of the senses, and with the split between conscious and unconscious, while also suggesting in that very multiplicity the possibility of embracing and transcending divisions through symbolic language.

From the very start Hesse creates a narrative structure that is not progressive and linear as in earlier works but multilayered through its unreliable narration. The bulk of the text consists of jottings supposedly left behind by one Harry Haller; these notes are presented to the reader by an "editor," the nephew of Haller's erstwhile landlady, who not only is unable to guarantee their authenticity but who also displays his own bourgeois limitations of insight so that the reader is doubly distanced from any trust in simple referentiality. Thus, the editor's revelations about Haller and the notes he edits are rendered suspect and unreliable. Similarly uncertain in status is a text within the jottings—the *Tractat vom Steppenwolf* (*Treatise on the Steppenwolf*). The Treatise was supposedly thrust into Haller's hand one dark night, and it remains ambiguous throughout the novel as Haller's possible own self-projection. Thus, the novel repeatedly draws attention to its own fictionality and opens up the possibility of multiple readings, uniting physical and psychic reality.

At one level there remains a kind of story. Haller is a man experiencing deep dislocation. Although highly cultured and contemptuous of bourgeois attitudes, he is yet drawn to bourgeois orderliness. He is fully aware also of a destructive bohemian streak in himself and is quite open in his attacks on the reawakened voices of German supremacism. In other respects, however, Haller is inhibited; he lives on the dark side of city life, yet hates the jazz culture of the 1920s. His notes record his depression and anguish over the ugly modern world and his own occasional compromises with it. They also disclose how, paradoxically, he finds ease for the pain within and without where he least expects it: a generous prostitute introduces him to the pleasures of the body, dance, and sex, and so Haller starts to become more at home in himself and in the world of modern urban life. Given the unreliable status of the narration, however, much richer readings are possible and are signaled specifically by the Treatise, with its theoretical delineation of endless coexisting polarities within the self. Just as this inner text may be read as Haller's own as yet unassimilated self-knowledge, so all the "real" figures and events of the text as a whole may be read as externalizations of inner processes, as Haller is released from his simplistic mind/body separation. Hermine the prostitute, as the name hints, is Haller's Jungian anima deconstructing gender divisions; Pablo the jazz musician recalls several of Jung's symbols of Self—wise man, divine musician. The magic theatre with which the text ends is both drug trip and journey into the Freudian unconscious, the fullest release yet of libidinal energies. Moreover, as this terminology shows, Hesse is not simply replacing physical realism with one alternative "story" of personality. The subtext is infinitely fluid and suggestive, and, although rich in the imagery of psychoanalysis, it may also be read as, for example, a quasi-Buddhist meditation on the illusory nature of all conceptual dualisms. The text itself introduces both music and mirrors as motifs and may also be construed in both contexts—as a complex musical harmony or a series of interreflecting mirrors. The reader, like Haller, has to learn to combine.

Earlier modernist texts in German (for example, the novels of Rainer Maria Rilke and Franz Kafka) had already made problematic the concepts of identity and narration. *Steppenwolf*'s originality is not only that it subverts traditional novel characterization through the rich agency of psychoanalytic theory but that it embodies in its very structure the possibility of therapeutic release from simplistic categorization. The text is open-ended, in that Haller lapses into judgmentalism; but his journey, like the reader's, can always begin again with new riches to discover. Not surprisingly, this novel has spoken to many readers in many ways. In its own time, its sexual explicitness was controversial, and it has been read diversely since, both as an examination of a specifically German issue—the split between culture and barbarism—and as a celebration of 1960s liberalism. It remains one of the most vibrant treatments in any language of 20th-century spiritual dislocation.

MARY E. STEWART

See also Hermann Hesse

Further Reading

Berman, Russell A., *The Rise of the Modern German Novel: Crisis and Charisma,* Cambridge, Massachusetts: Harvard University Press, 1986

Boulby, Mark, *Hermann Hesse: His Mind and Art,* Ithaca, New York: Cornell University Press, 1967

Freedman, Ralph, *Hermann Hesse, Pilgrim of Crisis: A Biography,* New York: Pantheon, 1978; London: Cape, 1979

Michels, Volker, *Materialien zu Hermann Hesses "Der Steppenwolf,"* Frankfurt am Main: Suhrkamp, 1972

Mileck, Joseph, *Hermann Hesse, Dichter, Sucher, Bekenner: Biographie,* Frankfurt am Main: Suhrkamp, 1987

Ziolkowski, Theodore, *The Novels of Hermann Hesse: A Study in Theme and Structure,* Princeton, New Jersey: Princeton University Press, 1965

Ziolkowski, Theodore, *Hesse: A Collection of Critical Essays,* Englewood Cliffs, New Jersey: Prentice-Hall, 1973

Laurence Sterne 1713–68

English

Laurence Sterne spent most of his working life in relative obscurity as a conscientious but minor Yorkshire vicar. Before *Tristram Shandy* (1759–67) made him something of a London celebrity in the 1760s, he had published only one anonymous poem, some uninspiring political journalism, two sermons, and a short satire on local church politics. By the time of his death in 1768, an eight-year literary career had won Sterne considerable renown in Britain and Europe and secured his place as an important and influential innovator in the history of the novel. Sterne wrote exuberantly inventive serio-comedy in which play with the possibilities of narrative form and voice illuminates his characteristic concerns. Potentially tragic issues—the limits of epistemological certainty, the human capacity for self delusion, the gaps between rhetoric and feeling, word and world, and self and other—are treated with a comic lightness that enhances rather than diminishes their importance.

In January 1759, Sterne published *A Political Romance* in York, and although he had it withdrawn from circulation almost immediately, the 60-page satire of a local ecclesiastical squabble seems to have been something of a catalyst for his writing career. Amusing, if generally unremarkable, *A Political Romance* adopts Jonathan Swift's strategy from *A Tale of a Tub* (1704), an allegory in which real-life arguments are made to seem trivial by a process of satiric diminishment. Interestingly, *A Political Romance* ends with a "key" in which members of a fictional political club debate the possible meanings of the allegory. The key, like the satire proper, is self-consciously in the Scriblerian mode, but it also partially prefigures *Tristram Shandy* in its presentation of humorous characters whose ruling passions inform the excesses of subjective and comically absurd interpretation.

Having given up hope of preferment in the church, and tired, as he put it, "of employing [his] brains for other people's advantage," Sterne spent the rest of 1759 working on what was to become *Tristram Shandy*. In a letter accompanying the manuscript he sent to Robert Dodsley in May, Sterne described his "Plan" as "a most extensive one,—taking in, not only, the Weak part of the Sciences, in w[hi]ch the true point of Ridicule lies—but every Thing else, which I find Laugh-at-able in my way." In considering *Tristram Shandy*'s place in the history of the novel form, then, it is worth remembering that its primarily satiric thrust affiliates it with the satires in narrative of Rabelais and the Scriblerians rather than with the fiction of, say, Daniel Defoe or Samuel Richardson. Where the latter exhibit considerable interest in character, Sterne tends to subordinate character development to his satiric ends. As one contemporaneous critic put it, "the story of the hero's life is the least part of the author's concern. It is . . .

nothing more than a vehicle for satire on a great variety of subjects." Nevertheless, in its humorous laying bare of the mechanisms of narrative representation, *Tristram Shandy* is one of the prototypes of the self-reflexive novel that has proved such a productive resource for 20th-century novelists around the world.

Alongside the publication of the five installments of *Tristram Shandy*, Sterne published four volumes of *The Sermons of Mr. Yorick*. In spite of adopting a pseudonym from the thinly veiled alter ego who appears as the parson in *Tristram Shandy*, the sermons themselves seem to have been little changed from those delivered by Sterne in his own parishes and in York Minster. Modern commentators have tended to approach the sermons through the fiction and have looked very hard for "Shandean" elements in what are orthodox and commonplace pulpit discourses. Yet there are real continuities between the concerns of the sermons and the fiction. The use of exemplary character sketches and pathos for didactic ends are common to both. Moreover, Sterne's efforts in *Tristram Shandy* to address and construct particular readers, as well as his creative use of typographical devices, take on new significance in the light of the habits of the sermonist. In his attempts to transpose into *Tristram Shandy* the kind of pathetic rhetoric typical of Anglican sermons, Sterne perhaps discovered some of the significant differences between an essentially public, spoken discourse and the fundamentally private and written character of prose fiction.

Just more than a year after the publication of the ninth and final volume of *Tristram Shandy*, the first two volumes of *A Sentimental Journey through France and Italy by Mr. Yorick* were published in 1768. Sterne's death two months later left *A Sentimental Journey* with the Italian section of Yorick's travels unwritten. For a narrative that begins and ends in mid-sentence, and for a writer for whom the unfinished and fragmentary are offered as a deliberate foil to the tyranny of efforts to totalize, *A Sentimental Journey* is fittingly incomplete. By comparison with the consistently surprising formal inventiveness of *Tristram Shandy*, *A Sentimental Journey* may seem ordinary. Nevertheless, in its parody of the conventions of travel writing, its subtle critique of English Francophobia, its searching analysis of sentimentalism, and its fluidity of form, *A Sentimental Journey* has its own distinct merits. Indeed, in the 18th century, reviewers greeted *A Sentimental Journey* with nearly unqualified enthusiasm. It was Sterne's final work, more than *Tristram Shandy*, that spread his reputation in France and Germany in particular.

Most influential in the decades after his death as a sentimentalist and creator of "stories painted to the heart," Sterne was nonetheless a favorite of such diverse figures as Honoré de Balzac, Johann Wolfgang von Goethe and Nikolai Gogol'. Sterne's influence on the novel form has been most felt, however, with the advent of modernist and postmodernist fiction. Where Virginia Woolf found in Sterne the kind of conversational prose best suited to her efforts to "record the atoms as they fall upon the mind," Milan Kundera, Salman Rushdie, and many others have found liberation from the demands of mimesis and "psychological realism." Inevitably, writers have often read their own preoccupations into Sterne, but his writing is sufficiently protean to suggest quite different things to different readers. Friedrich Nietzsche's assessment of Sterne in *Menshliches, Allzumenschliches* (1878; *Human, All Too Human*) is as insightful as any: "What is to be praised in him is not the closed and transparent but the 'endless melody' . . . an artistic style in which the

fixed form is constantly being broken up, displaced, transposed back into indefiniteness, so that it signifies one thing and at the same time another. . . . He, the supplest of authors, communicates something of this suppleness to his reader."

J.T. PARNELL

See also Tristram Shandy

Biography

Born 24 November 1713 in Clonmel, County Tipperary, Ireland, into an English Army family; spent childhood at various regimental posts in England and Ireland. Attended a school near Halifax, Yorkshire, 1723–31; Jesus College, Cambridge, 1733–36 (sizar, 1733; scholar, 1734), B.A. 1737, M.A. 1740. Ordained deacon, 1737: curate of St. Ives, Huntingdonshire, 1737; assistant curate, Catton, Yorkshire, 1738; ordained priest, 1738; rector of Sutton-on-the-Forest, Yorkshire, 1738, and the adjoining parish Stillington from 1743 (retained both livings all his life and lived in Sutton until 1760); prebendary of York Cathedral from 1741; traveled to London, 1760: charged by other writers with indecency for *Tristram Shandy*; received perpetual curacy of Coxwold, Yorkshire, and settled there, 1760; lived in France, 1762–64; traveled in France and Italy, 1765–66; met Mrs. Eliza Draper, 1767; lived in London, 1767. Died 18 March 1768.

Novels by Sterne

The Life and Opinions of Tristram Shandy, Gentleman, 9 vols., 1759–67
A Sentimental Journey through France and Italy by Mr. Yorick, 2 vols., 1768

Other Writings: one published poem ("The Unknown World") and a burst of political journalism in the 1740s; a short satire on petty church politics in York (*A Political Romance*, 1759); 45 sermons published as *The Sermons of Mr. Yorick*, 7 vols., 1760–69; a journal to a young woman with whom Sterne had a (probably) platonic "affair" in his last months (*The Journal to Eliza*, published posthumously in 1904).

Further Reading

Alter, Robert, *Partial Magic: The Novel as a Self-Conscious Genre*, Berkeley: University of California Press, 1975
Byrd, Max, *Tristram Shandy*, London and Boston: Allen and Unwin, 1985
Cash, Arthur H., *Laurence Sterne: The Early and Middle Years*, London: Methuen, 1975; New York: Routledge, 1992
Cash, Arthur H., *Laurence Sterne: The Later Years*, London and New York: Methuen, 1986
Howes, Alan B., editor, *Sterne: The Critical Heritage*, London: Routledge and Kegan Paul, 1971; as *Laurence Sterne: The Critical Heritage*, London and Boston: Routledge and Kegan Paul, 1974
Lamb, Jonathan, *Sterne's Fiction and the Double Principle*, Cambridge and New York: Cambridge University Press, 1989
Lanham, Richard, *"Tristram Shandy": The Games of Pleasure*, Berkeley: University of California Press, 1973
Loveridge, Mark, *Laurence Sterne and the Argument About Design*, London: Macmillan, and Totowa, New Jersey: Barnes and Noble, 1982

New, Melvyn, *"Tristram Shandy": A Book for Free Spirits,*
New York: Twayne, 1994

New, Melvyn, editor, *"Tristram Shandy": Contemporary Critical Essays,* New York: Macmillan, 1992

Stedmond, John M., *The Comic Art of Laurence Sterne: Convention and Innovation in "Tristram Shandy" and "A Sentimental Journey,"* Toronto: University of Toronto Press, 1967

Robert Louis Stevenson 1850–94

Scottish

When the young Robert Louis Stevenson, fresh from publishing his first novel, *Treasure Island* (1883), wrote a response to Henry James' "The Art of Fiction," he inaugurated a new phase in the understanding of the novel and narration. Ingratiatingly entitled "A Humble Remonstrance," Stevenson's article challenged the older and considerably more famous writer's conservative ideas. Certainly, the time was ripe for change. In the earlier part of the century, the realist novel had been dominant. Works about the effects of the Industrial Revolution—the "Condition of England" novels—chiefly addressed the social disruption, deprivation, and class inequalities in the move from country to city, issues often presented in a moral frame. But in the second half of the century, and particularly with Darwin's publication of *The Origin of Species* (1859), reality and its representation became more problematic. The new paradigm of evolution reflected a more objective way of understanding reality, which for writers like George Eliot and Thomas Hardy led to an increasing self-consciousness about their art. By the 1880s questions about the morality of the novel jostled with the new scientific naturalism of Émile Zola, and debates raged.

When Stevenson published his article in *Longman's Magazine* in December 1884, he entered the discussion that James had been conducting with Walter Besant about defining the "rules" of fiction writing. James rejected any prescriptive approach to the novel, as well as Besant's direction that artists should only write from personal experience. James argued that experience is never complete, that art competes with life, and that the novel is "organic." Stevenson challenged and expanded the debate by suggesting that any discussion of fiction had to address the question of *narrative*, a term applicable also to poetry, drama, biography, and history, all of which shared textual and structural problems with the novel. In dismissing James' claims for the "truth" of art as it competes with life, Stevenson wrote, "life is monstrous, infinite, illogical, abrupt and poignant; a work of art, in comparison, is neat, finite, self-contained, rational, flowing and emasculate." For Stevenson, the novel is not "a transcript of life" but a selection and reorganization of certain aspects of life. Furthermore, the choice of subject, whether "adventure," "character," or "drama" (passion), determines the form, insofar as each requires a different type of structure and emphasis.

In "A Gossip on Romance" (1882), Stevenson had explored the form of the novel by focusing on questions of realism and romance. Arguing against realism (Stevenson disliked realism in its extreme form of naturalism), he claimed that the romance of the adventure novel is not simply an escape from reality but a desire for particular experiences: "Stories may be nourished with the realities of life, but their true mark is to satisfy the nameless longings of the reader, and to obey the ideal laws of the daydream." In making these claims Stevenson was drawing on his own writing experience, but what is notable is his acute perception of the psychology of reading and writing. His pre-Freudian understanding of the role of dream and desire was realized in *Treasure Island,* his acclaimed "children's novel." Henry James recognized early that the skill of this work lay in its double-voicing, by which the grown-up narrator tells the story of his younger self retrospectively, a narrative method that, while it addresses child and adult readers simultaneously, also fractures relationships between "lived" and "remembered" experiences.

The use of voice, or more correctly voices, as a narrative technique is brilliantly exploited in *The Strange Case of Dr. Jekyll and Mr. Hyde* (1886), Stevenson's defining myth of the divided self. Jekyll's drive to experience primary instincts, his desire to know "the animal within licking the chops of memory," is told by various narrators, all of whom are disturbed by an experience that they cannot rationalize. But Jekyll's own account that "man is not really one but two" is itself a cacophony of voices, which dissolves finally into a primal whimper.

It is in "A Gossip on Romance," too, that Stevenson first described the Hawes Inn on the Firth of Forth, the setting for the dramatic opening of *Kidnapped* (1886), an adventure novel that explores the divisive nature of Scottish history and identity. The dispossessed Highlands culture of the post-1745 Jacobite Rebellion is represented by Alan Breck, now a fugitive in his own country. David Balfour is from the Lowlands and, as a fatherless boy (a recurring figure in Stevenson's novels), he is equally dispossessed by being denied his true history and inheritance. Both are locked in a struggle of mutual miscomprehension that is expressed through landscape, language, costume, and cultural and moral codes. As with its companion piece, *Catriona* (1893), Stevenson explores the dualities of his national culture within the form of the popular novel. The romance of these adventure tales makes them exciting reading, but they are also serious explorations of national, cultural, and psychological divisions. The historical theme is repeated in *The Master of Ballantrae* (1889), a "winter's tale" of two brothers on opposite sides in the 1745 rebellion. In this tale Stevenson explores further the theme of doubles, contraries, and the contaminating effects of evil, as related by two narrative voices of questionable reliability. Some critics have described the novel's dramatic ending as containing elements of magic realism.

Stevenson's life-long respiratory problems played a part in his decision to embark with his family on a cruise of the South Pacific in 1880. They then settled permanently in Samoa. With restored health, Stevenson began to write about life in the South Seas—not romances, but novels of a Zolaesque realism. The first of these, *The Wrecker* (1892), was based on the story of a strange cargo and a mysterious shipwreck that Stevenson and his stepson and collaborator, Lloyd Osbourne, had heard of in Honolulu. The work contains extraordinary passages concerning life in San Francisco, the opium trade, and the shipwreck, but its structure is difficult to define, particularly because the ending does not explain the mystery but, in a postmodernist way, deconstructs the story.

Another collaboration, *The Ebb-Tide: A Trio and a Quartette* (1894), is a pre-Conradian tale of colonial exploitation, in which a "trio" of beachcombers sailing a smallpox-infected ship get lost and land on an uncharted island owned by a Virgil-quoting English gentleman who is both a stern disciplinarian and a religious megalomaniac. The subtitle's musical analogy points to the characters' accented voices as they play out various postures of control and submission. These come to a climax in a perfectly composed chapter, "The Dinner Party," in which the game of power reaches its zenith.

Weir of Hermiston (1896), the Scottish historical novel Stevenson was working on when he died, is also about power clashes, this time intergenerational. Perhaps representative of Stevenson's own experience with an authoritarian father, the father-son confrontation also adumbrated a major social issue and literary theme of late 19th-century culture. Although the novel is only one-third complete, it is memorable for its title character. Adam Weir's vernacular voice, with its blend of the pulpit and the bench, defines the man. Again, Stevenson uses voice as a structuring principle in a way that reflects his belief that the novel "imitates not life but speech."

Stevenson died in Samoa at the age of 44. In his short life he challenged ideas about the content and purpose of the novel, used the concept of narrative to argue against the idea of fixed genres, experimented with structures, bridged the categories of the serious and the popular novel, expanded understanding about reading and reception, and understood and used voice in a way that was not surpassed until the 20th century in the novels of James Joyce.

CATHERINE KERRIGAN

See also Strange Case of Dr. Jekyll and Mr. Hyde

Biography

Born 13 November 1850 in Edinburgh. Attended Mr. Henderson's school, Edinburgh, 1855–61; Edinburgh Academy; a school in Isleworth; Mr. Thompson's school, Edinburgh; University of Edinburgh, 1867–72; studied law in the office of Skene Edwards and Gordon, Edinburgh: called to the Scottish bar, 1875. Lived in Europe, mainly in France, 1875–80; contributor, *Cornhill Magazine*, London, 1876–82; lived in the United States, 1879–80 and 1887–88, Scotland, 1881–82, Hyères, France, 1882–84, and Bournemouth, 1884–87; sailed on three cruises in the Pacific, 1888–89; settled in Vailima, Samoa, 1890. Died 3 December 1894.

Novels by Stevenson

Treasure Island, 1883
Prince Otto, 1885
The Strange Case of Dr. Jekyll and Mr. Hyde, 1886
Kidnapped, 1886
The Black Arrow, 1888
The Wrong Box (with Lloyd Osbourne), 1889
The Master of Ballantrae, 1889
The Wrecker (with Lloyd Osbourne), 1892
The Beach of Falesa, 1893
Catriona, 1893
The Ebb-Tide: A Trio and a Quartette (with Lloyd Osbourne), 1894
Weir of Hermiston, 1896
St. Ives, 1897

Other Writings: stories, plays, poetry, travel writings, essays (gathered in *The Centenary Edition of the Collected Works of Robert Louis Stevenson*, edited by Catherine Kerrigan, 1995–).

Further Reading

Balfour, Graham, *The Life of Robert Louis Stevenson*, 2 vols., New York: Scribner, 1901

Booth, Bradford A., and Ernest Mehew, editors, *The Letters of Robert Louis Stevenson*, 8 vols., New Haven, Connecticut, and London: Yale University Press, 1994–95

Eigner, Edwin M., *Robert Louis Stevenson and Romantic Tradition*, Princeton, New Jersey: Princeton University Press, 1966

Furnas, J.C., *Voyage to Windward: The Life of Robert Louis Stevenson*, New York: Sloane, 1951; London: Faber, 1952

Maixner, Paul, editor, *Robert Louis Stevenson: The Critical Heritage*, London and Boston: Routledge and Kegan Paul, 1981

McKay, George L., *A Stevenson Library: Catalogue of a Collection of Writings by and about Robert Louis Stevenson Formed by Edwin J. Beinecke*, 6 vols., New Haven, Connecticut: Yale University Press, 1951–64

Miller, Karl, *Doubles: Studies in Literary History*, Oxford and New York: Oxford University Press, 1985

Smith, Janet Adam, editor, *Henry James and Robert Louis Stevenson: A Record of Friendship and Criticism*, London: Hart-Davis, 1948

Swearingen, Roger G., *The Prose Writings of Robert Louis Stevenson*, London: Macmillan, and Hamden, Connecticut: Archon Books, 1980

Veeder, William, and Gordon Hirsch, editors, *Dr. Jekyll and Mr. Hyde after One Hundred Years*, Chicago: University of Chicago Press, 1988

Adalbert Stifter 1805–68

Austrian

Adalbert Stifter's prose fiction belongs largely to the Biedermeier era, a period of transition that produced its own distinctive poetic realism. He opened his literary career in 1840 with three novellas that treated the figure of the artist, *Der Condor* (The Condor), *Feldblumen* (Wild Flowers of the Field), and *Das Haidedorf* (The Village on the Heath), and went on to publish some 30 works of shorter fiction and three major novels, *Der Nachsommer* (1857; *Indian Summer*), *Witiko* (1865–67), and *Die Mappe meines Urgrossvaters* (published posthumously in 1939; My Great-Grandfather's Notebook). A most careful stylist who was seldom satisfied with his first efforts, Stifter was given to reworking his material. He republished much of his prose in two collections entitled *Studien* (1844–50; Studies) and *Bunte Steine* (1853; Colored Stones). The latter cycle, introduced by its famous preface, contains Stifter's aesthetic creed, which proclaims a revaluation of all that is commonly perceived as "great" in nature and mankind. Stifter, who was also a competent scientist, identified a principle that he called "the gentle law" acting within the universe, inconspicuously working toward preservation, growth, and restoration. Stifter specifies as "great" the all-pervading, unseen, yet omnipotent forces that are analogous to scientific law. The occasional disruptive appearance of volcanoes, earthquakes, and storms he designates as having lesser status, since these are merely effects and not the superior causes. Despite these avowed convictions, Stifter's work contains many striking and memorable depictions of natural catastrophes and violent eruptions that are the more impressive for breaking through unexpectedly and disrupting the calm control of his prose.

The three novels Stifter wrote in his maturer years show considerable originality in their striking differences of approach to the form. *Indian Summer* is ostensibly a novel of self-cultivation (Bildungsroman), in the tradition of Johann Wolfgang von Goethe's *Wilhelm Meisters Lehrjahre* (1795–1821; *Wilhelm Meister's Apprenticeship*), in that it explores a young man's growth to a fuller understanding of the world of science, art, and culture in general. Yet Stifter's work does not take us into the busy world of urban society, commerce, or institutions but into a sequestered, idyllic rural setting. As he wrote: "The whole situation, no less than the human characters must, in my view, be something higher which raises the reader above ordinary life." The novel's center of gravity is the figure of the young man's mentor and spiritual guide, Risach, who has laboriously built his ideal world—in the form of the "Rosenhaus," with its secluded garden and precious collections—upon the painful memory of a youthful passion. Risach's life's work, which outwardly manifests serene order and a high moral purpose, is nonetheless a monument to sacrificed youthful love. Stifter explores this underlying ambivalence through the ever-present symbol of the rose. The general tenor of the work is one of strenuous and lofty aspiration, which is equally expressed through its painstaking and polished style. The work cannot readily be compared with any contemporaneous European novel, for it was conceived in opposition to the literary fashions of its day and looks back rather toward neo-Platonic and Benedictine traditions, with their strong predilection for allegory and symbol.

The historical novel *Witiko*, which took 15 years to complete, is an ambitious attempt to create a grandiose epic in a modern prose form. Set in medieval Bohemia, it is avowedly faithful to historical events, yet Stifter subordinates his subject matter to rigorous formal patterning. He is concerned less with chronicling the events that led to the founding of the ruling house of Rosenberg than with perceiving a meaningful order in the course of history, which he called "the terrible majesty of the moral law." Although he depicts battles, conspiracies, lawless action, and usurpation of power, he does not seek to arouse interest by introducing conflict and suspense. Rather he looks to Homer for his model in staging the grand panorama of human struggle for supremacy over a nation and the establishment of justice and humanity. The work is conspicuously stylized in narrative technique, especially in its ceremonial use of language, which arranges description and dialogue to achieve the incantatory effect of litanies. Although Stifter wished to maintain a high level of diction so as "to create something that is not unworthy of the high excellence of poetic art," this rigidly formal style tends to become monotonous. What remains impressive is Stifter's innovative experimentation with problems of expression and form. In this way he is reminiscent of another perfectionist of the same era, Gustave Flaubert.

Stifter's last novel, *Die Mappe meines Urgrossvaters*, although unfinished at his death, is the formulation of a concept he had nurtured from his beginnings as a writer. The novel is set in his native landscape of Bohemia and has autobiographical accents. The narrative unfolds by way of diary installments written by a country doctor, who has learned from his friend, a retired colonel, that the act of recording each stage of one's life may help to bring order and direction to that life. After a painful breaking of faith with the woman he loves, the doctor must learn to regain mastery over his existence and heal the wound. Through his dedicated medical practice he gradually finds rewards, for in healing others he, too, is made whole. The intricate interdependence of theme and form achieved in this novel is one of perfect balance. This fourth and last version of his "favorite child," as Stifter called his final novel, shows the craftsman at the peak of his powers. He constantly filed down his material until he sensed that he had attained classical clarity and purity of form. This is particularly true of the sixth chapter ("Der sanftmütige Obrist"/The Gentle Colonel), a self-contained biography that entails a "lesson for life" and has therefore a crucial function in the design of the whole. The novel makes no concession to literary fashion and does not pander to any taste for the topical or the sensational, but rather it develops its own contemplative realism. Stifter's art was uncompromising in the pursuit of a truthfulness of content and purity of style, or, as he once put it, "simple, clear, transparent and a balm like the air."

ALEXANDER STILLMARK

Biography

Born 23 October 1805 in Oberplan, Bohemia, Austria (now Horné Planà, Czech Republic). Attended village school; Benedictine monastery school, Kremsmünster, 1818–26; law student at University of Vienna, 1828–30. Tutor and painter, and editor, *Der Wiener Bote*, 1849–50; school inspector, Upper Austria, 1850–65; art critic, *Linzer Zeitung*, 1852–57; Curator of Monuments for Upper Austria, 1853. Died (suicide) 28 January 1868.

Selected Fiction by Stifter
Studien [Studies], 6 vols., 1844–50; enlarged edition, 1855
Bunte Steine [Colored Stones], 1853
Der Nachsommer, 1857; as *Indian Summer*, translated by Wendell Freye, 1985
Witiko, 1865–67
Die Mappe meines Urgrossvaters [My Great-Grandfather's Notebook], 1939; final version, 1946

Other Writings: several volumes of Stifter's letters have been collected, including in the collected works, *Werke und Briefe*, edited by Alfred Doppler and Wolfgang Frühwald, 1978– .

Further Reading
Aspetsberger, Friedbert, "Die Aufschreibung des Lebens: Zu Stifters 'Mappe'," *Vierteljahresschrift des Adalbert-Stifter-Instituts des Landes Oberösterreich* 27:1–2 (1978)
Hohoff, Curt, *Adalbert Stifter: Seine dichterischen Mittel und die Prosa des neunzehnten Jahrhunderts,* Düsseldorf: Schwann, 1949
Kunisch, Hermann, *Adalbert Stifter: Mensch und Wirklichkeit: Studien zu seinem klassischen Stil,* Berlin: Duncker and Humblot, 1950
Lengauer, Hubert, "Konstitution und Selbstbeherrschung: Zum Verhältnis von Lebensgeschichte und Zeitgeschichte in Stifters Mappe," in *Adalbert Stifter Heute: Londoner Symposium 1983,* edited by Johann Lachinger, Alexander Stillmark, and Martin Swales, Linz/London: Adalbert-Stifter-Institut des Landes Oberösterreich, 1985
Schoenborn, Peter A., *Adalbert Stifter: Sein Leben und Werk,* Bern: Francke, 1992
Stillmark, Alexander, "Stifter's *Letzte Mappe* and the Idea of Wholeness," in *Tradition and Creation: Essays in Honour of Elizabeth Mary Wilkinson,* edited by C.P. Magill et al., Leeds: W.S. Maney, 1978
Swales, Martin, and Erika Swales, *Adalbert Stifter: A Critical Study,* Cambridge and New York: Cambridge University Press, 1984

The Stone Angel by Margaret Laurence

1964

The Stone Angel is the first of five books by Margaret Laurence that focus on the fictional town of Manawaka. On its publication in 1964, it established itself as an instant success, one of the most admired and best loved of Canadian novels. In Hagar Shipley, Laurence had created perhaps the most formidably memorable character in Canadian fiction—a character, moreover, worthy to take her place on the international literary stage. Hagar is not an especially likable figure—tough, proud, obstinate, selfish, independent, unyielding, a "holy terror" in the words of her elder son—but she is important historically in that she represents the mythic qualities of the original Canadian pioneer immigrants with their fabled grit, adaptability, and determination to establish themselves in a harsh and unfamiliar land. *The Stone Angel* was published at a time of rapid change, when Canadians were beginning to become aware of the significance—as well as the extent and complexity—of their history, and the novel was welcomed as an important contribution to the creation of a national literature.

By giving her heroine the biblical name of Hagar, Laurence associates her with even earlier pioneering peoples. While Laurence does not slavishly copy the story of Abraham and the handmaid from Genesis 16, biblical analogues and allusions occur frequently although unostentatiously within the text. In Hagar, Bram Shipley's second wife who flees "into the wilderness" in a frustrated attempt to give her second son a better chance in life, Laurence establishes echoes for readers aware of the biblical narrative and endows her story with a deeper significance.

Although complex in its implications, *The Stone Angel* is simple enough in its broad outlines. A first-person novel, it exists wholly within the mind of the 90-year-old Hagar, who is beginning to lose her bodily strength yet draws upon all her formidable powers of resistance to withstand plans by her elder son and daughter-in-law to place her in an old people's home. While planning a desperate escape, she simultaneously relives her earlier life, "remembering furiously" as she thinks back to her "lost men." As the novel's epigraph from Dylan Thomas indicates, Hagar's story is an extended "rage against the dying of the light." While planning (again like the biblical Hagar) to flee from unpleasant constraints, she finds herself casting up accounts, coming to terms with the manifold actions of a lifetime. She is, as she says, "rampant with memory," and the book's action alternates between her domestic present in British Columbia and the vividly recollected memories of her earlier life as a young woman on the Manitoba prairie.

The Stone Angel is most remarkable, perhaps, for its expert deployment of voice. Hagar tells her own story, and it was essential that Laurence should get her accents and cadences exactly right. In "Gadgetry or Growing," a lecture originally delivered at the University of Toronto, Laurence has testified to her satisfaction in successfully reproducing the speech rhythms of her grandparents' generation: "I felt when I was writing *The Stone Angel* an enormous conviction of the authenticity of Hagar's voice, and I experienced a strange pleasure in rediscovering an idiom I hardly knew I knew, as phrases from my grandparents coming back to me" (see Laurence, 1980). Hagar's speech is a combination of the formal and the vernacular. She dislikes slang and favors a racy exactitude, sharp, precise, and highly metaphorical, in telling contrast to what Clara Thomas has described as the "hackneyed commonplace in speech" characterized by her son Marvin (see Thomas, 1975). This effect is augmented as the Manawaka series proceeds, and Hagar's voice is replaced by the flatter, less eloquent, modern cadences of recent generations.

The Stone Angel stands firmly within the tradition of literary realism. We believe in Hagar as a living human character, and her Manawaka home strikes us as historically accurate. At the same time, of course, the novel is a verbal construct existing only within the words that Laurence assigns to Hagar so that she can articulate her story. And the ordering of these words, especially the arranging of narrative incidents, is the key to Laurence's art. Here she encountered her greatest challenge in writing the novel, as shown by her observations in "Gadgetry or Growing," which reveal a curious combination of insight and naïveté. While on the one hand she realized that the accounts of Hagar's earlier life would have to appear in chronological order if readers were not to become hopelessly confused, on the other hand she was troubled by what she felt to be an offense against realistic principles, since she feared that chronological ordering "diminishes the novel's resemblance to life."

Fortunately, however, her artistic instincts proved superior to her theorizing. In the event, she was able to devise a system whereby, as Hagar plans her final flight into the wilderness, she is continually reminded of incidents in her early life that are sparked off by a stray word, image, or sound. Much of the art of the novel consists in the way in which these shifts of temporal perspective are managed. Thus the sight of a nurse at the old people's home causes Hagar to remember and reenact an equivalent scene in a prairie hospital where her first son was born. Recognition of such effects constitutes one of the genuine pleasures of this text.

Margaret Laurence has been praised for many reasons: as a regional or prairie novelist, as a chronicler of women and women's attitudes, as a champion of Canadian nationalism and humane liberal causes, and even, in this novel, as a pioneer in the literary presentation of old age. But *The Stone Angel* is supreme as an imaginative human document transcending region, gender, nation, politics, or gerontology, and Laurence herself is best regarded as a writer primarily concerned with presenting the complexities of human behavior and the subtleties of the human condition.

W.J. KEITH

See also Margaret Laurence

Further Reading

Laurence, Margaret, "A Place To Stand On," in *Heart of a Stranger*, Toronto: McClelland and Stewart, 1976

Laurence, Margaret, "Gadgetry or Growing: Form and Voice in the Novel," *Journal of Canadian Fiction* 27 (1980)

New, W.H., "Every Now and Then: Voice and Language in Laurence's *The Stone Angel*," *Canadian Literature* 93 (Summer 1982)

Rooke, Constance, "Hagar's Old Age: *The Stone Angel* as Vollendungsroman," in *Fear of the Open Heart*, Toronto: Coach House Press, 1989

Thomas, Clara, *The Manawaka World of Margaret Laurence*, Toronto: McClelland and Stewart, 1975

Woodcock, George, *Introducing Margaret Laurence's "The Stone Angel,"* Toronto: ECW Press, 1989

Story. *See* Discourse Representation; Narrator; Plot; Point of View

---

The Story of an African Farm by Olive Schreiner

1883

Olive Schreiner's novel *The Story of an African Farm* was originally seen at the time as an expression of the crisis of religious faith brought about by the advent of evolutionary theory and the industrial revolution. To the British public its exotic setting in the South African karoo, amid ostriches and koppies, increased its appeal. So did the discovery that it was not in fact written by a man, the Ralph Iron whose name appeared on the first edition, but by a young woman newly arrived from South Africa. Reviewers recognized its passion for the issues it debated—religious faith and women's emancipation—as well as involvement in the landscapes of its origin, but were divided about the value of its conclusions and somberness of its atmosphere.

Contemporary readers responded to Schreiner's depiction of childhood, of the spiritual struggle in the young missionary's son Waldo, and of her spirited new woman, Lyndall, who articulated women's sense of reduced education and limited opportunities in the late Victorian era. Some complained that Schreiner interrupted her story to launch into disquisitions and long philosophical allegories. The novel's mixing of genres and its apparently arbitrary plot, including the causeless death of the hero in the closing pages, caused much critical concern, and for a long time the novel was judged wanting in terms of unity of action and of structure. Other critics explained away its unique structure in terms of poetry, arguing that its method was essentially lyric and so the book should not be judged as a novel. Schreiner added a preface to the second edition in which she responded to some of these criticisms. She argued that the method of the novel was that of the lives we all lead: arbitrary, random, with inexplicable appearances and disappearances, and with no controlling or redemptive creator. The novel's structure, thus, also bore testimony to the loss of stable structures of faith and meaning that had obtained within a Christian worldview. Schreiner also confronted the complaint that the novel did not offer the kind of adventure that British readers might expect of Africa (no lions and hairbreadth escapes) by arguing that the novel's crises were interior and spiritual, and that writers in South Africa should register the environment in which they find themselves, should paint with the pigments found all around them.

Schreiner thus formulated what later became enduring features of South African literature: its loyalty to the sometimes barren, but also efflorescent, features of the landscape, and its intransigent dedication to local problems of immediate relations between colonizer and colonized, Boer and Briton, missionary and farmer. Although her focus is on the aspirations of young white colonial men and women, and the life of servants and herdsmen is objectified, she nevertheless turns her attention to immediate problems of clashing cultures, racial misunderstanding, and violence. These remained the issues for subsequent generations of South African novelists, such as William Plomer, Alan Paton, Peter Abrahams, Dan Jacobson, Nadine Gordimer, Miriam Tlali, Sipho Sepamla, J.M. Coetzee, Sheila Roberts, and Peter Wilhelm. The bleakness of her view, her response to landscape, and her compassionate depiction of human suffering and disappointed aspirations in a climate with more conflict than cultural stimulus or aesthetic pleasure all set the scene for the development of the South African novel.

Schreiner's impact went beyond South Africa, however, especially in her rendition of characters as fluid amalgams of gender and consciousness, as states of being. She influenced writers such as D.H. Lawrence, who continued her worldview in the depiction of anguished, difficult relations between the sexes as the mark of modernity. Her strong focus on the consciousness of a young woman as the locus of the clash between aspiration and social constriction influenced generations of women writers, especially those, such as Doris Lessing and Nadine Gordimer, who have brought a South African consciousness to bear upon metropolitan concerns or readership. The young colonial woman who, with integrity and self-reliance, seeks honest answers to her quandaries amid a colonial heritage of violence, racism, gender privilege, and patriarchal structures (such characters as appear in Gordimer's and Lessing's novels), first steps forward in Lyndall, Schreiner's young heroine.

The Story of an African Farm is now understood within postcolonial frameworks as a fountainhead of counterhegemonic fictions that relate different forms of oppression, and that create aesthetic answers to the complicities of racial, class, and gender constructs. Although later fiction has foregrounded racial oppression much more strongly, as it was later foregrounded by successive South African political structures, *The Story of an African Farm* was the first South African novel of social protest. Its young protagonists also seek to realize their aspirations within a landscape that is on the verge of the huge dislocations brought about by urbanization and by the discovery of minerals. Schreiner's novel records a way of life on South African farms that was about to pass on, but whose mind-set created barriers to cultural harmony or growth that linger to this day. The inexplicable death of her young protagonist, Waldo, becomes a coda and a prophecy of the death of idealism and of political rationality that would follow in the long dark decades of racial segregation and white minority rule. Schreiner's contribution to the history of the novel was also a contribution to the voices of enlightenment that would ultimately prevail in South Africa.

CHERRY CLAYTON

Further Reading

Barsby, Christine, "Olive Schreiner: Towards a Redefinition of Culture," *Pretexts* 1:1 (1989)

Berkman, Joyce, *The Healing Imagination of Olive Schreiner: Beyond South African Colonialism,* Amherst: University of Massachusetts Press, 1989

Clayton, Cherry, *Olive Schreiner,* New York: Twayne, 1997

Gorak, Irene, "Olive Schreiner's Colonial Allegory: *The Story of an African Farm,*" *Ariel* 23:4 (1992)

Monsman, Gerald, *Olive Schreiner's Fiction: Landscape and Power,* New Brunswick, New Jersey: Rutgers University Press, 1991

Schoeman, Karel, *Olive Schreiner: 'n lewe in Suid-Afrika, 1855–1881,* Kaapstad: Human and Rousseau, 1989; as *Olive Schreiner: A Woman in South Africa, 1855–1881,* Johannesburg: Jonathan Ball, 1991

Voss, Tony, "Avatars of Waldo," *Alternation* 1:2 (1994)

Story of the Stone. *See* Six Classic Chinese Novels

The Story of Zahra by Ḥanān al-Shaykh

Ḥikāyat Zahrah 1980

During the period of Lebanon's civil war (1975–90), the impulse toward modernization began to be questioned by a new generation of Arab writers. With this questioning of cultural and political assumptions came another urgent and related questioning of sexual relations, particularly on the part of female writers. A sharp divergence in trajectory of modernist narrative development between male and female novelists appeared and began to widen.

At the outset of this period, the issue of national identity was perceived by many women writers as consonant with feminist issues. Women writers identified the struggle for national liberation with the feminist struggle and the soul of the Arab nation with the "eternal feminine," defending the ideal of a pluralistic society embodied in the cause of Palestinian nationalism. With the continuation of the Lebanese conflict into the 1980s, writers began to examine the ethic of violence in the pursuit of political objectives more critically. Women novelists began to distance themselves from the nationalist struggle and to view all types of politically motivated conflict as aspects of patriarchy. They presented femininity as something contrary to the process of armed conflict, regardless of its ideological motivation, and held women up as heroic symbols of resistance to a pattern of masculine self-destructiveness.

By the mid-1980s, however, a note of passivity, ennui, and despair crept into women's writing. In Ḥanān al-Shaykh's *The Story of Zahra,* we no longer find a bold female protagonist, either in the role of revolutionary or opponent of violence. Bewildered, passive, and directionless, the protagonist, Zahra, enacts a pattern of complicity with that violence. While still young, she enters into a lengthy affair with a married man that provides her with no genuine satisfaction. After two abortions, she decides to join her uncle, a political refugee who has fled to Africa. Although she repeatedly thwarts his sexual advances, she is propelled into a loveless marriage and immediately denounced by her husband because she is not a virgin. Returning to war-torn Beirut to live with her parents after the failure of her marriage, she gives herself freely to a sniper on the roof of an apartment building in a series of mute sexual encounters. For the first time she experiences sexual arousal and climax. Her descriptions of these sexual encounters combine the motif of dominance and submission with that of sexual awakening:

My back aches from lying on the ground. I want to rise, but the sniper never seems to have his fill of me. He drops down on me like a bat out of the air. Yet I like him weighing down on me. I clutch his back so that he weighs as much as possible. It is a weight that transforms itself into lightness until the sniper seems weightless, bodiless.

The contradictory images of weight and weightlessness reinforce the central paradox of the text. As a character, Zahra is a feminist's nightmare, and yet her narrative makes a disturbing impact, forcing us as readers to question at what point victimization becomes so complete that it is transformed into complicity. As Zahra sinks into sexual submission, her very acquiescence takes on the hue of rebellion, significantly against the patriarchal symbol of her father:

Oh, you sniper! You weigh on me like a vast but weightless mountain! Oh, you who dig these deep craters in my body, can't you dig deeper and deeper, can't you dig deeper and deeper until another orifice opens and sets free these old fearful moments, these images that have until now haunted all my days?

Oh, sniper, let me cry out in pleasure so that my father hears me and comes to find me sprawled out so. I am one with the dust in this building of death. Let my father see my legs spread wide in submission.

Zahra further rationalizes her experience, seeking to explain the sense of liberation that it brings:

This war has made beauty, money, terror and convention all equally irrelevant. It begins to occur to me that the war, with its miseries and destructiveness, has been necessary for me to start to return to being normal and human.

The war, which makes one expect the worst at any moment, has led me into accepting this new element in my life. Let it happen, let us witness it, let us open ourselves to accept the unknown, no matter what it may bring, disasters or surprises.

At the end of the narrative, Zahra informs the sniper that she is pregnant, only to be told that she should get an abortion. Her lover later seems to change his mind, implying that he will marry her, but as she leaves the rooftop where they have had their clandestine meetings, she suddenly feels an excruciating pain. The sniper has apparently shot her, and at this point she goes on to relate her own death:

A complete silence descends, for to scream has become an unbearable agony. My vocal chords are chained to my heart's root. The sniper is killing me. His first two bullets missed piercing my head. His third missed piercing the foetus inside me. I don't scream. I don't try to touch the streaming blood. Instead I lie silent in the rain. . . . The pain is terrible, but I grow accustomed to it, and to the darkness. As I close my eyes for an instant, I see the stars of pain. Then there are rainbows arching across white skies. He kills me. He kills me with the bullets that lay at his elbow as he made love to me.

In the last sentence, Zahra's thoughts juxtapose the beauty and transcendence of her own death with the horror of male aggression:

I see rainbows processing towards me across the white skies with their promises only of menace.

Zahra's narrative indeed represents a type of rebellion that resists any attempt to construct a heroic image. The ambivalence of the text, as well as its antiheroic stance, qualifies it as a quintessentially modernist text, and a watershed in the development of the Arabic novel.

STEFAN MEYER

See also Ḥanān al-Shaykh

Further Reading

Accad, Evelyne, *Sexuality and War: Literary Masks of the Middle East*, New York: New York University Press, 1990

Allen, Roger, *The Arabic Novel: An Historical and Critical Introduction*, Syracuse, New York: Syracuse University Press, and Manchester: Manchester University Press, 1982; 2nd edition, Syracuse, New York: Syracuse University Press, 1995

Cooke, Miriam, *War's Other Voices: Women Writers of the Lebanese Civil War*, Cambridge and New York: Cambridge University Press, 1988

Cooke, Miriam, *Women and the War Story*, Berkeley: University of California Press, 1996

Larson, Charles B., "The Fiction of Hanan al-Shaykh, Reluctant Feminist," *World Literature Today* (Winter 1991)

Sunderman, Paula W., "An Interview with Hanan al-Shaykh," *Michigan Quarterly Review* 31:4 (Fall 1992)

Zeidan, Joseph T., *Arab Women Novelists: The Formative Years and Beyond*, Albany: State University of New York Press, 1995

The Strange Case of Dr. Jekyll and Mr. Hyde by Robert Louis Stevenson

1886

The two-in-one protagonist of *The Strange Case of Dr. Jekyll and Mr. Hyde* has become proverbial for the divided self and, more superficially, for hypocrisy and duplicity. The immediate origins of the story, in a nightmare suffered when the author was seriously ill (an experience that also led to the book's rapid composition), are recounted by his first biographer, Graham Balfour (1901), but its sources go deep into Stevenson's childhood in Scotland, where the imagination of the weakly and sensitive boy fell under the influence of his Calvinist parents and a nurse who graphically described to him the torments of hell-fire that awaited sinners.

At the most obvious level, this novel is concerned with the struggle between good and evil and thus has affinities with such traditional genres as allegory and tragedy. Balfour notes that "A subject much in [Stevenson's] mind at this time was the duality of man's nature and the alternation of good and evil," and in this respect Stevenson's work may be compared with such familiar treatments of the Faust legend as Marlowe's *Dr. Faustus* and Goethe's *Faust*. (Jekyll's dying agonies on the last page of the story bear some resemblance to the final scene of Marlowe's tragedy.) However, whereas Faust was tempted by an external agent, Mephistopheles, Hyde—although described at the outset as "like Satan"—is an externalization of an aspect of Jekyll's own nature.

Despite its kinship with ancient forms of literature, in formal terms *The Strange Case of Dr. Jekyll and Mr. Hyde* is a product of its time and owes much to the newly emerged genres of mystery and detective fiction, with the sober and rational lawyer Gabriel Utterson playing the amateur detective. (Drawing explicit attention to the symbolic naming of the protagonist's darker self, Utterson observes that "If he be Mr. Hyde . . . I shall be Mr. Seek.") Like Wilkie Collins and other Victorian exponents of detective fiction, Stevenson uses a complex narrative method exploiting different points of view and incorporating documents such as letters.

The story is also of its time in its relationship to Darwinian ideas, since Hyde is not merely a projection of Jekyll's baser nature but seems to represent a reversal of the evolutionary process. Hyde, who is repeatedly referred to as "apelike" and "like a monkey," is subhuman in his physical aspect: an obvious counterpart of his moral degeneracy or deformity. As a monster created by a research scientist, he is also a descendant of Frankenstein's monster, described in Mary Shelley's famous novel of 1818. A later novel that also deals with a scientist's disastrous attempts to interfere with the order of nature, and that similarly bears comparison with Stevenson's story, is H.G. Wells' *The Island of Dr. Moreau* (1896).

The physical setting of the book—not Stevenson's favorite Edinburgh but a fogbound London strongly anticipatory of that evoked by Conan Doyle in his Sherlock Holmes stories, the first of which appeared in the following year—may owe something to Dickens, whose influence may perhaps also be detected in the use of the romantic motif of the alter ego, double, or doppelgänger. In his last novels, Dickens repeatedly explored the theme of the secret and shameful life hidden beneath the surface of respectability: a striking case in point is Jasper, the cathedral official and murderer in *The Mystery of Edwin Drood* (1870). Stevenson's Dr. Jekyll is a dignified, kind, and well-regarded pillar of society who nevertheless engages in secret indulgences (of an unspecified nature, although the implications are sexual) that lead to the emergence of Hyde, his second and baser self. Through this kind of doubling, Dickens and Stevenson both anticipate a prominent feature of modern fiction, to be found in writers from Conrad to Nabokov (the latter is the author of an interesting essay on this text).

Whereas earlier readings of the novel stressed its religious and metaphysical dimensions, many modern critics have preferred to adopt a psychoanalytic approach. In these terms Henry Jekyll becomes a study in repression, impelled to enact what he himself refers to in his final confession as a "duplicity of life": his self-described "almost morbid sense of shame" at his own secret indulgences finds release at first in the creation of Hyde, but this other self later gets out of control, commits appalling crimes, and ends by taking over his creator's personality.

The same approach has emphasized Stevenson's detailed description of the interior and exterior of Jekyll's house. There is in the English novel a strong tradition of using houses as symbolic objects, exemplified by a wide range of works from Jane Austen's *Mansfield Park* (1814) to Evelyn Waugh's *Brideshead Revisited* (1945), but Stevenson's pre-Freudian work lends itself more readily than most to psychoanalytical interpretation. The front of the house, representing Jekyll's public persona and better self, turns an imposing face on a spacious and elegant square, but hidden behind it in a narrow and gloomy "by-street" is a back entrance affording access to an untidy and neglected cellar. The Freudian symbolism of this description, combined with the fact that Hyde is a much younger man than the doctor whose secret self he represents, have led some interpreters to suggest the depiction of a coded or unconscious homosexual relationship between the two men. Suggestive analogies may be drawn with such texts as Wilde's *The Picture of Dorian Gray* (1891), published only five years later, as well as Conrad's *'Twixt Land and Sea* (1912).

One of the lesser manifestations of Hyde's incorrigibly evil nature is to annotate with "startling blasphemies" a work of piety that Jekyll is reading, and such details remind us that probably the deepest of all the many levels of this short but seminal text relates to the Calvinism of Stevenson's childhood. To this extent *The Strange Case of Dr. Jekyll and Mr. Hyde* may be seen as belonging to a distinctively Scottish tradition that is also represented by such works as James Hogg's remarkable *The Private Memoirs and Confessions of a Justified Sinner* (1824), while Stevenson's interest in the themes of possession and diabolism are evident in such earlier writings of his as the short stories "Thrawn Janet" and "Markheim."

NORMAN PAGE

See also Robert Louis Stevenson

Further Reading

Bell, Ian, *Robert Louis Stevenson: Dreams of Exile,* Edinburgh: Mainstream, 1992; New York: Holt, 1993

Calder, Jenni, editor, *Stevenson and Victorian Scotland,* Edinburgh: University of Edinburgh Press, 1981

Daiches, David, *Robert Louis Stevenson,* Norfolk, Connecticut: New Directions, and Glasgow: Maclellan, 1947

Eigner, Edwin M., *Robert Louis Stevenson and Romantic Tradition,* Princeton, New Jersey: Princeton University Press, 1966

Hammond, J.R., *A Robert Louis Stevenson Companion,* London and New York: Macmillan, 1984

Heath, Stephen, "Psychopathia Sexualis: Stevenson's *Strange Case,*" *Critical Quarterly* 28 (1986)

Nabokov, Vladimir, *Lectures on Literature,* London: Weidenfeld and Nicolson, and New York: Harcourt Brace, 1980

Smith, Janet Adam, *R.L. Stevenson,* London: Duckworth, 1937

The Stranger by Albert Camus

L'Étranger 1942

Albert Camus was still a relatively unknown journalist living in Algeria, where he was born, when *The Stranger* was published in 1942. It quickly became a best-seller in France, has sold more copies than any other French-language novel of the 20th century, and has been translated into more than 40 languages. The novel has inspired a large number of critical studies, commencing with a well-known article by Jean-Paul Sartre that analyzes *The Stranger* in light of Camus' philosophical essay "Le Mythe de Sisyphe" ("The Myth of Sisyphus"), which was published in the same year. Sartre's article was the first of a series of interpretations of the novel as a confrontation between an absurdist hero and a hostile universe. His analysis, however, tends to place Camus in the line of Sartre's own early work, and neglects the joyous acceptance of the natural world prevalent in all of Camus' writing. The first book-length study of *The Stranger,* by Robert Champigny (1959), sees Meursault, the main character of the novel, as a pagan hero. Two novelists associated with the *nouveau roman,* Nathalie Sarraute (1956) and Alain Robbe-Grillet (1963), perceived Camus' first novel as related to their own literary strategies. Sarraute identified Camus' refusal to create rounded characters as an instance of the "suspicion" with which mid-20th-century writers consider any attempt to understand others. Robbe-Grillet saw the first part of *The Stranger* as an instance of an absolute divorce between human actions and the external world.

The Stranger is a first-person monologue told by a narrator who refuses to analyze his feelings, to explain actions in normal logical terms, to make connections between events, or to judge himself or others. His monologue cannot be dated in terms of the events he describes, nor can we ever determine whether he has written or spoken it. The narrator uses the *passé composé*, the perfect tense normally used in conversational French but not in literary works. He begins his story with "Today" but quickly relates what happened after that opening day. There is no consistency in the narrative chronology.

This unconventional form of recounting a story is one clue to the character of Meursault, a shipping clerk in Algiers, who refuses to accept the conventional society of French Algeria or indeed of any Western bourgeois culture. He does not cry at his mother's funeral, agrees to marry his friend Marie but will not tell her he loves her, and gives up the chance for professional advancement and a job in Paris because he lacks ambition. He becomes involved in a fight on the beach that ends with the murder of an Arab. There is no logical explanation for the murder, which Meursault blames on the "sun." In the end, he is judged and condemned as much for his lack of emotion at his mother's funeral as for the murder.

The novel has often been read as an attack on the morality of middle-class society, in which outward displays of conventional feelings are the only criteria of judgment. It can also be seen as an ironic illustration of the absurdist hero of "The Myth of Sisyphus" in which Camus claims that a man aware of the absurd discrepancy between human aspirations to meaning and permanence and the absolute indifference of the external universe might be merely a clerk in an office rather than a Don Juan or a conqueror. In spite of his alienation from society, Meursault retains a feeling that life is worth living, that every sensual pleasure is worth more than any abstract reasoning, that every day he is alive is a victory over inevitable death. Meursault is not exemplary but is, as Camus later stated in a comment on his work, "the only Christ we deserve." Meursault may be an unassuming, unpretentious Everyman for an age without religious faith.

Interpretations of *The Stranger* have often centered on how to read the character of Meursault. Does he simply accept life or has he deliberately chosen to deny any transcendent meaning? Does he love his mother, whom he refers to by the rather childlike term "Maman," or is he indifferent to any human affection? Does he suddenly take on a heroic stance after his appeal has been rejected and he is condemned to die, when he hopes many people will greet him with jeers at his execution? Critics have offered divergent opinions of his comment that he killed because of the sun: was it just the glint on the knife blade that made him think the Arab was about to attack, or is the sun a symbol of the hostility of the external universe? (Robbe-Grillet felt that the novel diverged from his own concerns in the highly metaphoric description of the murder scene.) Other critical studies discuss the impossibility of determining exactly the chronological relationship between the events and the time of narration.

Camus termed *The Stranger* a *récit* (a narrative). He used a similar ambiguous first-person narrative voice in his later fiction, *La Chute* (1956; *The Fall*) and most of the stories in *L'Exil et le royaume* (1957; *Exile and the Kingdom*). He did not refer to any of his works as a novel until the unfinished book on which he was working at the time of his death in a car crash in 1960, *Le Premier Homme* (*The First Man*, published posthumously). This novel contains much more realistic detail than Camus' previous work.

The Stranger has influenced many US and European writers as well as writers from the developing world who have seen this story of an intelligent but unheroic character with few social ambitions and at odds with his society as a reflection of their own situation. Although some critics have viewed the book as showing a disregard for the Algerian Arab population, *The Stranger* and Camus' other early works have been a positive literary influence on many French-language writers of Arab origin in Algeria.

ADELE KING

Further Reading

Champigny, Robert, *Sur un heros paien*, Paris: Gallimard, 1959; as *A Pagan Hero: An Interpretation of Meursault in Camus' "The Stranger,"* Philadelphia: University of Pennsylvania Press, 1969

Fitch, Brian, *The Narcissistic Text: A Reading of Camus' Fiction*, Toronto and Buffalo, New York: University of Toronto Press, 1982

Gay-Crosier, Raymond, and Jacqueline Lévi-Valensi, editors, *Albert Camus: Oeuvre ouverte, Oeuvre fermée?* Paris: Gallimard, 1985

King, Adele, editor, *Camus' "L'Étranger": Fifty Years On*, London: Macmillan, 1992

Lévi-Valensi, Jacqueline, editor, *Les Critiques de notre temps et Camus*, Paris: Garnier, 1970

McCarthy, Patrick, *Albert Camus: The Stranger*, Cambridge and New York: Cambridge University Press, 1988

Robbe-Grillet, Alain, "Nature, Humanisme, Tragédie," in his *Pour un nouveau roman*, Paris: Editions de Minuit, 1963

Sarraute, Nathalie, "'Le Psychologique' dans *L'Étranger*," in *L'Ere du soupçon*, Paris: Gallimard, 1956

Todd, Olivier, *Albert Camus: Une vie*, Paris: Gallimard, 1996

Stream of Consciousness and Interior Monologue

The 18th- and 19th-century novel favored a narrative technique that foregrounds the directorial presence of the author as omniscient narrator. Thackeray, to give one example, observes the narrative on our behalf, so to speak:

> At sunset, from the lawn of Fairoaks, there was a pretty sight; it, and the opposite park of Clavering, were in the habit of putting on a rich golden tinge, which became them both wonderfully. The upper windows of the great house flamed so as to make your eyes wink (*The History of Pendennis*, 1849–50).

The author is plainly distinguishable, directing, stage-managing, even prompting. This use of the technique is in the confident tradition of Henry Fielding and Walter Scott, behind whom stand the Spanish writer Cervantes and his counterpart in French, Alain-René Lesage.

In the 20th-century novel, however, the landscape tends to exist in terms of what is seen by a given character. When Betty Flanders cries, in Virginia Woolf's *Jacob's Room* (1922), the tears in her eyes distort the landscape:

> Slowly welling from the point of her gold nib, pale blue ink dissolved the full stop; for there her pen stuck; her eyes fixed, and tears slowly filled them. The entire bay quivered; the lighthouse wobbled; and she had the illusion that the mast of Mr. Connor's little yacht was bending like a wax candle in the sun.

The landscape is not objectively "out there." Rather, it is the product of the character's vision and is expressed in interior monologue, a mode of expression closely associated with stream-of-consciousness writing. But more than the limitation of point of view to what a character sees, stream of consciousness is the attempt to create a verbal representation of a character's conscious awareness and all those (frequently random) things that impinge on it, including thoughts, associations, memories, perceptions, and sensations.

The term *stream of consciousness* derives from William James' *The Principles of Psychology* (1890). James argued that consciousness, in spite of its discontinuities, does not appear to itself to be chopped up into bits. Rather it flows effortlessly along, incorporating memories, associations, and external impressions into a never-ending "stream." But stream of consciousness was used in fiction even before James supplied the label. The English novelist George Meredith used long interior monologues representing the thoughts and emotions of his main characters, although he subordinated them to the superior objectivity and insight of the omniscient narrator. In 1888, Edouard Dujardin published *Les Lauriers sont coupés* (*We'll to the Woods No More*), a short novel that attempts to capture the movements of the protagonist's mind without supplying an omniscient narrative to relativize it. Dujardin was particularly interested in mental patterns, in the recurrence of particular images and thoughts through free association. Henry James, whose novels show an abiding interest in individual consciousness and its representation, also used interior monologue frequently.

Stream-of-consciousness writing came into its own with modernism, when the technique came to carry a philosophical burden. Convinced of the illusory nature of objectivity, the great modernist novelists eschewed omniscient narrative as a falsehood. They relied on interior monologue as the only possible approximation to truth, limited as it might be by individual subjectivity. Interior monologue, then, is modernism's version of realism. Its greatest practitioners in English include Dorothy Richardson (*Pointed Roofs*, 1915), James Joyce (*Ulysses*, 1922), Virginia Woolf (*Jacob's Room*, 1922; *Mrs Dalloway*, 1925), and William Faulkner (*The Sound and the Fury*, 1929; *As I Lay Dying*, 1930). The most notable French exponents of the technique are Marcel Proust (*À la Recherche du temps perdu*, 1913–27; translated as *Remembrance of Things Past* and also as *In Search of Lost Time*), and Valéry Larbaud (*Beauté, mon beau souci*, 1920). Virginia Woolf's essays, particularly "Mr Bennett and Mrs. Brown" and "The Modern Novel," are among the best theoretical expressions of modernism's interest in interiority.

Modernism's use of interior monologue was motivated also by the prevailing interest in psychology, particularly Freudian psychology. Stream of consciousness is used to explore mental patterns, including the recurrence of obsessional ideas, and to reveal such things as subconscious motivation, the mechanisms of free association, and the significance of repressed memory. Marcel Proust's use of the madeleine in *In Search of Lost Time*, as a prompter of long-lost memory through the process of association, is probably the most famous example of such explorations of mental functioning.

One consequence of the intense inwardness associated with interior monologue is a general simplification in plotting. By and large, very little happens in modernist novels, as their central focus shifts from the unfolding of events to the movements of the mind. Complexity is often provided by a richness of memory, Proust's *In Search of Lost Time* again being the paradigmatic example. In other cases, complexity derives from the juxtaposition of the interior worlds of different characters within one novel. Faulkner's *As I Lay Dying*, for instance, recounts the death and burial of Addie Bundren through a series of brief passages representing the thoughts and feelings of her grieving children and husband. The differences in the way they experience the same set of events illustrate the elusiveness of objective reality and allow the reader a better grasp of each character and of the particular subjective slant of his or her perceptions.

Interior monologue may be signaled by different linguistic "notations." Frequently associated with first-person narrative, stream of consciousness is sometimes also conveyed in the third person, as are Leopold Bloom's impressions in Joyce' *Ulysses*. The famous final section of the novel, however, gives Molly Bloom's nighttime thoughts in the first person. Differences in notation may be exploited to convey the qualitative differences between the characters' inner worlds. The monologues of Stephen Dedalus and Leopold Bloom in *Ulysses*, for instance, respect conventional grammar and punctuation. Molly Bloom's long monologue does not contain any punctuation whatsoever, a state of affairs that is considered by many to convey Molly's lack of sophistication. In other novels, contraventions of grammar serve a mimetic purpose, painting an even more realistic portrait of mental processes.

Although interior monologue is closely associated with the modernist novel, the technique has survived its hallmark period. It is now used in both realist and experimental fiction, as a viable mode for transcribing certain attitudes, especially those involving introspection and retrospection.

PHILIP HOBSBAUM AND MARIJKE RIJSBERMAN

See also Discourse Representation; Modernism; Narratology; Narrator; Point of View; Psychological Novel

Further Reading

Booth, Wayne C., *The Rhetoric of Fiction,* Chicago: University of Chicago Press, 1961; 2nd edition, Chicago: University of Chicago Press, and London: Penguin, 1983

Ellmann, Richard, and Charles Feidelson, Jr., editors, *The Modern Tradition: Backgrounds of Modern Literature,* New York: Oxford University Press, 1965

Genette, Gérard, *Discours du récit,* in *Figures III,* Paris: Seuil, 1972; as *Narrative Discourse,* Ithaca, New York: Cornell University Press, 1980

James, Henry, *The Art of the Novel: Critical Prefaces,* edited by R.P. Blackmur, New York: Scribner, 1934

James, William, *The Principles of Psychology,* New York: Holt, and London: Macmillan, 1890

Martin, Wallace, *Recent Theories of Narrative,* Ithaca, New York: Cornell University Press, 1986

Scholes, Robert, and Robert Kellogg, *The Nature of Narrative,* New York: Oxford University Press, 1966

Woolf, Virginia, *The Common Reader* (first series), London: Hogarth Press, and New York: Harcourt Brace, 1925

Woolf, Virginia, "Mr Bennett and Mrs Brown," in *The Captain's Death Bed and Other Essays,* edited by Leonard Woolf, London: Hogarth Press, and New York: Harcourt Brace, 1950

Structuralism, Semiotics, and the Novel

Although there are as many differences as there are commonalities between the two models of literary analysis prevalent during the 1950s and 1960s, structuralism and semiotics have often been used interchangeably to denote a systematic approach to all human discourses—including fictional narration—that treats "a set of phenomena . . . not as a mechanical agglomeration but as a structural whole, and the basic task is to reveal the inner . . . laws of this system" (Roman Jakobson, "Romantic Panslavism—New Slavic Studies," 1929). Structuralism and semiotics have at least one common originator, the Swiss linguist Ferdinand de Saussure (1857–1913), who in the posthumously published *Cours de linguistique générale* (1916; *Course in General Linguistics*) proposed a systematic reexamination of language structures and a "semiology" (from the Greek *semeîon,* sign), or "science of signs within society," based on it. Later representatives, such as Roman Jakobson, Claude Lévi-Strauss, or Roland Barthes, were themselves practitioners of both structuralism and semiotics, moving from the rigorous study of verbal texts to the ambitious task of establishing the general laws that govern all signs, from road signs to systems of food and clothing.

Particularly useful for the structuralist study of narration is Saussure's attempt to describe the smallest significant units in a discourse and their organization into two kinds of structure: temporal or "syntagmatic," unfolding according to a principle of combination; and spatial or "paradigmatic," organized according to the principle of selection. The paradigmatic structure places an item in relation to a whole system of conventions and choices available within a language (what Saussure called *langue*); the syntagmatic structure places an item in a temporal relation to items that precede or follow it, constituting what Saussure called *parole,* or individual "speech-events." According to this twofold organizational model, a narrative involves both a horizontal structure of temporal events and a vertical system of paradigmatic relationships among character types, plot situations, and thematic oppositions.

Drawing on Saussure's projected "semiology," but also on Charles Sanders Peirce's (1839–1914) logical description of signs, literary and cultural semiotics explore the nature, function, and effects of signs in human discourses. Central to Peirce's posthumously published *Collected Papers* (8 vols., 1931–35, 1958) is the idea that all thought is conducted through signs that do not designate directly an object, but relate to it through an "interpretant" (an interpretive idea). For Peirce, the interpretant was another sign that mediated logically the relationship between the original sign and its object; for Peirce's follower, Charles W. Morris (1903–79), the interpretant was a response produced in the interpreter. The advantage of Peirce's theory over Saussure's is that it allows a diversified treatment of signs (Peirce famously distinguished between "icons" that bear some resemblance to the object they represent, "indexes" that point to a particular object or meaning, and "symbols" that represent something by cultural convention), and it recognizes the open-endedness of interpretation, an "interpretant" being itself a sign that relates to other signs ad infinitum. This notion of semiotic open-endedness has been relevant for narrative criticism, informing such diverse perspectives as the phenomenological emphasis on the incomplete actualization of narrative works in reading (Roman Ingarden, Wolfgang Iser), the narratological concept of multicoded narratives (Roland Barthes, Christine Brooke-Rose), or the deconstructionist emphasis on the "indeterminacy" of narrative meaning (J. Hillis Miller, Paul de Man).

First applied to literature by the Prague structuralist Jan Mukařovsky (1891–1975), semiotics understands literature as a "semiological fact" ("Die Kunst als semiologisches Faktum,"

1934), at once a sign, a structure, and a value. As sign, a narrative is composed of a "perceivable signifier, created by the artist," a "'signification' registered in the collective consciousness," and "a relationship which refers to the total context of social phenomena." Mukařovsky further redefined the concept of structure, emphasizing its "energetic and dynamic character," subjecting each individual element/function and their interrelations to change ("Structuralism in Aesthetics and in the Study of Literature," 1940). Present only marginally in Mukařovsky's framework, the larger "context of social phenomena" was addressed by social anthropologists with semiotic leanings, such as Émile Durkheim and Marcel Mauss, who highlighted the relationship between symbolic representations and the social structures that facilitate them, and by Charles Morris who proposed a general science of signs subdivided into syntactics, which studies the relations of sign-vehicles within sign systems, semantics, which studies the relation of signs to the objects they represent, and pragmatics, which studies the uses and effects of signs in culture.

Accepted somewhat slowly into Anglo-American criticism, in which they had to defeat New Criticism's resistance to theory, structuralism and semiotics did not have time to establish long-term "schools," being almost immediately challenged by poststructuralist philosophies. The quasi-synchronous introduction of Russian formalism and French structuralism and poststructuralism (the first English translations of formalist texts were available in 1965, concurrently with translations from Tzvetan Todorov, Roland Barthes, and Claude Lévi-Strauss; they were followed a few years later by the poststructuralist texts of Barthes, Jacques Derrida, Julia Kristeva, and Jacques Lacan) explains why American narrative criticism has synthesized all three directions, juggling their terminologies and claims. Not only Barthes' structuralist work but also his later poststructuralist questionings have attracted American critics of various persuasions, from early structuralist advocates such as Robert Scholes (*Structuralism in Literature*, 1974) and Jonathan Culler (*Structuralist Poetics*, 1975) to post-Marxian critics such as Fredric Jameson, and from deconstructionists such as Ihab Hassan, Eugenio Donato, and J. Hillis Miller to "new historicists" such as Edward Said and Hayden White. The delayed American reception of structuralism and semiotics allowed a sharper awareness of their limitations, as well as a creative rethinking of their objectives, such as in Jameson's *The Prison-House of Language* (1972), which proposed to convert structuralism into a "study of superstructures or, in a more limited way of ideology."

One effect the dissemination of structuralist-semiotic ideas has had is the shift in fiction criticism from the "theory of the novel as central concern" to the "theory of narrative" (Martin, 1986). If the fiction criticism during the period 1945–60 elevated the novel to a position of literary prestige primarily by demonstrating that its forms and techniques were as subtle as those of drama and poetry, the following three decades redefined the issues of fiction by placing them within a broader theoretical perspective. Already in Northrop Frye's *Anatomy of Criticism* (1957), the novel was treated as one of several species of the genus "fiction," participating with romance, autobiography, and anatomy ("a vision of the world in terms of a single intellectual pattern") in a comprehensive intertextual system of literature. Wayne Booth in *The Rhetoric of Fiction* (1961) challenged the formalist focus on the novel as a self-contained structure of devices, proposing a rhetorical model of fiction that emphasized the commu-

nicational exchange between implied authors and their audience. The focus on the communicational and intertextual aspects of narration was consolidated during the 1960s under the impact of continental structuralism. The object of study expanded from literary narratives to oral tales, popular literature, and myths, and from finished texts to variants and "happenings." In lieu of the older thematic-historical discussion of novels, or the formalist analysis of single works, structuralism sought the underlying laws of narrative structure across different genres and media.

To the extent that structuralism concerns itself with the self-regulating structures of a particular narrative text, it is not very different from formalism or New Criticism. An early ambition of the Russian formalists (Boris Tomashevskii, Viktor Shklovskii, and Roman Jakobson) was to develop a poetics of fiction focused on its organizational units and devices (*fabula* and *syuzhet,* story time and reading time, types of motifs, types of expositions and endings, codes), but their primary concern was with the defamiliarizing effects these devices had in particular texts, breaking expected conventions such as those of verisimilitude. Structuralism comes into its own when it moves from the analysis of a particular textual system to the task of describing the general mechanisms and laws of an entire discursive system. The earliest manifestation of this structuralist agenda may be found in Vladimir Propp's *Morfologiia skazki* (1928; *Morphology of the Folktale*). Moving beyond the Russian formalists' work of classifying plot motifs, Propp constructed a rigorous "morphology" of narrative that sought "invariables" of action and character at a deeper level. Although he found a great number of motifs in the 100 Russian fairy tales studied, Propp reduced them to 31 basic functions, such as "a difficult task is proposed to the hero," "the hero acquires a magical agent," "the hero withstands a test," and so on. According to Propp, the basic order of these functions is always the same, so that a fairy tale may be defined as a story that moves from a function A (villainy) by way of intermediate functions to the problem-solving function W (wedding). Equally important was Propp's simplified typology of characters, which identified seven roles: dispatcher, hero, false hero, villain, donor or provider, helper, and princess or sought-for person.

In a 1960 review of the French translation of Propp's *Morphology of the Folktale*, Claude Lévi-Strauss called attention to Propp's pioneering work but also criticized it for overrating formal aspects. In his response, Propp admitted that "formal analysis, the precise description of the objective material studied" was the starting point of all historical research, but he dissociated his empirical structuralism from both the formalists' focus on heterogeneous devices and from Lévi-Strauss' compilation of random data into comprehensive patterns. In spite of their disagreement, there are obvious affinities between Lévi-Strauss and Propp. Lévi-Strauss' *Anthropologie structurale* (2 vols., 1958, 1973; *Structural Anthropology*) also sought to identify invariants in the structure of mythic texts and human institutions. Cuisine practices, class/clan relationships, cycles of mythic narratives—Lévi-Strauss treated all these systems as "languages," breaking them into basic units and charting the play of opposition and mediation between them. An earlier article influenced by his collaboration with Roman Jakobson, "L'analyse structurale en linguistique et en anthropologie" (1945), argues that kinship terms behave much like linguistic terms, deriving their meaning from their position within a system; and "The Structural Study of

Myth" (1955) lays down a rigorous method of analyzing mythic narratives, such as Oedipus, reading its variants both horizontally (chronologically) and vertically, in terms of their relationships of equivalence, opposition, and inversion. Lévi-Strauss' later work combined the structuralist perspective with the insights of Mauss' socioanthropology, seeking relationships of equivalences among the various spheres of the sociocultural world (technology, economy, aesthetics, religious rituals, and myths). Throwing away caution, Lévi-Strauss moved to the bold generalizations of *Mythologiques* (1964–71; translated as *The Raw and the Cooked,* 1969, *From Honey to Ashes,* 1973, *The Origin of Table Manners,* 1978, and *The Naked Man,* 1981), a four-volume opus that reduces the mythic tales of North and South American Indians to a few underlying oppositions, such as raw versus cooked, damp versus dry, naked versus clothed, and nature versus culture.

Combining Propp's syntagmatic charting with Lévi-Strauss' paradigmatic integration, A.-J. Greimas (1917–92) proposed in *Sémantique structurale* (1966; *Structural Semantics*) a bifocal model of narrative analysis. Simplifying Propp's chart of 31 functions, Greimas highlights their potential for binary groupings (prohibition/violation, command/acceptance, and so on), constructing around them a model of logical analysis known as the "semiotic square," which foregrounds the matrix of deep oppositions in a narrative. He also proposed an "actantial model," which maps three basic relationships between opposed "actants" (abstract character roles): a syntactic relationship driven by desire between subject and object, a communicational relationship between sender (dispatcher) and receiver (beneficiary), and an enabling relationship between "helper" and "opponent." Although Greimas was primarily interested in devising a "universal narrative grammar" based on simple traditional stories, his own testings on literary narratives, such as Guy de Maupassant's "Deux Amis" or the later applications of Culler, Scholes, or Jameson, revealed the capacity of his formalized models to deal with more complex thematic and ideological issues. In his own theoretical modeling of fairy tales ("La Logique des possibles narratifs" [1966; "The Logic of Narrative Possibilities"]; *Logique du récit,* 1973), Claude Bremond retained Propp's notion of functions but carried the level of abstraction even further, arguing that the most elementary sequence in narrative is composed of a function that opens up the possibility of an action, a function that realizes this potentiality, and a function that closes the process with a certain result. He also replaced Propp's idea of a unilinear chain of functions with a multilinear, branched structure according to which several alternatives remain open when a function is inserted (potentiality can lead to actualization or absence of actualization; if actualization is achieved, there may be either failure or success as the terminal function). Focused on the play of logical possibilities within interlaced sequences, Bremond's "grammar of narrative" also emphasizes the historicity and open-ended dynamics of narrative structures, amending the ahistorical views of Propp.

The two complementary approaches within the "grammar of narrative," abstract-logical and anthropologic-ideological, were dissociated in the subsequent work of Bulgarian-born Tzvetan Todorov, the only French structuralist influenced by both Propp and Lévi-Strauss, and the Russian formalists he helped translate. Taking his interest in poetics from Tomashevsky and Jakobson, but trying to purge it of extraneous concerns, Todorov argued in

Poétique de la prose (1971; *The Poetics of Prose*) and *Poétique* (1973; *Introduction to Poetics*) that the structuralist is a poetician rather than an interpreter, whose task is not to analyze particular narratives but to describe and classify general literary structures. In order to keep the extratextual interferences to a minimum, Todorov in *Grammaire du Décaméron* (1969) dropped the level of the *syuzhet* (discourse) entirely, dealing only with the syntactic aspects of the *fabula,* which he reduced to a relationship of subject, predication, and attribution. Other works of Todorov applied the abstract models of structuralist analysis to whole genres (*Introduction à la littérature fantastique* [1970; *The Fantastic: A Structural Approach to a Literary Genre*]; *Les Genres du discours* [1978; *Genres in Discourse*]), trying to define larger, transtextual categories of fiction. Todorov's formalistic interests were shared by Gerald Prince who, in *A Grammar of Stories: An Introduction* (1973) and *Narratology: The Form and Functioning of Narrative* (1982), developed a grammar of stories based on Noam Chomsky's transformational generative theories. His books define "minimal stories," describe the transformation rules that apply to simple narrative sentences, and devise formalized models for the representation of actions. By contrast, Pierre Macherey proposed in *Pour une théorie de la production littéraire* (1966; *A Theory of Literary Production*) a mode of structuralist criticism whose main purpose is to demystify the ideology of a text. The "objective metalanguage" of structuralism enabled the critic to perceive the incoherences and gaps of a text, to articulate its silences, and to reveal the unstated purposes of its ideology.

The reintegration of the grammatical and ideological models of analysis was persuasively achieved in the structuralist criticism of Roland Barthes. Well acquainted not only with Peirce, Saussure, the Prague structuralist school, Durkheim, Mauss, Lévi-Strauss, and Jakobson, but also with Karl Marx, Sigmund Freud, Jacques Lacan, and Maurice Merleau-Ponty, Barthes intelligently interplayed and expanded their perspectives. His influential early essay "Introduction à l'analyse structurale des récits" (1966; "Introduction to the Structural Analysis of Narratives," 1975) proposes a "functional syntax" capable of accounting for every type of narrative. Published in volume number eight of *Communications* (1966), a veritable manifesto of the French structuralist school with contributions from Greimas, Todorov, Metz, and Genette, Barthes' essay built on Propp's perspective as further formalized by the other contributors, improving upon it in several ways: adding a focus on "indices" (descriptive phrases containing information about characters and setting), integrating narrative instances into a vertical ("hierarchical") order, and replacing Propp's emphasis on the "subject" with a structuralist focus on agents. *Éléments de sémiologie* (1964; *Elements of Semiology*) continued Barthes' effort to devise a "second linguistics" capable of describing textual structures larger than a sentence, but supplemented it with an emphasis on the extralinguistic (semiotic and ideological) codifications of texts. He tested the capabilities of his analytic model that regarded each discourse as a functional system "of which one term is constant (the work), and the other is variable" (the world, the reaction of an age, the interpreter's response) on everything from stories to food, furniture, architecture, and garment systems. Along the same lines, Barthes' *S/Z* (1970) devised a comprehensive model of code analysis that reread Honoré de Balzac's story "Sarrasine" on five different levels (the proairetic code of action sequences, the hermeneutic code of enigmas, the code of cultural references, the semic code of connotations, and the symbolic code of binary oppositions) in order to "pluralize" interpretation. The analysis mimicks mathematical rigor (Balzac's story was divided into 561 "lexias," or units of reading, interspersed with 93 critical "divagations"), but this segmentation follows the idiosyncratic interests of the reader as much as the codes embedded in the text. In direct contrast to Barthes' earlier suggestion that all narrative texts had a precise grammar and lexicon of "semes" (units of meaning), *S/Z* suggests that meaning results as much from the differential play of the textual codes as from a reader's creative rewriting. Barthes in his later essays, *Le Plaisir du texte* (1973; *The Pleasure of the Text*), and the playful *Le Bruissement de la langue* (1984; *The Rustle of Language*), expanded his distinction between "readerly" (conventional) and "writerly" (experimental) texts.

A former student of Barthes and Lacan, Julia Kristeva argued in *Le Texte du roman: Approche sémiologique d'une structure discursive transformationnelle* (1970; The Text of the Novel) that the novel had to be approached through linguistic analysis because language formed its most important system of constraints, which further embedded the sociocultural codifications of the time and author. This early work also introduces the concept of intertextuality, arguing that the text of a novel is imbued in the culture's "supertext." Derived in part from Barthes' approach in *S/Z*, as well as from Mikhail Bakhtin, the anti-formalist Soviet theorist who described the novel as a "dialogic" art form, the theory of intertextuality asserts that no narrative text is autonomous or self-sufficient. The novel refracts the culture's ideological structures, but in so doing creates new forms of communication and modulations of discourse. As a method of analysis, intertextuality allows the structuralist to move from the system of a single text to the polysystem of culture. Kristeva's later work, from *La Révolution du langage poétique* (1974; *Revolution in Poetic Language*) and *Polylogue* (1977; partially translated as *Desire in Language*), to *Pouvoirs de l'horreur* (1980; *Powers of Horror*) and *Histoires d'amour* (1983; *Tales of Love*), clearly illustrates this move, expanding her brand of "semanalysis" with the cultural insights of feminism, poststructuralism, and Lacanian psychoanalysis. The influence of Bakhtin's dialogic model can be recognized not only in Kristeva's polyvalent semiotics, which defines narration as a cultural interlacing of texts and speaking subjects, but also in Michel Foucault's description of individual discourses as "nodes" in a field of "interdisciplinary discourses," or in Jameson's "symptomatic" analysis, which seeks the heterogeneous sign systems of a narrative in order to relate them "in a mode of structural difference and deterministic contradiction" to the larger socioeconomic structures.

The widely circulated work of Barthes and Kristeva contributed to a blurring of the dividing lines between semiotics and structuralism in the analysis of fiction. Leonard Orr (1987) points out that "as semioticians saw the necessity of expanding their models to include broader text structures, structuralists began to analyze "language systems" at work within texts, and both semioticians and structuralists branched out and began to include in their methods facets from other disciplines and methods." One result of this was the emergence during the 1970s of a new field called "narratology," opposed by Gérard Genot to "narrativics" (*Elements of Narrativics*, 1979) or the logical description of narrative. While Wolfgang Dressler, Siegfried J.

Schmidt, Teun A. van Dijk, János S. Petöfi, and Gérard Genot continued to seek abstract "text grammars," which established basic rules of transformation at surface and deep levels and described the competence of performers of narrativity, Gérard Genette, Gerald Prince, Mieke Bal, Seymour Chatman, and others supplemented the "universal models of narrative" with a more sophisticated repertory of analytic categories capable of dealing with complex literary narratives. Genette, in particular, undertook the task of conceptualizing the structures of a fictional text on the level of its "story" and "narrative" (discourse), describing tense, person, time relations between story and narrative, and modalities of representation (mood), focalization (point of view), and voice (levels of narration). Genette was very successful at developing a critical vocabulary of fine distinctions for the analysis of "constant literary forms," but he did not move beyond Saussure's classic binaries (signified and signifier, syntagmatic and paradigmatic) or Aristotle's more basic dichotomies of action (*praxis*) and story (*mythos*), mimesis (showing) and diegesis (telling). His formalist narratology has been refined and expanded by other scholars in two ways: by extrapolating his type of analysis from literary narratives to other media and genres, such as film (Chatman, David Bordwell, Teresa de Lauretis), oral narration and "ethnopoetics" (Alan Dundee, Eleazar Meletinsky, Heda Jason), or historical narration (A.C. Danto, Dominick LaCapra); and by enriching Genette's literary narratology with additional categories and concerns, such as those of implied authors (Chatman), implied and real readers (Iser, Shlomith Rimmon-Kenan, Meir Sternberg), narrative competence and naturalization (Culler), subject and object of focalization (Mieke Bal), narrative modes (Helmut Bonheim), narrative boundaries and crossings (Alexander Gelley), typologies of time (Paul Ricoeur, Julio C.M. Pinto) and of character (Paul Perron, Fernando Ferrara, James Phelan), and modes of representing character speech and consciousness (Dorrit Cohn, Roger Fowler, Monika Fludernik).

Other revisions have challenged the formalist-ahistorical bias of structuralist narratology more radically, proposing a non-Aristotelian (nonmimetic) model of fiction (Jean Ricardou, Brian McHale, Leonard Orr) or foregrounding components traditionally excluded from narratology, such as gender (Susan Sniader Lanser, Robyn Warhol, Teresa de Lauretis), semantic-cognitive aspects (Lubomír Dolezel, Thomas Pavel, Félix Martínez Bonati, Marie-Laure Ryan), communicational-rhetorical issues (Didier Coste, Lydia Polanyi, James Phelan), or ideological infrastructures (poststructuralist theories of narrative). The poststructuralist reaction of the late 1970s against universal grammars of narrative discontinued some of the structuralist models and practices, while introducing new concerns with narrative as a "socially symbolic act" (Jameson, Edward Said, Robert L. Caserio), driven by unconscious ideological-psychoanalytic infrastructures (de Lauretis, Peter Brooks, Ross Chambers, Nancy Armstrong), rhetorically and grammatically unstable (J. Hillis Miller, Paul de Man, Barbara Johnson), or open to creative rereading and rewriting (Umberto Eco, Peter Rabinowitz, Marcel Cornis-Pope). In this new poststructuralist version, narratology has become "a multi-disciplinary study of narrative which negotiates and incorporates the insights of many other critical discourses that involve narrative forms of representation" (Onega Jaen and Landa, 1996).

Parallels and models for this multidisciplinary broadening of narrative studies can be found in the "sociosemiology" of the Moscow-Tartu school (Jurii Lotman, Boris Uspenskii, A.M. Pjatigorskii, Jurii Levin). In *Poetika kompozitsii* (1970; *A Poetics of Composition*), Uspenskii discusses point of view within a broad communicational framework, distinguishing among ideological, phraseological (discursive), spatio-temporal, and psychological levels. Lotman's *Analiz poeticheskogo teksta* (1972; *Analysis of the Poetic Text*) and *Struktura khudozhestvennogo teksta* (1971; *The Structure of the Artistic Text*) challenge the structuralist idea of the autonomy of the work of art, relating the internal structure of the literary text to the sociocultural context through the different sets of cultural codes embedded in the text and the "language of the reader." His cultural semiotics has rehistoricized the narratological concepts of plot, point of view, and narrative function, showing for example that cultures have shifted between two modes of understanding the world narratively: one based on cyclic structures of myths, the other on "plot-texts" that perceive events in terms of isolated causes.

The recuperation of the subjective and sociocultural components of signification remains a major concern in narrative semiotics, for, as Kaja Silverman (1983) has argued, "Signification cannot be isolated from the human subject who uses it . . . or from the cultural system which generates it." Narratologists have also admitted that their field can be reinvigorated only by opening it up to traditionally excluded concerns about reference, speaking subjects, readers, and discursive ideology (see Rimmon-Kenan's stock-taking article, "How the Model Neglects the Medium," 1989). This does not mean that the structuralist base must be entirely rejected. Teresa de Lauretis' analysis of the relationship between narrative and desire combines structuralist insights with psychoanalysis, feminist theory, and cultural anthropology; Culler's more recent work (*The Pursuit of Signs,* 1980, *On Deconstruction,* 1982, and *Framing the Sign,* 1988) both adapts and criticizes European structuralism, foregrounding its potential for an analysis of political institutions. Finally, the theories of fictionality developed by a variety of scholars, some with structuralist connections (Lubomír Dolezel, Thomas Pavel, Félix Martínez Bonati, Michael Riffaterre, Marie-Laure Ryan, Cesare Segre, Siegfried Schmidt, and others) have managed to "crop the heritage of structuralism, and to partly rescue it from the multiple attacks it had to endure in the last quarter of a century, especially from poststructuralism and hermeneutics" (Mihailescu and Hamarneh, 1996). Using a broad interdisciplinary perspective that has integrated hermeneutics, possible-worlds semantics, reception theory, and the best of narratology, theories of fictionality have managed to challenge the simplified understanding of fictionality in other contemporary models, such as speech-act theory.

MARCEL CORNIS-POPE

See also Critics and Criticism (20th Century); Dialogism; Formalism; Mimesis; Narrative Theory; Narratology; Plot

Further Reading

Armstrong, Nancy, and Leonard Tennehouse, "History, Poststructuralism, and the Question of Narrative," *Narrative* 1:1 (January 1993)

Barthes, Roland, "Introduction à l'analyse structurale des récits," *Communications* 8 (1966); as "An Introduction to the Structural Analysis of Narrative," *New Literary History* 6 (1975)

Barthes, Roland, *S/Z,* Paris: Editions du Seuil, 1970, as *S/Z,* London: Cape, and New York: Hill and Wang, 1975

Berman, Art, *From New Criticism to Deconstruction: The Reception of Structuralism and Post-Structuralism,* Urbana: University of Illinois Press, 1988

Brooke-Rose, Christine, *Stories, Theories, and Things,* Cambridge and New York: Cambridge University Press, 1991

Cornis-Pope, Marcel, *Hermeneutic Desire and Critical Rewriting: Narrative Interpretation in the Wake of Poststructuralism,* London: Macmillan, and New York: St. Martin's Press, 1992

Culler, Jonathan, *Structuralist Poetics: Structuralism, Linguistics, and the Study of Literature,* London: Routledge and Kegan Paul, and Ithaca, New York: Cornell University Press, 1975

Deely, John, *Introducing Semiotic: Its History and Doctrine,* Bloomington: Indiana University Press, 1982

Fokkema, Douwe Wessel, and Elrud Ibsch, *Theories of Literature in the Twentieth-Century: Structuralism, Marxism, Aesthetics of Reception, Semiotics,* London: Hurst and New York: St. Martin's Press, 1977; with a new, extended preface, 1995

Genette, Gérard, *Discours du récit,* in *Figures III,* Paris: Editions du Seuil, 1972; as *Narrative Discourse,* Ithaca, New York: Cornell University Press, 1980

Genette, Gérard, *Nouveau discours du récit,* Paris: Editions du Seuil, 1983; as *Narrative Discourse Revisited,* Ithaca, New York: Cornell University Press, 1988

Hawkes, Terence, *Structuralism and Semiotics,* Berkeley: University of California Press, and London: Methuen, 1977

Martin, Wallace, *Recent Theories of Narrative,* Ithaca, New York: Cornell University Press, 1986

Mihailescu, Calin-Andrei, and Walid Hamarneh, editors, *Fiction Updated: Theories of Fictionality, Narratology, and Poetics,* Toronto and Buffalo, New York: University of Toronto Press, 1996

Onega Jaen, Susana, and José Ángel García Landa, editors, *Narratology: An Introduction,* London and New York: Longman, 1996

Orr, Leonard, *Semiotic and Structuralist Analyses of Fiction: An Introduction and a Survey of Applications,* Troy, New York: Whitson, 1987

Prince, Gerald, *A Dictionary of Narratology,* Lincoln: University of Nebraska Press, 1987; Aldershot: Scolar, 1988

Rimmon-Kenan, Shlomith, "How the Model Neglects the Medium: Linguistics, Language, and the Crisis of Narratology," *The Journal of Narrative Technique* 19:1 (Winter 1989)

Sebeok, Thomas, editor, *Encyclopedic Dictionary of Semiotics,* 3 vols., Berlin and New York: Mouton de Gruyter, 1986; 2nd edition, 1994

Silverman, Kaja, *The Subject of Semiotics,* New York: Oxford University Press, 1983

Subscription Libraries. *See* Libraries

Such Is Life by Joseph Furphy

1903

Such Is Life was finished in manuscript in 1897, but it was not published as a novel until 1903 after significant revision. It was very much a product of the literary movements in Australia in the last decades of the 19th century and a culmination of the literary ambitions of its 54-year-old author. The novel received mainly warm reviews in Australia and in the United Kingdom, but the intricacy of its plotting and ideas was apparent to only one reviewer, Joseph Furphy himself writing anonymously in the Sydney *Bulletin*. It was not until the 1940s that there was evidence that readers had become aware of its hidden plotlines. After an initial success, the novel's sale slowed, and it was not reprinted until 1937, when a British publisher brought out an abridged version. In 1944, the original version of the novel was republished in Australia, and it has not been out of print since.

Furphy's writing career before *Such Is Life* was confined to sketches, short stories, and poems published mainly in the "bushman's Bible," the Sydney *Bulletin,* which was the main outlet for radical and realist writing in the 1890s. It was not surprising, then, that *Such Is Life* was read by Furphy's contemporaries as a loose federation of realist stories and sketches of life in western New South Wales during the early 1880s that carried within them a strong socialist message. In the same way as many contemporary readers of *Gulliver's Travels* had believed in the authenticity of Gulliver and his travels, so, too, many readers believed that Furphy's novel was what it claimed to be: *Such Is Life: Being Certain Extracts from the Diary of Tom Collins,* with Tom Collins credited as the author. Tom Collins was one of Furphy's noms de plume—the name being taken from a mythical Australian rumormonger. Furphy's own name did not appear on the novel. Coincidentally, in 1915 the word *furphy* (meaning "a rumor") entered Australian English from wartime slang.

The overt form of Furphy's novel is a series of expanded diary entries from 1883 and 1884, selected at random by Tom Collins. In his prefatory remarks, Tom defends this aleatory method of organization on the grounds that it will show life as it really is, unlike the romantic novelist who bends reality to fit the demands of plot. Hence the title, which is repeated in differing and sometimes ironic contexts throughout the novel. Furphy, however, had a far more subtle program in mind, which he hoped would show that there was more to life than his pompous and deluded narrator saw in his annotations to his randomly chosen diary entries. That program involved weaving through the seven chapters (each based on a diary entry) several hidden stories.

The most significant of these interwoven stories tells of an accidentally disfigured girl who is jilted by her lover but disguises herself as a man and secretly follows her fiancé, now a bitter misanthrope full of self-hatred, around southwestern New South Wales. This romantic story is not evident to Tom, although from his scrupulous records of meetings with the protagonists very observant readers can put the pieces together. As a consequence, the book can be read as two artifacts: a realist account of life in the 1880s as recorded in diary form by Tom Collins and as a novel with deep undercurrents of romance. Each represents different notions of life—one purposeless and random, the other purposeful and manifesting grace. In creating this hybrid, Furphy believed that he had written a novel quite unlike any other. It is certainly unique in Australian literature, and, despite its importance, its idiosyncrasy is such that it has never been imitated, although the tradition of the naive or knowing unreliable narrator is well established in the national canon.

For many readers, the novel is not without its faults. In choosing to have the novel narrated by Tom, Furphy was committed to Tom's laborious and pompous prose style, which was complemented by Tom's accurate but pedantic rendering of the many dialects and voices of the immigrant society of New South Wales at that time. Many have found the style of the novel overworked and the 18th-century digressions on philosophical topics tedious. Nevertheless, its structural innovation and its comprehensive portrait of the social and intellectual world of its time have made it a classic of Australian literature. In its bulk and ambition, *Such Is Life* has often been seen as Australia's *Moby-Dick,* and like Melville's novel, *Such Is Life* embodies much of the national spirit at a time of intense change.

When *Such Is Life* was revised for publication in 1903, two sections Furphy had deleted were rewritten as two distinct novels. Neither was published in book form in Furphy's lifetime. *Rigby's Romance* was serialized in a miner's newspaper in 1905–06 and was published in an abridged form as a book in 1921 and republished in full in 1946, while *The Buln-Buln and the Brolga* was first published as a book in 1948. Neither work has achieved the fame or following of Furphy's sole masterpiece.

Joseph Furphy was an autodidact whose lifetime was spent in manual labor but whose intellectual ambitions were set at an early age. He was taught by his mother to read from the Bible and from the works of William Shakespeare, and those sources, together with his enthusiastic conversion to socialism in the 1880s, provided the basis of the novel that synthesized his life experiences and his beliefs. He was not able to repeat the achievement of *Such Is Life,* but his reputation as one of Australia's major novelists rests securely on his subtle but eccentric single work.

JULIAN CROFT

Further Reading

Barnes, John, *The Order of Things: A Life of Joseph Furphy,* Melbourne and New York: Oxford University Press, 1990

Croft, Julian, *The Life and Opinions of Tom Collins: A Study of the Works of Joseph Furphy,* St. Lucia and Portland, Oregon: University of Queensland Press, 1991

Devlin-Glass, Frances, editor, *The Annotated Such Is Life,* Oxford, Melbourne, and New York: Oxford University Press, 1991

Franklin, Miles (in association with Kate Baker), *Joseph Furphy: The Legend of a Man and His Book,* Sydney: Angus and Robertson, 1944

White, R.S., *Furphy's Shakespeare,* Perth: Centre for Studies in Australian Literature, University of Western Australia, 1989

Wilkes, G.A., *Joseph Furphy's "Such Is Life,"* Melbourne: Shillington House, 1985

The Sufferings of Young Werther by Johann Wolfgang von Goethe

Die Leiden des jungen Werthers 1774; revised edition 1787

Published anonymously, *The Sufferings of Young Werther* immediately became an international best-seller and is still, despite the greater renown of his *Faust,* Goethe's most frequently printed and translated work. In Germany, where Goethe was already a rising star and the novel's authorship no secret, its biographical and autobiographical elements were quickly identified and adduced in criticism of it; elsewhere it aroused curiosity about its author and its genesis that marked the beginning of Goethe's worldwide fame. Countless readers have recognized in Werther's thoughts and feelings aspects of their own experience (see Barthes, 1977): contemporaries discussed Werther as if he were an actual person, praising his virtues, condemning his insufficiencies, and scrutinizing his character and motives with passionate interest, and in the never diminishing spate of critical discussions of the novel until now the psychological complexity of its protagonist is always a central theme.

Werther's frank self-revelation through his own words—chiefly letters to his friend Wilhelm—until the novel's fictive editor introduces third-person narrative a week before his suicide (1774 text; a few days earlier in the text of 1787) was for 18th-century sentimentalists *prima facie* evidence of moral worth. In passages variously narrative, ironic, lyrical, reflective, elegiac, satiric, and idyllic, Werther writes prose that, from his very first letter, continually reveals traits of character that can and will be self-destructive and in which discerning readers have always recognized symptoms of a dangerous emotional and philosophical solipsism.

Werther's unhappiness in love may at first seem the main theme of Goethe's novel, but it is the complexity of his sorrows, his complicated character, and the subtly complex disintegration of his personality that make his story so much more compelling than that of other sentimental heroes. As Goethe declared on completing *Werther* (but prior to its publication), this is a story in which he depicts "a young person endowed with depth of pure feeling and genuine intellectual acumen who gets lost in fantastic dreams and is weakened by speculative thinking until, unhinged by further unhappy passions, in particular an inordinate love, he finally puts a bullet through his head."

If read in biographical terms, the intellectual dreamer is Goethe, who in 1772, during a summer stay in the diplomat-filled, rather stuffy town of Wetzlar, had been strongly attracted to the fiancée (Lotte) of a friend (Albert) and who, after a sad parting from this soon-to-be married couple, was much taken with another young woman after whose marriage in early 1774 he soon found himself unwelcome as a houseguest. The speculative thinker is a young embassy secretary whom Goethe had also known in Wetzlar; unhappy in his work and hopelessly in love with a woman whose husband had forbidden him their house, he committed suicide in mid-autumn 1772, when Lotte's husband sent Goethe an account of the affair, verbatim details of which were ultimately incorporated in the dénouement of Werther's story. The conflation of these two figures is the artistic achievement that differentiates *Werther* fundamentally from any transparently autobiographical first novel as well as from the mere literary exploitation of a sensational suicide some contemporaries considered it.

Werther is unlike other 18th-century novels not because it chiefly comprises one person's letters to one addressee—such novels had long been common—but because its letters and reflections, supplemented by editorial comment, annotation, and narration ranging from documentary objectivity to evaluative omniscience, do not constitute a melodramatic story: there are no mistaken identities, no villainous intrigues, no abductions or seductions, and no criminal assaults to advance its action. Until he violently embraces Lotte at their final meeting, Werther is never seen to be guilty of any grave impropriety. What makes a novel of such brevity and simplicity unique is the dense complexity with which its protagonist is characterized as he continually reveals more and more about himself. If his very first letter displays Werther as an attractive, sensitive, idealistic, intelligent, and nonconforming sentimentalist, it also reveals his irresoluteness, his dilettantism, his narcissism, and his fatalistic, self-exculpatory irresponsibleness; the letters that follow show how his sympathetic traits, no less than his weaknesses, lead to an alienation from society that culminates in a self-punitive, yet simultaneously sadistic, suicide—a last desperate devaluing of reality masked as liberation from a world to which he cannot adapt.

Goethe's mastery of dramatic irony—his model was Oliver Goldsmith, whose *Vicar of Wakefield* (1766) he, like his characters Lotte and Werther, greatly admired—makes possible a protagonist who remains a sympathetic figure despite unconscious revelations of such character traits as petulance, self-pity, and arrogant condescension toward inferiors, equals, and superiors alike. His economical use of parallel episodes (the instance of the seduced girl's suicide, the madness of the clerk who hopelessly loved Lotte, and—new in 1787—the farmhand's murder of the man who has won his former mistress' affections) permits Goethe to foreshadow the pathological forces that will destroy Werther. Technically most important, however, for conveying the novel's sense of tragic inevitability is the motival inversion in Book II of elements that in Book I have positive connotations: thus the godless gloom of Ossian supplants the *Odyssey* in Werther's favor; trees are destroyed that had afforded pleasant shade; flood ravishes a valley once a great beauty spot; Werther chafes in an urban courtly society of tense class distinctions that has supplanted the rural middle-class idyll of a spring and summer seeming to move directly from the winter of 1771 into the fall and December of 1772, when he shoots himself at a desk on which lies Lessing's tragedy *Emilia Galotti*, the antithesis of the light-hearted novel by Goldsmith that he had admired with Lotte. Also effective technically is the introduction from the very start of the novel of references to fate and omens of death that become insistently cumulative as it progresses and, like its parallelisms and motival inversions, contribute to the plausible motivation of Werther's death no less than does psychological verisimilitude.

Despite reservations about the noncondemnatory way in which suicide is presented in it, an overwhelmingly positive reception of *Werther* is documented in hundreds of imitations (not only novels, but also plays, ballets, operas, cantatas), by countless testimonials in the form of critical observation or poetic effusion, and—particularly until the end of the romantic period—by a wealth of songs, ballads, and *objets d'art* it inspired. With French romanticism *Werther* became a world-literary influence and has ever since remained a canonical depiction of tragic maladjustment and unhappy love. No precise influence of *Werther* on the subsequent development of the novel form has been convincingly identified, although it has been plausibly claimed (by Altman, 1982) that its success reversed an 18th-century trend of replacing a single letter writer in epistolary novels with a circle of correspondents. To the extent that it inspired its best emulators—e.g., Ugo Foscolo, Chateaubriand, Benjamin Constant, Charles Nodier—to avoid melodrama and concentrate on a single figure's inner life, *Werther* undoubtedly contributed significantly to the central place of psychological development in subsequent novels.

STUART ATKINS

See also Johann Wolfgang von Goethe

Further Reading

Abbot, Porter H., *Diary Fiction: Writing as Action,* Ithaca, New York: Cornell University Press, 1984

Altman, Janet Gurkin, *Epistolarity: Approaches to a Form,* Columbus: Ohio State University Press, 1982

Atkins, Stuart Pratt, *The Testament of Werther in Poetry and Drama,* Cambridge, Massachusetts: Harvard University Press, 1949

Atkins, Stuart Pratt, *Essays on Goethe,* Columbia, South Carolina: Camden House, 1995

Barthes, Roland, *Fragments d'un discours amoureux,* Paris: Editions du Seuil, 1977; as *A Lover's Discourse: Fragments,* New York: Hill and Wang, 1978

Blackall, Eric A., *Goethe and the Novel,* Ithaca, New York: Cornell University Press, 1976

Boyle, Nicholas, *Goethe: The Poet and the Age,* Oxford: Clarendon Press, 1991; New York: Oxford University Press, 1992

Lewes, George Henry, *The Life and Works of Goethe: With Sketches of His Age and Contemporaries, from Published and Unpublished Sources,* 2 vols., London: D. Nutt, 1855; Boston: Ticknor and Fields, 1856

Reiss, Hans Siegbert, *Goethes Romane,* Bern: Francke, 1963; as *Goethe's Novels,* London: Macmillan, and New York: St. Martin's Press, 1969

Vincent, Dierdre, *Werther's Goethe: The Game of Literary Creativity,* Toronto and Buffalo, New York: University of Toronto Press, 1992

Sult. *See* Hunger

The Sun Also Rises by Ernest Hemingway

1926

The Sun Also Rises was Hemingway's first major novel following the publication of his short-story collection *In Our Time* in 1925 and the satirical novel *The Torrents of Spring* in 1926. While in the latter work he had established his literary independence from the preceding generation of US authors, in particular Sherwood Anderson, with the publication of *The Sun Also Rises* the nature of prose writing, especially in the United States, was altered forever. Hemingway's position as the dominant new force among US authors was firmly established by the time the novel reached its third printing in 1926. The minimalist prose style that so marked Hemingway's short stories had developed to accommodate his analyses of the postwar expatriate experience of a group of disconnected American males, their rivalry over an English woman, Lady Brett Ashley, and the annual fiesta of San Fermin in Pamplona, Spain. Motifs that were to become staple Hemingway characteristics in his later fictional works—male codes of honor, heavy drinking, and bullfighting—are all contained within the tightly ordered and controlled narrative of this novel. Indeed, whereas Hemingway's later fiction may be rightly criticized for its loose construction and its overdependence on these central motifs, *The Sun Also Rises* stands out as the prime example of Hemingway's textual style and storytelling techniques at their honed and deliberately sparse best.

In a *Paris Review* interview in 1958, Hemingway revealed that his method of literary construction was analogous to the movement and structure of an iceberg, seven-eighths of which is concealed beneath the surface of the water. Consequently, a Hemingway text functions as a smoothly structured narrative surface that conceals the framework of the major elements essential to the development of its narrative. In his first-draft notebook he commented that "none of the significant things are going to have any literary signs marking them" (see Svoboda, 1984). Furthermore, in the novella *A Moveable Feast* (1964), Hemingway acknowledged his debt to Impressionist art, emphasizing the importance of Cézanne. His practice of maintaining clean, unadorned sentence construction allowed him to present an apparently purely objective viewpoint to his readers. However, Hemingway's use of metonymy and metaphor regarding certain recurring images, such as the bullfight (indicating the sublimation of desire) and the war (male codes of honor), introduces into the tight narrative structure of *The Sun Also Rises* the combative themes that intersect underneath. This pared and clipped journalistic narrative style is a thoroughly male fictional form in the tradition of Stephen Crane. This style, in turn, influenced the hard-boiled, nonpsychological narrative of US detective-fiction writers, an approach that was not challenged until 1944 when Saul Bellow published his first novel, *Dangling Man*.

Hemingway's analysis of the expatriate lifestyle relies heavily on personal experience. As a result, the novel is often considered a roman à clef, although it was much more so in earlier drafts before he established a chronological ordering of the narrative and added a much more fictionalized account of Paris and Pamplona circa 1925. For better or worse, the success of this novel ensured Hemingway's close identification with the so-called Lost Generation of the 1920s. The novel explores the disintegrating lives of expatriate individuals who seek temporary excitement and opportunities to displace the moral and spiritual voids that define their lives. The barren sexual tussles between the males over Lady Brett have inspired some critics to characterize Brett as a vamp or, as Edmund Wilson concluded, as "one of those international sirens who flourished in the cafés of the postwar period and whose ruthless and uncontrollable infidelities in such a circle as that depicted by Hemingway have made any sort of security impossible for the relations between men and women" (see Wilson, 1941). Such conclusions, however, are erroneous as they fail to incorporate all the details concealed by and within Hemingway's tight narrative style.

One also must take into account the importance of the war in altering the behavior and the social and sexual roles of the characters. Jake Barnes' war wound, for example, has destroyed any hope of a fruitful union with Brett, and Hemingway employs him as a postwar Fisher King, a man robbed of his sexual potency who is forced to witness and record the sexual jousting of the other male protagonists. A reassessment of value systems has occurred in the wake of the war. Because Brett behaves like, and indeed physically resembles, a male, her emancipation is offered on exclusively male terms. Prior to the war, she had been a passive sexual object; after the war, as an active one, she attempts to participate in the games and codes of the males and does so in the (dis)guise of a male. Her continual denigration as a sexual pawn results from her position as an "other" within this small male society. Hemingway marginalizes her; he introduces her to the reader in the company of homosexual males, and later she is excluded from participating in the fiesta by the male dancers who make of her a figure to be idolized. She is denied full and equal participation in the male world, even though she functions socially as a male. Her femininity is concealed beneath a visibly male social identity, while her social emancipation is constrained by tightly ordered male discourse and behavior.

The complex interweaving layers of Jake's first-person narrative, which alternates between personal revelations of his opinions of other characters, the recounting of their conversations, and a minimal presentation of the physical environments in which the action occurs, produces a text of immense complexity, resonating power, and enduring relevance.

PHILIP McGOWAN

See also Ernest Hemingway

Further Reading

Donaldson, Scott, editor, *The Cambridge Companion to Hemingway,* Cambridge and New York: Cambridge University Press, 1996

Lodge, David, *The Modes of Modern Writing: Metaphor, Metonymy, and the Typology of Modern Literature,* London: Arnold, and Ithaca, New York: Cornell University Press, 1977

Mandel, Miriam B., *Reading Hemingway: The Facts in the Fictions,* Metuchen, New Jersey: Scarecrow Press, 1995

Rudat, Wolfgang E.H., *Alchemy in "The Sun Also Rises":*

Hidden Gold in Hemingway's Narrative, Lewiston, New York: Edwin Mellen Press, 1992

Scafella, Frank, editor, *Hemingway: Essays of Reassessment*, New York: Oxford University Press, 1991

Svoboda, Frederic Joseph, *Hemingway and "The Sun Also Rises": The Crafting of a Style*, Lawrence: University Press of Kansas, 1984

Wagner-Martin, Linda, editor, *New Essays on "The Sun Also Rises,"* Cambridge and New York: Cambridge University Press, 1987

Wilson, Edmund, *The Wound and the Bow: Seven Studies in Literature*, New York: Oxford University Press, 1941; revised edition, London: Methuen, 1961

Surrealist Novel

"To write false novels"—from "Secrets of the Magical Surrealist Art," André Breton, *Manifesto of Surrealism*, 1924

The surrealists were better known for poetry than prose and were as a movement highly critical of the novel, especially in its traditional form. And yet the most well known text by the leader of the movement, André Breton, is his prose work *Nadja*, published in 1928. Indeed, despite many of the surrealists' professed dislike of the novel, surrealism exerted an undeniable influence on the inter- and postwar innovations of the genre, especially in France. Bearing stylistic and historic relationships to the magic realist and the postmodern novel, surrealist prose could be said to begin with writers such as Laurence Sterne and Denis Diderot and continue through John Hawkes and Angela Carter. Moreover, as many critics have pointed out, the surrealist dismissal of the novel genre was in no way as rarefied as it might seem, taking part in a general critical view of naturalism within the postsymbolist current in France at the beginning of the 20th century. Surrealism's critique of representation is analogous to contemporary art's dismissal of imitation: rather than represent the spectacle of the world, the surrealists focused on the spectacle of the creative process; writing for them became an explosive writing of the mental *image* (see Devésa, 1993). The surrealists, whose lifelong goals were to enlarge the boundaries of reality, were critical of what they perceived to be the novel's tendencies to limit and classify experience and to reinforce social norms and cliched worldviews. Surrealist procedures for expanding consciousness included the systematic exploration of the psyche, the celebration of eroticism, the cultivation of objective chance, and the alchemy of language (see Balakian, 1970). In short, whether fully "fictional" or not, surrealist prose extols the liberating forces of desire over the calculated and arranged world of representation, eschewing classification and categorization for a journey into the marvelously unknown. And yet surrealist prose is not "fantasy," in that it is not escapist literature; on the contrary it is an urgent search for self-knowledge as a stepping stone to societal transformation.

As a movement, surrealism came into existence in Paris during the years following World War I. The early part of the movement was strongly influenced by Dada, which was founded in Zurich in early 1916 but spread to Berlin, New York, Hannover, Cologne, and finally to Paris with the arrival of Tristan Tzara in January 1920. The atmosphere of early surrealism reflects the postwar mentality of much of the youth of Western Europe and the United States through its combination of extreme bitterness and derision regarding established institutions, along with a heady sense of freedom stemming in part from such extreme nihilism. These libertarian sentiments were hardly conducive to novel writing in the traditional sense. On the contrary, the surrealists were relatively uninterested in generic categories and, if anything, sought to destroy them. For the surrealists it was no longer a question of imitating life through writing but of making writing an actual trace of lived experience (Béhar and Carassou, 1984). Thus the early surrealists were as concerned with gathering experience as with writing: the young friends roamed the streets of Paris or else sat talking for hours in cafés and played experimental thought and language games, especially dream speaking and writing. Louis Aragon did write some dadaist novels, such as *Anicet* (1921) and *Les Aventures de Télémaque* (1922; *The Adventures of Telemachus*), which reflect the atmosphere in Paris after the war with their cavalier mix of philosophy, autobiography, fiction, eroticism, and anecdote. It was only shortly after this that Robert Desnos wrote his *Deuil pour deuil* (1924; *Mourning for Mourning*), Michel Leiris *Le Point Cardinal* (1927; *The Cardinal Point*) and Benjamin Péret *La Brébis galante* (1949; *The Elegant Ewe*), which was begun in the early 1920s and finished in 1949. These short, poetical texts could be called automatic novels, in that they permit the unconscious a chance to reveal itself within a highly imagistic, dreamlike narrative construct. Of course, the surrealist attempt to expand the realms of consciousness through "scientific" examination of the unconscious did not sit very well with Sigmund Freud, who found their goals suspiciously literary. The surrealists, however, did not consider themselves in this early stage as literary writers, and indeed the name of their journal, *Littérature* (founded in 1919), was meant to express this disdain in an ironic fashion.

The early-middle—or "heroic"—years of surrealism continued the surrealists' interest in oneiric consciousness with the clear formulation of a theory of automatic writing in Breton's *Manifesto of Surrealism*. The surrealists had gradually rejected what they considered to be the more negative aspects of dada, wishing rather to formulate their critique of society into a theoretical platform. They also gradually became more explicitly political during this time, turning *Littérature* into *La Révolution surréaliste* and protesting France's involvement in Spain's war against Morocco in 1925. They hooked up with the left-wing magazine *Clarté* and eventually began reading Marx and Hegel. It was during the mid-to-late 1920s that Breton's *Nadja* and

Louis Aragon's *Le Paysan de Paris* (*Paris Peasant*) were written (appearing in 1928 and 1926, respectively).

The later stages of the movement show the surrealists struggling to integrate their goals for the liberated imagination into the narrow confines of the communist party. This struggle eventually led to Breton's abandonment of communism and Aragon's, Tzara's, and Paul Eluard's abandonment of surrealism. During World War II, Breton went into exile and many others went into hiding and resistance; although surrealism did regroup after the war, it was superceded as the critical voice of its time by the more sober and "prosaic" existentialism. However, the spirit of surrealism has never died out completely and was found not only in movements such as May '68, the sexual revolution, fluxus, and "happenings" but continues in certain currents of postmodernism and fantasy, and even in esoteric elements of New Age thought: wherever there is a combination of protest and dream.

Surrealism officially began in 1924 with the publication of Breton's *Manifeste du surréalisme* (the first *Manifesto of Surrealism*) but in surrealist lore bloomed in 1919 when Breton and Philippe Soupault collaborated on a lyric dream-piece entitled *Les Champs magnétiques* (*The Magnetic Fields*). Considered a work "with two heads" in which it was impossible to distinguish clearly between authorial voices, *The Magnetic Fields* contains key elements of surrealism pertaining to their view of literature: namely, an attention to the voice of the unconscious, which was felt to have a universal truth-value, and a disdain for the type of writing the goals of which were either "merely" literary or escapist. By the time the first *Manifesto* was published five years later, Breton defined surrealism in the following way:

SURREALISM, n. Psychic automatism in its pure state, by which one proposes to express—verbally, by means of the written word, or in any other manner—the actual functioning of thought. Dictated by thought, in the absence of any control exercised by reason, exempt from any aesthetic or moral concern.

This definition helps separate the surrealist novel from the magic realist one, which seeks to expand the limits of everyday experience rather than concern itself with a psychological, philological, or philosophical imperative. However, not all surrealist prose fits into the mold of what is known as "psychic automatism."

To understand the notion of surrealist prose writing, it is necessary to begin with Breton's famous critique of the novel form, which seems to be at the crux of the surrealist experience; indeed the first pages of Breton's *Manifesto* contain a diatribe against the "realistic attitude, inspired by positivism, from Saint Thomas Aquinas to Anatole France," which is made up, according to Breton, of "mediocrity, hate and dull conceipt." Breton cites a description of Raskolnikov's room from Fedor Dostoevskii's *Prestuplenie i nakazanie* (1867; *Crime and Punishment*), exclaiming that his own mind has no desire to occupy itself with such trivia and declaring grandly that he simply will not *enter* that room. The opposition made by Breton between realism and "the reverse side" of realism, or surrealism, is that the latter does not consist of the "worthless moments" of life but rather only of the experiences of the breathtakingly marvelous, moments in which antinomies such as dream and waking are reconciled, and which in turn can reconcile the individual to life itself. The traditional realist novel was perceived as too limiting in its fixed psy-

chological attributions of motivation, which in retrospect always seem predetermined and fatalistic. (However, authors such as Raymond Roussel were to teach the surrealists that realism's techniques could be "inverted and made to defend an antirealist presentation"; see Matthews, 1966.) Thus, in *Nadja*, Breton claims to desire books the "doors" of which are left banging; that is, in which attempts to answer the mysteries of identity are not sealed into pat, finished analyses.

Yet it would be wrong to equate Breton's criticism of the realist novel with an outright rejection of the novel form. While Breton did tend to consider the novel inferior to poetry, he did not spend much time formulating the terms of that preference. Instead, Breton, who attempted ever since that first manifesto to create a tradition into which the surrealists could place themselves, preferred to concentrate on the spirit motivating the creative enterprise. He declared the following writers to be surrealist: the Marquis de Sade, Chateaubriand, Benjamin Constant, Victor Hugo, Edgar Allan Poe, Germain Nouveau, Alfred Jarry, and Roussel. Breton also praised the Gothic novel for its liberation of the marvelous, especially M.G. Lewis' *The Monk* (1796). (Breton also discusses the Gothic novel in *Les Vases Communicants* [1932; *Communicating Vessels*].) The surrealists were also influenced by the novels of Joris-Karl Huysmans. And no work held more importance for the surrealists than Le Comte de Lautréamont's *Les Chants de Maldoror* (1868–69; *The Lay of Maldoror*), which, while transgressing numerous novelistic (and an even greater number of social) conventions, could still be considered a novel. Thus, as Jacqueline Chénieux-Gendron (1983) argues, it is less the novel itself that came under attack with that first manifesto than the "realistic attitude." Indeed, it could be said that the manifesto laid open the possibility of writing a novel with a "surrealistic" attitude.

Surrealism played an active role in the novel's transition from a genre with more or less codified rules at the end of the 19th century to a protean *écriture,* combining lyricism, testimony, confession, essay, and manifesto, forms that were better suited to examine the mind thinking and the hand writing than to create characters or describe "slices of life." The surrealist novel is ultimately a means rather than an end in itself (Matthews, 1966), refusing absolutely the anodyne aesthetic. In spite of surrealism's interest in Freud (and indeed its basis in psychoanalytic thought), the surrealist novel is antipsychological, claiming no need for any sort of logical or rational justification for action outside of desire itself. Surrealist writing is playful and always celebrates the erotic. Whereas the novel could generally be considered the genre of extended time (with its patient unfoldings and use of duration), the surrealists demanded the writing of the moment/ous. Chénieux-Gendron speaks of the participational or magical aspect of surrealist thought: it is meant to actualize itself in the experience, whether as fable (which privileges life-beyond-the-text) or fiction (which creates a separate, highly imagined, and often absurd world where normal logical rules no longer apply).

There are two basic tenets in "classical" surrealism: Breton's and Louis Aragon's. The former's "analogical prose" (so called by Anna Balakian, 1970), exemplified by *Nadja* but also including texts such as *L'Amour fou* (1937; *Mad Love*) and *Arcane 17* (1944; *Arcanum 17*), approaches autobiographical fiction. In these texts, Breton attempts to write the magical moments of revelation offered to him by the women in his life, who save him from the despair of the "worthless moments" of everyday existence—the seeming glorification of which comprises the realist novel he so despises. The texts are not automatic writing but seem, on the contrary, laboriously written, in a style rejecting easy identification or assimilation on the reader's part. What is "surrealist" about these texts (especially the first two) is their insistence on the key importance of objective chance (*le hasard objectif*), the uncanny convergence of individual volition and exterior circumstances to create situations that resonate with significance. In *Nadja,* photographs are used to spare the narrator the necessity of going into the dull detail of description, but rather than giving one the sense of plenitude and understanding, they leave the reader more perplexed; the images often seem arbitrary and poorly chosen, illustrating many of the objects surrounding Nadja but leaving out any portrait of her. In fact, they bely the autobiographical aspects of the text: the formal portrait of a stiff-looking Breton at the end only serves to subvert the notion of authorial "presence." Indeed, all of Breton's texts deal with the phenomenology of presence and absence, and objective chance serves as a rare glimmer of presence—or intimations thereof—in an otherwise dull desert of boredom and futility. And yet because of these chance (and, hence, *significant*) happenings, Breton remains an essentially optimistic writer. This is most striking in *Arcanum 17,* which seeks to create a myth to be used as a foundation for a post-war Europe. In his text, Breton uses the old Celtic myth of Melusine, overlapping her story to that of his and his new wife's visit to the tip of the Gaspé Peninsula in Canada shortly before the end of World War II. The story is essentially an exploration of overcoming disaster, of living after the unlivable: "Mélusine après le cri" (Melusina after the cry). Myth was seen as a way to reformulate the universe poetically, through image and analogy, combining this formulation with narrative elements, such as in the tale (conte). For Breton, writing was always an act of communication; he always strove to "see, and make see" (*voir et faire voir*) only what was of sublime importance: *le merveilleux.*

The strand of surrealist prose exemplified by Louis Aragon also reflects the breathtakingly marvelous, but with more wit and less awe. (It is not without irony that Aragon eventually, as a dedicated member of the Communist Party, became a staunch proponent of socialist realism and wrote long traditional novels exposing complex social relations.) Aragon's great surrealist prose work, *Paris Peasant,* published around the same time as *Nadja,* is a piece of baroque exuberance, a fascination with language and the language of description. Consisting of several parts dating from several periods, *Paris Peasant* includes philosophical musings, discourses proffered by allegorical figures, detailed descriptions of shady Parisian arcades and nocturnal outings, and reproductions of, among other bits of *realia,* a menu from a dadaist-frequented café, and plaques on statues in a famous Parisian park. Like *Nadja, Paris Peasant* is autobiographical, and it also subverts the genre. But its view of language and representation differ from Breton's. Chénieux-Gendron (1983) speaks of Aragon's fascination with a "magical" language, one in which the signified melts away and leaves behind only the word. Whereas Breton seeks an altered state prior to writing—a surrealist resolution of binaries, a truth beyond language and description—Aragon seems to fixate on the myriad possibilities in the conjunction of the word and the world.

The two strands of the surrealist novel illustrate well not only the poles of the genre but also the similarities. For both, faithful representation of quotidian life is secondary to some other aspect: in Breton, it is heightened reality, in Aragon, language. But both focus the authorial gaze on an allegorical urban landscape (or what Walter Benjamin called "second nature": the return to a magical environment that consists of signs to be decoded for revelation, much as in a fairy tale), both manifest a romantic fascination with the creative power of the imagination, both idealize sexual love as crucial to the unleashing of the imagination, and both closely examine the interstices between subjective and objective worlds. The surrealist novel could be called an attempt to explore and enlarge the scope of the world beyond what has been represented by the "realist attitude." To that extent, surrealist novelists rarely employed third-person narrators since such omniscience appeared to them too artificial and contained too many presuppositions about identity.

Thus Robert Desnos' *La Liberté ou l'amour!* (1927; *Liberty or Love!*), which differs from the texts above in that it "tells" the story of the star-crossed lovers Corsair Sanglot and Louise Lame, also jumps from a seeming third-person narration to a first-person narrator, who occasionally interrupts the story at unexpected points to complain of his own loneliness, and who wonders what will happen to the characters whose story he is telling. The intent is thus less to affirm the God-like status of the storyteller than to explore human consciousness and the limits of knowledge. In a similar fashion, the book manifests no traditional unfolding of the story but rather sudden metamorphoses, and an incantatory and repetitive style: one critic calls Desnos' novels "long narrative poems in prose" (Caws, 1977). Moreover, the characters are "obstinately one-dimensional" (Matthews, 1966), figuring as emblems of revolt and desire, and thus psychological motivation is replaced by a mutually reflective discourse of passion and freedom on both the level of character "formation" and of narrative voice.

Such one-dimensional characters appear in other surrealist works, for example those of René Crevel, who once rivaled Desnos for the most interesting trance-pronouncements and whose suicide in 1935 shook up the group on the eve of the First International Writer's Congress. Crevel used the point of view of a young child in his 1927 *Babylone (Babylon)* to contrast the fresh innocence and creative "credulity" of the surrealist imaginative vision with the petrified stultification of bourgeois rationality. As a contrast to both of these views, the dazzling, red-headed figure of Cynthia, like many other surrealist heroines (Aurora in the eponymous novel by Leiris, Heide in Julien Gracq's *Au Chateau d'Argol* [1938; *The Castle of Argol*], and Desnos' Louise Lame), represents desire in its most absolute and socially destructive form. Crevel wrote several other novels before his death, all of which address the painful issues of identity, sexuality, and revolt not only against social norms but against life itself.

One of the greatest novels of desire and revolt is Gracq's *The Castle of Argol.* Gracq's first novel is a surrealist homage to the Gothic novel praised by Breton in the first *Manifesto,* and it creates an atmosphere of mystery and terror, sacrifice and redemption, interwoven with the theme of the quest for the Grail. In Gracq's novel, the three main characters are allegorical and antipsychological: neither types nor particulars, they resonate with the conjoined powers of desire and destiny.

Thus another route taken by the surrealists in their refusal of false psychological depth is that of myth. Many of the surrealists lived or traveled in the Americas, and all celebrated "primitive" over occidental values. Benjamin Péret, an important but virtually unread (and until recently unpublished) member of the core surrealist movement, is perhaps most widely known for his interest in the Native American population of Mexico, where he lived from 1941 to 1948. His *Anthologie des mythes, légendes et contes populaires d'Amérique* (Myths, Legends and Folk Tales of America) was published the year following his death in 1960, but previous to that his own *Histoire naturelle* (1958; Natural History) showed the fruitful conjunction between automatic writing (which he never abandoned) and myth's attention to the cosmic and the elemental. Péret never wavered in his commitment to surrealism in either his ficton or poetry and was one of many who ended up turning to myth as a model for prose forms.

Another surrealist interested in myth was Michel Leiris, well-known autobiographer and ethnographer, considered the modern-day Montaigne and known also as the former director of the Musée de l'Homme in Paris. Like Péret, Leiris remained faithful to surrealism's goals until the end of his life (in 1990), although unlike Péret he was no longer officially associated with the movement, having moved on in 1929 to work with Georges Bataille and later to coedit *Les Temps modernes* with Jean-Paul Sartre. Leiris' prose is always autobiographical; he recognized in himself the "incapacity" to move beyond the first-person singular. Indeed, he ran into problems as an ethnographer with his belief in the impossibility of assuming an objective gaze. And yet his great autobiographical work *La Règle du jeu* (1948; *Rules of the Game*), of which *L'Age d'homme* (1939; *Manhood*) was the springboard, seems almost like a scientific enterprise, and indeed could be called an ethnography of the self. Leiris' texts are often haunted and oneiric; indeed, he was a thorough and detailed chronicler of his own dreams and often used them as the groundwork for his prose writings. But he was equally interested in the functioning of language, to which his creation of a personalized dictionary, *Glossaire j'y serre mes gloses* (1939), attests. In this, he was greatly inspired by the strange experimental novelist Raymond Roussel, whose *Impressions d'Afrique* (1910; *Impressions of Africa*) combined intense verbal play with virtually hermetic imaginary activity. Leiris' early surrealist novel *Aurora* (not published until 1946), also in the form of a travelogue, combines wordplay and dream recounting in a narrative whose characters all wear different sides of the author's self, and which recounts his own journeys in a thinly veiled, albeit highly mythical and fabulous, way.

Like Leiris (and also Marcel Duchamp and Robert Desnos), the experimental writer Raymond Queneau is widely known for his attempts to liberate language from traditional dictionary significations. Queneau achieved fame in France and abroad for his *Zazie dans le métro* (1959; *Zazie*). In his novels Queneau manifests a surrealist taste for humor and the absurd, which he projects onto the ordinary life of the working classes. He combines an apparently childlike worldview with a sophisticated interest in mathematics and linguistics, and his sense of play is most serious, concealing a pessimistic worldview. An admirer of Gustave Flaubert, especially of *Bouvard et Pécuchet*, Queneau shares Flaubert's wry amusement at human folly and pomposity, and his delight in chronicling them.

It is, interestingly enough, the women associated with surrealism, albeit primarily its post-"heroic" period—Leonora Carrington, Joyce Mansour, and Gisèle Prassinos—who display the most remarkable dips into the darkness of the unconscious realms: their visions are generally haunted, often dealing with insanity and the dissolution of identity (Carrington, Prassinos) and intense sado-masochism (Mansour). Mansour's 1958 novel *Les Gisants satisfaits* is a vivid exploration of pain and transcendence; like the Marquis de Sade, Antonin Artaud, and Georges Bataille, Mansour suggests that the experience of bodily sacrifice allows one to overcome the limits of ordinary space-time consciousness.

The surrealists have influenced some of the most important and internationally recognized avant-garde writers and theorists, such as Bataille, Maurice Blanchot, and Louis-René des Forêts, whose haunting, experimental, and erotic prose resists any easy generic categorization. The *nouveau roman* (New Novel) also owes something to the surrealists' decontextualizing and privileging of the object, and although its scope and point of view are generally more limited than surrealism's life-and-death stakes, an author such as Robbe-Grillet reveals a certain surrealist sensibility.

While the writers discussed here display a remarkable diversity of talents, they tend generally to be concerned first and foremost with the exploration of the deeper layers of the self and psyche through their interest in the unconscious and the dream state. They all deal more closely with linguistic *signification* than with *representation*, and their prose is highly imagistic. Surrealist writers manifest a concern for currents that transcend the mundane and the particular, seeking support in the realm of myth, legend, and folk or fairy tale. They most emphatically exalt the revolutionary powers of love and sexual desire in the frankest manner. Many surrealists attempt to recover the lost innocence of the child's mind and reflect a childlike awe toward the world of things. A good number of surrealist novels have picaresque qualities, the early works especially, and their meanderings are often set in the streets of Paris, where the wanderers seek out the magical and *merveilleux* behind the facade of everyday reality. And yet literary critics of surrealism generally agree that it is not a particular theme or technique that makes the surrealist novel, but the *spirit* informing it. One could say that all surrealist texts proclaim, along with André Breton (quoting Rimbaud and Marx), the freedom and power of the imagination to "transform life" and "change the world."

ELIZABETH BRERETON ALLEN

See also French Novel (1914–45); Magic Realism

Further Reading

Balakian, Anna, *Surrealism: The Road to the Absolute*, New York: Noonday Press, 1959; revised edition, London: Unwin, 1970; 3rd edition, Chicago: University of Chicago Press, 1986

Béhar, Henri, and Michel Carassou, editors, *Le Surréalisme*, Paris: Le Livre de poche, 1984

Breton, André, *Las Vases Communicants*, Paris: Les Editions de Noel et Steele, 1932; as *Communicating Vessels*, Lincoln: University of Nebraska Press, 1990

Breton, André, *Manifestes du surréalisme* (contains the first and second manifestos), Paris: Pauvert, 1962; as *Manifestoes of Surrealism*, Ann Arbor: University of Michigan Press, 1969

Caws, Mary Ann, *The Surrealist Voice of Robert Desnos*, Amherst: University of Massachusetts Press, 1977

Chénieux-Gendron, Jacqueline, *Le Surréalisme et le roman: 1922–1950*, Lausanne: L'Age d'homme, 1983

Devésa, Jean-Michel, *René Crevel et le roman*, Amsterdam and Atlanta, Georgia: Rodopi, 1993

Hoog, Armand, "The Surrealist Novel," *Yale French Studies* (1951)

Hubert, Renée Riese, *Surrealism and the Book*, Berkeley: University of California Press, 1988

Matthews, J.H., *Surrealism and the Novel*, Ann Arbor: University of Michigan Press, 1966

Nadeau, Maurice, *Le Roman français depuis la guerre*, Paris: Gallimard, 1963; as *The French Novel Since the War*, London: Methuen, 1963; New York: Grove Press, 1969

Polizzotti, Mark, *Revolution of the Mind: The Life of André Breton*, New York: Farrar, Straus, and Giroux, and London: Bloomsbury, 1995

The Swallower Swallowed by Réjean Ducharme

L'Avalée des avalés 1966

Réjean Ducharme's first novel, *The Swallower Swallowed* created enormous controversy and attracted much critical attention in North America and Europe. Written by a then-unknown Québécois author notorious for fleeing public attention, *The Swallower Swallowed* is a masterfully original novel, unlike any work ever produced in Quebec or Canada, full of hyperbole, fantasy, irony, puns, and neologisms. In 1967, *The Swallower Swallowed* was awarded the Prix du Gouverneur du Canada and came very close to winning France's much sought-after literary prize, the Prix Goncourt.

That Ducharme's manuscript was rejected by publishing firms in Quebec may be explained by the nature of the novel. *The Swallower Swallowed* is neither a product of the dominant 1960s ideology espoused by those members of Quebec's intelligentsia and artistic community who wished to achieve Quebec's secession from Canada, nor a work that, through the principles of social realism, paints a portrait of society. Ducharme's profound originality lies in his extravagant vision, in which the realistic and fantastic are closely intertwined. One of his central themes is the quest for personal freedom. His main characters tend to be marginalized: observing society from the outside, they exhibit a supremely lucid understanding of life, an all-encompassing iconoclasm, and a striking wisdom.

The protagonist of *The Swallower Swallowed*, Bérénice Einberg, is an eloquent and typical example of Ducharme's characters. Age nine at the beginning of the novel, wise beyond her years, rebellious yet also neurasthenic, Bérénice exemplifies the anguish from which all of Ducharme's characters suffer. Unwilling to integrate herself into the insincere world of the adult, she disowns her parents, rejects the religious education imposed upon her, and attempts to repress her sexuality. Like Ducharme's other female characters, she stands apart from her own reality, acting as an external observer, a witness to the disintegration of conjugal relationships and family life as well as to the weaknesses and hypocrisy of social institutions.

As suggested by the title, Ducharme uses the metaphor of being swallowed or overpowered to describe Bérénice's relationships with those who would wish to dominate her. Thus, she is the swallower who is swallowed, that is, the headstrong individual over whom, at different times, adults triumph. However, she is also the swallower who swallows others, the victorious individual who retains her autonomy. Her struggle to preserve her independence and her perseverance in protecting herself from the corrupting influence of adulthood make her a symbol of the idealistic individual who is repressed by an autocratic force that she ultimately learns to manipulate. In Israel, at the end of the novel, Bérénice draws gunfire from Syrian soldiers and uses her friend Gloria as a human shield. In death, Gloria becomes a heroine, while Bérénice relishes her own triumph in deception.

Ducharme's use of puns, as in the title, and hyperbole are distinct traits of his style, consistently dazzling, poetic, and unpredictable. Sometimes the play with language serves to exaggerate the description of an outlandish character. Sometimes Ducharme seems merely to be toying with words in an apparently gratuitous repetition of prefixes or suffixes. Sometimes his playfulness seems driven by sheer delight in neologisms. Bérénice creates her own language, "le bérénicien," which is particularly rich in invective, such as "estanglobular spetermatorinx," for adult.

Her mastery of language makes it easy to forget that Bérénice is a child. Her ability to communicate overpowering emotions goes far beyond that of a typical nine-year-old: "Everything swallows me. When my eyes are shut it's my inside that swallows me, it's in my inside I stifle. When my eyes are open I'm swallowed because I see, it's in the inside of what I see that I suffocate. I'm swallowed by the river that's too big, the sky that's too high, the flowers that are too fragile." Bérénice Einberg is Ducharme's most hideous creation. Revolt, aggression, and hostility are liberating forces over which the child rejoices. No one is spared her tongue lashings. Her parents, Rabbi Schneider from the synagogue she attends, her brother, Christian, and close friends all suffer, to varying degrees, her fits of outrage. Madame Einberg, her mother, is described by her daughter as "hideous and repulsive as a dead cat that's being devoured by worms." The family home, an abandoned abbey on an island, exemplifies Ducharme's intention to create a largely imaginary world that readers could not possibly construe as an image of an independent Quebec, often evoked in Québécois literature of the 1960s. Turning his back on the dominant concerns of contemporary Canadian literature and refusing to participate in political debate, Ducharme created new artistic and technical openings for the development of the Canadian novel.

The Swallower Swallowed, unique through its use of word play, its dense texture of allusions to history, literature, and philosophy, and its portrayal of a diabolical and iconoclastic character, marks a turning point in the modern Québécois and Canadian novel. Together with the work of Hubert Aquin and Marie-Claire Blais, *The Swallower Swallowed* expanded the limits of the Québécois novel's use of language and discourse. Ducharme is considered one of the most innovative contributors to the modern francophone novel, and his distinctly recognizable voice resonates on each page, underlining his passion for language, irony, and innovation.

KENNETH W. MEADWELL

Further Reading

Bond, David, "The Search for Identity in the Novels of Réjean Ducharme," *Mosaic* 9:2 (1976)

Imbert, Patrick, "Révolution culturelle et clichés chez Réjean Ducharme," *Journal of Canadian Fiction* 25–26 (1979)

La Bossière, Camille, "Réjean Ducharme's Devilish Children," in her *The Dark Age of Enlightenment: An Essay on Québec Literature,* Fredericton, New Brunswick: York Press, 1980

Leduc-Park, Renée, *Réjean Ducharme: Nietzsche et Dionysos,* Quebec: Presses de l'Université Laval, 1982

Meadwell, Kenneth W., "Réjean Ducharme," in *Profiles in Canadian Literature,* volume 6, edited by Jeffrey Heath, Toronto: Dundurn Press, 1980

Meadwell, Kenneth W., "Ludisme et clichés dans *L'Avalée des avalés* de Réjean Ducharme," *Voix et Images* 41 (1989)

Meadwell, Kenneth W., *"L'Avalée des avalés," "L'Hiver de force" et "Les Enfantômes" de Réjean Ducharme: Une fiction mot à mot et sa littérarité,* Lewiston, New York, and Queenston, Ontario: Edwin Mellen Press, 1990

Swedish Novel. *See* Scandinavian Novel

Swiss Novel

German Language

When one looks at the stunning richness of the contemporary Swiss novel, it seems hard to believe that the genre has only been a major literary force in Switzerland since the latter 19th century. Although Heinrich Wittenweiler's *Ring* (c. 1410; Ring), a comic epic in the vein of François Rabelais and Luigi Pulci, can hardly qualify as a modern novel, it should nevertheless be mentioned here for its outstanding literary complexity, one that makes it a forerunner of Miguel de Cervantes' *Don Quixote* (1605–15). The only genuine Swiss contribution to the history of the novel until the 18th century, however, is Gotthard Heidegger's *Mythoscopia romantica* (1698), a sharp and witty attack on the novel as a genre in the spirit of Calvinistic theology. Heidegger's criticism is based on a thorough knowledge of the examples of the European novel, including its developing theory in Huet and Boileau, and it proved to be fairly influential. In fact, Switzerland's involvement in the Protestant Reformation and the rigid morality of the two major confessions are certainly responsible for the retarded emergence of a genuinely Swiss novel. Only a few cities could be regarded as cultural centers big enough to foster such a development, but the backwardness of the country at large nevertheless effectively prohibited such an enterprise.

After the peace of 1712, however, the situation looked to be more promising.

Without a genuine novelistic tradition in the 17th century, the Swiss-German reading public was satisfied with the narratives that came in from Germany and the multitude of German translations from English and French. Swiss readers also tapped into the cultural history of their immediate neighbors, with French and, to a lesser degree, Italian being accessible languages—particularly before the unification of the German Reich in 1871. For most of its history, then, Switzerland could have regarded itself simply as an autonomous part of the German-speaking world, a point of view that even influenced the francophone, although dominantly Protestant, west of the country. Only after a new federal state was formed in Switzerland in 1847 did the powers of the cantons become weakened and the Swiss novel fully emerge.

Each of Albrecht von Haller's didactic novels, *Usong* (1771), *Alfred* (1773), and *Fabius und Cato* (1774), discusses a particular type of government. Haller's novels reflect Switzerland's distinctive situation in the 18th century, insofar as after the 1647 declaration of political neutrality and the peace of 1712, confessional parity between the Catholics and the Reformed was achieved. As a result the ideas and ideals of the Enlightenment were allowed to take root. Haller himself was one of Europe's foremost modern scientists, and his novels are part of an unbiased, albeit primarily conservative, application of a common-sense attitude to society and culture at large. The ideals of the *citoyen* actively promoting the well-being of the commonwealth found ready expression in the attempts to reform education and to secure some sort of basic welfare for the numerous needy. The *Helvetische Gesellschaft* (Helvetic Society, 1712) soon became the focus of many reformist ideas aimed at advocating tolerance and establishing programs to raise the level of intellectual and material wealth. Haller's novels were not favored by the general reading public, however. It is perhaps not surprising that as much as Haller's pedantic doctrine and didacticism scared away Swiss readers, so did the blatant adventurousness and sometimes erotic characters of Heinrich Daniel Zschokke's narratives tend to attract them.

Zschokke, a naturalized Swiss since 1798, was certainly the most popular Swiss novelist of his day, capitalizing on his facility to produce the standard variety of the "Storm and Stress" sword and dagger novel. Although his novels do not qualify as particularly Swiss in character, rather more international, Zschokke is nevertheless important for his prominent involvement in Swiss politics and his advocacy of public enlightenment. These themes are the dominant topic of literary and social discourses in the late 18th century, and they constitute the primary perspective of the early Swiss novel of social reform. The Enlightenment in the second half of the 18th century fused the notion of public education with the growing desire of liberal intellectuals and businessmen to form a unified Swiss state. With the cantons still in power, the national ideal found an outlet in the multitude of "moral" and "economic" societies that promoted reformist ideas.

Johann Heinrich Pestalozzi is certainly the best-known social reformer and educator of his time. He shared a deeply felt commitment to help and teach the poor and to work with many of his compatriots toward the betterment of society in general. The education of the poor is the main topic of Pestalozzi's major literary achievement, the "novel for the people" *Lienhard und Gertrud* (1781; *Leonard and Gertrude*). Its author tries to emulate the numerous "contes moraux" (moral tales) of the Enlightenment, and he succeeds in transforming the genre into something quite unique. Pestalozzi does not use the literary form to demonstrate an abstract truth, like Voltaire or Johnson, but attempts instead to show, through the psychology of a repenting sinner, how the power of self-reform manages to lift his protagonists out of their poverty. The circumspect and morally upright Gertrud helps her husband to stay away from alcohol and to rebuild their lives through thriftiness, moral sincerity, honesty, and trust in God's grace. With the help of the idealized figure of a benign aristocrat, Arner, Lienhard and Gertrud become paragons for the entire village.

Although readers neglected to apply Pestalozzi's maxims, the book's simple story and uncommonly open pedagogical narrative style set the tone for a number of important followers until very recently. The novel uses dialogue to ease the impact of its pedagogical tenets and thus develops a style that closely resembles the naïveté of instructional manuals for children. This simplicity is of course not natural but carefully crafted, and corresponds to an idealization of pure and unspoiled nature in

the tradition of Pestalozzi's compatriot Jean-Jacques Rousseau. Unlike Rousseau, however, Pestalozzi allows for habit-forming institutions such as schools to exist, and in fact argues for a network of religious and educational institutions as a means for social welfare.

Both Pestalozzi and Rousseau write with the aim of applying their ideas against a background of rather bleak poverty and distress. The life of the poor farmers, farmhands, and workers was dismal, and often despair drove the poorest of the poor into alcohol, which became a standard topic throughout the late 18th and well into the 19th century. Nevertheless, the new sentimentalism and its preference for the genius of nature produced idealized idylls such as Salomon Gessner's, but it also successfully romanticized the personal accounts of a life under dire straits such as that presented in Ulrich Bräker's *Lebensgeschichte und natürliche Ebentheuer des Armen Mannes im Tockenburg* (1780; *The Life Story and Real Adventures of the Poor Man of Toggenburg*).

Bräker was the son of a poor farmer, and, destitute of any instruction, succeeded only later in life in achieving some education, mostly self-taught from books. His autobiography achieved fame not only for its Pestalozzi-like simplicity of description and its convincing representation of a destitute childhood and youth, but also and foremost for the descriptive beauty of its natural setting. The terror of poverty, it seems, was mitigated by the delights Swiss nature afforded the young shepherd, whose only education was provided by the magnificent vistas of the Alps and later on by the cunning of his fellows. Just as with Pestalozzi, Bräker's account was used by most Swiss readers for the purpose of creating an unreal scenery in which the hardships of life can be set off with the delight of nature.

The desire to advance the social conditions of the population at large led in the second half of the century to the foundation of the *Ökonomische Gesellschaft* (1759). This society tried to propagate modern methods of farming in a country that produced enough wheat for only 290 days of the year. Given these efforts and the ensuing economic pressures, it is perhaps not surprising that the farmhouse emerged as the focus of much of the novel writing of the day. This idea was dealt with in Hans Casper Hirzel's report on Jakob Guyer in 1762, the model farmer of Zurich who became known as the philosopher-farmer, or *Socrates rustique*. Hirzel's "Kleinjogg" thus became the forerunner not only of Pestalozzi and Bräker but also of the numerous rural protagonists in the work of the oldest of Switzerland's three great novelists, Jeremias Gotthelf (pseudonym for Albert Bitzius).

Gotthelf, a reformed clergyman, published alongside 70 tales some 13 novels and may be regarded as the first truly Swiss novelist (his forerunners, excluding Rousseau, did not see themselves as such, and the reading audience neglected their didactic and moral intentions). Gotthelf is the first to impress his readers as being distinctively Swiss—and yet also different. To be sure, his popularity never measured up with the authors of modern sentimental novels as mass entertainment; however, Gotthelf became the paradigm of the Swiss novelist by virtue of his use of Swiss dialect forms, mixed in with an essentially High German diegetic plot description and the thematic continuation of the didactic novel. As with Pestalozzi, social problems form Gotthelf's main thematic resource, and he succeeded in integrating a "simple" style, reminiscent of earlier religious and pedagogic treatises, with complex psychological descriptions in often beautiful language. His goals in his early writings are not much different from the programs of the moral and economic societies: to show the roots of evil and to point out a virtuous pathway to happiness. *Der Bauernspiegel* (1837; The Farmer's Mirror), his first novel, gained fame for its stark description of the miserable life of a farmhand who eventually reforms himself. If one were to compare Gotthelf's work to that of the contemporary German novelists of the period, one would find it far less cautious in its depiction of social problems, such as the depressing poverty and alcoholism then prevalent in Switzerland. A large part of the societal spectrum is represented in his novels, although village and farm life conditions his topics. In novels such as *Wie Uli der Knecht glücklich wird* (1841; How Uli the Farmhand Becomes Happy), *Geld und Geist; oder, Die Versöhnung* (1843–44; Money and the Spirit; or, The Reconciliation), *Der Geltstag* (1845; The Payday), *Uli der Pächter* (1847; Uli, the Tenant Farmer), and *Erlebnisse eines Schuldenbauers* (1852; Experiences of a Farmer in Debt), Gotthelf analyzes the roots of poverty (as he sees them) and propagates renunciation and hard work, combined with an unflinching trust in God, as the only way out of distress. His central hero, Uli, overcomes his initial problems by attempting to do his best. In the process of applying honesty to both his professional work and his conduct of life, Uli learns what is best for himself as well as for nature and society. Gotthelf's Biedermeier-solution for the ills of the world revolves around the idea of infusing secular behavior with religious and moral standards. His anachronistic rigorism resembles Pestalozzi's similarly simplistic and highly crafted rhetorics; both mix the blunt didactic maxim and direct moralization with a very refined way of psychologizing the protagonists.

Gotthelf's novels, written explicitly for service people—farmhands and maids—were in fact hardly ever read by their intended audience, as Gottfried Keller, his more famous and less popular contemporary, once bitingly observed. And yet if Gotthelf's moral vision and didactic measures were lost on an audience that utilized the author's conservatism to affirm its own self-righteous hypocrisy, Keller's often bitter liberal criticism of Swiss society kept him from becoming equally popular. The common misreading of Gotthelf at the time declared poverty an obstacle to be overcome, or endured as a basically idyllic situation without the dangers of material wealth. Keller, too, attacked the overestimation of the material world, without, however, losing sight of the necessary social reforms; unlike Gotthelf, his main complement was not religion but art. More widely traveled than Gotthelf and a thorough failure according to bourgeois standards, the one-time painter Keller had known artists and industrialists such as Richard Wagner and the magnate Alfred Escher, communists, liberal poets, and exiled politicians, and consequently his *Weltanschauung* and novelistic world was much broader than Gotthelf's. Of his novels, *Der grüne Heinrich* (1853–55, revised edition 1880; *Green Henry*) is regarded by most as Keller's major work, one in which he presents the story of a failing artist, drawing both on his own experiences and on earlier models of the *Entwicklungsroman* such as Goethe's *Wilhelm Meisters Lehrjahre* (1795–96; *Wilhelm Meister's Apprenticeship*).

After the settlement of the last interior conflict a year earlier, the *Sonderbundkrieg* of 1848, Switzerland had created a new and truly liberal constitution. The basis of this process had begun before the revolutions of 1848 in Europe, but was neverthe-less enhanced by them. The peace of 1847 had been a final defeat for the conservative-clerical factions, and the dominating discourses changed the interpretive paradigms from the dichotomy between secular materialism and religious spiritualism to the more precise antagonism between soulless capitalism and artistic individualism. Keller (and every critical writer since) attacks the sometimes brutal capitalist development that quickly transformed Swiss society and was as much of a hindrance to the individual's development of identity as was the clericalism of the *ancien régime*. However, Keller remained a staunch liberal democrat and supported the forces of liberalism in his fight against his pusillanimous contemporaries, their *ressentiment*, egotism, and lack of artistic feeling. Still, the old interpretive paradigm that tried to solve problems by returning to an essentially Christian state (employed by authors such as Gotthelf, among others) endured during this period. Its supporters succeeded in blocking the cultural and societal developments of modernization in the dominantly Catholic regions, and violent reactions among the basically Protestant and liberal population elsewhere showed that they too were not prepared to accept radical anticlericalism.

Keller became in retrospect the single most important writer in his country because he witnessed both the neglect of the cultural sphere in the new state and the growing estrangement between artists and intellectuals as well as that of society at large. The year 1848 had created a new but still very traditional society: the leading role of the liberal bourgeoisie ensured better political representation, more democratic institutions, and a better life. That was where the pact with the supporting intellectuals ended; their more visionary programs and often utopian hopes were not part of the practical programs of liberal politicians. As it turned out, then, society had changed, even in the right direction, but with little consequence for the creative artist. During his 15 years of service as a *Stadtschreiber,* a well-paid administrative officer in Zurich, Keller came to recognize the limitations of the 1848 watershed. But even as his political views softened, he could not help observing an ever-growing gap between the spirit of business and the spirit of art, and his last novel, *Martin Salander* (1886; *Martin Salander*), reflects this estrangement. Keller never regarded himself as a *local* Swiss author; *Green Henry* was not published in Switzerland and was intended for a broader reading public. In this respect, too, it remained important to be published by a German company for both financial success and a degree of popularity.

This was also the case for Conrad Ferdinand Meyer, the third well-known Swiss prose author of the 19th century. Meyer's only novel, *Jürg Jenatsch* (1874), deals with the conflicting spheres of politics and ethics. The author makes use of historical themes and personalities in his novels, and he presents his readers with a panorama of the present in the disguise of the Renaissance. As does Keller, Meyer utilizes local Swiss themes to mark the boundaries encountered by the autonomous subject—the "artist's" limitations that have appeared as a result of the economic success of the Swiss *Kleinstaat* (small state). Genuinely Swiss novels dealing with specific local themes first appeared after Meyer's death at the end of the century. Ernst Zahn (1867–1952) and Jakob Christoph Heer (1859–1925) both wrote in the conservative tradition that emphasized the bonds of nature and religion over the anonymous economic pressures increasingly apparent in Swiss society. Virtues associated with a rural life are combined in the work of these authors with both a love of *Heimat* and a religious work ethic. The result is an anti-materialistic program of self-imposed austerity. Of greater literary quality are the novels of Carl Spitteler, who was awarded the Nobel prize in 1919. Spitteler combined conventional narrative strategies with naturalistic themes (as for example in *Conrad der Leutnant* [1898; Lieutenant Conrad]), and in his most famous novel, the autobiographical *Imago* (1906; Imago), which dealt with the then-popular theme of artist versus bourgeois.

The advent of modern politics, with its concurrent economic and political polarizations, played a part in the development of the increasingly vitriolic positions of the period. On the other hand, after 1880 there appeared for the first time in Switzerland a type of art subsidy maintained by the various ministers of state. In 1887 the *Eidgenössische Kunstkommission* was founded. This was followed by the opening of the national museum in Zurich in 1898 and the opening of the national library in Bern in 1900. The *Lesezirkel Hottingen,* established in 1882, had proven itself to be the forum for the quickly developing literary scene, and its popular readings contributed to both its own success and to an increased literary awareness in the Swiss reading public as a whole. In the years that followed, this appreciation became the basis of a genuine Swiss readership for the various Swiss literary journals. Joseph Victor Widmann, editor-in-chief of the *Sonntagsblatt* of Bern's daily *Der Bund* from 1880 to 1910, took upon himself the role of advocate for the literature of his Swiss contemporaries, and helped to develop a critical style much in the same way as did Eduard Korrodi from 1915 to 1950 in the feuilletons of the influential *Neue Zürcher Zeitung.* In 1912 the *Schweizerische Schriftstellerverein* (SSV, Swiss Writer's Association) was founded. Its various roles included that of a *Schutzbund* (Writer's Protectorate) for authors affected by the increasingly adverse economic conditions in Switzerland.

The period between Spitteler's *Imago* (1906) and World War I produced a literary *embarras de richesse* in Switzerland, one that came to be known as the *epische Dekade.* Robert Walser's novels *Geschwister Tanner* (1907; The Tanner Siblings), *Der Gehülfe* (1908; The Assistant), and *Jakob von Gunten* (1909; Jakob von Gunten) are examples of the successful combination of traditional Swiss prose and the European avant-garde. Walser, whose work is decidedly unconventional and at times even bizarre, is today considered in rank alongside Franz Kafka and Thomas Mann. His work presents a sharp critique of bourgeois pedantry and narrow-mindedness in the form of an extremely ironic self-criticism. Walser's protagonists embody a self-chosen marginalization, as well as a cynical form of understatement, all in the form of a perspective from below. Swiss provincialism and an overestimation of material profit are the negative background for the novels of Albert Steffen (1884–1963), Carl Albrecht Loosli (1877–1955), Paul Ilg (1875–1957), and Jakob Schaffner (1875–1944). In his later novel *Ein Rufer in der Wüste* (1921; A Prophet in the Desert) Jakob Bosshart vividly presents a panorama of Swiss social problems in the form of a rebellion, not only against the father, capitalism, and an insensitive bourgeoisie, but also against a soulless international socialism. Bosshart's wayward protagonist eventually fails as a result of his love for mankind.

In addition to the problems of art and the artist, the struggle for social justice begins to appear as a theme more frequently in the Swiss novel of this period. This is, for example, indicative of the socialist novels of Jakob Bührer, which make use of a style borrowed from Walser and Loosli in order to further the interests of the proletariat. It is perhaps not surprising, then, that Bührer's major novel, *Im Roten Feld* (written 1938–51; In the Red Field), was first published in the former German Democratic Republic in 1973. More impressive in this vein, however, is the novel *Die Sticker* (1938; The Embroiderers) by Elisabeth Gerter, with its depiction of a worker's attempt to survive in a constantly changing world. Although a proletarian literature neither developed nor played a significant role in Switzerland, the economic instability of the 1920s and 1930s and the growth of fascism in Europe intensified a feeling of crisis among Swiss authors. Their attempts to work through the attendant feelings of mutability and a lack of rootedness did not, however, help them to counter the state-sponsored program of *Geistige Landesverteidigung* (Intellectual Cultural Defense). The most significant attempt to mobilize Switzerland's cultural forces found expression in the *Schweizerische Landesausstellung* (Swiss Exhibit) of 1939. Carl Spitteler had already attempted to define a program for cultural and intellectual neutrality during World War I. As was the case then, broad sections of Swiss society now chose to support the *Geistige Landesverteidigung,* with its disavowal of extreme political polarizations in favor of an engagement for Switzerland.

However, what was politically expedient was not necessarily favorable to the development of Swiss literature. The official position of the readership, and perhaps more importantly the authorities in Switzerland, tended toward the genre of the *Heimatliteratur,* and the tradition of a critical expressionistic avant-garde novel was neglected. It became difficult for authors of unconventional works that expressed criticism of contemporary morality to find publishers and an audience. Max Pulver's novel *Himmelpfortgasse* (1927; Heaven's Gate Street) describes an existence on the margins of society, and Hans Morgenthaler presents in his autobiographical novels (*Ich selbst-Gefühle* [1923; Myself-Feelings] and *Woly, Sommer im Süden* [1924; Woly, Summer in the South]) an often frightening depiction of private existential angst and social indictment. Even Otto Wirz's novels (*Gewalten eines Toren* [1923; Powers of a Fool] and *Die geduckte Kraft* [1928; Cringing Power]), with their unconventional presentation of a rebel's failed attempt to change social mores, did not find resonance among the Swiss readership. Nevertheless, these novels are indicative of the period. One of the most talented authors of this group, Albin Zollinger, depicts in his novels *Der halbe Mensch* (1929; Man Cut in Half), *Die grosse Unruhe* (1939; The Big Restlessness), and *Pfannenstiel: Die Geschichte eines Bildhauers* (1940; Pfannenstiel, The History of a Sculptor) the uncompromising counterarguments of the artist and bourgeois society. Zollinger's fragmented and modern style of presentation mirrors the aimlessness and sense of homelessness of this period. The lack of resonance of this ambitious and critical literature is no doubt also a result of its constant variations on the theme of the artist, and its corresponding stereotypical depictions of the bourgeoisie and its morality.

Felix Moeschlin, president of the *Schweizerische Schriftstellerverband* from 1924 to 1943, succeeded in alternatively reaching a broader public with a less complex narrative style and a more balanced approach in his choice of themes. But whereas Moeschlin remains close to the tradition of *Heimatliteratur,* the harmonious relationship between man and nature is treated as being somewhat more precarious in the works of

Meinrad Inglin. Inglin's protagonists are eccentrics who find themselves in the middle ground between rebellion and affirmation but are not pulled in either direction. His novels *Die Welt in Ingoldau* (1922; The World of Ingoldau), *Wendel von Euw* (1924), and *Grand Hotel Excelsior* (1928) testify to this resignation. In Inglin's novel *Schweizerspiegel* (1938), it is precisely the circumvention of these extremes that allows for the development and strengthening of integration. In spite of this, Inglin did not have a readership of any significance. His novel was published in Germany and remained—as did his earlier works—without resonance.

This was not the case for the germanophile Jakob Schaffner, who successfully mixed both expressionistic and realistic styles in his novels. In his *Johannes* tetralogy (1922–36), Schaffner depicts the somewhat thorny road, taken by a young man with a desire for *Heimat* and its stability, from an orphanage to Hitler's National Socialist movement. Schaffner earned the reputation of a devout Nazi with these novels and became a persona non grata in Switzerland, although his work did win him a broad readership in Germany. In spite of this, and in addition to the *Johannes* novels, Schaffner's earlier works, such as *Hans Himmelhoch* (1909), *Unter stählernen Bestien* (1905; Among Beasts of Steel), and *Konrad Pilater* (1910), are notable literary documents of their time. The Swiss readership tended in their preferences toward this type of *reichsdeutsche* literature of the period and that of the mass-produced *Heimatromane,* contrary to the efforts of the *Geistige Landesverteidigung.* Stories dealing with the *Vaterland,* Swiss nationalism, nature, and the rural classes are dominant themes in the works of these often second-rate authors. Those Swiss authors such as Rudolf Jakob Humm who offered a more complex and critical literature were not able to compete at this time with their *deutschtuemelnde* (hyper-German) compatriots. Humm's autobiographical novel *Die Inseln* (1936; The Islands) remained as unsuccessful as his *Das Linsengericht* (1927; The Dish of Lentils) and *Carolin* (1944). The socially critical murder mysteries of Friedrich Glauser (1896–1938) only achieved a renaissance 30 years after they were written, a fate similar to that of Traugott Vogel's novel *Der blinde Seher* (1930; The Blind Prophet), a protest against bourgeois quiescence.

There is, then, a coexistence of both affirmative and critical novels characteristic of Swiss literature of the 1920s, 1930s, and 1940s. After 1945, the *Heimat* literature developed into the conservative generations novel (for example with Robert Faesi and Kurt Guggenheim). Even Inglin's later works (*Werner Amberg,* 1949, and *Urwang,* 1954) presented less of a new beginning than a recollection of traditional values. This was also the case for as interesting a novel as Hans Albrecht Moser's *Vineta* (1955).

The changed political situation at the end of World War II first found expression in the works of Max Frisch. Already active as a writer in the 1930s, Frisch became, in a sense, the cultural conscience of Switzerland in the postwar period with his *Tagebücher 1946–49, 1966–71* (1983; Diaries 1946–49, 1966–71), his dramas, and his novels. The protagonists of his novels (*Stiller* [1954; I'm Not Stiller], *Homo faber* [1957; Homo Faber], and *Mein Name sei Gantenbein* [1964; Gantenbein]) are all prototypes of Switzerland's problematic consciousness. Unsure of their identities, and plagued by an existential angst, these characters are unable to make those basic decisions required to change their essentially bourgeois lives that they consider both devoid of meaning and unfulfilling. In addition to this, Frisch developed an open narrative form that both adequately presented this fragmented consciousness and actively drew the reader into the construction of his protagonists. Friedrich Dürrenmatt, on the other hand, continued in his novels the tradition of the socially critical detective story begun by Glauser. By adding an ethical element, Dürrenmatt developed a type of "philosophical" detective story that combined moral indecisiveness with contemporary Swiss politics. The result was Dürrenmatt's own theoretically grounded critique of Western logocentrism. His novels (*Der Richter und sein Henker* [1952; The Judge and His Hangman], *Der Verdacht* [1953; The Quarry], *Das Versprechen* [1958; The Pledge], and *Justiz* [1985; The Execution of Justice]) were just as successful internationally as those of Frisch and helped to achieve a high level of recognition for Swiss literature.

The political and literary battles of the postwar period in Switzerland helped to draw considerable attention to its writers. When the conservative novelist Kurt Guggenheim warned against the *Überfremdung* (too many immigrants) of Switzerland and its culture in 1966, the literary critic Emil Staiger responded in kind with a concurring essay that garnered international recognition. Staiger's essay also helped a younger generation of authors (younger, in fact, than both Frisch and Dürrenmatt) to come to a critical understanding of their predecessors. As a result of the negative resonance produced by Staiger's essay, even the influential critic for the *Neue Zürcher Zeitung,* Werner Weber, could not bring the two sides together in 1970. Maurice Zermatten, then president of the *Schweizerische Schriftstellerverband,* became well known for his anti-communist military propaganda, and as a result a number of Swiss authors left the SSV and founded the *Gruppe Olten.* Also, a number of politically oriented literary journals appeared in Switzerland during the 1970s in response to the increased politicization among Swiss intellectuals (important to note in this respect is the popularity of Walther Mathias Diggelmann's novel *Die Hinterlassenschaft* [1965; The Inheritance]). These journals acted as a forum for the younger generation of authors who could not make a living from their writing alone, particularly since the reading public in the BRD, in Austria, and in the DDR did not pay much attention to their work.

Swiss novelists of the 1960s developed a marked tendency toward a modern narrative style with avant-garde elements, one that helped them to combine a newfound awareness of their own geographical regionalism with a cultural internationalism. Otto F. Walter's novels *Der Stumme* (1959; The Mute), *Herr Tourel* (1962; Mister Tourel), and *Die ersten Unruhen: Ein Konzept* (1972; The First Troubles: A Plan) are early examples of this experimental form. Jörg Steiner's novel *Strafarbeit* (1962; Correctional Work) also makes use of these new narrative techniques to depict the repressive realities of a penal institution, as does Paul Nizon, whose refined literary depictions (in novels such as *Canto,* 1962, and *Das Jahr der Liebe* [1981; The Year of Love]) help him to escape reality's complexities. The legacy of both Steiner's eye for detail and Nizon's autobiographical psychology can be found in the *Heimatromanen* of Silvio Blatter. In *Zunehmendes Heimweh* (1978; Increasing Homesickness), *Kein schöner Land* (1983; No Land More Beautiful), and *Das sanfte Gesetz* (1988; The Gentle Law), Blatter fuses a political awareness with regional identification.

The most important, and visible, representative of contemporary Swiss literature is Adolf Muschg. Muschg has integrated virtually all of the literary traditions of postwar Switzerland in novels such as *Albissers Grund* (1974; Albisser's Reason) and *Baiyun; oder, Die Freundschaftsgesellschaft* (1980; Baiyun; or, The Society of Friends), which combine a critical evaluation of Swiss politics and culture with creative narrative techniques. The environmental, peace, and youth movements of the 1970s all helped to provide material for Muschg's novels. The climate of heightened political engagement among Switzerland's artists and intellectuals during this period exploded with the youth revolts in Zurich in 1981, and has been recorded in the work of Reto Hänny. Gerhard Meier, who began to write only later in his life, also influenced this younger generation of writers with works such as the trilogy *Baur und Bindschädler* (1979–85; Baur and Bindschädler), which used contemporary problems to point out issues of literary representation.

Swiss literature has always had a strong contingent of noteworthy female authors (Regina Ullmann, Cecile Ines Loos, Cecile Lauber, Erika Burkart, and Gertrud Wilker) and in the 1970s a new group appeared. In the works of authors such as Laure Wyss, Margrit Schriber, Elisabeth Meylan, and Hanna Johansen, among others, there appears alongside feminist texts devoted specifically to women's problems and experiences more general depictions of society and the individual. Erica Pedretti's novels are worth noting in that she constructs the identity problems of her narrators as a configuration of the different levels of narrative. A similar approach can be found in Helen Meier's later novel *Lebenleben* (1989; Living Life). This is also the case for the novels of Getrud Leutenegger in which the search for an autonomous identity is pertinent to the narrative's construction. With their progressive narrative techniques, Leutenegger's work may be viewed in the same tradition of experimental novels as E.Y. Meyer's *In Trubschachen* (1973) and those of Christoph Geiser, who incorporates a complex familial experience into his novels.

Practically all modern Swiss authors have been influenced in one way or another by the work of Robert Walser. The marginalized protagonists of Franz Böni's novels show a particular affinity in their restless observations of modern society. However, whereas Böni's texts attempt to present the realities of Switzerland as a timeless encroachment upon the individual's autonomy, those of Gerold Späth transform them into a baroque panorama filled with picaresque characters. Novels such as *Unschlecht* (1970; A Prelude to the Long Happy Life of Maximilian Goodman), *Stimmgänge* (1972; Voice Trails), *Balzapf; oder, Als ich auftauchte* (1977; Balzapf; or, When I Showed Up), *Commedia* (1980), and *Sindbadland* (1984; Land of Sindbad) all document a postmodern sensibility toward narrative and language. In this respect, Späth's novels are surpassed in their postmodernist techniques only by those of Hermann Burger. Burger's novel *Schilten: Schulbericht zuhanden der Inspektorenkonferenz* (1976; Schilten: School Report Addressed to the Inspector's Conference) is a breathtaking journey that combines linguistic and artistic craftmanship with a pronounced artificiality, as are his other novels *Die künstliche Mutter* (1982; The Artificial Mother), *Blankenburg* (1986), and *Brenner* (1989). Burger's work, with its virtual exhaustion of narrative and linguistic possibilities, nevertheless also marks the end of an era.

The most recent generation of authors in Switzerland is marked by the "No-Future" experience of the 1980s and 1990s. The works of Martin R. Dean, Matthias Zschokke, and Hansjörg Schertenleib all give voice to the new *Unübersichtlichkeit* of this period: no goals, no ideals, and no identity. Their protagonists are often victims of their own resignation and the stagnant effects of the consumer society in which they live. Dean's novel *Der Mann ohne Licht* (1988; Man Without Light) is a dense composition filled with postmodern intertextuality. However, in Switzerland, as in the BRD, a new impulse has appeared, carried by multicultural and multilingual authors. Dante Andrea Franzetti has made use of the political problems surrounding national identity and multilingualism in his novel *Cosimo und Hamlet* (1987), as has Francesco Micieli and Flurin Spescha in *Das Gewicht der Hügel* (1986; The Weight of Hills).

These writers are bridging the gap between the contemporary Italian-Swiss novel and its predecessors in the late 19th century. Focusing mainly on local and regional themes, this form of Swiss literature achieved a degree of autonomy only in the 20th century. The leading figure of Italian literature in Switzerland is without a doubt Francesco Chiesa. Originally a successful lyricist, it was only later that he turned to prose and developed his own simple and elegant use of language. This can be seen particularly in his autobiographical works (*Racconti puerili* [1920; Stories of Youth] and *Tempo di marzo* [1925; Time of March]), whereas Chiesa's novels *Villadorna* (1928), *Sant' Amarillide* (1938), and *Io e i miei* (1944; Myself and My Folks) are more constructed and less convincing. Chiesa's novel *Italianita* is written in a distanced conservative-classicist style, and, although it was received well critically, it did not influence later writers.

In *Il fondo del sacco* (1970; The Bottom of the Barrel) and *Requiem per zia Domenica* (1976; Requiem for Aunt Domenica), Plinio Martini convincingly combines realism and social criticism, particularly when it is based on the author's own experiences. Giovanni Orelli also successfully uses the city/countryside dichotomy in his novels *L'anno della valanga* (1965; Year of the Avalanche) and *La festa del ringraziamento* (1972; Feast of Thankfulness). More modern narrative strategies can be found in the works of Felice Fillipini and Giovanni Bonalumi, but perhaps most clearly in those of Giorgio Orelli and Grytzko Mascioni. In fact, Mascioni's novel *Carta d'autunno* (1973; Map of Autumn) is an example of a mostly ignored Italian postmodernism. Fleur Jaeggy, on the other hand, has attracted much more attention in recent years with her precise and penetrating autobiographical works.

ANDREAS SOLBACH

See also Gottfried Keller

Further Reading

Calgari, Guido, *Die vier Literaturen der Schweiz,* Olten: Walter, 1966

Ermatinger, Emil, *Dichtung und Geistesleben der deutschen Schweiz,* Munich: Beck, 1933

Fehr, Karl, *Der Realismus in der schweizerischen Literatur,* Bern: Francke, 1965

Flood, John L., editor, *Modern Swiss Literature: Unity and Diversity,* London: Wolff, and New York: St. Martin's Press, 1985

Greiner, Trudi, *Der literarische Verkehr zwischen der deutschen und welschen Schweiz seit 1848,* Bern and Leipzig: Haupt, 1940

Grossenbacher, Thomas, *Studien zum Verhältnis von Literatur und Moral an ausgewählten Werken des schweizerischen bürgerlichen Realismus,* Bern: Haupt, 1984

Gsteiger, Manfred, editor, *Die zeitgenössischen Literaturen der Schweiz,* Munich: Kindler, 1974

Günther, Werner, *Dichter der neueren Schweiz,* 3 vols., Bern: Francke, 1963–86

Huonker, Gustav, *Literaturszene Zürich: Menschen, Geschichten und Bilder 1914 bis 1945,* Zurich: Union, 1985

Köchli, Yvonne-Denise, *Themen in der neueren schweizerischen Literatur,* Bern: Peter Lang, 1982

Matt, Beatrice von, editor, *Antworten: Die Literatur der deutschsprachigen Schweiz in den achtziger Jahren,* Zurich: Neue Zürcher Zeitung, 1991

Mühlethaler, Hans, *Die Gruppe Olten: Das Erbe einer rebellierenden Schriftstellergeneration,* Aarau: Sauerlander, 1989

Pezold, Klaus, editor, *Geschichte der deutschsprachigen Schweizer Literatur im 20. Jahrhundert,* Berlin: Volk and Wissen, 1991

Schiltknecht, Wilfred, *Le roman contemporain en Suisse allemande,* Lausanne: L'Age d'homme, 1974

Spiegelberg, Sven, *Diskurs in der Lehre: Aufsätze zur aktuellen Literatur der Schweiz,* Bern and New York: Peter Lang, 1990

Straumann, Reinhard, *Literarischer Konservatismus in der Schweiz um 1848,* Bern and New York: Peter Lang, 1984

Walzer, Pierre Olivier, editor, *Lexikon der Schweizer Literaturen,* Basel: Lenos, 1991

Zäch, Alfred, *Die Dichtung der deutschen Schweiz,* Zurich: Speer, 1951

Zeller, Rosamarie, *Der neue Roman in der Schweiz: Die Unerzählbarkeit der modernen Welt,* Freiburg: Universitätsverlag, 1992

Zeltner-Neukomm, Gerda, *Das Ich ohne Gewähr: Gegenwartsautoren aus der Schweiz,* Zurich: Suhrkamp, 1980

Swiss Novel

Francophone

Extending from the Jura mountains in northwest Switzerland south to Lake Geneva and on to the alpine peaks of the Valais, French-speaking Switzerland has contributed much to both the Swiss and the French literary traditions. While the inhabitants of the *Suisse romande* are outnumbered by their German-speaking compatriots nearly three to one, a viable francophone literary presence has marked this multilingual nation since the Reformation. Serving as a refuge for Huguenots fleeing persecution in France, French-speaking Switzerland represented a bittersweet exile, one that permitted religious freedom but simultaneously isolated its inhabitants from Paris and its culture. Even today, the *Suisse romande* suffers from the same sort of literary and sometimes political schizophrenia, as French-speaking Switzerland and its authors seek to establish their own cultural identity, independent from Zurich or Paris. This constant struggle for identity, a potential reconciliation between Switzerland's European, multicultural roots and the parochial narrowness of the mountain villages, may indeed best define the novel and its development in the *Suisse romande.*

The origins of the Swiss-French novel trace back to Jean-Jacques Rousseau of Geneva. Prior to Rousseau, the Protestant population of French-speaking Switzerland did not favor the novel. As Bertil Galland (1986) notes, it is impossible to exaggerate the influence of the Reformation in French-speaking Switzerland. It made its mark on the language. Schools, present in every Protestant village as early as the 17th century, primarily taught the Bible. Such was the literature that nourished the people of French-speaking Switzerland for several hundred years. Rousseau's *Julie; ou, La Nouvelle Héloïse* (1761; *Julie; or, The New Eloise*), the most popular novel written in French in the 18th century, grew from and transformed this Protestant heritage. *Julie* is indeed a Swiss novel in the broadest sense: although Rousseau composed and published his psychological novel in France, it embraces themes that came to characterize the novel in Switzerland. The story of Julie and her lover St. Preux unfurls on the shores of Lake Geneva, highlighting the importance of religious tolerance promoted by the Reformation. At the same time, this epistolary novel links deeply felt sentiment with the natural world, reconciling passion and resignation, while foreshadowing the romantic movement that swept France and all of Europe in the first half of the 19th century.

Much like Rousseau, Madame de Staël and Benjamin Constant can most readily be situated in a European context, but both can trace their roots back to the Swiss literary tradition. Madame de Staël, the daughter of a wealthy Genevan banker, grew up in the salons of Paris. Exiled by Napoléon at the start of the 19th century, Madame de Staël sought to re-create the atmosphere of these salons at Coppet on the shores of Lake Geneva. Her novels *Delphine* (1802) and *Corinne; ou, L'Italie* (1807; *Corinne; or, Italy*), like *Julie,* attest to the importance of the Enlightenment specifically with regard to the education of women while at the same time moving toward romanticism. Benjamin Constant, known for his analytical novel *Adolphe* (1816), as well as for his volatile love affair with Madame de Staël, shows the influence of the 18th-century classics and highlights the *mal de siècle* that would come to characterize the French romantic movement. *Adolphe*, like *Der grüne Heinrich* (1853–55, revised edition 1880; *Green Henry*) by the Swiss-German author Gottfried Keller, is an autobiographical model for the Bildungsroman that traces the psychological and moral development of its protagonist. Like Madame de Staël, Benjamin Constant fell into disfavor with Napoléon and returned temporarily to his native Switzerland. It was thus at Coppet that Constant learned and developed his liberal philosophy. Through both their liberal politics and their written works, Benjamin Constant and Madame de Staël helped to create the elite literary circles that further favored the development of the novel in French-speaking Switzerland.

Never reaching the same international stature as Madame de Staël and Benjamin Constant, Madame de Charrière and Rodolphe Töpffer nonetheless made significant contributions to the Swiss-French world of letters in the late 18th and early 19th centuries. Indeed, they picked up many of the traces left by their predecessors. Madame de Charrière, who was born in Holland but lived in Colombier in the canton of Neuchâtel, published her *Lettres neuchâteloises* (1784; Letters from Neuchâtel) in the epistolary tradition of *Julie* some 20 years after Rousseau. Her novel *Trois femmes* (1798; Three Women) touched on the key issues of French and German nationalism later raised by Madame de Staël in her theoretical essays entitled *De l'Allemagne* (1810; *On Germany*). Rodolphe Töpffer, best known for his invention of the comic book, defended the idyllic natural world of Rousseau in his novel *Le Presbytère* (1839). The 19th century also witnessed the careers of minor figures such as Eugène Rambert and popular novelist Urbain Olivier, both of whom extolled the so-called Swiss virtues of moderation and simplicity while advocating a return to nature in their works. As Roger Francillon notes in his essay in *The Four Literatures of Switzerland*: "What is striking about these by now forgotten texts is their constant exhortation to return to rural simplicity, their nostalgia for a remote past, their rejection of passion and excess, and their lack of any form of aesthetic perspective" (see Calgari, 1988). This regional and moralistic tradition that marked the 19th century in French-speaking Switzerland sparked a revolution of sorts in the early 20th century, a revolution that engendered the emergence of a strong, independent novelistic tradition in the *Suisse romande*.

The literary debut of the magazine *La Voile latine* in 1904 in Geneva—launched by the painter Alexandre Cingria and several young writers, including novelist C.F. Ramuz—marked the beginning of a new era in Swiss-French letters. On a mission to renew Swiss letters through art, *La Voile latine* served as a starting point for the literary transformation that swept French-speaking Switzerland in 1913–14. Indeed, although *La Voile latine* disappeared in 1910, the publication of the new review *Les Cahiers vaudois* soon took its place.

Les Cahiers vaudois sought to liberate Swiss letters from the confines of its traditional past while at the same time emphasizing its anti-university, anti-intellectual stance. Indeed, *Les Cahiers* articulated the need and desire for a vibrant, invigorating Swiss cultural life, one that expressed a Swiss-French cultural identity without resorting to nostalgic longing for mythical, rural roots. This literary renewal in French-speaking Switzerland

simultaneously mirrored a similar phenomenon in France with the publication of Guillaume Apollinaire's *Alcools: Poèmes 1898–1913* (1913) and Marcel Proust's *Du côté de chez Swann* (1913; *Swann's Way*). It is perhaps no coincidence, then, that although Ramuz had already published his first novel *Aline* in 1905, his critically acclaimed *Vie de Samuel Belet* (The Life of Samuel Belet) emerged in 1913, along with fellow Swiss Blaise Cendrars' prose poem *La Prose du Transsibérien et de la petite Jehanne de France* (1913; *The Trans-Siberian*).

Perhaps Ramuz and Blaise Cendrars best represent the divergent paths in the quest for literary identity expressed by writers in French-speaking Switzerland in the first half of the 20th century. They certainly represent the best-known literary figures in the *Suisse romande* in the last 100 years: Ramuz is considered the cornerstone of modern Swiss-French literature, the reference point for all later Swiss writers. Indeed, Swiss-French literature is commonly categorized as pre- or post-Ramuz.

Although Ramuz lived in Paris from 1901–14, he studied literature in Lausanne and spent most of his life in the canton of Vaud, amid the high mountains and small villages that inspired him. Blaise Cendrars, on the other hand, did his best to shed his Swiss identity: born in the small city of La Chaux-de-Fonds as Frédéric Sauser, educated in Neuchâtel, Basle, and Bern, Cendrars left his studies and his name behind as he traveled the world, eventually migrating to Paris, where he adopted French citizenship. Considered along with Apollinaire as one of the inventors of modern French poetry, Cendrars also established himself as a first-class novelist in the 1920s, using his travels as a point of departure for his own inner, literary exploration. Aesthetically and stylistically, Cendrars and Ramuz move the Swiss-French novel from the regional to the universal, from a nostalgic past to a vigorous and innovative present.

Ramuz and Cendrars present, however, vastly different understandings of their own literary identities. During his sojourn in Paris, Ramuz recognized that his Swiss background and perspective defined him as a writer, setting him apart from his French colleagues. Indeed, Ramuz examines the ramifications of this realization for the artist in his novels *Aimé Pache, peintre vaudois* (1910; Aimé Pache, Vaudois Painter) and *Vie de Samuel Belet*. His lyrical prose often explores the impact of inexplicable or mysterious natural forces on the human community, as in *La Grande peur dans la montagne* (1925; *Terror on the Mountain*) and *Derborence* (1936; *When the Mountain Fell*). Cendrars, in contrast, defined his own literary self not in his Swiss origins, but rather in his cosmopolitan wanderings. While *L'Or* (1925; *Gold*) ostensibly tells the story of Johann August Sutter in California, it more effectively narrates, at least in part, the autobiography of Blaise Cendrars. As Roger Francillon explains, "This pseudo-autobiography, written in the present tense to dramatize the adventurer's extraordinary fate, discloses Cendrars' passion for life as a dream, a perpetual escape into the offensive." *L'Homme foudroyé* (1945; *The Astonished Man*) and *Bourlinger* (1948; *Planus*) continue in this autobiographical mode, transforming his travels and adventures into a springboard for the exploration of the inner self.

The renaissance of 1913 that launched the careers of writers such as Cendrars and Ramuz faded into World War I and its aftermath. Ramuz returned home to Switzerland from Paris in 1914; Cendrars joined the French Foreign Legion and lost his right arm in combat. Geneva, home of the International Red

Cross, filled its hospitals with wounded soldiers from all over Europe. Neutral Switzerland, although not directly engaged in the war, was nonetheless slow to recover. It was not until 1936 that Albert Mermoud breathed new life into the Swiss-French literary world by founding the publishing house La Guilde du livre in Lausanne. Run by Ramuz and others, La Guilde du livre dedicated itself to the promotion of literature in French-speaking Switzerland and to living authors. Beginning with Ramuz's *When the Mountain Fell* as the first title in its collection, La Guilde du livre paved the way for a new generation of Swiss-French novelists and writers. An alternative to Parisian and French publishing companies, La Guilde du livre proved to be an innovation for readers as well, making authors from the *Suisse romande* more accessible to the reading public.

Women writers were some of the first authors to benefit from the establishment of the new publishing house, emerging as some of the most exciting and innovative voices in prose in French-speaking Switzerland as early as the 1930s. Monique Saint-Hélier, in her cycle of novels on the Alérac family, beginning with *Bois-mort* (1934; Dead Wood) and ending with *L'Arrosoir rouge* (1955; The Red Watering Can), explores the inner world of memory, while Catherine Colomb, in her trilogy *Chateaux en enfance* (1945; Castles in Childhood), *Les Esprits de la terre* (1953; The Spirits of the Earth), and *Le Temps des anges* (1962; The Time of Angels), probes the often troubled relationship between children and adults. Alice Rivaz evokes the life of the working class in French-speaking Switzerland in general and women in particular, thus giving voice to a segment of the population that had previously gone unheard. Her many novels, including *Nuages dans la main* (1940; Clouds in One's Hand) and *La Paix des ruches* (1947; The Peace of the Hives), deal specifically with the reality of women's lives in a society marked by conservative, traditional values. S. Corinna Bille expresses the influence of French surrealism in works such as her novel *Théoda* (1944), deftly crossing the line between fantasy and reality while invoking the landscapes of the Valais. As Doris Jakubec accurately observes in her esssay in *The Four Literatures of Switzerland*: "It is thanks to these authors—writers who set aside considerations of genre and established form, revealed their interior world and introduced new voices and approaches—that the women writers of today need not restrict themselves to recounting life stories" (see Calgari, 1988).

Women's writing, in fact, makes up some of the most dynamic prose in contemporary Switzerland. In a country where women did not vote in national elections until 1971, where the women's movement and women's studies exist only as a pale shadow of the feminist movement and feminist theory in France, female authors have nonetheless come to the forefront, engaging themselves and the French-speaking community in a dialogue on the unique situation of women in Switzerland. Monique Laederach in *La Femme séparée* (1982; The Separated Woman) and Anne-Lise Grobéty in *Zéro positif* (1975), for example, each undertake the quest for the female self in the specific context of the social unrest of the 1970s. Questioning woman's role in marriage, at work, at home, and among friends, these novels highlight the specific need to broaden and redefine the accepted notions of woman's role in the *Suisse romande*. Amélie Plume probes similar subjects in her witty, burlesque novels such as *Les Aventures de Plumette et de son premier amant* (1981; The Adventures of Plumette and Her First Lover), creating an innovative style that visually is closer to poetry than prose, prompting the reader to look beyond the comic exterior to the darker vision of the world that lies below.

Women writers are not, however, alone in furthering the search for self in the context of a Swiss-French literary identity. On the contrary, Grobéty, Laederach, and Plume share much in common with many of their male colleagues, including the need to define their own literary space, one specific to the *Suisse romande*. The post-Ramuzian version of this dilemma can be traced to the aftermath of World War II, which left Swiss-French writers in a quandary: no longer wishing to identify with Paris, much like their Swiss-German colleagues who refused to identify with Germany, these authors struggled to define their relationship to language and society. The Swiss magazine *Rencontre* (1950–53) dealt with such issues, grappling with questions of engagement and Swiss neutrality, thus following the lead of Jean-Paul Sartre and the existentialists in France. The 1960s brought to the forefront the need for Swiss-French publishing houses independent of French and Parisian influence and resulted in the establishment of L'Aire-Rencontre, l'Age d'Homme, and Bertil Galland, as well as the Center for Swiss-French Literary Research in Lausanne, instituted in 1964. Ideological and practical changes in the writing and publishing of literary texts thus set the stage for new generations of novelists in the *Suisse romande*.

Indeed, the contemporary novel in French-speaking Switzerland, much like the contemporary novel in France, is characterized by the wide variety of approaches it engenders. Jacques Chessex, who won the Prix Goncourt for *L'Ogre* (1973; A Father's Love), recalls 19th-century French realism while setting his novels in rural, French-speaking Switzerland. He plays on the stark contrasts of the mountain setting and reacts against the Swiss, Calvinist heritage by highlighting the universality of the erotic. Georges Haldas, known for the fragmented, disjointed style of his novels and chronicles, analyzes and reanalyzes life experiences in *La Confession d'une graine: l'Emergence* (1983) and *Conquête matinale* (1986; Morning Conquest). He asks pointed questions about himself as a writer and poet, about Geneva, and about French-speaking Switzerland in order to come to terms with personal and community identity. Robert Pinget, born in Geneva but a resident of Paris since World War II, remains one of the foremost authors of the *nouveau roman* in France. His novels, including *Quelqu'un* (1965; Someone), winner of the Prix Fémina, and *Cette voix* (1971; That Voice), affirm the influence of Samuel Beckett: the constant search for meaning leads to nothingness, a void that Pinget advocates be filled by laughter. Other significant contributors include Yves Velan, author of several novels, such as *Je* (1959; I) and *Soft Goulag* (1977), and Agota Kristof, whose trilogy is composed of *Le Grand cahier* (1986; Big Notebook), *La Preuve* (1988; The Proof), and *Le Troisième mensonge* (1991; The Third Lie). Both Velan and Kristof look to literature as a means of reinventing language and the written word. For Velan this involves perfecting every detail down to its most minor point so that his novels are ripe with multiple significations. Kristof, on the other hand, takes a minimalist approach in which language says as little as possible, few details are provided, and the text is left wide open for interpretation. Finally, Nicolas Bouvier follows in the footsteps of Cendrars, choosing to travel the world and chronicle the inner journey in his travel narratives. Travels to Japan and the

Far East, as recounted in *Chronique japonaise* (1975; *The Japanese Chronicles*) and *Le Poisson-scorpion* (1981; *The Scorpion Fish*), serve as points of departure for reflection; as Doris Jakubec observes, "After he returns to Geneva, sometimes long after, Bouvier begins writing—sifting memories and notes about life, identity and otherness, openness and mystery, departure and return."

It is precisely this need for reflection about the independent self that may indeed be what best defines the novel in French-speaking Switzerland. The specific situation of the novelist in the *Suisse romande* is a unique one: while linguistically linked to France, politically Swiss-French writers find themselves tied to multilingual Switzerland, where they are clearly a minority. The Swiss-French novel reveals how Swiss writers navigate this imposed marginality, creating a literary culture that reflects their French and Swiss ties. At the same time, this quest for identity is hardly unique to the *Suisse romande* and serves to situate Swiss-French writers in both a Western European and global context.

SARA STEINERT BORELLA

See also Julie, or, The New Eloise

Further Reading

Barilier, Etienne, *Soyons médiocres! Essai sur le milieu littéraire romand*, Lausanne: L'Age d'Homme, 1989

Berchtold, Alfred, *La Suisse romande au cap du XXe siècle: Portrait littéraire et moral*, Lausanne: Payot, 1963

Boulanger, Mousse, and Henri Corbat, *Littératures de Suisse romande et aspects des littératures suisses non francophones: Anthologie et guide*, Bordas: Saved, 1988

Calgari, Guido, *Storia delle quattro litterature della Svizzera*, Milan: Nuova academia, 1958; as *The Four Literatures of Switzerland*, Zurich: Pro Helvetia, 1988

Chessex, Jacques, editor, *Les Saintes écritures*, Lausanne: Bertil Galland, 1972

Francillon, Roger, Clair Jaquier, and Adrien Pasquali, *Filations et filatures: Littérature et critique en Suisse romande*, Geneva: Zoé, 1991

Galland, Bertil, *La Littérature de la Suisse romande expliquée en un quart d'heure: Suivi d'une Anthologie lyrique de poche*, Geneva: Zoé, 1986

Jakubec, Doris, editor, *Solitude surpeuplée: Femmes écrivains suisses de langue française*, Lausanne: Editions d'en bas, 1990; new edition, 1997

Maggetti, Daniel, *L'Invention de la littérature romande, 1830–1910*, Lausanne: Payot, 1995

Nicollier, Alain, and Henri-Charles Dahlem, editors, *Dictionnaire des écrivains suisses d'expression française*, 2 vols., Geneva: GVA, 1994

T

Tale of Genji by Murasaki Shikibu

Genji monogatari (early 11th century)

The 11th-century *Genji monogatari,* written by the Heian (794–1185) Japanese court attendant Murasaki Shikibu, is not, strictly speaking, a novel. The most influential work of the "golden age" of Japanese literature, it is an innovative mixed-genre work that incorporates aspects of *monogatari* (dismissed by many as mere stories), personal diaries, poetry (both Japanese court poetry, *waka,* and Chinese "learned" poetry), as well as histories and scripture. Produced serially in 54 chapters, Murasaki's text probably worked audience feedback into the development of her "plot." Often referred to as the world's first psychological novel because of its layering of character and experience, the *Genji* focuses on the semi-royal Genji and his acknowledged and unacknowledged progeny in their relationships to a series of extraordinary women.

At the time the *Genji* was written, Chinese was the "official" language in Japan, much like Latin or French in relation to vernacular English in pre-Chaucerian England. Learned works by male courtiers, whose supposed preserve Chinese was, were often constrained and highly artificial. *Monogatari,* and works in Japanese in general (with the exception of *waka*), were considered unlearned and vernacular in nature. This is one of the reasons that the early canonical works were produced for the most part by women, and the script in which the texts were written is known as *onna-de,* or woman's hand.

The *Genji* has had an enormous influence in almost all areas of Japanese literature, theatre, and art. By the end of the 12th century, it was almost impossible to write poetry without making reference to this text, which was believed to represent the epitome of *miyabi,* or courtliness. The *Genji's* influence was felt most strongly in this area for quite a long period of time, even though the work provides a strong defense of fiction, parts of which read as follows:

There is, it seems, an art of so fitting each part of the narrative into the next that, though all is mere invention, the reader is persuaded that such things might easily have happened and is as deeply moved as though they were actually going on around him. . . . Even its practical value is immense. Without it what should we know of how people lived in the past. . . . We may indeed go so far as to say

that there is an actual mixture of Truth and Error. . . . Viewed in this light the novel is seen to be not, as is usually supposed, a mixture of useful truth with idle invention, but something which at every stage and in every part has a definite and serious purpose.

Critical responses to Murasaki's work focused initially on ways in which the text could be incorporated into Buddhist or Confucian readings of the world. The series of commentaries that explicated the text historically, socially, and allusively also began very early on. The *Genji* became the subject of many Nō plays when that art form developed in the 14th century. The critical tradition was ineluctably altered, however, by Motoori Norinaga (1730–1801), who favored an analysis based on the valorization of the poignancy of human experience. Norinaga read the *Genji* as a work of *mono no aware* (roughly, the term refers to the "ah-ness" of life—the wonder and sadness of human existence) and valorized the "feminine" aesthetics of the text. Norma Field (1987) indicates that "from the late nineteenth century on, the *Genji* has been dissected and reconstructed with a rich and bewildering variety of tools. It became the standard subject of experimentation for disciplines newly imported from the West."

Translations into modern Japanese (the Heian Japanese is almost unintelligible to modern Japanese readers; contemporary English-speaking readers might have similar difficulties with Old English) have been undertaken during the 20th century by the poet Yosano Akiko and the novelists Tanizaki Jun'ichirō and Enchi Fumiko. Kawabata Yasunari has gone so far as to suggest that all Japanese authors have been influenced by the *Genji.*

With Arthur Waley's first full translation of the *Genji monogatari* into English between 1925 and 1933, the work began to have an influence in the West. Virginia Woolf, for instance, reviewed the first book favorably for *Vogue* and also began referring to Murasaki Shikibu as one of her literary foremothers. Attention is often drawn to the fact that Murasaki might have been the Shakespeare's sister for whom Woolf searched in *A Room of One's Own.* Waley's very Bloomsbury translation makes skilled use of the free indirect style to convey some of the verbal patterns of the original. A second, unexpurgated

English-language version was published by Edward Seidensticker in 1976.

The most recent English-language analyses of the *Genji* focus on a debate about the position of women and their intervention in Heian politics, substituting a reading of the politically subversive and "feminist" nature of the work for earlier aesthetic or religious readings. In part, these readings focus on the way in which the vast panoramas of history (which have identifiable historical analogues) in this work are closely tied to the intimate details of life as seen from a privileged, but insecure, woman's perspective. These readings are well grounded in research on the Heian background, as well as in postmodernist, linguistic, and cross-cultural analyses. The *Genji*'s astounding multiplicity of perspectives and influences lends itself easily to such readings.

CATHERINE NELSON-MCDERMOTT

Further Reading

Bowring, Richard, *Murasaki Shikibu: Her Diary and Poetic Memoirs*, Princeton, New Jersey: Princeton University Press, 1982

Bowring, Richard, "The Female Hand in Heian Japan: A First Reading," in *The Female Autograph*, edited by Domna C. Stanton, New York: New York Literary Forum, 1984

Bowring, Richard, *Murasaki Shikibu: "The Tale of Genji,"* Cambridge and New York: Cambridge University Press, 1988

Field, Norma, *The Splendour of Longing in the "Tale of Genji,"* Princeton, New Jersey: Princeton University Press, 1987

Goff, Janet, *Noh Drama and "The Tale of Genji,"* Princeton, New Jersey: Princeton University Press, 1991

Morris, Ivan, *The World of the Shining Prince: Court Life in Ancient Japan,* New York: Knopf, and London: Oxford University Press, 1964

Okada, H. Richard, *Figures of Resistance: Language, Poetry and Narrating in "The Tale of Genji" and Other Mid-Heian Works,* Durham, North Carolina: Duke University Press, 1991

Shirane, Haruo, *The Bridge of Dreams: A Poetics of the "Tale of Genji,"* Stanford, California: Stanford University Press, 1987

Woolf, Virginia, review of Arthur Waley's translation of Murasaki Shikibu's *The Tale of Genji,* in *Vogue* (July 1925)

Tanizaki Jun'ichirō 1886–1965

Japanese

Tanizaki Jun'ichirō was a persistent defender of fictionality in a literary culture that valued a literal idea of the truth. Literary genres in Japan do not correspond directly with those in the West, and the *shōsetsu*, or prose fiction, genre in which Tanizaki excelled cannot immediately be equated with the novel, although it often is translated as such. The *shōsetsu* can vary in length, from the shortest short story to the longest novel, and often crosses the boundaries of the memoir and the essay. The *shishōsetsu*, or personal fiction, subgenre most privileged by high-culture readers and critics in Japan specifically blurs such borders by relying upon autobiographical material and by employing a rhetoric that allows textual material to be read as the truthful representation of an actual experience. In such a literary milieu, Tanizaki stood out for constructing long narratives whose imaginative content, amplitude, and structure can rightly be called novelistic. He eschewed the *shishōsetsu*, choosing instead to call attention to the fictionality of his texts.

A noteworthy essayist, Tanizaki plainly enunciated his ideas on fiction in "Jōzetsuroku" (1927; "Garrulous Jottings"), an essay in which he carried on his side of a public debate with friend and fellow writer Akutagawa Ryūnosuke. The latter advocated stories that dispensed with the "vulgar interest" of plot and conveyed what was registered by the "perceptive eyes" and "sensitive heart" of the artist. Tanizaki replied that plot was indispensable to fiction, whose purpose was "relating entertaining stories to the public." With the novel specifically in mind, Tanizaki argued that plot had aesthetic value as a source of "ar-chitectonic beauty" achieved through narrative expansiveness. Elsewhere in "Jōzetsuroku," Tanizaki forcefully stated his adherence to fabrication as the basis for fiction, adding that in both his reading and his writing he was "uninterested in anything but lies."

Tanizaki's novels were true to such a credo. He cultivated the artful lie in novels that persistently returned to certain themes: the erotics of cultural aspiration in a society pulled between East and West, the male desire to achieve such an aspiration either through reunion with a culturally immutable mother or through reconstructing women to represent cultural ideals, and the illusive yet powerful nature of desire. In *Chijin no ai* (1924; *Naomi*), Tanizaki's first successful novel, the narrator/protagonist recounts his attempt to train a young Japanese bar hostess, who happens to resemble Mary Pickford, in the skills and attitudes of a Western woman. He succeeds so admirably that his creation learns to despise him for being too Japanese and begins to take foreign lovers. Tanizaki remarked that *Naomi* was a kind of *watakushi shōsetsu* (another name for personal fiction), ironically calling attention to his audacious narrative strategy in which a clearly fabricated narrator uses a confessional mode of storytelling to revel in a patently preposterous story.

After the Kanto earthquake of 1923 forced the Tokyo-born Tanizaki to move to Kansai, an area encompassing the older cities of Kyoto, Osaka, and Kobe, his writing began to display a turn toward traditionalism. His fiction showed, however, that the writer understood tradition not as a fixed or preexisting phenomenon, but as the created product of a modern longing. In *Manji* (1931; *Quicksand*), one of the few Japanese novels narrated in dialect, the female narrator uses the age-old rhythms of Kansai speech to tell an unlikely tale of lesbian love and betrayal, in which the truth of her statements is constantly undermined by her own later revelations. In *Tade kuu mushi* (1928; *Some Prefer Nettles*) a Westernized Japanese caught in a passionless marriage finds himself drawn to a woman who represents an older model of femininity. Although the most conventionally told of Tanizaki's novels, *Some Prefer Nettles* flaunts its fictionality in its masterful use of imagery and careful plot development that employs the cultural topography of the novel's Kansai setting.

The 1930s were Tanizaki's years of immersion in Japanese history. He wrote masterful novellas and also translated into modern Japanese the 11th-century classic, the *Genji monogatari* (*The Tale of Genji*). In 1943 he began to serialize *Sasameyuki* (*The Makioka Sisters*), a long, elegiac chronicle of a prewar merchant family in decline. Completed in 1948, the work stands as Tanizaki's paean to a cultural ideal—a graceful way of life that balanced an appreciation of tradition with a striking cosmopolitanism. *The Makioka Sisters* is distinguished by its focus on a refined yet bourgeois female protagonist, and by its lyrical control of time, which echoes *The Tale of Genji* in balancing the cyclicity of seasonal observances against the inexorable march of history.

Tanizaki's two major postwar novels clarified what was implicit in his prior treatments of desire: that desire is anchored in isolated subjectivities ever in pursuit of illusions. *Kagi* (1956; *The Key*) and *Fūten rōjin nikki* (1962; *Diary of a Mad Old Man*) make inventive use of the diary-novel form to explore the intersection of aging and eroticism. In the former work, a college professor sets out to inflame his flagging sexual desires by encouraging his wife to take a younger lover. The novel is told in the form of two parallel diaries, one by the professor and the other by his wife. The narrative strategy places the work at the boundaries of epistolary fiction and the diary-novel, for the two characters use their diaries as a means of communication by tacitly agreeing to read each other's diaries while outwardly pretending that they do not. The diaries reveal both the manipulative nature of language and the solitary nature of subjectivity, even when what is at issue is the seemingly shared activity of sexual union. *Diary of a Mad Old Man* is a radical and Rabelaisian affirmation of desire told by an aged diarist who records both past desires and his current efforts to bribe his daughter-in-law to provide sexual favors in return for Western baubles. When the passionate diarist is struck down by a stroke caused by an excess of sexual excitement, however, his story is brought to an end by the records kept by medical personnel and a practical-minded daughter, who turn the old man's longings into dull pathologies.

Such an acknowledgment of the contingencies of subjectivity and language was a fitting insight for Tanizaki, an unsparing analyst of passion and a writer committed to the illusions made possible through words.

KEN K. ITO

Biography
Born 24 July 1886 in Tokyo. Attended Tokyo Imperial University, 1908–10. Lived in Yokohama and Tokyo; moved to Kansai, near Osaka, after Kanto earthquake in 1923; traveled in China, 1918. Died 30 July 1965.

Novels by Tanizaki
Kami to hito to no aida [Between God and Man], 1924
Chijin no ai, 1924; as *Naomi*, translated by Anthony H. Chambers, 1985
Kōjin [Shark-Man], 1926
Tade kuu mushi, 1928; as *Some Prefer Nettles*, translated by Edward G. Seidensticker, 1955
Manji, 1931; as *Quicksand*, translated by Howard Hibbett, 1994
Bushūkō hiwa, 1935; as *The Secret History of the Lord of Musashi*, translated by Anthony H. Chambers, 1982
Sasameyuki, 1948; as *The Makioka Sisters*, translated by Edward G. Seidensticker, 1957
Rangiku monogatari [Story of Tangled Chrysanthemums], 1949
Kagi, 1956; as *The Key*, translated by Howard Hibbett, 1960
Fūten rōjin nikki, 1962; as *Diary of a Mad Old Man*, translated by Howard Hibbett, in *Seven Japanese Tales*, 1963

Other Writings: short stories, novellas, essays, plays, screenplays, and memoirs (including *Yōshō jidai*, translated by Paul McCarthy as *Childhood Years*, 1988); other writings, as well as the novels, are collected in the complete works, *Tanizaki Jun'ichirō zenshū*, Tokyo: Chūōkōronsha, 1981–83.

Further Reading
Chambers, Anthony Hood, *The Secret Window: Ideal Worlds in Tanizaki's Fiction,* Cambridge, Massachusetts: Council on East Asian Studies, Harvard University, 1994
Chiba Shunji, *Tanizaki Jun'ichirō: Kitsune to mazohizumu,* Tokyo: Ozawa Shoten, 1994
Chiba Shunji, editor, *Tanizaki Jun'ichirō: Monogatari no hōhō,* volume 18 of *Nihon bungaku kenkyū shiryō shinshū,* Tokyo: Yūseidō, 1990
Gessel, Van C., *Three Modern Novelists: Sōseki, Tanizaki, Kawabata,* Tokyo and New York: Kodansha International, 1993
Ito, Ken K., *Visions of Desire: Tanizaki's Fictional Worlds,* Stanford, California: Stanford University Press, 1991
Kōno Taeko, *Tanizaki bungaku to kōtei no yokubō,* Tokyo: Bungei Shunjū, 1976
Nihon Bungaku Kenkyū Shiryō Kankōkai, editors, *Tanizaki Jun'ichirō,* Tokyo: Yūseidō, 1972
Noguchi Takehiko, *Tanizaki Jun'ichirō ron,* Tokyo: Chūōkōronsha, 1973
Nomura Shōgo, *Denki Tanizaki Jun'ichirō,* Tokyo: Rokkō Shuppan, 1974
Petersen, Gwenn Boardman, *The Moon in the Water: Understanding Tanizaki, Kawabata, and Mishima,* Honolulu: University Press of Hawaii, 1979

Temporality. *See* Tense in Narrative; Time in the Novel

Tense in Narrative

In his commentary on Albert Camus' *L'Étranger* (*The Stranger*), which in 1942 broke from established novelistic protocol in French by casting narration almost entirely in the *passé composé* (the past tense of speech although not of fictional narration), Jean-Paul Sartre suggested that the *tense* of a text holds the key to its special strangeness (*Situations*, 1947). Indeed, the choice of a verb tense—in literature as in natural language—is clearly more than just a grammatical agenda. Like pronoun choice (relevant to narrative "voice"), tense is a deictic grammatical category that links up with, and relates to, the position of a speaker in the act of producing an utterance. In the case of tense that deictic position is a temporal one, anchoring the events of a fictional world (if we limit consideration here to the utterances of narrative fiction) to the "now" of the text's speaker, the narrator in conventional fiction. (In light of the controversy in narratology over whether all texts have a speaker, the term *speaker function* may be preferable.)

Conventional fiction also assumes that *telling* comes after *experiencing*, whence the traditional role of past tense as the "unmarked" or default tense of fiction and of narration generally. But since tense in narrative is to a large extent decoupled from its temporal function of establishing story-world chronology, some narratologists have denied that the past tense in fiction is temporal at all (Hamburger, Weinrich), preferring to regard it as simply an index of fictionality, a metatextual signpost conveying the information: "let us pretend for the duration of this textual transaction that such and such events occurred in some (past) world." This association of past tense with fictionality did not always hold, however. In *Tense and the Novel* (1970), Bronzwaer recalls the dilemma of 18th-century novelists responding to the new challenge of writing in prose: "in a nutshell, the question was how to reconcile the preterite, traditionally the vehicle of historical narration, with a fictive story that had, when all was said and done, not really happened." Nor is it the case today that fiction relies on the past tense. With the exception of specific genres (historical novels, autobiography, detective fiction), and with some variation across languages, narrative fiction no longer preferentially adopts a retrospective viewpoint, opting instead for a "poetics of immediacy" that calls for the on-the-scene or in-the-mind present tense, and even licenses tense alternations of the type Wolfson (1979), Schiffrin (1981), and other discourse-oriented linguists have studied in the spontaneous storytelling of ordinary conversation (so-called "natural narrative"): "So there I *was* stopped at a red light when all of a sudden this guy *comes up* to the window and *points a gun* in my face." Tense-switching of this type, notably involving use of the present tense, has long been observed in the early narrative texts of various literary traditions (romances, epics, hagiography, chronicles, sundry tales), produced when the cultures were still predominantly oral. Only recently, however, has this premodern phenomenon of tense alternation been studied in the light of research into "natural narrative" and been shown, moreover, to be an antecedent of the modern "historical present" phenomenon of literary and historiographic narrative.

Contemporary fiction also has experimented with other tenses of the "discours" (Benveniste) or "commentative" (Weinrich) mode (for purposes of this discussion I ignore the differences between the two). Michael Frayn's *A Very Private Life* (1968) offers up a utopia set in the future and relies accordingly on the future tense ("Once upon a time there will be a little girl named Uncumber. Uncumber will have a brother called Sulpice . . .") before lapsing into the present tense; future is also the tense choice of Albert Vanasco's *Sin embargo Juan vivía* (1947; And Juan Lived After All). As noted above, Camus created a tempest in a linguistic teapot by choosing for *The Stranger* not the novelistic *passé simple* (simple past tense) but the *passé composé*, a tense of spoken discourse. Part of the oddity derived from the fact that the *passé composé*, in addition to being the past tense of ordinary speech, also functions in French as a present perfect, a tense universally absent from narrative, since it focuses on the present world of the speaker/narrator rather than on the past world of the story. Yet on a thematic level, for the first-person narrator of *The Stranger* the *passé composé* is appropriate, since the past is of no consequence to him except insofar as it bears on his present circumstances (his trial and imprisonment); moreover, the only past that exists for him is a recent past. The distance separating his past from his present is minimal, whence the *passé composé*, whose basic meaning is to establish a connection between a past situation and the speaker's present.

Among other "innovative" tenses of contemporary fiction we find, as a predominant option in Marguerite Duras' *La Maladie de la mort* (1982; *The Malady of Death*), the conditional tense, motivated presumably by the novel's highly fantastic plot, which the protagonist imagines rather than actually lives through. Claude Simon's *La Route des Flandres* (1960; *The Flanders Road*) tries to avoid tense—and the temporal anchoring of events—altogether by relying on the present participle, a nonfinite form that cannot by itself locate events in time. In the absence of tensed verbs, events in Simon's novel remain temporally ambiguous. Nonfinite too is the imperative tense, used in John Updike's "How to Love America and Leave It at the Same Time" (1979), Lorrie Moore's collection *Self-Help* (1985), and much second-person fiction.

In traditional narrative, a time reference is established at the outset of a text (explicitly or through vague temporal markers such as "Once upon a time . . ."), and time advances largely according to a principle of "iconic sequence" (i.e., the order of the telling is assumed to mirror the order of events in the world modeled by the text). Only in the case of anachrony (or discordance between the order in which events are reported to have occurred and the order in which they are recounted) is time reference signaled, by means of tenses and/or time adverbials (". . . whereas *the year before* life *had presented* no such interruptions"). Time reference, then, need not in principle be marked in each new sentence of a text. Yet as the philosopher of language Willard van Orman Quine has observed (in *Word and Object*, 1960):

> Our ordinary language shows a tiresome bias in its treatment of time. . . . The form it takes—that of requiring that every verb form show a tense—is peculiarly productive of needless complications, since it demands lip service to time even when time is farthest from our thoughts.

Fortunately, human language is not as uneconomical as Quine's statement suggests. Since tense is not necessary for conveying the chronology of events or other plot material (in novels that have plots and events), and given the efficiency with which language makes use of available grammatical resources, tense information is commonly "exapted" (a concept of biological recycling introduced into linguistics by Roger Lass in "How to Do Things With Junk," *Journal of Linguistics* 26 [1990]) from its basic temporal function into a variety of other, nontemporal functions. These include: manipulating the textual foreground and background (a contrast traditionally construed as synonymous with that between events and description) through the use of perfective versus imperfective tenses (in languages that formally express this aspectual contrast); creating a sense of immediacy, whether on the scene of events (via the narrative, or historical, present) or inside a character's consciousness (via the present of interior monologue or the imperfective tenses of represented speech and thought); distinguishing the narrator-self from the character-self in first-person fiction; and signaling point of view and focalization.

For many of the above functions tense works in concert with aspect, a (nondeictic) grammatical category that reports on the "boundedness" of predicated situations, i.e., whether they are presented as having endpoints (*at breakfast he read the newspaper*) or not (*he was reading the newspaper when . . .*). Most crucial here is the perfective/imperfective contrast, which distinguishes, e.g., the French *passé simple* (past tense + perfective aspect), the event tense par excellence, from the descriptive *imparfait* (past tense + imperfective aspect). The English progressive tenses also are aspectually imperfective. In certain languages one way of identifying represented speech and thought (also known as free indirect discourse, or *discours indirect libre*) is through a characteristic use of imperfective tenses, which also constitute a distinguishing grammatical mark of "irrealis" domains such as dream visions, hallucinations, and other departures from rational consciousness.

The qualifiers "conventional" or "traditional" have been used frequently in this essay in reference to narrative. This is because literary narrative—contemporary fiction in particular—often fails to conform to, indeed violates, basic tenets of "normative" narration. Yet the rhetorical and stylistic effects produced by the violations are possible precisely *because* a narrative norm, or

prototype, is in place. That is, the notion of a narrative norm is not invalidated by the fact that contemporary fiction frequently deviates from story chronology (through flashbacks, prolepses, repetitions of the same event) or obliterates chronology altogether, or that some texts foreground description rather than events, or obliterate events altogether in favor of a temporally chaotic journey through consciousness. To the contrary, without such a norm as part of our literary competence, the deviations could not produce the effects they do on readers. Narrative fiction continually plays with its own conventions, experimenting with its linguistic and discursive protocols; and over the centuries tense has played a significant role in these quiet revolutions in narrative language.

SUZANNE FLEISCHMAN

See also Description; Diegesis and Diegetic Levels of Narration; Discourse Representation; Narratology; Narrator; Person in Narrative; Plot; Point of View; Time in the Novel

Further Reading

Bache, Carl, "Tense and Aspect in Fiction," *Journal of Literary Semantics* 15 (1986)

Benveniste, Emile, "Les Relations de temps dans le verbe français," *Bulletin de la Société Linguistique de Paris* 54 (1959); reprint, *Problèmes de linguistique générale*, Paris: Gallimard, 1966; as *Problems in General Linguistics*, Coral Gables, Florida: University of Miami Press, 1971

Bronzwaer, W.J.M., *Tense in the Novel: An Investigation of Some Potentialities of Linguistic Criticism*, Groningen: Wolters-Noordhoff, 1970

Casparis, Christian Paul, *Tense Without Time: The Present Tense in Narration*, Bern: Francke, 1975

Fleischman, Suzanne, *Tense and Narrativity: From Medieval Performance to Modern Fiction*, Austin: University of Texas Press, and London: Routledge, 1990

Fleischman, Suzanne, "Toward a Theory of Tense-Aspect in Narrative Discourse," in *The Function of Tense in Texts*, edited by J. Gvozdanovic and T. Janssen, Amsterdam: North Holland, 1991

Fludernik, Monika, "The Historical Present Tense in English Literature: An Oral Pattern and Its Literary Adaptation," *Language and Literature* 17 (1992)

Fludernik, Monika, *Towards a "Natural" Narratology*, London and New York: Routledge, 1996

Hamburger, Käte, *Die Logik der Dichtung*, Stuttgart: Klett, 1957; 2nd edition, 1968; 2nd edition translated as *The Logic of Literature*, Bloomington: Indiana University Press, 1973

Schiffrin, Deborah, "Tense Variation in Narrative," *Language* 57 (1981)

Weinrich, Harald, *Tempus: Besprochene und erzählte Welt*, Stuttgart: Kohlhammer, 1964; 5th edition, 1994; also published as *Le Temps*, Paris: Éditions du Seuil, 1973

Wolfson, Nessa, "The Conversational Historical Present Alternation," *Language* 55 (1979)

Terra Nostra by Carlos Fuentes

1975

One of the most important works of Latin American fiction, Carlos Fuentes' *Terra Nostra* breaks new ground both thematically and technically. Synthesizing 2,000 years of civilization, ranging from Tiberius' first-century Rome to the oppressively abstemious and orderly confines of Philip II's 16th-century Escorial, to the Aztec myths of the New World, and to the apocalyptic atmosphere of the late 20th century, *Terra Nostra* is a profound exploration of the conflict between tyranny and liberty in the Hispanic soul.

The novel begins in Paris on a day of liberation, Bastille Day, 1999, when a young man named Polo Febo meets a woman named Celestina who asks him to explain to her the mysteries of modern civilization. Polo slips and falls into the Seine, and the narrative eventually shifts to the 16th century of Philip II and his wife Isabel, the main characters of the first part of the novel, "The Old World." Philip's religious and imperial fanaticism causes him to oppress and neglect both his wife and his empire. In the cold, stark architecture of his palace, El Escorial, Philip's tyrannical zeal never allows him to know or love either the queen or the New World. In contrast, the joyous physical and spiritual union of Polo Febo and Celestina in Paris at the end of the novel represents the end of Philip's legacy of tyranny. *Terra Nostra* is a compendium of many of the themes of Fuentes' earlier novels: the doppelgänger, the transmigration of souls; the relationship between individuals and nations, between Spain and the New World, between fate and freedom; and the importance of the indigenous past as a means of understanding the New World present.

Terra Nostra is also a compendium of innovative narrative techniques. While most experimental novels develop new techniques in one or two areas, *Terra Nostra* does so in numerous ways—linguistic invention, temporal shifts, multivocal narrative, and fictionalized history. The novel may also be read as a traditional adventure story, that of Polo Febo's journey through time and space. Fuentes himself has stated that *Terra Nostra* is a blending of the two novels that he believes define the narrative ideal, Alexandre Dumas' *The Count of Monte-Cristo* (the ultimate traditional adventure story) and James Joyce's *Ulysses* (the ideal experimental novel).

Even the title of the novel is an example of its linguistic complexity. It has at least three possible interpretations. First, *terra nostra* (our world) has a negative connotation, referring to Spain's imperial perception of the New World and all things indigenous to it as something to be dominated and exploited. This view makes Philip's Spain an extension of Tiberius' Rome, which regarded the Mediterranean Sea as its *mare nostrum* (our sea). Second, from the perspective of the New World, *terra nostra* is a positive term used to express its independence. Third, the title also refers to the new literary territory mapped out by Latin American writers of the 20th century such as Fuentes, Jorge Luis Borges, Alejo Carpentier, Gabriel García Márquez, Julio Cortázar, and Mario Vargas Llosa.

Terra Nostra is in many ways the technical and thematic culmination of Fuentes' narrative career. Like his *La región más transparente* (1958; *Where the Air Is Clear*), *Terra Nostra* consists of a series of juxtapositions of the indigenous past with the modern world. Like *La muerte de Artemio Cruz* (1962; *The Death of Artemio Cruz*), *Terra Nostra* is an extremely organized novel constructed of many layers of meaning, although *Terra Nostra* is constructed out of layers of history rather than personality as is the case in *Artemio Cruz*. As in *Cambio de piel* (1967; *A Change of Skin*), the narrative voices of *Terra Nostra* "change their skin," forcing the reader to chase a constantly changing narrator throughout the novel. Just as Philip II is unable to "read" the events of his time according to his narrow, unified scheme, the reader of *Terra Nostra* is unable to read the novel by means of a single, clearly defined narrator. According to Fuentes, truth is multiple and complex. In *Cervantes; o, La crítica de la lectura* (*Don Quixote; or, The Critique of Reading*), published a year after *Terra Nostra*, Fuentes reiterates this idea of multiple readings in his analysis of Miguel de Cervantes' protagonist: "the knight will continue to live only in the book that recounts his story . . . in the multiple readings life took from him in reality but granted him forever in the book."

Terra Nostra is a totalizing novel, that is, it attempts to include all times, all places, all narrators. It is similar in certain ways to three other important Latin American novels of the 20th century: Alejo Carpentier's *Los pasos perdidos* (1953; *The Lost Steps*), Julio Cortázar's *Rayuela* (1963; *Hopscotch*), and Gabriel García Márquez's *Cien años de soledad* (1967; *One Hundred Years of Solitude*). Like these three novels, *Terra Nostra* fuses history and myth, religion and philosophy, Old World and New World. The novel is also an interesting example of a theme common to several Latin American works of fiction—dictatorship. Fuentes has said that *Terra Nostra*, *Yo el Supremo* (1974; *I the Supreme*) by Augusto Roa Bastos, *El recurso del método* (1974; *Reasons of State*) by Carpentier, and *El otoño del patriarca* (1975; *The Autumn of the Patriarch*) by García Márquez form a kind of imaginary museum of Latin American dictators. In *Terra Nostra*, Fuentes explores the Iberian origins of this despotic tradition.

Although generally considered one of the most significant works of contemporary Latin American fiction, *Terra Nostra* has received a mixed critical response. Most critics have praised the carnivalesque richness of its historico-fictional world, the strength of its mythic symbology, and the abundance of its narrative innovations, but a few have complained of weak characterization, a tediously baroque plot structure, and excessive theoretical exposition. Nevertheless, *Terra Nostra* is certainly one of the most important Latin American novels of the 20th century for its technical as well as thematic originality.

J. PATRICK DUFFEY

See also Carlos Fuentes

Further Reading

Alazraki, Jaime, "*Terra Nostra*: Coming to Grips with History," *World Literature Today* 57 (1983)

Faris, Wendy B., *Carlos Fuentes*, New York: Ungar, 1983

Goytisolo, Juan, "*Terra Nostra*: Our New Old World," *Review* 19 (1976)

Gyurko, Lanin A., "Carlos Fuentes," in *Latin American Writers,* New York: Scribner, 1989

Hernández de López, Ana María, *La obra de Carlos Fuentes: Una visión múltiple,* Madrid: Pliegos, 1988

Janes, Regina, "*Terra Nostra*: Charting the Terrain," *The Literary Review* 23 (Winter 1980)

Julseth, David Charles, "The Millennium of Carlos Fuentes in

Terra Nostra," Ph.D. diss., University of Texas at Austin, 1992

Kundera, Milan, "Esch is Luther," *Review of Contemporary Fiction* 8:2 (1988)

Zamora, Lois Parkinson, *Writing the Apocalypse: Historical Vision in Contemporary U.S. and Latin American Fiction,* Cambridge and New York: Cambridge University Press, 1989

Tess of the d'Urbervilles by Thomas Hardy

1891

In 1888 Thomas Hardy was asked by Tillotson's Fiction Bureau to write a novel for serialization. That novel was to become *Tess of the d'Urbervilles.* The request came at a significant point in Hardy's life. He was nearly 50 years old and a well-known, even famous, literary figure who was becoming increasingly impatient with the moral conventions of the Victorian reading public. During 1889, while he was working on *Tess,* he wrote an essay for the *New Review* entitled "Candour in English Fiction," in which he made public what he had already privately noted, namely, that "the besetting sin of modern literature is its insincerity," and argued that the honest portrayal of life "must largely be concerned with . . . the relations of the sexes."

It is not surprising, then, that, strengthened by his reputation and the ideas he had so recently voiced publicly, Hardy refused to comply with Tillotson's demand for the withdrawal of two specific episodes—Tess' seduction by Alec d'Urberville and the midnight baptism of her illegitimate child—before publication. However, when the manuscript was also rejected by two other magazines, Hardy rewrote the sexual elements of the narrative to ensure publication, and the *Graphic* began serialization in July 1891. In this first version of the novel, the sexual theme is presented less explicitly. Tess is not seduced but goes through a bogus marriage ceremony; she does not have a child, and her relationship with Alec at the end of the novel is platonic. The overt eroticism of such scenes as the one in which Angel Clare carries the milkmaids over the stream is softened or distanced, perhaps absurdly, by his pushing them in a wheelbarrow. The serialized version was never published in book form and the first edition (which was virtually the same as Hardy's original) came out in 1891, although he continued to amend and add to the text, which was not finalized until 1912.

Because of its provocative content, *Tess of the d'Urbervilles* was an immediate sensation and catapulted Hardy into public view in a way he found uncomfortable and disturbing. The reviews ranged from unqualified praise for his courage and artistry to furious attacks on his morality. In the preface to the fifth edition, Hardy coolly summarized the general spirit of these attacks: that the subject of sexual relations between men and women was not a fit subject for art; that the novel was an argument for immoral behavior; that the word "pure" in the novel's subtitle, *A Pure Woman,* was a distortion of civilized morals. He

dismissed the charges by claiming that the novel was "oftener charged with impressions than convictions" and that the volume and intensity of reader response provided a measure of the novel's capacity to shock and to arouse public debate. In fact, *Tess of the d'Urbervilles* dealt with topics that were engaging many other writers, serious and sensational, at the time: the position of women, the nature of female sexuality, and the hypocrisy of contemporary sexual moral codes. Hardy's novel caught the mood of the moment, and the years that followed saw the publication of many novels dealing with similar themes, such as George Gissing's *The Odd Women* (1893), George Moore's *Esther Waters* (1894), and Grant Allen's *The Woman Who Did* (1895).

Although Hardy's contemporaries found his treatment of sexual issues controversial, in hindsight *Tess of the d'Urbervilles* seems to be in many ways a traditional Victorian novel. The narrative draws on the ballad tradition of the deserted maiden who murders her seducer, and Alec d'Urberville has all the makings of a Victorian villain. Hardy relies heavily on narrative interest and conventionally structures the novel around the events of Tess' life, which begins in youthful innocence and ends with her death. Although most novelists of his era were concerned with urban themes, Hardy set his narrative in the rural England of his recent past as a way of chronicling the changing landscape and vanishing ways of life. Many incidents in the novel, such as the Saturday night outing of the Trantbridge workers to Chaseborough, draw on Hardy's childhood experiences. Hardy's much-criticized reference at the end of the novel to the "President of the Immortals"—for its impiety, according to early critics; for its vague fatalism, according to modern critics—is the culmination of a traditional textual tapestry of classical and biblical allusions that highlight Tess' vulnerability and impermanence.

Yet for all the novel's traditional structure—F.R. Leavis in *The Great Tradition* (1948) found it amusing that anyone could judge Hardy as representative of the "modern consciousness"— the abiding impression of the novel today is its modernity. What is still shocking about *Tess of the d'Urbervilles* is not the social critique of late Victorian England but Hardy's transformation of the literary pastoral into an arena of alienation and his transformation of Tess' moral and social dilemmas into the "ache of modernism." Tess' "phases," as Hardy calls each section of her life and each part of the novel, initially appear in harmony with nature, since her actions and personality often merge with and are incorporated into descriptions of the weather, the countryside, and rural rituals. Her beauty, her youthful energy, and her intrinsic eroticism, for instance, are intensified and mirrored by the descriptions of the Talbothays' dairy, while her spiritual and physical exhaustion are both created and mirrored by the bitter conditions at Flintcomb-Ash Farm later in the novel. But Hardy's idea of being in harmony with nature is not Wordsworthian but rather a Darwinian recognition that Tess *is* nature and demonstrates nature's beauty and fruitfulness as well as its brutal, amoral imperatives.

This sense of modernity is deepened by what Malcolm Bradbury calls "a prevailing sense of dislocation from the past" (*Modernism: 1890–1930*, 1976). Mechanical innovations like the steam-powered threshing machine described in chapter 47 are changing people's relationship to the land. Old Lady-Day, or hiring day, has become a destabilizing circus for migrant workers. The major characters in the novel, notably Tess herself, have lost "knowable communities," as Raymond Williams has remarked (see Williams, 1970); they journey backward and forward across a landscape indifferent to human joys and suffering. Yet *Tess of the d'Urbervilles* is not a tragic novel in the classical sense. The denial of Tess' experience (by her family, by the men who claim to love her, by the society that decides her class, and by the changing world she inhabits), which destroys her child and then herself, may be considered a tragedy of social determinism; Tess' destiny as woman, lover, and mother may amount to a tragedy of biological determinism. Hardy, however, would not have called his novel "tragic" but simply "'questionings' in the exploration of reality."

LYNNE HAPGOOD

See also Thomas Hardy

Further Reading

Boumelha, Penny, *Thomas Hardy and Women: Sexual Ideology and Narrative Form*, Madison: University of Wisconsin Press, 1985

Brady, Kristin, "Tess and Alec: Rape or Seduction?" in *Hardy, the Tragic Novels: "The Return of the Native," "The Mayor of Casterbridge," "Tess of the d'Urbervilles" and "Jude the Obscure": A Casebook*, edited by R.P. Draper, London: Macmillan, 1975; revised edition, 1991

Goode, John, *Thomas Hardy: The Offensive Truth*, Oxford and New York: Blackwell, 1988

Gregor, Ian, *The Great Web: The Form of Hardy's Major Fiction*, London: Faber, and Totowa, New Jersey: Rowman and Littlefield, 1974

Kettle, Arnold, *An Introduction to the English Novel*, volume 2: *Henry James to 1950*, 2nd edition, London: Hutchinson, 1967

Kramer, Dale, *Thomas Hardy: The Forms of Tragedy*, Detroit, Michigan: Wayne State University Press, and London: Macmillan, 1975

Laird, J.T., *The Shaping of "Tess of the d'Urbervilles,"* Oxford: Clarendon Press, 1975

Lodge, David, "Tess, Nature, and the Voices of Hardy," in *Hardy, the Tragic Novels: "The Return of the Native," "The Mayor of Casterbridge," "Tess of the d'Urbervilles" and "Jude the Obscure": A Casebook*, edited by R.P. Draper, London: Macmillan, 1975; revised edition, 1991

Meisel, Perry, *Thomas Hardy: The Return of the Repressed: A Study of the Major Fiction*, New Haven, Connecticut: Yale University Press, 1972

Morgan, Rosemarie, *Women and Sexuality in the Novels of Thomas Hardy*, London and New York: Routledge, 1988

Tanner, Tony, "Colour and Movement in *Tess of the d'Urbervilles*," in *Hardy, the Tragic Novels: "The Return of the Native," "The Mayor of Casterbridge," "Tess of the d'Urbervilles" and "Jude the Obscure": A Casebook*, edited by R.P. Draper, London: Macmillan, 1975; revised edition, 1991

Van Ghent, Dorothy, "On *Tess of the d'Urbervilles*," in *Hardy: A Collection of Critical Essays*, edited by Albert J. Guerard, Englewood Cliffs, New Jersey: Prentice-Hall, 1963

Williams, Raymond, *The English Novel from Dickens to Lawrence*, London: Chatto and Windus, and New York: Oxford University Press, 1970

William Makepeace Thackeray 1811–63

English

Thackeray at one time was seen as the equal of his contemporary Dickens, or even as his superior. George Eliot regarded him, "as I suppose the majority of people with any intellect do, [as] the most powerful of living novelists." Even in his lifetime, however, reservations were occasionally voiced. Some readers felt that Thackeray was old-fashioned, and certainly his works—with the exception of *Vanity Fair* (1848)—have proved less than compelling to modern readers. Yet it is possibly the "old-fashioned" qualities of Thackeray that make him interesting, for his

is an awkward voice resisting the new assumptions at the heart of much mid-Victorian fiction.

Thackeray's reputation was established with *Vanity Fair*, subtitled "A Novel Without A Hero," which begins to suggest his scepticism about the commitment to the middle-class hero that we see in the works of his contemporaries. The reader is invited to consider the trials of Jane Eyre or David Copperfield with a great deal of seriousness. Thackeray's central character, Becky Sharp, on the other hand, is presented as a scheming adventuress making her way in the world, and we are not at all required to have much sympathy for her. Thackeray's approach to characterization is comic and external. *Vanity Fair* as a whole amounts to a satiric representation of a society consumed by a new desire for material goods, most of the characters being motivated by greed and self-interest.

Setting the novel at the time of Waterloo, Thackeray gives himself an opportunity to reflect, through his plot, on the tremendous social change associated with the Industrial Revolution. At a time when novels were serving a vital role in creating a sense of middle-class identity and self-worth, Thackeray fails to oblige. Rather than finding a new moral energy in middle-class experience, as many of his contemporaries did, he castigates it as selfish. Even Dobbin, the most honorable character in *Vanity Fair*, and the nearest we get to a middle-class hero, is viewed patronizingly. And most of the fun in this very funny novel derives from behavior that violates the code of conduct of the older, obsolete social order.

His lack of commitment to the middle-class subject, together with a lack of commitment to the associated values of marriage and family, establishes Thackeray as the awkward outsider in the mid-Victorian novel. His distance from the norm is particularly apparent in *The History of Pendennis* (1850), which appeared in the same year as *David Copperfield*. The novels feature similar stories, but whereas *David Copperfield* is centrally concerned with the construction of a successful middle-class identity, *Pendennis* concentrates on the hero's loss of a role and direction in his life. The leisurely pace of *Pendennis*, which can prove off-putting to modern readers, is possibly an important part of its achievement—that it establishes a rhythm at odds with the new rhythm of Victorian life.

It is in *The History of Henry Esmond* (1852) that Thackeray engages most directly with new Victorian ideas about individual identity. Set in the reign of Queen Anne, an old order—associated with a masculine culture of war and dueling, a commitment to the Stuart cause, and Catholicism—is yielding to a new order in which the individual is at the center, acting in accordance with the dictates of individual conscience. The novel may be read, therefore, as an articulation of a more sensitive set of values that is replacing a defunct male code. This reading is in line with the traditional response to Thackeray, seeing him as redefining the idea of the gentleman for a middle-class age. But Henry Esmond is not necessarily a positive figure. It is possible to see him as totally self-absorbed, setting himself up as a kind of god at the center of his own world. In that reading, *Henry Esmond* exposes the shortcomings of the new Victorian emphasis on the self.

The disintegration of an old military-based male culture is always at the heart of Thackeray's fiction. Starting with Becky Sharp, there are always strong women characters who threaten the males. Not surprisingly, Thackeray—who seems to share his characters' fear of these strong women—engineers their defeat in the end, but this does nothing to disguise the fact that his "heroes" are often emasculated. Perhaps the best indication of Thackeray's inability to envision a viable male identity in the rising bourgeois culture of the 19th century is the supernumerary gentleman who makes an appearance in every novel. This figure, dependent on inherited wealth and bereft of a purpose in life, is characterized by an inability—made up of both powerlessness and refusal—to construct a new social identity, to participate fully in middle-class culture.

This refusal to participate is often accompanied, as in *Vanity Fair*, by a devastating critique of materialism. In *The Newcomes* (1855), the most disturbing character is Barnes Newcome, a banker and wife-beater, who seems to set the tone for the mid-Victorian age. But he is only the most extreme character in a novel that takes apart the period's faith in marriage, home, and the family. What Thackeray sets against Barnes Newcome is the limp, ineffectual Clive Newcome, a dandy and an artist, not a person who is in any way qualified to challenge or change middle-class ideals. This pattern repeats itself in Thackeray's novels: the past yields to a corrupt present, but there is no sense of a possible move to a better future, no sense of that new moral energy that we see in other novels of the period.

By the end of his career, Thackeray's disillusionment with contemporary culture seems to have deepened. In *The Adventures of Philip* (1862), for example, he takes a reactionary stand not unlike the "muscular Christianity" of the period. Philip is a clumsy character awkwardly out of place in a world that does not accommodate his vision of masculinity. As is the case with some "muscular Christian" novels, *Philip* descends into violence and racism. But the crudeness of *Philip* in fact helps us appreciate the subtlety and elusiveness of Thackeray's position in the earlier novels. There, having lost confidence in the old order, Thackeray remains teasingly sceptical about the new values of Victorian Britain as reflected—and even created—in the novels of his contemporaries.

JOHN PECK

See also Vanity Fair

Biography

Born 18 July 1811 in Calcutta, India, of English parents; sent to England, 1817. Attended schools in Southampton and Chiswick, London; Charterhouse, London, 1822–28; Trinity College, Cambridge, 1829–30; traveled abroad and visited Goethe at Weimar, 1830–31; law student at the Middle Temple, London, 1831–32. Owner and editor, *National Standard*, London, 1833–34; lived in Paris, and studied painting, 1834–37; Paris correspondent, *Constitutional*, London, 1836–37; moved back to England, 1837, and began writing full-time; contributor, the *Times* and *Fraser's Magazine*, beginning in 1837; contributed articles and illustrations to *Punch*, 1842–54; delivered lectures on English humorists, in Britain, 1851, and in the United States, 1852–53; delivered lectures on the Hanoverian monarchs, in Britian and the United States, 1855–57; Independent parliamentary candidate for Oxford, 1857; editor, *Cornhill Magazine*, London, 1859–62. Died 24 December 1863.

Novels by Thackeray

Vanity Fair, 1848
The History of Pendennis, 1850
The History of Henry Esmond, Esq., 1852
The Luck of Barry Lyndon, 1853; revised edition, as *The Memoirs of Barry Lyndon, Esq.*, 1856
The Newcomes, 1855
The Virginians, 1859
Lovel the Widower, 1860
The Adventures of Philip on His Way Through the World, 1862
Denis Duval, 1864

Other Writings: stories, sketches, travel writings, journalism, and lectures.

Further Reading

Carey, John, *Thackeray: Prodigal Genius*, London: Faber, 1977

Colby, Robert A., *Thackeray's Canvass of Humanity: An Author and His Public*, Columbus: Ohio State University Press, 1979

Gilmour, Robin, *The Idea of the Gentleman in the Victorian Novel*, London and Boston: Allen and Unwin, 1981

Hardy, Barbara Nathan, *The Exposure of Luxury: Radical Themes in Thackeray*, London: Owen, and Pittsburgh, Pennsylvania: University of Pittsburgh Press, 1972

Lund, Michael, *Reading Thackeray*, Detroit, Michigan: Wayne State University Press, 1988

McMaster, Rowland, *Thackeray's Cultural Frame of Reference: Allusion in "The Newcomes,"* London: Macmillan, 1990; Montreal and Buffalo, New York: McGill-Queen's University Press, 1991

Thomas, Deborah A., *Thackeray and Slavery*, Athens: Ohio University Press, 1993

That Awful Mess on Via Merulana by Carlo Emilio Gadda

Quer pasticciaccio brutto de via Merulana 1957

Ostensibly a detective story, *That Awful Mess on Via Merulana* is set in Rome in 1927, with frequent and scathing reference to the omnipresence of Mussolini and the byzantine machinations of the bureaucracy of his regime. Written in the immediate aftermath of the fall of Fascism, it was published in part in serial form in 1946, appearing in its present form only in 1957.

Gadda introduces a recognizably modern—and now postmodern—figure, the police investigator with the characteristics of the private eye of popular fiction: at once an idealist, a loner, and a judgmental sceptic, without illusions and with impulses he recognizes as having in common with the criminal. He is a figure whose ancestry can be seen in G.K. Chesterton and Edgar Allan Poe and whose progeny can be found—in the Italian context—in the "mafia" novels of Leonardo Sciascia or (although with less serious intentions) in those of writing team Fruttero and Lucentini.

Police Commissioner Francesco Ingravallo, 35 and single, known as Don Ciccio, is assigned to a burglary case: the theft of some jewelry from an apartment at No. 219 Via Merulana, in a part of Rome that is simultaneously on the way up and on the way down. Resident in the same apartment block are middleclass friends of the commissioner, Remo and Liliana Balducci, a couple who often include him among guests at their Sunday lunches. For Ingravallo, Liliana is the epitome of womanly grace and loveliness, and, whether he knows it or not, he is in love with her.

The robbery enquiries are in their early stages when Ingravallo is sent to the scene of another, more serious, crime at the same address in Via Merulana, to find that Liliana has been murdered. This crime and the earlier robbery may be connected, particularly as Liliana's jewel box is missing. There are few leads, or, rather, there are too many.

In the Fascist era of law-enforced public decency, Gadda's Rome in 1926–27 is a city rife with unsolved murders, rapes, and robberies. The plot of the novel is the pursuit by the inspector, his grief and shock "professionally" sublimated, of some of the most promising leads across Rome at all levels of society, and out into its squalid semi-rural purlieus.

Suspicion rests at different times on various tenants of No. 219, giving rise to a network of inconclusive leads, among them Liliana's handsome nephew, not many years younger than she. Unsuspected complex realities emerge from behind smooth social exteriors. Dr. Valdarena, the nephew, is about to depart to take up a professional appointment in Genoa, where he is also to be married; it will be an end to his life as a gigolo in Rome, where he maintains an elegant and expensive lifestyle by exploiting lone foreign female tourists. He reveals, with tact and a creditable reluctance, a different and (to Ingravallo) disturbing Liliana. A childless woman, aware that her time is running out, desperate for motherhood, she had turned to a compliant Valdarena—but was it as a surrogate son or potential lover? In her obsession she also brought into her house a succession of "orphaned" or otherwise homeless girls from the country, whom Ingravallo recalls from his visits as inept helpers, not quite maids, about the luncheon table. Had they been on trial as "daughters," or—the suggestion is barely insinuated—was the desperate wife in some sense procuring them for her husband, in between his absences on business and hunting trips, in the hope of having a child from him by this means?

From a prostitute the police get a lead to a house on the outskirts of Rome, run by a former prostitute who now coordinates a variety of activities in the black market. The discovery, on the finger of one of her working girls, of a topaz ring belonging to Liliana leads to an apparent widening and tightening of the investigative net. The police find the cache of stolen jewelry in a chamber pot under an old woman's bed; Ingravallo questions one of Liliana's former charges, Assunta, now married, like others before her, with Liliana's help. Leads proliferate, the enquiry proceeds, but the novel concludes without anything having been established or proven, or any likely murderer identified. No event is ever clear in itself: Ingravallo must question Assunta, for instance, in distracting circumstances at her father's deathbed. Everywhere the investigative eye alights, there is an overplus— an "awful mess"—of information. The narrative itself takes part in this, as its attention roves and lingers on irrelevant objects described in exhaustive detail, to grotesque effect.

The *pasticciaccio* (awful mess) of the title has more than one reference. It is the crime itself, as an unsuturable rent in the social fabric. It is also the human body, in this case object, evidence, and even—it is obscurely suggested—instrument and cause of the crime; it is a body for which desire is overlaid (or overcome) by pity, horror, and disgust. Through Ingravallo's analytical, investigative, and professionally "objectifying" eyes, the common body's mucus, sweat, and rheum attract a coating of grime seen as a suitable interface for the realities beneath the skin, an occasion for revulsion and contempt. Added to this is the shocking fact of the blood from the savage neck wound on the one body he loved and considered untouchable. The open gash, described in objective forensic detail and, at the same time, in ambiguously suggestive sexual terms, is mirrored emblematically in the "black, vertical crease" in Assunta's forehead as, under the commissioner's "furious" and "haunted" questioning, she protests her ignorance and innocence. Inconclusively, the novel ends here.

The "mess" is carried into what—for a writer—is the heart of things, language. Gadda devises a pastiche of Latin, Spanish, invented words, slang, and dialects, including Roman (his title, *Quer pasticciaccio brutto de via Merulana,* is in Roman) and others up and down the Italian peninsula (much is made of "Don Ciccio" Ingravallo's origins outside the capital, in Molise, and of his dark, "southern" appearance). The prime motivation for Gadda's characteristic resort to a linguistic pastiche that is destructive to the formal body of language is an anguished revolt against the very fact of human existence. The novel posits existence as having evil at its core; the multiplicity and murkiness of human motivations are incommensurable with any human capacity to discover or explain them. The attempt to trace or verify any single event leads to immobilization in the "mess," the "tangled skein" of human affairs, for which Gadda-Ingravallo has a variety of terms in a variety of languages, dialects, and jargons, from the abstruse to the obscene, none of them readily translatable.

SUZANNE KIERNAN

See also Carlo Emilio Gadda

Further Reading

Adams, Robert Martin, *After Joyce: Studies in Fiction after "Ulysses,"* New York: Oxford University Press, 1977

Calvino, Italo, introduction to *That Awful Mess on Via Merulana,* by Carlo Emilio Gadda, translated by William Weaver, New York: Braziller, 1984

Cattaneo, Giulio, *Bisbetici e bizzarri nella letteratura italiana,* Milan: Fabbri, 1957

De Benedictis, Maurizio, *La piega nera: Groviglio stilistica ed enigma della femminilita in C.E. Gadda,* Anzio: De Rubeis, 1991

Dombroski, Robert S., "Carlo Emilio Gadda: Travesties," in *Properties of Writing: Ideological Discourse in Modern Italian Fiction,* Baltimore: Johns Hopkins University Press, 1994

Their Eyes Were Watching God by Zora Neale Hurston

1937

Zora Neale Hurston's *Their Eyes Were Watching God* is a remarkable novel narrating a woman's quest for identity in a racist and sexist society. Portraying the life and three marriages of Janie Crawford, the novel may be seen as an attempt to translate the concept of the self-assertive "New Negro," one of the main tenets of the Harlem Renaissance, into the everyday experience of black southern women. With the death of her controlling second husband, Janie finds herself well off economically and refuses to become the prototypical widow. Instead, she entertains a liberating relationship with Tea Cake, a much younger migrating worker and gambler, provocatively transgressing social and sexist conventions. She joins him "on the muck" and their picaresque journey takes them into the fertile Florida Evergreens and the hidden world of black work camps. In its setting, the novel also portrays the establishment of an autonomous black township in Florida, critically reflecting upon the validity and deficiencies of a self-regulated black culture. Written in a black folkloric idiom, the work projects not only a new image of black women and of a self-sufficient black community but also a new understanding of black folk vernacular, acknowledging its rich poetic resources and its vital force as a communal discourse.

Their Eyes Were Watching God has an equally remarkable reception history. This history documents not only the changes in academic institutions and refinements in literary criticism but also the ways in which American culture produces, represents, and reflects upon questions of race and gender and their complex overlapping. Published in 1937, *Their Eyes Were Watching God* was greeted initially with mixed reviews, the strongest criticism coming from black male critics who accused Hurston of presenting a one-sided idyllic view of black folk life. Richard Wright's well known review of the work, printed in the *New Masses,* was the most severe in its assessment, charging Hurston with "voluntarily [continuing] in her novel the tradition which was forced upon the Negro in the theatre, that is, the minstrel technique that makes the 'white folks' laugh" (see Wright, 1937). Similarly, Alain Locke (1938) pointed out that her portraits of "these entertaining pseudo-primitives" had not yet "come to grips with motive fiction and social document fiction." Later critical commentary by Langston Hughes, Nathan Huggins, Wallace Thurman, and Dwight Turner helped to transfer this picture of the "perfect darkie" to Hurston herself, who was portrayed as an opportunist who pandered to wealthy whites in order to please them and further her career.

Virtually forgotten, *Their Eyes Were Watching God* had an astonishing revival with the rise of feminist and African American studies in the 1970s. Black feminist scholars and writers like Alice Walker saw in the novel's inimitable heroine, as well as in the life of Hurston herself, a reflection of their own struggles for identity. These feminists were especially taken with what Walker calls Hurston's unique and "undiminished sense of racial health." "Here, finally," writes Mary Helen Washington (1987) of Janie, "was a woman on a quest for her own identity and, unlike so many other questing figures in black literature, her journey would take her, not away from, but deeper and deeper into blackness, the descent into the Everglades with its rich black soil, wild cane, and communal life representing immersion into black traditions." The reprinting of *Their Eyes Were Watching God* in 1978, the publication of Robert Hemenway's critically acclaimed biography (1977), and a collection of the artist's writing edited by Walker (1979) all helped to recover this neglected work and acknowledge Hurston as the predominant forerunner to contemporary female African American writers. In the 1980s *Their Eyes Were Watching God* secured its presence in American literary history, establishing Hurston as both a canonical and popular best-seller writer. Following and responding to Hurston's feminist literary criticism, works by Henry Louis Gates, Houston Baker, Barbara Johnson, and Michael Awkward further underscored the validity of her work as a diasporic writer rooted deeply in the African oral tradition that challenges a Western and Eurocentric model of writing.

After this triumphant revival, Hurston and her novel came under critical scrutiny once again in the 1990s. Hazel Carby (in Awkward, 1990), for instance, returned to Wright's criticism and argued that *Their Eyes Were Watching God,* like all of the author's work of the 1920s and 1930s, reveals an underlying exotic ethnography that turns black folk life into an aesthetic device, producing an unchanging definition of blackness that excludes the very real existence of urban misery. Carby's criticism also extends to the literary academy, which in its uncritical reception of the novel likewise perpetuates and reproduces a discourse that upholds the authenticity of black folk life and ignores a racist social order. Just as Hurston's early work displaces the mass migration of blacks to urban areas, claims Carby, so too does that of academic critics who privilege Hurston and celebrate black identity "at a moment of intense urban crisis and conflict" and when black presence in the academy is by no means secure. In a similar critical vein, Cornel West (in *Race Matters,* 1993) states the need to consider more carefully Hurston's often overlooked conservative politics (she supported segregation and publicly denounced the 1954 Supreme Court desegregation decision and Thurgood Marshall). And even a sympathetic critic like Mary Helen Washington, who played a significant role in reviving Hurston, is now asking "new questions about *Their Eyes*" that reveal the writer's ambivalence toward both her heroine and women in general. Returning to Robert Stepto's (1979) earlier criticism that Janie's power to speak is illusionary, Washington notes disturbing moments in the text when Hurston subverts her protagonist's voice.

Rather than receding in appeal and in spite of (or because of) such criticism, the popularity of *Their Eyes Were Watching God* remains strong, promising further debates and compelling questions concerning the politics of race, class, and gender. Its rich and revealing reception history illustrates the extent to which the culture industry produces and frames an author from within its own varying and historically changing ideological interests. Hurston's acclaimed novel thus also serves as a cultural indicator of the growing and expanding discourse on race and gender in America, and points at the same time to the troublesome and problematic commodification of these identities.

DELIA CAPAROSO KONZETT

Further Reading

Awkward, Michael, *Inspiriting Influences: Tradition, Revision, and Afro-American Women's Novels,* New York: Columbia University Press, 1989

Awkward, Michael, editor, *New Essays on "Their Eyes Were Watching God,"* Cambridge and New York: Cambridge University Press, 1990 (includes Hazel Carby's essay "The Politics of Fiction, Anthropology, and the Folk: Zora Neale Hurston")

Baker, Houston A., *Blues, Ideology, and Afro-American Literature: A Vernacular Theory,* Chicago: University of Chicago Press, 1984

Baker, Houston A., *Modernism and the Harlem Renaissance,* Chicago: University of Chicago Press, 1987

Gates, Henry Louis, Jr., "Zora Neale Hurston and the Speakerly Text," in *The Signifying Monkey,* New York: Oxford University Press, 1988

Hemenway, Robert E., *Zora Neale Hurston: A Literary Biography,* Urbana: University of Illinois Press, 1977

Johnson, Barbara, "Metaphor, Metonymy, and Voice in *Their Eyes,*" in *Black Literature and Literary Theory,* edited by Henry Louis Gates, Jr., New York: Methuen, 1984

Johnson, Barbara, "Thresholds of Difference: Structures of Address in Zora Neale Hurston," in *A World of Difference,* Baltimore: Johns Hopkins University Press, 1987

Locke, Alain, untitled review of *Their Eyes Were Watching God,* in *Opportunity* (1 June 1938); reprinted in *Zora Neale Hurston: Critical Perspectives Past and Present,* edited by Henry Louis Gates, Jr., and Anthony Appiah, New York: Amistad, 1993

Stepto, Robert B., *From Behind the Veil: A Study of Afro-American Narrative,* Urbana: University of Illinois Press, 1979; 2nd edition, 1991

Walker, Alice, "In Search of Zora Neale Hurston," *Ms.* (March 1975); reprinted in *I Love Myself When I Am Laughing . . . and Then Again When I Am Looking Mean and Impressive: A Zora Neale Hurston Reader,* edited by Alice Walker, New York: The Feminist Press, 1979

Washington, Mary Helen, "'I Love the Way Janie Crawford Left Her Husbands': Zora Neale Hurston's Emergent Hero," in *Invented Lives: Narratives of Black Women, 1860–1960,* Garden City, New York: Anchor Press, 1987

Wright, Richard, "Between Laughter and Tears," *New Masses* 25 (5 October 1937); reprinted in *Zora Neale Hurston: Critical Perspectives Past and Present,* edited by Henry Louis Gates, Jr., and Anthony Appiah, New York: Amistad, 1993

Things Fall Apart by Chinua Achebe

1958

Things Fall Apart marked the beginning of modern African literary tradition. With it Chinua Achebe became a pacesetter for African novelists in the second half of the 20th century. One of the novel's enduring distinctions is that, from its inception, it became a model of the Africanization of the novel, traditionally a Western art form. A handful of novels had been written by Africans before the publication of *Things Fall Apart,* but the novel's imagistic force and thematic realism reached out and overshadowed its forebears and peers. Its impact has been felt across many disciplines, including history, political science, literature, anthropology, and linguistics. Thus 1958 became a landmark not only for African writing and African literature but also for sociocultural and political development in Africa. Today, *Things Fall Apart* is without doubt the most famous novel in Africa and among the most widely read 20th-century novels in the English language. Few modern classics can compete with or match its singular distinction of being translated into 55 world languages, with the English edition selling 8 million copies within four decades of its publication.

Things Fall Apart reflects the enlightened African intellectual's pointed reaction against Western ethnocentrism and distortion of African reality during the colonial period. Achebe has consistently maintained that in Africa there is no "art for art's sake." Art has purpose. Art has meaning. Art has function. The message embodied is as important and essential as the medium. Both are interdependent, but when the message is monumental and urgent the artist must define clearly and unambiguously the cause that he or she seeks to espouse. Through eloquent theoretical essays, Achebe has defined the cause and burden that his first novel was meant to carry: "I would be quite satisfied if my novels (especially the ones I set in the past) did no more than teach my readers that their past—with all its imperfections—was not one long night of savagery from which the first Europeans acting on God's behalf delivered them" (see Achebe, 1965).

The African past of which Achebe speaks was the subject of two preceding narratives by Europeans: "Heart of Darkness" (1902) by Joseph Conrad and *Mister Johnson* (1939) by Joyce Cary. The majority of Achebe's youth was spent in the 1940s and 1950s, the decades of active colonial rule in Africa. Achebe was old enough to understand the dislocations brought about in the African social environment by imperialism. He witnessed firsthand the struggles of his people under colonial rule and observed with youthful impression the nationalist movements to dismantle the imperialistic yoke. The university curriculum for arts and humanities students during that time in Africa contained an essential literature component. Achebe read a surfeit of distortions and caricatures of African topography and people, but none affected him as stunningly as those he found in "Heart of Darkness" and *Mister Johnson*. Achebe resolved unequivocably, before he left the university, to depict the truth about Africa. *Things Fall Apart* was his fulfillment of that pledge. It represents the first noble effort to tell the African perspective of the European colonization of Africa

In 1953, when he began writing *Things Fall Apart*, Achebe had his objective clearly before him: "I was quite certain that I was going to try my hand at writing, and one of the things that set me thinking was Joyce Cary's novel, set in Nigeria, *Mister Johnson* which was praised so much, and it was clear to me that it was a most superficial picture of—not only of the country—but even of the Nigerian character, and so I thought if this was famous, then perhaps someone ought to try and look at this from the inside" (see Pieterse and Duerden, 1972). Achebe's impetus resulted in his writing a prodigious novel that he subdivided into two main novels—*Things Fall Apart* and *No Longer at Ease* (1960). He later developed a remnant of this original effort into yet another phenomenal novel, *Arrow of God* (1964). Although Achebe's five novels to date have enjoyed enormous success each in its own right, the special artistic features of *Things Fall Apart* mark it as his most seminal work.

Achebe's success in achieving his stated mission has made *Things Fall Apart* relevant to both African and Western audiences and a popular reference point for scholars and critics alike. In fact, *Things Fall Apart* was so totally different in craftsmanship from the known stereotypes of the Western novel that it forced a redefinition of the "English novel" as an entity different from the "novel in English." It also opened a plethora of critical debates on the definition of the "African novel" in particular and African literature in general. By forcing a comparison, *Things Fall Apart* called into question the message of African novels and novels about Africa that came before. It also revolutionized the art of the novel in Africa—especially in the domain of language usage and linguistic devices. Bruce King (1971) has summed up these distinguishing attributes quite succinctly:

> *Things Fall Apart* begins a tradition not only because its influence can be detected on subsequent Nigerian novelists . . . but also because it was the first solid achievement upon which others could build. Achebe was the first Nigerian writer to successfully transmute the conventions of the novel, a European art form, into African Literature. His craftsmanship can be seen in the way he creates a totally Nigerian texture for his fiction: Ibo idioms translated into English are used freely; European character study is subordinated to the portrayal of communal life; European economy of form is replaced by an aesthetic appropriate to the rythms [sic] of traditional tribal life. Achebe's themes reflect the cultural traits of the Ibo, the impact of European civilization upon traditional African society, and the role of tribal values in modern urban life.

Things Fall Apart is a story of the African colonial encounter with overzealous, egocentric European colonizers, set in a small Igbo village in Nigeria between 1895 and 1905. Today *Things Fall Apart* is the story of all colonial encounters the world over: Korea, India, the West Indies, the United States, Latin America, and many other regions.

No other novel conceived in Africa in the second half of the 20th century has traveled so fast and so appealingly to all corners of the globe. Initial critical reactions to it were not entirely palatable. Some European critics viewed it as nothing more than a transient sociological response to racism and colonialism by a reactionary ingrate who forgot so soon the source of his Western education, Western dress, and even the gift of a common language for the multilingual and multi-ethnic communities of his country. This view soon disappeared when several later critics could no longer deny the immensity of articulate literary qualities intrinsic to Achebe's novel. *Things Fall Apart* is no longer merely an African classic; it has become so universally relevant that today it is indeed a world classic.

ERNEST N. EMENYONU

See also Chinua Achebe

Further Reading

Achebe, Chinua, "The Novelist as Teacher," *New Statesman* (29 January 1965)

Achebe, Chinua, *Morning Yet on Creation Day,* London: Heinemann, and Garden City, New York: Anchor Press, 1975

Carroll, David, *Chinua Achebe,* New York: Twayne, 1970; 2nd edition, New York: St. Martin's Press, 1980; London: Macmillan, 1990

Emenyonu, Ernest, *The Rise of the Igbo Novel,* Oxford and New York: Oxford University Press, 1978

Killam, G.D., *The Novels of Chinua Achebe,* London: Heinemann, and New York: Africana, 1969; revised edition

as *The Writings of Chinua Achebe,* London: Heinemann, 1977

King, Bruce Alvin, editor, *Introduction to Nigerian Literature,* New York: Africana, and London: Evans Brothers, 1971

Lindfors, Bernth, editor, *Approaches to Teaching Achebe's "Things Fall Apart,"* New York: Modern Language Association of America, 1991

Lindfors, Bernth, and Catherine Lynette Innes, editors, *Critical Perspectives on Chinua Achebe,* Washington D.C.: Three Continents Press, 1978; London: Heinemann, 1979

Nnolim, Charles E., *Approaches to the African Novel: Essays in Analysis,* London: Saros International, 1992

Petersen, Kirsten Holst, and Anna Rutherford, *Chinua Achebe: A Celebration,* Oxford and Portsmouth, New Hampshire: Heinemann, 1991

Pieterse, Cosmo, and Dennis Duerden, editors, *African Writers Talking: A Collection of Radio Interviews,* London: Heinemann, and New York: Africana, 1972

Ravenscroft, Arthur, *Chinua Achebe,* Harlow: Longman, 1969; 2nd revised edition, 1977

Ugah, Ada, *In the Beginning: Chinua Achebe at Work,* Ibadan, Nigeria: Heinemann, 1990

Wren, Robert M., *Achebe's World: The Historical and Cultural Context of the Novels of Chinua Achebe,* Washington D.C.: Three Continents Press, 1980; Harlow: Longman, 1981

The Thousand and One Nights

Although *The Thousand and One Nights* (or *Arabian Nights*) is often cited as a work of Arabic literature, this is only partially true. The various Western texts that circulate under that name are only tenuously related to the medieval Arabic work from which they derive. *The Thousand and One Nights* was restructured and greatly expanded from 281 nights to 1001 during the 18th and 19th centuries by Europeans who added stories indiscriminately from a multitude of other sources. Indeed, perhaps no other single work of fiction contains elements drawn from so many different places and periods. Western redactors ultimately transformed it from a work that in Arabic had never been considered more than an entertaining collection of somewhat vulgar tales into a commodity marketed to Western audiences variously as a masterpiece of Arabic literature, an ethnographic guide to daily life in the Middle East, and even a classic work of Victorian erotica. However, most editions of *The Thousand and One Nights* are mostly fabulous forgeries that reflect Western fantasies about the exotic East more than they reflect traditional Arabic narratives or Islamic culture.

In the ninth century A.D., a work entitled *Hazār Afsān* (The Thousand Stories) was translated from Middle Persian (Pahlavi) into Arabic and renamed Ar. *Alf laylah wa-laylah* (*Thousand and One Nights*). It contained the famous frame-tale of Scheherazade, which has survived essentially unchanged. The frame-tale, however, was probably adapted from, or inspired by,

Indian models. The Persian tales it once contained have been lost or altered beyond recognition and replaced with tales from Arabic popular tradition. Most of the stories in the Arabic manuscripts depict Baghdad of the ninth and tenth centuries or Cairo of the 12th and 15th centuries. None of these Arabic manuscripts, which achieved only a modicum of popularity in the Middle East, contains more than 282 nights; most, in fact, contain only 200.

The astonishing impact of *The Thousand and One Nights* in Europe is due in great part to the work of the Frenchman Antoine Galland (1646–1715). Galland lived and traveled in the Middle East for nearly 15 years, during which time, despite being an avid bibliophile and collector, he never came in contact with *The Thousand and One Nights*. At home in France, having failed to procure a professorship in Arabic as he had hoped, he began to translate a manuscript of the *Voyages of Sindbad*. When he had nearly completed this project, Galland announced to his patron that he had discovered that these tales formed part of a larger collection called *The Thousand and One Nights*. It remains a mystery how Galland "discovered" this while residing in rural Normandy, since the two cycles had in fact never formed a single work.

Galland sent to Syria for a copy of *The Thousand and One Nights*. In his correspondence of 1701 Galland refers to a manuscript of five volumes, in 1702 a manuscript of four volumes, and after his death there were only three—another mystery. Galland began to publish his translation in 1704 and with each additional volume the stories grew more popular. Galland's translation follows the Arabic manuscript quite closely in parts, but he also inserted into the collection first the Sindbad cycle and then—yet another mystery—several "orphan" tales of unknown origin. His publisher later unscrupulously released a volume of tales from a different writer as part of *The Thousand and One Nights*. Eventually, Galland himself began to collect stories and publish them as new volumes. Some were stories he had heard at fashionable dinner parties from a visiting Syrian Maronite Christian named Hanna, including "Ali Baba" and "Aladdin," the two tales which have most come to symbolize *The Thousand and One Nights*. Of the 21 tale cycles in Galland's completed version, only nine were from the original Arabic manuscript. Having reached the number 1001, the Western version was complete.

Despite its mongrel lineage, most subsequent editions represent reworkings of the Galland text complete with the fraudulent tales. Only one English translation (Haddawy, 1990) reflects the text of a single authentic medieval Arabic manuscript.

The evolution of the tale did not stop there, however: Sir Richard Burton later released an additional 1001 "supplementary" nights; other collections such as *The Thousand and One Days, The Hundred and One Nights,* and so forth, continued to appear throughout the 19th century. *The Nights* became, in the words of British literary critic Leigh Hunt, "the most popular book in the world."

A handful of new translations from Arabic manuscripts were also completed in the 19th century. The British Arabist Edward Lane published a version couched in heavy, almost biblical, prose that was so thoroughly expurgated that it included no more than two-fifths of the Arabic text. The "translation" commonly referred to as the Richard Burton edition was in fact brazenly plagiarized almost entirely from an earlier translation by John Payne, then filled out with Burton's erotic and scatological commentary, thereby assuring its commercial success. The astonishing popularity of *The Nights* in the West eventually even led to printed editions in the Arab world that included the many tales (translated from European texts) that were never part of the original Arabic work in the first place.

The Nights appeared in France while the popularity of Charles Perrault's *Mother Goose Tales* (1697) and the rage for Madame D'Aulnoy's *contes de fées* were at their peak. The captivating tale of Scheherazade, the frame-tale device, and the exotic imagery of *The Nights* soon engendered a wave of imitations in a new, related genre, the Oriental tale. *The Nights* became the lens through which most Westerners perceived the Middle East; references to it permeate 19th-century travelers' accounts and journalism. Read by nearly every Western literary and political figure of the 18th and 19th centuries, it became a palette of devices and images for an astonishingly wide spectrum of Western writing. Authors as diverse as Voltaire, Samuel Johnson, Sir Walter Scott, William Beckford, Benjamin Disraeli, Washington Irving, Charles Dickens, Alexandre Dumas, Aleksandr Pushkin, Herman Melville, Edgar Allan Poe, Marcel Proust, Jorge Luis Borges, John Barth, Salman Rushdie, and many others have inscribed, directly or indirectly, the influence of *The Nights* in their works.

Although the popularity of *The Thousand and One Nights* is indisputable, its contribution to the development of the novel is a point of contention. Many of the most prominent elements in *The Nights* were already present in European literatures, particularly in the French literary fairy tale, such as the use of frame-tale devices, sumptuousness of detail, the "marvelous" as setting, and even the presence of a central female narrator, but *The Nights* seem to have given added impetus to all of these elements. In addition, *The Nights* provided an escape from the pseudo-classical models of Boileau, Pope, and Addison, and contributed to a growing appreciation of complex plots, leading one critic to note that the "*Arabian Nights* was the fairy godmother of the English novel" (see Conant, 1908).

DWIGHT REYNOLDS

Further Reading

Abdel-Halim, Mohamed, *Antoine Galland, sa vie et son oeuvre,* Paris: Nizet, 1964

Caracciolo, Peter L., editor, *The Arabian Nights in English Literature,* London: Macmillan, and New York: St. Martin's Press, 1988

Conant, Martha Pike, *The Oriental Tale in England in the Eighteenth Century,* New York: Columbia University Press, 1908; reprinted, New York: Octagon, and London: Cass, 1966

Gerhardt, Mia I., *The Art of Story-Telling: A Literary Study of the Thousand and One Nights,* Leiden: Brill, 1963

Hovannisian, Richard G., and Georges Sabagh, editors, *The Thousand and One Nights in Arabic Literature and Society,* Cambridge and New York: Cambridge University Press, 1997

Irwin, Robert, *The Arabian Nights: A Companion,* London: Allen Lane, 1994; New York: Penguin, 1995

Musawi, Muhsin Jasim, *Scheherazade in England: A Study of 19th-Century English Criticism of the Arabian Nights,* Washington, D.C.: Three Continents Press, 1981

Pinault, David, *Story-Telling Techniques in the Arabian Nights,* Leiden and New York: Brill, 1992

Three Kingdoms. *See* Six Classic Chinese Novels

Three Lives by Gertrude Stein

1909

Gertrude Stein's *Three Lives* is a stylistically remarkable example of early modernist writing. Consisting of three stories, "The Good Anna," "Melanctha," and "The Gentle Lena," the book is based on the model of Gustave Flaubert's *Trois Contes* (1877; *Three Tales*), but the sequence is closer to a novel than Flaubert's volume in that the stories act as oblique commentaries on each other. Stein reflects her position as an American drawn to European aesthetic models by, on the one hand, developing American naturalism and the psychological principles of her college professor William James and, on the other hand, inflecting American subject matter with Flaubertian irony and the painterly techniques of Paul Cézanne. Like Flaubert's tales, the apparent simplicity of the narratives disguises a complicated relationship between narrator, character, and reader.

Stein's three tales are marked by an unsettling narrative tone that is neither univocally judgmental nor critical, but is always shifting and radically uncertain. For example, "The Good Anna" is related in third person, but the narrator repeatedly uses phrases and offers perspectives that are characteristic of Anna's sensibility. In this way, Stein breaks away from the tenets of literary realism (in which the narrator and reader share an unproblematic sense of fictional "reality") and moves toward a position that exploits shifting perspectives, linguistic repetition, impressionistic features, and the use of free indirect speech later refined by James Joyce and Virginia Woolf. Stein did not fully develop her notion of "continuous present" until her voluminous work *The Making of Americans* (1925), but *Three Lives* is characterized by a narrative rhythm that derives from her use of phrases and paragraphs as basic structural units: the repetition and modulation of phrases lend the prose a fluidity that creates a retrospective dynamic at the same time as the narrative progresses. This fluid continuum of moments represents one of the most successful attempts to apply William James' description of "The Stream of Thought" (*The Principles of Psychology*, 1890) to literary prose.

If the theme and tone of *Three Lives* is reminiscent of Flaubert, then Stein's depiction of what Edith Wharton in her 1922 introduction to *Ethan Frome* calls "the deep rooted reticence and inarticulateness of the people" is a development of the American naturalism of Theodore Dreiser and Frank Norris. All three tales introduce characters as identifiable types—the well-meaning but domineering Anna, the uneducated but sensitive Melanctha, and the gentle yet feebleminded Lena—who are incapable of introspection. Because none of these characters undergoes much psychological development, the tales are little more than interesting explorations of the characteristics described in the titles. For example, the initially casual use of the epithet *good* to describe Anna, which defines and determines her character as a morally upright and industrious German serving-woman, is destabilized by its continuous use in different contexts: the good Anna does chores for other people's "own good" (defined by her moral standards), she cannot tolerate any opposition to her authority, and she contrasts her ideal of goodness with what she considers to be bad (Mrs. Lehntman's affair) or evil (the corrupting influence of the doctor). Moreover, Anna's rigid polarities—she divides the world into categories of good and bad, thin and fat—actually

transform *her* into a rigid type: "already the temper and the humor showed sharply in her clean blue eyes, and the thinning was begun about the lower jaw, that was so often strained with the upward pressure of resolve." Stein's use of connotation is analogous to the manner in which Flaubert exploits the negative implications of simple in "Un coeur simple" ("A Simple Heart," the first story in *Trois Contes*), but it becomes a dominant motif in *Three Lives,* which serves to undermine bourgeois notions of morality and to question habitual ways of seeing the world. Indeed, the impression of flux and change created by the use of narrative fluidity and shifting point of view acts as a countercheck to the sense of stasis and paralysis that grips all three characters.

As a collection, *Three Lives* undermines two other literary conventions. First, the narrators of the tales do not maintain the omniscient presence of the 19th-century realist narrator; as Marianne DeKoven (1983) discerns, at times Stein's narrators appear knowing and insightful and at other times "childish, whimsical, consciously naïve." For example, the beginning of "The Gentle Lena" reads like a fairy story: "Lena was patient, gentle, sweet and german. She had been a servant for four years and had liked it very well." Within a few lines the prose style becomes much more complex and the narrator more insightful: Lena "would call and wait a long time and then call again, always even, gentle, patient, while the young ones fell back often into that precious, tense, last bit of sleeping that gives a strength of joyous vigor in the young, over them that have come to the readiness of middle age, in their awakening." By varying the relative knowledge possessed by the narrators, Stein emphasizes the unstable boundaries between innocence and experience, ignorance and wisdom. Second, the tales reverse the upward and prospective trajectory of the realistic novel by closing with the deaths of the three women while in the hospital. "The Good Anna" and "The Gentle Lena" both begin in serenity and chart the decline in prospects of the two women. Similarly, although the opening scene of "Melanctha" depicts the death of Rose Johnson's baby, Melanctha is described as "patient, submissive, soothing and untiring," in stark contrast to Rose's "sullen, childish, cowardly" behavior and the negligence that leads to her baby's death. Anna and Lena die because their virtues—goodness and gentleness—stimulate their downfall, and Melanctha seeks "rest and quiet" but only gets herself into "trouble" with a series of men, including Rose Johnson's husband. Although Stein brutally exposes the foibles of the women, she actually seems less critical of her characters and more interested in exploring the social, cultural, and linguistic forces that determine them both as particular racial types (Anna and Lena are German and Melanctha is "a real black negress") and as subservient women.

MARTIN HALLIWELL

See also Gertrude Stein

Further Reading

Berry, Ellen E., *Curved Thought and Textual Wandering: Gertrude Stein's Postmodernism,* Ann Arbor: University of Michigan Press, 1992

Copeland, Carolyn Faunce, *Language & Time & Gertrude Stein,* Iowa City: University of Iowa Press, 1975

DeKoven, Marianne, *A Different Language: Gertrude Stein's Experimental Writing,* Madison: University of Wisconsin Press, 1983

Dubnick, Randa, *The Structure of Obscurity: Gertrude Stein, Language, and Cubism,* Urbana: University of Illinois Press, 1984

Glazener, Nancy, "Dialogic Subversion: Bakhtin, the Novel, and Gertrude Stein," in *Bakhtin and Cultural Theory,* edited by Ken Hirschkop, Manchester: Manchester University Press, and New York: St. Martin's Press, 1989

Neuman, Shirley, and Ira B. Nadel, *Gertrude Stein and the Making of Literature,* London: Macmillan, and Boston: Northeastern University Press, 1988

Pizer, Donald, *American Expatriate Writing and the Paris Moment: Modernism and Place,* Baton Rouge: Louisiana State University Press, 1996

Steiner, Wendy, *Exact Resemblance to Exact Resemblance: The Literary Portraiture of Gertrude Stein,* New Haven, Connecticut: Yale University Press, 1978

Walker, Jayne L., *The Making of a Modernist: Gertrude Stein from "Three Lives" to "Tender Buttons,"* Amherst: University of Massachusetts Press, 1984

Weinstein, Norman, *Gertrude Stein and the Literature of Modern Consciousness,* New York: Ungar, 1970

Through the Looking Glass. *See* Alice's Adventures in Wonderland

Tikhii Don. *See* Quiet Flows the Don

Time in the Novel

Time, in the ordinary, commonsense meaning of the term for post-Enlightenment European culture, is practically synonymous with "the novel." What is new about the 19th-century novel form is that it supplies a common temporal denominator for the human world, treating time as a neutral, objective measurement. This treatment of time is a crucial aspect of 19th-century realism and reflects its preference for inscribing the value of neutrality at the heart of narrative method.

The familiar exemplars of this high era of the novel form appear mainly in the 19th century across European culture in such writers as Sir Walter Scott, Stendhal, Anthony Trollope, George Eliot, Lev Tolstoi, Honoré de Balzac, George Gissing, Henry James, and, at the turn of the 20th century, even in writers like Dorothy Richardson, James Joyce, and Virginia Woolf. Among these, English novelists like Eliot, Trollope, and Woolf especially acknowledge their debt to Walter Scott, whose astonishing originality provided for a revolutionary Europe, a new form that left behind once and for all the traditions of epic and satire for the sake of a new historicism.

Scott provided for narrative, from his first novel onward, the temporal counterpart of single-point perspective: an apparently neutral realism that derives from an objective, universally applicable system of coordinates of time and consciousness. Conven-tionally we call this "history," but that term masks the complex discursive gesture implied by the construction of temporal neutrality. *Waverley; or, 'Tis Sixty Years Since* (1814) presents that construction of time in which the key gesture of the text links past and present. Particular events and characters of the novel act primarily as carriers for the communication about the mutual relevance between past and present, here and there, us and them. Nothing like it exists in Daniel Defoe, Samuel Richardson, Laurence Sterne, Henry Fielding, or Jane Austen. For that matter, nothing like it exists in W.M. Thackeray or the Brontës. But by the middle of the 19th century, there is nothing else.

To describe this familiar form may seem like belaboring the obvious, especially because it has become the form of most second-rank fiction in the 20th century—that is, fiction that aims to show how some particular problem like race or gender prejudice has a bearing on everyone by incorporating it into a universalizing medium. But belaboring the obvious becomes necessary precisely because its very popularity obscures the relative uniqueness of the realist novel form in general. Time in the historical novel differs radically from time in preceding and subsequent narrative conventions and traditions.

Historical time is the time in which, because it is neutral, identities emerge serially, not as end results that leave their pasts behind but as cumulative forms-in-process. George Eliot, Anthony Trollope, and Virginia Woolf often and explicitly emphasize this condition. Trollope's Plantagenet Palliser, for example, "is" at the end of several very long and delightful books a liberal aristocrat, with all the contradictions and functional importance that has. But his identity is not a product at the end of a series of events; it exists distributed in the series itself. And that series in turn, and the characters entwined with it, can be perceived as emergent forms, both identifiable and capable of change, only because they can be measured according to a single temporal system that the novel maintains as a crucial common denominator: a single, neutral time that contains the potentiality for mutual informativeness that makes the historical novel so impressive and so useful a form for social messages.

What was "novel" about this form was not primarily, as has often been claimed, new kinds of content and readership: for example, a new interest in ordinary life, a newly powerful middle class, a new emphasis on the domestic order of things as distinct from the public, a new role for women as readers and writers, and a new concern for privacy. Certainly such things distinguish the European novel from epic traditions of narrative from Homer to Milton. But subject matter alone does not make an art form, as can be seen from the range of material treated by realist painters, from the Virgins of Piero della Francesca to the horses of George Stubbs. What is "novel" about the narrative form that Walter Scott disseminated in Europe is its commitment to a common denominator in time. This time-coordination, which has often been associated with the development of railroads, actually preceded this new narrative and served the far more powerful end of literally objectifying the world, of unifying the social arena in an era when democratic politics was being renewed on a massive scale across Europe. The realist and historical novel became an experimental laboratory for those political and social changes.

Prior to the early 19th century, the familiar forms of narrative wander in varying degrees quite far from the normative venture of Scott's historicism. Common denominator time is not a primary issue in the epistolary novel or in satire. In Defoe and Richardson, for example, episodic form, lack of development, and circularities favoring moral messages about providence work away from the temporal neutrality and objectivity that Scott and his heirs were concerned to establish. The central characters of *Robinson Crusoe* (1719) and *Clarissa; or, The History of a Young Lady* (1747–48) quite conspicuously resist the change that time can bring. For very different reasons, Defoe and Richardson reinscribe the value of sameness and depreciate the value of travel and capitalization, both values of the historical convention. Defoe's novel is one long joke at the expense of such values, and Richardson's epistolary form renders impossible the kind of process-management that he associates with "encroaching" males like the evil Lovelace and the odious Solmes.

Henry Fielding presents a similar case, but from a tradition with a richer literary past, the tradition of Miguel de Cervantes. Fielding's *Tom Jones* (1749), for example, renders irrelevant the problem of keeping time and making links. For reasons that have to do with traditions of satiric undercut and dramatic reversal, the key revelations occur in time to prevent comedy from turning to tragedy at the end of this big book. But the interest of the text is episodic and its format ultimately epic, consisting of six volumes, two at each of three locations, and each volume subdivided in thirds. The text has the orderliness and symmetry of the epic, in its classical and mock-epic guises. (The work of Richardson, Defoe, and Fielding is characterized by a new attention to the quotidian, described so well by Ian Watt in *The Rise of the Novel*. This attention to the trivia of everyday life marks a new departure from the mythologized and idealized forms of an earlier and epic tradition, and in this sense the 18th-century novel pulls away from the heroic tradition and toward historical narrative. But such quotidian detail still supports the providential explanation of sequence and outcome.)

The resistance to realism and to historicism in Homer or Cervantes stems from their preoccupation with timeless heroic values in which the keynotes are repetition and exhaustive expression. No history in the modern sense can be possible in Homer's world, where the population consists of heroes and gods and where every life is extraordinary and preordained by the Erynnes or Furies or Spinners weaving all the strands of fate. Time is not the neutral medium of history, but instead the period allotted to fulfill a preordained plan. Hector can only be fully Hector; he cannot develop lateral interests like a soap-opera hero, or even like Plantagenet Palliser. In the Homeric world, for a hero to slip out of his original shape into something else is to betray destiny. It is unthinkable.

Cervantes' mock-epic *Don Quixote* (1605–15), on the other hand, does present the modern idea of history in the margins of the heroic enterprise, where it acts as a perpetual companion and undercutting agent in the person of Sancho Panza. While the Knight of the Sad Countenance attempts to live up to various heroic precedents that he knows largely from romances, Sancho Panza is left to deal with the quotidian problems of food, shelter, and safety in travel. Don Quixote's interpretations belong to one code, Sancho Panza's to quite another, and the disparity between them not only mocks the epic form and its cosmology, but also sets up an alternative parodic medium in which one plot comments on the other.

From this internal play among elements much of the best subsequent narrative is made. It has been argued in fact that the historicist and realist novel of the 19th century is the anomaly that proves the parodic rule in the rest of what is called "the novel." Certainly the 18th-century novel in English emphasizes the quixotic over the historical. Laurence Sterne's novels, while they may appear to be unlike *Tom Jones* or *Clarissa,* actually consist of the same episodic and quixotic element supported on conventional epic plots. Development is incidental and arbitrary, even random. Richardson and Sterne may internalize the action of their novels, but they share the same ahistorical suppositions about the nature of identity and sequence that characterized the era of timeless values.

Nineteenth-century writers explore historical values and their democratic social and political implications in many variations, but always with a mediating narrative voice that is altogether new and that enables the neutralization of temporality. The historical or realist novel neutralizes time and makes it into a universal common denominator by the simple, profoundly powerful expedient of synchronizing all possible moments into a common system. It is the *system* that speaks in realist (historical) time, just as it is the system that speaks in realist painting: the assertion that every perspective, every act, every thought, every omission must have general systemic value and import. The objects and subjects of realism and history exist not because they are there, but because they specify a system that is affirmed by a massive cultural act of faith.

After the disjunctive temporality of 18th-century epistolary, satiric, and journalistic narrative, the neutral homogeneous time of the 19th-century realist and historical narrative calls attention to the presence of the mediating system. But it is important to recognize that it is a perspective *system*, and not just a singular narrative perspective, that is at stake. To personalize this added narrative value as "the narrator," reliable or otherwise, is to miss the most powerful inscription of the narrative medium. The added narrative value, the effect that neutralizes time and makes "history" and modern selfhood fully possible, is systemic and depends upon certain values and rules that are discursive and not individual at all. To insist on discussing "the narrator," as Jonathan Culler long ago noted, is to naturalize what is artificial and to miss the shift in discursive formation. What is at stake in narrative that purports to be history—that is, in the narrative largely written after Walter Scott—is nothing less than the affirmation of the belief in the existence of "the individual" and of "society" as an entity. "In" time, emergent identity can develop so as to support constructions of "individual" and "society" that were relatively new to Europe and that were being explored both in narrative and "on the ground" in one revolution after another from 1848 to the Paris Commune. Narrative action, aligned with other cultural manifestations, confirms the existence of a single system of measurement common to all, based on a common denominator time.

By the end of World War II, however, this neutrality had come into serious question across a range of cultural practices: in physics, where time as the constant measure gives way to the speed of light after 1905; in various political conflicts that put the lie to universal shared values; in narrative, where the most original 20th-century novelists in all languages (Franz Kafka, James Joyce, Samuel Beckett, Marguerite Duras, Alain Robbe-Grillet, Julio Cortázar, Gabriel García Márquez) turn away from history and its neutralities and toward a newly poetic form, a newly inflected play of elements. But it is not a play "in" time. In fact, from a postmodern perspective, play constitutes its own time and is thus at odds with the sweeping objectivity of historical conventions. Where the novel of high modernity, especially in the 19th and early 20th centuries, emphasized the mediated unity of a single system of temporal coordinates, postmodern novels emphasize the unmediatable plurality of systems and the variety of times. Such writing moves beyond *relativism* to *relativity,* beyond a plurality that can be mediated by a single system of temporal or spatial coordinates to a plurality that is itself systemic and based in fundamentally irreducible languages or discourses. This move closes some opportunities and opens others, most tellingly in its reconstruction of temporality. Neutrality is no longer possible; no single system of coordinates could apply.

Such narrative has flourished in Latin languages, especially French (Raymond Queneau, Robbe-Grillet, Duras, Hélène Cixous) and Spanish (Jorge Luis Borges, Cortázar, José Donoso, García Márquez). And many of the issues about identity and sequence, and about time generally, issues that used to be the province of literary narrative, have become the province of cinema. So, for instance, some of the most innovative and splendid examples of postmodern narrative time may be found in the joint productions between the director Alain Resnais and two of the most important postwar French writers, Alain Robbe-Grillet and Marguerite Duras (e.g., *Last Year at Marienbad* [1961] and *Hiroshima Mon Amour* [1960]). In English, the most distinguished postmodern writer and expert on time is Vladimir Nabokov, by far the most distinguished writer of English (perhaps also Russian) of his generation. All postmodern writers of narrative accomplish in their different ways the same dismantling of time in its humanist phase: historical and neutral time, the homogeneous, unproblematic medium that provided the common denominator for so many personal and political, not to mention scientific, measurements. To read Nabokov, for example, is to experience a new kind of time, one in which finitude is a blessing, not a disaster, but one which, by comparison with either the histories of the 19th century or the providential novels of the 18th, requires very different acts of attention.

Elizabeth Deeds Ermarth

See also Historical Novel; Historical Writing and the Novel; Narrative Theory; Narratology; Plot; Postmodernism; Realism; Space; Tense in Narrative

Further Reading

Benjamin, Walter, "Theses on the Philosophy of History," in *Illuminations,* translated by Harry Zohn, New York: Schocken Books, 1969

Burke, Peter, *The Renaissance Sense of the Past,* London: Arnold, and New York: St. Martin's Press, 1969

Butterfield, Herbert, *The Whig Interpretation of History,* London: G. Bell, 1931; New York: Scribner, 1951

Casparis, Christian Paul, *Tense Without Time: The Present Tense in Narration,* Bern: Francke, 1975

Davies, P.C.W., *About Time: Einstein's Unfinished Revolution,* New York: Simon and Schuster, and London: Penguin, 1995

Ermarth, Elizabeth Deeds, "Ph(r)ase Time: Chaos Theory and Postmodern Reports on Knowledge," *Social Time* 4:1 (February 1995)

Ermarth, Elizabeth Deeds, *Realism and Consensus in the English Novel,* Princeton, New Jersey: Princeton University Press, 1983; new edition, with subtitle *The Construction of Time in Narrative,* Edinburgh: Edinburgh University Press, 1998

Ermarth, Elizabeth Deeds, *Sequel to History: Postmodernism and the Crisis of Representational Time,* Princeton, New Jersey: Princeton University Press, 1992

Forman, Frieda, editor, with Caoran Sowton, *Taking Our Time: Feminist Perspectives on Temporality,* Oxford and New York: Pergamon Press, 1989

Foucault, Michel, *Les Mots et les choses: Une Archéologie des sciences humaines,* Paris: Gallimard, 1966; as *The Order of Things: An Archaeology of the Human Sciences,* New York: Pantheon, and London: Tavistock, 1970

Gould, Stephen Jay, *Wonderful Life: The Burgess Shale and the Nature of History,* New York: Norton, and London: Hutchinson Radius, 1989

Huppert, George, *The Idea of Perfect History: Historical Erudition and Historical Philosophy in Renaissance France,* Urbana: University of Illinois Press, 1970

Lloyd, Genevieve, *Being in Time: Selves and Narrators in*

Philosophy and Literature, London and New York: Routledge, 1993

Löwith, Karl, *Meaning in History: The Theological Implications of the Philosophy of History,* Chicago: University of Chicago Press, 1949

Meyerhoff, Hans, *Time in Literature,* Berkeley: University of California Press, 1955

Poulet, Georges, *Études Sur le temps humain,* Edinburgh: Edinburgh University Press, 1949; as *Studies in Human Time,* Baltimore: Johns Hopkins University Press, 1956

Tin Drum. *See* Danzig Trilogy

The Tin Flute by Gabrielle Roy

Bonheur d'occasion 1945

The first novel by Canadian Gabrielle Roy was an immediate success. It launched Roy's career as a writer of international stature and garnered a number of important awards in North America and Europe. The original French version, entitled *Bonheur d'occasion,* appeared in Montreal in two volumes and was awarded the Richelieu medal of the Académie canadienne-française. Published in Paris in 1946, it was the first Canadian work to win a major literary prize in France, the Prix Fémina. Hanna Josephson's English translation, *The Tin Flute,* was named Book of the Month for May 1947 by the Literary Guild of America, and the movie rights were purchased in June 1947 by the Hollywood studio Universal Pictures for US$75,000. In Canada, *The Tin Flute* won the Governor General's Award and the Royal Academy's Lorne Pierce Medal, earning for its author the distinction of being the first woman elected to the Royal Society of Canada.

The Tin Flute played an important role in the development of the Quebec novel in several respects. As the first major urban novel, it signaled the end of the rural novel idealizing the land ("roman du terroir") and introduced social realism. As an indictment of the capitalist system, it can further be seen as the progenitor of the protest literature that swept Quebec in the 1960s during the Quiet Revolution. *The Tin Flute* also contributed to the development of the Quebec novel in terms of its narrative techniques. Finally, modern feminist readings of the novel have demonstrated Roy's subversion of the traditional role of women in contemporary Quebec society, which was dominated by the patriarchal structures of state and church.

The Tin Flute moved the Quebec novel away from the cult of traditional values and turned it toward social realism. Distancing itself from the prevalent ideology of conservatism represented by the novel of rural life such as Ringuet's *Trente arpents* (1938; *Thirty Acres*) and the historical novels of Léo-Paul Desrosiers, Roy's work deals with the social and economic problems of contemporary urban life. The novel is rooted in Saint-Henri, a working-class area in southwest Montreal, where Roy settled in 1939 on her return to Canada after a two-year sojourn in France and England. The stories and articles she wrote as a journalist at that time (in particular, a series of four articles entitled "Tout Montréal") were instrumental in shaping her powers of observation and the documentary style that inform her novel's urban social realism.

Taking place from February to June 1940, *The Tin Flute* chronicles the end of the Depression and the beginning of World War II, which brings a measure of prosperity to this impoverished neighborhood. The novel follows the fortunes of the Lacasse family, focusing on daughter Florentine's attempts to escape her family's poverty and to find love and security. Florentine's lover, the ambitious young engineer Jean Lévesque, finds unprecedented opportunities for work and advancement. For Florentine's father, Azarius, there is the chance of employment with regular army pay to support his wife Rose-Anna and their large family. Brother Eugène also enlists, while another brother, Philippe, finds work in a munitions factory. War is thus shown ironically as the salvation of the socially disadvantaged and economically deprived. Roy's social protest is apparent in the depiction of the humiliation and powerlessness of the French-Canadian workers of Saint-Henri in the face of the wealthy anglophone owners.

As Monique Lafortune points out in *Le roman québecois* (1985), Roy's development of two simultaneous actions (the Lacasse family's excursion to the country and Jean and Florentine's sexual encounter) makes *The Tin Flute* one of the first Quebec novels to depart from strictly linear narration. Another innovation is the writer's use of a variety of levels and registers of speech, including the "joual" of the inhabitants of Saint-Henri, a popular form of Quebec speech later used by Jacques Godbout and playwright Michel Tremblay. Despite the traditional third-person narrative, the text interweaves so many voices it effectively becomes a polyvocal novel. The representation of speech is in fact a key element in Roy's much-acclaimed talent for characterization.

Recently, critical attention has focused on the female characters, Rose-Anna and Florentine, as well as their relationship. A kind of Mother Courage, mainstay of her family, Rose-Anna accepts her role as the quintessential Quebec wife and mother with love and fortitude. However, Roy deconstructs that image by demonstrating that Rose-Anna's personal aspirations are sacrificed to her family's needs. Florentine's reluctance to follow in her mother's footsteps and sister Yvonne's decision to become a nun confirm that Roy does not subscribe to the view of love and marriage as fulfilling roles for women. Indeed, as the family disperses and disintegrates, the writer subtly but unmistakably shows the unenviable lot of women in Quebec society.

Since its publication in 1945, *The Tin Flute* has been translated into nine languages and continues to stimulate critical attention. Roy went on to write more than a dozen novels and collections of short stories, including three books for children, a collection of essays, and her autobiography, *La détresse et l'enchantement* (*Enchantment and Sorrow*), published posthumously in 1984. Although she won many more prizes and awards, including both the Medal of the Arts Council of Canada and Quebec's Prix David for lifetime achievements, none of her subsequent works had such a significant impact on her own career or on the development of the Quebec novel as *The Tin Flute*. Ushering in the modernist era, the work added a new dimension to Quebec literature.

CAROL J. HARVEY

See also Gabrielle Roy

Further Reading

Babby, Ellen, *The Play of Language and Spectacle: A Structural Reading of Selected Texts by Gabrielle Roy,* Toronto: ECW Press, 1985

Lafortune, Monique, *Le roman québecois: Reflet d'une société,* Montreal: Mondia, 1985

Lewis, Paula Gilbert, *Traditionalism, Nationalism and Feminism: Women Writers of Quebec,* Westport, Connecticut: Greenwood Press, 1985

Marcotte, Gilles, "*Bonheur d'occasion* et le 'grand réalisme'," *Voix et images* 14:3 (Spring 1989)

Romney, Claude, and Estelle Dansereau, *Portes de communications: Études discursives et stylistiques de l'oeuvre de Gabrielle Roy,* Quebec: Les Presses de l'Université Laval, 1995

Shek, Ben-Zion, *Social Realism in the French-Canadian Novel,* Montreal: Harvest House, 1976

Shek, Ben-Zion, *French-Canadian and Quebecois Novels,* Toronto and New York: Oxford University Press, 1991

Smart, Patricia, *Writing in the Father's House: The Emergence of the Feminine in the Quebec Literary Tradition,* Toronto: University of Toronto Press, 1991

Stépan, Andrée, "La femme et la guerre dans *Bonheur d'occasion* de Gabrielle Roy," *Gabrielle Roy: Voies nouvelles, Cahiers franco-canadiens de l'Ouest* 3:1 (Spring 1991)

Whitfield, Agnès, "Gabrielle Roy as Feminist: Re-Reading the Critical Myths," *Canadian Literature* 126 (1990)

To the Lighthouse by Virginia Woolf

1927

Virginia Woolf wrote *To the Lighthouse* when she was at the height of her career. The success of *Mrs. Dalloway* (1925), which brought her recognition as an important avant-garde writer, gave her the confidence to experiment further with her newfound techniques, the result of which was the daring design of *To the Lighthouse*. Woolf determined to write a book about her childhood and family, but, as she noted in her diary, she did not want it to be sentimental, and she did want it to contain greater depth, which she achieved through creating multiple viewpoints. The central and structuring image of the novel, however, is the figure of Mrs. Ramsay, who is based on Woolf's mother.

The novel has a tripartite structure. Parts 1 ("The Window") and 3 ("The Lighthouse") with their time scheme of a few hours are separated by Part 2 ("Time Passes"), which covers a ten-year period. The technical difficulty that Virginia Woolf confronted here was how to make a satisfying whole out of a narrative that she had deliberately broken at its center. She employed various obvious devices to accomplish this, such as the structuring theme of the journey, with its symbolic implications: the novel begins with the Ramsays' little son James desiring to row out to the lighthouse, and ends with the completed journey to it. In Part 1 Lily Briscoe, an artist, is absorbed by her painting, which she is unable to finish: it is completed at the end of the novel just as Mr. Ramsay with James reaches the lighthouse rock. The disrupted narrative is brought to a satisfying closure at all levels, and the whole is controlled literally by the sea and the dominant presence of the lighthouse, and also by the symbolic meaning of both. Less obvious, however, is the symbolic significance of the break itself in the theme of the novel's structural meaning. On one level, the work as a whole reflects the discontinuity of English life brought about by World War I, the shift from late Victorian/Edwardian security to the 1920s world of change and loss.

Part 1 presents the idyllic aura of Victorian family life. The novel recalls the author's own summer holidays spent at St. Ives in Cornwall and evokes the security of childhood, with her mother at the center of her world. Virginia Woolf's deeply felt affection for her characters, together with the idyllic life she has created for them—"The house seemed full of children sleeping and Mrs. Ramsay listening; of shaded lights and regular breathing"—makes *To the Lighthouse* among the most appealing of all her novels. "The Window" section is shot through with images of light, such as the lighthouse beam with which Mrs. Ramsay identifies herself, or the lighting of the candles at the dinner party that draws everyone closer together. The culmination of the first part of the novel is the dinner party. Mrs. Ramsay sees her task as a harmonizing one, and she endeavors to draw each character out of his or her isolation at the table. Mrs. Ramsay creates out of life the kind of wholeness that Lily Briscoe does vicariously in her painting. Part 2 is about the absence of all that was gloriously present in Part 1. It is about public and private disaster.

The first part of *To the Lighthouse* is a close-up of life, a few hours in the life of a specific family. The second part places the family in the long continuum of time. Beginning with the absence of all light in the "downpouring of immense darkness," Virginia Woolf opens the dense poetic abstract narrative in which she explores imagistically the nature of cosmic chaos and national disaster in which the death of Mrs. Ramsay is revealed in a parenthesis and the death of Andrew Ramsay in the war and of Prue Ramsay in childbirth are merely referred to. Her theme of destruction and restoration is personified in the deterioration of the house that, after reaching the precarious moment of almost complete disintegration, is lovingly restored by the hard work of Mrs. McNab. In Part 3 the world of "The Window" is revisited mentally; the past is finally understood and can be relinquished. Ghosts are laid to rest and journeys are completed.

Lily Briscoe's role in the novel is significant for the way in which her new kind of painting, not a representational work but one in which reality is presented structurally, reflects what Virginia Woolf was herself attempting to do through language in her novel. As Lily explains to William Bankes, her picture is a tribute to Mrs. Ramsay through its "relations of masses, of light and shadows." Here Lily is expressing the ideas of the Blooms-bury painters and art theorists Clive Bell and Roger Fry. Virginia Woolf has, in other words, positioned in this novel a clear articulation of Bloomsbury aesthetics, of the tenets of her own fictional manifesto in particular, and also of modernist fiction in general.

STELLA McNICHOL

See also Virginia Woolf

Further Reading

Abel, Elizabeth, *Virginia Woolf and the Fictions of Psychoanalysis*, Chicago: University of Chicago Press, 1989

Bennett, Joan, *Virginia Woolf: Her Art as a Novelist,* Cambridge: Cambridge University Press, and New York: Harcourt Brace, 1945

Brower, Reuben Arthur, *The Fields of Light: An Experiment in Critical Reading,* New York: Oxford University Press, 1951

Fleishman, Avrom, *Virginia Woolf, A Critical Reading,* Baltimore: Johns Hopkins University Press, 1975

Laurence, Patricia Ondek, *The Reading of Silence: Virginia Woolf in the English Tradition*, Stanford, California: Stanford University Press, 1991

Leaska, Mitchell A., *Virginia Woolf's Lighthouse: A Study in Critical Method,* London: Hogarth Press, and New York: Columbia University Press, 1970

Marcus, Jane, editor, *New Feminist Essays on Virginia Woolf,* London: Macmillan, and Lincoln: University of Nebraska Press, 1981

McLaurin, Allen, *Virginia Woolf: The Echoes Enslaved,* Cambridge: Cambridge University Press, 1973

McNichol, Stella, *Virginia Woolf and the Poetry of Fiction,* London and New York: Routledge, 1990

Mepham, John, *Virginia Woolf: A Literary Life,* London: Macmillan, and New York: St. Martin's Press, 1991

Richter, Harvena, *Virginia Woolf: The Inward Voyage,* Princeton, New Jersey: Princeton University Press, 1970

Tod des Vergil. *See* Death of Virgil

Lev Tolstoi 1828–1910

Russian

Lev Tolstoi is the author of *Voina i mir* (1863–69; *War and Peace*) and *Anna Karenina* (1875–77) and a host of short stories, plays, short novels, essays, religious writings, and letters, as well as a late third novel, *Voskresenie* (1899; *Resurrection*). He wrote in an age when critics were polarized by political and social questions, approving or disapproving of a work based partly on the attitudes it expressed. Situating himself in that context, Tolstoi wrote in a letter to a fellow writer, "The goals of art are incommensurate (as mathematicians say) with social goals. The goal of the artist is not to solve a question irrefutably, but to force people to love life in all its innumerable, inexhaustible manifestations." In spite of this apolitical stance, Tolstoi's novels proved more acceptable to conservative than to liberal or radical critics, although in his profound examination of human behavior and institutions he was as radical as any thinker in his milieu.

All of Tolstoi's work is characterized by lambent style, careful construction, deft characterization, and deep insight into human nature. He saw each of his works as having a central core of linked ideas that structures its apparent shapelessness. In 1876, he wrote to a friend, "every idea expressed by itself in words loses its meaning, becomes terribly debased when it is taken alone, out of the linking in which it is found." He added that the underlying connections could be expressed only indirectly, "with words describing images, actions, situations." Recreating the period of the Napoleonic invasion of Russia in his masterpiece *War and Peace*, he explores myriad related ideas, including ideas about the cause of war, the meaning of life, the significance of death, the meaning of marriage and family, the links between nature and human life, and a host of other ideas. The work is so vast and so complex that it breaks the bounds of what one might conventionally call a novel. Indeed, the Russians call it a "novel-epic."

Even though the scope of *Anna Karenina* is narrower, concentrating on an adulterous affair in Tolstoi's own times, it is capacious enough for comments on many social and philosophical ideas. It, too, is unconventional in construction, containing two stories that alternate throughout the book. Tolstoi said that he took pride in the architecture of *Anna Karenina*. "The vaults are thrown up in such a way that one cannot notice where the link is. . . . The unity in the structure is created not by action and not by relationships between the characters, but by an inner continuity."

Although Tolstoi stressed the central complex of ideas behind his work, much of his claim to literary preeminence derives from his ability to create living characters, like Natasha and Andrei in *War and Peace* or Stiva and Dolly in *Anna Karenina*. He does not create them through extensive physical description but by focusing on significant detail, such as the short downy upper lip of Andrei's wife Lise. Nor does he give extensive biographical information, although he does show traits shared by relatives, such as the amoral beauty of Helene and Anatol in *War and Peace* or the easy charm of Stiva and Anna in *Anna Karenina*. Instead he brings them alive on the page in scene after scene, talking and acting and thinking to themselves, revealing and endearing themselves to us as equals, fallible and fully human. His characters are so alive that we can accept Anna's repentance when she lies near death in childbirth and understand her change of mind when she wants to be reunited with Vronsky. Tolstoi even manages to penetrate the minds of animals, making us know how horses and dogs must feel. One aspect of Tolstoi's gift is his acute observation: no detail is too small to escape his attention, and each is telling and carefully chosen. Another aspect is his unflinching willingness to examine himself honestly and reveal the human traits we all share but prefer to conceal. He is particularly good at showing how people may act according to social convention, even while they disagree with it.

Tolstoi is also known for the extraordinary simplicity of his style. He wrote in very short chapters grouped into larger segments, which in turn move between various sets of characters or locations in both novels. *Anna Karenina* is shorter and less complex than *War and Peace*, under the influence of Tolstoi's study

of ancient Greek and the works of Aleksandr Pushkin. The apparently effortless grace of the resulting novel is the result of endless editing, of "taking the veils off" the object until it stands revealed in its purity.

Tolstoi's art stands at the summit of Russian realism. His creation of an illusion of reality through the use of typical events and characters set against a carefully described social background is characteristic, as is his use of an omniscient narrator. The introduction of contemporary social issues in *Anna Karenina* is also typical of Russian realism. Even so, *War and Peace* diverges from realist conventions in significant ways, particularly in being set a half century in the past. Tolstoy also stretches realist conventions through his interpolation of philosophical commentary into *War and Peace*, devoting whole chapters to his ideas on history and determinism. Although *War and Peace* takes liberties with realism, these freedoms do not undermine the realist illusion or the underlying tenets of the realist novel.

Anna Karenina, however, also experiments with some literary practices outside realism. For example, this novel makes more extensive use of symbols and meaningful dreams, although with such subtlety that much of it went unnoticed by critics until well into the 20th century. Tolstoi also experimented with a device known as "ostranenie" or "making strange." In the best-known example, Tolstoi renders an opera performance on stage as it really is, rather than by the impression it conveys, thus forcing us to look at the action with fresh eyes. A few lines will show how he does this: "One very fat girl in a white silk dress sat apart on a low bench to which a piece of green cardboard was glued. They all sang something. When they had finished their song the girl in white went up to the prompter's box." This is realism, but a realism of a new order. The effect is to show the unnaturalness of the action on stage (Tolstoi despised anything unnatural in art), all glittery show and no actual substance. The reader is meant to see that beautiful superficial Helene sitting in the audience is just the same as the action on stage, all glitter and no substance.

Tolstoi's artistry has never been in doubt, and today his ideas as expressed in the novels are receiving more respect than they have in the past. His views on war, on fatalism, on the natural life, on religion, on feminism, and other topics are the subjects of new study. Yet his third novel, *Resurrection*, which is heavier on ideas and lighter on artistry, does not come alive and "infect" the reader as Tolstoi thought good art should, and remains decidedly in the second rank of his production.

SYDNEY SCHULTZE

See also Anna Karenina; War and Peace

Biography

Born in Iasnaia Poliana, near Tula, 9 September 1828, the fourth of five children. Educated by private tutors; attended Kazan University first in the Faculty of Eastern Languages, then Faculty of Law, 1844–47: did not graduate; studied law for a brief period at St. Petersburg University, 1849. Traveled to the Caucasus with his brother Nikolai, 1851; served in the Russian Army, 1852–56: saw action in Caucasus where he was nearly killed by grenade, 1852, and at Sebastopol: retired as lieutenant; began to publish, 1852; participated in St. Petersburg intellectual life, 1855–59; first serious romance, with V.V. Arsen'eva, 1856; traveled to Western Europe twice, 1857,

1860–61; affair with Aksinia Bazykina, one of the peasants on his estate, 1858: possibly continued to marriage, at least one child; established a school at Iasnaia Poliana for the children of his serfs, 1859–62; eldest brother Nikolai died, 1860; lived continuously at Iasnaia Poliana throughout 1860s and 1870s, with occasional summer trips to Samara from 1871; reopened school at Iasnaia Poliana, 1872; wrote and compiled materials for a complete elementary education course: published it as the primer *Azbuka*, 1872, revised and reissued as *Novaia azbuka*, 1875 (ran to 28 editions in his lifetime); petitioned the new tsar asking him to pardon the assassins of Alexander II; took up winter residence, Moscow, 1881; took part in Moscow census, 1882; met V.G. Chertkov, subsequently his closest disciple, 1883; first attempted to leave home, 1884; founded popular press, "Posrednik" (Intermediary), 1885; after unsuccessful attempts, finally gave up meat, alcohol, and tobacco, 1888; in 1892 he renounced his copyright on works published after 1881; participated in famine relief in Riazan Province, 1891–93; published novel *Voskresenie* (*Resurrection*) to raise money for Dukhobors, 1899; International Tolstoi Society founded, 1900; excommunicated from the Orthodox Church, 1901; serious illness and recuperation in Crimea, 1901; left home, 1910. Died at Astapovo railway station, 7 November 1910. Buried at Iasnaia Poliana, 20 November 1910.

Novels by Tolstoi

Voina i mir, 1863–69; as *War and Peace*, translated by Clara Bell, 1886; numerous subsequent translations including by Constance Garnett, 1925, and Rosemary Edmonds, 1957; also translated by Louise and Aylmer Maude, edited by Henry Gifford, 1991

Anna Karenina, 1875–77; numerous translations, including as *Anna Karenin*, translated by Rosemary Edmonds, 1954; also translated as *Anna Karenina*, by Louise and Aylmer Maude, edited by John Bayley, 1980

Voskresenie, 1899; as *Resurrection*, translated by Vera Traill, 1899, Louise Maude, 1899, and Rosemary Edmonds, 1966; also translated by Louise Maude, edited by Richard F. Gustafson

Other Writings: short novels, stories, plays, letters, diaries, essays, religious writings.

Further Reading

Bayley, John, *Tolstoy and the Novel*, London: Chatto and Windus, and New York: Viking Press, 1966

Bayley, John, *Tolstoy*, Plymouth: Northcote House, 1997

Bloom, Harold, editor, *Leo Tolstoy*, New York: Chelsea House, 1986

Christian, Reginald Frank, *Tolstoy: A Critical Introduction*, London: Cambridge University Press, 1969

Eikhenbaum, Boris, *Tolstoi in the Sixties*, Ann Arbor, Michigan: Ardis, 1982

Eikhenbaum, Boris, *Tolstoi in the Seventies*, Ann Arbor, Michigan: Ardis, 1982

Gifford, Henry, editor, *Leo Tolstoy, A Critical Anthology*, Harmondsworth: Penguin, 1971

Matlaw, Ralph, editor, *Tolstoy: A Collection of Critical Essays*, Englewood Cliffs, New Jersey: Prentice-Hall, 1967

Shklovskii, Viktor, *Lev Tolstoi*, Moscow: Molodaia gvardiia, 1963; in English as *Lev Tolstoy*, Moscow: Progress, 1978

Wasiolek, Edward, editor, *Critical Essays on Tolstoy*, Boston: G.K. Hall, 1986

Tom Jones by Henry Fielding

1749

The History of Tom Jones, A Foundling is widely regarded as Henry Fielding's greatest achievement in fiction and as one of the most significant and influential of the early English novels. It is a novel of simple and elegant structure but complex referentiality, drawing on earlier forms and paving the way for many future developments.

Fielding's previous fiction was obviously reactive in one way or another. *Shamela* (1741) and *Joseph Andrews* (1742) are fueled with humorous contempt for Samuel Richardson; *Jonathan Wild* (1743) is based on the real life and death of a robber and satirizes specific individuals and institutions of Fielding's own day. *Tom Jones* also contains important historical and political allusions—notably to the second Jacobite Rebellion of 1745—but is more obviously self-justifying and self-propelled.

Like Fielding's earlier works, and like most other novels of the period, the narrative of *Tom Jones* is tied to the adventures of its eponymous hero. But the tie is a rather loose one, allowing for the introduction of many lively characters. Moreover, Fielding steps back from the narrative, continually reflecting on his own enterprise in introductory chapters to each of the novel's 18 books and discussing the imagined reader, his own literary ambitions, and wide questions of aesthetics—especially the potential of the novel form itself—and morality. But *Tom Jones* is not calculatedly meandering and mind-boggling in the manner of Laurence Sterne's *Tristram Shandy* (1759–67). The narratorial disquisitions are arranged rather as the invocations in a classical epic. They mark stages in the progress of the narrative, which goes forth, meanwhile, in a controlled and orderly fashion.

This control, however, encompasses a kind of necessary disorder in the life of the hero. *Tom Jones* can be seen as a primitive type of Bildungsroman. There is little doubt, from the start, that it is about the making, moral and economic, of its hero, but that making apparently requires some licensed misbehavior. Tom goes astray, committing acts of ill-judged generosity, brave but unwise pugnacity, and unpremeditated sex, and he nearly falls afoul of the moral standards set up by the textual world through which he moves, but these are necessary steps, it seems, for him to become a complete and worthy man (*man* being the operative word, since *Tom Jones* is unsurprisingly less tolerant of female transgressions).

The highest standard of moral probity is represented in the novel by Mr. Allworthy (as his name suggests), the affluent land-owner who adopts Tom as a baby at the beginning of the narra-tive. Allworthy is a type of benign dictator, whose moral validity has been questioned by some 20th-century interpreters (rather along the lines of Milton's God), but who, for Fielding's narra-tor, clearly represents the standard to which a man should as-pire—someone who had something of Tom's recklessness in his youth, we are encouraged to suspect, but who has learned to control that part of himself, becoming upright but not intoler-ant, sober but not puritanical. The characterization of Allworthy clearly owes much to Fielding's experience as a magistrate and to his own attempts to find solutions to the realities of 18th-centu-ry crime and public disorder.

The novel's moralism may seem schematic and impersonal, in-sofar as Tom Jones can be taken as an exemplary young man, with general virtues and vices such as good nature, sincerity, choler, and lust. His ultimate goal throughout the narrative is the love of Sophia, a spotless beauty who, beyond her bodily pres-ence (the reward, implicitly, for carnal Tom, the fortunate mor-tal) is also (as her name indicates) Wisdom, the goal of Tom the philosopher, who has learned about his own weaknesses and the ways of the world. But the moral quest is also mocked, to some extent. *Tom Jones* owes a good deal to *Don Quixote*—a point underlined by the fact that Tom is accompanied in his travels by the comic schoolmaster Partridge (a kind of combination of the Don and Sancho Panza)—and, like Cervantes' novel, *Tom Jones* suggests in the end a certain shedding of illusions, a coming down to earth, more than an accession to wisdom. The good na-ture advocated in the narratorial prefaces to *Tom Jones* extends to a tolerance throughout the text of different moral structures: "Allworthy" and "Sophia," together with the caricaturish vil-lains that Tom has to contend with on his way (such as his cousin Blifil and the tutor Thwackum), might seem to belong to a stern allegorical system in the mold of Bunyan's *Pilgrim's Prog-ress* (1678, 1684), but this is a type of rake's progress as well—only much more forgiving and indulgent than the graphic narrative of that title (the work of Fielding's friend, William Hogarth).

It is important not to underestimate the extent to which *Tom Jones,* for all its moral overtones, is driven by enjoyment: Field-ing's own, as is very obvious from the jovial, self-confident pref-aces, and that anticipated by Fielding in the reader. This novel was a commercial enterprise and a very successful one—selling 10,000 copies in its first nine months, despite costing 18 shillings for each six-volume set. It catered to a public taste for moral or-der, delivering an ending in which the recognizably good charac-ters are rewarded and the recognizably bad punished, but it catered, too, to a public taste for the comedy of short-term *dis*-order, embarrassment, and farce. Through Tom, the novel flirts with immoralism before returning to right thinking in the end.

More generally, the narrative is powered by uncertainty—with regard to Tom's future, above all, but also with regard to his past. The secret of Tom's parentage remains undiscovered until the closing chapters, a common device in the period (compare Smollett's *Roderick Random,* 1748), whereby the novel becomes an allegory of finding a place in the world, even reconciling one-self to the fact of having been born—a type of ontological romance.

Tom Jones was an immensely significant work in its own time, not least in terms of its commercial success: with a few other mid-century best-sellers, it helped establish the novel as a form with a high cultural profile much prized, much purchased, and much discussed. In addition, it widened the sense of what could be done with the novel in terms of social perspective and allu-siveness, and it encouraged, through the prefaces, reflection on the novel as art and on the novelist and reader as significant en-tities in the progress of that art—entities between whom the text mediates capriciously, making space for solicitation, cajolement, flattery, and offense. Fielding's focus on a central, flawed but en-gaging hero has been perpetuated in countless subsequent nov-els, and his combination of this focus with a broad social view and a knowing, comic sense of his own novelistic enterprise was the necessary and avowed foundation for the work of Charles Dickens, William Makepeace Thackeray, and other subsequent leaders in the comic/moralistic tradition.

DOMINIC RAINSFORD

See also Henry Fielding

Further Reading

Alter, Robert, *Fielding and the Nature of the Novel,* Cambridge, Massachusetts: Harvard University Press, 1968

Bender, John, *Imagining the Penitentiary: Fiction and the Architecture of Mind in Eighteenth-Century England,* Chicago: University of Chicago Press, 1987

Bloom, Harold, editor, *Henry Fielding's "Tom Jones,"* New York: Chelsea House, 1987

Campbell, Jill, *Natural Masques: Gender and Identity in Fielding's Plays and Novels,* Stanford, California: Stanford University Press, 1995

Harding, James M., "'He's a Gallus Un': Excess, Restriction, and Narrative Reprieve at the Gallows in *Tom Jones,*" *Eighteenth-Century Life* 18:2 (1994)

Harrison, Bernard, *Henry Fielding's "Tom Jones": The Novelist as Moral Philosopher,* London: published for Sussex University Press by Chatto and Windus, 1975

Lamb, Jonathan, "Exemplarity and Excess in Fielding's Fiction," *Eighteenth-Century Fiction* 1 (1989)

Miller, Henry Knight, *Henry Fielding's "Tom Jones" and the Romance Tradition,* Victoria, British Columbia: English Literary Studies, University of Victoria, 1976

Richetti, John, "The Old Order and the New Novel of the Mid-Eighteenth Century: Narrative Authority in Fielding and Smollett," *Eighteenth-Century Fiction* 2 (1990)

Spacks, Patricia Ann Meyer, *Desire and Truth: Functions of Plot in Eighteenth-Century English Novels,* Chicago: University of Chicago Press, 1990

Michel Tournier 1924–

French

Michel Tournier is something of a rarity among contemporary French novelists; his work has enjoyed great popularity among the general public, while at the same time literary critics have taken it very seriously. In an essay that appeared in his *Le Vent Paraclet* (1977; *The Wind Spirit*), Tournier points out the reason for his success and situates himself within the history of contemporary French fiction: "My goal is not to innovate form, but to express in a form as traditional, safe and reassuring as possible a content that possesses none of these qualities."

The major influence on postwar French fiction was the *nouveau roman* (new novel), which initially received considerable critical acclaim, both in France and abroad. However, the difficulty of this style of writing, with its propensity to favor description over dramatization, its avoidance of character analysis, and the absence of clear narrative development largely alienated the reading public. When Tournier began publishing novels, on the other hand, his work corresponded to what general yet educated audiences were seeking. *Vendredi; ou, Les Limbes du Pacifique* (1967; *Friday; or, The Other Island*) retells the story of Robinson Crusoe (winning for the author the *Grand Prix du Roman de l'Académie Française*). *Le Roi des Aulnes* (1970; *The Erl-King*) provides a mythic context to a Frenchman's adventures as a prisoner of war in Nazi Germany (receiving the even more prestigious *Prix Goncourt*). *Les Météores* (1975; *Gemini*) may be read as a contemporary version of Jules Verne's *Around the World in Eighty Days*; it recounts the story of twins, Jean and Paul. Jean sets out on a bizarre journey of self-discovery that takes him from Europe to Japan and Canada and eventually to the Berlin Wall, where disastrous events befall his brother Paul. *Gaspard, Melchior et Balthazar* (1980; *The Four Wise Men*) retells the tale of the Magi. As these brief descriptions indicate, Tournier appeared to have discovered the secret of refurbishing old stories and using traditional (mythic) structures to tell apparently undemanding stories the public liked to read.

Tournier's approach to the novel, however, is a matter of quiet subversion. Rather than recycle old stories and well-known methods, he parodies both in order to comment upon the contemporary world. His Robinson's enthusiasm to create order on his island leads to the collapse of the very Eurocentric and racist values he seeks to uphold. Abel Tiffauges, the main character in *The Erl-King*, discovers, much to the chagrin of Tournier's French readers, that he loves Nazi Germany, "this country of black and white," and his efforts to explore his mythic identity lead him both to examine the ambiguity of sexual stereotypes and to recreate in miniature his own version of the Third Reich. The "perfect twinship" that Paul tries to maintain in *Gemini* turns out to be a refusal to accept the separateness and individuality that adulthood entails. The Christ child the Magi discover in the manger is black, a fact that propels the syrupy Christmas story into an attack on racism and the inability of many to accept differences among peoples.

After the publication of *The Four Wise Men*, Tournier was at the height of his career, considered to be France's leading novelist. Since then his career has declined somewhat. His literary autobiography, *The Wind Spirit*, was considered pretentious by some critics, even though it provides valuable insights into the author's methods and thinking. His last major work of fiction, *La Goutte d'or* (1985; *The Golden Droplet*), was intended in part as an attack on France's racist attitudes toward its African migrant workers, but many found that he had romanticized the plight of these laborers. His most recent work, *Eléazar; ou, La Source et le buisson* (1996; Eléazar; or, The Bush and the Spring) recounts the journey of a family of 19th-century Irish settlers to a new home in California and explores the question of God's refusal to allow Moses to enter the Promised Land. In this brief novel, Tournier toys with the possibility that a writer (himself?) may fulfill his destiny within his lifetime and must depart the scene, much like Moses. However, Tournier intends to publish a long-awaited novel on Saint Sebastian in the near future and seems anything but ready to retire.

Tournier is hardly the first novelist to subvert traditional fictional formats and challenge his readers' literary and intellectual assumptions. Yet he did so at a time when the French novel was searching for a new direction. While many of his contemporaries believed that that would require abandoning the past and pushing resolutely forward even at readers' expense, Tournier chose to revitalize tradition, if only to show that elements of the past remain useful tools for a compelling exploration of the present.

WILLIAM CLOONAN

Biography

Born 19 December 1924 in Paris. Attended Collège Saint-Erembert and Collège Municipal, Saint-Germain-en-Laye; the Sorbonne; University of Tübingen. Producer and director, Radio-diffusion-Télévision Française (RTF), Paris, 1949–54; press attaché, Europe No. 1 radio, 1955–58; director of literary services, Plon publishers, Paris, 1958–68; hosted the television series *La Chambre Noir*, 1960–65.

Novels by Tournier

Vendredi; ou, Les Limbes du Pacifique, 1967; as *Friday; or, The Other Island,* translated by Norman Denny, 1969
Le Roi des Aulnes, 1970; as *The Erl-King,* translated by Barbara Bray, 1972; also translated as *The Ogre*
Les Météores, 1975; as *Gemini,* translated by Anne Carter, 1981
Gaspard, Melchior et Balthazar, 1980; as *The Four Wise Men,* translated by Ralph Mannheim, 1982
Gilles et Jeanne, 1983; as *Gilles and Jeanne,* translated by Alan Sheridan, 1987
La Goutte d'or, 1985; as *The Golden Droplet,* translated by Barbara Wright, 1987
Eléazar; ou, La Source et le buisson [Eléazar; or, The Bush and the Spring], 1996

Other Writings: short fiction, a play, autobiography, travel writing, literature for children, and essays.

Further Reading

Bouloumié, Arlette, *Michel Tournier: Le Roman mythologique,* Paris: José Corti, 1988

Bouloumié, Arlette, and Maurice de Gandillac, editors, *Images et signes de Michel Tournier*, Paris: Gallimard, 1991

Cloonan, William, *Michel Tournier*, Boston: Twayne, 1985

Krell, Jonathan, *Tournier élémentaire*, West Lafayette, Indiana: Purdue University Press, 1995

Merllié, Françoise, *Michel Tournier*, Paris: Belfond, 1988

Milne, Lorna, *L'Evangile selon Michel: La Trinité initiatique dans l'oeuvre de Tournier*, Amsterdam: Rodopi, 1994

Petit, Susan, *Michel Tournier's Metaphysical Fictions*, Amsterdam and Philadelphia: John Benjamins, 1991

Roberts, Martin, *Michel Tournier: Bricolage and Cultural Mythology*, Stanford, California: Anma Libri, 1994

Rosello, Mireille, *L'In-différence chez Michel Tournier*, Paris: José Corti, 1990

Worton, Michael, *Michel Tournier: La Goutte d'or*, Glasgow: University of Glasgow French and German Publications, 1992

Worton, Michael, editor, *Michel Tournier*, London: Longman, 1995

Translation of Novels

The Role of Translations in the Development and Spread of the Novel

The relative fortunes of different literary genres in the course of history have depended on a number of complex social, as well as political, factors. The theatre in England, to take a notable case, enjoyed immense popularity in Shakespeare's day, although theatres were closed in the country later in the 17th century. The use of classical models for drama and poetry since the Renaissance paralleled the teaching of classical languages and their currency within elite circles, which must be set against the growth in importance of vernacular languages and their standardization through printing, leading in the 18th century to the creation of a strongly hierarchical vision of literature that placed poetry at the pinnacle of literary achievement. Yet by the 18th century, prose, in the form of the essay, the letter, the journal, and the novel—the novelty that was not quite new—had also become well established, as had the apparatus of literary criticism. It is the age often associated with the early development of the novel, and the dominance of English novelists in particular is reflected in their popularity overseas, particularly in the rest of Europe, where there was a close relationship between printers, writers, translators, and booksellers. Amsterdam seems particularly important as a distribution center for more than just Dutch translations, as it is today.

It is difficult nonetheless to elaborate a causal connection between translation and the development of the novel as a form. A number of social factors strongly influenced its development: the relationship between book production and the development of a reading public, the move toward private reading, and the decline of the poet as a public orator were all highly significant. Ian Watt, in *The Rise of the Novel* (1957), suggests that while the 18th-century English novelists had their imitators in France, French writers of the period resisted the novel's claim to realism, and that Pierre Laclos and Mme de Lafayette were in fact too stylized, too tied to classical drama to be compared to their English contemporaries. The other major factor affecting the spread of the novel as a popular form has to do with changes in the philosophical climate that increasingly stressed both individualism and rationalism. Translation was of course highly significant in the spread of philosophical ideas since the beginning of Renaissance humanism, and in the 18th century the climate in which the novel grew was set by the spread of ideas and the consolidation of rational principles.

In fact, the early development of the novel starts long before the 18th century, and—keeping the question of translation in mind—two figures stand out: François Rabelais and Miguel de Cervantes. (Others have argued for much earlier origins—in the prose romances of 1st and 2nd century Greece and Rome, for example. But these early performances, for all they may have claim to inaugurating certain narrative techniques and approaches and anticipating the directions the novel would take throughout Europe in the 17th and 18th centuries, do not figure prominently in the role that textual translations played in the dissemination of the novel during this period.) Rabelais and Cervantes stand out in particular in relation to translation but also, especially in the case of *Don Quixote,* in the creation of main characters who broke free from the confines of earlier prose fictional narrative, with its rather narrow dependence on plot, to create myths of the heroes. According to Ian Watt's *Myths of Modern Individualism* (1996), there were 29 translated versions within the first 50 years of *Don Quixote*'s appearance in 1605, and there have been 928 overall. Thomas Shelton published Part I of *Don Quixote* in 1612 in English and both parts in 1620, to be followed by J. Philips' translation of 1687. Later significant translators were Motteux, Ozell, Jarvis, and Tobias Smollett in the 18th century, not forgetting Edward Ward's version, "Merrily translated into Hudibrastik verse," of 1711. César Oudin's French translation appeared in Paris in 1614, Filleau de Saint-Martin's in 1681, Mortier's (published in Amsterdam) in 1696. It was produced in Italian by Lorenzo Franciosimi Fiorentino in 1622, with following editions to 1795, in Dutch from 1657, and in German from 1669, although later German translations tended toward re-translations from the French, which was also true of Russian versions until 1838. The early international popularity of *Don Quixote* owed in large part to a widespread boredom with what Watt calls "sentimental and pastoral romances." The timing was perfect: the more fantastic elements in the medieval romances were no longer to the public's taste, and parody allowed intolerance to be released in laughter. The reversal of the model in which Fate is the mainspring of the action was the first step toward the novel, where the action springs from character. *Don Quixote* was poised between the two, although many structural elements of the novel predate not only works such as *Tristram Shandy* (1759–67), which was enormously influenced by it, but 20th-century experiments in fiction. The hints at intertextuality in *Don Quixote,* as in chapter 8 of Part I, where the narration is interrupted until a fragment of Arabic manuscript that happens to contain more of Don Quixote's story has been translated, is a device that points to the very heart of current theoretical concerns about translation, adaptation, and rewriting (see Lefevere, 1992).

Rabelais' *Pantagruel* appeared in 1532, followed in 1534 by *Gargantua.* Sir Thomas Urquhart's English translation of both texts appeared in London in 1653, with the names Motteux and Ozell reappearing in 1694 and 1737, respectively, as translators of Rabelais as well as Cervantes, and these continued to be popular into the 19th century. J. Fischart, under the pseudonym of H.E. Reznem, produced a German version in Strasbourg in 1575.

The other major mythical figures Watt considers in *Myths of Modern Individualism* are Faust, Don Juan, and Robinson Crusoe. In each of these cases, too, the central figure has clearly taken on an importance reaching far beyond the original works in which they appeared. Tirso de Molina is hardly known in the English-speaking world, but Don Juan is a universal figure—in addition to Dutch, Italian, French, and English versions, a total of 1,727 versions in other languages had been produced up to 1965. In relation to translation, the fluidity of the passage of the figure of Don Juan through a range of literary forms suggests that where, as here, the core structural element is based on a tight bonding between story and character (as in *Hamlet,* where the story springs from ambiguities in Hamlet's character), adaptation can be freer; and it is adaptation more than text-based translation that ensures the survival of the myth and its openness to further reworking. Faust underwent many transformations before Goethe treated the subject—there were 24 foreign language translations since the appearance of the *Faustbuch* in 1587, and the myth has continued to evolve up to the 1947 novel by Thomas Mann, *Doktor Faustus.* Indeed, Mann saw himself as being at the end of a line of development of the novel that had started with *Don Quixote.*

Daniel Defoe's *Robinson Crusoe* (1719), as well as being highly significant in terms of the development of the novel, made its mark because of its verisimilitude. Ian Watt points out in *The Rise of the Novel* that "Defoe and Richardson are the first great writers in our literature who did not take their plots from mythology, history, legend or previous literature," and yet Crusoe himself, of course, has become an almost mythical figure. William-Edward Mann, in his *Robinson Crusoë en France,* a doctoral dissertation published in 1916, points out that the book was first accepted in France as a true account of a shipwreck. There were 27 translations in Europe between 1719 and 1769, with the first French translation, variously attributed to Themiseul de Saint-Hyacinthe and Juste van Effen, appearing in 1720. The book was seen by the French as providing suitable moral guidance and self-help principles for the young, and children's versions were produced. *Robinson Crusoe* best illustrates the links provided by the underlying European philosophy of rationalism, which allowed for the possibility of its acceptance across a wide readership in Europe. Of

course philosophy and science were equally dependent on translation and international contacts to establish themselves as "universal." In *The Art of the Novel* (1988), Milan Kundera suggests that Defoe follows René Descartes in taking the thinking self as his starting point, and clearly the attention to realistic descriptive detail contributes to the progressive realism that characterized the novel in the 19th century. Kundera traces the development of the novel to the progressive closure of the world's horizons following the freedom and open-endedness suggested by *Don Quixote;* through Defoe's rationalism, with a different, more contingent understanding of time; to a growing materialism as the age of the "bourgeois realist" novel, typified by Honoré de Balzac, emerges in the 19th century. Finally in the mid–19th century psychology opens up new possibilities for the novel to explore the inner self, which leads not only to a new kind of novel but also to complexities regarding freedom and fictional space. In the 20th century this has led to attempts to reverse the structural impositions of the novel form. Michel Tournier, in *Vendredi; ou, Les Limbes du Pacifique* (1967; *Friday; or, The Other Island*), has further developed the Crusoe story and challenged many of the rationalist underpinnings of Defoe's work, and in so doing has challenged traditional "realist" principles in the construction of novels. While not a translation in any conventional sense, it is a radical transformation/rewriting of the story, as is *Foe* (1986) by J.M. Coetzee, who upsets the premise of the "original" story along gender lines.

Translation parallels and provides new paradigms for the development of the novel. Every translation offers the possibility of re-creation, and with each translation into a new language comes a renegotiation with meaning that will be brought out through an engagement with a new culture. Translation points toward the idea of the open-ended text.

Much debate about the novel as a genre has revolved around the question of realism, and in the 20th century in Europe and North and South America, the novel has gone far beyond 19th-century ideas, with so-called magic realism being a potent blend of myth, individual consciousness, and reversals of linear views of time. But just as the reception of South American literature in North America and its translation into other European languages has brought to the attention of new readers only a part of a much greater body of literary production, much of which may well not fit the magic-realist category, it is clear how publishers and translators can offer a partial view and make it seem like a totality. The general point is that translation is often piecemeal, and the appearance of a handful of novels in translation does not necessarily constitute a "literature," or more especially engage with the social and philosophical issues raised by the writers, although the act of translation in itself should open up possibilities for debate. Particularly in the 20th century, the experimental and innovative nature of much that has gone on in relation to Western fiction has not itself always been "translated" or received into some cultures. In a kind of reversal of this situation, Sujit Mukherjee (1981) has pointed out that in India, where there is an Indo-English literature, literary debate does not engage with European concerns about literary theory but does provide a pan-Indian forum about Indian literature through the medium of the English language. While debate on translation is limited, translators seemingly take great liberties with Indian novels in the hope of selling them in the West. Also, according to Mukherjee, students in India are not given access to English translations of European works because of conservative attitudes in university language departments. So much Indo-English literature and translations from works written in the various Indian languages remain unknown outside India, and works in some Indian languages are better represented than others. The novel as a form has been particularly strong in India since the mid–19th century, focusing on India's social problems prior to independence. Since independence, however, the symbiotic relationship between English and Anglo-Indian literature has been broken, making way for the emergence of a new kind of "home-grown" prose fiction. The problem is that translation has not been extensive or systematic. As Mukherjee points out,

> using what is available and without getting sidetracked into elusive issues such as "Indian-ness," it ought to be useful to try and analyse the formal aspects of such works as *Panther pancali, Godan, The Vigil, The Wild Bapu of Garambi, Chemmeen, Samskara,* etc., in order to determine whether these novels achieve formal completion by fulfilling the requirements of the western concept of the novel form or by violating such requirements.

The term *requirements* should not be misread: Mukherjee wants an Indian literature to be recognized for what it is through a more sensitive understanding of translation issues and problems in India.

The situation in China is rather different. Lennart Lundberg's *Lu Xun as a Translator* (1989) points out that interest in the Western novel grew from the end of the 19th century, and that translation from the West was linked to demands for political reform. It was also linked to the problem of language, as the older, classical Chinese was rather restrictive. A review entitled *New Fiction* appeared from 1902. Lu Xun was particularly interested in translation from Russian and Eastern European writers, as they dealt with the common people, unlike writing in the classical Chinese tradition. He also translated from Japanese works that already showed Western influence. Lin Shu (1852–1924) had already translated many Western classics, such as Alexandre Dumas, Sir Arthur Conan Doyle, Charles Dickens, Lev Tolstoi, and even Cervantes, but into the form of the classical Chinese novel, whereas Lu Xun was part of the reformist May Fourth movement that sought to introduce Western ideas to a wider audience. Translation in China, against preexisting, highly conservative structures, was then closely allied to political reform, and the novel was seen, as it had been in 19th-century Europe in the hands of Dickens, Zola, and George Eliot, as a vehicle for raising social awareness.

Through translation, publishing, and printing, Europe has been a reality for much longer than nationalist concerns would suggest. Romanticism, with its associated development of national identities and literatures, is more often associated with poetry, although there were significant transnational texts such as Mme de Staël's *De l'Allemagne* (1810; *On Germany*), and much cross-fertilization of ideas in this period. The novel has suffered from the identification of "literature" with poetry, which has been perpetuated through the growth of English literature, especially as a taught subject, from the late 19th century. And yet the novel has survived and continues to develop partly through its attachment to social concerns and, if the translation of European novels is a guide, to the commonality of experience at a deep level—the comic, the burlesque, the parodic. Just as there is a duality in the novel's

claims to truth, novel translation seems to perform a double function—on the one hand emphasizing differences and readdressing common assumptions about personal and social relations, and on the other bringing the fundamentals of humanity to the fore. The novel has survived because its ragbag nature opens up endless debate about what it should be doing, and how it engages with the culture that produces it. The translator as rewriter and the novelist are both engaged in that argument. If Thomas Mann was right in assuming that he stood at the end of an era that began with Cervantes, he was so only in relation to a certain empirical view of realism—it is the anarchist in Cervantes, not the realist, that has survived, and his interrogation of his own text parallels the work of the translator with every reworking. The translator, through rewriting, has aided the development of the novel by extending its relevance through different cultures, reengaging with each language to see where it adheres to myth, to stories that have undergone retellings and re-creations over a vast sweep of time.

Theoretical Issues and Problems

The theoretical issues arising specifically from the translation of novels have been largely overlooked in the rapid expansion of work in the field of translation studies since the 1980s. A large part of the reason for this must be pedagogical: in the seminar or classroom it is easier to focus on relatively short texts to illustrate theoretical points, and this limitation tends to favor the use of extracts from larger texts (for all the dangers inherent in that practice), short stories, or poems. The specificity of issues arising in poetry translation, often related to the peculiarly hermetic nature of poetic texts, has led to a wealth of material about the difficulties of translating poetry. The problems of translating prose fiction have been seen as minor in comparison. Yet there are a number of problems inherent in the translation of novels, some relating directly to the translator's task, and some, such as publishing policy, reception, and criticism, relating both indirectly to the work of the practicing translator and more widely to issues of cultural transferability or nontransferability.

Since the 18th century, the history of the translation of the novel has paralleled and indeed been part of the reason for the growth and popularity of the novel as a genre. In the 20th century, the growing self-consciousness of texts and the questioning of the realist novel as a form and as a socially determined construct often have been connected to issues raised in translation and language theory. The connection between the translation (and indeed the nontranslation) of the novel and publishing and marketing policy, the importance of which may be seen more clearly in the late 20th century, in fact has a long history that tells us much about cultural politics on a global scale.

With regard to the mechanics of fiction translation, the translator, in addition to criteria that would be applied universally, has to pay attention to the macro-structures of the novel: the overall shape, the dramatic structure and its relation to time or other competing elements, such as the use of memory, interior monologue, stream-of-consciousness techniques, or the like. Novelistic conventions, such as beginnings and endings, especially where these are ironized for the purposes of comedy or some more serious intent (as, for example, in Italo Calvino's *Se una notte d'inverno un viaggiatore* [1979; *If on a winter's night a traveler*]), need to be respected. The register of spoken discourse within the novel, particularly if it varies significantly between characters, may present particular difficulties where, as so often in the English novel throughout its history, language is a prime indicator of social class and power relations. Novels may include specific discourses of a technical or specialist nature, as in historical novels relating to naval warfare in the age of Nelson, for example, where the translator has to have access to a specialist vocabulary. Sometimes the specialist element is limited to a part of the overall text, as in the references to trajectories and rocket science in the work of Thomas Pynchon.

More theoretical consideration has been given to the history and politics of prose fiction translation, and to genre shifts and their bearing on the matter. The activities of critics, especially in the 18th and early 19th centuries, when they asserted themselves as judges of taste, holding sway over a relatively small reading public, were surely influential in dictating the activities of publishers and therefore of translators of major literary works; whereas in early and mid-18th-century Europe, the common concern in relation to translation seems to have focused on the classics, as the romantic movement led to a flurry of interest in the translation of contemporary works and in translation theories, notably those of Goethe, Schlegel, and Tytler. Laurence Sterne's *Tristram Shandy* in Ugo Foscolo's translation became well known in Italy, but while the best of the English novelists were known in Europe (Tobias Smollett's *The Expedition of Humphrey Clinker* [1771] was translated into German in 1775, with *The Adventures of Peregrine Pickle* [1751] following in 1787 and 1802; Henry Fielding's complete works were published in France in 1804, and many of his works were already known in French, Dutch, and German), the debate about translation still centered mainly on poetry. Yet commercial gains from the growing popular market for lurid or Gothic tales among women readers would have been uppermost in publishers' minds. As Josephine Grieder (1975) has pointed out, demand for "stories of love and passion, oriental tales, historical romances, pastorals, and didactic novels" led to a market for hack translators.

The novel as a form satisfied both the general taste and a more refined readership. French writers who became popular in late 18th-century England include Baculard d'Arnaud, Mme de Genlis, and Le Chevalier de Florian. The cult of sensibility was taken to extremes and coincided with the brief absence, after the death of Smollett in 1771, of major literary prose writers. Critics tried but failed to deter the almost totally female readership from reading material that was "too French" and charged the translators with immorality. The fad died quickly after 1790 and became a target for ridicule from the pens of William Beckford, Mary Charlton (in *Rosella, or Modern Occurrences* [1799]), and Maria Edgeworth, who attacked the oversentimentality of the French works.

The next fad in England for the Gothic tale, which drew on central European sources, was not primarily generated by translation, although references to the translation of, for example, lost manuscripts were often part of the fiction. As André Lefevere (1992) has pointed out, Horace Walpole's *The Castle of Otranto* (1764) contained two prefaces. The first preface, published before the success of the novel, disguises the tale as a translation (in case it should fail to be a success), while the second preface, written once success was established, apologizes for the deception and reveals the author as the writer of an original work. The novel was, of course, central to establishing the Gothic tale as a specific subgenre. This kind of fictional translation, where there is no source text, has been mentioned in an essay by

G.C. Kalman (in Lambert and Lefevere, 1993). In another development from the Gothic novel, Lawrence Venuti (1995) refers to the case of the Italian novelist Tarchetti (1839–69), who performed a kind of translation in adapting the tales of E.T.A. Hoffmann, Edgar Allan Poe, Gérard de Nerval, and Théophile Gautier into his narratives, thus using the foreign elements to subvert the dominant realism of the bourgeois novel. Elsewhere he, like Walpole, hid his identity as a translator in order to present himself as the author of texts by foreign writers that he wanted to use in his antibourgeois, antirealist attacks on the novel.

In global terms, it is interesting to look at what fiction is translated, and for what markets. The reception of Russian fiction in the West in the 20th century illustrates the politics of translation in maintaining the focus on 19th-century classics, almost to the exclusion of post-revolutionary work, until the smuggling out of Aleksandr Solzhenitsyn's *Odin den' Ivana Denisovicha* (1962; *One Day in the Life of Ivan Denisovitch*), which exposes the harsh reality of the Soviet labor camps. Despite the enormous impact of this slim text in the West, there was a tendency among Western publishers to cast Solzhenitsyn's larger works in the mold of his 19th-century predecessors, thus perpetuating an already fixed image of the so-called great Russian novel, and in this case perhaps limiting the force of the Western attack on the repression of Soviet authors. Solzhenitsyn played along with what was essentially a Western publisher's construct: while his work was banned in the Soviet Union, his English-language translators and their publishers were vital to him.

Another interesting case history is offered by the situation in India. The translation of the novel has been highly significant in the development of an Indian national literature, and as English has been adopted as the common language of letters in India, much work from the various Indian languages has been translated into English. However, the literature has mainly circulated within India and only secondarily sought a market elsewhere, which is unlike, for example, the case of much African fiction. The quality of translation tends to be poor, according to Sujit Mukherjee (1994) because English is not the first language of the translators. There is also a certain amount of Indian-Indian translation supported by the National Book Trust's *Aadan-Pradan* (exchange) program. Authors such as Krishna Balder Vaid have preferred to translate their own work, in this case from Hindi into English, because of the poverty of the translations in general, but perhaps Vaid and those like him find themselves rewriting their novels in the process. In India there has been very little respect for authorship and copyright owing to the traditional self-effacement of the author, and Mukherjee notes that until the advent of Western culture in India, translation had always been regarded as new writing, which is interesting in terms of the current struggle by translators in the West to have their creative status recognized. In the case of the Bangla novel *Pather Panchali* by Bibhutibhushana Bandyopadhyaya, the cutting out of the third part of the novel when it was translated into English and French was influenced by the book's film version by Satyajit Ray (1955). Another film, *Aparajito*, was made out of this third part of the novel and another work with that title by Bandyopadhyaya, and this gave rise to a third film, *Apur Sansar*.

This kind of relationship between film and novel is increasingly important in the West and reveals another form of translation and indeed re-creation that is liable to excite debate and controversy. India has been open to modern Western literature, some of which, even including E.M. Forster's *Passage to India* (1924), has been translated into the main Indian languages, following the modernist influence of Rabindranath Tagore. Traditionally, however, the West has focused only on classical or Sanskrit texts, or the major epic tales, and has largely ignored contemporary Indian fiction. More recently, however, the success of writers such as Salman Rushdie, Vikram Seth, and Rohinton Mistry has brought India into closer focus, although their cross-cultural experience dominates their mostly English-language narratives. So much from writers living and working in India remains untranslated and therefore unknown in the West.

The relationship between the author and the translator is one that often invites debate, particularly in the West, where copyright is strictly monitored and where the translator, although recognized legally as creating a new original work, is nevertheless bound to respect the text and remain faithful to it. Cases of major disputes between authors and translators are rare, but Piotr Kuhiwczak (in Bassnett and Lefevere, 1990) has highlighted the case of Milan Kundera's novel *Žert* (1967; *The Joke*), where the author was outraged by the liberties taken by the translator in its first English-language edition. The offending translation in this case was the first British translation of *The Joke* published in 1969, where gross liberties were taken with the text, mainly in the form of omissions, which were replaced in the 1970 edition. The author then demanded a completely new translation, which did not appear in Britain and the United States until 1983. This case illustrates what may happen when a translation of a previously unknown author from a little-known culture is introduced into a culture with firm ideas about literature and a strong sense of its own cultural and political values. The critical reception of the work in Britain in 1969–70 had made assumptions about the political content of the book, given the situation in Czechoslovakia at the time, which had slanted the reading of the novel. In the author's terms, the novel was intended to give a much more nuanced view of his characters' emotional and intellectual responses to the situations in which they were placed than could be covered by the term *political opposition*. The human element was vital to Kundera.

This is one of the rare instances in which the translator's activity takes center stage, but it is significant that it should be because of an attack by the author. The translator of fiction and the role he or she performs in transforming the text and presenting it for a target audience is rarely acknowledged, a point that is central to Lawrence Venuti's argument in *The Translator's Invisibility* (1995). More generally, however, in his examination of Paul Blackburn's translations of Julio Cortázar's *End of the Game and Other Stories* (1967), Venuti shows that translations are normally free to emerge in a target culture only if they conform to the dominant aesthetics of the time; in this case the very fluency of the translation went some way toward undermining some of the radical, antirealist and antibourgeois elements in the Spanish text. Against the general opening up during the 1960s toward Latin American radicalism because of the "boom" in Latin American writing that was too big for North American publishers to ignore, there was a more conservative, anti-modernist tendency. Blackburn was seen as a modernist (largely because of his preoccupation with Ezra Pound) in an age when Cold War politics was forcing the majority opinion back toward more traditional views of the novel. The suggestion in this case is

that, when it comes to emergent or radical writing, in which the translation of novels from other literatures has been central since the 1950s, Western critical opinion (as controlled by publishers, the media, critics, etc.) is conservative and appropriative, tending to bring the radical into the fold and domesticate it as far as possible while marketing its radicalism as newness.

Translation scholars have their own perspectives on the business of translation that cannot be generalized. While new translations of well-established works are sometimes commissioned, the comparative study of various translations of the work of contemporary or established novelists is generally confined to niche scholarship. A contemporary publisher will perhaps seek to create a new vogue for an area of literature, and while the work of the translator may be central to this in practice, larger political forces may bring about changes in public perceptions that publishers need to be aware of. This has happened in Britain in relation to Eastern Europe, for example. Publishers will seek out the opinions of other publishers to get an eye for a trend. Publishers of translated fiction tend to be small, but individual works may transfer to the mainstream market and become popular; the search for new fiction worldwide has led to the expansion of the fiction lists of previously more marginalized houses. Novelists writing in English, such as Salman Rushdie and Ben Okri, can be a help in indirectly inviting interest in the fiction of India or Africa. This, along with the increased popularity of travel literature that has in turn increased general awareness of other cultures, helps to create a publishing climate in which translations, particularly of young authors, can emerge. Translation prizes, such as the European *Aristeion* prize, are important in bringing public recognition to the work of the translator. Only slowly is the translator's importance in creating new markets for fiction coming to be recognized in commercial terms.

What does not get translated is significant; only a tiny proportion of the quantity of South American fiction post-1950s is known in the West, for example, and, as already noted, India is translating its fiction into English but only for a domestic market. As the world becomes more connected, it will become increasingly cosmopolitan but also less stable. Out of that instability, translations will emerge reflecting the experience of cultural difference, and good translations always carry trace elements of the source culture, which are embedded in language. Outside travel literature, which has its own limitations, the novel seems likely to preserve its popularity as the chosen form in which human experience finds a voice. Its translation from and to as many languages as possible is central to getting that voice heard.

JOHN S. DIXON

Further Reading

Bassnett, Susan, *Translation Studies,* London: Methuen, 1980; revised edition, London and New York: Routledge, 1991

Bassnett, Susan, and André Lefevere, *Translation: History and Culture,* London and New York: Pinter, 1990

Britt, Linda, "Translation, Criticism or Subversion? The Case of *Like Water for Chocolate,*" *Translation Review* 48 and 49 (1995)

Gentzler, Edwin, *Contemporary Translation Theories,* London and New York: Routledge, 1993

Grieder, Josephine, *Translations of French Sentimental Prose Fiction in Late 18th-Century England: The History of a*

Literary Vogue, Durham, North Carolina: Duke University Press, 1975

Hermans, Theo, editor, *The Manipulation of Literature, Studies in Literary Translation,* London: Croom Helm, and New York: St. Martin's Press, 1985

Lambert, José, and André Lefevere, editors, *La Traduction dans le développement des littératures (Actes du XIe. Congrès de l'Association Internationale de Littérature Comparée)/Translation in the development of literatures,* Bern: Peter Lang, and New York and Louvain: Leuven University Press, 1993

Lefevere, André, *Translation, Rewriting and the Manipulation of Literary Fame,* London and New York: Routledge, 1992

Mann, William Edward, *Robinson Crusoë en France,* Paris: Davy, 1916

Mukherjee, Sujit, *Translation as Discovery and Other Essays on Indian Literature in English Translation,* New Delhi: Allied, 1981; new edition, London: Sangam, 1994

Venuti, Lawrence, *The Translator's Invisibility: A History of Translation,* London and New York: Routledge, 1995

Venuti, Lawrence, editor, *Rethinking Translation: Discourse, Subjectivity, Ideology,* London and New York: Routledge, 1992

Watt, Ian, *The Rise of the Novel,* London: Chatto and Windus, and Berkeley: University of California Press, 1957

Watt, Ian, *Myths of Modern Individualism: Faust, Don Quixote, Don Juan, Robinson Crusoe,* Cambridge and New York: Cambridge University Press, 1996

Williamson, Edwin, editor, *Cervantes and the Modernists: The Question of Influence,* London: Tamesis, 1994

Travel Narrative. *See* Prose Novelistic Forms

Travels of Lao Can by Liu E

Lao Can youji 1904–07

Travels of Lao Can was the only novel Liu E (1857–1909) ever wrote, but it has become generally recognized as the first truly great novel of 20th-century China, particularly as a model of strikingly original narrative description. Although the vastness of China's literary heritage has generally been a boon to Chinese writers of recent centuries, these writers have had such a broad assortment of ready-made descriptive phrases from which to choose that their descriptive passages often seem little more than rearrangements of hackneyed classical phraseology, most commonly of four characters with the same number of syllables. The monotony of an overly parallel prose rhythm and the lack of originality and freshness of description dogged many a traditional Chinese literatus, who typically produced a kind of studio art far removed from direct observation of life in its fullness. Liu E (also known as Liu Tieyun) instead emphasized prose description based on personal observation, and his vivid descriptions of natural landscapes and a drum-singer performance in *Travels of Lao Can* make for a more personalized diction and individual expressiveness than earlier Chinese novels could consistently sustain. Hu Shi, the prominent scholarly advocate of vernacular Chinese literature over its classical counterpart, edited a definitive 1925 Chinese edition of *Travels of Lao Can* that helped this novel become a kind of textbook prose model for novelist and ordinary student alike.

Liu E's unconventional career directly contributed to his break with traditional Chinese patterns of prose description. Although his father served as a high official and Liu E himself successfully directed a major government flood-control project along the Yellow River, he mostly eschewed the comfortable drudgery and mediocrity of officialdom in favor of initiating the collection of archaic Shang dynasty oracle-bone writing and daring entrepreneurial ventures in areas such as mining and railroads. Liu E worked for a time as a traditional Chinese doctor, but China's crushing defeat in the Sino-Japanese War of 1895–96 and the Boxer Rebellion debacle of 1900 gave his reformist inclinations a strong sense of urgency; China, gradually becoming known as "the sick man of Asia," desperately needed the aid of individuals intelligent enough to prescribe an effective cure.

Having been swept up in the tide of Chinese intellectual ferment that began during the last few years of the 19th century, Liu E opens his novel with a famous allegory of a giant but crowded and leaky sailing ship whose officers arrogantly refuse the sound and well-meaning advice offered by the physician-protagonist, Lao Can, and other reformist friends who have paddled a small dinghy up alongside the huge vessel. Details such as the length of the ship and the number of its masts reveal it as clearly standing for China in Liu E's allegorical scheme. The desire to influence high-level officials to choose policies that improve the lives of ordinary people continues to animate Lao Can's strivings throughout much of the novel, even though by temperament he is quite reflective and not at all status conscious.

The allegory that dominates chapter one mostly dissolves into the novel's dominant mode of a mildly satiric realism as Lao Can befriends officials, such as Governor Zhuang, who values Lao Can's talent and counsel and struggles to reverse the harm done by ignorant and cruel officials such as Gang Bi and Yu Xian. The only major exception to the dominant texture of the novel's realism after the first chapter is an idyllic interlude of a few chapters in the middle of the novel in which a series of occasionally abstruse philosophical discourses takes place deep within a mountain retreat. This philosophical interlude serves mainly to expound the author's view that a careful synthesis of selected ideas from the three dominant Chinese traditions of Confucianism, Daoism, and Buddhism offers China its best hope to establish a foundation on which Western innovations can be productively added. The author's alter-ego protagonist and the hermit savant Yellow Dragon join in disapproving of the extreme antiforeignism of the Boxers and reactionary officials on the one hand and the overly Westernizing tendencies of Chinese revolutionaries on the other. An example of Lao Can's desire for China's selective Westernization is his belief that his country urgently needs to import the kind of legal incentive for technological invention that patent law represents. Pointing to an ingeniously designed Chinese opium lamp whose inventor was anonymous, Lao Can notes that whatever one might feel about opium smoking per se, it is definitely wrong for the inventor of such a device to have received no sanctioned recognition or patent rights for his invention.

Liu E's ability to maintain his equanimity within satirical sections of the novel represents a considerable advance over other late Qing dynasty satirical novelists, who tended to vent so much bitterness that a tone of self-righteousness prevailed. For example, among the more than 100 officials portrayed in Li Baojia's 1906 novel *Guanchang xianxing ji* (*A Record of Revelations from Officialdom*), not a single one is upright and incorruptible. While Liu E is well aware of the problem of official corruption and malfeasance, he focuses instead on an infrequently satirized but similarly serious betrayal of the public trust: the incorruptible official who hankers after promotion and fame rather than mere monetary gain and whose conscience remains clear even while imposing the most cruel and draconian measures on the populace.

The two main targets of Liu E's satire, Yu Xian and Gang Bi, are both "honest" officials in this careerist mold. Lao Can must use both his personal contacts with relatively wise officials and Holmesian detective gambits to right the gross miscarriages of justice perpetrated by these overzealous officials. As a mere commoner, Lao Can risks his life when daring to oppose Yu Xian and Gang Bi, yet he brilliantly succeeds in providing succor to these officials' innocent victims of imprisonment and torture.

In spite of portraying a number of harrowing incidents resulting from devastating floods and the two officials' cruel punishment of many innocent people, *Travels of Lao Can* is basically comic in structure. Aside from neutralizing the worst injustices perpetrated by the two officials, Lao Can and his close friend Huang Renrui both save former flood victims from the fate of prostitution by marrying them at the close of the novel. Unfortunately, the author himself could not survive the rigors of punitive exile visited on him in 1909 by cruel late Qing officials such as Yuan Shikai, and Liu E died that very year in faraway Chinese Turkestan. It is an irony of Chinese literary history that the warmest and most genial satire of the late Qing dynasty was written by the very man who would soon suffer the cruelest fate dispensed to his generation of novelists.

PHILIP F. WILLIAMS

Further Reading

Doleželová-Velingerová, Milena, editor, *The Chinese Novel at the Turn of the Century,* Toronto and Buffalo, New York: University of Toronto Press, 1980

Hsia, C.T., "*The Travels of Lao Ts'an*: An Exploration of Its Art and Meaning," *Tsing Hua Journal of Chinese Studies* 2:2 (1969)

Plaks, Andrew H., editor, *Chinese Narrative: Critical and Theoretical Essays,* Princeton, New Jersey: Princeton University Press, 1977

Wang, David Der-wei, *Cong Liu E dao Wang Zhenhe: Zhongguo xiandai xieshi xiaoshuo sanlun* (From Liu E to Wang Zhenhe: Essays on Modern Chinese Realist Fiction), Taipei: Shibao chuban gongsi, 1986

Wei Shaochang, *Lao Can youji ziliao* (Research Materials on *Travels of Lao Can*), Shanghai: Zhonghua shuju, 1962

Yang, Winston L.Y., Peter Li, and Nathan K. Mao, *Classical Chinese Fiction: A Guide to Its Study and Appreciation: Essays and Bibliographies*, Boston: G.K. Hall, and London: Prior, 1978

Zhao, Henry Y.H., *The Uneasy Narrator: Chinese Fiction from the Traditional to the Modern*, Oxford: Oxford University Press, 1995

The Trial by Franz Kafka

Der Prozess 1925

Like Kafka's other novels, *The Trial* is a fragment. He wrote most of it during 1914–15. In 1924 he directed his friend Max Brod to destroy the manuscript along with all his other unpublished material after his death. We owe four-fifths of Kafka's work to Brod's decision not to comply. When Brod began editing *The Trial* he found not a manuscript but an unorganized pile of unnumbered chapters, sketches, and notations. Using his own judgment, he arranged the chapters and coined the title. Scholarship has since established a more accurate sequence. Whatever the arrangement, the meaning remains unaffected; owing to the repetitive nature of the episodes, many are indeed interchangeable. And it is generally agreed that the novel can never be finished; Kafka could have invented new episodes *ad infinitum,* since Josef K., the hero, never changes. He repeats his basic pattern of behavior over and over with each cast of characters.

The Trial displays Kafka's lifelong fascination with the nature of reality. In his 20s he had studied the theories of Franz Brentano (1838–1917), the founder of empirical psychology. He was particularly intrigued by his claim that in the act of perception there is an interdependent relationship between the viewer and the object, that both are partially altered by the act of perceiving. Brentano argued further that whatever we experience— true, imagined, or hallucinated—is actual. Hence, reality is subjective. Interest in the nature of reality situates Kafka within that generation of similarly concerned authors and thinkers: William James, Gertrude Stein, R.M. Rilke, James Joyce, Hermann Broch, Marcel Proust, Virginia Woolf, and others affected by the Brentano school.

Similar to many of Kafka's other heroes, K. cannot cope with objective reality. So he escapes into one of his own creation where he is the innocent victim. The novel is therefore not a reflection of reality but of K.'s distortion of it. The author's narrative technique is to force us to experience this deformed reality as K. does. Kafka's narrator makes no intrusions into the narrative to help us out; he does not want to provide us a secure basis from which to formulate a rational explanation. He draws us into a malevolent universe with no stable core, where we endure baffling conversations and undergo exasperating experiences that defy common sense. In large part this accounts for the nightmarish, anxiety-riven tenor. The incidents present no definite point of view. They are essentially rootless, an exercise in possibilities without affirming or denying a single one. No wonder that reading a Kafka novel has been likened to having an illness.

The Trial's first sentence announces that the novel will explore the theme of guilt and innocence: "Someone must have denounced Josef K., for without having done anything bad, he was arrested one morning." As the novel progresses, however, we see that K. is legally innocent but morally guilty. In Kafka's world there is no such thing as a state of innocence. Simply by living we inflict pain and misfortune. Such instances occur throughout the book: after his arrest he apologizes to his landlady for upsetting the household; he begs pardon of Fraulein Burstner that her room was used for his interrogation without permission; he complains to the Court about the two warders' actions at his arrest and becomes responsible for the beating they get from the Whipper. He is guilty of bringing disgrace on his family; he neglects his clients at the bank. Directly or indirectly, he brings misfortune to almost everyone he meets. We learn that moral transgressions attract the Court.

For Kafka, the only authentic way to deal with guilt is to regard it as one of life's inevitabilities. The inauthentic reaction is to project it onto someone else. This is K.'s procedure. Again in the novel's first sentence, he "awakens" to the fact of his guilt, but he immediately blames the "someone" who denounced him. At first, he does admit to the possibility of culpability when he considers whether to draw up a written defense for the Court in which he would justify his life. But he soon concludes that to win his case "it was imperative to banish from his mind once and for all the idea of possible guilt." In rejecting responsibility he rejects freedom.

The book is also a grotesque distortion of the Bildungsroman (novel of education). In that genre the hero is often aided by one or more mentors who assist him in his quest for enlightenment. Yet K. surrounds himself with people who have neither power nor influence. What he is really doing is thrusting the responsibility onto their shoulders. He recruits Fraulein Burstner because she will soon become a legal secretary; instead of approaching the court usher directly, he appeals to his wife; he cultivates his lawyer's maid in the mistaken notion that she has influence. Toward the end, the priest at the cathedral warns him that he is relying too heavily on others and that he is seeking the wrong kind of help. This is the message of his parable about the Man from the Country who seeks entry to the Law and finds a guard at the door. Like K., he does not take the direct approach and simply walk through. Instead, he appeals to the fleas in the guard's fur collar.

Kafka makes it clear that the only way K. can gain redemption and thus win his case is to accept the burden of responsibility. The last of his many chances occurs at the very end as the two executioners pass the knife back and forth over his head. K. knows that he is being given the opportunity to do the job himself. Of course, his reluctance is not his fault: "The responsibility for this last failure of his lay with the one who had denied him the remnant of strength necessary for the deed."

JOHN D. SIMONS

See also Franz Kafka

Further Reading

Emrich, Wilhelm, *Franz Kafka,* Frankfurt: Athenaum, 1958
Flores, Angel, and Homer Swander, editors, *Franz Kafka Today,* Madison: University of Wisconsin Press, 1958
Heidsieck, Arnold, *The Intellectual Contexts of Kafka's Fiction: Philosophy, Law, Religion,* Columbia, South Carolina: Camden House, 1994
Karl, Frederick, *Franz Kafka: Representative Man,* New York: Ticknor and Fields, 1991
Koelb, Clayton, *Kafka's Rhetoric: The Passion of Reading,* Ithaca, New York: Cornell University Press, 1989
Kraft, Herbert, *Someone Like K.: Kafka's Novels,* Wurzburg: Konigshausen and Neumann, 1991
Pascal, Roy, *The German Novel,* Manchester: Manchester University Press, and Toronto: University of Toronto Press, 1956
Politzer, Heinrich, *Franz Kafka: Parable and Paradox,* Ithaca, New York: Cornell University Press, 1962; revised and expanded edition, 1966

Tristram Shandy by Laurence Sterne

1759–67

When the first installment of *Tristram Shandy* was published in December 1759, it became an almost overnight success. Laurence Sterne was lionized as one of the first literary celebrities and his work engendered numerous imitations, pamphlet responses, and offshoots such as "Shandean" card games, recipes, and dances. Although for some readers its novelty and surprise had worn off by the time the final volumes appeared in 1765 and 1767, *Tristram Shandy* remained a best-seller into the next century. Yet, in spite of the popularity that led one anonymous pamphleteer to describe *Tristram Shandy* as "the pocket-companion of the nation," the critical responses were mixed from the outset.

In the wake of Samuel Richardson's success in the 1740s and 1750s, critics in influential periodicals both responded to, and helped create, an increasing taste for the decorous and sentimental in fiction. In this context, Sterne's willingness to intermingle pathos with robust satire and bawdy Rabelaisian comedy at times provoked extreme responses from reviewers. *Tristram Shandy* was praised for its sentimental beauties and blamed for what were considered lapses into obscenity. While critics were ambivalent about the work's moral integrity, its apparent formal chaos proved still more problematic as readers and commentators sought to solve the puzzle of *Tristram Shandy*'s labyrinthine digressions and freedom from the constraints of chronology.

Although Dr. Johnson famously remarked of *Tristram Shandy* that "nothing odd will do long," its oddness has often been overstressed. Because literary historians have traditionally presented only selective accounts of 18th-century fiction, *Tristram Shandy* may appear unique and remarkably prescient. Placed starkly alongside the embryonic realisms of Daniel Defoe, Richardson, Henry Fielding, and Tobias Smollett, *Tristram Shandy* may appear as either a sui generis freak or a knowingly parodic anti-novel. But this is to ignore what *Tristram Shandy* shares with Menippean satires of the 17th and early 18th centuries, and to elide the consistently varied and experimental nature of 18th-century prose fiction. That Sterne may not have read what we now regard as the landmarks of the 18th-century novel—let alone have felt confident enough to parody diverse and still emergent novelistic conventions—suggests that *Tristram Shandy* only appears retrospectively as an anti-novel.

Tristram Shandy's distinctiveness is, perhaps, best revealed by paying some attention to its typicality. The satire on systems that informs *Tristram Shandy* has a lineage that stretches back to classical literature, but Sterne's more particular models are the narrative satires of François Rabelais and Jonathan Swift. If satiric and didactic ends dominate *Tristram Shandy* in a way alien to the novel as it was to develop in the 19th and 20th centuries, Sterne's novel still shares much with contemporary prose fiction whose aims are not primarily satiric. Indeed, as J. Paul Hunter remarks in *Before Novels: The Cultural Contexts of Eighteenth-Century English Fiction* (1990), *Tristram Shandy*'s "anxieties about the past, lineage, and time, and . . . its frustrated inability to locate individuals . . . in full intersubjectivity," make it "the paradigm of the eighteenth-century novel." *Tristram Shandy* is concerned, too, about questions of virtue and sociality in ways that make it comparable to numerous mid-cen-

tury narratives. Similarly, Sterne's much misunderstood deployment of pathetic rhetoric, and his consistent approval of natural "simplicity" at the expense of "art," partake of the same broad social and cultural trends that we associate with mid-century novels of sentiment and sensibility.

When Sterne described *Tristram Shandy* as a "ludicrous Satyr," Miguel de Cervantes was the model invoked with undiluted approbation, and the debt to *Don Quixote* (1605–15) is an important one. Sterne especially valued *Don Quixote* for a kind of mock-heroic voice that he described as "Cervantic humor," but Cervantes' influence may also be felt both in Sterne's tendency to embed tales within tales and in his approach to character. The relationship between Uncle Toby and Corporal Trim, for example, echoes that of the Don and Sancho, and the Shandy brothers' hobby-horses are figured as quixotic aberrations. The key, however, to the relationship with Cervantes is a shared Christian scepticism that is also the hallmark of Sterne's other favorites in the tradition of what D.W. Jefferson has called "learned wit." Just as the Menippean satires of Robert Burton, Desiderius Erasmus, Rabelais, and Swift and the sceptical and serpentine discourse of Michel de Montaigne's *Essais* (1580; *Essays*) enact their scepticism of worldly truths, so *Tristram Shandy* and *Don Quixote* enact theirs in a wholesale rejection of the certainties implied by linear, dogmatic narrative.

Interestingly, the discursive hybridity that Mikhail Bakhtin saw as a defining characteristic of "novelness" is foregrounded in *Tristram Shandy* in a number of significant ways. By including nonfictional texts within the fabric of the fiction—one of his own sermons, a 12th-century curse of excommunication, and a 1733 "memoire" by the doctors of the Sorbonne, for example—Sterne raises questions about the boundaries between world and text. More broadly, *Tristram Shandy* combines a hodgepodge of genres and discursive characteristics into a whole that still retains the integrity of its distinct discourses. The mixing of discourses; the typographical devices (drawing attention to both the limits of language and the materiality of the book); the digressions; the leisurely movement of the time scheme backward and forward; and the novel "ending" five years before the birth of the hero narrator all contribute to Sterne's efforts to counter monolithic certainty. Beginning on the night of Tristram's conception and ending without even attempting to tie up many of the narrative loose ends begun in the course of the nine volumes, Sterne creates an open text that manages, for all its conservative satire, to escape closure.

In the 18th century, *Tristram Shandy*'s impact was substantial, but it was limited in terms of any development of Sterne's narrative techniques. Apart from Denis Diderot's brilliant *Jacques le fataliste* (1796; *Jacques the Fatalist*), Sterne's immediate influence bore fruit in fragmentary, sentimental narratives typified by Henry Mackenzie's *Man of Feeling* (1771). The full impact of *Tristram Shandy* on the subsequent history of the novel awaited the 20th century, when modernists like Virginia Woolf and postmodernists like Carlos Fuentes, Milan Kundera, and Salman Rushdie found inspiration in the possibilities opened up by Sterne's prose, his artful use of unreliable and self-conscious narration, and the broader suggestiveness of narrative play and experiment peculiarly congenial to the various scepticisms of the 20th century.

J.T. PARNELL

See also Laurence Sterne

Further Reading

Byrd, Max, *Tristram Shandy,* London and Boston: Allen and Unwin, 1985

Holtz, William V., *Image and Immortality: A Study of "Tristram Shandy,"* Providence, Rhode Island: Brown University Press, 1970

Lamb, Jonathan, *Sterne's Fiction and the Double Principle,* Cambridge and New York: Cambridge University Press, 1989

Lanham, Richard, *"Tristram Shandy": The Games of Pleasure,* Berkeley: University of California Press, 1973

Mullan, John, "Laurence Sterne and the 'Sociality' of the Novel," in *Sentiment and Sociability: The Language of Feeling in the Eighteenth Century,* Oxford: Clarendon Press, and New York: Oxford University Press, 1988

New, Melvyn, *Laurence Sterne as Satirist: A Reading of "Tristram Shandy,"* Gainesville: University of Florida Press, 1969

New, Melvyn, editor *"Tristram Shandy": Contemporary Critical Essays,* New York: Macmillan, 1992

Pierce, David, and Peter Jan de Voogd, editors, *Laurence Sterne in Modernism and Postmodernism,* Amsterdam and Atlanta, Georgia: Rodopi, 1996

Traugott, John, *Tristram Shandy's World: Sterne's Philosophical Rhetoric,* Berkeley: University of California Press, 1954

Traugott, John, editor, *Laurence Sterne: A Collection of Critical Essays,* Englewood Cliffs, New Jersey: Prentice-Hall, 1968

Anthony Trollope 1815–82

English

Anthony Trollope is probably the most underappreciated of Victorian novelists. He has been stigmatized by both writers and critics for what appears to be his consummate conventionality. Ironically, one of the targets of this indictment has always been Trollope's own boast that his compositional methods were regular to the point of being robotic. In his *An Autobiography* (1883), which contains more commentary on the art of fiction than any other of Trollope's works, he compares writing novels to making shoes and claims that he always produced prose with factory-like methodicalness (a self-description that biographers have since proved to be a misrepresentation—not so much the confessions of a hack as Trollope's misguided attempt to distinguish himself from what he saw as the formal self-indulgence of less craftsmanlike novelists). Trollope has also been taken as a stodgy moralist—partly, again, because of misleading self-descriptions in *An Autobiography* and partly because his narrator often breaks the plane of the narrative to moralize quite openly.

In formal terms Trollope's realistic style has been disparaged for being unrelievedly plain. While some have found the dense ordinariness of his realism compelling—Nathaniel Hawthorne wrote that Trollope's world was "just as real as if some giant had hewn a great lump out of the earth, and put it under a glass case, with all its inhabitants going about their daily business, and not suspecting that they were made a show of"—others have complained about the nondescript prose style, the absence of symbolism, and the lack of dramatic or tragic action. Trollope's love for the conventions of romantic comedy has also given the novels an appearance of formal and thematic complacency. Recently, that complacency has been described in ideological terms as well, with Trollope cast as the most bourgeois of 19th-century novelists. Bradford Booth (1958) called him "the apotheosis of normality," and Mario Praz scorned him for being "the most typical representative . . . of the Biedermeier spirit." Trollope's antiquated set of favorite topics—the English clergy, foxhunting, the nature of the "true gentleman," the value of honesty—have only served to confirm these judgments.

Over the last century Trollope has been viewed, as George Saintsbury put it, as the exemplary writer of "the *average* novel of the third quarter of the century." He has often been singled out as the quintessential representative of a Victorian realistic tradition that modern novelists have sought at all costs to reject. Virginia Woolf observed that "if fiction had remained what it was to . . . Trollope, fiction would by this time be dead." More so than any other Victorian novelist, Trollope has been seen as the embodiment of the mainstream tradition of the novel and has been reviled for his fidelity to the values of that tradition.

Over the last three decades, however, a dramatic critical revaluation of Trollope's artistic stature and of his contributions to the history of the novel has taken place. This new scholarly appreciation has focused on Trollope's subtle but nevertheless extraordinary complexity, both thematic and formal—a complexity that cannot be grasped locally, in one particular passage or even in one particular novel, but which only accrues over the course of his work. As the historian of the English novel Walter Allen put it, Trollope's art is an "art of the cumulative," and the immense size of his oeuvre thus has serious aesthetic implications. Most important, Trollope's reputation as a moralist has risen greatly, as critics have pointed out the complex ironies and ambiguities his plots build up over the course of narrative time and over the course of his multinovel chronicles. The great complexities of moral action that result have caused some critics to see Trollope as an exemplar of "situation ethics" rather than as a strict moralist. In terms of style, a parallel preference for complex counterpointing enabled Trollope to produce an art that mixes realism and self-conscious artificiality to an extreme degree. As a result, Trollope has proved particularly stimulating for those interested in the relationship between ethics and aesthetics.

The formal means by which Trollope produces fictional complexity are both simple and unique. Trollope complicated the straightforward action of his main plots with disruptive subplots, for one thing, and, for another, he complicated the novels' moral implications through the reflections of his narrator's interventions, which, although reviled by many for being reductive, are actually qualified or even undermined by narrative events. Trollope's subplots always counter the main action rather than reinforce it, often parodying the moral or thematic lessons of the main plot by means of mirrored themes and motifs instead of through narrative action. These reversals make it very difficult to reduce the meaning of any particular novel to a single, noncontradictory moral position. Trollope developed his use of these subplots in increasingly sophisticated ways over the course of his career, and they eventually allowed him to conceal unorthodox ideas beneath the conventional surface of his narratives, as in his subtle but systematic championing of female independence in the later novels (a good example is the flattering treatment of the minor character Mrs. Hurtle in *The Way We Live Now* [1875]). Trollope's narrator, while intrusively moralistic, often intervenes to point out how wrong predictable judgments can be and how likely it is that his readers have already drawn the wrong conclusions—interventions that are themselves often qualified by later events in the novels. The effect of these techniques—subplot reversals and dramatized narratorial intervention—is to complicate readerly responses without necessarily overturning them. In this way, Trollope's narrative style both sustains traditions of formal realism and undermines them. As Walter Kendrick (1980) has put it, "The realized novel, for Trollope, is never a static structure to be contemplated or reflected upon. It is always dynamic, a process rather than an object." From being regarded as the naïve victim of an outmoded realistic tradition, then, Trollope has lately come to be seen as a writer who sheds a great deal of light on realism's complex potentials and thus as someone who occupies an intriguing position between traditional and modern forms of the novel.

Trollope is also notable for having developed the chronicle form of fiction. The Barsetshire and Palliser chronicles are his two official series, but characters from one Trollope novel often turn up in the pages of another. Trollope has been praised for his psychological portraits of character, and the scope of his chronicles is largely responsible for his ability to portray the shifting aspects of character psychology as well as the evolutionary changes that define both continuity and discontinuity between an individual self at different life stages—a perspective that further contributes to the moral complexity of his art.

In these ways, Trollope's work has been central to the critical revaluation of Victorian realism that has taken place recently, and increasing regard for him as a writer of great formal dexterity has helped critics revise the caricatures of Victorian realism often deployed by modernist writers in their attempts to distance themselves from the forms of the past. The rediscovery of Trollope's aesthetic sophistication has also clarified his importance in the development of techniques of narrative, thematic, and formal complication that were later adopted by other novelists.

JOHN KUCICH

See also Barsetshire Novels

Biography

Born 24 April 1815 in London, son of writer Frances Trollope. Attended Harrow School, Middlesex, 1822–25 and 1831–33; Winchester College, Hampshire, 1825–30. Classical usher at a school in Brussels, 1834; worked for the British Post Office, 1834–67; surveyor's clerk, later deputy surveyor, in Bangher, Clonmel, and Belfast, Northern Ireland, 1841–54; chief surveyor, Dublin, 1854–59; chief surveyor of the Eastern District, London, 1859–67; proposed the use of letter boxes; made official visits to Egypt, 1858, the West Indies, 1858–59, and the United States, 1861–62, 1868; lived at Waltham House, Hertfordshire, 1859–71, in London from 1872, and at Harting Grange, Sussex, until 1882; one of the founders of *Fortnightly Review*, 1865; editor, *Pall Mall Gazette*, 1865–66, and *St. Paul's Magazine*, 1867–70; Liberal parliamentary candidate for Beverley, 1868; traveled in Australia and New Zealand, 1871–72, Australia, 1875, and South Africa, 1877. Died 6 December 1882.

Novels by Trollope

The Macdermots of Ballycloran, 1847
The Kellys and the O'Kellys; or, Landlords and Tenants: A Tale of Irish Life, 1848
La Vendée, 1850
The Warden, 1855
Barchester Towers, 1857
The Three Clerks, 1858
Doctor Thorne, 1858
The Bertrams, 1859
Castle Richmond, 1860
Framley Parsonage, 1861
Orley Farm, 1862
The Struggles of Brown, Jones, and Robinson, by One of the Firm, 1862
Rachel Ray, 1863
The Small House at Allington, 1864
Can You Forgive Her?, 1864
Miss Mackenzie, 1865
The Belton Estate, 1866
Nina Balatka, 1867
The Last Chronicle of Barset, 1867
The Claverings, 1867
Linda Tressel, 1868
Phineas Finn, The Irish Member, 1869
He Knew He Was Right, 1869
The Vicar of Bullhampton, 1870
Sir Harry Hotspur of Humblethwaite, 1871
Ralph the Heir, 1871
The Golden Lion of Granpère, 1872
The Eustace Diamonds, 1872
Lady Anna, 1873
Phineas Redux, 1874
Harry Heathcote of Gangoil, 1874
The Way We Live Now, 1875
The Prime Minister, 1876
The American Senator, 1877
Is He Popenjoy?, 1878
An Eye for an Eye, 1879
John Caldigate, 1879

Cousin Henry, 1879
The Duke's Children, 1880
Dr. Wortle's School, 1881
Ayala's Angel, 1881
The Fixed Period, 1882
Marion Fay, 1882
Kept in the Dark, 1882
Mr. Scarborough's Family, 1883
The Landleaguers, 1883
An Old Man's Love, 1884

Other Writings: short stories, plays, journalism, travel books, an autobiography, lectures, and letters.

Further Reading

ApRoberts, Ruth, *The Moral Trollope,* Athens: Ohio University Press, and London: Chatto and Windus, 1971

Booth, Bradford A., *Anthony Trollope: Aspects of His Life and Art,* London: Hulton, and Bloomington: Indiana University Press, 1958

Herbert, Christopher, *Trollope and Comic Pleasure,* Chicago: University of Chicago Press, 1987

Kendrick, Walter M., *The Novel-Machine: The Theory and Fiction of Anthony Trollope,* Baltimore: Johns Hopkins University Press, 1980

Kincaid, James, *The Novels of Anthony Trollope,* Oxford: Clarendon Press, 1977

Miller, D.A., "The Novel as Usual: Trollope's *Barchester Towers,*" in *Sex, Politics, and Science in the Nineteenth-Century Novel,* edited by Ruth Bernard Yeazell, Baltimore: Johns Hopkins University Press, 1986

Miller, J. Hillis, *The Form of Victorian Fiction: Thackeray, Dickens, Trollope, George Eliot, Meredith, and Hardy,* Notre Dame, Indiana: University of Notre Dame Press, 1968

Nardin, Jane, *He Knew She Was Right: The Independent Woman in the Novels of Anthony Trollope,* Carbondale: Southern Illinois University Press, 1989

Ivan Turgenev 1818–83

Russian

Ivan Turgenev stands at the beginning of the 19th-century Russian tradition of the novel in several important respects: he was the first Russian novelist to treat the genre as an evolving form (developing it in a way that has come to be called "Turgenevan"), the first to achieve an international reputation as a "Russian" novelist, and the first to demonstrate how the novel in a Russian context could be uniquely relevant to contemporary social and political life. The work of his immediate predecessors—Aleksandr Pushkin's *Evgenii Onegin* (1833; *Eugene Onegin*), Mikhail Lermontov's *Geroi nashego vremeni* (1840; *A Hero of Our Time*), and Nikolai Gogol's *Mertvye dushi* (1842; *Dead Souls*), to name the principal examples—created the beginnings of the Russian novel as we now know it, but this hardly constituted a tradition. Turgenev may have adopted from Pushkin, for example, a classical objectivity and a love-story format, from Lermontov a concern with psychological portraiture, from Gogol' the importance of setting, social parody, and linguistic enrichment, but what he contributed principally to the genre was social and political relevance through his manner of portraying types representative of the Russian intelligentsia during the middle decades of the 19th century.

Although born to privilege as a member of the serf-owning nobility, Turgenev as a teenager swore a "Hannibal's oath" against serfdom and all other forms of tyranny. As a student educated abroad, where he "plunged," as he put it, "into the German Sea," he acquired a lasting admiration for liberal Western values. If in a personal sense this infatuation took the form of a lifelong love for the famous singer Pauline Viardot, in a political sense it developed into a conviction that the gradual implementation of liberal reforms, not revolution, was the only means to ensure the true freedom of the individual. He sought always to bridge the differences between classes and generations, between Russia and Europe; as an agnostic, he saw the tragedy of the human condition while never abandoning an optimistic faith in human idealism.

Artistically Turgenev achieved in his own work a special blend of social commentary and love story that was always notable for its style, especially in descriptions of nature. Formally speaking, he evolved a distinctive type of novel from the short-story form and from his experience as a playwright. Miniaturist by comparison with the novels of Walter Scott, Honoré de Balzac, and Charles Dickens, more akin to George Sand's novels and the German Romantic *Novellen,* the Turgenevan novel began as portraiture bordering on biography but objectified by ensuring that the characters of the novel's setting were each introduced with varying degrees of biographical detail, as if they were dramatis personae given roles to play in predominantly dialogue-based scenes. As a consequence, the portrayal of the "stranger" from outside through gradual revelation of his strengths and weaknesses became the novel's main purpose.

Rudin (1856; *Rudin*) set the tone for this kind of short novel. Turgenev's mastery in creating ambience, always the hallmark of his "month in the summer" novels, was evident in his portrayal of the stranger Rudin, a Hamlet-like "superfluous man" of cosmopolitan background, entering a country-estate setting to profess new ideas about love, politics, and the intelligentsia's social role. While portraiture and failed love story were the staple ingredients of Turgenev's fiction, his novels had a strong political dimension as well. Turgenev became the chronicler of Russian intelligentsia types representative of the 1840s, 1850s, and 1860s. His second novel, *Dvorianskoe gnezdo* (1859; *Home of the Gentry*), illustrated the plight of Turgenev's own generation of the 1840s, Westernized by their education and upbringing but unable to find any true "home" or "nest" in their own country.

The emergence of a younger intelligentsia in the post–Crimean War period (1855–61) demanded new types, and Turgenev responded with his first essay in Quixotic portraiture (based on the contrast of types described in his lecture "Hamlet and Don Quixote") in the figure of the independent-minded Elena, heroine of his third novel, *Nakanune* (1860; *On the Eve*). Looser in construction and memorable more for individual scenes than as a whole, this novel engaged the issue of the "positive hero" of the 1860s in the frankly unsuccessful image of a Bulgarian patriot; yet it was paradoxically both more topical in its relevance to Russia on the eve of reforms and more pessimistic in its implications that all human hopes for change were foredoomed.

Turgenev's masterpiece, *Ottsy i deti* (1862; *Fathers and Sons*), brought his particular techniques as a novelist to perfection. It demonstrated not only a nearly seamless blending of the compositional elements—character development, "staged" dialogue scenes, love story—but, more importantly, a mastery in the portrayal of the hero, Bazarov, through placing him in a variety of locales to illuminate differing aspects of his personality. Turgenev succeeded in so objectifying his portrayal of his "nihilist" hero that Bazarov's emergence as a sociopolitical type and his tragic image as the epitome of practical, hard-headed scientific man brought low by his fallible humanity have tantalized generations of readers.

Turgenev's final two novels, *Dym* (1867; *Smoke*) and *Nov'* (1877; *Virgin Soil*), show no further marked evolution in his art as a novelist, although the former, set unusually in Baden-Baden, enjoyed great popularity in Western Europe and helped to establish his international reputation. For the last 20 years of his life he lived mostly abroad, settling finally in Paris, where he became the close friend of Gustave Flaubert and the admired mentor of Henry James.

Turgenev's enormous reputation in late 19th-century Europe (never quite so marked in North America) owed partly to his being a Russian novelist who had, with a distinctive type of short novel blending politics, historical authenticity, and poignant love story, not only matched but in many ways transformed the predominantly European genre of the novel. The subtlety, the "mixture of fact and vision," as Virginia Woolf called it, the balance, the wit and objectivity, all held a deep appeal for writers as diverse as Joseph Conrad and Thomas Mann. Despite the much larger reputations since acquired by Dostoevskii and Tolstoi, Turgenev's qualities as an artist justified in its time Henry James' description of Turgenev as "the novelist's novelist" and Isaiah Berlin's claim a century later that "the figure of the well-meaning, troubled, self-questioning liberal" had become Turgenev's universal legacy.

RICHARD FREEBORN

See also Fathers and Sons

Biography

Born in Orel, Russia, 9 November 1818. Attended Moscow University, 1833–34; St. Petersburg University, 1834–37; University of Berlin, 1838–41; completed master's exam in St. Petersburg, 1842. Worked for the Ministry of the Interior, 1843–45; thereafter concentrated on country pursuits, writing, and travel; intimate relationship with the singer Pauline Garcia Viardot; traveled to France with her and her husband, 1845–46 and 1847–50; coined the phrase "superfluous man" in a story of 1850; arrested and confined to his country estate for writing a commemorative article on Gogol's death, 1852–53; left Russia to live in Western Europe, 1856: first in Baden-Baden, then in Paris with the Viardots, 1871–83. Died in Bougival, near Paris, 3 September 1883.

Novels by Turgenev

Rudin, 1856; edited by Galina Stilman, 1955; as *Dmitri Roudine,* 1873; as *Rudin,* translated by Richard Freeborn, 1975; also translated by Kathleen Cook, with *A Nest of the Gentry,* 1985

Dvorianskoe gnezdo, 1859; as *A Nest of Gentlefolk,* 1869; as *Lisa,* 1872; as *A House of Gentlefolk,* translated by Constance Garnett, 1897; as *A Nest of Hereditary Legislators,* translated by Franz Davidovitch Davies, 1913; as *A Nest of the Gentry,* translated by Bernard Isaacs, 1947; also translated by Kathleen Cook, with *Rudin,* 1985; as *Home of the Gentry,* translated by Richard Freeborn, 1970

Nakanune, 1860; as *On the Eve,* translated by C.E. Turner, 1871; also translated by Isabel F. Hapgood, 1903

Ottsy i deti, 1862; as *Fathers and Sons,* translated by Eugene Schuyler, 1867; numerous subsequent translations including by Barbara Makanowitzky, 1959, Rosemary Edmonds, 1965, Ralph E. Matlaw, 1989, Richard Freeborn, 1991, and Michael R. Katz, 1994; as *Fathers and Children,* translated by Avril Pyman, 1991

Dym, 1867; translated as *Smoke,* 1868

Nov', 1877; as *Virgin Soil,* translated by T.S. Perry, 1877; also translated by Constance Garnett, 1896

Other Writings: short stories, plays, poetry, memoirs, and letters.

Further Reading

Allen, Elizabeth Cheresh, *Beyond Realism: Turgenev's Poetics of Secular Salvation,* Stanford, California: Stanford University Press, 1992

Berlin, Isaiah, *Fathers and Children: Turgenev and the Liberal Predicament,* Oxford: Clarendon Press, 1972

Costlow, Jane T., *Worlds within Worlds: The Novels of Ivan Turgenev,* Princeton, New Jersey: Princeton University Press, 1990

Freeborn, Richard, *Turgenev: The Novelist's Novelist,* London: Oxford University Press, 1960

Garnett, Edward, *Turgenev: A Study,* London: Collins, 1917

Kagan-Kans, Eva Cherniavsky, *Hamlet and Don Quixote: Turgenev's Ambivalent Vision,* The Hague: Mouton, 1975

Lowe, David Allan, *Turgenev's "Fathers and Sons,"* Ann Arbor, Michigan: Ardis, 1983

Seeley, Frank F., *Turgenev: A Reading of His Fiction,* Cambridge and New York: Cambridge University Press, 1991

Turton, Glyn, *Turgenev and the Context of English Literature 1850–1900,* London and New York: Routledge, 1992

Waddington, Patrick, *Turgenev and England,* London: Macmillan, 1980; New York: New York University Press, 1981

Wasiolek, Edward, *Fathers and Sons: Russia at the Cross-roads,* New York: Twayne, 1993

Woodward, James B., *Turgenev's "Fathers and Sons,"* London: Bristol Classic Press, 1996

Turkish Novel

The development of the novel in Turkey has paralleled the development of the modern Turkish state itself. The introduction of the novel into the Turkish language in the second half of the 19th century was but a small part of the massive transformation of Turkish society from the closed theocracy of the Ottoman Empire into a democratic, secular nation comprised of Western-style social and political institutions.

The intimate connection between the novel and broader historical and political trends has had two major effects on the development of Turkish literature since the mid–19th century. First, the predominant form of the novel in Turkey has been realist, a fact that is especially true of the 20th-century novel. The predominance of this form can be traced both to the historical period during which European novels first made their appearance in Turkey as well as to uses that were made of translated Western texts and the first Turkish novels. Although a wide variety of Western novels were translated into Turkish, the Turkish novel quickly assumed the dominant characteristics of late 19th-century realist and naturalist fiction. Realism suited the use of the novel as a pedagogical, didactic tool to familiarize Turks with the values of modernity. Second, just as Turkish civil society has continued to struggle to find its identity at the tense intersection of traditional Islamic conservatism and liberal Western modernism, the Turkish novel also has had to find its own identity between the heavy influence of foreign models and the traditions of its own literary heritage.

Although a variety of narrative forms existed in the Turkish language prior to the *Tanzimat* (Reorganization) period of Turkish history—including both verse and prose narratives—no genre existed that approximated the novel either in its form or in its mass popularity. Classical narratives in verse (*mesnevi*), which largely had been adapted from the Persian literary tradition, were rhetorically and formally fixed, and limited thematically to a few subjects, such as the epic quests of lovers for their beloveds. These themes would become the basis for the very first Turkish novels. Prose narratives were adaptations of these *mesnevi*s and constituted a relatively minor literary form. In comparison to the legends, epics, folk stories, moral fables and popularized histories disseminated orally or read by storytellers, which were widely known and formed a shared cultural tradition, these classical narrative forms were extremely obscure and exerted relatively little influence either on the development of the Turkish novel or on Turkish literature more generally. This was due not only to the traditional identification of literary writing with poetry and with the use of prose for the writing of history, but to the gradual subsumption of storytelling to an emphasis on style in the historical development of these narratives. As Ahmet Evin has written, "sense was subordinated to sound, so much so that rhyming words punctuated phrases regardless of whether they made any sense at all. This futile obsession with prose style rendered stories written in the classical tradition nearly incomprehensible" (see Evin, 1983). Although writers did make appeals to the classical narrative tradition in constructing the first indigenous novels, the degree of outright "borrowing" was thus limited from the outset. The Turkish novel had to be constructed almost out of nothing, and so it is not surprising that the challenges of this early period are among the most interesting in the history of Turkish literature.

Initiated in 1839 by the proclamation of the Noble Rescript of the Rose Chamber, the *Tanzimat* was the first of many attempts to formally bring about the modernization of Turkish society through the establishment of Western-style political institutions. This period of Turkish history ushered in an openness toward the outside world, which was seen as a positive source of ideas and trends that could be put to use in reorganizing Turkish politics and society. One of the outcomes of the *Tanzimat* was the establishment of a civil bureaucracy, which produced a middle-class from whose ranks rose an intelligentsia strongly committed to the modernizing ideology of the West. The creation of several governmental institutions in the 19th century was important to the eventual introduction of the novel in Turkey, although perhaps none more so than the establishment of the Translation Office in 1933. The Office performed an essential role in the modernization of Turkey. While its official role was to train translators in European languages, particularly in French, it became unofficially a training school for an emergent class of Westernized statesmen and writers, including those writers and translators who first introduced the novel into Turkey.

The novel first appeared in Turkish in the form of translations of French texts. The very first such translation, the Grand Vizier Yusuf Kâmil Paşa's version of Abbé Fénelon's *Télémaque* (1699), *Tercüme-i Telemak* (1859; The Translation of *Télémaque*), introduced some of the basic structures of the novel, especially its attention to the prosaic instead of the fabulous. As was the case with many of these translations, Pasa's translation was hardly literal: some parts of Fénelon's book were summarized, others written in poetic form. The early difficulty of rendering a genre as alien as the novel into a form that could be understood by the Turkish reading public, and the linguistic problems raised by apparently untranslatable words and concepts, led to significant modifications and alterations of the novels that were translated. For example, an abridged version of Victor Hugo's *Les Misérables* was serialized in the leading Turkish independent paper of the period, *Tercüman-i Ahval* (The Interpreter of Events), in a style Saliha Parker describes as "the same as that of the standard police report of the time" and "abridged to the point of reducing the novel to a crime story" (Parker in Ostle, 1991). From the beginning, then, these translations involved an adaptation of the genre to local purposes rather than a straightforward adoption of foreign literary models. The apparently random choice of the early translations, which ranged from acknowledged masterpieces of contemporary European literature to forgotten historical curiosities to the popular texts of the day (including detective stories by Xavier de Montepin and the Parisian stories of Paul de Kock), can in this respect also be seen in terms of their utility in communicating and explaining the values and ideas of the Enlightenment to members of the Turkish intelligentsia and the public at large.

The issue of readership was thus established early as an important concern for the novel in Turkey. Perhaps more than in any other literature, the novel in Turkey has always been produced with the aim of reaching a broad readership, which has had an impact on form and theme. The simplicity of style and language required by the translations in order to secure an audience for this unusual form became a feature of the first Turkish novels as well. So, too, did the necessity for prose to relate to the immediate problems faced by a society undergoing a radical transformation. The amount of conscious aestheticism in Turkish literature—that is, literature written in terms of "art for art's sake"—has been a feature of only a limited number of novels throughout its history.

The first Turkish novel has sometimes been identified as Şemseddin Sami's *Taaşşuk-i Talât ve Finat* (1872; The Love of Talat and Finat), although this work is actually more of a hybrid text, a transitional form between classical prose narrative and the novel as such; the same may be said of the series of long, connected stories in Emin Nihat's *Müsameretname* (1872; Night Entertainment), which imitates *The Decameron* in form. In these two works, and in the stories of Ahmed Midhat, a thematic concern with the immediate problems of society is introduced for the first time in Turkish prose; however, other elements normally associated with the novel are missing, particularly any form of character development.

It is, therefore, with Namik Kemal's *Intibah: Sergüzeşt-i Ali Bey* (1876; The Awakening: Ali Bey's Adventures) that the Turkish novel proper begins. Kemal was aware of the shortcomings of his novel, including the relative simplicity of its plot, which relies on a pattern provided by classical Turkish narrative: Ali Bey, a government bureaucrat, embarks on a dangerous affair with a courtesan belonging to a rich merchant, with disastrous results for all involved. Nevertheless, Kemal in many respects achieved his stated intention in writing *Intibah*. For Kemal, the novel constituted a self-conscious experiment in the creation of a Turkish literary language appropriate to the novel. *Intibah*'s great attention to detail and to the psychological experience of the characters makes it a landmark in Turkish fiction, even if it is also a text that is formally incoherent—a pastiche of devices, techniques, and narrative models adopted from a variety of different novelistic subgenres.

The period immediately following the introduction of the novel into Turkey was marked by political events that had an important effect on consequent attempts to indigenize the genre. Chief among these events were the end of the *Tanzimat* in 1876, with the establishment of an Ottoman constitution and parliamentary democracy, and the almost immediate reversal of these gains as a result of the dispersal of parliament by Abdülhamid II in 1878. Hamidian censorship had a chilling effect on the political preoccupations of early Turkish novels. In place of an explicit attention to politics, writers began to explore social issues in Turkish society. The novel continued to be used as a way of introducing Western ideas into Turkish society, although increasingly it was used to argue for an appropriate Westernization that would be integrated with traditional beliefs and structures. The many novels of this period that satirized and criticized Turkish elites for their Western pretensions attest to the frustration of the *Tanzimat*-era literary elite with the direction of social change, and with the barriers that had been erected to Westernization.

The best example of this kind of satirical text is perhaps Recaizade Mahmut Ekrem's *Araba Sevdast* (1889; Obsession with a Carriage). The protagonist of this novel, Bihruz Bey, is an extreme version of the figure of the Westernized dandy—a favorite figure for the novelists of this period. Educated superficially in Western ways, Bihruz Bey sees himself as a romantic hero in French novels, and does little except shop, search for lovers in public parks, and travel about in his expensive new carriage. Ekrem's novel, and those by Halid Ziya [Uşakligil], beginning with *Bir Ölünün Defteri* (1889; Diary of a Dead Man), signaled the beginning of a greater attention to individual character development in the novels of the 1880s. Ziya's protagonist in *Bir Ölünün Defteri*, Vecdi, is altered by his experiences in the novel, and works actively to shape his destiny, as opposed to the hero of classical prose, who was static and accepted his fate as a matter of necessity. Perhaps the greatest influence on the development of Turkish literature during this period, which helped to turn the genre away from its earlier, didactic incarnations, was the introduction of Émile Zola's naturalism. The distinctions that existed in Europe between naturalism and realism were collapsed in Turkey, with the result that Zola was read as a realist writer. Therefore, it was Zola's *realism* that was explicitly and coherently argued for as the appropriate form of the Turkish novel by Beşir Fuat in *Victor Hugo* (1885). Ziya's *Hikaye* (1889; Fiction), which traced the development of the novel from its origins up to the 1880s and is perhaps the very best example of literary criticism in the 19th century in Turkey, also argues for the appropriateness of Zola's realism for Turkish literature. Significantly, Hiya argued that the novel should not simply detail events but should also depict its characters' feelings. This approach stands in stark contrast to Ahmed Midhat's *Müşahedat* (1890; Observations), which, although also influenced by Zola, retains a documentary style and a didacticism that represents a step backward in the development of the novel in Turkey.

The development of a true literary realism at the end of the 19th century was nevertheless in some respects impeded by the change of political fortune. For the older generation of writers who tended to belong to the elites employed in government ministries, the novel became one of the only ways to express their political discontent with the Hamidian regime that had put an end to their political aims. What is evident in Midhat's *Müşahedat* is true of other works as well: the novel was used as a platform to directly express political or philosophical positions. In other respects, however, Hamidian censorship perhaps inadvertently aided the growth of realism in Turkish literature. For the generation of writers born in the 1860s, Hamidian censorship, which was limited to Turkish texts, ironically made French texts even more appealing and accessible, especially as French had become the core of elite education. The French novel was in many respects the beginning point for a writer such as Sami Paşazade Sezai. Additionally, this newer generation had greater access to the work of their immediate predecessors than to the classical literary tradition. Sezai, for example, felt that Namik Kemal was the greatest Turkish writer; he discovered the works of the classical prose tradition only in the latter part of his career. It is also with this generation of writers that writing became a profession of its own. At the very least, writers were no longer almost exclusively employed by the government, but had other professions within the ranks of the middle classes that had developed by the end of the century.

A number of significant novels were written during this period. Sezai's *Sergüzeşt* (1889; The Adventure) critiques the institution of slavery through the tragic tale of the slave girl Dilber; it was the last major literary work written prior to the end of slavery in Turkey. Nabizade Nazim's *Karabibik* (1891), named after the novel's protagonist, explores the harsh realities of rural life.

Nazim's novel has been seen as a precursor of "village fiction," even though his depiction of villagers is not entirely sympathetic and at times even appears to be condescending. The novels written by Ziya toward the end of the century include two of his best: *Mai ve Siyah* (1897; The Blue and the Black) and *Aşk-i Memmu* (1900; Forbidden Love). *Mai ve Siyah* is the story of a struggling writer and his problems, and can be read as more generally representative of the tribulations of Turkish writers during this period. It is one of the first novels in the Turkish tradition to focus specifically on the self-development on an individual character. *Aşk-i Memmu* has been described as the high point of literary realism in Turkish letters. Around the central theme of an adulterous affair linking two families in Istanbul's high society, Ziya presents a vivid picture of the social contradictions and tensions with which Turkey entered the 20th century. Other notable writers writing around the turn of the century include Mehmet Rauf, Hüseyin Rahmi Gürpinar, Ahmet Rasim, and Ebubekir Hazim Tepeyran, who also wrote a novel that has been seen as a forerunner of village fiction.

The most significant event of the early part of the century for both Turkish literature and Turkish society was the 1908 Young Turk Revolution and the consequent establishment of the Turkish Republic in 1923 by Mustafa Kemal (who later became Kemal Atatürk). The Young Turk Revolution spawned numerous literary movements. The most significant of these for the novel was the *Genc kalemler* (Young Authors') movement, revolving around the literary magazine of the same name started in 1911. In the 1910s and 1920s prior to the formal establishment of the Republic, nationalism became the dominant ideological preoccupation of both fiction and poetry. Under the influence of nationalism, a didacticism quickly returned to the novel. The debates of the later part of the 19th century about the responsibility of the novel to society, which had been waged with particular vehemence between Namik Kemal and Ekrem, tipped decisively away from Ekrem's position that art/literature should be written for its own sake rather than primarily to instruct or to criticize. Nationalism introduced two other elements to the novel. The first was a thematic shift from an emphasis on upper-class city life to the lives of the poor in rural parts of the country. Related to this was the position advocated by the Young Authors' movement that literary language should be simple, direct, and accessible to the Turkish populace at large. This stood in sharp contrast to the *Servet-i Fünen* (Treasure of the Arts) movement started in 1891, whose attempt to introduce decadence into Turkish writing had more impact on poetry than prose in any case. This populist orientation characterizes the stories of Ömer Seyfettin, the major literary figure connected with the Young Authors. Seyfettin's stories are satirical examinations of rural and urban neighborhoods, with an eye toward defining and defending the unique characteristics and virtues of Turkish society. The example of Seyfettin would be an influence on the novelists of the Republican period.

The fiction of the 1920s and 1930s remained nationalist in orientation. With the establishment of the Republic, writers once again examined the implications of these enormous changes for Turkish society. The novels of Yakup Kadri Karaosmanoğlu, the most important novelist of this period, explore the breakdown of the traditional institutions of Turkish life under the renewed Westernization introduced by Atatürk, and the enormous material and psychological distance separating the urban and rural

parts of the Turkish nation. His best-known novel, *Yaban* (1932; The Stranger), is nevertheless unapologetically nationalist, locating the heart and soul of the nation in the folkloric culture of rural Anatolia. Halide Edid Adivar's *Ateşten Gömlek* (1922; The Shirt of Fire) is typical of the romantic nationalism in the novels of this period. Adivar, the first major female novelist in Turkey and an outspoken advocate for women's rights, is better known for *The Clown and His Daughter* (1935), which was written first in English before being translated into Turkish as *Sinekli Bakkal*. Peyami Safa's *Fatih-Harbiye* (1931), named for the old district of Istanbul (Fatih) and one of its newer, richer, Westernized sections (Harbiye), investigates the problems of the two mutually incompatible worlds that were beginning to emerge out of a modernizing Turkish state. Refik Halit Karay's short stories in *Memleket hikâyeleri* (1919; Stories from the Country) and Reşat Nuri Güntekin's *Çalikuşu* (1922; The Autobiography of a Turkish Girl) are also set in Anatolia, and examine the virtues and problems of peasant life. Mahmut Yesari and Sadri Ertem also emerged as significant novelists of this period.

It is with the novels published since the 1940s that Turkish fiction has been most readily identified internationally. From the 1940s up to the present, the Turkish novel has increasingly been used as a means of alerting society to its most pressing problems. While depictions of rural life for the writers of the Republican period were used to support the development of nationalism through the mining of a primordial, folkloric past, it was the misery and abject poverty of the countryside that became a thematic preoccupation of novelists following World War II. Socialist realism became the dominant form. Sabahaddin Ali's short stories and Mahmut Makal's nonfiction book *Bizim Köy* (1950; A Village in Anatolia), which were among the first literary works to protest the conditions of the peasants, were an important formative influence on the writers of "village fiction." Significantly, the writers of village fiction were often villagers themselves, or were educated in the "village institutes" or People's Houses established by the Republican Party to promote nationalism and to provide financial assistance to the artistic community. The only writer of village fiction and, perhaps with the exception of the poet Nazim Hikmet, the only contemporary writer of international stature in Turkey remains Yashar Kemal. Kemal established his reputation with his very first book, *Ince Memed* (1955; Memed, My Hawk), which offers an extremely vivid, realistic, and despairing view of life in rural Anatolia. Kemal has continued to explore Turkish rural life in all of its complexity, in a language notable for being stripped of all literary pretensions: his audience remains, first and foremost, the peasants themselves, and not an international, cosmopolitan reading public.

Many other writers of village fiction, while less well known, have provided remarkable accounts of Turkish village life. Fakir Baykurt's *Yilanlarin öcü* (1959; Revenge of the Snakes) shows the corruption that exists within the peasant community itself, as local leaders conspire with wealthy outsiders to strip the peasantry of what little they possess. Other writers of village fiction include Samim Kocagöz, Kemal Bilbasar, Talip Apaydin, and Mehmet Basaran. While Orhan Kemal also has been identified as belonging to this group, his subject was the other impoverished, marginal group in Turkish society that village fiction all but forgot: the urban poor, whose ranks have swelled as villagers have fled to the city to improve their living conditions. His *Mur-*

taza (1952) does for the urban poor what *Memed* accomplished for the peasantry: it makes their suffering a real and undeniable fact that must be dealt with if Turkish Westernization is ever truly to be called a success.

In the contemporary period, developments in Turkish literature have increasingly paralleled developments in US and European literature. There are no dominant literary forms or trends, but instead a literary pluralism has flourished, with representative novels written in all of the major forms of 20th-century literary experimentation, i.e., stream of consciousness, surrealism, modernism, postmodernism, and so on. While contemporary Turkish literature has been identified primarily with the work of the realist "village writers," and with the work of Yashar Kemal in particular, this is owing more to the limited availability of Turkish work in English translation (including recent writing by members of the Turkish diaspora living in Germany) than to village fiction qualifying as a dominant literary trend. With the exception of the excellent work of a few dedicated scholars, English-language literary critical research on Turkish literature has been extremely limited in size and scope, impeding a more nuanced understanding of the contemporary literary scene.

These circumstances may be changing somewhat with the work of Turkey's most respected contemporary novelist, Orhan Pamuk. Pamuk's first novel, *Cevdet Bey ve Ogullari* (1982; *Cevdet Bey and His Sons*), is a realist exploration of Western influences on Turkish life. Pamuk's last three novels have all been translated into English, and have been wildly and justly praised, earning him comparisons to Jorge Luis Borges and Italo Calvino. *Beyaz Kale* (1985; *The White Castle*), *Kara Kitap* (1990; *The Black Book*), and *Yeni Hayat* (1995; *New Life*) are postmodern explorations of identity, the confrontation between modernity and tradition, and the shattering of preconceived dichotomies. Full of elaborate ontological puzzles, stunning verbal games, and extravagantly, fascinatingly complex narratives, Pamuk's novels mark a wholesale break with the realist tradition and a renewed attention to the literary aspects of the novel in Turkey.

IMRE SZEMAN

See also Yashar Kemal; Southern Balkan Novel

Further Reading

Birnbaum, Eleazar, "Turkish Literature through the Ages," in *Introduction to Islamic Civilisation,* edited by Roger Savory, Cambridge and New York: Cambridge University Press, 1976

Evin, Ahmet Ö., "Turkish Literature," in *Encyclopedia of World Literature in the 20th Century,* revised edition, edited by Leonard S. Klein, New York: Ungar, 1981

Evin, Ahmet Ö., *Origins and Development of the Turkish Novel,* Minneapolis: Bibliotheca Islamica, 1983

Finn, Robert, "The Early Turkish Novel," Ph.D. diss., Princeton University, 1978

Halman, Talat Sait, "Turkish Literature in the 1960's," *The Literary Review* 15 (1972)

Halman, Talat Sait, "Turkish Literature," in *Columbia Dictionary of Modern European Literature,* 2nd edition, edited by Jean-Albert Bédé and William B. Edgerton, New York: Columbia University Press, 1980

Halman, Talat Sait, editor, *Contemporary Turkish Literature,* Rutherford, New Jersey: Fairleigh Dickinson University Press, 1982

Karpat, K., "Social Themes in Contemporary Turkish Literature," *Middle East Journal* 14 (1960)

Ostle, Robin, editor, *Modern Literature and the Near and Middle East,* London and New York: Routledge, 1991

Parker, Saliha, "Turkey," in *Modern Literature and the Near and Middle East,* edited by Robin Ostle, London and New York: Routledge, 1991

Rathburn, Carol, *The Village in the Turkish Novel and Short Story,* The Hague: Mouton, 1973

Amos Tutuola 1920–

Nigerian

Amos Tutuola's first published novel, *The Palm-Wine Drinkard and His Dead Palm-Wine Tapster in the Deads' Town* (1952), is the tale of a journey from the world of the "alives" to "the Deads' Town" undertaken by an incurable "drinkard." The drinkard is in search of his tapster, who has fallen to his death while tapping palm-wine. Tutuola was already world famous before his compatriot Chinua Achebe, the writer who would later be identified as the inaugurator of modern sub-Saharan African writing, published his seminal *Things Fall Apart* (1958).

Because of his rather slight education and his uncertain command of English (the language he nonetheless chose for his writing), early critics were most sceptical about his long-term prospects as a writer. Some critics in fact expressed misgivings, even apprehension, that his initial success might encourage him to continue writing. But in spite of those doubts Tutuola's productivity has been durable, spanning almost the entire second half of the 20th century. To date, he has published nine novels, two collections of short stories, and a volume of Yoruba folktales. Some of these have been well enough received to have merited translation into several European languages.

From the start, his sources have been Yoruba folktale materials and published Yoruba fictional texts, especially those of D.O. Fagunwa. Innocent of the copyright regulations governing the use of previously published materials, he has freely lifted whole episodes from Fagunwa's work, especially *Ògbójú Ode Nínú Igbó Irúnmalè* (1938; translated by Wole Soyinka as *The Forest of a Thousand Daemons: A Hunter's Saga*), for repeated use in his own tales.

Tutuola's novels have been so consistent in their major characteristics—the complement of characters, the plot, and the language, for example—as to have prompted critics to remark that to have read one book by him is to have read them all. Typically, a hero or heroine departs from home, sometimes with the flimsiest of excuses, to achieve a sometimes most unlikely goal, and in the process encounters a multitude of obstacles that he or she successfully overcomes before returning home in triumph. Thus, in *The Palm-Wine Drinkard,* the objective is to seek out the hero's dead palm-wine tapster in the land of the dead and secure his return. In *Simbi and the Satyr of the Dark Jungle* (1955), the heroine leaves the home of her wealthy and pampering mother to venture into the wilds in search of "the meanings of the 'Poverty' and of the 'Punishment'." In *The Witch-Herbalist of the Remote Town* (1981), a husband undertakes a perilous pilgrimage to the abode of an omniscient and omnipotent Witch Mother in search of medication that would cure his wife of her barrenness.

More often than not, the hero or heroine triumphs in many episodic encounters with adversaries that are characteristically as outlandishly grotesque as the author can make them and in situations calculated to elicit maximum shock or repulsion (many of these reprised in the same work or repeated in different works). Eventually, both hero and author seem to lose sight of the original objective, with the result that the ending bears little relationship to the premise for the adventure. *The Palm-Wine Drinkard* ends not with the return of the tapster or the magic egg he gives to the hero, but with the settling of a dispute between Earth and Heaven and the ending of the famine the dispute had engendered. Simbi returns from her adventure with three "gods" that represent a boon for her people, reforms a habitual kidnapper, and spends the rest of her time going from door to door cautioning young women against emulating her. The ending of *The Witch-Herbalist* has little to do with the barrenness of the hero's wife.

Tutuola was evidently aware of his limitations as a writer. Of his style, he once told an interviewer, "The grammar is not correct at all. I made many mistakes." Paradoxically it was precisely that infelicity of style that proved one of Tutuola's greatest assets upon his introduction to the European reading public. Dylan Thomas, whose positive review many credit with making Tutuola's reputation for all time, described it as "young English . . . always terse and direct, strong, wry, flat and savoury," while V.S. Pritchett characterized his voice as "like the beginning of man on earth, man emerging, wounded and growing" (both in Lindfors, 1975).

Tutuola has remained outside the mainstream of modern African writing. His peers are characteristically university educated and enjoy frequent invitations to speak at university and other fora around the world, sometimes occupying distinguished chairs of literature in European or American universities, but Tutuola is a loner. He is out of place among other African literati and painfully uncommunicative in interviews and on the few occasions that he has accepted invitations to venture abroad, a trait observers attribute to extreme shyness.

Moreover, he is quite untouched by the sociopolitical preoccupations of his contemporaries. Instead of their anticolonial awareness and sensibilities, Tutuola harbors and advocates what amount to reactionary, Eurocentric, colonialist sentiments. An example is his breezy demonization of "Pigmies" (whose liquidation is one of the main objectives of Adebisi, the heroine of

The Brave African Huntress, 1958). Furthermore, he is quite drawn to terms like "witch-herbalist," "witch-doctor," and the like, and he feels no discomfort in describing Yoruba peoples as "primitive" (as he does the people of Laketu in *Pauper, Brawler, and Slanderer,* 1987), or alluding to the people of the Rocky Town (Abeokuta) as "heathens" for worshiping "gods, idols, images, etc." in *The Witch-Herbalist,* or yet at characterizing Dogo, the kidnapper of *Simbi,* as a native of "Sinners' town," so-called because "only sinners and worshippers of gods" lived there. By contrast he is most approving of Christianity and other appurtenances of Westernism, features that he celebrates at great length especially in *My Life in the Bush of Ghosts* (1954), *The Wild Hunter in the Bush of Ghosts* (1982), *The Witch-Herbalist,* and *Ajaiyi and His Inherited Poverty* (1967).

OYEKAN OWOMOYELA

See also Palm-Wine Drinkard

Biography
Born in Abeokuta, Western Nigeria, in June 1920. Attended the Salvation Army School and the Anglican Central School, Abeokuta. Served as a blacksmith in the Royal Air Force, Lagos, 1943–46; from 1956 stores officer, Nigerian (later Federal) Broadcasting Corporation, Ibadan; visiting research fellow, University of Ife, 1979; founder, Mbari Club of Nigerian Writers; now retired.

Novels by Tutuola
The Palm-Wine Drinkard and His Dead Palm-Wine Tapster in the Deads' Town, 1952
My Life in the Bush of Ghosts, 1954
Simbi and the Satyr of the Dark Jungle, 1955
The Brave African Huntress, 1958
Feather Woman of the Jungle, 1962
Ajaiyi and His Inherited Poverty, 1967
The Witch-Herbalist of the Remote Town, 1981
The Wild Hunter in the Bush of Ghosts, 1982
Pauper, Brawler, and Slanderer, 1987

Other Writings: short stories and folktales.

Further Reading
Collins, Harold R., *Amos Tuuola,* New York: Twayne, 1969
Fagunwa, D.O., *Ògbójú Ode Nínú Igbó Irúnmalè,* Lagos: Church Missionary Society Bookshop, 1938; as *The Forest of a Thousand Daemons: A Hunter's Saga,* translated by Wole Soyinka, London: Nelson, 1968
Ibitokun, B.M., "Amos Tutuola," in *Perspectives on Nigerian Literature: 1700 to the Present,* volume 2, edited by Yemi Ogunbiyi, Lagos: Guardian, 1988
Lindfors, Bernth, "Amos Tutuola: Literary Syncretism and the Yoruba Folk Tradition," in *European-Language Writing in Sub-Saharan Africa,* edited by Albert S. Gérard, Budapest: Akadémiai Kiadó, 1986
Lindfors, Bernth, editor, *Critical Perspectives on Amos Tutuola,* Washington, D.C.: Three Continents Press, 1975; London: Heinemann, 1980

Mark Twain 1835–1910

United States

From 1865, when he first announced his intention to pursue a career in literature "of a low order—i.e., humorous," until his collaboration on an inauspicious novel, *The Gilded Age,* with Charles Dudley Warner in 1873, Samuel L. Clemens, alias Mark Twain, showed remarkably little interest in fiction. He had received his literary education in print shops, pilot houses, newsrooms, and bars from Washington, D.C., to San Francisco during the raucous 1850s and 1860s. His early notoriety as a Washoe journalist and lecturer culminated in 1869, when the name Mark Twain suddenly became famous throughout the English-speaking world as the plain-talking itinerant narrator of *The Innocents Abroad* (1869), a hilariously irreverent collection of travel writings. Twain followed that success with a second travel narrative, *Roughing It* (1872), this time chronicling his adventures and misadventures as a fortune hunter and journalist in the far western United States and Hawaii. Convinced he had found his literary niche, he made arrangements for fact-finding trips to Cuba, England, South Africa, and elsewhere, planning to gather material at each stop for subsequent comic travelogues.

Had these trips served their intended purpose, there is every reason to believe that Mark Twain would be known today as one of several globe-trotting literary comedians, alongside Dunn Browne and similarly forgettable contemporaries. For a variety of reasons, however, including his marriage to Olivia Langdon and his newfound desire to stay at home, these trips did not avail, and Mark Twain found himself uncomfortably saddled with the responsibility to invent stories rather than report them. It was a responsibility that he neither invited nor ever fully accepted. With the publication of *The Adventures of Tom Sawyer* in 1876, Twain immediately enjoyed magnificent popularity as a novelist, yet he remained convinced throughout his career that he lacked the analytical sensibility necessary to the novelist's art. He frequently returned to travel writing when other creative faculties failed him, as in *A Tramp Abroad* (1880), *Life on the Mississippi* (1883), and *Following the Equator* (1897). Many of his finest novels, including *The Adventures of Huckleberry Finn* (1884) and *A Connecticut Yankee in King Arthur's Court* (1889), are themselves thinly veiled travelogues, which reproduce the comic impulse of *The Innocents Abroad* by describing the experiences of a vernacular American narrator as he travels through corrupt, antiquated civilizations. The point to be drawn from this analogy between Mark Twain's wanderlust and his creative achievement in the domain of the 19th-century novel is not that he failed to develop his art beyond the crude structural imperatives of comic travel writing; rather, the point is that Twain's consistent antipathy for the novel and its tradition lies ironically at the heart of his achievement as one of the form's great 19th-century innovators.

Twain's antipathy was always more pronounced than were his efforts at innovation. As a reader, he registered his dislike of novels in countless letters and essays, complaining at one point to his close friend William Dean Howells that to pick up a book by Jane Austen made him feel "like a barkeeper entering the kingdom of heaven." He found George Eliot's "labored and tedious analyses of feelings and motives" even more oppressive, noting that he bored through *Middlemarch* and "nearly died from the effort." "I can't stand George Eliot, and [Nathaniel] Hawthorne, and those people," he told Howells, "and as for [Henry James'] *The Bostonians,* I would rather be damned to John Bunyan's heaven than read that." If Austen, Eliot, "and those people" were too excruciatingly analytical for Twain's journalistic taste, he expressed even greater disdain for the adventure novels of Sir Walter Scott and James Fenimore Cooper. His famous broadsides against these writers in *Life on the Mississippi* and "Fenimore Cooper's Literary Offenses" hinged on the implausibility of romantic escapades in the Waverley and Leatherstocking novels. Scott's tiresome "artificialities" and Cooper's romantically conceived Native Americans offered poor alternatives to the droning introspection of Henry James, against which Twain preferred works of nonfiction, like General Ulysses S. Grant's memoirs, which he claimed to read "with a delight I've failed to find in novels."

From the very beginning of his journalistic career, when he followed Bret Harte's example by publishing "condensed" versions of popular novels, Twain enjoyed poking fun at novelistic conventions. This antithetical relation to the genre emerged as a central theme in *Roughing It,* where Twain's hapless narrator, nurtured on a steady diet of Cooper and Emerson Bennett, arrives in the western United States with utterly distorted expectations. After cursing "the lying books" that "betrayed us" with their fantastically implausible representations of western life, the narrator becomes a novelist himself, joining a team of writers to compose a serial romance. His efforts are abandoned, however, when a drunk contributor exposes the novel-writing enterprise for what it really is: a kind of imaginative debauchery, in which the writer's fantasy completely obscures his and the reader's contact with everyday life.

When Mark Twain embarked a few years later on his own novelistic career, intending to extend the immense popular success of his travel writing, he did not substantially alter this playfully hostile characterization of the genre. Both *The Adventures of Tom Sawyer* and its sequel, *The Adventures of Huckleberry Finn,* are spiced with allusions to a novelistic tradition that stretches from Miguel de Cervantes to Scott, but Twain typically invokes the history of the novel in order to disavow his own participation in conventional literary fantasy. Tom Sawyer's muddled literary imagination, which inspires him to impose bookish conventions on Jim's quest for freedom in the controversial final chapters of *Huckleberry Finn,* largely structures both his and Huck's adventures, providing much of the fun and a great deal of the cruelty that always results in Twain's world when fiction is allowed to stand in for fact. In his late masterpiece, *Pudd'nhead Wilson* (1894), it is again a fiction—this time a "fiction of law and custom"—that distorts human understanding and leads in the end to tragedy.

Twain did not always adopt an antinovelistic pose, nor was he always so insistent about his ironic opposition to the novel as a form characterized by inauthenticity and excess. In *The Prince and the Pauper* (1881) and *Personal Recollections of Joan of Arc* (1896), he assumes the novelist's role apparently without hesitation, and in a late essay entitled "What Paul Bourget Thinks of Us," he goes so far as to praise the figure he calls "the native novelist," calling him "the one expert who is qualified to examine the souls and the life of a people and make a valuable report." These comments must seem perverse coming from a man who could count on one hand the number of actual novelists he admired (Howells and Charles Dickens were among the few he consistently praised), but in fact Twain's characterization of "the native novelist" only resumes his ongoing, tongue-in-cheek attack on the genre, albeit in a new key. The "native novelist," as Twain imagines this figure, is really an ideal antithesis to Cooper, Scott, Austen, and James, the writers against whom Twain repeatedly sought to position his craft, for the "native novelist" invents nothing, imagines nothing. Instead, this figure merely observes the people and events around him, unconsciously absorbing his culture's "soul, its life, its speech, its thought." Like the "jackleg novelist" of "Those Extraordinary Twins" (1894), the misbegotten companion to *Pudd'nhead Wilson,* the "native novelist" lacks "the novel-writing gift," and remains a rank amateur in literary technique. His narrative flows naturally, artlessly, capturing the soul, life, speech, and thought of his region with candid authenticity.

This idealized image of the "native novelist" as non-novelist offers a wonderfully apt description of Mark Twain's relationship with the genre he loved to assail, and that in assailing he thoroughly engaged. Twain was of course describing himself when he characterized the "native novelist" as the antitype of the novelist per se, a sort of natural man of letters. Like the unadorned poetry of Huck Finn, another natural man of letters, Mark Twain's voice hovers unpredictably between the literary and the nonliterary, drawing heavily on convention in order to disavow its use, straining the limits of the novel in order to energize the form with vernacular cadences. It is a testament both to his artistic achievement and to the uncanny capaciousness of the novel as a form that Twain continues to be regarded as one of America's foremost practitioners of the genre.

HENRY B. WONHAM

See also Adventures of Huckleberry Finn

Biography

Born 30 November 1835 in Florida, Missouri; moved with family to Hannibal, Missouri, 1839. Worked as a printer's apprentice and typesetter for Hannibal newspapers, 1847–50; assisted brother with Hannibal *Journal,* 1850–52; typesetter and printer in St. Louis, New York, Philadelphia, for Keokuk *Saturday Post,* Iowa, 1853–56, and in Cincinnati, 1857; apprentice river pilot, on the Mississippi, 1857–58; licensed as pilot, 1859–60; went to Nevada as secretary to his brother, then served on the staff of the Governor, and also worked as goldminer, 1861; staff member, Virginia City *Territorial Enterprise,* Nevada, 1862–64; first used pseudonym Mark Twain, 1863; reporter, San Francisco *Morning Call,* 1864; correspondent, Sacramento *Union,* 1866, and San Francisco *Alta California,* 1866–69; traveled to Sandwich (i.e. Hawaiian) Islands, 1866, and France, Italy, and Palestine, 1867; lecturer from 1867; editor, *Express,* Buffalo, New York, 1869–71; moved to Hartford, Connecticut, and began a relationship with Charles L. Webster Publishing Company, 1884; invested in unsuccessful Paige typesetter and went bankrupt, 1894 (paid off all debts by 1898); resided mainly in Europe, 1896–1900, New York, 1900–07, and Redding, Connecticut, 1907–10. Died 21 April 1910.

Novels by Twain

The Gilded Age, with Charles Dudley Warner, 1873
The Adventures of Tom Sawyer, 1876
The Prince and the Pauper, 1881
The Adventures of Huckleberry Finn, 1884
A Connecticut Yankee in King Arthur's Court, 1889
The American Claimant, 1892
The Tragedy of Pudd'nhead Wilson and the Comedy of Those Extraordinary Twins, 1894
Personal Recollections of Joan of Arc, 1896

Other Writings: verse, short stories, plays, and a vast assortment of other prose writings, including journalism, travel writings, autobiography, letters, notebooks, and essays.

Further Reading

Blair, Walter, *Mark Twain & Huck Finn,* Berkeley: University of California Press, 1960
Brooks, Van Wyck, *The Ordeal of Mark Twain,* New York: Dutton, 1920; London: Heinemann, 1922; new and revised edition, New York: Dutton, 1933
Cox, James M., *Mark Twain: The Fate of Humor,* Princeton, New Jersey: Princeton University Press, 1966
Gibson, William M., *The Art of Mark Twain,* New York: Oxford University Press, 1976
Howells, William Dean, *My Mark Twain: Reminiscences and Criticisms,* New York: Harper, 1910
Kaplan, Justin, *Mr. Clemens and Mark Twain,* New York: Simon and Schuster, and London: Cape, 1966
Rogers, Franklin R., *Mark Twain's Burlesque Patterns: As Seen in the Novels and Narratives, 1855–1885,* Dallas: Southern Methodist University Press, 1960
Smith, Henry Nash, *Mark Twain: The Development of a Writer,* Cambridge: Belknap Press of Harvard University Press, 1962
Wonham, Henry B., *Mark Twain and the Art of the Tall Tale,* New York: Oxford University Press, 1993

U

Ulysses by James Joyce

1922

James Joyce's *Ulysses* is arguably the most commented upon, most admired, and most reviled novel in any language to have been published in the 20th century.

In many ways, *Ulysses* is very much a work of its time—in part because it is an unrepeatable, self-consciously epoch-making performance. It is a principal text of high modernism alongside, for example, Ezra Pound's *Cantos* (1925), T.S. Eliot's *The Waste Land* (also published in 1922), and the novels of Virginia Woolf and Wyndham Lewis. *Ulysses* is a modernist text in its fragmented, complicated, at times aggressively difficult style—although it remains broadly intelligible to new readers in a way that Joyce's later *Finnegans Wake* (1939) does not—and it is modernist, too, in its comprehensive engagement with the world of the early 20th century, from the rising power of commercial advertising to the newly unstable and multilayered sense of the human mind propagated by Freudian psychoanalysis.

In looking for analogues to *Ulysses* in the earlier history of the novel, one is driven, paradoxically, to a list of works that resemble one another in each being remorselessly idiosyncratic: Laurence Sterne's *Tristram Shandy* (1759–67), for example, or Herman Melville's *Moby-Dick* (1851). *Ulysses* resembles these texts in egregiously seeking to move beyond contemporary ideas of the nature and capacity of the novel as a genre. It is this presumptuousness that accounts for the irritation that *Ulysses*, just like Sterne's and Melville's wonderful monstrosities, creates in many of its readers. It is a quality not shared by the novelist from whom Joyce probably learned most (although Joyce would not have admitted this), namely Charles Dickens, whose depictions of city life (as in *Bleak House*, 1853), quasi-autobiographical characterizations (*David Copperfield*, 1850), and extraordinary skill with names, puns, idiolects, and other linguistic modes and devices are all subsumed, mocked, but, above all, imitated in Joyce's vast, voracious text.

At the same time, *Ulysses* relates to a much earlier culture. As its title suggests, it is grounded in classical literature, particularly in the adventures of Odysseus (the Greek original of the Roman Ulysses) as related by Homer. Each episode of *Ulysses* bears a Homeric name—"Telemachus," "Nestor," "Proteus," and so on—and, in each case, the events of the episode may be illuminated to some degree by comparison with the *Odyssey*, although

the result is often parodic or mock-heroic: Joyce's "sirens," for example, are barmaids, his "Cyclops" a drunken and bigoted nationalist. In fact, these episode titles did not appear in the original edition: Stuart Gilbert first published them in his pioneering critical work, *James Joyce's "Ulysses"* (1930), together with an elaborate schema that assigns each episode a whole set of totemic keys, including a particular body organ. Such authentically Joycean complications of the original text have since been compounded by a hugely energetic critical industry, which has generated many volumes of annotation, encyclopedias of allusions, inventories of characters, maps, and pictorial guides to Joyce's Dublin. Thus, the Homeric schema is just one example of the intertextual kleptomania and invasiveness of *Ulysses*; to follow up all its threads would be impossible, and there is no end in sight to original critical readings.

However, the classicism of *Ulysses* has a more manageable significance within the fictional world of the novel. A relatively minor character, Buck Mulligan, declares his desire to "Hellenize" Ireland, and in so doing he seems to remind the very obviously Joyce-like young protagonist, Stephen Dedalus, of the project that a slightly younger Stephen had announced at the end of Joyce's *A Portrait of the Artist as a Young Man* (1916): namely, "to forge . . . the uncreated conscience of my race." *Ulysses* may be read as a celebration of many aspects of Dublin life, but it also seems designed to link Ireland with the wider history and culture of the world—for Ireland's own good. The classical allusions, in particular, function both as a reproach to modern Ireland for its lack of artistic and philosophical achievement (and, perhaps, of heroism) and as a gesture of faith in a kind of mythic splendor that is always there, if one can see it, in ordinary life, however shabby it may appear on the surface. Thus, Joyce's erudition and at times bewilderingly abstruse allusiveness are accompanied by a very close attention to the daily realities of Dublin and to the events and ideas of Irish political history. *Ulysses* is a work that strives to link the parochial with the cosmopolitan, the mundane with the mythic, to an extent that had probably never before been attempted.

However, there are clear continuities between *Ulysses* and the classic form of the novel as established in the 19th century. Within all its complexities, *Ulysses* harbors a fairly simple plot, concerning the activities of Stephen, who seems uncertain of his status in the world, alienated from his family, oscillating between a grandiose sense of artistic destiny and a mildly debauched ennui, and of Leopold Bloom, the Jewish advertising agent. Bloom gets by in a Dublin that treats him with some suspicion, as an outsider, but which, from time to time, acknowledges that he shows traces of cultural sophistication, hidden potentialities that seem to take bodily form in his immensely impressive opera-singer wife, Molly, the character who delivers the entire last chapter of *Ulysses* as a stream-of-consciousness monologue, who thus puts all the foregoing material in a new perspective, and who literally has the last word. This word, famously, is *yes,* which suits the generally upbeat sense of life that Joyceans typically derive from *Ulysses.* However, there are plenty of problems for all the characters: Molly Bloom, for example, may be unfaithful to Leopold; Stephen, like Telemachus, seems at a loss for a father—a role that Bloom may be able to fill. In other words, the characters are linked to one another by patterns of trust, suspicion, love, and betrayal in ways that echo the novels of George Eliot, say, or Gustave Flaubert, or Fedor Dostoevskii.

Joyce, however, took the radically innovative step of setting all the novel's events on a single day—June 16th, 1904 (now the occasion for many and various "Bloomsday" celebrations). This fact in itself determines much about the technique of the work. In order to explore many years in the lives of several characters during the course of a single (narrated) day, Joyce employs dreams, visions, memories, and, overall, a type of montage effect that compares to modernist cinematography (in the films of Sergei Eisenstein, for example), or cubist painting: techniques for producing a fuller picture of the perceptual world than that afforded by flat, linear, typically 19th-century modes of representation.

For many early readers, the technical innovations of *Ulysses* were overshadowed by the novel's treatment of sexuality and scatology, which was far from unprecedented in the history of the novel (Sterne springs to mind, once again, along with Tobias Smollett, Jonathan Swift, and, going farther back, François Rabelais), but which had few parallels in highbrow fiction of the 19th century. Even Virginia Woolf, whose own formal experiments had a good deal in common with Joyce's, reacted to these aspects of *Ulysses* with uncomprehending hostility, while in the United States the novel was banned until 1932, when it was finally judged not to be obscene. The famous scenes in which Bloom defecates and masturbates, for example, still surprise many readers, not the least because Joyce presents these acts through Bloom's own consciousness, so that some degree of self-identification with the character is impossible to avoid. But, if anything, this will be regarded nowadays as a sign of moral strength in the novel: a necessary honesty. More generally, Joyce stands out in current assessments as the most enlightened, and even the most likable, of the modernists. He was the artist who exposed and arguably denounced anti-Semitism, for example (through Bloom), while Eliot and Conrad, among others, arguably fostered it.

Ulysses has had a hugely enriching effect on the language and scope of 20th-century culture. More particularly, its influence is clear in the work of many contemporary novelists who seek to combine an encyclopedic range of reference—politics, history, literature, science, and religion—with adventurous modes of discourse and narrative. Examples include Thomas Pynchon and Salman Rushdie. Almost uniquely, *Ulysses* has also had a powerful and direct influence on contemporary literary theory: in the work of Jacques Derrida, for example, and of Hélène Cixous. Three-quarters of a century after its first publication, *Ulysses* remains surprisingly at home alongside the decentered postmodern (non)subject and in the mobile spaces of *écriture feminine.*

DOMINIC RAINSFORD

See also James Joyce

Further Reading

Arnold, Bruce, *The Scandal of "Ulysses": The Sensational Life of a Twentieth-Century Masterpiece,* London: Sinclair-Stevenson, 1991; New York: St. Martin's Press, 1992

Benstock, Bernard, *Narrative Con/Texts in "Ulysses,"* Urbana: University of Illinois Press, and London: Macmillan, 1991

Budgen, Frank, *James Joyce and the Making of "Ulysses" and Other Writings,* London: Oxford University Press, 1972

Davison, Neil R., *James Joyce, "Ulysses," and the Construction of Jewish Identity,* Cambridge and New York: Cambridge University Press, 1996

Gifford, Don, *"Ulysses" Annotated: Notes for James Joyce's "Ulysses,"* 2nd edition, Berkeley: University of California Press, 1988

Henke, Suzette A., *James Joyce and the Politics of Desire,* New York: Routledge, 1990

Kenner, Hugh, *"Ulysses,"* revised edition, Baltimore: Johns Hopkins University Press, 1987

Lawrence, Karen, *The Odyssey of Style in "Ulysses,"* Princeton, New Jersey: Princeton University Press, 1981

Roughley, Alan, *James Joyce and Critical Theory: An Introduction,* Hemel Hempstead: Harvester Wheatsheaf, 1991

Spoo, Robert E., *James Joyce and the Language of History: Dedalus's Nightmare,* New York: Oxford University Press, 1994

Miguel de Unamuno y Jugo 1864–1936

Spanish

Miguel de Unamuno was the most important writer of the so-called Generation of '98, the group of Spanish authors who were preoccupied with the future of Spain and who rejuvenated Spanish letters during the time of the Spanish-American War. His novels, as well as his essays, poetry, short stories, and plays, treat the philosophical themes of the essence of Spanishness. Unamuno's work also reflected his interest in questions of reason versus faith, immortality, the hereafter, and existentialist agony (Søren Kierkegaard was his spiritual mentor). Unamuno's beliefs, while earning him the castigation of the Church in a strongly Catholic society, were loudly voiced and strongly pronounced in spite of monarchical protest, dictatorial threats, exile and the revocation of his position as President of the University of Salamanca, and house arrest by the same Franco regime he had previously supported. His personal philosophy of life was intellectually based and existentially engaged and centered on the theory that humanity's need for immortality proves the existence of God, but that a faith only passively accepted is no faith at all.

Unamuno's first novel, *Paz en la guerra* (1897; *Peace in War*), is a thinly disguised autobiographical account of Bilbao, his childhood home, during the second Carlist War. Although the novel details the geography, actions, and personalities of that conflict, the presentation of the community as the hero is a step toward the author's later novelistic endeavors and developments in his analyses of the maladies of Spanish society. The novel, then, becomes a collection of isolated moments of description and action frozen in the dialogue, conversation, and thoughts of ordinary people.

Unamuno's *Amor y pedagogía* (1902; Love and Education), his second novel, is a novel of transition from the 19th-century realist tradition seen in his first novel to his later more developed style of examining the conflict between ideas and the forces of destiny. This catharsis is carried out through criticism of the ignorance of the Spanish people and a corresponding portrayal of the pedagogical methodology of positivism that was common to Spanish educational institutions of the day.

Perhaps Unamuno's greatest contribution to the genre lies in his existentialist *nivolas*, as outlined in *Niebla* (1914; *Mist*). As explained by the novelist himself, the basic characteristic of the *nivola* is a lack of detailed description of the scenery, the characters, and their lives; in addition, the plot works "a lo que salga" (as it goes along). The essence of the work may be found in the conversations, dialogues, and speeches of the principal characters. The descriptions that do exist incorporate symbolic meaning. That is, this literature makes a full break with the 19th-century idea of the novel as entailing realistic, detailed description of action. Unamuno preferred to call the principal characters *agonistas* (agonists) instead of protagonists, as he saw his works as psychologically dialogued studies of his characters' spiritual anguish.

In *Mist*, Augusto Pérez, the main character, visits the author Unamuno for advice but becomes involved in a dispute with the novelist over his ability to choose what he will, and can, do. *Mist* also has as revolutionary characteristics a prologue in which Víctor Goti, a fictional character created by Unamuno, explains the cause of death of Augusto Pérez. However, Unamuno's post-prologue offers another explanation of the same death, and an epilogue "written" by Orfeo, the character's dog, discourses on the pathetic state of mankind and what follows death.

Abel Sánchez (1917; *Abel Sánchez*) continues the previously examined literary technique of character development through dialogue and is a study of envy that bears some resemblance to the biblical story of Cain and Abel. The succinctness and forcible delivery of the narrative reveal more than a mere homicidal attitude on the part of Joaquín; the angst he suffers leads him to the brink of an emotional breakdown.

San Manuel Bueno, mártir y tres historias más (1933; *San Manuel Bueno*) examines the essence of Christianity and faith. Manuel, a priest who no longer believes the doctrine of life after death, faces the dilemma of whether to continue to perform his duties, hiding his true beliefs and serving the parishioners in their quest for eternal life, or whether he should admit his lack of belief and perhaps destroy what little hope remains for his parishioners. Evidently, the former is the better option, since by making his choice, Manuel becomes a saint and a martyr, dying so that others might achieve happiness and continue steadfast in their beliefs.

Unamuno's contributions to the novel have reverberated throughout the Western world. His existentialist engagement is not only evident in his novels and essays but further detailed in *Cómo se hace una novela* (1927; *How to Make a Novel*), a work he completed while in exile. In this work, he affirms that the novel is a means of expressing a thesis of conviction with social implications. His technical contributions to the genre include the development of the importance of dialogue and authorial displacement from a work, which aids in the novel's forcefulness and credibility and elicits the emotional involvement of the reader.

JEFFREY OXFORD

Biography

Born 29 September 1864 in Bilbao, Spain. Attended Colegio de San Nicolás, and Instituto Vizcaíno, both in Bilbao; University of Madrid, 1880–84, Ph.D. 1884. Professor of Greek, 1891–1924, 1930–34, and rector, 1901–14, 1934–36, University of Salamanca; banished to Canary Islands for criticizing Primo de Rivera government, 1924; lived in Paris, 1924, and Hendaye, 1925–30; placed under house arrest for criticizing Franco government, 1936. Died 31 December 1936.

Novels by Unamuno

Paz en la guerra, 1897; as *Peace in War,* translated by Allen
    Lacy, Martin Nozick, and Anthony Kerrigan, 1983
Amor y pedagogía [Love and Education], 1902
Niebla, 1914; as *Mist,* translated by Warner Fite, 1929
Abel Sánchez, 1917; as *Abel Sánchez,* translated 1947
Tres novelas ejemplares y un prólogo, 1920; as *Three
    Exemplary Novels,* translated by Angel Flores, 1930
La tía Tula, 1921; translated by Anthony Kerrigan, 1976
San Manuel Bueno, mártir y tres historias más, 1933; as *San*

Manuel Bueno, translated by Mario J. and María Elena de Valdés, 1973

Other Writings: short stories, plays, poetry, and essays.

Further Reading

Basdekis, Demetrios, *Unamuno and the Novel,* Madrid: Castalia, 1974

Marías, Julián, *Miguel de Unamuno,* Madrid: Espasa-Calpe, 1943; translated by Frances M. López-Morillas, Cambridge, Massachusetts: Harvard University Press, 1966

Nozick, Martin, *Miguel de Unamuno,* New York: Twayne, 1971

Roberts, Gemma, *Unamuno, afinidades y coincidencias kierkegaardianas,* Boulder, Colorado: Society of Spanish and Spanish-American Studies, 1986

Rubia Barcía, José, and M.A. Zeitlin, editors, *Unamuno: Creator and Creation,* Berkeley: University of California Press, 1967

Sánchez Barbudo, Antonio, editor, *Miguel de Unamuno,* Madrid: Taurus, 1974; 2nd edition, 1990

La Torre, Revista General de la Universidad de Puerto Rico (journal) 9:35–36 (1961)

Watson, Peggy, *Intra-historia in Miguel de Unamuno's Novels: A Continual Presence,* Potomac, Maryland: Scripta Humanistica, 1993

Zubizarreta, Armando F., *Unamuno en su "Nivola,"* Madrid: Taurus, 1960

Uncle Tom's Cabin by Harriet Beecher Stowe

1852

Initially published as a serial in the abolitionist paper *The National Era* (1851–52) and then in book form (1852), *Uncle Tom's Cabin* immortalized Harriet Beecher Stowe as "the little lady who made this big war," in Abraham Lincoln's famous description in 1863. The novel was written in reaction to the Fugitive Slave Act of 1850, which made it illegal to assist an escaped slave, and effectively transformed the whole of the United States into a slave-holding nation. It quickly became a runaway bestseller, probably proportionately the best-selling novel of all time. It was the first American novel to sell more than a million copies and was quickly translated into 37 languages. However, *Uncle Tom's Cabin* does not appear in any of the classic works of American literary criticism until the 1980s for three reasons: it was written by a woman for women, it had a cultural and propagandist function, and it was popular. *Uncle Tom's Cabin,* therefore, offers the absolute test case for the definition of aesthetic values in literature. Its effectiveness as abolitionist propaganda is unparalleled. The history of its reception also offers a history of American literary and cultural criticism.

Arguably, *Uncle Tom's Cabin* was also the most popular play of the 19th century, repeatedly adapted to provide "Tom Shows," volatile mixtures of song and dance, special effects, minstrelsy, and not-so-covert racism. The accent fell heavily on spectacle—Eliza escaping across dry ice, pursued onstage by live bloodhounds, little Eva ascending to heaven on wires, novelty performances on ice or on horseback. The play survived the Civil War, and in 1900 some 500 troupes were performing it on the road. It was still going strong in the 1930s. As a result it often has been difficult, at least in the popular mind, to separate the novel from its worst dramatic embodiments. Although Stowe had no hand in the adaptations, nor indeed in the mass of commercial memorabilia they spawned (Topsy dolls, poems, songs, dioramas, plates, and busts), the legend was propagated that she had created a stereotypical image of the docile, subservient black man, who gave the American language the term *Uncle Tom,* to mean a traitor to his race.

The early 20th century saw a decline in the popularity of Stowe's novel in the face of modernist assumptions that literature should not aim to effect social change, that it should eschew accessibility in favor of "literary" language, and that it should not readily follow conventions. *Uncle Tom's Cabin* failed on all counts. (By contrast, it remained enormously popular in the Soviet Union. Originally smuggled into Russia in Yiddish to evade the czarist censor, it speedily found an audience that responded to Stowe's indictment of slavery as a criticism of capitalism.) In America, the novel's comeback began, inauspiciously, in 1949, with James Baldwin's ringing condemnation of Stowe as portraying whites in blackface, employing a racist vocabulary equating black with evil, and creating in Uncle Tom a fleshless figure, "robbed of his humanity and divested of his sex." The rise of the "New Americanists" and particularly of feminist criticism in the 1970s finally led to a major reassessment. Where Baldwin saw emasculation, feminist critics such as Jane Tompkins saw feminization. In the comprehensive revaluation of the sentimental novel that followed, *Uncle Tom's Cabin* was a major focus. Critics defended its radical Christian vision based on matriarchal values (the novel extols motherhood in every chapter), its strong female characters (both black and white), its emphasis on family and domesticity as utopian ideals, and its feminist revision of Eve into Evangel in the figure of little Eva. In Tompkins' argument, *Uncle Tom's Cabin* supports the view that the popular domestic novel of the 19th century represented a massive attempt to reorganize culture from a feminine point of view. The novel may be a "three-handkerchief" tearjerker—in 1852 Congressman Horace Greeley cried so hard over it on a railway journey from Boston to Washington that he had to get off in Springfield and spend the night in a hotel to recover—but contemporary readers are less likely to reject it as a mere lachrymose denial of reality. The bodily nature of sentimental fiction's effects (as witness the unhappy congressman) unavoidably highlights the physical and effectively combats the sleight of hand by which apologists for slavery erased the black body from American culture. In a nation divided according to the body, physicality is fundamental to resistance against oppression.

Revaluations of Stowe's treatment of race are still in process. On the positive side of the argument, Stowe was steeped in black history and benefited in *Uncle Tom's Cabin* from her wide reading of slave narratives. After the example of Gandhi in India and following the Civil Rights Movement in the United States, Tom's passivity has been reinterpreted as a strategy of passive resistance. The example of Topsy has been examined as tending to support environmentalism over essentialism, and attention has been drawn to Cassey's creative use of the Gothic to achieve her liberty. Recent scholarship on minstrelsy has located the novel's political slipperiness in the ambiguity of the signifiers borrowed from the minstrel show, which provided terms, images, characters, and style that could be exploited by both pro- and antislavery forces. While it is true that the novel envisages a future for its characters only outside America (Canada, Africa, or heaven, in ascending order of value) and that later feminists have had reservations about the glorification of the home (even a politically dynamic one), *Uncle Tom's Cabin* nonetheless raises pressing questions about race, gender politics, and aesthetic assumptions.

Amid the welter of ideological readings, the formal features of the novel have been comparatively neglected. Sacvan Bercovitch's *The American Jeremiad* (1978), for example, managed to ignore *Uncle Tom's Cabin* entirely, although Stowe's novel offers the clearest example of this quintessentially American form, linking social criticism with spiritual renewal. Critics have applauded the variety of Stowe's characterization, her gift for dialogue and comedy, the narrative pace, and the encyclopedic range of settings, but the case for the novel is always made on political rather than formal grounds.

Uncle Tom's Cabin remained the high point of Stowe's career. Few of its readers are even aware that it was followed by a second antislavery novel, *Dred: A Tale of the Great Dismal Swamp* (1856). Perhaps the best corrective to any easy ideological dismissal of Stowe as favoring passivity, undermining the black male, and extolling the domestic angel is a reading of the latter novel, with its violent black insurrectionist (based on Nat Turner), its thinly disguised portrait of Sojourner Truth, its evocation of white mobocracy, and its forthright rejection of any reparatory fantasy of North-South reconciliation.

JUDIE NEWMAN

Further Reading

Ammons, Elizabeth, editor, *Critical Essays on Harriet Beecher Stowe,* Boston: G.K. Hall, 1980
Baldwin, James, "Everybody's Protest Novel," *Partisan Review* (June 1949)
Gossett, Thomas F., *Uncle Tom's Cabin and American Culture,* Dallas, Texas: Southern Methodist University Press, 1985
Hedrick, Joan D., *Harriet Beecher Stowe: A Life,* New York: Oxford University Press, 1994
Hovet, Theodore R., *The Master Narrative: Harriet Beecher Stowe's Subversive Story of Master and Slave in "Uncle Tom's Cabin" and "Dred,"* Lanham, Maryland: University Press of America, 1988
Moers, Ellen, *Harriet Beecher Stowe and American Literature,* Hartford, Connecticut: Stowe-Day Foundation, 1978
Sundquist, Eric, editor, *New Essays on "Uncle Tom's Cabin,"* Cambridge and New York: Cambridge University Press, 1986
Tompkins, Jane P., "Sentimental Power: *Uncle Tom's Cabin* and the Politics of Literary History," *Glyph* 8 (1981)

Under the Volcano by Malcolm Lowry

1947

The life of Malcolm Lowry was a shabby spectacle of drink and disaster, justified by one apotheosis: the publication of *Under the Volcano* and its gradual recognition as a literary masterpiece. Lowry wrote other things: an early novel, *Ultramarine* (1933), some reasonable short stories, an uneven corpus of poetry, an aborted screenplay. Yet during the post-*Volcano* years Lowry dissipated his energies and talents in alcohol and an outpouring of impossible writings, some recently rescued from oblivion by excellent scholarship but significant ultimately only in relation to the one great novel.

Under the Volcano took ten years to reach its final form. When Lowry arrived in Mexico in 1936, not on the Day of the Dead as he claimed, he found in Cuernavaca and its annexes a Faustian landscape awaiting exploration. In the nearby volcanoes (brought a little closer in his fictional geography) he saw the perfect emblems of his ambition to write a drunken Divine Comedy. The snowy peak of Popocatepetl represented aspiration, but the fiery heart of the volcanoes with the surrounding dark woods and deep barrancas formed a psychomachic symbol for one who, attempting the heights, abuses his human and mystical responsibilities and is instead thrown into the lower depths. This imaginative cosmology did not change through the novel's subsequent revisions, but everything else would.

By the time Lowry left Mexico, his first marriage in ruins, he had a manuscript of sorts, which he worked on intermittently in Los Angeles, where he met his second wife Margerie, and Vancouver, where the bulk of the writing was done. By 1940 he had produced a text recognizably that of the later novel, but, as the recent edition of the 1940 version indicates, at that date unpublishable and rightly turned down. Lowry acknowledged its shortcomings and set out to fix them. The next five years of constant revision and painful rewriting saw the transformation of a crude fictional construct into a poetic masterpiece.

What happened in that lustrum is a kind of literary miracle, but one largely explicable because of the body of notes and materials that somehow survived fire and firewater, and that are now in the library of the University of British Columbia. These document a complex textual and creative evolution, details of which are explored in Frederick Asals' meticulous study (1997). Lowry would write, Margerie would type, and Lowry would annotate and rewrite, infusing new details and working the passages over and over until they were "right," in the sense of being polished prose-poems. The book thus took shape rather like an erratic coral reef, cell by cell. There were major changes in characterization, the Consul, the novel's agonized protagonist, evolving from William Ames to Geoffrey Firmin, his wife Priscilla and daughter Yvonne blending into one figure, itself a composite of Lowry's two wives, Jan and Margerie, and Hugh becoming more complex as Firmin's doppelgänger.

Another major change concerned the magical and mystical elements, which were rather half-baked in the 1940 version. At a critical point, Lowry met a Cabbalist, Charles Stansfield-Jones, spiritual son of Aleister Crowley. Arguably, the novel came into focus upon Lowry's discovery of Stansfield-Jones' mysticism, which suggested a way to express without silliness the interpenetration of the material and spiritual worlds (the "depths" as he later called them in his magnificent "Letter to Jonathan Cape") that explains the forces driving the fiction. The key to the "Mysteries" was twofold: to make such preoccupations the Consul's and leave them obscure to Hugh and Yvonne; and to frame the action of the novel by mediating chapters 2 through 12 through the consciousness of Jacques Laruelle, failed filmmaker and adulterous lover, whose structural importance now became more subtle. The coincidences for which the novel is often criticized became explicable in terms of the novel's own controlling aesthetic, as a "projection" in the dark cinema of Laruelle's mind.

Like many of his generation, Lowry had been enchanted by the possibilities opening from the allusive techniques of Eliot and Joyce, or, more directly, Conrad Aiken, whose unappreciated *Blue Voyage* (1927) and *Great Circle* (1933) overwhelmed him—as did film and Expressionist art. *Under the Volcano* has a central place in the modernist tradition, which (in the words of Edmund Wilson) made the distinction between poetry and prose increasingly meaningless. Close scrutiny of the text reveals how much it is a mosaic compiled from other writings (Lowry's fears of plagiarism are a saga in themselves), but shaped into something strange and new. In a spirit deriving partly from Eliot's seminal essay on the modern writer's predicament in the face of literary tradition, "Tradition and the Individual Talent," Lowry felt a mystical affinity to the writers of the past, with whom he might thus connect in "the unimaginable library of the dead." He felt that his place in that ideal order was affirmed by the bond with those from whom he borrowed. He would have approved of the way that such diverse writers as Gabriel García Márquez (Colombia), J.G. Farrell (Ireland), and Cabrera Infante (Cuba) have acknowledged *Under the Volcano* as a masterpiece of world literature and paid tribute in their own fiction to its complexity and passion.

CHRIS ACKERLEY

Further Reading

Ackerley, Chris, and Lawrence J. Clipper, *A Companion to "Under the Volcano,"* Vancouver: University of British Columbia Press, 1984

Asals, Frederick, *The Making of Malcolm Lowry's "Under the Volcano,"* Athens: University of Georgia Press, 1997

Bowker, Gordon, *Pursued by Furies: A Life of Malcolm Lowry,* London: HarperCollins, and New York: St. Martin's Press, 1993

Day, Douglas, *Malcolm Lowry: A Biography,* New York: Oxford University Press, 1973

Kilgallin, Tony, *Lowry,* Erin, Ontario: Porcèpic, 1973

McCarthy, Patrick, *Forests of Symbols: World, Text and Self in Malcolm Lowry's Fiction,* Athens and London: University of Georgia Press, 1994

McCarthy, Patrick, and Paul Tiessen, editors, *Joyce/Lowry: Critical Perspectives,* Lexington: University Press of Kentucky, 1997

Salloum, Sheryl, *Malcolm Lowry: Vancouver Days,* Madeira Park, British Columbia: Harbour Publishing, 1987

Tiessen, Paul, and Miguel Mota, editors, *The 1940 "Under the Volcano,"* Waterloo, Ontario: MLR Editions, 1994

Woodcock, George, editor, *Malcolm Lowry: The Man and His Work,* Vancouver: University of British Columbia Press, 1971

Sigrid Undset 1882–1949

Norwegian

Between 1907 and 1940, when she went into wartime exile in the United States, the Norwegian author Sigrid Undset wrote 18 novels set both in her own time and in the distant past. Her major contribution to world literature is her two epic cycles of historical novels about life in medieval Norway, *Kristin Lavransdatter* (1920–22) and *Olav Audunssøn i Hestviken* (1925–27; *The Master of Hestviken*), which won her the 1928 Nobel prize.

The Norwegian tradition of historical fiction has roots in the 13th-century Icelandic sagas, histories of the Norwegian kings and expatriate families who settled Iceland in the ninth century. Undset called *Njals Saga,* which she read at age ten, "the book that was the turning point in my life," and her historical work is deeply influenced by the salient features of the medieval genre: a vigorous, sometimes brutal realism, a laconic style, unusual attention to domestic detail, and vivid, individualized portraits of men, children, and strong-minded women. Her writing is also stamped with the earthy lyricism of the Danish ballads, which she described at age 19 as "gloriously healthy" tales of farmer-knights and maidens whose deep love for home and their native soil was instinctive, sensual, almost erotic (see Undset, 1979).

The pride of Norway's recent independence (1905) and prospects of rapid social change after World War I stimulated a flush of Norwegian historical fiction in the 1920s. Undset broke new ground both with her choice of subject matter and her method of developing it. The prototype established by Walter Scott depicts the impact of momentous upheaval, such as revolution or war, on fictional characters. Undset's aim was both grander and more intimate, grander because the "revolution" that most concerned her, Norway's gradual transition from a pagan blood-feud society to European Christian culture, took centuries to accomplish, and more intimate because she was interested in the impact of that change on points where personal relations and social justice intersect—relations between the sexes, marriage and inheritance customs, medical practices, crime and punishment.

For this project Undset invented the "domestic epic," a sweeping story painted on a broad social canvas, set at a time devoid of political drama. Using legal documents and ecclesiastical records, literature, legends, material culture, and her own penetrating grasp of human behavior, she imaginatively reconstructed the inner lives of men and women wrestling with fundamental change. She was particularly concerned with two psychological shifts: adjustment to the Christian emphasis on forgiveness and protection of the weak, which radically reversed the Viking standard of honor based on vengeance and conquest; and the new cult of romantic love, in which affection-based liaisons—together with the canon law requiring female consent in marriage—could sabotage arrangements traditionally made by men.

Undset, who had decided to write about the Middle Ages while still in her teens, was determined not to indulge in the sentimental chauvinism of the national romantic style. She wanted to re-create the psychological realism of the Icelandic sagas, exposing elemental human passions—desire, jealousy, pride, hate, love, and fear, passions that drove people to transgress legal and ethical bounds—and examine ways those transgressions were dealt with in the past. She wanted to write so realistically, she explained, that "everything that seems romantic from here—murder, violence, etc. becomes ordinary—comes to life" (Undset, 1979). To collapse time between eras she aimed for natural, everyday speech, avoiding intrusive archaisms (an effort sabotaged by the Archer translation of *Kristin Lavransdatter*), keeping a tone of the past by selecting only words based on Old Danish. Her vivid descriptions of nature and everyday life in the physical world give sensuous immediacy to a distant time.

Undset's earliest historical work is *Fortællingen om Viga-Ljot og Vigdis* (1909; *Gunnar's Daughter*), a terse, swiftly moving tale about a woman's pursuit of vengeance set in Norway and Iceland in the Viking Age. Usually described as a "saga-pastiche" because of its explicit borrowings from well-known Icelandic models, it is actually a sophisticated conversation between the Saga Age and Undset's own time concerning cultural tensions common to both. The novel includes what may be the first literary treatment of the psychological effects of rape from a woman's viewpoint.

Her masterpiece is *Kristin Lavransdatter,* set in the first half of

the 14th century. The book was written at a major transition point in Undset's life. In 1919 she separated from her husband and moved with her three children from Oslo to Lillehammer. In 1924, two years after completing the trilogy, she was received as a Roman Catholic, and her 12-year marriage was annulled. *Kristin Lavransdatter* crystallizes much of the intellectual and emotional energy Undset devoted to marriage, parenthood, and Christianity during this period of crisis and commitment in her life.

The *Olav Audunssøn* cycle shares many of *Kristin Lavransdatter*'s strengths, although the story is darker and artistically less well balanced. Set in 13th-century Norway, it includes a remarkable episode in London in which Undset merges visionary experience and realism with full medieval assurance. Its triumph is a complex psychological portrait of a troubled child who ransoms his father's heart.

With the exception of *Madame Dorthea* (1939; *Madame Dorthea*), the only completed volume of a planned trilogy set in the 18th century, Undset's other novels are all set in her own time. Most explore the same themes that appear in her historical works: the anarchic power of erotic desire, disappointments in romantic love, and the responsibilities of marriage and parenthood. They also raise, but do not answer, questions about the role of religion in modern life. These modern works were seldom experimental in form but broke new ground in content. Undset became notorious for her frank descriptions of female eroticism in *Jenny* (1911; *Jenny*), a sensitive but overwrought work in which the heroine's physical and emotional needs eclipse and destroy her artistic career. Different objections were raised (particularly in staunchly Lutheran Scandinavia) to *Gymnadenia* (1929; *The Wild Orchid*) and *Den brændende busk* (1930; *The Burning Bush*), a set of novels treating a young man's conversion to Catholicism, which include theological digressions.

Undset's finest contemporary work is *Elleve år* (1934; *The Longest Years*), an autobiographical novel about her childhood to age 11, where interplay between memory and the senses illuminates the intellectual, moral, and sexual development of a preadolescent child.

SHERRILL HARBISON

See also Kristin Lavransdatter

Biography

Born 20 May 1882 in Kalundborg, Denmark, but raised in Oslo, Norway. Attended Commercial College, Oslo, graduated 1898. Married the painter Anders C. Svarstad in 1912 (marriage annulled 1924). Worked in office of electrical firm, Oslo, 1899–1909; converted to Catholicism, 1924; lived in the United States during World War II. Awarded Nobel prize for literature, 1928. Died 10 June 1949.

Novels by Undset

Fru Marta Oulie [Mrs. Marta Oulie], 1907
Fortællingen om Viga-Ljot og Vigdis, 1909; as *Gunnar's Daughter*, translated by Arthur G. Chater, 1936; with introduction and notes by Sherrill Harbison, 1998
Jenny, 1911; as *Jenny,* translated by A. Grippenwald, 1920; translated by W. Emmë, 1920
Vaaren [Spring], 1914
Splinten av troldspeilet [Splinters from a Magic Mirror], 1917;

first half translated by Arthur G. Chater as *Images in a Mirror,* 1938

Kristin Lavransdatter, I: Kransen, 1920; *II: Husfrue,* 1921; *III: Korset,* 1922; as *I: The Bridal Wreath* (in England, *The Garland*), translated by Charles Archer and J.S. Scott, 1923; as *II: The Mistress of Husaby,* translated by Charles Archer, 1925; as *III: The Cross,* 1927; as *Kristin Lavransdatter,* 1929; as *I: The Wreath,* translated by Tiina Nunnally, 1997

Olav Audunssøn i Hestviken, 1925; *Olav Audunssøn og hans børn,* 1927; as *The Master of Hestviken,* translated by Arthur G. Chater (includes *The Axe; The Snake Pit; In the Wilderness; The Son Avenger*), 1934

Gymnadenia, 1929; as *The Wild Orchid,* translated by Arthur G. Chater, 1931

Den brændende busk, 1930; as *The Burning Bush,* translated by Arthur G. Chater, 1932

Ida Elisabeth, 1932; translated by Arthur G. Chater, 1933

Elleve år, 1934; as *The Longest Years,* translated by Arthur G. Chater, 1935

Den trofaste hustru, 1936; as *The Faithful Wife,* translated by Arthur G. Chater, 1937

Madame Dorthea, 1939; translated by Arthur G. Chater, 1941

Other Writings: poetry, plays, stories, essays, reviews, memoirs, biography, history, hagiography, theology, children's books, antifascist polemics.

Further Reading

Bayerschmidt, Carl Frank, *Sigrid Undset,* New York: Twayne, 1970

Bliksrud, Liv, *Natur og normer hos Sigrid Undset,* Oslo: Aschehoug, 1988

Deschamps, Nicole, *Sigrid Undset, ou la morale de la passion,* Montreal: Presses de l'Université de Montréal, 1966

Gustafson, Alrik, "Christian Ethics in a Pagan World: Sigrid Undset," in *Six Scandinavian Novelists,* Princeton, New Jersey: Princeton University Press, and Minneapolis: University of Minnesota Press for the American Scandinavian Foundation, 1940

Harbison, Sherrill, "Medieval Aspects of Narcissism in Sigrid Undset's Modern Novels," *Scandinavian Studies* 63:4 (Autumn 1991)

Larsen, Hanna Astrup, "Sigrid Undset: Modern Works," *The American-Scandinavian Review* 17:6 (June 1929)

Larsen, Hanna Astrup, "Sigrid Undset: Medieval Works," *The American-Scandinavian Review* 17:7 (July 1929)

McFarlane, James Walter, "Sigrid Undset," in *Ibsen and the Temper of Norwegian Literature,* Oxford and New York: Oxford University Press, 1960

Solbakken, Elisabeth, *Redefining Integrity: The Portrayal of Women in the Contemporary Novels of Sigrid Undset,* Frankfurt and New York: Peter Lang, 1992

Undset, Sigrid, *Kjære Dea,* Oslo: Cappelen, 1979

Vinde, Victor, *Sigrid Undset: A Nordic Moralist,* Seattle: University of Washington Book Store, 1930

Winsnes, Andreas Hofgaard, *Sigrid Undset: A Study in Christian Realism,* New York: Sheed and Ward, 1953

United States Novel

18th Century

Although it emerged after the Revolutionary War, the 18th-century American novel nevertheless remained substantially subordinated to its British heritage. Even the allegorical pamphlet novel *A Pretty Story* (1774), written by Francis Hopkinson to convince colonial delegates to break from Britain, was not significantly distinguishable from its satiric Scottish prototype, John Arbuthnot's *Law Is a Bottom-less Pit* (1727). Several reasons accounted for the weak development of fiction in the new republic. That the English novel, which many consider to have commenced with Daniel Defoe's *Robinson Crusoe* (1719), was still a young genre of indefinite form was a factor. Other important reasons included the steady supply of books from abroad and, in the absence of international copyright laws, the ease with which such works were pirated by American printers. Germane, too, were such matters as the difficulty of competing with well-known British novelists, the relatively small number of presses in the new nation, the limited opportunities for local book pro-

motion, and the practice of subscription-based publication in America.

The retarded development of the novel in the new republic was also the result of an abiding cultural scepticism, more entrenched in the colonies than in the homeland, about the propriety of fiction. There was a general suspicion that fiction promoted idleness and immorality. This sentiment was the legacy of both early Puritan attitudes toward romance and, later, the Scottish Common Sense philosophers' hostility toward fiction. These responses disparaged fictional writing as a stimulator of the imagination, that deceiving "feminine" faculty of the mind so reviled by the defenders of "masculine" reason. In such an environment, the early American novel customarily protested its own innocence and, whatever the truth of the matter, insisted on its difference from the pernicious fiction said to ruin young women.

Such authorial protestations were undermined by publishers

who promoted novels by emphasizing the most sensational and scandalous features of their portraits of tempted or seduced women. William Hill Brown's epistolary *Power of Sympathy* (1789) was advertised in this manner. Doubtless the sensationalist elements of this book (incest, female abduction, suicide) had a greater impact on its small number of readers than did its message about education as a protection for female virtue. Many likely read *Power of Sympathy,* as they later read Hannah Webster Foster's *The Coquette* (1797), for scandalous details about the actual people whose lives were believed to be the basis for the novel. Such marketing strategies reinforced 18th-century American doubts concerning the legitimacy of the novel as a literary genre.

Cultural scepticism aside, there certainly was a demand for early American fiction. More than a century of colonial consumption of British chapbooks—inexpensive stitched pamphlets of popular fare—prepared for this sizable American market for fiction. The slow, unsteady emergence of regional magazines, usually short-lived ventures that included serialized fiction, augmented the indigenous appetite for the novel. At first, the high cost of nonpirated works resulted in publications aimed at wealthier patrons, who valued books as prized possessions. Soon the formation of subscription and circulation libraries, based on a model recommended by Benjamin Franklin, made more novels available to more people. By 1800, there were about 376 circulation libraries, of which 266 had been established during the 1790s. Thus, despite cultural scepticism about the genre and the expense of book production, a surprising number of early American novels were printed, several in fact becoming best-sellers after the turn of the century, when local presses were more available in small towns as well as big cities.

It is difficult to determine who primarily read this fiction. The novels themselves most frequently implied white, literate, unmarried young women as their principal readers. Women were also the putative victims of the genre. While signatures in extant copies of some of these works suggest that there were a number of novels avidly read by both women and men, women were likely the main consumers of fiction. Women conversed with one another about novels at social gatherings and in letters. They also exchanged copies of these books and read aloud from them in each other's presence. Women, who as a group had lagged behind men in literacy for more than a century, doubtless enhanced their reading and writing skills, not to mention their general knowledge, by reading 18th-century novels. Moreover, these books fostered, in women and men alike, an egalitarian sense of self-worth that emerged with the rise of national identity in post-Revolutionary America.

Although the novel in general has always been a polymorphous form resistant to a handy taxonomy, these 18th-century works are especially hard to classify. They include allegories, satires, picaresque adventures, colloquies, epistles, captivity narratives, travelogues, textbook subjects, biographical or historical chronicles, sentimental accounts, and Gothic or sensational romances. Early American novels commonly combine these diverse forms in nearly a haphazard manner, resulting in wildly erratic productions eliciting disparate responses from the reader without apparent authorial regard for consistency or other aesthetic concerns.

Early American novels imitating Gothic fiction, featuring frightening episodes involving extraordinary human abilities or supernatural events, are especially muddled. Sarah Wood's moral concern in *Julia* (1800), a novel indebted to Ann Radcliffe's English romances, is so freighted with such Gothic devices as deception, incest, murder, and supernatural forces that her moral intention is overwhelmed. Consequently, it is difficult to decode her symbolic use of mistaken and hidden identities as a warning about the threat that subversive religious and political ideas pose to an ideal classless new republic identity. Charles Brockden Brown's exceptional use of Gothic conventions, including impersonation and insanity, in his dark romances *Wieland* (1798), *Ormond* (1799), and *Edgar Huntly* (1799) also leads to uncertain, even contradictory interpretations. On one level, these conventions seem to contribute to conservative cautionary tales by Brown advising the need for personal and cultural restraint in an unsettled and unsettling new nation. On another level, the Gothic devices appear to serve Brown's challenge to the Lockean esteem for reason, method, and order, the neoclassical values of his day; these devices further suggest that the inscrutability of cause and motive undermines prevailing idealized rationalist versions of America's national identity, such as proposed by Wood. This level of Brown's apparent scepticism concerning humanity's understanding of reality deeply influenced the work of Edgar Allan Poe and Nathaniel Hawthorne.

The evident disorder of Brown's and other early American fiction participated in the unsystematic emergence of national identity, a subject of explicit public concern after the Treaty of Paris (1783). Since the new nation was characterized by varying regional speech, customs, and interests, the identity of America as a union arose very uncertainly. Reflecting this instability in its own disorganization, new republic fiction situated the quest for national identity within a host of contrary anxieties that included fears of rapid change, social chaos, and tyrannical power. Typically these works adapted the former colonial valuation of marriage and family order to the perceived needs of the new republic; yet at the same time these works (both by accident and design) often suggested problems with patriarchal authority and female inequality in a nation celebrating independence as a virtue.

The idealization of the family in the early American novel was reinforced by representations of orphans and incest, themes borrowed from Daniel Defoe's *Moll Flanders* (1722) and other English fiction. The motif of the waif in the anonymous *The Hapless Orphan* (1793), Wood's *Julia,* Brown's *Ormond,* and many other stories emphasized the unpredictable destiny of America, an orphan-like new nation recently separated from its motherland. Portraits of republican youth and families put at risk through orphaning and incest cut against the grain of the national optimism expressed in early American fiction, for these portraits symbolically suggested actual menacing instabilities in the new nation. A similar crosscurrent arose in crime fiction, typified by the anonymous picaresque *Memoirs of Stephen Burroughs* (1798), which associated social deviance with self-determination, criminal disguise with an unformed national identity. Nor was democracy itself exempt from such antipodal perspectives in early American fiction. Hugh Henry Brackenridge's *Modern Chivalry* (1792–1805), a five-volume picaresque satire indebted to English author Henry Fielding and Spanish author Miguel de Cervantes, coalesced democracy and mob rule in its dramatization of the misadventures of Teague O'Regan, an Irish servant traveling on the frontiers of American settlement. The numerous follies resulting from O'Regan's irrepressible ambition indicated that the unbridled democratic enthusiasm of the ignorant masses could permanently harm the new republic.

Such satiric fiction in the mock-heroic tradition was not the only hortative response to the instability of early America. There were also moralistic novels in the sentimental tradition, usually addressed to young women, that relied on the prevalent 18th-century belief in reward and punishment as social guides to human reason. The literary models of these works were European, with Samuel Richardson's *Pamela* (1740), *Clarissa* (1747–48), and *The History of Sir Charles Grandison* (1753–54) among the most influential of the epistolary novels that had been read widely throughout the colonies. Stereotypical characters, inconsistent or vague motivation, predictable plots, haphazard structure, meandering digressions, and authorial intrusions were characteristic of these early American imitations of British sentimental fiction.

Yet sometimes their setting and detail reflected American cultural matter, as in Gilbert Imlay's *The Emigrants* (1793), partially set on the Kentucky frontier; Ann Eliza Bleecker's *The History of Maria Kittle* (1793), set along Lake Champlain; and Susanna Haswell Rowson's *Reuben and Rachel* (1798), set in New Hampshire. Each of these works incorporated the Indian captivity narrative, a specifically American literary genre of enormous popularity at home and abroad during the 18th century. Anticipating the later American development of local color tradition, Imlay's *Emigrants* and Brown's *Edgar Huntly,* among other stories, sometimes indicated the beneficial effects of specific features of the American landscape on personal and cultural transformations in the new nation. In this regard, at least, such works paralleled an explicit theme of Michel Guillaume Jean de Crèvecoeur's *Letters from an American Farmer* (1782), which included some features of the epistolary novel.

Rowson's *Charlotte* (1791), while not the most original, was the most widely read of American sentimental novels. This book relates the story of a naive 15-year-old girl victimized by male irresponsibility and villainy; seduced and abandoned, she dies pitifully after giving birth to a daughter. The public demand for *Charlotte Temple,* as the book became known, was enormous for more than a century. Most readers perceived a morality tale in this short novel, but the sincerity, or at least efficacy, of Rowson's prefatory insistence that she designed this novel to warn "the thoughtless of the fair sex" about their "morals and conduct" is debatable. Sentimental novelists such as Rowson speak in this way to legitimize writing in a genre often associated in their day with immorality. Their usually brief messages about female virtue seem frail by comparison with the prolonged drama of their spirited heroine's downfall. Moreover, specific plot elements associating fallen women with the values of republican national identity—rebellion against authority, independence, and personal expression—appear to overpower an author's expressed moralistic admonitions concerning the propriety of female submission, dependence, and silent self-denial.

In some ways, then, these novels did not support the status quo, whatever their authors' admonitions about female nonconformity. Doubts about the genuineness of the expressed punishment theme of sentimental fiction emerged early in such contemporary novels as Foster's *Coquette* and Tabitha Tenney's *Female Quixotism* (1801), both best-sellers that at once utilized and undermined the moralistic conventions of the sentimental tradition. These novels related the theme of seduction to the in-

equality of power between men and women. In fact, the early American sentimental novel routinely attributed women's shortcomings and victimization to their inadequate education.

The didactic impulse informing both sentimental and satiric early American fiction was related to a widespread national belief in the need for an educated citizenry if the new republic was to prevail. Concern about an educated electorate inspired Brackenridge's mock rendering of male discourse and behavior in *Modern Chivalry,* and it specifically explained the plight of women as depicted in Rowson's *Charlotte* and Tenney's *Female Quixotism.* Enos Hitchcock's *Memoirs of the Bloomsgrove Family* (1790), an epistolary novel likely indebted to Thomas Day's *Sandford and Merton* (1783), alerted parents (the implied readers of the book) about the educational needs of new republic children; it particularly emphasized the vulnerability of daughters deprived of a sound formal schooling. Similar concerns, addressed to mothers and female teachers, informed *The Boarding School* (1798), in which Hannah Webster Foster presented an exchange of student letters as testaments to a widow's educational use of the fine arts and rational conversation in successfully preparing girls for early republican life. In *Story of Margaretta* (1798) reformer Judith Sargent Murray (under the pseudonym Constantia) presented a nonsentimental heroine who prevails precisely because she has been exposed to learning. The schoolmaster protagonist of Charles Brockden Brown's dialogue novel *Alcuin* (1798), evidently influenced by Mary Wollstonecraft's *A Vindication of the Rights of Woman* (1792), participates in a conversation that impugns the sentimental tradition for veiling the equality of men and women. Not only did these novels incorporate matter drawn from school books, but in turn early national textbooks sometimes included epistolary and dialogic fictional devices when presenting student lessons or precepts.

The early American novel was as concerned with informal as with formal education. There were, accordingly, novels written for young readers that addressed general social mores. These works, more often serious than humorous in manner, tended to be comprised of scenes that dramatized good and bad conduct. In *The Art of Courting* (1795), for example, Ebenezer Bradford resorted to tableaux, including scenes of a Christian woman refuting her suitor's Deistic notions, to create a guidebook on marriage designed for young readers who enjoyed reading novels.

Educating readers at home and abroad about the physical and cultural resources of the republic technically fell to textbooks but was also a goal of various kinds of travelogues. The travel narrative was already an established form in 18th-century Britain, as typified by James Boswell's *The Journal of a Tour to the Hebrides* (1785). In America these works also had an indigenous ancestor, the semifictitious descriptions reported in 17th-century promotion literature designed to foster settlement in the North American colonies. This advertisement tradition was reinforced by the characteristic wit and observation of the later travelogue tradition, and both readily blended with the discursive epistolary manner evident in many 18th-century American novels. Instead of directly promoting immigration, these post-Revolutionary works encouraged the formation of national self-awareness at home. In *The Algerine Spy in Pennsylvania* (1787), for example, Peter Markoe extols the physical and cultural resources of the new nation through the eyes of a fictional outsider; this spy's numerous observations, including reports on fashions and dancing, lead to a paean of national pride culminating with the foreigner's becoming a citizen of the new republic. Such a rosy portrait contravenes the dark Federalist admonitions associated with the early American picaresque journeys described in *Modern Chivalry*. It also contradicts the cultural implications of Royall Tyler's *The Algerine Captive* (1797), in which the recounted journeys of an American subjugated in Algers raises questions about the apparent virtue of an America that supports slavery.

The goal of the early American novel was the 18th-century standard parroted by Julia Coles, a young Connecticut girl who wrote in her diary that she found *Memoirs of the Bloomsgrove Family* to be both entertaining and instructive. Her parents would presumably have been pleased, for their early American culture valued art for its usefulness, specifically its service to social stability. Ideally, then, the entertaining art of the novel remained subordinate to, merely the medium of, socially endorsed rational enlightenment. Such indeed was the intention frequently declared in early American fiction, which nevertheless often presented characters and plots that at times apparently revised, resisted, or even subverted this very criterion.

WILLIAM J. SCHEICK

See also Epistolary Novel; Gothic Novel; Libraries; Regional Novel; Sentimental Novel; Sex, Gender, and the Novel

Further Reading

Brown, Herbert Ross, *The Sentimental Novel in America, 1789–1860,* Durham, North Carolina: Duke University Press, 1940

Cowie, Alexander, *The Rise of the American Novel,* New York: American Book Company, 1948

Davidson, Cathy N., *Revolution and the Word: The Rise of the Novel in America,* New York: Oxford University Press, 1986

Davidson, Cathy N., editor, *Reading in America: Literature and Social History,* Baltimore: Johns Hopkins University Press, 1989

Fennimore, Keith J., editor, *Short Stories from Another Day: Eighteenth-Century Periodical Fiction,* East Lansing: Michigan State University Press, 1989

Grabo, Norman S., *The Coincidental Art of Charles Brockden Brown,* Chapel Hill: University of North Carolina Press, 1981

Parker, Patricia L., *Charles Brockden Brown: A Reference Guide,* Boston: G.K. Hall, 1980

Parker, Patricia L., *Early American Fiction: A Reference Guide,* Boston: G.K. Hall, 1984

Pattee, Fred Lewis, *The First Century of American Literature, 1770–1870,* New York: Appleton-Century, 1935

Petter, Henri, *The Early American Novel,* Columbus: Ohio State University Press, 1971

Pitcher, Edward W.R., *Fiction in American Magazines Before 1800,* Schenectady, New York: Union College Press, 1993

Rosenthal, Bernard, editor, *Critical Essays on Charles Brockden Brown,* Boston: G.K. Hall, 1981

Spengemann, William C., *The Adventurous Muse: The Poetics of American Fiction, 1789–1900,* New Haven, Connecticut: Yale University Press, 1977

Tyler, Moses Coit, *The Literary History of the American Revolution, 1763–1783,* 2 vols., New York and London: Putnam, 1897

Watts, Steven, *The Romance of Real Life: Charles Brockden Brown and the Origins of American Culture,* Baltimore: Johns Hopkins University Press, 1994

Yannella, Donald, and John H. Roch, editors, *American Prose to 1820: A Guide to Information Sources,* Detroit, Michigan: Gale Research, 1979

United States Novel

1800–1850

The early 19th-century American novel developed within a milieu of increasing literary nationalism and substantial changes in book publishing practices. During the first three decades of the century, sales of American novels were relatively meager, but by the 1830s a mass readership for the American novel had evolved as substantial obstacles to widespread book distribution were surmounted. Aside from technological and economic impediments, publishers faced persistent suspicions regarding the moral propriety of the novel; meanwhile, writers had to overcome the pervasive sense that American literary culture was inferior to that of the British.

American authors effectively challenged notions of cultural inferiority by producing works that attained transatlantic prominence. The first American writer to achieve European renown, along with some prosperity from book sales, was Washington Irving, who secured his reputation with *The Sketch Book of Geoffrey Crayon* (1819–20) and subsequent histories that were translated into German and French. Although *The Sketch Book* features the short fiction for which Irving is largely remembered, one of his early works, *A History of New York* (1809), displays a novelistic response to the widespread scepticism toward fiction. *A History of New York,* despite its title and assurances of truthfulness, blends satire with history. Moreover, as is suggested by the subtitle—*From the Beginning of the World to the End of the Dutch Dynasty*—Irving was willing to parody American self-importance while undermining clear-cut distinctions between supposedly edifying nonfictional works and purportedly corrupting fictions. As the first major 19th-century American author, Irving served as an exemplar for literary nationalists, at the same time that he helped establish history as a typical subject for the American novel.

The idea that historical fiction could be instructional no doubt enhanced the reception given Sir Walter Scott's historical novels, which enjoyed great popularity during the first quarter of the 19th century. Scott's novels were enthusiastically greeted by American publishers largely because there were no effective international copyright laws to protect authors' interests. Accordingly, British authors generally could expect no royalties from American printers, who often competed among themselves to produce pirated editions of the newest novels as quickly as possible. The commercial benefits of distributing British rather than American novels were clear to American publishers, and almost half the best-sellers during this period were thus appropriated, a situation that a victimized Charles Dickens assailed in his *American Notes for General Circulation* (1842). Despite the obvious disadvantage this situation initially posed to American writers, the publication of British fiction eventually helped expand the market for all novels, including those by Americans.

James Fenimore Cooper was the American writer who most clearly benefited from the increasing taste for historical fiction. His first best-selling novel, *The Spy* (1821), is set during the American Revolution, and his most famous novels, the five Leatherstocking tales—*The Pioneers* (1823), *The Last of the Mohicans* (1826), *The Prairie* (1827), *The Pathfinder* (1840), and *The Deerslayer* (1841)—rely on specifically American backgrounds and history for their depictions of a frontiersman's life. The most financially successful of these works, *The Last of the Mohicans*, incorporates the motif of captivity by Native Americans, an abiding American preoccupation, within the context of pre-Revolutionary military and political conflict. The demagoguery of a particularly misanthropic Native American leader propels the plot, revealing yet another preoccupation—an apprehension about possible manipulation of mobs within a democracy that mirrors the fears of factionalism expressed by the *Federalist Papers*. Cooper repeatedly turned to political argumentation in his later writings, which eventually diminished his popularity. His publishers repeatedly, and fruitlessly, urged him to return to the themes that had enabled him to become the first American to support himself by writing novels.

Fictional attention to American situations arose alongside polemics on behalf of American literary nationalism. The desire for a literature that expressed an alleged national character dovetailed with the older concern that literature serve a social function. Of antebellum statements advocating literary nationalism, the most frequently recalled is Emerson's "The American Scholar" (1837), yet given the limited distribution of Emerson's essays before the Civil War, American readers seeking such sentiments would have discovered them in, for example, William Ellery Channing's "Remarks on National Literature" (1823). Channing affirmed the value of literature as a means of forming national character and improving society, much as William Cullen Bryant, in his "Lectures on Poetry" (1825–26), linked literary patriotism with domesticity and, thus, social stability.

In what appears as a general endorsement of literary nationalism, a number of early 19th-century authors achieved popular success writing historical novels. James Kirke Paulding's *Koningsmarke* (1823) satirized Scott's rhetorical and stylistic excesses, and *The Dutchman's Fireside* (1831), set in 18th-century

upstate New York, inspired sufficient enthusiasm to generate European translations. Stylistically undistinguished historical romances were offered by John Pendleton Kennedy in *Horse-Shoe Robinson* (1835) and *Quodlibet* (1840), which used the device of an imaginary history to satirize Andrew Jackson. Another writer of self-consciously nationalist works, John Neal, presented conflicts with Native Americans in *Logan* (1822) and focused on the American Revolution in *Seventy-Six* (1823). Neal, like Kennedy and Paulding, shared not only Cooper's interest in historical subjects but also the tendency toward compositional haste and carelessness. Neal additionally treated life in Puritan New England, writing of witchcraft trials in *Rachel Dyer* (1828), as did Harriet Vaughan Cheney in *A Peep at the Pilgrims in Sixteen Hundred Thirty-Six* (1824). An absorption with the ways Puritanism continued to inform contemporary New England culture may be found in Catharine Maria Sedgwick's *A New-England Tale* (1822). Inspiring interest largely for its portrayals of local manners, *A New-England Tale* critically regarded the tenacity of Calvinism. In this respect, it resembles contemporary attacks on the theological remnants of Puritanism, such as William Ellery Channing's "The Moral Argument Against Calvinism" (1820).

Sedgwick was one of several women novelists who used their portrayals of regional history and culture to advance criticisms of American society. In a later novel, *Hope Leslie* (1827), Sedgwick extends her critique of Calvinism to its American sources in 17th-century Puritan New England. Her fictional account of Puritan rigidity, a typical early 19th-century characterization, conceptualizes female moral agency manifesting itself in a protest against patriarchal Puritan authority. Sedgwick's critique of religious hypocrisy resembles another contemporary work, Catharine Williams' *Fall River* (1833), which tells the sensational story of a clergyman tried for the murder of a young woman. But *Hope Leslie* goes further when it treats Puritan relations with Native Americans. Suggesting that the colonists initiated violence, Sedgwick's account of a ruthless Puritan attack on a Native American settlement presents itself as a response to the Native American massacre of unarmed victims in Cooper's *The Last of the Mohicans*. In a similarly critical vein, Lydia Maria Child's *Hobomok* (1824) introduces a story of interracial marriage that dramatizes the unjust treatment of Native Americans. Sedgwick and Child base their treatment of historical themes on the notion of the superior ethical judgment of women. Like Cooper's fictional considerations of political organization, their work demands substantive reflection on the proper basis of American society.

Such novelistic attention to politics and ethics coincided with widespread concerns about the integrity of the republic during an era of increasing immigration. The American capacity to attract European immigrants led to an increasingly diverse populace that in turn engendered the kind of elitist anxieties voiced by Cooper. State-financed public schooling was in part developed as a conscious attempt to exercise a degree of social control over a lower-class public that, in the case of white males, often voted. By the 1840s, school enrollment in New York and Massachusetts stood close to 70 percent. Although difficult to gauge, white literacy rates in the East appeared to range from approximately 50 percent in the South to 75 percent in New England.

With the growth of a reading public and a potential market for literature came a series of profound changes in the publishing industry. In the early 1800s, the industry had been fairly decentralized, but by 1840 the vast majority of novels were published in New York, Boston, and Philadelphia. New York's ascent as a publishing center resulted from its position as a port city—where printers quickly received new English works—and its access to inland trade routes. Technological developments between 1825 and 1850, such as improvements in paper manufacture, the development of lighter book bindings, the invention of mechanical typesetting, and an increasing division of labor, altered the publishing industry. The most striking single change may have been the development of high-speed cylindrical presses that could produce printed work a hundred times faster than could their hand-operated precursors. One result of these composite changes was the first boom in paperback book production during the 1830s. But of particular importance to the growth of the novel was the serialization of pirated English novels, such as those of Dickens, which then led to the publication of complete novels inexpensively distributed because of subsidized postal rates.

Among the pirated English novels of the period were those of Frederick Marryat, whose nautical narratives, including *Frank Mildmay* (1829) and *Mr. Midshipman Easy* (1836), helped to popularize the genre. Cooper previously had written *The Pilot* (1823), set during the American Revolution, as well as *The Red Rover* (1827) and *The Water Witch* (1830), historical novels of seafaring life. A more fantastic nautical story that resists simple interpretation, Edgar Allan Poe's convoluted short novel *The Narrative of Arthur Gordon Pym of Nantucket* (1838), chronicles the strange adventures that lead the narrator to Antarctica, abruptly ending with a postscript that reports the narrator's death along with the disappearance of the final chapters.

The most enduring 19th-century nautical novels were those of Herman Melville, whose first work, *Typee: A Peep at Polynesian Life* (1846), established his fame in the United States and England. Although based on his own experiences during a Pacific voyage, *Typee* was not an autobiographical account like Richard Henry Dana's *Two Years Before the Mast* (1840), a young man's coming-of-age story. Melville's novel instead foregrounds confrontations with conventional American mores created by the narrator's admiration for the mutually supportive Typee people, who, despite their friendliness, remain the narrator's captors. The publisher's anxieties over prudish and pietistic responses to the sexual suggestiveness and criticisms of Christian missionaries in *Typee* induced Melville to expurgate the second American edition. He did, however, continue to criticize missionaries and the effects of colonialism in his next novel, *Omoo: A Narrative of Adventures in the South Seas* (1847).

Melville's subsequent work became more experimental and consequently less appealing to an audience anticipating simple sea stories. After a cool critical reception to the more allegorical *Mardi* (1849), Melville tried to return to conventional accounts, producing *Redburn: His First Voyage* (1849) and *White-Jacket; or, The World in a Man-of-War* (1850). Although these resemble ordinary sea stories, both novels feature caustic descriptions of social injustices, with *Redburn* treating class differences and *White-Jacket* ironically discussing American ideals. Of immense interest to readers during the 20th century, *Moby-Dick* (1851) may be understood as Melville's miscalculation of the desires of his 19th-century audience, which responded unfavorably to his philosophical speculations and his experimentation with novelistic form. In later novels, *Pierre* (1852), *Israel Potter* (1855), and

The Confidence-Man (1857), Melville persisted with formal experimentation and ideological critique. He eventually succumbed to discouragement over public indifference to his work.

Melville's recurrent depictions of travel—his use of a riverboat as a setting in *The Confidence-Man* is typical—reflects the American interest in geographical regionalism exhibited in the works of Irving, Sedgwick, and Paulding, among others. Life along the frontier furnished the basis for *Greyslaer: A Romance of the Mohawk* (1840) by Charles Fenno Hoffman, who had achieved some status with an earlier narrative of his travels, *A Winter in the West* (1835). The South supplied the setting for Johnson Jones Hooper's *Some Adventures of Captain Simon Suggs* (1845), a picaresque novel that derives its humor from the protagonist's unprincipled behavior. The novels of the prolific William Gilmore Simm represented to other regions the antebellum South. *The Yemassee* (1835) features adventures in the South Carolina setting typical of Simms's fiction, including *The Partisan* (1835) and *The Forayers* (1855). Another remarkably prolific teller of southern adventure tales, often set in Louisiana and Mississippi, was Joseph Holt Ingraham. Between 1839 and 1847, Ingraham produced more than 75 novels of approximately 100 pages in length. Designed for production on high-speed presses and cheap distribution, each could be sold for a quarter. His most successful novel, *Lafitte, the Pirate of the Gulf* (1836), later republished as *The Pirate* in 1839, remained in print into the 20th century, and *The Prince of the House of David* (1855) became the first best-selling piece of religious fiction in the US.

Religion more routinely constituted a background element in fiction. It was important as a perceived element of either reform or stability during an era of societal turbulence. Among the more profound antebellum changes was the economic transformation of the northeast, as primarily rural and maritime economies were supplanted by water-powered manufacture and industry. This rapid development radically altered the economic base of the region and has been associated with corresponding changes in politics and ideals of public virtue. The new industrial morality, generally identified as the Protestant work ethic, revered such behaviors as punctuality, abstinence from alcohol, and, perhaps most significantly, the notion that work is valuable for its own sake. This style of moralism, which may readily be associated with middle-class mores, proved an effective means of subordinating working-class interests to those of manufacturers.

Occasional dissent from class domination may be discerned, as in Melville's accounts of sailors' lives or his pointed description of factory workers in "The Paradise of Bachelors and The Tartarus of Maids" (1855). The most well-known antebellum protest against capitalist domination of workers, however, was George Lippard's best-seller *The Quaker City* (1844), which sold 60,000 copies during its first year and was published in numerous subsequent editions. The enthusiastic reception of Lippard's narrative of a secret capitalist cabal scheming to enslave workers eventually led him to diminish his literary output—he had written historical novels as well as other renderings of violent, degraded city life—and devote himself entirely to social reform efforts.

Lippard's vision of the horrors attending the urban milieu somewhat resembles the Gothicism of his friend Poe. Their depictions of human psychology are also similar. Such ideas as unconscious motivation or physiological determinism, far more prevalent during the 20th century, were not prominently featured within the dominant school of psychological thought during the antebellum era, that of Scottish Common Sense realism. Common Sense psychologists instead focused on moralism and character formation, areas that might seem alien to the novelists's purview given antebellum suspicions toward fiction and its purported ability to lead young people astray. The writers who, with their chronicles of women's moral development, most directly responded to questions about the psychological effects of aesthetic pleasures were practitioners of the sentimental novel.

The most popular sentimental novel of this period, Susan Warner's *The Wide, Wide World* (1851), tells the story of an orphan's moral and religious formation. The account of the protagonist's development assigns a sense of subjective agency to the young woman, which creates an alternative, female version of the Bildungsroman, which in its male variant, such as the sea story, tended to focus on the acquisition of skills and worldly knowledge. In Warner's novel, following maternal and biblical guidance allows one to regulate one's own impulses in the face of debased, unspiritual authority. But Warner's emphasis on the Christian moralism of Scottish Common Sense thought is developed simultaneously with an implied critique of a patriarchy that subordinates ethics and feeling to conventional, materialistic values and power. Along corresponding lines, Warner's lengthy *Queechy* (1852) features a protagonist who effectively displays her abilities to deal with economic and domestic difficulties.

The sentimental critique of patriarchal authority is noteworthy in its own right, but it also serves as an index of the recurrent antebellum preoccupation with questions about the proper basis of American society. In *The Scarlet Letter* (1850), Nathaniel Hawthorne positions sympathy as a middle ground between, on the one hand, the harsh judgments and behaviors he associates with Puritan intellectualism and, on the other, his protagonists' passionate excesses. Hawthorne disparages both conventional authority and the psychological distortions he associates with isolated individualism. He posits sympathy as the proper basis for social cohesion, an idea typical of mainstream thought as well as the sentimental critique of patriarchy. Moreover, like the work of sentimental novelists, Hawthorne's most famous historical novel further suggests that even though by the middle of the 19th century earlier concerns about the legitimacy and proper subject matter for the novel had somewhat diminished, apprehensions about American culture and its ethical and political bases largely underlay the plots and characterizations of early 19th-century American novels.

Antebellum malaise over the state of American society would culminate in what would become the best-selling novel of the 19th century, Harriet Beecher Stowe's abolitionist and antipatriarchal *Uncle Tom's Cabin* (1852).

JOSEPH ALKANA

See also American Western Novel; James Fenimore Cooper; Nathaniel Hawthorne; Herman Melville; Regional Novel; Uncle Tom's Cabin

Further Reading

Baym, Nina, *Woman's Fiction: A Guide to Novels by and about Women in America, 1820–1870,* Ithaca, New York: Cornell University Press, 1978; 2nd edition, Urbana: University of Illinois Press, 1993

Bellis, Peter, *No Mysteries Out of Ourselves: Identity and Textual Form in the Novels of Herman Melville,* Philadelphia: University of Pennsylvania Press, 1990

Bercovitch, Sacvan, *The Office of the Scarlet Letter,* Baltimore: Johns Hopkins University Press, 1991

Charvat, William, *The Profession of Authorship in America, 1800–1870,* Columbus: Ohio State University Press, 1968

Dimock, Wai-Chee, *Empire for Liberty: Melville and the Poetics of Individualism,* Princeton, New Jersey: Princeton University Press, 1989

Fiedler, Leslie, *Love and Death in the American Novel,* New York: Dell, 1960; London: Cape, 1967

Gilmore, Michael T., *American Romanticism and the Marketplace,* Chicago: University of Chicago Press, 1985

Harris, Susan K., *19th-Century American Women's Novels: Interpretive Strategies,* Cambridge and New York: Cambridge University Press, 1990

Matthiessen, F.O., *American Renaissance: Art and Expression in the Age of Emerson and Whitman,* London and New York: Oxford University Press, 1941

Railton, Stephen, *Authorship and Audience: Literary Performance in the American Renaissance,* Princeton, New Jersey: Princeton University Press, 1991

Reynolds, David, *Beneath the American Renaissance: The Subversive Imagination in the Age of Emerson and Melville,* New York: Knopf, 1988

Sellers, Charles Grier, *The Market Revolution: Jacksonian America, 1815–1846,* New York: Oxford University Press, 1991

Tompkins, Jane, *Sensational Designs: The Cultural Work of American Fiction, 1790–1860,* New York: Oxford University Press, 1985

Zboray, Ronald J., *A Fictive People: Antebellum Economic Development and the American Reading Public,* New York: Oxford University Press, 1993

Ziff, Larzer, *Literary Democracy: The Declaration of Cultural Independence in America,* New York: Viking Press, 1981; London: Penguin, 1982

United States Novel

1850–1900

To witness the death throes of antebellum American culture, a time traveler might visit Pfaff's restaurant-saloon on Broadway some evening in the 1850s. Reacting against the increasing rigidity and commercialization of American society, the Bohemians at Pfaff's tried desperately to cling to the almost childish innocence of simpler times, laughing and singing even as they watched their world come to an end. Here a visitor might see actresses, artists, comedians, poets, and novelists shouting to one another, telling jokes, drinking beer, puffing on cigars. The writers present might include Walt Whitman, as well as Fitz-James O'Brien and Charles D. Gardette, two fiction writers who patterned their work after Edgar Allan Poe's. Indeed, the recently deceased Poe, whose novel *The Narrative of Arthur Gordon Pym of Nantucket* (1838) describes a young man's flight from commerce and respectability, figured as a sort of patron saint for the merry cynics at Pfaff's.

Their forced gaiety and underlying gloom mirrors the emotions of Pym himself, who prefers the risk of starvation and cannibalism in the South Pacific to what he sees as the living death of the lawyer and businessman he will become if he stays in Nantucket. As Americans bade goodbye to a largely agrarian world, the Industrial Revolution moved into its maturity, with an attendant need for the increasingly complex and narrow roles played by workers-turned-specialists. In literature and the arts, now-familiar boundaries between high, middle-brow, and popular culture began to appear, to rigidify after the Civil War. Earlier, Shakespeare was performed on the same stage as farces and minstrel shows; political rallies included poetry and musical performance; and popular songs were derived from operatic arias, just as classical compositions incorporated folk music. David S. Reynolds compares antebellum utopian life at Brook Farm, depicted in Nathaniel Hawthorne's *The Blithedale Romance* (1852), with the more hierarchical way of life described in Edward Bellamy's novel *Looking Backward 2000–1887* (1888). In the former, people live communally, enjoying poetry readings, concerts, and *tableaux vivants* along with their daily work, whereas in the latter, life is more rigidly ordered, music is piped into separate living compartments, and much of the work is done by machines (see Reynolds, 1995).

A glance back, and then forward, at the careers of two very different authors, reveals two very different Americas. In 1839, Herman Melville published his first professional work, "Fragments from a Writing Desk," in a newspaper in Lansingburgh, New York. He also shipped as a deckhand on the *St. Lawrence,* a medium-sized merchant vessel bound for Liverpool; later, he would base his novel *Redburn* (1849) on that trip. Over the course of the next 20 years, in fact, Melville would produce a dozen volumes, including *Moby-Dick* (1851) and some of the finest short fiction in US literature. Not yet, however: once he came home from England, Melville was employed as a schoolteacher at the Greenbush Academy in Greenbush, New York. That a sailor whose own schooling had stopped at age 15 could become a teacher—indeed, that one person could be author, sailor, and teacher in the same year—is a powerful reminder of the unsettled state of Melville's America and, in particular, of the laxity with which the professions were viewed.

By contrast, by the century's end, Henry James, a novelist as representative of that time as Melville was of his, reflected a changed view of the professions, including authorship, in his preface to *The Wings of the Dove* (1902), where he compares the novelist to a civil engineer who erects a bridge and then, as "rueful builder," passes beneath it, watching and listening as others use a creation that is no longer his. Earlier, engineers had organized themselves into such regional associations as New York's American Society of Civil Engineers (1852), which admitted interested amateurs as well as practicing professionals. By 1867, the ASCE had begun to expand geographically and regulate its membership more thoroughly. In 1895, membership was restricted to those who actually designed machinery or public works.

James had begun his career in the 1870s. His first major novel, *Roderick Hudson,* appeared in 1875, and *The Portrait of a Lady,* which many critics regard as his finest work, was published in 1881. Thus James' career as a novelist was approaching its peak at a time when the profession of engineering, which he obviously looked to as a source of metaphors for his own work, was evolving out of its loosely conceived amateur stage and entering one of marked rigidification.

Similar changes were taking place in every profession. For example, medical practitioners, a more or less disreputable group until the mid–19th century, organized themselves into the American Medical Association in 1847 and, by putting into effect strict requirements for education, licensing, and practice, created the demi-god image of "the doctor," with its connotations of power, privilege, and esteem. Likewise, the American Bar Association was founded in 1878 and made possible the rise of lawyers to a position in American culture second only to that of physicians. And in 1857, educators formed the National Education Association, a group that, presumably, would have denied a teaching certificate to young Herman Melville, fresh from the decks of the *St. Lawrence.*

Among writers, of course, there was no such formal organizing, although, as James' ruminations show, there was, during the second half-century, a pronounced and often anxious awareness on the part of writers that the production, packaging, and promotion of literature had changed radically. Perhaps there is no more famous comment on the new situation than the one made by Nathaniel Hawthorne in an 1855 letter to his publisher, William D. Ticknor, in which the novelist complained that "America is now wholly given over to a d____d mob of scribbling women." The novel whose success particularly incensed Hawthorne was an 1854 moralistic romance by Maria Susanna Cummins about a Boston orphan girl who is befriended by a virtuous lamplighter. "What is the mystery of these innumerable editions of *The Lamplighter,*" asked Hawthorne, "and other books neither better nor worse?" Of course, Hawthorne's own novel *The Scarlet Letter* (1850) hovers in the background of this query. *The Scarlet Letter* was published by the firm of Ticknor and Fields, while *The Lamplighter* had been published by John P. Jewett, which had also published another best-selling book of the decade, Harriet Beecher Stowe's *Uncle Tom's Cabin* (1852). So in complaining about the "d____d mob," Hawthorne may have been taking a not-so-subtle dig at the relatively poor performance of his own publisher.

Indeed, Jewett had accomplished a small miracle in his packaging and promotion of *The Lamplighter,* mainly by increasing the number of potential buyers through targeting additional readerships. The plot of the novel was custom-made for consumption by 19th-century fiction's target audience, middle-class women. Its story of self-sacrifice and feminine virtue fulfilled the Horatian requirement that art both entertain and instruct; thus it was a novel that a woman could recommend to her friends as a productive way to fill their leisure hours. What Jewett did was extend the book's appeal to readerships beyond this traditional middle-class female group. Soon after *The Lamplighter* first appeared, it became available in a number of different formats: as a child's book with an abridged plot and pictures; as a lavishly illustrated deluxe edition for art lovers; and as an inexpensive "railroad edition" intended for travelers. Such manipulations of the market aside, Cummins' work is largely unread today, while Hawthorne, despite poor sales, had established his niche in the literary pantheon with *The Scarlet Letter* and would secure it with *The House of the Seven Gables* (1851), *The Blithedale Romance,* and *The Marble Faun* (1860). For the moment, however, he was quite eclipsed by Cummins's moralistic fable and Jewett's clever promotions.

New sales strategies were complemented and made even more successful by a fundamental change in the reviewing industry, one that reflects the increasing rigidification of American industry generally. The mid-century growth of the audience for fiction was paralleled by an increase in newspaper and periodical publication. The two phenomena were joined by a strong moral bond, to judge by the comments of most reviewers. The prevailing view was that fiction was a didactic medium with a clear mandate to instruct readers. After all, the novel as it is known now was then but a few decades old, at least in the United States, and therefore somewhat suspect, especially in contrast to the more venerable essay and poem. So novelists, publishers, reviewers, and readers interested in increasing the odds of survival for this vulnerable form resorted to various strategies designed to give it a fighting chance in the market. One such strategy was to pretend that the work of fiction was factual or at least fact-based. Poe's *Narrative of Arthur Gordon Pym* was passed off as an autobiography, for example, and Hawthorne's *The Scarlet Letter* is preceded by a lengthy preface detailing the author's "discovery" of the actual letter in an old trunk. Where the pretense of veracity was pointless, the case was often made that the book in question was fiction, yes, but of a highly moral kind unlikely to lead the reader astray (especially the young or female reader) and capable of delivering an uplifting moral message.

The principal task allotted to reviewers was to provide direction for readers, a significant portion of whom were thought incapable of making informed decisions on their own. Worse, fiction readers were assumed to be less intellectually endowed than readers of nonfiction and more indolent and desultory in their reading habits. A writer in the November 1859 number of *DeBow's Review* described the fiction-reading public as one that "cannot understand or appreciate . . . refined or elevated sentiment, original and profound thought," adding that "the commonplace, the superficial, the sensual, the gross, and the gaudy, are alone adapted to their torpid intellectual tastes." Even as late

as April 1865 these sentiments are echoed in the *Ladies' Repository,* where it is reported that "hurrying, uncultured, every-day people . . . will not read heavy, labored, theological works"; the masses "must have easy reading, or they will not read at all."

Inevitably, this untenable situation changed as both lay readers and reviewers became more discriminating in their choices and less enchanted with the shoddy offerings of the publishing industry. Susan S. Williams (1996) quotes an excerpt from *The American Publishers' Circular and Literary Gazette* (1855) that describes this reformation:

> A few years since . . . the nation seemed, for a time, in danger of becoming a land of novelists. . . . Bookmaking became contagious. One successful production . . . called into existence from ten to forty trashy and stupid imitations of it. They were all puffed, and, probably, all sold. But the public at length awoke; it discovered the deception. Then came the reaction. A great many books were published, but no system of puffery or advertising could induce men to buy them.

Slower to react, the reviewing industry nonetheless came around as well to this view of the proliferation of shoddy work:

> The critics, too, gradually assumed a tone of caution. They found their opinions disrespected; they resolved to change their tactics; and although we are now, as it were, but in one period of transition, it is not difficult, we think, to behold the dawn of a more healthful and secure existence.

During the transition, reviewers took pains not only to discriminate more carefully between good fiction and bad but also to describe more precisely the books that came across their desks. The critical reception of *The Lamplighter* reveals both an awareness of the contemporary moralizing condescension toward readers as well as the reviewers' desire to improve their own standards and acquire the rigor (and the public respect that accompanied it) that had become the hallmark of other professions. At the time, as Nina Baym observes, it was commonplace to categorize popular novels as belonging to one of three classes: the metropolitan novel, or novel of low life; the domestic novel; and the fashionable novel, or novel of high life (see Baym, 1984). Nominally, *The Lamplighter* belonged to the middle group, although reviewers, aware of the disrepute into which their trade had fallen, were careful to distinguish it from similar novels that were merely melodramatic or sensational. In the 28 March 1854 number of the *New York Tribune,* for example, it is noted that Cummins has dealt "with the materials at hand less with the view of enforcing a moral, than as the legitimate subjects of literary art." Thus, the aggressive and ingenious publishing strategies of John P. Jewett, combined with reviewers' awareness of the growing sophistication of the audience as well as their own need for higher standards, helped to make *The Lamplighter* extraordinarily successful. Add to this the popular stage productions of the work in Boston and, later, London, and it is easy to see the importance of one work that not only typified the mass-appeal novel that dominated the mid-century but also anticipated the novel of "literary art" that achieved greater prominence as the century went on.

As readers and reviewers became more sophisticated, both groups began to think of fiction as art and not merely moral instruction. With this change came an increase in interest in such writerly conventions as character and the rise of the novel that was character-driven rather than plot-driven. James L. Machor reports that, in the early days of American book reviewing, it was assumed that novels were narrated by the novelists themselves, and therefore the novelist should be a moral authority whom the reader could trust (see Machor, 1992). Certainly this was said of Maria Cummins, who was taken by readers to be a good woman telling a story in which goodness prevails. But for a later novelist like Mark Twain, for example, authorial morality is much less important than character complexity. Hence the appeal of the Tom Sawyer who not only dominated the story of his own adventures (published in 1876) but also played a crucial role in *The Adventures of Huckleberry Finn* (1884) and then returned in *Tom Sawyer Abroad* (1894) and *Tom Sawyer, Detective* (1896). Richard Hill points out that Tom may not be popular in contemporary academe, but he was an unadulterated hero to both the fictional citizens of St. Petersburg and the readers of Twain's day: the bravest, smartest kid in town, the one who not only saves the judge's daughter from a horrible death but wins the pot of robber's gold, a literary authority and, as the premier practitioner of the imaginative hoax, a *non pareil* performance artist. In Hill's words, Tom is "full of the heroic pioneer spirit, the give-me-liberty-or-give-me-death, I-only-regret-I-have-one-life-to-give-for-my-country, damn-the-torpedoes-full-speed-ahead American Right Stuff" (see Hill, 1991).

Contemporary reviewers of *Huckleberry Finn,* whose hero was billed as "Tom Sawyer's Comrade" on the cover, were so taken with Tom that they were blind to the racism of the novel's last chapters. In examining dozens of reviews written between 1885 and 1900, Hill found only one that condemned the ending; more typical was the review that read, "The romantic side of Tom Sawyer is shown in most delightfully humorous fashion in the account of his difficult devices to aid in the easy escape of Jim, a runaway negro." African-American novelists, too, had to take into account prevailing racial attitudes in the presentation of their characters. In Frederick Douglass' short novel *The Heroic Slave* (1853), the black hero is introduced by an authoritative white character who, in effect, vouches for him, simultaneously empowering and limiting his voice. As late as 1899, this same frame technique is used in Charles Waddell Chesnutt's *The Conjure Woman,* in which a white Northerner buys a plantation and inherits an ex-slave named Uncle Julius, whose buffoonish tales comprise the novel. Characters like Uncle Julius strike readers as embarrassing now, although, in Chesnutt's day, they represented a calculated authorial response to a contemporary readership's resistance to anything remotely resembling black aggression.

In the course of the 19th century, then, the novel underwent a far-reaching transformation: viewed at first more or less amateurishly by writer, reader, and reviewer alike, it was accorded the status of "literature" by century's end. With success, however, comes first self-consciousness and then anxiety: fear that one has failed to live up to one's own standards, nervousness about the reception of one's work. Henry James was not only one of the greatest novelists of any country or time; he was also one of the great worriers and a prodigious recorder of his own concerns. In contrast to Hawthorne's occasional muttering on the subject, James fretted constantly about audience, sales, and every conceivable aspect of the publishing process, as his journals and letters reveal. And in one of his novels, he dramatizes his fear that perhaps the novel had become too successful, that the new strategies for sales, distribution, and review had created a kind of novel so highly evolved that it had become estranged from its original audience.

James' early novels, such as *Roderick Hudson* and *The American* (1877), reflect his mastery of the romance techniques of his acknowledged master, Hawthorne. And with such novels as *Washington Square* (1881) and *The Portrait of a Lady,* James showed that, like his friend and fellow writer William Dean Howells, he had become a committed realist in the tradition of Flaubert. But in mid-career, he detoured into naturalism, an unusual mode for a novelist whose work dealt almost exclusively with the aristocratic and the wealthy. *The Princess Casamassima* (1886) is the story of Hyacinth Robinson, a cultured if impoverished bookbinder who joins a band of revolutionaries but kills himself when ordered to assassinate a duke. Margaret Scanlan (1992) points out that Hyacinth, the illegitimate son of a poor Frenchwoman and an English nobleman, contains within himself the struggle between political action and high culture, and, although he leans more toward the latter than the former, it is not mere fastidiousness that keeps him from his bloody deed. Instead, Hyacinth's suicide is an admission of the failure of revolutionaries who cannot win an audience they claim to represent—like a novelist whom no one reads.

Writers, readers, and publishers had not only succeeded in making fiction respectable and profitable but had conferred upon it the status of high art. At the peak of his career, James was competing with best-selling popular writers as well as so-called art novelists like himself. The industry had never been healthier, but then the field had never been more crowded, the demands for excellence never higher. No wonder one novelist, at least, was wondering whether all this success was worth it.

DAVID KIRBY

See also Awakening; Henry James; Little Women; Herman Melville; Naturalism; Reviewers and the Popular Press; Mark Twain; Uncle Tom's Cabin

Further Reading

Baym, Nina, *Novels, Readers, and Reviewers: Responses to Fiction in Antebellum America,* Ithaca, New York: Cornell University Press, 1984

Bell, Ian F.A., editor, *Henry James: Fiction as History,* London: Vision Press, and Totowa, New Jersey: Barnes and Noble, 1984

Brown, Gillian, *Domestic Individualism: Imagining Self in Nineteenth-Century America,* Berkeley: University of California Press, 1990

Machor, James L., "Fiction and Informed Reading in Early Nineteenth-Century America," *Nineteenth-Century Fiction* 47 (1992)

Machor, James L., editor, *Readers in History: Nineteenth-Century American Literature and the Contexts of Response,* Baltimore: Johns Hopkins University Press, 1993

Reynolds, David S., *Walt Whitman's America: A Cultural Biography,* New York: Knopf, 1995

Scanlan, Margaret, "Terrorism and the Realistic Novel: Henry

James and *The Princess Casamassima*," *Texas Studies in Literature and Language* 34 (1992)

Seltzer, Mark, *Henry James and the Art of Power*, Ithaca, New York: Cornell University Press, 1984

Smith, Henry Nash, *Democracy and the Novel: Popular*

Resistance to Classic American Writers, New York: Oxford University Press, 1978

Williams, Susan S., "'Promoting an Extensive Sale': The Production and Reception of *The Lamplighter*," *New England Quarterly* 69 (1996)

United States Novel

1900–1945

In the first part of the 20th century, the American novel became the popularly preferred literary genre. At the same time, it diversified to keep pace with an increasingly rapid process of cultural and economic change. The modern novel was called upon to give voice to issues of nationalism, expatriation, and immigration; the rise of science and technology; the decline of religion and increasing influence of psychology and psychoanalysis; the emphatic shift to urban lifestyles; racial and class conflict; polarized political views of the Left and Right; increasingly acute perceptions of social violence; women's issues; the foregrounding of commercial and business interests in everyday life; such literary movements as modernism and naturalism; literary renaissances in Harlem and in the South; socialism and communism; the increasing popularity of formula fictions like the romance, the crime novel, and the Western; and events like World War I, Prohibition, the Jazz Age, the Great Depression, the New Deal, and World War II. It is not surprising that this was a period of great novelistic diversification and innovation.

However, at the beginning of the century, the novel continued in the styles established by 19th-century masters. The late works of Henry James, for example, look back to the psychological and spiritual concerns of Nathaniel Hawthorne, Herman Melville, and the great European novelists of the Victorian period, but novels like *The Wings of the Dove* (1902), *The Ambassadors* (1903), and *The Golden Bowl* (1904) also anticipate the modern interest in the complexities of individual psychology and, after the impact of Freud was felt in the United States, the power of the unconscious mind. In the novels that crown his artistic achievement, James immerses the reader in the minutiae of his characters' thoughts, perceptions, and judgments. External realities become elaborate metaphors expressing the inner consciousness of the characters, who are placed in immensely complex moral situations. In *The Golden Bowl,* for example, Maggie Verver discovers that her husband and her father's wife are lovers. In *The Wings of the Dove,* Milly Theale is courted by a suitor who already has a lover and wants only Milly's fortune, although he is unable to accept it when it is given to him. In *The Ambassadors,* Lambert Strether is sent to Paris to save a young American from a designing European woman but finds that the young man is improved by his European experience. In these novels, the "international theme" of James' earlier work is given an intensely emblematic rendering, where all details of setting, manners, and social environment serve to dramatize the internal lives that are the subject of the fiction.

An abiding theme in James' fiction is the clashing of cultures. Edith Wharton's novels of the early part of the century share this concern, although Wharton wrote less from an international perspective than from the point of view of class and gender differences. Wharton was a bitter critic of Gilded Age America, where women were ornaments for rich men and the only alternative to its corrupt consumerism was abject poverty. In her first major novel, *The House of Mirth* (1905), Wharton creates the tragic heroine Lily Bart who can discover no alternative to marrying into the privileged classes. She despises them for their moral and spiritual superficiality, but Lily herself is like a hothouse orchid—bred for no other purpose than to please and unable, ultimately, to break free from the value system of her class. Wharton uses narrative images and motifs not so much to dramatize the characters' consciousness as to place them in a claustrophobic social framework. The realistic texture of the narrative reveals the imprisonment of the characters in roles defined by their class and gender. The complexity of moral judgment and the subtleties of individual psychology, as well as the portrayal of the constricting nature of society also characterize Wharton's subsequent novels. These also combine psychological and moral inquiry with the form of the novel of manners: *Ethan Frome* (1911), *The Custom of the Country* (1913), *Summer* (1917), and *The Age of Innocence* (1920).

In the main, Wharton's characters occupy a privileged place within the moneyed classes, who move in a world distanced from the ugly realities of urban life. The city slum was home to many of the immigrants arriving at this time, bringing about widespread and profound demographic change. Overcrowding, poverty, poor working conditions, crime, violence, racial conflict—these became the subjects of literary naturalism, which, from its origin in 19th-century fiction, was most commonly chosen as the novelistic style best suited for the representation of the ugly circumstances of urban slum-dwelling. Theodore Dreiser's achievement in *Sister Carrie* (1900), *Jennie Gerhardt* (1911), and *An American Tragedy* (1925) was to turn his early experience as a newspaperman to the precise rendering of narrative detail in order to support the critical images of American society he constructs. Dreiser's work was controversial when first published. The manner in which his impoverished characters rise, or seek to rise, in society was found scandalous by early reviewers, who were also shocked by Dreiser's frank recognition of female sexuality. The situation was perhaps exacerbated by Dreiser's sympathy for poor immigrant and other proletarian characters.

In his trilogy of Cowperwood novels, *The Financier* (1912), *The Titan* (1914), and *The Stoic* (1947), Dreiser came closest to the style of the Muckrakers—journalists who exposed the dark underside of American wealth and privilege. The rise to prominence of a powerful individual offered a narrative structure around which to organize an indictment of corruption and immorality at the highest levels of corporate culture. Muckraking fiction was inspired by a strong reformist motive. An allied development was the emergence of the immigrant or slum novel, notably Henry Roth's *Call It Sleep* (1934), Abraham Cahan's *The Rise of David Levinsky* (1917), and Anzia Yezierska's *Bread Givers* (1925). The most sensational of the muckraking novels was Upton Sinclair's *The Jungle* (1906), the story of the declining fortunes of a poor immigrant meatpacker who loses all he has. The novel calls for sweeping socialist reforms. Frank Norris in *The Octopus* (1901) and *The Pit* (1903) and Jack London in *People of the Abyss* (1903), *The Iron Heel* (1908), and *Burning Daylight* (1910) expose the true nature of working conditions in different industries to argue the socialist cause.

Jack London is best remembered for his semi-autobiographical adventure novels. *The Call of the Wild* (1902) and *White Fang* (1906) are based upon his experiences as a prospector in the Klondike. *The Sea-Wolf* (1904) focuses on his time as a sailor aboard a sealer, while his development as a writer forms the subject of *Martin Eden* (1909). The increasingly urban nature of modern American life gave rise to a nostalgia for the American wilderness, seen in the popularity of London's famous dog stories and the rise of the Western. Owen Wister, in *The Virginian: A Horseman of the Plains* (1902), created a novelistic genre that combined adventure with romance to celebrate the superiority of rough, uncultivated cowboys over the sophisticates of the East Coast. To press home this point, Wister chooses a tenderfoot as the narrator of the story of the unnamed Virginian, who defeats in a duel the forces of evil—represented by cattle rustlers—using his own natural instinct for justice rather than book learning. These motifs were developed by writers like Zane Grey in *Riders of the Purple Sage* (1912) and other Western writers who collectively created an enduring genre of popular fiction. Not only Westerns, but also the work of regionalists, like Willa Cather's Nebraska novels *O Pioneers!* (1913) and *My Ántonia* (1918), Marjorie Kinnan Rawlings' Florida writings, including *The Yearling* (1938), and Carl Carmer's *Stars Fell on Alabama* (1934), met a yearning for an alternative to the brash city life of 20th-century America.

The influx of blacks seeking to escape the Jim Crow laws and the renewed activities of the Ku Klux Klan in the post-Reconstruction South altered the racial constitution of American cities. In the cities of the North, African Americans formed literary and cultural societies as well as such institutions for reform as the National Association for the Advancement of Colored People (NAACP). Among black literary expression at that time were Charles Chesnutt's novels *The House Behind the Cedars* (1900), *The Marrow of Tradition* (1901), and *The Colonel's Dream* (1905), which combine black culture and folklore with a sophisticated literary style. The Southern racial vision was expressed by writers like Thomas Dixon, Jr., whose novels *The Leopard's Spots* (1902), *The Clansman* (1905), and *The Traitor* (1907) achieved national prominence after the blockbuster film *The Birth of a Nation* (1914) dramatized Dixon's glorification of Klan activities.

World War I caused the first of a number of major upheavals that were to rock American literary culture in the first half of the century. The enormous suffering and devastation of the war, the meaninglessness of the destruction, the hypocrisy of the official rhetoric, and the disjunction between those fighting the war and those directing it led Henry James to describe the conflict as "the crash of civilization." Edith Wharton served in Paris as a relief worker and translated her experience to the novels *The Marne* (1918) and *A Son at the Front* (1923).

For a generation of younger writers, the war was a formative experience that functioned as the starting-point for their writing careers. John Dos Passos, who was a volunteer at Verdun and later served with the Red Cross in Italy, wrote *One Man's Initiation: 1917* (1920) and *Three Soldiers* (1921). His antiwar sentiment became a more general dissatisfaction with the promises held out by American society in the experimental novel *Manhattan Transfer* (1925). In this novel and later in his *U.S.A.* trilogy (*The 42nd Parallel*, 1930; *1919*, 1932; and *The Big Money*, 1936), Dos Passos dispenses with linear narrative in favor of a montage technique that uses fragments from newsreels, prose poems, impressionistic slices of life or journalistic reportage, and popular songs to break up and to refigure discontinuous story lines. (Dos Passos' experimentation with discontinuity in the narrative is akin to Thornton Wilder's modernistic *The Bridge of San Luis Rey* of 1927.) Because of its stylistic innovation and condemnation of commercial culture, *U.S.A.* has become a classic of American modernism.

Ernest Hemingway also began his novelistic career writing of his experiences as an ambulance driver on the Italian front in *A Farewell to Arms* (1929) and *The Sun Also Rises* (1926). In these novels, the need and ability to deal with death and other harrowing events transfigure the individual. It is the transformative power of the imagination that endows characters like Jake Barnes and the bullfighter Romero in *The Sun Also Rises* with the grace that distinguishes them from the rest of humanity. The random destructiveness and malignance of the war, symbolized by the bullfight, is projected onto life in general. This vision results in a perception of irremediable meaninglessness, which becomes the most salient characteristic of Hemingway's fictional "Lost Generation." The modernist quality of Hemingway's fiction lies in his emphasis on the ordering power of the imagination in a world devoid of order and reason. The sparse minimalist style Hemingway cultivated is itself emblematic of the artistic imagination's power to bring order into being.

F. Scott Fitzgerald became the modernist chronicler of the madness of the Jazz Age in the novels *This Side of Paradise* (1920), *The Beautiful and Damned* (1922), *The Great Gatsby* (1925), and *Tender Is the Night* (1934). *The Great Gatsby*, generally considered his finest achievement, is a narrative of great economy and symbolic richness that charts the rise of a man who invents himself, in the tradition of the American Dream, in order to win the love of Daisy Buchanan. He is destroyed when he comes up against the closing ranks of inherited power and privilege and is forced to confront his own hollowness. The posthumous fragment *The Last Tycoon* (1941) uses Fitzgerald's experience as a Hollywood scriptwriter to explore the decadence of modern life.

A different approach to modernist experimentation is taken by Nathaneal West who, like Fitzgerald, was a writer in Hollywood before his early death and shared Fitzgerald's acute perception of the emptiness and decay at the heart of the American Dream. West excels at using imagery and symbolism to depict the frustration and rage of those who are disappointed in their ambitions in novels like *Miss Lonelyhearts* (1933) and *The Day of the Locust* (1939), the latter of which culminates in a surrealistic portrayal of a riot at a movie premier. The vulgarity of American life in the 1920s preoccupied Sinclair Lewis. In *Main Street* (1920) he satirized the provincialism and dullness of small-town America. The eponymous hero of his next novel, *Babbitt* (1922), became a byword for small-town attitudes and mediocrity. Lewis refused the Pulitzer Prize for *Arrowsmith* (1925), which he felt was being rewarded for wholesomeness rather than literary merit, and returned to the satirical style of his earlier novels in *Dodsworth* (1929) and especially *Elmer Gantry* (1927).

The 1920s were also the decade of the Harlem Renaissance, an outpouring of black creativity that coincided with a popular interest in black folklore and the exotic. However, the Harlem Renaissance was compromised as an authentic expression of African-American cultural identity by the issues of white patronage and the accommodation of black subject matter to a white audience. These issues were intensified by the popularity of *Nigger Heaven* (1926) by Carl Van Vechten, the principal white spokesman for the artists of the Harlem Renaissance. Among the novels praised for authenticity were Wallace Thurman's *Infants of the Spring* (1932) and Arna Bontemps' *Black Thunder* (1936). Zora Neale Hurston was criticized, most powerfully by Richard Wright, for her representation of a self-sufficient black community without reference to racial conflict in her novel *Their Eyes Were Watching God* (1937). Hurston used her training as an anthropologist to recreate the verbal nuances of black English as the basis for a portrait of Eatonville, Florida, as a community rooted in its own history and traditions, although deeply affected by white culture and racist ideology.

The Great Depression of the 1930s put an end to the white patronage that had supported the Harlem Renaissance. The bleak economic outlook turned many away from social realism toward the escapism of historical romances. Hervey Allen's *Anthony Adverse* (1933) was a best-seller, as were Kenneth Roberts' *Northwest Passage* (1937) and Margaret Mitchell's *Gone with the Wind* (1936). Other popular formula genres included the adventure novel and the science-fiction novel. Edgar Rice Burroughs, one of the most successful popular novelists, produced both these genres in series, starting with *Tarzan of the Apes* (1914) and *A Princess of Mars* (1917). But the Depression also saw the rise of proletarian novels, such as Giacomo Patri's *White Collar* (1940), Tom Kromer's *Waiting for Nothing* (1935), Jack Conroy's *The Disinherited* (1933) and *A World to Win* (1935), Edward Dahlberg's *Bottom Dogs* (1929) and *From Flushing to Calvary* (1932), Albert Halper's *Union Square* (1933), Robert Cantwell's *Land of Plenty* (1934), and Richard Wright's *Native Son* (1940). The condemnation of American capitalism, a common motif in modernism, social realism, and naturalism, now intensified into a call for sweeping political change. The style of these novels, however, was for the most part conventional, adhering to novelistic realism and narrative continuity.

Less radical novels of social protest include James T. Farrell's *Studs Lonigan* trilogy (1932–35), Erskine Caldwell's *Tobacco Road* (1932) and *God's Little Acre* (1933), and the work of John Steinbeck. In *Tortilla Flat* (1935), *In Dubious Battle* (1936), *Of*

Mice and Men (1937), and *The Grapes of Wrath* (1939), which was awarded the Pulitzer Prize, Steinbeck expresses a sympathy with simple folk who are uncorrupted by materialism and are close to an unspoiled nature. The conditions under which these people live and labor, particularly in the fruit industry of California, obscure the fundamental solidity of humanity and the sanctity of all life, motivating Steinbeck's call for reform. Steinbeck's masterpiece, *The Grapes of Wrath* tells the story of the Joad family's migration to California from the Oklahoma Dust Bowl. The narrative relies on a conventional realism interspersed with lyrical passages of narrative commentary. Steinbeck's commentary and the symbolic motifs that represent the Joads' kinship with nature elevate their plight and lend the story a universal significance.

The regional interest of Steinbeck's fiction, most of which is set in Monterey County, California, is shared by Willa Cather's Nebraska novels. However, the most popular regional fiction in the early 20th century emerged from the South, which experienced a veritable literary renaissance. Ellen Glasgow's early work includes a series of novels, among them *The Deliverance* (1904), *Virginia* (1913), and *Life and Gabriella* (1916), that represent a social history of Virginia from the antebellum period to World War I and chart the passing of power from the planter aristocracy to the new bourgeoisie. In the novels that followed, including *Barren Ground* (1925) and the Queenborough trilogy (*The Romantic Comedians*, 1926; *They Stooped to Folly*, 1929; *The Sheltered Life*, 1932), Glasgow continued to use the form of the novel of manners to depict the particular historical and social conditions of her region.

The Yoknapatawpha novels of William Faulkner combine an intense regional interest with wide-ranging novelistic innovation. In particular, Faulkner takes the stream-of-consciousness style, characteristic of much modernist fiction, to new heights. In *The Sound and the Fury* (1929), the voices of the three Compson brothers (Quentin, Jason, and the "idiot" Benji), interspersed with the authorial reporting of the black servant Dilsey's story, combine in a structure of recollected memory to represent the decline of a once-great planter family. The story of *As I Lay Dying* (1930) is told in 59 short interior monologues shared among 15 narrators, excluding an authorial point of view but including the dead woman Addie Bundren, whose body the family is transporting to Jefferson, Mississippi, for burial. In *Light in August* (1932), Faulkner employs a modified multiple-narrative style, and in *Absalom, Absalom!* (1936) he uses three narrative voices but no reliable narrative point of view, leaving the reader to piece together the complications of the story from the available subjective versions.

The novelistic achievement of Thomas Wolfe is compromised by the interventions of his editor, Maxwell Perkins. Wolfe broke with Perkins in 1937 but died suddenly the following year; his later work was published posthumously. Wolfe aimed for stylistic innovation in his novelistic saga of the Southern Gant family, *Look Homeward, Angel* (1929) and *Of Time and the River* (1935). Condemned by contemporary critics for formlessness, Wolfe used a modernist-inspired style to explore a range of discourses, from the documentary to the rhapsodic, within a symbolic or mythopoeic narrative structure. The sociological and psychological observation of Wolfe's writing is framed by the influence of the grotesque in Carson McCullers' novels of the 1940s, including *The Heart Is a Lonely Hunter* (1940), *Reflec-*

tions in a Golden Eye (1941), and *The Member of the Wedding* (1946).

World War II interrupted these continuities, preparing the ground for an equally tumultuous second half of the century.

DEBORAH L. MADSEN

See also African-American Novel; American Western Novel; Call It Sleep; Willa Cather; Theodore Dreiser; William Faulkner; F. Scott Fitzgerald; Grapes of Wrath; Ernest Hemingway; Henry James; Jewish-American Novel; Modernism; Native Son; Naturalism; Proletarian Novel; Regional Novel; Gertrude Stein; Their Eyes Were Watching God; U.S.A. Trilogy; Nathaneal West; Edith Wharton

Further Reading

Aaron, Daniel, *Writers on the Left: Episodes in American Literary Communism,* New York: Harcourt, Brace and World, 1961

Cowley, Malcolm, *Exile's Return: A Literary Odyssey of the 1920s,* New York: Viking Press, 1951

Hoffman, Frederick J., *The Twenties: American Writing in the Postwar Decade,* New York: Viking Press, 1955; revised edition, New York: Collier Books, 1962

Huggins, Nathan, *Harlem Renaissance,* New York: Oxford University Press, 1971

King, Richard H., *A Southern Renaissance: The Cultural Awakening of American South, 1930–1955,* New York: Oxford University Press, 1980

Klein, Marcus, *Foreigners: The Making of American Literature, 1900–1940,* Chicago: University of Chicago Press, 1981

Lewis, David L., *When Harlem Was in Vogue,* New York: Knopf, 1981

Massa, Ann, *American Literature in Context: 1900–1930,* London and New York: Methuen, 1982

Millgate, Michael, *American Social Fiction: James to Cozzens,* New York: Barnes and Noble, and Edinburgh: Oliver and Boyd, 1964

O'Brien, Michael, *The Idea of the American South, 1920–1941,* Baltimore: Johns Hopkins University Press, 1979

Rideout, Walter B., *The Radical Novel in the United States, 1900–1954: Some Interrelations of Literature and Society,* Cambridge, Massachusetts: Harvard University Press, 1956

Wilson, Edmund, *The American Earthquake: A Documentary of the Twenties and Thirties,* Garden City, New York: Doubleday, and London: W.H. Allen, 1958

United States Novel

1945–

The half century following World War II is notable in American history for both its scope and rate of change. Transformations of everything from the conception of space and time to the values and standards of culture were experienced with an intensity that threatened to destabilize the country itself. At the same time, the American novel was undergoing massive changes, many of them driven by these new conditions. Critics noted the same sense of instability, to the extent that some proclaimed "the death of the novel," given traditional fiction's apparent unsuitability for dealing with such a disrupted state of reality. Yet by the century's last years, the United States was stronger than ever, having weathered domestic turmoil and international transition to find itself the world's last genuine superpower. And the novel, instead of dying, incorporated aesthetic versions of these same challenges in order to address a broader array of concerns.

The massive war effort had done much to change the social reality of American lives. To increase production, women had entered the workforce in numbers never before imagined; and although such industrial conditions of employment did not survive into peacetime, a precedent had been set. African Americans, long subject to segregation in the South and to more subtle discrimination elsewhere in the country, returned from proud service in the military to demand equal respect at home. Even the so-called average man had his status changed, thanks to new possibilities of college education opened up by benefits of the G.I. Bill, a piece of legislation that altered American universities as well, making them much more democratic institutions. Apart from these new advantages, a new concern cast a shadow over the lives of all Americans: that of living under the threat of nuclear annihilation, as the massive destructive power that won the war for the United States now posed a constant threat to life on earth. For all the new things people were able to do, they also had to contemplate a possibility of apocalypse never reckoned with before.

It is no accident, then, that postwar novels are very ambitious. The war made Norman Mailer, for instance, believe that the great American novel of his generation would have to encompass and elucidate that conflict. In *The Naked and the Dead* (1948), he reasons the war as a contest of personal wills. Without such will, individuals are powerless before the larger forces that shape existence, the novel suggests. But this very ferocity of intent can itself be destructive, and that gives Mailer the scope to tell a much larger story within his focus on a single military unit. For Mailer's visceral focus, there is an intellectual equivalent, the equally combative moral drama of the philosophical and metaphysical rivalries that form the core of Saul Bellow's fiction. Early efforts such as *Dangling Man* (1944) and *The Victim* (1947) are relatively trim mental exercises compared to the massive impact of *The Adventures of Augie March* (1953), *Herzog* (1964), and *Humboldt's Gift* (1975), novels that analyze man's fate with the breadth and intensity otherwise characteristic of 19th-century Russian fiction. Only in postwar America could such a style of novel writing be both immensely popular and sufficiently valued to merit the Nobel prize for literature (1976), in spite of the fact that the country's lofty position is interrogated at every turn by Bellow's challenges to traditional order.

Great physical scope and metaphysical range characterize another important postwar novel, *Invisible Man* (1952) by Ralph Ellison. In this book, African-American fiction takes on new dimensions, moving beyond the socially pertinent depiction of ghetto life (typified by Richard Wright's work of 1940, *Native Son*) in order to treat the psychological and spiritual aspects of oppression. Beginning with the narrator's childhood in the American South, episodes from life in that region are recounted in a manner that emphasizes the ridiculous, often surreal nature of bigotry. When the action moves north, conditions are even more bizarre, forcing the narrator to live an underground life that gives the novel its title. Many mainstream critics, most prominently the socially committed Irving Howe, attacked Ellison for isolationism, for abandoning his own people. Yet Ellison's independence empowered a generation of minority writers to adopt an entirely new style of writing. In the years following Ellison's success, novelist James Baldwin was able to address the previously taboo topic of homosexuality, for instance, while authors such as William Demby and William Melvin Kelley were encouraged to write lyrically experimental novels in the tradition of James Joyce and other great literary artificers rather than in the confining mode of naturalism. In African-American writing, this development came to full fruition with the novels of Ishmael Reed, particularly *Mumbo-Jumbo* (1972) and *The Last Days of Louisiana Red* (1974), with their rich mix of Haitian voodoo and American popular culture. This same valuation of a culture's imaginative properties, instead of just its social and political impact, enabled Native American novelists such as N. Scott Momaday and Leslie Marmon Silko to transcend purely anthropological dictates and also helped Maxine Hong Kingston work free of mainstream cultural expectations that Chinese-American writers were only of interest for their colorful autobiographies. Her novel *Tripmaster Monkey* (1989) has much ethnic color, but, more importantly, its protagonist stands firmly within the larger tradition of American questers and literary experimenters.

Literary naturalism being eclipsed by these self-consciously artistic commitments, the more conservative mode of mannered realism also underwent change after the war. The fiction of John O'Hara had at first set the standard. By the 1960s, his role had been taken over by two other writers who came to prominence through *The New Yorker* magazine, John Cheever and John Updike. Their short stories and novels coincide with O'Hara's interest in the manners and morals of city dwellers and suburbanites in the thickly settled, culturally rich American Northeast. Yet, for each of these new writers fresh interests were evident, interests that reflected the deeper appreciation of larger issues. For Cheever, these changes involved replacing psychological concerns with suggestions of fabulation and even magic. Beneath the surface of the upper-middle-class Westchester County lives that Cheever depicts run strangely dark currents that ultimately shift the limits of conventional space and time. His most representative short story, "The Swimmer," takes a novel idea—that of a protagonist leaving a friend's pool party to swim his way home across the county, from one pool to another—and

uses its apparently clear-cut narrative to disrupt material standards and the order of the seasons. His novels *The Wapshot Chronicle* (1957) and *The Wapshot Scandal* (1964) set the social stage for the more disruptive *Bullet Park* (1969), a work in which wealth and envy generate their own malevolent potency for decay. John Updike's fiction adds to the world of social manners a mythic subtext (as in *The Centaur*, 1963) and an elegantly crafted, almost self-indulgent, style that the author deploys for musings both sexual (*Couples*, 1968) and theological (*A Month of Sundays*, 1975). Together, Cheever and Updike take the novel of manners into a world that might otherwise seem unsuitable for the narrative nuances of a Henry James or Edith Wharton, two American pioneers of the form.

By the 1960s, more than one novelist had complained that social reality was outpacing fiction's ability to depict it. Philip Roth's *Goodbye, Columbus* (1959), through its focus on suburban materialism and the sexual freedom allowed by easy and effective contraception, had anticipated the new tenor of life. However, Roth found the coming decade's disruptions impossible to contain within the quiet mannerism of his earlier work. Thus, in *The Breast* (1972) and *The Great American Novel* (1973), he turned to outrageous parody before finding a new subject in the probing self-examinations of the Zuckerman trilogy, *The Ghost Writer* (1979), *Zuckerman Unbound* (1981), and *The Anatomy Lesson* (1983).

Roth acknowledged the philosophical and aesthetic developments of the age in his 1987 novel, *The Counterlife*, in which rival versions of a narrative compete for the reader's credence. This turn is part of the cultural reorientation known as postmodernism. Its nature is part and parcel of the transformative conditions so evident during the 1960s and afterward. Its principal critical device, deconstruction, is one of radical interrogation, questioning the previously accepted standards that underlie value judgments and attitudes. Major reorientations in American life had begun with the redistributions of power mandated by the civil-rights movement and the beginnings of concern for women's rights and feminism. During the 1960s, what had begun as limited assistance from US military advisers grew into a full-fledged war in Vietnam, a war that aroused popular dissent even as its nature confounded previous paradigms of both politics and armed conflict. A sexual revolution was underway as well, criticized by some for its permissiveness and praised by others for its new honesty and frankness. Public life was traumatically disrupted by the assassination of President John F. Kennedy late in 1963, a disruption compounded by the 1968 killings of presidential candidate Robert Kennedy and civil-rights leader Dr. Martin Luther King. African-American neighborhoods burned; college campuses seethed with protest, protest that, on occasion, became violent and destructive. With so many traditions overturned and common practices abandoned, larger concepts such as postmodernism and deconstruction fitted in with the times and were embraced by the new generation of critics and intellectuals.

These concepts were not limited to ethereal realms of thought and disputation. Instead, the shift from modernism to postmodernism was a bottom-up, essentially democratic, affair. The novel has long been considered the most popular of the literary arts, and it was the first to show evidence of the postmodern transformation, most obviously in the US via the popularity of three key authors. Ken Kesey, Joseph Heller, and Kurt Vonnegut began as underground favorites, reaching a young and disaffected audience through paperback publication, but having to wait years for a best-seller and even longer for academic study. Although all three novelists overturn formal conventions, it was for their thematic challenges that they were first celebrated. Kesey's *One Flew Over the Cuckoo's Nest* (1962) is set in a madhouse, but its action soon reveals that the larger society is insane, particularly in its practice of institutional confinement. Heller's indictment in *Catch-22* (1961) is even more severe, complaining that resisting death (in warfare) is considered insane even as corporate business policies turn logic inside-out in waging global conflict. Most popular with the same group of readers was Kurt Vonnegut, whose *Cat's Cradle* (1963) deconstructed modernist notions of everything from science and religion to geopolitics and personal morals. Of the three, Vonnegut showed the most development throughout the period; the 1969 success of his *Slaughterhouse-Five* with much broader segments of the reading public signaled a new and widespread receptiveness for both postmodern ideas and reinventive literary practices; in subsequent decades Vonnegut was to expand his influence by becoming a major public spokesperson on the same issues that dominate his fiction.

During the 1960s, the novel underwent changes as massive as any in its long history. The most obvious challenge to tradition was the one mounted by authors no longer satisfied with suspending disbelief in the service of realism. By calling new attention to fiction's conditions and practices, writers who came to prominence in the 1960s and 1970s such as John Barth, William H. Gass, Raymond Federman, and Ronald Sukenick were able to parallel the achievements of an earlier generation of Abstract Expressionist painters (among them Jackson Pollock, Willem de Kooning, and Hans Hofmann) who saw the canvas not as a surface upon which to represent but rather an arena within which to act. This appreciation for the workings of words themselves, rather than for what they signify, is central to postmodernism. For three decades novelists of this persuasion dominated critical debate. Some of these writers were lyrical fabulators (John Barth, John Hawkes), others were flamboyant comedians (Robert Coover, Donald Barthelme), and still others were purveyors of such massive narrative overkill that their works are often referred to as meganovels or novels of excess (Thomas Pynchon, William Gaddis).

Although realistic fiction continued to be written during the 1980s and 1990s, in few cases was it done in ignorance of the great technical and theoretical advances made by the innovative writers of the two previous decades. Instead, there was a new awareness of textuality and the storymaking power of history, both of which inform the new narratives of African-American women, particularly Alice Walker's *The Color Purple* (1982) and Toni Morrison's *Beloved* (1987). Writers who wished to make sense of the Vietnam War and who were frustrated by the now-inappropriate conventions of traditional fiction found that metafictive devices do a much better job of expressing their relationship to the war. One of the best, Michael Herr's *Dispatches* (1977), takes advantage of the techniques of "new journalism," which applies fictional practices to reporting. Even traditional reporting became less influenced by the conventional novel than by metafiction itself, as in the self-focused excesses of Hunter S. Thompson's *Fear and Loathing in Las Vegas* (1971).

By the end of the 1990s, no assumptions about novel writing or the subjects of novels goes unquestioned. The most realistic appearing stories (by Raymond Carver) and novels (by Ann Beattie) are not realistic at all, but instead practice a rigorous "minimalism" that limits itself to a strictly phenomenological surface. The effect is much like that of photorealism in art, whereby such anti-hierarchical commitment to an even surface yields a painting that, instead of being conventionally realistic, shares every principle of abstract expressionism. Wide-ranging novels by a younger group, among them William T. Vollmann, Chris Mazza, and David Foster Wallace, challenge the suspension of disbelief by their exhaustive investigations of global topics.

The five-and-a-half decades following World War II wrought immense change. African Americans have held mayoral offices in major cities, including cities in the South. Women are presidents of some of the largest corporations. The country lost the first war in its history, yet two decades later was ranked as the last surviving superpower on earth, its one-time rival, the Soviet Union, no longer existing as a single state. As for lifestyles and personal values, the transformation has been as radical as anything in the country's history. In similar manner, the novel changed too; Norman Mailer's goal of totalizing an experience as vast as World War II would now seem preposterous, and Mailer himself has retreated to quasi-journalistic fiction in which his own limitations of view are considered advantages.

Following Kesey, Heller, and Vonnegut, not to mention Barthelme and Coover and the more radical innovators, a novel typical of the end of the century might well have been unreadable in 1945. With the millennial change looming ahead, the most common assumption seems to be nevertheless that, in terms of a novelist's ability to respond to major transformation, the biggest adjustments had already been made.

JEROME KLINKOWITZ

See also African-American Novel; James Baldwin; Saul Bellow; Catch-22; Catcher in the Rye; Invisible Man; Jewish-American Novel; Latino-American Novel; Norman Mailer; Bernard Malamud; Metafiction; Toni Morrison; Vladimir Nabokov; Naked Lunch; New Journalism; On the Road; Portnoy's Complaint; Postmodernism; Thomas Pynchon; Isaac Bashevis Singer

Further Reading

Bradbury, Malcolm, *The Modern American Novel*, Oxford and New York: Oxford University Press, 1983; new edition, 1993

Chénetier, Marc, *Beyond Suspicion: New American Fiction Since 1960*, Philadelphia: University of Pennsylvania Press, and Liverpool: Liverpool University Press, 1996

Friedman, Melvin J., and Ben Siegel, editors, *Traditions, Voices, and Dreams: The American Novel Since the 1960s,* Newark: University of Delaware Press, and London: Associated University Presses, 1995

Gordon, Avery, and Christopher Newfield, editors, *Mapping Multiculturalism,* Minneapolis: University of Minnesota Press, 1996

Hassan, Ihab, *Radical Innocence: The Contemporary American Novel*, Princeton, New Jersey: Princeton University Press, 1961

Karl, Frederick, *American Fictions, 1940–1980*, New York: Harper and Row, 1983

Klinkowitz, Jerome, *Literary Disruptions: The Making of a*

Post-Contemporary American Fiction, Urbana: University of Illinois Press, 1975; 2nd edition, 1980

LeClair, Tom, *The Novel of Excess,* Urbana: University of Illinois Press, 1989

Lupack, Barbara Tepa, *Insanity as Redemption in Contemporary American Fiction: Inmates Running the Asylum,* Gainesville, University Press of Florida, 1995

McCaffery, Larry, editor, *Some Other Frequency: Interviews with Innovative American Authors,* Philadelphia: University of Pennsylvania Press, 1996

Saltzman, Arthur M., *Designs of Darkness in Contemporary American Fiction,* Philadelphia: University of Pennsylvania Press, 1990

Saltzman, Arthur M., *The Novel in the Balance,* Columbia: University of South Carolina Press, 1993

Scholes, Robert, *Fabulation and Metafiction,* Urbana: University of Illinois Press, 1979

Siegle, Robert, *Suburban Ambush: Downtown Writing and the Fiction of Insurgency,* Baltimore: Johns Hopkins University Press, 1989

Tanner, Tony, *City of Words: American Fiction 1950–1970,* New York: Harper and Row, and London: Cape, 1971

Walker, Nancy A., *Feminist Alternatives: Irony and Fantasy in the Contemporary Novel by Women,* Jackson: University Press of Mississippi, 1990

Unnamable. *See* Molloy trilogy

Unreliable Narrator

Ever since Wayne C. Booth first proposed the unreliable narrator as a concept, it has been considered among the basic and indispensable categories of textual analysis. Hardly anyone to date has modified or challenged Booth's well-known formulation, which has become the canonized definition of the term: "I have called a narrator reliable when he speaks for or acts in accordance with the norms of the work (which is to say the implied author's norms), unreliable when he does not" (see Booth, 1961). According to Booth, the distinction between reliable and unreliable narrators is based on "the degree and kind of distance" that separates a given narrator from the implied author of a work.

A comparison of the definitions provided in standard narratological works, in scholarly articles, and in glossaries of literary terms shows that the great majority of narratologists have followed Booth, providing almost identical definitions of the unreliable narrator. The definition given by Gerald Prince in his *Dictionary of Narratology* is representative. An unreliable narrator is a "narrator whose norms and behavior are not in accordance with the implied author's norms; a narrator whose values (tastes, judgments, moral sense) diverge from those of the implied author's; a narrator the reliability of whose account is undermined by various features of that account" (see Prince, 1987). What most critics seem to have forgotten, however, is that Booth himself freely admitted that "[the terminology for] this kind of distance in narrators is almost hopelessly inadequate" (see Booth, 1961). There is indeed a peculiar discrepancy between the importance generally attributed to the question of

reliability in narrative and the unresolved issues surrounding the concept of the unreliable narrator (see Yacobi, 1981).

The narratological use of the term *unreliability* is not only vague but also fails to distinguish between moral and epistemological issues. Most definitions in the wake of Booth have emphasized that unreliability consists of a moral distance between the norms and values of the implied author and those articulated by the narrator. But other theorists have pointed out that what is at stake is not a question of moral norms but of the veracity of the account a narrator gives. It is also unclear whether unreliability is primarily a matter of misrepresenting the events or facts of the story or whether unreliability may result from the narrator's deficient understanding, dubious judgments, or flawed interpretations. The report a narrator gives of the events may be heavily flawed although the narrator himself may appear to be absolutely trustworthy (see Hof, 1984), while a "narrator may be quite trustworthy in reporting events but not competent in interpreting them" (see Lanser, 1981). One can, therefore, distinguish between an unreliable narrator—a narrator whose rendering of the story the reader has reasons to suspect—and an untrustworthy one, a narrator whose commentary does not accord with conventional notions of sound judgment. Moreover, there may be a number of different reasons for unreliability, including "the narrator's limited knowledge, his personal involvement, and his problematic value-scheme" (see Rimmon-Kenan, 1983). Depending on the reason for unreliability, one can distinguish different types of unreliable narrators such as the madman, the naive narrator, the hypocrite, the pervert, the morally debased narrator, the picaro, the liar, the trickster, or the clown (see Riggan, 1981).

One of the central problems in defining unreliable narration is the unresolved question of what standards allow the reader to recognize an unreliable narrator. Most theorists who have written on the unreliable narrator take the implied author for granted and consider it as the only standard according to which unreliability may be determined. The trouble with all of the definitions that are based on the implied author, however, is that they try to define unreliability by relating it to a concept that is itself vague and open to question. Critics who argue that a narrator's unreliability is to be gauged in comparison to the norms of the implied author simply shift the burden of determination onto a critical catch-all category that is itself notoriously ill-defined.

To explain what stands behind the impression that a narrator is of questionable reliability, it is not necessary to postulate an implied author. It is simply necessary to have recourse to the concept of structural or dramatic irony. With an unreliable narrator, dramatic irony results from the discrepancy between what a narrator actually tells the reader and the divergent state of affairs, or "true version," which the reader can grasp or infer. Unreliable narrators continually and unwittingly give the reader indirect information about their idiosyncratic state of mind, intentions, and value systems. The general effect of unreliable narration is the redirecting of the reader's attention from the level of the story to the speaker, to "the narrator's mental processes" (see Wall, 1994). In the case of unreliably narrated stories it is often difficult to determine whether what the narrator says provides facts about the fictional world or only clues to his or her distorted and evaluating consciousness.

Instead of postulating an essentialized and anthropomorphized entity designated "unreliable narrator," it may be more sensible to conceptualize the relevant phenomena in the context of semantics (see Amorós, 1991) or frame theory (see Nünning, 1998). Amorós and Nünning argue that unreliability is not so much a character trait of a narrator as it is an interpretive strategy of the reader, who tries to resolve textual inconsistencies and ambiguities by attributing them to the narrator's unreliability. In the context of frame theory, the reader's projection of unreliability may be understood as an interpretive strategy or a cognitive process of the sort that has come to be known as "naturalization" (see Fludernik, 1996). The reader accounts for whatever incongruity she may have detected as an instance of dramatic irony and by projecting an unreliable narrator as an integrative hermeneutic device.

To understand how unreliable narrators unwittingly reveal their own self-deceptions and delusions, one must explore the signals that allow the reader to apprehend narrational unreliability. The identification of an unreliable narrator does not depend solely on the reader's intuition or ability to "read between the lines," as some theorists suggest (see Chatman, 1978), but on a broad range of identifiable clues (see Wall, 1994; Nünning, 1997). It is possible to distinguish between textual signals and contextual clues to a narrator's unreliability. Textual indications of unreliability include such features as internal inconsistencies, conflicts between story and discourse, multiperspectival accounts of the same event, and verbal idiosyncrasies of the narrator.

Despite the importance of such textual clues, however, the question of whether a narrator is unreliable cannot be resolved on the basis of textual data alone. Readers also draw on extra-textual frames of reference in the attempt to gauge a narrator's unreliability. The identification of unreliable narrators depends, for instance, on the norms, cultural models, world knowledge, personality theory, and standards of normality that readers bring to the text. Narrators who violate agreed-upon moral and ethical norms or the standards that a given culture holds to be constitutive of normal psychological behavior are generally taken to be unreliable. The narrators in Ambrose Bierce's macabre tall tales, the child molester Humbert Humbert in Vladimir Nabokov's *Lolita* (1955), or the mad monologuists of Ian McEwan's and Patrick McGrath's neo-Gothic novels are cases in point.

In both critical practice and in theoretical work on unreliable narration, however, these different sets of norms are usually not explicitly set out but merely introduced in passing, and they seldom if ever receive any theoretical examination. In the only book-length study of the unreliable first-person narrator, William Riggan, for instance, suggests that the narrator's unreliability may be revealed by the "unacceptability of his [moral] philosophy in terms of normal moral standards or of basic common sense and human decency" (see Riggan, 1981). The trouble with seemingly self-explanatory yardsticks like "normal moral standards" and "basic common sense," however, is that no generally accepted standard of normality exists that could serve as the basis for impartial judgments. In a pluralist and multiculturalist age it has become more difficult than ever to determine what may count as "normal" moral or psychological standards. A narrator may be perfectly reliable, for instance, when compared to one person's notions of moral normality but quite unreliable by the standards of other people. In the end, it is both textual data like the structure and norms established by the respective work itself and the reader's conceptual knowledge of the world, psychological disposition, and system of norms and values that form the ultimate basis for deciding whether a narrator is reliable or not.

Although the history of the development of the narrative technique known as unreliable narration has yet to be written, it is clear that the unreliable narrator is by no means an ahistorical phenomenon. Rather, like other narrative techniques, it must be seen in the context of broader cultural developments. The history of the unreliable narrator goes back to the end of the 18th century, although it is not the case that unreliable narration originates in the works of the major 18th-century novelists like Defoe, Richardson, and Fielding. One of the earliest instances in British fiction of a full-fledged unreliable narrator is to be found in Maria Edgeworth's *Castle Rackrent* (1800). In the 19th-century British novel, unreliable narration is still very much the exception. The realist novel added little to the technique known as unreliable narration except for works cast in the comic variety of the fictional autobiography (see Riggan, 1981). There are, however, some noteworthy examples of unreliable narration in Victorian fiction, the most notorious of which is Emily Brontë's *Wuthering Heights* (1847), which features two unreliable narrators, Mr. Lockwood and Nelly Dean.

The unreliable narrator finally comes into his—or rather its—own in the period of transition from late Victorian to modern fiction. In the late 19th- and early 20th-century novel, one finds a broad range of individualized first-person narrators whose reliability the reader has reasons to suspect. The key author in this context is Henry James. Neither the equally deceiving and self-deceived narrator-scholar in *The Aspern Papers* (1888) nor the impressionable governess in *The Turn of the Screw* (1898) are reliable reporters of events. Other notable novels featuring unreliable narrators are Charlotte Perkins Gilman's *The Yellow Wallpaper* (1892), Joseph Conrad's *Lord Jim* (1900) and *Under Western Eyes* (1911), and Ford Madox Ford's *The Good Soldier* (1915).

Since the end of World War II, the unreliable narrator has enjoyed unprecedented popularity in the novel. Many contemporary authors no longer portray accepted norms of social relationships and human behavior but rather focus on various forms of deviance. On the basis of Kazuo Ishiguro's *The Remains of the Day* (1989), Kathleen Wall has demonstrated that contemporary fiction often even challenges conventional notions of unreliable narration because it "deconstructs the notion of truth, and consequently questions both 'reliable' and 'unreliable' narration and the distinctions we make between them" (see Wall, 1994). The same observation may be made with respect to many other postwar novels that employ first-person narrators, including William Golding's *Free Fall* (1959), Martin Amis' *Money* (1984), Julian Barnes' *Flaubert's Parrot* (1984), Nigel Williams' *Star Turn* (1985), William Boyd's *The New Confessions* (1987), and Jeanette Winterson's *Sexing the Cherry* (1989).

Although discussion of unreliable narration has focused almost exclusively on narrative fiction, it needs to be noted that its provenance and generic scope extend far beyond first-person narrators in novels or short stories. The dramatic monologues of 19th-century English literature, for instance, provide ample evidence of the use of unreliable narration in poetry. The same is true of the dramatic genre known as the "memory play," which typically features an unreliable first-person narrator, as Tom Stoppard's *Travesties* (produced in 1974) and Peter Shaffer's *Amadeus* (produced in 1979) illustrate. But the study of such novelistic devices as unreliable narration, point of view, and focalization in poetry and drama has received very little attention to date. Still a very fertile area of investigation, the question of unreliable narration needs to be reviewed in the light of both the renewed controversy about the relationship between ethics and aesthetics and the current attempt to enrich literary criticism through new theoretical approaches including feminism, cognitive theory, and cultural studies.

ANSGAR NÜNNING

See also Framing and Embedding; Implied Author; Narratology; Narrator; Point of View

Further Reading

Amorós, José Antonio Alvarez, "Possible-World Semantics, Frame Text, Insert Text, and Unreliable Narration: The Case of *The Turn of The Screw*," *Style* 25 (1991)

Booth, Wayne, *The Rhetoric of Fiction*, Chicago: University of Chicago Press, 1961; 2nd edition, Chicago: University of Chicago Press, and London: Penguin, 1983

Chatman, Seymour, *Story and Discourse: Narrative Structure in Fiction and Film*, Ithaca, New York: Cornell University Press, 1978

De Reuck, J., "Stereoscopic Perspectives: Transmission and Reception in Unreliable Homodiegetic Narration," *Journal of the Australasian Universities Language and Literature Association* 74 (1990)

Fludernik, Monika, *Towards a "Natural" Narratology*, London and New York: Routledge, 1996

Hof, Renate, *Das Spiel des "unreliable narrator": Aspekte unglaubwürdigen Erzählens im Werk von Vladimir Nabokov*, Munich: Fink, 1984

Lanser, Susan Sniader, *The Narrative Act: Point of View in Prose Fiction*, Princeton, New Jersey: Princeton University Press, 1981

Nünning, Ansgar, "'But why will you say that I am mad?' On the Theory, History, and Signals of Unreliable Narration in British Fiction," *Arbeiten aus Anglistik und Amerikanistik* 22 (1997)

Nünning, Ansgar, "Unreliable, Compared to What? Towards a Cognitive Theory of Unreliable Narration: Prolegomena and Hypotheses," in *Narratologie, Rhetorik, Textlinguistik: Ein Integrationsversuch*, edited by Walter Grünzweig and Andreas Solbach, Tübingen: Narr Verlag, 1998

Prince, Gerald, *A Dictionary of Narratology*, Lincoln: University of Nebraska Press, 1987; Aldershot: Scolar, 1988

Richardson, Brian, "Point of View in Drama: Diegetic Monologue, Unreliable Narrators, and the Author's Voice on Stage," *Comparative Drama* 22:3 (1988)

Riggan, William, *Picaros, Madmen, Naifs, and Clowns: The Unreliable First-Person Narrator*, Norman: University of Oklahoma Press, 1981

Rimmon-Kenan, Shlomith, *Narrative Fiction: Contemporary Poetics*, London and New York: Methuen, 1983

Wall, Kathleen, "*The Remains of the Day* and Its Challenges to Theories of Unreliable Narration," *Journal of Narrative Technique* 24 (1994)

Yacobi, Tamar, "Fictional Reliability as a Communicative Problem," *Poetics Today* 2 (1981)

Untouchable by Mulk Raj Anand

1935

Unlike Indian poets writing in English in the late 19th century, early practitioners of the English-language novel in India did not so obviously set out to mimic the form and style of their English counterparts. Instead, Indian English novelists, while clearly appropriating the form of the European novel and being influenced thematically and structurally by some of the great European practitioners of the genre, soon began to adapt it to suit their own literary and political purposes. From the late 19th century and through the early decades of the 20th, Indian novelists began to develop their own forms of the novel, drawing on Sanskrit and Persian narrative forms and on India's oral narrative traditions as well as on European literary examples.

If the ground had been prepared in the 50 or so years following the publication of Bankim Chandra Chaterjee's *Rajmohan's Wife* (1864), the foundations of the modern Indian novel were laid in the 1930s with the work of Mulk Raj Anand, Raja Rao, and R.K. Narayan, who are frequently referred to as the "founding fathers" of the Indian English novel. The impact of these three writers has been phenomenal, and it would be fair to say that it was their work that first prompted critics to take the Indian English novel seriously. While predominantly realist in form, the novels of Anand, Rao, and Narayan nevertheless provide the literary antecedents of the magic realist and other experimental innovations seen half a century later in the works of writers like Salman Rushdie.

Mulk Raj Anand's early fiction, which marks a shift from the Scott-like romance of *Rajmohan's Wife* to an almost Dickensian realism, is overtly political in both a nationalist and social sense. In his first three novels, *Untouchable* (1935), *Coolie* (1936), and *Two Leaves and a Bud* (1937), Anand sets out to reveal social injustices based on the caste system, child labor, and the exploitation of tea plantation workers, respectively. In these and in later works he successfully adapts both the English language and the form of the novel to articulate Indian life from an Indian perspective.

Untouchable is certainly Anand's best known and probably his best work, as well as his most controversial. It is a short, compassionate, unsentimental, and meticulously crafted study of a single day in the life of Bakha, an Untouchable, a sweeper and cleaner of latrines. But as E.M. Forster recognized in his preface, the reverberations of Anand's novel extend well beyond the circle of Bakha's life: "His Indian day is over and the next day will be like it, but on the surface of the earth if not in the depths of the sky, a change is at hand." In this sense, there is a distinct difference between Forster's own novel of colonial India, *A Passage to India,* published 11 years earlier in 1924, and Anand's novel. Whereas Forster's novel ends on a pessimistic note and offers little hope of meaningful interaction between the races, or even of independence for India in the near future, Anand's novel closes with at least the possibility of future reform and progress toward freedom for both Bakha and India.

The controlling design behind *Untouchable* is Anand's attack on colonial power structures based on the opposition between the colonizer and the colonized. If this serves a clear political agenda that aligns him with the nationalist movement of the

1930s, the other point of the novel's two-pronged attack reveals Anand's social agenda. In *Untouchable*, he suggests that colonial power structures are reproduced in Indian society in the binary opposition that exists between caste Hindus and Untouchables. His critique of this second opposition anticipates recent fiction such as Mahasweta Devi's "Doulati the Bountiful," which maps the relationship between the urban Indian elite and the tribals for whom independence remains a dream.

Untouchable is a novel without a story in the conventional sense. Rather it is made up of a series of incidents that occur during the course of Bakha's day. Two of the most important incidents, which serve to highlight the opposition between caste Hindus and Untouchables, are the humiliating touching scenes involving first Bakha, and then his sister, Sohini. In the first, Bakha accidentally touches a caste Hindu after having forgotten to call out the obligatory "*posh, posh, sweeper coming*" to warn of his presence. As a result he is abused by the crowd and slapped by the touched Lalla. Later, in a parallel incident, a priest molests Sohini and then, when she screams, he accuses her of polluting him. And although from this point on Anand adopts the structural pattern of alternating pleasant and unpleasant incidents as Bakha's day continues, these two humiliating incidents cast a shadow over every other incident in the novel and deny Bakha any true joy later in the hockey match he plays or the wedding he witnesses. Significantly, the reader's response to the opposition between colonizer and colonized is tempered by these incidents.

Mulk Raj Anand's *Untouchable* occupies an enormously important position in the tradition of the novel. Behind it lies the influence of the European novel, and in particular writers such as Lev Tolstoi and Charles Dickens, Maksim Gor'kii and James Joyce. Ahead of it stretches the whole tradition of the modern Indian English novel.

RALPH J. CRANE

See also Mulk Raj Anand

Further Reading

Cowasjee, Saros, *So Many Freedoms: A Study of the Major Fiction of Mulk Raj Anand,* New Delhi: Oxford University Press, 1977; Oxford: Oxford University, 1978

Dhawan, R.K., editor, *The Novels of Mulk Raj Anand,* New Delhi: Prestige, 1992

Mukherjee, Arun P., "The Exclusion of Postcolonial Theory and Mulk Raj Anand's *Untouchable*: A Case Study," *Ariel: A Review of International English Literature* 22:3 (July 1991)

Niven, Alastair, *The Yoke of Pity: A Study of the Fictional Writings of Mulk Raj Anand,* New Delhi: Arnold-Heinemann, 1978

Sharma, K.K., editor, *Perspectives on Mulk Raj Anand,* Ghaziabad: Vimal, 1978; Atlantic Highlands, New Jersey: Humanities Press, 1982

Sinha, Krishna Nandan, *Mulk Raj Anand,* New York: Twayne, 1972

Urban Origins of the Novel. *See* City and the Novel

U.S.A. Trilogy by John Dos Passos

1930–36

Together, the volumes of the *U.S.A.* trilogy (including *The 42nd Parallel*, first published in 1930, *1919*, published in 1932, and *The Big Money*, in 1936) constitute one of the central works of modern American literature. The trilogy is remarkable for the encyclopedic scope of its panoramic historical narration of the dramatic changes taking place in American society during the first three decades of the 20th century. The characters come from virtually all walks of life, while the action ranges over most of the continental United States, as well as extending into Latin America and Europe. As such, the novel has been seen as an American national epic, even though it is highly sceptical in its treatment of the myth of America.

Dos Passos presents this encyclopedic matter via a range of innovative narrative techniques that make the *U.S.A.* trilogy one of the most important works of modernist fiction. Among other things, the trilogy stands as an effective rejoinder to the many critics who have argued that modernist texts tend to be disengaged from history and politics. *U.S.A.* is also one of the major works of modern leftist fiction, participating in the attempt to develop a genuinely proletarian novel that occupied many writers in the 1930s. Many of the book's most enthusiastic early supporters were leftist critics, such as V.F. Calverton, and the book became an important model for leftist writers worldwide.

Although lacking a well-defined theoretical foundation, the trilogy at least begins from a clearly leftist perspective. Its most prominent theme is the death of the American Dream beneath the onslaught of modern consumer capitalism, which leads the nation to disavow its original ideals in the interest of a ruthless and greedy quest for profit. At the same time, however, the trilogy is a critique of American leftist political movements for failing to oppose this process. Dos Passos himself seems to drift gradually to the right in the course of the trilogy, so that *The Big Money* is far more sceptical in its treatment of leftist politics than is *The 42nd Parallel*. This process continued as Dos Passos grew older. He eventually became a conservative Republican, thus in a sense enacting the very failure of leftist politics recounted in the trilogy.

The narrative of *U.S.A.* is presented through a series of relatively brief textual segments of four different types. The bulk of the text consists of fairly straightforward, almost naturalistic, narrative segments. Donald Pizer thus argues that *U.S.A.* (along with Steinbeck's *The Grapes of Wrath* [1939] and James T. Farrell's *Studs Lonigan* trilogy [1935]) is one of the most important works of modern American naturalist fiction (see Pizer, 1982). However, these narrative segments tend toward modernism in the complex way they interweave the points of view of a variety of different characters. The variation in point of view occurs in

style as well as content, as Dos Passos seeks to capture the speech rhythms of different social groups. As the narrator puts it in the brief introductory section to *The 42nd Parallel*, "mostly *U.S.A.* is the speech of the people."

U.S.A. is a complex multigeneric work that differs substantially from the usual conventions of naturalist fiction by supplementing these narrative segments with "Newsreel" segments, "Camera Eye" segments, and brief (generally ironic) biographies of important figures in American history. As such, the book illustrates Mikhail Bakhtin's argument (in *The Dialogic Imagination*, 1981) that the novel is a unique genre in part because of its ability to incorporate a variety of different generic forms, both literary and nonliterary, within a single text. The Newsreel segments supplement the narrative with bits and pieces of headlines and news stories derived largely from actual contemporaneous newspaper reports. They also suggest the complicity of the media in the phenomena they report. Commenting on the Newsreels, David Seed notes that they draw "attention to the ways in which the media bombard the consumer with more information than he can digest" (see Seed, 1984). In addition, Seed observes that there is a "constant but unobtrusive emphasis" on the media throughout the trilogy, expanding beyond print to include radio, film, and advertising. Seed's view is typical of most critics, who generally read *U.S.A.* as a powerful critique of American media culture. However, Thomas Strychacz has argued that Dos Passos' own writing strategies often resemble the advertising practices that he seems to be criticizing and suggests the possibility that, especially in the Newsreels, "Dos Passos is setting out to identify the richness and potential complexity not just of the popular mind but of the newspaper idiom" (see Strychacz, 1993). In any case, the Newsreels, together with the biographies, serve to connect the various strands of the fictional narration with contemporary history. The biographies are largely critiques of "great men" in American history and include scathing indictments of figures such as Minor C. Keith, Andrew Carnegie, Woodrow Wilson, J.P. Morgan, Henry Ford, and William Randolph Hearst. Some figures, however, are presented in a positive light, including Eugene V. Debs, Big Bill Haywood, and (especially) Thorstein Veblen, whose biography, as Barbara Foley argues, "sets the tone for this critique of bourgeois ideology with his searing indictment of American capitalism. . . . Veblen provides the most explicit moral and political touchstone to Dos Passos' own grim assessment of the U.S.A. of this era" (see Foley, 1980). The highly impressionistic Camera Eye segments (the most modernist segments of the book) are a series of extremely subjective reactions to various private experiences, largely Dos Passos' own. Noting the autobiographical nature of the Camera

Eye segments, Westerhoven concludes that they gain "credibility as the impression not of an invented persona, but of the author himself" (see Westerhoven, 1976).

The title of *The 42nd Parallel* refers to the powerful jet stream winds that sweep across the American continent at that parallel. It suggests the anticipation of great change that was in the air in 1900 at the book's opening. This anticipation has much to do with the hope of political and social transformation under the pressure of socialism, syndicalism, and other leftist political movements that were gaining strength at the time. For example, the first narrative protagonist introduced is Mac, a young man who becomes involved with the IWW (Industrial Workers of the World), a radical labor union that was gaining significant strength at the beginning of the 20th century. But Mac's political commitment arises more from emotional reaction to injustice than from theoretical understanding. Anticipating the trajectory of the rest of the trilogy, Mac's personal problems surrounding his marriage interfere with his political activism, and he eventually moves to Mexico, where the revolution offers more opportunities for successful participation. In Mexico, however, Mac again becomes entangled in a sexual relationship, and his immersion in personal matters again limits his ability to contribute to the revolution. As Pizer points out, Mac's experiences are typical: "for the working-class radical, sex is a trap, since it can lead to the confinement of belief and action within the prison of middle-class marriage" (see Pizer, 1988).

The next narrative protagonist introduced in *The 42nd Parallel* is Janey Williams, a young woman from a lower-class background, who later becomes the private secretary of the advertising mogul J. Ward Moorehouse. Moorehouse himself (based loosely on Ivy Lee, one of the founders of the public-relations industry in America) is introduced next. Moorehouse rises from humble beginnings and early personal troubles to achieve great power and wealth as an advertising executive. Moorehouse, Pizer argues, is "the thematic center of *U.S.A.*," and his work in public relations and advertising "epitomizes the manipulation and corruption of language and therefore of belief in American life" (see Pizer, 1988). As Landsberg notes, "almost all of Dos Passos' fiction . . . is concerned with the role of deliberately manufactured opinion in America" (see Landsberg, 1972). *The 42nd Parallel* also introduces Eleanor Stoddard, an interior decorator and the would-be lover of Moorehouse. However, their relationship is stunted by their inability to establish a genuine emotional connection. The volume then ends with the introduction of Charley Anderson, a "composite tinkerer/inventor/entrepreneur American type" (see Pizer, 1988), who will become a major figure later in the trilogy.

As the first volume closes, Charley is talked into joining the ambulance corps and going to France shortly before the beginning of the official American involvement in World War I. That war is then the major event hovering over *1919*, which clearly presents the war as a capitalist plot to disrupt the rise of socialism. Moreover, American involvement in the war is depicted as a betrayal of the American people, especially given the fact that President Wilson, one of the major villains of the trilogy, had been elected on the promise to keep America out of the conflict. A major character in *1919* is Joe Williams, who appears marginally in *The 42nd Parallel* as the brother of Janey. Indeed, many of the events involving the Williams family in the earlier volume are retold in the second volume, but now from the point

of view of Joe. Joe eventually joins the navy, then deserts in Buenos Aires after a fight with a petty officer. His troubles continue from there. In the course of the book, he meets and marries the American woman Della (who turns out to be an ambitious gold-digger), then eventually breaks up with her because of her infidelity. After numerous other misadventures, including multiple arrests, bouts with gonorrhea, and sinkings of his ships by German mines and submarines, Joe is killed in a barfight on Armistice Night. His death makes him a striking symbol of lost promise and lost dreams. Also introduced in *1919* is Richard Ellsworth Savage, who, like Charley Anderson, goes to Europe to join the ambulance corps in the war. His Harvard education does little to prevent him from an eventual life of unscrupulous relations with women and dishonest dealings in business, especially while working for Moorehouse. His moral collapse eventually complete, we last see Savage being rolled by two black male prostitutes. The other major characters in *1919* include Eveline Hutchins, an attractive woman who spends her life seeking happiness in love affairs but who finds little but misery in the disappointment of her romantic expectations. Similar disappointments await Daughter Trent, an idealistic young woman whose love for Richard Savage is met with rejection once she becomes pregnant by him, making her a figure of the "victimization of the naive and openhearted by the more ruthless and circumspect" (see Pizer, 1988). Her death in a plane crash is one of the many disappointed lives that end suddenly in the trilogy. The socialist activist Ben Compton is the protagonist of only one narrative segment in *1919* but appears briefly in segments centering on Janey, Charley, Daughter, and Mary French. He is brutally beaten for his work in support of free speech and organized labor and often arrested, finally getting a 20-year sentence for speaking out against American involvement in World War I.

Charley Anderson reemerges as a major figure in *The Big Money*. A pilot and war hero, Charley returns to much acclaim but finds that his actual opportunities in the country he has fought to protect are rather limited. He eventually has some success as an engineering executive for an aeronautics firm in Detroit. He becomes vice president of the firm and marries a rich woman, but his adoption of a rich lifestyle leads to mounting debts. Both his marriage and his finances collapse. Meanwhile, he becomes involved in an affair with the actress Margo Dowling (herself a major character and an emblem of the role of American popular culture in the phenomena Dos Passos is describing) and dies after a car crash in Florida. The final major character in *The Big Money* is Mary French, an idealistic woman whose dedicated work in support of leftist causes leads to little but frustration and personal hardship. She has love affairs with Ben Compton and Don Stevens (another leftist activist), but both affairs end badly because the men put their political work ahead of private concerns. She also works actively in support of Sacco and Vanzetti, whose eventual executions function as a final image of the death of the American Dream and of the failure of leftist political activism in America. As Alfred Kazin puts it in *On Native Grounds* (1942), "out of the bitter realization that this society . . . could grind two poor Italian anarchists to death for their opinions, came the conception of the two nations, the two Americas, that is the scaffolding of *U.S.A.*"

At the end of the book, Mary is still determined to work for justice and is about to move to Pittsburgh to support a strike there. The last section, however, focuses on an allegorical figure called Vag (for vagrant) whose pursuit of the myth of success for all who seek it has resulted in nothing but poverty and misery. Indeed, the contrast between this ragged figure and the promises of the American Dream is perhaps the central message of the entire trilogy. As Foley notes, this final segment and the biographies of Hearst and Samuel Insull that come shortly before it "signal the decadence and inhumanity of capitalist economy in its decline" (see Foley, 1980). In particular, these segments together "focus our attention upon the causes and effects of the crisis in the capitalist system." That the trilogy ends on such a somber and pessimistic note is perhaps inevitable given the real course of modern American history and the seeming inability of Dos Passos to envision any human action that might have made it otherwise. As Foley points out, Dos Passos is "a progressive locked into a bourgeois system of thought," and he seems unable to "reconcile his commitment to personal action with his conviction that such action is rendered useless by the inexorable grinding of the machine of history." Dos Passos' limitations also extend to the treatment of issues surrounding race and gender, and his depictions of women and people of color often descend into stereotype. Nevertheless, the trilogy remains one of the most striking literary documents we have of the dramatic changes that swept across America in the first decades of this century. It is also an important document in the development of the modern novel and in the troubled history of the American left.

M. KEITH BOOKER

Further Reading
Foley, Barbara, "From *U.S.A.* to *Ragtime*: Notes on the Forms of Historical Consciousness in Modern Fiction," *American Literature* 50:1 (1978)
Foley, Barbara, "The Treatment of Time in *The Big Money*: An Examination of Ideology and Literary Form," *Modern Fiction Studies* 26:3 (1980)
Landsberg, Melvin, *Dos Passos' Path to "U.S.A.": A Political Biography, 1912–1936*, Boulder, Colorado: Associated University Press, 1972
Luddington, Townsend, *John Dos Passos: A Twentieth Century Odyssey*, New York: Dutton, 1980
Pizer, Donald, *Twentieth-Century American Literary Naturalism: An Interpretation*, Carbondale: Southern Illinois University Press, 1982
Pizer, Donald, *Dos Passos' "U.S.A.": A Critical Study*, Charlottesville and London: University Press of Virginia, 1988
Seed, David, "Media and Newsreels in Dos Passos' *U.S.A.*," *Journal of Narrative Technique* 14 (Fall 1984)
Strychacz, Thomas, *Modernism, Mass Culture, and Professionalism*, Cambridge and New York: Cambridge University Press, 1993
Weeks, Robert P., "The Novel as Poem: Whitman's Legacy to Dos Passos," *Modern Fiction Studies* 26:3 (1980)
Westerhoven, James N., "Autobiographical Elements in the Camera Eye," *American Literature* 48:3 (1976)

Utopian and Dystopian Novel

Utopian fiction takes its name from the book *Utopia* (1516) by Sir Thomas More. The title of More's work is derived from two Greek words, *outopia* (no place) and *eutopia* (good place). It describes the imaginary voyage of Raphael Hythlodaeus to a distant island in the newly discovered Americas. More ingeniously mixes fantasy and fact and has kept readers guessing what his motives were in writing the book. Some claim that there are enough signs in the work to indicate that More intended his audience to take Utopian society seriously as a superior vision of how Western society should be organized. The most famous critic to argue this case is the Austrian Marxist Karl Kautsky in *Thomas More and His Utopia* (1888). Some have alleged that More is tempting his audience with a vision of a false, rational society that has to be rejected because the pagan Utopians lack the true knowledge brought by Christian revelation. Others have read *Utopia* as a test that requires the reader to decide exactly when the Utopians should be admired and when they should be condemned. Related to this debate is the question of whether the text is meant to be taken seriously at all, or whether it is a humorous game inspired by the works of More's favorite writer, Lucian (c. A.D. 115–200).

More divides his work into two books. The first is a dialogue in which the traveler, Raphael, is introduced to a learned company, among whom is a fictionalized version of More himself. The participants discuss the merits of a society that has managed to dispense with property. In the second book, which has had a far greater impact on subsequent writing, Raphael describes what he saw during his time with the Utopians. The Utopians live an ascetic life that allows little time for frivolity: they all wear the same clothes, change houses every 10 years, study edifying literature in their hours of leisure, and are never idle. They laugh at European greed and are bemused at the value placed upon gold. In philosophy, they are Epicurians, believing that life should be based upon the rational pursuit of pleasure, as defined by the state. When they learn of Christianity, many are converted, as they are convinced of its superiority to their own beliefs. Their punishments for wrongdoing, especially sexual, are harsh, but so pleasant is Utopia deemed by those who have visited it that they invariably prefer a life of slavery there to freedom in their native lands. Despite Raphael's praise of Utopia and his plans to return, the book ends with the fictional More condemning the country as ridiculous because the communistic social system of the Utopians would undermine European greatness.

Utopia, an important work of humanist thought by a learned scholar with a sophisticated knowledge of Greek and Latin writings, is as much a work of political theory as it is fiction. More's text owes much to the discussion of the ideal commonwealth in Plato's *Republic* and of the lost continent of Atlantis in *Timaeus* and aligns itself with the philosophical tradition. Nevertheless, More's use of a fictional narrative has given impetus to an open-ended genre of writing that presents an alternative world to the reader and leaves open the question of its significance, political or otherwise. Utopian fiction is usually assumed to present a world that is more or less good, even though it is by no means clear whether that is the case in *Utopia.* Its opposite, dystopian fiction, presents a dark vision of an evil world. Just as these two types of writing are not easy to separate, neither is utopian or dystopian fiction always easy to distinguish from other related genres, notably satirical representations of fictional lands (such as Jonathan Swift's *Gulliver's Travels* [1726], science fiction, or pastoral literature. One should also note the tradition of political thought enshrined in such popular literary visions as the land of Cockaigne, a recent form of which can be found in the song, "The Big Rock Candy Mountain." In the land of Cockaigne nobody is forced to labor and all food and drink is free, to the extent that roast pigs run around with carving knives in their sides demanding to be eaten (see Morton, 1952).

In general, utopian fiction and utopian thought perform three interrelated functions. Some works make political recommendations by constructing an ideal republic, usually without explaining how such a state actually developed. Tommaso Campanella's *La città del sole* (written in 1602; *The City of the Sun*) is an example. Others show what the consequences of implementing a political ideal would be, often with the purpose of exposing the ideology behind such an ideal as dangerous and harmful (as in Aldous Huxley's *Brave New World,* 1932). Finally, utopian works often use a supposedly ideal republic to reflect on existing forms of government, *Utopia* itself being an instance as well as most forms of feminist utopian fiction.

A significant response was made to More's *Utopia* by Sir Francis Bacon in *The New Atlantis* (1626). Bacon's text is much more scientific in focus, and the tour of the island granted the travelers by the mysterious Jew, Joabin, provides a vehicle for Bacon's own predictions of future inventions, illustrating the close connection between utopias and science fiction. Responding to the earlier work, Bacon proposes an interesting correction to the marriage practices described in *Utopia.* In that work, couples were permitted to see each other naked before they agreed to marry. Joabin reports that this practice is regarded as cruel and that rejections after such familiarity are highly embarrassing. Instead, the inhabitants of the New Atlantis have Adam and Eve's pools where friends of the man and woman can see the prospective spouses without clothes and report back on any defects.

Much early European utopian fiction is related to religion in a more direct way, many works being expressions of apocalyptic or millenarian hopes and visions. Johann Eberlin von Gunzburg wrote *Wolfaria* (1521) after he became a follower of Luther. The text consists of a series of laws and statutes introduced by an imaginary state that suffers from the same evils as Gunzburg's Germany, including the excessive power of monks and priests,

the impossibility of marriage for ministers of the Gospel, excessive rites and sacraments that obscure the message of the Gospels, and too many holidays. *Wolfaria* is a work of revolutionary zeal, but it also contains many sensible recommendations concerning the duties of the state toward its citizens with respect to education, health, and general welfare.

Ludovico Agonistini is usually credited as the writer of the first Counter-Reformation utopia. Sections from his dialogues, *L'infinito* (1585–90), are often collected as "Repubblica Immaginaria" by modern scholars. The ideal state that emerges from these writings represents a religious ideal based on an ascetic lifestyle. Between these two extreme is the state described in the anonymous *Histoire du grand et Admirable Royaume d'Antangil,* published in France in 1616. This work describes an imaginary voyage to the kingdom of Antangil supposedly near Java, where the traveler encounters a society based on a series of rigid hierarchies. Classes are separated rather than abolished, and the austerity of More's *Utopia* (which the author had read) has given way to splendor and theatrical display. Works by Francesco Patrizi da Cherso, Anton Francesco Doni, Gasparus Stibinus, and Johann Valentin Andreae, all roughly contemporary with Agonistini, illustrate the European scope of the genre, as well as the variety of its manifestations (see Eliav-Feldon, 1982).

Probably the most frequently reproduced early utopian work is Campanella's *City of the Sun,* cast in the form of a dialogue between a Genoese sea captain who has been to the remote city of the sun and a grand master of the Knights Hospitalers. Campanella was an Italian theologian and poet who spent much of his life in prison for heresy and for his attempts to overthrow Spanish rule in southern Italy and to set up a more equal society. *The City of the Sun* is based on the principle of love, which abolishes all traces of self-love. Everything comes to be shared equally, including all property and children. Campanella's visionary city has much in common with More's Utopian society, but is less ambiguously presented.

In direct contrast is the work of Joseph Hall, the satirist whose *Mundus Alter et Idem* (1605; *Another World and Yet the Same*) has been described as the first dystopian novel. It describes a voyage to the southern hemisphere aboard the ship *Fantasy.* Here we are introduced to Crapula, the land of inebriate excess, which has two provinces, Pamphagonia (omnivorous gluttony) and Yvronia (drunkenness). Their latitudes and longitudes correspond exactly to those of England and Germany. In the former country (capital, Marzipan), everyone has rotten teeth and halitosis, and citizenship can only be gained by those of spectacular girth. In the latter, every town has a special series of ropes that lead from the market square to each citizen's house, so that returning from parties is less difficult (mistakes still happen, however).

The large number of utopian fictions written during and after the English Civil War of the 1640s resemble those produced after the Reformation in their religious and social hopes and expectations. One of the most important is Samuel Gott's *Nova Solyma* (1648), which represents an ideal society created after the resettlement of the Jews in a future Jerusalem from which the Turks have been banished. The two protagonists, Politian and Eugenius, gentlemen from Cambridge, catalogue the society they have visited, paying particular attention to the religion observed by the Nova Solymans. Eventually, a commercial treaty is signed between England and Nova Solyma. Gott depicts the islanders' religion as the best to which humans could ever aspire. Although reason has its limits in unlocking the mysteries of God, true happiness and enlightenment will come to whoever renounces sensual pleasures and the lure of romantic love in favor of devotion to Christian principles. Also of significance is John Sadler's *Olbia: The New Island Lately Discovered* (1660), which is the dialogue of a hermit and a shipwrecked sailor on an isolated island and expounds various theories of numerology and other forms of mysticism at great length. James Harrington's *Oceana* (1656) is an important work of republican political theory, which argues that private property should be limited rather than abolished. By way of contrast, *New Atlantis, Begun by the Lord Verulam, Viscount St. Albans: and Continued by R.H. Esquire, Wherein is set forth a Platform of Monarchical Government* (1660), is a robust defense of monarchy and privilege.

These are followed by a spate of utopian novels in the 18th century that are far less optimistic. Joseph Hall's satire may have served as an example for the imaginary lands represented in Swift's *Gulliver's Travels*, Book III. The Academy of Lagado and its perverse scientific experiments may be an attack on the optimistic visions of inevitable scientific progress contained in Bacon's *New Atlantis*. The flying island of Laputa, which oppresses the impoverished island of Balnibari, is a clear satire of the English oppression of Ireland. This section of Swift's work may be read as dystopian fiction, as may the first voyage to Lilliput. Both are balanced against the more temperate vision of the second voyage to Brobdignag. Book IV, presenting the encounter between Gulliver and the Houyhnhnms and Yahoos, may be read as either utopian or dystopian, depending on one's interpretation of the ending. Have the Houyhnhnms established an ideal society, or is their faith in their own reason an arrogance that makes them even worse than the violent and fallible societies encountered in the course of Gulliver's earlier travels? In a sense, the question for the reader is the same as the one posed by *Utopia*, which is why *Gulliver's Travels* demands to be read within the utopian tradition of fiction.

Similar questions might be asked of Samuel Johnson's *The History of Rasselas, Prince of Abyssinia* (1759), which describes the restless wanderings of the young protagonist when he tires of his idyllic kingdom. Johnson's point would appear to be that there can be no earthly utopia, because man is far too restless ever to be satisfied even with happiness. "The Conclusion, in which nothing is concluded" forces the reader to relate the book to his or her life, a recurring motif of utopian fiction. In general, 18th-century utopian fiction tended to be highly satirical, another notable example being Bernard de Mandeville's *Fable of the Bees* (1714), which portrays the earth as a giant hive populated with self-interested bees who thrive on greed.

A further development in the history of utopian fiction came with the rise of socialism and communism in the 19th century. The new social beliefs were often implicitly or explicitly utopian, notably those of Robert Owen (1771–1858), Claude-Henri Saint-Simon (1760–1825), and François Fourier (1772–1837). The most celebrated socialist utopia is probably William Morris' *News from Nowhere* (1890). The author falls asleep in his Hammersmith house and dreams that he has woken up in a communist society in the 21st century. He discovers a nonindustrial rural society where handicrafts are valued and practiced by everyone. (Morris was a craftsman, and it has been rather cruelly remarked that the world imagined in *News from Nowhere* appears to have been designed by Morris himself.) There is no money, no central government (the Houses of Parliament have become a dung market), no legal structure, and a religion of humanity holds sway. Also important, and partly inspired by Morris, are H.G. Wells' *A Modern Utopia* (1905) and *The New Machiavelli* (1911). Wells' science-fiction novella *The Time Machine* (1895) describes the opposite case, exposing a false pastoral vision of human evolution gone terribly wrong. It depicts a future world that appears idyllic until it is discovered that the beautiful, but rather vacuous, Eloi are in fact at the mercy of the terrifying Morlocks, descendants of underground laborers. A similar theme is explored in E.M. Forster's long short story "The Machine Stops" (1908).

News from Nowhere is an attack on the increasing industrialization of Western society in the 19th century, as well as what the author views as repressive political developments. Many dystopian novels of the 20th century share Morris' concerns, most notably Aldous Huxley's *Brave New World* and George Orwell's *Nineteen Eighty-Four* (1949). The former novel is set in the year 632 After Ford (the 26th century—time is now dated after the first major producer of the motor car rather than a religious figure), in a world where everything is regulated by the state to the extent that humans are biologically engineered and kept happy and docile by the administration of psychedelic drugs. This dystopia is challenged by the Savage from the American Indian reservations who takes up the ideals of freedom and passion, debating these with the World Controller Mustapha Mond. The novel ends with the Savage's suicide. Orwell's novel is equally bleak; it represents a world where Britain has become a minor part of the superstate Oceania, ruled by a single party and perpetually at war with the other superstates Eurasia and Eastasia. Whereas in Huxley's novel the drug Soma is used to quell any individuality and rebellious spirit, in Orwell's obedience is achieved through the extensive use of propaganda, citizens being encouraged to love Big Brother, whose image is omnipresent. The novel tells the story of Winston Smith, a minor government official who dares to challenge the state by committing "thought-crimes" and daring to fall in love. Smith is eventually betrayed, broken by his experience in room 101 where he faces his ultimate horror (being eaten by rats), and learns to love Big Brother. Both Huxley and Orwell were influenced by *My* (written in 1920; *We*), by the Russian novelist Evgenii Zamiatin (1884–1937), a satire on a future totalitarian state.

Probably the most significant development in the history of utopian/dystopian fiction in recent years has been the rediscovery and revival of a tradition of feminist utopian writing. Works by pioneering feminist writers such as Katherine Philips (1632–64), Jane Barker (1652–c.1727), and Sarah Scott (1723–95) have received renewed attention. As *The Feminist Companion to Literature in English* (1990) comments, "Utopian fiction is imagined in the face of contemporary social realities: women's peculiar oppression thus became the backdrop for a distinctive series of female utopian visions." Important recent fiction has attempted to imagine a future feminist world. Marge Piercy's *Woman on the Edge of Time* (1976) tells the story of a Chicana woman imprisoned in a mental hospital who is transported to a future society attempting to abolish sexism, racism, and heterosexism. Ursula Le Guin's *The Dispossessed: An Ambiguous Utopia* (1974) portrays an anarchist moon colony. In a more dystopian vein is her *The New Atlantis* (1975), which represents a totalitarian United States of the future. Doris Lessing's experimental science-fiction novels *Canopus in Argus: Archives* (1979–83) and Margaret Atwood's *The Handmaid's Tale* (1985) are similarly dystopian.

ANDREW HADFIELD

See also Pastoralism in the Novel; Science-Fiction Novel

Further Reading

Albanese, Denise, "*The New Atlantis* and the Uses of Utopia," *Literary History* 57 (1990)

Chambers, R.W., *Thomas More*, London: Cape, and New York: Harcourt Brace, 1935

Davis, J.C., *Utopia and the Ideal Society: A Study of English Utopian Writing, 1516–1700*, Cambridge and New York: Cambridge University Press, 1981

Donawerth, Jane L., and Carol A. Kolmerten, editors, *Utopian and Science Fiction by Women: Worlds of Difference*, Liverpool: Liverpool University Press, and Syracuse, New York: Syracuse University Press, 1994

Eliav-Feldon, Miriam, *Realistic Utopias: The Ideal Imaginary Societies of the Renaissance, 1516–1630*, Oxford: Clarendon Press, and New York: Oxford University Press, 1982

Fox, Alistair, *Thomas More: History and Providence*, Oxford: Blackwell, 1982; New Haven, Connecticut: Yale University Press, 1983

Hertzler, Joyce Oramel, *The History of Utopian Thought*, New York: Macmillan, and London: Allen and Unwin, 1923

Knapp, Jeffrey, *An Empire Nowhere: England, America, and Literature from "Utopia" to "The Tempest,"* Berkeley: University of California Press, 1992

Kumar, Krishan, *Utopianism*, Milton Keynes: Open University Press, and Minneapolis: University of Minnesota Press, 1991

Levitas, Ruth, *The Concept of Utopia*, London: Philip Allan, and Syracuse, New York: Syracuse University Press, 1990

Logan, George M., *Meaning of More's "Utopia,"* Princeton, New Jersey: Princeton University Press, 1983

Manuel, Frank E., editor, *Utopias and Utopian Thought*, Boston: Houghton Mifflin, 1966; London: Souvenir Press, 1973

Mellor, Anne K., "On Feminist Utopias," *Feminist Studies* 9 (1982)

Morley, Henry, editor, *Ideal Commonwealths*, London: Routledge, and New York: Dutton, 1895

Morton, A.L., *The English Utopia*, London: Lawrence and Wishart, 1952

V

Vanity Fair by William Makepeace Thackeray

1848

Vanity Fair was Thackeray's second novel (although the first published). It was followed by several novels that were well received in their own time, but by large margins it stands out as the one work for which Thackeray is now chiefly remembered. At the time of writing *Vanity Fair,* Thackeray was a regular contributor to *Punch* and was well established as a journalist and sketch artist in the vein of humorous social satire. The first novel he wrote, *The Luck of Barry Lyndon* (1853), revealed a capacity for sustained satire of an unusually harsh, astringent character. In *Vanity Fair,* he constructs a complex, unified action that extends over a period of several years and involves dozens of characters in multiple settings. These standard features of the big Victorian novel continue to appear in such later works as *Pendennis* (1850), *The Newcomes* (1855), and *The Virginians* (1859), but never again did Thackeray achieve the classic symmetry and power of *Vanity Fair.*

The symmetry of *Vanity Fair* is of a peculiar kind. The central organizing principle of the novel is its tonal structure, which is unusually complex and equivocal. In contrast to both his neoclassical predecessors and many of his contemporaries, Thackeray does not aim at investing his story with a single, coherent set of values and beliefs. He does not seek to resolve his own internal emotional tensions or eliminate confusions and uncertainties of judgment. Instead, in *Vanity Fair* he suspends his tonal perspective between the poles of satiric contempt and sentimental indulgence. These polar elements are not, as in Fielding, segregated as discrete generic modules; nor are they merely set in tension with one another; rather, they interact perpetually in a fluid, dynamic way, constantly undercutting and problematizing—but never wholly canceling—one another.

More than in most novels, even most Victorian novels, the narrator of *Vanity Fair* is himself an active presence, more prominent as a personality than any of his characters. Thackeray follows Fielding in amplifying his narrative with overt essayistic commentary, but whereas Fielding kept his essays separate, as discrete chapters, Thackeray intermingles commentary and narrative in a casual and colloquial fashion, taking the events of the story as occasions for his meditative and rhetorical improvisations. One tradition of criticism, affiliated with a Jamesian creed of objectivist narrative, has disparaged this method as "intrusive." A more dis-

cerning criticism recognizes that in this novel, to an exceptional degree, the characters, story, and tonally charged commentary are integrated as part of a total artistic design.

The two main characters, Becky Sharp and Amelia Sedley, embody the tonal elements that constitute the polar aspects of Thackeray's own narrative persona. Rebecca is a brilliant and charming woman, but she is also a sociopathic adventurer, heartless and faithless. She instantly sees through the vanities and delusions of every character she meets and is thus able to manipulate most of them with virtuoso facility. She is a satirist by nature, and she frequently stands in for Thackeray, as an internal agent of the narrator's own perspective, doing the work for him of amused revelation and mocking contempt.

Amelia is a figure of pathos, weak, passive, and soft, but generating quietly a vast and continuous devotion. She is devoted first to her husband, George, and then after his death to her memory of him and to their son Georgy. She also cares dutifully and tenderly for her peevish and impoverished parents. She thus exemplifies the nucleus of domestic bonds that for Thackeray form the medium of sentiment. In contrast to traditional figures of sentiment—including her neoclassical namesake, Fielding's eponymous Amelia, and the sentimental figures in Thackeray's contemporary, Dickens—Thackeray's Amelia is a problematic character. She is foolishly obtuse about the moral quality of the people around her; she idealizes and falsifies the objects of her attachment; and she selfishly exploits the devotion of William Dobbin, who is much worthier, but less glamorous, than her dead husband. In its extravagance and self-indulgence, Amelia's pathos constantly verges on parodic excess. Her paroxysms of sentiment are grotesque, mawkish, and vaguely obscene. As a form of introverted and self-indulgent excess, Amelia's emotional life finds a ludicrous physical counterpart in the figure of her brother Jos, who is timid, vain, and corpulent.

In the tonally equivocal resolutions of the story, Becky functions as a satiric agent in both benevolent and comically sinister ways, but she establishes no norms as alternatives to those of domestic comedy. In her benevolent aspect, she intervenes in Amelia's love life, puncturing her delusions about her dead husband and thus facilitating Amelia's marriage to Dobbin. In her more sinister aspect, Becky takes possession of "our fat friend" Jos, absorbing his property, ushering him to his grave under shady circumstances, and collecting on his insurance. Although she has no respect for the moral or emotional substance of social relations, she remains in thrall to the game of social positioning, and she dedicates her remaining life to sustaining a false social persona. Domestic comedy is shorn of romance, and satire empties itself of value.

In his great, climactic speech renouncing his devotion to Amelia, Dobbin shifts the balance of power between them. He thus gains his heart's desire, but only after he has become disenchanted with it. Dobbin's disillusionment and Amelia's regret serve as the culminating instances in Thackeray's survey of vanities, and they motivate his final, definitive apostrophe to the world as a scene of delusions and frustrations. "Ah! *Vanitas Vanitatum!* Which of us is happy in this world? Which of us has his desire? Or, having it, is satisfied?" Although he is in some ways typically Victorian, Thackeray's world-weary disillusionment and his peculiar capacity for equivocally ironized and self-reflexive moral judgment seem distinctly modern. He is the first novelist to achieve this particular form of tonal sophistication, and there are no others until Conrad.

JOSEPH CARROLL

See also William Makepeace Thackeray

Further Reading

Cecil, David, *Early Victorian Novelists,* London: Constable, 1934; Indianapolis: Bobbs-Merrill, 1935; also published as *Victorian Novelists*

Ferris, Ina, *William Makepeace Thackeray,* Boston: Twayne, 1983

McMaster, Juliet, *Thackeray: The Major Novels,* Toronto: University of Toronto Press, and Manchester: Manchester University Press, 1971

Peters, Catherine, *Thackeray's Universe: Shifting Worlds of Imagination and Reality,* New York: Oxford University Press, and London: Faber, 1987

Phelan, James, "*Vanity Fair*: Listening as a Rhetorician—and a Feminist," in *Out of Bounds: Male Writers and Gender(ed) Criticism,* edited by Laura P. Claridge and Elizabeth Langland, Amherst: University of Massachussetts Press, 1990

Ray, Gordon Norton, *Thackeray: The Uses of Adversity,* New York: McGraw-Hill, and London: Oxford University Press, 1955

Ray, Gordon Norton, *Thackeray: The Age of Wisdom,* New York: McGraw-Hill, and London: Oxford University Press, 1958

Tillotson, Geoffrey, and Donald Hawes, editors, *Thackeray: The Critical Heritage,* London: Routledge, and New York: Barnes and Noble, 1968

Trollope, Anthony, *Thackeray,* London: Macmillan, and New York: Harper, 1879

Mario Vargas Llosa 1936–

Peruvian

Mario Vargas Llosa is one of the most significant writers in the Hispanic world, and his work has been translated into numerous languages. He is a playwright, essayist, journalist, and literary critic, but it is as a novelist that he has earned most international acclaim. Since 1963 he has written 12 novels and a novella, all of them set in his native Peru except for *La guerra del fin del mundo* (1981; *The War of the End of the World*). Although he has experimented with various novelistic modes (historical, political, detective, autobiographical, comic, anthropological), his overriding ambition has always been to write a "totalizing" novel, that is, to create a fictional reality that rivals the world in all its complex, multifaceted layers of existence (visible and invisible, objective and subjective, psychological and social, actual and imaginary, scientific and magical). While perhaps no one novel in particular achieves this goal, his novelistic oeuvre does succeed in portraying with rare skill, dramatic power, and narrative persuasion what Honoré de Balzac called the *comédie humaine* of existence.

On more than one occasion Vargas Llosa has been dubbed the "Peruvian Flaubert," and not without reason. As he makes clear in his study *La orgía perpetua: Flaubert y "Madame Bovary"*

(1975; *The Perpetual Orgy: Flaubert and "Madame Bovary"*), his formula for the novel is borrowed from the French master: sex, violence, rebellion, and vulgarity. Each of his novels, from his first, *La çiudad y los perros* (1963; *The Time of the Hero*), to his latest, *Los cuadernos de don Rigoberto* (1997; *The Notebooks of Don Rigoberto*), contains these ingredients in varying doses. *The Time of the Hero*, in which sex and rebellion predominate, offers a savage portrayal of the physical, sexual, moral, and mental degradation of adolescent cadets in a military academy in Lima. Vulgarity prevails in *La tía Julia y el escribidor* (1977; *Aunt Julia and the Scriptwriter*). In this work the novelist turns his own story into a soap opera, in which his father threatens to shoot him in the middle of the street "as if he were a rabid dog" should he dare to marry his Aunt Julia. Violence of the most virulent and gory kind is the hallmark of *Lituma en los Andes* (1993; *Death in the Andes*), in which the members of a primitive Amerindian cult, roving bands of brainwashed terrorists, and squads of brutal soldiers combine to turn the majestic Andean countryside into a sea of blood.

While Vargas Llosa's international reputation as a storyteller is undisputed, his contribution to the development of the novel form is not as widely appreciated. In fact, there is probably no living Hispanic writer who has exercised the role of "practicing critic," in T.S. Eliot's phrase, with as much distinction as Vargas Llosa. Since completing his doctoral dissertation, "García Márquez: Historia de un deicidio" (1971; García Márquez: History of a Deicide), he has gone on to compile an impressive record of articles, essays, and books of literary criticism on such major 19th- and 20th-century prose writers as Gustave Flaubert, Victor Hugo, Jean-Paul Sartre, Albert Camus, Jorge Luis Borges, Julio Cortázar, William Faulkner, Ernest Hemingway, and José María Arguedas, among many others. In addition, he has written important articles on Miguel de Cervantes and on the Catalan Joannot Martorell, author of the classic chivalric romance *Tirant lo Blanc* (1511), which Vargas Llosa hails as a precursor of the "totalizing novel." These critical writings not only offer provocative and illuminating criticism of some of the most important novelists of the Western canon but also help to shed significant light upon Vargas Llosa's own theory and practice as a novelist.

The fundamental concept of Vargas Llosa's theory is that of the daemon, a metaphor utilized originally by Johann Wolfgang von Goethe and developed subsequently by César Moro and Georges Bataille to describe the secret, predominantly unconscious obsessions that are transformed into a novelist's themes. Personal, cultural, or historical, the daemon ultimately gives shape and meaning to a novel. It is not normally chosen by the novelist. Rather it imposes itself upon him or her because of some deep, abiding fear, trauma, neurosis, or preoccupation. Thus, Hemingway's obsession with machismo becomes a major theme in his novels. With respect to Vargas Llosa himself, it is apparent that his fictional universe is dominated by one overwhelming daemon: the painful memory of his bitter relationship with his father, which he records with disarming candor in his memoirs, *El pez en el agua* (1993; *A Fish in the Water*). In this sense all his novels are symptomatic of what Freudians call "father fear." Every one of them records or reflects the almost primeval feud between a son and a father, in a real or figurative sense. On the one hand, the battle is waged at a private level, as in the case of Marito and his tyrannical father in *Aunt Julia and the Scriptwriter*. On the other hand, as in *La casa verde* (1966; *The Green House*), *Conversación en La Catedral* (1969; *Conversation in The Cathedral*), and *Historia de Mayta* (1984; *The Real Life of Alejandro Mayta*), this Oedipal confrontation has a political corollary in the conflict between an oppressive patriarchy (the oligarchy, the army, the church) and the dependent sectors of society (the Indians, the proletariat, the poor).

In real life Vargas Llosa has undergone a well-documented evolution from Marxist fellow-traveler in the 1960s to conservative candidate for the Peruvian presidency in 1990. As the millennium approaches, he is a high-profile proponent of a radical neoliberal revolution in Latin America. What is remarkable in this regard is that it is almost impossible to discern the privileging of a particular political point of view in any of his novels. This narrative neutrality is a salient feature of his novelistic theory, which holds that a novel should never preach or propound but only show or re-create a particular aspect of reality. A novel must never be utilized as a vehicle for political propaganda or moral expostulation, or it will run the risk of prostituting its artistic integrity. It is ultimately up to the reader to interpret the novel from whatever point of view she may consider most appropriate, be it political, social, psychological, or moral.

While Vargas Llosa argues that the choice of themes very often escapes the novelist's rational control, he argues that the contrary should occur with respect to a novel's language, style, and technique, which convince a reader that the fiction is true. The art of the novel hinges on the ability to overcome the reader's critical defenses so as to make him believe that it is possible "to turn a white whale into a demon." In his critical writings, Vargas Llosa has identified a series of "tricks" used by the best novelists, from Joannot Martorell to Flaubert, from Proust to Faulkner and García Márquez, to pass off fictional lies as truths. Among the most important tricks are "el dato escondido" (the omission or postponement of an important fact in the story); "los vasos comunicantes" (the surprising conjunction of two or more scenes or episodes); "la muda or salto cualitativo" (abrupt changes in point of view, narrative voice, or level of reality); and "las cajas chinas" (a story within a story). All these devices—with elaborate variations, as in *Conversation in The Cathedral,* where at one stage 18 conversations are recorded simultaneously—are employed by Vargas Llosa with almost mathematical precision in his novels. Indeed, from a formal perspective, there is probably no more self-conscious novelist in the world today. In a nutshell, it could be said that his is indeed the story of a literary theory put into practice.

ROY C. BOLAND

See also War of the End of the World

Biography

Born in Arequipa, Peru, 28 March 1936; parents separated, and so brought up by mother and maternal grandparents in Cochabamba, Bolivia, 1937–45, Piura, northern Peru, 1945–46, then in Lima. Educated in Bolivia to 1945; parents reconciled when he was about eight years old; attended Leoncio Prado Military Academy, Lima, 1950–52; Colegio Nacional San Miguel de Piura, 1952; studied literature and law at the University of San Marcos, 1955–57; University of Madrid, 1957–59, Ph.D., 1959. Held several part-time jobs while a student, including: journalist for *La Industria,* Piura, c. 1952; coeditor of the literary journals *Cuadernos de Conversación,* 1957, and *Literatura,* 1959; journalist for Radio Panamericana and *La Crónica,* both in Lima; moved to Paris in 1959 because he felt that in Peru he could not earn his living as a serious writer; precarious existence in Paris working as Spanish teacher, journalist for Agence-France-Presse, and broadcaster for Radio Télévision Française, early 1960s; visited Peru in 1964; member of the editorial board, *Casa de las Américas,* Havana, 1965; contributor to the magazine *Caretas,* Lima, 1966; moved to Barcelona, 1970; established permanent residence in Peru, 1975; Fredemo (Democratic Front) candidate in Peruvian presidential elections, 1990.

Novels by Vargas Llosa

La ciudad y los perros, 1963; as *The Time of the Hero,* translated by Lysander Kemp, 1966

La casa verde, 1966; as *The Green House,* translated by Gregory Rabassa, 1968

Los cachorros, 1967; as *The Cubs,* translated by Gregory Kolovakos and Ronald Christ, published in *The Cubs and Other Stories,* 1979

Conversación en La Catedral, 1969; as *Conversation in The
Cathedral,* translated by Gregory Rabassa, 1975
Pantaleón y las visitadoras, 1973; as *Captain Pantoja and the
Special Service,* translated by Gregory Kolovakos and Ronald
Christ, 1978
La tía Julia y el escribidor, 1977; as *Aunt Julia and the
Scriptwriter,* translated by Helen Lane, 1982
La guerra del fin del mundo, 1981; as *The War of the End of
the World,* translated by Helen Lane, 1984
Historia de Mayta, 1984; as *The Real Life of Alejandro Mayta,*
translated by Alfred MacAdam, 1986
¿Quién mató a Palomino Molero?, 1986; as *Who Killed
Palomino Molero?,* translated by Alfred MacAdam, 1987
El hablador, 1987; as *The Storyteller,* translated by Helen Lane,
1989
Elogio de la madrastra, 1988; as *In Praise of the Stepmother,*
translated by Helen Lane, 1990
Lituma en los Andes, 1993; as *Death in the Andes,* translated
by Edith Grossman, 1996
Los cuadernos de don Rigoberto, 1997; as *The Notebooks of
Don Rigoberto,* translated by Edith Grossman, 1998

Other Writings: plays, essays, journalism, memoirs, film scripts;
a selection of his essays and journalistic articles has been published in *Making Waves* (1996).

Further Reading

Boland, Roy C., *Mario Vargas Llosa: Oedipus and the "Papa"
State,* Madrid: Voz, 1988; 3rd edition, 1990
Boland, Roy C., editor, *Mario Vargas Llosa: From "Pantaleón y
las visitadoras" to "Elogio de la madrastra,"* Madrid:
Antípodas I, and Auckland: Department of Romance
Languages, University of Auckland, 1988
Boland, Roy C., editor, *Specular Narratives: Critical
Perspectives on Carlos Fuentes, Juan Goytisolo, and Mario
Vargas Llosa,* Madrid: Antípodas VIII/IX, 1997
Booker, M. Keith, *Vargas Llosa among the Postmodernists,*
Gainesville: University Press of Florida, 1994
Castro-Klaren, Sara, *Understanding Mario Vargas Llosa,*
Columbia: University of South Carolina Press, 1990
Enkvist, Inger, *On Translating Mario Vargas Llosa,* Madrid:
VOX/AHS, 1993
Gerdes, Dick, *Mario Vargas Llosa,* Boston: Twayne, 1985
Oviedo, José Miguel, *Mario Vargas Llosa,* Madrid: Taurus,
1981
Oviedo, José Miguel, *Mario Vargas Llosa: La invención de una
realidad,* Barcelona: Seix Barral, 1982
Williams, Raymond L., *Mario Vargas Llosa,* New York: Ungar,
1986

Giovanni Verga 1840–1922

Italian

Giovanni Verga is the principal representative of Italian *verismo,* which was influenced by French realism and naturalism.
There are no biographical treatments of any length of Giovanni
Verga in English, and there are fewer in Italian than one might
expect, given the position accorded him in this century as a
writer in some sense "produced" by the Risorgimento and the
subsequent political unification of Italy in 1861.

Verga's career is marked by a notable silence: from the age of
49—that is to say for the last 33 years of his life—he published
nothing new or of substance. But before 1889, he published 11
novels and 8 short-story collections. He was also the author of 7
plays adapted from the stories, the most successful being *Cavalleria rusticana,* the basis for Mascagni's perennially popular opera
of the same name. After two historical novels (one never published in full, the other published in four volumes at his father's
expense), Verga began by writing derivative romantic novels
about "the passions" and "society novels," to be distinguished
from the "novels of society" on which his reputation now rests.

The shift to the more substantial, later work took place in the
early 1870s with the story *Nedda,* subtitled "a Sicilian sketch," a
generic hybrid of sketch, essay, and short story, compounded with elements of the contemporary journalistic news item, that
Verga was to make his own. *Nedda* was followed by
"Fantasticheria" ("A Reverie") and "L'amante di Gramigna"
("Gramigna's Mistress"), both collected in *Vita dei campi* (*Caval-*

leria Rusticana and Other Tales of Sicilian Peasant Life) in 1880.
All three show the writer in search of his true subject matter,
form, method, and style. The opening of "Gramigna's Mistress"
stands as a manifesto of *verismo* and the cultivation of impersonality that shows Verga's admiration for Gustave Flaubert and
Émile Zola. Verga used "naturalism" and "realism" interchangeably, but he has come to be identified with *verismo* on the basis of
the strong nonfiction influence on his later novels.

In his mature realist fiction, set for the most part in Sicily—in
his native Catania and its surroundings, to be more precise—Verga dealt with the impact of modernity on Italian society. Verga's
verismo looks to history, to anthropology, and to the positivistic
sciences in general. The influence of journalism in Verga's handling of detail and perspective was considerable. Interestingly,
Verga never wrote as a professional journalist, and the journalistic influence came to him indirectly through the mid-19th-century
French realist writers. Their work reflects a society whose knowledge of itself is constituted to a significant degree by the *faits-
divers* (news items) that were the stock-in-trade of newspapers.

Verga's true originality lies in his use of free indirect discourse,
elaborated in his work with Sicilian settings after *Nedda* and often thought of by Italian critics as achieving a choral effect of a
collective voice, as well as an objective stance. What passes for
Verga's objectivity, however, is revealed on closer inspection as a
kind of roving, dispersed collective subjectivity, a decentered

point of view that does not admit of authorial judgment on characters, events, or conditions. As the opening of "Gramigna's Mistress" proclaims, the work of literature should seem to narrate itself, without the intrusive presence of an author.

Within his free indirect discourse, Verga's language bordered on the experimental. Writing about a specifically Sicilian reality—the concrete and economic experience of the rural proletariat of peasants and fishermen—Verga could have resorted to dialect, in conformity with the realist imperative. However, dialect would have limited his readership in the newly unified Italy. Verga's solution was to write in the national language, Tuscan, and to make it *imitate* dialect, giving an impression of unmediated "natural" speech. The result was an apparently nonliterary language rich in expressive possibilities, and its ungrammatical elements did not have the sole function of representing "real" speech but were the foundation of a poetic style.

Verga is best known for his incomplete novel cycle *I vinti* (The Vanquished/Defeated). It was to consist of five novels, each representing a different level of society and phase of development. Verga described it as "a sort of phantasmagoria of the struggle for existence, extending from the rag-picker to the cabinet minister and to the artist, taking all forms, from ambition to greed, and lending itself to a thousand representations of the great tragi-comedy of humanity." Only two volumes were completed: *I Malavoglia* (1881; *The House by the Medlar Tree*) and *Mastro Don Gesualdo* (1889; *Master Don Gesualdo*). The first deals with a family of poor Sicilian fisher-folk and their efforts to survive in the newly unified Italy. The second, set in Sicily around 1820, is the story of a town-based manual laborer compelled to attain not merely economic self-sufficiency but to amass capital and to rise to a higher level of society through marriage, only to lose his wealth to the class that had never truly accepted him. The projected cycle did not go beyond the initial chapters of *La Duchessa di Leyra* (The Duchess of Leyra) and the titles of the remaining two novels, *L'onorevole Scipioni* (Scipioni, MP) and *L'uomo di lusso* (The Man of Luxury).

In the immediate post-Unification years, ideas of progress and of the struggle for existence were part of the cultural climate. Modern capitalism was about to change the relation of the "humble folk" to the basic means of existence. While it is difficult to attribute a specific politics to Verga, his work exhibits the apolitical conservatism of a man who has internalized the social Darwinism of his day and sees the social world in terms of anthropology or "social biology." For his stoic pessimism, relieved only by pathos and an occasional leap to the sublime, Verga is often compared with his coeval Thomas Hardy, and with the great Italian romantic poet Giacomo Leopardi. He can be described as a "Risorgimental patriot," to the extent of being prepared to obfuscate matters of historical fact with important consequences for our understanding of the Risorgimento, as in the case of "Libertà," a technically brilliant story in *Novelle rusticane* (1882; *Little Novels of Sicily*) about the peasant revolt at Bronte, Sicily, in 1860.

Verga's work has undergone several revaluations since his death in 1922. When Cesare Pavese and other neo-realists in the immediate post–World War II years opted to write about regional reality rather than the national myths favored by the fascist culture, they adopted Verga's simulated dialect. In the 1964 preface to his own postwar neo-realist novella *Il sentiero dei nidi di ragno* (1947; *The Path to the Nest of Spiders*), Calvino saw Verga's *The House by the Medlar Tree* as a useful example for his

generation: "We had devised a line for ourselves, consisting of *I Malavoglia*, [Elio Vittorini's] *Conversazione in Sicilia*, [Pavese's] *Paesi tuoi*, as a point of departure."

SUZANNE KIERNAN

See also House by the Medlar Tree

Biography
Born 2 September 1840 in Catania, Sicily. Schooled at home, and privately, 1851–60; studied law at University of Catania, 1860–65. Lived in Florence, 1865–70, Milan, 1870–85, and later in Catania. Made a senator, 1920. Died 27 January 1922.

Selected Fiction by Verga
Nedda, 1874; translated as *Nedda*, 1888
Vita dei campi, 1880; as *Cavalleria Rusticana and Other Tales of Sicilian Peasant Life*, translated by A. Strettell, 1893; as *Under the Shadow of Etna*, translated by N.H. Dole, 1896; as *Cavalleria Rusticana and Other Stories*, translated by D.H. Lawrence, 1928
I vinti [The Vanquished/Defeated]
  I Malavoglia, 1881; as *The House by the Medlar Tree*, translated by M.A. Craig, 1890; also translated by Eric Mosbacher, 1950; Raymond Rosenthal, 1964; L. Landry, 1991
  Mastro Don Gesualdo, 1889; as *Master Don Gesualdo*, translated by M.A. Craig, 1893, and by Giovanni Cecchetti, 1979; as *Mastro-Don Gesualdo*, translated by D.H. Lawrence, 1923
Novelle rusticane, 1882; as *Little Novels of Sicily*, translated by D.H. Lawrence, 1925, reprinted as *Short Sicilian Novels*, 1984

Other Writings: stories, plays adapted from his fiction, and letters.

Further Reading
Alexander, Alfred, *Giovanni Verga: A Great Writer and His World*, London: Grant and Cutler, 1972
Bergin, Thomas Goddard, *Giovanni Verga*, New Haven, Connecticut: Yale University Press, 1931; reprinted, Westport, Connecticut: Greenwood Press, 1969
Borsellino, Nino, *Storia di Verga*, Bari: Laterza, 1982; 2nd edition, 1992
Cambon, G., "Verga's Mature Style," *Comparative Literature* 14:2 (1962)
Cecchetti, Giovanni, *Giovanni Verga*, Boston: Twayne, 1978
Hazantonis, E., "The Permutation of the Narrator in Verga's pre-Malavoglia Novels," *Italica* 61:2 (1984)
Hemmings, F.W.J., editor, *The Age of Realism*, Harmondsworth and Baltimore: Penguin, 1974
Pacifici, Sergio, editor, *From Verismo to Experimentalism: Essays on the Modern Italian Novel*, Bloomington: Indiana University Press, 1969
Patruno, Nicholas, *Language in Giovanni Verga's Early Novels*, Chapel Hill: University of North Carolina Press, 1977
Ragusa, Olga, *Verga's Milanese Tales*, New York: Vanni, 1964
Raya, Gino, *Vita di Giovanni Verga*, Rome: Herder, 1990
Woolf, D., *The Art of Verga: A Study in Objectivity*, Sydney: Sydney University Press, 1977

Verisimilitude. *See* Critics and Criticism; Genre Criticism; Historical Novel; Historical Writing and the Novel; Mimesis; Realism

---

Verse Narrative and the Novel

The relationship between fictional narrative in verse and prose is relatively simple in theory, but in practice it has been complex and varied. The narrative poem and the novel may share the same themes and the same formal elements, including narrative voice and method, plot, character, setting, description, incident, dialogue, use of allusion and quotation, and so on. Both the narrative poem and the novel may also use poetic elements conventionally associated with lyric (or non-narrative) poetry, such as self-reflexive language, verbal complexity, figurative richness, polysemic imagery, symbolism, allegory, and others. In theory, the irreducible difference between the narrative poem and the novel is that the former is written in verse and the latter in prose. Reducing this difference to its compositional minimum, in the printed narrative poem the writer chooses the line ending, whereas in the novel (historically located in print culture) the line ends by accident of page size or typesetting. In works that were originally composed orally, "verse" or a structured line is signaled by audible effects (such as rhyme, alliteration, assonance, or metrical pattern), whereas in prose these effects are absent or appear accidental. Such differences apparently give the narrative poet just one resource of form not also available to the prose artist, or novelist. In practice, however, various narrative poets and novelists have at different times over centuries availed themselves of all the elements available to the other, although the nature and direction of such common practices and interaction have varied according to cultural and literary time and place.

Historically and culturally, the narrative poem seems to have preceded the novel, as a form of extended (as distinct from brief) narrative, in all cultures. Very broadly, the history of relatively extended fictitious or semifictitious narrative seems to have been a millennia-long, complex shift from verse and oral culture to prose and writing culture. Especially in preliterate or nonliterate societies, oral narrative was often improvised in various kinds of verse as a structuring device that enabled the oral poet, or bard, to recompose for particular occasions and performances the familiar stories that embodied a particular culture's legends, myths, history, and beliefs. These oral narratives, of varying lengths, were sometimes linked or grouped into cycles or into considerably extended narratives, later named epics, especially when the advent of writing in a particular culture and language enabled these narratives to be recorded, as with the Greek poems known as the *Iliad* and the *Odyssey* attributed to the (probably mythical, or at best quasi-historical) poet Homer.

There were also oral verse narratives among European peoples outside the Roman Empire, and later displacing the empire, that embodied their values and beliefs and legendary or mythic forms of their historical experience. These narrative poems, largely about the heroic exploits of the dominant warrior class, were also sometimes blended together, as in the Germanic poem known as *Beowulf,* written down in a dialect of Anglo-Saxon used in post-Roman England. Similar narrative "poems" are still performed in parts of Central Asia. These verse narratives seem to have reflected at least the culture of the dominant warrior-class in such societies, if not the culture of the entire society, and in that sense to have been popular narratives. This kind of popularity differs, of course, from that of the novel in later, market-driven literary cultures. These kinds of verse narratives had an important relationship with drama in classical Greece, providing many plots for tragedies, for example, but they did not have a significant relationship with prose fiction narrative.

In the centralized imperial culture of the Romans, imitations of the Greek epics, as of most everything Greek, had high cultural prestige, useful to demarcate a cultural, social, and, hence, political elite, and they became part of imperial court culture, as with the "secondary" epic written by Virgil, the *Aeneid.* Thus, extended verse narrative, or the epic, moved from a common to an elite cultural property. The largely illiterate common people of the empire probably retained certain forms of oral narrative, in verse or prose, and there seems to have been an elite readership for prose fiction that resembles the modern novel in certain respects, such as the *Satyricon* of Petronius. In certain parts of the empire, such as the Greek-speaking eastern Mediterranean, what would now be called novellas or short romances, erotic in character, such as Longus' *Daphnis and Chloe* (late 2nd century A.D.), seem to have been popular with a middle-class and urban readership. Occasionally these stories were extended in length and imitated epic matter, as with Heliodorus' *An Ethiopian Story* (sometime between the 2nd and 4th century A.D.).

The relationship between verse and prose narrative developed steadily after the decline of the Roman Empire. The dispersal of centralized Roman imperial power in the western regions of what is now Europe by various Germanic and other tribes resulted in the rise of court administrations with local or wide geographical power and with increasing dependence on writing. In this culture, verse narratives that were ultimately derived from the oral narratives of the Germanic and other peoples were written down, recomposed, or purposely composed in writing for court societies and their culture. Such court societies could be regional or even "national," although the nation in the modern sense, which the novel helped facilitate, did not yet exist. Court societies could also be relatively local, however, as with the court that apparently commissioned the major 14th-century English narrative poem *Gawain and the Green Knight*. Such narratives, although derived from the oral narratives of various Germanic tribes invading and settling in the western Roman Empire, came to be known as romances, as they were composed, in most cases, in the romance languages derived from Latin, as distinct from the classical epics written in Latin and Greek. These romances seem to have been read very much as later cultures would read novels—as guides to values and conduct for their intended readers. Such romances consequently had considerable social and cultural influence: the Spanish soldiers who followed Hernan Cortes to overthrow the Aztec empire of Mexico in the early 16th century apparently thought of themselves as chivalric heroes of the kind found in the widely read romance *Amadis de Gaul*. To some extent the verse narratives also had a cross-cultural life, adapted and translated from one European language and culture to another, as with the many poems concerning the semi-mythical British ruler King Arthur and his knights. This large and complex body of romances would be superseded by prose romance, and both eventually would be displaced by the novel as such. Meanwhile, a large body of short oral verse narratives appears to have survived or indeed flourished among the largely illiterate common people, later to be "discovered," denominated *ballads*, and, like the written romance literature, appropriated into the novel.

Different cultures and societies around the globe had their own versions of these repertories of oral and written verse narrative, later transformed or subsumed into prose and eventually into what would be known as the novel. In India, for example, such large story cycles as the Bhagavad Gita and the Rig Veda seem to have been composed from what were originally oral narratives. Many of the individual stories in these cycles turn up in European folktale repertories later collected by 19th- and 20th-century antiquarians and folklorists, suggesting that there was a large body of narratives of various kinds common to societies and cultures across a considerable geographical area from Asia through Europe. These narratives were composed or performed according to various structural formulas, sometimes in verse and sometimes closer to what we would recognize as prose. Some of these stories also turn up in written verse or prose narrative versions. Collections of such versions (often cast in a frame narrative) were produced for well-to-do clientele from the Middle Ages on. These include both verse forms, such as Giovanni Boccaccio's *Decameron* (around 1350) and Geoffrey Chaucer's *Canterbury Tales* (late 14th century), and prose forms, including Renaissance collections of novellas such as the *Cent nouvelles nouvelles* (around 1460) and Marguerite de Navarre's *L'Heptaméron* (1558–59; *Heptameron*), and they were reframed yet again in 17th- and 18th-century collections such as Miguel de Cervantes' *Novelas ejemplares* (1613; *Exemplary Novels*) and the *Contes de ma mère l'Oye* (1697; *Mother Goose Tales*) by Charles Perrault. In some instances, verse romances were rendered in prose, such as the medieval French verse romance *Valentine and Orson,* and ballad matter was similarly transposed, as in the case of English narrative songs about Robin Hood. In these cases, however, the movement from verse form to prose seems also to have been a movement "down market": the prose *Valentine and Orson* and Robin Hood tales were meant for the chapbook market, or cheap "street literature" sold by peddlars (chapmen) and petty shopkeepers for lower-class and lower-middle-class readers.

Throughout the Middle Ages and Renaissance in Western Europe, then, there appears to have been some traffic back and forth from verse to prose narrative. Nevertheless, verse remained the dominant narrative form, enjoying higher cultural status and influence than prose until the 18th century in Western Europe and the Europeanized colonies, and even later elsewhere. During the late Middle Ages and Renaissance, however, there seems to have been a movement away from verse to prose in the courtly romance written for upper-class readership and consequently representing an idealized form of their culture and reflecting their interests. This movement may have been part of a larger process of a widening readership that steadily extended into the middle classes, accelerated by the advent of printing. Presumably this widening middle-class readership was interested in the culture and reading matter of its social superiors for various reasons, including simple curiosity, social emulation, and the benefits of understanding the mentality of the hegemonic social class. In this process of demographic change in the readership for verse and prose narrative, verse narrative seems to have retained its association with elite culture, and prose narrative became associated with a broader and more middle-class and even plebeian readership. This shift conditioned the different paths of development and the changing relations between verse and prose narrative and also conditioned the factors that made possible the rise of what came to be the novel in the modern sense—an extended work of prose fiction dealing centrally, if not exclusively, with individual subjectivity.

During the 17th and 18th centuries, verse romances of earlier periods continued to be read, apparently by anyone who could gain access to them. During the 17th century, lengthy French prose *romans héroïques* (or *romans de longue haleine*: "long-winded romances"), by Madeleine de Scudéry (*Artamène; ou, Le Grand Cyrus* [1649–53; *Artamenes; or, The Grand Cyrus*]; *Clélie,* 1654) and Gaulthier de Coste, Seigneur de La Calprenède (*Cassandre* [1642–45; *Cassandra*]; *Cléopatre* [1646–57; *Cleopatra*]), gave representations of courtly amorous culture and adventures of earlier verse romances. These works were widely read in Western Europe by the well-to-do upper and middle classes into the 18th century, in original French as well as in translations and imitations. Other writers of verse narrative continued to work in or against both the classical epic tradition and the medieval and Renaissance romance tradition. The English poet John Milton seems to have written his *Paradise Lost* (1667, 1674) and *Paradise Regained* (1671), comprising a blank verse secondary classical epic, as a republican and Christian riposte to both verse and prose romance of upper-class and courtly culture. Thereafter, the epic, especially in blank verse and with Miltonic echoes, retained something of an association with reformist and classical republican upper- and middle-class cultures.

During the 18th century, however, prose fiction rapidly outstripped verse narrative in popularity. The relationship between the forms developed in two main ways during this century. Novelists devised versions of romances of adventure and amorous intrigue that increasingly reflected middle-class values of subjective self-mastery, against the historic emphasis of verse and prose romance on manners and conduct in upper-class life. The so-called rise of the novel in the 18th century has been equated with this development in the ways of representing subjectivity, or "psychological realism," a development of a language and of figures for the newly created authentic subjective self that would continue to be a central topic in middle-class ideology and culture. The major innovator was Samuel Richardson, who adapted the epistolary narrative form, historically an expressive and even lyric mode (thus contiguous to lyric expressive poetry), to dramatize personal consciousness, and who also borrowed from forms once dependent on upper-class culture, such as the heroic drama (a 17th-century dramatic version of the upper-class verse romance) and the *roman héroïque*. Richardson aimed to create a form of narrative that subsumed elements of upper-class courtly romance (which retained a certain glamour with the reading public) imbued with or subverted by middle-class values. His work was highly influential throughout Europe, especially in France, where his focus on the drama of subjectivity in a society dominated by "merely" social forms of identity was imitated by a number of novelists.

Richardson developed a kind of novel designed to displace both verse and prose romance and thus reduce its ideological and cultural influence on the increasingly middle-class readership for narrative. His opponent Henry Fielding used elements of epic and heroic verse narrative in a mode of narration designed to represent more of a dialectic or coalition of upper- and middle-class values and practices—founded in the historic humanist education and assuming knowledge of classical literature—that had been the common cultural ground of upper- and middle-class males for some centuries. Fielding's mock-heroic narrative method in his major novels *Joseph Andrews* (1742) and *Tom Jones* (1749) relies on this humanist literary and cultural background for its full appreciation, but it also relies on the anti-romance prose fiction tradition of Cervantes' *Don Quixote* (1605–15) as well as the earlier mock-heroic verse narrative tradition represented by such works as Samuel Butler's anti-Puritan narrative verse satire, *Hudibras* (1662–78). Fielding's design was at least in part to displace Richardson's displacement of historic fictitious verse and prose narrative by using a different adaptation of historic verse narrative. Richardson's approach proved the more influential for most of the century; Fielding's approach, drastically adapted, was the more influential in the following century.

As the late 18th and early 19th centuries saw increased interest in the verse and prose narratives of the common people, in this era of romantic cultural nationalism middle-class writers and intellectuals began avidly collecting oral narratives in prose (called *folktales*) and verse (often called *ballads*), writing them down, editing them, imitating them, counterfeiting them, and, in some cases, assembling them into national epics, as in the case of the *Kalevala* in Finland. In the same period, writers, led by Sir Walter Scott, appropriated various versions of these centuries-old, widely distributed verse or prose narratives for the new genre of the historical novel. These activities were repeated in other societies and emergent nations around the world throughout the 19th and 20th centuries. Narrative poets and novelists in different countries and cultures availed themselves of these materials to construct their own historical fictions for reading publics each eager for representations (or fabrications) of its "national" history, identity, and culture, cast in the commercialized forms of narrative verse or novel and thus also validated with the cultural authority of "literature." The eagerness of the reading public for such fictions, abetted by an increasingly adventurous and entrepreneurial publishing business, contributed to a resurgence in the market for verse narrative of various kinds. The fact that most novels were still widely regarded as subliterary, and even morally and intellectually corrupting, also tempted narrative artists to use the more prestigious form of verse, including revived and adapted forms of the verse stanzas used by Renaissance writers of verse romance.

The vogue for such verse narrative, often in pseudo-archaic language and form, which lasted from the end of the 18th through the first two and a half decades of the 19th century, included great variety and usually had correlative forms in the novel. There were, for example, the heroic and symbolic verse narrative "prophecies" of William Blake, influenced variously by Biblical prose narrative, Milton's *Paradise Lost*, and the antiquarian James Macpherson's prose "translations" (largely fabrications) of Gaelic oral poems supposedly by the bard Ossian (reputedly Napoléon's favorite "poet"). By their nature, these cryptic and difficult narrative poems had little chance of being cast in the form of the novel, which was much more dependent on obtaining a wide readership.

There were the philosophical narratives, some published at the time and some not for years later, such as William Wordsworth's *The Recluse* (1814) and *The Prelude* (1850), and Lord Byron's *Childe Harold's Pilgrimage* (1812–18). Again, such poems were not readily adaptable to novel form, although certain of the "silver-fork" novels of the late 1820s and 1830s did include some elements of the philosophical narrative, such as the reflective, often world-weary (Byronic) protagonist.

There were a host of satirical social survey verse narratives, such as William Combe's Dr. Syntax poems, Byron's *Don Juan* (1819–24), and Aleksandr Pushkin's *Evgenii Onegin* (1833; *Eugene Onegin*), that looked back to mock-heroic novels such as Fielding's *Tom Jones* and reflexive novels such as Laurence Sterne's *Tristram Shandy* (1759–67). This form of narrative was already well developed by novelists of manners in the 18th century and continued to be developed by men and women novelists of the romantic period, from Jane Austen to Stendhal. There were numerous Orientalist narrative poems, by writers such as Robert Southey, Walter Savage Landor, and Thomas Moore, which often employed certain historic clashes of East and West as figures for the clash of old and new orders, monarchic and reformist regimes, in European and Napoleonic Europe. These poems also had novelistic (and indeed dramatic) analogues, such as Thomas Hope's *Anastasius* (1819) and James Morier's *Hajji Baba* (1823). Thomas Moore's *Lalla Rookh* (1817) is actually a prose novel with several inset verse tales and was quite popular.

There were a further host of more or less historical verse narratives, many ostensibly incorporating folk-ballad themes and situations, using a repertory of poeticisms and archaisms and designed to provide readers with representations of imagined community, glamorized by poetry and supposedly authenticated by "fact." Although women writers were among the pioneers in this genre, Sir Walter Scott was the best-selling master of such narratives. The task of such poems was shared by the new literary invention of the historical novel—again pioneered by women writers such as Jane Porter but, again, made into a best-selling genre on a European—indeed global—scale by Scott.

Thus the romantic period, or rather the period of romantic nationalism, saw perhaps the most intense moment of exchange and overlap between verse narrative and the novel, with some writers moving back and forth between these discourses; Scott, for example, was the master of both forms in world-literary terms and had an outstanding career first in historical verse narrative and then in the historical novel. Significantly, perhaps, the end of the parallel popularity of certain forms of verse narrative and the novel seems to have been signaled by the financial crisis in the publishing business during the later 1820s. In any case, verse narrative thereafter did not enjoy the same popularity as the novel and, with some exceptions, became increasingly restricted to "high" or artistically and intellectually serious literature, with some exceptions. Verse narratives also seem to have become shorter in length and more dependent on effects associated historically with lyric poetry, such as rich patterns of imagery and symbolism, brevity of descriptive and narrative elements, ambiguity and complexity in language, intricacy and experiment in verse or stanza form, and other evident markers of literariness.

After the romantic period, through the 19th and 20th centuries, narrative verse, and especially narrative poems of any great length, steadily lost ground in cultural and literary prestige and in popularity to lyric poetry of various kinds. Avant-garde modernist novels turned to devices of lyric poetry, as in the lyric novels of Virginia Woolf and in James Joyce's *Ulysses* (1922), with its dense, poem-like allusions and symbolism. Indeed, verse narrative nowadays circulates most often in books and anthologies for children. The novel became the dominant narrative form of any length in terms of prestige and especially popularity. Narrative verse was largely shorter and still popular to a degree, especially when put to music as commercialized popular song—still the most common form of narrative verse. Lyric poets since the romantic period, if not before, often turned to the everyday and to common life, conventionally the domain of prose and prose fiction, to demonstrate the "poetry" of the commonplace, sometimes in opposition to what was coming to seem the grandiosity and pomposity of "high" literary art. Avant-garde poets produced prose poems, to demonstrate the conventionality of distinctions between prose and verse, and avant-garde novelists, following Woolf, turned to techniques of lyric poetry. The casualty in this long history of changing relationship between verse narrative and the novel, with lyric verse complicating the relationship, would seem to be verse narrative. Certainly long verse narratives, or even "novels in verse," continue to be written, such as Craig Raine's *History: The Home*

Movie (1994) or Vikram Seth's *Golden Gate* (1986), but by far the form of verse narrative most widely distrubuted—more so even than the novel—is in the form of commercialized popular music. This now seems to be, and will likely continue to be, the form of verse narrative in most frequent and fertile relationship with the novel.

GARY KELLY

See also Epic and Novel; Genre Criticism; Greek and Roman Narrative; Medieval Narrative; Renaissance Narrative; Romance

Further Reading

Barron, W.R.J., *English Medieval Romance*, London and New York: Longman, 1987

Clements, Robert J., and Joseph Gibaldi, *Anatomy of the Novella: The European Tale Collection from Boccaccio and Chaucer to Cervantes*, New York: New York University Press, 1977

Hägg, Tomas, *Den antika romanen*, Stockholm: Carmina, 1980; as *The Novel in Antiquity*, Oxford: Blackwell, and Berkeley: University of California Press, 1983

Haviland, Thomas Philip, *The Roman de Longue Haleine on English Soil*, Philadelphia: University of Pennsylvania, 1931

Jackson, W.T.H., *The Literature of the Middle Ages*, New York: Columbia University Press, 1960 (see chapter 5)

Ker, W.P., *Epic and Romance: Essays on Medieval Literature*, London: Macmillan, 1896; 2nd edition, 1908

Kinney, Clare Regan, *Strategies of Poetic Narrative: Chaucer, Spenser, Milton, Eliot*, Cambridge and New York: Cambridge University Press, 1992

Lawrence, William Witherle, *Medieval Story and the Beginnings of the Social Ideals of English-Speaking People*, New York: Columbia University Press, 1911; 2nd edition, 1926

Richmond, Velma Bourgeois, *The Popularity of Middle English Romance*, Bowling Green, Ohio: Bowling Green University Popular Press, 1975

Wittig, Susan, *Stylistic and Narrative Structures in the Middle English Romances*, Austin: University of Texas Press, 1978

The Vicar of Wakefield by Oliver Goldsmith

1766

Published in 1766, although apparently written at least two years earlier, *The Vicar of Wakefield* appeared after all the main developments of the so-called "Rise of the Novel" were in place: it is not even mentioned in Ian Watt's classic study by that name. The novel form was beginning to stabilize and find respectability during the 1760s, and Goldsmith's only novel, a domestic story

set in the country, did not in itself produce major changes. *The Vicar of Wakefield* is in some ways a conservative response to the obscenity and impertinence with which (Goldsmith thought) Laurence Sterne had attempted to subvert the form of the autobiographical novel in *Tristram Shandy* (1759–67). Nonetheless, *The Vicar of Wakefield* has always been regarded as an anomaly:

several early reviewers referred to it as "singular" or "peculiar" and were puzzled by its curious mix of literary forms. With its naive but good-hearted vicar, the innocently named Dr. Primrose, it draws on the comic parsons of Henry Fielding; in its rueful examples of worldly trickery it echoes the novels of Tobias Smollett; in its crushing sequence of stock sentimental disasters (loss of fortune and home, the abduction of one daughter, the apparent seduction and death of another, and false imprisonment) it is part of the world of Samuel Richardson. It combines a plausible hero with a wildly implausible plot; it falls into two symmetrical halves of quite different tone; it is a domestic idyll, which, nonetheless, begins and ends in aristocratic fortune. It draws on or encompasses several other literary genres and types (romance, confession, essay, drama, ballad, sermon, tract, and Christian journey). Critics retreated to a position of moral admiration: whatever else the novel did, it promoted "universal benevolence" and was therefore to be recommended. More entertaining and cheerful than Sarah Fielding's exploration of domestic amity in *David Simple* (1744–53), shorter, and cleaner, than any other canonical novel of the period except Samuel Johnson's *Rasselas* (1759), it appeared to supply an appropriately classic fiction for an adolescent reading public. "The thing has succeeded by its incomparable amenity," wrote a bemused Henry James.

Until recently, *The Vicar of Wakefield* has been praised more or less in Goldsmith's own terms as exhibiting in a morally positive light a hero who "unites in himself the three greatest characters upon earth; he is a priest, an husbandman, and the father of a family." The first-person autobiographical narrative voice ("written by himself," the subtitle tells us) establishes the monologic, or single-voiced, authoritative text of print culture. *The Vicar of Wakefield* relates the vicar's misfortunes (and their eventual redemption) from marriage onward, and his authority as narrator is conceived as analogous to his authority as patriarch and parson, schooling his family, parishioners and (when maliciously imprisoned for debt) his fellow prisoners. He espouses the virtues of patience and cheerfulness in the face of accumulating disaster. The novel has been taken as a benign and warm-hearted version of the Job legend in which passive obedience is rewarded by full restoration of fortune and family. The essayistic chapter headings, often delivered in the form of a moral precept to be exemplified in the narrative (in the manner of *Rasselas*), easily encouraged a homiletic reading of the text in which the vicar's voice is conflated with that of Goldsmith, who was better known as a critic and journalist.

The first-person narrative mode, so intimately linked through Daniel Defoe to the early realist novel, has, however, always faced intrinsic difficulties: the problem of hindsight, the distinction between the self that narrates and the self that is narrated in action, and the lack of overview. These problems are conspicuously fended off in Defoe's fiction, and as conspicuously foregrounded in Sterne's. In Goldsmith's narrative, the conflation of narrating and narrated selves has come to look less stable than it once did. Although it eschews the realm of childhood, where the problem is most acute, the full subtitle of the vicar's narrative is "a tale, supposed to be written by himself," which introduces a note of orality and romance, perhaps an irony. More than one-tenth of the book is actually occupied by the quoted first-person narratives of other characters, notably Primrose's eldest son. The relation of this novel to sentimental literature has come to look more like diminution or burlesque than intense identification (in

the light of Goldsmith's stated privileging of "laughing" comedy over "sentimental" comedy and his dislike of contemporary modes of fiction).

More extremely, the narrative is fissured with a number of discontinuities and inconsistencies of detail (in chronology, in amounts of money, in slips in the disguise of the narrator's patron) and other moments of reticence that seem at odds with the narrator's supposed control. Once ascribed to convention or carelessness (Goldsmith confessed "there are an hundred faults in this Thing" and presciently observed that "an hundred things might be said to prove them beauties"), these cracks in the narrative have been argued to represent a deliberate destabilization of the vicar's narrative authority: he is not telling the whole truth, and his mistakes reveal him as Quixotic, self-deceiving, and pompous. The shift in tone from comedy of manners to melodramatic pathos, also once played down as a change of intention, has been argued to signify the vicar's own moral downfall. His character has suffered much of late: Primrose has been taken as a wholly ironic Gulliver figure who displays unconscious worldliness and inefficiency as paterfamilias. More recently still, this argument for the satiric nature of the text has been reviewed as a last-ditch attempt to salvage aesthetic unity and transparency for a novel fractured less by slips of the pen or narrative self-deception than by an incomplete shift in contemporary ideology. John Bender (1987) holds that the novel is both reformist and nostalgic, seeking authority in the impersonal totality and transparency of the state but clinging to personalized notions of virtuous intervention: hence the prison reforms instituted by the vicar and the impromptu court convened to mete out punishments and rewards by the savior of the family, the noble Sir William Thornhill (present throughout as a friend in disguise). Bender associates this emergent shift and the moments of narrative awkwardness with a tentative reaching forward from personalized narrative to the pervasive or omniscient narrative authority of free indirect discourse and the later realist novel.

The Vicar of Wakefield was admired by Sir Walter Scott, Lord Byron, Friedrich Schlegel, and Johann Wolfgang von Goethe, and its influence has been detected in fictions as various as Charlotte Brontë's *Jane Eyre* (1847), George Eliot's *Scenes of Clerical Life* (1858), and William Beckford's *Vathek* (1912). Most importantly, Jane Austen's *Pride and Prejudice* (1813) manages to encompass a great deal of the family dynamics and narrative situations of Goldsmith's novel while moving much closer to the kind of architectural authority and pervasive psychological observation that Bender has in mind

PAUL BAINES

Further Reading

Backman, Sven, *This Singular Tale: A Study of "The Vicar of Wakefield" and Its Literary Background,* Lund: Gleerup, 1971

Bender, John, "Prison Reform and the Sentence of Narration in *The Vicar of Wakefield,*" in *The New Eighteenth Century: Theory, Politics, English Literature,* edited by Felicity Nussbaum and Laura Brown, New York: Methuen, 1987

Bloom, Harold, editor, *Oliver Goldsmith,* New York: Chelsea House, 1987

Dussinger, John A., *The Discourse of the Mind in Eighteenth-Century Fiction,* The Hague: Mouton, 1974

Dykstal, Timothy, "The Story of O: Politics and Pleasure in *The*

Vicar of Wakefield," *English Literary History* 62:2 (Summer 1995)

Grudis, Paul, "The Narrator and *The Vicar of Wakefield,*" *Essays in Literature* 1:1 (1973)

Hilliard, Raymond F., "The Redemption of Fatherhood in *The Vicar of Wakefield,*" *Studies in English Literature* 23:3 (Summer 1983)

Hopkins, Robert H., *The True Genius of Oliver Goldsmith,* Baltimore: Johns Hopkins University Press, 1969

Jefferson, D.W., "Observations on *The Vicar of Wakefield,*" *Cambridge Journal* 3 (1950)

Rousseau, G.S., editor, *Goldsmith: The Critical Heritage,* Boston and London: Routledge and Kegan Paul, 1974

Victorian Novel of Social Criticism. *See* Social Criticism

Vie mode d'emploi. *See* Life, a User's Manual

Voina i mir. *See* War and Peace

Voltaire [François-Marie Arouet] 1694–1778

French

Voltaire was one of the central figures of the French Enlightenment. His varied and voluminous oeuvre—with contributions in history, drama, poetry, and fiction—stood in the service of his Enlightenment philosophy. An indefatigable champion of rationality and a biting satirist, Voltaire attacked irrationality, obscurantism, and intolerance wherever he found it, but particularly in the Church and secular government. Never a favorite of the authorities, he was imprisoned in the Bastille for a year in his early 20s, upon which he adopted the name Voltaire. He spent much of the rest of his life in exile from Paris, with prolonged stays in England, Prussia, and Switzerland.

Although he was most celebrated in his lifetime for his drama and poetry, he is now mostly read for his *contes philosophiques,* or philosophical tales, a genre he developed fairly late in his career. The *conte philosophique* bears little resemblance to the 17th- and 18th-century French novel (*roman*), which is characterized at its best by subtle psychological analysis. Even *Candide; ou, l'Optimisme* (1759; *Candide; or, Optimism*), which

approximates the novel form in length, remains quite far from its narrative traditions. Strictly speaking, then, Voltaire is a *conteur* rather than a novelist.

Standard collections of Voltaire's work usually include 26 texts under the category of "romans et contes," following the classification by an early editor, Antoine-Nicolas de Condorcet, who grouped some very short, miscellaneous writings with the longer narratives. "Petite digression" (1766; "The Blind Judges of Colors"), for instance, is barely a page in length. Many of the shorter pieces are exempla, parables, or beast fables—a genre that had distanced itself in France from its folk origins and was cultivated with a great deal of conscious artistry. Their center of gravity lies in the moral rather than in the character development and careful plot construction that are more typical of the novel. Even the full-fledged *contes,* including the early and already highly accomplished *Zadig; ou, La Destinée* (1748; *Zadig; or, The Book of Fate*), *Candide,* and *La Princesse de Babylone* (1768; *The Princess of Babylon*), share traits with the parable, particularly in the central focus on the moral of the story. Sometimes the moral is given explicitly, at length, or in the form of a wry observation or maxim, as in the famous conclusion of *Candide,* in which Voltaire recommends "cultivating one's garden" and observes that work keeps away the evils of boredom, necessity, and vice. Elsewhere, moral precepts are scattered throughout the tale or can be derived from the events. However, characters in the longer tales gain in complexity over the figures in the shorter pieces: while they do not evolve in the modern, psychological sense, they do learn from their experience.

All Voltaire's tales comprise fantastical (or simply implausible) elements, usually to illustrate a moral or philosophical point. Uninterested in the conventions of realism, the best stand out for their wit, inspired sarcasm, range of characters and situations, insights into human behavior, and political, social, and moral satire. He drew on a wide variety of sources, including Savinien de Cyrano de Bergerac's *Histoire comique . . . contenant les états et empires de la lune* (1657; *Voyages to the Moon and the Sun*), a kind of proto–science fiction that directly informs Voltaire's fantastical *Micromégas: Histoire philosophique* (1752; *Micromegas*). The structural device of the journey that appears in *Micromegas* has antecedents, beyond Cyrano's *Voyages to the Moon and the Sun*, in the epic tradition and should be read metaphorically as well as literally, representing the journey of life. Another important model is Alain-René Lesage's picaresque *Histoire de Gil Blas de Santillane* (1715–35; *The Adventures of Gil Blas*), from which Voltaire's tales borrow their highly episodic narrative strategies. Charles-Louis de Secondat de Montesquieu is another significant precursor, particularly with his *Les Lettres persanes* (1721; *The Persian Letters*). In several of his longer works, Voltaire adopted Montesquieu's use of the epistolary format to illustrate a philosophical position, and he used exotic settings to similar effect—to evade the censors and to illuminate European society by presenting its mores through the incredulous incomprehension of members of a foreign culture.

This exoticism certainly has some entertainment value, but its primary purpose is satirical. For instance, India, a favorite setting, gave Voltaire a pretext to praise its ancient and reasonable moral and religious traditions (drawing an unspoken but biting contrast with Catholicism). Other exotic settings include a tropical paradise and the American wilderness. In both cases, native peoples are held up as a model, practicing natural religion and leading pure, healthy lives free from the corruption and vice of European society. *L'Ingénu* (1767; translated as *The Huron* and *The Pupil of Nature*), dealing with the confrontation of native and European mores, is an example of a tale with a North American setting. To put it charitably, Voltaire's anthropology is best forgotten, but it functions admirably as a device to expose corruption, folly, and the oppressiveness of 18th-century European institutions. His favorite targets are the Catholic Church, which he considered a social scourge for its intellectual tyrannies, encouragement of superstition and fanaticism, and extortionist financial practices; the absurdity of the Hebrew Bible; the Jesuits, whom he loathed with a special passion; monasticism; the papacy; and the Sorbonne. The Spanish Inquisition appears as the epitome of all the evils of organized Christianity, not only in *Candide* but in several other tales. Although he avoids criticism of monarchy in and of itself, the abuses of absolutism come in for frequent attack. In a slightly different category lies his generally unfavorable treatment of women, in whom he finds a great deal of vanity, superficiality, and treachery.

All Voltaire's work is notable for its rhetorical brilliance. In fact, one of his achievements is his ability to say succinctly and memorably what others said at greater length and less cleverly. His contribution to fiction lies in his development of a viable alternative to the realistic novel. His tales illustrate the narrative and cognitive possibilities of an antirealist aesthetic, including a serious presentation of ideas; the mixing of narrative means, levels of plausibility and seriousness, and wide ranges of tone; and violations of the illusion of the real by authorial intervention and commentary on the narrative process itself.

Romantic fiction had little use for Voltaire's rationality or satire. While he was admired by some, especially Victor Hugo, others considered him destructive. Alfred de Musset, for instance, accused him of having destroyed the hopes of an entire generation by attacking its faith. Several 19th-century authors, including Honoré de Balzac, Philippe-Auguste de Villiers de l'Isle-Adam, and Joris-Karl Huysmans, wrote philosophical fiction, but theirs tended toward occultism, idealism, and the mystical—anathema to Voltaire. His closest heirs among writers of fiction belong to the 20th century: André Gide, Jean-Paul Sartre, and Albert Camus.

CATHARINE SAVAGE BROSMAN

See also Candide; Conte Philosophique

Biography

Born François-Marie Arouet in Paris, February or November 1694. Attended Collège Louis-le-Grand, Paris, 1704–11; studied law, 1711–13. Articled by his father to a lawyer, 1714; ran into trouble for his satiric writings: arrested and banished from Paris for five months, 1716, and imprisoned in the Bastille, 1717–18; ill relations with the Chevalier de Rohan-Chabot led to another term in the Bastille and departure for England, 1726–28; retired to Château de Cirey with Madame Du Châtelet, 1734–40; Courtier with Frederick of Prussia, Berlin, 1750–53; lived in Colmar, 1753–54, at Les Délices, near Geneva, 1755–59, and at Ferney, 1759–78; traveled to Paris and received triumphant welcome, 1778. Died 30 May 1778.

Collections of Works by Voltaire
The Best Known Works of Voltaire, New York: Blue Ribbon Books, 1927; reprinted, New York: Book League, 1940
The Writings of Voltaire: Philosophical Novels, Romances, Short Stories, Dialogues, Poems, 4 vols., New York: W.H. Wise, 1931
Romans et contes, edited by Henri Bénac, Paris: Garnier, 1949
Romans et contes, edited by René Pomeau, Paris: Garnier-Flammarion, 1966
The Complete Tales of Voltaire, 3 vols., translated by William Walton, New York: Howard Fertig, 1990

Further Reading
Bonneville, Douglas A., "Voltaire and the Form of the Novel," *Studies on Voltaire and the Eighteenth Century* 158 (1976)
Gay, Peter, *Voltaire's Politics: The Poet as Realist,* Princeton, New Jersey: Princeton University Press, 1959; 2nd edition, New Haven, Connecticut: Yale University Press, 1988

Mason, Haydn, *Voltaire*, New York: St. Martin's Press, and London: Hutchinson, 1975

McGhee, Dorothy, *Voltairian Narrative Devices as Considered in the Author's Contes philosophiques*, Manasha, Wisconsin: George Banta, 1933

Pearson, Roger, *The Fables of Reason: A Study of Voltaire's*

"Contes philosophiques," Oxford: Clarendon Press, and New York: Oxford University Press, 1993

Ridgway, Ronald S., *Voltaire and Sensibility*, Montreal: McGill-Queen's University Press, 1973

Topazio, Virgil W., *Voltaire: A Critical Study of His Major Works*, New York: Random House, 1967

Voss by Patrick White

1957

By any measure, *Voss* is central to the work of the Australian Nobel laureate Patrick White and to Australian literature in general. It is also a masterwork of world literature.

The fifth of 12 novels White produced before his death in 1990, *Voss* marked the beginning of a major phase in his writing, in which he found and explored central themes such as the quest of the visionary loner, the nonduality of spiritual/physical existence, the nature of Australian identity, and the redemptive possibilities of failure. The novel fulfills the promise of its immediate predecessor, *The Tree of Man* (1955), an epic chronicle of white settlement of the virgin bush. One of the masterpieces of Australian modernism, *Voss* opened the door to postmodernism, which would dominate Australian and other literatures during the final decades of the 20th century. As Mark Williams states succinctly, "*Voss* is White's most important novel [and] one of the key novels to be written since the war. It is at once his most Australian novel and that which secures his status as an international modernist novelist" (see Williams, 1993).

Published first in the United States, then England, and finally in Australia, *Voss* was greeted by the kind of critical stammering that has been typical of initial responses to White's fiction. Although no one descended to the level of Australian poet A.D. Hope in his famously dismissive review of *The Tree of Man,* in which he accused White of writing "pretentious and illiterate verbal sludge," reviews of *Voss* were decidedly mixed and often very puzzled. In a letter, White attributes the bad reviews to a lack of understanding and to a sort of desperate "nostalgia" for his most recent work. Nonetheless, the novel was praised in many quarters. It was named a Book-of-the-Month Club selection in the United States and a Book Society choice in England and became a best-seller in Australia. In addition, it was the first recipient of the prestigious Miles Franklin Prize for the best Australian novel of the year and was presented the first W.H. Smith Award for the most outstanding contribution to English literature in 1957–58. The well-known Australian painter Sidney Nolan was persuaded to do the book jacket for the English edition and plans were almost immediately made to film the novel. An impressive opera with a libretto by the award-winning Australian novelist David Malouf is based on *Voss*. Obviously, many believed that White had become a literary voice to be reckoned with.

Voss is an epic of sorts, sprouted from the same dry and unpromising clay as *The Tree of Man*. Both novels grew out of

White's disgruntlement with his native land upon his return after World War II. He complained that Australia had become vacuous, mediocre, and materialistic. To counteract the creeping spiritual leprosy of modernity, White set out to "discover the extraordinary behind the ordinary, the mystery and poetry," as he put it in a 1958 essay entitled "The Prodigal Son." Thematically, such an attempt required that he revalue and often remythologize icons of Australian history, folklore, and myth: the prosperous burgher clinging to the coast and to his dreams of riches, the nouveau riche of the "squattocracy," the immigrant hesitant to put down new roots, the pioneer who settles the bush, the Aborigine who is displaced, the convict emancipator or escapee, the child (or woman) lost in the bush, the explorer who only imagines himself less lost. Stylistically, White wrote in "The Prodigal Son" (1958), the challenge of locating the poetry in Australian life demanded that he force prose to reproduce "the textures of music, the sensuousness of paint." His task was "to prove that the Australian novel is not necessarily the dreary, dun-coloured offspring of journalistic realism." This undertaking would preoccupy him throughout the following decade.

Perhaps the audacity of his creative goal accounts in part for the critical mystification it often produced. In the case of *Voss*, which tells the story of a 19th-century explorer of the Australian interior, White creates a kind of collage of genres and traditions that turns back to 19th-century realism, stakes unmistakable ground for 20th-century modernism, and—by employing elements of magic realism and metafictionality—looks ahead to postmodernism.

As a number of critics have noticed, *Voss* seems initially to locate the reader in the world of social-realist fiction, particularly that of the comedy of manners. The novel begins in colonial Sydney, with the first meeting between Voss and Laura Trevelyan, niece and ward of the prosperous and vapid merchant Mr. Bonner, who has offered to organize the financing for Voss' expedition into Australia's uncharted interior. Mr. Bonner's motives are purely commercial, and his rampant materialism and that of his newly rich social class become the first objects of White's increasingly trenchant satirical wit. Other targets are the lack of learning and the even more glaring lack of any genuine metaphysical or philosophical inquiry in colonial society, its indefensible pretensions to culture, its slavish reliance on English manners and customs inappropriately transplanted from "home," and its boredom with anything other than itself. It is this very satiric edge that finally subverts the realism of the novel. Its bourgeois subjects "become grotesques, figures of contempt, judged and condemned from the standpoint of the sensitive, alienated . . . 'outsider'" (see Wilding, 1997).

The novel concentrates on two such outsiders—Voss and Laura Trevelyan. When Voss' expedition departs for the interior of sand and soul-searching, the novel leaves behind the long-standing Australian tradition of realist fiction for the territory of modernist allegory. White evokes a monumental landscape for the purpose of objectifying Voss' monumental but doomed self-aggrandizing quest. As Voss and his party approach both illumination and annihilation, Laura enacts a similar interior journey within the confines of the Bonner establishment in Sydney, and the two communicate their growing understanding of life and love for each other, first through letters, and then by dreams, visions, and a sort of telepathy that has long disturbed the novel's critics. This mode of communication can be understood, however, as a development of a modernist use of interior monologue or stream of consciousness. White has the two loners communicate and eventually merge with each other, so that Voss (who dies in the desert) survives in Laura as well as in legend. Yet the author does not permit the kind of union that Jane Austen, Charles Dickens, or William Makepeace Thackeray might have allowed in their novels. Other modernist features include a fascination with point of view, which manifests itself in the layered construction of characters who have to be continuously reassessed by other characters, the narrator, and the reader. The narrative modulates into and out of *style indirect libre* to the extent that point of view is often unattributable.

Patrick White did not invent Australian modernism—an honor shared by Chester Cobb, Christina Stead, and Henry Handel Richardson—but he did secure its place in Australian letters. But *Voss* also anticipates postmodernism. Character treatment approaches magic realism in the insistence that the miraculous and the illuminating sometimes flower in the midst of the mundane. The novel's self-conscious awareness of how texts create history and reality, and of the fictionality and self-interestedness of all such texts, is common to postmodern fiction. Some critics have argued that the novel deconstructs personality, and postcolonial readings concentrate on the fact that Voss is a German invader of an English colony that itself has displaced and devalued indigenous inhabitants and their culture.

On the other hand, recent criticism of White has tended to voice displeasure at the fact that his work is not postmodernist or postcolonial enough. He has been accused of a lack of empathy and comprehension with regard to indigenous peoples, women, the working classes, and the whole of Australia's uneasy history as simultaneously colonized and colonizer. He has been faulted for too much modernist fascination with the alienated loner and too little confidence in social solutions to the modern malaise. But Julian Croft applauds precisely White's hopefulness, finding in him and in Australian literary modernism generally a paradoxical "celebration of . . . meaning beyond mere deterministic explanation" and in *Voss* in particular a discovery that "journeys to the interior might confront a vacuum and death, but insight resulted" (see Croft, 1988). The insight is probably that of Le Mesurier, one of Voss' several alter egos in the novel, who remarks, "The mystery of life is not solved by success, which is an end in itself, but in failure, in perpetual struggle, in becoming."

CAROLYN BLISS

See also Patrick White

Further Reading

Bliss, Carolyn, *Patrick White's Fiction: The Paradox of Fortunate Failure,* New York: St. Martin's Press, and London: Macmillan, 1986

Collier, Gordon, *The Rocks and Sticks of Words: Style, Discourse and Narrative Structure in the Fiction of Patrick White,* Amsterdam and Atlanta, Georgia: Rodopi, 1992

Croft, Julian, *Penguin New Literary History of Australia,* New York and Ringwood, Victoria: Penguin, 1988

Edgecombe, Rodney Stenning, *Vision and Style in Patrick White: A Study of Five Novels,* Tuscaloosa: University of Alabama Press, 1989

Kiernan, Brian, *Patrick White,* London: Macmillan, and New York: St. Martin's Press, 1980

Marr, David, *Patrick White: A Life,* London: Cape, 1991; New York: Knopf, 1992

Marr, David, editor, *Patrick White: Letters,* London: Cape, 1994

Morley, Patricia, *The Mystery of Unity: Theme and Technique in the Novels of Patrick White,* Montreal: McGill-Queen's University Press, and St. Lucia: University of Queensland Press, 1972

Tacey, David J., *Patrick White: Fiction and the Unconscious,* Melbourne and New York: Oxford University Press, 1988

White, Patrick, *Flaws in the Glass: A Self-Portrait,* London: Cape, 1981; New York: Viking, 1982

Wilding, Michael, *Studies in Classic Australian Fiction,* Sydney: Sydney Studies, and Nottingham: Shoestring Press, 1997

Williams, Mark, *Patrick White,* London: Macmillan, and New York: St. Martin's Press, 1993

Wolfe, Peter, *Laden Choirs: The Fiction of Patrick White,* Lexington: University Press of Kentucky, 1983

Voyage au bout de la nuit. *See* Journey to the End of the Night

W

Wahlverwandtschaften. *See* Elective Affinities

Wang Anyi 1954–

Chinese

The importance of Wang Anyi as a novelist stems not only from her extensive documentation of the changing Chinese society and consciousness in the last quarter of the century but also from her continual experimentation with fiction itself. Few contemporary novelists of her time have engaged as many critical subjects as Wang, and few have sustained the same passion with which she pursues her vocation as a writer. Arguably the most widely read, certainly the most anthologized and respected woman writer of her generation, Wang has established herself as a prominent intellectual figure in contemporary China through an extraordinarily wide range of novels, stories, essays, and literary commentaries.

Perhaps because of Wang's constant self-reflection, clearly demarcated stages can be observed in her development as a writer, each with its specific intellectual concerns and orientations. Various issues and moods may support her narratives and generate enormous creative energy, although it is also evident that the modern condition of an uneventful, if not anticlimactic, life has been the ultimate horizon of her literary landscape. Most of her early writings, including her first two novels, *69 jie chuzhong sheng* (1984; Junior High Class of '69) and *Huanghe gudao ren* (1986; People along the Ancient Yellow River), are largely based on her personal experiences during and in the wake of the Cultural Revolution (1966–76). While a sense of disillusionment permeates these stories—some of which are autobiographically framed around a young woman named Wenwen—there is ultimately an affirmation of meaning and positive values, such as integrity and dedication. From the outset of her work, Wang demonstrates a remarkable sensitivity in probing the emotions of human experience, especially when her characters are what she calls "ordinary folks," weighed down by the reality of life:

sympathetic portrayals of individual psychology define her narrative style and strength. She is also known for her ability to re-create a situation and mood swings through thick description, yet her interest does not lie in spinning sensational plots. *Weisheng* (1981; Coda) and *Liushi* (1982; *Lapse of Time*) are two novellas typical of this first, realistic period in her development.

In the last months of 1983, Wang, already an accomplished writer, attended an international writing camp in the United States and returned with considerable changes in her views on the purpose of fiction. To paraphrase her own words, she had been up until that point relying on an intuitive grasp of the meaning of life without being able to endow her narrative with a philosophical depth. Driven by the need for a more intense truth, she wanted her future novels to "condense within a short time a long history, within a small space a large world, and contain the most abstract of philosophies within the most concrete of things." This rethinking allowed Wang to contribute significantly to the then rising literary movement of "root-seeking." The two novellas she wrote in a deliberately allegorical mode, *Xiao Baozhuang* (1985; *Baotown*) and *Da Liuzhuang* (1985; Liutown), underscore a contemplative distance between narrative and narrator. More abstract forces, such as cultural habits and human nature, now play a formidable part in shaping the characters' destiny; the choice of a secluded village as the inescapable setting and the depiction of tradition-bound peasants highlight the "root-seeking" movement's conception of the modern Chinese condition.

At this point, thanks in no small part to Wang's famed productivity, the novella as a preferred medium in contemporary Chinese literature reached its height. What distinguishes the novellas of Wang Anyi of this period is a move away from realism toward daring psychological exploration. Her 1986–87 trilogy on love and sexuality sent shock waves through her readers by then well accustomed to more mainstream and socially conscientious material. The detailed, symbolic, and evocative depiction of sexual awakening and passion in these romances was unparalleled at the time, as Bonnie S. McDougall observes in the introduction to *Brocade Valley* (1992), her translation of *Jinxiugu zhi lian*.

The extended controversy over her fables about sexuality in contemporary life gave Wang the opportunity to better articulate her intellectual and literary pursuits. Gender difference and relations set against the backdrop of a mundane but demanding city life would become the dominant subject matter in her fiction. A new interest in women's life stories underlies her 1991 novel *Mi Ni*, the 1993 novella *Xianggang de qing yu ai* (Love and Sentiment in Hong Kong), and the monumental 1995 novel *Changhen ge* (Song of Unending Regret). This last novel adroitly enmeshes a realistic invocation of a lost world with a melancholy commentary on the muted sufferings and aspirations of a beauty queen in modern-day Shanghai: it presents a contemplative, post-romantic narrative style at its most powerful and penetrating. *Changhen ge* also brings to the fore a certain nostalgia that Wang develops in her late narratives regarding the uncertain effects of the cityscape, in particular that of Shanghai, on human life and emotions.

At the same time that she dealt with different intellectual and historical topics in her fiction, Wang also experimented with new narrative techniques. The most successful example of this is her 1990 novella *Shushu de gushi* (Our Uncle's Story), a metafictional story about storytelling. This parodic structure allows the self-questioning narrator ample room to make cultural criticisms and historical observations. Critics have noted that in this work Wang skillfully deconstructs the division between history and fictionality with this postmodern exercise and ultimately rethinks the process of myth-making.

Indeed, a mythical family genealogy appears to be a new form of historical novel, in which the writer's vision becomes much more global and multifocal. Alongside *Shangxin Taipingyang* (1993; Sadness for the Pacific), the novel *Jishi yu xugou* (1993; Records and Fiction) combines legends, fantasies, personal memoirs, historical accounts, and re-created texts to fashion a tapestry of private narrative that interweaves grand and diasporic history. The central thesis, which Wang states both in the subtitle of the novel and in an epigraph, is that "fiction can create history" and "history can be created like fiction." In this much-acclaimed novel, exhibiting the ethos of a classical Bildungsroman, Wang offers an intimate account of inner life and intellectual growth as a novelist. Its introspective, if not slightly narcissistic, first-person narrator is similar to that of the autobiographical "I-novel" that was popular in early 20th-century Japan but that has yet to take hold in modern Chinese fiction. Technical innovations aside, *Jishi yu xugou* confirms Wang's image as a "restless explorer" of historical memory and cultural complexes. It is also an aptly emblematic text, testimony to a body of work that stands as an expansive record of evolving Chinese self-consciousness.

XIAOBING TANG

Biography

Born 6 March 1954 in Nanjing. Moved to Shanghai with her family in July 1955; sent to the countryside in 1970 (during the Cultural Revolution); returned to Shanghai in 1978 to become a literary editor, and has lived in Shanghai ever since; in 1980 she became a member of the Chinese Association of Writers and is currently a professional writer.

Novels and Novellas by Wang Anyi

Weisheng [Coda], 1981
Liushi, 1982; as *Lapse of Time*, translation sponsored by Panda Books, 1988
69 jie chuzhong sheng [Junior High Class of '69], 1984
Da Liuzhuang [Liutown], 1985
Xiao Baozhuang, 1985; as *Baotown*, translated by Martha Avery, 1989
Huanghe gudao ren [People along the Ancient Yellow River], 1986
Huangshan zhi lian, 1986; as *Love on a Barren Mountain*, translated by Eva Hung, 1991
Xiaocheng zhi lian, 1986; as *Love in a Small Town*, translated by Eva Hung, 1988
Jinxiugu zhi lian, 1987; as *Brocade Valley*, translated by Bonnie S. McDougall and Chen Maiping, 1992
Liushui sanshi zhang, 1988
Gang shang de shiji, 1989
Shushu de gushi [Our Uncle's Story], 1990
Mi Ni, 1991
Shangxin Taipingyang [Sadness for the Pacific], 1993
Xianggang de qing yu ai [Love and Sentiment in Hong Kong], 1993
Jishi yu xugou [Records and Fiction], 1993
Changhen ge [Song of Unending Regret], 1995

Other Writings: short stories, essays, journalism, travel writings (including accounts of her trip to the United States and Western Europe), literary criticism (on language, literary techniques, and women's issues), letters to other writers, memoirs.

Further Reading

Bian Ying, editor, *The Time Is Not Yet Ripe: Contemporary China's Best Writers and Their Stories*, Beijing: Foreign Languages Press, 1991
Hongzhen Ji, "Wang Anyi," in *Zhong shen de xiaoxiang*, Beijing: Renmin wenxue chubanshe, 1996
Laifong Leung, *Morning Sun: Interviews with Chinese Writers of the Lost Generation*, Armonk, New York, and London: M.E. Sharpe, 1994
Ling Tun Ngai, "Politics of Sexuality: The Fiction of Zhang Xianliang, Mo Yan and Wang Anyi," Ph.D. diss., University of Wisconsin, Madison, 1994
Solmecke, Ulrike, *Zwischen ausserer und innerer Welt: Erzahlprosa der chinesischen Autorin Wang Anyi von 1980–1990*, Dortmund: Projekt Verlag, 1995
Tang, Xiaobing, "Melancholy Against the Grain: Approaching Postmodernity in Wang Anyi's Contemporary Tales of Sorrow," *boundary 2* 24 (Fall 1997)
Thakur, Ravni, *Rewriting Gender: Reading Contemporary Chinese Women*, London and Atlantic Highlands, New Jersey: Zed Books, 1997

War and Peace by Lev Tolstoi

Voina i mir 1863–69

War and Peace is a massive work in which many traditions come into play. The peace section of the novel echoes the English novel of family life, as written by Charles Dickens, William Makepeace Thackeray, and Anthony Trollope. The plot has the shape of a multiple sentimental education or Bildungsroman, tracing the journey from innocence to experience of five characters. The war section is a national history, recounting Russian experience through the Napoleonic campaigns to the eve of the Decembrist revolt. Here War and Peace achieves the epic magnitude of Homer (Tolstoi's favorite author), while its ironies recall Stendhal's La Chartreuse de Parme (1839; The Charterhouse of Parma). Nor should we neglect the importance of two genres that stand at the boundaries of belles lettres, the journalistic sketch and the personal diary, which also enrich Tolstoi's novel. In his early sketches of men at war, Tolstoi sharpened his eye for significant detail; in his diaries he cultivated his extraordinary talent for conveying the intimacies of everyday life.

Tolstoi wrote of War and Peace that "it is not a novel because I cannot and do not know how to confine the characters I have created within given limits." Indeed, from its publication to our times, readers have complained about the work's looseness of structure, especially its digressions into theorizing about war, history, freedom, and necessity: "he mounts his hobby-horse and is off!" Turgenev moaned; "baggy monsters" and "fluid puddings," Henry James fretted. However, novels have rarely been the tidy affairs some critics pretend. For every Jane Austen and Flaubert, we have had a Dickens or a Melville.

Tolstoi's refusal to recognize the conventional climaxes of narrative—"the death of one character only aroused interest in other characters, a marriage seemed . . . like a source of complication"—is one of the many strengths of his marvelous creation. The work captures the openness of experience—it begins in the middle of a conversation and some 1,300 pages later ends (in the first epilogue) in the middle of a sentence. Andrei dies, and Pierre marries. Vibrant Natasha finds love and grows plump. Restless Nikolai settles into tranquil domesticity with Princess Maria. Pierre is apparently on his way to fight in the Decembrist uprising and enter a new stream of complication. Life is a baggy monster in rather the same way that War and Peace is, and the novel's formlessness is the consequence of Tolstoi's pursuit of a superrealism that eschews tidy beginnings and endings.

As Tolstoi conveys the continuity of life in time, he stretches his canvas in space. Besides the five main characters, a host of secondary figures are introduced, many historical, others fictional. The novel moves from the familiarities of family life to the vast panorama of war, from a focus on young people trying to find their way in the world to a focus on the court of Alexander, the headquarters of Napoléon, the battlefields of Austerlitz and Borodino. The enormous cast is integrated through parallels and antitheses—of war and peace, city and country, gentry Moscow and courtly St. Petersburg, generals, politicians, emperors, and ordinary men and women. The reigning opposition that organizes all others is that of public and private life.

A unifying rhythm informs this vast composition. Russia begins to throw off the yoke of Napoléon at the decisive battle of Borodino as the lives of the main figures come to resolution, however tentatively. Even Andrei, at his death, discovers pity and the satisfaction of self-knowledge. These closures do not depend on the working out of a dramatic intrigue—Tolstoi detested these as false to life—but are the fulfillment of a process of growth. A Russia fighting not for abstract principle (like Napoléon) but for land and home has matured into a great power. Andrei, Pierre, and Nikolai have finally outgrown adolescent fantasies of glory and the latter two are ready to assume the responsibilities of marriage, as are Natasha and Maria.

The novel's theoretical interludes contribute to its epic magnitude. Nations are on the march and great issues are at stake. The reader may not agree with Tolstoi's answers, but many will be provoked by his questions: What is the role of the individual in history? What causes historical events? Why do usually decent men slaughter each other by the thousands in war? Tolstoi once wrote that his real hero is truth, and War and Peace, like all his fiction, is a quest for knowledge.

Despite certain inconsistencies (especially the second epilogue), the argument is in harmony with the action. The novel extends outward in space and forward in theoretically unbounded time because no single event, not even the War of 1812, exists in isolation. We are but links in a great chain of being, Tolstoi tells us, particles in a vast universe. Our every action is determined by an incalculable multitude of events before us and around us. Man is certainly free to raise or lower his arm, in Tolstoi's example, but in the immense arena of history, where he is affected by the actions of millions, this freedom is trivial.

This historical nihilism is the backdrop for Tolstoi's praise of the family. The family, especially the family of the Russian gentry, secluded on its country estates or in its Moscow winter homes, can to some extent escape the sledgehammer of history, the babble of politicians, the schemes of reformers, the ambitions of the mighty. The sustaining principle of family life, War and Peace argues, is not power, but love, which offers respite from the impersonal forces of history.

The villain of War and Peace is Napoléon, because he would impose his rational will on history. His opposite is the Russian general Kutuzov, who accepts the order of the world and swims with the tides. War and Peace largely dispenses with clashes of motive, confrontation, and final judgment, moving instead through a series of sacramental moments—Andrei contemplating the infinite sky, the wolf hunt, Natasha and Nikolai at "Uncle's"—that reveals the oneness of the universe and the interconnectedness of all life.

Probably every writer with the ambition to embrace the whole of life has seen himself as emulating Tolstoi. Those whose subject is war owe him a special debt—a notable instance is Hemingway in A Farewell to Arms (1929). Tolstoi's fiction is the acme of realism; yet his fascination with processes of thought led to modernist experiments with stream of consciousness. Proust is a distant cousin. His influence in Russia has been more direct and powerful, especially in the Soviet period. Mikhail Sholokhov's Tikhii Don (1928–40; Quiet Flows the Don), Boris Pasternak's Doktor Zhivago (1957; Doctor Zhivago), and Aleksandr Solzhenitsyn's

Avgust chetyrnadtsatogo (1971; *August 1914*) are but three of many attempts to capture the national experience and define the national identity in Tolstoi's footsteps.

MILTON EHRE

See also Lev Tolstoi

Further Reading

Bayley, John, *Tolstoy and the Novel,* London: Chatto and Windus, 1966; New York: Viking Press, 1967

Berlin, Isaiah, *The Hedgehog and the Fox: An Essay on Tolstoy's View of History,* New York: Simon and Schuster, and London: Weidenfeld and Nicolson, 1953

Christian, Reginald Frank, *Tolstoy's "War and Peace": A Study,* Oxford: Clarendon Press, 1962

Eikhenbaum, Boris, *Tolstoi in the Sixties,* Ann Arbor, Michigan: Ardis, 1982

Knowles, A.V., editor, *Tolstoy: The Critical Heritage,* London and Boston: Routledge and Kegan Paul, 1978

Lubbock, Percy, *The Craft of Fiction,* New York: Scribner, and London: Cape, 1921; revised edition, New York: Peter Smith, 1947

Matlaw, Ralph, editor, *Tolstoy: A Collection of Critical Essays,* Englewood Cliffs, New Jersey: Prentice-Hall, 1967

Mirsky, D.S., *A History of Russian Literature: Comprising a History of Russian Literature and Contemporary Russian Literature,* New York: Knopf, and London: Routledge and Kegan Paul, 1949

Morson, Gary Saul, *Hidden in Plain View: Narrative and Creative Potentials in "War and Peace,"* Stanford, California: Stanford University Press, 1987; Aldershot: Scolar, 1988

Shklovskii, Viktor, *Material i stil' v romane Lva Tolstogo "Voina i mir,"* Moscow: Federatsiia, 1928

Steiner, George, *Tolstoy and Dostoevsky: An Essay in the Old Criticism,* New York: Knopf, 1959; 2nd edition, New Haven, Connecticut: Yale University Press, 1996

Wasiolek, Edward, *Tolstoy's Major Fiction,* Chicago: University of Chicago Press, 1978

War Novel

Representations of War in the Novel

War is one of the universals of human social experience, and a major war is the most important public event of its time. Accordingly, war is a central feature in much canonical literature. *The Iliad,* most of *The Aeneid,* and many sequences in the Old Testament tell stories of war. The plays of Shakespeare frequently involve battles, and even *Paradise Lost* (1667), ethereal and theological as it may be, features a war in heaven, complete with cannons, between the loyal and rebellious hosts of angels.

War has special attractions as a subject of narrative. Virtually all narratives are agonistic—they present scenes of struggle in which protagonists seek to overcome obstacles and opponents in order to gain some goal. War reduces the agonistic situation to stark simplicity: groups of men trying to kill each other. Conflict is concrete and literal, and action usually reaches decisive closure in victory or defeat. Emotions and social interactions are elemental and intense. Characters are moved by the terror of injury and death, murderous hostility toward their enemies, and desperate dependence on their comrades. Combat returns men to a more primal, instinctive condition, but war is also a highly organized social activity, and military life imposes mass discipline. Men are usually separated from women, placed in prolonged intimacy with one another, and rigidly organized in hierarchies of power. The individual is required to sacrifice his own safety for the needs of a social group, and he is also expected as a matter of duty to assault other human beings. War thus involves elemental issues in the relations between the individual and the larger social order.

It is possible to make a rough distinction between three basic structural principles in war novels: the objective, the subjective, and the social. Objective war novels take their dominant structural principle from the course of an action—a whole war or some more limited part of it. Subjective novels take their dominant structural principle not from a sequence of actions but rather from the moral and emotional experience of individuals. In novels governed by the social principle, objective events and psychological processes are subordinated to some larger social theme; the characters and events symbolize the larger social order or depict the effect of war on a society. These three principles are not mutually exclusive, and in some of the greatest war novels, such as Lev Tolstoi's *Voina i mir* (1863–69; *War and Peace*), all three principles are fully operative. As descriptive categories, the principles can nonetheless serve to identify the kinds of interest invoked by any given novel. War novels may be regarded as a subgenre of historical fiction, and of all fictional forms the objective novel is the closest to actual history. We can distinguish three specific forms: the panoramic novel, the novel focused on a single, well-defined action, and the novel of episodic combat.

The panorama is a form in which characters are located at strategic points for the purpose of offering a comprehensive survey of the major theatres of action and the major phases of the conflict. Several of the better-known novels of the American Civil War are panoramic: J.E. Cooke's *The Hammer and the Rapier* (1870), Evelyn Scott's *The Wave* (1929), Joseph Pennell's *The History of Rome Hanks* (1944), and Ben Ames Williams' *House*

Divided (1947). In *Saigon* (1982), Anthony Grey uses a group of characters to trace the developments of Vietnamese conflicts from the early decades of the 20th century through the withdrawal of American troops in 1973. In one form of the panorama, the characters are fictional, relatively minor participants in the war who serve to register its dramatic course or provide representative perspectives on it. Edith Pargeter's trilogy of World War II—*The Eighth Champion of Christendom* (1945), *Reluctant Odyssey* (1946), and *Warfare Accomplished* (1947)—follows this pattern. In another form, the panorama intermingles fictional characters with major historical figures. The most illustrious instance is *War and Peace*. Tolstoi's characters include Napoléon, the czar, and the Russian general Kutuzov. The main fictional characters are also involved in the major events of the war, including the battles of Austerlitz and Borodino, the occupation and burning of Moscow, and the disastrous French retreat. In *The Winds of War* (1971) and *War and Remembrance* (1978), Herman Wouk uses the members of a military family, connected with historical figures, as a nexus for depicting the worldwide theatre of World War II.

The interweaving of fictional and real characters also may be used in battle novels and in novels that take their main structure not from the historical sequence of events, but from the more narrowly focused moral and emotional concerns of the participants. In *The Killer Angels* (1974), one of the finest of all battle novels, Michael Shaara uses a wide array of characters, some fictional and some historical, to re-create the Battle of Gettysburg. Each character is fully individualized, and the thoughts of each, as he responds to events and makes decisions, both delineate the course of the battle and convey a sense of its human dimensions. In her trilogy about World War I, *Regeneration* (1991), *The Eye in the Door* (1993), and *The Ghost Road* (1995), Pat Barker interweaves historical and fictional characters, including the poet and novelist Siegfried Sassoon, for the purpose of evoking a sense of moral and emotional ambivalence among the soldiers.

The panorama has close affinities with a perennial form of popular fiction, the historical romance. The two can be distinguished by identifying historical romance as a type of personal drama that uses war as a setting but that is not primarily concerned with the war as a subject. The motivating concerns are the common problems of romance and social station. Instances of historical romance include James Fenimore Cooper's *The Last of the Mohicans* (1826), a love story that takes place during the French and Indian Wars; William Makepeace Thackeray's *The Luck of Barry Lyndon* (1853), which includes sequences from the Seven Years' War; James Boyd's *Drums* (1925), set against the American Revolutionary War, and *Marching On* (1927), which has the American Civil War as a backdrop; and Ernest Hemingway's *A Farewell to Arms* (1929), Susan Hill's *Strange Meeting* (1971), and Sebastian Faulks' *Birdsong* (1993), all three about World War I.

Several important novels occupy the borderline between the historical romance, the panorama, and the novel of social impact. *War and Peace* is seriously attentive to the social significance of Napoléon's invasion of Russia, but the central motivating concerns of the main fictional characters are more moral and romantic than military and historical. Ford Madox Ford's tetralogy *Parade's End* (1924–28), about World War I, and Evelyn Waugh's trilogy *Sword of Honour* (1952–61), about World War II, both situate their wars within longer narrative spans that center on romantic, domestic, and social entanglements. In Margaret Mitchell's *Gone with the Wind* (1936), the characters operate at the level of historical romance, but the novel also depicts the socioeconomic and cultural changes wrought by the war. Robert Penn Warren's *Band of Angels* (1955) depicts the effects of the Civil War on the American South and explores racial conflicts through sexual and domestic complications. In *Tikhii Don* (1928–40; *Quiet Flows the Don*), Mikhail Sholokhov embeds World War I within a larger historical narrative that includes both the romantic intrigues of individuals and the mass struggles of a political revolution.

Narratives that take their shape from a single, well-defined action include, in addition to Shaara's *The Killer Angels*, Upton Sinclair's *Manassas* (1904) MacKinlay Kantor's *Long Remember* (1934; about Gettysburg), Shelby Foote's *Shiloh* (1952), Jules Romains' *Prelude to Verdun* (1938), James Jones' *The Thin Red Line* (1962; about Guadalcanal), and John Del Vecchio's *The Thirteenth Valley* (1981; a Vietnam operation). Novels limited to a single action can of course have other dominant concerns and structural principles. Stephen Crane's *The Red Badge of Courage* (1894) is less concerned with the Battle of Chancellorsville than with the thoughts and sensations of a boy fighting in it. Norman Mailer's *The Naked and the Dead* (1948) limits its action to the campaign to take a single island in the Pacific during World War II, but the main structure of meaning in the novel derives not from the action itself but from the symbolic patterning of moral and ideological relations among the characters.

In stories about World War I and Vietnam, single, well-defined actions are far less common than tales that involve a ragged series of engagements—in Vietnam sporadic ambushes and firefights, and in World War I raids or episodes within larger actions such as the First Battle of the Somme, which lasted for months, involved millions of combatants, had no distinct structure of action, and accomplished nothing. From World War I, signal depictions of diffuse combat include Henri Barbusse's *Le Feu: Journal d'une escouade* (1916; *Under Fire: The Story of a Squad*), Roland Dorgelès' *Les Croix de bois* (1919; *Wooden Crosses*), Thomas Boyd's *Through the Wheat* (1923), Erich Maria Remarque's *Im Westen nichts Neues* (1929; *All Quiet on the Western Front*), and Frederic Manning's *The Middle Parts of Fortune: Somme and Ancre, 1916* (1929). Novels of Vietnam that have particular merit in registering the quality of combat action include James Crumley's *One to Count Cadence* (1969), William Pelfrey's *The Big V* (1972), Larry Heinemann's *Close Quarters* (1977), Steven Phillip Smith's *American Boys* (1975), James Webb's *Fields of Fire* (1978), Gustav Hasford's *The Short Timers* (1979), and Charles Nelson's *The Boy Who Picked the Bullets Up* (1981).

Novels that take the emotional and moral experience of individuals as a dominant structural principle adopt a wide range of stances toward the experience of war, and the best of them tend to evoke a complex and often confused mixture of feelings: fear, anger, resentment, self-pity, guilt, horror, pride, and the exaltation of combat. *All Quiet on the Western Front* offers a classic instance. In the prologue, Remarque declares that the novel is "neither an accusation, nor a confession, and least of all an adventure." It is rather a story of men who "were destroyed by the war." In reality, it is all four of these things. Like many war novels, it expresses bitter resentment at the victimization of the soldiers, shame at their moral degradation, fascination with the artificial primitivism of their conditions, admiration for their courage and skill, and a deep love for their comradeship.

War can be a proving ground, providing the context for a story about coming of age, or alternatively, it can be an occasion for disillusionment and alienation. Some of the best war novels written for a youthful audience take the form of the Bildungsroman: Esther Forbes' *Johnny Tremain* (1943), Keith Harold's *Rifles for Watie* (1957), and Irene Hunt's *Across Five Aprils* (1964). Novels for adults that take this form include *The Red Badge of Courage*, Herman Wouk's *The Caine Mutiny* (1951), and Del Vecchio's *The Thirteenth Valley*. The majority of novels from World War I and Vietnam take as their themes the disillusionment and alienation brought about by war.

In one common form, the novel of accusation depicts situations in which the incompetence, heedless ambition, or inhumanity of officers endanger their men or bring about military disasters. Examples include Henry Morford's *The Coward* (1864), Fritz Unruh's *Opfergang* (1919; *The Way of Sacrifice*), Arnold Zweig's *Der Streit um den Sergeanten Grischa* (1928; *The Case of Sergeant Grischa*), Humphrey Cobb's *Paths of Glory* (1935), Wouk's *The Caine Mutiny*, Joseph Heller's *Catch-22* (1961), Jennifer Johnston's *How Many Miles to Babylon?* (1974), and Winston Groom's *Better Times Than These* (1978). In another form, accusation directs attention to the condition of civilians victimized by war. Kurt Vonnegut's *Slaughterhouse Five* (1969) records the bombing of Dresden, and John Hersey's *Hiroshima* (1946) graphically describes the effects of a nuclear explosion. Many novels of Vietnam feature scenes in which soldiers brutalize civilians—scenes evidently deriving from firsthand observation—and for most writers these experiences appear to have produced lasting sensations of moral nausea.

One distinct line of war novels concentrates attention on soldiers who have been irreparably damaged by war. William Faulkner's *Soldiers' Pay* (1926) describes the homecoming of a dying, brain-damaged soldier. The main character in Dalton Trumbo's *Johnny Got His Gun* (1939) has lost his arms and legs, his sight, his hearing, and his power of speech. The title character in Larry Heinemann's *Paco's Story* (1987) lives with chronic severe pain, muted by constant sedation, and the two central characters in Larry Brown's *Dirty Work* (1989) lie in adjacent hospital beds, one without a face and the other without arms and legs. Heinemann's Paco combines the physical pain of catastrophic wounds with the mental suffering occasioned by his memory of participating in a scene of rape and murder. In *Paco's Story,* as in many novels, the story of victimization thus blends insensibly into a story of confession. Other novels depicting moral degradation include Hersey's *The War Lover* (1959), T. Jeff Williams' *The Glory Hole* (1977), Dominic Certo's *The Valor of Francesco D'Amini* (1979), Smith's *American Boys,* and Barker's *The Eye in the Door.* In *The Young Lions* (1948), Irwin Shaw uses the form of the Bildungsroman for his American protagonists and consigns his German protagonist to moral degradation.

The experience of disillusionment and degradation has a sequel in stories of desertion or mutiny. Two of Dos Passos' soldiers in *Three Soldiers* (1921) desert. The protagonist of *A Farewell to Arms* says good-bye to all that. Siegfried Sassoon's experiences in World War I, fictionally rendered in *The Complete Memoirs of George Sherston* (1937), lead from martial enthusiasm to disillusionment and open revolt. William Faulkner's *A Fable* (1954) turns a soldier's conscientious refusal to fight into an elaborate allegory of the crucifixion and resurrection of Christ. *Catch-22* culminates in desertion, and among Vietnam novels desertion is a main theme in Victor Kolpacoff's *The Prisoners of Quai Dong* (1967), George Davis' *Coming Home* (1971), and Tim O'Brien's *Going After Cacciato* (1978).

Admiration for military valor is common in novels of war, even when this admiration is combined with resentment, selfpity, and guilt. Like many characters who have experienced combat, the protagonist of Hemingway's *A Farewell to Arms* repudiates the abstractions of heroic rhetoric, but *For Whom the Bell Tolls* (1940), about the Spanish Civil War, culminates in a quietly heroic act, as the protagonist sacrifices himself for a cause in which he believes. *The Red Badge of Courage,* after all the peripeties of cowardice and pretense, concludes in a triumphal affirmation of the protagonist's courage. In *Miss Ravenel's Conversion from Secession to Loyalty* (1867), a realist novel about the American Civil War, John William DeForest expresses overt contempt for cowardice in battle. In *The Killer Angels,* Shaara conveys the heroic courage of both sides at Gettysburg, and in *Shiloh,* as in his monumental history of the Civil War, Shelby Foote makes valor a central theme. Adrien Bertrand's *L'Appel du sol* (1916; *The Call of the Soil*) invokes the rhetoric of patriotism and heroism for World War I. Harry Brown's *A Walk in the Sun* (1944), about a minor action during World War II, concludes in a lyric evocation of grace under fire, and Leon Uris' *Battle Cry* (1953) is suffused with the esprit de corps of the United States Marines. Wouk's panoramas of World War II sound the themes of patriotism and heroic sacrifice, and in *The Bridges at Toko-Ri* (1953), James A. Michener takes a similar perspective on the Korean War. In *Das Boot* (1973; *The Boat*), Lothar-Günther Buchheim celebrates the valor of a German submarine crew during World War II, and in *Die verratene Armee* (1957; *The Forsaken Army*), Heinrich Gerlach pays homage to the determination of German soldiers at Stalingrad. Even among the novels of Vietnam—a war in which disaffection and the sense of futility loom very large—military pride is seldom wholly absent. David Halberstam's *One Very Hot Day* (1967), Pelfrey's *The Big V*, Webb's *Fields of Fire,* and Del Vecchio's *The Thirteenth Valley* all take the soldierly ethos as a dominant norm.

Among novels that take social order as their governing theme, a few are primarily concerned with the military as a society. James Jones' *From Here to Eternity* (1951) presents the community of enlisted men in the peacetime army as a relatively selfcontained social order, and Nicholas Proffitt's *Gardens of Stone* (1983) treats a similar subject during the Vietnam era. James Gould Cozzens' *Guard of Honor* (1948) concerns itself with the political and personal interaction among Army Air Corps officers during World War II. The same subject is treated satirically and with comic genius in Heller's *Catch-22.*

Many war novels use war to symbolize aspects of the larger social order. Ford in *Parade's End* and Waugh in *Sword of Honour* use their wars as touchstones for the degeneration of an ideal of honor among the governing classes. Dos Passos in *Three Soldiers* and D.H. Lawrence in *Lady Chatterley's Lover* (1928) both treat World War I as a manifestation of the dehumanizing mechanization of modern industrial society. In *Kaputt* (1944), Curzio Malaparte regards the cataclysmic disruption of World

War II as a reflex of cultural anarchy. Heller's *Catch-22* represents the army as a continuation of civilian life, with all its greed, ambition, ideological intimidation, and bureaucratic tyranny. In *The Naked and the Dead*, Mailer arranges his characters, in parallel order among enlisted men and officers, to symbolize the political tensions in American society. In *Dog Soldiers* (1974), Robert Stone superimposes the moral chaos of Vietnam and the underworld of American civilian life.

American war novels often use squads and platoons to represent a cross section of American society, with representative figures from different classes, regions, ethnic groups, and (in Vietnam) different races. Dos Passos' *Three Soldiers,* Heller's *Catch-22,* Mailer's *The Naked and the Dead,* Webb's *Fields of Fire,* and Del Vecchio's *The Thirteenth Valley* all employ this device. In William March's *Company K* (1933), all 113 members of an infantry company give brief, first-person narratives of their experiences during World War I, sometimes about the same events. Such a technique is similar to that of the panorama but is directed less toward delineating the shape of an action than toward displaying the multiplicity of possible perspectives within a shared set of circumstances.

Commentary on war novels has focused on the problems of style, figurative structure, literary relations (genres, movements, and traditions), and ethical and social stance. The central problem of style is that of finding a language appropriate to experiences usually conceived as monstrous and horrific. Straightforward, objective narration fails to evoke the emotional intensity and moral complexity of war experiences. Language that is too abstract and rhetorical, or too ornate and poetic, draws away from the sense of a raw, elemental reality that is basic to the experience of war. Figurative structure involves such matters as point of view, the interplay between individual experience and large-scale action, the relationship between realism and symbolism, and the analysis of tone. Many war novels are written in a basic realist mode, but some, like *Catch-22* and *Going After Cacciato,* employ complex narrative structures that invite close critical analysis. Studies of literary relations sometimes situate war novels within larger movements of literary history— for instance, the novels of World War I within the movements of naturalism and modernism. Some studies consider the way in which previous literary models shape the expectations of writers, provide ironic foils for them, or have to be adapted by them. For instance, commentators on Vietnam novels often consider these novels in relation to works by predecessors such as Hemingway, Mailer, Jones, and Heller. Critics also concern themselves with the relationships between war novels and contiguous genres such as history, journalism, autobiography, poetry, and film. Many critics of war novels, while paying some attention to problems of style, form, and literary relations, are preoccupied with ethical and social concerns. The majority of contemporary critics categorically disapprove of war. They tend both to emphasize the element of protest in war novels and to give this element a predominating place in their judgments of literary merit. For re-

viewers and common readers, the question of ideological stance has often been subsumed within more elementary considerations of imaginative power.

JOSEPH CARROLL

See also Adventure Novel and Imperial Romance

Further Reading

Aaron, Daniel, *The Unwritten War: American Writers and the Civil War,* New York: Knopf, 1973; London: Oxford University Press, 1975

Aldridge, John W., *After the Lost Generation: A Critical Study of the Writers of Two Wars,* New York: McGraw-Hill, 1951; London: Vision Press, 1959

Beidler, Philip D., *American Literature and the Experience of Vietnam,* Athens: University of Georgia Press, 1982

Benson, Frederick R., *Writers in Arms: The Literary Impact of the Spanish Civil War,* New York: New York University Press, 1967; London: University of London Press, 1968

Cooperman, Stanley, *World War One and the American Novel,* Baltimore: Johns Hopkins University Press, 1967

Cruickshank, John, *Variations on Catastrophe: Some French Responses to the Great War,* Oxford: Clarendon Press, and New York: Oxford University Press, 1982

Fussell, Paul, *The Great War and Modern Memory,* New York and London: Oxford University Press, 1975

Gilman, Owen W., Jr., and Lorrie Smith, editors, *America Rediscovered: Critical Essays on Literature and Film of the Vietnam War,* New York and London: Garland, 1990

Hager, Philip E., and Desmond Taylor, *The Novels of World War I: An Annotated Bibliography,* New York: Garland, 1981

Jones, Peter G., *War and the Novelist: Appraising the American War Novel,* Columbia: University of Missouri Press, 1976

Klein, Holger, editor, *The First World War in Fiction: A Collection of Critical Essays,* London: Macmillan, and New York: Barnes and Noble, 1976

Klein, Holger, with J.E. Flower and Eric Homberger, editors, *The Second World War in Fiction,* London: Macmillan, 1984

Lively, Robert A., *Fiction Fights the Civil War: An Unfinished Chapter in the Literary History of the American People,* Chapel Hill: University of North Carolina Press, 1957

Miller, Wayne Charles, *An Armed America: Its Face in Fiction: A History of the American Military Novel,* New York: New York University Press, and London: University of London Press, 1970

Newman, John, et al., *Vietnam War Literature: An Annotated Bibliography of Imaginative Works about Americans Fighting in Vietnam,* 3rd edition, Lanham, Maryland, and London: Scarecrow Press, 1996

Taylor, Desmond, *The Novels of World War II: An Annotated Bibliography,* New York and London: Garland, 1993

The War of the End of the World by Mario Vargas Llosa

La guerra del fin del mundo 1981

The War of the End of the World is a fictionalized account of a real historical event—the late 19th-century revolt of a religious cult in the town of Canudos against the Brazilian government and the resultant brutal response of the ruling authorities. The book recalls the great historical novels of the 19th century, such as Tolstoi's *Voina i mir* (1863–69; *War and Peace*). Indeed, as Michael Valdez Moses argues, *The War of the End of the World* may be usefully read through the perspective of Georg Lukács' discussions of the historical novel, especially in the way Vargas Llosa's text builds upon real historical events and attempts to present a sweeping view of the totality of Brazilian society at the time of these events (see Moses, 1995). There are, however, important differences between *The War of the End of the World* and the historical novels of Tolstoi, Walter Scott, and the other writers admired by Lukács. For one thing, the rebellion depicted by Vargas Llosa is not part of any sweeping historical transformation. For another, its failure to effect lasting change is reflected in the way Vargas Llosa presents the rebellion in Canudos not just as a predecessor to the various rebellions still underway in Latin America but in fact as a sort of allegorical stand-in for contemporary rebellions such as that conducted by Peru's *Sendero luminoso*.

The War of the End of the World lacks any obvious examples of the irony, parody, and reflexivity that mark many of Vargas Llosa's earlier novels. In fact, Vargas Llosa seems to aspire to a straightforward retelling of the events in such a way that technique will be transparent and not interfere with the story. However, the apparently conventional realism of the novel may be somewhat deceiving. Vargas Llosa's book is not directly based on the real historical events it describes, but on the account of those events published by Euclides da Cunha as *Os sertões* in 1902, available in English translation as *Rebellion in the Backlands* (1944). The resulting intertextual dialogue is of particular interest because da Cunha and his book occupy such a prominent position in the history of Brazilian letters, not to mention the fact that one of the main figures in Vargas Llosa's book is a "nearsighted journalist," loosely based on da Cunha, who observes many of the events in Canudos, later to write about them. This direct depiction of the writer in confrontation with reality acts in conjunction with the dialogue between Vargas Llosa and da Cunha to raise important questions concerning authorship and the relationship between history as the unfolding of events and history as the narrative inscription of those events.

Vargas Llosa relies quite directly on *Rebellion in the Backlands* as a source, and the character in the novel who most closely represents Vargas Llosa's own point of view is the journalist based on da Cunha. Almost the entire second half of *The War of the End of the World* comes to us through this reporter's accounts of the events, which are presumably valuable because the reporter was in Canudos with the rebels during the final siege and is one of the few surviving eyewitnesses of the last days of the rebellion. On the other hand, his observations are called into question by the fact that he is virtually blind without his glasses, which are destroyed during his trip to Canudos. The reporter's "eyewitness" accounts thus raise questions concerning the relia-

bility of historical records. Vargas Llosa supplements da Cunha's account with numerous insertions of his own, including graphic and horrifying accounts of the massacre that ends the Canudos revolt. In addition, Vargas Llosa introduces entirely new elements into his text. For example, where da Cunha merely mentions rumors that the Canudos rebellion may have involved a collaboration with foreign anti-Republican elements, Vargas Llosa dramatizes these rumors with the fictional story of Galileo Gall, a Scottish revolutionary anarchist who happens to be in Brazil at the time of the rebellion. Gall's presence gives the Republican newspaper editor Epaminondas Gonçalves an opportunity to manufacture "evidence" of a pro-monarchist conspiracy by claiming that Gall is a British agent sent to stir the rebellion. Gall is in fact anything but a British agent, but he himself contributes to the conspiracy theory with his avowed sympathy for the rebels, a sympathy that arises because his fanatical dedication to revolutionary ideals blinds him to the real nature of what is going on at Canudos. Indeed, Vargas Llosa carefully parallels the story of Gall with that of the religious fanaticism of the Canudos rebels as part of a rejection of fanaticism of all kinds.

All of the various fanatics depicted in the book have in common an unwavering belief that their vision of the world is correct and a faith that their views will ultimately win out in the establishment of a utopian paradise. Implicated in this portrayal of fanaticism are almost all of the great utopian metanarratives of the Western tradition, whether they involve the traditional Christian faith in ultimate salvation, the Marxist belief in the establishment of an ideal communism, or the Enlightenment faith in the power of science and reason to understand and control nature. The novel suggests that all of these worldviews are based on the Christian apocalyptic paradigm, a paradigm that authorizes its believers to commit any and all atrocities in the march toward the promised paradise. The novel's scepticism toward the possibility of positive radical social and political change identifies *The War of the End of the World* as a document of Vargas Llosa's increasing political conservatism. Its scepticism toward the reliability of narrative *per se* marks it as a work of postmodernism.

M. KEITH BOOKER

See also Mario Vargas Llosa

Further Reading

Beals, Carleton, "Latin American Literature," in *The Writer in a Changing World,* edited by Henry Hart, New York: Equinox Press, and London: Lawrence and Wishart, 1937

Booker, M. Keith, *Vargas Llosa among the Postmodernists,* Gainesville: University Press of Florida, 1994

Cunha, Euclides da, *Rebellion in the Backlands,* Chicago: University of Chicago Press, 1944

Lukács, Georg, *A történelmi regény,* Budapest: Hungaria, 1937; as *The Historical Novel,* London: Merlin Press, 1962; New York: Humanities Press, 1965

MacAdam, Alfred J., "Mario Vargas Llosa and Euclides da Cunha: Some Problems of Intertextuality," in *Proceedings of the Tenth Congress of the International Comparative*

Literature Association, Volume III: Inter-American Literary Relations, edited by M.J. Valdés, New York: Garland, 1985

Moses, Michael Valdez, *The Novel and the Globalization of Culture,* New York: Oxford University Press, 1995

Wasserman, Renata R. Mautner, "Mario Vargas Llosa, Euclides da Cunha, and the Strategy of Intertextuality," *PMLA* 108:3 (1993)

Williams, Raymond L., *Mario Vargas Llosa,* New York: Ungar, 1986

Zamora, Lois Parkinson, *Writing the Apocalypse: Historical Vision in Contemporary U.S. and Latin American Fiction,* New York and Cambridge: Cambridge University Press, 1989

Warden. *See* Barsetshire Novels

Water Margin. *See* Six Classic Chinese Novels

Waverley by Sir Walter Scott

1814

Walter Scott's *Waverley; or, 'Tis Sixty Years Since* is important to the history of the novel less for its own merit than as the first, pattern-setting work in the series known collectively as the Waverley novels, arguably the most influential novel series in world literature. The series was a best-selling publishing phenomenon in Britain in its own time, showing the ideological power and literary potential of this popular but hitherto disregarded literary genre. More important, the characteristics of the Waverley novels were imitated and appropriated by writers in many countries for the purpose of constructing romantic nationalism, or what Benedict Anderson calls the "imagined community" of the modern nation-state (*Imagined Communities,* 1983, expanded 1991). Finally, to a Marxist critic like Georg Lukács (1937), the Waverley novels founded the historical novel that embodied and disseminated the ideology of the bourgeoisie as a world-historical revolutionary class.

Waverley and the Waverley novels had diverse sources. One source was Enlightenment "philosophical history," or historiography, presenting a critique of the premodern customary economy and social structure of the *anciens régimes.* Another source was literary romance, from medieval and Renaissance chivalric romances through 18th-century novels of adventure, picaresque novels, satirical anti-romance, and Gothic novels. A third source included historical romances of the late 18th and early 19th centuries, pioneered by women novelists, from Harriet and Sophia Lee to Sydney Owenson (Lady Morgan), from Clara Reeve to Maria Edgeworth. Scott acknowledged some of these predecessors; others he did not. Finally, the Waverley novels were informed by Scott's knowledge of plebeian culture, especially ballads, folktales, "folksay" (or proverbial lore), and traditional chapbook tales. Scott combined elements of these sources first in his best-selling historical narrative poems; he then turned to the novel as an even better way to reach the reading public with his vision of what Britain and its empire should become in the aftermath of the French Revolution and Napoleonic Wars.

This vision is fully represented in *Waverley,* although less powerfully and artistically than in some other Waverley novels. In devising his formal method, Scott was keenly aware that the novel had been deployed politically during and after the revolutionary 1790s, and that certain formal devices had become associated with particular political positions. For example, *Waverley* uses omniscient third-person narration, as do almost all the Waverley novels. During the French Revolution debate in Britain, first-person confessional narration, especially in stories of victimization by the established social and political order, had become a favorite device of novelists with pro-revolutionary sympathies. Third-person narration had become associated with counter-revolutionary novelists, for whom this authoritative form represented their politics of social and political authority, if not authoritarianism. Scott's narrator resembles the Enlightenment philosophical historian, relating events from a position of transhistorical wisdom, implying that the individual, like the individual fictional character, only partly understands the momentous historical processes in which he is caught up and which he can do little to influence. It is the implied consciousness of the narrator, with whom the reader is meant to identify, who has the knowledge necessary to understand the past, and thus also the present and future.

The narrator constructs the novel's setting as a plausible, if not completely factual, version of a past place and time. This approach involves much description. Scott did not originate the romantic description novel, which was largely the work of the Gothic novelist Ann Radcliffe. Radcliffe mainly uses description of place, especially landscape, to represent the subjective response of her protagonist. Scott uses a wider range of description, including society, politics, costume, furniture, customs, and topography, to establish the narrator's authority on the past and thus, implicitly, on the past's implications for the present. He uses landscape description to exemplify the Enlightenment principle that natural environment forms individual and national character, for better and worse. So powerful are Scott's representations of Scotland, in particular, that many claim Scott to have invented the modern image of Scotland and its tourist industry.

Temporal historical setting as employed by Scott, and by earlier novelists and historical dramatists, is designed less for its own sake than as an analogy for the present depicted in the novel. Scott chooses a variety of moments of collision and conflict in the long historical "progress," as envisaged by Enlightenment philosophical historians, from barbarism to civil society. In *Waverley,* the Scottish Highlands represent the past, while the Lowlands and England represent the future. Scott uses historical setting as an analogy to the post-revolutionary, post-Napoleonic condition of Britain and Europe. In *Waverley,* the moment is the Jacobite rebellion of 1745—the last gesture of a feudal, customary, and regionalist society against modernization and the rise of civil and commercial society in the composite state of Great Britain under the Hanoverian government. Throughout the Waverley novels Scott turned to other similarly instructive moments from the past.

Setting was an aspect of major innovation by Scott; his use of plot and character was less so. In 18th-century novels of manners, minor characters provide a cross section of society and are presented through authoritative description and dialogue that is often idiolect and sociolect. With Scott's use of a standardized form of Scottish dialect for certain characters, he pioneered a major technique in the social historical novel of "imagined community." Scott's minor characters provide the social and historical context for the protagonist's progress. Scott's protagonists all resemble Edward Waverley in being immature young men (occasionally a young woman, such as Jeanie Deans in *Heart of Mid-Lothian,* 1818) who embark on a journey of experience and enlightenment, from youth to adulthood, from the domestic to the wider public sphere, returning wiser but sadder.

This journey is the classic pattern of romance. Whereas earlier, chivalric romance represented the testing of aristocratic values and culture, Scott's version of romance, like that of his contemporaries and immediate predecessors, represents the testing of middle-class values: moral self-restraint, appropriate knowledge and intellectual judgment, and ethical consistency. The test occurs in a world of conflict dominated by what are shown to be outmoded, if still glamorous, aristocratic practices on the one hand (Prince Charles and Fergus Mac-Ivor) and, on the other hand, dangerous and unpredictable plebeian practices (the Highlanders). In representing this journey, however, Scott invokes a tradition of anti-romance originated by Miguel de Cervantes' *Don Quixote* (1605–15) but used widely in the 1790s and early 1800s to discredit revolutionary enthusiasm as seductively and dangerously romantic. Thus, Edward Waverley's youthful reading in chivalric romance makes him vulnerable to seduction by the aristocratic and plebeian Jacobite cause in the Jacobite rebellion, represented by the fictional characters of the courtly Mac-Ivor and his sister Flora and their colorful but murderous Highland retainers, and led by the glamorous historical figure of "Bonnie Prince Charlie." Waverley is shocked by the reality of warfare and political violence, however, and enlightened to the futility of the Jacobite resistance to Hanoverian order in Britain. In the end, Waverley settles down in his new home of Tully-Veolan with the unglamorous but feminine and domestic Rose Bradwardine; their marriage anticipates the blending of English and Scottish identities into a new British identity.

This myth, ostensibly based on historical fact and promising national harmony after a generation of revolution and global warfare, was precisely what many Britons wanted to read in 1814 and, as it turned out, in other variations by Scott and his successors and imitators for many decades to come.

GARY KELLY

See also Sir Walter Scott

Further Reading

Brown, David, *Walter Scott and the Historical Imagination,* London and Boston: Routledge and Kegan Paul, 1979

Cottom, Daniel, *The Civilized Imagination: A Study of Ann Radcliffe, Jane Austen, and Sir Walter Scott,* Cambridge and New York: Cambridge University Press, 1985

Crawford, Thomas, *Scott,* Edinburgh: Scottish Academic Press, 1982

Fleishman, Avrom, *The English Historical Novel: Walter Scott to Virginia Woolf,* Baltimore and London: Johns Hopkins University Press, 1971

Lukács, Georg, *A történelmi regény,* Budapest: Hungaria, 1937; as *The Historical Novel,* London: Merlin Press, 1962; New York: Humanities Press, 1965

Millgate, Jane, *Walter Scott: The Making of the Novelist,* Edinburgh: Edinburgh University Press, and Toronto: University of Toronto Press, 1984

Wilt, Judith, *Secret Leaves: The Novels of Walter Scott,* Chicago: University of Chicago Press, 1985

We by Evgenii Zamiatin

My 1924

We is Evgenii Zamiatin's only completed novel, and its controversial nature with regard to the incipient, ideologically sensitive Soviet state caused it to undergo a bizarre publishing history. Written in 1920, it was immediately considered to be a malicious pamphlet on Soviet society; consequently its first publication came in an English translation (New York, 1924). An unauthorized and bastardized Russian version (with which Zamiatin was not involved, although this did not save him from severe tribulations, leading to his emigration to Paris in 1931) appeared in Prague in 1927. It was not until 1952, 15 years after Zamiatin's death, that a genuine Russian edition of the novel appeared (once again published in New York). *We* remained banned, and indeed virtually unmentionable, in Soviet Russia until 1988, well into the Gorbachev era of *glasnost'*.

In addition to being the author of *We*, Zamiatin is well known as a story writer and a literary essayist. His essays, written shortly after the Russian Revolution, first collected as *Litsa* (1955) and translated as *A Soviet Heretic* (1970), form a programmatic statement for his own fiction, and for the hoped-for direction of Russian literature; as well, they serve as a warning of the dangers he foresaw for Soviet culture. Since before the Revolution, he had been developing an innovative "neorealist" style in his prose fiction: this involved the use of grotesque elements, distortive imagery, satire, primitivism, distinctive methods of characterization, ellipsis, and other striking linguistic effects. He predicted and advocated this development as a dialectical synthesis of what had been the two dominant literary trends of the early part of the century—symbolism and naturalism—in an ongoing process that would superimpose the stylistic flights and imagery of the one onto the materialist base of the other. In his stories, such as "Mamai" (Mamay) and "Peshchera" (The Cave), he employed systems of imagery that tended almost to dominate the entire narrative. Zamiatin used such systems to similar effect in his novel *We*.

Although Zamiatin remained a confirmed revolutionary, having been a Bolshevik activist in his youth, his dialectical system quickly led him to question the direction taken by the Russian Revolution. This critical standpoint also sprang from his philosophy of heresy (best seen, perhaps, as a kind of renegade Marxism), which held that there must always be a "voice in the wilderness" inveighing against the status quo in order to continue the dialectical progression of history: today's truth inevitably becomes tomorrow's fallacy. Zamiatin the subversive recognized no final revolution, just as Zamiatin the mathematician could recognize no final number: he discerned a cosmic struggle between energy and entropy. Zamiatin therefore opposed the reification of any established system, not least one initiated through revolutionary change. Stagnation and philistinism remained his eternal foes. These views, expressed in a number of pungent works, were on especially prominent display in his futuristic novel. He soon aroused the antipathy of the new Soviet cultural overlords and was removed from Soviet life, and literature, as an "internal émigré" before spending the last six years of his life in France.

We, set in the 30th century, depicts an apparently unsuccessful uprising against a totalitarian, glass-enclosed city-state, ruthlessly ruled over by "the Benefactor" and his secret police, the "Guardians," who administer the "Tables of Daily Commandment." Built on extreme rationalist and collectivist principles, "The Single [or One] State," which treats its populace as mere organized "numbers," decides to eradicate all remaining individuality by a compulsory operation of "fantasiectomy," which would remove the imagination. At the same time, a spaceship named the "Integral" is designed to spread the state's gospel to neighboring worlds. Nevertheless, even this highly regulated society is still far from stable. Narrated in diary form by a key mathematician called (in licence-plate style) D–503, who develops doubts during the course of his own narrative, *We* displays Zamiatin's innovative techniques to mature effect, using systems of imagery built on mathematical terminology and color symbolism. The novel also provides an imaginative psychological analysis of a distant, dystopian society.

We looks backward for inspiration to the stylistic methods of Andrei Belyi, to the irrational philosophizing of Dostoevskii, and to the science-fiction projections of Zamiatin's favorite English author, H.G. Wells. At the same time, it may be seen as the first in a series of innovative, modernist anti-utopian European fictions. Its assumed influence on Huxley's *Brave New World* (1932) is probably erroneous; however, George Orwell did acknowledge its impact, via a French translation, on his *Nineteen-Eighty-Four* (1949). Parallels may also be drawn with near-contemporaneous speculative works by Karel Čapek and Georg Kaiser and with Fritz Lang's film *Metropolis* (1926). *We* may be read as a prophetic warning against tyranny of all types; as a strikingly innovative and advanced work of science fiction; and as a penetrating analysis of alienation and schizophrenia (Christopher Collins [1973] brings to bear on *We* a Jungian methodology). Edith W. Clowes (1996) has proclaimed it a confrontation of discourses: between the technological, the philosophical, and the poetic. The concept of "fantasiectomy" and Zamiatin's creed of heresy resonate anew today in the light of the Rushdie affair.

We has long been recognized in the West as a masterpiece of European innovative fiction. Zamiatin was a leading representative of Russian modernism, a prominent organizational figure in early Soviet culture, and an important mentor to the prose writers of the 1920s. Only in the last decade, however, has his influence begun to be rediscovered in Russia itself.

NEIL CORNWELL

Further Reading

Barratt, Andrew, "Revolution as Collusion: The Heretic and the Slave in Zamyatin's *My*," *Slavonic and East European Review* 62 (1984)

Barratt, Andrew, "The X-Factor in Zamyatin's *We*," *Modern Language Review* 80 (1985)

Clowes, Edith W., "Zamiatin's 'Experiment in Literary-Philosophical Synthesis'," in *After the Watershed: Russian*

Prose 1917–1992: Selected Essays, edited by N.J.L. Luker, Nottingham: Astra Press, 1996

Collins, Christopher, *Evgenij Zamjatin: An Interpretive Study*, The Hague: Mouton, 1973

Edwards, T.R.N., *Three Russian Writers and the Irrational: Zamyatin, Pil'nyak, and Bulgakov*, Cambridge and New York: Cambridge University Press, 1982

Hoyles, John, *The Literary Underground: Writers and the Totalitarian Experience, 1900–1950*, London: Harvester Wheatsheaf, 1990; New York: St. Martin's Press, 1991

Kern, Gary, editor, *Zamyatin's "We": A Collection of Critical Essays*, Ann Arbor, Michigan: Ardis, 1988

Russell, Robert, *Zamiatin's "We,"* London: Bristol Classical Press, 1998

Shane, Alex M., *The Life and Works of Evgenii Zamjatin*, Berkeley: University of California Press, 1968

Sicher, Efraim, "The Last Utopia: Entropy and Revolution in the Poetics of Evgeny Zamjatin," *History of European Ideas* 13 (1991)

Wei cheng. *See* Fortress Besieged

H.G. Wells 1866–1946

English

H.G. Wells published more than 100 works during his lifetime. Considered by many to be the inventor of science fiction, he was a polymath, a creator of utopian visions, a writer of social comedies and discussion novels, and an influential thinker. He became known in the 1890s through his literary and scientific journalistic writings, culminating in the brilliant achievement of *The Time Machine* (1895).

Wells built into his early fictions an analytic account of fin-de-siècle unease together with an ambivalent attitude toward science that runs through his entire oeuvre. His evolutionary preoccupations—he had studied under Huxley and Tindale—made him pessimistic about the future. Yet he was a man of immense energy and imaginative inventiveness and a lover of life. These seemingly contradictory aspects of his personality contributed to the creative tension of his best works. He worked for social change and world peace, joining the Fabians in 1903 and publishing articles and pamphlets advocating a league of nations. *The Outline of History* (1920) was the culmination of this phase of his career. This best-seller was followed by "outlines" of biology and economics.

The Time Machine is, on one level, an adventure story. The Time Traveler, having invented a machine that will enable him to travel into the fourth dimension of time, journeys into the future, to the year 802701. What he first takes to be utopia turns out to be a terrible world of degeneracy. Society is divided into two classes—the beautiful but ineffectual Eloi who live above ground and the ugly and cruel Morlocks, the workers, who live underground. (The eventual irony of the tale is that the Morlocks are actually in control.) The Traveler interprets what he sees as a present-day social system pushed to its logical conclu-sion. Having had a vision of the "outcome of the last surgings of the now purposeless energy of mankind," he returns to the present to tell his tale to a captive audience.

On a deeper level, *The Time Machine* is a story about the ultimate evolution of mankind. Its futuristic ideas are fantastic, but the tale is made plausible by the realistic responses of the Traveler to his circumstances and by the complex narrative frames within which Wells reveals his tale. The whole is beautifully written and full of inventiveness. A dream, a work of science fiction, a social allegory, a study in alienation, the novel is Wells' greatest work and arguably one of the most important works of modern fiction.

The Island of Doctor Moreau (1896) concerns the abuse of science. The scientist at the center of the story is a notorious vivisectionist who turns animals into human form. The whole is framed by the perceptions of the narrator, Prendick, who, back in England, is too profoundly disturbed by what he has experienced on the island to be able to adjust psychologically. This powerfully written narrative was disliked by critics. It was followed by the more light-hearted *The Invisible Man* (1897).

In *The War of the Worlds* (1898), in which Martians attempt to colonize earth because their own planet is cooling, Wells draws parallels between their invasion and European colonialism. The story proceeds through carefully arranged scenes of excitement and terror as Wells uses journalistic techniques to maintain narrative momentum. The story may be read as a version of modern warfare. The mass panic created by Orson Welles' adaptation of it for American radio attests to both its prophetic nature and imaginative potency.

Kipps (1905) and *The History of Mr. Polly* (1910) were the most popular of the social comedies, and they have survived the best. In the former, Wells satirized the English class system, and in the latter, he created a utopian vision. Kipps is an inarticulate innocent who, when he comes into a fortune, falls into the hands of predatory socialites. He is saved in the end by true love when he rejects social pretension. Mr. Polly escapes from social and economic pressures and a poor indigestion to the freedom, comfort, and security of a plump woman who owns a country pub. The liveliness of these texts is maintained by the exploration of the emotional ups and downs of lovable characters and the humor they generate.

Tono-Bungay (1908), Wells' weightiest Edwardian novel, is a "condition of England" novel that traces social change. Its central character, George Ponderevo, pins his hope for the future on science. Ironically, however, the novel's symbolism suggests a disturbing future. When George collects radioactive material from Mordet Island, it behaves like a cancer that "creeps and lives by destroying." Finally, he invents a destroyer, and the novel ends as the ship moves down the Thames, out to sea.

When Wells turned from social comedy to the discussion novel in the 1920s, he fell out of critical favor; by the 1930s he began to lose his readership. Wells is difficult to assess as a literary figure. His celebrated disagreement with Henry James put him at odds with the literary establishment and initiated early 20th-century debates about the nature of fiction. For Wells, the novel was a means to an end; for James, it was a work of art. James created avant-garde novels, Wells lively traditional narratives. Their discussions came to an end, effectively, with the publication of Wells' Boon (1915), a miscellany of stories and jottings remembered now because it contains Wells' mockery of James. Wells wrote to James (8 July 1915) that he would rather be a journalist than an artist. A generation later, Virginia Woolf dismissed Wells, along with John Galsworthy and Arnold Bennett, as realist novelists writing in an outmoded style: these writers, Woolf felt, had failed to understand and adopt the new techniques of modernist fiction. Wells is now remembered for the artistry of his scientific romances and social comedies.

STELLA McNICHOL

See also Science Fiction Novel

Biography

Born 21 September 1866 in Bromley, Kent. Attended Mr. Morley's Bromley Academy until age 13: certificate in bookkeeping; apprentice draper, Rodgers and Denyer, Windsor, 1880; pupil-teacher at a school in Wookey, Somerset, 1880; apprentice chemist in Midhurst, Sussex, 1880–81; apprentice draper, Hyde's Southsea Drapery Emporium, Hampshire, 1881–83; student/assistant, Midhurst Grammar School, 1883–84; student, Normal School (now Imperial College) of Science, London (editor, Science School Journal), 1884–87; teacher, Holt Academy, Wrexham, Wales, 1887–88, and at Henley House School, Kilburn, London, 1889; B. Sc. (honors) in zoology 1890, and D. Sc. 1943, University of London. Tutor, University Tutorial College, London, 1890–93; began writing full-time in 1893; theatre critic, Pall Mall Gazette, London, 1895; Fabian Society member, 1903–08; Labour candidate for Parliament, for the University of London, 1922, 1923; resided primarily in France, 1924–33. International president, PEN, 1934–46. Died 13 August 1946.

Selected Fiction by Wells

The Time Machine: An Invention, 1895
The Wonderful Visit, 1895
The Island of Dr. Moreau, 1896
The Wheels of Chance, 1896
The Invisible Man: A Grotesque Romance, 1897
The War of the Worlds, 1898
When the Sleeper Wakes: A Story of the Years to Come, 1899; revised edition as The Sleeper Wakes, 1910
Love and Mr. Lewisham, 1900
The First Men in the Moon, 1901
The Sea Lady: A Tissue of Moonshine, 1902
The Food of the Gods, and How It Came to Earth, 1904
A Modern Utopia, 1905
Kipps, 1905
In the Days of the Comet, 1906
The War in the Air, and Particularly How Mr. Bert Smallways Fared While It Lasted, 1908
Tono-Bungay, 1908
Ann Veronica, 1909
The History of Mr. Polly, 1910
The New Machiavelli, 1911
Marriage, 1912
The Passionate Friends, 1913
The World Set Free: A Story of Mankind, 1914
The Wife of Sir Isaac Harman, 1914
Boon, 1915
Bealby, 1915
The Research Magnificent, 1915
Mr. Britling Sees It Through, 1916
The Soul of a Bishop, 1917
Joan and Peter, 1918
The Undying Fire, 1919
The Secret Places of the Heart, 1922
Tales of the Unexpected [of Life and Adventure, of Wonder], 3 vols., 1922–23
Men Like Gods, 1923
The Dream, 1924
Christina Alberta's Father, 1925
The World of William Clissold, 1926
Meanwhile: The Picture of a Lady, 1927
Mr. Blettsworthy on Rampole Island, 1928
The King Who Was a King: The Book of a Film, 1929
The Autocracy of Mr. Parham, 1930
The Bulpington of Blup, 1932
The Shape of Things to Come: The Ultimate Resolution, 1933; revised edition as Things to Come (film story), 1935
The Croquet Player, 1936
Star Begotten: A Biological Fantasia, 1937
Brynhild, 1937
The Camford Visitation, 1937
The Brothers, 1938
Apropos of Dolores, 1938
The Holy Terror, 1939
Babes in the Darkling Wood, 1940
All Aboard for Ararat, 1940
You Can't Be Too Careful: A Sample of Life, 1901–1951, 1941
The Valley of Spiders, 1964
The Cone, 1965
The Wealth of Mr. Waddy, 1969

Other Writings: plays adapted from his fiction, screenplays, and a vast production of assorted nonfiction.

Further Reading

Batchelor, John, *H.G. Wells,* Cambridge and New York: Cambridge University Press, 1985

Bergonzi, Bernard, *The Early H.G. Wells,* Manchester: Manchester University Press, and Toronto: University of Toronto Press, 1961

Brooks, Van Wyck, *The World of H.G. Wells,* New York: Kennedy, and London: T. Fisher Unwin, 1915

Crossley, Robert, *A Reader's Guide to H.G. Wells,* Mercer Island, Washington: Starmont House, 1986

Huntington, John, editor, *Critical Essays on H.G. Wells,* Boston: G.K. Hall, 1991

McConnell, Frank, *The Science Fiction of H.G. Wells,* New York: Oxford University Press, 1981

Parrinder, Patrick, editor, *H.G. Wells: The Critical Heritage,* London and Boston: Routledge and Kegan Paul, 1972

West, Geoffrey, *H.G. Wells: A Sketch for a Portrait,* London: Howe, 1930

Zamiatin, Evgenii, *Gerbert Vells,* Leningrad: Epoka, 1922

Werther. *See* Sufferings of Young Werther

Nathanael West 1903–40

United States

Nathanael West wrote devastatingly funny, bleakly surrealist satires. Inspired by Edgar Allan Poe and Charles Baudelaire, and despising the "muddle-class" realism of Sinclair Lewis and Theodore Dreiser, West championed the formally experimental, short "lyric novel," which he recognized as a potently "distinct form," particularly appropriate for American use. "Forget the epic, the master work," he advised in defense of his second novel, *Miss Lonelyhearts* (1933), "In America fortunes do not accumulate, the soil does not grow, families have no history. Leave slow growth to the book reviewers, you only have time to explode. Remember William Carlos Williams' description of pioneer women who shot their children against the wilderness like cannonballs. Do the same with your novels."

In West's writing European modernism combusts with the violence of an American comic strip, a technique whereby "each chapter instead of going forward in time," he explains, "also goes backward, forward, up and down, in space like a picture. Violent images are used to illustrate commonplace events. Violent acts are left almost bald." This technique is perhaps best exemplified in the fast-moving, scatological, and collagistic narrative of his first novel, *The Dream Life of Balso Snell* (1931), the fruit of West's formative 1926 pilgrimage to Paris where he met with surrealists such as Max Ernst, Louis Aragon, and Philippe Soupault. This virtuoso parody of high modernism begins with the anal penetration of the Trojan horse, and then tours its intestine "inhabited solely by authors in search of an audience," whose numerous "tales are elephantine close-ups of various literary positions and their technical methods." The novel ends in onanistic orgasm. West's advertisement for *The*

Dream Life of Balso Snell boasts his surpassing the German avant-garde collagist Kurt Schwitters' definition, "Tout ce que l'artiste crache, c'est l'art" (Anything the artist expectorates is art). If his own joyous pretensions as aesthete and connoisseur are celebrated in the bookplate designed for him by his friend S.J. Perelman (a motto from Goethe, "Do I love what others love?"), then *The Dream Life of Balso Snell* and an unpublished short story, "The Impostor," lampooning the Parisian art scene suggest West's glorious ambivalence toward high modernist aesthetics.

West collaged (apparently genuine) letters to a New York columnist from "the seriously injured of our civic life" (William Carlos Williams' phrase) into the narrative of *Miss Lonelyhearts,* a savage satire on the role of the Hearst newspapers within the ideological frame of Depression America. His editorial collaboration on the magazine *Americana* with the exiled German dadaist George Grosz as "the laughing morticians of the present" may have sharpened his satiric vision, but West's achievement lay primarily in adapting European avant-garde techniques to American traditions for distinctively American use. This was emphasized by the task he and William Carlos Williams defined for their literary magazine, *Contact,* "to cut a trail through the American jungle without the use of a European compass." West saw their work as "not only in but against the American grain." The all-American rags-to-riches fantasies of Horatio Alger became his target in the antifascist satire *A Cool Million: The Dismantling of Lemuel Pitkin* (1934), whose protagonist literally falls apart in his attempt to become president. Toothless, eyeless, thumbless, bald, and one-legged, Lemuel

Pitkin eventually dies a fascist martyr. During one episode American consumerism is memorably figured as "a surfeit of shoddy" in the scathing invective of Chief Satinpenny, who scalps Pitkin and leaves a young brave to loot his "bloody head of its store teeth and glass eye."

West defended the excessive violence in his work as a reflection of American experience: "In America violence is idiomatic." This position earned him the postwar reputation of nihilist, which was enhanced by his writing's refusal of psychological depth. His grotesquely dehumanized and semi-reified characters often resemble "mechanical drawings." Earl Shoop, the stock cowboy in *The Day of the Locust* (1939), for example, has "a two-dimensional face that a talented child might have drawn with a ruler and compass." Another character is described as "a badly made automaton." West nevertheless mined psychology as a mythic resource ("Freud is your Bulfinch; you cannot learn from him.")—a narrative strategy apparently baffling to a generation of 1950s critics who searched in vain for depth of character and signs of spiritual redemption, and whose fears culminated in W.H. Auden's diagnosis of "West's disease" as manifest immorality and spiritual decay. Noting West's uneasy relationship with his Jewish background, some critics have attempted to read West's work in relation to Jewish prophetic traditions. West himself thought of his work as "moral satire" but recognized it was doomed to be misunderstood by his contemporaries on the left and right alike. Although politically sympathetic with the left, his work was deplored by the exponents of socialist realism. "My books fall between the different schools of writing," he told George Milburn: "The radical press, although I consider myself on their side, doesn't like my particular kind of joking, and think it even Fascist sometimes, and the literature boys whom I detest, detest me in turn. The high brow press finds that I avoid the big significant things and the lending library touts in the daily press think me shocking."

West's experience as a screenwriter in Hollywood formed the basis for his last and, for some, most successful work, *The Day of the Locust*. Often compared with F. Scott Fitzgerald's *The Last Tycoon* (1941), this coruscating satire on the Hollywood dream factory (originally entitled *The Cheated*) focuses on a seedy panorama of the grotesque, displaced, and marginalized—the losers at the fringes rather than the success stories at the center. This is the California of prostitution, violence, and sleaze, where people "come to die." In the final apocalyptic chapter the artist-hero Tod Hackett, in the midst of a mindless and bloody mob riot, imagines completing his painting, "The Burning of Los Angeles." Intertextual links between Hackett's painting and West's poem "Burn the Cities" (1933), a strange celebration of the ascendancy of Marxism over Christianity, have been acknowledged, but their significance for readings of West's work remains a vexed point of debate. Recent criticism (see Barnard, 1995; Roberts, 1996) has moved beyond the previous despondency over West's "bleak and absurd vision" and dark irony to offer more sophisticated readings of his negative critique of consumerism and the culture industry. More importantly, West's brief *oeuvre* has been recognized for its enormous impact on 20th-century writing. His influence has been acknowledged by many writers, including Carson McCullers, Flannery O'Connor, Joseph Heller, Saul Bellow, Thomas Pynchon, and Ishmael Reed. Philippe Soupault's 1946 French edition of *Miss Lonelyhearts* is also considered a significant landmark in European postwar fiction.

JANE GOLDMAN

Biography

Born Nathan Weinstein in New York City, 17 October 1903; Attended DeWitt Clinton High School, New York; Tufts College, Medford, Massachusetts, 1921; Brown University, Providence, Rhode Island, 1922–24, Ph.B. 1924. Worked for his father in real estate business, 1924–25; changed name, 1926; lived in Paris, 1926–27; night manager, Kenmore Hall Hotel and Suffolk Club Hotel, New York, 1927–31; associate editor, to William Carlos Williams, *Contact: An American Quarterly*, 1931–32; screenwriter for Columbia, 1933, 1938, Republic, 1936–38, Universal, 1938, and RKO, 1938–40, all Hollywood. Died 22 December 1940.

Novels by West

The Dream Life of Balso Snell, 1931
Miss Lonelyhearts, 1933
A Cool Million: The Dismantling of Lemuel Pitkin, 1934
The Day of the Locust, 1939

Other Writings: a couple of unsuccessful plays ("Even Stephen" with S.J. Perelman, "Good Hunting: A Satire in 3 Acts" with Joseph Schrank), short stories (mostly unpublished—see appendices to Wisker, 1990), a few poems (most notably, "Burn the Cities"), film scripts (including *Advice to the Lovelorn, Five Came Back, I Stole a Million, Lonelyhearts, Spirit of Calver*); West's brief statements on his novels, and on violence, are reproduced in Jay Martin's *Nathanael West: A Collection of Critical Essays* (1971).

Further Reading

Barnard, Rita, *The Great Depression and the Culture of Abundance: Kenneth Fearing, Nathanael West, and Mass Culture in the 1930s*, Cambridge and New York: Cambridge University Press, 1995
Bloom, Harold, editor, *Nathanael West*, New York: Chelsea House, 1986
Edenbaum, Robert I., "Dada and Surrealism: A Literary Instance," *Arts in Society* 5 (1986)
Long, Robert Emmet, *Nathanael West*, New York: Ungar, 1985
Martin, Jay, *Nathanael West: The Art of His Life*, New York: Farrar, Straus and Giroux, 1970; London: Secker and Warburg, 1971
Martin, Jay, editor, *Nathanael West: A Collection of Critical Essays*, Englewood Cliffs, New Jersey: Prentice-Hall, 1971
Roberts, Matthew, "Bonfire of the Avant-Garde: Cultural Rage and Readerly Complicity in *The Day of the Locust*," *Modern Fiction Studies* 42:1 (Spring 1996)
Siegel, Ben, editor, *Critical Essays on Nathanael West*, New York: G.K. Hall/Macmillan, 1994
Widmer, Kingsley, *Nathanael West*, Boston: Twayne, 1982
Vannatta, Dennis P., *Nathanael West: An Annotated Bibliography of the Scholarship and Works*, New York: Garland, 1976
White, William, *Nathanael West: A Comprehensive Bibliography*, Kent, Ohio: Kent State University Press, 1975
Wisker, Alistair, *The Writing of Nathanael West*, London: Macmillan, and New York: St. Martin's Press, 1990

Western Novel. *See* American Western Novel

Edith Wharton 1862–1937

United States

Edith Wharton is one of the most well known and renowned women writers in the American literary tradition. She is best known for her two major novels, *The House of Mirth* (1905) and *The Age of Innocence* (1920), but she wrote 14 other novels (including *The Buccaneers* [1938], which was unfinished at the time of her death in 1937), three novellas (including *Ethan Frome*, 1911), as well as numerous volumes of short stories, two volumes of poetry, travel writings, memoirs, and art criticism. Most of her novels examine American social manners and cultural conflict in the tradition of Henry James, to whom she is often unfavorably compared, and the Southern writer Ellen Glasgow. However, Wharton distinguishes herself from James in that her narrative style is characterized by clarity and a sharpness of wit that is often lost in the complexity of James' sentences and abstruse syntax. Nevertheless, both Wharton and James share a satirical impulse to expose the distinctive traits of East Coast culture and the idiosyncrasies of the American class system.

Wharton is a broadly realistic writer who examines the manner in which individuals are shaped and often victimized by their economic environments. However, this naturalistic focus does not detract from the dominant stylistic qualities of her novels. In one of her more interesting late essays entitled "Visibility in Fiction" (1929), she argues that style is the crucial consideration for unifying the form and content of a novel: not only does style lend a story the "enduring semblance of vitality" but it is necessary for the creation of "visible" characters. She comments on her troubled attempts to render the "visual intensity" of characters when she admits that "the gift of giving visibility to the characters of fiction is the rarest in the novelist's endowment." She warns that such visibility is often overstated, as in the cases of Charles Dickens and Honoré de Balzac, who persistently associate their characters with "the same physical or mental oddities." By way of contrast, she aspires to the manner in which Lev Tolstoi and Gustave Flaubert interweave realistic physical descriptions with subtle renderings of the emotional and mental complexities of their characters. In a similar manner, many of Wharton's novels present engaging characters faced with emotionally limiting or debilitating circumstances.

Wharton's popular early novel *The House of Mirth* (although she was 42 on its publication) establishes many of the themes that she develops in her later work: a serious reflection upon the etiquette and cultural tastes adopted by the New York gentility; an intimate examination of domestic, public, and economic relationships; a critique of repressed and barely articulated sexuality; and a forceful criticism of the entrapment that social expectations can impose on individuals. *The House of Mirth* and *The Age of Innocence* both explore the emergence of a new economic order that challenged the inherited assumptions and modes of living of the New York gentry. Changes to the economic order and the urban environment were distasteful to Wharton, whose general sympathy with the leisure class and reverence for the past are discernible throughout her novels. As she claimed in a 1927 article on the "The Great American Novel": "in inheriting an old social organization which provided for nicely shaded degrees of culture and conduct, modern America has simplified . . . it out of existence, forgetting that in such matters the process is necessarily one of impoverishment." *The House of Mirth* dramatizes the conflict between the fragile innocence of the novel's protagonist, Lily Bart, and the crass materialistic society into which she is immersed. Ill-equipped to contend with the values of modern society, Lily's sensibility is compromised as gradually she becomes corrupted by the seductions of luxury. For these reasons *The House of Mirth* is often compared with Theodore Dreiser's novel of urban corruption, *Sister Carrie* (1900). It also develops some of the observations made by the American sociologist Thorstein Veblen in *The Theory of the Leisure Class* (1899).

Despite her affection for the past and tradition, in *The Age of Innocence* Wharton's satire is directed at the false values and social restrictions displayed by the leisure class and at the unwelcome emergence of the nouveau riche in the late 19th century. While living in France in the 1910s, Wharton directly experienced the brutality of war and the shocking consequences of modern technology as she contributed to the Allied war relief effort. World War I represented a devastating shock to the sheltered, idealized, and innocent past of her American childhood. For Wharton, war symbolized both the crumbling of traditional culture and a fall from innocence into the chaotic and meaningless world of modernity. This conflict between innocence and experience is transposed into the late-19th-century world of *The Age of Innocence* in the guise of the two leading female characters, May Welland and Ellen Olenska: the former is the innocent and childlike product of Old New York society and the latter is perceived by the parochial Old New Yorkers as the embodiment of a decadent and fallen Europe. The male protagonist Newland Archer is the progeny of Old New York caught uncomfortably between May and Ellen, who represent, respectively, his sense of obligation and his unfulfilled passion. However, Archer's hesitation and his inability to challenge his class values contribute to his final realization that he has missed out on the possibilities of life. By dramatizing the tensions between these three characters the novel questions the currency of innocence in the modern world and explores America's ambivalent relationship to Europe in the early 20th century.

In her other novels Wharton persists with this group of core themes but extends her fictional interests to historical studies of European culture (*The Valley of Decision*, 1902); to challenging traditional representations of New England—what T.S. Eliot called the "stunted firs" and "granite boulders" novel (*Summer*, 1917); to dramatizing the possibilities and limitations of artistic freedom in the modern world (*Hudson River Bracketed*, 1929); and to analyzing the continued tensions between wealthy American society and the British aristocracy (*The Buccaneers*).

MARTIN HALLIWELL

See also Age of Innocence

Biography

Born 24 January 1862 in New York City. Traveled in Italy, Spain, and France as a child; educated privately. Lived in Newport, Rhode Island, after her marriage, and in Europe from 1907, where she maintained a close friendship with Henry James; assisted in organizing the American Hostel for Refugees, and the Children of Flanders Rescue Committee, during World War I. Died 11 August 1937.

Novels by Wharton

The Valley of Decision, 1902
The House of Mirth, 1905
The Fruit of the Tree, 1907
The Reef, 1912
The Custom of the Country, 1913
Summer, 1917
The Marne, 1918
The Age of Innocence, 1920
The Glimpses of the Moon, 1922
A Son at the Front, 1923
The Mother's Recompense, 1925
Twilight Sleep, 1927
The Children, 1928; as *The Marriage Playground*, 1930
Hudson River Bracketed, 1929

The Gods Arrive, 1932
The Buccaneers, 1938

Other Writings: short stories, plays, verse, a pioneer work in interior design (*The Decoration of Houses*, 1897), travel writings, an autobiography (*A Backward Glance*, 1934), and a book on fiction writing.

Further Reading

Ammons, Elizabeth, *Edith Wharton's Argument with America*, Athens: University of Georgia Press, 1980

Bell, Millicent, *Edith Wharton and Henry James: The Story of Their Friendship*, New York: Braziller, 1965; London: Owen, 1966

Bell, Millicent, editor, *The Cambridge Companion to Edith Wharton*, Cambridge and New York: Cambridge University Press, 1995

Benstock, Shari, *No Gifts from Chance: A Biography of Edith Wharton*, New York: Scribner, and London: Hamish Hamilton, 1994

Fryer, Judith, *Felicitous Space: The Imaginative Structures of Edith Wharton and Willa Cather*, Chapel Hill: University of North Carolina Press, 1986

Howe, Irving, editor, *Edith Wharton: A Collection of Critical Essays*, Englewood Cliffs, New Jersey: Prentice Hall, 1962

Lewis, R.W.B., *Edith Wharton: A Biography*, New York: Harper and Row, and London: Constable, 1975

Showalter, Elaine, *Sister's Choice: Tradition and Change in American Women's Writing*, Oxford: Clarendon Press, and New York: Oxford University Press, 1991

Wershoven, Carol, *The Female Intruder in the Novels of Edith Wharton*, Rutherford, New Jersey: Fairleigh Dickinson University Press, and London: Associated University Presses, 1982

Wharton, Edith, "The Great American Novel," *Yale Review* (1927)

Wharton, Edith, "Visibility in Fiction," *Life and Letters* (1929)

Wolff, Cynthia Griffin, *A Feast of Words: The Triumph of Edith Wharton*, New York: Oxford University Press, 1977; Oxford: Oxford University Press, 1978; 2nd edition, Reading, Massachusetts: Addison-Wesley, 1995

What Is To Be Done? by Nikolai Chernyshevskii

Chto delat'? 1863

Nikolai Chernyshevskii's *What Is To Be Done?* is arguably one of the most subversive and most influential novels ever written and has the rare distinction of being written and published while its author was incarcerated by government authorities. *What Is To Be Done?* became an instant success among a younger generation of Russians, many of whom consciously imitated the actions of the novel's protagonists. The novel influenced numerous young Russians to enter into so-called "fictitious marriages," which liberated young women to pursue an education and/or career and found cooperative/communal ventures. Familiarity with Chernyshevskii's novel came to be considered by Russian youth as the hallmark of an advanced man or woman.

If the reaction of young Russia was overwhelmingly positive, that of mainstream Russia was passionately negative. Conservatives, in particular, denounced the novel for its supposed immorality, claiming that it propagated the doctrine of free love.

Official Russia outlawed the novel and forbade the mention of its author's name in print. In fact, *What Is To Be Done?* did not appear legally in Russia for the remainder of the 19th century. Despite the official proscription, however, *What Is To Be Done?* continued to exert considerable influence on young Russians for decades. It was particularly revered by the various groups of the Russian left. Lenin, for example, claimed it as his favorite novel and attributed his transition to radicalism to its influence. After the Bolsheviks came into power in 1917 the novel took a place in the Soviet pantheon of great books. When the doctrine of socialist realism was declared in 1932, *What Is To Be Done?* was hailed as an important predecessor and, hence, an important model for Soviet writers. It was published regularly and was required reading in Soviet schools. With the dissolution of the Soviet Union, however, the novel has lost much of its previous status in Russia.

In writing the novel Chernyshevskii drew heavily upon previous Russian and Western European literary traditions, for thematics and for formal elements. Primary influences included Jean-Jacques Rousseau's *Julie; ou, La Nouvelle Héloïse* (1761; *Julie; or, The New Eloise*), Charles Dickens' *Hard Times* (1854), and George Sand's *Jacques* (1834; *Jacques*) and *La Comtesse de Rudolstadt* (1844; *The Countess of Rudolstadt*). In drawing on such works, however, Chernyshevskii did not simply rely on a work itself but also drew on its reception in Russia. For example, the novel's conflict centering on a love triangle draws not only on a similar conflict in the Sand novels but also on how this theme was further developed in Aleksandr Druzhinin's *Polin'ka Saks* (1847; *Polinka Saks*) and Aleksandr Herzen's *Kto vinovat?* (1847; *Who Is To Blame?*). *What Is To Be Done?* also makes use of other Western European works to a lesser degree, often referring directly to them (Boccaccio's *Decameron*, Saxo Grammaticus' legend of Hamlet).

From the Russian literary tradition Chernyshevskii drew on the most diverse sources. For example, medieval hagiography, especially *Zhitie Alekseia, cheloveka bozhiia* (The Life of Aleksei, a Man of God), greatly conditions Rakhmetov's story. For many formal elements Chernyshevskii drew on the three great novels of the first half of the 19th century: Aleksandr Pushkin's *Evgenii Onegin* (1833; *Eugene Onegin*), Mikhail Lermontov's *Geroi nashego vremeni* (1840; *Hero of Our Time*), and Nikolai Gogol's *Mertvye dushi* (1842; *Dead Souls*). In terms of thematics *What Is To Be Done?* is part and parcel of the polemics that raged in Russian literature in the middle of the century. Its very title recalls these polemics as expressed by Herzen in *Who Is To Blame?* and Ivan Turgenev in *Nakanune* (1860; *On the Eve*) and *Ottsy i deti* (1862; *Fathers and Sons*). The character Mar'ia Aleksevna, who resembles Mar'ia Aleksandrovna in Fedor Dostoevskii's *Diadushkin son* (1859; *Uncle's Dream*), provides a good example of literary polemic. Both Mar'ias are negative characters, but the attitudes of their respective narrators to them differs greatly. Not only did *What Is To Be Done?* respond to works by contemporary writers, the novel itself provoked a stream of parodies and responses by other writers. Indeed, a whole series of "anti-nihilist" works appeared in the 1860s, including Lev Tolstoi's "Zarazhennoe semeistvo" (1863–64; The Infected Family), Aleksei Pisemskii's *Vzbalamuchennoe more* (1863; Troubled Sea), and Nikolai Leskov's *Nekuda* (1864; *No Way Out*), which were aimed at both Chernyshevskii's novel and at the actions of his self-professed followers. The best known of these responses, however, remains Dostoevskii's *Zapiski iz podpol'ia* (1864; *Notes from Underground*), which draws heavily upon *What Is To Be Done?* both for thematics and plot situations. Many elements drawn from *What Is To Be Done?*, ranging from brief plot episodes to larger philosophical questions, also appear throughout Dostoevskii's later works.

In terms of innovation, *What Is To Be Done?* is notable in several respects. Although Chernyshevskii was not the first author to deal with the new social group of the *raznochintsy* (a term designating those intellectuals who originated not from the aristocracy but from other various ranks of Russian society) that rose to prominence in the 19th century, *What Is To Be Done?* presents this group and its milieu from its own point of view and in a positive light. The novel is also unique because of its treatment of a female member of the group. Far from appearing as a mere adjunct to a central male figure, the novel focuses on the heroine, Vera Pavlovna, and her quest for personal development. *What Is To Be Done?* is to a large extent concerned with the theme of women's emancipation and thus quickly became a cornerstone of the "woman question" in 19th-century Russia. Indeed, the novel marked an important point of departure for the treatment of women in Russian literature in general. Finally, Chernyshevskii breaks from previous tradition by portraying his main characters as "positive heroes"; they are not fundamentally flawed as were so many of their predecessors. Chernyshevskii's introduction of positive heroes into literature forced many of his contemporaries to respond. Although most of the well-known writers of the period disapproved of Chernyshevskii's particular formulations, the question of the positive hero began to occupy a larger role in their works, particularly those of Dostoevskii. Chernyshevskii's positive heroes, especially Rakhmetov (rightly or wrongly), also came to serve as a prototype for those of socialist realism during the Soviet period.

ANDREW M. DROZD

Further Reading

Andrew, Joe, *Women in Russian Literature, 1780–1863*, London: Macmillan, and New York: St. Martin's Press, 1988.

Clark, Katerina, *The Soviet Novel: History as Ritual*, Chicago: University of Chicago Press, 1981; 2nd edition, 1985

Drozd, Andrew M., "N.G. Chernyshevskii's *What Is To Be Done?*: A Reevaluation," Ph.D. diss., Indiana University, 1995

Katz, Michael R., "English Translations of *What Is To Be Done?*" *Slavic Review* 46:1 (Spring 1987)

Katz, Michael R., "Vera Pavlovna's Dreams in Chernyshevskii's *What is to be Done?*" in *Issues in Russian Literature Before 1917*, edited by J. Douglas Clayton, Columbus, Ohio: Slavica, 1989

Klenin, Emily, "On the Ideological Sources of *Čto delat'?*: Sand, Družinin, Leroux," *Zeitschrift für slavische Philologie* 51:2 (1991)

Paperno, Irina, *Chernyshevsky and the Age of Realism: A Study in the Semiotics of Behavior*, Stanford, California: Stanford University Press, 1988

Randall, Francis B., *N.G. Chernyshevskii*, New York: Twayne, 1967

Patrick White 1912–90

Australian

The first (and still the only) Australian to win the Nobel prize for literature, Patrick White became his country's dominant writer in the mid-1950s and remained so until his death 35 years later. As well as the novels that won him his wide international reputation (and have been translated into many languages), he published two very early volumes of poetry, three collections of short stories, eight plays, and an autobiography. In an essay, "The Prodigal Son" (*Australian Letters*, 1958), White described himself as opposing the mainstream of Australian fiction, which he saw as "the dreary, dun-coloured off-spring of journalistic realism." At that time in Australia his work was hailed, or damned, for its departures from the prevailing mode of realism—for its modernist stylistic experimentation and preoccupation with individual, and religious, consciousness. What would become more apparent later was that White was extending the range of Australian realism through his social comedy and satire and simultaneously engaging in highly self-conscious literary play.

His first novel, *Happy Valley* (1939), set in a small rural community in New South Wales, and *The Living and the Dead* (1941), set in London during the Spanish Civil War, are perhaps most interesting today for the influences they reveal of the first generation of modernists: James Joyce, T.S. Eliot, D.H. Lawrence, and Virginia Woolf. (Like all his subsequent novels they were published initially in New York and London.) *The Aunt's Story* (1948) is the first of White's novels to display a distinct idiom, which alternates ironically between presenting often sharply satiric (and realistic) social comedy and his central characters' epiphanies and search for transcendence. However, the quest of Theodora Goodman (the aunt of the title) ends in an hallucinatory surrealism, and White's explicit intention with his next novel (as he wrote in "The Prodigal Son") was "to discover the extraordinary behind the ordinary, the mystery and poetry" in the lives of an ordinary couple.

The Tree of Man (1955), White's stylized reworking of the conventional (and "dun-coloured") saga of Australian pioneering, was the first novel to win him considerable international attention—and consequently attention in Australia. By turns accessible (which the surrealistic sections of *The Aunt's Story* were not) and difficult (with its echoes of Genesis, *Madame Bovary*, the English novel of rural life, and modernist recoils from contemporary urban life), *The Tree of Man* combined a variety of styles ranging from the comic to spiritual allegory.

Voss (1957) similarly drew upon another staple of earlier Australian fiction—the novel of exploration—for an historically based allegory of spiritual search. But to compare this novel with *The Tree of Man* is to appreciate the extraordinary protean nature of White's literary imagination. Whereas the preceding novel engages with the ordinary, *Voss* engages with the heroic, romantic spirit—and the spirit of European, specifically German, romanticism. Structured around the metaphor of the desert (both the actual interior of Australia and the aridity of colonial society for the questing individual), *Voss* sets multiple levels of irony, and literary parody, in play. Its final irony is to leave the reader to answer the question of whether Australian society has transcended its colonial past.

These two internationally acclaimed novels of the mid-1950s were followed by *Riders in the Chariot* (1961), which engaged directly with contemporary Australian urban life. Set in Sarsaparilla (a Faulknerian caricature of the outer suburb in which White was living at that time and which also was a setting for his stories and plays), *Riders in the Chariot* also presents an allegory. It implies, through the crucifixion of a refugee German Jew by a group of his factory work "mates," a correspondence between "the banality of evil" under the Third Reich and what is satirized as the mindless conformity and tasteless materialism of postwar Australia. Another of the novel's "riders," or visionaries, and also a victim of the prevailing ethos, is an Aboriginal painter. Today's official policies of multiculturalism and reconciliation with Aborigines have made *Riders in the Chariot*'s moral engagement with this society seem much less eccentric than when it first appeared.

Also set in Sarsaparilla is *The Solid Mandala* (1966), which, instead of assuming the epic framework of its predecessor, offers an overtly playful version of domestic Gothic and, through the lives of the twin brothers Arthur and Waldo Brown, an allegory of intuition versus intellect. Arthur is mentally retarded but enjoys supernatural experiences unavailable to the coldly rational, and monstrously egotistical, Waldo (a less oblique self-portrait than that of Theodora in *The Aunt's Story*).

White completed *The Solid Mandala* after he had moved to Centennial Park in the inner suburbs of Sydney, and the first novel he began there departed from his earlier, and conventionally literary, recoil from that city as an image of the fallen modern world. *The Vivisector* (1970) is a study of a Sydney painter and of art as "vivisection"—as the artist's ruthless exploitation, even destruction of others in his pursuit of truth. Its critique (and self-critique) of artistry was said to have alarmed the Nobel committee, who postponed awarding White the prize until *The Eye of the Storm* (1973) appeared. Again set in contemporary Sydney, and also celebrating the city in which White spent his early childhood, *The Eye of the Storm* presents in rich and comic detail the perceptions of family members and others attending the death of an elderly matriarch. What none of the widely varied cast of characters realizes is that once in her long and selfish life Mrs. Hunter had glimpsed momentarily that transcendence, that "pure being," sought by all White's protagonists.

A Fringe of Leaves (1976), loosely based on the story of Eliza Fraser (and of considerable interest to postcolonial critics today), seemed a return to the historical mode of *Voss*. In fact, White had conceived the work much earlier, before setting it aside to write his "Sydney" novels. The direction in which his fiction was moving, toward more overtly parodic and self-parodic "postmodern" play, was made abundantly clear by *The Twyborn Affair* (1979), whose protagonist leads different lives in different milieux (some of them sites from White's earlier fictions) as Eudoxia/Eddie/Eadith—the last being the "madam" of a London brothel. Playing freely with signification, especially with gender signifiers, *The Twyborn Affair* offered an all-but-explicit autobiographical allegory. This autobiographical context became obvious when the autobiography *Flaws in the Glass*

(1981) followed. In it, the once-reclusive White, now a public personality, acknowledged his homosexuality and elaborated on his lifelong love/hate relationship with Australia. Postmodern narrative playfulness, including self-parody, characterize his final novel, the slight (and, it must be said, silly) *Memoirs of Many in One* (1986).

Over a writing career that spanned half a century, White continued to move with the times—from a somewhat belated high modernism with his first novels to postmodern play and pastiche with his last. Through the decades, critics argued whether he was really an "Australian" novelist at all, whether he was a traditionalist or an experimentalist, whether a conventional Christian or a Gnostic (or even a sceptic). But such arguments reflect shifts in critical interests more than they illuminate White's multilayered texts. Current interests in gender construction, postcolonial critique, multiculturalism, and writing as the endless deferral of meaning have recontextualized his work, so that (as Alan Lawson has shown in an article in *Antipodes*) even as early a novel as *The Aunt's Story* may be reread as freshly "postmodern." White's high literary awareness and virtuoso command of modes, combined with his undeniable, if constantly shifting, search for ultimate values, mean that his novels partially fit, but finally transcend, the various categories in which successive generations of commentators have attempted to place them.

BRIAN KIERNAN

See also Voss

Biography

Born 28 May 1912 in London; taken to Australia, 1912. Attended Tudor House, Moss Vale, and other schools in Australia, 1919–25; Cheltenham College, England, 1925–29; King's College, Cambridge, 1932–35, B.A. in modern languages, 1935. Served in the Royal Air Force, in Sudan and Egypt, during World War II: intelligence officer. Worked on sheep stations in New South Wales, 1929–32; lived in London and traveled in Europe, 1935–38; traveled in the United States, 1939–40; after the war lived with Manoly Lascaris in Castle Hill, New South Wales, and later Sydney. Awarded Nobel prize for literature, 1973. Died 30 September 1990.

Novels by White

Happy Valley, 1939
The Living and the Dead, 1941
The Aunt's Story, 1948
The Tree of Man, 1955
Voss, 1957
Riders in the Chariot, 1961
The Solid Mandala, 1966
The Vivisector, 1970
The Eye of the Storm, 1973
A Fringe of Leaves, 1976
The Twyborn Affair, 1979
Memoirs of Many in One, 1986

Other Writings: three collections of stories, a novella, seven plays, an autobiography (*Flaws in the Glass*, 1981), two collections of verse, a collection of speeches.

Further Reading

Bliss, Carolyn, *Patrick White's Fiction: The Paradox of Fortunate Failure*, London: Macmillan, and New York: St. Martin's Press, 1986
Kiernan, Brian, *Patrick White*, New York: St. Martin's Press, and London: Macmillan, 1980
Lawson, Alan, "Bound to Dis-integrate—Narrative and Interpretation in *The Aunt's Story*," *Antipodes: A North American Journal of Australian Literature* 6:1 (June 1992)
Marr, David, *Patrick White: A Life*, London: Cape, and Milson's Point, New South Wales: Random House, 1991
Wilkes, G.A., editor, *Ten Essays on Patrick White from Southerly (1964–67)*, Sydney: Angus and Robertson, 1970
Williams, Mark, *Patrick White*, New York: St. Martin's Press, and London: Macmillan, 1993
Wolfe, Peter, editor, *Critical Essays on Patrick White*, Boston: G.K. Hall, 1990

Christa Wolf 1929–

German

Without question, Christa Wolf is one of the most prominent postwar German writers and a writer of world stature. Yet with the 1990 publication of her novella *Was bleibt* (*What Remains*), a literary and political storm was unleashed. Written in 1979 in the form of a journal, *What Remains* is about a period of Wolf's life when she was under surveillance by East Germany's secret police. During the ensuing literary debate, critics and writers in the West German literary establishment accused Wolf of cowardice and opportunism for not risking publication before the East German government was toppled. They attempted to relegate her to the status of a privileged "state author." The attack became more intense in 1993, when Wolf's brief alignment with the secret police at the beginning of her writing career was made public. In the early 1990s Wolf became a scapegoat, as the moral authority of East German writers was widely questioned. However, much recent scholarship on Wolf has focused on a productive new reading of her work, which has led to a revaluation of her literary merits. However, her far-reaching aesthetic contributions through innovative narrative techniques cannot be separated from her politics—a hope for the realization of a socialist utopia—and her view of literature as a visionary power that can play a role in the realization of that utopia.

Wolf's utopian socialism is fundamental to an understanding of her work and at the same time essential for understanding the contradictions in its reception. West German critics have tried to relegate her work to the genre of affirmative functional literature with no serious criticism of the system, whereas East German authorities discredited her as a writer for ignoring and undermining socialist realism, with its emphasis on a positive hero, the setting of an example, the focus on the successful integration of the individual into the collective, the narrator's partisanship, and the accessibility and popularity of the text.

Wolf's first short narrative, *Moskauer Novelle* (1961; Moscow Novella), about a love affair between a Berlin doctor and a Russian interpreter, was entirely conventional, adhering largely to socialist realist criteria. However, Wolf's ambiguous and elusive *Der geteilte Himmel* (1963; *Divided Heaven*), which established her as East Germany's foremost woman writer, went far beyond the state-mandated form. Set in August 1961, during the time of the building of the Berlin Wall, the novel is an intricate retrospective analysis of the female protagonist's decision not to follow her lover to the West. The text abruptly alternates between omniscient narrative and interior monologue. The narrative shifts between two temporal planes, the present and the time of the couple's first meeting in 1959. The shifts are an expansion of the formal possibilities of socialist realism and its emphasis on linear progression. With her next novel, *Nachdenken über Christa T.* (1968; *The Quest for Christa T.*), Wolf achieved recognition in the West. Here she continued more radically with her experimentation with narrative perspective and her subversion of the prescriptions of socialist realism. In reconstructing the life of her friend Christa T. after her death of leukemia (death was considered a taboo in socialist realist literature), the narrator draws on friends' letters, diaries, and papers to bring her own memories and fantasies about her friend into sharper focus. Christa T.'s continual fight against conformity and repressive systems becomes a source of anxiety and self-doubt for the narrator. Modernist concerns with the problematics of language replace the forms and themes of socialist realism.

Wolf describes her experience in writing *The Quest for Christa T.* in her essay "The Reader and the Writer" (in the collection of essays entitled *Lesen und Schreiben* [1972], translated as *The Reader and the Writer*), in which she makes clear that experience and reflection form the crux of her writing. An unconditional demand for truth in dealing with one's own experiences informs her concept of *inner* or *subjective authenticity*, a term she first used in a 1973 interview. This concept calls for a new relationship to reality and, by necessity, a break with the prevailing doctrine of socialist realism. Instead of attempting an objective reproduction of facts, in which subjective elements, such as self-doubts, are hidden or suppressed, Wolf wishes to bring the subjective element out into the open. This focus on subjectivity involves the experience of the writing process as well as personal evaluations and thoughts. Subjective authenticity is also closely tied to Wolf's term *fourth dimension*, the dimension of the author, a concept she developed before subjective authenticity. In calling for a new realism that surpasses mere reproduction of the surfaces of things, she dismisses character, plot, linear time, and 19th-century conventions as clichés. She asks the prose writer to add a fourth dimension, the "coordinate of depth," to the three dimensions of surface. Blurring the distinction between author and narrator, Wolf dethrones the omniscient narrator or "reader's guide" of socialist realism. For Wolf, literature should provide the reader with stimuli for growth.

Kindheitsmuster (1976; *A Model Childhood*) is a multilayered investigation into her childhood in Nazi Germany, focusing particularly on a visit with her family to Poland. Wolf's reflections on the writing experience bring the past into the present and challenge reader and writer to reflect on the period of national socialism in the context of persisting fascist structures. In *Kein Ort, Nirgends* (1979; *No Place on Earth*), an imagined meeting takes place between two 19th-century literary figures in a repressive system, Heinrich von Kleist and Karoline von Günderrode. The existential crisis that both writers experience and share with each other is structurally and thematically related to Wolf's other texts depicting the romantic era and to her later artist-narratives, *Sommerstück* (1989; Summer Piece) and *What Remains*—works in which the relationship between artistic and personal integrity and cultural-political estrangement undergoes intense scrutiny. Drawing on Greek mythology, Wolf situates the female characters in her novels *Medea: Stimmen* (1996; *Medea: A Modern Retelling*) and *Kassandra* (1983; *Cassandra*) in political environments that test power structures and boundaries between freedom of choice and subjugation to authority.

Wolf's emphasis on the writer's experience and her notions of subjective authenticity have created spaces for reflection and dialogical dimensions in her novels, narratives, and essays. Her manifold contributions to the development of the novel are as much in the area of experimentation with form and perspective as with reflective self-confrontation and literary responsibility. For Wolf, writing should reveal an individual's subjective vision of reality as "playing with open possibilities."

BARBARA MABEE

Biography

Born 18 March 1929 in Landsberg an der Warthe, Germany (now Gorzow, Poland). Attended schools in Landsberg, Schwerin, and Bad Frankenhausen, graduated 1949; universities of Jena and Leipzig, 1949–53, diploma 1953. Secretary to the mayor of Gammelin, 1945–46; technical assistant, East German Writers' Union, 1953–59; editor, *Neue deutsche Literatur*, 1958–59; reader for Mitteldeutscher Verlag, Halle, 1959–62, and Verlag Neues Leben, Berlin; resident writer in a freight car manufacturing company, 1959–62; freelance writer from 1962; resigned membership in the German Communist Party, 1989, after 40 years as a party member.

Novels by Wolf

Moskauer Novelle [Moscow Novella], 1961
Der geteilte Himmel, 1963; as *Divided Heaven*, translated by Joan Becker, 1965
Nachdenken über Christa T., 1968; as *The Quest for Christa T.*, translated by Christopher Middleton, 1970
Kindheitsmuster, 1976; as *A Model Childhood*, translated by Ursula Molinaro and Hedwig Rappolt, 1980
Kein Ort, Nirgends, 1979; as *No Place on Earth*, translated by Jan Van Heurck, 1982
Kassandra, 1983; as *Cassandra: A Novel and Four Essays*, translated by Jan Van Heurck, 1984

Störfall: Nachrichten eines Tages, 1987; as *Accident: A Day's News*, translated by Heike Schwarzbauer and Rick Takvorian, 1989

Sommerstück [Summer Piece], 1989

Was bleibt, 1990; as *What Remains and Other Stories*, translated by Heike Schwarzbauer and Rick Takvorian, 1993

Medea: Stimmen, 1996; as *Medea: A Modern Retelling*, translated by John Cullen, 1998

Other Writings: short narratives, essays, journals, speeches, narratives for a film, letter exchanges, conversations.

Further Reading

Ankum, Katharina von, *Die Rezeption von Christa Wolf in Ost und West: Von "Moskauer Novelle" bis "Selbstversuch,"* Amsterdam and Atlanta, Georgia: Rodopi, 1991

Fehervary, Helen, "Christa Wolf's Prose: A Landscape of Masks," *New German Critique* 27 (1982)

Fries, Marilyn Sibley, editor, *Responses to Christa Wolf: Critical Essays*, Detroit, Michigan: Wayne State University Press, 1989

Hilzinger, Sonja, *Christa Wolf*, Stuttgart: Metzler, 1986

Lennox, Sara, "Christa Wolf und Ingeborg Bachmann: Über die Schwierigkeiten beim Schreiben der Wahrheit," in *Zwischen gestern und morgen: Schriftstellerinnen der DDR aus amerikanischer Sicht*, edited by Ute Thoss Brandes, Berlin and New York: Peter Lang, 1992

Sauer, Klaus, *Christa Wolf, Materialienbuch*, Darmstadt and Neuwied: Luchterhand, 1979

Schuler, Brigitta, *Phantastische Autentizität: Wirklichkeit im Werk Christa Wolfs*, Frankfurt am Main and New York: Peter Lang, 1988

Stephan, Alexander, *Christa Wolf*, Munich: Beck, 1976

Teupe, Peter, *Christa Wolfs "Kein Ort, Nirgends" als Paradigma der DDR-Literatur der siebziger Jahre*, Frankfurt am Main and New York: Peter Lang, 1992

Wallace, Ian, editor, *Christa Wolf in Perspective*, Amsterdam and Atlanta, Georgia: Rodopi, 1994

Woman at Point Zero by Nawāl al-Saʿdāwī

Emra'ah ʿinda nuqṭat al-ṣifr 1975

Nawāl al-Saʿdāwī's *Woman at Point Zero* is a novel of social protest that searingly indicts the treatment of women in Egypt's male-dominated economic system. At the same time, the novel displays preoccupations with individual awareness and self-conscious narration, reflecting the deep-seated conflict of the Arab intellectual caught between issues of gender and class, politics and art.

Saʿdāwī's protagonist, Firdaws, is a former prostitute who has murdered a despicable pimp, has been sentenced to death, and is awaiting execution, at which point she is interviewed by a female psychologist whose own narrative frames the text. Even before the two actually meet, Firdaws is invested with a charismatic aura by virtue of the imperial aloofness with which she resides in her jail cell, refusing all visitors. The warder and prison doctor speak of her complete indifference to everything. The psychologist is initially shocked upon entering Firdaws' cell: there is not a stick of furniture. As Firdaws tells her to sit on the ground, the psychologist describes the naked, cold touch of the floor. The bareness of the cell underscores Firdaws' apartness, her isolation from society and its values, and the psychologist's disorientation in the face of Firdaws' condition as a condemned prisoner.

Firdaws subsequently narrates a search for freedom that is also a growth into greater political and individual awareness. Beginning at the very bottom rung of society, she gradually becomes more independent. Each stage of her independence is marked by a new awareness that takes the form of an epiphany, a feeling on her part that she has finally discovered the highest truth. When her uncle first gives her a piastre, the truth is the power of money. When she first adopts the life of a prostitute, it is physical comfort and sensuality. When she abandons prostitution, it is respectability. When she is attracted to a man, it is love. When she goes back to prostitution, it is independence. And when she commits murder, it is courage. Each time she converts her new realization into a type of ethic, and each time she eventually comes to a point of disillusionment, which causes her to admit the limitations of her previous assumptions, reevaluate her experience, and grasp for a greater measure of freedom.

One of the most striking aspects of the narrative is Firdaws' relationship to money. She starts at the bottom of the economic ladder, and from her earliest childhood recollections money is charged with power and significance. When she earns her first £10 as a prostitute, she clutches the £10 note in her hand:

> The sudden contact sent a strange tautness through my body, an inner contraction as though something had jumped inside me and shaken my body with a violence that was almost painful.

As a prostitute, Firdaws presents herself to men as a commodity, yet in so doing she also obtains a degree of control both over herself and the volatile power of money. She dictates her terms to her clients, and experiments carefully with charging larger amounts for her services, testing the limits of her power to handle money in greater quantities and feeling the greater sense of her own worth that accrues with it. Significantly, toward the end of her narrative, Firdaws must confront the assumption with which she began. In a crucial scene, she snatches the money offered by a rich client out of his hand and tears it up into little pieces with a pent-up fury:

The feel of the notes under my fingers was the same as that of the first piastre ever held between them. . . . I tore the money to pieces, tore off . . . the last remaining veil from my eyes, to reveal the whole enigma which had puzzled me throughout . . . my life. . . . It was as though I was destroying all the money I had ever held . . . and at the same time destroying all the men I had ever known.

Thus, in Firdaws' final epiphany, she rediscovers and emphatically rejects money as a source of freedom and even power, based on her recognition that money underlies the entire oppressive, male-dominated system. More importantly, however, in her utter rejection of money as power, she rejects power itself. In a sense, she removes herself completely from the material realm, looking forward only to death:

I have triumphed over both life and death because I no longer desire to live, nor do I any longer fear to die. I want nothing. I hope for nothing. I fear nothing. Therefore I am free. For during our life it is our wants, our hopes, our fears that enslave us.

It is at this point that Saʿdāwī transfers the momentum of the narrative from Firdaws back to the psychologist, who, after listening to Firdaws' story, feels indecisive:

I got into my little car, my eyes on the ground. Inside of me was a feeling of shame. I felt ashamed of myself, of my life, of my fears, and my lies. . . . I rammed my foot down on the accelerator as though in a hurry to run over the world, to stamp it out. But the next moment I quickly lifted my foot and braked hard, and the car came to a halt.

The psychologist's self-conscious awareness of herself as a member of the social elite puts her in a quandary, which is a stark contrast to the deep conviction and certainty that characterizes Firdaws. At the same time, however, her hesitation throws Firdaws' role as exemplar and social conscience into question. Because Firdaws has always gone from one epiphany to another, we must doubt whether she has really arrived at the ultimate truth. While she presents a devastating political critique of Egyptian society, her example does not offer a solution. Firdaws allies herself with no cause, no movement. She gives no hint of espousing any type of collective action. Her statement that "It is our wants, our hopes, our fears that enslave us" is a profoundly nonpolitical sentiment, reflecting the ambivalence of the author more than that of the social class that she means to represent and defend.

STEFAN MEYER

See also Nawāl al-Saʿdāwī

Further Reading

Accad, Evelyne, *Sexuality and War: Literary Masks of the Middle East,* New York: New York University Press, 1990

Hafez, Sabry, "Woman's Narrative in Modern Arabic Literature: A Typology," in *Love and Sexuality in Modern Arabic Literature,* edited by Roger Allen and Hilary Kilpatrick, London: Saqi Press, 1995

Malti-Douglas, Fedwa, *Woman's Body, Woman's Word: Gender and Discourse in Arabo-Islamic Writing,* Princeton, New Jersey: Princeton University Press, 1991

Malti-Douglas, Fedwa, *Men, Women, and God(s): Nawal El Saadawi and Arab Feminist Poetics,* Berkeley: University of California Press, 1995

Zeidan, Joseph T., *Arab Women Novelists: The Formative Years and Beyond,* Albany: State University of New York Press, 1995

Women in Love by D.H. Lawrence

1920

D.H. Lawrence was never out of battle with the attitudes that dominated book culture in his time. It is a wonder that he was able to get himself in print. The recent Cambridge Editions of Lawrence's work have produced his texts and their history, in particular the textual history of *Women in Love,* with an uncompromised thoroughness Lawrence himself could not have managed in his conflicted state.

In the Cambridge Edition of *Women in Love* (1987), David Farmer, Lindeth Vasey, and John Worthen elaborate the story— already known in a rough way—of how "The Sisters" began as a single novel to follow *Sons and Lovers* (1913). The story then grew so comprehensive in scope that Lawrence first published *The Rainbow* (1915), which narrated the early life of the Brangwen family and the two Brangwen sisters, and then added *Women in Love* to tell the story of their loves; the latter novel was published in slightly different versions in 1920 and 1921.

The too-vivid actualities of personal life, as Joyce called them, can always be called to account for what Lawrence published, what he was warned not to publish, and what he was forced to rescind. His friend and editor Edward Garnett clearly cut into the early prose of Lawrence as he did that of Conrad; manuscripts of *Women in Love* were held hostage by competing publishers, and Lawrence was forced to adjust two characters in the novel to avoid libel. Yet Lawrence was the kind of writer who answered back to pressure, and he found more elaborate (and perhaps even more powerful) means to season his bitter stew.

As E.M. Forster suggested, English writing often aspires to prophecy. If *King Lear* is pre-biblical, at best an English *figura* for revealing the rivalrous violence that has been hidden since the foundation of the world, *The Rainbow* is post-biblical, depicting an English family reared up ripe for revelation. Paul Morel in *Sons and Lovers* has a reason to blame his problems on his parents' problems, but *The Rainbow*'s genealogy is more hopeful: it implies that an English family could come through to spiritual life, not death. Both *Sons and Lovers* and *The Rainbow* (along with James Joyce's *A Portrait of the Artist as a Young Man,* 1916) end with their heroes resolutely refusing a death that the novel's structure (as the form of history) has prepared for them. Against the novel's form is the lyrical narrative voice with which we are invited to identify, and which successfully wishes Paul and Ursula (and Stephen) well.

Ursula is reborn at the end of *The Rainbow* as a woman more than fit for Birkin, a man without any family at all to drag him down, a self-generated being. She knows about Birkin what the novels know about Lawrence's heroes: their self-regarding posturing before women. In *Women in Love,* Birkin has been continuing with a relationship that is rotting him, and has been unable to break clear for Ursula alone. Dialectic in the homely form of domestic quarreling, which is the technique of discovery in Lawrence's greatest fiction, saves Birkin from himself:

> "Go to your spiritual brides—but don't come to me as well, because I'm not having any, thank you. . . . I know your dirty little game." Suddenly a flame ran over her, and she stamped her foot madly on the road, and he winced, afraid that she would strike him.

This is from the "Excurse" chapter of *Women in Love,* where Birkin and Ursula drive out for a picnic. In this scene, Birkin is reckless behind the wheel in the same way Gerald Crich, his counterpart, runs the machines at the colliery, with a taste for self-destruction. The argument beautifully crystallizes Birkin and Ursula as a couple; by chapter's end the auto becomes a haven, not an instrument of self-destruction, where they spend the evening together in Sherwood Forest.

In general, *Women in Love* depicts the way in which people transform themselves into new beings; as such, it poses two major questions (for Lawrence as well, since he was always on the lookout for people capable of transformation, and always disappointed): Where do such new beings come from? And how do they recognize each other?

In *The Rainbow,* Ursula is reborn in the university laboratory, looking through a microscope. Under her own eyes she sees being change form, according to its own inscape. Like the most successful species, she then mimics this transmogrification. Like many writers of his time, Lawrence believed humans could change their lives in more than conscious ways, but he found Freud tawdry and sacrilegious to the mysterious new beings forming and collecting in the modern world. This view forced Lawrence to write his own psychology, twice-over, in *Psychoanalysis and the Unconscious* (1921) and *Fantasia of the Unconscious* (1922), just after the publication of *Women in Love.*

Gerald Crich and Gudrun Brangwen (Ursula's sister), like Birkin and Hermione (Birkin's lover before Ursula), show by contrast bad mimesis, the imitation and reciprocity of conflict. In these relationships, each individual wants to absorb the other's being. When Ursula and Gudrun see Gerald brutally reining in his red Arab mare to the regulated horsepower of an oncom-

ing train, in the "Coaldust" chapter early in the novel, Ursula is furious, but Gudrun is fascinated. (Later, Gudrun and Gerald arouse each other under a viaduct to the rhythm of one of Gerald's trains passing overhead.) A proper feminism would see in this episode the end of any further sorority implied in the title ("The Sisters") of the novel's first draft, and of its first chapter. Women must distinguish themselves in love with the men they choose.

The "Industrial Magnate" chapter analyzes Gerald's lineage and casts his future. The chapter beautifully weaves personal and social relations together. Gerald's father dallied with his men, pretending to serve them rather than to possess them. Gerald, however, makes the intuitive leap of futurism, seeing in machines and industry the ultimate reduction of other beings (his employees) to be appropriated in his own being. Bored with hand-to-hand combat in imperialism's wilder shores (late capitalism's version of the gentleman's cultural tour), he has returned home to struggle with matter itself.

With similar self-deception, Mr. Crich senior demands the sole possession of his wife's being; the life-long struggle poisons him and crazes her. In love, Gerald likewise passes beyond his father. Gerald's initial campy erotic entanglement with an art model, however, seems to refer to the contemporaneous studies of primitive and perverted sexual behavior as manuals for modern erotic practice; their coupling parodies as well the sensuous electricity of Lawrence's earlier work. If there is something theoretical or manmade in this sexual electricity, Gerald follows this inclination to a more serious and profound contest with Gudrun, whose art student guise hides a superior understanding of the possibilities of possessing other beings.

Gudrun sees beyond Gerald's rough appropriation of labor to the artist's more comprehensive reduction of sexuality into representations. In the end she changes out the supermasculine Gerald for the more theoretical (and more dangerous) Loerke. In the magnificent "Continental" chapter, Ursula (and Lawrence) stands alone against the reigning aesthetic orthodoxy of art's indifference represented by Loerke. Even Birkin pretends not to see what is there in Loerke's art for all to see.

> The statuette was of a naked girl, small, finely made, sitting on a great naked horse. The girl was young and tender, a mere bud. She was sitting sideways on the horse, her face in her hands, as if in shame and grief, in a little abandon.

As in the "Coaldust" chapter, Gudrun is fascinated, Ursula is again furious. She is ridiculed by everyone as aesthetically naive for confusing representations with real horses, for questioning the morality of this representation by insisting that horses really are sensitive, not brutal creatures. It takes Ursula a long pause to give back a reply no one else could: If one allows the artist to represent horses as stupid and brutal, what follows?

In defiance of the false sophistication of others, Ursula insists on answering her own question publicly. Her question, however, reveals that Loerke's brutality is commodified for all to possess privately, autoerotically. Aesthetic practice follows world market practices, selves being absorbed like little nations, third-world labor forces. Loerke condenses rare erotics for later reconstitution. Loerke's *cénacle* handle easily a photogravure reproduction of a statuette, and are exonerated in advance from consumer guilt over sweated labor. This particular statue or representation suggests that victims are dramatic "masochists," only posing "as if in shame and grief, in a little abandon." Despite all their denials, and embarrassment at Ursula's clumsiness, Gudrun subsequently asks Loerke (once Ursula is no longer present) who the girl really was.

Women in Love, having come so far, ends more diffidently than either *Sons and Lovers* or *The Rainbow.* Ursula and Birkin end the novel in disagreement about whether they have enough in each other. The promise of the future, which all true modern novels carry, is borne solely by their practice, by their success in finding each other through argument.

WILLIAM A. JOHNSEN

See also D.H. Lawrence

Further Reading

Bloom, Harold, editor, *D.H. Lawrence's "Women in Love,"* New York: Chelsea House, 1988

Carpenter, Lucas, "The Name 'Minette' in *Women in Love,"* *English Language Notes* 32:1 (September 1994)

Clarke, Colin (Colin C.), editor, *D.H. Lawrence: "The Rainbow" and "Women in Love": A Casebook,* London: Macmillan, 1969

Craft, Christopher, *Another Kind of Love: Male Homosexual Desire in English Discourse, 1850–1920,* Berkeley: University of California Press, 1994

Davies, Alistair, "Contexts of Reading: The Reception of D.H. Lawrence's *The Rainbow* and *Women in Love,"* in *The Theory of Reading,* edited by Frank Gloversmith, Brighton, Sussex: Harvester, and Totowa, New Jersey: Barnes and Noble, 1984

Doherty, Gerald, "The Salvator Mundi Touch: Messianic Typology in D.H. Lawrence's *Women in Love,"* *ARIEL: A Review of International English Literature* 13:3 (July 1982)

Doherty, Gerald, "Ars Erotica or Scientia Sexualis? Narrative Vicissitudes in D.H. Lawrence's *Women in Love,"* *Journal of Narrative Technique* 26:2 (Spring 1996)

Erzgraber, Willi, "Formen des Bewusstseins im technologischen Zeitalter: Zu D.H. Lawrences Roman *Women in Love,"* in *Das Natur/Kultur-Paradigma in der englischsprachigen Erzahlliteratur des 19. und 20. Jahrhunderts: Festschrift zum 60. Geburtstag von Paul Goetsch,* edited by Konrad Gross, Kurt Muller, and Meinhard Winkgens, Tübingen: Günter Narr, 1994

Gordon, David J., "D.H. Lawrence's Dual Myth of Origin," *Sewanee Review* 89:1 (Winter 1981)

Hayles, Nancy Katherine, "The Ambivalent Approach: D.H. Lawrence and the New Physics," *Mosaic: A Journal for the Interdisciplinary Study of Literature* 15:3 (September 1982)

Heywood, Christopher, "The Image of Africa in *Women in Love,"* *D.H. Lawrence: The Journal of the D.H. Lawrence Society* 4:1 (1986)

Holderness, Graham, *"Women in Love,"* Philadelphia and Milton Keynes: Open University Press, 1986

Hyde, Virginia, "Architectural Monuments: Centers of Worship in *Women in Love,"* *Mosaic: A Journal for the Interdisciplinary Study of Literature* 17:4 (Fall 1984)

Ingersoll, Earl, "Staging the Gaze in D.H. Lawrence's *Women in Love,"* *Studies in the Novel* 26:3 (Fall 1994)

Jewinski, Ed, "The Phallus in D.H. Lawrence and Jacques Lacan," *The D.H. Lawrence Review* 21:1 (Spring 1988)

Katz-Roy, Ginette, "Le dialogue avec les avant-gardes dans *Women in Love,"* *Etudes Lawrenciennes* 5 (1990)

Leavis, F.R., *D.H. Lawrence, Novelist,* New York: Norton, 1947; London: Chatto and Windus, 1955

Mackillop, Ian, "Women in Love, Class War, and School Inspectors," in *D.H. Lawrence: New Studies,* edited by Christopher Heywood, London: Macmillan, and New York: St. Martin's Press, 1987

McLean, Celia, "The Entropic Artist: Loerke's Theories of Art in *Women in Love,"* *The D.H. Lawrence Review* 20:3 (Fall 1988)

Miko, Stephen J., editor, *Twentieth Century Interpretations of "Women in Love": A Collection of Critical Essays,* Englewood Cliffs, New Jersey: Prentice-Hall, 1969

New, Peter, *Fiction and Purpose in "Utopia," "Rasselas," "The Mill on the Floss," and "Women in Love,"* London: Macmillan, and New York: St. Martin's Press, 1985

O'Hara, Daniel, "The Power of Nothing in *Women in Love,"* *Bucknell Review: A Scholarly Journal of Letters, Arts and Sciences* 28:2 (1983)

Ross, Charles H., "Editorial Principles in the Penguin and Cambridge Editions of *Women in Love,"* *The D.H. Lawrence Review* 21:2 (Summer 1990)

Sagar, Keith, *D.H. Lawrence: Life into Art,* London: Viking, and Athens: University of Georgia Press, 1985

Topia, Andre, "*Women in Love*: L'Espace, le corps, la machine," in *L'Espace littéraire dans la littérature et la culture anglo-saxonnes,* edited by Bernard Brugiere, Paris: Presses de la Sorbonne Nouvelle, 1995

Torgovnick, Mariana, "Closure and the Shape of Fictions: The Example of *Women in Love,"* in *The Study of Time IV,* edited by J.T. Fraser, Berlin and New York: Springer, 1981

Wright, Anne, *Literature of Crisis, 1910–22: "Howards End," "Heartbreak House," "Women in Love," and "The Waste Land,"* London: Macmillan, 1984

Zapf, Herbert, "Taylorism in D.H. Lawrence's *Women in Love,"* *The D.H. Lawrence Review* 15:1–2 (Spring–Summer 1982)

Virginia Woolf 1882–1941

English

Virginia Woolf occupies two different roles in the history of the novel: she is a founder of modernism and an important feminist social critic. The conjunction of these two roles defines what is most distinctive about her. In her literary works, as in those of few other modernists, formal innovations function as social commentary and as acts of resistance. Modernism is usually considered a purely aesthetic movement, identified by the use of distinctive literary techniques such as fragmentation, stream of consciousness, images, and nonreferential prose. Critics who view Woolf as a modernist describe her as a writer who creates beautiful, mythic, and poetic patterns, presenting consciousness as what she called a "luminous halo" surrounding everything.

Yet Woolf's novels also contain powerful social criticism, and her formal innovations support that assessment. In one of the most important essays in the history of feminist theory, *A Room of One's Own* (1929), Woolf argued that a change in the forms of literature was necessary because most literature had been "made by men out of their own needs for their own uses." She developed innovative literary forms in order to speak from and to women's experiences. This literary project was part of a vast dream of social change involving economics and politics as well as gender roles: she and her husband Leonard supported the socialist agenda of the British Labour party, and they were pacifists.

One way to understand the social project in Woolf's novels is to say that she seeks to reveal an alternative to the conventional ways we view reality. She complains in one essay that novelists have sought to portray people too much in terms of their external surroundings, as if knowing a person's house is sufficient to know the contours of that person's life and mind. Instead, Woolf argues, authors must recognize that "In one day . . . thousands of emotions have met, collided, and disappeared in astonishing disorder." Using the stream-of-consciousness technique to reveal the astonishing disorder inside her characters, Woolf unveils impulses people have never acted upon because of social constraints. She thereby disrupts what had been a central characteristic of novels: the growth and revelation of a distinct, coherent character. Woolf's works imply that the process that makes individuals seem coherent is largely one of limitation and repression. In *To the Lighthouse* (1927), the streams of thought reveal the unpursued desires of the characters, and the dullness of everyday conversation is at least in part a result of vast restrictive social forces that squeeze out of life that which is most vibrant and exciting, that which Woolf's luminous prose seeks to restore.

Woolf's distinctive style emerges in the last quarter of her first novel, *The Voyage Out* (1915): after many pages of a witty love story, the young heroine comes down with a mysterious fever, and Woolf changes style to delve into the distortions of fevered perception, creating a mysterious world beyond the limits of Victorian psychology and social conventions. After *The Voyage Out,* Woolf wrote a fairly traditional novel, *Night and Day* (1919), and then began a series of experiments that became her major novels. *Mrs. Dalloway* (1925) follows the thoughts of several groups of people whose paths overlap but never cross over the course of a single day, until the social order seems a giant web in which all the separate minds are caught. Woolf implies in this novel that, in order to fulfill the social roles assigned to them, both men and women have to repress and deaden their feelings: Clarissa Dalloway, an intelligent, passionate woman, finds that her world becomes "narrow" when she marries, and Woolf parallels that narrowness to the suicidal emptiness felt by a young man after the trauma of fighting in World War I.

In the novels after *Mrs. Dalloway* Woolf creates multiple perspectives by using a double structure of chronology: the longest passages consist of acutely observed moments, sometimes only a few minutes long, during which we see the dense web of subconscious thoughts occurring simultaneously in many persons' minds; the text then leaps from one such moment to another, years apart, bridging the leaps with short descriptions of changes that occur independent of what the characters are doing (for example, seasons shifting and wars breaking out). Her books thus confront us with the problem of how to combine two kinds of time: the rich emotional density of momentary experience and the vast impersonal flow of history.

Her most well known novel, *To the Lighthouse,* is divided into three parts: in the first section, we watch the Ramsay family and some friends during a few evening hours at a vacation house; then the characters all leave for a very short section entitled "Time Passes," during which there is a mysterious, impersonal flow of time, including World War I and the death of Mrs. Ramsay; the last chapter is another long account of a morning ten years later. Woolf described the book as having a "broken unity": it enacts the shift from the Victorian to the modern era as the breaking of the unified flow of the traditional novel. The novel focuses on a young woman's struggle to become an artist, suggesting what Woolf wrote in *A Room of One's Own,* that changes in the social order around the time of the war altered the very fabric of consciousness, the way people experience everyday life, and thereby led to new forms of expression, a process that she hoped would someday remove the constrictions on women's writing. In *The Waves* (1931), Woolf carries much further the double structure of time. The book consists of two quite different styles: each chapter begins with a brief "interlude," a lush description of a setting that slowly changes throughout the novel (for example, flowers start to grow in the first interlude, blossom in a middle interlude, and wither at the end); after each interlude, there are monologues given by each of six friends, with no narration or description at all. Each chapter picks up the six characters at different stages in their lives—as little children, as students at school together, as workers, as middle-aged adults, and, finally, as individuals facing death. The characters do not discuss conventionally important elements of lives—marriage, childbirth, success at work, or war. Rather, they focus on powerful moments of sensation and shared feelings, so that their speeches often seem more like lyric poetry than novelistic dialogue. Critics have regarded *The Waves* as Woolf's most mystical work, suggesting either the isolation of all modern life or a deep spiritual unity that remains invisible most of the time. The book also is an acute analysis of the ways that each generation is molded so that it repeats the behaviors and thoughts of previous generations. The radical structure of the novel reflects Woolf's radical hope for a new generation that would not follow the pattern of her own, a new generation that could perhaps appreciate intensity of feeling more than success.

Woolf's later novels extend the double structure beyond single lifetimes to ponder how ages do sometimes change. *Orlando* (1928) turns to fantasy: Orlando is a small boy in the Elizabethan era who falls asleep one night, waking as a young man in the 18th century; later he undergoes an equally surprising transition to become a young woman in the 19th century and later still a 30-year-old woman in 1928. The book is illustrated with pictures of Woolf's lover, Vita Sackville-West, dressed as Orlando at various ages. The novel is a playful tribute to Vita as well as an effort to understand and revise the history of gender roles. Woolf's last novel, *Between the Acts* (1941), occurs in one day, during which a pageant written by a lesbian author presents an overview of English history. The pageant ends in the present day, represented by actors who carry dozens of mirrors on stage, creating a fragmented reflection of the audience. One might say that Woolf's career culminates in this image of the fragmented form of modernist literature becoming a part of the public ceremony of life, breaking up not only aesthetics but also social rituals.

Woolf drowned herself in 1941. Her suicide has colored interpretations of her works. In her memoirs, Woolf draws attention to traumas she suffered in her childhood: both her parents died when she was just entering adolescence, leading to episodes of mental breakdown, and she was sexually abused by her half-brother. Her struggle with these traumas and with her own experiences of abnormal psychology are depicted in her works, but she drew far more than personal meaning out of them. Woolf found both horror and beauty in what was left out of everyday consciousness, and she modified the form of the novel to reveal that rich complexity.

MICHAEL TRATNER

See also Mrs. Dalloway; To the Lighthouse

Biography

Born 25 January 1882 in London; daughter of the scholar and writer Leslie Stephen, and younger sister of the painter Vanessa Bell. Educated privately; attended Kings College, London, as an external student, 1898–1902. Married the writer Leonard Woolf in 1912. Moved to Bloomsbury, London, 1905, and began her association with what later became known as the Bloomsbury Group, consisting of her sister, the economist J.M. Keynes, the art critic Roger Fry, the painter Duncan Grant, the writers E.M. Forster and David Garnett, and others; also at this time began contributing articles to the *Times Literary Supplement* and various other journals; teacher of adult education classes, Morley College, London, 1905; founder, with Leonard Woolf, Hogarth Press, Richmond, Surrey, later London, 1917–41. Died 28 March 1941.

Novels by Woolf

The Voyage Out, 1915
Night and Day, 1919
Jacob's Room, 1922
Mrs. Dalloway, 1925
To the Lighthouse, 1927
Orlando, 1928
The Waves, 1931
Flush, 1933
The Years, 1937
Between the Acts, 1941

Other Writings: essays, criticism, short stories, and letters; prominent works include *A Room of One's Own* (1929), *Three Guineas* (1938), and *Roger Fry: A Biography* (1940).

Further Reading

Abel, Elizabeth, *Virginia Woolf and the Fictions of Psychoanalysis,* Chicago: University of Chicago Press, 1989

Bazin, Nancy Topping, *Virginia Woolf and the Androgynous Vision,* New Brunswick, New Jersey: Rutgers University Press, 1973

Bell, Quentin, *Virginia Woolf: A Biography,* New York: Harcourt, Brace, Jovanovich, and London: Hogarth Press, 1972; revised edition, London: Pimlico, 1996

Bowlby, Rachel, *Virginia Woolf: Feminist Destinations,* New York: Blackwell, 1988

DeSalvo, Louise, *Virginia Woolf: The Impact of Childhood Sexual Abuse on Her Life and Work,* London: Women's Press, and Boston: Beacon Press, 1989

Hussey, Mark, editor, *Virginia Woolf and War: Fiction, Reality, and Myth,* Syracuse, New York: Syracuse University Press, 1991

Laurence, Patricia Ondek, *The Reading of Silence: Virginia Woolf in the English Tradition,* Stanford, California: Stanford University Press, 1991

Love, Jean O., *Worlds in Consciousness: Mythopoetic Thought in the Novels of Virginia Woolf,* Berkeley: University of California Press, 1970

Marcus, Jane, *Virginia Woolf and the Languages of Patriarchy,* Bloomington: Indiana University Press, 1987

Marcus, Jane, editor, *Virginia Woolf, a Feminist Slant,* Lincoln: University of Nebraska Press, 1983

Mepham, John, *Virginia Woolf: A Literary Life,* London: Macmillan, and New York: St. Martin's Press, 1991

Minow-Pinkney, Makiko, *Virginia Woolf and the Problem of the Subject,* Brighton: Harvester, and New Brunswick, New Jersey: Rutgers University Press, 1987

Naremore, James, *The World Without a Self: Virginia Woolf and the Novel,* New Haven, Connecticut: Yale University Press, 1973

Rose, Phyllis, *Woman of Letters: A Life of Virginia Woolf,* New York: Oxford University Press, and London; Routledge and Kegan Paul, 1978

Ruotolo, Lucio, *The Interrupted Moment: A View of Virginia Woolf's Novels,* Stanford, California: Stanford University Press, 1986

Squier, Susan Merrill, *Virginia Woolf and London: The Sexual Politics of the City,* Chapel Hill: University of North Carolina Press, 1985

Zwerdling, Alex, *Virginia Woolf and the Real World,* Berkeley: University of California Press, 1986

Working-Class Novel. *See* Proletarian Novel

World of Wonders. *See* Deptford Trilogy

Wuthering Heights by Emily Brontë

1847

The initial reception of Emily, Charlotte, and Anne Brontë's first novels (all published in 1847) is part of Brontë lore. Charlotte's *Jane Eyre* was an instant success, Anne's *Agnes Grey* was noticed in passing, and Emily's *Wuthering Heights* elicited critical responses indicating that the reviewers, while noting its originality and power, had difficulty assessing a novel that appeared to defy the conventions of current fiction. The excessive behavior of the principal characters seemed unrealistic, and the complex time scheme of the novel was taken as evidence that Emily Brontë had not achieved full formal control over her narrative materials.

After her sisters' deaths, Charlotte Brontë edited a second edition of their novels, with prefatory commentary aimed at correcting what she saw as the reviewers' misunderstanding of *Wuthering Heights*, and at presenting the novel as at least partly realistic—not, as some critics had suggested, the product of an overluxuriant imagination creating a fictional world out of whole cloth. When, after Charlotte's death, her father, Patrick Brontë, solicited her friend and fellow novelist Elizabeth Gaskell to write Charlotte's biography, Gaskell also took pains to persuade readers unfamiliar with Yorkshire that the behavior of the characters in the Brontës' novels was an accurate reflection of Yorkshire life; as such, Gaskell sought to locate their novels within the then-current expectations for realistic fiction. Where *Wuthering Heights* is concerned, the reason both for initial critical incomprehension and the efforts of Charlotte Brontë and Gaskell to resituate the novel within the conventions of fictional realism may lie in Emily Brontë's extremely sophisticated handling of first-person narrative and, to a lesser degree, in her departure from conventional linear narrative.

First-person narration, used by all of the Brontës in their first novels, had a long history by 1847. In the mid–18th century, Samuel Richardson had freed first-person narrative from the limitations of the monologic, or single narrative voice, typical of the novels of Defoe; Richardson introduced multivocalism through the device of the continuing exchange of letters among characters. Whereas both Anne and Charlotte Brontë reverted to the monologic autobiographical form, Emily reintroduced multivocal first-person narration—not, however, through an ex-change of letters, but by layering narrative within narrative. Her model may have been Mary Shelley's *Frankenstein* (1818), which *is* epistolary, but which layers Dr. Frankenstein's and the Monster's oral narratives within the letters of the principal narrator, Walton, to his sister.

In contrast to Charlotte and Anne, whose novels take the form of autobiographies written by authoritative and reliable narrators, Emily introduces an unreliable narrator, Lockwood, a cosmopolitan outsider who is so baffled by the behavior of Heathcliff, his Yorkshire landlord, and the other inhabitants of Wuthering Heights, that he consistently misinterprets their reactions to him as well as their own relationships and interactions. From a combination of frustration, curiosity, and irritation, Lockwood asks Nelly Dean, his housekeeper, who has lived for two generations with the novel's two principal families, the Earnshaws and the Lintons, to recount their histories, which he records in his journal. Nelly Dean thus becomes the main narrator of the novel. Since Brontë does not superimpose an omniscient authorial voice as check or corrective for either of her first-person narrators, Lockwood and Nelly, she places the reader in a position similar to Lockwood's in the initial chapters. Both as chronicler and interpreter of the history of the two families, Nelly stands as mediator between the reader and the raw data from which her narrative is composed. The reader, therefore, must depend on Nelly's reliability as historical chronicler as well as on her ability to shape the data of the chronicle into an articulated narrative structure promising the possibility of meaning.

The opening chapters of *Wuthering Heights* stage a confrontation between the modern/sophisticated and the archaic/primitive: the self-conscious, educated language of Lockwood against its extreme opposite, the Yorkshire dialect of the old servant, Joseph. Between these two poles is situated the enigmatic young Catherine, who speaks Lockwood's standard English, but who, the narrative suggests, may also be an adept at black magic. This confrontation reaches an early and uncanny climax in the famous dream scene, in which Lockwood, marooned at Wuthering Heights by a snow storm, spends the night in an ancient closed bed, where he is visited by two absurd and terrifying nightmares. In each of these nightmares, Lockwood is forced into confrontations to which he reacts with belligerence, terror, and violence, implying that Lockwood's civilized behavior is a veneer that masks primitive, irrational forces within him of which he has been unaware but which may erupt in moments of extreme stress. This sequence has provoked a wide range of interpretive responses, on the assumption that unlocking the meaning of the dreams is crucial to the interpretation of the novel as a whole.

But the eruption of the primitive through the veneer of civilization is relevant as well to the novel's peculiar kind of discourse. Nelly Dean's narrative is a sustained oral performance, an archaic form dependent on memory that has survived into the modern world, and as such it predates both the written narrative of Lockwood's diary and the print culture of the novel itself. Its physical analogue is Wuthering Heights, a house dating from 1500, in distinct contrast to the modern Thrushcross Grange, the estate rented by Lockwood. Since Nelly's history is oral, and thus can survive only by being transposed to writing in Lockwood's journal, it is tempting to assume that Brontë's text subordinates the archaic to the modern, so that Lockwood's journal becomes a kind of archaeological exercise, retrieving a past that would otherwise vanish. But Nelly's narrative, while oral, is not folkloric. It adopts the conventions of realistic narrative: linear narration unfolded as an almost seamless sequence of cause and effect, psychological individualization of character, and novelistic development by scene and summary. From this perspective, it is possible to see Nelly as dominant, and Lockwood serving merely as her scribe.

While Nelly's presentation is that of the contemporary realist narrator, the materials of her history are strangely resistant to continuous linear narrative. It is not the eruption of violence in some of the scenes, evoking a primitive substratum beneath the appearance of civility, that measures this resistance to linearity. It is rather a pattern of cyclical repetition suggesting the persistence of the archaic that refuses to be defined by, explained by, or reduced to the rational, irreversible sequence of cause and effect. Thus, not only the plot of the novel, but also the conflicted form of Nelly's narrative reproduces a crisis of historical transition, and the ambiguity of the novel's ending, suggesting that on the one hand the story's dead rest peacefully in their graves, and on the other that they inhabit the landscape as ghosts, suspends the reader between the atavistic primitive and the rational modern.

If *Wuthering Heights* had any immediate influence on the novel form, one might locate that influence in the development of the sensationalist novels of the 1860s, particularly in Wilkie Collins' experiments with multivocal first-person narratives in such works as *The Woman in White* (1860) and *The Moonstone* (1868). Not until Conrad, however, did a novelist explore the tensions between the primitive and the modern with such a sophisticated control of narrative voice, or with a similar refusal to reduce ambiguity to simplistic clarity, as Brontë did in *Wuthering Heights*.

JAMES L. HILL

Further Reading

Armstrong, Nancy, "Emily Brontë: In and Out of Her Time," *Genre* 15 (1982)

Davies, Stevie, *Emily Brontë*, New York and London: Harvester Wheatsheaf, 1988

Eagleton, Terry, *Myths of Power: A Marxist Study of the Brontës,* London: Macmillan, and New York: Barnes and Noble, 1975; 2nd edition, London: Macmillan, 1988

Homans, Margaret, *Bearing the Word: Language and Female Experience in Nineteenth-Century Women's Writing,* Chicago: University of Chicago Press, 1986

Jacobs, Carol, *Uncontainable Romanticism: Shelley, Brontë, Kleist,* Baltimore: Johns Hopkins University Press, 1989

Jameson, Fredric, *The Political Unconscious: Narrative as a Socially Symbolic Act,* Ithaca, New York: Cornell University Press, and London: Methuen, 1981

Knoepflmacher, U.C., *Emily Brontë: Wuthering Heights,* Cambridge and New York: Cambridge University Press, 1989

Tayler, Irene, *Holy Ghosts: The Male Muses of Emily and Charlotte Brontë,* New York: Columbia University Press, 1990

Van Ghent, Dorothy, *The English Novel: Form and Function,* New York: Rinehart, 1953

X

Xiao Hong 1911–42

Chinese

During a writing career that spanned less than a decade, Xiao Hong (pseudonym of Zhang Naiying) furthered the development of the novel in China as few other novelists were able to do. After depicting the harsh realities of village life in Manchuria and the brutalities of war in her first novel, she capped her career in Hong Kong shortly before her death there with an autobiographical novel that set the standard for the genre.

Few women wrote fiction during the early decades of the Republican era in China, which began politically with the fall of the Manchu (Qing) dynasty in 1911 and culturally with the May 4th Movement (1919), a complete rupture with the classical traditions that had held sway for millennia; none but Xiao Hong tried her hand at the novel. The publication of *Sheng si chang* (1935; *The Field of Life and Death*), written shortly after Xiao Hong fled the city of Harbin for the coastal city of Qingdao with fellow novelist Xiao Jun, made such an impact on leftist literary circles and urban readers that Xiao Hong gained instant fame. Initially, that fame grew out of her treatment of a part of China little known south of the Great Wall. She was heralded by Lu Xun, China's most revered cultural figure, who wrote the preface for *The Field of Life and Death*, lauding its author for her graphic evocation of Manchurian village life and for giving full artistic expression to the effects of war on the northeastern peasantry, as Japanese encroachments increased. The novel opens with starkly vivid domestic conflicts centering on the young female protagonist, replete with animal imagery and uncharacteristically coarse language. However, a wrenching shift in tone and perspective occurs two-thirds of the way through the novel: suddenly, as war comes to Manchuria somewhere beyond the village, darkly cinematic scenes are replaced by hearsay and shadowy musings on the future of the village. This, of course, is how women learned of the cruelties of war outside their homes, and a palpable sense of foreboding informs the writing from that point on.

The inexorable progress of the Japanese army southward and inland forced Xiao Hong to spend the last seven years of her life on the run, driven by approaching war from the cities of Qingdao, Shanghai, Wuhan, and Chongqing to Hong Kong on the eve of its fall. During that time, ideologically driven stories and essays—long on patriotic fervor but short on artistry, interspersed occasionally with nostalgic re-creations of life in Manchuria—were published under Xiao Hong's name.

After arriving in Hong Kong, desperately ill and emotionally spent, Xiao Hong surprised (and, for the most part, displeased) her readers and the writing community by publishing the first volume of a planned trilogy, a comic satire entitled *Ma Bole* (1940; Ma Bo-le); the second volume appeared in serialized form on the eve of the author's death several months later. Satire, an underdeveloped form in China, has generally appeared only in novels of fantasy. Xiao Hong, however, created a comical (eponymous) character who mocks the patriotism of his era and trivializes the war raging around him. It would take nearly half a century before other Chinese authors would feel sufficiently confident of their comic vision and secure enough politically to break free of Sinocentric realist conventions (socialist and otherwise) and treat contemporary life in China with this sort of barbed humor.

Yet for all her successes and innovations in realistic and satirical novels, Xiao Hong is best known as a writer of fictionalized memoirs, a body of lyrical re-creations of the author/narrator's life as a child in Manchuria. This facet of her oeuvre, which surfaced periodically throughout her short career, was capped by the novel *Hulanhe zhuan* (1941; *Tales of Hulan River*). Set in Xiao Hong's hometown in the years immediately following the collapse of the last imperial dynasty, the novel succeeds brilliantly in evoking quotidian domestic images through the eyes of the narrator/protagonist, investing the narrative with childlike innocence and unmediated observations of place, people, and a way of life. This is accomplished through simple yet poetic language and revealing descriptions of ordinary events, in contrast to the simplistic bombast preferred by most of Xiao Hong's peers. *Tales of Hulan River* was characterized as a genre painting by Mao Dun, the foremost literary critic of the early Republican era. Given the contemporary preference for more "functional" literature, Xiao Hong's impact on the development of the novel in China would not be felt until 40 years after her death, when the nation's wars with foreign and domestic enemies had run their course, and writers were once again free to experiment with artistic forms and narrative strategies.

Xiao Hong was nearly alone in grasping the concept that both form and content are mutually informing. Her three novels, and the stories upon which the last two were based, display an intuitive understanding that a variety of narrative styles and generic forms must be employed to successfully treat diverse materials. While most of her peers were content to paint heroic or uncommonly bleak pictures of China through the medium of "hardcore" realism—humorless and heavily didactic—she was driven to experiment with all the colors in her literary palette. Satire, reminiscence, and imprecise descriptions of likely events, while frowned upon by most wartime writers, established her reputation, albeit belatedly, as one of the most innovative novelists of the Republican era. As a result, her works have stood as models for later generations of writers.

HOWARD GOLDBLATT

Biography
Born 2 June 1911 to a landlord family in Heilongjiang province in Northeast China (Manchuria). After attending school in Harbin, began submitting stories and poems to local newspapers; driven from her homeland by the Japanese invasion in 1932, she traveled to Shanghai with fellow Northeastern novelist Xiao Jun, where they came under the wing of China's foremost literary figure, Lu Xun; over the next several years she kept one step ahead of Japanese advances, traveling from Wuhan to Chongqing and finally to Hong Kong, where she died of respiratory problems in January 1942, shortly after the colony fell to the Japanese.

Novels by Xiao Hong
Sheng si chang, 1935; as *The Field of Life and Death*, translated by Howard Goldblatt, 1979
Ma Bole [Ma Bo-le], 1940; sequel [Ma Bo-le, Part II], 1941
Hulanhe zhuan, 1941; as *Tales of Hulan River*, translated by Howard Goldblatt, 1979

Other Writings: stories and poems.

Further Reading
Cros-Morea, Simone, "Women and Sexuality in Xiao Hong's *Sheng Sichang*," in *Woman and Literature in China*, edited by Anna Gerstlacher, Bochum: Brockmeyer, 1985
Goldblatt, Howard, *Hsiao Hung*, Boston: Twayne, 1976
Goldblatt, Howard, "Life as Art: Xiao Hong and Autobiography," in *Woman and Literature in China*, edited by Anna Gerstlacher, Bochum: Brockmeyer, 1985
Liu, Lydia H., "The Female Body and Nationalist Discourse: Manchuria in Xiao Hong's *Field of Life and Death*," in *Body, Subject & Power in China*, edited by Angelo Zito and Tani E. Barlow, Chicago: University of Chicago Press, 1994
Shuying Tsao, "Xiao Hong and Her Novel *Tales of Hulan River*," in *Woman and Literature in China*, edited by Anna Gerstlacher, Bochum: Brockmeyer, 1985

Xiyou ji. *See* Six Classic Chinese Novels

Y

Yang ko. *See* Rice Sprout Song

A.B. Yehoshua 1936–

Israeli

Avraham B. Yehoshua is a leading Israeli author from a generation that came of age after the establishment of the State of Israel in 1948. He is acclaimed both in Israel and abroad, and his short stories have been adapted to film, television, and theatre.

Striking in the depth of their psychological portrayals, Yehoshua's novels probe a number of moral, social, and political problems arising from modern Israeli statehood and the Jewish condition. His realistic depiction of different lifestyles is punctuated by ironic and humorous insights into human behavior. His characters, without being stereotypes, range in age, gender, ethnicity, and religious affiliation, representing most sectors of Israeli society. Typically, they lead normal lifestyles until the fantasies and obsessions at the core of their personalities suffuse and transform their lives.

Owing to their compulsiveness, Yehoshua's complex-ridden characters are usually caught in absurd situations. Having facilitated his wife's adultery, Adam, the middle-aged husband in Yehoshua's first novel, *Hame'ahev* (1977; *The Lover*), obsessively searches for her lover, who vanishes at the onset of the Yom Kippur war. *The Lover*'s opening lines introduce the comical absurdity of its plot as the cuckolded husband himself announces in plural, "And in the last [war] we lost a lover. We used to have a lover, and since the war he is gone." In *Shivah me-Hodu* (1994; *Open Heart*), a struggling young doctor falls in love with an overweight, middle-aged wife and mother rather than with her attractive young daughter, whom he is asked to rescue from India. In Yehoshua's most recent novel, *Masa el tom ha-elef* (1997; *Voyage to the End of the Millennium*), a Sephardic businessman travels perilously across the ocean to try to convince his nephew's wife that bigamy is not an abomination.

Similar combinations of obsession and absurdity mounted upon a realistic frame of reference to daily life hallmark Yeho-

shua's novels together with a distinguishing array of characters ranging panoramically across Jewish history and contemporary Israeli society. In *The Lover*, Yehoshua's dynamic portrayal of an intelligent and eloquent young Israeli-Arab contrasts sharply with an earlier depiction of a mute old Arab arsonist in his classical short story "Mul haye'arot" (1968; "Facing the Forest"). Yehoshua's ability to render empathetically many sectors of Israeli society has expanded over the course of his writing career.

Since he began writing novels in the mid-1970s, Yehoshua increasingly has turned toward explorations of the mores and behavior of Sephardic Jews, who trace their cultural heritage to Spain and the Mediterranean. As a Sephardic Jerusalemite educated among Ashkenazic Jews, at the onset of his literary career Yehoshua wrote short stories centering on troubled Ashkenazic intellectuals. Particularly in the last decade, however, he has veered toward representations of Sephardic Jews living in a world dominated by Western culture. Like Yehoshua himself, most of the Sephardic characters in his novels belong to the "old settlement" of Jews in Israel, dating back several generations and thus differing both from Ashkenazic Jews and more recent Middle Eastern immigrants. The protagonist of *Molcho* (1987; *Five Seasons*) is a Sephardic man whose dutiful adherence to home and family symbolizes a patient acceptance of the hardships of the land of Zion; this scenario contrasts with the fickleness of the Ashkenazic protagonist of *Gerushim me'uharim* (1982; *A Late Divorce*), who leaves Israel and his family when his marital life takes a bad turn.

Evident in all of Yehoshua's novels is a preoccupation with the "illness of Diaspora," as Yehoshua calls it, as well as with a variety of political and existential issues related to Zionism. Yet the main subjects of his novels are the universal themes of obsession, isolation, curiosity, age, illness, death, and passion. All his plots involve some form of marital calamity, dysfunctional family life, and tension between the generations.

Yehoshua is also a superb stylist who enjoys playing with the structural possibilities of the novel. He favors the use of staggered monologue and dialogue narratives that enable him to display conflicting points of view without allowing any to dominate over the others. *The Lover* and *A Late Divorce* are constructed as a series of alternating and overlapping monologues; stream-of-consciousness narration is used intermittently. *Mar Mani* (1990; *Mr. Mani*), a structural tour de force, presents five conversations in which only the words of one interlocutor appear on the page, yet the reader easily reconstructs the words of the absent interlocutor from the arguments, apologies, and requests of the first speaker. Yehoshua is William Faulkner's faithful student, respecting the employment of multiple narrating consciousnesses that give equal weight to conflicting points of view. His keen psychological insight, ironic social criticism, and intelligent humor are further reminiscent of Fedor Dostoevskii, Charles Dickens, and S.Y. Agnon, while a Kafkaesque dimension may be gleaned from his blend of realism and the absurd.

In *Mr. Mani*, realistic details and milestones of more than 200 years of Jewish history are chronicled *backward* through conversations about a Sephardic family perpetually tottering on the verge of extinction. Since its series of conversations starting in 1982 and ending in 1848 take place mostly between Ashkenazic Jews who are strangers to the family, this novel has been described as an *anti*-historical novel and an *anti*-family saga that skillfully subverts the genres and techniques it uses. With *Masa el tom ha-elef*, a historical novel set in the year 1000 A.D., Yehoshua reaches further into the origins of the distinctions between Sephardic and Ashkenazic worldviews by placing his story at a key juncture in Jewish history, during which the cultural demography of the Jewish people was forever altered.

Compared to the ideological optimism of early Zionist writers, Yehoshua's historical and political vision may seem pessimistic. Yet, since he confronts the perennial troubles of Jews and Israel in a playful style imbued with empathy and high humor, Yehoshua should not be pigeon-holed as either a prophet of doom or a humorist, as purely a realist or a fantasist. Structurally and thematically, Yehoshua has revolutionized Israeli literature by balancing all these impulses.

YAEL HALEVI-WISE

See also Mr. Mani

Biography

Born 9 December 1936 in Jerusalem. Attended Jerusalem Hebrew Gymnasium; Hebrew University, Jerusalem, B.A. 1961; Teachers College, graduated 1962. Served in the Israeli Army, 1954–57; teacher, Hebrew University High School, Jerusalem, 1961–63; director, Israeli School, Paris, 1963–64; secretary-general, World Union of Jewish Students, Paris, 1963–67; dean of students, 1967–72, and from 1972 professor of comparative literature, Haifa University; visiting fellow, St. Cross College, Oxford, 1975–76; guest professor, Harvard University,

Cambridge, Massachusetts, 1977, University of Chicago, 1988, and Stanford University, Stanford, California, 1990; member of board of art, Haifa Municipal Theatre; adviser to drama editorial board, Israeli Television Network; member of editorial board, *Keshet* literary magazine, 1967–74; editorial consultant, *Siman Kria, Tel-Aviv Review,* and *Mifgash.*

Novels by Yehoshua

Hame'ahev, 1977; as *The Lover,* translated by Philip Simpson, 1977

Gerushim me'uharim, 1982; as *A Late Divorce,* translated by Hillel Halkin, 1984

Molcho, 1987; as *Five Seasons,* translated by Hillel Halkin, 1989

Mar Mani, 1990; as *Mr. Mani,* translated by Hillel Halkin, 1992

Shivah me-Hodu, 1994; as *Open Heart,* translated by Dalya Bilu, 1996

Masa el tom ha-elef [Voyage to the End of the Millennium], 1997

Other Writings: several volumes of short stories, a novella (*Bithilat kayits 1970* [1972; *Early in the Summer of 1970*]), plays (including *Laylah beMai* [1969; *A Night in May*] and *Tipolim acharonim* [1973; *Last Treatment*]), and political essays (*Bizechut hanormaliyut* [1980; *Between Right and Right*] and *Hakir vehahar: Metsi'uto hasifrutit shel hasofer be Yisrael* [1989; *The Wall and the Mountain: The Literary Reality of the Writer in Israel*]).

Further Reading

Ben-Dov, Nitza, editor, *Ba-Kivun Ha-Negdi: Kovets Mekarim Al "Mar Mani" Le-A.B. Yehoshua* (In the Opposite Direction: Articles on *Mr. Mani*), Tel Aviv: Ha-Kibuts Ha-meuhad, 1995

Hakak, Lev, "Israeli Society as Depicted in the Novels of A.B. Yehoshua," in his *Equivocal Dreams: Studies in Modern Hebrew Literature,* Hoboken, New Jersey: Ktav, 1993

Horn, Bernard, *Facing the Fires: Conversations with A.B. Yehoshua,* Syracuse, New York: Syracuse University Press, 1997

Itzjaki, Yedidya, *Ha-Pesukim Ha-Semuyim Min Ha-Ayin: Al Yetsirat A.B. Yehoshua* (The Concealed Verses), Ramat-Gan: Bar-Ilan University, 1992

Morahg, Gilead, "Outraged Humanism: The Fiction of A.B. Yehoshua," *Hebrew-Annual Review* 3 (1979)

Morahg, Gilead, "Reality and Symbol in the Fiction of A.B. Yehoshua," *Prooftexts* 2 (1982)

Sadan-Lovenshtein, Nili, *A.B. Yehoshua: A Monograph,* Tel Aviv: Sifriyat Poa'alim, 1981

Shohet, Meiri, *Al Hatzhok Ba-Sifrut Ha-Israelit: A.B. Yehoshua, Nathan Zach, Yehuda Amichai* (Laughter in Israeli Literature: A.B. Yehoshua, Nathan Zach, Yehuda Amichai), Tel Aviv: Sifriyat Poa'alim, 1973

Yugoslavian Novel

From the beginning of their existence in southeastern Europe, around the tenth century, Slavic tribes developed their cultures independently, just as they formed their national identities separately. Only after World War I were they united in one state called Yugoslavia (meaning, roughly, "South Slavs"). Even then, Yugoslav literatures continued their separate existence despite the ethnic, linguistic, and historical kinship. Therefore, it is best to discuss the history of the Yugoslav novel of the main literatures—Serbian, Croatian, and Slovenian—separately, following their independent developments, even after 1918, while highlighting their common features. (*For a discussion of the Macedonian novel, see the entry* Southern Balkan Novel.)

Serbia

The Serbian novel traces its crude beginnings to the 12th century, when in the only seats of learning at that time, churches and monasteries, a number of biographies of Serbian rulers and saints were written in a form that resembles the novel. During the five-century-long occupation by the Turks, only oral literature was permitted and numerous epic poems were composed, to be written down later. These also bear a crude resemblance to the novel. One of these poetry cycles describes the prehistory, the event itself, and the aftermath of the fateful battle of Kosovo, in which Serbia lost its independence. In another cycle, the adventures and superhuman feats of the greatest Serbian mythical hero, Kraljević Marko, were depicted with a rather novelistic unity of plot and character development. Although the direct influence of these epic poems on the later development of the Serbian novel is not immediately clear, there is no doubt that it was significant.

During the centuries of Turkish rule, when the only manifestation of national identity was the Serbian Church, several medieval novels were translated into the liturgical language. Such novels as *The Trojan War, Alexander the Great, Varlaam and Joasaf,* and other historical and religious stories, were the only contact the Serbs had with world literature. In the 18th century would come translations of French, German, and other novels and stories. Inasmuch as they are not original creations, these translations properly belong to the prehistory of the Serbian novel, although they, too, exerted a significant influence on the first novelists. Again, it is very difficult to ascertain the nature and extent of this influence.

It was not until the beginning of the 19th century that the Serbian novel had its real beginning with the work of Milovan Vidaković. He possessed limited artistic skills but unlimited ambitions, imitating the European baroque adventure novel and the Greek love novels of late antiquity. He wrote several novels of scant artistic value, yet they were popular with readers. His best known works, *Usamljeni junoša* (1810; Lonely Youth) and *Ljubomir in Elisium* (1814; Ljubomir in Elysium), display the main features of his art: a pervasive sentimentality, especially in matters of love and romantic adventure, and a general disregard for realism, expressed in unrestrained flights of imagination, unlikely events, inconsistencies, and even contradictions. Despite these shortcomings, Vidaković succeeded in arousing in Serbian readers an appetite for novels written in their own language. For this, the noted Serbian critic Jovan Skerlić called him "the founder of the Serbian novel," indicating his historical, if not artistic, significance.

The period of romanticism that followed, lasting approximately four decades (1830–70), emphasized poetry and drama. Few novels were written, and those that were clearly rejected the romantic spirit in literature. The only novel of Jovan Sterija Popović, *Roman bez romana* (1832; A Novel without a Story), demonstrates even in its title the author's rejection of sentimental romanticism, even while satirizing the failings of Vidaković and other writers of his time. Bogoboj Atanacković employed in his *Dva idola* (1851–52; Two Idols) the staple romantic themes of love and patriotism, but turned his attention primarily to the contemporary life of Serbs under Hungarian rule and their suffering in the 1848 revolution. Both of these novels are still read today, primarily for their historical flavor.

The Serbian novel began to mature in the second half of the 19th century. The writer who made great strides in bringing the novel to the sophistication and popularity of poetry and the short story was Jakov Ignjatović. Starting with historical novels, he soon turned to the realistic depiction of life in his native region, Voyvodina in Austria-Hungary. His seven novels on contemporary themes form a rich repository of the ethnic and social mores of his people. Even though romanticism still dominated Serbian literature at the time he wrote most of his novels, his attention to the details of everyday life (learned from the French realists) made him the founder of the realist novel in Serbian literature. His first work, an ambitious two-volume undertaking, *Milan Narandžić* (1860–62; Milan Narandzhich), is a picaresque story about a young man of humble origins who finds his place in society mainly by unscrupulous means. Ignjatović also portrays the life of the prosperous middle class in Austria-Hungary around the middle of the 19th century, particularly their materialism and social climbing. Thus Ignjatović succeeds, as Jovan Deretić points out, in degrading and vulgarizing the idealistic and noble impulses while at the same time praising and poeticizing the low and vulgar ones (see Deretić, 1981). Other novels by Ignjatović—*Čudan svet* (1869; Strange World), *Trpen spasen* (1874–75; Endurance Is Deliverance), *Vasa Rešpekt* (1875; Vasa the Respected), *Veciti mladoženja* (1878; The Perennial Bridegroom), and *Patnica* (1885; The Sufferer)—reveal a writer of sharp observation and boundless energy. His novels formed a firm basis for the further development of the Serbian novel. They enjoyed wide popularity and are still read with interest.

Ignjatović's achievements were not fully appreciated by the critics of his time, mainly because realism supplanted romanticism only after the arrival of other realist novelists in the last decade of the 19th century. While these novelists may have resembled Ignjatović in their realistic approach and in their trend toward regionalism, they differed from him in other ways. For the most part they depicted Serbian village life, following the lead of the short story, which in this period developed into an original literary genre, often referred to as the Serbian village short story. It is no coincidence that most of these novelists were also well known as short-story writers. The best of them is Janko Veselinović, a prolific short-story writer who portrayed the Serbian village of his native region, northwestern Serbia, in an exaggerated, idealized fashion. His principal novels, *Seljanka* (1893; A Peasant Woman) and *Hajduk Stanko* (1896; The Rebel Stanko), are actually long short stories with novelistic features. Simo Matavulj presents Dalmatia and Montenegro in his two novels, *Uskok* (1892; The Rebel) and *Bakonja fra Brne* (1892; Bakonja Fratar Brne), but with greater artistic skill. His second novel is a fine psychological portrait of life in a Catholic monastery, the monks being portrayed with all their virtues and weaknesses. Stevan Sremac wrote about southeastern Serbia around the town of Niš, where the old ways of life were in constant conflict with the new. Several of his novels—*Ivkova slava* (1895; Ivko's House Patron's Day), *Limunacija na selu* (1896; Fireworks in the Village), *Pop Ćira i pop Spira* (1898; Father Ćira and Father Spira), *Vukadin* (1903; Vukadin), and *Zona Zamfirova* (1907; Zamphir's Zona)—have enjoyed immense popularity ever since they were published. The main reasons are to be found in Sremac's realistic portrayal of life, in his close identification with the common people, and above all in his gentle and genuine humor. His novels have strong dramatic qualities, and practically all of them have been made into plays and, later, movies. All these qualities show Sremac's strong kinship with Gogol'.

Another realist novelist of note, Svetolik Ranković, attempted a series of ambitious psychological character studies, which suffer from a general lack of sophistication and artistic excellence. Under the influence of Russian realists, especially Tolstoi and Dostoevskii, he wrote three psychologically and socially poignant novels. *Gorski car* (1897; The Mountain Czar), the story of an outlaw who meets his inevitable end at the hand of justice, de-romanticizes a pattern of antisocial behavior that goes back to medieval Serbian history, when it was justified in the struggle against the Turks. *Seoska učiteljica* (1898; The Village Teacher) presents the tragedy of a young schoolmistress whose life is destroyed by the backward and often cruel villagers who have not yet reached the civilized stage to which she aspires. *Porušeni ideali* (1900; Shattered Ideals) treats the disillusionment and tragic end of a young idealist in a monastery. Ranković's novels illustrate the rapid advances of the Serbian novel as well as the limitations that prevented it from reaching greater heights.

The realist tradition persisted for a while into the 20th century. At the same time, modernist tendencies began to make inroads. Changes in narrative technique were not dramatic at first, but in time modernist approaches became dominant. The best representative of the new generation is Borislav Stanković, who depicted the town of Vranje at the border of two worlds—the Serbian, therefore European, and the Turkish, whose influence still lingered in parts of the Balkans. His best novel, *Nečista krv* (1911; Sophka), brought new tones into Serbian literature by dwelling on sensuality in his characters, both young and old, and by showing the changes brought about by the struggle between the old and new ways of life. Other novelists of the time, including Svetozar Ćorović and Ivo Ćipiko, brought little new in their novels. The new element was ushered in by Milutin Uskoković, whose two novels, *Došljaci* (1910; Newcomers) and *Čedomir Ilić* (1914; Chedomir Ilich), depicted life in Belgrade, in contrast to practically the entire existing literature, which concerned itself with either village or small-town life.

Modernist features became fully noticeable only after World War I, when an entirely new generation of writers entered the literary arena. Of many novelists, two stand apart: Rastko Petrović and Miloš Crnjanski. Their work belongs to the best in Serbian literature. Their efforts to break with the traditional approach to the novel and to replace it with avant-garde innovations resulted partly from the horrors of war they had experienced and partly from a desire to catch up with modernism in Western European literatures. In his first novel, *Burleska gospodina Peruna boga groma* (1921; The Burlesque of Mr. Perun, the God of Thunder), Petrović erases the boundaries between the real and unreal, between the possible and impossible, between logic and nonsense, for the purpose of shocking the reader and exploring new possibilities in literature. His most important novel, *Dan šesti* (1961; The Sixth Day), is much more down to earth, yet it, too, is not free of excesses and uncontrolled flights of fantasy. The novel is organized around a large number of loosely connected events and characters, which convey the idea that life and death constantly alternate in an endless renewal, foreshadowing Boris Pasternak's *Doktor Zhivago* (1957; *Doctor Zhivago*) in certain ways. Many of Crnjanski's novels also deal with the basic questions of life and death. *Dnevnik o Čarnojeviću* (1921; A Diary about Charnojevich) voices a protest against a senseless war and human cruelty. However, war serves primarily as the background of the protagonist's maturation. *Seobe* (1929; Migrations) delves into the history of the Serbs in Austria-Hungary around the middle of the 18th century, when they were sent to Western Europe to fight and die for an empire they did not consider their own. The Serbs serve in the Austro-Hungarian army hoping to improve their lot through their sacrifices. When they are disappointed, they see their salvation only in migrating to another Slavic country, Russia. Thus Crnjanski touches upon one of the basic facts in the history of his people—constant migrations which fate forces upon them. Petrović and Crnjanski, both accomplished poets, imbued their novels with a poetic atmosphere hitherto unknown in Serbian fiction.

Of other novels in the interwar period, a few deserve brief mention. *Crvene magle* (1922; Red Fogs) by Dragiša Vasić, one of the first post–World War I novels, vividly depicts the horrible suffering in that war, both physical and psychological (the latter turmoil referred to by the "red fog" of the title). *Nevidbog* (1933; The Invisible God) by Risto Ratković is also about the war but as seen by common men preoccupied primarily with their personal problems. *Srpska trilogija* (1934–36; Serbian Trilogy) by Stevan Jakovljević is the most popular epic saga about World War I, treating the war as a heroic effort rather than as meaningless suffering. *Pokošeno polje* (1936; The Mowed Field) by Branimir Ćosić begins in the prewar era and ends with the disillusionment of the postwar period, with the war seen from the point of view of a social critic. *Selo* (1937; A Village) by Dušan Radić is one of the best novels about Serbian village life in the 1930s, with all its joys and sorrows. *Dukljanska zemlja* (1939; The Land of Duclea) by Dušan Djurović describes the hard life in Montenegro around World War I, realistically and poetically, but mostly critically. The overall novelistic output between the world wars reflects a great variety of approaches and efforts to continue in the realistic tradition and strike out along new, modernist paths at the same time. Although not on the same artistic level as the novels by Petrović and Crnjanski, these works contributed to the overall development of the Serbian novel as it moved away from self-centered regionalism and toward more universal perspectives.

The Serbian novel after World War II received a strong impetus from the publication of three novels by Ivo Andrić in 1945: *Na Drini ćuprija* (*The Bridge on the Drina*), *Travnička hronika* (translated as *Bosnian Story* and also as *Bosnian Chronicle* and *The Days of the Consuls*), and *Gospodjica* (*The Woman from Sarajevo*). The first two rank among the best novels in Serbian literature, and it is largely on their strength that Andrić received the Nobel prize for literature in 1961. *The Bridge on the Drina* is of epic proportions, spanning some of the most fateful events in the history of the southern Slavs from the early 16th century to the beginning of World War I. It shows generations of Serbs, Croats, and Bosnians, belonging to the Orthodox, Catholic, Muslim, and Jewish faiths, caught in the turbulent storms of Balkan history. It is more a chronicle than a true novel. The unifying feature is the bridge, built by a Turkish vizier of south Slavic origin. The bridge serves metaphorically as a link joining various nationalities living around it—joining East and West. In Andrić's words, "Life is an incomprehensible miracle because it is constantly being consumed and eroded and yet it lasts and stands firmly like the bridge on the Drina." By presenting the bridge as a national shrine, Andrić has also created the most meaningful and beautiful metaphor in all of Yugoslav literature. *Bosnian Story,* which some critics consider to be Andrić's best work, also resembles a chronicle, although it is more limited in scope. Confined to the beginning of the 19th century, it shows history at work in the backwater region of Bosnia during the period of Napoléon. Andrić is again concerned with the interaction of forces that shape history, attempting to prove the impossibility of a historical transplantation, which the big powers are trying to achieve on Balkan soil.

The most recent decades of Serbian fiction are marked by a significantly increased output, by an improved artistic quality, and by a continuation of the tradition coupled with adaptations to the developments in other literatures. These trends followed upon a brief flirtation with socialist realism. *Svadba* (1950; Wedding) by Mihailo Lalić was the first in a steady stream of excellent Serbian novels to appear since the 1950s. This novelist's crowning achievement actually came a few years later with *Lelejska gora* (1959; *The Wailing Mountain*), which deals with the trials and tribulations of a young partisan leader in Montenegro during World War II. Cut off from his comrades and surrounded by the enemy, he is forced to improvise in order to survive. Lalić uses this existentialist setting to probe into the mind and soul of the main character. He is concerned as much with the reactions of his hero to everyday situations as he is with the war. The combination of realistic, often naturalistic, descriptions with psychological probing, achieved by way of dreams, hallucinations, and reminiscences, gives the work immediacy and a deeper significance rivaled by few other novels.

Dobrica Ćosić also began with a successful novel about the partisan war, *Daleko je sunce* (1951; Far Away Is the Sun), and over the next three decades he developed into a major novelist. His tetralogy *Vreme smrti* (1972–79; *This Land, This Time*) follows the struggle of the Serbs against their opponents in World War I. Eschewing for the most part the gory aspects of the war, Ćosić is primarily interested in finding answers to such age-old questions as: Why do people war with each other? When does a man have the right to kill another? His skillful blending of universal questions with descriptions of the heroic feats of his people at a time when their survival was at stake, coupled with

objectivity and dramatic flair, makes *This Time, This Land* one of the best novels in all of Serbian literature. Ćosić continued with novels about various periods in modern Serbian history. A three-volume artistic exposition of the communists' struggle for power is depicted in *Vreme zla* (1985–90; A Time of Evil), and the horrible experience of the Yugoslav communists loyal to Moscow in the post-1948 concentration camps is treated in the ongoing set of novels, *Vreme vlasti* (1996– ; A Time of Power). In these novels, Ćosić is a sharp critic of his own former comrades. His work is in the nature of a *roman-fleuve,* depicting Serbian society in the 20th century by tracing the story of one family, the Katićes, in all of his novels.

Among other Serbian novels, mention should be made of *Pesma* (1952; Poem) by Oskar Davičo, a highly artistic account of the underground struggle of the young communists against the Germans during the occupation in Belgrade. Branko Ćopić wrote several novels, with variable success, about the partisan war and its aftermath. Miloš Crnjanski, in a sequel to his *Migrations* entitled *Druga knjiga Seoba* (1962; The Second Book of Migrations), has his wandering Serbs finally arrive in Russia, where they are slowly assimilated. The sequel continues the bleak and pessimistic, yet eerily poetic, atmosphere of the first volume. Crnjanski's last novel, *Roman o Londonu* (1971; Novel about London), ostensibly about a Russian émigré, is in reality about the author's own physical and emotional hardships during his stay in London as an émigré after World War II. These novels confirmed Crnjanski's reputation as a leading Serb novelist.

The 1960s and the 1970s brought a large number of gifted new novelists. Meša Selimović distinguished himself with several successful works, especially *Derviš i smrt* (1966; *Death and the Dervish*). This thoughtful novel grapples with the basic problems of human existence: death, the contemplative versus the active life, and the effects of power on humans, both the rulers and the ruled. The treatment of these problems, suffused with philosophical, psychological, and poetic overtones, elevate the novel to the point of grandeur. Miodrag Bulatović published three provocative novels: *Crveni petao leti prema nebu* (1959; *The Red Cock Flies to Heaven*), *Heroj na magarcu* (1964; *A Hero on a Donkey*), and *Rat je bio bolji* (1968; *The War Was Better*). Bulatović uses these novels to voice a protest against war and other inhumane behavior. Later, in his novels about organized crime, *Ljudi sa četiri prsta* (1975; People with Four Fingers) and *Peti prst* (1977; The Fifth Finger), he seems to lose some of the creative power of his earlier work.

The most accomplished writers of recent decades are Danilo Kiš and Milorad Pavić. Kiš represents an objectivist movement in Serbian fiction that is influenced by Jorge Luis Borges. It produces "the prose of things," paying attention to things, details and historical facts. In his early works, he concentrated on the tragedy of his relatives who perished in great numbers at the hands of the Nazis. He built a particularly poignant memorial to his father in his first novel, *Bašta, pepeo* (1965; *Garden, Ashes*). The author's yearning for his lost childhood and for his eccentric but elusive father—a dreamer, a poet, a frustrated genius, and a proud squanderer of his many gifts—is a recurring theme in Kiš' fiction, most notably *Peščanik* (1972; *Hourglass*). Later he turned to a theme that would preoccupy him for the rest of his life—the cruelty of man to man as exemplified in the Nazi atrocities of World War II and the Stalinist purges. Both his last novel, *Grobnica za Borisa Davidoviča* (1976; *A Tomb for Boris*

Davidovich), and a collection of short stories, *Enciklopedija mrtvih* (1983; *The Encyclopedia of the Dead*), focus on communist atrocities.

Just as accomplished and innovative as Kiš, Milorad Pavić embodies the postmodernist tendencies in Serbian literature. His first novel, *Hazarski rečnik* (1984; *Dictionary of the Khazars*), which he subtitled a "novel lexicon in 100,000 words," was a worldwide success, owing primarily to its whimsical qualities. Pavić's mastery of form and language, his brilliant metaphors and other images, his studied playfulness, and his interest in basic philosophical questions concerning the nature of truth and reality—all have contributed to his success. He displays those characteristics in his other novels as well—*Predeo slikan čajem* (1988; *Landscape Painted with Tea*), *Unutrašnja strana vetra ili Roman o Heri i Leandru* (1991; *The Inner Side of the Wind; or, The Novel of Hero and Leander*), and *Poslednja ljubav u Carigradu* (1994; *Last Love in Constantinople*). Each of his novels has an innovative twist (*Landscape Painted with Tea*, for example, works like a crossword puzzle). Both Kiš and Pavić have been very successful abroad, adding substantially to the international exposure of Serbian literature and helping to engineer the end of provincialism.

Other notables among contemporary novelists are Borislav Pekić, Aleksandar Tišma, Dragoslav Mihailović, and Slobodan Selenić. Erudite, thoughtful, and indefatigable, Pekić is the author of many novels and plays. His first novel, *Vreme čuda* (1965; *The Time of Miracles*), presents an unorthodox, occasionally sacrilegious "gospel" in the name of Judas Iscariot, commenting on important events in the life of Jesus. His multivolume novels *Hodo čašće Arsenija Njegovana* (1970–81; *The Houses of Belgrade*) and *Zlatno runo* (1978–81; Golden Fleece) are studies of remarkable historical characters. Tišma also has several novels to his credit. Perhaps his best, *Upotreba čoveka* (1976; *The Use of Man*), tells the tragic story of a Jewish girl who was used for medical experiments by the Nazi doctors in Novi Sad. Mihailović burst upon the literary scene with a powerful novel, *Kad su cvetale tikve* (1968; *When the Pumpkins Bloomed*), which set a new trend with his merciless depiction of the alienation of youth and his criticism of social ills at a time when it was dangerous to do so. Before his untimely death in 1995, Selenić established a reputation as one of the best Serbian novelists. Each of his six novels—*Memoari Pere Bogalja* (1968; Memoirs of Pera the Cripple), *Prijatelji* (1980; Friends), *Pismoglava* (1982; Heads or Tails), *Očevi i oci* (1985; Fathers and Paters), *Timor mortis* (1989), and *Ubistvo s predumišljajem* (1994; *Premeditated Murder*)—represents a solid novelistic achievement with memorable characters and penetrating issues.

Novelists who were writing in the last years of the 20th century and who have contributed significantly to the genre include Erih Koš, Pavle Ugrinov, Živojin Pavlović, Mirko Kovač, Vidosav Stevanović, and Miroslav Josić Višnjić. Younger novelists whose work was just beginning to receive critical attention included David Albahari, Dragan Velikić, Svetislav Basara, and Vladimir Arsenijević.

The recent tragic events in Bosnia have had an effect on Serbian literature, most notably in Slobodan Selenić's *Premeditated Murder* and Vladimir Arsenijević's *U potpalublju* (1995; *In the Hold*). Both authors refrain from passing judgment on the conflict. Instead, they show its devastating effects on the psyche of the people, especially the young. Of late, many novelists are re-examining recent Serbian history, especially the circumstances of the communists' rise to power and their rule in the last 50 years—something writers were either unwilling or afraid to do before. Thus, Slobodan Selenić depicts in *Timor mortis* the immediate, harsh justice meted out to the domestic "traitors" in World War II, as does Svetlana Velmar Janković in her novel *Lagum* (1990; *Dungeon*). Vuk Drašković reconstructs in *Noć djenerala* (1994; The General's Night) the last night of General Draža Mihailović before his execution by the communists. Such revaluations are likely to occupy Serbian novelists for some time to come.

Croatia

Croatian fiction had a very early beginning when Petar Zoranić wrote the novel *Planine* (1569; Mountains). However, this work was to remain a solitary achievement, more an illustration of a highly polished literary culture that thrived in Dubrovnik in the Middle Ages than the beginning of a genre. When the next novelist appeared three centuries later, he had little beyond nationality in common with Zoranić. August Šenoa, the true founder of the Croatian novel, wrote several enduring novels in his relatively short life. Even though his work shows some romantic features, such as plots based on a sentimental love story, he approached everyday life almost like a realist, especially when he described social conditions in the bourgeois society of his time. Šenoa is often called the Croatian Walter Scott, and his best novels are on historical subjects: *Zlatorovo zlato* (1871; The Goldsmith's Gold), *Seljačka buna* (1878; *The Peasant Rebellion*), *Diogenes* (1878), and *Kletva* (1881; The Curse). Historical events and figures from the 14th to the 18th century were used by Šenoa as an inspiration to the Croatian people in their struggle for independence and a just social order. Toward the end of his life, he turned entirely to topics from everyday life and wrote *Prosjak Luka* (1879; The Beggar Luka) and *Branka* (1881; Branka), but these novels are weaker than the historical ones. They show him gravitating toward realism, in sync with Croatian literature generally.

The only other novelist in this period worth mentioning is Josip Eugen Tomić, who lived and worked in Šenoa's shadow and could never match Šenoa's popularity. Nevertheless, Tomić left behind some interesting novels, especially his best work, *Melita* (1899; Melita), a novel about social conditions in Croatia toward the end of the century.

The realistic features in the work of Šenoa and Tomić gave the next generation a head start. In the last two decades of the 19th century—at about the same time as in Serbian fiction—several realists put their stamp on Croatian fiction. Perhaps the most prominent among them was Ante Kovačić. A protégé of Šenoa, he wrote at first in the romantic vein, but later turned to realism. Coming from a poor peasant family and having to fight for survival his entire life, he developed a keen eye for, and deep understanding of, social and political problems in Croatian society during the second half of the 19th century, especially with respect to the relationship between the village and the city. Kovačić describes the processes of urbanization in three novels, *Baroničina ljubav* (1877; The Baroness's Love), *Fiškal* (1882; The Solicitor), and his best work, *U registraturi* (1888; At the Registrar's). Kovačić, who possessed a great deal of raw talent but lacked literary sophistication, offered a broad panorama of Croatian social structure. He painted a number of well-executed characters from all walks of life and a starkly realistic presentation of everyday life. He was especially successful in presenting women as symbols of the protagonists' destinies.

Other realist writers of the time include Eugen Kumičić, Josip Kozarac, Vjenceslav Novak, Ksaver Šandor Djalski, and Janko Leskovar. Most of them wrote only one or two successful novels, but they all helped in establishing a tradition in Croatian fiction that would later bring forth outstanding works. Eugen Kumičić brought naturalism into Croatian literature following his studies in France. A native of Istria, he wrote his best works about his own region. An ardent patriot and active politician (as was Šenoa before him and Djalski after him), he lashed out against the sources of arbitrary power—Rome, Vienna, and Budapest—which kept his people, whom he idealized, in perpetual bondage. Most of his novels deal with the evils of contemporary life: *Začudjeni svatovi* (1883; The Astounded Wedding Guests), *Gospodja Sabina* (1884; Madame Sabina), *Sirota* (1885; The Orphan). His later novels on historical themes, *Urota Zrinsko-Frankopanska* (1892–93; The Zrinski-Frankopan Conspiracy) and *Kraljica Lepa* (1902; Queen Lepa), express his devotion to the Croatian people, especially the peasants, and his dislike for foreigners. Although Kumičić's artistic power was not exceptional, he nevertheless excelled in narration and in plot construction.

Josip Kozarac was also interested in social and economic problems and, unfortunately, often subordinated artistry to those concerns. In his two novels, *Mrtvi kapitali* (1889; Dead Capitals) and *Medju svjetlom i tminom* (1891; Between Light and Darkness), he depicted the sometimes too rapid economic development of his native Slavonia, which often resulted in the gradual demise of the traditional life of the peasants, in their ill-fated movement to the cities, and in the accompanying deterioration of their morals. He blamed his own people for these calamities, as well as foreigners, yet he offered no workable solution to the problem. Even though Kozarac approached his literary subjects often as an economist and sociologist and allowed that perspective to influence his writing, he also produced fine psychological portraits and poetic descriptions of the beauty of Slavonia, the richest Croatian region.

Vjenceslav Novak was, like all realists, interested primarily in everyday life, and in his numerous works he presented all facets of life in his native region of Senj—both the city and the surrounding villages. He is sometimes called the Croatian Balzac, because of his focus on daily life. In his best novels, *Poslednji Stipančići* (1899; The Last of the Stipanchich) and *Tito Dorčić* (1906; Tito Dorchich), he dwells on the conditions of the poor and on the inevitably tragic results of their poverty. This "poet of the poor," as Antun Barac calls him in his *History of Yugoslav Literature* (1973), approached his subject matter emotionally, despite his seeming detachment as a realist. The overall effect of his work is that of a passionate chronicler of reality.

In his long creative life Ksaver Šandor Djalski wrote many novels. A descendant of an old aristocratic family, he was a very cultured man, unlike most of his fellow realists. His origin, however, occasionally led to confusion as he tried to reconcile his allegiance to the old order with his desire to understand and accept the new. Nevertheless, his work exhibits a penetrating understanding of the social, political, and psychological make-up of the Croats in the last decades of the 19th century, especially in his best novel, *U noći* (1886; In the Night). His other novels—*Djurdjica Agićeva* (1889; Djurdjica Agich), *Osvit* (1892; Dawn), and *Za materinsku riječ* (1906; For a Motherly Word)—reveal his broad erudition and the influence of Turgenev, Balzac, and Flaubert. The artistic quality of Djalski's work is uneven and his emotional attachment was to a vanishing world, but he remains one of the most encompassing writers and the first "European" in Croatian literature.

Around the turn of the century profound changes took place in Croatian literature. Realism lost its vitality, and new currents, spurred by developments in Western European literatures, especially the French, began to take hold. A movement called *Moderna* ("Modern") established itself as the leading literary trend, just as it did in Serbian literature on a smaller scale. Although *Moderna* was more prominent in other genres, especially in poetry, there were some modernist novels as well. Among the novelists of this period are Milutin Cihlar Nehajev, Dinko Šimunović, and Janko Polić Kamov. Nehajev advocated close ties with European literatures and what they represented at this juncture—pessimism, fin-de-siècle weariness, and decadence. His best novel, *Bijeg* (1909; Flight), expresses these attitudes as experienced by a decadent intellectual. Šimunović, on the other hand, was not as closely tied with *Moderna* as others were. In his novels *Tudjinac* (1911; The Stranger) and *Porodica Vinčić* (1923; The Family Vinchich) he presents his native region, Dalmatia, not in the realistic fashion as his not-too-distant predecessors had done, but through the subjective prism of an artist who considers the form of his art just as important as its content.

Polić Kamov was a writer of revolt who rejected established norms and demanded that the artist follow his own dictates. Unfortunately, his dictates led him to the verge of total chaos and insanity. In his brief life, he left behind a fiery trail of feverish imagination and introspection, along with bold innovations. His only novel, *Isušena kaljuža* (1957; A Dried-Out Mudhole), published almost half a century after his death, shows that he was far ahead of his time. His works are only now being properly studied and appreciated.

The dominant figure in Croatian literature between the two world wars—and one of the most powerful writers in all of Yugoslav literature of the 20th century—was Miroslav Krleža. The author of numerous poems, short stories, plays, novels, essays, and political writings, Krleža dominated the literary scene as no other writer had. His political activism, based on "communism with a human face," colored his approach to literature as well, primarily in his selection of subjects and in his treatment of social problems. In his novels, *Povratak Filipa Latinovicza* (1932; The Return of Philip Latinovicz), *Na rubu pameti* (1938; On the Edge of Reason), *Banket u Blitvi* (1938–39, 1962; Banquet in Blitva), and *Zastave* (1967; Banners), he offers variations on the same theme, the rise and fall of a bourgeois society and its death throes. Spawned during the glory days of the Austro-Hungarian Empire, the Croatian part of the empire continued to live in mud, rot, and perfidy. Krleža frequently chose this stagnation as the subject and background of his fiction, most memorably in *The Return of Philip Latinovicz*.

The other important novelist of the interwar period was August Cesarec. A contemporary as well as a political and literary ally of Krleža, he limited his scope to a criticism of Croatian society in Zagreb after World War I. Under the influence of Dostoevskii and Krleža, Cesarec added fine psychological portraiture to his social criticism and imbued his characters with credible motivation in their social and political activism. All his novels,

Careva kraljevina (1925; The Czar's Kingdom), *Zlatni mladić* (1928; The Golden Youth), and *Bjegunci* (1933; Fugitives), display the same mixture of psychological realism, social criticism, and expressionistic style.

Other novelists of note writing at this time included Vjekoslav Majer, Hasan Kikić, Ivo Kozarčanin, Novak Simić, Milan Begović, Vladimir Nazor, and Viktor Car Emin. They all wrote in the shadow of Krleža and contributed, to varying degrees, to the period's lively atmosphere and literary ferment. Croatian literature of this time was more preoccupied with social and political problems than were other Yugoslav literatures, and the main reasons for this were Krleža's influence and the specific conditions found in the Croatian part of Yugoslavia after the common state was formed in 1918.

After World War II, Croatian literature saw some experiments in socialist realism, but the main trend in the novel was a continuation of prewar forms. The most striking feature of the contemporary Croatian novel is perhaps its versatility. For the first time the novel equaled the sophistication of the short story, which had long dominated Croatian fiction. Although most of the new novelists were, until recently, under the influence of Krleža, many of them freed themselves of this influence in their later development.

Among contemporary novelists, several deserve to be singled out. Petar Šegedin concentrates in all of his novels on the inner world of his characters, especially in the early *Djeca božja* (1946; God's Children) and *Osamljenici* (1947; Lonely People). The tendency toward psychological realism may be considered an important feature of the modern Croatian novel, which stands in sharp contrast to earlier fiction, which was more interested in social and political realities. This concentration on the inner world may be found also in the work of Vladan Desnica. His novels, *Zimsko ljetovanje* (1950; The Winter Holiday) and *Proljeća Ivana Galeba* (1957; The Springtimes of Ivan Galeb), show the subtle transformation of Desnica into a writer of great intellectual and psychological acuity and of an increasing preoccupation with the basic issues of human existence, told in a modernist fashion that has become the trademark of contemporary Croatian fiction. Another writer who first appeared before the war but came into his own only later is Ranko Marinković. A fine short-story writer and playwright, he also has written *Kiklop* (1965; Cyclops), a novel about the plight, alienation, and fears of a modern-day intellectual in Zagreb. His interpretation of human existence is, in the words of Miroslav Vaupotić in his *Hrvatska suvremena književnost—Contemporary Croatian Literature* (1966), cynically destructive and yet compassionately humanistic. *Kiklop* is perhaps the most modern of Croatian novels, indicating the direction in which contemporary Croatian fiction is moving.

Vjekoslav Kaleb employs the theme of the partisan war in *Divota prašine* (1954; Glorious Dust) and *Bijeli kamen* (1955; White Stone), offering a realistic description of the war but also searching for the human being in the warrior and for the relationship between the inner and the outside world of the soldier. Mirko Božić writes about the same region as Kaleb, the Dalmatian hinterland, in a unique way, in both content and form. His best novels, *Kurlani* (1952; The Kurlans) and *Neisplakani* (1955; The Unwept), probe the relationship of man to nature in a bold formalist style that reveals a wide span of lexical possibilities. Vojin Jelić also began with the war theme (*Andjeli lijepo pjevaju* [1953; Angels Sing Beautifully]), but in later novels he has turned to urban life and to the world of childhood, thus widening his field of interest and deepening his penetration into the psyche of his characters. His later novel, *Doživotni grešnici* (1981; Life-Long Sinners), is about the life and tribulations of the people from the Dalmatian hinterland, written in a form that blends biography, chronicle, memoir, fantasy, and folklore. Jelić's work speaks for the diversity and experimentation of modern Croatian fiction.

Among the more important novels written in the past 30 years include works by Ivan Raos, Slobodan Novak, Antun Šoljan, Jozo Laušić, and Zvonimir Majdak, to name a few. Raos was a prolific fiction writer and playwright, whose best work, the trilogy *Vječno žalosni smijeh* (1965; Eternally Sorrowful Laughter), combines autobiographical and fictional elements told in a lyrical and humorous vein. Novak has written only one novel, *Mirisi, zlato i tamjan* (1968; Gold, Frankincense and Myrrh), but it ranks as one of the best contemporary Croatian novels. It is a bittersweet story of childhood and lost innocence, set on a Dalmatian island and projected against the cruel reality of war and betrayed expectations. A prominent poet, short-story writer, and playwright, Šoljan also wrote the novels *Izdajice* (1961; Traitors), *Luka* (1974; Harbor), and *Drugi ljudi na mjesecu* (1978; Other Men on the Moon), in which he analyzes the inability of mostly young individuals to find a common ground. Laušić, another prolific writer, prefers the subject matter of World War II and the devastation it has wreaked upon individuals. His best works, *Kostolomi* (1960; Bone Breaking) and *Opsada* (1965; Siege), reflect the rift between the warring sides and the ethical dilemmas that are felt long after the war. Majdak's favorite themes are individual destinies and personal relationships, especially among the young. His numerous novels, notably *Mladić* (1965; The Youth) and *Kužiš, stari moj* (1970; Get the Hang of It, Old Boy), represent the Croatian brand of the so-called "blue-jeans fiction."

A new generation of novelists is making their voices heard on the Croatian novelistic scene. The leading figures among them are Ivan Aralica, Pavao Pavličić, Goran Tribuson, and Dubravka Ugrešić. A native of Dalmatia, Aralica uses historical themes to comment on contemporary problems. His best novels, *Psi u trgovištu* (1979; Dogs at the Market), *Put bez sna* (1982; Journey Without Sleep), *Duše robova* (1984; The Souls of Slaves), and *Okvir za mržnju* (1987; A Frame for Hatred), are both traditional and modernist, combining the elements of medieval chronicles, oral folklore, and contemporary jargon. Pavličić often opts for urban, unusual, almost esoteric subject matter and he writes in a light, entertaining style bolstered by the curiosity of a modern intellectual, especially in his best novel, *Večernji akt* (1981; Evening Act). Somewhat similar to Pavličić, Tribuson also writes about urban everyday reality, often in the form of the mystery novel. One of his best novels, *Istorija pornografije* (1988; History of Pornography), depicts childhood in a provincial Croatian town. Ugrešić achieved her greatest success with *Forsiranje romana-reke* (1988; Fording the Stream of Consciousness), a spoof detective novel about an international literary conference in Zagreb, replete with humorous and ironic remarks about an artificial world of self-aggrandizement, soon to be buried in the catacombs of history. These writers are reaching their full potential only now and the final assessment of their works is yet to come. One thing is certain: like their Serbian counterparts, Croatian novelists of today are showing great versatility, maturity, and familiarity—even affinity—with the tendencies of contemporary world fiction.

Slovenia

It took the Slovenian novel even longer than the Serbian and Croatian to make its appearance. Because the Slovenes achieved their independence only in 1918 and had to fight for centuries for sheer survival as a nation, it was not until 1866 that their first novel, *Deseti brat* (The Tenth Brother) by Josip Jurčič, was published. Jurcic, considered the founder of Slovene fiction, wrote at the time of late romanticism in Slovenian literature. His work is closely related to folklore, which had survived through the dark times of Slovenian history. *Deseti brat* itself is based on the folk belief that the tenth child in a family is destined to go through extraordinary and mostly tragic experiences.

Without any other narrative tradition to draw upon, Jurčič and other early Slovenian fiction writers mined the rich folklore tradition. However, they did not simply borrow, but transformed the folklore material into genuine works of literature. While the short story was the dominant form of fiction, the novel, once inaugurated, made quick and significant strides. Jurčič himself wrote several novels after *Deseti brat,* the best of which are *Cvet in sad* (1867; The Flower and the Garden) and *Doktor Zober* (1876; Doctor Zober). Born in an impoverished village, he wrote mostly about the hard life of the Slovenian peasants, although later he also described city life as well. In all his works he approached his subject matter in a romantic vein, but realistic features are present as well. A contemporary of Jurčič, Josip Stritar wrote very much in the same vein, mixing romanticism and realism. Much more versatile and eventually more influential than Jurčič, Stritar wrote in other genres besides fiction. His main novels are *Zorin* (1870; Zorin) and *Gospod Mirodolski* (1876; Mr. Mirodolski).

The realist period in Slovene fiction followed hard on the heels of romanticism. Coming at about the same time as it did in Serbian and Croatian literatures, Slovene realism and was similarly influenced by French and Russian examples. The leading realists, Janko Kersnik and Ivan Tavčar, published their novels soon after Jurčič and Stritar. Kersnik, a descendant of a land-owning family and a well-educated intellectual, dwelled on the emergence of the Slovenian intellectual and the problems he faced being torn between the impoverished peasants and their foreign rulers. He too wrote about the life of the peasants, not as an outside observer but as a compassionate compatriot. In his novels—*Na Žerinjah* (1876; At Zherinje), *Ciklamen* (1883; Cyclamen), *Agitator* (1885; The Agitator), and *Jara gospoda* (1893; The Upstarts)—he did not completely reject romantic features, although his selection of themes and his treatment of social problems reveal in him the true realist.

Ivan Tavčar developed in the opposite direction. From a peasant origin, he rose socially and became a lawyer and an influential politician. It is interesting that even though he wrote mostly about the aristocracy and higher social strata (*Izza kongresa* [1906–07; After the Congress]), he wrote most successfully about the peasants, as evident in his best work, a historical novel *Visoška kronika* (1919; The Chronicles of Visoko), which treats the religious struggle during the Reformation.

The writer who put an end to both romanticism and realism at the beginning of the 20th century was Ivan Cankar, one of the greatest of Slovene writers. He was a leader of the *Moderna* movement, which, as in Croatia and Serbia, brought fundamental changes. A prolific and versatile writer, Cankar wrote several novels that belong to the highest achievements of the genre: *Tujci* (1901; Foreigners), *Na klancu* (1902; On the Cliff), and *Martin Kačur* (1906; Martin Kachur), to mention only the most important ones. He showed great sympathy for the downtrodden, championing the cause of social justice, human understanding, and compassion. At first affected by the spirit of decadence and symbolism at the turn of the century, he later developed his own unique style, not severing ties with the *Moderna,* yet going beyond its purely artistic objectives. A highly sensitive and basically lyrical writer and an activist in matters of social justice, he portrayed a great variety of characters from all walks of life, young and old, men and women. Most of his characters lead a rather unhappy life and are seemingly beyond help. Cankar also lashed out at the rich, the philistines, and the hypocrites—all those who were insensitive to the plight of their fellow man. Thus Cankar, the best Slovene fiction writer—on a par with Ivo Andrić and Miroslav Krleža—brought a new spirit into Slovene literature and, with his high artistic achievements, lighted the way for the generations after *Moderna.*

Two other fiction writers, whose creativity spanned several decades but who made their appearance approximately at the same time as Cankar, are František Saleški Finžgar and Alois Kraigher. Even though they wrote in Cankar's shadow, even after his death, they made their own contributions, especially Finžgar with his epic novel, *Pod svobodnim soncem* (1906–07; Under the Sun of Freedom), in which he lionized the struggle and victory of the sixth-century Slavs against Byzantium.

The end of World War I brought additional changes in Slovene literature. Cankar's death in 1918 marked a natural watershed, closing one chapter and opening another. The interwar period, however, saw many of the older writers continuing their activity, trying to coexist with, or adapt to, the new spirit, which was characterized by a great variety of approaches and styles, including realism, socialist realism, naturalism, neoromanticism, symbolism, futurism, and expressionism. Among writers of the period, Prežihov Voranc stands out. He published his most important novels on the eve and at the end of World War II: *Požganica* (1939), *Doberdob* (1940), and *Jamnica* (1945). Of proletarian origin and active in the political struggle between the two world wars (he spent World War II in a concentration camp), he wrote mostly of peasants and their hard life, using that theme to expound his ideas and the social programs he supported. Fortunately, Voranc subordinated his political activism to artistic considerations and, in the process, wrote some of the best works in Slovene literature. He illuminates his characters with fine psychological insight, he narrates with facility and directness, and he is objective in his depiction of the problems that beset his characters.

Many novelists, most of whom continued to be active after World War II, first published during the interwar period: Ivan Pregelj, Juš Kozak, France Bevk, Anton Ingolič, Ciril Kosmač, and Miško Kranjec. Ivan Pregelj's novel *Tolminci* (1927; The People of Tolmin) goes back to the peasant rebellion of 1712, but in most of his other novels he deals in an expressionistic style with the spiritual and intellectual themes relating to the present. Similarly, Juš Kozak treats in his ambitious novel *Šenpeter* (1931; St. Peter) the theme of urban life in one of

Ljubljana's suburbs before World War II. France Bevk, a very prolific and perhaps the most popular Slovene author, wrote about his native region on the border with Italy in a realistic manner. He was interested primarily in the content and he used literature in order to put forward his progressive ideas in artistic fashion. His best work is the novel *Kaplan Martin Čedermac* (1938; The Curate Martin Chedermats). Anton Ingolič, another strict realist, was nevertheless open to new ideas and themes, and he knew how to narrate interestingly and skillfully. Ciril Kosmač was primarily a short-story writer. His only novel, *Pomladni dan* (1953; A Day in Spring), deals with his staple theme, the struggle of his people against Italian rule before and during World War II. He, too, deployed his basically socialist-realist approach with considerable artistry. Miško Kranjec, the author of many long novels, describes the life of the peasants in a style that is realistic, even naturalistic, but at the same time often lyrical. His last work, *Strici so mi povedali* (1975; My Uncles Told Me), is an autobiographical account of his long and fruitful career. The work of these writers shows an increasing interest in psychology and in existential problems after World War II, together with a pronounced intellectualism.

Novelists who first became active after the war took these developments one step further in leaving regionalism largely behind. They include Vitomil Zupan, Andrej Hieng, Vladimir Kavčič, Peter Božič, Pavle Zidar, and Drago Jančar. Political activist and maverick, Zupan wrote several novels, two of which, *Minuet za kitaro* (1975; Minuet for the Guitar) and *Levitan* (1983; Leviathan), belong to some of the best of Slovene contemporary novels, offering an unconventional picture of life in Slovenia in the last 50 years. Hieng's first novel, *Gozd in pečina* (1966; The Forest and the Cave), reveals the author's profound understanding of human suffering and yearnings and displays a variety of stylistic techniques, achieving a unity of universal themes and everyday considerations. Hieng's other novels are *Orfeum* (1972; Orpheum) and *Čarodej* (1976; The Magician). Kavčič writes reflexive and analytical novels, stressing man's loneliness, powerlessness, and alienation. Božič's best novel, *Zemlja* (1976; The Earth), is about the history of the earth itself, yet the perceptive reader recognizes references to our time. The novel foreshadows Milorad Pavić's appeal to the reader to be a creative partner with the author. Most productive and popular among Slovene novelists, Zidar published more than 20 novels, most of which deal with the complex moral dilemmas facing modern man. An accomplished playwright, Jančar has been successful with his novels *Galjot* (1978; Galliot) and *Severni sij* (1984; Polar Light). Other novelists worth mentioning are Alojz Rebula, Beno Zupančič, Lojze Kovačič, Branko Hofman, and Rudi Šeligo.

Although the contemporary Slovenian novel is not as strongly represented as its Serbian and Croatian counterparts, it is still contributing significantly to the overall development of modern Slovenian literature.

VASA D. MIHAILOVICH

See also Ivo Andrić; Dictionary of the Khazars; Miroslav Krleža; Migrations; Southern Balkan Novel

Further Reading

Bandić, Miloš I., *Vreme romana*, Belgrade: Nolit, 1958

Barac, Antun, *A History of Yugoslav Literature*, translated by Petar Mijuskovic, Ann Arbor: Michigan Slavic Publications, 1973

Coote, Mary P., "Evgenij Kumičić and the Croatian Novel," *Scottish Slavonic Review* 2 (1984)

Davison, Milena, "The Waste Land in the State of Siege: Comments on the Contemporary Slovene Novel," *Slovene Studies* 3:2 (1981)

Deretić, Jovan, *Srpski roman 1800–1950*, Belgrade: Nolit, 1981

Donat, Branimir, "Postwar Croatian Novel," *The Bridge* 10 (1968)

Eekman, Thomas, *Thirty Years of Yugoslav Literature 1945–1975*, Ann Arbor: Michigan Slavic Publications, 1978

Goy, E.D., "The Serbian and Croatian Novel Since 1948," *The Slavonic and East European Review* 40:94 (1961)

Jeremić, Ljubiša, "The Novel at the Close of the Twentieth Century," *Relations* 2 (1981)

Jovanović, Aleksandar, "The Contemporary Serbian Novel and the Break with the Traditionalist Narration," *Relations* 2 (1982)

Korać, Stanko, "Dvadeset godina hrvatskog romana 1895–1914," *Rad JAZU* 333 (1963)

Korać, Stanko, *Srpski roman izmedju dva rata 1918–1941*, Belgrade: Nolit, 1982

Marković, Milivoje, *Raskršća romana: Jugoslovenski roman 1975–1981*, Priština: Jedinstvo, 1982

Matejić, Mateja, "On the Contemporary Yugoslav Novel," *Canadian Slavic Studies* 5:3 (1971)

Mihailovich, Vasa D., "On the Contemporary Serbian Novel," *The International Fiction Review* 2:1 (1975)

Mihailovich, Vasa D., and Mateja Matejić, editors, *A Comprehensive Bibliography of Yugoslav Literature in English, 1593–1980*, Columbus, Ohio: Slavica, 1984; *First Supplement, 1981–1985*, 1988; *Second Supplement, 1986–1990*, 1992

Moravcevich, Nicholas, "Epic Dimension in the Contemporary Serbian Novel," *Southeastern Europe* 9:1–2 (1982)

Palavestra, Predrag, "Elements of Neutral Temporality and Critical Realism in the Contemporary Serbian Novel," *Fiction and Drama in Eastern and Southeastern Europe*, edited by Henrik Birnbaum and Thomas Eekman, Columbus, Ohio: Slavica, 1980

Peleš, Gajo, *Poetika suvremenog jugoslavenskog romana 1945–1961*, Zagreb: Naprijed, 1966

Petrov, Aleksandar, editor, *Moderni roman*, Belgrade: Nolit, 1975

Zorić, Pavle, "The Contemporary Serbian Novel," *Literary Quarterly* 1:2 (1965)

Yukiguni. *See* Snow Country

Z

Zauberberg. *See* Magic Mountain

Zhang Ailing. *See* Eileen Chang

Zhang Xianliang 1936–

Chinese

Although some of Zhang Xianliang's novels are strictly contemporary in setting and have no connection with prison life, his best-known fiction portrays a semi-autobiographical protagonist whose memories of arduous stints in Mao-era prison camps frequently come back to absorb him in his later years of relative freedom. Far from serving simply as a bitter indictment of the regime that for no good reason made him languish some 20 years in the camps, Zhang Xianliang's fiction lays more emphasis on the emotional and intellectual reconstruction of a personality shattered by two decades of politically motivated imprisonment beginning in early manhood. This process of emotional and intellectual reintegration never achieves final closure but moves forward owing to his protagonists' powers of memory and observation, their ability to recall and apply their broad grounding in Chinese and Western literary and philosophical classics, and their tenacity in adapting to harsh or unfamiliar circumstances in and out of the camps.

Lühua shu (1985; *Mimosa*) portrays protagonist Zhang Yonglin's struggle during the early 1960s to ward off both starvation in the camps and emotional aridity after being released to work on a government farm near the camp. A chaste engagement with a resourceful but illiterate local woman, Ma Yinghua, helps him recover a semblance of normalcy, but he is thrown back into the camps before they can get married. *Nanren de yiban shi nüren* (1985; *Half of Man Is Woman*) is set in the 1970s and deals with the sexual frustration of an older and more sardonic Zhang Yonglin as a prisoner and the impotence that plagues his early marital life with fellow ex-inmate Huang Xiangjiu after their release. Zhang Xianliang originally planned to make *Mimosa* and *Half of Man Is Woman* two of the early installments of a multivolume series to be entitled *Weiwulun de qishilu* (Revelations of a Materialist), which would amount to a sort of Bildungsroman, charting Zhang Yonglin's emotional and intellectual development from adolescence through two decades in labor camps. However, the author later shifted to a first-person approach based on diary narration and larded with Rousseauistic confession in *Xiguan siwang* (1989; *Getting Used to Dying*), *Fannao jiu shi zhihui* (1992; *Grass Soup*), and *Wode putishu* (1994; *My Bodhi Tree*).

Zhang Xianliang has advanced a persuasive argument that the major defect of late 20th-century Chinese fiction in the People's Republic of China (PRC) is the relatively low level of literary and artistic knowledge in writers, who enjoyed few opportunities for wide reading and untrammeled public discussion during the three decades of stringent political controls under Mao Zedong. The scion of a wealthy and cultured family, Zhang Xianliang's fine childhood education during the 1940s provided the foundation on which he continued a life of literary and artistic cultivation whenever not confined within the camps (1958–79), where literary classics and other vehicles of "bourgeois" or "reactionary" ideology were outlawed in favor of government propaganda tracts. Zhang's broad familiarity with artistic classics from China and Europe is apparent in references to them throughout his oeuvre. In just one brief chapter of *Mimosa*, one finds a number of well-integrated references to European poets, such as Aleksandr Pushkin and Mikhail Lermontov, and excerpts from classical poets, such as Li Bo and Lu Lun, along with various borderland folksongs and even the musical score of selected melodic lines in those songs.

In a similar vein, the end of part three of *Half of Man Is Woman* finds a still impotent Zhang Yonglin in a quandary as to how to react when he discovers that the party secretary has cuckolded him. Without a ready and trusted friend in whom to confide, Zhang Yonglin conjures forth Othello, the famous outlaw chief Song Jiang, the ancient philosopher Zhuangzi, and Karl Marx, each of whom engages in a spirited dialogue with Zhang Yonglin. Since the author had been banished to the arid and impoverished northwestern borderlands, he naturally found intellectuals in short supply and even fewer trustworthy educated confidantes. In spite of his admiration for many facets of the local folk culture, there was no alternative to his personal store of book learning when it came to analyzing many of life's most puzzling questions.

Sometimes Zhang Yonglin's store of learning fails him, as when he bases various negative generalizations about women in *Half of Man Is Woman* on what little he knows about the mostly illiterate women of the impoverished northwest. His impotence is political rather than marital in origin, however, for it stems from his partial internalization of two decades of emotional and physical mistreatment in the party-state's prison system: because the government is so powerful and intolerant of criticism, the cuckold dares vent his anger only on his wife, Huang Xiangjiu, rather than on the official who committed adultery with her. Furthermore, the lopsided relationship between the educated husband of good family and the relatively illiterate wife of humble origin is merely the modern continuation of the scholar-meets-courtesan motif that has been prominent for many centuries in Chinese literature.

The relatively experimental quality of the later three novels in Zhang Xianliang's oeuvre can be explained by his decision during the mid-1980s to draw on various non-naturalistic techniques rarely encountered in the realism and romanticism that have served as the mainstay of 20th-century Chinese novelists. *Getting Used to Dying* is a series of abrupt juxtapositions of encounters with death and suffering in the Chinese camps on the one hand and a spate of speaking engagements and sexual relationships in the West on the other. Abrupt transitions between decades-old memories and the narrative present give the novel a fast-paced rhythm. *Grass Soup* and *My Bodhi Tree* take the unusual form of frank 1990s commentaries on elusively laconic diary passages from the 1960s, when Zhang Xianliang was still in a labor camp and thus constrained from writing anything that the camp authorities could seize upon as the basis for further prosecution or punishment. Memory is again dominant, but the mood is relatively reflective; the author is less concerned with confession than with the preservation of a chunk of personal and national history that has been fading from public awareness.

Zhang Xianliang's penchant for elaborate metaphors resonates with the English metaphysical poets' fondness for the conceit, such as John Donne's likening of two lovers to the dual points of a drafter's compass. For instance, hollow-tipped dum-dum bullets that shatter and splinter after entering flesh, causing a jagged and gaping wound, have long been referred to as *kaihua dan* or "bullets that [make penetrated flesh] bloom." When the People's Liberation Army soldiers are firing this type of bullet into prisoners' heads during the collective execution of a few dozen counter-revolutionaries and other convicts in a scene from *Getting Used to Dying*, the participant-narrator describes the gory mixture of red blood and white brain tissue in floral terms as "a field of China Pinks," the same red and white flower whose appearance the narrator has repeatedly recalled following episodes of lovemaking. Having barely escaped death from both starvation and political crackdowns during his decades in the camps, the ex-prisoner burdened by survivor's guilt seems impelled to conceive of sex as a form of expiatory self-immolation; the bloody but voluptuous conceit of China Pinks links sex to death as twin preoccupations of this novel's participant-narrator.

Because Zhang Xianliang's father, formerly a wealthy Nationalist official and industrialist, died in a Maoist prison during the 1950s, the fact that Zhang Xianliang and his semi-autobiographical protagonists, such as Zhang Yonglin, manage to emerge from China's gulag alive provides extremely fertile ground for survivor's guilt. This form of guilt may be compounded by the belief that the ex-inmate's promiscuity in *Getting Used to Dying* derives from an impulse to return to the maternal womb, the imagination of which pervades the participant-narrator's thoughts. "The great fuss men make in the world," agrees one of the narrator's better-educated lovers, "is only so much twisting and turning in their mother's womb." As a rare example of a major writer who is a second-generation PRC political prisoner, Zhang Xianliang has launched an unprecedentedly comprehensive literary engagement with Chinese prison camp life and its aftermath—a preoccupation that may be explicable in large part as a family matter.

Philip F. Williams

Biography

Born 8 December 1936 in Nanjing. Attended schools in Beijing, expelled 1954. Farm worker in Ningxia region, 1955; teacher, school for government cadres, 1956; imprisoned for writing: held in labor camps, state farms, and prisons, 1958–79; committee member, China People's Consultative Conference, 1983, and China Writers' Association, 1986; chair, Ningxia Federation of Literary and Art Circles, from 1986.

Selected Novels by Zhang

Nanren de yiban shi nüren, 1985; as *Half of Man Is Woman*, translated by Martha Avery, 1988

Lühua shu, 1985; as *Mimosa*, translated by Gladys Yang, in *Mimosa and Other Stories*, 1985

Xiguan siwang, 1989; as *Getting Used to Dying*, translated by Martha Avery, 1991

Fannao jiu shi zhihui, 1992; as *Grass Soup*, translated by Martha Avery, 1994

Wode putishu, 1994; as *My Bodhi Tree*, translated by Martha Avery, 1996

Other Writings: short stories, including those collected in *Ling yu rou* (1981; Body and Soul), and screenplays.

Further Reading

Gunn, Edward, *Rewriting Chinese: Style and Innovation in Twentieth-Century Chinese Prose,* Stanford, California: Stanford University Press, 1991

He Yuhuai, *Cycles of Repression and Relaxation: Politico-Literary Events in China, 1976–1989,* Bochum: Brockmeyer, 1992

Hualing Nieh, editor, *Literature of the Hundred Flowers,* volume 2, New York: Columbia University Press, 1981

Kinkley, Jeffrey C., "A Bettelheimian Interpretation of Zhang Xianliang's Concentration Camp Novels," *Asia Major* 4:2 (1991)

Lei Da, *Tuibian yu xin chao* (Transformation and the New Tide), Beijing: Zhongguo wenlian chuban gongsi, 1987

Martin, Helmut, and Jeffrey C. Kinkley, editors, *Modern Chinese Writers: Self-Portrayals,* Armonk, New York: M.E. Sharpe, 1992

Williams, Philip F., "'Remolding' and the Chinese Labor Camp Novel," *Asia Major* 4:2 (1991)

Wu, Yenna, "Women as Sources of Redemption in Zhang Xianliang's Labor-Camp Novels," *Asia Major* 4:2 (1991)

Zhang Fang, *Dalu xin shiqi xiaoshuo lun* (On the Mainland's New Era Fiction), Taipei: Dongda chuban, 1992

Zola, Émile. *See* Rougon-Macquart

INDEXES

TITLE INDEX

This index lists all the titles in the "Novels by" sections of the entries on individual writers. The name in parentheses directs the reader to the appropriate entry, where more complete information is provided. Items in bold indicate that a separate entry has been provided on that novel. The encyclopedia contains a number of entries on novels by writers who have not been given a separate writer entry; these novels are shown below in italics. A date appearing in brackets represents the year a novel appeared in its original language. Thus, for example, *Doctor Zhivago* **(Pasternak)**, *1958 [1957]* tells the reader that this novel is discussed in its own entry (it is in bold type), that there is no writer entry under Pasternak (it is also in italics), and that the book was originally published in 1957 (1958 being the year the translation "Doctor Zhivago" appeared). The reader may turn to the entry itself for the original title. In cases where the English title is identical to the original title, the date of original publication only is given.

GENERAL INDEX

Page numbers in **boldface** indicate subjects with their own entries.

narrative symbolism of, 763
as postmodernist writer, 860, 1035
satire usage, 1164
temporal relativity of, 1335
Thousand and One Nights influence on, 1331
Universal History of Infamy, 796
Born, Nicolas, 78, 477
Borodino, Battle of (1812), 1413, 1415
Boron, Robert de, 825
Borschette, Albert, 104
Bosboom Toussaint, A.L.G. (Geertrui)
  Het huis Lauerness (House of Lauernesse), 923
  Leycester trilogy, 923
  Majoor Frans (Major Frans), 923
Bosch, Hieronymus, 956
Bosch, Juan, 745
Bosco, Monique, 160, 161
Bosnia, 133, 1448
Bosshart, Jakob, 1309
Boston (Massachusetts), 1085
Boston Athenaeum, 772
Boston Library Society, 772, 773
Boston Public Library, 772
Boswell, James
  Journal of a Tour to the Hebrides, 1372
  Life of Samuel Johnson, 245, 261
Botev, Khristo, 1255
Botswana, 32–33
Boucicault, Dion, 614
Boucq, François, 507
Boudier-Bakker, Ina, 925
Boukhedenna, Sakinna, 23
Boullosa, Carmen
  Duerme (Sleep), 707
  metahistorical novels of, 707
  They're Cows, We're Pigs, 707
Bouraoui, Hédi, 21
  Retour à Thyna (Return to Thyna), 22–23
Bouraoui, Nina, *Forbidden Vision,* 24
Bourbon dynasty, 544
Bourdeilles de Brântomes, Pierre de, *Mémoires,* 1089
Bourdouxhe, Madeleine, 103
bourgeois novel
  in German novel development, 470
  and Marxist criticism, 818
  See also middle class
bourgeoisie. *See* middle class
Bourgeon, François, 507
Bourget, Paul, 449, 450, 1058
  André Cornélius, 1058
  Cruelle énigme (Love's Cruel Enigma), 1058
  Disciple, 1058
Bouvier, Nicolas, 1314–15
Bowen, Elizabeth, 130–31, 376
  Big House background of, 619
  Collected Stories, 131
  Death of the Heart, 130, **288–89**
  Demon Lover, 288
  English Novelists, 130
  Friends and Relations, 130
  Heat of the Day, 130, 288, 376

Hotel, 130
House in Paris, 130, 288
Ivy Gripped the Steps, 130
Last September, 130, 288, 619
Little Girls, 130
To the North, 130
World of Love, 130
Bowen, Marjorie, 520
Bower, B.M., 1029
  Chip of the Flying U, 48
Bowering, George, 150
Bowlby, Rachel, 293–94
Bowles, Paul, 414
Boxer Rebellion (1900), 1348, 1349
Boyd, Brian, 889, 890
Boyd, James
  Drums, 1415
  Marching On, 1415
Boyd, Martin, 430
  Langton tetralogy, 70
Boyd, Thomas, *Through the Wheat,* 1415
Boyd, William
  New Confessions, 1388
  unreliable narrator usage, 1388
Boyer, Jean-Baptiste de (Marquis d'Argens), *Thérèse philosophe* (Philosophical Thérèse), 768–69
Boylan, Clare, 619
Boyle, Karin, *Kallocain,* 1180–81
Boyle, Roger, *Parthenissa,* 1046, 1091
Boyne, Battle of the (1690), 613
Boys of England (publication), 318
Boy's Own Paper (publication), 318
Boz (pseud. of Charles Dickens), 282
Bozic, Mirko, 1450
Bozic, Peter, *Zemlja* (Earth), 1452
Bozic, Streten, 72
Bozveli, Neofit, 1255
Braak, Menno ter, 925
Brabner, Joyce, 508
Brackenridge, Hugh Henry, *Modern Chivalry,* 1371–72, 1373
Bradbury, Malcolm
  campus novels by, 786
  on Hardy, 1324
  on Huxley, 374
  Possibilities: Essays on the State of the Novel, 466
Bradbury, Ray, *Fahrenheit 451,* 413
Bradbury and Evans (British publisher), 992
Braddon, Mary Elizabeth, 258, 884, 992, 993, 1109
Bradford, Ebenezer, *Art of Courting,* 1372
Bradford, Thomas, 773
Bradley, David, 10
Bradley, Marion Zimmer, 826
Braine, John, 786
Bräker, Ulrich, *Life Story and Real Adventures of the Poor Man of Toggenburg,* 1307
Bram, Christopher, 1213
Bramón, Francisco, *Sirgueros de la Virgen sin original pecado* (Linnets of the Virgin without Original Sin), 697
Brañas, César, 732
Brand, Dionne, 153

Brand, Max (pseud. of Frederick Faust), 48
Brandes, Georg, 1166, 1174
Brandys, Kazimierz, 1019–20
  Sons and Comrades, 1019
Branner, Hans Christian, 1168
Brasillach, Robert, 452
Brathwaite, Edward Kamau, *Arrivants,* 170
Brathwaite, Errol, 931
Brau, Salvador, 744
Braun, Volker, 476
Brautigan, Richard, 846
Bravo, José Antonio, *Cuando la gloria agoniza* (When Glory Goes into Agony), 717
Bray, Bernard, 386
Brazilian Academy of Letters, 727, 728, 729
Brazilian Historical and Geographic Institute, 726
Brazilian novel, 44, 304–05, 328, 330–31, 724–30
  magic realism, 696
  modernismo, 695
  romanticism, 694
  social justice and regional themes, 775
  Vargas Llosa's *War of the End of the World* as social panorama, 1418
Breban, Nicolae, 1123, 1124
Brecht, Bertolt, 76, 475, 1270
  Lukács debate, 819
  Mother Courage and Her Children, 1224
Bredel, Willi, 475, 476
Brehm, Alfred Edmund, 110
Breiner, Laurence A., 605
Bremer, Fredrika, 1178
Bremond, Claude, 900, 1294
Brentano, Clemens, 472
Brentano, Franz, 1350
Breton, André, 498, 939
  amour fou in works by, 812
  Arcanum 17, 1302, 1303
  Communicating Vessels, 1302
  definition of surrealism, 1302
  as founder of surrealism, 452, 1301, 1302, 1304
  listing of surrealist writers, 1302
  Mad Love, 1302
  Magnetic Fields, 1302
  Manifesto of Surrealism, 1301, 1302
  on Maturin, 827
  Nadja, 452, 1301, 1302, 1303
Bretonne, Restif de la, 444
Brett, Edward J., 318
Brett-Young, Francis, 1083
Brierley, Walter, 375
  Means Test Man, 1043
Briggs, Raymond, 508
Brik, Osip, 422, 423
Brin, David, 381
Brink, André, 134–35, 493
  Chain of Voices, 134
  First Life of Adamastor, 134
  Imaginings of Sand, 34
  Instant in the Wind, 134
  Land Apart (ed.), 34
  Looking on Darkness, 134

Coleridge, Samuel Taylor, 7, 422, 498, 499, 500, 1107
    on Bunyan, 1006
    on canon, 163
    on Defoe, 1105
    Peacock's caricature of, 1164
Coles, Julia, 1373
Colet, Louise, 792
Colette, 449, 453, 857, 859
    Cheri, 451
    My Mother's House, 451
    portrayals of feminine condition, 451
    Vagabond, 449
collaboration, 251, 338, 491, 1109, 1113, 1282
Collection of Poems Ancient and Modern, 633
college novel, 466
    Lodge (David) as author of, 786
    Lucky Jim as first, 786
    of Malamud, 802
Collett, Camilla, *Amtmandens Døtre* (District Governor's Daughters), 1175
Colletta, Cristina Della, 757
Collier, Jane, 1100
Collier's (magazine), 648, 994
Collins, Christopher, 1421
Collins, Merle, 171
    Angel, 171
Collins, Tom (pseud.). *See* Furphy, Joseph
Collins, Wilkie, 499, 559
    British colonialism as influence on, 597
    Dead Secret, 992
    detective and crime fiction, 125, 144, 257, 865, 1288
    Moonstone, 144, 257, 334, 597, **865–66**, 992, 1113, 1115, 1439
    narrative framing usage, 434
    New Zealand novelistic imitations of, 929
    Rogue's Life, 992
    as romance writer, 1113
    as sensationalist novel pioneer, 528, 884, 1115, 1439
    serialization of works, 865, 992, 993, 994
    Woman in White, 257, 434, 500, 865, 884, 992, 994, 1212, 1439
Collins, William, 1114
Collodi, Carlo, *Adventures of Pinocchio*, 10–11, 202, 625
Colman, George (the elder), 770
Colomb, Catherine, 1314
Colombian novel, 694, 718–21, 962–63
colonialism. *See* adventure novel and imperial romance; postcolonial narrative and criticism
Colonna, Francesco, 437
    Hypnerotomachia Poliphili, 626
Columbus, Christopher, 178, 742, 746, 1073
Colunje, Gil, 738
Colwell, D.J., 792
Combe, William, 1404
comedy and humor, 231–33
    Austen's *Emma* as social comedy, 355
    in Cervantes' *Don Quixote*, 329, 330
    in China, 1227

in Dickens' works, 231, 232, 233, 311–12, 1004
in English novel, 363
in French novel, 441, 442
Frye on, 467
in Gogol's work, 485
New Humor novel, 926–27
in 19th-century realistic novel, 853
in novel of manners, 353
parody as, 975–77
in Proust's works, 593
in Prus' works, 1051
in Rabelais' works, 1067
in Swedish novel, 1180
of Twain, 1361
See also satirical novel
comic books. *See* graphic novel
comic novel. *See* comedy and humor
Comics Code (1954), 507
"coming-out" experiences, 81–82
Common, Jack
    Ampersand, 1044
    Kiddar's Luck, 1044
common sense realism (Scottish), 1376
Communications (French journal), 1294
communism
    in China, 1098, 1217
    in Czechoslovakia, 563
    in Germany, 476
    in Hollywood, 1274
    in Israel, 761
    Kundera and, 682
    Lessing and, 758
    Orwell's denunciation of, 1163
    in Poland, 1019, 1020
    in Romania, 1123, 1124
    in Soviet Union, 961, 1007, 1153, 1239
    surrealists and, 1302, 1303
    utopian fiction and, 1394
    See also Marxism; Marxist criticism; socialist realism
Communist Party of Australia, 70, 1273
Communist Party of China, 212, 213, 214, 215, 852
Communist Party of the Soviet Union, 961, 1018, 1020, 1148, 1149
Communist Party of the United States, 607, 912, 1044
Communist Revolution (China), 1217
Compendium of Prodigies (British periodical), 991
Compère, Gaston, 103
Comte, Auguste, 916, 1166
Conan, Laure (Félicité Anger), *Angéline de Montbrun*, 154–55
Conan Doyle, Sir Arthur, 91, 144
    and adventure novel, 6, 8, 370, 597
    Case-Book of Sherlock Holmes, 558
    fogbound London setting, 1288
    historical novels by, 559
    Hound of the Baskervilles, 558–59
    Lost World, 6, 559
    science fiction by, 559
    Sherlock Holmes series, 252, 257, 558–59, 1288

Sir Nigel, 559
Study in Scarlet, 558
translations of works, 1345
White Company, 559
concluding lines. *See* beginnings and endings
Concurso Ricardo Miró (Ricard Miró Competition), 739
Condé, Maryse, 176, 233–35
    Colonie du Nouveau Monde (Colony of the New World), 234
    Crossing the Mangrove, 234
    Derniers Rois Mages (Last of the Wise Men), 234
    Hérémakhonon, 176, 234
    I, Tituba, Black Witch of Salem, 176, 234
    Migration des coeurs (Migration of Hearts), 234
    Season in Rihata, 234
    Ségou, 234
    Tree of Life, 234
Condé, Prince of, 544
conditional tense, 1320
condition-of-England novels, 1234, 1281
Condon, Matthew, 73
Condorcet, Antoine-Nicolas, marquis de, 697, 1407
confessional autobiography
    in Germany, 477
    in Japan, 123, 1232
    libertine novel as, 768
    Sadeh as pioneer of, 622
    See also autobiographical novel
Confiant, Raphaël, 175
Confucian Civil Service Examination, 211, 212
Confucianism, 191, 206, 207, 208, 209, 210, 211, 678
    in six classic Chinese novels, 1226, 1228, 1229
Congo, Democratic Republic of (formerly Zaire), 109
Congress of Soviet Writers, 1022
Congreve, William
    on Bunyan, 1006
    Incognita, 259, 321
Conill, Alejandro Santa María, *Ciudad de barro* (Mud City), 711
Conrad, Joseph, 143, 237–38, 311, 353, 373, 412, 417, 514, 630, 663, 690, 839, 872, 891, 918, 1028, 1119, 1200, 1355, 1364, 1398, 1439
    Achebe's critique of, 237, 886–87, 1029, 1329
    adventure novels by, 7, 8, 9
    Almayer's Folly, 237, 371
    Apocalypse Now as film adaptation of "Heart of Darkness," 413
    birth name, 1016
    in canon, 164
    Chance, 266, 371, 994
    chronological shifts in works, 491
    conception of fiction, 266
    doubling as theme, 1288
    exposure of discriminatory and unfair practices, 648

on *Misérables*, 847
Tarchetti adaptation, 1346
Gavidia, Francisco, 733
Gawain and the Green Knight (narrative
poem), 1403
Gay, John, 1006
gay literature. *See* homosexuality
Gaytán, Nery Alexis, 736
Gazette des tribunaux (crime periodical), 1109
Gazzetta del Popolo, 868
gCopaleen, Myles n (pseud.), *Poor Mouth*,
616
GDR. *See* German Democratic Republic
Ge Fei, 214
Gee, Maurice, 931
Plumb trilogy, 932
Geering, R.G., 1274
Geertz, Clifford, 546
Geijerstam, Gustaf, 1179
Erik Grane, 1179
Geiser, Christoph, 1311
gekiga (Japanese dramatic pictures), 506
Gelfant, Blanche, 220
Gellert, Christian Fürchtegott, 470
Gelley, Alexander, 1295
genbun itchi, 634
Genc kalemler (Turkish Young Authors'
movement), 1358
gender, 1209–13
book marketing and, 974
in Carter (Angela) works, 179
character's social roles and, 199
children's novels and, 201–02, 203
critical approaches and, 271
decadency as role reversal, 291–92
in Eliot (George) works, 353
in English novel, 368, 369
and epistolary novel, 387
in Hawthorne's *The Scarlet Letter*, 1184
in Lessing's work, 758, 1044
narrative significance of, 904
national identification relationship, 910
and Oliphant's cultural identity, 1197
in Poniatowska's work, 705
in Sa'dawi's works, 1155
in Sand's works, 446, 602–03
and science, 1185
sexism in Caribbean francophone novel,
176
as Woolf's *Orlando* focus, 1437
See also feminist criticism; feminist novel;
homosexuality; sexuality; women; women
writers
gender-neutral language, 973
Generación Comprometida (Committed
Generation), 734
General Society of Mechanics and Tradesmen
(New York), 774
General Strike of 1926, 374, 765
Generation of 1880 (Argentina), 708, 710
Generation of 1880 (Belgium), 102
Generation of 1898 (Spain), 1268
Generation of 1900 (Costa Rica), 737
Generation of 1920 (Guatemala), 732
Generation of 1938 (Chile), 723
Generation of 1940 (El Salvador), 737

Generation of 1950 (Chile), 723
Generation of 1968 (Spain), 1272
Generation of '45 (Indonesia), 1036
Generation of the '50s (Indonesia), 1249
Generation of '98 (Spain), 859, 1365
Genet, Jean, 81, 404, 595, 657
Genette, Gérard, 62, 316–17, 396, 1012, 1294
on framing in narrative, 434
on historical vs. fictional narratives, 551
on implied author, 590
on narrative levels, 901, 902
and narratology development, 900, 1295
on Plato's and Aristotle's interpretation of
mimesis, 845
study of chronological frequency, 903
on temporality of narrative, 903
Genlis, Félicité (Madame de), 444, 554, 1128,
1346
Genot, Gérard, 1295
genre criticism, **465–69**
canon formation and, 163–65
on novel's middle-class origins, 224–26,
244, 255, 382, 405, 441, 470, 471,
1403–04
on parody, 975–77
See also critics and criticism
Gentleman's Magazine, 991
Geoffrey of Monmouth, 823
Geoffroy Saint-Hilaire, 448, 568, 985
geographical novel, historical novel as, 545
George III, king of Great Britain, 366, 613,
615
George, Stefan, 938
Geramys, Anna, 103
Gerdes, Dick, 716, 717
Gérin-Lajoie, Antoine, *Jean Rivard*, 154
Gerlach, Heinrich, *Forsaken Army*, 1416
German Democratic Republic (East Germany),
472, 476, 477, 478, 1430
German language, Swiss novels written in,
1306–12
German novel, **469–79**
Bildungsroman origins, 118–23
for children, 202, 204
double as theme of romantics, 1057
etymology of novella, 942
and expressionism, 859
irony in, 809
Korean novel and, 676
national identity and, 1082
nationalistic naturalism, 265
naturalist tradition of, 916
novella, 948–49, 950
paperbacks, 973
picaresque, 1002
prose fiction, 1088, 1090
Renaissance narrative, 1090
reviewers of, 1095
and *roman-fleuve* origins, 1111
romanticism, development of, 1126
satirical, 1090, 1164
utopian, 1393
Volksbücher, 117
war novels, 1416
women's 18th-century works, 1209
See also Nazism

German Occupation. *See under* World War II
Gernsback, Hugo, 1189, 1192, 1193
Gerter, Elisabeth, 1309
Gertner, María Elena, *Islas en la ciudad*
(Islands in the City), 723
gesaku (Japanese popular fiction), 634
Gessner, Salomon, 1307
Gettysburg, Battle of (1863), 1415
Geulincx, Arnold, 879
Geuss, Raymond, 582
Gevers, Marie, 103
Madame Orpha, 103
Ghallab, 'Abd al-Karim, 22
Al-Mu'allim 'Ali, 22
Sa'at Abwab, 22
Ghana, 16, 17, 18, 19, 59–61
Ghelderode, Michel de, 103
Ghiano, Juan Carlos, 708
Ghica, I., 1118
Ghica, Pantazi, 1118, 1120
Ghitani, Jamal al-, 25, 1156
Kitab al-Tajalliyat (Revelations), 25
Zayni Barakat, 349
Ghose, Zulfikar, 797
Ghosh, Amitav, *Shadow Lines*, 598, 599, 600
ghost stories. *See* supernatural
Giangiacomo Feltrinelli (publisher), 756
Giardina, Denise, *Storming Heaven*, 1044
Giardinelli, Mempo, 42, 713
Qué solos se quedan los muertos (How
Lonely the Dead Ones Stay), 713
Santo oficio de la memoria (Holy Office of
Memory), 713
Gibbon, Edward, 545
Gibbon, Lewis Grassic, *Scots Quair* trilogy,
1043, 1200, 1201
Gibbons, Dave, *Watchmen*, 508
Gibbons, Kaye, 184
Gibbons, Stella, *Cold Comfort Farm*, 375
Gibbs, A.C., 824
Gibran, Kahlil, 760, 763
Gibson, William, 221, 500, 511
Neuromancer, 1188, 1193
Gide, André, 81, 174, 315, 449, 450, 451,
452, 453, **480–81**, 1027, 1041, 1067,
1180
Counterfeiters, 252–53, 449, 451, 452, 473,
481, 554, 855, 858, 1187
deviant subcultures as theme, 892
diary form refinement, 480
Geneviève, 452
and Hogg, 1041
and homosexuality, 449, 480, 1213
Immoralist, 449, 480, 481, 659, 764
Isabelle, 481
Journal, 480
Logbook of the Coiners, 253
Lovers' Attempt, 480
Marshlands, 449, 480, 919
and Mexican *contemporáneos*, 702
mimesis usage, 252, 253
as modernist, 402, 855, 858, 859, 1187
notebooks of, 480, 481
Notebooks of André Walter, 480
Pastoral Symphony, 451, 481
prewar fiction, 449

as romance writer, 1113, 1116, 1183–84
Scarlet Letter, 327, 531–32, 639, 829, 1094, 1095, **1183–84,** 1376, 1377, 1378
Septimus, 993
serializations of work, 993
Twain on, 1361
Twice-Told Tales, 532
on women writers' popularity, 1086, 1377, 1378
Hay, John MacDougall, 1201
Haya de la Torre, Raúl, 715
Haycox, Ernest, 48
Haydar, Haydar, *Walimah li A'shab al-Bahr* (Feast for the Vegetation of the Sea), 761–62
Haydn, Franz Joseph, 388
Hayes, Harold, 927
Haykal, Muhammad Husayn, *Zaynab,* 347
Hays, Mary, 1210
Memoirs of Emma Courtney, 385
Haywood, Big Bill, 1390
Haywood, Eliza, 260, 358–59, 360, 862
Anti-Pamela, 359
comic and domestic narratives, 360
Defoe's *Moll Flanders* compared with *Love in Excess,* 862
Fortunate Foundlings, 360
History of Jemmy and Jenny Jessamy, 360
History of Miss Betsy Thoughtless, 360, 392, 1209
Idalia, 359
Injur'd Husband, 359
Lasselia, 359
Life's Progress Through the Passions, 360
Love in Excess, 358, 862
Manley imitation, 358
Memoirs of a Certain Island Adjacent to the Kingdom of Utopia, 358
picaresque novels of, 360
Hayworth, Rita, 1060
Hazell, Stephen, 265
Hazlitt, William, 143, 499, 862, 1100
He Jingzhi, 213
Head, Bessie, 32–33
Bewitched Crossroad, 33
Maru, 32–33
Question of Power, 32–33
Serowe, 32–33
When Rain Clouds Gather, 32
Head, Richard, 470, 1047
English Rogue, 1091
Hearne, John, 170
Sure Salvation, 170
Hearst, William Randolph, 1390, 1392
Hébert, Anne, 159, **533–35**
Aurélian, Clara, Mademoiselle, and the English Lieutenant, 534
Burden of Dreams, 533
Children of the Black Sabbath, 533, 534
First Garden, 533–34
Heloise, 533
In the Shadow of the Wind, 533, 534
Kamouraska, 533, 534
Silent Rooms, 533, 534
Hébert, Louis, 534

Hebrew Semitic Union, 622
Hebrew writing, 55–56, 131–32
of Grossman (David), 522–23
history of, 621
Heckerling, Amy, 413
Hedayat, Sadeq, 609
Blind Owl, 609
Heer, Jakob Christoph, 1308
Heffner, Avraham, *Sefer hameforash* (Explicated Book), 623
Hegel, G.W.F., 539
Aesthetics, 121, 478
generic definition of Bildungsroman by, 121, 122
Phenomenology of Spirit, 121, 122
view of history, 468
Heian society, 633, 634, 1317, 1318
Heidegger, Gotthard, *Mythoscopia romantica,* 1306
Heidegger, Martin, 112, 269, 282, 680, 709, 804
Heidenreich, Gerd, 478
Heidenstam, Verner von, 1179
Charles Men, 1179
Hans Alienus, 1179
Tree of the Folkungs, 1179
Heijermans, Herman, 924
Kamertjeszonde (Chamber Sin), 924
Heimat novel, 136
Heimatliteratur tradition, 1309–10
Heimburg, E., 1110
Hein, Christoph, 476
Heine, Maurice, 657
Heinemann (publisher), 370, 429
African Writers Series, 27, 29, 31
Heinemann, Larry
Close Quarters, 1415
Paco's Story, 1416
Heinesen, William, 1174
Heinlein, Robert A., 1190, 1193
Heinse, Wilhelm, 471
Heiseler, Bernd von, 474
Heiserman, Arthur, 516
Hejazi, Mohammad, 608
Heldt, Barbara, 391
Heliade, 1118
Heliodorus, 516, 517, 518, 519
Ethiopian Story, 515, 516, 624, 980, 1264, 1402
extended travel as theme, 517
German translations of, 470
portrayal of women, 518
Hellema (pseud. of Alexander Bernard van Praag), 925
Hellenistic age. *See* Greek and Roman narrative
Hellens, Franz, 102–03
Heller, Joseph, 190, 311, 1425
Catch-22, 98, 182–83, 232, 311, 893, 1385, 1416, 1417
comic novels, 232–33
as postmodern writer, 1384–85
Hellström, Gustaf, 1179
Helvetic Society, 1307
Hemenway, Robert, 1328
Hemingway, Ernest, 10, 14, 105, 151, 276,

462, 535–37, 618, 800, 918, 1022, 1058, 1245, 1267, 1399
Across the River and into the Trees, 535
critical approaches to, 268
dialogic description, 302
dismissal of Cather as writer, 185
Farewell to Arms, 96, 99, **399–400,** 536, 1175, 1381, 1415, 1416
For Whom the Bell Tolls, 287, 536, 649, 1022, 1044, 1416
Garden of Eden, 399
In Our Time, 399, 1275, 1300
as journalist, 648, 649
"Killers," 908
as Latino-American novel influence, 749
Men Without Women, 399
minimalist style, 857–58
as model for Mulgan (John) novel, 931
Moveable Feast, 1300
objective narrator usage, 908
Old Man and the Sea, 462, 536, 949
Phelan on, 898
proletarian movement's influence on, 1044
realism of, 182
roman à clef usage, 1107
as screenwriter, 412
and Stein (Gertrude), 857
Sun Also Rises, 302, 399, 535, 1107, 1300–01, 1381
thematic obsessions, 1399
themes of modernist novels, 856
To Have and Have Not, 536
Torrents of Spring, 535, 1300
World War I experiences, 1300, 1381, 1415
Hemlow, Joyce, 392
Hemmer, Jarl, *Fool of Faith,* 1173
Hémon, Louis, *Maria Chapdelaine,* 155
Hemyng, Bracebridge, 318
Henley, W.E., 164, 994
Hennique, Léon, 916
Henriot, Émile, 455
Henry II, king of England, 824
Henry II, king of France, 544, 1039
Henry III, king of France, 440
Henry IV, king of England, 438, 439
Henry IV, king of France, 543
Henry VII, king of England, 498
Henry VIII, king of England, 1047
Henryson, Robert, *Testament of Cressid,* 826
Henty, G.A., 6, 546, 597
Heptameron, 1090
Herben, Jan, 274
Herbert, A.P., 654
Herbert, Frank, *Dune,* 1193
Herbert, Xavier, 71
Capricornia, 71
Poor Fellow My Country, 71
Herbst, Josephine, *Rope of Gold,* 1044
Herbster, Madame, *Cavern of Roseville,* 546
Herburger, Günter, 477, 478
Herculano, Alexandre, 724–25, 1129
Herder, Johann Gottfried von, 119, 470
Hergé (Georges Rémi), 507
Herling-Grudzinski, Gustaw, 1020
Herman, Jan, 387
Hermans, Willem Frederik, 925

Ishiguro, Kazuo, 947
  Remains of the Day, 1388
Ishimure Michiko, 636
Isis (deity), 518
Isla, José Francisco de, *History of the Famous
    Preacher, Friar Gerund de Campazas,
    Otherwise Gerund Zotes,* 1265
Islam, 23, 346, 379
  and Egyptian novel, 346, 347, 1155,
    1156
  Fundamentalist censorship, 191, 192–93
  and Iranian novel, 608
  and Rushdie's death sentence, 1030, 1137
  and Sa'dawi's death sentence, 1155
Islamic Revolution (Iran), 610, 611
Islas, Arturo, 748
  Rain God, 749
Israeli novel, **621–23**
Istrati, Panait, 1121, 1122, 1123
  Codin, 1121
  Kirah Kiralinah, 1121
  Thistles of Baragan, 1121
Italian novel, **624–27**
  modernists, 859
  and national identity, 1082
  naturalistic elements in, 916
  novella, 948, 949
  pornographic, 1024
  postmodern writing, 1034
  prose fiction, 1088
  verismo, 1134, 1186, 1400–01
Ivanov, Anatolii, *Eternal Call,* 1238
Ivanov, Viacheslav, 1000
Ivanov, Vsevolod, 1149, 1236, 1238
Ivasiuc, Alexandru, 1123, 1124
Ivins, William J., Jr., 1073
Ivory, James, 414
Ivy, James, 911
Iwan Simatupang
  Drought, 1246
  Merahnya Merah (Red of the Red), 1246
  Pilgrim, 1246
Iyayi, Festus, 20, 32
Izaguirre, Carlos, 735
Izco, Ayguals de, 1265

Jabiri, Muhammad Salih, 22
Jabiri, Shakib al-, 760
Jabra, Jabra Ibrahim
  Hunters in a Narrow Street, 760
  Passage in the Silent Night, 760
  Ship, 761
Jackson, Andrew, 1374
Jackson, Jack, 507
Jackson, Michael, 933
Jackson, Robert L., 332
Jackson, Shirley
  Haunting of Hill House, 556
  We Have Always Lived in the Castle,
    557
Jacob, Christian, 437
Jacob, Violet, 1200
Jacobite rebellion of 1745 (Scotland), 364,
    411, 545, 1281, 1340, 1420
Jacobs, W.W., 926
Jacobsen, Hans Jacob. *See* Brú, Hedín

Jacobsen, Jens Peter, 1166, 1174
  Marie Grubbe, 1166
  Niels Lyhne, 1166
Jacobsen, Jørgen-Frantz, *Barbara,* 1174
Jacobson, Dan, 34, 1286
Jacobson, J.P., 1211
Jadrah, Rashid Abu, 21, 23
Jaeger, Frank, 1168–69
Jaeggy, Fleur, 1311
Jaén, Jeremías, 739
jagunços (Brazilian folk character), 306
Jahnn, Hans Henry, 473, 474, 477
Jakobs, Karl-Heinz, 476
Jakobsdóttir, Svava, 175
Jakobson, Roman, 424
  as Russian formalist, 422, 423, 860, 1293,
    1294
  structuralism and semiotics of, 1292,
    1293–94
  on syntactic approach to narrative, 896
Jakovljevic, Stevan, *Srpska trilogija* (Serbian
    Trilogy), 1446
Jakubec, Doris, 1314, 1315
Jalandoni, Magdalena, 1251
Jamaica, 168, 169, 171, 172, 173
Jamalzadeh, Mohammad Ali, 609, 612
  Once Upon a Time, 609
Jam'at Taht al-Sur (Tunisian writers group),
    22
James I, king of England, 309, 613
James II, king of England, 100, 965
James, C.L.R., 168–69
  Minty Alley, 169
James, Carol, 605
James, G.P.R., 363, 1115
James, Henry, 36, 37, 90, 130, 220, 289, 308,
    311, 355, 371, 373, 412, 416, 425, 426,
    491, 514, 532, 535, **629–31,** 710, 845,
    857, 918, 1116, 1261
  Ambassadors, **45–46,** 487, 630, 854, 907,
    994, 1057, 1380
  American, 466, 629, 947, 994, 995, 1028,
    1379
  "Art of Fiction," 265–66, 267, 487, 843,
    1281
  Art of the Novel, 266, 630
  Aspern Papers, 630, 1388
  Awkward Age, 630, 994
  Bostonians, 413, 629, 1095, 1184, 1361
  in canon, 164
  caricatures of, 372
  characterizations, 1012
  on Conrad, 237, 266
  and consciousness novel, 319, 654
  as critic, 264–66, 267, 268, 629, 1059
  critical approaches to, 268, 270
  culture-clash as theme, 180
  Daisy Miller, 413, 630, 949, 1028
  decline in sales of works by, 1094
  on Dostoevskii and Tolstoi, 255
  as dramatist, 629–30
  editorial pressure on, 995
  on effects of World War I, 1381
  Eliot (George) as model for, 352, 353, 839
  Europeans, 413, 1028
  experimentation in late work, 630

Felman on, 1059
film adaptations of works, 413
as Flaubertian artistry advocate, 371,
    466–67, 792
on Flaubert's *Madame Bovary,* 265
framing in narrative by, 433
Golden Bowl, **487–88,** 630, 946, 1057,
    1380
on Goldsmith's *Vicar of Wakefield,* 1406
Gothic writing of, 499
Guy Domville, 629
Hawthorne, 630
on Hawthorne's *Scarlet Letter,* 1184
as high-art novel champion, 370
horror usage, 557
interior monologue usage, 1291
"Jolly Corner," 1057
mastery of short form, 949
melodrama usage, 829
as modernist writer, 856
as Murdoch influence, 877
on *Nana,* 265
narrative complexity, 520, 854, 856, 907,
    908
on narrative theory, 1012, 1397
on novel as art form, 164
as novelist of manners, 945, 946, 947,
    1039
novelistic periods, 487
novellas by, 949–50
on *Père Goriot,* 986
on point of view, 413, 487, 1012
Portrait of a Lady, 38, 164, 270, 353, 413,
    487, 629, 994, **1028–29,** 1057, 1095,
    1184, 1377, 1379
Princess Casamassima, 629, 1095, 1379
and professionalization of authorship, 1377,
    1379
psychobiography of, 1055
as psychological novelist, 1057
realism standards, 853
as realist novelist, 1077
reviewers on, 1095
Roderick Hudson, 629, 994, 1028, 1377,
    1379
on romance vs. realism, 466
Sacred Fount, 630
and scenic novel, 630
serializations of works, 993–94, 995
Spoils of Poynton, 630, 1095
Stevenson's response to "Art of Fiction,"
    1281
temporal neutrality usage, 1333
Tragic Muse, 629
on Trollope, 91–92, 93
Turgenev as literary mentor, 1355
Turn of the Screw, 433, 557, 630, 949, 958,
    1388
Twain's negative view of, 1361, 1362
unreliable narrators usage, 1388
Washington Square, 487, 994, 1379
Watch and Ward, 993
Wells (H.G.) dispute with, 1191, 1423
Wharton comparison, 38, 1426
What Maisie Knew, 487, 630, 908, 994,
    1095

NOTES ON ADVISERS
AND CONTRIBUTORS

Ablow, Rachel Karol. Graduate Instructor in English, Johns Hopkins University, Baltimore, Maryland. **Essay:** *David Copperfield* (Dickens).

Abramson, Edward A. Senior Lecturer and Head of the Department of American Studies, University of Hull; Visiting Professor, College of William and Mary, Virginia, 1986–87. Author of *The Immigrant Experience in American Literature* (1982), *Chaim Potok* (1986), *Bernard Malamud Revisited* (1993), and of articles in *Studies in American Jewish Literature* and *Yearbook of English Studies*. **Essays:** *Call It Sleep* (Henry Roth); Jewish-American Novel; Bernard Malamud; *Portnoy's Complaint* (Philip Roth).

Ackerley, Chris. Senior Lecturer in English, University of Otago, Dunedin, New Zealand. Author of *A Companion to "Under the Volcano"* (1984) and *The Bridging of Troy* (1986) and many articles on modernism and 20th-century fiction. Member of Editorial Boards, *Malcolm Lowry Review* (since 1986) and *Journal of Beckett Studies* (since 1996). **Essays:** Graham Greene; *Murphy* (Beckett); Flann O'Brien; *Passage to India* (Forster); *Under the Volcano* (Lowry).

Adams, Edward A. Assistant Professor of English, Washington and Lee University, Lexington, Virginia. **Essay:** Epic and Novel.

Albright, Angela K. Graduate Instructor in English, University of Arkansas, Fayetteville. Assistant Editor of *The Ogalala Review*. **Essay:** *Native Son* (Wright).

Alkana, Joseph. Associate Professor of English, University of Miami, Coral Gables, Florida. Author of *The Social Self: Hawthorne, Howells, William James, and 19th-Century Psychology* (1997); coeditor of *Cohesion and Dissent in America* (1994). **Essay:** United States Novel: 1800–1850.

Allain, Mathé. Professor of French and Francophone Studies, University of Southwestern Louisiana, Lafayette. Author of *Not Worth a Straw: French Colonial Policy and the Founding of the Louisiana Colony* (1988) and of articles in *Studies in Voltaire and the 18th Century,* among other journals. Assistant Editor, *Études francophones.* **Essay:** *Manon Lescaut* (Prévost).

Allen, Elizabeth Brereton. Lecturer in French and Comparative Literature, Washington University, St. Louis, Missouri. Author of *Transforming Impact: The Shock Experience in Dada and Surrealist Poetry* (1995). **Essay:** Surrealist Novel.

Allen, Elizabeth Cheresh. Associate Professor of Russian and Comparative Literature, Bryn Mawr College, Pennsylvania. Author of *Beyond Realism: Turgenev's Poetics of Secular Salvation* (1992). **Essay:** *Hero of Our Time* (Lermontov).

Allen, Roger (adviser). Professor of Arabic Literature, University of Pennsylvania, Philadelphia. Author of numerous books on the Arabic novel, including *The Arabic Novel: An Historical and Critical Introduction* (1982, 2nd edition 1995) and *The Arabic Literary Heritage* (1998); editor of *Modern Arabic Literature* (1987). Also translator of Arabic novels into English.

Amell, Alma. Professor of Spanish and Head of Latin American Studies Program, Pontifical College Josephinum, Columbus, Ohio. Author of *La preocupación por España en Larra* (1990), *Rosa Montero's Odyssey* (1994) and of articles on *La Regenta* in *The Feminist Encyclopedia of Spanish Literature,* edited by Janet Pérez (1996), and *Actas del I Congreso de la Asociación Hispánica de Humanidades* (1996). Member of Editorial Board, *España Contemporánea.* **Essays:** Miguel de Cervantes; *Regenta* (Clarín).

Andries, Lise. Chargée de Recherches, CNRS, Université de Paris IV-Sorbonne. Author of *La Bibliothèque bleu au 18e siècle: Une tradition Editoriale* (1989) and *Le grand Livre des Secrets: Le colportage en France aux 17e et 18e siècles* (1994); coeditor of *Contes bleues* (1983). **Essay:** Bibliothèque bleue.

Armstrong, Katherine A. Lecturer in English, University College Chester. Author of *Defoe: Writer as Agent* (1996). **Essays:** Daniel Defoe; *Evelina* (Burney); Libraries: England; Prose Novelistic Forms; *Robinson Crusoe* (Defoe).

Arrington, Melvin S., Jr. Professor of Modern Languages, University of Mississippi, University. Author of numerous articles on 20th-century Spanish American Literature in journals and reference books. Member of Editorial Board, *Romance Monographs.* **Essay:** *Obscene Bird of Night* (Donoso).

Atkins, Stuart. Professor Emeritus of German, University of California, Santa Barbara. Author of *The Testament of Werther in Poetry and Drama* (1949) and of numerous articles on Goethe in *Modern Language Review, Modern Language Quarterly,* and

PMLA. Editor, *The German Quarterly,* 1952–57. **Essay:** *Sufferings of Young Werther* (Goethe).

Augenbraum, Harold. Director, The Mercantile Library of New York. Author of *Growing Up Latino: Memoirs and Stories* (1993), *Bendíceme, América* (1993), and *Teaching U.S. Latino Literature* (1998); editor of *Latinos in English: A Bibliography* (1992) and *The Latino Reader: An American Literary Tradition 1542 to the Present* (1997). **Essay:** Latino-American Novel.

Baines, Paul. Lecturer in English, University of Liverpool. Author of numerous articles on 18th-century writers in journals and reference books. **Essay:** *Vicar of Wakefield* (Goldsmith).

Bamia, Aida A. Associate Professor in the Department of African and Asian Languages and Literatures, University of Florida, Gainesville. Author of *Tatawwur al-Adab al-Qasasi al-Jaz'iri, 1925–1967* (1982) and several articles on North African literature; contributor to the *Encyclopedia of World Literature in the Twentieth Century* (volume 5, 1993) and the *Encyclopedia of the Modern Middle East* (volume 3, 1996). **Essays:** African Novel: Northern Africa; ʿAbd al-Raḥmān Munīf.

Barber, Samantha J. Graduate Instructor in English, University of Sheffield. **Essay:** *Love in the Time of Cholera* (García Márquez).

Barbosa, Maria José Somerlate. Assistant Professor of Spanish and Portuguese, University of Iowa, Iowa City. Author of *Clarice Lispector: Spinning the Webs of Passion* (1997). **Essays:** Clarice Lispector; Joaquim Maria Machado de Assis.

Bartolomeo, Joseph F. Associate Professor of English, University of Massachusetts, Amherst. Author of *A New Species of Criticism: 18th-Century Discourse on the Novel* (1994). Eighteenth-century field editor for the Twayne English Authors Series, since 1994. **Essay:** Critics and Criticism: 18th Century.

Beebee, Thomas O. Associate Professor of German and Comparative Literature, Pennsylvania State University, University Park. Author of *Clarissa on the Continent: Translation and Seduction* (1990), *The Ideology of Genre: Comparative Essays in Generic Instability* (1994), and of essays on epistolary fiction published in *Revue de Littérature Comparée, Clio,* and *Journal of English and Germanic Philology.* **Essay:** Epistolary Novel.

Bennett, Bruce (adviser). Professor of English, Australian Defence Force Academy, Canberra. Author of *Place, Region, and Community* (1984), *An Australian Compass: Essays on Place and Direction in Australian Literature* (1991), and *Spirit in Exile: Peter Porter and His Poetry* (1991); coeditor of *Crossing Cultures* (1996) and the *Oxford Literary History of Australia* (1998).

Besner, Neil K. Professor and Chair of English, University of Winnipeg, Manitoba. Author of *The Light of Imagination: Mavis Gallant's Fiction* (1988) and *Introducing Alice Munro's "Lives of Girls and Women": A Reader's Guide* (1990); coeditor of *The Short Story in English* (with David Staines, 1991) and *Uncommon Wealth: An Anthology of Poetry in English* (with

Deborah Schnitzer and Alden Rolfe Turner, 1997). **Essays:** Jorge Amado; Canadian Novel: Anglophone; *Dona Flor and Her Two Husbands* (Amado).

Betensky, Carolyn. Adjunct Assistant Professor of French, Vassar College, Poughkeepsie, New York. Managing Editor, *Romantic Review.* **Essay:** Ideology and the Novel.

Bishop, Neil B. Professor of Canadian and French Literature, Memorial University of Newfoundland, St. Johns. Author of *Anne Hébert: Son oeuvre, leurs exils* (1993) and of numerous articles on Hébert in journals and books. **Essay:** Anne Hébert.

Blair, Ruth M. Lecturer in English, University of Queensland, Brisbane. Author of Introduction and Notes in *Typee* by Herman Melville (Oxford World's Classics, 1996) and of articles on American literature in journals. **Essays:** Environmental Novel; *Last of the Mohicans* (Cooper).

Bliss, Carolyn. Guest Professor of English, University of Utah, Salt Lake City. Author of *Patrick White's Fiction: The Paradox of Fortunate Failure* (1986) and of numerous articles on White and Australian literature in books and journals. President, American Association of Australian Literary Studies. **Essays:** Peter Carey; *Voss* (White).

Boland, Roy C. Professor of Spanish, LaTrobe University, Bundoora, Australia. Author of *Mario Vargas Llosa: Oedipus and the "Papa" State* (1988; 3rd edition, 1990); editor of two special issues of *Antípodas,* "Mario Vargas Llosa" (1988) and "Specular Narratives: Critical Perspectives on Carlos Fuentes, Juan Goytisolo and Mario Vargas Llosa" (1997). **Essay:** Mario Vargas Llosa.

Booker, M. Keith. Professor of English, University of Arkansas, Fayetteville. Author of *Techniques of Subversion in Modern Literature: Transgression, Abjection, and the Carnivalesque* (1991), *Literature and Domination: Sex, Knowledge, and Power in Modern Fiction* (1993), *Vargas Llosa Among the Postmodernists* (1994), *The Dystopian Impulse in Modern Literature: Fiction as Social Criticism* (1994), *Dystopian Fiction: A Theory and Research Guide* (1994), *Bakhtin, Stalin, and Modern Russian Fiction: Carnival, Dialogism, and History* (with Dubravka Juraga, 1995), *Flann O'Brien, Bakhtin, and Menippean Satire* (1995), *Joyce, Bakhtin, and the Literary Tradition: Toward a Comparative Cultural Poetics* (1996), *A Practical Introduction to Literary Theory and Criticism* (1996), *Colonial Power, Colonial Texts: India in the Modern British Novel* (1997), and *A Practical Introduction to the African Novel* (1998). **Essays:** African Novel: South Africa; *Gravity's Rainbow* (Pynchon); Alex La Guma; Marxist Criticism of the Novel; Proletarian Novel; Ousmane Sembène; *U.S.A.* Trilogy (Dos Passos); *War of the End of the World* (Vargas Llosa).

Borella, Sara Steinert. Assistant Professor of French, Pacific University, Forest Grove, Oregon. Author of articles on Swiss women writers in *Women in History* and *The Translation Review.* **Essay:** Swiss Novel: Francophone.

Bradbury, Malcolm (adviser). Professor Emeritus, School of English and American Studies, University of East Anglia, Norwich.

Author of *Evelyn Waugh* (1964), *What Is a Novel* (1969), *The Social Context of Modern English Literature* (1971), *Possibilities* (1973), *The Outland Dart: American Writers and European Modernism* (1978), *The Expatriate Tradition in American Literature* (1982), *Saul Bellow* (1983), *The Modern American Novel* (1983, revised editon 1991), *My Strange Quest for Mensonge: Structuralism's Hidden Hero* (1987), *No, Not Bloomsbury* (1987), *The Modern World: Ten Great Writers* (1989), *From Puritanism to Postmodernism: The Story of American Literature* (with Richard Ruland, 1991), *The Modern British Novel* (1993), and *Dangerous Pilgrimages: Trans-Atlantic Mythologies and the Novel* (1997), and many novels, plays, radio dramas, and television and film screenplays, including the screenplay of John Schlesinger's *Cold Comfort Farm;* editor, *Modernism, 1890–1930* (with James McFarlane, 1976), and *The Novel Today: Contemporary Writers on Modern Fiction* (1977, revised edition 1990).

Brantly, Susan. Associate Professor and Chair, Scandinavian Department, University of Wisconsin-Madison. Author of *The Life and Writings of Laura Marholm* (1991) and "Into the 20th Century, 1890–1950," in *A History of Swedish Literature,* edited by Lars Warme (1996). **Essay:** Pär Lagerkvist.

Briggs, A.D.P. Professor of Russian Language and Literature, University of Birmingham. Author of *Vladimir Mayakovsky: A Tragedy* (1979), *Alexander Pushkin: A Critical Study* (1983), *A Wicked Irony: The Rhetoric of Lermontov's "A Hero of Our Time"* (with Andrew Barratt, 1989), *A Comparative Study of Pushkin's "The Bronze Horseman," Nekrasov's "Red-Nosed Frost," and Blok's "The Twelve"* (1990), *Eugene Onegin* (1992), and *Alexander Pushkin* (1997). Also editor and translator of works by Pushkin. **Essay:** Aleksandr Pushkin.

Brooks, Peter (adviser). Tripp Professor of Humanities, Yale University, New Haven, Connecticut. Author of several book-length works including *The Melodramatic Imagination: Balzac, Henry James, Melodrama, and the Mode of Excess* (1976), *Reading for the Plot: Design and Intention in Narrative* (1984), *Body Work: Objects of Desire in Modern Narrative* (1993), and *Psychoanalysis and Storytelling* (1994); editor of *Père Goriot: A Norton Critical Edition* (1998).

Brosman, Catharine Savage. Kathryn B. Gore Professor of French Emeritus, Tulane University, New Orleans, Louisiana, and Honorary Research Professor, Department of French, University of Sheffield. Author of *André Gide: L'évolution de sa pensée religieuse* (1962), *Malraux, Sartre, and Aragon as Political Novelists* (1964), *Roger Martin du Gard* (1968), *Jean-Paul Sartre* (1983) *An Annotated Bibliography of Criticism on André Gide, 1973–88* (1990); editor of *French Novelists 1900–30, French Novelists 1930–60,* and *French Novelists Since 1960* (3 volumes in the Dictionary of Literary Biography series, 1988–89); also editor and principal contributor to *Twentieth-Century French Culture 1900–75* (1995). Managing Editor (1977–80) and member of Editorial Board (since 1984), *French Review;* Comité de lecture, *Bulletin des Amis d'André Gide.* **Essays:** *Counterfeiters* (Gide); French Novel: 1914–1945; André Gide; *Nausea* (Sartre); Voltaire.

Brothers, Robyn. Received Ph.D. in French from Brown University, Providence, Rhode Island, 1997. Her dissertation is entitled "Literary Liberalism: Proust, Sartre, and the Private/Public Dialectic." Author of "Cyborg Identities and the Relational Web: Recasting 'Narrative Identity' in Moral and Political Theory," in *Metaphilosophy* (July 1997). **Essay:** Marcel Proust.

Burdan, Judith. Assistant Professor of English, Purdue University Calumet, Hammond, Indiana. **Essays:** *Frankenstein* (Shelley); *Oroonoko* (Behn); *Pilgrim's Progress* (Bunyan); *Pride and Prejudice* (Austen).

Cahalan, James M. Professor of English, Indiana University of Pennsylvania. Author of many books and articles on Irish literature, including *Great Hatred, Little Room: The Irish Historical Novel* (1983), *The Irish Novel: A Critical History* (1988), *Liam O'Flaherty: A Study of the Short Fiction* (1991), and *Modern Irish Literature and Culture: A Chronology* (1993). **Essay:** Irish Novel.

Canuel, Mark. Assistant Professor of English, University of Illinois-Chicago. Author of "Holy Hypocricy and the Government of Belief: Religion and Nationalism in the Gothic," in *Studies in Romanticism* (Winter 1995). **Essays:** *Caleb Williams* (Godwin); Canon.

Carpenter, Kenneth E. Assistant Director for Research Resources, Widener Library, Harvard University, Cambridge, Massachusetts. Author of *The Harvard University Library: A Documentary History* (1990), *Readers and Libraries: Toward a History of Libraries and Culture in America* (1996); editor of *Books and Society in History* (1983). Editor of *Harvard Library Bulletin,* since 1980. **Essay:** Libraries: United States.

Carroll, Joseph. Professor of English, University of Missouri-St. Louis. Author of *The Cultural Theory of Matthew Arnold* (1982), *Wallace Stevens' Supreme Fiction: A New Romanticism* (1987), and *Evolution and Literary Theory* (1995). **Essays:** George Eliot; *Middlemarch* (Eliot); *Vanity Fair* (Thackeray); War Novel.

Case, Frederick Ivor. Professor of French, New College, University of Toronto. Author of *The Crisis of Identity: Studies in the Guadeloupean and Martiniquan Novel* (1985). **Essay:** Caribbean Novel: Francophone.

Caudle, David J. Ph.D. in English, University of North Texas, Denton. Author of *Kate Chopin: An Annotated Bibliography of Critical Works* (with Suzanne D. Green, 1998). **Essay:** Regional Novel: United States.

Chambers, Helen. Senior Lecturer in German, Leeds University. Author of *Supernatural and Irrational Elements in the Works of Theodor Fontane* (1980) and *The Changing Image of Theodor Fontane* (1997). **Essay:** Theodor Fontane.

Charters, Ann. Professor of English, University of Connecticut, Storrs. Author of *Kerouac: A Biography* (1973); editor of *The Kerouac Reader* (1996) and *Selected Letters of Jack Kerouac* (1996). **Essay:** *On the Road* (Kerouac).

Chatman, Seymour. Professor of Rhetoric Emeritus, University of California, Berkeley. Author of numerous books and articles, including *Story and Discourse: Narrative Structure in Fiction and Film* (1978) and *Coming to Terms: The Rhetoric of Narrative in Fiction and Film* (1990). **Essays:** Narrator; Point of View.

Claridge, Henry. Senior Lecturer in English, University of Kent, Canterbury. Regular contributor on American literature to *The Year's Work in English Studies;* editor of *F. Scott Fitzgerald: Critical Assessments* (4 vols., 1992) and *William Faulkner: Critical Assessments* (4 vols., 1997). **Essays:** Critics and Criticism: 19th Century; Theodore Dreiser; *Moby-Dick* (Melville); Naturalism.

Clayton, Cherry. Lecturer in English, University of Guelph, Ontario. Author of numerous articles and two books on Olive Schreiner (1983 and 1997); editor of collections of Schreiner's writings and of *Women and Writing in South Africa: A Critical Anthology* (1989). **Essays:** *Emma* (Austen); *Story of an African Farm* (Schreiner).

Cloonan, William. Professor of French, Florida State University, Tallahassee. Author of *Michel Tournier* (1985) and of numerous articles on Tournier and contemporary French fiction. **Essays:** *Liaisons dangereuses* (Laclos); Michel Tournier.

Cloy, John D. Bibliographer for the Humanities, J.D. Williams Library, University of Mississippi, University. Author of *Pensive Jester: The Literary Career of W.W. Jacobs* (1996) and of "Turn-of-the-Century British Humorists: Some Bibliographic Difficulties," in *Editor's Notes* (Spring/Fall 1993). **Essay:** New Humor Novel.

Clune, Anne. Senior Lecturer in English, Trinity College, Dublin. Author of *Flann O'Brien: A Critical Introduction to His Writing* (1975) and of several articles on O'Brien and other Irish novelists. **Essays:** *At Swim-Two-Birds* (O'Brien); *Melmoth the Wanderer* (Maturin).

Cohen, Debra Rae. Instructor in English, University of Mississippi, University. **Essay:** English Novel: 1920–1950.

Cohen, Monica F. Assistant Professor of Literature, California Institute of Technology, Pasadena. Author of *Professional Domesticity in the Victorian Novel: Women, Work, and Home* (1998) and of articles on Victorian novelists in *Studies in the Novel, Victorian Literature and Culture, Dickens Quarterly,* and *Novel.* **Essay:** *Persuasion* (Austen).

Conley, Tom. Professor of Romance Languages, Harvard University, Cambridge, Massachusetts. Author of numerous books and articles on French literature and culture, including *The Graphic Unconscious in Early Modern French Writing* (1992) and *The Self-Made Map: Cartographic Writing in Early Modern France* (1996). **Essay:** French Novel: 16th and 17th Centuries.

Coppola, Carlo (adviser). Professor, Department of Modern Languages and Literature, and Director, Center for International Programs, Oakland University, Rochester, Michigan. Author of *Marxist Influences and South Asian Literature* (1988) and of numerous articles on South Asian writers. Member of the Board of

Directors, Michigan Psychoanalytic Foundation and guest faculty member, Michigan Psychoanalytic Institute. Founding Editor, *Journal of South Asian Literature.* **Essays:** Magic Realism; Psychoanalytic Models of Narrative and Criticism of the Novel; Salman Rushdie.

Cornis-Pope, Marcel. Professor of English and Comparative Literature, Virginia Commonwealth University, Richmond. Author of *Anatomy of the White Whale: A Poetics of the American Symbolist Epic* (1982), *Hermeneutic Desire and Critical Rewriting: Narrative Interpretation in the Wake of Poststructuralism* (1992), *The Unfinished Battles: Romanian Postmodernism Before and After 1989* (1996), as well as articles on contemporary Romanian fiction; editor of *Violence and Mediation in Contemporary Literature and Culture* (with Ronald Bogue, 1995). Editor, since 1991, of *The Comparatist,* and Associate Editor, since 1984, of *The European Studies Journal.* **Essays:** Romanian Novel; Structuralism, Semiotics, and the Novel.

Cornwell, Neil. Professor of Russian and Comparative Literature, University of Bristol. Author of *The Literary Fantastic: From Gothic to Postmodernism* (1990); editor of *Reference Guide to Russian Literature* (1998). Translator of fiction by Zamiatin, Odoevskii, and Kharms. **Essay:** *We* (Zamiatin).

Costlow, Jane. Associate Professor of Russian, Bates College, Lewiston, Maine. Author of *Worlds within Words: The Novels of Ivan Turgenev* (1990); editor of *Representations of the Body and Sexuality in Russian Culture* (with Stephanie Sandler and Judith Vowles, 1993). **Essay:** *Fathers and Sons* (Turgenev).

Cox, J. Randolph. Professor Emeritus of English, St. Olaf College, Northfield, Minnesota. Author of *Man of Magic and Mystery: The Work of Walter B. Gibson* (1988), *H.G. Wells: A Reference Guide* (with William Scheick, 1988), and of several articles on dime novels. Editor and Publisher, since 1994, of *Dime Novel Round-Up.* **Essay:** Dime Novels and Penny Dreadfuls.

Craft, Linda J. Lecturer in Spanish, Northwestern University, Evanston, Illinois. Author of *Novels of Testimony and Resistance from Central America* (1997) and "Testinovela/Telenovela: Latin American Popular Culture and Contemporary Women's Narrative," in *Indiana Journal of Hispanic Literatures* 8. **Essay:** Latin American Novel: Central America.

Crane, Ralph J. Senior Lecturer in English, University of Waikato, New Zealand. Author of *Inventing India: A History of India in English-Language Fiction* (1992) and *Ruth Prawer Jhabvala* (1992); editor of *Passages to Ruth Prawer Jhabvala* (1991) and *Ending the Silences: Critical Essays on the Works of Maurice Shadbolt* (1995). Coeditor of *SPAN—The Journal of the South Pacific Association of Commonwealth Literature and Language Studies.* **Essays:** R.K. Narayan; Maurice Shadbolt; *Untouchable* (Anand).

Cremers Pearson, Martine. Associate Professor of French, Shorter College, Rome, Georgia. **Essay:** *Man's Fate* (Malraux).

Croft, Julian. Professor of English, University of New England, Armidale, New South Wales. Author of *T.H. Jones* (1976), *The*

Life and Opinions of Tom Collins: A Study of the Works of Joseph Furphy (1991), as well as other books of scholarship and poetry. **Essay:** *Such Is Life* (Furphy).

Cruz, Isagani R. Alfredo E. Litiatco Professor of Literature, De La Salle University, Manila, Philippines. Author of *Beyond Futility: The Filipino as Critic* (1984); editor, *Manila: History, People, and Culture: The Proceedings of the Manila Studies Conference* (with others, 1989), and *Reading Bienvenido N. Santos* (with David Jonathan Bayot, 1994). **Essay:** Southeast Asian Novel: Philippines.

Čulík, Jan. Lecturer in Czech Studies, University of Glasgow. Author of *Knihy za ohradou: česká literatura v exilových nakladatelstvích, 1971–1989* (1991; Books Behind the Fence: Czech Literature in Emigré Publishing Houses) and "Bohumil Hrabal—Looking Back," in *Scottish Slavonic Review* 10 (Spring 1988). **Essays:** Czech Novel; *Good Soldier Švejk* (Hašek); Bohumil Hrabal; Milan Kundera.

Davis, Lennard J. (adviser). Professor of English, State University of New York, Binghamton. Author of *Factual Fictions: Origins of the English Novel* (1983) and *Resisting Novels: Fiction and Ideology* (1987); coeditor of *Left Politics and the Literary Profession* (1991). **Essay:** Journalism and the Novel.

Davis, Liselotte M. Senior Lecturer in German, Yale University, New Haven, Connecticut. Author of articles on Thomas Mann, Fritz Reuter, Uwe Johnson, Heimito von Doderer, and Joseph von Eichendorff. **Essays:** *Doctor Faustus* (Mann); Uwe Johnson.

Denton, Kirk A. Associate Professor of East Asian Languages and Literatures, Ohio State University, Columbus. Editor of *Modern Chinese Literary Thought: Writings on Literature 1893–1945* (1996). **Essay:** Lu Xun.

Dixon, John S. University of Warwick, Coventry. **Essay:** Translation of Novels.

Dixon, Paul B. Professor of Spanish, Purdue University, West Lafayette, Indiana. Author of *Reversible Readings: Ambiguity in Four Modern Latin American Novels* (1985), *Retired Dreams: Dom Casmurro, Myth, and Modernity* (1989), and *Oscontos de Machado de Assis: mais do que sonha a filosofia* (1992), as well as several articles on Machado de Assis. **Essays:** *Devil to Pay in the Backlands* (Guimarães Rosa); *Dom Casmurro* (Machado de Assis).

Dixon, Simon. Ph.D. candidate in the Department of English, University of Iowa, Iowa City. **Essay:** Film and the Novel.

Draper, R.P. Regius Chalmers Professor of English Emeritus, University of Aberdeen. Author of numerous books, including *Lyric Tragedy* (1985), *Sons and Lovers* (1986), and *An Annotated Critical Bibliography of Thomas Hardy* (1989); editor of *Hardy: The Tragic Novels* (1975, revised 1991), *"The Mill on the Floss" and "Silas Marner": A Casebook* (1977), *Tragedy: Developments in Criticism* (1980), *Hardy: Three Pastoral Novels* (1987), *The Literature of Region and Nation* (1989), *The Epic: Developments in Criticism* (1990), and *A Spacious Vision:*

Essays on Hardy (with Phillip V. Mallett, 1994). **Essays:** *Golden Bowl* (James); *Jude the Obscure* (Hardy); Pastoralism in the Novel.

Drozd, Andrew M. Assistant Professor of Russian, University of Alabama, Tuscaloosa. Author of *N.G. Chernyshevskii's "What Is To Be Done?": A Reevaluation* (1995). **Essay:** *What Is To Be Done?* (Chernyshevskii).

Duffey, J. Patrick. Assistant Professor of Spanish, Austin College, Sherman, Texas. Author of *De la pantalla al texto: La influencia del cine en la narrativa mexicana del siglo XX* (1997). **Essays:** Latin American Novel: Mexico; *Terra Nostra* (Fuentes).

Duncan, Ian (adviser). Barbara and Carlisle Moore Professor of English, University of Oregon, Eugene. Author of *Modern Romance and Transformations of the Novel: The Gothic, Scott, Dickens* (1992). **Essays:** *Private Memoirs and Confessions of a Justified Sinner* (Hogg); Romance; Sir Walter Scott; Scottish Novel.

Duval, Edwin M. Professor of French, Yale University, New Haven, Connecticut. Author of numerous books and articles on Rabelais and French Renaissance literature, including *Poesis and Poetic Tradition in the Early Works of Saint-Amant: Four Essays in Contextual Reading* (1981), *The Design of Rabelais's Pantagruel* (1991), *The Design of Rabelais's Tiers Livre de Pantagruel* (1997), and *The Design of Rabelais's Quart Livre de Pantagruel* (1998). **Essay:** François Rabelais.

Duyfhuizen, Bernard. Professor of English, University of Wisconsin-Eau Claire. Author of *Narratives of Transmission* (1992) and of numerous articles on Pynchon in journals. Coeditor of *Pynchon Notes*. **Essays:** Diegesis and Diegetic Levels of Narration; Framing and Embedding in Narrative; Thomas Pynchon.

Earle, Scott. Graduate Instructor in English, University of Arkansas, Fayetteville. **Essay:** *Grapes of Wrath* (Steinbeck).

Easterling, Thomas. Graduate Instructor in English, University of Mississippi, University. Associate Editor, *The Oxford American*. **Essay:** *Absalom, Absalom!* (Faulkner).

Easton, Fraser. Assistant Professor of English, University of Waterloo, Ontario. **Essay:** *Moll Flanders* (Defoe).

Ehre, Milton. Professor of Slavic Languages and Literatures, University of Chicago. Author of numerous books and articles, including "Ivan Goncharov on Art, Literature, and the Novel" (1970, reprinted 1981), *Oblomov and His Creator: The Life and Art of Ivan Goncharov* (1973), and *Isaac Babel* (1986); editor of *The Theater of Nikolay Gogol: Plays and Selected Writings* (with Fruma Gottschalk, 1980); translator of *Chekhov for the Stage* (1992). **Essays:** *Oblomov* (Goncharov); *War and Peace* (Tolstoi).

Eile, Stanislaw. Senior Lecturer in Polish, School of Slavonic and East European Studies, University of London. Author of *Modernist Trends in Twentieth-Century Polish Fiction* (1996) and articles in Polish, English, and French on 19th- and 20th-century

Polish literature; coeditor and contributor, *New Perspectives in Twentieth-Century Polish Literature* (1992). **Essays:** Witold Gombrowicz; Bolesław Prus; Henryk Sienkiewicz.

Elliott, Dorice Williams. Assistant Professor of English, University of Kansas, Lawrence. Author of articles in *Nineteenth-Century Literature, Nineteenth-Century Contexts,* and *Studies in English Literature 1500–1900.* **Essays:** Feminist Criticism of Narrative; Social Criticism.

Emenyonu, Ernest N. Visiting Professor, African and Afro-American Studies Department, Brandeis University, Waltham, Massachusetts. Author of numerous books and articles on African writers, including *Cyprian Ekwensi* (1974); *The Rise of the Igbo Novel* (1978), *Studies on the Nigerian Novel* (1991) and *Flora Nwapa's Writings for Children: Visions of Innocence and Regeneration* (1997). Editorial Consultant for the journal *Kunapipi,* and Contributing Editor, *Okike*; West African Regional Representative, *Journal of Commonwealth Literature.* **Essays:** Cyprian Ekwensi; Flora Nwapa; *Things Fall Apart* (Achebe).

Ermarth, Elizabeth Deeds. Saintsbury Professor of English Literature and Director of the Postgraduate School, University of Edinburgh. Author of numerous books and articles, including *Realism and Consensus in the English Novel* (1983; new edition, with subtitle *The Construction of Time in Narrative,* 1998), *George Eliot* (1985), *Sequel to History: Postmodernism and the Crisis of Representational Time* (1992), "The Crisis of Realism in Postmodern Time," in *Realism and Representation,* edited by George Levine (1993), and *The Novel in History 1840–95* (1997). **Essays:** English Novel: 1840–1880; Vladimir Nabokov; Postmodernism and the Novel; Realism; Time in the Novel.

Ermolaev, Herman. Professor of Russian and Soviet Literature, Princeton University, New Jersey. Author of *Mikhail Sholokhov and His Art* (1982) and of numerous articles on Sholokhov. President of the American Association of Teachers of Slavic and East European Languages, 1970–72. **Essay:** *Quiet Flows the Don* (Sholokhov).

Falconer, Graham. Professor Emeritus of French, University of Toronto; Director, Centre d'Études Romantiques J. Sablé, St. Michael's College, University of Toronto. Author of numerous articles on French 19th-century writers, and editor of *La Lecture Sociocritique du Texte Romanesque* (1975), *Écriture/Réécriture: La Genèse du Texte* (1988), and *Kaleidoscope: Essays in 19th-Century French Literature* (with M. Donaldson-Evans, 1996). Editorial Boards of *Novel* (1968–75), *University of Toronto Quarterly* (since 1990), *Texte* (since 1995), and *Nineteenth-Century French Studies* (since 1995). **Essays:** *Human Comedy* (Balzac); Libraries: France; *Madame Bovary* (Flaubert).

Ferreira, César. Assistant Professor of Spanish, University of North Texas, Denton. Editor of *Los mundos de Alfredo Bryce Echenique* (with Ismael P. Márquez, 1994) and *Asedios a Julio Ramón Ribeyro* (with Marquez, 1996). **Essay:** *Pedro Páramo* (Rulfo).

Ferrier, Carole. Associate Professor of English, University of Queensland, Brisbane. Editor of *Gender, Politics and Fiction:*

20th-Century Australian Women's Novels (1985; new edition 1992), *The Janet Frame Reader* (1995), and *The Point of Change: Marxism, Australia, History, Theory* (with Rebecca Pelan, 1998). **Essay:** Janet Frame.

Finney, Brian. Adjunct Professor of English, California State University, Long Beach. Author of numerous books and articles on 20th-century novelists, including *Since How It Is: A Study of Samuel Beckett's Later Fiction* (1972) and "Beckett's Postmodern Fictions," in *The Columbia History of the British Novel,* edited by John Richetti (1994); also editor of several editions of the works of D.H. Lawrence for Penguin and for *The Cambridge Edition of the Works of D.H. Lawrence.* **Essays:** Samuel Beckett; *Midnight's Children* (Rushdie); *Molloy, Malone Dies, The Unnamable* (Beckett); *Sons and Lovers* (Lawrence).

Fleischman, Suzanne. Professor of French and Romance Philology, University of California, Berkeley. Author of *Tense and Narrativity: From Medieval Performance to Modern Fiction* (1990) and of numerous articles in journals on the issue of tense and time in narrative; editor of *Discourse Pragmatics and the Verb: The Evidence from Romance* (with Linda R. Waugh, 1991) and *Modality in Grammar and Discourse* (with Joan L. Bybee, 1995). Member of Editorial Boards of *Romance Philology* (1982–95), *Probus* (since 1987), *Tenso* (since 1986), *Journal of French Language Studies* (1990–96), *Publications of the Modern Language Association* (1991–95), and *Hispanic Review* (since 1994). **Essay:** Tense in Narrative.

Fludernik, Monika. Professor of English Literature, University of Freiburg. Author of *The Fictions of Language and the Languages of Fiction: The Linguistic Representations of Speech and Consciousness* (1993) and *Towards a "Natural" Narratology* (1996), as well as numerous articles on fiction and narratology. Guest Editor, *Second-Person Narrative,* a special issue of *Style* (28:3 [1994]). Series Editor, *Handbücher zum literaturwissenschaftlichen Studium* (with Ansgar Nünning). Editorial Board, *Style,* since 1994, and *Language and Literature,* since 1997. **Essays:** Discourse Representation; Fable; Narratology.

Fortier, Paul A. University Distinguished Professor of French, University of Manitoba, Winnipeg. Author of *Une Lecture de Camus: La Valeur des éléments descriptifs dans l'œuvre romanesque* (1977), *Structures et Communication dans "La Jalousie" d'Alain Robbe-Grillet* (1981), *Le Métro émotif: Étude du fonctionnement des structures thématiques dans "Voyage au bout de la nuit"* (1981), and *Décor et dualism: "L'Immoraliste" d'André Gide* (1988), as well as numerous articles on Céline. **Essay:** *Voyage to the End of the Night* (Céline).

Foster, David William (adviser). Regents' Professor of Spanish, Interdisciplinary Humanities, and Women's Studies, and Chair, Languages-Literatures, Arizona State University, Tempe. Author of numerous works including *Currents in the Contemporary Argentine Novel: Arlt, Mallea, Sabato, and Cortázar* (1975), *Cultural Diversity in Latin American Literature* (1994), and *Sexual Textualities: Essays on Queer/ing Latin American Writing* (1997). Has also edited numerous volumes including *Handbook of Latin American Literature* (1987, 2nd edition 1992) and

Mexican Literature: A History (1994). Editor, *Chasqui; revista de literatura latinoamericana.*

Foster, Ian. Lecturer in German, University of Salford. Author of *The Image of the Habsburg Army in Austrian Prose Fiction* (1991). **Essay:** *Radetzky March* (Joseph Roth).

Foulcher, Keith. Lecturer in Southeast Asian Studies, University of Sydney. Author of "Historical Past and Political Present in Recent Indonesian Novels" (1987), "The Early Fiction of Pramoedya Ananta Toer" and "Literature, Cultural Politics and the Indonesian Revolution," both in *Text/Politics in Island Southeast Asia,* edited by D.M. Roskies (1992), "Post-Modernism or the Question of History: Some Trends in Indonesian Fiction Since 1965," in *Culture and Society in New Order Indonesia,* edited by Virginia Hooker (1993), and "In Search of the Postcolonial in Indonesian Literature" (1995). **Essay:** Southeast Asian Novel: Indonesia.

Freeborn, Richard (adviser). Professor of Russian, School of Slavonic and East European Studies, University of London. Author of *Turgenev: The Novelist's Novelist* (1960), *A Short History of Modern Russia* (1966), *The Rise of the Russian Novel: Studies in the Russian Novel from "Eugene Onegin" to "War and Peace"* (1973), *Russian Literary Attitudes from Pushkin to Solzhenitsyn* (1976), and *The Russian Revolutionary Novel: Turgenev to Pasternak* (1982); editor of *Ideology in Russian Literature* (1990). Translator, *Rudin, Home of the Gentry, A Month in the Country, Sketches from a Hunter's Album, Love and Death: Six Stories,* and *Fathers and Sons* by Ivan Turgenev and *An Accidental Family* by Fedor Dostoevskii. **Essays:** *Doctor Zhivago* (Pasternak); Maksim Gor'kii; Russian Novel: 1855–1900; Ivan Turgenev.

Fulton, Bruce. Ph.D. candidate, Seoul National University, Korea. Author of articles on Korean literature in *Korean Culture, Koreana,* and *Manoa.* Translator, *The Moving Castle* (with Ju-Chan Fulton, 1985), by Hwang Sun-won; compiler and translator of *Words of Farewell: Stories by Korean Women Writers* (with Ju-Chan Fulton, 1989), *Land of Exile: Contemporary Korean Fiction* (with Ju-Chan Fulton and Marshall Pihl), *Wayfarer: New Women's Fiction from Korea* (with Ju-Chan Fulton, 1997), and *A Ready-Made Life: Early Masters of Modern Korean Fiction* (with Kim Chong-un, 1998). Director of Publications, International Korean Literature Association (since 1992). **Essay:** Korean Novel.

Fusso, Susanne. Associate Professor of Russian Language and Literature, Wesleyan University, Middletown, Connecticut. Author of *Designing Dead Souls: An Anatomy of Disorder in Gogol* (1993); editor of *Essays on Gogol: Logos and the Russian Word* (with Priscilla Meyer, 1992) and of the revised and annotated edition of *Dead Souls,* translated by Bernard G. Guerney (1996). **Essay:** *Dead Souls* (Gogol').

Gafaiti, Hafid. Jeanne Charnier-Qualia Professor of French and Francophone Literature, Texas Tech University, Lubbock. Author of *Kateb Yacine: Un homme, une œuvre, un pays* (1986), *Boudjedra, ou la passion de la modernité* (1987), *Les femmes dans le roman algérien: Histoire, discours et texte* (1996), and

"Between God and the President: Literature and Censorship in North Africa" (forthcoming in *Diacritics*). **Essay:** Censorship and the Novel.

Gardiner, Allan. Lecturer in English, Queensland University of Technology, Brisbane. Author of articles on Australian socialist-realist writers. **Essay:** *Golden Notebook* (Lessing).

Gardner, Colin. Professor of English, University of Natal, Pietermaritzburg, South Africa. Author of several articles on Alan Paton and editor of *Knocking on the Door: Shorter Writings of Alan Paton* (1975). **Essay:** *Cry, the Beloved Country* (Paton).

Gaspar, Christine. Ph.D. candidate in French, Brown University, Providence, Rhode Island. Writing a dissertation on Marguerite Duras and Maryse Condé. **Essay:** Marguerite Duras.

Ghandour, Sabah. Senior Lecturer, Asian and Middle Eastern Studies, University of Pennsylvania, Philadelphia. Author of articles on Arabic writers and of the Forewords to the English translations of Khūrī's *Gates of the City* (1993) and *Journey of Little Gandhi* (1994). **Essays:** *Journey of Little Gandhi* (Khūrī); Ilyās Khūrī; Ḥanān al-Shaykh.

Ghanoonparvar, M.R. Associate Professor of Persian and Comparative Literature, University of Texas at Austin. Author of *Prophets of Doom: Literature as a Socio-Political Phenomenon in Modern Iran* (1984), *In a Persian Mirror: Images of the West and Westerners in Contemporary Iranian Fiction* (1993), and numerous articles on Iranian literature. **Essay:** Iranian Novel.

Gibbs, James. Special Lecturer, University of the West of England, Bristol. Author of *Wole Soyinka* (1986). Reviews Editor, *African Literature Today.* **Essay:** *Interpreters* (Soyinka).

Gikandi, Simon. Professor of English and Comparative Literature, University of Michigan, Ann Arbor. Author of several works on African and Caribbean literature, including *The East African Novel in Its Historical Perspective* (1978), *Reading the African Novel* (1987), *Reading Chinua Achebe: Language and Ideology in Fiction* (1991), *Writing in Limbo: Modernism and Caribbean Literature* (1992), *Maps of Englishness: Writing Identity in the Culture of Colonialism* (1996), and *Ngugi wa Thiong'o* (1998). Associate Editor, *Cambridge History of African and Caribbean Literature,* and Associate Editor, *African Literature Today.* **Essay:** Ngugi wa Thiong'o.

Ginsburg, Michal Peled (adviser). Professor of French and Comparative Literature, and Chair, Department of French and Italian, Northwestern University, Evanston, Illinois. Author of *Flaubert Writing: A Study in Narrative Strategies* (1986) and *Economies of Change: Form and Transformation in the 19th-Century Novel* (1997). **Essays:** *Red and the Black* (Stendhal); *Sentimental Education* (Flaubert).

GoGwilt, Chris. Associate Professor of English, Fordham University, Bronx, New York. Author of *The Invention of the West: Joseph Conrad and the Double-Mapping of Europe and Empire* (1995) and "Pramoedya's Fiction and History: An Interview with Indonesian Novelist Pramoedya Ananta Toer," in *Yale Journal of Criticism* (1996). **Essay:** Pramoedya Ananta Toer.

Goldblatt, Howard. Professor of Chinese, University of Colorado, Boulder. Author of articles and monographs on Chinese writers. Translator of numerous Chinese novels for Viking Press and others, including *The Field of Life and Death* and *Tales of Hulan River* by Xiao Hong (both 1979), and *Red Sorghum* (1993) and *The Garlic Ballads* (1995), both by Mo Yan. Founding Editor, *Modern Chinese Literature* (since 1984). **Essays:** Mo Yan; Xiao Hong.

Goldman, Jane. Lecturer in English, University of Dundee. Author of "'Miss Lonelyhearts and the Party Dress': Cross-Dressing and Collage in the Satires of Nathaneal West" (1993), "Dada Goes West: Re-Reading Revolution in *The Day of the Locust*" (1996), and *The Feminist Aesthetics of Virginia Woolf: Modernism, Post-Impressionism and the Poetics of the Visual* (forthcoming). **Essay:** Nathanael West.

Gömöri, George. Lecturer in Slavonic Studies, University of Cambridge. Author of several articles on Hungarian and Polish writers. Member of the editorial board, *World Literature Today,* since 1969. **Essays:** Peter Esterházy; *Ferdydurke* (Gombrowicz); Hungarian Novel; György Konrád.

Gordon, David J. Professor of English, Hunter College and the CUNY Graduate Center, New York. Author of *Iris Murdoch's Fables of Unselfing* (1995). **Essay:** Iris Murdoch.

Graham, Colin. Lecturer in English, University of Huddersfield. Author of "History, Gender, and the Colonial Moment: *Castle Rackrent*," in *Irish Studies Review* 14 (1996); editor of *Ireland and Cultural Theory: The Mechanics of Authenticity* (with Richard Kirkland, 1998). **Essays:** *Castle Rackrent* (Edgeworth); *Dracula* (Stoker).

Green, Sharon. Lecturer in the Department of Near and Middle Eastern Studies, University of Toronto. Author of "The Golden Age of Yiddish Literature: From the Late 19th Century Until the Outbreak of World War II," in *Yiddish Panorama: A Thousand Years of Yiddish Language, Literature, and Culture* (1995), and *Love in Exile: A Key to the Work of S.Y. Agnon* (1997); editor and translator of *And They Will Call Us: Poems of the Holocaust* (with others, 1982). **Essays:** *Bridal Canopy* (Agnon); Isaac Bashevis Singer.

Green, Suzanne D. Assistant Professor of English, Northwestern State University of Louisiana, Natchitoches. Author of *Kate Chopin: An Annotated Bibliography of Critical Works* (with David J. Caudle, 1998). **Essays:** *Awakening* (Chopin); Willa Cather; Regional Novel: United States.

Greetham, David. Distinguished Professor of English and Interdisciplinary Studies, CUNY Graduate School, New York. Author of *Textual Scholarship: An Introduction* (1992; revised 1994), *Scholarly Editing: A Guide to Research* (1995), *Theories of the Text* (1997), *Textual Transgression* (1997), and "Rights to Copy," in *Text* 10 (1997); editor of *Margins of the Text* (1997). Coeditor of the journal *Text*. **Essay:** Copyright.

Grice, Helena. Tutor in English, University of Wales, Aberystwyth. Coeditor of *I'm Telling You Stories: Jeanette Winterson and the Politics of Reading* (1997). **Essay:** *Rice Sprout Song* (Chang).

Griffiths, Gareth. Professor of English, University of Western Australia, Nedlands, Perth. Author of numerous books and articles, including *A Double Exile: African and West Indian Writing Between Two Cultures* (1978), *The Empire Writes Back: The Theory and Practice of Post-Colonial Literatures* (with others, 1989), and "Writing, Literacy, and History in Africa," in *Writing in Africa Today,* edited by Mphalevi Hangson Msiska and Paul Hyland (1996); editor of *Post-Colonial Drama* (special issue of *New Literatures Review,* 1990) and *The Post-Colonial Studies Reader* (with others, 1994). **Essay:** African Novel: Western Africa.

Grossman, Kathryn M. Professor of French, Pennsylvania State University, University Park. Author of *The Early Novels of Victor Hugo: Towards a Poetics of Harmony* (1986), *Figuring Transcendence in "Les Misérables": Hugo's Romantic Sublime* (1994) *"Les Misérables": Conversion, Revolution, Redemption* (1996), as well as numerous articles on Hugo and 19th-century French literature in journals. Member of the Editorial Board, *Comparative Literature Studies.* **Essays:** Victor-Marie Hugo; *Misérables* (Hugo).

Gunn, Edward. Professor of Chinese Literature and Associate Director of the East Asia Program, Cornell University, Ithaca, New York. Book-length publications include *Unwelcome Muse: Chinese Literature in Shanghai and Peking 1937–45* (1980) and *Rewriting Chinese: Style and Innovation in Twentieth-Century Chinese Prose* (1991). **Essay:** Chinese Novel: 20th Century.

Guntsche, Marina. Assistant Professor of Spanish, Ball State University, Muncie, Indiana. Author of *Novela argentina del siglo XX: entre la locura y la cordura* (1997) and of articles on the Argentine novel in journals. **Essay:** Latin American Novel: Argentina.

Hadfield, Andrew. Senior Lecturer in English, University of Wales, Aberystwyth. Author of *Literature, Politics and National Identity: Reformation to the Renaissance* (1994); editor of *Representing Ireland: Literature and the Origins of Conflict, 1534–1660* (with Brendan Bradshaw and others, 1993) and *"Strangers to That Land": British Perceptions of Ireland from the Reformation to the Famine* (with John McVeagh, 1994). **Essays:** Renaissance Narrative; Utopian and Dystopian Novel.

Hagiioannu, Andrew. Tutor in English, University of Leicester. **Essay:** *Nostromo* (Conrad).

Haig, Stirling. Professor of French, University of North Carolina, Chapel Hill. Author of *Flaubert and the Gift of Speech: Dialogue and Discourse in Four "Modern" Novels* (1986) and *The Madame Bovary Blues: The Pursuit of Illusion in Nineteenth-Century French Fiction* (1987). Editor-in-Chief, *The French Review,* 1974–86. **Essays:** Gustave Flaubert; *Père Goriot* (Balzac).

Halen, Pierre. Professor of French and Francophone Literature, University of Metz, France. Author of numerous books and articles on Belgian literature, including *Marcel Thiry: Une poétique de l'imparfait* (1990) and *"Le petit Belge avait vu grand": Une littérature coloniale* (1993). Managing Editor, *Textyles: Revue des lettres belges de langue française.* **Essay:** Belgian and Luxembourgeois Novel.

Halevi-Wise, Yael. Visiting Scholar and Lecturer in Comparative Literature, Romance Languages and Near Eastern Studies, Cornell University, Ithaca, New York. Author of articles including "Storytelling in *Like Water for Chocolate*," in *The Other Mirror: Women's Narrative in Mexico, 1980–1995* (1997), and "The Rhetoric of Silence in Conrad's *Lord Jim*," in *Anatomies of Silence* (1998). **Essays:** *Mr. Mani* (Yehoshua); A.B. Yehoshua.

Hall, N. John. Distinguished Professor of English, Bronx Community College and the Graduate School, CUNY, New York. Author of numerous books and articles, including *Trollope and His Illustrators* (1980) and *Trollope: A Biography* (1991); editor of *The Trollope Critics* (1981) as well as several editions of Trollope's works, including *Selected Works of Anthony Trollope* (1981) and *The Letters of Anthony Trollope* (1983). **Essay:** Barsetshire Novels (Trollope).

Halliwell, Martin. Lecturer in English and American Studies, De Montfort University, Leicester. Contributor to *Borderlines: Studies in American Culture, The Journal of American Studies,* and *Over Here: A European Journal of American Culture.* **Essays:** *Confessions of Zeno* (Svevo); Description; *Invisible Cities* (Calvino); Franz Kafka; Picaresque; Gertrude Stein; *Three Lives* (Stein); Edith Wharton.

Hamarneh, Walid. Professor of Arabic and Comparative Literature, University of Texas at Austin. Author of the forthcoming *Problems of Aesthetic Transfer: The Modern Novel Between the Western Center and Arabic Periphery* and numerous articles on Arabic literature; editor of *Fiction Updated: Theories of Fictionality, Narratology, and Poetics* (with Calin-Andrei Mihailescu, 1996). **Essays:** Egyptian Novel; Ghassān Kanafānī; Nagīb Maḥfūẓ.

Hapgood, Lynne. Head of English, Nottingham Trent University. Author of "Urban Utopias: Socialism, Religion and the City, 1880–1900," in *Cultural Politics and the Fin-de-Siècle* (1995) and "'The Reconceiving of Christianity': Secularisation, Realism and the Religious Novel, 1888–1900," in *Literature and Theology* 10:4 (December 1996). **Essays:** Politics and the Novel; *Tess of the d'Urbervilles* (Hardy).

Harbison, Sherrill. Independent scholar. Author of "Aspects of Narcissism in Sigrid Undset's Modern Novels," in *Scandinavian Studies* 63:4 (Autumn 1991) and "Sigrid Undset and Willa Cather: The Uses of Catholicism," in *Nordic Experiences* (1997). **Essays:** *Kristin Lavransdatter* (Undset); Sigrid Undset.

Hargraves, John A. Assistant Professor of German, Connecticut College, New London. Translator of *Notes from Hampstead: The Writer's Notes, 1954–71* (1998), by Elias Canetti. **Essays:** Hermann Broch; *Death of Virgil* (Broch).

Hart, Thomas R. Professor Emeritus of Comparative Literature, University of Oregon, Eugene. Author of *Cervantes and Ariosto: Renewing Fiction* (1989) and *Cervantes' Exemplary Fictions* (1994). Editor, *Comparative Literature, 1972–95.* **Essays:** *Celestina* (Rojas); *Don Quixote* (Cervantes); *Lazarillo de Tormes.*

Harvey, Carol J. Professor of French, University of Winnipeg, Manitoba. Author of *Le Cycle manitobain de Gabrielle Roy* (1993), *La Littérature au féminin* (1995), and several articles on Gabrielle Roy. **Essay:** *Tin Flute* (Roy).

Hassall, Anthony J. Professor of English Literature, James Cook University, Townsville, Australia. Author of *Henry Fielding's Tom Jones* (1979), *Strange Country: A Study of Randolph Stow* (1986), and *Dancing on Hot Macadam: Peter Carey's Fiction* (1994). Founding General Editor, University of Queensland Press' Studies in Australian Literature Series, since 1987. **Essay:** *Lucky Jim* (Amis).

Hegel, Robert E. Professor of Chinese and Comparative Literature and Chair of Comparative Literature, Washington University, St. Louis, Missouri. Author of numerous works on the Chinese novel, including *The Novel in Seventeenth-Century China* (1981) and *Reading Illustrated Fiction in Late Imperial China* (1997). Coeditor, *Chinese Literature: Essays, Articles, Reviews* (annual journal). **Essay:** Chinese Novel: Beginnings to the 20th Century.

Henderson, Margaret. Tutorial Assistant, Department of English, University of Queensland, Brisbane. Author of "Magical Transformations: Angela Carter's *The Passion of New Eve* and *Nights at the Circus*," in *Australian Feminist Studies* 22 (1995). Brisbane correspondent, *Overland* journal. **Essay:** Angela Carter.

Hewitt, Nicholas. Professor of French, University of Nottingham. Author of *Henri Troyat* (1984), *The Golden Age of Louis-Ferdinand Céline* (1987), *"Les Maladies du siècle": The Image of Malaise in French Fiction and Thought in the Interwar Years* (1988), and *Literature and the Right in Postwar France: The Story of the "Hussards"* (1996); editor, *The Culture of Reconstruction: European Literature, Thought and Film 1945–1950* (1989), *France and the Mass Media* (with Brian Rigby, 1991), *Popular Culture and Communication in Twentieth-Century France* (with Rosemary Chapman, 1992), and *Controlling Broadcasting: Access Policy and Practice in North America and Europe* (with Meryl Aldridge, 1994). **Essay:** Roman-Fleuve.

Heyworth, Gregory. Doctoral candidate, Princeton University, New Jersey. **Essay:** Novel and Romance: Etymologies.

Hill, James L. (adviser). Professor of English, Michigan State University, East Lansing. Author of articles on 19th-century English literature in *English Literary History, Studies in English Literature,* and *Journal of Aesthetics and Art Criticism.* **Essays:** Elizabeth Gaskell; *Mill on the Floss* (Eliot); *Moonstone* (Collins); *Wuthering Heights* (Emily Brontë).

Hobsbaum, Philip. Professor of English Literature, University of Glasgow. Author of numerous books on fiction, criticism, and poetry, including *A Theory of Criticism* (1970), *A Theory of Communication* (1970), *A Reader's Guide to Charles Dickens* (1973), *Tradition and Experiment in English Poetry* (1979), *A Reader's Guide to D.H. Lawrence* (1981), and *Essentials of Literary Criticism* (1983); also editor or coeditor of several volumes of poetry. Editor, *The Glasgow Review*, 1993–94. **Essays:** D.H. Lawrence; Stream of Consciousness and Interior Monologue.

Hoffman, Anne Golomb. Professor of English and Comparative Literature, Fordham University, Lincoln Center, New York. Author of *Between Exile and Return: S.Y. Agnon and the Drama of Writing* (1991) and several other articles on Agnon; editor of *A Book That Was Lost and Other Stories by S.Y. Agnon* (with Alan Mintz, 1995). Associate Editor, *Prooftexts: A Journal of Jewish Literary History*. **Essay:** S.Y. Agnon.

Holman, J. Martin. Head of the Japanese program, Huron College, University of Western Ontario, London. Translator, *The Old Capital* (1987), *Palm-of-the-Hand Stories* (with Lane Dunlop, 1988), and *The Dancing Girl of Izu and Other Stories* (1997), all by Kawabata Yasunari. Translator and editor, *The Book of Masks* (1990) and *Shadows of Sounds* (1990) by Hwang Sun-Won and *The House of Twilight* (1990) by Yun Heung-gil. **Essays:** Kawabata Yasunari; *Snow Country* (Kawabata).

Hooker, Virginia Matheson. Reader, Faculty of Asian Studies, Australian National University, Canberra. Author of "Transmission through Practical Example: Women and Islam in 1920s Malay Fiction" (*Journal of the Malaysian Branch of the Royal Asiatic Society* 67:2 [1994]) and "Developing a Rhetoric for Malay Society: The Writings of the Generation of the 1950s (ASAS 50)" (*Malay Literature* 8:2 [1995]); editor and contributor, *Culture and Society in New Order Indonesia* (1993). Consulting Editor, *Journal of Malay Literature*. Member, advisory committee, *Journal of Malay Studies*, and international advisory board, *South-East Asia Research*. Correspondent, *Indonesia Circle*. **Essay:** Southeast Asian Novel: Malaysia.

Horowitz, Louise K. Professor of French, Rutgers University-Camden, New Jersey. Author of *Honoré d'Urfé* (1984), "Where Have All the 'Old Knights' Gone?: *L'Astrée*," in *Romance: Generic Transformation from Chrétien de Troyes to Cervantes* (1985), and "Pastoral Parenting: *L'Astrée*," in *The Pastoral Landscape* (1992). Advisory board, *Studies in Early Modern France*. Book review editor, *The French Review*, 1977–80. **Essay:** *Astrée* (d'Urfé).

Hsia, C.T. (adviser). Professor Emeritus of Chinese, Columbia University, New York. Author of several important studies of Chinese literature, including *A History of Modern Chinese Fiction* (1961, 2nd edition 1971) and *The Classic Chinese Novel: A Critical Introduction* (1968, Cornell East Asia Series reprint, 1996).

Huber, Lothar. Lecturer in German, Birkbeck College, University of London. Author of articles on Austrian and German literature, including "Satire and Irony in Musil's *Der Mann ohne Eigenschaften*" (1982); editor and contributor, *Musil in Focus* (with J.J. White, 1982) and editor, *Franz Werfel: An Austrian Writer Reassessed* (1989). **Essay:** *Man Without Qualities* (Musil).

Humble, Malcolm. Lecturer, Department of German, University of St. Andrews. Author of *Introduction to German Literature 1871–1990* (1994), *A Companion to Twentieth Century German Literature* (2nd edition 1997; both with Raymond Furness), and various articles on German novels of the 20th century. Editor, *Forum for Modern Language Studies*, since 1989. **Essays:** *Berlin Alexanderplatz* (Döblin); German Novel.

Hunt, Peter. Professor of English Literature, University of Wales, Cardiff. Author of *Approaching Arthur Ransome* (1992), *An Introduction to Children's Literature* (1994), *The Wind in the Willows: A Fragmented Arcadia* (1994), and numerous articles on children's literature as well as author of children's novels; editor, *Children's Literature: The Development of Criticism* (1990), *Literature for Children: Contemporary Criticism* (1992), *Children's Literature: An Illustrated History* (1995), and *International Companion Encyclopedia of Children's Literature* (1996). **Essay:** Children's Novel.

Hutchinson, Peter (adviser). Lecturer in German, and Director of Studies in Modern Languages, Trinity Hall, University of Cambridge. Author of *Literary Representations of a Divided Germany* (1977), *Games Authors Play* (1983), and *Stefan Heym: The Perpetual Dissident* (1992). Has also edited numerous critical editions of modern German writers. German Series Editor, Bristol Classical Press. **Essay:** Novella.

Huters, Theodore. Professor of East Asian Languages and Cultures, University of California, Los Angeles. Author of *Qian Zhongshu* (1982). Editor, *Reading the Modern Chinese Short Story* (1990) and *Culture and State in Chinese History* (with Bin Wong and Pauline Yu, 1997). **Essay:** *Fortress Besieged* (Qian Zhongshu).

Ito, Ken K. Associate Professor of Japanese Literature, University of Michigan, Ann Arbor. Author of "Seven Japanese Tales," in *Masterworks of Asian Literature in Comparative Perspective: A Guide for Teaching* (1994) and *Visions of Desire: Tanizaki's Fictional Worlds* (1991). **Essay:** Tanizaki Jun'ichirō.

Johnsen, William A. Professor of English, Michigan State University, East Lansing. Author of "Myth, Ritual, and Literature after Girard," in *Literary Theory's Future* (1989), and numerous other articles on literature. **Essays:** Joseph Conrad; E.M. Forster; Myth and the Novel; *Women in Love* (Lawrence).

Johnson-Woods, Toni. Lecturer/Curriculum Developer, Bachelor of Contemporary Studies, University of Queensland, Brisbane. **Essay:** Roman-Feuilleton.

Jones, Lawrence. Professor of English, University of Otago, New Zealand. Author of *Barbed Wire and Mirrors: Essays on New Zealand Prose* (1987, 2nd edition 1990) and numerous articles on New Zealand literature. Coeditor, *Journal of New Zealand Literature*, since 1990. **Essays:** New Zealand Novel; *Owls Do Cry* (Frame); Periodicals and the Serialization of Novels.

Jones, Malcolm V. Emeritus Professor of Slavonic Studies, University of Nottingham. Author of *Dostoevsky: The Novel of Discord* (1976), *Dostoevsky after Bakhtin* (1990), and a host of articles on Russian literature; editor of *New Essays on Tolstoy* (1978) and *Dostoevsky and the 20th Century* (1993); coeditor, *New Essays on Dostoyevsky* (1983). Formerly General Editor of Cambridge Studies in Russian Literature. Currently President of the International Dostoevsky Society. **Essay:** Fedor Dostoevskii.

Joshi, Priya. Assistant Professor of English, University of California, Berkeley. Author of "Culture and Consumption: Fiction, the Reading Public, and the British Novel in Colonial India," *Book History* 1:1 (1998) and a forthcoming book on the Indian novel. **Essay:** Indian Novel.

Juraga, Dubravka. Independent scholar and writer. Author of *Bakhtin, Stalin, and Modern Russian Literature: Dialogism, Carnival, and History* (with M. Keith Booker, 1995). **Essays:** Mulk Raj Anand; *Master and Margarita* (Bulgakov); Novel of Ideas; Socialist Realism.

Kahn, Andrew. Fellow and Tutor in Russian, St. Edmund Hall, University of Oxford. Editor of *"Institutiones Rhetorical": A Treatise of a Russian Sentimentalist* (1995), by M.N. Murav'ev, and *The Queen of Spades and Other Stories* (1997), by Aleksandr Pushkin. **Essay:** Russian Novel: 1750–1830.

Kanes, Martin. Professor Emeritus of French, State University of New York, Albany. Author of *Zola's "La Bête humaine": A Study in Literary Creation* (1962), *L'Atelier de Zola* (1963), *Balzac's Comedy of Words* (1975), *Critical Essays on Honoré de Balzac* (1990), *Père Goriot: Anatomy of a Troubled World* (1993), and numerous articles on French literature. **Essay:** *Rougon-Macquart* (Zola).

Kavanagh, Thomas M. Professor of French, University of California, Berkeley. Author of *The Vacant Mirror: A Study of Mimesis Through Diderot's "Jacques le fataliste"* (1972), *Writing the Truth: Authority and Desire in Rousseau* (1987), *The Limits of Theory* (1989), *Enlightenment and the Shadows of Chance: The Novel and the Culture of Gambling in Eighteenth-Century France* (1993), and *Esthetics of the Moment: Literature and Art in the French Enlightenment* (1997). **Essay:** Conte Philosophique.

Keith, W.J. (adviser). Professor Emeritus of English and Canadian Literature, University College, University of Toronto. Author and editor of several books on Canadian writers, including *Canadian Literature in English* (1985), *A Sense of Style: Studies in the Art of Fiction in English-Speaking Canada* (1989), *An Independent Stance: Essays on English-Canadian Criticism and Fiction* (1991), *Literary Images of Ontario* (1992), and *Life Struggle: Hugh MacLennan's "The Watch That Ends the Night"* (1993). **Essays:** *Deptford Trilogy* (Davies); Margaret Laurence; Hugh MacLennan; *Stone Angel* (Laurence).

Kelly, Gary. Professor of English, University of Alberta, Edmonton. Author of *The English Jacobin Novel 1780–1805* (1976), *English Fiction of the Romantic Period 1789–1830* (1989), *Revolutionary Feminism: The Mind and Career of Mary Wollstonecraft* (1991), and *Women, Writing, and Revolution 1790–1827* (1992). General Editor, *Longman's History of Women's Writing in English*. **Essays:** Jane Austen; English Novel:

1800–1840; Regional Novel; Romantic Novel; Verse Narrative and the Novel; *Waverley* (Scott).

Kerrigan, Catherine. Professor of English, University of Guelph, Ontario. Author of *Travelling Hopefully: Robert Louis Stevenson* (1994), *Robert Louis Stevenson's "The Ebb-Tide"* (with Peter Hinchcliffe, 1995), *Robert Louis Stevenson's "Weir of Hermiston"* (1995), and various articles on Scottish literature. General Editor, the Centenary Edition of the Collected Works of Robert Louis Stevenson. **Essay:** Robert Louis Stevenson.

Kershner, R. Brandon. Professor of English, University of Florida, Gainesville. Author of *Joyce, Bakhtin, and Popular Literature* (1989), *The Twentieth-Century Novel: An Introduction* (1997), and articles on 20th-century English and Irish novelists; editor, Bedford Books edition of *A Portrait of the Artist as a Young Man* (1992) and *Joyce and Popular Culture* (1996). **Essays:** Elizabeth Bowen; *Death of the Heart* (Bowen); Dialogism; Modernism; *Portrait of the Artist as a Young Man* (Joyce).

Khoury, Martha. Independent scholar and writer. Author of "Entre mémoire et oubli: Fin de sens ou fin d'un sens?" in *Recyclages: Économies de l'appropriation culturelle* (1996). **Essay:** *Cities of Salt* (Munif).

Kiernan, Brian. Associate Professor of English, University of Sydney. Author of *Images of Society and Nature: Seven Essays on Australian Novels* (1971) and *Patrick White* (1980). **Essays:** Australian Novel; Patrick White.

Kiernan, Suzanne. Lecturer, Department of Italian, University of Sydney. Author of various articles on Italian literature. **Essays:** Carlo Emilio Gadda; *House by the Medlar Tree* (Verga); *That Awful Mess on Via Merulana* (Gadda); Giovanni Verga.

Killam, Douglas. Professor of English, University of Guelph, Ontario. Author of *Africa in English Fiction, 1874–1939* (1968), *The Novels of Chinua Achebe* (1969; revised edition as *The Writings of Chinua Achebe,* 1977), and *An Introduction to the Writings of Ngugi* (1980); editor, *African Writers on African Writing* (1973), *The Writing of East and Central Africa* (1984), and *Critical Perspectives on Ngugi wa Thiong'o* (1984). **Essay:** Chinua Achebe.

King, Adele. Professor of French, Ball State University, Muncie, Indiana. Author of *Camus* (1964), *Proust* (1968), *Paul Nizan: Écrivain* (1976), *The Writings of Camara Laye* (1980), and *French Women Novelists: Defining a Female Style* (1989); editor of *Camus's L'Étranger: Fifty Years On* (1992). **Essays:** *Mission to Kala* (Beti); *Radiance of the King* (Camara Laye); *Stranger* (Camus).

King, Andrew L. Currently teaches literature at the University of Bucharest; formerly taught at universities in Catania (Italy), Warsaw, Manila, and City University in London. Completing a dissertation on *The London Journal*, the best-selling fiction weekly of the mid–19th century in which many of Sue's novels appeared. **Essay:** *Mysteries of Paris* (Sue).

Kinkley, Jeffrey C. Professor of History, St. John's University, New York. Author of *The Odyssey of Shen Congwen* (1987); editor of *After Mao: Chinese Literature and Society, 1978–81* (1985), *Chen Xuezhao: Surviving the Storm* (1990), and *Shen Congwen: Imperfect Paradise* (1995); coeditor, *Modern Chinese Writers: Self-Portrayals* (1992). Assistant Editor, China and Inner Asia, *The Journal of Asian Studies,* 1991–94. **Essay:** Shen Congwen.

Kirby, David. W. Guy McKenzie Professor of English, Florida State University, Tallahassee. Author of *American Fiction to 1900: A Guide to Information Sources* (1975), *America's Hive of Honey, or Foreign Influences on American Fiction through Henry James: Essays and Bibliographies* (1980), *"The Portrait of a Lady" and "The Turn of the Screw": Henry James and Melodrama* (1991), and *Herman Melville* (1993); editor of *Individual and Community: Variations on a Theme in American Fiction* (with Kenneth Baldwin, 1975). **Essays:** *Adventures of Huckleberry Finn* (Twain); Critics and Criticism: 20th Century; Reviewers, the Popular Press, and Their Impact on the Novel; United States Novel: 1850–1900.

Klein, Scott W. Associate Professor of English, Wake Forest University, Winston-Salem, North Carolina. Author of *The Fictions of James Joyce and Wyndham Lewis: Monsters of Nature and Design* (1994) and of articles on Joyce and Lewis including "Searching for Lost Keys: Epic and Linguistic Dislocations in *Ulysses*" in *Approaches to Teaching Joyce's "Ulysses"* (1993) and "The Experiment of Vorticist Drama: Wyndham Lewis and 'Enemy of the Stars'" in *Twentieth Century Literature* 37:2 (Summer 1991). **Essays:** *Good Soldier* (Ford); James Joyce; Wyndham Lewis; *Lord Jim* (Conrad).

Klinkowitz, Jerome. Professor of English and University Distinguished Scholar, University of Northern Iowa, Cedar Falls. Author of *Kurt Vonnegut Jr.: A Descriptive Bibliography and Annotated Secondary Checklist* (with Asa B. Pieratt Jr., 1974), *Literary Disruptions* (1975, revised edition 1980), *The Life of Fiction* (1977), *Donald Barthelme: A Comprehensive Bibliography* (1977), *The Practice of Fiction in America* (1980), *The American 1960s* (1980), *Kurt Vonnegut* (1982), *Peter Handke and the Postmodern Transformation* (with James Knowlton, 1983), *The Self-Apparent Word: Fiction as Language/Language as Fiction* (1984), *Literary Subversions* (1985), *The New American Novel of Manners* (1986), *Kurt Vonnegut: A Comprehensive Bibliography* (with Judie Huffman-Klinkowitz, 1987), *Rosenberg/Barthes/Hassan: The Postmodern Habit of Thought* (1988), *"A Short Season" and Other Stories* (1988), *Their Finest Hours: Narratives of the Raf and Luftwaffe in World War II* (1989), *Slaughterhouse-Five: Reinventing the Novel and the World* (1990), *Listen: Gerry Mulligan/An Aural Narrative in Jazz* (1991), *Donald Barthelme: An Exhibition* (1991), *Structuring the Void* (1992), *Basepaths* (1995), *Yanks over Europe: American Flyers in World War II* (1996), and *Here at Ogallala State U.* (1997); editor of *Innovative Fiction* (with John Somers, 1972), *The Vonnegut Statement* (with Somers, 1973), *Vonnegut in America* (with Donald L. Lawler, 1977), *Writing under Fire: Stories of the Vietnam War* (with Somers, 1978), *The Diaries of Willard Motley* (1979), *Nathaniel Hawthorne* (1984), and *Writing Baseball* (1991). General Editor, Crosscurrents/Modern Cri-

tiques, Southern Illinois University Press; editor, "Prose Since 1945," *Norton Anthology of American Literature,* 5th edition; advisory editor, *Critique, Resources for American Literary Study,* and Southern Illinois University Press Baseball and Literature Series. **Essays:** Norman Mailer; Metafiction; New Journalism and the Nonfiction Novel; United States Novel: 1945–.

Knapp, Liza. Associate Professor, Department of Slavic Languages and Literatures, University of California, Berkeley. Author of *Dostoevsky as Reformer: The Petrashevsky Case* (1987) and *The Annihilation of Inertia: Dostoevsky and Metaphysics* (1996). **Essay:** *Brothers Karamazov* (Dostoevskii).

Kong, Haili. Professor, Department of Modern Languages and Literatures, Swarthmore College, Pennsylvania. Author of "Symbolism through Zhang Yimou's Subversive Lens in His Early Films," *Asian Cinema* 8:2 (Winter 1996), "The Spirit of 'Native-Soil' in the Fictional World of Duanmu Hongliang and Mo Yan," *China Information* 6:4 (Spring 1997), and *Duanmu Hongliang zhuan* (1998; a critical biography of Duanmu Hongliang); editor of *Duanmu Hongliang sishi niandai zuopin xuan* (with C.T. Hsia, 1996; The Forties: The Selected Works of Duanmu Hongliang). **Essay:** Ba Jin.

Konzett, Delia Caparoso. Part-time Instructor, Departments of English and Film Studies, Yale University, New Haven, Connecticut. Author of "Administered Identities and Linguistic Assimilation: The Politics of Immigrant English in Anzia Yezierska's *Hungry Hearts*," in *American Literature* 69:3 (September 1997). **Essays:** *Catch-22* (Heller); *Their Eyes Were Watching God* (Hurston).

Konzett, Matthias. Assistant Professor of German Literature, Yale University, New Haven, Connecticut. Author of "Cultural Amnesia and the Banality of Human Tragedy: Peter Handke's *Wunschloses Unglück* and Its Post-Ideological Aesthetics," in *The Germanic Review* 80:2 (Spring 1995), "*Publikumsbeschimpfung*: Thomas Bernhard's Provocations of the Austrian Public Sphere," in *The German Quarterly* 68:3 (Summer 1995), and "The Politics of Recognition in Contemporary Austrian Jewish Literature," in *Monatshefte* 90:1 (Spring 1998); editor of *Encyclopedia of German Literature,* (forthcoming, 1999). **Essays:** Austrian Novel; Thomas Bernhard; *Notebooks of Malte Laurids Brigge* (Rilke).

Kopper, Edward A., Jr. Distinguished Commonwealth Professor of English, Slippery Rock University, Pennsylvania. Author of *John Millington Synge: A Reference Guide* (1979), *James Joyce: New Glances* (1980), *A J.M. Synge Literary Companion* (1988), and *Lady Gregory: A Review of the Criticism* (1991), among other books and monographs. Editor and publisher, *Notes on Modern Irish Literature*; member of the editorial board, *Studies in the Humanities.* **Essay:** *Finnegans Wake* (Joyce).

Krueger, Kurt J. Associate Professor of English, Concordia University, Irvine, California. **Essay:** Ernest Hemingway.

Krzyżanowski, Jerzy R. Professor Emeritus of Slavic Languages and Literatures, Ohio State University, Columbus. Author of *Ernest Hemingway* (1963), *Wladyslaw Stanislaw Reymont* (1972), *General Leopold Okulicki* (1980), *Diana* (1986), *Legen-*

da Somosierry (1987), *Banff* (1988), *U Szarugi* (1995), and *General "Niedzwiadek"* (1996); editor of *A Modern Polish Reader* (1970), *Janta* (1982), and *Katyn w literaturze* (1995). **Essays:** Polish Novel; Władysław Stanisław Reymont.

Kucich, John. Professor of English, University of Michigan, Ann Arbor. Author of *Excess and Restraint in the Novels of Charles Dickens* (1981), *Repression in Victorian Fiction: Charlotte Brontë, George Eliot, and Charles Dickens* (1987), *The Power of Lies: Transgression in Victorian Fiction* (1994), and numerous articles on Victorian fiction in journals such as *PMLA, ELH, Nineteenth-Century Fiction,* and *Victorian Studies.* **Essays:** Charles Dickens; Anthony Trollope.

Langen, Timothy Colin. Recently completed Ph.D. in Russian literature at Northwestern University, Evanston, Illinois. Author of an article on Russian literature and music in *Intersections and Transpositions: Russian Music, Literature, and Society,* edited by Andrew Wachtel (1998). **Essay:** *Petersburg* (Belyi).

Larson, Wendy. Associate Professor, East Asian Languages and Literatures, University of Oregon, Eugene. Author of *Literary Authority and the Chinese Writer: Ambivalence and Autobiography* (1991) and *Women and Writing in Modern China* (1997); editor of *Inside Out: Modernism and Post-Modernism in Contemporary China* (with Anne Wedell-Wedellsborg, 1993). Translator, *Bolshevik Salute: A Modernist Chinese Novel* (1989), by Wang Meng. **Essay:** Eileen Chang.

Lee, A. Robert. Professor of American Literature, Nihon University, Tokyo. Author of *Black American Fiction Since Richard Wright* (1983), *A Permanent Etcetera: Cross-Cultural Perspectives on Post-War America* (1993), *Other Britain, Other British: Contemporary Multicultural Fiction* (1995), *Beat Generation Writers* (1996), and *Designs of Blackness: Studies in the Literature of Afro-America* (1997); editor of *Black Fiction: New Studies in the Afro-American Novel Since 1945* (1980), *Nathaniel Hawthorne: New Critical Essays* (1982), *Herman Melville: Reassessments* (1984), and *William Faulkner: The Yoknapatawpha Fiction* (1990); also editor of the Everyman editions of Melville's *Moby-Dick* (1975, 1992, 1993), *Typee* (1993), and *Billy Budd and Other Stories* (1993). **Essays:** James Baldwin; William Faulkner; Herman Melville; *Scarlet Letter* (Hawthorne).

Lee, Wai Sum Amy. Doctoral candidate, University of Warwick. Editor, *Cultural Criticism* 2 (February 1995). **Essay:** Autobiographical Novel.

Lever, Susan. Associate Professor, School of English, University College, University of New South Wales. Author of *A Question of Commitment: Australian Literature in the Twenty Years after the War* (1989); editor of *Bengala or Some Time Ago* by Mary Theresa Vidal (1990), *Oxford Book of Australian Women's Verse* (1995), and *Henry Handel Richardson: The Getting of Wisdom, Stories, Selected Prose and Correspondence* (with Catherine Pratt, 1997). **Essays:** *Man Who Loved Children* (Stead); Christina Stead.

Li, Peter. Associate Professor of Chinese and Comparative Literature, Rutgers University, New Brunswick, New Jersey. Author of *Modern Chinese Fiction: A Guide to Its Study and Appreciation* (1981), *Understanding Asian Americans* (1990), and *Culture and Politics in China: The Anatomy of Tiananmen Square* (1991). Book Review Editor, *Journal of the Chinese Language Teachers Association.* **Essays:** Lao She; Mao Dun.

Li-Chun Lin, Sylvia. Instructor, Department of East Asian Languages and Literatures, University of Colorado, Boulder. **Essay:** Pai Hsien-yung.

Lindfors, Bernth (adviser). Professor of English, University of Texas at Austin. Author of numerous books and articles, including, most recently, *Comparative Approaches to African Literatures* (1994), *Long Drums and Canons: Teaching and Researching African Literatures* (1995), *Loaded Vehicles: Studies in African Literary Media* (1996), and *African Textualities: Texts, Pre-Texts, and Contexts of African Literature* (1997).

Lindstrom, Naomi. Professor of Spanish and Portuguese, University of Texas at Austin. Author of *Women's Voice in Latin American Literature* (1989), *Jewish Issues in Argentine Literature: From Gerchunoff to Szichman* (1989), *Jorge Luis Borges: A Study of the Short Fiction* (1990), and *Twentieth-Century Spanish American Fiction* (1994). Translator, *Woman between Mirrors* (with Fred P. Ellison, 1989), by Brazilian novelist Helena Parente Cunha. Editorial Board Member, *Chasqui, Studies in Twentieth Century Literature, Studies in Latin American Popular Culture.* **Essay:** Latin American Novel: Overview.

Loloi, Parvin. Independent scholar and writer. Author of "Ghazal and Fable in Persian Poetry," in *Acumen* (1987), "Byron in Persian Costume," in *Swansea Review* (1988), "The Merchant and His Parrot," in *Acumen* (1988), and "Grocer and the Parrot," in *An Anthology of Contemporary Poetry and Prose: A Literary Festchrift for James Hogg* (1996). **Essay:** Fable.

López Cotín, Olga. Head of Spanish Program, Residential College, University of Michigan, Ann Arbor. Author of "*El tono menor del deseo* de Pia Barros: Territorios de identidad, tortura y resistencia," in *La Chispa '95: Selected Proceedings* (1995) and "Maldita yo entre las mujeres de Mercedes Valdineso: Una arqueología del diabolismo femenino," in *Cincinnati Romance Review* 15 (1996). **Essay:** Latin American Novel: Chile.

Löschnigg, Martin. Teaches literature at the University of Graz, Austria. Author of *Der Erste Weltkrieg in deutscher und englischer Dichtung* (1994); editor of *Intimate Enemies: English and German Literary Reactions to the Great War 1914–1918* (with F.K. Stanzel, 1994). **Essay:** Mimesis: Representation and Referentiality in the Novel.

Luis, William. Professor, Department of Spanish and Portuguese, Vanderbilt University, Nashville, Tennessee. Author of *Literary Bondage: Slavery in Cuban Narrative* (1990) and *Dance Between Two Cultures: Latino Caribbean Literature Written in the United States* (1997); editor of *Voices from Under: Black Narrative in Latin America and the Caribbean* (1984), *Translating Latin America: Culture as Text* (with Julio Rodríguez, 1991), *Modern Latin American Fiction Writers, First Series* (1992), *Modern Latin American Fiction Writers, Second Series* (with

Ann Gónzalez, 1994), and *Antología: Poesía hispano-Caribeña escrita en los Estados Unidos* (1995). **Essay:** Latin American Novel: Hispanic Caribbean.

Lydon, Mary. Professor of French, University of Wisconsin-Madison. Author of *Perpetuum Mobile: A Study of the Novels and Aesthetics of Michel Butor* (1980), *Skirting the Issue: Essays in Literary Theory* (1995), and articles on 20th-century French writers. **Essay:** French Novel: 1945–.

Lynch, Deidre. Assistant Professor of English, State University of New York at Buffalo. Editor of *Cultural Institutions of the Novel* (with William B. Warner, 1996). **Essay:** Alice Munro.

Mabee, Barbara. Associate Professor of German, Oakland University, Rochester, Michigan. Author of *Die Poetik von Sarah Kirsch: Erinnerungsarbeit und Geschichtsbewusstsein* (1989) and numerous articles on German literature, with a particular emphasis on women writers. **Essays:** Ingeborg Bachmann; *Buddenbrooks* (Mann); Christa Wolf.

Macpherson, Sandra. Assistant Professor of English, Ohio State University, Columbus. Author of "Matrimonial Risk, 'Matrimonial Murther': Central Planning and the Logic of Liability in Defoe's Marriage Novels," in *Eighteenth-Century Life* (Spring 1997). Assistant Editor, *English Literary History,* 1993–95. **Essay:** Samuel Richardson.

Madsen, Deborah L. Professor of English, South Bank University, London. Author of *The Postmodernist Allegories of Thomas Pynchon* (1991), *Rereading Allegory: A Narrative Approach to Genre* (1994), *Visions of America Since 1492* (1994), and *Allegory in America: From Puritanism to Postmodernism* (1996). Executive Editor, *The Year's Work in English Studies.* **Essays:** *Beloved* (Morrison); Genre Criticism; Nathaniel Hawthorne; Toni Morrison; United States Novel: 1900–1945.

Mainil, Jean. Lecturer in French literature at the University of Nottingham. Author of *Dans les règles du plaisir: Théories de la différence dans le discours obscène, romanesque et médical de l'Ancien Régime* (1996) and articles on the libertine novel. **Essay:** Libertine Novel.

Mallett, Phillip. Senior Lecturer in English, University of St. Andrews. Editor, *Limits and Renewals* (1987), by Rudyard Kipling, *Kipling Considered* (1989), and *A Spacious Vision: Essays on Hardy* (with R.P. Draper, 1994). **Essay:** *Kim* (Kipling).

Maloney, Edward. Doctoral candidate, Ohio State University, Columbus. **Essay:** *Catcher in the Rye* (Salinger).

Mandal, A.A. Research Student, University of Wales, Cardiff. **Essays:** *Against Nature* (Huysmans); Decadent Novel; *Mysteries of Udolpho* (Radcliffe).

Mandrell, James. Associate Professor of Spanish, Comparative Literature, and Film Studies, Brandeis University, Waltham, Massachusetts. Author of "The Prophetic Voice in Garro, Morante, and Allende" in *Comparative Literature* 42 (1990),

Don Juan and the Point of Honor: Seduction, Patriarchal Society, and Literary Tradition (1992) and numerous articles on Spanish and Latin American literature. **Essay:** *House of the Spirits* (Allende).

Mangum, Bryant. Professor of English, Virginia Commonwealth University, Richmond. Author of *A Fortune Yet: Money in the Art of F. Scott Fitzgerald's Short Stories* (1991) and contributor to numerous edited critical volumes and literary journals. **Essays:** F. Scott Fitzgerald; *Great Gatsby* (Fitzgerald).

Marcus, Sharon. Assistant Professor, Department of English, University of California, Berkeley. Author of *Restless Houses: Domestic Architecture and Urban Culture in Paris and London, 1830–1880* (1995) and *Apartment Stories: City and Home in Nineteenth-Century Paris and London* (1998). **Essay:** Space.

Margolin, Uri. Professor of Comparative Literature, University of Alberta, Edmonton. Author of numerous articles including "Characters in Literary Narrative: Representation and Signification," in *Semiotica* 106 (1995) and "Telling Our Story: On 'We' Literary Narratives," in *Language and Literature* 5 (1996). **Essays:** Character; Person in Narrative.

Márquez, Ismael P. Professor, Department of Modern Languages, Literatures, and Linguistics, University of Oklahoma, Norman. Author of *La retórica de la violencia en tres novelas peruanas* (1994). Editor of *Los mundos de Alfredo Bryce Echenique—Obra crítica* (with César Ferreira, 1994) and *Asedios a Julio Ramón Ribeyro* (with Ferreira, 1996). **Essay:** Latin American Novel: Peru.

Martin, Gerald. Andrew W. Mellon Professor of Modern Languages, University of Pittsburgh, Pennsylvania. Author of *Journey Through the Labyrinth: Latin American Fiction in the Twentieth Century* (1989). Translator, critical edition of *Men of Maize* (1993), by Miguel Ángel Asturias. Editor, Pittsburgh Editions of Latin American Literature in Translation, since 1992. Member of the International Committee, Association of Latin American, Caribbean, and African 20th-Century Literature (University of Paris, UNESCO), since 1983. **Essays:** Miguel Ángel Asturias; Gabriel García Márquez; *Men of Maize* (Asturias).

Mason, Hugh J. Associate Professor and Undergraduate Coordinator, Department of Classics, University of Toronto. Author of articles on classical literature including "The Literature of Classical Lesbos and the Fiction of Stratis Myrivilis," in *Classical and Modern Literature* 9 (1989) and "Romance in a Limestone Landscape," *Classical Philology* 90 (1995). **Essay:** Greek and Roman Narrative.

Maxwell, Richard. Professor of English, Valparaiso University, Indiana. Author of *The Mysteries of Paris and London* (1992). **Essays:** *Betrothed* (Manzoni); *Count of Monte-Cristo* (Dumas); Historical Novel; Alessandro Manzoni.

May, Gita. Professor of French and Romance Philology, Columbia University, New York. Author of *Madame Roland and the*

Age of Revolution (1970), *Diderot et Baudelaire, critiques d'art* (3rd edition 1973*)*, *De Jean-Jacques Rousseau à Madame Roland: Essai sur la sensibilité préromantique et révolutionnaire* (2nd edition 1974), and *Stendhal and the Age of Napoleon* (1977). General Editor, The Age of Revolution and Romanticism Series, Peter Lang Publishing, since 1991. **Essays:** *Candide* (Voltaire); Denis Diderot; *Julie, or, The New Eloise* (Rousseau); *Princesse de Clèves* (Lafayette).

Mazzeno, Laurence W. President, Ursuline College, Pepper Pike, Ohio. Author of *Victorian Poetry: A Bibliography of Criticism* (1989), *The Victorian Novel: A Bibliography of Criticism* (1994), *Herman Wouk* (1994). Managing Editor, *Arnoldian Review* (1980–84); Editor/Managing Editor of *Nineteenth-Century Prose* (1986–92). **Essays:** *Ambassadors* (James); Nikos Kazantzakis.

McAlpin, Mary. Assistant Professor of French, University of Tennessee, Knoxville. **Essay:** Alexandre Dumas *père*.

McCall, Anne E. Assistant Professor, Department of French and Italian, Tulane University, New Orleans, Louisiana. Author of *De l'être en lettres: L'Autobiographie épistolaire de George Sand* (1996), and of articles on George Sand in *Esprit Créateur, Auto/Biography Studies*, and *George Sand Studies*. Guest Editor, *George Sand Studies*, 1997 and 1998. **Essays:** *Corinne* (de Staël); George Sand.

McCormick, Ian. Senior Lecturer in English Studies, Nene University College, Northampton. Author of *Secret Sexualities: Seventeenth and Eighteenth Century Writings* (1997). **Essay:** *Gulliver's Travels* (Swift).

McGowan, Philip. American Literature Tutor, Trinity College, Dublin. Author of "The Intemperate Irish in American Reform Literature," in *Irish Journal of American Studies* (1995). **Essay:** *Sun Also Rises* (Hemingway).

McMillin, Arnold. Professor of Russian Literature, School of Slavonic and East European Studies, University of London. Author of various articles on Russian literature. Editor of *From Pushkin to "Palisandriia": Essays on the Russian Novel in Honour of Richard Freeborn* (1990). Chairman of Editorial Board, *Slavonic and East European Review*, since 1995. **Essays:** Russian Novel: 1945–; Aleksandr Solzhenitsyn.

McNab, Christopher. Ph.D. Researcher, Department of English, University of Wales, Aberystwyth. Author of "Derrida, Rushdie and the Ethics of Mortality," in *Literature and Ethics* (1997). **Essays:** Psychological Novel and Roman d'analyse; Sex, Gender, and the Novel.

McNichol, Stella. Senior Lecturer, Lancaster University. Author of *Mrs. Dalloway's Party* (1972) and *Virginia Woolf and the Poetry of Fiction* (1989); editor of Macmillan's *Collected Novels of Virginia Woolf: Mrs. Dalloway, To the Lighthouse, The Waves* (with an introduction and notes, 1992) and the three Penguin volumes of *Mrs. Dalloway, To the Lighthouse*, and *Between the Acts* (all 1992). **Essays:** *Mrs. Dalloway* (Woolf); *Portrait of a Lady* (James); *Sound and the Fury* (Faulkner); *To the Lighthouse* (Woolf); H.G. Wells.

Meadwell, Kenneth W. Chair, Department of French Studies, University of Winnipeg, Manitoba. Author of "*L'Avalée des avalés*," "*L'Hiver de force*" et "*Les Enfantômes*" de Réjean Ducharme: Une Fiction mot à mot et sa littérarité* (1990) and various articles on French-Canadian literature. **Essays:** Hubert Aquin; *Swallower Swallowed* (Ducharme).

Meuser, Frances. Assistant Professor of Spanish, Oakland University, Rochester, Michigan. Author of articles on literature and pedagogy. **Essay:** *Diana* (Montemayor).

Mews, Siegfried. Professor of German, University of North Carolina, Chapel Hill. Author of various articles on German literature, including "From Admiration to Confrontation: Günter Grass and the United States," in *University of Dayton Review* 17:3 (1985–86) and "Heinrich Böll and Günter Grass as Political Writers," in *Coping with the Past: Germany and Austria after 1945* (1990); editor of "The Fisherman and His Wife": Günter Grass's The Flounder in Critical Perspective* (1983). **Essays:** Heinrich Böll; *Danzig Trilogy* (Grass).

Meyer, Stefan. Independent scholar and writer. **Essays:** Levantine Arabic Novel; *Men in the Sun* (Kanafānī); *Story of Zahra* (al-Shaykh); *Woman at Point Zero* (al-Sa'dāwī).

Michel-Mansour, Thérèse. Assistant Professor, New College, University of Toronto. Author of "Croisement de discours: Le Cas de Naoual el Saadaoui," in *Synthèses* 1 (1992), "La Spécificité du féminisme du Machrek au Maghreb," in *La Problématique de l'implicite* (1992), and *La Portée esthétique du signe dans le texte maghrébin* (1994). **Essay:** Nawāl al-Sa'dāwī.

Midgley, David. University Lecturer in German, University of Cambridge. Author of *Arnold Zweig* (1987); editor of *The German Novel in the Twentieth Century: Beyond Realism* (1993). **Essays:** Alfred Döblin; Robert Musil; Joseph Roth.

Mihailovich, Vasa D. Professor Emeritus of Yugoslavian literature, University of North Carolina, Chapel Hill. Author of *A Comprehensive Bibliography of Yugoslav Literature in English, 1593–1980* (with Mateja Matejić, 1984; supplements 1988, 1992) and numerous articles on Yugoslavian literature, including "Parable of Nationhood: Milorad Pavić, *Dictionary of the Khazars*," in *The World and I* 3:11 (1988), and "Fiction or Faction in *A Tomb for Boris Davidovich*: The Literary Affair," in *The Review of Contemporary Fiction* 14:1 (1994); editor of *Dictionary of Literary Biography: South Slavic Writers Before World War II* (1994). **Essays:** *Bridge on the Drina* (Andrić); *Dictionary of the Khazars* (Pavić); Miroslav Krleža; *Migrations* (Crnjanski); Yugoslavian Novel.

Minden, Michael. University Lecturer in German, University of Cambridge. Author of *Arno Schmidt: A Critical Study of His Prose* (1982) and *The German Bildungsroman: Incest and Inheritance* (1997); editor of *Thomas Mann* (1995). **Essays:** Bildungsroman; Günter Grass; Thomas Mann.

Molina Gavilán, Yolanda. Assistant Professor, Comparative Cultures, Eckard College, St. Petersburg, Florida. Author of "Latin American Science Fiction," in *Encyclopedia of Latin American Literature* (1996). Assistant Editor, *Chasqui: Revista de literatura latinoamericana.* **Essay:** Science and the Novel.

Montgomery-Crawford, Maxine Lavon. Associate Professor, Department of English, Florida State University, Tallahassee. Author of *The Apocalypse in African-American Fiction* (1996) and several articles on African-American novels. **Essay:** African-American Novel.

Moretti, Franco (adviser). Professor of English and Comparative Literature, Columbia University, New York. Author of *Signs Taken for Wonders: Essays in the Sociology of Literary Forms* (1983, revised edition 1988), *The Way of the World: The Bildungsroman in European Culture* (1987), *Modern Epic: The World-System from Goethe to García Márquez* (1996), and *Atlas of the European Novel 1800–1900* (1998).

Motte, Warren. Professor of French and Comparative Literature, University of Colorado, Boulder. Author of *The Poetics of Experiment: A Study of the Work of Georges Perec* (1984), *Questioning Edmond Jabès* (1990), and *Playtexts: Ludics in Contemporary Literature* (1995); editor of *Literary Ludics* (special issue of *L'Esprit Créateur* 31:4 [1991]) and *Alteratives* (with Gerald Prince, 1993); editor and translator, *Oulipo: A Primer of Potential Literature* (1986). **Essays:** *Life, a User's Manual* (Perec); Georges Perec.

Murav, Harriet. Associate Professor of Russian and Comparative Literature, University of California, Davis. Author of *Holy Foolishness: Dostoevsky's Novels and the Poetics of Cultural Critique* (1992) and numerous articles on Russian literature. **Essay:** *Devils* (Dostoevskii).

Musschoot, Anne Marie. Professor of Dutch Literature, University of Gent, Belgium. Author of *Het Judith-thema in de Nederlandse letterkunde* (1972), *Karel van de Woestijne en het symbolisme* (1975), and *Contemporary Fiction of the Low Countries* (with Jaap Goedegebuure, 1991); editor of *Cyriel Buysse, Verzameld werk* (with A. van Elslander, 7 vols., 1974–82), *Van Nu en Straks 1893–1901: Bloemlezing met inleiding en toelichtingen* (1982), and *Karel van de Woestijne, Brieven aan Lode Ontrop* (1985). **Essay:** Netherlandish Novel.

Naess, Harald S. Professor Emeritus of Scandinavian Studies, University of Wisconsin-Madison. Author of *Knut Hamsun og Amerika* (1969) and *Knut Hamsun* (1984); editor of numerous volumes including, most recently, *A History of Norwegian Literature* (1993) and *Knut Hamsuns brev. I–III* (1994–96). **Essay:** Knut Hamsun.

Napier, Susan J. Professor, Department of Asian Studies, University of Texas at Austin. Author of *Escape from the Wasteland: Romanticism and Realism in the Fiction of Mishima Yukio and Oe Kenzaburo* (1991). **Essays:** Mishima Yukio; Ōe Kenzaburō.

Nelson, T.G.A. Associate Professor, Department of English and Communication Studies, University of New England, New South Wales. Author of *Comedy: An Introduction to Comedy in Literature, Drama and Cinema* (1990) and *Children, Parents, and the Rise of the Novel* (1995). **Essay:** Comedy and Humor in the Novel.

Nelson-McDermott, Catherine. Sessional Lecturer in English, University of British Columbia, Vancouver. Author of "Virginia Woolf and Murasaki Shikibu: A Question of Perception," in *Virginia Woolf Miscellanies: Proceedings of the First Annual Conference on Virginia Woolf* (1992). **Essay:** *Tale of Genji* (Murasaki).

Nettelbeck, Amanda. Lecturer in English and Drama, Flinders University of South Australia. Author of *Reading David Malouf* (1995) and of articles on Malouf; editor of *Provisional Maps: Critical Essays on David Malouf* (1994). **Essay:** David Malouf.

Newman, Judie. Professor of American and Postcolonial Literature, Department of English, University of Newcastle. Author of *Saul Bellow and History* (1984), *Nadine Gordimer* (1988), *John Updike* (1988), and *The Ballistic Bard: Postcolonial Fictions* (1995); editor of *Dred: A Tale of the Great Dismal Swamp* (with introduction and notes, 1992), by Harriet Beecher Stowe. Chair, British Association for American Studies, 1995–98. Editorial Board, *Journal of American Studies, Rethinking History,* and *Over Here.* **Essays:** Saul Bellow; *Conservationist* (Gordimer); *Herzog* (Bellow); *Little Women* (Alcott); *Uncle Tom's Cabin* (Stowe).

Newton, K.M. Professor of English, University of Dundee. Author of *George Eliot: Romantic Humanist* (1981), *In Defence of Literary Interpretation: Theory and Practice* (1986), and *Interpreting the Text* (1990); editor of *Twentieth-Century Literary Theory: A Reader* (1988), *George Eliot* (a Longman Critical Reader, 1991), and *Theory into Practice: A Reader in Modern Literary Criticism* (1992). Editor, *English* (Journal of the English Association). **Essay:** *Daniel Deronda* (Eliot).

Nünning, Ansgar. Professor of English and American Literature, Institut für Anglistik und Amerikanistik, Justus-Liebig-Universität Giessen. Author of *Von historischer Fiktion zu historiographischer Metafiktion: Bd. 1.: Theorie, Typologie und Poetik des historischen Romans* (1995, translated as *From Historical Fiction to Historiographic Metafiction: Volume 1: Theory, Typology, and Poetics of the Historical Novel*) and *Bd. 2: Erscheinungsformen und Entwicklungstendenzen des historischen Romans in England seit 1950* (1995, translated as *Volume 2: Kinds of Developments of the Historical Novel in England since 1950*); also author of articles on the concepts of implied author and unreliable narrator, including "The Resurrection of an Anthropomorphicized Passepartout or the Obituary of a Critical Phantom? Deconstructing and Reconceptualizing the 'Implied Author'," in *Anglistik: Organ des Verbandes Deutscher Anglisten* 8 (1997), "'But why will you say that I am mad?' On the Theory, History, and Signals of Unreliable Narration in British Fiction," *Arbeiten aus Anglistik und Amerikanistik* 22 (1997), and "Unreliable, Compared to What? Towards a Cognitive Theory of Unreliable Narration: Prolegomena and Hypotheses," in *Narratologie, Rhetorik, Textlinguistik: Ein Integrationsversuch,* edited by Walter Grünzweig and Andreas Solbach (1998). **Es-**

says: Historical Writing and the Novel; Implied Author; Unreliable Narrator.

O'Brien, George. Professor, Department of English, Georgetown University, Washington, D.C. Author of *The Village of Longing* (1987), *Dancehall Days* (1988), *Brian Friel* (1989), and *Brian Friel: A Reference Guide* (1995); coeditor, *The Ireland Anthology* (1997). **Essay:** Maria Edgeworth.

Okonkwo, Chidi. Senior Lecturer in English, University College Chester. Author of *Race, Colonialism and the Novel* (1995) and a host of articles on African literature. **Essays:** *Bend in the River* (Naipaul); *Palm-Wine Drinkard* (Tutuola); *People of the City* (Ekwensi); Postcolonial Narrative and Criticism of the Novel.

Oropesa, Salvador A. Associate Professor, Department of Modern Languages, Kansas State University, Manhattan. Author of *La obra de Ariel Dorfman: Ficción y crítica* (1992) and numerous essays on Spanish and Latin American literature. Editorial Board, *Chasqui* and *Studies in Twentieth Century Literature,* since 1995. **Essays:** *Fortunata and Jacinta* (Pérez Galdós); *Hive* (Cela).

Owomoyela, Oyekan. Professor, Department of English, University of Nebraska, Lincoln. Author of numerous works on African literature including *African Literatures: An Introduction* (1979), *Visions and Revisions: Essays on African Literatures and Criticism* (1981), and *Yoruba Trickster Tales* (1997); editor of *A History of Twentieth-Century African Literatures* (1993). **Essay:** Amos Tutuola.

Oxford, Jeffrey. Assistant Professor of Spanish, University of North Texas, Denton. **Essay:** Miguel de Unamuno y Jugo.

Page, Norman. Emeritus Professor of Modern English Literature, University of Nottingham. Author of many books, including *The Language of Jane Austen* (1972), *Speech in the English Novel* (1973, revised 1987), *Thomas Hardy* (1977), *E.M. Forster's Posthumous Fiction* (1977), *A.E. Housman: A Critical Biography* (1983), *A Dickens Companion* (1983), *A Kipling Companion* (1984), *A Conrad Companion* (1986), *Muriel Spark* (1990), *Tennyson: An Illustrated Life* (1992); editor of *Dickens: "Hard Times," "Great Expectations," "Our Mutual Friend": A Casebook* (1979), *The Language of Literature: A Casebook* (1984), *The Literature of Place* (with Peter Preston, 1993), as well as numerous collections of essays, interviews, and editions of works by various novelists. Former editor of *Thomas Hardy Journal* and *Thomas Hardy Annual.* **Essays:** *Great Expectations* (Dickens); Thomas Hardy; *Pickwick Papers* (Dickens); *Strange Case of Dr. Jekyll and Mr. Hyde* (Stevenson).

Parnell, J.T. Lecturer in English, Goldsmiths College, University of London. Author of "Swift, Sterne and the Skeptical Tradition," in *Studies in Eighteenth-Century Culture* 23 (1994), "'Que scais-je?' Montaigne's *Apology, Hamlet* and *Tristram Shandy*: Enquiry and Sceptical Response," in *Eighteenth-Century Ireland* 10 (1995), "Sterne and Kundera: The Novel of Variations and the 'Noisy Foolishness of Human Certainty'," in *Laurence Sterne in Modernism and Postmodernism* (1996). **Essays:** Laurence Sterne; *Tristram Shandy* (Sterne).

Peace, Richard. Professor Emeritus of Russian literature, University of Bristol. Author of *Dostoyevsky: An Examination of the Major Novels* (1971), *The Enigma of Gogol* (1981), *Chekhov: A Study of the Four Major Plays* (1983), *"Oblomov": A Critical Examination of Goncharov's Novel* (1991), and *Dostoevsky's "Notes from Underground"* (1993). **Essay:** Russian Novel: 1830–1855.

Peck, John. Senior Lecturer, School of English, University of Wales, Cardiff. Author of several books, including *How to Study a Novel* (1983, revised edition 1995) and articles on Thackeray's novels in *English, English Studies,* and *Dionysos;* editor of *"Middlemarch": A New Casebook* (1992) and *"David Copperfield" and "Hard Times": A New Casebook* (1995). **Essay:** William Makepeace Thackeray.

Pelan, Rebecca. Assistant Lecturer in English, University of Queensland, Brisbane. Author of articles including "Contemporary Irish Women's Literary Work," in *Takahe* 26 (Autumn 1996), and "Edna O'Brien's 'Irishness': An 'Act' of Resistance," in *Canadian Journal of Irish Studies* 19:1 (July 1993); editor of *The Point of Change: Marxism, Australia, History, Theory* (with Carole Ferrier, 1998). Editor, *Irish-Australian Studies: Proceedings from the 7th Irish-Australian Conference* (1994). **Essays:** George Moore; Pornographic Novel.

Pender, Anne. Research Fellow in English, University College, University of New South Wales. **Essays:** Satirical Novel; Christina Stead.

Pérez, Genaro J. Professor of Spanish, Texas Tech University, Lubbock. Author of *Formalist Elements in the Novels of Juan Goytisolo* (1979). Editor and Publisher, *Monographic Review.* Book Review Editor, *Hispania.* **Essays:** *Death of Artemio Cruz* (Fuentes); Juan Goytisolo; Manuel Puig.

Pérez, Janet. Paul Whitfield Horn Professor of Spanish and Associate Graduate Dean, Texas Tech University, Lubbock. Author of several books and articles on Spanish writers, including *Ana María Matute* (1971), *Miguel Delibes* (1972), *Novelistas femeninas de la postguerra española* (1983), *Gonzalo Torrente Ballester* (1984), and *Women Writers of Contemporary Spain* (1984); editor or coeditor of more than 100 volumes in the Twayne World Authors Series/Spain. **Essays:** Camilo José Cela; Spanish Novel.

Pesaresi, Massimo Mandolini. Assistant Professor of Italian, Columbia University, New York. Author of *Grecian Vistas: Giacomo Leopardi and Romantic Hellas* (1998) and a host of articles on Italian literature. **Essay:** Italian Novel.

Petrey, Sandy. Professor of French and Comparative Literature, State University of New York at Stony Brook. Author of *History in the Text* (1980), *Realism and Revolution: Balzac, Stendhal, Zola, and the Performances of History* (1988), and *Speech Acts and Literary Theory* (1990); editor of *The French Revolution, 1789–1989 : Two Hundred Years of Rethinking* (1989). **Essays:** French Novel: 1800–1850; *Indiana* (Sand).

Phelan, James. Professor of English, Ohio State University, Columbus. Author of *Worlds from Words* (1981), *Reading Peo-*

ple, *Reading Plots: Character, Progression, and the Interpretation of Narrative* (1989), and *Narrative as Rhetoric: Technique, Audiences, Ethics, Ideology* (1996); editor of *Reading Narrative: Form, Ethics, and Ideology* (1989) and *Understanding Narrative* (with Peter J. Rabinowitz, 1994). Editor of the journal *Narrative*. **Essays:** Beginnings and Endings; *Farewell to Arms* (Hemingway); Plot.

Pierce, Peter. Professor of Australian Literature, James Cook University of North Queensland, Australia. Author of *Australian Melodramas: Thomas Keneally's Fiction* (1995). General Editor, *The Oxford Literary Guide to Australia* (1987) and *Xavier Herbert* (with Frances de Groen, 1992). **Essays:** Adventure Novel and Imperial Romance; Thomas Keneally; Melodrama.

Pietralunga, Mark. Professor of Italian, Florida State University, Tallahassee. Author of *Beppe Fenoglio and English Literature: A Study of the Writer as Translator* (1987) and numerous articles on Italian literature. Editorial Board, *Canadian Journal of Italian Studies*. **Essays:** Italo Calvino; *Johnny the Partisan* (Fenoglio); *Leopard* (Lampedusa).

Pitchford, Nicola. Assistant Professor of English, Fordham University, Bronx, New York. Author of "Reading Feminism's Pornography Conflict: Implications for Postmodernist Reading Strategies," in *Genders* 25 (March 1997). **Essay:** English Novel: 1950–.

Poovey, Mary (adviser). Professor of English, Johns Hopkins University, Baltimore, Maryland. Author of several works including *The Proper Lady and the Woman Writer: Ideology as Style in the Works of Mary Wollstonecraft, Mary Shelley, and Jane Austen* (1984), *Uneven Developments: The Ideological Work of Gender in Mid-Victorian England* (1988), *Post-Structuralism, History, and Feminism: A Crisis in Politics* (1990), *Making a Social Body: British Cultural Formation, 1830–1864* (1995), and *A History of the Modern Fact: Problems of Knowledge in the Sciences of Wealth and Society* (1998).

Porter, Charles. Professor of French, Yale University, New Haven, Connecticut. Author of *Restif's Novels, or An Autobiography in Search of an Author* (1967), *Chateaubriand: Composition, Imagination, and Poetry* (1978), and several articles on French literature. **Essay:** *René* (Chateaubriand).

Poulson, Sally-Ann. Postgraduate student at the University of Warwick. **Essay:** Alberto Moravia.

Praeger, Michèle. Associate Professor of French, Department of French and Italian, University of California, Davis. Author of articles on French literature in *French Forum, Etudes Littéraires, Critique,* and *French Review*. **Essay:** Alain Robbe-Grillet.

Pratt, Catherine. Lecturer, School of English, University College, Australian Defence Force Academy, Canberra. Author of "'What had she to do with angels?': Gender and Narrative in *The Fortunes of Richard Mahony*," in *Australian Literary Studies* 16:2 (1993), "Fictions of Development: Richardson's *The Getting of Wisdom*," in *Antipodes* 9:1 (1995); editor of *Henry*

Handel Richardson: The Getting of Wisdom, Stories, Selected Prose and Correspondence (with Susan Lever, 1997). **Essay:** *Fortunes of Richard Mahony* (Richardson).

Prince, Gerald (adviser). Professor of French, University of Pennsylvania, Philadelphia. Author of numerous works on French literature, narrative, and narratology, including *Métaphysique et technique dans l'oeuvre romanesque de Sartre* (1968), *A Grammar of Stories: An Introduction* (1973), *Narratology: The Form and Functioning of Narrative* (1982), *A Dictionary of Narratology* (1987), and *Narrative As Theme: Studies in French Fiction* (1992).

Punday, Daniel. Assistant Professor of English, Purdue University Calumet, Hammond, Indiana. Author of articles including "Ishmael Reed's Rhetorical Turn: Uses of 'Signifying' in *Reckless Eyeballing*," in *College English* 54:4 (April 1992), and "Narrative After Deconstruction: Structure and the Negative Poetics of *Cities of the Red Night*," in *Style* 29:1 (Spring 1995). **Essay:** Narrative Theory.

Quazi, Moumin. Doctoral candidate at the University of North Texas, Denton. Assistant Editor, *Grasslands Review*. **Essay:** *Last Temptation of Christ* (Kazantzakis).

Rabkin, Eric S. Professor of English, University of Michigan, Ann Arbor. Author of *The Fantastic in Literature* (1976), *Science Fiction: History, Science, Vision* (with Robert Scholes, 1977) and several other works; editor or coeditor of numerous books on fantastic, science-fiction, and utopian/dystopian literature, including most recently *Science Fiction and Market Realities* (with George Slusser and Gary Westfahl, 1996) and *Foods of the Gods: Eating and the Eaten in Fantasy and Science Fiction* (with Slusser and Westfahl, 1996). **Essay:** Science-Fiction Novel.

Rainsford, Dominic. Research Fellow in English, University of Wales, Aberystwyth. Author of *Authorship, Ethics, and the Reader: Blake/Dickens/Joyce* (1997). **Essays:** *Bleak House* (Dickens); *Hound of the Baskervilles* (Conan Doyle); *Tom Jones* (Fielding); *Ulysses* (Joyce).

Ratner, Tsila. Lecturer in Hebrew and Jewish Studies, University College London. **Essay:** Amos Oz.

Reynolds, Dwight. Associate Professor of Religious Studies, University of California, Santa Barbara. Author of *Heroic Poets, Poetic Heroes : The Ethnography of Performance in an Arabic Oral Epic Tradition* (1995); editor of *Interpreting the South: Autobiography in the Arabic Literary Tradition* (1999). **Essay:** *Thousand and One Nights*.

Richetti, John. Leonard Sugarman Term Professor of English, University of Pennsylvania, Philadelphia. Author of several books on English fiction, including *Popular Fiction Before Richardson: Narrative Patterns 1700–1739* (1969, reprint 1992), *Defoe's Narratives: Situations and Structures* (1975), *Philosophical Writing: Locke, Berkeley, Hume* (1983), and *Daniel Defoe* (1987); editor of *The Columbia History of the British Novel* (1995) and *The Cambridge Companion to the Eighteenth-Century Novel* (1996). Coeditor, Cambridge Studies in Eighteenth-Century Literature and Thought. **Essay:** English Novel: 18th Century.

Rijsberman, Marijke. Managing Web Editor, International Network Services, Sunnyvale, California. Completed her Ph.D. in Comparative Literature, Yale University, New Haven, Connecticut, 1995. Assistant Editor of the *Encyclopedia of the Novel.* **Essays:** coauthor of Autobiographical Novel; *Don Quixote* (Cervantes); *One Day in the Life of Ivan Denisovich* (Solzhenitsyn); Science and the Novel; Stream of Consciousness and Interior Monologue; translator of Belgian and Luxembourgeois Novel.

Robbeson, Angela. Doctoral candidate in English, University of Ottawa. **Essay:** Mordecai Richler.

Rodgers, Eamonn. Professor of Spanish and Latin American Studies, University of Strathclyde, Glasgow. Author of *Benito Pérez Galdós, "Miau"* (1978) and *From Enlightenment to Realism: The Novels of Galdós, 1870–1887* (1987). **Essay:** Benito Pérez Galdós.

Rosenshield, Gary. Professor of Slavic Languages, University of Wisconsin-Madison. Author of *"Crime and Punishment": The Techniques of the Omniscient Author* (1978) and numerous articles on Dostoevskii, including *"The Bronze Horseman* and *The Double*: The Depoetization of the Myth of Petersburg in the Young Dostoevskii," in *Slavic Review* 55:2 (1996), and "Dostoevskii's 'The Funeral of the Universal Man' and 'An Isolated Case' and Chekhov's 'Rothschild's Fiddle': The Jewish Question," in *Russian Review* 56:4 (October 1997). **Essays:** *Crime and Punishment* (Dostoevskii); *Idiot* (Dostoevskii).

Rowland, Susan. Lecturer in Literary Studies, University of Greenwich, London. Author of "The Body's Sacred: Romance and Sacrifice in Religious and Jungian Narratives," in *Literature and Theology* (June 1996). Contributor to *British Women Writing Fiction* (1997). **Essay:** Margaret Atwood.

Royle, Nicholas. Reader in English Studies, University of Stirling. Author of *Telepathy and Literature: Essays on the Reading Mind* (1991), *After Derrida* (1995), *An Introduction to Literature, Criticism and Theory: Key Critical Concepts* (with Andrew Bennett, 1995), and *Elizabeth Bowen and the Dissolution of the Novel: Still Lives* (with Bennett, 1995). Editor, *The Oxford Literary Review.* **Essays:** *Alice's Adventures in Wonderland* (Carroll); *Hunger* (Hamsun).

Rydel, Christine A. Professor of Russian, Grand Valley State University, Allendale, Michigan. Editor of *The Ardis Anthology of Russian Romanticism* (1984) and two volumes in the series *Dictionary of Literary Biography: Russian Literature in the Age of Pushkin and Gogol, Volume I: Prose* and *Volume II: Poetry and Drama* (1998). **Essays:** *Eugene Onegin* (Pushkin); Formalism; *Gift* (Nabokov); Nikolai Gogol'.

Sadlier, Darlene. Professor of Spanish and Portuguese, Indiana University, Bloomington. Author of *Imagery and Theme in the Poetry of Cecília Meireles: A Study of Mar Absoluto* (1983), *Cecília Meireles e João Alphonsus* (1984), and *The Question of How: Women Writers and New Portuguese Literature* (1989);

editor of *New Perspectives in Brazilian Literary Studies: Symbolism Today* (1984); editor and translator, *One Hundred Years After Tomorrow: Brazilian Women's Fiction in the 20th Century* (1992). General Editor, *Indiana Journal of Hispanic Literatures.* **Essay:** Latin American Novel: Brazil.

Sage, Victor. Reader in English Literature, School of English and American Studies, University of East Anglia, Norwich. Author of *Horror Fiction in the Protestant Tradition* (1988); editor of *The Gothick Novel: A Casebook* (1990), *Gothick Origins and Innovations* (with Allan Lloyd Smith, 1994), and *Modern Gothic: A Reader* (with Allan Lloyd Smith, 1996). **Essays:** Gothic Novel; Parody and Pastiche.

Saint-Martin, Lori. Associate Professor, Department of Literary Studies, University of Quebec, Montreal. Author of *Malaise et révolte des femmes dans la littérature québécoise depuis 1945* (1989) and the short-story collection *Lettre imaginaire à la femme de mon amant* (1991). Translator, *Ana historique* (with Paul Gagné, 1992), by Daphne Marlatt, and *Le Cas d'Emily V.* (with Gagné, 1996), by Keith Oatley; editor of *L'Autre Lecture: La Critique au féminin et les textes québécois,* volumes I and II (with introductions, 1992, 1994). **Essay:** Gabrielle Roy.

Sammons, Jeffrey L. Leavenworth Professor of German, Yale University, New Haven, Connecticut. Author of numerous books on German literature including, most recently, *Heinrich Heine* (1991) and *The Shifting Fortunes of Wilhelm Raabe: A History of Criticism as a Cautionary Tale* (1992). **Essay:** Gottfried Keller.

Sanderson, Heather. Lecturer, Department of English, University of British Columbia, Vancouver. Author of "Robert and Taffler: Homosexuality and the Discourse of Gender in Timothy Findley's *The Wars,*" in *Textual Studies in Canada* 8 (1996) and "God This and God That and Amen: Religion in the Fiction of Timothy Findley," in *And Birds Began to Sing: Religion and Literature in Post-Colonial Cultures* (1996). **Essay:** Robertson Davies.

Sarkonak, Ralph. Professor of French, University of British Columbia, Vancouver. Author of *Claude Simon: Les Carrefours du texte* (1986), *Understanding Claude Simon* (1990), and *Les Trajets de l'écriture: Claude Simon* (1994); editor of *À la recherche du référent . . .* (1994). Editor of the journal *Claude Simon.* **Essays:** *In Search of Lost Time* (Proust); Claude Simon.

Schade, Richard E. Professor, Department of Germanic Languages and Literatures, University of Cincinnati, Ohio. Author of "Text and Images: Representation in Grimmelshausen's *Continuatio,*" *The German Quarterly* 64 (1991) and "Simplicissimus in Paris: The Allegory of the Beautiful Lutenist," *Monatshefte* 88 (1996). **Essay:** *Simplicius Simplicissimus* (Grimmelshausen).

Scheick, William J. J.R. Millikan Centennial Professor, University of Texas at Austin. Author of numerous books on American literature including *Two Mather Biographies: "Life and Death" and "Parentator"* (1989), *Design in Puritan American Literature* (1992), and *Paine, Scripture, and Authority: "The Age of*

Reason" as Religious and Political Idea (1994). Editor, *Society of Early Americanists Newsletter.* **Essay:** United States Novel: 18th Century.

Schoolfield, George C. Professor Emeritus of German and Scandinavian Literature, Yale University, New Haven, Connecticut. Author, editor, or translator of a host of works on German and Scandinavian literature including, most recently, *A History of Finland's Literature* (volume 4 of *History of Scandinavian Literatures,* 1998), *European Decadent Novels* (1998), and *Understanding Karen Blixen* (1998). **Essay:** Scandinavian Novel.

Schor, Naomi. Professor of French, Harvard University, Cambridge, Massachusetts. Author of *Zola's Crowds* (1978), *Breaking the Chain: Women, Theory, and French Realist Fiction* (1985), *Reading in Detail: Aesthetics and the Feminine* (1987), *George Sand and Idealism* (1993), and *Bad Objects: Essays Popular and Unpopular* (1995). Coeditor, with Elizabeth Weed, of *Differences: A Journal of Feminist Cultural Studies.* **Essay:** French Novel: 1850–1914.

Schultze, Sydney. Professor of Classical and Modern Languages, University of Louisville, Kentucky. Author of *Structure of "Anna Karenina"* (1982) and articles on Tolstoi; editor of *Meyerhold, the Director* (1981), by Konstantin Rudnitskii. Associate Editor, *Russian Literature Triquarterly.* **Essays:** *Anna Karenina* (Tolstoi); Lev Tolstoi.

Seed, David. Reader in English, Liverpool University. Author of *The Fictional Labyrinths of Thomas Pynchon* (1988), *The Fiction of Joseph Heller: Against the Grain* (1989) and *James Joyce's "A Portrait of the Artist as a Young Man"* (1992). **Essay:** City and the Novel.

Seifrid, Thomas. Associate Professor, Department of Slavic Languages and Literatures, University of Southern California. Author of *Andrei Platonov: Uncertainties of Spirit* (1992) and articles on Platonov. **Essay:** Andrei Platonov.

Sellin, Eric. Professor of Modern French and Francophone Literature and Chair of the Department of French and Italian at Tulane University, New Orleans, Louisiana. Author of *The Dramatic Concepts of Antonin Artaud* (1968), *Reflections on the Aesthetics of Futurism, Dadaism, and Surrealism: A Prosody beyond Words* (1993), and more than 150 scholarly articles and translations, mostly involving French and francophone literature. **Essays:** *Jealousy* (Robbe-Grillet); *Nedjma* (Kateb); Nouveau Roman; *Sand Child* and *Sacred Night* (Ben Jelloun).

Shek, Ben-Z. Professor Emeritus of French Language and Literature, University of Toronto. Author of *Social Realism in the French-Canadian Novel* (1977) and *French-Canadian and Québécois Novels* (1991); editor of *The Arts in Canada: The Last Fifty Years* (with W.J. Keith, 1980). Contributor to *Dictionnaire des oeuvres littéraires du Québec, Volume II: 1900–1939* (1980), *The Oxford Companion to Canadian Theatre* (1983), and *Dictionnaire des oeuvres du XXe siècle: Littérature française et francophone* (1995). **Essay:** Canadian Novel: Francophone.

Shieff, Sarah. Lecturer, Department of English, University of Waikato, Hamilton, New Zealand. **Essay:** *Bone People* (Hulme).

Sholty, Janet P. Graduate Teaching Fellow, University of North Texas, Denton. **Essays:** *Adventures of Pinocchio* (Collodi); Horror Novel; Medieval Narrative; Saga.

Siefken, Hinrich. Emeritus Professor of German, University of Nottingham. Author of *Überindividuelle Formen und der Aufbau des Kudrunepos* (1967), *Kafka: "Ungeduld und Lässigkeit": Zu den Romanen "Der Prozess" und "Das Schloss"* (1977), and *Thomas Mann, Goethe, "Ideal der Deutschheit": Wiederholte Spiegelungen, 1893–1949* (1981); editor of *"Tag- und Nachtbücher 1939–1945"* (1989) by Theodor Haecker, *Die Weisse Rose und ihre Flugblätter* (1994), and *Theodor Haecker, Leben und Werk: Texte, Briefe, Erinnerungen, Würdigungen* (with Bernard Hanssler, 1995). **Essay:** *Effi Briest* (Fontane).

Simms, Norman. Senior Lecturer, English Department, Waikato University, Hamilton, New Zealand. Author of *Invisibility and Silence: A Study of the New Literatures of the Pacific* (1986), *Points of Contact: A Study of the Interplay and Intersection of Traditional and Non-Traditional Literatures, Cultures, and Mentalities* (1990), *Writers from the South Pacific: A Bio-Bibliographical Encyclopedia* (1992), *The Humming Tree: History of Mentalities* (1992), and *My Cow Comes to Haunt Me: European Explorers, Travellers and Novelists Constructing Textual Selves and Imagining the Unthinkable in Lands and Islands beyond the Sea, from Christopher Columbus to Alexander von Humboldt* (1995). Founding editor, *Mentalities: Mentalités.* **Essay:** Biblical Narrative and the Novel.

Simons, John D. Professor of German, Florida State University, Tallahassee. Author of *Schiller's Influence on Dostoevsky* (1966), *Hermann Hesse's "Steppenwolf": A Critical Commentary* (1972), *Günter Grass' "The Tin Drum": A Critical Commentary* (1974), *Dostoevsky's "Crime and Punishment": A Critical Commentary* (1976), and *Friedrich Schiller* (1981). **Essays:** Hermann Hesse; *Magic Mountain* (Mann); *Trial* (Kafka).

Simpkins, Scott (adviser). Associate Professor of English and Editor, *Studies in the Novel,* University of North Texas, Denton.

Simpson, Harriet. Research Student in English Literature, University College Chester. **Essay:** *Fanny Hill* (Cleland).

Smith, Angela. Director, Centre of Commonwealth Studies, University of Stirling. Author of *East African Writing in English* (1989). **Essay:** African Novel: East and Central Africa.

Smylie, John. Editor at the *Journal of Philosophy,* Columbia University, New York. **Essay:** Graphic Novel.

Snyder, Stephen. Assistant Professor of Japanese, University of Colorado, Boulder. Editor of *In Pursuit of Contemporary East Asian Culture* (with Xiaobing Tang, 1996). **Essay:** *Black Rain* (Ibuse).

Soestwohner, Bettina. Research Associate and Lecturer, Department of English and Comparative Literature, University of California-Irvine. Author of "Uprooting Antillean Identity: Maryse Condé's *La Colonie du nouveau monde*," in *Callaloo* 18:3 (1995), and "La Puissance de l'eau: Dissolution et recherche de forme dans l'oeuvre de Werewere Liking," in *Histoires d'eaux: Émergence d'une écriture dans les textes d'écrivaines francophones* (1996). **Essay:** Maryse Condé.

Sokoloff, Naomi. Associate Professor, Near Eastern Languages and Civilization, University of Washington, Seattle. Author of *Imagining the Child in Modern Jewish Fiction* (1992); editor of *Gender and Text in Modern Hebrew and Yiddish Literature* (with Anne Lapidus Lerner and Anita Norich, 1992) and *Infant Tongues: The Voice of the Child in Literature* (with Elizabeth Goodenough and Mark Heberle, 1994). **Essay:** David Grossman.

Solbach, Andreas. Professor, Department of Germanic Languages and Literature, University of Toronto. Author of *Gesellschaftsethik und Romantheorie: Studien zu Grimmelshausen, Weise und Beer* (1994) and *Evidentia und Erzähltheorie: Die Rhetorik anschaulichen Erzählens in der Frühmoderne und ihre antiken Quellen* (1994). **Essay:** Swiss Novel: German Language.

Spacks, Patricia Ann Meyer (adviser). Professor of English, University of Virginia, Charlottesville. Author of numerous works including *The Female Imagination* (1975), *The Adolescent Idea: Myths of Youth and the Adult Imagination* (1981), *Desire and Truth: Functions of Plot in Eighteenth-Century English Novels* (1990), *Boredom: The Literary History of a State of Mind* (1995), and *Imagining a Self: Autobiography and Novel in Eighteenth-Century England* (1995); editor of *Contemporary Women Novelists: A Collection of Critical Essays* (1977), and of *Sense and Sensibility* (critical edition, 1982) and *Persuasion: Authoritative Text, Backgrounds and Contexts, Criticism* (1995), both by Jane Austen.

Stevenson, John Allen. Associate Professor and Chair, Department of English, University of Colorado, Boulder. Author of *The British Novel: Defoe to Austen, A Critical History* (1990) and numerous articles on the 18th-century novel. **Essays:** *Clarissa* (Richardson); Crime, Detective, and Mystery Novel; Henry Fielding.

Stevenson, Richard C. Associate Professor of English, University of Oregon, Eugene. Author of articles on George Meredith in *Harvard English Studies, Texas Studies in Literature and Language,* and *Nineteenth-Century Fiction.* **Essays:** George Meredith; *Ordeal of Richard Feverel* (Meredith).

Stewart, Joan Hinde. Professor of French, North Carolina State University, Raleigh. Author of *The Novels of Mme Riccoboni* (1976) and *Gynographs: French Novels by Women of the Late Eighteenth Century* (1993); editor of *Lettres de Mistriss Fanni Butlerd* (1979), by Mme Riccoboni, and *Lettres de Mistriss Henley publiées par son amie* (with Philip Stewart, 1993), by Isabelle de Charrière. **Essay:** *Adolphe* (Constant).

Stewart, Mary E. University Lecturer in German and Fellow of Robinson College, University of Cambridge. Author of "The Re-

fracted Self: Hermann Hesse, *Der Steppenwolf*," in *The German Novel in the Twentieth Century: Beyond Realism* (1993) and of articles on Hesse in journals and reference books. **Essay:** *Steppenwolf* (Hesse).

Stewart, Philip. Professor of French, Duke University, Durham, North Carolina. Author of *Imitation and Illusion in the French Memoir-Novel, 1700–1750: The Art of Make-Believe* (1969), *Le Masque et la parole: Le Langage de l'amour au XVIIIe siècle* (1973), *Rereadings: Eight Early French Novels* (1984), *Half-Told Tales: Dilemmas of Meaning in Three French Novels* (1987), and *Engraven Desire: Eros, Image, and Text in the French Eighteenth Century* (1992). Translator, *Letters of Mistress Henley Published by Her Friend* (with Jean Vaché, 1993), by Isabelle de Charrière; editor of *Lettres de Mistriss Henley publiées par son amie* (with Joan Hinde Stewart, 1993), by Isabelle de Charrière. Editorial Board, *Eighteenth-Century Life* and *Studies on Voltaire and the Eighteenth Century*. **Essay:** French Novel: 18th Century.

Stillmark, Alexander. Reader in German, University College London. Editor of several volumes on German literature, including *Kritische Wege der Landnahme: Ingeborg Bachmann im Blickfeld der Neunziger Jahre* (with R. Pichl, 1994) and *Joseph Roth: Der Sieg über die Zeit, Stuttgarter Arbeiten zur Germanistik* (1996). **Essay:** Adalbert Stifter.

Striff, Erin. Graduate student at University of Wales, Cardiff. **Essay:** *Handmaid's Tale* (Atwood).

Swales, Martin. Professor of German, University College London. Author of *Arthur Schnitzler: A Critical Study* (1971), *The German Novelle* (1977), *The German Bildungsroman* (1978), *Thomas Mann* (1980), *Goethe, "The Sorrows of Young Werther"* (1987), *Buddenbrooks: Family Life as the Mirror of Social Change* (1991), and *Studies of German Prose Fiction in the Age of European Realism* (1995). Joint Editor of Cambridge Studies in German and of Publications of the English Goethe Society. **Essays:** *Elective Affinities* (Goethe); Johann Wolfgang von Goethe.

Szeman, Imre. Doctoral candidate, Literature Program, Duke University, Durham, North Carolina. Author of articles published in *Reverse Shot* (May 1994), *Re-Naming the Landscape* (edited by Bruce Butterfield and Jurgen Kleist, 1994), and *Constructing Nations, Constructing Selves* (edited by Lynn Domina and Peter Naccarato, 1997). Founding editor of *Prosthesis: A Graduate Journal of Theory and Criticism*. **Essays:** *Apprenticeship of Duddy Kravitz* (Richler); Yashar Kemal; Turkish Novel.

Taglieri, Gina L. Assistant Professor of English (adjunct), Fashion Institute of Technology/State University of New York. **Essays:** *Age of Innocence* (Wharton); *Invisible Man* (Ellison).

Talbot, Emile J. Professor of French and Comparative Literature, University of Illinois, Urbana-Champaign. Author of *La Critique stendhalienne de Balzac à Zola* (1979), *Stendhal and Romantic Aesthetics* (1985), and *Stendhal Revisited* (1993). **Essay:** Stendhal.

Tang, Xiaobing. Associate Professor of Chinese, University of Chicago. Author of *Global Space and the Nationalist Discourse of Modernity: The Historical Thinking of Liang Qichao* (1996) and "Melancholy Against the Grain: Approaching Postmodernity in Wang Anyi's Contemporary Tales of Sorrow," in *boundary 2 24* (Fall 1997); editor of *Politics, Ideology, and Literary Discourse in Modern China: Theoretical Interventions and Cultural Critique* (with Liu Kang, 1993) and *In Pursuit of Contemporary East Asian Culture* (with Stephen Snyder, 1996). **Essays:** *Cold Nights* (Ba Jin); Wang Anyi.

Teahan, Sheila. Associate Professor of English, Michigan State University, East Lansing. Author of *The Rhetorical Logic of Henry James* (1995) and of articles on James. **Essay:** Henry James.

Terras, Victor. Professor Emeritus of Slavic Languages and Comparative Literature, Brown University, Providence, Rhode Island. Author of more than a dozen books on Russian literature, including *A History of Russian Literature* (1991). **Essay:** Russian Novel: 1900–1945.

Thieme, John. Professor of New Literatures in English, University of Hull. Author of *V.S. Naipaul, "The Mimic Men"* (1985) and *The Web of Tradition: Uses of Allusion in V.S. Naipaul's Fiction* (1987); editor of *The Arnold Anthology of Post-Colonial Literatures in English* (1996). **Essays:** Caribbean Novel: Anglophone; Wilson Harris; George Lamming; *Man-Eater of Malgudi* (Narayan); V.S. Naipaul.

Thomas, Kathleen Smith. Professor of Humanities, Florida State University, Tallahassee. **Essay:** Mikhail Bulgakov.

Todd, Janet. Professor of English, University of East Anglia, Norwich. Author of *Women's Friendship in Literature* (1980), *Sensibility: An Introduction* (1986), *The Sign of Angellica: Women, Writing and Fiction* (1989), *Gender, Art and Death* (1993), and *The Secret Life of Aphra Behn* (1996); editor of *The Complete Works of Aphra Behn* (1992–96) and *Aphra Behn Studies* (1995). Joint Editor, *Women's Writing,* since 1993. **Essays:** Aphra Behn; Sentimental Novel.

Toker, Leona. Associate Professor of English, The Hebrew University of Jerusalem. Author of *Nabokov: The Mystery of Literary Structures* (1989) and *Eloquent Reticence: Withholding Information in Fictional Narrative* (1993); editor of *Commitment in Reflection: Essays in Literature and Moral Philosophy* (1994). **Essay:** *One Day in the Life of Ivan Denisovich* (Solzhenitsyn).

Tratner, Michael. Associate Professor of English, Bryn Mawr College, Pennsylvania. Author of *Student Writers at Work and in the Company of Other Writers* (with Nancy Sommers and Donald McQuade, 3rd edition, 1989) and *Modernism and Mass Politics: Joyce, Woolf, Eliot, Yeats* (1995). **Essays:** Class and the Novel; Virginia Woolf.

Trumpener, Katie. Associate Professor, Germanic Studies, Comparative Literature, and English, University of Chicago. Author of *Bardic Nationalism: The Romantic Novel and the British Empire* (1997). Editorial Board, *Modern Philology* and *Public Culture.* **Essays:** Alice Munro; National Tale.

Vassar, Andrew P. Graduate Instructor, University of Arkansas, Fayetteville. **Essay:** American Western Novel.

Virkus, Andres. Independent scholar and writer. **Essays:** Miguel de Cervantes; *Naked Lunch* (Burroughs).

Viscarri, Dionisio. Assistant Professor, Department of Spanish and Classics, University of New Hampshire, Durham. **Essay:** Clarín [Leopoldo Alas].

Wachtel, Andrew. Professor, Department of Slavic Languages and Literatures, Northwestern University, Evanston, Illinois. Author of "Imagining Yugoslavia: The Historical Archeology of Ivo Andric," in *Ivo Andric Revisited: The Bridge Still Stands* (1995), and *Making a Nation, Breaking a Nation: Literature and Cultural Politics in Yugoslavia* (1998); editor of *Intersections and Transpositions: Russian Music, Literature, and Society* (1998). **Essay:** Ivo Andrić.

Wagner, Kathy. Instructor in English, Middlesex County College, Edison, New Jersey. Author of *Rereading Nadine Gordimer* (1994). **Essay:** Nadine Gordimer.

Washburn, Dennis C. Assistant Professor of Asian Studies, Dartmouth College, Hanover, New Hampshire. Author of *The Dilemma of the Modern in Japanese Fiction* (1995). **Essay:** Natsume Sōseki.

Watkins, Susan. Lecturer in English Literature, University College Chester. Author of *Studying Literature: A Practical Introduction* (1995). **Essays:** *Jane Eyre* (Charlotte Brontë); Doris Lessing.

Watts, Philip. Assistant Professor, Department of French and Italian, University of Pittsburgh, Pennsylvania. Author of *Allegories of the Purge: How Literature Responded to the Postwar Trials of Writers and Intellectuals in France* (1999). **Essay:** Louis-Ferdinand Céline.

Weaver, William. Recently completed Ph.D. in English, Johns Hopkins University, Baltimore, Maryland. Author of "Identifying Men at Ida's University: Education, Gender, and Male/Male Identification in Tennyson's *The Princess,*" in *Nineteenth-Century Contexts* (forthcoming). **Essays:** Illustrations and Engravings; Roman à clef.

Weed, Edwin. Doctoral student in English at Johns Hopkins University, Baltimore, Maryland. **Essay:** James Fenimore Cooper.

Wheelock, Jennifer. Instructor of English, Florida State University, Tallahassee. Contributor to the *Encyclopedia of American Literature* (1997). **Essay:** Paperpack.

Wilcox, Shane. Medical student, University of Queensland, Brisbane. Author of "The Sacrificial Body," in *The Body in the Library* (1997). **Essay:** *Justine* (Sade).

Williams, Mark (adviser). Senior Lecturer in Japanese Studies, University of Leeds. Author of numerous articles in journals and coeditor of *Japan and Christianity: Impacts and Responses* (1996). **Essays:** Endō Shūsaku; Japanese Novel; *Silence* (Endō).

Williams, Philip F. Associate Professor of Chinese Literature and Humanities, Arizona State University, Tempe. Author of *Village Echoes: The Fiction of Wu Zuxiang* (1993). Translator, "Body and Soul" by Zhang Xianliang, in *Prize-Winning Stories from China, 1980–81* (1985). Executive Board, American Association of Chinese Comparative Literature, since 1995. **Essays:** *Camel Xiangzi* (Lao She); *Travels of Lao Can* (Liu E); Zhang Xianliang.

Williams, Raymond Leslie. Professor and Chair, Department of Spanish and Portuguese, University of California-Riverside. Author of *Una década de la novela colombiana: La experiencia de los setenta* (1981), *Gabriel García Márquez* (1984), *The Colombian Novel 1844–1987* (1991), *The Postmodern Novel in Latin America* (1995), and *The Writings of Carlos Fuentes* (1996). **Essays:** Carlos Fuentes; *Hopscotch* (Cortázar); Latin American Novel: Colombia; *One Hundred Years of Solitude* (García Márquez).

Wilt, Judith. Professor of English, Boston College, Massachusetts. Author of *The Readable People of George Meredith* (1975), *Ghosts of the Gothic, Austen, Eliot, and Lawrence* (1980), *Secret Leaves: The Novels of Walter Scott* (1986), and *Abortion, Choice, and Contemporary Fiction: The Armageddon of the Maternal Instinct* (1991). **Essay:** *Ivanhoe* (Scott).

Winnett, Susan. Teaches in the Department of English and American Literature, University of Hamburg, Germany. Author of *Terrible Sociability: The Text of Manners in Laclos, Goethe, and James* (1993). **Essay:** Novel of Manners.

Winnifrith, Tom. Professor, Department of English and Comparative Literary Studies, University of Warwick. Author of *The Brontës and Their Background: Romance and Reality* (1973, 2nd edition 1988), *The Brontës* (1977), *Brontë Facts and Problems* (with Edward Chitham, 1983), *A New Life of Charlotte Brontë* (1987), *Fallen Women in the Nineteenth-Century Novel* (1994), *Shattered Eagles, Balkan Fragments* (1995), and *The Sayings of Charlotte Brontë* (1996); editor of *The Poems of Charlotte Brontë* (1983) and *The Philosophy of Literature* (with others, 1989). **Essays:** Charlotte Brontë; Southern Balkan Novel.

Wollaeger, Mark A. Associate Professor of English, Vanderbilt University, Nashville, Tennessee. Author of *Joseph Conrad and the Fictions of Skepticism* (1990); editor of *Joyce and the Subject of History* (1996). **Essay:** English Novel: 1880–1920.

Wonham, Henry B. Professor of English, University of Oregon, Eugene. Author of *Mark Twain and the Art of the Tall Tale* (1993) and scholarly articles on Twain. **Essay:** Mark Twain.

Woods, Tim S. Lecturer in English and American Studies, University of Wales, Aberystwyth. Author of *New Literatures and History* (with Peter Middleton, forthcoming). **Essays:** André Brink; *Grain of Wheat* (Ngugi).

Wright, Derek. Department of English, University of Queensland, Brisbane. Author of *Ayi Kwei Armah's Africa: The Sources of His Fiction* (1989), *Wole Soyinka Revisited* (1993), *The Novels of Nuruddin Farah* (1994), *Wole Soyinka: Life, Work and Criticism* (1996), and *New Directions in African Fiction 1970–1995* (1997); editor of *Critical Perspectives on Ayi Kwei Armah* (1992) and *Contemporary African Fiction: A Critical Anthology* (1997). Advisory Editor, *New Literatures Review*, since 1994. Contributing Editor, *World Literatures Written in English*, since 1994. **Essays:** Ayi Kwei Armah; J.M. Coetzee; Anita Desai; *Lolita* (Nabokov).

Wu, Yenna. Associate Professor of Chinese, University of California, Riverside. Author of *The Chinese Virago: A Literary Theme* (1995) and *The Lioness Roars: Shrew Stories from Late Imperial China* (1995). **Essay:** Six Classic Chinese Novels.

Young, Richard A. Professor of Spanish, University of Alberta, Edmonton. Author of *Agustín Yáñez y sus cuentos* (1978), *La figura del rey y la institución real en la comedia lopesca* (1979), *Alejo Carpentier: El reino de este mundo* (1983), *Carpentier ante la crítica: Bibliografía comentada* (with Patricia Rubio, 1985), and *Octaedro en cuatro tiempos (texto y tiempo en un libro de Cortázar)* (1993). Editor, *Revista canadiense de estudios hispánicos.* **Essays:** Alejo Carpentier; Julio Cortázar; *Lost Steps* (Carpentier).

Yudkin, Leon I. Lecturer in Hebrew, University College London. Author of several works on Hebrew and Jewish literature including *Jewish Writing and Identity in the 20th Century* (1982), *1948 and After: Aspects of Israeli Fiction* (1984), *Else Lasker-Schüler: A Study in German Jewish Literature* (1991), *Beyond Sequence: Current Israeli Fiction and Its Context* (1992), and *A Home Within: Varieties of Jewish Expression in Modern Fiction* (1996). **Essay:** Israeli Novel.

Zapata, Celia Correas. Professor of Contemporary Latin American Literature, San Jose State University, California. Author of *Isabel Allende: Vida y espíritus: Una biografía literaria* (1998); editor of *Detrás de la reja* (1980), an anthology of short stories by Latin American women writers, and *The Magic and the Real: Latin American Women Writers* (1990), also an anthology. **Essay:** Isabel Allende.

Zeraschi, Deborah. Research student (Ph.D.), University of Wales, Cardiff. **Essay:** *His Natural Life* (Clarke).

Zierler, Wendy. Postdoctoral Research Fellow, University of Hong Kong. Author of articles on various Israeli and Jewish American writers. **Essay:** Aharon Appelfeld.

Zohn, Harry. Professor of German Emeritus, Brandeis University, Waltham, Massachusetts. Author of *Ich bin ein Sohn der deutschen Sprache nur: Jüdisches Erbe in der österreichischen Literatur* (1986) and *Austriaca and Judaica: Essays and Translations* (1995). General Editor, Austrian Culture Series, Peter Lang Publishing. Editorial Board, *Modern Austrian Literature.* **Essay:** *Badenheim 1939* (Appelfeld).